The GREAT INTERNATIONAL ATLAS

The GREAT INTERNATIONAL ATLAS

PORTLAND HOUSE
NEW YORK

Edited by
B. M. Willett Director and Cartographic Editor,
George Philip and Son Ltd

David Gaylard, Joan Russell, Ray Smith and Amanda
Wells

Maps prepared by George Philip Cartographic Services
under the direction of A. G. Poynter, Director of
Cartography

Printed in Italy

This 1987 edition published by Portland House,
distributed by Crown Publishers, Inc., 225 Park
Avenue South, New York, New York 10003.

Library of Congress Cataloging in Publication Data

Great international atlas
    Includes index.
    1. Atlases.
G1021.G688   1987   912   86-675541
ISBN 0-517-63579-8

H G F E D C B A

PREFACE

The core of this Atlas is the maps and index and around it are sections giving more information about the World and its countries.

The maps are physically colored, that is, they portray the land with contours, layer colors, and hill-shading, and it is on this physical background that the roads, railroads, boundaries, and cities and towns are shown. There is a map at the beginning of each continental part that is politically colored so as to clearly portray individual countries that collectively make up the continent.

The maps are arranged by continents, starting in Europe, proceeding to Asia, Oceania and Africa, and then crossing the Pacific to the Americas and, finally, there are maps of the Polar regions. Each continent opens with a pair of facing pages, one showing the physique of the land and the other map colored to individual countries. There follows a series of physical maps of various scales. There are maps of the larger regions of each continent and then maps on a greater scale and showing more detail for the more densely populated areas. Thus, to give one example of this map sequence, there is a map of North America, separate maps of Canada and the U.S.A., and then the U.S.A. is shown by three double-page spreads on a scale of 1:4.8 million, with the more densely populated parts on maps with a scale of 1:2 million. This pattern of series of maps on various scales is repeated throughout the world and can be clearly seen and understood by looking at the layout maps which accompany the list of contents.

The topographical maps are preceded by maps, diagrams, and illustrations explaining in concise form the Universe, the Earth, and Man's place on it and his activities. The contents list gives more detail of each page-topic.

Following the topographical maps are two parts of the atlas concerned with economic information. There are a series of world maps showing various agricultural and industrial productions. Diagrams and tables give the amounts of these productions and the contribution to world totals made by the individual countries. There is then an economic statistical section which lists the major countries of the World and gives information for them concerning such features as their demography, agriculture, mining and industrial production, and trade. More is said about the aims and content of this section on its introductory page.

International boundaries have been drawn to show the de facto situation where there are rival claims to territory.

The reader is encouraged to enter into the bank of information that is stored in the atlas in various ways. The contents pages and the layout maps will take the reader to specific areas. The selected reference list likewise takes the reader to the page where countries, islands, or regions, for example, will be found. The index is the obvious and very precise way for a particular place to be found; this takes the reader to the page number and, with the geographical co-ordinates, to the exact location.

Finally, a word about the name forms that appear on the maps and in the index. The main form of the names is always given in the local form, which is the spelling used by the people of that particular country. Where necessary, the English conventional name form is given in brackets on the maps and cross-referenced in the index. Thus the city of Munich, Germany, is rendered as München, but the English form, Munich, is given in brackets, and cross-referenced to the main form in the index. For countries that do not use a Roman script, place names have been transcribed according to the standard systems adopted by the British and U.S. Geographic Name authorities. For Chinese place names, the modern Pinyin system has been used, with some of the more well known forms in brackets; Beijing (Peking) is an example, and both of these spellings will be in the index.

B.M. Willett

TABLE OF CONTENTS

OVERVIEW

ILLUSTRATED SECTION

MAPS

The World

Europe

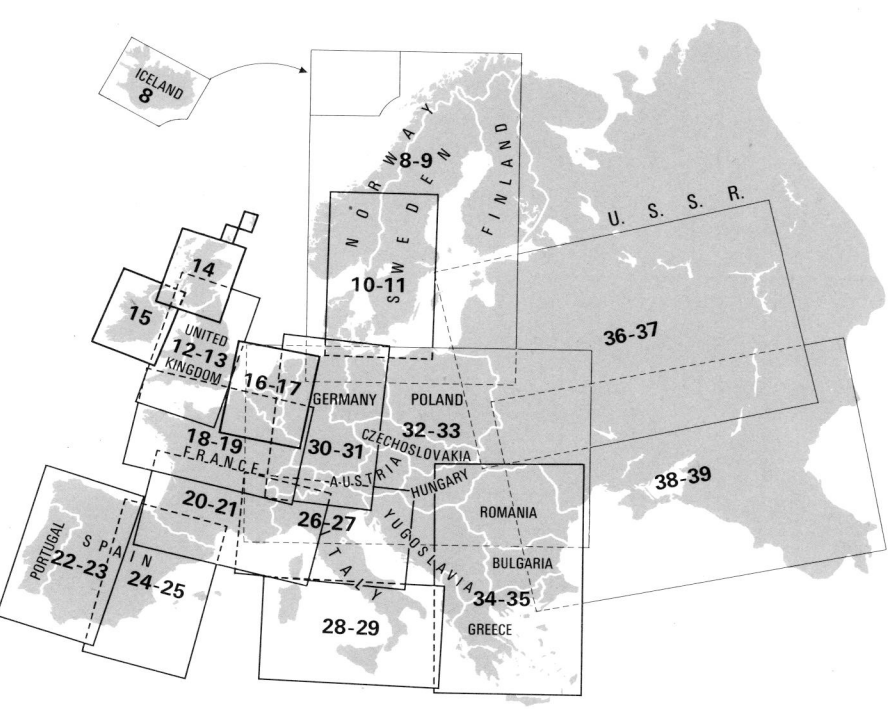

ICELAND
8
8-9
NORWAY
SWEDEN
FINLAND
U. S. S. R.
10-11
14
15
UNITED
12-13
KINGDOM
16-17
GERMANY
POLAND
32-33
36-37
18-19
FRANCE
30-31
CZECHOSLOVAKIA
AUSTRIA
HUNGARY
ROMANIA
38-39
20-21
26-27
YUGOSLAVIA
BULGARIA
PORTUGAL
SPAIN
22-23
24-25
ITALY
34-35
GREECE
28-29

Asia

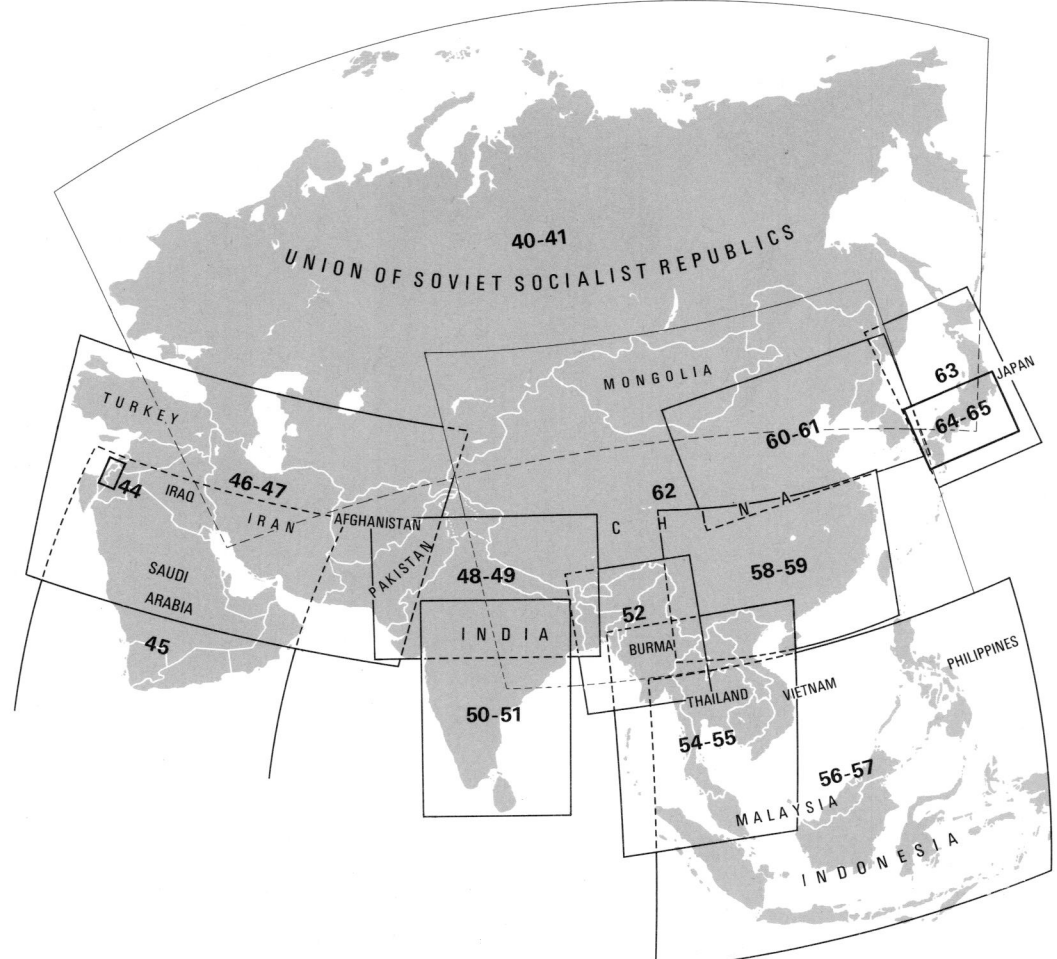

Oceania

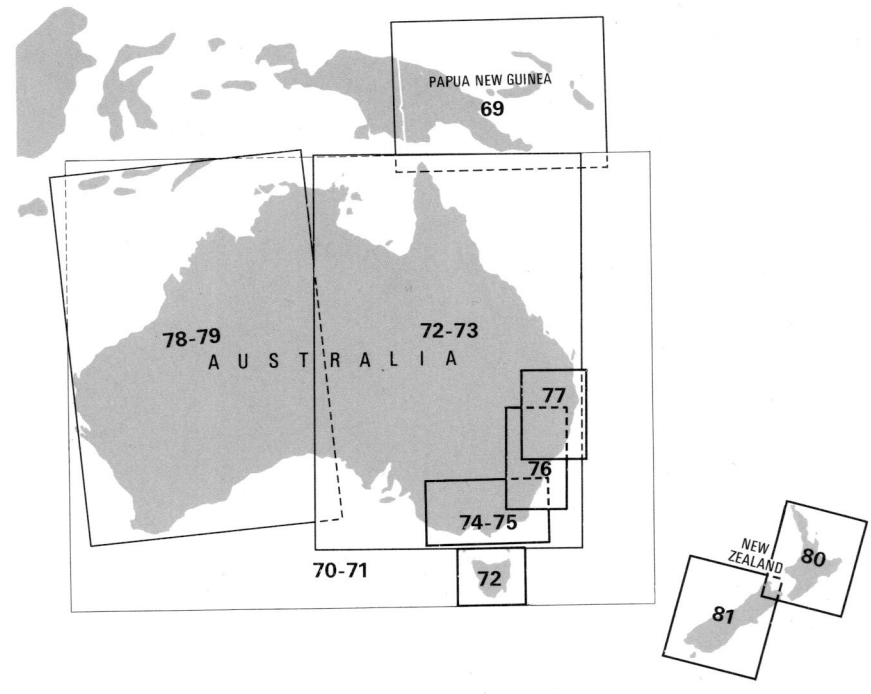

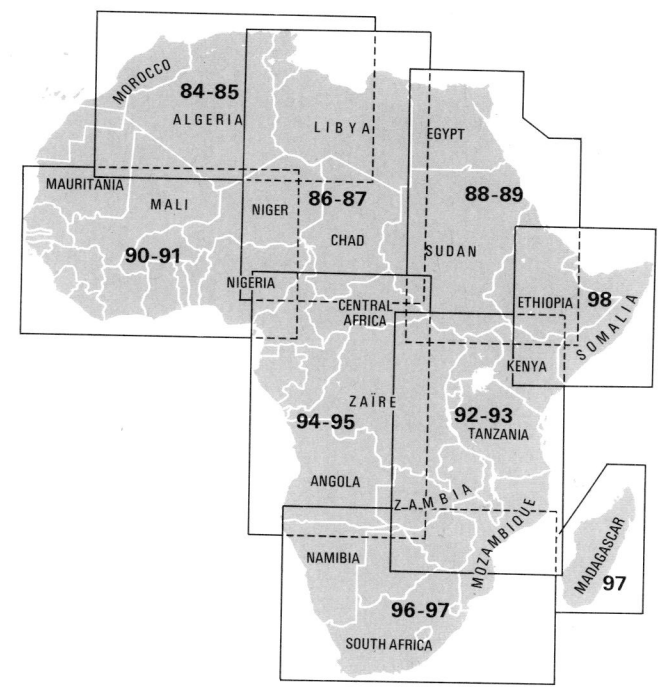

Africa

North America

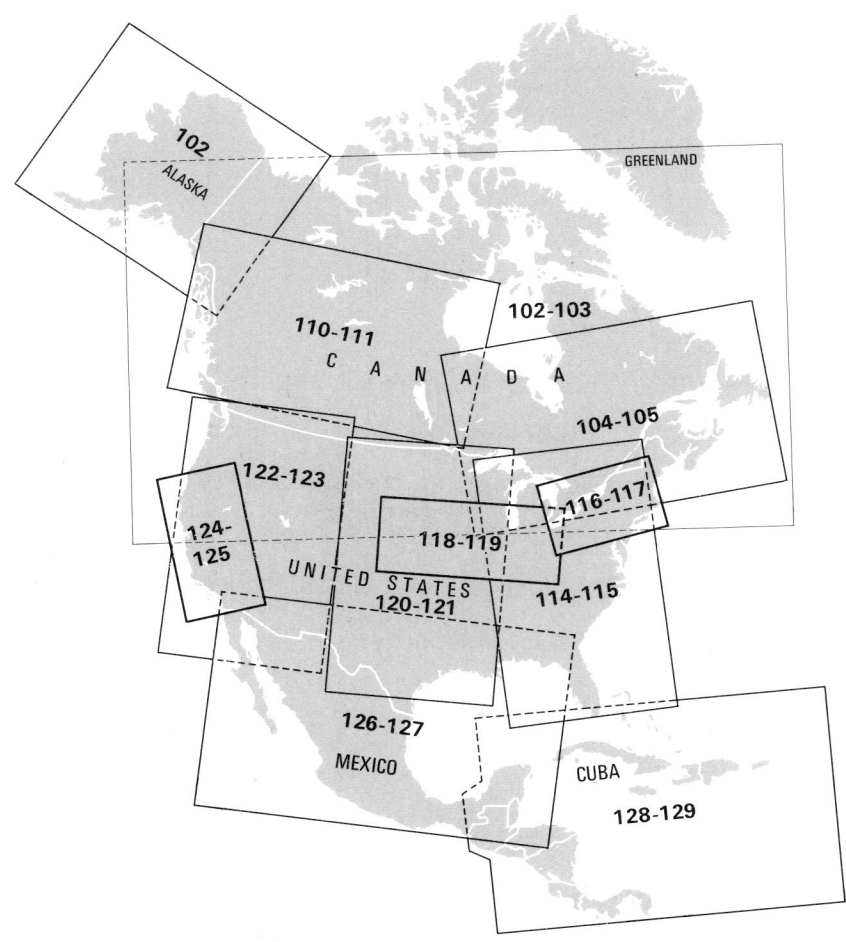

South America

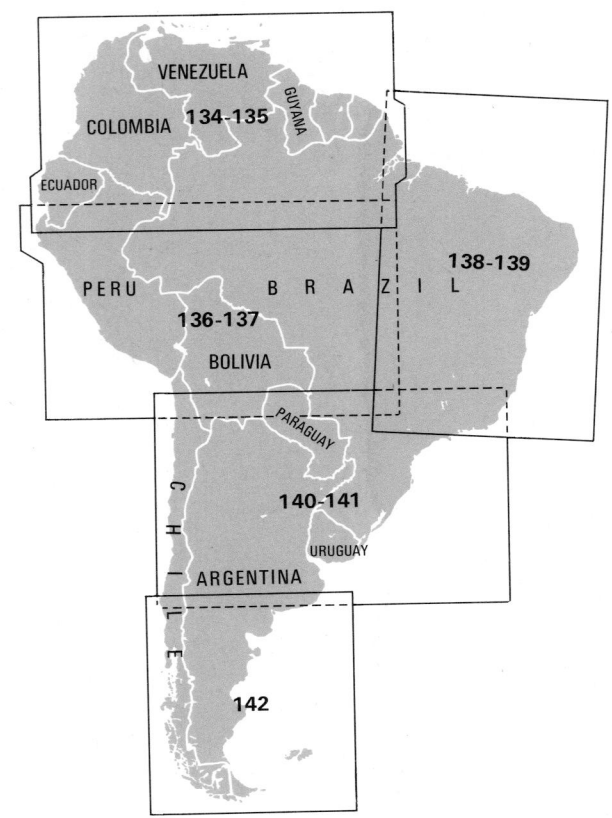

THEMATIC MAPS

ECONOMIC SECTION

INDEX

POPULATION OF COUNTRIES

Country	Area in thousands of square km.	Population in thousands	Density of population per sq. km.	Capital Population in thousands
Afghanistan	648	18 136	28	Kābul (1 127)
Albania	29	2 962	102	Tiranë (202)
Algeria	2 382	21 718	9	Algiers (1 740)
Angola	1 247	8 754	7	Luanda (700)
Argentina	2 767	30 564	11	Buenos Aires (9 927)
Australia	7 687	15 752	2	Canberra (256)
Austria	84	7 555	90	Vienna (1 531)
Bangladesh	144	98 657	685	Dacca (3 459)
Belgium	33	9 903	300	Brussels (989)
Belize	23	166	7	Belmopan (3)
Benin	113	3 932	35	Porto-Novo (208)
Bhutan	47	1 417	30	Thimphu (60)
Bolivia	1 099	6 429	6	Sucre (64) La Paz (881)
Botswana	600	1 085	2	Gaborone (79)
Brazil	8 512	135 564	16	Brasilia (1 177)
Brunei	6	224	37	Bandar Seri Begawan (58)
Bulgaria	111	8 957	81	Sofia (1 094)
Burkina Faso	274	6 639	24	Ouagadougou (286)
Burma	677	37 154	55	Rangoon (2 459)
Burundi	28	4 718	169	Bujumbura (141)
Cambodia (Kampuchea)	181	7 284	40	Phnom Penh (500)
Cameroon	475	10 106	21	Yaoundé (485)
Canada	9 976	25 379	3	Ottawa (738)
Central African Rep.	623	2 608	4	Bangui (382)
Chad	1 284	5 108	4	Ndjamena (303)
Chile	757	12 074	16	Santiago (4 132)
China	9 597	1 059 521	110	Peking (9 330)
Colombia	1 139	28 624	25	Bogotá (4 486)
Congo	342	1 740	5	Brazzaville (422)
Costa Rica	51	2 600	51	San José (245)
Cuba	111	10 090	91	Havana (1 951)
Cyprus	9	665	74	Nicosia (161)
Czechoslovakia	128	15 500	121	Prague (1 190)
Denmark	43	5 114	119	Copenhagen (1 366)
Djibouti	22	430	20	Djibouti (150)
Dominican Republic	49	6 243	127	Santo Domingo (1 313)
Ecuador	284	9 378	33	Quito (1 110)
Egypt	1 001	48 503	48	Cairo (6 818)
El Salvador	21	4 819	229	San Salvador (884)
Equatorial Guinea	28	392	14	Rey Malabo (37)
Ethiopia	1 222	43 350	35	Addis Ababa (1 478)
Fiji	18	696	39	Suva (71)
Finland	337	4 908	15	Helsinki (932)
France	547	55 172	101	Paris (8 510)
French Guiana	91	82	1	Cayenne (38)
Gabon	268	1 151	4	Libreville (350)
Gambia	11	643	58	Banjul (103)
Germany, East	108	16 644	154	East Berlin (1 173)
Germany, West	249	61 015	245	Bonn (293)
Ghana	239	13 588	57	Accra (965)
Greece	132	9 935	75	Athens (3 027)
Greenland	2 176	53	0.02	Godthaab (10)
Guatemala	109	7 963	73	Guatemala (1 300)
Guinea	246	6 075	25	Conakry (763)
Guinea-Bissau	36	890	25	Bissau (109)
Guyana	215	790	4	Georgetown (188)
Haiti	28	6 585	235	Port-au-Prince (888)
Honduras	112	4 372	39	Tegucigalpa (534)
Hong Kong	1	5 423	5 423	Hong Kong (1 184)
Hungary	93	10 649	115	Budapest (2 064)
Iceland	103	241	2	Reykjavík (124)
India	3 288	750 900	228	Delhi (5 729)
Indonesia	1 905	163 393	86	Jakarta (6 503)
Iran	1 648	44 212	27	Tehrān (4 589)
Iraq	435	15 898	37	Baghdād (2 969)
Irish Republic	70	3 552	51	Dublin (915)
Israel	21	4 233	202	Jerusalem (429)
Italy	301	57 128	190	Rome (2 831)
Ivory Coast	322	9 810	30	Abidjan (1 850)
Jamaica	11	2 337	212	Kingston (671)
Japan	372	120 754	325	Tōkyō (11 676)
Jordan	98	3 515	36	'Ammān (681)
Kenya	583	20 333	35	Nairobi (1 200)
Korea, North	121	20 385	168	Pyŏngyang (1 500)
Korea, South	98	41 209	421	Seoul (8 367)
Kuwait	18	1 710	95	Kuwait (775)
Laos	237	4 117	17	Vientiane (120)
Lebanon	10	2 668	267	Beirut (702)
Lesotho	30	1 528	51	Maseru (45)
Liberia	111	2 189	20	Monrovia (425)
Libya	1 760	3 605	2	Tripoli (980)
Luxembourg	3	366	122	Luxembourg (79)
Madagascar	587	9 985	17	Antananarivo (400)
Malawi	118	7 058	60	Lilongwe (99)
Malaysia	330	15 557	47	Kuala Lumpur (938)
Mali	1 240	8 206	7	Bamako (419)
Malta	0.3	383	1 277	Valletta (14)
Mauritania	1 031	1 888	2	Nouakchott (135)
Mauritius	2	1 020	510	Port Louis (150)
Mexico	1 973	78 524	40	Mexico (14 750)
Mongolia	1 565	1 891	1	Ulan Bator (419)
Morocco	447	21 941	49	Rabat (842)
Mozambique	802	13 961	17	Maputo (384)
Namibia	824	1 550	2	Windhoek (61)
Nepal	141	16 625	118	Katmandu (235)
Netherlands	37	14 484	391	Amsterdam (994)
New Zealand	269	3 254	12	Wellington (343)
Nicaragua	130	3 272	25	Managua (615)
Niger	1 267	6 115	5	Niamey (225)
Nigeria	924	95 198	103	Lagos (1 477)
Norway	324	4 153	13	Oslo (643)
Oman	212	1 242	6	Muscat (25)
Pakistan	804	96 180	120	Islamabad (201)
Panama	77	2 180	28	Panamá (655)
Papua New Guinea	462	3 329	7	Port Moresby (124)
Paraguay	407	3 681	9	Asunción (708)
Peru	1 285	19 698	15	Lima (5 258)
Philippines	300	54 378	181	Manila (1 630)
Poland	313	37 203	119	Warsaw (1 649)
Portugal	92	10 229	111	Lisbon (1612)
Puerto Rico	9	3 451	383	San Juan (1 086)
Romania	238	23 017	97	Bucharest (1 979)
Rwanda	26	6 070	233	Kigali (157)
Saudi Arabia	2 150	11 542	5	Riyadh (667)
Senegal	196	6 444	33	Dakar (799)
Sierra Leone	72	3 602	50	Freetown (316)
Singapore	0.6	2 558	4 263	Singapore (2 517)
Somali Republic	638	4 653	7	Mogadishu (600)
South Africa	1 221	32 392	27	Pretoria (739) Cape Town (1 491)
Spain	505	38 602	76	Madrid (3 188)
Sri Lanka	66	15 837	240	Colombo (1 412)
Sudan	2 506	21 550	9	Khartoum (476)
Surinam	163	375	2	Paramaribo (151)
Swaziland	17	647	38	Mbabane (23)
Sweden	450	8 350	19	Stockholm (1 420)
Switzerland	41	6 374	155	Bern (301)
Syria	185	10 267	55	Damascus (1 112)
Taiwan	36	19 012	528	Taipei (2 271)
Tanzania	945	21 733	23	Dodoma (46)
Thailand	514	51 301	100	Bangkok (5 468)
Togo	57	2 960	52	Lomé (283)
Trinidad and Tobago	5	1 185	237	Port of Spain (60)
Tunisia	164	7 081	43	Tunis (774)
Turkey	781	49 272	63	Ankara (2 276)
Uganda	236	15 477	66	Kampala (332)
United Arab Emirates	84	1 327	16	Abu Dhabi (243)
U.S.S.R.	22 402	278 618	12	Moscow (8 537)
United Kingdom	245	56 125	229	London (6 767)
United States	9 373	239 283	26	Washington (3 429)
Uruguay	176	3 012	17	Montevideo (1 362)
Venezuela	912	17 317	19	Caracas (2 944)
Vietnam	330	59 713	181	Hanoi (2 571)
Western Samoa	3	159	53	Apia (32)
Yemen, North	195	6 849	35	Sana' (278)
Yemen, South	333	2 294	7	Aden (264)
Yugoslavia	256	23 123	90	Belgrade (1 407)
Zaïre	2 345	30 363	13	Kinshasa (2 444)
Zambia	753	6 666	9	Lusaka (538)
Zimbabwe	391	8 300	21	Harare (681)

POPULATION OF CITIES

The population figures used are from censuses or more recent estimates and are given in thousands for towns and cities over 200,000 (over 500,000 in China, India, United States and U.S.S.R. and 250,000 in Brazil and Japan). Where possible the population of the metropolitan area is given e.g. Greater London, Greater New York etc.

AFRICA

ALGERIA (1977)
Algiers	1 740
Oran	543
Constantine	379
Annaba	246
Tizi-Ouzou	224

ANGOLA (1982)
Luanda	700

BENIN (1982)
Cotonou	487
Porto-Novo	208

BURKINA FASO (1982)
Ouagadougou	286

CAMEROON (1983)
Douala	708
Yaoundé	485

CANARY ISLANDS (1981)
Las Palmas	360

CENTRAL AFRICAN REPUBLIC (1981)
Bangui	387

CHAD (1979)
Ndjamena	303

CONGO (1980)
Brazzaville	422

EGYPT (1976)
Cairo	6 818
Alexandria	2 318
El Giza	1 230
Shubra el Kheima	394
El Mahalla el Kubra	292
Tanta	285
Port Said	263
El Mansûra	259
Asyût	214
Zagazig	203

ETHIOPIA (1983)
Addis Ababa	1 478
Asmera	491

GABON (1983)
Libreville	350

GHANA (1984)
Accra	965
Kumasi	489

GUINEA (1980)
Conakry	763

IVORY COAST (1982)
Abidjan	1 850
Bouaké	640
Man-Danane	450
Korhogo	280

KENYA (1983)
Nairobi (1985)	1 200
Mombasa	410

LIBERIA (1984)
Monrovia	425

LIBYA (1982)
Tripoli	980
Benghazi	650
Misrâtah	285

MADAGASCAR (1978)
Antananarivo	400

MALAWI (1977)
Blantyre	219

MALI (1976)
Bamako	419

MOROCCO (1981)
Casablanca	2 409
Rabat-Salé	842
Fès	562
Marrakesh	549
Meknès	487
Oujda	470
Kénitra	450
Tétouan	372
Tangier	304
Safi	256
Agadir	246
Khouribga	229
Béni-Mellal	204

MOZAMBIQUE (1970)
Maputo	384

NIGER (1977)
Niamey	225

NIGERIA (1975)
Lagos	1 477
Ibadan	847
Ogbomosho	432
Kano	399
Ilorin	282
Oshogbo	282
Abeokuta	253
Port Harcourt	242
Ilesha	224
Zaria	224
Onitsha	220
Iwo	214
Ado-Ekiti	213
Kaduna	202

SENEGAL (1979)
Dakar	799

SIERRA LEONE (1982)
Freetown	316

SOMALI REP. (1982)
Mogadishu	600

SOUTH AFRICA (1980)
Johannesburg	1 726
Cape Town	1 491
Durban	961
Pretoria	739
Port Elizabeth	585
Vanderbijlpark/ Vereeniging	448

SUDAN (1983)
Omdurman	526
Khartoum	476
Khartoum North	341
Port Sudan	207

TANZANIA (1978)
Dar-es-Salaam	757

TOGO (1980)
Lomé	283

TUNISIA (1984)
Tunis	774
Sfax	232

UGANDA (1975)
Kampala	332

ZAÏRE (1976)
Kinshasa	2 444
Kananga	704
Lubumbashi	451
Mbuji Mayi	383
Kisangani	339
Bukavu	209

ZAMBIA (1980)
Lusaka	538
Kitwe	315
Ndola	282

ZIMBABWE (1983)
Harare	681
Bulawayo	429

ASIA

AFGHANISTAN (1982)
Kābul	1 127

BANGLADESH (1982)
Dacca	3 459
Chittagong	1 388
Khulna	623
Narayanganj	298

BURMA (1977)
Rangoon (1983)	2 459
Mandalay	458
Kanbe (1973)	254

CAMBODIA (KAMPUCHEA) (1983)
Phnom Penh	500

CHINA (1982)
Shanghai	11 940
Beijing	9 330
Tianjin	7 850
Shenyang	4 080
Wuhan	3 280
Guangzhou	3 160
Chongqing	2 690
Harbin	2 560
Chengdu	2 510
Zibo	2 264
Xi'an	2 220
Nanjing	2 170
Taiyuan	1 790
Changchun	1 770
Dalian	1 520
Zhengzhou	1 517
Lanzhou	1 430
Jinan	1 360
Tangshan	1 351
Guiyang	1 330
Kunming	1 320
Anshan	1 240
Qiqihar	1 232
Qingdao	1 210
Hangzhou	1 201
Fushun	1 200
Fuzhou	1 142
Changsha	1 100
Jilin	1 099
Shijiazhuang	1 098
Nanchang	1 061
Baotou	1 051
Huainan	1 017
Ürümqi	944
Xuzhou	793
Suzhou (1970)	730
Wuxi (1970)	650
Hefei (1970)	630
Benxi (1970)	600
Luoyang (1970)	580
Nanning (1970)	550
Hohhot (1970)	530
Xining (1970)	500

HONG KONG (1981)
Kowloon	2 450
Hong Kong	1 184
Tsuen Wan	599

INDIA (1981)
Calcutta	9 194
Bombay	8 243
Delhi	5 729
Madras	4 289
Bangalore	2 922
Ahmadabad	2 548
Hyderabad	2 546
Pune	1 686
Kanpur	1 639
Nagpur	1 302
Jaipur	1 015
Lucknow	1 008
Coimbatore	920
Patna	919
Surat	914
Madurai	908
Indore	829
Varanasi	797
Jabalpur	757
Agra	747
Vadodara	744
Cochin	686
Dhanbad	678
Bhopal	671
Jamshedpur	670
Allahabad	650
Ulhasnagar	649
Tiruchchirappalli	610
Ludhiana	606
Srinagar	606
Vishakhapatnam	604
Amritsar	595
Gwalior	556
Calicut	546
Vijayawada	543
Meerut	537
Dharwad	527
Trivandrum	520
Salem	519
Solapur	515
Jodhpur	506
Ranchi	503

INDONESIA (1980)
Jakarta	6 503
Surabaya	2 028
Bandung	1 462
Medan	1 379
Semarang	1 026
Palembang	787
Ujung Pandang	709
Malang	512
Padang	481
Surakarta	470
Yogyakarta	399
Banjarmasin	381
Pontianak	305
Tanjung Karang	284
Balikpapan	281
Samarinda	265
Bogor	247
Jambi	230
Cirebon	224
Kediri	222
Manado	217
Ambon	209

IRAN (1976)
Tehrān	4 589
Esfahān	842
Mashhad	743
Tabrīz	715
Shirāz	448
Ahvāz	340
Bākhtarān	336
Abadan	308
Qom	247
Hamadan	230
Karaj	214

IRAQ (1970)
Baghdād	2 969
Basra	371
Mosul	293
Kirkūk	208

ISRAEL (1983)
Jerusalem	429
Tel Aviv-Jaffa	327
Haifa	226

JAPAN (1982)
Tōkyō	11 676
Yokohama	2 848
Ōsaka	2 623
Nagoya	2 093
Kyōto	1 480
Sapporo	1 465
Kobe	1 383
Fukuoka	1 121
Kitakyūshū	1 065
Kawasaki	1 055
Hiroshima	898
Sakai	809
Chiba	756
Sendai	662
Okayama	551
Kumamoto	522
Kagoshima	514
Amagasaki	510
Higashiōsaka	501
Hamamatsu	500
Funabashi	488
Shizuoka	462
Niigata	458
Sagamihara	455
Nagasaki	449
Hameji	448
Yokosuka	429
Matsuyama	413
Kanazawa	412
Matsudo	411
Kurashiki	410
Nishinoyama	410
Gifu	409
Wakayama	404
Toyonaka	397
Hachiōji	395
Kawaguchi	391
Utsunomiya	389
Ichikawa	374
Hirakata	368
Oita	367
Urawa	366
Omiya	361
Asahikawa	359
Fukuyama	353
Iwaki	352
Takatsuki	340
Suita	333
Nagano	328
Hakodate	321
Takamatsu	320
Fujisawa	313
Toyohashi	311
Nara	309
Toyama	308
Kōchi	305
Naha	302
Machida	301
Aomori	291
Akita	290
Kōriyama	290
Toyota	287
Maebashi	271
Okazaki	269
Shimonoseki	269
Miyazaki	267
Yao	266
Fukushima	265
Kawagoe	265
Yokkaichi	258
Akashi	257
Neyagawa	255
Ichinomiya	253
Sasebo	253
Tokushima	251

JORDAN (1981)
'Ammān	681
Az-Zarqā	234

KOREA, NORTH (1972)
Pyŏngyang	1 500
Hamhung	420
Chongjin	265
Kimchaek	265

KOREA, SOUTH (1980)
Seoul	8 367
Pusan	3 160
Taegu	1 607
Inchŏn	1 085
Kwangju	728
Taejon	652
Ulsan	418
Masan	387
Songnam	376
Chonju	367
Suwŏn	311

KUWAIT (1980)
Kuwait	775

LEBANON (1980)
Beirut	702

MACAU (1981)
Macau	250

MALAYSIA (1980)
Kuala Lumpur	938
Ipoh	301
Pinang	251

MONGOLIA (1980)
Ulan Bator	419

NEPAL (1981)
Katmandu	235

PAKISTAN (1981)
Karachi	5 103
Lahore	2 922
Faisalabad	1 092
Rawalpindi	806
Hyderabad	795
Multan	730
Gujranwala	597
Peshawar	555
Sialkot	296
Sargodha	294
Quetta	243
Islamabad	201

PHILIPPINES (1980)
Manila	1 630
Quezon City	1 166
Davao	610
Cebu	490
Caloocan	468
Zamboanga	344
Pasay	288
Bacolod	262
Iloilo	245
Cagayan de Oro	227

SAUDI ARABIA (1974)
Riyadh	667
Jedda	561
Mecca	367
Taif	205

SINGAPORE (1983)
Singapore	2 517

SRI LANKA (1982)
Colombo	1 412

SYRIA (1982)
Damascus	1 112
Aleppo	985
Homs	354

TAIWAN (1981)
Taipei	2 271
Kaohsiung	1 227
Taichung	607
Tainan	595
Chilung	348
Sanchung	335
Chiai	252
Hsinchu	243
Fengshan	227
Chunli	215
Yungho	214

THAILAND (1982)
Bangkok	5 468

TURKEY (1982)
İstanbul	2 949
Ankara	2 276
İzmir	1 083
Adana	864
Konya	691
Bursa	658
Gaziantep	526
Mersin	440
Kayseri	394
Diyarbakir	390
Samsun	354
Balikesir	352
Eskişehir	352
İzmit	328
Zonguldak	321
Erzurum	292
Maras	292
Antalya	290
Urfa	285
Sivas	279
Malatya	245
Denizli	211

UNITED ARAB EMIRATES (1980)
Dubai	266
Abu Dhabi	243

VIETNAM (1973)
Ho Chi Minh City (1979)	3 420
Hanoi (1979)	2 571
Haiphong (1979)	1 279
Da-Nang	492
Nha-Trang	216
Qui-Nhon	214
Hue	209

YEMEN, NORTH (1981)
Sana'	278

YEMEN, SOUTH (1981)
Aden	264

AUSTRALIA AND NEW ZEALAND

AUSTRALIA (1983)
Sydney	3 335
Melbourne	2 865
Brisbane	1 138
Adelaide	969
Perth	969
Newcastle	414
Canberra	256
Wollongong	235

NEW ZEALAND (1983)
Auckland	864
Wellington	343
Christchurch	322

EUROPE

ALBANIA (1982)
Tiranë	202

AUSTRIA (1984)
Vienna	1 531
Graz	243

BELGIUM (1983)
Brussels 989
Antwerp 491
Ghent 237
Charleroi 216
Liège 207

BULGARIA (1984)
Sofia 1 094
Plovdiv 373
Varna 295

CZECHOSLOVAKIA (1984)
Prague 1 190
Bratislava 409
Brno 383
Ostrava 325
Kosice 218

DENMARK (1984)
Copenhagen 1 366

FINLAND (1983)
Helsinki 932
Turku 257
Tampere 250

FRANCE (1982)
Paris 8 510
Lyons 1 170
Marseilles 1 080
Lille 935
Bordeaux 628
Toulouse 523
Nantes 465
Nice 449
Toulon 410
Grenoble 392
Rouen 380
Strasbourg 373
Valenciennes 337
Lens 323
St-Étienne 317
Grasse-Cannes 296
Nancy 278
Clermont-Ferrand 256
Le Havre 255
Tours 255
Rennes 234
Montpellier 221
Mulhouse 220
Orléans 220
Dijon 209
Douai 202

GERMANY, EAST (1982)
East Berlin 1 173
Leipzig 557
Dresden 521
Karl-Marx-Stadt 320
Magdeburg 288
Rostock 239
Halle 235
Erfurt 213

GERMANY, WEST (1983)
West Berlin 1 860
Hamburg 1 618
Munich 1 284
Cologne 953
Essen 635
Frankfurt 615
Dortmund 595
Düsseldorf 580
Stuttgart 571
Bremen 545
Duisburg 542
Hanover 524
Nuremberg 476
Bochum 391
Wuppertal 386
Bielefeld 308
Mannheim 300
Gelsenkirchen 295
Bonn 293
Munster 273
Wiesbaden 273
Karlsruhe 270
Mönchengladbach 258
Braunschweig 257
Kiel 248
Augsburg 247
Aachen 244
Oberhausen 226
Krefeld 222
Lübeck 216
Hagen 212

GREECE (1981)
Athens 3 027
Thessaloníki 871

HUNGARY (1984)
Budapest 2 064
Miskolc 211

IRISH REPUBLIC (1981)
Dublin 915

ITALY (1983)
Rome 2 831
Milan 1 561
Naples 1 209
Turin 1 069
Genoa 747
Palermo 712
Bologna 448
Florence 441
Catánia 380
Bari 370
Venice 341
Messina 264
Verona 262
Trieste 246
Táranto 243
Padua 231
Cágliari 225
Bréscia 204

NETHERLANDS (1984)
Rotterdam 1 025
Amsterdam 994
The Hague 672
Utrecht 501
Eindhoven 374
Arnhem 291
Heerlen-Kerkrade 266
Enschede-Hengelo 248
Tilburg 234
Nijmegen 222
Haarlem 217
Groningen 207

NORWAY (1984)
Oslo 643
Bergen 208

POLAND (1984)
Warsaw 1 649
Lodz 849
Kraków 740
Wrocław 636
Poznań 574
Gdansk 467
Szczecin 391
Katowice 363
Bydgoszcz 361
Lublin 324
Sosnowiec 254
Częstochowa 247
Białystok 245
Gdynia 243
Bytom 238
Radom 213
Gliwice 206

PORTUGAL (1981)
Lisbon 1 612
Oporto 1 315

ROMANIA (1982)
Bucharest 1 979
Braşov 334
Constanţa 307
Timişoara 302
Cluj-Napoca 301
Iaşi 295
Galaţi 279
Craiova 253
Ploieşti 228
Brăila 225
Oradea 201

SPAIN (1981)
Madrid 3 188
Barcelona 1 755
Valencia 752
Seville 654
Zaragoza 591
Málaga 503
Bilbao 433
Valladolid 330
Palma de Mallorca 304
Hospitalet 294
Murcia 289
Córdoba 285
Granada 262
Vigo 259
Gijón 256
Alicante 251
La Coruña 232
Badalona 228

SWEDEN (1983)
Stockholm 1 420
Göteborg 699
Malmö 455

SWITZERLAND (1983)
Zürich 840
Geneva 372
Basle 365
Bern 301
Lausanne 225

U.S.S.R. (1983-84)
Moscow 8 537
Leningrad 4 827
Kiev 2 409
Tashkent 1 986
Baku 1 661
Kharkov 1 536
Minsk 1 442
Gorki 1 392
Novosibirsk 1 384
Sverdlovsk 1 286
Kuybyshev 1 250
Dnepropetrovsk 1 140
Tbilisi 1 140
Yerevan 1 114
Odessa 1 113
Omsk 1 094
Chelyabinsk 1 086
Donetsk 1 064
Perm 1 048
Ufa 1 048
Alma-Ata 1 046
Kazan 1 039
Rostov 983
Volgograd 969
Saratov 893
Riga 875
Krasnoyarsk 857
Zaporozhye 844
Voronezh 840
Lvov 728
Krivoy Rog 680
Yaroslavl 623
Karaganda 608
Kishinev 605
Krasnodar 603
Ustinov 603
Frunze 590
Vladivostok 590
Irkutsk 589
Novokuznetsk 572
Barnaul 568
Khabarovsk 568
Dushanbe 539
Vilnius 535
Tula 529
Ulyanovsk 524
Penza 522
Zhdanov 520
Samarkand 515
Orenburg 513

UNITED KINGDOM (1981)
London (1985) 6 767
Birmingham (1985) 1 007
Glasgow 762
Liverpool 510
Leeds 449
Manchester 449
Sheffield 447
Edinburgh 419
Bristol 388
Belfast 374
Coventry 314
Leicester 283
Bradford 281
Cardiff 274
Nottingham 271
Hull 268
Stoke-on-Trent 252
Wolverhampton 252
Plymouth 244
Derby 216
Southampton 204

YUGOSLAVIA (1981)
Belgrade 1 407
Zagreb 1 175
Skopje 507
Sarajevo 449
Ljubljana 305
Novi Sad 258
Split 236
Niš 231
Priština 216

NORTH AMERICA

CANADA (1983)
Toronto 3 067
Montréal 2 862
Vancouver 1 311
Ottawa 738
Edmonton 699
Calgary 634
Winnipeg 601
Québec 580
Hamilton 548
St. Catherines 304
Kitchener 294
London 287
Halifax 281
Windsor 245
Victoria 240

COSTA RICA (1984)
San José 245

CUBA (1982)
Havana 1 951
Santiago de Cuba 349
Camagüey 251

DOMINICAN REP. (1981)
Santo Domingo 1 313
Santiago 279

EL SALVADOR (1983)
San Salvador 884

GUATEMALA (1983)
Guatemala 1 300

HAITI (1982)
Port-au-Prince 888

HONDURAS (1982)
Tegucigalpa 534
San Pedro Sula 398

JAMAICA (1980)
Kingston 671

MEXICO (1979)
Mexico 14 750
Guadalajara 2 468
Netzahualcóyotl 2 331
Monterrey 2 019
Puebla 711
Ciudad Juárez 625
León 625
Tijuana 566
Acapulco 462
Torreón 407
Tampico 390
Chihuahua 386
Mexicali 349
San Luis Potosi 327
Culiacán 324
Hermosillo 319
Veracruz 307
Mérida 270
Saltillo 258
Aguascalientes 257
Morelia 251
Toluca 242
Cuernavaca 241
Reynosa 231
Durango 229
Nuevo Laredo 224
Jalapa 201

NICARAGUA (1981)
Managua 615

PANAMA (1981)
Panama 655

PUERTO RICO (1980)
San Juan 1 086
Ponce 253
Bayamón 209

UNITED STATES (1984)
New York 17 807
Los Angeles 12 373
Chicago 8 035
Philadelphia 5 755
San Francisco 5 685
Detroit 4 577
Boston 4 027
Houston 3 566
Washington 3 429
Dallas 3 348
Miami 2 799
Cleveland 2 788
St. Louis 2 398
Atlanta 2 380
Pittsburgh 2 372
Baltimore 2 245
Minneapolis 2 231
Seattle 2 208
San Diego 2 064
Tampa 1 811
Denver 1 791
Phoenix 1 715
Cincinnati 1 673
Milwaukee 1 568
Kansas City 1 477
Portland 1 341
New Orleans 1 319
Columbus 1 279
Sacramento 1 220
Buffalo 1 205
Indianapolis 1 195
San Antonio 1 188
Providence 1 095
Norfolk 1 026
Salt Lake City 1 025
Rochester 989
Louisville 963
Oklahoma 963
Memphis 935
Dayton 930
Birmingham 895
Nashville-Davidson 890
Greensboro 886
Albany 843
Orlando 824
Honolulu 805
Richmond 796
Jacksonville 795
Hartford 729
Scranton 727
Tulsa 726
West Palm Beach 692
Syracuse 650
Charlotte 647
Austin 645
Allentown 635
Grand Rapids 626
Toledo 611
Raleigh 609
Omaha 607
Greenville 593
Knoxville 589
Fresno 565
Baton Rouge 538
Las Vegas 536
Tucson 531
El Paso 526
Youngstown 518
Springfield 516

SOUTH AMERICA

ARGENTINA (1980)
Buenos Aires 9 927
Córdoba 982
Rosario 955
Mendoza 597
La Plata 560
San Miguel de Tucuman 497
Mar del Plata 407
San Juan 290
Santa Fé 287
Salta 260
Bahia Blanca 221
Resistencia 218

BOLIVIA (1982)
La Paz 881
Santa Cruz 377
Cochabamba 282

BRAZIL (1980)
São Paulo 8 493
Rio de Janeiro 5 091
Belo Horizonte 1 781
Salvador 1 502
Fortaleza 1 308
Recife 1 204
Brasilia 1 177
Pôrto Alegre 1 125
Nova Iguaçu 1 095
Curitiba 1 025
Belém 933
Goiánia 717
Campinas 665
Manaus 633
São Gonçalo 615
Duque de Caxias 576
Santo André 553
Guarulhos 533
Osasco 474
São Luis 449
São Bernardo do Campo 426
Natal 417
Santos 417
Maceió 399
São João de Meriti 399
Niterói 397
Teresina 378
Campos 348
Jaboatao 330
João Pessoa 330
Ribeirão Preto 318
Juiz de Fora 307
Londrina 302
Aracaju 293
Campo Grande 292
Feira de Santana 292
São José dos Campos 288
Olinda 282
Sorocaba 269
Pelotas 260
Jundiaí 259

CHILE (1983)
Santiago 4 132
Viña del Mar 299
Valparaiso 268
Talcahuano 213
Concepción 210

COLOMBIA (1980)
Bogotá 4 486
Medellin 1 812
Cali 1 232
Barranquilla 900
Bucaramanga 459
Cartagena 368
Pereira 309
Manizales 302
Cucuta 272
Ibagué 238

ECUADOR (1982)
Guayaquil 1 301
Quito 1 110

PARAGUAY (1983)
Asunción 708

PERU (1981)
Lima (1983) 5 258
Arequipa 447
Callao 441
Trujillo 355
Chiclayo 280
Chimbote 216

URUGUAY (1981)
Montevideo 1 362

VENEZUELA (1980)
Caracas 2 944
Maracaibo 901
Valencia 506
Barquisimento 489
Maracay 344
Barcelona-Puerto La Cruz 275
San Cristóbal 272

SELECTED REFERENCES

These selected references are additional to the contents list on the previous pages and are included to take the reader directly to the page required for certain well known and used names. The list includes all country names and names of large geographical features, mountains and seas for example. The page(s) quoted will be the one(s) where the feature appears as a whole and at the largest scale.

CHART OF THE STARS

Northern Stars

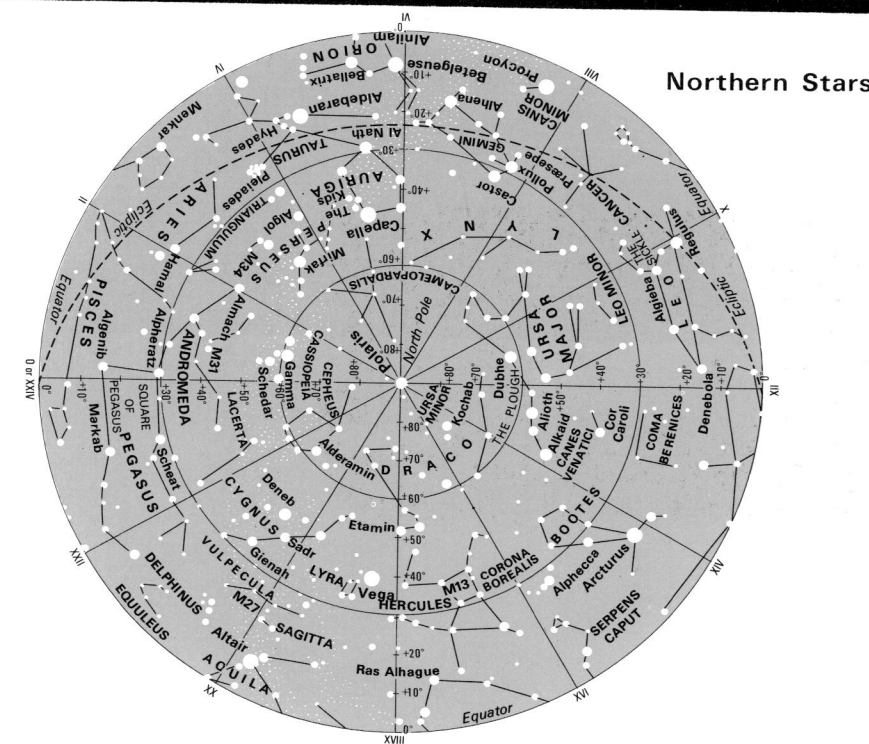

Above: Rosette Nebula in Monoceros.

Stars of the Middle Heavens

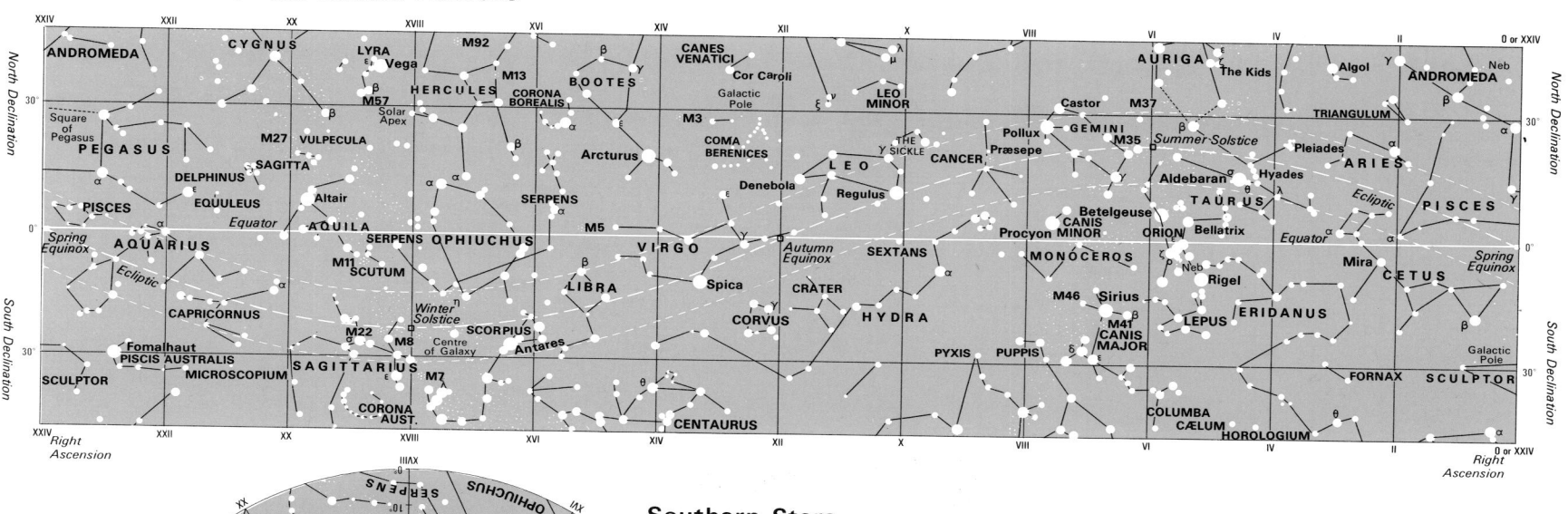

Southern Stars

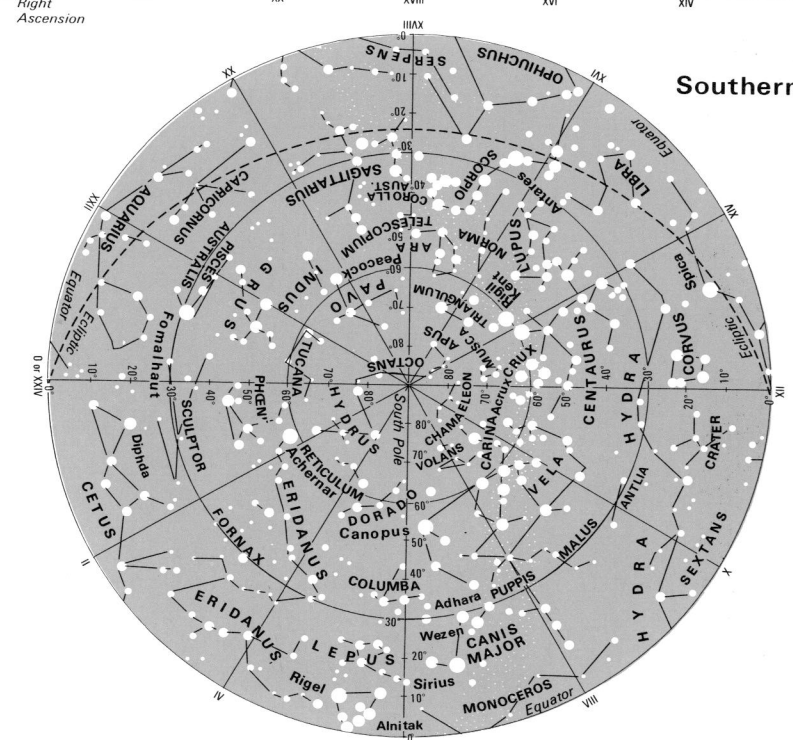

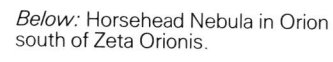

Below: Horsehead Nebula in Orion south of Zeta Orionis.

Above: The Trifid Nebula consists mainly of glowing hydrogen gas. 'Dark lanes' of silhouetted dust can be seen crossing the disc making the nebula resemble a pansy.

THE SOLAR SYSTEM

The solar system is a minute part of one of the billions of galaxies that make up the universe. **Our galaxy** is represented in the top drawing at the right, with our **solar system** (S) lying 27 000 light years from its center. The system consists of a central sun with planets, moons, asteroids, comets, meteors, meteorites, dust, and gases in orbit around it. It is at least 4 700 million years old. As depicted at the bottom right, the sun's diameter is 109 times that of the earth.

We can consider the solar system as having two parts: the **inner region planets** and the **outer region planets**. The inner planets are (from the sun outward): Mercury, Venus, Earth, and Mars. The outer ones are: Jupiter, Saturn, Uranus, Neptune, and Pluto.

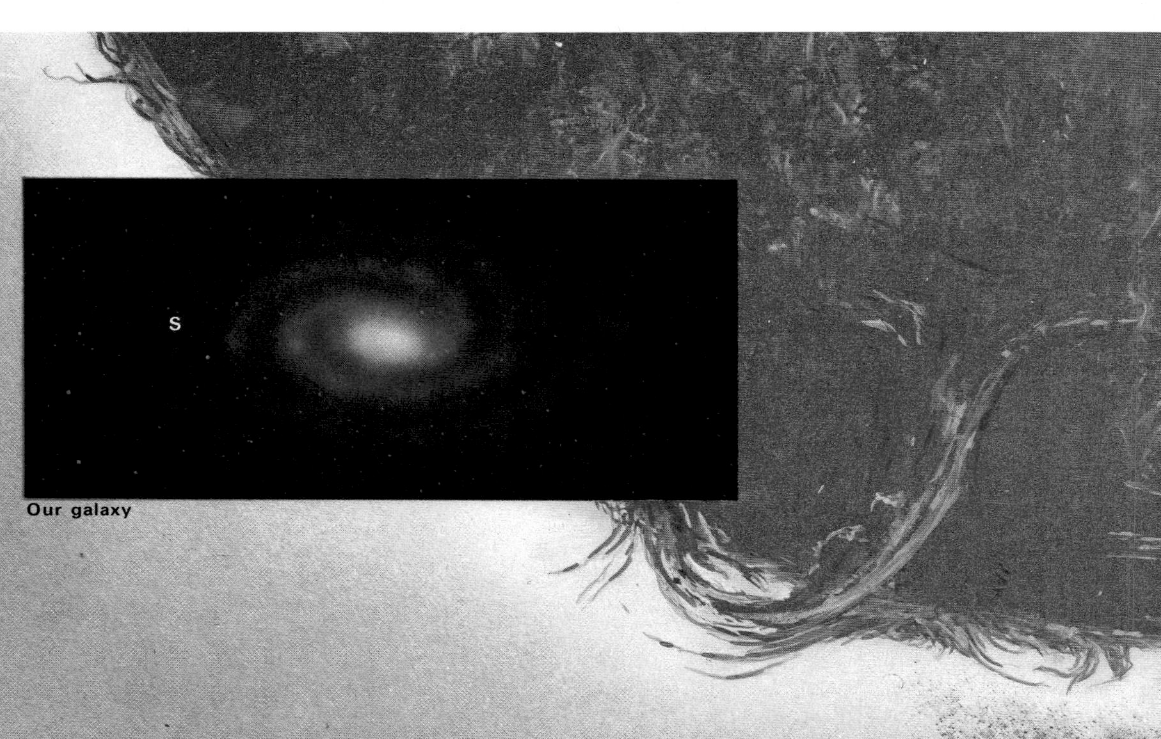

Our galaxy

Inner region planets

Mercury
Venus
Earth
Mars

Outer region planets

Mars
Jupiter
Saturn
Uranus
Neptune
Pluto

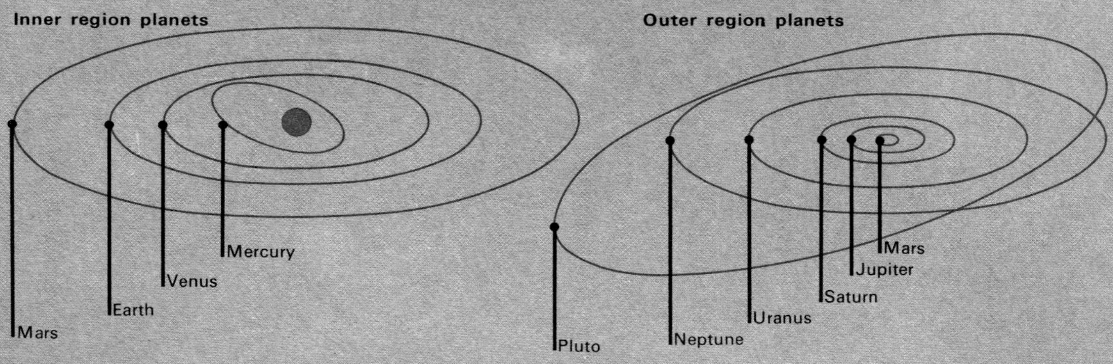

All the planets revolve around the sun in the same direction, and mostly in the same plane. The diagrams at the left show the planets' orbits; their paths are not perfectly circular.

The table below summarizes their dimensions and movements.

The interior of the sun has a temperature of about 15 million degrees Celsius, brought about by continuous thermonuclear fusion of hydrogen to helium. This immense energy is transferred by radiation to the surrounding layers of gas, the outer surface of which is called the chromosphere. Solar prominences, or flares, leap from the chromosphere, forming a diffuse corona. The corona can best be seen at times of **total solar eclipse,** as shown in the top photograph. The temperature of the sun's surface is calculated to be about 6 000°C. The bottom photograph shows the **surface of the sun** with sunspots prominent. Sunspots are sites of great disturbance.

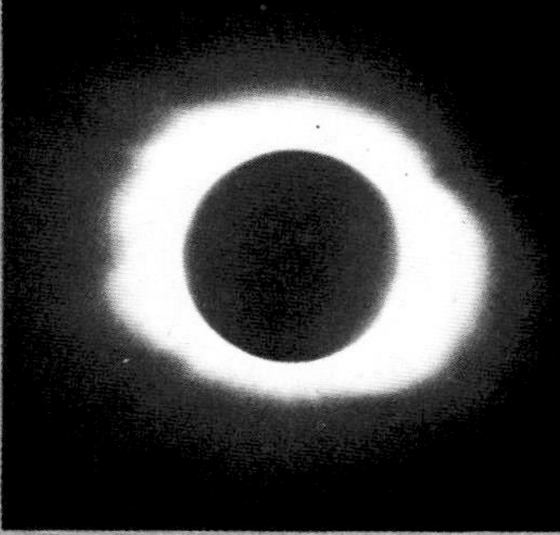

Total eclipse of the sun

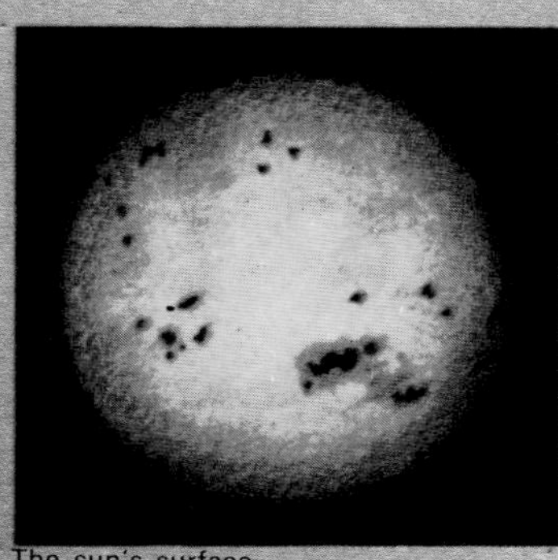

The sun's surface

	Equatorial diameter in km	Mass (earth = 1)	Mean distance from sun in millions km	Mean radii of orbit (earth = 1)	Orbital inclination	Mean sidereal period (days)	Mean period of rotation on axis (days)	Number of satellites
Sun	1 392 000	332 946	—	—	—	—	25·38	—
Mercury	4 878	0·05	57·9	0·38	7°	87·9	58·6	0
Venus	12 104	0·81	108·2	0·72	3°23'	224·7	243	0
Earth	12 756	1·00	149·6	1·00	—	365·2	0·99	1
Mars	6 794	0·10	227·9	1·52	1°50'	686·9	1·02	2
Jupiter	142 800	317·9	778·3	5·20	1°18'	4332·5	0·41	14 ?
Saturn	120 000	95·1	1 427	9·53	2°29'	10759·2	0·42	11
Uranus	52 000	14·5	2 869	19·17	0°46'	30684·8	0·45	5
Neptune	48 400	17·2	4 496	30·05	1°46'	60190·5	0·67	2
Pluto	3 000 ?	0·001	5 900	39·43	17°1'	91628·6	6·38	1 ?

The Sun's diameter is 109 times greater than that of the Earth.

Distances from sun in millions km

57·9 — Mercury
108·2 — Venus
149·6 — Earth
227·9 — Mars

778·3 — Jupiter

1427 — Saturn

2869 — Uranus

4496 — Neptune

5900 — Pluto

Mercury, the smallest planet, is nearest to the sun. It is made mostly of metals and has an atmosphere of inert gases.

Venus is similar in size to Earth, and probably in composition. But Venus is much hotter and has a dense atmosphere of carbon dioxide.

Earth, largest of the inner planets, has a dense iron and nickel core that is surrounded by layers of rock. Its surface is about three-eighths land and five-eighths water. The lower atmosphere consists of a life-supporting mixture of nitrogen, oxygen, carbon dioxide, and other gases plus water vapor. Surface temperatures usually range between $-50°C$ and $+40°C$.

Mars, smaller than Earth, has a noticeably red appearance. Recent photographs sent back by spacecraft show clearly the cratered surface and ice areas at the poles. The planet is a vast wasteland.

The Asteroids orbit the sun mainly between Mars and Jupiter. They consist of thousands of bodies of varying sizes with diameters ranging from yards to hundreds of miles.

Jupiter is the largest planet of the solar system. It shines brightly, having a magnitude of -2.5, and is notable for its many belts and great red spot.

Saturn, the second largest planet, consists of hydrogen, helium, and other gases. Its density is less than that of water. It is unique in appearance because of its equatorial rings, believed to be made of ice-covered particles.

Uranus was discovered in 1781 by Herschel. It is extremely remote yet faintly visible to the naked eye. Methane in its atmosphere gives it a slightly greenish appearance.

Neptune is even more remote than Uranus and larger. It is composed of gases and has a bluish-green appearance through a telescope. As with Uranus, little detail can be observed on its surface.

Pluto is the most distant and second smallest planet. Little is known of its surface and composition. Its existence was first surmised in a computed hypothesis, which was tested by repeated searches with large telescopes. The planet was finally found in 1930.

THE EARTH

The **seasons, solstices, and equinoxes** are shown in the top drawing. The earth revolves around the sun once a year, rotating once daily on its axis. Its axis is inclined at 66.5° to the orbital plane and always points into space in the same direction. In summer, the North Pole (N) points toward the sun; in winter, it points away from the sun. At the spring and autumn equinoxes, day and night are of equal length.

The second drawing below compares the **length of day and night** in the northern and southern hemispheres. At the summer solstice in the northern hemisphere, the Arctic has total daylight, and the Antarctic total darkness. The opposite occurs at the winter solstice. At the equator, the length of day and night are almost equal all the year. At 30° latitude, the length of the day varies from about 14 to 10 hours and at 50°, from about 16 to 8 hours.

The diagrams in the third and fourth rows on the page show the **apparent path of the sun** at various latitudes in different seasons. In diagram A, at the equator; B, in mid-latitudes; C, at the Arctic Circle; and D, at the North Pole. At the North Pole, there is a six-month period of continuous daylight followed by six months of continuous darkness.

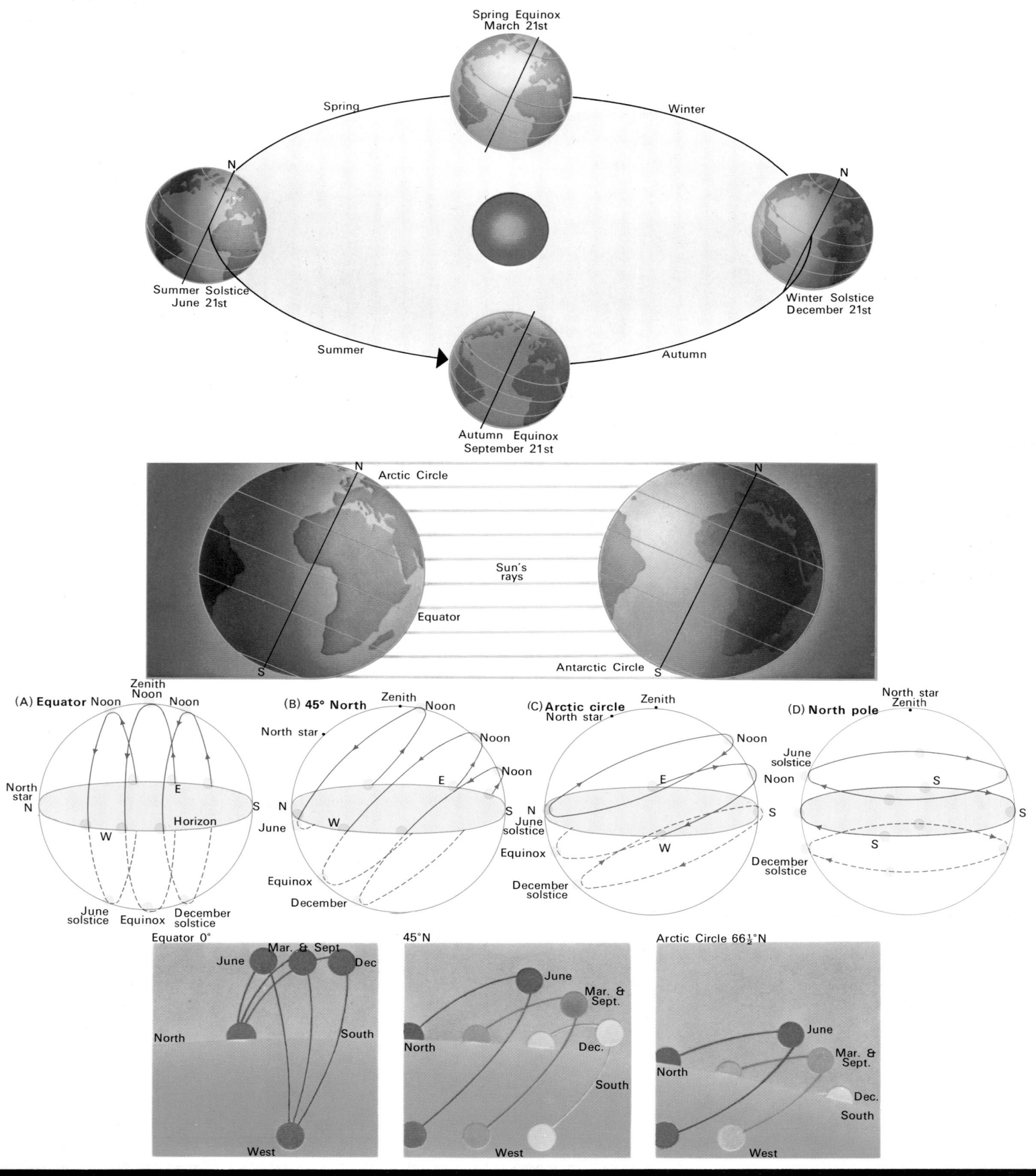

THE MOON

The moon rotates slowly, making one complete turn on its axis in just over 27 days. This rotation period corresponds to one **revolution of the moon around the earth** (top diagram). Thus, the moon always presents to us the same hemisphere or face. We never see the far side of the moon. The composite photograph beneath the diagram shows the **phases of the moon**, which are numbered to match the diagram. The interval between one full moon and the next is about 29½ days. The apparent changes in the shape of the moon arise from its changing position in relation to the earth.

The bottom drawing at the right depicts the relative **size of the moon and the earth**. The illustration above it shows the **landing sites of U. S. Apollo missions** 11 (Sea of Tranquility, 1969), 12 (Ocean of Storms, 1969), 14 (Fra Mauro, 1971), 15 (Hadley Rill, 1971), 16 (Descartes, 1972), 17 (Sea of Serenity, 1972). The astronauts had to cope with an environment devoid of water and atmosphere and temperatures approximating +200°C. The moon's mean diameter is 3 473 km. Its mass approximates 1/81 that of the earth. Its distance from the earth varies from 356 410 to 406 685 km.

The top diagram on the lower half of the page depicts **eclipses of the sun and moon**. When the moon passes between the sun and the earth, it causes a partial eclipse (1) of the sun if the earth passes through the moon's outer shadow (P). It causes a total eclipse (2) if the inner cone shadow crosses the earth's surface. In a lunar eclipse, the earth's shadow crosses the moon and gives either a total or partial eclipse.

The bottom diagram shows **the moon's effect on tides**. When solar and lunar gravitational forces pull together near new and full moon, high spring tides result. At the quarters, neap tides occur.

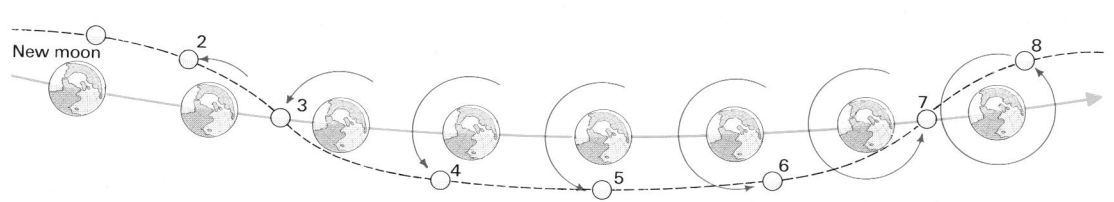

Crescent moon(2) Half moon, first quarter(3) Gibbous moon (4) Full moon (5) The waning moon (6) Half moon, last quarter(7) The old moon (8)

Landings on the Moon

Apollo 11 Sea of Tranquility (1°N 23°E) 1969
Apollo 12 Ocean of Storms (3°S 24°W) 1969
Apollo 14 Fra Mauro (4°S 17°W) 1971
Apollo 15 Hadley Rill (25°N 4°E) 1971
Apollo 16 Descartes (9°S 15°E) 1972
Apollo 17 Sea of Serenity (20°N 31°E) 1972

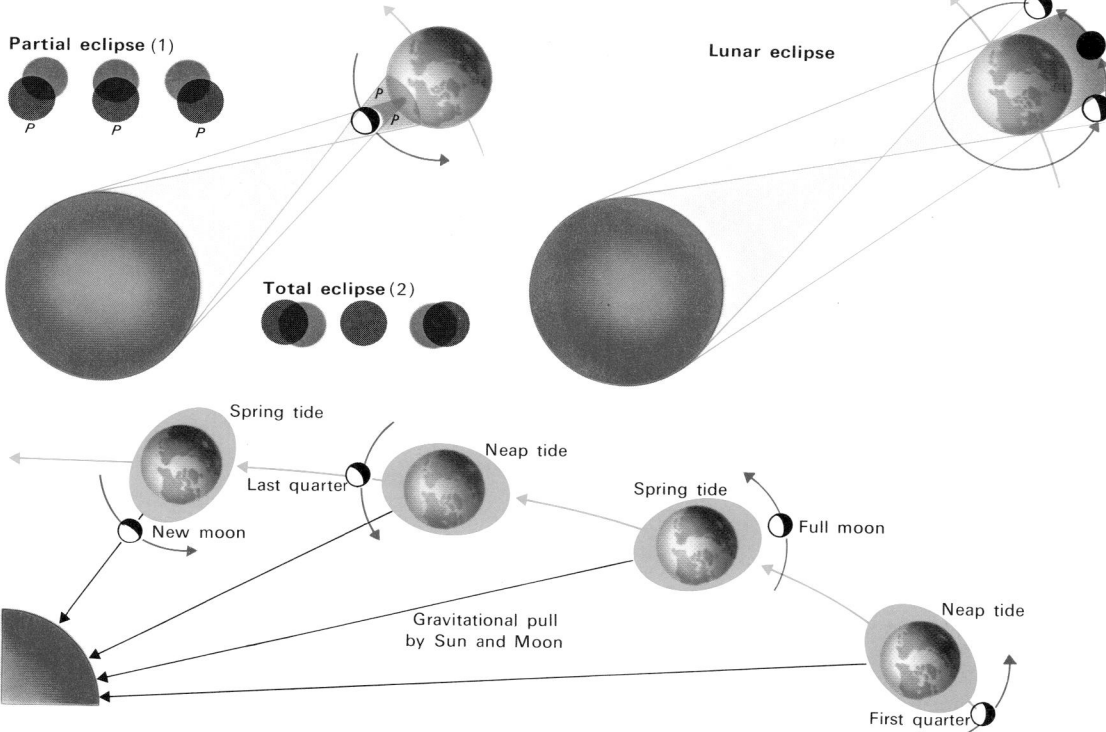

Partial eclipse (1)

Total eclipse (2)

Lunar eclipse

Spring tide

Neap tide

Last quarter

New moon

Spring tide

Full moon

Gravitational pull by Sun and Moon

Neap tide

First quarter

Moon data

Distance from Earth 356 410 km
                    to 406 685 km
Mean diameter 3 473 km
Mass approx. $\frac{1}{81}$ of that of Earth
Surface gravity $\frac{1}{6}$ of that of Earth
Atmosphere - none, hence no clouds,
            no weather, no sound.
Diurnal range of temperature at
the Equator +200°C

TIME

The basic unit of time measurement is the day, one **rotation of the earth** on its axis, as depicted immediately below. The subdivision of the day into hours and minutes is arbitrary and simply for our convenience. Our present calendar is based on the solar year of 365.25 days, the time taken by the earth to orbit the sun. As the earth rotates from west to east, the sun appears to rise in the east and set in the west. When the sun is setting in Shanghai, on the directly opposite side of the earth New York is just emerging into sunlight. Noon, when the sun is directly overhead, is coincident at all places on the same meridian, with shadows pointing directly toward the poles, as shown in the second diagram of the earth below.

Astronomers distinguish between **solar time** (see diagram at bottom, left) and **sidereal time** (bottom, right). Solar time has to do with the time taken by the earth to rotate on its axis. One rotation defines a solar day. But the speed of the earth along its orbit around the sun is inconstant. The length of day, or "apparent solar day," as defined by the apparent successive transits of the sun is irregular because the earth must complete more than one rotation before the sun returns to the same meridian. The constant sidereal day is defined as the interval between two successive apparent transits of a star, or the first point of Aries, across the same meridian. If the sun is at the equinox and overhead at a meridian one day, then the next day the sun will be to the east by approximately 1°. Thus, the sun will not cross the meridian until about 4 minutes after the sidereal noon.

From the diagrams at bottom right it is possible to find out the time of sunrise or sunset on a given date and for latitudes between 60°N and 60°S.

Rotation of the Earth

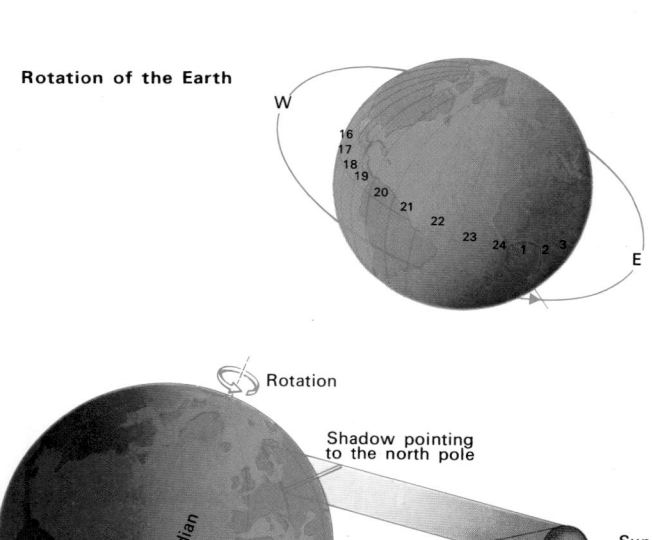

Greenwich Observatory

Astronomical clock, Delhi

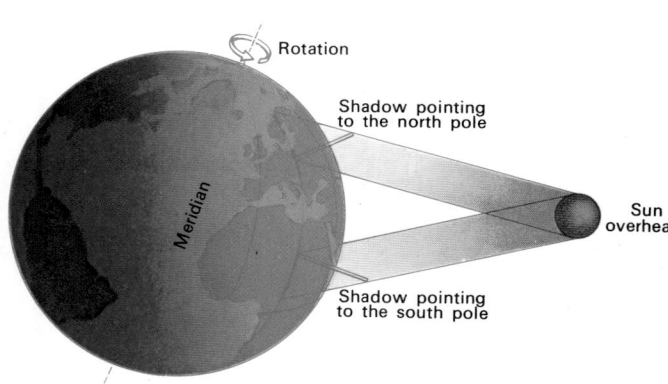

Prime Meridian

Kendall's chronometer

Time

The Year – the time taken by the Earth to revolve around the Sun, or 365¼ days.

The Month – the approximate time taken by the Moon to revolve around the Earth. The twelve months of the year in fact vary from 28 (29 in a Leap Year) to 31 days.

The Week – an artificial period of 7 days, not based on astronomical time.

The Day – the time taken by the Earth to complete one rotation on its axis.

The Hour – 24 hours make one day. Usually the day is divided into hours A.M. (ante meridiem or before noon) and P.M. (post meridiem or after noon), although most timetables now use the 24-hour system, from midnight to midnight, for example, 1p.m. = 13.00 hours.

International date line

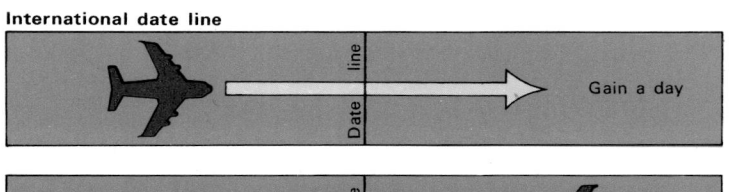

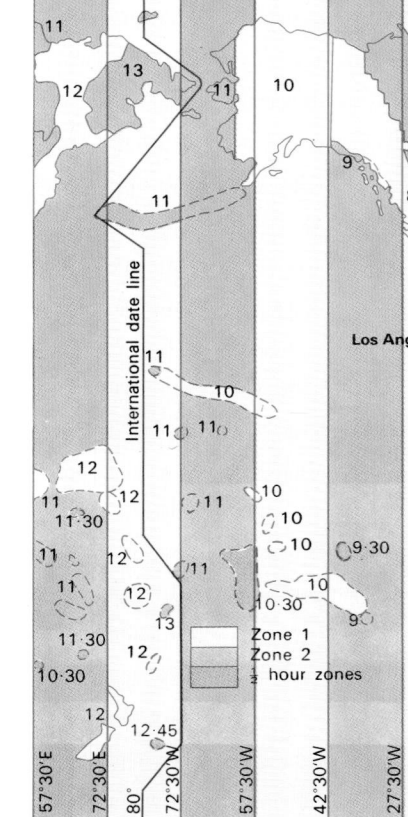

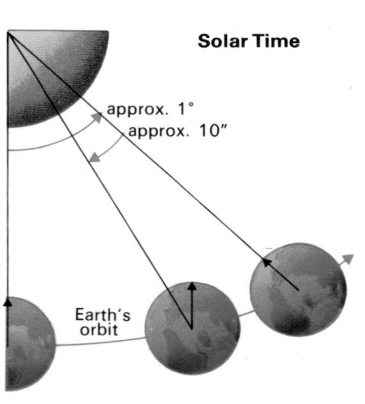

Solar Time

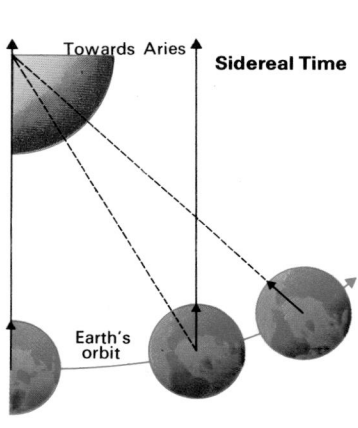

Sidereal Time

Sunrise

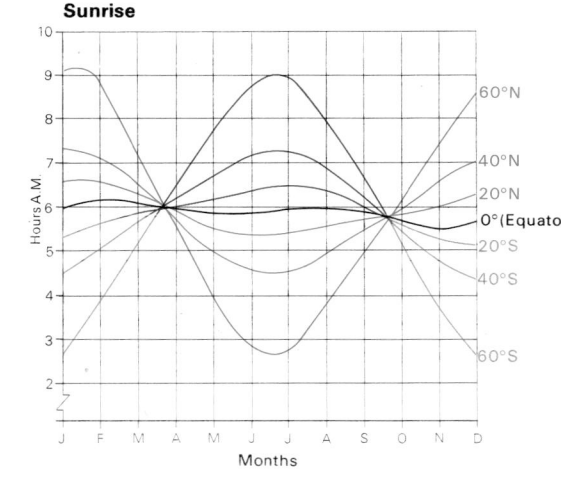

Sunset

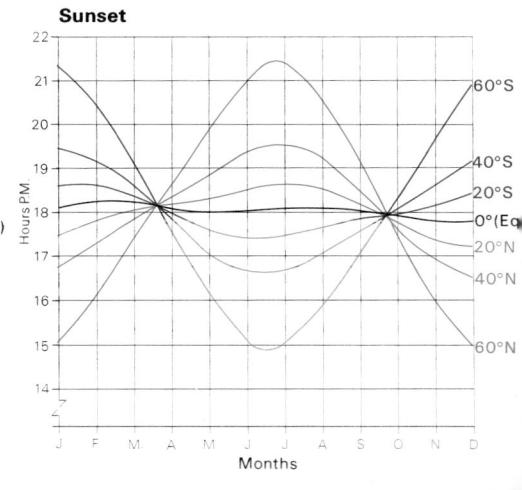

As shown on the map below, the world is divided into 24 **time zones**. Each zone is centered at 15° intervals, the longitudinal distance the sun appears to travel every hour. The meridian running through Greenwich Observatory in England passes through the middle of the first zone. At 0° longitude, it is called the Prime Meridian. Successive zones to the east of the Greenwich zone are ahead of Greenwich time by one hour for every 15° of longitude, whereas zones to the west are behind by one hour.

When it is noon at the Greenwich meridian, at a point 180° east it is midnight of the same day, and at 180° west the day is only just beginning. To overcome this discrepancy, the **International Dateline** (see map) was established, approximately following the 180° meridian. Thus, for example, traveling eastward from Japan (140 east) to Samoa (170 west), one would pass from Sunday night into Sunday morning. A plane or ship crossing the dateline from west to east gains a day; crossing in the opposite direction, it would lose a day. The chart at the right below shows **time differences when traveling by air**.

The graph at the left below shows the **progress of the accuracy of timekeepers** over the past 700 years. Inventive genius replaced the sundial with a variety of devices, including the chronometer and chronograph of the 18th and 19th centuries, topping them all with the 20th century atomic clocks. The quartz crystal clock, for example, can measure small units of time and radio frequencies. The connection between quartz clocks and the natural vibrations of atoms and molecules means that the unchanging frequencies emitted by atoms can be used to control the quartz clock. The diagram at the center below depicts the **vibration of a quartz ring**. A recent version of an atomic clock is accurate to one second in 300 years.

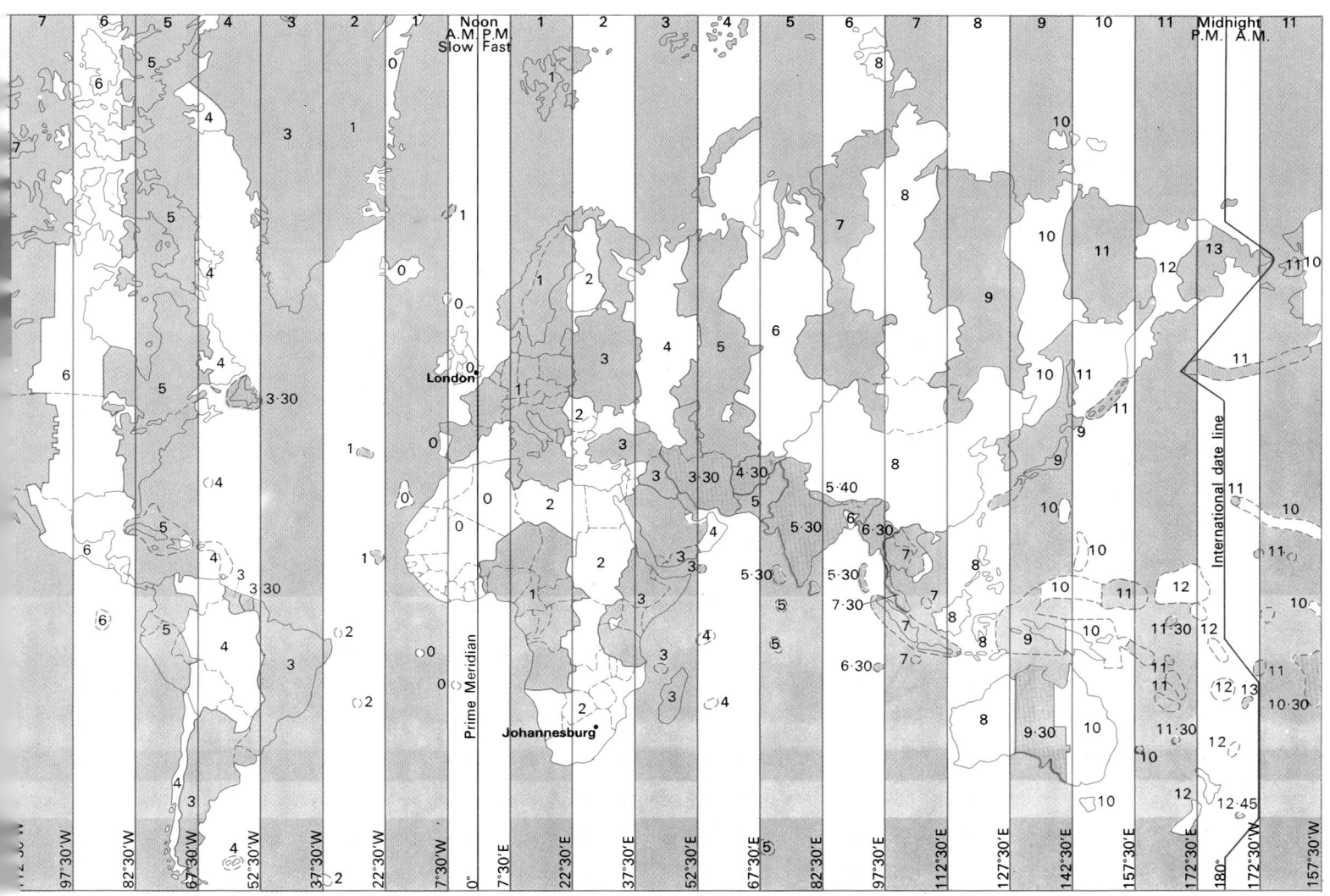

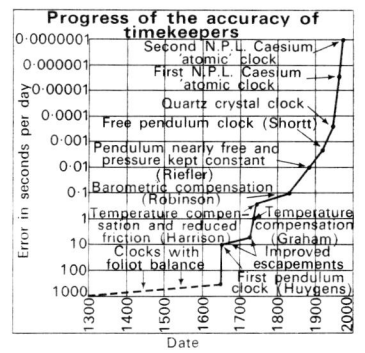

Progress of the accuracy of timekeepers

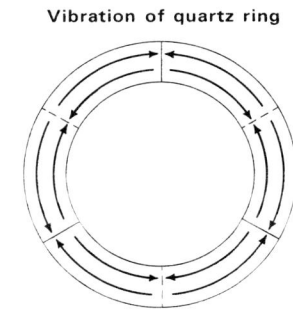

Vibration of quartz ring

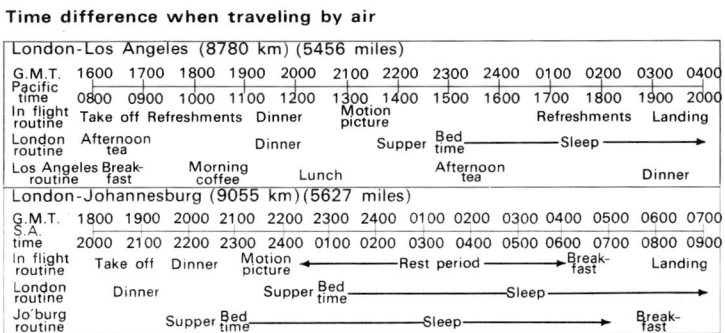

Time difference when traveling by air

London-Los Angeles (8780 km) (5456 miles)													
G.M.T.	1600	1700	1800	1900	2000	2100	2200	2300	0100	0200	0300	0400	
Pacific time	0800	0900	1000	1100	1200	1300	1400	1500	1600	1700	1800	1900	2000
In flight routine	Take off	Refreshments	Dinner		Motion picture					Refreshments	Landing		
London routine	Afternoon tea			Dinner			Supper	Bed time	Sleep				
Los Angeles routine	Break-fast		Morning coffee		Lunch			Afternoon tea		Dinner			

London-Johannesburg (9055 km)(5627 miles)													
G.M.T.	1800	1900	2000	2100	2200	2300	2400	0100	0200	0300	0400	0500	0600	0700
S.A. time	2000	2100	2200	2300	2400	0100	0200	0300	0400	0500	0600	0700	0800	0900
In flight routine	Take off	Dinner	Motion picture		Rest period					Break-fast	Landing			
London routine	Dinner			Supper	Bed time	Sleep								
Jo'burg routine			Supper	Bed time		Sleep					Break-fast			

THE ATMOSPHERE AND CLOUDS

Earth's atmosphere is a blanket of protective gases, as shown below at the left, that provide insulation against otherwise extreme alternations in temperature. The earth's gravitational pull increases the density of the atmosphere near the earth's surface so that five-sixths of the atmospheric mass is in the first 15 km. This blanket of air is a very thin layer compared with the earth's diameter of 12 680 km. The **physical and chemical structure of the atmosphere** are illustrated at the center and right below.

Four main layers comprise the atmosphere: **exosphere**, **ionosphere**, **stratosphere**, and **troposphere**. The highest layer, exosphere, merges with the interplanetary medium. Although there is no definite boundary with the next layer, the ionosphere, the exosphere starts at a height of about 600 km. Its rarefied air consists mainly of a small amount of atomic oxygen and equal proportions of hydrogen and helium at the 600-km level, but with hydrogen predominating above 2 400 km. Air particles of the ionosphere are electrically charged by the sun's radiation and congregate in four main layers — D, E, F-1, and F-2 — which can reflect radio waves. Auroras, caused by charged particles deflected toward the poles of the earth's magnetic field, are a phenomenon of the ionosphere. It is in the lower ionosphere that meteors from outer space burn up as they meet increased air resistance.

The stratosphere contains a thin layer of ozone which absorbs ultra-violet light, giving off heat. This warmer region of the stratosphere, just above the ozone layer, is called the **mesosphere**. These layers are separated from the troposphere by the **tropopause**.

Cloud formation is a major characteristic of

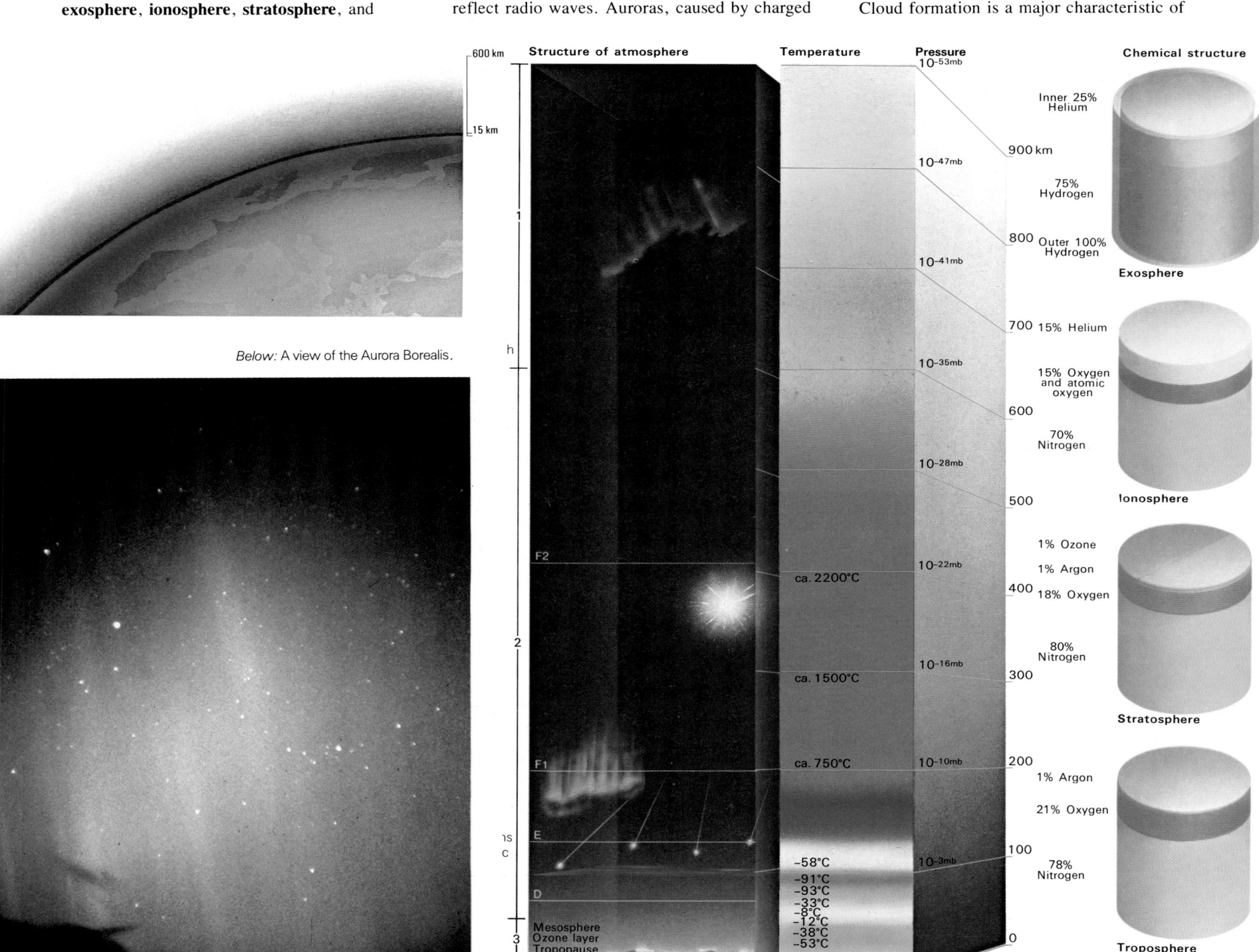

Below: A view of the Aurora Borealis.

Structure of atmosphere

Temperature

Pressure

Chemical structure

the troposphere. The two photographs at the lower left show the paths of prevailing winds in **cloud patterns over the Pacific Ocean**. The origin of these winds is shown in the two drawings beneath the photographs. The drawing on the left shows the **circulation of the air** set up by the high temperatures of the equatorial regions of the earth. Hot air expands and rises, producing a low pressure belt. As the air cools at high altitudes, it loses moisture, spreads out, and sinks, thus forming high pressure belts. The **interaction of high and low pressure belts** to produce prevailing winds is shown in the diagram at the bottom right.

Clouds form when damp, usually rising, air is cooled. Thus, they form when a wind rises to cross hills or mountains; when a mass of air rises over, or is pushed up by, another mass of denser air; or when local heating of the ground causes convection currents. The nine **types of clouds** are classified according to altitude as high, middle, or low. The high ones are **cirrus** (1), **cirrostratus** (2), and **cirrocumulus** (3). These clouds are made up of ice crystals. The middle clouds are **altostratus** (4), a gray or bluish striated, fibrous, or uniform sheet

producing light drizzle, and **altocumulus** (5), a thicker and fluffier version of cirrocumulus. The low clouds include **nimbostratus** (6), a dark gray layer that brings almost continuous rain or snow; **cumulus** (7), a detached heap — brilliant white in sunlight but dark and flat at the base; **stratus** (8), which forms dull, overcast skies at low altitudes; and **cumulonimbus** (9), associated with storms and rain, heavy and dense with flat base and a high, fluffy outline.

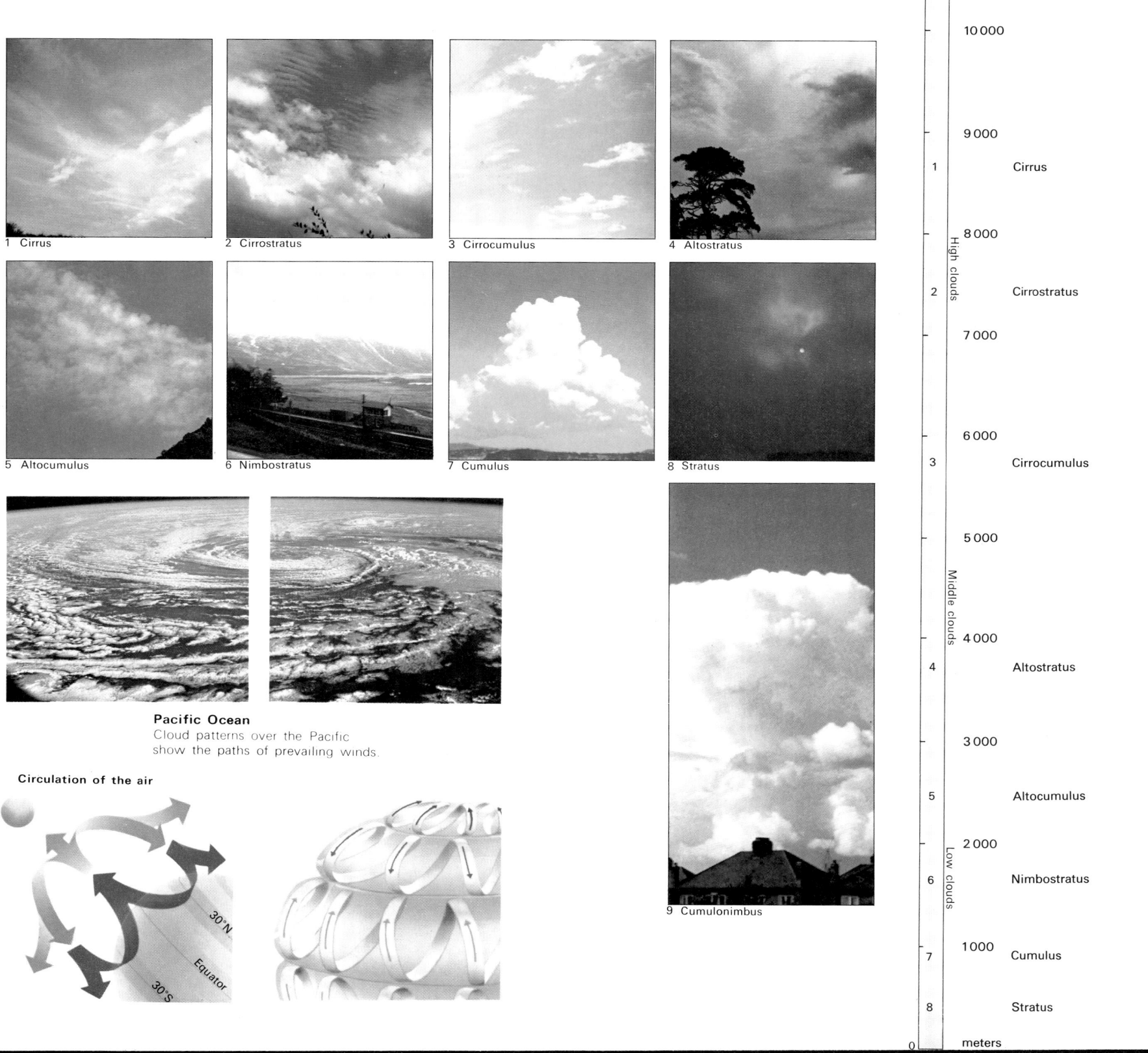

1 Cirrus
2 Cirrostratus
3 Cirrocumulus
4 Altostratus
5 Altocumulus
6 Nimbostratus
7 Cumulus
8 Stratus
9 Cumulonimbus

Pacific Ocean
Cloud patterns over the Pacific show the paths of prevailing winds.

Circulation of the air

30°N
Equator
30°S

Altitude at which clouds are formed

10 000
9 000
8 000
7 000
6 000
5 000
4 000
3 000
2 000
1 000
0
meters

High clouds
Middle clouds
Low clouds

1 Cirrus
2 Cirrostratus
3 Cirrocumulus
4 Altostratus
5 Altocumulus
6 Nimbostratus
7 Cumulus
8 Stratus

CLIMATE AND WEATHER

Weather has been defined as the condition of the atmosphere at any place at a specific time with respect to various elements: temperature, precipitation, pressure, winds, and so on. Climate is the average of weather elements over previous months and years. Each of the **climate graphs** below typifies the kind of climatic conditions one would experience in the region to which the graph is related by color on the world climate map at the right. The scale refers to degrees Celsius for temperature and millimeters for rainfall, shown by bars.

The small map at the right below shows **tropical storm tracks**. A tropical cyclone, or storm, has winds of gale force (60 kph) but less than hurricane force (120 kph). It is a homogeneous air mass with upward spiralling currents around a windless center, or eye.

The diagrams labeled (i) through (iv) at the lower left show the **development of a depression**, or low-pressure center. In an equilibrium front (i), a wave of disturbance develops as cold air undercuts warm air (ii). Cyclone circulation is created (iii). Occlusion occurs as the warm air is pinched out (iv). **Kinds of precipitation** are shown at the bottom of the page.

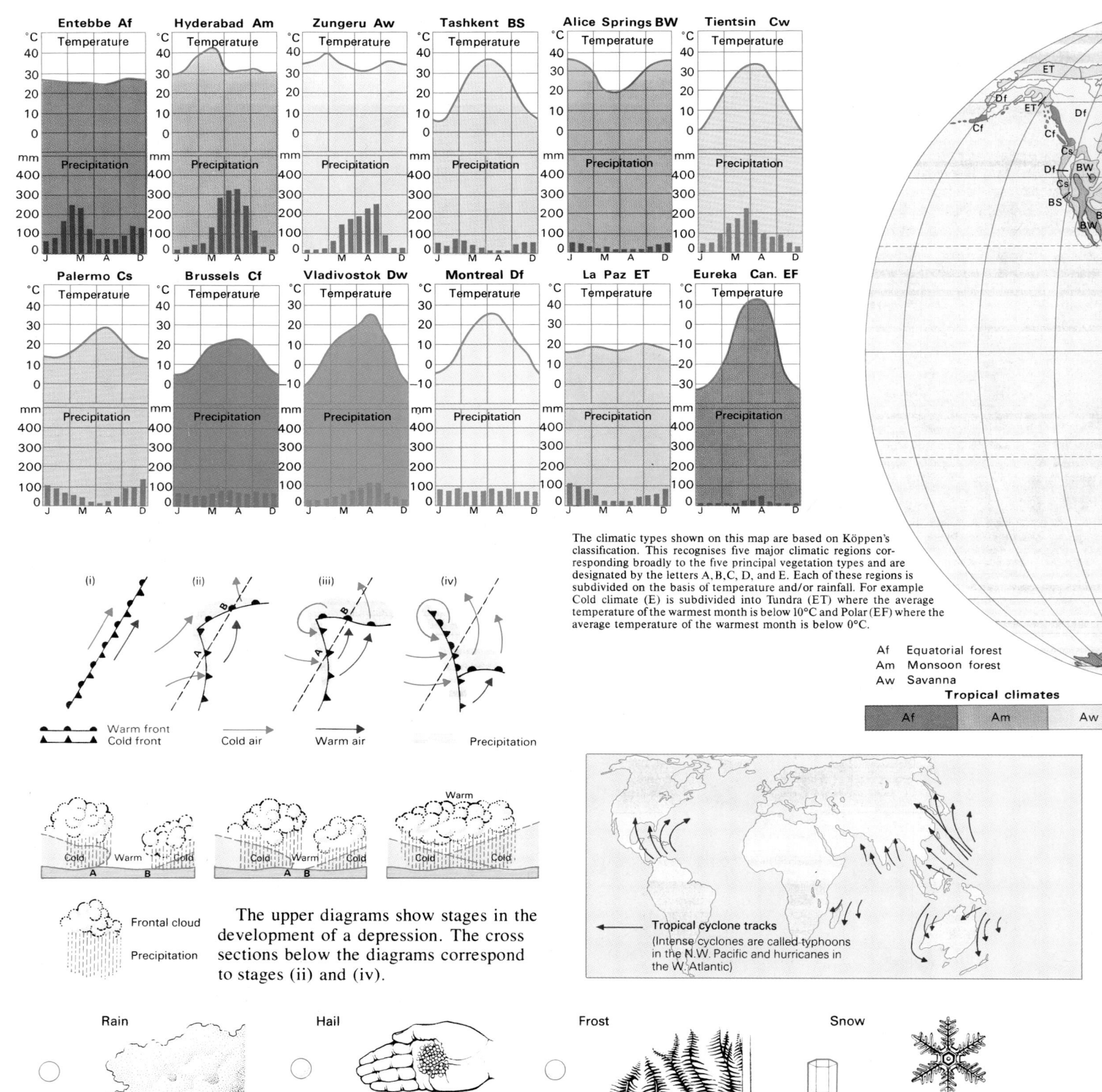

The climatic types shown on this map are based on Köppen's classification. This recognises five major climatic regions corresponding broadly to the five principal vegetation types and are designated by the letters A, B, C, D, and E. Each of these regions is subdivided on the basis of temperature and/or rainfall. For example Cold climate (E) is subdivided into Tundra (ET) where the average temperature of the warmest month is below 10°C and Polar (EF) where the average temperature of the warmest month is below 0°C.

Af Equatorial forest
Am Monsoon forest
Aw Savanna
Tropical climates

Warm front
Cold front
Cold air
Warm air
Precipitation

Frontal cloud
Precipitation

The upper diagrams show stages in the development of a depression. The cross sections below the diagrams correspond to stages (ii) and (iv).

Tropical cyclone tracks
(Intense cyclones are called typhoons in the N.W. Pacific and hurricanes in the W. Atlantic)

Rain   Hail   Frost   Snow

The water vapor contained in the atmosphere returns to earth as various forms of precipitation. It condenses on microscopic particles of dust, sulfur, soot, or ice to form water particles. These combine until they are heavy enough to fall as **rain**. Water particles carried to a great height freeze into ice particles that fall and become coated with fresh moisture. They are swept upward and refrozen repeatedly until heavy enough to fall as **hail**. Hoar, the most common type of **frost**, is precipitated instead of dew when water vapor changes directly to ice crystals on the surface of objects that have cooled below freezing point. **Snow** is the precipitate of ice directly from water vapor in the form of flakes, or clusters, of basically hexagonal ice crystals.

The four photographs below relate to the **extremes of weather and climate**: left to right, **hurricane devastation**; **hot desert**; **tornado**; **Arctic dwellings**. Tropical high temperatures and polar low temperatures combined with wind systems, altitude, and unequal rainfall distribution result in the extremes of climate. If these causative factors fluctuate sharply, catastrophic heat waves, floods, frosts, or storms could occur.

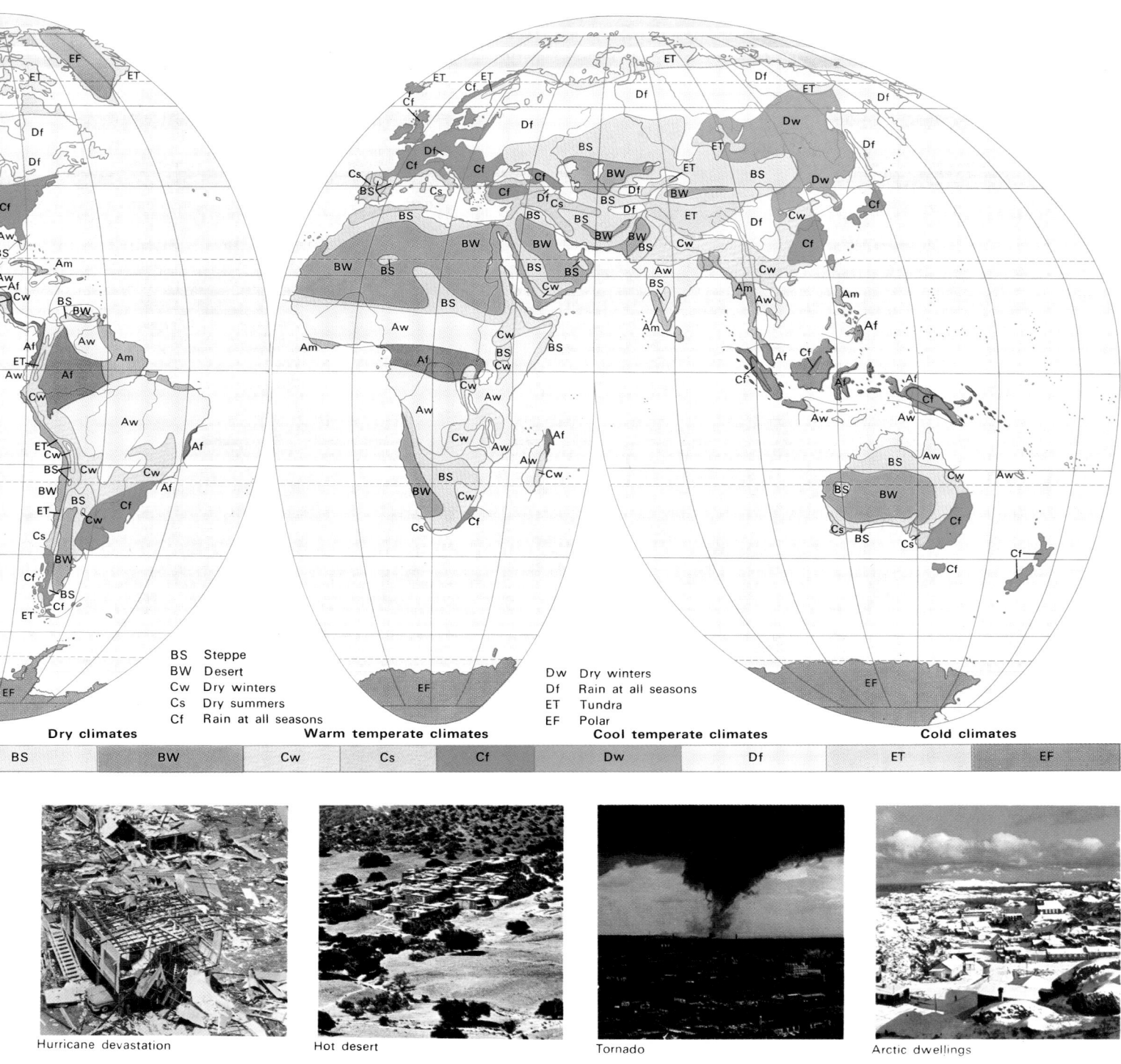

BS	Steppe	Dw	Dry winters
BW	Desert	Df	Rain at all seasons
Cw	Dry winters	ET	Tundra
Cs	Dry summers	EF	Polar
Cf	Rain at all seasons		

Dry climates · **Warm temperate climates** · **Cool temperate climates** · **Cold climates**

| BS | BW | Cw | Cs | Cf | Dw | Df | ET | EF |

Hurricane devastation

Hot desert

Tornado

Arctic dwellings

THE EARTH FROM SPACE

Photographs taken with cameras mounted in U. S. spacecraft have provided detailed views of the earth's topography. The top row, left to right, shows the **River Brahmaputra**, **India**, looking westward with the Himalayas on the right and the Khasi Hills of Assam to the left; the River Tachin in the mountainous region of **Szechwan**, **China**; infra-red photograph of the western end of Long Island, **New York** and the entrance to the Hudson River. The gray area is metropolitan New York; the red shows vegetation. Middle row, left: a view from Apollo IX of the **eastern Himalayas**, **Asia**; right, infra-red view of **Mount Etna**, **Sicily** at the top of the photograph with the Mediterranean to the right. Bottom row, left: **Canterbury Plains**, **New Zealand** right, **Hawaii**, the largest of the Hawaiian Islands, in the central Pacific Ocean.

River Brahmaputra, India

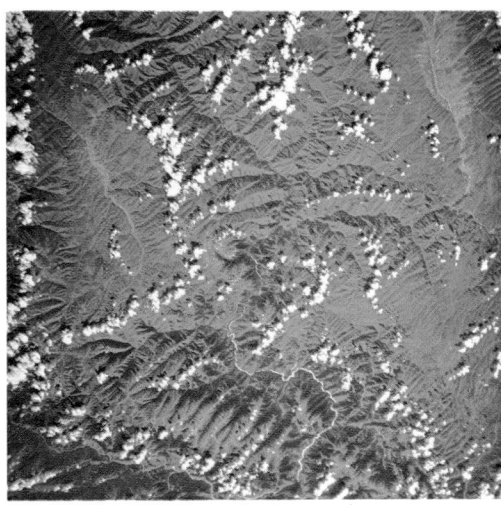
Szechwan, China

New York, U.S.A.

Eastern Himalayas, Asia

Mount Etna, Sicily

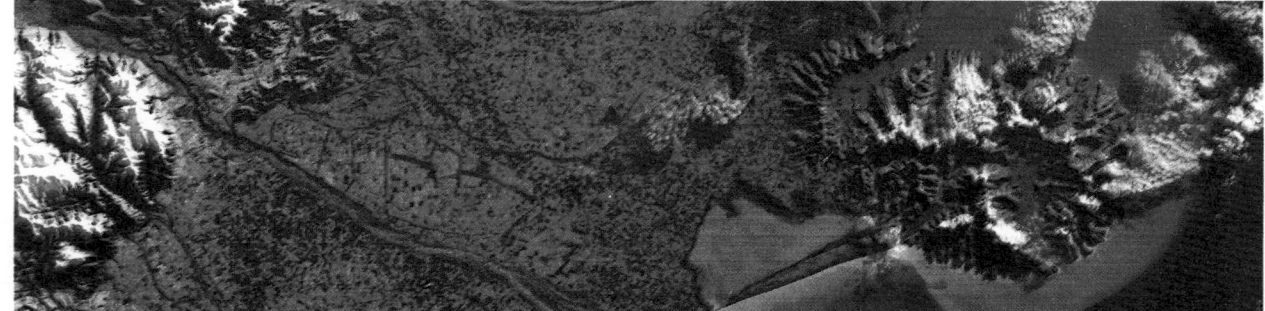
Canterbury Plains, New Zealand

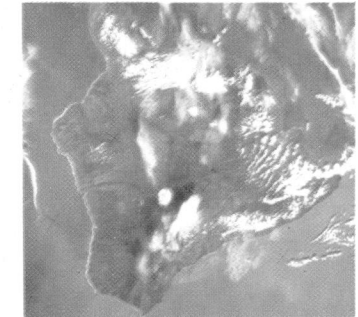
Hawaii, Pacific Ocean

Below, left, the top photograph is of the **Great Barrier Reef of Australia** and the Queensland coast from Cape Melville to Cape Flattery. Smoke from a number of forest fires can be seen in the lower center of the photograph. Left, center, the **Atacama Desert, Chile**. This view looks eastward from the Pacific over the Mejillones peninsula with the Andes in the background. The city of Antofagasta can be seen in the bay at the lower center of the picture.

The Alps of Europe are shown in the top photograph at the right. The photograph shows the snow-covered mountains and glaciers of the Alps along the Swiss-Italian-French border.

Hong Kong is the light gray area on the extreme right of the photograph shown at bottom, left. The photograph at the bottom, right, is part of a Thematic Mapper image showing **Detroit, Michigan**.

The Great Barrier Reef, Australia

Atacama Desert, Chile

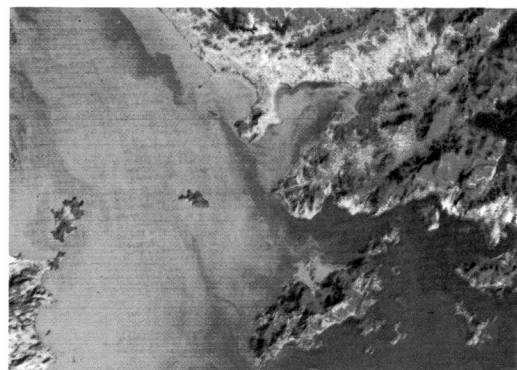

Hong Kong

The Alps, Europe

Detroit, Michigan

13

THE EVOLUTION OF THE CONTINENTS

The origin of the earth is still open to much conjecture, although the most widely accepted theory is that it was formed from a solar cloud consisting mainly of hydrogen. Under gravitation, the cloud condensed and shrank to form our planets orbiting around the sun. Gravitation forced the lighter elements to the surface of the earth, where they cooled to form a crust while the inner material remained hot and molten. Earth's first rocks formed over 3 500 million years ago. Since then the surface has been constantly altered.

Until comparatively recently, the view that the primary units of the earth had remained essentially fixed throughout geological time was regarded as common sense. However, the concept of moving continents has been traced back to references in the Bible of breakup of the land after Noah's flood. The continental drift theory was first developed by Antonio Snider in 1858, but probably the most important single advocate was Alfred Wegener who, in 1915, published evidence from geology, climatology, and biology. His conclusions are very similar to those reached by current research, although he was wrong about the speed of breakup.

The measurement of fossil magnetism found in rocks has probably proved the most influential evidence. Whereas originally these drift theories were openly mocked, they are now considered to be standard doctrine. As knowledge of the shape and structure of the earth's surface grew, several of the early geographers noted a relationship in the shape of the coasts bordering the Atlantic. For example, the east coast of South America would fit the contour of the west coast of Africa, as shown in the small center drawing below. It was this remarkable coincidence that led to the first detailed geological and structural comparisons. Even more accurate fits can be made by placing the edges of the continental shelves in juxtaposition.

The four maps below show the progression of the splitting of the original single land mass into continents. Top left, **180 million years ago**, the original Pangaea land mass had split into

two major continental groups. The southern group, Gondwanaland, had itself started to break up, isolating India and Antarctica-Australia. The rift had begun to appear between South America and Africa; and, in the east, Africa was closing up the Tethys Sea. Top right, **135 million years** ago, both Gondwanaland and Laurasia, the northern group, continued to drift northward, but the widening rifts in the North Atlantic and Indian Oceans persisted. The South Atlantic continued to lengthen, and a further perpendicular rift appeared, which would eventually separate Greenland from North America. India continued heading northward toward Asia. Bottom left, **65 million years ago**, South America moved quickly north and westward. Madagascar broke free from Africa, but there was no sign of the Red Sea rift that was to split Africa from the Arabian Peninsula. The Mediterranean Sea was already forming. Australia was still connected to Antarctica. Bottom right, **today**, India had moved northward and collided with Asia, crumpling up the sediments to form the Himalayas. South America had moved westward to connect with North America, and Australia had separated from Antarctica.

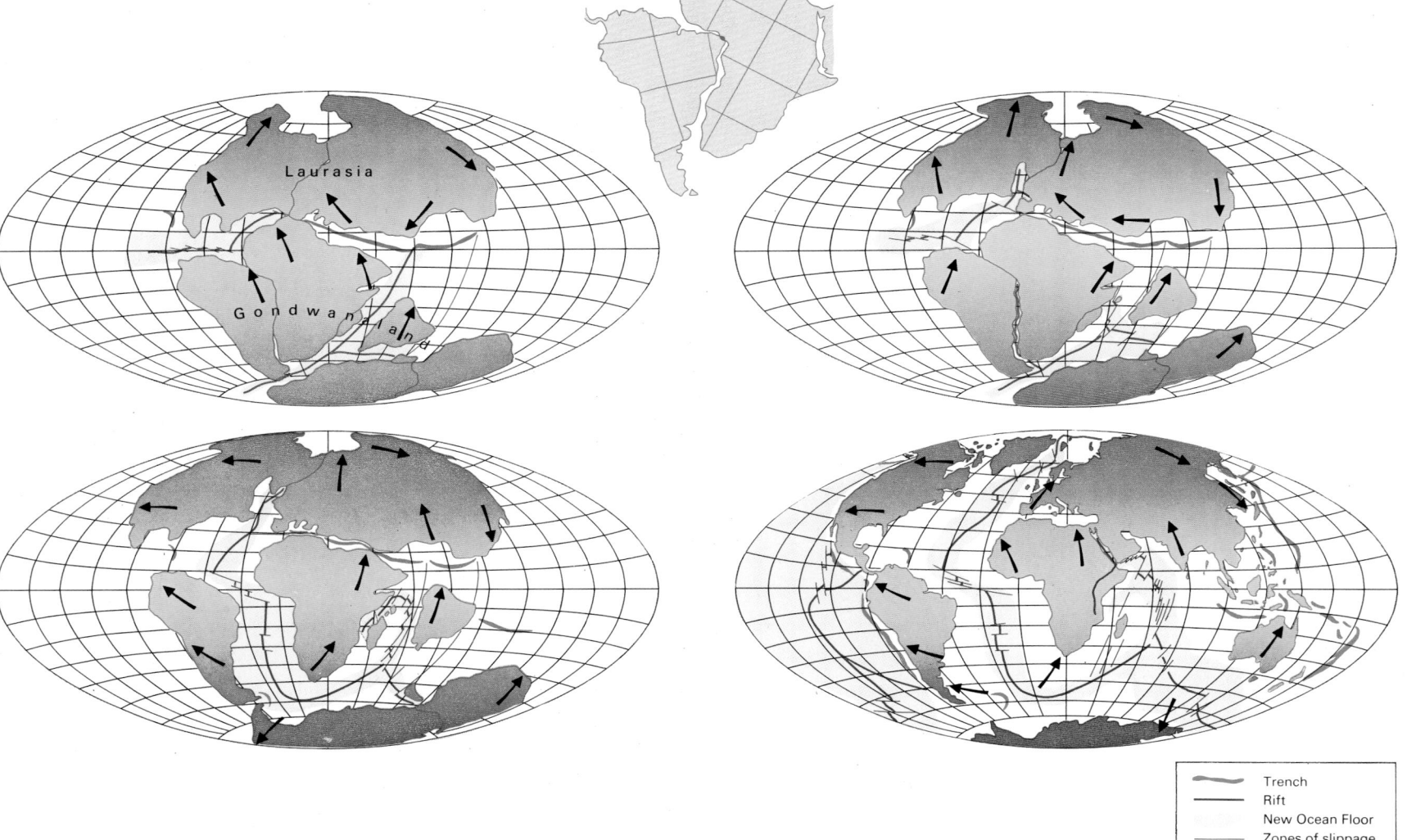

	Trench
	Rift
	New Ocean Floor
	Zones of slippage

The original debate about continental drift was only a prelude to a more radical idea: **plate tectonics**. (See distribution of tectonic plates represented on the world map below.) The basic theory here is that the earth's crust is made up of a series of rigid plates that float on a soft layer of the mantle and are moved about by convection currents in the earth's interior. These plates converge and diverge along margins marked by earthquakes, volcanoes, and other seismic activity. Plates diverge from mid-ocean ridges where molten lava pushes upward and forces the plates apart at a rate of about 30 mm a year. Converging plates form either a trench, where the oceanic plate sinks below the lighter continental rock, or mountain ranges where two continents collide. This explains the paradox that whereas there have always been oceans, none of the present oceans contains sediments more than 150 million years old.

The present explanation for the comparative youth of the ocean floors is that where an ocean and a continent meet, the ocean plate dips under the less dense continental plate at an angle of 45°. All previous crust is then ingested at the **trench boundary**, top left below, by downward convection currents. In the Japanese trench, this occurs at a rate of 120 mm a year.

The recent identification of the **transform, or transverse fault**, second left below, proved to be one of the crucial preliminaries to the investigation of plate tectonics. Such faults occur when two plates slip alongside each other without parting or approaching to any great extent. They complete the outline of the plates delineated by the ridges and trenches and demonstrate large-scale movements of parts of the earth's surface.

The third diagram at the left below illustrates a **ridge boundary**. One plate can ease itself away from another; and, when that happens, hot molten rock rises from below to fill in the incipient rift and form a ridge. These ridges trace a line almost exactly through the center of the major oceans. The bottom drawing on the left shows the **destruction of ocean plates**. As the ocean plate sinks below the continental plate, some of the sediment on its surface is scraped off and piled up on the landward side. The sediment is later incorporated in a folded mountain range, which usually appears on the edge of the continent, such as the Andes. Similarly, if two continents collide, the sediments are squeezed up into new mountains.

The map at the lower right illustrates **sea floor spreading**. Reversals in the earth's magnetic field have occurred throughout history. As new rock emerges at the ocean ridges, it cools and is magnetized in the direction of the prevailing magnetic field. By mapping the magnetic patterns on either side of the ridge, a symmetrical striped pattern of alternating fields can be observed (see inset area in map). As the dates for the last few reversals are known, the rate of spreading can be calculated.

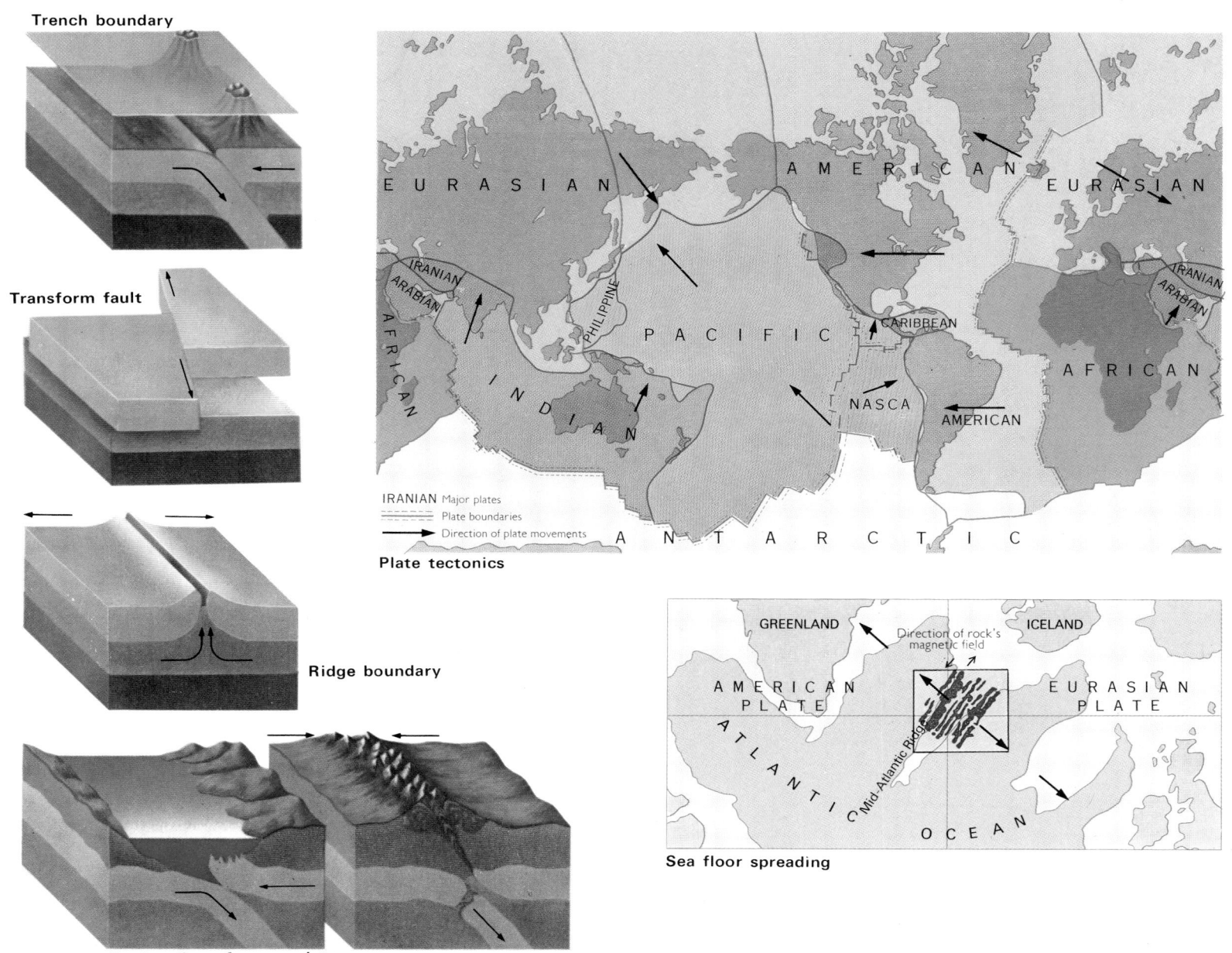

Trench boundary

Transform fault

Ridge boundary

Destruction of ocean plates.

IRANIAN Major plates
Plate boundaries
Direction of plate movements

Plate tectonics

Sea floor spreading

THE UNSTABLE EARTH

The earth's surface is slowly but continually being rearranged. Some changes, such as erosion and deposition, are extremely slow, but they upset the balance, which causes other more abrupt changes that often originate deep within the earth's interior. The constant movements vary in intensity, often with stresses building up to a climax — such as a particularly violent volcanic eruption or earthquake.

The earth's crust, shown below in cross section (left) and in the cutaway sphere (right), consists of a comparatively low density, brittle material varying from 5 km to 50 km deep beneath the continents. Under the crust is a layer of rock consisting predominantly of silica

and aluminum; hence, it is called "sial." Extending under the ocean floors and below the sial is a basaltic layer known as "sima," since it consists mainly of silica and magnesium.

In the earth's **mantle**, the rock layer immediately below the crust shows a distinct change in density and chemical properties. The mantle is made up of iron and magnesium silicates and has temperatures that reach 1600°C. The rigid upper mantle extends down to a depth of about 1 000 km, below which is the more viscous lower mantle, which is about 1 900 km thick. The **core** of the earth consists of two layers. The outer core, approximately 2 100 km thick, is made up of molten iron and

nickel at 2000°C to 5000°C. About 5 000 km below the surface there is a liquid transition zone, just above the solid inner core. The inner core is a sphere 2 740 km in diameter. It is three times as dense as the crust.

A **volcano** occurs when hot liquefied rock moves to the earth's surface, pouring out as lava. Ash and cinders form a cone around the volcano's vent. (See center photograph.) The map at the bottom shows the **world distribution of volcanoes**. The diagrams beside the map show, top to bottom, five types of volcano: **shield, composite, cinder-cone, hornit-cone,** and **caldera**. The caldera forms when a violent eruption blows off the top of an existing cone.

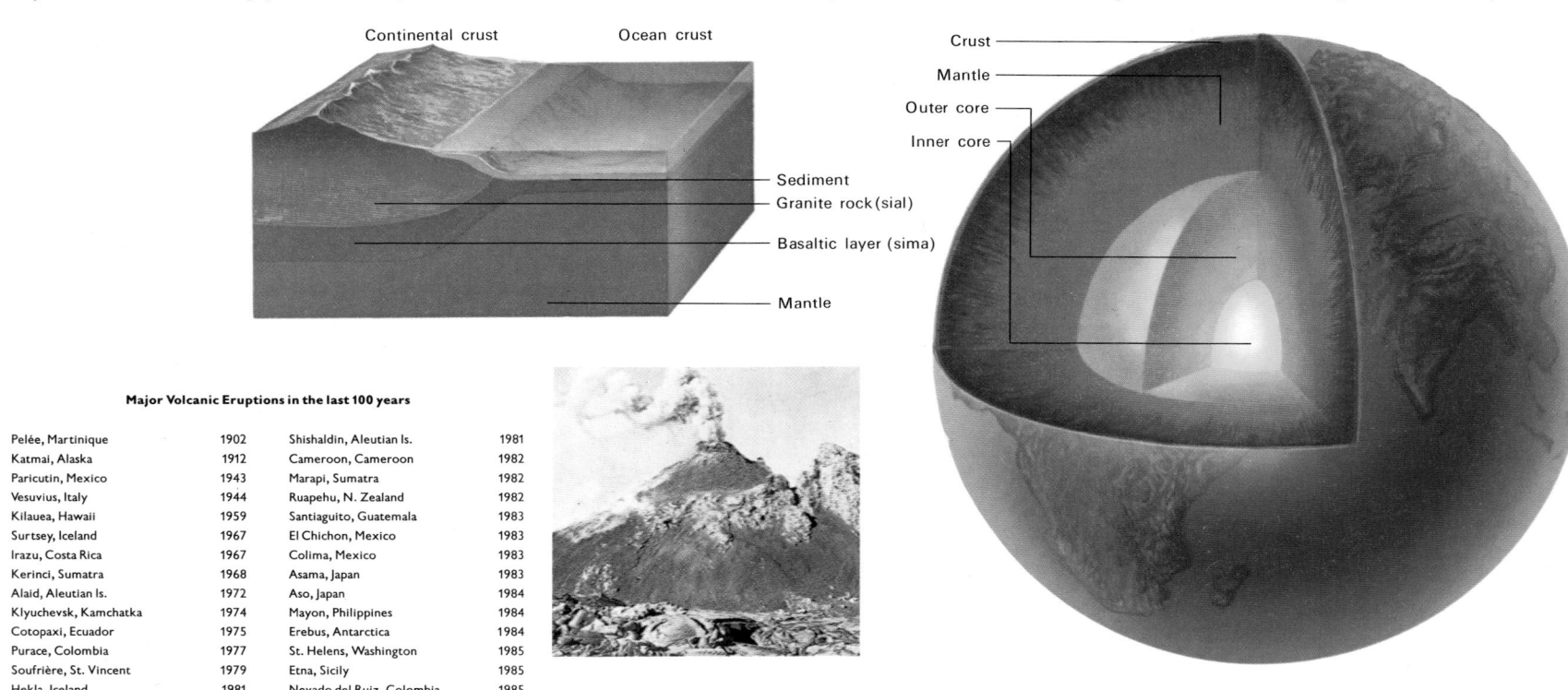

Continental crust	Ocean crust

Crust — Mantle — Outer core — Inner core

Sediment
Granite rock (sial)
Basaltic layer (sima)
Mantle

Major Volcanic Eruptions in the last 100 years

Pelée, Martinique	1902	Shishaldin, Aleutian Is.	1981
Katmai, Alaska	1912	Cameroon, Cameroon	1982
Paricutin, Mexico	1943	Marapi, Sumatra	1982
Vesuvius, Italy	1944	Ruapehu, N. Zealand	1982
Kilauea, Hawaii	1959	Santiaguito, Guatemala	1983
Surtsey, Iceland	1967	El Chichon, Mexico	1983
Irazu, Costa Rica	1967	Colima, Mexico	1983
Kerinci, Sumatra	1968	Asama, Japan	1983
Alaid, Aleutian Is.	1972	Aso, Japan	1984
Klyuchevsk, Kamchatka	1974	Mayon, Philippines	1984
Cotopaxi, Ecuador	1975	Erebus, Antarctica	1984
Purace, Colombia	1977	St. Helens, Washington	1985
Soufrière, St. Vincent	1979	Etna, Sicily	1985
Hekla, Iceland	1981	Nevado del Ruiz, Colombia	1985

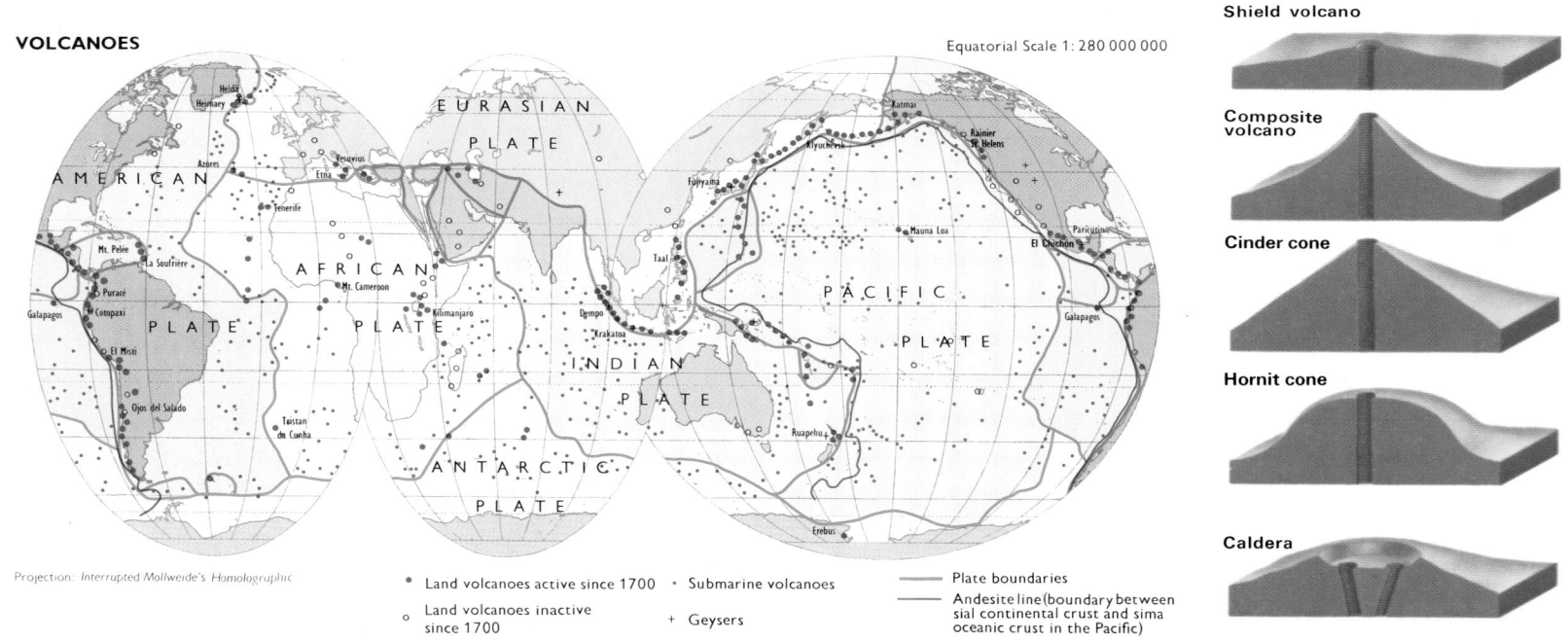

VOLCANOES

Equatorial Scale 1: 280 000 000

Shield volcano

Composite volcano

Cinder cone

Hornit cone

Caldera

Projection: Interrupted Mollweide's Homolographic

• Land volcanoes active since 1700   · Submarine volcanoes

○ Land volcanoes inactive since 1700   + Geysers

—— Plate boundaries

—— Andesite line (boundary between sial continental crust and sima oceanic crust in the Pacific)

The large map below shows the **world distribution of earthquakes** and their foci. The chart to the right of the map lists major earthquakes and their toll of human lives. An earthquake is a series of rapid vibrations originating (at an epicenter) from the slipping or faulting of parts of the earth's crust when stresses within build up to breaking point. The diagram at the left center below shows **how shock waves travel** through the earth.

Severe earthquakes may cause extensive damage destroying structures and severing communications, as in the **Alaska quake of 1964** (bottom left). Most loss of life occurs as a result of secondary causes — falling masonry,

fires, or tsunami waves. The small map at the bottom of the page shows how **tsunami waves** travel from the epicenter of an earthquake. A sudden slump in the ocean bed during an earthquake forms a trough, followed by a crest and smaller waves. A more marked change in the level of the sea can start forming a tsunami crest that travels up to 600 km/h with waves up to 60 m high. **Seismographic detectors**, diagramed below at the right, continuously record earthquake shocks and warn of the tsunami waves. As shown, P waves cause the first tremors, S the second, and L waves the main shock.

The two diagrams at the center right show

how **seismic waves** spread through the earth. The shock waves sent out from the epicenter are of three main kinds. Primary (P) waves are compressional waves that can be transmitted through both solids and liquids and therefore will pass through the earth's liquid core. Secondary (S) waves are shear waves and pass only through solids. They are reflected at the liquid core-mantle boundary, taking a concave course back to the surface. But the surface refracts the P waves. The net result is the formation of a shadow zone that is free from P and S waves at a certain distance from the epicenter. The third main kind of wave is a long (L) wave, which travels slowly along the earth's surface, either vertically or horizontally.

EARTHQUAKES

Equatorial Scale 1 : 280 000 000

Major Earthquakes

		Nos. killed
1556	Shaanxi, China	830 000
1730	Hokkaido, Japan	137 000
1737	Calcutta, India	300 000
1755	Lisbon, Portugal	60 000
1868	Ecuador and N. Peru	40 000
1906	Valparaiso, Chile	22 000
1906	San Francisco, U.S.A.	450
1908	Messina, Italy	77 000
1915	Avezzano, Italy	30 000
1920	Gansu, China	180 000
1923	Yokohama, Japan	143 000
1927	Nan Shan, China	200 000
1931	Napier, N. Zealand	250
1932	Gansu, China	70 000
1934	Nepal	11 700
1935	Quetta, Pakistan	30 000
1939	Erzincan, Turkey	30 000
1960	Agadir, Morocco	12 000
1962	Khorasan, Iran	10 000
1963	Skopje, Yugoslavia	1 000
1964	Anchorage, Alaska	100
1968	N.E. Iran	12 000
1970	N. Peru	67 000
1972	Managua, Nicaragua	7 000
1974	N. Pakistan	10 000
1976	Tangshan, China	650 000
1978	Tabas, Iran	11 000
1980	El Asnam, Algeria	20 000
1985	Mexico	20 000

• 1906 Principal earthquakes and their dates

— Oceanic marginal troughs

Mobile land areas

Submarine zones of mobile land areas

Stable land platforms

Submarine extensions of stable land platforms

Mid-oceanic volcanic ridges

Oceanic platforms

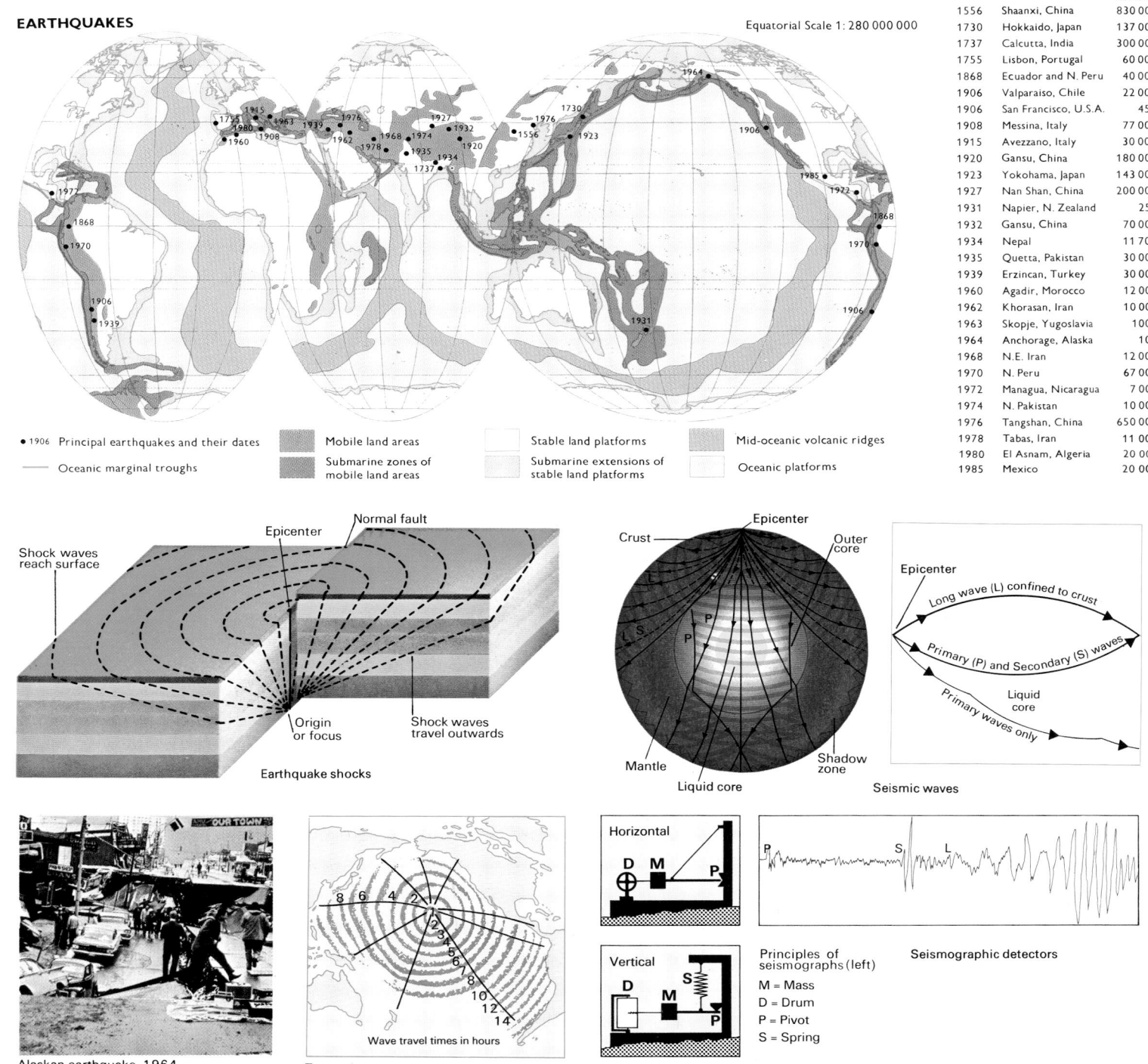

Earthquake shocks

Shock waves reach surface · Epicenter · Normal fault · Origin or focus · Shock waves travel outwards

Seismic waves

Crust · Epicenter · Outer core · Mantle · Liquid core · Shadow zone · L S P P

Epicenter · Long wave (L) confined to crust · Primary (P) and Secondary (S) waves · Liquid core · Primary waves only

Alaskan earthquake, 1964

Tsunami waves

Wave travel times in hours

Seismographic detectors

Horizontal · D M P

Vertical · D M S P

Principles of seismographs (left)

M = Mass
D = Drum
P = Pivot
S = Spring

P S L

17

THE MAKING OF LANDSCAPE

The major forces that shape our land act very slowly in comparison with the average human life-span; but in geological terms the erosion of rock is, in fact, very fast. Land goes through a **cycle of transformation**. It is broken up by earthquakes and other earth movements, temperature changes, and the action of water, wind, and ice. Rock debris is then transported by water, wind, and glaciers and deposited on lowlands and on the sea floor (top left below). Here it builds up and by pressure of its own weight is converted into new rock strata (second left below). These in turn can be uplifted, either gently as plains or plateaus or more irregularly

to form mountains. In either case, the new higher land is eroded as the cycle begins again. (Top right, a peneplain; second right, an uplifted peneplain.)

Rivers shape the land by three basic processes: erosion, transportation, and deposition. The three **stages in the life of a river** are shown in the three-part drawing at the right center below. Left to right: a youthful river flows fast, eroding downward to form a narrow valley; as it matures, it deposits some debris and erodes laterally to widen the valley; finally, it meanders across a wide, flat flood plain, depositing fine particles of alluvium.

The drawing at the bottom right explains the storage of **underground water**. Water enters porous and permeable rocks from the surface, moving downward until it reaches a layer of impermeable rock. Joints in the underground rock, such as limestone, are eroded to form underground caves and caverns. When the roof of a cave collapses, a gorge is formed. The illustrations at the center and bottom left show the effect of wind on the surface of the earth. **Wind erosion** (bottom left) caused by blasting of rock wastes against rock strata, can produce weird shapes. Wind also builds barchan sand dunes which slowly travel forward, horns first.

A Peneplain

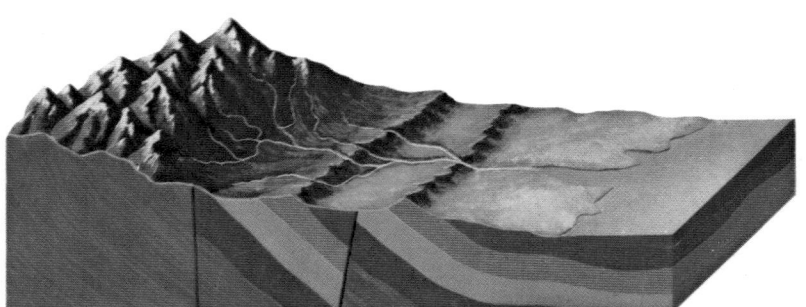

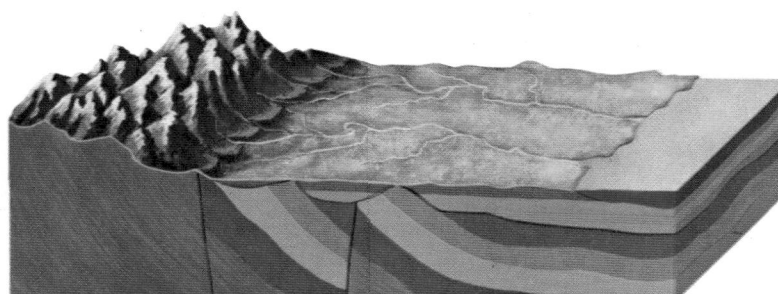

Uplifted peneplain

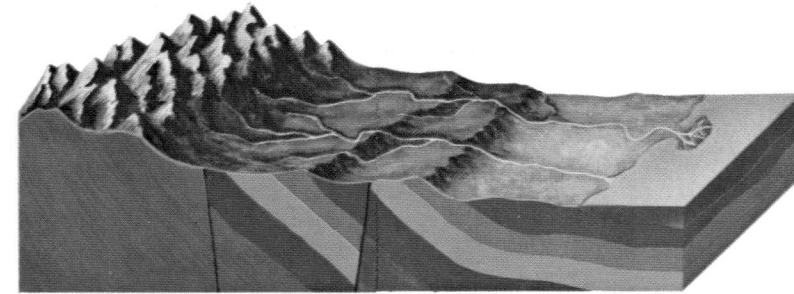

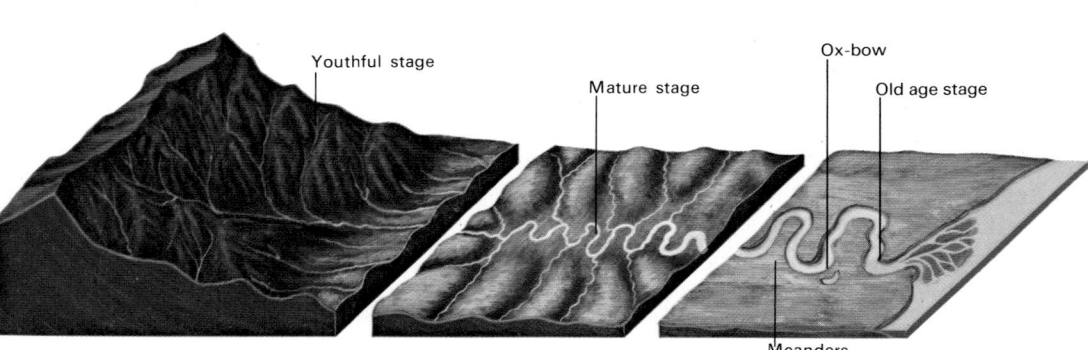

Youthful stage / Mature stage / Ox-bow / Old age stage / Meanders

Natural bridge / Limestone gorge

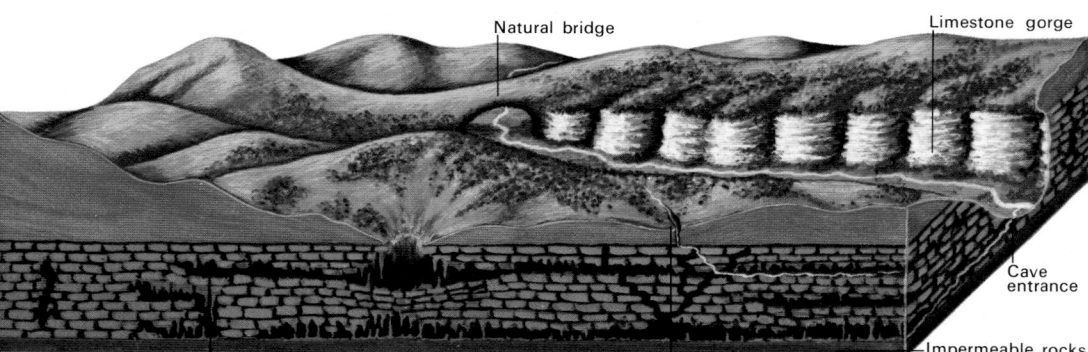

Wind

Cave with stalactites and stalagmites / River disappears down swallow hole / Cave entrance / Impermeable rocks

The earth's landscape can be altered greatly by **volcanic activity**, top left, below. When pressure on rocks beneath the earth's crust is released, the normally semi-solid hot rock becomes liquid magma. The magma forces its way into cracks in the crust and may either reach the surface to form a volcano, or collect in the crust as sills, dikes, or laccoliths. When magma reaches the surface, it cools to form lava.

Mountainous landscapes may result from **folding and faulting**, below, top right. A vertical displacement in the earth's crust is called a **normal fault** or a **reverse fault**, a lateral displacement is a **tear fault**. An uplifted block is called a **horst**, the reverse of which is a **rift valley**. Compressed horizontal layers of sedimentary rock fold to form mountains. The layers that bend up form an **anticline**; those bending down form a **syncline**. Continued pressure forms an **overfold anticline**, an **overfold syncline**, and an **overthrust fold**.

The two drawings in the second row below show how **waves change the landscape**. Some coasts retreat under wave erosion; others advance with wave deposition. Steep cliffs and wave-cut platforms develop, and eroded debris deposits as terraces. Wave action also creates **odd features** such as those at the right. The next two drawings below show how **ice changes the landscape**, forming a glaciated valley. As the glacier deepens, it straightens and widens the valley. Intervalley divides are frost shattered to form sharp aretes and pyramidal peaks. Hanging valleys mark the entry of tributary rivers, and eroded rocks form moraines.

The bottom drawing depicts **subsidence and uplift**. As the land surface is eroded, it may eventually become a level plain — a peneplain, broken only by low hills that are remnants of previous mountains. In turn, this peneplain may be uplifted to form a plateau with steep edges. At the coast, a coastal plain may form.

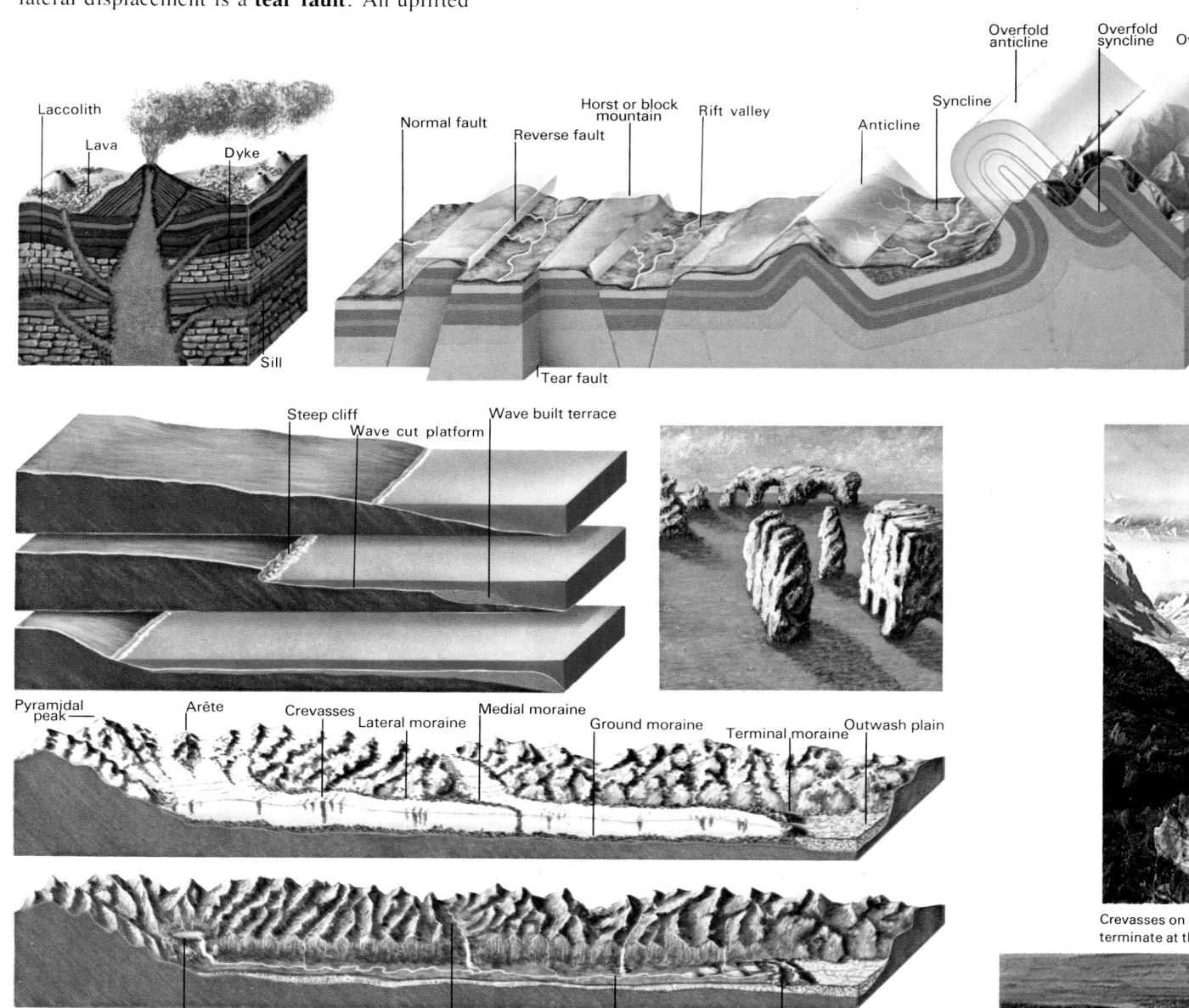

Crevasses on one of the several glaciers which terminate at the sea in Glacier Bay, Alaska.

The Fish River Canyon, Namibia is 1.5 km deep and is the second largest canyon in the world.

THE EARTH: PHYSICAL DIMENSIONS

The figure of the earth can be expressed as a geoid, an imaginary sea-level surface, everywhere at right angles to the direction of gravity. By measuring at different places the angles from plumb lines to a fixed star, scientists found the geoid to be an oblate spheroid. Observations from satellites have now provided even more accurate data. Below, **land and sea hemispheres** are shown. About 85% of the land is contained in the hemisphere centered on a point between Paris and Brussels.

The two maps at the right below present the major **oceans and seas** (top map) and the major **lakes and inland seas** (bottom map). The accompanying data give the areas of these water bodies in 1000 km². Other **long rivers** not shown below are: Mekong, Asia; Niger, Africa; Mackenzie, N. America; Ob, Asia; and Yenisei, Asia.

High mountains and ocean depths are fascinating physical features of the earth's

Its surface

Highest point on the earth's surface: Mt. Everest, Tibet - Nepal boundary   8 848 m
Lowest point on the earth's surface: The Dead Sea, Jordan   below sea level 395 m
Greatest ocean depth.: Challenger Deep, Mariana Trench   11 022 m
Average height of land   840 m
Average depth of seas and oceans   3 808 m

Dimensions

Superficial area	510 000 000 km²
Land surface	149 000 000 km²
Land surface as % of total area	29·2 %
Water surface	361 000 000 km²
Water surface as % of total area	70·8 %
Equatorial circumference	40 077 km
Meridional circumference	40 009 km
Equatorial diameter	12 756·8 km
Polar diameter	12 713·8 km
Equatorial radius	6 378·4 km
Polar radius	6 356·9 km
Volume of the Earth	1 083 230 x 10⁶ km³
Mass of the Earth	5·9 x 10²¹ tonnes

Oceans and Seas
Area in 1000 km²

Pacific Ocean	165 721	North Sea	575
Atlantic Ocean	81 660	Black Sea	448
Indian Ocean	73 442	Red Sea	440
Arctic Ocean	14 351	Baltic Sea	422
Mediterranean Sea	2 966	Persian Gulf	238
Bering Sea	2 274	St. Lawrence, Gulf of	236
Caribbean Sea	1 942	English Channel & Irish Sea	179
Mexico, Gulf of	1 813	California, Gulf of	161
Okhotsk, Sea of	1 528		
East China Sea	1 248		
Hudson Bay	1 230		
Japan, Sea of	1 049		

Lakes and Inland Seas
Areas in 1000 km²

Caspian Sea, Asia	424·2	Lake Ontario, N.America	19·5
Lake Superior, N.America	82·4	Lake Ladoga, Europe	18·4
Lake Victoria, Africa	69·5	Lake Balkhash, Asia	17·3
Aral Sea (Salt), Asia	63·8	Lake Maracaibo, S.America	16·3
Lake Huron, N.America	59·6	Lake Onega, Europe	9·8
Lake Michigan, N.America	58·0	Lake Eyre (Salt), Australia	9·6
Lake Tanganyika, Africa	32·9	Lake Turkana (Salt), Africa	9·1
Lake Baikal, Asia	31·5	Lake Titicaca, S.America	8·3
Great Bear Lake, N.America	31·1	Lake Nicaragua, C.America	8·0
Great Slave Lake, N.America	28·9	Lake Athabasca, N.America	7·9
Lake Nyasa, Africa	28·5	Reindeer Lake, N.America	6·3
Lake Erie, N.America	25·7	Issyk-Kul, Asia	6·2
Lake Winnipeg, N.America	24·3	Lake Torrens (Salt), Australia	6·1
Lake Chad, Africa	20·7	Koko Nor (Salt), Asia	6·0
		Lake Urmia, Asia	6·0
		Vänern, Europe	5·6

Longest rivers

	km.
Nile, Africa	6 690
Amazon, S.America	6 280
Mississipi - Missouri,N.America	6 270
Yangtze, Asia	4 990
Zaïre, Africa	4 670
Amur, Asia	4 410
Hwang Ho (Yellow), Asia	4 350
Lena, Asia	4 260
Mekong, Asia	4 180
Niger, Africa	4 180
Mackenzie, N.America	4 040
Ob, Asia	4 000
Yenisei, Asia	3 800

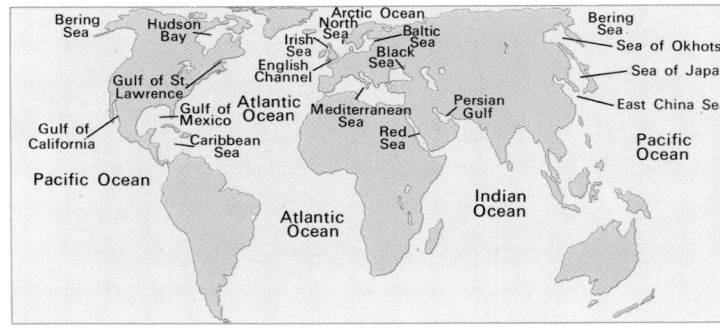

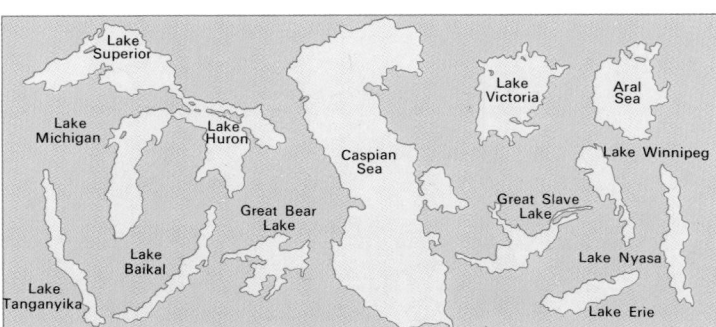

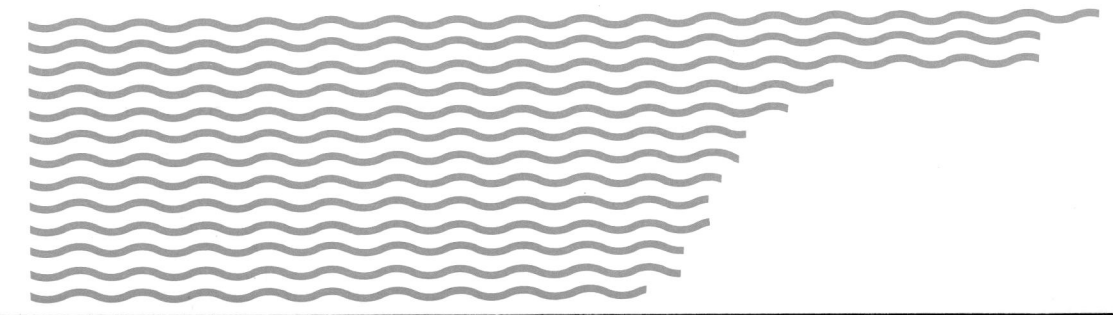

surface. **Mountain heights** (in meters) are shown below in the top chart. Trenches represent less than 2% of the total area of the sea-bed, but they are of great interest as lines of structural weakness in the earth's crust and as areas of frequent earthquakes. The greatest ocean trenches are the Puerto Rico deep (9 200 m), the Tonga (10 822 m), Mindanao (10 497 m), and Mariana (11 022 m) trenches. These **ocean depths** are shown at the right below in the second row. To the left of the chart is the **Bathyscaphe**, the vessel that made exploration of the greatest depths possible. The remaining photographs show a **waterfall** and a **dam**, natural and man-made physical features of the earth. The map at the bottom locates the mountains and trenches represented in the charts.

High mountains

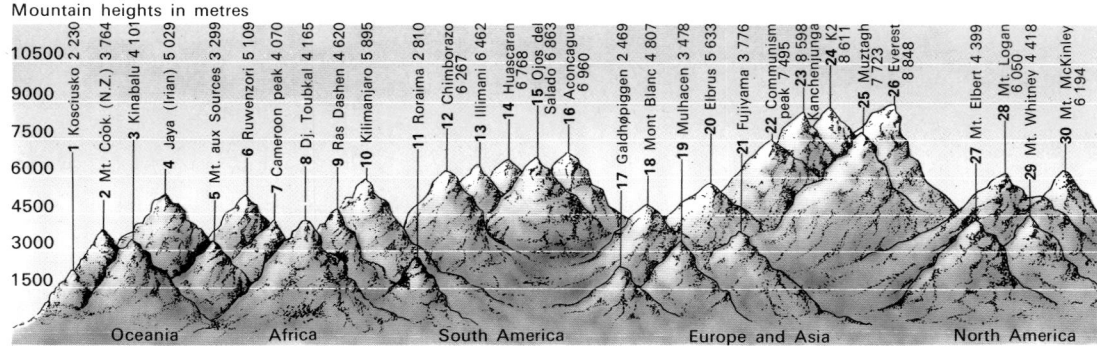

Mountain heights in metres

Oceania — Africa — South America — Europe and Asia — North America

1 Kosciusko 2 230; 2 Mt. Cook (N.Z.) 3 764; 3 Kinabalu 4 101; 4 Jaya (Irian) 5 029; 5 Mt. aux Sources 3 299; 6 Ruwenzori 5 109; 7 Cameroon peak 4 070; 8 Dj. Toubkal 4 165; 9 Ras Dashen 4 620; 10 Kilimanjaro 5 895; 11 Roraima 2 810; 12 Chimborazo 6 267; 13 Illimani 6 462; 14 Huascaran 6 768; 15 Ojos del Salado 6 863; 16 Aconcagua 6 960; 17 Galdhøpiggen 2 469; 18 Mont Blanc 4 807; 19 Mulhacen 3 478; 20 Elbrus 5 633; 21 Fujiyama 3 776; 22 Communism peak 7 495; 23 8 598; 24 K2 8 611; 25 Muztagh 7 723; 26 Everest 8 848; Kanchenjunga; 27 Mt. Elbert 4 399; 28 Mt. Logan 6 050; 29 Mt. Whitney 4 418; 30 Mt. McKinley 6 194

Ocean depths in metres

Sea level

Indian Ocean — Pacific Ocean — Atlantic Ocean

31 Mauritius basin 6 400; 32 W. Australian basin 6 459; 33 Java trench 7 450; 34 Mindanao trench 10 497; 35 Mariana trench 11 022; 36 Japan trench 10 554; 37 Bougainville deep 9 140; 38 Kuril trench 10 542; 39 Aleutian trench 7 822; 40 Kermadec trench 10 047; 41 Tonga trench 10 822; 42 Cayman trough 7 680; 43 Puerto Rico trough 9 200; 44 S. Sandwich trench 8 428; 45 Romanche deep 7 758

Bathyscaphe

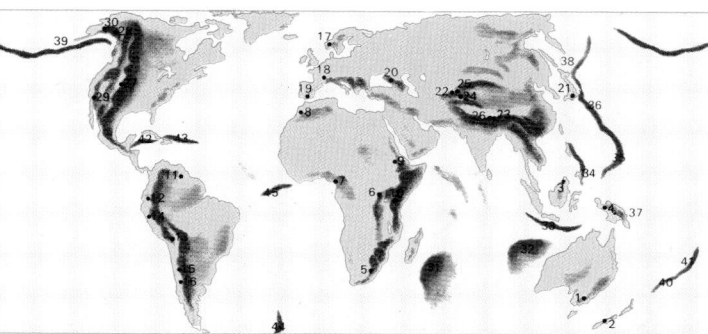
Waterfall

Dam

Notable Waterfalls
heights in metres

Angel, Venezuela	980
Tugela, S. Africa	853
Mongefossen, Norway	774
Yosemite, California	738
Mardalsfossen, Norway	655
Cuquenan, Venezuela	610
Sutherland, N.Z.	579
Reichenbach, Switzerland	548
Wollomombi, Australia	518
Ribbon, California	491
Gavarnie, France	422
Tyssefallene, Norway	414
Krimml, Austria	370
King George VI, Guyana	366
Silver Strand, California	356
Geissbach, Switzerland	350
Staubbach, Switzerland	299
Trümmelbach, Switzerland	290
Chirombo, Zambia	268
Livingstone, Zaire	259
King Edward VIII, Guyana	256
Gersoppa, India	253
Vettifossen, Norway	250
Kalambo, Zambia	240
Kaieteur, Guyana	226
Maletsunyane, Lesotho	192
Terui, Italy	180
Kabarega, Uganda	122
Victoria, Zimbabwe-Zambia	107
Cauvery, India	97
Boyoma, Zaire	61
Niagara, N.America	51
Schaffhausen, Switzerland	30

Notable Dams
heights in metres
Africa

Cabora Bassa, Zambezi R.	168
Akosombo Main Dam, Volta R.	141
Kariba, Zambezi R.	128
Aswan High Dam, Nile R.	110

Asia

Nurek, Vakhsh R., U.S.S.R.	317
Sayano-Shushensk, U.S.S.R.	245
Bhakra, Sutlej R., India	226
Toktogul, U.S.S.R.	215
Kurobegawa, Kurobe R., Jap.	186
Charvak, Chirchik R., U.S.S.R.	168
Okutadami, Tadami R., Jap.	157
Bratsk, Angara R., U.S.S.R.	125

Oceania

Warragamba, N.S.W., Australia	137
Eucumbene, N.S.W., Australia	116

Europe

Grande Dixence, Switz.	284
Inguri R., U.S.S.R.	272
Vajont, Vajont, R., Italy	261
Mauvoisin, Drance R., Switz.	237
Chirkei, U.S.S.R.	233
Contra , Verzasca R., Switz.	230
Mratinje, Yugoslavia	220
Luzzone, Brenno R., Switz.	208
Tignes, Isère R., France	180
Amir Kabir, Karadj R., U.S.S.R.	180
Vidraru, Argeş R., Rom.	165
Kremasta, Acheloos R., Greece	165

North America

Chicoasén, Mexico	261
Alvaro Obregon, Mexico	260
Mica, Columbia R., Can.	242
Oroville, Feather R.,	235
Hoover, Colorado R.,	221
Dworshak, Idaho	219
Glen Canyon, Colorado R.,	216
Daniel Johnson, Can.	214
New Bullards Bar, N. Yuba R.	194
Mossyrock, Cowlitz R.,	184
Shasta, Sacramento R.,	183
W.A.C. Bennett, Canada.	183

Central and South America

Chivor, Colombia	237
Guri, Caroni R., Venezuela.	106

The Dead Sea, 396m below sea level, is the lowest place on the surface of the earth.

Mt. Everest, at 8 848m, the highest point on earth.

DISTANCES

London
51 28N 0 27W

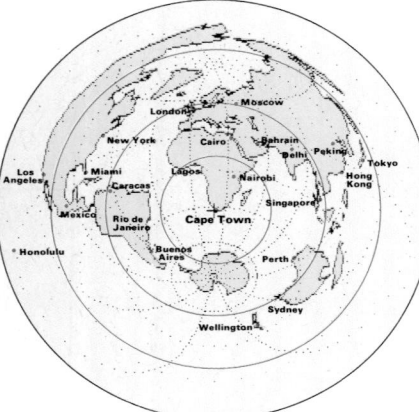

Cape Town
33 58S 18 36E

Mexico City
19 26N 99 4W

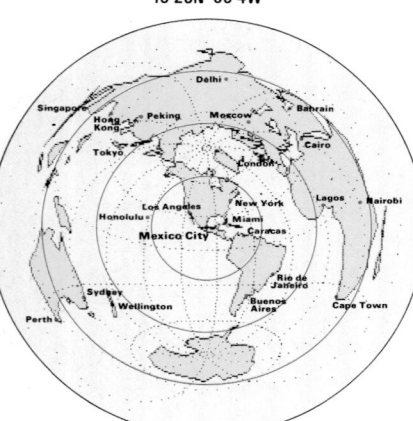

Rio de Janeiro
22 50S 43 15W

Kms — distance table (lower-left triangle)

	Berlin	Bombay	Buenos Aires	Cairo	Calcutta	Caracas	Chicago	Copenhagen	Darwin	Hong Kong	Honolulu	Johannesburg	Lagos	Lisbon	London
Berlin															
Bombay	6288														
Buenos Aires	11909	14925													
Cairo	2890	4355	11814												
Calcutta	7033	1664	16524	5699											
Caracas	8435	14522	5096	10203	15464										
Chicago	7084	12953	9011	3206	12839	4027									
Copenhagen	357	6422	12067	9860	7072	8392	6840								
Darwin	12946	7257	14693	11612	6047	18059	15065	12903							
Hong Kong	8754	4317	18478	8150	2659	16360	12526	8671	4271						
Honolulu	11764	12914	12164	14223	11343	9670	6836	11407	8640	8921					
Johannesburg	8870	6974	8088	6267	8459	11019	13984	9225	10639	10732	19206				
Lagos	5198	7612	7916	3915	9216	7741	9612	5530	14222	11845	16308	4505			
Lisbon	2311	8018	9600	3794	9075	6501	6424	2478	15114	11028	12587	8191	3799		
London	928	7190	11131	3508	7961	7507	6356	952	13848	9623	11632	9071	5017	1588	
Los Angeles	9311	14000	9852	12200	13120	5812	2804	9003	12695	11639	4117	16676	12414	9122	875…
Mexico City	9732	15656	7389	12372	15280	3586	2726	9514	14631	14122	6085	14585	11071	8676	893…
Moscow	1610	5031	13477	2902	5534	9938	8000	1561	11350	7144	11323	9161	6254	3906	249…
Nairobi	6370	4532	10402	3536	6179	11544	12883	6706	10415	8776	17282	2927	3807	6461	681…
New York	6385	12541	8526	9020	12747	3430	1145	6188	16047	12950	7980	12841	8477	5422	557…
Paris	876	7010	11051	3210	7858	7625	6650	1026	13812	9630	11968	8732	4714	1454	34…
Peking	7822	4757	19268	7544	3269	14399	10603	7202	6011	1963	8160	11710	11457	9668	813…
Reykjavik	2385	8335	11437	5266	8687	6915	4757	2103	13892	9681	9787	10938	6718	2948	188…
Rio de Janeiro	10025	13409	1953	9896	15073	4546	8547	10211	16011	17704	13342	7113	6035	7734	929…
Rome	1180	6175	11151	2133	7219	8363	7739	1531	13265	9284	12916	7743	4039	1861	143…
Singapore	9944	3914	15879	8267	2897	18359	15078	9969	3349	2599	10816	8660	11145	11886	1085…
Sydney	16096	10160	11800	14418	9138	15343	14875	16042	3150	7374	8168	11040	15519	18178	1699…
Tokyo	8924	6742	18362	9571	5141	14164	10137	8696	5431	2874	6202	13547	13480	11149	956…
Toronto	6497	12488	9093	9233	12561	3873	700	6265	15498	12569	7465	13374	8948	5737	570…
Wellington	18140	12370	9981	16524	11354	13122	13451	17961	5325	9427	7513	11761	16050	19575	1881…

Upper-right triangle (columns cut off at right edge)

Diagonal labels shown: Berlin, Bombay, Buenos Aires, Cairo, Calcutta, Caracas, Chicago, Copenhagen, Darwin, Hong Kong, Honolulu, Johannesburg, Lagos, Lisbon, London.

```
         3907  7400  1795  4370  5241  4402   222  8044  5440  7310  5511  3230  1436   5…
         9275  2706  1034  9024  8048  3990  4510  2683  8024  4334  4730  4982   44…
         7341 10268  3167  5599  7498  9130 11481  7558  5025  4919  5964   69…
         3541  6340  6127  1992  7216  5064  8838  3894  2432  2358  218…
Berlin   9609  7978  4395  3758  1653  7048  5256  5727  5639  494…
Bombay   2502  5215 11221 10166  6009  6847  4810  4044  460…
Buenos Aires  4250  9361  7783  4247  8689  5973  3992   39…
Cairo    8017  5388  7088  5732  3436  1540   5…
Calcutta 2654  5369  6611  8837  9391   86…
Caracas  5543  6669  7360  6853  598…
Chicago 11934 10133  7821  722…
Copenhagen 2799  5089   56…
Darwin   2360   31…
Hong Kong  98…
```

Azimuthal maps

These circular maps are drawn on an Azimuthal Equidistant projection with its origin, its center, at the city shown. The whole world is shown and so there are some strange distortions of the coastline at the edges, for example, in that of Singapore. The principal property of the projection is that all distances measured through the center of the circle are true to scale, and so a straight-line passing from the center to any other point is a great circle and shows the shortest distance between the cities. Also that line is correct for direction/bearing and shows the great circle flight path. The three circle[s] drawn at radius 5000 km (3 100 miles), 10 000 km (6 200 miles) and 15 000 km (9 300 miles) from the central city.

Los Angeles	Mexico City	Moscow	Nairobi	New York	Paris	Peking	Reykjavik	Rio de Janeiro	Rome	Singapore	Sydney	Tokyo	Toronto	Wellington	
785	6047	1000	3958	3967	545	4860	1482	6230	734	6179	10002	5545	4037	11272	**Berlin**
700	9728	3126	2816	7793	4356	2956	5179	8332	3837	2432	6313	4189	7760	7686	**Bombay**
122	4591	8374	6463	5298	6867	11972	7106	1214	6929	9867	7332	11410	5650	6202	**Buenos Aires**
580	7687	1803	2197	5605	1994	4688	3272	6149	1325	5137	8959	5947	5737	10268	**Cairo**
152	9494	3438	3839	7921	4883	2031	5398	9366	4486	1800	5678	3195	7805	7055	**Calcutta**
612	2228	6175	7173	2131	4738	8947	4297	2825	5196	11407	9534	8801	2406	8154	**Caracas**
742	1694	4971	8005	711	4132	6588	2956	5311	4809	9369	9243	6299	435	8358	**Chicago**
594	5912	970	4167	3845	638	4475	1306	6345	951	6195	9968	5403	3892	11160	**Copenhagen**
888	9091	7053	6472	9971	8582	3735	8632	9948	8243	2081	1957	3375	9630	3309	**Darwin**
232	8775	4439	5453	8047	5984	1220	6015	11001	5769	1615	4582	1786	7810	5857	**Hong Kong**
558	3781	7036	10739	4958	7437	5070	6081	8290	8026	6721	5075	3854	4638	4669	**Honolulu**
362	9063	5692	1818	7979	5426	7276	6797	4420	4811	5381	6860	8418	8310	7308	**Johannesburg**
713	6879	3886	2366	5268	2929	7119	4175	3750	2510	6925	9643	8376	5560	9973	**Lagos**
668	5391	2427	4015	3369	903	6007	1832	4805	1157	7385	11295	6928	3565	12163	**Lisbon**
442	5552	1552	4237	3463	212	5057	1172	5778	889	6743	10558	5942	3545	11691	**London**
	1549	6070	9659	2446	5645	6251	4310	6310	6331	8776	7502	5475	2170	6719	**Los Angeles**
		6664	9207	2090	5717	7742	4635	4780	6365	10321	8058	7024	2018	6897	**Mexico City**
			3942	4666	1545	3600	2053	7184	1477	5237	9008	4651	4637	10283	**Moscow**
				7358	4029	5727	5395	5548	3350	4635	7552	6996	7570	8490	**Nairobi**
					3626	6828	2613	4832	4280	9531	9935	6741	356	8951	**New York**
493						5106	1384	5708	687	6671	10539	6038	3738	11798	**Paris**
769	10724						4897	10773	5049	2783	5561	1304	6557	6700	**Peking**
544	14818	6344						6135	2048	7155	10325	5469	2600	10725	**Reykjavik**
936	3364	7510	11842						5725	9763	8389	11551	5180	7367	**Rio de Janeiro**
085	9200	2486	6485	5836						6229	10143	6127	4399	11523	**Rome**
060	12460	5794	9216	10988	8217						3915	3306	9350	5298	**Singapore**
936	7460	3304	8683	4206	2228	7882						4861	9800	1383	**Sydney**
155	7693	11562	8928	7777	9187	17338	9874						6410	5762	**Tokyo**
188	10243	2376	5391	6888	1105	8126	3297	9214						8820	**Toronto**
123	16610	8428	7460	15339	10737	4478	11514	15712	10025						**Wellington**
073	12969	14497	12153	15989	16962	8949	16617	13501	16324	6300					**Miles**
811	11304	7485	11260	10849	9718	2099	8802	18589	9861	5321	7823				
492	3247	7462	12183	574	6015	10552	4184	8336	7080	15047	15772	10316			
814	11100	16549	13664	14405	18987	10782	17260	11855	18545	8526	2226	9273	14194		

Distance table

These distances are the great circle distances between the cities (international airports). Great circle distances are the shortest distances between two points on the globe. They are the normal flight paths for aircraft where they are free from the restrictions of air corridors or national airspace.

Tokyo
35 33N 139 46E

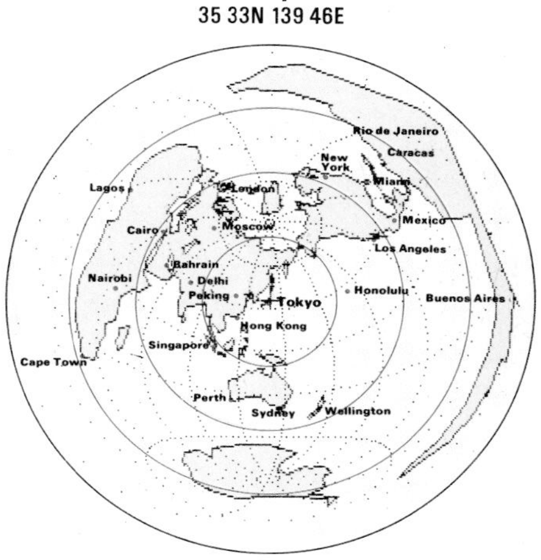

Sydney
33 56S 151 10E

Delhi
28 34N 77 7E

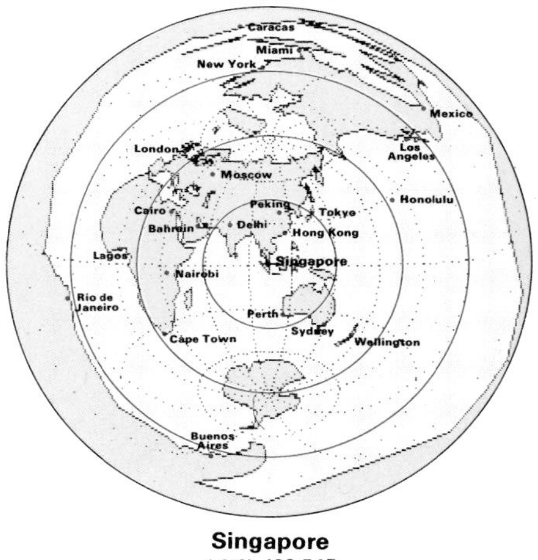

Singapore
1 21N 103 54E

WATER RESOURCES AND VEGETATION

Fresh water is essential for life, and in some parts of the world it is a most precious commodity. Since it is easy for industrialized states to take water's existence for granted, our increasing demands may yet require the desalination of the earth's 1 250 million cubic kilometers of water. The drawing at the left below shows the global **distribution of water**. The drawing at the upper right depicts the **hydrologic cycle**, in which water is continually absorbed into the atmosphere as vapor, which in turn condenses or freezes and falls as rain, hail, or snow. As shown, vegetation plays an important part in this cycle.

The map and photographs on the opposite page show the earth's natural vegetation by climate. The photographs show: (1) tundra, (2) coniferous forest, (3) broad-leaved forest, (4) tropical rain forest, (5) monsoon forest, (6) Mediterranean scrub, (7) grassland, (8) savanna, (9) steppe, and (10) desert.

Water Availability in Selected Countries 1985

	Per Capita (thousand cubic meters per year)
Water-Rich Countries	
1 Canada	121.93
2 Panama	66.06
3 Nicaragua	53.48
4 Brazil	38.28
5 Ecuador	33.48
6 Malaysia	29.32
7 Sweden	22.11
8 Cameroon	21.41
9 Finland	21.33
10 U.S.S.R.	16.93
11 Indonesia	15.34
12 Austria	12.02
13 United States	10.43
Water-Poor Countries	
1 Malta	0.07
2 Libya	0.19
3 Barbados	0.20
4 Oman	0.54
5 Kenya	0.72
6 Egypt	1.20
7 Belgium	1.27
8 South Africa	1.54
9 Poland	1.57
10 Haiti	1.67
11 Peru	2.03
12 India	2.43
13 China	2.52

Source: Forkasiewicz and Margat, 1980

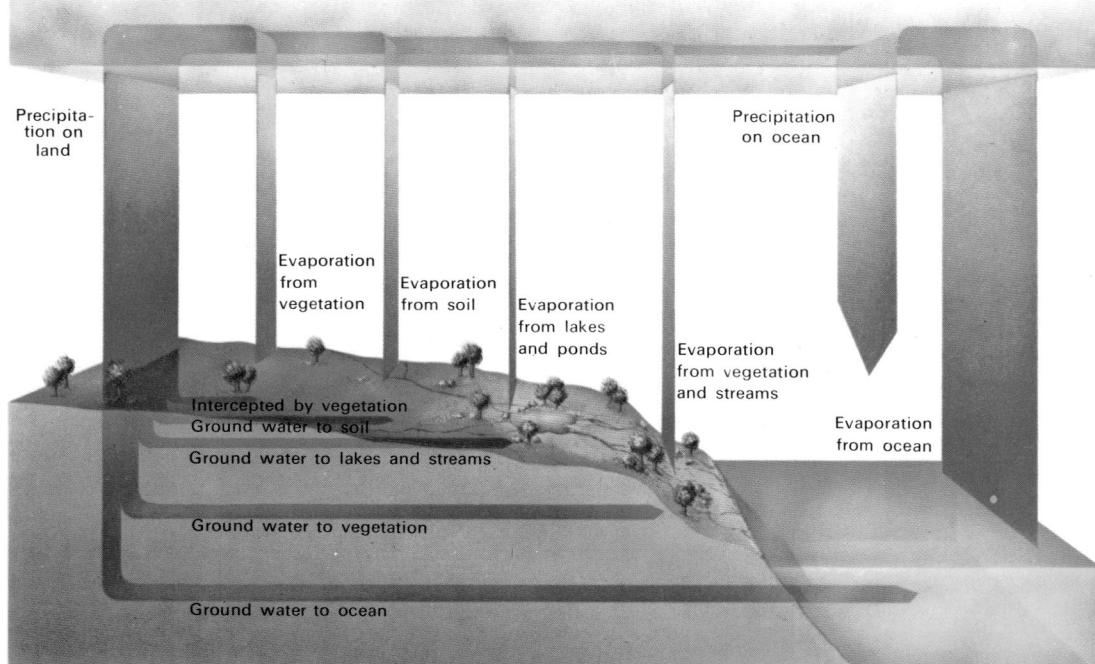

Precipitation on land

Precipitation on ocean

Evaporation from vegetation

Evaporation from soil

Evaporation from lakes and ponds

Evaporation from vegetation and streams

Evaporation from ocean

Intercepted by vegetation

Ground water to soil

Ground water to lakes and streams

Ground water to vegetation

Ground water to ocean

Domestic consumption of water

An area's level of industrialisation, climate and standard of living are all major influences in the consumption of water. On average Europe consumes 636 liters per head each day of which 180 liters is used domestically. In the U.S.A. domestic consumption is slightly higher at 270 liters per day. The graph (right) represents domestic consumption in the U.K. in 1970.

Drinking and eating 3%
Garden 3%
Laundry 9%
Dishwashing 10%
Waste in distribution 13%
Personal hygiene 30%
Toilet 32%

Distribution of water

Oceans and seas 97.29%
Ice caps and glaciers 2.09%
Underground aquifers 0.6054%
Lakes and rivers 0.0136%
Atmosphere 0.00094%
Biosphere 0.00004%

Average Annual Water Use in Selected Countries

Country	Water Withdrawal (km³)	Percentage Share Withdrawn (by Sector)			
		Public	Industry	Electric Cooling	Agriculture/Irrigation
United States	472.000	10	11	38	41
Canada	30.000	13	39	39	10
Egypt	45.000	1	0	0	98
Finland	4.610	7	85	0	8
Belgium	8.260	6	37	47	10
U.S.S.R.	226.000	8	15	14	63
Panama	1.300	12	11	0	77
India	380.000	3	1	3	93
China	460.000	6	7	0	87
Poland	15.900	14	21	40	25
Libya	1.470	17	0	0	83
Oman	0.043	2	0	0	98
South Africa	9.200	17	0	0	83
Nicaragua	0.890	18	45	0	37
Barbados	0.027	45	35	0	20
Malta	0.023	100	0	0	0

Source: Forkasiewicz and Margat, 1980

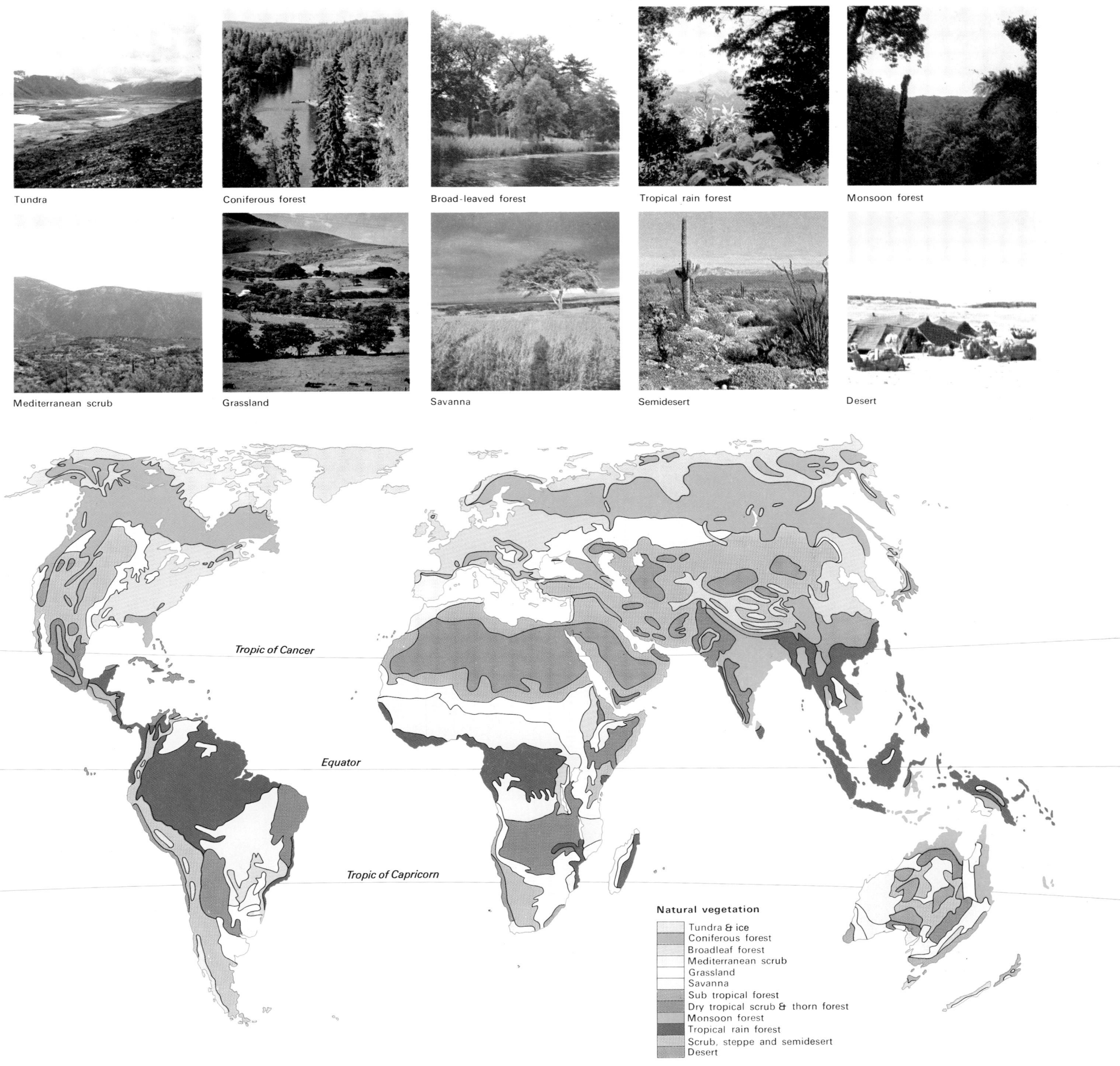

Tundra

Coniferous forest

Broad-leaved forest

Tropical rain forest

Monsoon forest

Mediterranean scrub

Grassland

Savanna

Semidesert

Desert

Tropic of Cancer

Equator

Tropic of Capricorn

Natural vegetation

Tundra & ice
Coniferous forest
Broadleaf forest
Mediterranean scrub
Grassland
Savanna
Sub tropical forest
Dry tropical scrub & thorn forest
Monsoon forest
Tropical rain forest
Scrub, steppe and semidesert
Desert

POPULATION

World population distribution is shown on the maps at the right and on the chart below the map at the far right. The most densely populated regions are in India, China, and Europe where the average density is between 100 and 200 per square kilometer, although there are pockets of extremely high density elsewhere. In contrast, Australia has only 1.5 people per square kilometer. The countries have been drawn on the chart to make their areas proportional to their populations.

The graphs at the left below present **age distribution** for six countries in the mid 1980s. The U.K. shows many demographic characteristics of European countries where birth and death rates have declined, with moderate population growth and nearly as many old as young. The maps below show **life expectancy** and the **birth** and **death rates** for the regions of the world.

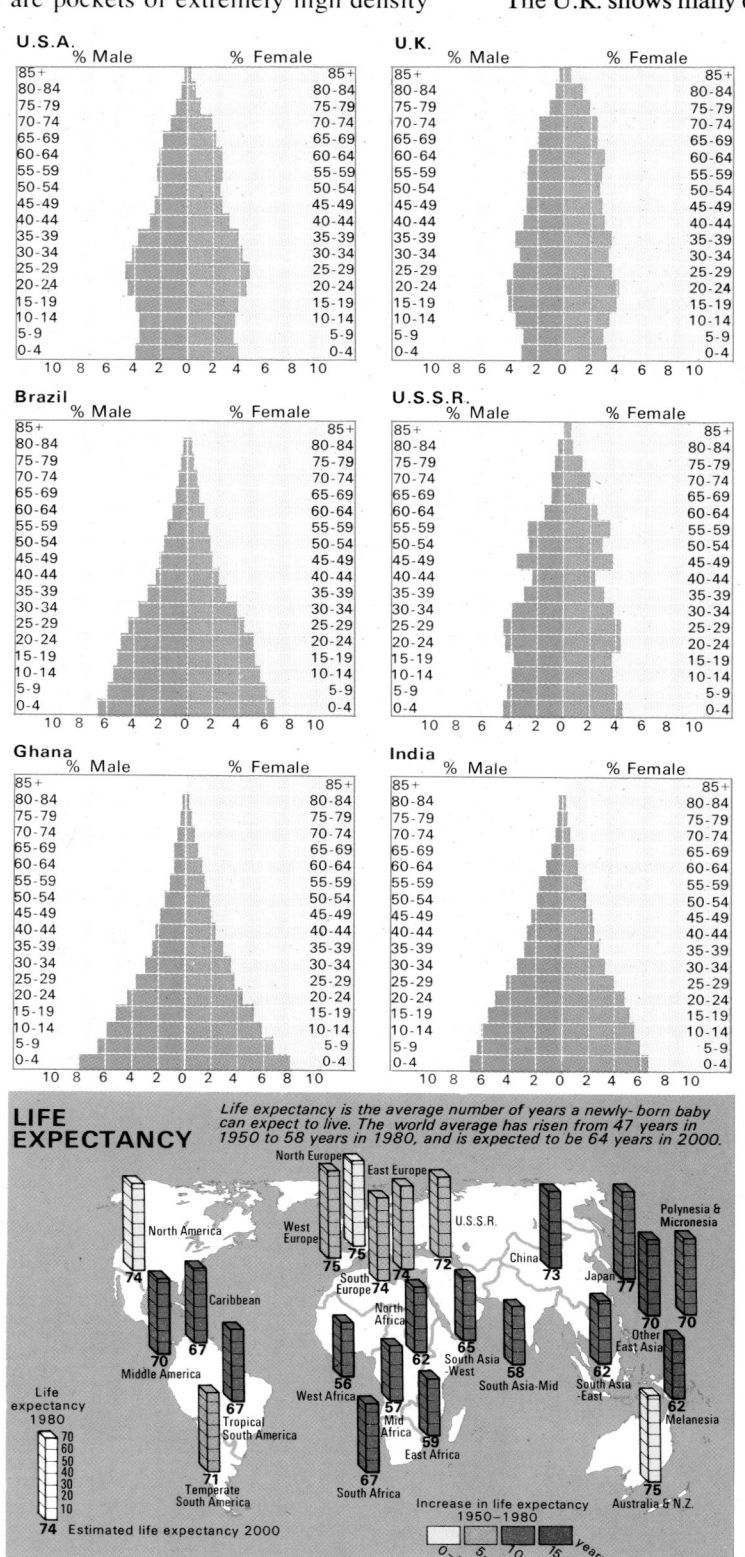

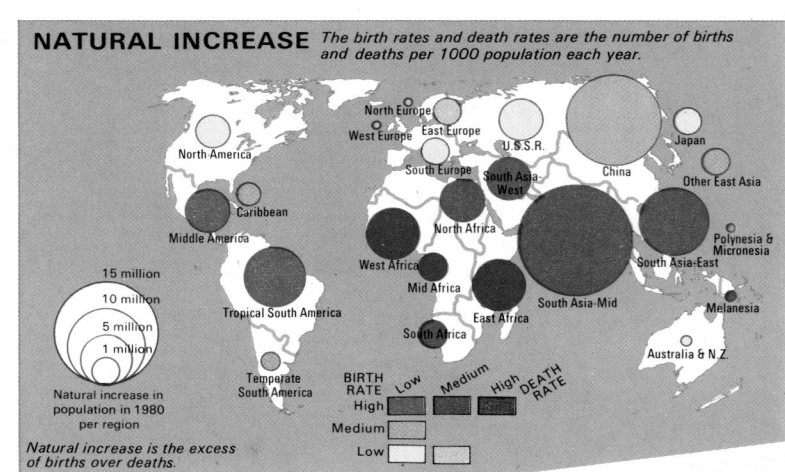

People have always been unevenly distributed in the world. Europe has for centuries contained nearly 20% of the world's population; but, after the 16–19th century explorations and consequent migrations, this proportion was rapidly reduced. In 1750, the Americas had 2% of the world's total; by A.D. 2000, they will contain 16%. This increase is reflected in the graph at the bottom of the page, on which population is given as millions. As shown on the graph, until recently there was little increase in world population. About 6000 B.C. there were probably about 200 million people in all. This level increased just over 100 million in the next 7 000 years. By the 1800s, there were about 1 000 million people. At present, world population is approximating 4 000 million. It is expected that this figure will be over 6 000 million by the year 2000.

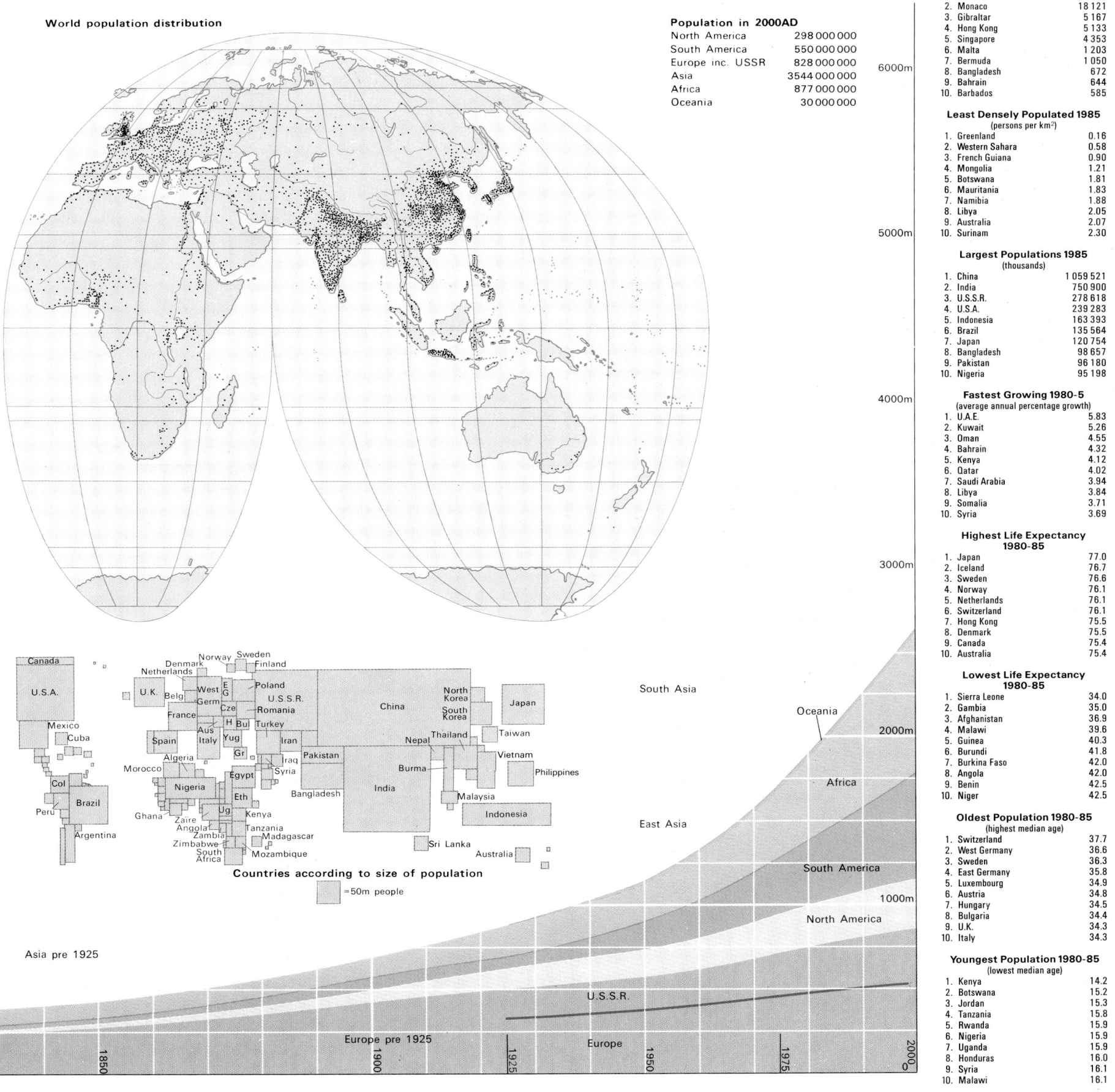

World population distribution

Population in 2000AD

North America	298 000 000
South America	550 000 000
Europe inc. USSR	828 000 000
Asia	3 544 000 000
Africa	877 000 000
Oceania	30 000 000

Countries according to size of population

= 50m people

Most Densely Populated (1985)
(persons per km²)

1.	Macau	21 431
2.	Monaco	18 121
3.	Gibraltar	5 167
4.	Hong Kong	5 133
5.	Singapore	4 353
6.	Malta	1 203
7.	Bermuda	1 050
8.	Bangladesh	672
9.	Bahrain	644
10.	Barbados	585

Least Densely Populated 1985
(persons per km²)

1.	Greenland	0.16
2.	Western Sahara	0.58
3.	French Guiana	0.90
4.	Mongolia	1.21
5.	Botswana	1.81
6.	Mauritania	1.83
7.	Namibia	1.88
8.	Libya	2.05
9.	Australia	2.07
10.	Surinam	2.30

Largest Populations 1985
(thousands)

1.	China	1 059 521
2.	India	750 900
3.	U.S.S.R.	278 618
4.	U.S.A.	239 283
5.	Indonesia	163 393
6.	Brazil	135 564
7.	Japan	120 754
8.	Bangladesh	98 657
9.	Pakistan	96 180
10.	Nigeria	95 198

Fastest Growing 1980-5
(average annual percentage growth)

1.	U.A.E.	5.83
2.	Kuwait	5.26
3.	Oman	4.55
4.	Bahrain	4.32
5.	Kenya	4.12
6.	Qatar	4.02
7.	Saudi Arabia	3.94
8.	Libya	3.84
9.	Somalia	3.71
10.	Syria	3.69

Highest Life Expectancy 1980-85

1.	Japan	77.0
2.	Iceland	76.7
3.	Sweden	76.6
4.	Norway	76.1
5.	Netherlands	76.1
6.	Switzerland	76.1
7.	Hong Kong	75.5
8.	Denmark	75.5
9.	Canada	75.4
10.	Australia	75.4

Lowest Life Expectancy 1980-85

1.	Sierra Leone	34.0
2.	Gambia	35.0
3.	Afghanistan	36.9
4.	Malawi	39.6
5.	Guinea	40.3
6.	Burundi	41.8
7.	Burkina Faso	42.0
8.	Angola	42.0
9.	Benin	42.5
10.	Niger	42.5

Oldest Population 1980-85
(highest median age)

1.	Switzerland	37.7
2.	West Germany	36.6
3.	Sweden	36.3
4.	East Germany	35.8
5.	Luxembourg	34.9
6.	Austria	34.8
7.	Hungary	34.5
8.	Bulgaria	34.4
9.	U.K.	34.3
10.	Italy	34.3

Youngest Population 1980-85
(lowest median age)

1.	Kenya	14.2
2.	Botswana	15.2
3.	Jordan	15.3
4.	Tanzania	15.8
5.	Rwanda	15.9
6.	Nigeria	15.9
7.	Uganda	15.9
8.	Honduras	16.0
9.	Syria	16.1
10.	Malawi	16.1

LANGUAGE

To a degree, language differences may be blamed for the division and lack of understanding between nations. Whereas a common language binds countries, it also isolates them from other countries and groups. Thus beliefs, inventions, and ideas remain exclusive to these groups and different cultures develop.

The map below shows the **worldwide distribution of language**. As a result of colonization and the spread of internationally accepted languages, many countries have superimposed a language completely unrelated to their own in order to combine isolated national groups and to facilitate international understanding. Examples are the use of Spanish in South America and English in India. Certain languages that show marked similarities are thought to have developed from a common parent language, such as Latin. After the retreat of the Roman Empire, Latin remained as the released nation's new language wherever it had been firmly established. Where there was no unifying center, divergent development took place, and Latin evolved into a new language.

Written language (see chart below) originated with a series of pictures which gradually changed in style, influenced by the writing tools used. Carved alphabets tended to be angular; painted ones tended to be curved.

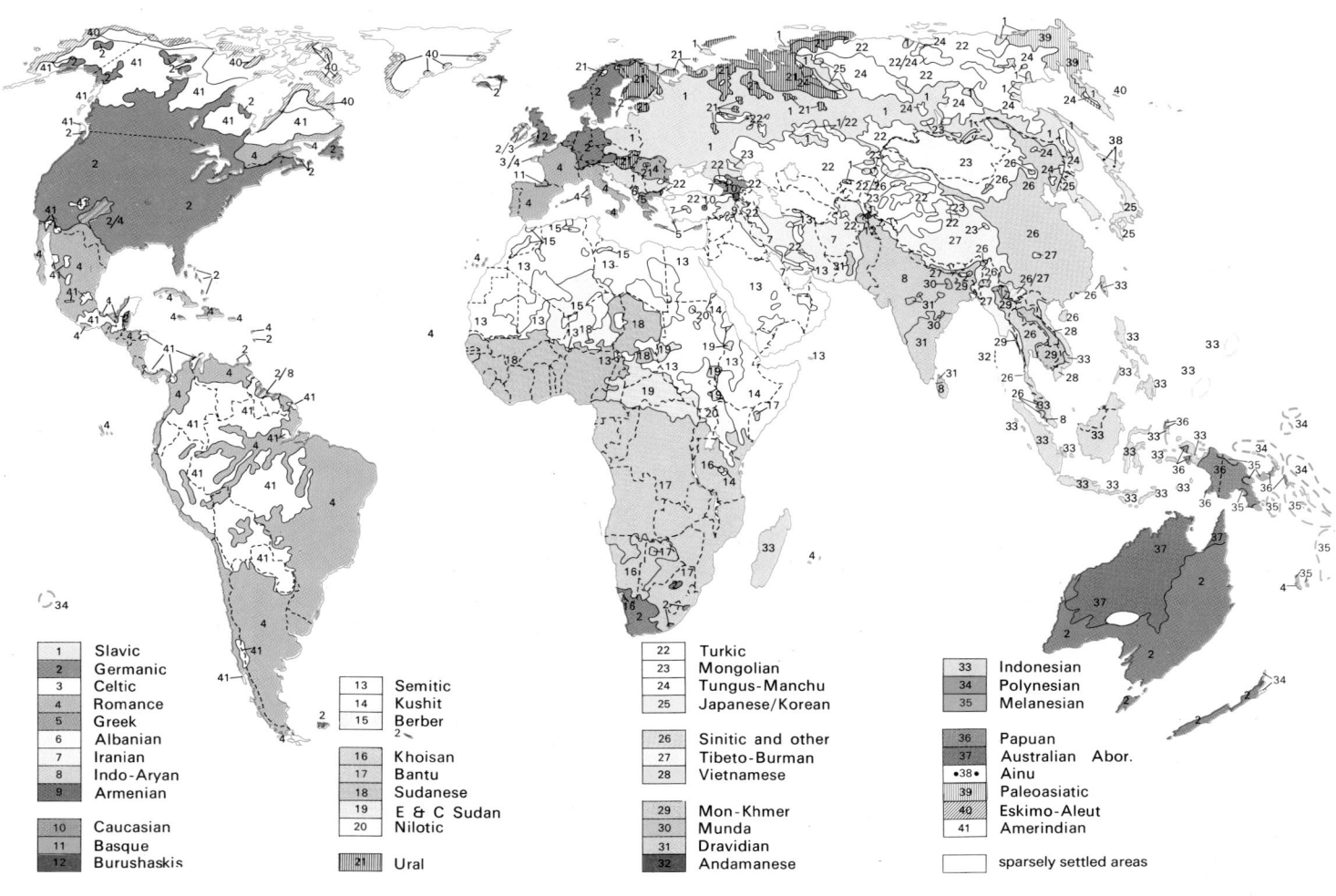

1	Slavic
2	Germanic
3	Celtic
4	Romance
5	Greek
6	Albanian
7	Iranian
8	Indo-Aryan
9	Armenian
10	Caucasian
11	Basque
12	Burushaskis

13	Semitic
14	Kushit
15	Berber
16	Khoisan
17	Bantu
18	Sudanese
19	E & C Sudan
20	Nilotic
21	Ural

22	Turkic
23	Mongolian
24	Tungus-Manchu
25	Japanese/Korean
26	Sinitic and other
27	Tibeto-Burman
28	Vietnamese
29	Mon-Khmer
30	Munda
31	Dravidian
32	Andamanese

33	Indonesian
34	Polynesian
35	Melanesian
36	Papuan
37	Australian Abor.
38	Ainu
39	Paleoasiatic
40	Eskimo-Aleut
41	Amerindian
	sparsely settled areas

Assyrian (carved)

Ancient Hebrew (painted)

Egyptian hieroglyphic (painted)

Some modern non-latin type faces

Greek
ΑΒΓΔΕΖΗΘΙΚΛΜΝΞΟΠΡΣΤΥΦΧΨΩΣ

Cyrillic
АБВГДЕЖЗИЙІКЛМНОПРСТУФХЦЏЧШ

Arabic
فى عام ١٨٩٧ وصل إلى إنجلترا أ نموذج

Bengali
১৮৯৭ খ্রীস্টাব্দে আধুনিক মডেলের একটি

Telugu
నిస్స సాయింటకి వచ్చిన యతిథ యెమియు

Japanese
国 土 の 位 置 と 地 形

Chinese
司 父
在 獨
提 子
印 出
芬 有
刷 之
奧 限
業 地
司 位
上 司，
有 能

ILLITERACY

Percentage of population in each country who are illiterate

80–100%	
60–80%	
40–60%	
20–40%	
0–20%	

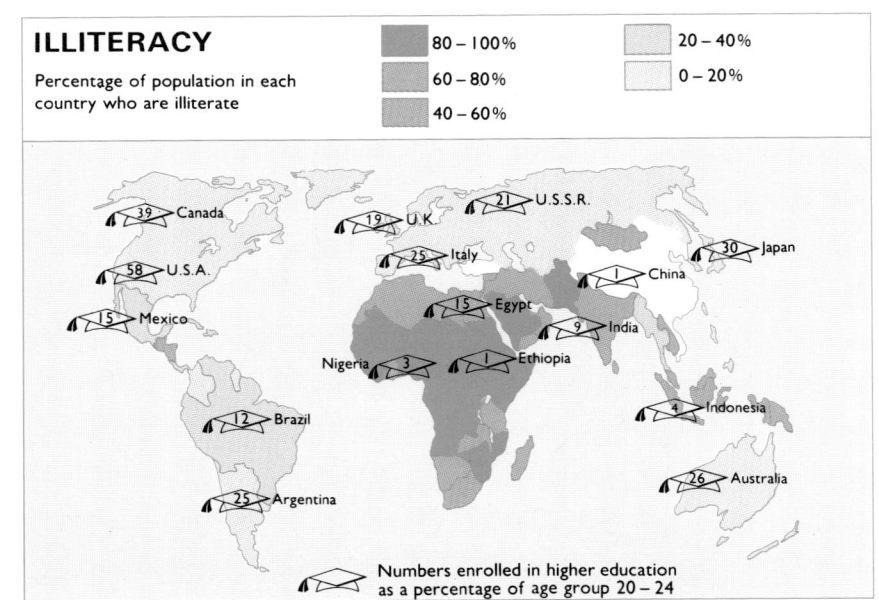

Numbers enrolled in higher education as a percentage of age group 20–24

RELIGION

Throughout history, people have held belief in supernatural powers based on the forces of nature. They expressed this belief by worshipping a supreme being or several gods. **Hinduism**, for example, honors many gods and goddesses, all manifestations of the one Spirit, Brahma. This religion incorporates the doctrine of reincarnation and espouses the caste system. **Buddhism**, founded in northeast India by

Gautama Buddha (563-483 B.C.), teaches that spiritual and moral discipline are essential to the achievement of supreme peace. **Confucianism**, a mixture of Buddhism and Confucius' teachings, provided a moral basis for the political structure of Imperial China and supported existing forms of ancestor worship. **Judaism**, which dates back many centuries, recognized but one God. Expelled from the

Holy Land in A.D. 70, its adherents (Jews) were reinstated there as the state of Israel in 1948. **Islam**, founded in Mecca by Muhammad (A.D. 570-632), spread across Asia and Africa, where it still thrives. **Christianity** was founded almost 2,000 years ago. Photographs below: **Christian monastery, Jewish holy place, Hindu temple, Mohammedan mosque, Buddhist temple.**

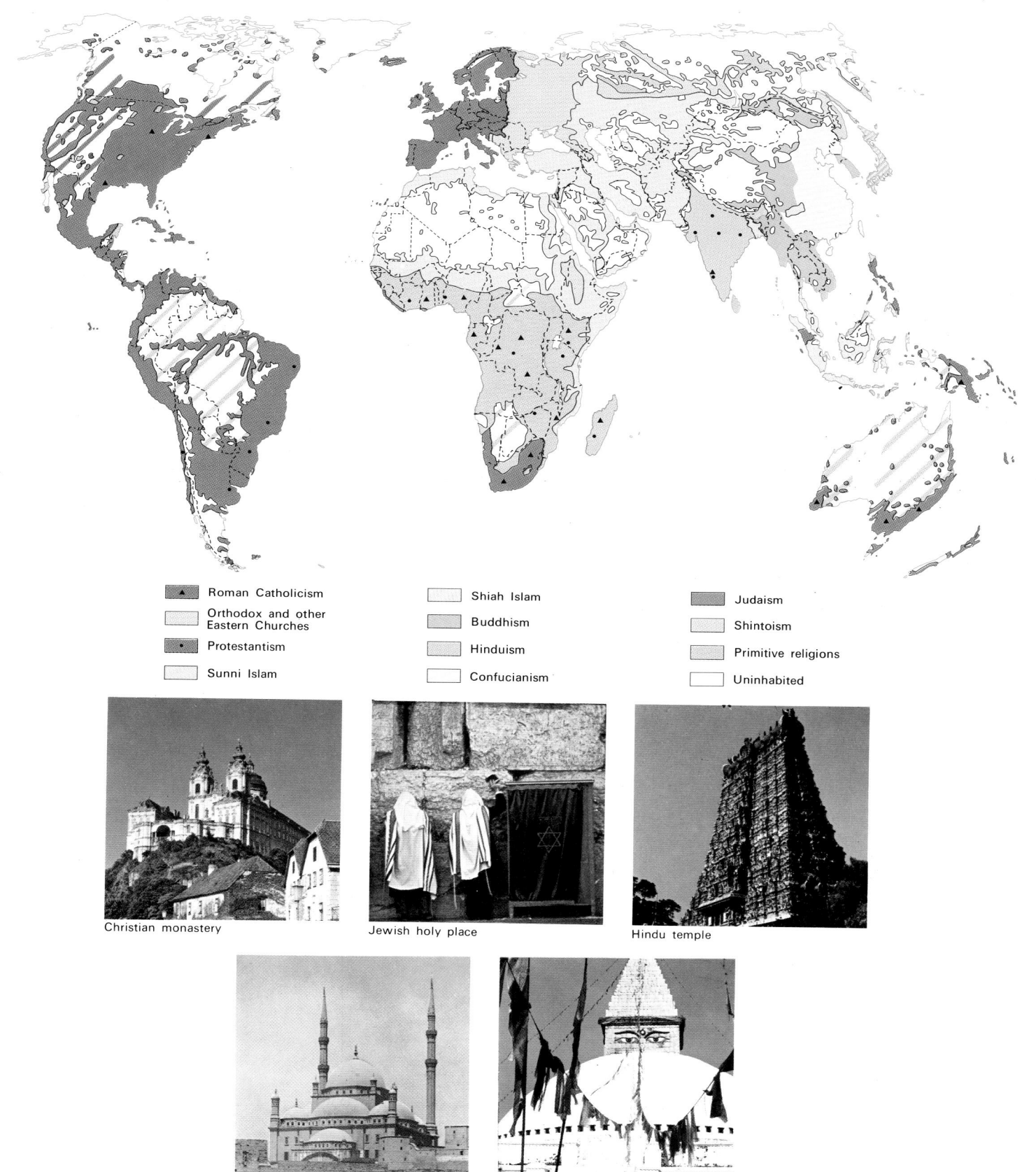

▲ Roman Catholicism		Shiah Islam		Judaism
Orthodox and other Eastern Churches		Buddhism		Shintoism
• Protestantism		Hinduism		Primitive religions
Sunni Islam		Confucianism		Uninhabited

Christian monastery

Jewish holy place

Hindu temple

Mohammedan mosque

Buddhist temple

THE GROWTH OF CITIES

The evolution of the semi-permanent Neolithic settlement into a city took 15 centuries (from 5000 to 3500 B.C.). Efficient communications and exchange systems were developed as population densities rose as high as 30 000 to 50 000 per square kilometer by 2000 B.C. in Egypt and Babylonia. New York City today has a density of 10 000 per square kilometer. The series of maps below shows the shift in location of the largest city in the world and in the distribution of the 25 largest cities between 200 B.C. and A.D. 1900. The graph at the left immediately below depicts the **increase in urbanization** from 1920 to 1980.

The increase in urbanization resulted primarily from better sanitation and health, which fostered population growth, and from the movement of people off the land into industry and service occupations in the cities. Generally, the most highly developed industrial nations are the most urbanized, although Switzerland and Norway are exceptions. The graph at the right shows the total **population of the 20 largest cities** of the world in the 1980s. Modern cities have a large metropolitan area of many communities linked to the central city.

The large illustrated map at the right shows the **distribution of the major cities** of today's world. The concentration of population in temperate regions is clearly shown. Normally, these major cities are not only major centers of population and wealth; they are also centers of political power and trade. Today, they are the sites of international airports and characteristically are great ports through which imported and exported goods can flow. These goods move along roads and railways that focus on the city. The staple trades and industries of these cities are varied and flexible.

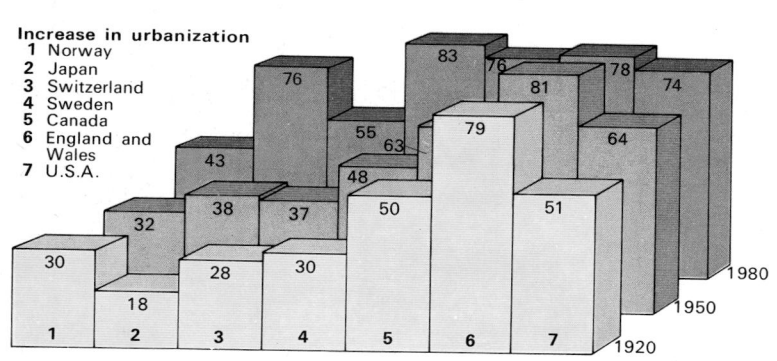

Increase in urbanization
1 Norway
2 Japan
3 Switzerland
4 Sweden
5 Canada
6 England and Wales
7 U.S.A.

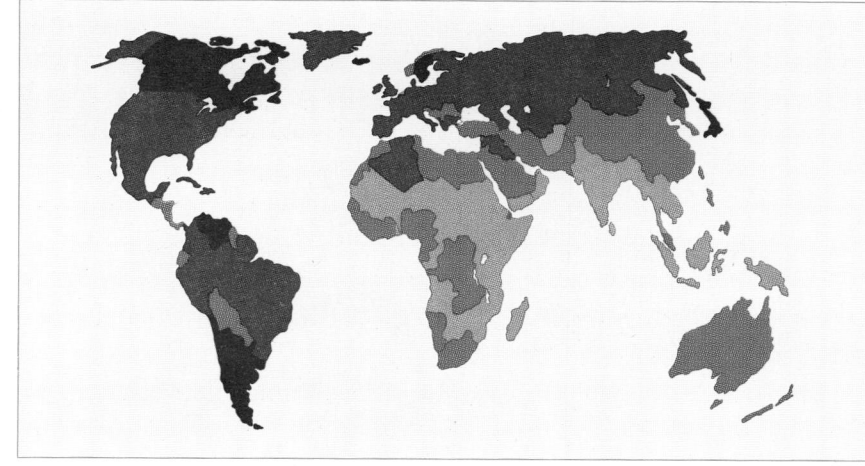

Percentage of population living in towns and cities in each country

- 75 – 100%
- 50 – 75%
- 25 – 50%
- 0 – 25%

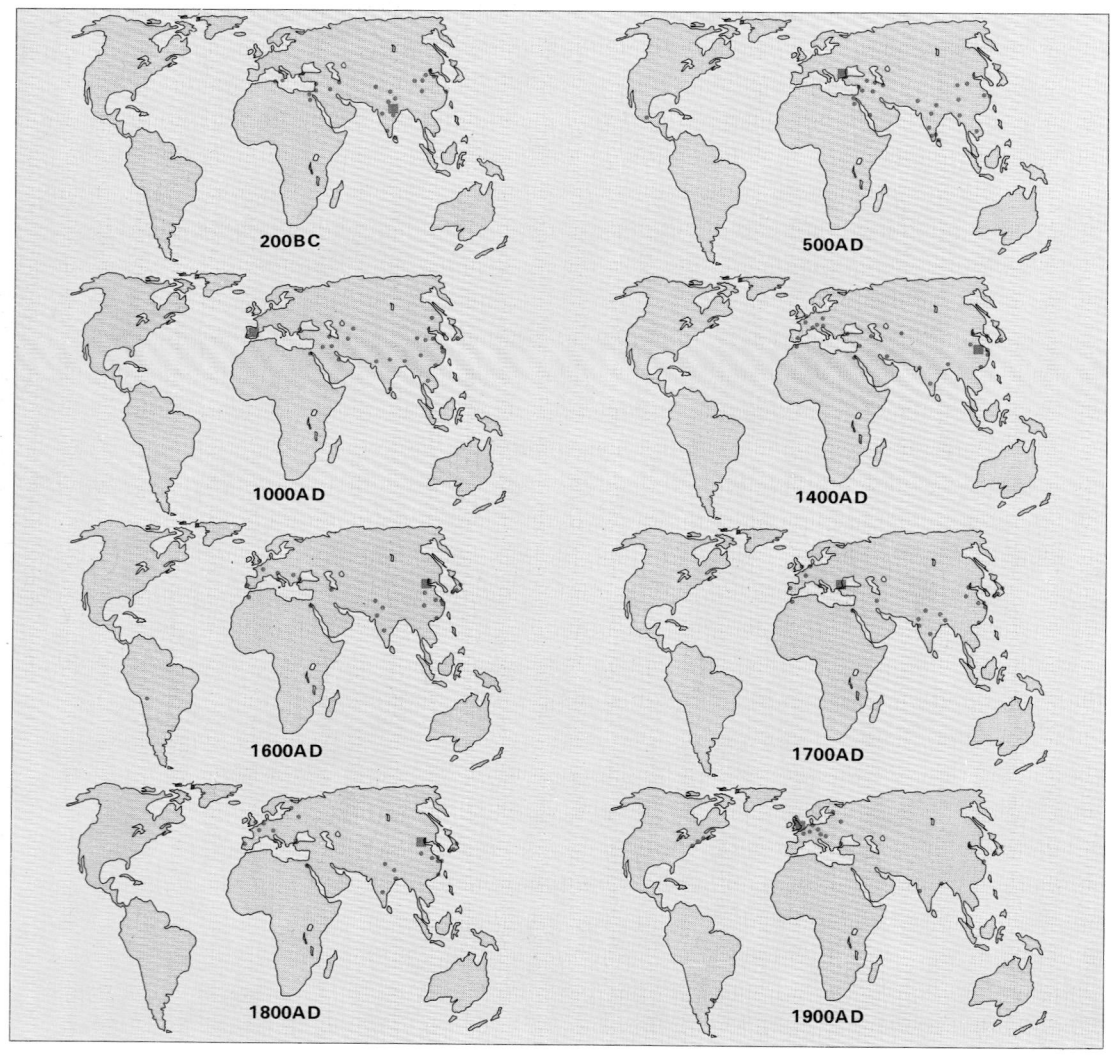

200BC 500AD 1000AD 1400AD 1600AD 1700AD 1800AD 1900AD

10 Most Urbanized Countries (urban as % of total population)		10 Least Urbanized Countries (urban as % of total population)	
1. Belgium	94.6	1. Rwanda	4.7
2. Kuwait	92.0	2. Bhutan	5.0
3. Hong Kong	91.7	3. Lesotho	6.0
4. Israel	89.6	4. Cape Verde	6.0
5. Iceland	89.0	5. Nepal	6.4
6. Netherlands	88.3	6. Burkina Faso	6.4
7. Qatar	88.0	7. Burundi	7.1
8. U.K.	87.7	8. Oman	9.0
9. West Germany	86.0	9. Ethiopia	11.3
10. Uruguay	84.5	10. Malawi	11.7

Population of the World's 20 largest cities			
	1950	1983-5	Projection 2000
1. New York	14 830 192	17 687 400	22 773 000
2. Mexico City	2 967 000	14 750 182	31 025 000
3. Los Angeles	4 046 000	12 190 600	14 154 000
4. São Paulo	2 227 512	12 183 634	25 796 000
5. Tokyo	6 275 190	11 746 190	24 172 000
6. Shanghai	4 300 630	11 185 100	22 677 000
7. Buenos Aires	5 251 000	9 967 826	12 104 000
8. Seoul	1 446 019	9 200 000	14 246 000
9. Calcutta	4 446 000	9 194 018	16 678 000
10. Beijing	2 163 000	9 179 660	19 931 000
11. Rio de Janeiro	2 937 000	8 821 845	18 961 000
12. Paris	5 525 000	8 706 963	11 330 000
13. Moscow	4 841 000	8 642 000	9 087 000
14. Bombay	2 901 000	8 243 405	17 056 000
15. Chicago	3 620 962	8 015 900	9 411 000
16. Tianjin	2 392 000	7 790 160	9 200 000
17. Cairo	2 466 000	7 464 000	13 058 000
18. London	8 348 023	7 379 014	6 860 200
19. Chongqing	1 573 000	6 511 130	4 247 000
20. Jakarta	1 725 000	6 503 449	16 591 000

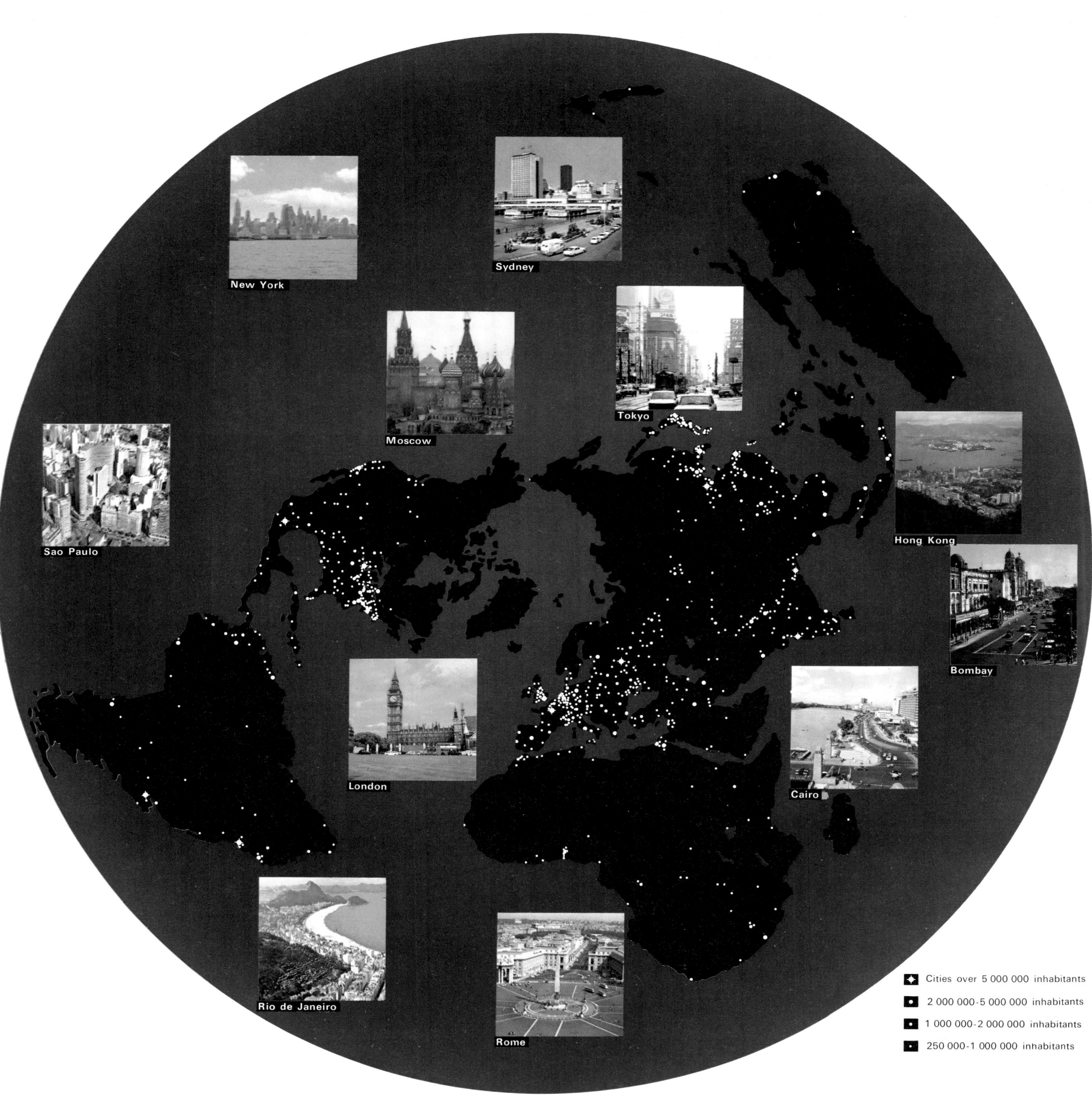

New York

Sydney

Moscow

Tokyo

Sao Paulo

Hong Kong

London

Bombay

Cairo

Rio de Janeiro

Rome

◆ Cities over 5 000 000 inhabitants

■ 2 000 000-5 000 000 inhabitants

■ 1 000 000-2 000 000 inhabitants

■ 250 000-1 000 000 inhabitants

FOOD RESOURCES: VEGETABLE

Cocoa, tea , coffee

These tropical or sub-tropical crops are grown mainly for export to the economically advanced countries. Tea and coffee are the world's principal beverages. Cocoa is used more in the manufacture of chocolate.

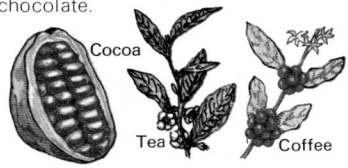

Sugar beet, sugar cane

Cane Sugar - a tropical crop - accounts for the bulk of the sugar entering into international trade. Beet Sugar, on the other hand, demands a temperate climate and is produced primarily for domestic consumption.

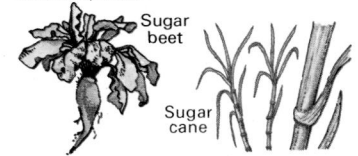

Fruit, wine

With the improvements in canning, drying and freezing, and in transport and marketing, the international trade and consumption of deciduous and soft fruits, citrus fruits and tropical fruits has greatly increased.
Over 80% of grapes are grown for wine and over a half in countries bordering the Mediterranean.

Vegetable oilseeds and oils

Despite the increasing use of synthetic chemical products and animal and marine fats, vegetable oils extracted from these crops grow in quantity, value and importance. Food is the major use- in margarine and cooking fats.

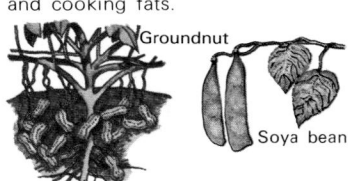

Groundnuts are also a valuable subsistence crop and the meal is used as animal feed. Soya-bean meal is a growing source of protein for humans and animals. The Mediterranean lands are the prime source of olive oil.

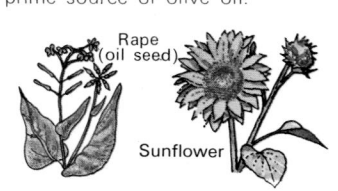

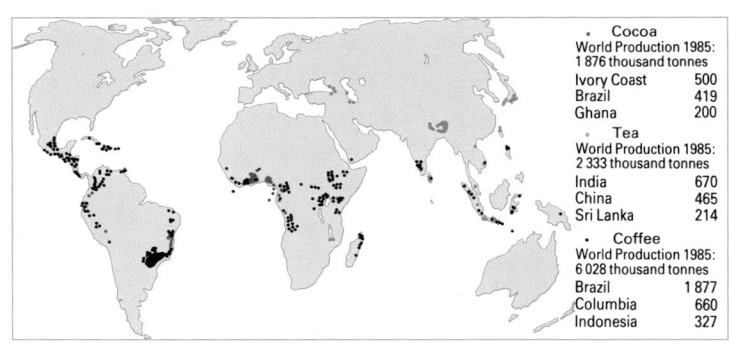

- **Cocoa**
World Production 1985:
1 876 thousand tonnes
Ivory Coast | 500
Brazil | 419
Ghana | 200
- **Tea**
World Production 1985:
2 333 thousand tonnes
India | 670
China | 465
Sri Lanka | 214
- **Coffee**
World Production 1985:
6 028 thousand tonnes
Brazil | 1 877
Columbia | 660
Indonesia | 327

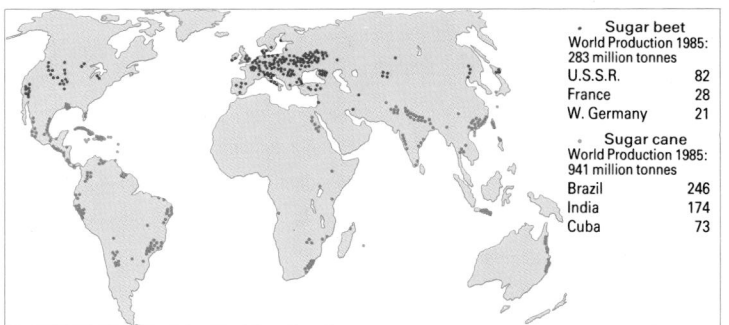

- **Sugar beet**
World Production 1985:
283 million tonnes
U.S.S.R. | 82
France | 28
W. Germany | 21
- **Sugar cane**
World Production 1985:
941 million tonnes
Brazil | 246
India | 174
Cuba | 73

- Temperate fruit
World Production 1985:
165 million tonnes
U.S.S.R. | 21
Italy | 16
China | 14
- Citrus fruit
World Production 1985:
59 million tonnes
Brazil | 15
U.S.A. | 9
Spain | 3
- Limits of the vine

- **Groundnuts**
World Production 1985:
21 260 thousand tonnes
China | 6 757
India | 5 600
U.S.A. | 1 800
- **Soya beans**
World Production 1985:
101 million tonnes
U.S.A. | 57
Brazil | 18
China | 11

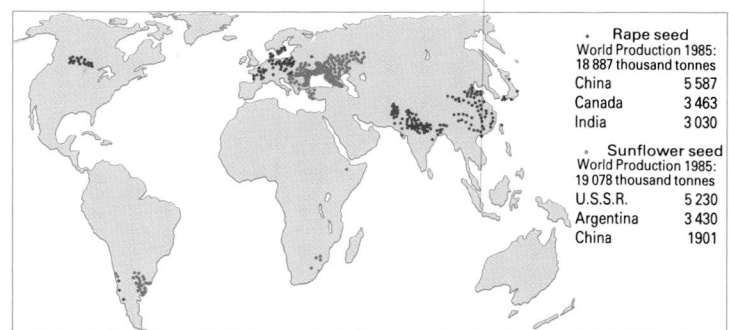

- **Rape seed**
World Production 1985:
18 887 thousand tonnes
China | 5 587
Canada | 3 463
India | 3 030
- **Sunflower seed**
World Production 1985:
19 078 thousand tonnes
U.S.S.R. | 5 230
Argentina | 3 430
China | 1901

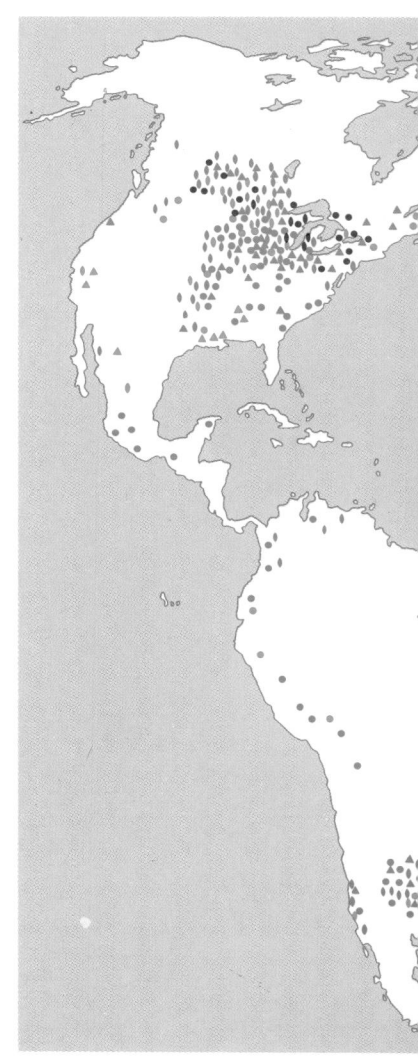

The vegetable kingdom has always been of prime importance to the food supply of the world. All parts of the plant contribute to this supply, but perhaps none is as important as the seed, from which all our cereals are derived and our food oils extracted. Fruits and the wines made from them also contribute to the overall food supply.

Tropical and sub-tropical crops such as cocoa, tea, and coffee are grown mostly for export. Another tropical crop, cane sugar, accounts for the bulk of the sugar entering the international trade. Beet sugar, which requires a temperate climate, is produced primarily for domestic consumption. Vegetable oils extracted from soya beans, peanuts (ground nuts), and rape and sunflower seeds are used widely, as shown on the maps. Cereals and potatoes are the principal sources of food for modern civilizations.

Maize (or Corn)
Needs plenty of sunshine, summer rain or irrigation and frost free for 6 months. Important as animal feed and for human food in Africa, Latin America and as a vegetable and breakfast cereal.

World production 1985 490 million tonnes

Barley
Has the widest range of cultivation requiring only 8 weeks between seed time and harvest. Used mainly as animal-feed and by the malting industry.

World production 1985 178 million tonnes

Oats
Widely grown in temperate regions with the limit fixed by early autumn frosts. Mainly fed to cattle. The best quality oats are used for oatmeal, porridge and breakfast foods.

World production 1985 45.6 million tonnes

Rice
Needs plains or terraces which can be flooded and abundant water in the growing season. The staple food of half the human race. In the husk, it is known as paddy.

World production 1985 466 million tonnes

Wheat
The most important grain crop in the temperate regions though it is also grown in a variety of climates e.g. in Monsoon lands as a winter crop.

World production 1985 510 million tonnes

Rye
The hardiest of cereals and more resistant to cold, pests and disease than wheat. An important foodstuff in Central and E. Europe and the U.S.S.R.

World production 1985 29.6 million tonnes

Millets
The name given to a number of related members of the grass family, of which sorghum is one of the most important. They provide nutritious grain.

World production 1985 109 million tonnes

Potato
An important food crop though less nutritious weight for weight than grain crops. Requires a temperate climate with a regular and plentiful supply of rain.

World production 1985 299 million tonnes

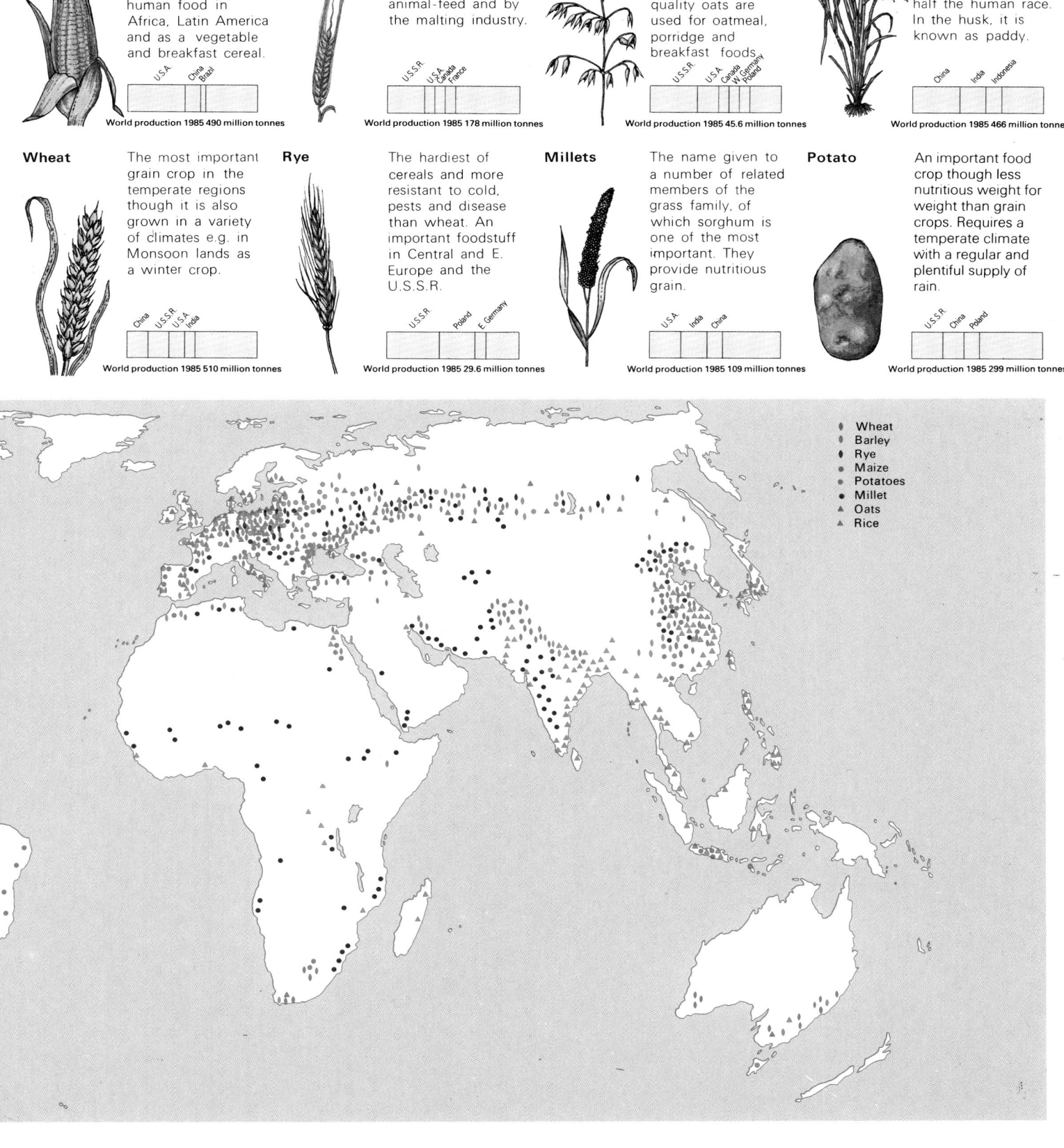

- ● Wheat
- ● Barley
- ● Rye
- ● Maize
- ● Potatoes
- ● Millet
- ▲ Oats
- ▲ Rice

FOOD RESOURCES: ANIMAL

Meat, milk, and allied foods are prime protein providers as well as sources of vitamins. Meat is mainly a product of continental and savanna grasslands and of the cool west coasts, particularly in Europe. (See map below.) Milk, cheese, eggs, and fish — though found in some quantity throughout the world — are primarily products of the temperate zones. Commercial fishing requires large shoals of fish of one species within reach of markets. The graphs below show **world production of major animal food resources**. Top row, left to right: sheep, beef cattle, dairy cattle, cheese; second row, pigs, fish, and butter.

Australia, New Zealand, and Argentina provide the major part of international beef

exports, whereas western U.S.A. and Europe produce much beef for their high local demand. Dairying, which requires a rich diet for the herd as well as nearby markets for its products, is carried on in densely populated areas of the temperate zones — U.S.A., N.W. Europe, New Zealand, and S.E. Australia. As shown on the map, production of sheep is worldwide. They are raised mostly for wool and meat. The merino yields a fine wool, but crossbreds are best for meat. The skins of sheep and the cheese made from sheep's milk are important products in some countries. World production of all kinds of cheese is well over ten million tons annually, the principal producers being U.S.A., India, W. Europe, and U.S.S.R. The chief

exporters are the Netherlands, New Zealand, Denmark, and France.

As indicated on the map, pigs can be reared in most climates, from monsoon to cool temperate. They are abundant in China, in the corn belt of the U.S.A., northwest and central Europe, Brazil, and in the U.S.S.R. Fish raised on fish farms as well as those caught in the wild are becoming an increasingly valuable source of protein. In addition to marine fishing, which is a worldwide enterprise, freshwater fishing is also important commercially. Long an important food source, butter still ranks high as a provider of calories and vitamin A. The biggest butter producers are U.S.S.R., W. Europe, U.S.A., New Zealand, and Australia.

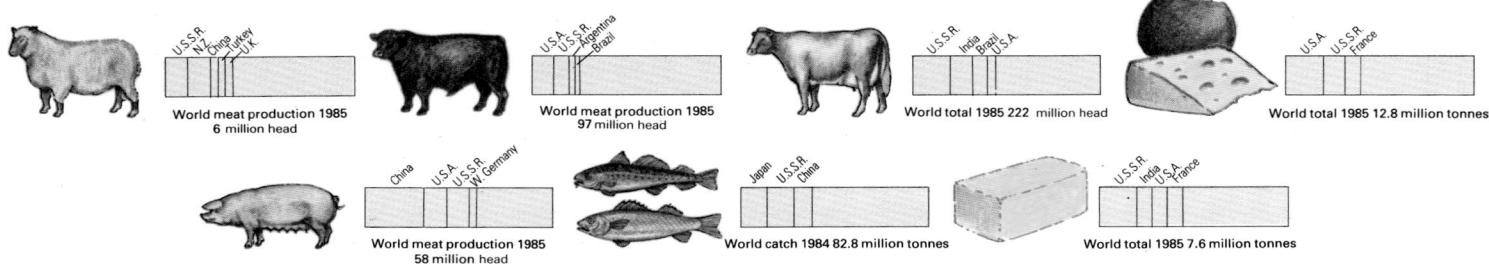

World meat production 1985
6 million head

World meat production 1985
97 million head

World total 1985 222 million head

World total 1985 12.8 million tonnes

World meat production 1985
58 million head

World catch 1984 82.8 million tonnes

World total 1985 7.6 million tonnes

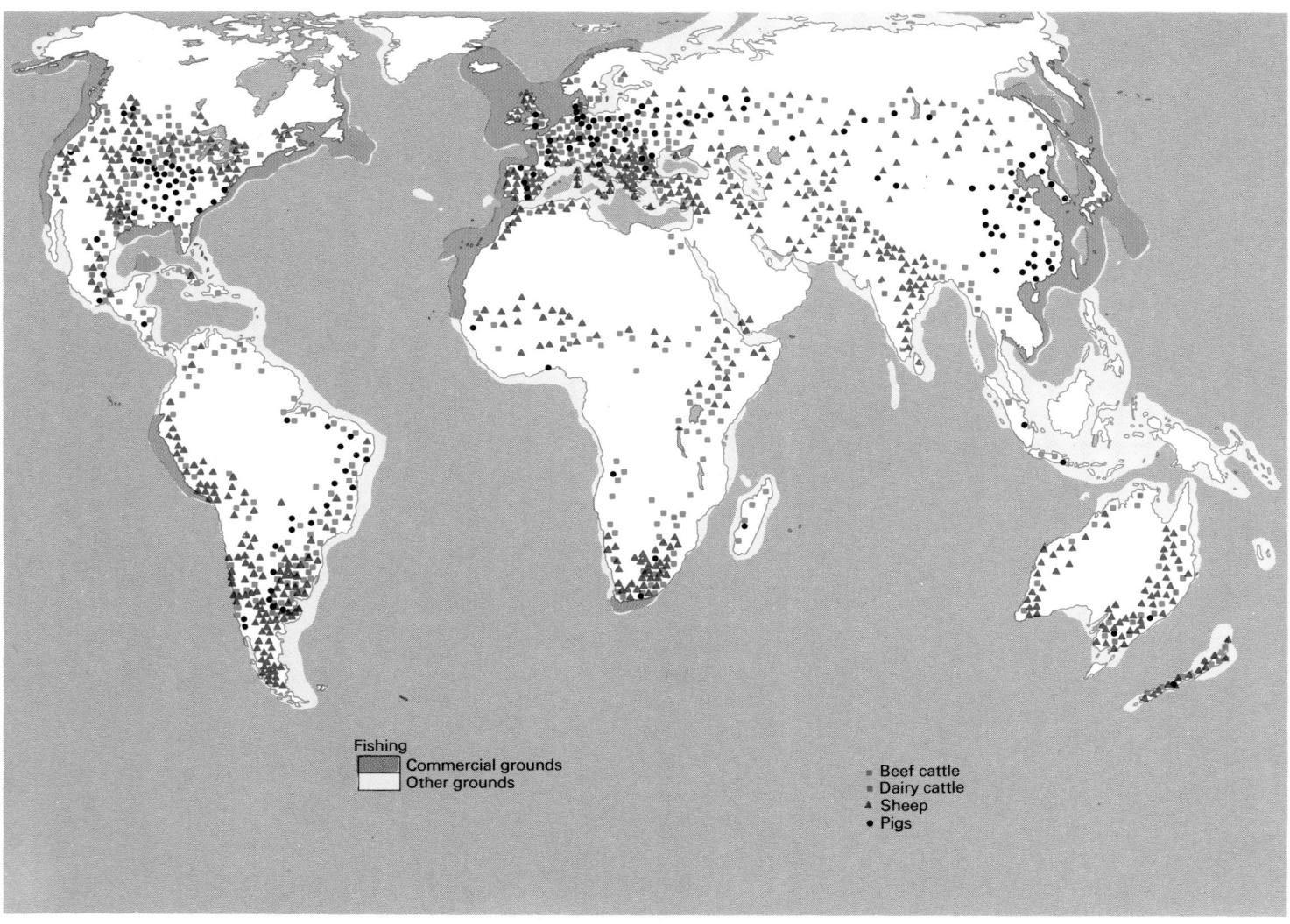

Fishing
Commercial grounds
Other grounds

■ Beef cattle
● Dairy cattle
▲ Sheep
● Pigs

NUTRITION

Foodstuffs fall, nutritionally, into three groups – providers of energy, protein, and vitamins. Cereals and oil-seeds provide energy and second-class protein; milk, meat and allied foods provide protein and vitamins; fruit and vegetables provide vitamins, especially Vitamin C, and some energy. To avoid malnutrition, a minimum level of these three groups of foodstuffs is required; the maps and diagrams show how unfortunately widespread are low standards of nutrition and even malnutrition.

Comparison of daily diets

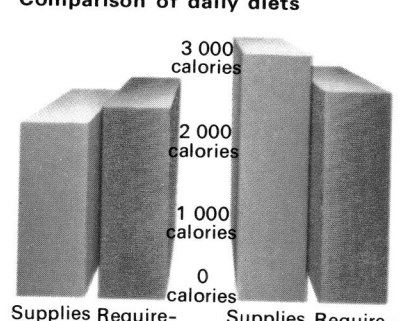

3 000 calories

2 000 calories

1 000 calories

0 calories

Supplies Require-ments

Supplies Require-ments

Far East, Near East, Africa & Latin America

Europe, Oceania & North America

Proportions of calories

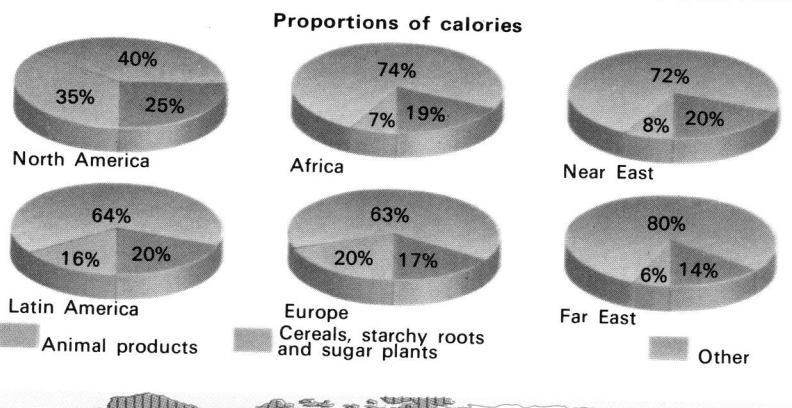

North America — 40%, 35%, 25%

Africa — 74%, 7%, 19%

Near East — 72%, 8%, 20%

Latin America — 64%, 16%, 20%

Europe — 63%, 20%, 17%

Far East — 80%, 6%, 14%

Animal products

Cereals, starchy roots and sugar plants

Other

Malnutrition

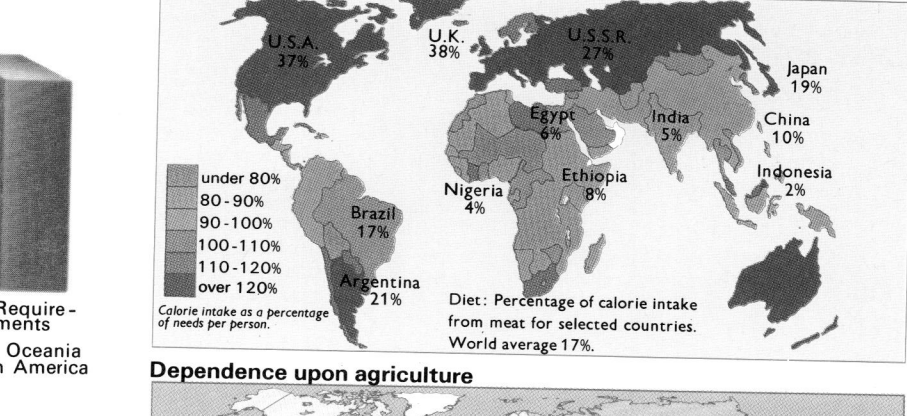

U.S.A. 37% U.K. 38% U.S.S.R. 27% Japan 19%

Egypt 6% India 5% China 10%

Brazil 17% Nigeria 4% Ethiopia 8% Indonesia 2%

Argentina 21%

under 80%
80 - 90%
90 - 100%
100 - 110%
110 - 120%
over 120%

Calorie intake as a percentage of needs per person.

Diet: Percentage of calorie intake from meat for selected countries. World average 17%.

Dependence upon agriculture

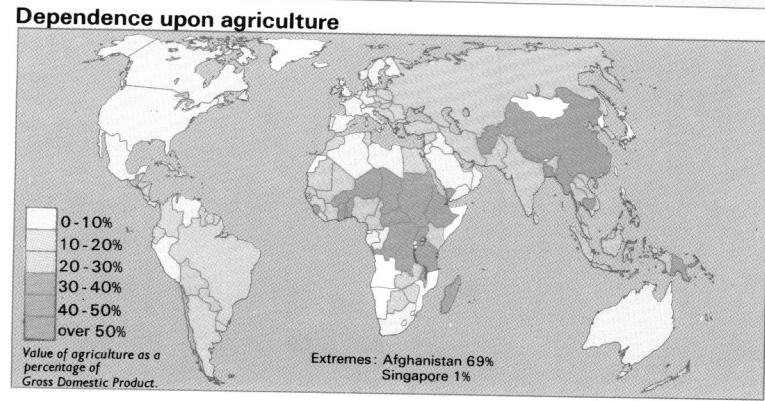

0 - 10%
10 - 20%
20 - 30%
30 - 40%
40 - 50%
over 50%

Value of agriculture as a percentage of Gross Domestic Product.

Extremes: Afghanistan 69% Singapore 1%

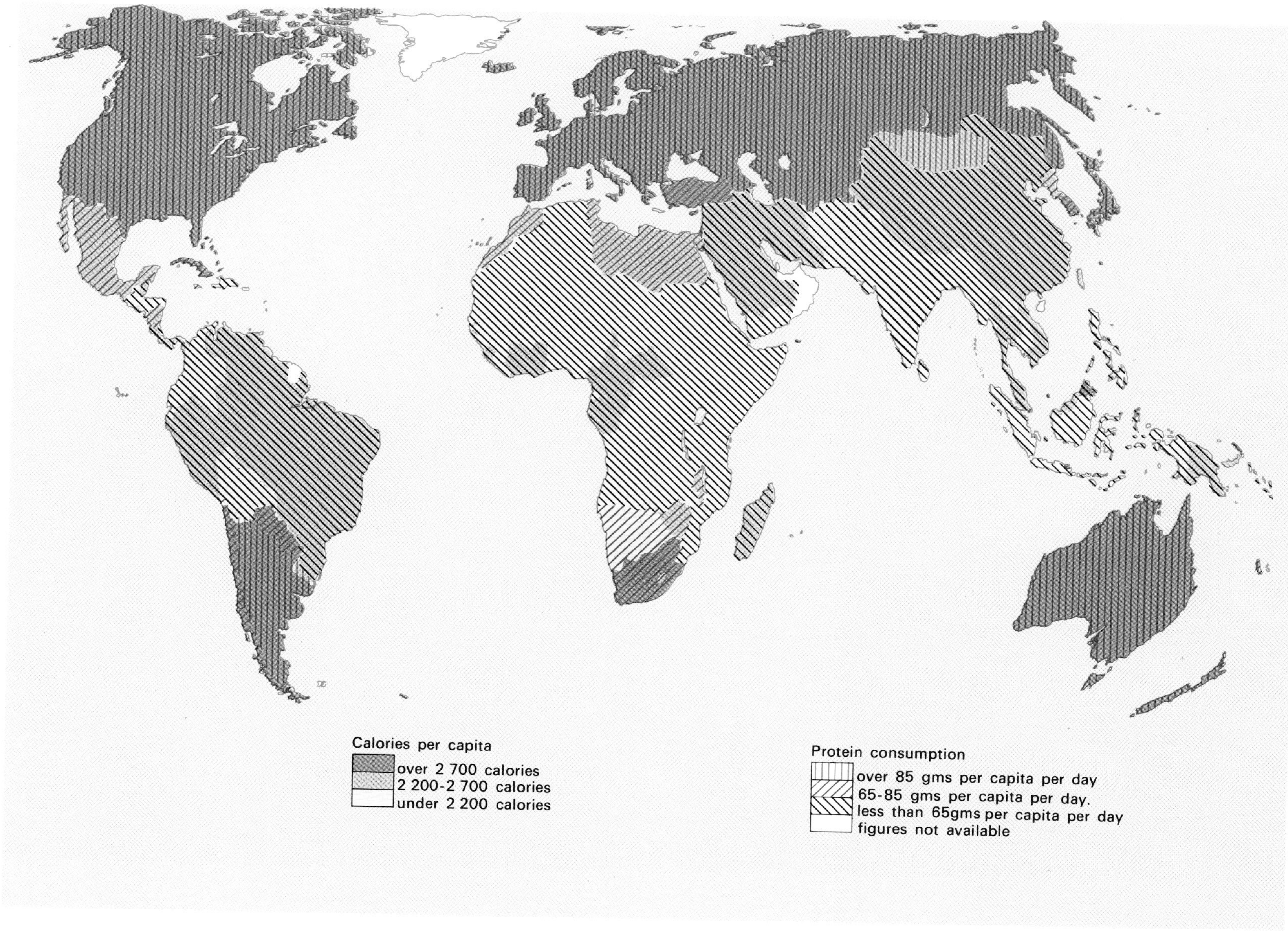

Calories per capita

over 2 700 calories
2 200 - 2 700 calories
under 2 200 calories

Protein consumption

over 85 gms per capita per day
65 - 85 gms per capita per day.
less than 65gms per capita per day
figures not available

Primitive man used iron for tools and vessels and its use extended gradually until iron, and later steel, became the backbone of the Modern World with the Industrial Revolution in the late 18th Century. At first, local ores were used, whereas today richer iron ores in huge deposits have been discovered and are mined on a large scale, often far away from the areas where they are used; for example, in Western Australia, Northern Sweden, Venezuela and Liberia. Iron smelting plants are today increasingly located at coastal sites, where the large ore carriers can easily discharge their cargo.

Steel is refined iron with the addition of other minerals, giving to the steel their own special properties; for example, resistance to corrosion (chromium, nickel, cobalt), hardness (tungsten, vanadium), elasticity (molybdenum), magnetic properties (cobalt), high tensile strength (manganese) and high ductility (molybdenum).

Production of metal ores used in ferro-alloys

Molybdenum 1984 95 000 tonnes — U.S.A., Chile, U.S.S.R., Canada

Chrome 1984 9 300 000 tonnes — South Africa, U.S.S.R., Albania, Turkey, Zimbabwe, India

Nickel 1984 738 000 tonnes — U.S.S.R., Canada, Australia, New Caledonia, Indonesia, Cuba

Cobalt 1984 23 100 tonnes — Zaïre, Zambia, U.S.S.R., Canada, New Caledonia, Australia

Tungsten 1984 45 000 tonnes — China, U.S.S.R., Canada, S. Korea, Bolivia, Australia, Portugal

Manganese 1984 8 861 000 tonnes — U.S.S.R., South Africa, Gabon, Brazil, Australia, China, India

Vanadium 1984 31 000 tonnes — South Africa, U.S.S.R., China, Finland

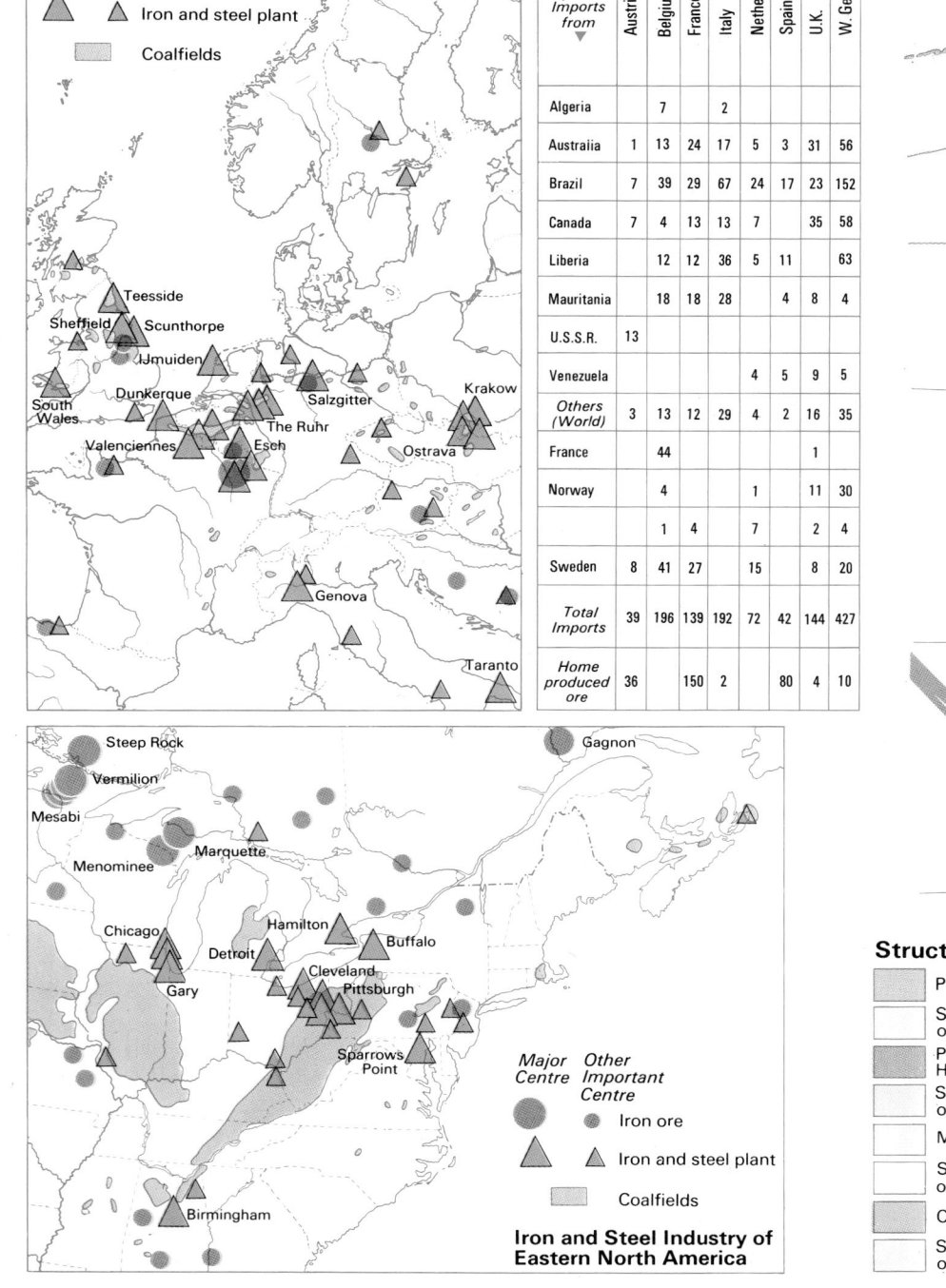

Iron and Steel Industry of Western Europe

Major Centre / *Other Important Centre*

- ● / ∘ Iron ore
- ▲ / △ Iron and steel plant
- ▨ Coalfields

Sources of Iron ore imported into Western Europe
hundred thousand tonnes

Imports from ▼	Austria	Belgium-Lux	France	Italy	Netherlands	Spain	U.K.	W. Germany
Algeria		7		2				
Australia	1	13	24	17	5	3	31	56
Brazil	7	39	29	67	24	17	23	152
Canada	7	4	13	13	7		35	58
Liberia		12	12	36	5	11		63
Mauritania		18	18	28		4	8	4
U.S.S.R.	13							
Venezuela					4	5	9	5
Others (World)	3	13	12	29	4	2	16	35
France		44					1	
Norway		4			1		11	30
		1	4		7		2	4
Sweden	8	41	27		15		8	20
Total Imports	39	196	139	192	72	42	144	427
Home produced ore	36		150	2		80	4	10

Iron and Steel Industry of Eastern North America

Major Centre / *Other Important Centre*

- ● / ∘ Iron ore
- ▲ / △ Iron and steel plant
- ▨ Coalfields

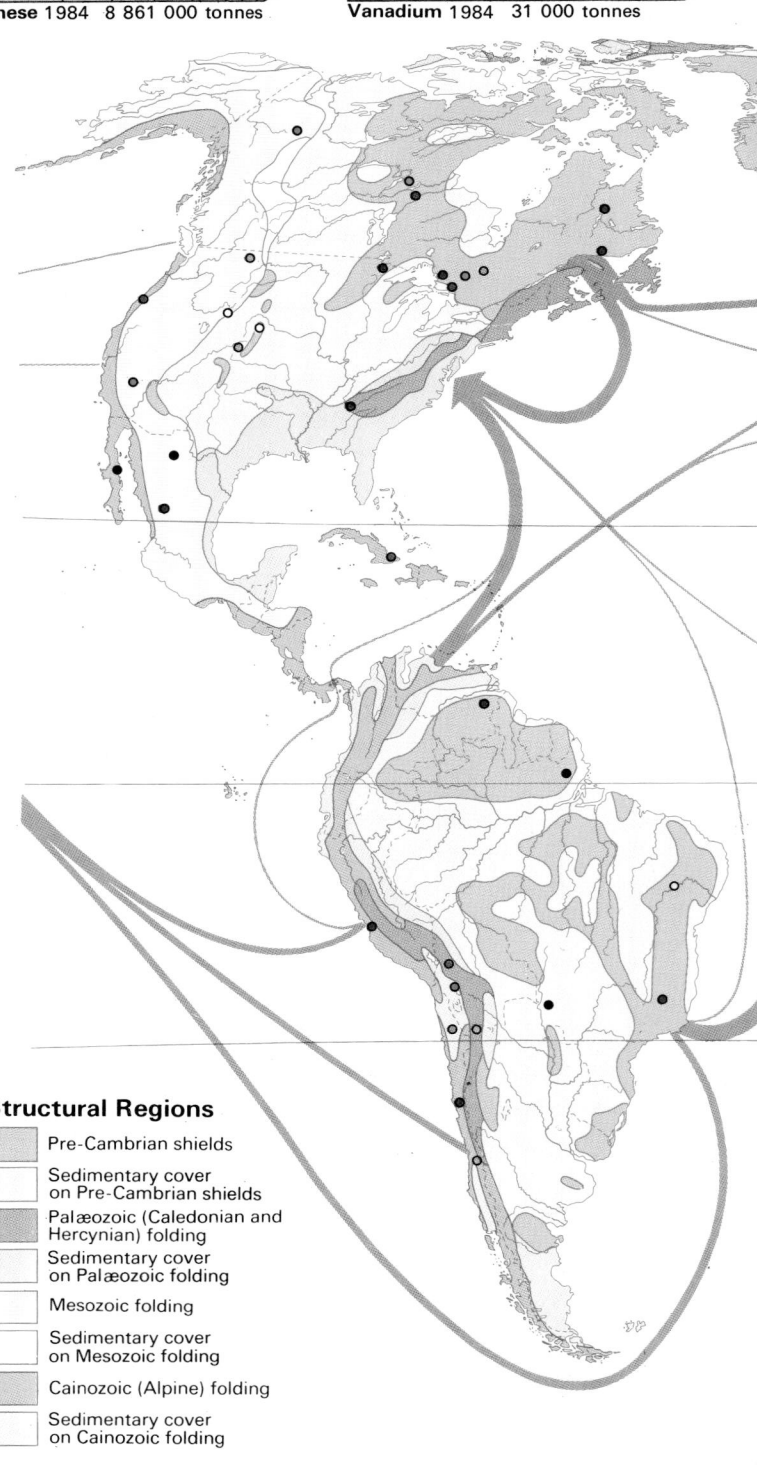

Structural Regions

- Pre-Cambrian shields
- Sedimentary cover on Pre-Cambrian shields
- Palæozoic (Caledonian and Hercynian) folding
- Sedimentary cover on Palæozoic folding
- Mesozoic folding
- Sedimentary cover on Mesozoic folding
- Cainozoic (Alpine) folding
- Sedimentary cover on Cainozoic folding

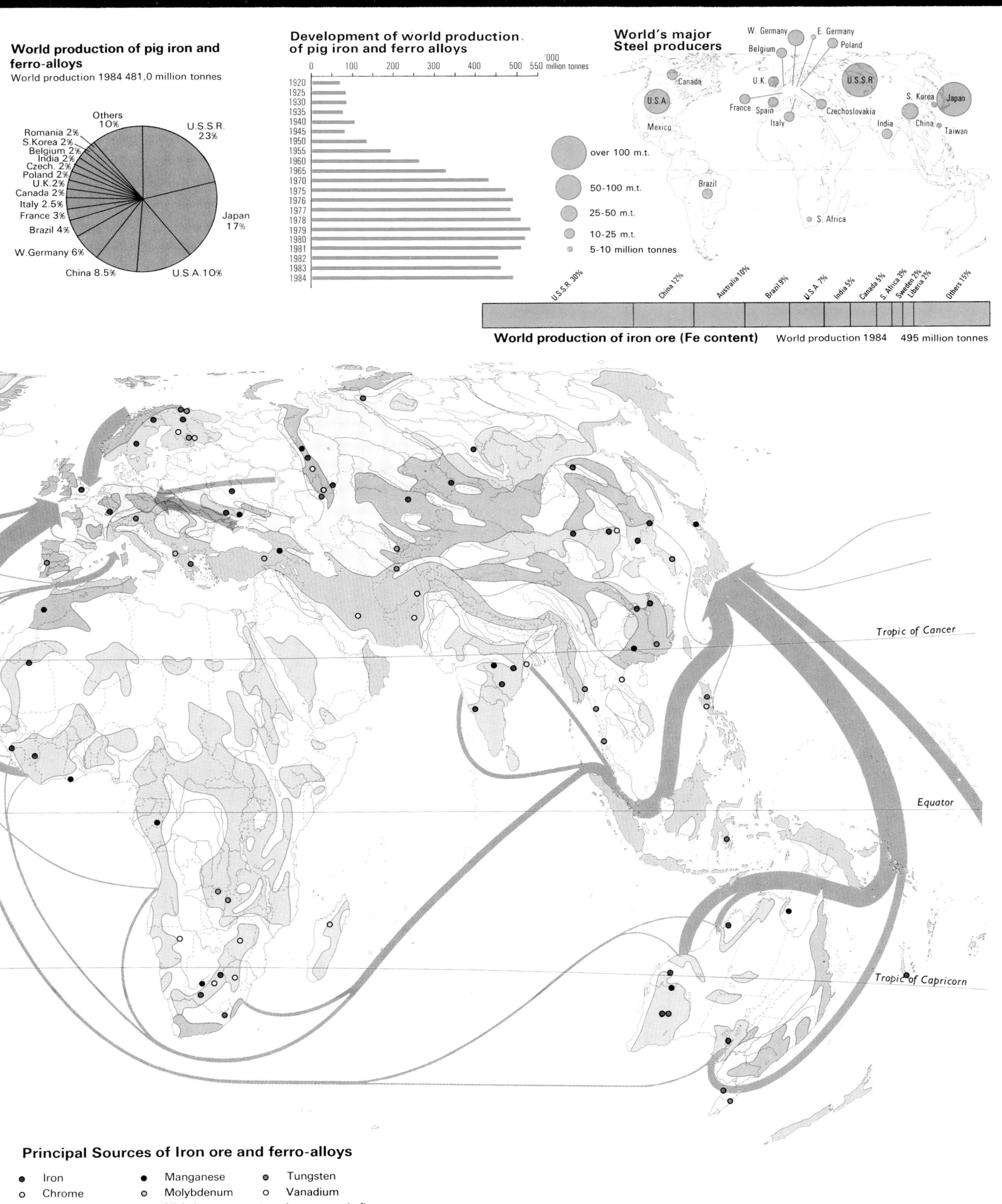

World production of pig iron and ferro-alloys
World production 1984 481,0 million tonnes

Others 10%
U.S.S.R. 23%
Romania 2%
S.Korea 2%
Belgium 2%
India 2%
Czech. 2%
Poland 2%
U.K.2%
Canada 2%
Italy 2.5%
France 3%
Brazil 4%
W.Germany 6%
China 8.5%
U.S.A.10%
Japan 17%

Development of world production of pig iron and ferro alloys

'000 million tonnes

	0	100	200	300	400	500	550

1920
1925
1930
1935
1940
1945
1950
1955
1960
1965
1970
1975
1976
1977
1978
1979
1980
1981
1982
1983
1984

World's major Steel producers

W. Germany
E. Germany
Belgium
Poland
Canada
U.K.
U.S.S.R.
U.S.A.
France
Spain
Italy
Czechoslovakia
S. Korea
Japan
Mexico
India
China
Taiwan
Brazil
S. Africa

over 100 m.t.
50-100 m.t.
25-50 m.t.
10-25 m.t.
5-10 million tonnes

U.S.S.R. 30% China 12% Australia 10% Brazil 9% U.S.A 7% India 5% Canada 5% S. Africa 3% Sweden 2% Liberia 2% Others 15%

World production of iron ore (Fe content)   World production 1984   495 million tonnes

Tropic of Cancer

Equator

Tropic of Capricorn

Principal Sources of Iron ore and ferro-alloys

- ● Iron
- ○ Chrome
- ◉ Cobalt
- ● Manganese
- ◉ Molybdenum
- ◉ Nickel
- ◉ Tungsten
- ○ Vanadium
- ▬ Iron ore trade flow

Antimony — imparts hardness when alloyed to other metals, especially lead. Uses: type metal, pigments (paints, glass, enamels), fireproofing textiles.

World production 1984 51 600 tonnes

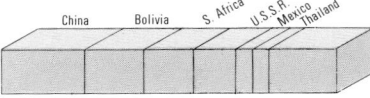

Copper — excellent conductor of electricity and heat, durable, strong, ductile, resistant to corrosion. Uses: wire, tubing, making brass and bronze.

World production 1984 8 300 000 tonnes

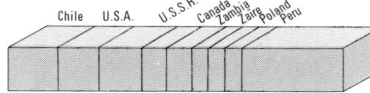

Lead — heavy, soft, malleable, acid-resistant. Uses: storage batteries, sheeting and piping, cable covering, ammunition, type metal, weights, gasoline additive.

World production 1984 3.4 million tonnes

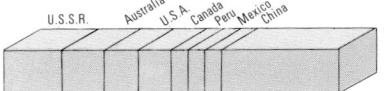

Mercury — liquid metal, excellent conductor. Uses: thermometers, drugs, pigments, in dentistry, electrical industry, gold and silver extraction.

World production 1984 5.5 million kg.

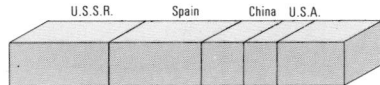

Tin — resistant to organic acids, malleable. Uses: canning containers, foils, as an alloy in bronze and brass.

World production 1984 194 000 tonnes

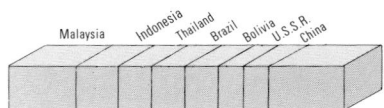

Zinc — hard metal, low corrosion factor. Uses: brass making, galvanizing, die-casting; in medicines, paints, and dyes.

World production 1984 6.8 million tonnes

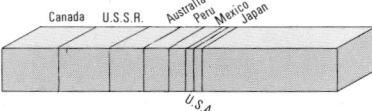

Aluminum — lightweight, resistant to corrosion, good conductor. Uses: aircraft, road and rail vehicles, utensils, cables, light and strong alloys.

World production 1984 91 million tonnes (of Bauxite)

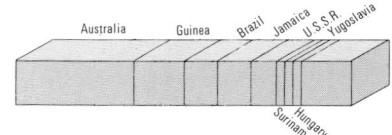

Diamonds — very hard and resistant to chemical attack; high luster; very rare. Uses: jewelry; cutting and abrading.

World production 1984 63 million carats

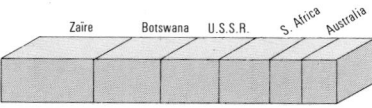

Gold — untarnishable and resistant to corrosion, highly ductile and malleable, good conductor. So soft it must be alloyed to harden it. Uses: bullion, coins, jewelry.

World production 1984 1 400 tonnes

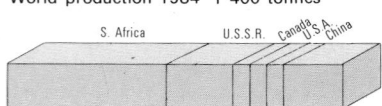

Silver — ductile and malleable; soft (must be alloyed in coins). Uses: coins, jewelry, photography, electronics, medicines.

World production 1984 12 779 tonnes

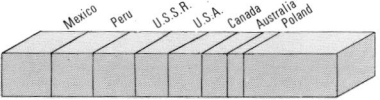

World consumption of non-ferrous metals

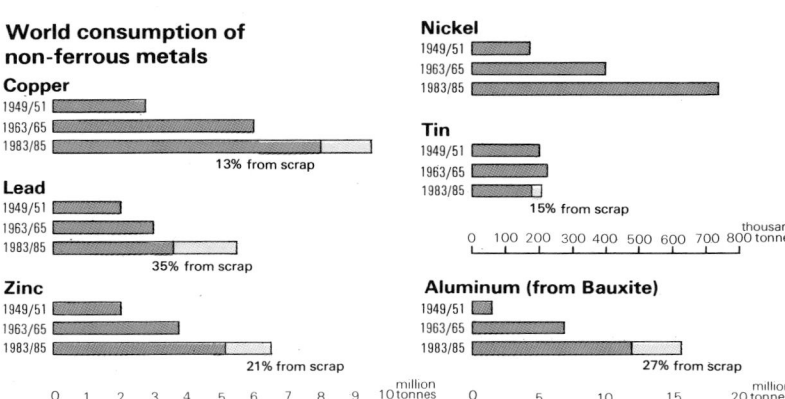

Copper
1949/51
1963/65
1983/85 13% from scrap

Lead
1949/51
1963/65
1983/85 35% from scrap

Zinc
1949/51
1963/65
1983/85 21% from scrap

0 1 2 3 4 5 6 7 8 9 10 million tonnes

Nickel
1949/51
1963/65
1983/85

Tin
1949/51
1963/65
1983/85 15% from scrap

0 100 200 300 400 500 600 700 800 thousand tonnes

Aluminum (from Bauxite)
1949/51
1963/65
1983/85 27% from scrap

0 5 10 15 20 million tonnes

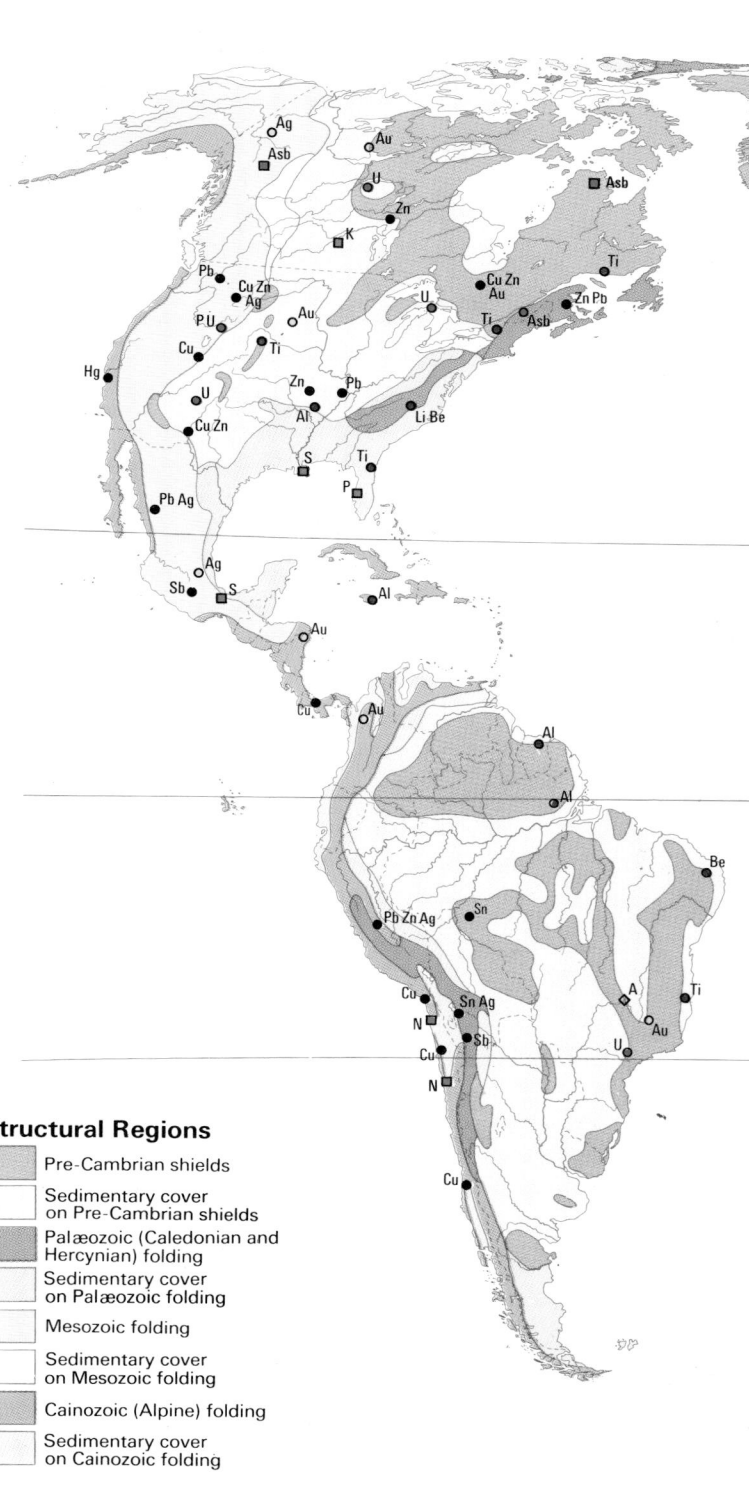

Structural Regions

- Pre-Cambrian shields
- Sedimentary cover on Pre-Cambrian shields
- Palæozoic (Caledonian and Hercynian) folding
- Sedimentary cover on Palæozoic folding
- Mesozoic folding
- Sedimentary cover on Mesozoic folding
- Cainozoic (Alpine) folding
- Sedimentary cover on Cainozoic folding

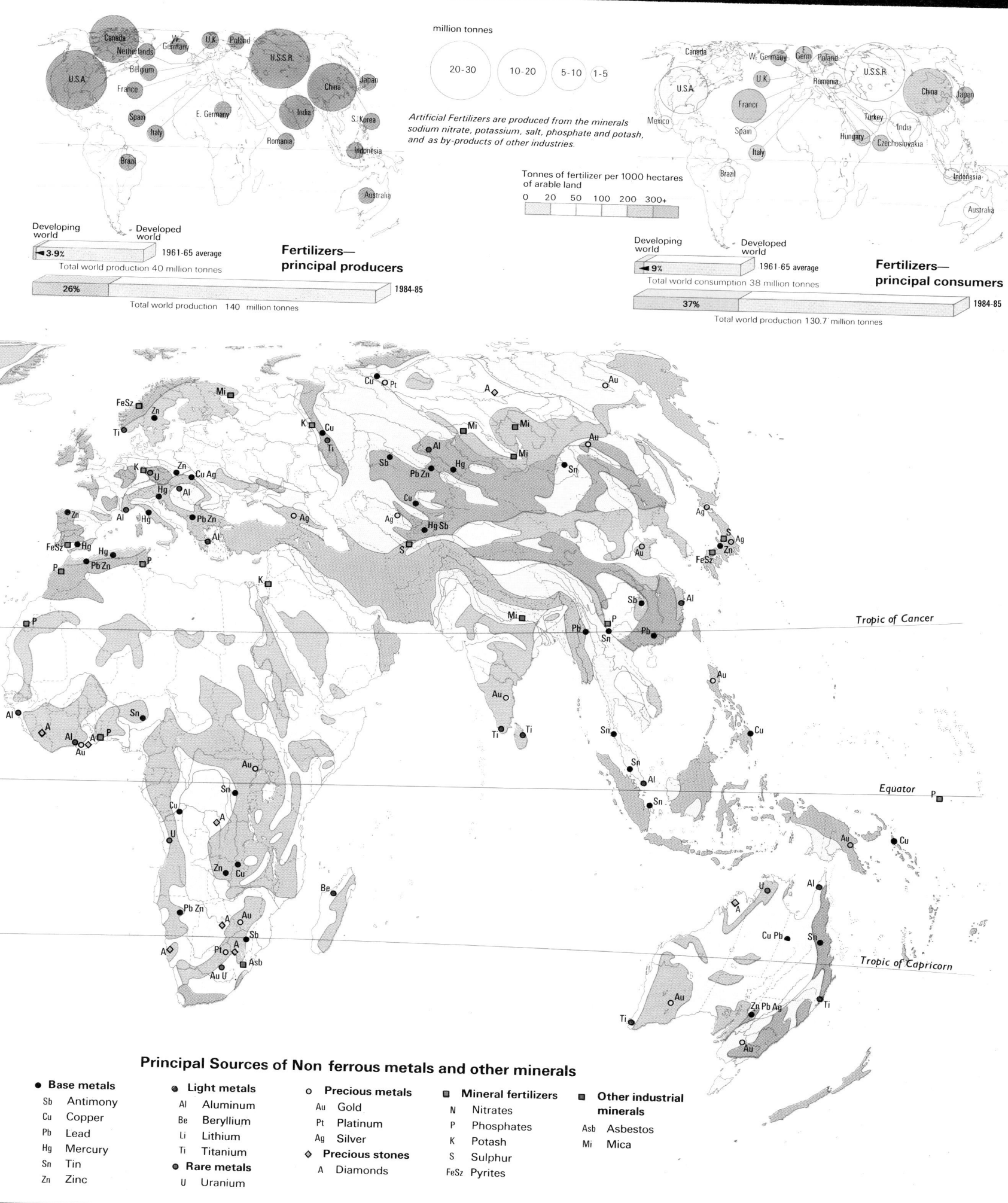

million tonnes

20-30　　10-20　　5-10　　1-5

Artificial Fertilizers are produced from the minerals
sodium nitrate, potassium, salt, phosphate and potash,
and as by-products of other industries.

Tonnes of fertilizer per 1000 hectares
of arable land

0　　20　　50　　100　　200　　300+

**Fertilizers—
principal producers**

Developing
world　　　　Developed
　　　　　　world

◄ 3·9%　　　　　　　　1961-65 average

Total world production 40 million tonnes

26%　　　　　　　　　　　　　　1984-85

Total world production　140　million tonnes

**Fertilizers—
principal consumers**

Developing
world　　　　Developed
　　　　　　world

◄ 9%　　　　　　　　1961-65 average

Total world consumption 38 million tonnes

37%　　　　　　　　　　　　1984-85

Total world production 130.7 million tonnes

Principal Sources of Non-ferrous metals and other minerals

● Base metals		● Light metals		○ Precious metals		▣ Mineral fertilizers		▣ Other industrial minerals	
Sb	Antimony	Al	Aluminum	Au	Gold	N	Nitrates	Asb	Asbestos
Cu	Copper	Be	Beryllium	Pt	Platinum	P	Phosphates	Mi	Mica
Pb	Lead	Li	Lithium	Ag	Silver	K	Potash		
Hg	Mercury	Ti	Titanium	◇ Precious stones		S	Sulphur		
Sn	Tin			A	Diamonds	FeSz	Pyrites		
Zn	Zinc	● Rare metals							
		U	Uranium						

Tropic of Cancer

Equator

Tropic of Capricorn

FUEL AND ENERGY

Coal is the result of the accumulation of vegetation over millions of years. Under pressure from overlying sediments, it hardened through four stages: peat, lignite, bituminous coal, and finally anthracite. The map at the top lists the major coal producers and shows world distribution of coal production. The photograph at the far right, a coal mine. Coal is important in the production of electricity, plastics, and many chemicals. **Oil**, which is derived from the remains of marine animals and plants, has replaced coal as an energy source in many areas. Oil is a complex mixture of hydrocarbons, which are refined to extract various constituents such as gasoline, kerosene, and heavy fuel oils. Photograph at the far right, an oil derrick.

Natural gas, or methane, has become one of the largest sources of energy. By liquefaction, its volume can be reduced to 1/600 of that of gas and hence be easily transported. At the far right, a North Sea gas rig. **Hydro-electric power** stations use moving water to drive turbines that generate electricity. The ideal site for such a station is one in which a consistently large volume of water falls a considerable height, as in mountainous areas. At the far

right, a hydro-electric power station. Potential sources of hydro-electricity using ocean waves or tides are yet to be exploited widely.

The map at the bottom of the page shows world production of **nuclear energy**. A nuclear power station is shown in the photograph to the right of the map. Here energy is obtained from heat generated by splitting atoms of certain elements, of which uranium and plutonium are the most important. Although the installation costs are high, actual running costs are low because of the slow consumption of fuel.

Tidal Power

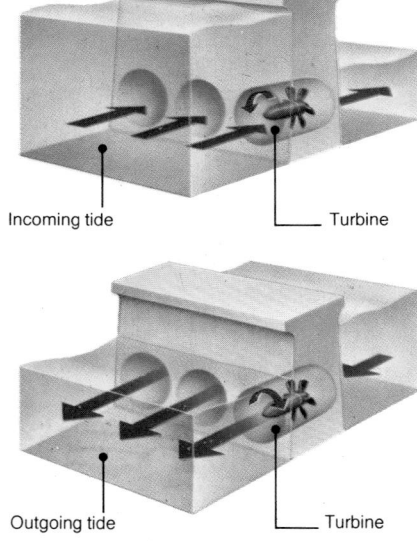

Incoming tide — Turbine

Outgoing tide — Turbine

A basin reservoir is created by constructing a barrage across a tidal estuary. Seawater enters and leaves the basin through ducts containing turbines that power generators. Such schemes are restricted to estuaries whose tidal range between high and low water is extremely large, such as the Rance estuary in northwestern France. The Severn estuary in England is a possible site for the future development of tidal power.

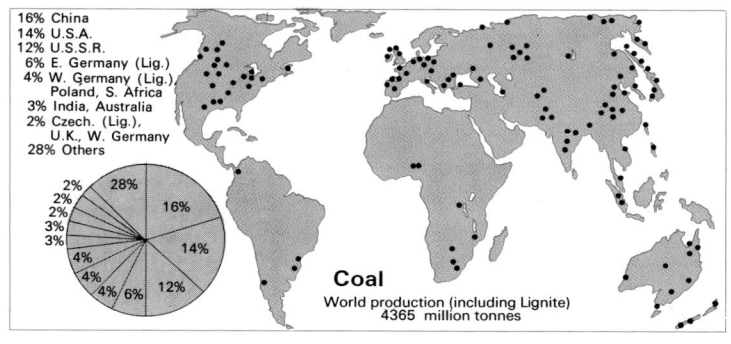

16% China
14% U.S.A.
12% U.S.S.R.
6% E. Germany (Lig.)
4% W. Germany (Lig.)
Poland, S. Africa
3% India, Australia
2% Czech. (Lig.)
U.K., W. Germany
28% Others

Coal
World production (including Lignite)
4365 million tonnes

Coal mine

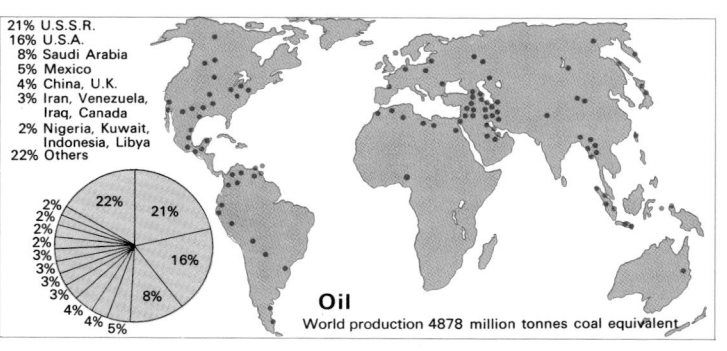

21% U.S.S.R.
16% U.S.A.
8% Saudi Arabia
5% Mexico
4% China, U.K.
3% Iran, Venezuela,
Iraq, Canada
2% Nigeria, Kuwait,
Indonesia, Libya
22% Others

Oil
World production 4878 million tonnes coal equivalent

Oil derrick

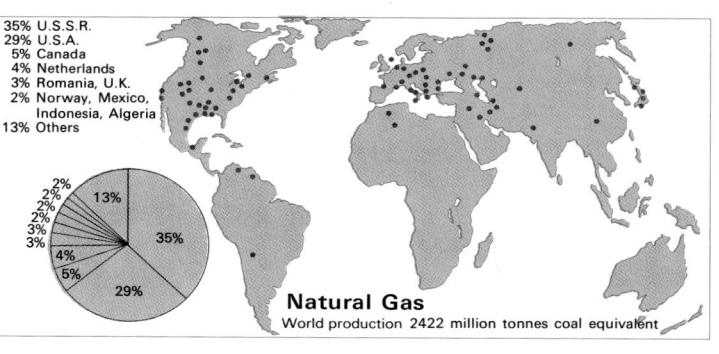

35% U.S.S.R.
29% U.S.A.
5% Canada
4% Netherlands
3% Romania, U.K.
2% Norway, Mexico,
Indonesia, Algeria
13% Others

Natural Gas
World production 2422 million tonnes coal equivalent

North sea gas rig

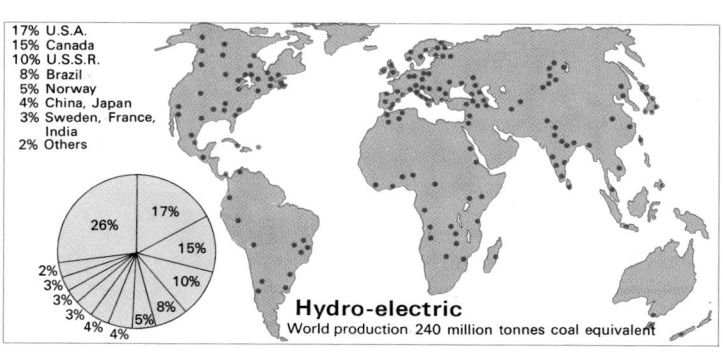

17% U.S.A.
15% Canada
10% U.S.S.R.
8% Brazil
5% Norway
4% China, Japan
3% Sweden, France,
India
2% Others

Hydro-electric
World production 240 million tonnes coal equivalent

Water power

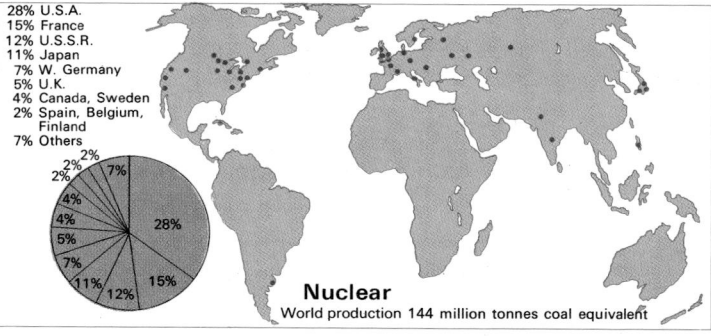

28% U.S.A.
15% France
12% U.S.S.R.
11% Japan
7% W. Germany
5% U.K.
4% Canada, Sweden
2% Spain, Belgium,
Finland
7% Others

Nuclear
World production 144 million tonnes coal equivalent

Nuclear power station

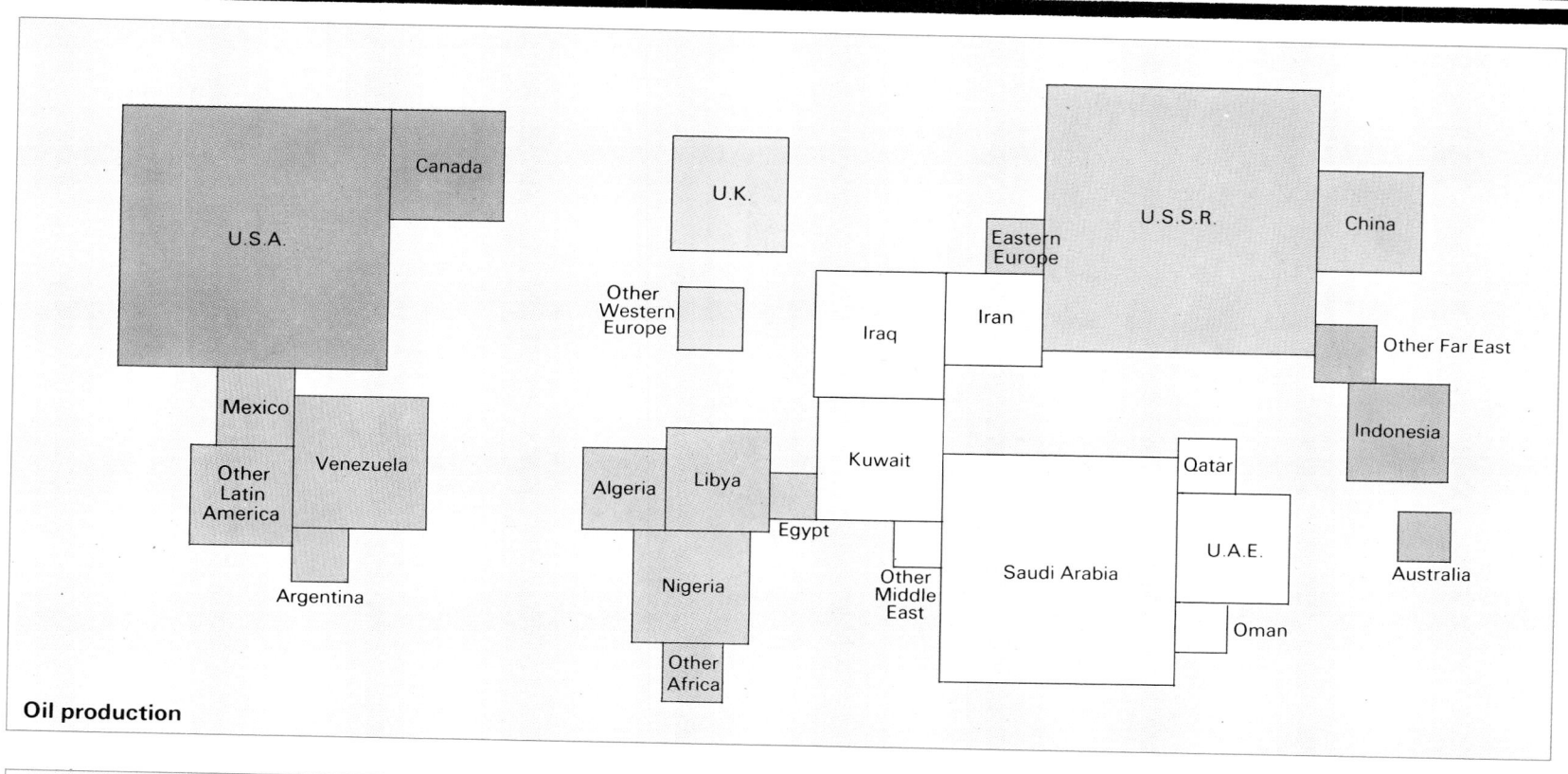

Oil production

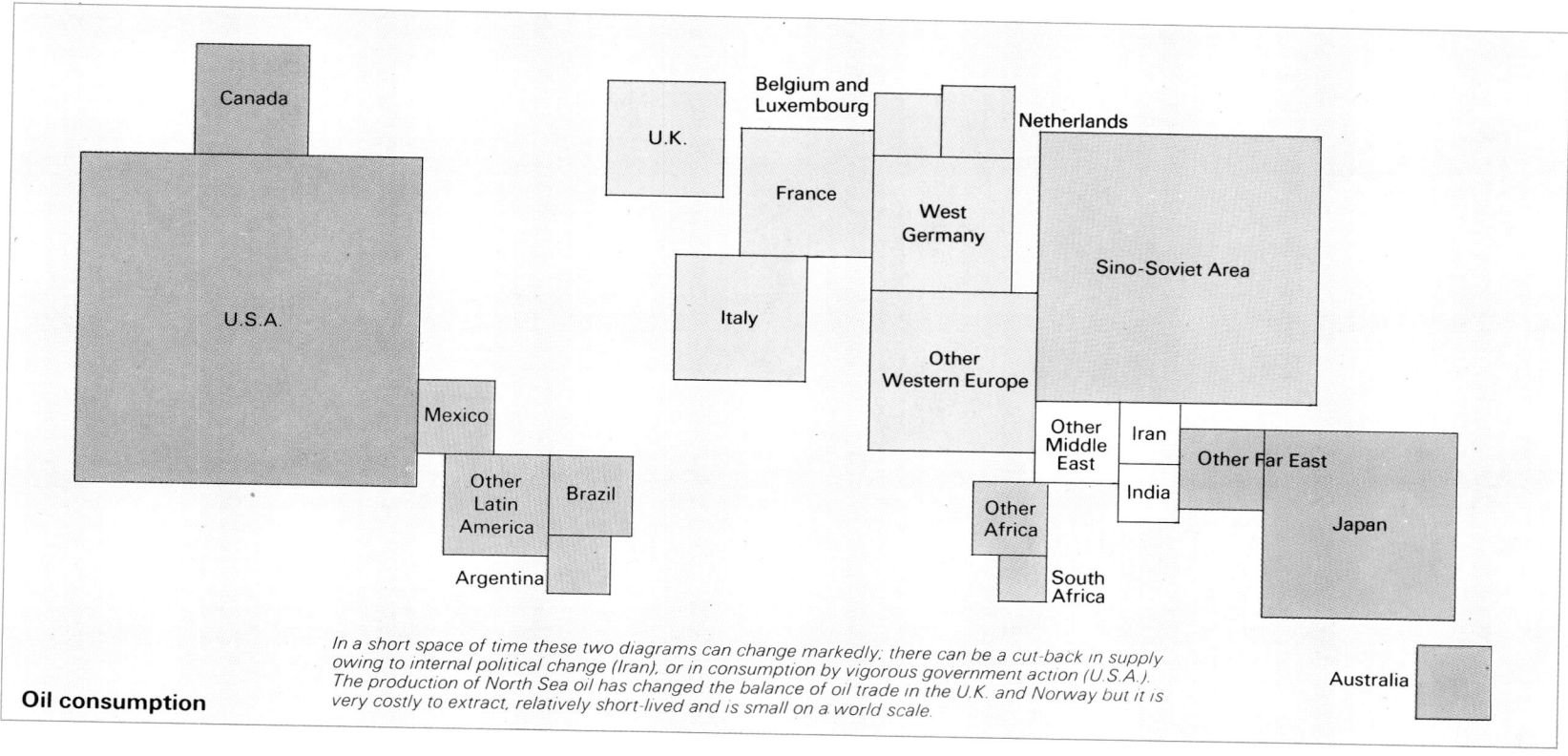

In a short space of time these two diagrams can change markedly; there can be a cut-back in supply owing to internal political change (Iran), or in consumption by vigorous government action (U.S.A.). The production of North Sea oil has changed the balance of oil trade in the U.K. and Norway but it is very costly to extract, relatively short-lived and is small on a world scale.

Oil consumption

Oil's new super-powers *above*
When countries are scaled according to their production and consumption of oil they take on new dimensions. At present, large supplies of oil are concentrated in a few countries of the Caribbean, the Middle East and North Africa, except for the vast indigenous supplies of the U.S.A. and U.S.S.R. The Middle East, with 58% of the world's reserves, produces 19% of the world's supply and yet consumes only 3%. The U.S.A. despite its great production, has a deficiency of nearly 155 million tons a year, consuming 25% of the world's total. The U.S.S.R. with 9% of world reserves, produces 23% of world output and consumes 15%. Soviet production continues to grow annually although at a decreased rate since the mid-1970's. Japan is the world's third largest oil consumer but 98% of this has to be imported, making it the worlds largest importer.

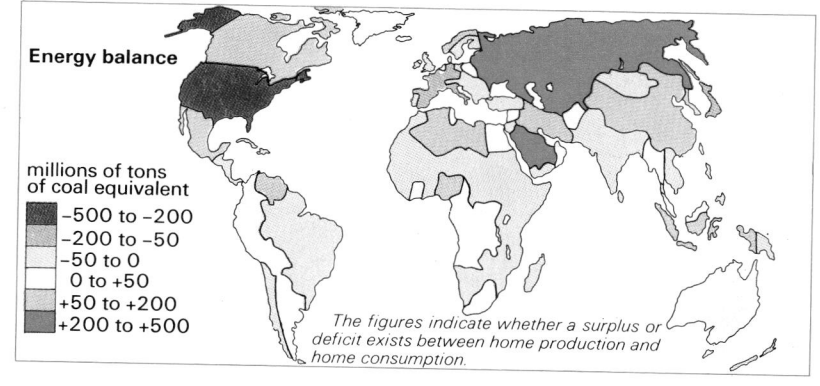

Energy balance

millions of tons of coal equivalent

- −500 to −200
- −200 to −50
- −50 to 0
- 0 to +50
- +50 to +200
- +200 to +500

The figures indicate whether a surplus or deficit exists between home production and home consumption.

OCCUPATIONS

Part of the assembly line in a cigarette factory

Manufacturing Employment

The number of people employed in each manufacturing sector is given as a percentage of total manufacturing employment within each country.

Manufacturing Sector	India	Mexico	Japan
Food & tobacco	14.6%	24.1%	10.8%
Precision instruments	0.4%	—	2.3%
Transport equipment	7.0%	9.8%	8.5%
Electrical machinery	5.9%	6.8%	12.8%
General machinery	6.7%	1.1%	11.1%
Non-ferrous metals	0.7%	2.9%	1.4%
Iron & steel	7.0%	11.0%	4.2%
Ceramics & glass	1.3%	4.2%	1.4%
Oil refining & its products	0.5%	0.8%	0.4%
Chemicals & rubber	9.4%	14.1%	5.3%
Paper & paper products	2.0%	5.2%	2.7%
Wood products	0.8%	1.0%	4.1%
Leather goods	0.4%		0.4%
Textiles	30.4%	10.0%	7.4%
Others	12.9%	9.0%	27.2%

The table is comparing the manufacturing industries of a low income economy (India), an upper middle income economy (Mexico), and an industrial market economy (Japan)

Percentage of Economically Active Population Engaged in Agriculture, 1965 and 1985

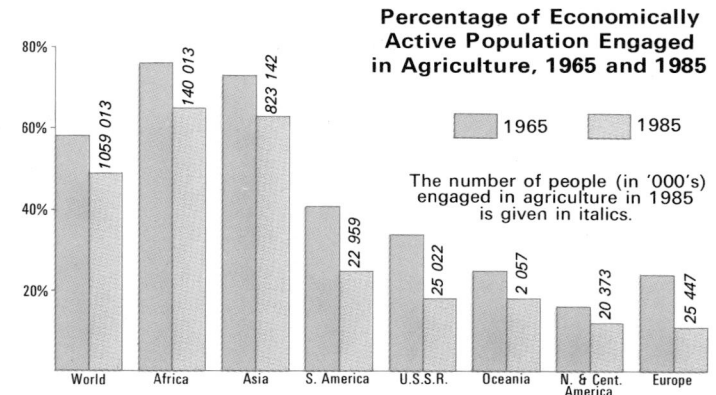

■ 1965   ■ 1985

The number of people (in '000's) engaged in agriculture in 1985 is given in italics.

EMPLOYMENT

Employment by Sector in 1980
Key to Map Colours

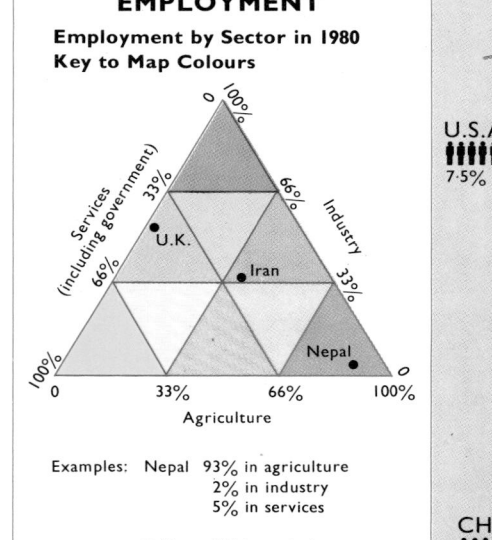

Examples:

Nepal   93% in agriculture
         2% in industry
         5% in services

U.K.   2% in agriculture
       42% in industry
       56% in services

Iran   38% in agriculture
       33% in industry
       29% in services

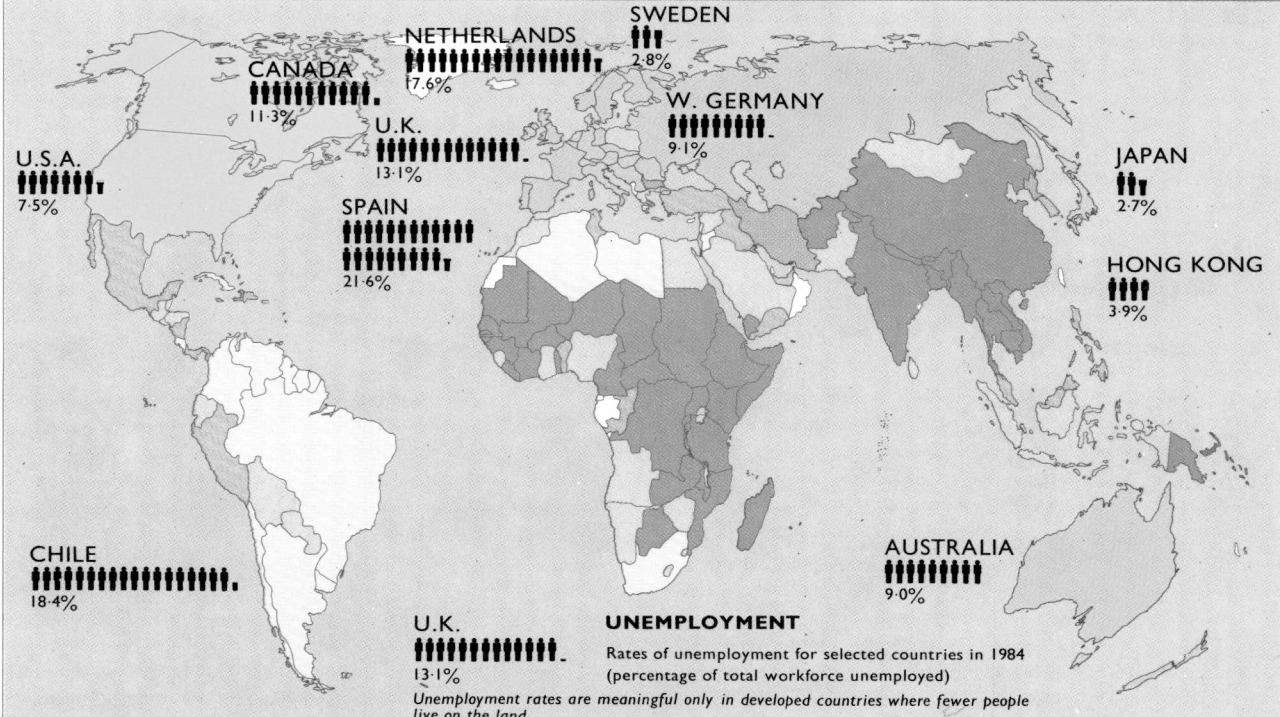

CANADA 11.3%
U.S.A. 7.5%
NETHERLANDS 7.6%
SWEDEN 2.8%
U.K. 13.1%
W. GERMANY 9.1%
SPAIN 21.6%
JAPAN 2.7%
HONG KONG 3.9%
CHILE 18.4%
AUSTRALIA 9.0%
U.K. 13.1%

UNEMPLOYMENT

Rates of unemployment for selected countries in 1984 (percentage of total workforce unemployed)

Unemployment rates are meaningful only in developed countries where fewer people live on the land.

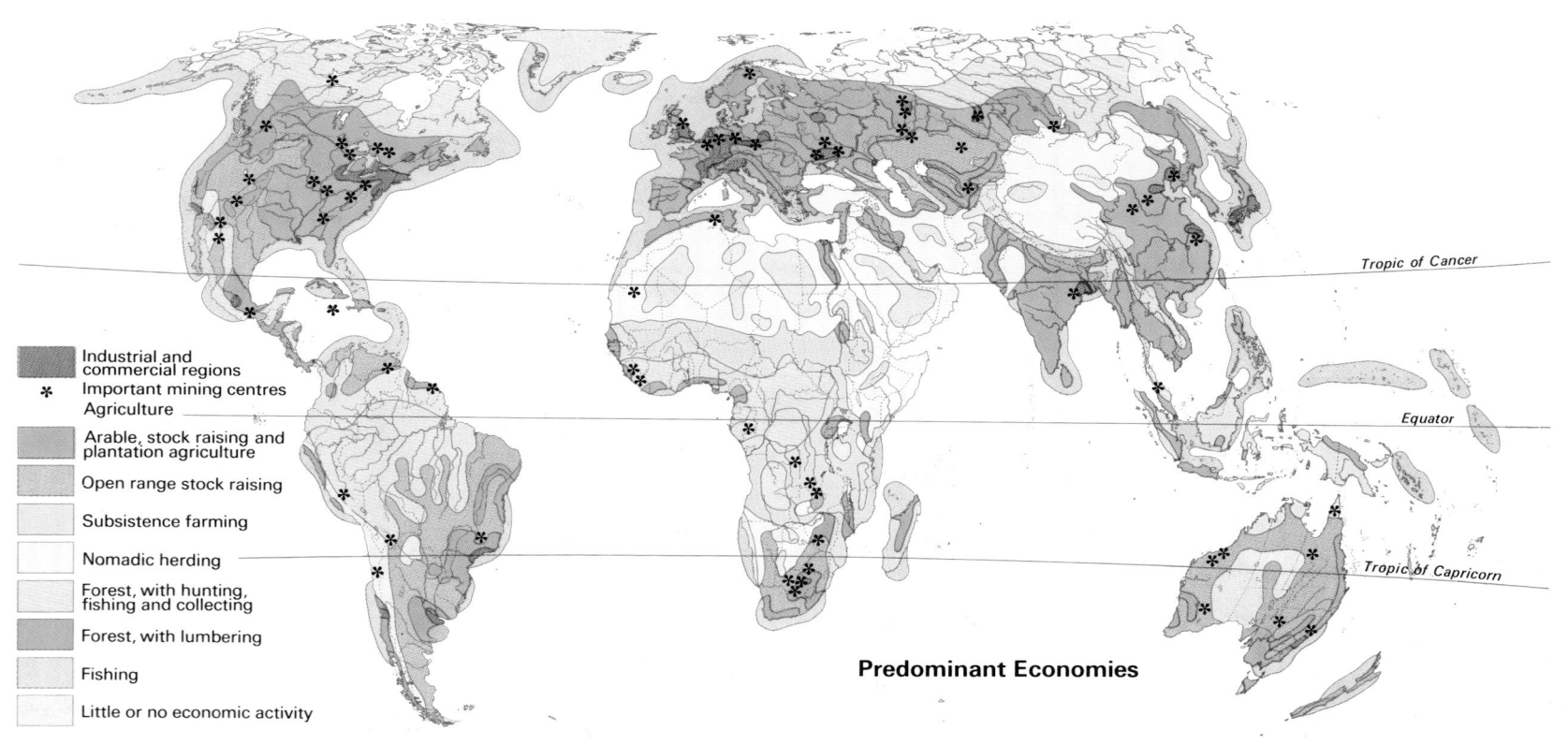

- Industrial and commercial regions
- ✳ Important mining centres
- Agriculture
- Arable, stock raising and plantation agriculture
- Open range stock raising
- Subsistence farming
- Nomadic herding
- Forest, with hunting, fishing and collecting
- Forest, with lumbering
- Fishing
- Little or no economic activity

Tropic of Cancer
Equator
Tropic of Capricorn

Predominant Economies

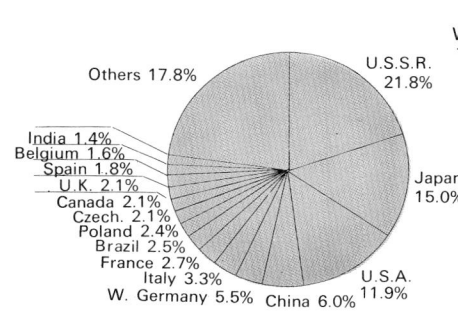

Casting steel ingots

World Steel production

Others 17.8%
India 1.4%
Belgium 1.6%
Spain 1.8%
U.K. 2.1%
Canada 2.1%
Czech. 2.1%
Poland 2.4%
Brazil 2.5%
France 2.7%
Italy 3.3%
W. Germany 5.5%
China 6.0%
U.S.A. 11.9%
Japan 15.0%
U.S.S.R. 21.8%

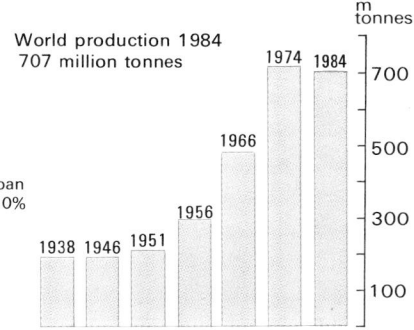

Growth of World Steel production

World production 1984
707 million tonnes

m tonnes

1938 1946 1951 1956 1966 1974 1984

World Steel production per capita

tonnes/capita
Belgium 1.10
Japan 0.90
W. Germany 0.64
Canada 0.58
U.S.S.R. 0.56
Poland 0.45
Australia 0.37
France 0.35
U.K. 0.27
China 0·04

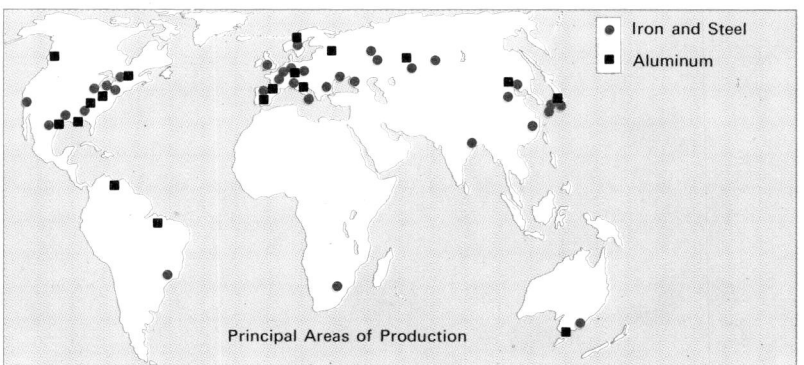

- ● Iron and Steel
- ■ Aluminum

Principal Areas of Production

Aluminum

World production 1984 15.9 million tonnes

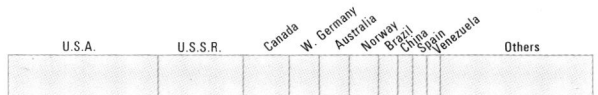

U.S.A.   U.S.S.R.   Canada   W. Germany   Australia   Norway   Brazil   China   Spain   Venezuela   Others

When compared with bauxite production on p. 38 it is evident that those countries mining bauxite do not necessarily produce proportional quantities of aluminum. For example the U.S.A. mines only 1% of the world's bauxite but is the greatest producer of aluminum. The refining is done where there are abundant sources of cheap electricity, hydro-electricity for example. It takes 15 000 kWh to convert 2 tonnes of alumina to 1 tonne of aluminum.

- ○ Chemicals
- ■ Cement

Principal Areas of Production

Chemicals

Synthetic Rubber

World production 1983
8257.6 thousand tonnes

U.S.A.	1 985
U.S.S.R.	1 970
Japan	1 003
France	514
W. Germany	432
U.K.	253

Caustic Soda

World production 1983
30.4 million tonnes

U.S.A.	9.3
W. Germany	3.4
U.S.S.R.	2.9
Japan	2.8
China	2.1
Canada	1.5
France	1.4

Cement

World production 1984
890 million tonnes

U.S.S.R.	130.1	Spain	25.5
China	121.1	France	22.7
Japan	78.9	S. Korea	20.4
U.S.A.	70.5	Brazil	19.5
Italy	38.3	Mexico	18.4
India	29.0	Poland	16.6
W. Germany	28.7	U.K.	15.7

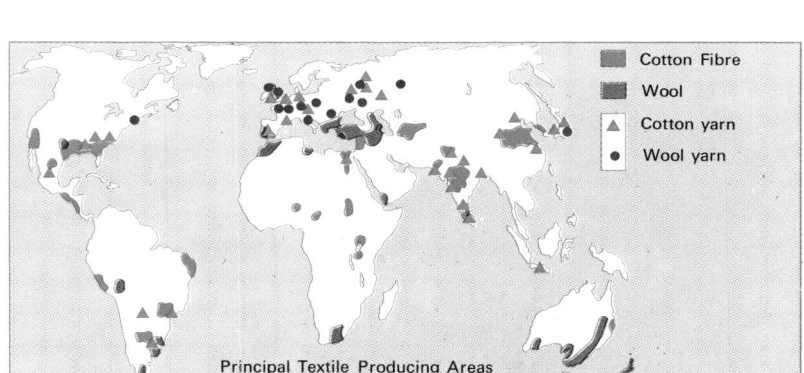

- ▨ Cotton Fibre
- ▧ Wool
- ▲ Cotton yarn
- ● Wool yarn

Principal Textile Producing Areas

Textiles

Cotton Yarn		Cotton Lint		Wool-greasy		Woollen Yarn	
World production 1983 11 623.8 thousand tonnes		World production 1984 17 794 thousand tonnes		World production 1984 2 888 thousand tonnes		No world total available Thousand tonnes 1983	
China	3 270	China	6 077	Australia	729	U.S.S.R.	447.0
U.S.S.R.	1 659	U.S.A.	2 894	U.S.S.R.	463	Italy	290.8
India	1 180	U.S.S.R.	2 400	New Zealand	363	U.K.	121.2
U.S.A.	1 064	India	1 250	China	187	Japan	110.0
S. Korea	477	Pakistan	990	Argentine	155	France	107.9
Pakistan	448	Brazil	618	S. Africa	109	China	101.0
Japan	438	Turkey	586	Uruguay	91	Belgium	86.7
Egypt	229	Egypt	390	Turkey	63	Poland	81.3
Italy	217	Mexico	257	U.K.	51	Romania	78.8
Poland	177	Sudan	219	U.S.A.	46	W. Germany	76.4

Timber and Paper

Roundwood-coniferous		Roundwood-non-coniferous		Wood Pulp		Paper and Paper Board	
World production 1983 1 187 million m³		World production 1983 1 741 million m³		World production 1983 128 million tonnes		World production 1983 175 million tonnes	
U.S.S.R.	296	India	214	U.S.A.	47.7	U.S.A.	58.8
U.S.A.	277	U.S.A.	158	Canada	19.2	Japan	18.4
Canada	129	Brazil	153	U.S.S.R.	9.2	Canada	13.4
China	111	China	121	Japan	8.8	U.S.S.R.	8.9
Sweden	45	Indonesia	121	Sweden	8.6	W. Germany	8.3
Brazil	37	Nigeria	79	Finland	7.2	Finland	6.4
Finland	31	U.S.S.R.	60	Brazil	3.4	Sweden	6.3
Poland	21	Malaysia	40	W. Germany	2.1	France	5.3
W. Germany	21	Tanzania	39	France	1.9	Italy	4.3
Japan	21	Thailand	37	Norway	1.6	Brazil	3.4

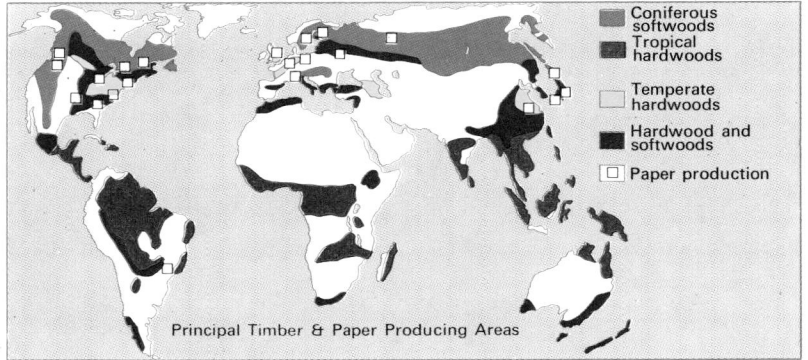

- ▨ Coniferous softwoods
- ▨ Tropical hardwoods
- ☐ Temperate hardwoods
- ■ Hardwood and softwoods
- ☐ Paper production

Principal Timber & Paper Producing Areas

TRANSPORT

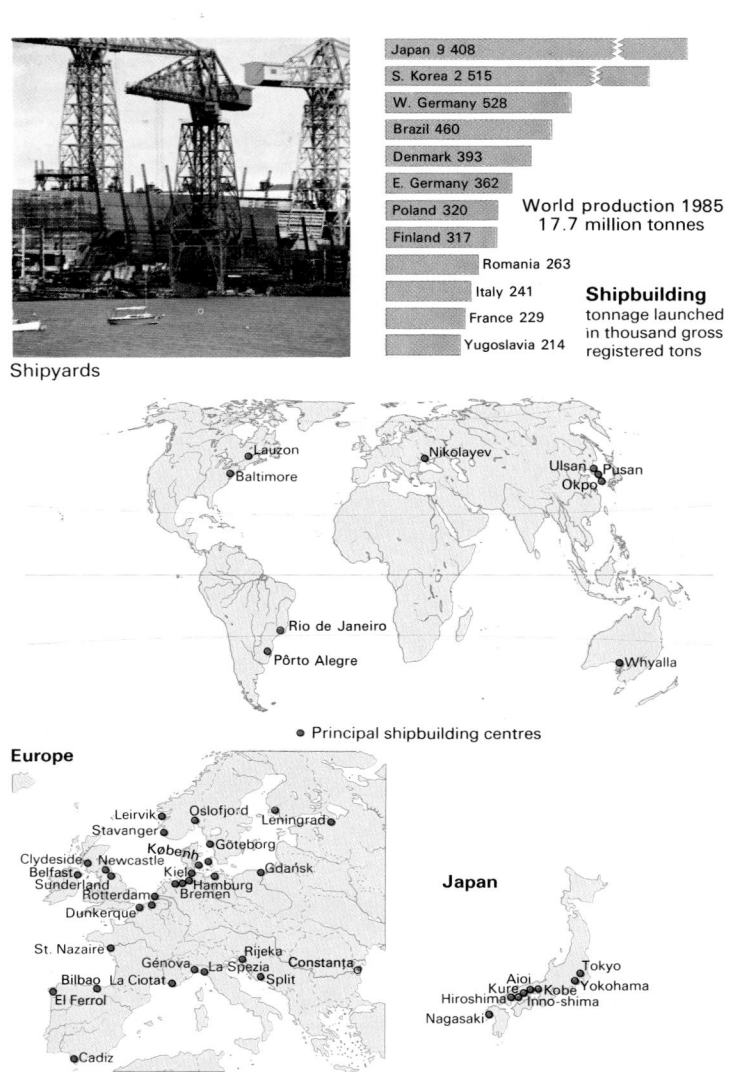

Shipyards

Japan 9 408
S. Korea 2 515
W. Germany 528
Brazil 460
Denmark 393
E. Germany 362
Poland 320
Finland 317
Romania 263
Italy 241
France 229
Yugoslavia 214

World production 1985
17.7 million tonnes

Shipbuilding
tonnage launched
in thousand gross
registered tons

- Principal shipbuilding centres

Europe

Japan

Concorde and Boeing 747

Aircraft Industry

In 1985 there were approximately
9 400 civil passenger airliners in
service. This diagram shows where the
were built.

U.S.A. 53%	U.S.S.R. 33%	U.K. 6% Netherlands 3% France 2%

Trade in Aircraft

	Exports *million U.S. $*		Imports
U.S.A.	11076	W. Germany	3670
W. Germany	3817	U.S.A.	3042
U.K.	2853	U.K.	1699
France	2801	Canada	1192
Italy	1072	Japan	939
Canada	1004	S. Arabia	921
Netherlands	533	Italy	885

- Principal aircraft manufacturing centres

Locomotive works

Railway vehicles

Exports *million U.S. $*		Imports *million U.S. $*	
U.S.A.	587.3	U.S.A.	365.7
W. Germany	549.4	Iraq	174.4
Japan	517.4	Indonesia	146.9
France	321.5	Canada	146.9
Canada	173.3	Iran	141.1
U.K.	168.9	Netherlands	94.2
Italy	127.0	Brazil	77.8
Belg.-Lux.	60.0	Egypt	74.1
Switzerland	45.3	W. Germany	70.6
S. Korea	33.8	Yugoslavia	68.8
Sweden	28.9	Tunisia	55.6
Spain	16.2	S. Africa	49.2
Portugal	13.9	Mexico	47.3

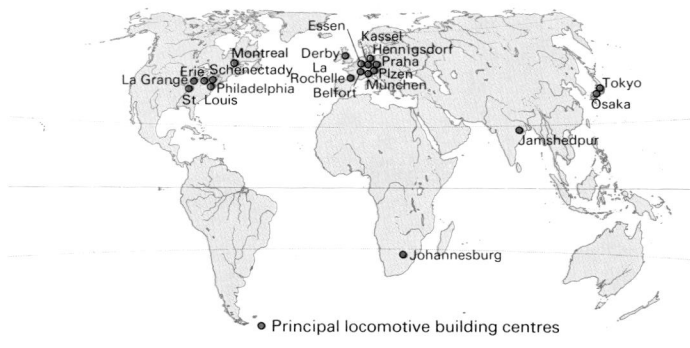

- Principal locomotive building centres

Motor vehicles World production 1985 43 660 614 vehicles

Production *thousand units*	Exports *million U.S. $*	Imports *million U.S. $*
Japan 11 465	32 798	619
U.S.A. 10 925	14 621	37 587
W. Germany 4045	26 657	7 601
France 3062	9 626	6 987
U.S.S.R. 1900	2 299	2 682
Canada 1829	16 482	14 129
Italy 1601	4 700	4 328
Spain 1309	2 401	1 013
U.K. 1134	4 666	8 721

Car assembly line

Europe

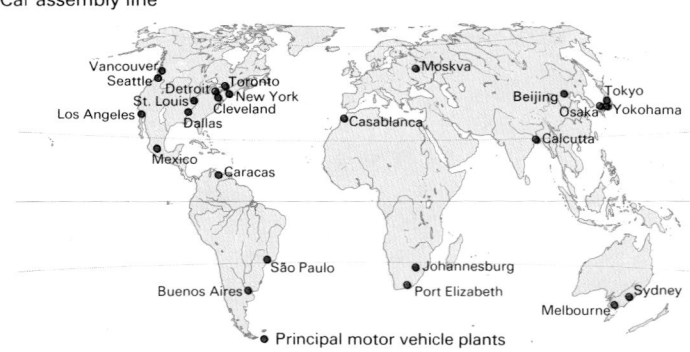

- Principal motor vehicle plants

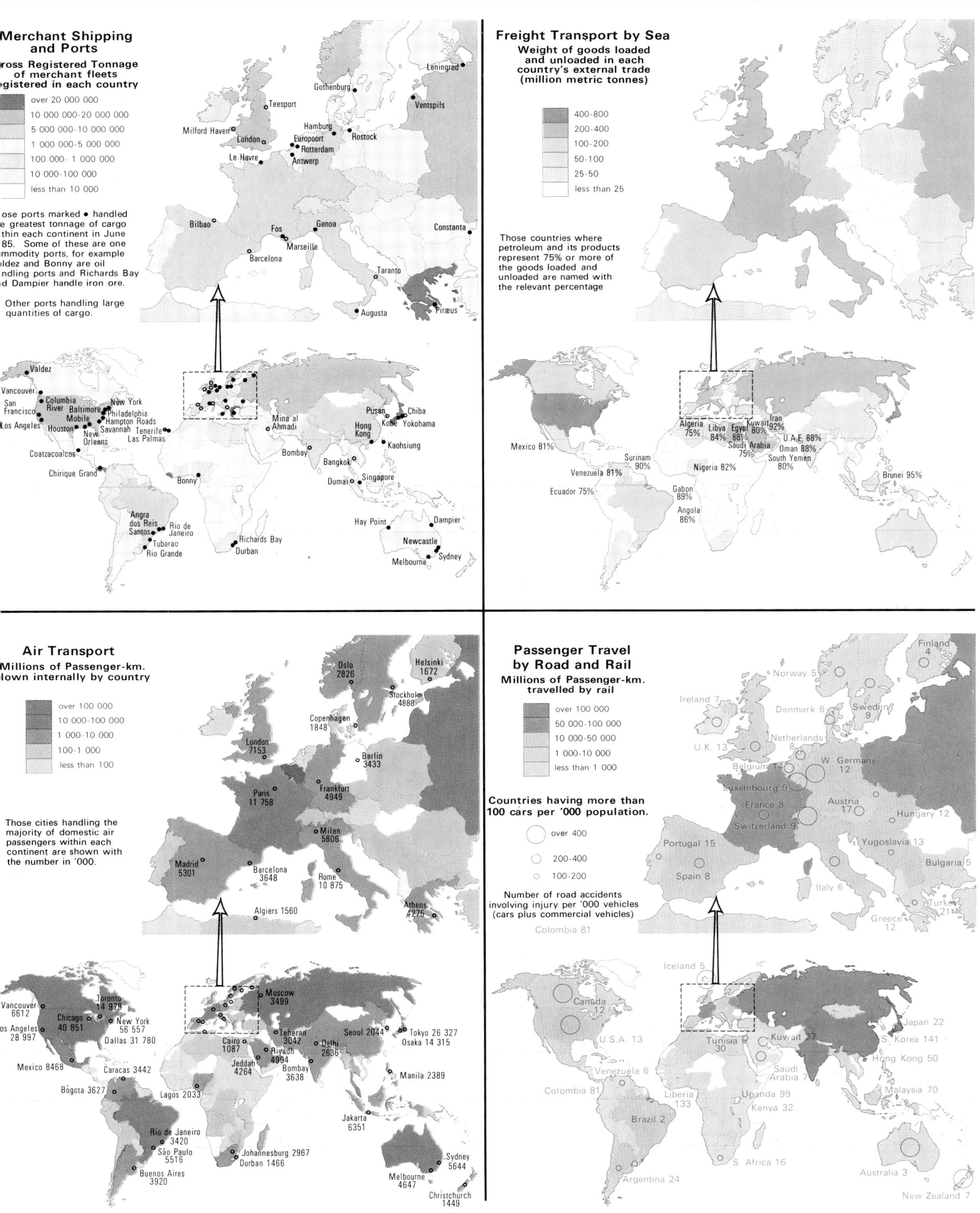

Merchant Shipping and Ports

Gross Registered Tonnage of merchant fleets registered in each country

- over 20 000 000
- 10 000 000–20 000 000
- 5 000 000–10 000 000
- 1 000 000–5 000 000
- 100 000–1 000 000
- 10 000–100 000
- less than 10 000

Those ports marked ● handled the greatest tonnage of cargo within each continent in June 1985. Some of these are one commodity ports, for example Valdez and Bonny are oil handling ports and Richards Bay and Dampier handle iron ore.

○ Other ports handling large quantities of cargo.

Leningrad
Gothenburg
Teesport
Hamburg
Milford Haven
London
Europoort
Rostock
Rotterdam
Le-Havre
Antwerp
Bilbao
Fos
Genoa
Marseille
Constanta
Barcelona
Taranto
Augusta
Piræus

Valdez
Vancouver
Columbia River
New York
San Francisco
Baltimore
Los Angeles
Mobile
Philadelphia
Houston
Hampton Roads
New Orleans
Savannah
Tenerife
Las Palmas
Coatzacoalcos
Chirique Grand
Bonny
Angra dos Reis
Santos
Rio de Janeiro
Tubarao
Rio Grande
Richards Bay
Durban
Mina al Ahmadi
Bombay
Bangkok
Dumai
Singapore
Pusan
Kobe
Chiba
Yokohama
Hong Kong
Kaohsiung
Hay Point
Dampier
Newcastle
Melbourne
Sydney

Freight Transport by Sea

Weight of goods loaded and unloaded in each country's external trade (million metric tonnes)

- 400–800
- 200–400
- 100–200
- 50–100
- 25–50
- less than 25

Those countries where petroleum and its products represent 75% or more of the goods loaded and unloaded are named with the relevant percentage

Mexico 81%
Surinam 90%
Venezuela 81%
Ecuador 75%
Gabon 89%
Angola 86%
Algeria 75%
Libya 84%
Egypt 88%
Kuwait 92%
Iran 92%
Saudi Arabia 75%
U.A.E 88%
Oman 88%
South Yemen 80%
Nigeria 82%
Brunei 95%

Air Transport

Millions of Passenger-km. flown internally by country

- over 100 000
- 10 000–100 000
- 1 000–10 000
- 100–1 000
- less than 100

Those cities handling the majority of domestic air passengers within each continent are shown with the number in '000.

Oslo 2826
Helsinki 1672
Stockholm 4888
Copenhagen 1848
London 7153
Berlin 3433
Paris 11 758
Frankfurt 4949
Milan 5806
Madrid 5301
Barcelona 3648
Rome 10 875
Algiers 1560
Athens 4279

Vancouver 6612
Toronto 14 979
Chicago 40 851
New York 56 557
Los Angeles 28 997
Dallas 31 780
Mexico 8468
Caracas 3442
Bogotá 3627
Lagos 2033
Rio de Janeiro 3420
São Paulo 5516
Buenos Aires 3920
Johannesburg 2967
Durban 1466
Moscow 3499
Teheran 3042
Cairo 1087
Riyadh 4994
Jeddah 4264
Delhi 2636
Bombay 3638
Seoul 2044
Tokyo 26 327
Osaka 14 315
Manila 2389
Jakarta 6351
Sydney 5644
Melbourne 4647
Christchurch 1449

Passenger Travel by Road and Rail

Millions of Passenger-km. travelled by rail

- over 100 000
- 50 000–100 000
- 10 000–50 000
- 1 000–10 000
- less than 1 000

Countries having more than 100 cars per '000 population.

- over 400
- 200–400
- 100–200

Number of road accidents involving injury per '000 vehicles (cars plus commercial vehicles)

Finland 4
Norway 5
Ireland 7
Denmark 6
Sweden 9
U.K 13
Netherlands 8
Belgium 14
W. Germany 12
Luxembourg 9
France 8
Austria 17
Hungary 12
Portugal 15
Switzerland 9
Yugoslavia 13
Bulgaria 5
Spain 8
Italy 6
Turkey 21
Greece 12
Colombia 81
Iceland 5
Canada 12
U.S.A. 13
Tunisia 30
Kuwait 37
Japan 22
Venezuela 6
Saudi Arabia 7
S. Korea 141
Liberia 133
Uganda 99
Kenya 32
Hong Kong 50
Malaysia 70
Brazil 2
S. Africa 16
Argentina 24
Australia 3
New Zealand 7

TRADE

Road container lorry.

Oil tanker.

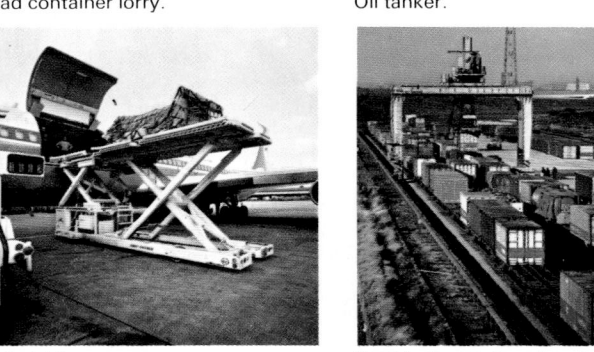

Airfreight.

Road/rail container depot.

The Trade of Europe

The circles on this map are at the same scale as those on the World map below. See the legend to the latter.

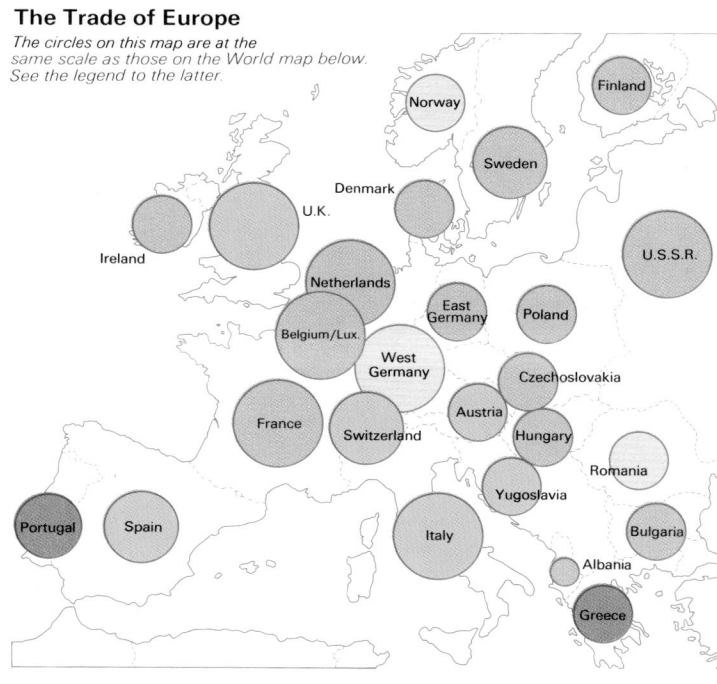

Value of Trade in Goods
(Imports plus exports)

thousand million U.S. $

- Over 100
- 50-100
- 10-50
- 2-10
- 1-2
- Less than 1

Balance of Trade in Goods

Exports exceed imports by :
- more than 50%
- 10-50%
- 10% either side of balance

Imports exceed exports by :
- 10-50%
- more than 50%

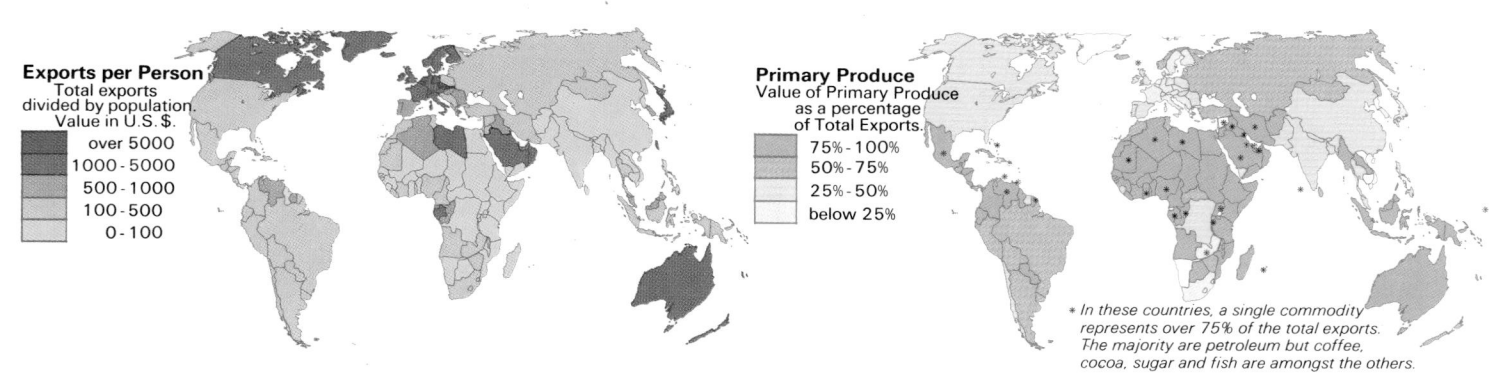

Exports per Person
Total exports divided by population. Value in U.S. $.
- over 5000
- 1000 - 5000
- 500 - 1000
- 100 - 500
- 0 - 100

Primary Produce
Value of Primary Produce as a percentage of Total Exports.
- 75% - 100%
- 50% - 75%
- 25% - 50%
- below 25%

In these countries, a single commodity represents over 75% of the total exports. The majority are petroleum but coffee, cocoa, sugar and fish are amongst the others.

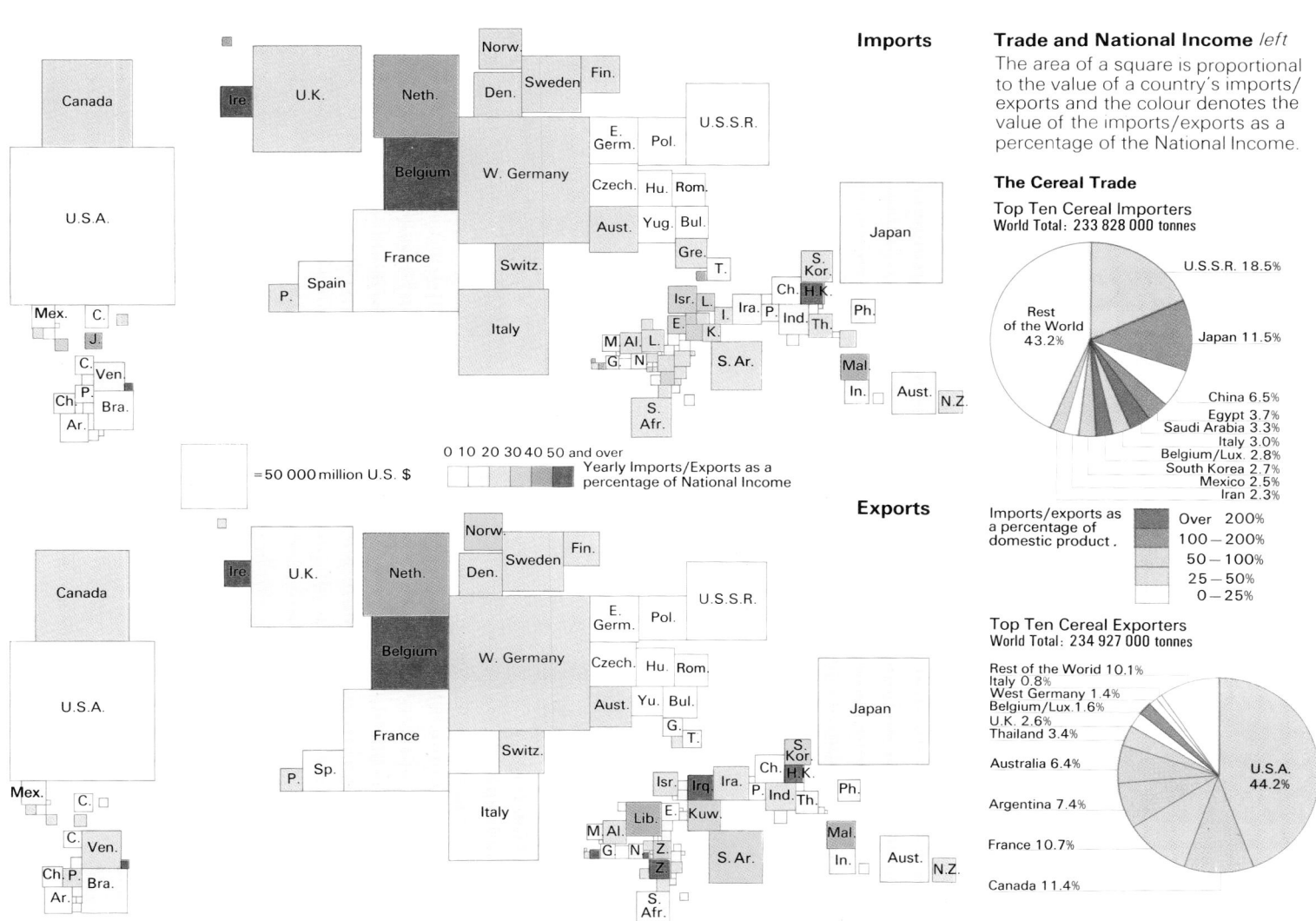

Imports

Trade and National Income *left*
The area of a square is proportional to the value of a country's imports/exports and the colour denotes the value of the imports/exports as a percentage of the National Income.

Canada
U.K. Ire. Norw. Sweden Fin. Neth. Den.
E. Germ. Pol. U.S.S.R.
Belgium W. Germany Czech. Hu. Rom.
U.S.A.
Aust. Yug. Bul.
France Gre.
P. Spain Switz. T.
Isr. L. Ira. P. Ind. Th. S. Kor. Ch. H.K. Ph. Japan
Italy E. K. I.
Mex. C. J. M. Al. L. Mal.
C. Ven. G. N. S. Ar. In. Aust. N.Z.
Ch. P. Bra. S. Afr.
Ar.

The Cereal Trade

Top Ten Cereal Importers
World Total: 233 828 000 tonnes

U.S.S.R. 18.5%
Japan 11.5%
China 6.5%
Egypt 3.7%
Saudi Arabia 3.3%
Italy 3.0%
Belgium/Lux. 2.8%
South Korea 2.7%
Mexico 2.5%
Iran 2.3%
Rest of the World 43.2%

= 50 000 million U.S. $

0 10 20 30 40 50 and over
Yearly Imports/Exports as a percentage of National Income

Exports

Imports/exports as a percentage of domestic product.
Over 200%
100 — 200%
50 — 100%
25 — 50%
0 — 25%

Top Ten Cereal Exporters
World Total: 234 927 000 tonnes

Rest of the World 10.1%
Italy 0.8%
West Germany 1.4%
Belgium/Lux. 1.6%
U.K. 2.6%
Thailand 3.4%
Australia 6.4%
Argentina 7.4%
France 10.7%
Canada 11.4%
U.S.A. 44.2%

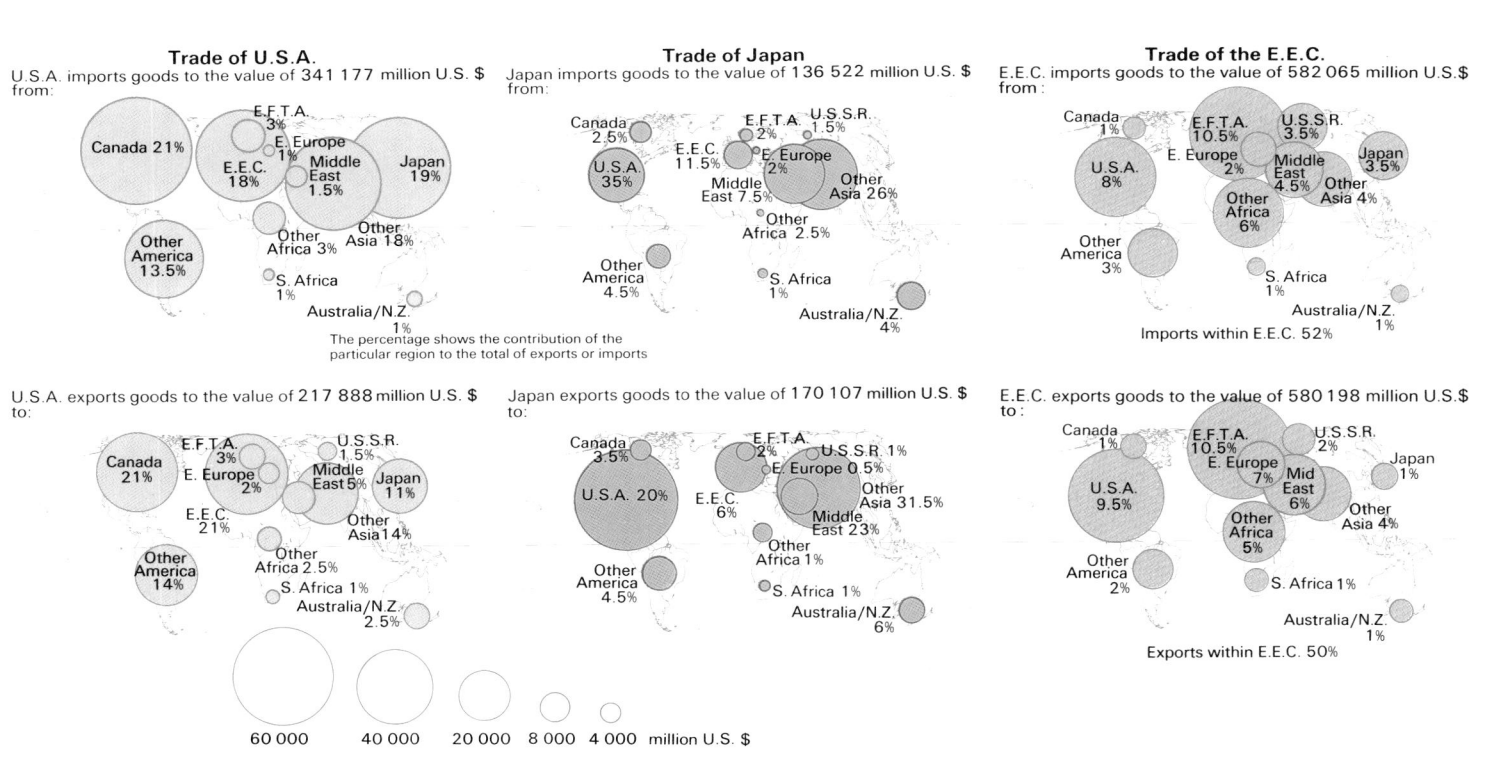

Trade of U.S.A.
U.S.A. imports goods to the value of 341 177 million U.S. $ from:

Canada 21%
E.F.T.A. 3%
E. Europe 1%
E.E.C. 18%
Middle East 1.5%
Japan 19%
Other America 13.5%
Other Africa 3%
Other Asia 18%
S. Africa 1%
Australia/N.Z. 1%

The percentage shows the contribution of the particular region to the total of exports or imports

U.S.A. exports goods to the value of 217 888 million U.S. $ to:

Canada 21%
E.F.T.A. 3%
E. Europe 2%
U.S.S.R. 1.5%
Middle East 5%
Japan 11%
E.E.C. 21%
Other Asia 14%
Other America 14%
Other Africa 2.5%
S. Africa 1%
Australia/N.Z. 2.5%

Trade of Japan
Japan imports goods to the value of 136 522 million U.S. $ from:

Canada 2.5%
E.F.T.A. 2%
U.S.S.R. 1.5%
E.E.C. 11.5%
E. Europe 2%
U.S.A. 35%
Middle East 7.5%
Other Asia 26%
Other Africa 2.5%
Other America 4.5%
S. Africa 1%
Australia/N.Z. 4%

Japan exports goods to the value of 170 107 million U.S. $ to:

Canada 3.5%
E.F.T.A. 2%
U.S.S.R. 1%
E. Europe 0.5%
U.S.A. 20%
E.E.C. 6%
Middle East 23%
Other Asia 31.5%
Other Africa 1%
Other America 4.5%
S. Africa 1%
Australia/N.Z. 6%

Trade of the E.E.C.
E.E.C. imports goods to the value of 582 065 million U.S.$ from:

Canada 1%
E.F.T.A. 10.5%
U.S.S.R. 3.5%
E. Europe 2%
Japan 3.5%
U.S.A. 8%
Middle East 4.5%
Other Africa 6%
Other Asia 4%
Other America 3%
S. Africa 1%
Australia/N.Z. 1%
Imports within E.E.C. 52%

E.E.C. exports goods to the value of 580 198 million U.S.$ to:

Canada 1%
E.F.T.A. 10.5%
U.S.S.R. 2%
E. Europe 7%
Japan 1%
U.S.A. 9.5%
Mid East 6%
Other Africa 5%
Other Asia 4%
Other America 2%
S. Africa 1%
Australia/N.Z. 1%
Exports within E.E.C. 50%

60 000 40 000 20 000 8 000 4 000 million U.S. $

WEALTH

The living standard of a few highly developed, urbanized, industrialized countries is a complete contrast to the conditions of the vast majority of economically undeveloped, agrarian states. It is this contrast which divides humanity into rich and poor, well fed, and hungry. The developing world is still an overwhelmingly agricultural world. Over 70% of all its people live off the land and yet the output from that land remains pitifully low. Many Africans, South Americans, and Asians struggle with the soil but the bad years occur only too frequently and they seldom have anything left over to save. The need for foreign capital then arises.

National Income
The gap between developing and developed worlds is in fact widening eg. in 1938 the incomes for the United States and India were in the proportions of 1:15: now they are 1:53.

Development aid
The provision of foreign aid defined as assistance on concessional terms for promoting development, is today an accepted, though controversial aspect of the economic policies of most advanced countries towards less developed countres. Aid for development is based not merely on economic considerations but also on social, political, and historical factors. The most important international committee

set up after the war was that of the U.N.; practically all aid however has been given bilaterally direct from an industrialized country to an under-developed country. Although aid increased during the 1950's the donated proportion of industrialized countries GNP has diminished from 0·5 to 0·4%. Less developed countries share of world trade also decreased and increased population invalidated any progress made.

Incomes per capita in U.S. dollars

- Africa $722
- Carribean & Latin America $1686
- U.S.S.R. $2588
- Asia $3933
- Oceania $6727
- Europe $8652
- North America $14 335

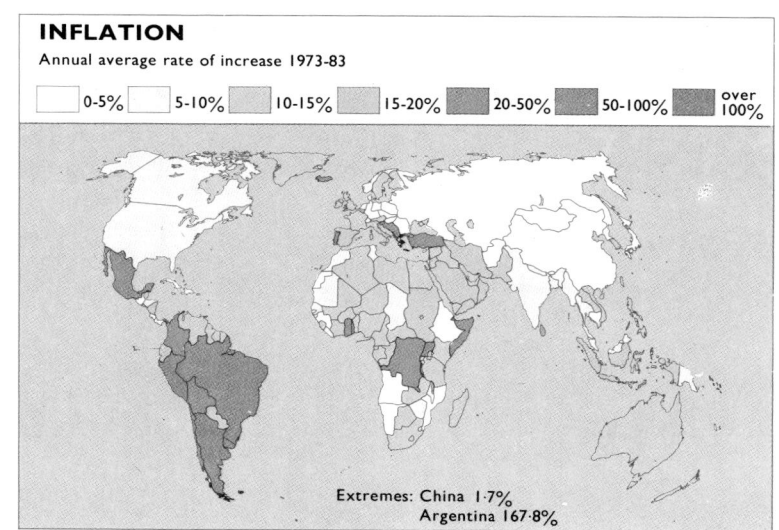

INFLATION
Annual average rate of increase 1973-83

| 0-5% | 5-10% | 10-15% | 15-20% | 20-50% | 50-100% | over 100% |

Extremes: China 1·7%
Argentina 167·8%

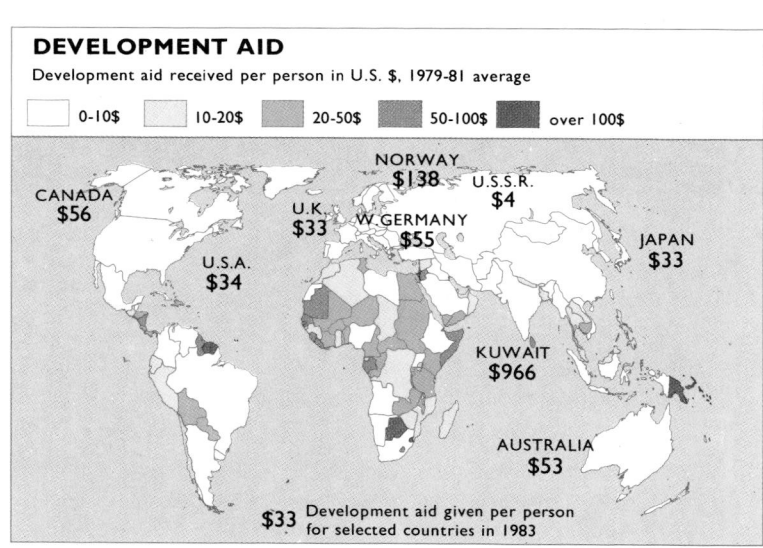

DEVELOPMENT AID
Development aid received per person in U.S. $, 1979-81 average

| 0-10$ | 10-20$ | 20-50$ | 50-100$ | over 100$ |

- CANADA $56
- NORWAY $138
- U.S.S.R. $4
- U.K. $33
- W. GERMANY $55
- JAPAN $33
- U.S.A. $34
- KUWAIT $966
- AUSTRALIA $53

$33 Development aid given per person for selected countries in 1983

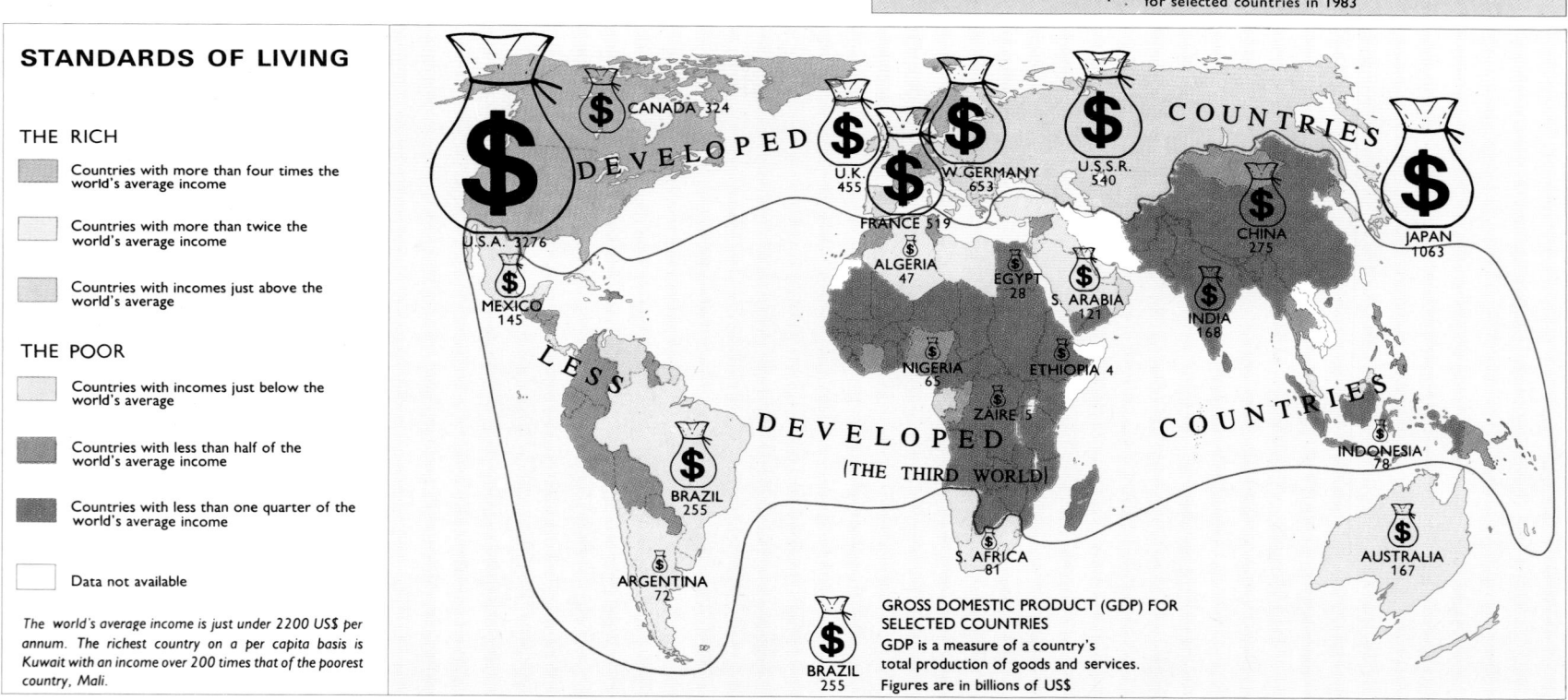

STANDARDS OF LIVING

THE RICH

- Countries with more than four times the world's average income
- Countries with more than twice the world's average income
- Countries with incomes just above the world's average

THE POOR

- Countries with incomes just below the world's average
- Countries with less than half of the world's average income
- Countries with less than one quarter of the world's average income

- Data not available

The world's average income is just under 2200 US$ per annum. The richest country on a per capita basis is Kuwait with an income over 200 times that of the poorest country, Mali.

DEVELOPED COUNTRIES

- CANADA 324
- U.K. 455
- W. GERMANY 653
- U.S.S.R. 540
- FRANCE 519
- U.S.A. 3276
- CHINA 275
- JAPAN 1063
- MEXICO 145
- ALGERIA 47
- EGYPT 28
- S. ARABIA 121
- INDIA 168
- NIGERIA 65
- ETHIOPIA 4
- ZAIRE 5
- LESS DEVELOPED COUNTRIES (THE THIRD WORLD)
- INDONESIA 78
- BRAZIL 255
- S. AFRICA 81
- ARGENTINA 72
- AUSTRALIA 167

BRAZIL 255

GROSS DOMESTIC PRODUCT (GDP) FOR SELECTED COUNTRIES
GDP is a measure of a country's total production of goods and services.
Figures are in billions of US$

SETTLEMENTS

Settlement symbols in order of size

◻ NEW YORK   ▣ Minsk   ◉ Katmandu   ⊚ Prince Rupert   ⊙ Bayt Lahm   ○ Penzance   ○ Monte-Carlo

Settlement symbols and type styles vary according to the scale of each map and indicate the importance of towns on the map rather than specific population figures

∴ Sites of Archæological or Historical importance

BOUNDARIES

————— International Boundaries

— — — International Boundaries (Undemarcated or Undefined)

⋯⋯⋯ Internal Boundaries

International boundaries show the *de facto* situation where there are rival claims to territory

National and Provincial Parks

COMMUNICATIONS

═══ Freeways

◇ Principal Railroads

⋯⋯ Principal Canals

═══ Freeways under construction

◇ Other Railroads

┼─┼ Principal Oil Pipelines

⊸⊶ Trans-Canada Highway

⌇ Railroads under construction

_3386_ Principal Shipping Routes (Distances in Nautical Miles)

——— Principal Roads

╕╌╌╒ Railroad Tunnels

⏑ Passes

◡ Other Roads

╕╌╌╒ Highway Tunnels

✈ + ☼ Airports

⌇ Trails and Seasonal Roads

PHYSICAL FEATURES

◡ Perennial Streams

◠ Seasonal Lakes, Salt Flats

Permanent Ice

⋯ Seasonal Streams

Swamps, Marshes

◡ Wells in Desert

▲ 8848 Spot Height in meters

▼ 8050 Sea Depths in meters

_1134_ Height of Lake Surface Above Sea Level, in meters

Height of Land Above Sea Level, in meters and feet

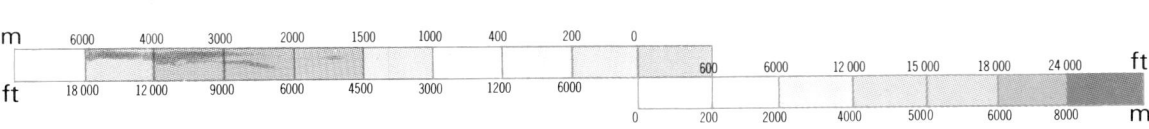

m 6000 4000 3000 2000 1500 1000 400 200 0

ft 18 000 12 000 9000 6000 4500 3000 1200 6000

600 6000 12 000 15 000 18 000 24 000 ft

0 200 2000 4000 5000 6000 8000 m Depth of Sea in meters and feet

Some of the maps have different contours to highlight and clarify the principal relief features

Abbreviations of measures used   ft Feet   m Meters   Mi. Miles   Km Kilometers

ARCTIC OCEAN

BEAUFORT

SEA

ELLESMERE I.

Greenland

SVALBARD

QUEEN ELIZABETH IS

PARRY IS.

DEVON I.

BANKS I.

BAFFIN

BAY

VICTORIA

DAVIS STR.

Arctic Circle

Great Bear L.

ICELAND

Great Slave L.

HUDSON BAY

C. Farewell

ALEXANDER ARCH.

Labrador

British
Isles

NORTH

NORTH

IRELAND

GREAT

SEA

L. Winnipeg

AMERICA

NEWFOUNDLAND

BRITAIN

VANCOUVER I.

L. Superior

C. Race

L. Huron

L. Michigan

L. Ontario

L. Erie

AZORES

MEDI

AMERICA

MADEIRA

BERMUDA

CANARY IS.

Tropic of Cancer

GULF OF
MEXICO

BAHAMAS

ATLANTIC

Sahara

HAWAIIAN IS.

CUBA

West
Indies

9200

HISPANIOLA

AFR

JAMAICA

C. VERDE IS.

CARIBBEAN SEA

PACIFIC

LEEWARD IS.

WINDWARD IS.

CHRISTMAS I.

Equator

GALAPAGOS IS.

OCEAN

GULF OF
GUINEA

Galapagos

MARQUESAS IS.

Selvas

ASCENSION

Mato
Grosso

SOUTH

SOCIETY IS.

TUAMOTU ARCH.

ST. HELENA

COOK IS.

AMERICA

L. Titicaca

Tropic of Capricorn

8050

TUBUAI IS.

San Chaco

OCEAN

Pampas

Río de la Plata

TRISTAN DA CUNHA

FALKLAND IS.

TIERRA
DEL FUEGO

S. GEORGIA

SOUTH

C. Horn

ARCTIC OCEAN

FRANZ JOSEPH LAND

SEVERNAYA
ZEMLYA

BARENTS

LAPTEV

NEW SIBERIAN IS.

NOVAYA
ZEMLYA

KARA

SEA

Taimyr
Pen.

WRANGEL I.

North C.

SEA

SEA

BERING STR.

WHITE SEA

Ob

BERING

SEA

L. Ladoga

Siberia

SEA OF
OKHOTSK

ALEUTIAN IS

RUSSIA

Russia

Steppe

Volga

L. Balkhash

Gobi

SAKHALIN

Stanovoy
Range

KURIL IS.

BLACK
SEA

ARAL
SEA

A   S   I   A

HOKKAIDŌ

Danube

CASPIAN SEA

SEA OF
JAPAN

RANEAN SEA

Mesopotamia

HONSHŪ

Arabia

Tien Shan

HUANG

YELLOW
SEA

KYŪSHŪ

10 554

RED SEA

THE GULF

RYUKYU IS.

Tropic of Cancer

CA

India

TAIWAN

ARABIAN
SEA

BAY OF
BENGAL

Chad

ANDAMAN
IS.

LUZON

MARIANA IS.

PACIFIC

Ras Asir

LACCADIVE IS.

Mekong

SOUTH CHINA SEA

Philippines

GUAM

11 022

10 497

CEYLON

Malay
Pen.

MINDANAO

MARSHALL IS.

MALDIVES

CAROLINE IS.

Congo
Basin

INDIAN

MOLUCCAS

GILBERT IS.

Equator

L. Tanganyika

ZANZIBAR

SEYCHELLES

CHAGOS ARCH.

East Indies

SUMATRA

NEW
GUINEA

BISMARK
ARCH.

OCEAN

SUNDA

JAVA

CELEBES

OCEAN

SOLOMON IS.

SAMOA

MOZAMBIQUE CHANNEL

COCOS OR
KEELING IS.

TIMOR

TIMOR
SEA

CORAL
SEA

FIJI

MADAGASCAR

MAURITIUS
RÉUNION

AUSTRALIA

NEW
CALEDONIA

TONGA

Tropic of Capricorn

Kalahari

10 822

of
Good Hope

TASMAN
SEA

NORTH I.

2230

New
Zealand

CROZET IS.

TASMANIA

3764

SOUTH I.

N   OCEAN

KERGUELEN

MACQUARIE IS.

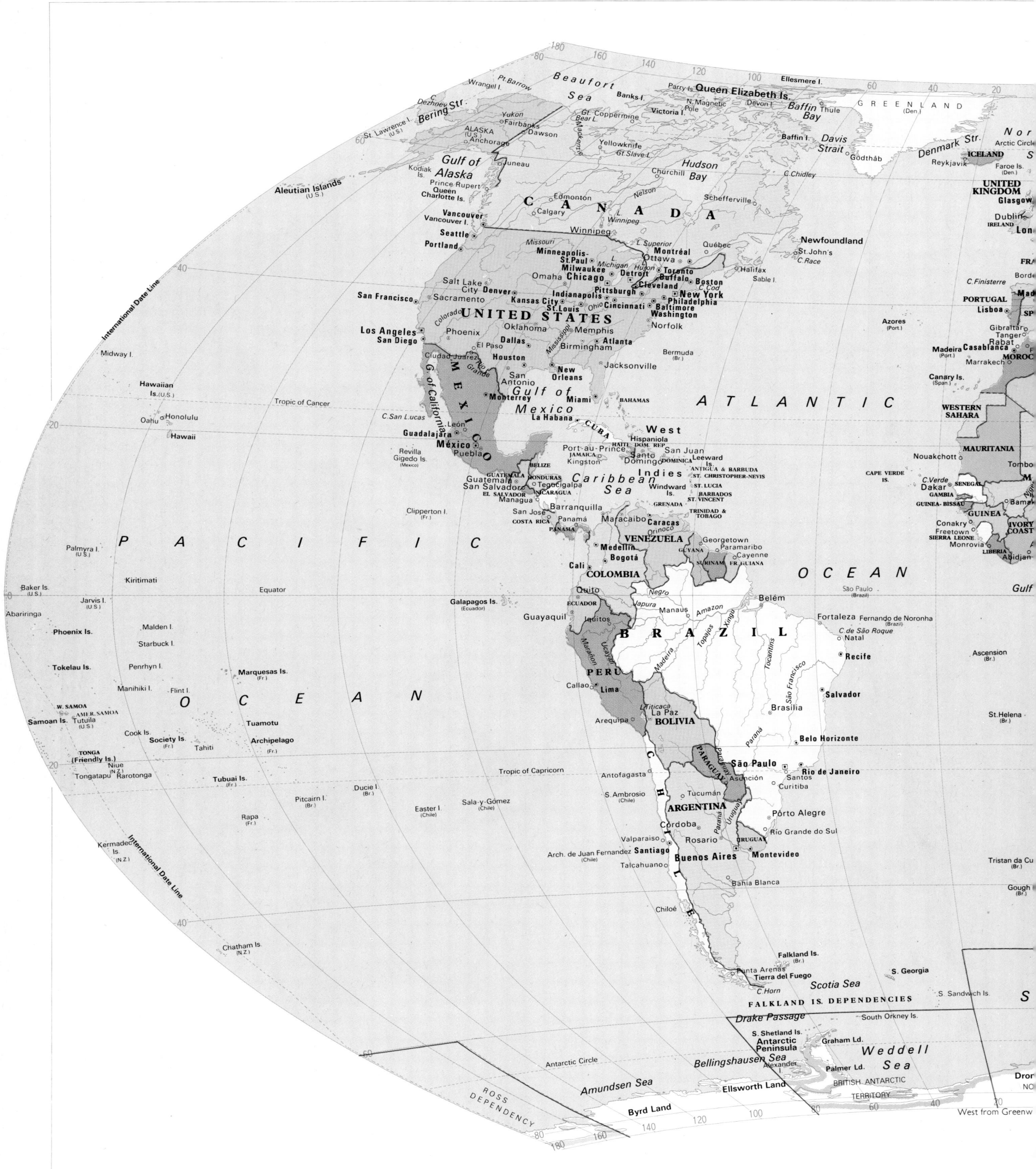

ARCTIC OCEAN
UNION OF SOVIET SOCIALIST REPUBLICS
MONGOLIA
CHINA
JAPAN
PACIFIC OCEAN
INDIAN OCEAN
SOUTHERN OCEAN
INDIA
PAKISTAN
IRAN (PERSIA)
SAUDI ARABIA
LIBYA
EGYPT
SUDAN
CHAD
NIGER
NIGERIA
ETHIOPIA
KENYA
ZAÏRE (CONGO)
TANZANIA
ANGOLA
ZAMBIA
MOZAMBIQUE
MADAGASCAR
NAMIBIA
BOTSWANA
SOUTH AFRICA
INDONESIA
MALAYSIA
PHILIPPINES
AUSTRALIA
NEW ZEALAND
TRUST TERRITORY OF THE PACIFIC ISLANDS (U.S.)
Tropic of Cancer
Equator
Tropic of Capricorn
Antarctic Circle
AUSTRALIAN DEPENDENCY
East from Greenwich

1 : 16 000 000

100   1   100   200   300   400   500 miles
100   0   200   400   600   800 km

ATLANTIC OCEAN

NORWEGIAN SEA

NORTH SEA

BALTIC SEA

BLACK SEA

CASPIAN SEA −28

MEDITERRANEAN SEA

ADRIATIC SEA

Aegean Sea

Ionian Sea

Tyrrhenian Sea

Ligurian Sea

White Sea

Ural Mountains

Obshchi Syrt

Volga Uplands

Central Russian Uplands

Ukraine

Finland

Lapland

Tundra

Scandinavia

Pripyat Marshes

Carpathians

Transylvanian Alps

Wallachia

Balkans

Balkan Peninsula

Pindus

Anatolia

Taurus

Caucasus

Plain of Hungary

Dinaric Alps

Apennines

Alps

Pyrenees

Iberian Peninsula

Meseta

Old Castile

New Castile

Sierra Morena

Andalusia

Sa. Nevada

Cantabrian Mts.

Maritime Atlas

Plateau of the Shotts

Iceland

British Isles

Great Britain

Ireland

North Cape

Kola Peninsula

Kanin Peninsula

Crimea

Crete

Cyprus

Corsica

Sardinia

Sicily

Calabria

Malta

Balearic Is.

Hebrides

Shetland Is.

Orkney Is.

Faroe Is.

Rockall

Gotland

Vesterålen

Lofoten

Dogger Bank

Fisher Bank

English Channel

Irish Sea

Bay of Biscay

Gulf of Bothnia

Gulf of Finland

G. of Riga

Skagerrak

Kattegat

Sea of Azov

G. of Lions

Str. of Gibraltar

Str. of Otranto

Str. of Messina

Str. of Bonifacio

Bosporus

Jutland

Brittany

ft   m
12 000 — 4000
6000 — 2000
3000 — 1000
1200 — 600
600 — 200
0
200 — 600
4000 — 2000
12 000 — 4000

Projection : Bonne   West from Greenwich   0   East from Greenwich

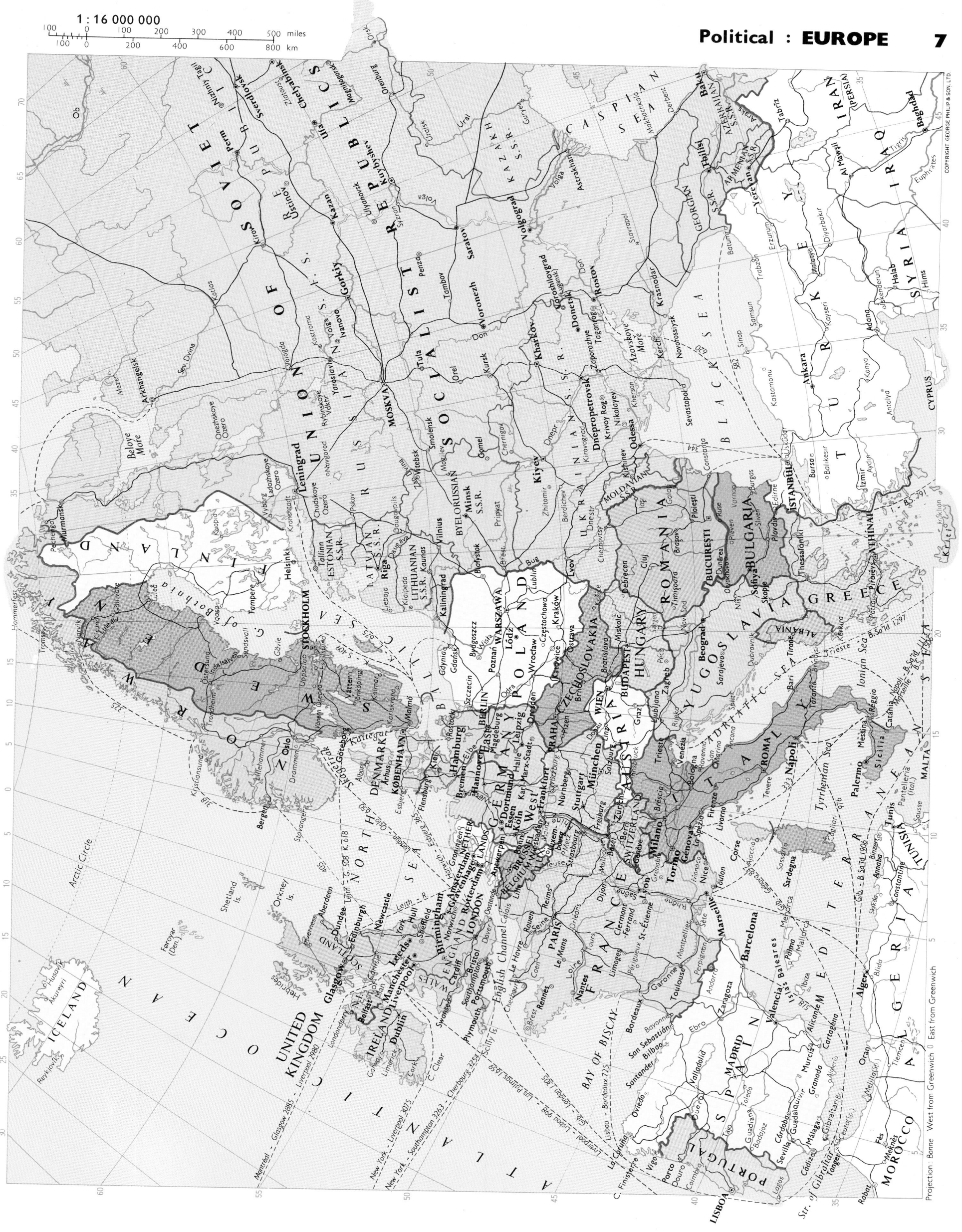
1 : 16 000 000
100 0 100 200 300 400 500 miles
100 0 200 400 600 800 km
UNION OF SOVIET SOCIALIST REPUBLICS
R. S. F. S. R.
KAZAKH S.S.R.
UKRAINIAN S.S.R.
BYELORUSSIAN S.S.R.
ESTONIAN S.S.R.
LATVIAN S.S.R.
LITHUANIAN S.S.R.
MOLDAVIAN S.S.R.
GEORGIAN S.S.R.
ARMENIAN S.S.R.
AZERBAIJAN S.S.R.
CASPIAN SEA
BLACK SEA
Azovskoye More
TURKEY
SYRIA
IRAQ
IRAN (PERSIA)
CYPRUS
FINLAND
SWEDEN
NORWAY
DENMARK
POLAND
GERMANY
East
West
CZECHOSLOVAKIA
AUSTRIA
HUNGARY
ROMANIA
BULGARIA
YUGOSLAVIA
ALBANIA
GREECE
ITALY
SWITZERLAND
FRANCE
BELGIUM
NETHERLANDS
UNITED KINGDOM
IRELAND
ICELAND
SPAIN
PORTUGAL
MOROCCO
ALGERIA
TUNISIA
MALTA
ATLANTIC OCEAN
NORTH SEA
BALTIC SEA
G. of Bothnia
MEDITERRANEAN SEA
ADRIATIC SEA
Tyrrhenian Sea
Ionian Sea
BAY OF BISCAY
English Channel
Arctic Circle
Beloye More
MOSKVA
Leningrad
Kiyev
Minsk
Riga
Vilnius
Tallinn
Helsinki
STOCKHOLM
Oslo
KØBENHAVN
BERLIN
WARSZAWA
PRAHA
WIEN
BUDAPEST
BUCUREŞTI
Sofiya
Beograd
ATHINAI
ISTANBUL
Ankara
ROMA
LONDON
PARIS
MADRID
LISBOA
Dublin
Baghdad
Tbilisi
Baku
Yerevan
Sverdlovsk
Perm
Ufa
Chelyabinsk
Kazan
Gorkiy
Kuybyshev
Saratov
Volgograd
Voronezh
Kharkov
Donetsk
Rostov
Dnepropetrovsk
Odessa
Zaporozhye
Krasnodar
Arkhangelsk
Murmansk
Milano
Torino
Genova
Napoli
Palermo
Marseille
Lyon
Barcelona
Valencia
Hamburg
München
Frankfurt
Glasgow
Edinburgh
Manchester
Liverpool
Birmingham
Leeds
Belfast
Projection: Bonne West from Greenwich 0 East from Greenwich
COPYRIGHT GEORGE PHILIP & SON, LTD.

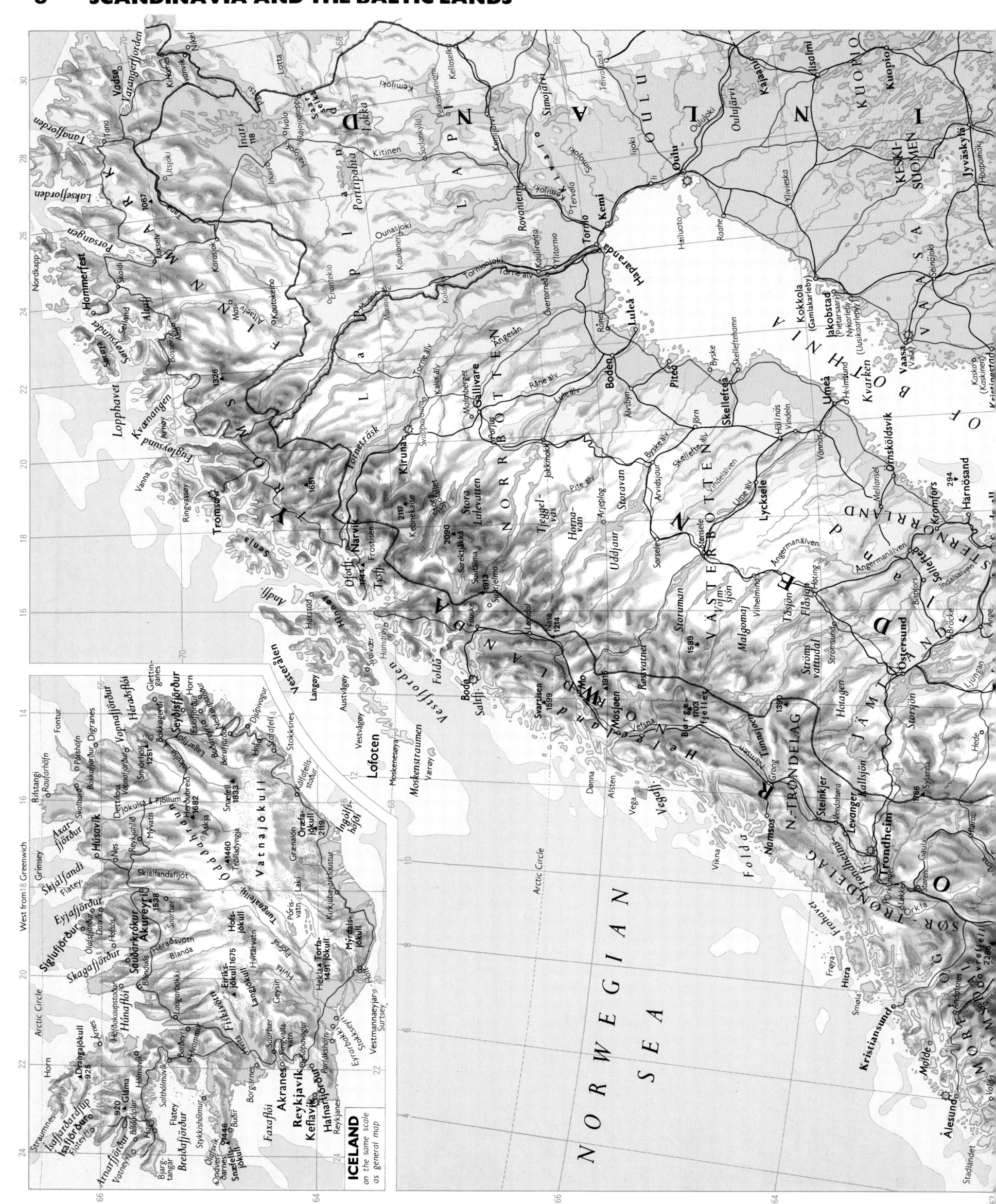
ICELAND
on the same scale
as general map
West from 18 Greenwich
Arctic Circle
NORWEGIAN
SEA
Vestfjorden
Lofoten
Vesterålen
Nordkapp
Hammerfest
Tromsø
Narvik
Kiruna
Gällivare
Luleå
Boden
Piteå
Skellefteå
Umeå
Vaasa
Kokkola
Oulu
Kemi
Tornio
Haparanda
Rovaniemi
Kuopio
Jyväskylä
Östersund
Trondheim
Namsos
Steinkjer
Levanger
Mosjøen
Bodø
Kristiansund
Molde
Ålesund
Härnösand
Kramfors
Lycksele
Örnsköldsvik
Reykjavík
Keflavík
Hafnarfjörður
Akranes
Akureyri
Húsavík
Ísafjörður
Vatnajökull
Faxaflói
Breiðafjörður
Húnaflói
Skagafjörður
Eyjafjörður
Seyðisfjörður
Vestmannaeyjar
Surtsey
Inari
Vadsø
Tana
Porsangen
Lakselv
Alta
Kautokeino
Karasjok
Kvænangen
Lopphavet
Senja
Andøy
Hinnøy
Harstad
Ofotfj.
Tysfj.
Saltfj.
Svartisen
Storavan
Uddjaur
Hornavan
Storuman
Malgomaj
Ströms vattudal
Storsjön
Kallsjön
Hitra
Frøya
Smøla
Vega
Vikna
Folda
Frohavet
Kvarken
Fauske
Rana
Røssvatnet
Gaula
Orkla
Torne älv
Lule älv
Pite älv
Ume älv
Angermanälven
Indalsälven
Kemijoki
Ounasjoki
Tornionjoki
Muonio älv
Kokemäenjoki
Oulujärvi
Oulujoki
Kajaani
Iisalmi
Ylivieska
Raahe
Jakobstad
Kaskö
Vindeln
Vilhelmina
Sorsele
Arvidsjaur
Jokkmokk
Arjeplog
Kebnekaise
2117
Sarektjåkkå
2090
Stora Lulevatten
Sulitjelma
1913
Dovrefjell
2286
Sylarna
Stadlandet
Kristinestad

1 : 4 000 000

20 10 0 100 miles
40 20 0 40 80 120 160 km

FINLAND

Tampere · Hämeenlinna · HELSINKI (Helsingfors) · Porvoo · Loviisa · Kotka · Kundo · Rakvere

Pori · Rauma · Uusikaupunki · Turku (Åbo) · Hangö (Hanko) · Tallinn · Haapsalu · Rakvere

ESTONIAN S.S.R. · Valga · Viljandi · Pärnu · Moisaküla

TURUN · PORI · HÄME · UUSIMAA · Salo · Hyvinkää

Hiiumaa (Dagö) · Saaremaa (Ösel) · Kingissepp · Ruhnu

LATVIAN S.S.R. · Valmiera · Cēsis · Riga · Bauska · Jelgava · Tukums · Ventspils · Kuldiga · Liepaja · Telšiai · Klaipeda

LITHUANIAN S.S.R. · Šiauliai · Panevėžys · Ukmergė · Kaunas · Vilnius · Grodno · Sovetsk · Chernyakhovsk · Kaliningrad · Gusev · Suwałki · Augustów · Łomża · Białystok

Åland (Ahvenanmaa) · Mariehamn (Maarianhamina)

SEA · **BALTIC**

GULF OF BOTHNIA

Hudiksvall · Söderhamn · Bollnäs · Gävle · Sandviken · Borlänge · Falun · Hedemora · Avesta · Fagersta · Västerås · Uppsala · STOCKHOLM · Södertälje · Nynäshamn · Eskilstuna · Köping · Örebro · Kumla · Katrineholm · Norrköping · Nyköping · Oxelösund · Söderköping

Gotska Sandön · Fårö · Gotland · Visby · Roma · Hemse · Burgsvik · Hoburgen

GÄVLEBORG · **KOPPARBERG** · **VÄSTMANLAND** · **SÖDERMANLAND** · **UPPSALA**

Motala · Mjölby · Linköping · Vadstena · Skövde · Lidköping · Falköping · Jönköping · Tranås · Nässjö · Eksjö · Vetlanda · Västervik · Oskarshamn · Kalmar · Öland · Borgholm

ÖSTERGÖTLAND · **JÖNKÖPING** · **KALMAR** · **KRONOBERG** · **BLEKINGE**

Växjö · Värnamo · Ljungby · Nybro · Karlskrona · Karlshamn · Sölvesborg · Kristianstad

Bornholm · Nexö · Rønne · Ystad · Trelleborg

Karlstad · Arvika · Filipstad · Kristinehamn · Karlskoga · Kongsvinger · Åmål · Säffle · Vänern · Mariestad · Lidköping · Skara · Vänersborg · Trollhättan · Alingsås · Borås · Mölndal · GÖTEBORG · Uddevalla · Strömstad · Kungsbacka

VÄRMLAND · **ÄLVSBORG** · **GÖTEBORG OCH BOHUS** · **SKARABORG** · **HALLAND**

Vänersborg · Varberg · Falkenberg · Halmstad · Laholm · Ängelholm · Helsingborg · Landskrona · Helsingör · MALMÖ · KØBENHAVN (Copenhagen) · Roskilde · Køge

MALMÖHUS · **Sjælland** · **The Sound**

NORWAY

Bergen · Hardangerfjorden · Haugesund · Kopervik · Stavanger · Sandnes · Egersund (Eigersund) · Flekkefjord · Farsund · Lista · Kristiansand · Mandal · Lillesand · Grimstad · Arendal · Risør · Kragerø · Skien · Larvik · Tønsberg · Drammen · OSLO · Drøbak · Moss · Fredrikstad · Sarpsborg · Halden

SOGN OG FJORDANE · **HORDALAND** · **ROGALAND** · **VEST-AGDER** · **AUST-AGDER** · **TELEMARK** · **BUSKERUD** · **OPPLAND** · **HEDMARK**

Galdhøpiggen 2468 · Glittertind 2465 · Lillehammer · Gjøvik · Hamar · Elverum · Kongsberg · Hønefoss · Tyristand

Galdhøpiggen · Gausta 1883 · 1920

DENMARK

Thisted · Ålborg · Limfjorden · Hjørring · Skagen · Frederikshavn · Læsø · Anholt · Grenå · Randers · Viborg · Herning · Silkeborg · Århus · Horsens · Vejle · Kolding · Fredericia · Esbjerg · Ribe · Åbenrå · Sønderborg · Flensburg · Odense · Svendborg · Nyborg · Korsør · Slagelse · Næstved · Vordingborg · Nykøbing · Lolland · Falster · Gedser

Jylland · **Fyn** · **Kattegat** · **Skagerrak** · **Store Bælt** · **Lille Bælt**

POLAND

Elbląg · Malbork · Gdynia · Gdańsk · Zatoka Gdańska · Słupsk · Koszalin · Kołobrzeg · Wolin · Szczecin (Stettin) · Toruń · Bydgoszcz · Grudziądz · Chełmno · Chojnice

WEST GERMANY · **EAST GERMANY**

Rostock · Warnemünde · Stralsund · Greifswald · Rügen · Schwerin · Lübeck · Kiel · Hamburg · Lüneburg · Bremen · Bremerhaven · Wilhelmshaven · Oldenburg · Emden · Groningen

NETHERLANDS

East from Greenwich

Projection. Conical with two standard parallels

m ft · 6000 4500 3000 1200 600 200 0

Gulf of Bothnia

JÄMTLANDS LÄN

VÄSTERNORRLANDS LÄN

GÄVLEBORGS LÄN

KOPPARBERGS LÄN

VÄRMLANDS LÄN

VÄSTMANLANDS LÄN

UPPSALA LÄN

STOCKHOLMS LÄN

SÖDERMANLANDS LÄN

ÖREBRO LÄN

TRØNDELAG

SØR TRØNDELAG FYLKE

MØRE OG ROMSDAL FYLKE

HEDMARK FYLKE

OPPLAND FYLKE

BUSKERUD FYLKE

AKERSHUS FYLKE

ØSTFOLD

VESTFOLD

TELEMARK FYLKE

miles
km

COPYRIGHT. GEORGE PHILIP & SON, LTD.

POLAND

Stupsk
Ustka
Darłowo
Sławno
Szczecin

BALTIC SEA

Gotland
Visby
Klintehamn

Öland
Kalmar

KALMAR LÄN

Oskarshamn
Västervik

Nyköping
Oxelösund
Norrköping
Linköping
Motala
Mjölby

ÖSTERGÖTLANDS LÄN

JÖNKÖPINGS LÄN

Jönköping
Huskvarna
Nässjö
Tranås
Värnamo
Ljungby

KRONOBERGS LÄN

Växjö
Älmhult

BLEKINGE LÄN

Karlskrona
Ronneby
Karlshamn

CHRISTIANSTADS LÄN

Kristianstad
Hässleholm
Simrishamn
Ystad

MALMÖHUS LÄN

Malmö
Lund
Landskrona
Helsingborg
Ängelholm
Trelleborg

Bornholm
Rønne
Nexø

HALLANDS LÄN

Halmstad
Falkenberg
Varberg

GÖTEBORGS OCH BOHUS LÄN

Göteborg
Mölndal
Kungsbacka
Borås
Alingsås
Trollhättan
Uddevalla
Vänersborg

SKARABORGS LÄN

Lidköping
Skara
Falköping
Skövde
Mariestad

ÄLVSBORGS LÄN

Arendal
Risør
Tvedestrand

Kattegat

Anholt
Læsø

GERMANY

Rügen
Hiddensee
Kiel
Flensburg
Schleswig
Husum
Rendsburg

Kieler Bucht
Fehmarn

DENMARK

Skagen
Frederikshavn
Hjørring

NORDJYLLANDS AMT
Ålborg
Ålborg Bugt
Limfjorden
Brønderslev

Thisted
Nykøbing Mors

JYLLAND

Viborg
VIBORG AMT
Skive
Holstebro

RINGKØBING AMT
Ringkøbing
Herning
Ikast

ÅRHUS AMT
Århus
Randers
Grenå
Djursland
Silkeborg
Skanderborg
Horsens

VEJLE AMT
Vejle
Kolding
Fredericia
Grindsted

RIBE AMT
Esbjerg
Varde
Ribe

HADERSLEV AMT
Haderslev

SØNDERJYLLANDS AMT
Åbenrå
Sønderborg
Tønder

FYN
Odense
Svendborg
Middelfart
Nyborg
Assens
Fåborg
Ærø

Store Bælt
Lille Bælt

SJÆLLAND
København (Copenhagen)
Roskilde
Helsingør
Hillerød
Frederiksværk
Frederikssund
Køge
Slagelse
Korsør
Næstved
Ringsted
Sorø
Kalundborg

VESTSJÆLLANDS AMT
FREDERIKSBORG AMT

STORSTRØMS AMT

LOLLAND
Nakskov
Maribo
Rødby

FALSTER
Nykøbing
Gedser

Møn
Møns Klint

Femer Bælt
Langelands Bælt

Rostock
Darsser Ort

East from Greenwich

Projection: Conical with two standard parallels

ft   m
6000   2000
4500   1500
3000   1000
1200   400
600   200
0   0

Holmsland Klit

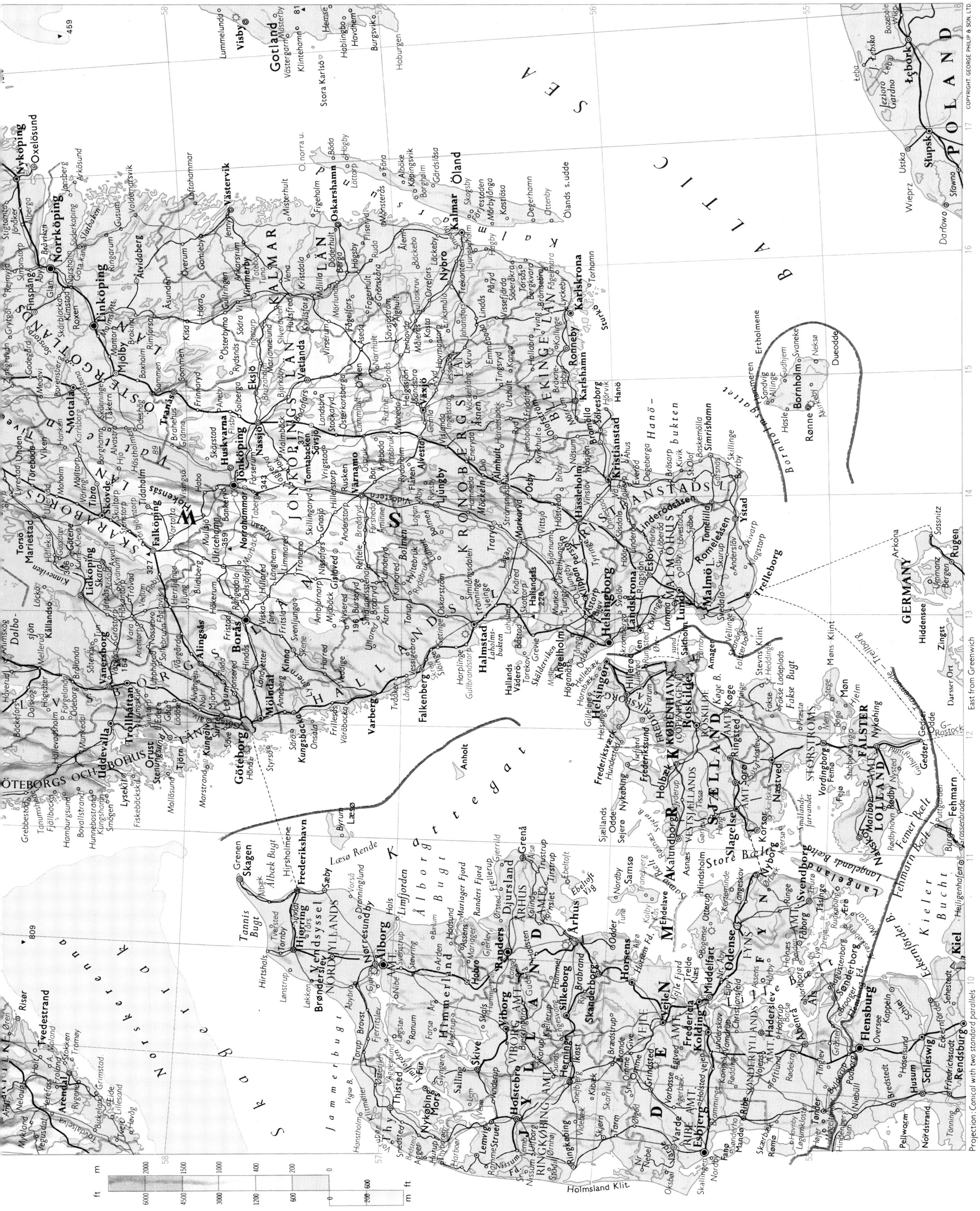

NORTH SEA
IRISH SEA
North Channel
SCOTLAND
Southern Uplands
Pennines
CUMBRIA
Cumbrian Mts.
NORTHUMBERLAND
DURHAM
CLEVELAND
TYNE & WEAR
N. York Moors
NORTH YORKSHIRE
W. YORKSHIRE
SOUTH YORKSHIRE
HUMBERSIDE
LANCASHIRE
MERSEYSIDE
CHESHIRE
DERBY
NOTTS
LINCOLN
NORFOLK
STAFFORD
CLWYD
GWYNEDD
ISLE OF MAN
Anglesey
The Wash
Edinburgh
Glasgow
Newcastle
Carlisle
Leeds
Bradford
Sheffield
Manchester
Liverpool
Hull
York
Middlesbrough
(Teesside)
Sunderland
Blackpool
Preston
Nottingham
Derby
Lincoln
Stoke-on-Trent
Norwich
Great Yarmouth
Kings Lynn
Douglas
Belfast

1 : 1 600 000

10   0   10   20   30   40   50 miles
10   0   10   20   30   40   50   60   70   80 km

SCILLY ISLES
On same Scale

Isles of Scilly

St. Ives
Penzance
Land's End
St. Mary's

ENGLISH   CHANNEL

F R A N C E

Rouen
Dieppe
Le Havre
Cherbourg
Guernsey
Channel Islands
Jersey
St. Helier
St. Peter Port
Sark
Alderney

Bristol Channel

Cardigan Bay

SUFFOLK
ESSEX
KENT
EAST SUSSEX
WEST SUSSEX
SURREY
HANTS
DORSET
DEVON
CORNWALL
SOMERSET
WILTS
BERKS
OXFORD
BUCKS
BEDFORD
CAMBRIDGE
NORTHANTS
WARWICK
WEST MIDLANDS
HEREFORD & WORCESTER
SHROPSHIRE
GLOUCESTER
AVON
GWENT
MID GLAMORGAN
WEST GLAMORGAN
SOUTH GLAMORGAN
DYFED
POWYS
HERTFORD

Lowestoft
Ipswich
Colchester
Southend
Cambridge
Peterborough
Leicester
Northampton
Bedford
Milton Keynes
Luton
London
Oxford
Reading
Southampton
Portsmouth
Bournemouth
Brighton
Hove
Worthing
Eastbourne
Hastings
Dover
Folkestone
Margate
Ramsgate
Canterbury
Maidstone
Chatham
Gillingham
Rochester
Gravesend
Basildon
Chelmsford
Birmingham
Coventry
Wolverhampton
Walsall
Dudley
West Bromwich
Gloucester
Cheltenham
Bristol
Bath
Cardiff
Newport
Swansea
Plymouth
Exeter
Torquay (Torbay)
Paignton
Weston-super-Mare
Salisbury
Winchester
Guildford
Crawley
Weymouth
Poole
Dorchester
Merthyr Tydfil
St. Austell
Truro
Penzance
Falmouth
Newquay

ISLE OF WIGHT
Newport
Cowes
Ryde
Ventnor

Projection: Conical with two standard parallels.
East from Greenwich   COPYRIGHT GEORGE PHILIP & SON LTD.

m   ft
1000   3000
400   1200
200   600
100   300
150
50
ft   m

1 : 1 600 000

10   0   10   20   30   40   50 miles

10   0   10   20   30   40   50   60   70   80 km

ORKNEY IS.
On same scale

Hoy · Scapa Flow · South Ronaldsay · North Ronaldsay
Westray · Eday · Sanday · Stronsay · Rousay
Stromness · Mainland · Shapinsay · ORKNEY · Kirkwall · Scapa Flow · Hoy · South Ronaldsay
Pentland Firth · Dunnet Hd. · John O'Groats

Orkney Is. · Pentland Firth · Dunnet Hd. · John O'Groats · Strathy Pt. · Thurso · Dounreay · Halladale · Wick · Noss Hd. · Lybster · Ord of Caithness

Butt of Lewis · Flannan Is. · L. Roag · Broad Bay · Stornoway · Eye Pen. · Lewis · Tarbert · Harris · WESTERN ISLES · Monach Is. · North Uist · Lochmaddy · Benbecula · South Uist · Lochboisdale · Barra · Barra Hd.

C. Wrath · Durness · L. Laxford · Eddrachillis Bay · Lochinver · Enard Bay · Ben Hope 927 · Tongue · Naver · Rear Forest · L. Shin · Lairg · Helmsdale · Brora · Golspie · Dornoch · Dornoch Firth · Tain · Tarbat Ness

Rubha Hunish · Trotternish · L. Gairloch · L. Maree · L. Broom · Ullapool · Oykell · Bonar Bridge · NORTH WEST HIGHLANDS · B. More Assynt · B. Dearg 1081

Portree · Raasay · Rona · L. Torridon · Stromeferry · Strathpeffer · Dingwall · Conon · Cromarty · Moray Firth · Lossiemouth · Cullen · Portsoy · Banff · Macduff · Kinnaird's Head · Fraserburgh · Rattray Head · Peterhead · Buchan Ness

Cuillin Hills · Kyle of Lochalsh · Dornie · Glen Affric · Beauly · Inverness · Nairn · Forres · Elgin · Keith · Dufftown · Huntly · Turriff · Ellon · Deveron · Ythan

Ben More 620 · Canna · Rhum · Eigg · Muck · L. Hourn · Glen Garry · Fort Augustus · L. Oich · Newtonmore · Kingussie · Aviemore · Monadhliath Mts. · Cairn Gorm 1245 · Cairngorm Mts. · Cairn Toul 1292 · Ben Macdhui 1311 · Grantown-on-Spey · Strath Spey · GRAMPIAN · Tomintoul · Alford · Inverurie · Don · Aberdeen · Girdle Ness

Mallaig · L. Morar · Arisaig · L. Arkaig · Glen Spean · Badenoch · GRAMPIAN HIGHLANDS · Braemar · Balmoral · Lochnagar 1154 · Braes of Angus · Laurencekirk · Inverbervie · Stonehaven

Coll · Tobermory · Pt. of Ardnamurchan · MORVERN · Ardgour · Fort William · Ben Nevis 1343 · Rannoch Moor · Forest of Atholl · Blair Atholl · Pass of Killiecrankie · Pitlochry · Kirriemuir · Forfar · Brechin · Montrose

Tiree · Staffa · Mull · Ben More 966 · Iona · Sound of Mull · Lismore · Ballachulish · Loch Etive · Ben Cruachan 1124 · Glen Orchy · Killin · Ben Lawers 1214 · L. Tay · Aberfeldy · Dunkeld · Blairgowrie · Alyth · Sidlaw Hills · Arbroath · Broughty Ferry · NORTH SEA

ATLANTIC OCEAN · Colonsay · Oban · L. Awe · Inveraray · Ben More 1174 · B. Vorlich 983 · Crieff · Breadalbane · TAYSIDE · Scone · Perth · Firth of Tay · Tayport · St. Andrews · Fife Ness

Rubh a' Mhail · Crinan · B. Vorlich 943 · Ben Lomond 974 · L. Katrine · Trossachs · Callander · Dunblane · CENTRAL · Stirling · Bannockburn · FIFE · Kinross · Leven · Cowdenbeath · Glenrothes · Buckhaven · Anstruther

Islay · Bowmore · Port Ellen · Gigha · Jura · Tarbert · Lochgilphead · Helensburgh · Dumbarton · Clydebank · Greenock · Port Glasgow · Paisley · Glasgow · Airdrie · Coatbridge · Motherwell · Wishaw · Cumbernauld · Falkirk · Grangemouth · Bo'ness · Linlithgow · Edinburgh · Leith · Musselburgh · Haddington · LOTHIAN · North Berwick · Dunbar · St. Abb's Hd. · Eyemouth

Ailsa Craig · Ardrossan · Saltcoats · Troon · Prestwick · Ayr · Kilmarnock · Irvine · E. Kilbride · Hamilton · Carstairs · Lanark · STRATHCLYDE · Pentland Hills · Moorfoot Hills · Peebles · Galashiels · Melrose · Lammermuir Hills · Duns · Coldstream · Berwick-upon-Tweed · Holy I.

Campbeltown · Mull of Kintyre · KINTYRE · Goat Fell 874 · Arran · Brodick · Dalmellington · Cumnock · Sanquhar · Leadhills · Broad Law 840 · Tweed · Moffat · Selkirk · Hawick · Jedburgh · The Cheviot 816 · CHEVIOT HILLS · Coquet

SHETLAND IS. · On same scale · Unst · Fetlar · Yell · Yell Sound · Whalsay · Mainland · Bressay · Lerwick · Scalloway · Foula · Sumburgh Hd. · SHETLAND

NORTHERN IRELAND · Belfast · Bangor · Newtownards · Belfast Lough · Larne · Ballymena · Portpatrick · Stranraer · L. Ryan · Merrick 843 · Trostan 554 · Ballycastle · Rathlin · Fair Hd. · N. CHANNEL · NORTH CHANNEL · Firth of Clyde

DUMFRIES AND GALLOWAY · Newton Stewart · Wigtown · Whithorn · Wigtown Bay · Kirkcudbright · Castle Douglas · Dalbeattie · Dumfries · Annan · Gretna Green · Lockerbie · Langholm · Mull of Galloway · Luce Bay · SOUTH UPLANDS · BORDERS · Kelso · Flodden · Till

Solway Firth · Carlisle · HADRIAN'S WALL · Hexham · S. Tyne · N. Tyne · Alston · Cross Fell 893 · Workington · Skiddaw 931 · Ullswater · Penrith · Wear · CUMBRIAN MTS. · Tees · Barnard Castle · ENGLAND · Derwent

ft · m · 3000 · 1000 · 1200 · 400 · 600 · 200 · 300 · 100 · 0 · 50 · 150 · 100 · 300 · m · ft

1 : 1 600 000

Projection: Conical with two standard parallels.

West from Greenwich

COPYRIGHT. GEORGE PHILIP & SON. LTD.

Towns underlined in Northern Ireland give their names to the Districts in which they stand

The remaining Districts are:—

1 Fermanagh   5 Castlereagh
2 Moyle   6 Ards
3 Newtownabbey 7 Down
4 North Down   8 Newry & Mourne

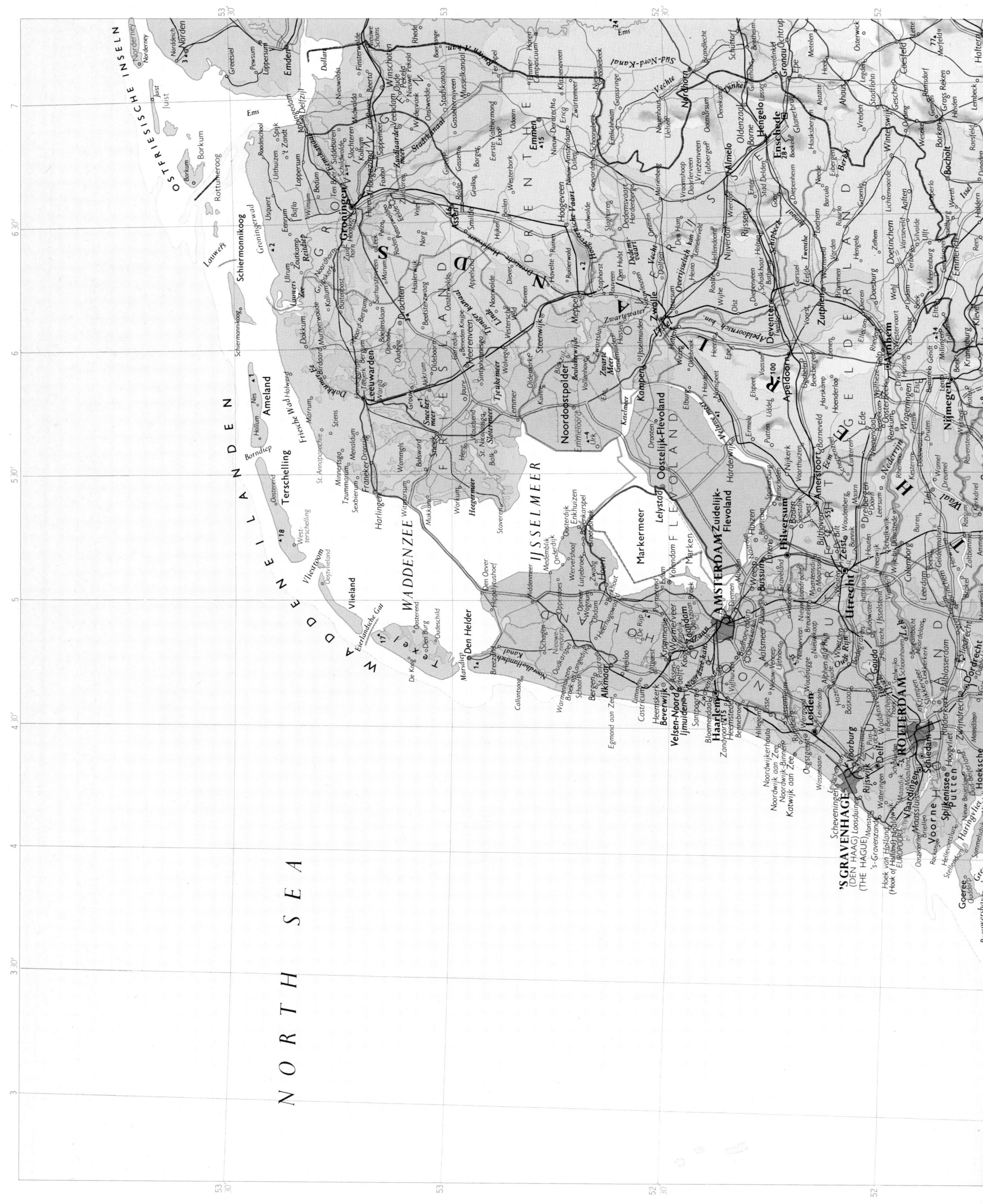
NORTH SEA
WADDENEILANDEN
OSTFRIESISCHE INSELN
WADDENZEE
IJSSELMEER
AMSTERDAM
'S GRAVENHAGE (DEN HAAG) (THE HAGUE)
ROTTERDAM

1 : 1 000 000

Projection : Conical with two standard parallels 3.30'

East from Greenwich

DÉPARTEMENTS IN THE PARIS AREA
1 Ville de Paris   3 Val-de-Marne
2 Seine-St-Denis   4 Hauts-de-Seine

Projection: Conical with two standard parallels

West from Greenwich   East from Greenwich

1 : 2 000 000

COPYRIGHT GEORGE PHILIP & SON LTD.

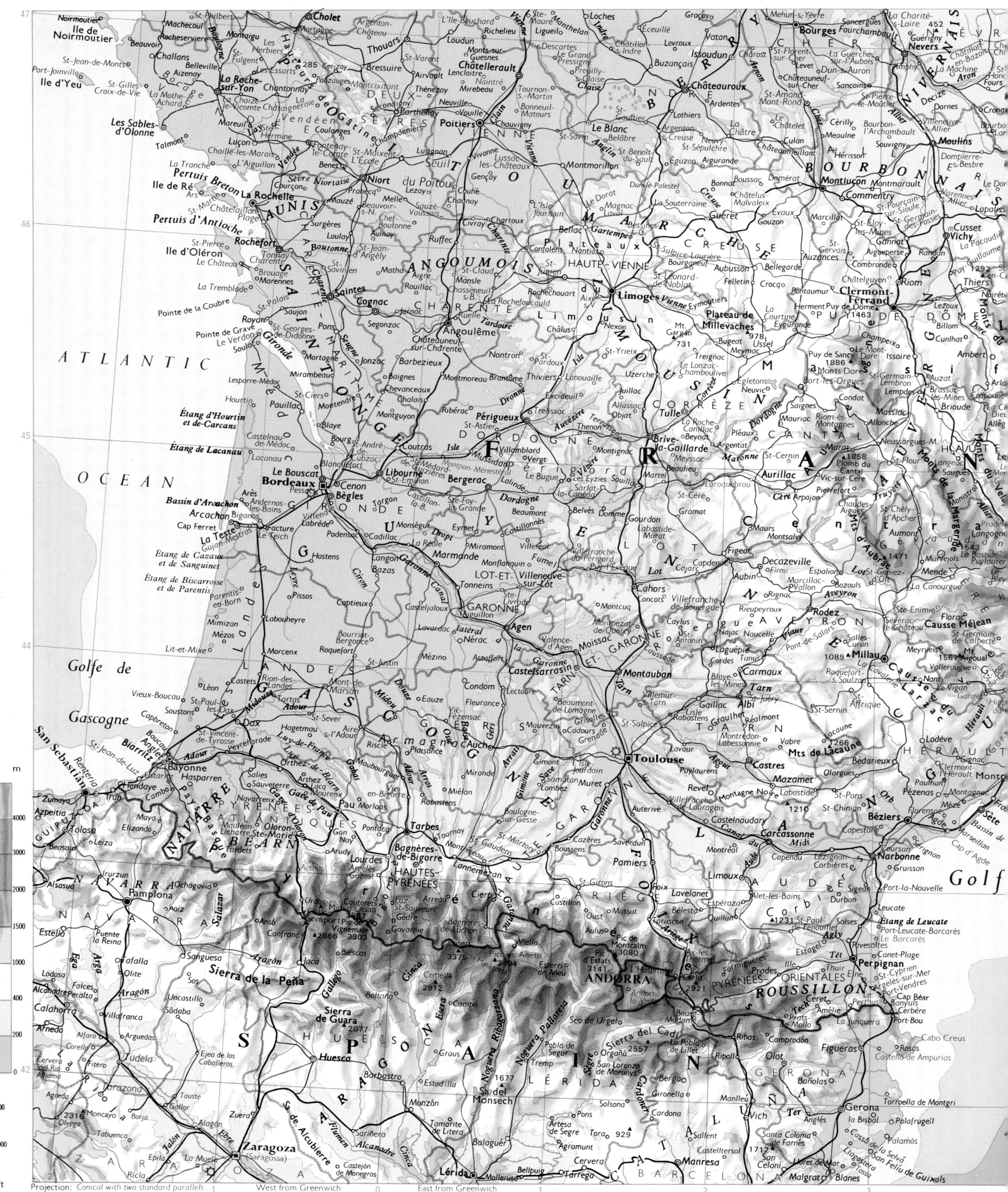

Projection: Conical with two standard parallels
West from Greenwich   East from Greenwich

1 : 2 000 000

10   0   10   20   30   40   50 miles
10   0   10   20   30   40   50   60   70   80 km

SWITZERLAND

FRANCE

ITALY

LYON

Genève

Lausanne

Bern

Luzern

Schwyz

GRAUBÜNDEN

VALAIS

Milano

Bergamo

Brescia

Torino

Grenoble

Valence

Asti

Alessandria

Parma

La Spezia

Massa

Livorno

ALPES-DE-HAUTE-PROVENCE

ALPES-MARITIMES

VAUCLUSE

BOUCHES DU RHÔNE

Avignon

Nîmes

Arles

Aix-en-Provence

MARSEILLE

Toulon

Hyères

ILES D'HYÈRES

Nice

Monaco

Monte-Carlo

Cannes

San Remo

Imperia (Maurizio-Oneglia)

Savona

GENOVA

Golfo di Génova

LIGURIAN SEA

Côte d'Azur

MEDITERRANEAN SEA

Golfe du Lion

C. Corse

Capraia

Elba

Pianosa

Gorgona

Bastia

HAUTE-CORSE

CORSICA

Ajaccio

CORSE DU SUD

Bonifacio

I. de Cavallo

COPYRIGHT. GEORGE. PHILIP & SON. LTD.

BAY OF BISCAY
ATLANTIC OCEAN
SPAIN
San Sebastián
Bilbao
Santander
Gijón
Oviedo
La Coruña (Corunna)
El Ferrol
Santiago de Compostela
Lugo
Orense
Vigo
León
Burgos
Vitoria
Logroño
Palencia
Valladolid
Zamora
Salamanca
Segovia
Avila
MADRID
Guadalajara
Alcalá de Henares
Getafe
Aranjuez
Porto (Oporto)
Vila Nova de Gaia
Braga
Bragança
Viseu
Guarda
Coimbra
Aveiro
Picos de Europa
Sierra de Gredos
Sierra de Guadarrama
Duero
Douro
Miño

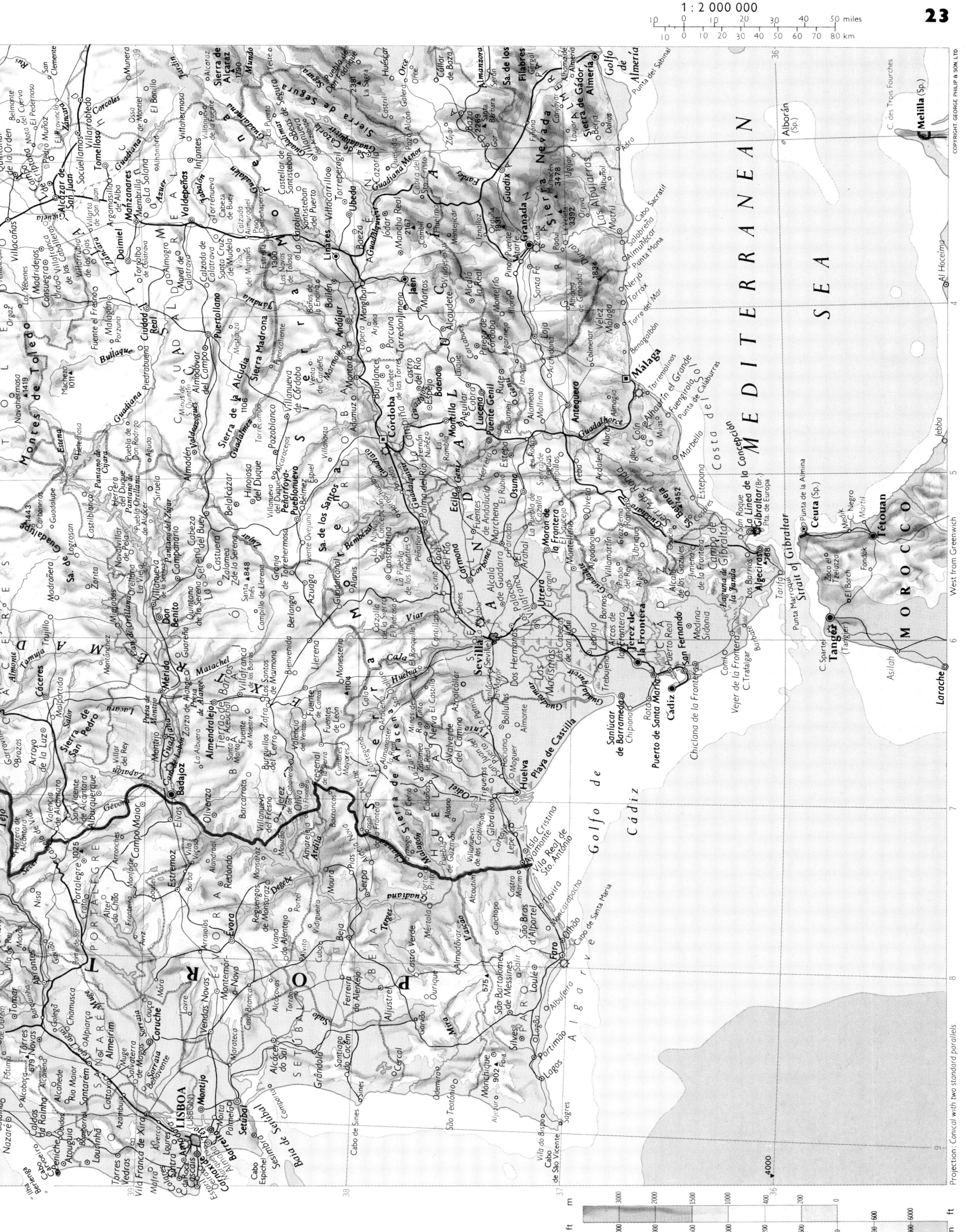

1 : 2 000 000

MEDITERRANEAN SEA

MOROCCO

PORTUGAL

ANDALUCÍA

Projection - Conical with two standard parallels

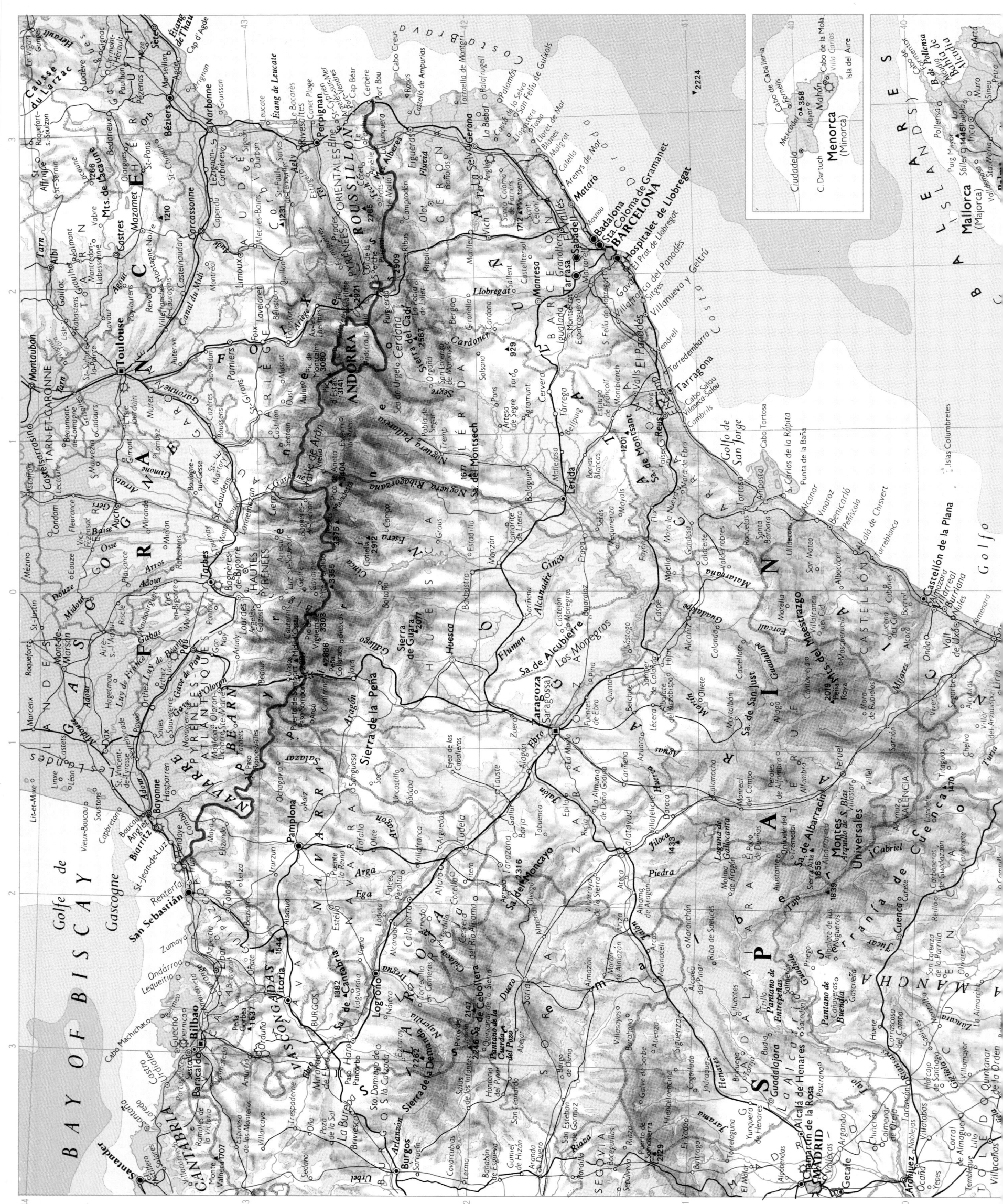
BAY OF BISCAY
Golfe de Gascogne
FRANCE
SPAIN
Costa Brava
Costa Dorada
Golfo de San Jorge
Menorca (Minorca)
Mallorca (Majorca)
BALEARES (ISLANDS)
ANDORRA
ROUSSILLON
PYRÉNÉES ORIENTALES
HAUTES PYRÉNÉES
PYRÉNÉES-ATLANTIQUES
NAVARRE
BEARN
NAVARRA
VASCONGADAS
CANTABRIA
LA RIOJA
ARAGÓN
CATALUÑA
GASCOGNE
TARN-ET-GARONNE
BARCELONA
Toulouse
Montauban
Carcassonne
Perpignan
Narbonne
Béziers
Bayonne
Biarritz
San Sebastián
Bilbao
Santander
Vitoria
Pamplona
Logroño
Burgos
Zaragoza (Saragossa)
Huesca
Lérida
Tarragona
Reus
Manresa
Sabadell
Tarrasa
Badalona
Mataró
Gerona
Figueras
Castellón de la Plana
Teruel
Cuenca
Guadalajara
Alcalá de Henares
MADRID
Getafe
Aranjuez
Soria
Calatayud
Tudela
Tarbes
Lourdes
Pau
Auch
Sierra de la Peña
Sierra de Guara
Sa. del Moncayo
Sa. de Cebollera
Sierra de la Demanda
Montes Universales
Sa. de Albarracín
Mts. del Maestrazgo
Sa. de San Just
Sa. de Montsant
Sa. del Montsech
Serranía de Cuenca
Los Monegros
Sa. de Alcubierre
Ebro
Segre
Cinca
Jalón
Tajo
Duero
Garonne
Adour
Tarn

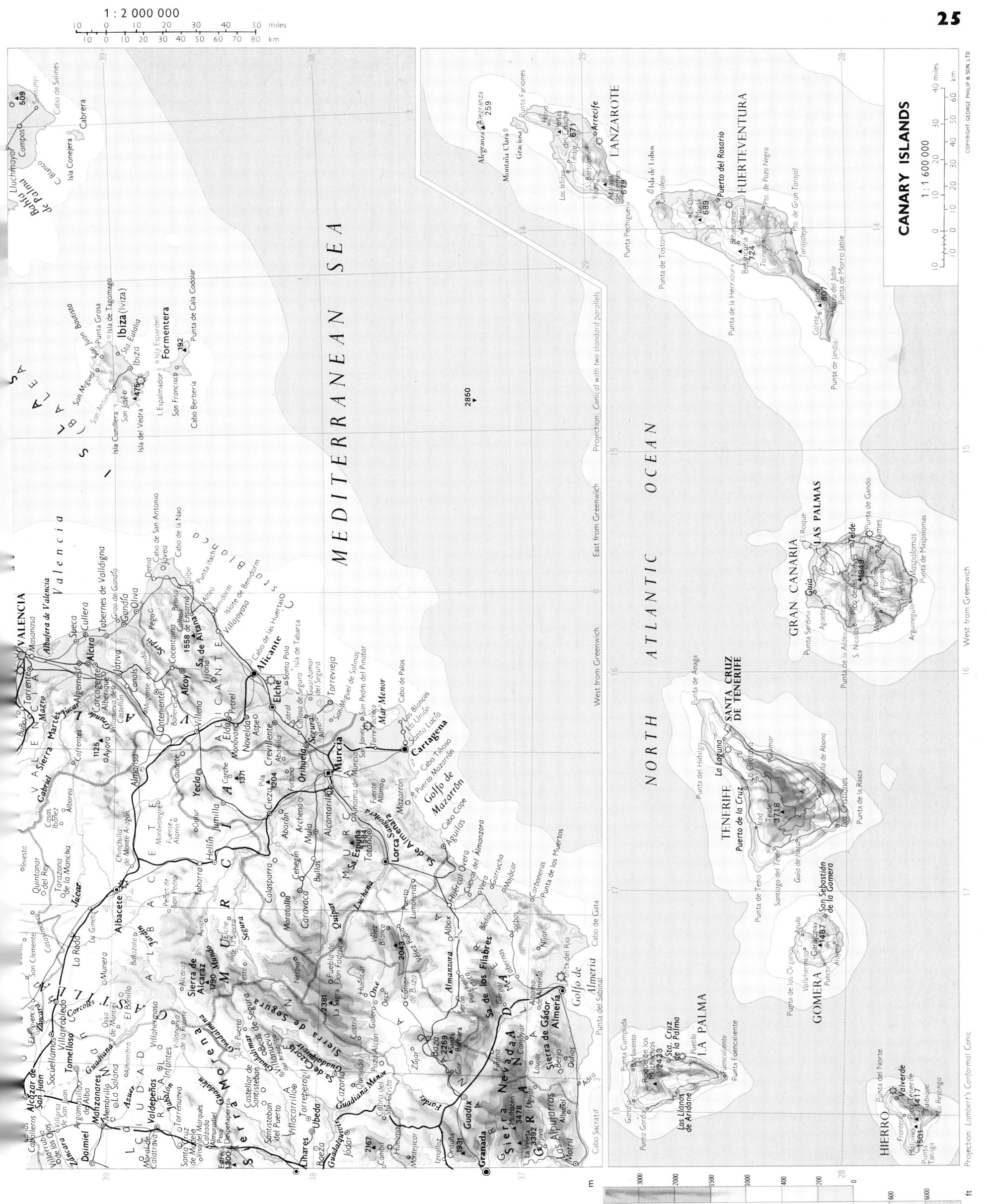

CANARY ISLANDS

1:2 000 000

1:1 600 000

MEDITERRANEAN SEA

NORTH ATLANTIC OCEAN

COPYRIGHT GEORGE PHILIP & SON LTD

Projection: Conical with two standard parallels

Projection: Lambert's Conformal Conic

East from Greenwich

West from Greenwich

LANZAROTE

Arrecife

FUERTEVENTURA

Puerto del Rosario

GRAN CANARIA

LAS PALMAS

Telde

TENERIFE

SANTA CRUZ DE TENERIFE

La Laguna

Puerto de la Cruz

GOMERA

San Sebastián de la Gomera

LA PALMA

Sta. Cruz de la Palma

Los Llanos de Aridane

HIERRO

Valverde

VALENCIA

Albufera de Valencia

Ibiza (Iviza)

Formentera

Alicante

Elche

Murcia

Orihuela

Cartagena

Lorca

Granada

Almería

Sierra Nevada

Mulhacén 3478

Guadix

Albacete

Valdepeñas

Daimiel

LIGURIAN SEA

Golfo di Génova

CORSE
(CORSICA)

HAUTE CORSE

CORSE DU SUD

ILES D'HYERES

MARSEILLE
(Marseilles)

SWITZERLAND

MILANO
(Milan)

TORINO
Turin

Livorno
(Leghorn)

Projection: Conical with two standard parallels

East from Greenwich

CORSICA
CORSE
CORSE-DU-SUD
Ajaccio
G.d'Ajaccio
Bonifacio
Bouches de Bonifacio
Porto-Vecchio
Iles Cerbicales
Maddalena
La Maddalena
Caprera
Costa Smeralda
Golfo dell' Asinara
Asinara
Sássari
Alghero
Olbia
G.di Ólbia
Tavolara
Posada
Núoro
Golfo di Orosei
SARDEGNA
SARDINIA
Monti del Gennargentu
1834
Oristano
Golfo di Oristano
Iglésias
Carbonia
San Pietro
Sant' Antíoco
Cágliari
Golfo di Cágliari
C. Spartivento
C. Carbonara
TYRRHENIAN
SEA
3719
3589
ROMA
(Rome)
Vatican City
Tívoli
Latina
Terracina
Golfo di Gaeta
Ísole Ponziane
Ponza
Ventotene
Íschia
Ustica
PALERMO
Trápani
Érice
Ísole Égadi
Marettimo
Favignana
Marsala
Castelvetrano
Mazara del Vallo
Sciacca
Agrigento
SICI
Sicilian Channel
Iles de la Galite
C. Serrat
Bizerte
(Binzert)
Menzel-Bourguiba
Zembra
Golfe de Tunis
C. Bon
TUNIS
Halq el Oued
Mateur
Tabarka
El Kala
ALGERIA
Béja
Medjerda
Menzel-Temime
Kelibia
Nabeul
Hammamet
Zaghouan
Téboursouk
TUNISIA
Pantelleria
836
1319
MEDITE
ft m
9000 3000
6000 2000
4500 1500
3000 1000
1200 400
600 200
37
0 0
200 600
2000 6000
4000 12 000
m ft
Projection: Conical with two standard parallels
East from Greenwich

1 : 2 000 000

10   0   10   20   30   40   50 miles
10 0 10 20 30 40 50 60 70 80 km

BRUZZI

MOLISE

ADRIATIC

SEA

ALBANIA

Sangro

Trigno

Montenero

di Bisaccia

L. di Lésina

Rodi Gargánico

Vico del Gargano

Vieste

Drini

K. iMyzhllit

te Skénderbeut

TIRANA-

DURRËSI

Agnone

Castelmáuro

Serracapriola

Cagnano

Carpino

Testa del Gargano

Shëngjini

Lezha

Rubiku

Rrësheni

Trivento

Casacalenda

Bonefro

Santa Croce

di Magliano

S. Páolo di Civitate

Monte Gargano

S'SEVERO

MARCO

1056

Monte Sant'Angelo

S. Giovanni

Rotondo

Bishti i Palles

Ishmi

Krujä

Kavaja

(Tiranë)

Durrës

(Durazzo)

Campobasso

Volturara

Appula

Lucera

Cervaro

Zapponeta

Kalaja e Turrës

ISERNIA

Cercemaggiore

Riccia

FÓGGIA

Garapelli

G. di Manfredónia

Manfredónia

Shkumbini

ELBASANI

Frosolone

Piedimonte

d'Alife

S. Bartolomeo

in Galdo

Colle Sannita

Biccari

Tróia

Trinitápoli

Margherita di Savoia

Fieri

Semani

Q. Stalin

BERATI

Teano

Cáserta

MADDALONI

Benevento

Ariano

Irpino

Candela

Cerignola

S. Fernando

di Púglia

Barletta

Trani

Biscéglie

Molfetta

Giovinazzo

Levani

Seleníca

Berat

Afrógola

Nola

Avellino

Grottamináro

Orsara di Púglia

Bovino

Canosa

Andria

Corato

Terlizzi

Bitonto

BARI

Vlora (Vlonë)

Kanina

Oríkum

POLI

Vesuvio

1277

Boscatrécase

Sarno

Mirabella

Eclano

Calitri

Lavello

Ofanto

Minérvino

Murge

686

Spinazzola

Ruvo

di Púglia

Palo

del Colle

Palo di Bari

Grumo

Appula

Bitetto

Modúgno

Noicáttaro

Rutigliano

Mola di Bari

Conversano

Polignano a Mare

VLORA

2130

Dukati

Himari

Torre del Greco

Nocera

Inferiore

Campagna

Melfi

Rionero

in Vúlture

Palazzo S. Gérvasio

Gravina

di Púglia

Altamura

Gioia

del Colle

Acquaviva

delle Fonti

Casamássima

Sannicandro

Castellana

Grotte

Putignano

Alberobello

Fasano

Monópoli

SALERNO

Éboli

Batipáglia

Montella

Forenza

Acerenza

Irsina

Santéramo

Nocí

Martina

Franca

Locoroto ndo

Cisternino

Ostuni

Ceglie

Messápico

Céllino S. Marco

Carovigno

Bríndisi

C. d'Otranto

Kérkira

(Corfu)

Gastoúri

G. di Salerno

Sele

Campagna

POTENZA

Pisticci

Basento

Bernalda

Ginosa

Palagiano

Mássafra

GROTTÁGLIE

TÁRANTO

Sava

S. Pietro Vernótico

Mesagne

Latiano

Squinzano

Francavilla

Fontana

Manduria

LECCE

Copertino

Nardó

Galatina

Martano

Otranto

Áyios Matthaíos

Argyrádhes

Levkimmi

Agrópoli

Rocca d'Aspíde

Teggiano

Sala

Consilina

M. Sirino

1836

BASILICATA

Mársico

Nuovo

Corleto

Perticara

Stigliano

Ferrandina

Montalbano Iónico

S. Giórgio Iónico

Lizzano

Campi

Salentina

Maruggio

Leverano

Veglie

Móglie

Galátone

Parábita

Casarano

Poggiardo

Ugento

Tricase

Presícce

Gagliano del Capo

C. Santa Maria di Leuca

Othonoí

Erikoúsa

Karousádhes

Samothráki

Korakiánou

Liapádhes

Kassiópi

Kérkira

Castellabate

Punta Licosa

Póllica

Pisciotta

Agri

S. Arcángelo

Senise

Tursi

Rotondella

Sinni

Golfo di

Táranto

Rá15cale

Gallípoli

C. Palinuro

Camerota

1225

Sopri

Lagónegro

2005

Lauria

Latrónico

Murate

Mormanno

Monte Pollino

2271

Amendolaro

Trebisacce

G. di

Policastro

Scalea

Laos

Castrovíllari

Cassano

Albo

Crati

Oríolo

Scaled

Morano

Cálabro

Verbícaro

Roggiano

Gravina

Spezzano

Albanese

S. Demétrio

Corone

Corigliano

Cálabro

C. Trionto

Rossano

Belvedere

Maríttimo

Fagnano

Castello

S. Marco

Argen

Bisignano

Acri

Longobucco

Cirò

Cetraro

Montalto

Uffugo

Fuscaldo

Páola

S. Lúcido

Luzzi

CALABRIA

S. Giovanni

in Fiore

Strôngoli

Pta. dell'Alice

Marina di Cirò

Fiumefreddo Brúzio

COSENZA

Aprigliano

La Sila

1929

Neto

Petilia

Policastro

Amantea

Rogliano

Cotroíei

Mésoraca

Crotone

C. delle Colonne

Nocera Terinese

Décollatura

Nicastro

Gízzeria

Tiriolo

Gimigliano

Sersale

Cutro

Ísola di Capo Rizzuto

C. Rizzuto

Sambiase

Maída

Bôrgia

Girifalco

CATANZARO

Tacina

IONIAN

Strómboli

926

Isole Eólie o Lípari (Æolian Is.)

Golfo di

Sant'Eufémia

Pizzo

S. Onofrio

Filadélfia

Golfo di Squillace

Chiaravalle

Centrale

3065

Filicudi

Malfa

Salina

Panarea

Tropea

Capo Vaticano

Vibo Valéntia

1423

Mileto

Serra S. Bruno

Guardavalle

Alicudi

962

Lípari

602

Lípari

Nicótera

Laureana

di Borrello

Capo Stilo

499

Vulcano

G. di Gióia

Rosarno

Gióia Táuro

Taurianova

Polistena

Mámmola

Coulónia

S. Ágata

di Militello

Sant'Agata

d'Orlando

C. Calavà

Pirdino

Pozzo di Gotto

Milazzo

Barcellona

S. Giovanni

Palmi

Bagnara

Oppido

Mamertino

Cittanova

Roccella Iónica

Gioiosa Iónica

Siderno Marina

San Fratello

Naso

Patti

Castroreale

Mi. Peloritani

1279

Mi. Peloro Cálabro

Aspromonte

1956

Locri

Bovalino

Marina

Santo Stefano

di Camastra

Mistretta

Tortorici

Santa Teresa

di Riva

Str. di Messina

MESSINA

Villa S. Gio.

RÉGGIO

di Cálabria

Péllaro

Capo dell'Armi

Mélito

di Porto Salvo

Bova Marina

C. Spartivento

Monti Nébrodi

1847

Cesarò

Rándazzo

Taormina

Nicosía

Tróina

Capizzi

Bronte

Etna

3340

Giarre

Riposto

SEA

Pétralia

Alimena

Agira

Regalbuto

Adrano

Biancavilla

Belpasso

Paternó

Acireale

SIGILIA

Enna

916

Valguarnera Caropepe

Centúripe

Misterbianco

CATÁNIA

Golfo di

Catánia

Pietraperzia

Aidone

Ramacca

Palagonía

Scordia

Leontini

Simeto

Bartafranca

Piazza

Armerina

Mazzarino

Militello

in Val di Catánia

Carlentini

Augusta

Caltagirone

Grammichele

Vizzini

Francofonte

Sortino

Monti Iblei

986

Siracusa

Butera

Niscemi

Chiaramonte

Gulfi

Floridia

Palazzolo

Acréide

Canicattini

Gela

Vittória

Cómiso

RAGUSA

Módica

Noto

Avola

G. di

Noto

Santa Croce

Camerina

Scicli

Rosolini

Íspica

Pachino

C. Passero

Pozzallo

Channel

RANEAN SEA

4116

COPYRIGHT, GEORGE PHILIP & SON, LTD.

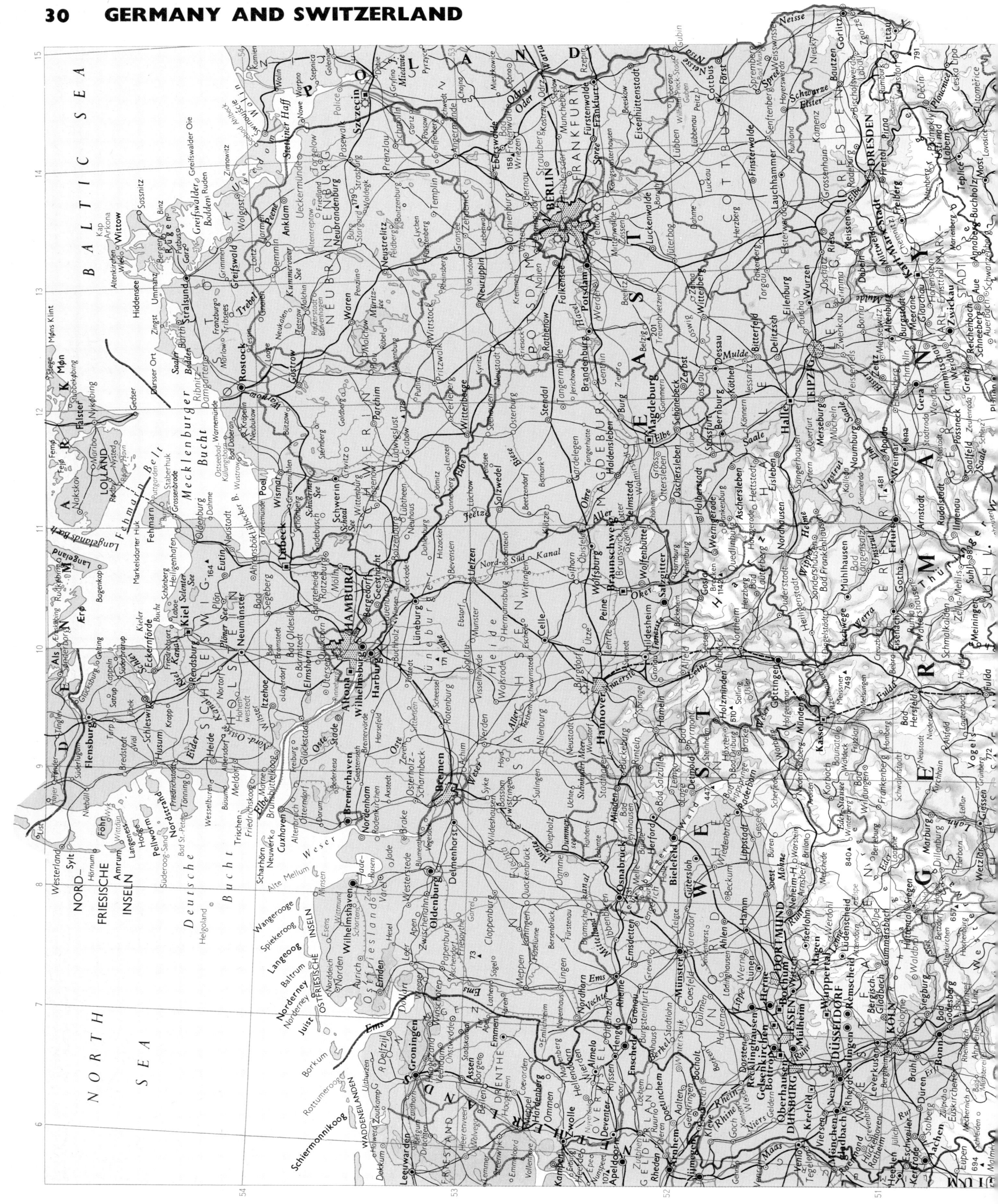
BALTIC SEA
NORTH SEA
Mecklenburger Bucht
Deutsche Bucht
NORD-FRIESISCHE INSELN
OSTFRIESISCHE INSELN
BERLIN
HAMBURG
Bremen
Hannover
DRESDEN
LEIPZIG
Magdeburg
Rostock
Kiel
Lübeck
Szczecin
Groningen
KÖLN
DÜSSELDORF
DORTMUND
ESSEN

1 : 2 000 000

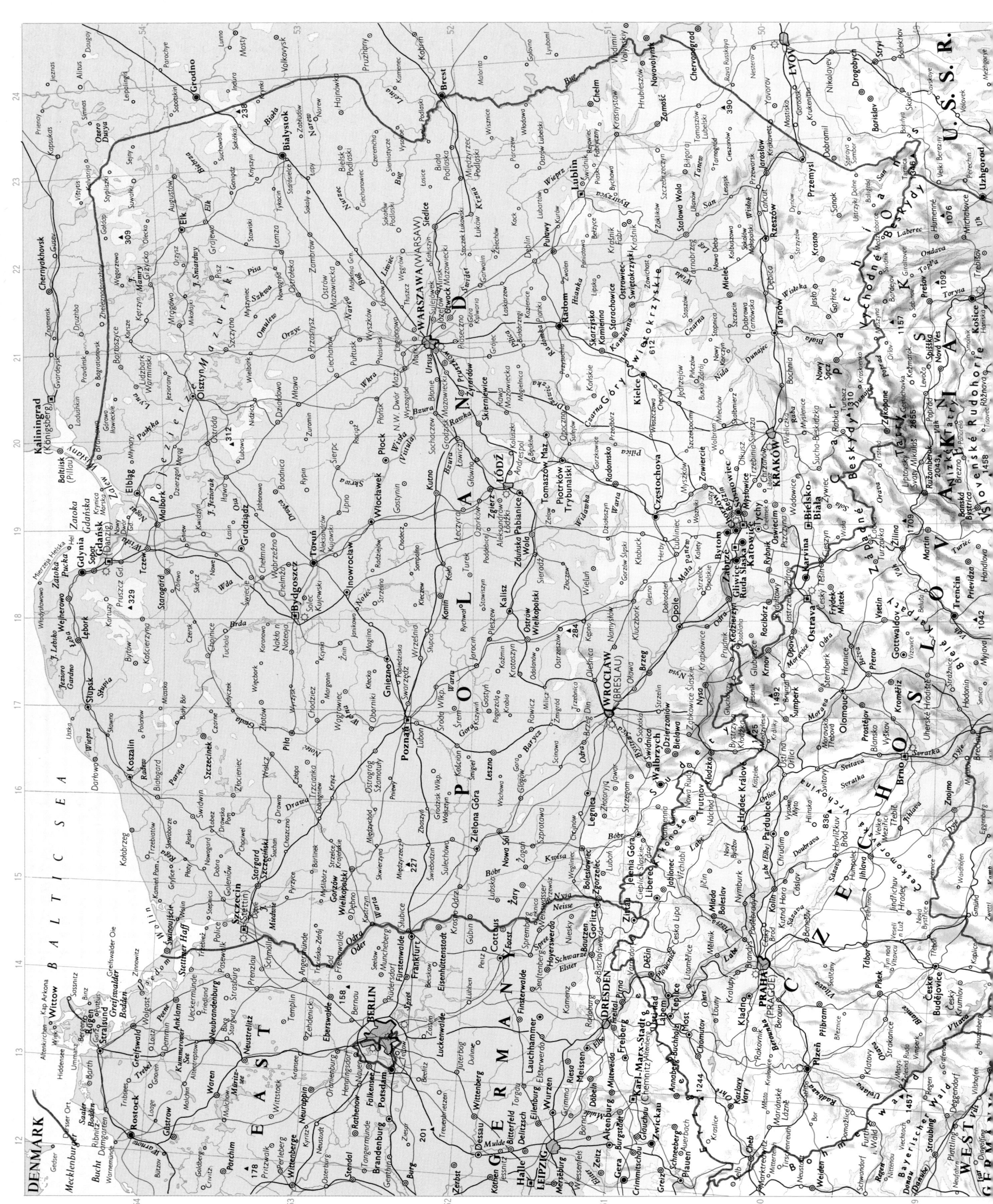
DENMARK
BALTIC SEA
EAST
GERMANY
POLAND
CZECHOSLOVAKIA
U.S.S.R.
WEST GERMANY
Kaliningrad (Königsberg)
Gdańsk (Danzig)
Gdynia
Szczecin (Stettin)
Rostock
Stralsund
Grodno
Białystok
Brest
LVOV
WARSZAWA (WARSAW)
ŁÓDŹ
Poznań
Bydgoszcz
Toruń
WROCŁAW (BRESLAU)
KRAKÓW
Katowice
Lublin
BERLIN
Potsdam
Frankfurt
LEIPZIG
DRESDEN
Karl-Marx-Stadt (Chemnitz)
PRAHA (PRAGUE)
Brno
Ostrava
Plzeň
Košice
Uzhgorod

1 : 2 800 000

10   0   100 miles

10   0   10 20 30 40 50   100   150 km

COPYRIGHT GEORGE PHILIP & SON, LTD

East from Greenwich

Projection: Conical with two standard parallels

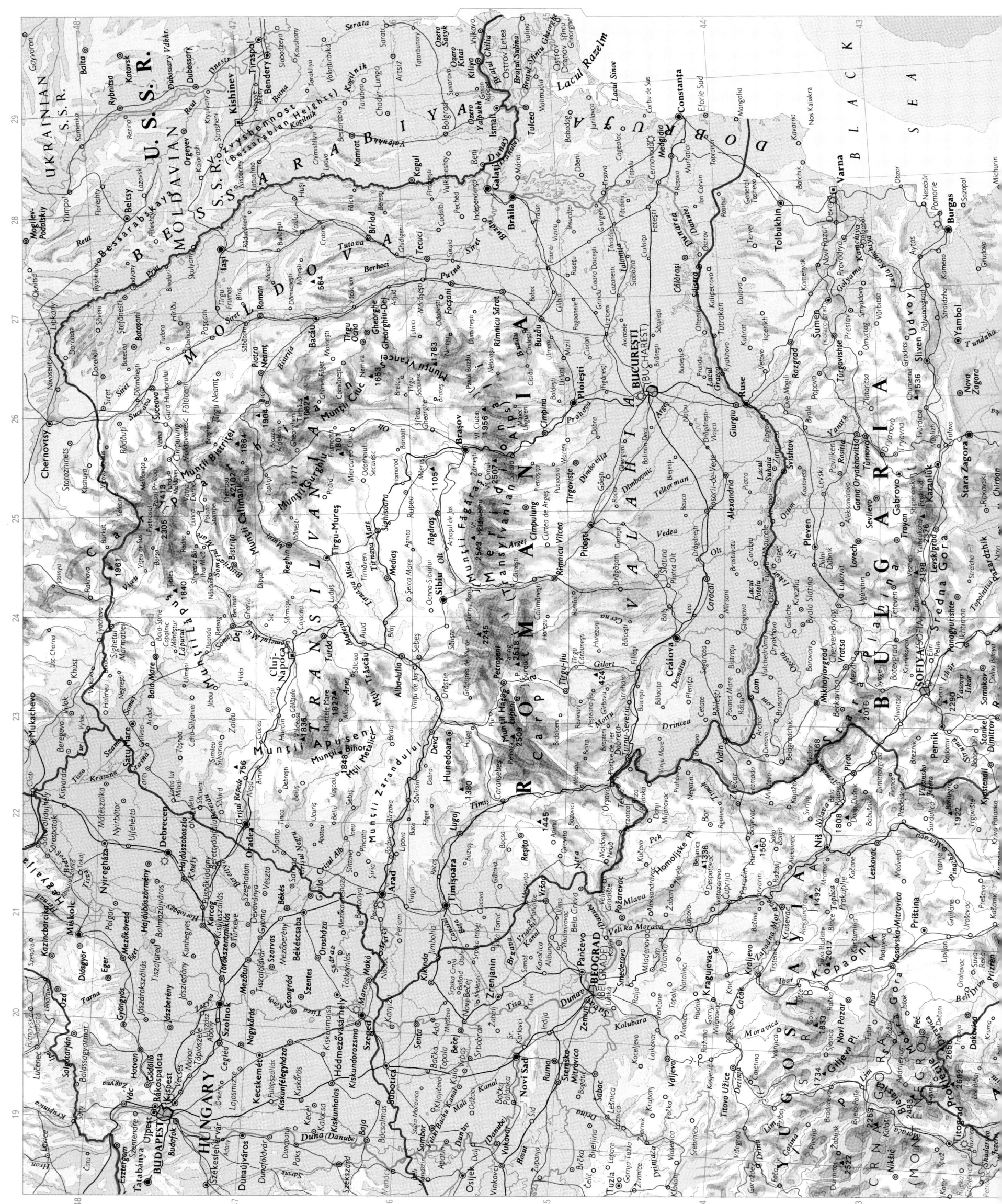
BLACK SEA
U.S.S.R.
UKRAINIAN S.S.R.
MOLDAVIAN S.S.R.
BESSARABIYA
MOLDOVA
TRANSILVANIA
ROMANIA
VALAHIA
DOBRUJA
BULGARIA
HUNGARY
YUGOSLAVIA
CRNA GORA (MONTENEGRO)
Carpaţi Meridionali (Transylvanian Alps)
BUCUREŞTI (BUCHAREST)
BEOGRAD (BELGRADE)
SOFIYA (SOFIA)
BUDAPEST
Kishinev
Constanţa
Varna
Burgas
Cluj-Napoca
Braşov
Iaşi
Galaţi
Brăila
Ploieşti
Craiova
Timişoara
Debrecen
Szeged
Novi Sad
Ruse
Dunărea (Danube)
Lacul Razelm

1 : 2 800 000

10 0 10 20 30 40 50 ___ 100 miles
10 0 10 20 30 40 50 ___ 100 ___ 150 km

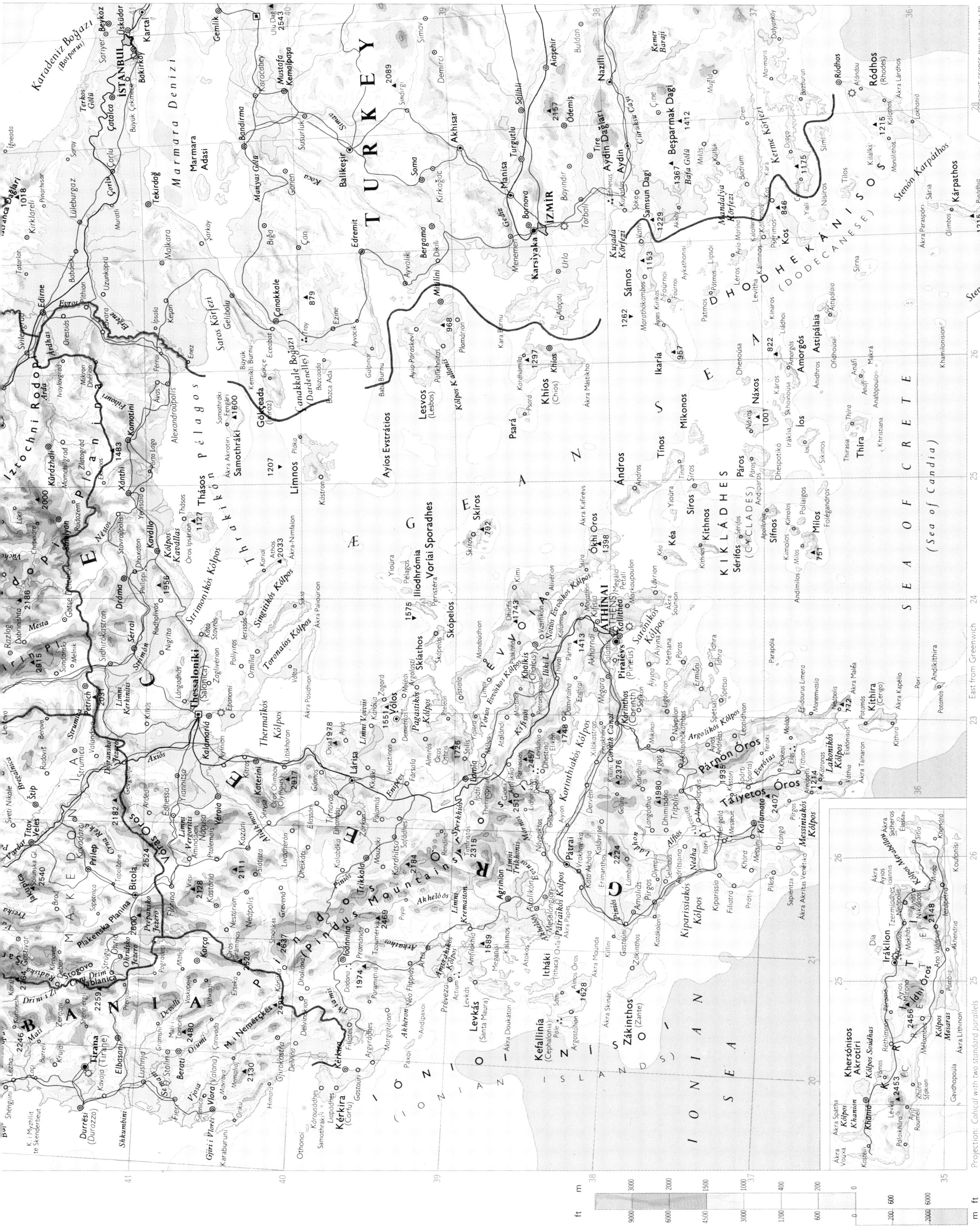

COPYRIGHT GEORGE PHILIP & SON LTD

TURKEY

Karadeniz Boğazı (Bosporus)
İSTANBUL
Üsküdar
Beykoz
Kartal
Sarıyer
Bebek
Çatalca
Terkos Gölü

Marmara Denizi
Marmara Adası
Tekirdağ
Çorlu
Kırklareli
Lüleburgaz

Edirne
Keşan
Gelibolu
Saros Körfezi
Çanakkale
Çanakkale Boğazı (Dardanelles)
Gökçeada (İmroz)
Samothráki
Limnos
Ayios Evstrátios

Bandırma
Biga
Çan
Edremit
Ayvalık
Bergama
Dikili
Soma
Balıkesir
Akhisar
Manisa
Bornova
İZMIR
Karşıyaka
Menemen

Lesvos (Lesbos)
Mitilíni
Psará
Khíos (Chios)

Turgutlu
Salihli
Ödemiş
Aydın Dağları
Aydın
Nazilli
Tire

Sámos
İkaría
Samsun Dağı

DHODHEKÁNISOS (DODECANESE)
Ródhos (Rhodes)
Kos
Pátmos
Léros
Kálimnos
Astipálaia
Amorgós
Kárpathos
Kásos

AEGEAN SEA

Skíros
Vóriai Sporádhes
Skópelos
Skíathos

Évvoia
Khalkís
ATHÍNAI
ATHENS
Piraiévs (Piraeus)
Saronikós Kólpos

KIKLÁDHES (CYCLADES)
Ándros
Tínos
Míkonos
Náxos
Páros
Íos
Síros
Kéa
Kíthnos
Sérifos
Sífnos
Mílos
Thíra
Folégandros

SEA OF CRETE (Sea of Candia)

Thessaloníki (Salonika)
Kateríni
Lárisa
Vólos
Pagasitikós Kólpos
Thermaïkós Kólpos

Kozáni
Tríkkala
Trnovos
Kardhítsa
Lamía

ÍPIROS
Ioánnina
Árta
Préveza

PÍNDOS MOUNTAINS (Pindus Mountains)

Agrínion
Mesolóngion
Patraï
Pátraikós Kólpos
Korinthiakós Kólpos
Kórinthos (Corinth)
Corinth Canal

Pelopónnisos
Trípolis
Kalámai
Taíyetos Óros
Párnon Óros
Lakonikós Kólpos
Messiniakós Kólpos
Argolikós Kólpos
Náfplion

Levkás (Santa Maura)
Kefallínia (Cephalonia)
Zákinthos (Zante)
Itháki (Ithaca)

IONIAN ISLANDS
IONIAN SEA

Kérkira (Corfu)
Kérkira

ALBANIA
Tiranë (Tirana)
Durrës (Durazzo)
Elbasan
Vlorë (Valona)
Berat
Korçë

MAKEDONIJA
Bitola
Veles
Prilep
Štip
Strumica

Kavála
Dráma
Sérrai
Thásos
Thrakikón Pélagos
Xánthi
Komotiní
Alexandroúpolis

East from Greenwich

Iráklion
SEA OF CRETE
Khersónisos Akrotíri
Khaniá

Projection: Conical with two standard parallels

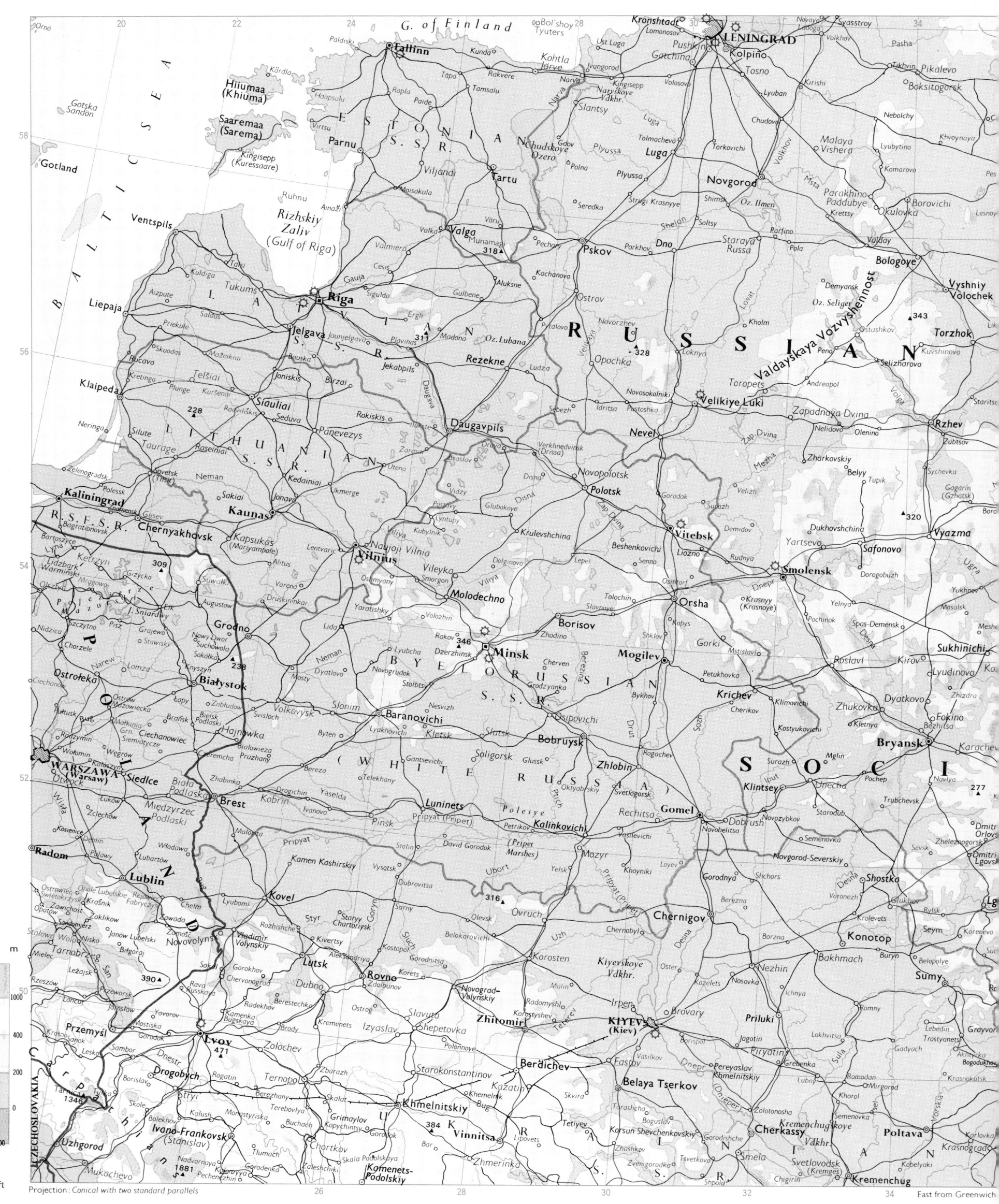
G. of Finland
BALTIC SEA
Gotland
Gotska Sandön
Hiiumaa (Khiuma)
Saaremaa (Sarema)
Kingisepp (Kuressaare)
Ruhnu
Rizhskiy Zaliv (Gulf of Riga)
Tallinn
Paldiski
Kunda
Rakvere
Kohtla Järve
Narva
Tartu
Viljandi
Parnu
Valga
Munamägi 318
ESTONIAN S.S.R.
Ventspils
Liepaja
Riga
Jelgava
Daugavpils
Rezekne
Madona
Jekabpils
LATVIAN S.S.R.
Klaipeda
Siauliai
Panevezys
Kaunas
Vilnius
LITHUANIAN S.S.R.
Kaliningrad
Sovetsk (Tilsit)
Chernyakhovsk
R.S.F.S.R.
Neman
Grodno
Lida
Molodechno
Minsk
Borisov
Baranovichi
Slonim
Bobruysk
Mogilev
Orsha
Vitebsk
Polotsk
Novopolotsk
Gomel
Mozyr
Pinsk
Brest
Luninets
Kalinkovichi
Rechitsa
BYELORUSSIAN S.S.R. (WHITE RUSSIA)
Pripyat (Pripet)
Polesye (Pripet Marshes)
Dnepr
Dvina
Białystok
Ostrołęka
WARSZAWA (Warsaw)
Siedlce
Biała Podlaska
Lublin
Radom
Chełm
Przemyśl
POLAND
CZECHOSLOVAKIA
Carpathians
Uzhgorod
Mukachevo
Ivano-Frankovsk (Stanislav)
Drogobych
Lvov
Ternopol
Khmelnitskiy
Vinnitsa
Rovno
Lutsk
Kovel
Zhitomir
Berdichev
KIYEV (Kiev)
Belaya Tserkov
Cherkassy
Kremenchug
Kremenchugskoye Vdkhr.
Poltava
Chernigov
Konotop
Sumy
Priluki
Kiyevskoye Vdkhr.
Nezhin
Korosten
Ovruch
Shostka
UKRAINIAN S.S.R.
LENINGRAD
Kronshtadt
Pushkin
Gatchina
Kolpino
Tosno
Luga
Novgorod
Oz. Ilmen
Pskov
Chudskoye Ozero
Staraya Russa
Dno
Ostrov
Opochka
Velikiye Luki
Nevel
Toropets
Valdayskaya Vozvyshennost
Bologoye
Vyshniy Volochek
Torzhok
Rzhev
Vyazma
Smolensk
Safonovo
Yartsevo
Roslavl
Bryansk
Klintsy
Sukhinichi
Tikhvin
Pikalevo
Borovichi
Okulovka
Valday
Ostashkov
Oz. Seliger
RUSSIAN SOVIET
Projection: Conical with two standard parallels
East from Greenwich
ft m
3000 1000
1200 400
600 200
0 0
200 600
m ft

1 : 4 000 000

50   0   50   100 miles

50   0   50   100   150 km

S O V I E T   F E D E R A T I V E   ...   L I S T   R E P U B L I C

Oz. Beloye
Belozersk
Kirillov
Ozero Kubenskoye
Sokol
Sukhona
Dyakovskaya
Totma
293
Nikolsk
Murashi
Nagorsk
Vyatka
Peskovka
Kama
Zalazna
329
Babayevo
Cherepovets
Chebsara
Vologda
Suda
Ustyuzhna
Gryazovets
Vokhtoga
Igoshevo
Krasnoye
Chernovskoye
Khalturin
Belaya Kholunitsa
Chernaya Kholunitsa
Omutninsk
Vesyegonsk
Vokhma
Vokhma
Kirov
Novovyatsk
Kirovo-Chepetsk
Zuyevka
Falenki
Glazov
58
Bezhetsk
Rybinskoye Vodokhranilishche
Krasnyy Kholm
Breytovo
Danilov
Lyubim
Buy
Antropovo
Manturovo
Sharya
Leninskoye
Kotelnich
Kumeny
Uni
Medveditsa
Sonkovo
Andropov (Rybinsk)
Volga
Tutayev
Kostromskoye Vdkhr.
Makaryev
Unzha
Shakhunya
Uren
Yaransk
Sovetsk
Urzhum
Malmyzh
Mozhga
UDMURT A.S.S.R.
Uva
Goritsy
Kashin
Kalyazin
293
Kostroma
Privolzhsk
Kineshma
Gorkovskoye Vdkhr.
Yuryevets
Vetluzhskiy
Krasnyye Baki
Tursha
Yoshkar Ola
Shurma
Kilmez
56
Kalinin
Kimry
Dubna
Pereslavl Zalesskiy
Yaroslavl
Rostov
Nerekhta
Volgorechensk
Zavolzhsk
Vichuga
Rodniki
Komsomolsk
Ivanovo
Shuya
Chkalovsk
Semenov
Gorodets
Pravdinsk
Borisoglebskiy
Voskresenskoye
MARI A.S.S.R.
Kozmodemyansk
Marlinskiy Posad
Cheboksary
Krasnogorskiy
Zelenodolsk
Kazan
TATAR A.S.S.R.
Mamadysh
Konakovo
Novo-Zavidovskiy
Krasnozavodsk
Aleksandrov
Yuryev-Polskiy
Suzdal
Teykovo
Kokhma
Gorbatov
Dzerzhinsk
GORKIY (Gorki)
Kstovo
Leninskaya Sloboda
Lyskovo
Yadrin
Tsivilsk
CHUVASH A.S.S.R.
Kanash
Kuybyshev
Bilyarsk
Chistopol
Klin
Solnechnogorsk
Dmitrov
Zagorsk
Pushkino
Elektrogorsk
Pokrov
Vladimir
Sobinka
Vyazniki
Gorokhovets
Volodarsk
Bogorodsk
Pavlovo
Sudogda
Krasnaya Gorbatka
Pyana
Sergach
Shumerlya
A.S.S.R.
Kamskoye Ustye
Tetyushi
Zelenograd
Mytishchi
Balashikha
Noginsk
Orekhovo-Zuyevo
Pavlovskiy-Posad
Gus-Khrustalnyy
Murom
Vyksa
Kulebaki
Arzamas
235
Gagino
Lukoyanov
Poretskoye
Kirya
Buinsk
Nurlat
MOSKVA (Moscow)
Lyubertsy
Elektrostal
Shatura
Kurlovskiy
Melenki
Oz. Velikoye
Tuma
Yelatma
Sarova
Pervomaysk
Pochinki
Alatyr
Ardatov
Alatyr
Kuybyshevskoye Vdkhr.
Odintsovo
Ramenskoye
Bronnitsy
Kurovskoye
Yegoryevsk
Voskresensk
Spas-Klepiki
Kasimov
Moksha
Temnikov
Romodanovo
Sura
Karsun
Ulyanovsk
Dimitrovgrad
Sernovodsk
54
Mozhaysk
Nara
Naro-Fominsk
Podolsk
Stolbovaya
Mikhnevo
Kolomna
Rybnoye
Solotcha
Kadom
Krasnoslobodsk
MORDOVIAN A.S.S.R.
Saransk
Cherdakly
Borovsk
Obninsk
Maloyaroslavets
Serpukhov
Stupino
Kashira
Zarаysk
Osyory
Oka
Spassk-Ryazanskiy
Shilovo
Sasovo
Pervomaysk
Ruzayevka
Kobylkino
Inza
Novodevichye
Sengiley
Togliatti
375
Zhigulevsk
Kinel
KUYBYSHEV
Novokuybyshevsk
Tarussa
Kaluga
Aleksin
Yesnogorsk (Laptevo)
Venev
Mikhaylov
Ryazhsk
Sapozhok
Shatsk
Bednodemyanovsk
Nizhniy Lomov
Lunino
Barysh
Oktyabrsk
Syzran
Chapayevsk
Privolzhye
Suvorov
Tula
Novotulskiy
Novomoskovsk
Kimovsk
Donskoy
Skopin
Pavelets
Ukholovo
Morshansk
Moksha
Gorodishche
Sura
Kuznetsk
351
Kashpirovka
Balshaya Glushitsa
Shchekino
Dedilovo
Uzlovaya
Bogoroditsk
Lev Tolstoy
Zametchino
Penza
Sursk
Serdobsk
Khvalynsk
Krasnyy Yar
Odoyevo
Krapivna
Tovarkovskiy
Plavsk
Dankov
Chaplygin
Chaplin
Kamenka
Belinskiy (Chembar)
Petrovsk
Bazarny Karabulak
Khvatovka
Volsk
Balakovo
Pugachev
Pestravka
Bolkhov
293
Mtsensk
Yefremov
Lebedyan
Gryazi
Rasskazovo
Kotovsk
Inzhavino
Rtishchevo
Petrovsk
Marks
Orel
Novosil
Verkhovye
Yelets
Lipetsk
Michurinsk
Tambov
Serdobsk
Balanda
Saratov
Engels
Yershov
Kamenka
52
Livny
Zadonsk
Usman
Mordovo
Uvarovo
Turki
Arkadak
Atkarsk
Privolzhskiy
Pushkino
Orlov Gay
Sosna
Ramon
Zherdevka
Muchkapskiy
Voronezh
Gribanovskiy
Arkhangelskoye
Anna
Balashov
Samoylovka
Volgogradskoye Vdkhr.
Krasnyy Kut
Gornyy
Staryy Oskol
276
Gubkin
Korotoyak
Ostrogozhsk
Georgiu-Dezh
239
Buturlinovka
Uryupinsk
Buzuluk
Kukvize
Novoannenskiy
Panfilovo
Krasnoarmeysk
Kamenskiy
Piterka
Novouzensk
Belgorod
Shebekino
Novyy Oskol
Alekseyevka
Oskol
Volokonovka
Valuyki
Pavlovsk
Kalach
Khrenovoye
Talovaya
Novokhopersk
Yelan
Zhirnovsk
Krasnyy Yar
Rovnoye
Aleksandrov Gay
Kharkov
Kupyansk
Volchansk
Pechenezhskoye Vdkhr.
Kupyansk-Uzlovoi
Yevstratovskiy
Rossosh
Kantemirovka
Boguchar
Ust Buzulukskaya
Kumylzhenskaya
Mikhaylovka
Nikolayevsk
Kaztalovka
Mal. Uzen
50
Sev. Donets
Dergachi
Balakleya
Starobelsk
Krasnyyoskolskoye Vdkhr.
Meshkovskaya
Kazanskaya
Veshenskaya
Serafimovich
Ilovlya
Bykovo
Dubovka
Kapustin Yar
Urda
KAZAKH S.S.R.
Rubezhnoye
Millerovo
Chertkovo
Kamenskiy
Kletskiy
Iouliya
Prichalnaya
Volzhskiy
Elton
Volgograd (Stalingrad)
Krasnoslobodsk
Leninsk
48   COPYRIGHT GEORGE PHILIP & SON LTD

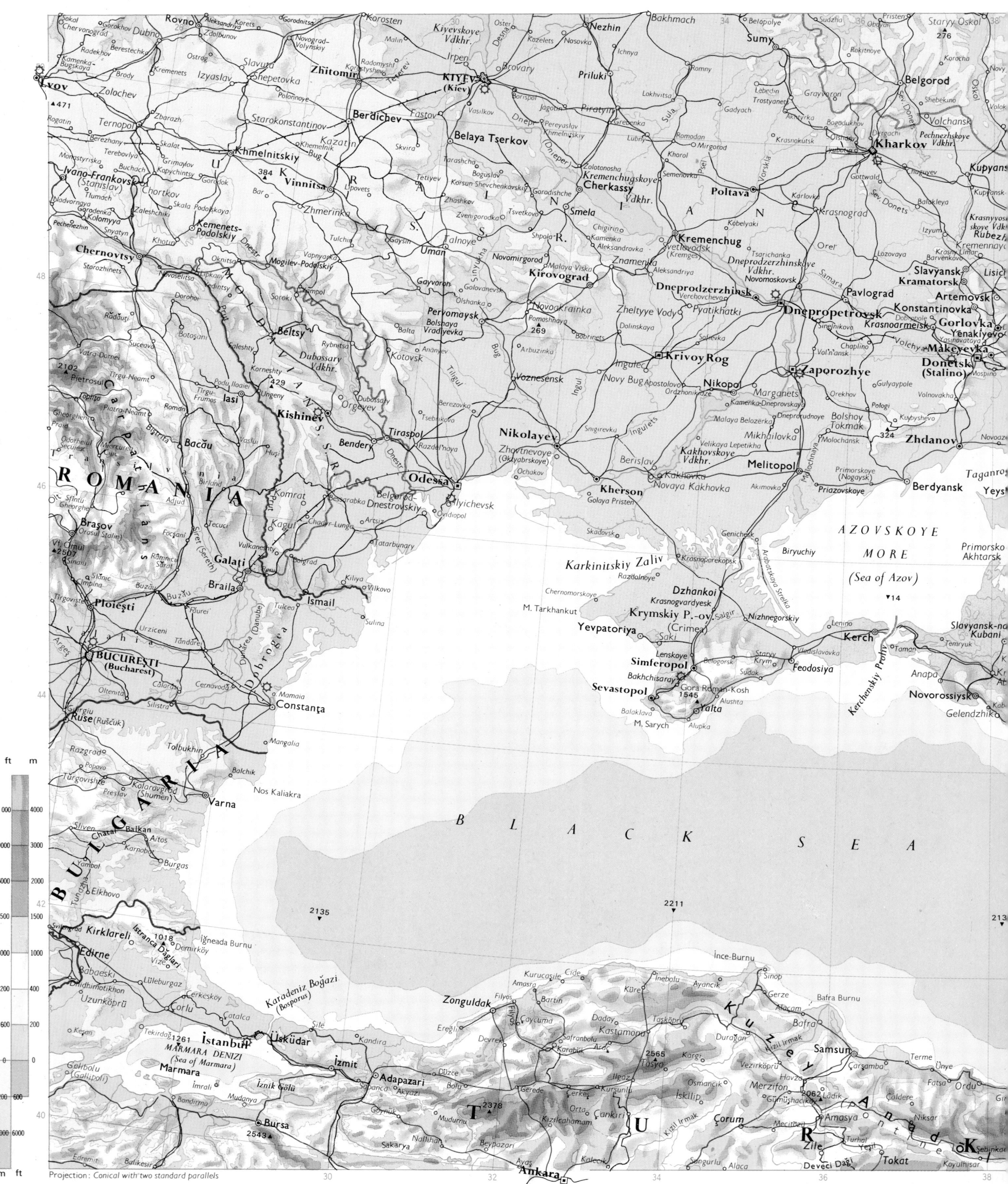

BLACK SEA

AZOVSKOYE MORE (Sea of Azov)

ROMANIA

BULGARIA

MARMARA DENIZI (Sea of Marmara)

Projection: Conical with two standard parallels

1 : 4 000 000

50   0   50   100 miles

50   0   50   100   150 km

Korotoyak · Yelan-Kolenovskiy · Povorino · Peski · Samoylovka · Krasnoarmeysk · Krasnyy Kut
Don · Khrenovoye · Talovaya · Novokhopersk · Zhirnovsk · Kamenka
Georgiu-Dezh · Buturlinovka · 239 · Uryupinsk · Buzuluk · Yelan · Krasnyy Yar · Rovnoye · Novouzensk
Ostrogozhsk · Kamenka · Novoannenskiy · Panfilovo · 358 · Vozvyshennost · Piterka · Oz. Chalkar · Chalkar
Alekseyevka · Pavlovsk · Khoper · Kukvidze · Medveditsa · Danilovka · Volgogradskoye · Aleksandrov Gay · Dzhambeyty
Yevstratovskiy · Rossosh · Boguchar · Kazanskaya · Mikhaylovka · Kamyshin · Nikolayevsk · Bykovo · Novouzensk · Karsha
K A Z A K H · S.S.R. · Mergenevskiy

Starobelsk · Meelovoye · Chertkovo · Don · Kletskaya · Volzhskaya · Dubovka · Pallasovka · Kaztalovka · Bazartobe
Severodonetsk · Millerovo · Veshenskaya · Serafimovich · Ilovlya · Volzhskiy · Elton · Inderborskiy
Kirovsk · Stakhanov · Glubokiy · Kletskiy · Volgograd (Stalingrad) · Leninsk · Urda · Zelenyy · Topol
Bryanka · Voroshilovgrad (Lugansk) · Kamensk-Shakhtinskiy · Kalach na Donu · Krasnoslobodsk · Kapustin Yar · Vladimirovka · Makhambet (Yamankhalinka)
Kommunarsk · Krasnodon · Lenin · Morozovsk · Chernyshkovskiy · Krasnoarmeysk · Volga · Akhtubinsk (Petropavlovsky) · Verkhniy Baskunchak · Novobogatinskoye
Thorez · Krasnyy Luch · Gukovo · Belaya Kalitva · Krasnodonetskaya · Tsimlyanskoye Vdkhr. · Shungay · P r i k a s p i y s k a y a
Novoshakhtinsk · Shakhty · Ust-Donetsk · Tsimlyansk · Kotelnikovo · Yenatayevka · N i z m e n n o s t · Guryev
Matveyev Kurgan · Novocherkassk · Konstantinovskiy · Dubovskoye · Obilnoye · Kopanovka · Novobogatinskoye · –28
Tuzlov · Rostov · Bolshaya Martynovka · Zimovniki · Zavetnoye · K A L M Y K · Kamyzyak · Chushkino
Taganrog · Batausk · Veselovskoye Vdkhr. · Manych · Kuberle · A.S.S.R. · Krasnyy Yar · Guryev
Azov · Zernograd · Mechetinskaya · Salsk · Oz. Manych-Gudilo · Elista (Stepnoi) · Astrakhan · Krasnoye
Port Katon · Proletarskaya · Remontnoye · Priyutnoye · Krasnoye · Mumra · Kultay
Staro-minskaya · Kushchevskaya · Yegorlykskaya · Gigant · Leninsk · Divnoye · Liman · O. Kulaly · Mangyshlakskiy Zaliv
Kanevskaya · Belaya Glina · Krasnogvardeyskoye · Kalaus · Arzgir · Kuma · Beloye Ozero · M. Tyub Karagan · P-ov
Timashevsk · Tikhoretsk · Kropotkin · Novoaleksandrovskaya · Svetlograd (Petrovskoye) · Blagodarnoye · Kaspiyskiy · Fort Shevchenko · Mangyshlak
Korenovsk · Izobil'nyy · Budennovsk · Staryy Biryuzyak · Shevchenko
Ust-Labinsk · Krasnodar · Armavir · Stavropol · 831 · Vladimirovka · Tyuleniy · Bryanskoye · C A S P I A N
Khadyzhensk · Maykop · Kurganinsk (Kurgannaya) · Nevinnomyssk · Zelenokumsk · Vorontsovo-Aleksandrovskoye · Aleksandriyskaya
Neftegorsk · Apsheronsk · Labinsk · Kuban · Kursavka · Cherkessk · Mineralnyye Vody · Lopatin · S E A
Jubga · Khadyzhensk · Dakhovskaya · Georgievsk · Kizlyar · Shevchenko
Tapse · B o l · s h · o y · Yessentuki · Pyatigorsk · Prokhladnyy · Mozdok · CHECHENO- · Sulak · 800
Sochi · Matsesta · Krasnaya Polyana · Kislovodsk · Karachayevsk · Nalchik · Mayskiy · Nartkala · INGUSH · Gudermes · Kizil Yurt · Makhachkala
Adler · K a v k a z · Teberda · Tyrnyauz · Elbrus 5633 · KABARDINO- · Malgobek · Groznyy · A.S.S.R. · Khasavyurt · Kaspiysk
Gagra · ABKHAZ · Gudata · 5203 · BALKAR A.S.S.R. · Beslan · Ordzhonikidze · Sagaysan · Kumtorkala · Buynaksk · Derbent
Novyy Afon · A.S.S.R. · Tkvarcheli · Kodori · Kartal · 5047 · Tebulos 4492 · Avtari · Khunzakh · Novokayakent · Akusha
Sukhumi · Dzhvari · Zugdidi · Rioni · Oni · Sadon · Kvareli · Agvali · Kokhib · Akhty · Akusha · Dagestanskiye Ogni
Ochamchire · Gali · Sachkhere · Tskhinvali (Staliniri) · Dushetti · Telavi · Tlyarata · Madzhalis · Derbent
Anaklia · Kutaisi · Chiatura · Zestafoni · Khashuri · Gori · Mtskheta · Gurdzhaani · Kubachi · Kasumkent
Poti · Mikha-Tskhakaya · Samtredia · Kaspi · Tbilisi · Signakhi · Alazan · Sheki (Nukha) · Akhty · Khachmas
Kobuleti · Makharadze · G E O R G I A · Borzhomi · Rustavi · Citeli Ckaro · Mirzaani · Zakatala · Bazar Dyuzi 4466 · Kuba · Mikhaylovka
Batumi · ADZHAR · S.S.R. · Khulo · Akhaltsikhe · Marneuli · Shaumyani · Iori · Kutkashen · Baba dag 3629 · Divichi
A.S.S.R. · Vale · Akhalkalaki · Khrami · Mingechaurskoye Vdkhr. · Siazan
Hopa · Pazar · Borcka · Ardahan · Alaverdi · Tauz · Kura · Agdash · Shemakha · Sumgait
Görele · Akcaabat · Artvin · Ardanuc · Cildir · 3192 · Kirovakan · Dzhanlar · Shemokha · Surakhany
Tirebolu · Trabzon · Surmene · Rize · Kackar 3437 · Olur · Sarikamis · Dilizhan · Kirovabad · Z E R B A I J A N · Baku
Harsit · Kaz · E g l a r i · Narman · Selim · Artik · Charentsavan · Ozero Sevan · Mir-Bashir · Berda · Kazi Magomed
Gumusane · 2063 · Oltu · 3192 · Kars · Digor · Aragats 4090 · A R M E N I A N · Dashkesan · Terter · Mashtaga
Bayburt · M o u n t a i n s · Tortum · Kagizman · Echmiadzin · Yerevan · S.S.R. · Kamo · Sabirabad · Imishly · Karachala
Alucra · Aras · Narman · Martuni · Agdzhabedi · M. Byandovan

COPYRIGHT. GEORGE PHILIP & SON LTD.

R.S.F.S.R.
1. Daghestan A.S.S.R.
2. Kabardino–Balkar A.S.S.R.
3. Mari A.S.S.R.
4. Mordovian A.S.S.R.
5. North Ossetian A.S.S.R.
6. Tatar A.S.S.R.
7. Udmurt A.S.S.R.
8. Chuvash A.S.S.R.
9. Checheno–Ingush A.S.S.R.
AZERBAIJAN
10. Nakhichevan A.S.S.R.
GEORGIA
11. Abkhaz A.S.S.R.
12. Adzhar A.S.S.R.

Projection: Conical Orthomorphic with two standard parallels   East from Greenwich

1 : 16 000 000

100   0   100   200   300   400   500 miles
100   0   200   400   600   800 km

OCEAN

Mys Dezhneva
(East C.)

St. Lawrence I.
(U.S.A.)

Severnaya
Zemlya

Ostrov
Komsomolets

Ostrov
Oktyabrskoy
Revolyutsii

Ostrov
Bolshevik

Laptev Sea

East Siberian Sea

Chukotskoye
More

Chukotskiy Khrebet

Ostrov Vrangelya

Koryakskiy Khrebet

Bering
Sea

Poluostrov
Taymyr

Ostrova Delong

Novosibirskiye Ostrova

Ostrova
Medvezhi

Sredinnyy

Poluostrov
Kamchatka

Nordvik

Tiksi

Verkhoyansk

Khrebet Cherskogo

Srednekolymsk

Okhotsko Kolymskoye

Petropavlovsk-
Kamchatskiy

Y A K U T

Verkhoyanskiy Khrebet

A. S. S. R.

Yakutsk

Magadan

Sea of
Okhotsk

Vilyuysk

Lena R.

Aldan

Okhotsk

Sakhalin

Olekminsk

Stanovoy Khrebet

Nikolayevsk-
na-Am.

Sovetskaya Gavan

Yuzhno-Sakhalinsk

Kirensk

Komsomolsk

Khrebet Sikhote Alin

Bratsk

Krasnoyarsk

Chita

Ulan Ude

Blagoveshchensk

Birobidzhan

Khabarovsk

Hokkaido

Sapporo

Hakodate

Irkutsk

B U R Y A T
A. S. S. R.

Amur

Harbin

Jiamusi

Ussuriysk

Vladivostok

Nakhodka

Sea of
JAPAN

Honshū

M O N G O L I A

Ulaanbaatar
(Ulan Bator)

Hulun Nur

Qiqihar

Dong bei

Changchun

Jilin

Chongjin

JAPAN

Niigata

Kanazawa

G O B I

Shenyang
Fushun

Anshan

Dandong

North

Wŏnsan

Baotou Hohhot

Zhangjiakou

Beijing

Dalian

P'yŏngyang

Seoul

South

Pusan

Taegu

Boundaries of U.S.S.R.
Boundaries of S.S.R.
Boundaries of A.S.S.R.

COPYRIGHT. GEORGE PHILIP & SON. LTD.

1 : 40 000 000

250   0   250   500   750   1000 miles
250   0   500   1000   1500   km

PACIFIC OCEAN

ARCTIC OCEAN

INDIAN OCEAN

Tropic of Cancer

Equator

Arctic Circle

East from Greenwich

Projection: Bonne

Seas and Oceans: Bering Sea, Sea of Okhotsk, Japan Sea, East China Sea, Yellow Sea, Korea Str., South China Sea, Celebes Sea, Sulu Sea, Java Sea, Banda Sea, Arafura Sea, Bay of Bengal, Arabian Sea, Red Sea, Mediterranean Sea, Adriatic Sea, Black Sea, Caspian Sea, Aral Sea, Kara Sea, Barents Sea, Laptev Sea, White Sea, Baltic Sea, North Sea, Dead Sea, G. of Aden, G. of Oman, The Gulf, G. of Thailand, Str. of Malacca, Macassar Strait, Sunda Str.

Land features: Greenland, Iceland, British Isles, Scandinavia, Finland, North European Plain, Ural Mountains, West Siberian Plain, Central Siberian Plateau, Plateau of Mongolia, Altai, Tien Shan, Pamir, Hindu Kush, Karakoram Ra., Kunlun Shan, Plateau of Tibet, Himalaya, Tarim Basin, Takla Makan, Turfan Basin, Lop Nor, Koko Nor, Great Plain of China, Manchurian Plain, Great Khingan Mts., Stanovoy Ra., Yablonovy Ra., Sayan Mts., Verkhoyansk Range, Sikhote Alin Ra., Taimyr Peninsula, Chelyuskin, Kamchatka Peninsula, Aleutians, Kuril Is., Hokkaido, Honshu, Shikoku, Kyushu, Korea, Formosa, Hainan, Luzon, Mindanao, Philippine Is., Palawan, Borneo, Celebes, Sumatra, Java, Bali, Timor, Flores, Ceram, Halmahera, Moluccas, Guam, Caroline Is., Palau Is., New Guinea, Australia

Plateau of Iran, Elburz Mts., Caucasus, Anatolia, Taurus Mts., Ararat, Arabia, Rub' al Khali, Somali Peninsula, Socotra, Mesopotamia, Syrian Desert, Libyan Desert, Great Salt Desert, Great Kavir, Thar Desert, Deccan, Western Ghats, Eastern Ghats, Ceylon, Laccadive Is., Maldive Is., Chagos Arch., Seychelles, Amirantes, Nicobar Is., Andaman Is., Malay Peninsula

Rivers: Lena, Ob, Irtysh, Tobol, Yenisei, Lower Tunguska, Angara, Selenga, Amur, Kolyma, Indigirka, Olenek, Kotuy, Volga, Ural, Don, Dnepr, Danube, Vistula, Oder, Elbe, Rhine, Syr Darya, Amu Darya, Indus, Ganga, Brahmaputra, Yamuna, Narmada, Godavari, Krishna, Tigris, Euphrates, Nile, Hwang-ho, Si-kiang, Yangtze, Mekong, Salween, Irrawaddy, Chao Phraya, Tsangpo

Heights: Belukha 4506, Mt. Communism Pk. 7495, Karakoram 8611, Demavend 5601, Elbrus 5633, Ararat 5165, Narodnaya 1894, Dezhneva 10 497, Kinabalu 4101

m   6000   4000   2000   1000   400   200   0
ft   18 000   12 000   6000   3000   1200   600   0   200   6000   12 000   18 000   24 000   ft
m   200   2000   4000   6000   8000   m

1 : 40 000 000

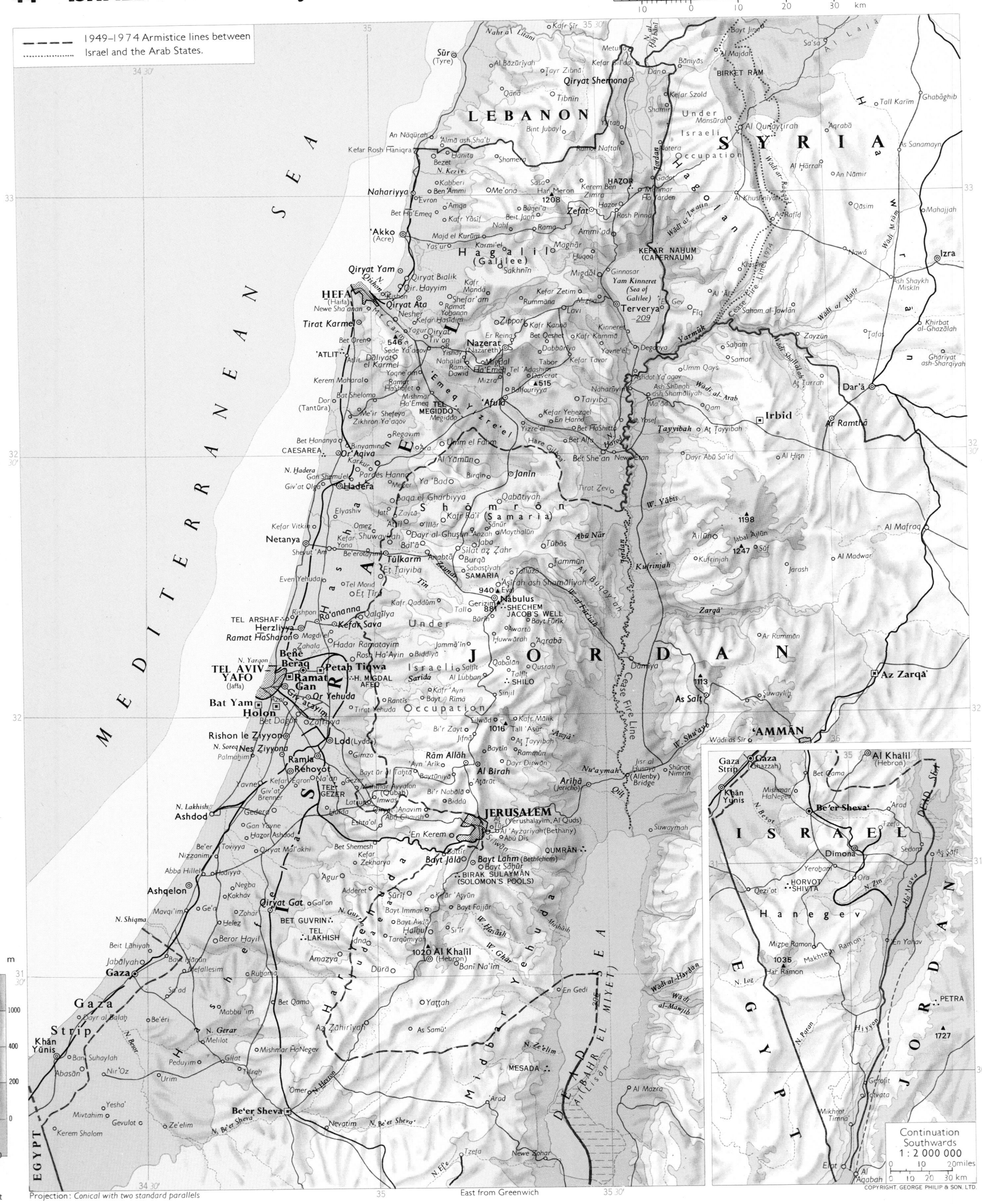
1 : 800 000
10 5 0 10 20 miles
10 0 10 20 30 km
1949–1974 Armistice lines between
Israel and the Arab States.
MEDITERRANEAN SEA
LEBANON
SYRIA
Under Israeli Occupation
ISRAEL
JORDAN
Under Israeli Occupation
Hagalil (Galilee)
Shomron (Samaria)
Yam Kinneret (Sea of Galilee)
DEAD SEA
(BAHR EL MIYET)
Midbar Yehuda
Gaza Strip
EGYPT
Sur (Tyre)
Qiryat Shemona
Nahariyya
'Akko (Acre)
HEFA (Haifa)
Zefat
Terverya
Nazerat (Nazareth)
'Afula
Hadera
Netanya
Tulkarm
Nablus
Herzliyya
TEL AVIV-YAFO (Jaffa)
Petah Tiqwa
Ramat Gan
Bat Yam
Holon
Rishon le Ziyyon
Lod (Lydda)
Ramla
Rehovot
Ashdod
Ashqelon
Gaza
Khan Yunis
Be'er Sheva
JERUSALEM
Ram Allah
Bayt Lahm (Bethlehem)
Al Khalil (Hebron)
Ariha (Jericho)
Irbid
Dar'a
Az Zarqa'
As Salt
'AMMAN
Continuation Southwards
1 : 2 000 000
0 10 20 miles
0 10 20 30 km
Projection: Conical with two standard parallels
East from Greenwich
COPYRIGHT. GEORGE PHILIP & SON. LTD.

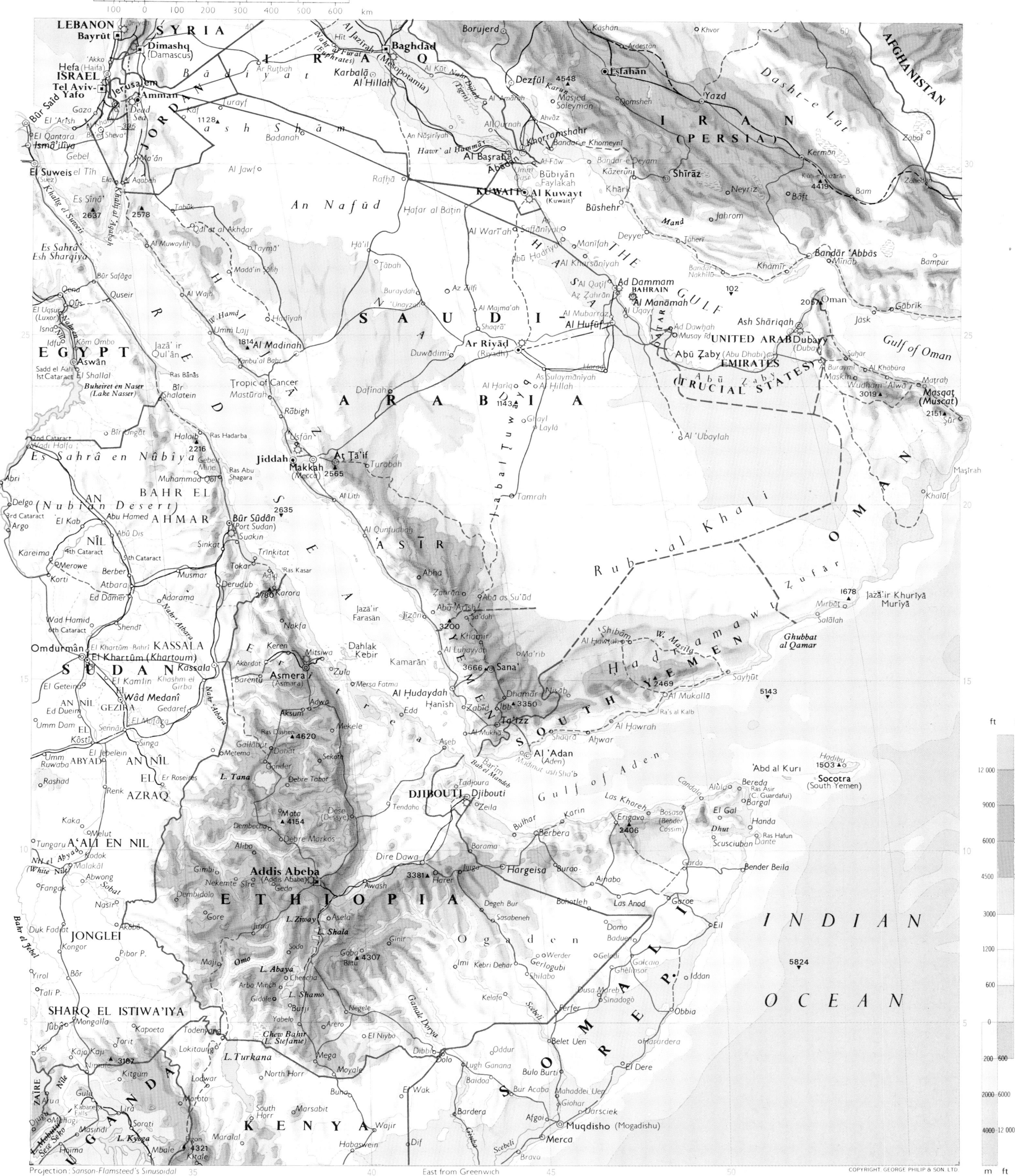

1:12 000 000

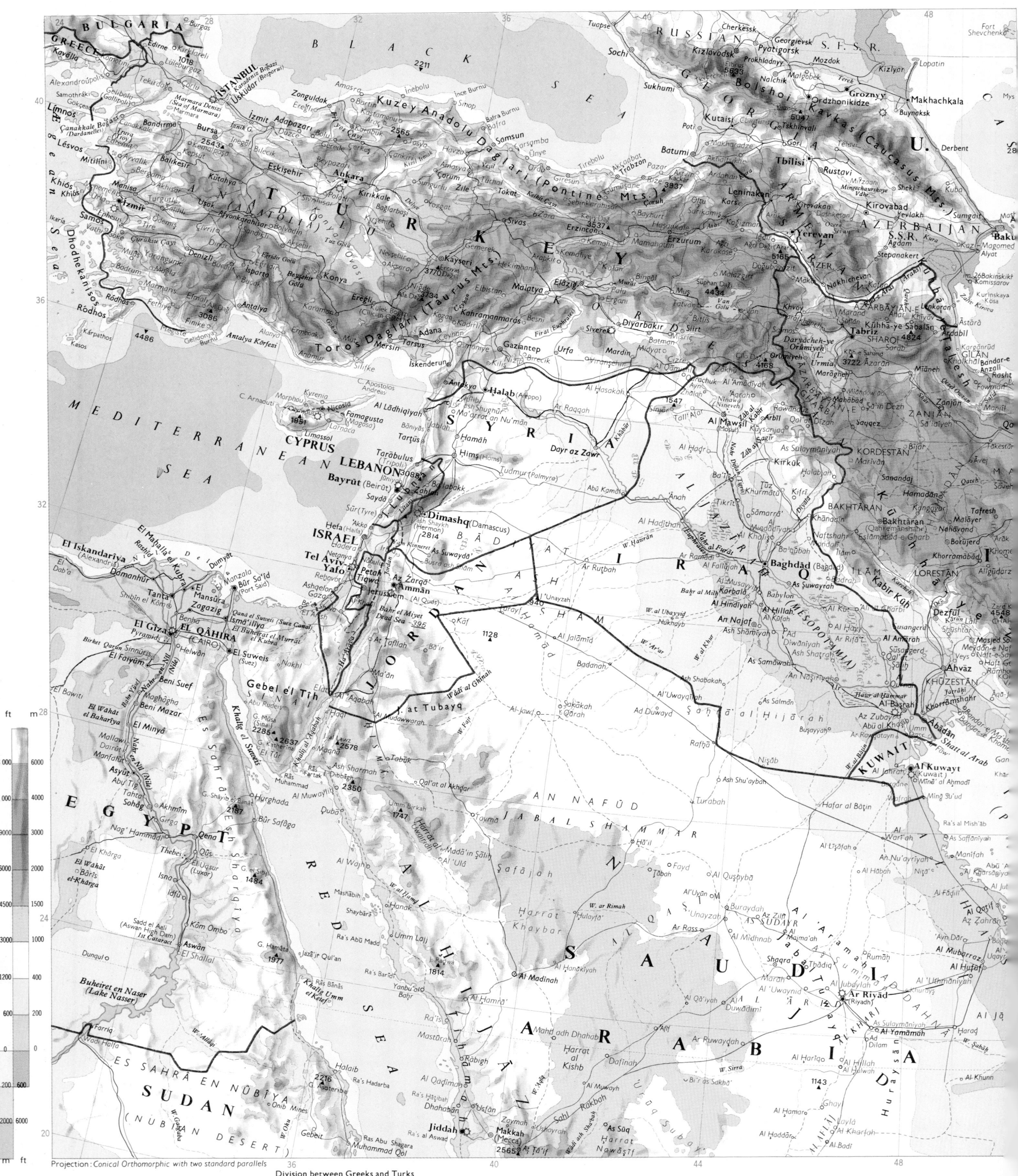

Projection: Conical Orthomorphic with two standard parallels

Division between Greeks and Turks
in Cyprus; Turks to the North.

100 0 100 200 300 miles
100 0 100 200 300 400 500 km

KAZAKH S.S.R.
Plato Ustyurt
Aralskoye More
Muynak
KARA-KALPAKISCHE A.S.S.R.
Kungrad
Chimbai
Nukus
PESKI KYZYLKUM
KAZAKH S.S.R.
Turkestan
Chimkent
Lenger 4488
Tashkent
Chirchik
Angren
KIRGIZ S.S.R.
Namangan
Andizhan
Margelan
Kokand
Fergana
Leninabad
Osh
Kashi Kashgar
CHINA
7579
7555
Tien Shan
Urgench
Turtkul
Khiva
Tashaus
Ozero Sarykamysh
UZBEKSTAN S.S.R.
Bukhara
Kagan
Samarkand
Dzhizak
2169
Kattakurgan
Karshi
5489
Dushanbe
TADZHIK S.S.R.
Pamir
7134
Pik Kommunisma 7495
Khorog
KARA KUM
Chardzhou
Kerki
Termez
Mazar-e-Sharif
BADAKHSHAN
7690
Feyzabad
7789
Kazakhskiy Zaliv
Sartas
Zaliv
Kara Bogaz Gol
Krasnovodski Poluostrov
Krasnovodsk
Nebit Dag 1880
Kizyl Arvat
TURKMEN S.S.R.
Ashkhabad
Mary (Mary)
Bairam Ali
Tedzhen
Serakhs
Qondoz
Taloqan
Baghlan
Kabul
KABUL
Peshawar
Islamabad
Rawalpindi
Kopeh Dagh
Quchan
Mashhad (Meshed)
3314
Kuh-e Binalud
AFGHANISTAN
Herat
3588
Safed Koh
3216
Ghazni
WARDAK
Gardez
Khost
FRONTIER
Bojnurd
Gorgan
Babol
Sari
Reshteh-ye Kuhha-ye Alborz
5604
Damavand
Tehran
SEMNAN
Semnan
DASHT-E KAVIR (Great Salt Desert)
Qom
Kashan
IRAN
Torbat-e Heydariyeh
Torbat-e Jam
KHORASAN
Birjand
2886
Tabas
Yazdan
Shindand
FARAH
4148
Farah
Qandahar
QANDAHAR
HELMAND
3787
Quetta 3593
Chaman
BALUCHISTAN
PAKISTAN
Esfahan
YAZD
Yazd
4075
KERMAN
Kerman
3992
Bam
4419
4042
Zahedan
Zabol
Seistan
Dasht-e Margow
Rigestan
NIMRUZ
Chah Gay
2462
Dalbandin
Kalat
INDIA
GREAT INDIAN DESERT
387
Shiraz
FARS
Sirjan
Daryacheh-ye Tashk
3280
Hamun-e Jaz Murian
SISTAN VA BALUCHESTAN
2146
Siahan Range
Central Makran Ra.
1580
Hyderabad
Bandar-e Abbas
2804
Qeshm
St. of Hormuz
Oman
2057
Minab
Kuhha-ye Bashakerd
2163
Turbat
Makran Coast Range
Gwadar
KARACHI
Mouths of the Indus
Gulf of Kachchh
Jamnagar
Porbandar
QATAR
Ad Dawhah
BAHRAIN
Abu Zaby (Abu Dhabi)
Dubayy (Dubai)
UNITED ARAB EMIRATES
Al Wahat al Buraymi
Masqat (Muscat)
OMAN
Gulf of Oman
Tropic of Cancer
4122
3019
2151
Ra's al Hadd
ARABIAN SEA

East from Greenwich

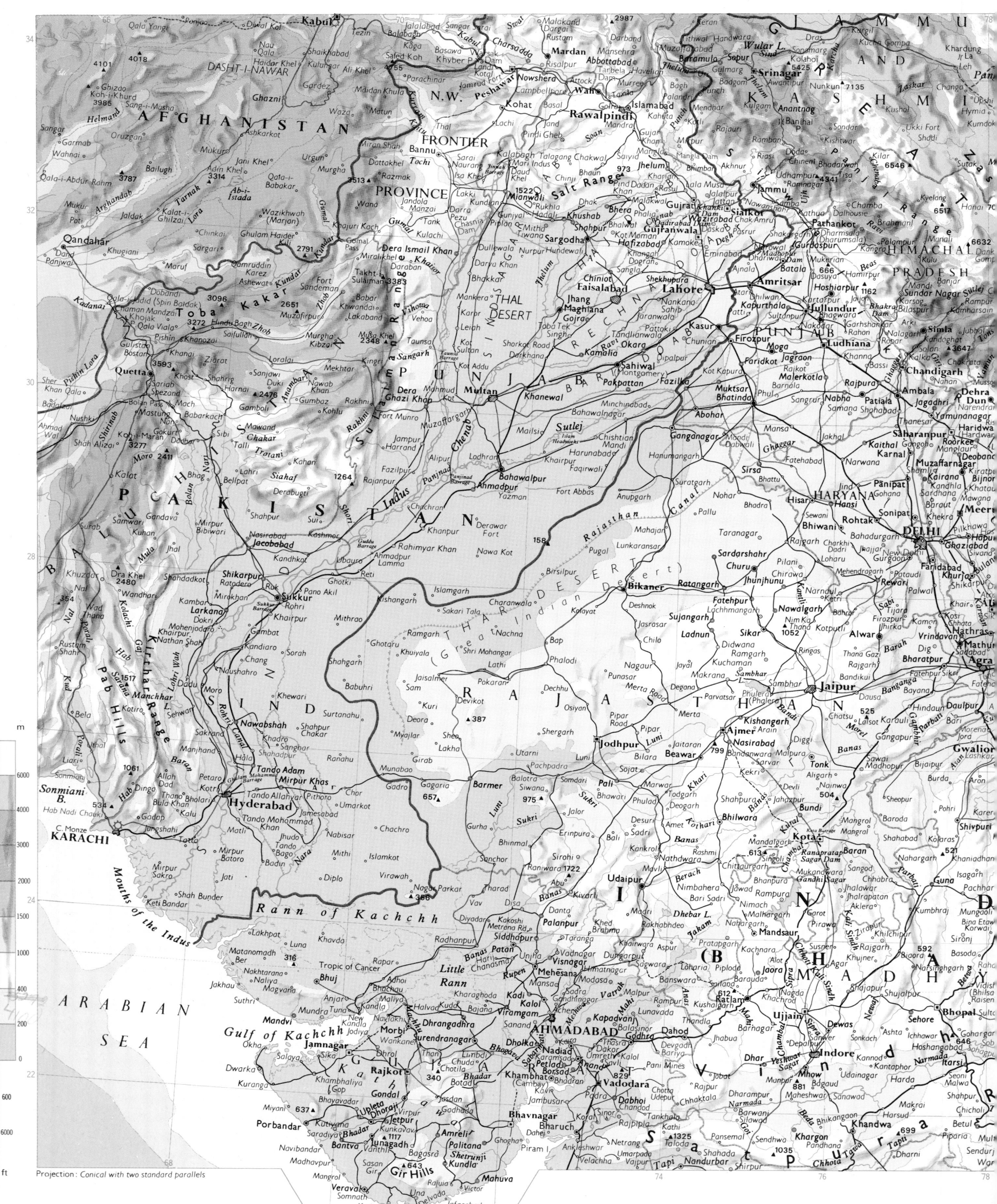
AFGHANISTAN
N.W. FRONTIER PROVINCE
PUNJAB
PAKISTAN
BALUCHISTAN
SIND
RAJASTHAN
THAR DESERT
(Great Indian Desert)
THAL DESERT
JAMMU AND KASHMIR
HIMACHAL PRADESH
HARYANA
PUNJAB
MADHYA PRADESH
GUJARAT
Kathiawar
DASHT-I-NAWAR
Toba Kakar
Sulaiman Range
Kirthar Range
Pab Hills
Salt Range
Pir Panjal Range
Zaskar
Rann of Kachchh
Little Rann
Gulf of Kachchh
Mouths of the Indus
ARABIAN SEA
Sonmiani B.
Tropic of Cancer
Gir Hills
Satpura
Vindhya
Kabul
Kandahar
Quetta
Peshawar
Islamabad
Rawalpindi
Srinagar
Lahore
Amritsar
Faisalabad
Multan
Bahawalpur
Sukkur
Hyderabad
KARACHI
Jodhpur
Bikaner
Jaipur
Ajmer
DELHI
Agra
Chandigarh
Ludhiana
Ahmadabad
Vadodara
Rajkot
Bhavnagar
Indore
Bhopal
Ujjain
Udaipur
Indus
Chenab
Jhelum
Ravi
Sutlej
Beas
Luni
Chambal
Narmada
Tapti
Mahi
Rajasthan Canal
ft m
18 000 6000
12 000 4000
9000 3000
6000 2000
4500 1500
3000 1000
1200 400
600 200
0 0
200 600
2000 6000
m ft
Projection: Conical with two standard parallels

1 : 4 800 000

50   0   50   100   150 miles
50   0   50   100   150   200   250 km

JAMMU AND KASHMIR
On same scale as Main Map

CHINESE REPUBLIC

N.W. FRONTIER PROVINCE

PUNJAB

JAMMU AND KASHMIR

HIMACHAL PRADESH

XIZANG

Mt. Everest 8848

SIKKIM

BHUTAN

ASSAM

U   T   T   A   R   P   R   A   D   E   S   H

M   A   D   H   Y   A   P   R   A   D   E   S   H

B   I   H   A   R

W   E   S   T   B   E   N   G   A   L

BANGLADESH

DHAKA

Kanpur
Lucknow
Allahabad
Varanasi
Jabalpur
Patna
Gaya
Ranchi
Jamshedpur
Raurkela
CALCUTTA
Kharagpur
Haora

Mouths of the Ganga

The Sandheads

East from Greenwich

COPYRIGHT. GEORGE PHILIP & SON. LTD.

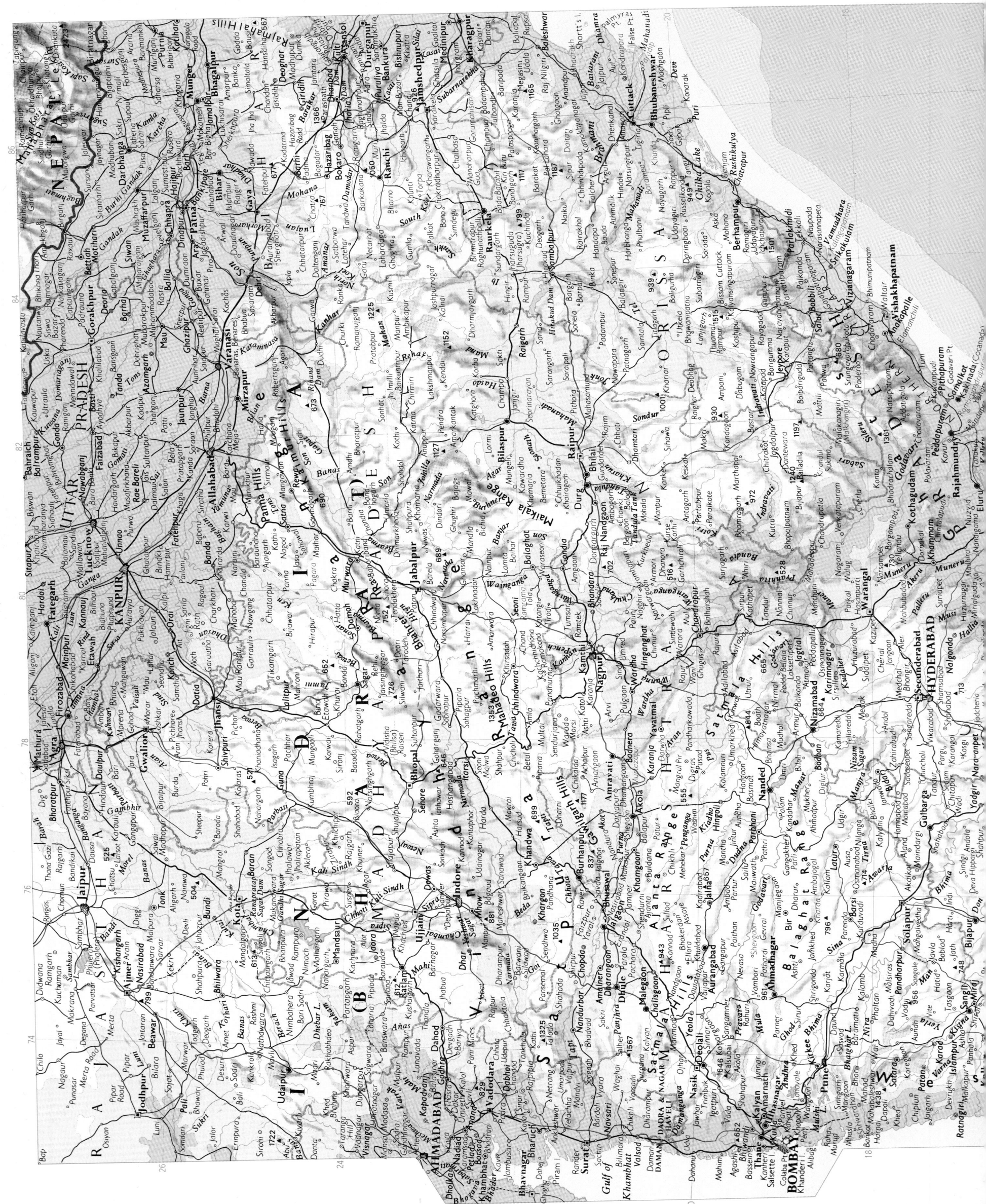
NEPAL
UTTAR PRADESH
KANPUR
Lucknow
Allahabad
Varanasi
Jaipur
Agra
Gwalior
Jhansi
AHMADABAD
Vadodara
Surat
Gulf of Khambhat
Indore
Bhopal
Jabalpur
Nagpur
Raipur
Bilaspur
Ranchi
Jamshedpur
Cuttack
Bhubaneshwar
ORISSA
Satpura Range
Vindhya Range
Kaimur Hills
Mahadeo Hills
Maikala Range
Ajanta Range
Balaghat Range
Nasik
Aurangabad
Pune
BOMBAY
Solapur
Gulbarga
Secunderabad
HYDERABAD
Warangal
Nizamabad
Vishakhapatnam
Rajahmundry
NORTHERN CIRCARS

1 : 4 800 000

East from 80 Greenwich

Projection: Conical with two standard parallels

1 : 4 800 000

50   0   50   100   150 miles
50 0 50 100 150 200 250 km

CHINESE REPUBLIC

XIZANG

ARUNACHAL PRADESH

INDIA

SIKKIM

BHUTAN

ASSAM

NAGALAND

KACHIN

MEGHALAYA

Garo Hills

Khasi Hills

Barail Range

MANIPUR

BANGLADESH

DHAKA

TRIPURA

MIZORAM
Tropic of Cancer

CHIN

SAGAING

CALCUTTA

Sunderbans

Mouths of the Ganga

The Sandheads

BAY   OF

BENGAL

Sittwe (Akyab)

Combermere
Bay

BURMA

SHAN

MANDALAY

KAYAH

THAILAND

ARAKAN

MAGWE

TENASSERIM

IRRAWADDY

PEGU

Rangoon

Bassein

Moulmein

G. of Martaban

Mouths of the Irrawaddy

Projection: Conical with two standard parallels

East from Greenwich

COPYRIGHT. GEORGE PHILIP & SON. LTD.

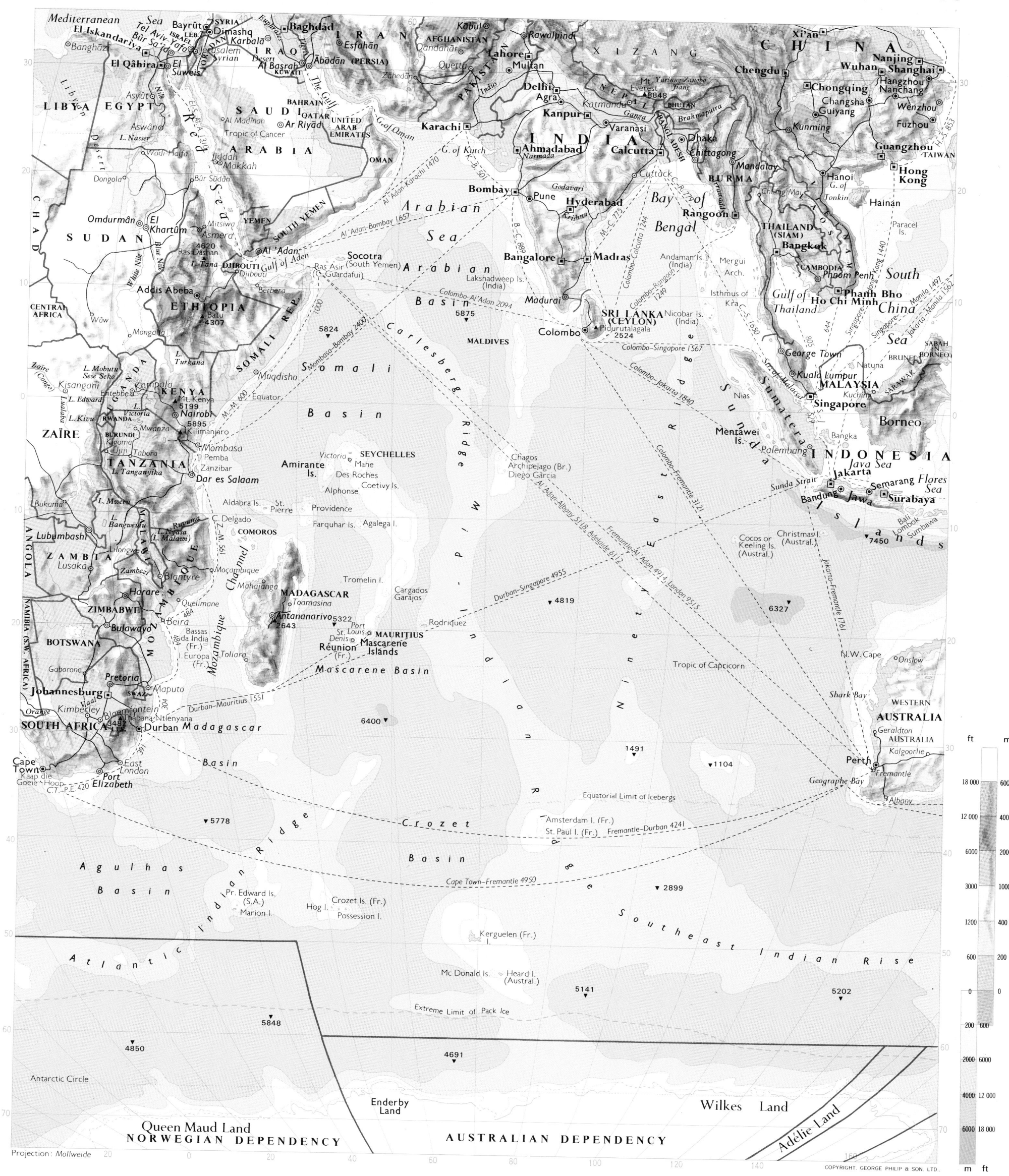
Arabian Sea
Bay of Bengal
Arabian Basin
Somali Basin
Carlesberg Ridge
Mid-Indian Ridge
Ninety East Ridge
Southeast Indian Rise
Atlantic Indian Ridge
Mascarene Basin
Madagascar Basin
Crozet Basin
Agulhas Basin
Mozambique Channel
SAUDI ARABIA
INDIA
CHINA
INDONESIA
AUSTRALIA
MADAGASCAR
SOUTH AFRICA
TANZANIA
KENYA
ETHIOPIA
SUDAN
Equatorial Limit of Icebergs
Extreme Limit of Pack Ice
Antarctic Circle
Tropic of Capricorn
Queen Maud Land
NORWEGIAN DEPENDENCY
AUSTRALIAN DEPENDENCY
Enderby Land
Wilkes Land
Adélie Land
Projection: Mollweide

YUNNAN
CHINA
GUANGXI ZHUANGZU ZIZHIQU
AUTONOMOUS REGION
Hainan
Leizhou Bandao
Gulf of Tonkin
Red River Delta
BAC-PHAN
TONKIN
VIETNAM
LAOS
Chaîne Annamitique
THAILAND (SIAM)
CAMBODIA
BURMA
SHAN STATE
KAYAH
KAWTHULE
TENASSERIM
Central Highlands
Cao Nguyen Tran Ninh
Cao Nguyen Boloven
Khorat
Phnom Dangrek
Dawna Range
Tanen Tong Dan
Mekong
Salween
Nanning
Zhanjiang
Haikou
Hanoi
Haiphong
Nam Dinh
Thanh Hoa
Vinh
Hue
Da Nang (Tourane)
Qui Nhon
Ban Me Thuot
Luang Prabang
Vientiane
Pakse
Savannakhet
Udon Thani
Khon Kaen
Nakhon Ratchasima (Khorat)
Ubon Ratchathani
Chiang Mai
Lampang
Phitsanulok
Nakhon Sawan
BANGKOK (Krung Thep)
Thon Buri
Chon Buri
Battambang
Tonle Sap (Great Lake)
Moulmein
Thaton
Pegu
Rangoon
Mandalay
Maymyo
Toungoo
Tavoy
Gulf of Martaban

1 : 4 800 000

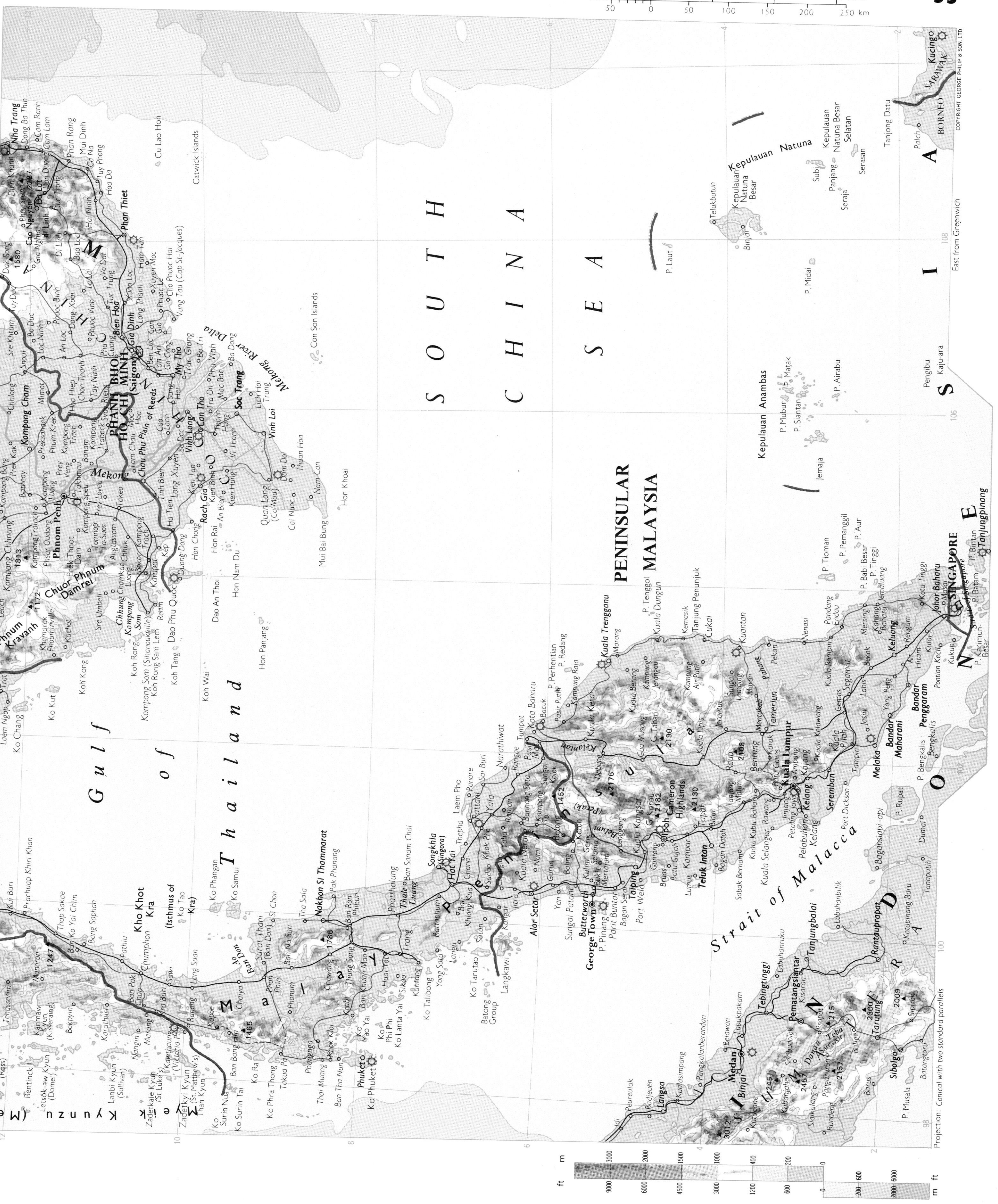

50　0　50　100　150 miles
50　0　50　100　150　200　250 km

COPYRIGHT GEORGE PHILIP & SON LTD

East from Greenwich

SOUTH CHINA SEA

Gulf of Thailand

Strait of Malacca

PENINSULAR MALAYSIA

Kepulauan Natuna

Kepulauan Anambas

Kepulauan Natuna Besar
Natuna Selatan

BORNEO
SARAWAK
Kucing
Tanjong Datu

Nha Trang
Phan Rang
Phan Thiet
Dien Bien Phu 2287
Cao Nguyen Di Linh
1580

PHANH BHO HO CHI MINH
Saigon
Bien Hoa
Gia Dinh
Kompong Cham
Phnom Penh
Mekong River Delta
Chau Phu Plain of Reeds
Can Tho
Vinh Long
Soc Trang
Rach Gia
Dao Phu Quoc
Chuor Phnum Damrei
Phnum Kravanh 1172
Kompong Som
Koh Rong
Koh Tang

Con Son Islands
Catwick Islands

Ko Chang
Ko Kut
Koh Kong

Bangkok region
Prachuap Khiri Khan
Chumphon
Bang Saphan
Ko Samui
Ko Phangan
Ko Tao
Surat Thani (Ban Don)
Nakhon Si Thammarat
Phatthalung
Trang
Songkhla (Singora)
Hat Yai
Pattani
Yala
Narathiwat
Ko Phuket
Phuket

Kho Khot Kra
(Isthmus of Kra)

Malay Peninsula

Ko Tarutao
Langkawi
Alor Setar
George Town
P. Pinang
Butterworth
Taiping
Ipoh
Cameron Highlands
Teluk Intan
Kelang
Kuala Lumpur
Seremban
Melaka
Bandar Penggaram
Bandar Maharani
Kota Baharu
Kuala Trengganu
Kuantan
Pekan
Mersing
Keluang
Johor Baharu
SINGAPORE
Tanjungpinang

G. Tahan 2190
2176
2182
2130

P. Tioman
P. Tenggol
P. Redang
P. Perhentian
P. Aur
P. Pemanggil
P. Babi Besar
P. Tinggi
P. Bintan
P. Batam

SUMATERA
Medan
Binjai
Langsa
Tebingtinggi
Pematangsiantar
Rantauprapat
Tanjungbalai
Sibolga
Tarutung 2009
Danau Toba
2157
2451
2151

Kyunzu (Mergui Archipelago)
Kawthaung (Victoria Point)
Thap Sakae

Projection: Conical with two standard parallels

ft m
9000 3000
6000 2000
4500 1500
3000 1000
1500 600
600 200
0 0
600 200
6000 2000

BURMA
THAILAND (SIAM)
LAOS
CAMBODIA
VIET-NAM
ANDAMAN SEA
Gulf of Thailand (Siam)
SOUTH CHINA SEA
MALAYSIA
PENINSULAR MALAYSIA
SINGAPORE
Strait of Malacca
SUMATERA
BORNEO
KALIMANTAN
SARAWAK
SABAH
BRUNEI
INDONESIA
JAVA (JAWA)
JAVA SEA
Greater Sunda Islands
INDIAN OCEAN
Java Trench
RANGOON
G. of Martaban
Moulmein
Vientiane
Nong Khai
Udon Thani
Uttaradit
Phitsanulok
Tak
Thaton
Savannakhet
Thakhek
Hue
Da Nang (Tourane)
Quang Ngai
Qui Nhon
Nha Trang
Phan Rang
Mui Ca Na
Nakhon Ratchasima (Khorat)
Ubon Ratchathani
Phnom Dangrek
Phra Nakhon Si Ayutthaya
BANGKOK
Chon Buri
Battambang
Siem Reap
Kompong Cham
Phnom Penh
PHANH BHO HO CHI MINH (Saigon)
Vung Tau
Kompong Som
Kampot
Phu Quoc
Chanthaburi
Tavoy
Mergui
Tenasserim
Chumphon
Kho Khot Kra
Ranong
Ko Samui
Surat Thani
Nakhon Si Thammarat
Phuket
Trang
Songkhla (Singora)
Pattani
Kota Baharu
Alor Setar
George Town (Pinang)
Kuala Trengganu
Ipoh
Taiping
Kuantan
Kuala Lumpur
Kelang
Seremban
Melaka
Johor Baharu
Tanjungpinang
Kepulauan Riau
Kepulauan Lingga
Singkep
Bintan
Batam
Sabang
Banda Aceh (Kutaraja)
ACEH
Medan
Belawan
Simeulue
Nias
Sibolga
Padang
Bukittinggi
Pekanbaru
Jambi
Palembang
Bengkulu
Siberut
Kepulauan Mentawai
Enggano
Kepulauan Natuna
Kepulauan Anambas
Kucing
Sibu
Bintulu
Miri
Kota Kinabalu (Jesselton)
Bandar Seri Begawan
Pontianak
Bangka
Pangkalpinang
Belitung (Billiton)
Banjarmasin
Tanjungkarang Telukbetung
JAKARTA
Serang
Bogor
Bandung
Cirebon
Semarang
Yogyakarta
Surakarta
Surabaya
Malang
Madiun
Madura
Kediri
Probolinggo
BALI
Lombok
Denpasar
Mataram
NUSA TENGGARA
Spratly I.
Palawan
Hsisha
Chuntao
Projection: Mercator
East from Greenwich

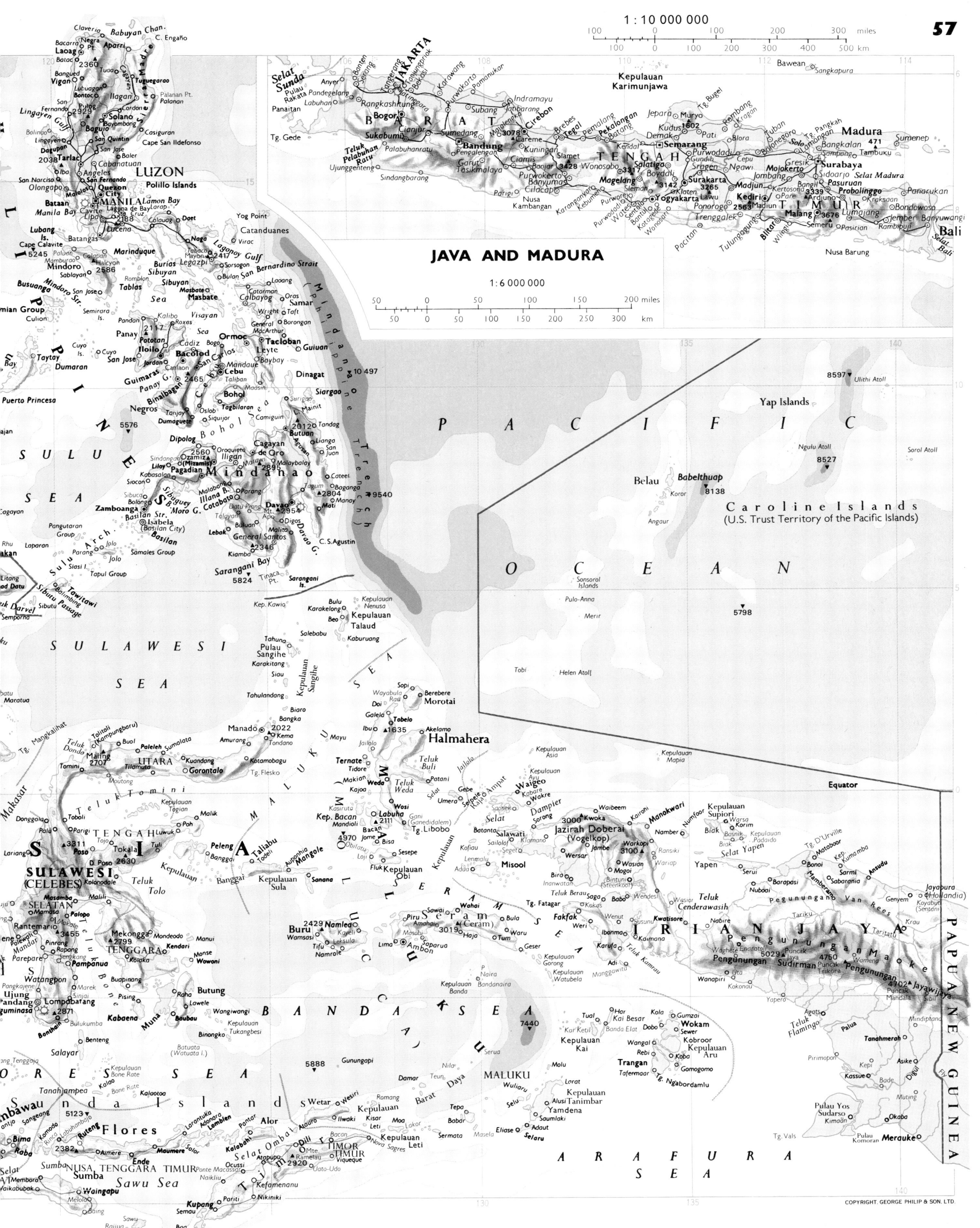

1 : 10 000 000

100   0   100   200   300 miles
100 0 100 200 300 400 500 km

JAVA AND MADURA

1 : 6 000 000

50   0   50   100   150   200 miles
50 0 50 100 150 200 250 300 km

LUZON

JAKARTA

BARAT

TENGAH

Bandung

Semarang

Surabaya

Madura

Surakarta
Yogyakarta

TIMUR

Malang

Bali

PACIFIC

OCEAN

Yap Islands

Belau   Babelthuap

Caroline Islands
(U.S. Trust Territory of the Pacific Islands)

Equator

SULU

SEA

Mindanao

Davao

Sarangani Bay

SULAWESI

SEA

Halmahera

Ternate
Tidore

IRIAN JAYA

PAPUA NEW GUINEA

Jayapura

SULAWESI
(CELEBES)

Misool

SELATAN

TENGGARA

Ujung
Pandang

Buru   Namlea

Seram (Ceram)

Ambon

BANDA   SEA

MALUKU

Kepulauan
Kai

Trangan

Kepulauan
Aru

Merauke

FLORES   SEA

Flores

TIMUR

TIMOR

NUSA TENGGARA TIMUR

Sumba

Kupang

Sawu Sea

ARAFURA

SEA

COPYRIGHT. GEORGE PHILIP & SON. LTD.

GANSU
SHAANXI
SICHUAN
GUIZHOU
YUNNAN
GUANGXI
KACHIN
BURMA
SHAN STATE
LAOS
VIETNAM
THAILAND
CHENGDU (Ch'engtu; Tch'eng-tou)
CHONGQING (Ch'ungch'ing; Tch'ong-k'ing)
Kunming
Guiyang (Kueiyang)
Nanning
Hanoi
Haiphong
Gulf of Tonkin
Leizhou Bandao
Projection: Conical with two standard parallels

HENAN · HUBEI · ANHUI · JIANGSU · HUNAN · JIANGXI · ZHEJIANG · FUJIAN · GUANGDONG · GUANGXI · TAIWAN (FORMOSA)

Major cities: Nanyang, Huainan, Bengbu, NANJING (Nanking; Nanching), Zhenjiang (Chenchiang), Changzhou (Ch'angchou), Wuxi (Wuhsi), Suzhou (Suchou), SHANGHAI (Changhai), Nantong, Hefei, Wuhu, Wuhan (Wou-han), Hankou, Hanyang, Huangshi, Anqing, Hangzhou (Hangchow), Ningbo (Ningpo), Shaoxing, Yichang (Ich'ang), Shashi, Changsha, Zhuzhou, Xiangtan, Hengyang, Nanchang, Jingdezhen, Wenzhou (Wenchow), Fuzhou (Foochow; Fuchou), Guilin, Ganzhou, Shaoguan, Xiamen (Hsiamen; Amoy), Quanzhou (Ch'uanchou), Zhangzhou, Shantou (Swatow), GUANGZHOU (Kwangchou; Canton), Foshan, Jiangmen, HONG KONG (U.K.), Kowloon, Macau (Macao) (Port.), Zhanjiang, Wuzhou, Gaoxiong (Kaohsiung), Tainan, TAIBEI (T'aipei), Jilong, Taizhong (T'aichung), Jiayi

Rivers / features: Chang Jiang (Yangtze), Huai He, Han Shui, Gan Jiang, Xiang Jiang, Min Jiang, Xi Jiang, Bei Jiang, Dong Jiang, Han Jiang, Dongting Hu, Poyang Hu, Chao Hu, Tai Hu, Hangzhou Wan

Tropic of Cancer

SOUTH CHINA SEA · Luzon Strait · Taiwan Strait · Formosa Strait

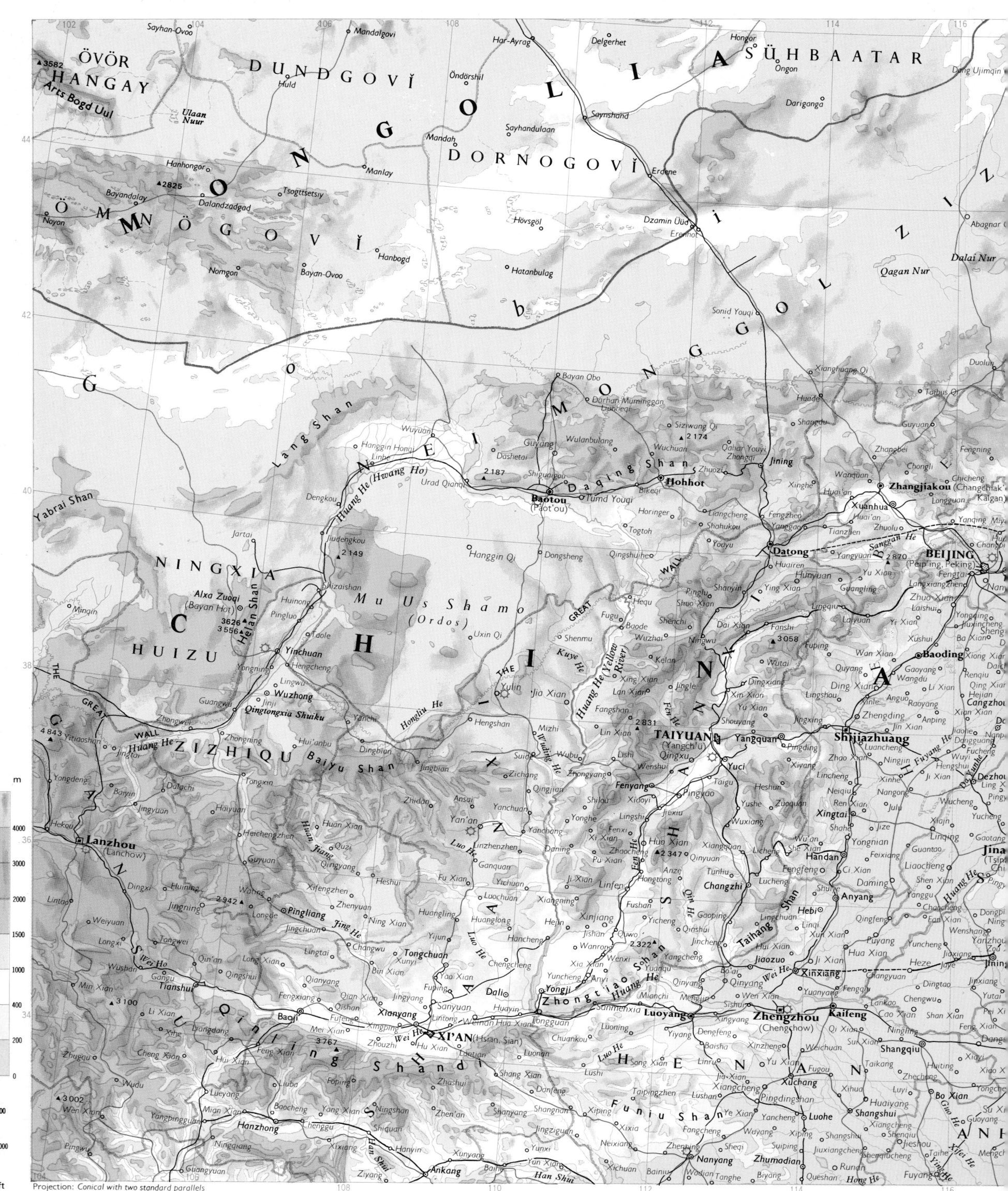

ft   m
12 000 4000
9000 3000
6000 2000
4500 1500
3000 1000
1200 400
600 200
0 0
200 600
2000 6000
m   ft

Projection: Conical with two standard parallels

1 : 4 800 000

50   0   50   100   150 miles
50   0   50   100   150   200   km

Horqin Youyi Qianqi
Zhenlai
Nen Jiang
HARBIN
(Haerhpin)
Bin Xian
Acheng
Yanshou
Turiy Rog
Linkou
Jixi
Ozero Khanka
HEILONGJIANG
U.S.S.R.

Maoxing Zhaoyang Jiang Shuangcheng Shangzhi Yimianpo Hengdaohezi Muling Suiyang Suifenhe
Tuquan Tao'an Songhua Fuyu Changchunling Lalin Wuchang Mudanjiang Hailin Ning'an Dongning Golenki
Qian Gorlos Shenjingzi Kuishan Yushu Shulan Shanhetun Zhangguangcailing 1690 Maqiaohe Pogranichnyy Ussuriysk (Voroshilov)
Nong'an Dehui Jiutai Gongzhuling Dongjingcheng Jingpo Hu Luozigou Razdolnoye
Changling Fulongquan Wulajie Gangyao Jiaohe Xinzhan Huangsongdian Dunhua Daxinggou Wangqing Tavrichanka Artem
Changchun Jilin (Kirin) Chili Songhua Hu Emu Antu 1677 Yanji Tumen Hunchan Kroshino Vladivostok
Shuangliao Maolin Huaidezhen Fantun Panshi Huadian Helong Musan Hoemdong Paksikori Posyet
Siping Liaoyuan Dongfeng Xifeng Huinan Erdao Jiang Fusong Paektu-san 2541 Puryong Pugodong Najin Slavyanka
Jargalang Zhangwu Hailong Jingyu Changbai Changbaishan Hyesan Kapsan Kilju Musudan
WALL Kaiyuan Shanchengzhen Dihua Linjiang Hapsu Irhyangdong Ondejin Songjin
Fuxin Xinlitun Zhangwu Liao He Tieling Qingyuan Tonghua Chunggang-up Huchang Kasan-dong Simpungdong
SHENYANG Fushun Xinbin Hwangye Pungsan Koson-ni
(Mukden) Heishan Huajiaozi 1845 Ji'an Manpojin Kanggye 2522 Kwangdoeri Changhung-ni Pukchong Tanchon
Benxi Qinghecheng Yalu Jiang Kuup-tong Changjin-chosuji Changjin
Liaoyang Anping Supung Sk. Chosan Koin-dong Sinhung Sohori
Jinzhou Panshan Niuzhuang Kuandian Cao He Taegwan **NORTH** Oro Hamhung Hongwon
Anshan Haicheng Liangshanguan Pyoktong Pukchin Hungnam
Yingkou Fengcheng Sakchu Taegwan **KOREA** Tongjoson Man
Gai Xian Xiuyan Uji Sinuiju Kujang Tongchon-ni
Liaodong Xiongyuecheng Wanfu 1131 **Dandong** Yongampo Chongju Anju Sinanju Tokchon Yonghung **Wonsan**
Wan. Donggou Yalu Jiang Sonchon Sunchon Kaechon Kowon
Fu Xian Gushan Zhuanghe Sukchon Yongchon Munchon Anbyon
Xinjin Pikou Kangdong Tongyang Singosan Kojo
P'yongyang Chunghwa Koksan Sepo-ri Hoeyang Koson
Jin Xian Chinnampo Songnim Pyonggang 1638 Changdo-ri Kansong
Lushun **DALIAN** Songhwa Suan Chiha-ri Hwachon-chosuji Yangyang
(Luda) Cho-do Sariwon Nam-chon 1578 Chumunjin
Korea Chaeryong Sinmak Chorwon Kumhwa Hwachon
Changyon Haeju Kaesong Panmunjom Uijongbu Chunchon Hongchon Kangnung
Bay Ongjin Yonan Munsan Hoengsong Samchok
Paengnyong-do Kanghwa **SEOUL** Wonju Yongwol Ulchin Ullung-do
Cease Fire Line Yongdungpo (Seoul) Hongchon
Inch'on Suwon Osan Yoju Chechon Uljin
Chungju **SOUTH** Yongju
Pyongtaek Chongju Chechon Yongwol
KOREA Andong Yongdok

Huang He Longkou Huang Xian Yantai
Huimin Zhanhua Penglai Daxindian Weihai
Wudi Beizhen Zhaoyuan Fushan Muping
Yangxin **Laizhou** Ye Xian Qixia Wendeng 923
Wan Shouguang Changyi 923 Rushan Nanhuang Shidao
Guangrao Changle Pingdu Laiyang Haiyang
Zibo Yidu Fangzi Laixi Qixia
Zhoucun Linzi Weifang Gaomi Jimo Chengyang
SHAN Boshan Linqu Anqiu Jiao Xian Zhucheng
DONG 1108 Jiaozhou Wan
QINGDAO
(Ch'ingtao)

HUANG HAI
(Yellow Sea)

Yesan Hongsong Nonsan Taejon Kumsan Sangju Sansong
Chochiwon Yongdong Kimchon Yongchon
Anmyon-do Chongju Okchon Waegwan **Taegu** Chongdo Ulsan
Tpechon- do Kanggyong Nonsan Koryong Miryang
Kunsan **Chonju** Iri Kochang Hamyang Chinju 1915 Tongnae
Puan Imsil Namwon Chinju Masan **PUSAN**
Chongup Namwon Sago-ri Chinhae
Sangjong-ni Tamyang Hadong Samchonpo Chungmu
Kwangju Suncheon Polgyo-ri Yosu
Mokpo Naju Posong
Changhung-ni Sasuna
Chindo Haenam

Cheju Cheju-do
Hallim 1950 Onpyong-ni
Mosulpo Sogwi-po
Nakadori-jima
JAPAN Sasebo

Bo Hai
(Gulf of Chihli)

Tangshan (Tientsin)
TIANJIN (T'ienching)
Tanggu
Dagu

SEA OF JAPAN

Korea Strait

Tsushima-kaikyo

Karatsu
Imari
Omura
Isahaya
Nagasaki Kuchinotsu

1 : 16 000 000

100   0   100   200   300   400 miles
100   0   100   200   300   400   500   600 km

COPYRIGHT GEORGE PHILIP & SON LTD.

U.S.S.R.

UNION OF SOVIET SOCIALIST REPUBLICS

KAZAKH S.S.R.

KIRGIZ S.S.R.

MONGOLIA

C H I N A

XIZANG (TIBET)

XINJIANG UYGUR (Aut. Reg.)

Tarim Pendi

Dzungar Pendi

NINGXIA HUIZU (Aut. Reg.)

NEI MONGOL

HEILONGJIANG

JILIN

LIAONING

HEBEI

SHANXI

SHAANXI

GANSU

QINGHAI

SICHUAN

YUNNAN

GUIZHOU

HUNAN

HUBEI

HENAN

SHANDONG

JIANGSU

ANHUI

ZHEJIANG

JIANGXI

FUJIAN

GUANGDONG

GUANGXI ZHUANG

HAINAN Dao

NORTH KOREA

SOUTH KOREA

JAPAN

TAIWAN (FORMOSA)

PHILIPPINES

Luzon

VIETNAM

LAOS

THAILAND (SIAM)

BURMA

ASSAM

BHUTAN

NEPAL

INDIA

BANGLADESH

KASHMIR

YELLOW SEA

EAST CHINA SEA

SOUTH CHINA SEA

Bo Hai

Korea Bay

RYUKYU-RETTO

BAY OF BENGAL

G. of Tonkin

Hainan Channel

Bushi Channel

Batan Is.

Tropic of Cancer

East from Greenwich

Projection: Bonne

BEIJING   SHANGHAI   TIANJIN   SHENYANG   WUHAN   GUANGZHOU   CHONGQING   CHENGDU   XI'AN   NANJING   HARBIN   QINGDAO   DALIAN   TAIYUAN   LANZHOU   KUNMING   HANOI   HONG KONG   Macau   Kowloon

Xiao Hinggan Ling

Da Hinggan Ling

Altun Shan

Kunlun Shan

Qilian Shan

Tien Shan

Altai Shan

Tanggula Shan

Bayan Har Shan

Daxue Shan

Dabie Shan

Nan Shan

Huang (river)

Chang (river)

m   ft
6000 18000
4000 12000
3000 9000
2000 6000
1500 4500
1000 3000
400 1200
200 600
0 0
200 600
2000 6000
4000 12000
6000 18000

1 : 6 000 000

50   0   50   100   150   200 miles
50   0   50   100   150   200   250   300 km

CHINA

U.S.S.R.

Mudanjiang
Ningan
Turii Rog
Ozero
Khanka
Spassk-Dalni
Varfolomeyevka
Verkhove
Tetyukhe
Ussurysk
(Voroshilov)
Uglovaya
Vladivostok
Suchan
Nakhodka
Tumen
Hunchun
Zaliv Petra
Velikogo
Najin

**NORTH
KOREA**

Chongjin

Songjin

Tanchon

Kosŏng

Samchok

**SOUTH
KOREA**

Ullung Do

Pusan

KOREA STRAIT

Tsushima

Tsushima-Kaikyō

Iki

HOKKAIDO

Rebun-Tō
Rishiri-Tō
Wakkanai
Teshio
Otoineppu
Enbetsu
Monbetsu
Yubetsu
Sea of Okhotsk

Teshio
Rumoi
Shibatsu
Kitami
Abashiri
Asahigawa
Daisetsu 2290
Nemuro-Kaikyō
Atsuta
Bibai
Yūbari
Obihiro
Nemuro
Iwanai
Otaru
Sapporo 2052
Poroshiri Dake
Kushiro
Kamui-Misaki
Tomakomai
Tokachi
Shiraoi
Mombetsu
Muroran
Urakawa
Samani
Ushibira-Wan
Erimo-Misaki

Okushiri-Tō
Esashi
Hakodate
Esan-Misaki
Matsumae
Tsugaru Kaikyō
Shiriya-Zaki
Mutsu
Mutsu-Wan
Aomori
Hirosaki
Towada-Ko
Odate
Noshiro
Yoneshiro
Iwate-San 2041
Akita
Omono
Morioka
Miyako
Hanamaki
Kitakami
Kamaishi
Honjō
Yokote
Ichinoseki
Sakata
Shinjō
TŌHOKU
Tsuruoka
Mogami
Kogota
Ishinomaki
Yamagata
Shiogama
Sendai
Iwanuma
Sado
Yonezawa
Fukushima
Niigata
Shibata
Agano
Bandai-San 1819
Aizuwakamatsu
Koriyama
Nagaoka
Tajima
Iwaki
Naoetsu
Nikkō
Takada
Hitachi
Nakaminato
Nagano
Maebashi
Kiryū
Utsunomiya
Ueda
Takasaki
Tochigi
Mito
Matsumoto
Chichibu
Gyoda
Tsuchiura
Suwa
Kawagoe
Omiya
KANTŌ
Ontake-San
Kōfu
Urawa
Sawara
3063
Kiso
Iida
Fuji-San
TOKYO
Chōshi
Gifu
3776
Yokohama
Yokosuka
Ichinomiya
Fuji-no-miya
Kawasaki
Nagoya
Shimizu
Fujisawa
Yokkaichi
Okazaki
Shizuoka
Numazu
Atami
Tsu
Toyohashi
Katsuura
Nara
Hamamatsu
Suruga-Wan
Tateyama
Ise-Wan
Matsusaka
Shimada
Toba
Ō-Shima
Owase
Nii-Jima
Daiō-Misaki
KINKI
Miyake-Jima
Wakayama
Shingū
Mikura-Jima

CHUBU
Wajima
Suzu-Misaki
Nanao
Himi
Toyama-Wan
Takaoka
Kanazawa
Toyama
Fukui
Takefu
Tsuruga
Kyō-ga-Saki
Wakasa-Wan
Maizuru
Biwa-Ko
Ōtsu
Ayabe
Hikone
Fukuchiyama
Kyōto
Amagasaki
Kōbe
Ōsaka
Sakai
Kishiwada

Hi-no-Misaki
Izumo
Matsue
Tottori
Toyooka
CHUGOKU
Yonago
Tsuyama
Hamada
Okayama
Himeji
Akashi
Masuda
Fukuyama
Kurashiki
Onomichi
Hiroshima
Miharai
Hōfu
Yamaguchi
Kure
Tokuyama
Shimonoseki
Ube

Suō-Nada
Seto-Naikai
Niihama
Matsuyama
Takamatsu
Marugame
Tokushima
SHIKOKU
Kōchi
Yawatahama
Bungo-Suidō
Uwajima
Kii-Suidō
Nakamura
Tosa-Wan
Muroto-Misaki
SHIKOKU
Ashizuri-zaki
Shio-no-Misaki

Nakadori-Jima
Fukuoka
Karatsu
Saga
Nakatsu
Kitakyūshū
Sasebo
Kurume
Beppu
Ōita
Isahaya
Kashima
Saiki
Usuki
Nagasaki
Omuta
Aso-zan 1592
Kumamoto
Shimabara
Yatsushiro
KYŪSHŪ
Shimo-Jima
Minamata
Nobeoka
Fukue-Jima
Sendai
Miyazaki
KYŪSHŪ
Kobayashi
Miyakonojō
Kagoshima
Kanoya
Makurazaki
Kagoshima-Wan
Shibushi-Wan
Ōsumi-Kaikyō
Nishinoomote
Ōsumi-Shotō
Tane-ga-Shima
Kuchinoerabu-Jima
Yaku-Jima
Tokara-Kaikyō
Naka-no-Shima
Suwanose-Jima

SEA   OF   JAPAN

PACIFIC

OCEAN

Aoga-Shima
Hachijo-Jima

RYŪKYŪ ISLANDS
Ōsumi-Shotō
Kuchinoerabu-Jima
Yaku-Jima
Tokara-Kaikyō
Naka-no-Shima
Suwanose-Jima
Kikai-Jima
Naze
Amami-Ō Shima
Setouchi
Tokunoshima
Okinoerabu-Jima
Okinawa-Jima
Ishikawa
Kerama-Shotō
Koza
Ginowan
Naha

Miyako-Jima
Hirara
Yaeyama-Shotō
Yonaguni-Jima
Ishigaki-Jima
Iriomote-Jima
Ishigaki

7507

Nansei-Shotō Trench

RYŪKYŪ ISLANDS
Continuation southwards
in same scale

ft   m

4500   1500

3000   1000

1200   400

600   200

0   0

200   600

m   ft

PACIFIC

OCEAN

Projection: Bonne

East from Greenwich

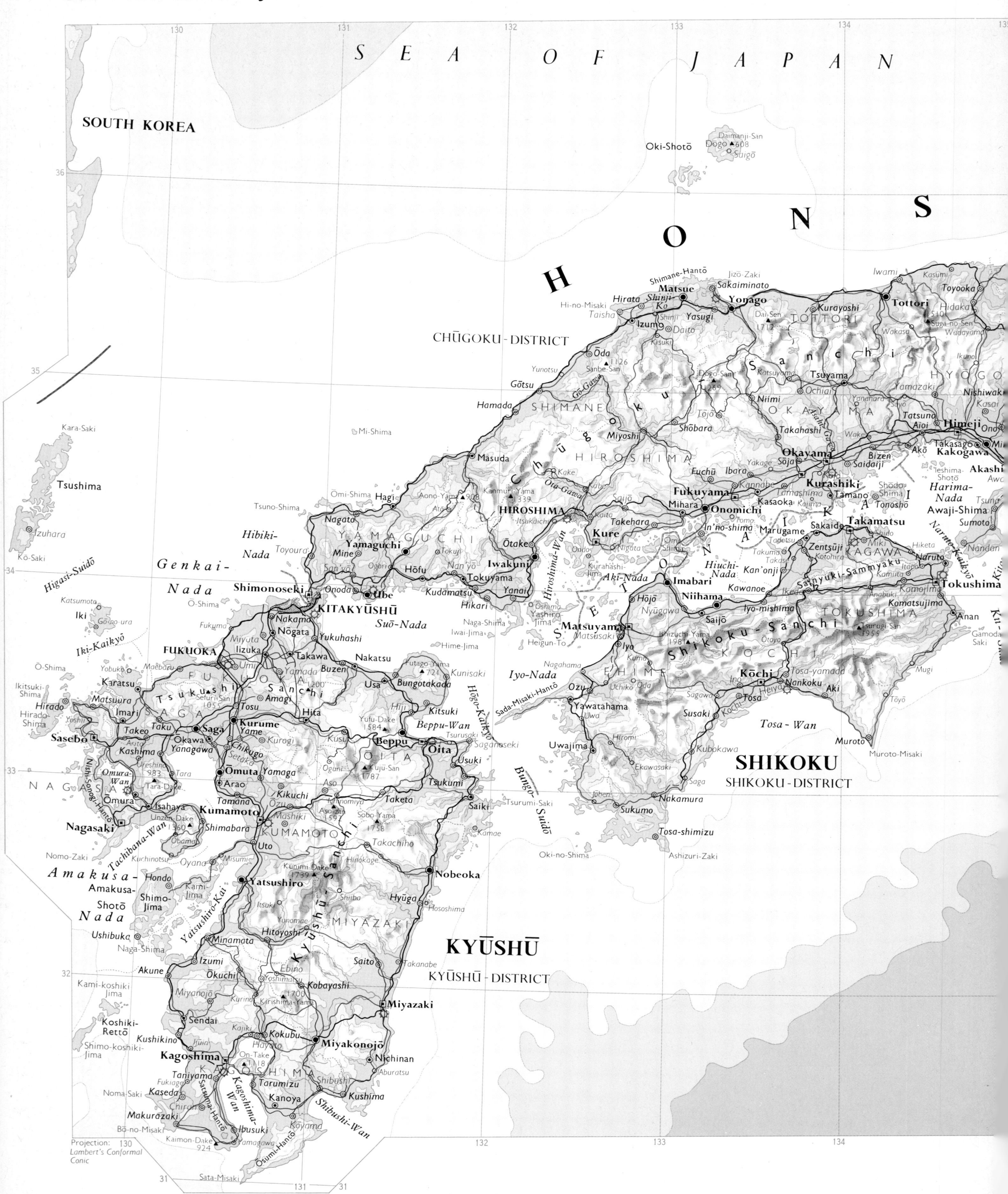

SEA OF JAPAN

SOUTH KOREA

Oki-Shotō
Daimanji-San
Dōgo ▲608
Saigō

HONS

CHŪGOKU-DISTRICT

Shimane-Hantō
Jizō-Zaki
Iwami
Kasumi
Toyooka
Hi-no-Misaki
Hirata
Shinji-
Ko
Sakaiminato
Yonago
Kurayoshi
Tottori
Hidaka
Taisha
Izumo
Yasugi
Dai-Sen
1712
TOTTORI
Wakasa
Suga-no-Sen
Wadayama

Ōda
Sanbe-San
1126
Dōgo-San
Katsuyama
Tsuyama
Yamazaki
Ikuno
HYŌGO

Yunotsu
Miyoshi
Tōjō
OKAYAMA
Yanahara
Nishiwaki
Kasai

Gōtsu
Gō-Gawa
Shōbara
Niimi
Takahashi
Wake
Tatsuno
Aioi
Himeji
Ono

Hamada
SHIMANE
Ibara
Kannabe
Sōja
Okayama
Bizen
Akō
Takasago
Kakogawa

Masuda
HIROSHIMA
Fuchū
Tamashima
Kurashiki
Tamano
Ieshima-Shotō
Akashi
Awa

Ōmi-Shima
Hagi
Aono-Yama
Kanmuri-Yama
Ōta-Gawa
Saijō
Mihara
Onomichi
Kasaoka
Kojima
Shōdo-
Shima
Tonoshō
Harima-
Nada
Awaji-Shima
Sumoto

Tsuno-Shima
Nagato
Aso
Itsukaichi
HIROSHIMA
Takehara
In'no-shima
Marugame
Takamatsu
Hiketa
Nandan

Hibiki-
Nada
YAMAGUCHI
Ōtake
Kure
Iwakuni
Ōmishima
Tadotsu
Zentsūji
KAGAWA
Naruto
Naruto-Kaikyō

Yamaguchi
Mine
Hōfu
Nan'yō
Tokuyama
Hiroshima-Wan
Yashiro-
Jima
Aki-Nada
Hōjō
Hiuchi-
Nada
Kan'onji
Sanuki-Sammyaku
Komatsujima
Tokushima

Shimonoseki
Onoda
Ube
Kudamatsu
Hikari
Yanai
Naga-Shima
Hime-Jima
Matsuyama
Nyūgawa
Niihama
Iyo-mishima
Anabuki
Kamojima

KITAKYŪSHŪ
Nakama
Suō-Nada
Heigun-To
Matsusaki
Iyo
Shizuchi-Yama
1981
Saijō
TOKUSHIMA-Sanchi
Tsurugi-San
1955
Anan
Gamōda-
Saki

FUKUOKA
Miyuta
Iizuka
Takawa
Nakatsu
Futago-Yama
721
Kunisaki
Iyo-Nada
Ōzu
Uchiko
Ōda
Sagawa
Kōchi
Tosa-yamada
Mugi

Yobuko
Karatsu
Umi
Nōgata
Yukuhashi
Buzen
Usa
Bungotakada
Uwa
Yawatahama
Susaki
Kōchi
Tosa
Aki
Muroto

Ō-Shima
FUKUOKA
Yamada
Sanchi
1200
Hita
Hiji
Kitsuki
Hōgo-Kaikyō
Uwajima
Hiromi
Kubokawa
Tosa-Wan
Muroto-Misaki

Ikitsuki-
Shima
Matsuura
SAGA
Sefuri-San
1055
Tosu
Amagi
Kusu
Yufu-Dake
1584
Beppu-Wan
Ekawasaki
Saga
Tosa-shimizu

Hirado
Imari
Taku
Saga
Yame
Kurogi
Beppu
Ōita
Saganoseki

Hirado-
Shima
Takeo
Okawa
Chikugo
Setaka
Kusu
Ōita
Usuki

SAGA
Kashima
Yanagawa
OITA
Oguni
1787
Tsukumi
Bungo-Suidō
Jōben
Nakamura

Sasebo
Ariake-Kai
Ōmuta
Yamaga
Aso
Enomiya
Saiki
Tsurumi-Saki

NAGASAKI
Tara
Tara-Dake
983
Arao
Tamana
Kikuchi
Aso-San
1592
Sobo-Yama
1758
Kamae
Tosa-shimizu

Omura-
Wan
Isahaya
Kumamoto
Mashiki
Takachiho
Oki-no-Shima
Sukumo

Nagasaki
Ōmura
Unzen-Dake
1360
Shimabara
Uto
KUMAMOTO
Hinokage
Nobeoka
Ashizuri-Zaki

Nishi-Sonogi-Hantō
Obama
Misumi
Kunimi-Dake
1739
Shiiba
Hyūga

Tachibana-Wan
Kuchinotsu
Oyano
Kyūshū-Sanchi
Itsuki
Hososhima

Amakusa-
Hondo
Kami-
Jima
Yatsushiro
Yunomae
MIYAZAKI
Nomo-Zaki
Amakusa-
Shotō
Nada
Shimo-
Jima
Yatsushiro-Kai
Hitoyoshi
Shiba
Saito
Takanabe

Ushibuka
Naga-Shima
Minamata
KYŪSHŪ
Izumi
Ebino
Saito
KYŪSHŪ-DISTRICT

Kami-koshiki-
Jima
Akune
Ōkuchi
Kobayashi
Yoshino
Shimo-koshiki-
Jima
Miyanojō
Kurino
1700
Kirishima-Yama
Miyakonojō
Nichinan

Koshiki-
Rettō
Sendai
Kaji
Kokubu
Miyazaki

Shimo-koshiki-
Jima
Kushikino
Ijūin
Hayato
Miyakonojō
Nichinan
Aburatsu

Kagoshima
On-Take
1118
KAGOSHIMA
Shibushi
Kushima

Taniyama
Fukiage
KAGOSHIMA
Tarumizu
Kanoya
Shibushi-Wan

Noma-Saki
Kaseda
Chiran
Kagoshima-
Wan
Koyama
Kōyama

Makurazaki
Ōsumi-Hantō

Bō-no-Misaki
Kaimon-Dake
924
Ibusuki
Yamagawa
Sata-Misaki

Genkai-
Nada

Higasi-Suidō

Kara-Saki

Tsushima

Izuhara

Kō-Saki

Iki

Iki-Kaikyō

Ō-Shima

Katsumoto

Fukuma

Mi-Shima

CHŪGOKU-DISTRICT

SHIKOKU

SHIKOKU-DISTRICT

EHIME

KŌCHI

SHIKOKU-Sanchi

Tosa-Wan

KYŪSHŪ

1 : 2 000 000

10   0   10   20   30   40   50 miles

10   0   20   40   60   80 km

CHŪBU-DISTRICT

KANTŌ-DISTRICT

KINKI-DISTRICT

Kashima-Nada

HŪ

H

Kanazawa   Matsutō   **Toyama**   **Takaoka**   Himi   Shinminato   Uozu   Namerikawa   Oyabe   Tsubata   Tonami   **Nagano**   Nakano   Suzaka   Nakanojō   Numata   Nikko   **Utsunomiya**   **Hitachi**   Daigo   Karasuyama   Hitachi-ota   Katsuta   Nakaminato   **Mito**   Ōarai

Komatsu   Kaga   ISHIKAWA   Yamanaka   Hakusan   Takayama   Furukawa   Kamioka   Ōmachi   Kōshoku   Shinonoi   Ueda   Asama-Yama   Shibukawa   **Kiryū**   **Ashikaga**   Tochigi   Kanuma   Kasama   Mo'oka

Fukui   Sabae   Ono   FUKUI   Katsuyama   **Matsumoto**   Saku   Komoro   **Maebashi**   **Takasaki**   Tomioka   Ōta   Isesaki   Honjō   Fukaya   Hanyū   Gyoda   Konosu   **Omiya**   **Kashiwa**   Tsuchiura   Ishioka   Hakota

Tsuruga   Takefu   Echizen-Misaki   Mikuni   Maruoka   Shiojiri   Okaya   Suwa   Chino   Chichibu   SAITAMA   Ageo   **Urawa**   Warabi   Kawaguchi   **Matsudo**   Narita   **Chiba**   **Chōshi**   Yokaichiba

Wakasa-Wan   Obama   GIFU   Hachiman   Gero   Ina   Komagane   **Kōfu**   Yamanashi   Enzan   Ōtsuki   **Hachiōji**   Tachikawa   **Kodaira**   Musashino   **TŌKYŌ**   Ichikawa   Sakura   Asahi   Naruto

Maizuru   Fukuchiyama   Ayabe   Nagahama   Mino   Seki   Inuyama   Mizunami   Akechi   Nakatsugawa   Iida   YAMANASHI   Fuji-yoshida   Tsuru   Tanzawa-Sanchi   Yamato   Machida   **KAWASAKI**   **YOKOHAMA**   Ichihara   Mobara

Gifu   **Ōgaki**   Hashima   **Ichinomiya**   Mino-Kamo   Tajimi   Komaki   **Toyota**   Sagamihara   KANAGAWA   Fujisawa   Kamakura   **Yokosuka**   Kisarazu   Ōhara

KYOTO   Ōtsu   Hikone   Inazawa   Kuwana   Kasugai   **NAGOYA**   Seto   Mino-Mikawa-Kōgen   Gotemba   Hiratsuka   Chigasaki   Odawara   Mishima   Atami

Takatsuki   Uji   Kusatsu   SHIGA   Tōkai   Kariya   **Okazaki**   Toyokawa   Shinshiro   Fuji-no-miya   **Fuji**   Numazu   Ito   Sagami-Nada   Tateyama

Yamashina   **Yokkaichi**   Suzuka   Tokoname   Anjō   Hekinan   Shimada   Kakegawa   **Shizuoka**   **Shimizu**   Su-no-Saki   Nojima-Zaki

Nara   Ueno   Kameyama   Tsu   Handa   Gamagori   **Toyohashi**   Hamakita   Tenryū   Yaizu   Suruga-Wan

OSAKA   **Sakai**   Matsubara   Tenri   Nabari   MIE   Ise-Wan   **Matsusaka**   Tahara   **Hamamatsu**   Iwata   Fukuroi   Sagara   Omae-Zaki   Enshū-Nada

Wakayama   Arida   Gojō   Hashimoto   NARA   Ise   Toba   Shima-Hantō   Ago   Irako-Zaki   Daiō-Misaki

Tanabe   Shirahama   Kushimoto   Shio-no-Misaki   Kumano   Owase   Nachikatsuura   Shingū   Kii-Hantō   WAKAYAMA   Kumano-Nada

Mihara-Yama   755   Ō-Shima   Shimoda   To-Shima   Nii-Jima   Shikine-Jima   Kōzu-Shima   Miyake-Jima

Mikura-Jima   Aoga-Shima   Hachijō-Jima

PACIFIC OCEAN

Sumisu-Jima

m
9000   3000
6000   2000
4500   1500
3000   1000
1200   400
600   200
0   0
200   600
2000   6000
4000   12 000
m ft

East from Greenwich

COPYRIGHT. GEORGE PHILIP & SON, LTD.

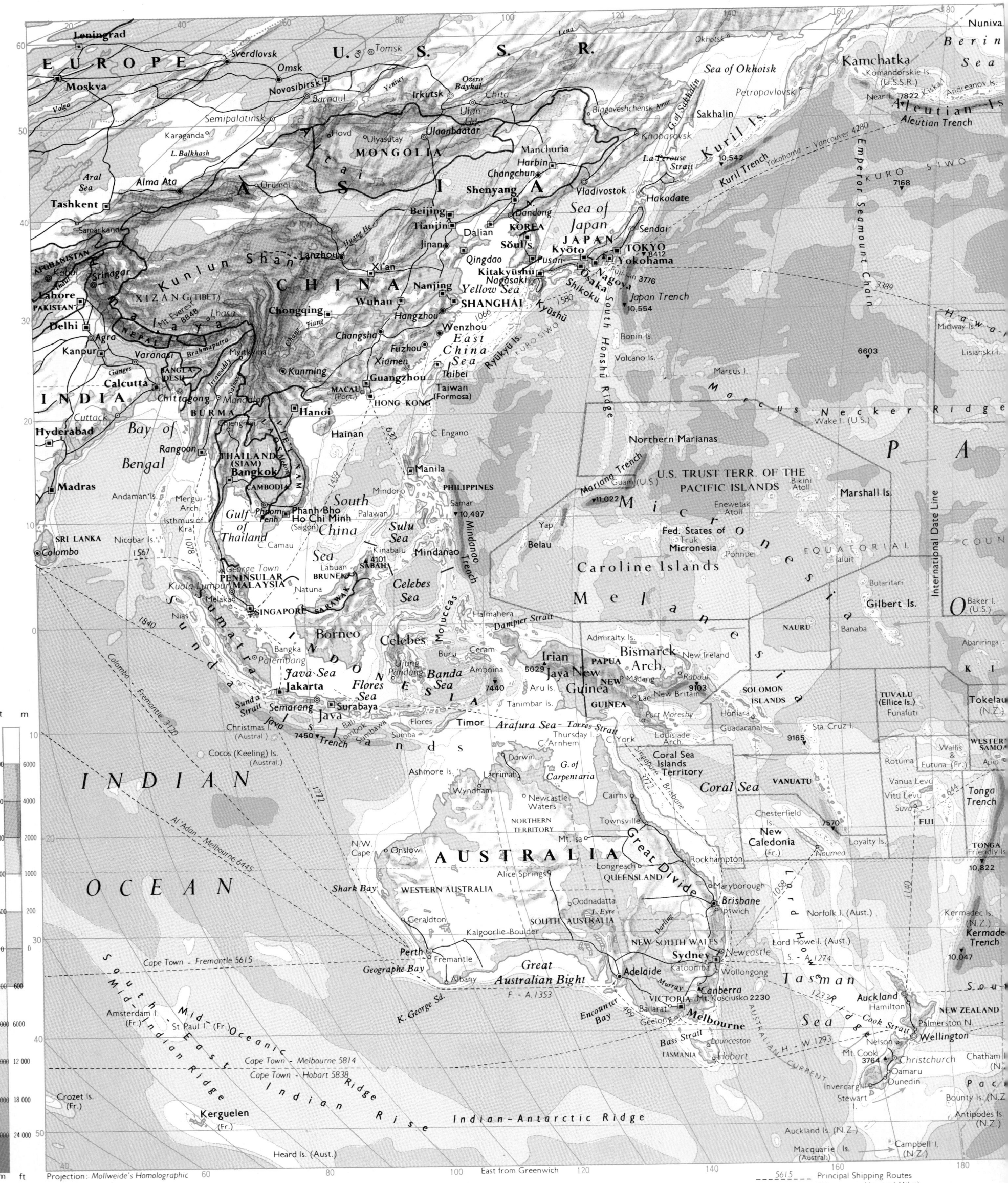
EUROPE
Leningrad
Moskva
Volga
Sverdlovsk
Omsk
U. S. S. R.
Tomsk
Ob
Novosibirsk
Barnaul
Semipalatinsk
Karaganda
L. Balkhash
Aral Sea
Tashkent
Alma Ata
Samarkand
Irkutsk
Ozero Baykal
Yenisey
Lena
Chita
Ulan Ude
Hovd
Ulyasutay
Ulaanbaatar
MONGOLIA
Altai
ASIA
Urumqi
Blagoveshchensk
Amur
Khabarovsk
Manchuria
Harbin
Changchun
Shenyang
Vladivostok
Beijing
Tianjin
Dalian
N. KOREA
Dandong
Jinan
Huang He
Lanzhou
Xi'an
Qingdao
Sŏul
S. KOREA
Pusan
Kitakyūshū
Nagasaki
Sea of Japan
JAPAN
Kyōto
Ōsaka
Nagoya
TŌKYŌ
Yokohama
Fuji-san 3776
Shikoku
Kyūshū
Sendai
Hakodate
Sea of Okhotsk
Okhotsk
G. of Sakhalin
Sakhalin
La Perouse Strait
Kuril Is.
10,542
Kuril Trench
Kamchatka
Petropavlovsk
Komandorskie Is. (U.S.S.R.)
Near I.
7822
Kiska I.
Andreanof Is.
Aleutian Is.
Aleutian Trench
Bering Sea
Nuniva
Yokohama - Vancouver 4280
Emperor Seamount Chain
KURO SIWO
7168
3389
AFGHANISTAN
Kabul
Indus
Srinagar
Lahore
PAKISTAN
Delhi
Agra
Kanpur
Varanasi
Ganges
Kunlun Shan
XIZANG (TIBET)
Lhasa
Mt. Everest 8848
Himalaya
NEPAL
Brahmaputra
BANGLADESH
Calcutta
Chittagong
INDIA
Cuttack
Hyderabad
Bay of Bengal
Madras
SRI LANKA
Colombo
CHINA
Chongqing
Chang Jiang
Wuhan
Nanjing
SHANGHAI
Hangzhou
Yellow Sea
Changsha
Wenzhou
East China Sea
Fuzhou
Xiamen
Taibei
Taiwan (Formosa)
Guangzhou
MACAU (Port.)
HONG KONG
Kunming
Myitkyina
Irrawaddy
Salween
Mandalay
BURMA
Rangoon
Hanoi
Hainan
LAOS
VIETNAM
Mekong
Chiengmai
THAILAND (SIAM)
Bangkok
KAMPUCHEA
Phnom Penh
Ho Chi Minh (Saigon)
Gulf of Thailand
Andaman Is.
Mergui Arch.
Isthmus of Kra
Nicobar Is.
1567
1078
C. Camau
South China Sea
George Town
PENINSULAR MALAYSIA
Kuala Lumpur
Melaka
SINGAPORE
Natuna
Labuan
BRUNEI
SABAH
Kinabalu 4101
SARAWAK
Borneo
Sumatra
Nias
Bangka
Palembang
Java Sea
Jakarta
Sunda Strait
Semarang
Surabaya
Java
Bali
Lombok
Sumbawa
Flores Sea
Flores
Sumba
Timor
Java Trench
7450
Sunda Islands
INDONESIA
Celebes
Ujung Pandang
Banda Sea
Buru
Ceram
Amboina
7440
Aru Is.
Tanimbar Is.
Moluccas
Halmahera
Celebes Sea
Sulu Sea
Mindanao
Mindanao Trench
Manila
Mindoro
Palawan
PHILIPPINES
Samar
10,497
C. Engano
Ryukyu Is.
KURO SIWO
1066
1580
1459
630
Dampier Strait
Irian Jaya
5029
PAPUA NEW GUINEA
New Guinea
Madang
Lae
Port Moresby
Bismarck Arch.
New Ireland
Rabaul
New Britain
9103
SOLOMON ISLANDS
Honiara
Guadacanal
Louisiade Arch.
Arafura Sea
Torres Strait
Thursday I.
C. York
C. Arnhem
Darwin
G. of Carpentaria
Ashmore Is.
Larrimah
Wyndham
Newcastle Waters
NORTHERN TERRITORY
Cairns
Townsville
Mt. Isa
AUSTRALIA
N.W. Cape
Onslow
Alice Springs
Longreach
QUEENSLAND
Great Divide
Rockhampton
Maryborough
Brisbane
Ipswich
WESTERN AUSTRALIA
Shark Bay
Oodnadatta
L. Eyre
SOUTH AUSTRALIA
Darling
Geraldton
Kalgoorlie-Boulder
NEW SOUTH WALES
Perth
Fremantle
Geographe Bay
Albany
Great Australian Bight
F. - A. 1353
K. George Sd.
Adelaide
Murray
Sydney
Newcastle
Katoomba
Wollongong
Canberra
Mt. Kosciusko 2230
VICTORIA
Ballarat
Geelong
Melbourne
Encounter Bay
499
Bass Strait
Launceston
TASMANIA
Hobart
AUSTRALIAN CURRENT
Coral Sea Islands Territory
Coral Sea
Singapore - Brisbane 3772
VANUATU
Chesterfield Is.
7570
New Caledonia (Fr.)
Noumea
Loyalty Is.
Lord Howe Rise
Norfolk I. (Aust.)
Lord Howe I. (Aust.)
S. - A. 1274
Tasman Sea
1233
H. - W. 1293
Auckland
Hamilton
NEW ZEALAND
Palmerston N.
Cook Strait
Wellington
Nelson
Mt. Cook 3764
Christchurch
Oamaru
Dunedin
Invercargill
Stewart I.
Chatham Is.
Bounty Is. (N.Z.)
Antipodes Is. (N.Z.)
Auckland Is. (N.Z.)
Macquarie Is. (Austral.)
Campbell I. (N.Z.)
Kermadec Is. (N.Z.)
Kermadec Trench
10,047
TONGA Friendly Is.
Tonga Trench
10,822
FIJI
Vanua Levu
Vitu Levu
Suva
644
Rotuma
Wallis & Futuna (Fr.)
WESTERN SAMOA
Apia
Tokelau (N.Z.)
TUVALU (Ellice Is.)
Funafuti
Sta. Cruz I.
9165
NAURU
Banaba
Abariringa
Gilbert Is.
Butaritari
Baker I. (U.S.)
Marshall Is.
Bikini Atoll
Enewetak Atoll
Jaluit
EQUATORIAL COUNTER CURRENT
Pohnpei
Truk
Fed. States of Micronesia
Caroline Islands
Micronesia
Melanesia
Belau
Yap
Guam (U.S.)
11,022
Mariana Trench
Northern Marianas
U.S. TRUST TERR. OF THE PACIFIC ISLANDS
Marcus Necker Ridge
Wake I. (U.S.)
Marcus I.
Volcano Is.
Bonin Is.
South Honshu Ridge
Japan Trench
10,554
8412
6603
Hawaiian Is.
Midway Is.
Lisianski I.
International Date Line
PACIFIC OCEAN
INDIAN OCEAN
Christmas I. (Austral.)
Cocos (Keeling) Is. (Austral.)
1840
1772
Colombo - Fremantle 3120
Al 'Adan - Melbourne 6445
Cape Town - Fremantle 5615
Cape Town - Melbourne 5814
Cape Town - Hobart 5838
South-East Indian Ridge
Mid-Oceanic Ridge
Mid-Indian Ridge
Indian Rise
Indian-Antarctic Ridge
Amsterdam I. (Fr.)
St. Paul I. (Fr.)
Crozet Is. (Fr.)
Kerguelen (Fr.)
Heard Is. (Aust.)
ft
m
18 000
6000
12 000
4000
6000
2000
3000
1000
600
200
0
0
200
600
2000
6000
4000
12 000
6000
18 000
8000
24 000
m
ft
Projection: Mollweide's Homolographic
East from Greenwich
5615 Principal Shipping Routes
(Distances in Nautical Miles)

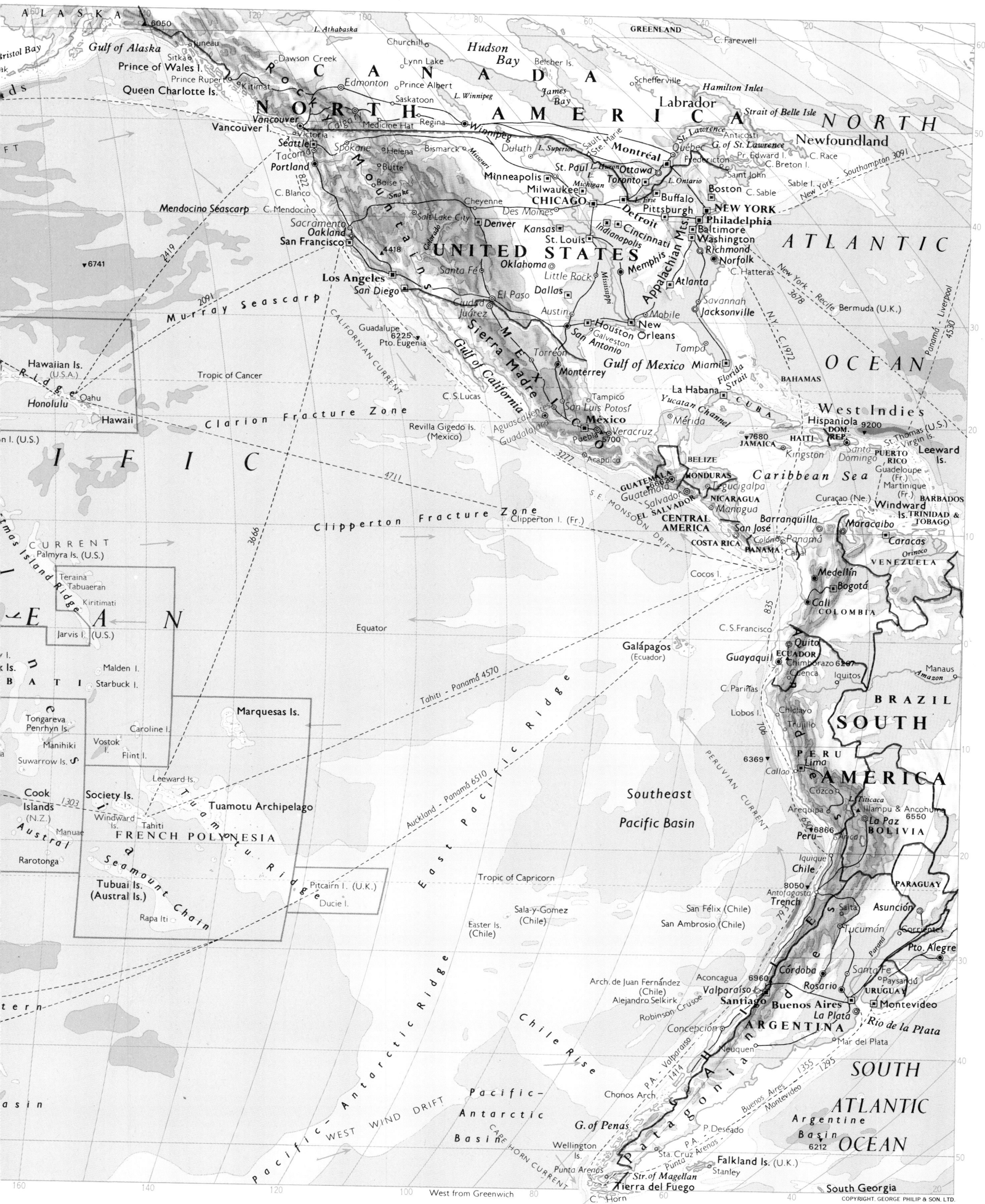

ALASKA
6050
Gulf of Alaska
Bristol Bay
Juneau
Sitka
Prince of Wales I.
Prince Rupert
Queen Charlotte Is.
Kitimat
Vancouver
Vancouver I.
Victoria
Seattle
Tacoma
Portland
C. Blanco
Mendocino Seascarp
C. Mendocino
Sacramento
Oakland
San Francisco
6741
Los Angeles
San Diego

CANADA
NORTH AMERICA
Dawson Creek
Edmonton
Prince Albert
Saskatoon
Medicine Hat
Regina
Winnipeg
L. Athabaska
Churchill
Lynn Lake
L. Winnipeg
Bismarck
Helena
Butte
Boise
Cheyenne
Salt Lake City
Denver
4418
UNITED STATES
Santa Fé
Oklahoma
El Paso
Ciudad Juárez
Dallas
Austin
Torreón
Houston
San Antonio
Galveston

Hudson Bay
Belcher Is.
James Bay
Scheffervilie
Hamilton Inlet
St. Lawrence
Anticosti
G. of St. Lawrence
Newfoundland
C. Race
Southampton 3091

GREENLAND
C. Farewell

NORTH

Labrador
Strait of Belle Isle

Duluth
L. Superior
Ste. Marie
Montréal
Québec
Fredericton
Pr. Edward I.
C. Breton I.
Sable I.
Saint John
Minneapolis
St. Paul
Milwaukee
L. Michigan
Ottawa
Toronto
L. Huron
L. Ontario
L. Erie
Buffalo
Boston
New York
CHICAGO
Detroit
Pittsburgh
Philadelphia
Cincinnati
Indianapolis
Baltimore
Washington
Richmond
Norfolk
St. Louis
Memphis
Little Rock
Atlanta
C. Hatteras
Mobile
Savannah
Jacksonville
New Orleans
Tampa
Miami

ATLANTIC

OCEAN

New York - Recife 3678
Bermuda (U.K.)

Tropic of Cancer
Hawaiian Is. (U.S.A.)
Oahu
Honolulu
Hawaii

Murray Seascarp
2091
CALIFORNIAN CURRENT
Guadalupe
6225
Pto. Eugenia
C. S. Lucas
Gulf of California
Sierra Madre
MEXICO
Aguascalientes
Guadalajara
Revilla Gigedo Is. (Mexico)
San Luis Potosí
México
3277
Puebla 5700
Veracruz
Acapulco
Tampico
Monterrey
Gulf of Mexico
Mérida
Yucatán Channel
La Habana
CUBA
Florida Strait
BAHAMAS
West Indies
Hispaniola
HAITI
JAMAICA
9200
DOM. REP.
Kingston
Santo Domingo
PUERTO RICO
St. Thomas (U.S.)
Virgin Is.
Leeward Is.

Clarion Fracture Zone
4711

PACIFIC
OCEAN
Clipperton Fracture Zone
3666
Clipperton I. (Fr.)
S.E. MONSOON DRIFT
BELIZE
GUATEMALA
6882
Guatemala
San Salvador
EL SALVADOR
CENTRAL AMERICA
HONDURAS
Tegucigalpa
NICARAGUA
Managua
COSTA RICA
San José
PANAMA
Colón
Panamá
Panama Canal
Caribbean Sea
Curaçao (Ne.)
Barranquilla
Maracaibo
Martinique (Fr.)
Guadeloupe (Fr.)
Windward Is.
BARBADOS
TRINIDAD & TOBAGO
Caracas
VENEZUELA
Orinoco

Hawaiian Ridge
Palmyra Is. (U.S.)
KIRIBATI
Teraina Tabuaeran
Kiritimati
Jarvis I. (U.S.)
Malden I.
Starbuck I.
Cocos I.
C. S. Francisco
Medellín
Bogotá
Cali
COLOMBIA
835
Quito
ECUADOR
Guayaquil
Chimborazo 6207
Cuenca
Iquitos
Manaus
Amazon
BRAZIL
SOUTH
AMERICA
C. Pariñas
Lobos Is.
Chiclayo
Trujillo
706
PERU
6369
Callao
Lima
Cozco

Equator

Galápagos (Ecuador)

Tongareva Penrhyn
Manihiki
Suwarrow Is.
Vostok
Flint I.
Caroline I.
Marquesas Is.
Tuamotu Archipelago
Society Is.
Leeward Is.
Windward Is.
Tahiti
FRENCH POLYNESIA
Manuae
Cook Islands (N.Z.)
Rarotonga
Austral
Tubuai Is. (Austral Is.)
Rapa Iti
Seamount Chain
Pitcairn I. (U.K.)
Ducie I.

Tahiti - Panamá 4570
Auckland - Panamá 6510
East Pacific Ridge
Southeast
Pacific Basin
PERUVIAN CURRENT
Arequipa
Titicaca
Illampu & Ancohuma 6550
6866
La Paz
BOLIVIA
Peru
Iquique
Chile
Antofagasta
8050
Trench
6960
Aconcagua
Córdoba
Rosario
Santa Fé
PARAGUAY
Asunción
Tucumán
Salta
Corrientes
URUGUAY
Paysandú
Pto. Alegre

Tropic of Capricorn
Sala-y-Gomez (Chile)
Easter Is. (Chile)
San Félix (Chile)
San Ambrosio (Chile)
Arch. de Juan Fernández (Chile)
Alejandro Selkirk
Robinson Crusoe
Valparaíso
Santiago
Buenos Aires
La Plata
Montevideo
Concepción
ARGENTINA
Río de la Plata
Mar del Plata
Neuquén

Chile Rise
Chonos Arch.
Patagonia
1414
1355
1795
SOUTH
Argentine
Basin
ATLANTIC
OCEAN
6212
G. of Penas
P. Deseado
Sta. Cruz Arenas
Falkland Is. (U.K.)
Stanley
Wellington
Punta Arenas
Str. of Magellan
Tierra del Fuego
C. Horn
CAPE HORN CURRENT
South Georgia

Pacific-Antarctic Ridge
WEST WIND DRIFT
Pacific-Antarctic Basin

West from Greenwich
COPYRIGHT. GEORGE PHILIP & SON. LTD.

1 : 4 000 000

50 0 50 100 miles
50 0 50 100 150 km

FIJI

VANUATU

Great Sea Reef
Undu Pt.
Ringgold Isles
Vanua Levu
1031
Rambi
Nggamea
Savusavu
Nambouwalu
Somosomo Str.
Taveuni
Nanuku Passage
Lomaloma
Vanua Mbalavu
Mango
Thithia
Tuvutha
Nayau
Koro
Ngau
Lakemba Passage
Lakemba
Moala
Matuku
Totoya
Kambara
Namuka-i-Lau
Ongea Levu

Yasawa Group
Yasawa
Naviti
Waya
Bligh Water
Mamanutha Group
Lautoka
Tavua
1322 Tomaniivi
Nandi
Viti Levu
Navua
Singatoka
Nausori
Suva
Ovalau
Levuka
Mbengga
Vatulele
Kandavu
Ono
Vunisea
Kandavu Passage

Koro Sea
Lau (Eastern) Group

Torres Is.
Hiu
Tegua
Loh
Toga
Ureparapara
Mota Lava
Mota
Banks Is.
Vanua Lava
951
Gaua
Tarasag
797
Mera Lava
1030

Espíritu Santo
C. Cumberland
Nokuku 1372
C. Queiros
Molau
Mt. Tabwemasana 1810
Pusei
Sora
326 Malo
Maewo (Aurora)
811
Nasawa
Lolowai
Nduindui 1496
Aoba
Patteson Passage
614
Norsup Lakatoro
Mt. Penot 863
Malekula (Mallicolo)
Lamap
Maskelyne Is.
5303
1279 Mt. Marum
Ambrym
Paama
Lopevi 1413
833 Epi
Valesdir
Tongoa
Shepherd Is.
Emaï
Mataso
Nguna
Moso
Efate (Vaté)
Mt. Macdonald 647
Manouro Pt.
Devil's Pt.
Vila
886
Erromango
Ipota
Aniwa
Tanna 1084
Isangel
Whitesands
Aneityum
Aname
Pentecost (Pentecôte) 946
3334

PAPUA NEW GUINEA
Bougainville
Shortland
Mono
Treasury Is.
Vella Lavella
New Georgia Is.
Ganongga
Rendova

C. Alexander
Momarana
Nukiki
Choiseul
Sasamungga 1067
Luti
Shortland Is.
Rob Roy
Wagina
Barorafa
Kia
Barora Ite
Santa Isabel
Gatere
Dadali 1219 Buala
Susubona
Tataba
Sepi

Maravari
Vella
Moungga
Gizo
Kula Gulf
Munda
Segi
Vangunu
Gatukai
Lokuru
New Georgia
San Jorge
Russell Is.
Yandina
Pavuvu
Florida Is.
Savo
C. Esperance
Visale
Honiara 2439
Guadalcanal
C. Hunter
Avu Avu

Malaita
Malu'u
Dala
Auki
Anaano 1432
Su'u
Takataka
Maramasike
Sa'a
C. Zelee
Ulawa

C. Astrolabe
C. Aracides
Indispensable Strait

Ubuna
Ugi
Three Sisters Is.
Moroga 1250
Kira Kira
Wainoni
San Cristóbal
Hagaruhu
Santa Ona

TONGA

'Uta Vava'u
Hunga
Vava'u
Neiafu Group
Fonualei
Toku
Late
Home Reef
Disney Reef
Kao
Tofua
Fotuha'a
Kotu Group
Nomuka Group
Fonuafo'ou
Hunga Ha'apai
Ha'ano
Foa
Lifuka
Uiha
Ha'aleva
Oto Tolu Group
Tonumea
Nuku'alofa
Tongatapu Group
Eua

GUAM
Ritidian Pt.
Upi
Pati Pt.
Orote Peninsula
Agat
Agana
Mt. Lamlam 405 Guam
Umatac
Inarajan
Cocos I.
Ajayan Pt.

ÎLES DU VENT
Moorea
Papetoai
Papenoo
Afareaitu
Punavia
Papeete
Tahiti
Papeari
Mt. Roonui 1332
Tautira
Presqu'île de Taiarapu
Pte. Fareara

TAHITI AND MOORÉA

WESTERN SAMOA
Sataua
Fagamalo
Pu'apu'a
Falelima 1858
Taga
Faga
Savai'i
Satupa'itea
Safata Bay
Mulifanua
Falelatai
Lotofaga 1100
Upolu
Apia
Ti'avea
Amaile

AMERICAN SAMOA (U.S.A.)
Ofu
Tau
Tutuila
Pago Pago
Pago Pago Hbr.
Manua Is.
Vaitogi

SAMOAN ISLANDS

SOLOMON ISLANDS

Bellona
Rennell

NEW CALEDONIA AND LOYALTY ISLANDS
Yandé
Î. Baaba
Balabio
Pte. Nendiarene
Récif de la Gazelle
Î. Neba
Poum
Ouegoa
Oubatche
Î. Beautemps-Beaupré
Paagoumène
Koumac
Kaala-Gomén
Mt. Panié 1628
Hienghène
Touho
Is. Loyauté (Loyalty Is.)
Uvéa
St.-Joseph
Fayaoué
C. Escarpé
Chépénéhe
Ouaco
Voh 1385
Poindimié
Wé
Î. Lifu
Massif de Tchingou
Ponérihouen
Koné
Pouembout
Mé Maoya 1508
Houailou
Tiga
3566
Poya
Kouaoua
C. de Flotte
Bourail
Canala
Tadine
Î. Maré
Moindou
Thio
C. Wabao
La Foa 1441 1610
Massif du Humbolt
C. Boyer
Boulouparis
2212
Pavitou
Dumbéa
Barrage Yaté
Nouméa
Mont Dore
Île Ouen
Cap N'dua
Île des Pins

Projection: Mercator

COPYRIGHT. GEORGE PHILIP & SON. LTD.

ft m
6000 2000
4500 1500
3000 1000
1200 400
600 200
0 0
200 600
2000 6000
4000 12 000
6000 18 000
m ft

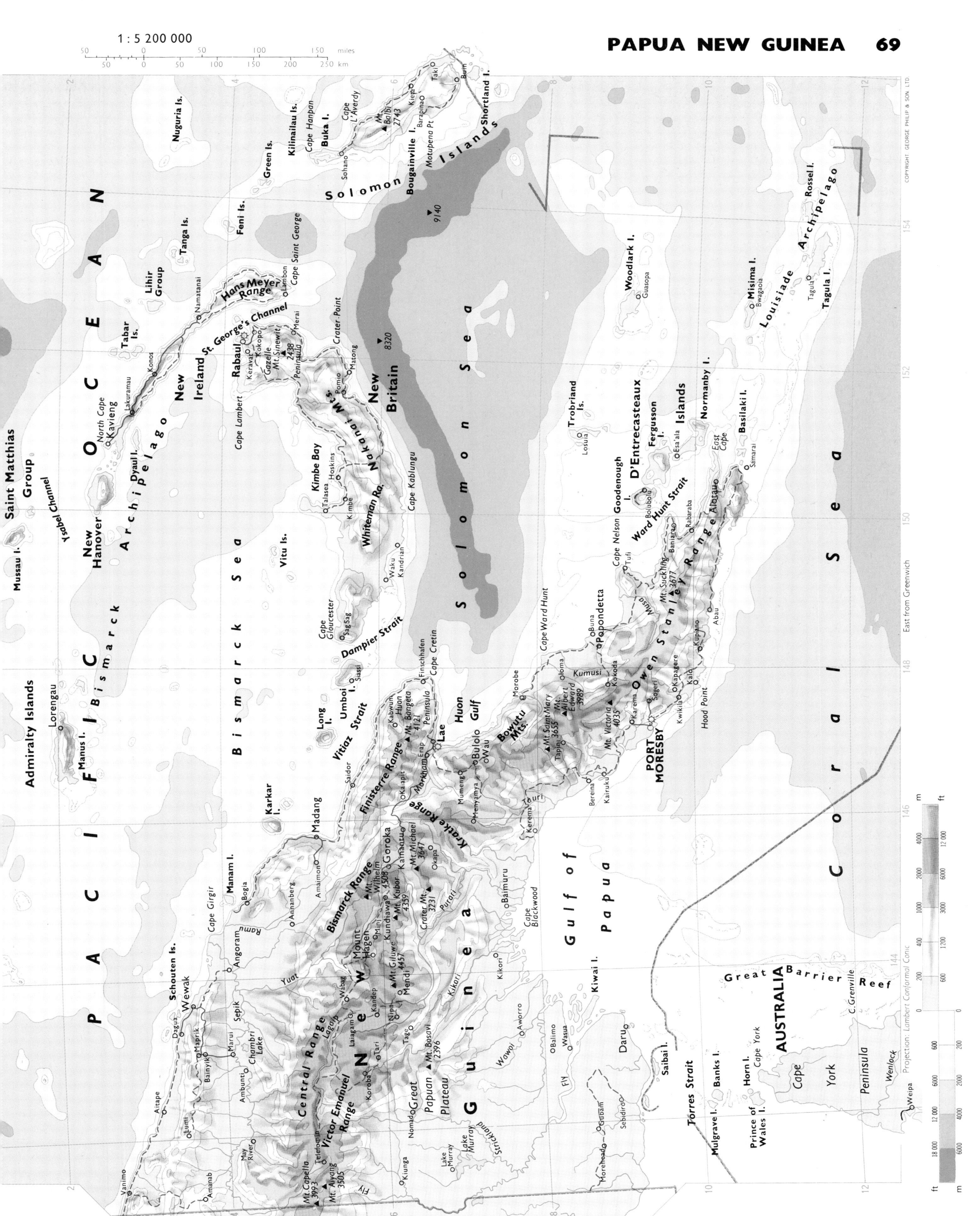

1 : 5 200 000

COPYRIGHT GEORGE PHILIP & SON. LTD.

East from Greenwich

Projection: Lambert Conformal Conic

Java Trench
TIMOR SEA
INDIAN OCEAN
WESTERN AUSTRALIA
NORTHERN TERRITORY
SOUTH AUSTRALIA
Great Sandy Desert
Gibson Desert
Great Victoria Desert
Tanami Desert
Nullarbor Plain
Great Australian Bight
Kimberley
Darling Range
Hamersley Ra.
Macdonnell Ras.
Musgrave Ranges
Perth
Fremantle
Kalgoorlie-Boulder
Darwin
Geraldton
Carnarvon
Albany
Esperance
Broome
Derby
Port Hedland
Bunbury
Projection: Bonne
East from Greenwich
ft m
6000 2000
4500 1500
3000 1000
1200 400
600 200
0 0
200 600
2000 6000
4000 12 000
6000 18 000
m ft

1 : 11 200 000

100 50 0   100   200   300   400 miles
100   0   100   200   300   400   500   600 km

C O R A L   S E A

CORAL SEA

CORAL   SEA   ISLANDS

TERRITORY

P A C I F I C   O C E A N

QUEENSLAND

Great Dividing Range

Great Dividing Range

Grey Range

NEW SOUTH WALES

New England Range

VICTORIA

Australian Alps

MELBOURNE

TASMANIA

Hobart

Bass Strait

T A S M A N   S E A

Gulf of Carpentaria

Cape York Peninsula

Groote Eylandt

Thursday I.
Prince of Wales I.
C. York
Endeavour Str.
Banks I.
P. Musgrave
Cape Wenlock
Shelburne B.
C. Grenville
Temple B.
Weipa
Duifken Pt.
Albatross B.
Archer
Holroyd
Coleman
Coen
Princess Charlotte B.
Bathurst B.
C. Melville
Normanby
C. Direction
C. Weymouth
C. Flattery
Cooktown
C. Bedford
C. Tribulation
Mossman
Cairns
C. Grafton
Atherton
Bartle Frere 1612
Innisfail
Chillagoe Mareeba
Ravenshoe
Croydon
Einasleigh
Forsayth
Hinchinbrook I.
Ingham
Palm Is.
Halifax B.
Normanton
Gilbert
Norman
Gregory Ra.
Cleveland B.
C. Bowling Green
Townsville
Ayr
Charters Towers
Home Hill
Bowen
Whitsunday I.
Proserpine
Collinsville
Cumberland Is.
Netherdale
Mackay
Palmerston
C. Townshend
Townshend I.
Swain Rfs.
Pentland
Hughenden
Richmond
Belyando
Denham Ra.
Connors Ra.
Broad Sd.
Winton
Muttaburra
Aramac
Clermont
Emerald
Nogoa
Rockhampton
Keppel B.
C. Capricorn
Curtis I.
P. Curtis
Gladstone
Longreach
Barcaldine
Alpha
Peak Downs
Mt. Morgan
Ilfracombe
Blackall
Springsure
Biloela
Theodore
Monto
Bundaberg
Sandy C.
Hervey Bay Fraser I.
Jundah
Yaraka
Augathella
Childers
Pialba
Maryborough
Windorah
Adavale
Injune
Taroom Wandoan
Gayndah
Wondai
Gympie
Yambum
Quilpie
Charleville
Mitchell
Roma Miles
Murgon
Kingaroy Nanango
Dalby
Caboolture
Bribie I.
Moreton I.
N. Stradbroke I.
Brisbane
Ipswich
Moonie
Toowoomba
Southport
Gold Coast
Warwick
Murwillumbah
Byron Bay
C. Byron
Lismore
Ballina
Casino
Kyogle
Tenterfield
Clarence
Glen Innes
Grafton
Inverell
Round Mt.
Coffs Harbour
Nambucca Heads
Armidale
Macleay
Tamworth
Kempsey
Barrington Tops
Port Macquarie
Gunnedah
Liverpool Plains
Muswellbrook
Singleton
Maitland
P. Stephens
Newcastle
Cessnock
Lithgow
SYDNEY
Katoomba
Hawkesbury R.
Penrith
Liverpool
Wollongong
Shellharbour
Bathurst
Orange
Cowra
Young
Goulburn
CANBERRA
Queanbeyan
Jervis B.
Cooma
Batemans B.
Bombala
Twofold B.
Mt. Kosciusko 2230
Bega
Eden
Disaster B.
C. Howe
Mallacoota Inlet
Snowy
Everard
Ninety Mile Beach
Wilsons Promontory
King I.
Flinders I.
Furneaux Group
Cape Barren I.
Clarke I.
Devonport
George Town
Scottsdale
Launceston
Ben Lomond
St. Marys
Freycinet Pen.
Burnie
Zeehan 1517
Mt. Ossa 1527
Great L.
Queenstown
Glenorchy
Tasman Penin.
Bruny I.
S.E. Cape
P. Davey
Low Rocky Pt.
Storm B.

Louisiade Archipelago
Misima I.
Rossel I.
Tagula I.
San Cristobal
Rennell
Avon Is.
Chesterfield Is.
Kenn Reef
Bellona Rfs.
Cato I.
Tropic of Capricorn
Bird I.
Lord Howe I.
Lihou Rfs. & Cays.
Saumarez Rf.
Osprey Rf.
Lihou Rfs.

Wessel Is.
The English Co. Is.
Wilberforce
Melville B.
Gove
C. Arnhem
P. Bradshaw
Caledon B.
C. Grey
Blue Mud B.
Angurugu
C. Beatrice
Limmen Bight
Sir Edward Pellew Group
Vanderlin I.
Borroloola
Mornington I.
C. van Diemen
Bentinck I.
Wellesley Is.
Burketown
Camooweal
Austral Downs
Mount Isa
Cloncurry
Julia Cr.
Kajabbi
Mary Kathleen
Duchess
Selwyn Ra.
Selwyn
Urandangi
Dajarra
Boulia
Bedourie
Birdsville
Diamantina
Thomson
Barcoo
Borgeo
Thargomindah
Cunnamulla
St. George
Dirranbandi
Goondiwindi
Mungindi
Macintyre
Moree
Gwydir
Narrabri
Coonamble
Walgett
Bourke
Barwon
Bogan
Coonabarabran
Gilgandra
Wellington
Dubbo
Narromine
Parkes
Forbes
Condobolin
Cargelligo
Hillston
Griffith
Leeton
Narrandera
Junee
Wagga Wagga
Albury
Cootamundra
Gundagai
Tumut
Yass
Deniliquin
Echuca
Bendigo
Shepparton
Benalla
Wangaratta
Mt. Bogong 1986
Mt. Hotham
Bairnsdale
Sale
Gippsland
Morwell
Traralgon
Warragul
Wonthaggi
Phillip I.
Port Phillip B.
Geelong
Colac
Warrnambool
Port Fairy
Portland
C. Bridgewater
C. Nelson
Discovery B.
C. Northumberland
Mt. Gambier
Millicent
Penola
Naracoorte
Hamilton
Mt. William
Ballarat
Maryborough
Castlemaine
Ararat
Stawell
Horsham
Kaniva
Bordertown
Kingston S.E.
Keith
Tailem Bend
Murray Bridge
Coorong
The Coorong
Encounter B.
Victor Harbor
Kangaroo I.
C. Jervis
Yankalilla
Adelaide
Elizabeth
Gawler
Port Pirie
Jamestown
Peterborough
Burra
Broken Hill
Wilcannia
Menindee
Ivanhoe
Hay
Balranald
Swan Hill
Kerang
Mildura
Wentworth
Renmark
Loxton
Pinnaroo
Ouyen
Murray
Murrumbidgee
Lachlan
Darling
Barrier Ra.
Barrier
Whyalla
Port Augusta
Quorn
Mt. Brown 934
Hawker
St. Mary's Pk.
Flinders Ranges
Mt. Bryan
L. Frome
L. Blanche
L. Callabonna
Tibooburra
Paroo
Warrego
Condamine
Balonne
Moonie
Macquarie
Castlereagh
Namoi
Gwydir
Liverpool
Macdonald
Lachlan
Murray
Hume
Eildon

Cooper Creek
Strzelecki Cr.
L. Yamma Yamma
L. Machattie
Eyre Cr.
Simpson Desert
Warburton
The Macumba
L. Eyre (North) -52
L. Eyre (South)
L. Gregory
Leigh Creek South
Marree
Lyndhurst
L. Torrens
Pimba
Woomera
Harris
L. Gairdner
Kimba
Iron Knob
Cowell
Cleve
Spencer Gulf
Port Lincoln
C. Spencer
Investigator Str.
Kangaroo I.
Yorke Penin.
Wallaroo
Kadina
Moonta
G. St. Vincent
Gawler Ranges

QUEENSLAND
NEW SOUTH WALES
SOUTH AUSTRALIA
VICTORIA

COPYRIGHT GEORGE PHILIP & SON LTD.

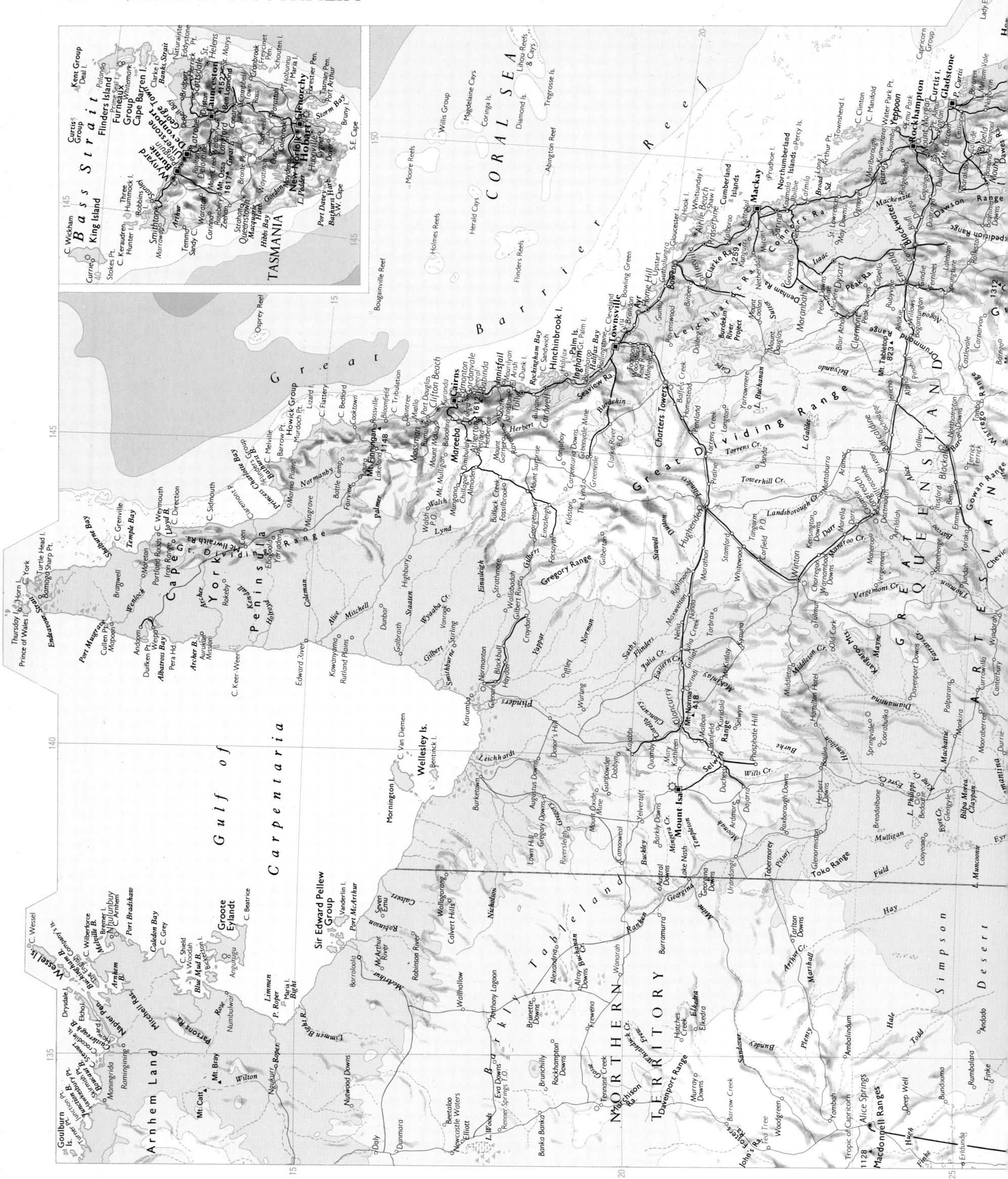
CORAL SEA
Great Barrier Reef
Gulf of Carpentaria
Bass Strait
TASMANIA
King Island
Flinders Island
Hobart
Launceston
NORTHERN TERRITORY
QUEENSLAND
Great Dividing Range
Cape York Peninsula
Arnhem Land
Barkly Tableland
Simpson Desert
Townsville
Cairns
Mackay
Rockhampton
Gladstone
Mount Isa
Charters Towers
Alice Springs
Macdonnell Ranges
Wellesley Is.
Groote Eylandt
Sir Edward Pellew Group
Hinchinbrook I.
Cumberland Islands
Northumberland Islands
Wessel Is.
Tropic of Capricorn

1 : 6 400 000

50   100   150   200 miles

50   0   50   100   150   200   250   300 km

TASMAN

SEA

Projection: Bonne   East from Greenwich

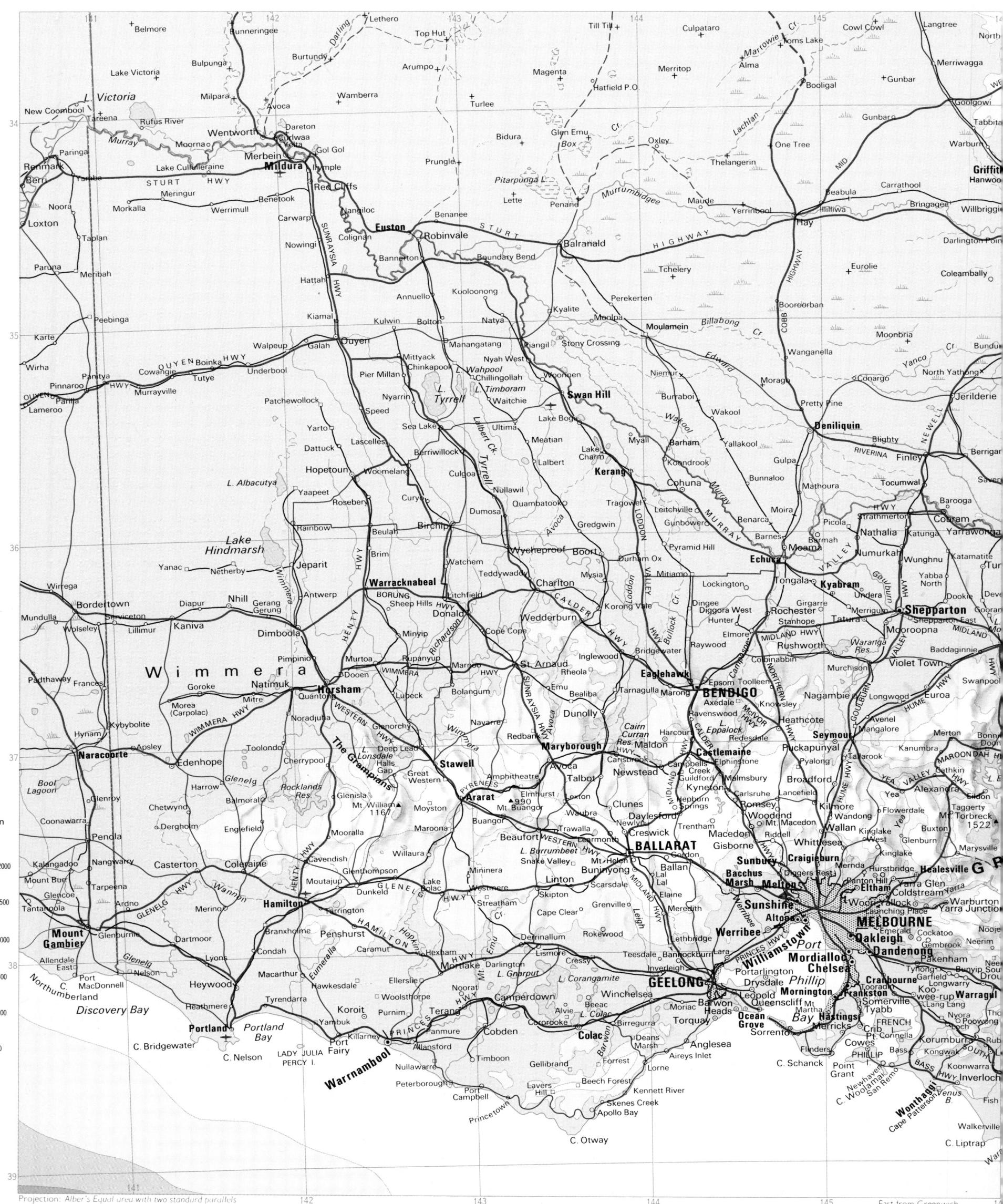

Projection: *Alber's Equal area with two standard parallels*

East from Greenwich

1 : 2 000 000

10   0   10   20   30   40   50 miles
10   0   20   40   60   80 km

SYDNEY
WOLLONGONG
Woy Woy
Broken Bay
Richmond   Kurrajong
Springwood   Penrith   Blacktown   Hornsby
Katoomba   Parramatta   Manly
Mt. Victoria   Blackheath   Oberon   Hampton
Ben Chifley   Glenbrook   St. Marys   Port Jackson
Wallacia   Fairfield   Liverpool   Sutherland
Camden   Botany Bay
Campbelltown   Cronulla
Picton   Helensburgh
Appin   Stanwell Park
Buxton   Bulli   Woonona
Mittagong   Cordeaux Res.   Port Kembla
Bowral   Moss Vale   Dapto   Shellharbour
Robertson   Albion Park   Kiama
Bundanoon   Berry   Gerringong
Kangaroo Valley   Bomaderry
Nowra

Gubbata   Ungarie
Kikoira   Garema   Cabowindra
West Wyalong   Wyalong   Cowra   Woodstock
Narriah   Tallimba
Leeton   Temora   Young   Harden   Cootamundra
Narrandera   Coolamon   Junee   Gundagai   Yass
Wagga Wagga   Tumut   Murrumbateman   Goulburn
Adelong   CANBERRA   Queanbeyan
AUSTRALIAN CAPITAL TERRITORY
Tumbarumba   Cooma
Albury   Cabramurra   Batemans Bay
Wodonga   Mt. Kosciusko 2230   Moruya
Wangaratta   Thredbo Village   Narooma
Bright   Mt. Bogong 1986   Bombala   Bega   Tathra
Mt. Buffalo 1806   Merimbula
Omeo   Delegate   Eden   Pambula
Bruthen   Orbost   Twofold Bay
Bairnsdale   Genoa   C. Howe
Sale   Lakes Entrance   Mallacoota
Traralgon   Morwell   Yarram

GREAT DIVIDING RANGE
Cullaring Range
Snowy Mts.
Australian Alps
Gippsland
DIVIDING RANGE

SOUTH   PACIFIC   OCEAN

TASMAN SEA

Wilsons Promontory
C. Wellington

COPYRIGHT GEORGE PHILIP & SON LTD

147   148   149   150   151

34
35
36
37
38
39

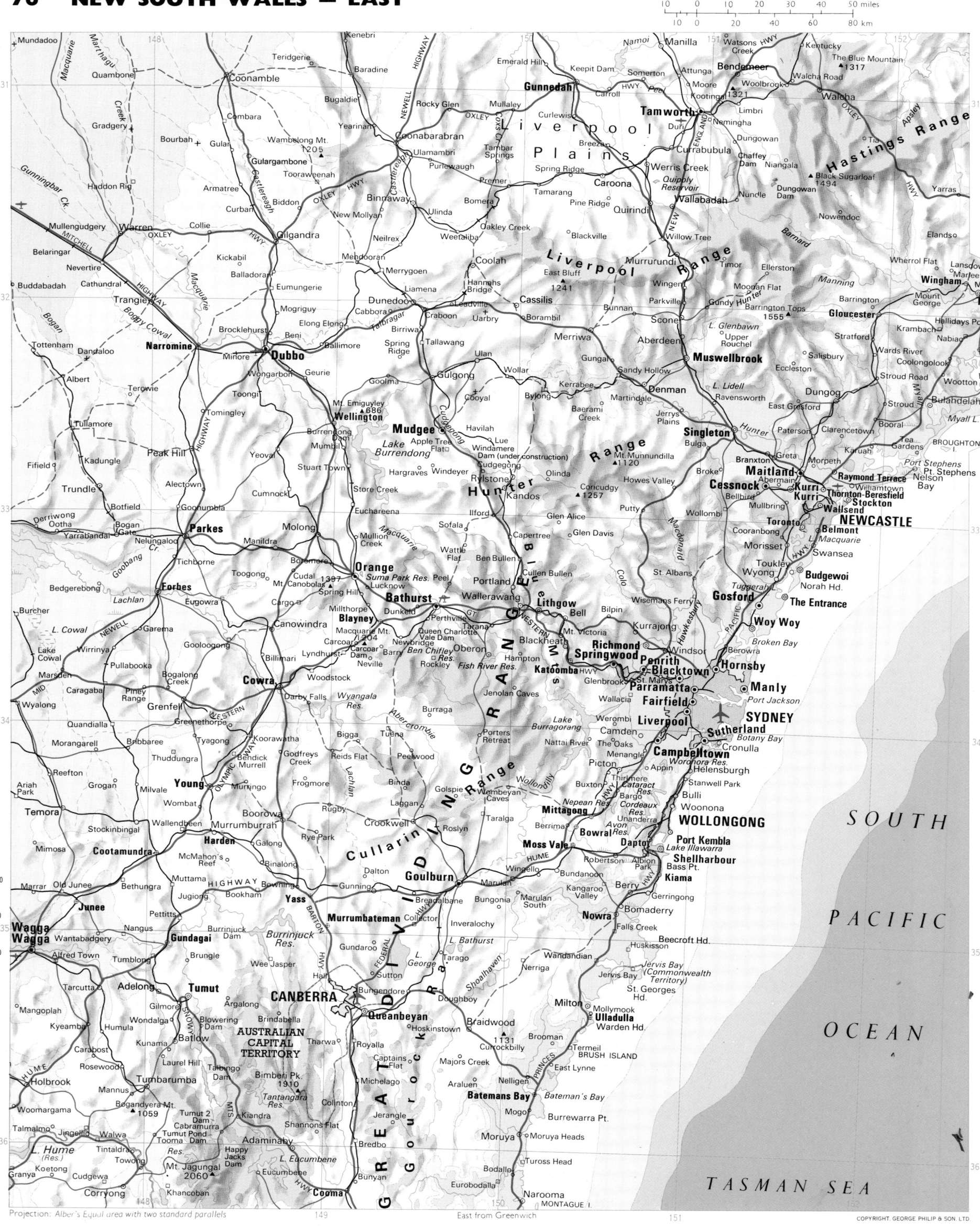

1 : 2 000 000

SOUTH

PACIFIC

OCEAN

TASMAN SEA

Projection: Alber's Equal area with two standard parallels

East from Greenwich

COPYRIGHT. GEORGE PHILIP & SON. LTD.

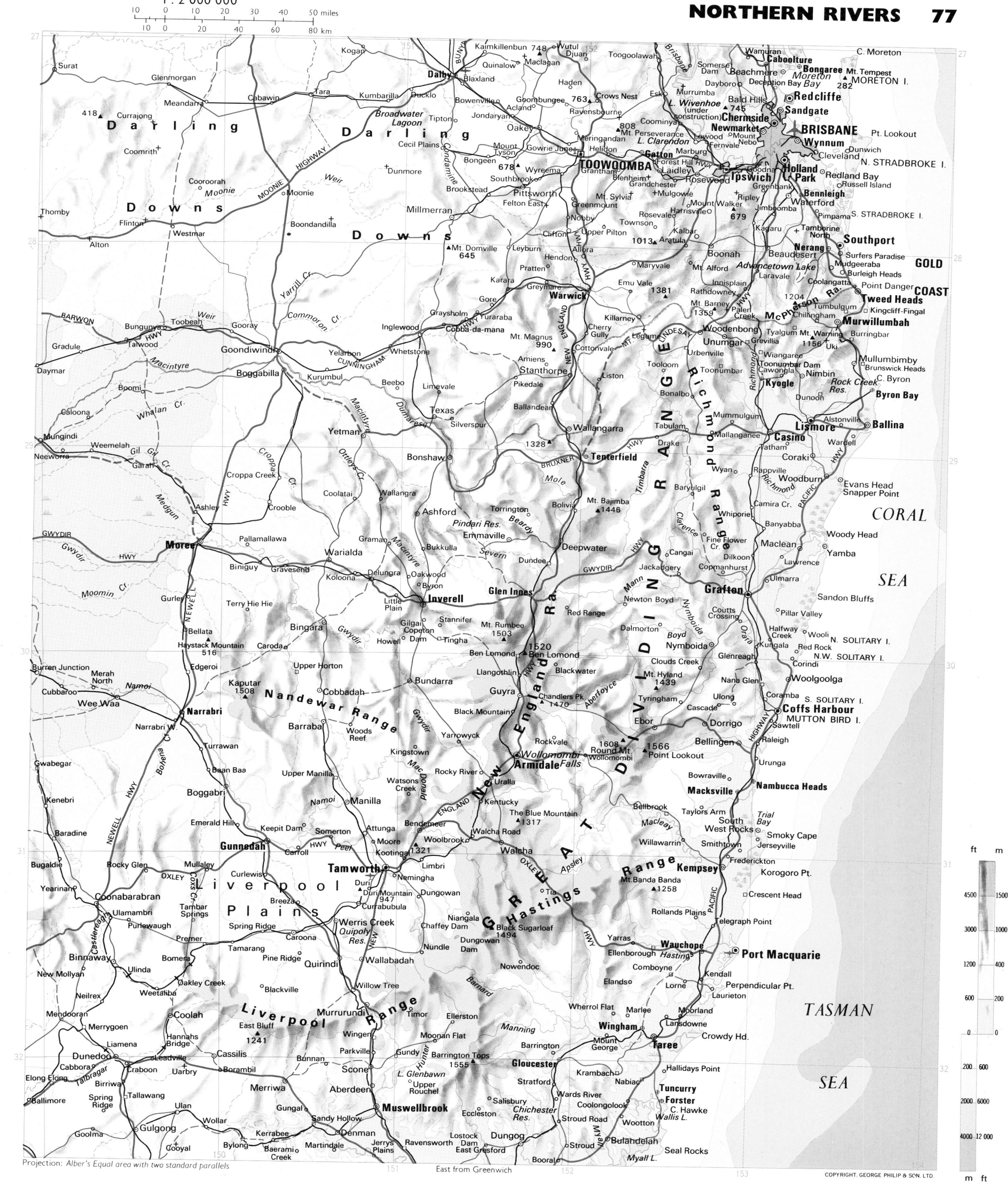

1 : 2 000 000

Projection: Alber's Equal area with two standard parallels

East from Greenwich

COPYRIGHT. GEORGE PHILIP & SON. LTD.

INDONESIA
TIMOR SEA
INDIAN OCEAN
NORTHERN TERRITORY
Timor
Roti
Sawa
Sumba
Lombok
Melville I.
Bathurst I.
Darwin
Port Darwin
Katherine
Tanami Desert
Great Sandy Desert
Gibson Desert
Joseph Bonaparte Gulf
Cambridge Gulf
Wyndham
Kununurra
Halls Creek
Fitzroy Crossing
Derby
Broome
Roebuck B.
King Sound
Buccaneer Archipelago
Bonaparte Archipelago
King Leopold Ranges
Durack Range
Eighty Mile Beach
Port Hedland
Dampier
Karratha
Roebourne
Onslow
Exmouth
Exmouth Gulf
Hamersley Range
Newman
Tom Price
Marble Bar
Nullagine
Lake Mackay
Lake Disappointment
Tropic of Capricorn
Macdonnell Ranges
Rowley Shoals
Scott Reef
Ashmore Reef
Cartier I.
Lacepede Is.
Dampier Archipelago
Monte Bello Is.
Barrow I.

1 : 6 400 000

50   0   50   100   150   200 miles
50   0   50   100   150   200   250   300   km

SOUTH   AUSTRALIA

WESTERN

S O U T H E R N   O C E A N

Great Australian Bight

Great Victoria Desert

Nullarbor Plain

Hampton Tableland

Mt. Olga 1069 ▲   Ayers Rock 868 ▲
Musgrave Ranges   Mt. Woodroffe 1549 ▲
Everard Ranges   Everard Park
Mann Ras. Mt. Morris 1387 ▲   The Officer   1174
Mt. Aloysius 1058 ▲   Mt. Blackstone   Tomkinson Ras.
Mt. Forrest   Carnegie Ra.
Barrow Ra.   Warburton   Mt. Squires 705 ▲
Warburton Ra.   Pt. Lillian 466
Macintosh Ra.   Saunders Pt. 466

L. Meramangye   Wynbring   L. Dey-Dey
Wilkinson Lakes   L. Maurice   30
Serpentine Lakes   Nurrari Lakes
Oldea   Barton
Ooldea   Cook   Fisher   Watson
Hughes   Deakin   Reid
Loongana   Forrest   Cook
Rawlinna   Naretha
Kitchener   Zanthus   Wilson Bluff
Euclid Motel   Mundrabilla Low Pt.
Madura Motel   Red Rocks Pt.
Pt. Culver   Pt. Dover
Eyre

L. Breaden   L. Buchanan   Baker L.
L. Gillen   L. Throssell   L. Yeo   L. Ell
L. Blair   Jubilee L.   Shell Lakes
L. Wells   Cosmo Newberry   Rason L.
Ernest Giles Ra. 712   L. Minigwal
L. Carnegie   L. Rebecca
Kirgella Rocks   Cundeelee
Broad Arrow   Kanowna   L. Yindarlgooda
L. Cowan   L. Dundas   L. Lefroy
L. Gilmore   Salmon Gums   Mt. Ridley

Mt. Essendon 906   Carnarvon Ra.
Montague Ra.   Bates Ra.   Robinson Ra.
Mt. Redcliffe 576   Mt. Alexander
Mt. Barlee   Mt. Marmion
Kalgoorlie-Boulder 554   Mt. Burges
Norseman   Mt. Hope   Peak Eleanora 503
Mt. Ragged 585   Esperance
Archipelago of the Recherche
Eastern Group   C. Arid   C. Pasley   Pt. Malcolm
Middle I.   South East Is.   Sandy Bight

Mt. Augustus 1105   Mt. Fraser 799   Peak Hill
Mount Magnet   L. Austin   L. Way
Barr Smith Ra.   Wiluna   Depot Springs
Yowergabbie   Wyemandoo 543
Cue   Mount Magnet   Sandstone   Cashmere Downs
L. Moore   Bencubbin   Southern Cross

Murchison R.   Mt. Narryer   Meekatharra
Nicholson Ra.   Dividing Ra. Tallering Peak 439
Geraldton   Greenough   Moora   Northam
Dongara   New Norcia   Toodyay
Houtman Abrolhos   Wongan Hills   Merredin
Moorine Rock   Bruce Rock
Narrogin   Wagin   Katanning
Albany   Stirling Ra. 1073   Mt. Barker
Bald Hd.   West C. Howe

PERTH
Rottnest I.   Fremantle   New Town
Kwinana   Rockingham   Mandurah
Pinjarra   Harvey   Bunbury   Busselton
C. Leeuwin   C. Naturaliste   Manjimup
Bridgetown   Nannup   Northcliffe   Pt. D'Entrecasteaux

Gascoyne   Carnarvon   Shark Bay
Denham   Denham Sound   Hamelin Pool
Dirk Hartog I.   Steep Pt.   Peron   Useless Loop
C. Cuvier   C. Ronsard   Bernier I.   Dorre I.
Geographe Channel   Kennedy Ra.   Minnie Creek
Lyons R.   Mount Phillip   Gascoyne Junction
Three Rivers   Collier Ra.   Mt. Vernon

COPYRIGHT GEORGE PHILIP & SON LTD.

East from Greenwich   115   120   125   130   35

Projection. Bonne

m   ft
3000
1200
600
0
2000   6000   12 000
m   ft
1000   4000
600   2000
400   1200
200   600
0   0

1 : 2 800 000

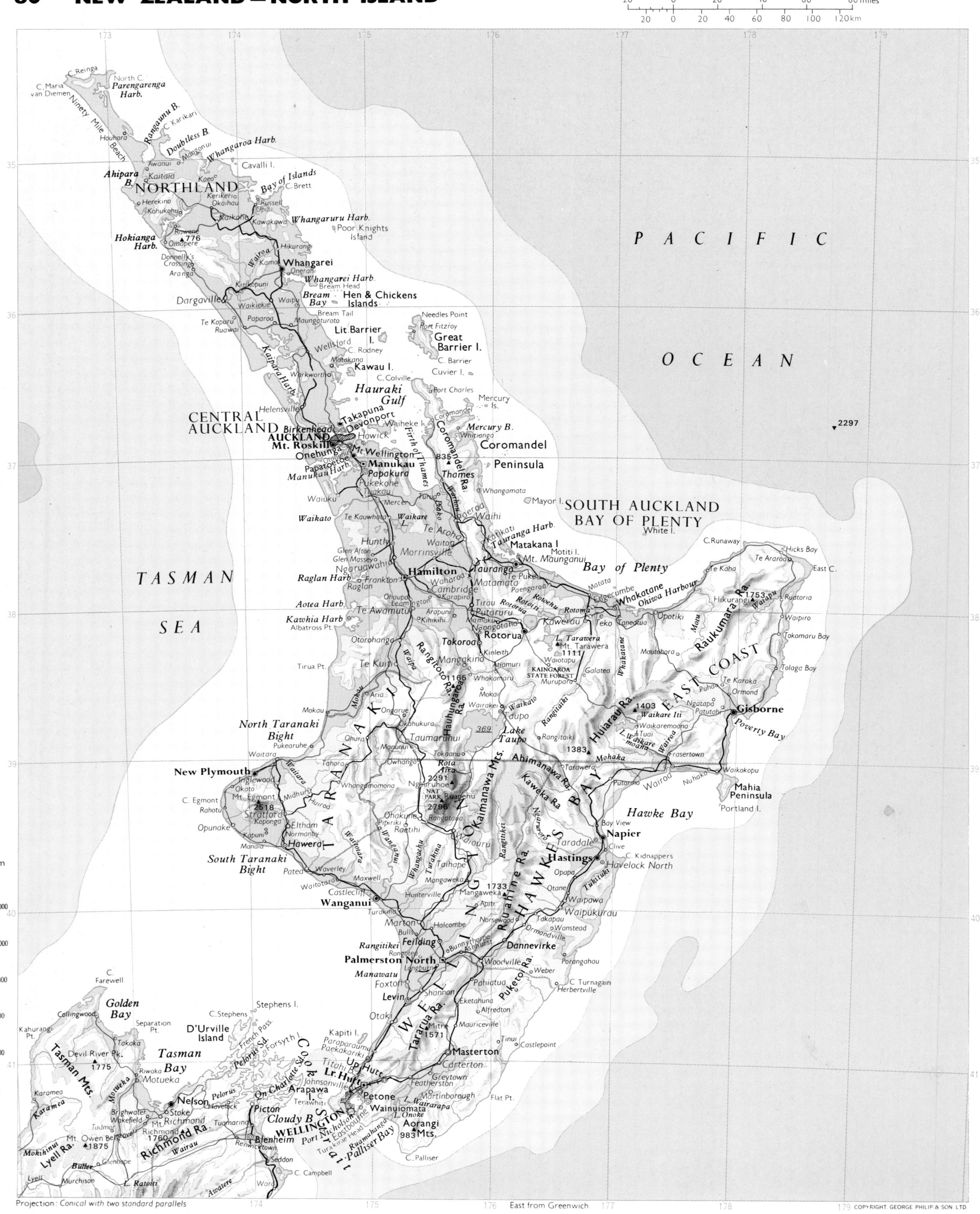

Projection: Conical with two standard parallels

East from Greenwich

COPYRIGHT GEORGE PHILIP & SON LTD.

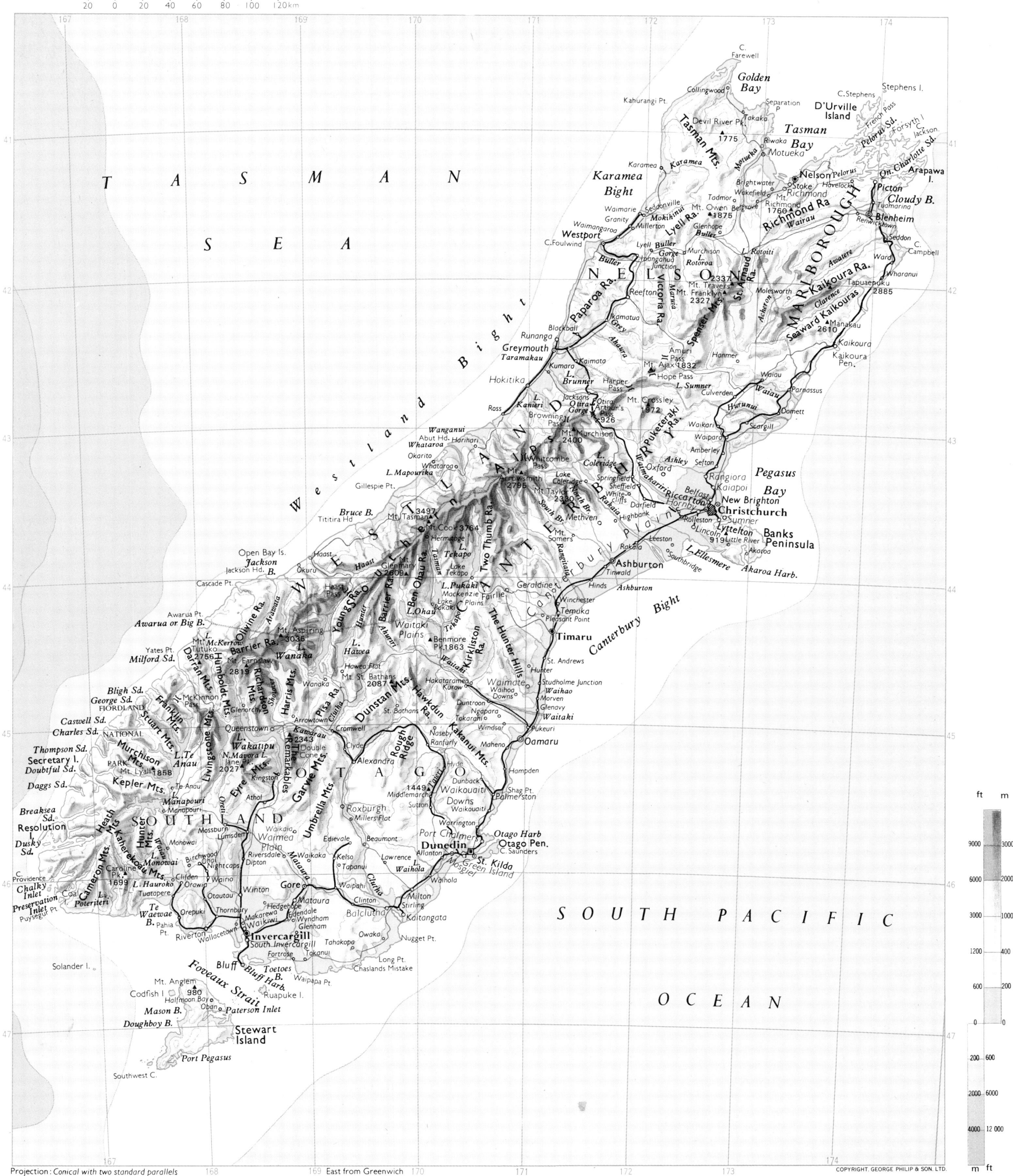

1 : 2 800 000

20   0   20   40   60   80 miles
20   0   20   40   60   80   100   120km

TASMAN   SEA

T A S M A N   S E A

Golden Bay
Tasman Bay
D'Urville Island
Karamea Bight
Tasman Mts.
NELSON
MARLBOROUGH
Nelson
Picton
Blenheim
Cloudy B.
Richmond Ra.
Westport
Buller
Greymouth
Paparoa Ra.
Victoria Ra.
Spenser Mts.
St. Arnaud Ra.
Seaward Kaikoura Ra.
Kaikoura
Kaikoura Pen.
Hokitika
L. Brunner
Arthur's Pass
Hurunui
WESTLAND
CANTERBURY
Pegasus Bay
Christchurch
New Brighton
Lyttelton
Banks Peninsula
Mt. Cook 3764
Mt. Tasman 3497
Hermitage
L. Tekapo
L. Pukaki
L. Ohau
Mackenzie Plains
Canterbury Plain
Ashburton
Timaru
Canterbury Bight
WESTLAND
Haast
Jackson
Open Bay Is.
Bruce B.
Milford Sd.
Awarua or Big B.
L. Wanaka
L. Hawea
Mt. Aspiring 3035
Waitaki Plains
Oamaru
FIORDLAND
Te Anau
L. Te Anau
L. Manapouri
Queenstown
L. Wakatipu
OTAGO
Dunstan Mts.
Waikouaiti Downs
Palmerston
Waitaki
SOUTHLAND
Waimea Plain
Invercargill
Gore
Dunedin
Otago Pen.
Otago Harb.
St. Kilda
Bluff
Foveaux Strait
Stewart Island
Paterson Inlet
Port Pegasus
Solander I.
Codfish I.

SOUTH   PACIFIC

O C E A N

ft   m
9000   3000
6000   2000
3000   1000
1200   400
0   0
200   600
2000   6000
4000   12 000
m   ft

Projection: Conical with two standard parallels   East from Greenwich   COPYRIGHT. GEORGE PHILIP & SON, LTD.

1 : 32 000 000

200   0   200   400   600   800   1000 miles
200   0   200   400   600   800   1000 1200 1400 1600 km

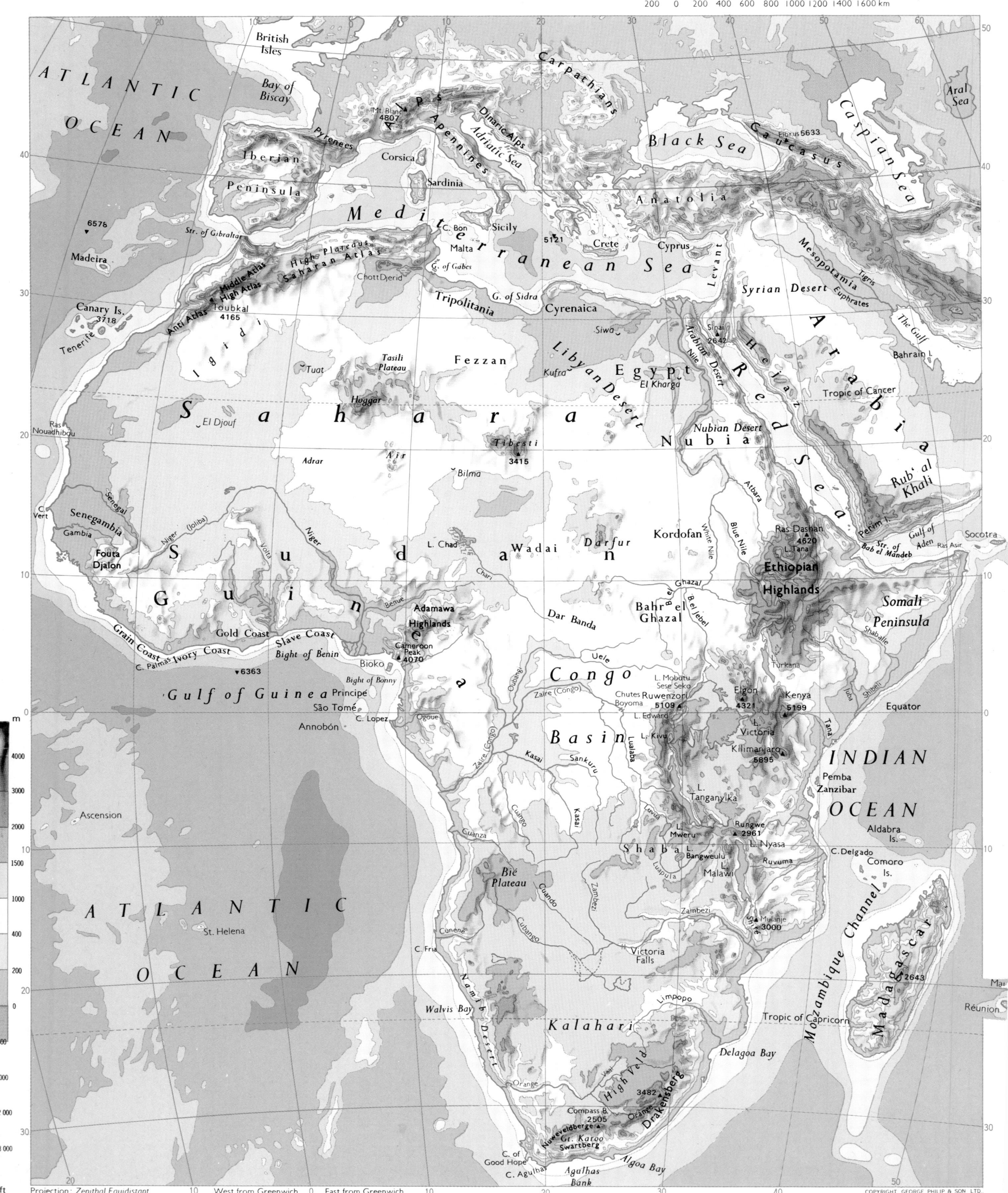

ATLANTIC OCEAN

British Isles

Bay of Biscay

Alps
Mt. Blanc 4807
Pyrenees
Iberian Peninsula
Apennines
Dinaric Alps
Adriatic Sea
Carpathians
Caucasus
Elbrus 5633
Black Sea
Caspian Sea
Aral Sea

6576
Corsica
Sardinia
Anatolia

Str. of Gibraltar
Madeira
Sicily
Malta
Crete
Cyprus
Mesopotamia
Tigris
Euphrates

Mediterranean Sea

Canary Is.
Tenerife
Middle Atlas
High Atlas
High Plateaus
Saharan Atlas
Anti Atlas
Toubkal 4165
Chott Djerid
C. Bon
G. of Gabes
Tripolitania
G. of Sidra
Cyrenaica
5121
Siwa
Levant
Syrian Desert
Sinai 2642
Hejaz
Arabia
The Gulf
Bahrain I.

Ras Nouadhibou
Igidi
Tuat
Tasili Plateau
Fezzan
Kufra
Libyan Desert
Egypt
El Kharga
Nile
Arabian Desert
Red Sea
Tropic of Cancer

Sahara

Hoggar
Air
Tibesti 3415
Bilma
Nubian Desert
Nubia
Rub' al Khali
Petrin I.
Gulf of Aden
Ras Asir
Socotra
Str. of Bab el Mandeb

C. Vert
Senegal
Adrar
L. Chad
Wadai
Darfur
Kordofan
White Nile
Blue Nile
Atbara
Ras Dashan 4620
L. Tana

Senegambia
Gambia
Niger (Joliba)
Sudan
Chari
Bahr el Ghazal
Ethiopian Highlands
Somali Peninsula

Fouta Djalon
Volta
Niger
Benue
Dar Banda
Bahr el Ghazal
B. el Jebel
Shabelle

Guinea
Gold Coast
Slave Coast
Bight of Benin
Adamawa Highlands
Uele
Oubangi
Congo (Zaire)
L. Mobutu Sese Seko
Ruwenzori
Turkana
Elgon 4321
Kenya 5199
Iba
Shabeli
Equator

Grain Coast
Ivory Coast
C. Palmas
Cameroon Peak 4070
Bioko
6363
Bight of Bonny
Zaire (Congo)
Chutes Boyoma 5109
L. Edward
L. Kivu

Gulf of Guinea
Príncipe
São Tomé
Annobón
C. Lopez
Ogoue
Congo Basin
Kasai
Lualaba
L. Victoria
Kilimanjaro 5895
Tana
INDIAN OCEAN
Pemba
Zanzibar

Ascension
Zaire (Congo)
Kasai
Sankuru
L. Tanganyika
Lomami
Aldabra Is.

St. Helena
ATLANTIC OCEAN
Cuango
Cuanza
Kasai
L. Mweru
Rungwe 2961
L. Nyasa
Bangweulu
Ruvuma
C. Delgado
Comoro Is.

Bié Plateau
Shaba
Malawi
Luapula
Madagascar
Mozambique Channel

Cunene
Zambezi
Zambezi
Mulanje 3000
2643
Réunion

Victoria Falls
Cubango
Cuando
Limpopo
Réunion

Kalahari
Namib Desert
Walvis Bay
C. Fria
Delagoa Bay
Tropic of Capricorn

Orange
High Veld 3482
Drakensberg
Compass B. 2505
Nieuweveldberge
Gt. Karoo
Swartberg
Orange
Algoa Bay
Agulhas Bank

C. of Good Hope
C. Agulhas
Delagoa Bay

ft   m
12 000   4000
9000   3000
6000   2000
4500   1500
3000   1000
1200   400
600   200
0   0
200   600
2000   6000
4000   12 000
6000   18 000
m   ft

Projection: Zenithal Equidistant.   10   West from Greenwich   0   East from Greenwich   10   20   30   40   50

COPYRIGHT. GEORGE PHILIP & SON LTD.

1 : 32 000 000

200 0 200 400 600 800 1000 miles
200 0 200 400 600 800 1000 1200 1400 1600 km

ATLANTIC OCEAN

UNITED KINGDOM London NETH. GERMANY POLAND Warszawa
Bay of Biscay FRANCE BELG. Praha CZECHOSLOVAKIA Kiyev U. S. S. R.
Paris SWITZ. AUSTRIA Wien HUNGARY Volgograd
ROMANIA Odessa
Madeira (Port) Madrid SPAIN ITALY YUGOSLAVIA BULGARIA Istanbul Black Sea Aral Sea
Lisboa PORTUGAL Corse Roma Sardegna Athínai GREECE Kriti TURKEY Ankara Baku Caspian Sea
Tanger Alger Annaba Bizerte Sicilia MALTA CYPRUS Halab Al Mawşil Tehrān
Tétouan Constantine Tunis Malta Bûr Saïd 936 SYRIA Dimashq Baghdād Eşfahān
Casablanca Rabat Fès Oran Sfax TUNISIA El Iskandarîya Tel Aviv-Yafo Jerusalem IRAN Al Başrah
MOROCCO Marrakech ALGERIA Tarābulus Banghāzi EGYPT Bûr Saïd JORDAN ISRAEL KUWAIT The Gulf BAHRAIN
Essaouira EL QÂHIRA El Suweis SAUDI- QATAR
Ifni Ghudāmis In Salah LIBYA Sahrâ' El Faiyûm Asyût Nile ARABIA Al Madinah Tropic of Cancer
WESTERN SAHARA Marzûq Ghat Al Jawf Aswân Makkah ASIR
S a h a r a Wadi Halfa Es Sahrâ en Nûbiya Bûr Sûdân YEMEN SOUTH YEMEN
Dakhla Fdérik Dongola Atbara Kassala Asmera Mitsiwa Socotra
MAURITANIA Nouakchott Tombouctou Gaô Agadez Omdurmân El Khartûm L. Tana DJIBOUTI Berbera
St. Louis Kayes NIGER CHAD Abéché SUDAN El Fâsher El Obeid Addis Abeba Al 'Adan (Aden)
Dakar SENEGAL MALI Bamako Niamey Sokoto Kano Ndjamena (Ft.-Lamy) Bousso Malakâl Harer Hargeisa Ras Asir Dante
GAMBIA Banjul BURKINA FASO Ouagadougou Maiduguri Bauchi NIGERIA El Obeid Wâw ETHIOPIA SOMALI REP
GUINEA BISSAU Bissau GUINEA Kankan Kaduna Sarh CENTRAL AFRICAN REPUBLIC Mongalla L. Turkana
Conakry Freetown SIERRA LEONE TOGO BENIN Ibadan Enugu Bangui Muqdisho
LIBERIA IVORY COAST GHANA Kumasi Lagos Port Harcourt CAMEROON Yaoundé Kisangani KENYA Equator
Monrovia Bouake Accra Porto Novo Douala Zaïre (Congo) L. Mobutu Sese Seko UGANDA Kampala Nairobi INDIAN
Abidjan Sekondi-Takoradi Bight of Benin Malabo Bioko EQUATORIAL GUINEA Mbandaka L. Edward L. Victoria Kisumu Mombasa
Gulf of Guinea SÃO TOMÉ & PRINCIPE Libreville GABON CONGO ZAÏRE L. Kivu RWANDA BURUNDI Mwanza Pemba
Annobón Brazzaville Kinshasa Kasai Ilebo Kigoma Tabora TANZANIA Zanzibar Dar-es-Salaam
Pointe-Noire Cabinda Mbuji-Mayi Kananga Shaba Kalemie Dodoma
Luanda Boma Bukama L. Tanganyika L. Mweru OCEAN
ANGOLA Likasi Lubumbashi Kitwe L. Nyasa Cabo Delgado COMOROS Antsiranana
Benguela Lobito ZAMBIA MALAWI Lilongwe Ruvuma Aldabra Is.
Huambo Lusaka Kafue Zomba Blantyre Moçambique Mahajanga
Namibe Kuando Livingstone Harare Quelimane MOZAMBIQUE MADAGASCAR Toamasina
NAMIBIA (SOUTH WEST AFRICA) Windhoek BOTSWANA ZIMBABWE Bulawayo Beira Antananarivo
Swakopmund Walvis-baai Kalahari Gaborone Tropic of Capricorn Toliara MAURITIUS Réunion (Fr)
Lüderitz TRANSVAAL Pretoria Maputo (Lourenço Marques) Fianarantsoa
Johannesburg SWAZ. Mozambique Channel
Oranje Kimberley Bloem. O.F.S. LES. NATAL Durban
SOUTH AFRICA CAPE PROVINCE
Cape Town East London
Kaap die Goeie Hoop (Cape of Good Hope) Port Elizabeth

ATLANTIC OCEAN
Ascension (Br.)
St. Helena (Br.)

LES. Lesotho
O.F.S. Orange Free State
SWAZ. Swaziland

Projection: Zenithal Equidistant. West from Greenwich 0 East from Greenwich

COPYRIGHT. GEORGE PHILIP & SON. LTD.

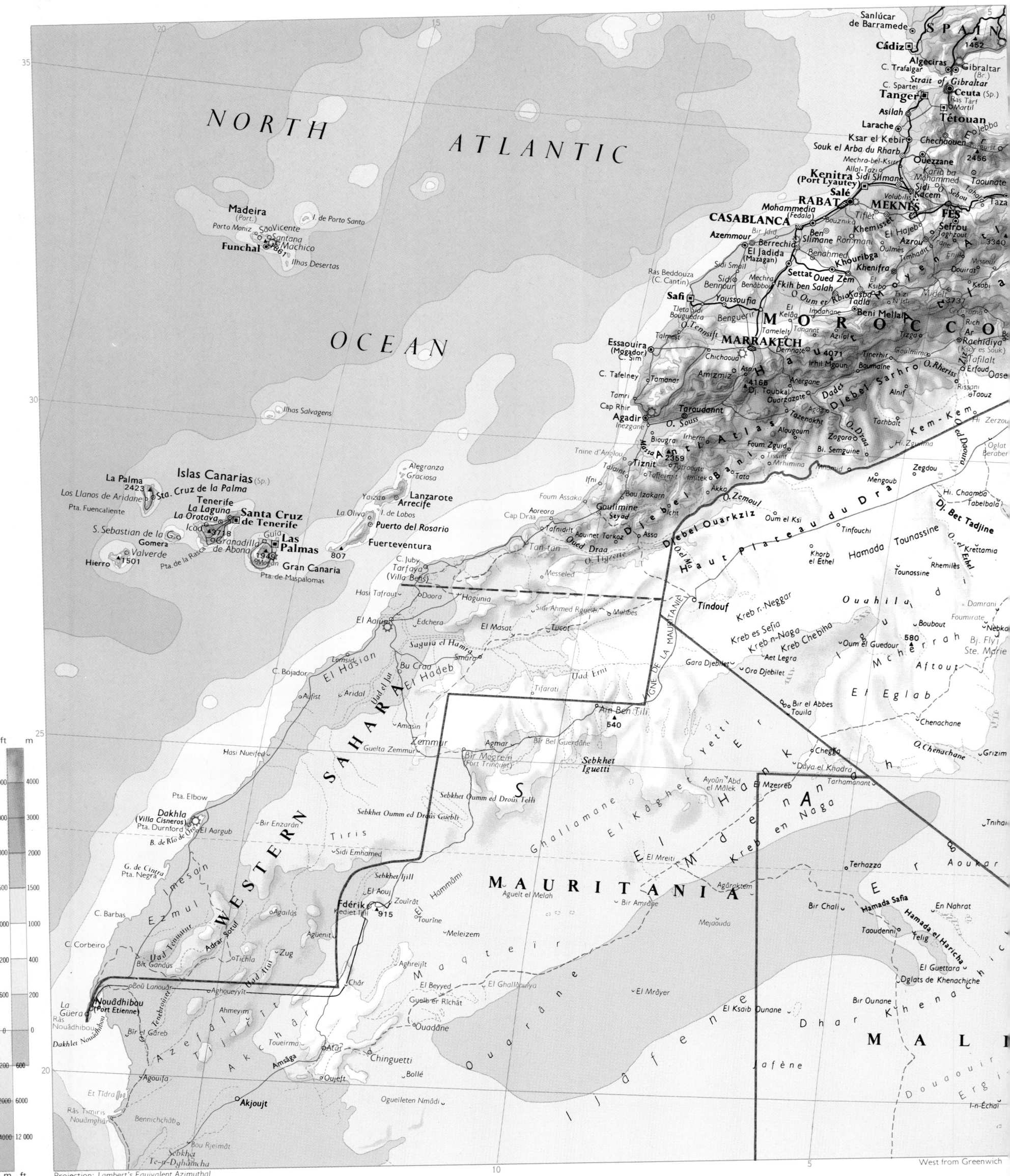
NORTH ATLANTIC OCEAN
Madeira (Port.)
Funchal
Islas Canarias (Sp.)
La Palma
Tenerife
Santa Cruz de Tenerife
Las Palmas
Gran Canaria
Lanzarote
Fuerteventura
Gomera
Hierro
SPAIN
Cádiz
Gibraltar
Strait of Gibraltar
Ceuta (Sp.)
Tanger
Tétouan
Kenitra (Port Lyautey)
RABAT
MEKNES
FES
CASABLANCA
Safi
Essaouira (Mogador)
MARRAKECH
Agadir
MOROCCO
Haut Atlas
Anti Atlas
Tindouf
Hamada du Draa
El Aaiún
WESTERN SAHARA
Dakhla (Villa Cisneros)
Nouâdhibou (Port Etienne)
Fdérik
Akjoujt
Atar
Chinguetti
MAURITANIA
MALI
El Djouf
Erg Iguidi
Projection: Lambert's Equivalent Azimuthal
West from Greenwich

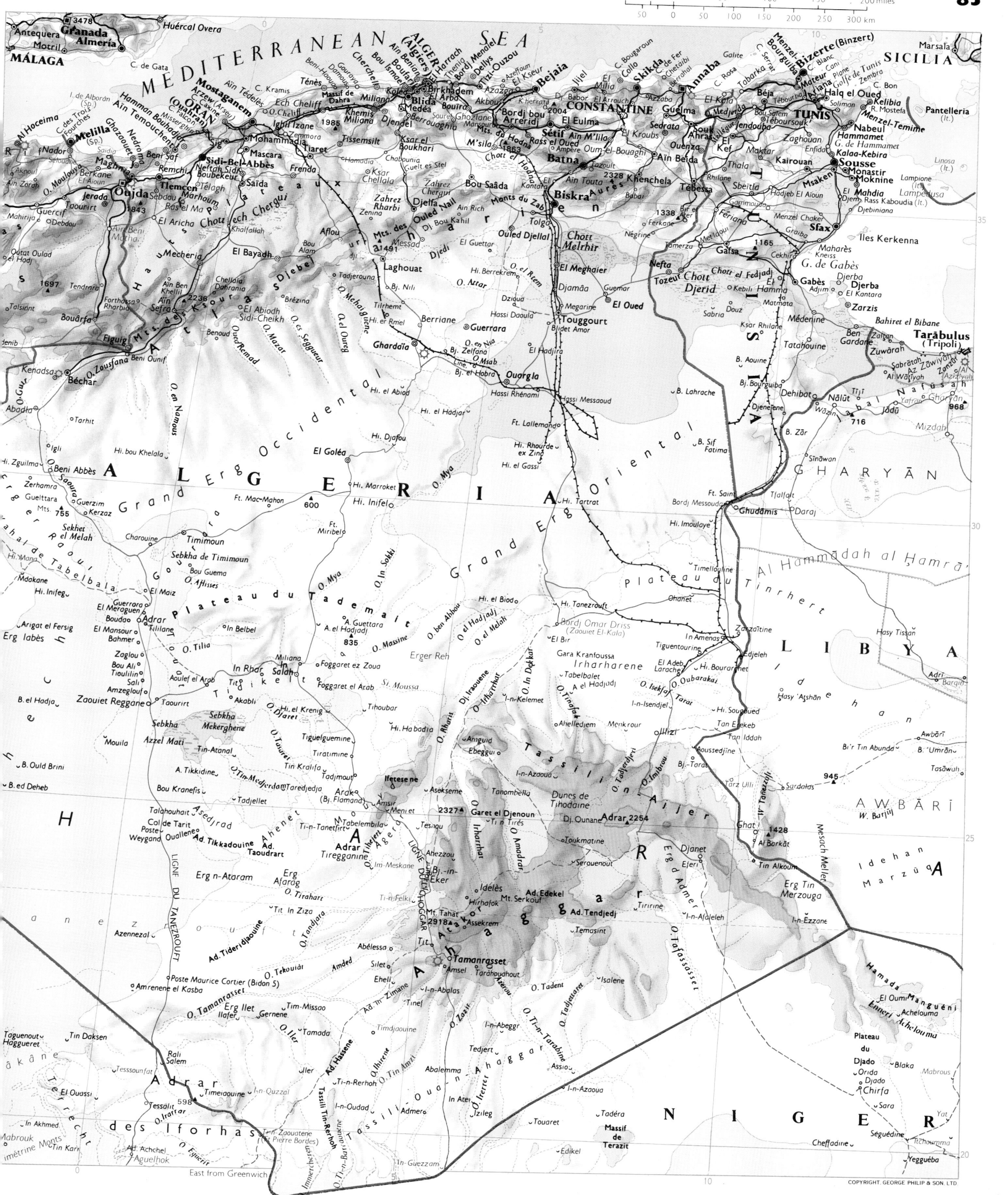

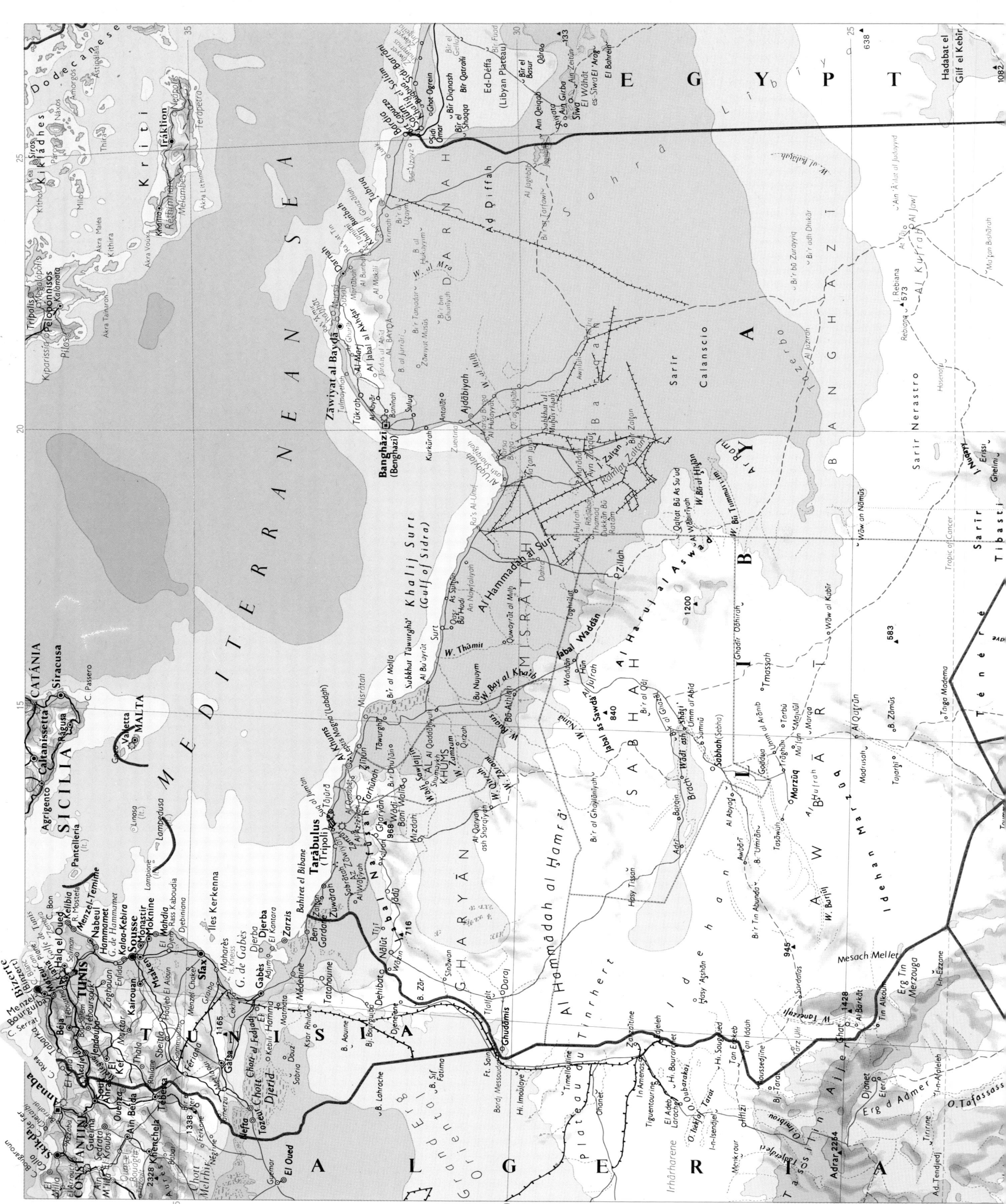
MEDITERRANEAN SEA
Khalij Surt (Gulf of Sidra)
SICILIA
CATÁNIA
Siracusa
Caltanissetta
Agrigento
Ragusa
C. Passero
MALTA
Valletta
Gozo
Pantelleria
Lampedusa
Linosa
Lampione
Kriti
Iráklion
Kikládhes
Dodecanese
Pelopónnisos
Tripolis
Kalamata
TUNISIA
TUNIS
Bizerte (Binzert)
Sousse
Sfax
Kairouan
Gabès
Djerba
Zarzis
Médenine
Tatahouine
Gafsa
Tozeur
Chott Djerid
Chott el Fedjadj
Monastir
Moknine
Mahdia
Nabeul
Hammamet
Menzel-Temime
Kelibia
C. Bon
Îles Kerkenna
G. de Gabès
Bahiret el Bibane
ALGERIA
CONSTANTINE
Skikda
Annaba
Tébessa
Khenchela
El Oued
Grand Erg Oriental
Plateau du Tinrhert
Ghudāmis
In Amenas
Tassili n'Ajjer
Adrar 2254
Erg d'Admer
Djanet
LIBYA
Tarābulus (Tripoli)
Az Zāwiyah
Zuwārah
Al Khums
Leptis Magna (Labdah)
Zlīṭan
Miṣrātah
Surt
Banghāzī (Benghazi)
Zāwiyat al Bayḍā
Al Marj
Darnah
Ṭubruq
Ajdābiyah
Jabal Nafūsah
Gharyān
Ghadāmis
Al Ḥammādah al Ḥamrā'
Jabal as Sawdā'
Al Harūj al Aswad
Jabal Waddān
Sabhah (Sebha)
Marzūq
Ghāt
Awbārī
Idehan Marzūq
Zillah
Waddān
Hūn
Sarīr Calanscio
Sarīr Tibasti
Sarir Nerastro
Al Kufrah
Al Jawf
Ad Diffah
EGYPT
Sīwa
Al Jaghbūb
Bardia
Es Salûm
Ed-Déffa (Libyan Plateau)
Hadabat el Gilf el Kebîr
Ténéré
Tropic of Cancer

1 : 6 400 000

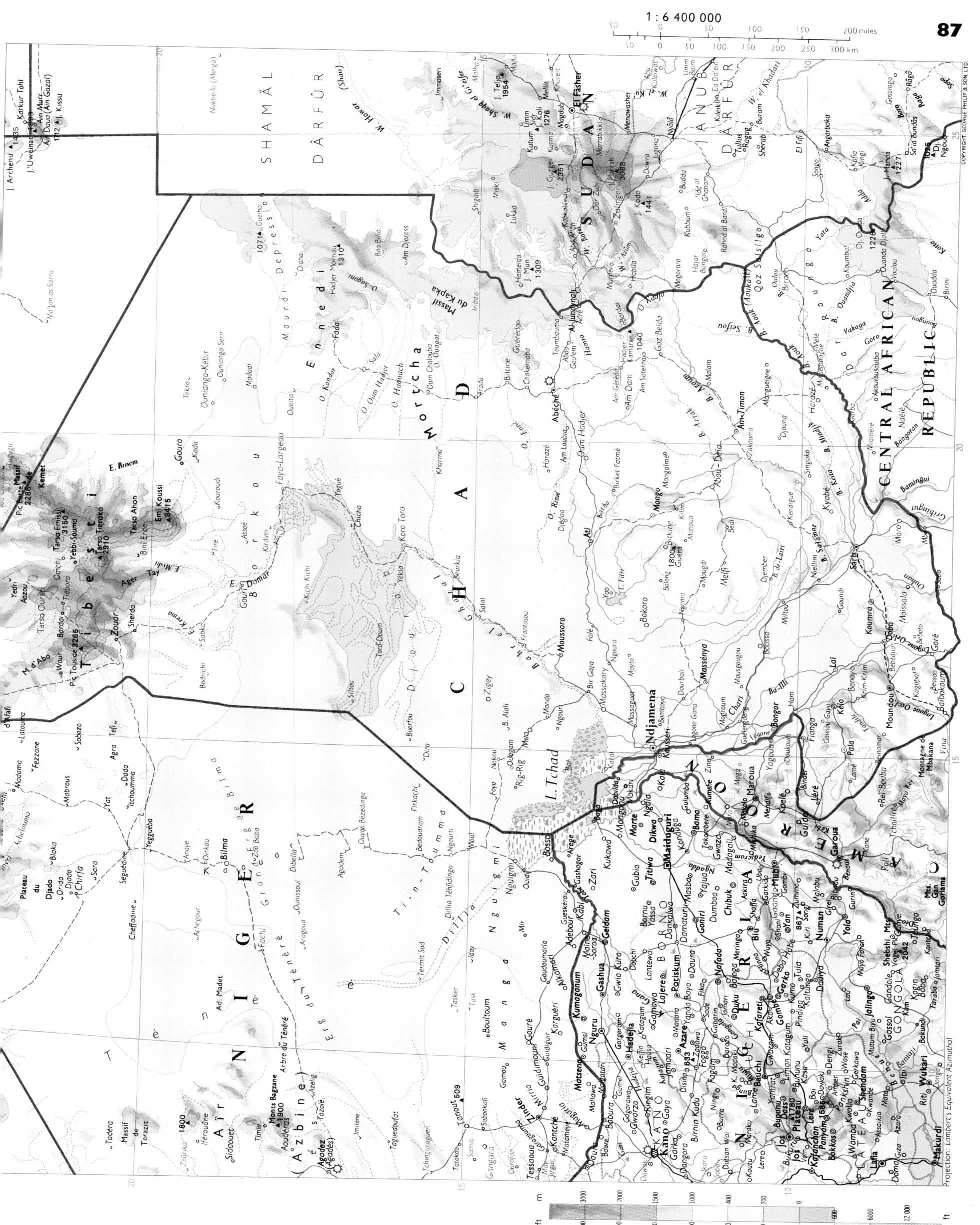
50 0 50 100 150 200 miles
50 0 50 100 150 200 250 300 km
CHAD
SUDAN
NIGER
NIGERIA
CAMEROON
CENTRAL AFRICAN REPUBLIC
Tibesti
Ennedi
SHAMÂL DÂRFÛR
JANUB DÂRFÛR
BORNO
BAUCHI
KANO
PLATEAU
GONGOLA
Aïr (Azbine)
Ténéré
Erg du Ténéré
Grand Erg de Bilma
Mourdi Depression
Djourab
Borkou
Mortcha
Manga
Massif du Kapka
Plateau du Djado
L. Tchad
Ndjamena
Abéché
Moundou
Sarh
Bongor
Am-Timan
Mongo
Ati
Moussoro
Faya-Largeau
Zouar
Fada
El Fâsher
Nyâlâ
Kutum
Agadez (Agadès)
Zinder
Bilma
Tanout
Maiduguri
Kano
Jos
Bauchi
Yola
Garoua
Maroua
Kousseri
Emi Koussi 3415
Pic Tousidé 3265
Pic Bette 2286
Tarso Emissi 3150
Tarso Tieroko 2910
Marrah 3088
Monts Bagzane 1900
Guera 1800
J. Kissu
Kemet
Chari
Bahr el Ghazal
COPYRIGHT, GEORGE PHILIP & SON, LTD.
Projection: Lambert's Equivalent Azimuthal
ft m
9000 3000
6000 2000
4500 1500
3000 1000
1200 400
600 200
0 0
200 600
2000 6000
4000 12 000
m ft

THE NILE DELTA
1:3 200 000
MEDITERRANEAN SEA
EL ISKANDARÎYA (Alexandria)
EL QÂHIRA (Cairo)
Bûr Sa'îd (Port Said)
Dumyât (Damietta)
El Suweis (Suez)
East from Greenwich
EGYPT
SAUDI ARABIA
JORDAN
ISRAEL
Ammân
Jerusalem (Al Quds)
Tel Aviv-Yafo
Gaza
Makkah (Mecca)
Jiddah
Al Madinah (Medina)
Bûr Sûdân (Port Sudan)
Aswân
Asyût
El Minyâ
Beni Suef
El Faiyûm
El Uqsur (Luxor)
Qena
Buheiret en Naser (Lake Nasser)
Khalîg el Suweis
Tropic of Cancer
Es Sahrâ' El Gharbîya
(Western Desert)
Es Sahrâ en Nûbîya
(Nubian Desert)
Hadabat el Gilf el Kebîr
Munkhafed el Qattâra (Qattâra Depression)
Second Cataract
Third Cataract
Fourth Cataract
Fifth Cataract
Atbara
Berber
Wadi Halfa
Harrat Khaybar
Harrat al Kishb
Tel Aviv-Yafo
Gebel Abyad

1 : 6 400 000

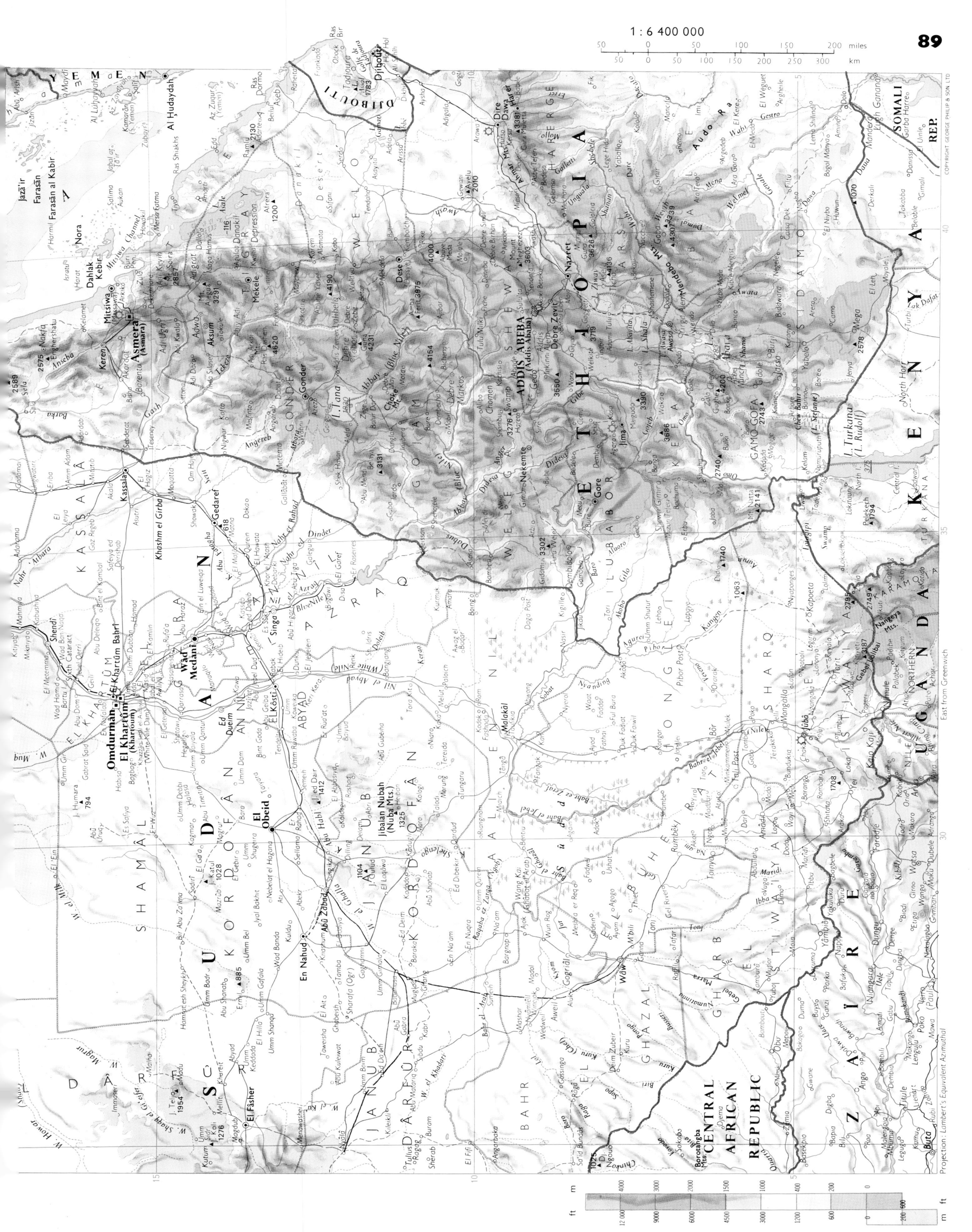

0 50 100 150 200 miles
0 50 100 150 200 250 300 km
YEMEN
DJIBOUTI
ETHIOPIA
SUDAN
KENYA
UGANDA
ZAÏRE
CENTRAL AFRICAN REPUBLIC
SOMALI REP.
ADDIS ABEBA (Addis Ababa)
Asmera (Asmara)
Omdurmân
El Khartûm (Khartoum)
Wad Medani
El Obeid
Kassala
Gonder
Dese
Dire Dawa
Harer
Nazret
Jima
Nekemte
Gore
Malakâl
Jûbâ
Wâw
En Nahud
El Fâsher
Mitsiwa
Keren
Mekele
Aksum
Djibouti
Al Hudaydah
L. Tana
L. Turkana (L. Rudolf)
Nil el Abyad (White Nile)
Abbay (Blue Nile)
Dahlak Kebir
Jibalan Nubah (Nuba Mts.)
COPYRIGHT GEORGE PHILIP & SON LTD
Projection: Lambert's Equivalent Azimuthal
East from Greenwich
m 4000 3000 2000 1500 1000 400 200 0
ft 12 000 9000 6000 4500 3000 1200 600 0

Projection: Lambert's Equivalent Azimuthal

West from Gree

1 : 6 400 000

ALGERIA

NIGER

N. E. NIGERIA
on same scale
as general map

CHAD

Lac Tchad

Maiduguri

Maroua

Garoua

Massif de Terazit

Aïr

(Azbine)

Monts Bagzane 1900

Agadez (Agadès)

Tahoua

Zinder

Maradi

Niamey

Sokoto

Katsina

Kano

Zaria

KADUNA

Kaduna

SOKOTO

Birnin Kebbi

Gusau

Azare

Potiskum

BORNO

NIGER

Minna

Abuja

Jos

Plateau

Bauchi

Gombe

Numan

Yola

CAMEROON

BURKINA

Bolgatanga

Tamale

GHANA

BENIN

TOGO

Lomé

ACCRA

Accra

Abomey

Cotonou

Porto-Novo

LAGOS

Lagos

Ilorin

OYO

Ogbomosho

Oyo

IBADAN

Ibadan

Abeokuta

Ife

Ilesha

Ado-Ekiti

Akure

Benin City

BENDEL

Warri

Onitsha

ANAMBRA

Enugu

ANAMBRA

Owerri

Aba

Port-Harcourt

Calabar

CROSS RIVER

Makurdi

BENUE

Lafia

PLATEAU

GONGOLA

Wukari

Bamenda

DOUALA

Douala

Yaoundé

BIOKO
(FERNANDO POO)

EQUATORIAL GUINEA

Bight of Bonny

Niger Delta

Bight of Benin

Slave Coast

G U L F   O F   G U I N E A

East from Greenwich

COPYRIGHT GEORGE PHILIP & SON LTD.

SOMALI REP.

ETHIOPIA

KENYA

UGANDA

SUDAN

ZAIRE

TANZANIA

RWANDA

BURUNDI

CENTRAL AFRICAN REPUBLIC

NAIROBI

MOMBASA

DAR ES SALAAM

Kampala

Entebbe

Kisangani

Juba

Zanzibar

Pemba I.

Mafia I.

Lake Victoria

L. Tanganyika

L. Turkana (L. Rudolf)

L. Kyoga

L. Albert

L. Kivu

Dodoma

Tabora

Arusha

Moshi

Nakuru

Eldoret

Kitale

Bukavu

1 : 6 400 000

50   0   50   100   150   200 miles
50   0   100   200   300 km

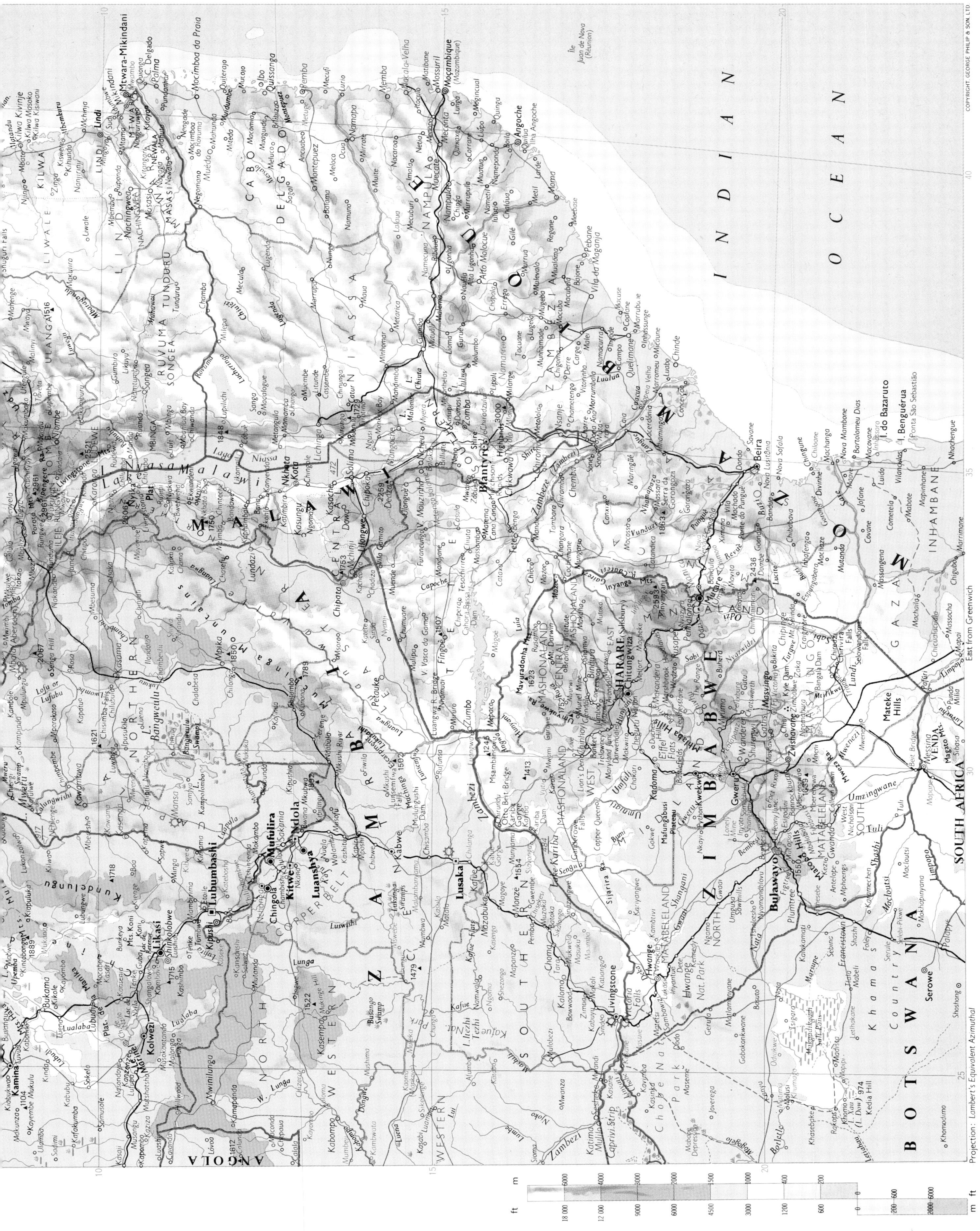

I N D I A N   O C E A N

A N G O L A

Z A M B I A

M A L A W I

M O Z A M B I Q U E

Z I M B A B W E

B O T S W A N A

SOUTH AFRICA

HARARE

Lusaka

Blantyre

Beira

Bulawayo

Gweru

Livingstone

Kolwezi

Likasi

Lubumbashi

Mufulira

Kitwe

Ndola

Chingola

Kabwe

Kamina

Serowe

NORTHERN

WESTERN

SOUTHERN

CENTRAL

MASHONALAND

MATABELELAND

COPPER BELT

NYASA

L. Nyasa (Malawi)

L. Bangweulu

L. Kariba

Zambezi

Luangwa

Lualaba

Victoria Falls

Hwange Nat. Park

East from Greenwich

COPYRIGHT GEORGE PHILIP & SON LTD

Projection: Lambert's Equivalent Azimuthal

ft   18 000   12 000   9000   6000   4500   3000   1200   600   0   200   600   6000 m

m   6000   4000   3000   2000   1500   1000   500   400   200   0   ft

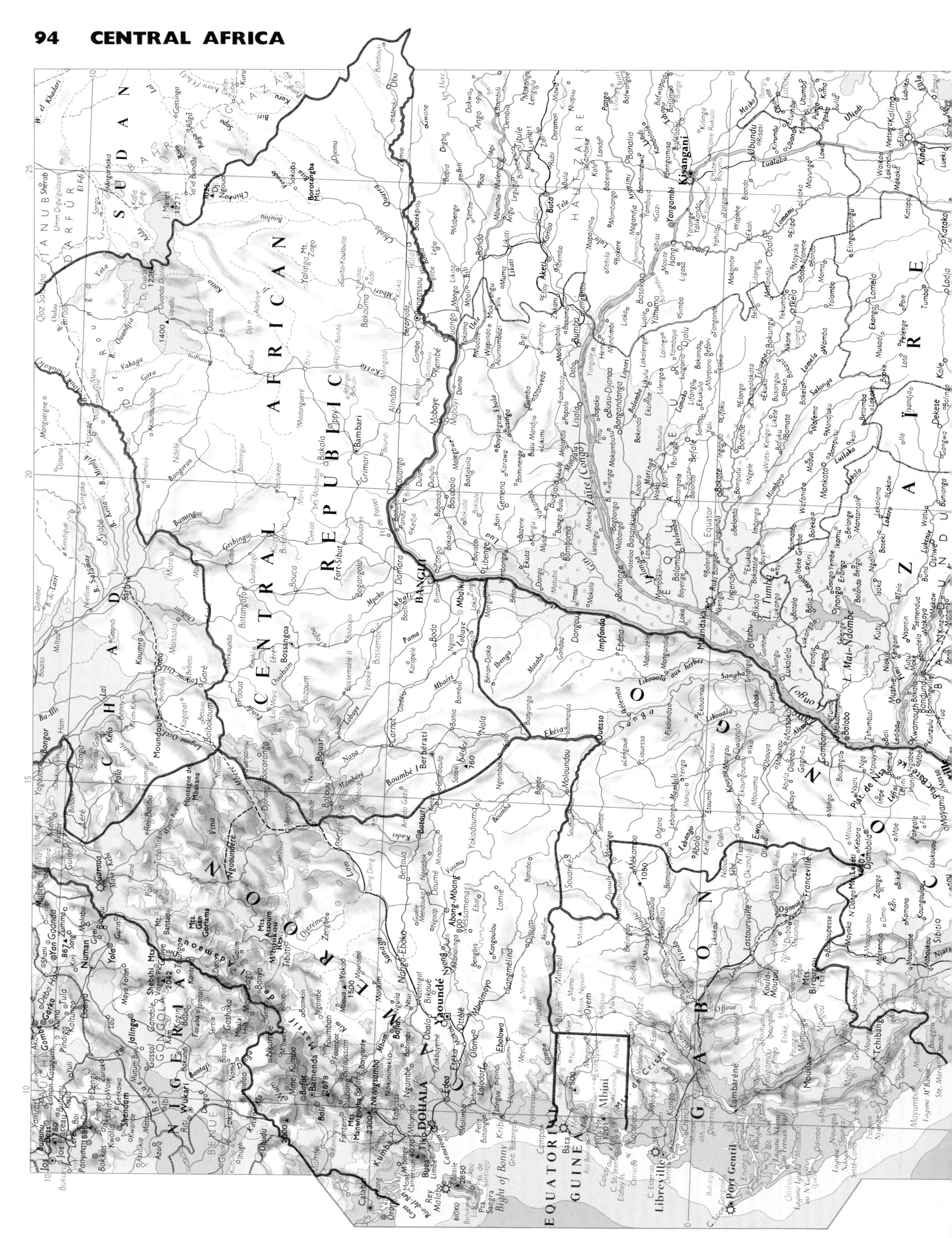
CENTRAL AFRICAN REPUBLIC
CHAD
SUDAN
CAMEROON
NIGERIA
EQUATORIAL GUINEA
GABON
CONGO
ZAÏRE
BANGUI
Yaoundé
DOUALA
Libreville
Port Gentil
Kisangani
Bight of Bonny

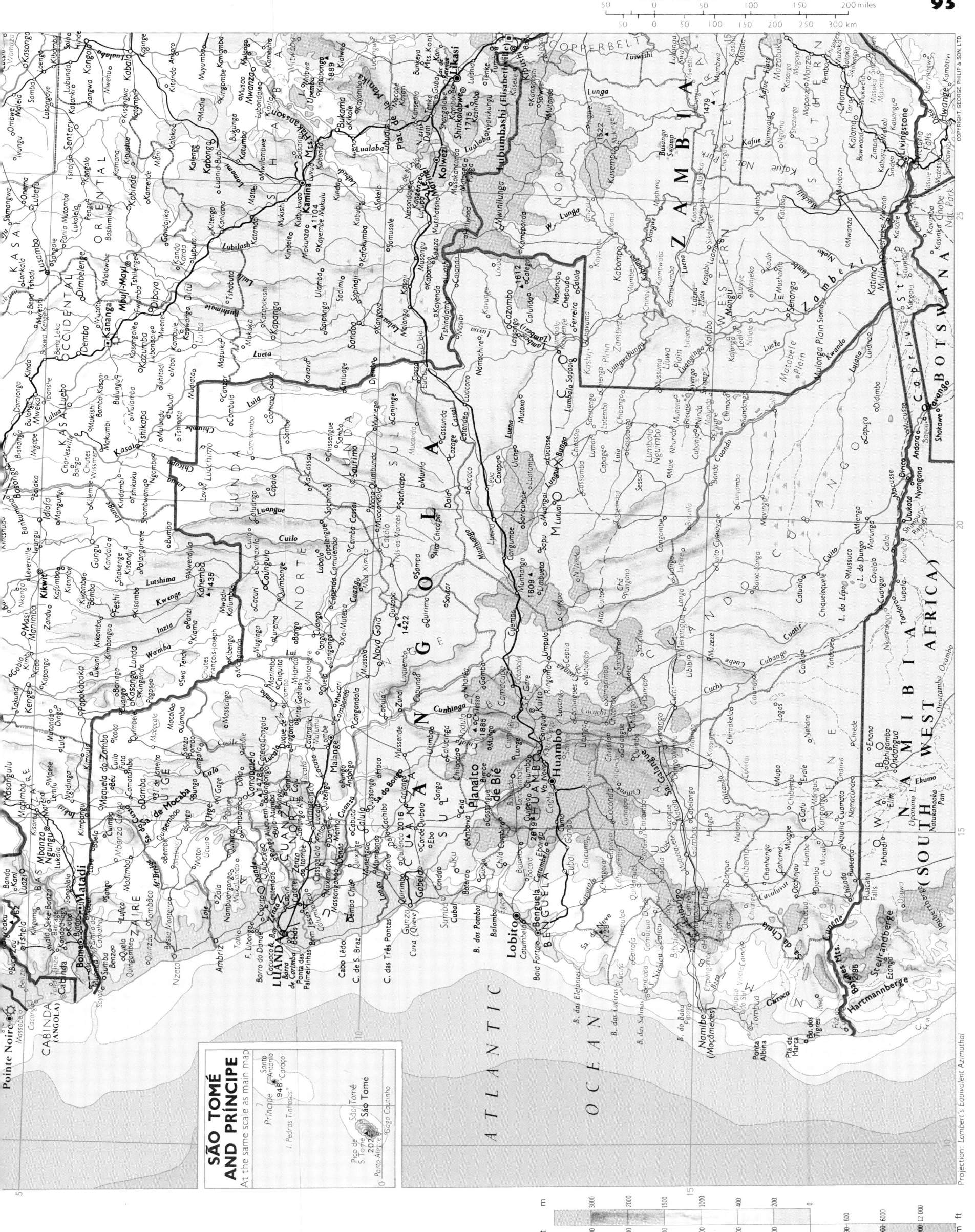

1 : 6 400 000

50   0   50   100   150   200 miles
50   0   50   100   150   200   250   300 km

COPYRIGHT GEORGE PHILIP & SON, LTD.

SÃO TOMÉ AND PRÍNCIPE

At the same scale as main map

Príncipe
Santa António
948
I. Pedras Tinhosas

São Tomé

Pico de
S. Tomé
2024▲
Porto Alegre
Ilhéo Gago Coutinho

Projection: Lambert's Equivalent Azimuthal

ft   m
9000   6000   4500   3000   1500   600   m   0   200   600   1200   2000   4000   6000   12 000   ft
         3000   2000   1500   1000   400   200   0   600

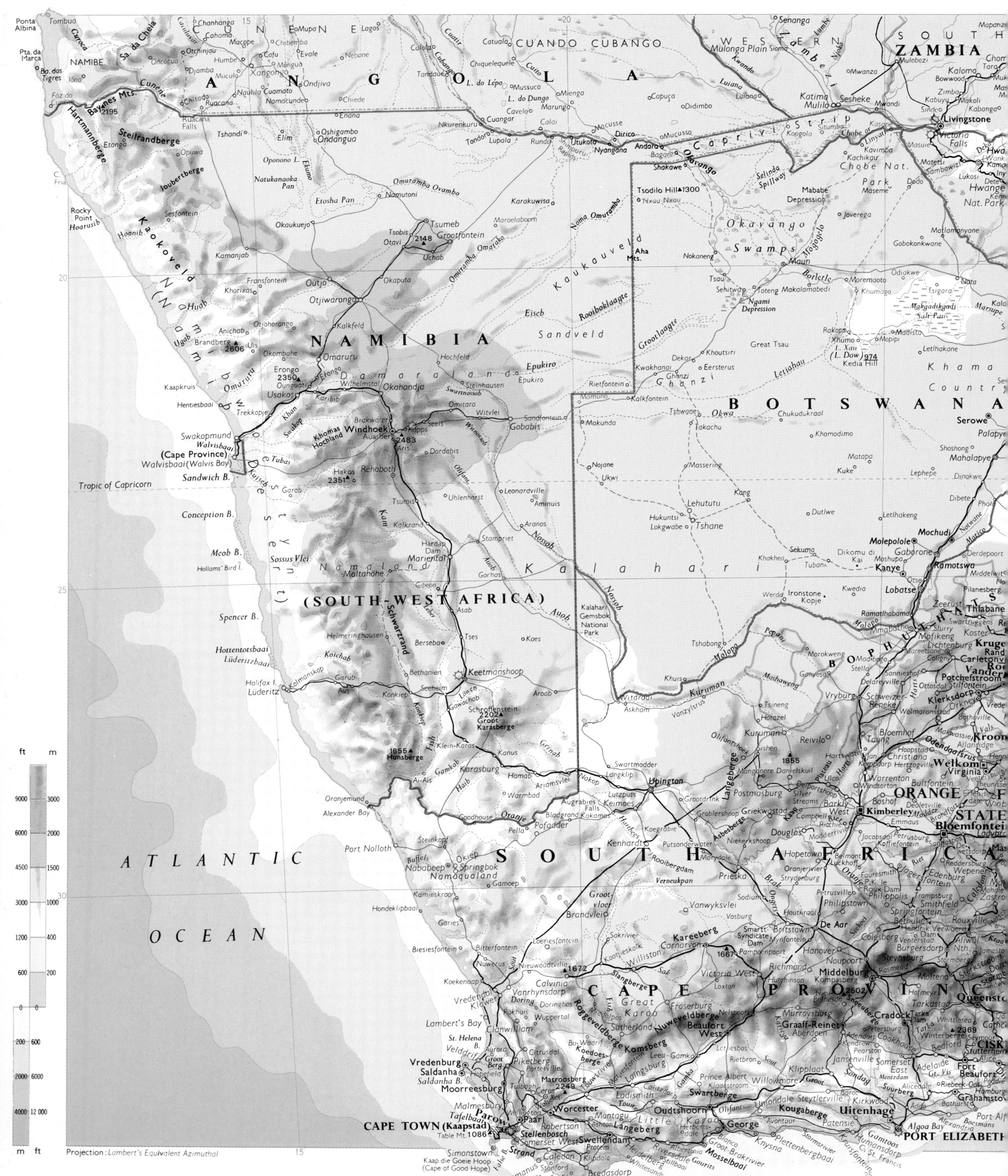
ANGOLA
CUANDO CUBANGO
ZAMBIA
WESTERN
SOUTH
Caprivi Strip
NAMIBIA
(SOUTH-WEST AFRICA)
BOTSWANA
SOUTH AFRICA
CAPE PROVINCE
ORANGE FREE STATE
BOPHUTHATSWANA
ATLANTIC OCEAN
Tropic of Capricorn
Namib Desert
Kalahari
Damaraland
Namaland
Kaokoveld
Okavango Swamps
Makgadikgadi Salt Pan
Etosha Pan
Ngami Depression
Great Karoo
Little Karoo
Namaqualand
Windhoek
Walvisbaai (Walvis Bay)
(Cape Province)
Swakopmund
Lüderitz
Keetmanshoop
Tsumeb
Grootfontein
Otjiwarongo
Rehoboth
Mariental
Gobabis
Livingstone
Victoria Falls
Maun
Serowe
Mahalapye
Molepolole
Gaborone
Kanye
Lobatse
Mafikeng
Kimberley
Bloemfontein
Welkom
Upington
Springbok
Calvinia
Beaufort West
Middelburg
Graaff-Reinet
Cradock
Oudtshoorn
George
Worcester
Paarl
Stellenbosch
CAPE TOWN (Kaapstad)
Table Mt. 1086
Kaap die Goeie Hoop (Cape of Good Hope)
C. Agulhas
Mosselbaai
Uitenhage
PORT ELIZABETH
Algoa Bay
Saldanha
Vredenburg
Port Nolloth
Alexander Bay
Oranjemund
Orange
Molopo
Nossob
Auob
Fish
Projection: Lambert's Equivalent Azimuthal
ft m
9000 3000
6000 2000
4500 1500
3000 1000
1200 400
600 200
0 0
200 600
2000 6000
4000 12 000
m ft

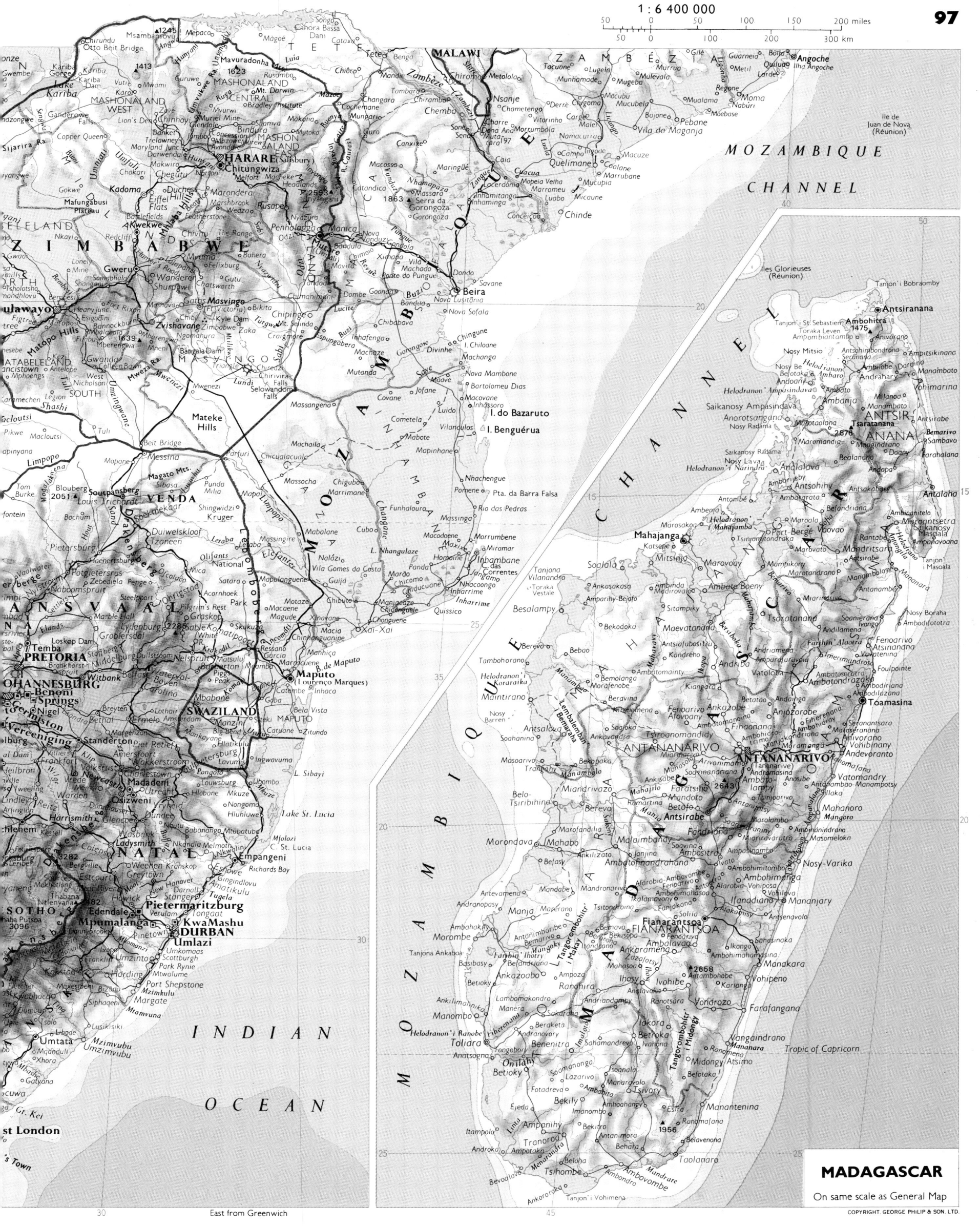

1 : 6 400 000

50   100   150   200 miles

50   0   100   200   300 km

MALAWI

ZAMBÉZIA

MOZAMBIQUE

CHANNEL

MOZAMBIQUE CHANNEL

ZIMBABWE

MASHONALAND
CENTRAL

HARARE

MASHONALAND

TETE

Ile de
Juan de Nova
(Réunion)

Iles Glorieuses
(Réunion)

Antsiranana

MADAGASCAR

Mahajanga

ANTANANARIVO

Antsirabe

Toamasina

FIANARANTSOA

Toliara

INDIAN

OCEAN

VENDA

TRANSVAAL

PRETORIA

JOHANNESBURG

SWAZILAND

MAPUTO

Maputo
(Lourenço Marques)

NATAL

DURBAN

Pietermaritzburg

LESOTHO

Umtata

East London

Tropic of Capricorn

East from Greenwich

MADAGASCAR

On same scale as General Map

COPYRIGHT. GEORGE PHILIP & SON. LTD.

1 : 6 400 000

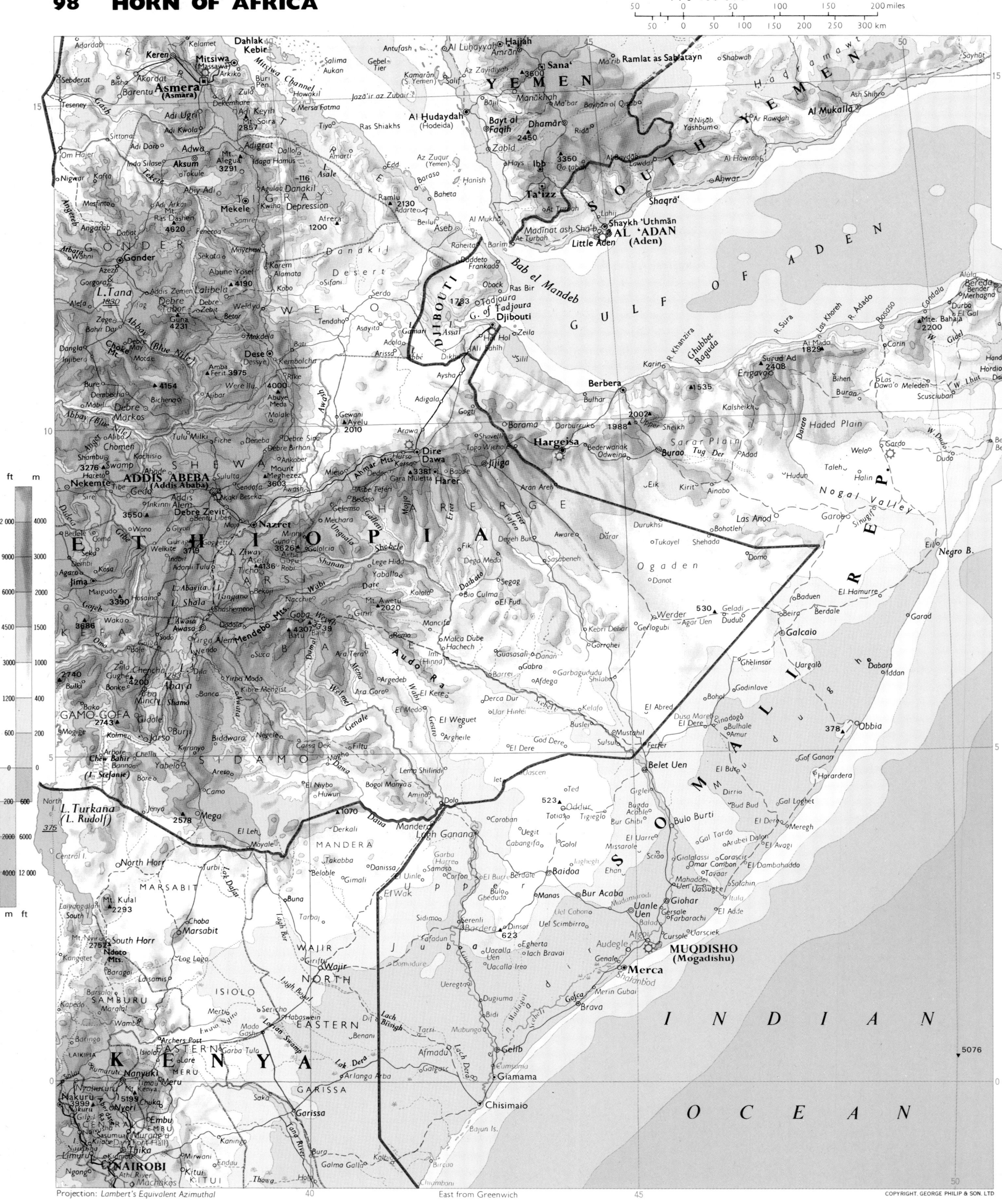
ETHIOPIA
SOMALI REP.
KENYA
YEMEN
SOUTH YEMEN
DJIBOUTI
GULF OF ADEN
INDIAN OCEAN
Bab el Mandeb
ADDIS ABEBA (Addis Ababa)
Asmera (Asmara)
Mitsiwa (Massawa)
Djibouti
Berbera
Hargeisa
Dire Dawa
Harer
Nazret
Gonder
Dese (Dessye)
Mekele
Aksum
Jima
Nekemte
Sana'
Al Hudaydah (Hodeida)
Ta'izz
AL 'ADAN (Aden)
Al Mukalla
MUQDISHO (Mogadishu)
Merca
Brava
Chisimaio
Belet Uen
Baidoa
Galcaio
Obbia
Garissa
Nairobi
Nanyuki
Ogaden
Haded Plain
Nogal Valley
L. Tana
L. Turkana (L. Rudolf)
Danakil Depression
Abbay (Blue Nile)
Shebele
Genale
Dawa
Juba
Tana River
Projection: Lambert's Equivalent Azimuthal
East from Greenwich

1 : 48 000 000

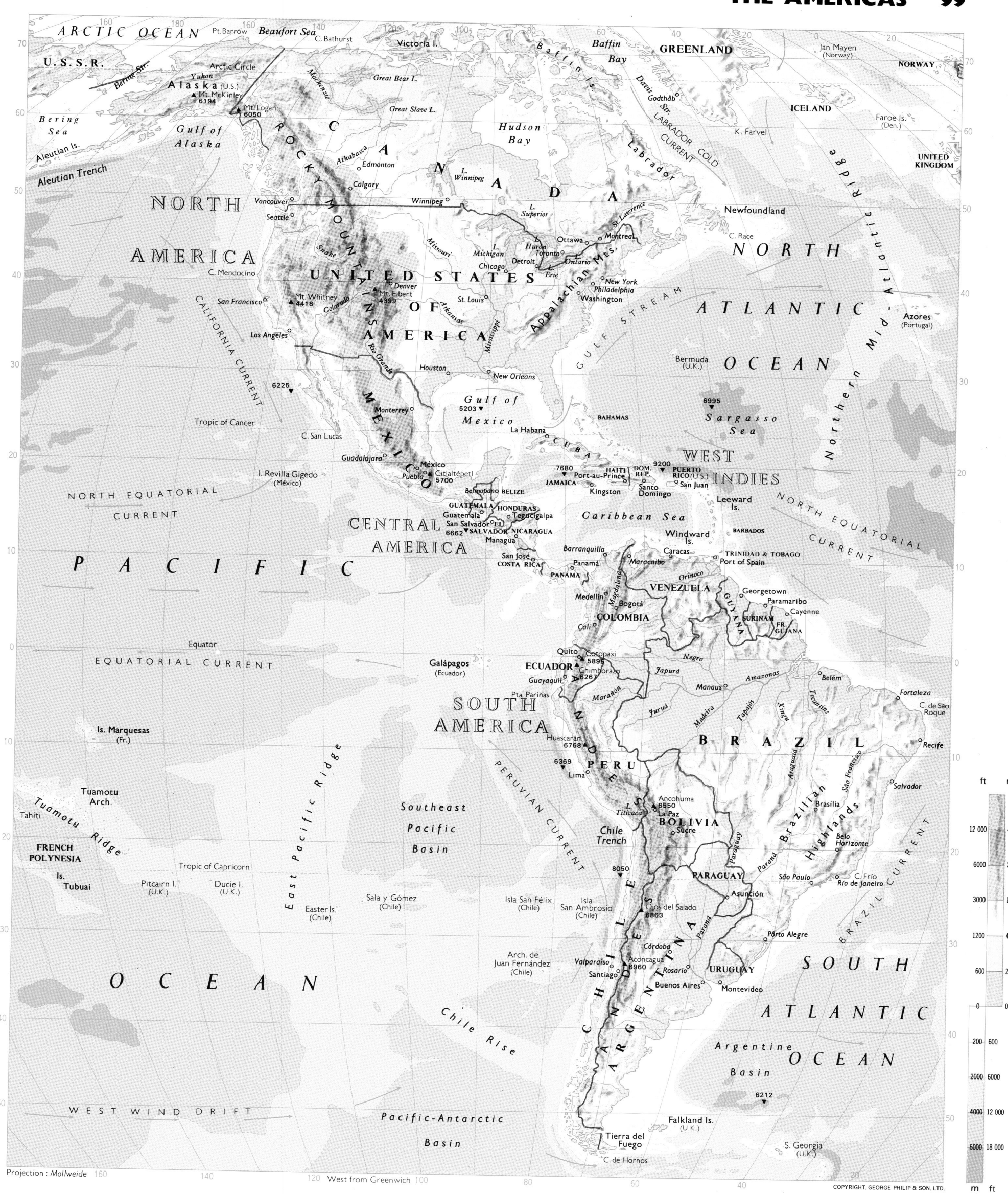
ARCTIC OCEAN
U.S.S.R.
Alaska (U.S.)
Beaufort Sea
Victoria I.
Baffin Bay
GREENLAND
Hudson Bay
CANADA
NORTH AMERICA
UNITED STATES OF AMERICA
ROCKY MOUNTAINS
Gulf of Alaska
Bering Sea
Aleutian Trench
Gulf of Mexico
MEXICO
CENTRAL AMERICA
Caribbean Sea
WEST INDIES
NORTH ATLANTIC OCEAN
Sargasso Sea
Northern Mid-Atlantic Ridge
GULF STREAM
CALIFORNIA CURRENT
NORTH EQUATORIAL CURRENT
EQUATORIAL CURRENT
PACIFIC OCEAN
SOUTH AMERICA
BRAZIL
ANDES
PERUVIAN CURRENT
Southeast Pacific Basin
East Pacific Ridge
Chile Rise
Pacific-Antarctic Basin
WEST WIND DRIFT
SOUTH ATLANTIC OCEAN
Argentine Basin
BRAZIL CURRENT
Tropic of Cancer
Equator
Tropic of Capricorn
Projection : Mollweide
West from Greenwich

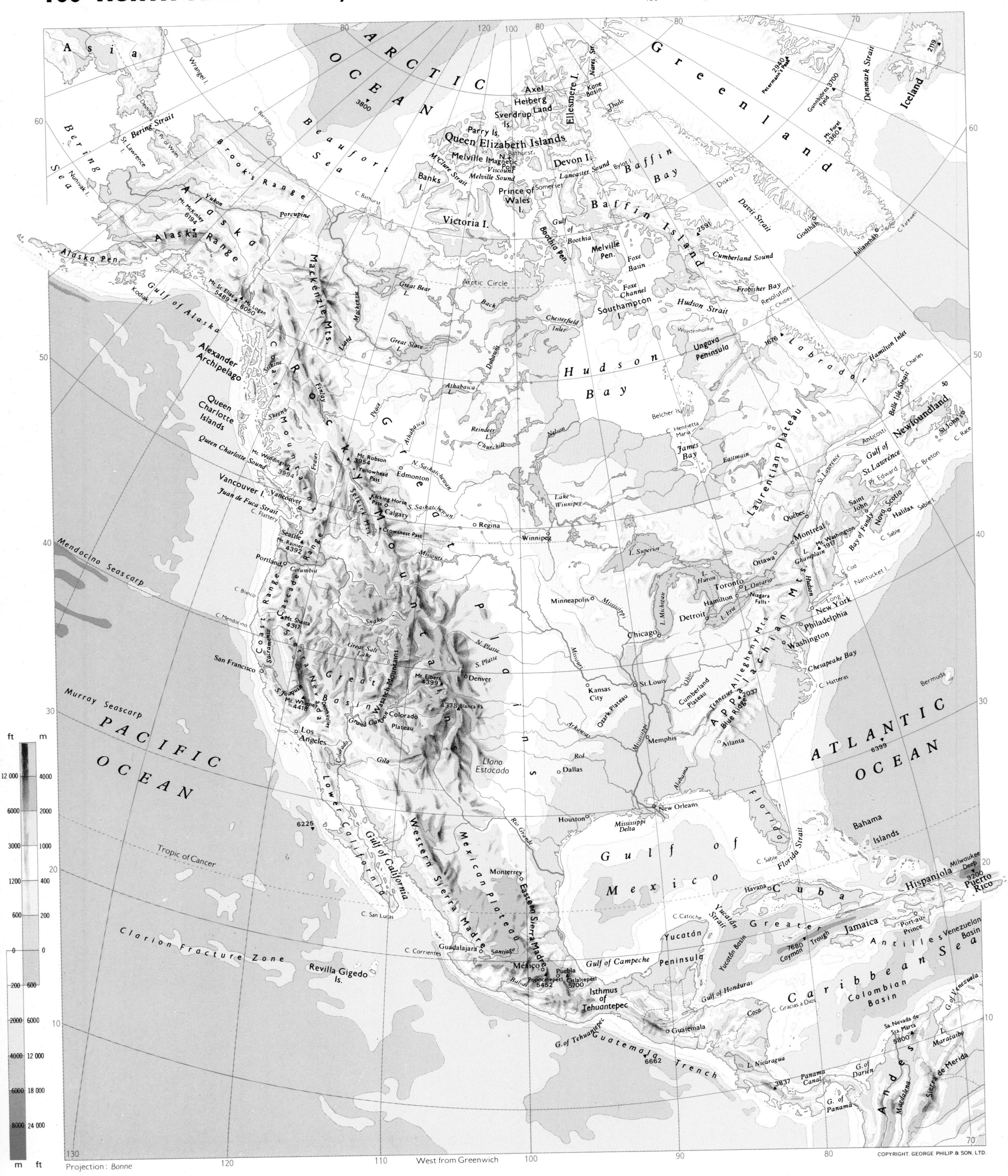

1 : 28 000 000

Projection: Bonne

West from Greenwich

COPYRIGHT. GEORGE PHILIP & SON. LTD.

1 : 28 000 000

200 0 200 400 600 800 miles
400   0   400   800   1200 km

U.S.S.R.

ARCTIC OCEAN

GREENLAND (Denmark)

Bering Sea
Bering Strait

Beaufort Sea

Queen Elizabeth Is.

Ellesmere I.

Baffin Bay

Denmark Strait

ICELAND
Reykjavík

Arctic Circle
ALASKA
Yukon
Fairbanks
Anchorage
Gulf of Alaska
Juneau
Whitehorse

INUVIK
YUKON TERRITORY
FORT SMITH
Mackenzie
Yellowknife
Great Bear L.
Great Slave L.

KITIKMEOT
Victoria I.
Back
KEEWATIN

NORTHWEST TERRITORIES

Baffin I.

Hudson Strait

C. Farewell
Godthåb
Davis Strait

BRITISH COLUMBIA
Finlay
Skeena
Fraser
Peace
Athabasca
ALBERTA
Edmonton
N. Saskatchewan
Calgary

CANADA

SASKATCHEWAN
Athabasca
S. Saskatchewan
Regina

MANITOBA
Churchill
Nelson
L. Winnipeg
Winnipeg

Hudson Bay

Eastmain

QUÉBEC

NEWFOUNDLAND

Labrador

St. Lawrence
Québec
NEW BRUNSWICK
PRINCE EDWARD
Charlottetown
NOVA SCOTIA
Halifax
SPM
St. John's

Victoria
Vancouver
WASHINGTON
Olympia
Seattle
Columbia
Portland
Salem
OREGON

MONTANA
Missouri
Helena

NORTH DAKOTA
Bismarck

MINNESOTA
St. Paul
Minneapolis
Madison
WISCONSIN
L. Superior
L. Michigan
MICHIGAN
Lansing

ONTARIO
Ottawa
Montréal
Toronto
L. Huron
L. Ontario
Buffalo
Detroit
Cleveland
Montpelier
MAINE
Augusta
N.H.
VER.
Concord
NEW YORK
Albany
MASS.
Boston
Hartford
R.I.
Providence

IDAHO
Boise
Snake

WYOMING
Cheyenne
N. Platte
NEBRASKA
Lincoln

SOUTH DAKOTA
Pierre

IOWA
Des Moines

ILLINOIS
Springfield
Chicago
Milwaukee
INDIANA
Indianapolis
OHIO
Columbus
Frankfort
Cincinnati
Toledo
Pittsburgh
PENNSYLVANIA
Harrisburg
Trenton
Philadelphia
NEW YORK
NEW JERSEY
Dover
D.C.
Annapolis
Baltimore
Washington
WEST VIRGINIA
Charleston
Richmond
VIRGINIA

Sacramento
San Francisco
San Jose
CALIFORNIA
NEVADA
Carson City
Salt Lake City
UTAH
Denver
COLORADO
Arkansas
KANSAS
Topeka
Kansas City
MISSOURI
Jefferson City
St. Louis
KENTUCKY
Frankfort
TENNESSEE
Nashville
Tennessee
NORTH CAROLINA
Raleigh
Columbia
SOUTH CAROLINA

Las Vegas
LOS ANGELES
San Diego
Colorado
Gila
ARIZONA
Phoenix
Tucson
Santa Fe
Albuquerque
NEW MEXICO
El Paso
OKLAHOMA
Oklahoma City
Red River
Little Rock
ARKANSAS
Memphis
MISSISSIPPI
Birmingham
ALABAMA
Jackson
Montgomery
GEORGIA
Atlanta
Charleston
Jacksonville
FLORIDA

UNITED STATES

PACIFIC OCEAN

ATLANTIC OCEAN

Bermuda

TEXAS
Dallas
Austin
Houston
LOUISIANA
Baton Rouge
New Orleans
Mississippi
Tallahassee
Tampa
Miami
C. Sable
Str. of Florida
Nassau
BAHAMAS

Rio Grande
Monterrey

Gulf of Mexico

Tropic of Cancer

MEXICO

Guadalajara
MEXICO

Havana
CUBA

HAITI
Port-au-Prince
DOMINICAN REP.
Santo Domingo
San Juan
PUERTO RICO

JAMAICA
Kingston

Caribbean Sea

BELIZE
Belmopan
GUATEMALA
Guatemala
San Salvador
EL SALVADOR
HONDURAS
Tegucigalpa
NICARAGUA
Managua
L. Nicaragua
COSTA RICA
San José
PANAMA
Panamá

Maracaibo
Barranquilla
VENEZUELA
Medellín
COLOMBIA
Bogotá

SOUTH AMERICA

State capital ⊙

C.	CONNECTICUT
D.	DELAWARE
D.C.	DISTRICT OF COLUMBIA
M.	MARYLAND
MASS.	MASSACHUSETTS
N.H.	NEW HAMPSHIRE
N.J.	NEW JERSEY
R.I.	RHODE ISLAND
VER.	VERMONT
SPM	ST. PIERRE ET MIQUELON

Projection: Bonne

West from Greenwich

COPYRIGHT. GEORGE PHILIP & SON. LTD.

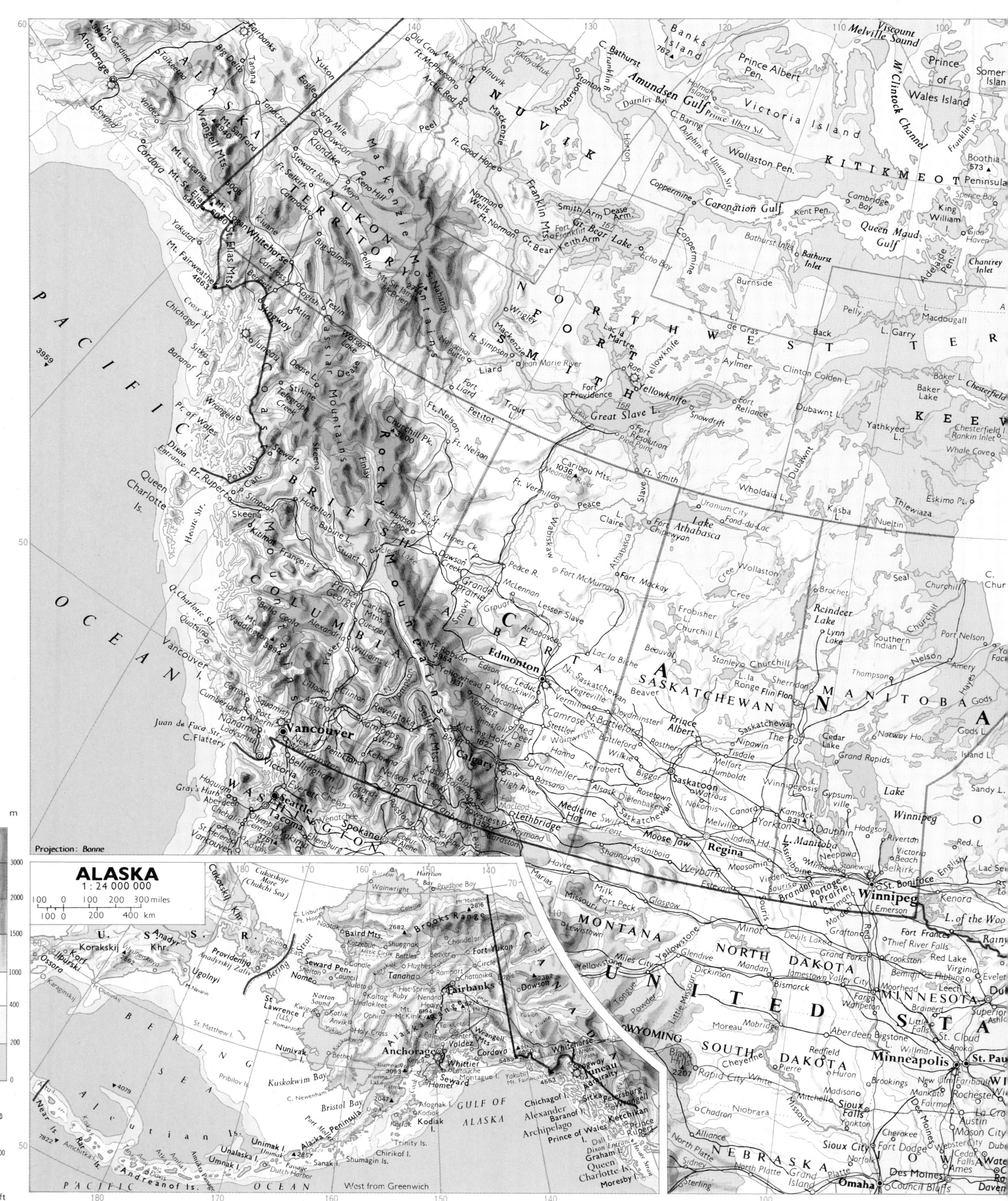

ALASKA

1 : 24 000 000

100 0 100 200 300 miles

100 0 200 400 km

Projection: Bonne

100 50 0   100   200   300   400 miles
100   0   100   200   300   400   500   600 km

Devon Island
Lancaster Sound
2136
1890
Arctic Bay
Bylot I.
Brodeur
Peninsula
Milne
Inlet
Pond Inlet
Pond Inlet
Scott I.
Clyde
C. Hewett
Baffin Bay

GREENLAND
Angmagssalik
Svartenhuk Halvø
Disko
Christianshåb
Disko B.
Sandre Stromfjord
Holsteinsborg
2850
Kong Frederik VI's Kyst
Sukkertoppen
Godthåb
Eskenæsset
Frederikshåb
Julianehåb
Ivigtut
Nanortalik
Kap Farvel

B   a   f   f   i   n
Fury & Hecla Str.
Igloolik
Island
Hall
Lake
Prince
Charles
I.
Foxe
Peninsula
Melville
Peninsula
Pelly
Bay
Committee B.
Home B.
Broughton
Island
Padloping Island
C. Dyer
Cape
Dyer
2591
Cumberland
Peninsula
Pangnirtung
Hoare B.
C. Mercy

Davis Strait

Wager B.
Rae Isthmus
Repulse Bay
Southampton I.
Coral Harbour
Bell Pen.
Ross Welcome Sd.
Foxe
Basin
Nettilling
L.
Foxe
Channel
C. Dorchester
Foxe
Penin.
Amadjuak
L.
Amadjuak
Lake
Harbour
Cape Dorset
Frobisher
Bay
Frobisher Bay
Resolution I.

Hudson   Strait

Coats
I.
Digges Is.
Mansel
I.
Invujivik
(Sugluk)
Saglouc
(Sugluk)
Maricourt
(Wakeham)
Koartac
(Notre Dame
de Koartac)
Akpatok
I.
C. Chidley
Hudson
Bay
Ottawa Is.
257
Portland
Promontory
Inoucdjouac
(Port Harrison)
Payne L.
Arnaud (Bellin)
(Payne Bay)
Ungava Bay
Ungava
Bay
P e n i n s u l a
Feuilles
Loksoak
Kuujjuaq
George
Whale
Nain
C. Harrison
Hopedale
Indian Harbour
Mélèzes
Kaniapiskau
Nutak
Hebron

Sleeper Is.
King
George Is.
King George Is.
Baker's
Dozen
Is.
Belcher
Is.
L. Minto
Rigolet
L. Magpie
Cartwright
Belle Isle
Bottle Harb.
North West R.
COAST OF LABRADOR
Schefferville
Petitsikapau L.
Churchill
Falls
Churchill
Natashquan

D
Winisk
Severn
Big
Trout L.
C. Henrietta
Maria
Pte.
Louis-XIV
L'Eau Claire
Grand Baleine
Poste-de-
la-Baleine
(Great Whale River)
Kanaaupscow
Ft. George
La Grande
Kaniapiskau
1128
Gagnon
QUEBEC
Moisie
Ashuanipi
Romaine
Natashquan
St-Augustin-
Saguenay
NEWFOUNDLAND
814
Notre Dame B.
Twillingate
Lewisporte
Gander
Bonavista
Trinity B.
St. John's
Grand Falls
Harbour Grace
Carbonear
Placentia
Trepassey
C. Race

James Bay
Akimiski
I.
Charlton I.
Nouveau Comptoir
(Paint Hills)
Eastmain
Ft. Albany
Fort Rupert
(Rupert House)
Rupert
Mistassini
L. Albanel
Péribonca
Manicouagan
Sept Îles
Moisie
Port-Cartier
Îs. de la Madeleine
Î. d'Anticosti
Gulf of
St. Lawrence
Cabot Str.
Cape Breton I.
Glace Bay
Sydney
Port Hawkesbury
ST-PIERRE
et MIQUELON
(Fr.)
Placentia B.
Ray

TARIO
Winisk
L. St. Joseph
Attawapiskat
Albany
Moosonee
Harricana
Nottaway
Chibougamau
Baie-Comeau
R. St. Lawrence
Matane
Pen. de Gaspé
C. de Gaspé
Rimouski
Campbellton
Bathurst
Chatham
PR. EDWARD I.
Summerside
Charlottetown
Northumberland Str.
Pictou
New Glasgow
Mulgrave
Sable I.
(Nova Scotia)

Thunder Bay
Nipigon
L. Nipigon
Longlac
Hearst
Kapuskasing
Cochrane
Timmins
Kirkland Lake
Noranda
Rouyn
Senneterre
Val d'Or
La Tuque
Shawinigan
Trois-Rivières
Québec
Lévis
Thetford Mines
Woodstock
1917
NEW
BRUNSWICK
Moncton
Amherst
Springhill
Truro
NOVA SCOTIA
Windsor
Dartmouth
Halifax
Bridgewater
Liverpool
Shelburne
C. Sable
Yarmouth
6309

Nakina
Geraldton
Heron Bay
Franz
Oba
Michipicoten
Haileybury
Cobalt
Témiscamingue
Rés. de
Cabonga
Joliette
Sorel
St. Hyacinthe
Sherbrooke
MAINE
Bangor
Saint
John
B. of Fundy
Digby
Annapolis

Thunder Bay
Calumet
Laurium
Keweenaw
Bay
L. Gogebic
Marquette
Michipicoten
Sault Ste. Marie
Sault Ste. Marie
North Chan.
Sudbury
Copper Cliff
North Bay
Pembroke
Ottawa
Hull
Lachine
MONTRÉAL
Cornwall
L. Champlain
VERMONT
NEW
HAMPSHIRE
Manchester
Portland
Augusta
Lewiston

Ironwood
Ironwood
Antigo
Menominee
Wausau
Green
Bay
Appleton
Escanaba
Manistique
Cheboygan
Petoskey
Georgian
Bay
Parry
Sound
Lake
Huron
Orillia
Peterboro
Belleville
Kingston
Burlington
Watertown
Glens
Utica
Concord
Lowell
Manchester
MASS.
Boston
C. Cod

WISCONSIN
Sheboygan
Manitowoc
Ludington
Saginaw
Muskegon
Owen Sound
TORONTO
Guelph
Kitchener
Oshawa
L. Ontario
Rochester
Syracuse
Albany
Springfield
CONN.
Providence
New Haven

Milwaukee
Racine
Kenosha
Waukegan
Evanston
Grand
Rapids
Kalamazoo
London
Brantford
Hamilton
St. Catharines
Niagara
Falls
Buffalo
NEW YORK
Binghamton
Elmira
Scranton
Waterbury
Bridgeport
Newark
Jersey City
NEW YORK

CHICAGO
Gary
INDIANA
South Bend
Toledo
DETROIT
Windsor
Cleveland
Youngstown
Akron
Erie
Jamestown
Williamsport
PENNSYLVANIA
Allentown
Reading
Trenton
NEW JERSEY
ILLINOIS
OHIO

ATLANTIC   OCEAN

3809

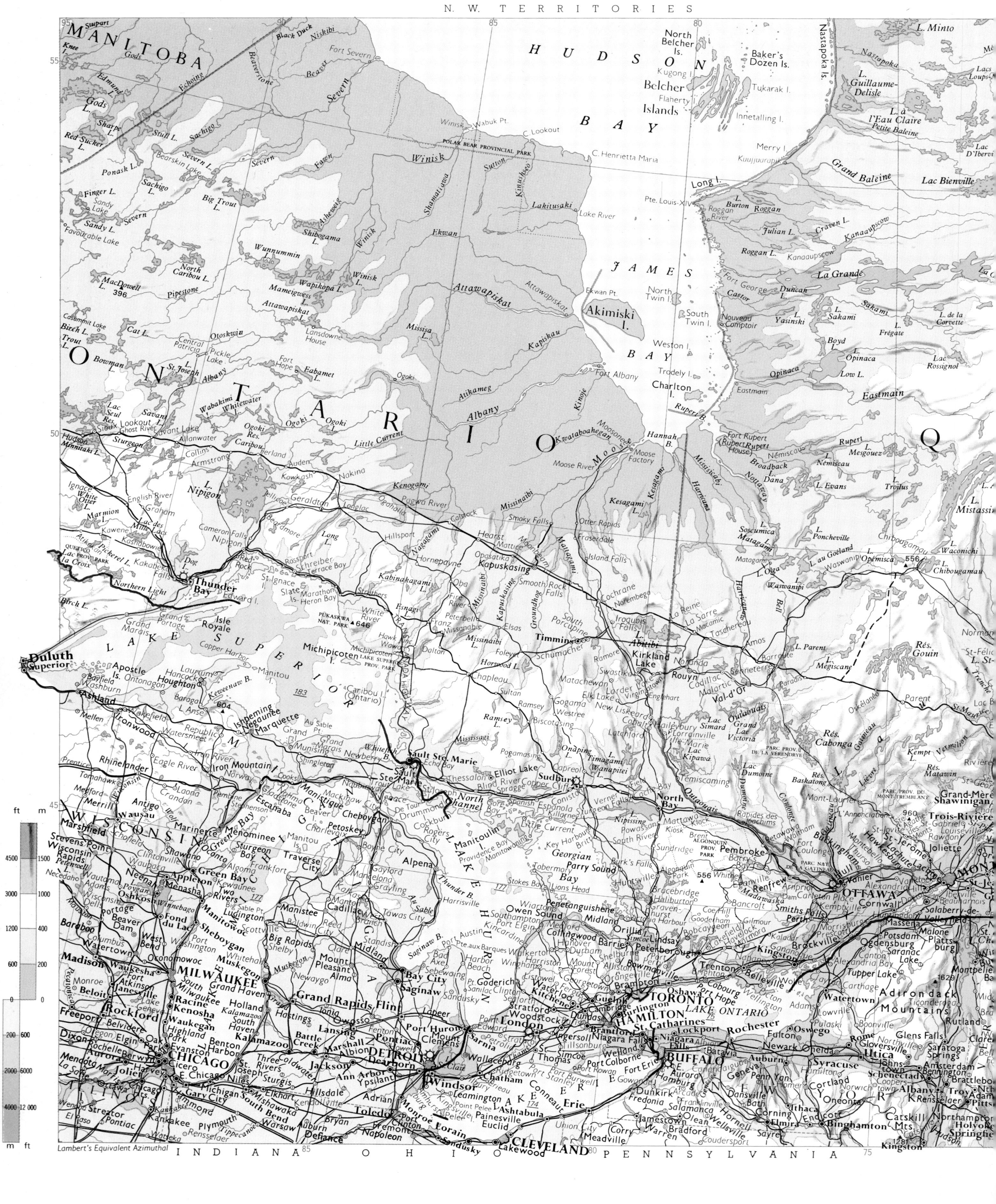

N. W. TERRITORIES

MANITOBA

ONTARIO

HUDSON BAY

JAMES BAY

QUEBEC

Belcher Islands
Flaherty I.
Akimiski I.
North Twin I.
South Twin I.
Charlton
Weston I.

North Belcher Is.
Baker's Dozen Is.
Kugong I.
Tukarak I.
Innetalling I.
Merry I.

L. Minto
Nastapoka Is.
L. Guillaume-Delisle
Lac Bienville
Grand Baleine
Petite Baleine

Polar Bear Provincial Park
Winisk
Severn
Fort Severn
Black Duck
Niskibi

Attawapiskat
Ekwan
Albany
Fort Albany
Moosonee
Moose Factory
Moose River

La Grande
Fort George
Eastmain
Fort Rupert (Rupert House)
Rupert R.

Kapuskasing
Hearst
Cochrane
Timmins
Kirkland Lake
Rouyn
Val-d'Or

Thunder Bay
LAKE SUPERIOR
Isle Royale
Duluth
Superior

Sault Ste. Marie
Sudbury
North Bay
Elliot Lake

WISCONSIN
Green Bay
LAKE MICHIGAN
LAKE HURON
Georgian Bay
Manitoulin I.
Parry Sound

MILWAUKEE
Madison
Rockford
CHICAGO

DETROIT
Windsor
London
Hamilton
TORONTO
St. Catharines
Niagara Falls
BUFFALO

LAKE ONTARIO
Kingston
Ottawa
Brockville

Toledo
CLEVELAND
LAKE ERIE
Rochester
Syracuse
Utica

NEW YORK
Adirondack Mountains
Albany

INDIANA   OHIO   PENNSYLVANIA

Lambert's Equivalent Azimuthal

1 : 5 600 000

50 0 50 100 150 200 miles
50 0 50 100 150 200 250 300 km
COAST OF LABRADOR
NEWFOUNDLAND
QUEBEC
NEW BRUNSWICK
NOVA SCOTIA
MAINE
PRINCE EDWARD ISLAND
GULF OF ST. LAWRENCE
ATLANTIC OCEAN
St. Lawrence
Cabot Strait
Str. of Belle Isle
Bay of Fundy
Î. d'Anticosti
Dét. de Jacques-Cartier
Dét. d'Honguedo
Mts. Chic-Chocs
Pén. de Gaspé
Chaleur Bay
Îs. de la Madeleine (Quebec)
Cape Breton Island
SAINT-PIERRE ET MIQUELON (Fr.)
Sable I. (Nova Scotia)
Avalon Peninsula
Long Range Mts.
Mealy Mts.
Kaniapiskau Lake
Michikamau Lake
Rés. Manicouagan
Labrador City
Schefferville
Churchill Falls
Happy Valley-Goose Bay
North-West River
L. Melville
Hopedale
Nain
Sept-Îles
Port-Cartier
Baie-Comeau
Rimouski
Matane
Gaspé
Chicoutimi
Jonquière
Arvida
Alma
Rivière-du-Loup
Lauzon
Lévis
Thetford Mines
Sherbrooke
Coaticook
Edmundston
Campbellton
Dalhousie
Bathurst
Newcastle
Chatham
Moncton
Fredericton
Saint John
Summerside
Charlottetown
Amherst
Truro
New Glasgow
Stellarton
Halifax
Dartmouth
Yarmouth
Sydney
Glace Bay
New Waterford
Sydney Mines
Corner Brook
Stephenville
Gander
Grand Falls
Botwood
Lewisporte
Clarenville
St. John's
Bangor
Augusta
Portland
Lewiston
Auburn
Waterville
Biddeford
Saco
Portsmouth
Manchester
Nashua
Haverhill
Lawrence
Lowell
Lynn
Gloucester
BOSTON
Brockton
Presque Isle
Houlton
Millinocket
Caribou
70
65
60
55
50
45
West from Greenwich

L. Obamsca
L. Paul-Sauvé
L. Montreuil
L. Soscumica
L. Porcheville
L. Bouchier
Opataca
L. Lemieux
Brock
Sauva
L. Grasset
L. la Trève
Opémisca
Maicasagi
50
Matagami
L. au Goéland
Waswanipi
Chibougameau
Chapais
Matagami
L. Olga
Waswanipi
L. Opawica
Miquelon
Waswanipi
Desmaraisville
Rés.
Goé
Kattawagami L.
Bell
Surprise
L. Turgeon
L. Quévillon
Bigniba
Lebel-sur-Quévillon
49
Cochrane
Norembega
Normétal
Desméloizes
La Reine
L. Chicobi
Obalski
Lallamne
L. Parent
Rochebaucourt
Obedjwan
Iroquois Falls
Lake Abitibi
Dupuy
La Sarre
Macamic
Taschereau
Villemontel
Champneuf
L. Mégiscane
Frederick House L.
Connaught
Val Gagné
Matheson
Palmarolle
Duparquet
Amos
andrienne
Barraute
Belcourt
Senneterre
Timmins
Hoyle
KETTLE LAKES PROV. PK.
Holtyre
L. Duparquet
PARC AIGUEBELLE
la Motte
Faillon
Porcupine
South Porcupine
Ramore
Watabeag L.
Bourkes
ESKER LAKES PROV. PARK
Dasserat
L. Preissac
Barraute
Belcourt
Senneterre
Redstone
Whitefish
Kirkland Lake
Swastika
Arntfield
Évain
Noranda
Rouyn
Cadillac
L. Malartic
Paradis
Forsythe
Mégiscane
48
Matachewan
Larder Lake
Virginiatown
Larder L.
L. Opasatica
Malartic
Sullivan
Val-d'Or
Guéguen
Soucy
Clova
Oskélanéo
Charlton
Englehart
Rollet
L. Roger
Lemoine
L. Matchi-Manitou
Gowganda
Elk Lake
Earlton
Belle Vallée
Rémigny
Outaouais
Réservoir Decelles
L. Sabourin
L. Villebon
Camachigama
Thornloe
Notre-Dame-du-Nord
L. Simard
L. Granet
L. Échouani
Makobe L.
New Liskeard
Angliers
Rapide-Sept
Réservoir Dozois
Bazin
Smoothwater L.
Haileybury
Guigues
L. des Quinze
Laforce
Grand Lac Victoria
L. des Augustines
47
Burwash L.
Cobalt
Laverlochère
Latulipe
Réservoir Cabonga
Némiscachi
Latchford
Ville Marie
Lorrainville
Belleterre
L. à la Truite
Rés. Mitchinamé
Obabika L.
Timagami
Béarn
Fabre
L. Ostaboningue
L. Ogascanane
PARC PROV. DE LA VÉRENDRYE
Bear Island
L. Sasaginaga
Timagami
Lac Kipawa
L. aux Foins
Gatineau
L. de l'Écorce
Wanapitei L.
Wanapitei L.
Sturgeon
Timiskanning
Kipawa
L. Sairs
L. Dumoine
Capreol
Marten River
Témiscaming
Tee Lake
L. Pin-Blanc
Ste-Anne-du-Lac
Réservoir Baskatong
Val Caron
Hanmer
River Valley
Field
L. Beauchêne
L. du Fils
Ferme-Neuve
Lièvre
Sudbury
Azilda
Falconbridge
Markstay
Tomiko
L. Bleu
Ottawa
St-Patrice
PARC PONTIAC
Montcerf
Mont-Laurier
Lac-des-Écorces
Copper Cliff
Coniston
Warren
Verner
Sturgeon Falls
Feronia
Outaouais
Dumoine
Val-Barrette
L. Nomin
Burwash
Cache Bay
North Bay
Lake Nipissing
Mattawa
Messine
Maniwaki
L'Ann
Rutter
Notre Dame du Lac
Bonfield
Deux-Rivières
Bouchette
Lac des Trente et un Milles
L. du Cerf
Labelle
46
Noelville
Callander
Astorville
Rapides des Joachims
Rolphton
Gracefield
L. Gagnon
La Conception
St-Jov
Key Harbour
French River
Powassan
Kiosk
Brent
Deep River
Noire
Lac-Ste-Marie
Venosta
Val-des-Bois
PAPINEAU
Britt
Port Loring
Commanda
Cedar L.
Chalk River
Chapeau
Waltham Sta.
Low
Ripon
Byng Inlet
Drocourt
Sundridge
Trout Creek
South River
ALGONQUIN PROV. PARK
Lavieille
Petawawa
Fort-Coulonge
Poltimore
Chénéville
Pointe au Baril Sta.
Ardbeg
Dunchurch
Magnetawan
Bernard L.
Big Trout L.
Opeongo L.
Pembroke
Alice
Bryson
Campbell's Bay
Glen Almond
St-André-Av
Montebe
Shawanaga
McKellar
Emsdale
Burk's Falls
Kearney
Algonquin Park
Bonnéchère
Round L.
Beachburg
Cobden
Shawville
PARC DE LA GATINEAU
Buckingham
Thurso
Waubamik
Nobel
Spruce dale
Novar
Whitney
Aylen L.
Killaloe Sta.
Golden Lake
Bristol
Pointe Gatineau
Masson
Angers
Rockland
Parry Sound
Huntsville
Dwight
Kawagama L.
Madawaska
Barry's Bay
Golden Eganville
Quyon
Renfrew
Hull
Gatineau
Cumberland
Hawkesbu
45
Georgian Bay
Rosseau
L. of Bays
Dorset
Lake St. Peter
L. Clear
Combermere
Calabogie
Arnprior
Braeside
OTTAWA
Bourget
Joseph
MacTier
Port Carling
Baysville
Eagle Lake
Madawaska
Griffith
Pakenham
Aylmer
Deschènes
Vars
Limoges
Alexandre
Bala
GEORGIAN BAY ISLANDS NATIONAL PARK
Muskoka
Denbigh
White L.
Almonte
Richmond
Bells Corner
Casselman
Moose Creek
Maxvi
HOPE I.
Honey Harbour
Gravenhurst
Bracebridge
Wilberforce
Bancroft
Flower Sta.
North Gower
Osgoode
Avonmore
GRIFFITH I.
CHRISTIAN I.
Muskoka
Minden
Gooderham
Weslemkoon L.
Plevna
Lavant Sta.
Mississippi
Carleton Place
Kemptville
Lanark
Winchester
Cornwall
Masse

Projection: Bonne

10   0   10   20   30   40   50 miles
10   0   20   40   60   80 km

PARC PROV. DE MISTASSINI
Baie-du-Poste
L. File Axe
L. Waconichi
Chibougamau
R. du Chef
Nestaocano
Mistassibi
Mistassibi Nord-Est
Manouane
L. De La Blanche
Ste-Anne
St-Pierre

L. Péribonca
Chute-des-Passes
L. du Goéland
Réservoir Pipmuacan
L. du Brochet
L. Dionne
Godbout

PARC PROV. DE CHIBOUGAMAU
L. Poutrincourt
Bochart
L. Chigoubiche
L. Marquette
Girardville
Albanel
Mistassibi
Péribonca
Réservoir La Mothe
Moncouche
L. Poulin-de-Courval
Portneuf
Outardes
Franquelin
Godbout

Rouvray
Itomamo
Réservoir Pipmuacan
Labrieville
Betsiamites
Baie-Comeau
Hauterive
Pointe-Lebel

Sault aux Cochons
Rivière-Bersimis
Pointe-aux-Outardes
Betsiamites
Colombier
St-Ulric

Mistassini
Milot
Ste-Monique
St-Cœur-de-Marie
St-Ambroise
Normandin
Péribonka
L'Ascension
Onatchiway
Portneuf
St-Paul-du-Nord
Forestville
Métis-sur-Mer
St-Noël
Price
Mont-Joli
Luceville
Sayabec
Ste-Angèle-de-Mérici

N.D.-de la Doré
St-Félicien
St-Prime
Lac St-Jean
Alma
Roberval
St-Gédéon
St-Bruno
Kénogami
Arvida
St-Fulgence
Chicoutimi
La Baie
Bagotville
Jonquière
Saguenay
Sacré-Cœur-de-Jésus
Les Escoumins
Grandes-Bergeronnes
Tadoussac
Baie-Ste-Catherine
Rimouski-Est
Rimouski
St-Anaclet
St-Gabriel-de-Rimouski
Bic
ÎLE DU BIC
St-Fabien
Ste-Blandine

Chambord
Desbiens
St-Jérôme
L. Kénogami
Lac Bouchette
Petit-Saguenay
Trois-Pistoles
St-Simon-de-Rimouski
Ste-Françoise
St-Éloi
PARC PROV. DE RIMOUSKI

B E C
L. des Commissaires
Van Bruyssel
ISLE VERTE
L'Isle Verte
St-Jean-de-Dieu

St-Maurice
Windigo
Trenche
St-Georges-de-Cacouna
St-Siméon
Squatec

NEW BRUNSW.

Rapide-Blanc
Lac Édouard
PARC PROV. DES LAURENTIDES
L. Jacques-Cartier
Clermont
Notre-Dame-du-Portage
Rivière-du-Loup
St-Antonin
Andreville
St-Alexandre
Cabano
Lejeune
Notre-Dame-du-Lac

Châteauvert
La Malbaie
Kamouraska
Pelletier Sta.
St-Eusèbe
Dégelis
Green

La Tuque
Batiscan
St-Hilarion
Pointe-au-Pic
Les Eboulements
Baie-St-Paul
Mont-Carmel
St-Éleuthère
St-Joseph-de-la-Rivière-Bleue
St-Jacques
Edmundston
St-Basile
Rivière-Verte

Kempt Lake
Mondonac
Vermilion
Wayagamac
Linton
L. Batiscan
La Pocatière
St-Roch
Rivière-Ouelle
St-Pacôme
Estcourt
Les Etroits
Clair
Madawaska
Frenchville
Ste-Anne-de-Madawaska
St-Léonard
Van Buren

L. Devenyns
Mékinac
Rivière-aux-Rats
PARC PROV. DE PORTNEUF
Rivière-à-Pierre
St-Jean-Port-Joli
St-Aubert
Lefebvre
St-Omer
St-Pamphile
St-Francis
St John
Dickey
Allagash
Eagle Lake
Winterville
Caribou

Matawin
Ste-Thècle
Lac-aux-Sables
Stoneham
Ste-Anne-de-Beaupré
Ste-Famille
St-Joachim
Cap-St-Ignace
St-Cyrille-de-L'Islet
St-Adalbert
Portage Lake
Washburn
Mapleton

Réservoir Matawin
St-Raymond
St-Léonard-de-Portneuf
Charlesbourg
Giffard
Beauport
St-François
ÎLE D'ORLEANS
Montmagny
St-Raphaël
Ste-Apolline
St-Paul-de-Montminy
Clayton Lake
Ashland
Presque Isle

PARC NAT. DE LA MAURICIE
Pont-Rouge
Loretteville
QUÉBEC
Lauzon
St-Pierre
St-Philémon
Masardis
Westfield

Grandes-Piles
St-Basile-Sud
Ste-Foy
Lévis
St-Romuald
St-Henri
St-Anselme
Ste-Claire
St-Maglöire
St-Sabine
St-Justine
Lac-Etchemin

Grand-Mère
St-Tite
St-Casimir
Portneuf
Donnacona
Charny
St-Agapitville
Scott-Jonction
Eagle L.
M A I N E

Shawinigan
Shawinigan-Sud
Deschambault
Ste-Croix
St-Isidore
Laurier-Station
Dosquet
Ste-Agathe
Ste-Marie
Vallée-Jonction
St-Joseph-de-Beauce
Allagash
Chamberlain L.

Cap-de-la-Madeleine
Batiscan
Val-Alain
Lyster
Manseau
Caucomgomoc L.
BAXTER STATE PARK

PARC PROV. DE JOLIETTE
St-Alexis-des-Monts
St-Paulin
Charette
Trois-Rivières
St-Donat-de-Montcalm
St-Gabriel
Louiseville
Lemieux
Laurierville
Tring-Jonction
East Broughton Station
Beauceville
Seboomook L.
Mt. Katahdin 1605
Smyrna Mills
Oakfield
Island Falls
Patten

St-Côme
St-Barthélemy
Maskinongé
Nicolet
Plessisville
Princeville
Robertsonville
St-Georges Ouest
St-George
Linière
Chesuncook L.
Sherman

Carré
St-Félix-de-Valois
Berthierville
Baieville
St-François-du-Lac
Bernierville
Black Lake
Thetford Mines
St-Ephrem-de-Tring
Seboomook
Mt. Katahdin
Stacyville

Ste-Agathe-des-Monts
Rawdon
St-Joseph-de-Sorel
Sorel
Pierreville
Victoriaville
La Guadeloupe
St-Gédéon-de-Beauce
Brassua L.
Rockwood
Millinocket
East Millinocket
Kingman

Joliette
Lanoraie
Tracy
Yamaska
Notre-Dame-du-Bon-Conseil
Disraëli
Lambton
Kokad-jo
White Cap Mt. 1130
Medway

St-Jacques
Lavaltrie
St-Ours
Massueville
St-Cyrille
Beaulac
St-Gérard
St-Ludger
Jackman
Pemadumcook L.
Millinocket

L'Epiphanie
L'Assomption
Contrecœur
St-Guillaume
St-Germain-de-Grantham
Kingsey Falls
Drummondville
Asbestos
St-Sébastien
Moosehead L.
Greenville
Brownville Junction
Brownville
Winn
Carroll

Mascouche
Terrebonne
Verchères
St-Jude
St-Nazaire
Wickham
Wottonville
Weedon-Centre
Lac-Mégantic
Shirley Mills
Milo
Lincoln

Repentigny
Rosemère
Pointe-aux-Trembles
Upton
Acton Vale
Richmond
Marbleton
Bishopton
Mégantic
Scotstown
Tumbledown Mt. 1080
Coburn Mt. 1133
Monson
Dover-Foxcroft
Howland
Enfield

Blainville
Laval
Beloeil
St-Hyacinthe
Roxton Falls
Windsor
E. Angus
Bury
Mégantic
Mt. 1105
Snow Mt. 1203
Abbot Village
Guilford
Sangerville
Springfield

MONTREAL
Longueuil
Ste-Prudentienne
Valcourt
Bromptonville
Cookshire
La Patrie
Notre-Dame-des-Bois
Rump Mt. 1112
Flagstaff L.
Stratton
Bingham
Dexter
Corinna
Bradford
Old Town
Orono

Pointe-Claire
Chambly
Marieville
St-Césaire
Granby
Sherbrooke
Lennoxville
Eastman
Waterville
North Hatley
Compton
Sawyerville
NEW HAMP.
Kennebago Lake
Sugarloaf Mt. 1291
Bangor
Brewer

Dorion
Salaberry-de-Valleyfield
St-Jean
St-Luc
Iberville
Farnham
Foster
Knowlton
Magog
Coaticook
Mt. Hereford 841
Rangeley L.
Harmony
Hartland
Newport
Carmel
Amherst

Ormstown
Huntingdon
Hemmingford
Cowansville
Bedford
Napierville
Henryville
L. Memphremagog
Ayer's Cliff
Rock Island
Dixville
Rangeley
Newport

St-Chrysostôme
Lacolle
Rouses Point
Philipsburg
Sutton 972
Beebe Plain
Derby Line
N. Troy 1177
Jay Peak 1176
Newport

St. Lawrence (Saint-Laurent)

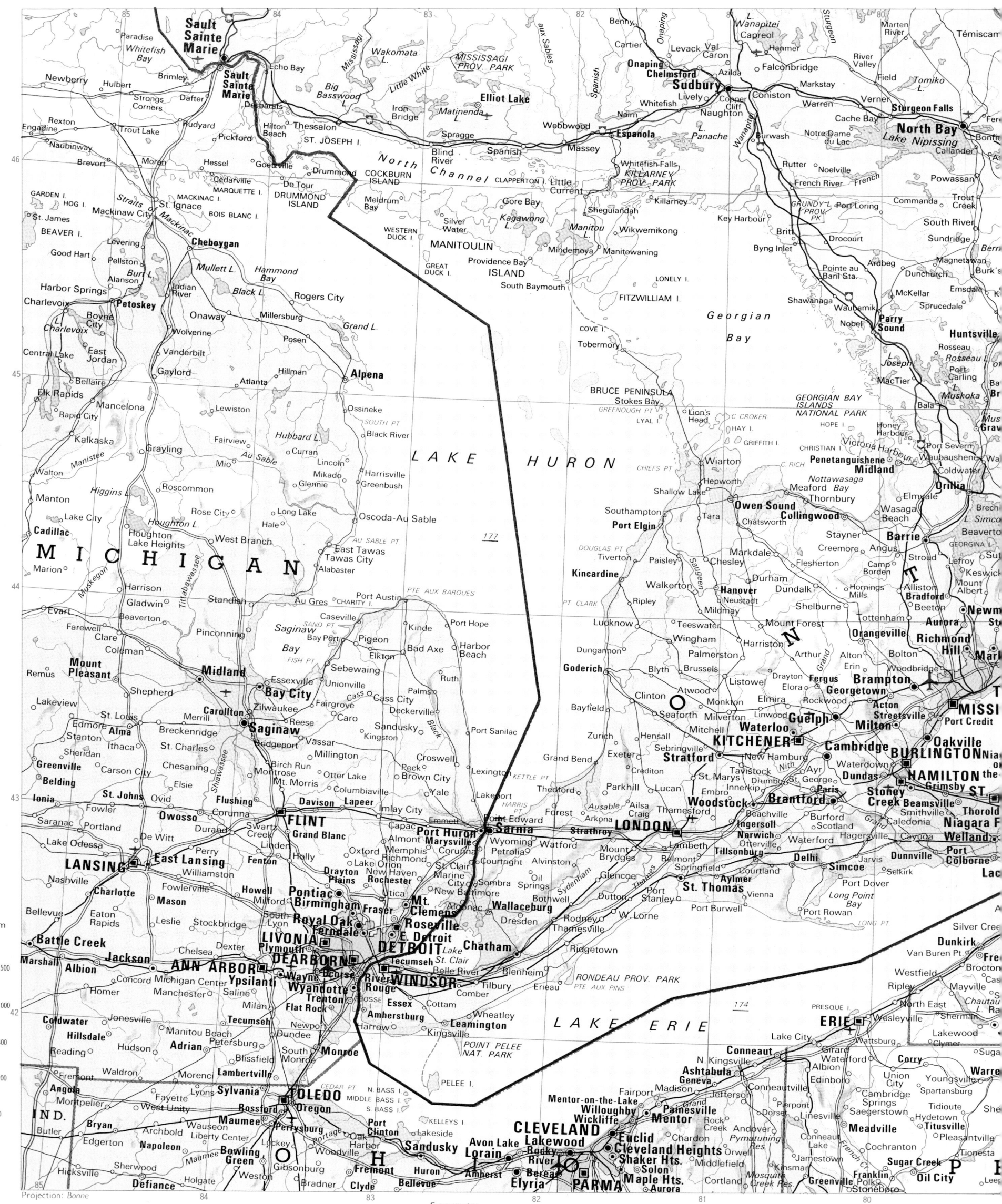

Projection: Bonne

Ferry routes

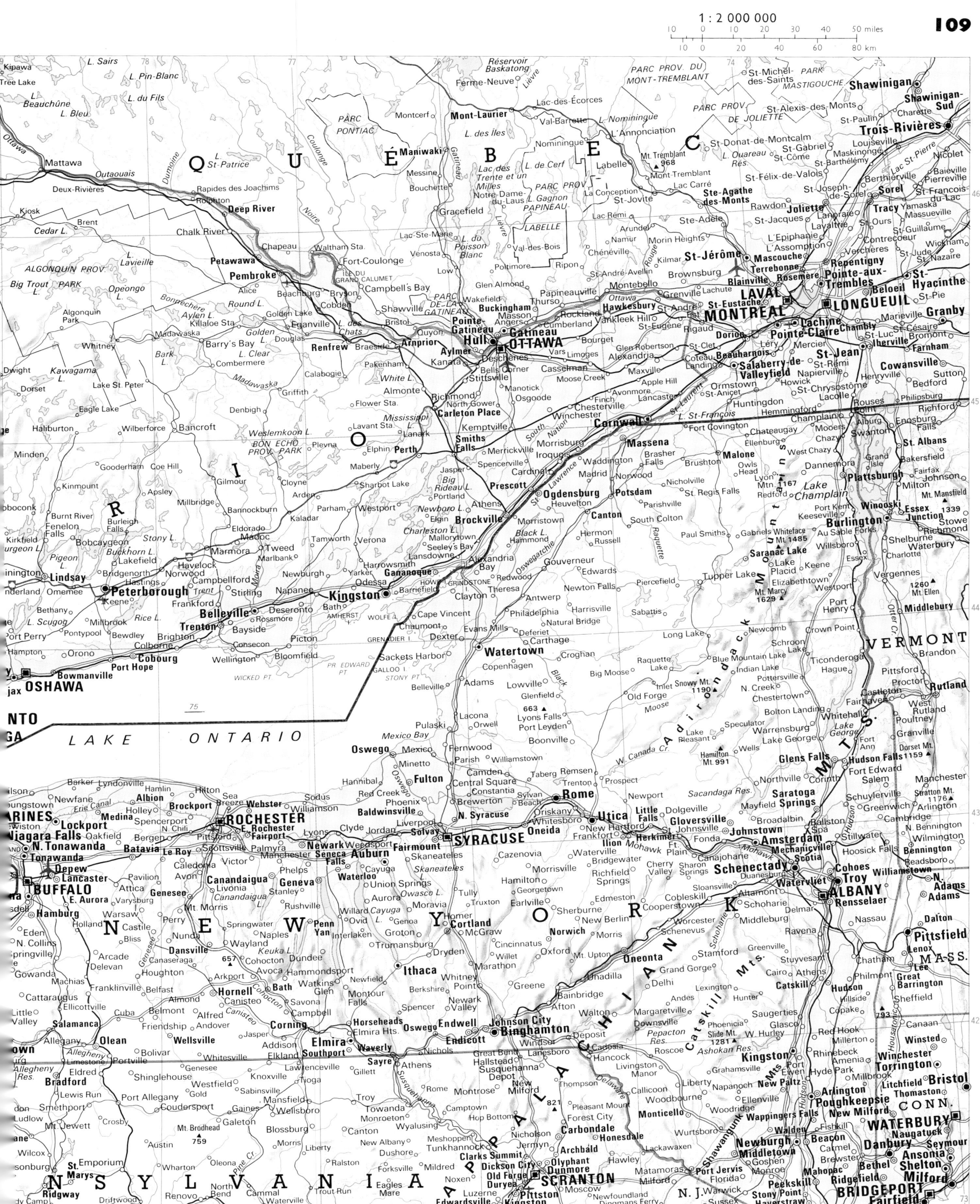
1 : 2 000 000
10 0 10 20 30 40 50 miles
10 0 20 40 60 80 km
QUÉBEC
ONTARIO
NEW YORK
VERMONT
MASS.
CONN.
N. J.
NSYLVANIA
LAKE ONTARIO
APPALACHIAN MTS.
Adirondack Mountains
Catskill Mts.
Lake Champlain
PARC PROV. DU MONT-TREMBLANT
PARC PROV. DE JOLIETTE
PARC PONTIAC
PARC PROV. PAPINEAU-LABELLE
ALGONQUIN PROV. PARK
BON ECHO PROV. PARK
Réservoir Baskatong
Ottawa
Outaouais
St. Lawrence
Mattawa
Deep River
Pembroke
Petawawa
Renfrew
Arnprior
Hull
Gatineau
OTTAWA
Smiths Falls
Perth
Carleton Place
Brockville
Prescott
Kingston
Belleville
Trenton
Peterborough
Lindsay
Cobourg
Port Hope
OSHAWA
Cornwall
MONTRÉAL
LAVAL
LONGUEUIL
Trois-Rivières
Shawinigan
Sorel
St-Jérôme
St-Jean
Granby
Mont-Laurier
Maniwaki
Plattsburgh
Burlington
Middlebury
Rutland
Bennington
Pittsfield
Massena
Ogdensburg
Potsdam
Watertown
Oswego
Rome
Utica
ROCHESTER
SYRACUSE
BUFFALO
Niagara Falls
Lockport
Auburn
Geneva
Ithaca
Cortland
Elmira
Corning
Binghamton
Oneonta
Schenectady
Albany
Troy
Amsterdam
Glens Falls
Saratoga Springs
Kingston
Poughkeepsie
Newburgh
SCRANTON
WATERBURY
Danbury
BRIDGEPORT
Bristol
Torrington
West from Greenwich
78
77
76
75
74
73
46
45
44
43
42
COPYRIGHT, GEORGE PHILIP & SON, LTD.

YUKON TERRITORY
NORTHWEST TERRITORIES
FORT SMITH
FORT MACKENZIE
BRITISH COLUMBIA
ALBERTA
ALASKA
WASHINGTON
IDAHO
PACIFIC OCEAN
ROCKY MOUNTAINS
Coast Mountains
Skeena Mountains
Cariboo Mountains
Selkirk Mountains
Cassiar Mountains
Caribou Mts.
Birch Mountains
Buffalo Head Hills
QUEEN CHARLOTTE ISLANDS
VANCOUVER ISLAND
Whitehorse
Yellowknife
Prince Rupert
Prince George
Dawson Creek
Kamloops
VANCOUVER
Victoria
EDMONTON
Calgary
Lethbridge
Red Deer
SEATTLE
GREAT SLAVE LAKE
Projection: Lambert's Equivalent Azimuthal
West from Greenwich
ft
m
12 000
9000
6000
4500
3000
1200
600
0
200
2000
4000
3000
2000
1500
1000
400
200
0
600
6000
m
ft

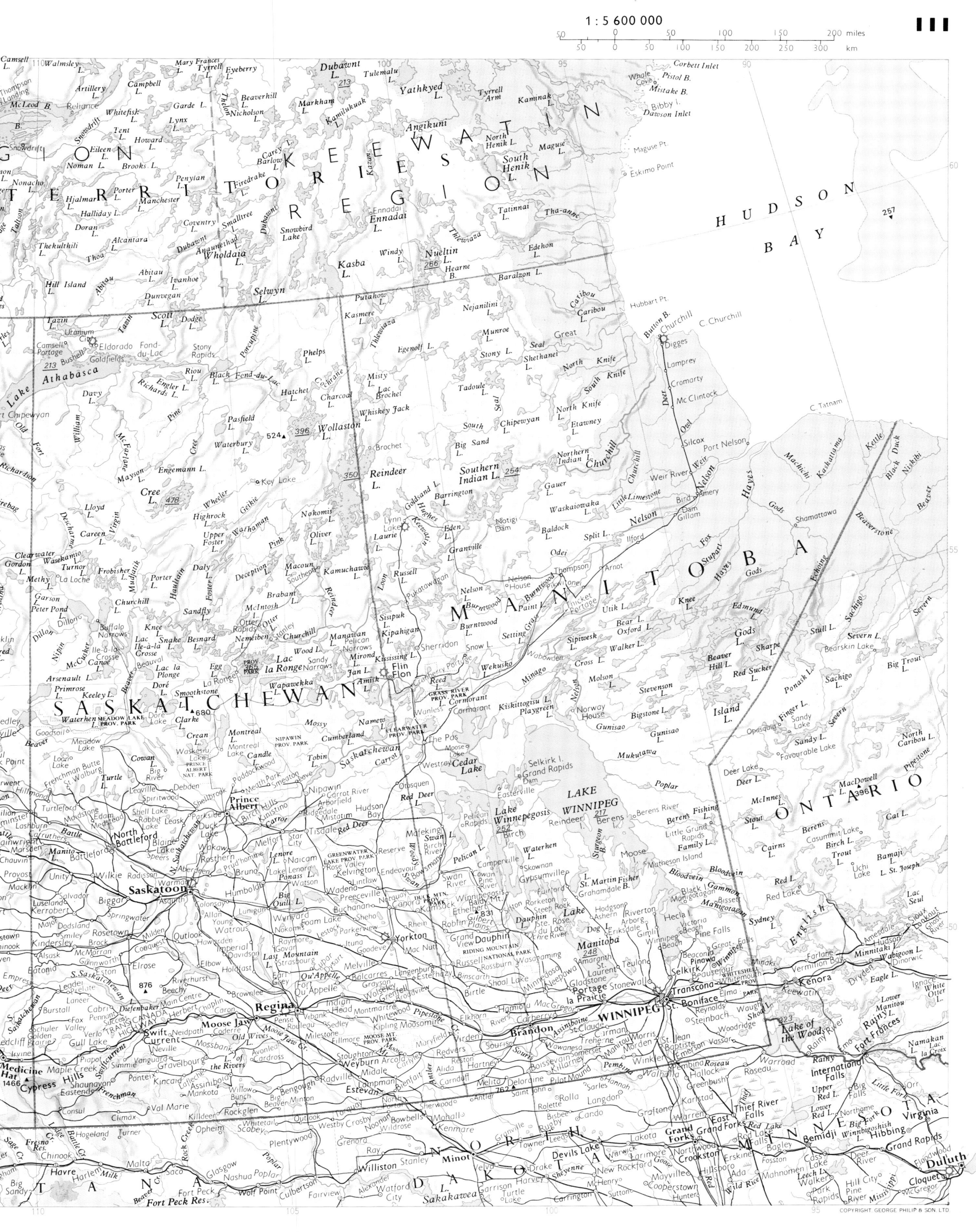

1:5 600 000

50   100   150   200 miles
50   0   50   100   150   200   250   300 km

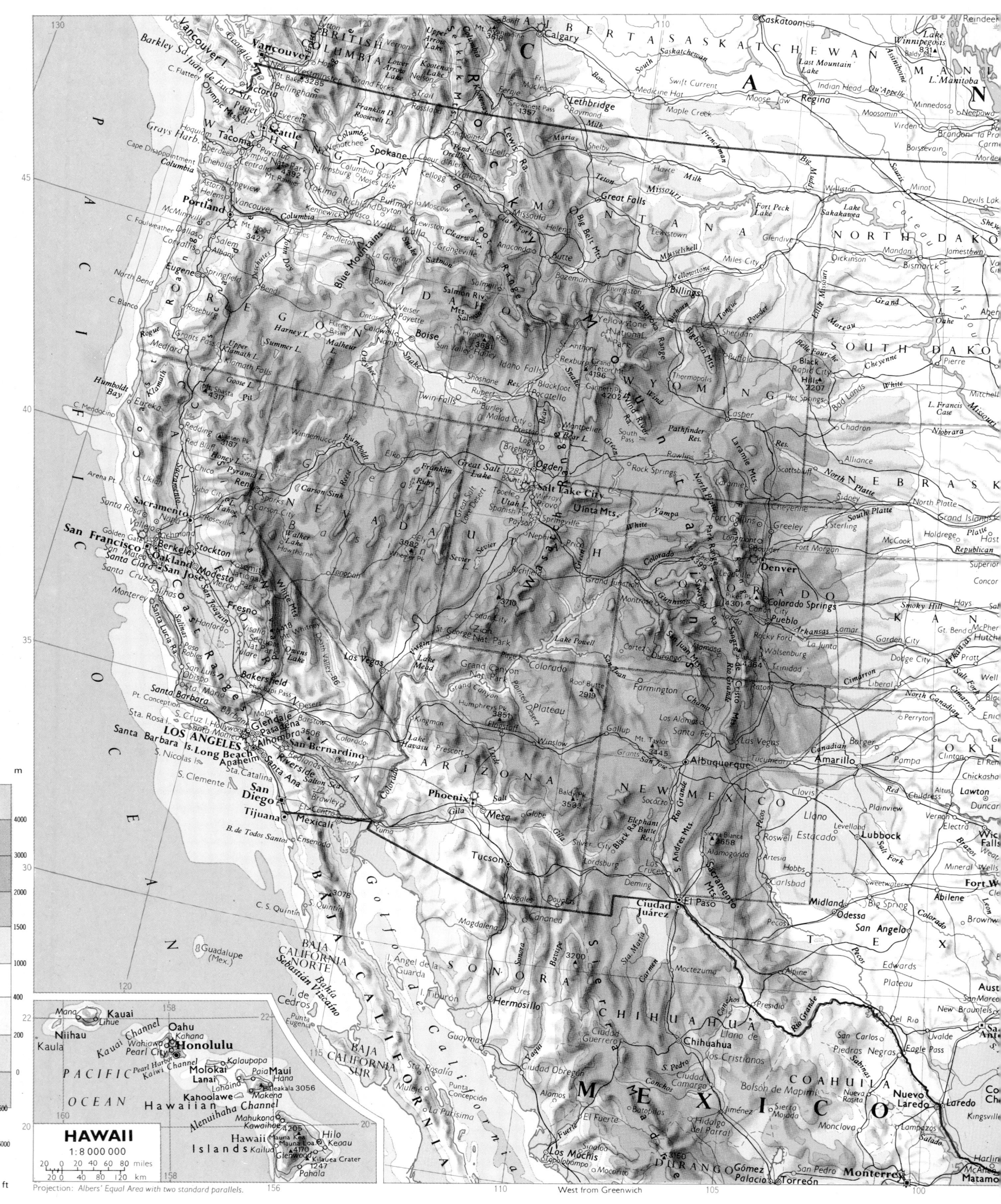

HAWAII
1:8 000 000
Projection: Albers' Equal Area with two standard parallels.

West from Greenwich

1 : 9 600 000

ONTARIO
QUEBEC
NEW YORK
PENNSYLVANIA
OHIO
INDIANA
MICHIGAN
WISCONSIN
ILLINOIS
KENTUCKY
WEST VIRGINIA
VIRGINIA
MARYLAND
NEW JERSEY
DELAWARE
VERMONT
NEW HAMPSHIRE
MASS.
LAKE SUPERIOR
LAKE HURON
LAKE ERIE
LAKE ONTARIO
Georgian Bay
Chesapeake Bay

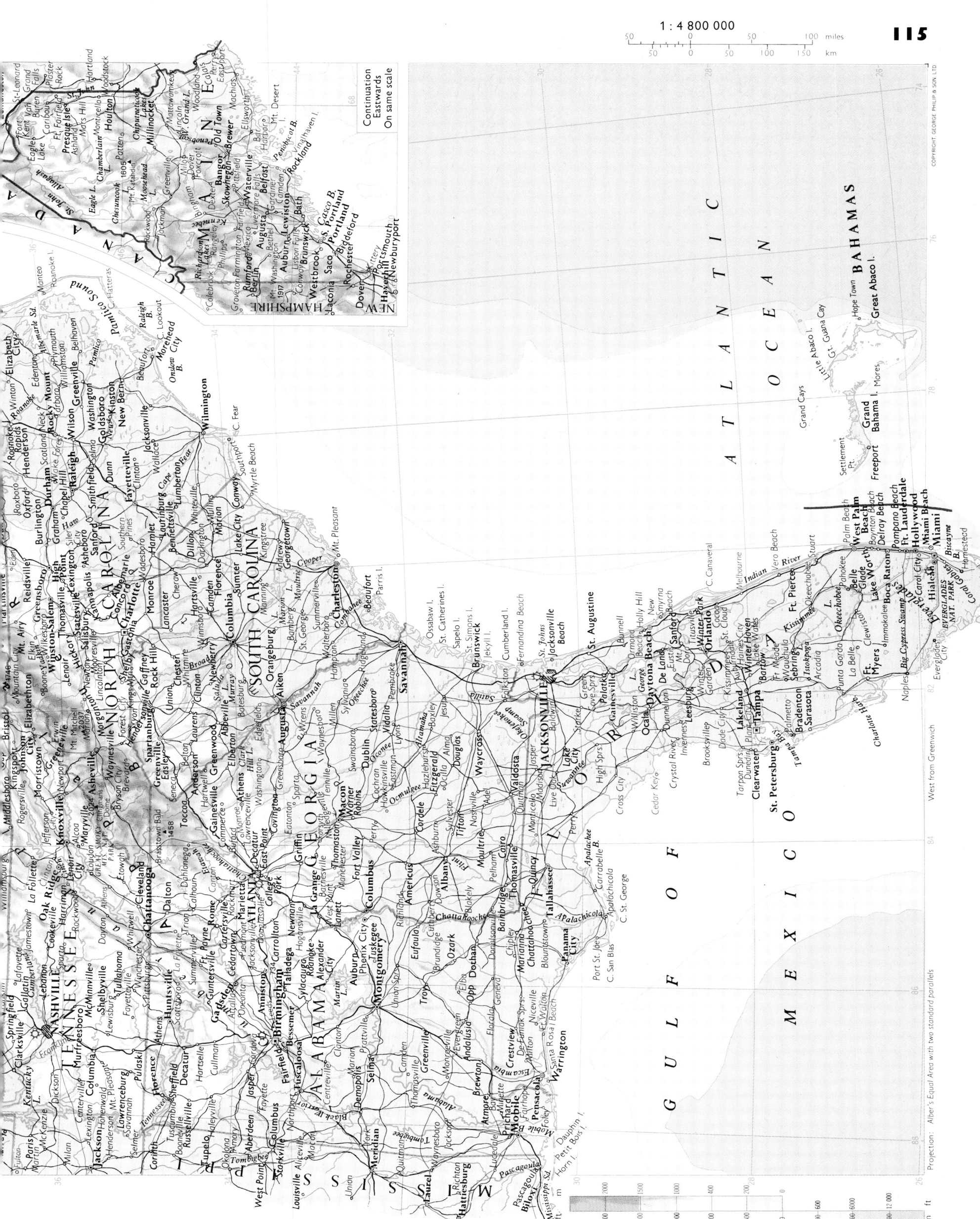

1 : 4 800 000

50   0   50   100 miles

50   0   50   100   150 km

COPYRIGHT GEORGE PHILIP & SON LTD.

Continuation
Eastwards
On same scale

MAINE

NEW HAMPSHIRE

CANADA

Bangor
Old Town
Brewer
Waterville
Augusta
Lewiston
Auburn
Brunswick
S. Casco B.
Portland
Biddeford

Portsmouth
Newburyport

BAHAMAS

Hope Town
Great Abaco I.

Gt. Guana Cay
Little Abaco I.

Grand Cays

Grand
Bahama I.
Freeport

Settlement
Pt.

A T L A N T I C   O C E A N

NORTH CAROLINA

Raleigh
Durham
Greensboro
Wilmington
C. Fear
C. Lookout
C. Hatteras

SOUTH CAROLINA

Columbia
Charleston
Myrtle Beach

GEORGIA

Atlanta
Savannah
Macon
Columbus
Augusta

TENNESSEE

Nashville
Knoxville
Chattanooga

ALABAMA

Birmingham
Montgomery
Mobile

MISSISSIPPI

Meridian
Hattiesburg
Biloxi

FLORIDA

Jacksonville
St. Augustine
Daytona Beach
Orlando
Tampa
St. Petersburg
Palm Beach
West Palm Beach
Ft. Lauderdale
Hollywood
Miami
Everglades
NAT. PARK
Key West

C. Canaveral
Cape Kennedy

Okeechobee
L. Okeechobee

G U L F   O F   M E X I C O

West from Greenwich

Projection: Alber's Equal Area with two standard parallels

ft
7000
6000
4500
3000
1500
1200
600
200
0

m
2000
1500
1000
400
200
0
600
6000
12 000

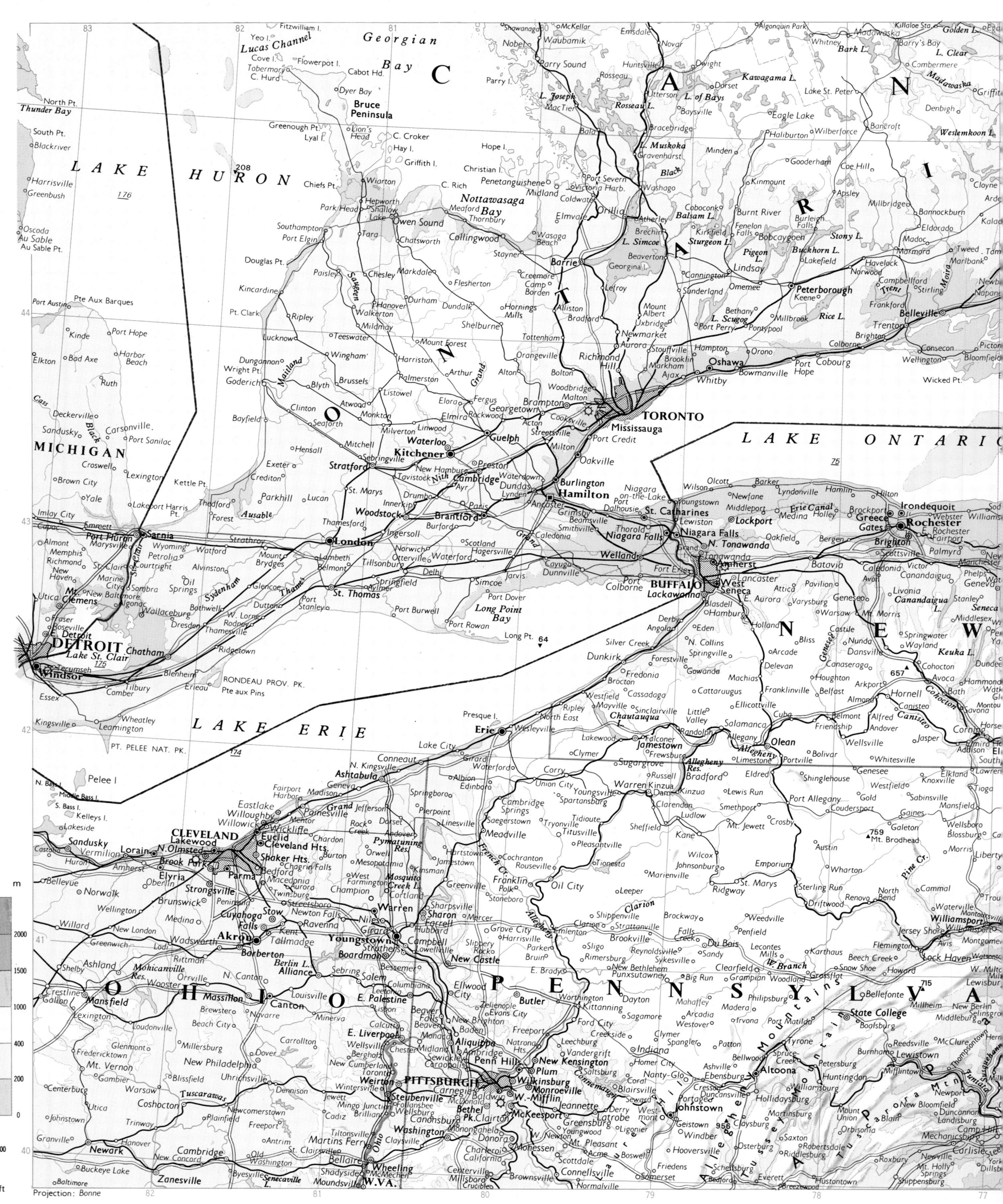
Georgian Bay
CANADA
ONTARIO
LAKE HURON
LAKE ONTARIO
LAKE ERIE
MICHIGAN
OHIO
PENNSYLVANIA
NEW YORK
Bruce Peninsula
Nottawasaga Bay
Thunder Bay
L. Simcoe
Long Point Bay
TORONTO
Mississauga
Hamilton
Kitchener
Waterloo
Guelph
London
Brantford
St. Catharines
Niagara Falls
BUFFALO
Rochester
DETROIT
Windsor
Sarnia
Port Huron
CLEVELAND
Akron
Canton
Youngstown
Erie
Jamestown
Olean
Warren
PITTSBURGH
Wheeling
W.VA.
Johnstown
Altoona
State College
Williamsport
Lock Haven
Peterborough
Oshawa
Belleville
Allegheny Mountains
Tuscarora Mtn
RONDEAU PROV. PK.
PT. PELEE NAT. PK.
Projection: Bonne
ft
m
6000
4500
3000
1200
600
0
200
2000
1500
1000
400
200
0
600

1 : 2 000 000

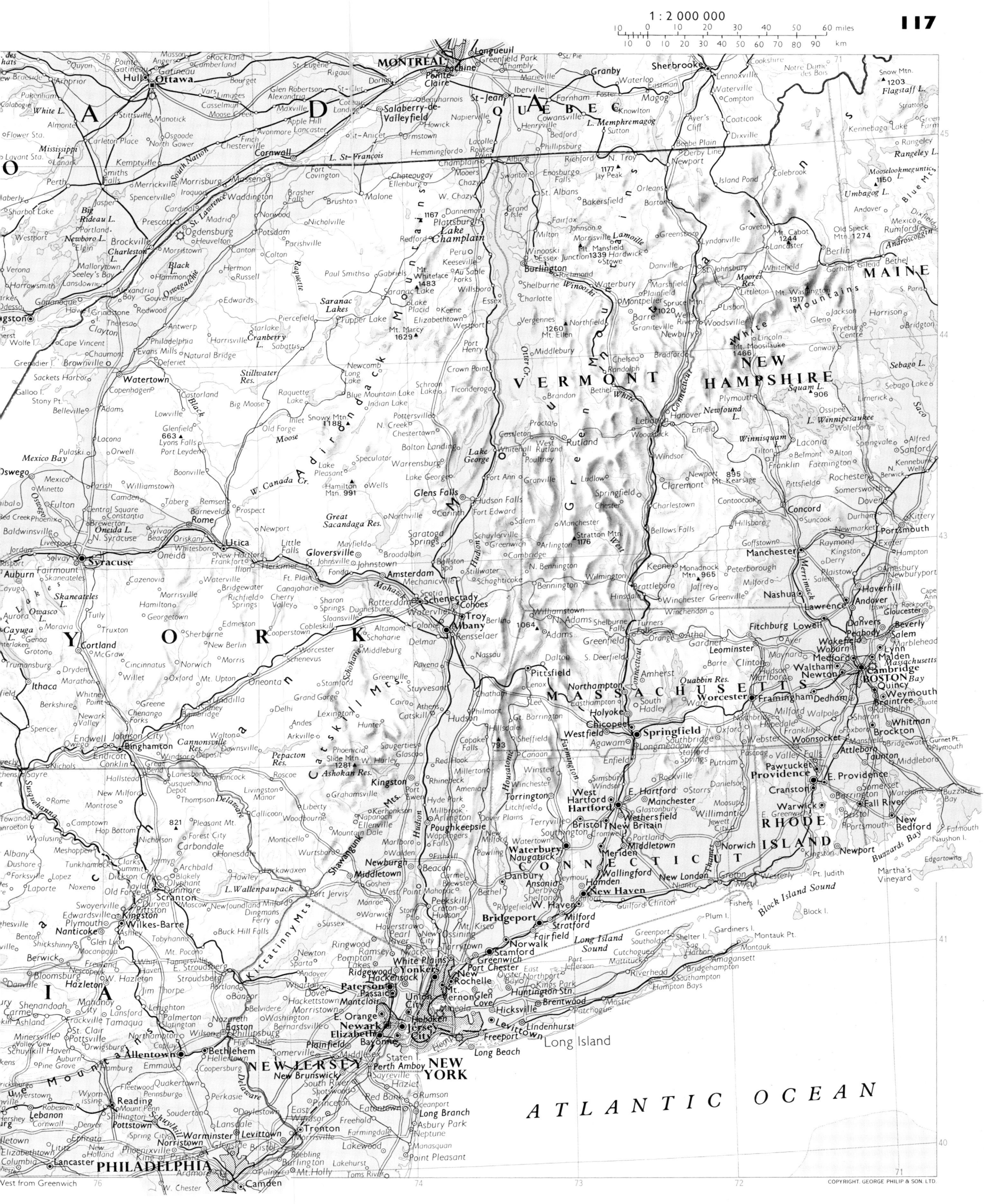

10 0 10 20 30 40 50 60 miles
10 0 10 20 30 40 50 60 70 80 90 km
C A N A D A
Q U E B E C
MONTREAL
Ottawa
Hull
Sherbrooke
Granby
St-Jean
Salaberry-de-Valleyfield
Cornwall
Kingston
Watertown
Syracuse
Utica
Rome
Oswego
Auburn
Ithaca
Cortland
Binghamton
Scranton
Wilkes-Barre
Allentown
Bethlehem
Reading
Lancaster
PHILADELPHIA
Camden
Trenton
NEW JERSEY
NEW YORK
Newark
Jersey City
Paterson
Yonkers
White Plains
Stamford
Norwalk
Bridgeport
New Haven
Hartford
Waterbury
Springfield
Worcester
Providence
BOSTON
Cambridge
Manchester
Concord
Portsmouth
Burlington
Montpelier
Rutland
Albany
Schenectady
Troy
Saratoga Springs
Glens Falls
Plattsburgh
Poughkeepsie
Newburgh
Kingston
VERMONT
NEW HAMPSHIRE
MAINE
MASSACHUSETTS
CONNECTICUT
RHODE ISLAND
Y O R K
Lake Champlain
Lake George
L. Memphremagog
L. Winnipesaukee
Adirondack Mountains
Green Mountains
White Mountains
Catskill Mts.
Long Island
Long Island Sound
Block Island Sound
Martha's Vineyard
Mt. Marcy 1629
Mt. Washington 1917
A T L A N T I C   O C E A N
West from Greenwich
76
74
73
72
71
45
44
43
41
40

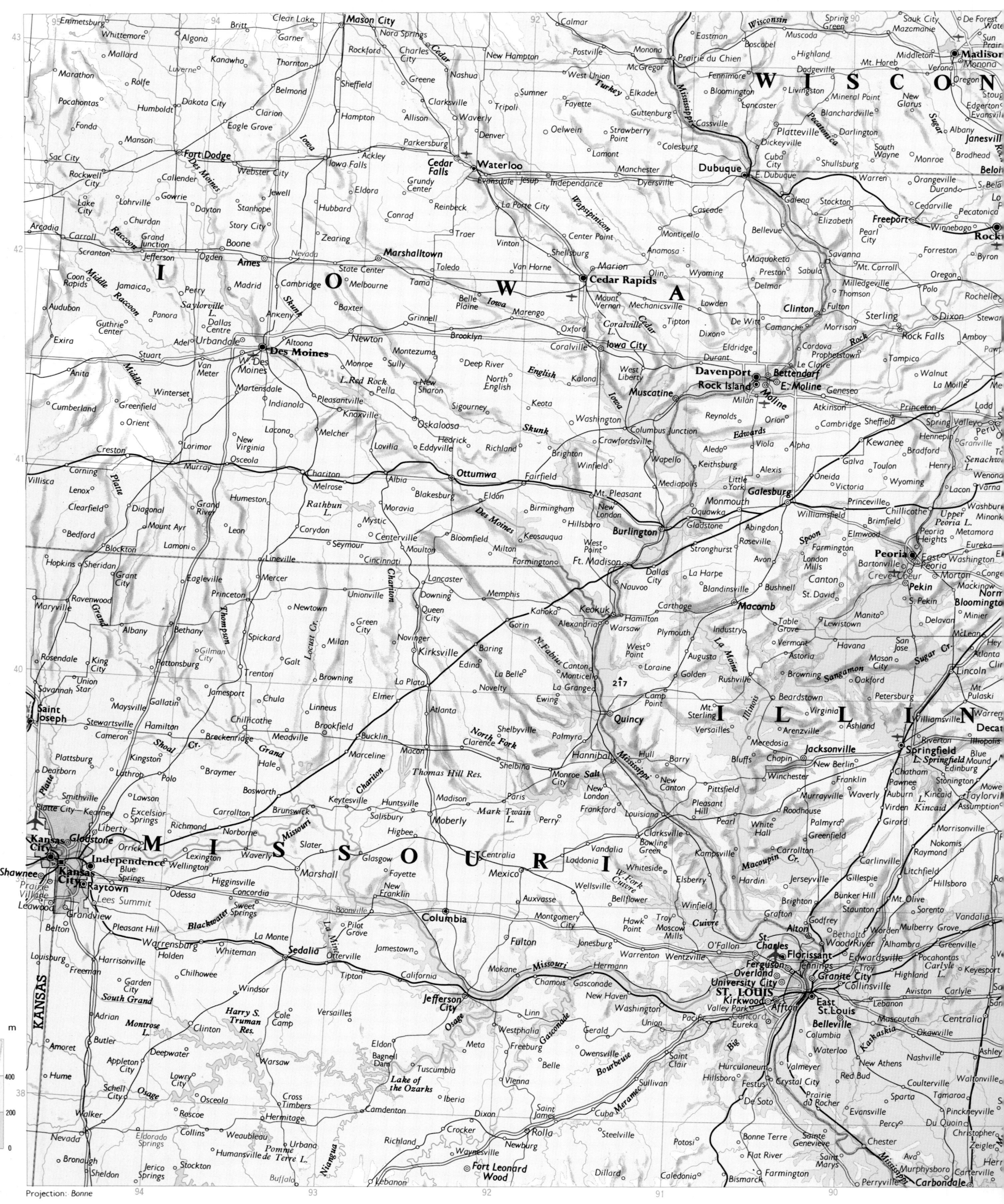
I O W A
W I S C O N
I L L I N
M I S S O U R I
KANSAS
Mason City
Waterloo
Cedar Falls
Fort Dodge
Ames
Marshalltown
Cedar Rapids
Iowa City
Des Moines
W. Des Moines
Dubuque
Davenport
Bettendorf
Rock Island
Moline
E. Moline
Muscatine
Clinton
Burlington
Keokuk
Ottumwa
Oskaloosa
Newton
Fairfield
Mt. Pleasant
Ft. Madison
Galesburg
Peoria
Pekin
Macomb
Quincy
Hannibal
Springfield
Jacksonville
Decatur
Lincoln
Bloomington
Kewanee
Freeport
Rockford
Madison
Janesville
Beloit
Saint Joseph
Kansas City
Independence
Gladstone
Liberty
Raytown
Lees Summit
Shawnee
Prairie Village
Leawood
Grandview
Belton
Columbia
Jefferson City
Sedalia
Moberly
Mexico
Kirksville
Fulton
St. Charles
Florissant
St. Louis
East St.Louis
University City
Kirkwood
Affton
Belleville
Alton
Granite City
Edwardsville
Collinsville
Fort Leonard Wood
Rolla
Carbondale
Lake of the Ozarks
Harry S. Truman Res.
Thomas Hill Res.
Mark Twain L.
Rathbun L.
Saylorville L.
Coralville L.
Red Rock L.
Mississippi
Missouri
Des Moines
Iowa
Cedar
Skunk
Wapsipinicon
Rock
Illinois
Sangamon
Osage
Gasconade
Meramec
Kaskaskia
Chariton
Grand
Platte
Spoon
Projection: Bonne
ft m
1200 400
600 200
0 0

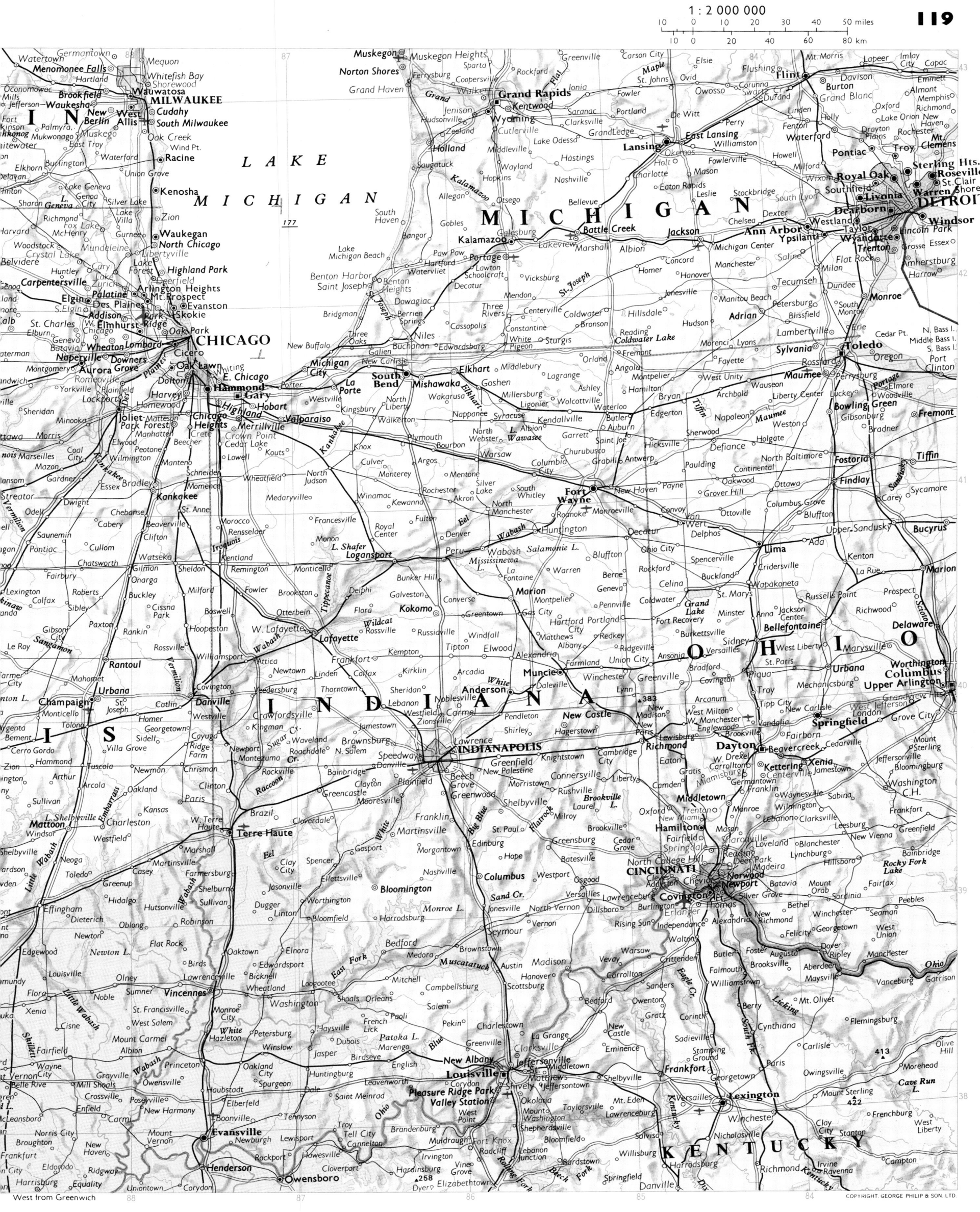

1 : 2 000 000

10 0 10 20 30 40 50 miles
10 0   20   40   60   80 km

LAKE

MICHIGAN

177

MICHIGAN

OHIO

INDIANA

KENTUCKY

West from Greenwich

COPYRIGHT GEORGE PHILIP & SON LTD

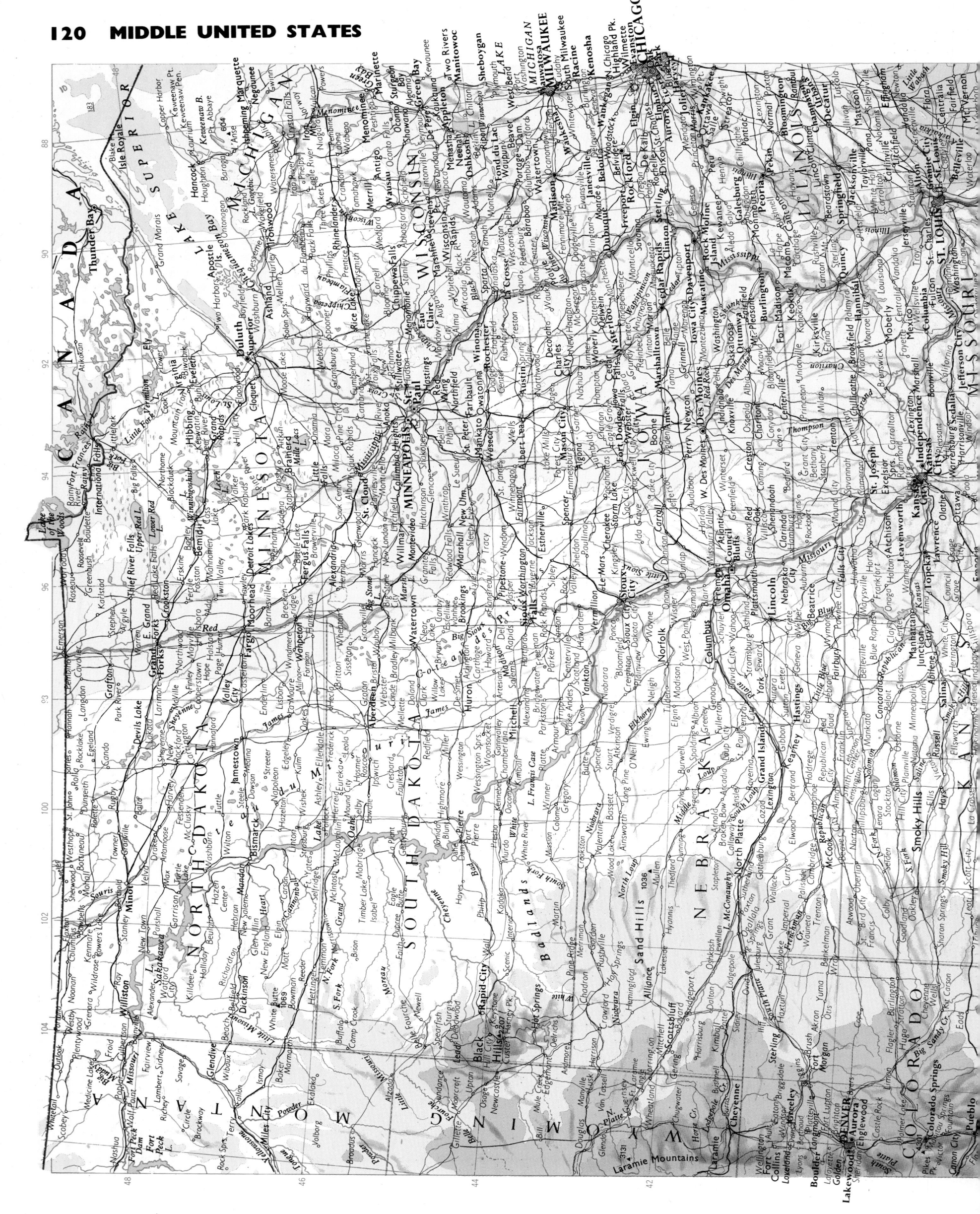
CANADA
LAKE SUPERIOR
LAKE MICHIGAN
MICHIGAN
WISCONSIN
MINNESOTA
IOWA
ILLINOIS
MISSOURI
NORTH DAKOTA
SOUTH DAKOTA
NEBRASKA
KANSAS
MONTANA
WYOMING
COLORADO
MILWAUKEE
CHICAGO
MINNEAPOLIS
St. Paul
ST. LOUIS
DENVER
Laramie Mountains
Sand Hills
Badlands
Black Hills
Lake of the Woods

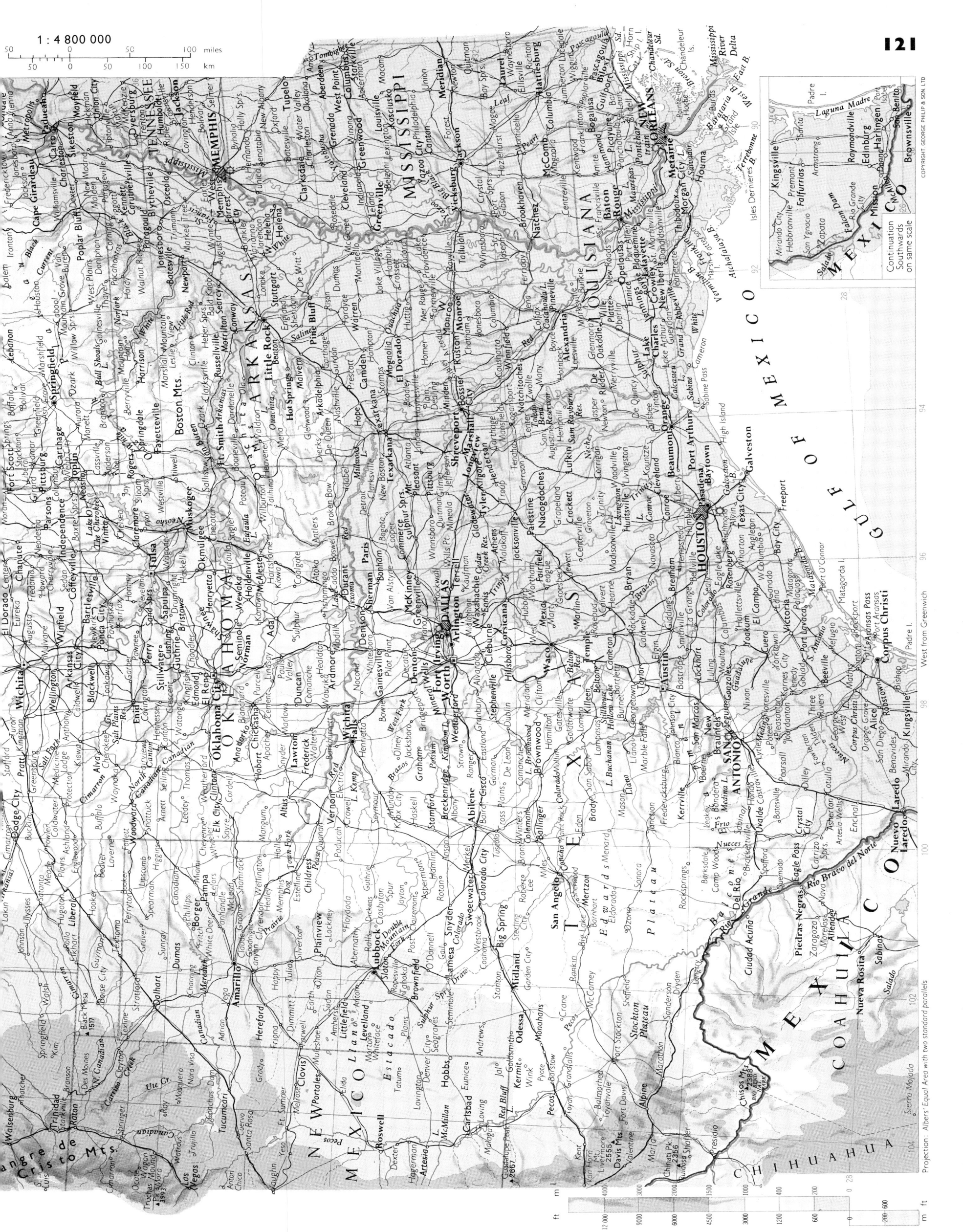
1 : 4 800 000
miles
km
OKLAHOMA
ARKANSAS
MISSISSIPPI
LOUISIANA
TENNESSEE
TEXAS
NEW MEXICO
MEXICO
COAHUILA
CHIHUAHUA
GULF OF MEXICO
DALLAS
HOUSTON
SAN ANTONIO
NEW ORLEANS
MEMPHIS
Oklahoma City
Little Rock
Shreveport
Fort Worth
Austin
Corpus Christi
Continuation Southwards on same scale
West from Greenwich
Projection: Albers' Equal Area with two standard parallels
COPYRIGHT GEORGE PHILIP & SON, LTD

1 : 4 800 000

50 · · · · 0 · · · · · 50 · · · · · · · 100 miles
50 · · · 0 · 50 · · · 100 · · · 150 km

SASKATCHEWAN

ALBERTA

BRITISH COLUMBIA

MONTANA

WASHINGTON

IDAHO

OREGON

WYOMING

NEVADA

CALIFORNIA

VANCOUVER

SEATTLE

Spokane

PORTLAND

Salem

Billings

Great Falls

Butte

Helena

Bozeman

Boise

Salt Lake City

Ogden

Reno

Sacramento

YELLOWSTONE NAT. PARK

GREAT SALT LAKE

Bighorn Mountains

Medicine Bow Mts.

Wind River Range

Salmon River Mountains

Bitterroot Range

Lewis Range

Columbia

Missouri

Snake

Olympic Mts.

Columbia Plateau

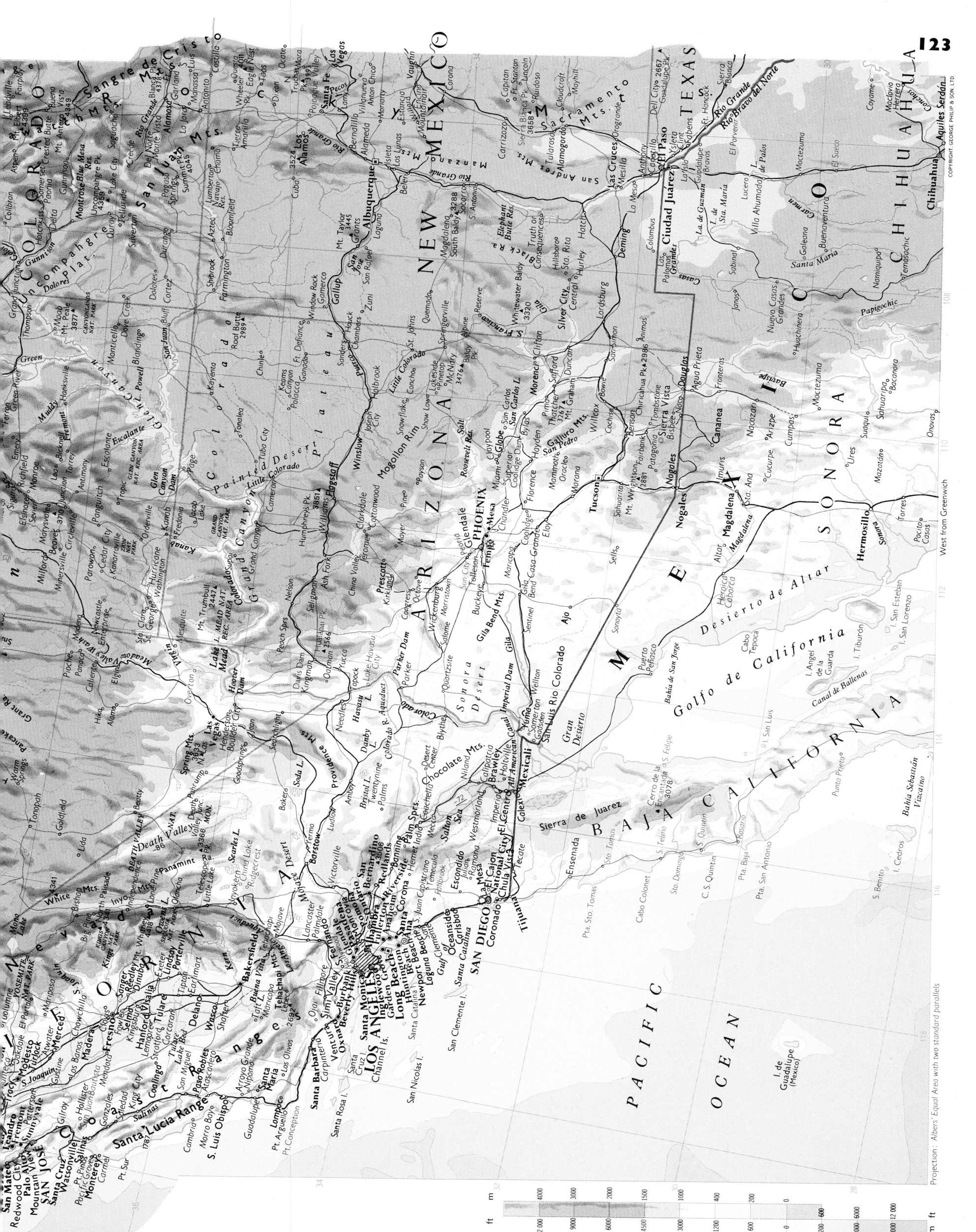

Projection: Albers' Equal Area with two standard parallels

West from Greenwich

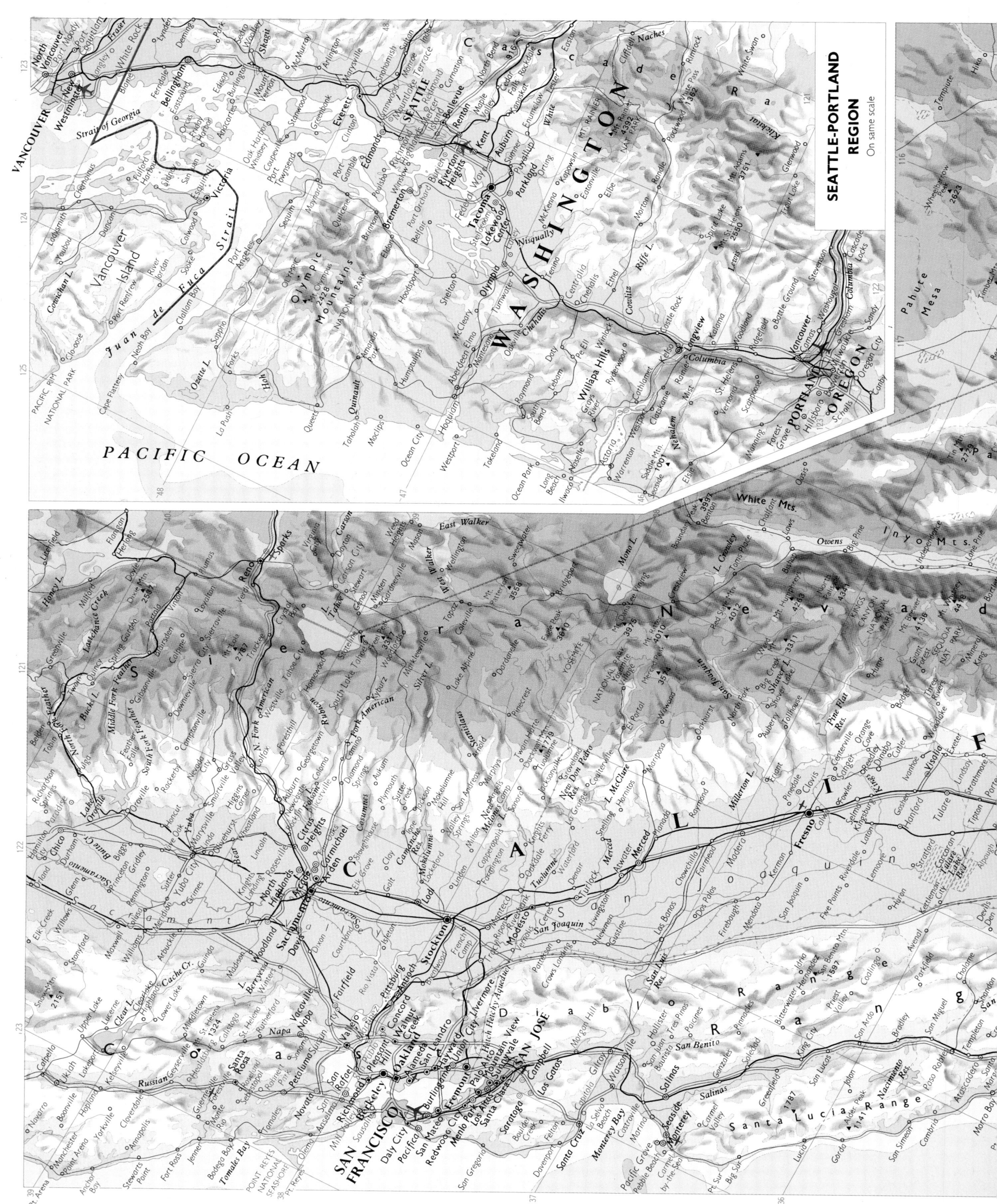
SEATTLE-PORTLAND REGION
On same scale
PACIFIC OCEAN
WASHINGTON
OREGON
VANCOUVER
SEATTLE
PORTLAND
SAN FRANCISCO
SAN JOSE
Vancouver Island
Strait of Georgia
Juan de Fuca Strait
Olympic Mountains
White Mts.
Inyo Mts.
Santa Lucia Range

1 : 2 000 000

10 0 10 20 30 40 50 miles

10 0 20 40 60 80 km

COPYRIGHT GEORGE PHILIP & SON LTD.

West from Greenwich

Projection: Bonne

N E V A D A

A R I Z O N A

M E X I C O

P A C I F I C O C E A N

Lake Mead

LAKE MEAD NATIONAL RECREATION AREA

Meadow Valley Wash

North Las Vegas
Las Vegas
Sunrise Manor
Paradise
Henderson
Hoover Dam
Boulder City

Amargosa Range

Death Valley

Amargosa

M O J A V E   D E S E R T

S O N O R A N   D E S E R T

Chocolate Mts.

Colorado R. Aqueduct

Coachella Canal

Imperial Valley

Salton Sea

JOSHUA TREE NAT. MON.

San Bernardino Mts.

SAN BERNARDINO

Riverside

LOS ANGELES

Pasadena
Glendale
Burbank
Santa Monica
Inglewood
Torrance
Long Beach
Huntington Beach
Newport Beach
Santa Ana
Anaheim
Orange
Costa Mesa

Bakersfield

Lancaster
Palmdale

San Rafael Mts.

Santa Barbara Channel

Santa Barbara

Ventura
Oxnard
Thousand Oaks
Simi Valley
Beverly Hills

Channel Islands

Santa Cruz I.
Santa Rosa I.
San Miguel I.
Santa Barbara I.
San Nicolas I.
Santa Catalina I.
San Clemente I.

San Pedro Channel

Gulf of Santa Catalina

SAN DIEGO

Oceanside
Carlsbad
Encinitas
Escondido
El Cajon
Chula Vista
National City
Coronado
Imperial Beach

Tijuana

Mexicali

El Centro

Imperial Dam

Yuma

ANZA BORREGO DESERT STATE PARK

Palm Springs

Indio
Coachella

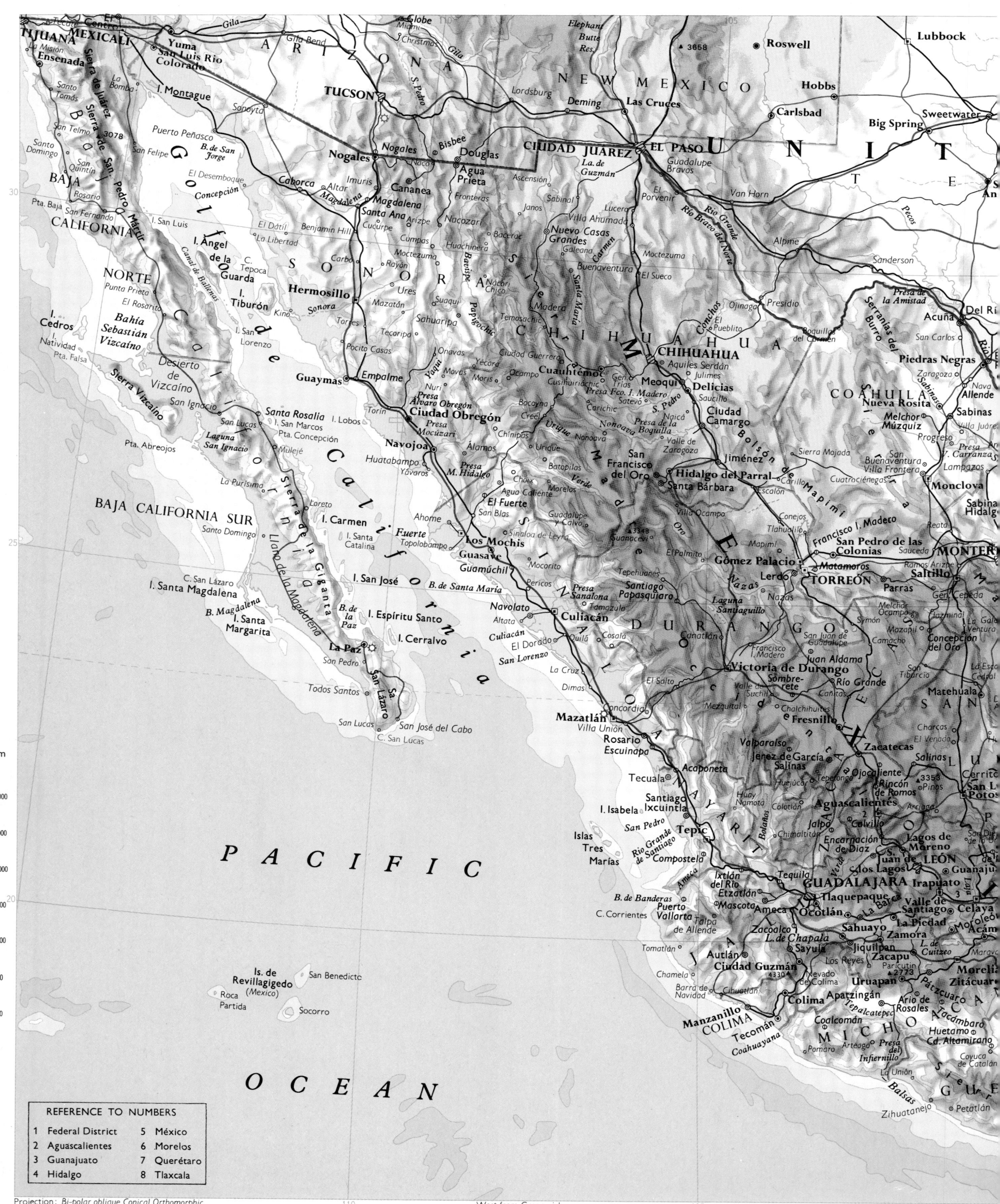

UNITED STATES

ARIZONA
NEW MEXICO
TEXAS

Tijuana
Mexicali
Ensenada
Yuma
San Luis Rio Colorado
Tucson
Lubbock
Roswell
Hobbs
Carlsbad
Big Spring
Sweetwater
Las Cruces
Deming
El Paso
Ciudad Juarez

BAJA CALIFORNIA NORTE
SONORA
CHIHUAHUA
COAHUILA

Hermosillo
Guaymas
Ciudad Obregón
Navojoa
Los Mochis
Culiacán
Chihuahua
Delicias
Hidalgo del Parral
Piedras Negras
Nueva Rosita
Sabinas
Monclova
Saltillo
Monterrey
Torreón
Gómez Palacio
Lerdo

BAJA CALIFORNIA SUR
La Paz
San José del Cabo

DURANGO
Victoria de Durango
Mazatlán
Rosario
Zacatecas
Aguascalientes
San Luis Potosí

PACIFIC

OCEAN

Is. de Revillagigedo (Mexico)
San Benedicto
Socorro
Roca Partida

Tepic
Guadalajara
León
Guanajuato
Irapuato
Celaya
Colima
Manzanillo
Uruapan
Morelia

REFERENCE TO NUMBERS
1 Federal District   5 México
2 Aguascalientes   6 Morelos
3 Guanajuato   7 Querétaro
4 Hidalgo   8 Tlaxcala

Projection: Bi-polar oblique Conical Orthomorphic   West from Greenwich

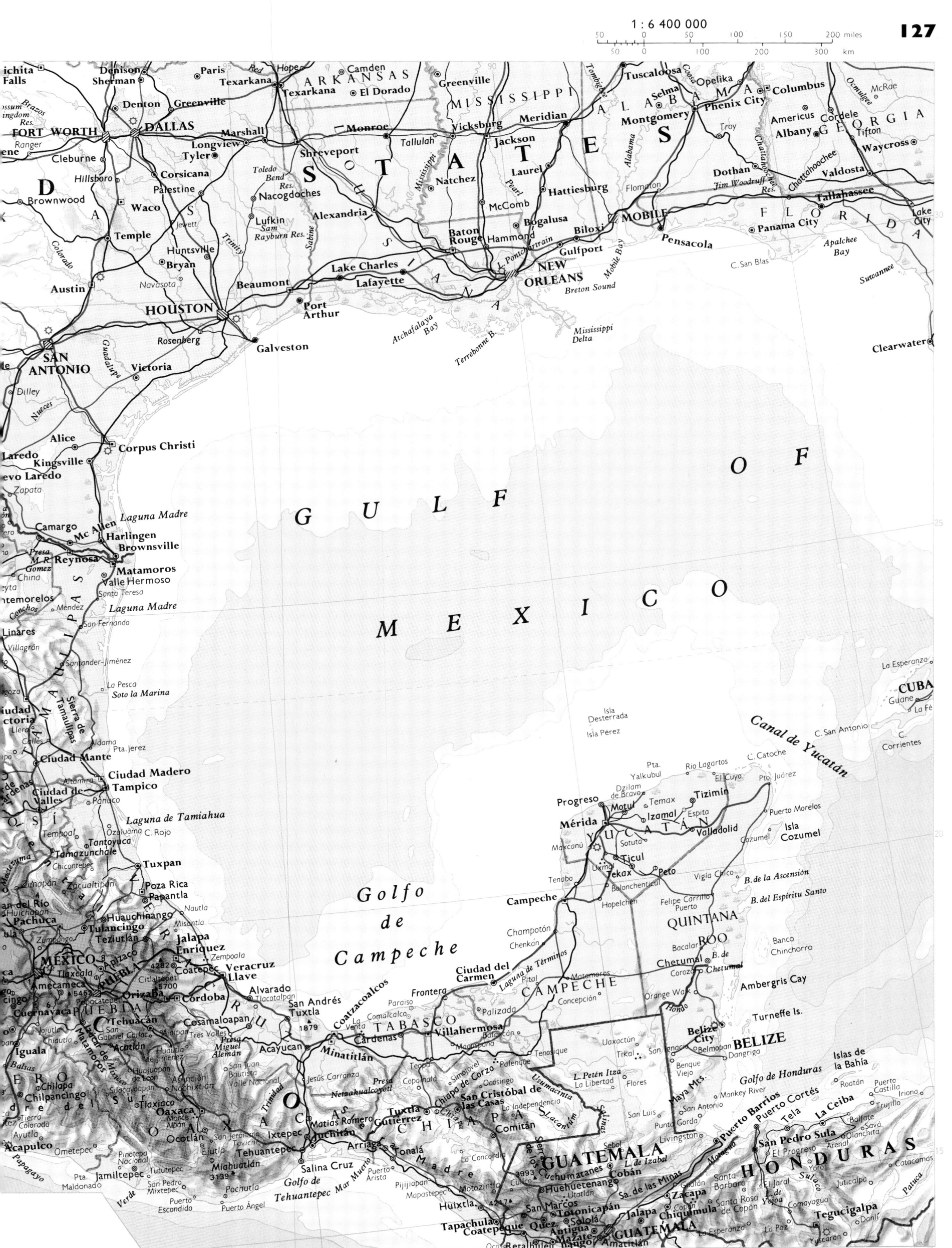

GULF OF MEXICO

Golfo de Campeche

UNITED STATES

TEXAS

ARKANSAS

MISSISSIPPI

ALABAMA

GEORGIA

FLORIDA

LOUISIANA

CUBA

YUCATÁN

QUINTANA ROO

CAMPECHE

TABASCO

CHIAPAS

GUATEMALA

HONDURAS

BELIZE

OAXACA

MÉXICO

PUEBLA

VERACRUZ

TAMAULIPAS

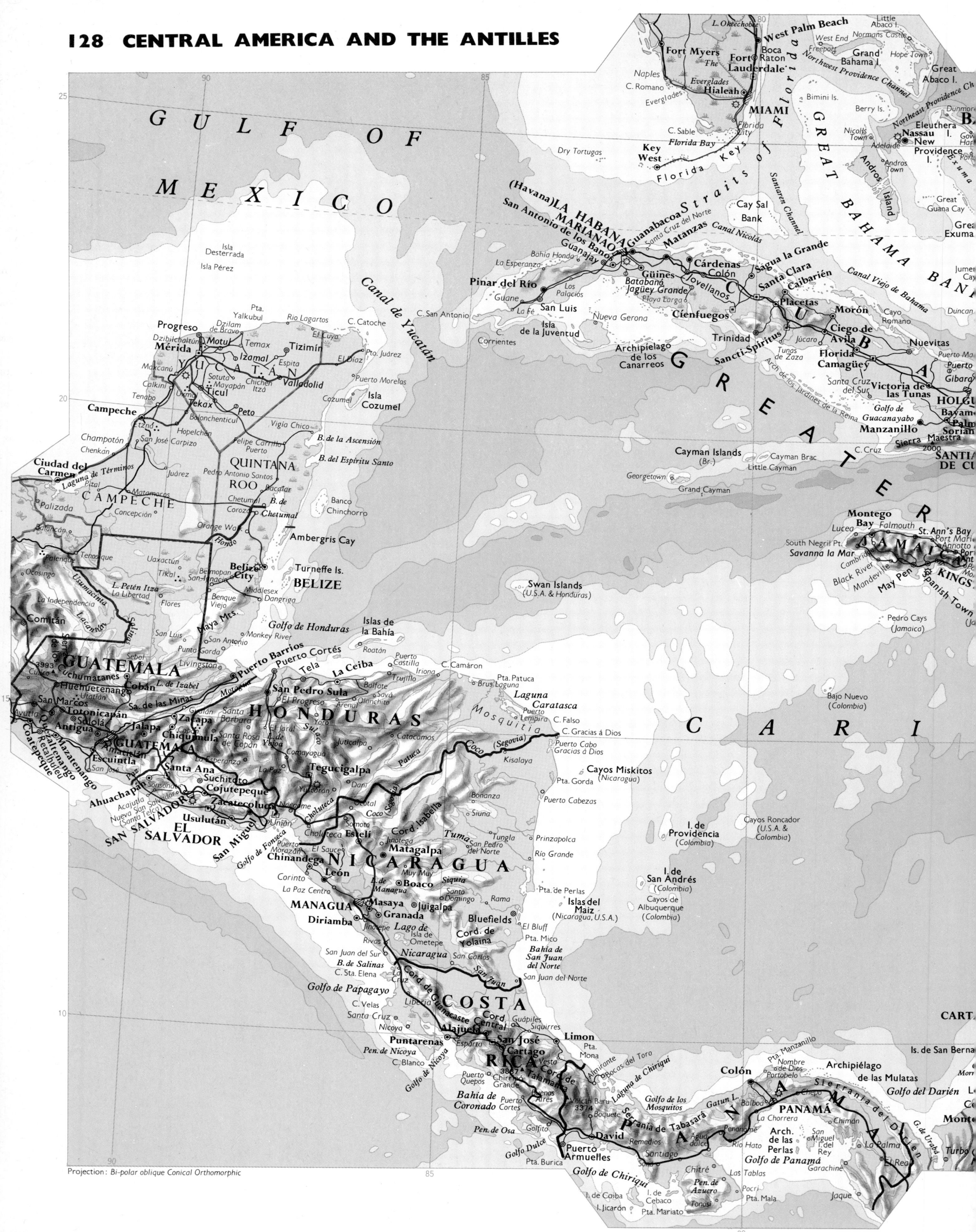

GULF OF MEXICO

GREAT BAHAMA BANK

West Palm Beach
Fort Myers
Boca Raton
Fort Lauderdale
Naples
Hialeah
MIAMI
Key West

Isla Desterrada
Isla Pérez

Progreso
Mérida
YUCATAN
Campeche
CAMPECHE
Ciudad del Carmen
QUINTANA ROO
Chetumal

BELIZE
Belize City

GUATEMALA
HONDURAS
EL SALVADOR
SAN SALVADOR

NICARAGUA
MANAGUA

COSTA RICA
San José

PANAMÁ

(Havana) LA HABANA
MARIANAO
Matanzas
Cárdenas
Santa Clara
Cienfuegos
Trinidad
Sancti Spíritus
Ciego de Avila
Camagüey
CUBA

Cayman Islands (Br.)
Grand Cayman

Montego Bay
JAMAICA
KINGSTON

CARIBBEAN

Golfo de Panamá

1 : 6 400 000

50   100   150   200 miles
50   0   50   100   150   200   250   300 km

A T L A N T I C

O C E A N

Tropic of Cancer

ft   m

12 000   4000

9000   3000

6000   2000

4500   1500

3000   1000

1200   400

600   200

0   0

200   600

2000   6000

4000   12 000

6000   18 000

8000   24 000

m   ft

MAS

's Town

he Bight
Cat I.
San Salvador
(Watling I., Guanahani)
Conception I.
Rum Cay

Long I.
Clarence
Town
Atwood or
Samana Cay
Crooked I. Passage
Richmond
Albert
Town
Snug
Corner
Plana Cays
Crooked I.
Mayaguana I.
Verde
Acklins I.
Mira por vos Cay
Santa
go

Hogsty Reef
Caicos Passage
Little Inagua I.
Caicos
Islands
(Br.)
Turks Islands
(Br.)
Lake Rose
Great
Inagua I.
Matthew
Town
Moa
Baracoa
Pta. de
Maisí
Î. de la
Tortue
Cap-Haïtien
Monte Cristi
Fort-Liberté
La Isabela
Puerto Plata
C. Frances Viejo
Port-de-Paix
Santiago de
los Caballeros
San Francisco de Macorís
Nagua
Vega
tánamo
Paso de los Vientos
(Windward Passage)
Jean-Rabel
Cap-à-Foux
Golfe de la
Gonâve
St.-Marc
Gonaïves
Hinche
Cordi
Central
3175
Sánchez
Sabana de La Mar
HAITI
DOMINICAN
REP.
Hato Mayor
Bayamón SAN JUAN
Virgin Gorda
Virgin Is.
St. Thomas
Tortola
(Br.)
Anegada
Sombrero (Anguilla)
Jérémie
Î. de la Gonâve
PORT-
AU-PRINCE
San Juan
San Pedro
de Macorís
Higüey
C. Engano
Aguadilla
Arecibo
Road Town
Anegada Passage
Anguilla (Br.)
St.-Martin (Guad.)
St.-Barthélemy (Fr.)
Barbuda
a I.
Dame
Marie
Les Cayes
Massif de la Hotte
Aquin
2280
Jacmel
L.
Enriquillo
Azua de
Compostela
Bani
San Cristóbal
SANTO DOMINGO
B. de
Yuma
I. Saona
Canal de la Mona
Mayagüez
Ponce
Caguas
Carolina
Fajardo
Virgin Is.
(U.S.A.)
Charlotte Amalie
St. Maarten
(Neth.)
St. Eustatius
(Neth.)
Saba (Neth.)
St.
CHRISTOPHER-
NEVIS
ANTIGUA
& BARBUDA
St. Johns
Antigua
C. Carcasse
Pointe-à-Gravois
Î.-à-Vache
Pedernales
Barahona
I. Beata
C. Beata
Isla
Mona
(U.S.A.)
PUERTO
RICO
(U.S.A.)
Guayama
1338
Christiansted
Frederiksted
St. Croix
Basseterre
NEVIS
Nevis
Redonda
Montserrat
HISPANIOLA

A N T I L L E S

Guadeloupe Passage

Ste-Rose
Moule
Désirade
(Fr.) GUADELOUPE
Pointe-à-Pitre
Basse-Terre
Marie-Galante (Fr.)
Grand-Bourg
I. des Saintes
(Guad.)
Dominica Passage
Portsmouth
DOMINICA
I. de Aves (Bird I.)
(Venezuela)
Roseau
Martinique Passage
Mt. Pelée
1397
Ste-Marie
François
Rivière-Pilot
Fort-de-France
MARTINIQUE
St. Lucia Channel (Fr.)
Castries
ST. LUCIA
Soufrière
B E A N   S E A

St. Vincent Passage
Soufrière 1234 ST. VINCENT
Speightstown
Kingstown
Bridgetown
THE BARBADOS
Hillsborough
The Grenadines
GRENADINES
St. George's GRENADA

L E S S E R   A N T I L L E S

Aruba
(Neth.)
Curaçao
(Neth.)
Bonaire (Neth.)
I. Blanquilla (Ven.)
I. Los Hermanos
(Ven.)
Tobago
Scarborough
Pta. Gallinas
C. San Román
Willemstad
NETH.
ANTILLES
Is. de Aves
(Ven.)
I. Orchila
(Ven.)
Is. Los Testigos
(Ven.)
Galera
Pt.
Port of
Spain
Arima
Pen. de la
Guajira
Pta.
Espada
Pen. de
Paraguaná
Punta
Cardón
Puerto
Cumarebo
Is. Los Roques
(Ven.)
I. Margarita
La Asunción
NUEVA
ESPARTA
Porlamar
Pen. de Paria
Dragon's Mouth
Trinidad
TRINIDAD
& TOBAGO
Ríohacha
Uribia
Golfo de
Venezuela
Punto Fijo
Puerto
Cabello
Maiquetía
La Guaira
CARACAS
DISTRITO
FEDERAL
I. La Tortuga
(Ven.)
C. Codera
Higuerote
Río Chico
Carúpano
Río
Caribe
Güíria
Golfo de Paria
San Fernando
Serpent's Mouth
Río Claro
C. San Juan
de Guía
GUAJIRA
San
Rafael
Altagracia
Mene de Mauroa
FALCÓN
Coro
La Vela de Coro
Tucacas
CARAMON
Maracay
Valencia
MIRANDA
ARAGUA
Los Teques
Ocumare del Tuy
Puerto
La Cruz
Cumaná
Caripito
SUCRE
Cantaura
Maturín
MONAGAS
DELTA-
Santa
Marta
Cienaga
Sierra de
Santa Marta
5800
La
Concepción
MARACAIBO
Santa Rita
Barquaa
Baragua
San Felipe
YARACUY
Barquisimeto
El Tocuyo
LARA
Villa
de Cura
S. Juan de
los Morros
GUÁRICO
San Carlos
El Sombrero
Aragua de
Barcelona
Barcelona
Caicara
Anaco
El Tigre
ANZOÁTEGUI
Ciudad Guayana
AMACUR
Tucupita
RAN-
ILLA
Soledad
Sabanalarga
Fundación
Calamar
MAGDALENA
Plato
Zambrano
Agustín
Codazzi
Valledupar
CÉSAR
Villa del
Rosario
Machiques
Lago de
Maracaibo
La Ceiba
ZULIA
Cuidad
Ojeda
Cabimas
Mene
Grande
TRUJILLO
Trujillo
Valera
Betijoque
Acarigua
PORTUGUESA
Guanare
Portuguesa
COJEDES
El Baúl
Calabozo
Valle de la
Pascua
Santa María
de Ipire
Pariaguán
Soledad
El Pao
Ciudad
Bolívar
Sierra Imataca
Upata
Guasipati
El Callao
Tumeremo
rmen
C
Sahagún
Majagual
Corozal
Caucasia
BOLÍVAR
Ayapel
Magangué
Mompós
Banco
Ocaña
NORTE
Cúcuta
SANTANDER
Simití
Catatumbo
El
Carmen
San Carlos
del Zulia
Encontrados
TÁCHIRA
Arauca
Encon-
MÉRIDA
de Mérida
Cord.
Santa
Bárbara
BARINAS
Barinas
Libertad
Ciudad
Bolivia
Bruzual
Achaguas
Ptes. de Nutrias
San
Fernando de
Apure
Apure
Mapire
Caicara
Emb. de Guri
Caroni
Orinoco
V E N E Z U E L A

West from Greenwich

75   70   65   60

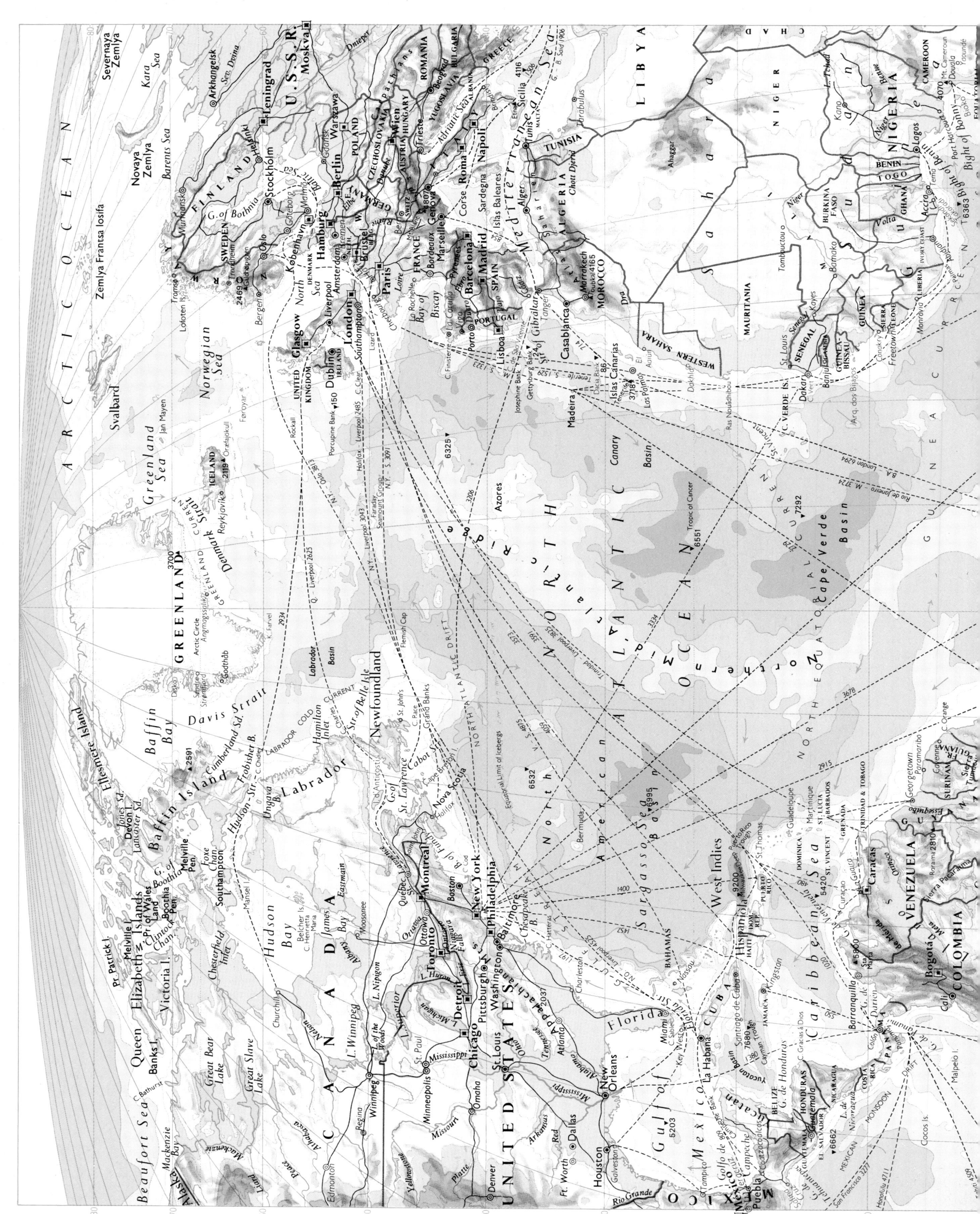
ARCTIC OCEAN
Greenland Sea
Norwegian Sea
Baffin Bay
Davis Strait
Hudson Bay
Labrador Basin
GREENLAND
ICELAND
Svalbard
Jan Mayen
Azores
Madeira
Bermuda
NORTH ATLANTIC OCEAN
Northern Mid-Atlantic Ridge
North American Basin
Sargasso Sea
Canary Basin
Cape Verde Basin
West Indies
Caribbean Sea
Gulf of Mexico
Mediterranean Sea
CANADA
UNITED STATES
MEXICO
U.S.S.R.
UNITED KINGDOM
IRELAND
FRANCE
SPAIN
PORTUGAL
MOROCCO
ALGERIA
TUNISIA
LIBYA
MAURITANIA
WESTERN SAHARA
SENEGAL
NIGERIA
VENEZUELA
COLOMBIA
CUBA
Newfoundland
Labrador
Baffin Island
London
Paris
Madrid
Lisboa
Roma
Berlin
Moskva
Leningrad
Stockholm
New York
Montreal
Toronto
Chicago
Washington
Philadelphia
New Orleans
Houston
Miami
Caracas
Bogotá
Tropic of Cancer
Arctic Circle
NORTH ATLANTIC DRIFT
LABRADOR COLD CURRENT
EAST GREENLAND CURRENT
NORTH EQUATORIAL CURRENT

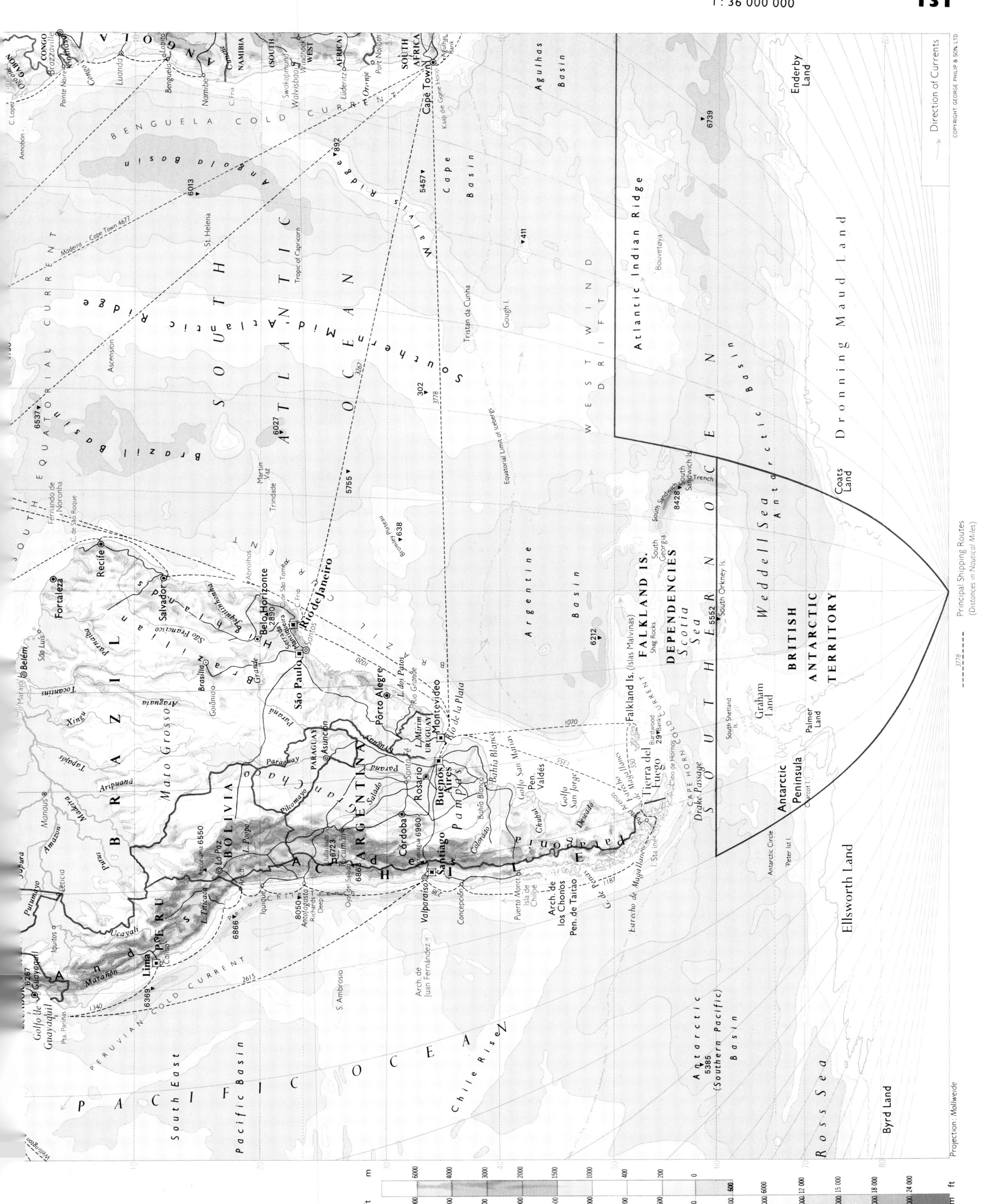
SOUTH ATLANTIC OCEAN
PACIFIC OCEAN
SOUTHERN OCEAN
BRAZIL
ARGENTINA
BOLIVIA
PERU
PARAGUAY
URUGUAY
FALKLAND IS.
DEPENDENCIES
BRITISH ANTARCTIC TERRITORY
NAMIBIA
SOUTH AFRICA
South East Pacific Basin
Brazil Basin
Angola Basin
Cape Basin
Agulhas Basin
Argentine Basin
Mid-Atlantic Ridge
Walvis Ridge
Atlantic Indian Ridge
Chile Rise
Scotia Sea
Weddell Sea
Ross Sea
Drake Passage
Antarctic (Southern Pacific) Basin
Antarctic Peninsula
Graham Land
Palmer Land
Ellsworth Land
Byrd Land
Coats Land
Dronning Maud Land
Enderby Land
Tierra del Fuego
SOUTH EQUATORIAL CURRENT
BENGUELA COLD CURRENT
PERUVIAN COLD CURRENT
BRAZIL CURRENT
WEST WIND DRIFT
CAPE HORN COLD CURRENT
Tropic of Capricorn
Antarctic Circle
Equatorial Limit of Icebergs
Rio de Janeiro
São Paulo
Buenos Aires
Montevideo
Santiago
Lima
Salvador
Recife
Fortaleza
Belém
Belo Horizonte
Brasília
Pôrto Alegre
Asunción
Córdoba
Rosario
Valparaíso
La Paz
Cape Town
Tristan da Cunha
Gough I.
St. Helena
Ascension
Trindade
Falkland Is. (Islas Malvinas)
South Georgia
South Sandwich Is.
South Orkney Is.
South Shetland Is.
Bouvetøya
Principal Shipping Routes
(Distances in Nautical Miles)
Direction of Currents
Projection: Mollweide
COPYRIGHT GEORGE PHILIP & SON LTD.
ft m
18 000 6000
12 000 4000
9000 3000
6000 2000
4500 1500
3000 1000
1200 400
600 200
0 0
200 600
2000 6000
4000 12 000
5000 15 000
6000 18 000
8000 24 000
m ft

1 : 24 000 000

100   0   100   200   300   400   500 miles
100   0   200   400   600   800 km

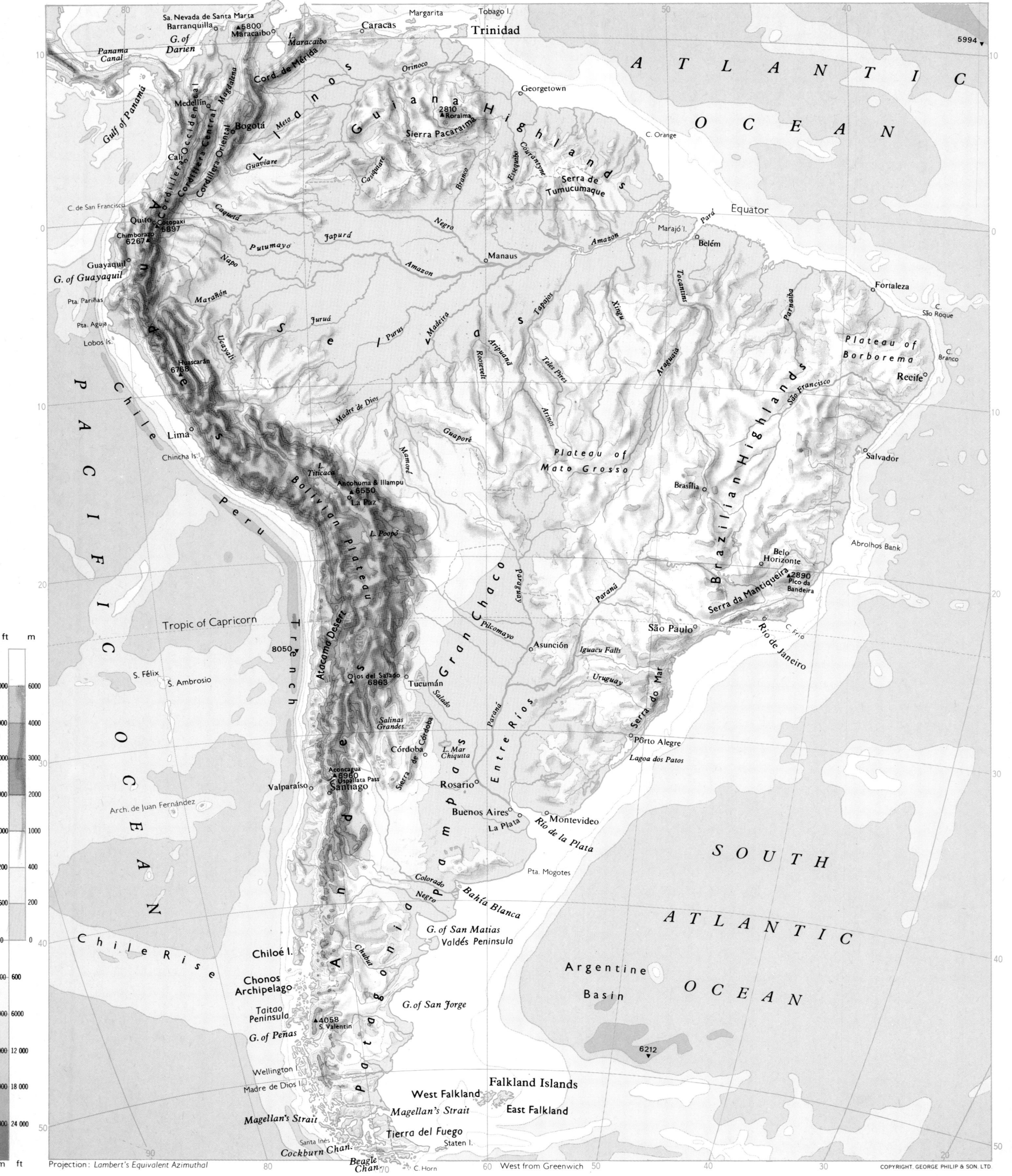

5994

ATLANTIC

OCEAN

Sa. Nevada de Santa Marta
Barranquilla
▲5800
Maracaibo
L. Maracaibo
Caracas
Margarita
Tobago I.
Trinidad
Panama Canal
G. of Darien
Medellín
Cord. de Mérida
Orinoco
Georgetown
C. Orange
Cali
Bogotá
Cordillera Occidental
Cordillera Central
Cordillera Oriental
Llanos
Meta
Guaviare
Guiana Highlands
2810 ▲Roraima
Sierra Pacaraima
Casiquiare
Branco
Essequibo
Courantyne
Serra de Tumucumaque
C. de San Francisco
Quito
Cotopaxi
5897
Chimborazo
6267 ▲
Caquetá
Putumayo
Japurá
Negro
Equator
Pará
Marajó I.
Amazon
Belém
Guayaquil
G. of Guayaquil
Napo
Marañón
Amazon
Manaus
Fortaleza
C. São Roque
Pta. Pariñas
Pta. Aguja
Lobos Is.
Juruá
Purus
Madeira
Roosevelt
Tapajós
Xingu
Tocantins
Parnaíba
Plateau of Borborema
C. Branco
Recife
Huascarán
6768 ▲
Ucayali
Madre de Dios
Aripuanã
Teles Pires
Arinos
São Francisco
Lima
Guaporé
Plateau of Mato Grosso
Brazilian Highlands
Chincha Is.
L. Titicaca
Ancohuma & Illampu
6550
La Paz
Brasília
Salvador
Bolivian Plateau
L. Poopó
Abrolhos Bank
Belo Horizonte
2890 Pico da Bandeira
Serra da Mantiqueira
Tropic of Capricorn
8050
Gran Chaco
Pilcomayo
Paraguay
Paraná
São Paulo
C. Frio
Rio de Janeiro
Ojos del Salado 6863 ▲
Tucumán
Salado
Asunción
Iguaçu Falls
Uruguay
Pôrto Alegre
Serra do Mar
Salinas Grandes
Córdoba
Sierra de Córdoba
L. Mar Chiquita
Entre Ríos
Lagoa dos Patos
Aconcagua 6960
Uspallata Pass
Santiago
Valparaíso
Rosario
Paraná
Arch. de Juan Fernández
Buenos Aires
La Plata
Montevideo
Rio de la Plata
Pampas
Colorado
Negro
Bahía Blanca
Pta. Mogotes
G. of San Matias
Valdés Peninsula
Chiloé I.
Chonos Archipelago
Patagonia
G. of San Jorge
Taitao Peninsula
4058
S. Valentin
G. of Peñas
6212
Wellington I.
Madre de Dios I.
Falkland Islands
West Falkland
East Falkland
Magellan's Strait
Tierra del Fuego
Santa Inés I.
Cockburn Chan.
Staten I.
Beagle Chan.
C. Horn

PACIFIC

OCEAN

Chile Rise

Chile

Peru

Atacama Desert

Trench

S. Félix
S. Ambrosio

S. Ambrosio

SOUTH

ATLANTIC

OCEAN

Argentine Basin

ft   m
18 000 6000
12 000 4000
9000   3000
6000   2000
3000   1000
1200   400
600   200
0   0
200   600
2000   6000
4000   12000
6000   18000
8000   24000
m   ft

Projection: Lambert's Equivalent Azimuthal

West from Greenwich

COPYRIGHT. GEORGE PHILIP & SON LTD

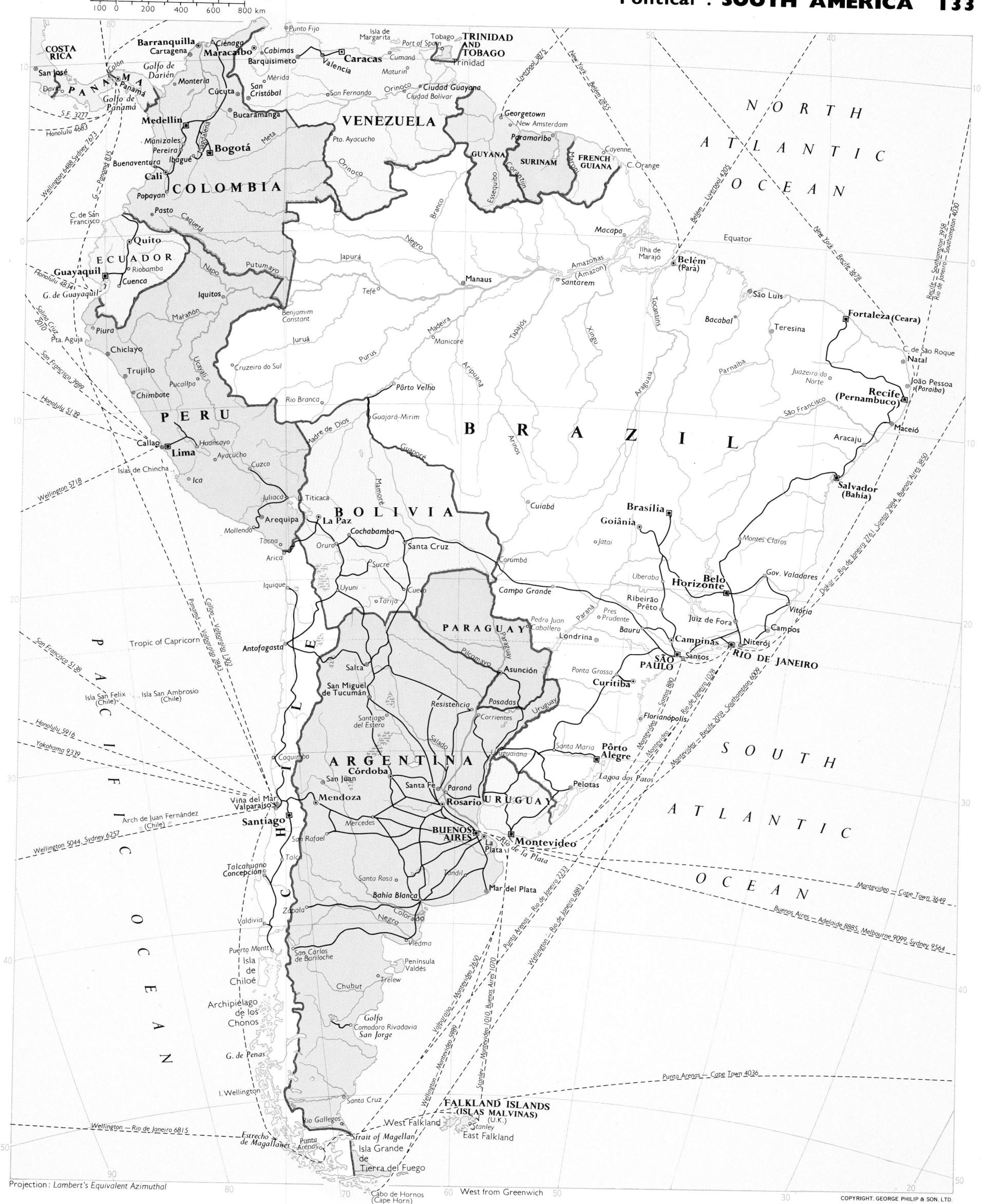

1 : 24 000 000

100   0   100   200   300   400   500 miles
100   0   200   400   600   800 km

COSTA
RICA

PANAMA

Barranquilla
Cartagena
Ciénaga
Maracaibo
Barquisimeto
Valencia
Caracas

Punto Fijo
Isla de
Margarita
Port of Spain
Cumaná

TRINIDAD
AND
TOBAGO
Trinidad

San José
Golfo de
Darién
Golfo de
Panamá
Colón
Panamá

Montería
Cúcuta
Mérida
San
Cristóbal
San Fernando

Maturín
Orinoco

VENEZUELA

Medellín
Bucaramanga

Pto. Ayacucho

Ciudad Guayana
Ciudad Bolívar

Georgetown
New Amsterdam
Paramaribo
Cayenne
C. Orange

Manizales
Pereira
Ibagué
Bogotá

GUYANA
SURINAM
FRENCH
GUIANA

Buenaventura
Cali
Popayán

COLOMBIA

Orinoco

Branco

Esequibo

C. de San
Francisco
Pasto

Caquetá

Macapa

Equator

Quito
ECUADOR
Riobamba

Napo
Putumayo

Japurá

Amazonas
(Amazon)

Santarem

Ilha de
Marajó
Belém
(Pará)

São Luís

Guayaquil
Cuenca

G. de Guayaquil

Iquitos

Marañón

Benjamim
Constant

Tefé

Manaus

NORTH
ATLANTIC
OCEAN

Fortaleza (Ceara)

Piura
Pta. Aguja

Chiclayo

Trujillo

Chimbote

Cruzeiro do Sul

Juruá
Purus

Madeira

Manicoré

Tapajós

Xingu

Bacabal

Teresina

Parnaíba

C. de São Roque
Natal
João Pessoa
(Paraíba)
Recife
(Pernambuco)

PERU

Pucallpa

Rio Branca

Pôrto Velho

Guajará-Mirim

Guaporé

Aripuanã

B   R   A   Z   I   L

Araguaia

Tocantins

São Francisco

Maceió

Callao
Lima

Huancayo
Ayacucho

Cuzco

Andre de Dios

Mamoré

Aracaju

Islas de Chincha
Ica

Juliaca
Titicaca

BOLIVIA

Cuiabá

Brasília
Goiânia

Jatai

Montes Claros

Salvador
(Bahia)

Arequipa
Mollendo
Tacna
Arica

La Paz
Cochabamba

Oruro

Sucre

Santa Cruz

Corumbá

Campo Grande

Uberaba

Belo
Horizonte

Gov. Valadares

Iquique

Uyuni

Tarija

Cueto

PARAGUAY

Pedro Juan
Caballero

Londrina

Bauru

Ribeirão
Prêto

Juiz de Fora

Campinas

Vitória

Campos
Niterói
RIO DE JANEIRO

Tropic of Capricorn

Antofagasta

Salta

Paraguay

Asunción

Parana

Pres.
Prudente

Ponta Grossa

SÃO
PAULO

Santos

Isla San Félix
(Chile)
Isla San Ambrosio
(Chile)

San Miguel
de Tucumán

Pilcomayo

Posadas

Resistencia
Corrientes

Uruguay

CURITIBA

Florianópolis

Honolulu 5916
Yokahama 9339

Santiago
del Estero

Salado

ARGENTINA

Córdoba

San Juan

Santa Fe

Paraná
Rosario

Uruguaiana

Santa María

Pôrto
Alegre

Lagoa dos Patos

Arch de Juan Fernández
(Chile)

CHILE

Coquimbo

Viña del Mar
Valparaíso
Santiago

Mendoza

San Rafael

Mercedes

Pelotas

SOUTH

ATLANTIC

OCEAN

Talcahuano
Concepción

Talca

Santa Rosa

Buenos
Aires
La
Plata

URUGUAY
Montevideo

Rio de la Plata

Valdivia

Zapala

Colorado
Negro

Tandil

Bahía Blanca

Mar del Plata

OCEAN

Puerto Montt
I. Isla
de
Chiloé

San Carlos
de Bariloche

Viedma

Península
Valdés
Trelew

PACIFIC

Archipiélago
de los
Chonos

Chubut

Golfo
Comodoro Rivadavia
San Jorge

G. de Penas

I. Wellington

Santa Cruz

Rio Gallegos

Estrecho
de Magallanes
Punta
Arenas

FALKLAND ISLANDS
(ISLAS MALVINAS)
(U.K.)

West Falkland
Stanley
East Falkland

Strait of Magellan
Isla Grande
de
Tierra del Fuego

Cabo de Hornos
(Cape Horn)

West from Greenwich

Projection: Lambert's Equivalent Azimuthal

COPYRIGHT. GEORGE PHILIP & SON. LTD.

C A R I B B E A N S E A
PACIFIC OCEAN
C O L O M B I A
V E N E Z
ECUADOR
P E R U
NETH. ANTILLES
Aruba (Neth.)
Curaçao (Neth.)
Bonaire (Neth.)
Willemstad
Is. de Aves (Ven.)
Is. Los Roques
Pta. Gallinas
Península de la Guajira
Cabo de la Vela
Golfo de Venezuela
Punto Fijo
Punta Cardón
Paraguaná
Coro
Puerto Cumarebo
FALCÓN
DISTRITO FEDERAL
Maiquetía
La Guaira
CARACAS
Los Teques
MIRANDA
Maracay
Valencia
Pto. Cabello
Barquisimeto
LARA
Carora
San Felipe
YARACUY
ARAGUA
GUÁRICO
COJEDES
San Carlos
Acarigua
Araure
Guanare
PORTUGUESA
Barinas
BARINAS
Mérida
MÉRIDA
TRUJILLO
Trujillo
Valera
TÁCHIRA
San Cristóbal
San Fernando de Apure
APURE
Calabozo
Valle de la Pascua
ZULIA
MARACAIBO
Lago de Maracaibo
Cabimas
Ciudad Ojeda
Machiques
Villa del Rosario
La Concepción
GUAJIRA
Ríohacha
Maicao
Santa Marta
Ciénaga
BARRANQUILLA
ATLÁNTICO
CARTAGENA
BOLÍVAR
MAGDALENA
Valledupar
CÉSAR
Sierra Nevada de Santa Marta
Golfo de Morrosquillo
Sincelejo
SUCRE
Montería
CÓRDOBA
Colón
PANAMÁ
PANAMA
Golfo de Panamá
Arch. de las Perlas
Golfo del Darién
DARIÉN
Golfo de Urabá
NORTE DE SANTANDER
Cúcuta
Pamplona
BUCARAMANGA
SANTANDER
Barrancabermeja
ANTIOQUIA
MEDELLÍN
Golfo de Cupica
Golfo de Tibugá
Quibdó
CHOCÓ
MANIZALES
CALDAS
Pereira
Armenia
Ibagué
TOLIMA
BOGOTÁ
CUNDINAMARCA
Tunja
BOYACÁ
Sogamoso
Duitama
Villavicencio
META
ARAUCA
Arauca
CASANARE
VICHADA
Puerto Ayacucho
Orinoco
Meta
Guaviare
GUAINÍA
VAUPÉS
Mitú
CAQUETÁ
Florencia
PUTUMAYO
AMAZONAS
Leticia
Buenaventura
VALLE
CALI
Palmira
Tuluá
Buga
HUILA
Neiva
CAUCA
Popayán
NARIÑO
Pasto
Tumaco
Ipiales
Tulcán
CARCHI
Esmeraldas
ESMERALDAS
IMBABURA
Ibarra
QUITO
PICHINCHA
MANABÍ
Manta
Portoviejo
COTOPAXI
Latacunga
Ambato
TUNGURAHUA
Riobamba
CHIMBORAZO
GUAYAQUIL
GUAYAS
Golfo de Guayaquil
Cuenca
AZUAY
Machala
EL ORO
Loja
LOJA
NAPO
PASTAZA
MORONA-SANTIAGO
ZAMORA-CHINCHIPE
Tumbes
TUMBES
Sullana
PIURA
Iquitos
L O R E T O
Amazonas
Marañón
Putumayo
Caquetá
Japurá
Napo
Benjamin Constant
Requena
A M A Z
Projection: Lambert's Equivalent Azimuthal

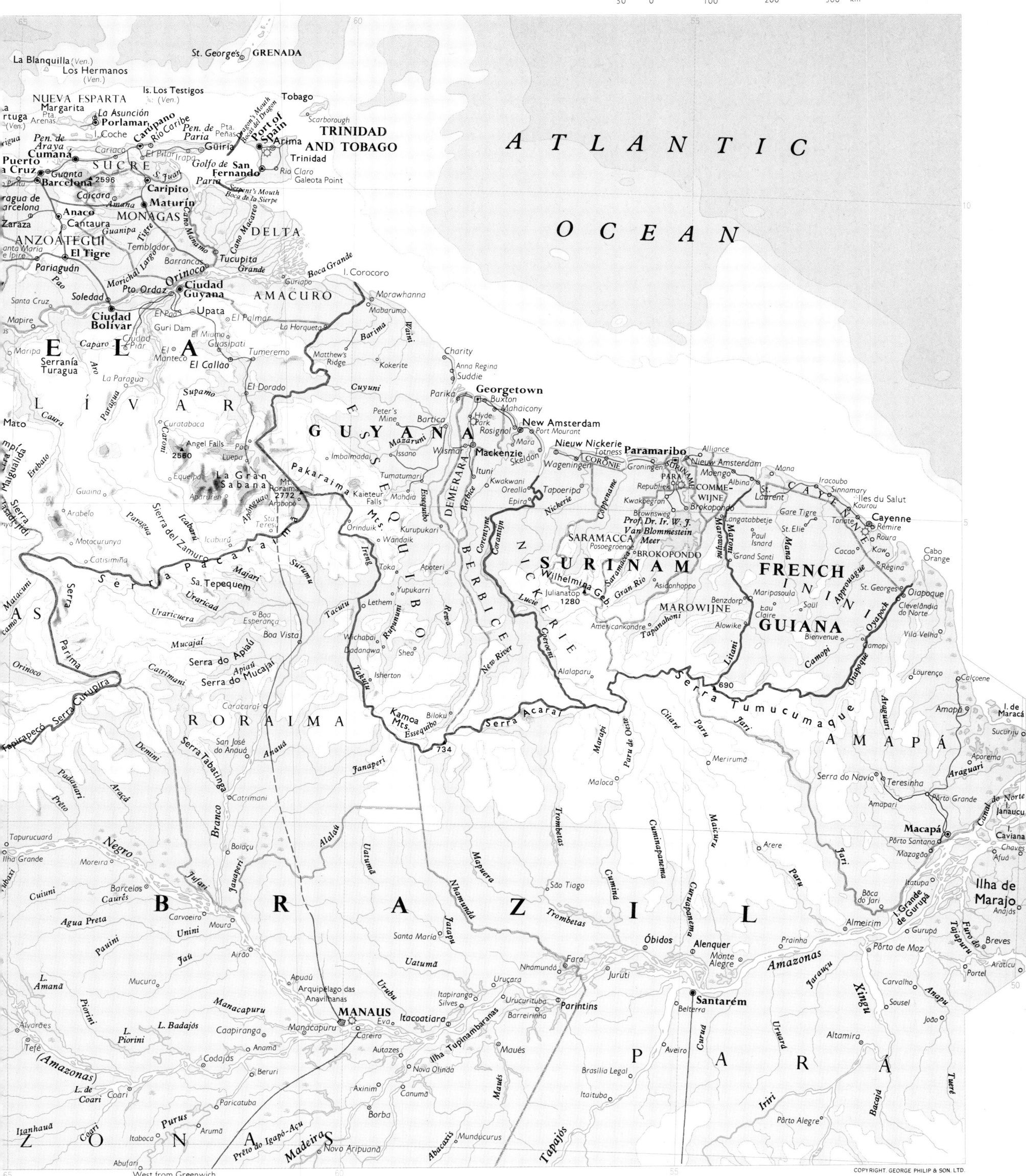

1 : 6 400 000

ATLANTIC

OCEAN

La Blanquilla (Ven.)
Los Hermanos (Ven.)
St. George's GRENADA

Is. Los Testigos (Ven.)

Tobago
Scarborough

NUEVA ESPARTA
Margarita
Pta.
La Asunción
Porlamar
Coche

TRINIDAD AND TOBAGO

Caripano
Río Caribe
Pen. de Paria
Port of Spain
Arima

Trinidad

Pen. de Araya
Cumaná
SUCRE
Cariaco
S.Juan
Güiria
Golfo de Paria
San Fernando
Río Claro
Galeota Point

Puerto la Cruz
Guanta
Barcelona 2596
Caripito
Maturín
MONAGAS
Amana
Tucupita
DELTA
I. Corocoro

Anaco
Cantaura
Guanipa
ANZOATEGUI
El Tigre
Temblador
Tigre
Barrancas
Orinoco
Ciudad Guayana
AMACURO
Morawhanna
Mabaruma

Pariaguán
Pao
Morichal Largo
Pto. Ordaz
Ciudad Guayana
Guriapo
Boca Grande

Soledad
Ciudad Bolívar
Guri Dam
El Pao
Upata
Barima
Wini
Charity
Anna Regina
Suddie

VENEZUELA

BOLÍVAR

GUYANA

ATLANTIC

Georgetown

SURINAM

FRENCH GUIANA

Paramaribo

Cayenne

BRAZIL

MANAUS

AMAZONAS

RORAIMA

PARÁ

AMAPÁ

Ilha de Marajó

Macapá

Santarém

West from Greenwich

PACIFIC OCEAN

PERU

CHILE

BOLIVIA

Selected place and feature names:

Tumbes, Pto. Mancora, TUMBES, El Alto, Talara, Brea, Colón, Paita, Pijura, Catacaos, Sechura, Punta Negra, Reventazón, I. Lobos de Tierra, LAMBAYEQUE, Jayanca, Ferreñafe, Chiclayo, Pimentel, Monsefú, Chepén, Guadalupe, Pacasmayo, San Pedro de Lloc, Paiján, Trujillo, Chan Chan, Salaverry, LA LIBERTAD, Chimbote, Península de Ferrol, Casma, Huaraz, ANCASH, Huarmey, Barranca, Supe, Huacho, Punta Lachay, Huaral, Chancay, Ancón, CALLAO, I. San Lorenzo, LIMA, Pachacamac, Mala, Imperial, Cañete, Chincha Alta, Tambo de Mora, Pisco, Península Paracas, Punta Carretas, Ica, ICA, Palpa, Nasca, Marcona, Punta Parada, San Juan, Acari, Chala, Atico, Ocoña, Camaná, Mollendo, Ilo, Punta Coles, TACNA, Tacna, Arica, Iquique, Pisagua, Tocopila, ANTOFAGASTA

Loja, LOJA, Zamora, Macará, Sullana, PIURA, Chulucanas, Pijura, Castilla, Cajamarca, SAN MARTIN, Moyobamba, Tarapoto, Yurimaguas, Chachapoyas, Lamas, Juanjui, HUÁNUCO, Huánuco, Cerro de Pasco, PASCO, JUNIN, La Oroya, Tarma, Huancayo, Jauja, Concepción, Huancavelica, HUANCAVELICA, Ayacucho, AYACUCHO, APURIMAC, Abancay, CUZCO, Cuzco, Machu Picchu, Urubamba, Pisac, Sicuani, Ayaviri, Azángaro, Juliaca, Puno, Lago Titicaca, PUNO, AREQUIPA, Arequipa, MOQUEGUA, Moquegua, Corocoro, LA PAZ, Oruro, ORURO, Lago de Poopó, Salar de Coipasa, Salar de Uyuni

Marañón, AMAZONAS, Huallaga, Ucayali, Pucallpa, LORETO, MADRE DE DIOS, Puerto Maldonado, Río de las Piedras, Manu, PANDO, Cobija, Rio Branco, ACRE, Cruzeiro do Sul

Elevation scale:
ft / m
18 000 / 6000
12 000 / 4000
9 000 / 3000
6 000 / 2000
4500 / 1500
3000 / 1000
1200 / 400
600 / 200
0 / 0
200 / 600
2000 / 6000
4000 / 12 000
6000 / 18 000
m / ft

Projection: Lambert's Equivalent Azimuthal

1 : 6 400 000

50 0 50 100 150 200 miles
50 0 100 200 300 km

Z O N A S

L. de Coari Coari Paricatuba Axinim Canumã Itaituba Iriri Pôrto Alegre Bacajá

Itanhauá Purus Itaboca Arumã Borba Maués Abacaris Munducurus Tucunaré Entre Rios Nazaré

Coari Tapauá Itatuba Tapauá Manicoré Santa Maria dos Marmeles Madeira Novo Aripuanã Capoeira Miriti São Cinza Crepori São Félix

Pinhua Purus Lábrea Abufari Itapinima Prainha Samaúma Canudos Cururú Tapajós Xingu Riosinho

B R A S I L

Coari Canutama Carandapatuba Três Casas Aripuanã Teles Pires Recreio Serra do Cachimbo Cachimba Curuá

Ituxi Majuriã Mucuim Humaitá Madeira Calama Barracão do Barreto S. Benedito Cachimba Alto Iriri

Madeira Jamari Tabajara Aripuanã Peixoto de Azeredo Serra Formosa Campo de Diauarum Iriri Novo

Pôrto Velho Jaciparaná Caritianas Pôrto Cajueiro Manitsaud-Missu Liberdade

404 comércio Abunã Ariquemes Rondônia Serra dos Apiacás Pousa Alegre Suiá Missu Serra do Roncador

Manoa Nova Vida Jaru Jaru Presidente Hermes Serra do Norte Arinos Xingu Pôrto dos Meinacos

Guajará-Mirim Sa. dos Pacaás Novos Pimenta Bueno Barão de Melgaço Serra do Tombador Serra dos Caiabis Ronuro Coliseu

Guayaramerin Rondônia Camararé Nhambiquara Juruena Teles Pires Verde

Príncipe da Beira Serra Apidiá 663 Vilhena Utiariti Planalto

Puerto Siles Versalles Pedras Negras Mato Grosso M A T O G R O S S O do

Lago Rogoaguado San Joaquin Mategua Magdalena Guaporé Nortelândia Diamântino Cuiabá Chavantina

xoltación San Ramón Baures Puerto Villazón Serranía de Huanchaca Arenápolis Alto Paraguai Serra Azul

Lago de San Luis El Carmen Mato Grosso 915 Aruanã

E N I Mamoré San Javier San Martín Jauru Chapada dos Guimarães Mortes

Trinidad Blanco Negro Perseverancia 1995 Guaporé Tapirapuã Rosário Oeste Acorizal Barra do Bugres

s de Mojos San Francisco Añez Santa Rosa de la Roca Pôrto Esperidião Várzea Grande Cuiabá Coronel Ponce Barro do Garças

lorenzo Loreto Nossa Senhora do Livramento Cáceres Santo Antônio do Leverger Poxoréu Rio das Garças Araguaiana Araguaia

O L I V I A Grande Yapacani San Javier Concepción San Ignacio San Matías Poconé Barão de Melgaço Jaciara Tesouro Baliza

habamba Portachuelo Montero Santa Ana Cuiabá Ródonópolis Ponte Branca Iporá Ivolândia

Punata San Carlos Warnes San Miguel São Lourenço Itiquira Guiratinga Araguaia Catopônia

Santa Cruz Buena Vista S A N T A C R U Z El Cerro Laguna Concepción Lagoa Uberaba Pôrto Jofre Alto Garças Santa Rita do Araguaia Sa. das Divisões

Pampa Grande Cotoca San José Pantanal do São Lourenço Itiquira Serra do Caiapó Mineiros Rio Verde

Samaipata El Palmar Llanos de Chiquitos Santo Corazón Correntes Itiquira Alto Araguaia Jataí

Villagrande Santa Rosa del Palmar 1425 Serr. Santiago La Cal Lagoa Mandioré Taquari Baús Claro

Sucre Abapó Bañados de Izozog Roboré Santa Ana Pôrto Suárez M A T O G R O S S O Verde Itarumã

Terebuco Gutiérrez Puerto Suárez Corumbá Pantanal do Rio Negro Rio Verde de Mato Grosso Paraíso Cassilândia Aporé

Padilla Lagunillas Charagua Fortín General Pando Ladário Nhecolândia D O S U L Alto Sucuriú Paranaíba

Monteagudo Camiri Fortín Ingavi Albuquerque Pôrto Esperança Negro Corguinho Paraná Inocência

Azurduy Olimpo Coimbra Miranda Rochedo Verde Aparecida do Taboado

CHUQUISACA Camargo Carandaiti Fortín Coronel Eugenio Garay Bahía Negra Miranda Aquidauana Terenos Jaraguari Agua Clara Rubinéia

Chaco Boreal Fortín P. Madrejón Jango Campo Grande Ribas do Rio Pardo Pereira Barreto

Tarija Huacaya Villa Montes Fuerte Olimpo Paraguay P A R A G U A Y Bonito Sidrolândia Garcias Três Lagoas Andradina

5603 Entre Rios Fortín Garrapatal Puerto Guaraní B O Q U E R Ó N Pilcomayo Jardim Nioaque Guia Lopes da Laguna Maracaju Anhandui Xavantina Mirandópolis Panorama

Tarija Yacuiba La Esmeralda Pôrto Murtinho Aguapeí

Tartagal West from Greenwich COPYRIGHT GEORGE PHILIP & SON LTD.

S A L T A

ATLANTIC OCEAN
AMAPÁ
Macapá
Ilha de Marajó
BELÉM (Pará)
SÃO LUÍS
FORTALEZA (Ceará)
NATAL
João Pessoa (Paraíba)
RECIFE (Pernambuco)
MACEIÓ
Aracaju
Teresina
Caxias
Parnaíba
Sobral
Mossoró
Campina Grande
Juàzeiro do Norte
Crato
Petrolina
Juàzeiro
Imperatriz
Marabá
Carolina
Floriano
PARÁ
MARANHÃO
CEARÁ
RIO GRANDE DO NORTE
PARAÍBA
PERNAMBUCO
ALAGOAS
SERGIPE
PIAUÍ
BRAZIL
Tocantins
Xingu
Serra dos Carajás
Serra do Gurupi
Serra do Estrondo
Chapada das Mangabeiras

1 : 6 400 000
50 0 50 100 150 200 miles
50 0 100 200 300 km
ATLANTIC OCEAN
ESPIRITO SANTO
Tropic of Capricorn
West from Greenwich
BAHIA
GOIÁS
MINAS GERAIS
SÃO PAULO
PARANÁ
RIO DE JANEIRO
DISTRITO FEDERAL
BRASÍLIA
BELO HORIZONTE
RIO DE JANEIRO
SÃO PAULO
SALVADOR (Bahia)
CURITIBA
GOIÂNIA
CAMPINAS
SANTOS
NITERÓI
CAMPOS
Projection: Lambert's Equivalent Azimuthal
m ft
2000 6000
1500 4500
1000 3000
400 1200
200 600
0 0
200 600
2000 6000
4000 12 000
m ft

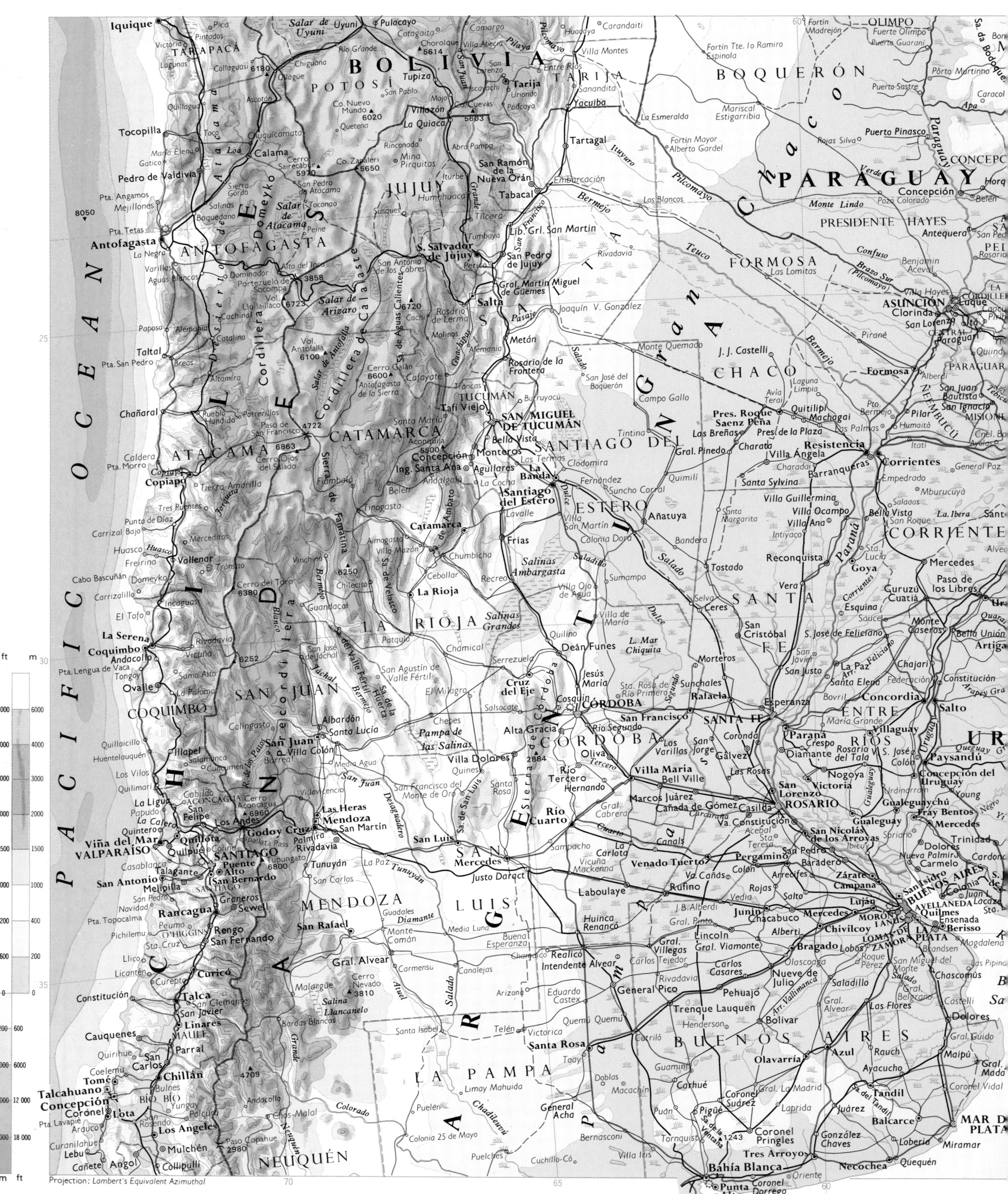

Projection: Lambert's Equivalent Azimuthal

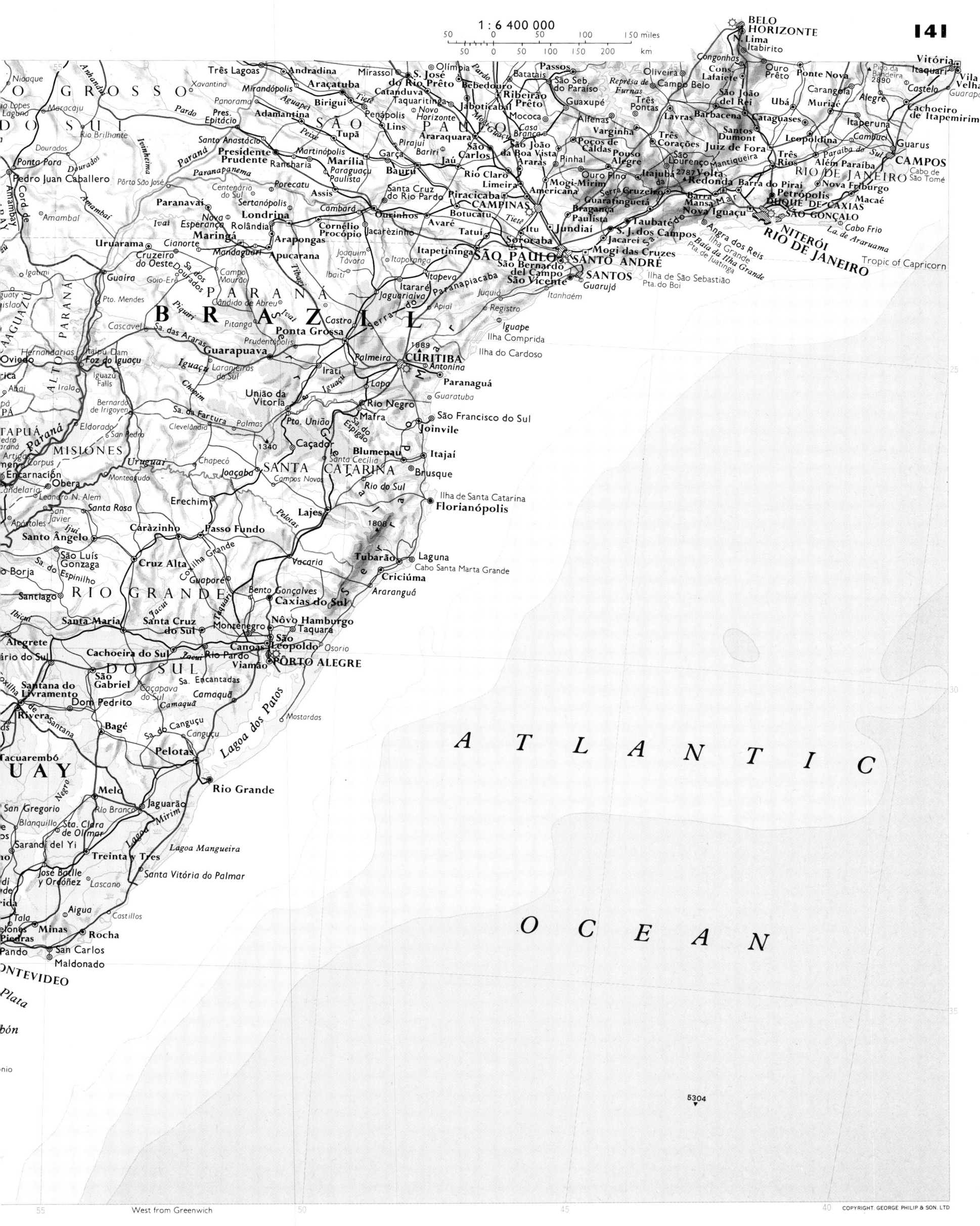

1 : 6 400 000

50   0   50   100   150 miles

50   0   50   100   150   200 km

BELO HORIZONTE

ATLANTIC

OCEAN

West from Greenwich

COPYRIGHT. GEORGE PHILIP & SON, LTD

1 : 6 400 000

50 0 50 100 150 miles
50 0 50 100 200 km

LA PAMPA

BUENOS AIRES

Juárez
Coronel Pringles
González Chaves
Balcarce
Loberia
Quequén
Necochea
Tres Arroyos
Bahía Blanca
Punta Alta
Coronel Dorrego
B. Blanca
I. Trinidad
Médanos
Mayor Buratovich
Tornquist 1243
Villa Iris
Bernasconi
Cuchillo-Có

ARAUCO
Cañete
Angol
Mulchén
Collipulli
Victoria
Paso Copahue 2980
Loncopué
Colonia 25 de Mayo
Puelches
Anelo
Neuquén
Cipolletti
Chelforó
Fortín Uno
Allen Gral. Roca
Choele Choel
Lamarque
Río Colorado
Colorado
Capitán Pastene
I. Mocha
Traiguén
Curacautín
Lautaro 3124
Temuco
Paso Pino Hachado 1824
Zapala
Cutral-Có
Las Lajas
Paso de los Indios
Barda del Medio
Negro
RÍO NEGRO
Gral. Conesa
Stroeder
B. Anegada
Pta. Rasa

Puerto Saavedra
Nueva Imperial
Cunco
Cherquenco
Freire
NEUQUÉN
Picún Leufú
Limay
Gen. Lorenzo Vintter
Viedma
Carmen de Patagones

ARAUCANIA
Pitrufquén
Toltén
Loncoche
Villarrica
Paso Mamuil Malal 1253
3776
Junín de los Andes
Piedra del Aguila
El Cuy
Valcheta
Aguada Cecilio
San Antonio Oeste

Valdivia
Corral
Pta. Galera
Los Lagos
San Martín de los Andes
1314
La Esperanza
Sa. Colorada
Los Menucos
Maquinchao
Salina Gualicho

Golfo San Matías

La Unión
Osorno
Río Bueno
Puyehue
L. Ranco
Futrono
Lago Ranco
L. Nahuel Huapi
Comallo
Ingeniero Jacobacci
El Caín
Cona Niyeu
Meseta de Somuncurá
Sierra Grande
Verde
Pta. Norte
G. San José
Pen. Valdés
Puerto Pirámides
Punta Delgada

LOS LAGOS
Río Negro
Vol. Osorno 2660 3554
La Ensenada Mte. Tronador
Puerto Varas
L. Llanquihue
Puerto Montt
Maullín
G. de los Coronados
Pta. Huechucuicui
Ancud 820
G. de Ancud
Isla de Chiloé
Castro
Achao
Puerto Quellón
C. Quilán
I. Guafo
Boca del Guafo
Islas Guaitecas

San Carlos de Bariloche
El Bolsón
Norquinco
El Maitén
Leleque
Gualjaina
Gan Gan
Telsen
1879
Puerto Lobos
Golfo Nuevo
Puerto Madryn

CHUBUT
Esquel 2470
L. Menéndez
Chaitén 2440
Tecka
Gaiman
Trelew
Rawson
Chubut
El Corcovado 2300
L. Yelcho 2075
Pampa de Agnia
Perdido
Las Plumas
Mesa de Montemayor
C. Raso

Archipiélago de los Chonos
I. Guamblin
Magdalena
Canal Moraleda
Palena
L. Gral. Vintter
Río Pico
José de San Martín
1245
Genoa
Chico
Gran Laguna Salada
Camarones
B. Camarones
C. Dos Bahías

La Plata 2020
L. Fontana
Alto Río Senguer
Facundo
Senguer
L. Musters
L. Colhué Huapi
Sarmiento
B. Bústamante

Golfo San Jorge

Coihaique
Puerto Aisén
Mayo
Río Mayo
Holdich
Comodoro Rivadavia

Balmaceda
L. Buenos Aires
Perito Moreno
Colonia Las Heras
Caleta Olivia
Los Monos

C. Taitao 1372
Mte. San Valentín 4058
Chile Chico
L. Gral. Carrera
Los Antiguos
Pico Truncado
Mazarredo
C. Tres Puntas
C. Blanco

Península de Taitao
Arenales 3437
Cochrane
L. Pueyrredón
Lago Posadas
Fitz Roy
Jaramillo
1335
Puerto Deseado
Deseado

Golfo de Penas
Archipiélago Guayaneco
I. Javier
Co. San Lorenzo 3700
Las Horquetas
Pta. Medanosa

I. Campana
Canal Baker
Melliza Sur 3050
Mte. Melizo 2280
Mt. Inés 1120
Gob. Gregores
Bahía Laura

I. Patricio Lynch
I. Esmeralda
I. Wellington
Canal Messier
SANTA CRUZ
L. San Martín
L. Cardiel
Gran Altiplanicie Central
San Julián

I. Madre de Dios
I. Duque de York
C. Santiago
B. Salvación
I. Hanover
Mte. Fitzroy 3375
L. Viedma
Tres Lagos
Shehuen
Chico

Arch. Reina Adelaida
I. Mornington
G. Trinidad
G. Ladrillero
Co. Murallón 3600
Lago Argentino
Santa Cruz
Cmte. Luis Piedrabuena

Bahía Grande

Calafate
Esperanza
Coig
Puerto Coig

Puerto Natales
El Turbio
Gallegos
Guer Aike
Río Gallegos
Monte Dinero
C. Virgenes

FALKLAND ISLANDS (ISLAS MALVINAS)
Jason Is.
Pebble I.
C. Dolphin
King George B.
Queen Charlotte B.
Mt. Adam 700
Mt. Usborne 705
Weddell I.
Port Darwin
Stanley
West Falkland
East Falkland
C. Meredith
Beauchêne I.

G. Almirante Montt
Seno Skyring
Cerro Sombrero
Strait of Magellan
Isla Grande de Tierra del Fuego
San Sebastián
Río Grande

Pen. Muñoz
Gamero
C. Deseado
I. Riesco
Seno de Otway
Porvenir
TIERRA DEL FUEGO
Misión Fagnano
C. San Diego

Punta Arenas
Pen. Brunswick
Canal Magallanes
Dawson
Whiteside
L. Fagnano
I. de los Estados (Staten I.)

Santa Inés
Clarence
Capt. Aracena
Pen. Breacknock
2469 Mte. Darwin
Ushuaia
Gordon
Canal Beagle
I. Navarino
I. Picton
I. Nueva
Est. de Le Maire

I. Stewart
I. Londonderry
B. Cook
I. Hoste
B. Nassau
I. Lennox
Pen. Hardy
Islas Wollaston
Is. Hermite
Cabo de Hornos (Cape Horn)
Islas Diego Ramírez

PACIFIC OCEAN
SOUTH ATLANTIC OCEAN

ft m
9000 3000
6000 2000
4500 1500
3000 1000
1200 400
600 200
0 0
200 600
2000 6000
4000 12000
m ft

Projection: Lambert's Equivalent Azimuthal

COPYRIGHT. GEORGE PHILIP & SON. LTD.

West from Greenwich

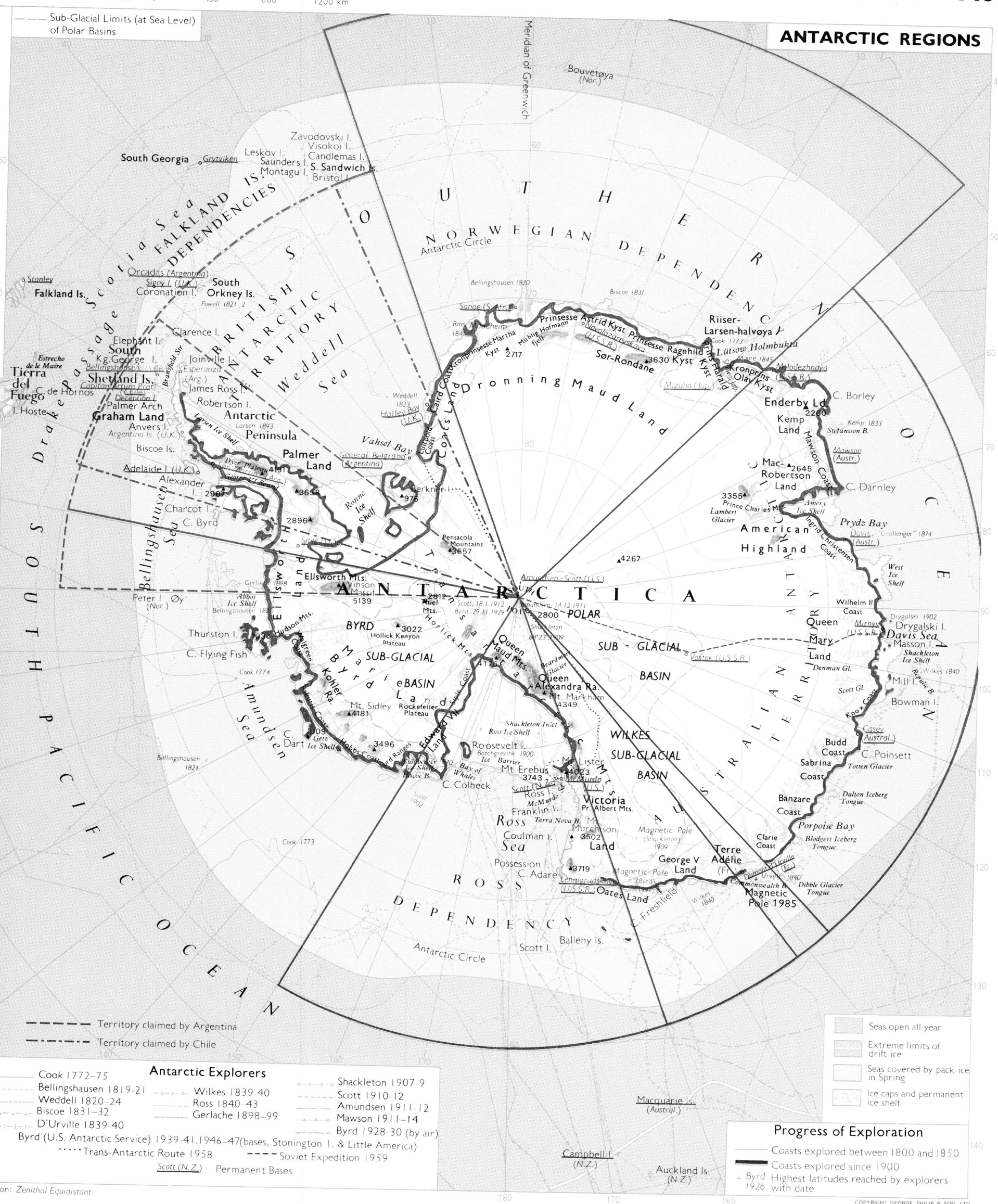

1 : 28 000 000

Sub-Glacial Limits (at Sea Level)
of Polar Basins

--- Territory claimed by Argentina

-·-·- Territory claimed by Chile

Antarctic Explorers

Cook 1772-75
Bellingshausen 1819-21
Weddell 1820-24   Wilkes 1839-40
Biscoe 1831-32   Ross 1840-43
D'Urville 1839-40   Gerlache 1898-99

Shackleton 1907-9
Scott 1910-12
Amundsen 1911-12
Mawson 1911-14
Byrd 1928-30 (by air)

Byrd (U.S. Antarctic Service) 1939-41, 1946-47 (bases, Stonington I. & Little America)
···· Trans-Antarctic Route 1958   ---- Soviet Expedition 1959
Scott (N.Z.) Permanent Bases

ion: *Zenithal Equidistant*

Seas open all year
Extreme limits of
drift-ice
Seas covered by pack-ice
in Spring
Ice caps and permanent
ice shelf

Progress of Exploration

Coasts explored between 1800 and 1850
Coasts explored since 1900
+ Byrd Highest latitudes reached by explorers
  1926 with date

COPYRIGHT GEORGE PHILIP & SON LTD.

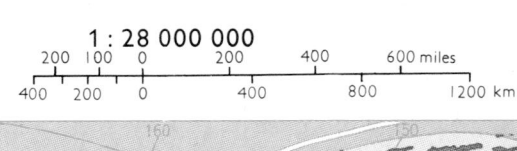

1 : 28 000 000

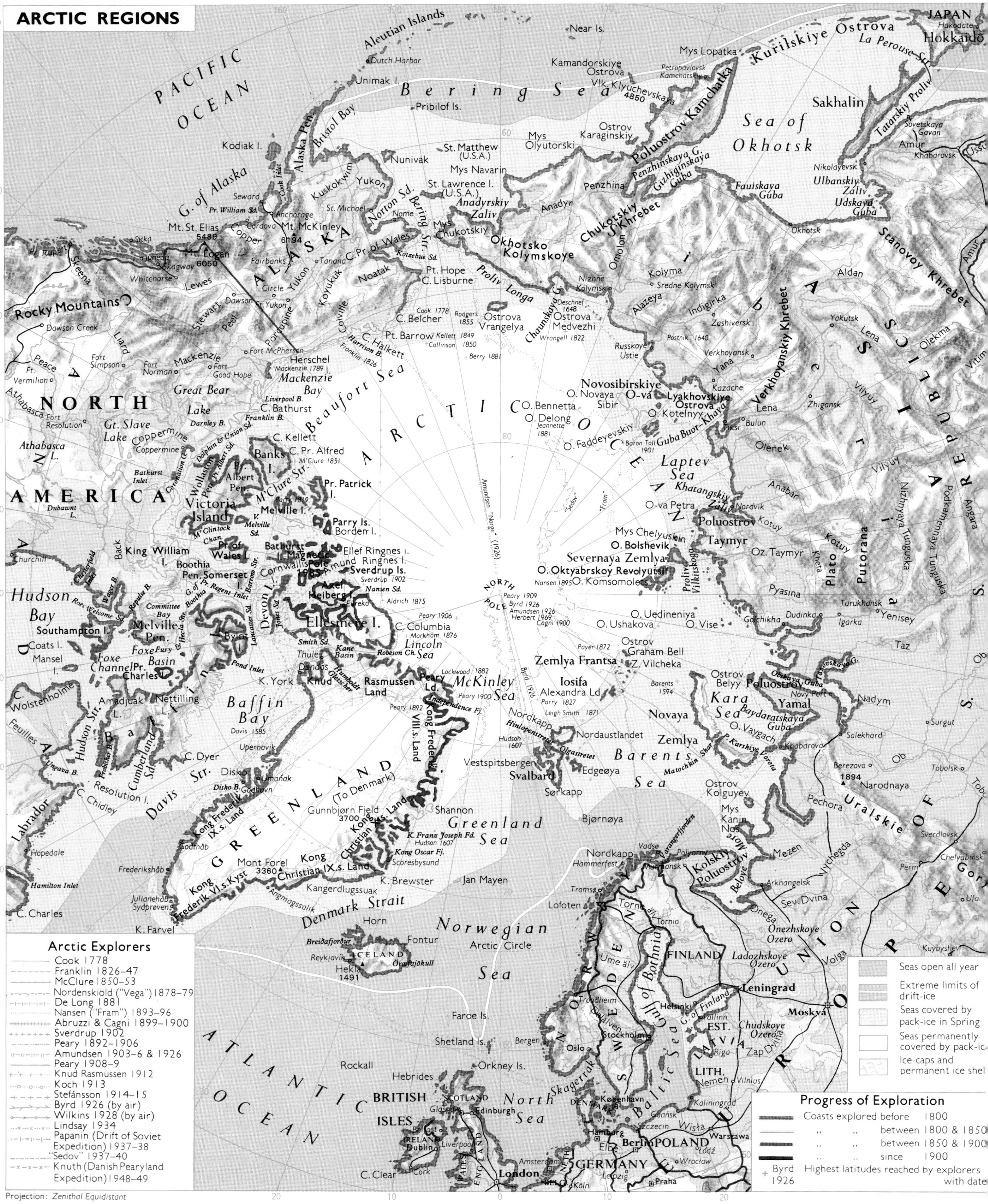

200 100 0 200 400 600 miles
400 200 0 400 800 1200 km

ARCTIC REGIONS

PACIFIC OCEAN

JAPAN
Hokkaidō
Hakodate

Aleutian Islands
Near Is.
Kamandorskiye Ostrova
Kurilskiye Ostrova
La Perouse Str.

Unimak I.
Dutch Harbor
Pribilof Is.

Bering Sea

Mys Lopatka
Petropavlovsk-Kamchatskiy
Vlk. Klyuchevskaya 4850
Poluostrov Kamchatka

Sakhalin
Sovetskaya Gavan
Tatarskiy Proliv

Sea of Okhotsk

Kodiak I.

G. of Alaska
Mt. St. Elias 5489
Sitka
Juneau
Skagway
Whitehorse

Alaska Pen.
Bristol Bay
St. Matthew (U.S.A.)
St. Lawrence I. (U.S.A.)

Nunivak

Kuskokwim

Mys Olyutorski
Mys Navarin

Karaginskiy
Ostrov Karaginskiy
Penzhina

Penzhinskaya G.
Gizhiginskaya Guba
Fauiskaya Guba

Nikolayevsk
Ulbanskiy Zaliv
Udskaya Guba

Amur
Khabarovsk

Seward
Anchorage
Cordova Mt. McKinley 6194

ALASKA
Fairbanks
Tanana

Yukon
Nome
St. Michael
Norton Sd.
C. Pr. of Wales
Kotzebue Sd.
Bering Str.

Mys Chukotskiy
Anadyrskiy Zaliv

Chukotskiy Khrebet

Okhotsko Kolymskoye
Okhotsk

Mt. Logan 6050

Copper
Mt. McKinley

Circle Yukon
Ft. Yukon
Porcupine
Koyukuk

Pt. Hope
C. Lisburne
Proliv Longa

Nizhne Kolymsk
Kolyma

Sredne Kolymsk
Omolon

Aldan
Stanovoy Khrebet

Rocky Mountains
Dawson Creek

Liard
Peace
Ft. Vermilion

Stewart
Dawson
Peel

Colville
Harrison B.
Franklin 1826

Cook 1778
Rodgers 1855
C. Belcher
Ostrova Vrangelya
Chaunskaya

Deschnef 1648
Russkoye Ustie
Alazeya
Indigirka

Yakutsk
Verkhoyansk
Verkhoyanskiy Khrebet

Lena
Zhigansk

NORTH
Fort Norman
Fort Good Hope
Mackenzie

Herschel
Mackenzie Bay
C. Bathurst
Liverpool B.
Darnley B.
Franklin B.

Kellett 1849
Collinson 1850
Pt. Barrow
C. Halkett
Berry 1881
Wrangell 1822

Ostrov Medvezhi
Zashiversk

Postnik 1640

Kazache
Yana

Olenek

Great Bear Lake
Coppermine
C. Kellett

Beaufort Sea

Novosibirskiye O-va
O. Novaya Sibir
O. Kotelnyy

Lyakhovskiye Ostrova
Baron Toll 1901

Tiksi
Bulun

AMERICA

Gt. Slave Lake
Coppermine
C. Pr. Alfred
M'Clure 1851

Banks I.
Pr. Patrick I.

ARCTIC OCEAN

O. Bennetta
O. Delong
Jeannette 1881

O. Faddeyevskiy
Guba Buor-Khaya

Laptev Sea

Khatangskiy Zaliv
Nordvik
Kotuy

Lena

Athabasca L.
Fort Resolution
Dubawnt

Victoria Island
Mt Clintock
Melville I.
Melville Sd.

Parry Is.
Borden I.
Ellef Ringnes I.
Amund Ringnes I.

"Norge" (1926)

O-va Petra
Mys Chelyuskin
O. Bolshevik

Severnaya Zemlya
O. Oktyabrskoy Revolyutsii
O. Komsomolets

Nansen 1895

Poluostrov Taymyr
Oz. Taymyr

Pyasina

Kheta
Anabar

Turukhansk
Yenisey
Igarka

Churchill
King William I.
Boothia Pen.
Somerset
Pr. of Wales

Bathurst
Magnetic Pole 1831
Cornwallis I.
Sverdrup Is.
Sverdrup 1902

NORTH POLE
Peary 1909
Byrd 1926
Amundsen 1926
Herbert 1969
Cogni 1900

Nansen 1895
Fram

O. Uedineniya
O. Ushakova
O. Vise

Golchikha
Dudinka

Hudson Bay
Southampton I.
Coats I.
Mansel

Melville Pen.
Foxe Channel
Foxe Basin
Pr. Charles

Axel Heiberg
Eureka

Devon I.
Nansen Sd.
Aldrich 1875

Peary 1906

Pr. Charles
Foxe Basin
Fury

Ellesmere I.
C. Columbia
Markham 1876
Lincoln Sea
Robeson Ch.

Peary 1909
Byrd 1926

Payer 1872
Zemlya Frantsa Iosifa

Ostrov Graham Bell
Z. Vilcheka

Barents 1594

Novaya Zemlya

Kara Sea

Ostrov Belyy
Poluostrov Yamal
Obskaya Guba

Nadym

Labrador
C. Wolstenholme

Baffin Bay
Davis 1585
Upernavik

Smith Sd.
Thule
Kane Basin
Humboldt Gletscher

K. York
Knud
Rasmussen Land

Peary Ld.
Lockwood 1882
Peary 1900

McKinley

Iosifa
Alexandra Ld.
Parry 1827
Leigh Smith 1871

Nordkapp
Zemlya

Novaya
Zemlya

Barents Sea

P. Karskiye Vorota

Ostrov Kolguyev

Narodnaya
Uralskie

Berezovo
Salekhard

Ob
Tobolsk
Surgut

Feuilles
Ungava B.

Resolution I.
C. Chidley

Hudson Str.

Davis Str.
C. Dyer

Disko
Disko B.
Godhavn
Umanak

Godthab
Frederikshåb

GREENLAND
(To Denmark)

Gunnbjørn Field 3700
Kong Frederik IX.s Land
Kong Christian IX.s Land

Mont Forel 3360
Kong Frederik VI.s Kyst
Frederik VI.s Kyst

Peary 1892
Independence Fj.
Vll.s Land

Long Frederik

Hinlopenstretet
Nordkapp
Hudson 1607
Olgastretet

Vestspitsbergen
Svalbard
Edgeøya
Sørkapp

K. Franz Joseph Fd.
Hudson 1607
Kong Oscar Fj.
Scoresbysund
K. Brewster

Shannon

Greenland Sea

Jan Mayen

Bjørnøya

Nordaustlandet

Matochkin Shar
P. Karskiye Vorota
O. Vaygach

Khabarovo

Novy Port

Mys Kanin Nos

Pechora

1894

Sverdlovsk
Chelyabinsk

Julianehåb
Sydprøven

Kong Frederik VI.s Kyst
Angmagssalik
Kangerdlugssuak

Denmark Strait

Nordkapp
Vadsø
Varangerfjorden
Polyarnyy

Hammerfest
Murmansk

Mys Kanin Nos

Bel"e
More

Mezen
Ntchegda

Onega
Sev. Dvina
Arkhangelsk

Kolskiy Poluostrov
Onezhskoye Ozero

Ufa

C. Charles
C. Farvel
K. Farvel

Breiðafjörður
ICELAND
Reykjavik
Hekla 1491
Öræfajökull

Horn
Fontur

Norwegian Sea
Arctic Circle

Tromsø
Lofoten

Trondheim

Torne
Tornio

Gulf of Bothnia

FINLAND
Helsinki

Leningrad

Ladozhskoye Ozero
Volga

Kuybyshev

UNION OF

ft   m
12 000   4000
9000   3000
6000   2000
3000   1000
1200   400
600   200
0   0

Faroe Is.

SWEDEN
NORWAY

Bergen
Oslo
Stockholm

EST.
Tallinn
Chudskoye Ozero
Zap Dvina

Moskva

Faroe Is.

Shetland Is.

Rockall

Hebrides
Orkney Is.

BRITISH ISLES
SCOTLAND
Glasgow
Edinburgh

North Sea

DENMARK
København
Oslo

Gulf of Finland
Riga
LATVIA
LITH.
Nemen
Vilnius

Kaliningrad

IRELAND
Dublin
Liverpool
ENGLAND

London
C. Clear
Cork

NETH.
Amsterdam

GERMANY
BELG.
Köln
Hamburg
Berlin
Leipzig
Praha

POLAND
Gdansk
Szczecin
Wisła
Wrocław
Warszawa

ATLANTIC OCEAN

Projection: Zenithal Equidistant

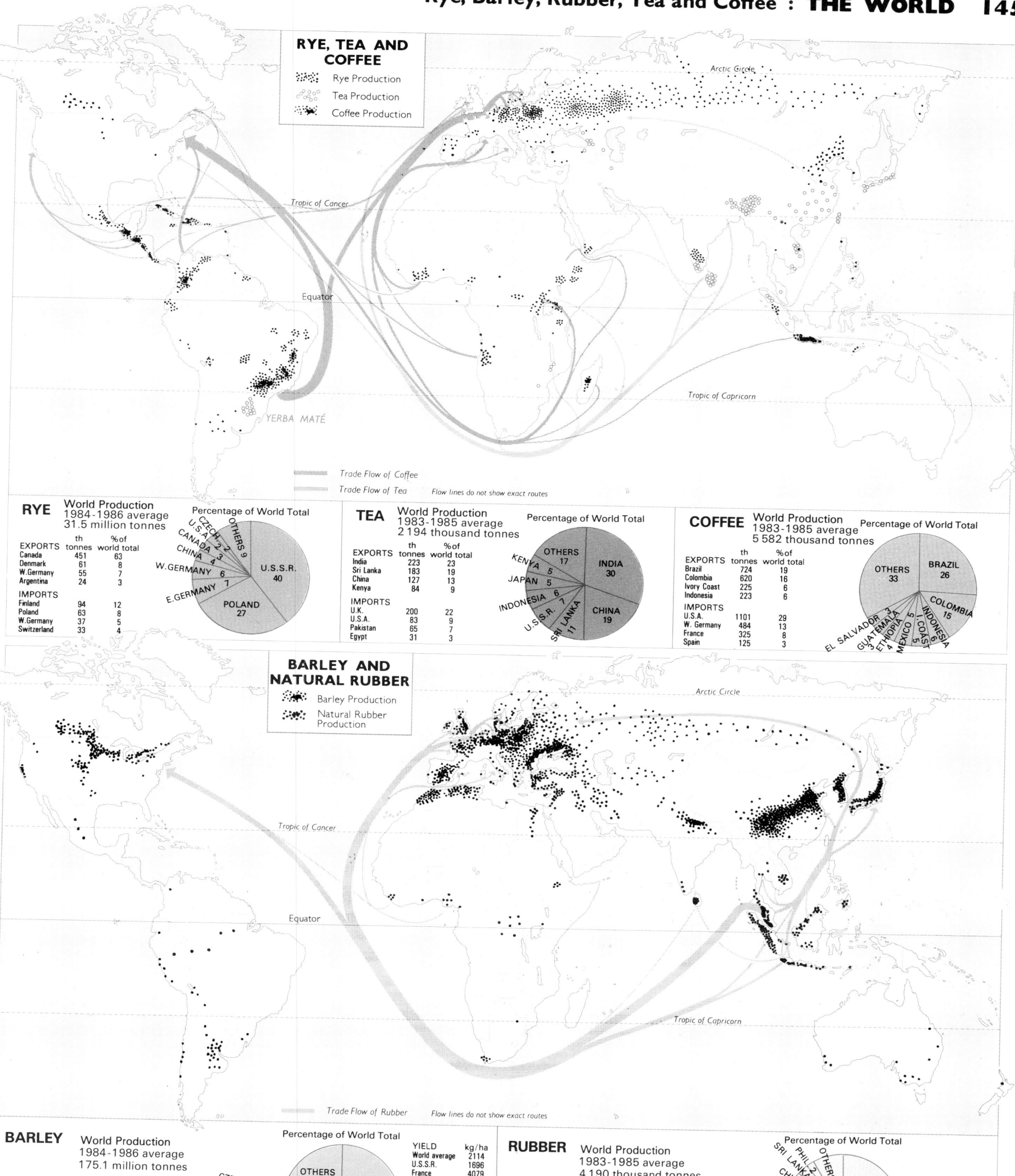

RYE, TEA AND COFFEE
- Rye Production
- Tea Production
- Coffee Production

Arctic Circle

Tropic of Cancer

Equator

Tropic of Capricorn

YERBA MATÉ

Trade Flow of Coffee
Trade Flow of Tea   Flow lines do not show exact routes

RYE World Production
1984-1986 average
31.5 million tonnes

EXPORTS	th tonnes	%of world total
Canada	451	63
Denmark	61	8
W.Germany	55	7
Argentina	24	3
IMPORTS		
Finland	94	12
Poland	63	8
W.Germany	37	5
Switzerland	33	4

Percentage of World Total

U.S.S.R. 40
POLAND 27
E.GERMANY 7
W.GERMANY 6
CHINA 4
CANADA 4
U.S.A. 3
CZECH. 2
OTHERS 9

TEA World Production
1983-1985 average
2 194 thousand tonnes

EXPORTS	th tonnes	%of world total
India	223	23
Sri Lanka	183	19
China	127	13
Kenya	84	9
IMPORTS		
U.K.	200	22
U.S.A.	83	9
Pakistan	65	7
Egypt	31	3

Percentage of World Total

INDIA 30
CHINA 19
SRI LANKA 11
U.S.S.R. 7
INDONESIA 6
JAPAN 5
KENYA 5
OTHERS 17

COFFEE World Production
1983-1985 average
5 582 thousand tonnes

EXPORTS	th tonnes	%of world total
Brazil	724	19
Colombia	620	16
Ivory Coast	225	6
Indonesia	223	6
IMPORTS		
U.S.A.	1101	29
W. Germany	484	13
France	325	8
Spain	125	3

Percentage of World Total

BRAZIL 26
COLOMBIA 15
INDONESIA 6
I. COAST 5
MEXICO 5
ETHIOPIA 5
GUATEMALA 4
EL SALVADOR 3
OTHERS 33

BARLEY AND
NATURAL RUBBER
- Barley Production
- Natural Rubber Production

Arctic Circle

Tropic of Cancer

Equator

Tropic of Capricorn

Trade Flow of Rubber   Flow lines do not show exact routes

BARLEY World Production
1984-1986 average
175.1 million tonnes

EXPORTS	th tonnes	%of world total	IMPORTS	th tonnes	%of world total
Canada	5722	30	Saudi Arabia	3860	21
France	3019	16	Belgium-Lux	1453	8
U.K.	2426	13	Japan	1330	7
Australia	1795	10	Italy	1294	7
			W. Germany	1084	6

Percentage of World Total

U.S.S.R. 29
CANADA 8
U.K. 7
U.S.A. 7
FRANCE 6
W. GERMANY 5
DENMARK 4
SPAIN 4
TURKEY 4
E.GERM. 2
CZECHOSLOVAKIA 2
OTHERS 21

YIELD	kg/ha
World average	2114
U.S.S.R.	1696
France	4079
U.K.	4751
Canada	2380
U.S.A.	2819
W.Germany	4377
Denmark	3289
Spain	1808
E. Germany	4377
Czechoslovakia	4379
Turkey	2036

RUBBER World Production
1983-1985 average
4 190 thousand tonnes

EXPORTS	th tonnes	%of world total	IMPORTS	th tonnes	%of world total
Malaysia	1553	35	U.S.A.	685	20
Indonesia	885	27	Japan	428	12
Thailand	316	10	China	266	7
			U.S.S.R.	216	6
			France	180	5
			W. Germany	179	5

Percentage of World Total

MALAYSIA 40
INDONESIA 26
THAILAND 13
INDIA 4
CHINA 4
SRI LANKA 3
PHIL. 2
OTHERS 8

Maps based on Modified Homolographic Projection

COPYRIGHT GEORGE PHILIP & SON LTD.

1 ha (hectare) = 2.47 acres
1 kg/ha = 0.89 pounds/acres

1 tonne (metric ton) = 0.98 tons = 2204.62 pounds
1 kg (kilogram) = 2.20 pounds

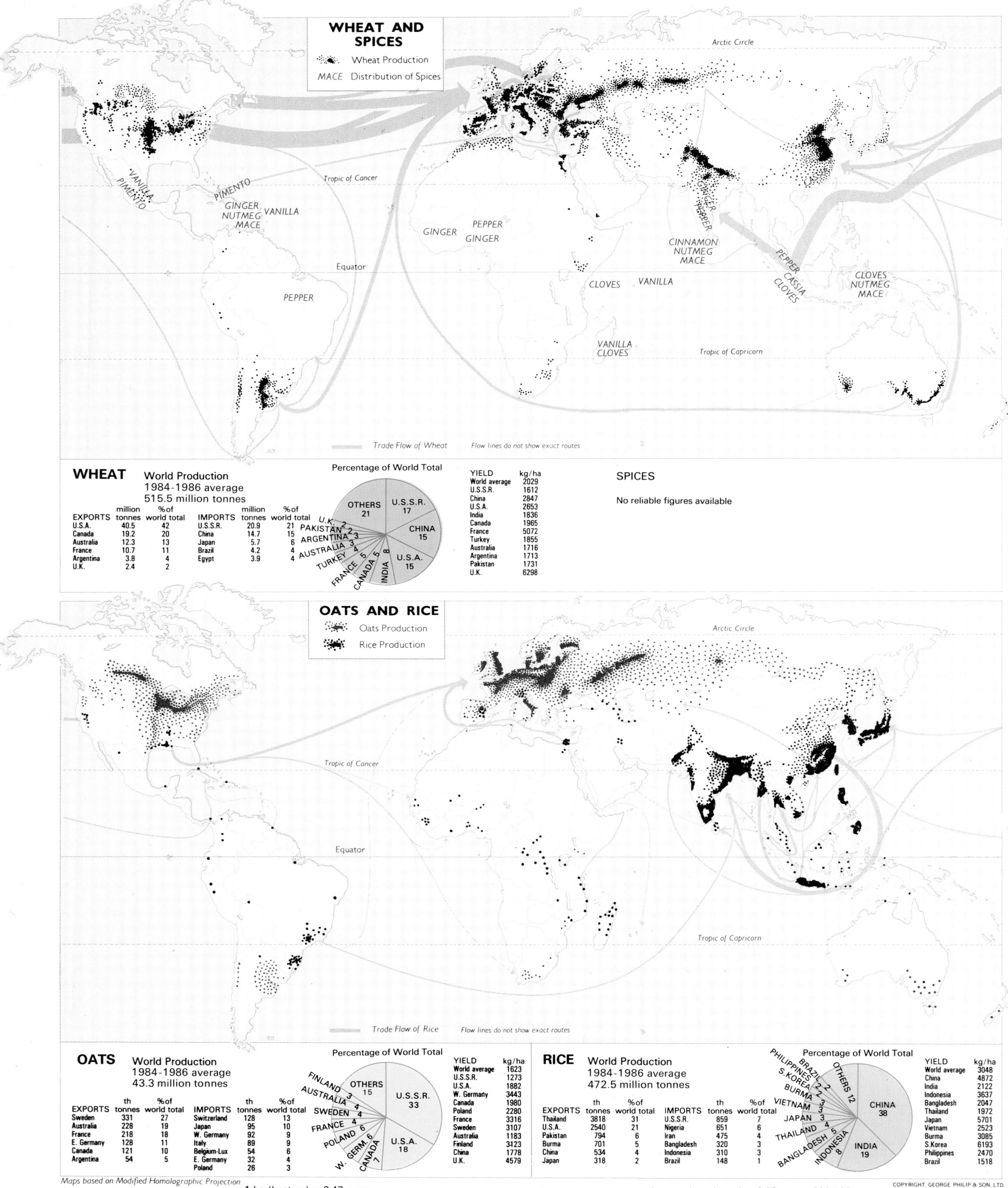

WHEAT AND SPICES

- Wheat Production
- *MACE* Distribution of Spices

VANILLA PIMENTO
PIMENTO
GINGER NUTMEG MACE VANILLA
GINGER PEPPER GINGER
PEPPER
CINNAMON NUTMEG MACE
GINGER PEPPER
PEPPER CASSIA CLOVES
CLOVES NUTMEG MACE
CLOVES VANILLA
VANILLA CLOVES

Arctic Circle
Tropic of Cancer
Equator
Tropic of Capricorn

Trade Flow of Wheat   Flow lines do not show exact routes

WHEAT World Production
1984-1986 average
515.5 million tonnes

EXPORTS	million tonnes	%of world total	IMPORTS	million tonnes	%of world total
U.S.A.	40.5	42	U.S.S.R.	20.9	21
Canada	19.2	20	China	14.7	15
Australia	12.3	13	Japan	5.7	6
France	10.7	11	Brazil	4.2	4
Argentina	3.8	4	Egypt	3.9	4
U.K.	2.4	2			

Percentage of World Total

OTHERS 21 · U.S.S.R. 17 · CHINA 15 · U.S.A. 15 · INDIA 8 · CANADA 5 · FRANCE 5 · TURKEY 4 · AUSTRALIA 4 · ARGENTINA 3 · PAKISTAN 2 · U.K. 2

YIELD	kg/ha
World average	2029
U.S.S.R.	1612
China	2847
U.S.A.	2653
India	1836
Canada	1965
France	5072
Turkey	1855
Australia	1716
Argentina	1713
Pakistan	1731
U.K.	6298

SPICES

No reliable figures available

OATS AND RICE

- Oats Production
- Rice Production

Arctic Circle
Tropic of Cancer
Equator
Tropic of Capricorn

Trade Flow of Rice   Flow lines do not show exact routes

OATS World Production
1984-1986 average
43.3 million tonnes

EXPORTS	th tonnes	%of world total	IMPORTS	th tonnes	%of world total
Sweden	331	27	Switzerland	128	13
Australia	228	19	Japan	95	10
France	218	18	W. Germany	92	9
E. Germany	128	11	Italy	89	9
Canada	121	10	Belgium-Lux	54	6
Argentina	54	5	E. Germany	32	4
			Poland	26	3

Percentage of World Total

FINLAND 3 · AUSTRALIA 3 · OTHERS 15 · U.S.S.R. 33 · SWEDEN 4 · FRANCE 5 · POLAND 6 · W. GERM. 6 · CANADA 7 · U.S.A. 18

YIELD	kg/ha
World average	1623
U.S.S.R.	1273
U.S.A.	1882
W. Germany	3443
Canada	1980
Poland	2280
France	3316
Sweden	3107
Australia	1183
Finland	3123
China	1778
U.K.	4579

RICE World Production
1984-1986 average
472.5 million tonnes

EXPORTS	th tonnes	%of world total	IMPORTS	th tonnes	%of world total
Thailand	3818	31	U.S.S.R.	859	7
U.S.A.	2540	21	Nigeria	651	6
Pakistan	794	6	Iran	475	4
Burma	701	5	Bangladesh	320	3
China	534	4	Indonesia	310	3
Japan	318	2	Brazil	148	1

Percentage of World Total

PHILIPPINES 2 · BRAZIL 2 · S.KOREA 2 · BURMA 3 · OTHERS 12 · VIETNAM 3 · JAPAN 3 · CHINA 38 · THAILAND 4 · BANGLADESH 5 · INDONESIA 8 · INDIA 19

YIELD	kg/ha
World average	3048
China	4872
India	2122
Indonesia	3637
Bangladesh	2047
Thailand	1972
Japan	5701
Vietnam	2523
Burma	3085
S.Korea	6193
Philippines	2470
Brazil	1518

Maps based on Modified Homolographic Projection

1 ha (hectare) = 2.47 acres
1 kg/ha = 0.89 pounds/acres

1 tonne (metric ton) = 0.98 tons = 2204.62 pounds
1 kg (kilogram) = 2.20 pounds

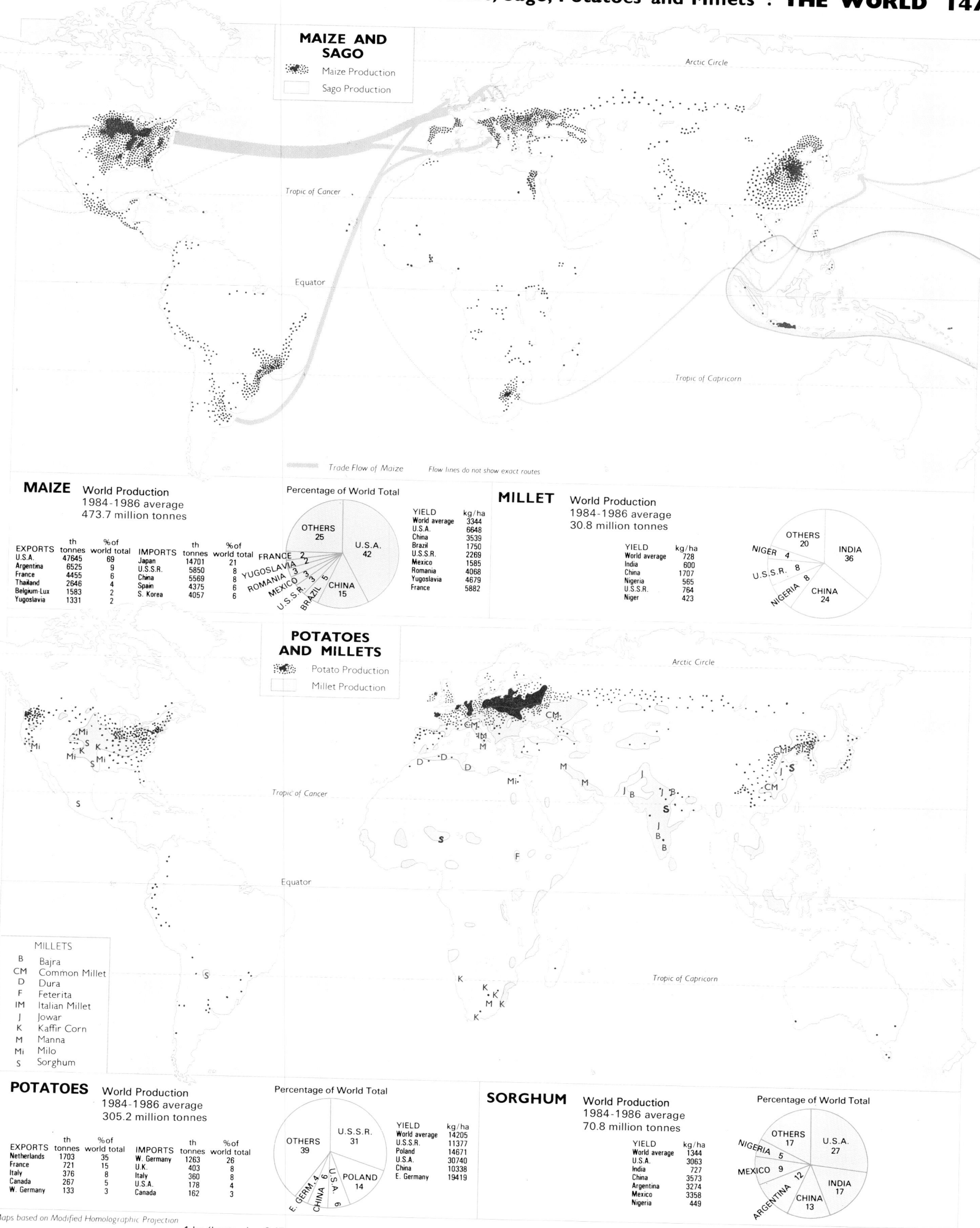

MAIZE AND SAGO

- Maize Production
- Sago Production

POTATOES AND MILLETS

- Potato Production
- Millet Production

Trade Flow of Maize   Flow lines do not show exact routes

MAIZE
World Production
1984-1986 average
473.7 million tonnes

EXPORTS	th tonnes	%of world total	IMPORTS	th tonnes	%of world total
U.S.A.	47645	69	Japan	14701	21
Argentina	6525	9	U.S.S.R.	5850	8
France	4455	6	China	5569	8
Thailand	2646	4	Spain	4375	6
Belgium-Lux	1583	2	S. Korea	4057	6
Yugoslavia	1331	2			

Percentage of World Total

OTHERS 25
U.S.A. 42
FRANCE 2
YUGOSLAVIA 2
ROMANIA 3
MEXICO 3
U.S.S.R. 3
BRAZIL 5
CHINA 15

MILLET
World Production
1984-1986 average
30.8 million tonnes

YIELD	kg/ha
World average	3344
U.S.A.	6648
China	3539
Brazil	1750
U.S.S.R.	2269
Mexico	1585
Romania	4068
Yugoslavia	4679
France	5882

YIELD	kg/ha
World average	728
India	600
China	1707
Nigeria	565
U.S.S.R.	764
Niger	423

Percentage of World Total

OTHERS 20
INDIA 36
NIGER 4
U.S.S.R. 8
NIGERIA 8
CHINA 24

MILLETS
B	Bajra
CM	Common Millet
D	Dura
F	Feterita
IM	Italian Millet
J	Jowar
K	Kaffir Corn
M	Manna
Mi	Milo
S	Sorghum

POTATOES
World Production
1984-1986 average
305.2 million tonnes

EXPORTS	th tonnes	%of world total	IMPORTS	th tonnes	%of world total
Netherlands	1703	35	W. Germany	1263	26
France	721	15	U.K.	403	8
Italy	376	8	Italy	360	8
Canada	267	5	U.S.A.	178	4
W. Germany	133	3	Canada	162	3

YIELD	kg/ha
World average	14205
U.S.S.R.	11377
Poland	14671
U.S.A.	30740
China	10338
E. Germany	19419

Percentage of World Total

OTHERS 39
U.S.S.R. 31
POLAND 14
CHINA 6
E. GERM. 4

SORGHUM
World Production
1984-1986 average
70.8 million tonnes

YIELD	kg/ha
World average	1344
U.S.A.	3063
India	727
China	3573
Argentina	3274
Mexico	3358
Nigeria	449

Percentage of World Total

OTHERS 17
U.S.A. 27
NIGERIA 5
MEXICO 9
ARGENTINA 12
INDIA 17
CHINA 13

Maps based on Modified Homolographic Projection

1 ha (hectare) = 2.47 acres
1 kg/ha = 0.89 pounds/acres

1 tonne (metric ton) = 0.98 tons = 2204.62 pounds
1 kg (kilogram) = 2.20 pounds

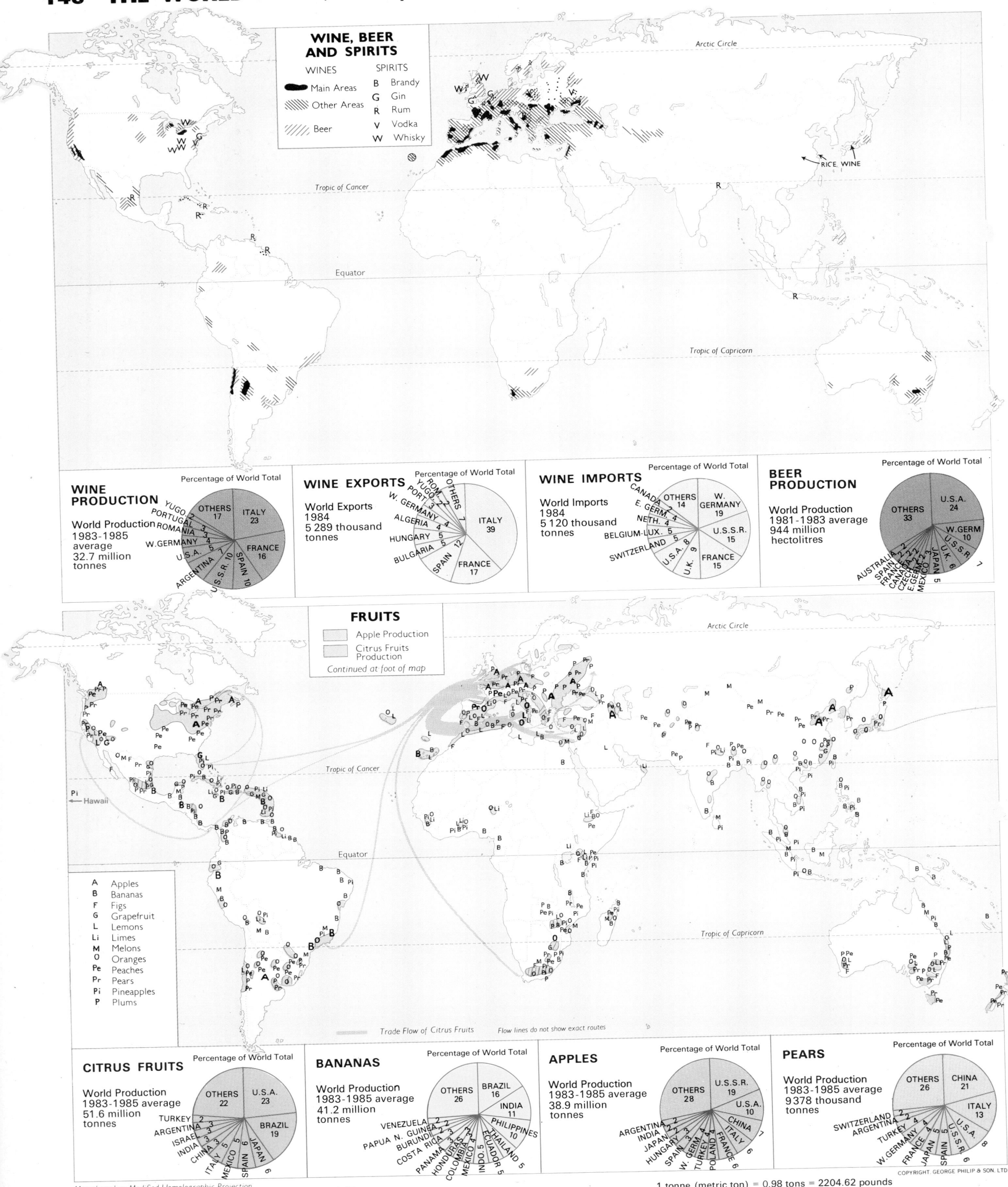

WINE, BEER AND SPIRITS

WINES
- ⬛ Main Areas
- ▨ Other Areas
- ▧ Beer

SPIRITS
- B Brandy
- G Gin
- R Rum
- V Vodka
- W Whisky

Arctic Circle

Tropic of Cancer

Equator

Tropic of Capricorn

RICE WINE

WINE PRODUCTION

World Production 1983-1985 average 32.7 million tonnes

Percentage of World Total

OTHERS 17 · ITALY 23 · FRANCE 16 · SPAIN 10 · U.S.S.R. 10 · ARGENTINA 7 · U.S.A. 4 · W.GERMANY 3 · ROMANIA 3 · PORTUGAL 3 · YUGO. 3

WINE EXPORTS

World Exports 1984 5 289 thousand tonnes

Percentage of World Total

OTHERS 7 · ITALY 39 · FRANCE 17 · SPAIN 12 · BULGARIA 5 · HUNGARY 5 · ALGERIA 4 · W.GERMANY 4 · PORT. 3 · YUGO. 2 · ROM. 2

WINE IMPORTS

World Imports 1984 5 120 thousand tonnes

Percentage of World Total

OTHERS 14 · W. GERMANY 19 · U.S.S.R. 15 · FRANCE 15 · U.K. 9 · U.S.A. 8 · SWITZERLAND · BELGIUM-LUX. 5 · NETH. 4 · E. GERM. 4 · CANADA 2

BEER PRODUCTION

World Production 1981-1983 average 944 million hectolitres

Percentage of World Total

OTHERS 33 · U.S.A. 24 · W.GERM. 10 · U.S.S.R. · JAPAN 5 · U.K. 6 · MEXICO · E.GERM. · CZECH. · CANADA 2 · FRANCE 2 · SPAIN 2 · AUSTRALIA 2

FRUITS

- ▨ Apple Production
- ▨ Citrus Fruits Production

Continued at foot of map

Arctic Circle

Tropic of Cancer

← Hawaii

Equator

Tropic of Capricorn

- A Apples
- B Bananas
- F Figs
- G Grapefruit
- L Lemons
- Li Limes
- M Melons
- O Oranges
- Pe Peaches
- Pr Pears
- Pi Pineapples
- P Plums

Trade Flow of Citrus Fruits   Flow lines do not show exact routes

CITRUS FRUITS

World Production 1983-1985 average 51.6 million tonnes

Percentage of World Total

OTHERS 22 · U.S.A. 23 · BRAZIL 19 · JAPAN 6 · SPAIN 6 · MEXICO 5 · ITALY 5 · CHINA 3 · INDIA 3 · ISRAEL 3 · ARGENTINA 3 · TURKEY 2

BANANAS

World Production 1983-1985 average 41.2 million tonnes

Percentage of World Total

OTHERS 26 · BRAZIL 16 · INDIA 11 · PHILIPPINES 11 · THAILAND 10 · ECUADOR 5 · INDO. 5 · MEXICO 3 · COLOMBIA 3 · HONDURAS · PANAMA · COSTA RICA · BURUNDI · PAPUA N. GUINEA 2 · VENEZUELA 2

APPLES

World Production 1983-1985 average 38.9 million tonnes

Percentage of World Total

OTHERS 28 · U.S.S.R. 19 · U.S.A. 10 · CHINA · ITALY 7 · FRANCE 6 · POLAND · TURKEY 4 · W. GERM. · HUNGARY · SPAIN 3 · JAPAN · INDIA · ARGENTINA 2

PEARS

World Production 1983-1985 average 9378 thousand tonnes

Percentage of World Total

OTHERS 26 · CHINA 21 · ITALY 13 · U.S.A. · U.S.S.R. 8 · SPAIN · JAPAN 5 · FRANCE 4 · W. GERMANY · TURKEY · ARGENTINA 4 · SWITZERLAND 2

COPYRIGHT. GEORGE PHILIP & SON. LTD

Maps based on Modified Homolographic Projection

1 ha (hectare) = 2.47 acres
1 kg/ha = 0.89 pounds/acres

1 tonne (metric ton) = 0.98 tons = 2204.62 pounds
1 kg (kilogram) = 2.20 pounds

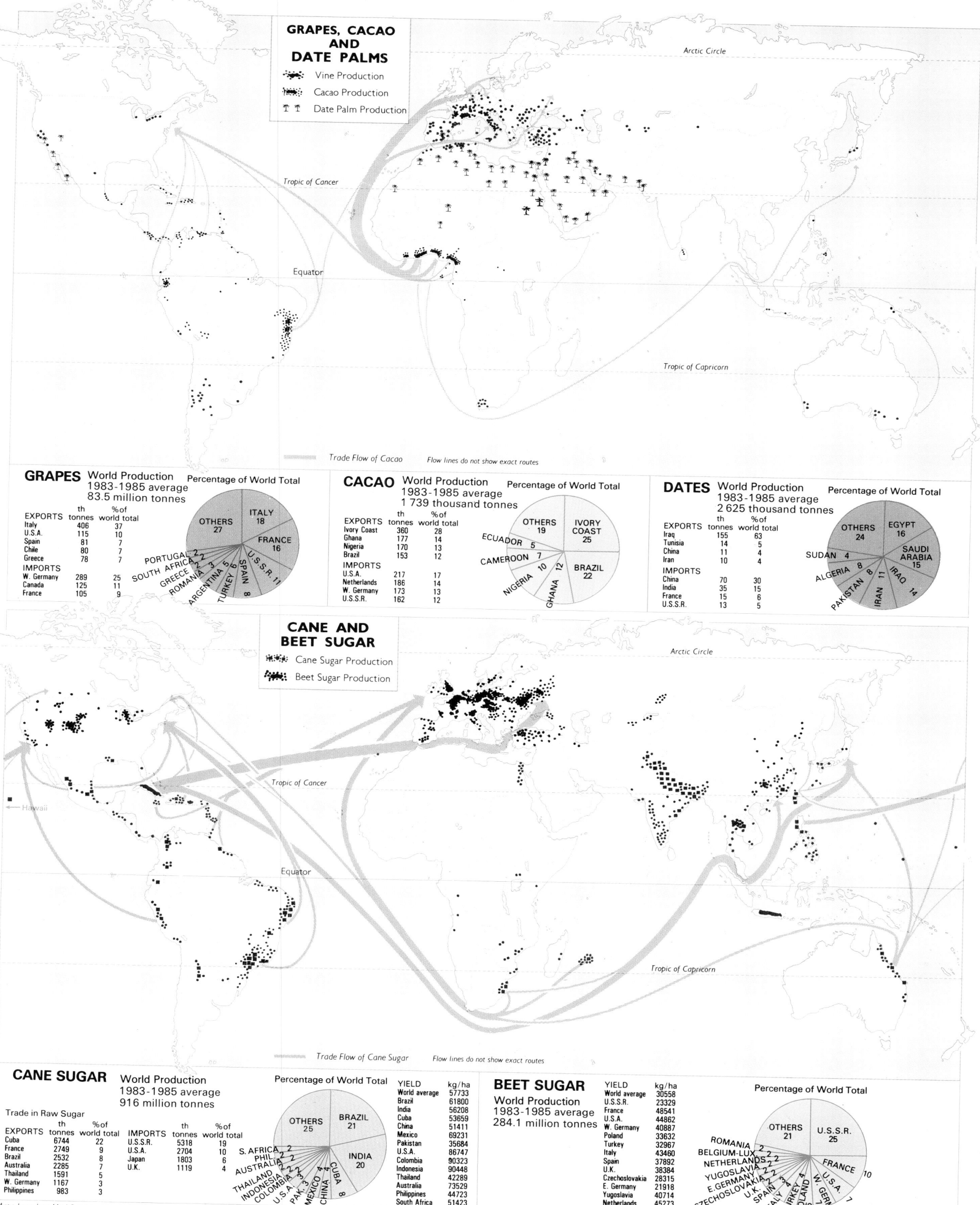

GRAPES, CACAO AND DATE PALMS

- Vine Production
- Cacao Production
- Date Palm Production

Arctic Circle

Tropic of Cancer

Equator

Tropic of Capricorn

Trade Flow of Cacao   Flow lines do not show exact routes

GRAPES World Production
1983-1985 average
83.5 million tonnes

Percentage of World Total

EXPORTS	th tonnes	%of world total
Italy	406	37
U.S.A.	115	10
Spain	81	7
Chile	80	7
Greece	78	7
IMPORTS		
W. Germany	289	25
Canada	125	11
France	105	9

OTHERS 27 / ITALY 18 / FRANCE 16 / U.S.S.R. 11 / SPAIN 8 / TURKEY 5 / ARGENTINA 3 / ROMANIA 3 / GREECE 3 / SOUTH AFRICA 2 / PORTUGAL 2

CACAO World Production
1983-1985 average
1 739 thousand tonnes

Percentage of World Total

EXPORTS	th tonnes	%of world total
Ivory Coast	360	28
Ghana	177	14
Nigeria	170	13
Brazil	153	12
IMPORTS		
U.S.A.	217	17
Netherlands	186	14
W. Germany	173	13
U.S.S.R.	162	12

OTHERS 19 / IVORY COAST 25 / ECUADOR 5 / CAMEROON 7 / BRAZIL 22 / GHANA 12 / NIGERIA 10

DATES World Production
1983-1985 average
2 625 thousand tonnes

Percentage of World Total

EXPORTS	th tonnes	%of world total
Iraq	155	63
Tunisia	14	5
China	11	4
Iran	10	4
IMPORTS		
China	70	30
India	35	15
France	15	6
U.S.S.R.	13	5

OTHERS 24 / EGYPT 16 / SAUDI ARABIA 15 / IRAQ 14 / IRAN 11 / PAKISTAN 8 / ALGERIA 8 / SUDAN 4

CANE AND BEET SUGAR

- Cane Sugar Production
- Beet Sugar Production

Arctic Circle

← Hawaii

Tropic of Cancer

Equator

Tropic of Capricorn

Trade Flow of Cane Sugar   Flow lines do not show exact routes

CANE SUGAR World Production
1983-1985 average
916 million tonnes

Trade in Raw Sugar

EXPORTS	th tonnes	%of world total	IMPORTS	th tonnes	%of world total
Cuba	6744	22	U.S.S.R.	5318	19
France	2749	9	U.S.A.	2704	10
Brazil	2532	8	Japan	1803	6
Australia	2285	7	U.K.	1119	4
Thailand	1591	5			
W. Germany	1167	3			
Philippines	983	3			

Percentage of World Total

OTHERS 25 / BRAZIL 21 / INDIA 20 / CUBA 8 / CHINA 7 / MEXICO 4 / PAK. 3 / U.S.A. 3 / COLOMBIA 2 / INDONESIA 2 / THAILAND 2 / AUSTRALIA 2 / PHIL. 2 / S. AFRICA 2

YIELD	kg/ha
World average	57733
Brazil	61800
India	56208
Cuba	53659
China	51411
Mexico	69231
Pakistan	35684
U.S.A.	86747
Colombia	90323
Indonesia	90448
Thailand	42289
Australia	73529
Philippines	44723
South Africa	51423

BEET SUGAR

World Production
1983-1985 average
284.1 million tonnes

YIELD	kg/ha
World average	30558
U.S.S.R.	23329
France	48541
U.S.A.	44862
W. Germany	40887
Poland	33632
Turkey	32967
Italy	43460
Spain	37892
U.K.	38384
Czechoslovakia	28315
E. Germany	21918
Yugoslavia	40714
Netherlands	45273

Percentage of World Total

OTHERS 21 / U.S.S.R. 25 / FRANCE 10 / U.S.A. 7 / W. GERM. 7 / POLAND 5 / TURKEY 4 / ITALY 4 / SPAIN 3 / U.K. 3 / CZECHOSLOVAKIA 2 / E. GERMANY 2 / YUGOSLAVIA 2 / NETHERLANDS 2 / BELGIUM-LUX. 2 / ROMANIA 2

Maps based on Modified Homolographic Projection

1 ha (hectare) = 2.47 acres
1 kg/ha = 0.89 pounds/acres

1 tonne (metric ton) = 0.98 tons = 2204.62 pounds
1 kg (kilogram) = 2.20 pounds

COPYRIGHT. GEORGE PHILIP & SON. LTD

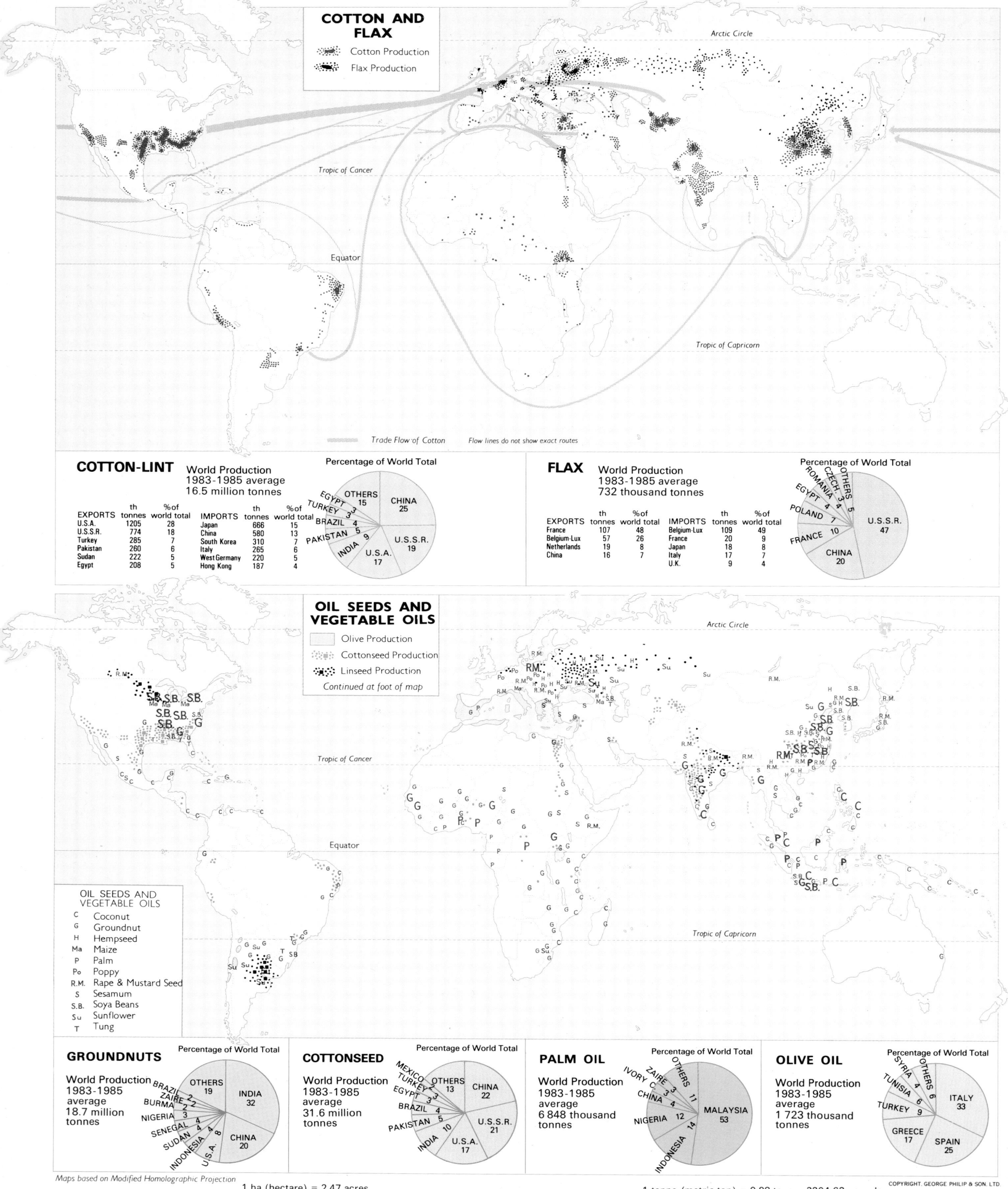

COTTON AND FLAX

Cotton Production
Flax Production

Arctic Circle

Tropic of Cancer

Equator

Tropic of Capricorn

Trade Flow of Cotton   Flow lines do not show exact routes

COTTON-LINT

World Production
1983-1985 average
16.5 million tonnes

Percentage of World Total

EXPORTS	th tonnes	%of world total	IMPORTS	th tonnes	%of world total
U.S.A.	1205	28	Japan	666	15
U.S.S.R.	774	18	China	580	13
Turkey	285	7	South Korea	310	7
Pakistan	260	6	Italy	265	6
Sudan	222	5	West Germany	220	5
Egypt	208	5	Hong Kong	187	4

OTHERS 15
CHINA 25
EGYPT 3
TURKEY 3
BRAZIL 4
PAKISTAN 5
INDIA 9
U.S.A. 17
U.S.S.R. 19

FLAX

World Production
1983-1985 average
732 thousand tonnes

Percentage of World Total

EXPORTS	th tonnes	%of world total	IMPORTS	th tonnes	%of world total
France	107	48	Belgium-Lux	109	49
Belgium-Lux	57	26	France	20	9
Netherlands	19	8	Japan	18	8
China	16	7	Italy	17	7
			U.K.	9	4

OTHERS 5
ROMANIA 4
CZECH. 3
EGYPT 4
POLAND 7
FRANCE 10
U.S.S.R. 47
CHINA 20

OIL SEEDS AND VEGETABLE OILS

Olive Production
Cottonseed Production
Linseed Production
Continued at foot of map

Arctic Circle

Tropic of Cancer

Equator

Tropic of Capricorn

OIL SEEDS AND VEGETABLE OILS

C	Coconut
G	Groundnut
H	Hempseed
Ma	Maize
P	Palm
Po	Poppy
R.M.	Rape & Mustard Seed
S	Sesamum
S.B.	Soya Beans
Su	Sunflower
T	Tung

GROUNDNUTS

World Production
1983-1985
average
18.7 million
tonnes

Percentage of World Total

OTHERS 19
INDIA 32
BRAZIL 2
ZAIRE 2
BURMA
NIGERIA 3
SENEGAL 4
SUDAN 4
INDONESIA 4
U.S.A. 8
CHINA 20

COTTONSEED

World Production
1983-1985
average
31.6 million
tonnes

Percentage of World Total

OTHERS 13
CHINA 22
MEXICO
TURKEY 3
EGYPT 3
BRAZIL 4
PAKISTAN 5
INDIA 10
U.S.A. 17
U.S.S.R. 21

PALM OIL

World Production
1983-1985
average
6 848 thousand
tonnes

Percentage of World Total

OTHERS 11
ZAIRE 3
IVORY C. 3
CHINA 4
MALAYSIA 53
NIGERIA 12
INDONESIA 14

OLIVE OIL

World Production
1983-1985
average
1 723 thousand
tonnes

Percentage of World Total

OTHERS 6
SYRIA 4
TUNISIA
TURKEY 9
ITALY 33
GREECE 17
SPAIN 25

Maps based on Modified Homolographic Projection

COPYRIGHT. GEORGE PHILIP & SON. LTD.

1 ha (hectare) = 2.47 acres
1 kg/ha = 0.89 pounds/acres

1 tonne (metric ton) = 0.98 tons = 2204.62 pounds
1 kg (kilogram) = 2.20 pounds

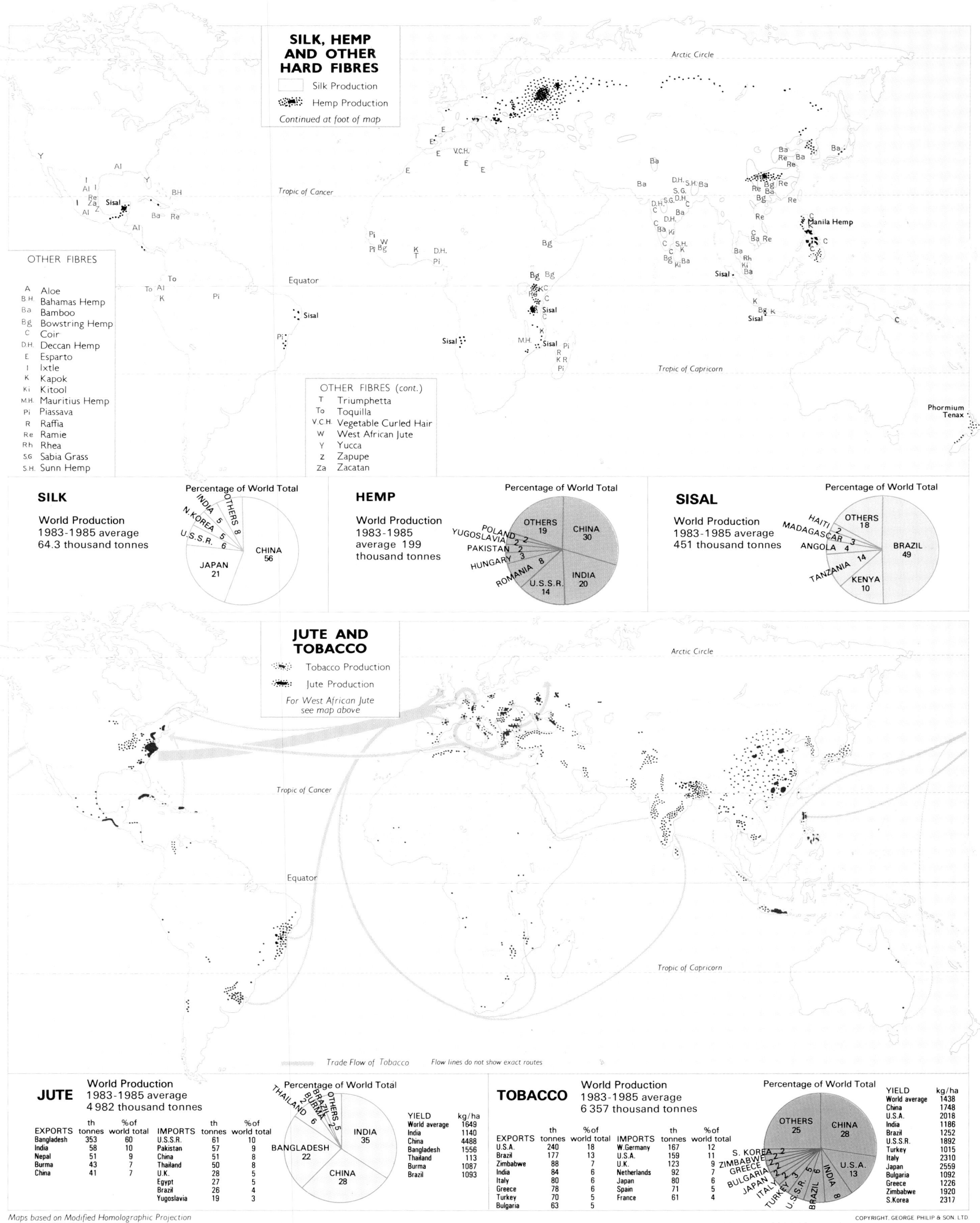

SILK, HEMP AND OTHER HARD FIBRES

☐ Silk Production

▓ Hemp Production

Continued at foot of map

OTHER FIBRES

A	Aloe
B.H.	Bahamas Hemp
Ba.	Bamboo
Bg	Bowstring Hemp
C	Coir
D.H.	Deccan Hemp
E	Esparto
I	Ixtle
K	Kapok
Ki	Kitool
M.H.	Mauritius Hemp
Pi	Piassava
R	Raffia
Re	Ramie
Rh	Rhea
S.G.	Sabia Grass
S.H.	Sunn Hemp

OTHER FIBRES (cont.)

T	Triumphetta
To	Toquilla
V.C.H.	Vegetable Curled Hair
W	West African Jute
Y	Yucca
Z	Zapupe
Za	Zacatan

SILK

World Production
1983-1985 average
64.3 thousand tonnes

Percentage of World Total

CHINA 56
JAPAN 21
U.S.S.R. 6
N.KOREA 5
INDIA 5
OTHERS 8

HEMP

World Production
1983-1985 average 199 thousand tonnes

Percentage of World Total

CHINA 30
INDIA 20
OTHERS 19
U.S.S.R. 14
ROMANIA 8
HUNGARY 3
PAKISTAN 2
YUGOSLAVIA 2
POLAND 2

SISAL

World Production
1983-1985 average
451 thousand tonnes

Percentage of World Total

BRAZIL 49
OTHERS 18
TANZANIA 14
KENYA 10
ANGOLA 4
MADAGASCAR 3
HAITI 2

JUTE AND TOBACCO

▓ Tobacco Production

▓ Jute Production

For West African Jute see map above

Trade Flow of Tobacco   Flow lines do not show exact routes

JUTE

World Production
1983-1985 average
4 982 thousand tonnes

EXPORTS	th tonnes	%of world total	IMPORTS	th tonnes	%of world total
Bangladesh	353	60	U.S.S.R.	61	10
India	58	10	Pakistan	57	9
Nepal	51	9	China	51	8
Burma	43	7	Thailand	50	8
China	41	7	U.K.	28	5
			Egypt	27	5
			Brazil	26	4
			Yugoslavia	19	3

Percentage of World Total

INDIA 35
CHINA 28
BANGLADESH 22
THAILAND 6
BURMA 2.5
BRAZIL 2
OTHERS 2.5

YIELD	kg/ha
World average	1649
India	1140
China	4488
Bangladesh	1556
Thailand	113
Burma	1087
Brazil	1093

TOBACCO

World Production
1983-1985 average
6 357 thousand tonnes

EXPORTS	th tonnes	%of world total	IMPORTS	th tonnes	%of world total
U.S.A.	240	18	W.Germany	167	12
Brazil	177	13	U.S.A.	159	11
Zimbabwe	88	7	U.K.	123	9
India	84	6	Netherlands	92	7
Italy	80	6	Japan	80	6
Greece	78	6	Spain	71	5
Turkey	70	5	France	61	4
Bulgaria	63	5			

Percentage of World Total

CHINA 28
OTHERS 25
U.S.A. 13
INDIA 8
BRAZIL 6
U.S.S.R. 4
TURKEY 3
ITALY 2
JAPAN 2
BULGARIA 2
GREECE 2
ZIMBABWE 2
S. KOREA 2

YIELD	kg/ha
World average	1438
China	1748
India	1186
U.S.S.R.	1892
Turkey	1015
Brazil	1252
U.S.A.	2018
Italy	2310
Japan	2559
Bulgaria	1092
Greece	1226
Zimbabwe	1920
S.Korea	2317

Maps based on Modified Homolographic Projection

1 ha (hectare) = 2.47 acres
1 kg/ha = 0.89 pounds/acres

1 tonne (metric ton) = 0.98 tons = 2204.62 pounds
1 kg (kilogram) = 2.20 pounds

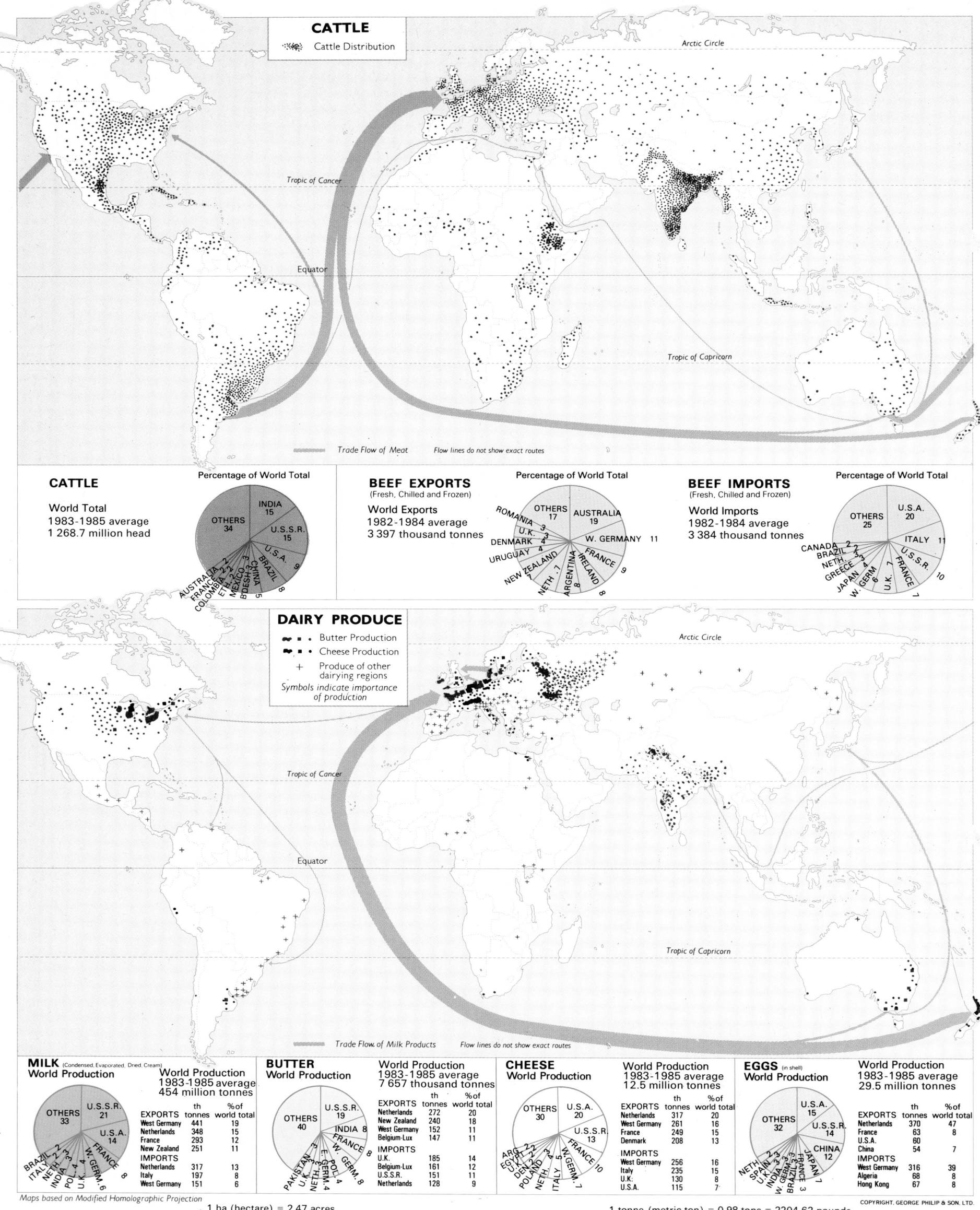

CATTLE
Cattle Distribution

Arctic Circle

Tropic of Cancer

Equator

Tropic of Capricorn

Trade Flow of Meat   Flow lines do not show exact routes

CATTLE
World Total
1983-1985 average
1 268.7 million head

Percentage of World Total

INDIA 15
OTHERS 34
U.S.S.R. 15
U.S.A. 9
BRAZIL 8
CHINA 5
BDESH 3
MEXICO 3
ETH. 2
FRANCE 2
COLOMBIA 2
AUSTRALIA 2

BEEF EXPORTS
(Fresh, Chilled and Frozen)
World Exports
1982-1984 average
3 397 thousand tonnes

Percentage of World Total

AUSTRALIA 19
OTHERS 17
ROMANIA 3
U.K. 3
DENMARK 4
URUGUAY 4
NEW ZEALAND 7
ARGENTINA 8
IRELAND 9
FRANCE 7
W. GERMANY 11
NETH. 7

BEEF IMPORTS
(Fresh, Chilled and Frozen)
World Imports
1982-1984 average
3 384 thousand tonnes

Percentage of World Total

U.S.A. 20
OTHERS 25
ITALY 11
U.S.S.R. 10
FRANCE 7
U.K. 7
W. GERM. 4
JAPAN 4
GREECE 3
NETH. 3
BRAZIL 2
CANADA 2

DAIRY PRODUCE
Butter Production
Cheese Production
Produce of other dairying regions
Symbols indicate importance of production

Arctic Circle

Tropic of Cancer

Equator

Tropic of Capricorn

Trade Flow of Milk Products   Flow lines do not show exact routes

Maps based on Modified Homolographic Projection

MILK (Condensed, Evaporated, Dried, Cream)
World Production
1983-1985 average
454 million tonnes

U.S.S.R. 21
OTHERS 33
U.S.A. 14
FRANCE 8
W. GERM. 6
U.K. 4
POL. 3
INDIA 3
NETH. 3
ITALY 2
BRAZIL 2

EXPORTS	th tonnes	%of world total
West Germany	441	19
Netherlands	348	15
France	293	12
New Zealand	251	11
IMPORTS		
Netherlands	317	13
Italy	197	8
West Germany	151	6

BUTTER
World Production
1983-1985 average
7 657 thousand tonnes

U.S.S.R. 19
OTHERS 40
INDIA 8
FRANCE 8
W. GERM. 8
POL. 4
E. GERM. 4
NETH. 3
PAKISTAN 3

EXPORTS	th tonnes	%of world total
Netherlands	272	20
New Zealand	240	18
West Germany	152	11
Belgium-Lux	147	11
IMPORTS		
U.K.	185	14
Belgium-Lux	161	12
U.S.S.R.	151	11
Netherlands	128	9

CHEESE
World Production
1983-1985 average
12.5 million tonnes

U.S.A. 20
OTHERS 30
U.S.S.R. 13
FRANCE 10
W. GERM. 7
ITALY 7
NETH. 5
DEN. 4
POLAND 3
U.K. 2
EGYPT 2
ARG. 2

EXPORTS	th tonnes	%of world total
Netherlands	317	20
West Germany	261	16
France	249	15
Denmark	208	13
IMPORTS		
West Germany	256	16
Italy	235	15
U.K.	130	8
U.S.A.	115	7

EGGS (in shell)
World Production
1983-1985 average
29.5 million tonnes

U.S.A. 15
OTHERS 32
U.S.S.R. 14
CHINA 12
JAPAN 7
FRANCE 3
BRAZIL 3
INDIA 3
U.K. 3
SPAIN 3
NETH. 2

EXPORTS	th tonnes	%of world total
Netherlands	370	47
France	63	8
U.S.A.	60	
China	54	7
IMPORTS		
West Germany	316	39
Algeria	68	8
Hong Kong	67	8

1 ha (hectare) = 2.47 acres
1 kg/ha = 0.89 pounds/acres

1 tonne (metric ton) = 0.98 tons = 2204.62 pounds
1 kg (kilogram) = 2.20 pounds

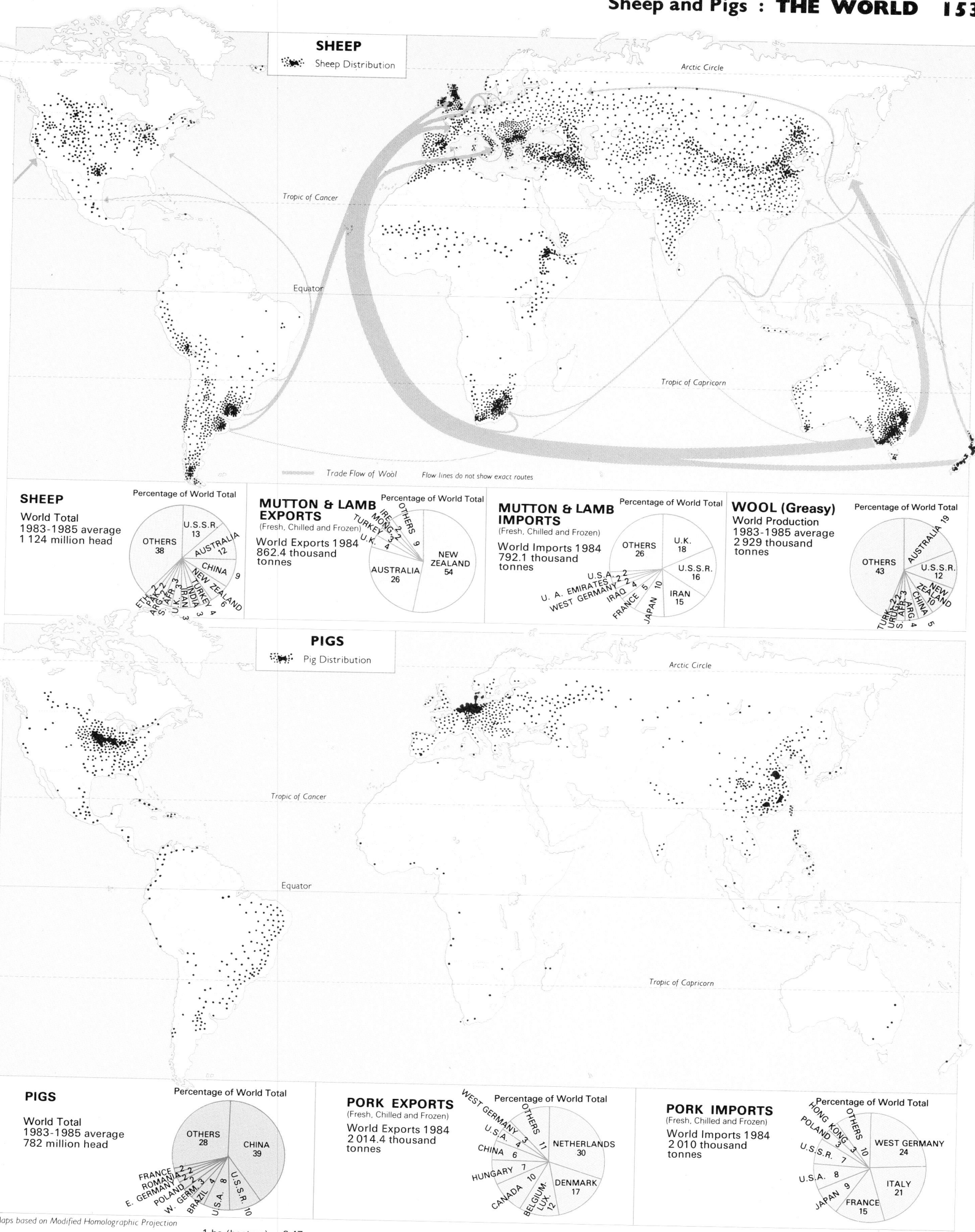

SHEEP

Sheep Distribution

SHEEP

World Total
1983-1985 average
1 124 million head

Percentage of World Total

U.S.S.R. 13
OTHERS 38
AUSTRALIA 12
CHINA 9
NEW ZEALAND
ETH. 3
PAK. 2
ARG. 3
S. AFR. 3
U.K. 3
INDIA 3
IRAN 6
TURKEY 4

MUTTON & LAMB EXPORTS
(Fresh, Chilled and Frozen)

World Exports 1984
862.4 thousand
tonnes

Percentage of World Total

OTHERS 9
IRE. 2
MONG. 3
TURKEY 2
U.K. 4
NEW ZEALAND 54
AUSTRALIA 26

MUTTON & LAMB IMPORTS
(Fresh, Chilled and Frozen)

World Imports 1984
792.1 thousand
tonnes

Percentage of World Total

OTHERS 26
U.K. 18
U.S.S.R. 16
U.S.A. 2
U. A. EMIRATES 2
WEST GERMANY 4
IRAQ 2
FRANCE 5
JAPAN 10
IRAN 15

WOOL (Greasy)

World Production
1983-1985 average
2 929 thousand
tonnes

Percentage of World Total

OTHERS 43
AUSTRALIA 19
U.S.S.R. 12
NEW ZEALAND 10
CHINA 5
ARG. 4
S. AFR. 3
URUG. 2
TURK. 2

PIGS

Pig Distribution

PIGS

World Total
1983-1985 average
782 million head

Percentage of World Total

OTHERS 28
CHINA 39
U.S.S.R. 10
U.S.A. 8
BRAZIL 4
W. GERM. 3
POLAND 2
E. GERMANY 2
ROMANIA 2
FRANCE 2

PORK EXPORTS
(Fresh, Chilled and Frozen)

World Exports 1984
2 014.4 thousand
tonnes

Percentage of World Total

WEST GERMANY 3
OTHERS 11
U.S.A. 4
NETHERLANDS 30
CHINA 6
HUNGARY 7
CANADA 10
BELGIUM-LUX. 12
DENMARK 17

PORK IMPORTS
(Fresh, Chilled and Frozen)

World Imports 1984
2 010 thousand
tonnes

Percentage of World Total

HONG KONG 3
OTHERS 10
POLAND 3
WEST GERMANY 24
U.S.S.R. 7
U.S.A. 8
JAPAN 9
FRANCE 15
ITALY 21

Trade Flow of Wool   Flow lines do not show exact routes

Maps based on Modified Homolographic Projection

1 ha (hectare) = 2.47 acres
1 kg/ha = 0.89 pounds/acres

1 tonne (metric ton) = 0.98 tons = 2204.62 pounds
1 kg (kilogram) = 2.20 pounds

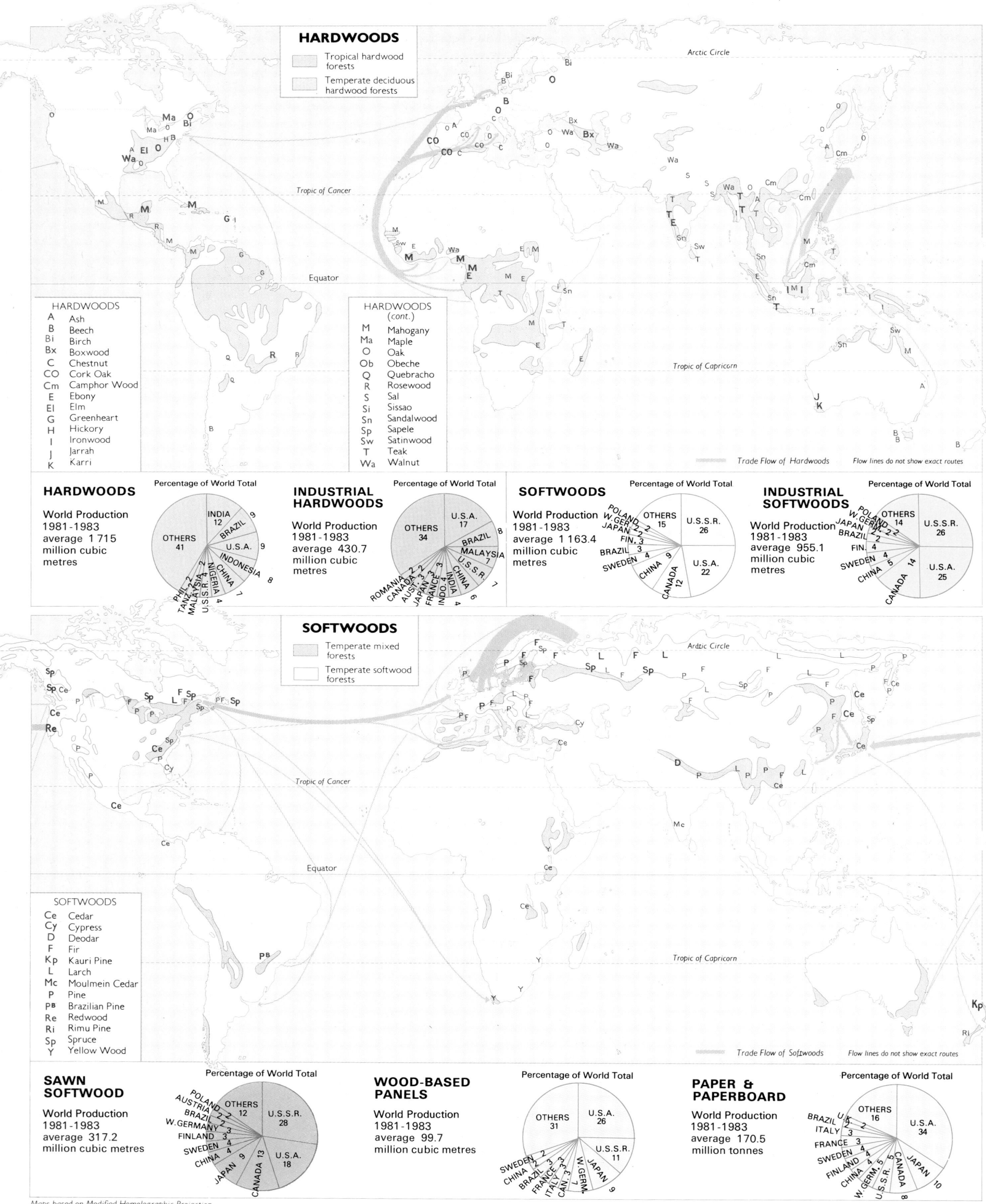

HARDWOODS

- Tropical hardwood forests
- Temperate deciduous hardwood forests

Arctic Circle

Tropic of Cancer

Equator

Tropic of Capricorn

HARDWOODS	
A	Ash
B	Beech
Bi	Birch
Bx	Boxwood
C	Chestnut
CO	Cork Oak
Cm	Camphor Wood
E	Ebony
El	Elm
G	Greenheart
H	Hickory
I	Ironwood
J	Jarrah
K	Karri

HARDWOODS (cont.)	
M	Mahogany
Ma	Maple
O	Oak
Ob	Obeche
Q	Quebracho
R	Rosewood
S	Sal
Si	Sissao
Sn	Sandalwood
Sp	Sapele
Sw	Satinwood
T	Teak
Wa	Walnut

Trade Flow of Hardwoods · Flow lines do not show exact routes

HARDWOODS
World Production 1981-1983 average 1 715 million cubic metres

Percentage of World Total
INDIA 12, BRAZIL, U.S.A. 9, INDONESIA, CHINA 7, NIGERIA 4, U.S.S.R. 4, MALAYSIA 2, TANZ. 2, PHIL. 2, OTHERS 41, INDIA 9, 8

INDUSTRIAL HARDWOODS
World Production 1981-1983 average 430.7 million cubic metres

Percentage of World Total
U.S.A. 17, BRAZIL, MALAYSIA 7, U.S.S.R. 7, INDIA 6, CHINA, INDO. 4, FRANCE 3, JAPAN 3, AUST. 3, CANADA 2, ROMANIA 2, OTHERS 34

SOFTWOODS
World Production 1981-1983 average 1 163.4 million cubic metres

Percentage of World Total
U.S.S.R. 26, U.S.A. 22, CANADA 12, CHINA 9, SWEDEN, BRAZIL 3, FIN. 3, JAPAN, W. GER. 2, POLAND 2, OTHERS 15

INDUSTRIAL SOFTWOODS
World Production 1981-1983 average 955.1 million cubic metres

Percentage of World Total
U.S.S.R. 26, U.S.A. 25, CANADA 14, CHINA 14, SWEDEN 5, FIN. 4, BRAZIL, JAPAN, W. GERM., POLAND 2, OTHERS 14

SOFTWOODS

- Temperate mixed forests
- Temperate softwood forests

Arctic Circle

Tropic of Cancer

Equator

Tropic of Capricorn

SOFTWOODS	
Ce	Cedar
Cy	Cypress
D	Deodar
F	Fir
Kp	Kauri Pine
L	Larch
Mc	Moulmein Cedar
P	Pine
PB	Brazilian Pine
Re	Redwood
Ri	Rimu Pine
Sp	Spruce
Y	Yellow Wood

Trade Flow of Softwoods · Flow lines do not show exact routes

SAWN SOFTWOOD
World Production 1981-1983 average 317.2 million cubic metres

Percentage of World Total
U.S.S.R. 28, U.S.A. 18, CANADA 13, JAPAN 9, CHINA 4, SWEDEN 4, FINLAND 3, W. GERMANY, BRAZIL, AUSTRIA 2, POLAND 2, OTHERS 12

WOOD-BASED PANELS
World Production 1981-1983 average 99.7 million cubic metres

Percentage of World Total
U.S.A. 26, U.S.S.R. 11, JAPAN 9, W. GERM. 7, CAN., ITALY 3, FRANCE 3, BRAZIL 3, CHINA, SWEDEN 2, OTHERS 31

PAPER & PAPERBOARD
World Production 1981-1983 average 170.5 million tonnes

Percentage of World Total
U.S.A. 34, JAPAN 10, CANADA 8, U.S.S.R. 5, W. GERM. 5, CHINA 4, FINLAND 4, SWEDEN 3, FRANCE 3, ITALY 3, BRAZIL 2, U.S., OTHERS 16

Maps based on Modified Homolographic Projection

1 ha (hectare) = 2.47 acres
1 kg/ha = 0.89 pounds/acres

1 tonne (metric ton) = 0.98 tons = 2204.62 pounds
1 kg (kilogram) = 2.20 pounds

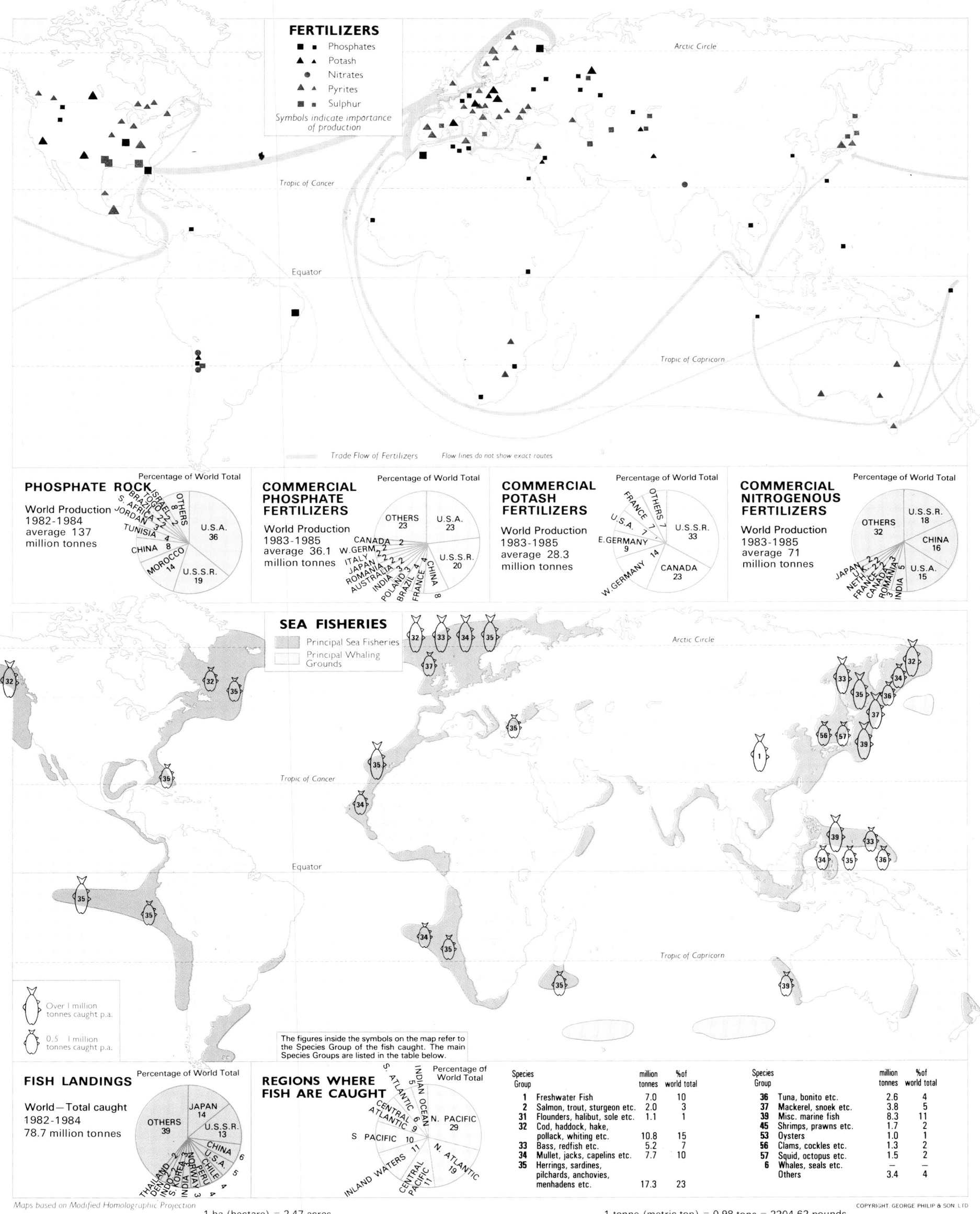

FERTILIZERS

- ■ Phosphates
- ▲ Potash
- ● Nitrates
- ▲ Pyrites
- ■ Sulphur

Symbols indicate importance of production

―――― *Trade Flow of Fertilizers*   *Flow lines do not show exact routes.*

PHOSPHATE ROCK

World Production
1982-1984
average 137
million tonnes

Percentage of World Total

OTHERS
U.S.A. 36
U.S.S.R. 19
MOROCCO 14
CHINA 8
TUNISIA 4
JORDAN 3
S.AFRICA 2
BRAZIL 2
ISRAEL 2

COMMERCIAL PHOSPHATE FERTILIZERS

World Production
1983-1985
average 36.1
million tonnes

Percentage of World Total

OTHERS 23
U.S.A. 23
U.S.S.R. 20
CHINA 8
FRANCE 4
BRAZIL 3
POLAND 3
INDIA 3
AUSTRALIA 2
ROMANIA 2
JAPAN 2
ITALY 2
W.GERM 2
CANADA 2

COMMERCIAL POTASH FERTILIZERS

World Production
1983-1985
average 28.3
million tonnes

Percentage of World Total

OTHERS 7
U.S.S.R. 33
CANADA 23
W.GERMANY 14
E.GERMANY 9
U.S.A. 7
FRANCE 7

COMMERCIAL NITROGENOUS FERTILIZERS

World Production
1983-1985
average 71
million tonnes

Percentage of World Total

OTHERS 32
U.S.S.R. 18
CHINA 16
U.S.A. 15
INDIA 5
ROMANIA 3
CANADA 3
FRANCE 2
NETH. 2
U.K. 2
JAPAN 2

SEA FISHERIES

▨ Principal Sea Fisheries
▢ Principal Whaling Grounds

Over 1 million tonnes caught p.a.

0.5 - 1 million tonnes caught p.a.

The figures inside the symbols on the map refer to the Species Group of the fish caught. The main Species Groups are listed in the table below.

FISH LANDINGS

World—Total caught
1982-1984
78.7 million tonnes

Percentage of World Total

JAPAN 14
U.S.S.R. 13
CHINA 6
CHILE 5
U.S.A. 5
PERU 4
NORWAY 3
INDIA 3
S.KOREA 3
INDONESIA 2
DEN. 2
THAILAND 2
OTHERS 39

REGIONS WHERE FISH ARE CAUGHT

Percentage of World Total

N. PACIFIC 29
N. ATLANTIC 19
CENTRAL PACIFIC 11
INLAND WATERS 11
S PACIFIC 10
CENTRAL ATLANTIC 9
INDIAN OCEAN 6
S. ATLANTIC 5

Species Group		million tonnes	%of world total
1	Freshwater Fish	7.0	10
2	Salmon, trout, sturgeon etc.	2.0	3
31	Flounders, halibut, sole etc.	1.1	1
32	Cod, haddock, hake, pollack, whiting etc.	10.8	15
33	Bass, redfish etc.	5.2	7
34	Mullet, jacks, capelins etc.	7.7	10
35	Herrings, sardines, pilchards, anchovies, menhadens etc.	17.3	23

Species Group		million tonnes	%of world total
36	Tuna, bonito etc.	2.6	4
37	Mackerel, snoek etc.	3.8	5
39	Misc. marine fish	8.3	11
45	Shrimps, prawns etc.	1.7	2
53	Oysters	1.0	1
56	Clams, cockles etc.	1.3	2
57	Squid, octopus etc.	1.5	2
6	Whales, seals etc.	—	—
	Others	3.4	4

Maps based on Modified Homolographic Projection

1 ha (hectare) = 2.47 acres
1 kg/ha = 0.89 pounds/acres

1 tonne (metric ton) = 0.98 tons = 2204.62 pounds
1 kg (kilogram) = 2.20 pounds

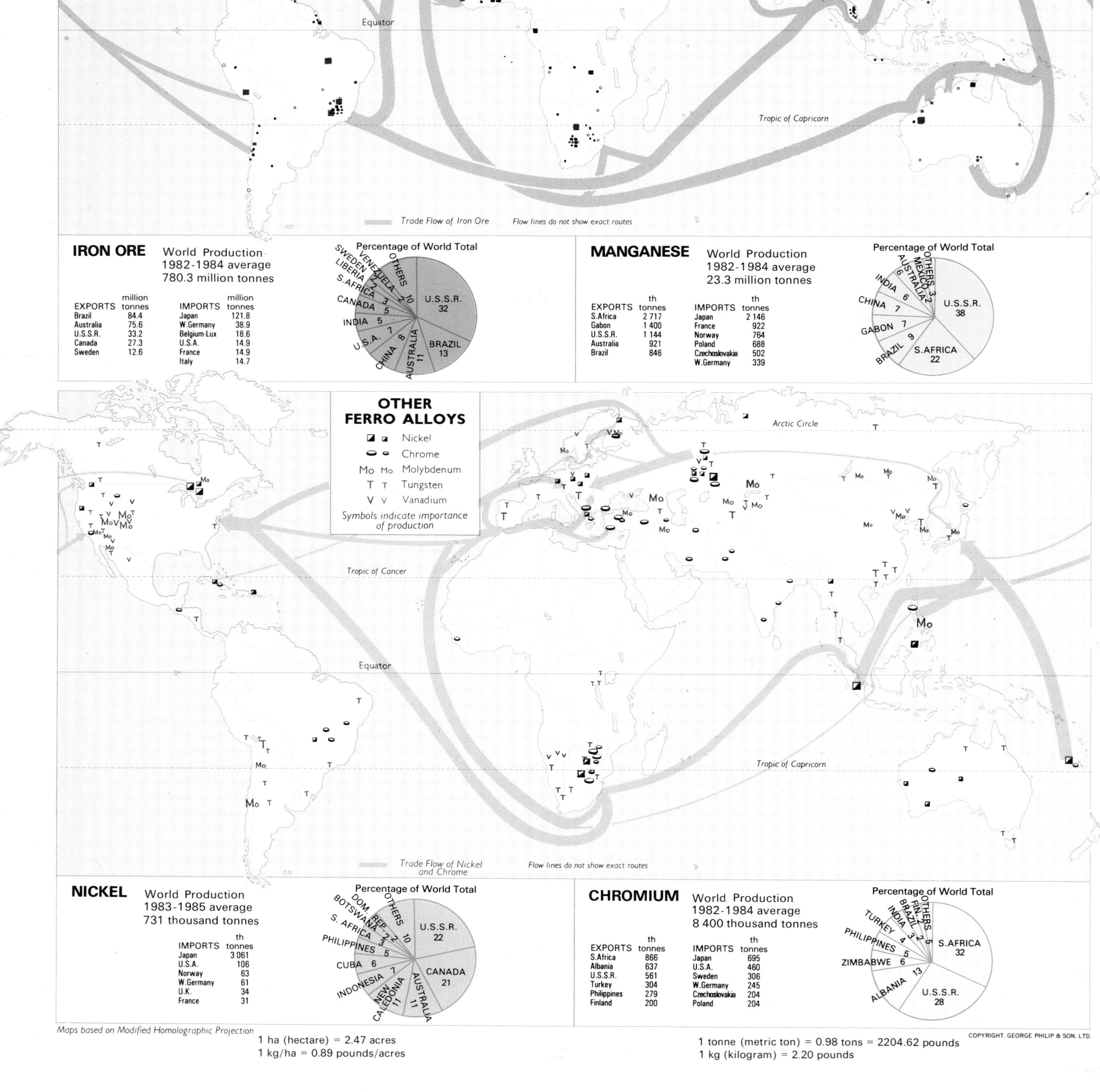

IRON ORE MANGANESE

- Iron Ore
- Manganese

Symbols indicate importance of production

Trade Flow of Iron Ore   *Flow lines do not show exact routes*

IRON ORE

World Production
1982-1984 average
780.3 million tonnes

EXPORTS	million tonnes	IMPORTS	million tonnes
Brazil	84.4	Japan	121.8
Australia	75.6	W.Germany	38.9
U.S.S.R.	33.2	Belgium-Lux	18.6
Canada	27.3	U.S.A.	14.9
Sweden	12.6	France	14.9
		Italy	14.7

Percentage of World Total

U.S.S.R. 32
BRAZIL 13
AUSTRALIA 11
CHINA 8
U.S.A. 7
INDIA 5
CANADA 4
S.AFRICA 3
LIBERIA 2
SWEDEN 2
VENEZUELA 2
OTHERS 10

MANGANESE

World Production
1982-1984 average
23.3 million tonnes

EXPORTS	th tonnes	IMPORTS	th tonnes
S.Africa	2 717	Japan	2 146
Gabon	1 400	France	922
U.S.S.R.	1 144	Norway	764
Australia	921	Poland	688
Brazil	846	Czechoslovakia	502
		W.Germany	339

Percentage of World Total

U.S.S.R. 38
S.AFRICA 22
BRAZIL 9
GABON 7
CHINA 7
INDIA 6
AUSTRALIA 3
MEXICO 2
OTHERS 3

OTHER FERRO ALLOYS

- Nickel
- Chrome
- Mo   Molybdenum
- T   Tungsten
- V   Vanadium

Symbols indicate importance of production

Trade Flow of Nickel and Chrome   *Flow lines do not show exact routes*

NICKEL

World Production
1983-1985 average
731 thousand tonnes

IMPORTS	th tonnes
Japan	3 061
U.S.A.	106
Norway	63
W.Germany	61
U.K.	34
France	31

Percentage of World Total

U.S.S.R. 22
CANADA 21
AUSTRALIA 11
NEW CALEDONIA 7
INDONESIA 7
CUBA 6
PHILIPPINES 5
S. AFRICA 5
BOTSWANA 2
DOM. REP. 2
OTHERS 10

CHROMIUM

World Production
1982-1984 average
8 400 thousand tonnes

EXPORTS	th tonnes	IMPORTS	th tonnes
S.Africa	866	Japan	695
Albania	637	U.S.A.	460
U.S.S.R.	561	Sweden	306
Turkey	304	W.Germany	245
Philippines	279	Czechoslovakia	204
Finland	200	Poland	204

Percentage of World Total

S.AFRICA 32
U.S.S.R. 28
ALBANIA 13
ZIMBABWE 6
PHILIPPINES 5
TURKEY 4
INDIA 3
BRAZIL 2
FIN. 2
OTHERS 5

Maps based on Modified Homolographic Projection

1 ha (hectare) = 2.47 acres
1 kg/ha = 0.89 pounds/acres

1 tonne (metric ton) = 0.98 tons = 2204.62 pounds
1 kg (kilogram) = 2.20 pounds

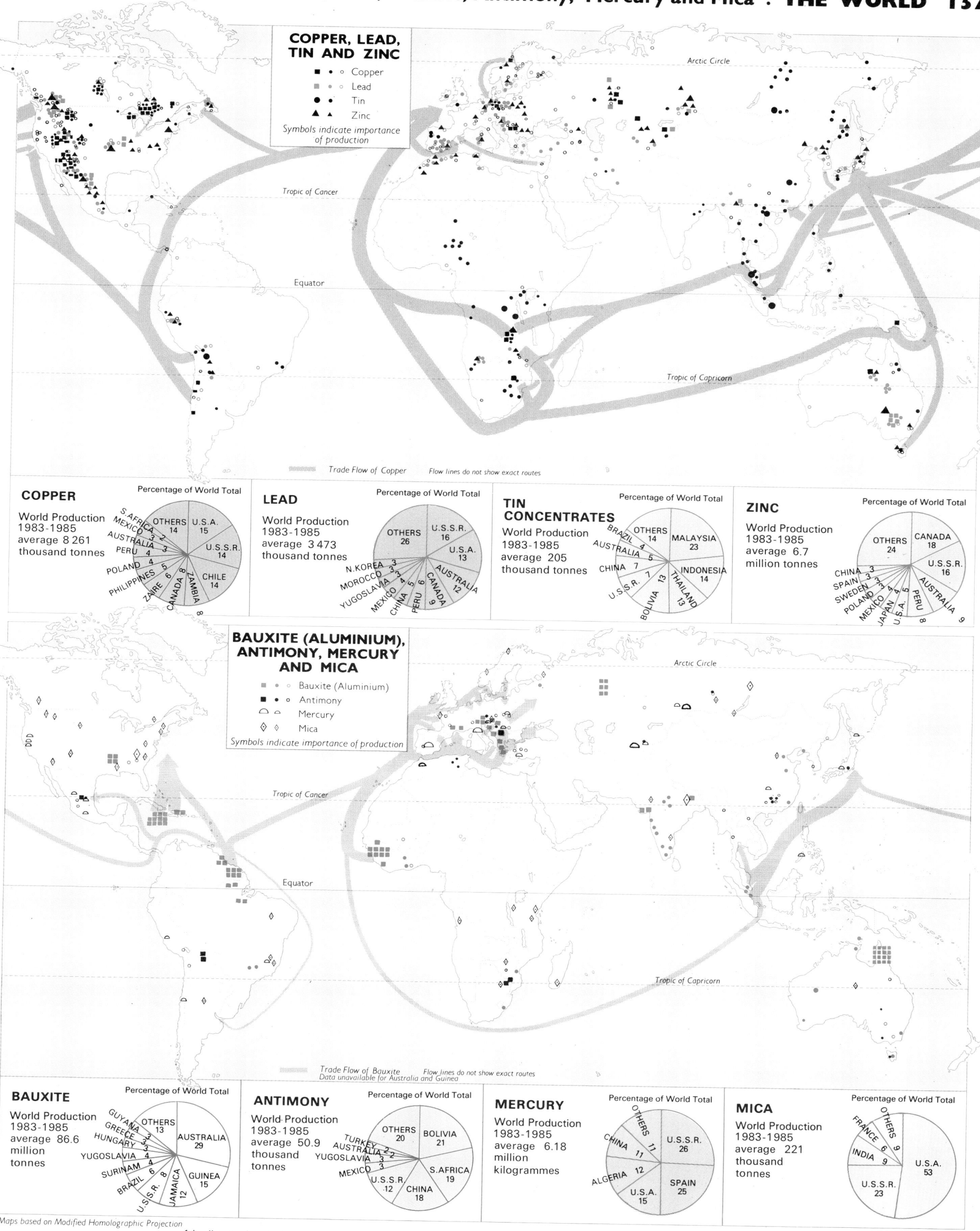

COPPER, LEAD, TIN AND ZINC

- Copper
- Lead
- Tin
- Zinc

Symbols indicate importance of production

Trade Flow of Copper   Flow lines do not show exact routes

COPPER

Percentage of World Total

World Production
1983-1985
average 8 261
thousand tonnes

S. AFRICA 3 · MEXICO 3 · AUSTRALIA 3 · PERU 4 · POLAND 4 · PHILIPPINES 5 · ZAIRE 6 · CANADA 8 · ZAMBIA 8 · CHILE 14 · U.S.S.R. 14 · U.S.A. 15 · OTHERS 14

LEAD

Percentage of World Total

World Production
1983-1985
average 3 473
thousand tonnes

U.S.S.R. 16 · U.S.A. 13 · AUSTRALIA 12 · CANADA 9 · PERU 6 · CHINA 5 · MEXICO 4 · YUGOSLAVIA 3 · MOROCCO 3 · N.KOREA 3 · OTHERS 26

TIN CONCENTRATES

Percentage of World Total

World Production
1983-1985
average 205
thousand tonnes

MALAYSIA 23 · INDONESIA 14 · THAILAND 13 · BOLIVIA 13 · U.S.S.R. 7 · CHINA 7 · AUSTRALIA 5 · BRAZIL 5 · OTHERS 14

ZINC

Percentage of World Total

World Production
1983-1985
average 6.7
million tonnes

CANADA 18 · U.S.S.R. 16 · AUSTRALIA 9 · PERU 8 · U.S.A. 5 · JAPAN 4 · MEXICO 4 · POLAND 3 · SWEDEN 3 · SPAIN 3 · CHINA 3 · OTHERS 24

BAUXITE (ALUMINIUM), ANTIMONY, MERCURY AND MICA

- Bauxite (Aluminium)
- Antimony
- Mercury
- Mica

Symbols indicate importance of production

Trade Flow of Bauxite   Flow lines do not show exact routes
Data unavailable for Australia and Guinea

BAUXITE

Percentage of World Total

World Production
1983-1985
average 86.6
million
tonnes

AUSTRALIA 29 · GUINEA 15 · JAMAICA 12 · U.S.S.R. 8 · BRAZIL 6 · SURINAM 4 · YUGOSLAVIA 4 · HUNGARY 3 · GREECE 3 · GUYANA 3 · OTHERS 13

ANTIMONY

Percentage of World Total

World Production
1983-1985
average 50.9
thousand
tonnes

BOLIVIA 21 · S.AFRICA 19 · CHINA 18 · U.S.S.R. 12 · MEXICO 3 · YUGOSLAVIA 3 · AUSTRALIA 2 · TURKEY 2 · OTHERS 20

MERCURY

Percentage of World Total

World Production
1983-1985
average 6.18
million
kilogrammes

U.S.S.R. 26 · SPAIN 25 · U.S.A. 15 · ALGERIA 12 · CHINA 11 · OTHERS 11

MICA

Percentage of World Total

World Production
1983-1985
average 221
thousand
tonnes

U.S.A. 53 · U.S.S.R. 23 · INDIA 9 · FRANCE 6 · OTHERS 9

Maps based on Modified Homolographic Projection

1 ha (hectare) = 2.47 acres
1 kg/ha = 0.89 pounds/acres

1 tonne (metric ton) = 0.98 tons = 2204.62 pounds
1 kg (kilogram) = 2.20 pounds

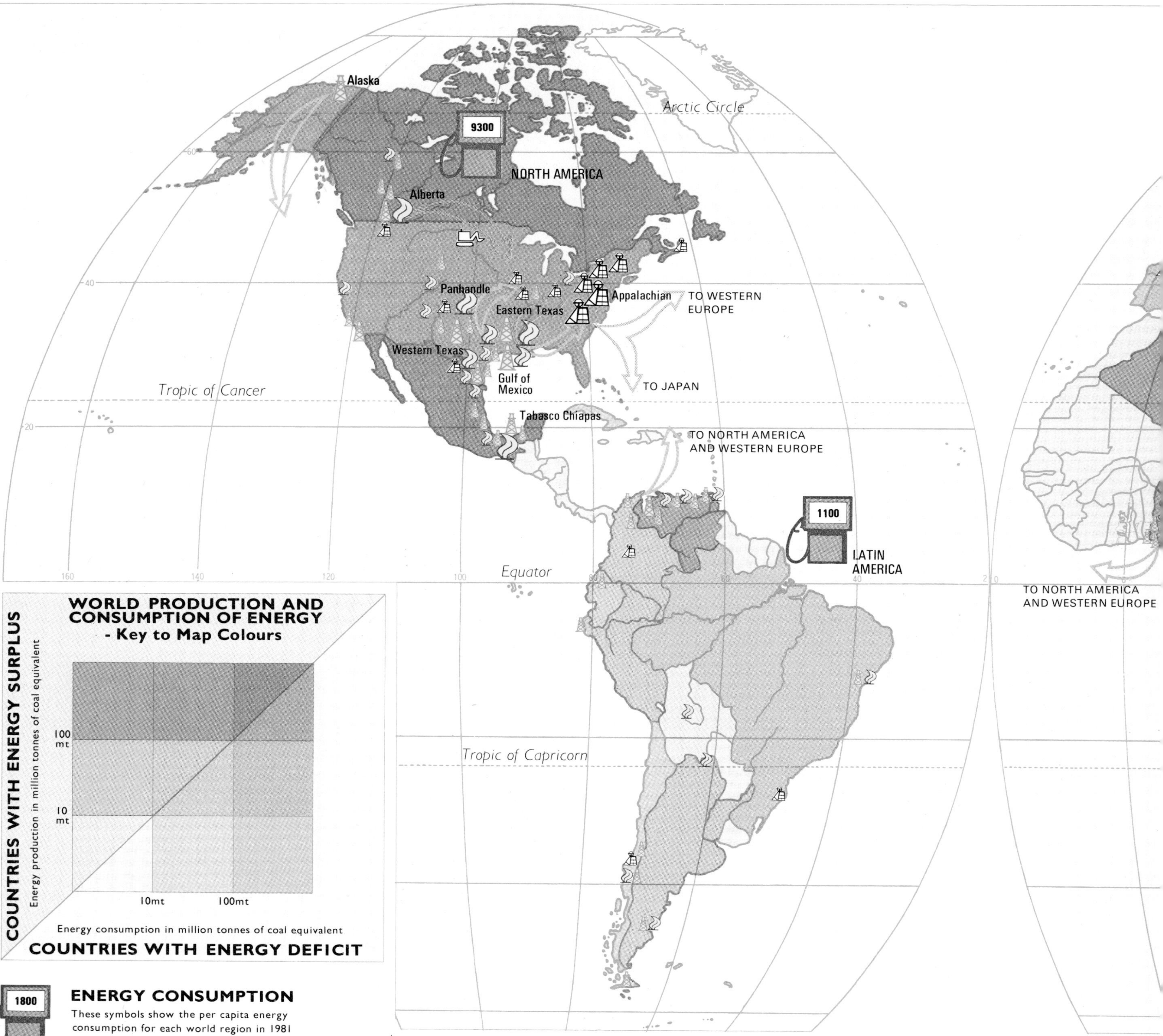

Alaska

9300

NORTH AMERICA

Arctic Circle

Alberta

Panhandle

Eastern Texas

Appalachian

TO WESTERN EUROPE

Western Texas

Gulf of Mexico

Tropic of Cancer

TO JAPAN

Tabasco Chiapas

TO NORTH AMERICA AND WESTERN EUROPE

1100

LATIN AMERICA

Equator

TO NORTH AMERICA AND WESTERN EUROPE

Tropic of Capricorn

WORLD PRODUCTION AND CONSUMPTION OF ENERGY
- Key to Map Colours

COUNTRIES WITH ENERGY SURPLUS

Energy production in million tonnes of coal equivalent

100 mt

10 mt

10mt 100mt

Energy consumption in million tonnes of coal equivalent

COUNTRIES WITH ENERGY DEFICIT

ENERGY CONSUMPTION

1800

These symbols show the per capita energy consumption for each world region in 1981 (in litres of oil equivalent)

OIL-CRUDE PETROLEUM

Principal oilfields

Direction of oil exports (by land and sea)

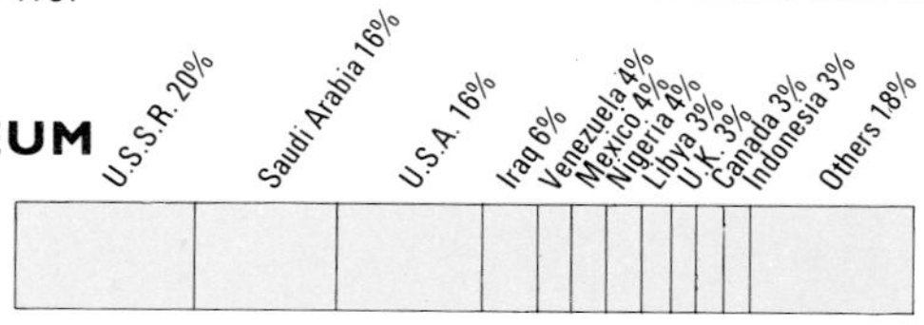

U.S.S.R. 20% | Saudi Arabia 16% | U.S.A. 16% | Iraq 6% | Venezuela 4% | Mexico 4% | Nigeria 4% | Libya 3% | U.K. 3% | Canada 3% | Indonesia 3% | Others 18%

World production 1982-1984 average 2 678 million tonnes

NATURAL GAS

Principal gasfields

Direction of gas exports (by land and sea)

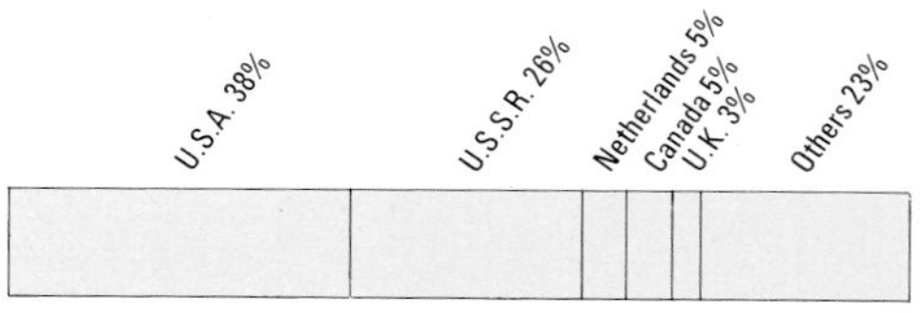

U.S.A. 38% | U.S.S.R. 26% | Netherlands 5% | Canada 5% | U.K. 3% | Others 23%

World production 1982-1984 average 55 653 petajoule

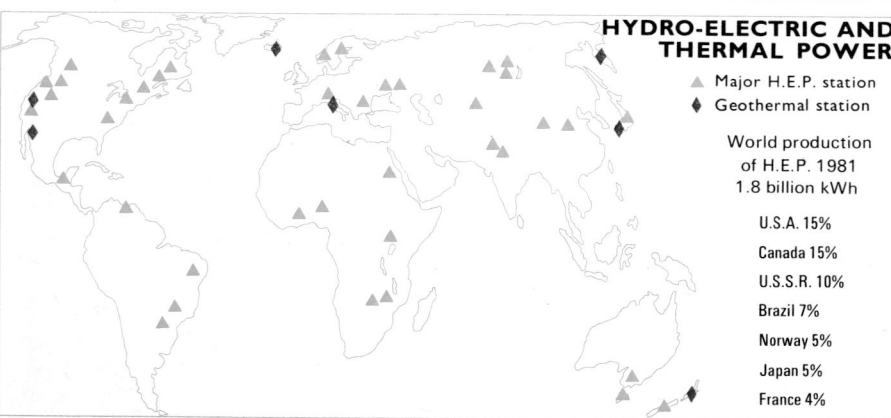

HYDRO-ELECTRIC AND THERMAL POWER

▲ Major H.E.P. station
◆ Geothermal station

World production of H.E.P. 1981 1.8 billion kWh

U.S.A. 15%
Canada 15%
U.S.S.R. 10%
Brazil 7%
Norway 5%
Japan 5%
France 4%

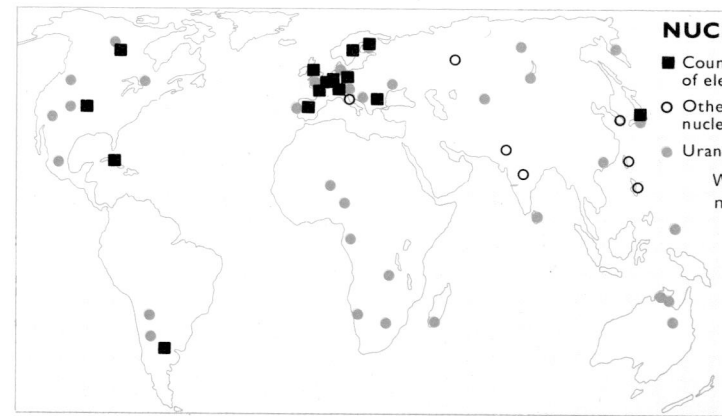

NUCLEAR POWER

■ Countries where over 5 of electric power is nuc
○ Other countries with nuclear power stations
● Uranium production

World production o nuclear power 198 0.8 billion kWh

U.S.A. 34%
France 12%
U.S.S.R. 10%
Japan 10%
W. Germany 6%
U.K. 6%

1 ha (hectare) = 2.47 acres
1 kg/ha = 0.89 pounds/acres

1 tonne (metric ton) = 0.98 tons = 2204.62 pounds
1 kg (kilogram) = 2.20 pounds

* 1 petajoule = 10^{15} watts per se

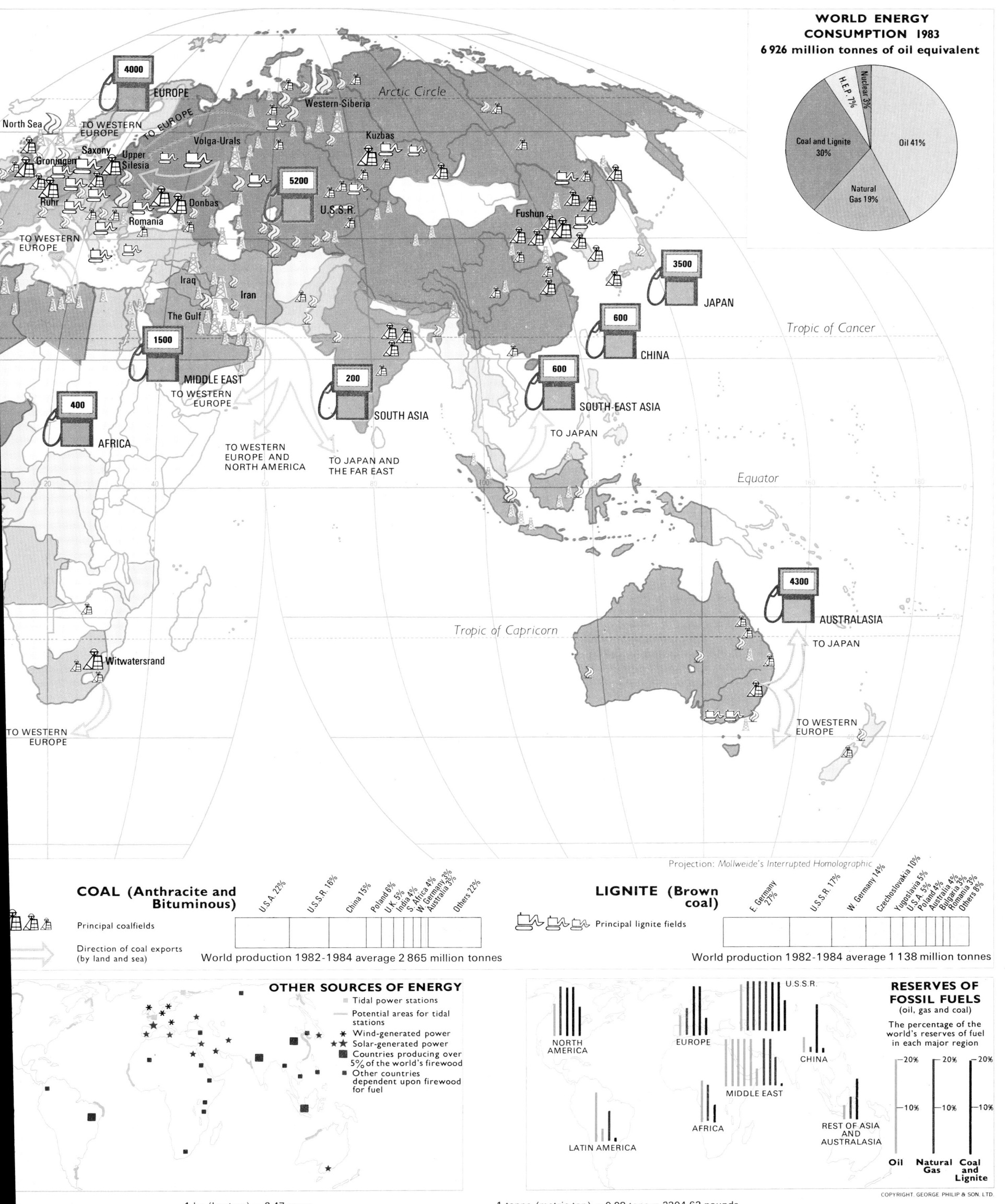

WORLD ENERGY CONSUMPTION 1983
6 926 million tonnes of oil equivalent

Oil 41%
Natural Gas 19%
Coal and Lignite 30%
H.E.P. 7%
Nuclear 3%

4000 EUROPE
North Sea
TO WESTERN EUROPE
TO EUROPE
Groningen
Saxony
Upper Silesia
Ruhr
Romania
Donbas
Volga-Urals
Western-Siberia
Kuzbas
5200 U.S.S.R.
Fushun
Arctic Circle

Iraq
Iran
The Gulf
1500 MIDDLE EAST
TO WESTERN EUROPE

400 AFRICA
TO WESTERN EUROPE

200 SOUTH ASIA
TO WESTERN EUROPE AND NORTH AMERICA
TO JAPAN AND THE FAR EAST

600 CHINA
600 SOUTH-EAST ASIA
TO JAPAN

3500 JAPAN
Tropic of Cancer

Equator

Witwatersrand

Tropic of Capricorn
4300 AUSTRALASIA
TO JAPAN
TO WESTERN EUROPE

Projection: Mollweide's Interrupted Homolographic

COAL (Anthracite and Bituminous)

Principal coalfields

Direction of coal exports (by land and sea)

U.S.A. 22% U.S.S.R. 16% China 15% Poland 6% U.K. 5% India 4% S. Africa 4% W. Germany 3% Australia 3% Others 22%

World production 1982-1984 average 2 865 million tonnes

LIGNITE (Brown coal)

Principal lignite fields

E. Germany 27% U.S.S.R. 17% W. Germany 14% Czechoslovakia 10% Yugoslavia 5% U.S.A. 5% Poland 4% Australia 4% Bulgaria 3% Romania 3% Others 8%

World production 1982-1984 average 1 138 million tonnes

OTHER SOURCES OF ENERGY

- Tidal power stations
- Potential areas for tidal stations
- * Wind-generated power
- ★ Solar-generated power
- ■ Countries producing over 5% of the world's firewood
- ■ Other countries dependent upon firewood for fuel

RESERVES OF FOSSIL FUELS
(oil, gas and coal)

The percentage of the world's reserves of fuel in each major region

NORTH AMERICA
EUROPE
U.S.S.R.
CHINA
MIDDLE EAST
AFRICA
REST OF ASIA AND AUSTRALASIA
LATIN AMERICA

Oil Natural Gas Coal and Lignite

1 ha (hectare) = 2.47 acres
1 kg/ha = 0.89 pounds/acres

1 tonne (metric ton) = 0.98 tons = 2204.62 pounds
1 kg (kilogram) = 2.20 pounds

COPYRIGHT. GEORGE PHILIP & SON. LTD.

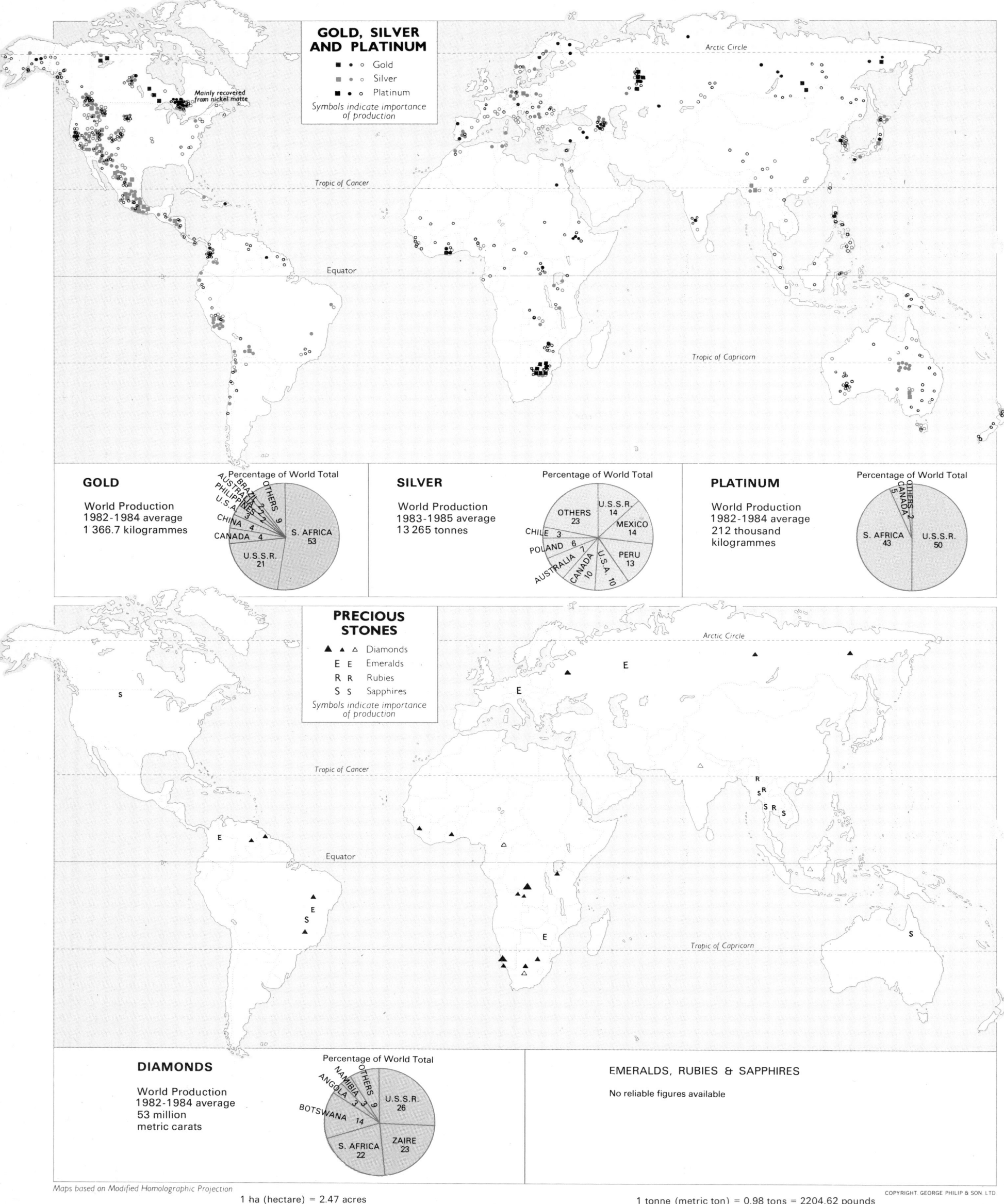

GOLD, SILVER AND PLATINUM

- ■ ● ○ Gold
- ■ ● ○ Silver
- ■ ● ○ Platinum

Symbols indicate importance of production

Mainly recovered from nickel matte

GOLD

World Production
1982-1984 average
1 366.7 kilogrammes

Percentage of World Total

OTHERS 9
BRAZIL 2
AUSTRALIA 2
PHILIPPINES 3
U.S.A. 3
CHINA 4
CANADA 4
U.S.S.R. 21
S. AFRICA 53

SILVER

World Production
1983-1985 average
13 265 tonnes

Percentage of World Total

OTHERS 23
CHILE 3
POLAND 6
AUSTRALIA 7
CANADA 10
U.S.A. 10
PERU 13
MEXICO 14
U.S.S.R. 14

PLATINUM

World Production
1982-1984 average
212 thousand kilogrammes

Percentage of World Total

OTHERS 2
CANADA 5
S. AFRICA 43
U.S.S.R. 50

PRECIOUS STONES

- ▲ ▲ △ Diamonds
- E E Emeralds
- R R Rubies
- S S Sapphires

Symbols indicate importance of production

DIAMONDS

World Production
1982-1984 average
53 million
metric carats

Percentage of World Total

OTHERS 9
NAMIBIA 3
ANGOLA 3
BOTSWANA 14
S. AFRICA 22
ZAIRE 23
U.S.S.R. 26

EMERALDS, RUBIES & SAPPHIRES

No reliable figures available

Maps based on Modified Homolographic Projection

1 ha (hectare) = 2.47 acres
1 kg/ha = 0.89 pounds/acres

1 tonne (metric ton) = 0.98 tons = 2204.62 pounds
1 kg (kilogram) = 2.20 pounds

ECONOMIC SECTION

Introduction

It is the aim of these statistics to present for the largest countries a picture of their character and position in the world in such a way that comparisons between countries may be made and a wide variety of basic questions answered.

The chosen items of information are the most important within the general categories of area and demography, natural resources, industrial production and trade. The arrangement of columns corresponds to these categories, the first column being general and the rest refer to the four categories.

In case some of the terms are unfamiliar, explanations are given below in the appropriate part of the Notes.

Table Arrangement

Country
1. Form of Government.
2. Language.
3. Currency.
4. Exchange rates (Spring 1986).

Area and population
1. Area (thousand sq. km.)
2. Population (thousands) and density (Estimates, 1985).
3. Birth and Death rates per thousand population Annual Increase (percentage, 1980-84).
4. Urban population (thousands) Percentage of total population.
5. Capital and population (thousands).

Production
1. GDP (million $) 1982/84 and average annual growth rate, 1975-81; GDP per capita 1982/84 and annual growth rate, 1975-81. Industrial origin of GDP, percentage distribution.
2. Agricultural production, thousand tonnes.
3. Livestock, thousand head.
4. Fish caught, thousand tonnes, 1983.
5. Roundwood 1983, thousand cubic m.
6. Minerals mined, thousand tonnes.
   Gas in terajoules
   Coal – million tonnes
   Gold – tonnes
   Silver – tonnes
   Diamonds – thousand carats
   Uranium – tonnes
   Iron ore – million tonnes
   Lignite – million tonnes
   Crude petroleum – million tonnes.

Manufactures
1. Production/Consumption of all energy, million tonnes of coal equivalent 1983. Electricity production, million kWh (percentage hydro-electricity, nuclear, geothermal).
2. Manufactures, (thousand tonnes)
   (a) Agricultural 1983/84
   (b) Industrial 1982/84
   Sawnwood, thousand cubic m.
3. Communications: telephones and cars in use (thousands) 1981/82. Railway, passenger-km and tonne-km (millions) 1983/84 Airlines, passenger-km and tonne-km (thousands) 1983/84. Sea cargo, loaded and unloaded (thousand tonnes).

Trade
Export and Import totals, million $.
List of major items.
Main trading partners in order of importance.
Invisible trade balance, million $, 1983-84.
Revenue from tourism, million $, 1982.
Aid given or received, million $ (Annual average 1979-81)

General Notes

As far as possible the figures refer to 1983/84. When they are for different years or periods, for example, for the Exchange Rate or the GDP growth figures, the appropriate date is mentioned in the table description above. For the urban and capital populations the most recent estimates or figures from the latest censuses are given; these may be 5-10 years old.

Column One
The exchange rates for the £ and U.S. $ are shown.
The C.F.A. franc is the unit of currency used throughout the African countries associated with France. (C.F.A. = Communauté Financière Africaine.)

Column Two
The area figure is for the total area of the country, including inland water bodies.
The birth and death rates are the latest figures that are available. The annual rate of change in the population is expressed as an average for the years 1980-84. The figure includes the natural net balance of births and deaths and also migration.

Column Three
The GDP in line 1 is the Gross Domestic Product. In Communist countries the best similar measure is the NMP, the Net Material Product.
The Gross Domestic Product is a measure of a country's total production of goods and services. The figures are expressed in 'purchaser's values' which means the cost in the market of goods and services on delivery to the purchaser; that is the cost of materials, production, trade and transport charges. Imported goods and services are excluded.
The Net Material Product is not wholly comparable to the GDP; it is the total net value of goods and production services, including taxes, in one year. Excluded are public administration, defence, personal and professional services. The figure should be used with caution and treated as a general indicator.
A second figure is given for the GDP expressed per capita, and an annual average rate of change is added after both.
The Industrial Origin of the GDP comes in the next line and is divided into three categories, Agriculture, Industry and Other. The percentage figures show which part of the GDP is contributed by each category.
Roundwood refers to the forest output of wood in its natural state as felled.

Column Four
The production and consumption of various types of energy has been converted to one measure – the heat energy obtained from burning one tonne of coal, – the 'coal equivalent'. The production figure is based on the home production of coal, lignite, crude petroleum, natural gas and hydro- and nuclear electricity. Imported energy sources are included in the consumption figure.
Sawnwood is timber in its first state of processing.
Energy Petroleum Products include particular products obtained from crude petroleum or shale oil. These products are motor and aviation gasolenes, jet fuels and kerosene, gas, diesel and residual oils and liquefied petroleum gas.

Column Five
Exports are f.o.b. and imports c.i.f.
Trade partners are listed in order of importance.
f.o.b. (free on board)   A valuation of the cost of goods, plus insurance and freight to the border of the exporting country.
c.i.f. (cost, insurance, freight)   A valuation of the cost of goods, plus insurance and freight to the border of the importing country.
The invisible trade balance is the net balance of earnings from, and expenditure on the exchange of non-physical ('invisible') goods. The most important activities are international banking, investment, insurance, shipping and tourism.
The revenue from tourism is the total income, not a net balance.
Aid is a general term for all planned assistance to the developing countries. Aid comes from governments and from private organisations.
A second distinction can be made between bilateral and multilateral aid. Bilateral aid is arranged between two governments according to their own arrangements; this method accounts for just over 80% of all aid. Multilateral aid is given through institutions such as the World Bank, the E.E.C., regional institutions like the Colombo plan and other U.N. agencies.

Abbreviations

. . .	data not available	c	carats (thousand)	m²	square metres	hydr	hydro-electric
t	tonnes, –the metric tonne	grt	gross registered tons (thousand)	m³	cubic metres	geo	geothermal
kg	kilogrammes	hl	hectolitres (thousand)	kWh	kilowatt-hour	M	million
km	kilometres	m	metres	nucl	nuclear	T	thousand

Country	Area and Population	Production	Manufactures	Trade

AFGHANISTAN

1. Republic
2. Pashto, Persian
3. Afghani
4. $1 = 65.50
   £1 = 99.00

1. 648 th. sq. km.
2. 18 136; 28 per sq. km.
3. BR 48; DR 22; AI 0.04%
4. Urb. pop.: 2 376 (16%)
5. Kabul 1 127

1. GDP $1 858 (. . .); $111 (. . .)
   Agric. 69%, Indust. 14%, Others 17%
2. Wheat 2 850   Maize 800
   Cottonseed 44   Cotton lint 22
3. Sheep 20 000   Cattle 3 750
   Goats 3 000
5. Roundwood 6 681
6. Coal 0.1   Natural gas 99.5
   Salt 30

1. 3.6/0.9; 1 025 kWh (80% hydr.)
2a. Sugar 6   Sawnwood 400
   Meat 252
b. Cement 87   Cotton woven 23Mm
3. Telephones 32; Cars 37
   Air: 231 pass.-km.; 39 ton-km.

Exports: $708   Imports: $695
Cotton   Food
Natural gas   Textiles
Dried fruit   Petroleum products
Fresh fruit   Machinery
Exports to: U.S.S.R., U.K., Pakistan
Imports from: U.S.S.R., Japan, Iran
Aid received (net): $44.2

ALBANIA

1. Republic
2. Albanian
3. Lek
4. $1 = 6.75
   £1 = 10.20

1. 29 th. sq. km.
2. 2 962; 102 per sq. km.
3. BR 26; DR 6; AI 2.2%
4. Urb. pop.: 961 (34%)
5. Tirana 202

1. NMP . . . (9.2%); . . . (6.2%)
2. Wheat 600   Maize 400
   Cottonseed 10   Cotton lint 6
3. Sheep 1 200   Goats 700
5. Roundwood 2 330
6. Lignite 1 020   Crude petroleum 3.5
   Chrome 900   Copper 14.0
   Nickel 9.0

1. 6.8/3.6; 2 885 kWh (68% hydr.)
2a. Sugar 40   Sawnwood 200
b. Cement 1 088   Copper 10
   Cotton woven . . .   Wool woven . . .

Exports: . . .   Imports: . . .
Fuels and Minerals
Exports to: India, Czechoslovakia, Poland, E. Germany
Imports from: India, Czechoslovakia, Poland, E. Germany

ALGERIA

1. Republic
2. Arabic, French
3. Algerian Dinar
4. $1 = 4.80
   £1 = 7.25

1. 2 382 th. sq. km.
2. 21 718; 9 per sq. km.
3. BR 47; DR 13; AI 3.3%
4. Urb. pop.: 9 785 (46%)
5. Algiers 1 740

1. GDP $44 926 (8.7%); $2 262 (5.3%)
   Agric. 6%, Indust. 40%, Other 54%
2. Wheat 1 200   Barley 588
   Grapes 360   Oranges 228
3. Sheep 14 700   Goats 3 000
4. Fish 70
5. Roundwood 1 685
6. Crude petroleum 30.3   Natural gas 516
   Iron ore 2.0   Phosphates 893
   Lead 5

1. 85.1/12.8; 8 520 kWh (4% hydr.)
2a. Wine 215   Meat 192
   Sawnwood 13
b. Cotton yarn 19.9   Cement 4 500
   Petroleum products 28.8
3. Telephones 607; Cars 574
   Rail: 1 506 pass.-km.; 2 016 ton-km.
   Air: 2 610 pass.-km.; 253 ton-km.
   Sea: 44 824 loaded; 13 299 unloaded

Exports: $11 861   Imports: $10 286
Crude petroleum   Machinery
Wine   Iron and steel
Natural gas   Food
Exports to: France, W. Germany, U.S.A., Italy
Imports from: France, W. Germany, Italy, U.S.A.
Revenue from tourism: $167
Aid received (net): $187.9

ANGOLA

1. Republic
2. Portuguese
3. Kwanza
4. $1 = 28.98
   £1 = 43.80

1. 1 247 th. sq. km.
2. 8 754; 7 per sq. km.
3. BR 48; DR 24; AI 2.5%
4. Urb. pop.: 1 964 (23%)
5. Luanda 700

1. GDP $2 701 (. . .); $432 (. . .)
2. Coffee 27   Sugar cane 360
   Maize 260   Palm oil 40
3. Cattle 3 350   Goats 955
4. Fish 112
5. Roundwood 9 003
6. Crude petroleum 10.3   Diamonds 920c

1. 12.4/1.0; 1 740 kWh (74% hydr.)
2a. Sugar 34   Sawnwood 160
b. Cement 3 600   Cotton yarn 3
3. Telephones 28; Cars 40
   Rail: 858 pass.-km.; 96 ton-km.
   Sea: 5 590 loaded; 1 608 unloaded

Exports: $2 029   Imports: $636
Coffee   Machinery
Diamonds   Metals
Crude petroleum
Exports to: U.S.A., Portugal, Canada, Japan
Imports from: Portugal, W. Germany, South Africa, U.S.A.
Aid received (net): $53.4

ARGENTINA

1. Republic
2. Spanish
3. Austral
4. $1 = 0.83
   £1 = 1.25

1. 2 767 th. sq. km.
2. 30 564; 11 per sq. km.
3. BR 24; DR 8; AI 1.3%
4. Urb. pop.: 27 398 (83%)
5. Buenos Aires 9 927

1. GDP $122 195 (1.3%); $4 124 (1.0%)
   Agric. 13%, Indust. 35%, Others 52%
2. Wheat 13 000   Maize 9 500
   Linseed 703   Oranges 580
   Wool 155   Grapes 2 759
3. Cattle 53 500   Sheep 30 000
4. Fish 416
5. Roundwood 10 520
6. Coal 0.5   Zinc 35
   Crude petroleum 23.2   Lead 29
   Natural gas 427   Silver 62

1. 56.8/50.9; 42 998 kWh (43% hydr., 8% nucl.)
2a. Meat 3 482   Wine 2 000
   Sugar 1 450   Sawnwood 1 163
b. Cotton yarn 91.2   Steel 2 508
   Petroleum products 21.9   Vehicles:
   Cement 5 220   pass. 144, comm. 30
   Iron 2 600
3. Telephones 2 767; Cars 2 368
   Rail: 10 524 pass.-km.; 11 244 ton-km.
   Air: 6 252 pass.-km.; 722 ton-km.
   Sea: 35 184 loaded; 5 568 unloaded

Exports: $8 107   Imports: $4 583
Meat   Machinery
Cereals   Iron and steel
Wool   Non-ferrous metals
Exports to: Italy, Netherlands, Brazil, U.S.A.
Imports from: U.S.A., W. Germany, Brazil, Japan
Invisible trade balance: −$6 479
Revenue from tourism: $516
Aid received (net): $149.1

AUSTRALIA

1. Commonwealth
2. English
3. Australian Dollar
4. $1 = 1.38
   £1 = 2.08

1. 7 687 th. sq. km.
2. 15 752; 2 per sq. km.
3. BR 15; DR 7; AI 1.2%
4. Urb. pop.: 13 368 (86%)
5. Canberra 256

1. GDP $166 691 (2.6%); $10 981 (1.3%)
   Agric. 6%, Indust. 27%, Others 67%
2. Wheat 18 580   Barley 5 470
   Oats 1 470   Wool 729
   Oranges 380   Other fruits 3 000
3. Sheep 139 242   Cattle 22 161
4. Fish 169
5. Roundwood 16 015
6. Coal 124.5   Lead 440
   Crude petroleum 23.9   Zinc 657
   Natural gas 463   Manganese 1 033
   Gold 39   Iron ore 57.6
   Nickel 76.9   Bauxite 32 182
   Copper 240   Silver 1 063
   Diamonds 5 700c   Uranium 3 211t

1. 135.4/92.0; 106 287 kWh (12% hydr.)
2a. Meat 2 304   Sugar 3 550
   Sawnwood 2 794   Butter & cheese 279
b. Wool yarn 20   Cement 5 100
   Steel 6 168   Radios 143
   Petroleum products 26.3   Vehicles:
       pass. 371, comm. 29
3. Telephones 7 153; Cars 6 819
   Rail: . . .; 39 444 ton-km.
   Air: 26 124 pass.-km.; 2 953 ton-km.
   Sea: 209 832 loaded; 22 572 unloaded

Exports: $23 998   Imports: $23 424
Wool   Machinery
Cereals   Vehicles
Metals   Textiles
Meat   Crude petroleum
Exports to: Japan, U.S.A., New Zealand
Imports from: U.S.A., Japan, U.K., W. Germany
Invisible trade balance: −$6 740
Revenue from tourism: $1 097
Aid given (net): $812

AUSTRIA

1. Federal Republic
2. German
3. Austrian Schilling
4. $1 = 15.53
   £1 = 23.48

1. 84 th. sq. km.
2. 7 555; 90 per sq. km.
3. BR 12; DR 12; AI 0.0%
4. Urb. pop.: 3 927 (52%)
5. Vienna 1 531

1. GDP $58 490 (3.0%); $7 747 (3.0%)
   Agric. 4%, Indust. 28%, Others 68%
2. Wheat 1 501   Barley 1 517
   Potatoes 1 138   Rye 380
   Maize 1 542   Pears 151
3. Pigs 3 881   Cattle 2 633
5. Roundwood 13 670
6. Lignite 219   Iron ore 1.1
   Crude petroleum 1.3   Magnesite 1 006
   Natural gas 49   Antimony 0.5
   Salt 501   Lead 4
   Zinc 21

1. 8.6/26.7; 42 625 kWh (72% hydr.)
2a. Wine 252   Sugar 457
   Sawnwood 6 308   Meat 763
b. Cotton yarn 16.8   Wool yarn 5.1
   Steel 5 316   Aluminium 94
   Petroleum products 6.8
3. Telephones 3 178; Cars 2 361
   Rail: 7 217 pass.-km.; 11 244 ton-km.
   Air: 1 404 pass.-km.; 135 ton-km.

Exports: $15 741   Imports: $19 631
Machinery   Machinery
Iron and steel   Food
Textiles   Textiles
Sawnwood   Vehicles
    Chemical products
Exports to: W. Germany, Italy, Switzerland, U.K.
Imports from: W. Germany, Switzerland, Italy, France
Invisible trade balance: +$2 865
Revenue from tourism: $5 649
Aid given (net): $285

BANGLADESH

1. Republic
2. Bengali
3. Taka
4. $1 = 29.87
   £1 = 45.15

1. 144 th. sq. km.
2. 98 657; 685 per sq. km.
3. BR 47; DR 19; AI 2.4%
4. Urb. pop.: 9 673 (10%)
5. Dacca 3 459

1. GDP $15 298 (. . .); $158 (. . .)
   Agric. 48%, Indust. 9%, Others 43%
2. Rice 21 500   Bananas 680
   Tea 46   Jute 733
3. Cattle 36 300   Goats 12 050
4. Fish 729
5. Roundwood 32 051
6. Natural gas 79.0

1. 2.8/4.6; 3 758 kWh (18% hydr.)
2a. Sugar 165   Sawnwood 196
b. Cotton yarn 46.8   Cement 326
3. Telephones 122; Cars 44
   Rail: 5 366 pass.-km.; 831 ton-km.
   Air: 1 430 pass.-km.; 149 ton-km.
   Sea: 1 056 loaded; 6 948 unloaded

Exports: $934   Imports: $2 042
Exports to: U.S.A., Pakistan, U.S.S.R., U.K.
Imports from: Japan, U.S.A., U.K.
Revenue from tourism: $10
Aid received (net): $1 142.7

Country	Area and Population	Production	Manufactures	Trade

BELGIUM

1. Kingdom
2. French, Flemish, German
3. Belgian Franc
4. $1 = 45.48
   £1 = 68.75

1. 33 th. sq. km.
2. 9 903; 300 per sq. km.
3. BR 12; DR 11; AI 0.1%
4. Urb. pop.: 8 790 (89%)
5. Brussels 989

1. GDP $75 306 (2.3%); $7 638 (2.2%)
   Agric. 2%, Indust. 25%, Others 73%
2. Wheat 1 330   Barley 935
   Potatoes 1 650   Apples 260
3. Pigs 5 300   Cattle 3 171
4. Fish 49
5. Roundwood 3 041
6. Coal 6.3

1. 10.0/48.9; 52 706 kWh (2% hydr., 46% nucl.)
2a. Sugar 900   Sawnwood 695
   b. Cotton yarn 46.8   Wool yarn 92
   Steel 11 304   Copper 418
   Coke oven coke 5 106   Plastics 2 000
   Petroleum products 19.3   Vehicles:
   Iron 8 964   pass. 890, comm. 39
3. Telephones 3 819; Cars 3 231
   Rail: 6 456 pass.-km.; 7 884 ton-km.
   Air: 5 652 pass.-km.; 967 ton-km.
   Sea: 47 052 loaded; 72 096 unloaded

Exports: $51 699   Imports: $55 247
(incl. Luxembourg)   (incl. Luxembourg)
Iron and steel   Machinery
Vehicles   Vehicles
Machinery   Non-ferrous metals
Non-ferrous metals   Diamonds
Textiles   Petrol
Trade is principally with: W. Germany, France, Netherlands, U.K.
Invisible trade balance (incl. Luxembourg): +$2 281
Revenue from tourism: $1 578
Aid given (net): $2 274

BENIN

1. Republic
2. French
3. C.F.A. Franc
4. $1 = 352.13
   £1 = 532.25

1. 113 th. sq. km.
2. 3 932; 35 per sq. km.
3. BR 51; DR 25; AI 3.5%
4. Urb. pop.: 1 314 (39%)
5. Porto-Novo 208

1. GDP $1 035 (−4.3%); $303 (−6.3%)
   Agric. 44%, Indust. 6%, Others 50%
2. Cassava 639   Palm oil 40
   Maize 379   Cottonseed 34
   Groundnuts 58
3. Goats 1 000   Cattle 875
4. Fish 21
5. Roundwood 4 210

1. . . ./0.2; 5 kWh
2a. Sawnwood 9
3. Telephones 9; Cars 17
   Rail: 83 pass.-km.; 94 ton-km.
   Air: 212 pass.-km.; 41 ton-km.
   Sea: 110 loaded; 749 unloaded

Exports: $43   Imports: $476
Palm oil   Manufactured
Oilseeds   products
Cotton   Machinery
Cocoa
Exports to: France, Netherlands, U.K.
Imports from: France, W. Germany, Netherlands, U.K.
Aid received (net): $87.1

BOLIVIA

1. Republic
2. Spanish
3. Bolivian Peso
4. $1 = 1.9 mill.
   £1 = 2.88 mill.

1. 1 099 th. sq. km.
2. 6 429; 6 per sq. km.
3. BR 47; DR 18; AI 2.7%
4. Urb. pop.: 2 822 (46%)
5. La Paz 881, Sucre 64

1. GDP $6 238 (3.2%); $1 054 (0.4%)
   Agric. 22%, Indust. 23%, Others 55%
2. Maize 489   Barley 40
   Potatoes 650   Oranges 95
3. Sheep 9 200   Cattle 4 300
5. Roundwood 1 272
6. Antimony 9.3   Crude petroleum 1.6
   Tin 19.9   Silver 142t
   Tungsten 3 997t   Zinc 38
   Natural gas 88.5   Copper 2
   Lead 7

1. 4.9/2.1; 1 698 kWh (72% hydr.)
2a. Sugar 198   Sawnwood 97
   Cement 325   Tin 14
3. Telephones 49; Cars 50
   Rail: 529 pass.-km.; 646 ton-km.
   Air: 876 pass.-km.; 95 ton-km.

Exports: $773   Imports: $631
Tin ore   Cars
Crude petroleum   Flour
Exports to: U.K., Argentina, U.S.A.
Imports from: U.S.A., Japan, Argentina, Brazil
Invisible trade balance: −$436
Aid received (net): $211.3

BRAZIL

1. Federal Republic
2. Portuguese
3. Cruzado
4. $1 = 13.79
   £1 = 20.84

1. 8 512 th. sq. km.
2. 135 564; 16 per sq. km.
3. BR 32; DR 9; AI 2.2%
4. Urb. pop.: 86 611 (68%)
5. Brasilia 1 306

1. GDP $283 076 (6.5%); $2 232 (3.9%)
   Agric. 10%, Indust. 25%, Others 65%
2. Maize 21 174   Rice 9 023
   Cassava 21 275   Soya beans 15 537
   Bananas 6 968   Oranges 13 372
   Cottonseed 1 179   Tobacco 415
3. Cattle 132 801   Pigs 33 000
4. Fish 845
5. Roundwood 220 248
6. Coal 7.5   Crude petroleum 12.8
   Iron ore 66.0   Natural gas 64.8
   Manganese 941   Asbestos 159
   Gold 55.1   Tin 20.0
   Bauxite 6 271   Zinc 79
   Copper 26   Silver 69

1. 50.3/85.7; 161 970 kWh (94% hydr.)
2a. Meat 4 847   Sugar 9 100
   Sawnwood 15 852
   b. Cotton fabric 1 207Mm   Iron 17 904
   Steel 18 384   Aluminium 400
   Cement 19 488   Petroleum products 43.2
   Vehicles:
   .pass. 536, comm. 384
3. Telephones 8 536; Cars 9 922
   Rail: 13 133 pass.-km.; 79 269 ton-km.
   Air: 17 229 pass.-km.; 2 229 ton-km.
   Sea: 141 732 loaded; 53 856 unloaded

Exports: $27 005   Imports: $15 210
Coffee   Machinery
Cotton   Crude petroleum
Iron ore   Cereals
Machinery   Non-ferrous metals
Exports to: U.S.A., W. Germany, Netherlands, Japan
Imports from: U.S.A., W. Germany, Japan, Saudi Arabia, Iraq
Invisible trade balance: −$13 414
Revenue from tourism: $1 608
Aid received (net): $556.4

BULGARIA

1. Republic
2. Bulgar
3. Lev
4. $1 = 0.91
   £1 = 1.37

1. 111 th. sq. km.
2. 8 957; 81 per sq. km.
3. BR 14; DR 11; AI 0.4%
4. Urb. pop.: 5 775 (68%)
5. Sofia 1 094

1. NMP $34 000 (6.0%); $3 800 (5.8%)
   Agric. 18%, Indust. 57%, Others 25%
2. Wheat 3 600   Maize 3 000
   Tobacco 125   Grapes 1 000
3. Sheep 10 978   Pigs 3 769
4. Fish 121
5. Roundwood 4 756
6. Coal 0.2   Crude petroleum 0.6
   Lignite 32.1   Zinc 65
   Iron ore 0.6   Lead 95
   Silver 26   Copper 73

1. 18.8/50.2; 42 534 kWh (8% hydr., 29% nucl.)
2a. Meat 722   Sawnwood 1 345
   Wine 510   Sugar 145
   b. Cotton yarn 82.8   Iron 1 584
   Steel 2 868   Cement 5 712
   Petroleum products 11.4
3. Telephones 1 513; Cars 480
   Rail: 7 536 pass.-km.; 18 132 ton-km.
   Air: 980 pass.-km.; 99 ton-km.
   Sea: 4 488 loaded; 24 750 unloaded

Exports: $12 829   Imports: $12 668
Cigarettes   Machinery
Alcoholic drinks   Ferrous metals
Clothing   Petroleum products
The principal trade is with U.S.S.R. and E. Germany
Revenue from tourism: $265

BURKINA FASO

1. Republic
2. French
3. C.F.A. Franc
4. $1 = 352.13
   £1 = 532.25

1. 274 th. sq. km.
2. 6 639; 24 per sq. km.
3. BR 48; DR 24; AI 2.3%
4. Urb. pop.: 362 (6%)
5. Ouagadougou 286

1. GDP $1 079 (6.6%); $163 (4.7%)
   Agric. 37%, Indust. 11%, Others 52%
2. Millet/sorghum 1 150   Maize 60
   Rice 40   Groundnuts 77
3. Cattle 2 800   Goats 2 600
5. Roundwood 7 281
6. Gold . . .

1. . . ./0.2; 115 kWh
2a. Meat 60
3. Telephones 6; Cars 12
   Air: 215 pass.-km.; 41 ton-km.

Exports: $57   Imports: $288
Livestock   Manufactured goods
Cotton   Foods
Exports to: Ivory Coast, France, China
Imports from: France, U.S.A., Ivory Coast
Aid received (net): $208.7

BURMA

1. Republic
2. Burmese
3. Kyat
4. $1 = 7.28
   £1 = 11

1. 677 th. sq. km.
2. 37 154; 55 per sq. km.
3. BR 39; DR 14; AI 2.5%
4. Urb. pop.: 8 455 (24%)
5. Rangoon 2 459

1. GDP $6 176 (6.3%); $165 (3.5%)
   Agric. 50%, Indust. 11%, Others 39%
2. Rice 14 500   Groundnuts 601
   Tobacco 62   Jute 55
3. Cattle 9 550   Buffaloes 2 100
4. Fish 586
5. Roundwood 19 254
6. Crude petroleum 1.5   Zinc 4
   Lead 8   Silver 18
   Tin 1.9

1. 3.0/2.5; 1 872 kWh (60% hydr.)
2a. Sugar 56   Sawnwood 415
   b. Lead 8   Cotton yarn 8.4
3. Telephones 37; Cars 48
   Rail: 4 008 pass.-km.; 648 ton-km.
   Air: 239 pass.-km.; 23 ton-km.
   Sea: 1 248 loaded; 528 unloaded

Exports: $310   Imports: $239
Sawnwood   Machinery
Rice   Textiles
Exports to: Japan, Indonesia, Vietnam
Imports from: Japan, China, W. Germany, U.K., Singapore
Invisible trade balance: −$73.2
Aid received (net): $318.9

CAMBODIA

1. Republic
2. French, Cambodian
3. Riel
4. $1 = ?
   £1 = ?

1. 181 th. sq. km.
2. 7 284; 40 per sq. km.
3. BR 30; DR 40; AI 2.9%
4. Urb. pop.: 714 (10%)
5. Phnom Penh 500

1. GDP $592 (. . .); $83 (. . .)
   Agric. 41%, Indust. 17%, Others 42%
2. Rice 1 300   Maize 75
   Rubber 14   Bananas 84
3. Cattle 1 466   Pigs 1 008
4. Fish 64
5. Roundwood 5 229

1. . . ./0.02; 140 kWh (41% hydr.)
2a. Sawnwood 43
3. Telephones 71; Cars 25

Exports: . . .   Imports: . . .
Rubber   Machinery
Rice   Textiles
Cattle   Iron and steel
Exports to: Vietnam, Hong Kong, Singapore
Imports from: France, Japan, China, Thailand, U.S.A.
Aid received (net): $172.8

For detailed table headings and notes see first page of this section

163

Country	Area and Population	Production	Manufactures	Trade

CAMEROON

1. Republic
2. French, English
3. C.F.A. Franc
4. $1 = 352.13
   £1 = 532.25

1. 475 th. sq. km.
2. 10 106; 21 per sq. km.
3. BR 43; DR 19; AI 2.5%
4. Urb. pop.: 1 984 (28%)
5. Yaoundé 485

1. GDP $7 786 (3.7%); $871 (1.8%)
   Agric. 23%, Indust. 26%, Others 51%
2. Coffee 127   Groundnuts 80
   Cocoa 115   Palm oil 81
3. Goats 2 000   Cattle 3 730
4. Fish 84
5. Roundwood 9 904

1. 8.4/4.1; 1 804 kWh (95% hydr.)
2a. Sawnwood 426
b. Aluminium 77
3. Telephones 22; Cars 55
   Rail: 492 pass.-km.; 864 ton-km.
   Air: 581 pass.-km., 99 ton-km.
   Sea: 996 loaded; 3 000 unloaded

Exports: $883   Imports: $1 107
Cocoa   Manufactured goods
Coffee   Machinery
Exports to: France, Netherlands, W. Germany
Imports from: France, W. Germany, U.S.A.
Aid received (net): $263.5

CANADA

1. Commonwealth
2. English, French
3. Canadian Dollar
4. $1 = 1.39
   £1 = 2.10

1. 9 976 th. sq. km.
2. 25 379; 3 per sq. km.
3. BR 15; DR 7; AI 1.2%
4. Urb. pop.: 18 435 (76%)
5. Ottawa 738

1. GDP $327 555 (3.1%); $13 034 (2.0%)
   Agric. 3%, Indust. 23%, Others 74%
2. Wheat 21 199   Barley 10 252
   Oats 2 670   Maize 7 024
3. Cattle 12 284   Pigs 10 760
4. Fish 1 337
5. Roundwood 141 502
6. Iron ore 22.6   Crude petroleum 71.2
   Coal 32.1   Natural gas 2 740
   Copper 712   Zinc 1 207
   Nickel 174.2   Asbestos 829
   Gold 81.3   Salt 7 542
   Lead 307   Silver 1 171
   Lignite 25.3   Uranium 6 758

1. 281.0/238.6; 408 443 kWh (65% hydr., 12% nucl.)
2a. Sawnwood 48 469   Wood pulp 19 295
   Paper 13 353   Sugar 14
b. Iron 9 840   Steel 14 700
   Aluminium 1 091   Copper 465
   Televisions 450   Petroleum products 75.3
   Vehicles: Cement 8 856
   pass. 1 033, comm. 809
3. Telephones 16 944; Cars 10 199
   Rail: 2 088 pass.-km.; 244 668 ton-km.
   Air: 32 140 pass.-km.; 3 813 ton-km.
   Sea: 125 000 loaded; 49 000 unloaded

Exports: $86 817   Imports: $73 999
Vehicles   Machinery
Machinery   Vehicles
Paper and cardboard   Iron and steel
Non-ferrous metals   Textiles
Wood pulp   Crude petroleum
Sawnwood   Fruit and vegetables
Crude petroleum
Wheat
Trade is principally with: U.S.A., U.K., Japan
Invisible trade balance: −$15 414
Revenue from tourism: $2 447
Aid given (net): $2 721

CENTRAL AFRICAN REPUBLIC

1. Republic
2. French
3. C.F.A. Franc
4. $1 = 352.13
   £1 = 532.25

1. 623 th. sq. km.
2. 2 608; 4 per sq. km.
3. BR 44; DR 23; AI 2.2%
4. Urb. pop.: 834 (35%)
5. Bangui 387

1. GDP $796 (6.2%); $342 (3.2%)
   Agric. 32%, Indust. 15%, Others 53%
2. Maize 43   Cassava 900
   Bananas 147   Coffee 15
   Groundnuts 130   Cottonseed 20
3. Goats 960   Cattle 1 500
5. Roundwood 3 049
6. Diamonds 300

1. . . ./0.1; 68 kWh (96% hydr.)
2a. Meat 42   Sawnwood 63
3. Telephones 5; Cars 14
   Air: 220 pass.-km.; 42 ton-km.

Exports: $109   Imports: $127
Diamonds   Machinery
Cotton   Vehicles
Coffee
Exports to: France, Belgium, Luxembourg
Imports from: France, W. Germany, Japan
Aid received (net): $97.6

CHAD

1. Republic
2. French
3. C.F.A. Franc
4. $1 = 352.13
   £1 = 532.25

1. 1 284 th. sq. km.
2. 5 108; 4 per sq. km.
3. BR 44; DR 24; AI 2.3%
4. Urb. pop.: 882 (18%)
5. N'Djamena 303

1. GDP $665 (−4.5%); $165 (−6.6%)
   Agric. 41%, Indust. 17%, Others 42%
2. Millet 320   Groundnuts 80
   Cottonseed 72   Cotton 40
3. Cattle 3 400   Goats 2 000
4. Fish 110
5. Roundwood 8 112

1. . . ./0.1; 65 kWh
2a. Meat 46
3. Telephones 6; Cars 10
   Air: 229 pass.-km.; 43 ton-km.

Exports: $58   Imports: $109
Cotton   Petroleum products
Meat   Machinery

Exports to: France, Nigeria, Cameroon
Imports from: France, Nigeria, Netherlands
Aid received (net): $58.2

CHILE

1. Republic
2. Spanish
3. Chilean Peso
4. $1 = 186.83
   £1 = 282.48

1. 757 th. sq. km.
2. 12 074; 16 per sq. km.
3. BR 21; DR 6; AI 1.6%
4. Urb. pop.: 9 653 (83%)
5. Santiago 4 132

1. GDP $17 796 (7.6%); $1 524 (5.8%)
   Agric. 6%, Indust. 31%, Others 63%
2. Wheat 988   Grapes 1 050
   Wool 21   Tobacco 8
3. Sheep 6 300   Cattle 3 870
4. Fish 3 978
5. Roundwood 12 849
6. Coal 1.2   Iron ore 3.4
   Crude petroleum 1.8   Copper 1 290
   Natural gas 36.7   Molybdenum 15.3
   Gold 18.0   Nickel 12.7
   Silver 487   Lead 1

1. 6.5/10.6; 12 624 kWh (70% hydr.)
2a. Meat 361   Sawnwood 1 610
   Sugar 332   Wood pulp 796
   Wine 520
b. Iron 600   Steel 684
   Copper 833   Fertilizers 139
   Cement 1 296
3. Telephones 595; Cars 562
   Rail: 1 428 pass.-km.; 2 304 ton-km.
   Air: 1 824 pass.-km.; 315 ton-km.
   Sea: 11 832 loaded; 5 268 unloaded

Exports: $3 657   Imports: $3 191
Copper, Iron ore,   Machinery
Fishmeal, Saltpetre   Food
    Manufactured
    products
    Chemical products
Exports to: Japan, W. Germany, U.K., Argentina, U.S.A., Brazil
Invisible trade balance: −$2 452
Revenue from tourism: $123
Aid received (net): $22.5

CHINA

1. Republic
2. Chinese and others
3. Renminbi Yuan
4. $1 = 3.32
   £1 = 4.88

1. 9 597 th. sq. km.
2. 1 059 521; 110 per sq. km.
3. BR 22; DR 8; AI 1.2%
4. Urb. pop.: 252 360 (24%)
5. Peking 9 330

1. GDP $224 263 (. . .); $218 (. . .)
   Agric. 45%, Indust. 42%, Others 13%
2. Rice 181 028   Wheat 87 682
   Maize 72 690   Soya beans 9 710
   Groundnuts 4 900   Oranges 1 495
   Tobacco 1 526   Sorghum 8 532
   Tea 435   Cotton lint 6 077
   Rye 1 500   Cottonseed 12 162
   Jute 1 489
3. Pigs 304 424   Sheep 98 916
4. Fish 5 213
5. Roundwood 231 650
6. Coal 736.2   Manganese 480
   Crude petroleum 112.5   Natural gas 475
   Tungsten 12.5   Iron ore 37.0
   Tin 17.5   Salt 15 875
   Lead 165   Bauxite 2 000
   Copper 180   Zinc 190
   Gold 65.0   Nickel 175
   Silver 90

1. 682.6/629.1; 351 440 kWh (25% hydr.)
2a. Meat 18 335   Sawnwood 244.10
   Sugar 5 119
b. Iron 41 160   Steel 43 320
   Aluminium 425   Cement 121 000
   Cotton yarn 3 226   Petroleum products 75.4
3. Telephones 4 425; Cars 283
   Rail: 203 604 pass.-km.; 722 316 ton-km.
   Air: 5 750 pass.-km.; 603 ton-km.
   Sea: 47 268 loaded; 57 192 unloaded

Exports: $24 278   Imports: $25 495
Agricultural products   Grain
Textiles   Cotton products
Minerals   Machinery
Crude petroleum   Primary materials
    Petrol
Exports to: Hong Kong, U.S.S.R., Japan, Singapore
Imports from: Japan, Australia, U.S.S.R., Canada
Revenue from tourism: $843

COLOMBIA

1. Republic
2. Spanish
3. Columbian Peso
4. $1 = 183.99
   £1 = 278.10

1. 1 139 th. sq. km.
2. 28 624; 25 per sq. km.
3. BR 32; DR 8; AI 2.2%
4. Urb. pop.: 18 632 (66%)
5. Bogotá 4 486

1. GDP $32 414 (5.7%); $1 149 (2.8%)
   Agric. 18%, Indust. 24%, Others 58%
2. Maize 874   Rice 1 696
   Palm oil 121   Cassava 2 000
   Bananas 3 500   Coffee 780
   Cottonseed 200   Tobacco 37
   Cotton lint 107
3. Cattle 23 860   Pigs 2 386
4. Fish 56
5. Roundwood 16 553
6. Coal 5.6   Silver 3t
   Natural gas 181   Gold 21.3
   Crude petroleum 8.2   Iron ore 0.2

1. 26.3/25.0; 27 100 kWh (72% hydr.)
2a. Meat 878   Paper 366
   Sugar 1 176   Sawnwood 721
b. Iron 246   Steel 276
   Petroleum products 8.5   Cement 5 280
3. Telephones 1 842; Cars 599
   Rail: 192 pass.-km.; 720 ton-km.
   Air: 550 pass.-km.; 714 ton-km.
   Sea: 7 128 loaded; 6 636 unloaded

Exports: $3 462   Imports: $4 052
Coffee   Machinery
Crude petroleum   Vehicles
Cotton   Iron and steel
Bananas   Organic chemicals
Sugar and honey
Exports to: U.S.A., W. Germany, Venezuela
Imports from: U.S.A., W. Germany, Venezuela
Invisible trade balance: −$1 754
Revenue from tourism: $624
Aid received (net): $265.6

CONGO

1. Popular Republic
2. French
3. C.F.A. Franc
4. $1 = 352.13
   £1 = 532.25

1. 342 th. sq. km.
2. 1 740; 5 per sq. km.
3. BR 45; DR 19; AI 2.6%
4. Urb. pop.: 932 (55%)
5. Brazzaville 422

1. GDP $1 918 (. . .); $1 128 (. . .)
   Agric. 8%, Indust. 48%, Others 44%
2. Cassava 600   Palm oil 15
3. Goats 182   Cattle 68
4. Fish 32
5. Roundwood 2 238
6. Diamonds. . .   Crude petroleum 5.9

1. 7.8/0.2; 185 kWh (92% hydr.)
2a. Sugar 21   Sawnwood 66
3. Telephones 17; Cars 27
   Rail: 408 pass.-km.; 480 ton-km.
   Air: 247 pass.-km.; 45 ton-km.
   Sea: 3 084 loaded; 600 unloaded

Exports: $1 066   Imports: $806
Timber   Machinery
    Manufactured
    products
Exports to: France, Italy, U.S.A., Brazil, Spain
Imports from: France, U.S.A., Gabon, W. Germany
Aid received (net): $75.1

Country	Area and Population	Production	Manufactures	Trade

CUBA

1. Republic 2. Spanish 3. Cuban Peso 4. $1 = 0.68 £1 = 1.29	1. 111 th. sq. km. 2. 10 090; 91 per sq. km. 3. BR 17; DR 6; AI 0.6% 4. Urb. pop.: 6 861 (70%) 5. Havana 1 951	1. NMP $15 244 (. . .); $1 526 (. . .) Agric. 10%, Indust. 35%, Others 55% 2. Rice 555 Cassava 340 Coffee 21 Oranges 374 Sugar cane 75 000 Tobacco 45 3. Cattle 6 400 Pigs 2 300 4. Fish 198 5. Roundwood 3 193 6. Chrome 34 Nickel 38.0 Copper 3 Crude petroleum 0.7	1. 1.1/1.3; 11 551 kWh (0.5% hydr.) 2a. Meat 343 Sawnwood 108 Sugar 8 331 b. Petroleum products 6.0 Cotton, woven 138Mm^2 Cement 3 348 3. Telephones 406; Cars 182 Rail: 2 352 pass.-km.; 2 808 ton-km. Air: 1 100 pass.-km.; 112 ton-km. Sea: 2 208 loaded; 2 712 unloaded	Exports: $6 172 Imports: $8 144 Sugar Machinery Minerals Cereals Tobacco Fertilizers Petroleum products Exports to: U.S.S.R., Japan, Spain Imports from: U.S.S.R., Japan Aid received (net): $28.1

CYPRUS

1. Republic (split between Greek and Turkish parts) 2. Greek, Turkish and English 3. Cypriot Pound 4. $1 = 0.51 £1 = 0.77	1. 9 th. sq. km. 2. 665; 74 per sq. km. 3. BR 20; DR 9; AI 1.2% 4. Urb. pop.: 276 (42%) 5. Nicosia 161	1. GDP $2 009 (9.3%); $3 043 (8.7%) Agric. 9%, Indust. 17%, Others 74% 2. Barley 90 Potatoes 180 Grapes 205 Oranges 147 3. Sheep 500 Goats 360 5. Roundwood 5.74 6. Copper 1.1 Chrome 17 Asbestos 17.3	1. . . ./1.2; 1 221 kWh 2a. Wine 56 Sawnwood 55 b. Cement 852 3. Telephones 128; Cars 106 Air: 851 pass.-km.; 18 ton-km. Sea: 1 812 loaded; 3 168 unloaded	Exports: $575 Imports: $1 364 Vegetables Machinery Citrus fruits Textiles Copper Vehicles Exports to: U.K., Saudi Arabia, Lebanon Imports from: U.K., W. Germany, Italy, Iraq, Greece Revenue from tourism: $292

CZECHOSLOVAKIA

1. Socialist Republic 2. Czech, Slovak 3. Koruna 4. $1 = 10.08 £1 = 15.23	1. 128 th. sq. km. 2. 15 500; 121 per sq. km. 3. BR 15; DR 12; AI 0.4% 4. Urb. pop.: 10 357 (67%) 5. Prague 1 190	1. GDP $44 112 (3.2%); $2 853 (2.6%) Agric. 8%, Indust. 59%, Others 33% 2. Barley 3 677 Wheat 6 170 Oats 479 Potatoes 3 978 Apples 378 Tomatoes 79 Pigs 7 070 Cattle 5 190 5. Roundwood 19 206 6. Coal 26.4 Silver 32t Lignite 104.7 Crude petroleum 0.5 Iron ore 0.5 Antimony 1 Natural gas 0.8 Lead 3 Tin 0.2	1. 67.7/96.9; 76 275 kWh (5% hydr., 8% nucl.) 2a. Meat 1 460 Sawnwood 5 143 Sugar 815 Butter and cheese 344 Beer 24.9 Mhl b. Iron 9 624 Steel 14 832 Aluminium 32 Plastics 1 034 Wool yarn 57 Petroleum products 13.5 Cotton yarn 140 3. Telephones 3 226; Cars 2 442 Rail: 19 320 pass.-km.; 73 992 ton-km. Air: 1 592 pass.-km.; 164 ton-km.	Exports: $17 196 Imports: $17 080 Machinery Machinery Manufactured goods Petroleum Iron and steel Non-ferrous metals Vehicles Iron and steel Main trade is with: U.S.S.R., E. Germany, Poland, Hungary Revenue from tourism: $243

DENMARK

1. Kingdom 2. Danish 3. Danish Krone 4. $1 = 8.15 £1 = 12.33	1. 43 th. sq. km. 2. 5 114; 119 per sq. km. 3. BR 10; DR 11; AI 0.1% 4. Urb. pop.: 4 243 (83%) 5. Copenhagen 1 366	1. GDP $50 252 (2.1%); $9 834 (1.8%) Agric. 5%, Indust. 18%, Others 77% 2. Barley 6 072 Oats 150 Rye 608 Wheat 2 446 Potatoes 1 121 Apples 116 Rape seed 517 3. Pigs 9 000 Cattle 2 900 4. Fish 1 862 5. Roundwood 2 953 6. Crude petroleum 2.1	1. 3.1/22.2; 22 186 kWh 2a. Pork 1 041 Beef 248 Butter and cheese 400 Sugar 595 b. Cotton yarn 2.0 Steel 528 Petroleum products 6.5 Ships (grt.) 376 3. Telephones 3 453; Cars 1 367 Rail: 48 036 pass.-km.; 18 888 ton-km. Air: 3 193 pass.-km.; 412 ton-km. Sea: 11 784 loaded; 31 020 unloaded	Exports: $16 349 Imports: $16 973 Machinery Machinery Pork Manufactured products Other meat Iron and steel Fish Textiles Exports to: Sweden, U.K., W. Germany Imports from: W. Germany, Sweden, U.K. Invisible trade balance: −$1 499 Revenue from tourism: $1 305 Aid given (net): $774

ECUADOR

1. Republic 2. Spanish 3. Sucre 4. $1 = 125.25 £1 = 189.49	1. 284 th. sq. km. 2. 9 378; 33 per sq. km. 3. BR 42; DR 10; AI 3.1% 4. Urb. pop.: 3 978 (45%) 5. Quito 1 110	1. GDP $11 684 (6.0%); $1 283 (2.5%) Agric. 14%, Indust. 36%, Others 50% 2. Maize 300 Rice 470 Bananas/Plantains 2 600 Oranges 350 Cocoa 60 Coffee 90 3. Cattle 3 300 Sheep 2 311 4. Fish 307 5. Roundwood 7 795 6. Crude petroleum 12.6 Gold 5.4 Nickel 16.5	1. 17.8/5.8; 4 289 kWh (40% hydr.) 2a. Meat 238 Sawnwood 980 Sugar 328 b. Petroleum products 3.6 3. Telephones 290; Cars 70 Rail: 230 pass.-km.; 625 ton-km. Air: 862 pass.-km.; 117 ton-km. Sea: 5 319 loaded; 2 451 unloaded	Exports: $2 581 Imports: $1 716 Bananas Machinery Coffee Vehicles Cocoa Chemical products Exports to: U.S.A., Panama, Colombia, Chile Imports from: U.S.A., W. Germany, Japan Invisible trade balance: −$1 085 Revenue from tourism: $131 Aid received (net): $126.8

EGYPT

1. Republic 2. Arabic 3. Egyptian Pound 4. $1 = 0.83 £1 = 2.06	1. 1 001 th. sq. km. 2. 48 503; 48 per sq. km. 3. BR 38; DR 10; AI 2.5% 4. Urb. pop.: 19 255 (44%) 5. Cairo 6 818	1. GDP $31 750 (8.7%); $711 (6.0%) Agric. 19%, Indust. 29%, Others 52% 2. Maize 3 600 Wheat 1 815 Rice 2 300 Tomatoes 2 600 Oranges 1 450 Dates 450 Cotton lint 390 Cottonseed 677 3. Cattle 1 825 Buffaloes 2 410 4. Fish 140 5. Roundwood 1 935 6. Iron ore 1.1 Salt 853 Crude petroleum 39.3 Phosphates 647	1. 56.5/25.9; 23 520 kWh (50% hydr.) 2a. Meat 543 Sugar 780 b. Cotton yarn 244 Iron 700 Wool yarn 14.3 Steel 1 000 Fertilizers 600 Cement 4 595 Petroleum products 16.9 3. Telephones 522; Cars 461 Rail: 10 995 pass.-km.; 2 472 ton-km. Air: 3 643 pass.-km.; 395 ton-km. Sea: 10 944 loaded; 33 084 unloaded	Exports: $3 215 Imports: $10 274 Cotton Machinery Rice Manufactured products Cotton lint Wheat Fruit and vegetables Vehicles Exports to: U.S.S.R., Italy, Netherlands Imports from: U.S.A., France, Italy, U.K., W. Germany Invisible trade balance: −$277 Revenue from tourism: $386 Aid received (net): $1 477.5

ETHIOPIA

1. Republic 2. Amharic 3. Ethiopian Birr 4. $1 = 2.09 £1 = 3.16	1. 1 222 th. sq. km. 2. 43 350; 35 per sq. km. 3. BR 49; DR 23; AI 2.6% 4. Urb. pop.: 4 719 (14%) 5. Addis-Ababa 1 478	1. GDP $4 429 (. . .); $135 (. . .) Agric. 45%, Indust. 10%, Others 45% 2. Barley 848 Millet 145 Coffee 240 Maize 1 275 3. Cattle 26 000 Sheep 23 450 5. Roundwood 29 764 6. Gold 400kg Salt 124	1. 0.07/0.84; 753 kWh (75% hydr.) 2a. Sugar 198 Sawnwood 45 b. Cotton yarn 9.2 Cement 159 3. Telephones 86; Cars 43 Rail: 310 pass.-km.; 131 ton-km. Air: 762 pass.-km.; 97 ton-km. Sea: 547 loaded; 1 753 unloaded	Exports: $416 Imports: $942 Coffee Machinery Hides Manufactured products Exports to: U.S.A., Djibouti, Saudi Arabia Imports from: Japan, W. Germany, Kuwait, Italy, Saudi Arabia Aid received (net): $201.8

FINLAND

1. Republic 2. Finnish, Swedish 3. Markka 4. $1 = 4.99 £1 = 7.54	1. 337 th. sq. km. 2. 4 908; 15 per sq. km. 3. BR 13; DR 9; AI 0.3% 4. Urb. pop.: 2 873 (60%) 5. Helsinki 932	1. GDP $47 148 (3.4%); $9 661 (3.1%) Agric. 7%, Indust. 24%, Others 69% 2. Wheat 478 Barley 1 715 Oats 1 321 Potatoes 745 3. Cattle 1 620 Pigs 1 383 4. Fish 157 5. Roundwood 38 439 6. Iron ore 0.7 Chrome 170 Titanium 164 Copper 31 Zinc 60 Gold 784kg Silver 27t	1. 4.1/21.6; 40 236 kWh (33% hydr., 42% nucl.) 2a. Meat 320 Butter and cheese 152 Sawnwood 8 023 Wood pulp 7 200 b. Paper 6 400 Newsprint 1 556 Iron 2 028 Steel 2 628 Cotton yarn 7.2 Ships (grt.) 315 Petroleum products 9.2 3. Telephones 2 511; Cars 1 352 Rail: 3 276 pass.-km.; 7 980 ton-km. Air: 2 589 pass.-km.; 297 ton-km. Sea: 20 724 loaded; 30 260 unloaded	Exports: $13 505 Imports: $12 443 Paper and cardboard Machinery Wood pulp Crude petroleum Sawnwood Petroleum products Machinery Iron and steel Ships and boats Textiles Clothing Vehicles Exports to: U.K., Sweden, U.S.S.R., W. Germany Imports from: Sweden, W. Germany, U.S.S.R., U.K. Invisible trade balance: −$1 323 Revenue from tourism: $579 Aid given (net): $150

For detailed table headings and notes see first page of this section

Country	Area and Population	Production	Manufactures	Trade

FRANCE

1. Republic
2. French
3. French Franc
4. $1 = 7.04
   £1 = 10.65

1. 547 th. sq. km.
2. 55 172; 101 per sq. km.
3. BR 14; DR 10; AI 0.3%
4. Urb. pop.: 43 958 (80%)
5. Paris 8 510

1. GDP $445 913 (2.8%); $8 115 (2.4%)
   Agric. 4%, Indust. 26%, Others 70%
2. Wheat 32 884 — Barley 11 543
   Oats 1 875 — Maize 10 321
   Potatoes 6 200 — Sugarbeet 27 790
   Apples 2 935 — Grapes 9 400
   Tomatoes 790 — Pears 485
   Tobacco 37 — Wool 23
   Rape seed 1 354
3. Cattle 23 570 — Pigs 11 400
   Sheep 12 260 — Goats 1 200
   Horses 310
4. Fish 784
5. Roundwood 39 839
6. Coal 16.6 — Iron ore 4.5
   Crude petroleum 1 680 — Lead 2
   Natural gas 231 — Zinc 36
   Salt 6 579 — Potash 1 651
   Bauxite 1 530 — Nickel 6.9
   Silver 24 — Uranium 3 299

1. 57.0/208.2; 283 400 kWh (25% hydr., 48% nucl.)
2a. Meat 5 585 — Butter and cheese 1 855
    Wine 6 447 — Beer 22.4 Mhl
    Sugar 4 340 — Sawnwood 9 367
b. Iron 15 420 — Steel 19 020
   Aluminium 510 — Cement 22 716
   Plastics 2 694 — Paper 5 300
   Synthetic fibres 38 — Petroleum products 68.2
   Cotton yarn 193 — Wool yarn 107
   Ships (grt.) 221 — Radios 2 733
   Vehicles:
   pass. 2 910, comm. 424
3. Telephones 26 940; Cars 19 300
   Rail: 60 276 pass.-km.; 60 120 ton-km.
   Air: 37 916 pass.-km.; 5 670 ton-km.
   Sea: 52 284 loaded; 172 332 unloaded

Exports: $93 276 — Imports: $103 807
Machinery — Machinery
Vehicles — Petrol
Iron and steel — Iron and steel
Textiles — Non-ferrous metals
Wheat — Vehicles
Organic chemical — Textile fibres
products — Meat
Non-ferrous metals — Fruits
Petroleum products
Petrol
Wine
Exports to: W. Germany, Belgium-Luxembourg, Italy, U.K.
Imports from: W. Germany, Italy, Belgium-Luxembourg, U.S.A.
Invisible trade balance: +$5 190
Revenue from tourism: $6 991
Aid given (net): $9 418

FRENCH GUIANA

1. French Overseas Dept.
2. French
3. Franc
4. $1 = 7.04
   £1 = 10.65

1. 91 th. sq. km.
2. 82; 1 per sq. km.
3. BR 30; DR 7; AI 3.4%
4. Urb. pop.: 48 (67%)
5. Cayenne 38

2. Cassava 8 — Bananas 1
3. Pigs 10 — Cattle 14
5. Roundwood 254
6. Gold 160kg

1. . . ./0.19; 150 kWh
2a. Sugar. . . — Sawnwood 19
3. Telephones 18; Cars 10
   Sea: 25 loaded; 219 unloaded

Exports: $37 — Imports: $249
Timber — Machinery
Exports to: France, U.S.A., Japan
Imports from: France, Trinidad and Tobago
Aid received (net): $95.4

GABON

1. Republic
2. French, Bantu
3. C.F.A. Franc
4. $1 = 352.13
   £1 = 532.25

1. 268 th. sq. km.
2. 1 151; 4 per sq. km.
3. BR 33; DR 19; AI 1.6%
4. Urb. pop.: 367 (32%)
5. Libreville 350

1. GDP $3 603 (. . .); $3 246 (. . .)
   Agric. 5%, Indust. 49%, Others 46%
2. Cassava 265 — Bananas 178
   Cocoa 2
3. Goats 60 — Sheep 80
4. Fish 52
5. Roundwood 2 608
6. Crude petroleum 7.5 — Gold 20kg
   Manganese 928 — Uranium 1 007

1. 11.8/1.1; 535 kWh (48% hydr.)
2a. Sawnwood 108 — Beer 0.6Mhl
b. Petroleum products 1.3
3. Telephones 7; Cars 22
   Air: 430 pass.-km.; 67 ton-km.
   Sea: 8 040 loaded; 631 unloaded

Exports: $1 975 — Imports: $853
Petrol — Manufactured
Sawnwood — products
Manganese ores — Machinery
Vehicles
Exports to: France, U.S.A., Argentina
Imports from: France, U.S.A., Japan
Aid received (net): $47.8

GERMANY (EAST)

1. Republic
2. German
3. Ostmark
4. $1 = 2.21
   £1 = 3.34

1. 108 th. sq. km. (including E. Berlin)
2. 16 644; 154 per sq. km.
3. BR 14; DR 13; AI −0.1%
4. Urb. pop.: 12 784 (77%)
5. Berlin (East) 1 173

1. GDP $72 820 (3.3%); $4 368 (3.4%)
   Agric. 9%, Indust. 74%, Others 17%
2. Barley 4 400 — Rye 2 300
   Wheat 4 100 — Potatoes 8 000
   Apples 500 — Rape seed 303
3. Pigs 13 058 — Cattle 5 908
   Sheep 2 359
4. Fish 240
5. Roundwood 10 908
6. Lignite 296.3 — Natural gas 145
   Copper 12 — Potash 3 431
   Salt 3 126 — Tin 2.5
   Coal 1.0 — Silver 40

1. 91.7/121.8; 104 928 kWh (12% hydr., 1.6% nucl.)
2a. Meat 1 812 — Butter 297
    Sugar 690 — Beer 25.4Mhl
    Sawnwood 2 446
b. Cotton yarn 134 — Wool yarn 37
   Iron 2 352 — Steel 7 572
   Ships (grt.) 350 — Petroleum products 19.4
   Vehicles: — Radios 900
   pass. 202, comm. 41
3. Telephones 3 252; Cars 3 000
   Rail: 22 920 pass.-km.; 56 652 ton-km.
   Air: . . . pass.-km.; . . . ton-km.
   Sea: 4 000 loaded; 15 500 unloaded

Exports: $24 836 — Imports: $22 940
Machinery — Machinery
Vehicles — Crude petroleum
Consumer goods — Iron ore
Coal
Fuels
The principal trade is with: U.S.S.R., Czechoslovakia, W. Germany, Poland

---

GERMANY (WEST)

1. Federal Republic
2. German
3. Deutschmark
4. $1 = 2.21
   £1 = 3.34

1. 249 th. sq. km. (including W. Berlin)
2. 61 015; 245 per sq. km.
3. BR 10; DR 11; AI −0.2%
4. Urb. pop.: 52 616 (86%)
5. Bonn 293

1. GDP $554 511 (3.5%); $9 064 (3.6%)
   Agric. 2%, Indust. 31%, Others 67%
2. Barley 10 284 — Wheat 10 223
   Rye 1 930 — Potatoes 7 753
   Apples 1 752 — Grapes 1 066
3. Pigs 23 449 — Cattle 15 552
4. Fish 306
5. Roundwood 29 485
6. Coal 84.0 — Zinc 113
   Lignite 127.3 — Natural gas 635
   Iron ore 0.3 — Crude petroleum 0.3
   Salt 11 266 — Potash 2 419
   Silver 38 — Lead 27

1. 157.8/339.7; 373 813 kWh (5% hydr., 18% nucl.)
2a. Meat 5 239 — Butter and cheese 1 444
    Sugar 3 150 — Sawnwood 9 500
    Wine 810 — Beer 91.2Mhl
b. Cotton yarn 194 — Wool yarn 48
   Iron 30 360 — Steel 39 384
   Aluminium 1 219 — Radios 2 864
   Vehicles: — Petroleum products 76.6
   pass. 3 788, comm. 264 — Ships (grt.) 489
   Synthetic fibres 143
3. Telephones 30 122; Cars 25 036
   Rail: 38 616 pass.-km.; 59 844 ton-km.
   Air: 21 625 pass.-km.; 3 746 ton-km.
   Sea: 43 632 loaded; 84 984 unloaded

Exports: $169 784 — Imports: $151 246
Machinery — Machinery
Vehicles — Non-ferrous metals
Iron and steel — Crude petroleum
Textiles — Iron and steel
Organic chemicals — Textiles
— Food
Exports to: France, Netherlands, U.S.A., Belgium-Luxembourg, Italy
Imports from: Netherlands, France, Belgium-Luxembourg, Italy, U.S.A.
Invisible trade balance: −$5 200
Revenue from tourism: $5 614
Aid given (net): $7 467

GHANA

1. Republic
2. English
3. Cedi
4. $1 = 90.39
   £1 = 136.62

1. 239 th. sq. km.
2. 13 588; 57 per sq. km.
3. BR 47; DR 16; AI 3.3%
4. Urb. pop.: 4 044 (31%)
5. Accra 965

1. GDP $8 182 (2.3%); $668 (−1.2%)
   Agric. 51%, Indust. 6%, Others 43%
2. Cassava 1 900 — Cocoa 188
   Groundnuts 90 — Maize 534
3. Sheep 2 000 — Goats 2 000
4. Fish 228
5. Roundwood 9 803
6. Bauxite 64 — Manganese 76.2
   Gold 11.6 — Diamonds 350

1. 0.4/1.2; 2 589 kWh (98% hydr.)
2a. Sawnwood 381 — Beer 0.3Mhl
3. Telephones 70; Cars 108
   Rail: 314 pass.-km.; 92 ton-km.
   Air: 291 pass.-km.; 31 ton-km.
   Sea: 1 471 loaded; 2 493 unloaded

Exports: $57 — Imports: $247
Cocoa — Manufactured goods
Aluminium — Machinery
Exports to: U.K., U.S.A., W. Germany, U.S.S.R., Netherlands
Imports from: U.S.A., U.K., W. Germany, Nigeria
Invisible trade balance: −$219
Aid received (net): $175.2

GREECE

1. Republic
2. Greek
3. Drachma
4. $1 = 140.1
   £1 = 211.76

1. 132 th. sq. km.
2. 9 935; 75 per sq. km.
3. BR 13; DR 9; AI 0.6%
4. Urb. pop.: 6 432 (65%)
5. Athens 3 027

1. GDP $29 361 (3.7%); $2 966 (2.5%)
   Agric. 15%, Indust. 19%, Others 66%
2. Wheat 2 646 — Potatoes 980
   Olives 1 400 — Tomatoes 2 250
   Grapes 1 565 — Tobacco 137
3. Sheep 8 500 — Goats 4 650
4. Fish 100
5. Roundwood 2 624
6. Bauxite 2 386 — Lignite 32.4
   Chrome 35 — Magnesite 891
   Zinc 23 — Lead 22
   Nickel 13.6

1. 7.9/21.4; 22 262 kWh (10% hydr.)
2a. Olive oil 285 — Wine 540
    Butter and cheese 262 — Sawnwood 390
b. Cotton yarn 119 — Steel 900
   Cement 13 320 — Aluminium 136
   Petroleum products 12.8
3. Telephones 2 957; Cars 999
   Rail: 1 536 pass.-km.; 768 ton-km.
   Air: 4 924 pass.-km.; 507 ton-km.
   Sea: 20 328 loaded; 28 224 unloaded

Exports: $4 811 — Imports: $9 434
Tobacco — Machinery
Iron and steel — Ships and boats
Raisins — Vehicles
Aluminium — Iron and steel: Crude
Cotton — petroleum
Exports to: W. Germany, Italy, France, Saudi Arabia
Imports from: W. Germany, Italy, Japan
Invisible trade balance: +$466
Revenue from tourism: $1 527

Country	Area and Population	Production	Manufactures	Trade

GUINEA

1. Republic
2. French
3. Guinean Franc
4. $1 = 339.89
   £1 = 513.74

1. 246 th. sq. km.
2. 6 075; 25 per sq. km.
3. BR 47; DR 25; AI 2.3%
4. Urb. pop.: 1 378 (26%)
5. Conakry 763

1. GDP $1 910 (. . .); $369 (. . .)
2. Cassava 650 — Rice 400
   Coffee 15 — Bananas 350
   Sweet potatoes 73 — Palm oil 45
3. Sheep 455 — Cattle 1 850
5. Roundwood 3 644
6. Bauxite 14 738 — Diamonds 40

1. 0.01/0.42; 500 kWh (16% hydr.)
2a. Sawnwood 90
3. Telephones 10; Cars 10
   Air: 144 pass.-km.; 14 ton-km.
   Sea: 10 000 loaded; 545 unloaded

Exports: $70 — Imports: $100
Bauxite and — Machinery
aluminium — Manufactured goods
Iron ore — Foods
Coffee
Main trade is with: Portugal, Sweden
Aid received (net): $82.3

HAITI

1. Republic
2. French, Creole
3. Gourde
4. $1 = 5.00
   £1 = 7.56

1. 28 th. sq. km.
2. 6 585; 235 per sq. km.
3. BR 42; DR 16; AI 2.5%
4. Urb. pop.: 1 452 (28%)
5. Port-au-Prince 888

1. GDP $1 029 (4.1%); $199 (2.3%)
   Agric. 32%, Indust. 17%, Others 51%
2. Bananas 550 — Sisal 11
   Cocoa 3 — Coffee 38
3. Pigs 500 — Goats 1 100
5. Roundwood 5 624
6. Bauxite 377

1. 0.03/0.3; 373 kWh (70% hydr.)
2a. Meat 64 — Sugar 35
3. Telephones 18; Cars 17
   Sea: 723 loaded; 561 unloaded.

Exports: $187 — Imports: $314
Coffee — Foods
Bauxite — Textiles
Sugar — Machinery
Sisal — Mineral oils
Exports to: U.S.A, France, Belgium-Luxembourg
Imports from: U.S.A., Neth. Antilles, Japan, Canada,
Aid received (net): $101.5

HONG KONG

1. British colony
2. English, Chinese
3. Hong Kong Dollar
4. $1 = 7.77
   £1 = 11.74

1. 1.04 th. sq. km.
2. 5 423; 5 423 per sq. km.
3. BR 14; DR 5; AI 2.1%
4. Urb. pop.: 4 573 (92%)
5. Hong Kong 1 184

1. GDP $26 786 (12.0%); $4 997 (8.8%)
   Agric. 1%, Indust. 21%, Others 78%
2. Rice 1
3. Pigs 500 — Cattle 5
4. Fish 189
5. Roundwood 180
6. Iron ore . . .

1. . . ./102; 16 482 kWh
2a. Cotton yarn 137 — Wool yarn 6
   Sawnwood 262
3. Telephones 1 823; Cars 228
   Rail: 1 476 pass.-km.; 96 ton-km.
   Sea: 13 980 loaded; 33 504 unloaded

Exports: $28 317 — Imports: $28 567
Clothing — Textiles
Textiles — Machines
Toys and games — Diamonds
Radios — Cotton
Exports to: U.S.A., U.K., Japan, W. Germany
Imports from: Japan, China, U.S.A., U.K., Singapore
Revenue from tourism: $1 457
Aid received (net): $19.8

HUNGARY

1. Republic
2. Hungarian
3. Forint
4. $1 = 45.84
   £1 = 69.29

1. 93 th. sq. km.
2. 10 649; 115 per sq. km.
3. BR 12; DR 14; AI 0.7%
4. Urb. pop.: 5 810 (54%)
5. Budapest 2 064

1. NMP $15 705 (3.4%); $1 473 (3.1%)
   Agric. 13%, Indust. 38%, Others 49%
2. Maize 6 700 — Wheat 7 300
   Potatoes 1 300 — Tobacco 17
   Apples 1 144 — Grapes 850
3. Pigs 9 844 — Sheep 2 977
4. Fish 44
5. Roundwood 6 396
6. Coal 2.6 — Bauxite 2 994
   Lignite 22.5 — Manganese 17.6
   Natural gas 249 — Crude petroleum 27.0

1. 22.4/39.8; 25 775 kWh (0.6% hydr., 10% nucl.)
2a. Sugar 533 — Sawnwood 1 180
   Wine 535 — Beer 7.9 Mhl
b. Iron 2 100 — Steel 3 744
   Aluminium 74 — Cotton yarn 56.4
   Wool yarn 11 — Petroleum products 7.4
3. Telephones 1 297; Cars 1 182
   Rail: 10 512 pass.-km.; 22 308 ton-km.
   Air: 1 208 pass.-km.; 130 ton-km.

Exports: $8 563 — Imports: $8 109
Machinery — Machinery
Vehicles — Vehicles
Fruit and vegetables — Iron and steel
Iron and steel — Crude petroleum
Medicinal products — Petroleum products
— Chemical products
Main trade is with: U.S.S.R., W. Germany, E.Germany,
Czechoslovakia
Invisible trade balance: −$609
Revenue from tourism: $394

ICELAND

1. Republic
2. Icelandic
3. Icelandic Krona
4. $1 = 41.25
   £1 = 62.35

1. 103 th. sq. km.
2. 241; 2 per sq. km.
3. BR 18; DR 7; AI 1.1%
4. Urb. pop.: 207 (89%)
5. Reykjavik 124

1. GDP $2 636 (4.1%); $10 983 (3.1%)
2. Potatoes 13
3. Sheep 770
4. Fish 839 — Whaling 352

1. 0.5/1.1; 3 781 kWh (95% hydr., 4.8% geo.)
2a. Meat 25
b. Aluminium 82
3. Telephones 111; Cars 95
   Air: 1 405 pass.-km.; 151 ton-km.
   Sea: 502 loaded; 1 358 unloaded

Exports: $728 — Imports: $820
Fish, frozen and fresh — Machinery
Fish, salted and — Petroleum products
smoked — Textiles
Fish meal — Iron and steel
Aluminium — Paper and cardboard
Cod liver oil
Exports to: U.S.A., U.K., W. Germany
Imports from: W. Germany, U.K., U.S.S.R., Denmark,
Sweden

INDIA

1. Federal Republic
2. Hindi, English
3. Indian Rupee
4. $1 = 12.29
   £1 = 18.57

1. 3 288 th. sq. km.
2. 750 900; 228 per sq. km.
3. BR 34; DR 12; AI 2.0%
4. Urb. pop.: 159 727 (23%)
5. Delhi 5 729

1. GDP $173 883 (3.7%); $233 (1.7%)
   Agric. 29%, Indust. 17%, Others 54%
2. Wheat 45 148 — Millet 11 800
   Rice 91 000 — Tea 645
   Coffee 103 — Tobacco 497
   Sorghum 1 180 — Rubber 185
   Jute 1 404 — Cotton lint 1 250
   Cottonseed 2 500
3. Cattle 182 160 — Goats 80 800
4. Fish 2 520
5. Roundwood 232 537
6. Coal 144.7 — Manganese 442
   Iron ore 25.8 — Chrome 390
   Bauxite 2 306 — Crude petroleum 25.8
   Copper 47 — Lead 19
   Zinc 44 — Diamonds 14
   Gold 2.0 — Silver 25

1. 159.8/169.3; 147 952 kWh (35% hydr., 1.4% nucl.)
2a. Sugar 6 420 — Butter 740
   Sawnwood 10 976
b. Iron 9 588 — Steel 10 344
   Aluminium 268 — Zinc 55
   Cement 29 028 — Cotton yarn 1 093
   Radios 1 563 — Petroleum products 26.7
3. Telephones 2 982; Cars 1 068
   Rail: 220 464 pass.-km.; 172 536 ton-km.
   Air: 13 259 pass.-km.; 1 625 ton-km.
   Sea: 38 900 loaded; 40 380 unloaded

Exports: $8 474 — Imports: $13 501
Jute products — Machinery
Tea — Wheat
Iron ore — Petrol
Iron and steel — Cotton
Cotton goods — Iron and steel
Exports to: U.S.A., Japan, U.S.S.R., U.K.
Imports from: U.S.A., U.K., Japan, W. Germany
Invisible trade balance: −$621
Revenue from tourism: $800
Aid received (net): $1 933.4

INDONESIA

1. Republic
2. Bahasa Indonesia
3. Rupiah
4. $1 = 1 123.63
   £1 = 1 698.36

1. 1 905 th. sq. km.
2. 163 393; 86 per sq. km.
3. BR 36; DR 15; AI 1.8%
4. Urb. pop.: 32 845 (22%)
5. Jakarta 6 503

1. GDP $79 994 (7.9%); $500 (6.0%)
   Agric. 25%, Indust. 30%, Others 45%
2. Cassava 14 000 — Groundnuts 820
   Rice 37 500 — Copra 800
   Coffee 329 — Tea 115
   Palm oil 1 000 — Tobacco 118
   Rubber 1 150
3. Cattle 6 800 — Goats 7 910
4. Fish 2 112
5. Roundwood 122 249
6. Coal 1.1 — Tin 23.2
   Bauxite 1 003 — Natural gas 690
   Nickel 47.8 — Crude petroleum 66.3
   Diamonds 2.7 — Copper 86
   Silver 35

1. 120.1/38.3; 15 280 kWh (10% hydr.)
2a. Meat 537 — Sawnwood 6 314
   Sugar 1 675
b. Cement 6 612 — Tin 23
   Petroleum products 20.8
3. Telephones 584; Cars 791
   Rail: 6 384 pass.-km.; 1 176 ton-km.
   Air: 8 044 pass.-km.; 875 ton-km.
   Sea: 107 124 loaded; 24 876 unloaded

Exports: $21 858 — Imports: $13 882
Crude petroleum — Machinery
Petroleum products — Textiles
Rubber — Iron and steel
Coffee — Vehicles
Tin — Rice
Spices
Exports to: Japan, Singapore, U.S.A.,
Trinidad and Tobago
Imports from: U.S.A., W. Germany, Japan, Singapore
Aid received (net): $1 176.4

IRAN

1. Islamic Republic
2. Persian
3. Rial
4. $1 = 78.56
   £1 = 118.75

1. 1 648 th. sq. km.
2. 44 212; 27 per sq. km.
3. BR 43; DR 12; AI 3%
4. Urb. pop.: 20 774 (50%)
5. Teheran 4 589

1. GDP $128 921 (−4.7%); $3 161 (−7.0%)
   Agric. 18%, Indust. 26%, Others 56%
2. Wheat 5 500 — Cottonseed 180
   Rice 1 230 — Cotton lint 95
   Dates 330 — Tea 45
   Raisins 52 — Tobacco 25
3. Sheep 34 000 — Goats 13 600
5. Roundwood 5 721
6. Natural gas 264 — Crude petroleum 107.9
   Chrome 40 — Zinc 30
   Lead 20 — Salt 750
   Silver 30

1. 190.8/47.3; 29 900 kWh (22% hydr.)
2a. Sugar 725 — Sawnwood 163
b. Cotton yarn 88 — Wool yarn 19
   Cement 10 270 — Petroleum products 25.5
3. Telephones 1 049; Cars 933
   Rail: 2 526 pass.-km.; 3 861 ton-km.
   Air: 1 852 pass.-km.; 215 ton-km.
   Sea: 80 000 loaded; 6 000 unloaded

Exports: $19 414 — Imports: $11 539
Crude petroleum — Machinery
Petroleum products — Iron and steel
Carpets — Vehicles
— Textiles
Exports to: U.S.S.R., W. Germany, U.S.A., Italy,
Saudi Arabia
Imports from: W. Germany, U.S.A., Japan, U.K.
Invisible trade balance: −$3 442

For detailed table headings and notes see first page of this section

167

Country	Area and Population	Production	Manufactures	Trade

IRAQ

Country
1. Republic
2. Arabic
3. Iraq Dinar
4. $1 = 0.31 £1 = 0.47

Area and Population
1. 435 th. sq. km.
2. 15 898; 37 per sq. km.
3. BR 47; DR 13; AI 3.5%
4. Urb. pop.: 8 683 (68%)
5. Bagdad 2 969

Production
1. GDP $48 879 (. . .); $3 700 (. . .) Agric. 7%, Indust. 60%, Others 33%
2. Barley 300 — Rice 95; Wheat 300 — Dates 115; Cottonseed 6
3. Sheep 8 300 — Goats 2 300
5. Roundwood 113
6. Natural gas 17 — Crude petroleum 60.7

Manufactures
1. 69.1/9.2; 13 700 kWh (4% hydr.)
2b. Petroleum products 7.7
3. Telephones 185; Cars 170; Rail: 797 pass.-km.; 2 254 ton-km.; Air: 1 470 pass.-km.; 187 ton-km.; Sea: 95 750 loaded; 4 004 unloaded

Trade
Exports: $10 530 — Imports: $7 903
Crude petroleum / Manufactured goods
Dates / Machinery / Food
Exports to: India, China, Kuwait
Imports from: U.K., W. Germany, Japan
Revenue from tourism: $170
Aid received (net): $12.4

IRELAND

Country
1. Republic
2. Irish, English
3. Irish pound
4. $1 = 0.73 £1 = 1.10

Area and Population
1. 70 th. sq. km.
2. 3 552; 51 per sq. km.
3. BR 19; DR 9; AI 2.0%
4. Urb. pop.: 1 914 (56%)
5. Dublin 915

Production
1. GDP $16 613 (3.7%); $4 733 (2.5%) Agric. 11%, Indust. 24%, Others 65%
2. Barley 1 600 — Wheat 660; Potatoes 1 000 — Wool 10; Tomatoes 19
3. Cattle 6 759 — Sheep 3 754
4. Fish 203
5. Roundwood 1 026
6. Lead 37 — Zinc 206; Coal 0.06 — Natural gas 83

Manufactures
1. 4.3/11.2; 11 178 kWh (11% hydr.)
2a. Meat 638 — Sawnwood 247; Butter and cheese 216
b. Wool yarn 5.2 — Petroleum products 0.7; Cotton yarn 20
3. Telephones 720; Cars 714; Rail: 816 pass.-km.; 552 ton-km.; Air: 2 343 pass.-km.; 285 ton-km.; Sea: 5 000 loaded; 14 500 unloaded

Trade
Exports: $9 629 — Imports: $9 663
Cattle / Machinery
Beef / Textiles
Dairy products / Vehicles
Non-ferrous metals / Iron and steel
Machinery / Crude petroleum
Main trade is with U.K.
Exports to: U.S.A., France, W. Germany, Netherlands, Belgium-Lux
Imports from: U.S.A., W. Germany, France, Italy, Japan
Invisible trade balance: –$1 589
Revenue from tourism: $477

ISRAEL

Country
1. Republic
2. Hebrew, Arabic
3. Shekel
4. $1 = 1.49 £1 = 2.25

Area and Population
1. 21 th. sq. km.
2. 4 233; 202 per sq. km.
3. BR 24; DR 7; AI 2.1%
4. Urb. pop.: 3 525 (87%)
5. Jerusalem 429

Production
1. GDP $24 483 (3.1%); $6 075 (0.8%) Agric. 4%, Indust. 23%, Others 73%
2. Wheat 130 — Cottonseed 187; Oranges 921 — Cotton lint 94; Grapefruits 409 — Tomatoes 359
3. Cattle 330 — Sheep 240
4. Fish 22
5. Roundwood 118
6. Phosphates 1 966 — Potash 1 000; Salt 145 — Crude petroleum 0.02

Manufactures
1. 0.1/10.2; 14 578 kWh
2a. Meat 234 — Butter and cheese 66; Wine 33
b. Cotton yarn 16.8 — Wool yarn 5.6; Cement 1 884
3. Telephones 1 230; Cars 519; Rail: 221 pass.-km.; 827 ton-km.; Air: 4 648 pass.-km.; 720 ton-km.; Sea: 7 080 loaded; 9 576 unloaded

Trade
Exports: $5 804 — Imports: $8 411
Diamonds / Machinery
Fruit / Diamonds
Clothing / Iron and steel
Exports to: U.S.A., W. Germany, U.K., Hong Kong
Imports from: U.S.A., W. Germany, U.K., Netherlands, Switzerland
Invisible trade balance: –$2 213
Revenue from tourism: $900
Aid received (net): $957.3

ITALY

Country
1. Republic
2. Italian
3. Italian Lira
4. $1 = 1 512.40 £1 = 2 286.00

Area and Population
1. 301 th. sq. km.
2. 57 128; 190 per sq. km.
3. BR 10; DR 9; AI 0.3%
4. Urb. pop.: 40 453 (71%)
5. Rome 2 831

Production
1. GDP $316 190 (3.6%); $5 549 (3.2%) Agric. 5%, Indust. 27%, Others 68%
2. Wheat 10 005 — Maize 6 781; Tomatoes 6 143 — Grapes 11 200; Olives 2 050 — Tobacco 153; Oranges 1 700 — Apples 2 050; Pears 1 070 — Lemons 690
3. Cattle 9 113 — Sheep 9 228
4. Fish 478
5. Roundwood 5 658
6. Lignite 1 950 — Natural gas 501; Zinc 43 — Crude petroleum 2.2; Asbestos 139 — Bauxite 13; Lead 24

Manufactures
1. 27.6/172.6; 182 880 kWh (24% hydr., 3.1% nucl., 1.4% geo.)
2a. Meat 3 732 — Butter and cheese 731; Sugar 1 370 — Wine 7 000; Olives 430 — Sawnwood 2 264
b. Iron 11 892 — Steel 23 076; Aluminium 513 — Woven silk 20; Cotton yarn 150 — Wool yarn 319; Televisions 1 719 — Ships (grt.) 233; Petroleum products 71.4 — Vehicles:; Synthetic fibres 595 — pass. 1 439, comm. 160
3. Telephones 20 453; Cars 18 603; Rail: 37 128 pass.-km.; 17 868 ton-km.; Air: 15 143 pass.-km.; 1 953 ton-km.; Sea: 34 512 loaded; 187 584 unloaded

Trade
Exports: $73 303 — Imports: $84 215
Machinery / Machinery
Vehicles / Petroleum
Textiles / Non-ferrous metals
Clothing / Iron and steel
Petroleum products / Textile fibres
Shoes / Cereals
Iron and steel / Vehicles
Fruit / Meat
Exports to: France, W. Germany, U.S.A., U.K.
Imports from: W. Germany, France, U.S.A.
Invisible trade balance: +$2 026
Revenue from tourism: $8 234
Aid given (net): $3 676

IVORY COAST

Country
1. Republic
2. French
3. C.F.A. Franc
4. $1 = 352.13 £1 = 532.25

Area and Population
1. 322 th. sq. km.
2. 9 810; 30 per sq. km.
3. BR 46; DR 20; AI 3.4%
4. Urb. pop.: 4 169 (44%)
5. Abidjan 1 850

Production
1. GDP $7 586 (7.1%); $856 (2.9%) Agric. 27%, Indust. 11%, Others 62%
2. Rice 490 — Coffee 285; Cassava 800 — Cocoa 411
3. Sheep 1 400 — Goats 1 400
4. Fish 94
5. Roundwood 11 839
6. Diamonds 70

Manufactures
1. 1.9/1.8; 1 932 kWh (90% hydr.)
2a. Sawnwood 805 — Petroleum products 2.7
3. Telephones 88; Cars 167; Rail: 852 pass.-km.; 576 ton-km.; Air: 316 pass.-km.; 51 ton-km.; Sea: 4 536 loaded; 4 848 unloaded

Trade
Exports: $2 067 — Imports: $1 340
Cocoa / Machinery
Coffee / Vehicles
Exports to: France, U.S.A., Italy, Netherlands
Imports from: France, W. Germany, U.S.A
Invisible trade balance: –$1 172
Aid received (net): $224.4

JAMAICA

Country
1. Commonwealth
2. English
3. Jamaica Dollar
4. $1 = 5.83 £1 = 8.82

Area and Population
1. 11 th. sq. km.
2. 2 337; 212 per sq. km.
3. BR 23; DR 5; AI 1.4%
4. Urb. pop.: 1 191 (52%)
5. Kingston 671

Production
1. GDP $3 185 (–2.5%); $1 428 (–3.6%) Agric. 7%, Indust. 22%, Others 71%
2. Bananas 185 — Copra 7; Oranges 32 — Sugar cane 2 655
3. Goats 420 — Cattle 318
4. Fish 9
5. Roundwood 39
6. Bauxite 8 735

Manufactures
1. 0.02/3.0; 2 350 kWh (6% hydr.)
2a. Meat 50 — Sugar 193
b. Petroleum products 1.2
3. Telephones 60; Cars 124; Rail: 83 pass.-km.; 186 ton-km.; Air: 1 230 pass.-km.; 129 ton-km.; Sea: 8 335 loaded; 4 018 unloaded

Trade
Exports: $781 — Imports: $1 178
Bauxite and aluminium / Machinery
Sugar / Textiles
Bananas / Petroleum
Exports to: U.S.A., U.K., Canada, Norway
Imports from: U.S.A., Venezuela, U.K.
Revenue from tourism: $338
Aid received (net): $166.2

JAPAN

Country
1. Constitutional Monarchy
2. Japanese
3. Japanese Yen
4. $1 = 172.01 £1 = 260.00

Area and Population
1. 372 th. sq. km. (incl. Ryukyu Arch.)
2. 120 754; 325 per sq. km.
3. BR 13; DR 6; AI 0.6%
4. Urb. pop.: 89 187 (74%)
5. Tokyo 11 676

Production
1. GDP $1 183 975 (5.0%); $9 928 (4.1%) Agric. 3%, Indust. 31%, Others 66%
2. Rice 14 848 — Potatoes 3 584; Tomatoes 791 — Apples 986; Pears 480; Tea 102 — Oranges/mandarines 2 552; Tobacco 137
3. Pigs 10 423 — Cattle 4 682
4. Fish 11 250
5. Roundwood 32 813
6. Coal 16.6 — Lead 49; Natural gas 90 — Manganese 27; Crude petroleum 0.2 — Zinc 253; Iron ore 0.3 — Gold 3.0; Copper 43 — Silver 324

Manufactures
1. 43.8/403.9; 602 357 kWh (14% hydr., 18% nucl.)
2a. Meat 3 344 — Sugar 905; Beer 48.4 Mhl — Sawnwood 29 670
b. Iron 81 816 — Steel 105 588; Aluminium 1 106 — Plastics 5 701; Cotton yarn 436 — Wool yarn 122; Silk 10 500 — Newsprint 2 715; Synthetic fibres 425 — Petroleum products 153.8; Vehicles: — Radios 14 318; pass. 7 073, comm. 4 037 — TV receivers 12 796; Ships (grt.) 9 395
3. Telephones 56 284; Cars 25 539; Rail: 325 008 pass.-km.; 23 184 ton-km.; Air: 55 731 pass.-km.; 6 986 ton-km.; Sea: 94 320 loaded; 602 664 unloaded

Trade
Exports: $170 132 — Imports: $136 492
Iron and steel / Crude petroleum
Electrical machinery / Machinery
Textiles / Sawnwood
Other machinery / Iron ore
Vehicles / Textile fibres
Ships and boats / Non-ferrous metals / Cereals
Exports to: U.S.A., S. Korea, W. Germany
Imports from: U.S.A., Australia, Saudi Arabia, Indonesia
Invisible trade balance: –$7 750
Revenue from tourism: $763
Aid given (net): $8 593

KENYA

Country
1. Republic
2. Swahili, English
3. Kenyan Shilling
4. $1 = 15.85 £1 = 23.95

Area and Population
1. 583 th. sq. km.
2. 20 333; 35 per sq. km.
3. BR 56; DR 14; AI 4.1%
4. Urb. pop.: 2 382 (15%)
5. Nairobi 1 200

Production
1. GDP $5 442 (5.4%); $279 (1.2%) Agric. 27%, Indust. 11%, Others 62%
2. Maize 1 275 — Cottonseed 17; Coffee 95 — Tea 116
3. Cattle 12 000 — Goats 8 300; Sheep 6 700
4. Fish 97
5. Roundwood 29 330
6. Salt 83 — Soda ash 153

Manufactures
1. 0.2/1.8; 2 166 kWh (68% hydr.)
2a. Sugar 391 — Sawnwood 181
b. Cement 1 140 — Petroleum products 2.8
3. Telephones 217; Cars 115; Rail: 8 665 pass.-km.; 3 536 ton-km. (incl. Tanzania and Uganda); Air: 942 pass.-km.; 110 ton-km.; Sea: 1 512 loaded; 3 792 unloaded

Trade
Exports: $1 084 — Imports: $1 501
Coffee / Machinery
Tea / Vehicles
Petroleum products / Petroleum
Pyrethrum / Iron and steel
Exports to: U.K., W. Germany, Uganda
Imports from: U.K., Japan, W. Germany, U.S.A., Iran
Revenue from tourism: $185
Aid received (net): $445.6

For detailed table headings and notes see first page of this section

Country	Area and Population	Production		Manufactures		Trade	

KOREA (NORTH)

1. Republic
2. Korean
3. Won
4. $1 = 0.94
   £1 = 1.42

1. 121 th. sq. km.
2. 20 385; 168 per sq. km.
3. BR 33; DR 8; AI 2.3%
4. Urb. pop.: 12 171 (62%)
5. Pyongyang 1 500

2. Rice 5 400 — Maize 2 580
   Potatoes 1 700 — Tobacco 52
3. Pigs 2 700 — Cattle 1 025
4. Fish 1 600
5. Roundwood 6 200
6. Coal 37.1 — Zinc 150
   Lead 110 — Tungsten 500t
   Iron ore 4.8 — Copper 10
   Gold 5.0 — Silver 50

1. 47.8/52.3; 41 000 kWh (64% hydr.)
2a. Sawnwood 280
   b. Cotton . . . — Lead 95
      Steel 6 500 — Zinc 115
      Iron 3 000 — Fertilizers 860
      Petroleum products 2.9
3. Sea: 1 300 loaded; 2 000 unloaded

Exports: . . . — Imports: . . .
   Minerals — Machinery
   Metal products
Main trade is with U.S.S.R.

KOREA (SOUTH)

1. Republic
2. Korean
3. Won
4. $1 = 888.82
   £1 = 1 343.45

1. 98 th. sq. km.
2. 41 209; 421 per sq. km.
3. BR 23; DR 6; AI 1.4%
4. Urb. pop.: 21 434 (53%)
5. Seoul 8 367

1. GDP $81 129 (7.2%); $1 999 (5.6%)
   Agric. 14%, Indust. 30%, Others 56%
2. Rice 7 970 — Barley 804
   Potatoes 436 — Cottonseed 2
3. Pigs 3 649 — Cattle 2 215
4. Fish 2 400
5. Roundwood 10 189
6. Coal 20.6 — Gold 2.2
   Iron ore 0.7 — Tungsten 2.5
   Zinc 54 — Silver 70

1. 13.9/57.8; 53 047 kWh (5% hydr., 17% nucl.)
2a. Meat 679 — Sawnwood 3 518
   b. Cotton yarn 275 — Steel 5 016
      Radios 5 500 — Iron 8 904
      Petroleum products 22.7 — Cars 167
3. Telephones 2 898; Cars 360
   Rail: 21 227 pass.-km.; 10 625 ton-km.
   Air: 12 101 pass.-km.; 2 180 ton-km.
   Sea: 26 292 loaded; 79 020 unloaded

Exports: $29 245 — Imports: $30 631
   Clothing — Machinery
   Plywood — Rice
   Textiles — Petrol
Exports to: U.S.A., Japan, Saudi Arabia
Imports from: Japan, U.S.A., Saudi Arabia
Invisible trade balance: –$876
Revenue from tourism: $502
Aid received (net): $531.8

LAOS

1. Democratic Republic
2. Laotian, French
3. Kip
4. $1 = 34.99
   £1 = 52.89

1. 237 th. sq. km.
2. 4 117; 17 per sq. km.
3. BR 43; DR 17; AI 2.5%
4. Urb. pop.: 647 (15%)
5. Vientiane 120

1. GDP $300 (. . .); $87 (. . .)
2. Rice 1 322 — Coffee 4
   Cottonseed 14 — Tobacco 4
3. Pigs 1 350 — Buffaloes 915
5. Roundwood 3 920
6. Tin 0.6

1. 0.1/0.3; 1 250 kWh (95% hydr.)
2a. Sawnwood 41
   b. Woven silk. . .
3. Telephones 6; Cars 15
   Air: 10 pass.-km.; 2 ton-km.

Exports: $33 — Imports: $125
   Sawnwood — Agricultural products
   Tin — Petroleum products
   — Vehicles
Exports to: Thailand, Malaysia, Hong Kong
Imports from: Thailand, Japan, France, W. Germany
Aid received (net): $43.3

LEBANON

1. Republic
2. Arabic, French
3. Lebanese pound
4. $1 = 24.69
   £1 = 37.32

1. 10 th. sq. km.
2. 2 668; 267 per sq. km.
3. BR 30; DR 13; AI –0.01%
4. Urb. pop.: 2 062 (78%)
5. Beirut 702

1. GDP $3 438 (. . .); $1 273 (. . .)
   Agric. 8%, Indust. 13%, Others 79%
2. Wheat 18 — Oranges 200
   Apples 128 — Grapes 160
   Tomatoes 125 — Tobacco 4
3. Goats 440 — Sheep 130
5. Roundwood 252
6. Salt 5

1. 0.1/2.0; 1 220 kWh (46% hydr.)
2a. Sugar 12 — Sawnwood 33
   b. Cotton yarn. . . — Petroleum products 0.7
3. Telephones 192; Cars 315
   Rail: 2 pass.-km.; 42 ton-km.
   Air: 968 pass.-km.; 555 ton-km.
   Sea: 2 000 loaded; 2 500 unloaded

Exports: $886 — Imports: $3 615
   Fruit — Machinery
   Machinery — Textiles
   Vegetables — Vehicles
   Eggs — Petroleum products
Exports to: Saudi Arabia, Syria, Libya, Kuwait
Imports from: U.S.A., W. Germany, France, Italy, U.K.
Aid received (net): $77.2

LIBYA

1. People's Republic
2. Arabic
3. Libyan Dinar
4. $1 = 0.30
   £1 = 0.45

1. 1 760 th. sq. km.
2. 3 605; 2 per sq. km.
3. BR 38; DR 9; AI 3.9%
4. Urb. pop.: 2 211 (61%)
5. Tripoli 980

1. GDP $29 885 (7.7%); $8 974 (3.5%)
   Agric. 2%, Indust. 52%, Others 46%
2. Barley 70 — Tomatoes 245
   Dates 98 — Olives 110
   Tobacco 1 — Groundnuts 14
3. Sheep 4 800 — Goats 1 500
5. Roundwood 631
6. Crude petroleum 54.3 — Natural gas 384

1. 91.9/19.1; 7 150 kWh
2a. Olive oil 16
   b. Petroleum products 4.9
3. Telephones 41; Cars 400
   Air: 1 473 pass.-km.; 121 ton-km.
   Sea: 53 530 loaded; 12 680 unloaded

Exports: $11 136 — Imports: $7 175
   Crude petroleum — Machinery
   — Vehicles
Exports to: W. Germany, Italy, U.S.A, France, Spain
Imports from: Italy, U.K., W. Germany, France, Japan
Aid received (net): $13.7

LUXEMBOURG

1. Grand Duchy
2. Luxembourgeois, French, German
3. Luxembourg Franc
4. $1 = 45.05
   £1 = 68.10

1. 2.6 th. sq. km.
2. 366; 122 per sq. km.
3. BR 12; DR 11; AI –0.1%
4. Urb. pop.: 283 (78%)
5. Luxembourg 79

1. GDP $3 344 (2.7%); $9 289 (2.7%)
   Agric. 3%, Indust. 29%, Others 68%
2. Oats 33
6. Iron ore 0.3

1. 0.1/3.8; 797 kWh (55% hydr.)
2a. Wine 16 — Beer 0.7 Mhl
   Sawnwood 917
   b. Iron 2 772 — Steel 3 948
3. Telephones 228; Cars 138
   Rail: 288 pass.-km.; 588 ton-km.
   Air: 92 pass.-km.; 9 ton-km.

Exports: (See Belgium) — Imports: (See Belgium)

MADAGASCAR

1. Republic
2. Malagasy, French
3. Malagasy Franc
4. $1 = 571.31
   £1 = 863.53

1. 587 th. sq. km.
2. 9 985; 17 per sq. km.
3. BR 45; DR 18; AI 2.8%
4. Urb. pop.: 1 239 (16%)
5. Antananarivo 400

1. GDP $2 991 (1.8%); $325 (–0.8%)
   Agric. 33%, Indust. 19%, Others 48%
2. Rice 2 132 — Cassava 2 047
   Bananas 224 — Sisal 20
   Coffee 81 — Groundnuts 32
3. Cattle 10 400 — Goats 1 800
4. Fish 55
5. Roundwood 6 262
6. Graphite 13 — Gold 3kg
   Chrome 45

1. 0.03/0.6; 450 kWh (55% hydr.)
2a. Sugar 99 — Sawnwood 234
   b. Cotton yarn. . . — Cement 36
3. Telephones 38; Cars 61
   Rail: 275 pass.-km.; 216 ton-km.
   Air: 506 pass.-km.; 75 ton-km.
   Sea: 312 loaded; 756 unloaded

Exports: $296 — Imports: $387
   Coffee — Manufactured goods
   Spices — Machinery
Exports to: France, U.S.A., Indonesia
Imports from: France, W. Germany, China
Invisible trade balance: –$97
Aid received (net): $159.6

MALAWI

1. Republic
2. Bantu, English
3. Kwacha
4. $1 = 1.78
   £1 = 2.69

1. 118 th. sq. km.
2. 7 058; 60 per sq. km.
3. BR 49; DR 25; AI 3.2%
4. Urb. pop.: 752 (11%)
5. Lilongwe 99

1. GDP $1 334 (5.7%); $208 (3.0%)
   Agric. 37%, Indust. 13%, Others 50%
2. Maize 1 400 — Groundnuts 180
   Tea 34 — Tobacco 70
   Cottonseed 18 — Cotton lint 7
3. Goats 770 — Cattle 910
4. Fish 58
5. Roundwood 6 458

1. 0.06/0.3; 486 kWh (94% hydr.)
2a. Sawnwood 43 — Beer 0.6Mhl
3. Telephones 29; Cars 14
   Rail: 108 pass.-km.; 120 ton-km.
   Air: 96 pass.-km.; 10 ton-km.

Exports: $292 — Imports: $279
   Tobacco — Machinery
   Tea — Textiles
   Groundnuts — Vehicles
Exports to: U.K., U.S.A., W. Germany, Netherlands
Imports from: U.K., Japan, South Africa
Invisible trade balance: –$128
Aid received (net): $162.6

MALAYSIA

1. Federation
2. Malay, Chinese, English and others
3. Ringgit
4. $1 = 2.54
   £1 = 3.84

1. 330 th. sq. km.
2. 15 557; 47 per sq. km.
3. BR 31; DR 7; AI 2.3%
4. Urb. pop.: 4 713 (31%)
5. Kuala Lumpur 938

1. GDP $23 796 (8.2%); $1 566 (4.8%)
   Agric. 20%, Indust. 31%, Others 49%
2. Rice 1 755 — Palm oil 3 717
   Copra 212 — Bananas 450
   Pineapples 181 — Rubber 1 497
3. Pigs 2 050 — Cattle 575
4. Fish 741
5. Roundwood 41 877
6. Iron ore 0.1 — Tin 41.3
   Crude petroleum 23.0 — Tungsten 49
   Gold 185kg — Copper 28

1. 28.2/13.3; 12 135 kWh (11% hydr.)
2a. Meat 245 — Sawnwood 6 050
   b. Cement 3 468 — Petroleum products 8.4
      Tin 47
3. Telephones 717; Cars 900
   Rail: 1 500 pass.-km.; 1 056 ton-km. (incl. Singapore)
   Air: 5 418 pass.-km.; 658 ton-km.
   Sea: 30 108 loaded; 22 140 unloaded

Exports: $13 917 — Imports: $13 987
   Rubber — Machinery
   Tin — Crude petroleum
   Sawnwood — Vehicles
   Fish — Textiles
   Palm oil — Rice
   — Iron and steel
   — Foods
Exports to: Singapore, Japan, U.S.A., U.K., Netherlands
Imports from: Japan, U.K., Singapore, Australia, W. Germany
Aid received (net): $218.4

For detailed table headings and notes see first page of this section

169

Country	Area and Population	Production	Manufactures	Trade

MALI

1. Republic
2. French, Arabic
3. Mali Franc
4. $1 = 352.13
   £1 = 532.25

1. 1 240 th. sq. km.
2. 8 206; 7 per sq. km.
3. BR 43; DR 18; AI 2.7%
4. Urb. pop.: 1 331 (18%)
5. Bamako 419

1. GDP $2 179 (. . .); $297 (. . .)
2. Millet 800   Rice 142
   Groundnuts 100   Cottonseed 96
3. Sheep 6 300   Cattle 6 000
4. Fish 33
5. Roundwood 4 583

1. 0.01/0.20; 110 kWh (46% hydr.)
2a. Sugar 10   Meat 118
3. Telephones 5; Cars 20
   Rail: 156 pass.-km.; 132 ton-km.
   Air: 110 pass.-km.; 11 ton-km.

Exports: $167   Imports: $344
Cattle   Manufactured goods
Fish   Machinery
Cotton   Vehicles
Exports to: France, Ivory Coast, China, U.K.
Imports from: France, Ivory Coast, China, Senegal
Aid received (net): $214.6

MALTA

1. Commonwealth
2. Maltese, English
3. Maltese Pound
4. $1 = 0.40
   £1 = 0.60

1. 0.3 th. sq. km.
2. 383; 1 277 per sq. km.
3. BR 15; DR 8; AI 0.7%
4. Urb. pop.: 357 (94%)
5. Valetta 14

1. GDP $937 (10.2%); $2 466 (8.0%)
   Agric. 4%, Indust. 31%, Others 65%
2. Potatoes 13   Wheat 5
   Tomatoes 15   Grapes 3
3. Pigs 54   Goats 5

1. . . ./0.5; 675 kWh
2a. Wine 2
3. Telephones 91; Cars 75
   Air: 644 pass.-km.; 60 ton-km.
   Sea: 168 loaded; 1 404 unloaded

Exports: $394   Imports: $717
Clothing   Foods
Textiles   Manufactured goods
Exports to: U.K., Libya, W. Germany
Imports from: U.K., Italy, W. Germany, U.S.A
Revenue from tourism: $185

MAURITANIA

1. Republic
2. Arabic, French
3. Ouguiya
4. $1 = 76.98
   £1 = 116.35

1. 1 031 th. sq. km.
2. 1 888; 2 per sq. km.
3. BR 50; DR 23; AI 2.9%
4. Urb. pop.: 421 (23%)
5. Nouakchott 135

1. GDP $811 (0.7%); $483 (−2.1%)
   Agric. 22%, Indust. 19%, Others 59%
2. Millet 15   Dates 10
3. Sheep 5 000   Cattle 1 300
4. Fish 54
5. Roundwood 54
6. Iron ore 5.9

1. . . ./0.29; 102 kWh
3. Telephones . . .; Cars 8
   Air: 251 pass.-km.; 45 ton-km.
   Sea: 7 022 loaded; 294 unloaded

Exports: $294   Imports: $194
Iron ore   Machinery
Fish   Foods
Exports to: France, U.K., W. Germany, Spain, Italy, Belgium
Imports from: France, U.S.A., U.K., Senegal
Aid received (net): $113.3

MEXICO

1. Federal Republic
2. Spanish
3. Mexican Peso
4. $1 = 503.14
   £1 = 760.75

1. 1 973 th. sq. km.
2. 78 524; 40 per sq. km.
3. BR 38; DR 6; AI 2.6%
4. Urb. pop.: 50 683 (66%)
5. Mexico 14 750

1. GDP $171 267 (7.1%); $2 284 (4.0%)
   Agric. 7%, Indust. 31%, Others 62%
2. Maize 14 050   Copra 120
   Bananas 1 500   Sorghum 6 729
   Wheat 4 262   Tomatoes 1 320
   Oranges 1 600   Coffee 262
   Pineapples 400   Cottonseed 395
   Tobacco 62
3. Cattle 37 500   Pigs 18 370
4. Fish 1 070
5. Roundwood 19 805
6. Crude petroleum 136.6   Lead 183
   Natural gas 1 048   Zinc 290
   Coal 5.8   Silver 1 987
   Iron ore 5.3   Gold 6.9
   Copper 189   Mercury 275t
   Tin 0.5

1. 259.8/130.4; 82 343 kWh (25% hydr., 1.6% geo.)
2a. Meat 1 871   Sugar 3 260
   Sawnwood 1 539
b. Iron 5 544   Steel 7 284
   Aluminium 64   Radios 663
   Cotton yarn . . .   Cement 18 384
   Petroleum products 63.8   Vehicles:
   pass. 246, comm. 62
3. Telephones 5 511; Cars 5 221
   Rail: 5 808 pass.-km.; 44 640 ton-km.
   Air: 13 465 pass.-km.; 1 330 ton-km.
   Sea: 72 108 loaded; 10 932 unloaded

Exports: $11 207   Imports: $23 462
Cotton   Vehicles
Sugar   Organic chemical
Tomatoes   products
Coffee   Iron and steel
Cattle   Paper and cardboard
Machinery   Petroleum products
Exports to: U.S.A., Spain, Japan, W. Germany, Brazil
Imports from: U.S.A., W. Germany, Japan, France
Invisible trade balance: −$9 654
Revenue from tourism: $1 406
Aid received (net): $542.5

MONGOLIA

1. People's Republic
2. Mongol
3. Tugrik
4. $1 = 3.35
   £1 = 5.07

1. 1 565 th. sq. km.
2. 1 891; 1 per sq. km.
3. BR 37; DR 8; AI 2.7%
4. Urb. pop.: 928 (51%)
5. Ulan-Bator 419

2. Wheat 459   Potatoes 123
3. Sheep 14 400   Goats 4 549
5. Roundwood 2 390
6. Coal 0.4   Lignite 4.1
   Tin 1.0   Copper 128
   Molybdenum 700t

1. 1.8/2.8; 1 975 kWh
2a. Wool. . .   Meat 229
   Sawnwood 470
b. Cement 106
3. Telephones 31; Cars. . .
   Rail: 297 pass.-km.; 3 449 ton-km.

Exports: $436   Imports: $655
Livestock   Consumer goods
Wool   Machinery
Meat   Raw materials

MOROCCO

1. Kingdom
2. Arabic, French, Spanish
3. Dirham
4. $1 = 9.06
   £1 = 13.70

1. 447 th. sq. km.
2. 21 941; 49 per sq. km.
3. BR 45; DR 14; AI 3.3%
4. Urb. pop.: 8 444 (42%)
5. Rabat 842

1. GDP $14 697 (4.3%); $687 (1.2%)
   Agric. 14%, Indust. 23%, Others 63%
2. Barley 1 405   Wheat 1 989
   Oranges 746   Grapes 230
   Dates 40   Olives 250
3. Sheep 12 000   Goats 4 500
4. Fish 440
5. Roundwood 1 695
6. Coal 0.4   Cobalt 773t
   Iron ore 0.1   Lead 101
   Antimony 1.0   Phosphates 20 106
   Copper 22   Silver 127

1. 1.0/6.6; 6 010 kWh (9% hydr.)
2a. Meat 300   Wine 45
   Olive oil 34   Sawnwood 149
   Sugar 451
b. Petroleum products 4.0   Wool yarn . . .
   Cement 3 336
3. Telephones 241; Cars 447
   Rail: 1 608 pass.-km.; 4 572 ton-km.
   Air: 1 827 pass.-km.; 203 ton-km.
   Sea: 19 428 loaded; 11 244 unloaded

Exports: $2 095   Imports: $3 861
Phosphates   Machinery
Oranges   Manufactured goods
Vegetables
Exports to: France, W. Germany, Italy, Spain
Imports from: France, U.S.A., W. Germany, Italy, Spain
Revenue from tourism: $425
Aid received (net): $350.8

MOZAMBIQUE

1. People's Republic
2. Portuguese, Bantu
3. Metica
4. $1 = 40.38
   £1 = 61.03

1. 802 th. sq. km.
2. 13 961; 17 per sq. km.
3. BR 45; DR 17; AI 3.1%
4. Urb. pop.: 1 539 (13%)
5. Maputo 384

1. GDP $3 272 (. . .); $322 (. . .)
2. Cassava 3 150   Maize 330
   Copra 65   Groundnuts 70
   Cottonseed 35   Sisal 4
3. Cattle 1 320   Goats 355
5. Roundwood 14 585
6. Coal 0.5

1. 1.1/1.3; 6 426 kWh (94% hydr.)
2a. Sugar 95   Sawnwood 33
   Beer 0.5Mhl
b. Petroleum products 0.7
3. Telephones 56; Cars 110
   Rail: 570 pass.-km.; 1 509 ton-km.
   Air: 614 pass.-km.; 67 ton-km.
   Sea: 2 613 loaded; 1 260 unloaded

Exports: $86   Imports: $487
Cotton   Machinery
Cashew nuts   Vehicles
Sugar   Iron and steel
Tea   Petroleum
Exports to: Portugal, S. Africa, U.K., U.S.A
Imports from: Portugal, S.Africa, W. Germany, U.K.
Aid received (net): $148.5

NAMIBIA

1. Mandated Territory
2. English, African dialects
3. Rand
4. $1 = 1.99
   £1 = 3.01

1. 824 th. sq. km.
2. 1 550; 2 per sq. km.
3. BR 45; DR 19; AI 2.8%
4. Urb. pop.: 407 (27%)
5. Windhoek 61

1. (incl. with South Africa)
2. Maize 40   Millet 20
3. Sheep 6 000   Cattle 2 000
4. Fish 341
5. Roundwood . . .
6. Copper 50   Zinc 31
   Lead 43   Diamonds 930
   Vanadium. . .   Tin 0.8
   Silver 106   Uranium 3 713

2a. Meat 68
b. Copper . . .   Lead 29
3. Telephones 57; Cars. . .
   Rail: see South Africa

Exports: . . . (Trade included with South Africa)   Imports: . . .

NEPAL

1. Kingdom
2. Nepalese, Hindu
3. Nepalese Rupee
4. $1 = 20.50
   £1 = 30.98

1. 141 th. sq. km.
2. 16 625; 118 per sq. km.
3. BR 44; DR 21; AI 2.3%
4. Urb. pop.: 956 (51%)
5. Katmandu 235

1. GDP $2 212 (2.6%); $141 (−0.4%)
   Agric. 53%, Indust. 4%, Others 43%
2. Rice 2 760   Maize 751
   Wheat 634   Jute 25
3. Cattle 7 000   Goats 2 600
5. Roundwood 14 684

1. 0.02/0.2; 257 kWh (80% hydr.)
2a. Sugar 23   Sawnwood 220
3. Telephones 11; Cars. . .
   Air: 250 pass.-km.; 24 ton-km.

Exports: $97   Imports: $163
Food grains   Textiles
Livestock   Petroleum products
Jute   Iron and steel
Timber   Machinery
Tea
Main trade is with India
Aid received (net): $153.4

For detailed table headings and notes see first page of this section

Country	Area and Population	Production	Manufactures	Trade

NETHERLANDS

1. Kingdom
2. Dutch
3. Gilder
4. $1 = 2.49
   £1 = 3.77

1. 37 th. sq. km.
2. 14 484; 391 per sq. km.
3. BR 12; DR 8; AI 0.4%
4. Urb. pop.: 12 591 (88%)
5. Amsterdam 994, The Hague 672

1. GDP $111 259 (2.5%); $7 716 (1.8%)
   Agric. 4%, Indust. 26%, Others 70%
2. Barley 192   Wheat 1 133
   Tomatoes 491   Apples 400
   Pears 96   Potatoes 6 673
3. Pigs 11 000   Cattle 5 500
4. Fish 503
5. Roundwood 905
6. Crude petroleum 2.5 Natural gas 2 691
   Salt 3 124   Coal 4.3

1. 109.7/91.9; 59 639 kWh (6% nucl.)
2a. Meat 2 264 (Pork 1 100)   Sugar 1 000
    Sawnwood 312   Butter and cheese 772
b. Iron 4 920   Steel 3 736
   Wool yarn 6.5   Cotton yarn 7.2
   Petroleum products 47.1   Vehicles:
   Plastics 2 500   pass. 108, comm. 19
   Ships (grt.) 151
3. Telephones 7 697; Cars 4 650
   Rail: 8 940 pass.-km.; 3 120 ton-km.
   Air: 16 282 pass.-km.; 2 589 ton-km.
   Sea: 80 676 loaded; 244 056 unloaded

Exports: $65 881   Imports: $62 136
Machinery   Machinery
Textiles   Crude petroleum
Chemical products   Textiles
Petroleum   Vehicles
Meat   Iron and steel
Iron and steel   Clothing
Vegetables   Non-ferrous metals
Exports to: W. Germany, Belgium-Luxembourg, France, U.K., Italy, U.S.A
Imports from: W. Germany, Belgium-Luxembourg, U.S.A., France, U.K., Italy
Invisible trade balance: +$394
Revenue from tourism: $520
Aid given (net): $1 818

NEW ZEALAND

1. Commonwealth
2. English
3. New Zealand Dollar
4. $1 = 1.75
   £1 = 2.64

1. 269 th. sq. km.
2. 3 254; 12 per sq. km.
3. BR 16; DR 8; AI 0.8%
4. Urb. pop.: 2 683 (83%)
5. Wellington 343

1. GDP $21 554 (. . .); $6 736 (. . .)
   Agric. 10%, Indust. 25%, Others 65%
2. Barley 589   Pears 15
   Apples 200   Wheat 294
   Tomatoes 60   Wool 363
3. Sheep 70 344   Cattle 7 910
4. Fish 142
5. Roundwood 10 021
6. Coal 1.8   Lignite 0.2
   Natural gas 85   Gold 0.3
   Crude petroleum 0.7 Silver 7

1. 8.4/11.7; 25 527 kWh (77% hydr., 4% geo.)
2a. Meat 1 212   Butter and cheese 410
    Sawnwood 2 154   Wood pulp 1 043
    Wine 58
b. Petroleum products 2.3   Vehicles:
   Cement 828   pass. 79, comm. 25
   Wool yarn 19
3. Telephones 1 730; Cars 1 405
   Rail: 396 pass.-km.; 3 168 ton-km.
   Air: 5 900 pass.-km.; 784 ton-km.
   Sea: 9 012 loaded; 7 464 unloaded

Exports: $5 358   Imports: $6 010
Meat   Machinery
Wool   Textiles
Butter   Vehicles
Cheese   Iron and steel
                         Petroleum products
Exports to: U.K., Japan, Australia
Imports from: U.K., Australia, U.S.A., Japan
Invisible trade balance: –$1 416
Revenue from tourism: $226
Aid given (net): $87

NICARAGUA

1. Republic
2. Spanish
3. Cordoba
4. $1 = 27.95
   £1 = 42.24

1. 130 th. sq. km.
2. 3 272; 25 per sq. km.
3. BR 46; DR 12; AI 3.3%
4. Urb. pop.: 1 459 (46%)
5. Managua 615

1. GDP $2 955 (1.7%); $998 (−1.9%)
   Agric. 25%, Indust. 21%, Others 54%
2. Maize 219   Rice 162
   Bananas 213   Coffee 46
   Cottonseed 126   Cotton lint 85
3. Cattle 2 000   Pigs 540
5. Roundwood 3 370
6. Gold 1.5

1. 0.07/0.9; 1 080 kWh (49% hydr., 2.7% geo.)
2a. Sugar 258   Meat 87
    Sawnwood 222
b. Cement 100
3. Telephones 43; Cars 38
   Rail: 21 pass.-km.; 19 ton-km.
   Air: 120 pass.-km.; 12 ton-km.
   Sea: 366 loaded; 1 000 unloaded

Exports: $385   Imports: $826
Cotton   Machinery
Meat   Textiles
Coffee   Iron and steel
Exports to: U.S.A., Japan, Costa Rica, W. Germany
Imports from: U.S.A., Guatemala, Costa Rica, W. Germany, Japan, Venezuela
Aid received (net): $171.4

NIGER

1. Republic
2. Arabic, French
3. C.F.A. Franc
4. $1 = 352.13
   £1 = 532.25

1. 1 267 th. sq. km.
2. 6 115; 5 per sq. km.
3. BR 51; DR 25; AI 2.8%
4. Urb. pop.: 832 (14%)
5. Niamey 225

1. GDP $2 513 (. . .); $473 (. . .)
   Agric. 43%, Indust. 16%, Others 41%
2. Groundnuts 74   Millet 900
3. Goats 7 500   Cattle 3 500
5. Roundwood 3 731
6. Tin 50t   Uranium 2 906

1. 0.04/0.3; 252 kWh
2a. Meat 108
3. Telephones 10; Cars 13
   Air: 225 pass.-km.; 42 ton-km.

Exports: $333   Imports: $442
Groundnuts   Manufactured goods
Exports to: France, Italy, Nigeria
Imports from: France, Ivory Coast, W. Germany
Aid received (net): $189.0

NIGERIA

1. Federal Republic
2. English, W. African
3. Naira
4. $1 = 1.00
   £1 = 1.52

1. 924 th. sq. km.
2. 95 198; 103 per sq. km.
3. BR 51; DR 25; AI 3.3%
4. Urb. pop.: 20 248 (22%)
5. Lagos 1 477

1. GDP $64 956 (1.7%); $730 (−1.5%)
   Agric. 25%, Indust. 25%, Others 50%
2. Cassava 11 800   Millet 3 000
   Rubber 55   Cocoa 160
   Groundnuts 550   Cottonseed 32
   Sorghum 3 000
3. Goats 26 000   Cattle 11 800
4. Fish 515
5. Roundwood 85 760
6. Coal 0.2   Natural gas 220
   Tin 1.3   Crude petroleum 70.4

1. 96.8/17.0; 8 500 kWh (29% hydr.)
2a. Meat 810   Sugar 58
    Sawnwood 2 703
b. Petroleum products 6.9   Cement 3 600
3. Telephones 128; Cars 115
   Rail: 784 pass.-km.; 970 ton-km.
   Air: 2 252 pass.-km.; 230 ton-km.
   Sea: 58 088 loaded; 15 497 unloaded

Exports: $11 317   Imports: $13 440
Petroleum   Machinery
Cocoa   Textiles
Groundnuts   Vehicles
Tin   Iron and steel
Exports to: Bermuda, U.S.A., Netherlands
Imports from: U.K., W. Germany, U.S.A., Japan
Invisible trade balance: −$2 146
Aid received (net): $76.8

NORWAY

1. Kingdom
2. Norwegian
3. Norwegian Krone
4. $1 = 7.04
   £1 = 10.64

1. 324 th. sq. km.
2. 4 153; 13 per sq. km.
3. BR 12; DR 10; AI 0.3%
4. Urb. pop.: 2 893 (71%)
5. Oslo 643

1. GDP $49 149 (4.2%); $11 872 (3.8%)
   Agric. 3%, Indust. 32%, Others 65%
2. Barley 700   Apples 48
   Oats 527   Potatoes 470
3. Sheep 2 351   Cattle 976
4. Fish 2 822
5. Roundwood 9 553
6. Coal 0.5   Molybdenum 303
   Iron ore 2.5   Vanadium 100
   Copper 22   Zinc 29
   Titanium 544   Natural gas 1 032
   Crude petroleum 34.2 Lead 4
   Silver 7

1. 93.3/23.8; 106 243 kWh (99.4% hydr.)
2a. Butter and cheese 94   Sawnwood 2 362
    Canned fish 32   Wood pulp 1 641
b. Iron 1 368   Steel 888
   Magnesium 48   Aluminium 768
   Paper 1 400   Wool yarn 3.2
   Ships (grt.) 99   Petroleum products 7.0
3. Telephones 1 992; Cars 1 337
   Rail: 2 184 pass.-km.; 2 652 ton-km.
   Air: 4 118 pass.-km.; 498 ton-km.
   Sea: 47 088 loaded; 17 616 unloaded

Exports: $18 892   Imports: $13 889
Non-ferrous metals   Machinery
(mainly aluminium)   Ships and boats
Ships and boats   Vehicles
Machinery   Iron and steel
Paper and cardboard   Textiles
Fish   Non-ferrous metals
Iron and steel   Petroleum products
Exports to: U.K., Sweden, W. Germany, Denmark, U.S.A.
Imports from: Sweden, W. Germany, U.K., U.S.A., Denmark
Invisible trade balance: −$1 381
Aid given (net): $702

PAKISTAN

1. Republic
2. Urdu, English
3. Pakistan Rupee
4. $1 = 16.14
   £1 = 24.40

1. 804 th. sq. km.
2. 96 180; 120 per sq. km.
3. BR 42; DR 10; AI 3.1%
4. Urb. pop.: 26 082 (29%)
5. Islamabad 201

1. GDP $31 138 (6.4%); $334 (3.6%)
   Agric. 22%, Indust. 19%, Others 59%
2. Rice 5 009   Wheat 11 053
   Dates 225   Maize 1 100
   Tobacco 75   Rape seed 251
   Cotton lint 990   Cottonseed 1 980
3. Cattle 16 352   Sheep 24 272
4. Fish 343
5. Roundwood 19 095
6. Coal 1.2   Salt 796
   Natural gas 319   Crude petroleum 0.7
   Chrome 7

1. 14.3/21.7; 19 636 kWh (53% hydr., 1% nucl.)
2a. Meat 973   Sugar 1 258
    Sawnwood 55   Jute 1
b. Petroleum products 4.1   Cotton yarn 414
   Cement 4 500
3. Telephones 358; Cars 301
   Rail: 18 288 pass.-km.; 7 368 ton-km.
   Air: 6 425 pass.-km.; 820 ton-km.
   Sea: 2 352 loaded; 12 408 unloaded

Exports: $2 592   Imports: $5 873
Textiles   Machinery
Cotton   Iron and steel
Leather   Fertilizer
Rice   Crude petroleum
                         Vehicles
Exports to: China, Japan, Iran, U.K.
Imports from: U.S.A., U.K., Japan, W. Germany
Invisible trade balance: −$635
Aid received (net): $730.8

PANAMA

1. Republic
2. Spanish
3. Balboa
4. $1 = 1.0
   £1 = 1.51

1. 77 th. sq. km.
2. 2 180; 28 per sq. km.
3. BR 26; DR 6; AI 2.2%
4. Urb. pop.: 899 (49%)
5. Panama 655

1. GDP $4 541 (6.1%); $2 132 (3.6%)
   Agric. 9%, Indust. 9%, Others 82%
2. Rice 175   Bananas 1 183
   Coffee 9   Oranges 66
3. Cattle 1 470   Pigs 200
4. Fish 166
5. Roundwood 2 047

1. 0.1/1.5; 2 239 kWh (39% hydr.)
2a. Meat 73   Sugar 180
    Sawnwood 53
b. Petroleum products 2.4
3. Telephones 185; Cars 104
   Air: 400 pass.-km.; 51 ton-km.
   Sea: 79 512 loaded; 63 204 unloaded

Exports: $256   Imports: $1 423
Bananas   Manufactured goods
Petroleum products   Petroleum
                         Machinery
Exports to: U.S.A., W. Germany
Imports from: U.S.A., Ecuador, Venezuela, Saudi Arabia
Invisible trade balance: +$631
Aid received (net): $68.1

For detailed table headings and notes see first page of this section

Country	Area and Population	Production	Manufactures	Trade

PERU

1. Republic
2. Spanish
3. Intl (1 000 Sol)
4. $1 = 13.92
   £1 = 21.05

1. 1 285 th. sq. km.
2. 19 698; 15 per sq. km.
3. BR 38; DR 12; AI 2.6%
4. Urb. pop.: 11 108 (64%)
5. Lima 5 258

1. GDP $11 428 (2.1%); $595 (−0.7%)
   Agric. 8%, Indust. 36%, Others 56%
2. Maize 576   Rice 8 280
   Oranges 155 Coffee 92
   Cottonseed 165 Potatoes 1 515
3. Sheep 14 500 Cattle 2 825
4. Fish 1 487
5. Roundwood 7 775
6. Iron ore 2.5 Gold 5.4t
   Antimony 0.5 Silver 1 773
   Copper 364 Zinc 568
   Lead 198 Tungsten 720
   Molybdenum 2 563 Crude petroleum 10.0
   Tin 3.0

1. 14.7/11.8; 9 328 kWh (78% hydr.)
2a. Meat 423 Fish meal
    Sugar 532 Sawnwood 577
b. Cotton yarn. . . Copper 219
3. Telephones 475; Cars 300
   Rail: 651 pass.-km.; 612 ton-km.
   Air: 1 685 pass.-km.; 246 ton-km.
   Sea: 8 298 loaded; 3 199 unloaded

Exports: $3 131 Imports: $1 870
Copper Machinery
Fish meal Chemical products
Iron ore Wheat
Cotton Iron and steel
Exports to: U.S.A., Japan, Italy
Imports from: U.S.A., Ecuador, Venezuela
Invisible trade balance: −$1 417
Revenue from tourism: $465
Aid received (net): $329.4

PHILIPPINES

1. Republic
2. Tagalog, English
3. Philippine Peso
4. $1 = 20.08
   £1 = 30.35

1. 300 th. sq. km.
2. 54 378; 181 per sq. km.
3. BR 34; DR 8; AI 2.5%
4. Urb. pop.: 17 943 (37%)
5. Manila 1 630

1. GDP $27 750 (6.0%); $520 (3.2%)
   Agric. 25%, Indust. 27%, Others 48%
2. Maize 3 400 Rice 8 280
   Bananas 4 380 Pineapples 1 200
   Coffee 145 Copra 1 400
   Tobacco 55
3. Pigs 7 779 Buffaloes 2 900
4. Fish 1 837
5. Roundwood 35 787
6. Coal 0.4 Copper 233
   Iron ore 2.6 Gold 34.1
   Chrome 360 Silver 50
   Nickel 15.6

1. 2.6/16.3; 20 761 kWh (20% hydr., 14% geo.)
2a. Meat 761 Sawnwood 1 222
    Salted fish 48 Sugar 2 400
b. Plastics . . . Cotton yarn 39
   Petroleum products 7.8 Cement 3 660
   Copper 99
3. Telephones 731; Cars 561
   Rail: 228 pass.-km.; 12 ton-km.
   Air: 7 369 pass.-km.; 881 ton-km.
   Sea: 12 672 loaded; 18 972 unloaded

Exports: $5 005 Imports: $7 980
Wood Machinery
Sugar Petroleum
Copra Vehicles
Copper Iron and steel
Exports to: U.S.A., Japan, Netherlands
Imports from: Japan, U.S.A., Saudi Arabia
Invisible trade balance: −$958
Revenue from tourism: $450
Aid received (net): $648.2

POLAND

1. People's Republic
2. Polish
3. Złoty
4. $1 = 166.46
   £1 = 251.60

1. 313 th. sq. km.
2. 37 203; 119 per sq. km.
3. BR 19; DR 9; AI 0.9%
4. Urb. pop.: 21 493 (59%)
5. Warsaw 1 649

1. NMP $58 867 (−0.8%); $1 595 (−1.6%)
   Agric. 17%, Indust. 50%, Others 33%
2. Barley 3 555 Wheat 6 010
   Rye 9 540 Oats 2 604
   Potatoes 37 437 Apples 1 566
   Tobacco 100 Rape seed 911
3. Pigs 16 657 Cattle 11 197
4. Fish 735
5. Roundwood 24 681
6. Coal 191.6 Nickel 2
   Lignite 50.4 Zinc 191
   Copper 431 Natural gas 166
   Lead 53 Salt 4 326
   Silver 744

1. 170.9/161.4; 125 821 kWh (2.6% hydr.)
2a. Meat 2 299 Sawnwood 6 764
    Butter and cheese 721 Sugar 1 891
    Salted fish 18
b. Iron 9 624 Steel 16 536
   Aluminium 46 Plastics 671
   Cotton yarn 179 Wool yarn 79.2
   Petroleum products 9.9 Vehicles:
   Ships (grt.) 317 pass. 280, comm. 55
3. Telephones 3 506; Cars 2 871
   Rail: 53 184 pass.-km.; 123 504 ton-km.
   Air: 778 pass.-km.; 72 ton-km.
   Sea: 22 406 loaded; 15 844 unloaded

Exports: $11 687 Imports: $10 633
Coal Dairy products
Ships and boats Iron ore
Meat Crude petroleum
Dairy products Cotton
Machinery Wheat
Clothing Iron and steel
  Petroleum products
  Machinery
Main trade is with: U.S.S.R., W. Germany,
Czechoslovakia, E.Germany
Revenue from tourism: $65

PORTUGAL

1. Republic
2. Portuguese
3. Escudo
4. $1 = 144.23
   £1 = 218.0

1. 92 th. sq. km.
2. 10 229; 111 per sq. km.
3. BR 14; DR 10; AI 0.7%
4. Urb. pop.: 2 905 (30%)
5. Lisbon 1 612

1. GDP $23 811 (4.9%); $2 344 (4.1%)
   Agric. 8%, Indust. 30%, Others 62%
2. Wheat 475 Maize 530
   Grapes 1 020 Olives 300
   Tomatoes 881 Wool 9
3. Sheep 5 000 Pigs 3 450
4. Fish 246
5. Roundwood 8 278
6. Coal 0.2 Tin 0.3
   Iron ore 22.7 Tungsten 1 187
   Copper 2.6 Gold 2t

1. 1.2/13.2; 18 161 kWh (45% hydr.)
2a. Meat 448 Sawnwood 2 360
    Canned fish 47 Salted fish 15
    Wine 730 Olive oil 50
b. Iron 468 Steel 400
   Petroleum products 7.2 Vehicles:
   Cotton yarn 107 pass. 55, comm. 35
   Wool yarn 3.5
3. Telephones 1 456; Cars 1 346
   Rail: 5 448 pass.-km.; 1 236 ton-km.
   Air: 4 174 pass.-km.; 483 ton-km.
   Sea: 4 100 loaded; 19 000 unloaded

Exports: $5 184 Imports: $7 797
Textiles Machinery
Clothing Vehicles
Wine Iron and steel
Diamonds Cotton
Machinery Diamonds
Fish Cereals
Cork Crude petroleum
Exports to: U.K., France, W. Germany
Imports from: W. Germany, U.K., U.S.A., France
Invisible trade balance: −$665
Revenue from tourism: $878

ROMANIA

1. Socialist Republic
2. Romanian
3. Leu
4. $1 = 12.55
   £1 = 18.98

1. 238 th. sq. km.
2. 23 017; 97 per sq. km.
3. BR 14; DR 10; AI 0.8%
4. Urb. pop.: 10 905 (49%)
5. Bucharest 1 979

1. NMP $17 915 (7.2%); $843 (6.3%)
   Agric. 15%, Indust. 58%, Others 27%
2. Maize 13 000 Wheat 7 900
   Grapes 1 020 Tomatoes 1 800
   Tobacco 32 Sunflower seed 890
3. Sheep 18 451 Pigs 14 347
4. Fish 243
5. Roundwood 22 953
6. Coal 7.8 Lead 20
   Lignite 36.0 Manganese 18
   Iron ore 0.5 Natural gas 1 570
   Bauxite 460 Crude petroleum 12.5
   Zinc 39 Copper 30
   Silver 23

1. 92.4/101.4; 70 260 kWh (14% hydr.)
2a. Meat 1 744 Sawnwood 4 948
    Sugar 610 Butter and cheese 155
b. Iron 8 184 Steel 13 800
   Petroleum products 21.6 Cotton yarn 172
   Silk 120 Wool yarn 74
   Fertilizers 2 600 Aluminium 215
3. Telephones 1 196; Cars 235
   Rail: 25 578 pass.-km.; 71 110 ton-km.
   Air: 1 145 pass.-km.; 102 ton-km.
   Sea: 10 000 loaded; 22 000 unloaded

Exports: $13 241 Imports: $9 959
Machinery Machinery
Consumer goods Iron ore
Petroleum products Coke
Cereals Vehicles
  Iron goods
Exports to: U.S.S.R., E. Germany, W. Germany
Imports from: U.S.S.R., E. Germany, W. Germany
Revenue from tourism: $280

SAUDI ARABIA

1. Kingdom
2. Arabic
3. Rial
4. $1 = 3.64
   £1 = 5.51

1. 2 150 th. sq. km.
2. 11 542; 5 per sq. km.
3. BR 46; DR 14; AI 3.9%
4. Urb. pop.: 7 685 (71%)
5. Ar Riyāḍ 667

1. GDP $120 937 (8.7%); $12 094 (4.1%)
   Agric. 2%, Indust. 53%, Others 45%
2. Wheat 1 300 Millet/Sorghum 112
   Dates 450 Tomatoes 350
3. Sheep 3 600 Goats 2 350
6. Crude petroleum 226.3 Natural gas 50

1. 385.3/37.4; 32 000 kWh
2b. Petroleum products 40.4 Cement 5 263
3. Telephones 789; Cars 153
   Rail: 105 pass.-km.; 393 ton-km.
   Air: 12 277 pass.-km.; 1 478 ton-km.
   Sea: 299 257 loaded; 30 000 unloaded

Exports: $36 834 Imports: $33 696
Crude petroleum Machinery
Petroleum products Vehicles
  Food
Exports to: Japan, Italy, France, U.S.A.
Imports from: U.S.A., Japan, W. Germany
Invisible trade balance: −$25 123

SENEGAL

1. Republic
2. French, West African
3. C.F.A. Franc
4. $1 = 352.13
   £1 = 532.25

1. 196 th. sq. km.
2. 6 444; 33 per sq. km.
3. BR 55; DR 23; AI 2.7%
4. Urb. pop.: 1 713 (34%)
5. Dakar 799

1. GDP $2 117 (1.1%); $331 (−1.5%)
2. Millet 471 Rice 120
   Bananas 2 Groundnuts 682
3. Cattle 2 200 Goats 1 000
4. Fish 213
5. Roundwood 3 894
6. Phosphates 1 254 Salt 170
   Titanium. . . Zirconium. . .

1. . . ./1.0; 631 kWh
2a. Sawnwood 11
b. Petroleum products 1.0 Cement 375
3. Telephones 40; Cars 65
   Rail: 426 pass.-km.; 158 ton-km.
   Air: 229 pass.-km.; 42 ton-km.
   Sea: 2 448 loaded; 2 880 unloaded

Exports: $416 Imports: $1 039
Groundnut oil Food
Groundnuts Manufactured goods
  Machinery

Main trade is with France
Aid received (net): $323.7

SINGAPORE

1. Republic
2. English, Chinese, Malay, Tamil
3. Singapore Dollar
4. $1 = 2.18
   £1 = 3.29

1. 0.6 th. sq. km.
2. 2 558; 4 263 per sq. km.
3. BR 16; DR 5; AI 1.2%
4. Urb. pop.: 2 529 (100%)
5. Singapore 2 517

1. GDP $17 848 (9.0%); $7 083 (7.6%)
   Agric. 1%, Indust. 25%, Others 74%
3. Pigs 1 310 Cattle 1
4. Fish 20

1. . . ./13.4; 8 626 kWh
2a. Meat 105 Sawnwood 418
b. Petroleum products 29.2
3. Telephones 775; Cars 195
   Rail: see Malaysia
   Air: 18 161 pass.-km.; 2 466 ton-km.
   Sea: 35 665 loaded; 59 995 unloaded

Exports: $24 108 Imports: $28 712
Rubber Machinery
Petroleum products Textiles
Machinery Rubber
Exports to: Malaysia, U.S.A., Japan
Imports from: Japan, Malaysia, U.S.A., Saudi Arabia
Invisible trade balance: +$3 594
Revenue from tourism: $1 916
Aid received (net): $11.4

For detailed table headings and notes see first page of this section

Country	Area and Population	Production	Manufactures	Trade

SOUTH AFRICA

1. Republic
2. English, Afrikaans
3. Rand
4. $1 = 1.99
   £1 = 3.01

1. 1 221 th. sq. km.
2. 32 392; 27 per sq. km.
3. BR 38; DR 15; AI 2.5%
4. Urb. pop.: 17 372 (55%)
5. Pretoria 739; Cape Town 1 491

Production
1. GDP $73 556 (3.5%); $2 448 (0.7%) Agric. 5%, Indust. 38%, Others 57%
2. Maize 4 440 — Wheat 2 150
   Oranges 495 — Pineapples 153
   Grapes 1 700 — Cottonseed 58
   Tobacco 37 — Wool 109
3. Sheep 31 650 — Cattle 12 895
4. Fish 600
5. Roundwood 20 524
6. Coal 158 — Manganese 3 181
   Iron 15.6 — Asbestos 221
   Copper 212 — Antimony 7.5
   Chrome 2 870 — Nickel 22.5
   Gold 683.3 — Diamonds 9 800
   Tin 2.3 — Zinc 103
   Lead 95 — Silver 218
   Uranium 6 045

Manufactures
1. 105.9/99.9; 109 185 kWh (0.7% hydr.)
2a. Meat 1 206 — Sugar 2 500
   Wine 896 — Beer 9.2Mhl
   Sawnwood 1 550
   b. Iron 8 580 — Steel 7 824
   Copper 148 — Cotton yarn 38
   Wool yarn 20 — Petroleum products 14.3
   Vehicles: — Cement 8 112
   pass. 273, comm. 114
3. Telephones 2 933; Cars 2 499
   Rail: . . . pass.-km.; 82 052 ton-km.
   Air: 9 287 pass.-km.; 1 175 ton-km.
   Sea: 69 276 loaded; 26 758 unloaded

Trade
Exports: $9 334 — Imports: $14 956
Diamonds — Machinery
Fruit — Vehicles
Wool — Textiles
Gold — Crude petroleum
Copper — Petroleum products
Iron and steel — Chemical products
Cereals
Exports to: U.K., Japan, U.S.A., W. Germany
Imports from: U.K., U.S.A., W. Germany, Japan
Invisible trade balance: −$3 297

SPAIN

1. Monarchy
2. Spanish
3. Spanish Peseta
4. $1 = 140.59
   £1 = 212.50

1. 505 th. sq. km.
2. 38 602; 76 per sq. km.
3. BR 13; DR 7; AI 0.8%
4. Urb. pop.: 34 500 (91%)
5. Madrid 3 188

Production
1. GDP $149 193 (1.6%); $3 853 (0.7%) Agric. 6%, Indust. 27%, Others 67%
2. Barley 10 695 — Wheat 6 044
   Tomatoes 2 553 — Oranges 1 310
   Grapes 5 569 — Olives 3 418
   Cottonseed 87 — Cotton lint 55
   Tobacco 44 — Wool 23
3. Sheep 16 600 — Pigs 12 400
4. Fish 1 240
5. Roundwood 14 823
6. Coal 15.1 — Lead 96
   Lignite 24.4 — Tungsten 550t
   Iron ore 3.7 — Mercury 1 416t
   Copper 64 — Zinc 228
   Crude petroleum 3.2 — Tin 0.4
   Silver 221

Manufactures
1. 27.7/81.8; 115 450 kWh (24% hydr., 8% nucl.)
2a. Meat 2 635 — Sugar 1 328
   Olive oil 727 — Wine 3 554
   Sawnwood 2 720
   b. Cotton yarn 69 — Wool yarn 30
   Silk 13 — Copper 156
   Iron 5 364 — Steel 13 572
   Aluminium 421 — Ships (grt.) 141
   Petroleum products 39.8 — Vehicles:
   Cement 25 500 — pass. 1 174, comm. 32
3. Telephones 12 386; Cars 8 354
   Rail: 15 576 pass.-km.; 11 820 ton-km.
   Air: 16 457 pass.-km.; 1 960 ton-km.
   Sea: 44 652 loaded; 88 752 unloaded

Trade
Exports: $23 544 — Imports: $28 812
Machinery — Machinery
Fruits — Crude petroleum
Vegetables — Iron and steel
Footwear — Organic chemicals
Petroleum products — Maize
Textiles — Soya
Ships and boats — Sawnwood
Olive oil — Copper
Exports to: U.S.A., W. Germany, France, U.K
Imports from: U.S.A., W. Germany, France, Saudi Arabia
Invisible trade balance: +$5 217
Revenue from tourism: $7 126

SRI LANKA

1. Republic
2. Sinhalese, English, Tamil
3. Sri Lanka Rupee
4. $1 = 27.72
   £1 = 41.90

1. 66 th. sq. km.
2. 15 837; 240 per sq. km.
3. BR 26; DR 6; AI 2.0%
4. Urb. pop.: 3 194 (20%)
5. Colombo 1 412

Production
1. GDP $4 768 (5.6%); $309 (3.8%) Agric. 26%, Indust. 16%, Others 58%
2. Rice 2 270 — Cassava 650
   Tea 230 — Copra 100
   Rubber 145 — Tobacco 17
3. Cattle 1 738 — Buffaloes 951
4. Fish 222
5. Roundwood 8 363
6. Graphite 8 — Salt 129
   Titanium 90

Manufactures
1. 0.2/2.1; 2 114 kWh (58% hydr.)
2a. Meat 35 — Sawnwood 418
   b. Cotton yarn 7.2 — Petroleum products 1.2
3. Telephones 110; Cars 132
   Rail: 2 256 pass.-km.; 240 ton-km.
   Air: 1 947 pass.-km.; 210 ton-km.
   Sea: 1 932 loaded; 3 588 unloaded

Trade
Exports: $1 454 — Imports: $1 845
Tea — Machinery
Rubber — Rice
Copra — Sugar
Coconuts — Flour
Coconut fibre — Textiles
— Petroleum products
Exports to: U.K., Pakistan, China, U.S.A.
Imports from: Saudi Arabia, Iran, U.S.A.
Revenue from tourism: $147
Aid received (net): $355.4

SUDAN

1. Republic
2. Arabic, Hamitic, English
3. Sudanese Pound
4. $1 = 2.50
   £1 = 3.78

1. 2 506 th. sq. km.
2. 21 550; 9 per sq. km.
3. BR 47; DR 19; AI 2.9%
4. Urb. pop.: 4 153 (20%)
5. Khartoum 476

Production
1. GDP $6 634 (. . .); $345 (. . .) Agric. 36%, Indust. 10%, Others 54%
2. Millet 2 340 — Wheat 162
   Dates 115 — Groundnuts 420
   Sorghum 1 450 — Cottonseed 416
   Cotton lint 219
3. Cattle 19 600 — Sheep 20 000
4. Roundwood 38 157
5. Chrome 20 — Salt 150

Manufactures
1. 0.06/1.6; 1 010 kWh (50% hydr.)
2a. Meat 469 — Sugar 462
   b. Cement 211 — Petroleum products 1.5
   Cotton fabrics . . .
3. Telephones 68; Cars 55
   Rail: . . . pass.-km.; 2 285 ton-km.
   Air: 657 pass.-km.; 70 ton-km.
   Sea: 916 loaded; 2 642 unloaded

Trade
Exports: $624 — Imports: $1 354
Cotton — Machinery
Gum arabic — Cotton fabrics
Sesame — Petroleum products
Groundnuts
Exports to: Saudi Arabia, China, Japan, Italy
Imports from: U.K., W. Germany, Japan, India
Aid received (net): $434.9

SWEDEN

1. Kingdom
2. Swedish
3. Krona
4. $1 = 7.11
   £1 = 10.75

1. 450 th. sq. km.
2. 8 350; 19 per sq. km.
3. BR 11; DR 11; AI 0.01%
4. Urb. pop.: 6 920 (83%)
5. Stockholm 1 420

Production
1. GDP $88 048 (1.2%); $10 570 (1.0%) Agric. 3%, Indust. 21%, Others 76%
2. Oats 1 904 — Barley 2 733
   Wheat 1 776 — Apples 121
   Potatoes 1 307 — Rape seed 382
3. Pigs 2 670 — Cattle 1 875
4. Fish 265
5. Roundwood 53 294
6. Iron ore 11.8 — Lead 81
   Copper 86 — Zinc 207
   Gold 3.4 — Silver 180

Manufactures
1. 13.0/38.3; 109 635 kWh (59% hydr., 37% nucl.)
2a. Meat 562 — Butter and cheese 194
   Sugar 411 — Sawnwood 11 762
   Wood pulp 8 600
   b. Iron 2 208 — Steel 4 704
   Aluminium 114 — Copper 64
   Paper 6 300 — Ships (grt.) 178
   Petroleum products 13.1 — Vehicles:
   pass. 314, comm. 36
3. Telephones 6 888; Cars 2 936
   Rail: 6 480 pass.-km.; 16 944 ton-km.
   Air: 5 573 pass.-km.; 683 ton-km.
   Sea: 42 876 loaded; 48 780 unloaded

Trade
Exports: $29 781 — Imports: $26 572
Machinery — Machinery
Iron and steel — Petroleum products
Paper and cardboard — Vehicles
Wood pulp — Textiles
Vehicles — Iron and steel
Sawnwood — Non-ferrous metals
Ships and boats — Clothing
Iron ore — Crude petroleum
Exports to: U.K., W. Germany, Denmark, Norway
Imports from: W. Germany, U.K., U.S.A., Denmark
Invisible trade balance: −$2 530
Aid given (net): $1 397

SWITZERLAND

1. Federal Republic
2. German, French, Italian
3. Swiss Franc
4. $1 = 1.85
   £1 = 2.79

1. 41 th. sq. km.
2. 6 374; 155 per sq. km.
3. BR 12; DR 9; AI −0.3%
4. Urb. pop.: 3 801 (59%)
5. Bern 301

Production
1. GDP $97 120 (1.9%); $15 081 (1.9%) Agric. 2%, Indust. 21%, Others 77%
2. Potatoes 944 — Apples 360
   Wheat 577 — Pears 135
3. Cattle 1 943 — Pigs 2 004
5. Roundwood 4 295
6. Salt 272

Manufactures
1. 6.3/23.6; 51 819 kWh (70% hydr., 28% nucl.)
2a. Meat 480 — Butter and cheese 169
   Wine 118 — Beer 4.2 Mhl
   Sawnwood 1 760
   b. Iron 10 — Steel 900
   Aluminium 102 — Cotton yarn 49
   Petroleum products 4.2
3. Telephones 4 802; Cars 2 473
   Rail: 8 964 pass.-km.; 6 888 ton-km.
   Air: 11 773 pass.-km.; 1 550 ton-km.

Trade
Exports: $25 863 — Imports: $29 469
Machinery — Machinery
Watches — Vehicles
Textiles — Iron and steel
Medicines — Textiles
Organic chemical products — Petroleum products
Exports to: W. Germany, France, U.S.A., Italy, U.K.
Imports from: W. Germany, France, Italy, U.S.A., U.K.
Invisible trade balance: +$7 505
Revenue from tourism: $3 015
Aid given (net): $2 268

SYRIA

1. Republic
2. Arabic
3. Syrian Pound
4. $1 = 5.95
   £1 = 9.00

1. 185 th. sq. km.
2. 10 267; 55 per sq. km.
3. BR 45; DR 9; AI 3.7%
4. Urb. pop.: 4 370 (47%)
5. Damascus 1 112

Production
1. GDP $19 140 (5.9%); $1 927 (2.0%) Agric. 20%, Indust. 17%, Others 63%
2. Barley 302 — Wheat 1 051
   Grapes 440 — Olives 370
   Tomatoes 740 — Tobacco 15
   Cottonseed 300
3. Sheep 14 000 — Goats 1 000
4. Roundwood 44
6. Crude petroleum 8.0 — Salt 88
   Phosphates 1 231

Manufactures
1. 14.1/9.1; 4 428 kWh (70% hydr.)
2a. Meat 201 — Sugar 85
   Olive oil 85
   b. Cement 4 284 — Cotton, woven 35
   Petroleum products 8.0
3. Telephones 429; Cars 45
   Rail: 756 pass.-km.; 960 ton-km.
   Air: 947 pass.-km.; 98 ton-km.
   Sea: 7 656 loaded; 11 124 unloaded

Trade
Exports: $1 853 — Imports: $4 116
Cotton — Machinery
Livestock — Iron and steel
Crude petroleum — Vehicles
Vegetables — Textiles
Wheat — Crude petroleum
Exports to: France, Italy, Greece, U.S.A.
Imports from: W. Germany, Italy, France, Iraq, Romania
Aid received (net): $162.7

For detailed table headings and notes see first page of this section

Country	Area and Population	Production	Manufactures	Trade

TAIWAN

1. Republic
2. Chinese
3. New Dollar
4. $1 = 38.60
   £1 = 58.34

1. 36 th. sq. km.
2. 19 012; 528 per sq. km.
3. BR 20; DR 5; AI 2.1%
4. Urb. pop.: 11 407 (60%)
5. Tai-pei 2 271

1. GDP $58 000 (. . .); $3 146 (. . .)
   Agric. 6%, Indust. 36%, Others 58%
2. Rice 2 244 Bananas 203
   Groundnuts 86 Citrus fruits 354
   Pineapples 245 Tea 24
   Soya beans 9.5
3. Pigs 6 569 Cattle 130
4. Fish 1 003
5. Roundwood 700
6. Coal 4.2 Gold 1.6t

1. 6 029/48 527; 49 286 kWh (3% hydr., 18% nucl.)
2a. Sugar 619 Sawnwood 563
   Meat . . .
b. Steel 5 627 Aluminium 38
   Cotton yarn . . . Televisions 5 165
   Petroleum products 20
3. Telephones 4 855; Cars 688
   Rail: 7 321 pass.-km.; 2 685 ton-km.
   Air: 866 pass.-km.; 3.2 ton.-km.
   Sea: 36 887 loaded; 62 440 unloaded

Exports: $30 456 Imports: $21 959
Textiles Machinery
Electrical goods Crude petroleum
Timber products Iron and steel
Plastics Chemicals
Exports to: U.S.A., Japan, Saudi Arabia
Imports from: Japan, U.S.A., Kuwait

TANZANIA

1. Federal Republic
2. Swahili
3. Tanzanian Shilling
4. $1 = 18.72
   £1 = 28.30

1. 945 th. sq. km.
2. 21 733; 23 per sq. km.
3. BR 51; DR 17; AI 3.5%
4. Urb. pop.: 2 412 (14%)
5. Dodoma 46

1. GDP $5 127 (2.7%); $299 (–0.4%)
   Agric. 46%, Indust. 9%, Others 45%
2. Maize 1 131 Cassava 5 600
   Bananas 2 000 Coffee 50
   Cottonseed 91 Cotton lint 47
   Tobacco 10 Sisal 40
3. Cattle 14 500 Goats 6 100
4. Fish 272
5. Roundwood 39 770
6. Gold 0.2 Diamonds 360

1. 0.06/0.9; 705 kWh (77% hydr.)
2a. Meat 220 Sawnwood 34
   Sugar 143 Beer 0.6Mhl
3. Telephones 66; Cars 44
   Rail: see Kenya
   Air: 210 pass.-km.; 20 ton-km.
   Sea: 1 080 loaded; 3 180 unloaded

Exports: $366 Imports: $822
Coffee Machinery
Cotton Vehicles
Diamonds Textiles
Sisal Petroleum products
Cashew nuts Iron and steel
Exports to: U.K., W. Germany, U.S.A., Italy
Imports from: U.K., Japan, Netherlands, W. Germany
Aid received (net): $651.5

THAILAND

1. Kingdom
2. Thai
3. Baht
4. $1 = 26.17
   £1 = 39.56

1. 514 th. sq. km.
2. 51 301; 100 per sq. km.
3. BR 31; DR 8; AI 2.1%
4. Urb. pop.: 7 632 (17%)
5. Bangkok 5 468

1. GDP $36 529 (7.4%); $725 (5.0%)
   Agric. 20%, Indust. 21%, Others 59%
2. Maize 4 150 Rice 19 200
   Bananas 2 045 Pineapples 1 650
   Jute 199 Rubber 580
   Cottonseed 82 Tobacco 90
   Cassava 19 985 Palm oil 81
3. Buffaloes 6 150 Cattle 4 620
4. Fish 2 250
5. Roundwood 40 415
6. Lignite 2.3 Natural gas 57
   Tungsten 562 Iron ore 1.9
   Tin 21.6 Antimony 2.9
   Manganese 3.0 Lead 20

1. 3.5/17.4; 18 875 kWh (22% hydr.)
2a. Meat 783 Sawnwood 930
   Sugar 2 350
b. Cotton yarn 101 Petroleum products 7.8
   Cement 8 244 Tin 20
   Vehicles:
   pass. 36, comm. 75
3. Telephones 529; Cars 451
   Rail: 9 231 pass.-km.; 2 421 ton-km.
   Air: 8 611 pass.-km.; 1 095 ton-km.
   Sea: 17 760 loaded; 17 484 unloaded

Exports: $7 413 Imports: $10 398
Rice Machinery
Maize Vehicles
Rubber Iron and steel
Fruit and vegetables Crude petroleum
Tin
Exports to: Japan, U.S.A., Singapore, Netherlands, Indonesia
Imports from: Japan, U.S.A., W. Germany, Saudi Arabia
Invisible trade balance: –$1 226
Revenue from tourism: $972
Aid received (net): $624.4

TOGO

1. Republic
2. Bantu, Hamitic, French
3. C.F.A. Franc
4. $1 = 352.13
   £1 = 532.25

1. 57 th. sq. km.
2. 2 960; 52 per sq. km.
3. BR 46; DR 17; AI 2.9%
4. Urb. pop.: 624 (22%)
5. Lomé 283

1. GDP $815 (2.7%); $296 (0.2%)
   Agric. 27%, Indust. 15%, Others 58%
2. Cassava 345 Cocoa 15
   Coffee 6 Groundnuts 20
   Palm oil 14
3. Goats 740 Sheep 840
5. Roundwood 745
6. Phosphates 2 081

1. . . ./0.6; 173 kWh (16% hydr.)
2a. Food industries
3. Telephones 10; Cars 2
   Rail: 104 pass.-km.; 13 ton-km.
   Air: 153 pass.-km.; 14 ton-km.
   Sea: 704 loaded; 995 unloaded

Exports: $162 Imports: $284
Cocoa Cotton fabric
Phosphates Machinery
Coffee Food
 Vehicles
Exports to: France, W. Germany, Netherlands
Imports from: France, W. Germany, U.K, U.S.A.
Aid received (net): $107

TRINIDAD & TOBAGO

1. Commonwealth
2. English
3. Trinidad and Tobago Dollars
4. $1 = 3.60
   £1 = 5.44

1. 5 th. sq. km.
2. 1 185; 237 per sq. km.
3. BR 25; DR 7; AI 0.9%
4. Urb. pop.: 243 (22%)
5. Port of Spain 60

1. GDP $8 115 (6.2%); $7 056 (4.6%)
   Agric. 2%, Indust. 29%, Others 69%
2. Rice 18 Bananas 8
   Oranges 7 Grapefruits 7
   Cocoa 2 Coffee 2
   Copra 6
3. Cattle 76 Pigs 62
5. Roundwood 67
6. Natural gas 119 Crude petroleum 8.4

1. 16.1/6.4; 2 300 kWh
2a. Beer 71 Beer 0.3 Mhl
b. Petroleum products 4.2
3. Telephones 67; Cars 132
   Air: 1 540 pass.-km.; 149 ton-km.
   Sea: 12 798 loaded; 11 094 unloaded

Exports: $2 194 Imports: $2 101
Petroleum products Crude petroleum
Petroleum Manufactured goods
Exports to: U.S.A., Netherlands, Surinam
Imports from: U.S.A., U.K., Saudi Arabia, Indonesia
Revenue from tourism: $163
Aid received (net): $5

TUNISIA

1. Republic
2. Arabic, French
3. Dinar
4. $1 = 0.72
   £1 = 1.09

1. 164 th. sq. km.
2. 7 081; 43 per sq. km.
3. BR 33; DR 11; AI 2.5%
4. Urb. pop.: 2 779 (50%)
5. Tunis 774

1. GDP 8 132 (6.4%); $1 208 (3.8%)
   Agric. 13%, Indust. 23%, Others 64%
2. Wheat 711 Tomatoes 430
   Oranges 130 Olives 400
   Grapes 112 Dates 50
3. Sheep 5 230 Cattle 600
4. Fish 67
5. Roundwood 2 673
6. Lead 6 Crude petroleum 5.7
   Iron ore 0.2 Phosphates 5 796
   Natural gas 17.6

1. 8.7/4.3; 3 531 kWh (1% hydr.)
2a. Sugar 7 Wine 70
   Meat 107 Olive oil 90
b. Petroleum products 1.8
3. Telephones 200; Cars 102
   Rail: 744 pass.-km.; 1 692 ton-km.
   Air: 1 531 pass.-km.; 154 ton-km.
   Sea: 2 856 loaded; 6 744 unloaded

Exports: $1 618 Imports: $2 420
Petroleum Machinery
Olive oil Wheat
Phosphates Textiles
Fertilizer Iron and steel
Exports to: France, Italy, Greece, W. Germany
Imports from: France, W. Germany, Italy
Revenue from tourism: $555
Aid received (net): $257.3

TURKEY

1. Republic
2. Turkish
3. Lira
4. $1 = 656.62
   £1 = 992.48

1. 781 th. sq. km.
2. 49 272; 63 per sq. km.
3. BR 35; DR 10; AI 2.3%
4. Urb. pop.: 20 673 (43%)
5. Ankara 2 276

1. GDP $40 551 (3.4%); $858 (1.3%)
   Agric. 18%, Indust. 28%, Others 54%
2. Barley 6 500 Wheat 17 235
   Apples 1 900 Oranges 744
   Rye 360 Grapes 3 300
   Tomatoes 4 000 Cottonseed 938
   Cotton lint 586 Wool 63
   Tobacco 210
3. Sheep 48 630 Goats 16 732
4. Fish 567
5. Roundwood 19 193
6. Coal 7.1 Zinc 51
   Lignite 24.3 Crude petroleum 2.0
   Iron ore 1.9 Antimony 0.2
   Chrome 520 Mercury 161t
   Bauxite 128 Copper 27

1. 15.5/35.5; 27 321 kWh (42% hydr.)
2a. Meat 900 Sawnwood 4 117
   Sugar 1 630 Wine 37
   Olive oil 143
b. Iron 228 Steel 2 748
   Cotton yarn 54 Wool yarn 5.3
   Petroleum products 14.2 Copper 39
   Cement 15 154
3. Telephones 2 104; Cars 472
   Rail: 6 624 pass.-km.; 7 680 ton-km.
   Air: 1 177 pass.-km.; 126 ton-km.
   Sea: 45 144 loaded; 36 312 unloaded

Exports: $7 086 Imports: $10 822
Cotton Machinery
Nuts Vehicles
Tobacco Fertilizer
Raisins Crude petroleum
 Iron and steel
Exports to: W. Germany, U.S.A., Italy, France
Imports from: W. Germany, U.S.A., Iran, Italy, France
Revenue from tourism: $370

UGANDA

1. Republic
2. English, Bantu
3. Ugandan Shilling
4. $1 = 1 422.00
   £1 = 2 149.00

1. 236 th. sq. km.
2. 15 477; 66 per sq. km.
3. BR 50; DR 16; AI 5.5%
4. Urb. pop.: 1 061 (7%)
5. Kampala 332

1. GDP $3 360 (–0.4%); $238 (–3.7%)
   Agric. 73%, Indust. 6%, Others 21%
2. Cassava 1 650 Millet/Sorghum 980
   Coffee 204 Tea 3
   Cottonseed 42 Groundnuts 100
3. Cattle 5 200 Goats 2 500
4. Fish 172
5. Roundwood 26 255
6. Tin 0.1 Tungsten 20t
   Lead 8

1. 0.08/0.3; 650 kWh (99% hydr.)
2a. Meat 156 Sugar 6
   Sawnwood 24
3. Telephones 43; Cars 35
   Rail: see Kenya
   Air: 125 pass.-km.; 41 ton-km.

Exports: $399 Imports: $293
Coffee Manufactured goods
Cotton Machinery
Copper Vehicles
Exports to: U.K., U.S.A., Spain, France
Imports from: U.K., W. Germany, Kenya, Brazil
Aid received (net): $99.7

For detailed table headings and notes see first page of this section

Country	Area and Population	Production	Manufactures	Trade

UNITED KINGDOM

Area and Population
1. Kingdom
2. English
3. English Pound
4. $1 = 0.66

1. 245 th. sq. km.
2. 56 125; 229 per sq. km.
3. BR 13; DR 12; AI –0.0%
4. Urb. pop.: 50 618 (91%)
5. London 6 767

Production
1. GDP $367 983 (0.8%); $6 514 (0.8%)
   Agric. 2%, Indust. 29%, Others 69%
2. Barley 10 958 / Wheat 14 960
   Oats 550 / Potatoes 7 398
   Apples 344 / Wool 51
   Sheep 34 802 / Cattle 13 213
3. Fish 847
4. Roundwood 3 950
5. Coal 51.3
   Iron ore 0.1 / Natural gas 1 628
   Tin 5.0 / Crude petroleum 122.1
   Lead 4 / Salt 6 311

Manufactures
1. 328.7/260.2; 276 227 kWh (2% hydr., 18% nucl.)
2a. Meat 3 199 / Sawnwood 1 691
    Butter and cheese 450 / Sugar 1 400
    Beer 59.8 Mhl
b. Iron 9 672 / Steel 15 120
   Aluminium 462 / Lead 338
   Copper 137 / Plastics 2 051
   Cotton yarn 89 / Wool yarn 126
   Synthetic fibres 175 / Paper 3 200
   Radios 407 / Petroleum products 69.9
   Vehicles: / Ships (grt.) 204
   pass. 910, comm. 224 / Cement 13 488
3. Telephones 27 784; Cars 15 910
   Rail: 30 084 pass.-km.; 12 456 ton-km.
   Air: 53 645 pass.-km.; 6 606 ton-km.
   Sea: 136 140 loaded; 136 128 unloaded

Trade
Exports: $101 332 / Imports: $109 270
Machinery / Machinery
Vehicles / Crude petroleum
Textiles / Non-ferrous metals
Diamonds / Fruit and vegetables
Non-ferrous metals / Diamonds
Iron and steel / Minerals
Alcoholic drinks / Cereals
Aircraft / Butter
/ Meat
/ Textiles
Exports to: U.S.A., W. Germany, France, Ireland, Belgium-Luxembourg, Netherlands
Imports from: U.S.A., W. Germany, France, Netherlands
Invisible trade balance: +$9 690
Revenue from tourism: $5 144
Aid given (net): $11 615

UNITED STATES

Area and Population
1. Federal Republic
2. English
3. U.S. Dollar
4. £1 = 1.51

1. 9 373 th. sq. km.
2. 239 283; 26 per sq. km.
3. BR 16; DR 9; AI 0.8%
4. Urb. pop.: 167 050 (71%)
5. Washington 3 061

Production
1. GDP $3 276 000 (3.1%); $13 968 (2.1%)
   Agric. 2%, Indust. 24%, Others 74%
2. Barley 12 988 / Potatoes 16 404
   Maize 194 475 / Wheat 70 638
   Sorghum 21 994 / Rye 823
   Oranges 6 566 / Grapefruit 1 945
   Wine 1 620 / Soya beans 50 643
   Cottonseed 4 811 / Tobacco 791
   Rice 6 216 / Cotton 2 894
3. Cattle 114 040 / Pigs 55 819
4. Fish 4 143
5. Roundwood 437 762
6. Coal 750.3
   Iron ore 32.8 / Tungsten 980t
   Bauxite 856 / Vanadium 1 969t
   Copper 1 091 / Natural gas 15 879
   Gold 71.5 / Crude petroleum 435.8
   Lead 333 / Potash 1 429
   Molybdenum 15 / Phosphates 42 573
   Zinc 278 / Silver 1 382
   Lignite 57.3 / Uranium 8 138

Manufactures
1. 1 904.6/2 174.8; 2 367 634 kWh (14% hydr., 12% nucl., 0.2% geo.)
2a. Meat 25 627 / Butter and cheese 2 910
    Sugar 5 394 / Wine 1 620
    Sawnwood 78 110 / Wood pulp 47 700
b. Cotton yarn 1 064 / Wool yarn 58
   Synthetic fibres 286 / Silk fabric 83 863 M ft[2]
   Paper 58 800 / Copper 1 500
   Magnesium 144 / Iron 47 088
   Steel 82 716 / Aluminium 5 759
   Plastics 12 418 / Petroleum products 604
   Vehicles: / Radios 7 661
   pass. 7 622, comm. 3 076 / Ships (grt.) 118
3. Telephones 181 892; Cars 123 461
   Rail: 17 695 pass.-km.; 1 341 717 ton-km.
   Air: 408 997 pass.-km.; 47 144 ton-km.
   Sea: 327 768 loaded; 332 424 unloaded

Trade
Exports: $217 888 / Imports: $341 177
Machinery / Vehicles
Vehicles / Machinery
Aircraft / Iron and steel
Cereals / Non-ferrous metals
Chemical products / Crude petroleum
Iron and steel / Petroleum products
Non-ferrous metals / Clothing
Soya / Paper and cardboard
Metals / Textiles
Coal / Metals
Textiles
Exports to: Canada, Japan, U.K., W. Germany, Mexico
Imports from: Canada, Japan, W. Germany, U.K., Mexico
Invisible trade balance: +$18 750
Revenue from tourism: $11 293
Aid given (net): $17 870

URUGUAY

Area and Population
1. Republic
2. Spanish
3. Uruguayan Peso
4. $1 = 139.69
   £1 = 211.14

1. 176 th. sq. km.
2. 3 012; 17 per sq. km.
3. BR 18; DR 9; AI 3.3%
4. Urb. pop.: 2 502 (84%)
5. Montevideo 1 362

Production
1. GDP $3 980 (3.9%); $1 331 (3.4%)
   Agric. 12%, Indust. 22%, Others 66%
2. Maize 120 / Wheat 450
   Grapes 117 / Oranges 50
   Linseed 8 / Wool 91
3. Sheep 23 337 / Cattle 9 491
4. Fish 144
5. Roundwood 2 975

Manufactures
1. 0.9/2.1; 7 343 kWh (98% hydr.)
2a. Meat 438 / Sawnwood 16
    Sugar 91
b. Petroleum products 2.2
3. Telephones 294; Cars 281
   Rail: 339 pass.-km.; 205 ton-km.
   Air: 293 pass.-km.; 28 ton-km.
   Sea: 570 loaded; 454 unloaded

Trade
Exports: $925 / Imports: $736
Beef / Machinery
Wool / Vehicles
Hides and skins / Crude petroleum
Exports to: W. Germany, Brazil, U.S.A.
Imports from: Argentina, Brazil, U.S.A., Iraq
Aid received (net): $17.1

U.S.S.R.

Area and Population
1. Socialist Republic
2. Russian and others
3. Rouble
4. $1 = 0.71
   £1 = 1.07

1. 22 402 th. sq. km.
2. 278 618; 12 per sq. km.
3. BR 20; DR 11; AI 0.9%
4. Urb. pop.: 173 185 (64%)
5. Moscow 8 537

Production
1. NMP $711 818 (4.1%); $2 588 (3.2%)
   Agric. 20%, Indust. 46%, Others 34%
2. Barley 42 000 / Wheat 76 000
   Maize 13 000 / Potatoes 85 300
   Grapes 7 500 / Rye 10 500
   Flax 480 / Cotton 2 400
   Tomatoes 7 500 / Cottonseed 5 350
   Tobacco 360
3. Sheep 145 265 / Cattle 119 558
4. Fish 9 757
5. Roundwood 355 900
6. Coal 483.3 / Tungsten 9 100t
   Iron ore 148.2 / Zinc 980
   Bauxite 6 200 / Natural gas 18 638
   Chrome 2 500 / Crude petroleum 613.0
   Copper 1 020 / Phosphates 27 700
   Lead 570 / Potash 9 294
   Manganese 3 457 / Salt 16 200
   Molybdenum 11 / Asbestos 2 250
   Nickel 175 / Diamonds 12 000
   Gold 270.0 / Tin 10.0
   Lignite 153.0 / Silver 1 600

Manufactures
1. 2 065.5/1 611.5; 1 408 100 kWh (13% hydr., 6% nucl.)
2a. Meat 16 839 / Sawnwood 109 200
    Butter and cheese 3 269 / Sugar 8 350
    Wine 3 800
b. Iron 110 496 / Steel 153 996
   Aluminium 2 300 / Copper 1 380
   Magnesium 80 / Paper 8 900
   Cotton yarn 1 658 / Wool yarn 457
   Synthetic fibres 645 / Radios 8 906
   Petroleum products 420 / Vehicles:
   / pass. 1 296, comm. 866
3. Telephones 25 069; Cars 9 631
   Rail: 347 852 pass.-km.; 3 464 480 ton-km.
   Air: 172 206 pass.-km.; 18 517 ton-km.
   Sea: 162 000 loaded; 63 000 unloaded

Trade
Exports: $91 649 / Imports: $80 624
Machinery / Machinery
Iron and steel / Clothing
Crude petroleum / Ships
Non-ferrous metals / Iron and steel
Petroleum products / Minerals
Sawnwood / Railway rolling stock
Cotton / Shoes
Vehicles
Main trade is with: E.Germany, Poland, Czechoslovakia, Bulgaria, Hungary

VENEZUELA

Area and Population
1. Republic
2. Spanish
3. Bolivar
4. $1 = 19.33
   £1 = 29.21

1. 912 th. sq. km.
2. 17 317; 19 per sq. km.
3. BR 37; DR 6; AI 3.3%
4. Urb. pop.: 10 936 (65%)
5. Caracas 2 944

Production
1. GDP $46 461 (2.8%); $2 757 (–0.2%)
   Agric. 7%, Indust. 40%, Others 53%
2. Maize 547 / Bananas 1 403
   Oranges 362 / Tomatoes 127
   Cocoa 21 / Coffee 61
   Cottonseed 25 / Sesame 38
3. Cattle 12 283 / Pigs 2 584
4. Fish 227
5. Roundwood 1 300
6. Iron ore 8.1 / Natural gas 645
   Gold 863kg / Crude petroleum 85.9
   Diamonds 300 / Coal 0.04

Manufactures
1. 165.9/50.1; 41 700 kWh (41% hydr.)
2a. Meat 778 / Sawnwood 210
    Sugar 423
b. Iron 2 400 / Steel 2 772
   Cotton yarn . . . / Synthetic fibres 17
   Cement 6 000 / Vehicles:
   Petroleum products 40.4 / pass. 235, comm. 66
3. Telephones 789; Cars 1 643
   Rail: 19 pass.-km.; 29 ton-km.
   Air: 5 031 pass.-km.; 563 ton-km.
   Sea: 60 821 loaded; 12 093 unloaded

Trade
Exports: $7 792 / Imports: $6 676
Crude petroleum / Machinery
Petroleum products / Vehicles
Iron ore / Iron and steel
Coffee / Cereals
/ Manufactured goods
Exports to: U.S.A., Neth. Antilles, Canada
Imports from: U.S.A., W. Germany, Japan
Invisible trade balance: –$3 524

VIETNAM

Area and Population
1. Democratic Republic
2. Vietnamese
3. Dông
4. $1 = 12.46
   £1 = 18.83

1. 330 th. sq. km.
2. 59 713; 181 per sq. km.
3. BR 39; DR 12; AI 2.0%
4. Urb. pop.: 11 661 (20%)
5. Hanoi 2 571

Production
1. GDP $4 682 (. . .); $98 (. . .)
   Agric. 29%, Indust. 7%, Others 64%
2. Rice 15 416 / Cassava 2 900
   Groundnuts 87 / Tea 29
   Maize 475 / Tobacco 27
3. Cattle 2 010 / Pigs 11 202
4. Fish 710
5. Roundwood 23 676
6. Coal 5.3 / Phosphates 220
   Salt 900 / Tin 0.5

Manufactures
1. 6.2/7.2; 4 200 kWh (38% hydr.)
2a. Sawnwood 520
b. Cotton yarn 36 / Cement 798
3. Telephones 47; Cars 66
   Rail: 4 043 pass.-km.; 980 ton-km.
   Air: 389 pass.-km.; 5 ton-km.
   Sea: 680 loaded; 5 000 unloaded

Trade
Exports: $440 / Imports: $1 210
Main trade is with:
U.S.S.R. and other Communist countries, Japan, France, Singapore, Hong Kong
Aid received (net): $266

For detailed table headings and notes see first page of this section

YEMEN, NORTH

1. Republic
2. Arabic
3. Riyal
4. $1 = 7.02
   £1 = 10.61

1. 195 th. sq. km.
2. 6 849; 35 per sq. km.
3. BR 49; DR 24; AI 2.3%
4. Urb. pop.: 1 149 (18%)
5. Sana 278

1. GDP $1 122 (5.4%); $212 (3.4%)
   Agric. 61%, Indust. 3%, Others 36%
2. Wheat 50   Coffee 3
   Cottonseed 3
3. Sheep 1 823   Cattle 950

1. . . ./1.2; 285 kWh
3. Telephones 4; Cars. . .
   Air: 490 pass.-km.; 49 ton-km.
   Sea: 40 loaded; 2 000 unloaded

Exports: $39   Imports: $1 521
Exports to: China, S. Yemen, Italy, Saudi Arabia
Imports from: Saudi Arabia, Japan, India
Aid received (net): $137.5

YEMEN, SOUTH

1. People's Republic
2. Arabic
3. South Yemen Dinar
4. $1 = 0.34
   £1 = 0.52

1. 333 th. sq. km.
2. 2 294; 7 per sq. km.
3. BR 48; DR 23; AI 1.9%
4. Urb. pop.: 823 (37%)
5. Aden 264

1. GDP $290 (. . .); $176 (. . .)
   Agric. 19%, Indust. 17%, Others 64%
2. Millet 80   Wheat 15
   Dates 10   Cottonseed 10
3. Goats 1 380   Sheep 1 000
4. Fish 74
5. Roundwood 270

1. . . ./1.7; 180 kWh
2b. Petroleum products 3.1
3. Telephones 9; Cars 11
   Sea: 1 426 loaded; 2 204 unloaded

Exports: $430   Imports: $673
Petroleum products   Petroleum
Cotton   Cotton fabric
                      Cereals
Exports to: U.K., Yemen, South Africa
Imports from: Iran, Kuwait, Japan
Aid received (net): $51.0

YUGOSLAVIA

1. Federal Republic
2. Croatian, Serbian
3. Yugoslavian Dinar
4. $1 = 337.47
   £1 = 510.08

1. 256 th. sq. km.
2. 23 123; 90 per sq. km.
3. BR 16; DR 9; AI 0.8%
4. Urb. pop.: 10 333 (45%)
5. Belgrade 1 407

1. NMP $49 736 (5.4%); $2 196 (4.5%)
   Agric. 14%, Indust. 42%, Others 44%
2. Maize 11 265   Wheat 5 596
   Grapes 1 560   Wool 10
   Tobacco 75
3. Sheep 7 458   Pigs 9 337
4. Fish 80
5. Roundwood 15 381
6. Coal 0.3   Gold 4.2
   Lignite 54.5   Lead 114
   Iron ore 1.8   Silver 128
   Antimony 0.9   Zinc 86
   Bauxite 3 347   Copper 138
   Crude petroleum 4.0 Natural gas 105

1. 33.5/52.9; 71 571 kWh (30% hydr., 5% nucl., 9% geo)
2a. Meat 1 629   Sawnwood 4 413
    Sugar 985   Wine 750
b. Iron 3 264   Steel 1 956
   Copper 128   Lead 120
   Cotton yarn 119   Wool yarn 50
   Synthetic fibres 58 Ships (grt.) 199
   Petroleum products 12.3
3. Telephones 2 303; Cars 2 568
   Rail: 11 508 pass.-km.; 28 476 ton-km.
   Air: 2 870 pass.-km.; 318 ton-km.
   Sea: 6 312 loaded; 22 080 unloaded

Exports: $9 811   Imports: $11 538
Machinery   Machinery
Non-ferrous metals   Iron and steel
Ships and boats   Vehicles
Clothing   Textile fibres
Meat   Textiles
Textiles   Non-ferrous metals
Iron and steel   Chemical products
Shoes   Crude petroleum
Exports to: Italy, U.S.S.R., W. Germany
Imports from: W. Germany, Italy, U.S.S.R
Invisible trade balance: +$2 144
Revenue from tourism: $844

ZAÏRE

1. Democratic Republic
2. French, Kiswahili, etc
3. Zaïre
4. $1 = 54.52
   £1 = 82.42

1. 2 345 th. sq. km.
2. 30 363; 13 per sq. km.
3. BR 46; DR 17; AI 2.9%
4. Urb. pop.: 9 010 (34%)
5. Kinshasa 2 444

1. GDP $5 443 (−3.7%); $180 (−6.7%)
   Agric. 26%, Indust. 16%, Others 58%
2. Cassava 14 800   Maize 680
   Coffee 80   Groundnuts 380
   Palm oil 140   Rubber 24
   Bananas 1 805   Cottonseed 50
3. Goats 2 910   Cattle 1 300
4. Fish 102
5. Roundwood 31 265
6. Cobalt 11   Tin 2.4
   Copper 501   Zinc 75
   Manganese . . .   Diamonds 18 500
   Gold 6.0   Tungsten 85t
   Crude petroleum 1.3 Silver 25

1. 2.3/2.1; 4 213 kWh (99% hydr.)
2a. Sugar 45   Beer 5.0Mhl
    Sawnwood 121
b. Copper 225   Zinc 66
   Petroleum products 0.6 Cement 400
3. Telephones 27; Cars 40
   Rail: 467 pass.-km.; 2 203 ton-km.
   Air: 683 pass.-km.; 93 ton-km.
   Sea: 845 loaded; 1 513 unloaded

Exports: $1 004   Imports: $682
Copper   Machinery
Diamonds   Vehicles
Cobalt   Petroleum products
Coffee   Cotton fabric
Palm oil   Cereals
Exports to: Belgium-Luxembourg, U.K., U.S.A.
Imports from: Belgium-Luxembourg, U.S.A., France, W. Germany
Aid received (net): $410.9

ZAMBIA

1. Republic
2. English
3. Kwacha
4. $1 = 7.09
   £1 = 10.72

1. 753 th. sq. km.
2. 6 666; 9 per sq. km.
3. BR 48; DR 17; AI 3.3%
4. Urb. pop.: 3 029 (47%)
5. Lusaka 538

1. GDP $2 767 (−1.6%); $443 (−4.5%)
   Agric. 14%, Indust. 35%, Others 51%
2. Maize 857   Tobacco 3
   Millet/sorghum 27 Groundnuts 19
   Cattle 2 400   Goats 355
4. Fish 67
5. Roundwood 9 171
6. Coal 0.5   Tin . . .
   Cobalt 2.4t   Gold 0.3
   Copper 565   Silver 28
   Lead 19   Zinc 41

1. 1.6/2.2; 10 071 kWh (99% hydr.)
2a. Meat 88   Sugar 141
    Sawnwood 42
b. Copper 523   Zinc 29
   Lead 9   Cement 252
3. Telephones 61; Cars 68
   Air: 557 pass.-km.; 74 ton-km.

Exports: $648   Imports: $566
Copper   Machinery
Zinc   Vehicles
Lead   Textiles
Cobalt   Iron and steel
Tobacco   Petroleum products
Exports to: Japan, U.K., W. Germany, U.S.A.
Imports from: U.K., Saudi Arabia, U.S.A.
Aid received (net): $290.1

ZIMBABWE

1. Republic
2. English
3. Zimbabwe Dollar
4. $1 = 1.60
   £1 = 2.42

1. 391 th. sq. km.
2. 8 300; 21 per sq. km.
3. BR 47; DR 14; AI 3.5%
4. Urb. pop.: 1 823 (24%)
5. Harare 681

1. GDP $6 612 (3.2%); $876 (0%)
   Agric. 13%, Indust. 27%, Others 60%
2. Maize 1 501   Millet/sorghum 132
   Groundnuts 70   Tobacco 118
3. Cattle 5 500   Goats 1 100
5. Roundwood 6 696
6. Coal 3.1   Gold 14.5t
   Iron ore 0.5   Nickel 11.1
   Chrome 420   Tin 1.2
   Copper 21   Asbestos 153
   Silver 38

1. 2.9/3.8; 4 426 kWh (84% hydr.)
2a. Meat 116   Sugar 457
    Sawnwood 131
b. Iron 420   Steel 528
   Copper 23   Cement 648
3. Telephones 224; Cars 176
   Rail: . . . pass.-km.; 6 259 ton-km.
   Air: 541 pass.-km.; 58 ton-km.

Exports: $1 008   Imports: $959
Tobacco   Machinery
Asbestos   Textiles
Copper   Vehicles
Gold   Mineral fuels
Main trade is with: U.K., W. Germany, U.S.A.
Aid received (net): $136.1

For detailed table headings and notes see first page of this section

INDEX

The number printed in bold type against each index entry indicates the map page where the feature will be found. The geographical coordinates which follow the name are sometimes only approximate but are close enough for the place name to be located. Rivers have been indexed to their mouth or confluence.

An open square □ signifies that the name refers to an administrative subdivision of a country while a solid square ■ follows the name of a country. An arrow → follows the name of a river.

The alphabetic order of names composed of two or more words is governed primarily by the first word and then by the second. This rule applies even if the second word is a description or its abbreviation, R., L., I. for example. Names composed of a proper name (Gibraltar) and a description (Strait of) are positioned alphabetically by the proper name. If the same place name occurs twice or more times in the index and all are in the same country, each is followed by the name of the administrative subdivision in which it is located. The names are placed in the alphabetical order of the subdivisions. If the same place name occurs twice or more in the index and the places are in different countries, the latter governs the alphabetical order. In a mixture of these situations the primary order is fixed by the alphabetical sequence of the countries and the secondary order by that of the country subdivisions.

Abbreviations used in the index

A.C.T. — Australian Capital Territory
A.R. — Autonomous Region
A.S.S.R. — Autonomous Soviet Socialist Republic
Afghan. — Afghanistan
Ala. — Alabama
Alta. — Alberta
Amer. — America(n)
And. P. — Andhra Pradesh
Arch. — Archipelago
Ariz. — Arizona
Ark. — Arkansas
Atl. Oc. — Atlantic Ocean
B. — Baie, Bahía, Bay, Bucht, Bugt
B.A. — Buenos Aires
B.C. — British Columbia
Baden-W. — Baden-Württemburg
Bangla. — Bangladesh
Barr. — Barrage
Bay. — Bayern
Beds. — Bedfordshire
Berks. — Berkshire
Br. — British
Bri. — Bridge
Bucks. — Buckinghamshire
C. — Cabo, Cap, Cape, Coast
C.A.R. — Central African Republic
C. Prov. — Cape Province
Calif. — California
Cambs. — Cambridgeshire
Cent. — Central
Chan. — Channel
Colo. — Colorado
Conn. — Connecticut
Cord. — Cordillera
Cr. — Creek
Cumb. — Cumbria
Czech. — Czechoslovakia
D.C. — District of Columbia
Del. — Delaware
Dep. — Dependency
Derby. — Derbyshire
Des. — Desert
Dist. — District
Dj. — Djebel
Domin. — Dominica
Dom. Rep. — Dominican Republic
Dumf. & Gall. — Dumfries & Galloway
E. — East
El Salv. — El Salvador
Eng. — England
Eq. Guin. — Equatorial Guinea
Fla. — Florida
Ft. — Fort
Falk. Is. — Falkland Is.
G. — Golfe, Golfo, Gulf, Guba
Ga. — Georgia
Gib. — Gibraltar
Gloucs. — Gloucester
Gt. — Great, Greater
Guinea-Biss. — Guinea-Bissau
H.K. — Hong Kong
H.P. — Himachal Pradesh
Hants. — Hampshire
Harb. — Harbor, Harbour
Hd. — Head
Hereford & Worcs. — Hereford & Worcester
Herts. — Hertfordshire
Hts. — Heights
I. of M. — Isle of Man
I.(s). — Île, Ilha, Insel, Isla, Island, Isle
Ill. — Illinois
Ind. — Indiana
Ind. Oc. — Indian Ocean
Ivory C. — Ivory Coast
J. — Jabal, Jebel, Jazira
Junc. — Junction
K. — Kap, Kapp
Kans. — Kansas
Kep. — Kepulauan
Ky. — Kentucky
L. — Lac, Lacul, Lago, Lagoa, Lake, Limni, Loch, Lough
La. — Louisiana
Lancs. — Lancashire
Leics. — Leicestershire
Liech. — Liechtenstein
Lim. — Limerick
Lincs. — Lincolnshire
Lit. — Little
Lr. — Lower
Lux. — Luxembourg
Mad. P. — Madhya Pradesh
Madag. — Madagascar
Man. — Manitoba
Mass. — Massachusetts
Md. — Maryland
Me. — Maine
Medit. S. — Mediterranean Sea
Mich. — Michigan
Minn. — Minnesota
Miss. — Mississippi
Mo. — Missouri
Mont. — Montana
Mozam. — Mozambique
Mt.(e). — Mont, Monte, Monti, Montaña, Mountain
N. — Nord, Norte, North, Northern, Nouveau
N.B. — New Brunswick
N.C. — North Carolina
N. Cal. — New Caledonia
N. Dak. — North Dakota
N.H. — New Hampshire
N.I. — North Island
N.J. — New Jersey
N. Mex. — New Mexico
N.S. — Nova Scotia
N.S.W. — New South Wales
N. Terr. — Northern Territory
N.W.T. — North West Territory
N.Y. — New York
N.Z. — New Zealand
Nat. — National
Nebr. — Nebraska
Neths. — Netherlands
Neth. Ant. — Netherlands Antilles
Nev. — Nevada
Nfld. — Newfoundland
Nic. — Nicaragua
Northants. — Northamptonshire
Northumb. — Northumberland
Notts. — Nottinghamshire
O. — Oued, Ouadi
Occ. — Occidentale
O.F.S. — Orange Free State
Okla. — Oklahoma
Ont. — Ontario
Or. — Orientale
Oreg. — Oregon
Os. — Ostrov
Oxon. — Oxfordshire
Oz. — Ozero
P. — Pass, Passo, Pasul, Pulau
P.E.I. — Prince Edward Island
P.O. — Post Office
Pa. — Pennsylvania
Pac. Oc. — Pacific Ocean
Papua N.G. — Papua New Guinea
Pass. — Passage
Pen. — Peninsula, Péninsule
Phil. — Philippines
Pk. — Park, Peak
Plat. — Plateau
P-ov. — Poluostrov
Prom. — Promontory
Prov. — Province, Provincial
Pt. — Point
Pta. — Ponta, Punta
Pte. — Pointe
Qué. — Québec
Queens. — Queensland
R. — Rio, River
R.I. — Rhode Island
R.S.F.S.R. — Russian Soviet Federative Socialist Republic
Ra.(s). — Range(s)
Raj. — Rajasthan
Reg. — Region
Rep. — Republic
Res. — Reserve, Reservoir
Rhld.-Pfz. — Rheinland-Pfalz
S. — San, South, Sea
Si. Arabia — Saudi Arabia
S. Austral. — South Australia
S.C. — South Carolina
S. Dak. — South Dakota
S.-Holst. — Schleswig-Holstein
S.I. — South Island
S. Leone — Sierra Leone
S.S.R. — Soviet Socialist Republic
Sa. — Serra, Sierra
Sard. — Sardinia
Sask. — Saskatchewan
Scot. — Scotland
Sd. — Sound
Sept. — Septentrionale
Sev. — Severnaya
Sib. — Siberia
Som. — Somerset
Sprs. — Springs
St. — Saint, Sankt, Sint
St.P. & M. — St. Pierre & Miquelon
Sta. — Santa, Station
Staffs. — Staffordshire
Ste. — Sainte
Sto. — Santo
Str. — Strait, Stretto
Switz. — Switzerland
T.O. — Telegraph Office
Tas. — Tasmania
Tenn. — Tennessee
Terr. — Territory
Tex. — Texas
Tg. — Tanjung
Tipp. — Tipperary
Trans. — Transvaal
Trin. & Tob. — Trinidad & Tobago
U.A.E. — United Arab Emirates
U.K. — United Kingdom
U.S.A. — United States of America
U.S.S.R. — Union of Soviet Socialist Republics
Ukr. — Ukraine
Ut. P. — Uttar Pradesh
Va. — Virginia
Vdkhr. — Vodokhranilishche
Vic. — Victoria
Vol. — Volcano
Vt. — Vermont
W. — Wadi, West
W. Austral. — Western Australia
W. Isles — Western Isles
W. Va. — West Virginia
Wall. & F. Is. — Wallis & Futuna Is.
Wash. — Washington
Wilts. — Wiltshire
Wis. — Wisconsin
Wlkp. — Wielkopolski
Wyo. — Wyoming
Yorks. — Yorkshire

A

Al Mish'āb

Agailás, Mauritania 84 22 37N 14 22W
Agana, Guam 68 13 28N 144 45 E
Agano →, Japan 63 37 57N 139 8 E
Agapa, U.S.S.R. 41 71 27N 89 15 E
Agar, India 48 23 40N 76 2 E
Agaro, Ethiopia 89 7 50N 36 38 E
Agartala, India 52 23 50N 91 23 E
Agassiz, Canada 110 49 14N 121 46W
Agats, Indonesia 57 5 33 S 138 0 E
Agbélouvé, Togo 91 6 35N 1 14 E
Agboville, Ivory C. 90 5 55N 4 15W
Agdam, U.S.S.R. 39 40 0N 46 58 E
Agdash, U.S.S.R. 39 40 44N 47 22 E
Agde, France 20 43 19N 3 28 E
Agde, C. d', France 20 43 16N 3 28 E
Agdz, Morocco 84 30 47N 6 30W
Agdzhabedi, U.S.S.R. 39 40 5N 47 27 E
Agen, France 20 44 12N 0 38 E
Ageo, Japan 65 35 58N 139 36 E
Ager Tay, Chad 87 20 0N 17 41 E
Agersø, Denmark 11 55 13N 11 12 E
Ageyevo, U.S.S.R. 37 54 10N 36 27 E
Agger, Denmark 11 56 47N 8 13 E
Ággius, Italy 28 40 56N 9 4 E
Aghil Mts., China 49 36 0N 77 0 E
Aghoueyyît, Mauritania 84 21 10N 15 6W
Aginskoye, U.S.S.R. 41 51 6N 114 32 E
Agira, Italy 29 37 40N 14 30 E
Agly →, France 20 42 46N 3 3 E
Agnibilékrou, Ivory C. 90 7 10N 3 11W
Agnita, Romania 34 45 59N 24 40 E
Agnone, Italy 29 41 49N 14 20 E
Ago, Japan 65 34 20N 136 51 E
Agofie, Ghana 91 8 27N 0 15 E
Agogna →, Italy 26 45 4N 8 52 E
Agogo, Sudan 89 7 50N 28 45 E
Agon, France 18 49 2N 1 34W
Agön, Sweden 10 61 34N 17 23 E
Agordo, Italy 27 46 18N 12 2 E
Agout →, France 20 43 47N 1 41 E
Agra, India 48 27 17N 77 58 E
Agramunt, Spain 24 41 48N 1 6 E
Agreda, Spain 24 41 51N 1 55W
Agri →, Italy 29 40 13N 16 44 E
Ağri Daği, Turkey 46 39 50N 44 15 E
Ağri Karakose, Turkey 46 39 44N 43 3 E
Agrigento, Italy 28 37 19N 13 33 E
Agrinion, Greece 35 38 37N 21 27 E
Agrópoli, Italy 29 40 23N 14 59 E
Água Branca, Brazil 138 5 50 S 42 40W
Agua Caliente, Baja Calif. N., Mexico 125 32 29N 116 59W
Agua Caliente, Sinaloa, Mexico 126 26 30N 108 20W
Agua Caliente Springs, U.S.A. 125 32 56N 116 19W
Água Clara, Brazil 137 20 25 S 52 45W
Agua Hechicero, Mexico 125 32 26N 116 14W
Agua Preta →, Brazil 135 1 41 S 63 48W
Agua Prieta, Mexico 126 31 20N 109 32W
Aguachica, Colombia 134 8 19N 73 38W
Aguada Cecilio, Argentina 142 40 51 S 65 51W
Aguadas, Colombia 134 5 40N 75 38W
Aguadilla, Puerto Rico 129 18 27N 67 10W
Aguadulce, Panama 128 8 15N 80 32W
Aguanga, U.S.A. 125 33 27N 116 51W
Aguanish, Canada 105 50 14N 62 2W
Aguanus →, Canada 105 50 13N 62 5W
Aguapeí, Brazil 137 16 12 S 59 43W
Aguapeí →, Brazil 139 21 0 S 51 0W
Aguapey →, Argentina 140 29 7 S 56 36W
Aguaray Guazú →, Paraguay 140 24 47 S 57 19W
Aguarico →, Ecuador 134 0 59 S 75 11W
Aguas →, Spain 24 41 20N 0 30W
Aguas Blancas, Chile 140 24 15 S 69 55W
Aguas Calientes, Sierra de, Argentina 140 25 26 S 66 40W
Águas Formosas, Brazil 139 17 5 S 40 57W
Aguascalientes, Mexico 126 21 53N 102 12W
Aguascalientes □, Mexico 126 22 0N 102 20W
Agudo, Spain 23 38 59N 4 52W
Águeda, Portugal 22 40 34N 8 27W
Agueda →, Spain 22 41 2N 6 56W
Aguié, Niger 91 13 31N 7 46 E
Aguilafuente, Spain 22 41 13N 4 7W
Aguilar, Spain 23 37 31N 4 40W
Aguilar de Campóo, Spain 22 42 47N 4 15W
Aguilares, Argentina 140 27 26 S 65 35W
Aguilas, Spain 25 37 23N 1 35W
Agüimes, Canary Is. 25 27 58N 15 27W
Aguja, C. de la, Colombia 134 11 18N 74 12W
Agulaa, Ethiopia 89 13 40N 39 40 E
Agulhas, C., S. Africa 96 34 52 S 20 0 E
Agulo, Canary Is. 25 28 11N 17 12W
Agung, Indonesia 56 8 20 S 115 28 E
'Agur, Israel 44 31 42N 34 55 E
Agur, Uganda 92 2 28N 32 55 E
Agusan →, Phil. 57 9 0N 125 30 E
Agustín Codazzi, Colombia 134 10 2N 73 14W
Agvali, U.S.S.R. 39 42 36N 46 8 E
Aha Mts., Botswana 96 19 45 S 21 0 E
Ahaggar, Algeria 85 23 0N 6 30 E
Ahamansu, Ghana 91 7 38N 0 35 E
Ahar, Iran 46 38 35N 47 0 E
Ahaura →, N.Z. 81 42 21 S 171 34 E
Ahaus, W. Germany 30 52 4N 7 1 E
Ahelledjem, Algeria 85 26 37N 6 58 E
Ahipara B., N.Z. 80 35 5 S 173 5 E
Ahiri, India 50 19 30N 80 0 E
Ahlen, W. Germany 30 51 45N 7 52 E
Ahmad Wal, Pakistan 48 29 18N 65 58 E
Ahmadabad, India 48 23 0N 72 40 E
Ahmadnagar, India 50 19 7N 74 46 E
Ahmadpur, Pakistan 48 29 12N 71 10 E
Ahmar Mts., Ethiopia 89 9 20N 41 15 E
Ahmedabad = Ahmadabad, India 48 23 0N 72 40 E
Ahmednagar = Ahmadnagar, India 50 19 7N 74 46 E
Ahoada, Nigeria 91 5 8N 6 36 E
Ahome, Mexico 126 25 55N 109 11W
Ahr →, W. Germany 30 50 33N 7 17 E
Ahrensbök, W. Germany 30 54 0N 10 34 E
Ahrweiler, W. Germany 30 50 31N 7 3 E
Ahuachapán, El Salv. 128 13 54N 89 52W
Ahuriri →, N.Z. 81 44 31 S 170 12 E
Åhus, Sweden 11 55 56N 14 18 E
Ahvāz, Iran 46 31 20N 48 40 E
Ahvenanmaa = Åland, Finland 9 60 15N 20 0 E
Aḥwar, S. Yemen 45 13 30N 46 40 E
Ahzar, Mali 91 15 30N 3 20 E
Aiari →, Brazil 134 1 22N 68 36W
Aichach, W. Germany 31 48 28N 11 9 E
Aichi □, Japan 65 35 0N 137 15 E
Aidone, Italy 29 37 26N 14 26 E
Aiello Cálabro, Italy 29 39 6N 16 12 E
Aigle, Switz. 31 46 18N 6 58 E
Aigle, L', France 18 48 46N 0 38 E
Aignay-le-Duc, France 19 47 40N 4 43 E
Aigoual, Mt., France 20 44 8N 3 35 E
Aigre, France 20 45 54N 0 1 E
Aigua, Uruguay 141 34 13 S 54 46W
Aiguebelle, Parc, Canada 106 48 30N 78 45W
Aigueperse, France 20 46 3N 3 13 E
Aigues →, France 21 44 7N 4 43 E
Aigues-Mortes, France 21 43 35N 4 12 E
Aigues-Mortes, G. d', France 21 43 31N 4 3 E
Aiguilles, France 21 44 47N 6 51 E
Aiguillon, France 20 44 18N 0 21 E
Aiguillon-sur-Mer, L', France 20 46 20N 1 18W
Aigurande, France 20 46 27N 1 49 E
Aihui, China 62 50 10N 127 30 E
Aija, Peru 136 9 50 S 77 45W
Aiken, U.S.A. 115 33 34N 81 50W
Ailao Shan, China 58 24 0N 101 20 E
Aillant-sur-Tholon, France 19 47 52N 3 20 E
Aillik, Canada 105 55 11N 59 18W
Ailly-sur-Noye, France 19 49 45N 2 20 E
Ailsa Craig, Canada 108 43 8N 81 33W
Ailsa Craig, U.K. 14 55 15N 5 7W
'Ailūn, Jordan 44 32 18N 35 47 E
Aim, U.S.S.R. 41 59 0N 133 55 E
Aimere, Indonesia 57 8 45 S 121 3 E
Aimogasta, Argentina 140 28 33 S 66 50W
Aimorés, Brazil 139 19 30 S 41 4W
Ain □, France 21 46 5N 5 20 E
Ain →, France 21 45 45N 5 11 E
Ain Banaiyan, Si. Arabia 47 23 0N 51 0 E
Aïn Beïda, Algeria 85 35 50N 7 29 E
Ain Ben Khellil, Algeria 85 33 15N 0 49W
Aïn Ben Tili, Mauritania 84 25 59N 9 27W
Aïn Beni Mathar, Morocco 85 34 1N 2 0W
Aïn Benian, Algeria 85 36 48N 2 55 E
Ain Dalla, Egypt 88 27 20N 27 23 E
Ain el Mafki, Egypt 88 27 30N 28 15 E
Ain Girba, Egypt 88 29 20N 25 14 E
Aïn M'lila, Algeria 85 36 2N 6 35 E
Ain Qeiqab, Egypt 88 29 42N 24 55 E
Aïn-Sefra, Algeria 85 32 47N 0 37W
Ain Sheikh Murzûk, Egypt 88 26 47N 27 45 E
Ain Sukhna, Egypt 88 29 32N 32 20 E
Aïn Tédelès, Algeria 85 36 0N 0 21 E
Aïn-Témouchent, Algeria 85 35 16N 1 8W
Aïn Touta, Algeria 85 35 26N 5 54 E
Ain Zeitûn, Egypt 88 29 10N 25 48 E
Aïn Zorah, Morocco 85 34 37N 3 32W
Ainabo, Somali Rep. 98 9 0N 46 25 E
Ainaži, U.S.S.R. 36 57 50N 24 24 E
Aínos Óros, Greece 35 38 10N 20 35 E
Ainsworth, U.S.A. 120 42 33N 99 52W
Aioi, Japan 64 34 48N 134 28 E
Aipe, Colombia 134 3 13N 75 15W
Aiquile, Bolivia 137 18 10 S 65 10W
Aïr, Niger 91 18 30N 8 0 E
Air Hitam, Malaysia 55 1 55N 103 11 E
Airaines, France 19 49 58N 1 55 E
Airão, Brazil 135 1 56 S 61 22W
Airdrie, U.K. 14 55 53N 3 57W
Aire →, France 19 49 18N 4 49 E
Aire →, U.K. 12 53 42N 0 55W
Aire, I. del, Spain 24 39 48N 4 16 E
Aire-sur-la-Lys, France 19 50 37N 2 22 E
Aire-sur-l'Adour, France 20 43 42N 0 15W
Aireys Inlet, Australia 74 38 29 S 144 5 E
Airlie Beach, Australia 72 20 16 S 148 43 E
Airvault, France 18 46 50N 0 8W
Aisch →, W. Germany 31 49 46N 11 1 E
Aisen □, Chile 142 46 30 S 73 0W
Aisne □, France 19 49 42N 3 40 E
Aisne →, France 19 49 26N 2 50 E
Aitana, Sierra de, Spain 25 38 35N 0 24W
Aitape, Papua N. G. 69 3 11 S 142 22 E
Aitkin, U.S.A. 120 46 32N 93 43W
Aitolikón, Greece 35 38 26N 21 21 E
Aiuaba, Brazil 138 6 38 S 40 7W
Aiud, Romania 34 46 19N 23 44 E
Aix-en-Provence, France 21 43 32N 5 27 E
Aix-la-Chapelle = Aachen, W. Germany 30 50 47N 6 4 E
Aix-les-Bains, France 21 45 41N 5 53 E
Aixe-sur-Vienne, France 20 45 47N 1 9 E
Aiyang, Mt., Papua N. G. 69 5 10 S 141 20 E
Aiyansh, Canada 110 55 17N 129 2W
Áíyina, Greece 35 37 45N 23 26 E
Aiyínion, Greece 35 40 28N 22 28 E
Aiyion, Greece 35 38 15N 22 5 E
Aizawl, India 52 23 40N 92 44 E
Aizenay, France 18 46 44N 1 38W
Aizpute, U.S.S.R. 36 56 43N 21 40 E
Aizuwakamatsu, Japan 63 37 30N 139 56 E
Ajaccio, France 21 41 55N 8 40 E
Ajaccio, G. d', France 21 41 52N 8 40 E
Ajaju →, Colombia 134 0 59N 72 20W
Ajalpan, Mexico 127 18 22N 97 15W
Ajanta Ra., India 50 20 28N 75 50 E
Ajax, Canada 109 43 50N 79 1W
Ajax, Mt., N.Z. 81 42 35 S 172 5 E
Ajayan Pt., Guam 68 13 15N 144 43 E
Ajdâbiyah, Libya 86 30 54N 20 4 E
Ajdovščina, Yugoslavia 27 45 54N 13 54 E
Ajibar, Ethiopia 89 10 35N 38 36 E
Ajka, Hungary 33 47 4N 17 31 E
'Ajmān, Asia 47 25 25N 55 30 E
Ajmer, India 48 26 28N 74 37 E
Ajo, U.S.A. 123 32 18N 112 54W
Ajok, Sudan 89 9 15N 28 28 E
Ak Dağ, Turkey 46 36 30N 30 0 E
Akaba, Togo 91 8 10N 1 2 E
Akabli, Algeria 85 26 49N 1 31 E
Akaishi-Dake, Japan 65 35 27N 138 9 E
Akaishi-Sammyaku, Japan 65 35 25N 138 10 E
Akaki Beseka, Ethiopia 89 8 55N 38 45 E
Akala, Sudan 89 15 39N 36 13 E
Akaroa, N.Z. 81 43 49 S 172 59 E
Akasha, Sudan 88 21 10N 30 32 E
Akashi, Japan 64 34 45N 135 0 E
Akbou, Algeria 85 36 31N 4 31 E
Akchâr, Mauritania 84 20 20N 14 28W
Akechi, Japan 65 35 18N 137 23 E
Akelamo, Indonesia 57 1 35N 129 40 E
Akershus fylke □, Norway 10 60 0N 11 10 E
Akeru →, India 50 17 25N 80 0 E
Aketi, Zaïre 94 2 38N 23 47 E
Akhalkalaki, U.S.S.R. 39 41 27N 43 25 E
Akhaltsikhe, U.S.S.R. 39 41 40N 43 0 E
Akharnaí, Greece 35 38 5N 23 44 E
Akhelóös →, Greece 35 38 36N 21 14 E
Akhendria, Greece 35 34 58N 25 16 E
Akhéron →, Greece 35 39 20N 20 29 E
Akhisar, Turkey 46 38 56N 27 48 E
Akhladhókambos, Greece 35 37 31N 22 35 E
Akhmîm, Egypt 88 26 31N 31 47 E
Akhnur, India 49 32 52N 74 45 E
Akhtubinsk, U.S.S.R. 39 48 13N 46 7 E
Akhty, U.S.S.R. 39 41 30N 47 45 E
Akhtyrka, U.S.S.R. 36 50 25N 35 0 E
Aki, Japan 64 33 30N 133 54 E
Aki-Nada, Japan 64 34 5N 132 40 E
Akiéni, Gabon 94 1 11 S 13 53 E
Akimiski I., Canada 104 52 50N 81 30W
Akimovka, U.S.S.R. 38 46 44N 35 0 E
Åkirkeby, Denmark 11 55 4N 14 55 E
Akita, Japan 63 39 45N 140 7 E
Akjoujt, Mauritania 90 19 45N 14 15W
Akka, Morocco 84 29 22N 8 9W
'Akko, Israel 44 32 55N 35 4 E
Akkol, U.S.S.R. 40 45 0N 75 39 E
Akkrum, Neths. 16 53 3N 5 50 E
Aklampa, Benin 91 8 15N 2 10 E
Aklavik, Canada 102 68 12N 135 0W
Akmonte, Spain 23 37 13N 6 38W
Aknoul, Morocco 85 34 40N 3 55W
Akō, Japan 64 34 45N 134 24 E
Ako, Nigeria 91 10 19N 10 48 E
Akobo →, Ethiopia 89 7 48N 33 3 E
Akola, India 50 20 42N 77 2 E
Akonolinga, Cameroon 91 3 50N 12 18 E
Akordat, Ethiopia 89 15 30N 37 40 E
Akosombo Dam, Ghana 91 6 20N 0 5 E
Akot, India 50 21 10N 77 10 E
Akot, Sudan 89 6 31N 30 9 E
Akpatok I., Canada 103 60 25N 68 8W
Akranes, Iceland 8 64 19N 21 58W
Akreïjit, Mauritania 90 18 19N 9 11W
Akrítas Venétiko, Ákra, Greece 35 36 43N 21 54 E
Akron, Colo., U.S.A. 120 40 13N 103 15W
Akron, Ind., U.S.A. 119 41 2N 86 1W
Akron, Ohio, U.S.A. 116 41 7N 81 31W
Akrotíri, Ákra, Greece 35 40 26N 25 27 E
Aksai Chih, India 49 35 15N 79 55 E
Aksaray, Turkey 46 38 25N 34 2 E
Aksarka, U.S.S.R. 40 66 31N 67 50 E
Aksay, U.S.S.R. 40 51 11N 53 0 E
Akşehir, Turkey 46 38 18N 31 30 E
Aksenovo Zilovskoye, U.S.S.R. 41 53 20N 117 40 E
Akstafa, U.S.S.R. 39 41 7N 45 27 E
Aksu, China 62 41 5N 80 10 E
Aksum, Ethiopia 89 14 5N 38 40 E
Aktogay, U.S.S.R. 40 46 57N 79 40 E
Aktyubinsk, U.S.S.R. 40 50 17N 57 10 E
Aku, Nigeria 91 6 40N 7 18 E
Akula, Zaïre 94 2 22N 20 12 E
Akune, Japan 64 32 1N 130 12 E
Akure, Nigeria 91 7 15N 5 5 E
Akureyri, Iceland 8 65 40N 18 6W
Akusha, U.S.S.R. 39 42 18N 47 30 E
Akyab = Sittwe, Burma 52 20 18N 92 45 E
Al Abyār, Libya 86 32 9N 20 29 E
Al 'Adan, S. Yemen 45 12 45N 45 0 E
Al Aḥsā, Si. Arabia 46 25 50N 49 0 E
Al Amādīyah, Iraq 46 37 5N 43 30 E
Al Amārah, Iraq 46 31 55N 47 15 E
Al 'Aqabah, Jordan 44 29 31N 35 0 E
Al 'Aramah, Si. Arabia 46 25 30N 46 0 E
Al Ashkhara, Oman 47 21 50N 59 30 E
Al 'Ayzarīyah, Jordan 44 31 47N 35 15 E
Al 'Azīzīyah, Libya 86 32 30N 13 1 E
Al Badī', Si. Arabia 46 22 0N 46 35 E
Al Barkāt, Libya 86 24 56N 10 14 E
Al Başrah, Iraq 46 30 30N 47 50 E
Al Bayḍā □, Libya 86 32 0N 21 30 E
Al Bāzūrīyah, Lebanon 44 33 15N 35 16 E
Al Bīrah, Jordan 44 31 55N 35 12 E
Al Bu'ayrāt, Libya 86 31 24N 15 44 E
Al Buqay'ah, Jordan 44 32 15N 35 30 E
Al Fallūjah, Iraq 46 33 20N 43 55 E
Al Fāw, Iraq 46 30 0N 48 30 E
Al Fujayrah, Asia 47 25 7N 56 18 E
Al Gharīb, Libya 86 32 35N 21 11 E
Al Hābah, Si. Arabia 46 27 10N 47 0 E
Al Haddār, Si. Arabia 46 21 58N 45 57 E
Al Ḥadīthah, Iraq 46 34 0N 41 13 E
Al Hāmad, Si. Arabia 46 31 30N 39 30 E
Al Ḥamar, Si. Arabia 46 22 23N 46 6 E
Al Hammādah al Ḥamrā', Libya 86 29 30N 12 0 E
Al Ḥamrā', Si. Arabia 46 24 2N 38 55 E
Al Ḥarīq, Si. Arabia 46 23 29N 46 27 E
Al Harīr, W. →, Syria 44 32 44N 35 59 E
Al Harūj al Aswad, Libya 86 27 0N 17 10 E
Al Ḥasakah, Syria 46 36 35N 40 45 E
Al Ḥawrah, S. Yemen 45 13 50N 47 35 E
Al Ḥayy, Iraq 46 32 5N 46 5 E
Al Ḥijāz, Si. Arabia 46 26 0N 37 30 E
Al Ḥillah, Iraq 46 32 30N 44 25 E
Al Ḥillah, Si. Arabia 46 23 35N 46 50 E
Al Hindīyah, Iraq 46 32 30N 44 10 E
Al Ḥiṣn, Jordan 44 32 29N 35 52 E
Al Hoceïma, Morocco 84 35 8N 3 58W
Al Ḥudaydah, Yemen 45 14 50N 43 0 E
Al Ḥufrah, Awbārī, Libya 86 25 32N 14 1 E
Al Ḥufrah, Misrātah, Libya 86 29 5N 18 3 E
Al Hufūf, Si. Arabia 46 25 25N 49 45 E
Al Ḥulwah, Si. Arabia 46 23 24N 46 48 E
Al Husayyāt, Libya 86 30 24N 20 37 E
Al Irq, Libya 86 29 5N 21 35 E
Al Ittihad = Madīnat ash Sha'b, S. Yemen 45 12 50N 45 0 E
Al Jabal al Akhḍar, Libya 86 32 0N 21 30 E
Al Jāfūrah, Si. Arabia 46 25 0N 50 15 E
Al Jaghbūb, Libya 86 29 42N 24 38 E
Al Jahrah, Kuwait 46 29 25N 47 40 E
Al Jalāmīd, Si. Arabia 46 31 20N 39 45 E
Al Jawf, Libya 86 24 10N 23 24 E
Al Jawf, Si. Arabia 46 29 55N 39 40 E
Al Jazirah, Iraq 46 33 30N 44 0 E
Al Jazirah, Libya 86 26 10N 21 20 E
Al Jubayl, Si. Arabia 46 27 0N 49 50 E
Al Jubaylah, Si. Arabia 46 24 55N 46 25 E
Al Junaynah, Sudan 87 13 27N 22 45 E
Al Khābūra, Oman 47 23 57N 57 5 E
Al Khalīl, Jordan 44 31 32N 35 6 E
Al Khalūf, Oman 45 20 30N 58 13 E
Al Kharfah, Si. Arabia 46 22 0N 46 35 E
Al Kharj, Si. Arabia 46 24 0N 47 0 E
Al Khasab, Oman 47 26 14N 56 15 E
Al Khums, Libya 86 32 40N 14 17 E
Al Khums □, Libya 86 31 20N 14 10 E
Al Kufrah, Libya 86 24 17N 23 15 E
Al Kūt, Iraq 46 32 30N 46 0 E
Al Kuwayt, Kuwait 46 29 30N 48 0 E
Al Lādhiqīyah, Syria 46 35 30N 35 45 E
Al Līth, Si. Arabia 88 20 9N 40 15 E
Al Lubban, Jordan 44 32 9N 35 14 E
Al Luḥayyah, Yemen 45 15 45N 42 40 E
Al Madīnah, Si. Arabia 46 24 35N 39 52 E
Al-Mafraq, Jordan 44 32 17N 36 14 E
Al Majma'ah, Si. Arabia 46 25 57N 45 22 E
Al Makīlī, Libya 86 32 10N 22 17 E
Al Manāmah, Bahrain 47 26 10N 50 30 E
Al Marj, Libya 86 32 25N 20 30 E
Al Mawşil, Iraq 46 36 15N 43 5 E
Al Mazra, Jordan 44 31 16N 35 31 E
Al Midhnab, Si. Arabia 46 25 50N 44 18 E
Al Miqdādīyah, Iraq 46 34 0N 45 0 E
Al Mish'āb, Si. Arabia 46 28 12N 48 36 E

Al Mubarraz

Al Mubarraz, *Si. Arabia* **46** 25 30N 49 40 E
Al Muḩarraq, *Bahrain* **47** 26 15N 50 40 E
Al Mukallā, *S. Yemen* **45** 14 33N 49 2 E
Al Mukhā, *Yemen* **45** 13 18N 43 15 E
Al Musayyib, *Iraq* **46** 32 40N 44 25 E
Al Muwaylih, *Si. Arabia* **46** 27 40N 35 30 E
Al Owuho = Otukpa, *Nigeria* **91** 7 9N 7 41 E
Al Qaddāhīyah, *Libya* **86** 31 15N 15 9 E
Al Qadīmah, *Si. Arabia* **46** 22 20N 39 13 E
Al Qā'iyah, *Si. Arabia* **46** 24 33N 43 15 E
Al Qāmishli, *Turkey* **46** 37 10N 41 10 E
Al Qaryah ash Sharqīyah, *Libya* **86** 30 28N 13 40 E
Al Qaşabāt, *Libya* **86** 32 39N 14 1 E
Al Qaşīm, *Si. Arabia* **46** 26 0N 43 0 E
Al Qaţīf, *Si. Arabia* **46** 26 35N 50 0 E
Al Qaţrūn, *Libya* **86** 24 56N 15 3 E
Al Quaisūmah, *Si. Arabia* **46** 28 10N 46 20 E
Al Quds = Jerusalem, *Israel* **44** 31 47N 35 10 E
Al Qunfudhah, *Si. Arabia* **88** 19 3N 41 4 E
Al Qurayyāt, *Oman* **47** 23 17N 58 53 E
Al Qurnah, *Iraq* **46** 31 1N 47 25 E
Al 'Ulā, *Si. Arabia* **46** 26 35N 38 0 E
Al Uqaylah ash Sharqīgah, *Libya* **86** 30 12N 19 10 E
Al Uqayr, *Si. Arabia* **46** 25 40N 50 15 E
Al 'Uthmānīyah, *Si. Arabia* **46** 25 5N 49 22 E
Al 'Uwaynid, *Si. Arabia* **46** 24 50N 46 0 E
Al' 'Uwayqīlah, *Si. Arabia* **46** 30 30N 42 10 E
Al 'Uyūn, *Si. Arabia* **46** 26 30N 43 50 E
Al Wajh, *Si. Arabia* **88** 26 10N 36 30 E
Al Wakrah, *Qatar* **47** 25 10N 51 40 E
Al Wari'āh, *Si. Arabia* **46** 27 51N 47 25 E
Al Wātīyah, *Libya* **86** 32 28N 11 57 E
Al Yamāmah, *Si. Arabia* **46** 24 5N 47 30 E
Al Yāmūn, *Jordan* **44** 32 29N 35 14 E
Ala, *Italy* **26** 45 46N 11 0 E
Alabama □, *U.S.A.* **115** 33 0N 87 0W
Alabama →, *U.S.A.* **115** 31 8N 87 57W
Alaejos, *Spain* **22** 41 18N 5 13W
Alagna Valsésia, *Italy* **26** 45 51N 7 56 E
Alagoa Grande, *Brazil* **138** 7 3 S 35 35W
Alagoas □, *Brazil* **138** 9 0 S 36 0W
Alagoinhas, *Brazil* **139** 12 7 S 38 20W
Alagón, *Spain* **24** 41 46N 1 12W
Alagón →, *Spain* **23** 39 44N 6 53W
Alajero, *Canary Is.* **25** 28 3N 17 13W
Alajuela, *Costa Rica* **128** 10 2N 84 8W
Alakamisy, *Madag.* **97** 21 19 S 47 14 E
Alalapura, *Surinam* **135** 2 20N 56 25W
Alalaú →, *Brazil* **135** 0 30 S 61 9W
Alameda, *Spain* **23** 37 12N 4 39W
Alameda, *Calif., U.S.A.* **124** 37 46N 122 15W
Alameda, *N. Mex., U.S.A.* **123** 35 10N 106 43W
Alamo, *U.S.A.* **125** 36 21N 115 10W
Alamo Crossing, *U.S.A.* **125** 34 16N 113 33W
Alamogordo, *U.S.A.* **123** 32 59N 106 0W
Alamos, *Mexico* **126** 27 0N 109 0W
Alamosa, *U.S.A.* **123** 37 30N 106 0W
Åland, *Finland* **9** 60 15N 20 0 E
Aland, *India* **50** 17 36N 76 35 E
Alandroal, *Portugal* **23** 38 41N 7 24W
Ålands hav, *Sweden* **9** 60 0N 19 30 E
Alandur, *India* **51** 13 0N 80 15 E
Alange, Presa de, *Spain* **23** 38 45N 6 18W
Alanis, *Spain* **23** 38 3N 5 43W
Alanya, *Turkey* **46** 36 38N 32 0 E
Alaotra, Farihin', *Madag.* **97** 17 30 S 48 30 E
Alapayevsk, *U.S.S.R.* **40** 57 52N 61 42 E
Alar del Rey, *Spain* **22** 42 38N 4 20W
Alaraz, *Spain* **22** 40 45N 5 17W
Alaska □, *U.S.A.* **102** 65 0N 150 0W
Alaska, G. of, *Pac. Oc.* **102** 58 0N 145 0W
Alaska Highway, *Canada* **110** 60 0N 130 0W
Alaska Pen., *U.S.A.* **102** 56 0N 160 0W
Alaska Range, *U.S.A.* **102** 62 50N 151 0W
Alássio, *Italy* **26** 44 1N 8 10 E
Alataw Shankou, *China* **62** 45 5N 81 57 E
Alatri, *Italy* **28** 41 44N 13 21 E
Alatyr, *U.S.S.R.* **37** 54 45N 46 35 E
Alatyr →, *U.S.S.R.* **37** 54 52N 46 36 E
Alausi, *Ecuador* **134** 2 0 S 78 50W
Álava □, *Spain* **24** 42 48N 2 28W
Alava, C., *U.S.A.* **122** 48 10N 124 40W
Alaverdi, *U.S.S.R.* **39** 41 15N 44 37 E
Alawoona, *Australia* **73** 34 45 S 140 30 E
Alayor, *Spain* **24** 39 57N 4 8 E
Alazan →, *U.S.S.R.* **39** 41 5N 46 40 E
Alba, *Italy* **26** 44 41N 8 1 E
Alba de Tormes, *Spain* **22** 40 50N 5 30W
Alba Iulia, *Romania* **34** 46 8N 23 39 E
Albac, *Romania* **34** 46 28N 23 1 E
Albacete, *Spain* **25** 39 0N 1 50W
Albacete □, *Spain* **25** 38 50N 2 0W
Albacutya, L., *Australia* **74** 35 45 S 141 58 E
Ålbæk, *Denmark* **11** 57 36N 10 25 E
Ålbæk Bugt, *Denmark* **11** 57 35N 10 40 E
Albaida, *Spain* **25** 38 51N 0 31W
Albalate de las Nogueras, *Spain* **24** 40 22N 2 18W
Albalate del Arzobispo, *Spain* **24** 41 6N 0 31W
Albanel, *Canada* **107** 48 53N 72 27W
Albania ■, *Europe* **35** 41 0N 20 0 E
Albano Laziale, *Italy* **28** 41 44N 12 40 E
Albany, *Australia* **79** 35 1 S 117 58 E
Albany, *Ga., U.S.A.* **115** 31 40N 84 10W
Albany, *Ind., U.S.A.* **119** 40 18N 85 13W
Albany, *Minn., U.S.A.* **120** 45 37N 94 38W
Albany, *Mo., U.S.A.* **118** 40 15N 94 20W
Albany, *N.Y., U.S.A.* **117** 42 35N 73 47W
Albany, *Oreg., U.S.A.* **122** 44 41N 123 0W
Albany, *Tex., U.S.A.* **121** 32 45N 99 20W
Albany, *Wis., U.S.A.* **118** 42 43N 89 26W
Albany →, *Canada* **104** 52 17N 81 31W
Albardón, *Argentina* **140** 31 20 S 68 30W
Albarracín, *Spain* **24** 40 25N 1 26W
Albarracín, Sierra de, *Spain* **24** 40 30N 1 30W
Albatross B., *Australia* **72** 12 45 S 141 30 E
Albatross Pt., *N.Z.* **80** 38 7 S 174 44 E
Albegna →, *Italy* **27** 42 30N 11 11 E
Albemarle, *U.S.A.* **115** 35 27N 80 15W
Albemarle Sd., *U.S.A.* **115** 36 0N 76 30W
Albenga, *Italy* **26** 44 3N 8 12 E
Alberche →, *Spain* **22** 39 58N 4 46W
Alberdi, *Paraguay* **140** 26 14 S 58 20W
Alberes, Mts., *Spain* **24** 42 28N 2 56 E
Alberique, *Spain* **25** 39 7N 0 31W
Albersdorf, *W. Germany* **30** 54 8N 9 19 E
Albert, *Australia* **76** 32 22 S 147 30 E
Albert, *France* **19** 50 0N 2 38 E
Albert, L. = Mobutu Sese Seko, L., *Africa* **92** 1 30N 31 0 E
Albert, L., *Australia* **73** 35 30 S 139 10 E
Albert Canyon, *Canada* **110** 51 8N 117 41W
Albert Edward, Mt., *Papua N. G.* **69** 8 20 S 147 24 E
Albert Edward Ra., *Australia* **78** 18 17 S 127 57 E
Albert Lea, *U.S.A.* **120** 43 32N 93 20W
Albert Nile →, *Uganda* **92** 3 36N 32 2 E
Albert Town, *Bahamas* **129** 22 37N 74 33 E
Alberta □, *Canada* **110** 54 40N 115 0W
Alberti, *Argentina* **140** 35 1 S 60 16W
Albertinia, *S. Africa* **96** 34 11 S 21 34 E
Albertkanaal →, *Belgium* **17** 51 14N 4 26 E
Alberton, *Canada* **105** 46 50N 64 0W
Albertville = Kalemie, *Zaïre* **92** 5 55 S 29 9 E
Albertville, *France* **21** 45 40N 6 22 E
Albi, *France* **20** 43 56N 2 9 E
Albia, *U.S.A.* **118** 41 0N 92 50W
Albina, *Surinam* **135** 5 37N 54 15W
Albina, Ponta, *Angola* **95** 15 52 S 11 44 E
Albino, *Italy* **26** 45 47N 9 48 E
Albion, *Idaho, U.S.A.* **122** 42 21N 113 37W
Albion, *Ill., U.S.A.* **119** 38 23N 88 4W
Albion, *Ind., U.S.A.* **119** 41 24N 85 25W
Albion, *Mich., U.S.A.* **119** 42 15N 84 45W
Albion, *Nebr., U.S.A.* **120** 41 47N 98 0W
Albion, *Pa., U.S.A.* **116** 41 53N 80 21W
Albion Park, *Australia* **76** 34 36 S 150 45 E
Alblasserdam, *Neths.* **16** 51 52N 4 40 E
Albocácer, *Spain* **24** 40 21N 0 1 E
Alböke, *Sweden* **11** 56 57N 16 47 E
Alborán, *Medit. S.* **23** 35 57N 3 0W
Alborea, *Spain* **25** 39 17N 1 24W
Ålborg, *Denmark* **11** 57 2N 9 54 E
Ålborg Bugt, *Denmark* **11** 56 50N 10 35 E
Alborz, Reshteh-ye Kūhhā-ye, *Iran* **47** 36 0N 52 0 E
Albox, *Spain* **25** 37 23N 2 8W
Albreda, *Canada* **110** 52 35N 119 10W
Albuera, La, *Spain* **23** 38 45N 6 49W
Albufeira, *Portugal* **23** 37 5N 8 15W
Albula →, *Switz.* **31** 46 38N 9 30 E
Albuñol, *Spain* **25** 36 48N 3 11W
Albuquerque, *Brazil* **137** 19 23 S 57 26W
Albuquerque, *U.S.A.* **123** 35 5N 106 47W
Albuquerque, Cayos de, *Caribbean* **128** 12 10N 81 50W
Alburg, *U.S.A.* **117** 44 58N 73 19W
Alburno, Mte., *Italy* **29** 40 32N 15 15 E
Alburquerque, *Spain* **23** 39 15N 6 59W
Albury, *Australia* **75** 36 3 S 146 56 E
Alby, *Sweden* **10** 62 30N 15 28 E
Alcácer do Sal, *Portugal* **23** 38 22N 8 33W
Alcaçovas, *Portugal* **23** 38 23N 8 9W
Alcalá de Chisvert, *Spain* **24** 40 19N 0 13 E
Alcalá de Guadaira, *Spain* **23** 37 20N 5 50W
Alcalá de Henares, *Spain* **24** 40 28N 3 22W
Alcalá de los Gazules, *Spain* **23** 36 29N 5 43W
Alcalá la Real, *Spain* **23** 37 27N 3 57W
Alcamo, *Italy* **28** 37 59N 12 55 E
Alcanadre, *Spain* **24** 42 24N 2 7W
Alcanadre →, *Spain* **24** 41 43N 0 12W
Alcanar, *Spain* **24** 40 33N 0 28 E
Alcanede, *Portugal* **23** 39 25N 8 49W
Alcanena, *Portugal* **23** 39 27N 8 40W
Alcañices, *Spain* **22** 41 41N 6 21W
Alcañiz, *Spain* **24** 41 2N 0 8W
Alcântara, *Brazil* **138** 2 20 S 44 30W
Alcántara, *Spain* **23** 39 41N 6 57W
Alcantara L., *Canada* **111** 60 57N 108 9W
Alcantarilla, *Spain* **25** 37 59N 1 12W
Alcaracejos, *Spain* **23** 38 24N 4 58W
Alcaraz, *Spain* **25** 38 40N 2 29W
Alcaraz, Sierra de, *Spain* **25** 38 40N 2 20W
Alcarria, La, *Spain* **24** 40 31N 2 45W
Alcaudete, *Spain* **23** 37 35N 4 5W
Alcázar de San Juan, *Spain* **25** 39 24N 3 12W
Alcira, *Spain* **25** 39 9N 0 30W
Alcoa, *U.S.A.* **115** 35 50N 84 0W
Alcobaça, *Portugal* **23** 39 32N 9 0W
Alcobendas, *Spain* **24** 40 32N 3 38W
Alcolea del Pinar, *Spain* **24** 41 2N 2 28W
Alcora, *Spain* **24** 40 5N 0 14W
Alcoutim, *Portugal* **23** 37 25N 7 28W
Alcova, *U.S.A.* **122** 42 37N 106 52W
Alcoy, *Spain* **25** 38 43N 0 30W
Alcubierre, Sierra de, *Spain* **24** 41 45N 0 22W
Alcublas, *Spain* **24** 39 48N 0 43W
Alcudia, *Spain* **24** 39 51N 3 7 E
Alcudia, B. de, *Spain* **24** 39 47N 3 15 E
Alcudia, Sierra de la, *Spain* **23** 38 34N 4 30W
Aldabra Is., *Seychelles* **53** 9 22 S 46 28 E
Aldama, *Mexico* **127** 23 0N 98 4W
Aldan, *U.S.S.R.* **41** 58 40N 125 30 E
Aldan →, *U.S.S.R.* **41** 63 28N 129 35 E
Aldea, Pta. de la, *Canary Is.* **25** 28 0N 15 50W
Aldeburgh, *U.K.* **13** 52 9N 1 35 E
Aldeia Nova, *Portugal* **23** 37 55N 7 24W
Alder, *U.S.A.* **122** 45 27N 112 3W
Alder Pk., *U.S.A.* **124** 35 53N 121 22W
Alderney, *Chan. Is.* **18** 49 42N 2 12W
Aldershot, *U.K.* **13** 51 15N 0 43W
Alectown, *Australia* **76** 32 53 S 148 17 E
Aledo, *U.S.A.* **118** 41 10N 90 50W
Alefa, *Ethiopia* **89** 11 55N 36 55 E
Aleg, *Mauritania* **90** 17 3N 13 55W
Alegranza, *Canary Is.* **25** 29 23N 13 32W
Alegranza, I., *Canary Is.* **25** 29 23N 13 32W
Alegre, *Brazil* **139** 20 50 S 41 30W
Alegrete, *Brazil* **141** 29 40 S 56 0W
Aleisk, *U.S.S.R.* **40** 52 40N 83 0 E
Alejandro Selkirk, I., *Pac. Oc.* **67** 33 50 S 80 15W
Aleksandriya, *Ukraine S.S.R., U.S.S.R.* **36** 50 37N 26 19 E
Aleksandriya, *Ukraine S.S.R., U.S.S.R.* **38** 48 42N 33 3 E
Aleksandriyskaya, *U.S.S.R.* **39** 43 59N 47 0 E
Aleksandrov, *U.S.S.R.* **37** 56 23N 38 44 E
Aleksandrovac, *Yugoslavia* **33** 44 28N 21 13 E
Aleksandrovka, *U.S.S.R.* **38** 48 55N 32 20 E
Aleksandrovo, *Bulgaria* **34** 43 14N 24 51 E
Aleksandrovsk-Sakhalinskiy, *U.S.S.R.* **41** 50 50N 142 20 E
Aleksandrovskiy Zavod, *U.S.S.R.* **41** 50 40N 117 50 E
Aleksandrovskoye, *U.S.S.R.* **40** 60 35N 77 50 E
Aleksandrów Kujawski, *Poland* **32** 52 53N 18 43 E
Aleksandrów Łódźki, *Poland* **32** 51 49N 19 17 E
Alekseyevka, *U.S.S.R.* **37** 50 43N 38 40 E
Aleksin, *U.S.S.R.* **37** 54 31N 37 9 E
Aleksinac, *Yugoslavia* **33** 43 31N 21 42 E
Além Paraíba, *Brazil* **139** 21 52 S 42 41W
Alemania, *Argentina* **140** 25 40 S 65 30W
Alemania, *Chile* **140** 25 10 S 69 55W
Ålen, *Norway* **10** 62 51N 11 17 E
Alençon, *France* **18** 48 27N 0 4 E
Alenuihaha Chan., *U.S.A.* **112** 20 25N 156 0W
Aleppo = Ḩalab, *Syria* **46** 36 10N 37 15 E
Aléria, *France* **21** 42 5N 9 26 E
Alert Bay, *Canada* **110** 50 30N 126 55W
Alès, *France* **21** 44 9N 4 5 E
Aleşd, *Romania* **34** 47 3N 22 22 E
Alessándria, *Italy* **26** 44 54N 8 37 E
Ålestrup, *Denmark* **11** 56 42N 9 29 E
Ålesund, *Norway* **8** 62 28N 6 12 E
Alet-les-Bains, *France* **20** 42 59N 2 14 E
Aleutian Is., *Pac. Oc.* **102** 52 0N 175 0W
Aleutian Trench, *Pac. Oc.* **66** 48 0N 180 0 E
Alexander, *U.S.A.* **120** 47 51N 103 40W
Alexander, C., *Solomon Is.* **68** 6 35 S 156 30 E
Alexander, Mt., *Australia* **79** 28 58 S 120 16 E
Alexander Arch., *U.S.A.* **102** 57 0N 135 0W
Alexander B., *S. Africa* **96** 28 36 S 16 33 E
Alexander Bay, *S. Africa* **96** 28 40 S 16 30 E
Alexander City, *U.S.A.* **115** 32 58N 85 57W
Alexander I., *Antarctica* **143** 69 0 S 70 0W
Alexandra, *Australia* **74** 37 8 S 145 40 E
Alexandra, *N.Z.* **81** 45 14 S 169 25 E
Alexandra Falls, *Canada* **110** 60 29N 116 18W
Alexandretta = İskenderun, *Turkey* **46** 36 32N 36 10 E
Alexandria = El Iskandarîya, *Egypt* **88** 31 0N 30 0 E
Alexandria, *Australia* **72** 19 5 S 136 40 E
Alexandria, *B.C., Canada* **110** 52 35N 122 27W
Alexandria, *Ont., Canada* **109** 45 19N 74 38W
Alexandria, *Romania* **34** 43 57N 25 24 E
Alexandria, *S. Africa* **96** 33 38 S 26 28 E
Alexandria, *Ind., U.S.A.* **119** 40 18N 85 40W
Alexandria, *Ky., U.S.A.* **119** 38 58N 84 23W
Alexandria, *La., U.S.A.* **121** 31 20N 92 30W
Alexandria, *Minn., U.S.A.* **120** 45 50N 95 20W
Alexandria, *Mo., U.S.A.* **118** 40 27N 91 28W
Alexandria, *S. Dak., U.S.A.* **120** 43 40N 97 45W
Alexandria, *Va., U.S.A.* **114** 38 47N 77 1W
Alexandria Bay, *U.S.A.* **117** 44 20N 75 52W
Alexandrina, L., *Australia* **73** 35 25 S 139 10 E
Alexandroúpolis, *Greece* **35** 40 50N 25 54 E
Alexis, *U.S.A.* **118** 41 4N 90 33W
Alexis →, *Canada* **105** 52 33N 56 8W
Alexis Creek, *Canada* **110** 52 10N 123 20W
Alfambra, *Spain* **24** 40 33N 1 5W
Alfândega da Fé, *Portugal* **22** 41 20N 6 59W
Alfaro, *Spain* **24** 42 10N 1 50W
Alfeld, *W. Germany* **30** 52 0N 9 49 E
Alfenas, *Brazil* **141** 21 20 S 46 10W
Alfiós →, *Greece* **35** 37 40N 21 33 E
Alfonsine, *Italy* **27** 44 30N 12 1 E
Alford, *U.K.* **14** 57 13N 2 42W
Alfred, *Maine, U.S.A.* **117** 43 28N 70 40W
Alfred, *N.Y., U.S.A.* **116** 42 15N 77 45W
Alfred Town, *Australia* **76** 35 8 S 147 30 E
Alfredton, *N.Z.* **80** 40 41 S 175 54 E
Alfreton, *U.K.* **12** 53 6N 1 22W
Alfta, *Sweden* **10** 61 21N 16 4 E
Alga, *U.S.S.R.* **40** 49 53N 57 20 E
Algaba, La, *Spain* **23** 37 27N 6 1W
Algar, *Spain* **23** 36 40N 5 39W
Algarinejo, *Spain* **23** 37 19N 4 9W
Algarve, *Portugal* **23** 36 58N 8 20W
Algeciras, *Spain* **23** 36 9N 5 28W
Algemesí, *Spain* **25** 39 11N 0 27W
Alger, *Algeria* **85** 36 42N 3 8 E
Algeria ■, *Africa* **85** 28 30N 2 0 E
Alghero, *Italy* **28** 40 34N 8 20 E
Algiers = Alger, *Algeria* **85** 36 42N 3 8 E
Algoa B., *S. Africa* **96** 33 50 S 25 45 E
Algodonales, *Spain* **23** 36 54N 5 24W
Algodor →, *Spain* **22** 39 55N 3 53W
Algoma, *U.S.A.* **114** 44 35N 87 27W
Algona, *U.S.A.* **118** 43 4N 94 14W
Algonac, *U.S.A.* **116** 42 37N 82 32W
Algonquin Prov. Park, *Canada* **109** 45 50N 78 30W
Alhama de Almería, *Spain* **25** 36 57N 2 34W
Alhama de Aragón, *Spain* **24** 41 18N 1 54W
Alhama de Granada, *Spain* **23** 37 0N 3 59W
Alhama de Murcia, *Spain* **25** 37 51N 1 25W
Alhambra, *Spain* **25** 38 54N 3 4W
Alhambra, *Calif., U.S.A.* **125** 34 2N 118 10W
Alhambra, *Ill., U.S.A.* **118** 38 52N 89 45W
Alhaurín el Grande, *Spain* **23** 36 39N 4 41W
Alhucemas = Al Hoceïma, *Morocco* **84** 35 8N 3 58W
'Alī al Gharbī, *Iraq* **46** 32 30N 46 45 E
Ali Bayramly, *U.S.S.R.* **39** 39 59N 48 52 E
'Alī Khēl, *Afghan.* **48** 33 57N 69 43 E
Ali Sahîh, *Djibouti* **89** 11 10N 42 44 E
Ália, *Italy* **28** 37 47N 13 42 E
Aliaga, *Spain* **24** 40 40N 0 42W
Aliákmon →, *Greece* **35** 40 30N 22 36 E
Alibag, *India* **50** 18 38N 72 56 E
Alibo, *Ethiopia* **89** 9 52N 37 5 E
Alibunar, *Yugoslavia* **33** 45 5N 20 57 E
Alicante, *Spain* **25** 38 23N 0 30W
Alicante □, *Spain* **25** 38 30N 0 37W
Alice, *Canada* **109** 45 47N 77 14W
Alice, *S. Africa* **96** 32 48 S 26 55 E
Alice, *U.S.A.* **121** 27 47N 98 1W
Alice →, *Queens., Australia* **72** 24 2 S 144 50 E
Alice →, *Queens., Australia* **72** 15 35 S 142 20 E
Alice, Punta dell', *Italy* **29** 39 23N 17 10 E
Alice Arm, *Canada* **110** 55 29N 129 31W
Alice Downs, *Australia* **78** 17 45 S 127 56 E
Alice Springs, *Australia* **72** 23 40 S 133 50 E
Alicedale, *S. Africa* **96** 33 15 S 26 4 E
Aliceville, *U.S.A.* **115** 33 9N 88 10W
Alick Cr. →, *Australia* **72** 20 55 S 142 20 E
Alicudi, I., *Italy* **29** 38 33N 14 20 E

Amersfoort

Alida, *Canada* **111** 49 25N 101 55W
Aligarh, *Raj., India* **48** 25 55N 76 15 E
Aligarh, *Ut. P., India* **48** 27 55N 78 10 E
Aligüdarz, *Iran* **46** 33 25N 49 45 E
Alijó, *Portugal* **22** 41 16N 7 27W
Alimena, *Italy* **29** 37 42N 14 4 E
Alindao, *C.A.R.* **94** 5 2N 21 13 E
Alingsås, *Sweden* **11** 57 56N 12 31 E
Alipur, *Pakistan* **48** 29 25N 70 55 E
Alipur Duar, *India* **52** 26 30N 89 35 E
Aliquippa, *U.S.A.* **116** 40 38N 80 18W
Aliste →, *Spain* **22** 41 34N 5 58W
Alitus, *U.S.S.R.* **36** 54 24N 24 3 E
Alivérion, *Greece* **35** 38 24N 24 2 E
Aliwal North, *S. Africa* **96** 30 45 S 26 45 E
Alix, *Canada* **110** 52 24N 113 11W
Aljezur, *Portugal* **23** 37 18N 8 49W
Aljustrel, *Portugal* **23** 37 55N 8 10W
Alkamari, *Niger* **91** 13 27N 11 10 E
Alken, *Belgium* **17** 50 53N 5 18 E
Alkmaar, *Neths.* **16** 52 37N 4 45 E
All American Canal, *U.S.A.* **123** 32 45N 115 0W
Allada, *Benin* **91** 6 41N 2 9 E
Allah Dad, *Pakistan* **48** 25 38N 67 34 E
Allahabad, *India* **49** 25 25N 81 58 E
Allakh-Yun, *U.S.S.R.* **41** 60 50N 137 5 E
Allal Tazi, *Morocco* **84** 34 30N 6 20W
Allan, *Canada* **111** 51 53N 106 4W
Allanche, *France* **20** 45 14N 2 57 E
Allanmyo, *Burma* **52** 19 30N 95 17 E
Allanridge, *S. Africa* **96** 27 45 S 26 40 E
Allansford, *Australia* **74** 38 26 S 142 39 E
Allanton, *N.Z.* **81** 45 55 S 170 15 E
Allanwater, *Canada* **104** 50 14N 90 10W
Allaqi, Wadi →, *Egypt* **88** 23 7N 32 47 E
Allariz, *Spain* **22** 42 11N 7 50W
Allassac, *France* **20** 45 15N 1 29 E
Alle, *Belgium* **17** 49 51N 4 58 E
Allegan, *U.S.A.* **119** 42 32N 85 52W
Allegany, *U.S.A.* **116** 42 6N 78 30W
Allegheny →, *U.S.A.* **116** 40 27N 80 0W
Allegheny Mts., *U.S.A.* **114** 38 0N 80 0W
Allegheny Res., *U.S.A.* **116** 42 0N 78 55W
Allègre, *France* **20** 45 12N 3 41 E
Allen, *Argentina* **142** 38 58 S 67 50W
Allen, Bog of, *Ireland* **15** 53 15N 7 0W
Allen, L., *Ireland* **15** 54 12N 8 5W
Allenby Br. = Jisr al Ḩusayn, *Jordan* **44** 31 53N 35 33 E
Allende, *Mexico* **126** 28 20N 100 50W
Allentown, *U.S.A.* **117** 40 36N 75 30W
Alleppey, *India* **51** 9 30N 76 28 E
Aller →, *W. Germany* **30** 52 57N 9 10 E
Alleur, *Belgium* **17** 50 39N 5 31 E
Allevard, *France* **21** 45 24N 6 5 E
Alliance, *Surinam* **135** 5 50N 54 50W
Alliance, *Nebr., U.S.A.* **120** 42 10N 102 50W
Alliance, *Ohio, U.S.A.* **116** 40 53N 81 7W
Allier □, *France* **20** 46 25N 3 0 E
Allier →, *France* **19** 46 57N 3 4 E
Allingåbro, *Denmark* **11** 56 28N 10 20 E
Allinge, *Denmark* **11** 55 17N 14 50 E
Allison, *U.S.A.* **118** 42 45N 92 48W
Alliston, *Canada* **108** 44 9N 79 52W
Alloa, *U.K.* **14** 56 7N 3 49W
Allora, *Australia* **77** 28 2 S 152 0 E
Allos, *France* **21** 44 15N 6 38 E
Alma, *Canada* **107** 48 35N 71 40W
Alma, *Ga., U.S.A.* **115** 31 33N 82 28W
Alma, *Kans., U.S.A.* **120** 39 1N 96 22W
Alma, *Mich., U.S.A.* **104** 43 25N 84 40W
Alma, *Nebr., U.S.A.* **120** 40 10N 99 25W
Alma, *Wis., U.S.A.* **120** 44 19N 91 54W
'Almā ash Sha'b, *Lebanon* **44** 33 7N 35 9 E
Alma Ata, *U.S.S.R.* **40** 43 15N 76 57 E
Almada, *Portugal* **23** 38 40N 9 9W
Almaden, *Australia* **72** 17 22 S 144 40 E
Almadén, *Spain* **23** 38 49N 4 52W
Almagro, *Spain* **23** 38 50N 3 45W
Almanor, L., *U.S.A.* **122** 40 15N 121 11W
Almansa, *Spain* **25** 38 51N 1 5W
Almanza, *Spain* **22** 42 39N 5 3W
Almanzor, Pico de, *Spain* **22** 40 15N 5 18W
Almanzora →, *Spain* **25** 37 14N 1 46W
Almarcha, La, *Spain* **24** 39 41N 2 24W
Almas, *Brazil* **139** 11 33 S 47 9W
Almazán, *Spain* **24** 41 30N 2 30W
Almazora, *Spain* **24** 39 57N 0 3W
Almeirim, *Brazil* **135** 1 30 S 52 34W
Almeirim, *Portugal* **23** 39 12N 8 37W
Almelo, *Neths.* **16** 52 22N 6 42 E
Almenar, *Spain* **24** 41 43N 2 12W
Almenara, *Brazil* **139** 16 11 S 40 42W
Almenara, *Spain* **24** 39 46N 0 14W
Almenara, Sierra de, *Spain* **25** 37 34N 1 32W
Almendralejo, *Spain* **23** 38 41N 6 26W
Almería, *Spain* **25** 36 52N 2 27W
Almería □, *Spain* **25** 37 20N 2 20W
Almería, G. de, *Spain* **25** 36 41N 2 28W
Älmhult, *Sweden* **11** 56 33N 14 8 E
Almirante, *Panama* **128** 9 10N 82 30W
Almirante Montt, G., *Chile* **142** 51 52 S 72 50W
Almirós, *Greece* **35** 39 11N 22 45 E
Almodôvar, *Portugal* **23** 37 31N 8 2W
Almodóvar del Campo, *Spain* **23** 38 43N 4 10W
Almogia, *Spain* **23** 36 50N 4 32W
Almonaster la Real, *Spain* **23** 37 52N 6 48W
Almont, *U.S.A.* **116** 42 53N 83 2W
Almonte, *Canada* **106** 45 14N 76 12W
Almonte →, *Spain* **23** 39 41N 6 28W
Almora, *India* **49** 29 38N 79 40 E
Almoradi, *Spain* **25** 38 7N 0 46W
Almorox, *Spain* **22** 40 14N 4 24W
Almoustarat, *Mali* **91** 17 35N 0 8 E
Almuñécar, *Spain* **23** 36 43N 3 41W
Almunia de Doña Godina, La, *Spain* **24** 41 29N 1 23W
Alnif, *Morocco* **84** 31 10N 5 8W
Alnwick, *U.K.* **12** 55 25N 1 42W
Aloi, *Uganda* **92** 2 16N 33 10 E
Alon, *Burma* **52** 22 12N 95 5 E
Alor, *Indonesia* **57** 8 15 S 124 30 E
Alor Setar, *Malaysia* **55** 6 7N 100 22 E
Alora, *Spain* **23** 36 49N 4 46W
Alosno, *Spain* **23** 37 33N 7 7W
Alotau, *Papua N. G.* **69** 10 16 S 150 30 E
Alougoum, *Morocco* **84** 30 17N 6 56W
Aloysius Mt., *Australia* **79** 26 0 S 128 38 E
Alpaugh, *U.S.A.* **124** 35 53N 119 29W
Alpedrinha, *Portugal* **22** 40 6N 7 27W
Alpena, *U.S.A.* **104** 45 6N 83 24W
Alpercatas →, *Brazil* **138** 6 2 S 44 19W
Alpes-de-Haute-Provence □, *France* **21** 44 8N 6 10 E
Alpes-Maritimes □, *France* **21** 43 55N 7 10 E
Alpha, *Australia* **72** 23 39 S 146 37 E
Alpha, *U.S.A.* **118** 41 11N 90 23W
Alphen, *Neths.* **17** 51 29N 4 58 E
Alphen aan den Rijn, *Neths.* **16** 52 7N 4 40 E
Alphonse, *Seychelles* **53** 7 0 S 52 45 E
Alpiarça, *Portugal* **23** 39 15N 8 35W
Alpine, *Ariz., U.S.A.* **123** 33 57N 109 4W
Alpine, *Calif., U.S.A.* **125** 32 50N 116 46W
Alpine, *Tex., U.S.A.* **121** 30 25N 103 35W
Alps, *Europe* **6** 47 0N 8 0 E
Alpujarras, Las, *Spain* **25** 36 55N 3 20W
Alrø, *Denmark* **11** 55 52N 10 5 E
Alroy Downs, *Australia* **72** 19 20 S 136 5 E
Alsace, *France* **19** 48 15N 7 25 E
Alsask, *Canada* **111** 51 21N 109 59W
Alsásua, *Spain* **24** 42 54N 2 10W
Alsen, *Sweden* **10** 63 23N 13 56 E
Alsfeld, *W. Germany* **30** 50 44N 9 19 E
Alsten, *Norway* **8** 65 58N 12 40 E
Alstonville, *Australia* **77** 28 51 S 153 27 E
Alta, *Norway* **8** 69 57N 23 10 E
Alta, Sierra, *Spain* **24** 40 31N 1 30W
Alta Gracia, *Argentina* **140** 31 40 S 64 30W
Alta Lake, *Canada* **110** 50 10N 123 0W
Alta Sierra, *U.S.A.* **125** 35 42N 118 33W
Altaelva →, *Norway* **8** 69 46N 23 45 E
Altafjorden, *Norway* **8** 70 5N 23 5 E
Altagracia, *Venezuela* **134** 10 45N 71 30W
Altagracia de Orituco, *Venezuela* **134** 9 52N 66 23W
Altai = Aerht'ai Shan, *Mongolia* **62** 46 40N 92 45 E
Altamachi →, *Bolivia* **136** 16 8 S 66 50W
Altamaha →, *U.S.A.* **115** 31 19N 81 17W
Altamira, *Brazil* **135** 3 12 S 52 10W
Altamira, *Chile* **140** 25 47 S 69 51W
Altamira, *Colombia* **134** 2 3N 75 47W
Altamira, *Mexico* **127** 22 24N 97 55W
Altamira, Cuevas de, *Spain* **22** 43 20N 4 5W
Altamont, *Ill., U.S.A.* **119** 39 4N 88 45W
Altamont, *N.Y., U.S.A.* **117** 42 43N 74 3W
Altamura, *Italy* **29** 40 50N 16 33 E
Altanbulag, *Mongolia* **62** 50 16N 106 30 E
Altar, *Mexico* **126** 30 40N 111 50W
Altata, *Mexico* **126** 24 30N 108 0W
Altavista, *U.S.A.* **114** 37 9N 79 22W
Altay, *China* **62** 47 48N 88 10 E
Altdorf, *Switz.* **31** 46 52N 8 36 E
Alte Mellum, *W. Germany* **30** 53 45N 8 6 E
Altea, *Spain* **25** 38 38N 0 2W
Altenberg, *E. Germany* **30** 50 46N 13 47 E
Altenbruch, *W. Germany* **30** 53 48N 8 44 E
Altenburg, *E. Germany* **30** 50 59N 12 28 E
Altenkirchen, *E. Germany* **30** 54 38N 13 20 E
Altenkirchen, *W. Germany* **30** 50 41N 7 38 E
Altenteptow, *E. Germany* **30** 53 42N 13 15 E
Alter do Chão, *Portugal* **23** 39 12N 7 40W
Altiplano, *Bolivia* **136** 17 0 S 68 0W
Altkirch, *France* **19** 47 37N 7 15 E
Altmühl →, *W. Germany* **31** 48 54N 11 54 E
Alto Adige = Trentino-Alto Adige □, *Italy* **26** 46 30N 11 0 E
Alto Araguaia, *Brazil* **137** 17 15 S 53 20W
Alto Chindio, *Mozam.* **93** 16 19 S 35 25 E
Alto Cuchumatanes = Cuchumatanes, Sierra de los, *Guatemala* **128** 15 35N 91 25W
Alto Cuito, *Angola* **95** 13 27 S 18 49 E
Alto del Inca, *Chile* **140** 24 10 S 68 10W
Alto Garças, *Brazil* **137** 16 56 S 53 32W
Alto Iriri →, *Brazil* **137** 8 50 S 53 25W
Alto Ligonha, *Mozam.* **93** 15 30 S 38 11 E
Alto Molocue, *Mozam.* **93** 15 50 S 37 35 E
Alto Paraguai, *Brazil* **137** 14 30 S 56 31W
Alto Paraná □, *Paraguay* **141** 25 0 S 54 50W
Alto Parnaíba, *Brazil* **138** 9 6 S 45 57W
Alto Purús →, *Peru* **136** 9 12 S 70 28W
Alto Río Senguerr, *Argentina* **142** 45 2 S 70 50W
Alto Santo, *Brazil* **138** 5 31 S 38 15W
Alto Sucuriú, *Brazil* **137** 19 19 S 52 47W
Alto Turi, *Brazil* **138** 2 54 S 45 38W
Alton, *Australia* **77** 28 0 S 149 16 E
Alton, *Canada* **108** 43 54N 80 5W
Alton, *U.S.A.* **118** 38 55N 90 5W
Alton Downs, *Australia* **73** 26 7 S 138 57 E
Altona, *Australia* **74** 37 51 S 144 50 E
Altona, *W. Germany* **30** 53 32N 9 56 E
Altoona, *Iowa, U.S.A.* **118** 41 39N 93 28W
Altoona, *Pa., U.S.A.* **116** 40 32N 78 24W
Altopáscio, *Italy* **26** 43 50N 10 40 E
Altos, *Brazil* **138** 5 3 S 42 28W
Altötting, *W. Germany* **31** 48 14N 12 41 E
Altstätten, *Switz.* **31** 47 22N 9 33 E
Altun Shan, *China* **62** 38 30N 88 0 E
Alturas, *U.S.A.* **122** 41 36N 120 37W
Altus, *U.S.A.* **121** 34 30N 99 25W
Alucra, *Turkey* **39** 40 22N 38 47 E
Aluksne, *U.S.S.R.* **36** 57 24N 27 3 E
Alùla, *Somali Rep.* **98** 11 50N 50 45 E
Alunite, *U.S.A.* **125** 35 59N 114 55W
Alupka, *U.S.S.R.* **38** 44 23N 34 2 E
Alushta, *U.S.S.R.* **38** 44 40N 34 25 E
Alusi, *Indonesia* **57** 7 35 S 131 40 E
Alustante, *Spain* **24** 40 36N 1 40W
Alva, *U.S.A.* **121** 36 50N 98 50W
Alvaiázere, *Portugal* **22** 39 49N 8 23W
Älvängen, *Sweden* **11** 57 58N 12 8 E
Alvarado, *Mexico* **127** 18 40N 95 50W
Alvarado, *U.S.A.* **121** 32 25N 97 15W
Alvarães, *Brazil* **135** 3 12 S 64 50W
Alvaro Obregón, Presa, *Mexico* **126** 27 55N 109 52W
Alvdal, *Norway* **10** 62 6N 10 37 E
Alvear, *Argentina* **140** 29 5 S 56 30W
Alverca, *Portugal* **23** 38 56N 9 1W
Alveringen, *Belgium* **17** 51 1N 2 43 E
Alvesta, *Sweden* **11** 56 54N 14 35 E
Alvie, *Australia* **74** 38 14 S 143 30 E
Alvin, *U.S.A.* **121** 29 23N 95 12W
Alvinston, *Canada* **108** 42 49N 81 52W
Alvito, *Portugal* **23** 38 15N 8 0W
Älvkarleby, *Sweden* **9** 60 34N 17 26 E
Älvros, *Sweden* **10** 62 3N 14 38 E
Älvsborgs län □, *Sweden* **11** 58 30N 12 30 E
Älvsbyn, *Sweden* **8** 65 40N 21 0 E
Älvsered, *Sweden* **11** 57 14N 12 51 E
Alwar, *India* **48** 27 38N 76 34 E
Alwaye, *India* **51** 10 8N 76 24 E
Alxa Zuoqi, *China* **60** 38 50N 105 40 E
Alyaskitovyy, *U.S.S.R.* **41** 64 45N 141 30 E
Alyata, *U.S.S.R.* **39** 39 58N 49 25 E
Alyth, *U.K.* **14** 56 38N 3 15W
Alzada, *U.S.A.* **120** 45 3N 104 22W
Alzano Lombardo, *Italy* **26** 45 44N 9 43 E
Alzette →, *Lux.* **17** 49 45N 6 6 E
Alzey, *W. Germany* **31** 49 48N 8 4 E
Am Dam, *Chad* **87** 12 40N 20 35 E
Am Géréda, *Chad* **87** 12 53N 21 14 E
Am-Timan, *Chad* **87** 11 0N 20 10 E
Amacuro □, *Venezuela* **135** 8 50N 61 5W
Amadeus, L., *Australia* **79** 24 54 S 131 0 E
Amâdi, *Sudan* **89** 5 29N 30 25 E
Amadi, *Zaïre* **92** 3 40N 26 40 E
Amadjuak, *Canada* **103** 64 0N 72 39W
Amadjuak L., *Canada* **103** 65 0N 71 8W
Amadora, *Portugal* **23** 38 45N 9 13W
Amagasaki, *Japan* **65** 34 42N 135 20 E
Amager, *Denmark* **11** 55 37N 12 35 E
Amagi, *Japan* **64** 33 25N 130 39 E
Amaimon, *Papua N. G.* **69** 5 12 S 145 30 E
Amakusa-Nada, *Japan* **64** 32 35N 130 5 E
Amakusa-Shotō, *Japan* **64** 32 15N 130 10 E
Åmål, *Sweden* **10** 59 3N 12 42 E
Amalapuram, *India* **51** 16 35N 81 55 E
Amalfi, *Colombia* **134** 6 55N 75 4W
Amalfi, *Italy* **29** 40 39N 14 34 E
Amaliás, *Greece* **35** 37 47N 21 22 E
Amalner, *India* **50** 21 5N 75 5 E
Amambaí, *Brazil* **141** 23 5 S 55 13W
Amambaí →, *Brazil* **141** 23 22 S 53 56W
Amambay □, *Paraguay* **141** 23 0 S 56 0W
Amambay, Cordillera de, *S. Amer.* **141** 23 0 S 55 45W
Amana →, *Venezuela* **135** 9 45N 62 39W
Amanã, L., *Brazil* **135** 2 35 S 64 40W
Amanab, *Papua N. G.* **69** 3 40 S 141 14 E
Amanda Park, *U.S.A.* **124** 47 28N 123 55W
Amándola, *Italy* **27** 42 59N 13 21 E
Amangeldy, *U.S.S.R.* **40** 50 10N 65 10 E
Amantea, *Italy* **29** 39 8N 16 3 E
Amapá, *Brazil* **138** 2 5N 50 50W
Amapá □, *Brazil* **138** 1 40N 52 0W
Amapari, *Brazil* **135** 0 37N 51 39W
Amara, *Sudan* **89** 10 25N 34 10 E
Amarante, *Brazil* **138** 6 14 S 42 50W
Amarante, *Portugal* **22** 41 16N 8 5W
Amarante do Maranhão, *Brazil* **138** 5 36 S 46 45W
Amaranth, *Canada* **111** 50 36N 98 43W
Amarapura, *Burma* **52** 21 54N 96 3 E
Amaravati →, *India* **51** 11 0N 78 15 E
Amareleja, *Portugal* **23** 38 12N 7 13W
Amargosa, *Brazil* **139** 13 2 S 39 36W
Amargosa →, *U.S.A.* **125** 36 14N 116 51W
Amargosa Ra., *U.S.A.* **125** 36 25N 116 40W
Amarillo, *U.S.A.* **121** 35 14N 101 46W
Amarnath, *India* **50** 19 12N 73 22 E
Amaro, Mt., *Italy* **27** 42 5N 14 6 E
Amaro Leite, *Brazil* **139** 13 58 S 49 9W
Amarpur, *India* **49** 25 5N 87 0 E
Amasra, *Turkey* **46** 41 45N 32 30 E
Amassama, *Nigeria* **91** 5 1N 6 2 E
Amasya, *Turkey* **46** 40 40N 35 50 E
Amataurá, *Brazil* **134** 3 29 S 68 6W
Amatikulu, *S. Africa* **97** 29 3 S 31 33 E
Amatitlán, *Guatemala* **128** 14 29N 90 38W
Amatrice, *Italy* **27** 42 38N 13 16 E
Amay, *Belgium* **17** 50 33N 5 19 E
Amazon = Amazonas →, *S. Amer.* **135** 0 5 S 50 0W
Amazonas □, *Brazil* **136** 4 0 S 62 0W
Amazonas □, *Peru* **136** 5 0 S 78 0W
Amazonas □, *Venezuela* **134** 3 30N 66 0W
Amazonas →, *S. Amer.* **135** 0 5 S 50 0W
Ambad, *India* **50** 19 38N 75 50 E
Ambahakily, *Madag.* **97** 21 36 S 43 41 E
Ambala, *India* **48** 30 23N 76 56 E
Ambalangoda, *Sri Lanka* **51** 6 15N 80 5 E
Ambalapulai, *India* **51** 9 25N 76 25 E
Ambalavao, *Madag.* **97** 21 50 S 46 56 E
Ambalindum, *Australia* **72** 23 23 S 135 0 E
Ambam, *Cameroon* **94** 2 20N 11 15 E
Ambanja, *Madag.* **97** 13 40 S 48 27 E
Ambarchik, *U.S.S.R.* **41** 69 40N 162 20 E
Ambarijeby, *Madag.* **97** 14 56 S 47 41 E
Ambaro, Helodranon', *Madag.* **97** 13 23 S 48 38 E
Ambartsevo, *U.S.S.R.* **40** 57 30N 83 52 E
Ambasamudram, *India* **51** 8 43N 77 25 E
Ambato, *Ecuador* **134** 1 5 S 78 42W
Ambato, Sierra de, *Argentina* **140** 28 25 S 66 10W
Ambato Boeny, *Madag.* **97** 16 28 S 46 43 E
Ambatofinandrahana, *Madag.* **97** 20 33 S 46 48 E
Ambatolampy, *Madag.* **97** 19 20 S 47 35 E
Ambatondrazaka, *Madag.* **97** 17 55 S 48 28 E
Ambatosoratra, *Madag.* **97** 17 37 S 48 31 E
Ambenja, *Madag.* **97** 15 17 S 46 58 E
Amberg, *W. Germany* **31** 49 25N 11 52 E
Ambergris Cay, *Belize* **127** 18 0N 88 0W
Ambérieu-en-Bugey, *France* **21** 45 57N 5 20 E
Amberley, *N.Z.* **81** 43 9 S 172 44 E
Ambert, *France* **20** 45 33N 3 44 E
Ambidédi, *Mali* **90** 14 35N 11 47W
Ambikapur, *India* **49** 23 15N 83 15 E
Ambikol, *Sudan* **88** 21 20N 30 50 E
Ambilobé, *Madag.* **97** 13 10 S 49 3 E
Ambinanindrano, *Madag.* **97** 20 5 S 48 23 E
Ambjörnarp, *Sweden* **11** 57 25N 13 17 E
Ambleside, *U.K.* **12** 54 26N 2 58W
Amblève, *Belgium* **17** 50 21N 6 10 E
Amblève →, *Belgium* **17** 50 25N 5 45 E
Ambo, *Ethiopia* **89** 12 20N 37 30 E
Ambo, *Peru* **136** 10 5 S 76 10W
Ambodifototra, *Madag.* **97** 16 59 S 49 52 E
Ambodilazana, *Madag.* **97** 18 6 S 49 10 E
Ambohimahasoa, *Madag.* **97** 21 7 S 47 13 E
Ambohimanga, *Madag.* **97** 20 52 S 47 36 E
Ambohitra, *Madag.* **97** 12 30 S 49 10 E
Ambon, *Indonesia* **57** 3 35 S 128 20 E
Amboseli L., *Kenya* **92** 2 40 S 37 10 E
Ambositra, *Madag.* **97** 20 31 S 47 25 E
Ambovombé, *Madag.* **97** 25 11 S 46 5 E
Amboy, *Calif., U.S.A.* **125** 34 33N 115 51W
Amboy, *Ill., U.S.A.* **118** 41 44N 89 20W
Amboyna I., *S. China Sea* **56** 7 50N 112 50 E
Ambridge, *U.S.A.* **116** 40 36N 80 15W
Ambriz, *Angola* **95** 7 48 S 13 8 E
Ambrym, *Vanuatu* **68** 16 15 S 168 10 E
Ambunti, *Papua N. G.* **69** 4 13 S 142 52 E
Ambur, *India* **51** 12 48N 78 43 E
Amby, *Australia* **73** 26 30 S 148 11 E
Amchitka I., *U.S.A.* **102** 51 30N 179 0W
Amderma, *U.S.S.R.* **40** 69 45N 61 30 E
Ameca, *Mexico* **126** 20 30N 104 0W
Ameca →, *Mexico* **126** 20 40N 105 15W
Amecameca, *Mexico* **127** 19 7N 98 46W
Ameland, *Neths.* **16** 53 27N 5 45 E
Amélia, *Italy* **27** 42 34N 12 25 E
Amélie-les-Bains-Palalda, *France* **20** 42 29N 2 41 E
Amen, *U.S.S.R.* **41** 68 45N 180 0 E
Amendolaro, *Italy* **29** 39 58N 16 34 E
America, *Neths.* **17** 51 27N 5 59 E
American Falls, *U.S.A.* **122** 42 46N 112 56W
American Falls Res., *U.S.A.* **122** 43 0N 112 50W
American Highland, *Antarctica* **143** 73 0 S 75 0 E
American Samoa ■, *Pac. Oc.* **68** 14 20 S 170 40W
Americana, *Brazil* **141** 22 45 S 47 20W
Americus, *U.S.A.* **115** 32 0N 84 10W
Amersfoort, *Neths.* **16** 52 9N 5 23 E
Amersfoort, *S. Africa* **97** 26 59 S 29 53 E

Arcos de Valdevez

Anorotsangana, Madag. 97 13 56 S 47 55 E
Anping, Hebei, China 60 38 15N 115 30 E
Anping, Liaoning, China 61 41 5N 123 30 E
Anpu Gang, China 58 21 25N 109 50 E
Anqing, China 59 30 30N 117 3 E
Anqiu, China 61 36 25N 119 10 E
Anren, China 59 26 43N 113 18 E
Ans, Belgium 17 50 39N 5 32 E
Ansāb, Si. Arabia 46 29 11N 44 43 E
Ansai, China 60 36 50N 109 20 E
Ansbach, W. Germany 31 49 17N 10 34 E
Anse, L', U.S.A. 104 46 47N 88 28W
Anse au Loup, L', Canada 105 51 32N 56 50W
Anseba →, Ethiopia 89 16 0N 38 30 E
Anserma, Colombia 134 5 13N 75 48W
Anseroeul, Belgium 17 50 43N 3 32 E
Anshan, China 61 41 5N 122 58 E
Anshun, China 58 26 18N 105 57 E
Ansião, Portugal 22 39 56N 8 27W
Ansirabe, Madag. 97 19 55 S 47 2 E
Ansley, U.S.A. 120 41 19N 99 24W
Ansó, Spain 24 42 51N 0 48W
Anson, U.S.A. 121 32 46N 99 54W
Anson B., Australia 78 13 20 S 130 6 E
Ansongo, Mali 91 15 25N 0 35 E
Ansonia, Conn., U.S.A. 117 41 21N 73 6W
Ansonia, Ohio, U.S.A. 119 40 13N 84 38W
Anstruther, U.K. 14 56 14N 2 40W
Ansudu, Indonesia 57 2 11 S 139 22 E
Antabamba, Peru 136 14 40 S 73 0W
Antakya, Turkey 46 36 14N 36 10 E
Antalaha, Madag. 97 14 57 S 50 20 E
Antalya, Turkey 46 36 52N 30 45 E
Antalya Körfezi, Turkey 46 36 15N 31 30 E
Antananarivo, Madag. 97 18 55 S 47 31 E
Antananarivo □, Madag. 97 19 0 S 47 0 E
Antanimbaribe, Madag. 97 21 30 S 44 48 E
Antarctic Pen., Antarctica 143 67 0 S 60 0W
Antarctica 143 90 0 S 0 0 E
Antelope, Zambia 93 21 2 S 28 31 E
Antenor Navarro, Brazil 138 6 44 S 38 27W
Antequera, Paraguay 140 24 8 S 57 7W
Antequera, Spain 23 37 5N 4 33W
Antero Mt., U.S.A. 123 38 45N 106 15W
Anthony, Kans., U.S.A. 121 37 8N 98 2W
Anthony, N. Mex., U.S.A. 123 32 1N 106 37W
Anthony Lagoon, Australia 72 18 0 S 135 30 E
Anti Atlas, Morocco 84 30 0N 8 30W
Antibes, France 21 43 34N 7 6 E
Antibes, C. d', France 21 43 31N 7 7 E
Anticosti, I. d', Canada 105 49 30N 63 0W
Antifer, C. d', France 18 49 41N 0 10 E
Antigo, U.S.A. 120 45 8N 89 5W
Antigonish, Canada 105 45 38N 61 58W
Antigua, Canary Is. 25 28 24N 14 1W
Antigua, Guatemala 128 14 34N 90 41W
Antigua, W. Indies 129 17 0N 61 50W
Antigua & Barbuda ■, W. Indies 129 17 20N 61 48W
Antilla, Cuba 128 20 40N 75 50W
Antimony, U.S.A. 123 38 7N 112 0W
Antioch, U.S.A. 124 38 0N 121 45W
Antioche, Pertuis d', France 20 46 6N 1 20W
Antioquia, Colombia 134 6 40N 75 55W
Antioquia □, Colombia 134 7 0N 75 30W
Antipodes Is., Pac. Oc. 66 49 45 S 178 40 E
Antler, U.S.A. 120 48 58N 101 18W
Antler →, Canada 111 49 8N 101 0W
Antlers, U.S.A. 121 34 15N 95 35W
Antofagasta, Chile 140 23 50 S 70 30W
Antofagasta □, Chile 140 24 0 S 69 0W
Antofagasta de la Sierra, Argentina 140 26 5 S 67 20W
Antofalla, Argentina 140 25 30 S 68 5W
Antofalla, Salar de, Argentina 140 25 40 S 67 45W
Antoing, Belgium 17 50 34N 3 27 E
Anton, U.S.A. 121 33 49N 102 5W
Anton Chico, U.S.A. 123 35 12N 105 5W
Antongila, Helodrano, Madag. 97 15 30 S 49 50 E
Antonibé, Madag. 97 15 7 S 47 24 E
Antonibé, Presqu'île d', Madag. 97 14 55 S 47 20 E
Antonina, Brazil 141 25 26 S 48 42W
Antonito, U.S.A. 123 37 4N 106 1W
Antonovo, U.S.S.R. 39 49 25N 51 42 E
Antrain, France 18 48 28N 1 30W
Antrim, U.K. 15 54 43N 6 13W
Antrim □, U.K. 15 54 55N 6 20W
Antrim, Mts. of, U.K. 15 54 57N 6 8W
Antrim Plateau, Australia 78 18 8 S 128 20 E
Antrodoco, Italy 27 42 25N 13 4 E
Antropovo, U.S.S.R. 37 58 26N 42 51 E
Antsalova, Madag. 97 18 40 S 44 37 E
Antsiranana, Madag. 97 12 25 S 49 20 E
Antsohihy, Madag. 97 14 50 S 47 59 E
Antsohimbondrona Seranana, Madag. 97 13 7 S 48 48 E
Antu, China 61 42 30N 128 20 E
Antwerp = Antwerpen, Belgium 17 51 13N 4 25 E
Antwerp, Australia 74 36 17 S 142 4 E
Antwerp, N.Y., U.S.A. 117 44 12N 75 36W
Antwerp, Ohio, U.S.A. 119 41 11N 84 45W
Antwerpen, Belgium 17 51 13N 4 25 E
Antwerpen □, Belgium 17 51 15N 4 40 E
Anupgarh, India 48 29 10N 73 10 E
Anuradhapura, Sri Lanka 51 8 22N 80 28 E
Anvers = Antwerpen, Belgium 17 51 13N 4 25 E
Anvers I., Antarctica 143 64 30 S 63 40W
Anvik, U.S.A. 102 62 37N 160 20W
Anxi, Fujian, China 59 25 2N 118 12 E
Anxi, Gansu, China 62 40 30N 95 43 E
Anxiang, China 59 29 27N 112 11 E
Anxious B., Australia 73 33 24 S 134 45 E
Anyama, Ivory C. 90 5 30N 4 3W
Anyang, China 60 36 5N 114 21 E
Anyi, Jiangxi, China 59 28 49N 115 25 E
Anyi, Shanxi, China 60 35 2N 111 2 E
Anyuan, China 59 25 9N 115 21 E
Anza, U.S.A. 125 33 35N 116 39W
'Anzah, Jordan 44 32 22N 35 12 E
Anze, China 60 36 10N 112 12 E
Anzhero-Sudzhensk, U.S.S.R. 40 56 10N 86 0 E
Ánzio, Italy 28 41 28N 12 37 E
Anzoátegui □, Venezuela 135 9 0N 64 30W
Aoba, Vanuatu 68 15 25 S 167 50 E
Aoga-Shima, Japan 65 32 28N 139 46 E
Aoiz, Spain 24 42 46N 1 22W
Aomori, Japan 63 40 45N 140 45 E
Aonla, India 49 28 16N 79 11 E
Aono-Yama, Japan 64 34 28N 131 48 E
Aorangi Mts., N.Z. 80 41 28 S 175 22 E
Aosta, Italy 26 45 43N 7 20 E
Aoudéras, Niger 91 17 45N 8 20 E
Aouinet Torkoz, Morocco 84 28 31N 9 46W
Aoukar, Mali 84 23 50N 2 45W
Aouker, Mauritania 90 17 40N 10 0W
Aoulef el Arab, Algeria 85 26 55N 1 2 E
Apa →, S. Amer. 140 22 6 S 58 2W
Apache, U.S.A. 121 34 53N 98 22W
Apalachee B., U.S.A. 115 30 0N 84 0W
Apalachicola, U.S.A. 115 29 40N 85 0W
Apalachicola →, U.S.A. 115 29 40N 85 0W
Apapa, Nigeria 91 6 25N 3 25 E
Apaporis →, Colombia 134 1 23 S 69 25W
Aparecida do Taboado, Brazil 139 20 5 S 51 5W
Aparri, Phil. 57 18 22N 121 38 E
Aparurén, Venezuela 135 5 6N 62 8W
Apateu, Romania 34 46 36N 21 47 E
Apatin, Yugoslavia 33 45 40N 19 0 E
Apatzingán, Mexico 126 19 0N 102 20W
Apeldoorn, Neths. 16 52 13N 5 57 E
Apeldoornsch Kanal →, Neths. 16 52 29N 6 5 E
Apen, W. Germany 30 53 12N 7 47 E
Apere →, Bolivia 137 13 44 S 65 18W
Apia, W. Samoa 68 13 50 S 171 50W
Apiacás, Serra dos, Brazil 137 9 50 S 57 0W
Apiaú →, Brazil 135 2 39N 61 12W
Apiaú, Serra do, Brazil 135 2 30N 62 0W
Apidiá →, Brazil 137 11 39 S 61 11W
Apinajé, Brazil 139 11 31 S 48 18W
Apiti, N.Z. 80 39 58 S 175 54 E
Apizaco, Mexico 127 19 26N 98 9W
Aplao, Peru 136 16 0 S 72 40W
Apo, Mt., Phil. 57 6 53N 125 14 E
Apodi, Brazil 138 5 39 S 37 48W
Apolda, E. Germany 30 51 1N 11 30 E
Apollo Bay, Australia 74 38 45 S 143 40 E
Apollonia = Marsá Susah, Libya 86 32 52N 21 59 E
Apollonia, Greece 35 36 58N 24 43 E
Apolo, Bolivia 136 14 30 S 68 30W
Apónguao →, Venezuela 135 4 48N 61 36W
Aporé, Brazil 137 18 58 S 52 1W
Aporé →, Brazil 139 19 27 S 50 57W
Aporema, Brazil 138 1 14N 50 49W
Apostle Is., U.S.A. 120 47 0N 90 30W
Apóstoles, Argentina 141 28 0 S 56 0W
Apostolovo, U.S.S.R. 38 47 39N 33 39 E
Apoteri, Guyana 135 4 2N 58 32W
Appalachian Mts., U.S.A. 114 38 0N 80 0W
Appelscha, Neths. 16 52 57N 6 21 E
Appenines = Appennini, Italy 26 44 0N 11 0 E
Appennini, Italy 26 44 0N 11 0 E
Appennino Ligure, Italy 26 44 30N 9 0 E
Appenzell-Ausser Rhoden □, Switz. 31 47 23N 9 23 E
Appenzell-Inner Rhoden □, Switz. 31 47 20N 9 25 E
Appiano, Italy 27 46 27N 11 17 E
Appin, Australia 76 34 11 S 150 45 E
Appingedam, Neths. 16 53 19N 6 51 E
Apple Hill, Canada 109 45 13N 74 46W
Apple Tree Flat, Australia 76 32 40 S 149 36 E
Apple Valley, U.S.A. 125 34 30N 117 11W
Appleby, U.K. 12 54 35N 2 29W
Appleton, U.S.A. 114 44 17N 88 25W
Appleton City, U.S.A. 118 38 11N 94 2W
Approuague, Fr. Guiana 135 4 20N 52 0W
Approuague →, Fr. Guiana 135 4 30N 51 57W
Apricena, Italy 29 41 47N 15 25 E
Aprigliano, Italy 29 39 17N 16 19 E
Aprília, Italy 28 41 38N 12 38 E
Apsheronsk, U.S.S.R. 39 44 28N 39 42 E
Apsley, Australia 74 36 58 S 141 5 E
Apsley, Canada 109 44 45N 78 6W
Apt, France 21 43 53N 5 24 E
Apuane, Alpi, Italy 26 44 7N 10 14 E
Apuaú, Brazil 135 2 25 S 60 53W
Apucarana, Brazil 141 23 55 S 51 33W
Apulia = Púglia □, Italy 29 41 0N 16 30 E
Apure □, Venezuela 134 7 10N 68 50W
Apure →, Venezuela 134 7 37N 66 25W
Apurímac □, Peru 136 14 0 S 73 0W
Apurimac →, Peru 136 12 17 S 73 56W
Apuseni, Munţii, Romania 34 46 30N 22 45 E
Aqabah = Al 'Aqabah, Jordan 44 29 31N 35 0 E
'Aqabah, Khalīj al, Red Sea 46 28 15N 33 20 E
Āqcheh, Afghan. 47 37 0N 66 5 E
Aqîq, Sudan 88 18 14N 38 12 E
Aqîq, Khalîg, Sudan 88 18 20N 38 10 E
Aqrabā, Jordan 44 32 9N 35 20 E
Aqrah, Iraq 46 36 46N 43 45 E
Aquidauana, Brazil 137 20 30 S 55 50W
Aquidauana →, Brazil 137 19 44 S 56 50W
Áquila, L', Italy 27 42 21N 13 24 E
Aquiles Serdán, Mexico 126 28 37N 105 54W
Aquin, Haiti 129 18 16N 73 24W
Ar Rachidiya, Morocco 84 31 58N 4 20W
Ar Rafīd, Syria 44 32 57N 35 52 E
Ar Ramādī, Iraq 46 33 25N 43 20 E
Ar Raml, Libya 86 26 45N 19 40 E
Ar Ramthā, Jordan 44 32 34N 36 0 E
Ar Raqqah, Syria 46 36 0N 38 55 E
Ar Rass, Si. Arabia 46 25 50N 43 40 E
Ar Rifā'i, Si. Arabia 46 31 50N 46 10 E
Ar Riyāḍ, Si. Arabia 46 24 41N 46 42 E
Ar Rummān, Jordan 44 32 9N 35 48 E
Ar Ruṭbah, Iraq 46 33 0N 40 15 E
Ar Ruwayḍah, Si. Arabia 46 23 40N 44 40 E
Ara, India 49 25 35N 84 32 E
'Arab, Bahr el →, Sudan 89 9 0N 29 30 E
Arab, Khalîg el, Egypt 88 30 55N 29 0 E
Arab, Shatt al, Asia 46 30 0N 48 31 E
Arabatskaya Strelka, U.S.S.R. 38 45 40N 35 0 E
Arabba, Italy 27 46 30N 11 51 E
Arabelo, Venezuela 135 4 55N 64 13W
Arabia, Asia 45 25 0N 45 0 E
Arabian Desert = Es Sahrâ' Esh Sharqîya, Egypt 88 27 30N 32 30 E
Arabian Gulf = Gulf, The, Asia 47 27 0N 50 0 E
Arabian Sea, Ind. Oc. 42 16 0N 65 0 E
Araç, Turkey 46 41 15N 33 21 E
Aracaju, Brazil 138 10 55 S 37 4W
Aracataca, Colombia 134 10 38N 74 9W
Aracati, Brazil 138 4 30 S 37 44W
Araçatuba, Brazil 141 21 10 S 50 30W
Aracena, Spain 23 37 53N 6 38W
Aracena, Sierra de, Spain 23 37 50N 6 50W
Aracides, C., Solomon Is. 68 8 21 S 161 0 E
Araçuaí, Brazil 139 16 52 S 42 4W
Araçuaí →, Brazil 139 16 46 S 42 2W
'Arad, Israel 44 31 15N 35 12 E
Arad, Romania 34 46 10N 21 20 E
Arada, Chad 87 15 0N 20 20 E
Arafura Sea, E. Indies 57 9 0 S 135 0 E
Aragarças, Brazil 137 15 55 S 52 15W
Aragats, U.S.S.R. 39 40 30N 44 15 E
Aragón □, Spain 24 41 25N 1 0W
Aragón →, Spain 24 42 13N 1 44W
Aragona, Italy 28 37 24N 13 36 E
Aragua □, Venezuela 134 10 0N 67 10W
Aragua de Barcelona, Venezuela 135 9 28N 64 49W
Araguacema, Brazil 138 8 50 S 49 20W
Araguaçu, Brazil 139 12 49 S 49 51W
Araguaia →, Brazil 138 5 21 S 48 41W
Araguaiana, Brazil 137 15 43 S 51 51W
Araguaína, Brazil 138 7 12 S 48 12W
Araguari, Brazil 139 18 38 S 48 11W
Araguari →, Brazil 138 1 15N 49 55W
Araguatins, Brazil 138 5 38 S 48 7W
Araioses, Brazil 138 2 53 S 41 55W
Arak, Algeria 85 25 20N 3 45 E
Arāk, Iran 46 34 0N 49 40 E
Arakan □, Burma 52 19 0N 94 15 E
Arakan Yoma, Burma 52 20 0N 94 40 E
Arakkonam, India 51 13 7N 79 43 E
Araks = Aras, Rūd-e →, Iran 46 39 10N 47 10 E
Aral Sea = Aralskoye More, U.S.S.R. 40 44 30N 60 0 E
Aralsk, U.S.S.R. 40 46 50N 61 20 E
Aralskoye More, U.S.S.R. 40 44 30N 60 0 E
Araluen, Australia 76 35 36 S 149 49 E
Aramac, Australia 72 22 58 S 145 14 E
Arambag, India 49 22 53N 87 48 E
Aran Areh, Ethiopia 98 9 2N 43 54 E
Aran I., Ireland 15 55 0N 8 30W
Aran Is., Ireland 15 53 5N 9 42W
Aranda de Duero, Spain 24 41 39N 3 42W
Aranga, N.Z. 80 35 44 S 173 40 E
Arani, India 51 12 43N 79 19 E
Aranjuez, Spain 22 40 1N 3 40W
Aranos, Namibia 96 24 9 S 19 7 E
Aransas Pass, U.S.A. 121 27 55N 97 9W
Aranzazu, Colombia 134 5 16N 75 30W
Arao, Japan 64 32 59N 130 25 E
Araouane, Mali 90 18 55N 3 30W
Arapahoe, U.S.A. 120 40 22N 99 53W
Arapari, Brazil 138 5 34 S 49 15W
Arapey Grande →, Uruguay 140 30 55 S 57 49W
Arapiraca, Brazil 138 9 45 S 36 39W
Arapkir, Turkey 46 39 5N 38 30 E
Arapongas, Brazil 141 23 29 S 51 28W
Araracuara, Colombia 134 0 24 S 72 17W
Araranguá, Brazil 141 29 0 S 49 30W
Araraquara, Brazil 139 21 50 S 48 0W
Ararás, Serra das, Brazil 141 25 0 S 53 10W
Ararat, Australia 74 37 16 S 143 0 E
Ararat, Mt. = Ağri Daği, Turkey 46 39 50N 44 15 E
Arari, Brazil 138 3 28 S 44 47W
Araria, India 49 26 9N 87 33 E
Araripe, Chapada do, Brazil 138 7 20 S 40 0W
Araripina, Brazil 138 7 33 S 40 34W
Araruama, L. de, Brazil 139 22 53 S 42 12W
Araruna, Brazil 138 6 52 S 35 44W
Aras, Rūd-e →, Iran 46 39 10N 47 10 E
Araticu, Brazil 138 1 58 S 49 51W
Arauca, Colombia 134 7 0N 70 40W
Arauca □, Colombia 134 6 40N 71 0W
Arauca →, Venezuela 134 7 24N 66 35W
Arauco, Chile 140 37 16 S 73 25W
Arauco □, Chile 140 37 40 S 73 25W
Araújos, Brazil 139 19 56 S 45 14W
Arauquita, Colombia 134 7 2N 71 25W
Araure, Venezuela 134 9 34N 69 13W
Arawa, Ethiopia 89 9 57N 41 58 E
Arawata →, N.Z. 81 44 0 S 168 40 E
Araxá, Brazil 139 19 35 S 46 55W
Araya, Pen. de, Venezuela 135 10 40N 64 0W
Arba Minch, Ethiopia 89 6 0N 37 30 E
Arbatax, Italy 28 39 57N 9 42 E
Arbaza, U.S.S.R. 41 52 40N 92 30 E
Arbīl, Iraq 46 36 15N 44 5 E
Arboga, Sweden 10 59 24N 15 52 E
Arbois, France 19 46 55N 5 46 E
Arboletes, Colombia 134 8 51N 76 26W
Arbore, Ethiopia 89 5 3N 36 50 E
Arborea, Italy 28 39 46N 8 34 E
Arborfield, Canada 111 53 6N 103 39W
Arborg, Canada 111 50 54N 97 13W
Arbrå, Sweden 10 61 28N 16 22 E
Arbresle, L', France 21 45 50N 4 36 E
Arbroath, U.K. 14 56 34N 2 35W
Arbuckle, U.S.A. 124 39 3N 122 2W
Arbus, Italy 28 39 30N 8 33 E
Arbuzinka, U.S.S.R. 38 47 0N 31 59 E
Arc, France 19 47 28N 5 34 E
Arc →, France 21 45 34N 6 12 E
Arcachon, France 20 44 40N 1 10W
Arcachon, Bassin d', France 20 44 42N 1 10W
Arcade, Calif., U.S.A. 124 34 2N 118 15W
Arcade, U.S.A. 116 42 34N 78 25W
Arcadia, Fla., U.S.A. 115 27 20N 81 50W
Arcadia, Ind., U.S.A. 119 40 10N 86 1W
Arcadia, Iowa, U.S.A. 118 42 5N 95 3W
Arcadia, La., U.S.A. 121 32 34N 92 53W
Arcadia, Nebr., U.S.A. 120 41 29N 99 4W
Arcadia, Pa., U.S.A. 116 40 46N 78 54W
Arcadia, Wis., U.S.A. 120 44 13N 91 29W
Arcanum, U.S.A. 119 39 59N 84 33W
Arcata, U.S.A. 122 40 55N 124 4W
Arcévia, Italy 27 43 29N 12 58 E
Archangel = Arkhangelsk, U.S.S.R. 40 64 40N 41 0 E
Archar, Bulgaria 34 43 50N 22 54 E
Archbald, U.S.A. 117 41 30N 75 31W
Archbold, U.S.A. 119 41 31N 84 18W
Archena, Spain 25 38 9N 1 16W
Archer →, Australia 72 13 28 S 141 41 E
Archer B., Australia 72 13 20 S 141 30 E
Archers Post, Kenya 92 0 35N 37 35 E
Archidona, Spain 23 37 6N 4 22W
Arci, Monte, Italy 28 39 47N 8 44 E
Arcidosso, Italy 27 42 51N 11 30 E
Arcila = Asilah, Morocco 84 35 29N 6 0W
Arcis-sur-Aube, France 19 48 32N 4 10 E
Arckaringa, Australia 73 27 56 S 134 45 E
Arckaringa Cr. →, Australia 73 28 10 S 135 22 E
Arco, Italy 26 45 55N 10 54 E
Arco, U.S.A. 122 43 45N 113 16W
Arcola, Canada 111 49 40N 102 30W
Arcola, U.S.A. 119 39 41N 88 19W
Arcos, Spain 24 41 12N 2 16W
Arcos de los Frontera, Spain 23 36 45N 5 49W
Arcos de Valdevez, Portugal 22 41 55N 8 22W

Arcot

Arcot, *India* **51** 12 53N 79 20 E
Arcoverde, *Brazil* **138** 8 25 S 37 4W
Arcs, Les, *France* **21** 43 27N 6 29 E
Arctic Bay, *Canada* **103** 73 1N 85 7W
Arctic Ocean, *Arctic* **144** 78 0N 160 0W
Arctic Red River, *Canada* **102** 67 15N 134 0W
Arda →, *Bulgaria* **35** 41 40N 26 29 E
Arda →, *Italy* **26** 44 53N 9 52 E
Ardabīl, *Iran* **46** 38 15N 48 18 E
Ardahan, *Turkey* **46** 41 7N 42 41 E
Ardakān = Sepīdān, *Iran* **47** 30 20N 52 5 E
Ardales, *Spain* **23** 36 53N 4 51W
Årdalstangen, *Norway* **10** 61 14N 7 43 E
Ardatov, *U.S.S.R.* **37** 54 51N 46 15 E
Ardbeg, *Canada* **108** 45 38N 80 5W
Ardea, *Greece* **35** 40 58N 22 3 E
Ardèche □, *France* **21** 44 42N 4 16 E
Ardèche →, *France* **21** 44 16N 4 39 E
Ardee, *Ireland* **15** 53 51N 6 32W
Arden, *Canada* **109** 44 43N 76 56W
Arden, *Calif., U.S.A.* **124** 38 36N 121 33W
Arden, *U.S.A.* **125** 36 1N 115 14W
Arden Stby., *Denmark* **11** 56 46N 9 52 E
Ardenne, *Belgium* **19** 50 0N 5 10 E
Ardennes □, *France* **19** 49 35N 4 40 E
Ardentes, *France* **19** 46 45N 1 50 E
Ardestān, *Iran* **47** 33 20N 52 25 E
Ardgour, *U.K.* **14** 56 45N 5 25W
Árdhas →, *Greece* **35** 41 36N 26 25 E
Ardila →, *Portugal* **23** 38 12N 7 28W
Ardlethan, *Australia* **75** 34 22 S 146 53 E
Ardmore, *Australia* **72** 21 39 S 139 11 E
Ardmore, *Okla., U.S.A.* **121** 34 10N 97 5W
Ardmore, *Pa., U.S.A.* **117** 39 58N 75 18W
Ardmore, *S. Dak., U.S.A.* **120** 43 0N 103 40W
Ardnacrusha, *Ireland* **15** 52 43N 8 38W
Ardnamurchan, Pt. of, *U.K.* **14** 56 44N 6 14W
Ardno, *Australia* **74** 37 49 S 141 3 E
Ardooie, *Belgium* **17** 50 59N 3 13 E
Ardore Marina, *Italy* **29** 38 11N 16 10 E
Ardres, *France* **19** 50 50N 2 0 E
Ardrossan, *Australia* **73** 34 26 S 137 53 E
Ardrossan, *U.K.* **14** 55 39N 4 50W
Ards □, *U.K.* **15** 54 35N 5 30W
Ards Pen., *U.K.* **15** 54 30N 5 25W
Ardud, *Romania* **34** 47 37N 22 52 E
Ardunac, *Turkey* **39** 41 8N 42 5 E
Åre, *Sweden* **10** 63 22N 13 15 E
Arecibo, *Puerto Rico* **129** 18 29N 66 42W
Areia Branca, *Brazil* **138** 5 0 S 37 0W
Arena, Pt., *U.S.A.* **124** 38 57N 123 44W
Arenales, Cerro, *Chile* **142** 47 5 S 73 40W
Arenápolis, *Brazil* **137** 14 26 S 56 49W
Arenas, *Spain* **22** 43 17N 4 50W
Arenas de San Pedro, *Spain* **22** 40 12N 5 5W
Arendal, *Norway* **11** 58 28N 8 46 E
Arendonk, *Belgium* **17** 51 19N 5 5 E
Arendsee, *E. Germany* **30** 52 52N 11 27 E
Arenillas, *Ecuador* **134** 3 33 S 80 10W
Arenys de Mar, *Spain* **24** 41 35N 2 33 E
Arenzano, *Italy* **26** 44 24N 8 40 E
Arenzville, *U.S.A.* **118** 39 53N 90 22W
Areópolis, *Greece* **35** 36 40N 22 22 E
Arequipa, *Peru* **136** 16 20 S 71 30W
Arequipa □, *Peru* **136** 16 0 S 72 50W
Arere, *Brazil* **135** 0 16 S 53 52W
Arero, *Ethiopia* **89** 4 41N 38 50 E
Arès, *France* **20** 44 47N 1 8W
Arévalo, *Spain* **22** 41 3N 4 43W
Arezzo, *Italy* **27** 43 28N 11 50 E
Arga →, *Spain* **24** 42 18N 1 47W
Argalastí, *Greece* **35** 39 13N 23 13 E
Argalong, *Australia* **76** 35 18 S 148 27 E
Argamakmur, *Indonesia* **56** 3 35 S 102 0 E
Argamasilla de Alba, *Spain* **25** 39 8N 3 5W
Arganda, *Spain* **24** 40 19N 3 26W
Arganil, *Portugal* **22** 40 13N 8 3W
Argelès-Gazost, *France* **20** 43 0N 0 6W
Argelès-sur-Mer, *France* **20** 42 34N 3 1 E
Argens →, *France* **21** 43 24N 6 44 E
Argent-sur-Sauldre, *France* **19** 47 33N 2 25 E
Argenta, *Italy* **27** 44 37N 11 50 E
Argenta, *U.S.A.* **119** 39 59N 88 49W
Argentan, *France* **18** 48 45N 0 1W
Argentário, Mte., *Italy* **27** 42 23N 11 11 E
Argentat, *France* **20** 45 6N 1 56 E
Argentera, *Italy* **26** 44 23N 6 58 E
Argentera, Monte del, *Italy* **26** 44 12N 7 5 E
Argenteuil, *France* **19** 48 57N 2 14 E
Argentia, *Canada* **105** 47 18N 53 58W
Argentiera, C. dell', *Italy* **28** 40 44N 8 8 E
Argentière-la-Bessée, L', *France* **21** 44 47N 6 33 E
Argentina ■, *S. Amer.* **142** 35 0 S 66 0W
Argentina Is., *Antarctica* **143** 66 0 S 64 0W
Argentino, L., *Argentina* **142** 50 10 S 73 0W
Argenton-Château, *France* **18** 46 59N 0 27W
Argenton-sur-Creuse, *France* **20** 46 36N 1 30 E
Argeş →, *Romania* **34** 44 12N 26 14 E
Arghandab →, *Afghan.* **48** 31 30N 64 15 E
Argo, *Sudan* **88** 19 28N 30 30 E
Argolikós Kólpos, *Greece* **35** 37 20N 22 52 E
Argonne, *France* **19** 49 10N 5 0 E
Árgos, *Greece* **35** 37 40N 22 43 E
Argos, *U.S.A.* **119** 41 14N 86 15W
Argostólion, *Greece* **35** 38 12N 20 33 E
Arguedas, *Spain* **24** 42 11N 1 36W
Arguello, Pt., *U.S.A.* **125** 34 34N 120 40W
Arguineguín, *Canary Is.* **25** 27 46N 15 41W
Argun →, *U.S.S.R.* **41** 53 20N 121 28 E
Argungu, *Nigeria* **91** 12 40N 4 31 E
Argus Pk., *U.S.A.* **125** 35 52N 117 26W
Argyle, *U.S.A.* **120** 48 23N 96 49W
Argyle, L., *Australia* **78** 16 20 S 128 40 E
Argyrádhes, *Greece* **35** 39 27N 19 58 E
Århus, *Denmark* **11** 56 8N 10 11 E
Århus Amtskommune □, *Denmark* **11** 56 15N 10 15 E
Aria, *N.Z.* **80** 38 33 S 175 0 E
Ariah Park, *Australia* **76** 34 22 S 147 16 E
Ariamsvlei, *Namibia* **96** 28 9 S 19 51 E
Ariana, *Tunisia* **86** 36 52N 10 12 E
Ariano Irpino, *Italy* **29** 41 10N 15 4 E
Ariano nel Polèsine, *Italy* **27** 44 56N 12 5 E
Ariari →, *Colombia* **134** 2 35N 72 47W
Aribinda, *Burkina Faso* **91** 14 17N 0 52W
Arica, *Chile* **136** 18 32 S 70 20W
Arica, *Colombia* **134** 2 0 S 71 50W
Arico, *Canary Is.* **25** 28 9N 16 29W
Arid, C., *Australia* **79** 34 1 S 123 10 E
Arida, *Japan* **65** 34 5N 135 8 E
Aridh, *Si. Arabia* **46** 25 0N 46 0 E
Ariège □, *France* **20** 42 56N 1 30 E
Ariège →, *France* **20** 43 30N 1 25 E
Arieş →, *Romania* **34** 46 24N 23 20 E
Arima, *Trin. & Tob.* **129** 10 38N 61 17W
Arinos →, *Brazil* **137** 10 25 S 58 20W
Ario de Rosales, *Mexico* **126** 19 12N 102 0W
Aripuanã, *Brazil* **137** 9 25 S 60 30W
Aripuanã →, *Brazil* **137** 5 7 S 60 25W
Ariquemes, *Brazil* **137** 9 55 S 63 6W
Arisaig, *U.K.* **14** 56 55N 5 50W
Arîsh, W. el →, *Egypt* **88** 31 9N 33 49 E
Arismendi, *Venezuela* **134** 8 29N 68 22W
Arissa, *Ethiopia* **89** 11 10N 41 35 E
Aristazabal I., *Canada* **110** 52 40N 129 10W
Arita, *Japan* **64** 33 11N 129 54 E
Arivaca, *U.S.A.* **123** 31 37N 111 25W
Arivonimamo, *Madag.* **97** 19 1 S 47 11 E
Ariyalur, *India* **51** 11 8N 79 8 E
Ariza, *Spain* **64** 41 19N 2 3W
Arizaro, Salar de, *Argentina* **140** 24 40 S 67 50W
Arizona, *Argentina* **140** 35 45 S 65 25W
Arizona □, *U.S.A.* **123** 34 20N 111 30W
Arizpe, *Mexico* **126** 30 20N 110 11W
Årjäng, *Sweden* **10** 59 24N 12 8 E
Arjeplog, *Sweden* **8** 66 3N 18 2 E
Arjona, *Colombia* **134** 10 14N 75 22W
Arjona, *Spain* **23** 37 56N 4 4W
Arjuno, *Indonesia* **57** 7 49 S 112 34 E
Arka, *U.S.S.R.* **41** 60 15N 142 0 E
Arkadak, *U.S.S.R.* **37** 51 58N 43 19 E
Arkadelphia, *U.S.A.* **121** 34 5N 93 0W
Arkaig, L., *U.K.* **14** 56 58N 5 10W
Arkalyk, *U.S.S.R.* **40** 50 13N 66 50 E
Arkansas □, *U.S.A.* **121** 35 0N 92 30W
Arkansas →, *U.S.A.* **121** 33 48N 91 4W
Arkansas City, *U.S.A.* **121** 37 4N 97 3W
Árkathos →, *Greece* **35** 39 20N 21 4 E
Arkhangelsk, *U.S.S.R.* **40** 64 40N 41 0 E
Arkhangelskoye, *U.S.S.R.* **37** 51 32N 40 58 E
Arkiko, *Ethiopia* **89** 15 33N 39 30 E
Arklow, *Ireland* **15** 52 48N 6 10W
Arkona, *Canada* **108** 43 4N 81 50W
Arkona, Kap, *E. Germany* **30** 54 41N 13 26 E
Arkösund, *Sweden* **11** 58 29N 16 56 E
Arkticheskiy, Mys, *U.S.S.R.* **41** 81 10N 95 0 E
Arkul, *U.S.S.R.* **37** 57 17N 50 3 E
Arlanc, *France* **20** 45 25N 3 42 E
Arlanza →, *Spain* **22** 42 6N 4 9W
Arlanzón →, *Spain* **22** 42 3N 4 17W
Arlberg Pass, *Austria* **31** 47 9N 10 12 E
Arlee, *U.S.A.* **122** 47 10N 114 4W
Arles, *France* **21** 43 41N 4 40 E
Arlington, *S. Africa* **97** 28 1 S 27 53 E
Arlington, *Oreg., U.S.A.* **122** 45 48N 120 6W
Arlington, *S. Dak., U.S.A.* **120** 44 25N 97 4W
Arlington, *Va., U.S.A.* **114** 38 52N 77 5W
Arlington, *Wash., U.S.A.* **110** 48 11N 122 4W
Arlington Heights, *U.S.A.* **119** 42 5N 87 59W
Arlon, *Belgium* **17** 49 42N 5 49 E
Arlöv, *Sweden* **11** 55 38N 13 5 E
Arly, *Burkina Faso* **91** 11 35N 1 28 E
Armagh, *Canada* **107** 46 41N 70 32W
Armagh, *U.K.* **15** 54 22N 6 40W
Armagh □, *U.K.* **15** 54 18N 6 37W
Armagnac, *France* **20** 43 50N 0 10 E
Armançon →, *France* **19** 47 59N 3 30 E
Armavir, *U.S.S.R.* **39** 45 2N 41 7 E
Armenia, *Colombia* **134** 4 35N 75 45W
Armenian S.S.R. □, *U.S.S.R.* **39** 40 0N 44 0 E
Armentières, *France* **19** 50 40N 2 50 E
Armidale, *Australia* **77** 30 30 S 151 40 E
Armour, *U.S.A.* **120** 43 20N 98 25W
Armstrong, *B.C., Canada* **110** 50 25N 119 10W
Armstrong, *Ont., Canada* **104** 50 18N 89 4W
Armstrong, *U.S.A.* **121** 26 59N 97 48W
Armstrong Cr. →, *Australia* **78** 16 35 S 131 40 E
Armur, *India* **50** 18 48N 78 16 E
Arnaouti, C., *Cyprus* **46** 35 6N 32 17 E
Arnarfjörður, *Iceland* **8** 65 48N 23 40W
Arnaud →, *Canada* **103** 60 0N 70 0W
Arnay-le-Duc, *France* **19** 47 10N 4 27 E
Arnedillo, *Spain* **24** 42 13N 2 14W
Arnedo, *Spain* **24** 42 12N 2 5W
Arnemuiden, *Neths.* **17** 51 30N 3 40 E
Árnes, *Iceland* **8** 66 1N 21 31W
Årnes, *Norway* **10** 60 7N 11 28 E
Arnett, *U.S.A.* **121** 36 9N 99 44W
Arnhem, *Neths.* **16** 51 58N 5 55 E
Arnhem, C., *Australia* **72** 12 20 S 137 30 E
Arnhem B., *Australia* **72** 12 20 S 136 10 E
Arnhem Land, *Australia* **72** 13 10 S 134 30 E
Arno →, *Italy* **26** 43 41N 10 17 E
Arno Bay, *Australia* **73** 33 54 S 136 34 E
Arnold, *Calif., U.S.A.* **124** 38 15N 120 20W
Arnold, *Nebr., U.S.A.* **120** 41 29N 100 10W
Arnoldstein, *Austria* **33** 46 33N 13 43 E
Arnon →, *France* **19** 47 13N 2 1 E
Arnot, *Canada* **111** 55 56N 96 41W
Arnøy, *Norway* **8** 70 9N 20 40 E
Arnprior, *Canada* **109** 45 26N 76 21W
Arnsberg, *W. Germany* **30** 51 25N 8 2 E
Arnstadt, *E. Germany* **30** 50 50N 10 56 E
Arntfield, *Canada* **106** 48 12N 79 15W
Aro →, *Venezuela* **135** 8 1N 64 11W
Aroab, *Namibia* **96** 26 41 S 19 39 E
Aroche, *Spain* **23** 37 56N 6 57W
Aroeiras, *Brazil* **138** 7 31 S 35 41W
Arolsen, *W. Germany* **30** 51 23N 9 1 E
Aron →, *France* **20** 46 50N 3 28 E
Arona, *Italy* **26** 45 45N 8 32 E
Arosa, Ria de, *Spain* **22** 42 28N 8 57W
Arpajon, *France* **19** 48 36N 2 15 E
Arpajon-sur-Cère, *France* **20** 44 53N 2 28 E
Arpino, *Italy* **28** 41 40N 13 35 E
Arque, *Bolivia* **136** 17 48 S 66 23W
Arrabury, *Australia* **73** 26 45 S 141 0 E
Arraias, *Brazil* **139** 12 56 S 46 57W
Arraias →, *Mato Grosso, Brazil* **137** 11 10 S 53 35W
Arraias →, *Pará, Brazil* **138** 7 30 S 49 20W
Arraiolos, *Portugal* **23** 38 44N 7 59W
Arran, *U.K.* **14** 55 34N 5 12W
Arrandale, *Canada* **110** 54 57N 130 0W
Arras, *France* **19** 50 17N 2 46 E
Arrats →, *France* **20** 44 6N 0 52 E
Arreau, *France* **20** 42 54N 0 22 E
Arrecife, *Canary Is.* **25** 28 57N 13 37W
Arrecifes, *Argentina* **140** 34 6 S 60 9W
Arrée, Mts. d', *France* **18** 48 26N 3 55W
Arriaga, *Chiapas, Mexico* **127** 16 15N 93 52W
Arriaga, *San Luis Potosí, Mexico* **126** 21 55N 101 23W
Arrilalah P.O., *Australia* **72** 23 43 S 143 54 E
Arrino, *Australia* **79** 29 30 S 115 40 E
Arrojado →, *Brazil* **139** 13 24 S 44 20W
Arromanches-les-Bains, *France* **18** 49 20N 0 38W
Arronches, *Portugal* **23** 39 8N 7 16W
Arros →, *France* **20** 43 40N 0 2W
Arrou, *France* **18** 48 6N 1 8 E
Arrow, L., *Ireland* **15** 54 3N 8 20W
Arrow Rock Res., *U.S.A.* **122** 43 45N 115 50W
Arrowhead, *Canada* **110** 50 40N 117 55W
Arrowhead, L., *U.S.A.* **125** 34 16N 117 10W
Arrowsmith, Mt., *N.Z.* **81** 43 20 S 170 55 E
Arrowtown, *N.Z.* **81** 44 57 S 168 50 E
Arroyo de la Luz, *Spain* **23** 39 30N 6 38W
Arroyo Grande, *U.S.A.* **125** 35 9N 120 32W
Års, *Denmark* **11** 56 48N 9 30 E
Ars-en-Ré, *France* **20** 46 12N 1 31W
Ars-sur-Moselle, *France* **19** 49 5N 6 4 E
Arsenault L., *Canada* **111** 55 6N 108 32W
Arsi □, *Ethiopia* **89** 7 45N 39 0 E
Arsiero, *Italy* **27** 45 49N 11 22 E
Arsikere, *India* **51** 13 15N 76 15 E
Arsk, *U.S.S.R.* **37** 56 10N 49 50 E
Árta, *Greece* **35** 39 8N 21 2 E
Artá, *Spain* **24** 39 41N 3 21 E
Arteaga, *Mexico* **126** 18 50N 102 20W
Arteijo, *Spain* **22** 43 19N 8 29W
Artem, Ostrov, *U.S.S.R.* **39** 40 28N 50 20 E
Artemovsk, *R.S.F.S.R., U.S.S.R.* **41** 54 45N 93 35 E
Artemovsk, *Ukraine S.S.R., U.S.S.R.* **38** 48 35N 38 0 E
Artemovski, *U.S.S.R.* **39** 47 45N 40 16 E
Artenay, *France* **19** 48 5N 1 50 E
Artern, *E. Germany* **30** 51 22N 11 18 E
Artesa de Segre, *Spain* **24** 41 54N 1 3 E
Artesia = Mosomane, *Botswana* **96** 24 2 S 26 19 E
Artesia, *U.S.A.* **121** 32 55N 104 25W
Artesia Wells, *U.S.A.* **121** 28 17N 99 18W
Artesian, *U.S.A.* **120** 44 2N 97 54W
Arthez-de-Béarn, *France* **20** 43 29N 0 38W
Arthington, *Liberia* **90** 6 35N 10 45W
Arthur, *Canada* **108** 43 50N 80 32W
Arthur, *U.S.A.* **119** 39 43N 88 28W
Arthur →, *Australia* **72** 41 2 S 144 40 E
Arthur Cr. →, *Australia* **72** 22 30 S 136 25 E
Arthur Pt., *Australia* **72** 22 7 S 150 3 E
Arthur's Pass, *N.Z.* **81** 42 54 S 171 35 E
Arthur's Town, *Bahamas* **129** 24 38N 75 42W
Artigas, *Uruguay* **140** 30 20 S 56 30W
Artik, *U.S.S.R.* **39** 40 38N 43 58 E
Artillery L., *Canada* **111** 63 9N 107 52W
Artois, *France* **19** 50 20N 2 30 E
Artsiz, *U.S.S.R.* **38** 46 4N 29 26 E
Artvin, *Turkey* **46** 41 14N 41 44 E
Aru, Kepulauan, *Indonesia* **57** 6 0 S 134 30 E
Aru Meru □, *Tanzania* **92** 3 20 S 36 50 E
Arua, *Uganda* **92** 3 1N 30 58 E
Aruanã, *Brazil* **139** 14 54 S 51 10W
Aruba, *Neth. Ant.* **129** 12 30N 70 0W
Arucas, *Canary Is.* **25** 28 7N 15 32W
Arudy, *France* **20** 43 7N 0 28W
Arumã, *Brazil* **135** 4 44 S 62 8W
Arumpo, *Australia* **74** 33 48 S 142 55 E
Arun →, *Nepal* **49** 26 55N 87 10 E
Arunachal Pradesh □, *India* **52** 28 0N 95 0 E
Arundel, *Canada* **106** 45 58N 74 37W
Aruppukkottai, *India* **51** 9 31N 78 8 E
Arusha, *Tanzania* **92** 3 20 S 36 40 E
Arusha □, *Tanzania* **92** 4 0 S 36 30 E
Arusha Chini, *Tanzania* **92** 3 32 S 37 20 E
Aruvi →, *Sri Lanka* **51** 8 48N 79 53 E
Aruwimi →, *Zaïre* **92** 1 13N 23 36 E
Arvada, *U.S.A.* **122** 44 43N 106 6W
Arvakalu, *Sri Lanka* **51** 8 20N 79 58 E
Arvayheer, *Mongolia* **62** 46 15N 102 48 E
Arve →, *France* **21** 46 11N 6 8 E
Arvi, *India* **50** 20 59N 78 16 E
Arvida, *Canada* **107** 48 25N 71 14W
Arvidsjaur, *Sweden* **8** 65 35N 19 10 E
Arvika, *Sweden* **10** 59 40N 12 36 E
Arvin, *U.S.A.* **125** 35 12N 118 50W
Arxan, *China* **62** 47 11N 119 57 E
Arys, *U.S.S.R.* **40** 42 26N 68 48 E
Arzachena, *Italy* **28** 41 5N 9 27 E
Arzamas, *U.S.S.R.* **37** 55 27N 43 55 E
Arzew, *Algeria* **85** 35 50N 0 23W
Arzgir, *U.S.S.R.* **39** 45 18N 44 23 E
Arzignano, *Italy* **27** 45 30N 11 20 E
As, *Belgium* **17** 51 1N 5 35 E
'As Saffānīyah, *Si. Arabia* **46** 28 5N 48 50 E
Aş Şāfī, *Jordan* **44** 31 2N 35 28 E
As Salt, *Jordan* **44** 32 2N 35 43 E
As Samāwah, *Iraq* **46** 31 15N 45 15 E
As Samū', *Jordan* **44** 31 24N 35 4 E
As Sanamayn, *Syria* **44** 33 3N 36 10 E
As Sulaymānīyah, *Iraq* **46** 35 35N 45 29 E
As Sulaymānīyah, *Si. Arabia* **46** 24 9N 47 18 E
As Sulṭan, *Libya* **86** 31 4N 17 8 E
As Summān, *Si. Arabia* **46** 25 0N 47 0 E
As Sūq, *Si. Arabia* **46** 21 58N 42 3 E
As Suwaydā', *Syria* **46** 32 40N 36 30 E
As Suwayh, *Oman* **47** 22 10N 59 33 E
As Ṣuwayrah, *Iraq* **46** 32 55N 45 0 E
Asab, *Namibia* **96** 25 30 S 18 0 E
Asaba, *Nigeria* **91** 6 12N 6 38 E
Asafo, *Ghana* **90** 6 20N 2 40W
Asahi, *Japan* **65** 35 43N 140 39 E
Asahi-Gawa →, *Japan* **64** 34 36N 133 58 E
Asahigawa, *Japan* **63** 43 46N 142 22 E
Asale, L., *Ethiopia* **89** 14 0N 40 20 E
Asama-Yama, *Japan* **65** 36 24N 138 31 E
Asamankese, *Ghana* **91** 5 50N 0 40W
Asansol, *India* **49** 23 40N 87 1 E
Åsarna, *Sweden* **10** 62 39N 14 22 E
Asbe Teferi, *Ethiopia* **89** 9 4N 40 49 E
Asbesberge, *S. Africa* **96** 29 0 S 23 0 E
Asbestos, *Canada* **105** 45 47N 71 58W
Asbury Park, *U.S.A.* **117** 40 15N 74 1W
Ascensión, *Mexico* **126** 31 6N 107 59W
Ascensión, B. de la, *Mexico* **127** 19 50N 87 20W
Ascension I., *Atl. Oc.* **4** 8 0 S 14 15W
Aschaffenburg, *W. Germany* **31** 49 58N 9 8 E
Aschendorf, *W. Germany* **30** 53 2N 7 22 E
Aschersleben, *E. Germany* **30** 51 45N 11 28 E
Asciano, *Italy* **27** 43 14N 11 32 E
Áscoli Piceno, *Italy* **27** 42 51N 13 34 E
Áscoli Satriano, *Italy* **29** 41 11N 15 32 E
Ascope, *Peru* **136** 7 46 S 79 8W
Ascotán, *Chile* **140** 21 45 S 68 17W
Aseb, *Ethiopia* **89** 13 0N 42 40 E
Åseda, *Sweden* **11** 57 10N 15 20 E
Asedjrad, *Algeria* **85** 24 51N 1 29 E
Asela, *Ethiopia* **89** 8 0N 39 0 E

Autazes

Autazes, *Brazil* **135** 3 35 S 59 8W
Autelbas, *Belgium* **17** 49 39N 5 52 E
Auterive, *France* **20** 43 21N 1 29 E
Authie →, *France* **19** 50 22N 1 38 E
Authon-du-Perche, *France* **18** 48 12N 0 54 E
Autlán, *Mexico* **126** 19 40N 104 30W
Autun, *France* **19** 46 58N 4 17 E
Auvelais, *Belgium* **17** 50 27N 4 38 E
Auvergne, *Australia* **78** 15 39 S 130 1 E
Auvergne, *France* **20** 45 20N 3 15 E
Auvergne, Mts. d', *France* **20** 45 20N 2 55 E
Auvézére →, *France* **20** 45 12N 0 50 E
Auxerre, *France* **19** 47 48N 3 32 E
Auxi-le-Château, *France* **19** 50 15N 2 8 E
Auxonne, *France* **19** 47 10N 5 20 E
Auxvasse, *U.S.A.* **118** 39 1N 91 54W
Auzances, *France* **20** 46 2N 2 30 E
Auzat-sur-Allier, *France* **20** 45 27N 3 19 E
Ava, *U.S.A.* **118** 37 53N 89 30W
Avallon, *France* **19** 47 30N 3 53 E
Avalon, *U.S.A.* **125** 33 21N 118 20W
Avalon Pen., *Canada* **105** 47 30N 53 20W
Avanigadda, *India* **51** 16 0N 80 56 E
Avaré, *Brazil* **141** 23 4 S 48 58W
Ávas, *Greece* **35** 40 57N 25 56 E
Avawatz Mts., *U.S.A.* **125** 35 30N 116 20W
Aveiro, *Brazil* **135** 3 10 S 55 5W
Aveiro, *Portugal* **22** 40 37N 8 38W
Aveiro □, *Portugal* **22** 40 40N 8 35W
Āvej, *Iran* **46** 35 40N 49 15 E
Avelgem, *Belgium* **17** 50 47N 3 27 E
Avellaneda, *Argentina* **140** 34 50 S 58 10W
Avellino, *Italy* **29** 40 54N 14 46 E
Avenal, *U.S.A.* **124** 36 0N 120 8W
Avenel, *Australia* **74** 36 53 S 145 15 E
Averøya, *Norway* **10** 63 0N 7 35 E
Aversa, *Italy* **29** 40 58N 14 11 E
Avery, *U.S.A.* **122** 47 22N 115 56W
Aves, I. de, *W. Indies* **129** 15 45N 63 55W
Aves, Is. de, *Venezuela* **129** 12 0N 67 30W
Avesnes-sur-Helpe, *France* **19** 50 8N 3 55 E
Avesta, *Sweden* **10** 60 9N 16 10 E
Aveyron □, *France* **20** 44 22N 2 45 E
Aveyron →, *France* **20** 44 5N 1 16 E
Avezzano, *Italy* **27** 42 2N 13 24 E
Aviá Terai, *Argentina* **140** 26 45 S 60 50W
Aviano, *Italy* **27** 46 3N 12 35 E
Avigliana, *Italy* **26** 45 7N 7 13 E
Avigliano, *Italy* **29** 40 44N 15 41 E
Avignon, *France* **21** 43 57N 4 50 E
Ávila, *Spain* **22** 40 39N 4 43W
Ávila □, *Spain* **22** 40 30N 5 0W
Ávila, Sierra de, *Spain* **22** 40 40N 5 0W
Avila Beach, *U.S.A.* **125** 35 11N 120 44W
Avilés, *Spain* **22** 43 35N 5 57W
Avisio →, *Italy* **27** 46 7N 11 5 E
Aviston, *U.S.A.* **118** 38 36N 89 36W
Aviz, *Portugal* **23** 39 4N 7 53W
Avize, *France* **19** 48 59N 4 0 E
Avoca, *Australia* **74** 37 5 S 143 26 E
Avoca, *Ireland* **15** 52 52N 6 13W
Avoca, *U.S.A.* **116** 42 24N 77 25W
Avoca →, *Australia* **74** 35 40 S 143 43 E
Avola, *Canada* **110** 51 45N 119 19W
Avola, *Italy* **29** 36 56N 15 7 E
Avon, *Ill., U.S.A.* **118** 40 40N 90 26W
Avon, *N.Y., U.S.A.* **116** 42 55N 77 42W
Avon, *S. Dak., U.S.A.* **120** 43 0N 98 3W
Avon □, *U.K.* **13** 51 30N 2 40W
Avon →, *Australia* **79** 31 40 S 116 7 E
Avon →, *Avon, U.K.* **13** 51 30N 2 43W
Avon →, *Hants., U.K.* **13** 50 44N 1 45W
Avon →, *Warwick, U.K.* **13** 52 0N 2 9W
Avondale, *Zambia* **93** 17 43 S 30 58 E
Avonlea, *Canada* **111** 50 0N 105 0W
Avonmore, *Canada* **106** 45 10N 74 58W
Avonmouth, *U.K.* **13** 51 30N 2 42W
Avranches, *France* **18** 48 40N 1 20W
Avre →, *France* **18** 48 47N 1 22 E
Avu Avu, *Solomon Is.* **68** 9 50 S 160 22 E
Awag el Baqar, *Sudan* **89** 10 10N 33 10 E
Awaji, *Japan* **65** 34 32N 135 1 E
Awaji-Shima, *Japan* **64** 34 30N 134 50 E
'Awālī, *Bahrain* **47** 26 0N 50 30 E
Awantipur, *India* **49** 33 55N 75 3 E
Awanui, *N.Z.* **80** 35 4 S 173 17 E
Awarja →, *India* **50** 17 5N 76 15 E
'Awartā, *Jordan* **44** 32 10N 35 17 E
Awarua Pt., *N.Z.* **81** 44 15 S 168 5 E
Awasa, L., *Ethiopia* **89** 7 0N 38 30 E
Awash, *Ethiopia* **89** 9 1N 40 10 E
Awash →, *Ethiopia* **89** 11 45N 41 5 E
Awaso, *Ghana* **90** 6 15N 2 22W
Awatere →, *N.Z.* **81** 41 37 S 174 10 E
Awbārī, *Libya* **86** 26 46N 12 57 E
Awbārī □, *Libya* **86** 26 35N 12 46 E
Awe, L., *U.K.* **14** 56 15N 5 15W
Aweil, *Sudan* **89** 8 42N 27 20 E
Awgu, *Nigeria* **91** 6 4N 7 24 E
Awjilah, *Libya* **86** 29 8N 21 7 E
Aworro, *Papua N. G.* **69** 7 43 S 143 11 E
Ax-les-Thermes, *France* **20** 42 44N 1 50 E
Axarfjörður, *Iceland* **8** 66 15N 16 45W
Axedale, *Australia* **74** 36 47 S 144 30 E
Axel, *Neths.* **17** 51 16N 3 55 E
Axel Heiberg I., *Canada* **144** 80 0N 90 0W
Axim, *Ghana* **90** 4 51N 2 15W
Axinim, *Brazil* **135** 4 2 S 59 22W
Axintele, *Romania* **34** 44 37N 26 47 E
Axioma, *Brazil* **137** 6 45 S 64 31W
Axiós →, *Greece* **35** 40 57N 22 35 E
Axmarsbruk, *Sweden* **10** 61 3N 17 10 E
Axminster, *U.K.* **13** 50 47N 3 1W
Axstedt, *W. Germany* **30** 53 26N 8 43 E
Axvall, *Sweden* **11** 58 23N 13 34 E
Aÿ, *France* **19** 49 3N 4 0 E
Ayaantang, *Eq. Guin.* **94** 1 58N 10 24 E
Ayabaca, *Peru* **136** 4 40 S 79 53W
Ayabe, *Japan* **65** 35 20N 135 20 E
Ayacucho, *Argentina* **140** 37 5 S 58 20W
Ayacucho, *Peru* **136** 13 0 S 74 0W
Ayaguz, *U.S.S.R.* **40** 48 10N 80 0 E
Ayakudi, *India* **51** 10 28N 77 56 E
Ayamonte, *Spain* **23** 37 12N 7 24W
Ayan, *U.S.S.R.* **41** 56 30N 138 16 E
Ayancık, *Turkey* **38** 41 57N 34 18 E
Ayapel, *Colombia* **134** 8 19N 75 9W
Ayas, *Turkey* **38** 40 10N 32 14 E
Ayaviri, *Peru* **136** 14 50 S 70 35W
Āybak, *Afghan.* **47** 36 15N 68 5 E
Aye, *Belgium* **17** 50 14N 5 18 E
Ayenngré, *Togo* **91** 8 40N 1 1 E
Ayer's Cliff, *Canada* **117** 45 10N 72 3W
Ayers Rock, *Australia* **79** 25 23 S 131 5 E
Ayiá, *Greece* **35** 39 43N 22 45 E
Ayía Marína, *Greece* **35** 37 11N 26 48 E
Ayía Paraskeví, *Greece* **35** 39 14N 26 16 E
Ayía Rouméli, *Greece* **35** 35 14N 23 58 E
Áyios Andréas, *Greece* **35** 37 21N 22 45 E
Ayíos Evstrátios, *Greece* **35** 39 34N 24 58 E
Áyios Ioannis, Ákra, *Greece* **35** 35 20N 25 40 E
Áyios Kirikos, *Greece* **35** 37 34N 26 17 E
Áyios Mírono, *Greece* **35** 35 15N 25 1 E
Áyios Nikólaos, *Greece* **35** 35 11N 25 41 E
Aykathonisi, *Greece* **35** 37 28N 27 0 E
Aylen L., *Canada* **109** 45 37N 77 51W
Aylesbury, *U.K.* **13** 51 48N 0 49W
Aylmer, *Ont., Canada* **108** 42 46N 80 59W
Aylmer, *Qué., Canada* **106** 45 24N 75 51W
Aylmer L., *Canada* **102** 64 0N 110 8W
'Ayn al Ghazālah, *Libya* **86** 32 10N 23 20 E
'Ayn 'Arīk, *Jordan* **44** 31 54N 35 8 E
Ayn Dār, *Si. Arabia* **46** 25 55N 49 10 E
Ayn Zālah, *Iraq* **46** 36 45N 42 35 E
'Ayn Zaqqūt, *Libya* **86** 29 0N 19 30 E
Ayna, *Spain* **25** 38 34N 2 3W
Ayolas, *Paraguay* **140** 27 10 S 56 59W
Ayom, *Sudan* **89** 7 49N 28 23 E
Ayon, Ostrov, *U.S.S.R.* **41** 69 50N 169 0 E
Ayora, *Spain* **25** 39 3N 1 3W
Ayr, *Australia* **72** 19 35 S 147 25 E
Ayr, *Canada* **108** 43 17N 80 27W
Ayr, *U.K.* **14** 55 28N 4 37W
Ayr →, *U.K.* **14** 55 29N 4 40W
Ayre, Pt. of, *U.K.* **12** 54 27N 4 21W
Aysha, *Ethiopia* **89** 10 50N 42 23 E
Aytos, *Bulgaria* **34** 42 42N 27 16 E
Ayu, Kepulauan, *Indonesia* **57** 0 35N 131 5 E
Ayutla, *Guatemala* **128** 14 40N 92 10W
Ayutla, *Mexico* **127** 16 58N 99 17W
Ayvalık, *Turkey* **46** 39 20N 26 46 E
Aywaille, *Belgium* **17** 50 28N 5 40 E
Az Ẓahrān, *Si. Arabia* **46** 26 10N 50 7 E
Az Zarqā, *Jordan* **44** 32 5N 36 4 E
Az Zāwiyah, *Libya* **86** 32 52N 12 56 E
Az-Zilfī, *Si. Arabia* **46** 26 12N 44 52 E
Az Zubayr, *Iraq* **46** 30 20N 47 50 E
Azambuja, *Portugal* **23** 39 4N 8 51W
Azamgarh, *India* **49** 26 5N 83 13 E
Azangaro, *Peru* **136** 14 55 S 70 13W
Azaouak, Vallée de l', *Mali* **91** 15 50N 3 20 E
Āzarbāyjān-e Gharbī □, *Iran* **46** 37 0N 44 30 E
Āzarbāyjān-e Sharqī □, *Iran* **46** 37 20N 47 0 E
Azare, *Nigeria* **91** 11 55N 10 10 E
Azay-le-Rideau, *France* **18** 47 16N 0 30 E
Azazga, *Algeria* **85** 36 48N 4 22 E
Azbine = Aïr, *Niger* **91** 18 30N 8 0 E
Azefal, *Mauritania* **84** 21 0N 14 45W
Azeffoun, *Algeria* **85** 36 51N 4 26 E
Azemmour, *Morocco* **85** 33 20N 9 20W
Azerbaijan S.S.R. □, *U.S.S.R.* **39** 40 20N 48 0 E
Azezo, *Ethiopia* **89** 12 28N 37 15 E
Azilda, *Canada* **108** 46 33N 81 6W
Azimganj, *India* **49** 24 14N 88 16 E
Aznalcóllar, *Spain* **23** 37 32N 6 17W
Azogues, *Ecuador* **134** 2 35 S 78 0W
Azor, *Israel* **44** 32 2N 34 48 E
Azores, *Atl. Oc.* **4** 38 44N 29 0W
Azov, *U.S.S.R.* **39** 47 3N 39 25 E
Azov Sea = Azovskoye More, *U.S.S.R.* **40** 46 0N 36 30 E
Azovskoye More, *U.S.S.R.* **40** 46 0N 36 30 E
Azovy, *U.S.S.R.* **40** 64 55N 64 35 E
Azpeitia, *Spain* **24** 43 12N 2 19W
Azrou, *Morocco* **84** 33 28N 5 19W
Aztec, *U.S.A.* **123** 36 54N 108 0W
Azúa de Compostela, *Dom. Rep.* **129** 18 25N 70 44W
Azuaga, *Spain* **23** 38 16N 5 39W
Azuara, *Spain* **24** 41 15N 0 53W
Azuay □, *Ecuador* **134** 2 55 S 79 0W
Azuer →, *Spain* **23** 39 8N 3 36W
Azuero, Pen. de, *Panama* **128** 7 30N 80 30W
Azul, *Argentina* **140** 36 42 S 59 43W
Azul, Serra, *Brazil* **137** 14 50 S 54 50W
Azurduy, *Bolivia* **137** 19 59 S 64 29W
Azusa, *U.S.A.* **125** 34 8N 117 52W
Azzaba, *Algeria* **85** 36 48N 7 6 E
Azzano Décimo, *Italy* **27** 45 53N 12 46 E

B

Ba Don, *Vietnam* **54** 17 45N 106 26 E
Ba Dong, *Vietnam* **55** 9 40N 106 33 E
Ba Ngoi = Cam Lam, *Vietnam* **55** 11 54N 109 10 E
Ba Ria, *Vietnam* **55** 10 30N 107 10 E
Ba Tri, *Vietnam* **55** 10 2N 106 36 E
Ba Xian, *China* **60** 39 8N 116 22 E
Baa, *Indonesia* **57** 10 50 S 123 0 E
Baaba, I., *N. Cal.* **68** 20 3 S 164 59 E
Baamonde, *Spain* **22** 43 7N 7 44W
Baan Baa, *Australia* **77** 30 36 S 149 56 E
Baarle Nassau, *Belgium* **17** 51 27N 4 56 E
Baarlo, *Neths.* **17** 51 20N 6 6 E
Baarn, *Neths.* **16** 52 12N 5 17 E
Bab el Mandeb, *Red Sea* **45** 12 35N 43 25 E
Baba dag, *U.S.S.R.* **39** 41 0N 48 19 E
Babaçulândia, *Brazil* **138** 7 13 S 47 46W
Babadag, *Romania* **34** 44 53N 28 44 E
Babahoyo, *Ecuador* **134** 1 40 S 79 30W
Babakin, *Australia* **79** 32 7 S 118 1 E
Babana, *Nigeria* **91** 10 31N 3 46 E
Babar, *Algeria* **85** 35 10N 7 6 E
Babar, *Indonesia* **57** 8 0 S 129 30 E
Babar, *Pakistan* **48** 31 7N 69 32 E
Babarkach, *Pakistan* **48** 29 45N 68 0 E
Babayevo, *U.S.S.R.* **37** 59 24N 35 55 E
Babb, *U.S.A.* **122** 48 56N 113 27W
Babenhausen, *W. Germany* **31** 49 57N 8 56 E
Babi Besar, P., *Malaysia* **55** 2 25N 103 59 E
Babian Jiang →, *China* **58** 22 55N 101 47 E
Babile, *Ethiopia* **89** 9 16N 42 11 E
Babinda, *Australia* **72** 17 20 S 145 56 E
Babine, *Canada* **110** 55 22N 126 37W
Babine →, *Canada* **110** 55 45N 127 44W
Babine L., *Canada* **110** 54 48N 126 0W
Babo, *Indonesia* **57** 2 30 S 133 30 E
Bābol, *Iran* **47** 36 40N 52 50 E
Bābol Sar, *Iran* **47** 36 45N 52 45 E
Baboua, *C.A.R.* **94** 5 49N 14 58 E
Babura, *Nigeria* **91** 12 51N 8 59 E
Babusar Pass, *Pakistan* **49** 35 12N 73 59 E
Babušnica, *Yugoslavia* **33** 43 7N 22 27 E
Babuyan Chan., *Phil.* **57** 18 40N 121 30 E
Babylon, *Iraq* **46** 32 40N 44 30 E
Bac Can, *Vietnam* **54** 22 8N 105 49 E
Bac Giang, *Vietnam* **54** 21 16N 106 11 E
Bac Ninh, *Vietnam* **54** 21 13N 106 4 E
Bac Phan, *Vietnam* **54** 22 0N 105 0 E
Bac Quang, *Vietnam* **54** 22 30N 104 48 E
Bacabal, *Brazil* **138** 4 15 S 44 45W
Bacajá →, *Brazil* **135** 3 25 S 51 50W
Bacalar, *Mexico* **127** 18 50N 87 27W
Bacan, *Indonesia* **57** 8 27 S 126 27 E
Bacan, Kepulauan, *Indonesia* **57** 0 35 S 127 30 E
Bacan, Pulau, *Indonesia* **57** 0 50 S 127 30 E
Bacarra, *Phil.* **57** 18 15N 120 37 E
Bacău, *Romania* **34** 46 35N 26 55 E
Baccarat, *France* **19** 48 28N 6 42 E
Bacchus Marsh, *Australia* **74** 37 43 S 144 27 E
Bacerac, *Mexico* **126** 30 18N 108 50W
Băceşti, *Romania* **34** 46 50N 27 11 E
Bach Long Vi, Dao, *Vietnam* **54** 20 10N 107 40 E
Bachaquero, *Venezuela* **134** 9 56N 71 8W
Bacharach, *W. Germany* **31** 50 3N 7 46 E
Bachelina, *U.S.S.R.* **40** 57 45N 67 20 E
Bachuma, *Ethiopia* **89** 6 48N 35 53 E
Bačina, *Yugoslavia* **33** 43 42N 21 23 E
Back →, *Canada* **102** 65 10N 104 0W
Bačka Palanka, *Yugoslavia* **33** 45 17N 19 27 E
Bačka Topola, *Yugoslavia* **33** 45 49N 19 39 E
Bäckefors, *Sweden* **11** 58 48N 12 9 E
Backnang, *W. Germany* **31** 48 57N 9 26 E
Backstairs Passage, *Australia* **73** 35 40 S 138 5 E
Bacolod, *Phil.* **57** 10 40N 122 57 E
Bacqueville-en-Caux, *France* **18** 49 47N 1 0 E
Bácsalmás, *Hungary* **33** 46 8N 19 17 E
Bacuk, *Malaysia* **55** 6 4N 102 25 E
Bad →, *U.S.A.* **120** 44 22N 100 22W
Bad Axe, *U.S.A.* **116** 43 48N 82 59W
Bad Bergzabern, *W. Germany* **31** 49 6N 8 0 E
Bad Bramstedt, *W. Germany* **30** 53 56N 9 53 E
Bad Doberan, *E. Germany* **30** 54 6N 11 55 E
Bad Driburg, *W. Germany* **30** 51 44N 9 0 E
Bad Ems, *W. Germany* **31** 50 22N 7 44 E
Bad Frankenhausen, *E. Germany* **30** 51 21N 11 3 E
Bad Freienwalde, *E. Germany* **30** 52 47N 14 3 E
Bad Godesberg, *W. Germany* **30** 50 41N 7 4 E
Bad Hersfeld, *W. Germany* **30** 50 52N 9 42 E
Bad Hofgastein, *Austria* **33** 47 17N 13 6 E
Bad Homburg, *W. Germany* **31** 50 17N 8 33 E
Bad Honnef, *W. Germany* **30** 50 39N 7 13 E
Bad Ischl, *Austria* **33** 47 44N 13 38 E
Bad Kissingen, *W. Germany* **31** 50 11N 10 5 E
Bad Kreuznach, *W. Germany* **31** 49 47N 7 47 E
Bad Lands, *U.S.A.* **120** 43 40N 102 10W
Bad Langensalza, *E. Germany* **30** 51 6N 10 40 E
Bad Lauterberg, *W. Germany* **30** 51 38N 10 29 E
Bad Lippspringe, *W. Germany* **30** 51 47N 8 46 E
Bad Mergentheim, *W. Germany* **31** 49 29N 9 47 E
Bad Münstereifel, *W. Germany* **30** 50 33N 6 46 E
Bad Muskau, *E. Germany* **30** 51 33N 14 43 E
Bad Nauheim, *W. Germany* **31** 50 24N 8 45 E
Bad Oeynhausen, *W. Germany* **30** 52 16N 8 45 E
Bad Oldesloe, *W. Germany* **30** 53 48N 10 22 E
Bad Orb, *W. Germany* **31** 50 16N 9 21 E
Bad Pyrmont, *W. Germany* **30** 51 59N 9 15 E
Bad Reichenhall, *W. Germany* **31** 47 44N 12 53 E
Bad St.-Peter, *W. Germany* **30** 54 23N 8 32 E
Bad Salzuflen, *W. Germany* **30** 52 8N 8 44 E
Bad Segeberg, *W. Germany* **30** 53 58N 10 16 E
Bad Tölz, *W. Germany* **31** 47 43N 11 34 E
Bad Waldsee, *W. Germany* **31** 47 56N 9 46 E
Bad Wildungen, *W. Germany* **30** 51 7N 9 10 E
Bad Wimpfen, *W. Germany* **31** 49 12N 9 10 E
Bad Windsheim, *W. Germany* **31** 49 29N 10 25 E
Badagara, *India* **51** 11 35N 75 40 E
Badagri, *Nigeria* **91** 6 25N 2 55 E
Badajós, L., *Brazil* **135** 3 15 S 62 50W
Badajoz, *Spain* **23** 38 50N 6 59W
Badajoz □, *Spain* **23** 38 40N 6 30W
Badakhshān □, *Afghan.* **47** 36 30N 71 0 E
Badalona, *Spain* **24** 41 26N 2 15 E
Badalzai, *Afghan.* **48** 29 50N 65 35 E
Badampahar, *India* **50** 22 10N 86 10 E
Badanah, *Si. Arabia* **46** 30 58N 41 30 E
Badarinath, *India* **49** 30 45N 79 30 E
Badas, *Brunei* **56** 4 33N 114 25 E
Badas, Kepulauan, *Indonesia* **56** 0 45N 107 5 E
Baddaginnie, *Australia* **74** 36 34 S 145 52 E
Baddo →, *Pakistan* **47** 28 0N 64 20 E
Bade, *Indonesia* **57** 7 10 S 139 35 E
Baden, *Austria* **33** 48 1N 16 13 E
Baden, *Switz.* **31** 47 28N 8 18 E
Baden-Baden, *W. Germany* **31** 48 45N 8 15 E
Baden-Württemberg □, *W. Germany* **31** 48 40N 9 0 E
Badger, *Canada* **105** 49 0N 56 4W
Badger, *U.S.A.* **124** 36 38N 119 1W
Bādghīsāt □, *Afghan.* **47** 35 0N 63 0 E
Badgom, *India* **49** 34 1N 74 45 E
Badhoevedorp, *Neths.* **16** 52 20N 4 47 E
Badia Polèsine, *Italy* **27** 45 6N 11 30 E
Badin, *Pakistan* **48** 24 38N 68 54 E
Badnera, *India* **50** 20 48N 77 44 E
Badogo, *Mali* **90** 11 2N 8 13W
Badong, *China* **59** 31 1N 110 23 E
Baduen, *Somali Rep.* **98** 7 15N 47 40 E
Badulla, *Sri Lanka* **51** 7 1N 81 7 E
Badupi, *Burma* **52** 21 36N 93 27 E
Baena, *Spain* **23** 37 37N 4 20W
Baerami Creek, *Australia* **76** 32 27 S 150 27 E
Baexem, *Neths.* **17** 51 13N 5 53 E
Baeza, *Ecuador* **134** 0 25 S 77 53W
Baeza, *Spain* **25** 37 57N 3 25W
Bafang, *Cameroon* **91** 5 9N 10 11 E
Bafatá, *Guinea-Biss.* **90** 12 8N 14 40W
Baffin B., *Canada* **144** 72 0N 64 0W
Baffin I., *Canada* **103** 68 0N 75 0W
Bafia, *Cameroon* **91** 4 40N 11 10 E
Bafilo, *Togo* **91** 9 22N 1 22 E
Bafing →, *Mali* **90** 13 49N 10 50W
Baflo, *Neths.* **16** 53 22N 6 31 E
Bafoulabé, *Mali* **90** 13 50N 10 55W
Bafoussam, *Cameroon* **91** 5 28N 10 25 E
Bāfq, *Iran* **47** 31 40N 55 25 E

Ban Sangkha

Bafra, *Turkey* **38** 41 34N 35 54 E
Bafra, C., *Turkey* **38** 41 44N 35 58 E
Bāft, *Iran* **47** 29 15N 56 38 E
Bafut, *Cameroon* **91** 6 6N 10 2 E
Bafwasende, *Zaïre* **92** 1 3N 27 5 E
Bagalkot, *India* **51** 16 10N 75 40 E
Bagamoyo, *Tanzania* **92** 6 28 S 38 55 E
Bagamoyo □, *Tanzania* **92** 6 20 S 38 30 E
Bagan Datoh, *Malaysia* **55** 3 59N 100 47 E
Bagan Serai, *Malaysia* **55** 5 1N 100 32 E
Baganga, *Phil.* **57** 7 34N 126 33 E
Bagani, *Namibia* **96** 18 7 S 21 41 E
Bagansiapiapi, *Indonesia* **56** 2 12N 100 50 E
Bagasra, *India* **48** 21 30N 71 0 E
Bagata, *Zaïre* **94** 3 44 S 17 57 E
Bagawi, *Sudan* **89** 12 20N 34 18 E
Bagdad, *U.S.A.* **125** 34 35N 115 53W
Bagdarin, *U.S.S.R.* **41** 54 26N 113 36 E
Bagé, *Brazil* **141** 31 20 S 54 15W
Bagenalstown = Muine Bheag, *Ireland* **15** 52 42N 6 57W
Baggs, *U.S.A.* **122** 41 8N 107 46W
Bagh, *Pakistan* **49** 33 59N 73 45 E
Baghdād, *Iraq* **46** 33 20N 44 30 E
Bagherhat, *Bangla.* **52** 22 40N 89 47 E
Bagheria, *Italy* **28** 38 5N 13 30 E
Baghlān, *Afghan.* **47** 36 12N 69 0 E
Baghlān □, *Afghan.* **47** 36 0N 68 30 E
Bagley, *U.S.A.* **120** 47 30N 95 22W
Bagnacavallo, *Italy* **27** 44 25N 11 58 E
Bagnara Cálabra, *Italy* **29** 38 16N 15 49 E
Bagnell Dam, *U.S.A.* **118** 38 14N 92 36W
Bagnères-de-Bigorre, *France* **20** 43 5N 0 9 E
Bagnères-de-Luchon, *France* **20** 42 47N 0 38 E
Bagni di Lucca, *Italy* **26** 44 1N 10 37 E
Bagno di Romagna, *Italy* **27** 43 50N 11 59 E
Bagnoles-de-l'Orne, *France* **18** 48 32N 0 25W
Bagnoli di Sopra, *Italy* **27** 45 13N 11 55 E
Bagnolo Mella, *Italy* **26** 45 27N 10 14 E
Bagnols-sur-Cèze, *France* **21** 44 10N 4 36 E
Bagnorégio, *Italy* **27** 42 38N 12 7 E
Bagolino, *Italy* **26** 45 49N 10 28 E
Bagotville, *Canada* **107** 48 22N 70 54W
Bagua, *Peru* **136** 5 35 S 78 22W
Baguio, *Phil.* **57** 16 26N 120 34 E
Bahabón de Esgueva, *Spain* **24** 41 52N 3 43W
Bahadurabad Ghat, *Bangla.* **52** 25 11N 89 44 E
Bahadurgarh, *India* **48** 28 40N 76 57 E
Bahama, Canal Viejo de, *W. Indies* **128** 22 10N 77 30W
Bahamas ■, *N. Amer.* **129** 24 0N 75 0W
Baharampur, *India* **49** 24 2N 88 27 E
Bahariya, El Wâhât al, *Egypt* **88** 28 0N 28 50 E
Bahau, *Malaysia* **55** 2 48N 102 26 E
Bahawalnagar, *Pakistan* **48** 30 0N 73 15 E
Bahawalpur, *Pakistan* **48** 29 24N 71 40 E
Baheri, *India* **49** 28 45N 79 34 E
Bahi, *Tanzania* **92** 5 58 S 35 21 E
Bahi Swamp, *Tanzania* **92** 6 10 S 35 0 E
Bahía = Salvador, *Brazil* **139** 13 0 S 38 30W
Bahía □, *Brazil* **139** 12 0 S 42 0W
Bahía, Is. de la, *Honduras* **128** 16 45N 86 15W
Bahía Blanca, *Argentina* **140** 38 35 S 62 13W
Bahía de Caráquez, *Ecuador* **134** 0 40 S 80 27W
Bahía Honda, *Cuba* **128** 22 54N 83 10W
Bahía Laura, *Argentina* **142** 48 10 S 66 30W
Bahía Negra, *Paraguay* **137** 20 5 S 58 5W
Bahir Dar, *Ethiopia* **89** 11 37N 37 10 E
Bahmer, *Algeria* **85** 27 32N 0 10W
Bahönye, *Hungary* **33** 46 25N 17 28 E
Bahr Aouk →, *C.A.R.* **94** 8 40N 19 0 E
Bahr el Ahmar □, *Sudan* **88** 20 0N 35 0 E
Bahr el Ghazâl □, *Sudan* **89** 7 0N 28 0 E
Bahr Salamat →, *Chad* **87** 9 20N 18 0 E
Bahr Yûsef →, *Egypt* **88** 28 25N 30 35 E
Bahra el Burullus, *Egypt* **88** 31 28N 30 48 E
Bahraich, *India* **49** 27 38N 81 37 E
Bahrain ■, *Asia* **47** 26 0N 50 35 E
Bahror, *India* **48** 27 51N 76 20 E
Bai, *Mali* **90** 13 35N 3 28W
Bai Bung, Mui, *Vietnam* **55** 8 38N 104 44 E
Bai Duc, *Vietnam* **54** 18 3N 105 49 E
Bai Thuong, *Vietnam* **54** 19 54N 105 23 E
Baia Farta, *Angola* **95** 12 40 S 13 11 E
Baia Mare, *Romania* **34** 47 40N 23 35 E
Baia-Sprie, *Romania* **34** 47 41N 23 43 E
Baião, *Brazil* **138** 2 40 S 49 40W
Baïbokoum, *Chad* **87** 7 46N 15 43 E
Baicheng, *China* **61** 45 38N 122 42 E
Baidoa, *Somali Rep.* **98** 3 8N 43 30 E
Baie Comeau, *Canada* **105** 49 12N 68 10W
Baie-du-Poste, *Canada* **107** 50 24N 73 56W
Baie-St-Paul, *Canada* **107** 47 28N 70 32W
Baie-Ste-Catherine, *Canada* **107** 48 6N 69 44W
Baie Trinité, *Canada* **105** 49 25N 67 20W
Baie Verte, *Canada* **105** 49 55N 56 12W
Baieville, *Canada* **107** 46 8N 72 43W
Baignes-Ste.-Radegonde, *France* **20** 45 23N 0 25W
Baigneux-les-Juifs, *France* **19** 47 31N 4 39 E
Baihe, *China* **60** 32 50N 110 5 E
Baihe, *Taiwan* **59** 23 24N 120 24 E
Ba'ījī, *Iraq* **46** 35 0N 43 30 E
Baikal, L. = Baykal, Oz., *U.S.S.R.* **41** 53 0N 108 0 E
Bailadila, Mt., *India* **50** 18 43N 81 15 E
Baile Atha Cliath = Dublin, *Ireland* **15** 53 20N 6 18W
Bailei, *Ethiopia* **89** 6 44N 40 18 E
Bailén, *Spain* **23** 38 8N 3 48W
Băileşti, *Romania* **34** 44 1N 23 20 E
Baileux, *Belgium* **17** 50 2N 4 23 E
Bailhongal, *India* **51** 15 55N 74 53 E
Bailique, Ilha, *Brazil* **138** 1 2N 49 58W
Bailleul, *France* **19** 50 44N 2 41 E
Bailundo, *Angola* **95** 12 10 S 15 50 E
Baima, *China* **58** 33 0N 100 26 E
Baimuru, *Papua N. G.* **69** 7 35 S 144 51 E
Bain-de-Bretagne, *France* **18** 47 50N 1 40W
Bainbridge, *Ga., U.S.A.* **115** 30 53N 84 34W
Bainbridge, *Ind., U.S.A.* **119** 39 46N 86 49W
Bainbridge, *N.Y., U.S.A.* **117** 42 17N 75 29W
Bainbridge, *Ohio, U.S.A.* **119** 39 14N 83 16W
Baing, *Indonesia* **57** 10 14 S 120 34 E
Bainiu, *China* **60** 32 50N 112 15 E
Bainville, *U.S.A.* **120** 48 8N 104 10W
Bainyik, *Papua N. G.* **69** 3 40 S 143 4 E
Bā'ir, *Jordan* **46** 30 45N 36 55 E
Baird, *U.S.A.* **121** 32 25N 99 25W
Baird Mts., *U.S.A.* **102** 67 10N 160 15W
Bairin Youqi, *China* **61** 43 30N 118 35 E
Bairin Zuoqi, *China* **61** 43 58N 119 15 E
Bairnsdale, *Australia* **75** 37 48 S 147 36 E
Baisha, *China* **60** 34 20N 112 32 E
Baïsole →, *France* **20** 43 26N 0 25 E
Baissa, *Nigeria* **91** 7 14N 10 38 E
Baitadi, *Nepal* **49** 29 35N 80 25 E
Baixa Grande, *Brazil* **139** 11 57 S 40 11W
Baiyin, *China* **60** 36 45N 104 14 E
Baiyü, *China* **58** 31 16N 98 50 E
Baiyu Shan, *China* **60** 37 15N 107 30 E
Baiyuda, *Sudan* **88** 17 35N 32 7 E
Baj Baj, *India* **49** 22 30N 88 5 E
Baja, *Hungary* **33** 46 12N 18 59 E
Baja, Pta., *Mexico* **126** 29 50N 116 0W
Baja California, *Mexico* **126** 31 10N 115 12W
Bajana, *India* **48** 23 7N 71 49 E
Bajimba, Mt., *Australia* **77** 29 17 S 152 6 E
Bajo Nuevo, *Caribbean* **128** 15 40N 78 50W
Bajoga, *Nigeria* **91** 10 57N 11 20 E
Bajool, *Australia* **72** 23 40 S 150 35 E
Bakala, *C.A.R.* **94** 6 15N 20 20 E
Bakar, *Yugoslavia* **27** 45 18N 14 32 E
Bakchar, *U.S.S.R.* **40** 57 1N 82 5 E
Bakel, *Neths.* **17** 51 30N 5 45 E
Bakel, *Senegal* **90** 14 56N 12 20W
Baker, *Calif., U.S.A.* **125** 35 16N 116 8W
Baker, *Mont., U.S.A.* **120** 46 22N 104 12W
Baker, *Oreg., U.S.A.* **122** 44 50N 117 55W
Baker, Canal, *Chile* **142** 47 45 S 74 45W
Baker, L., *Australia* **79** 26 54 S 126 5 E
Baker, L., *Canada* **102** 64 0N 96 0W
Baker I., *Pac. Oc.* **66** 0 10N 176 35W
Baker Lake, *Canada* **102** 64 20N 96 3W
Baker Mt., *U.S.A.* **122** 48 50N 121 49W
Bakers Creek, *Australia* **72** 21 13 S 149 7 E
Baker's Dozen Is., *Canada* **104** 56 45N 78 45W
Bakersfield, *Calif., U.S.A.* **125** 35 25N 119 0W
Bakersfield, *Vt., U.S.A.* **117** 44 46N 72 48W
Bakhchisaray, *U.S.S.R.* **38** 44 40N 33 45 E
Bakhmach, *U.S.S.R.* **36** 51 10N 32 45 E
Bākhtarān, *Iran* **46** 34 23N 47 0 E
Bākhtarān □, *Iran* **46** 34 0N 46 30 E
Bakinskikh Komissarov, im. 26, *U.S.S.R.* **46** 39 20N 49 15 E
Bakırköy, *Turkey* **35** 40 59N 28 53 E
Bakkafjörður, *Iceland* **8** 66 2N 14 48W
Bakkagerði, *Iceland* **8** 65 31N 13 49W
Bakony →, *Hungary* **33** 47 35N 17 54 E
Bakony Forest = Bakony Hegyseg, *Hungary* **33** 47 10N 17 30 E
Bakony Hegyseg, *Hungary* **33** 47 10N 17 30 E
Bakori, *Nigeria* **91** 11 34N 7 25 E
Bakouma, *C.A.R.* **94** 5 40N 22 56 E
Baku, *U.S.S.R.* **39** 40 25N 49 45 E
Bakutis Coast, *Antarctica* **143** 74 0 S 120 0W
Bakwa-Kenge, *Zaïre* **95** 4 51 S 22 4 E
Bala, *Canada* **108** 45 1N 79 37W
Bal'ā, *Jordan* **44** 32 20N 35 6 E
Bala, L., *U.K.* **12** 52 53N 3 38W
Balabac, Str., *E. Indies* **56** 7 53N 117 5 E
Balabac I., *Phil.* **56** 8 0N 117 0 E
Balabagh, *Afghan.* **48** 34 25N 70 12 E
Balabakk, *Lebanon* **46** 34 0N 36 10 E
Balabalangan, Kepulauan, *Indonesia* **56** 2 20 S 117 30 E
Balabio, I., *N. Cal.* **68** 20 7 S 164 11 E
Bălăciţa, *Romania* **34** 44 23N 23 8 E
Balaghat, *India* **50** 21 49N 80 12 E
Balaghat Ra., *India* **50** 18 50N 76 30 E
Balaguer, *Spain* **24** 41 50N 0 50 E
Balakété, *C.A.R.* **94** 6 56N 19 54 E
Balakhna, *U.S.S.R.* **37** 56 25N 43 32 E
Balaklava, *Australia* **73** 34 7 S 138 22 E
Balaklava, *U.S.S.R.* **38** 44 30N 33 30 E
Balakleya, *U.S.S.R.* **38** 49 28N 36 55 E
Balakovo, *U.S.S.R.* **37** 52 4N 47 55 E
Balancán, *Mexico* **127** 17 48N 91 32W
Balanda, *U.S.S.R.* **37** 51 30N 44 40 E
Balangir, *India* **50** 20 43N 83 35 E
Balapur, *India* **50** 20 40N 76 45 E
Balashikha, *U.S.S.R.* **37** 55 49N 37 59 E
Balashov, *U.S.S.R.* **37** 51 30N 43 10 E
Balasinor, *India* **48** 22 57N 73 23 E
Balasore = Baleshwar, *India* **50** 21 35N 87 3 E
Balassagyarmat, *Hungary* **33** 48 4N 19 15 E
Balât, *Egypt* **88** 25 36N 29 19 E
Balaton, *Hungary* **33** 46 50N 17 40 E
Balazote, *Spain* **25** 38 54N 2 9W
Balbi, Mt., *Papua N. G.* **69** 5 55 S 154 58 E
Balboa, *Panama* **128** 9 0N 79 30W
Balbriggan, *Ireland* **15** 53 35N 6 10W
Balcarce, *Argentina* **140** 38 0 S 58 10W
Balcarres, *Canada* **111** 50 50N 103 35W
Balchik, *Bulgaria* **34** 43 28N 28 11 E
Balclutha, *N.Z.* **81** 46 15 S 169 45 E
Balcombe, *Australia* **74** 38 16 S 145 2 E
Bald Hd., *Australia* **79** 35 6 S 118 1 E
Bald I., *Australia* **79** 34 57 S 118 27 E
Bald Knob, *U.S.A.* **121** 35 20N 91 35W
Baldock L., *Canada* **111** 56 33N 97 57W
Baldwin, *Fla., U.S.A.* **115** 30 15N 82 10W
Baldwin, *Mich., U.S.A.* **114** 43 54N 85 53W
Baldwinsville, *U.S.A.* **117** 43 10N 76 19W
Bale, *Yugoslavia* **27** 45 4N 13 46 E
Bale □, *Ethiopia* **89** 6 20N 41 30 E
Baleares □, *Spain* **24** 39 30N 3 0 E
Baleares, Is., *Spain* **24** 39 30N 3 0 E
Balearic Is. = Baleares, Is., *Spain* **24** 39 30N 3 0 E
Baleia, Pta. da, *Brazil* **139** 17 40 S 39 7W
Balen, *Belgium* **17** 51 10N 5 10 E
Baler, *Phil.* **57** 15 46N 121 34 E
Baleshwar, *India* **50** 21 35N 87 3 E
Balfate, *Honduras* **128** 15 48N 86 25W
Balfe's Creek, *Australia* **72** 20 12 S 145 55 E
Balfour, *S. Africa* **97** 26 38 S 28 35 E
Balfour Channel, *Solomon Is.* **68** 8 43 S 157 27 E
Balfouriyya, *Israel* **44** 32 38N 35 18 E
Balharshah, *India* **50** 19 50N 79 23 E
Bali, *Cameroon* **91** 5 54N 10 0 E
Bali, *Indonesia* **56** 8 20 S 115 0 E
Bali □, *Indonesia* **56** 8 20 S 115 0 E
Bali, Selat, *Indonesia* **57** 8 18 S 114 25 E
Baligród, *Poland* **32** 49 20N 22 17 E
Balikesir, *Turkey* **46** 39 35N 27 58 E
Balikpapan, *Indonesia* **56** 1 10 S 116 55 E
Balimbing, *Phil.* **57** 5 5N 119 58 E
Balimo, *Papua N. G.* **69** 8 6 S 142 57 E
Baling, *Malaysia* **55** 5 41N 100 55 E
Baliza, *Brazil* **137** 16 0 S 52 20W
Balk, *Neths.* **16** 52 54N 5 35 E
Balkan Mts. = Stara Planina, *Bulgaria* **34** 43 15N 23 0 E
Balkan Pen., *Europe* **6** 42 0N 22 0 E
Balkh, *Afghan.* **47** 36 44N 66 47 E
Balkh □, *Afghan.* **47** 36 30N 67 0 E
Balkhash, *U.S.S.R.* **40** 46 50N 74 50 E
Balkhash, Ozero, *U.S.S.R.* **40** 46 0N 74 50 E
Ballachulish, *U.K.* **14** 56 40N 5 10W
Balladonia, *Australia* **79** 32 27 S 123 51 E
Balladoran, *Australia* **76** 31 52 S 148 39 E
Ballan, *Australia* **74** 37 35 S 144 13 E
Ballandean, *Australia* **77** 28 46 S 151 50 E
Ballarat, *Australia* **74** 37 33 S 143 50 E
Ballard, L., *Australia* **79** 29 20 S 120 10 E
Ballater, *U.K.* **14** 57 2N 3 2W
Ballenas, Canal de, *Mexico* **126** 29 10N 113 45W
Balleny Is., *Antarctica* **143** 66 30 S 163 0 E
Ballia, *India* **49** 25 46N 84 12 E
Ballidu, *Australia* **79** 30 35 S 116 45 E
Ballimore, *Australia* **76** 32 12 S 148 55 E
Ballina, *Australia* **77** 28 50 S 153 31 E
Ballina, *Mayo, Ireland* **15** 54 7N 9 10W
Ballina, *Tipp., Ireland* **15** 52 49N 8 27W
Ballinasloe, *Ireland* **15** 53 20N 8 12W
Ballinger, *U.S.A.* **121** 31 45N 99 58W
Ballinrobe, *Ireland* **15** 53 36N 9 13W
Ballinskelligs B., *Ireland* **15** 51 46N 10 11W
Ballon, *France* **18** 48 10N 0 14 E
Ballycastle, *U.K.* **15** 55 12N 6 15W
Ballymena, *U.K.* **15** 54 53N 6 18W
Ballymena □, *U.K.* **15** 54 53N 6 18W
Ballymoney, *U.K.* **15** 55 5N 6 30W
Ballymoney □, *U.K.* **15** 55 5N 6 23W
Ballyshannon, *Ireland* **15** 54 30N 8 10W
Balmaceda, *Chile* **142** 46 0 S 71 50W
Balmazújváros, *Hungary* **33** 47 37N 21 21 E
Balmoral, *Australia* **74** 37 15 S 141 48 E
Balmoral, *U.K.* **14** 57 3N 3 13W
Balmorhea, *U.S.A.* **121** 31 2N 103 41W
Balombo, *Angola* **95** 12 21 S 14 46 E
Balonne →, *Australia* **73** 28 47 S 147 56 E
Balrampur, *India* **49** 27 30N 82 20 E
Balranald, *Australia* **74** 34 38 S 143 33 E
Balş, *Romania* **34** 44 22N 24 5 E
Balsapuerto, *Peru* **136** 5 48 S 76 33W
Balsas, *Mexico* **127** 18 0N 99 40W
Balsas →, *Goiás, Brazil* **138** 9 58 S 47 52W
Balsas →, *Maranhão, Brazil* **138** 7 15 S 44 35W
Balsas →, *Mexico* **126** 17 55N 102 10W
Bålsta, *Sweden* **10** 59 35N 17 30 E
Balston Spa, *U.S.A.* **117** 43 0N 73 52W
Balta, *Romania* **34** 44 54N 22 38 E
Balta, *U.S.A.* **120** 48 12N 100 7W
Balta, *R.S.F.S.R., U.S.S.R.* **39** 42 58N 44 32 E
Balta, *Ukraine S.S.R., U.S.S.R.* **38** 48 2N 29 45 E
Baltanás, *Spain* **22** 41 56N 4 15W
Baltic Sea, *Europe* **9** 56 0N 20 0 E
Baltîm, *Egypt* **88** 31 35N 31 10 E
Baltimore, *Ireland* **15** 51 29N 9 22W
Baltimore, *U.S.A.* **114** 39 18N 76 37W
Baltit, *Pakistan* **49** 36 15N 74 40 E
Baltrum, *W. Germany* **30** 53 43N 7 25 E
Baluchistan □, *Pakistan* **47** 27 30N 65 0 E
Balurghat, *India* **49** 25 15N 88 44 E
Balygychan, *U.S.S.R.* **41** 63 56N 154 12 E
Balzar, *Ecuador* **134** 2 2 S 79 54W
Bam, *Iran* **47** 29 7N 58 14 E
Bama, *China* **58** 24 8N 107 12 E
Bama, *Nigeria* **91** 11 33N 13 41 E
Bamako, *Mali* **90** 12 34N 7 55W
Bamba, *Mali* **91** 17 5N 1 24W
Bamba, *Zaïre* **95** 5 45 S 18 23 E
Bambamarca, *Peru* **136** 6 36 S 78 32W
Bambari, *C.A.R.* **94** 5 40N 20 35 E
Bambaroo, *Australia* **72** 18 50 S 146 10 E
Bamberg, *U.S.A.* **115** 33 19N 81 1W
Bamberg, *W. Germany* **31** 49 54N 10 53 E
Bambesi, *Ethiopia* **89** 9 45N 34 40 E
Bambey, *Senegal* **90** 14 42N 16 28W
Bambili, *Zaïre* **92** 3 40N 26 0 E
Bambuí, *Brazil* **139** 20 1 S 45 58W
Bamenda, *Cameroon* **91** 5 57N 10 11 E
Bamfield, *Canada* **110** 48 45N 125 10W
Bāmīān □, *Afghan.* **47** 35 0N 67 0 E
Bamiancheng, *China* **61** 43 15N 124 2 E
Bamingui, *C.A.R.* **94** 7 34N 20 11 E
Bamkin, *Cameroon* **91** 6 3N 11 27 E
Bampūr, *Iran* **47** 27 15N 60 21 E
Ban Aranyaprathet, *Thailand* **54** 13 41N 102 30 E
Ban Ban, *Laos* **54** 19 31N 103 30 E
Ban Bang Hin, *Thailand* **55** 9 32N 98 35 E
Ban Chiang Klang, *Thailand* **54** 19 25N 100 55 E
Ban Chik, *Laos* **54** 17 15N 102 22 E
Ban Choho, *Thailand* **54** 15 2N 102 9 E
Ban Dan Lan Hoi, *Thailand* **54** 17 0N 99 35 E
Ban Don = Surat Thani, *Thailand* **55** 9 6N 99 20 E
Ban Don, *Vietnam* **54** 12 53N 107 48 E
Ban Don, Ao, *Thailand* **55** 9 20N 99 25 E
Ban Dong, *Thailand* **54** 19 30N 100 59 E
Ban Hong, *Thailand* **54** 18 18N 98 50 E
Ban Kaeng, *Thailand* **54** 17 29N 100 7 E
Ban Keun, *Laos* **54** 18 22N 102 35 E
Ban Khai, *Thailand* **54** 12 46N 101 18 E
Ban Kheun, *Laos* **54** 20 13N 101 7 E
Ban Khlong Kua, *Thailand* **55** 6 57N 100 8 E
Ban Khuan Mao, *Thailand* **55** 7 50N 99 37 E
Ban Khun Yuam, *Thailand* **54** 18 49N 97 57 E
Ban Ko Yai Chim, *Thailand* **55** 11 17N 99 26 E
Ban Kok, *Thailand* **54** 16 40N 103 40 E
Ban Laem, *Thailand* **54** 13 13N 99 59 E
Ban Lao Ngam, *Laos* **54** 15 28N 106 10 E
Ban Le Kathe, *Thailand* **54** 15 49N 98 53 E
Ban Mae Chedi, *Thailand* **54** 19 11N 99 31 E
Ban Mae Laeng, *Thailand* **54** 20 1N 99 17 E
Ban Mae Sariang, *Thailand* **54** 18 10N 97 56 E
Ban Mi, *Thailand* **54** 15 3N 100 32 E
Ban Muong Mo, *Laos* **54** 19 4N 103 58 E
Ban Na Mo, *Laos* **54** 17 7N 105 40 E
Ban Na San, *Thailand* **55** 8 53N 99 52 E
Ban Na Tong, *Laos* **54** 20 56N 101 47 E
Ban Nam Bac, *Laos* **54** 20 38N 102 20 E
Ban Nam Ma, *Laos* **54** 22 2N 101 37 E
Ban Ngang, *Laos* **54** 15 59N 106 11 E
Ban Nong Bok, *Laos* **54** 17 5N 104 48 E
Ban Nong Boua, *Laos* **54** 15 40N 106 33 E
Ban Nong Pling, *Thailand* **54** 15 40N 100 10 E
Ban Pak Chan, *Thailand* **55** 10 32N 98 51 E
Ban Phai, *Thailand* **54** 16 4N 102 44 E
Ban Pong, *Thailand* **54** 13 50N 99 55 E
Ban Ron Phibun, *Thailand* **55** 8 9N 99 51 E
Ban Sanam Chai, *Thailand* **55** 7 33N 100 25 E
Ban Sangkha, *Thailand* **54** 14 37N 103 52 E

Beaulieu

Barra do Dande, *Angola* 95 8 28 S 13 22 E
Barra do Mendes, *Brazil* 139 11 43 S 42 4W
Barra do Piraí, *Brazil* 139 22 30 S 43 50W
Barra Falsa, Pta. da, *Mozam.* 97 22 58 S 35 37 E
Barra Hd., *U.K.* 14 56 47N 7 40W
Barra Mansa, *Brazil* 141 22 35 S 44 12W
Barraba, *Australia* 77 30 21 S 150 35 E
Barracão do Barreto, *Brazil* 137 8 48 S 58 24W
Barrackpur = Barakpur, *India* 49 22 44N 88 30 E
Barrafranca, *Italy* 29 37 22N 14 10 E
Barranca, *Lima, Peru* 136 10 45 S 77 50W
Barranca, *Loreto, Peru* 134 4 50 S 76 50W
Barrancabermeja, *Colombia* 134 7 0N 73 50W
Barrancas, *Colombia* 134 10 57N 72 50W
Barrancas, *Venezuela* 135 8 55N 62 5W
Barrancos, *Portugal* 23 38 10N 6 58W
Barranqueras, *Argentina* 140 27 30 S 59 0W
Barranquilla, *Colombia* 134 11 0N 74 50W
Barras, *Brazil* 138 4 15 S 42 18W
Barras, *Colombia* 134 1 45 S 73 13W
Barraute, *Canada* 106 48 26N 77 38W
Barre, *U.S.A.* 117 44 15N 72 30W
Barre do Bugres, *Brazil* 137 15 0 S 57 11W
Barreal, *Argentina* 140 31 33 S 69 28W
Barrei, *Ethiopia* 98 6 10N 42 49 E
Barreiras, *Brazil* 139 12 8 S 45 0W
Barreirinha, *Brazil* 135 2 47 S 57 3W
Barreirinhas, *Brazil* 138 2 30 S 42 50W
Barreiro, *Portugal* 23 38 40N 9 6W
Barreiros, *Brazil* 138 8 49 S 35 12W
Barrême, *France* 21 43 57N 6 23 E
Barren, Nosy, *Madag.* 97 18 25 S 43 40 E
Barretos, *Brazil* 139 20 30 S 48 35W
Barrhead, *Canada* 110 54 10N 114 24W
Barrie, *Canada* 108 44 24N 79 40W
Barriefield, *Canada* 109 44 14N 76 28W
Barrier, C., *N.Z.* 80 36 25 S 175 32 E
Barrier Ra., *Australia* 73 31 0 S 141 30 E
Barrier Ra., *N.Z.* 81 44 5 S 169 42 E
Barrière, *Canada* 110 51 12N 120 7W
Barrington, *Australia* 77 31 58 S 151 55 E
Barrington, *U.S.A.* 117 41 43N 71 20W
Barrington L., *Canada* 111 56 55N 100 15W
Barrington Tops, *Australia* 77 32 6 S 151 28 E
Barringun, *Australia* 73 29 1 S 145 41 E
Barro do Garças, *Brazil* 137 15 54 S 52 16W
Barrow, *U.S.A.* 102 71 16N 156 50W
Barrow →, *Ireland* 15 52 10N 6 57W
Barrow Creek, *Australia* 72 21 30 S 133 55 E
Barrow I., *Australia* 78 20 45 S 115 20 E
Barrow-in-Furness, *U.K.* 12 54 8N 3 15W
Barrow Pt., *Australia* 72 14 20 S 144 40 E
Barrow Ra., *Australia* 79 26 0 S 127 40 E
Barrow Str., *Canada* 144 74 20N 95 0W
Barruecopardo, *Spain* 22 41 4N 6 40W
Barruelo, *Spain* 22 42 54N 4 17W
Barry, *Australia* 76 33 38 S 149 16 E
Barry, *U.K.* 13 51 23N 3 19W
Barry, *U.S.A.* 118 39 42N 91 2W
Barry's Bay, *Canada* 109 45 29N 77 41W
Barsalogho, *Burkina Faso* 91 13 25N 1 3W
Barsat, *Pakistan* 49 36 10N 72 45 E
Barsi, *India* 50 18 10N 75 50 E
Barsø, *Denmark* 11 55 7N 9 33 E
Barstow, *Calif., U.S.A.* 125 34 58N 117 2W
Barstow, *Tex., U.S.A.* 121 31 28N 103 24W
Barth, *E. Germany* 30 54 20N 12 36 E
Barthélemy, Col, *Vietnam* 54 19 26N 104 6 E
Bartica, *Guyana* 135 6 25N 58 40W
Bartin, *Turkey* 46 41 38N 32 21 E
Bartlesville, *U.S.A.* 121 36 50N 95 58W
Bartlett, *Calif., U.S.A.* 124 36 29N 118 2W
Bartlett, *Tex., U.S.A.* 121 30 46N 97 30W
Bartlett, L., *Canada* 110 63 5N 118 20W
Bartolomeu Dias, *Mozam.* 93 21 10 S 35 8 E
Barton, *Australia* 79 30 31 S 132 39 E
Barton-upon-Humber, *U.K.* 12 53 41N 0 27W
Bartonville, *U.S.A.* 118 40 39N 89 39W
Bartoszyce, *Poland* 32 54 15N 20 55 E
Bartow, *U.S.A.* 115 27 53N 81 49W
Barú, I. de, *Colombia* 134 10 15N 75 35W
Barú, Volcan, *Panama* 128 8 55N 82 35W
Barumba, *Zaïre* 92 1 3N 23 37 E
Baruth, *E. Germany* 30 52 3N 13 31 E
Barvaux, *Belgium* 17 50 21N 5 29 E
Barvenkovo, *U.S.S.R.* 38 48 57N 37 0 E
Barwani, *India* 48 22 2N 74 57 E
Barwon →, *Australia* 74 38 8 S 144 3 E
Barwon Heads, *Australia* 74 38 17 S 144 30 E
Barysh, *U.S.S.R.* 37 53 39N 47 8 E
Baryulgil, *Australia* 77 29 12 S 152 38 E
Bas-Rhin □, *France* 19 48 40N 7 30 E
Bašaid, *Yugoslavia* 33 45 38N 20 25 E
Bāsa'idū, *Iran* 47 26 35N 55 20 E
Basal, *Pakistan* 48 33 33N 72 13 E
Basankusa, *Zaïre* 94 1 5N 19 50 E
Basawa, *Afghan.* 48 34 15N 70 50 E
Bascharage, *Lux.* 17 49 34N 5 55 E
Bascuñán, C., *Chile* 140 28 52 S 71 35W
Basècles, *Belgium* 17 50 32N 3 39 E
Basel, *Switz.* 31 47 35N 7 35 E
Basel-Stadt □, *Switz.* 31 47 35N 7 35 E
Baselland □, *Switz.* 31 47 26N 7 45 E
Basento →, *Italy* 29 40 21N 16 50 E
Bashkir A.S.S.R. □, *U.S.S.R.* 40 54 0N 57 0 E
Basilaki I., *Papua N. G.* 69 10 35 S 151 0 E
Basilan, *Phil.* 57 6 35N 122 0 E
Basilan Str., *Phil.* 57 6 50N 122 0 E
Basildon, *U.K.* 13 51 34N 0 29 E
Basilicata □, *Italy* 29 40 30N 16 0 E
Basim = Washim, *India* 50 20 3N 77 0 E
Basin, *U.S.A.* 122 44 22N 108 2W
Basingstoke, *U.K.* 13 51 15N 1 5W
Basirhat, *Bangla.* 52 22 40N 88 54 E
Baška, *Yugoslavia* 27 44 58N 14 45 E
Baskatong, Rés., *Canada* 106 46 46N 75 50W
Basle = Basel, *Switz.* 31 47 35N 7 35 E
Basmat, *India* 50 19 15N 77 12 E
Basoda, *India* 48 23 52N 77 54 E
Basoka, *Zaïre* 92 1 16N 23 40 E
Basongo, *Zaïre* 95 4 15 S 20 20 E
Basque, Pays, *France* 20 43 15N 1 20W
Basque Provinces = Vascongadas □, *Spain* 24 42 50N 2 45W
Basra = Al Başrah, *Iraq* 46 30 30N 47 50 E
Bass, *Australia* 74 38 29 S 145 28 E
Bass Point, *Australia* 77 34 36 S 150 54 E
Bass Rock, *U.K.* 14 56 5N 2 40W
Bass Str., *Australia* 72 39 15 S 146 30 E
Bassano, *Canada* 110 50 48N 112 20W
Bassano del Grappa, *Italy* 27 45 45N 11 45 E
Bassar, *Togo* 91 9 19N 0 57 E
Basse Santa-Su, *Gambia* 90 13 13N 14 15W
Basse-Terre, *Guadeloupe* 129 16 0N 61 40W
Bassée, La, *France* 19 50 31N 2 49 E
Bassein, *Burma* 52 16 45N 94 30 E
Bassein, *India* 50 19 26N 72 48 E
Basseterre, *St. Christopher-Nevis* 129 17 17N 62 43W
Bassett, *Nebr., U.S.A.* 120 42 37N 99 30W
Bassett, *Va., U.S.A.* 115 36 48N 79 59W
Bassevelde, *Belgium* 17 51 15N 3 41 E
Bassi, *India* 48 30 44N 76 21 E
Bassigny, *France* 19 48 0N 5 30 E
Bassikounou, *Mauritania* 90 15 55N 6 1W
Bassilly, *Belgium* 17 50 40N 3 56 E
Bassum, *W. Germany* 30 52 50N 8 42 E
Båstad, *Sweden* 11 56 25N 12 51 E
Bastak, *Iran* 47 27 15N 54 25 E
Bastar, *India* 50 19 15N 81 40 E
Bastelica, *France* 21 42 1N 9 3 E
Basti, *India* 49 26 52N 82 55 E
Bastia, *France* 21 42 40N 9 30 E
Bastia Umbra, *Italy* 27 43 4N 12 34 E
Bastide-Puylaurent, La, *France* 20 44 35N 3 55 E
Bastogne, *Belgium* 17 50 1N 5 43 E
Bastrop, *U.S.A.* 121 30 5N 97 22W
Bat Yam, *Israel* 44 32 2N 34 44 E
Bata, *Eq. Guin.* 94 1 57N 9 50 E
Bata, *Romania* 34 46 1N 22 4 E
Bataan, *Phil.* 57 14 40N 120 25 E
Batabanó, *Cuba* 128 22 40N 82 20W
Batabanó, G. de, *Cuba* 128 22 30N 82 30W
Batac, *Phil.* 57 18 3N 120 34 E
Batagoy, *U.S.S.R.* 41 67 38N 134 38 E
Batak, *Bulgaria* 35 41 57N 24 12 E
Batalha, *Portugal* 23 39 40N 8 50W
Batama, *Zaïre* 92 0 58N 26 33 E
Batamay, *U.S.S.R.* 41 63 30N 129 15 E
Batang, *China* 58 30 1N 99 0 E
Batang, *Indonesia* 57 6 55 S 109 45 E
Batangafo, *C.A.R.* 94 7 25N 18 20 E
Batangas, *Phil.* 57 13 35N 121 10 E
Batanta, *Indonesia* 57 0 55 S 130 40 E
Batatais, *Brazil* 141 20 54 S 47 37W
Batavia, *Ind., U.S.A.* 119 41 55N 88 17W
Batavia, *N.Y., U.S.A.* 116 43 0N 78 10W
Batavia, *Ohio, U.S.A.* 119 39 5N 84 11W
Bataysk, *U.S.S.R.* 39 47 3N 39 45 E
Batchelor, *Australia* 78 13 4 S 131 1 E
Batéké, Plateau, *Congo* 94 3 30 S 15 45 E
Bateman's B., *Australia* 76 35 40 S 150 12 E
Batemans Bay, *Australia* 76 35 44 S 150 11 E
Batesburg, *U.S.A.* 115 33 54N 81 32W
Batesville, *Ark., U.S.A.* 121 35 48N 91 40W
Batesville, *Ind., U.S.A.* 119 39 18N 85 13W
Batesville, *Miss., U.S.A.* 121 34 17N 89 58W
Batesville, *Tex., U.S.A.* 121 28 59N 99 38W
Bath, *Canada* 109 44 11N 76 47W
Bath, *U.K.* 13 51 22N 2 22W
Bath, *Maine, U.S.A.* 105 43 50N 69 49W
Bath, *N.Y., U.S.A.* 116 42 20N 77 17W
Batheay, *Cambodia* 55 11 59N 104 57 E
Bathgate, *U.K.* 14 55 54N 3 38W
Bathmen, *Neths.* 16 52 15N 6 29 E
Bathurst = Banjul, *Gambia* 90 13 28N 16 40W
Bathurst, *Australia* 76 33 25 S 149 31 E
Bathurst, *Canada* 105 47 37N 65 43W
Bathurst, *S. Africa* 96 33 30 S 26 50 E
Bathurst, C., *Canada* 102 70 34N 128 0W
Bathurst B., *Australia* 72 14 16 S 144 25 E
Bathurst Harb., *Australia* 72 43 15 S 146 10 E
Bathurst I., *Australia* 78 11 30 S 130 10 E
Bathurst I., *Canada* 144 76 0N 100 30W
Bathurst Inlet, *Canada* 102 66 50N 108 1W
Bathurst L., *Australia* 76 35 3 S 149 44 E
Batie, *Burkina Faso* 90 9 53N 2 53W
Batinah, *Oman* 47 24 0N 56 0 E
Batiscan, *Canada* 107 46 30N 72 15W
Batiscan →, *Canada* 107 46 16N 72 15W
Batiscan, L., *Canada* 107 47 22N 71 55W
Batlow, *Australia* 76 35 31 S 148 9 E
Batman, *Turkey* 46 37 55N 41 5 E
Batna, *Algeria* 85 35 34N 6 15 E
Batoala, *Gabon* 94 0 48N 13 27 E
Batoka, *Zambia* 93 16 45 S 27 15 E
Baton Rouge, *U.S.A.* 121 30 30N 91 5W
Batong, Ko, *Thailand* 55 6 32N 99 12 E
Batopilas, *Mexico* 126 27 0N 107 45W
Batouri, *Cameroon* 94 4 30N 14 25 E
Battambang, *Cambodia* 54 13 7N 103 12 E
Batticaloa, *Sri Lanka* 51 7 43N 81 45 E
Battice, *Belgium* 17 50 39N 5 50 E
Battipáglia, *Italy* 29 40 38N 15 0 E
Battīr, *Israel* 44 31 44N 35 8 E
Battle, *U.K.* 13 50 55N 0 30 E
Battle →, *Canada* 111 52 43N 108 15W
Battle Camp, *Australia* 72 15 20 S 144 40 E
Battle Creek, *U.S.A.* 119 42 20N 85 6W
Battle Ground, *U.S.A.* 124 45 47N 122 32W
Battle Harbour, *Canada* 105 52 16N 55 35W
Battle Lake, *U.S.A.* 120 46 20N 95 43W
Battle Mountain, *U.S.A.* 122 40 45N 117 0W
Battlefields, *Zambia* 93 18 37 S 29 47 E
Battleford, *Canada* 111 52 45N 108 15W
Battonya, *Hungary* 33 46 16N 21 3 E
Batu, Kepulauan, *Indonesia* 56 0 30 S 98 25 E
Batu Caves, *Malaysia* 55 3 15N 101 40 E
Batu Gajah, *Malaysia* 55 4 28N 101 3 E
Batu Pahat, *Malaysia* 55 1 50N 102 56 E
Batuata, *Indonesia* 57 6 12 S 122 42 E
Batumi, *U.S.S.R.* 39 41 30N 41 30 E
Baturaja, *Indonesia* 56 4 11 S 104 15 E
Baturité, *Brazil* 138 4 28 S 38 45W
Bau, *Malaysia* 56 1 25N 110 9 E
Baubau, *Indonesia* 57 5 25 S 122 38 E
Bauchi, *Nigeria* 91 10 22N 9 48 E
Bauchi □, *Nigeria* 91 10 30N 10 0 E
Baud, *France* 18 47 52N 3 1W
Baudette, *U.S.A.* 120 48 46N 94 35W
Baudour, *Belgium* 17 50 29N 3 50 E
Bauer, C., *Australia* 73 32 44 S 134 4 E
Baugé, *France* 18 47 31N 0 8W
Bauhinia Downs, *Australia* 72 24 35 S 149 18 E
Baule, La, *France* 18 47 17N 2 24W
Baume-les-Dames, *France* 19 47 22N 6 22 E
Baunatal, *W. Germany* 30 51 13N 9 25 E
Baunei, *Italy* 28 40 2N 9 41 E
Baures, *Bolivia* 137 13 35 S 63 35W
Bauru, *Brazil* 141 22 10 S 49 0W
Baús, *Brazil* 137 18 22 S 52 47W
Bauska, *U.S.S.R.* 36 56 24N 25 15 E
Bautzen, *E. Germany* 30 51 11N 14 25 E
Baux-de-Provence, Les, *France* 21 43 45N 4 51 E
Bavaria = Bayern □, *W. Germany* 31 49 7N 11 30 E
Båven, *Sweden* 10 59 0N 16 56 E
Bavi Sadri, *India* 48 24 28N 74 30 E
Bavispe →, *Mexico* 126 29 30N 109 11W
Baw Baw, Mt., *Australia* 75 37 49 S 146 19 E
Bawdwin, *Burma* 52 23 5N 97 20 E
Bawean, *Indonesia* 56 5 46 S 112 35 E
Bawku, *Ghana* 91 11 3N 0 19W
Bawlake, *Burma* 52 19 11N 97 21 E
Bawolung, *China* 58 28 50N 101 16 E
Baxley, *U.S.A.* 115 31 43N 82 23W
Baxoi, *China* 58 30 1N 96 50 E
Baxter, *U.S.A.* 118 41 49N 93 9W
Baxter Springs, *U.S.A.* 121 37 3N 94 45W
Bay, L. de, *Phil.* 57 14 20N 121 11 E
Bay Bulls, *Canada* 105 47 19N 52 50W
Bay City, *Mich., U.S.A.* 104 43 35N 83 51W
Bay City, *Oreg., U.S.A.* 122 45 45N 123 58W
Bay City, *Tex., U.S.A.* 121 28 59N 95 55W
Bay de Verde, *Canada* 105 48 5N 52 54W
Bay Minette, *U.S.A.* 115 30 54N 87 43W
Bay St. Louis, *U.S.A.* 121 30 18N 89 22W
Bay Springs, *U.S.A.* 121 31 58N 89 18W
Bay View, *N.Z.* 80 39 25 S 176 50 E
Baya, *Zaïre* 93 11 53 S 27 25 E
Bayamo, *Cuba* 128 20 20N 76 40W
Bayamón, *Puerto Rico* 129 18 24N 66 10W
Bayan Har Shan, *China* 62 34 0N 98 0 E
Bayan Hot = Alxa Zuoqi, *China* 60 38 50N 105 40 E
Bayan Obo, *China* 60 41 52N 109 59 E
Bayan-Ovoo, *Mongolia* 60 42 55N 106 5 E
Bayana, *India* 48 26 55N 77 18 E
Bayanaul, *U.S.S.R.* 40 50 45N 75 45 E
Bayandalay, *Mongolia* 60 43 30N 103 29 E
Bayanhongor, *Mongolia* 62 46 8N 102 43 E
Bayard, *U.S.A.* 120 41 48N 103 17W
Bayázeh, *Iran* 47 33 30N 54 40 E
Baybay, *Phil.* 57 10 40N 124 55 E
Bayburt, *Turkey* 46 40 15N 40 20 E
Bayerischer Wald, *W. Germany* 31 49 0N 13 0 E
Bayern □, *W. Germany* 31 49 7N 11 30 E
Bayeux, *France* 18 49 17N 0 42W
Bayfield, *Canada* 108 43 34N 81 42W
Bayfield, *U.S.A.* 120 46 50N 90 48W
Baykal, Oz., *U.S.S.R.* 41 53 0N 108 0 E
Baykit, *U.S.S.R.* 41 61 50N 95 50 E
Baykonur, *U.S.S.R.* 40 47 48N 65 50 E
Baynes Mts., *Namibia* 96 17 15 S 13 0 E
Bayombong, *Phil.* 57 16 30N 121 10 E
Bayon, *France* 19 48 30N 6 20 E
Bayona, *Spain* 22 42 6N 8 52W
Bayonne, *France* 20 43 30N 1 28W
Bayonne, *U.S.A.* 117 40 41N 74 7W
Bayovar, *Peru* 136 5 50 S 81 0W
Bayram-Ali, *U.S.S.R.* 40 37 37N 62 10 E
Bayreuth, *W. Germany* 31 49 56N 11 35 E
Bayrischzell, *W. Germany* 31 47 39N 12 1 E
Bayrūt, *Lebanon* 46 33 53N 35 31 E
Bays, L. of, *Canada* 108 45 15N 79 4W
Bayside, *Canada* 109 44 7N 77 30W
Baysville, *Canada* 108 45 9N 79 7W
Bayt Awlá, *Jordan* 44 31 37N 35 2 E
Bayt Fajjār, *Jordan* 44 31 38N 35 9 E
Bayt Fūrīk, *Jordan* 44 32 11N 35 20 E
Bayt Ḩānūn, *Egypt* 44 31 32N 34 32 E
Bayt Jālā, *Jordan* 44 31 43N 35 11 E
Bayt Lahm, *Jordan* 44 31 43N 35 12 E
Bayt Rīma, *Jordan* 44 32 2N 35 6 E
Bayt Sāḩūr, *Jordan* 44 31 42N 35 13 E
Bayt Ummar, *Jordan* 44 31 38N 35 7 E
Bayt 'ūr al Taḩtā, *Jordan* 44 31 54N 35 5 E
Baytīn, *Jordan* 44 31 56N 35 14 E
Baytown, *U.S.A.* 121 29 42N 94 57W
Baytūniyā, *Jordan* 44 31 54N 35 10 E
Bayzo, *Niger* 91 13 52N 4 35 E
Baza, *Spain* 25 37 30N 2 47W
Bazar Dyuzi, *U.S.S.R.* 39 41 12N 47 50 E
Bazarny Karabulak, *U.S.S.R.* 37 52 15N 46 20 E
Bazarnyy Syzgan, *U.S.S.R.* 37 53 45N 46 40 E
Bazartobe, *U.S.S.R.* 39 49 26N 51 45 E
Bazaruto, I. do, *Mozam.* 97 21 40 S 35 28 E
Bazas, *France* 20 44 27N 0 13W
Bazhong, *China* 58 31 52N 106 46 E
Bazin →, *Canada* 106 47 29N 75 22W
Beach, *U.S.A.* 120 46 57N 103 58W
Beach City, *U.S.A.* 116 40 38N 81 35W
Beachburg, *Canada* 109 45 44N 76 51W
Beachport, *Australia* 73 37 29 S 140 0 E
Beachville, *Canada* 108 43 5N 80 49W
Beachy Head, *U.K.* 13 50 44N 0 16 E
Beacon, *Australia* 79 30 26 S 117 52 E
Beacon, *U.S.A.* 117 41 32N 73 58W
Beaconia, *Canada* 111 50 25N 96 31W
Beagle, Canal, *S. Amer.* 142 55 0 S 68 30W
Beagle Bay, *Australia* 78 16 58 S 122 40 E
Bealanana, *Madag.* 97 14 33 S 48 44 E
Bealiba, *Australia* 74 36 48 S 143 34 E
Beamsville, *Canada* 108 43 12N 79 28W
Bear →, *U.S.A.* 124 38 56N 121 36W
Béar, C., *France* 20 42 31N 3 8 E
Bear I., *Ireland* 15 51 38N 9 50W
Bear L., *B.C., Canada* 110 56 10N 126 52W
Bear L., *Man., Canada* 111 55 8N 96 0W
Bear L., *U.S.A.* 122 42 0N 111 20W
Bearcreek, *U.S.A.* 122 45 11N 109 6W
Beardmore, *Canada* 104 49 36N 87 57W
Beardmore Glacier, *Antarctica* 143 84 30 S 170 0 E
Beardstown, *U.S.A.* 118 40 0N 90 25W
Béarn, *Canada* 106 47 17N 79 20W
Béarn, *France* 20 43 20N 0 30W
Bearpaw Mts., *U.S.A.* 122 48 15N 109 30W
Bearskin Lake, *Canada* 104 53 58N 91 2W
Beas de Segura, *Spain* 25 38 15N 2 53W
Beasain, *Spain* 24 43 3N 2 11W
Beata, C., *Dom. Rep.* 129 17 40N 71 30W
Beata, I., *Dom. Rep.* 129 17 34N 71 31W
Beatrice, *U.S.A.* 120 40 20N 96 40W
Beatrice, *Zambia* 93 18 15 S 30 55 E
Beatrice, C., *Australia* 72 14 20 S 136 55 E
Beatton →, *Canada* 110 56 15N 120 45W
Beatton River, *Canada* 110 57 26N 121 20W
Beatty, *U.S.A.* 124 36 58N 116 46W
Beaucaire, *France* 21 43 48N 4 39 E
Beauce, Plaine de la, *France* 19 48 10N 1 45 E
Beauceville, *Canada* 107 46 13N 70 46W
Beauchêne, I., *Falk. Is.* 142 52 55 S 59 15W
Beauchûne, L., *Canada* 106 46 35N 78 55W
Beaudesert, *Australia* 77 27 59 S 153 0 E
Beaufort, *Australia* 74 37 25 S 143 25 E
Beaufort, *Malaysia* 56 5 30N 115 40 E
Beaufort, *N.C., U.S.A.* 115 34 45N 76 40W
Beaufort, *S.C., U.S.A.* 115 32 25N 80 40W
Beaufort Sea, *Arctic* 144 72 0N 140 0W
Beaufort West, *S. Africa* 96 32 18 S 22 36 E
Beaugency, *France* 19 47 47N 1 38 E
Beauharnois, *Canada* 107 45 20N 73 52W
Beaujeu, *France* 21 46 10N 4 35 E
Beaulac, *Canada* 107 45 50N 71 23W
Beaulieu →, *Canada* 110 62 3N 113 11W

Beaulieu-sur-Dordogne

Beaulieu-sur-Dordogne, *France* **20** 44 58N 1 50 E
Beaulieu-sur-Mer, *France* **21** 43 42N 7 20 E
Beauly, *U.K.* **14** 57 29N 4 27W
Beauly →, *U.K.* **14** 57 26N 4 28W
Beaumaris, *U.K.* **12** 53 16N 4 7W
Beaumetz-lès-Loges, *France* **19** 50 15N 2 38 E
Beaumont, *Belgium* **17** 50 15N 4 14 E
Beaumont, *France* **20** 44 45N 0 46 E
Beaumont, *N.Z.* **81** 45 50 S 169 33 E
Beaumont, *Calif., U.S.A.* **125** 33 56N 116 58W
Beaumont, *Tex., U.S.A.* **121** 30 5N 94 8W
Beaumont-de-Lomagne, *France* **20** 43 53N 1 0 E
Beaumont-le-Roger, *France* **18** 49 4N 0 47 E
Beaumont-sur-Oise, *France* **19** 49 9N 2 17 E
Beaumont-sur-Sarthe, *France* **18** 48 13N 0 8 E
Beaune, *France* **19** 47 2N 4 50 E
Beaune-la-Rolande, *France* **19** 48 4N 2 25 E
Beauport, *Canada* **107** 46 52N 71 11W
Beaupré, *Canada* **107** 47 3N 70 54W
Beaupréau, *France* **18** 47 12N 0 59W
Beauraing, *Belgium* **17** 50 7N 4 57 E
Beauséjour, *Canada* **111** 50 5N 96 35W
Beausset, Le, *France* **21** 43 12N 5 48 E
Beautemps-Beaupré, I., *N. Cal.* **68** 20 24 S 166 9 E
Beauvais, *France* **19** 49 25N 2 8 E
Beauval, *Canada* **111** 55 9N 107 37W
Beauvoir-sur-Mer, *France* **18** 46 55N 2 2W
Beauvoir-sur-Niort, *France* **20** 46 12N 0 30W
Beaver, *Alaska, U.S.A.* **102** 66 20N 147 30W
Beaver, *Okla., U.S.A.* **121** 36 52N 100 31W
Beaver, *Pa., U.S.A.* **116** 40 40N 80 18W
Beaver, *Utah, U.S.A.* **123** 38 20N 112 45W
Beaver →, *B.C., Canada* **110** 59 52N 124 20W
Beaver →, *Ont., Canada* **104** 55 55N 87 48W
Beaver →, *Sask., Canada* **111** 55 26N 107 45W
Beaver City, *U.S.A.* **120** 40 13N 99 50W
Beaver Dam, *U.S.A.* **120** 43 28N 88 50W
Beaver Falls, *U.S.A.* **116** 40 44N 80 20W
Beaver Hill L., *Canada* **111** 54 5N 94 50W
Beaver I., *U.S.A.* **104** 45 40N 85 31W
Beavercreek, *U.S.A.* **119** 39 43N 84 11W
Beaverhill L., *Alta., Canada* **110** 53 27N 112 32W
Beaverhill L., *N.W.T., Canada* **111** 63 2N 104 22W
Beaverlodge, *Canada* **110** 55 11N 119 29W
Beavermouth, *Canada* **110** 51 32N 117 23W
Beaverstone →, *Canada* **104** 54 59N 89 25W
Beaverton, *Canada* **108** 44 26N 79 9W
Beaverton, *U.S.A.* **124** 45 29N 122 48W
Beaverville, *U.S.A.* **119** 40 57N 87 39W
Beawar, *India* **48** 26 3N 74 18 E
Bebedouro, *Brazil* **141** 21 0 S 48 25W
Beboa, *Madag.* **97** 17 22 S 44 33 E
Bebra, *W. Germany* **30** 50 59N 9 48 E
Beccles, *U.K.* **13** 52 27N 1 33 E
Bečej, *Yugoslavia* **33** 45 36N 20 3 E
Becerreá, *Spain* **22** 42 51N 7 10W
Béchar, *Algeria* **85** 31 38N 2 18W
Beckley, *U.S.A.* **114** 37 50N 81 8W
Beckum, *W. Germany* **30** 51 46N 8 3 E
Bečva →, *Czech.* **32** 49 31N 17 40 E
Bédar, *Spain* **25** 37 11N 1 59W
Bédarieux, *France* **20** 43 37N 3 10 E
Bédarrides, *France* **21** 44 2N 4 54 E
Beddouza, Ras, *Morocco* **84** 32 33N 9 9W
Bedele, *Ethiopia* **89** 8 31N 36 23 E
Bederkesa, *W. Germany* **30** 53 37N 8 50 E
Bederwanak, *Somali Rep.* **98** 9 34N 44 23 E
Bedeso, *Ethiopia* **89** 9 58N 40 52 E
Bedford, *Canada* **107** 45 7N 72 59W
Bedford, *S. Africa* **96** 32 40 S 26 10 E
Bedford, *U.K.* **13** 52 8N 0 29W
Bedford, *Ind., U.S.A.* **119** 38 50N 86 30W
Bedford, *Iowa, U.S.A.* **118** 40 40N 94 41W
Bedford, *Ky., U.S.A.* **119** 38 36N 85 19W
Bedford, *Ohio, U.S.A.* **116** 41 23N 81 32W
Bedford, *Pa., U.S.A.* **116** 40 1N 78 30W
Bedford, *Va., U.S.A.* **114** 37 25N 79 30W
Bedford □, *U.K.* **13** 52 4N 0 28W
Bedford, C., *Australia* **72** 15 14 S 145 21 E
Bedford Downs, *Australia* **78** 17 19 S 127 20 E
Bedgerebong, *Australia* **76** 33 21 S 147 43 E
Bedi, *Chad* **87** 11 6N 18 33 E
Będków, *Poland* **32** 51 36N 19 44 E
Bednja →, *Yugoslavia* **27** 46 12N 16 25 E
Bednodemyanovsk, *U.S.S.R.* **37** 53 55N 43 15 E
Bedónia, *Italy* **26** 44 28N 9 36 E
Bedourie, *Australia* **72** 24 30 S 139 30 E
Bedum, *Neths.* **16** 53 18N 6 36 E
Będzin, *Poland* **32** 50 19N 19 7 E
Beeac, *Australia* **74** 38 13 S 143 37 E
Beebe Plain, *Canada* **107** 45 1N 72 9W
Beebo, *Australia* **77** 28 43 S 150 59 E
Beech Fork →, *U.S.A.* **119** 37 55N 85 50W
Beech Grove, *U.S.A.* **119** 39 40N 86 2W
Beecher, *U.S.A.* **119** 41 21N 87 38W
Beechworth, *Australia* **75** 36 22 S 146 43 E
Beechy, *Canada* **111** 50 53N 107 24W
Beecroft Head, *Australia* **77** 35 0 S 150 51 E
Beek, *Gelderland, Neths.* **16** 51 55N 6 11 E
Beek, *Limburg, Neths.* **17** 50 57N 5 48 E
Beek, *Noord-Brabant, Neths.* **17** 51 32N 5 38 E
Beekbergen, *Neths.* **16** 52 10N 5 58 E
Beelitz, *E. Germany* **30** 52 14N 12 58 E
Beenleigh, *Australia* **77** 27 43 S 153 10 E
Be'er Sheva', *Israel* **44** 31 15N 34 48 E
Be'er Sheva' →, *Israel* **44** 31 12N 34 40 E
Be'er Toviyya, *Israel* **44** 31 44N 34 42 E
Be'eri, *Israel* **44** 31 25N 34 30 E
Be'erotayim, *Israel* **44** 32 19N 34 59 E
Beersheba = Be'er Sheva', *Israel* **44** 31 15N 34 48 E
Beerta, *Neths.* **16** 53 11N 7 6 E
Beerze →, *Neths.* **16** 51 39N 5 20 E
Beesd, *Neths.* **16** 51 53N 5 11 E
Beeskow, *E. Germany* **30** 52 9N 14 14 E
Beeston, *U.K.* **12** 52 55N 1 11W
Beetaloo, *Australia* **72** 17 15 S 133 50 E
Beeton, *Canada* **108** 44 5N 79 47W
Beetsterzwaag, *Neths.* **16** 53 4N 6 5 E
Beetzendorf, *E. Germany* **30** 52 42N 11 6 E
Beeville, *U.S.A.* **121** 28 27N 97 44W
Befale, *Zaïre* **94** 0 25N 20 45 E
Befandriana, *Madag.* **97** 21 55 S 44 0 E
Befotaka, *Madag.* **97** 23 49 S 47 0 E
Bega, *Australia* **75** 36 41 S 149 51 E
Bega, Canalul, *Romania* **34** 45 37N 20 46 E
Bégard, *France* **18** 48 38N 3 18W
Bègles, *France* **20** 44 45N 0 35W
Begna →, *Norway* **10** 60 41N 10 0 E
Begonte, *Spain* **22** 43 10N 7 40W
Begusarai, *India* **49** 25 24N 86 9 E
Behara, *Madag.* **97** 24 55 S 46 20 E
Behbehān, *Iran* **46** 30 30N 50 15 E
Behshahr, *Iran* **47** 36 45N 53 35 E
Bei Jiang →, *China* **59** 23 2N 112 58 E
Bei'an, *China* **62** 48 10N 126 20 E
Beibei, *China* **62** 29 47N 106 22 E
Beigang, *Taiwan* **59** 23 38N 120 16 E
Beihai, *China* **58** 21 28N 109 6 E
Beijing, *China* **60** 39 55N 116 20 E
Beijing □, *China* **60** 39 55N 116 20 E
Beilen, *Neths.* **16** 52 52N 6 27 E
Beiliu, *China* **59** 22 41N 110 21 E
Beilngries, *W. Germany* **31** 49 1N 11 27 E
Beilpajah, *Australia* **73** 32 54 S 143 52 E
Beilul, *Ethiopia* **89** 13 2N 42 20 E
Beipiao, *China* **61** 41 52N 120 32 E
Beira, *Mozam.* **93** 19 50 S 34 52 E
Beira, *Somali Rep.* **98** 6 57N 47 19 E
Beirut = Bayrūt, *Lebanon* **46** 33 53N 35 31 E
Beit Lāhiyah, *Egypt* **44** 31 32N 34 30 E
Beitaolaizhao, *China* **61** 44 58N 125 58 E
Beitbridge, *Zambia* **93** 22 12 S 30 0 E
Beiuş, *Romania* **34** 46 40N 22 21 E
Beizhen, *Liaoning, China* **61** 41 38N 121 54 E
Beizhen, *Shandong, China* **61** 37 20N 118 2 E
Beizhengzhen, *China* **61** 44 31N 123 30 E
Beja, *Portugal* **23** 38 2N 7 53W
Béja, *Tunisia* **86** 36 43N 9 12 E
Beja □, *Portugal* **23** 37 55N 7 55W
Bejaia, *Algeria* **85** 36 42N 5 2 E
Béjar, *Spain* **22** 40 23N 5 46W
Bejestān, *Iran* **47** 34 30N 58 5 E
Bekasi, *Indonesia* **57** 6 14 S 106 59 E
Békés, *Hungary* **33** 46 47N 21 9 E
Békéscsaba, *Hungary* **33** 46 40N 21 5 E
Bekily, *Madag.* **97** 24 13 S 45 19 E
Bekkevoort, *Belgium* **17** 50 57N 4 58 E
Bekoji, *Ethiopia* **89** 7 40N 39 17 E
Bekok, *Malaysia* **55** 2 20N 103 7 E
Bekwai, *Ghana* **91** 6 30N 1 34W
Bela, *India* **49** 25 50N 82 0 E
Bela, *Pakistan* **48** 26 12N 66 20 E
Bela Crkva, *Yugoslavia* **33** 44 55N 21 27 E
Bela Palanka, *Yugoslavia* **33** 43 13N 22 17 E
Bela Vista, *Brazil* **140** 22 12 S 56 20W
Bela Vista, *Mozam.* **97** 26 10 S 32 44 E
Bélâbre, *France* **20** 46 34N 1 8 E
Belalcázar, *Spain* **23** 38 35N 5 10W
Belaringar, *Australia* **76** 31 45 S 147 34 E
Belas, *Angola* **95** 8 55 S 13 9 E
Belau Is., *Pac. Oc.* **66** 7 30N 134 30 E
Belavenona, *Madag.* **97** 24 50 S 47 4 E
Belawan, *Indonesia* **56** 3 33N 98 32 E
Belaya, Mt., *Ethiopia* **89** 11 25N 36 8 E
Belaya Glina, *U.S.S.R.* **39** 46 5N 40 48 E
Belaya Kalitva, *U.S.S.R.* **39** 48 13N 40 50 E
Belaya Kholunitsa, *U.S.S.R.* **37** 58 41N 50 13 E
Belaya Tserkov, *U.S.S.R.* **36** 49 45N 30 10 E
Belcher Is., *Canada* **104** 56 15N 78 45W
Belchite, *Spain* **24** 41 18N 0 43W
Belcourt, *Canada* **106** 48 24N 77 21W
Belden, *U.S.A.* **124** 40 2N 121 17W
Belém, *Brazil* **138** 1 20 S 48 30W
Belém de São Francisco, *Brazil* **138** 8 46 S 38 58W
Belén, *Argentina* **140** 27 40 S 67 5W
Belén, *Colombia* **134** 1 26N 75 56W
Belén, *Paraguay* **140** 23 30 S 57 6W
Belen, *U.S.A.* **123** 34 40N 106 50W
Bélesta, *France* **20** 42 55N 1 56 E
Belet Uen, *Somali Rep.* **98** 4 30N 45 5 E
Belev, *U.S.S.R.* **37** 53 50N 36 5 E
Belfair, *U.S.A.* **124** 47 27N 122 50W
Belfast, *N.Z.* **81** 43 27 S 172 39 E
Belfast, *S. Africa* **97** 25 42 S 30 2 E
Belfast, *U.K.* **15** 54 35N 5 56W
Belfast, *Maine, U.S.A.* **105** 44 30N 69 0W
Belfast, *N.Y., U.S.A.* **116** 42 21N 78 9W
Belfast □, *U.K.* **15** 54 35N 5 56W
Belfast, L., *U.K.* **15** 54 40N 5 50W
Belfeld, *Neths.* **17** 51 18N 6 6 E
Belfield, *U.S.A.* **120** 46 54N 103 11W
Belfort, *France* **19** 47 38N 6 50 E
Belfry, *U.S.A.* **122** 45 10N 109 2W
Belgaum, *India* **51** 15 55N 74 35 E
Belgioioso, *Italy* **26** 45 9N 9 21 E
Belgium ■, *Europe* **17** 50 30N 5 0 E
Belgorod, *U.S.S.R.* **38** 50 35N 36 35 E
Belgorod-Dnestrovskiy, *U.S.S.R.* **38** 46 11N 30 23 E
Belgrade = Beograd, *Yugoslavia* **33** 44 50N 20 37 E
Belgrade, *U.S.A.* **122** 45 50N 111 10W
Belgrove, *N.Z.* **81** 41 27 S 172 59 E
Belhaven, *U.S.A.* **115** 35 34N 76 35W
Beli Drim →, *Europe* **33** 42 6N 20 25 E
Beli Manastir, *Yugoslavia* **33** 45 45N 18 36 E
Belice →, *Italy* **28** 37 35N 12 55 E
Belin-Béliet, *France* **20** 44 29N 0 47W
Belinga, *Gabon* **94** 1 10N 13 2 E
Belinskiy, *U.S.S.R.* **37** 53 0N 43 25 E
Belinyu, *Indonesia* **56** 1 35 S 105 50 E
Belitung, *Indonesia* **56** 3 10 S 107 50 E
Beliu, *Romania* **34** 46 30N 22 0 E
Belize ■, *Cent. Amer.* **127** 17 0N 88 30W
Belize City, *Belize* **127** 17 25N 88 0W
Beljanica, *Yugoslavia* **33** 44 8N 21 43 E
Belkovskiy, Ostrov, *U.S.S.R.* **41** 75 32N 135 44 E
Bell, *Australia* **76** 33 28 S 150 17 E
Bell →, *Canada* **106** 49 48N 77 38W
Bell Bay, *Australia* **72** 41 6 S 146 53 E
Bell I., *Canada* **105** 50 46N 55 35W
Bell-Irving →, *Canada* **110** 56 12N 129 5W
Bell Peninsula, *Canada* **103** 63 50N 82 0W
Bell Ville, *Argentina* **140** 32 40 S 62 40W
Bella Bella, *Canada* **110** 52 10N 128 10W
Bella Coola, *Canada* **110** 52 25N 126 40W
Bella Flor, *Bolivia* **136** 11 9 S 67 49W
Bella Unión, *Uruguay* **140** 30 15 S 57 40W
Bella Vista, *Corrientes, Argentina* **140** 28 33 S 59 0W
Bella Vista, *Tucuman, Argentina* **140** 27 10 S 65 25W
Bellac, *France* **20** 46 7N 1 3 E
Bellágio, *Italy* **26** 45 59N 9 15 E
Bellaire, *U.S.A.* **116** 40 1N 80 46W
Bellary, *India* **51** 15 10N 76 56 E
Bellata, *Australia* **77** 29 53 S 149 46 E
Bellbird, *Australia* **76** 32 52 S 151 19 E
Bellbrook, *Australia* **77** 30 47 S 152 31 E
Belle, *U.S.A.* **118** 38 17N 91 43W
Belle, La, *Fla., U.S.A.* **115** 26 45N 81 22W
Belle, La, *Mo., U.S.A.* **118** 40 7N 91 55W
Belle Fourche, *U.S.A.* **120** 44 43N 103 52W
Belle Fourche →, *U.S.A.* **120** 44 25N 102 19W
Belle Glade, *U.S.A.* **115** 26 43N 80 38W
Belle-Ile, *France* **18** 47 20N 3 10W
Belle Isle, *Canada* **105** 51 57N 55 25W
Belle Isle, Str. of, *Canada* **105** 51 30N 56 30W
Belle-Isle-en-Terre, *France* **18** 48 33N 3 23W
Belle Plaine, *Iowa, U.S.A.* **118** 41 51N 92 18W
Belle Plaine, *Minn., U.S.A.* **120** 44 35N 93 48W
Belle Rive, *U.S.A.* **119** 38 14N 88 45W
Belle River, *Canada* **108** 42 18N 82 43W
Belle Yella, *Liberia* **90** 7 24N 10 0W
Belledonne, Chaîne de, *France* **21** 45 20N 6 10 E
Belledune, *Canada* **105** 47 55N 65 50W
Bellefontaine, *U.S.A.* **119** 40 20N 83 45W
Bellefonte, *U.S.A.* **116** 40 56N 77 45W
Bellegarde, *France* **19** 47 59N 2 26 E
Bellegarde-en-Marche, *France* **20** 45 59N 2 18 E
Bellegarde-sur-Valserine, *France* **21** 46 4N 5 50 E
Bellême, *France* **18** 48 22N 0 34 E
Belleoram, *Canada* **105** 47 31N 55 25W
Belleterre, *Canada* **106** 47 25N 78 41W
Belleville, *Canada* **109** 44 10N 77 23W
Belleville, *France* **21** 46 7N 4 45 E
Belleville, *Ill., U.S.A.* **118** 38 30N 90 0W
Belleville, *Kans., U.S.A.* **120** 39 51N 97 38W
Belleville, *N.Y., U.S.A.* **117** 43 46N 76 10W
Belleville-sur-Vie, *France* **18** 46 46N 1 25W
Bellevue, *Canada* **110** 49 35N 114 22W
Bellevue, *Idaho, U.S.A.* **122** 43 25N 114 23W
Bellevue, *Iowa, U.S.A.* **118** 42 16N 90 26W
Bellevue, *Mich., U.S.A.* **119** 42 27N 85 1W
Bellevue, *Ohio, U.S.A.* **116** 41 20N 82 48W
Bellevue, *Wash., U.S.A.* **124** 47 37N 122 12W
Belley, *France* **21** 45 46N 5 41 E
Bellflower, *U.S.A.* **118** 39 0N 91 21W
Bellin, *Canada* **103** 60 0N 70 0W
Bellingen, *Australia* **77** 30 25 S 152 50 E
Bellingham, *U.S.A.* **110** 48 45N 122 27W
Bellingshausen, *Antarctica* **143** 62 0 S 59 0W
Bellingshausen Sea, *Antarctica* **143** 66 0 S 80 0W
Bellinzona, *Switz.* **31** 46 11N 9 1 E
Bello, *Colombia* **134** 6 20N 75 33W
Bellona, *Solomon Is.* **68** 11 17 S 159 47 E
Bellows Falls, *U.S.A.* **117** 43 10N 72 30W
Bellpat, *Pakistan* **48** 29 0N 68 5 E
Bellpuig, *Spain* **24** 41 37N 1 1 E
Bells Corners, *Canada* **109** 45 19N 75 50W
Belluno, *Italy* **27** 46 8N 12 13 E
Bellville, *U.S.A.* **121** 29 58N 96 18W
Bellwood, *U.S.A.* **116** 40 36N 78 21W
Bélmez, *Spain* **23** 38 17N 5 17W
Belmond, *U.S.A.* **118** 42 51N 93 37W
Belmont, *Australia* **76** 33 4 S 151 42 E
Belmont, *Canada* **108** 42 53N 81 5W
Belmont, *S. Africa* **96** 29 28 S 24 22 E
Belmont, *U.S.A.* **116** 42 14N 78 3W
Belmonte, *Brazil* **139** 16 0 S 39 0W
Belmonte, *Portugal* **22** 40 21N 7 20W
Belmonte, *Spain* **24** 39 34N 2 43W
Belmopan, *Belize* **127** 17 18N 88 30W
Belmullet, *Ireland* **15** 54 13N 9 58W
Belo Horizonte, *Brazil* **139** 19 55 S 43 56W
Belo Jardim, *Brazil* **138** 8 20 S 36 26W
Belo-sur-Mer, *Madag.* **97** 20 42 S 44 0 E
Belo-Tsiribihina, *Madag.* **97** 19 40 S 44 30 E
Beloeil, *Canada* **107** 45 34N 73 12W
Belogorsk, *R.S.F.S.R., U.S.S.R.* **41** 51 0N 128 20 E
Belogorsk, *Ukraine S.S.R., U.S.S.R.* **38** 45 3N 34 35 E
Belogradchik, *Bulgaria* **34** 43 53N 22 15 E
Beloha, *Madag.* **97** 25 10 S 45 3 E
Beloit, *Kans., U.S.A.* **120** 39 32N 98 9W
Beloit, *Wis., U.S.A.* **118** 42 35N 89 0W
Belokorovichi, *U.S.S.R.* **36** 51 7N 28 2 E
Belomorsk, *U.S.S.R.* **40** 64 35N 34 30 E
Belonia, *India* **52** 23 15N 91 30 E
Belopolye, *U.S.S.R.* **36** 51 14N 34 20 E
Belovo, *U.S.S.R.* **40** 54 30N 86 0 E
Beloye More, *U.S.S.R.* **40** 66 30N 38 0 E
Beloye Ozero, *U.S.S.R.* **39** 45 15N 46 50 E
Belozersk, *U.S.S.R.* **37** 60 0N 37 30 E
Belpasso, *Italy* **29** 37 37N 15 0 E
Belsele, *Belgium* **17** 51 9N 4 6 E
Belsito, *Italy* **28** 37 50N 13 47 E
Beltana, *Australia* **73** 30 48 S 138 25 E
Belterra, *Brazil* **135** 2 45 S 55 0W
Beltinci, *Yugoslavia* **27** 46 37N 16 20 E
Belton, *S.C., U.S.A.* **115** 34 31N 82 39W
Belton, *Tex., U.S.A.* **121** 31 4N 97 30W
Belton Res., *U.S.A.* **121** 31 8N 97 32W
Beltsy, *U.S.S.R.* **38** 47 48N 28 0 E
Belturbet, *Ireland* **15** 54 6N 7 28W
Belukha, *U.S.S.R.* **40** 49 50N 86 50 E
Beluran, *Malaysia* **56** 5 48N 117 35 E
Belvedere Maríttimo, *Italy* **29** 39 37N 15 52 E
Belvès, *France* **20** 44 46N 1 0 E
Belvidere, *Ill., U.S.A.* **119** 42 15N 88 55W
Belvidere, *N.J., U.S.A.* **117** 40 48N 75 5W
Belvis de la Jara, *Spain* **23** 39 45N 4 57W
Belyando →, *Australia* **72** 21 38 S 146 50 E
Belyy, *U.S.S.R.* **36** 55 48N 32 51 E
Belyy, Ostrov, *U.S.S.R.* **40** 73 30N 71 0 E
Belyy Yar, *U.S.S.R.* **40** 58 26N 84 39 E
Belzig, *E. Germany* **30** 52 8N 12 36 E
Belzoni, *U.S.A.* **121** 33 12N 90 30W
Bemaraha, Lembalemban' i, *Madag.* **97** 18 40 S 44 45 E
Bemarivo, *Madag.* **97** 21 45 S 44 45 E
Bemarivo →, *Madag.* **97** 15 27 S 47 40 E
Bemavo, *Madag.* **97** 21 33 S 45 25 E
Bembéréke, *Benin* **91** 10 11N 2 43 E
Bembesi, *Zambia* **93** 20 0 S 28 58 E
Bembesi →, *Zambia* **93** 18 57 S 27 47 E
Bembézar →, *Spain* **23** 37 45N 5 13W
Bemboka, *Australia* **75** 36 38 S 149 34 E
Bement, *U.S.A.* **119** 39 55N 88 34W
Bemidji, *U.S.A.* **120** 47 30N 94 50W
Bemm River, *Australia* **75** 37 47 S 148 58 E
Bemmel, *Neths.* **16** 51 54N 5 54 E
Ben 'Ammi, *Israel* **44** 33 0N 35 7 E
Ben Bullen, *Australia* **76** 33 12 S 150 2 E
Ben Cruachan, *U.K.* **14** 56 26N 5 8W
Ben Dearg, *U.K.* **14** 57 47N 4 58W
Ben Gardane, *Tunisia* **86** 33 11N 11 11 E
Ben Hope, *U.K.* **14** 58 24N 4 36W
Ben Lawers, *U.K.* **14** 56 33N 4 13W
Ben Lomond, *N.S.W., Australia* **77** 30 1 S 151 43 E

Bhatghar L.

Ben Lomond, *Tas., Australia* **72** 41 38 S 147 42 E
Ben Lomond, *U.K.* **14** 56 12N 4 39W
Ben Luc, *Vietnam* **55** 10 39N 106 29 E
Ben Macdhui, *U.K.* **14** 57 4N 3 40W
Ben Mhor, *U.K.* **14** 57 16N 7 21W
Ben More, *Central, U.K.* **14** 56 23N 4 31W
Ben More, *Strathclyde, U.K.* **14** 56 26N 6 2W
Ben More Assynt, *U.K.* **14** 58 7N 4 51W
Ben Nevis, *U.K.* **14** 56 48N 5 0W
Ben Ohau Ra., *N.Z.* **81** 44 1 S 170 4 E
Ben Quang, *Vietnam* **54** 17 3N 106 55 E
Ben Slimane, *Morocco* **84** 33 38N 7 7W
Ben Tre, *Vietnam* **55** 10 3N 106 36 E
Ben Vorlich, *U.K.* **14** 56 22N 4 15W
Ben Wyvis, *U.K.* **14** 57 40N 4 35W
Bena, *Nigeria* **91** 11 20N 5 50 E
Bena Dibele, *Zaïre* **95** 4 4 S 22 50 E
Bena-Leka, *Zaïre* **95** 5 8 S 22 10 E
Bena-Tshadi, *Zaïre* **95** 4 40 S 22 49 E
Benadir □, *Somali Rep.* **98** 1 30N 44 30 E
Benagalbón, *Spain* **23** 36 45N 4 15W
Benagerie, *Australia* **73** 31 25 S 140 22 E
Benahmed, *Morocco* **84** 33 4N 7 9W
Benalla, *Australia* **74** 36 30 S 146 0 E
Benamejí, *Spain* **23** 37 16N 4 33W
Benares = Varanasi, *India* **49** 25 22N 83 0 E
Bénat, C., *France* **21** 43 5N 6 22 E
Benavente, *Portugal* **23** 38 59N 8 49W
Benavente, *Spain* **22** 42 2N 5 43W
Benavides, *Spain* **22** 42 30N 5 54W
Benavides, *U.S.A.* **121** 27 35N 98 28W
Benbecula, *U.K.* **14** 57 26N 7 21W
Benbonyathe, Mt., *Australia* **73** 30 25 S 139 11 E
Bencubbin, *Australia* **79** 30 48 S 117 52 E
Bend, *U.S.A.* **122** 44 2N 121 15W
Bendel □, *Nigeria* **91** 6 0N 6 0 E
Bendela, *Zaïre* **94** 3 18 S 17 36 E
Bendemeer, *Australia* **77** 30 53 S 151 8 E
Bender Beila, *Somali Rep.* **98** 9 30N 50 48 E
Bender Merchagno, *Somali Rep.* **98** 11 41N 50 34 E
Bendering, *Australia* **79** 32 23 S 118 18 E
Bendery, *U.S.S.R.* **38** 46 50N 29 30 E
Bendick Murrell, *Australia* **76** 34 8 S 148 28 E
Bendigo, *Australia* **74** 36 40 S 144 15 E
Bendorf, *W. Germany* **30** 50 26N 7 34 E
Benē Beraq, *Israel* **44** 32 6N 34 51 E
Beneden Knijpe, *Neths.* **16** 52 58N 5 59 E
Beneditinos, *Brazil* **138** 5 27 S 42 22W
Benedito Leite, *Brazil* **138** 7 13 S 44 34W
Bénéna, *Mali* **90** 13 9N 4 17W
Benenitra, *Madag.* **97** 23 27 S 45 5 E
Benešŏv, *Czech.* **32** 49 46N 14 41 E
Bénestroff, *France* **19** 48 54N 6 45 E
Benet, *France* **20** 46 22N 0 35W
Benetook, *Australia* **74** 34 22 S 142 0 E
Benevento, *Italy* **29** 41 7N 14 45 E
Benfeld, *France* **19** 48 22N 7 34 E
Benga, *Mozam.* **93** 16 11 S 33 40 E
Bengal, Bay of, *Ind. Oc.* **42** 15 0N 90 0 E
Bengbu, *China* **61** 32 58N 117 20 E
Benghazi = Banghāzī, *Libya* **86** 32 11N 20 3 E
Bengkalis, *Indonesia* **56** 1 30N 102 10 E
Bengkulu, *Indonesia* **56** 3 50 S 102 12 E
Bengkulu □, *Indonesia* **56** 3 48 S 102 16 E
Bengough, *Canada* **111** 49 25N 105 10W
Benguela, *Angola* **95** 12 37 S 13 25 E
Benguela □, *Angola* **95** 13 0 S 13 30 E
Benguerir, *Morocco* **84** 32 16N 7 56W
Benguérua, I., *Mozam.* **97** 21 58 S 35 28 E
Benha, *Egypt* **88** 30 26N 31 8 E
Beni, *Australia* **76** 32 11 S 148 43 E
Beni, *Zaïre* **92** 0 30N 29 27 E
Beni □, *Bolivia* **137** 14 0 S 65 0W
Beni →, *Bolivia* **137** 10 23 S 65 24W
Beni Abbès, *Algeria* **85** 30 5N 2 5W
Beni-Haoua, *Algeria* **85** 36 30N 1 30 E
Beni Mazâr, *Egypt* **88** 28 32N 30 44 E
Beni Mellal, *Morocco* **84** 32 21N 6 21W
Beni Ounif, *Algeria* **85** 32 0N 1 10W
Beni Saf, *Algeria* **85** 35 17N 1 15W
Beni Suef, *Egypt* **88** 29 5N 31 6 E
Beniah L., *Canada* **110** 63 23N 112 17W
Benicarló, *Spain* **24** 40 23N 0 23 E
Benicia, *U.S.A.* **124** 38 3N 122 9W
Benidorm, *Spain* **25** 38 33N 0 9W
Benidorm, Islote de, *Spain* **25** 38 31N 0 9W
Benin ■, *Africa* **91** 10 0N 2 0 E
Benin, Bight of, *W. Afr.* **91** 5 0N 3 0 E
Benin City, *Nigeria* **91** 6 20N 5 31 E
Benisa, *Spain* **25** 38 43N 0 3 E
Benjamin Aceval, *Paraguay* **140** 24 58 S 57 34W
Benjamin Constant, *Brazil* **134** 4 40 S 70 15W
Benjamin Hill, *Mexico* **126** 30 10N 111 10W
Benkelman, *U.S.A.* **120** 40 7N 101 32W
Benkovac, *Yugoslavia* **27** 44 2N 15 37 E
Benlidi, *Australia* **72** 24 35 S 144 50 E
Benmore Pk., *N.Z.* **81** 44 25 S 170 8 E
Bennebroek, *Neths.* **16** 52 19N 4 36 E
Bennekom, *Neths.* **16** 52 0N 5 41 E
Bennett, *Canada* **110** 59 56N 134 53W
Bennett, Ostrov, *U.S.S.R.* **41** 76 21N 148 56 E
Bennettsville, *U.S.A.* **115** 34 38N 79 39W
Bennington, *U.S.A.* **117** 42 52N 73 12W
Benny, *Canada* **108** 46 47N 81 38W
Bénodet, *France* **18** 47 53N 4 7W
Benoni, *S. Africa* **97** 26 11 S 28 18 E
Benoud, *Algeria* **85** 32 20N 0 16 E
Benoy, *Chad* **87** 8 59N 16 19 E
Benque Viejo, *Belize* **127** 17 5N 89 8W
Bensheim, *W. Germany* **31** 49 40N 8 38 E
Benson, *U.S.A.* **123** 31 59N 110 19W
Bent, *Iran* **47** 26 20N 59 31 E
Benteng, *Indonesia* **57** 6 10 S 120 30 E
Bentinck I., *Australia* **72** 17 3 S 139 35 E
Bentiu, *Sudan* **89** 9 10N 29 55 E
Bento Gonçalves, *Brazil* **141** 29 10 S 51 31W
Benton, *Ark., U.S.A.* **121** 34 30N 92 35W
Benton, *Calif., U.S.A.* **124** 37 48N 118 32W
Benton, *Ill., U.S.A.* **118** 38 0N 88 55W
Benton Harbor, *U.S.A.* **119** 42 10N 86 28W
Bentu Liben, *Ethiopia* **89** 8 32N 38 21 E
Bentung, *Malaysia* **55** 3 31N 101 55 E
Benue □, *Nigeria* **91** 7 30N 7 30 E
Benue →, *Nigeria* **91** 7 48N 6 46 E
Benxi, *China* **61** 41 20N 123 48 E
Benzdorp, *Surinam* **135** 3 44N 54 5W
Beo, *Indonesia* **57** 4 25N 126 50 E
Beograd, *Yugoslavia* **33** 44 50N 20 37 E
Beowawe, *U.S.A.* **122** 40 35N 116 30W
Bepan Jiang →, *China* **58** 24 55N 106 5 E
Beppu, *Japan* **64** 33 15N 131 30 E
Beppu-Wan, *Japan* **64** 33 18N 131 34 E
Bera, *Bangla.* **52** 24 5N 89 37 E
Berati, *Albania* **35** 40 43N 19 59 E
Berau, Teluk, *Indonesia* **57** 2 30 S 132 30 E
Berber, *Sudan* **88** 18 0N 34 0 E
Berbera, *Somali Rep.* **98** 10 30N 45 2 E
Berbérati, *C.A.R.* **94** 4 15N 15 40 E
Berberia, C. del, *Spain* **25** 38 39N 1 24 E
Berbice □, *Guyana* **135** 4 0N 58 0W
Berbice →, *Guyana* **135** 6 20N 57 32W
Berceto, *Italy* **26** 44 30N 10 0 E
Berchtesgaden, *W. Germany* **31** 47 37N 12 58 E
Berdale, *Somali Rep.* **98** 7 4N 47 51 E
Berdichev, *U.S.S.R.* **38** 49 57N 28 30 E
Berdsk, *U.S.S.R.* **40** 54 47N 83 2 E
Berdyansk, *U.S.S.R.* **38** 46 45N 36 50 E
Berea, *U.S.A.* **114** 37 35N 84 18W
Berebere, *Indonesia* **57** 2 25N 128 45 E
Bereda, *Somali Rep.* **98** 11 45N 51 0 E
Bereina, *Papua N. G.* **69** 8 39 S 146 30 E
Berekum, *Ghana* **90** 7 29N 2 34W
Berenice, *Egypt* **88** 24 2N 35 25 E
Berens →, *Canada* **111** 52 25N 97 2W
Berens I., *Canada* **111** 52 18N 97 18W
Berens River, *Canada* **111** 52 25N 97 0W
Berestechko, *U.S.S.R.* **36** 50 22N 25 5 E
Bereşti, *Romania* **34** 46 6N 27 50 E
Beretău →, *Romania* **34** 47 10N 21 50 E
Berettyo →, *Hungary* **33** 46 59N 21 7 E
Berettyóújfalu, *Hungary* **33** 47 13N 21 33 E
Berevo, *Mahajanga, Madag.* **97** 17 14 S 44 17 E
Berevo, *Toliara, Madag.* **97** 19 44 S 44 58 E
Bereza, *U.S.S.R.* **36** 52 31N 24 51 E
Berezhany, *U.S.S.R.* **36** 49 26N 24 58 E
Berezina →, *U.S.S.R.* **36** 52 33N 30 14 E
Berezna, *U.S.S.R.* **37** 51 35N 31 46 E
Berezniki, *U.S.S.R.* **40** 59 24N 56 46 E
Berezovka, *U.S.S.R.* **38** 47 14N 30 55 E
Berezovo, *U.S.S.R.* **40** 64 0N 65 0 E
Berga, *Spain* **24** 42 6N 1 48 E
Berga, *Sweden* **11** 57 14N 16 3 E
Bergama, *Turkey* **46** 39 8N 27 15 E
Bergambacht, *Neths.* **16** 51 56N 4 48 E
Bérgamo, *Italy* **26** 45 42N 9 40 E
Bergantiños, *Spain* **22** 43 20N 8 40W
Bergara, *Spain* **24** 43 9N 2 28W
Bergedorf, *W. Germany* **30** 53 28N 10 12 E
Bergeijk, *Neths.* **17** 51 19N 5 21 E
Bergen, *E. Germany* **30** 54 24N 13 26 E
Bergen, *Neths.* **16** 52 40N 4 43 E
Bergen, *Norway* **9** 60 23N 5 20 E
Bergen, *U.S.A.* **116** 43 5N 77 56W
Bergen-op-Zoom, *Neths.* **17** 51 30N 4 18 E
Bergerac, *France* **20** 44 51N 0 30 E
Bergheim, *W. Germany* **30** 50 57N 6 38 E
Berghem, *Neths.* **16** 51 46N 5 33 E
Bergisch-Gladbach, *W. Germany* **30** 50 59N 7 9 E
Bergkvara, *Sweden* **11** 56 23N 16 5 E
Bergschenhoek, *Neths.* **16** 51 59N 4 30 E
Bergsjö, *Sweden* **10** 61 59N 17 3 E
Bergues, *France* **19** 50 58N 2 24 E
Bergum, *Neths.* **16** 53 13N 5 59 E
Bergvik, *Sweden* **10** 61 16N 16 50 E
Bergville, *S. Africa* **97** 28 52 S 29 18 E
Berhala, Selat, *Indonesia* **56** 1 0 S 104 15 E
Berhampore = Baharampur, *India* **49** 24 2N 88 27 E
Berhampur, *India* **50** 19 15N 84 54 E
Berheci →, *Romania* **34** 46 7N 27 19 E
Bering Sea, *Pac. Oc.* **102** 58 0N 167 0 E
Bering Str., *U.S.A.* **102** 66 0N 170 0W
Beringen, *Belgium* **17** 51 3N 5 14 E
Beringovskiy, *U.S.S.R.* **41** 63 3N 179 19 E
Berislav, *U.S.S.R.* **38** 46 50N 33 30 E
Berisso, *Argentina* **140** 34 56 S 57 50W
Berja, *Spain* **25** 36 50N 2 56W
Berkane, *Morocco* **85** 34 52N 2 20W
Berkel →, *Neths.* **16** 52 8N 6 12 E
Berkeley, *U.K.* **13** 51 41N 2 28W
Berkeley, *U.S.A.* **124** 37 52N 122 20W
Berkeley Springs, *U.S.A.* **114** 39 38N 78 12W
Berkhout, *Neths.* **16** 52 38N 4 59 E
Berkner I., *Antarctica* **143** 79 30 S 50 0W
Berkovitsa, *Bulgaria* **34** 43 16N 23 8 E
Berkshire □, *U.K.* **13** 51 30N 1 20W
Berlaar, *Belgium* **17** 51 7N 4 39 E
Berland →, *Canada* **110** 54 0N 116 50W
Berlanga, *Spain* **23** 38 17N 5 50W
Berlare, *Belgium* **17** 51 2N 4 0 E
Berleburg, *W. Germany* **30** 51 3N 8 22 E
Berlenga, I., *Portugal* **23** 39 25N 9 30W
Berlin, *Germany* **30** 52 32N 13 24 E
Berlin, *Md., U.S.A.* **114** 38 19N 75 12W
Berlin, *N.H., U.S.A.* **117** 44 29N 71 10W
Berlin, *Wis., U.S.A.* **114** 43 58N 88 55W
Bermeja, Sierra, *Spain* **23** 36 30N 5 11W
Bermejo →, *Formosa, Argentina* **140** 26 51 S 58 23W
Bermejo →, *San Juan, Argentina* **140** 32 30 S 67 30W
Bermeo, *Spain* **24** 43 25N 2 47W
Bermillo de Sayago, *Spain* **22** 41 22N 6 8W
Bermuda ■, *Atl. Oc.* **4** 32 45N 65 0W
Bern, *Switz.* **31** 46 57N 7 28 E
Bern □, *Switz.* **31** 46 45N 7 40 E
Bernado, *U.S.A.* **123** 34 30N 106 53W
Bernalda, *Italy* **29** 40 24N 16 44 E
Bernalillo, *U.S.A.* **123** 35 17N 106 37W
Bernard L., *Canada* **108** 45 45N 79 23W
Bernardo de Irigoyen, *Argentina* **141** 26 15 S 53 40W
Bernardo O'Higgins □, *Chile* **140** 34 15 S 70 45W
Bernasconi, *Argentina* **140** 37 55 S 63 44W
Bernau, *E. Germany* **30** 52 40N 13 35 E
Bernau, *W. Germany* **31** 47 45N 12 20 E
Bernay, *France* **18** 49 5N 0 35 E
Bernburg, *E. Germany* **30** 51 40N 11 42 E
Berne = Bern, *Switz.* **31** 46 57N 7 28 E
Berne, *U.S.A.* **119** 40 39N 84 57W
Berne □ = Bern □, *Switz.* **31** 46 45N 7 40 E
Berneck, *E. Germany* **31** 51 3N 11 40 E
Berner Alpen, *Switz.* **31** 46 27N 7 35 E
Bernese Oberland = Oberland, *Switz.* **31** 46 30N 7 30 E
Bernier I., *Australia* **79** 24 50 S 113 12 E
Bernierville, *Canada* **107** 46 6N 71 34W
Bernina, Piz, *Switz.* **31** 46 20N 9 54 E
Bernissart, *Belgium* **17** 50 28N 3 39 E
Bernkastel-Kues, *W. Germany* **31** 49 55N 7 4 E
Beror Hayil, *Israel* **44** 31 34N 34 38 E
Beroroha, *Madag.* **97** 21 40 S 45 10 E
Béroubouay, *Benin* **91** 10 34N 2 46 E
Beroun, *Czech.* **32** 49 57N 14 5 E
Berounka →, *Czech.* **32** 50 0N 13 47 E
Berovo, *Yugoslavia* **35** 41 38N 22 51 E
Berrahal, *Algeria* **85** 36 54N 7 33 E
Berre, Étang de, *France* **21** 43 27N 5 5 E
Berrechid, *Morocco* **84** 33 18N 7 36W
Berri, *Australia* **73** 34 14 S 140 35 E
Berriane, *Algeria* **85** 32 50N 3 46 E
Berridale, *Australia* **75** 36 22 S 148 48 E
Berrien Springs, *U.S.A.* **119** 41 57N 86 20W
Berrima, *Australia* **76** 34 28 S 150 20 E
Berriwillock, *Australia* **74** 35 36 S 142 59 E
Berrouaghia, *Algeria* **85** 36 10N 2 53 E
Berry, *Australia* **76** 34 46 S 150 43 E
Berry, *France* **19** 46 50N 2 0 E
Berry, *U.S.A.* **119** 38 31N 84 23W
Berry Is., *Bahamas* **128** 25 40N 77 50W
Berryessa, L., *U.S.A.* **124** 38 31N 122 6W
Berryville, *U.S.A.* **121** 36 23N 93 35W
Bersenbrück, *W. Germany* **30** 52 33N 7 56 E
Berthierville, *Canada* **107** 46 5N 73 10W
Berthold, *U.S.A.* **120** 48 19N 101 45W
Berthoud, *U.S.A.* **120** 40 21N 105 5W
Bertincourt, *France* **19** 50 5N 2 58 E
Bertoua, *Cameroon* **94** 4 30N 13 45 E
Bertrand, *U.S.A.* **120** 40 35N 99 38W
Bertrange, *Lux.* **17** 49 37N 6 3 E
Bertrix, *Belgium* **17** 49 51N 5 15 E
Berufjörður, *Iceland* **8** 64 48N 14 29W
Beruri, *Brazil* **135** 3 54 S 61 22W
Berwick, *Australia* **74** 38 2 S 145 23 E
Berwick, *U.S.A.* **117** 41 4N 76 17W
Berwick-upon-Tweed, *U.K.* **12** 55 47N 2 0W
Berwyn Mts., *U.K.* **12** 52 54N 3 26W
Berzasca, *Romania* **34** 44 39N 21 58 E
Besal, *Pakistan* **49** 35 4N 73 56 E
Besalampy, *Madag.* **97** 16 43 S 44 29 E
Besançon, *France* **19** 47 15N 6 0 E
Besar, *Indonesia* **56** 2 40 S 116 0 E
Beshenkovichi, *U.S.S.R.* **36** 55 2N 29 29 E
Beslan, *U.S.S.R.* **39** 43 15N 44 28 E
Besnard L., *Canada* **111** 55 25N 106 0W
Besni, *Turkey* **46** 37 41N 37 52 E
Besor, N. →, *Egypt* **44** 31 28N 34 22 E
Bessa Monteiro, *Angola* **95** 7 7 S 13 44 E
Bessarabka, *U.S.S.R.* **38** 46 21N 28 58 E
Bessèges, *France* **21** 44 18N 4 8 E
Bessemer, *Ala., U.S.A.* **115** 33 25N 86 57W
Bessemer, *Mich., U.S.A.* **120** 46 27N 90 0W
Bessin, *France* **18** 49 18N 1 0W
Bessines-sur-Gartempe, *France* **20** 46 6N 1 22 E
Best, *Neths.* **17** 51 31N 5 23 E
Bet Alfa, *Israel* **44** 32 31N 35 25 E
Bet Dagan, *Israel* **44** 32 1N 34 49 E
Bet Guvrin, *Israel* **44** 31 37N 34 54 E
Bet Ha'Emeq, *Israel* **44** 32 58N 35 8 E
Bet Hashitta, *Israel* **44** 32 31N 35 27 E
Bet Qeshet, *Israel* **44** 32 41N 35 21 E
Bet She'an, *Israel* **44** 32 30N 35 30 E
Bet Shemesh, *Israel* **44** 31 44N 35 0 E
Bet Tadjine, Djebel, *Algeria* **84** 29 0N 3 30W
Bet Yosef, *Israel* **44** 32 34N 35 33 E
Betafo, *Madag.* **97** 19 50 S 46 51 E
Betancuria, *Canary Is.* **25** 28 25N 14 3W
Betanzos, *Bolivia* **137** 19 34 S 65 27W
Betanzos, *Spain* **22** 43 15N 8 12W
Bétaré Oya, *Cameroon* **94** 5 40N 14 5 E
Bétera, *Spain* **24** 39 35N 0 28W
Bethal, *S. Africa* **97** 26 27 S 29 28 E
Bethanien, *Namibia* **96** 26 31 S 17 8 E
Bethany = Al 'Ayzarīyah, *Jordan* **44** 31 47N 35 15 E
Bethany, *Canada* **109** 44 11N 78 34W
Bethany, *S. Africa* **96** 29 34 S 25 59 E
Bethany, *Ill., U.S.A.* **119** 39 39N 88 45W
Bethany, *Mo., U.S.A.* **118** 40 18N 94 0W
Bethel, *Alaska, U.S.A.* **102** 60 50N 161 50W
Bethel, *Ohio, U.S.A.* **119** 38 58N 84 5W
Bethel, *Vt., U.S.A.* **117** 43 50N 72 37W
Bethel Park, *U.S.A.* **116** 40 20N 80 2W
Bethlehem = Bayt Lahm, *Jordan* **44** 31 43N 35 12 E
Bethlehem, *S. Africa* **97** 28 14 S 28 18 E
Bethlehem, *U.S.A.* **117** 40 39N 75 24W
Bethulie, *S. Africa* **96** 30 30 S 25 59 E
Béthune, *France* **19** 50 30N 2 38 E
Béthune →, *France* **18** 49 53N 1 9 E
Bethungra, *Australia* **76** 34 45 S 147 51 E
Betijoque, *Venezuela* **134** 9 23N 70 44W
Betim, *Brazil* **139** 19 58 S 44 7W
Betioky, *Madag.* **97** 23 48 S 44 20 E
Beton-Bazoches, *France* **19** 48 42N 3 15 E
Betong, *Thailand* **55** 5 45N 101 5 E
Betoota, *Australia* **72** 25 45 S 140 42 E
Betroka, *Madag.* **97** 23 16 S 46 0 E
Betsiamites, *Canada* **107** 48 56N 68 40W
Betsiamites →, *Canada* **107** 48 56N 68 38W
Betsiboka →, *Madag.* **97** 16 3 S 46 36 E
Betsjoeanaland, *S. Africa* **96** 26 30 S 22 30 E
Bettembourg, *Lux.* **17** 49 31N 6 6 E
Bettendorf, *U.S.A.* **118** 41 32N 90 30W
Bettiah, *India* **49** 26 48N 84 33 E
Béttola, *Italy* **26** 44 42N 9 32 E
Betul, *India* **50** 21 58N 77 59 E
Betung, *Malaysia* **56** 1 24N 111 31 E
Betzdorf, *W. Germany* **30** 50 47N 7 53 E
Beuca, *Romania* **34** 44 14N 24 56 E
Beuil, *France* **21** 44 6N 6 59 E
Beulah, *Australia* **74** 35 58 S 142 29 E
Beulah, *U.S.A.* **120** 47 18N 101 47W
Beuvron →, *France* **18** 47 29N 1 15 E
Bevensen, *W. Germany* **30** 53 5N 10 34 E
Beveren, *Belgium* **17** 51 12N 4 16 E
Beverley, *Australia* **79** 32 9 S 116 56 E
Beverley, *U.K.* **12** 53 52N 0 26W
Beverlo, *Belgium* **17** 51 7N 5 13 E
Beverly, *Mass., U.S.A.* **117** 42 32N 70 50W
Beverly, *Wash., U.S.A.* **122** 46 55N 119 59W
Beverly Hills, *U.S.A.* **125** 34 4N 118 29W
Beverwijk, *Neths.* **16** 52 28N 4 38 E
Bewdley, *Canada* **109** 44 5N 78 19W
Bex, *Switz.* **31** 46 15N 7 0 E
Beyin, *Ghana* **90** 5 1N 2 41W
Beykoz, *Turkey* **35** 41 8N 29 7 E
Beyla, *Guinea* **90** 8 30N 8 38W
Beynat, *France* **20** 45 8N 1 44 E
Beyneu, *U.S.S.R.* **40** 45 10N 55 3 E
Beypazarı, *Turkey* **46** 40 10N 31 56 E
Beypore →, *India* **51** 11 10N 75 47 E
Beyşehir Gölü, *Turkey* **46** 37 40N 31 45 E
Bezet, *Israel* **44** 33 4N 35 8 E
Bezhetsk, *U.S.S.R.* **37** 57 47N 36 39 E
Bezhitsa, *U.S.S.R.* **36** 53 19N 34 17 E
Béziers, *France* **20** 43 20N 3 12 E
Bezwada = Vijayawada, *India* **51** 16 31N 80 39 E
Bhadarwah, *India* **49** 32 58N 75 46 E
Bhadra →, *India* **51** 14 0N 75 20 E
Bhadrakh, *India* **50** 21 10N 86 30 E
Bhadravati, *India* **51** 13 49N 75 40 E
Bhagalpur, *India* **49** 25 10N 87 0 E
Bhainsa, *India* **50** 19 10N 77 58 E
Bhairab →, *Bangla.* **52** 22 51N 89 34 E
Bhairab Bazar, *Bangla.* **52** 24 4N 90 58 E
Bhakkar, *Pakistan* **48** 31 40N 71 5 E
Bhakra Dam, *India* **48** 31 30N 76 45 E
Bhamo, *Burma* **52** 24 15N 97 15 E
Bhamragarh, *India* **50** 19 30N 80 40 E
Bhandara, *India* **50** 21 5N 79 42 E
Bhanrer Ra., *India* **48** 23 40N 79 45 E
Bharat = India ■, *Asia* **5** 20 0N 78 0 E
Bharatpur, *India* **48** 27 15N 77 30 E
Bharuch, *India* **50** 21 47N 73 0 E
Bhatghar L., *India* **50** 18 10N 73 48 E

Bhatiapara Ghat

Bhatiapara Ghat, *Bangla.* **52** 23 13N 89 42 E
Bhatinda, *India* **48** 30 15N 74 57 E
Bhatkal, *India* **51** 13 58N 74 35 E
Bhatpara, *India* **49** 22 50N 88 25 E
Bhattiprolu, *India* **51** 16 7N 80 45 E
Bhaun, *Pakistan* **48** 32 55N 72 40 E
Bhaunagar = Bhavnagar, *India* **48** 21 45N 72 10 E
Bhavani, *India* **51** 11 27N 77 43 E
Bhavani →, *India* **51** 11 0N 78 15 E
Bhavnagar, *India* **48** 21 45N 72 10 E
Bhawanipatna, *India* **50** 19 55N 80 10 E
Bhera, *Pakistan* **48** 32 29N 72 57 E
Bhilsa = Vidisha, *India* **48** 23 28N 77 53 E
Bhilwara, *India* **48** 25 25N 74 38 E
Bhima →, *India* **50** 16 25N 77 17 E
Bhimavaram, *India* **51** 16 30N 81 30 E
Bhimbar, *Pakistan* **49** 32 59N 74 3 E
Bhind, *India* **49** 26 30N 78 46 E
Bhiwandi, *India* **50** 19 20N 73 0 E
Bhiwani, *India* **48** 28 50N 76 9 E
Bhola, *Bangla.* **52** 22 45N 90 35 E
Bhongir, *India* **50** 17 30N 78 56 E
Bhopal, *India* **48** 23 20N 77 30 E
Bhor, *India* **50** 18 12N 73 53 E
Bhubaneshwar, *India* **50** 20 15N 85 50 E
Bhuj, *India* **48** 23 15N 69 49 E
Bhumibol Dam, *Thailand* **54** 17 15N 98 58 E
Bhusaval, *India* **50** 21 3N 75 46 E
Bhutan ■, *Asia* **52** 27 25N 90 30 E
Biá →, *Brazil* **134** 3 28 S 67 23W
Biafra, B. of = Bonny, Bight of, *Africa* **91** 3 30N 9 20 E
Biak, *Indonesia* **57** 1 10 S 136 6 E
Biała →, *Poland* **32** 50 3N 20 55 E
Biała Podlaska, *Poland* **32** 52 4N 23 6 E
Białogard, *Poland* **32** 54 2N 15 58 E
Białystok, *Poland* **32** 53 10N 23 10 E
Biancavilla, *Italy* **29** 37 39N 14 50 E
Biaro, *Indonesia* **57** 2 5N 125 26 E
Biarritz, *France* **20** 43 29N 1 33W
Biasca, *Switz.* **31** 46 22N 8 58 E
Biba, *Egypt* **88** 28 55N 31 0 E
Bibai, *Japan* **63** 43 19N 141 52 E
Bibala, *Angola* **95** 14 44 S 13 24 E
Bibane, Bahiret el, *Tunisia* **86** 33 16N 11 13 E
Bibassé, *Gabon* **94** 1 27N 11 37 E
Bibbenluke, *Australia* **75** 36 48 S 149 17 E
Bibbiena, *Italy* **27** 43 43N 11 50 E
Bibby I., *Canada* **111** 61 55N 93 0W
Biberach, *W. Germany* **31** 48 5N 9 49 E
Bibey →, *Spain* **22** 42 24N 7 13W
Bibiani, *Ghana* **90** 6 30N 2 8W
Bibile, *Sri Lanka* **51** 7 10N 81 25 E
Biboohra, *Australia* **72** 16 56 S 145 25 E
Bibungwa, *Zaïre* **92** 2 40 S 28 15 E
Bic, *Canada* **107** 48 20N 68 41W
Bic, Île du, *Canada* **107** 48 24N 68 52W
Bicaz, *Romania* **34** 46 53N 26 5 E
Biccari, *Italy* **29** 41 23N 15 12 E
Biche, La →, *Canada* **110** 59 57N 123 50W
Bichena, *Ethiopia* **89** 10 28N 38 10 E
Bickerton I., *Australia* **72** 13 45 S 136 10 E
Bicknell, *Ind., U.S.A.* **119** 38 50N 87 20W
Bicknell, *Utah, U.S.A.* **123** 38 16N 111 35W
Bida, *Nigeria* **91** 9 3N 5 58 E
Bida, *Zaïre* **94** 4 55N 19 56 E
Bidar, *India* **50** 17 55N 77 35 E
Biddeford, *U.S.A.* **105** 43 30N 70 28W
Biddiyā, *Jordan* **44** 32 7N 35 4 E
Biddon, *Australia* **76** 31 30 S 148 47 E
Biddū, *Jordan* **44** 31 50N 35 8 E
Biddwara, *Ethiopia* **89** 5 11N 38 34 E
Bideford, *U.K.* **13** 51 1N 4 13W
Bidon 5 = Poste Maurice Cortier, *Algeria* **85** 22 14N 1 2 E
Bidor, *Malaysia* **55** 4 6N 101 15 E
Bié □, *Angola* **95** 12 30 S 17 0 E
Bié, Planalto de, *Angola* **95** 12 0 S 16 0 E
Bieber, *U.S.A.* **122** 41 4N 121 6W
Biel, *Switz.* **31** 47 8N 7 14 E
Bielawa, *Poland* **32** 50 43N 16 37 E
Bielé Karpaty, *Czech.* **32** 49 5N 18 0 E
Bielefeld, *W. Germany* **30** 52 2N 8 31 E
Bielersee, *Switz.* **31** 47 6N 7 5 E
Biella, *Italy* **26** 45 33N 8 3 E
Bielsk Podlaski, *Poland* **32** 52 47N 23 12 E
Bielsko-Biała, *Poland* **32** 49 50N 19 2 E
Bien Hoa, *Vietnam* **55** 10 57N 106 49 E
Bienfait, *Canada* **111** 49 10N 102 50W
Bienne = Biel, *Switz.* **31** 47 8N 7 14 E
Bienvenida, *Spain* **23** 38 18N 6 12W
Bienvenue, *Fr. Guiana* **135** 3 0N 52 30W
Bienville, L., *Canada* **104** 55 5N 72 40W
Biescas, *Spain* **24** 42 37N 0 20W
Biese →, *E. Germany* **30** 52 53N 11 46 E
Biesiesfontein, *S. Africa* **96** 30 57 S 17 58 E
Bietigheim, *W. Germany* **31** 48 57N 9 8 E
Bievre, *Belgium* **17** 49 57N 5 1 E
Biferno →, *Italy* **29** 41 59N 15 2 E
Bifoum, *Gabon* **94** 0 20 S 10 23 E
Big →, *Canada* **105** 54 50N 58 55W
Big →, *U.S.A.* **118** 38 27N 90 37W
Big B., *Canada* **105** 55 43N 60 35W
Big Basswood L., *Canada* **108** 46 25N 83 23W
Big Bear City, *U.S.A.* **125** 34 16N 116 51W
Big Bear L., *U.S.A.* **125** 34 15N 116 56W
Big Beaver, *Canada* **111** 49 10N 105 10W
Big Belt Mts., *U.S.A.* **122** 46 50N 111 30W
Big Bend, *Swaziland* **97** 26 50 S 31 58 E
Big Bend Nat. Park, *U.S.A.* **121** 29 15N 103 15W
Big Black →, *U.S.A.* **121** 32 0N 91 5W
Big Blue →, *Ind., U.S.A.* **119** 39 12N 85 56W
Big Blue →, *Kans., U.S.A.* **120** 39 11N 96 40W
Big Cr. →, *Canada* **110** 51 42N 122 41W
Big Creek, *U.S.A.* **124** 37 11N 119 14W
Big Cypress Swamp, *U.S.A.* **115** 26 12N 81 10W
Big Falls, *U.S.A.* **120** 48 11N 93 48W
Big Fork →, *U.S.A.* **120** 48 31N 93 43W
Big Horn Mts. = Bighorn Mts., *U.S.A.* **122** 44 30N 107 30W
Big Lake, *U.S.A.* **121** 31 12N 101 25W
Big Moose, *U.S.A.* **117** 43 49N 74 58W
Big Muddy →, *Ill., U.S.A.* **118** 38 0N 89 0W
Big Muddy →, *Mont., U.S.A.* **120** 48 8N 104 36W
Big Pine, *U.S.A.* **124** 37 12N 118 17W
Big Piney, *U.S.A.* **122** 42 32N 110 3W
Big Quill L., *Canada* **111** 51 55N 104 50W
Big Rapids, *U.S.A.* **114** 43 42N 85 27W
Big Rideau L., *Canada* **109** 44 40N 76 15W
Big River, *Canada* **111** 53 50N 107 0W
Big Run, *U.S.A.* **116** 40 57N 78 55W
Big Sable Pt., *U.S.A.* **114** 44 5N 86 30W
Big Sand L., *Canada* **111** 57 45N 99 45W
Big Sandy, *U.S.A.* **122** 48 12N 110 9W
Big Sandy Cr. →, *U.S.A.* **120** 38 6N 102 29W
Big Sioux →, *U.S.A.* **120** 42 30N 96 25W
Big Spring, *U.S.A.* **121** 32 10N 101 25W
Big Springs, *U.S.A.* **120** 41 4N 102 3W
Big Stone City, *U.S.A.* **120** 45 20N 96 30W
Big Stone Gap, *U.S.A.* **115** 36 52N 82 45W
Big Stone L., *U.S.A.* **120** 45 30N 96 35W
Big Sur, *U.S.A.* **124** 36 15N 121 48W
Big Timber, *U.S.A.* **122** 45 53N 110 0W
Big Trout L., *Ont., Canada* **104** 53 40N 90 0W
Big Trout L., *Ont., Canada* **109** 45 46N 78 37W
Biganos, *France* **20** 44 39N 0 59W
Bigfork, *U.S.A.* **122** 48 3N 114 2W
Bigga, *Australia* **76** 34 4 S 149 9 E
Biggar, *Canada* **111** 52 4N 108 0W
Biggar, *U.K.* **14** 55 38N 3 31W
Bigge I., *Australia* **78** 14 35 S 125 10 E
Biggenden, *Australia* **73** 25 31 S 152 4 E
Biggs, *U.S.A.* **124** 39 24N 121 43W
Bighorn, *U.S.A.* **122** 46 11N 107 25W
Bighorn →, *U.S.A.* **122** 46 9N 107 28W
Bighorn Mts., *U.S.A.* **122** 44 30N 107 30W
Bigniba →, *Canada* **106** 49 18N 77 20W
Bignona, *Senegal* **90** 12 52N 16 14W
Bigorre, *France* **20** 43 10N 0 5 E
Bigstone L., *Canada* **111** 53 42N 95 44W
Bigwa, *Tanzania* **92** 7 10 S 39 10 E
Bihać, *Yugoslavia* **27** 44 49N 15 57 E
Bihar, *India* **49** 25 5N 85 40 E
Bihar □, *India* **49** 25 0N 86 0 E
Biharamulo, *Tanzania* **92** 2 25 S 31 25 E
Biharamulo □, *Tanzania* **92** 2 30 S 31 20 E
Bihor, Munţii, *Romania* **34** 46 29N 22 47 E
Bijagós, Arquipélago dos, *Guinea-Biss.* **90** 11 15N 16 10W
Bijaipur, *India* **48** 26 2N 77 20 E
Bijapur, *Karnataka, India* **50** 16 50N 75 55 E
Bijapur, *Mad. P., India* **50** 18 50N 80 50 E
Bījār, *Iran* **46** 35 52N 47 35 E
Bijeljina, *Yugoslavia* **33** 44 46N 19 17 E
Bijelo Polje, *Yugoslavia* **33** 43 1N 19 45 E
Bijie, *China* **58** 27 20N 105 16 E
Bijni, *India* **52** 26 30N 90 40 E
Bijnor, *India* **48** 29 27N 78 11 E
Bikaner, *India* **48** 28 2N 73 18 E
Bikapur, *India* **49** 26 30N 82 7 E
Bikeqi, *China* **60** 40 43N 111 20 E
Bikin, *U.S.S.R.* **41** 46 50N 134 20 E
Bikini Atoll, *Pac. Oc.* **66** 12 0N 167 30 E
Bikoro, *Zaïre* **94** 0 48 S 18 15 E
Bikoué, *Cameroon* **91** 3 55N 11 50 E
Bilara, *India* **48** 26 14N 73 53 E
Bilaspara, *India* **52** 26 13N 90 14 E
Bilaspur, *Mad. P., India* **49** 22 2N 82 15 E
Bilaspur, *Punjab, India* **48** 31 19N 76 50 E
Bilauk Taungdan, *Thailand* **54** 13 0N 99 0 E
Bilbao, *Spain* **24** 43 16N 2 56W
Bilbeis, *Egypt* **88** 30 25N 31 34 E
Bilbor, *Romania* **34** 47 6N 25 30 E
Bíldudalur, *Iceland* **8** 65 41N 23 36W
Bileća, *Yugoslavia* **33** 42 53N 18 27 E
Bilecik, *Turkey* **46** 40 5N 30 5 E
Biłgoraj, *Poland* **32** 50 33N 22 42 E
Bilibino, *U.S.S.R.* **41** 68 3N 166 20 E
Bilibiza, *Mozam.* **93** 12 30 S 40 20 E
Bilin, *Burma* **52** 17 14N 97 15 E
Bilir, *U.S.S.R.* **41** 65 40N 131 20 E
Bill, *U.S.A.* **120** 43 18N 105 18W
Billabalong, *Australia* **79** 27 25 S 115 49 E
Billiluna, *Australia* **78** 19 37 S 127 41 E
Billingham, *U.K.* **12** 54 36N 1 18W
Billings, *U.S.A.* **122** 45 43N 108 29W
Billingsfors, *Sweden* **10** 58 59N 12 15 E
Billiton Is. = Belitung, *Indonesia* **56** 3 10 S 107 50 E
Billom, *France* **20** 45 43N 3 20 E
Bilma, *Niger* **87** 18 50N 13 30 E
Bilo Gora, *Yugoslavia* **33** 45 53N 17 15 E
Biloela, *Australia* **72** 24 24 S 150 31 E
Biloku, *Guyana* **135** 1 50N 58 25W
Biloxi, *U.S.A.* **121** 30 24N 88 53W
Bilpa Morea Claypan, *Australia* **72** 25 0 S 140 0 E
Bilpin, *Australia* **76** 33 28 S 150 31 E
Bilthoven, *Neths.* **16** 52 8N 5 12 E
Biltine, *Chad* **87** 14 40N 20 50 E
Bilugyun, *Burma* **52** 16 24N 97 32 E
Bilyana, *Australia* **72** 18 5 S 145 50 E
Bilyarsk, *U.S.S.R.* **37** 54 58N 50 22 E
Bilzen, *Belgium* **17** 50 52N 5 31 E
Bima, *Indonesia* **57** 8 22 S 118 49 E
Bimban, *Egypt* **88** 24 24N 32 54 E
Bimberi Peak, *Australia* **76** 35 44 S 148 51 E
Bimbila, *Ghana* **91** 8 54N 0 5 E
Bimbo, *C.A.R.* **94** 4 15N 18 33 E
Bimini Is., *Bahamas* **128** 25 42N 79 25W
Bin Xian, *Heilongjiang, China* **61** 45 42N 127 32 E
Bin Xian, *Shaanxi, China* **60** 35 2N 108 4 E
Bina-Etawah, *India* **48** 24 13N 78 14 E
Binalbagan, *Phil.* **57** 10 12N 122 50 E
Bīnālūd, Kūh-e, *Iran* **47** 36 30N 58 30 E
Binatang, *Malaysia* **56** 2 10N 111 40 E
Binbee, *Australia* **72** 20 19 S 147 56 E
Binche, *Belgium* **17** 50 26N 4 10 E
Binchuan, *China* **58** 25 42N 100 38 E
Binda, *Australia* **73** 27 52 S 147 21 E
Binda, *Zaïre* **95** 5 52 S 13 14 E
Bindi Bindi, *Australia* **79** 30 37 S 116 22 E
Bindle, *Australia* **73** 27 40 S 148 45 E
Bindura, *Zambia* **93** 17 18 S 31 18 E
Bingara, *N.S.W., Australia* **77** 29 52 S 150 36 E
Bingara, *Queens., Australia* **73** 28 10 S 144 37 E
Bingen, *W. Germany* **31** 49 57N 7 53 E
Bingerville, *Ivory C.* **90** 5 18N 3 49W
Bingham, *U.S.A.* **105** 45 5N 69 50W
Bingham Canyon, *U.S.A.* **122** 40 31N 112 10W
Binghamton, *U.S.A.* **117** 42 9N 75 54W
Bingöl, *Turkey* **46** 38 53N 40 29 E
Binh Dinh = An Nhon, *Vietnam* **54** 13 55N 109 7 E
Binh Khe, *Vietnam* **54** 13 57N 108 51 E
Binh Son, *Vietnam* **54** 15 20N 108 40 E
Binhai, *China* **61** 34 2N 119 49 E
Biniguy, *Australia* **77** 29 34 S 150 14 E
Binjai, *Indonesia* **56** 3 20N 98 30 E
Binnaway, *Australia* **77** 31 28 S 149 24 E
Binongko, *Indonesia* **57** 5 55 S 123 55 E
Binscarth, *Canada* **111** 50 37N 101 17W
Bint Jubayl, *Lebanon* **44** 33 8N 35 25 E
Bintan, *Indonesia* **56** 1 0N 104 0 E
Bintulu, *Malaysia* **56** 3 10N 113 0 E
Bintuni, *Indonesia* **57** 2 7 S 133 32 E
Binyamina, *Israel* **44** 32 32N 34 56 E
Binyang, *China* **58** 23 12N 108 47 E
Binz, *E. Germany* **30** 54 23N 13 37 E
Binza, *Zaïre* **95** 4 21 S 15 14 E
Binzert = Bizerte, *Tunisia* **86** 37 15N 9 50 E
Bío Bío □, *Chile* **140** 37 35 S 72 0W
Biograd, *Yugoslavia* **27** 43 56N 15 29 E
Bioko, *Eq. Guin.* **91** 3 30N 8 40 E
Biougra, *Morocco* **84** 30 15N 9 14W
Biq'at Bet Netofa, *Israel* **44** 32 49N 35 22 E
Bir, *India* **50** 19 4N 75 46 E
Bir, Ras, *Djibouti* **89** 12 0N 43 20 E
Bîr Abu Hashim, *Egypt* **88** 23 42N 34 6 E
Bîr Abu M'nqar, *Egypt* **88** 26 33N 27 33 E
Bîr Adal Deib, *Sudan* **88** 22 35N 36 10 E
Bi'r al Malfa, *Libya* **86** 31 58N 15 18 E
Bir Aouine, *Tunisia* **86** 32 25N 9 18 E
Bîr 'Asal, *Egypt* **88** 25 55N 34 20 E
Bir Autrun, *Sudan* **88** 18 15N 26 40 E
Bi'r Dhu'fān, *Libya* **86** 31 59N 14 32 E
Bîr Diqnash, *Egypt* **88** 31 3N 25 23 E
Bir el Abbes, *Algeria* **84** 26 7N 6 9W
Bir el Ater, *Algeria* **85** 34 46N 8 3 E
Bîr el Basur, *Egypt* **88** 29 51N 25 49 E
Bîr el Gellaz, *Egypt* **88** 30 50N 26 40 E
Bîr el Shaqqa, *Egypt* **88** 30 54N 25 1 E
Bîr Fuad, *Egypt* **88** 30 35N 26 28 E
Bir Gara, *Chad* **87** 13 11N 15 58 E
Bîr Haimur, *Egypt* **88** 22 45N 33 40 E
Bir Jdid, *Morocco* **84** 33 26N 8 0W
Bîr Kanayis, *Egypt* **88** 24 59N 33 15 E
Bîr Kerawein, *Egypt* **88** 27 10N 28 25 E
Bir Lahrache, *Algeria* **85** 32 1N 8 12 E
Bîr Maql, *Egypt* **88** 23 7N 33 40 E
Bîr Misaha, *Egypt* **88** 22 13N 27 59 E
Bir Mogrein, *Mauritania* **84** 25 10N 11 25W
Bîr Murr, *Egypt* **88** 23 28N 30 10 E
Bi'r Nabālā, *Jordan* **44** 31 52N 35 12 E
Bîr Nakheila, *Egypt* **88** 24 1N 30 50 E
Bîr Qatrani, *Egypt* **88** 30 55N 26 10 E
Bîr Ranga, *Egypt* **88** 24 25N 35 15 E
Bîr Sahara, *Egypt* **88** 22 54N 28 40 E
Bîr Seiyâla, *Egypt* **88** 26 10N 33 50 E
Bir Semguine, *Morocco* **84** 30 1N 5 39W
Bîr Shalatein, *Egypt* **88** 23 5N 35 25 E
Bîr Shebb, *Egypt* **88** 22 25N 29 40 E
Bîr Shût, *Egypt* **88** 23 50N 35 15 E
Bîr Terfawi, *Egypt* **88** 22 57N 28 55 E
Bîr Umm Qubûr, *Egypt* **88** 24 35N 34 2 E
Bîr Ungât, *Egypt* **88** 22 8N 33 48 E
Bîr Za'farâna, *Egypt* **88** 29 10N 32 40 E
Bîr Zāmūs, *Libya* **86** 24 16N 15 6 E
Bi'r Zayt, *Jordan* **44** 31 59N 35 11 E
Bîr Zeidûn, *Egypt* **88** 25 45N 33 40 E
Bira, *Indonesia* **57** 2 3 S 132 2 E
Bîra, *Romania* **34** 47 2N 27 3 E
Birak Sulaymān, *Jordan* **44** 31 42N 35 7 E
Biramféro, *Guinea* **90** 11 40N 9 10W
Birao, *C.A.R.* **94** 10 20N 22 47 E
Birawa, *Zaïre* **92** 2 20 S 28 48 E
Bîrca, *Romania* **34** 43 59N 23 36 E
Birch Hills, *Canada* **111** 52 59N 105 25W
Birch I., *Canada* **111** 52 26N 99 54W
Birch L., *N.W.T., Canada* **110** 62 4N 116 33W
Birch L., *Ont., Canada* **104** 51 23N 92 18W
Birch L., *U.S.A.* **104** 47 48N 91 43W
Birch Mts., *Canada* **110** 57 30N 113 10W
Birch River, *Canada* **111** 52 24N 101 6W
Birchip, *Australia* **74** 35 56 S 142 55 E
Birchwood, *N.Z.* **81** 45 55 S 167 53 E
Bird, *Canada* **111** 56 30N 94 13W
Bird City, *U.S.A.* **120** 39 48N 101 33W
Bird I. = Aves, I. de, *W. Indies* **129** 15 45N 63 55W
Bird I., *S. Africa* **96** 32 3 S 18 17 E
Birdaard, *Neths.* **16** 53 18N 5 53 E
Birdlip, *U.K.* **13** 51 50N 2 7W
Birds, *U.S.A.* **119** 38 50N 87 40W
Birdseye, *U.S.A.* **119** 38 19N 86 42W
Birdsville, *Australia* **72** 25 51 S 139 20 E
Birdum, *Australia* **78** 15 39 S 133 13 E
Birecik, *Turkey* **46** 37 0N 38 0 E
Bireuen, *Indonesia* **56** 5 14N 96 39 E
Birifo, *Gambia* **90** 13 30N 14 0W
Birigui, *Brazil* **141** 21 18 S 50 16W
Birini, *C.A.R.* **94** 7 51N 22 24 E
Birkenfeld, *W. Germany* **31** 49 39N 7 11 E
Birkenhead, *N.Z.* **80** 36 49 S 174 46 E
Birkenhead, *U.K.* **12** 53 24N 3 1W
Birket Qârûn, *Egypt* **88** 29 30N 30 40 E
Birkhadem, *Algeria* **85** 36 43N 3 3 E
Bîrlad, *Romania* **34** 46 15N 27 38 E
Birmingham, *U.K.* **13** 52 30N 1 55W
Birmingham, *Ala., U.S.A.* **115** 33 31N 86 50W
Birmingham, *Iowa, U.S.A.* **118** 40 53N 91 57W
Birmitrapur, *India* **50** 22 24N 84 46 E
Birni Ngaouré, *Niger* **91** 13 5N 2 51 E
Birni Nkonni, *Niger* **91** 13 55N 5 15 E
Birnin Gwari, *Nigeria* **91** 11 0N 6 45 E
Birnin Kebbi, *Nigeria* **91** 12 32N 4 12 E
Birnin Kudu, *Nigeria* **91** 11 30N 9 29 E
Birobidzhan, *U.S.S.R.* **41** 48 50N 132 50 E
Birougou, Mts., *Gabon* **94** 1 51 S 12 20 E
Birqīn, *Jordan* **44** 32 27N 35 15 E
Birr, *Ireland* **15** 53 7N 7 55W
Birregurra, *Australia* **74** 38 20 S 143 46 E
Birrie →, *Australia* **73** 29 43 S 146 37 E
Birriwa, *Australia* **77** 32 7 S 149 28 E
Birsilpur, *India* **48** 28 11N 72 15 E
Birsk, *U.S.S.R.* **40** 55 25N 55 30 E
Birtin, *Romania* **34** 46 59N 22 31 E
Birtle, *Canada* **111** 50 30N 101 5W
Biryuchiy, *U.S.S.R.* **38** 46 10N 35 0 E
Birzai, *U.S.S.R.* **36** 56 11N 24 45 E
Bîrzava, *Romania* **34** 46 7N 21 59 E
Bisa, *Indonesia* **57** 1 15 S 127 28 E
Bisáccia, *Italy* **29** 41 0N 15 20 E
Bisacquino, *Italy* **28** 37 42N 13 13 E
Bisai, *Japan* **65** 35 16N 136 44 E
Bisalpur, *India* **49** 28 14N 79 48 E
Bisbal, La, *Spain* **24** 41 58N 3 2 E
Bisbee, *U.S.A.* **123** 31 30N 110 0W
Biscarrosse et de Parentis, Étang de, *France* **20** 44 21N 1 10W
Biscay, B. of, *Atl. Oc.* **130** 45 0N 2 0W
Biscayne B., *U.S.A.* **115** 25 40N 80 12W
Biscéglie, *Italy* **29** 41 14N 16 30 E
Bischofshofen, *Austria* **33** 47 26N 13 14 E
Bischofswerda, *E. Germany* **30** 51 8N 14 11 E
Bischwiller, *France* **19** 48 46N 7 50 E
Biscoe Bay, *Antarctica* **143** 77 0 S 152 0W
Biscoe Is., *Antarctica* **143** 66 0 S 67 0W
Biscostasing, *Canada* **106** 47 18N 82 9W
Biscucuy, *Venezuela* **134** 9 22N 69 59W
Biševo, *Yugoslavia* **27** 42 57N 16 3 E
Bisha, *Ethiopia* **89** 15 30N 37 31 E
Bishah, W. →, *Si. Arabia* **88** 21 24N 43 26 E
Bishan, *China* **58** 29 33N 106 12 E
Bishnupur, *India* **49** 23 8N 87 20 E
Bisho, *S. Africa* **97** 32 50 S 27 23 E
Bishop, *Calif., U.S.A.* **124** 37 20N 118 26W
Bishop, *Tex., U.S.A.* **121** 27 35N 97 49W
Bishop Auckland, *U.K.* **12** 54 40N 1 40W
Bishop's Falls, *Canada* **105** 49 2N 55 30W
Bishop's Stortford, *U.K.* **13** 51 52N 0 11 E
Bishopton, *Canada* **107** 45 35N 71 35W
Bisignano, *Italy* **29** 39 30N 16 17 E
Bisina, L., *Uganda* **92** 1 38N 33 56 E
Biskra, *Algeria* **85** 34 50N 5 44 E

Bogorodsk

Bislig, *Phil.* **57** 8 15N 126 27 E
Bismarck, *Mo., U.S.A.* **118** 37 46N 90 38W
Bismarck, *N. Dak., U.S.A.* **120** 46 49N 100 49W
Bismarck Arch., *Papua N. G.* **69** 2 30S 150 0 E
Bismarck Ra., *Papua N. G.* **69** 5 35S 145 0 E
Bismarck Sea, *Papua N. G.* **69** 4 10S 146 50 E
Bismark, *E. Germany* **30** 52 39N 11 31 E
Biso, *Uganda* **92** 1 44N 31 26 E
Bison, *U.S.A.* **120** 45 34N 102 28W
Bispfors, *Sweden* **8** 63 1N 16 37 E
Bispgården, *Sweden* **10** 63 2N 16 40 E
Bissagos = Bijagós, Arquipélago dos, *Guinea-Biss.* **90** 11 15N 16 10W
Bissau, *Guinea-Biss.* **90** 11 45N 15 45W
Bissett, *Canada* **111** 51 2N 95 41W
Bissikrima, *Guinea* **90** 10 50N 10 58W
Bistcho L., *Canada* **110** 59 45N 118 50W
Bistreţu, *Romania* **34** 43 54N 23 23 E
Bistrica = Ilirska-Bistrica, *Yugoslavia* **27** 45 34N 14 14 E
Bistriţa, *Romania* **34** 47 9N 24 35 E
Bistriţa →, *Romania* **34** 46 30N 26 57 E
Bistriţei, Munţii, *Romania* **34** 47 15N 25 40 E
Biswan, *India* **49** 27 29N 81 2 E
Bitam, *Gabon* **94** 2 5N 11 25 E
Bitburg, *W. Germany* **31** 49 58N 6 32 E
Bitche, *France* **19** 49 2N 7 25 E
Bitkine, *Chad* **87** 11 59N 18 13 E
Bitlis, *Turkey* **46** 38 20N 42 3 E
Bitola, *Yugoslavia* **35** 41 5N 21 10 E
Bitolj = Bitola, *Yugoslavia* **35** 41 5N 21 10 E
Bitonto, *Italy* **29** 41 7N 16 40 E
Bitter Creek, *U.S.A.* **122** 41 39N 108 36W
Bitter L. = Buheirat-Murrat-el-Kubra, *Egypt* **88** 30 15N 32 40 E
Bitterfeld, *E. Germany* **30** 51 36N 12 20 E
Bitterfontein, *S. Africa* **96** 31 1S 18 32 E
Bitterroot →, *U.S.A.* **122** 46 52N 114 6W
Bitterroot Range, *U.S.A.* **122** 46 0N 114 20W
Bitterwater, *U.S.A.* **124** 36 23N 121 0W
Bitti, *Italy* **28** 40 29N 9 20 E
Bittou, *Burkina Faso* **91** 11 17N 0 18W
Biu, *Nigeria* **91** 10 40N 12 3 E
Bivolari, *Romania* **34** 47 31N 27 27 E
Biwa-Ko, *Japan* **65** 35 15N 136 10 E
Biwabik, *U.S.A.* **120** 47 33N 92 19W
Bixad, *Romania* **34** 47 56N 23 28 E
Biyang, *China* **60** 32 38N 113 21 E
Biysk, *U.S.S.R.* **40** 52 40N 85 0 E
Bizana, *S. Africa* **97** 30 50S 29 52 E
Bizen, *Japan* **64** 34 43N 134 8 E
Bizerte, *Tunisia* **86** 37 15N 9 50 E
Bjargtangar, *Iceland* **8** 65 30N 24 30W
Bjelasica, *Yugoslavia* **33** 42 50N 19 40 E
Bjelovar, *Yugoslavia* **33** 45 56N 16 49 E
Bjerringbro, *Denmark* **11** 56 23N 9 39 E
Björbo, *Sweden* **10** 60 27N 14 44 E
Björneborg, *Sweden* **10** 59 14N 14 16 E
Bjørnøya, *Arctic* **144** 74 30N 19 0 E
Bjuv, *Sweden* **11** 56 5N 12 55 E
Blace, *Yugoslavia* **33** 43 18N 21 17 E
Blache, L. de la, *Canada* **107** 50 5N 69 29W
Black → = Da →, *Vietnam* **54** 21 15N 105 20 E
Black →, *Canada* **108** 44 42N 79 19W
Black →, *Ark., U.S.A.* **121** 35 38N 91 19W
Black →, *N.Y., U.S.A.* **117** 43 59N 76 4W
Black →, *Wis., U.S.A.* **120** 43 52N 91 22W
Black Diamond, *Canada* **110** 50 45N 114 14W
Black Forest = Schwarzwald, *W. Germany* **31** 48 0N 8 0 E
Black Hills, *U.S.A.* **120** 44 0N 103 50W
Black I., *Canada* **111** 51 12N 96 30W
Black L., *Canada* **111** 59 12N 105 15W
Black L., *U.S.A.* **114** 45 28N 84 15W
Black Lake, *Canada* **107** 46 1N 71 22W
Black Mesa, Mt., *U.S.A.* **121** 36 57N 102 55W
Black Mt. = Mynydd Du, *U.K.* **13** 51 45N 3 45W
Black Mountain, *Australia* **77** 30 18S 151 39 E
Black Mts., *U.K.* **13** 51 52N 3 5W
Black Range, *U.S.A.* **123** 33 30N 107 55W
Black River, *Jamaica* **128** 18 0N 77 50W
Black River Falls, *U.S.A.* **120** 44 23N 90 52W
Black Sea, *Europe* **38** 43 30N 35 0 E
Black Sugarloaf, Mt., *Australia* **77** 31 18S 151 35 E
Black Volta →, *Africa* **90** 8 41N 1 33W
Black Warrior →, *U.S.A.* **115** 32 32N 87 51W
Blackall, *Australia* **72** 24 25S 145 45 E
Blackball, *N.Z.* **81** 42 22S 171 26 E
Blackbull, *Australia* **72** 17 55S 141 45 E
Blackburn, *U.K.* **12** 53 44N 2 30W
Blackduck, *U.S.A.* **120** 47 43N 94 32W
Blackfoot, *U.S.A.* **122** 43 13N 112 12W
Blackfoot →, *U.S.A.* **122** 46 52N 113 53W
Blackfoot Res., *U.S.A.* **122** 43 0N 111 35W
Blackheath, *Australia* **76** 33 39S 150 17 E
Blackie, *Canada* **110** 50 36N 113 37W
Blackpool, *U.K.* **12** 53 48N 3 3W
Blackriver, *U.S.A.* **116** 44 46N 83 17W
Blacks Harbour, *Canada* **105** 45 3N 66 49W
Blacksburg, *U.S.A.* **114** 37 17N 80 23W
Blacksod B., *Ireland* **15** 54 6N 10 0W
Blackstone, *U.S.A.* **114** 37 6N 78 0W
Blackstone →, *Canada* **110** 61 5N 122 55W
Blackstone Ra., *Australia* **79** 26 0S 128 30 E
Blacktown, *Australia* **76** 33 48S 150 55 E
Blackville, *Australia* **77** 31 40S 150 15 E
Blackville, *Canada* **105** 46 44N 65 50W
Blackwater, *N.S.W., Australia* **77** 30 4S 151 53 E
Blackwater, *Queens., Australia* **72** 23 35S 148 53 E
Blackwater →, *Ireland* **15** 51 55N 7 50W
Blackwater →, *U.K.* **15** 54 31N 6 35W
Blackwater →, *U.S.A.* **118** 38 59N 92 59W
Blackwater Cr. →, *Australia* **73** 25 56S 144 30 E
Blackwell, *U.S.A.* **121** 36 55N 97 20W
Blackwells Corner, *U.S.A.* **125** 35 37N 119 47W
Blackwood, C., *Papua N. G.* **69** 7 49S 144 31 E
Bladel, *Neths.* **17** 51 22N 5 13 E
Blaenau Ffestiniog, *U.K.* **12** 53 0N 3 57W
Blagodarnoye, *U.S.S.R.* **39** 45 7N 43 37 E
Blagoevgrad, *Bulgaria* **35** 42 2N 23 5 E
Blagoveshchensk, *U.S.S.R.* **41** 50 20N 127 30 E
Blain, *France* **18** 47 29N 1 45W
Blaine, *U.S.A.* **110** 48 59N 122 43W
Blaine Lake, *Canada* **111** 52 51N 106 52W
Blainville, *Canada* **107** 45 40N 73 52W
Blainville-sur-l'Eau, *France* **19** 48 33N 6 23 E
Blair, *U.S.A.* **120** 41 38N 96 10W
Blair Athol, *Australia* **72** 22 42S 147 31 E
Blair Atholl, *U.K.* **14** 56 46N 3 50W
Blairgowrie, *U.K.* **14** 56 36N 3 20W
Blairmore, *Canada* **110** 49 40N 114 25W
Blairsden, *U.S.A.* **124** 39 47N 120 37W
Blairsville, *U.S.A.* **116** 40 27N 79 15W
Blaj, *Romania* **34** 46 10N 23 57 E
Blake Pt., *U.S.A.* **120** 48 12N 88 27W
Blakely, *U.S.A.* **115** 31 22N 85 0W
Blakesburg, *U.S.A.* **118** 40 58N 92 38W
Blâmont, *France* **19** 48 35N 6 50 E
Blanc, C., *Tunisia* **86** 37 15N 9 56 E
Blanc, Le, *France* **20** 46 37N 1 3 E
Blanc, Mont, *Alps* **21** 45 48N 6 50 E
Blanca, B., *Argentina* **142** 39 10S 61 30W
Blanca Peak, *U.S.A.* **123** 37 35N 105 29W
Blanchard, *U.S.A.* **121** 35 8N 97 40W
Blanchardville, *U.S.A.* **118** 42 48N 89 52W
Blanche, C., *Australia* **73** 33 1S 134 9 E
Blanche Channel, *Solomon Is.* **68** 8 30S 157 30 E
Blanche L., *S. Austral., Australia* **73** 29 15S 139 40 E
Blanche L., *W. Austral., Australia* **78** 22 25S 123 17 E
Blanchester, *U.S.A.* **119** 39 17N 83 59W
Blanco, *S. Africa* **96** 33 55S 22 23 E
Blanco, *U.S.A.* **121** 30 7N 98 30W
Blanco →, *Argentina* **140** 30 20S 68 42W
Blanco, C., *Costa Rica* **128** 9 34N 85 8W
Blanco, C., *Spain* **25** 39 21N 2 51 E
Blanco, C., *U.S.A.* **122** 42 50N 124 40W
Blanda →, *Iceland* **8** 65 20N 19 40W
Blandford Forum, *U.K.* **13** 50 52N 2 10W
Blanding, *U.S.A.* **123** 37 35N 109 30W
Blandinsville, *U.S.A.* **118** 40 33N 90 52W
Blanes, *Spain* **24** 41 40N 2 48 E
Blangy-sur-Bresle, *France* **19** 49 55N 1 37 E
Blanice →, *Czech.* **32** 49 10N 14 5 E
Blankenberge, *Belgium* **17** 51 20N 3 9 E
Blankenburg, *E. Germany* **30** 51 46N 10 56 E
Blanquefort, *France* **20** 44 55N 0 38W
Blanquilla, La, *Venezuela* **135** 11 51N 64 37W
Blanquillo, *Uruguay* **141** 32 53S 55 37W
Blansko, *Czech.* **32** 49 22N 16 40 E
Blantyre, *Malawi* **93** 15 45S 35 0 E
Blaricum, *Neths.* **16** 52 16N 5 14 E
Blarney, *Ireland* **15** 51 57N 8 35W
Blato, *Yugoslavia* **27** 42 56N 16 48 E
Blaubeuren, *W. Germany* **31** 48 24N 9 47 E
Blåvands Huk, *Denmark* **9** 55 33N 8 4 E
Blaydon, *U.K.* **12** 54 56N 1 47W
Blaye, *France* **20** 45 8N 0 40W
Blaye-les-Mines, *France* **20** 44 1N 2 8 E
Blayney, *Australia* **76** 33 32S 149 14 E
Blaze, Pt., *Australia* **78** 12 56S 130 11 E
Bleckede, *W. Germany* **30** 53 18N 10 43 E
Bled, *Yugoslavia* **27** 46 27N 14 7 E
Blednaya, Gora, *U.S.S.R.* **40** 76 20N 65 0 E
Bléharis, *Belgium* **17** 50 31N 3 25 E
Blejeşti, *Romania* **34** 44 19N 25 27 E
Blekinge län □, *Sweden* **11** 56 20N 15 20 E
Blenheim, *Canada* **108** 42 20N 82 0W
Blenheim, *N.Z.* **81** 41 38S 173 57 E
Bléone →, *France* **21** 44 5N 6 0 E
Blerick, *Neths.* **17** 51 22N 6 9 E
Bletchley, *U.K.* **13** 51 59N 0 44W
Bleu, L., *Canada* **106** 46 35N 78 24W
Bleymard, Le, *France* **20** 44 30N 3 42 E
Blida, *Algeria* **85** 36 30N 2 49 E
Blidet Amor, *Algeria* **85** 32 59N 5 58 E
Blidö, *Sweden* **10** 59 37N 18 53 E
Blidsberg, *Sweden* **11** 57 56N 13 30 E
Bligh Sound, *N.Z.* **81** 44 47S 167 32 E
Bligh Water, *Fiji* **68** 17 0S 178 0 E
Blind River, *Canada* **108** 46 10N 82 58W
Blissfield, *U.S.A.* **119** 41 50N 83 52W
Blitar, *Indonesia* **57** 8 5S 112 11 E
Blitta, *Togo* **91** 8 23N 1 6 E
Block I., *U.S.A.* **117** 41 11N 71 35W
Block Island Sd., *U.S.A.* **117** 41 17N 71 35W
Blockton, *U.S.A.* **118** 40 37N 94 29W
Blodgett Iceberg Tongue, *Antarctica* **143** 66 8S 130 35 E
Bloemendaal, *Neths.* **16** 52 24N 4 39 E
Bloemfontein, *S. Africa* **96** 29 6S 26 7 E
Bloemhof, *S. Africa* **96** 27 38S 25 32 E
Blois, *France* **18** 47 35N 1 20 E
Blokziji, *Neths.* **16** 52 43N 5 58 E
Blomskog, *Sweden* **10** 59 16N 12 2 E
Blönduós, *Iceland* **8** 65 40N 20 12W
Bloodvein →, *Canada* **111** 51 47N 96 43W
Bloody Foreland, *Ireland* **15** 55 10N 8 18W
Bloomer, *U.S.A.* **120** 45 8N 91 30W
Bloomfield, *Australia* **72** 15 56S 145 22 E
Bloomfield, *Canada* **109** 43 59N 77 14W
Bloomfield, *Ind., U.S.A.* **119** 39 1N 86 57W
Bloomfield, *Iowa, U.S.A.* **118** 40 44N 92 26W
Bloomfield, *Ky., U.S.A.* **119** 37 55N 85 19W
Bloomfield, *N. Mex., U.S.A.* **123** 36 46N 107 59W
Bloomfield, *Nebr., U.S.A.* **120** 42 38N 97 40W
Bloomingburg, *U.S.A.* **119** 39 36N 83 24W
Bloomington, *Ill., U.S.A.* **118** 40 27N 89 0W
Bloomington, *Ind., U.S.A.* **119** 39 10N 86 30W
Bloomington, *Wis., U.S.A.* **118** 42 53N 90 55W
Bloomsburg, *U.S.A.* **117** 41 0N 76 30W
Blora, *Indonesia* **57** 6 57S 111 25 E
Blossburg, *U.S.A.* **116** 41 40N 77 4W
Blouberg, *S. Africa* **97** 23 8S 28 59 E
Blountstown, *U.S.A.* **115** 30 28N 85 5W
Blowering Dam, *Australia* **76** 35 26S 148 16 E
Bludenz, *Austria* **31** 47 10N 9 50 E
Blue →, *U.S.A.* **119** 38 11N 86 18W
Blue Island, *U.S.A.* **114** 41 40N 87 40W
Blue Lake, *U.S.A.* **122** 40 53N 124 0W
Blue Mesa Res., *U.S.A.* **123** 38 30N 107 15W
Blue Mound, *U.S.A.* **118** 39 42N 89 7W
Blue Mts., *Australia* **76** 33 40S 150 0 E
Blue Mts., *Oreg., U.S.A.* **122** 45 15N 119 0W
Blue Mts., *Pa., U.S.A.* **117** 40 30N 76 30W
Blue Mud B., *Australia* **72** 13 30S 136 0 E
Blue Nile = An Nîl el Azraq □, *Sudan* **89** 12 30N 34 30 E
Blue Nile = Nîl el Azraq →, *Sudan* **89** 15 38N 32 31 E
Blue Rapids, *U.S.A.* **120** 39 41N 96 39W
Blue Ridge Mts., *U.S.A.* **115** 36 30N 80 15W
Blue Springs, *U.S.A.* **118** 39 1N 94 17W
Blue Stack Mts., *Ireland* **15** 54 46N 8 5W
Blueberry →, *Canada* **110** 56 45N 120 49W
Bluefield, *U.S.A.* **114** 37 18N 81 14W
Bluefields, *Nic.* **128** 12 20N 83 50W
Blueskin B., *N.Z.* **81** 45 44S 170 38 E
Bluff, *Australia* **72** 23 35S 149 4 E
Bluff, *N.Z.* **81** 46 37S 168 20 E
Bluff, *U.S.A.* **123** 37 17N 109 33W
Bluff Harbour, *N.Z.* **81** 46 36S 168 21 E
Bluff Knoll, *Australia* **79** 34 24S 118 15 E
Bluff Pt., *Australia* **79** 27 50S 114 5 E
Bluffs, *U.S.A.* **118** 39 45N 90 32W
Bluffton, *Ind., U.S.A.* **119** 40 43N 85 9W
Bluffton, *Ohio, U.S.A.* **119** 40 54N 83 54W
Bluford, *U.S.A.* **119** 38 20N 88 45W
Blumenau, *Brazil* **141** 27 0S 49 0W
Blumenthal, *W. Germany* **30** 53 5N 8 20 E
Blunt, *U.S.A.* **120** 44 32N 100 0W
Bly, *U.S.A.* **122** 42 23N 121 0W
Blyberg, *Sweden* **10** 61 9N 14 11 E
Blyth, *Canada* **108** 43 44N 81 26W
Blyth, *U.K.* **12** 55 8N 1 32W
Blythe, *U.S.A.* **125** 33 40N 114 33W
Bø, *Norway* **10** 59 25N 9 3 E
Bo, *S. Leone* **90** 7 55N 11 50W
Bo Duc, *Vietnam* **55** 11 58N 106 50 E
Bo Hai, *China* **61** 39 0N 120 0 E
Bō-no-Misaki, *Japan* **64** 31 15N 130 13 E
Bo Xian, *China* **60** 33 50N 115 45 E
Boa Esperança, *Brazil* **135** 3 21N 61 23W
Boa Nova, *Brazil* **139** 14 22S 40 10W
Boa Viagem, *Brazil* **138** 5 7S 39 44W
Boa Vista, *Brazil* **135** 2 48N 60 30W
Boaco, *Nic.* **128** 12 29N 85 35W
Bo'ai, *China* **60** 35 10N 113 3 E
Boal, *Spain* **22** 43 25N 6 49W
Boali, *C.A.R.* **94** 4 48N 18 7 E
Boardman, *U.S.A.* **116** 41 2N 80 40W
Boatman, *Australia* **73** 27 16S 146 55 E
Bobadah, *Australia* **73** 32 19S 146 41 E
Bobai, *China* **58** 22 17N 109 59 E
Bobbili, *India* **50** 18 35N 83 30 E
Bóbbio, *Italy* **26** 44 47N 9 22 E
Bobcaygeon, *Canada* **109** 44 33N 78 33W
Böblingen, *W. Germany* **31** 48 41N 9 1 E
Bobo-Dioulasso, *Burkina Faso* **90** 11 8N 4 13W
Boboc, *Romania* **34** 45 13N 26 59 E
Bobonaza →, *Ecuador* **134** 2 36S 76 38W
Bobov Dol, *Bulgaria* **34** 42 20N 23 0 E
Bóbr →, *Poland* **32** 52 4N 15 4 E
Bobraomby, Tanjon' i, *Madag.* **97** 12 40S 49 10 E
Bobrinets, *U.S.S.R.* **38** 48 4N 32 5 E
Bobrov, *U.S.S.R.* **37** 51 5N 40 2 E
Bobruysk, *U.S.S.R.* **36** 53 10N 29 15 E
Bobures, *Venezuela* **134** 9 15N 71 11W
Boca de Drago, *Venezuela* **135** 11 0N 61 50W
Boca de Uracoa, *Venezuela* **134** 9 8N 62 20W
Bôca do Acre, *Brazil* **136** 8 50S 67 27W
Bôca do Jari, *Brazil* **135** 1 7S 51 58W
Bôca do Moaco, *Brazil* **136** 7 41S 68 17W
Boca Grande, *Venezuela* **135** 8 40N 60 40W
Boca Raton, *U.S.A.* **115** 26 21N 80 5W
Bocaiúva, *Brazil* **139** 17 7S 43 49W
Bocanda, *Ivory C.* **90** 7 5N 4 31W
Bocaranga, *C.A.R.* **94** 7 0N 15 35 E
Bocas del Toro, *Panama* **128** 9 15N 82 20W
Boceguillas, *Spain* **24** 41 20N 3 39W
Bochart, *Canada* **107** 49 10N 73 30W
Bochnia, *Poland* **32** 49 58N 20 27 E
Bocholt, *Belgium* **17** 51 10N 5 35 E
Bocholt, *W. Germany* **30** 51 50N 6 35 E
Bochum, *W. Germany* **30** 51 28N 7 12 E
Bockenem, *W. Germany* **30** 52 1N 10 8 E
Bocognano, *France* **21** 42 5N 9 4 E
Boconó, *Venezuela* **134** 9 15N 70 16W
Boconó →, *Venezuela* **134** 8 43N 69 34W
Bocoyna, *Mexico* **126** 27 52N 107 35W
Bocq →, *Belgium* **17** 50 20N 4 55 E
Boda, *C.A.R.* **94** 4 19N 17 26 E
Böda, *Sweden* **11** 57 15N 17 3 E
Bodafors, *Sweden* **11** 57 48N 14 23 E
Bodalla, *Australia* **76** 36 4S 150 4 E
Bodaybo, *U.S.S.R.* **41** 57 50N 114 0 E
Boddington, *Australia* **79** 32 50S 116 30 E
Bodega Bay, *U.S.A.* **124** 38 20N 123 3W
Bodegraven, *Neths.* **16** 52 5N 4 46 E
Boden, *Sweden* **8** 65 50N 21 42 E
Bodensee, *W. Germany* **31** 47 35N 9 25 E
Bodenteich, *W. Germany* **30** 52 49N 10 41 E
Bodhan, *India* **50** 18 40N 77 44 E
Bodinayakkanur, *India* **51** 10 2N 77 10 E
Bodinga, *Nigeria* **91** 12 58N 5 10 E
Bodmin, *U.K.* **13** 50 28N 4 44W
Bodmin Moor, *U.K.* **13** 50 33N 4 36W
Bodoquena, Serra da, *Brazil* **137** 21 0S 56 50W
Bodoupa, *C.A.R.* **94** 5 43N 17 36 E
Bodrog →, *Hungary* **33** 48 15N 21 35 E
Bodrum, *Turkey* **46** 37 5N 27 30 E
Boechout, *Belgium* **17** 51 10N 4 30 E
Boegoebergdam, *S. Africa* **96** 29 7S 22 9 E
Boekelo, *Neths.* **16** 52 12N 6 49 E
Boelenslaan, *Neths.* **16** 53 10N 6 10 E
Boembé, *Congo* **94** 2 54S 15 39 E
Boën, *France* **21** 45 44N 4 0 E
Boende, *Zaïre* **94** 0 24S 21 12 E
Boerne, *U.S.A.* **121** 29 48N 98 41W
Boertange, *Neths.* **16** 53 1N 7 12 E
Boezinge, *Belgium* **17** 50 54N 2 52 E
Boffa, *Guinea* **90** 10 16N 14 3W
Bogale, *Burma* **52** 16 17N 95 24 E
Bogalong Creek, *Australia* **76** 33 50S 148 6 E
Bogalusa, *U.S.A.* **121** 30 50N 89 55W
Bogan →, *Australia* **76** 29 59S 146 17 E
Bogan Gate, *Australia* **76** 33 7S 147 49 E
Bogangolo, *C.A.R.* **94** 5 34N 18 15 E
Bogantungan, *Australia* **72** 23 41S 147 17 E
Bogata, *U.S.A.* **121** 33 26N 95 10W
Bogatić, *Yugoslavia* **33** 44 51N 19 30 E
Bogense, *Denmark* **11** 55 34N 10 5 E
Boggabilla, *Australia* **77** 28 36S 150 24 E
Boggabri, *Australia* **77** 30 45S 150 0 E
Boggeragh Mts., *Ireland* **15** 52 2N 8 55W
Boggy Cowal →, *Australia* **76** 32 10S 148 0 E
Bogia, *Papua N. G.* **69** 4 9S 145 0 E
Bognor Regis, *U.K.* **13** 50 47N 0 40W
Bogø, *Denmark* **11** 54 55N 12 2 E
Bogo, *Phil.* **57** 11 3N 124 0 E
Bogodukhov, *U.S.S.R.* **36** 50 9N 35 33 E
Bogong, Mt., *Australia* **75** 36 47S 147 17 E
Bogor, *Indonesia* **57** 6 36S 106 48 E
Bogoroditsk, *U.S.S.R.* **37** 53 47N 38 8 E
Bogorodsk, *U.S.S.R.* **37** 56 4N 43 30 E

Breteuil

Bossembélé II, *C.A.R.* **94** 5 41N 16 38 E
Bossier City, *U.S.A.* **121** 32 28N 93 48W
Bosso, *Niger* **91** 13 43N 13 19 E
Bosten Hu, *China* **62** 41 55N 87 40 E
Boston, *U.K.* **12** 52 59N 0 2W
Boston, *U.S.A.* **117** 42 20N 71 0W
Boston Bar, *Canada* **110** 49 52N 121 30W
Bosusulu, *Zaïre* **94** 0 50N 20 45 E
Bosut →, *Yugoslavia* **33** 45 20N 19 0 E
Boswell, *Canada* **110** 49 28N 116 45W
Boswell, *Ind., U.S.A.* **119** 40 30N 87 23W
Boswell, *Okla., U.S.A.* **121** 34 1N 95 50W
Boswell, *Pa., U.S.A.* **116** 40 9N 79 2W
Bosworth, *U.S.A.* **118** 39 28N 93 20W
Botad, *India* **48** 22 15N 71 40 E
Botany Bay, *Australia* **76** 34 0 S 151 14 E
Botene, *Laos* **54** 17 35N 101 12 E
Botevgrad, *Bulgaria* **34** 42 55N 23 47 E
Botfield, *Australia* **76** 33 1 S 147 46 E
Bothaville, *S. Africa* **96** 27 23 S 26 34 E
Bothnia, G. of, *Europe* **8** 63 0N 20 0 E
Bothwell, *Australia* **72** 42 20 S 147 1 E
Bothwell, *Canada* **108** 42 38N 81 52W
Boticas, *Portugal* **22** 41 41N 7 40W
Botletle →, *Botswana* **96** 20 10 S 23 15 E
Botoşani, *Romania* **34** 47 42N 26 41 E
Botro, *Ivory C.* **90** 7 51N 5 19W
Botswana ■, *Africa* **96** 22 0 S 24 0 E
Bottineau, *U.S.A.* **120** 48 49N 100 25W
Bottrop, *W. Germany* **17** 51 34N 6 59 E
Botucatu, *Brazil* **141** 22 55 S 48 30W
Botwood, *Canada* **105** 49 6N 55 23W
Bou Alam, *Algeria* **85** 33 50N 1 26 E
Bou Ali, *Algeria* **85** 27 11N 0 4W
Bou Djébéha, *Mali* **90** 18 25N 2 45W
Bou Guema, *Algeria* **85** 28 49N 0 19 E
Bou Ismael, *Algeria* **85** 36 38N 2 42 E
Bou Izakarn, *Morocco* **84** 29 12N 9 46W
Boû Lanouâr,
Mauritania **84** 21 12N 16 34W
Bou Saâda, *Algeria* **85** 35 11N 4 9 E
Bou Salem, *Tunisia* **86** 36 45N 9 2 E
Bouaké, *Ivory C.* **90** 7 40N 5 2W
Bouanga, *Congo* **94** 2 7 S 16 8 E
Bouar, *C.A.R.* **94** 6 0N 15 40 E
Bouârfa, *Morocco* **85** 32 32N 1 58W
Bouca, *C.A.R.* **94** 6 45N 18 25 E
Boucau, *France* **20** 43 32N 1 29W
Boucaut B., *Australia* **72** 12 0 S 134 25 E
Boucher →, *Canada* **107** 49 10N 69 6W
Bouches-du-Rhône □,
France **21** 43 37N 5 2 E
Bouchette, *Canada* **106** 46 12N 75 57W
Bouchier, L., *Canada* **106** 50 6N 77 48W
Bouda, *Algeria* **85** 27 50N 0 27W
Boudenib, *Morocco* **84** 31 59N 3 31W
Boufarik, *Algeria* **85** 36 34N 2 58 E
Bougainville C.,
Australia **78** 13 57 S 126 4 E
Bougainville I.,
Solomon Is. **69** 6 0 S 155 0 E
Bougainville Reef,
Australia **72** 15 30 S 147 5 E
Bougainville Str.,
Solomon Is. **68** 6 40 S 156 10 E
Bougaroun, C., *Algeria* **85** 37 6N 6 30 E
Bougie = Bejaia,
Algeria **85** 36 42N 5 2 E
Bougouni, *Mali* **90** 11 30N 7 20W
Bouillon, *Belgium* **17** 49 44N 5 3 E
Bouïra, *Algeria* **85** 36 20N 3 59 E
Boulder, *Colo., U.S.A.* **120** 40 3N 105 10W
Boulder, *Mont., U.S.A.* **122** 46 14N 112 4W
Boulder City, *U.S.A.* **125** 35 58N 114 50W
Boulder Creek, *U.S.A.* **124** 37 7N 122 7W
Boulder Dam =
Hoover Dam, *U.S.A.* **125** 36 0N 114 45W
Boulembo, *Gabon* **94** 1 26 S 12 0 E
Bouli, *Mauritania* **90** 15 17N 12 18W
Boulia, *Australia* **72** 22 52 S 139 51 E
Bouligny, *France* **19** 49 17N 5 45 E
Boulogne →, *France* **18** 47 12N 1 47W
Boulogne-sur-Gesse,
France **20** 43 18N 0 38 E
Boulogne-sur-Mer,
France **19** 50 42N 1 36 E
Bouloire, *France* **18** 47 59N 0 45 E
Bouloupari, *N. Cal.* **68** 21 52 S 166 4 E
Boulsa, *Burkina Faso* **91** 12 39N 0 34W
Boultoum, *Niger* **91** 14 45N 10 25 E
Boumalne, *Morocco* **84** 31 25N 6 0W
Boun Neua, *Laos* **54** 21 38N 101 54 E
Boun Tai, *Laos* **54** 21 23N 101 58 E
Bouna, *Ivory C.* **90** 9 10N 3 0W
Boundary Bend,
Australia **74** 34 43 S 143 8 E
Boundary Pk., *U.S.A.* **124** 37 51N 118 21W
Boundiali, *Ivory C.* **90** 9 30N 6 20W
Bountiful, *U.S.A.* **122** 40 57N 111 58W
Bounty I., *Pac. Oc.* **66** 48 0 S 178 30 E
Bourail, *N. Cal.* **68** 21 34 S 165 30 E
Bourbah, *Australia* **76** 31 18 S 148 20 E
Bourbeuse →, *U.S.A.* **118** 38 24N 90 54W
Bourbon, *U.S.A.* **119** 41 18N 86 7W
Bourbon-Lancy, *France* **20** 46 37N 3 45 E
Bourbon-
l'Archambault,
France **20** 46 36N 3 4 E
Bourbonnais, *France* **20** 46 28N 3 0 E
Bourbonne-les-Bains,
France **19** 47 54N 5 45 E
Bourem, *Mali* **91** 17 0N 0 24W
Bourg, *France* **20** 45 3N 0 34W
Bourg-Argental, *France* **21** 45 18N 4 32 E
Bourg-de-Péage, *France* **21** 45 2N 5 3 E
Bourg-en-Bresse,
France **21** 46 13N 5 12 E
Bourg-St.-Andéol,
France **21** 44 23N 4 39 E
Bourg-St.-Maurice,
France **21** 45 35N 6 46 E
Bourganeuf, *France* **20** 45 57N 1 45 E
Bourges, *France* **19** 47 9N 2 25 E
Bourget, *Canada* **106** 45 26N 75 9W
Bourget, L. du, *France* **21** 45 44N 5 52 E
Bourgneuf, B. de,
France **18** 47 3N 2 10W
Bourgneuf-en-Retz,
France **18** 47 2N 1 58W
Bourgneuf-la-Fôret, Le,
France **18** 48 10N 0 59W
Bourgogne, *France* **19** 47 0N 4 50 E
Bourgoin-Jallieu,
France **21** 45 36N 5 17 E
Bourgueil, *France* **18** 47 17N 0 10 E
Bourke, *Australia* **73** 30 8 S 145 55 E
Bournemouth, *U.K.* **13** 50 43N 1 53W
Bourriot-Bergonce,
France **20** 44 7N 0 14W
Bouscat, Le, *France* **20** 44 53N 0 37W
Bouse, *U.S.A.* **125** 33 55N 114 0W
Boussac, *France* **20** 46 22N 2 13 E
Boussens, *France* **20** 43 12N 0 58 E
Bousso, *Chad* **87** 10 34N 16 52 E
Boussu, *Belgium* **17** 50 26N 3 48 E
Boutilimit, *Mauritania* **90** 17 45N 14 40W
Bouvet I. = Bouvetøya,
Antarctica **143** 54 26 S 3 24 E
Bouvetøya, *Antarctica* **143** 54 26 S 3 24 E
Bouznika, *Morocco* **84** 33 46N 7 6W
Bouzonville, *France* **19** 49 17N 6 32 E
Bova Marina, *Italy* **29** 37 59N 15 56 E
Bovalino Marina, *Italy* **29** 38 9N 16 10 E
Bovec, *Yugoslavia* **27** 46 20N 13 33 E
Bovenkarspel, *Neths.* **16** 52 41N 5 14 E
Bovigny, *Belgium* **17** 50 12N 5 55 E
Bovill, *U.S.A.* **122** 46 58N 116 27W
Bovino, *Italy* **29** 41 15N 15 20 E
Bow Island, *Canada* **110** 49 50N 111 23W
Bowbells, *U.S.A.* **120** 48 47N 102 19W
Bowdle, *U.S.A.* **120** 45 30N 99 40W
Bowelling, *Australia* **79** 33 25 S 116 30 E
Bowen, *Australia* **72** 20 0 S 148 16 E
Bowen, Mt., *Australia* **75** 37 9 S 148 35 E
Bowen Mts., *Australia* **75** 37 0 S 148 0 E
Bowie, *Ariz., U.S.A.* **123** 32 15N 109 30W
Bowie, *Tex., U.S.A.* **121** 33 33N 97 50W
Bowland, Forest of,
U.K. **12** 54 0N 2 30W
Bowling Green, *Ky.,*
U.S.A. **114** 37 0N 86 25W
Bowling Green, *Mo.,*
U.S.A. **118** 39 21N 91 12W
Bowling Green, *Ohio,*
U.S.A. **119** 41 22N 83 40W
Bowling Green, C.,
Australia **72** 19 19 S 147 25 E
Bowman, *U.S.A.* **120** 46 12N 103 21W
Bowman I., *Antarctica* **143** 65 0 S 104 0 E
Bowmans, *Australia* **73** 34 10 S 138 17 E
Bowmanville, *Canada* **109** 43 55N 78 41W
Bowmore, *U.K.* **14** 55 45N 6 18W
Bowning, *Australia* **76** 34 46 S 148 50 E
Bowral, *Australia* **76** 34 26 S 150 27 E
Bowraville, *Australia* **77** 30 37 S 152 52 E
Bowron →, *Canada* **110** 54 3N 121 50W
Bowser, *Australia* **75** 36 19 S 146 23 E
Bowser L., *Canada* **110** 56 30N 129 30W
Bowsman, *Canada* **111** 52 14N 101 12W
Bowutu Mts.,
Papua N. G. **69** 7 45 S 147 10 E
Bowwood, *Zambia* **93** 17 5 S 26 20 E
Boxholm, *Sweden* **11** 58 12N 15 3 E
Boxmeer, *Neths.* **17** 51 38N 5 56 E
Boxtel, *Neths.* **17** 51 36N 5 20 E
Boyabat, *Turkey* **38** 41 28N 34 42 E
Boyabo, *Zaïre* **94** 3 43N 18 46 E
Boyaca □, *Colombia* **134** 5 30N 72 30W
Boyce, *U.S.A.* **121** 31 25N 92 39W
Boyer →, *Canada* **110** 58 27N 115 57W
Boyer, C., *N. Cal.* **68** 21 37 S 168 6 E
Boyle, *Ireland* **15** 53 58N 8 19W
Boyne →, *Ireland* **15** 53 43N 6 15W
Boyne City, *U.S.A.* **104** 45 13N 85 1W
Boyni Qara, *Afghan.* **47** 36 20N 67 0 E
Boynton Beach, *U.S.A.* **115** 26 31N 80 3W
Boyoma, Chutes, *Zaïre* **92** 0 35N 25 23 E
Boyup Brook, *Australia* **79** 33 50 S 116 23 E
Bozeman, *U.S.A.* **122** 45 40N 111 0W
Bozen = Bolzano, *Italy* **27** 46 30N 11 20 E
Bozene, *Zaïre* **94** 2 56N 19 12 E
Bozouls, *France* **20** 44 28N 2 43 E
Bozoum, *C.A.R.* **94** 6 25N 16 35 E
Bozovici, *Romania* **34** 44 56N 22 1 E
Bra, *Italy* **26** 44 41N 7 50 E
Brabant □, *Belgium* **17** 50 46N 4 30 E
Brabant L., *Canada* **111** 55 58N 103 43W
Brabrand, *Denmark* **11** 56 9N 10 7 E
Brač, *Yugoslavia* **27** 43 20N 16 40 E
Bracadale, L., *U.K.* **14** 57 20N 6 30W
Bracciano, *Italy* **27** 42 6N 12 10 E
Bracciano, L. di, *Italy* **27** 42 8N 12 11 E
Bracebridge, *Canada* **108** 45 2N 79 19W
Brach, *Libya* **86** 27 31N 14 20 E
Bracieux, *France* **19** 47 30N 1 30 E
Bräcke, *Sweden* **10** 62 45N 15 26 E
Brackettville, *U.S.A.* **121** 29 21N 100 20W
Bračk̆i Kanal,
Yugoslavia **27** 43 24N 16 40 E
Brad, *Romania* **34** 46 10N 22 50 E
Brádano →, *Italy* **29** 40 23N 16 51 E
Bradenton, *U.S.A.* **115** 27 25N 82 35W
Bradford, *Canada* **108** 44 7N 79 34W
Bradford, *U.K.* **12** 53 47N 1 45W
Bradford, *Ill., U.S.A.* **118** 41 11N 89 39W
Bradford, *Ohio, U.S.A.* **119** 40 8N 84 27W
Bradford, *Pa., U.S.A.* **116** 41 58N 78 41W
Bradford, *Vt., U.S.A.* **117** 43 59N 72 9W
Brădiceni, *Romania* **34** 45 3N 23 4 E
Bradley, *Ark., U.S.A.* **121** 33 7N 93 39W
Bradley, *Calif., U.S.A.* **124** 35 52N 120 48W
Bradley, *Ill., U.S.A.* **119** 41 9N 87 52W
Bradley, *S. Dak.,*
U.S.A. **120** 45 10N 97 40W
Bradley Institute,
Zambia **93** 17 7 S 31 25 E
Bradore Bay, *Canada* **105** 51 27N 57 18W
Bradshaw, *Australia* **78** 15 21 S 130 16 E
Brady, *U.S.A.* **121** 31 8N 99 25W
Brædstrup, *Denmark* **11** 55 58N 9 37 E
Braemar, *Australia* **73** 33 12 S 139 35 E
Braeside, *Canada* **106** 45 28N 76 24W
Braga, *Portugal* **22** 41 35N 8 25W
Braga □, *Portugal* **22** 41 30N 8 30W
Bragado, *Argentina* **140** 35 2 S 60 27W
Bragança, *Brazil* **138** 1 0 S 47 2W
Bragança, *Portugal* **22** 41 48N 6 50W
Bragança □, *Portugal* **22** 41 30N 6 45W
Bragança Paulista,
Brazil **141** 22 55 S 46 32W
Brahmanbaria, *Bangla.* **52** 23 58N 91 15 E
Brahmani →, *India* **50** 20 39N 86 46 E
Brahmaputra →, *India* **49** 24 2N 90 59 E
Braich-y-pwll, *U.K.* **12** 52 47N 4 46W
Braidwood, *Australia* **76** 35 27 S 149 49 E
Brăila, *Romania* **34** 45 19N 27 59 E
Braine-l'Alleud,
Belgium **17** 50 42N 4 23 E
Braine-le-Comte,
Belgium **17** 50 37N 4 8 E
Brainerd, *U.S.A.* **120** 46 20N 94 10W
Braintree, *U.K.* **13** 51 53N 0 34 E
Braintree, *U.S.A.* **117** 42 11N 71 0W
Brak →, *S. Africa* **96** 29 35 S 22 55 E
Brake, *Niedersachsen,*
W. Germany **30** 53 19N 8 30 E
Brake,
Nordrhein-Westfalen,
W. Germany **30** 51 43N 9 12 E
Brakel, *Neths.* **16** 51 49N 5 5 E
Bräkne-Hoby, *Sweden* **11** 56 14N 15 6 E
Brakwater, *Namibia* **96** 22 28 S 17 3 E
Brålanda, *Sweden* **11** 58 34N 12 21 E
Bralorne, *Canada* **110** 50 50N 122 50W
Bramberg, *W. Germany* **31** 50 6N 10 40 E
Bramminge, *Denmark* **11** 55 28N 8 42 E
Brämön, *Sweden* **10** 62 14N 17 40 E
Brampton, *Canada* **108** 43 45N 79 45W
Bramsche, *W. Germany* **30** 52 25N 7 58 E
Bramwell, *Australia* **72** 12 8 S 142 37 E
Branco →, *Brazil* **135** 1 20 S 61 50W
Branco, C., *Brazil* **138** 7 9 S 34 47W
Brande, *Denmark* **11** 55 57N 9 8 E
Brandenburg,
E. Germany **30** 52 24N 12 33 E
Brandenburg, *U.S.A.* **119** 38 0N 86 10W
Brandfort, *S. Africa* **96** 28 40 S 26 30 E
Brandon, *Canada* **111** 49 50N 99 57W
Brandon, *U.S.A.* **117** 43 48N 73 4W
Brandon, Mt., *Ireland* **15** 52 15N 10 15W
Brandon B., *Ireland* **15** 52 17N 10 8W
Brandsen, *Argentina* **140** 35 10 S 58 15W
Brandval, *Norway* **10** 60 19N 12 1 E
Brandvlei, *S. Africa* **96** 30 25 S 20 30 E
Brandýs, *Czech.* **32** 50 10N 14 40 E
Branford, *U.S.A.* **117** 41 15N 72 48W
Braniewo, *Poland* **32** 54 25N 19 50 E
Bransfield Str.,
Antarctica **143** 63 0 S 59 0W
Branson, *Colo., U.S.A.* **121** 37 4N 103 53W
Branson, *Mo., U.S.A.* **121** 36 40N 93 18W
Brantford, *Canada* **108** 43 10N 80 15W
Brantôme, *France* **20** 45 22N 0 39 E
Branxholme, *Australia* **74** 37 52 S 141 49 E
Branxton, *Australia* **76** 32 38 S 151 21 E
Branzi, *Italy* **26** 46 0N 9 46 E
Bras d'Or, L., *Canada* **105** 45 50N 60 50W
Brasil, Planalto, *Brazil* **132** 18 0 S 46 30W
Brasiléia, *Brazil* **136** 11 0 S 68 45W
Brasília, *Brazil* **139** 15 47 S 47 55W
Brasília Legal, *Brazil* **135** 3 49 S 55 36W
Braslav, *U.S.S.R.* **36** 55 38N 27 0 E
Braslovce, *Yugoslavia* **27** 46 21N 15 3 E
Braşov, *Romania* **34** 45 38N 25 35 E
Brass, *Nigeria* **91** 4 35N 6 14 E
Brass →, *Nigeria* **91** 4 15N 6 13 E
Brassac-les-Mines,
France **20** 45 24N 3 20 E
Brasschaat, *Belgium* **17** 51 19N 4 27 E
Brassey, Banjaran,
Malaysia **56** 5 0N 117 15 E
Brassey Ra., *Australia* **79** 25 8 S 122 15 E
Brasstown Bald, Mt.,
U.S.A. **115** 34 54N 83 45W
Bratislava, *Czech.* **33** 48 10N 17 7 E
Bratsk, *U.S.S.R.* **41** 56 10N 101 30 E
Brattleboro, *U.S.A.* **117** 42 53N 72 37W
Braţul Chilia →,
Romania **34** 45 25N 29 20 E
Bratul Sfîntu
Gheorghe →,
Romania **34** 45 0N 29 20 E
Braţul Sulina →,
Romania **34** 45 10N 29 20 E
Braunau, *Austria* **33** 48 15N 13 3 E
Braunschweig,
W. Germany **30** 52 17N 10 28 E
Braunton, *U.K.* **13** 51 6N 4 9W
Brava, *Somali Rep.* **98** 1 20N 44 8 E
Bråviken, *Sweden* **10** 58 38N 16 32 E
Bravo del Norte →,
Mexico **126** 25 57N 97 9W
Brawley, *U.S.A.* **125** 32 58N 115 30W
Bray, *Ireland* **15** 53 12N 6 6W
Bray, Mt., *Australia* **72** 14 0 S 134 30 E
Bray, Pays de, *France* **19** 49 46N 1 26 E
Bray-sur-Seine, *France* **19** 48 25N 3 14 E
Braymer, *U.S.A.* **118** 39 35N 93 48W
Brazeau →, *Canada* **110** 52 55N 115 14W
Brazil, *U.S.A.* **119** 39 32N 87 8W
Brazil ■, *S. Amer.* **139** 12 0 S 50 0W
Brazilian Highlands =
Brasil, Planalto,
Brazil **132** 18 0 S 46 30W
Brazo Sur →, *S. Amer.* **140** 25 21 S 57 42W
Brazos →, *U.S.A.* **121** 28 53N 95 23W
Brazzaville, *Congo* **95** 4 9 S 15 12 E
Brčko, *Yugoslavia* **33** 44 54N 18 46 E
Brea, *Peru* **136** 4 40 S 81 7W
Breadalbane, *N.S.W.,*
Australia **76** 34 48 S 149 28 E
Breadalbane, *Queens.,*
Australia **72** 23 50 S 139 35 E
Breadalbane, *U.K.* **14** 56 30N 4 15W
Breaden, L., *Australia* **79** 25 51 S 125 28 E
Breaksea Sd., *N.Z.* **81** 45 35 S 166 35 E
Bream Bay, *N.Z.* **80** 35 56 S 174 28 E
Bream Head, *N.Z.* **80** 35 51 S 174 36 E
Bream Tail, *N.Z.* **80** 36 3 S 174 36 E
Breas, *Chile* **140** 25 29 S 70 24W
Brebes, *Indonesia* **57** 6 52 S 109 3 E
Brechin, *Canada* **108** 44 32N 79 10W
Brechin, *U.K.* **14** 56 44N 2 40W
Brecht, *Belgium* **17** 51 21N 4 38 E
Breckenridge, *Colo.,*
U.S.A. **122** 39 30N 106 2W
Breckenridge, *Minn.,*
U.S.A. **120** 46 20N 96 36W
Breckenridge, *Mo.,*
U.S.A. **118** 39 46N 93 48W
Breckenridge, *Tex.,*
U.S.A. **121** 32 48N 98 55W
Brecknock, Pen., *Chile* **142** 54 35 S 71 30W
Břeclav, *Czech.* **32** 48 46N 16 53 E
Brecon, *U.K.* **13** 51 57N 3 23W
Brecon Beacons, *U.K.* **13** 51 53N 3 27W
Breda, *Neths.* **17** 51 35N 4 45 E
Bredaryd, *Sweden* **11** 57 10N 13 45 E
Bredasdorp, *S. Africa* **96** 34 33 S 20 2 E
Bredbo, *Australia* **76** 35 58 S 149 10 E
Bredene, *Belgium* **17** 51 14N 2 59 E
Bredstedt, *W. Germany* **30** 54 37N 8 59 E
Bree, *Belgium* **17** 51 8N 5 35 E
Breeza, *Australia* **77** 31 15 S 150 27 E
Breezand, *Neths.* **16** 52 53N 4 49 E
Bregalnica →,
Yugoslavia **35** 41 43N 22 9 E
Bregenz, *Austria* **31** 47 30N 9 45 E
Bréhal, *France* **18** 48 53N 1 30W
Bréhat, I. de, *France* **18** 48 51N 3 0W
Breiðafjörður, *Iceland* **8** 65 15N 23 15W
Breil-sur-Roya, *France* **21** 43 56N 7 31 E
Breisach, *W. Germany* **31** 48 2N 7 37 E
Brejinho de Nazaré,
Brazil **138** 11 1 S 48 34W
Brejo, *Brazil* **138** 3 41 S 42 47W
Bremen, *W. Germany* **30** 53 4N 8 47 E
Bremen □,
W. Germany **30** 53 6N 8 46 E
Bremer I., *Australia* **72** 12 5 S 136 45 E
Bremerhaven,
W. Germany **30** 53 34N 8 35 E
Bremerton, *U.S.A.* **124** 47 30N 122 38W
Bremervörde,
W. Germany **30** 53 28N 9 10 E
Bremsnes, *Norway* **10** 63 6N 7 40 E
Brenes, *Spain* **23** 37 32N 5 54W
Brenham, *U.S.A.* **121** 30 5N 96 27W
Brenner Pass, *Alps* **31** 47 0N 11 30 E
Breno, *Italy* **26** 45 57N 10 20 E
Brent, *Canada* **109** 46 2N 78 29W
Brent, *U.K.* **13** 51 33N 0 18W
Brenta →, *Italy* **27** 45 11N 12 18 E
Brentwood, *U.K.* **13** 51 37N 0 19 E
Brentwood, *U.S.A.* **117** 40 47N 73 15W
Bréscia, *Italy* **26** 45 33N 10 13 E
Breskens, *Neths.* **17** 51 23N 3 33 E
Breslau = Wrocław,
Poland **32** 51 5N 17 5 E
Bresle →, *France* **18** 50 4N 1 22 E
Bresles, *France* **19** 49 25N 2 13 E
Bressanone, *Italy* **27** 46 43N 11 40 E
Bressay I., *U.K.* **14** 60 10N 1 5W
Bresse, *France* **19** 46 50N 5 10 E
Bresse, La, *France* **19** 48 0N 6 53 E
Bressuire, *France* **18** 46 51N 0 30W
Brest, *France* **18** 48 24N 4 31W
Brest, *U.S.S.R.* **36** 52 10N 23 40 E
Bretagne, *France* **18** 48 0N 3 0W
Bretçu, *Romania* **34** 46 7N 26 18 E
Breteuil, *Eure, France* **18** 48 50N 0 53 E
Breteuil, *Oise, France* **19** 49 38N 2 18 E

Breton

Breton, *Canada* **110** 53 7N 114 28W
Breton, Pertuis, *France* **20** 46 17N 1 25W
Breton Sd., *U.S.A.* **121** 29 40N 89 12W
Brett, C., *N.Z.* **80** 35 10 S 174 20 E
Bretten, *W. Germany* **31** 49 2N 8 43 E
Breukelen, *Neths.* **16** 52 10N 5 0 E
Brevard, *U.S.A.* **115** 35 19N 82 42W
Breves, *Brazil* **138** 1 40 S 50 29W
Brevik, *Norway* **10** 59 4N 9 42 E
Brewarrina, *Australia* **73** 30 0 S 146 51 E
Brewer, *U.S.A.* **105** 44 43N 68 50W
Brewer, Mt., *U.S.A.* **124** 36 44N 118 28W
Brewster, *N.Y., U.S.A.* **117** 41 23N 73 37W
Brewster, *Wash., U.S.A.* **122** 48 10N 119 51W
Brewster, Kap, *Greenland* **144** 70 7N 22 0W
Brewton, *U.S.A.* **115** 31 9N 87 2W
Breyten, *S. Africa* **97** 26 16 S 30 0 E
Breytovo, *U.S.S.R.* **37** 58 18N 37 50 E
Brezhnev, *U.S.S.R.* **40** 55 42N 52 19 E
Brežice, *Yugoslavia* **27** 45 54N 15 35 E
Brézina, *Algeria* **85** 33 4N 1 14 E
Březnice, *Czech.* **32** 49 32N 13 57 E
Breznik, *Bulgaria* **34** 42 44N 22 50 E
Brezno, *Czech.* **32** 48 50N 19 40 E
Bria, *C.A.R.* **94** 6 30N 21 58 E
Briagolong, *Australia* **75** 37 51 S 147 5 E
Briançon, *France* **21** 44 54N 6 39 E
Briare, *France* **19** 47 38N 2 45 E
Bribbaree, *Australia* **76** 34 10 S 147 51 E
Bribie I., *Australia* **73** 27 0 S 152 58 E
Bricquebec, *France* **18** 49 28N 1 38W
Bridgehampton, *U.S.A.* **117** 40 56N 72 19W
Bridgend, *U.K.* **13** 51 30N 3 35W
Bridgenorth, *Canada* **109** 44 23N 78 23W
Bridgeport, *Canada* **108** 43 29N 80 29W
Bridgeport, *Calif., U.S.A.* **124** 38 14N 119 15W
Bridgeport, *Conn., U.S.A.* **117** 41 12N 73 12W
Bridgeport, *Nebr., U.S.A.* **120** 41 42N 103 10W
Bridgeport, *Tex., U.S.A.* **121** 33 15N 97 45W
Bridger, *U.S.A.* **122** 45 20N 108 58W
Bridgeton, *U.S.A.* **114** 39 29N 75 10W
Bridgetown, *Australia* **79** 33 58 S 116 7 E
Bridgetown, *Barbados* **129** 13 0N 59 30W
Bridgetown, *Canada* **105** 44 55N 65 18W
Bridgewater, *Australia* **74** 36 36 S 143 59 E
Bridgewater, *Canada* **105** 44 25N 64 31W
Bridgewater, *Mass., U.S.A.* **117** 41 59N 70 56W
Bridgewater, *S. Dak., U.S.A.* **120** 43 34N 97 29W
Bridgewater, C., *Australia* **74** 38 23 S 141 23 E
Bridgman, *U.S.A.* **119** 41 57N 86 33W
Bridgnorth, *U.K.* **13** 52 33N 2 25W
Bridgton, *U.S.A.* **117** 44 5N 70 41W
Bridgwater, *U.K.* **13** 51 7N 3 0W
Bridlington, *U.K.* **12** 54 6N 0 11W
Bridport, *Australia* **72** 40 59 S 147 23 E
Bridport, *U.K.* **13** 50 43N 2 45W
Brie, Plaine de la, *France* **19** 48 35N 3 10 E
Brie-Comte-Robert, *France* **19** 48 40N 2 35 E
Briec, *France* **18** 48 6N 4 0W
Brielle, *Neths.* **16** 51 54N 4 10 E
Brienne-le-Château, *France* **19** 48 24N 4 30 E
Brienon-sur-Armançon, *France* **19** 47 59N 3 38 E
Brienz, *Switz.* **31** 46 46N 8 2 E
Brienzersee, *Switz.* **31** 46 44N 7 53 E
Briey, *France* **19** 49 14N 5 57 E
Brig, *Switz.* **31** 46 18N 7 59 E
Brigg, *U.K.* **12** 53 33N 0 30W
Briggsdale, *U.S.A.* **120** 40 40N 104 20W
Brigham City, *U.S.A.* **122** 41 30N 112 1W
Bright, *Australia* **75** 36 42 S 146 56 E
Brighton, *Australia* **73** 35 5 S 138 30 E
Brighton, *Canada* **109** 44 2N 77 44W
Brighton, *U.K.* **13** 50 50N 0 9W
Brighton, *Colo., U.S.A.* **120** 39 59N 104 50W
Brighton, *Ill., U.S.A.* **118** 39 2N 90 8W
Brighton, *Iowa, U.S.A.* **118** 41 10N 91 49W
Brightwater, *N.Z.* **81** 41 22 S 173 9 E
Brignogan-Plage, *France* **18** 48 40N 4 20W
Brignoles, *France* **21** 43 25N 6 5 E
Brihuega, *Spain* **24** 40 45N 2 52W
Brikama, *Gambia* **90** 13 15N 16 45W
Brilliant, *Canada* **110** 49 19N 117 38W
Brilliant, *U.S.A.* **116** 40 15N 80 39W
Brilon, *W. Germany* **30** 51 23N 8 32 E
Brim, *Australia* **74** 36 3 S 142 27 E
Brimfield, *U.S.A.* **118** 40 50N 89 53W
Brindabella, *Australia* **76** 35 22 S 148 44 E
Bríndisi, *Italy* **29** 40 39N 17 55 E
Brinje, *Yugoslavia* **27** 45 0N 15 9 E
Brinkley, *U.S.A.* **121** 34 55N 91 15W
Brinkworth, *Australia* **73** 33 42 S 138 26 E
Brinnon, *U.S.A.* **122** 47 41N 122 54W
Brion, I., *Canada* **105** 47 46N 61 26W
Brionne, *France* **18** 49 11N 0 43 E
Brionski, *Yugoslavia* **27** 44 55N 13 45 E
Brioude, *France* **20** 45 18N 3 24 E
Briouze, *France* **18** 48 42N 0 23W
Brisbane, *Australia* **77** 27 25 S 153 2 E
Brisbane →, *Australia* **77** 27 24 S 153 9 E
Brisighella, *Italy* **27** 44 14N 11 46 E
Bristol, *Canada* **106** 45 32N 76 28W
Bristol, *U.K.* **13** 51 26N 2 35W
Bristol, *Conn., U.S.A.* **117** 41 44N 72 57W
Bristol, *Pa., U.S.A.* **117** 40 6N 74 52W
Bristol, *R.I., U.S.A.* **117** 41 40N 71 15W
Bristol, *S. Dak., U.S.A.* **120** 45 25N 97 43W
Bristol, *Tenn., U.S.A.* **115** 36 36N 82 11W
Bristol B., *U.S.A.* **102** 58 0N 160 0W
Bristol Channel, *U.K.* **13** 51 18N 4 30W
Bristol I., *Antarctica* **143** 58 45 S 28 0W
Bristol L., *U.S.A.* **123** 34 23N 116 50W
Bristow, *U.S.A.* **121** 35 55N 96 28W
British Antarctic Territory □, *Antarctica* **143** 66 0 S 45 0W
British Columbia □, *Canada* **110** 55 0N 125 15W
British Guiana = Guyana ■, *S. Amer.* **136** 5 0N 59 0W
British Honduras = Belize ■, *Cent. Amer.* **127** 17 0N 88 30W
British Isles, *Europe* **6** 55 0N 4 0W
Brits, *S. Africa* **97** 25 37 S 27 48 E
Britstown, *S. Africa* **96** 30 37 S 23 30 E
Britt, *Canada* **108** 45 46N 80 34W
Britt, *U.S.A.* **118** 43 6N 93 48W
Brittany = Bretagne, *France* **18** 48 0N 3 0W
Britton, *U.S.A.* **120** 45 50N 97 47W
Brive-la-Gaillarde, *France* **20** 45 10N 1 32 E
Briviesca, *Spain* **24** 42 32N 3 19W
Brixton, *Australia* **72** 23 32 S 144 57 E
Brlik, *U.S.S.R.* **40** 43 40N 73 49 E
Brno, *Czech.* **32** 49 10N 16 35 E
Bro, *Sweden* **10** 59 31N 17 38 E
Broach = Bharuch, *India* **50** 21 47N 73 0 E
Broad →, *U.S.A.* **115** 33 59N 82 39W
Broad Arrow, *Australia* **79** 30 23 S 121 15 E
Broad B., *U.K.* **14** 58 14N 6 16W
Broad Haven, *Ireland* **15** 54 20N 9 55W
Broad Law, *U.K.* **14** 55 30N 3 22W
Broad Sd., *Australia* **72** 22 0 S 149 45 E
Broadford, *Australia* **74** 37 14 S 145 4 E
Broadhurst Ra., *Australia* **78** 22 30 S 122 30 E
Broads, The, *U.K.* **12** 52 45N 1 30 E
Broadus, *U.S.A.* **120** 45 28N 105 27W
Broadview, *Canada* **111** 50 22N 102 35W
Broadwater, *Australia* **77** 28 59 S 153 29 E
Broager, *Denmark* **11** 54 53N 9 40 E
Broaryd, *Sweden* **11** 57 7N 13 15 E
Brochet, *Canada* **111** 57 53N 101 40W
Brochet, L., *Canada* **111** 58 36N 101 35W
Brochet, L. du, *Canada* **107** 49 40N 69 37W
Brock, *Canada* **111** 51 26N 108 43W
Brock →, *Canada* **106** 50 0N 75 5W
Brocken, *E. Germany* **30** 51 48N 10 40 E
Brocklehurst, *Australia* **76** 32 9 S 148 38 E
Brockport, *U.S.A.* **116** 43 12N 77 56W
Brockton, *U.S.A.* **117** 42 8N 71 2W
Brockville, *Canada* **109** 44 35N 75 41W
Brockway, *Mont., U.S.A.* **120** 47 18N 105 46W
Brockway, *Pa., U.S.A.* **116** 41 14N 78 48W
Brocton, *U.S.A.* **116** 42 25N 79 26W
Brod, *Yugoslavia* **35** 41 35N 21 17 E
Brodarevo, *Yugoslavia* **33** 43 14N 19 44 E
Brodeur Pen., *Canada* **103** 72 30N 88 10W
Brodhead, *U.S.A.* **118** 42 37N 89 22W
Brodick, *U.K.* **14** 55 34N 5 9W
Brodnica, *Poland* **32** 53 15N 19 25 E
Brodribb →, *Australia* **75** 37 29 S 148 35 E
Brody, *U.S.S.R.* **36** 50 5N 25 10 E
Broechem, *Belgium* **17** 51 11N 4 38 E
Broek, *Neths.* **16** 52 26N 5 0 E
Broek op Langedijk, *Neths.* **16** 52 41N 4 49 E
Brogan, *U.S.A.* **122** 44 14N 117 32W
Broglie, *France* **18** 49 0N 0 30 E
Broke, *Australia* **76** 32 45 S 151 7 E
Broken →, *Australia* **74** 36 24 S 145 24 E
Broken Bay, *Australia* **76** 33 30 S 151 15 E
Broken Bow, *Nebr., U.S.A.* **120** 41 25N 99 35W
Broken Bow, *Okla., U.S.A.* **121** 34 2N 94 43W
Broken Hill = Kabwe, *Zambia* **93** 14 30 S 28 29 E
Broken Hill, *Australia* **73** 31 58 S 141 29 E
Brokind, *Sweden* **11** 58 13N 15 42 E
Brokopondo, *Surinam* **135** 5 3N 54 59W
Brokopondo □, *Surinam* **135** 4 30N 55 30W
Bromfield, *U.K.* **13** 52 25N 2 45W
Bromley, *U.K.* **13** 51 20N 0 5 E
Bromölla, *Sweden* **11** 56 5N 14 28 E
Bromont, *Canada* **107** 45 17N 72 39W
Bromptonville, *Canada* **107** 45 28N 71 57W
Bronaugh, *U.S.A.* **118** 37 41N 94 28W
Brønderslev, *Denmark* **11** 57 16N 9 57 E
Brong-Ahafo □, *Ghana* **90** 7 50N 2 0W
Bronkhorstspruit, *S. Africa* **97** 25 46 S 28 45 E
Bronnitsy, *U.S.S.R.* **37** 55 27N 38 10 E
Bronson, *U.S.A.* **119** 41 52N 85 12W
Bronte, *Italy* **29** 37 48N 14 49 E
Bronte, *U.S.A.* **121** 31 54N 100 18W
Bronte Park, *Australia* **72** 42 8 S 146 30 E
Brook Park, *U.S.A.* **116** 41 24N 80 51W
Brookfield, *U.S.A.* **118** 39 50N 93 4W
Brookhaven, *U.S.A.* **121** 31 40N 90 25W
Brookings, *Oreg., U.S.A.* **122** 42 4N 124 10W
Brookings, *S. Dak., U.S.A.* **120** 44 20N 96 45W
Brooklin, *Canada* **116** 43 55N 78 55W
Brooklyn, *U.S.A.* **118** 41 44N 92 27W
Brookmere, *Canada* **110** 49 52N 120 53W
Brooks, *Canada* **110** 50 35N 111 55W
Brooks B., *Canada* **110** 50 15N 127 55W
Brooks L., *Canada* **111** 61 55N 106 35W
Brooks Ra., *U.S.A.* **102** 68 40N 147 0W
Brookston, *U.S.A.* **119** 40 36N 86 52W
Brooksville, *Fla., U.S.A.* **115** 28 32N 82 21W
Brooksville, *Ky., U.S.A.* **119** 38 41N 84 4W
Brookville, *U.S.A.* **119** 39 25N 85 0W
Brooloo, *Australia* **73** 26 30 S 152 43 E
Broom, L., *U.K.* **14** 57 55N 5 15W
Brooman, *Australia* **76** 35 29 S 150 17 E
Broome, *Australia* **78** 18 0 S 122 15 E
Broomehill, *Australia* **79** 33 51 S 117 39 E
Broons, *France* **18** 48 20N 2 16W
Brora, *U.K.* **14** 58 0N 3 50W
Brora →, *U.K.* **14** 58 4N 3 52W
Brösarp, *Sweden* **11** 55 43N 14 6 E
Brosna →, *Ireland* **15** 53 8N 8 0W
Broşteni, *Romania* **34** 47 14N 25 43 E
Brotas de Macaúbas, *Brazil* **139** 12 0 S 42 38W
Brothers, *U.S.A.* **122** 43 56N 120 39W
Brøttum, *Norway* **10** 61 2N 10 34 E
Brou, *France* **18** 48 13N 1 11 E
Broughton, *U.S.A.* **119** 37 56N 88 27W
Broughton I., *Australia* **76** 32 37 S 152 20 E
Broughton Island, *Canada* **103** 67 33N 63 0W
Broughty Ferry, *U.K.* **14** 56 29N 2 50W
Brouwershaven, *Neths.* **16** 51 45N 3 55 E
Brouwershavensche Gat, *Neths.* **16** 51 46N 3 50 E
Brovary, *U.S.S.R.* **36** 50 34N 30 48 E
Brovst, *Denmark* **11** 57 6N 9 31 E
Browerville, *U.S.A.* **120** 46 3N 94 50W
Brown, Pt., *Australia* **73** 32 32 S 133 50 E
Brown Willy, *U.K.* **13** 50 35N 4 34W
Brownfield, *U.S.A.* **121** 33 10N 102 15W
Browning, *Ill., U.S.A.* **118** 40 7N 90 22W
Browning, *Mo., U.S.A.* **118** 40 3N 93 12W
Browning, *Mont., U.S.A.* **122** 48 35N 113 0W
Brownlee, *Canada* **111** 50 43N 106 1W
Brownsburg, *Canada* **107** 45 41N 74 25W
Brownsburg, *U.S.A.* **119** 39 50N 86 26W
Brownstown, *U.S.A.* **119** 38 53N 86 3W
Brownsville, *Oreg., U.S.A.* **122** 44 29N 123 0W
Brownsville, *Tenn., U.S.A.* **121** 35 35N 89 15W
Brownsville, *Tex., U.S.A.* **121** 25 56N 97 25W
Brownsweg, *Surinam* **135** 5 5N 55 15W
Brownwood, *U.S.A.* **121** 31 45N 99 0W
Brownwood, L., *U.S.A.* **121** 31 51N 98 35W
Browse I., *Australia* **78** 14 7 S 123 33 E
Brozas, *Spain* **23** 39 37N 6 47W
Bruas, *Malaysia* **55** 4 30N 100 47 E
Bruay-en-Artois, *France* **19** 50 29N 2 33 E
Bruce, Mt., *Australia* **78** 22 37 S 118 8 E
Bruce B., *N.Z.* **81** 43 35 S 169 42 E
Bruce Pen., *Canada* **108** 45 0N 81 30W
Bruce Rock, *Australia* **79** 31 52 S 118 8 E
Bruche →, *France* **19** 48 34N 7 43 E
Bruchsal, *W. Germany* **31** 49 9N 8 39 E
Bruck an der Leitha, *Austria* **33** 48 1N 16 47 E
Bruck an der Mur, *Austria* **33** 47 24N 15 16 E
Brückenau, *W. Germany* **31** 50 17N 9 48 E
Brue →, *U.K.* **13** 51 10N 2 59W
Brugelette, *Belgium* **17** 50 35N 3 52 E
Bruges = Brugge, *Belgium* **17** 51 13N 3 13 E
Brugg, *Switz.* **31** 47 29N 8 11 E
Brugge, *Belgium* **17** 51 13N 3 13 E
Brühl, *W. Germany* **30** 50 49N 6 51 E
Bruinisse, *Neths.* **17** 51 40N 4 5 E
Brûlé, *Canada* **110** 53 15N 117 58W
Brûlon, *France* **18** 47 58N 0 15W
Brûly, *Belgium* **17** 49 58N 4 32 E
Brumado, *Brazil* **139** 14 14 S 41 40W
Brumado →, *Brazil* **139** 14 13 S 41 40W
Brumath, *France* **19** 48 43N 7 40 E
Brummen, *Neths.* **16** 52 5N 6 10 E
Brumunddal, *Norway* **10** 60 53N 10 56 E
Brunchilly, *Australia* **72** 18 50 S 134 30 E
Brundidge, *U.S.A.* **115** 31 43N 85 45W
Bruneau, *U.S.A.* **122** 42 57N 115 55W
Bruneau →, *U.S.A.* **122** 42 57N 115 58W
Brunei = Bandar Seri Begawan, *Brunei* **56** 4 52N 115 0 E
Brunei ■, *Asia* **56** 4 50N 115 0 E
Brunette Downs, *Australia* **72** 18 40 S 135 55 E
Brunflo, *Sweden* **10** 63 5N 14 50 E
Brungle, *Australia* **76** 35 8 S 148 13 E
Brunico, *Italy* **27** 46 50N 11 55 E
Brunkeberg, *Norway* **10** 59 26N 8 28 E
Brunna, *Sweden* **10** 59 52N 17 25 E
Brunnen, *Switz.* **31** 46 59N 8 37 E
Brunner, L., *N.Z.* **81** 42 37 S 171 27 E
Brunnsvik, *Sweden* **10** 60 12N 15 8 E
Bruno, *Canada* **111** 52 20N 105 30W
Brunsbüttelkoog, *W. Germany* **30** 53 52N 9 13 E
Brunssum, *Neths.* **17** 50 57N 5 59 E
Brunswick = Braunschweig, *W. Germany* **30** 52 17N 10 28 E
Brunswick, *Ga., U.S.A.* **115** 31 10N 81 30W
Brunswick, *Maine, U.S.A.* **105** 43 53N 69 50W
Brunswick, *Md., U.S.A.* **114** 39 20N 77 38W
Brunswick, *Mo., U.S.A.* **118** 39 26N 93 10W
Brunswick, *Ohio, U.S.A.* **116** 41 15N 81 50W
Brunswick, Pen. de, *Chile* **142** 53 30 S 71 30W
Brunswick B., *Australia* **78** 15 15 S 124 50 E
Brunswick Heads, *Australia* **77** 28 32 S 153 33 E
Brunswick Junction, *Australia* **79** 33 15 S 115 50 E
Bruntál, *Czech.* **32** 50 0N 17 27 E
Bruny I., *Australia* **72** 43 20 S 147 15 E
Brus Laguna, *Honduras* **128** 15 47N 84 35W
Brusartsi, *Bulgaria* **34** 43 40N 23 5 E
Brush, *U.S.A.* **120** 40 17N 103 33W
Brush Island, *Australia* **77** 35 32 S 150 25 E
Brushton, *U.S.A.* **117** 44 50N 74 32W
Brusio, *Switz.* **31** 46 14N 10 8 E
Brusque, *Brazil* **141** 27 5 S 49 0W
Brussel, *Belgium* **17** 50 51N 4 21 E
Brussels = Brussel, *Belgium* **17** 50 51N 4 21 E
Brussels, *Canada* **108** 43 44N 81 15W
Brustem, *Belgium* **17** 50 48N 5 14 E
Bruthen, *Australia* **75** 37 42 S 147 50 E
Bruxelles = Brussel, *Belgium* **17** 50 51N 4 21 E
Bruyères, *France* **19** 48 10N 6 40 E
Bryan, *Ohio, U.S.A.* **119** 41 30N 84 30W
Bryan, *Tex., U.S.A.* **121** 30 40N 96 27W
Bryan, Mt., *Australia* **73** 33 30 S 139 0 E
Bryanka, *U.S.S.R.* **39** 48 32N 38 45 E
Bryansk, *U.S.S.R.* **36** 53 13N 34 25 E
Bryanskoye, *U.S.S.R.* **39** 44 20N 47 10 E
Bryant, *U.S.A.* **120** 44 35N 97 28W
Bryne, *Norway* **9** 58 44N 5 38 E
Bryson, *Canada* **106** 45 41N 76 37W
Bryson City, *U.S.A.* **115** 35 28N 83 25W
Brza Palanka, *Yugoslavia* **33** 44 28N 22 27 E
Brzava →, *Yugoslavia* **33** 45 21N 20 45 E
Brzeg, *Poland* **32** 50 52N 17 30 E
Brzeg Din, *Poland* **32** 51 16N 16 41 E
Bū Athlah, *Libya* **86** 30 9N 15 39 E
Bu Craa, *W. Sahara* **84** 26 45N 12 50W
Bua Yai, *Thailand* **54** 15 33N 102 26 E
Buala, *Solomon Is.* **68** 8 10 S 159 35 E
Buangor, *Australia* **74** 37 20 S 143 10 E
Buangor, Mt., *Australia* **74** 37 16 S 143 13 E
Buapinang, *Indonesia* **57** 4 40 S 121 30 E
Buayan, *Phil.* **57** 6 3N 125 6 E
Buba, *Guinea-Biss.* **90** 11 40N 14 59W
Bubanda, *Zaïre* **94** 4 14N 19 38 E
Bubanza, *Burundi* **92** 3 6 S 29 23 E
Bucak, *Turkey* **46** 37 28N 30 36 E
Bucaramanga, *Colombia* **134** 7 0N 73 0W
Buccaneer Arch., *Australia* **78** 16 7 S 123 20 E
Bucchiánico, *Italy* **27** 42 20N 14 10 E
Bucecea, *Romania* **34** 47 47N 26 28 E
Buchach, *U.S.S.R.* **36** 49 5N 25 25 E
Buchan, *Australia* **75** 37 30 S 148 12 E
Buchan, *U.K.* **14** 57 32N 2 8W
Buchan →, *Australia* **75** 37 22 S 148 9 E
Buchan Ness, *U.K.* **14** 57 29N 1 48W
Buchanan, *Canada* **111** 51 40N 102 45W
Buchanan, *Liberia* **90** 5 57N 10 2W
Buchanan, *U.S.A.* **119** 41 50N 86 22W
Buchanan, L., *Queens., Australia* **72** 21 35 S 145 52 E
Buchanan, L., *W. Austral., Australia* **79** 25 33 S 123 2 E
Buchanan, L., *U.S.A.* **121** 30 50N 98 25W
Buchans, *Canada* **105** 48 50N 56 52W
Bucharest = Bucureşti, *Romania* **34** 44 27N 26 10 E
Buchholz, *W. Germany* **30** 53 19N 9 51 E
Buchloe, *W. Germany* **31** 48 3N 10 45 E
Buchon, Pt., *U.S.A.* **124** 35 15N 120 54W
Bückeburg, *W. Germany* **30** 52 16N 9 2 E
Buckeye, *U.S.A.* **123** 33 28N 112 40W
Buckhannon, *U.S.A.* **114** 39 2N 80 10W
Buckhaven, *U.K.* **14** 56 10N 3 2W
Buckhorn L., *Canada* **109** 44 29N 78 23W
Buckie, *U.K.* **14** 57 40N 2 58W
Buckingham, *Canada* **106** 45 37N 75 24W
Buckingham, *U.K.* **13** 52 0N 0 59W
Buckingham □, *U.K.* **13** 51 50N 0 55W
Buckingham B., *Australia* **72** 12 10 S 135 40 E
Buckingham Can., *India* **51** 14 0N 80 5 E
Buckland, *U.S.A.* **119** 40 37N 84 16W
Buckland Newton, *U.K.* **13** 50 45N 2 25W

Büsum

Buckle Hd., *Australia* . **78** 14 26 S 127 52 E
Buckleboo, *Australia* . **73** 32 54 S 136 12 E
Buckley, *Ill., U.S.A.* . . **119** 40 35N 88 2W
Buckley, *Wash., U.S.A.* **122** 47 10N 122 2W
Bucklin, *Kans., U.S.A.* **121** 37 37N 99 40W
Bucklin, *Mo., U.S.A.* . **118** 39 47N 92 53W
Bucks L., *U.S.A.* **124** 39 54N 121 12W
Buco Zau, *Angola* . . . . **95** 4 46 S 12 33 E
Bucquoy, *France* . . . . . **19** 50 9N 2 43 E
Buctouche, *Canada* . . . **105** 46 30N 64 45W
Bucureşti, *Romania* . . . **34** 44 27N 26 10 E
Bucyrus, *U.S.A.* **119** 40 48N 83 0W
Budafok, *Hungary* . . . . **33** 47 26N 19 2 E
Budalin, *Burma* . . . . . . **52** 22 20N 95 10 E
Budapest, *Hungary* . . . **33** 47 29N 19 5 E
Budaun, *India* . . . . **49** 28 5N 79 10 E
Budd Coast, *Antarctica* **143** 68 0 S 112 0 E
Buddabadah, *Australia* **76** 31 56 S 147 14 E
Budduso, *Italy* . . . . **28** 40 35N 9 18 E
Bude, *U.K.* **13** 50 49N 4 33W
Budel, *Neths.* . . . . **17** 51 17N 5 34 E
Budennovsk, *U.S.S.R.* **39** 44 50N 44 10 E
Budeşti, *Romania* . . . . **34** 44 13N 26 30 E
Budge Budge = Baj Baj, *India* . . . . **49** 22 30N 88 5 E
Budgewoi Lake, *Australia* . . . . **76** 33 13 S 151 34 E
Búðareyri, *Iceland* **8** 65 2N 14 13W
Búðir, *Iceland* **8** 64 49N 23 23W
Budia, *Spain* **24** 40 38N 2 46W
Budjala, *Zaïre* . . . . **94** 2 50N 19 40 E
Búdrio, *Italy* . . . . **27** 44 31N 11 31 E
Buea, *Cameroon* . . . . . **91** 4 10N 9 9 E
Buellton, *U.S.A.* **125** 34 37N 120 12W
Buena Vista, *Bolivia* . . **137** 17 27 S 63 40W
Buena Vista, *Colo., U.S.A.* **123** 38 56N 106 6W
Buena Vista, *Va., U.S.A.* **114** 37 47N 79 23W
Buena Vista L., *U.S.A.* **125** 35 15N 119 21W
Buenaventura, *Colombia* **134** 3 53N 77 4W
Buenaventura, *Mexico* **126** 29 50N 107 30W
Buenaventura, B. de, *Colombia* **134** 3 48N 77 17W
Buendía, Pantano de, *Spain* **24** 40 25N 2 43W
Buenópolis, *Brazil* . . . . **139** 17 54 S 44 11W
Buenos Aires, *Argentina* . . . . **140** 34 30 S 58 20W
Buenos Aires, *Colombia* **134** 1 36N 73 18W
Buenos Aires, *Costa Rica* **128** 9 10N 83 20W
Buenos Aires □, *Argentina* . . . . **140** 36 30 S 60 0W
Buenos Aires, L., *Chile* **142** 46 35 S 72 30W
Buesaco, *Colombia* . . . **134** 1 23N 77 9W
Buffalo, *Mo., U.S.A.* . **118** 37 40N 93 5W
Buffalo, *N.Y., U.S.A.* **116** 42 55N 78 50W
Buffalo, *Okla., U.S.A.* **121** 36 55N 99 42W
Buffalo, *S. Dak., U.S.A.* **120** 45 39N 103 31W
Buffalo, *Wyo., U.S.A.* **122** 44 25N 106 50W
Buffalo →, *Australia* . **75** 36 42 S 146 40 E
Buffalo →, *Canada* . . **110** 60 5N 115 5W
Buffalo Head Hills, *Canada* **110** 57 25N 115 55W
Buffalo L., *Canada* . . . **110** 52 27N 112 54W
Buffalo Narrows, *Canada* **111** 55 51N 108 29W
Buffels →, *S. Africa* . **96** 29 36 S 17 3 E
Buford, *U.S.A.* **115** 34 5N 84 0W
Bug →, *Poland* . . . . . . **32** 52 31N 21 5 E
Bug →, *U.S.S.R.* . . . . **38** 46 59N 31 58 E
Buga, *Colombia* **134** 4 0N 76 15W
Bugaldie, *Australia* . . . **77** 31 2 S 149 6 E
Buganda □, *Uganda* . . **92** 0 0 31 30 E
Buganga, *Uganda* . . . . **92** 0 3 S 32 0 E
Bugeat, *France* . . . . **20** 45 36N 1 55 E
Bugel, Tanjung, *Indonesia* . . . . **56** 6 26 S 111 3 E
Buggenhout, *Belgium* . **17** 51 1N 4 12 E
Bugsuk, *Phil.* . . . . **56** 8 15N 117 15 E
Bugue, Le, *France* . . . . **20** 44 55N 0 56 E
Buguma, *Nigeria* . . . . . **91** 4 42N 6 55 E
Buguruslan, *U.S.S.R.* . **40** 53 39N 52 26 E
Buhăeşti, *Romania* . . . **34** 46 47N 27 32 E
Buheirat-Murrat-el-Kubra, *Egypt* . . . . . . **88** 30 15N 32 40 E
Buhl, *Idaho, U.S.A.* . . **122** 42 35N 114 54W
Buhl, *Minn., U.S.A.* . . **120** 47 30N 92 46W
Buick, *U.S.A.* **121** 37 38N 91 2W
Builth Wells, *U.K.* **13** 52 10N 3 26W
Buin, *Papua N. G.* . . . **68** 6 48 S 155 42 E
Buinsk, *U.S.S.R.* . . . . . **37** 55 0N 48 18 E
Buíque, *Brazil* . . . . **138** 8 37 S 37 9W
Buir Nur, *Mongolia* . . **62** 47 50N 117 42 E
Buis-les-Baronnies, *France* . . . . **21** 44 17N 5 16 E
Buitenpost, *Neths.* . . . . **16** 53 15N 6 9 E
Buitrago, *Spain* **22** 41 0N 3 38W
Bujalance, *Spain* **23** 37 54N 4 23W
Buján, *Spain* **22** 42 59N 8 36W
Bujaraloz, *Spain* **24** 41 29N 0 10W
Buje, *Yugoslavia* . . . . . **27** 45 24N 13 39 E
Buji, *Papua N. G.* . . . . . **69** 9 8 S 142 11 E
Bujumbura, *Burundi* . . **92** 3 16 S 29 18 E
Buka I., *Papua N. G.* . . **69** 5 10 S 154 35 E
Bukachacha, *U.S.S.R.* **41** 52 55N 116 50 E
Bukama, *Zaïre* . . . . **93** 9 10 S 25 50 E
Bukavu, *Zaïre* . . . . **92** 2 20 S 28 52 E
Bukene, *Tanzania* . . . . **92** 4 15 S 32 48 E
Bukhara, *U.S.S.R.* . . . . **40** 39 48N 64 25 E
Bukima, *Tanzania* . . . . **92** 1 50 S 33 25 E
Bukit Mertajam, *Malaysia* . . . . **55** 5 22N 100 28 E
Bukittinggi, *Indonesia* . **56** 0 20 S 100 20 E
Bukkapatnam, *India* . . **51** 14 14N 77 46 E
Bukkulla, *Australia* . . . **77** 29 30 S 151 8 E
Bukoba, *Tanzania* . . . . **92** 1 20 S 31 49 E
Bukoba □, *Tanzania* . . . **92** 1 30 S 32 0 E
Bukuru, *Nigeria* . . . . . . **91** 9 42N 8 48 E
Bukuya, *Uganda* . . . . . **92** 0 40N 31 52 E
Bula, *Guinea-Biss.* **90** 12 7N 15 43W
Bula, *Indonesia* . . . . . . **57** 3 6 S 130 30 E
Bulahdelah, *Australia* . **76** 32 23 S 152 13 E
Bulan, *Phil.* . . . . **57** 12 40N 123 52 E
Bulandshahr, *India* . . . **48** 28 28N 77 51 E
Bûlâq, *Egypt* . . . . **88** 25 10N 30 38 E
Bulawayo, *Zambia* . . . . **93** 20 7 S 28 32 E
Buldana, *India* . . . . **50** 20 30N 76 18 E
Bulga, *Australia* . . . . . . **76** 32 39 S 151 2 E
Bulgan, *Mongolia* . . . . **62** 48 45N 103 34 E
Bulgaria ■, *Europe* . . . **34** 42 35N 25 30 E
Bulgroo, *Australia* . . . . **73** 25 47 S 143 58 E
Bulgunnia, *Australia* . . **73** 30 10 S 134 53 E
Bulhale, *Somali Rep.* . . **98** 5 20N 46 29 E
Bulhar, *Somali Rep.* . . . **98** 10 25N 44 30 E
Buli, Teluk, *Indonesia* . **57** 1 5N 128 25 E
Buliluyan, C., *Phil.* . . . **56** 8 20N 117 15 E
Bulki, *Ethiopia* . . . . **89** 6 11N 36 31 E
Bulkley →, *Canada* . . . **110** 55 15N 127 40W
Bull Shoals L., *U.S.A.* **121** 36 40N 93 5W
Bullange, *Belgium* . . . . **17** 50 24N 6 15 E
Bullaque →, *Spain* **23** 38 59N 4 17W
Bullara, *Australia* . . . . **78** 22 40 S 114 3 E
Bullaring, *Australia* . . . **79** 32 30 S 117 45 E
Bullas, *Spain* **25** 38 2N 1 40W
Bulle, *Switz.* . . . . **31** 46 37N 7 3 E
Buller →, *N.Z.* . . . . . . **81** 41 44 S 171 36 E
Buller, Mt., *Australia* . **75** 37 10 S 146 28 E
Buller Gorge, *N.Z.* . . . . **81** 41 40 S 172 10 E
Bulli, *Australia* . . . . **76** 34 15 S 150 57 E
Bullock Cr. →, *Australia* . . . . **74** 35 42 S 143 54 E
Bullock Creek, *Australia* . . . . **72** 17 43 S 144 31 E
Bulloo →, *Australia* . . **73** 28 43 S 142 30 E
Bulloo Downs, *Queens., Australia* . . **73** 28 31 S 142 57 E
Bulloo Downs, *W. Austral., Australia* **79** 24 0 S 119 32 E
Bulloo L., *Australia* . . **73** 28 43 S 142 25 E
Bulls, *N.Z.* . . . . **80** 40 10 S 175 24 E
Bully-les-Mines, *France* **19** 50 27N 2 44 E
Bulnes, *Chile* . . . . **140** 36 42 S 72 19W
Bulo Burti, *Somali Rep.* **98** 3 50N 45 33 E
Bulo Ghedudo, *Somali Rep.* . . . . **98** 2 52N 43 1 E
Buloke, L., *Australia* . **74** 36 15 S 142 58 E
Bulolo, *Papua N. G.* . . **69** 7 10 S 146 40 E
Bulongo, *Zaïre* . . . . . . **95** 4 45 S 21 30 E
Bulsar = Valsad, *India* **50** 20 40N 72 58 E
Bultfontein, *S. Africa* . **96** 28 18 S 26 10 E
Bulu Karakelong, *Indonesia* . . . . **57** 4 35N 126 50 E
Bulukumba, *Indonesia* **57** 5 33 S 120 11 E
Bulun, *U.S.S.R.* . . . . . . **41** 70 37N 127 30 E
Bulungu, *Zaïre* . . . . **95** 6 4 S 21 54 E
Bumba, *Zaïre* . . . . **94** 2 13N 22 30 E
Bumbiri I., *Tanzania* . . **92** 1 40 S 31 55 E
Bumhkang, *Burma* . . . **52** 26 51N 97 40 E
Bumhpa Bum, *Burma* . **52** 26 51N 97 14 E
Bumi →, *Zambia* . . . . **93** 17 0 S 28 20 E
Bumtang →, *Bhutan* . . **52** 26 56N 90 53 E
Buna, *Kenya* . . . . **92** 2 58N 39 30 E
Buna, *Papua N. G.* . . . . **69** 8 42 S 148 27 E
Bunazi, *Tanzania* . . . . . **92** 1 3 S 31 23 E
Bunbah, Khalīj, *Libya* **86** 32 20N 23 15 E
Bunbury, *Australia* . . . **79** 33 20 S 115 35 E
Buncrana, *Ireland* **15** 55 8N 7 28W
Bundaberg, *Australia* . **73** 24 54 S 152 22 E
Bundanoon, *Australia* . **76** 34 40 S 150 16 E
Bundarra, *Australia* . . . **77** 30 4 S 151 0 E
Bünde, *W. Germany* . . **30** 52 11N 8 33 E
Bundey →, *Australia* . **72** 21 46 S 135 37 E
Bundi, *India* . . . . **48** 25 30N 75 35 E
Bundooma, *Australia* . **72** 24 54 S 134 16 E
Bundoran, *Ireland* **15** 54 24N 8 17W
Bundukia, *Sudan* . . . . . **89** 5 14N 30 55 E
Bung Kan, *Thailand* . . . **54** 18 23N 103 37 E
Bungatakada, *Japan* . . **64** 33 35N 131 25 E
Bungil Cr. →, *Australia* . . . . **72** 27 5 S 149 5 E
Bungo-Suidō, *Japan* . . **64** 33 0N 132 15 E
Bungoma, *Kenya* . . . . . **92** 0 34N 34 34 E
Bungonia, *Australia* . . **76** 34 51 S 149 57 E
Bungu, *Tanzania* . . . . . **92** 7 35 S 39 0 E
Bungun Shara, *Mongolia* . . . . **62** 49 0N 104 0 E
Bungunya, *Australia* . . **77** 28 25 S 149 42 E
Bunia, *Zaïre* . . . . **92** 1 35N 30 20 E
Buninyong, *Australia* . **74** 37 36 S 143 54 E
Bunji, *Pakistan* . . . . . . **49** 35 45N 74 40 E
Bunker Hill, *Ill., U.S.A.* **118** 39 3N 89 57W
Bunker Hill, *Ind., U.S.A.* **119** 40 40N 86 6W
Bunkie, *U.S.A.* **121** 31 1N 92 12W
Bunnan, *Australia* . . . . **77** 32 2 S 150 37 E
Bunnell, *U.S.A.* **115** 29 28N 81 12W
Bunnik, *Neths.* . . . . **16** 52 4N 5 12 E
Bunnythorpe, *N.Z.* . . . **80** 40 16 S 175 39 E
Buñol, *Spain* **25** 39 25N 0 47W
Bunsbeek, *Belgium* . . . **17** 50 50N 4 56 E
Bunschoten, *Neths.* . . . **16** 52 14N 5 22 E
Buntok, *Indonesia* . . . . **56** 1 40 S 114 58 E
Bununu, *Nigeria* . . . . . **91** 9 51N 9 32 E
Bununu Dass, *Nigeria* . **91** 10 0N 9 31 E
Bunyan, *Australia* . . . . **76** 36 10 S 149 11 E
Bunyip, *Australia* . . . . . **74** 38 6 S 145 43 E
Bunyu, *Indonesia* . . . . . **56** 3 35N 117 50 E
Bunza, *Nigeria* . . . . **91** 12 8N 4 0 E
Buol, *Indonesia* . . . . . . **57** 1 15N 121 32 E
Buon Brieng, *Vietnam* **54** 13 9N 108 12 E
Buon Me Thuot, *Vietnam* . . . . **54** 12 40N 108 3 E
Buong Long, *Cambodia* **54** 13 44N 106 59 E
Buorkhaya, Mys, *U.S.S.R.* . . . . **41** 71 50N 132 40 E
Buqayq, *Si. Arabia* . . . **46** 26 0N 49 45 E
Buqbua, *Egypt* . . . . **88** 31 29N 25 29 E
Buqei'a, *Israel* . . . . **44** 32 58N 35 20 E
Bur Acaba, *Somali Rep.* . . . . **98** 3 12N 44 20 E
Bûr Fuad, *Egypt* . . . . . **88** 31 15N 32 20 E
Bur Ghibi, *Somali Rep.* **98** 3 56N 45 7 E
Bûr Safâga, *Egypt* . . . . **88** 26 43N 33 57 E
Bûr Sa'îd, *Egypt* . . . . . **88** 31 16N 32 18 E
Bûr Sûdân, *Sudan* . . . . **88** 19 32N 37 9 E
Bûr Taufiq, *Egypt* . . . . **88** 29 54N 32 32 E
Bura, *Kenya* . . . . **92** 1 4 S 39 58 E
Buran, *Somali Rep.* . . . **98** 10 14N 48 44 E
Burao, *Somali Rep.* . . . **98** 9 32N 45 32 E
Buras, *U.S.A.* **121** 29 20N 89 33W
Buraydah, *Si. Arabia* . . **46** 26 20N 44 8 E
Buraymī, Al Wāhāt al, *Oman* . . . . **47** 24 10N 55 43 E
Burbank, *U.S.A.* **125** 34 9N 118 23W
Burcher, *Australia* . . . . **76** 33 30 S 147 16 E
Burdekin →, *Australia* **72** 19 38 S 147 25 E
Burdett, *Canada* **110** 49 50N 111 32W
Burdur, *Turkey* . . . . . . **46** 37 45N 30 22 E
Burdwan = Barddhaman, *India* . **49** 23 14N 87 39 E
Bure, *Ethiopia* . . . . **89** 10 40N 37 4 E
Bure →, *U.K.* . . . . **12** 52 38N 1 45 E
Bureba, La, *Spain* **24** 42 36N 3 24W
Buren, *Neths.* . . . . **16** 51 55N 5 20 E
Büren, *W. Germany* . . . **30** 51 33N 8 34 E
Bureya →, *U.S.S.R.* . . **41** 49 27N 129 30 E
Burford, *Canada* **108** 43 7N 80 27W
Burg, *E. Germany* . . . . **30** 52 16N 11 50 E
Burg, *W. Germany* . . . . **30** 54 25N 11 10 E
Burg el Arab, *Egypt* . . **88** 30 54N 29 32 E
Burg et Tuyur, *Sudan* . **88** 20 55N 27 56 E
Burg Stargard, *E. Germany* . . . . **30** 53 29N 13 19 E
Burgas, *Bulgaria* . . . . . **34** 42 33N 27 29 E
Burgdorf, *Switz.* . . . . . **31** 47 3N 7 37 E
Burgdorf, *W. Germany* **30** 52 27N 10 0 E
Burgeo, *Canada* **105** 47 37N 57 38W
Burgersdorp, *S. Africa* **96** 31 0 S 26 20 E
Burges, Mt., *Australia* **79** 30 50 S 121 5 E
Burghausen, *W. Germany* . . . . **31** 48 10N 12 50 E
Búrgio, *Italy* . . . . **28** 37 35N 13 18 E
Burglengenfeld, *W. Germany* . . . . **31** 49 11N 12 2 E
Burgo de Osma, *Spain* **24** 41 35N 3 4W
Burgohondo, *Spain* . . . **22** 40 26N 4 47W
Burgos, *Spain* **24** 42 21N 3 41W
Burgos □, *Spain* **24** 42 21N 3 42W
Burgstädt, *E. Germany* **30** 50 55N 12 49 E
Burgsteinfurt, *W. Germany* . . . . **30** 52 9N 7 23 E
Burgsvik, *Sweden* . . . . **11** 57 3N 18 19 E
Burguillos del Cerro, *Spain* **23** 38 23N 6 35W
Burgundy = Bourgogne, *France* . **19** 47 0N 4 50 E
Burhanpur, *India* . . . . . **50** 21 18N 76 14 E
Burhou, *U.K.* **18** 49 45N 2 15W
Buri Pen., *Ethiopia* . . . **89** 15 25N 39 55 E
Burias, *Phil.* . . . . **57** 12 55N 123 5 E
Burica, Pta., *Costa Rica* **128** 8 3N 82 51W
Burigi, L., *Tanzania* . . **92** 2 2 S 31 22 E
Burin, *Canada* **105** 47 1N 55 14W
Būrīn, *Jordan* . . . . **44** 32 11N 35 15 E
Buriram, *Thailand* . . . . **54** 15 0N 103 0 E
Buriti Alegre, *Brazil* . . **139** 18 9 S 49 3W
Buriti Bravo, *Brazil* . . **138** 5 50 S 43 50W
Buriti dos Lopes, *Brazil* **138** 3 10 S 41 52W
Burji, *Ethiopia* . . . . **89** 5 29N 37 51 E
Burkburnett, *U.S.A.* . . . **121** 34 7N 98 35W
Burke, *U.S.A.* **122** 47 31N 115 56W
Burke →, *Australia* . . **72** 23 12 S 139 33 E
Burketown, *Australia* . . **72** 17 45 S 139 33 E
Burkettsville, *U.S.A.* . . **119** 40 21N 84 39W
Burkina Faso ■, *Africa* **90** 12 0N 1 0W
Burk's Falls, *Canada* . . **108** 45 37N 79 24W
Burleigh Falls, *Canada* **109** 44 33N 78 12W
Burleigh Heads, *Australia* . . . . **77** 28 5 S 153 25 E
Burley, *U.S.A.* **122** 42 37N 113 55W
Burlingame, *U.S.A.* . . . **124** 37 35N 122 21W
Burlington, *Canada* . . . **108** 43 18N 79 45W
Burlington, *Colo., U.S.A.* **120** 39 21N 102 18W
Burlington, *Ill., U.S.A.* **119** 42 43N 88 33W
Burlington, *Iowa, U.S.A.* **118** 40 50N 91 5W
Burlington, *Kans., U.S.A.* **120** 38 15N 95 47W
Burlington, *Ky., U.S.A.* **119** 39 2N 84 43W
Burlington, *N.C., U.S.A.* **115** 36 7N 79 27W
Burlington, *N.J., U.S.A.* **117** 40 5N 74 50W
Burlington, *Vt., U.S.A.* **117** 44 27N 73 14W
Burlington, *Wash., U.S.A.* **110** 48 29N 122 19W
Burlington, *Wis., U.S.A.* **114** 42 41N 88 18W
Burlyu-Tyube, *U.S.S.R.* **40** 46 30N 79 10 E
Burma ■, *Asia* . . . . **52** 21 0N 96 30 E
Burnaby I., *Canada* . . **110** 52 25N 131 19W
Burnet, *U.S.A.* **121** 30 45N 98 11W
Burney, *U.S.A.* **122** 40 56N 121 41W
Burngup, *Australia* . . . **79** 33 2 S 118 42 E
Burnham, *U.S.A.* **116** 40 37N 77 34W
Burnie, *Australia* . . . . . **72** 41 4 S 145 56 E
Burnley, *U.K.* **12** 53 47N 2 15W
Burns, *Oreg., U.S.A.* . . **122** 43 40N 119 4W
Burns, *Wyo., U.S.A.* . . **120** 41 13N 104 18W
Burns Lake, *Canada* . . **110** 54 20N 125 45W
Burnside →, *Canada* . **102** 66 51N 108 4W
Burnside, L., *Australia* **79** 25 22 S 123 0 E
Burnt River, *Canada* . **109** 44 41N 78 42W
Burntwood →, *Canada* **111** 56 8N 96 34W
Burntwood L., *Canada* **111** 55 22N 100 26W
Burpengary, *Australia* . **77** 27 10 S 152 57 E
Burqā, *Jordan* . . . . **44** 32 18N 35 11 E
Burqān, *Kuwait* . . . . . . **46** 29 0N 47 57 E
Burqin, *China* . . . . **62** 47 43N 87 0 E
Burra, *Australia* . . . . . . **73** 33 40 S 138 55 E
Burraga, *Australia* . . . . **76** 33 57 S 149 32 E
Burragate, *Australia* . . . **75** 37 2 S 149 38 E
Burragorang, L., *Australia* . . . . **76** 33 52 S 150 37 E
Burramurra, *Australia* . **72** 20 25 S 137 15 E
Burreli, *Albania* . . . . . . **35** 41 36N 20 1 E
Burren Junction, *Australia* . . . . **73** 30 7 S 148 59 E
Burrendong, L., *Australia* . . . . **76** 32 45 S 149 10 E
Burrendong Dam, *Australia* . . . . **76** 32 39 S 149 6 E
Burrewarra Pt., *Australia* . . . . **76** 35 50 S 150 15 E
Burriana, *Spain* **24** 39 50N 0 4W
Burringbar, *Australia* . **77** 28 25 S 153 29 E
Burrinjuck Dam, *Australia* . . . . **76** 35 0 S 148 34 E
Burrinjuck Res., *Australia* . . . . **76** 35 0 S 148 36 E
Burro, Serranías del, *Mexico* **126** 29 0N 102 0W
Burrumbeet, L., *Australia* . . . . **74** 37 30 S 143 39 E
Burrundie, *Australia* . . **78** 13 32 S 131 42 E
Burruyacú, *Argentina* . **140** 26 30 S 64 40W
Burry Port, *U.K.* **13** 51 41N 4 17W
Bursa, *Turkey* . . . . **46** 40 15N 29 5 E
Burseryd, *Sweden* . . . . **11** 57 12N 13 17 E
Burstall, *Canada* **111** 50 39N 109 54W
Burton, *U.S.A.* **119** 43 0N 83 40W
Burton L., *Canada* . . . **104** 54 45N 78 20W
Burton-upon-Trent, *U.K.* **12** 52 48N 1 39W
Burtundy, *Australia* . . . **74** 33 45 S 142 15 E
Buru, *Indonesia* . . . . . . **57** 3 30 S 126 30 E
Burullus, Bahra el, *Egypt* . . . . **88** 31 25N 31 0 E
Burundi ■, *Africa* . . . . **92** 3 15 S 30 0 E
Bururi, *Burundi* . . . . . . **92** 3 57 S 29 37 E
Burutu, *Nigeria* . . . . . . **91** 5 20N 5 29 E
Burwash, *Canada* **108** 46 14N 80 51W
Burwell, *U.S.A.* **120** 41 49N 99 8W
Bury, *Canada* **107** 45 28N 71 30W
Bury, *U.K.* **12** 53 36N 2 19W
Bury St. Edmunds, *U.K.* . . . . **13** 52 15N 0 42 E
Buryat A.S.S.R. □, *U.S.S.R.* . . . . **41** 53 0N 110 0 E
Buryn, *U.S.S.R.* . . . . . **36** 51 13N 33 50 E
Busalla, *Italy* . . . . **26** 44 34N 8 58 E
Busango Swamp, *Zambia* . . . . **93** 14 15 S 25 45 E
Buşayyah, *Iraq* . . . . . . **46** 30 0N 46 10 E
Busca, *Italy* . . . . **26** 44 31N 7 29 E
Būshehr, *Iran* . . . . **47** 28 55N 50 55 E
Būshehr □, *Iran* . . . . . **47** 28 20N 51 45 E
Bushell, *Canada* **111** 59 31N 108 45W
Bushenyi, *Uganda* . . . . **92** 0 35 S 30 10 E
Bushire = Būshehr, *Iran* . . . . **47** 28 55N 50 55 E
Bushnell, *Ill., U.S.A.* . **120** 40 32N 90 30W
Bushnell, *Nebr., U.S.A.* **120** 41 18N 103 50W
Busia □, *Kenya* . . . . . . **92** 0 25N 34 6 E
Busie, *Ghana* **90** 10 29N 2 22W
Businga, *Zaïre* . . . . **94** 3 16N 20 59 E
Buskerud fylke □, *Norway* . . . . **10** 60 13N 9 0 E
Busko Zdrój, *Poland* . . **32** 50 28N 20 42 E
Buslei, *Ethiopia* . . . . . . **89** 5 28N 44 25 E
Busoga □, *Uganda* . . . **92** 0 5N 33 30 E
Busovača, *Yugoslavia* . **33** 44 6N 17 53 E
Busra ash Shām, *Syria* **46** 32 30N 36 25 E
Bussang, *France* . . . . . **19** 47 50N 6 50 E
Busselton, *Australia* . . **79** 33 42 S 115 15 E
Busseto, *Italy* . . . . **26** 44 59N 10 2 E
Bussum, *Neths.* . . . . . . **16** 52 16N 5 10 E
Bustamante, B., *Argentina* . . . . **142** 45 5 S 66 18W
Busto, C., *Spain* **22** 43 34N 6 28W
Busto Arsizio, *Italy* . . . **26** 45 40N 8 50 E
Busu-Djanoa, *Zaïre* . . **94** 1 43N 21 23 E
Busuanga, *Phil.* . . . . . . **57** 12 10N 120 0 E
Büsum, *W. Germany* . **30** 54 7N 8 50 E

Buta, Zaïre 92 2 50N 24 53 E
Butare, Rwanda 92 2 31 S 29 52 E
Butaritari, Kiribati 66 3 30N 174 0 E
Bute, U.K. 14 55 48N 5 2W
Bute Inlet, Canada 110 50 40N 124 53W
Butemba, Uganda 92 1 9N 31 37 E
Butembo, Zaïre 92 0 9N 29 18 E
Butera, Italy 29 37 10N 14 10 E
Bütgenbach, Belgium 17 50 26N 6 12 E
Butha Qi, China 62 48 0N 122 32 E
Buthidaung, Burma 52 20 52N 92 32 E
Butiaba, Uganda 92 1 50N 31 20 E
Butler, Ind., U.S.A. 119 41 26N 84 52W
Butler, Ky., U.S.A. 119 38 47N 84 22W
Butler, Mo., U.S.A. 118 38 17N 94 18W
Butler, Pa., U.S.A. 116 40 52N 79 52W
Butte, Mont., U.S.A. 122 46 0N 112 31W
Butte, Nebr., U.S.A. 120 42 56N 98 54W
Butte Creek →, U.S.A. 124 39 12N 121 56W
Butterworth = Gcuwa, S. Africa 97 32 20 S 28 11 E
Butterworth, Malaysia 55 5 24N 100 23 E
Buttfield, Mt., Australia 79 24 45 S 128 9 E
Button B., Canada 111 58 45N 94 23W
Buttonwillow, U.S.A. 125 35 24N 119 28W
Butty Hd., Australia 79 33 54 S 121 39 E
Butuan, Phil. 57 8 57N 125 33 E
Butuku-Luba, Eq. Guin. 91 3 29N 8 33 E
Butung, Indonesia 57 5 0 S 122 45 E
Buturlinovka, U.S.S.R. 37 50 50N 40 35 E
Butzbach, W. Germany 30 50 24N 8 40 E
Bützow, E. Germany 30 53 51N 11 59 E
Buxar, India 49 25 34N 83 58 E
Buxton, N.S.W., Australia 76 34 15 S 150 32 E
Buxton, Vic., Australia 74 37 26 S 145 42 E
Buxton, Guyana 135 6 48N 58 2W
Buxton, S. Africa 96 27 38 S 24 42 E
Buxton, U.K. 12 53 16N 1 54W
Buxy, France 19 46 44N 4 40 E
Buy, U.S.S.R. 37 58 28N 41 28 E
Buyaga, U.S.S.R. 41 59 50N 127 0 E
Buynaksk, U.S.S.R. 39 42 48N 47 7 E
Büyük Çekmece, Turkey 35 41 2N 28 35 E
Buzançais, France 18 46 54N 1 25 E
Buzău, Romania 34 45 10N 26 50 E
Buzău →, Romania 34 45 26N 27 44 E
Buzău, Pasul, Romania 34 45 35N 26 12 E
Buzen, Japan 64 33 35N 131 5 E
Buzet, Yugoslavia 27 45 24N 13 58 E
Buzi →, Mozam. 93 19 50 S 34 43 E
Buziaş, Romania 34 45 38N 21 36 E
Buzuluk, U.S.S.R. 40 52 48N 52 12 E
Buzuluk →, U.S.S.R. 37 50 15N 42 7 E
Buzzards Bay, U.S.A. 117 41 45N 70 38W
Bwagaoia, Papua N. G. 69 10 40 S 152 52 E
Bwana Mkubwe, Zaïre 93 13 8 S 28 38 E
Byala, Bulgaria 34 43 28N 25 44 E
Byala Slatina, Bulgaria 34 43 26N 23 55 E
Byandovan, Mys, U.S.S.R. 39 39 45N 49 28 E
Bychawa, Poland 32 51 1N 22 36 E
Bydgoszcz, Poland 32 53 10N 18 0 E
Byelorussian S.S.R. □, U.S.S.R. 36 53 30N 27 0 E
Byers, U.S.A. 120 39 46N 104 13W
Byesville, U.S.A. 116 39 56N 81 32W
Byhalia, U.S.A. 121 34 53N 89 41W
Bykhov, U.S.S.R. 36 53 31N 30 14 E
Bykovo, U.S.S.R. 39 49 50N 45 25 E
Bylas, U.S.A. 123 33 11N 110 9W
Bylderup, Denmark 11 54 57N 9 6 E
Bylong, Australia 76 32 24 S 150 8 E
Bylot I., Canada 103 73 13N 78 34W
Byng Inlet, Canada 108 45 46N 80 33W
Byrd, C., Antarctica 143 69 38 S 76 7W
Byrd Land, Antarctica 143 79 30 S 125 0W
Byrd Sub-Glacial Basin, Antarctica 143 82 0 S 120 0W
Byro, Australia 79 26 5 S 116 11 E
Byrock, Australia 73 30 40 S 146 27 E
Byron, Australia 77 29 40 S 151 7 E
Byron, U.S.A. 118 42 8N 89 15W
Byron, C., Australia 77 28 38 S 153 40 E
Byron Bay, Australia 77 28 43 S 153 37 E
Byrranga, Gory, U.S.S.R. 41 75 0N 100 0 E
Byrum, Denmark 11 57 16N 11 0 E
Byske, Sweden 8 64 57N 21 11 E
Byske älv →, Sweden 8 64 57N 21 13 E
Bystrzyca Kłodzka, Poland 32 50 19N 16 39 E
Byten, U.S.S.R. 36 52 50N 25 27 E
Bytom, Poland 32 50 25N 18 54 E
Bytów, Poland 32 54 10N 17 30 E
Byumba, Rwanda 92 1 35 S 30 4 E

C

Ca →, Vietnam 54 18 45N 105 45 E
Ca Mau = Quan Long, Vietnam 55 9 7N 105 8 E
Ca Mau, Mui = Bai Bung, Mui, Vietnam 55 8 38N 104 44 E
Ca Na, Vietnam 55 11 20N 108 54 E
Caacupé, Paraguay 140 25 23 S 57 5W
Caála, Angola 95 12 46 S 15 30 E
Caamano Sd., Canada 110 52 55N 129 25W
Caapiranga, Brazil 135 3 18 S 61 13W
Caazapá, Paraguay 140 26 8 S 56 19W
Caazapá □, Paraguay 141 26 10 S 56 0W
Caballeria, C. de, Spain 24 40 5N 4 5 E
Cabana, Peru 136 8 25 S 78 5W
Cabanaconde, Peru 136 15 38 S 71 58W
Cabañaquinta, Spain 22 43 10N 5 38W
Cabanatuan, Phil. 57 15 30N 120 58 E
Cabanes, Spain 24 40 9N 0 2 E
Cabanillas, Peru 136 15 36 S 70 28W
Cabano, Canada 107 47 40N 68 56W
Čabar, Yugoslavia 27 45 36N 14 39 E
Cabazon, U.S.A. 125 33 55N 116 47W
Cabbora →, Australia 77 32 2 S 149 17 E
Cabedelo, Brazil 138 7 0 S 34 50W
Cabery, U.S.A. 119 40 59N 88 12W
Cabeza del Buey, Spain 23 38 44N 5 13W
Cabildo, Chile 140 32 30 S 71 5W
Cabimas, Venezuela 134 10 23N 71 25W
Cabinda, Angola 95 5 33 S 12 11 E
Cabinda □, Angola 95 5 0 S 12 30 E
Cabinet Mts., U.S.A. 122 48 0N 115 30W
Cabiri, Angola 95 8 52 S 13 39 E
Cabo Blanco, Argentina 142 47 15 S 65 47W
Cabo Frio, Brazil 139 22 51 S 42 3W
Cabo Pantoja, Peru 134 1 0 S 75 10W
Cabo Raso, Argentina 142 44 20 S 65 15W
Cabonga, Réservoir, Canada 106 47 20N 76 40W
Cabool, U.S.A. 121 37 10N 92 8W
Caboolture, Australia 73 27 5 S 152 58 E
Cabora Bassa Dam, Mozam. 93 15 20 S 32 50 E
Caborca, Mexico 126 30 40N 112 10W
Cabot, Mt., U.S.A. 117 44 30N 71 25W
Cabot Strait, Canada 105 47 15N 59 40W
Cabra, Spain 23 37 30N 4 28W
Cabra del Santo Cristo, Spain 25 37 42N 3 16W
Cabramurra, Australia 76 35 56 S 148 26 E
Cábras, Italy 28 39 57N 8 30 E
Cabrera, I., Spain 25 39 8N 2 57 E
Cabrera, Sierra, Spain 22 42 12N 6 40W
Cabri, Canada 111 50 35N 108 25W
Cabriel →, Spain 25 39 14N 1 3W
Cabruta, Venezuela 134 7 50N 66 10W
Cabuyaro, Colombia 134 4 18N 72 49W
Caçabelos, Spain 22 42 36N 6 44W
Čačak, Yugoslavia 33 43 54N 20 20 E
Cacao, Fr. Guiana 135 4 33N 52 26W
Cáceres, Brazil 137 16 5 S 57 40W
Cáceres, Colombia 134 7 35N 75 20W
Cáceres, Spain 23 39 26N 6 23W
Cáceres □, Spain 23 39 45N 6 0W
Cache Bay, Canada 108 46 22N 80 0W
Cache Cr. →, U.S.A. 124 38 45N 121 43W
Cachepo, Portugal 23 37 20N 7 49W
Cachéu, Guinea-Biss. 90 12 14N 16 8W
Cachi, Argentina 140 25 5 S 66 10W
Cachimbo, Brazil 137 8 57 S 54 54W
Cachimbo, Serra do, Brazil 137 9 30 S 55 0W
Cachingues, Angola 95 13 5 S 16 43 E
Cachoeira, Brazil 139 12 30 S 39 0W
Cachoeira Alta, Brazil 139 18 48 S 50 58W
Cachoeira de Itapemirim, Brazil 141 20 51 S 41 7W
Cachoeira do Sul, Brazil 141 30 3 S 52 53W
Cachoeiro do Arari, Brazil 138 1 1 S 48 58W
Cachopo, Portugal 23 37 20N 7 49W
Cachuela Esperanza, Bolivia 137 10 32 S 65 38W
Cacólo, Angola 95 10 9 S 19 21 E
Caconda, Angola 95 13 48 S 15 8 E
Cacongo, Angola 95 5 11 S 12 5 E
Caçu, Brazil 139 18 37 S 51 4W
Cacula, Angola 95 14 29 S 14 10 E
Caculé, Brazil 139 14 30 S 42 13W
Cacuso, Angola 95 9 25 S 15 45 E
Cadarache, France 21 43 41N 5 43 E
Čadca, Czech. 32 49 26N 18 45 E
Caddo, U.S.A. 121 34 8N 96 18W
Cadell Cr. →, Australia 72 22 35 S 141 51 E
Cader Idris, U.K. 12 52 43N 3 56W
Cadí, Sierra del, Spain 24 42 17N 1 42 E
Cadibarrawirracanna, L., Australia 73 28 52 S 135 27 E
Cadillac, Canada 106 48 14N 78 23W
Cadillac, France 20 44 38N 0 20W
Cadillac, U.S.A. 104 44 16N 85 25W
Cadiz, Phil. 57 10 57N 123 15 E
Cádiz, Spain 23 36 30N 6 20W
Cadiz, U.S.A. 116 40 13N 81 0W
Cádiz □, Spain 23 36 36N 5 45W
Cádiz, G. de, Spain 23 36 40N 7 0W
Cadney Park, Australia 73 27 55 S 134 3 E
Cadomin, Canada 110 53 2N 117 20W
Cadotte →, Canada 110 56 43N 117 10W
Cadours, France 20 43 44N 1 2 E
Cadoux, Australia 79 30 46 S 117 7 E
Caen, France 18 49 10N 0 22W
Caernarfon, U.K. 12 53 8N 4 17W
Caernarfon B., U.K. 12 53 4N 4 40W
Caernarvon = Caernarfon, U.K. 12 53 8N 4 17W
Caerphilly, U.K. 13 51 34N 3 13W
Caesarea, Israel 44 32 30N 34 53 E
Caeté, Brazil 139 19 55 S 43 40W
Caetité, Brazil 139 13 50 S 42 32W
Cafayate, Argentina 140 26 2 S 66 0W
Cafifi, Colombia 134 5 13N 71 4W
Cafu, Angola 95 16 30 S 15 8 E
Cagayan →, Phil. 57 18 25N 121 42 E
Cagayan de Oro, Phil. 57 8 30N 124 40 E
Cagli, Italy 27 43 32N 12 38 E
Cágliari, Italy 28 39 15N 9 6 E
Cágliari, G. di, Italy 28 39 8N 9 10 E
Cagnano Varano, Italy 29 41 49N 15 47 E
Cagnes-sur-Mer, France 21 43 40N 7 9 E
Caguán →, Colombia 134 0 8 S 74 18W
Caguas, Puerto Rico 129 18 14N 66 4W
Caha Mts., Ireland 15 51 45N 9 40W
Cahama, Angola 95 16 17 S 14 19 E
Caher, Ireland 15 52 23N 7 56W
Cahersiveen, Ireland 15 51 57N 10 13W
Cahore Pt., Ireland 15 52 34N 6 11W
Cahors, France 20 44 27N 1 27 E
Cahuapanas, Peru 136 5 15 S 77 0W
Cahuinari →, Colombia 134 1 21 S 70 44W
Cai Bau, Dao, Vietnam 54 21 10N 107 27 E
Cai Nuoc, Vietnam 55 8 56N 105 1 E
Caia, Mozam. 93 17 51 S 35 24 E
Caiabis, Serra dos, Brazil 137 11 30 S 56 30W
Caianda, Angola 93 11 2 S 23 31 E
Caiapó, Serra do, Brazil 137 17 0 S 52 0W
Caiapônia, Brazil 137 16 57 S 51 49W
Caibarién, Cuba 128 22 30N 79 30W
Caicara, Bolívar, Venezuela 134 7 38N 66 10W
Caicara, Monagas, Venezuela 135 9 52N 63 38W
Caicó, Brazil 138 6 20 S 37 0W
Caicos Is., W. Indies 129 21 40N 71 40W
Caicos Passage, W. Indies 129 22 45N 72 45W
Cailloma, Peru 136 15 9 S 71 45W
Caine →, Bolivia 137 18 23 S 65 21W
Caird Coast, Antarctica 143 75 0 S 25 0W
Cairn Curran Res., Australia 74 37 5 S 144 2 E
Cairn Gorm, U.K. 14 57 7N 3 40W
Cairn Toul, U.K. 14 57 3N 3 44W
Cairngorm Mts., U.K. 14 57 6N 3 42W
Cairns, Australia 72 16 57 S 145 45 E
Cairo = El Qâhira, Egypt 88 30 1N 31 14 E
Cairo, Ga., U.S.A. 115 30 52N 84 12W
Cairo, Ill., U.S.A. 121 37 0N 89 10W
Cairo Montenotte, Italy 26 44 23N 8 16 E
Caithness, Ord of, U.K. 14 58 9N 3 37W
Caiundo, Angola 95 15 50 S 17 28 E
Caiza, Bolivia 137 20 2 S 65 40W
Cajabamba, Peru 136 7 38 S 78 4W
Cajamarca, Peru 136 7 5 S 78 28W
Cajamarca □, Peru 136 6 15 S 78 50W
Cajapió, Brazil 138 2 58 S 44 48W
Cajarc, France 20 44 29N 1 50 E
Cajatambo, Peru 136 10 30 S 77 2W
Cajàzeiras, Brazil 138 6 52 S 38 30W
Čajetina, Yugoslavia 33 43 47N 19 42 E
Çakirgol, Turkey 39 40 33N 39 40 E
Čakovec, Yugoslavia 27 46 23N 16 26 E
Cal, La →, Bolivia 137 17 27 S 58 15W
Cala, Spain 23 37 59N 6 21W
Cala →, Spain 23 37 38N 6 5W
Cala Cadolar, Punta de, Spain 25 38 38N 1 35 E
Calabar, Nigeria 91 4 57N 8 20 E
Calabogie, Canada 109 45 18N 76 43W
Calabozo, Venezuela 134 9 0N 67 28W
Calábria □, Italy 29 39 24N 16 30 E
Calaburras, Pta. de, Spain 23 36 30N 4 38W
Calaceite, Spain 24 41 1N 0 11 E
Calacota, Bolivia 136 17 16 S 68 38W
Calafate, Argentina 142 50 19 S 72 15W
Calahorra, Spain 24 42 18N 1 59W
Calais, France 19 50 57N 1 56 E
Calais, U.S.A. 105 45 11N 67 20W
Calais, Pas de, France 19 51 0N 1 20 E
Calalaste, Cord. de, Argentina 140 25 0 S 67 0W
Calama, Brazil 137 8 0 S 62 50W
Calama, Chile 140 22 30 S 68 55W
Calamar, Bolívar, Colombia 134 10 15N 74 55W
Calamar, Vaupés, Colombia 134 1 58N 72 32W
Calamarca, Bolivia 136 16 55 S 68 9W
Calamian Group, Phil. 57 11 50N 119 55 E
Calamocha, Spain 24 40 50N 1 17W
Calañas, Spain 23 37 40N 6 53W
Calanda, Spain 24 40 56N 0 15W
Calandula, Angola 95 9 6 S 15 57 E
Calang, Indonesia 56 4 37N 95 37 E
Calangiánus, Italy 28 40 56N 9 12 E
Calanscio, Sarīr, Libya 86 27 0N 21 30 E
Calapan, Phil. 57 13 25N 121 7 E
Călăraşi, Romania 34 44 12N 27 20 E
Călăraşi □, Romania 34 44 10N 27 0 E
Calasparra, Spain 25 38 14N 1 41W
Calatafimi, Italy 28 37 56N 12 50 E
Calatayud, Spain 24 41 20N 1 40W
Calato = Kálathos, Greece 35 36 9N 28 8 E
Calauag, Phil. 57 13 55N 122 15 E
Calavà, C., Italy 29 38 11N 14 55 E
Calavite, Cape, Phil. 57 13 26N 120 20 E
Calbayog, Phil. 57 12 4N 124 38 E
Calbe, E. Germany 30 51 57N 11 47 E
Calca, Peru 136 13 22 S 72 0W
Calcasieu L., U.S.A. 121 30 0N 93 17W
Calci, Italy 26 43 44N 10 31 E
Calcutta, India 49 22 36N 88 24 E
Caldaro, Italy 27 46 23N 11 15 E
Caldas □, Colombia 134 5 15N 75 30W
Caldas da Rainha, Portugal 23 39 24N 9 8W
Caldas de Reyes, Spain 22 42 36N 8 39W
Caldas Novas, Brazil 139 17 45 S 48 38W
Calder →, U.K. 12 53 44N 1 21W
Caldera, Chile 140 27 5 S 70 55W
Caldwell, Idaho, U.S.A. 122 43 45N 116 42W
Caldwell, Kans., U.S.A. 121 37 5N 97 37W
Caldwell, Tex., U.S.A. 121 30 30N 96 42W
Caledon, S. Africa 96 34 14 S 19 26 E
Caledon →, S. Africa 96 30 31 S 26 5 E
Caledon B., Australia 72 12 45 S 137 0 E
Caledonia, Canada 108 43 7N 79 58W
Caledonia, Mo., U.S.A. 118 37 45N 90 46W
Caledonia, N.Y., U.S.A. 116 42 57N 77 54W
Calella, Spain 24 41 37N 2 40 E
Calemba, Angola 96 16 0 S 15 44 E
Calenzana, France 21 42 31N 8 51 E
Calera, La, Chile 140 32 50 S 71 10W
Caleta Olivia, Argentina 142 46 25 S 67 25W
Calexico, U.S.A. 125 32 40N 115 33W
Calf of Man, I. of Man 12 54 4N 4 48W
Calgary, Canada 110 51 0N 114 10W
Calhoun, U.S.A. 115 34 30N 84 55W
Cali, Colombia 134 3 25N 76 35W
Calicut, India 51 11 15N 75 43 E
Caliente, U.S.A. 123 37 36N 114 34W
California, Mo., U.S.A. 118 38 37N 92 30W
California, Pa., U.S.A. 116 40 5N 79 55W
California □, U.S.A. 123 37 25N 120 0W
California, Baja, Mexico 126 32 10N 115 12W
California, Baja, T.N. □, Mexico 126 30 0N 115 0W
California, Baja, T.S. □, Mexico 126 25 50N 111 50W
California, G. de, Mexico 126 27 0N 111 0W
California, Lr. = California, Baja, Mexico 126 32 10N 115 12W
California City, U.S.A. 125 35 7N 117 57W
California Hot Springs, U.S.A. 125 35 51N 118 41W
Călimăneşti, Romania 34 45 14N 24 20 E
Călimani, Munţii, Romania 34 47 12N 25 0 E
Călineşti, Romania 34 45 21N 24 18 E
Calingasta, Argentina 140 31 15 S 69 30W
Calipatria, U.S.A. 125 33 8N 115 30W
Calistoga, U.S.A. 124 38 36N 122 32W
Calitri, Italy 29 40 54N 15 25 E
Calitzdorp, S. Africa 96 33 33 S 21 42 E
Callabonna, L., Australia 73 29 40 S 140 5 E
Callac, France 18 48 25N 3 27W
Callan, Ireland 15 52 33N 7 25W
Callander, Canada 108 46 13N 79 22W
Callander, U.K. 14 56 15N 4 14W
Callantsoog, Neths. 16 52 50N 4 42 E
Callao, Peru 136 12 0 S 77 0W
Callaway, U.S.A. 120 41 20N 99 56W
Callender, U.S.A. 118 42 22N 94 17W
Calles, Mexico 127 23 2N 98 42W
Callide, Australia 72 24 18 S 150 28 E
Calling Lake, Canada 110 55 15N 113 12W
Calliope, Australia 72 24 0 S 151 16 E
Callosa de Ensarriá, Spain 25 38 40N 0 8W
Callosa de Segura, Spain 25 38 7N 0 53W
Calmar, U.S.A. 118 43 11N 91 52W
Calne, U.K. 12 51 26N 2 0W
Calola, Angola 95 16 25 S 17 48 E
Caloona, Australia 77 28 52 S 149 11 E
Calore →, Italy 29 41 11N 14 28 E
Caloundra, Australia 73 26 45 S 153 10 E
Calpe, Spain 25 38 39N 0 3 E
Calpella, U.S.A. 124 39 14N 123 12W
Calpine, U.S.A. 124 39 40N 120 27W
Calstock, Canada 104 49 47N 84 9W
Caltabellotta, Italy 28 37 36N 13 11 E
Caltagirone, Italy 29 37 13N 14 30 E
Caltanissetta, Italy 29 37 30N 14 3 E
Calucinga, Angola 95 11 18 S 16 12 E
Calulo, Angola 95 10 1 S 14 56 E
Calumet, U.S.A. 114 47 14N 88 27W
Calunda, Angola 95 12 7 S 23 36 E
Caluquembe, Angola 95 13 47 S 14 44 E
Caluso, Italy 26 45 18N 7 52 E
Calvados □, France 18 49 5N 0 15W
Calvert, U.S.A. 121 30 59N 96 40W
Calvert →, Australia 72 16 17 S 137 44 E
Calvert Hills, Australia 72 17 15 S 137 20 E
Calvert I., Canada 110 51 30N 128 0W
Calvert Ra., Australia 78 24 0 S 122 30 E
Calvi, France 21 42 34N 8 45 E
Calvillo, Mexico 126 21 51N 102 43W
Calvinia, S. Africa 96 31 28 S 19 45 E
Calw, W. Germany 31 48 43N 8 44 E
Calwa, U.S.A. 124 36 42N 119 46W
Calzada Almuradiel, Spain 25 38 32N 3 28W

Centralia

Cass City, U.S.A. 114 43 34N 83 24W
Cass Lake, U.S.A. 120 47 23N 94 38W
Cassá de la Selva, Spain 24 41 53N 2 52 E
Cassai, Angola 95 10 33 S 21 59 E
Cassamba, Angola 95 13 6 S 20 18 E
Cassano Iónio, Italy 29 39 47N 16 20 E
Cassel, France 19 50 48N 2 30 E
Casselman, Canada 106 45 19N 75 5W
Casselton, U.S.A. 120 47 0N 97 15W
Cassiar, Canada 110 59 16N 129 40W
Cassiar Mts., Canada 110 59 30N 130 30W
Cassilândia, Brazil 137 19 9 S 51 45W
Cassilis, Australia 77 32 3 S 149 58 E
Cassinga, Angola 95 15 5 S 16 4 E
Cassino, Italy 28 41 30N 13 50 E
Cassis, France 21 43 14N 5 32 E
Cassoalala, Angola 95 9 30 S 14 22 E
Cassoango, Angola 95 13 42 S 20 56 E
Cassopolis, U.S.A. 119 41 55N 86 1W
Cassunda, Angola 95 10 57 S 21 3 E
Cassville, Mo., U.S.A. 121 36 45N 93 52W
Cassville, Wis., U.S.A. 118 42 43N 90 59W
Cástagneto Carducci, Italy 26 43 9N 10 36 E
Castaic, U.S.A. 125 34 30N 118 38W
Castanhal, Brazil 138 1 18 S 47 55W
Casteau, Belgium 17 50 32N 4 2 E
Castéggio, Italy 26 45 1N 9 8 E
Castejón de Monegros, Spain 24 41 37N 0 15W
Castel di Sangro, Italy 27 41 47N 14 6 E
Castel San Giovanni, Italy 26 45 4N 9 25 E
Castel San Pietro, Italy 27 44 23N 11 30 E
Castelbuono, Italy 29 37 56N 14 4 E
Casteldelfino, Italy 26 44 35N 7 4 E
Castelfiorentino, Italy 26 43 36N 10 58 E
Castelfranco Emília, Italy 26 44 37N 11 2 E
Castelfranco Véneto, Italy 27 45 40N 11 56 E
Casteljaloux, France 20 44 19N 0 6 E
Castellabate, Italy 29 40 18N 14 55 E
Castellammare, G. di, Italy 28 38 5N 12 55 E
Castellammare del Golfo, Italy 28 38 2N 12 53 E
Castellammare di Stábia, Italy 29 40 47N 14 29 E
Castellamonte, Italy 26 45 23N 7 42 E
Castellana Grotte, Italy 29 40 53N 17 10 E
Castellane, France 21 43 50N 6 31 E
Castellaneta, Italy 29 40 40N 16 57 E
Castellar de Santisteban, Spain 25 38 16N 3 8W
Castelleone, Italy 26 45 19N 9 47 E
Castelli, Argentina 140 36 7 S 57 47W
Castelló de Ampurias, Spain 24 42 15N 3 4 E
Castellón □, Spain 24 40 15N 0 5W
Castellón de la Plana, Spain 24 39 58N 0 3W
Castellote, Spain 24 40 48N 0 15W
Castelltersol, Spain 24 41 45N 2 8 E
Castelmáuro, Italy 29 41 50N 14 40 E
Castelnau-de-Médoc, France 20 45 2N 0 48W
Castelnaudary, France 20 43 20N 1 58 E
Castelnovo ne' Monti, Italy 26 44 27N 10 26 E
Castelnuovo di Val di Cécina, Italy 26 43 12N 10 54 E
Castelo, Brazil 139 20 33 S 41 14W
Castelo Branco, Portugal 22 39 50N 7 31W
Castelo Branco □, Portugal 22 39 52N 7 45W
Castelo de Paiva, Portugal 22 41 2N 8 16W
Castelo de Vide, Portugal 23 39 25N 7 27W
Castelo do Piauí, Brazil 138 5 20 S 41 33W
Castelsarrasin, France 20 44 2N 1 7 E
Casteltérmini, Italy 28 37 32N 13 38 E
Castelvetrano, Italy 28 37 40N 12 46 E
Castendo, Angola 95 8 39 S 14 10 E
Casterton, Australia 74 37 30 S 141 30 E
Castets, France 20 43 52N 1 6W
Castiglione del Lago, Italy 27 43 7N 12 3 E
Castiglione della Pescáia, Italy 26 42 46N 10 53 E
Castiglione della Stiviere, Italy 26 45 23N 10 30 E
Castiglione Fiorentino, Italy 27 43 20N 11 55 E
Castilblanco, Spain 23 39 17N 5 5W
Castilla, Peru 136 5 12 S 80 38W
Castilla, Playa de, Spain 23 37 0N 6 33W
Castilla La Mancha □, Spain 23 39 30N 3 30W
Castilla La Nueva, Spain 23 39 45N 3 20W
Castilla La Vieja, Spain 22 41 55N 4 0W
Castilla y Leon □, Spain 22 42 0N 5 0W
Castillon, Barr. de, France 21 43 53N 6 33 E
Castillon-en-Couserans, France 20 42 56N 1 1 E
Castillon-la-Bataille, France 20 44 51N 0 2W
Castillonès, France 20 44 39N 0 37 E
Castillos, Uruguay 141 34 12 S 53 52W
Castle Dale, U.S.A. 122 39 11N 111 1W
Castle Douglas, U.K. 14 54 57N 3 57W
Castle Point, N.Z. 80 40 54 S 176 15 E
Castle Rock, Colo., U.S.A. 120 39 26N 104 50W
Castle Rock, Wash., U.S.A. 124 46 20N 122 58W
Castlebar, Ireland 15 53 52N 9 17W
Castleblaney, Ireland 15 54 7N 6 44W
Castlecliff, N.Z. 80 39 57 S 174 59 E
Castlegar, Canada 110 49 20N 117 40W
Castlemaine, Australia 74 37 2 S 144 12 E
Castlereagh, Ireland 15 53 47N 8 30W
Castlereagh □, U.K. 15 54 33N 5 53W
Castlereagh →, Australia 73 30 12 S 147 32 E
Castlereagh B., Australia 72 12 10 S 135 10 E
Castletown, I. of Man 12 54 4N 4 40W
Castletown Bearhaven, Ireland 15 51 40N 9 54W
Castlevale, Australia 72 24 30 S 146 48 E
Castor, Canada 110 52 15N 111 50W
Castres, France 20 43 37N 2 13 E
Castricum, Neths. 16 52 33N 4 40 E
Castries, St. Lucia 129 14 0N 60 50W
Castril, Spain 25 37 48N 2 46W
Castro, Brazil 141 24 45 S 50 0W
Castro, Chile 142 42 30 S 73 50W
Castro Alves, Brazil 139 12 46 S 39 33W
Castro del Río, Spain 23 37 41N 4 29W
Castro Marim, Portugal 23 37 13N 7 26W
Castro Urdiales, Spain 24 43 23N 3 11W
Castro Verde, Portugal 23 37 41N 8 4W
Castrojeriz, Spain 22 42 17N 4 9W
Castropol, Spain 22 43 32N 7 0W
Castroreale, Italy 29 38 5N 15 15 E
Castrovíllari, Italy 29 39 49N 16 11 E
Castroville, Calif., U.S.A. 124 36 46N 121 45W
Castroville, Tex., U.S.A. 121 29 20N 98 53W
Castrovirreyna, Peru 136 13 20 S 75 18W
Castuera, Spain 23 38 43N 5 37W
Casummit Lake, Canada 104 51 29N 92 22W
Cat Ba, Dao, Vietnam 54 20 50N 107 0 E
Cat I., Bahamas 129 24 30N 75 30W
Cat I., U.S.A. 121 30 15N 89 7W
Cat L., Canada 104 51 40N 91 50W
Catabola, Angola 95 12 9 S 17 16 E
Catacamas, Honduras 128 14 54N 85 56W
Catacáos, Peru 136 5 20 S 80 45W
Cataguases, Brazil 139 21 23 S 42 39W
Catahoula L., U.S.A. 121 31 30N 92 5W
Catalão, Brazil 139 18 10 S 47 57W
Catalina, Canada 105 48 31N 53 4W
Catalonia = Cataluña □, Spain 24 41 40N 1 15 E
Cataluña □, Spain 24 41 40N 1 15 E
Catamarca, Argentina 140 28 30 S 65 50W
Catamarca □, Argentina 140 27 0 S 65 50W
Catanduanes, Phil. 57 13 50N 124 20 E
Catanduva, Brazil 141 21 5 S 48 58W
Catánia, Italy 29 37 31N 15 4 E
Catánia, G. di, Italy 29 37 25N 15 8 E
Catanzaro, Italy 29 38 54N 16 38 E
Catarman, Phil. 57 12 28N 124 35 E
Cateau, Le, France 19 50 7N 3 32 E
Cateel, Phil. 57 7 47N 126 24 E
Catende, Angola 95 11 14 S 21 30 E
Catende, Brazil 138 8 40 S 35 43W
Catete, Angola 95 9 6 S 13 43 E
Cathcart, Australia 75 36 52 S 149 24 E
Cathcart, S. Africa 96 32 18 S 27 10 E
Cathkin, Australia 74 37 10 S 145 38 E
Cathlamet, U.S.A. 124 46 12N 123 23W
Cathundral, Australia 76 31 55 S 147 51 E
Catio, Guinea-Biss. 90 11 17N 15 15W
Catismiña, Venezuela 135 4 5N 63 40W
Catita, Brazil 138 9 31 S 43 1W
Catlettsburg, U.S.A. 114 38 23N 82 38W
Catlin, U.S.A. 119 40 4N 87 42W
Catoche, C., Mexico 127 21 40N 87 8W
Catolé do Rocha, Brazil 138 6 21 S 37 45W
Catral, Spain 25 38 10N 0 47W
Catria, Mt., Italy 27 43 28N 12 42 E
Catrimani, Brazil 135 0 27N 61 41W
Catrimani →, Brazil 135 0 28N 61 44W
Catskill, U.S.A. 117 42 14N 73 52W
Catskill Mts., U.S.A. 117 42 15N 74 15W
Catt, Mt., Australia 72 13 49 S 134 23 E
Cattaraugus, U.S.A. 116 42 22N 78 52W
Cattólica, Italy 27 43 58N 12 43 E
Cattólica Eraclea, Italy 28 37 27N 13 24 E
Catu, Brazil 139 12 21 S 38 23W
Catuala, Angola 95 16 25 S 19 2 E
Catumbela, Angola 95 12 25 S 13 34 E
Catur, Mozam. 93 13 45 S 35 30 E
Catwick Is., Vietnam 55 10 0N 109 0 E
Cauca □, Colombia 134 2 30N 76 50W
Cauca →, Colombia 134 8 54N 74 28W
Caucaia, Brazil 138 3 40 S 38 35W
Caucasia, Colombia 134 8 0N 75 12W
Caucasus Mts. = Bolshoi Kavkas, U.S.S.R. 39 42 50N 44 0 E
Caudebec-en-Caux, France 18 49 30N 0 42 E
Caudete, Spain 25 38 42N 1 2W
Caudry, France 19 50 7N 3 22 E
Caulnes, France 18 48 18N 2 10W
Caulónia, Italy 29 38 23N 16 25 E
Caúngula, Angola 95 8 26 S 18 38 E
Cauquenes, Chile 140 36 0 S 72 22W
Caura →, Venezuela 135 7 38N 64 53W
Caurés →, Brazil 135 1 21 S 62 20W
Cauresi →, Mozam. 93 17 8 S 33 0 E
Causapscal, Canada 105 48 19N 67 12W
Caussade, France 20 44 10N 1 33 E
Causse-Méjean, France 20 44 18N 3 42 E
Cauterets, France 20 42 52N 0 8W
Cautín □, Chile 142 39 0 S 72 30W
Caux, Pays de, France 18 49 38N 0 35 E
Cava dei Tirreni, Italy 29 40 42N 14 42 E
Cávado →, Portugal 22 41 32N 8 48W
Cavaillon, France 21 43 50N 5 2 E
Cavalaire-sur-Mer, France 21 43 10N 6 33 E
Cavalcante, Brazil 139 13 48 S 47 30W
Cavalerie, La, France 20 44 0N 3 10 E
Cavalese, Italy 27 46 17N 11 29 E
Cavalier, U.S.A. 120 48 50N 97 39W
Cavalla = Cavally →, Africa 90 4 22N 7 32W
Cavalli Is., N.Z. 80 35 0 S 173 58 E
Cavallo, I. de, France 21 41 22N 9 16 E
Cavally →, Africa 90 4 22N 7 32W
Cavan, Ireland 15 54 0N 7 22W
Cavan □, Ireland 15 53 58N 7 10W
Cavárzere, Italy 27 45 8N 12 6 E
Cave City, U.S.A. 114 37 13N 85 57W
Cavenagh Range, Australia 79 26 12 S 127 55 E
Cavendish, Australia 74 37 31 S 142 2 E
Caviana, I., Brazil 138 0 10N 50 10W
Cavite, Phil. 57 14 29N 120 55 E
Cavour, Italy 26 44 47N 7 22 E
Cavtat, Yugoslavia 33 42 35N 18 13 E
Cawasachouane, L., Canada 106 47 27N 77 45W
Cawndilla, L., Australia 73 32 30 S 142 15 E
Cawnpore = Kanpur, India 49 26 28N 80 20 E
Caxias, Brazil 138 4 55 S 43 20W
Caxias do Sul, Brazil 141 29 10 S 51 10W
Caxine, C., Algeria 85 35 56N 0 27W
Caxito, Angola 95 8 30 S 13 30 E
Caxopa, Angola 95 11 52 S 20 52 E
Cay Sal Bank, Bahamas 128 23 45N 80 0W
Cayambe, Ecuador 134 0 3N 78 8W
Cayambe, Vol., Ecuador 134 0 2N 77 59W
Cayenne, Fr. Guiana 135 5 0N 52 18W
Cayenne □, Fr. Guiana 135 4 0N 53 0W
Cayes, Les, Haiti 129 18 15N 73 46W
Cayeux-sur-Mer, France 19 50 10N 1 30 E
Caylus, France 20 44 15N 1 47 E
Cayman Brac, Cayman Is. 128 19 43N 79 49W
Cayman Is., W. Indies 128 19 40N 80 30W
Cayo Romano, Cuba 129 22 0N 78 0W
Cayuga, Canada 108 42 59N 79 50W
Cayuga, Ind., U.S.A. 119 39 57N 87 38W
Cayuga, N.Y., U.S.A. 117 42 54N 76 44W
Cayuga L., U.S.A. 117 42 45N 76 45W
Cazaje, Angola 95 11 2 S 20 45 E
Cazalla de la Sierra, Spain 23 37 56N 5 45W
Căzăneşti, Romania 34 44 36N 27 3 E
Cazaux et de Sanguinet, Étang de, France 20 44 29N 1 10W
Cazères, France 20 43 13N 1 5 E
Cazin, Yugoslavia 27 44 57N 15 57 E
Čazma, Yugoslavia 27 45 45N 16 39 E
Čazma →, Yugoslavia 27 45 35N 16 29 E
Cazombo, Angola 95 11 54 S 22 56 E
Cazorla, Spain 25 37 55N 3 2W
Cazorla, Venezuela 134 8 1N 67 0W
Cazorla, Sierra de, Spain 25 38 5N 2 55W
Cea →, Spain 22 42 0N 5 36W
Ceanannus Mor, Ireland 15 53 42N 6 53W
Ceará = Fortaleza, Brazil 138 3 45 S 38 35W
Ceará □, Brazil 138 5 0 S 40 0W
Ceará Mirim, Brazil 138 5 38 S 35 25W
Cebaco, I. de, Panama 128 7 33N 81 9W
Cebollar, Argentina 140 29 10 S 66 35W
Cebollera, Sierra de, Spain 24 42 0N 2 30W
Cebreros, Spain 22 40 27N 4 28W
Cebu, Phil. 57 10 18N 123 54 E
Ceccano, Italy 28 41 34N 13 18 E
Cechi, Ivory C. 90 6 15N 4 25W
Cecil Plains, Australia 77 27 30 S 151 11 E
Cécina, Italy 26 43 19N 10 33 E
Cécina →, Italy 26 43 19N 10 29 E
Ceclavin, Spain 22 39 50N 6 45W
Cedar →, U.S.A. 118 41 17N 91 21W
Cedar City, U.S.A. 123 37 41N 113 3W
Cedar Creek Res., U.S.A. 121 32 4N 96 5W
Cedar Falls, Iowa, U.S.A. 118 42 39N 92 29W
Cedar Falls, Wash., U.S.A. 124 47 25N 121 45W
Cedar Grove, U.S.A. 119 39 22N 84 56W
Cedar Key, U.S.A. 115 29 9N 83 5W
Cedar L., Man., Canada 111 53 10N 100 0W
Cedar L., Ont., Canada 109 46 2N 78 30W
Cedar Lake, U.S.A. 119 41 20N 87 25W
Cedar Point, U.S.A. 119 41 44N 83 21W
Cedar Rapids, U.S.A. 118 42 0N 91 38W
Cedartown, U.S.A. 115 34 1N 85 15W
Cedarvale, Canada 110 55 1N 128 22W
Cedarville, S. Africa 97 30 23 S 29 3 E
Cedarville, Calif., U.S.A. 122 41 37N 120 13W
Cedarville, Ill., U.S.A. 118 42 23N 89 38W
Cedarville, Ohio, U.S.A. 119 39 44N 83 49W
Cedeira, Spain 22 43 39N 8 2W
Cedral, Mexico 126 23 50N 100 42W
Cedrino →, Italy 28 40 23N 9 44 E
Cedro, Brazil 138 6 34 S 39 3W
Cedros, I. de, Mexico 126 28 10N 115 20W
Ceduna, Australia 73 32 7 S 133 46 E
Cefalù, Italy 29 38 3N 14 1 E
Cega →, Spain 22 41 33N 4 46W
Cegléd, Hungary 33 47 11N 19 47 E
Céglie Messápico, Italy 29 40 39N 17 31 E
Cehegín, Spain 25 38 6N 1 48W
Ceheng, China 58 24 58N 105 48 E
Cehu-Silvaniei, Romania 34 47 24N 23 9 E
Ceiba, La, Honduras 128 15 40N 86 50W
Ceira →, Portugal 22 40 13N 8 16W
Cekhira, Tunisia 86 34 20N 10 5 E
Cela, Angola 95 11 25 S 15 7 E
Celano, Italy 27 42 6N 13 30 E
Celanova, Spain 22 42 9N 7 58W
Celaya, Mexico 126 20 31N 100 37W
Celbridge, Ireland 15 53 20N 6 33W
Celebes = Sulawesi □, Indonesia 57 2 0 S 120 0 E
Celebes Sea, Indonesia 57 3 0N 123 0 E
Celendín, Peru 136 6 52 S 78 10W
Čelić, Yugoslavia 33 44 43N 18 47 E
Celica, Ecuador 134 4 7 S 79 59W
Celina, U.S.A. 119 40 32N 84 31W
Celje, Yugoslavia 27 46 16N 15 18 E
Celle, W. Germany 30 52 37N 10 4 E
Celles, Belgium 17 50 42N 3 28 E
Celorico da Beira, Portugal 22 40 38N 7 24W
Cement, U.S.A. 121 34 56N 98 8W
Cenepa →, Peru 134 4 40 S 78 10W
Cengong, China 58 27 13N 108 44 E
Cenis, Col du Mont, France 21 45 15N 6 55 E
Ceno →, Italy 26 44 4N 10 5 E
Centallo, Italy 26 44 30N 7 35 E
Centenário do Sul, Brazil 139 22 48 S 51 36W
Center, N. Dak., U.S.A. 120 47 9N 101 17W
Center, Tex., U.S.A. 121 31 50N 94 10W
Center Point, U.S.A. 118 42 12N 91 46W
Centerfield, U.S.A. 123 39 9N 111 56W
Centerville, Calif., U.S.A. 124 36 44N 119 30W
Centerville, Iowa, U.S.A. 118 40 45N 92 57W
Centerville, Mich., U.S.A. 119 41 55N 85 32W
Centerville, Pa., U.S.A. 116 40 3N 79 59W
Centerville, S. Dak., U.S.A. 120 43 10N 96 58W
Centerville, Tenn., U.S.A. 115 35 46N 87 29W
Centerville, Tex., U.S.A. 121 31 15N 95 56W
Cento, Italy 27 44 43N 11 16 E
Central, Brazil 138 11 8 S 42 8W
Central, U.S.A. 123 32 46N 108 9W
Central □, Kenya 92 0 30 S 37 30 E
Central □, Malawi 93 13 30 S 33 30 E
Central □, U.K. 14 56 10N 4 30W
Central □, Zambia 93 14 25 S 28 50 E
Central, Cordillera, Bolivia 137 18 30 S 64 55W
Central, Cordillera, Colombia 134 5 0N 75 0W
Central, Cordillera, Costa Rica 128 10 10N 84 5W
Central, Cordillera, Dom. Rep. 129 19 15N 71 0W
Central, Cordillera, Peru 136 7 0 S 77 30W
Central African Republic ■, Africa 94 7 0N 20 0 E
Central City, Ky., U.S.A. 114 37 20N 87 7W
Central City, Nebr., U.S.A. 120 41 8N 98 0W
Central I., Kenya 92 3 30N 36 0 E
Central Makran Range, Pakistan 47 26 30N 64 15 E
Central Patricia, Canada 104 51 30N 90 9W
Central Ra., Papua N. G. 69 5 0 S 143 0 E
Central Russian Uplands, Europe 6 54 0N 36 0 E
Central Siberian Plateau, U.S.S.R. 42 65 0N 105 0 E
Central Tilba, Australia 75 36 20 S 150 4 E
Centralia, Ill., U.S.A. 118 38 32N 89 5W
Centralia, Mo., U.S.A. 118 39 12N 92 6W
Centralia, Wash., U.S.A. 124 46 46N 122 59W

Centreville

Centreville, *Ala., U.S.A.* **115** 32 55N 87 7W
Centreville, *Miss., U.S.A.* **121** 31 10N 91 3W
Centúripe, *Italy* **29** 37 37N 14 41 E
Cephalonia = Kefallinía, *Greece* **35** 38 20N 20 30 E
Ceprano, *Italy* **28** 41 33N 13 30 E
Cepu, *Indonesia* **57** 7 9 S 111 35 E
Ceram = Seram, *Indonesia* **57** 3 10 S 129 0 E
Ceram Sea = Seram Sea, *Indonesia* **57** 2 30 S 128 30 E
Cerbère, *France* **20** 42 26N 3 10 E
Cerbicales, Is., *France* **21** 41 33N 9 22 E
Cercal, *Portugal* **23** 37 48N 8 40W
Cercemaggiore, *Italy* **29** 41 27N 14 43 E
Cerdaña, *Spain* **24** 42 22N 1 35 E
Cerdedo, *Spain* **22** 42 33N 8 23W
Cère →, *France* **20** 44 55N 1 49 E
Cerea, *Italy* **27** 45 12N 11 13 E
Ceres, *Argentina* **140** 29 55 S 61 55W
Ceres, *Brazil* **139** 15 17 S 49 35W
Ceres, *Italy* **26** 45 19N 7 22 E
Ceres, *S. Africa* **96** 33 21 S 19 18 E
Ceres, *U.S.A.* **124** 37 35N 120 57W
Céret, *France* **20** 42 30N 2 42 E
Cereté, *Colombia* **134** 8 53N 75 48W
Cerf, L. de, *Canada* **106** 46 16N 75 30W
Cerfontaine, *Belgium* **17** 50 11N 4 26 E
Cerignola, *Italy* **29** 41 17N 15 53 E
Cerigo = Kíthira, *Greece* **35** 36 9N 23 0 E
Cérilly, *France* **20** 46 37N 2 50 E
Cerisiers, *France* **19** 48 8N 3 30 E
Cerizay, *France* **18** 46 50N 0 40W
Çerkeş, *Turkey* **46** 40 49N 32 52 E
Cerknica, *Yugoslavia* **27** 45 48N 14 21 E
Cerna →, *Romania* **34** 44 45N 24 0 E
Cernavodă, *Romania* **34** 44 22N 28 3 E
Cernay, *France* **19** 47 44N 7 10 E
Cernik, *Yugoslavia* **33** 45 17N 17 22 E
Cerralvo, I., *Mexico* **126** 24 20N 109 45 E
Cerreto Sannita, *Italy* **29** 41 17N 14 34 E
Cerritos, *Mexico* **126** 22 27N 100 20W
Cerro Gordo, *U.S.A.* **119** 39 53N 88 44W
Cerro Sombrero, *Chile* **142** 52 45 S 69 15W
Certaldo, *Italy* **26** 43 32N 11 2 E
Cervaro →, *Italy* **29** 41 30N 15 52 E
Cervera, *Spain* **24** 41 40N 1 16 E
Cervera de Pisuerga, *Spain* **22** 42 51N 4 30W
Cervera del Río Alhama, *Spain* **24** 42 2N 1 58W
Cérvia, *Italy* **27** 44 15N 12 20 E
Cervignano del Friuli, *Italy* **27** 45 49N 13 20 E
Cervinara, *Italy* **29** 41 2N 14 36 E
Cervione, *France* **21** 42 20N 9 29 E
Cervo, *Spain* **22** 43 40N 7 24W
César □, *Colombia* **134** 9 0N 73 30W
Cesaro, *Italy* **29** 37 50N 14 38 E
Cesena, *Italy* **27** 44 9N 12 14 E
Cesenático, *Italy* **27** 44 12N 12 22 E
Cēsis, *U.S.S.R.* **36** 57 17N 25 28 E
Česká Lípa, *Czech.* **32** 50 45N 14 30 E
České Budějovice, *Czech.* **32** 48 55N 14 25 E
Ceskomoravská Vrchovina, *Czech.* **32** 49 30N 15 40 E
Český Brod, *Czech.* **32** 50 4N 14 52 E
Český Krumlov, *Czech.* **32** 48 43N 14 21 E
Český Těšin, *Czech.* **32** 49 45N 18 39 E
Cessnock, *Australia* **76** 32 50 S 151 21 E
Cestos →, *Liberia* **90** 5 40N 9 10W
Cétin Grad, *Yugoslavia* **27** 45 9N 15 45 E
Cetina →, *Yugoslavia* **27** 43 26N 16 42 E
Cetraro, *Italy* **29** 39 30N 15 56 E
Ceuta, *Morocco* **84** 35 52N 5 18W
Ceva, *Italy* **26** 44 23N 8 3 E
Cévennes, *France* **20** 44 10N 3 50 E
Ceyhan, *Turkey* **46** 37 4N 35 47 E
Ceylon = Sri Lanka ■, *Asia* **51** 7 30N 80 50 E
Cèze →, *France* **21** 44 6N 4 43 E
Cha-am, *Thailand* **54** 12 48N 99 58 E
Chá Pungana, *Angola* **95** 13 44 S 18 39 E
Chaam, *Neths.* **17** 51 30N 4 52 E
Chabeuil, *France* **21** 44 54N 5 3 E
Chablais, *France* **21** 46 20N 6 36 E
Chablis, *France* **19** 47 47N 3 48 E
Chabounia, *Algeria* **85** 35 30N 2 38 E
Chacabuco, *Argentina* **140** 34 40 S 60 27W
Chachapoyas, *Peru* **136** 6 15 S 77 50W
Chachasp, *Peru* **136** 15 30 S 72 15W
Chachoengsao, *Thailand* **54** 13 42N 101 5 E
Chachro, *Pakistan* **48** 25 5N 70 15 E
Chaco □, *Argentina* **140** 26 30 S 61 0W
Chad ■, *Africa* **87** 15 0N 17 15 E
Chad, L. = Tchad, L., *Chad* **87** 13 30N 14 30 E
Chadan, *U.S.S.R.* **41** 51 17N 91 35 E
Chadileuvú →, *Argentina* **140** 37 46 S 66 0W
Chadiza, *Zambia* **93** 14 45 S 32 27 E
Chadron, *U.S.A.* **120** 42 50N 103 0W
Chadyr-Lunga, *U.S.S.R.* **38** 46 3N 28 51 E
Chae Hom, *Thailand* **54** 18 43N 99 35 E
Chaem →, *Thailand* **54** 18 11N 98 38 E
Chagda, *U.S.S.R.* **41** 58 45N 130 38 E
Chagny, *France* **19** 46 57N 4 45 E
Chagoda, *U.S.S.R.* **36** 59 10N 35 15 E
Chagos Arch., *Ind. Oc.* **53** 6 0 S 72 0 E
Chāh Bahār, *Iran* **47** 25 20N 60 40 E
Chāh Gay Hills, *Afghan.* **47** 29 30N 64 0 E
Chahār Mahāll va Bakhtīarī □, *Iran* **46** 32 0N 49 0 E
Chahtung, *Burma* **52** 26 41N 98 10 E
Chaillé-les-Marais, *France* **20** 46 25N 1 2W
Chainat, *Thailand* **54** 15 11N 100 8 E
Chaise-Dieu, La, *France* **20** 45 18N 3 42 E
Chaitén, *Chile* **142** 42 55 S 72 43W
Chaiya, *Thailand* **55** 9 23N 99 14 E
Chaize-le-Vicomte, La, *France* **18** 46 40N 1 18W
Chaj Doab, *Pakistan* **48** 32 15N 73 0 E
Chajari, *Argentina* **140** 30 42 S 58 0W
Chakaria, *Bangla.* **52** 21 45N 92 5 E
Chake Chake, *Tanzania* **92** 5 15 S 39 45 E
Chakhānsūr, *Afghan.* **47** 31 10N 62 0 E
Chakonipau, L., *Canada* **105** 56 18N 68 30W
Chakradharpur, *India* **49** 22 45N 85 40 E
Chakwadam, *Burma* **52** 27 29N 98 31 E
Chakwal, *Pakistan* **48** 32 56N 72 53 E
Chala, *Peru* **136** 15 48 S 74 20W
Chalais, *France* **20** 45 16N 0 3 E
Chalakudi, *India* **51** 10 18N 76 20 E
Chalchihuites, *Mexico* **126** 23 29N 103 53W
Chalcis = Khalkís, *Greece* **35** 38 27N 23 42 E
Chaleur B., *Canada* **105** 47 55N 65 30W
Chalfant, *U.S.A.* **124** 37 32N 118 21W
Chalhuanca, *Peru* **136** 14 15 S 73 15W
Chalindrey, *France* **19** 47 43N 5 26 E
Chaling, *China* **59** 26 58N 113 30 E
Chalisgaon, *India* **50** 20 30N 75 10 E
Chalk River, *Canada* **109** 46 1N 77 27W
Chalkar, *U.S.S.R.* **39** 50 40N 51 53 E
Chalkar, Ozero, *U.S.S.R.* **39** 50 50N 51 50 E
Chalky Inlet, *N.Z.* **81** 46 3 S 166 31 E
Challans, *France* **18** 46 50N 1 52W
Challapata, *Bolivia* **136** 18 53 S 66 50W
Challis, *U.S.A.* **122** 44 32N 114 25W
Chalna, *India* **49** 22 36N 89 35 E
Chalon-sur-Saône, *France* **19** 46 48N 4 50 E
Chalonnes-sur-Loire, *France* **18** 47 20N 0 45W
Châlons-sur-Marne, *France* **19** 48 58N 4 20 E
Châlus, *France* **20** 45 39N 0 58 E
Chalyaphum, *Thailand* **54** 15 48N 102 2 E
Cham, *W. Germany* **31** 49 12N 12 40 E
Cham, Cu Lao, *Vietnam* **54** 15 57N 108 30 E
Chama, *U.S.A.* **123** 36 54N 106 35W
Chaman, *Pakistan* **47** 30 58N 66 25 E
Chamartín de la Rosa, *Spain* **24** 40 28N 3 40W
Chamba, *India* **48** 32 35N 76 10 E
Chamba, *Tanzania* **93** 11 37 S 37 0 E
Chambal →, *India* **49** 26 29N 79 15 E
Chamberlain, *U.S.A.* **120** 43 50N 99 21W
Chamberlain →, *Australia* **78** 15 30 S 127 54 E
Chambers, *U.S.A.* **123** 35 13N 109 30W
Chambersburg, *U.S.A.* **114** 39 53N 77 41W
Chambéry, *France* **21** 45 34N 5 55 E
Chambly, *Canada* **117** 45 27N 73 17W
Chambon-Feugerolles, Le, *France* **21** 45 24N 4 19 E
Chambord, *Canada* **107** 48 25N 72 6W
Chambri L., *Papua N. G.* **69** 4 15 S 143 10 E
Chamela, *Mexico* **126** 19 32N 105 5W
Chamical, *Argentina* **140** 30 22 S 66 27W
Chamkar Luong, *Cambodia* **55** 11 0N 103 45 E
Chamois, *U.S.A.* **118** 38 41N 91 46W
Chamonix-Mont-Blanc, *France* **21** 45 55N 6 51 E
Chamouchouane →, *Canada* **107** 48 37N 72 20W
Champa, *India* **49** 22 2N 82 43 E
Champagne, *Canada* **110** 60 49N 136 30W
Champagne, *France* **19** 48 40N 4 20 E
Champagne, Plaine de, *France* **19** 49 0N 4 30 E
Champagnole, *France* **19** 46 45N 5 55 E
Champaign, *U.S.A.* **119** 40 8N 88 14W
Champassak, *Laos* **54** 14 53N 105 52 E
Champaubert, *France* **19** 48 50N 3 45 E
Champdeniers, *France* **20** 46 29N 0 25W
Champeix, *France* **20** 45 37N 3 8 E
Champlain, *Canada* **104** 46 27N 72 24W
Champlain, *U.S.A.* **117** 44 59N 73 27W
Champlain, L., *U.S.A.* **117** 44 30N 73 20W
Champneuf, *Canada* **106** 48 35N 77 30W
Champotón, *Mexico* **127** 19 20N 90 50W
Chamrajnagar, *India* **51** 11 52N 76 52 E
Chamusca, *Portugal* **23** 39 21N 8 29W
Chan Chan, *Peru* **136** 8 7 S 79 0W
Chana, *Thailand* **55** 6 55N 100 44 E
Chañaral, *Chile* **140** 26 23 S 70 40W
Chanasma, *India* **48** 23 44N 72 5 E
Chancay, *Peru* **136** 11 32 S 77 25W
Chandalar, *U.S.A.* **102** 67 30N 148 35W
Chandannagar, *India* **49** 22 52N 88 24 E
Chandausi, *India* **49** 28 27N 78 49 E
Chandeleur Is., *U.S.A.* **121** 29 48N 88 51W
Chandeleur Sd., *U.S.A.* **121** 29 58N 88 40W
Chandigarh, *India* **48** 30 43N 76 47 E
Chandler, *Australia* **73** 27 0 S 133 19 E
Chandler, *Canada* **105** 48 18N 64 46W
Chandler, *Ariz., U.S.A.* **123** 33 20N 111 56W
Chandler, *Okla., U.S.A.* **121** 35 43N 96 53W
Chandlers Peak, *Australia* **77** 30 15 S 151 48 E
Chandless →, *Brazil* **136** 9 8 S 69 51W
Chandmani, *Mongolia* **62** 45 22N 98 2 E
Chandpur, *Bangla.* **52** 23 8N 90 45 E
Chandpur, *India* **48** 29 8N 78 19 E
Chandrapur, *India* **50** 19 57N 79 25 E
Chang, *Pakistan* **48** 26 59N 68 30 E
Chang, Ko, *Thailand* **55** 12 0N 102 23 E
Chang Jiang →, *China* **59** 31 48N 121 10 E
Changa, *India* **49** 33 53N 77 35 E
Changanacheri, *India* **51** 9 25N 76 31 E
Changane →, *Mozam.* **97** 24 30 S 33 30 E
Changbai, *China* **61** 41 25N 128 5 E
Changbai Shan, *China* **61** 42 20N 129 0 E
Changchiak'ou = Zhangjiakou, *China* **60** 40 48N 114 55 E
Ch'angchou = Changzhou, *China* **59** 31 47N 119 58 E
Changchun, *China* **61** 43 57N 125 17 E
Changchunling, *China* **61** 45 18N 125 27 E
Changde, *China* **59** 29 4N 111 35 E
Changfeng, *China* **59** 32 28N 117 10 E
Changhai = Shanghai, *China* **59** 31 15N 121 26 E
Changhua, *China* **59** 30 12N 119 12 E
Changjiang, *China* **54** 19 20N 108 55 E
Changjin-chŏsuji, *N. Korea* **61** 40 30N 127 15 E
Changle, *China* **59** 25 59N 119 27 E
Changli, *China* **61** 39 40N 119 13 E
Changling, *China* **61** 44 20N 123 58 E
Changlun, *Malaysia* **55** 6 25N 100 26 E
Changning, *Hunan, China* **59** 26 28N 112 22 E
Changning, *Yunnan, China* **58** 24 45N 99 30 E
Changping, *China* **60** 40 14N 116 12 E
Changsha, *China* **59** 28 12N 113 0 E
Changshan, *China* **59** 28 55N 118 27 E
Changshou, *China* **58** 29 51N 107 8 E
Changshu, *China* **59** 31 38N 120 43 E
Changshun, *China* **58** 26 3N 106 25 E
Changtai, *China* **59** 24 35N 117 42 E
Changting, *China* **59** 25 50N 116 22 E
Changwu, *China* **60** 35 10N 107 45 E
Changxing, *China* **59** 31 0N 119 55 E
Changyang, *China* **59** 30 30N 111 10 E
Changyi, *China* **61** 36 40N 119 30 E
Changyuan, *China* **60** 35 15N 114 42 E
Changzhi, *China* **60** 36 10N 113 6 E
Changzhou, *China* **59** 31 47N 119 58 E
Chanhanga, *Angola* **95** 16 0 S 14 8 E
Chanlar, *U.S.S.R.* **39** 40 25N 46 10 E
Channapatna, *India* **51** 12 40N 77 15 E
Channel Is., *U.K.* **18** 49 30N 2 40W
Channel Is., *U.S.A.* **125** 33 55N 119 26W
Channel-Port aux Basques, *Canada* **105** 47 30N 59 9W
Channing, *Mich., U.S.A.* **114** 46 9N 88 1W
Channing, *Tex., U.S.A.* **121** 35 45N 102 20W
Chantada, *Spain* **22** 42 36N 7 46W
Chanthaburi, *Thailand* **54** 12 38N 102 12 E
Chantilly, *France* **19** 49 12N 2 29 E
Chantonnay, *France* **18** 46 40N 1 3W
Chantrey Inlet, *Canada* **102** 67 48N 96 20W
Chanute, *U.S.A.* **121** 37 45N 95 25W
Chanza →, *Spain* **23** 37 32N 7 30W
Chao Hu, *China* **59** 31 30N 117 30 E
Chao Phraya →, *Thailand* **54** 13 32N 100 36 E
Chao Phraya Lowlands, *Thailand* **54** 15 30N 100 0 E
Chao Xian, *China* **59** 31 38N 117 50 E
Chao'an, *China* **59** 23 42N 116 32 E
Chaocheng, *China* **60** 36 4N 115 37 E
Chaoyang, *Guangdong, China* **59** 23 17N 116 30 E
Chaoyang, *Liaoning, China* **61** 41 35N 120 22 E
Chapada dos Guimarães, *Brazil* **137** 15 26 S 55 45W
Chapais, *Canada* **106** 49 47N 74 51W
Chapala, *Mozam.* **93** 15 50 S 37 35 E
Chapala, L. de, *Mexico* **126** 20 10N 103 20W
Chaparé →, *Bolivia* **137** 15 58 S 64 42W
Chaparmukh, *India* **52** 26 12N 92 31 E
Chaparral, *Colombia* **134** 3 43N 75 28W
Chapayevo, *U.S.S.R.* **39** 50 25N 51 10 E
Chapayevsk, *U.S.S.R.* **37** 53 0N 49 40 E
Chapeau, *Canada* **106** 45 54N 77 4W
Chapecó, *Brazil* **141** 27 14 S 52 41W
Chapel Hill, *U.S.A.* **115** 35 53N 79 3W
Chapelle d'Angillon, La, *France* **19** 47 21N 2 25 E
Chapelle-Glain, La, *France* **18** 47 38N 1 11W
Chapin, *U.S.A.* **118** 39 46N 90 24W
Chapleau, *Canada* **104** 47 50N 83 24W
Chaplin, *Canada* **111** 50 28N 106 40W
Chaplino, *U.S.S.R.* **38** 48 8N 36 15 E
Chaplygin, *U.S.S.R.* **37** 53 15N 40 0 E
Châr, *Mauritania* **84** 21 32N 12 45W
Chara, *U.S.S.R.* **41** 56 54N 118 20 E
Charadai, *Argentina* **140** 27 35 S 60 0W
Charagua, *Bolivia* **137** 19 45 S 63 10W
Charalá, *Colombia* **134** 6 17N 73 10W
Charambirá, Punta, *Colombia* **134** 4 16N 77 32W
Charaña, *Bolivia* **136** 17 30 S 69 25W
Charapita, *Colombia* **134** 0 37 S 74 21W
Charata, *Argentina* **140** 27 13 S 61 14W
Charcas, *Mexico* **126** 23 10N 101 20W
Charcoal L., *Canada* **111** 58 49N 102 22W
Chard, *U.K.* **13** 50 52N 2 59W
Chardara, *U.S.S.R.* **40** 41 16N 67 59 E
Chardon, *U.S.A.* **116** 41 34N 81 17W
Charduar, *India* **52** 26 51N 92 46 E
Chardzhou, *U.S.S.R.* **40** 39 6N 63 34 E
Charente □, *France* **20** 45 50N 0 16 E
Charente →, *France* **20** 45 57N 1 5W
Charente-Maritime □, *France* **20** 45 45N 0 45W
Charentsavan, *U.S.S.R.* **39** 40 35N 44 41 E
Charette, *Canada* **107** 46 27N 72 56W
Chari →, *Chad* **87** 12 58N 14 31 E
Chārīkār, *Afghan.* **47** 35 0N 69 10 E
Charité-sur-Loire, La, *France* **19** 47 10N 3 1 E
Chariton, *U.S.A.* **118** 41 1N 93 19W
Chariton →, *U.S.A.* **118** 39 19N 92 58W
Charity, *Guyana* **135** 7 24N 58 36W
Charkhari, *India* **49** 25 24N 79 45 E
Charkhi Dadri, *India* **48** 28 37N 76 17 E
Charleroi, *Belgium* **17** 50 24N 4 27 E
Charleroi, *U.S.A.* **116** 40 8N 79 54W
Charles, C., *U.S.A.* **114** 37 10N 75 59W
Charles City, *U.S.A.* **118** 43 2N 92 41W
Charles L., *Canada* **111** 59 50N 110 33W
Charles Town, *U.S.A.* **114** 39 20N 77 50W
Charlesbourg, *Canada* **107** 46 51N 71 16W
Charleston, *Ill., U.S.A.* **114** 39 30N 88 10W
Charleston, *Ill., U.S.A.* **119** 39 30N 88 10W
Charleston, *Miss., U.S.A.* **121** 34 2N 90 3W
Charleston, *Mo., U.S.A.* **121** 36 52N 89 20W
Charleston, *S.C., U.S.A.* **115** 32 47N 79 56W
Charleston, *W. Va., U.S.A.* **114** 38 24N 81 36W
Charleston L., *Canada* **109** 44 32N 76 0W
Charleston Park, *U.S.A.* **125** 36 17N 115 37W
Charleston Pk., *U.S.A.* **125** 36 16N 115 42W
Charlestown, *S. Africa* **97** 27 26 S 29 53 E
Charlestown, *U.S.A.* **119** 38 29N 85 40W
Charlesville, *Zaïre* **95** 5 27 S 20 59 E
Charleville = Rath Luirc, *Ireland* **15** 52 21N 8 40W
Charleville, *Australia* **73** 26 24 S 146 15 E
Charleville-Mézières, *France* **19** 49 44N 4 40 E
Charlevoix, *U.S.A.* **104** 45 19N 85 14W
Charlieu, *France* **21** 46 10N 4 10 E
Charlotte, *Mich., U.S.A.* **119** 42 36N 84 48W
Charlotte, *N.C., U.S.A.* **115** 35 16N 80 46W
Charlotte Amalie, *Virgin Is.* **129** 18 22N 64 56W
Charlotte Harbor, *U.S.A.* **115** 26 58N 82 4W
Charlottenberg, *Sweden* **10** 59 54N 12 17 E
Charlottesville, *U.S.A.* **114** 38 1N 78 30W
Charlottetown, *Canada* **105** 46 14N 63 8W
Charlton, *Australia* **74** 36 16 S 143 24 E
Charlton, *U.S.A.* **118** 40 59N 93 20W
Charlton I., *Canada* **104** 52 0N 79 20W
Charmes, *France* **19** 48 22N 6 17 E
Charny, *Canada* **107** 46 43N 71 15W
Charolles, *France* **21** 46 27N 4 16 E
Chârost, *France* **19** 46 58N 2 7 E
Charouine, *Algeria* **85** 29 0N 0 15W
Charre, *Mozam.* **93** 17 13 S 35 10 E
Charroux, *France* **20** 46 9N 0 25 E
Charsadda, *Pakistan* **48** 34 7N 71 45 E
Charters Towers, *Australia* **72** 20 5 S 146 13 E
Chartre-sur-le-Loir, La, *France* **18** 47 44N 0 34 E
Chartres, *France* **18** 48 29N 1 30 E
Chascomús, *Argentina* **140** 35 30 S 58 0W
Chasefu, *Zambia* **93** 11 55 S 33 8 E
Chaslands Mistake, *N.Z.* **81** 46 38 S 169 22 E
Chasovnya-Uchurskaya, *U.S.S.R.* **41** 57 15N 132 50 E
Chasseneuil-sur-Bonnieure, *France* **20** 45 52N 0 29 E
Châtaigneraie, La, *France* **20** 46 39N 0 44W
Chatal Balkan = Udvoy Balkan, *Bulgaria* **34** 42 50N 26 50 E
Château-Arnoux, *France* **21** 44 6N 6 0 E
Château-Chinon, *France* **19** 47 4N 3 56 E
Château-d'Oléron, Le, *France* **20** 45 54N 1 12W
Château-du-Loir, *France* **18** 47 40N 0 25 E
Château-Gontier, *France* **18** 47 50N 0 48W
Château-la-Vallière, *France* **18** 47 30N 0 20 E
Château-Landon, *France* **19** 48 8N 2 40 E

Chikhli

Château-Porcien, France 19 49 31N 4 13 E
Château-Renault, France 18 47 36N 0 56 E
Château-Salins, France 19 48 50N 6 30 E
Château-Thierry, France 19 49 3N 3 20 E
Châteaubourg, France 18 48 7N 1 25W
Châteaubriant, France 18 47 43N 1 23W
Châteaudun, France 18 48 3N 1 20 E
Châteaugiron, France 18 48 3N 1 30W
Châteaulin, France 18 48 11N 4 8W
Châteaumeillant, France 20 46 35N 2 12 E
Châteauneuf-du-Faou, France 18 48 11N 3 50W
Châteauneuf-en-Thymerais, France 18 48 35N 1 13 E
Châteauneuf-sur-Charente, France 20 45 36N 0 3W
Châteauneuf-sur-Cher, France 19 46 52N 2 18 E
Châteauneuf-sur-Loire, France 19 47 52N 2 13 E
Châteaurenard, Bouches-du-Rhône, France 21 43 53N 4 51 E
Châteaurenard, Loiret, France 19 47 56N 2 55 E
Châteauroux, France 19 46 50N 1 40 E
Châteauvert, L., Canada 107 47 39N 73 56W
Châtelaillon-Plage, France 20 46 5N 1 5W
Châtelaudren, France 18 48 33N 2 59W
Chatelet, Belgium 17 50 24N 4 32 E
Châtelet, Le, France 20 46 38N 2 16 E
Châtelet-en-Brie, Le, France 19 48 31N 2 48 E
Châtelguyon, France 20 45 55N 3 4 E
Châtellerault, France 18 46 50N 0 30 E
Châtelus-Malvaleix, France 20 46 18N 2 1 E
Chatfield, U.S.A. 120 43 15N 91 58W
Chatham, N.B., Canada 105 47 2N 65 28W
Chatham, Ont., Canada 108 42 24N 82 11W
Chatham, U.K. 13 51 22N 0 32 E
Chatham, Ill., U.S.A. 118 39 40N 89 42W
Chatham, La., U.S.A. 121 32 22N 92 26W
Chatham, N.Y., U.S.A. 117 42 21N 73 32W
Chatham, I., Chile 142 50 40 S 74 25W
Chatham Is., Pac. Oc. 66 44 0 S 176 40W
Chatham Str., U.S.A. 110 57 0N 134 40W
Chatillon, Italy 26 45 45N 7 40 E
Châtillon-Coligny, France 19 47 50N 2 51 E
Châtillon-en-Bazois, France 19 47 3N 3 39 E
Châtillon-en-Diois, France 21 44 41N 5 29 E
Châtillon-sur-Indre, France 18 46 59N 1 10 E
Châtillon-sur-Loire, France 19 47 35N 2 44 E
Châtillon-sur-Marne, France 19 49 6N 3 44 E
Châtillon-sur-Seine, France 19 47 50N 4 33 E
Chatmohar, Bangla. 49 24 15N 89 15 E
Chatra, India 49 24 12N 84 56 E
Chatrapur, India 50 19 22N 85 2 E
Châtre, La, France 20 46 35N 2 0 E
Chats, L. des, Canada 106 45 30N 76 20W
Chatsworth, Canada 108 44 27N 80 54W
Chatsworth, U.S.A. 119 40 45N 88 18W
Chatsworth, Zambia 93 19 38 S 31 13 E
Chatta-Hantō, Japan 65 34 45N 136 55 E
Chattahoochee →, U.S.A. 115 30 43N 84 51W
Chattanooga, U.S.A. 115 35 2N 85 17W
Chaturat, Thailand 54 15 40N 101 51 E
Chau Doc, Vietnam 55 10 42N 105 7 E
Chaudanne, Barr. de, France 21 43 51N 6 32 E
Chaudes-Aigues, France 20 44 51N 3 1 E
Chaudière →, Canada 107 46 45N 71 17W
Chauffailles, France 21 46 13N 4 20 E
Chauk, Burma 52 20 53N 94 49 E
Chaukan Pass, Burma 52 27 8N 97 10 E
Chaulnes, France 19 49 48N 2 47 E
Chaumont, France 19 48 7N 5 8 E
Chaumont, U.S.A. 117 44 4N 76 9W
Chaumont-en-Vexin, France 19 49 16N 1 53 E
Chaumont-sur-Loire, France 18 47 29N 1 11 E
Chaunay, France 20 46 13N 0 9 E
Chauny, France 19 49 37N 3 12 E
Chausey, Is., France 18 48 52N 1 49W
Chaussin, France 19 46 59N 5 22 E
Chautauqua L., U.S.A. 116 42 7N 79 30W
Chauvigny, France 18 46 34N 0 39 E
Chauvin, Canada 111 52 45N 110 10W
Chaux-de-Fonds, La, Switz. 31 47 7N 6 50 E
Chavantina, Brazil 137 14 40 S 52 21W
Chaves, Brazil 138 0 15 S 49 55W
Chaves, Portugal 22 41 45N 7 32W
Chavuma, Zambia 95 13 4 S 22 40 E
Chawang, Thailand 55 8 25N 99 30 E
Chazelles-sur-Lyon, France 21 45 39N 4 22 E
Chazuta, Peru 136 6 30 S 76 0W
Chazy, U.S.A. 117 44 52N 73 28W
Cheb, Czech. 32 50 9N 12 28 E
Chebanse, U.S.A. 119 41 0N 87 54W
Cheboksary, U.S.S.R. 37 56 8N 47 12 E
Cheboygan, U.S.A. 104 45 38N 84 29W
Chebsara, U.S.S.R. 37 59 10N 38 59 E
Chech, Erg, Africa 84 25 0N 2 15W
Chechaouen, Morocco 84 35 9N 5 15W
Chechen, Os., U.S.S.R. 39 43 59N 47 40 E
Checheno-Ingush A.S.S.R. □, U.S.S.R. 39 43 30N 45 29 E
Chęciny, Poland 32 50 46N 20 28 E
Checleset B., Canada 110 50 5N 127 35W
Checotah, U.S.A. 121 35 31N 95 30W
Chedabucto B., Canada 105 45 25N 61 8W
Cheduba I., Burma 52 18 45N 93 40 E
Cheepie, Australia 73 26 33 S 145 1 E
Chef, R. du →, Canada 107 49 21N 73 25W
Chef-Boutonne, France 20 46 7N 0 4W
Chegdomyn, U.S.S.R. 41 51 7N 133 1 E
Chegga, Mauritania 84 25 27N 5 40W
Chegutu, Zambia 93 18 10 S 30 14 E
Chehalis, U.S.A. 124 46 44N 122 59W
Cheiron, Mt., France 21 43 49N 6 58 E
Cheju Do, S. Korea 61 33 29N 126 34 E
Chekalin, U.S.S.R. 37 54 10N 36 10 E
Chekiang = Zhejiang □, China 59 29 0N 120 0 E
Chel = Kuru, Bahr el →, Sudan 89 8 10N 26 50 E
Chela, Sa. da, Angola 95 16 20 S 13 20 E
Chelan, U.S.A. 122 47 49N 120 0W
Chelan, L., U.S.A. 122 48 5N 120 30W
Cheleken, U.S.S.R. 40 39 26N 53 7 E
Chelforó, Argentina 142 39 0 S 66 33W
Chéliff, O. →, Algeria 85 36 0N 0 8 E
Chelkar, U.S.S.R. 40 47 48N 59 39 E
Chelkar Tengiz, Solonchak, U.S.S.R. 40 48 0N 62 30 E
Chellala Dahrania, Algeria 85 33 2N 0 1 E
Chelles, France 19 48 52N 2 33 E
Chełm, Poland 32 51 8N 23 30 E
Chełmek, Poland 32 50 6N 19 16 E
Chełmno, Poland 32 53 20N 18 30 E
Chelmsford, U.K. 13 51 44N 0 29 E
Chelmsford Dam, S. Africa 97 27 55 S 29 59 E
Chelmża, Poland 32 53 10N 18 39 E
Chelsea, Australia 74 38 5 S 145 8 E
Chelsea, Mich., U.S.A. 119 42 19N 84 1W
Chelsea, Okla., U.S.A. 121 36 35N 95 35W
Chelsea, Vt., U.S.A. 117 43 59N 72 27W
Cheltenham, U.K. 13 51 55N 2 5W
Chelva, Spain 24 39 45N 1 0W
Chelyabinsk, U.S.S.R. 40 55 10N 61 24 E
Chelyuskin, C., U.S.S.R. 42 77 30N 103 0 E
Chemainus, Canada 110 48 55N 123 42W
Chembar = Belinskiy, U.S.S.R. 37 53 0N 43 25 E
Chemillé, France 18 47 14N 0 45W
Chemnitz = Karl-Marx-Stadt, E. Germany 30 50 50N 12 55 E
Chemult, U.S.A. 122 43 14N 121 47W
Chen, Gora, U.S.S.R. 41 65 16N 141 50 E
Chen Xian, China 59 25 47N 113 1 E
Chenab →, Pakistan 48 30 23N 71 2 E
Chenachane, O. →, Algeria 84 25 20N 3 20W
Chenango Forks, U.S.A. 117 42 15N 75 51W
Chencha, Ethiopia 89 6 15N 37 32 E
Chenchiang = Zhenjiang, China 59 32 11N 119 26 E
Chênée, Belgium 17 50 37N 5 37 E
Chénéville, Canada 106 45 53N 75 3W
Cheney, U.S.A. 122 47 29N 117 34W
Cheng Xian, China 60 33 43N 105 42 E
Chengalpattu, India 51 12 42N 79 58 E
Chengbu, China 59 26 18N 110 16 E
Chengcheng, China 60 35 8N 109 56 E
Chengchou = Zhengzhou, China 60 34 45N 113 34 E
Chengde, China 61 40 59N 117 58 E
Chengdong Hu, China 59 32 15N 116 20 E
Chengdu, China 58 30 38N 104 2 E
Chengele, India 52 28 47N 96 16 E
Chenggong, China 58 24 52N 102 56 E
Chenggu, China 60 33 10N 107 21 E
Chengjiang, China 58 24 39N 103 0 E
Chengkou, China 58 31 54N 108 31 E
Ch'engtu = Chengdu, China 58 30 38N 104 2 E
Chengwu, China 60 34 58N 115 50 E
Chengxi Hu, China 59 32 15N 116 10 E
Chengyang, China 61 36 18N 120 21 E
Chenjiagang, China 61 34 23N 119 47 E
Chenkán, Mexico 127 19 8N 90 58W
Chenoa, U.S.A. 119 40 45N 88 42W
Chenxi, China 59 28 2N 110 12 E
Cheo Reo, Vietnam 54 13 25N 108 28 E
Cheom Ksan, Cambodia 54 14 13N 104 56 E
Chepelare, Bulgaria 35 41 44N 24 40 E
Chepén, Peru 136 7 15 S 79 23W
Chépénéhé, Vanuatu 68 20 47 S 167 9 E
Chepes, Argentina 140 31 20 S 66 35W
Chepo, Panama 128 9 10N 79 6W
Cheptsa →, U.S.S.R. 37 58 36N 50 4 E
Cheptulil, Mt., Kenya 92 1 25N 35 35 E
Chequamegon B., U.S.A. 120 46 40N 90 30W
Cher □, France 19 47 10N 2 30 E
Cher →, France 18 47 21N 0 29 E
Cheran, India 52 25 45N 90 44 E
Cherasco, Italy 26 44 39N 7 50 E
Cheratte, Belgium 17 50 40N 5 41 E
Cheraw, U.S.A. 115 34 42N 79 54W
Cherbourg, France 18 49 39N 1 40W
Cherchell, Algeria 85 36 35N 2 12 E
Cherdakly, U.S.S.R. 37 54 25N 48 50 E
Cherdyn, U.S.S.R. 40 60 24N 56 29 E
Cheremkhovo, U.S.S.R. 41 53 8N 103 1 E
Cherepanovo, U.S.S.R. 40 54 15N 83 30 E
Cherepovets, U.S.S.R. 37 59 5N 37 55 E
Chergui, Chott ech, Algeria 85 34 21N 0 25 E
Cherikov, U.S.S.R. 36 53 32N 31 20 E
Cherkassy, U.S.S.R. 38 49 27N 32 4 E
Cherkessk, U.S.S.R. 39 44 15N 42 5 E
Cherlak, U.S.S.R. 40 54 15N 74 55 E
Chernaya Kholunitsa, U.S.S.R. 37 58 51N 51 52 E
Cherni, Bulgaria 34 42 35N 23 18 E
Chernigov, U.S.S.R. 36 51 28N 31 20 E
Chernobyl, U.S.S.R. 36 51 13N 30 15 E
Chernogorsk, U.S.S.R. 41 53 49N 91 18 E
Chernomorskoye, U.S.S.R. 38 45 31N 32 40 E
Chernovskoye, U.S.S.R. 37 58 48N 47 20 E
Chernovtsy, U.S.S.R. 38 48 15N 25 52 E
Chernoye, U.S.S.R. 41 70 30N 89 10 E
Chernyakhovsk, U.S.S.R. 36 54 36N 21 48 E
Chernyshkovskiy, U.S.S.R. 39 48 30N 42 13 E
Chernyshovskiy, U.S.S.R. 41 63 0N 112 30 E
Cherokee, Iowa, U.S.A. 120 42 40N 95 30W
Cherokee, Okla., U.S.A. 121 36 45N 98 25W
Cherokees, L. O'The, U.S.A. 121 36 50N 95 12W
Cherquenco, Chile 142 38 35 S 72 0W
Cherry Creek, U.S.A. 122 39 50N 114 58W
Cherry Gully, Australia 77 28 25 S 152 1 E
Cherry Valley, U.S.A. 125 33 59N 116 57W
Cherrypool, Australia 74 37 7 S 142 13 E
Cherryvale, U.S.A. 121 37 20N 95 33W
Cherskiy, U.S.S.R. 41 68 45N 161 18 E
Cherskogo Khrebet, U.S.S.R. 41 65 0N 143 0 E
Chertkovo, U.S.S.R. 39 49 25N 40 19 E
Cherven, U.S.S.R. 36 53 45N 28 28 E
Cherven-Bryag, Bulgaria 34 43 17N 24 7 E
Chervonograd, U.S.S.R. 36 50 25N 24 10 E
Cherwell →, U.K. 13 51 46N 1 18W
Chesapeake, U.S.A. 114 36 43N 76 15W
Chesapeake Bay, U.S.A. 114 38 0N 76 12W
Cheshire □, U.K. 12 53 14N 2 30W
Cheshskaya Guba, U.S.S.R. 40 67 20N 47 0 E
Cheslatta L., Canada 110 53 49N 125 20W
Chesley, Canada 108 44 17N 81 5W
Chesne, Le, France 19 49 30N 4 45 E
Cheste, Spain 25 39 30N 0 41W
Chester, U.K. 12 53 12N 2 53W
Chester, Calif., U.S.A. 122 40 22N 121 14W
Chester, Ill., U.S.A. 118 37 58N 89 50W
Chester, Mont., U.S.A. 122 48 31N 111 0W
Chester, Pa., U.S.A. 114 39 54N 75 20W
Chester, S.C., U.S.A. 115 34 44N 81 13W
Chesterfield, U.K. 12 53 14N 1 26W
Chesterfield, Is., N. Cal. 66 19 52 S 158 15 E
Chesterfield Inlet, Canada 102 63 30N 90 45W
Chesterton Range, Australia 73 25 30 S 147 27 E
Chesterville, Canada 106 45 6N 75 14W
Chesuncook L., U.S.A. 105 46 0N 69 10W
Chetaibi, Algeria 85 37 1N 7 20 E
Chéticamp, Canada 105 46 37N 60 59W
Chetumal, Mexico 127 18 30N 88 20W
Chetumal, B. de, Mexico 127 18 40N 88 10W
Chetwynd, Australia 74 37 17 S 141 23 E
Chetwynd, Canada 110 55 45N 121 36W
Chevanceaux, France 20 45 18N 0 14W
Cheviot, U.S.A. 119 39 10N 84 37W
Cheviot, The, U.K. 12 55 29N 2 8W
Cheviot Hills, U.K. 12 55 20N 2 30W
Cheviot Ra., Australia 72 25 20 S 143 45 E
Chew Bahir, Ethiopia 89 4 40N 36 50 E
Chewelah, U.S.A. 122 48 17N 117 43W
Cheyenne, Okla., U.S.A. 121 35 35N 99 40W
Cheyenne, Wyo., U.S.A. 120 41 9N 104 49W
Cheyenne →, U.S.A. 120 44 40N 101 15W
Cheyenne Wells, U.S.A. 120 38 51N 102 10W
Cheylard, Le, France 21 44 55N 4 25 E
Cheyne B., Australia 79 34 35 S 118 50 E
Chhabra, India 48 24 40N 76 54 E
Chhapra, India 49 25 48N 84 44 E
Chhata, India 48 27 42N 77 30 E
Chhatak, Bangla. 52 25 5N 91 37 E
Chhatarpur, India 49 24 55N 79 35 E
Chhep, Cambodia 54 13 45N 105 24 E
Chhindwara, India 49 22 2N 78 59 E
Chhlong, Cambodia 55 12 15N 105 58 E
Chhuk, Cambodia 55 10 46N 104 28 E
Chi →, Thailand 54 15 11N 104 43 E
Chiamis, Indonesia 57 7 20 S 108 21 E
Chiamussu = Jiamusi, China 62 46 40N 130 26 E
Chiang Dao, Thailand 54 19 22N 98 58 E
Chiang Kham, Thailand 54 19 32N 100 18 E
Chiang Khan, Thailand 54 17 52N 101 36 E
Chiang Khong, Thailand 54 20 17N 100 24 E
Chiang Mai, Thailand 54 18 47N 98 59 E
Chiang Saen, Thailand 54 20 16N 100 5 E
Chiange, Angola 95 15 35 S 13 40 E
Chiapa →, Mexico 127 16 42N 93 0W
Chiapa de Corzo, Mexico 127 16 42N 93 0W
Chiapas □, Mexico 127 17 0N 92 45W
Chiaramonte Gulfi, Italy 29 37 1N 14 41 E
Chiaravalle, Italy 27 43 38N 13 17 E
Chiaravalle Centrale, Italy 29 38 41N 16 25 E
Chiari, Italy 26 45 31N 9 55 E
Chiatura, U.S.S.R. 39 42 15N 43 17 E
Chiautla, Mexico 127 18 18N 98 34W
Chiávari, Italy 26 44 20N 9 20 E
Chiavenna, Italy 26 46 18N 9 23 E
Chiba, Japan 65 35 30N 140 7 E
Chiba □, Japan 65 35 30N 140 20 E
Chibabava, Mozam. 97 20 17 S 33 35 E
Chibatu, Indonesia 57 7 6 S 107 59 E
Chibemba, Cunene, Angola 95 15 48 S 14 8 E
Chibemba, Huila, Angola 95 16 20 S 15 20 E
Chibia, Angola 95 15 10 S 13 42 E
Chibougamau, Canada 107 49 56N 74 24W
Chibougamau →, Canada 106 49 42N 75 57W
Chibougamau, Parc Prov. de, Canada 107 49 15N 73 45W
Chibougamau L., Canada 107 49 50N 74 20W
Chibuk, Nigeria 91 10 52N 12 50 E
Chic-Chocs, Mts., Canada 105 48 55N 66 0W
Chicacole = Srikakulam, India 50 18 14N 83 58 E
Chicago, U.S.A. 119 41 53N 87 40W
Chicago Heights, U.S.A. 119 41 29N 87 37W
Chichagof I., U.S.A. 110 58 0N 136 0W
Chichaoua, Morocco 84 31 32N 8 44W
Chicheng, China 60 40 55N 115 55 E
Chichester, U.K. 13 50 50N 0 47W
Chichibu, Japan 65 36 5N 139 10 E
Ch'ich'ihaerh = Qiqihar, China 62 47 26N 124 0 E
Chickasha, U.S.A. 121 35 0N 98 0W
Chiclana de la Frontera, Spain 23 36 26N 6 9W
Chiclayo, Peru 136 6 42 S 79 50W
Chico, U.S.A. 124 39 45N 121 54W
Chico →, Chubut, Argentina 142 44 0 S 67 0W
Chico →, Santa Cruz, Argentina 142 50 0 S 68 30W
Chicobi, L., Canada 106 48 53N 78 30W
Chicomo, Mozam. 97 24 31 S 34 6 E
Chicontepec, Mexico 127 20 58N 98 10W
Chicopee, U.S.A. 117 42 6N 72 37W
Chicoutimi, Canada 105 48 28N 71 5W
Chicoutimi, Parc Prov. de, Canada 107 48 30N 70 20W
Chicualacuala, Mozam. 97 22 6 S 31 42 E
Chidambaram, India 51 11 20N 79 45 E
Chidenguele, Mozam. 97 24 55 S 34 11 E
Chidley, C., Canada 103 60 23N 64 26W
Chiede, Angola 95 17 15 S 16 22 E
Chiefs Pt., Canada 108 44 41N 81 18W
Chiem Hoa, Vietnam 54 22 12N 105 17 E
Chiemsee, W. Germany 31 47 53N 12 27 E
Chiengi, Zambia 93 8 45 S 29 10 E
Chiengmai = Chiang Mai, Thailand 54 18 47N 98 59 E
Chiengo, Angola 95 13 20 S 21 55 E
Chienti →, Italy 27 43 18N 13 45 E
Chieri, Italy 26 45 0N 7 50 E
Chiers →, France 19 49 39N 5 0 E
Chiese →, Italy 26 45 8N 10 25 E
Chieti, Italy 27 42 22N 14 10 E
Chièvres, Belgium 17 50 35N 3 48 E
Chifeng, China 61 42 18N 118 58 E
Chigasaki, Japan 65 35 19N 139 24 E
Chigirin, U.S.S.R. 38 49 4N 32 38 E
Chignecto B., Canada 105 45 30N 64 40W
Chigorodó, Colombia 134 7 41N 76 42W
Chigoubiche, L., Canada 107 49 7N 73 30W
Chiguana, Bolivia 140 21 0 S 67 58W
Chihli, G. of = Bo Hai, China 61 39 0N 120 0 E
Chihuahua, Mexico 126 28 40N 106 3W
Chihuahua □, Mexico 126 28 40N 106 3W
Chiili, U.S.S.R. 40 44 20N 66 15 E
Chik Bollapur, India 51 13 25N 77 45 E
Chikhli, India 50 20 20N 76 18 E

Chikmagalur

Chikmagalur, India 51 13 15N 75 45 E
Chikodi, India 51 16 26N 74 38 E
Chikugo, Japan 64 33 14N 130 28 E
Chikuma-Gawa →, Japan 65 36 59N 138 35 E
Chikwawa, Malawi 93 16 2 S 34 50 E
Chilac, Mexico 127 18 20N 97 24W
Chilako →, Canada 110 53 53N 122 57W
Chilam Chavki, Pakistan 49 35 5N 75 5 E
Chilanga, Zambia 93 15 33 S 28 16 E
Chilapa, Mexico 127 17 40N 99 11W
Chilas, Pakistan 49 35 25N 74 5 E
Chilcotin →, Canada 110 51 44N 122 23W
Childers, Australia 73 25 15 S 152 17 E
Childress, U.S.A. 121 34 30N 100 15W
Chile ■, S. Amer. 142 35 0 S 72 0W
Chile Chico, Chile 142 46 33 S 71 44W
Chile Rise, Pac. Oc. 67 38 0 S 92 0W
Chilecito, Argentina 140 29 10 S 67 30W
Chilete, Peru 136 7 10 S 78 50W
Chilhowee, U.S.A. 118 38 36N 93 51W
Chililabombwe, Zambia 93 12 18 S 27 43 E
Chilin = Jilin, China 61 43 44N 126 30 E
Chilka L., India 50 19 40N 85 25 E
Chilko →, Canada 110 52 0N 123 40W
Chilko, L., Canada 110 51 20N 124 10W
Chillagoe, Australia 72 17 7 S 144 33 E
Chillán, Chile 140 36 40 S 72 10W
Chillicothe, Ill., U.S.A. 118 40 55N 89 32W
Chillicothe, Mo., U.S.A. 118 39 45N 93 30W
Chillicothe, Ohio, U.S.A. 114 39 20N 82 58W
Chillingham, Australia 77 28 20 S 153 17 E
Chillingollah, Australia 74 35 16 S 143 3 E
Chilliwack, Canada 110 49 10N 121 54W
Chilo, India 48 27 25N 73 32 E
Chiloane, I., Mozam. 97 20 40 S 34 55 E
Chiloé □, Chile 142 43 0 S 73 0W
Chiloé, I. de, Chile 142 42 30 S 73 50W
Chilonda, Angola 95 11 19 S 16 12 E
Chilpancingo, Mexico 127 17 30N 99 30W
Chiltern, Australia 75 36 10 S 146 36 E
Chiltern Hills, U.K. 13 51 44N 0 42W
Chilton, U.S.A. 114 44 1N 88 12W
Chiluage, Angola 95 9 30 S 21 50 E
Chilubula, Zambia 93 10 14 S 30 51 E
Chilumba, Malawi 93 10 28 S 34 12 E
Chilwa, L., Malawi 93 15 15 S 35 40 E
Chimaltitán, Mexico 126 21 46N 103 50W
Chimán, Panama 128 8 45N 78 40W
Chimay, Belgium 17 50 3N 4 20 E
Chimbay, U.S.S.R. 40 42 57N 59 47 E
Chimborazo, Ecuador 134 1 29 S 78 55W
Chimborazo □, Ecuador 134 1 0 S 78 40W
Chimbote, Peru 136 9 0 S 78 35W
Chimkent, U.S.S.R. 40 42 18N 69 36 E
Chimoio, Mozam. 93 19 4 S 33 30 E
Chimpembe, Zambia 93 9 31 S 29 33 E
Chin □, Burma 52 22 0N 93 0 E
Chin Hills, Burma 52 22 30N 93 30 E
Chin Ling Shan = Qinling Shandi, China 60 33 50N 108 10 E
China, Mexico 127 25 40N 99 20W
China ■, Asia 62 30 0N 110 0 E
China Lake, U.S.A. 125 35 44N 117 37W
Chinacota, Colombia 134 7 37N 72 36W
Chinan = Jinan, China 60 36 38N 117 1 E
Chinandega, Nic. 128 12 35N 87 12W
Chinati Pk., U.S.A. 121 30 0N 104 25W
Chincha Alta, Peru 136 13 25 S 76 7W
Chinchilla, Australia 73 26 45 S 150 38 E
Chinchilla de Monte Aragón, Spain 25 38 53N 1 40W
Chinchón, Spain 24 40 9N 3 26W
Chinchorro, Banco, Mexico 127 18 35N 87 20W
Chinchou = Jinzhou, China 61 41 5N 121 3 E
Chinchoua, Gabon 94 0 1N 9 48 E
Chincoteague, U.S.A. 114 37 58N 75 21W
Chinde, Mozam. 93 18 35 S 36 30 E
Chindwin →, Burma 52 21 26N 95 15 E
Chineni, India 49 33 2N 75 15 E
Chinga, Mozam. 93 15 13 S 38 35 E
Chingola, Zambia 93 12 31 S 27 53 E
Chingole, Malawi 93 13 4 S 34 17 E
Chingoroi, Angola 95 13 37 S 14 1 E
Ch'ingtao = Qingdao, China 61 36 5N 120 20 E
Chinguar, Angola 95 12 25 S 16 45 E
Chinguetti, Mauritania 84 20 25N 12 24W
Chingune, Mozam. 97 20 33 S 35 0 E
Chinhae, S. Korea 61 35 9N 128 47 E
Chinhanguanine, Mozam. 97 25 21 S 32 30 E
Chinhoyi, Zimbabwe 93 17 20 S 30 8 E
Chiniot, Pakistan 48 31 45N 73 0 E
Chínipas, Mexico 126 27 22N 108 32W
Chinju, S. Korea 61 35 12N 128 2 E
Chinkapook, Australia 74 35 11 S 142 57 E
Chinle, U.S.A. 123 36 14N 109 38W
Chinnamanur, India 51 9 50N 77 24 E
Chinnampo, N. Korea 61 38 52N 125 10 E
Chinnur, India 50 18 57N 79 49 E
Chino, Japan 65 35 59N 138 9 E
Chino, U.S.A. 125 34 1N 117 41W
Chino Valley, U.S.A. 123 34 54N 112 28W
Chinon, France 18 47 10N 0 15 E
Chinook, Canada 111 51 28N 110 59W
Chinook, U.S.A. 122 48 35N 109 19W
Chinsali, Zambia 93 10 30 S 32 2 E
Chintamani, India 51 13 26N 78 3 E
Chióggia, Italy 27 45 13N 12 15 E
Chíos = Khíos, Greece 35 38 27N 26 9 E
Chipata, Zambia 93 13 38 S 32 28 E
Chipatujah, Indonesia 57 7 45 S 108 0 E
Chipewyan L., Canada 111 58 0N 98 27W
Chipinge, Zambia 93 20 13 S 32 28 E
Chipiona, Spain 23 36 44N 6 26W
Chipley, U.S.A. 115 30 45N 85 32W
Chiplun, India 50 17 31N 73 34 E
Chipman, Canada 105 46 6N 65 53W
Chipoka, Malawi 93 13 57 S 34 28 E
Chippenham, U.K. 13 51 27N 2 7W
Chippewa →, U.S.A. 120 44 25N 92 10W
Chippewa Falls, U.S.A. 120 44 55N 91 22W
Chiquián, Peru 136 10 10 S 77 0W
Chiquimula, Guatemala 128 14 51N 89 37W
Chiquinquira, Colombia 134 5 37N 73 50W
Chiquitos, Llanos de, Bolivia 137 18 0 S 61 30W
Chir →, U.S.S.R. 39 48 30N 43 0 E
Chirala, India 51 15 50N 80 26 E
Chiramba, Mozam. 93 16 55 S 34 39 E
Chiran, Japan 64 31 22N 130 27 E
Chirawa, India 48 28 14N 75 42 E
Chirayinkil, India 51 8 41N 76 49 E
Chirchik, U.S.S.R. 40 41 29N 69 35 E
Chirfa, Niger 87 20 55N 12 22 E
Chirgua →, Venezuela 134 8 54N 67 58W
Chiricahua Pk., U.S.A. 123 31 53N 109 14W
Chirikof I., U.S.A. 102 55 50N 155 40W
Chiriquí, G. de, Panama 128 8 0N 82 10W
Chiriquí, L. de, Panama 128 9 10N 82 0W
Chirivira Falls, Zambia 93 21 10 S 32 12 E
Chirpan, Bulgaria 34 42 10N 25 19 E
Chirripó Grande, Cerro, Costa Rica 128 9 29N 83 29W
Chisamba, Zambia 93 14 55 S 28 20 E
Chisholm, Canada 110 54 55N 114 10W
Chishtian Mandi, Pakistan 48 29 50N 72 55 E
Chishui, China 58 28 30N 105 42 E
Chishui He →, China 58 28 49N 105 50 E
Chisimaio, Somali Rep. 98 0 22 S 42 32 E
Chisimba Falls, Zambia 93 10 12 S 30 56 E
Chisone →, Italy 26 44 49N 7 25 E
Chisos Mts., U.S.A. 121 29 20N 103 15W
Chistopol, U.S.S.R. 37 55 25N 50 38 E
Chita, Colombia 134 6 11N 72 28W
Chita, U.S.S.R. 41 52 0N 113 35 E
Chitado, Angola 95 17 10 S 14 8 E
Chitapur, India 50 17 10N 77 5 E
Chitembo, Angola 95 13 30 S 16 50 E
Chitipa, Malawi 93 9 41 S 33 19 E
Chitrakot, India 50 19 10N 81 40 E
Chitral, Pakistan 47 35 50N 71 56 E
Chitravati →, India 51 14 45N 78 15 E
Chitré, Panama 128 7 59N 80 27W
Chittagong, Bangla. 52 22 19N 91 48 E
Chittagong □, Bangla. 52 24 5N 91 0 E
Chittaurgarh, India 48 24 52N 74 38 E
Chittoor, India 51 13 15N 79 5 E
Chittur, India 51 10 40N 76 45 E
Chiumba, Angola 95 12 29 S 16 8 E
Chiume, Angola 95 15 3 S 21 14 E
Chiusa, Italy 27 46 38N 11 34 E
Chiusi, Italy 27 43 1N 11 58 E
Chiva, Spain 25 39 27N 0 41W
Chivacoa, Venezuela 134 10 10N 68 54W
Chivasso, Italy 26 45 10N 7 52 E
Chivay, Peru 136 15 40 S 71 35W
Chivhu, Zambia 93 19 2 S 30 52 E
Chivilcoy, Argentina 140 34 55 S 60 0W
Chiwanda, Tanzania 93 11 23 S 34 55 E
Chixi, China 59 22 0N 112 58 E
Chizela, Zambia 93 13 10 S 25 0 E
Chkalov = Orenburg, U.S.S.R. 40 51 45N 55 6 E
Chkolovsk, U.S.S.R. 37 56 50N 43 10 E
Chloride, U.S.A. 125 35 25N 114 12W
Cho Bo, Vietnam 54 20 46N 105 10 E
Cho Phuoc Hai, Vietnam 55 10 26N 107 18 E
Choba, Kenya 92 2 30N 38 5 E
Chobe National Park, Botswana 96 18 0 S 25 0 E
Chociwel, Poland 32 53 29N 15 21 E
Chocó □, Colombia 134 6 0N 77 0W
Chocontá, Colombia 134 5 9N 73 41W
Chodavaram, India 50 17 50N 82 57 E
Chodecz, Poland 32 52 24N 19 2 E
Chodziez, Poland 32 52 58N 16 58 E
Choele Choel, Argentina 142 39 11 S 65 40W
Chōfu, Japan 65 35 39N 139 33 E
Choiseul, Solomon Is. 68 7 0 S 156 40 E
Choisy-le-Roi, France 19 48 45N 2 24 E
Choix, Mexico 126 26 40N 108 23W
Chojnice, Poland 32 53 42N 17 32 E
Chojnów, Poland 32 51 18N 15 58 E
Choke Mts., Ethiopia 89 11 18N 37 15 E
Chokurdakh, U.S.S.R. 41 70 38N 147 55 E
Cholame, U.S.A. 124 35 44N 120 18W
Cholet, France 18 47 4N 0 52W
Choluteca, Honduras 128 13 20N 87 14W
Choluteca →, Honduras 128 13 0N 87 20W
Chom Bung, Thailand 54 13 37N 99 36 E
Chom Thong, Thailand 54 18 25N 98 41 E
Choma, Zambia 93 16 48 S 26 59 E
Chomen Swamp, Ethiopia 89 9 20N 37 10 E
Chomun, India 48 27 15N 75 40 E
Chomutov, Czech. 32 50 28N 13 23 E
Chon Buri, Thailand 54 13 21N 101 1 E
Chon Thanh, Vietnam 55 11 24N 106 36 E
Chonan, S. Korea 61 36 48N 127 9 E
Chone, Ecuador 134 0 40 S 80 0W
Chong Kai, Cambodia 54 13 57N 103 35 E
Chong Mek, Thailand 54 15 10N 105 27 E
Chong'an, China 59 27 45N 118 0 E
Chongde, China 59 30 32N 120 26 E
Chongjin, N. Korea 61 41 47N 129 50 E
Chŏngju, N. Korea 61 39 40N 125 5 E
Chŏngju, S. Korea 61 36 39N 127 27 E
Chongli, China 60 40 58N 115 15 E
Chongming, China 59 31 38N 121 23 E
Chongming Dao, China 59 31 40N 121 30 E
Chongoyape, Peru 136 6 35 S 79 25W
Chongqing, Sichuan, China 58 29 35N 106 25 E
Chongqing, Sichuan, China 58 30 38N 103 40 E
Chongren, China 59 27 46N 116 3 E
Chongzuo, China 58 22 23N 107 20 E
Chŏnju, S. Korea 61 35 50N 127 4 E
Chonos, Arch. de los, Chile 142 45 0 S 75 0W
Chopda, India 50 21 20N 75 15 E
Chopim →, Brazil 141 25 35 S 53 5W
Chorbat La, India 49 34 42N 76 37 E
Chorley, U.K. 12 53 39N 2 39W
Chorolque, Cerro, Bolivia 140 20 59 S 66 5W
Chorregon, Australia 72 22 40 S 143 32 E
Chorrera, La, Colombia 134 0 44 S 73 1W
Chortkov, U.S.S.R. 36 49 2N 25 46 E
Chŏrwŏn, S. Korea 61 38 15N 127 10 E
Chorzów, Poland 32 50 18N 18 57 E
Chos-Malal, Argentina 140 37 20 S 70 15W
Chosan, N. Korea 61 40 50N 125 47 E
Chōshi, Japan 65 35 45N 140 51 E
Choszczno, Poland 32 53 7N 15 25 E
Chota, Peru 136 6 33 S 78 39W
Choteau, U.S.A. 122 47 50N 112 10W
Chotila, India 48 22 23N 71 15 E
Chowchilla, U.S.A. 124 37 11N 120 12W
Chowkham, Burma 52 20 52N 97 28 E
Choybalsan, Mongolia 62 48 4N 114 30 E
Chrisman, U.S.A. 119 39 48N 87 41W
Christchurch, N.Z. 81 43 33 S 172 47 E
Christchurch, U.K. 13 50 44N 1 33W
Christian I., Canada 106 44 50N 80 12W
Christiana, S. Africa 96 27 52 S 25 8 E
Christiansfeld, Denmark 11 55 21N 9 29 E
Christiansted, Virgin Is. 129 17 45N 64 42W
Christie B., Canada 111 62 32N 111 10W
Christina →, Canada 111 56 40N 111 3W
Christmas Cr. →, Australia 78 18 29 S 125 23 E
Christmas Creek, Australia 78 18 29 S 125 23 E
Christmas I. = Kiritimati, Kiribati 67 1 58N 157 27W
Christmas I., Ind. Oc. 53 10 30 S 105 40 E
Christopher L., Australia 79 24 49 S 127 42 E
Chrudim, Czech. 32 49 58N 15 43 E
Chrzanów, Poland 32 50 10N 19 21 E
Chtimba, Malawi 93 10 35 S 34 13 E
Chu, U.S.S.R. 40 43 36N 73 42 E
Chu →, Vietnam 54 19 53N 105 45 E
Chu Chua, Canada 110 51 22N 120 10W
Chu Lai, Vietnam 54 15 28N 108 45 E
Chu Xian, China 59 32 19N 118 20 E
Chuadanga, Bangla. 52 23 38N 88 51 E
Ch'uanchou = Quanzhou, China 59 24 55N 118 34 E
Chuankou, China 60 34 20N 110 59 E
Chūbu □, Japan 65 36 45N 137 30 E
Chubut □, Argentina 142 43 30 S 69 0W
Chubut →, Argentina 142 43 20 S 65 5W
Chuchi L., Canada 110 55 12N 124 30W
Chudovo, U.S.S.R. 36 59 10N 31 41 E
Chudskoye, Oz., U.S.S.R. 36 58 13N 27 30 E
Chūgoku □, Japan 64 35 0N 133 0 E
Chūgoku-Sanchi, Japan 64 35 0N 133 0 E
Chuguyev, U.S.S.R. 38 49 55N 36 45 E
Chugwater, U.S.A. 120 41 48N 104 47W
Chukhloma, U.S.S.R. 37 58 45N 42 40 E
Chukotskiy Khrebet, U.S.S.R. 41 68 0N 175 0 E
Chukotskoye More, U.S.S.R. 41 68 0N 175 0W
Chula, U.S.A. 118 39 55N 93 29W
Chula Vista, U.S.A. 125 32 39N 117 8W
Chulman, U.S.S.R. 41 56 52N 124 52 E
Chulucanas, Peru 136 5 8 S 80 10W
Chulumani, Bolivia 136 16 24 S 67 31W
Chulym →, U.S.S.R. 40 57 43N 83 51 E
Chum Phae, Thailand 54 16 40N 102 6 E
Chum Saeng, Thailand 54 15 55N 100 15 E
Chuma, Bolivia 136 15 24 S 68 56W
Chumar, India 49 32 40N 78 35 E
Chumbicha, Argentina 140 29 0 S 66 10W
Chumerna, Bulgaria 34 42 45N 25 55 E
Chumikan, U.S.S.R. 41 54 40N 135 10 E
Chumphon, Thailand 55 10 35N 99 14 E
Chumpi, Peru 136 15 4 S 73 46W
Chumuare, Mozam. 93 14 31 S 31 50 E
Chuna →, U.S.S.R. 41 57 47N 94 37 E
Chun'an, China 59 29 35N 119 3 E
Chunchŏn, S. Korea 61 37 58N 127 44 E
Chunchura, India 49 22 53N 88 27 E
Chunga, Zambia 93 15 0 S 26 2 E
Chungking = Chongqing, China 58 29 35N 106 25 E
Chungt'iaoshan = Zhongtiao Shan, China 60 35 0N 111 10 E
Chunian, Pakistan 48 30 57N 74 0 E
Chunya, Tanzania 93 8 30 S 33 27 E
Chunya □, Tanzania 92 7 48 S 33 0 E
Chunyang, China 61 43 38N 129 23 E
Chuquibamba, Peru 136 15 47 S 72 44W
Chuquibambilla, Peru 136 14 7 S 72 41W
Chuquicamata, Chile 140 22 15 S 69 0W
Chuquisaca □, Bolivia 137 20 30 S 63 30W
Chur, Switz. 31 46 52N 9 32 E
Churachandpur, India 52 24 20N 93 40 E
Churchill, Australia 75 38 19 S 146 25 E
Churchill, Canada 111 58 47N 94 11W
Churchill →, Man., Canada 111 58 47N 94 12W
Churchill →, Nfld., Canada 105 53 19N 60 10W
Churchill, C., Canada 111 58 46N 93 12W
Churchill Falls, Canada 105 53 36N 64 19W
Churchill L., Canada 111 55 55N 108 20W
Churchill Pk., Canada 110 58 10N 125 10W
Churdan, U.S.A. 118 42 9N 94 29W
Churu, India 48 28 20N 74 50 E
Churubusco, U.S.A. 119 41 14N 85 19W
Chushal, India 49 33 40N 78 40 E
Chusovoy, U.S.S.R. 40 58 15N 57 40 E
Chute-aux-Outardes, Canada 107 49 7N 68 24W
Chute-des-Passes, Canada 107 49 52N 71 16W
Chuvash A.S.S.R. □, U.S.S.R. 37 55 30N 47 0 E
Chuxiong, China 58 25 2N 101 28 E
Ci Xian, China 60 36 20N 114 25 E
Ciacova, Romania 34 45 35N 21 10 E
Cianjur, Indonesia 57 6 49 S 107 8 E
Cibadok, Indonesia 57 6 53 S 106 47 E
Cibatu, Indonesia 57 7 8 S 107 59 E
Cibola, U.S.A. 125 33 17N 114 42W
Cicero, Ill., U.S.A. 119 41 51N 87 45W
Cicero, U.S.A. 114 41 48N 87 48W
Cícero Dantas, Brazil 138 10 36 S 38 23W
Cidacos →, Spain 24 42 21N 1 38W
Cide, Turkey 38 41 53N 33 1 E
Ciechanów, Poland 32 52 52N 20 38 E
Ciego de Avila, Cuba 128 21 50N 78 50W
Ciénaga, Colombia 134 11 1N 74 15W
Ciénaga de Oro, Colombia 134 8 53N 75 37W
Cienfuegos, Cuba 128 22 10N 80 30W
Cieplice Sląskie Zdrój, Poland 32 50 50N 15 40 E
Cierp, France 20 42 55N 0 40 E
Cíes, Is., Spain 22 42 12N 8 55W
Cieszyn, Poland 32 49 45N 18 35 E
Cieza, Spain 25 38 17N 1 23W
Cifuentes, Spain 24 40 47N 2 37W
Cihuatlán, Mexico 126 19 14N 104 35W
Cijara, Pantano de, Spain 23 39 18N 4 52W
Cijulang, Indonesia 57 7 42 S 108 27 E
Cikajang, Indonesia 57 7 25 S 107 48 E
Cikampek, Indonesia 57 6 23 S 107 28 E
Cilacap, Indonesia 57 7 43 S 109 0 E
Çıldır, Turkey 39 41 10N 43 20 E
Cili, China 59 29 30N 111 8 E
Cilician Gates P., Turkey 46 37 20N 34 52 E
Cima, U.S.A. 125 35 14N 115 30W
Cimahi, Indonesia 57 6 53 S 107 33 E
Cimarron, Kans., U.S.A. 121 37 50N 100 20W
Cimarron, N. Mex., U.S.A. 121 36 30N 104 52W
Cimarron →, U.S.A. 121 36 10N 96 17W
Cimone, Mte., Italy 26 44 10N 10 40 E
Cîmpina, Romania 34 45 10N 25 45 E
Cîmpulung, Argeş, Romania 34 45 17N 25 3 E
Cîmpulung, Suceava, Romania 34 47 32N 25 30 E
Cinca →, Spain 24 41 26N 0 21 E
Cincinnati, Iowa, U.S.A. 118 40 38N 92 56W
Cincinnati, Ohio, U.S.A. 119 39 10N 84 26W
Cîndeşti, Romania 34 45 15N 26 42 E
Ciney, Belgium 17 50 18N 5 5 E
Cîngoli, Italy 27 43 23N 13 10 E
Cinigiano, Italy 27 42 53N 11 23 E
Cinto, Mte., France 21 42 24N 8 54 E
Ciorani, Romania 34 44 45N 26 25 E
Ciotat, La, France 21 43 10N 5 37 E
Čiovo, Yugoslavia 27 43 30N 16 17 E
Cipó, Brazil 138 11 6 S 38 31W
Circeo, Monte, Italy 28 41 14N 13 3 E
Circle, Alaska, U.S.A. 102 65 50N 144 10W
Circle, Mont., U.S.A. 120 47 26N 105 35W
Circleville, Ohio, U.S.A. 114 39 35N 82 57W
Circleville, Utah, U.S.A. 123 38 12N 112 24W
Cirebon, Indonesia 57 6 45 S 108 32 E
Cirencester, U.K. 13 51 43N 1 59W

Cofrentes

Cirey-sur-Vezouze, *France* **19** 48 35N 6 57 E
Ciriè, *Italy* **26** 45 14N 7 35 E
Cirò, *Italy* **29** 39 23N 17 3 E
Ciron →, *France* **20** 44 36N 0 18W
Cisco, *U.S.A.* **121** 32 25N 99 0W
Ciskei □, *S. Africa* **97** 33 0 S 27 0 E
Cislău, *Romania* **34** 45 14N 26 20 E
Cisne, *U.S.A.* **119** 38 31N 88 26W
Cisneros, *Colombia* **134** 6 33N 75 4W
Cissna Park, *U.S.A.* **119** 40 34N 87 54W
Cisterna di Latina, *Italy* **28** 41 35N 12 50 E
Cisternino, *Italy* **29** 40 45N 17 26 E
Citaré →, *Brazil* **135** 1 11N 54 41W
Citeli-Ckaro, *U.S.S.R.* **39** 41 33N 46 0 E
Citlaltépetl, *Mexico* **127** 19 0N 97 20W
Citrus Heights, *U.S.A.* **124** 38 42N 121 17W
Citrusdal, *S. Africa* **96** 32 35 S 19 0 E
Città della Pieve, *Italy* **27** 42 57N 12 0 E
Città di Castello, *Italy* **27** 43 27N 12 14 E
Città Sant' Angelo, *Italy* **27** 42 32N 14 5 E
Cittadella, *Italy* **27** 45 39N 11 48 E
Cittaducale, *Italy* **27** 42 24N 12 58 E
Cittanova, *Italy* **29** 38 22N 16 5 E
Ciucaş, *Romania* **34** 45 31N 25 56 E
Ciudad Altamirano, *Mexico* **126** 18 20N 100 40W
Ciudad Bolívar, *Venezuela* **135** 8 5N 63 36W
Ciudad Camargo, *Mexico* **126** 27 41N 105 10W
Ciudad de Valles, *Mexico* **127** 22 0N 99 0W
Ciudad del Carmen, *Mexico* **127** 18 38N 91 50W
Ciudad Delicias = Delicias, *Mexico* **126** 28 10N 105 30W
Ciudad Guayana, *Venezuela* **135** 8 0N 62 30W
Ciudad Guerrero, *Mexico* **126** 28 33N 107 28W
Ciudad Guzmán, *Mexico* **126** 19 40N 103 30W
Ciudad Juárez, *Mexico* **126** 31 40N 106 28W
Ciudad Madero, *Mexico* **127** 22 19N 97 50W
Ciudad Mante, *Mexico* **127** 22 50N 99 0W
Ciudad Obregón, *Mexico* **126** 27 28N 109 59W
Ciudad Ojeda, *Venezuela* **134** 10 12N 71 19W
Ciudad Real, *Spain* **23** 38 59N 3 55W
Ciudad Real □, *Spain* **23** 38 50N 4 0W
Ciudad Rodrigo, *Spain* **22** 40 35N 6 32W
Ciudad Trujillo = Santo Domingo, *Dom. Rep.* **129** 18 30N 69 59W
Ciudad Victoria, *Mexico* **127** 23 41N 99 9W
Ciudadela, *Spain* **24** 40 0N 3 50 E
Ciulniţa, *Romania* **34** 44 26N 27 22 E
Cividale del Friuli, *Italy* **27** 46 6N 13 25 E
Cívita Castellana, *Italy* **27** 42 18N 12 24 E
Civitanova Marche, *Italy* **27** 43 18N 13 41 E
Civitavécchia, *Italy* **27** 42 6N 11 46 E
Civitella del Tronto, *Italy* **27** 42 48N 13 40 E
Civray, *France* **20** 46 10N 0 17 E
Çivril, *Turkey* **46** 38 20N 29 43 E
Cixerri →, *Italy* **28** 39 20N 8 40 E
Cizre, *Turkey* **46** 37 19N 42 10 E
Clackline, *Australia* **79** 31 40 S 116 32 E
Clacton-on-Sea, *U.K.* **13** 51 47N 1 10 E
Clain →, *France* **18** 46 47N 0 33 E
Claire, *Canada* **107** 47 15N 68 40W
Claire, L., *Canada* **110** 58 35N 112 5W
Claire, Le, *U.S.A.* **118** 41 36N 90 21W
Clairemont, *U.S.A.* **121** 33 9N 100 44W
Clairton, *U.S.A.* **116** 40 18N 79 54W
Clairvaux-les-Lacs, *France* **21** 46 35N 5 45 E
Clallam Bay, *U.S.A.* **124** 48 15N 124 16W
Clamecy, *France* **19** 47 28N 3 30 E
Clanton, *U.S.A.* **115** 32 48N 86 36W
Clanwilliam, *S. Africa* **96** 32 11 S 18 52 E
Clapperton I., *Canada* **108** 46 0N 82 14W
Clara, *Ireland* **15** 53 20N 7 38W
Clara →, *Australia* **72** 19 8 S 142 30 E
Claraville, *U.S.A.* **125** 35 24N 118 20W
Clare, *Australia* **73** 33 50 S 138 37 E
Clare, *U.S.A.* **104** 43 47N 84 45W
Clare □, *Ireland* **15** 52 20N 9 0W
Clare →, *Ireland* **15** 53 22N 9 5W
Clare I., *Ireland* **15** 53 48N 10 0W
Claremont, *Calif., U.S.A.* **125** 34 6N 117 43W
Claremont, *U.S.A.* **117** 43 23N 72 20W
Claremont Pt., *Australia* **72** 14 1 S 143 41 E
Claremore, *U.S.A.* **121** 36 40N 95 37W
Claremorris, *Ireland* **15** 53 45N 9 0W
Clarence, *U.S.A.* **118** 39 45N 92 16W
Clarence →, *Australia* **77** 29 25 S 153 22 E
Clarence →, *N.Z.* **81** 42 10 S 173 56 E
Clarence, I., *Chile* **142** 54 0 S 72 0W
Clarence I., *Antarctica* **143** 61 10 S 54 0W
Clarence Str., *Australia* **78** 12 0 S 131 0 E
Clarence Str., *U.S.A.* **110** 55 40N 132 10W
Clarence Town, *Bahamas* **129** 23 6N 74 59W
Clarencetown, *Australia* **76** 32 34 S 151 46 E
Clarendon, *Ark., U.S.A.* **121** 34 41N 91 20W
Clarendon, *Tex., U.S.A.* **121** 34 58N 100 54W
Clarenville, *Canada* **105** 48 10N 54 1W
Claresholm, *Canada* **110** 50 0N 113 33W
Clarie Coast, *Antarctica* **143** 68 0 S 135 0 E
Clarinda, *U.S.A.* **120** 40 45N 95 0W
Clarion, *Iowa, U.S.A.* **118** 42 41N 93 46W
Clarion, *Pa., U.S.A.* **116** 41 12N 79 22W
Clarion →, *U.S.A.* **116** 41 9N 79 41W
Clarion Fracture Zone, *Pac. Oc.* **67** 20 0N 120 0W
Clark, *U.S.A.* **120** 44 55N 97 45W
Clark, Pt., *Canada* **108** 44 4N 81 45W
Clark Fork, *U.S.A.* **122** 48 9N 116 9W
Clark Fork →, *U.S.A.* **122** 48 9N 116 15W
Clark Hill Res., *U.S.A.* **115** 33 45N 82 20W
Clarkdale, *U.S.A.* **123** 34 53N 112 3W
Clarke City, *Canada* **105** 50 12N 66 38W
Clarke I., *Australia* **72** 40 32 S 148 10 E
Clarke L., *Canada* **111** 54 24N 106 54W
Clarke Ra., *Australia* **72** 20 45 S 148 20 E
Clark's Fork →, *U.S.A.* **122** 45 39N 108 43W
Clark's Harbour, *Canada* **105** 43 25N 65 38W
Clarks Summit, *U.S.A.* **117** 41 31N 75 44W
Clarksburg, *U.S.A.* **114** 39 18N 80 21W
Clarksdale, *U.S.A.* **121** 34 12N 90 33W
Clarkston, *U.S.A.* **122** 46 28N 117 2W
Clarksville, *Ark., U.S.A.* **121** 35 29N 93 27W
Clarksville, *Iowa, U.S.A.* **118** 42 47N 92 40W
Clarksville, *Mich., U.S.A.* **119** 42 50N 85 15W
Clarksville, *Ohio, U.S.A.* **119** 39 24N 83 59W
Clarksville, *Tenn., U.S.A.* **115** 36 32N 87 20W
Clarksville, *Tex., U.S.A.* **121** 33 37N 94 59W
Claro →, *Brazil* **139** 19 8 S 50 40W
Clatskanie, *U.S.A.* **124** 46 9N 123 12W
Claude, *U.S.A.* **121** 35 8N 101 22W
Claveria, *Phil.* **57** 18 37N 121 4 E
Clay, *U.S.A.* **124** 38 17N 121 10W
Clay Center, *U.S.A.* **120** 39 27N 97 9W
Clay City, *Ind., U.S.A.* **119** 39 17N 87 7W
Clay City, *Ky., U.S.A.* **119** 37 52N 83 55W
Clayette, La, *France* **21** 46 17N 4 19 E
Claypool, *U.S.A.* **123** 33 27N 110 55W
Claysville, *U.S.A.* **116** 40 5N 80 25W
Clayton, *Idaho, U.S.A.* **122** 44 12N 114 31W
Clayton, *Ind., U.S.A.* **119** 39 41N 86 31W
Clayton, *N. Mex., U.S.A.* **121** 36 30N 103 10W
Cle Elum, *U.S.A.* **122** 47 15N 120 57W
Clear, C., *Ireland* **15** 51 26N 9 30W
Clear, L., *Canada* **109** 45 26N 77 12W
Clear I., *Ireland* **15** 51 26N 9 30W
Clear L., *U.S.A.* **124** 39 5N 122 47W
Clear Lake, *Iowa, U.S.A.* **118** 43 8N 93 23W
Clear Lake, *S. Dak., U.S.A.* **120** 44 48N 96 41W
Clear Lake, *Wash., U.S.A.* **122** 48 27N 122 15W
Clear Lake Res., *U.S.A.* **122** 41 55N 121 10W
Clearfield, *Iowa, U.S.A.* **118** 40 48N 94 29W
Clearfield, *Pa., U.S.A.* **114** 41 0N 78 27W
Clearfield, *Utah, U.S.A.* **122** 41 10N 112 0W
Clearlake Highlands, *U.S.A.* **124** 38 57N 122 38W
Clearmont, *U.S.A.* **122** 44 43N 106 29W
Clearwater, *Canada* **110** 51 38N 120 2W
Clearwater, *U.S.A.* **115** 27 58N 82 45W
Clearwater →, *Alta., Canada* **110** 52 22N 114 57W
Clearwater →, *Alta., Canada* **111** 56 44N 111 23W
Clearwater Cr. →, *Canada* **110** 61 36N 125 30W
Clearwater Mts., *U.S.A.* **122** 46 20N 115 30W
Clearwater Prov. Park, *Canada* **111** 54 0N 101 0W
Cleburne, *U.S.A.* **121** 32 18N 97 25W
Cleethorpes, *U.K.* **12** 53 33N 0 2W
Cleeve Cloud, *U.K.* **13** 51 56N 2 0W
Clelles, *France* **21** 44 50N 5 38 E
Clemency, *Lux.* **17** 49 35N 5 53 E
Clerke Reef, *Australia* **78** 17 22 S 119 20 E
Clermont, *Australia* **72** 22 49 S 147 39 E
Clermont, *Canada* **107** 47 41N 70 14W
Clermont, *France* **19** 49 23N 2 24 E
Clermont-en-Argonne, *France* **19** 49 5N 5 4 E
Clermont-Ferrand, *France* **20** 45 46N 3 4 E
Clermont-l'Hérault, *France* **20** 43 38N 3 26 E
Clerval, *France* **19** 47 25N 6 30 E
Clervaux, *Lux.* **17** 50 4N 6 2 E
Cléry-St-André, *France* **19** 47 50N 1 46 E
Cles, *Italy* **26** 46 21N 11 4 E
Cleveland, *Australia* **77** 27 30 S 153 15 E
Cleveland, *Miss., U.S.A.* **121** 33 43N 90 43W
Cleveland, *Ohio, U.S.A.* **116** 41 28N 81 43W
Cleveland, *Okla., U.S.A.* **121** 36 21N 96 33W
Cleveland, *Tenn., U.S.A.* **115** 35 9N 84 52W
Cleveland, *Tex., U.S.A.* **121** 30 18N 95 0W
Cleveland □, *U.K.* **12** 54 35N 1 8 E
Cleveland, C., *Australia* **72** 19 11 S 147 1 E
Cleveland Heights, *U.S.A.* **116** 41 32N 81 30W
Clevelândia, *Brazil* **141** 26 24 S 52 23W
Clevelândia do Norte, *Brazil* **135** 3 49N 51 52W
Cleves, *U.S.A.* **119** 39 10N 84 45W
Clew B., *Ireland* **15** 53 54N 9 50W
Clewiston, *U.S.A.* **115** 26 44N 80 50W
Clifden, *Ireland* **15** 53 30N 10 2W
Clifden, *N.Z.* **81** 46 1 S 167 42 E
Cliffdell, *U.S.A.* **124** 46 56N 121 5W
Clifton, *Australia* **77** 27 59 S 151 53 E
Clifton, *Ariz., U.S.A.* **123** 33 8N 109 23W
Clifton, *Ill., U.S.A.* **119** 40 56N 87 56W
Clifton, *Tex., U.S.A.* **121** 31 46N 97 35W
Clifton Beach, *Australia* **72** 16 46 S 145 39 E
Clifton Forge, *U.S.A.* **114** 37 49N 79 51W
Clifton Hills, *Australia* **73** 27 1 S 138 54 E
Climax, *Canada* **111** 49 10N 108 20W
Clinch →, *U.S.A.* **115** 36 0N 84 29W
Clingmans Dome, *U.S.A.* **115** 35 35N 83 30W
Clint, *U.S.A.* **123** 31 37N 106 11W
Clinton, *B.C., Canada* **110** 51 6N 121 35W
Clinton, *Ont., Canada* **108** 43 37N 81 32W
Clinton, *N.Z.* **81** 46 12 S 169 23 E
Clinton, *Ark., U.S.A.* **121** 35 37N 92 30W
Clinton, *Ill., U.S.A.* **120** 40 8N 89 0W
Clinton, *Ind., U.S.A.* **119** 39 40N 87 22W
Clinton, *Iowa, U.S.A.* **118** 41 50N 90 12W
Clinton, *Mass., U.S.A.* **117** 42 26N 71 40W
Clinton, *Mo., U.S.A.* **118** 38 20N 93 46W
Clinton, *N.C., U.S.A.* **115** 35 5N 78 15W
Clinton, *Okla., U.S.A.* **121** 35 30N 99 0W
Clinton, *S.C., U.S.A.* **115** 34 30N 81 54W
Clinton, *Tenn., U.S.A.* **115** 36 6N 84 10W
Clinton, *Wash., U.S.A.* **124** 47 59N 122 22W
Clinton, *Wis., U.S.A.* **119** 42 34N 88 52W
Clinton C., *Australia* **72** 22 30 S 150 45 E
Clinton Colden L., *Canada* **102** 63 58N 107 27W
Clintonville, *U.S.A.* **120** 44 35N 88 46W
Clipperton, I., *Pac. Oc.* **67** 10 18N 109 13W
Clipperton Fracture Zone, *Pac. Oc.* **67** 19 0N 122 0W
Clisson, *France* **18** 47 5N 1 16W
Clive, *N.Z.* **80** 39 36 S 176 58 E
Clive L., *Canada* **110** 63 13N 118 54W
Cliza, *Bolivia* **137** 17 36 S 65 56W
Cloates, Pt., *Australia* **78** 22 43 S 113 40 E
Clocolan, *S. Africa* **97** 28 55 S 27 34 E
Clodomira, *Argentina* **140** 27 35 S 64 14W
Clonakilty, *Ireland* **15** 51 37N 8 53W
Clonakilty B., *Ireland* **15** 51 33N 8 50W
Cloncurry, *Australia* **72** 20 40 S 140 28 E
Cloncurry →, *Australia* **72** 18 37 S 140 40 E
Clones, *Ireland* **15** 54 10N 7 13W
Clonmel, *Ireland* **15** 52 22N 7 42W
Cloppenburg, *W. Germany* **30** 52 50N 8 3 E
Cloquet, *U.S.A.* **120** 46 40N 92 30W
Clorinda, *Argentina* **140** 25 16 S 57 45W
Cloud Peak, *U.S.A.* **122** 44 23N 107 10W
Cloudcroft, *U.S.A.* **123** 33 0N 105 48W
Clouds Creek, *Australia* **77** 30 4 S 152 42 E
Cloudy B., *N.Z.* **81** 41 25 S 174 10 E
Clova, *Canada* **106** 48 7N 75 22W
Cloverdale, *Calif., U.S.A.* **124** 38 49N 123 0W
Cloverdale, *Ind., U.S.A.* **119** 39 31N 86 47W
Cloverport, *U.S.A.* **119** 37 50N 86 38W
Clovis, *Calif., U.S.A.* **124** 36 47N 119 45W
Clovis, *N. Mex., U.S.A.* **121** 34 20N 103 10W
Cloyes-sur-le-Loir, *France* **18** 48 0N 1 14 E
Cloyne, *Canada* **109** 44 49N 77 11W
Club Terrace, *Australia* **75** 37 35 S 148 58 E
Cluj-Napoca, *Romania* **34** 46 47N 23 38 E
Clunes, *Australia* **74** 37 20 S 143 45 E
Cluny, *France* **21** 46 26N 4 38 E
Cluses, *France* **21** 46 5N 6 35 E
Clusone, *Italy* **26** 45 54N 9 58 E
Clutha →, *N.Z.* **81** 46 20 S 169 49 E
Clwyd □, *U.K.* **12** 53 5N 3 20W
Clwyd →, *U.K.* **12** 53 20N 3 30W
Clyde, *N.Z.* **81** 45 12 S 169 20 E
Clyde, *U.S.A.* **116** 43 8N 76 52W
Clyde →, *U.K.* **14** 55 56N 4 29W
Clyde, Firth of, *U.K.* **14** 55 20N 5 0W
Clyde River, *Canada* **103** 70 30N 68 30W
Clydebank, *U.K.* **14** 55 54N 4 25W
Clymer, *U.S.A.* **116** 42 3N 79 39W
Côa →, *Portugal* **22** 41 5N 7 6W
Coachella, *U.S.A.* **125** 33 44N 116 13W
Coachella Canal, *U.S.A.* **125** 32 43N 114 57W
Coahoma, *U.S.A.* **121** 32 17N 101 20W
Coahuayana →, *Mexico* **126** 18 41N 103 45W
Coahuayutla, *Mexico* **126** 18 19N 101 42W
Coahuila □, *Mexico* **126** 27 0N 103 0W
Coal →, *Canada* **110** 59 39N 126 57W
Coal City, *U.S.A.* **119** 41 17N 88 17W
Coal I., *N.Z.* **81** 46 8 S 166 40 E
Coalane, *Mozam.* **93** 17 48 S 37 2 E
Coalcomán, *Mexico* **126** 18 40N 103 10W
Coaldale, *Canada* **110** 49 45N 112 35W
Coalgate, *U.S.A.* **121** 34 35N 96 13W
Coalinga, *U.S.A.* **124** 36 10N 120 21W
Coalville, *U.K.* **12** 52 43N 1 21W
Coalville, *U.S.A.* **122** 40 58N 111 24W
Coaraci, *Brazil* **139** 14 38 S 39 32W
Coari, *Brazil* **135** 4 8 S 63 7W
Coari →, *Brazil* **135** 4 30 S 63 33W
Coari, L. de, *Brazil* **135** 4 15 S 63 22W
Coast □, *Kenya* **92** 2 40 S 39 45 E
Coast Mts., *Canada* **110** 55 0N 129 20W
Coast Ranges, *U.S.A.* **124** 41 0N 123 0W
Coastal Plains Basin, *Australia* **79** 30 10 S 115 30 E
Coatbridge, *U.K.* **14** 55 52N 4 2W
Coatepec, *Mexico* **127** 19 27N 96 58W
Coatepeque, *Guatemala* **128** 14 46N 91 55W
Coatesville, *U.S.A.* **114** 39 59N 75 55W
Coaticook, *Canada* **107** 45 10N 71 46W
Coats I., *Canada* **103** 62 30N 83 0W
Coats Land, *Antarctica* **143** 77 0 S 25 0W
Coatzacoalcos, *Mexico* **127** 18 7N 94 25W
Cobalt, *Canada* **106** 47 25N 79 42W
Cobán, *Guatemala* **128** 15 30N 90 21W
Cobar, *Australia* **73** 31 27 S 145 48 E
Cobargo, *Australia* **75** 36 20 S 149 55 E
Cobba-da-mana, *Australia* **77** 28 24 S 151 14 E
Cobberas, Mt., *Australia* **75** 36 53 S 148 12 E
Cobden, *Australia* **74** 38 20 S 143 3 E
Cobden, *Canada* **109** 45 38N 76 53W
Cóbh, *Ireland* **15** 51 50N 8 18W
Cobham, *Australia* **73** 30 18 S 142 7 E
Cobija, *Bolivia* **136** 11 0 S 68 50W
Cobleskill, *U.S.A.* **117** 42 40N 74 30W
Coboconk, *Canada* **109** 44 39N 78 48W
Cobourg, *Canada* **109** 43 58N 78 10W
Cobourg Pen., *Australia* **78** 11 20 S 132 15 E
Cobram, *Australia* **74** 35 54 S 145 40 E
Cobre, *U.S.A.* **122** 41 6N 114 25W
Cóbué, *Mozam.* **93** 12 0 S 34 58 E
Coburg, *W. Germany* **31** 50 15N 10 58 E
Coca, *Spain* **22** 41 13N 4 32W
Coca →, *Ecuador* **134** 0 29 S 76 58W
Cocachacra, *Peru* **136** 17 5 S 71 45W
Cocal, *Brazil* **138** 3 28 S 41 34W
Cocanada = Kakinada, *India* **50** 16 57N 82 11 E
Cocentaina, *Spain* **25** 38 45N 0 27W
Cocha, La, *Argentina* **140** 27 50 S 65 40W
Cochabamba, *Bolivia* **137** 17 26 S 66 10W
Coche, I., *Venezuela* **135** 10 47N 63 56W
Cochem, *W. Germany* **31** 50 8N 7 7 E
Cochemane, *Mozam.* **93** 17 0 S 32 54 E
Cochin, *India* **51** 9 59N 76 22 E
Cochin China = Nam-Phan, *Vietnam* **55** 10 30N 106 0 E
Cochise, *U.S.A.* **123** 32 6N 109 58W
Cochran, *U.S.A.* **115** 32 25N 83 23W
Cochrane, *Alta., Canada* **110** 51 11N 114 30W
Cochrane, *Ont., Canada* **104** 49 0N 81 0W
Cochrane →, *Canada* **111** 59 0N 103 40W
Cochrane, L., *Chile* **142** 47 10 S 72 0W
Cockatoo, *Australia* **74** 37 57 S 145 32 E
Cockburn, *Australia* **73** 32 5 S 141 0 E
Cockburn, Canal, *Chile* **142** 54 30 S 72 0W
Cockburn I., *Canada* **108** 45 55N 83 22W
Cockburn Ra., *Australia* **78** 15 46 S 128 0 E
Cocklebiddy Motel, *Australia* **79** 32 0 S 126 3 E
Coco →, *Cent. Amer.* **128** 15 0N 83 8W
Coco, Pta., *Colombia* **134** 2 58N 77 43W
Cocoa, *U.S.A.* **115** 28 22N 80 40W
Cocobeach, *Gabon* **94** 0 59N 9 34 E
Côcos, *Brazil* **139** 14 10 S 44 33W
Côcos →, *Brazil* **139** 12 44 S 44 48W
Cocos I., *Guam* **68** 13 14N 144 39 E
Cocos I., *Pac. Oc.* **67** 5 25N 87 55W
Cocos Is., *Ind. Oc.* **53** 12 10 S 96 55 E
Cod, C., *U.S.A.* **113** 42 8N 70 10W
Codajás, *Brazil* **135** 3 55 S 62 0W
Codera, C., *Venezuela* **134** 10 35N 66 4W
Coderre, *Canada* **111** 50 11N 106 31W
Codigoro, *Italy* **27** 44 50N 12 5 E
Codó, *Brazil* **138** 4 30 S 43 55W
Codogno, *Italy* **26** 45 10N 9 42 E
Codpa, *Chile* **136** 18 50 S 69 44W
Codróipo, *Italy* **27** 45 57N 13 0 E
Cody, *U.S.A.* **122** 44 35N 109 0W
Coe Hill, *Canada* **109** 44 52N 77 50W
Coelemu, *Chile* **140** 36 30 S 72 48W
Coelho Neto, *Brazil* **138** 4 15 S 43 0W
Coen, *Australia* **72** 13 52 S 143 12 E
Coeroeni →, *Surinam* **135** 3 21N 57 31W
Coesfeld, *W. Germany* **30** 51 56N 7 10 E
Coetivy Is., *Seychelles* **53** 7 8 S 56 16 E
Cœur d'Alene, *U.S.A.* **122** 47 45N 116 51W
Cœur d'Alene L., *U.S.A.* **122** 47 32N 116 48W
Coevorden, *Neths.* **16** 52 40N 6 44 E
Cofete, *Canary Is.* **25** 28 6N 14 23W
Coffeyville, *U.S.A.* **121** 37 0N 95 40W
Coffs Harbour, *Australia* **77** 30 16 S 153 5 E
Cofrentes, *Spain* **25** 39 13N 1 5W

Courtenay

Contrexéville, *France* **19** 48 10N 5 53 E
Contumaza, *Peru* **136** 7 23 S 78 57W
Convención, *Colombia* **134** 8 28N 73 21W
Conversano, *Italy* **29** 40 57N 17 8 E
Converse, *U.S.A.* **119** 40 34N 85 52W
Convoy, *U.S.A.* **119** 40 55N 84 43W
Conway = Conwy, *U.K.* **12** 53 17N 3 50W
Conway = Conwy →, *U.K.* **12** 53 18N 3 50W
Conway, *Ark., U.S.A.* **121** 35 5N 92 30W
Conway, *N.H., U.S.A.* **117** 43 58N 71 8W
Conway, *S.C., U.S.A.* **115** 33 49N 79 2W
Conway, L., *Australia* **73** 28 17 S 135 35 E
Conwy, *U.K.* **12** 53 17N 3 50W
Conwy →, *U.K.* **12** 53 18N 3 50W
Cooch Behar = Koch Bihar, *India* **52** 26 22N 89 29 E
Coodardy, *Australia* **79** 27 15 S 117 39 E
Cook, *Australia* **79** 30 37 S 130 25 E
Cook, *U.S.A.* **120** 47 49N 92 39W
Cook, B., *Chile* **142** 55 10 S 70 0W
Cook, Mt., *N.Z.* **81** 43 36 S 170 9 E
Cook Inlet, *U.S.A.* **102** 59 0N 151 0W
Cook Is., *Pac. Oc.* **67** 17 0 S 160 0W
Cook Strait, *N.Z.* **81** 41 15 S 174 29 E
Cookeville, *U.S.A.* **115** 36 12N 85 30W
Cookhouse, *S. Africa* **96** 32 44 S 25 47 E
Cookshire, *Canada* **117** 45 25N 71 38W
Cookstown, *U.K.* **15** 54 40N 6 43W
Cookstown □, *U.K.* **15** 54 40N 6 43W
Cooksville, *Canada* **116** 43 36N 79 35W
Cooktown, *Australia* **72** 15 30 S 145 16 E
Coolabah, *Australia* **73** 31 1 S 146 43 E
Cooladdi, *Australia* **73** 26 37 S 145 23 E
Coolah, *Australia* **77** 31 48 S 149 41 E
Coolamon, *Australia* **76** 34 46 S 147 8 E
Coolangatta, *Australia* **77** 28 11 S 153 29 E
Coolatai, *Australia* **77** 29 15 S 150 45 E
Coolgardie, *Australia* **79** 30 55 S 121 8 E
Coolibah, *Australia* **78** 15 33 S 130 56 E
Coolidge, *U.S.A.* **123** 33 1N 111 35W
Coolidge Dam, *U.S.A.* **123** 33 10N 110 30W
Coolongolook, *Australia* **77** 32 12 S 152 20 E
Cooma, *Australia* **75** 36 12 S 149 8 E
Coon Rapids, *U.S.A.* **118** 41 53N 94 41W
Coonabarabran, *Australia* **76** 31 14 S 149 18 E
Coonamble, *Australia* **76** 30 56 S 148 27 E
Coonana, *Australia* **79** 31 0 S 123 0 E
Coondapoor, *India* **51** 13 42N 74 40 E
Coongie, *Australia* **73** 27 9 S 140 8 E
Coongoola, *Australia* **73** 27 43 S 145 51 E
Cooninie, L., *Australia* **73** 26 4 S 139 59 E
Coonoor, *India* **51** 11 21N 76 45 E
Cooper, *U.S.A.* **121** 33 20N 95 40W
Cooper →, *U.S.A.* **115** 33 0N 79 55W
Coopers Cr. →, *Australia* **73** 28 29 S 137 46 E
Cooperstown, *N. Dak., U.S.A.* **120** 47 30N 98 6W
Cooperstown, *N.Y., U.S.A.* **117** 42 42N 74 57W
Coopersville, *U.S.A.* **119** 43 4N 85 57W
Coorabie, *Australia* **79** 31 54 S 132 18 E
Coorabulka, *Australia* **72** 23 41 S 140 20 E
Cooranbong, *Australia* **76** 33 4 S 151 28 E
Coorong, The, *Australia* **73** 35 50 S 139 20 E
Coorow, *Australia* **79** 29 53 S 116 2 E
Cooroy, *Australia* **73** 26 22 S 152 54 E
Coos Bay, *U.S.A.* **122** 43 26N 124 7W
Cootamundra, *Australia* **76** 34 36 S 148 1 E
Cootehill, *Ireland* **15** 54 5N 7 5W
Cooyal, *Australia* **76** 32 25 S 149 45 E
Cooyar, *Australia* **73** 26 59 S 151 51 E
Cooyeana, *Australia* **72** 24 29 S 138 45 E
Copahue Paso, *Argentina* **140** 37 49 S 71 8W
Copainalá, *Mexico* **127** 17 8N 93 11W
Copán, *Honduras* **128** 14 50N 89 9W
Copatana, *Brazil* **134** 2 48 S 67 4W
Cope, *U.S.A.* **120** 39 44N 102 50W
Cope, C., *Spain* **25** 37 26N 1 28W
Cope Cope, *Australia* **74** 36 27 S 143 5 E
Copenhagen = København, *Denmark* **11** 55 41N 12 34 E
Copertino, *Italy* **29** 40 17N 18 2 E
Copiapó, *Chile* **140** 27 30 S 70 20W
Copiapó →, *Chile* **140** 27 19 S 70 56W
Copley, *Australia* **73** 30 36 S 138 26 E
Copmanhurst, *Australia* **77** 29 33 S 152 49 E
Copp L., *Canada* **110** 60 14N 114 40W
Coppadah, *Australia* **77** 30 12 S 150 34 E
Copparo, *Italy* **27** 44 52N 11 49 E
Coppename →, *Surinam* **135** 5 48N 55 55W
Copper Center, *U.S.A.* **102** 62 10N 145 25W
Copper Cliff, *Canada* **108** 46 28N 81 4W
Copper Harbor, *U.S.A.* **104** 47 31N 87 55W
Copper Queen, *Zambia* **93** 17 29 S 29 18 E
Copperbelt □, *Zambia* **93** 13 15 S 27 30 E
Coppermine, *Canada* **102** 67 50N 115 5W
Coppermine →, *Canada* **102** 67 49N 116 4W
Copperopolis, *U.S.A.* **124** 37 58N 120 38W
Coquet →, *U.K.* **12** 55 18N 1 45W
Coquilhatville = Mbandaka, *Zaïre* **94** 0 1N 18 18 E
Coquille, *U.S.A.* **122** 43 15N 124 12W
Coquimbo, *Chile* **140** 30 0 S 71 20W
Coquimbo □, *Chile* **140** 31 0 S 71 0W
Corabia, *Romania* **34** 43 48N 24 30 E
Coração de Jesus, *Brazil* **139** 16 43 S 44 22W
Coracora, *Peru* **136** 15 5 S 73 45W
Coradi, Is., *Italy* **29** 40 27N 17 10 E
Coraki, *Australia* **77** 28 59 S 153 17 E
Coral Gables, *U.S.A.* **115** 25 45N 80 16W
Coral Harbour, *Canada* **103** 64 8N 83 10W
Coral Sea, *Pac. Oc.* **66** 15 0 S 150 0 E
Coralville, *U.S.A.* **118** 41 42N 91 34W
Coralville Res., *U.S.A.* **118** 41 50N 91 40W
Coramba, *Australia* **77** 30 12 S 153 3 E
Corangamite, L., *Australia* **74** 38 0 S 143 30 E
Corantijn →, *Surinam* **135** 5 50N 57 8W
Coraopolis, *U.S.A.* **116** 40 30N 80 10W
Corato, *Italy* **29** 41 12N 16 22 E
Corbeil-Essonnes, *France* **19** 48 36N 2 26 E
Corbie, *France* **19** 49 54N 2 30 E
Corbières, *France* **20** 42 55N 2 35 E
Corbigny, *France* **19** 47 16N 3 40 E
Corbin, *U.S.A.* **114** 37 0N 84 3W
Corbion, *Belgium* **17** 49 48N 5 0 E
Corbones →, *Spain* **23** 37 36N 5 39W
Corby, *U.K.* **13** 52 49N 0 31W
Corcoles →, *Spain* **25** 39 40N 3 18W
Corcoran, *U.S.A.* **124** 36 6N 119 35W
Corcubión, *Spain* **22** 42 56N 9 12W
Cordele, *U.S.A.* **115** 31 55N 83 49W
Cordell, *U.S.A.* **121** 35 18N 99 0W
Cordenons, *Italy* **27** 45 59N 12 42 E
Cordes, *France* **20** 44 5N 1 57 E
Cordisburgo, *Brazil* **139** 19 7 S 44 21W
Córdoba, *Argentina* **140** 31 20 S 64 10W
Córdoba, *Mexico* **127** 18 50N 97 0W
Córdoba, *Spain* **23** 37 50N 4 50W
Córdoba □, *Argentina* **140** 31 22 S 64 15W
Córdoba □, *Colombia* **134** 8 20N 75 40W
Córdoba □, *Spain* **23** 38 5N 5 0W
Córdoba, Sierra de, *Argentina* **140** 31 10 S 64 25W
Cordon, *Phil.* **57** 16 42N 121 32 E
Cordova, *Ala., U.S.A.* **115** 33 45N 87 12W
Cordova, *Alaska, U.S.A.* **102** 60 36N 145 45W
Cordova, *Ill., U.S.A.* **118** 41 41N 90 19W
Corella, *Spain* **24** 42 7N 1 48W
Corella →, *Australia* **72** 19 34 S 140 47 E
Coremas, *Brazil* **138** 7 1 S 37 58W
Corentyne →, *Guyana* **135** 5 50N 57 8W
Corfield, *Australia* **72** 21 40 S 143 21 E
Corfu = Kérkira, *Greece* **35** 39 38N 19 50 E
Corgo, *Spain* **22** 42 56N 7 25W
Corguinho, *Brazil* **137** 19 53 S 54 52W
Cori, *Italy* **28** 41 39N 12 53 E
Coria, *Spain* **22** 40 0N 6 33W
Coricudgy, Mt., *Australia* **76** 32 51 S 150 24 E
Corigliano Cálabro, *Italy* **29** 39 36N 16 31 E
Corindi, *Australia* **77** 30 1 S 153 12 E
Corinella, *Australia* **74** 38 25 S 145 25 E
Coringa Is., *Australia* **72** 16 58 S 149 58 E
Corinna, *Australia* **72** 41 35 S 145 10 E
Corinth = Kórinthos, *Greece* **35** 37 56N 22 55 E
Corinth, *Ky., U.S.A.* **119** 38 30N 84 34W
Corinth, *Miss., U.S.A.* **115** 34 54N 88 30W
Corinth, *N.Y., U.S.A.* **117** 43 15N 73 50W
Corinth, G. of = Korinthiakós Kólpos, *Greece* **35** 38 16N 22 30 E
Corinth Canal, *Greece* **35** 37 58N 23 0 E
Corinto, *Brazil* **139** 18 20 S 44 30W
Corinto, *Nic.* **128** 12 30N 87 10W
Cork, *Ireland* **15** 51 54N 8 30W
Cork □, *Ireland* **15** 51 50N 8 50W
Cork Harbour, *Ireland* **15** 51 46N 8 16W
Corlay, *France* **18** 48 20N 3 5W
Corleone, *Italy* **28** 37 48N 13 16 E
Corleto Perticara, *Italy* **29** 40 23N 16 2 E
Çorlu, *Turkey* **46** 41 11N 27 49 E
Cormack L., *Canada* **110** 60 56N 121 37W
Cormóns, *Italy* **27** 45 58N 13 29 E
Cormorant, *Canada* **111** 54 14N 100 35W
Cormorant L., *Canada* **111** 54 15N 100 50W
Corn Is. = Maiz, Is. del, *Nic.* **128** 12 15N 83 4W
Cornélio Procópio, *Brazil* **141** 23 7 S 50 40W
Cornell, *Ill., U.S.A.* **119** 40 58N 88 43W
Cornell, *Wis., U.S.A.* **120** 45 10N 91 8W
Corner Brook, *Canada* **105** 48 57N 57 58W
Corner Inlet, *Australia* **75** 38 45 S 146 20 E
Corníglio, *Italy* **26** 44 29N 10 5 E
Corning, *Ark., U.S.A.* **121** 36 27N 90 34W
Corning, *Calif., U.S.A.* **122** 39 56N 122 9W
Corning, *Iowa, U.S.A.* **118** 40 57N 94 40W
Corning, *N.Y., U.S.A.* **116** 42 10N 77 3W
Corno, Monte, *Italy* **27** 42 28N 13 34 E
Cornwall, *Canada* **109** 45 2N 74 44W
Cornwall □, *U.K.* **13** 50 26N 4 40W
Cornwallis I., *Canada* **144** 75 8N 95 0W
Corny Pt., *Australia* **73** 34 55 S 137 0 E
Coro, *Venezuela* **134** 11 25N 69 41W
Coroaci, *Brazil* **139** 18 35 S 42 17W
Coroatá, *Brazil* **138** 4 8 S 44 0W
Coroban, *Somali Rep.* **98** 3 58N 42 44 E
Corocoro, *Bolivia* **136** 17 15 S 68 28W
Corocoro, I., *Venezuela* **135** 8 30N 60 10W
Coroico, *Bolivia* **136** 16 0 S 67 50W
Coromandel, *Brazil* **139** 18 28 S 47 13W
Coromandel, *N.Z.* **80** 36 45 S 175 31 E
Coromandel Coast, *India* **51** 12 30N 81 0 E
Coromandel Pen., *N.Z.* **80** 37 0 S 175 45 E
Coromandel Ra., *N.Z.* **80** 37 0 S 175 40 E
Corona, *Australia* **73** 31 16 S 141 24 E
Corona, *Calif., U.S.A.* **125** 33 49N 117 36W
Corona, *N. Mex., U.S.A.* **123** 34 15N 105 32W
Coronada, *U.S.A.* **125** 32 45N 117 9W
Coronado, B. de, *Costa Rica* **128** 9 0N 83 40W
Coronados, G. de los, *Chile* **142** 41 40 S 74 0W
Coronados, Is. los, *U.S.A.* **125** 32 25N 117 15W
Coronation, *Canada* **110** 52 5N 111 27W
Coronation Gulf, *Canada* **102** 68 25N 110 0W
Coronation I., *Antarctica* **143** 60 45 S 46 0W
Coronation I., *U.S.A.* **110** 55 52N 134 20W
Coronation Is., *Australia* **78** 14 57 S 124 55 E
Coronda, *Argentina* **140** 31 58 S 60 56W
Coronel, *Chile* **140** 37 0 S 73 10W
Coronel Bogado, *Paraguay* **140** 27 11 S 56 18W
Coronel Dorrego, *Argentina* **140** 38 40 S 61 10W
Coronel Fabriciano, *Brazil* **139** 19 31 S 42 38W
Coronel Murta, *Brazil* **139** 16 37 S 42 11W
Coronel Oviedo, *Paraguay* **140** 25 24 S 56 30W
Coronel Ponce, *Brazil* **137** 15 34 S 55 1W
Coronel Pringles, *Argentina* **140** 38 0 S 61 30W
Coronel Suárez, *Argentina* **140** 37 30 S 61 52W
Coronel Vidal, *Argentina* **140** 37 28 S 57 45W
Corongo, *Peru* **136** 8 30 S 77 53W
Coronie □, *Surinam* **135** 5 55N 56 20W
Coropuna, Nevado, *Peru* **136** 15 30 S 72 41W
Cororooke, *Australia* **74** 38 17 S 143 31 E
Çorovoda, *Albania* **35** 40 31N 20 14 E
Corowa, *Australia* **75** 35 58 S 146 21 E
Corozal, *Belize* **127** 18 23N 88 23W
Corozal, *Colombia* **134** 9 19N 75 18W
Corps, *France* **21** 44 50N 5 56 E
Corpus, *Argentina* **141** 27 10 S 55 30W
Corpus Christi, *U.S.A.* **121** 27 50N 97 28W
Corpus Christi, L., *U.S.A.* **121** 28 5N 97 54W
Corque, *Bolivia* **136** 18 20 S 67 41W
Corral, *Chile* **142** 39 52 S 73 26W
Corral de Almaguer, *Spain* **24** 39 45N 3 10W
Corralejo, *Canary Is.* **25** 28 43N 13 53W
Corréggio, *Italy* **26** 44 46N 10 47 E
Corrente, *Brazil* **138** 10 27 S 45 10W
Corrente →, *Brazil* **139** 13 8 S 43 28W
Correntes →, *Brazil* **137** 17 38 S 55 8W
Correntes, C. das, *Mozam.* **97** 24 6 S 35 34 E
Correntina, *Brazil* **139** 13 20 S 44 39W
Corrèze □, *France* **20** 45 20N 1 45 E
Corrèze →, *France* **20** 45 10N 1 28 E
Corrib, L., *Ireland* **15** 53 5N 9 10W
Corrientes, *Argentina* **140** 27 30 S 58 45W
Corrientes □, *Argentina* **140** 28 0 S 57 0W
Corrientes →, *Argentina* **140** 30 42 S 59 38W
Corrientes →, *Peru* **136** 3 43 S 74 35W
Corrientes, C., *Colombia* **134** 5 30N 77 34W
Corrientes, C., *Cuba* **128** 21 43N 84 30W
Corrientes, C., *Mexico* **126** 20 25N 105 42W
Corrigan, *U.S.A.* **121** 31 0N 94 48W
Corrigin, *Australia* **79** 32 20 S 117 53 E
Corrowidgie, *Australia* **75** 36 56 S 148 50 E
Corry, *U.S.A.* **116** 41 55N 79 39W
Corryong, *Australia* **75** 36 12 S 147 53 E
Corse, *France* **21** 42 0N 9 0 E
Corse, C., *France* **21** 43 1N 9 25 E
Corse-du-Sud □, *France* **21** 41 45N 9 0 E
Corsica = Corse, *France* **21** 42 0N 9 0 E
Corsicana, *U.S.A.* **121** 32 5N 96 30W
Corte, *France* **21** 42 19N 9 11 E
Corte do Pinto, *Portugal* **23** 37 42N 7 29W
Cortegana, *Spain* **23** 37 52N 6 49W
Cortez, *U.S.A.* **123** 37 24N 108 35W
Cortina d'Ampezzo, *Italy* **27** 46 32N 12 9 E
Cortland, *U.S.A.* **117** 42 35N 76 11W
Cortona, *Italy* **27** 43 16N 12 0 E
Coruche, *Portugal* **23** 38 57N 8 30W
Çorum, *Turkey* **46** 40 30N 34 57 E
Corumbá, *Brazil* **137** 19 0 S 57 30W
Corumbá →, *Brazil* **139** 18 19 S 48 55W
Corumbá de Goiás, *Brazil* **139** 16 0 S 48 50W
Corumbaíba, *Brazil* **139** 18 9 S 48 34W
Coruña, La, *Spain* **22** 43 20N 8 25W
Coruña, La □, *Spain* **22** 43 10N 8 30W
Corunna = Coruña, La, *Spain* **22** 43 20N 8 25W
Corunna, *Canada* **108** 42 53N 82 26W
Corunna, *U.S.A.* **119** 42 59N 84 7W
Corvallis, *U.S.A.* **122** 44 36N 123 15W
Corvette, L. de la, *Canada* **104** 53 25N 74 3W
Corydon, *Ind., U.S.A.* **119** 38 13N 86 7W
Corydon, *Iowa, U.S.A.* **118** 40 42N 93 22W
Corydon, *Ky., U.S.A.* **119** 37 44N 87 43W
Cosalá, *Mexico* **126** 24 28N 106 40W
Cosamaloapan, *Mexico* **127** 18 23N 95 50W
Cosenza, *Italy* **29** 39 17N 16 14 E
Coshocton, *U.S.A.* **116** 40 17N 81 51W
Cosmo Newberry, *Australia* **79** 28 0 S 122 54 E
Cosne-sur-Loire, *France* **19** 47 24N 2 54 E
Coso Junction, *U.S.A.* **125** 36 3N 117 57W
Coso Pk., *U.S.A.* **125** 36 13N 117 44W
Cospeito, *Spain* **22** 43 12N 7 34W
Cosquín, *Argentina* **140** 31 15 S 64 30W
Cossato, *Italy* **26** 45 34N 8 10 E
Cossé-le-Vivien, *France* **18** 47 57N 0 54W
Cosson →, *France* **18** 47 30N 1 15 E
Costa Blanca, *Spain* **25** 38 25N 0 10W
Costa Brava, *Spain* **24** 41 30N 3 0 E
Costa del Sol, *Spain* **23** 36 30N 4 30W
Costa Dorada, *Spain* **24** 40 45N 1 15 E
Costa Mesa, *U.S.A.* **125** 33 39N 117 55W
Costa Rica ■, *Cent. Amer.* **128** 10 0N 84 0W
Costa Smeralda, *Italy* **28** 41 5N 9 35 E
Costigliole d'Asti, *Italy* **26** 44 48N 8 11 E
Costilla, *U.S.A.* **123** 37 0N 105 30W
Cosumnes →, *U.S.A.* **124** 38 14N 121 25W
Coswig, *E. Germany* **30** 51 52N 12 31 E
Cotabato, *Phil.* **57** 7 14N 124 15 E
Cotacajes →, *Bolivia* **136** 16 0 S 67 1W
Cotagaita, *Bolivia* **140** 20 45 S 65 40W
Cotahuasi, *Peru* **136** 15 12 S 72 50W
Côte d'Azur, *France* **21** 43 25N 7 10 E
Côte d'Or, *France* **19** 47 10N 4 50 E
Côte-d'Or □, *France* **19** 47 30N 4 50 E
Côte-St.-André, La, *France* **21** 45 24N 5 15 E
Coteau des Prairies, *U.S.A.* **120** 44 30N 97 0W
Coteau du Missouri, *U.S.A.* **120** 47 0N 101 0W
Coteau Landing, *Canada* **117** 45 15N 74 13W
Cotegipe, *Brazil* **139** 12 2 S 44 15W
Cotentin, *France* **18** 49 15N 1 30W
Côtes de Meuse, *France* **19** 49 15N 5 22 E
Côtes-du-Nord □, *France* **18** 48 25N 2 40W
Cotiella, *Spain* **24** 42 31N 0 19 E
Cotina →, *Yugoslavia* **33** 43 36N 18 50 E
Cotoca, *Bolivia* **137** 17 49 S 63 3W
Cotonou, *Benin* **91** 6 20N 2 25 E
Cotopaxi □, *Ecuador* **134** 0 5 S 78 55W
Cotopaxi, Vol., *Ecuador* **134** 0 40 S 78 30W
Cotronei, *Italy* **29** 39 9N 16 45 E
Cotswold Hills, *U.K.* **13** 51 42N 2 10W
Cottage Grove, *U.S.A.* **122** 43 48N 123 2W
Cottam, *Canada* **108** 42 8N 82 45W
Cottbus, *E. Germany* **30** 51 44N 14 20 E
Cottbus □, *E. Germany* **30** 51 43N 13 30 E
Cottonvale, *Australia* **77** 28 31 S 151 57 E
Cottonwood, *U.S.A.* **123** 34 48N 112 1W
Cotulla, *U.S.A.* **121** 28 26N 99 14W
Coubre, Pte. de la, *France* **20** 45 42N 1 15W
Couches, *France* **19** 46 53N 4 30 E
Couço, *Portugal* **23** 38 59N 8 17W
Coudersport, *U.S.A.* **116** 41 45N 78 1W
Coudres, Île aux, *Canada* **107** 47 24N 70 23W
Couedic, C. du, *Australia* **73** 36 5 S 136 40 E
Couëron, *France* **18** 47 13N 1 44W
Couesnon →, *France* **18** 48 38N 1 32W
Couhé, *France* **20** 46 17N 0 11 E
Coulanges-sur-Yonne, *France* **19** 47 31N 3 33 E
Coulee City, *U.S.A.* **122** 47 36N 119 18W
Coulman I., *Antarctica* **143** 73 35 S 170 0 E
Coulommiers, *France* **19** 48 50N 3 3 E
Coulonge →, *Canada* **106** 45 52N 76 46W
Coulonges-sur-l'Autize, *France* **20** 46 29N 0 36W
Coulterville, *Calif., U.S.A.* **124** 37 42N 120 12W
Coulterville, *Ill., U.S.A.* **118** 38 11N 89 36W
Council, *Alaska, U.S.A.* **102** 64 55N 163 45W
Council, *Idaho, U.S.A.* **122** 44 44N 116 26W
Council Bluffs, *U.S.A.* **120** 41 20N 95 50W
Council Grove, *U.S.A.* **120** 38 41N 96 30W
Coupeville, *U.S.A.* **124** 48 13N 122 41W
Courantyne →, *S. Amer.* **136** 5 55N 57 5W
Courcelles, *Belgium* **17** 50 28N 4 22 E
Courçon, *France* **20** 46 15N 0 50W
Couronne, C., *France* **21** 43 19N 5 3 E
Cours-la-Ville, *France* **21** 46 7N 4 19 E
Coursan, *France* **20** 43 14N 3 4 E
Courseulles-sur-Mer, *France* **18** 49 20N 0 29W
Court-St.-Etienne, *Belgium* **17** 50 38N 4 34 E
Courtenay, *Canada* **110** 49 45N 125 0W

Dengi, *Nigeria* **91** 9 25N 9 55 E
Dengkou, *China* **60** 40 18N 106 55 E
Denham, *Australia* **79** 25 56 S 113 31 E
Denham Ra., *Australia* **72** 21 55 S 147 46 E
Denham Sd., *Australia* **79** 25 45 S 113 15 E
Denia, *Spain* **25** 38 49N 0 8 E
Denial B., *Australia* **73** 32 14 S 133 32 E
Deniliquin, *Australia* **74** 35 30 S 144 58 E
Denison, *Iowa, U.S.A.* **120** 42 0N 95 18W
Denison, *Tex., U.S.A.* **121** 33 50N 96 40W
Denison Plains, *Australia* **78** 18 35 S 128 0 E
Denizli, *Turkey* **46** 37 42N 29 2 E
Denman, *Australia* **76** 32 24 S 150 42 E
Denman Glacier, *Antarctica* **143** 66 45 S 99 25 E
Denmark, *Australia* **79** 34 59 S 117 25 E
Denmark ■, *Europe* **11** 55 30N 9 0 E
Denmark Str., *Atl. Oc.* **144** 66 0N 30 0W
Dennison, *U.S.A.* **116** 40 21N 81 21W
Denpasar, *Indonesia* **56** 8 45 S 115 14 E
Denton, *Mont., U.S.A.* **122** 47 25N 109 56W
Denton, *Tex., U.S.A.* **121** 33 12N 97 10W
D'Entrecasteaux Is., *Papua N. G.* **69** 9 0 S 151 0 E
D'Entrecasteaux Pt., *Australia* **79** 34 50 S 115 57 E
Denu, *Ghana* **91** 6 4N 1 8 E
Denver, *Colo., U.S.A.* **120** 39 45N 105 0W
Denver, *Ind., U.S.A.* **119** 40 52N 86 5W
Denver, *Iowa, U.S.A.* **118** 42 40N 92 20W
Denver City, *U.S.A.* **121** 32 58N 102 48W
Deoband, *India* **48** 29 42N 77 43 E
Deobhog, *India* **50** 19 53N 82 44 E
Deogarh, *India* **50** 21 32N 84 45 E
Deoghar, *India* **49** 24 30N 86 42 E
Deolali, *India* **50** 19 58N 73 50 E
Deoli = Devli, *India* **48** 25 50N 75 20 E
Deoria, *India* **49** 26 31N 83 48 E
Deosai Mts., *Pakistan* **49** 35 40N 75 0 E
Deping, *China* **61** 37 25N 116 58 E
Deposit, *U.S.A.* **117** 42 5N 75 23W
Depot Springs, *Australia* **79** 27 55 S 120 3 E
Deputatskiy, *U.S.S.R.* **41** 69 18N 139 54 E
Dêqên, *China* **58** 28 34N 98 51 E
Deqing, *China* **59** 23 8N 111 42 E
Dera Ghazi Khan, *Pakistan* **48** 30 5N 70 43 E
Dera Ismail Khan, *Pakistan* **48** 31 50N 70 50 E
Derbent, *U.S.S.R.* **38** 42 5N 48 15 E
Derby, *Australia* **78** 17 18 S 123 38 E
Derby, *U.K.* **12** 52 55N 1 28W
Derby, *Conn., U.S.A.* **117** 41 20N 73 5W
Derby, *N.Y., U.S.A.* **116** 42 40N 78 59W
Derby □, *U.K.* **12** 52 55N 1 28W
Derg →, *U.K.* **15** 54 42N 7 26W
Derg, L., *Ireland* **15** 53 0N 8 20W
Dergachi, *U.S.S.R.* **37** 50 9N 36 11 E
Dergholm, *Australia* **74** 37 24 S 141 14 E
Dernieres Isles, *U.S.A.* **121** 29 0N 90 45W
Dêrong, *China* **58** 28 44N 99 9 E
Derrinallum, *Australia* **74** 37 57 S 143 15 E
Derriwong, *Australia* **76** 33 6 S 147 21 E
Derry = Londonderry, *U.K.* **15** 55 0N 7 20W
Derryveagh Mts., *Ireland* **15** 55 0N 8 40W
Derudub, *Sudan* **88** 17 31N 36 7 E
Derval, *France* **18** 47 40N 1 41W
Dervéni, *Greece* **35** 38 8N 22 25 E
Derwent, *Canada* **111** 53 41N 110 58W
Derwent →, *Derby, U.K.* **12** 52 53N 1 17W
Derwent →, *N. Yorks., U.K.* **12** 53 45N 0 57W
Derwent Water, L., *U.K.* **12** 54 35N 3 9W
Des Moines, *Iowa, U.S.A.* **118** 41 35N 93 37W
Des Moines, *N. Mex., U.S.A.* **121** 36 50N 103 51W
Des Moines →, *U.S.A.* **120** 40 23N 91 25W
Des Plaines, *U.S.A.* **119** 42 3N 87 52W
Des Plaines →, *U.S.A.* **119** 41 23N 88 15W
Desaguadero →, *Argentina* **140** 34 30 S 66 46W
Desaguadero →, *Bolivia* **136** 16 35 S 69 5W
Desbarats, *Canada* **108** 46 20N 83 56W
Desbiens, *Canada* **107** 48 25N 71 57W
Descanso, Pta., *Mexico* **125** 32 21N 117 3W
Descartes, *France* **20** 46 59N 0 42 E
Deschaillons, *Canada* **107** 46 32N 72 7W
Deschambault, *Canada* **107** 46 39N 71 56W
Descharme →, *Canada* **111** 56 51N 109 13W
Deschênes, *Canada* **106** 45 23N 75 48W
Deschutes →, *U.S.A.* **122** 45 30N 121 0W
Dese, *Ethiopia* **89** 11 5N 39 40 E
Deseado, C., *Chile* **142** 52 45 S 74 42W
Desenzano del Gardo, *Italy* **26** 45 28N 10 32 E
Deseronto, *Canada* **109** 44 12N 77 3W
Desert Center, *U.S.A.* **125** 33 45N 115 27W
Desert Hot Springs, *U.S.A.* **125** 33 58N 116 30W
Désirade, I., *Guadeloupe* **129** 16 18N 61 3W
Deskenatlata L., *Canada* **110** 60 55N 112 3W
Desmaraisville, *Canada* **106** 49 32N 76 9W
Desméloizes, *Canada* **106** 48 57N 79 29W
Desna →, *U.S.S.R.* **36** 50 33N 30 32 E
Desnătui →, *Romania* **34** 44 15N 23 27 E
Desolación, I., *Chile* **142** 53 0 S 74 0W
Despeñaperros, Paso, *Spain* **25** 38 24N 3 30W
Despotovac, *Yugoslavia* **33** 44 6N 21 30 E
Dessau, *E. Germany* **30** 51 49N 12 15 E
Dessel, *Belgium* **17** 51 15N 5 7 E
Dessye = Dese, *Ethiopia* **89** 11 5N 39 40 E
D'Estrees B., *Australia* **73** 35 55 S 137 45 E
Desuri, *India* **48** 25 18N 73 35 E
Desvres, *France* **19** 50 40N 1 48 E
Det Udom, *Thailand* **54** 14 54N 105 5 E
Dete, *Zambia* **93** 18 38 S 26 50 E
Detinja →, *Yugoslavia* **33** 43 51N 19 45 E
Detmold, *W. Germany* **30** 51 55N 8 50 E
Detour Pt., *U.S.A.* **114** 45 37N 86 35W
Detroit, *Mich., U.S.A.* **116** 42 23N 83 5W
Detroit, *Tex., U.S.A.* **121** 33 40N 95 10W
Detroit Lakes, *U.S.A.* **120** 46 50N 95 50W
Deurne, *Belgium* **17** 51 12N 4 24 E
Deurne, *Neths.* **17** 51 27N 5 49 E
Deutsche Bucht, *W. Germany* **30** 54 0N 8 0 E
Deutschlandsberg, *Austria* **33** 46 49N 15 14 E
Deux-Sèvres □, *France* **18** 46 35N 0 20W
Deva, *Romania* **34** 45 53N 22 55 E
Devakottai, *India* **51** 9 55N 78 45 E
Devaprayag, *India* **49** 30 13N 78 35 E
Dévaványa, *Hungary* **33** 47 2N 20 59 E
Deveci Daği, *Turkey* **38** 40 10N 36 0 E
Devenish, *Australia* **74** 36 20 S 145 54 E
Deventer, *Neths.* **16** 52 15N 6 10 E
Devenyns, L., *Canada* **107** 47 5N 73 50W
Deveron →, *U.K.* **14** 57 40N 2 31W
Devgad, I., *India* **51** 14 48N 74 5 E
Devgadh Bariya, *India* **48** 22 40N 73 55 E
Devil River Pk., *N.Z.* **81** 40 56 S 172 37 E
Devils Den, *U.S.A.* **124** 35 46N 119 58W
Devils Lake, *U.S.A.* **120** 48 5N 98 50W
Devils Paw, *Canada* **110** 58 47N 134 0W
Devil's Pt., *Sri Lanka* **51** 9 26N 80 6 E
Devil's Pt., *Vanuatu* **68** 17 44 S 168 11 E
Devizes, *U.K.* **13** 51 21N 2 0W
Devli, *India* **48** 25 50N 75 20 E
Devnya, *Bulgaria* **34** 43 13N 27 33 E
Devolii →, *Albania* **35** 40 57N 20 15 E
Devon, *Canada* **110** 53 24N 113 44W
Devon I., *Canada* **144** 75 10N 85 0W
Devonport, *Australia* **72** 41 10 S 146 22 E
Devonport, *N.Z.* **80** 36 49 S 174 49 E
Devonport, *U.K.* **13** 50 23N 4 11W
Devonshire □, *U.K.* **13** 50 50N 3 40W
Dewas, *India* **48** 22 59N 76 3 E
Dewetsdorp, *S. Africa* **96** 29 33 S 26 39 E
Dewsbury, *U.K.* **12** 53 42N 1 38W
Dexing, *China* **59** 28 46N 117 30 E
Dexter, *Mich., U.S.A.* **119** 42 20N 83 53W
Dexter, *Mo., U.S.A.* **121** 36 50N 90 0W
Dexter, *N. Mex., U.S.A.* **121** 33 15N 104 25W
Dey-Dey, L., *Australia* **79** 29 12 S 131 4 E
Deyang, *China* **58** 31 3N 104 27 E
Deyhūk, *Iran* **47** 33 15N 57 30 E
Deyyer, *Iran* **47** 27 55N 51 55 E
Dezadeash L., *Canada* **110** 60 28N 136 58W
Dezfūl, *Iran* **46** 32 20N 48 30 E
Dezhneva, Mys, *U.S.S.R.* **41** 66 5N 169 40W
Dezhou, *China* **60** 37 26N 116 18 E
Dhafra, *Oman* **47** 23 20N 54 0 E
Dhahaban, *Si. Arabia* **88** 21 58N 39 3 E
Dhahira, *Oman* **47** 23 40N 57 0 E
Dhahran = Aẓ Ẓahrān, *Si. Arabia* **46** 26 10N 50 7 E
Dhaka, *Bangla.* **52** 23 43N 90 26 E
Dhaka □, *Bangla.* **52** 24 25N 90 25 E
Dhamangaon, *India* **50** 20 45N 78 15 E
Dhamar, *Yemen* **45** 14 30N 44 20 E
Dhamási, *Greece* **35** 39 43N 22 11 E
Dhampur, *India* **49** 29 19N 78 33 E
Dhamtari, *India* **50** 20 42N 81 35 E
Dhanbad, *India* **49** 23 50N 86 30 E
Dhankuta, *Nepal* **49** 26 55N 87 40 E
Dhanora, *India* **50** 20 20N 80 22 E
Dhar, *India* **48** 22 35N 75 26 E
Dharampur, *Gujarat, India* **50** 20 32N 73 17 E
Dharampur, *Mad. P., India* **48** 22 13N 75 18 E
Dharamsala = Dharmsala, *India* **48** 32 16N 76 23 E
Dharapuram, *India* **51** 10 45N 77 34 E
Dharmapuri, *India* **51** 12 10N 78 10 E
Dharmavaram, *India* **51** 14 29N 77 44 E
Dharmsala, *India* **48** 32 16N 76 23 E
Dharwad, *India* **51** 15 22N 75 15 E
Dhaulagiri, *Nepal* **49** 28 39N 83 28 E
Dhebar, L., *India* **48** 24 10N 74 0 E
Dhenkanal, *India* **50** 20 45N 85 35 E
Dhenoúsa, *Greece* **35** 37 8N 25 48 E
Dheskáti, *Greece* **35** 39 55N 21 49 E
Dhespotikó, *Greece* **35** 36 57N 24 58 E
Dhestina, *Greece* **35** 38 25N 22 31 E
Dhimitsána, *Greece* **35** 37 36N 22 3 E
Dhírfis, *Greece* **35** 38 40N 23 54 E
Dhodhekánisos, *Greece* **35** 36 35N 27 0 E
Dholiana, *Greece* **35** 39 54N 20 32 E
Dholka, *India* **48** 22 44N 72 29 E
Dhoraji, *India* **48** 21 45N 70 37 E
Dhoxáton, *Greece* **35** 41 9N 24 16 E
Dhrangadhra, *India* **48** 22 59N 71 31 E
Dhrol, *India* **48** 22 33N 70 25 E
Dhubaibah, *Oman* **47** 23 25N 54 35 E
Dhuburi, *India* **52** 26 2N 89 59 E
Dhulasar, *Bangla.* **52** 21 52N 90 14 E
Dhule, *India* **50** 20 58N 74 50 E
Dhupdhara, *India* **52** 26 10N 91 4 E
Di Linh, *Vietnam* **55** 11 35N 108 4 E
Di Linh, Cao Nguyen, *Vietnam* **55** 11 30N 108 0 E
Día, *Greece* **35** 35 26N 25 13 E
Diablo, Mt., *U.S.A.* **124** 37 53N 121 56W
Diablo Range, *U.S.A.* **124** 37 0N 121 5W
Diafarabé, *Mali* **90** 14 9N 4 57W
Diagonal, *U.S.A.* **118** 40 49N 94 20W
Diala, *Mali* **90** 14 10N 10 0W
Dialakoro, *Mali* **90** 12 18N 7 54W
Diallassagou, *Mali* **90** 13 47N 3 41W
Diamante, *Argentina* **140** 32 5 S 60 40W
Diamante →, *Argentina* **140** 34 30 S 66 46W
Diamantina, *Brazil* **139** 18 17 S 43 40W
Diamantina →, *Australia* **73** 26 45 S 139 10 E
Diamantino, *Brazil* **137** 14 30 S 56 30W
Diamond Harbour, *India* **49** 22 11N 88 14 E
Diamond Is., *Australia* **72** 17 25 S 151 5 E
Diamond Mts., *U.S.A.* **122** 40 0N 115 58W
Diamond Springs, *U.S.A.* **124** 38 42N 120 49W
Diamondville, *U.S.A.* **122** 41 51N 110 30W
Dianbai, *China* **59** 21 33N 111 0 E
Diancheng, *China* **59** 21 30N 111 4 E
Diano Marina, *Italy* **26** 43 55N 8 3 E
Dianópolis, *Brazil* **139** 11 38 S 46 50W
Dianra, *Ivory C.* **90** 8 45N 6 14W
Diapaga, *Burkina Faso* **91** 12 5N 1 46 E
Diapangou, *Burkina Faso* **91** 12 5N 0 10 E
Diapur, *Australia* **74** 36 19 S 141 29 E
Diariguila, *Guinea* **90** 10 35N 10 2W
Dībā, *Oman* **47** 25 45N 56 16 E
Dibaya, *Zaïre* **95** 6 30 S 22 57 E
Dibaya-Lubue, *Zaïre* **95** 4 12 S 19 54 E
Dibbi, *Ethiopia* **89** 4 10N 41 52 E
Dibble Glacier Tongue, *Antarctica* **143** 66 8 S 134 32 E
Dibete, *Botswana* **96** 23 45 S 26 32 E
Dibrugarh, *India* **52** 27 29N 94 55 E
Dickeyville, *U.S.A.* **118** 42 38N 90 36W
Dickinson, *U.S.A.* **120** 46 50N 102 48W
Dickson, *U.S.A.* **115** 36 5N 87 22W
Dickson, *U.S.S.R.* **40** 73 40N 80 5 E
Dickson City, *U.S.A.* **117** 41 29N 75 40W
Dicomano, *Italy* **27** 43 53N 11 30 E
Didam, *Neths.* **16** 51 57N 6 8 E
Didesa, W. →, *Ethiopia* **89** 10 2N 35 32 E
Didiéni, *Mali* **90** 13 53N 8 6W
Didsbury, *Canada* **110** 51 35N 114 10W
Didwana, *India* **48** 27 23N 74 36 E
Die, *France* **21** 44 47N 5 22 E
Diébougou, *Burkina Faso* **90** 11 0N 3 15W
Diefenbaker L., *Canada* **111** 51 0N 106 55W
Diego Garcia, *Ind. Oc.* **53** 7 50 S 72 50 E
Diekirch, *Lux.* **17** 49 52N 6 10 E
Diélette, *France* **18** 49 33N 1 52W
Diéma, *Mali* **90** 14 32N 9 12W
Diémbéring, *Senegal* **90** 12 29N 16 47W
Diemen, *Neths.* **16** 52 21N 4 58 E
Dien Ban, *Vietnam* **54** 15 53N 108 16 E
Dien Bien, *Vietnam* **54** 21 20N 103 0 E
Dien Khanh, *Vietnam* **55** 12 15N 109 6 E
Diepenbeek, *Belgium* **17** 50 54N 5 25 E
Diepenheim, *Neths.* **16** 52 12N 6 33 E
Diepenveen, *Neths.* **16** 52 18N 6 9 E
Diepholz, *W. Germany* **30** 52 37N 8 22 E
Dieppe, *France* **18** 49 54N 1 4 E
Dieren, *Neths.* **16** 52 3N 6 6 E
Dierks, *U.S.A.* **121** 34 9N 94 0W
Diessen, *Neths.* **17** 51 29N 5 10 E
Diest, *Belgium* **17** 50 58N 5 4 E
Dieterich, *U.S.A.* **119** 39 4N 88 23W
Dieulefit, *France* **21** 44 32N 5 4 E
Dieuze, *France* **19** 48 49N 6 43 E
Diever, *Neths.* **16** 52 51N 6 19 E
Differdange, *Lux.* **17** 49 31N 5 54 E
Dig, *India* **48** 27 28N 77 20 E
Digba, *Zaïre* **92** 4 25N 25 48 E
Digboi, *India* **52** 27 23N 95 38 E
Digby, *Canada* **105** 44 38N 65 50W
Diggers Rest, *Australia* **74** 37 38 S 144 43 E
Digges, *Canada* **111** 58 40N 94 0W
Digges Is., *Canada* **103** 62 40N 77 50W
Diggora West, *Australia* **74** 36 21 S 144 32 E
Dighinala, *Bangla.* **52** 23 15N 92 5 E
Dighton, *U.S.A.* **120** 38 30N 100 26W
Diglur, *India* **50** 18 34N 77 33 E
Digne, *France* **21** 44 5N 6 12 E
Digoin, *France* **20** 46 29N 3 58 E
Digos, *Phil.* **57** 6 45N 125 20 E
Digranes, *Iceland* **8** 66 4N 14 44W
Digras, *India* **50** 20 6N 77 45 E
Digul →, *Indonesia* **57** 7 7 S 138 42 E
Dijlah, Nahr →, *Asia* **46** 31 0N 47 25 E
Dijle →, *Belgium* **17** 50 58N 4 41 E
Dijon, *France* **19** 47 20N 5 0 E
Dikala, *Sudan* **89** 4 45N 31 28 E
Dikkil, *Djibouti* **89** 11 8N 42 20 E
Dikomu di Kai, *Botswana* **96** 24 58 S 24 36 E
Diksmuide, *Belgium* **17** 51 2N 2 52 E
Dikson = Dickson, *U.S.S.R.* **40** 73 40N 80 5 E
Dikwa, *Nigeria* **91** 12 4N 13 30 E
Dila, *Ethiopia* **89** 6 21N 38 22 E
Dilbeek, *Belgium* **17** 50 51N 4 17 E
Dili, *Indonesia* **57** 8 39 S 125 34 E
Dilizhan, *U.S.S.R.* **39** 40 46N 44 57 E
Dilkoon, *Australia* **77** 29 30 S 152 59 E
Dillard, *U.S.A.* **118** 37 44N 91 13W
Dillenburg, *W. Germany* **30** 50 44N 8 17 E
Dilley, *U.S.A.* **121** 28 40N 99 12W
Dilling, *Sudan* **89** 12 3N 29 35 E
Dillingen, *W. Germany* **31** 48 32N 10 29 E
Dillon, *Canada* **111** 55 56N 108 35W
Dillon, *Mont., U.S.A.* **122** 45 9N 112 36W
Dillon, *S.C., U.S.A.* **115** 34 26N 79 20W
Dillon →, *Canada* **111** 55 56N 108 56W
Dillsboro, *U.S.A.* **119** 39 1N 85 4W
Dilolo, *Zaïre* **95** 10 28 S 22 18 E
Dilsen, *Belgium* **17** 51 2N 5 44 E
Dilston, *Australia* **72** 41 22 S 147 10 E
Dimapur, *India* **52** 25 54N 93 45 E
Dimas, *Mexico* **126** 23 43N 106 47W
Dimashq, *Syria* **46** 33 30N 36 18 E
Dimbaza, *S. Africa* **97** 32 50 S 27 14 E
Dimbelenge, *Zaïre* **95** 5 33 S 23 7 E
Dimbokro, *Ivory C.* **90** 6 45N 4 46W
Dimboola, *Australia* **74** 36 28 S 142 7 E
Dîmboviţa →, *Romania* **34** 44 5N 26 35 E
Dîmbovnic →, *Romania* **34** 44 28N 25 18 E
Dimbulah, *Australia* **72** 17 8 S 145 4 E
Dimitrovgrad, *Bulgaria* **35** 42 5N 25 35 E
Dimitrovgrad, *U.S.S.R.* **37** 54 14N 49 39 E
Dimitrovgrad, *Yugoslavia* **33** 43 0N 22 48 E
Dimitrovo = Pernik, *Bulgaria* **34** 42 35N 23 2 E
Dimmitt, *U.S.A.* **121** 34 36N 102 16W
Dimo, *Sudan* **89** 5 19N 29 10 E
Dimona, *Israel* **44** 31 2N 35 1 E
Dimovo, *Bulgaria* **34** 43 43N 22 50 E
Dinagat, *Phil.* **57** 10 10N 125 40 E
Dinajpur, *Bangla.* **52** 25 33N 88 43 E
Dinan, *France* **18** 48 28N 2 2W
Dinant, *Belgium* **17** 50 16N 4 55 E
Dinapur, *India* **49** 25 38N 85 5 E
Dinar, *Turkey* **46** 38 5N 30 15 E
Dinara Planina, *Yugoslavia* **27** 44 0N 16 30 E
Dinard, *France* **18** 48 38N 2 6W
Dinaric Alps = Dinara Planina, *Yugoslavia* **27** 44 0N 16 30 E
Dinder, Nahr ed →, *Sudan* **89** 14 6N 33 40 E
Dindi →, *India* **51** 16 24N 78 15 E
Dindigul, *India* **51** 10 25N 78 0 E
Ding Xian, *China* **60** 38 30N 114 59 E
Dingbian, *China* **60** 37 35N 107 32 E
Dingee, *Australia* **74** 36 22 S 144 15 E
Dingelstädt, *E. Germany* **30** 51 19N 10 19 E
Dinghai, *China* **59** 30 1N 122 6 E
Dingle, *Ireland* **15** 52 9N 10 17W
Dingle B., *Ireland* **15** 52 3N 10 20W
Dingmans Ferry, *U.S.A.* **117** 41 13N 74 55W
Dingnan, *China* **59** 24 45N 115 0 E
Dingo, *Australia* **72** 23 38 S 149 19 E
Dingolfing, *W. Germany* **31** 48 38N 12 30 E
Dingtao, *China* **60** 35 5N 115 35 E
Dinguiraye, *Guinea* **90** 11 18N 10 49W
Dingwall, *U.K.* **14** 57 36N 4 26W
Dingxi, *China* **60** 35 30N 104 33 E
Dingxiang, *China* **60** 38 30N 112 58 E
Dingyuan, *China* **59** 32 32N 117 41 E
Dinh, Mui, *Vietnam* **55** 11 22N 109 1 E
Dinh Lap, *Vietnam* **54** 21 33N 107 6 E
Dinhata, *India* **52** 26 8N 89 27 E
Dinkel →, *Neths.* **16** 52 30N 6 58 E
Dinokwe, *Botswana* **96** 23 29 S 26 37 E
Dinosaur National Monument, *U.S.A.* **122** 40 30N 108 58W
Dinslaken, *W. Germany* **17** 51 34N 6 41 E
Dinsor, *Somali Rep.* **98** 2 24N 42 59 E
Dintel →, *Neths.* **17** 51 39N 4 22 E
Dinteloord, *Neths.* **17** 51 38N 4 22 E
Dinuba, *U.S.A.* **124** 36 31N 119 22W
Dinxperlo, *Neths.* **16** 51 52N 6 30 E
Dio, *Sweden* **11** 56 37N 14 15 E
Diósgyör, *Hungary* **33** 48 7N 20 43 E
Diourbel, *Senegal* **90** 14 39N 16 12W
Diphu Pass, *India* **52** 28 9N 97 20 E
Diplo, *Pakistan* **48** 24 35N 69 35 E
Dipolog, *Phil.* **57** 8 36N 123 20 E
Dipşa, *Romania* **34** 46 58N 24 27 E
Dipton, *N.Z.* **81** 45 54 S 168 22 E
Dir, *Pakistan* **47** 35 8N 71 59 E
Diré, *Mali* **90** 16 20N 3 25W
Dire Dawa, *Ethiopia* **89** 9 35N 41 45 E
Diriamba, *Nic.* **128** 11 51N 86 19W
Dirico, *Angola* **95** 17 50 S 20 42 E
Dirk Hartog I., *Australia* **79** 25 50 S 113 5 E
Dirkou, *Niger* **87** 19 1N 12 53 E
Dirranbandi, *Australia* **73** 28 33 S 148 17 E
Disa, *India* **48** 24 18N 72 10 E

Disa, *Sudan* **89** 12 5N 34 15 E
Disappointment, C., *U.S.A.* **122** 46 20N 124 0W
Disappointment L., *Australia* **78** 23 20 S 122 40 E
Disaster B., *Australia* **75** 37 15 S 150 0 E
Discovery B., *Australia* **74** 38 10 S 140 40 E
Disentis, *Switz.* **31** 46 42N 8 50 E
Dishna, *Egypt* **88** 26 9N 32 32 E
Disina, *Nigeria* **91** 11 35N 9 50 E
Disko, *Greenland* **144** 69 45N 53 30W
Disko Bugt, *Greenland* **144** 69 10N 52 0W
Disna, *U.S.S.R.* **36** 55 32N 28 11 E
Disna →, *U.S.S.R.* **36** 55 34N 28 12 E
Disney Reef, *Tonga* **68** 19 17 S 174 7W
Dison, *Belgium* **17** 50 37N 5 51 E
Disraëli, *Canada* **107** 45 54N 71 21W
Disteghil Sar, *Pakistan* **49** 36 20N 75 12 E
Distrito Federal □, *Brazil* **139** 15 45 S 47 45W
Distrito Federal □, *Venezuela* **134** 10 30N 66 55W
Disûq, *Egypt* **88** 31 8N 30 35 E
Ditu, *Zaïre* **95** 5 23 S 21 27 E
Diu, *India* **48** 20 45N 70 58 E
Dives →, *France* **18** 49 18N 0 7W
Dives-sur-Mer, *France* **18** 49 18N 0 8W
Divi Pt., *India* **51** 15 59N 81 9 E
Divichi, *U.S.S.R.* **39** 41 15N 48 57 E
Divide, *U.S.A.* **122** 45 48N 112 47W
Dividing Ra., *Australia* **79** 27 45 S 116 0 E
Divinópolis, *Brazil* **139** 20 10 S 44 54W
Divisões, Serra dos, *Brazil* **139** 17 0 S 51 0W
Divnoye, *U.S.S.R.* **39** 45 55N 43 21 E
Divo, *Ivory C.* **90** 5 48N 5 15W
Dīwāl Kol, *Afghan.* **48** 34 23N 67 52 E
Dix →, *U.S.A.* **119** 37 49N 84 44W
Dixie Mt., *U.S.A.* **124** 39 55N 120 16W
Dixon, *Calif., U.S.A.* **124** 38 27N 121 49W
Dixon, *Ill., U.S.A.* **118** 41 50N 89 30W
Dixon, *Iowa, U.S.A.* **118** 41 45N 90 47W
Dixon, *Mo., U.S.A.* **118** 37 59N 92 6W
Dixon, *Mont., U.S.A.* **122** 47 19N 114 25W
Dixon, *N. Mex., U.S.A.* **123** 36 15N 105 57W
Dixon Entrance, *U.S.A.* **110** 54 30N 132 0W
Dixonville, *Canada* **110** 56 32N 117 40W
Dixville, *Canada* **107** 45 4N 71 46W
Diyarbakir, *Turkey* **46** 37 55N 40 18 E
Diz Chah, *Iran* **47** 35 30N 55 30 E
Djado, *Niger* **87** 21 4N 12 14 E
Djado, Plateau du, *Niger* **87** 21 29N 12 21 E
Djakarta = Jakarta, *Indonesia* **57** 6 9 S 106 49 E
Djamâa, *Algeria* **85** 33 32N 5 59 E
Djamba, *Angola* **95** 16 45 S 13 58 E
Djambala, *Congo* **94** 2 32 S 14 30 E
Djanet, *Algeria* **85** 24 35N 9 32 E
Djaul I., *Papua N. G.* **69** 2 58 S 150 57 E
Djawa = Jawa, *Indonesia* **57** 7 0 S 110 0 E
Djebiniana, *Tunisia* **86** 35 1N 11 0 E
Djédaa, *Chad* **87** 13 31N 18 34 E
Djelfa, *Algeria* **85** 34 40N 3 15 E
Djema, *C.A.R.* **92** 6 3N 25 15 E
Djember, *Chad* **87** 10 25N 17 50 E
Djendel, *Algeria* **85** 36 15N 2 25 E
Djeneïene, *Tunisia* **86** 31 45N 10 9 E
Djenné, *Mali* **90** 14 0N 4 30W
Djenoun, Garet el, *Algeria* **85** 25 4N 5 31 E
Djerba, *Tunisia* **86** 33 52N 10 51 E
Djerid, Chott, *Tunisia* **86** 33 42N 8 30 E
Djiba, *Gabon* **94** 1 20 S 13 9 E
Djibo, *Burkina Faso* **91** 14 9N 1 35W
Djibouti, *Djibouti* **89** 11 30N 43 5 E
Djibouti ■, *Africa* **89** 12 0N 43 0 E
Djolu, *Zaïre* **94** 0 35N 22 5 E
Djougou, *Benin* **91** 9 40N 1 45 E
Djoum, *Cameroon* **94** 2 41N 12 35 E
Djourab, *Chad* **87** 16 40N 18 50 E
Djugu, *Zaïre* **92** 1 55N 30 35 E
Djúpivogur, *Iceland* **8** 64 39N 14 17W
Djursholm, *Sweden* **10** 59 25N 18 6 E
Djursland, *Denmark* **11** 56 27N 10 45 E
Dmitriev-Lgovskiy, *U.S.S.R.* **36** 52 10N 35 0 E
Dmitriya Lapteva, Proliv, *U.S.S.R.* **41** 73 0N 140 0 E
Dmitrov, *U.S.S.R.* **37** 56 25N 37 32 E
Dmitrovsk-Orlovskiy, *U.S.S.R.* **36** 52 29N 35 10 E
Dnepr →, *U.S.S.R.* **38** 46 30N 32 18 E
Dneprodzerzhinsk, *U.S.S.R.* **38** 48 32N 34 37 E
Dneprodzerzhinskoye Vdkhr., *U.S.S.R.* **38** 49 0N 34 0 E
Dnepropetrovsk, *U.S.S.R.* **38** 48 30N 35 0 E
Dneprorudnoye, *U.S.S.R.* **38** 47 21N 34 58 E
Dnestr →, *U.S.S.R.* **38** 46 18N 30 17 E
Dnestrovski = Belgorod, *U.S.S.R.* **38** 50 35N 36 35 E
Dnieper = Dnepr →, *U.S.S.R.* **38** 46 30N 32 18 E
Dniester = Dnestr →, *U.S.S.R.* **38** 46 18N 30 17 E
Dno, *U.S.S.R.* **36** 57 50N 29 58 E
Doan Hung, *Vietnam* **54** 21 30N 105 10 E
Doba, *Chad* **87** 8 40N 16 50 E
Dobbiaco, *Italy* **27** 46 44N 12 13 E
Dobbyn, *Australia* **72** 19 44 S 140 2 E
Döbeln, *E. Germany* **30** 51 7N 13 10 E
Doberai, Jazirah, *Indonesia* **57** 1 25 S 133 0 E
Dobiegniew, *Poland* **32** 52 59N 15 45 E
Doblas, *Argentina* **140** 37 5 S 64 0W
Dobo, *Indonesia* **57** 5 45 S 134 15 E
Doboj, *Yugoslavia* **33** 44 46N 18 6 E
Dobra, *Dîmbovita, Romania* **34** 44 52N 25 40 E
Dobra, *Hunedoara, Romania* **34** 45 54N 22 36 E
Dobreta-Turnu-Severin, *Romania* **34** 44 39N 22 41 E
Dobrinishta, *Bulgaria* **35** 41 49N 23 34 E
Dobrodzień, *Poland* **32** 50 45N 18 25 E
Dobropole, *U.S.S.R.* **38** 48 25N 37 2 E
Dobruja, *Romania* **34** 44 30N 28 15 E
Dobrush, *U.S.S.R.* **37** 52 28N 30 19 E
Dobtong, *Sudan* **89** 6 25N 31 40 E
Doc, Mui, *Vietnam* **54** 17 58N 106 30 E
Doce →, *Brazil* **139** 19 37 S 39 49W
Doda, *India* **49** 33 10N 75 34 E
Dodecanese = Dhodhekánisos, *Greece* **35** 36 35N 27 0 E
Dodewaard, *Neths.* **16** 51 55N 5 39 E
Dodge Center, *U.S.A.* **120** 44 1N 92 50W
Dodge City, *U.S.A.* **121** 37 42N 100 0W
Dodge L., *Canada* **111** 59 50N 105 36W
Dodgeville, *U.S.A.* **118** 42 55N 90 8W
Dodo, *Sudan* **89** 5 10N 29 57 E
Dodola, *Ethiopia* **89** 6 59N 39 11 E
Dodoma, *Tanzania* **92** 6 8 S 35 45 E
Dodoma □, *Tanzania* **92** 6 0 S 36 0 E
Dodsland, *Canada* **111** 51 50N 108 45W
Dodson, *U.S.A.* **122** 48 23N 108 16W
Doesburg, *Neths.* **16** 52 1N 6 9 E
Doetinchem, *Neths.* **16** 51 59N 6 18 E
Dog Creek, *Canada* **110** 51 35N 122 14W
Dog L., *Man., Canada* **111** 51 2N 98 31W
Dog L., *Ont., Canada* **104** 48 48N 89 30W
Dogger Bank, *N. Sea* **6** 54 50N 2 0 E
Dogliani, *Italy* **26** 44 35N 7 55 E
Dōgo, *Japan* **64** 36 15N 133 16 E
Dōgo-San, *Japan* **64** 35 2N 133 13 E
Dogondoutchi, *Niger* **91** 13 38N 4 2 E
Dogran, *Pakistan* **48** 31 48N 73 35 E
Doguéraoua, *Niger* **91** 14 0N 5 31 E
Doi, *Indonesia* **57** 2 14N 127 49 E
Doi Luang, *Thailand* **54** 18 30N 101 0 E
Doi Saket, *Thailand* **54** 18 52N 99 9 E
Doig →, *Canada* **110** 56 25N 120 40W
Dois Irmãos, Sa., *Brazil* **138** 9 0 S 42 30W
Dokka, *Norway* **9** 60 49N 10 7 E
Dokka →, *Norway* **10** 61 7N 10 0 E
Dokkum, *Neths.* **16** 53 20N 5 59 E
Dokkumer Ee →, *Neths.* **16** 53 18N 5 52 E
Dokri, *Pakistan* **48** 27 25N 68 7 E
Dol-de-Bretagne, *France* **18** 48 34N 1 47W
Doland, *U.S.A.* **120** 44 55N 98 5W
Dolbeau, *Canada* **107** 48 53N 72 18W
Dole, *France* **19** 47 7N 5 31 E
Doleib, Wadi →, *Sudan* **89** 12 10N 33 15 E
Dolgellau, *U.K.* **12** 52 44N 3 53W
Dolgelley = Dolgellau, *U.K.* **12** 52 44N 3 53W
Dolginovo, *U.S.S.R.* **36** 54 39N 27 29 E
Dolianova, *Italy* **28** 39 23N 9 11 E
Dolinskaya, *U.S.S.R.* **38** 48 6N 32 46 E
Dollart, *Neths.* **16** 53 20N 7 10 E
Dolna Banya, *Bulgaria* **34** 42 18N 23 44 E
Dolni Dŭbnik, *Bulgaria* **34** 43 24N 24 26 E
Dolo, *Ethiopia* **89** 4 11N 42 3 E
Dolo, *Italy* **27** 45 25N 12 4 E
Dolomites = Dolomiti, *Italy* **27** 46 30N 11 40 E
Dolomiti, *Italy* **27** 46 30N 11 40 E
Dolores, *Argentina* **140** 36 20 S 57 40W
Dolores, *Uruguay* **140** 33 34 S 58 15W
Dolores, *U.S.A.* **123** 37 30N 108 30W
Dolores →, *U.S.A.* **123** 38 49N 108 17W
Dolphin, C., *Falk. Is.* **142** 51 10 S 59 0W
Dolphin and Union Str., *Canada* **102** 69 5N 114 45W
Dolton, *U.S.A.* **119** 41 38N 87 36W
Dom Joaquim, *Brazil* **139** 18 57 S 43 16W
Dom Pedrito, *Brazil* **141** 31 0 S 54 40W
Dom Pedro, *Brazil* **138** 4 59 S 44 27W
Doma, *Nigeria* **91** 8 25N 8 18 E
Domasi, *Malawi* **93** 15 15 S 35 22 E
Domazlice, *Czech.* **32** 49 28N 13 0 E
Dombarovskiy, *U.S.S.R.* **40** 50 46N 59 32 E
Dombås, *Norway* **9** 62 4N 9 8 E
Dombasle-sur-Meurthe, *France* **19** 48 38N 6 21 E
Dombes, *France* **21** 46 0N 5 0 E
Dombóvár, *Hungary* **33** 46 21N 18 9 E
Domburg, *Neths.* **17** 51 34N 3 30 E
Domérat, *France* **20** 46 21N 2 32 E
Domett, *N.Z.* **81** 42 53 S 173 12 E
Domeyko, *Chile* **140** 29 0 S 71 0W
Domeyko, Cordillera, *Chile* **140** 24 30 S 69 0W
Domfront, *France* **18** 48 37N 0 40W
Dominador, *Chile* **140** 24 21 S 69 20W
Dominica ■, *W. Indies* **129** 15 20N 61 20W
Dominica Passage, *W. Indies* **129** 15 10N 61 20W
Dominican Rep. ■, *W. Indies* **129** 19 0N 70 30W
Domiongo, *Zaïre* **95** 4 37 S 21 15 E
Dömitz, *E. Germany* **30** 53 9N 11 13 E
Domme, *France* **20** 44 48N 1 12 E
Dommel →, *Neths.* **17** 51 30N 5 20 E
Domo, *Ethiopia* **98** 7 50N 47 10 E
Domodóssola, *Italy* **26** 46 6N 8 19 E
Dompaire, *France* **19** 48 14N 6 14 E
Dompierre-sur-Besbre, *France* **20** 46 31N 3 41 E
Dompim, *Ghana* **90** 5 10N 2 5W
Domrémy-la-Pucelle, *France* **19** 48 26N 5 40 E
Domsjö, *Sweden* **10** 63 16N 18 41 E
Domville, Mt., *Australia* **77** 28 1 S 151 15 E
Domvraína, *Greece* **35** 38 15N 22 59 E
Domžale, *Yugoslavia* **27** 46 9N 14 35 E
Don →, *India* **51** 16 20N 76 15 E
Don →, *England, U.K.* **12** 53 41N 0 51W
Don →, *Scotland, U.K.* **14** 57 14N 2 5W
Don →, *U.S.S.R.* **39** 47 4N 39 18 E
Don, C., *Australia* **78** 11 18 S 131 46 E
Don Benito, *Spain* **23** 38 53N 5 51W
Don Duong, *Vietnam* **55** 11 51N 108 35 E
Don Martín, Presa de, *Mexico* **126** 27 30N 100 50W
Dona Ana, *Mozam.* **93** 17 25 S 35 5 E
Donaghadee, *U.K.* **15** 54 38N 5 32W
Donald, *Australia* **74** 36 23 S 143 0 E
Donalda, *Canada* **110** 52 35N 112 34W
Donaldsonville, *U.S.A.* **121** 30 2N 91 0W
Donalsonville, *U.S.A.* **115** 31 3N 84 52W
Donau →, *Austria* **33** 48 10N 17 0 E
Donaueschingen, *W. Germany* **31** 47 57N 8 30 E
Donauwörth, *W. Germany* **31** 48 42N 10 47 E
Doncaster, *U.K.* **12** 53 31N 1 9W
Dondo, *Angola* **95** 9 45 S 14 25 E
Dondo, *Mozam.* **93** 19 33 S 34 46 E
Dondo, *Zaïre* **94** 4 11N 21 39 E
Dondo, Teluk, *Indonesia* **57** 0 29N 120 30 E
Dondra Head, *Sri Lanka* **51** 5 55N 80 40 E
Donegal, *Ireland* **15** 54 39N 8 8W
Donegal □, *Ireland* **15** 54 53N 8 0W
Donegal B., *Ireland* **15** 54 30N 8 35W
Donets →, *U.S.S.R.* **39** 47 33N 40 55 E
Donetsk, *U.S.S.R.* **38** 48 0N 37 45 E
Dong Ba Thin, *Vietnam* **55** 12 8N 109 13 E
Dong Dang, *Vietnam* **54** 21 54N 106 42 E
Dong Giam, *Vietnam* **54** 19 25N 105 31 E
Dong Ha, *Vietnam* **54** 16 55N 107 8 E
Dong Hene, *Laos* **54** 16 40N 105 18 E
Dong Hoi, *Vietnam* **54** 17 29N 106 36 E
Dong Jiang →, *China* **59** 23 6N 114 0 E
Dong Khe, *Vietnam* **54** 22 26N 106 27 E
Dong Ujimqin Qi, *China* **60** 45 32N 116 55 E
Dong Van, *Vietnam* **54** 23 16N 105 22 E
Dong Xoai, *Vietnam* **55** 11 32N 106 55 E
Donga, *Nigeria* **91** 7 45N 10 2 E
Dong'an, *China* **59** 26 23N 111 12 E
Dongara, *Australia* **79** 29 14 S 114 57 E
Dongargarh, *India* **50** 21 10N 80 40 E
Dongbei, *China* **61** 42 0N 125 0 E
Dongchuan, *China* **58** 26 8N 103 1 E
Dongen, *Neths.* **17** 51 38N 4 56 E
Donges, *France* **18** 47 18N 2 4W
Dongfang, *China* **54** 18 50N 108 33 E
Dongfeng, *China* **61** 42 40N 125 34 E
Donggala, *Indonesia* **57** 0 30 S 119 40 E
Donggan, *China* **58** 23 22N 105 9 E
Donggou, *China* **61** 39 52N 124 10 E
Dongguan, *China* **59** 22 58N 113 44 E
Dongguang, *China* **60** 37 50N 116 30 E
Donghai Dao, *China* **59** 21 0N 110 15 E
Dongjingcheng, *China* **61** 44 0N 129 10 E
Donglan, *China* **58** 24 30N 107 21 E
Dongliu, *China* **59** 30 13N 116 55 E
Dongmen, *China* **58** 22 20N 107 48 E
Dongning, *China* **61** 44 2N 131 5 E
Dongnyi, *China* **58** 28 3N 100 15 E
Dongo, *Angola* **95** 14 36 S 15 48 E
Dongola, *Sudan* **88** 19 9N 30 22 E
Dongou, *Congo* **94** 2 0N 18 5 E
Dongping, *China* **60** 35 55N 116 20 E
Dongshan, *China* **59** 23 43N 117 30 E
Dongsheng, *China* **60** 39 50N 110 0 E
Dongshi, *Taiwan* **59** 24 18N 120 49 E
Dongtai, *China* **61** 32 51N 120 21 E
Dongting Hu, *China* **59** 29 18N 112 45 E
Dongxiang, *China* **59** 28 11N 116 34 E
Dongxing, *China* **58** 21 34N 108 0 E
Dongyang, *China* **59** 29 13N 120 15 E
Dongzhi, *China* **59** 30 9N 117 0 E
Donington, C., *Australia* **73** 34 45 S 136 0 E
Doniphan, *U.S.A.* **121** 36 40N 90 50W
Donja Stubica, *Yugoslavia* **27** 45 59N 16 0 E
Donji Dušnik, *Yugoslavia* **33** 43 12N 22 5 E
Donji Miholjac, *Yugoslavia* **33** 45 45N 18 10 E
Donji Milanovac, *Yugoslavia* **33** 44 28N 22 6 E
Donji Vakuf, *Yugoslavia* **33** 44 8N 17 24 E
Donjon, Le, *France* **20** 46 22N 3 48 E
Dønna, *Norway* **8** 66 6N 12 30 E
Donna, *U.S.A.* **121** 26 12N 98 2W
Donnaconna, *Canada* **107** 46 41N 71 41W
Donnelly's Crossing, *N.Z.* **80** 35 42 S 173 38 E
Donnybrook, *Australia* **79** 33 34 S 115 48 E
Donnybrook, *S. Africa* **97** 29 59 S 29 48 E
Donora, *U.S.A.* **116** 40 11N 79 50W
Donor's Hill, *Australia* **72** 18 42 S 140 33 E
Donque, *Angola* **95** 15 28 S 14 6 E
Donskoy, *U.S.S.R.* **37** 53 55N 38 15 E
Donya Lendava, *Yugoslavia* **27** 46 35N 16 25 E
Donzère, *France* **21** 44 28N 4 43 E
Donzère-Mondragon, Barr. de, *France* **21** 44 13N 4 42 E
Donzy, *France* **19** 47 20N 3 6 E
Dooen, *Australia* **74** 36 39 S 142 16 E
Dookie, *Australia* **74** 36 20 S 145 41 E
Doon →, *U.K.* **14** 55 26N 4 41W
Doorn, *Neths.* **16** 52 2N 5 20 E
Dor, *Israel* **44** 32 37N 34 55 E
Dora, L., *Australia* **78** 22 0 S 123 0 E
Dora Báltea →, *Italy* **26** 45 11N 8 5 E
Dora Riparia →, *Italy* **26** 45 5N 7 44 E
Dorada, La, *Colombia* **134** 5 30N 74 40W
Doran L., *Canada* **111** 61 13N 108 6W
Dorat, Le, *France* **20** 46 14N 1 5 E
Dorchester, *U.K.* **13** 50 42N 2 28W
Dorchester, C., *Canada* **103** 65 27N 77 27W
Dordogne □, *France* **20** 45 5N 0 40 E
Dordogne →, *France* **20** 45 2N 0 36W
Dordrecht, *Neths.* **16** 51 48N 4 39 E
Dordrecht, *S. Africa* **96** 31 20 S 27 3 E
Dore →, *France* **20** 45 50N 3 35 E
Dore, Mts., *France* **20** 45 32N 2 50 E
Doré L., *Canada* **111** 54 46N 107 17W
Doré Lake, *Canada* **111** 54 38N 107 36W
Dores do Indaiá, *Brazil* **139** 19 27 S 45 36W
Dorfen, *W. Germany* **31** 48 16N 12 10 E
Dorgali, *Italy* **28** 40 18N 9 35 E
Dori, *Burkina Faso* **91** 14 3N 0 2W
Doring →, *S. Africa* **96** 31 54 S 18 39 E
Doringbos, *S. Africa* **96** 31 59 S 19 16 E
Dorion, *Canada* **107** 45 23N 74 3W
Dormaa-Ahenkro, *Ghana* **90** 7 15N 2 52W
Dormo, Ras, *Ethiopia* **89** 13 14N 42 35 E
Dornberg, *Yugoslavia* **27** 45 45N 13 50 E
Dornbirn, *Austria* **31** 47 25N 9 45 E
Dornes, *France* **19** 46 48N 3 18 E
Dornoch, *U.K.* **14** 57 52N 4 0W
Dornoch Firth, *U.K.* **14** 57 52N 4 0W
Dornogovĭ □, *Mongolia* **60** 44 0N 110 0 E
Doro, *Mali* **91** 16 9N 0 51W
Dorogobuzh, *U.S.S.R.* **36** 54 50N 33 18 E
Dorohoi, *Romania* **34** 47 56N 26 30 E
Döröö Nuur, *Mongolia* **62** 48 0N 93 0 E
Dorre I., *Australia* **79** 25 13 S 113 12 E
Dorrigo, *Australia* **77** 30 20 S 152 44 E
Dorris, *U.S.A.* **122** 41 59N 121 58W
Dorset, *Canada* **106** 45 14N 78 54W
Dorset, *U.S.A.* **116** 41 4N 80 40W
Dorset □, *U.K.* **13** 50 48N 2 25W
Dorsten, *W. Germany* **30** 51 40N 6 55 E
Dortmund, *W. Germany* **30** 51 32N 7 28 E
Dorum, *W. Germany* **30** 53 40N 8 33 E
Doruma, *Zaïre* **92** 4 42N 27 33 E
Dos Bahías, C., *Argentina* **142** 44 58 S 65 32W
Dos Hermanas, *Spain* **23** 37 16N 5 55W
Dos Palos, *U.S.A.* **124** 36 59N 120 37W
Dosquet, *Canada* **107** 46 28N 71 32W
Dosso, *Niger* **91** 13 0N 3 13 E
Dothan, *U.S.A.* **115** 31 10N 85 25W
Dottignies, *Belgium* **17** 50 44N 3 19 E
Doty, *U.S.A.* **124** 46 38N 123 17W
Douai, *France* **19** 50 21N 3 4 E
Douala, *Cameroon* **91** 4 0N 9 45 E
Douarnenez, *France* **18** 48 6N 4 21W
Double Island Pt., *Australia* **73** 25 56 S 153 11 E
Doubrava →, *Czech.* **32** 49 40N 15 30 E
Doubs □, *France* **19** 47 10N 6 20 E
Doubs →, *France* **19** 46 53N 5 1 E
Doubtful Sd., *N.Z.* **81** 45 20 S 166 49 E
Doubtless B., *N.Z.* **80** 34 55 S 173 26 E
Doudeville, *France* **18** 49 43N 0 47 E
Doué-la-Fontaine, *France* **18** 47 11N 0 16W
Douentza, *Mali* **90** 14 58N 2 48W
Doughboy, *Australia* **76** 35 15 S 149 38 E
Douglas, *Canada* **109** 45 31N 76 56W
Douglas, *S. Africa* **96** 29 4 S 23 46 E
Douglas, *U.K.* **12** 54 9N 4 29W
Douglas, *Alaska, U.S.A.* **110** 58 23N 134 24W
Douglas, *Ariz., U.S.A.* **123** 31 21N 109 30W
Douglas, *Ga., U.S.A.* **115** 31 32N 82 52W
Douglas, *Wyo., U.S.A.* **120** 42 45N 105 20W
Douglas Pt., *Canada* **108** 44 19N 81 37W
Douglastown, *Canada* **105** 48 46N 64 24W
Douglasville, *U.S.A.* **115** 33 46N 84 43W
Douirat, *Morocco* **84** 33 2N 4 11W
Doukáton, Ákra, *Greece* **35** 38 34N 20 30 E

Dutton

Doulevant-le-Château, France 19 48 23N 4 55 E
Doullens, France 19 50 10N 2 20 E
Doumé, Cameroon 94 4 15N 13 25 E
Douna, Mali 90 13 13N 6 0W
Dounan, Taiwan 59 23 41N 120 26 E
Dounguila, Congo 94 2 53 S 11 58 E
Dounreay, U.K. 14 58 34N 3 44W
Dour, Belgium 17 50 24N 3 46 E
Dourada, Serra, Brazil 139 13 10 S 48 45W
Dourados, Brazil 141 22 9 S 54 50W
Dourados →, Brazil 141 21 58 S 54 18W
Dourdan, France 19 48 30N 2 1 E
Douro →, Europe 22 41 8N 8 40W
Douvaine, France 21 46 19N 6 16 E
Douz, Tunisia 86 33 25N 9 0 E
Douze →, France 20 43 54N 0 30W
Dove →, U.K. 12 52 51N 1 36W
Dove Creek, U.S.A. 123 37 46N 108 59W
Dover, Australia 72 43 18 S 147 2 E
Dover, U.K. 13 51 7N 1 19 E
Dover, Del., U.S.A. 114 39 10N 75 31W
Dover, Ky., U.S.A. 119 38 43N 83 52W
Dover, N.H., U.S.A. 117 43 12N 70 51W
Dover, N.J., U.S.A. 117 40 53N 74 34W
Dover, Ohio, U.S.A. 116 40 32N 81 30W
Dover, Pt., Australia 79 32 32 S 125 32 E
Dover, Str. of, Europe 18 51 0N 1 30 E
Dover-Foxcroft, U.S.A. 105 45 14N 69 14W
Dover Plains, U.S.A. 117 41 43N 73 35W
Dovey →, U.K. 13 52 32N 4 0W
Dovrefjell, Norway 10 62 15N 9 33 E
Dowa, Malawi 93 13 38 S 33 58 E
Dowagiac, U.S.A. 119 41 58N 86 8W
Dowlat Yār, Afghan. 47 34 30N 65 45 E
Dowlatābād, Iran 47 28 20N 56 40 E
Down □, U.K. 15 54 20N 6 0W
Downers Grove, U.S.A. 119 41 49N 88 1W
Downey, Calif., U.S.A. 125 42 26N 112 7W
Downey, U.S.A. 122 42 29N 112 3W
Downham Market, U.K. 13 52 36N 0 22 E
Downieville, U.S.A. 124 39 34N 120 50W
Downing, U.S.A. 118 40 29N 92 22W
Downpatrick, U.K. 15 54 20N 5 43W
Downpatrick Hd., Ireland 15 54 20N 9 21W
Dowshī, Afghan. 47 35 35N 68 43 E
Doyle, U.S.A. 124 40 2N 120 6W
Doylestown, U.S.A. 117 40 21N 75 10W
Dozois, Rés., Canada 106 47 30N 77 5W
Draa, C., Morocco 84 28 47N 11 0W
Draa, Oued →, Morocco 84 28 40N 11 10W
Drac →, France 21 45 12N 5 42 E
Drachten, Neths. 16 53 7N 6 5 E
Drăgănești, Romania 34 44 9N 24 32 E
Drăgănești-Viașca, Romania 34 44 5N 25 33 E
Dragaš, Yugoslavia 33 42 5N 20 35 E
Drăgășani, Romania 34 44 39N 24 17 E
Dragonera, I., Spain 24 39 35N 2 19 E
Draguignan, France 21 43 32N 6 27 E
Drain, U.S.A. 122 43 45N 123 17W
Drake, Australia 77 28 55 S 152 25 E
Drake, U.S.A. 120 47 56N 100 21W
Drake Passage, S. Ocean 143 58 0 S 68 0W
Drakensberg, S. Africa 97 31 0 S 28 0 E
Dráma, Greece 35 41 9N 24 10 E
Drammen, Norway 10 59 42N 10 12 E
Drangajökull, Iceland 8 66 9N 22 15W
Drangedal, Norway 10 59 6N 9 3 E
Dranov, Ostrov, Romania 34 44 55N 29 30 E
Dras, India 49 34 25N 75 48 E
Drau = Drava →, Yugoslavia 33 45 33N 18 55 E
Drava →, Yugoslavia 33 45 33N 18 55 E
Draveil, France 19 48 41N 2 25 E
Dravograd, Yugoslavia 27 46 36N 15 5 E
Drawa →, Poland 32 52 52N 15 59 E
Drawno, Poland 32 53 13N 15 46 E
Drayton, Canada 108 43 46N 80 40W
Drayton Plains, U.S.A. 119 42 42N 83 23W
Drayton Valley, Canada 110 53 12N 114 58W
Dreibergen, Neths. 16 52 3N 5 17 E
Drenthe □, Neths. 16 52 52N 6 40 E
Drentsche Hoofdvaart, Neths. 16 52 39N 6 4 E
Dresden, Canada 108 42 35N 82 11W
Dresden, E. Germany 30 51 2N 13 45 E
Dresden □, E. Germany 30 51 12N 14 0 E
Dreux, France 18 48 44N 1 23 E
Drexel, U.S.A. 119 39 45N 84 18W
Driel, Neths. 16 51 57N 5 49 E
Driffield, U.K. 12 54 0N 0 25W
Driftwood, U.S.A. 116 41 22N 78 9W
Driggs, U.S.A. 122 43 50N 111 8W
Drin i zi →, Albania 35 41 37N 20 28 E
Drina →, Yugoslavia 33 44 53N 19 21 E
Drincea →, Romania 34 44 20N 22 55 E
Drini →, Albania 34 42 20N 20 0 E
Drinjača →, Yugoslavia 33 44 15N 19 8 E
Drivstua, Norway 10 62 26N 9 47 E
Drniš, Yugoslavia 27 43 51N 16 10 E
Drøbak, Norway 10 59 39N 10 39 E
Drocourt, Canada 108 45 46N 80 21W
Drogheda, Ireland 15 53 45N 6 20W
Drogichin, U.S.S.R. 36 52 15N 25 8 E
Drogobych, U.S.S.R. 36 49 20N 23 30 E
Droichead Nua, Ireland 15 53 11N 6 50W
Droitwich, U.K. 13 52 16N 2 10W
Dromana, Australia 74 38 22 S 144 57 E
Drôme □, France 21 44 38N 5 15 E
Drôme →, France 21 44 46N 4 46 E
Dromedary, C., Australia 75 36 17 S 150 10 E
Dronero, Italy 26 44 29N 7 22 E
Dronfield, Australia 72 21 12 S 140 3 E
Dronne →, France 20 45 2N 0 9W
Dronning Maud Land, Antarctica 143 72 30 S 12 0 E
Dronninglund, Denmark 11 57 10N 10 19 E
Dronrijp, Neths. 16 53 11N 5 39 E
Dropt →, France 20 44 35N 0 6W
Drouin, Australia 74 38 10 S 145 53 E
Drumbo, Canada 108 43 16N 80 35W
Drumheller, Canada 110 51 25N 112 40W
Drummond, U.S.A. 122 46 40N 113 4W
Drummond I., U.S.A. 104 46 0N 83 40W
Drummond Pt., Australia 73 34 9 S 135 16 E
Drummond Ra., Australia 72 23 45 S 147 10 E
Drummondville, Canada 107 45 55N 72 25W
Drumright, U.S.A. 121 35 59N 96 38W
Drunen, Neths. 17 51 41N 5 8 E
Druskininkai, U.S.S.R. 36 54 3N 23 58 E
Drut →, U.S.S.R. 36 53 3N 30 42 E
Druten, Neths. 16 51 53N 5 36 E
Druya, U.S.S.R. 36 55 45N 27 28 E
Druzhina, U.S.S.R. 41 68 14N 145 18 E
Drvar, Yugoslavia 27 44 21N 16 23 E
Drvenik, Yugoslavia 27 43 27N 16 3 E
Dry Tortugas, U.S.A. 128 24 38N 82 55W
Dryanovo, Bulgaria 34 42 59N 25 28 E
Dryden, Canada 111 49 47N 92 50W
Dryden, U.S.A. 121 30 3N 102 3W
Drygalski I., Antarctica 143 66 0 S 92 0 E
Drysdale, Australia 74 38 11 S 144 32 E
Drysdale →, Australia 78 13 59 S 126 51 E
Drysdale I., Australia 72 11 41 S 136 0 E
Dschang, Cameroon 91 5 32N 10 3 E
Du Bois, U.S.A. 116 41 8N 78 46W
Du Quoin, U.S.A. 118 38 0N 89 10W
Duanesburg, U.S.A. 117 42 45N 74 11W
Duaringa, Australia 72 23 42 S 149 42 E
Ḍubā, Si. Arabia 46 27 10N 35 40 E
Dubai = Dubayy, U.A.E. 47 25 18N 55 20 E
Dubawnt →, Canada 111 64 33N 100 6W
Dubawnt, L., Canada 111 63 4N 101 42W
Dubayy, U.A.E. 47 25 18N 55 20 E
Dubbeldam, Neths. 16 51 47N 4 43 E
Dubbo, Australia 76 32 11 S 148 35 E
Dubele, Zaïre 92 2 56N 29 35 E
Dubica, Yugoslavia 27 45 11N 16 48 E
Dublin, Ireland 15 53 20N 6 18W
Dublin, Ga., U.S.A. 115 32 30N 82 34W
Dublin, Tex., U.S.A. 121 32 0N 98 20W
Dublin □, Ireland 15 53 24N 6 20W
Dublin B., Ireland 15 53 18N 6 5W
Dubna, R.S.F.S.R., U.S.S.R. 37 54 8N 36 59 E
Dubna, R.S.F.S.R., U.S.S.R. 37 56 44N 37 10 E
Dubno, U.S.S.R. 36 50 25N 25 45 E
Dubois, Idaho, U.S.A. 122 44 7N 112 9W
Dubois, Ind., U.S.A. 119 38 26N 86 48W
Dubossary, U.S.S.R. 38 47 15N 29 10 E
Dubossary Vdkhr., U.S.S.R. 38 47 30N 29 0 E
Dubovka, U.S.S.R. 39 49 5N 44 50 E
Dubovskoye, U.S.S.R. 39 47 28N 42 46 E
Dubrajpur, India 49 23 48N 87 25 E
Dubréka, Guinea 90 9 46N 13 31W
Dubrovitsa, U.S.S.R. 36 51 31N 26 35 E
Dubrovnik, Yugoslavia 33 42 39N 18 6 E
Dubrovskoye, U.S.S.R. 41 58 55N 111 10 E
Dubulu, Zaïre 94 4 18N 20 16 E
Dubuque, U.S.A. 118 42 30N 90 41W
Duchang, China 59 29 18N 116 12 E
Duchesne, U.S.A. 122 40 14N 110 22W
Duchess, Australia 72 21 20 S 139 50 E
Ducie I., Pac. Oc. 67 24 40 S 124 48W
Duck Cr. →, Australia 78 22 37 S 116 53 E
Duck Lake, Canada 111 52 50N 106 16W
Duck Mt. Prov. Parks, Canada 111 51 45N 101 0W
Duckwall, Mt., U.S.A. 124 37 58N 120 7W
Düdelange, Lux. 17 49 29N 6 5 E
Duderstadt, W. Germany 30 51 30N 10 15 E
Dudhnai, India 52 25 59N 90 47 E
Dudinka, U.S.S.R. 41 69 30N 86 13 E
Dudley, U.K. 13 52 30N 2 5W
Dudna →, India 50 19 17N 76 54 E
Dudo, Somali Rep. 98 9 20N 50 12 E
Dudub, Ethiopia 98 6 55N 46 43 E
Dueñas, Spain 22 41 52N 4 33W
Dueodde, Denmark 11 54 59N 15 4 E
Dueré, Brazil 139 11 20 S 49 17W
Duero → = Douro →, Europe 22 41 8N 8 40W
Duffel, Belgium 17 51 6N 4 30 E
Dufftown, U.K. 14 57 26N 3 9W
Dugger, U.S.A. 119 39 4N 87 16W
Dugi, Yugoslavia 27 44 0N 15 0 E
Dugiuma, Somali Rep. 98 1 15N 42 34 E
Dugo Selo, Yugoslavia 27 45 51N 16 18 E
Duifken Pt., Australia 72 12 33 S 141 38 E
Duisburg, W. Germany 30 51 27N 6 42 E
Duitama, Colombia 134 5 50N 73 2W
Duiveland, Neths. 17 51 38N 4 0 E
Duiwelskloof, S. Africa 97 23 42 S 30 10 E
Duke I., U.S.A. 110 54 50N 131 20W
Dukhān, Qatar 47 25 25N 50 50 E
Dukhovshchina, U.S.S.R. 36 55 15N 32 27 E
Duku, Bauchi, Nigeria 91 10 43N 10 43 E
Duku, Sokoto, Nigeria 91 11 11N 4 55 E
Dulce →, Argentina 140 30 32 S 62 33W
Dulce, G., Costa Rica 128 8 40N 83 20W
Dŭlgopol, Bulgaria 34 43 3N 27 22 E
Dulit, Banjaran, Malaysia 56 3 15N 114 30 E
Duliu, China 60 39 2N 116 55 E
Dullewala, Pakistan 48 31 50N 71 25 E
Dülmen, W. Germany 30 51 49N 7 18 E
Dulovo, Bulgaria 34 43 48N 27 9 E
Dululu, Australia 72 23 48 S 150 15 E
Duluth, U.S.A. 120 46 48N 92 10W
Dum Dum, India 49 22 39N 88 33 E
Dum Hadjer, Chad 87 13 18N 19 41 E
Dumaguete, Phil. 57 9 17N 123 15 E
Dumai, Indonesia 56 1 35N 101 28 E
Dumaran, Phil. 57 10 33N 119 50 E
Dumaresq →, Australia 77 28 40 S 150 29 E
Dumas, Ark., U.S.A. 121 33 52N 91 30W
Dumas, Tex., U.S.A. 121 35 50N 101 58W
Dumbarton, U.K. 14 55 58N 4 35W
Dumbea, N. Cal. 68 22 10 S 166 27 E
Dumbleyung, Australia 79 33 17 S 117 42 E
Dumbo, Angola 95 14 6 S 17 24 E
Dumfries, U.K. 14 55 4N 3 37W
Dumfries & Galloway □, U.K. 14 55 0N 4 0W
Dumka, India 49 24 12N 87 15 E
Dümmersee, W. Germany 30 52 30N 8 21 E
Dumoine →, Canada 106 46 13N 77 51W
Dumoine L., Canada 106 46 55N 77 55W
Dumosa, Australia 74 35 54 S 143 13 E
Dumraon, India 49 25 33N 84 8 E
Dumyât, Egypt 88 31 24N 31 48 E
Dumyât, Masabb, Egypt 88 31 28N 31 51 E
Dun Laoghaire, Ireland 15 53 17N 6 9W
Dun-le-Palestel, France 20 46 18N 1 39 E
Dun-sur-Auron, France 19 46 53N 2 33 E
Duna →, Hungary 33 45 51N 18 48 E
Dunaföldvár, Hungary 33 46 50N 18 57 E
Dunaj →, Czech. 33 47 50N 18 50 E
Dunajec →, Poland 32 50 15N 20 44 E
Dunajska Streda, Czech. 33 48 0N 17 37 E
Dunapatai, Hungary 33 46 39N 19 4 E
Dunărea →, Romania 34 45 20N 29 40 E
Dunaújváros, Hungary 33 47 0N 18 57 E
Dunav →, Yugoslavia 33 44 47N 21 20 E
Dunback, N.Z. 81 45 23 S 170 36 E
Dunbar, Australia 72 16 0 S 142 22 E
Dunbar, U.K. 14 56 0N 2 32W
Dunblane, U.K. 14 56 10N 3 58W
Duncan, Canada 110 48 45N 123 40W
Duncan, Ariz., U.S.A. 123 32 46N 109 6W
Duncan, Okla., U.S.A. 121 34 25N 98 0W
Duncan, L., Canada 104 53 29N 77 58W
Duncan L., Canada 110 62 51N 113 58W
Duncan Town, Bahamas 128 22 15N 75 45W
Duncannon, U.S.A. 116 40 23N 77 2W
Dunchurch, Canada 108 45 39N 79 51W
Dundalk, Canada 108 44 10N 80 24W
Dundalk, Ireland 15 54 1N 6 25W
Dundalk Bay, Ireland 15 53 55N 6 15W
Dundas, Canada 108 43 17N 79 59W
Dundas, L., Australia 79 32 35 S 121 50 E
Dundas I., Canada 110 54 30N 130 50W
Dundas Str., Australia 78 11 15 S 131 35 E
Dundee, Australia 77 29 33 S 151 50 E
Dundee, S. Africa 97 28 11 S 30 15 E
Dundee, U.K. 14 56 29N 3 0W
Dundee, U.S.A. 119 41 57N 83 40W
Dundgovĭ □, Mongolia 60 45 10N 106 0 E
Dundoo, Australia 73 27 40 S 144 37 E
Dundrum, U.K. 15 54 17N 5 50W
Dundrum B., U.K. 15 54 12N 5 40W
Dundwara, India 49 27 48N 79 9 E
Dunedin, N.Z. 81 45 50 S 170 33 E
Dunedin, U.S.A. 115 28 1N 82 45W
Dunedin →, Canada 110 59 30N 124 5W
Dunedoo, Australia 77 32 0 S 149 25 E
Dunfermline, U.K. 14 56 5N 3 28W
Dungannon, Canada 108 43 51N 81 36W
Dungannon, U.K. 15 54 30N 6 47W
Dungannon □, U.K. 15 54 30N 6 55W
Dungarpur, India 48 23 52N 73 45 E
Dungarvan, Ireland 15 52 6N 7 40W
Dungarvan Bay, Ireland 15 52 5N 7 35W
Dungeness, U.K. 13 50 54N 0 59 E
Dungo, L. do, Angola 95 17 15 S 19 0 E
Dungog, Australia 76 32 22 S 151 46 E
Dungowan, Australia 77 31 13 S 151 8 E
Dungu, Zaïre 92 3 40N 28 32 E
Dungunâb, Sudan 88 21 10N 37 9 E
Dungunâb, Khalij, Sudan 88 21 5N 37 12 E
Dunhinda Falls, Sri Lanka 51 7 5N 81 6 E
Dunhua, China 61 43 20N 128 14 E
Dunhuang, China 62 40 8N 94 36 E
Dunières, France 21 45 13N 4 20 E
Dunk I., Australia 72 17 59 S 146 29 E
Dunkeld, Australia 74 37 40 S 142 22 E
Dunkeld, U.K. 14 56 34N 3 36W
Dunkerque, France 19 51 2N 2 20 E
Dunkery Beacon, U.K. 13 51 15N 3 37W
Dunkirk = Dunkerque, France 19 51 2N 2 20 E
Dunkirk, U.S.A. 116 42 30N 79 18W
Dunkuj, Sudan 89 12 50N 32 49 E
Dunkwa, Central, Ghana 90 6 0N 1 47W
Dunkwa, Central, Ghana 91 5 30N 1 0W
Dunlap, U.S.A. 120 41 50N 95 36W
Dúnleary = Dun Laoghaire, Ireland 15 53 17N 6 9W
Dunmanus B., Ireland 15 51 31N 9 50W
Dunmara, Australia 72 16 42 S 133 25 E
Dunmore, U.S.A. 117 41 27N 75 38W
Dunmore Hd., Ireland 15 52 10N 10 35W
Dunmore Town, Bahamas 128 25 30N 76 39W
Dunn, U.S.A. 115 35 18N 78 36W
Dunnellon, U.S.A. 115 29 4N 82 28W
Dunnet Hd., U.K. 14 58 38N 3 22W
Dunning, U.S.A. 120 41 52N 100 4W
Dunnville, Canada 108 42 54N 79 36W
Dunolly, Australia 74 36 51 S 143 44 E
Dunoon, Australia 77 28 42 S 153 20 E
Dunoon, U.K. 14 55 57N 4 56W
Dunqul, Egypt 88 23 26N 31 37 E
Duns, U.K. 14 55 47N 2 20W
Dunseith, U.S.A. 120 48 49N 100 2W
Dunsmuir, U.S.A. 122 41 10N 122 18W
Dunstable, U.K. 13 51 53N 0 31W
Dunstan Mts., N.Z. 81 44 53 S 169 35 E
Dunster, Canada 110 53 8N 119 50W
Duntroon, N.Z. 81 44 51 S 170 40 E
Dunvegan L., Canada 111 60 8N 107 10W
Duolun, China 60 42 12N 116 28 E
Duong Dong, Vietnam 55 10 13N 103 58 E
Duparquet, Canada 106 48 30N 79 14W
Duparquet, L., Canada 106 48 28N 79 16W
Dupree, U.S.A. 120 45 4N 101 35W
Dupuy, Canada 106 48 50N 79 21W
Dupuyer, U.S.A. 122 48 11N 112 31W
Duque de Caxias, Brazil 139 22 45 S 43 19W
Duque de York, I., Chile 142 50 37 S 75 25W
Dūrā, Jordan 44 31 31N 35 1 E
Durack →, Australia 78 15 33 S 127 52 E
Durack Range, Australia 78 16 50 S 127 40 E
Durance →, France 21 43 55N 4 45 E
Durand, Ill., U.S.A. 118 42 26N 89 20W
Durand, Mich., U.S.A. 119 42 54N 83 58W
Durango, Spain 24 43 13N 2 40W
Durango, U.S.A. 123 37 16N 107 50W
Durango □, Mexico 126 25 0N 105 0W
Duranillin, Australia 79 33 30 S 116 45 E
Durant, Iowa, U.S.A. 118 41 36N 90 54W
Durant, Okla., U.S.A. 121 34 0N 96 25W
Duratón →, Spain 22 41 37N 4 7W
Durazno, Uruguay 140 33 25 S 56 31W
Durazzo = Durrësi, Albania 35 41 19N 19 28 E
Durban, France 20 42 59N 2 49 E
Durban, S. Africa 97 29 49 S 31 1 E
Durbo, Somali Rep. 98 11 37N 50 20 E
Dúrcal, Spain 23 37 0N 3 34W
Düren, W. Germany 30 50 48N 6 30 E
Durg, India 50 21 15N 81 22 E
Durgapur, India 49 23 30N 87 20 E
Durham, Canada 108 44 10N 80 49W
Durham, U.K. 12 54 47N 1 34W
Durham, Calif., U.S.A. 124 39 39N 121 48W
Durham, N.C., U.S.A. 115 36 0N 78 55W
Durham □, U.K. 12 54 42N 1 45W
Durham Downs, Australia 73 26 6 S 141 47 E
Durham Ox, Australia 74 36 6 S 143 57 E
Duri, Australia 77 31 10 S 150 51 E
Duri Mountain, Australia 77 31 12 S 150 44 E
Durmitor, Yugoslavia 33 43 10N 19 0 E
Durness, U.K. 14 58 34N 4 45W
Durrësi, Albania 35 41 19N 19 28 E
Durrie, Australia 72 25 40 S 140 15 E
Durtal, France 18 47 40N 0 18W
Duru, Zaïre 92 4 14N 28 50 E
D'Urville, Tanjung, Indonesia 57 1 28 S 137 54 E
D'Urville I., N.Z. 81 40 50 S 173 55 E
Duryea, U.S.A. 117 41 20N 75 45W
Dusa Mareb, Somali Rep. 98 5 30N 46 15 E
Dûsh, Egypt 88 24 35N 30 41 E
Dushak, U.S.S.R. 40 37 13N 60 1 E
Dushan, China 58 25 48N 107 30 E
Dushanbe, U.S.S.R. 40 38 33N 68 48 E
Dusheti, U.S.S.R. 39 42 10N 44 42 E
Dusky Sd., N.Z. 81 45 47 S 166 30 E
Dussejour, C., Australia 78 14 45 S 128 13 E
Düsseldorf, W. Germany 30 51 15N 6 46 E
Dussen, Neths. 16 51 44N 4 59 E
Dutch Harbor, U.S.A. 102 53 54N 166 35W
Dutlwe, Botswana 96 23 58 S 23 46 E
Dutsan Wai, Nigeria 91 10 50N 8 10 E
Dutton, Canada 108 42 39N 81 30W

Dutton

Dutton →, *Australia* . **72** 20 44 S 143 10 E
Duved, *Sweden* . . . . . . **10** 63 24N 12 55 E
Duvno, *Yugoslavia* . . . **33** 43 42N 17 13 E
Duwādimi, *Si. Arabia* . **46** 24 35N 44 15 E
Duyun, *China* . . . . **58** 26 18N 107 29 E
Duzce, *Turkey* . . . . **46** 40 50N 31 10 E
Duzdab = Zāhedān, *Iran* . . . . **47** 29 30N 60 50 E
Dvina, Sev. →, *U.S.S.R.* . . . . **40** 64 32N 40 30 E
Dvinsk = Daugavpils, *U.S.S.R.* . . . . **36** 55 53N 26 32 E
Dvor, *Yugoslavia* . . . . . **27** 45 4N 16 22 E
Dwarka, *India* . . . . **48** 22 18N 69 8 E
Dwellingup, *Australia* . **79** 32 43 S 116 4 E
Dwight, *Canada* **106** 45 20N 79 1W
Dwight, *U.S.A.* **119** 41 5N 88 25W
Dyakovskoya, *U.S.S.R.* **37** 60 5N 41 12 E
Dyatkovo, *U.S.S.R.* . . **36** 53 40N 34 27 E
Dyatlovo, *U.S.S.R.* . . . **36** 53 28N 25 28 E
Dyer, *U.S.A.* **119** 37 24N 86 13W
Dyer, C., *Canada* **103** 66 40N 61 0W
Dyer Plateau, *Antarctica* . . . . **143** 70 45 S 65 30W
Dyersburg, *U.S.A.* **121** 36 2N 89 20W
Dyersville, *U.S.A.* **118** 42 29N 91 8W
Dyfed □, *U.K.* **13** 52 0N 4 30W
Dyje →, *Czech.* . . . . . **32** 48 37N 16 56 E
Dyle →, *Belgium* . . . . **17** 50 58N 4 41 E
Dynevor Downs, *Australia* . . . . **73** 28 10 S 144 20 E
Dynów, *Poland* . . . . . . **32** 49 50N 22 11 E
Dysart, *Canada* **111** 50 57N 104 2W
Dzamin Üüd, *Mongolia* **60** 43 50N 111 58 E
Dzerzhinsk, *Byelorussian S.S.R., U.S.S.R.* . . . . **36** 53 40N 27 1 E
Dzerzhinsk, *R.S.F.S.R., U.S.S.R.* . . . . **37** 56 14N 43 30 E
Dzhalinda, *U.S.S.R.* . . **41** 53 26N 124 0 E
Dzhambeyty, *U.S.S.R.* **39** 50 16N 52 35 E
Dzhambul, *U.S.S.R.* . . **40** 42 54N 71 22 E
Dzhankoi, *U.S.S.R.* . . **38** 45 40N 34 20 E
Dzhanybek, *U.S.S.R.* . **39** 49 25N 46 50 E
Dzhardzhan, *U.S.S.R.* **41** 68 10N 124 10 E
Dzhelinde, *U.S.S.R.* . . **41** 70 0N 114 20 E
Dzhetygara, *U.S.S.R.* . **40** 52 11N 61 12 E
Dzhezkazgan, *U.S.S.R.* **40** 47 44N 67 40 E
Dzhikimde, *U.S.S.R.* . **41** 59 1N 121 47 E
Dzhizak, *U.S.S.R.* . . . . **40** 40 6N 67 50 E
Dzhugdzur, Khrebet, *U.S.S.R.* . . . . **41** 57 30N 138 0 E
Dzhvari, *U.S.S.R.* . . . . **39** 42 42N 42 4 E
Działdowo, *Poland* . . . **32** 53 15N 20 15 E
Działoszyn, *Poland* . . . **32** 51 6N 18 50 E
Dzierzgoń, *Poland* . . . **32** 53 58N 19 20 E
Dzierzoniów, *Poland* . . **32** 50 45N 16 39 E
Dzilam de Bravo, *Mexico* **127** 21 24N 88 53W
Dzioua, *Algeria* . . . . . . **85** 33 14N 5 14 E
Dzungaria = Junggar Pendi, *China* . . . . **62** 44 30N 86 0 E
Dzungarian Gate = Alataw Shankou, *China* . . . . **62** 45 5N 81 57 E
Dzuumod, *Mongolia* . . **62** 47 45N 106 58 E

E

Eabamet, L., *Canada* . **104** 51 30N 87 46W
Eads, *U.S.A.* **120** 38 30N 102 46W
Eagle, *Alaska, U.S.A.* **102** 64 44N 141 7W
Eagle, *Colo., U.S.A.* . **122** 39 39N 106 55W
Eagle →, *Canada* **105** 53 36N 57 26W
Eagle Butt, *U.S.A.* . . . **120** 45 1N 101 12W
Eagle Cr. →, *U.S.A.* . **119** 38 36N 85 4W
Eagle Grove, *U.S.A.* . . **118** 42 37N 93 53W
Eagle L., *Calif., U.S.A.* **122** 40 35N 120 50W
Eagle L., *Maine, U.S.A.* **105** 46 23N 69 22W
Eagle Lake, *Canada* . . **109** 45 8N 78 29W
Eagle Lake, *U.S.A.* . . . **121** 29 35N 96 21W
Eagle Mountain, *U.S.A.* **125** 33 52N 115 26W
Eagle Nest, *U.S.A.* . . . **123** 36 33N 105 13W
Eagle Pass, *U.S.A.* . . . **121** 28 45N 100 35W
Eagle Pk., *U.S.A.* **124** 38 10N 119 25W
Eagle Pt., *Australia* . . . **78** 16 11 S 124 23 E
Eagle River, *U.S.A.* . . **120** 45 55N 89 17W
Eagleville, *U.S.A.* **118** 40 28N 93 59W
Ealing, *U.K.* **13** 51 30N 0 19W
Earaheedy, *Australia* . **79** 25 34 S 121 29 E
Earl Grey, *Canada* . . . **111** 50 57N 104 43W
Earle, *U.S.A.* **121** 35 18N 90 26W
Earlimart, *U.S.A.* **125** 35 53N 119 16W
Earlville, *U.S.A.* **119** 41 35N 88 55W
Earn →, *U.K.* **14** 56 20N 3 19W
Earn, L., *U.K.* **14** 56 23N 4 14W
Earnslaw, Mt., *N.Z.* . . **81** 44 32 S 168 27 E
Earoo, *Australia* . . . . . **79** 29 34 S 118 22 E
Earth, *U.S.A.* **121** 34 18N 102 30W
Easley, *U.S.A.* **115** 34 52N 82 35W
East Angus, *Canada* . . **107** 45 30N 71 40W
East Aurora, *U.S.A.* . . **116** 42 46N 78 38W
East B., *U.S.A.* **121** 29 2N 89 16W
East Beskids = Vychodné Beskydy, *Europe* . . . . **32** 49 30N 22 0 E
East Bluff, Mt., *Australia* . . . . **77** 31 53 S 150 13 E
East Brady, *U.S.A.* . . . **116** 40 59N 79 36W
East Broughton Station, *Canada* **107** 46 14N 71 5W
East C., *N.Z.* . . . . **80** 37 42 S 178 35 E
East C., *Papua N. G.* . **69** 10 13 S 150 53 E
East Chicago, *U.S.A.* . **119** 41 40N 87 30W
East China Sea, *Asia* . **62** 30 5N 126 0 E
East Coast Bays, *N.Z.* **80** 36 40 S 174 40 E
East Coulee, *Canada* . **110** 51 23N 112 27W
East Dubuque, *U.S.A.* **118** 42 29N 90 39W
East Falkland, *Falk. Is.* **142** 51 30 S 58 30W
East Germany ■, *Europe* . . . . **30** 52 0N 12 0 E
East Grand Forks, *U.S.A.* **120** 47 55N 97 5W
East Greenwich, *U.S.A.* **117** 41 39N 71 27W
East Gresford, *Australia* . . . . **76** 32 25 S 151 31 E
East Hartford, *U.S.A.* . **117** 41 45N 72 39W
East Helena, *U.S.A.* . . **122** 46 37N 111 58W
East Indies, *Asia* . . . . . **56** 0 0 120 0 E
East Jordan, *U.S.A.* . . **114** 45 10N 85 7W
East Kilbride, *U.K.* . . . **14** 55 46N 4 10W
East Lansing, *U.S.A.* . . **119** 42 44N 84 29W
East Liverpool, *U.S.A.* **116** 40 39N 80 35W
East London, *S. Africa* **97** 33 0 S 27 55 E
East Lynne, *Australia* . **76** 35 35 S 150 16 E
East Main = Eastmain, *Canada* **104** 52 10N 78 30W
East Moline, *U.S.A.* . . **118** 41 31N 90 25W
East Orange, *U.S.A.* . . **117** 40 46N 74 13W
East Pacific Ridge, *Pac. Oc.* . . . . **67** 15 0 S 110 0W
East Pakistan = Bangladesh ■, *Asia* **52** 24 0N 90 0 E
East Palestine, *U.S.A.* **116** 40 50N 80 32W
East Peoria, *U.S.A.* . . **118** 40 40N 89 34W
East Pine, *Canada* . . . **110** 55 48N 120 12W
East Pt., *Canada* **105** 46 27N 61 58W
East Point, *U.S.A.* . . . **115** 33 40N 84 28W
East Providence, *U.S.A.* **117** 41 48N 71 22W
East Retford, *U.K.* . . . **12** 53 19N 0 55W
East St. Louis, *U.S.A.* **118** 38 37N 90 4W
East Schelde → = Oosterschelde, *Neths.* **17** 51 33N 4 0 E
East Siberian Sea, *U.S.S.R.* . . . . **41** 73 0N 160 0 E
East Stroudsburg, *U.S.A.* **117** 41 1N 75 11W
East Sussex □, *U.K.* . . **13** 51 0N 0 20 E
East Tawas, *U.S.A.* . . . **114** 44 17N 83 31W
East Toorale, *Australia* **73** 30 27 S 145 28 E
East Troy, *U.S.A.* **119** 42 47N 88 24W
East Walker →, *U.S.A.* **124** 38 52N 119 10W
Eastbourne, *N.Z.* . . . . **80** 41 19 S 174 55 E
Eastbourne, *U.K.* . . . . **13** 50 46N 0 18 E
Eastend, *Canada* **111** 49 32N 108 50W
Easter Islands, *Pac. Oc.* **67** 27 0 S 109 0W
Eastern □, *Kenya* . . . . **92** 0 0 38 30 E
Eastern □, *Uganda* . . . **92** 1 50N 33 45 E
Eastern Cr. →, *Australia* . . . . **72** 20 40 S 141 35 E
Eastern Ghats, *India* . . **51** 14 0N 78 50 E
Eastern Group = Lau, *Fiji* . . . . **68** 17 0 S 178 30W
Eastern Group, *Australia* . . . . **79** 33 30 S 124 30 E
Eastern Province □, *S. Leone* **90** 8 15N 11 0W
Easterville, *Canada* . . **111** 53 8N 99 49W
Easthampton, *U.S.A.* . **117** 42 15N 72 41W
Eastland, *U.S.A.* **121** 32 26N 98 45W
Eastleigh, *U.K.* **13** 50 58N 1 21W
Eastmain, *Canada* **104** 52 10N 78 30W
Eastmain →, *Canada* . **104** 52 27N 78 26W
Eastman, *Canada* **117** 45 18N 72 19W
Eastman, *Ga., U.S.A.* . **115** 32 13N 83 20W
Eastman, *Wis., U.S.A.* **118** 43 10N 91 1W
Easton, *Md., U.S.A.* . . **114** 38 47N 76 7W
Easton, *Pa., U.S.A.* . . **117** 40 41N 75 15W
Easton, *Wash., U.S.A.* **124** 47 14N 121 8W
Eastport, *U.S.A.* **105** 44 57N 67 0W
Eastsound, *U.S.A.* . . . **124** 48 42N 122 55W
Eaton, *Colo., U.S.A.* . . **120** 40 35N 104 42W
Eaton, *Ohio, U.S.A.* . . **119** 39 45N 84 38W
Eaton Rapids, *U.S.A.* **119** 42 31N 84 39W
Eatonia, *Canada* **111** 51 13N 109 25W
Eatonton, *U.S.A.* **115** 33 22N 83 24W
Eatontown, *U.S.A.* . . . **117** 40 18N 74 7W
Eatonville, *Canada* . . . **107** 47 20N 69 41W
Eatonville, *U.S.A.* . . . **124** 46 52N 122 16W
Eau Claire, *Fr. Guiana* **135** 3 30N 53 40W
Eau Claire, *U.S.A.* . . . **120** 44 46N 91 30W
Eauze, *France* . . . . **20** 43 53N 0 7 E
Ebagoola, *Australia* . . . **72** 14 15 S 143 12 E
Eban, *Nigeria* . . . . **91** 9 40N 4 50 E
Ebangalakata, *Zaïre* . . **94** 0 29 S 21 29 E
Ebbw Vale, *U.K.* **13** 51 47N 3 12W
Ebden, *Australia* . . . . . **75** 36 10 S 147 1 E
Ebebiyín, *Eq. Guin.* . . . **94** 2 9N 11 20 E
Ebeggui, *Algeria* . . . . . **85** 26 2N 6 0 E
Ebel, *Gabon* . . . . **94** 0 7N 11 5 E
Ebeltoft, *Denmark* . . . . **9** 56 12N 10 41 E
Ebensburg, *U.S.A.* . . . **116** 40 29N 78 43W
Ebensee, *Austria* . . . . . **33** 47 48N 13 46 E
Eberbach, *W. Germany* **31** 49 27N 8 59 E
Eberswalde, *E. Germany* . . . . **30** 52 49N 13 50 E
Ebian, *China* . . . . **58** 29 11N 103 13 E
Ebingen, *W. Germany* **31** 48 13N 9 1 E
Ebino, *Japan* . . . . **64** 32 2N 130 48 E
Eboli, *Italy* . . . . **29** 40 39N 15 2 E
Ebolowa, *Cameroon* . . **91** 2 55N 11 10 E
Ebor, *Australia* . . . . . . **77** 30 22 S 152 27 E
Eboulements, Les, *Canada* **107** 47 28N 70 21W
Ebrach, *W. Germany* . **31** 49 50N 10 30 E
Ébrié, Lagune, *Ivory C.* **90** 5 12N 4 26W
Ebro →, *Spain* . . . . . . **24** 40 43N 0 54 E
Ebro, Pantano del, *Spain* **22** 43 0N 3 58W
Ebstorf, *W. Germany* . **30** 53 2N 10 23 E
Ecaussines-d' Enghien, *Belgium* . . . . **17** 50 35N 4 11 E
Eccleston, *Australia* . . **76** 32 14 S 151 30 E
Ech Cheliff, *Algeria* . . **85** 36 10N 1 20 E
Échelles, Les, *France* . **21** 45 26N 5 46 E
Echeng, *China* . . . . **59** 30 23N 114 50 E
Echizen-Misaki, *Japan* **65** 35 59N 135 57 E
Echmiadzin, *U.S.S.R.* . **39** 40 12N 44 19 E
Echo Bay, *N.W.T., Canada* **102** 66 5N 117 55W
Echo Bay, *Ont., Canada* **108** 46 29N 84 4W
Echoing →, *Canada* . . **111** 55 51N 92 5W
Échouani, L., *Canada* **106** 47 46N 75 42W
Echt, *Neths.* . . . . **17** 51 7N 5 52 E
Echternach, *Lux.* . . . . . **17** 49 49N 6 25 E
Echuca, *Australia* . . . . **74** 36 10 S 144 20 E
Ecija, *Spain* **23** 37 30N 5 10W
Eckernförde, *W. Germany* . . . . **30** 54 26N 9 50 E
Eclipse Is., *Australia* . . **78** 13 54 S 126 19 E
Écommoy, *France* . . . . **18** 47 50N 0 17 E
Ecoporanga, *Brazil* . . . **139** 18 23 S 40 50W
Écorce, L. de l', *Canada* **106** 47 5N 76 24W
Écos, *France* . . . . **19** 49 9N 1 35 E
Écouché, *France* **18** 48 42N 0 10W
Ecuador ■, *S. Amer.* . **134** 2 0 S 78 0W
Écueillé, *France* . . . . . . **18** 47 5N 1 21 E
Ed, *Sweden* . . . . **11** 58 55N 11 55 E
Ed Dabbura, *Sudan* . . **88** 17 40N 34 15 E
Ed Dâmer, *Sudan* . . . . **88** 17 27N 34 0 E
Ed Debba, *Sudan* . . . . **88** 18 0N 30 51 E
Ed-Déffa, *Egypt* . . . . . **88** 30 40N 26 30 E
Ed Deim, *Sudan* . . . . . **89** 10 10N 28 20 E
Ed Dueim, *Sudan* . . . . **89** 14 0N 32 10 E
Edah, *Australia* . . . . . . **79** 28 16 S 117 10 E
Edam, *Canada* **111** 53 11N 108 46W
Edam, *Neths.* . . . . **16** 52 31N 5 3 E
Edapally, *India* . . . . . . **51** 11 19N 78 3 E
Eday, *U.K.* **14** 59 11N 2 47W
Edd, *Ethiopia* . . . . **89** 14 0N 41 38 E
Eddrachillis B., *U.K.* . . **14** 58 16N 5 10W
Eddystone, *U.K.* **13** 50 11N 4 16W
Eddystone Pt., *Australia* . . . . **72** 40 59 S 148 20 E
Eddyville, *U.S.A.* **118** 41 9N 92 38W
Ede, *Neths.* . . . . **16** 52 4N 5 40 E
Ede, *Nigeria* . . . . **91** 7 45N 4 29 E
Édea, *Cameroon* . . . . . **91** 3 51N 10 9 E
Edegem, *Belgium* . . . . **17** 51 10N 4 27 E
Edehon L., *Canada* . . . **111** 60 25N 97 15W
Edekel, Adrar, *Algeria* **85** 23 56N 6 47 E
Eden, *Australia* . . . . . . **75** 37 3 S 149 55 E
Eden, *N.C., U.S.A.* . . . **115** 36 29N 79 53W
Eden, *N.Y., U.S.A.* . . . **116** 42 39N 78 55W
Eden, *Tex., U.S.A.* . . . **121** 31 16N 99 50W
Eden, *Wyo., U.S.A.* . . . **122** 42 2N 109 27W
Eden →, *U.K.* **12** 54 57N 3 2W
Eden L., *Canada* **111** 56 38N 100 15W
Edenburg, *S. Africa* . . **96** 29 43 S 25 58 E
Edendale, *N.Z.* . . . . . . **81** 46 19 S 168 48 E
Edendale, *S. Africa* . . . **97** 29 39 S 30 18 E
Edenderry, *Ireland* . . . **15** 53 21N 7 3W
Edenhope, *Australia* . . **74** 37 4 S 141 19 E
Edenton, *U.S.A.* **115** 36 5N 76 36W
Edenville, *S. Africa* . . . **97** 27 37 S 27 34 E
Eder →, *W. Germany* **30** 51 15N 9 25 E
Ederstausee, *W. Germany* . . . . **30** 51 11N 9 0 E
Edgar, *U.S.A.* **120** 40 25N 98 0W
Edgartown, *U.S.A.* . . . **117** 41 22N 70 28W
Edge Hill, *U.K.* **13** 52 7N 1 28W
Edgecumbe, *N.Z.* . . . . **80** 37 59 S 176 47 E
Edgefield, *U.S.A.* **115** 33 50N 81 59W
Edgeley, *U.S.A.* **120** 46 27N 98 41W
Edgemont, *U.S.A.* **120** 43 15N 103 53W
Edgeøya, *Svalbard* . . . **144** 77 45N 22 30 E
Edgeroi, *Australia* . . . . **77** 30 7 S 149 50 E
Edgerton, *Ohio, U.S.A.* **119** 41 27N 84 45W
Edgerton, *Wis., U.S.A.* **118** 42 50N 89 4W
Edgewood, *U.S.A.* . . . **119** 38 55N 88 40W
Edhessa, *Greece* . . . . . **35** 40 48N 22 5 E
Edievale, *N.Z.* . . . . **81** 45 49 S 169 22 E
Edina, *Liberia* **90** 6 0N 10 10W
Edina, *U.S.A.* **118** 40 6N 92 10W
Edinburg, *Ill., U.S.A.* . . **118** 39 39N 89 23W
Edinburg, *Ind., U.S.A.* . **119** 39 21N 85 58W
Edinburg, *Tex., U.S.A.* . **121** 26 22N 98 10W
Edinburgh, *U.K.* **14** 55 57N 3 12W
Edirne, *Turkey* . . . . **46** 41 40N 26 34 E
Edison, *U.S.A.* **124** 48 33N 122 27W
Edithburgh, *Australia* . **73** 35 5 S 137 43 E
Edjeleh, *Algeria* . . . . . . **85** 28 38N 9 50 E
Edjudina, *Australia* . . . **79** 29 48 S 122 23 E
Edmeston, *U.S.A.* **117** 42 42N 75 15W
Edmond, *U.S.A.* **121** 35 37N 97 30W
Edmonds, *U.S.A.* **124** 47 47N 122 22W
Edmonton, *Australia* . . **72** 17 2 S 145 46 E
Edmonton, *Canada* . . . **110** 53 30N 113 30W
Edmund L., *Canada* . . **111** 54 45N 93 17W
Edmundston, *Canada* . **105** 47 23N 68 20W
Edna, *U.S.A.* **121** 29 0N 96 40W
Edna Bay, *U.S.A.* **110** 55 55N 133 40W
Edolo, *Italy* . . . . **26** 46 10N 10 21 E
Edremit, *Turkey* . . . . . **46** 39 34N 27 0 E
Edsbyn, *Sweden* . . . . . **10** 61 23N 15 49 E
Edsel Ford Ra., *Antarctica* . . . . **143** 77 0 S 143 0W
Edsele, *Sweden* . . . . . . **10** 63 25N 16 32 E
Edson, *Canada* **110** 53 35N 116 28W
Eduardo Castex, *Argentina* . . . . **140** 35 50 S 64 18W
Edward →, *Australia* . **74** 35 0 S 143 30 E
Edward, L., *Africa* . . . **92** 0 25 S 29 40 E
Edward I., *Canada* . . . **104** 48 22N 88 37W
Edward VII Land, *Antarctica* . . . . **143** 80 0 S 150 0W
Edwards, *U.S.A.* **125** 34 55N 117 51W
Edwards →, *U.S.A.* . . **118** 41 10N 90 59W
Edwards Plateau, *U.S.A.* **121** 30 30N 101 5W
Edwardsburg, *U.S.A.* . **119** 41 48N 86 6W
Edwardsport, *U.S.A.* . **119** 38 49N 87 15W
Edwardsville, *Ill., U.S.A.* **118** 38 49N 89 57W
Edwardsville, *Pa., U.S.A.* **117** 41 15N 75 56W
Edzo, *Canada* **110** 62 49N 116 4W
Eefde, *Neths.* . . . . **16** 52 10N 6 13 E
Eekloo, *Belgium* . . . . . **17** 51 11N 3 33 E
Eel →, *Ind., U.S.A.* . **119** 39 7N 86 58W
Eel →, *Ind., U.S.A.* . **119** 40 45N 86 22W
Eelde, *Neths.* . . . . **16** 53 8N 6 34 E
Eem →, *Neths.* . . . . . . **16** 52 16N 5 20 E
Eems →, *Neths.* . . . . . **16** 53 26N 6 57 E
Eems Kanaal, *Neths.* . **16** 53 18N 6 46 E
Eenrum, *Neths.* . . . . . . **16** 53 22N 6 28 E
Eernegem, *Belgium* . . . **17** 51 8N 3 2 E
Eerste Valthermond, *Neths.* . . . . **16** 52 53N 6 58 E
Efate, I., *Vanuatu* . . . . **68** 17 40 S 168 25 E
Ef'e, Nahal, *Israel* . . . . **44** 31 9N 35 13 E
Eferi, *Algeria* . . . . **85** 24 30N 9 28 E
Effingham, *U.S.A.* **119** 39 8N 88 30W
Eforie Sud, *Romania* . . **34** 44 1N 28 37 E
Ega →, *Spain* **24** 42 19N 1 55W
Égadi, Ísole, *Italy* . . . . **28** 37 55N 12 16 E
Eganville, *Canada* **109** 45 32N 77 5W
Egeland, *U.S.A.* **120** 48 42N 99 6W
Egenolf L., *Canada* . . . **111** 59 3N 100 0W
Eger = Cheb, *Czech.* . **32** 50 9N 12 28 E
Eger, *Hungary* . . . . **33** 47 53N 20 27 E
Eger →, *Hungary* . . . . **33** 47 38N 20 50 E
Egersund, *Norway* . . . . **9** 58 26N 6 1 E
Egg L., *Canada* **111** 55 5N 105 30W
Eggenburg, *Austria* . . . **32** 48 38N 15 50 E
Eggenfelden, *W. Germany* . . . . **31** 48 24N 12 46 E
Egherta, *Somali Rep.* . . **98** 2 4N 43 11 E
Éghezée, *Belgium* . . . . **17** 50 35N 4 55 E
Eginbah, *Australia* . . . . **78** 20 53 S 119 47 E
Egito, *Angola* . . . . **95** 12 4 S 13 58 E
Égletons, *France* . . . . . **20** 45 24N 2 3 E
Egmond-aan-Zee, *Neths.* . . . . **16** 52 37N 4 38 E
Egmont, C., *N.Z.* . . . . **80** 39 16 S 173 45 E
Egmont, Mt., *N.Z.* . . . . **80** 39 17 S 174 5 E
Eğridir, *Turkey* . . . . **46** 37 52N 30 51 E
Eğridir Gölü, *Turkey* . . **46** 37 53N 30 50 E
Egtved, *Denmark* . . . . **11** 55 38N 9 18 E
Eguas →, *Brazil* . . . . **139** 13 26 S 44 14W
Egume, *Nigeria* . . . . . . **91** 7 30N 7 14 E
Éguzon, *France* . . . . . . **20** 46 27N 1 33 E
Egvekinot, *U.S.S.R.* . . **41** 66 19N 179 50W
Egypt ■, *Africa* . . . . . . **88** 28 0N 31 0 E
Eha Amufu, *Nigeria* . . . **91** 6 30N 7 46 E
Ehime □, *Japan* . . . . . **64** 33 30N 132 40 E
Ehingen, *W. Germany* . **31** 48 16N 9 43 E
Ehrenberg, *U.S.A.* **125** 33 36N 114 31W
Ehrwald, *Austria* . . . . . **31** 47 24N 10 56 E
Eibar, *Spain* **24** 43 11N 2 28W
Eibergen, *Neths.* . . . . . **16** 52 6N 6 39 E
Eichstatt, *W. Germany* **31** 48 53N 11 12 E
Eider →, *W. Germany* **30** 54 19N 8 58 E
Eidsvold, *Australia* . . . **73** 25 25 S 151 12 E
Eidsvoll, *Norway* . . . . . **9** 60 19N 11 14 E
Eifel, *W. Germany* . . . **31** 50 10N 6 45 E
Eiffel Flats, *Zambia* . . **93** 18 20 S 30 0 E
Eigg, *U.K.* **14** 56 54N 6 10W
Eighty Mile Beach, *Australia* . . . . **78** 19 30 S 120 40 E
Eil, *Somali Rep.* . . . . . **98** 8 0N 49 50 E
Eil, L., *U.K.* **14** 56 50N 5 15W
Eildon, *Australia* . . . . . **74** 37 14 S 145 55 E
Eildon, L., *Australia* . . **74** 37 10 S 146 0 E
Eileen L., *Canada* **111** 62 16N 107 37W
Eilenburg, *E. Germany* **30** 51 28N 12 38 E
Ein el Luweiqa, *Sudan* **89** 14 5N 33 50 E
Einasleigh, *Australia* . . **72** 18 32 S 144 5 E
Einasleigh →, *Australia* **72** 17 30 S 142 17 E
Einbeck, *W. Germany* . **30** 51 48N 9 50 E
Eindhoven, *Neths.* . . . . **17** 51 26N 5 30 E
Einsiedeln, *Switz.* . . . . **31** 47 7N 8 46 E
Eire ■, *Europe* **15** 53 0N 8 0W
Eiríksjökull, *Iceland* . . **8** 64 46N 20 24W
Eirlandsche Gat, *Neths.* **16** 53 12N 4 54 E
Eirunepé, *Brazil* . . . . . **136** 6 35 S 69 53W
Eisden, *Belgium* . . . . . . **17** 50 59N 5 42 E
Eisenach, *E. Germany* . **30** 50 58N 10 18 E
Eisenberg, *E. Germany* **30** 50 59N 11 50 E
Eisenerz, *Austria* . . . . . **33** 47 32N 14 54 E
Eisenhüttenstadt, *E. Germany* . . . . **30** 52 9N 14 41 E

Elten

Eisenstadt, *Austria* ... **33** 47 51N 16 31 E
Eiserfeld, *W. Germany* **30** 50 50N 7 59 E
Eisfeld, *E. Germany* .. **30** 50 25N 10 54 E
Eisleben, *E. Germany* .. **30** 51 31N 11 31 E
Ejby, *Denmark* ...... **11** 55 25N 9 56 E
Eje, Sierra del, *Spain* . **22** 42 24N 6 54W
Ejea de los Caballeros,
Spain **24** 42 7N 1 9W
Ejutla, *Mexico* **127** 16 34N 96 44W
Ekalaka, *U.S.A.* **120** 45 55N 104 30W
Ekalla, *Gabon* .... **94** 1 27 S 14 0 E
Ekanga, *Zaïre* .... **94** 2 23 S 23 14 E
Ekawasaki, *Japan* .... **64** 33 13N 132 46 E
Ekeren, *Belgium* ..... **17** 51 17N 4 25 E
Eket, *Nigeria* .... **91** 4 38N 7 56 E
Eketahuna, *N.Z.* ..... **80** 40 38 S 175 43 E
Ekhínos, *Greece* ...... **35** 41 16N 25 1 E
Ekibastuz, *U.S.S.R.* .. **40** 51 50N 75 10 E
Ekimchan, *U.S.S.R.* .. **41** 53 0N 133 0 E
Ekoli, *Zaïre* .... **92** 0 23 S 24 13 E
Eksel, *Belgium* .... **17** 51 9N 5 24 E
Eksjö, *Sweden* .... **11** 57 40N 14 58 E
Ekwan →, *Canada* ... **104** 53 12N 82 15W
Ekwan Pt., *Canada* ... **104** 53 16N 82 7W
El Aaiún, *W. Sahara* . **84** 27 9N 13 12W
El Aargub, *Mauritania* **84** 23 37N 15 52W
El Aat, *Syria* .... **44** 32 50N 35 45 E
El Abiodh-Sidi-Cheikh,
Algeria .... **85** 32 53N 0 31 E
El Adde, *Somali Rep.* **98** 2 35N 46 9 E
El Aïoun, *Morocco* ... **85** 34 33N 2 30W
El 'Aiyat, *Egypt* ..... **88** 29 36N 31 15 E
El Alamein, *Egypt* ... **88** 30 48N 28 58 E
El Alto, *Peru* .... **136** 4 15 S 81 14W
El 'Arag, *Egypt* ...... **88** 28 40N 26 20 E
El Arahal, *Spain* **23** 37 15N 5 33W
El Aricha, *Algeria* **85** 34 13N 1 10W
El Arīhā, *Jordan* ..... **44** 31 52N 35 27 E
El Arish, *Australia* ... **72** 17 35 S 146 1 E
El 'Arîsh, *Egypt* ..... **88** 31 8N 33 50 E
El Arrouch, *Algeria* .. **85** 36 37N 6 53 E
El Asnam = Ech
Cheliff, *Algeria* ..... **85** 36 10N 1 20 E
El Astillero, *Spain* **22** 43 24N 3 49W
El Badâri, *Egypt* ..... **88** 27 4N 31 25 E
El Bahrein, *Egypt* .... **88** 28 30N 26 25 E
El Ballâs, *Egypt* ...... **88** 26 2N 32 43 E
El Balyana, *Egypt* .... **88** 26 10N 32 3 E
El Banco, *Colombia* .. **134** 9 0N 73 58W
El Baqeir, *Sudan* ..... **88** 18 40N 33 40 E
El Barco de Ávila,
Spain **22** 40 21N 5 31W
El Barco de
Valdeorras, *Spain* .. **22** 42 23N 7 0W
El Bauga, *Sudan* ..... **88** 18 18N 33 52 E
El Baúl, *Venezuela* ... **134** 8 57N 68 17W
El Bawiti, *Egypt* ..... **88** 28 25N 28 45 E
El Bayadh, *Algeria* ... **85** 33 40N 1 1 E
El Bierzo, *Spain* **22** 42 45N 6 30W
El Bluff, *Nic.* **128** 11 59N 83 40W
El Bolsón, *Argentina* . **142** 41 55 S 71 30W
El Bonillo, *Spain* **25** 38 57N 2 35W
El Buheirat □, *Sudan* . **89** 7 0N 30 0 E
El Bur, *Somali Rep.* .. **98** 4 40N 46 37 E
El Caín, *Argentina* ... **142** 41 38 S 68 19W
El Cajon, *U.S.A.* **125** 32 49N 117 0W
El Callao, *Venezuela* .. **135** 7 18N 61 50W
El Camp, *Spain* ...... **24** 41 5N 1 10 E
El Campo, *U.S.A.* **121** 29 10N 96 20W
El Carmen, *Bolivia* ... **137** 13 40 S 63 55W
El Carmen, *Venezuela* **134** 1 16N 66 52W
El Castillo, *Spain* **23** 37 41N 6 19W
El Centro, *U.S.A.* **125** 32 50N 115 40W
El Cerro, *Bolivia* ..... **137** 17 30 S 61 40W
El Cerro, *Spain* **23** 37 45N 6 57W
El Cocuy, *Colombia* .. **134** 6 25N 72 27W
El Compadre, *Mexico* . **125** 32 20N 116 14W
El Corcovado,
Argentina .... **142** 43 25 S 71 35W
El Coronil, *Spain* **23** 37 5N 5 38W
El Cuy, *Argentina* .... **142** 39 55 S 68 25W
El Cuyo, *Mexico* **127** 21 30N 87 40W
El Dab'a, *Egypt* ...... **88** 31 0N 28 27 E
El Dambahaddo,
Somali Rep. .... **98** 3 17N 46 40 E
El Deir, *Egypt* .... **88** 25 25N 32 20 E
El Dere, *Ethiopia* .... **98** 5 6N 43 5 E
El Dere, *Somali Rep.* . **98** 3 50N 47 8 E
El Dere, *Somali Rep.* . **98** 5 22N 46 11 E
El Descanso, *Mexico* . **125** 32 12N 116 58W
El Desemboque,
Mexico **126** 30 30N 112 57W
El Dilingat, *Egypt* .... **88** 30 50N 30 31 E
El Diviso, *Colombia* .. **134** 1 22N 78 14W
El Djem, *Tunisia* ..... **86** 35 18N 10 42 E
El Dorado, *Ark.*,
U.S.A. **121** 33 10N 92 40W
El Dorado, *Kans.*,
U.S.A. **121** 37 55N 96 56W
El Dorado, *Venezuela* **135** 6 55N 61 37W
El Eglab, *Algeria* **84** 26 20N 4 30W
El Escorial, *Spain* **22** 40 35N 4 7W
El Eulma, *Algeria* .... **85** 36 9N 5 42 E
El Faiyûm, *Egypt* .... **88** 29 19N 30 50 E
El Fâsher, *Sudan* .... **89** 13 33N 25 26 E
El Fashn, *Egypt* ...... **88** 28 50N 30 54 E
El Ferrol, *Spain* **22** 43 29N 8 15W
El Fifi, *Sudan* .... **89** 10 4N 25 0 E
El Fud, *Ethiopia* ..... **98** 7 15N 42 52 E
El Fuerte, *Mexico* **126** 26 30N 108 40W
El Gal, *Somali Rep.* .. **98** 10 58N 50 20 E
El Gebir, *Sudan* ...... **89** 13 40N 29 40 E
El Gedida, *Egypt* ..... **88** 25 40N 28 30 E
El Geteina, *Sudan* .... **89** 14 50N 32 27 E
El Gezira □, *Sudan* .. **89** 15 0N 33 0 E
El Gîza, *Egypt* ...... **88** 30 0N 31 10 E
El Goléa, *Algeria* .... **85** 30 30N 2 50 E
El Guettar, *Algeria* ... **85** 34 5N 4 38 E
El Hadeb, *W. Sahara* . **84** 25 51N 13 0W
El Hadjira, *Algeria* ... **85** 32 36N 5 30 E
El Hagiz, *Sudan* ...... **89** 15 15N 35 50 E
El Hajeb, *Morocco* ... **84** 33 43N 5 13W
El Hammam, *Egypt* .. **88** 30 52N 29 25 E
El Hammâmi,
Mauritania **84** 23 3N 11 30W
El Hamurre,
Somali Rep. .... **59** 7 13N 48 54 E
El Hank, *Mauritania* .. **84** 24 30N 7 0W
El Harrach, *Algeria* ... **85** 36 45N 3 5 E
El Hasian, *W. Sahara* . **84** 26 20N 14 0W
El Hawata, *Sudan* .... **89** 13 25N 34 42 E
El Heiz, *Egypt* .... **88** 27 50N 28 40 E
El 'Idisât, *Egypt* ..... **88** 25 30N 32 35 E
El Iskandarîya, *Egypt* . **88** 31 0N 30 0 E
El Jadida, *Morocco* ... **84** 33 11N 8 17W
El Jebelein, *Sudan* ... **89** 12 40N 32 55 E
El Kab, *Sudan* .... **88** 19 27N 32 46 E
El Kala, *Algeria* ...... **85** 36 50N 8 30 E
El Kalâa, *Morocco* ... **84** 32 4N 7 27W
El Kamlin, *Sudan* .... **89** 15 3N 33 11 E
El Kantara, *Algeria* ... **85** 35 14N 5 45 E
El Kantara, *Tunisia* ... **86** 33 45N 10 58 E
El Karaba, *Sudan* .... **88** 18 32N 33 41 E
El Kef, *Tunisia* ...... **86** 36 12N 8 47 E
El Khandaq, *Sudan* ... **88** 18 30N 30 30 E
El Khârga, *Egypt* ..... **88** 25 30N 30 33 E
El Khartûm, *Sudan* ... **89** 15 31N 32 35 E
El Khartûm □, *Sudan* **89** 16 0N 33 0 E
El Khartûm Bahrî,
Sudan .... **89** 15 40N 32 31 E
El-Khroubs, *Algeria* .. **85** 36 10N 6 55 E
El Kseur, *Algeria* ..... **85** 36 46N 4 49 E
El Ksiba, *Morocco* ... **84** 32 45N 6 1W
El Kuntilla, *Egypt* .... **88** 30 1N 34 45 E
El Laqâwa, *Sudan* .... **89** 11 25N 29 1 E
El Laqeita, *Egypt* .... **88** 25 50N 33 15 E
El Leiya, *Sudan* ...... **89** 16 15N 35 28 E
El Mafâza, *Sudan* .... **89** 13 38N 34 30 E
El Mahalla el Kubra,
Egypt .... **88** 31 0N 31 0 E
El Mahârîq, *Egypt* .... **88** 25 35N 30 35 E
El Mahmûdîya, *Egypt* . **88** 31 10N 30 32 E
El Maitén, *Argentina* . **142** 42 3 S 71 10W
El Maiz, *Algeria* **85** 28 19N 0 9W
El-Maks el-Bahari,
Egypt .... **88** 24 30N 30 40 E
El Manshâh, *Egypt* ... **88** 26 26N 31 50 E
El Mansour, *Algeria* .. **85** 27 47N 0 14W
El Mansûra, *Egypt* ... **88** 31 0N 31 19 E
El Mantico, *Venezuela* **135** 7 38N 62 45W
El Manzala, *Egypt* .... **88** 31 10N 31 50 E
El Marâgha, *Egypt* ... **88** 26 35N 31 10 E
El Masid, *Sudan* ..... **89** 15 15N 33 0 E
El Matariya, *Egypt* ... **88** 31 15N 32 0 E
El Meghaier, *Algeria* . **85** 33 55N 5 58 E
El Meraguen, *Algeria* . **85** 28 0N 0 7W
El Metemma, *Sudan* .. **89** 16 50N 33 10 E
El Miamo, *Venezuela* . **135** 7 39N 61 46W
El Milagro, *Argentina* . **140** 30 59 S 65 59W
El Milia, *Algeria* ..... **85** 36 51N 6 13 E
El Minyâ, *Egypt* ..... **88** 28 7N 30 33 E
El Molar, *Spain* **24** 40 42N 3 45W
El Mreyye, *Mauritania* **90** 18 0N 6 0W
El Obeid, *Sudan* ..... **89** 13 8N 30 10 E
El Odaiya, *Sudan* .... **89** 12 8N 28 12 E
El Oro, *Mexico* **127** 19 48N 100 8W
El Oro □, *Ecuador* ... **134** 3 30 S 79 50W
El Oued, *Algeria* ..... **85** 33 20N 6 58 E
El Palmar, *Bolivia* .... **137** 17 50 S 63 9W
El Palmar, *Venezuela* . **135** 7 58N 61 53W
El Palmito, Presa,
Mexico **126** 25 40N 105 30W
El Panadés, *Spain* .... **24** 41 10N 1 30 E
El Pardo, *Spain* **22** 40 31N 3 47W
El Paso, *Ill., U.S.A.* .. **118** 40 44N 89 1W
El Paso, *Tex., U.S.A.* . **123** 31 50N 106 30W
El Paso Robles, *U.S.A.* **124** 35 38N 120 41W
El Pedernoso, *Spain* .. **25** 39 29N 2 45W
El Pedroso, *Spain* **23** 37 51N 5 45W
El Pobo de Dueñas,
Spain **24** 40 46N 1 39W
El Portal, *U.S.A.* **124** 37 44N 119 49W
El Porvenir, *Mexico* .. **126** 31 15N 105 51W
El Prat de Llobregat,
Spain .... **24** 41 18N 2 3 E
El Progreso, *Honduras* **128** 15 26N 87 51W
El Provencío, *Spain* .. **25** 39 23N 2 35W
El Pueblito, *Mexico* .. **126** 29 3N 105 4W
El Pueblo, *Canary Is.* . **25** 28 36N 17 47W
El Qâhira, *Egypt* ..... **88** 30 1N 31 14 E
El Qantara, *Egypt* .... **88** 30 51N 32 20 E
El Qasr, *Egypt* .... **88** 25 44N 28 42 E
El Quseima, *Egypt* ... **88** 30 40N 34 15 E
El Qusîya, *Egypt* ..... **88** 27 29N 30 44 E
El Râshda, *Egypt* .... **88** 25 36N 28 57 E
El Reno, *U.S.A.* **121** 35 30N 98 0W
El Ribero, *Spain* **22** 42 30N 8 30W
El Rîdisiya, *Egypt* .... **88** 24 56N 32 51 E
El Rio, *U.S.A.* **125** 34 14N 119 10W
El Ronquillo, *Spain* .. **23** 37 44N 6 10W
El Roque, Pta.,
Canary Is. **25** 28 10N 15 25W
El Rosarito, *Mexico* .. **126** 28 38N 114 4W
El Rubio, *Spain* **23** 37 22N 5 0W
El Saff, *Egypt* .... **88** 29 34N 31 16 E
El Salto, *Mexico* **126** 23 47N 105 22W
El Salvador ■,
Cent. Amer. **128** 13 50N 89 0W
El Sancejo, *Spain* **23** 37 4N 5 6W
El Sauce, *Nic.* **128** 13 0N 86 40W
El Shallal, *Egypt* ..... **88** 24 0N 32 53 E
El Simbillawein, *Egypt* **88** 30 48N 31 13 E
El Sombrero, *Venezuela* **134** 9 23N 67 3W
El Suweis, *Egypt* ..... **88** 29 58N 32 31 E
El Thamad, *Egypt* .... **88** 29 40N 34 28 E
El Tigre, *Venezuela* ... **135** 8 44N 64 15W
El Tocuyo, *Venezuela* . **134** 9 47N 69 48W
El Tofo, *Chile* .... **140** 29 22 S 71 18W
El Tránsito, *Chile* .... **140** 28 52 S 70 17W
El Tûr, *Egypt* .... **88** 28 14N 33 36 E
El Turbio, *Argentina* .. **142** 51 45 S 72 5W
El Uinle, *Somali Rep.* **98** 3 4N 41 42 E
El Uqsur, *Egypt* ...... **88** 25 41N 32 38 E
El Vado, *Spain* **24** 41 2N 3 18W
El Vallés, *Spain* ..... **24** 41 35N 2 20 E
El Venado, *Mexico* ... **126** 22 56N 101 10W
El Vigía, *Venezuela* ... **134** 8 38N 71 39W
El Wak, *Kenya* ...... **92** 2 49N 40 56 E
El Wak, *Somali Rep.* . **98** 2 44N 41 1 E
El Waqf, *Egypt* ...... **88** 25 45N 32 15 E
El Wâsta, *Egypt* ..... **88** 29 19N 31 12 E
El Weguet, *Ethiopia* .. **89** 5 28N 42 17 E
El Wuz, *Sudan* ...... **89** 15 0N 30 7 E
Elafónisos, *Greece* .... **35** 36 29N 22 56 E
Elaine, *Australia* ..... **74** 37 44 S 144 2 E
Elamanchili, *India* .... **50** 17 33N 82 50 E
Elands, *Australia* ..... **77** 31 37 S 152 20 E
Elandsvlei, *S. Africa* . **96** 32 19 S 19 31 E
Élassa, *Greece* .... **35** 35 18N 26 21 E
Elassón, *Greece* ...... **35** 39 53N 22 12 E
Elat, *Israel* .... **44** 29 30N 34 56 E
Elâzığ, *Turkey* .... **46** 38 37N 39 14 E
Elba, *Italy* .... **26** 42 48N 10 15 E
Elba, *U.S.A.* **115** 31 27N 86 4W
Elbasani, *Albania* .... **35** 41 9N 20 9 E
Elbe, *U.S.A.* **124** 46 45N 122 10W
Elbe →, *Europe* ..... **30** 53 50N 9 0 E
Elberfeld, *U.S.A.* **119** 38 10N 87 27W
Elbert, Mt., *U.S.A.* .. **123** 39 5N 106 27W
Elberta, *U.S.A.* **114** 44 35N 86 14W
Elberton, *U.S.A.* **115** 34 7N 82 51W
Elbeuf, *France* .... **18** 49 17N 1 2 E
Elbidtan, *Turkey* ..... **46** 38 13N 37 12 E
Elbing = Elbląg,
Poland .... **32** 54 10N 19 25 E
Elbląg, *Poland* .... **32** 54 10N 19 25 E
Elbow, *Canada* **111** 51 7N 106 35W
Elbrus, *U.S.S.R.* ..... **39** 43 21N 42 30 E
Elburg, *Neths.* .... **16** 52 26N 5 50 E
Elburn, *U.S.A.* **119** 41 54N 88 28W
Elburz Mts. = Alborz,
Reshteh-ye Kūhhā-
ye, *Iran* .... **47** 36 0N 52 0 E
Elche, *Spain* **25** 38 15N 0 42W
Elche de la Sierra,
Spain **25** 38 27N 2 3W
Elcho I., *Australia* .... **72** 11 55 S 135 45 E
Elda, *Spain* **25** 38 29N 0 47W
Eldon, *Mo., U.S.A.* .. **118** 38 20N 92 38W
Eldon, *Wash., U.S.A.* **124** 47 32N 123 4W
Eldora, *U.S.A.* **118** 42 20N 93 5W
Eldorado, *Argentina* .. **141** 26 28 S 54 43W
Eldorado, *Ont., Canada* **109** 44 35N 77 31W
Eldorado, *Sask.*,
Canada **111** 59 35N 108 30W
Eldorado, *Mexico* **126** 24 20N 107 22W
Eldorado, *Ill., U.S.A.* **119** 37 50N 88 25W
Eldorado, *Tex., U.S.A.* **121** 30 52N 100 35W
Eldorado Springs,
U.S.A. **118** 37 54N 93 59W
Eldoret, *Kenya* ...... **92** 0 30N 35 17 E
Eldred, *U.S.A.* **116** 41 57N 78 24W
Eldridge, *U.S.A.* **118** 41 39N 90 35W
Electra, *U.S.A.* **121** 34 0N 99 0W
Elefantes →, *Mozam.* **97** 24 10 S 32 40 E
Elefantes, G., *Chile* .. **142** 46 28 S 73 49W
Elektrogorsk, *U.S.S.R.* **37** 55 56N 38 50 E
Elektrostal, *U.S.S.R.* . **37** 55 41N 38 32 E
Elele, *Nigeria* .... **91** 5 5N 6 50 E
Elephant Butte Res.,
U.S.A. **123** 33 45N 107 30W
Elephant I., *Antarctica* **143** 61 0 S 55 0W
Elephant Pass,
Sri Lanka .... **51** 9 35N 80 25 E
Elesbão Veloso, *Brazil* **138** 6 13 S 42 8W
Eleuthera, *Bahamas* .. **128** 25 0N 76 20W
Elgepiggen, *Norway* .. **10** 62 10N 11 21 E
Elgeyo-Marakwet □,
Kenya .... **92** 0 45N 35 30 E
Elgin, *N.B., Canada* .. **105** 45 48N 65 10W
Elgin, *Ont., Canada* .. **109** 44 36N 76 13W
Elgin, *U.K.* **14** 57 39N 3 20W
Elgin, *Ill., U.S.A.* **119** 42 0N 88 20W
Elgin, *N. Dak., U.S.A.* **120** 46 24N 101 46W
Elgin, *Nebr., U.S.A.* .. **120** 41 58N 98 3W
Elgin, *Nev., U.S.A.* .. **123** 37 21N 114 20W
Elgin, *Oreg., U.S.A.* .. **122** 45 37N 118 0W
Elgin, *Tex., U.S.A.* .. **121** 30 21N 97 22W
Elgon, Mt., *Africa* ... **92** 1 10N 34 30 E
Eliase, *Indonesia* ..... **57** 8 21 S 130 48 E
Elida, *U.S.A.* **121** 33 56N 103 41W
Elikón, Mt., *Greece* .. **35** 38 18N 22 45 E
Elim, *S. Africa* ...... **96** 34 35 S 19 45 E
Elisabethville =
Lubumbashi, *Zaïre* . **93** 11 40 S 27 28 E
Eliseu Martins, *Brazil* . **138** 8 13 S 43 42W
Elista, *U.S.S.R.* ...... **39** 46 16N 44 14 E
Elizabeth, *Australia* ... **73** 34 42 S 138 41 E
Elizabeth, *Ill., U.S.A.* **118** 42 19N 90 13W
Elizabeth, *N.J., U.S.A.* **117** 40 37N 74 12W
Elizabeth City, *U.S.A.* **115** 36 18N 76 16W
Elizabethton, *U.S.A.* . **115** 36 20N 82 13W
Elizabethtown, *Ky.*,
U.S.A. **114** 37 40N 85 54W
Elizabethtown, *N.Y.*,
U.S.A. **117** 44 13N 73 36W
Elizabethtown, *Pa.*,
U.S.A. **117** 40 8N 76 36W
Elizondo, *Spain* **24** 43 12N 1 30W
Elk, *Poland* .... **32** 53 50N 22 21 E
Elk City, *U.S.A.* **121** 35 25N 99 25W
Elk Creek, *U.S.A.* ... **124** 39 36N 122 32W
Elk Grove, *U.S.A.* ... **124** 38 25N 121 22W
Elk Island Nat. Park,
Canada **110** 53 35N 112 59W
Elk Lake, *Canada* **106** 47 40N 80 25W
Elk Point, *Canada* **111** 53 54N 110 55W
Elk River, *Idaho*,
U.S.A. **122** 46 50N 116 8W
Elk River, *Minn.*,
U.S.A. **120** 45 17N 93 34W
Elkader, *U.S.A.* **118** 42 51N 91 24W
Elkedra, *Australia* .... **72** 21 9 S 135 33 E
Elkedra →, *Australia* . **72** 21 8 S 136 22 E
Elkhart, *Ind., U.S.A.* . **119** 41 42N 85 55W
Elkhart, *Kans., U.S.A.* **121** 37 3N 101 54W
Elkhart →, *U.S.A.* ... **119** 41 41N 85 58W
Elkhorn, *Canada* **111** 49 59N 101 14W
Elkhorn, *U.S.A.* **119** 42 40N 88 33W
Elkhorn →, *U.S.A.* .. **120** 41 7N 98 15W
Elkhotovo, *U.S.S.R.* .. **39** 43 19N 44 15 E
Elkhovo, *Bulgaria* .... **34** 42 10N 26 40 E
Elkin, *U.S.A.* **115** 36 17N 80 50W
Elkins, *U.S.A.* **114** 38 53N 79 53W
Elko, *Canada* **110** 49 20N 115 10W
Elko, *U.S.A.* **122** 40 50N 115 50W
Ell, L., *Australia* ..... **79** 29 13 S 127 46 E
Ellecom, *Neths.* ...... **16** 52 2N 6 6 E
Ellef Ringnes I.,
Canada **144** 78 30N 102 2W
Ellenborough, *Australia* **77** 31 27 S 152 28 E
Ellendale, *Australia* ... **78** 17 56 S 124 48 E
Ellendale, *U.S.A.* **120** 46 3N 98 30W
Ellensburg, *U.S.A.* ... **122** 47 0N 120 30W
Ellenville, *U.S.A.* **117** 41 42N 74 23W
Ellerslie, *Australia* .... **74** 38 10 S 142 44 E
Ellerston, *Australia* ... **77** 31 49 S 151 20 E
Ellery, Mt., *Australia* . **75** 37 28 S 148 47 E
Ellesmere I., *Canada* . **144** 79 30N 80 0W
Ellesworth Land,
Antarctica .... **143** 76 0 S 89 0W
Ellettsville, *U.S.A.* ... **119** 39 14N 86 38W
Ellezelles, *Belgium* ... **17** 50 44N 3 42 E
Ellice Is. = Tuvalu ■,
Pac. Oc. .... **66** 8 0 S 178 0 E
Ellinwood, *U.S.A.* **120** 38 27N 98 37W
Elliot, *Australia* ...... **72** 17 33 S 133 32 E
Elliot, *S. Africa* ...... **97** 31 22 S 27 48 E
Elliot Lake, *Canada* .. **108** 46 25N 82 35W
Elliotdale = Xhora,
S. Africa .... **97** 31 55 S 28 38 E
Ellis, *U.S.A.* **120** 39 0N 99 39W
Ellisville, *U.S.A.* **121** 31 38N 89 12W
Ellon, *U.K.* **14** 57 21N 2 5W
Ellore = Eluru, *India* . **50** 16 48N 81 8 E
Ells →, *Canada* **110** 57 18N 111 40W
Ellsworth, *U.S.A.* **120** 38 47N 98 15W
Ellsworth Land,
Antarctica .... **143** 76 0 S 89 0W
Ellsworth Mts.,
Antarctica .... **143** 78 30 S 85 0W
Ellwangen,
W. Germany .... **31** 48 57N 10 9 E
Ellwood City, *U.S.A.* . **116** 40 52N 80 19W
Elm, *Switz.* .... **31** 46 54N 9 10 E
Elma, *Canada* **111** 49 52N 95 55W
Elma, *U.S.A.* **124** 47 0N 123 30W
Elmalı, *Turkey* .... **46** 36 44N 29 56 E
Elmer, *U.S.A.* **118** 39 57N 92 39W
Elmhurst, *Australia* ... **74** 37 13 S 143 16 E
Elmhurst, *U.S.A.* **119** 41 52N 87 58W
Elmina, *Ghana* **91** 5 5N 1 21W
Elmira, *Canada* **108** 43 36N 80 33W
Elmira, *U.S.A.* **116** 42 8N 76 49W
Elmore, *Australia* .... **74** 36 30 S 144 37 E
Elmore, *Calif., U.S.A.* **125** 33 7N 115 49W
Elmore, *Minn., U.S.A.* **119** 43 29N 83 18W
Elmshorn, *W. Germany* **30** 53 44N 9 40 E
Elmvale, *Canada* **108** 44 35N 79 52W
Elmwood, *U.S.A.* **118** 40 47N 90 0W
Elne, *France* .... **20** 42 36N 2 58 E
Elnora, *U.S.A.* **119** 38 53N 87 5W
Elong Elong, *Australia* **77** 32 8 S 149 3 E
Elora, *Canada* **108** 43 41N 80 26W
Elorza, *Venezuela* **134** 7 3N 69 31W
Eloy, *U.S.A.* **123** 32 46N 111 33W
Éloyes, *France* .... **19** 48 6N 6 36 E
Elphin, *Canada* **109** 44 55N 76 37W
Elphinstone, *Australia* **74** 37 5 S 144 22 E
Elrose, *Canada* **111** 51 12N 108 0W
Elsas, *Canada* **104** 48 32N 82 55W
Elsie, *U.S.A.* **124** 45 52N 123 35W
Elsinore = Helsingør,
Denmark .... **11** 56 2N 12 35 E
Elsinore, *U.S.A.* **123** 38 40N 112 2W
Elspe, *W. Germany* ... **30** 51 10N 8 1 E
Elspeet, *Neths.* ...... **16** 52 17N 5 48 E
Elst, *Neths.* .... **16** 51 55N 5 51 E
Elster →, *E. Germany* **30** 51 25N 11 57 E
Elsterwerda,
E. Germany .... **30** 51 27N 13 32 E
Elten, *Neths.* .... **16** 51 52N 6 9 E

Espinilho, Serra do, *Brazil* **141** 28 30 S 55 0W
Espino, *Venezuela* **134** 8 34N 66 1W
Espinosa de los Monteros, *Spain* **22** 43 5N 3 34W
Espírito Santo □, *Brazil* **139** 20 0 S 40 45W
Espíritu Santo, *Vanuatu* **68** 15 15 S 166 50 E
Espíritu Santo, B. del, *Mexico* **127** 19 15N 87 0W
Espíritu Santo, I., *Mexico* **126** 24 30N 110 23W
Espita, *Mexico* **127** 21 1N 88 19W
Esplanada, *Brazil* **139** 11 47 S 37 57W
Espluga de Francolí, *Spain* **24** 41 24N 1 7 E
Espuña, Sierra, *Spain* **25** 37 51N 1 35W
Espungabera, *Mozam.* **97** 20 29 S 32 45 E
Esquel, *Argentina* **142** 42 55 S 71 20W
Esquina, *Argentina* **140** 30 0 S 59 30W
Essaouira, *Morocco* **84** 31 32N 9 42W
Essarts, Les, *France* **18** 46 47N 1 12W
Essebie, *Zaïre* **92** 2 58N 30 40 E
Essen, *Belgium* **17** 51 28N 4 28 E
Essen, *W. Germany* **30** 51 28N 6 59 E
Essequibo □, *Guyana* **135** 7 0N 59 0W
Essequibo →, *Guyana* **135** 6 50N 58 30W
Essex, *Canada* **108** 42 10N 82 49W
Essex, *Calif., U.S.A.* **125** 34 44N 115 15W
Essex, *Ill., U.S.A.* **119** 41 11N 88 11W
Essex, *N.Y., U.S.A.* **117** 44 17N 73 21W
Essex □, *U.K.* **13** 51 48N 0 30 E
Esslingen, *W. Germany* **31** 48 43N 9 19 E
Essonne □, *France* **19** 48 30N 2 20 E
Essvik, *Sweden* **10** 62 18N 17 24 E
Estaca, Pta. del, *Spain* **22** 43 46N 7 42W
Estadilla, *Spain* **24** 42 4N 0 16 E
Estados, I. de Los, *Argentina* **142** 54 40 S 64 30W
Estagel, *France* **20** 42 47N 2 40 E
Estância, *Brazil* **138** 11 16 S 37 26W
Estancia, *U.S.A.* **123** 34 50N 106 1W
Estarreja, *Portugal* **22** 40 45N 8 35W
Estats, Pic d', *Spain* **24** 42 40N 1 24 E
Estcourt, *Canada* **107** 47 28N 69 14W
Estcourt, *S. Africa* **97** 29 0 S 29 53 E
Este, *Italy* **27** 45 12N 11 40 E
Esteban, *Spain* **22** 43 33N 6 5W
Estelí, *Nic.* **128** 13 9N 86 22W
Estella, *Spain* **24** 42 40N 2 0W
Estelline, *S. Dak., U.S.A.* **120** 44 39N 96 52W
Estelline, *Tex., U.S.A.* **121** 34 35N 100 27W
Estena →, *Spain* **23** 39 23N 4 44W
Estepa, *Spain* **23** 37 17N 4 52W
Estepona, *Spain* **23** 36 24N 5 7W
Esterhazy, *Canada* **111** 50 37N 102 5W
Esternay, *France* **19** 48 44N 3 33 E
Esterri de Aneu, *Spain* **24** 42 38N 1 5 E
Estevan, *Canada* **111** 49 10N 102 59W
Estevan Group, *Canada* **110** 53 3N 129 38W
Estherville, *U.S.A.* **120** 43 25N 94 50W
Estissac, *France* **19** 48 16N 3 48 E
Eston, *Canada* **111** 51 8N 108 40W
Estonian S.S.R. □, *U.S.S.R.* **36** 58 30N 25 30 E
Estoril, *Portugal* **23** 38 42N 9 23W
Estouk, *Mali* **91** 18 14N 1 2 E
Estrada, La, *Spain* **22** 42 43N 8 27W
Estrêla, Serra da, *Portugal* **22** 40 10N 7 45W
Estrella, *Spain* **25** 38 25N 3 35W
Estremoz, *Portugal* **23** 38 51N 7 39W
Estrondo, Serra do, *Brazil* **138** 7 20 S 48 0W
Esztergom, *Hungary* **33** 47 47N 18 44 E
Et Tîdra, *Mauritania* **90** 19 45N 16 20W
Eţ Ţīra, *Israel* **44** 32 14N 34 56 E
Étables-sur-Mer, *France* **18** 48 38N 2 51W
Etadunna, *Australia* **73** 28 43 S 138 38 E
Etah, *India* **49** 27 35N 78 40 E
Étain, *France* **19** 49 13N 5 38 E
Etalle, *Belgium* **17** 49 40N 5 36 E
Etamamu, *Canada* **105** 50 18N 59 59W
Étampes, *France* **19** 48 26N 2 10 E
Étang-sur-Arroux, *France* **21** 46 51N 4 11 E
Etanga, *Namibia* **96** 17 55 S 13 0 E
Étaples, *France* **19** 50 30N 1 39 E
Etawah, *India* **49** 26 48N 79 6 E
Etawah →, *U.S.A.* **115** 34 20N 84 15W
Etawney L., *Canada* **111** 57 50N 96 50W
Ete, *Nigeria* **91** 7 2N 7 28 E
Éthe, *Belgium* **17** 49 35N 5 35 E
Ethel, *U.S.A.* **124** 46 32N 122 46W
Ethel, Oued el →, *Algeria* **84** 28 31N 3 37W
Ethel Creek, *Australia* **78** 23 5 S 120 11 E
Ethelbert, *Canada* **111** 51 32N 100 25W
Ethiopia ■, *Africa* **45** 8 0N 40 0 E
Ethiopian Highlands, *Ethiopia* **82** 10 0N 37 0 E
Etive, L., *U.K.* **14** 56 30N 5 12W
Etna, *Italy* **29** 37 45N 15 0 E
Etoile, *Zaïre* **93** 11 33 S 27 30 E
Etolin I., *U.S.A.* **110** 56 5N 132 20W
Etosha Pan, *Namibia* **96** 18 40 S 16 30 E
Etoumbi, *Congo* **94** 0 1 S 14 57 E
Etowah, *U.S.A.* **115** 35 20N 84 30W
Étrépagny, *France* **19** 49 18N 1 36 E
Étretat, *France* **18** 49 42N 0 12 E
Étroits, Les, *Canada* **107** 47 24N 68 54W
Ettelbruck, *Lux.* **17** 49 51N 6 5 E
Etten, *Neths.* **17** 51 34N 4 38 E
Ettlingen, *W. Germany* **31** 48 58N 8 25 E
Ettrick Water, *U.K.* **14** 55 31N 2 55W
Etuku, *Zaïre* **92** 3 42 S 25 45 E
Etzatlán, *Mexico* **126** 20 48N 104 5W
Eu, *France* **18** 50 3N 1 26 E
Eua, *Tonga* **68** 21 22 S 174 56W
Euboea = Évvoia, *Greece* **35** 38 30N 24 0 E
Euchareena, *Australia* **76** 32 57 S 149 6 E
Euclid, *U.S.A.* **116** 41 32N 81 31W
Euclides da Cunha, *Brazil* **138** 10 31 S 39 1W
Eucumbene, *Australia* **75** 36 8 S 148 38 E
Eucumbene, L., *Australia* **75** 36 2 S 148 40 E
Eudora, *U.S.A.* **121** 33 5N 91 17W
Eufaula, *Ala., U.S.A.* **115** 31 55N 85 11W
Eufaula, *Okla., U.S.A.* **121** 35 20N 95 33W
Eufaula, L., *U.S.A.* **121** 35 15N 95 28W
Eugene, *U.S.A.* **122** 44 0N 123 8W
Eugowra, *Australia* **76** 33 22 S 148 24 E
Eulo, *Australia* **73** 28 10 S 145 3 E
Eumeralla →, *Australia* **74** 38 18 S 142 0 E
Eumungerie, *Australia* **76** 31 56 S 148 36 E
Eunice, *La., U.S.A.* **121** 30 35N 92 28W
Eunice, *N. Mex., U.S.A.* **121** 32 30N 103 10W
Eupen, *Belgium* **17** 50 37N 6 3 E
Euphrates = Furāt, Nahr al →, *Asia* **46** 31 0N 47 25 E
Eure □, *France* **18** 49 10N 1 0 E
Eure →, *France* **18** 49 18N 1 12 E
Eure-et-Loir □, *France* **18** 48 22N 1 30 E
Eureka, *Canada* **144** 80 0N 85 56W
Eureka, *Calif., U.S.A.* **122** 40 50N 124 0W
Eureka, *Ill., U.S.A.* **118** 40 43N 89 16W
Eureka, *Kans., U.S.A.* **121** 37 50N 96 20W
Eureka, *Mo., U.S.A.* **118** 38 30N 90 38W
Eureka, *Mont., U.S.A.* **122** 48 53N 115 6W
Eureka, *Nev., U.S.A.* **122** 39 32N 116 2W
Eureka, *S. Dak., U.S.A.* **120** 45 49N 99 38W
Eureka, *Utah, U.S.A.* **122** 40 0N 112 9W
Eureka, Mt., *Australia* **79** 26 35 S 121 35 E
Euroa, *Australia* **74** 36 44 S 145 35 E
Eurobodalla, *Australia* **76** 36 9 S 149 59 E
Europa, Picos de, *Spain* **22** 43 10N 4 49W
Europa, Pta. de, *Gib.* **23** 36 3N 5 21W
Europa Pt. = Europa, Pta. de, *Gib.* **23** 36 3N 5 21W
Europe **6** 50 0N 20 0 E
Europoort, *Neths.* **16** 51 57N 4 10 E
Euskirchen, *W. Germany* **30** 50 40N 6 45 E
Eustis, *U.S.A.* **115** 28 54N 81 36W
Eutin, *W. Germany* **30** 54 7N 10 38 E
Eutsuk L., *Canada* **110** 53 20N 126 45W
Eva, *Brazil* **135** 3 9 S 59 56W
Eva Downs, *Australia* **72** 18 1 S 134 52 E
Évain, *Canada* **106** 48 14N 79 8W
Eval, *Jordan* **44** 32 15N 35 15 E
Evale, *Angola* **95** 16 33 S 15 44 E
Evans, *U.S.A.* **120** 40 25N 104 43W
Evans Head, *Australia* **77** 29 7 S 153 27 E
Evans L., *Canada* **104** 50 50N 77 0W
Evans Mills, *U.S.A.* **117** 44 6N 75 48W
Evansdale, *U.S.A.* **118** 42 30N 92 17W
Evanston, *Ill., U.S.A.* **119** 42 0N 87 40W
Evanston, *Wyo., U.S.A.* **122** 41 10N 111 0W
Evansville, *Ill., U.S.A.* **118** 38 5N 89 56W
Evansville, *Ind., U.S.A.* **119** 38 0N 87 35W
Evansville, *Wis., U.S.A.* **118** 42 47N 89 18W
Évaux-les-Bains, *France* **20** 46 12N 2 29 E
Eveleth, *U.S.A.* **120** 47 29N 92 46W
Even Yahuda, *Israel* **44** 32 16N 34 53 E
Evensk, *U.S.S.R.* **41** 62 12N 159 30 E
Evenstad, *Norway* **10** 61 25N 11 7 E
Everard, L., *Australia* **73** 31 30 S 135 0 E
Everard Ras., *Australia* **79** 27 5 S 132 28 E
Evere, *Belgium* **17** 50 52N 4 25 E
Everest, Mt., *Nepal* **49** 28 5N 86 58 E
Everett, *Pa., U.S.A.* **116** 40 2N 78 24W
Everett, *Wash., U.S.A.* **124** 48 0N 122 10W
Evergem, *Belgium* **17** 51 7N 3 43 E
Everglades, *U.S.A.* **115** 26 0N 80 30W
Everglades City, *U.S.A.* **115** 25 52N 81 23W
Everglades Nat. Park., *U.S.A.* **115** 25 27N 80 53W
Evergreen, *U.S.A.* **115** 31 28N 86 55W
Everson, *U.S.A.* **122** 48 57N 122 22W
Everton, *Australia* **75** 36 25 S 146 33 E
Evesham, *U.K.* **13** 52 6N 1 57W
Évian-les-Bains, *France* **21** 46 24N 6 35 E
Evinayong, *Eq. Guin.* **94** 1 26N 10 35 E
Évinos →, *Greece* **35** 38 27N 21 40 E
Évisa, *France* **21** 42 15N 8 48 E
Évora, *Portugal* **23** 38 33N 7 57W
Évora □, *Portugal* **23** 38 33N 7 50W
Évreux, *France* **18** 49 0N 1 8 E
Évron, *France* **18** 48 10N 0 24W
Evrótas →, *Greece* **35** 36 50N 22 40 E
Évvoia, *Greece* **35** 38 30N 24 0 E
Évvoia □, *Greece* **35** 38 40N 23 40 E
Ewe, L., *U.K.* **14** 57 49N 5 38W
Ewing, *Mo., U.S.A.* **118** 40 0N 91 43W
Ewing, *Nebr., U.S.A.* **120** 42 18N 98 22W
Ewo, *Congo* **94** 0 48 S 14 45 E
Exaltación, *Bolivia* **137** 13 10 S 65 20W
Excelsior Springs, *U.S.A.* **118** 39 20N 94 10W
Excideuil, *France* **20** 45 20N 1 4 E
Exe →, *U.K.* **13** 50 38N 3 27W
Exeter, *Canada* **108** 43 21N 81 29W
Exeter, *U.K.* **13** 50 43N 3 31W
Exeter, *Calif., U.S.A.* **124** 36 17N 119 9W
Exeter, *N.H., U.S.A.* **117** 43 0N 70 58W
Exeter, *Nebr., U.S.A.* **120** 40 43N 97 30W
Exira, *U.S.A.* **118** 41 35N 94 52W
Exloo, *Neths.* **16** 52 53N 6 52 E
Exmes, *France* **18** 48 45N 0 10 E
Exmoor, *U.K.* **13** 51 10N 3 59W
Exmouth, *Australia* **78** 21 54 S 114 10 E
Exmouth, *U.K.* **13** 50 37N 3 26W
Exmouth G., *Australia* **78** 22 15 S 114 15 E
Expedition Range, *Australia* **72** 24 30 S 149 12 E
Extremadura □, *Spain* **23** 39 30N 6 5W
Exuma Sound, *Bahamas* **128** 24 30N 76 20W
Eyasi, L., *Tanzania* **92** 3 30 S 35 0 E
Eyeberry L., *Canada* **111** 63 8N 104 43W
Eyemouth, *U.K.* **14** 55 53N 2 5W
Eygurande, *France* **20** 45 40N 2 26 E
Eyjafjörður, *Iceland* **8** 66 15N 18 30W
Eymet, *France* **20** 44 40N 0 25 E
Eymoutiers, *France* **20** 45 40N 1 45 E
Eyrarbakki, *Iceland* **8** 63 52N 21 9W
Eyre, *Australia* **79** 32 15 S 126 18 E
Eyre (North), L., *Australia* **73** 28 30 S 137 20 E
Eyre (South), L., *Australia* **73** 29 18 S 137 25 E
Eyre Cr. →, *Australia* **73** 26 40 S 139 0 E
Eyre Mts., *N.Z.* **81** 45 25 S 168 25 E
Eyre Pen., *Australia* **73** 33 30 S 137 17 E
Eyzies-de-Tayac-Sireuil, Les, *France* **20** 44 56N 1 1 E
Ez Zeidab, *Sudan* **88** 17 25N 33 55 E
Ezcaray, *Spain* **24** 42 19N 3 0W
Ezmul, *Mauritania* **84** 22 15N 15 40W

F

Fabens, *U.S.A.* **123** 31 30N 106 8W
Fåborg, *Denmark* **11** 55 6N 10 15 E
Fabre, *Canada* **106** 47 12N 79 22W
Fabriano, *Italy* **27** 43 20N 12 52 E
Făcăeni, *Romania* **34** 44 32N 27 53 E
Facatativá, *Colombia* **134** 4 49N 74 22W
Fachi, *Niger* **87** 18 6N 11 34 E
Facture, *France* **20** 44 39N 0 58W
Fada, *Chad* **87** 17 13N 21 34 E
Fada-n-Gourma, *Burkina Faso* **91** 12 10N 0 30 E
Faddeyevskiy, Ostrov, *U.S.S.R.* **41** 76 0N 150 0 E
Fāḍilī, *Si. Arabia* **46** 26 55N 49 10 E
Fadlab, *Sudan* **88** 17 42N 34 2 E
Faenza, *Italy* **27** 44 17N 11 53 E
Fafa, *Mali* **91** 15 22N 0 48 E
Fafe, *Portugal* **22** 41 27N 8 11W
Faga, *W. Samoa* **68** 13 39 S 172 8W
Fagam, *Nigeria* **91** 11 1N 10 1 E
Fagamalo, *W. Samoa* **68** 13 25 S 172 21W
Făgăras, *Romania* **34** 45 48N 24 58 E
Făgăras, Munţii, *Romania* **34** 45 40N 24 40 E
Fågelsjö, *Sweden* **10** 61 50N 14 35 E
Fagerhult, *Sweden* **11** 57 8N 15 40 E
Fagernes, *Norway* **9** 60 59N 9 14 E
Fagersta, *Sweden* **10** 60 1N 15 46 E
Făget, *Romania* **34** 45 52N 22 10 E
Fagnano, L., *Argentina* **142** 54 30 S 68 0W
Fagnano Castello, *Italy* **29** 39 31N 16 4 E
Fagnières, *France* **19** 48 58N 4 20 E
Fahraj, *Iran* **47** 29 0N 59 0 E
Fahūd, *Oman* **47** 22 18N 56 28 E
Faillon, L., *Canada* **106** 48 21N 76 39W
Fair Hd., *U.K.* **15** 55 14N 6 10W
Fair Oaks, *U.S.A.* **124** 38 39N 121 16W
Fairbank, *U.S.A.* **123** 31 44N 110 12W
Fairbanks, *U.S.A.* **102** 64 50N 147 50W
Fairborn, *U.S.A.* **119** 39 52N 84 2W
Fairbury, *Ill., U.S.A.* **119** 40 45N 88 31W
Fairbury, *Nebr., U.S.A.* **120** 40 5N 97 5W
Fairfax, *Ohio, U.S.A.* **119** 39 5N 83 37W
Fairfax, *Okla., U.S.A.* **121** 36 37N 96 45W
Fairfield, *Australia* **76** 33 53 S 150 57 E
Fairfield, *Ala., U.S.A.* **115** 33 30N 87 0W
Fairfield, *Calif., U.S.A.* **124** 38 14N 122 1W
Fairfield, *Conn., U.S.A.* **117** 41 8N 73 16W
Fairfield, *Idaho, U.S.A.* **122** 43 21N 114 46W
Fairfield, *Ill., U.S.A.* **119** 38 20N 88 20W
Fairfield, *Iowa, U.S.A.* **118** 41 0N 91 58W
Fairfield, *Mont., U.S.A.* **122** 47 40N 112 0W
Fairfield, *Ohio, U.S.A.* **119** 39 21N 84 34W
Fairfield, *Tex., U.S.A.* **121** 31 40N 96 0W
Fairford, *Canada* **111** 51 37N 98 38W
Fairholme, *Australia* **76** 33 14 S 147 22 E
Fairhope, *U.S.A.* **115** 30 35N 87 50W
Fairlie, *N.Z.* **81** 44 5 S 170 49 E
Fairmead, *U.S.A.* **124** 37 5N 120 10W
Fairmont, *Minn., U.S.A.* **120** 43 37N 94 30W
Fairmont, *W. Va., U.S.A.* **114** 39 29N 80 10W
Fairmount, *U.S.A.* **125** 34 45N 118 26W
Fairplay, *U.S.A.* **123** 39 9N 105 40W
Fairport, *N.Y., U.S.A.* **116** 43 8N 77 29W
Fairport, *Ohio, U.S.A.* **116** 41 45N 81 17W
Fairview, *Australia* **72** 15 31 S 144 17 E
Fairview, *Canada* **110** 56 5N 118 25W
Fairview, *N. Dak., U.S.A.* **120** 47 49N 104 7W
Fairview, *Okla., U.S.A.* **121** 36 19N 98 30W
Fairview, *Utah, U.S.A.* **122** 39 50N 111 0W
Fairweather, Mt., *U.S.A.* **102** 58 55N 137 45W
Faisalabad, *Pakistan* **48** 31 30N 73 5 E
Faith, *U.S.A.* **120** 45 2N 102 4W
Faizabad, *India* **49** 26 45N 82 10 E
Faizpur, *India* **50** 21 14N 75 49 E
Fajardo, *Puerto Rico* **129** 18 20N 65 39W
Fakfak, *Indonesia* **57** 3 0 S 132 15 E
Fakobli, *Ivory C.* **90** 7 23N 7 23W
Fakse, *Denmark* **11** 55 15N 12 8 E
Fakse B., *Denmark* **11** 55 11N 12 15 E
Fakse Ladeplads, *Denmark* **11** 55 11N 12 9 E
Faku, *China* **61** 42 32N 123 21 E
Falaise, *France* **18** 48 54N 0 12W
Falaise, Mui, *Vietnam* **54** 19 6N 105 45 E
Falam, *Burma* **52** 23 0N 93 45 E
Falces, *Spain* **24** 42 24N 1 48W
Fălciu, *Romania* **34** 46 17N 28 7 E
Falcón □, *Venezuela* **134** 11 0N 69 50W
Falcon, C., *Algeria* **85** 35 50N 0 50W
Falcon Dam, *U.S.A.* **121** 26 50N 99 20W
Falconara Marittima, *Italy* **27** 43 37N 13 23 E
Falconbridge, *Canada* **108** 46 35N 80 45W
Falconer, *U.S.A.* **116** 42 7N 79 13W
Faléa, *Mali* **90** 12 16N 11 17W
Falelatai, *W. Samoa* **68** 13 55 S 171 59W
Falelima, *W. Samoa* **68** 13 32 S 172 41W
Falenki, *U.S.S.R.* **37** 58 22N 51 35 E
Faleshty, *U.S.S.R.* **38** 47 32N 27 44 E
Falfurrias, *U.S.A.* **121** 27 14N 98 8W
Falher, *Canada* **110** 55 44N 117 15W
Falkenberg, *E. Germany* **30** 51 34N 13 13 E
Falkenberg, *Sweden* **11** 56 54N 12 30 E
Falkensee, *E. Germany* **30** 52 35N 13 6 E
Falkenstein, *E. Germany* **30** 50 27N 12 24 E
Falkirk, *U.K.* **14** 56 0N 3 47W
Falkland, East, I., *Falk. Is.* **142** 51 40 S 58 30W
Falkland, West, I., *Falk. Is.* **142** 51 40 S 60 0W
Falkland Is., *Atl. Oc.* **142** 51 30 S 59 0W
Falkland Is. Dependency □, *Atl. Oc.* **143** 57 0 S 40 0W
Falkland Sd., *Falk. Is.* **142** 52 0 S 60 0W
Falköping, *Sweden* **11** 58 12N 13 33 E
Fall River, *U.S.A.* **117** 41 45N 71 5W
Fall River Mills, *U.S.A.* **122** 41 1N 121 30W
Fallbrook, *U.S.A.* **123** 33 25N 117 12W
Fallbrook, *U.S.A.* **125** 33 23N 117 15W
Fallon, *Mont., U.S.A.* **120** 46 52N 105 8W
Fallon, *Nev., U.S.A.* **122** 39 31N 118 51W
Falls City, *Nebr., U.S.A.* **120** 40 0N 95 40W
Falls City, *Oreg., U.S.A.* **122** 44 54N 123 29W
Falls Creek, *N.S.W., Australia* **76** 34 58 S 150 36 E
Falls Creek, *Vic., Australia* **75** 36 52 S 147 17 E
Falls Creek, *U.S.A.* **116** 41 8N 78 49W
Falmouth, *Jamaica* **128** 18 30N 77 40W
Falmouth, *U.K.* **13** 50 9N 5 5W
Falmouth, *U.S.A.* **119** 38 40N 84 20W
False B., *S. Africa* **96** 34 15 S 18 40 E
False Divi Pt., *India* **51** 15 43N 80 50 E
Falset, *Spain* **24** 41 7N 0 50 E
Falso, C., *Honduras* **128** 15 12N 83 21W
Falster, *Denmark* **11** 54 45N 11 55 E
Falsterbo, *Sweden* **11** 55 23N 12 50 E
Fălticeni, *Romania* **34** 47 21N 26 20 E
Falun, *Sweden* **10** 60 37N 15 37 E
Famagusta, *Cyprus* **46** 35 8N 33 55 E
Famatina, Sierra de, *Argentina* **140** 27 30 S 68 0W
Family L., *Canada* **111** 51 54N 95 27W
Famoso, *U.S.A.* **125** 35 37N 119 12W
Fan Xian, *China* **60** 35 55N 115 38 E
Fana, *Mali* **90** 13 0N 6 56W
Fandriana, *Madag.* **97** 20 14 S 47 21 E
Fang, *Thailand* **54** 19 55N 99 13 E
Fang Xian, *China* **59** 32 3N 110 40 E
Fangchang, *China* **59** 31 5N 118 4 E
Fangcheng, *Guangxi Zhuangzu, China* **58** 21 42N 108 21 E
Fangcheng, *Henan, China* **60** 33 18N 112 59 E
Fangliao, *Taiwan* **59** 22 22N 120 38 E
Fangshan, *China* **60** 38 3N 111 25 E
Fangzi, *China* **61** 36 33N 119 10 E
Fani i Madh →, *Albania* **35** 41 56N 20 16 E
Fanjiatun, *China* **61** 43 40N 125 0 E
Fannich, L., *U.K.* **14** 57 40N 5 0W
Fanny Bay, *Canada* **110** 49 37N 124 48W
Fanø, *Denmark* **11** 55 25N 8 25 E
Fano, *Italy* **27** 43 50N 13 0 E
Fanshaw, *U.S.A.* **110** 57 11N 133 30W
Fanshi, *China* **60** 39 12N 113 20 E
Fao = Al Fāw, *Iraq* **46** 30 0N 48 30 E

Faqirwali

Faqirwali, *Pakistan* ... **48** 29 27N 73 0 E
Fara in Sabina, *Italy* .. **27** 42 13N 12 44 E
Faradje, *Zaïre* .... **92** 3 50N 29 45 E
Farafangana, *Madag.* .. **97** 22 49 S 47 50 E
Farâfra, El Wâhât el-, *Egypt* .... **88** 27 15N 28 20 E
Farāh, *Afghan.* .... **47** 32 20N 62 7 E
Farāh □, *Afghan.* ..... **47** 32 25N 62 10 E
Farahalana, *Madag.* .. **97** 14 26 S 50 10 E
Faraid, Gebel, *Egypt* . **88** 23 33N 35 19 E
Faramana, *Burkina Faso* **90** 11 56N 4 45W
Faranah, *Guinea* **90** 10 3N 10 45W
Farasān, Jazā'ir, *Si. Arabia* .... **45** 16 45N 41 55 E
Faratsiho, *Madag.* ..... **97** 19 24 S 46 57 E
Farbarachi, *Somali Rep.* **98** 2 30N 45 30 E
Fardes →, *Spain* **25** 37 35N 3 0W
Fareara, Pte., *Tahiti* .. **68** 17 52 S 149 9W
Fareham, *U.K.* **13** 50 52N 1 11W
Farewell, C., *N.Z.* ... **81** 40 29 S 172 43 E
Farewell C. = Farvel, Kap, *Greenland* **144** 59 48N 43 55W
Farewell Spit, *N.Z.* ... **81** 40 35 S 173 0 E
Fargo, *U.S.A.* **120** 46 52N 96 40W
Fari'a →, *Jordan* .... **44** 32 12N 35 27 E
Faribault, *U.S.A.* **120** 44 15N 93 19W
Faridkot, *India* .... **48** 30 44N 74 45 E
Faridpur, *Bangla.* ..... **49** 23 15N 89 55 E
Färila, *Sweden* .... **10** 61 48N 15 50 E
Farim, *Guinea-Biss.* .. **90** 12 27N 15 9W
Farīmān, *Iran* .... **47** 35 40N 59 49 E
Farina, *Australia* ..... **73** 30 3 S 138 15 E
Faringe, *Sweden* ...... **10** 59 55N 18 7 E
Farinha →, *Brazil* ... **138** 6 51 S 47 30W
Fariones, Pta., *Canary Is.* **25** 29 13N 13 28W
Fâriskûr, *Egypt* ...... **88** 31 20N 31 43 E
Farmer City, *U.S.A.* .. **119** 40 15N 88 39W
Farmersburg, *U.S.A.* . **119** 39 15N 87 23W
Farmerville, *U.S.A.* .. **121** 32 48N 92 23W
Farmington, *Calif., U.S.A.* **124** 37 56N 121 0W
Farmington, *Ill., U.S.A.* **118** 40 42N 90 0W
Farmington, *Iowa, U.S.A.* **118** 40 38N 91 44W
Farmington, *Mo., U.S.A.* **118** 37 47N 90 25W
Farmington, *N.H., U.S.A.* **117** 43 25N 71 7W
Farmington, *N. Mex., U.S.A.* **123** 36 45N 108 28W
Farmington, *Utah, U.S.A.* **122** 41 0N 111 12W
Farmington →, *U.S.A.* **117** 41 51N 72 38W
Farmland, *U.S.A.* **119** 40 15N 85 5W
Farmville, *U.S.A.* **114** 37 19N 78 22W
Farnborough, *U.K.* ... **13** 51 17N 0 46W
Farne Is., *U.K.* **12** 55 38N 1 37W
Farnham, *Canada* **117** 45 17N 72 59W
Faro, *Brazil* .... **135** 2 10 S 56 39W
Faro, *Portugal* **23** 37 2N 7 55W
Fårö, *Sweden* .... **9** 57 55N 19 5 E
Faro □, *Portugal* **23** 37 12N 8 10W
Faroe Is. = Føroyar, *Atl. Oc.* **130** 62 0N 7 0W
Farquhar, C., *Australia* **79** 23 50 S 113 36 E
Farquhar Is., *Seychelles* **53** 11 0 S 52 0 E
Farrar →, *U.K.* **14** 57 30N 4 30W
Farrars Cr. →, *Australia* .... **72** 25 35 S 140 43 E
Farrāshband, *Iran* .... **47** 28 57N 52 5 E
Farrell, *U.S.A.* **116** 41 13N 80 29W
Farrell Flat, *Australia* . **73** 33 48 S 138 48 E
Farrukhabad-cum-Fatehgarh, *India* ... **49** 27 30N 79 32 E
Fārs □, *Iran* .... **47** 29 30N 55 0 E
Fársala, *Greece* ...... **35** 39 17N 22 23 E
Farsø, *Denmark* ...... **11** 56 46N 9 19 E
Farsund, *Norway* ..... **9** 58 5N 6 55 E
Fartak, Râs, *Si. Arabia* **46** 28 5N 34 34 E
Fartura, Serra da, *Brazil* .... **141** 26 21 S 52 52W
Faru, *Nigeria* .... **91** 12 48N 6 12 E
Farum, *Denmark* ..... **11** 55 49N 12 21 E
Farvel, Kap, *Greenland* **144** 59 48N 43 55W
Farwell, *U.S.A.* **121** 34 25N 103 0W
Fāryāb □, *Afghan.* ... **47** 36 0N 65 0 E
Fasā, *Iran* .... **47** 29 0N 53 39 E
Fasano, *Italy* .... **29** 40 50N 17 20 E
Fashoda, *Sudan* ...... **89** 9 50N 32 2 E
Fastnet Rock, *Ireland* . **15** 51 22N 9 37W
Fastov, *U.S.S.R.* ..... **36** 50 7N 29 57 E
Fatagar, Tanjung, *Indonesia* .... **57** 2 46 S 131 57 E
Fatehgarh, *India* ..... **49** 27 25N 79 35 E
Fatehpur, *Raj., India* . **48** 28 0N 74 40 E
Fatehpur, *Ut. P., India* **49** 25 56N 81 13 E
Fatesh, *U.S.S.R.* ..... **37** 52 8N 35 57 E
Fatick, *Senegal* **90** 14 19N 16 27W
Fatima, *Canada* **105** 47 24N 61 53W
Fátima, *Portugal* **23** 39 37N 8 39W
Fatoya, *Guinea* **90** 11 37N 9 10W
Faucille, Col de la, *France* .... **21** 46 22N 6 2 E
Faulkton, *U.S.A.* **120** 45 4N 99 8W
Faulquemont, *France* . **19** 49 3N 6 36 E
Fauquembergues, *France* .... **19** 50 36N 2 5 E
Faure I., *Australia* .... **79** 25 52 S 113 50 E
Făurei, *Romania* ..... **34** 45 6N 27 19 E
Fauresmith, *S. Africa* . **96** 29 44 S 25 17 E
Fauro, *Solomon Is.* .... **68** 6 55 S 156 7 E
Fauske, *Norway* ...... **8** 67 17N 15 25 E
Fauvillers, *Belgium* ... **17** 49 51N 5 40 E
Favara, *Italy* .... **28** 37 19N 13 39 E
Favignana, *Italy* ...... **28** 37 56N 12 18 E
Favignana, I., *Italy* ... **28** 37 56N 12 18 E
Favourable Lake, *Canada* **104** 52 50N 93 39W
Fawn →, *Canada* **104** 55 20N 87 35W
Fawnskin, *U.S.A.* **125** 34 16N 116 56W
Faxaflói, *Iceland* **8** 64 29N 23 0W
Faya-Largeau, *Chad* .. **87** 17 58N 19 6 E
Fayaoué, *Vanuatu* .... **68** 20 38 S 166 33 E
Fayd, *Si. Arabia* ..... **46** 27 1N 42 52 E
Fayence, *France* ...... **21** 43 38N 6 42 E
Fayette, *Ala., U.S.A.* . **115** 33 40N 87 50W
Fayette, *Iowa, U.S.A.* **118** 42 51N 91 48W
Fayette, *Mo., U.S.A.* . **118** 39 10N 92 40W
Fayette, *Ohio, U.S.A.* **119** 41 40N 84 20W
Fayetteville, *Ark., U.S.A.* **121** 36 0N 94 5W
Fayetteville, *N.C., U.S.A.* **115** 35 0N 78 58W
Fayetteville, *Tenn., U.S.A.* **115** 35 8N 86 30W
Fayón, *Spain* .... **24** 41 15N 0 20 E
Fazenda Libongo, *Angola* .... **95** 8 24 S 13 24 E
Fazenda Nova, *Brazil* . **139** 16 11 S 50 48W
Fazilka, *India* .... **48** 30 27N 74 2 E
Fazilpur, *Pakistan* .... **48** 29 18N 70 29 E
Fdérik, *Mauritania* ... **84** 22 40N 12 45W
Fé, La, *Cuba* **128** 22 2N 84 15W
Feale →, *Ireland* **15** 52 26N 9 40W
Fear, C., *U.S.A.* **115** 33 51N 78 0W
Feather →, *U.S.A.* ... **122** 38 47N 121 36W
Feather Falls, *U.S.A.* . **124** 39 36N 121 16W
Featherston, *N.Z.* .... **80** 41 6 S 175 20 E
Featherstone, *Zambia* . **93** 18 42 S 30 55 E
Feathertop, Mt., *Australia* .... **75** 36 53 S 147 7 E
Fécamp, *France* ...... **18** 49 45N 0 22 E
Fedala = Mohammedia, *Morocco* **84** 33 44N 7 21W
Federación, *Argentina* **140** 31 0 S 57 55W
Fedjadj, Chott el, *Tunisia* .... **86** 33 52N 9 14 E
Fehmarn, *E. Germany* **30** 54 26N 11 10 E
Fei Xian, *China* ...... **61** 35 18N 117 59 E
Feijó, *Brazil* .... **136** 8 9 S 70 21W
Feilding, *N.Z.* .... **80** 40 13 S 175 35 E
Feira de Santana, *Brazil* .... **139** 12 15 S 38 57W
Feixiang, *China* ...... **60** 36 30N 114 45 E
Fejø, *Denmark* .... **11** 54 55N 11 30 E
Felanitx, *Spain* .... **25** 39 28N 3 9 E
Feldberg, *E. Germany* **30** 53 20N 13 26 E
Feldberg, *W. Germany* **31** 47 51N 7 58 E
Feldkirch, *Austria* .... **31** 47 15N 9 37 E
Felicity, *U.S.A.* **119** 38 51N 84 6W
Felipe Carrillo Puerto, *Mexico* **127** 19 38N 88 3W
Felixlândia, *Brazil* .... **139** 18 47 S 44 55W
Felixstowe, *U.K.* ..... **13** 51 58N 1 22 E
Felletin, *France* ...... **20** 45 53N 2 11 E
Felton, *U.S.A.* **124** 37 3N 122 4W
Feltre, *Italy* .... **27** 46 1N 11 55 E
Femø, *Denmark* ...... **11** 54 58N 11 53 E
Femunden, *Norway* ... **10** 62 10N 11 53 E
Fen He →, *China* .... **60** 35 36N 110 42 E
Fenelon Falls, *Canada* **109** 44 32N 78 45W
Feneroa, *Ethiopia* .... **89** 13 5N 39 3 E
Feng Xian, *Jiangsu, China* .... **60** 34 43N 116 35 E
Feng Xian, *Shaanxi, China* .... **60** 33 54N 106 40 E
Fengári, *Greece* ...... **35** 40 25N 25 32 E
Fengcheng, *Jiangxi, China* .... **59** 28 12N 115 48 E
Fengcheng, *Liaoning, China* .... **61** 40 28N 124 5 E
Fengdu, *China* .... **58** 29 55N 107 41 E
Fengfeng, *China* ..... **60** 36 28N 114 8 E
Fenggang, *China* ..... **58** 27 57N 107 47 E
Fenghua, *China* ...... **59** 29 40N 121 25 E
Fenghuang, *China* .... **58** 27 57N 109 29 E
Fenghuangzui, *China* . **58** 33 30N 109 23 E
Fengjie, *China* .... **58** 31 5N 109 36 E
Fengkai, *China* .... **59** 23 24N 111 30 E
Fengle, *China* .... **59** 31 29N 112 29 E
Fengning, *China* ..... **60** 41 10N 116 33 E
Fengqing, *China* ..... **58** 24 38N 99 55 E
Fengqiu, *China* ...... **60** 35 2N 114 25 E
Fengrun, *China* ...... **61** 39 48N 118 8 E
Fengshan, *Guangxi Zhuangzu, China* .... **58** 24 39N 109 15 E
Fengshan, *Guangxi Zhuangzu, China* .... **58** 24 31N 107 3 E
Fengtai, *Anhui, China* **59** 32 50N 116 40 E
Fengtai, *Beijing, China* **60** 39 50N 116 18 E
Fengxian, *China* ..... **59** 30 55N 121 26 E
Fengxiang, *China* .... **60** 34 29N 107 25 E
Fengxin, *China* ...... **59** 28 41N 115 18 E
Fengyang, *China* ..... **61** 32 51N 117 29 E
Fengyi, *China* .... **58** 25 37N 100 20 E
Fengzhen, *China* ..... **60** 40 25N 113 2 E
Feni Is., *Papua N. G.* . **69** 4 0 S 153 40 E
Fenit, *Ireland* **15** 52 17N 9 51W
Fennimore, *U.S.A.* ... **118** 42 58N 90 41W
Fenny, *Bangla.* .... **52** 22 55N 91 32 E
Feno, C. de, *France* .. **21** 41 58N 8 33 E
Fenoarivo Afovoany, *Madag.* .... **97** 18 26 S 46 34 E
Fenoarivo Atsinanana, *Madag.* .... **97** 17 22 S 49 25 E
Fens, The, *U.K.* ..... **12** 52 45N 0 2 E
Fenton, *U.S.A.* **104** 42 47N 83 44W
Fenxi, *China* .... **60** 36 40N 111 31 E
Fenyang, *China* ...... **60** 37 18N 111 48 E
Fenyi, *China* .... **59** 27 45N 114 47 E
Feodosiya, *U.S.S.R.* .. **38** 45 2N 35 28 E
Fer, C. de, *Algeria* ... **85** 37 3N 7 10 E
Ferdows, *Iran* .... **47** 33 58N 58 2 E
Fère, La, *France* ..... **19** 49 39N 3 21 E
Fère-Champenoise, *France* .... **19** 48 45N 4 0 E
Fère-en-Tardenois, *France* .... **19** 49 10N 3 30 E
Ferentino, *Italy* ...... **28** 41 42N 13 14 E
Ferfer, *Somali Rep.* ... **98** 5 4N 45 9 E
Fergana, *U.S.S.R.* ... **40** 40 23N 71 19 E
Fergus, *Canada* **108** 43 43N 80 24W
Fergus Falls, *U.S.A.* .. **120** 46 18N 96 7W
Ferguson, *U.S.A.* **118** 38 45N 90 18W
Fergusson I., *Papua N. G.* .... **69** 9 30 S 150 45 E
Fériana, *Tunisia* ...... **86** 34 59N 8 33 E
Feričanci, *Yugoslavia* . **33** 45 32N 18 0 E
Ferkane, *Algeria* ..... **85** 34 37N 7 26 E
Ferkéssédougou, *Ivory C.* **90** 9 35N 5 6W
Ferlach, *Austria* ...... **33** 46 32N 14 18 E
Ferland, *Canada* **104** 50 19N 88 27W
Ferlo, Vallée du, *Senegal* **90** 15 15N 14 15W
Fermanagh □, *U.K.* .. **15** 54 21N 7 40W
Ferme-Neuve, *Canada* **106** 46 42N 75 27W
Fermo, *Italy* .... **27** 43 10N 13 42 E
Fermoselle, *Spain* **22** 41 19N 6 27W
Fermoy, *Ireland* **15** 52 4N 8 18W
Fernán Nuñéz, *Spain* . **23** 37 40N 4 44W
Fernández, *Argentina* . **140** 27 55 S 63 50W
Fernandina Beach, *U.S.A.* **115** 30 40N 81 30W
Fernando de Noronha, *Brazil* .... **138** 4 0 S 33 10W
Fernando Póo = Bioko, *Eq. Guin.* .... **91** 3 30N 8 40 E
Fernandópolis, *Brazil* . **139** 20 16 S 50 14W
Ferndale, *Calif., U.S.A.* **122** 40 37N 124 12W
Ferndale, *Wash., U.S.A.* **124** 48 51N 122 41W
Fernie, *Canada* **110** 49 30N 115 5W
Fernlees, *Australia* ... **72** 23 51 S 148 7 E
Fernley, *U.S.A.* **122** 39 36N 119 14W
Feroke, *India* .... **51** 11 9N 75 46 E
Feronia, *Canada* **108** 46 22N 79 19W
Ferozepore = Firozpur, *India* .... **48** 30 55N 74 40 E
Férrai, *Greece* .... **35** 40 53N 26 10 E
Ferrandina, *Italy* ..... **29** 40 30N 16 28 E
Ferrara, *Italy* .... **27** 44 50N 11 36 E
Ferrato, C., *Italy* ..... **28** 39 18N 9 39 E
Ferreira do Alentejo, *Portugal* **23** 38 4N 8 6W
Ferreñafe, *Peru* ...... **136** 6 42 S 79 50W
Ferret, C., *France* **20** 44 38N 1 15W
Ferrette, *France* ..... **19** 47 30N 7 20 E
Ferriday, *U.S.A.* **121** 31 35N 91 33W
Ferrières, *France* ..... **19** 48 5N 2 48 E
Ferriete, *Italy* .... **26** 44 40N 9 30 E
Ferrol, Pen. de, *Peru* . **136** 9 10 S 78 35W
Ferron, *U.S.A.* **123** 39 3N 111 3W
Ferros, *Brazil* .... **139** 19 14 S 43 2W
Ferryland, *Canada* **105** 47 2N 52 53W
Ferrysburg, *U.S.A.* ... **119** 43 5N 86 13W
Ferté-Bernard, La, *France* .... **18** 48 10N 0 40 E
Ferté-Macé, La, *France* **18** 48 35N 0 22W
Ferté-St.-Aubin, La, *France* .... **19** 47 42N 1 57 E
Ferté-sous-Jouarre, La, *France* .... **19** 48 56N 3 8 E
Ferté-Vidame, La, *France* .... **18** 48 37N 0 53 E
Fertile, *U.S.A.* **120** 47 31N 96 18W
Fertília, *Italy* .... **28** 40 37N 8 13 E
Fès, *Morocco* **84** 34 0N 5 0W
Feschaux, *Belgium* ... **17** 50 9N 4 54 E
Feshi, *Zaïre* .... **95** 6 8 S 18 10 E
Fessenden, *U.S.A.* ... **120** 47 42N 99 38W
Festus, *U.S.A.* **118** 38 13N 90 24W
Feteşti, *Romania* ..... **34** 44 22N 27 51 E
Fethiye, *Turkey* ...... **46** 36 36N 29 10 E
Fetlar, *U.K.* **14** 60 36N 0 52W
Feuilles →, *Canada* .. **103** 58 47N 70 4W
Feurs, *France* .... **21** 45 45N 4 13 E
Feyzābād, *Afghan.* ... **47** 37 7N 70 33 E
Fezzan, *Libya* .... **82** 27 0N 15 0 E
Ffestiniog, *U.K.* **12** 52 58N 3 56W
Fiambalá, *Argentina* .. **140** 27 45 S 67 37W
Fianarantsoa, *Madag.* . **97** 21 26 S 47 5 E
Fianarantsoa □, *Madag.* .... **97** 19 30 S 47 0 E
Fianga, *Cameroon* .... **87** 9 55N 15 9 E
Fichtelgebirge, *W. Germany* .... **31** 50 10N 12 0 E
Ficksburg, *S. Africa* .. **97** 28 51 S 27 53 E
Fidenza, *Italy* .... **26** 44 51N 10 3 E
Fiditi, *Nigeria* .... **91** 7 45N 3 53 E
Field, *Canada* **108** 46 31N 80 1W
Field →, *Australia* ... **72** 23 48 S 138 0 E
Field I., *Australia* .... **78** 12 5 S 132 23 E
Fieri, *Albania* .... **35** 40 43N 19 33 E
Fife □, *U.K.* **14** 56 13N 3 2W
Fife Ness, *U.K.* **14** 56 17N 2 35W
Fifield, *Australia* ..... **76** 32 47 S 147 28 E
Fifth Cataract, *Sudan* . **88** 18 22N 33 50 E
Figeac, *France* .... **20** 44 37N 2 2 E
Figline Valdarno, *Italy* **27** 43 37N 11 28 E
Figtree, *Zambia* ...... **93** 20 22 S 28 20 E
Figueira Castelo Rodrigo, *Portugal* .. **22** 40 57N 6 58W
Figueira da Foz, *Portugal* **22** 40 7N 8 54W
Figueiró dos Vinhos, *Portugal* **22** 39 55N 8 16W
Figueras, *Spain* ...... **24** 42 18N 2 58 E
Figuig, *Morocco* **85** 32 5N 1 11W
Fihaonana, *Madag.* ... **97** 18 36 S 47 12 E
Fiherenana, *Madag.* .. **97** 18 29 S 48 24 E
Fiherenana →, *Madag.* **97** 23 19 S 43 37 E
Fiji ■, *Pac. Oc.* ...... **68** 17 20 S 179 0 E
Fika, *Nigeria* .... **91** 11 15N 11 13 E
Filabres, Sierra de los, *Spain* **25** 37 13N 2 20W
Filadelfia, *Bolivia* .... **136** 11 20 S 68 46W
Filadélfia, *Brazil* ..... **138** 7 21 S 47 30W
Filadélfia, *Italy* ...... **29** 38 47N 16 17 E
File Axe, L., *Canada* . **107** 50 18N 73 34W
Filer, *U.S.A.* **122** 42 30N 114 35W
Filey, *U.K.* **12** 54 13N 0 18W
Filiaşi, *Romania* ...... **34** 44 32N 23 31 E
Filiátes, *Greece* ...... **35** 39 38N 20 16 E
Filiatrá, *Greece* ...... **35** 37 9N 21 35 E
Filicudi, *Italy* .... **29** 38 35N 14 33 E
Filiourí →, *Greece* ... **35** 41 15N 25 40 E
Filipstad, *Sweden* ..... **10** 59 43N 14 9 E
Filisur, *Switz.* .... **31** 46 41N 9 40 E
Fillmore, *Canada* **111** 49 50N 103 25W
Fillmore, *Calif., U.S.A.* **125** 34 23N 118 58W
Fillmore, *Utah, U.S.A.* **123** 38 58N 112 20W
Filottrano, *Italy* ...... **27** 43 28N 13 20 E
Fils, L. du, *Canada* ... **106** 46 37N 78 7W
Filyos, *Turkey* .... **38** 41 34N 32 4 E
Filyos →, *Turkey* .... **46** 41 35N 32 10 E
Finale Lígure, *Italy* ... **26** 44 10N 8 21 E
Finale nell' Emília, *Italy* **27** 44 50N 11 18 E
Fiñana, *Spain* **25** 37 10N 2 50W
Finch, *Canada* **106** 45 11N 75 7W
Findhorn →, *U.K.* ... **14** 57 38N 3 38W
Findlay, *U.S.A.* **119** 41 0N 83 41W
Fine Flower Creek, *Australia* .... **77** 29 24 S 152 42 E
Finger L., *Canada* **111** 53 33N 93 30W
Fíngõe, *Mozam.* ..... **93** 14 55 S 31 50 E
Finike, *Turkey* .... **46** 36 21N 30 10 E
Finistère □, *France* ... **18** 48 20N 4 0W
Finisterre, *Spain* **22** 42 54N 9 16W
Finisterre, C., *Spain* .. **22** 42 50N 9 19W
Finisterre Ra., *Papua N. G.* .... **69** 6 0 S 146 30 E
Finke, *Australia* ...... **72** 25 34 S 134 35 E
Finke →, *Australia* ... **73** 27 0 S 136 10 E
Finland ■, *Europe* ... **9** 63 0N 27 0 E
Finland, G. of, *Europe* **9** 60 0N 26 0 E
Finlay →, *Canada* ... **110** 57 0N 125 10W
Finley, *Australia* ..... **74** 35 38 S 145 35 E
Finley, *U.S.A.* **120** 47 35N 97 50W
Finn →, *Ireland* **15** 54 50N 7 55W
Finnigan, Mt., *Australia* **72** 15 49 S 145 17 E
Finniss, C., *Australia* . **73** 33 8 S 134 51 E
Finnmark fylke □, *Norway* .... **8** 69 30N 25 0 E
Finschhafen, *Papua N. G.* .... **69** 6 33 S 147 50 E
Finsteraarhorn, *Switz.* **31** 46 31N 8 10 E
Finsterwalde, *E. Germany* .... **30** 51 37N 13 42 E
Finsterwolde, *Neths.* .. **16** 53 12N 7 6 E
Fiora →, *Italy* .... **27** 42 20N 11 35 E
Fiordland National Park, *N.Z.* .... **81** 45 0 S 167 50 E
Fiorenzuola d'Arda, *Italy* .... **26** 44 56N 9 54 E
Fiq, *Syria* .... **44** 32 46N 35 41 E
Fire River, *Canada* ... **104** 48 47N 83 21W
Firebag →, *Canada* .. **111** 57 45N 111 21W
Firebaugh, *U.S.A.* **124** 36 52N 120 27W
Firedrake L., *Canada* . **111** 61 25N 104 30W
Firenze, *Italy* .... **27** 43 47N 11 15 E
Firmi, *France* .... **20** 44 33N 2 19 E
Firminy, *France* ...... **21** 45 23N 4 18 E
Firozabad, *India* ..... **49** 27 10N 78 25 E
Firozpur, *India* .... **48** 30 55N 74 40 E
Fīrūzābād, *Iran* ...... **47** 28 52N 52 35 E
Fīrūzkūh, *Iran* .... **47** 35 50N 52 50 E
Firvale, *Canada* **110** 52 27N 126 13W
Fish →, *Namibia* .... **96** 28 7 S 17 10 E
Fish →, *S. Africa* .... **96** 31 30 S 20 16 E
Fish Creek, *Australia* . **74** 38 43 S 146 7 E
Fisher, *Australia* ..... **79** 30 30 S 131 0 E
Fisher B., *Canada* **111** 51 35N 97 13W
Fishguard, *U.K.* **13** 51 59N 4 59W
Fishing L., *Canada* ... **111** 52 10N 95 24W
Fismes, *France* ...... **19** 49 20N 3 40 E
Fitchburg, *U.S.A.* **117** 42 35N 71 47W
Fitero, *Spain* **24** 42 4N 1 52W
Fitri, L., *Chad* .... **87** 12 50N 17 28 E
Fitz Roy, *Argentina* ... **142** 47 0 S 67 0W
Fitzgerald, *Canada* ... **110** 59 51N 111 36W
Fitzgerald, *U.S.A.* ... **115** 31 45N 83 16W
Fitzmaurice →, *Australia* .... **78** 14 45 S 130 5 E
Fitzroy →, *Queens., Australia* .... **72** 23 32 S 150 52 E

Fortuna

Fitzroy →, W. Austral., Australia 78 17 31 S 123 35 E
Fitzroy Crossing, Australia 78 18 9 S 125 38 E
Fitzwilliam I., Canada 108 45 30N 81 45W
Fiume = Rijeka, Yugoslavia 27 45 20N 14 21 E
Fiumefreddo Brúzio, Italy 29 39 14N 16 4 E
Five Points, U.S.A. 124 36 26N 120 6W
Fivizzano, Italy 26 44 12N 10 11 E
Fizi, Zaïre 92 4 17 S 28 55 E
Fjellerup, Denmark 11 56 29N 10 34 E
Fjerritslev, Denmark 11 57 5N 9 15 E
Fkih ben Salah, Morocco 84 32 32N 6 45W
Flå, Norway 10 63 13N 10 18 E
Flagler, U.S.A. 120 39 20N 103 4W
Flagstaff, U.S.A. 123 35 10N 111 40W
Flaherty I., Canada 104 56 15N 79 15W
Flåm, Norway 9 60 50N 7 7 E
Flambeau →, U.S.A. 120 45 18N 91 15W
Flamborough Hd., U.K. 12 54 8N 0 4W
Flaming Gorge Dam, U.S.A. 122 40 50N 109 46W
Flaming Gorge Res., U.S.A. 122 41 15N 109 30W
Flamingo, Teluk, Indonesia 57 5 30 S 138 0 E
Flanagan, U.S.A. 119 40 53N 88 52W
Flanders = West-Vlaanderen □, Belgium 17 51 0N 3 0 E
Flandre Occidentale □ = West-Vlaanderen □, Belgium 17 51 0N 3 0 E
Flandre Orientale □ = Oost-Vlaanderen □, Belgium 17 51 5N 3 50 E
Flandreau, U.S.A. 120 44 5N 96 38W
Flanigan, U.S.A. 124 40 10N 119 53W
Flåsjön, Sweden 8 64 5N 15 40 E
Flat →, Canada 110 61 33N 125 18W
Flat →, U.S.A. 119 42 56N 85 20W
Flat River, U.S.A. 121 37 50N 90 30W
Flat Rock, Ill., U.S.A. 119 38 54N 87 40W
Flat Rock, Mich., U.S.A. 119 42 4N 83 15W
Flatey, Barðastrandarsýsla, Iceland 8 66 10N 17 52W
Flatey, Suður-þingeyjarsýsla, Iceland 8 65 22N 22 56W
Flathead L., U.S.A. 122 47 50N 114 0W
Flatrock →, U.S.A. 119 38 46N 86 10W
Flattery, C., Australia 72 14 58 S 145 21 E
Flattery, C., U.S.A. 124 48 21N 124 43W
Flavy-le-Martel, France 19 49 43N 3 12 E
Flaxton, U.S.A. 120 48 52N 102 24W
Flèche, La, France 18 47 42N 0 4W
Fleetwood, U.K. 12 53 55N 3 1W
Flekkefjord, Norway 9 58 18N 6 39 E
Flémalle, Belgium 17 50 36N 5 28 E
Flemingsburg, U.S.A. 119 38 25N 83 45W
Flemington, U.S.A. 116 41 7N 77 28W
Flensborg Fjord, W. Germany 11 54 50N 9 40 E
Flensburg, W. Germany 30 54 46N 9 28 E
Flers, France 18 48 47N 0 33W
Flesherton, Canada 108 44 16N 80 33W
Flesko, Tanjung, Indonesia 57 0 29N 124 30 E
Fletton, U.K. 13 52 34N 0 13W
Fleurance, France 20 43 52N 0 40 E
Fleurier, Switz. 31 46 54N 6 35 E
Fleurus, Belgium 17 50 29N 4 32 E
Flevoland □, Neths. 16 52 30N 5 30 E
Flin Flon, Canada 111 54 46N 101 53W
Flinders, Australia 74 38 30 S 145 2 E
Flinders →, Australia 72 17 36 S 140 36 E
Flinders B., Australia 79 34 19 S 115 19 E
Flinders Group, Australia 72 14 11 S 144 15 E
Flinders I., Australia 72 40 0 S 148 0 E
Flinders Ranges, Australia 73 31 30 S 138 30 E
Flinders Reefs, Australia 72 17 37 S 148 31 E
Flint, U.K. 12 53 15N 3 7W
Flint, U.S.A. 104 43 5N 83 40W
Flint →, U.S.A. 115 30 52N 84 38W
Flint I., Kiribati 67 11 26 S 151 48W
Flinton, Australia 77 27 55 S 149 32 E
Fliseryd, Sweden 11 57 6N 16 15 E
Flix, Spain 24 41 14N 0 32 E
Flixecourt, France 19 50 0N 2 5 E
Flobecq, Belgium 17 50 44N 3 45 E
Flodden, U.K. 12 55 37N 2 8W
Floodwood, U.S.A. 120 46 55N 92 55W
Flora, Norway 10 63 27N 11 22 E
Flora, Ill., U.S.A. 114 38 40N 88 30W
Flora, Ind., U.S.A. 119 40 33N 86 31W
Florac, France 20 44 20N 3 37 E
Florala, U.S.A. 115 31 0N 86 20W
Florânia, Brazil 138 6 8 S 36 49W
Floreffe, Belgium 17 50 26N 4 46 E
Florence = Firenze, Italy 27 43 47N 11 15 E
Florence, Ala., U.S.A. 115 34 50N 87 40W
Florence, Ariz., U.S.A. 123 33 0N 111 25W
Florence, Colo., U.S.A. 120 38 26N 105 0W
Florence, Oreg., U.S.A. 122 44 0N 124 3W
Florence, S.C., U.S.A. 115 34 12N 79 44W
Florence, L., Australia 73 28 53 S 138 9 E
Florennes, Belgium 17 50 15N 4 35 E
Florensac, France 20 43 23N 3 28 E
Florenville, Belgium 17 49 40N 5 19 E
Flores, Brazil 138 7 51 S 37 59W
Flores, Guatemala 128 16 59N 89 50W
Flores, Indonesia 57 8 35 S 121 0 E
Flores I., Canada 110 49 20N 126 10W
Flores Sea, Indonesia 56 6 30 S 124 0 E
Floresta, Brazil 138 8 40 S 37 26W
Floresville, U.S.A. 121 29 10N 98 10W
Floriano, Brazil 138 6 50 S 43 0W
Florianópolis, Brazil 141 27 30 S 48 30W
Florida, Cuba 128 21 32N 78 14W
Florida, Uruguay 141 34 7 S 56 10W
Florida □, U.S.A. 115 28 30N 82 0W
Florida, Straits of, U.S.A. 128 25 0N 80 0W
Florida B., U.S.A. 128 25 0N 81 20W
Florida Is., Solomon Is. 68 9 55 S 160 15 E
Florida Keys, U.S.A. 128 25 0N 80 40W
Florídia, Italy 29 37 6N 15 9 E
Floridsdorf, Austria 33 48 14N 16 22 E
Flórina, Greece 35 40 48N 21 26 E
Florissant, U.S.A. 118 38 48N 90 20W
Florø, Norway 9 61 35N 5 1 E
Flower Sta., Canada 106 45 10N 76 41W
Flowerdale, Australia 74 37 20 S 145 19 E
Flower's Cove, Canada 105 51 14N 56 46W
Floydada, U.S.A. 121 33 58N 101 18W
Fluk, Indonesia 57 1 42 S 127 44 E
Flumen →, Spain 24 41 43N 0 9W
Flumendosa →, Italy 28 39 26N 9 38 E
Fluminimaggiore, Italy 28 39 25N 8 30 E
Flushing = Vlissingen, Neths. 17 51 26N 3 34 E
Flushing, U.S.A. 119 43 4N 83 51W
Fluviá →, Spain 24 42 12N 3 7 E
Fly →, Papua N. G. 69 8 25 S 143 0 E
Flying Fish, C., Antarctica 143 72 6 S 102 29W
Foa, Tonga 68 19 45 S 174 18W
Foa, La, N. Cal. 68 21 43 S 165 50 E
Foam Lake, Canada 111 51 40N 103 32W
Foča, Yugoslavia 33 43 31N 18 47 E
Focşani, Romania 34 45 41N 27 15 E
Fogang, China 59 23 52N 113 30 E
Foggaret el Arab, Algeria 85 27 13N 2 49 E
Foggaret ez Zoua, Algeria 85 27 20N 2 53 E
Fóggia, Italy 29 41 28N 15 31 E
Foggo, Nigeria 91 11 21N 9 57 E
Foglia →, Italy 27 43 55N 12 54 E
Fogo, Canada 105 49 43N 54 17W
Fogo I., Canada 105 49 40N 54 5W
Fohnsdorf, Austria 33 47 12N 14 40 E
Föhr, W. Germany 30 54 40N 8 30 E
Foia, Portugal 23 37 19N 8 37W
Foins, L. aux, Canada 106 47 5N 78 11W
Foix, France 20 42 58N 1 38 E
Fokino, U.S.S.R. 36 53 30N 34 22 E
Folda, Nord-Trøndelag, Norway 8 64 41N 10 50 E
Folda, Nordland, Norway 8 67 38N 14 50 E
Foleyet, Canada 104 48 15N 82 25W
Folgefonn, Norway 9 60 3N 6 23 E
Foligno, Italy 27 42 58N 12 40 E
Folkestone, U.K. 13 51 5N 1 11 E
Folkston, U.S.A. 115 30 55N 82 0W
Follett, U.S.A. 121 36 30N 100 12W
Follette, La, U.S.A. 115 36 23N 84 9W
Follónica, Italy 26 42 55N 10 45 E
Follónica, G. di, Italy 26 42 50N 10 40 E
Folsom Res., U.S.A. 124 38 42N 121 9W
Fond-du-Lac, Canada 111 59 19N 107 12W
Fond du Lac, U.S.A. 120 43 46N 88 26W
Fond-du-Lac →, Canada 111 59 17N 106 0W
Fonda, Iowa, U.S.A. 118 42 35N 94 51W
Fonda, N.Y., U.S.A. 117 42 57N 74 23W
Fondi, Italy 28 41 21N 13 25 E
Fonfría, Spain 22 41 37N 6 9W
Fongen, Norway 10 63 11N 11 38 E
Fonni, Italy 28 40 5N 9 16 E
Fonsagrada, Spain 22 43 8N 7 4W
Fonseca, G. de, Cent. Amer. 128 13 10N 87 40W
Fontaine, La, U.S.A. 119 40 40N 85 43W
Fontaine-Française, France 19 47 32N 5 21 E
Fontainebleau, France 19 48 24N 2 40 E
Fontana, L., Argentina 142 44 55 S 71 30W
Fontas →, Canada 110 58 14N 121 48W
Fonte Boa, Brazil 134 2 33 S 66 0W
Fontem, Cameroon 91 5 32N 9 52 E
Fontenay-le-Comte, France 20 46 28N 0 48W
Fontur, Iceland 8 66 23N 14 32W
Fonuafo'ou, Tonga 68 20 19 S 175 25W
Fonualei, Tonga 68 18 1 S 174 19W
Fonyód, Hungary 33 46 44N 17 33 E
Foochow = Fuzhou, China 59 26 5N 119 16 E
Foping, China 60 33 41N 108 0 E
Foppiano, Italy 26 46 21N 8 24 E
Föra, Sweden 11 57 1N 16 51 E
Forbach, France 19 49 10N 6 52 E
Forbes, Australia 76 33 22 S 148 0 E
Forbesganj, India 49 26 17N 87 18 E
Forcados, Nigeria 91 5 26N 5 26 E
Forcados →, Nigeria 91 5 25N 5 19 E
Forcall →, Spain 24 40 51N 0 16W
Forcalquier, France 21 43 58N 5 47 E
Forchheim, W. Germany 31 49 42N 11 4 E
Ford City, Calif., U.S.A. 125 35 10N 119 27W
Ford City, Pa., U.S.A. 116 40 47N 79 31W
Ford's Bridge, Australia 73 29 41 S 145 29 E
Fordyce, U.S.A. 121 33 50N 92 20W
Forécariah, Guinea 90 9 28N 13 10W
Forel, Mt., Greenland 144 66 52N 36 55W
Foremost, Canada 110 49 26N 111 34W
Forenza, Italy 29 40 50N 15 50 E
Forest, Belgium 17 50 49N 4 20 E
Forest, Canada 108 43 6N 82 0W
Forest, U.S.A. 121 32 21N 89 27W
Forest City, Iowa, U.S.A. 120 43 12N 93 39W
Forest City, N.C., U.S.A. 115 35 23N 81 50W
Forest City, Pa., U.S.A. 117 41 39N 75 29W
Forest Grove, U.S.A. 124 45 31N 123 4W
Forestburg, Canada 110 52 35N 112 1W
Foresthill, U.S.A. 124 39 1N 120 49W
Forestier Pen., Australia 72 43 0 S 148 0 E
Forestville, Canada 107 48 48N 69 2W
Forestville, Calif., U.S.A. 124 38 28N 122 54W
Forestville, Wis., U.S.A. 114 44 41N 87 29W
Forez, Mts. du, France 20 45 40N 3 50 E
Forfar, U.K. 14 56 40N 2 53W
Forges-les-Eaux, France 19 49 37N 1 30 E
Forks, U.S.A. 124 47 56N 124 23W
Forlì, Italy 27 44 14N 12 2 E
Forman, U.S.A. 120 46 9N 97 43W
Formazza, Italy 26 46 23N 8 26 E
Formby Pt., U.K. 12 53 33N 3 7W
Formentera, Spain 25 38 43N 1 27 E
Formentor, C. de, Spain 24 39 58N 3 13 E
Fórmia, Italy 28 41 15N 13 34 E
Formiga, Brazil 139 20 27 S 45 25W
Formigine, Italy 26 44 37N 10 51 E
Formiguères, France 20 42 37N 2 5 E
Formosa = Taiwan ■, Asia 59 23 30N 121 0 E
Formosa, Argentina 140 26 15 S 58 10W
Formosa, Brazil 139 15 32 S 47 20W
Formosa □, Argentina 140 25 0 S 60 0W
Formosa, Serra, Brazil 137 12 0 S 55 0W
Formosa Bay, Kenya 92 2 40 S 40 20 E
Formoso →, Brazil 139 10 34 S 49 56W
Fornells, Spain 24 40 3N 4 7 E
Fornos de Algodres, Portugal 22 40 38N 7 32W
Fornovo di Taro, Italy 26 44 42N 10 7 E
Føroyar, Atl. Oc. 130 62 0N 7 0W
Forres, U.K. 14 57 37N 3 38W
Forrest, Vic., Australia 74 38 33 S 143 47 E
Forrest, W. Austral., Australia 79 30 51 S 128 6 E
Forrest, Mt., Australia 79 24 48 S 127 45 E
Forrest City, U.S.A. 121 35 0N 90 50W
Forreston, U.S.A. 118 42 8N 89 35W
Forrières, Belgium 17 50 8N 5 17 E
Fors, Sweden 10 60 14N 16 20 E
Forsa, Sweden 10 61 44N 16 55 E
Forsayth, Australia 72 18 33 S 143 34 E
Forserum, Sweden 11 57 42N 14 30 E
Forshaga, Sweden 10 59 33N 13 29 E
Forskacka, Sweden 10 60 39N 16 54 E
Forsmo, Sweden 10 63 16N 17 11 E
Forst, E. Germany 30 51 43N 14 37 E
Forster, Australia 77 32 12 S 152 31 E
Forsyth, Ga., U.S.A. 115 33 4N 83 55W
Forsyth, Mont., U.S.A. 122 46 14N 106 37W
Forsyth I., N.Z. 81 40 58 S 174 5 E
Forsythe, Canada 106 48 14N 76 26W
Fort Albany, Canada 104 52 15N 81 35W
Fort Apache, U.S.A. 123 33 50N 110 0W
Fort Assiniboine, Canada 110 54 20N 114 45W
Fort Atkinson, U.S.A. 119 42 56N 88 50W
Fort Augustus, U.K. 14 57 9N 4 40W
Fort Beaufort, S. Africa 96 32 46 S 26 40 E
Fort Benton, U.S.A. 122 47 50N 110 40W
Fort Bragg, U.S.A. 122 39 28N 123 50W
Fort Bridger, U.S.A. 122 41 22N 110 20W
Fort Chipewyan, Canada 111 58 42N 111 8W
Fort Collins, U.S.A. 120 40 30N 105 4W
Fort-Coulonge, Canada 106 45 50N 76 45W
Fort Davis, U.S.A. 121 30 38N 103 53W
Fort-de-France, Martinique 129 14 36N 61 2W
Fort de Possel = Possel, C.A.R. 94 5 5N 19 10 E
Fort Defiance, U.S.A. 123 35 47N 109 4W
Fort Dodge, U.S.A. 120 42 29N 94 10W
Fort Edward, U.S.A. 117 43 16N 73 35W
Fort Frances, Canada 111 48 36N 93 24W
Fort Franklin, Canada 102 65 10N 123 30W
Fort Garland, U.S.A. 123 37 28N 105 30W
Fort George, Canada 104 53 50N 79 0W
Fort Good-Hope, Canada 102 66 14N 128 40W
Fort Hancock, U.S.A. 123 31 19N 105 56W
Fort Hertz = Putao, Burma 52 27 28N 97 30 E
Fort Hope, Canada 104 51 30N 88 0W
Fort Irwin, U.S.A. 125 35 16N 116 34W
Fort Jameson = Chipata, Zambia 93 13 38 S 32 28 E
Fort Kent, U.S.A. 105 47 12N 68 30W
Fort Klamath, U.S.A. 122 42 45N 122 0W
Fort Knox, U.S.A. 119 37 54N 85 57W
Fort Lallemand, Algeria 85 31 13N 6 17 E
Fort-Lamy = Ndjamena, Chad 87 12 10N 14 59 E
Fort Laramie, U.S.A. 120 42 15N 104 30W
Fort Lauderdale, U.S.A. 115 26 10N 80 5W
Fort Leonard Wood, U.S.A. 118 37 46N 92 11W
Fort Liard, Canada 110 60 14N 123 30W
Fort Liberté, Haiti 129 19 42N 71 51W
Fort Lupton, U.S.A. 120 40 8N 104 48W
Fort Mackay, Canada 110 57 12N 111 41W
Fort McKenzie, Canada 105 57 20N 69 0W
Fort Macleod, Canada 110 49 45N 113 30W
Fort MacMahon, Algeria 85 29 43N 1 45 E
Fort McMurray, Canada 110 56 44N 111 7W
Fort McPherson, Canada 102 67 30N 134 55W
Fort Madison, U.S.A. 118 40 39N 91 20W
Fort Meade, U.S.A. 115 27 45N 81 45W
Fort Miribel, Algeria 85 29 25N 2 55 E
Fort Morgan, U.S.A. 120 40 10N 103 50W
Fort Myers, U.S.A. 115 26 39N 81 51W
Fort Nelson, Canada 110 58 50N 122 44W
Fort Nelson →, Canada 110 59 32N 124 0W
Fort Norman, Canada 102 64 57N 125 30W
Fort Payne, U.S.A. 115 34 25N 85 44W
Fort Peck, U.S.A. 122 48 1N 106 30W
Fort Peck Dam, U.S.A. 122 48 0N 106 38W
Fort Peck L., U.S.A. 122 47 40N 107 0W
Fort Pierce, U.S.A. 115 27 29N 80 19W
Fort Pierre, U.S.A. 120 44 25N 100 25W
Fort Pierre Bordes = Ti-n-Zaouaténe, Algeria 85 20 0N 2 55 E
Fort Plain, U.S.A. 117 42 56N 74 39W
Fort Portal, Uganda 92 0 40N 30 20 E
Fort Providence, Canada 110 61 3N 117 40W
Fort Qu'Appelle, Canada 111 50 45N 103 50W
Fort Recovery, U.S.A. 119 40 25N 84 47W
Fort Resolution, Canada 110 61 10N 113 40W
Fort Rixon, Zambia 93 20 2 S 29 17 E
Fort Roseberry = Mansa, Zambia 93 11 13 S 28 55 E
Fort Ross, U.S.A. 124 38 32N 123 13W
Fort Rousset = Owando, Congo 94 0 29 S 15 55 E
Fort Rupert, Canada 104 51 30N 78 40W
Fort Saint, Tunisia 86 30 19N 9 31 E
Fort St. James, Canada 110 54 30N 124 10W
Fort St. John, Canada 110 56 15N 120 50W
Fort Sandeman, Pakistan 48 31 20N 69 31 E
Fort Saskatchewan, Canada 110 53 40N 113 15W
Fort Scott, U.S.A. 121 37 50N 94 40W
Fort Severn, Canada 104 56 0N 87 40W
Fort Shevchenko, U.S.S.R. 39 43 40N 51 20 E
Fort-Sibut, C.A.R. 94 5 46N 19 10 E
Fort Simpson, Canada 110 61 45N 121 15W
Fort Smith, Canada 110 60 0N 111 51W
Fort Smith, U.S.A. 121 35 25N 94 25W
Fort Stanton, U.S.A. 123 33 33N 105 36W
Fort Stockton, U.S.A. 121 30 54N 102 54W
Fort Sumner, U.S.A. 121 34 24N 104 16W
Fort Thomas, U.S.A. 119 39 5N 84 27W
Fort Trinquet = Bir Mogrein, Mauritania 84 25 10N 11 25W
Fort Valley, U.S.A. 115 32 33N 83 52W
Fort Vermilion, Canada 110 58 24N 116 0W
Fort Walton Beach, U.S.A. 115 30 25N 86 40W
Fort Wayne, U.S.A. 119 41 5N 85 10W
Fort William, U.K. 14 56 48N 5 8W
Fort Worth, U.S.A. 121 32 45N 97 25W
Fort Yates, U.S.A. 120 46 8N 100 38W
Fort Yukon, U.S.A. 102 66 35N 145 20W
Fortaleza, Bolivia 136 12 6 S 66 49W
Fortaleza, Brazil 138 3 45 S 38 35W
Forteau, Canada 105 51 28N 56 58W
Forth, Firth of, U.K. 14 56 5N 2 55W
Forthassa Rharbia, Algeria 85 32 52N 1 18W
Fortín Coronel Eugenio Garay, Paraguay 137 20 31 S 62 8W
Fortín Garrapatal, Paraguay 137 21 27 S 61 30W
Fortín General Pando, Paraguay 137 19 45 S 59 47W
Fortín Madrejón, Paraguay 137 20 45 S 59 52W
Fortín Uno, Argentina 142 38 50 S 65 18W
Fortore →, Italy 27 41 55N 15 17 E
Fortrose, N.Z. 81 46 38 S 168 45 E
Fortrose, U.K. 14 57 35N 4 10W
Fortuna, Spain 25 38 11N 1 7W
Fortuna, Calif., U.S.A. 122 40 38N 124 8W

Fortuna

Fortuna, N. Dak., U.S.A. 120 48 55N 103 48W
Fortune B., Canada 105 47 30N 55 22W
Forūr, Iran 47 26 20N 54 30 E
Fos-sur-Mer, France 21 43 26N 4 56 E
Foshan, China 59 23 4N 113 5 E
Fossacesia, Italy 27 42 15N 14 30 E
Fossano, Italy 26 44 33N 7 40 E
Fosses-la-Ville, Belgium 17 50 24N 4 41 E
Fossil, U.S.A. 122 45 0N 120 9W
Fossilbrook, Australia 72 17 47 S 144 29 E
Fossombrone, Italy 27 43 41N 12 49 E
Fosston, U.S.A. 120 47 33N 95 39W
Foster, Australia 75 38 40 S 146 15 E
Foster, Canada 117 45 17N 72 30W
Foster, U.S.A. 119 38 48N 84 13W
Foster →, Canada 111 55 47N 105 49W
Fosters Ra., Australia 72 21 35 S 133 48 E
Fostoria, U.S.A. 119 41 8N 83 25W
Fotuha'a, Tonga 68 19 49 S 174 44W
Fougamou, Gabon 94 1 16 S 10 30 E
Fougères, France 18 48 21N 1 14W
Foul Pt., Sri Lanka 51 8 35N 81 18 E
Foulness I., U.K. 13 51 36N 0 55 E
Foulpointe, Madag. 97 17 41 S 49 31 E
Foum Assaka, Morocco 84 29 8N 10 24W
Foum Zguid, Morocco 84 30 2N 6 59W
Foumban, Cameroon 91 5 45N 10 50 E
Foundiougne, Senegal 90 14 5N 16 32W
Fountain, Colo., U.S.A. 120 38 42N 104 40W
Fountain, Utah, U.S.A. 122 39 41N 111 37W
Fountain Springs, U.S.A. 125 35 54N 118 51W
Fourchambault, France 19 47 0N 3 3 E
Fourchu, Canada 105 45 43N 60 17W
Fouriesburg, S. Africa 96 28 38 S 28 14 E
Fourmies, France 19 50 1N 4 2 E
Foúrnoi, Greece 35 37 36N 26 32 E
Fours, France 19 46 50N 3 42 E
Fouta Djalon, Guinea 90 11 20N 12 10W
Foux, Cap-à-, Haiti 129 19 43N 73 27W
Foveaux Str., N.Z. 81 46 42 S 168 10 E
Fowey, U.K. 13 50 20N 4 39W
Fowler, Calif., U.S.A. 124 36 41N 119 41W
Fowler, Colo., U.S.A. 120 38 10N 104 0W
Fowler, Ind., U.S.A. 119 40 37N 87 19W
Fowler, Kans., U.S.A. 121 37 28N 100 7W
Fowler, Mich., U.S.A. 119 43 0N 84 45W
Fowlers B., Australia 79 31 59 S 132 34 E
Fowlerton, U.S.A. 121 28 26N 98 50W
Fowlerville, U.S.A. 119 42 40N 84 4W
Fox →, Canada 111 56 3N 93 18W
Fox Valley, Canada 111 50 30N 109 25W
Foxe Basin, Canada 103 66 0N 77 0W
Foxe Chan., Canada 103 65 0N 80 0W
Foxe Pen., Canada 103 65 0N 76 0W
Foxen, Sweden 10 59 25N 11 55 E
Foxhol, Neths. 16 53 10N 6 43 E
Foxpark, U.S.A. 122 41 4N 106 6W
Foxton, N.Z. 80 40 29 S 175 18 E
Foyle, Lough, U.K. 15 55 6N 7 8W
Foynes, Ireland 15 52 37N 9 5W
Foz, Spain 22 43 33N 7 20W
Fóz do Cunene, Angola 95 17 15 S 11 48 E
Foz do Gregório, Brazil 136 6 47 S 70 44W
Foz do Iguaçu, Brazil 141 25 30 S 54 30W
Foz do Riosinho, Brazil 136 7 11 S 71 50W
Frackville, U.S.A. 117 40 46N 76 15W
Fraga, Spain 24 41 32N 0 21 E
Fraire, Belgium 17 50 16N 4 31 E
Frameries, Belgium 17 50 24N 3 54 E
Framingham, U.S.A. 117 42 18N 71 26W
Franca, Brazil 139 20 33 S 47 30W
Francavilla al Mare, Italy 27 42 25N 14 16 E
Francavilla Fontana, Italy 29 40 32N 17 35 E
France ■, Europe 18 47 0N 3 0 E
Frances, Australia 73 36 41 S 140 55 E
Frances →, Canada 110 60 16N 129 10W
Frances L., Canada 110 61 23N 129 30W
Francés Viejo, C., Dom. Rep. 129 19 40N 70 0W
Francesville, U.S.A. 119 40 59N 86 53W
Franceville, Gabon 94 1 40 S 13 32 E
Franche-Comté, France 19 46 50N 5 55 E
Francisco de Orellana, Ecuador 134 0 28 S 76 58W
Francisco I. Madero, Coahuila, Mexico 126 25 48N 103 18W
Francisco I. Madero, Durango, Mexico 126 24 32N 104 22W
Francisco Sá, Brazil 139 16 28 S 43 30W
Francistown, Botswana 97 21 7 S 27 33 E
Francofonte, Italy 29 37 13N 14 50 E
François, Canada 105 47 35N 56 45W
François, Martinique 129 14 38N 60 57W
François L., Canada 110 54 0N 125 30W
Francorchamps, Belgium 17 50 27N 5 57 E
Franeker, Neths. 16 53 12N 5 33 E
Frankado, Djibouti 89 12 30N 43 12 E
Frankenberg, W. Germany 30 51 3N 8 47 E
Frankenthal, W. Germany 31 49 32N 8 21 E
Frankenwald, W. Germany 31 50 18N 11 36 E
Frankford, Canada 109 44 12N 77 36W
Frankford, U.S.A. 118 39 29N 91 19W
Frankfort, S. Africa 97 27 17 S 28 30 E
Frankfort, Ind., U.S.A. 119 40 20N 86 33W
Frankfort, Kans., U.S.A. 120 39 42N 96 26W
Frankfort, Ky., U.S.A. 119 38 12N 84 52W
Frankfort, Mich., U.S.A. 114 44 38N 86 14W
Frankfort, Ohio, U.S.A. 119 39 24N 83 11W
Frankfurt □, E. Germany 30 52 30N 14 0 E
Frankfurt am Main, W. Germany 31 50 7N 8 40 E
Frankfurt an der Oder, E. Germany 30 52 20N 14 31 E
Fränkische Alb, W. Germany 31 49 20N 11 30 E
Fränkische Rezal →, W. Germany 31 49 11N 11 1 E
Fränkische Saale →, W. Germany 31 50 30N 9 42 E
Fränkische Schweiz, W. Germany 31 49 45N 11 10 E
Frankland →, Australia 79 35 0 S 116 48 E
Franklin, Ill., U.S.A. 118 39 37N 90 3W
Franklin, Ind., U.S.A. 119 39 29N 86 3W
Franklin, Ky., U.S.A. 115 36 40N 86 30W
Franklin, La., U.S.A. 121 29 45N 91 30W
Franklin, Mass., U.S.A. 117 42 4N 71 23W
Franklin, N.H., U.S.A. 117 43 28N 71 39W
Franklin, Nebr., U.S.A. 120 40 9N 98 55W
Franklin, Ohio, U.S.A. 119 39 34N 84 18W
Franklin, Pa., U.S.A. 116 41 22N 79 45W
Franklin, Tenn., U.S.A. 115 35 54N 86 53W
Franklin, Va., U.S.A. 115 36 40N 76 58W
Franklin, W. Va., U.S.A. 114 38 38N 79 21W
Franklin, L., U.S.A. 122 40 20N 115 26W
Franklin B., Canada 102 69 45N 126 0W
Franklin D. Roosevelt L., U.S.A. 122 48 30N 118 16W
Franklin I., Antarctica 143 76 10 S 168 30 E
Franklin Mts., Canada 102 65 0N 125 0W
Franklin Mts., N.Z. 81 44 55 S 167 45 E
Franklin Str., Canada 102 72 0N 96 0W
Franklinton, U.S.A. 121 30 53N 90 10W
Franklinville, U.S.A. 116 42 21N 78 28W
Franklyn Mt., N.Z. 81 42 4 S 172 42 E
Franks Peak, U.S.A. 122 43 50N 109 5W
Frankston, Australia 74 38 8 S 145 8 E
Frankton Junc., N.Z. 80 37 47 S 175 16 E
Fränsta, Sweden 10 62 30N 16 11 E
Frantsa Iosifa, Zemlya, U.S.S.R. 40 82 0N 55 0 E
Franz, Canada 104 48 25N 84 30W
Franz Josef Land = Frantsa Iosifa, Zemlya, U.S.S.R. 40 82 0N 55 0 E
Franzburg, E. Germany 30 54 9N 12 52 E
Frascati, Italy 28 41 48N 12 41 E
Fraser →, B.C., Canada 110 49 7N 123 11W
Fraser →, Nfld., Canada 105 56 39N 62 10W
Fraser, Mt., Australia 79 25 35 S 118 20 E
Fraser I., Australia 73 25 15 S 153 10 E
Fraser Lake, Canada 110 54 0N 124 50W
Fraserburg, S. Africa 96 31 55 S 21 30 E
Fraserburgh, U.K. 14 57 41N 2 0W
Fraserdale, Canada 104 49 55N 81 37W
Frasertown, N.Z. 80 38 58 S 177 28 E
Frasne, France 19 46 50N 6 10 E
Frauenfeld, Switz. 31 47 34N 8 54 E
Fray Bentos, Uruguay 140 33 10 S 58 15W
Frazier Downs, Australia 78 18 48 S 121 42 E
Frechilla, Spain 22 42 8N 4 50W
Fredericia, Denmark 11 55 34N 9 45 E
Frederick, Md., U.S.A. 114 39 25N 77 23W
Frederick, Okla., U.S.A. 121 34 22N 99 0W
Frederick, S. Dak., U.S.A. 120 45 55N 98 29W
Frederick Sd., U.S.A. 110 57 10N 134 0W
Fredericksburg, Tex., U.S.A. 121 30 17N 98 55W
Fredericksburg, Va., U.S.A. 114 38 16N 77 29W
Frederickstown, U.S.A. 121 37 35N 90 15W
Frederickton, Australia 77 31 0 S 152 53 E
Frederico I. Madero, Presa, Mexico 126 28 7N 105 40W
Fredericton, Canada 105 45 57N 66 40W
Fredericton Junc., Canada 105 45 41N 66 40W
Frederikshavn, Denmark 11 57 28N 10 31 E
Frederikssund, Denmark 11 55 50N 12 3 E
Frederiksted, Virgin Is. 129 17 43N 64 53W
Fredonia, Ariz., U.S.A. 123 36 59N 112 36W
Fredonia, Kans., U.S.A. 121 37 34N 95 50W
Fredonia, N.Y., U.S.A. 116 42 26N 79 20W
Fredrikstad, Norway 10 59 13N 10 57 E
Freeburg, U.S.A. 118 38 19N 91 56W
Freehold, U.S.A. 117 40 15N 74 18W
Freel Pk., U.S.A. 124 38 52N 119 53W
Freeland, U.S.A. 117 41 3N 75 48W
Freels, C., Canada 105 49 15N 53 30W
Freeman, Calif., U.S.A. 125 35 35N 117 53W
Freeman, Mo., U.S.A. 118 38 37N 94 30W
Freeman, S. Dak., U.S.A. 120 43 25N 97 20W
Freeport, Bahamas 128 26 30N 78 47W
Freeport, Canada 105 44 15N 66 20W
Freeport, Ill., U.S.A. 118 42 18N 89 40W
Freeport, N.Y., U.S.A. 117 40 39N 73 35W
Freeport, Tex., U.S.A. 121 28 55N 95 22W
Freetown, S. Leone 90 8 30N 13 17W
Frégate, L., Canada 104 53 15N 74 45W
Fregenal de la Sierra, Spain 23 38 10N 6 39W
Fregene, Italy 28 41 50N 12 12 E
Fregeneda, La, Spain 22 40 58N 6 54W
Fréhel, C., France 18 48 40N 2 20W
Freiberg, E. Germany 30 50 55N 13 20 E
Freibourg = Fribourg, Switz. 31 46 49N 7 9 E
Freiburg, Baden-W., W. Germany 31 48 0N 7 52 E
Freiburg, Niedersachsen, W. Germany 30 53 49N 9 17 E
Freire, Chile 142 38 54 S 72 38W
Freirina, Chile 140 28 30 S 71 10W
Freising, W. Germany 31 48 24N 11 47 E
Freistadt, Austria 32 48 30N 14 30 E
Freital, E. Germany 30 51 0N 13 40 E
Fréjus, France 21 43 25N 6 44 E
Fremantle, Australia 79 32 7 S 115 47 E
Fremont, Calif., U.S.A. 124 37 32N 122 1W
Fremont, Ind., U.S.A. 119 41 44N 84 56W
Fremont, Mich., U.S.A. 114 43 29N 85 59W
Fremont, Nebr., U.S.A. 120 41 30N 96 30W
Fremont, Ohio, U.S.A. 119 41 20N 83 5W
Fremont →, U.S.A. 123 38 15N 110 20W
Fremont, L., U.S.A. 122 43 0N 109 50W
French →, Canada 108 46 2N 80 34W
French Camp, U.S.A. 124 37 53N 121 16W
French Cr. →, U.S.A. 116 41 22N 79 50W
French Guiana ■, S. Amer. 135 4 0N 53 0W
French I., Australia 74 38 20 S 145 22 E
French Lick, U.S.A. 119 38 33N 86 37W
French Polynesia □, Pac. Oc. 67 20 0 S 145 0 E
French River, Canada 108 46 2N 80 34W
French Terr. of Afars & Issas = Djibouti ■, Africa 89 12 0N 43 0 E
Frenchburg, U.S.A. 119 37 57N 83 38W
Frenchglen, U.S.A. 122 42 48N 119 0W
Frenchman →, N. Amer. 122 48 24N 107 5W
Frenchman Butte, Canada 111 53 35N 109 38W
Frenchman Creek →, U.S.A. 120 40 13N 100 50W
Frenda, Algeria 85 35 2N 1 1 E
Fresco →, Brazil 137 7 15 S 51 30W
Freshfield, C., Antarctica 143 68 25 S 151 10 E
Fresnay-sur-Sarthe, France 18 48 17N 0 1 E
Fresnillo, Mexico 126 23 10N 103 0W
Fresno, U.S.A. 124 36 47N 119 50W
Fresno Alhandiga, Spain 22 40 42N 5 37W
Fresno Res., U.S.A. 122 48 40N 110 0W
Freudenstadt, W. Germany 31 48 27N 8 25 E
Freux, Belgium 17 49 59N 5 27 E
Frévent, France 19 50 15N 2 17 E
Frew →, Australia 72 20 0 S 135 38 E
Frewena, Australia 72 19 25 S 135 25 E
Freycinet Pen., Australia 72 42 10 S 148 25 E
Freyming-Merlebach, France 19 49 8N 6 48 E
Freyung, W. Germany 31 48 48N 13 33 E
Fria, Guinea 90 10 27N 13 38W
Fria, C., Namibia 96 18 0 S 12 0 E
Fría, La, Venezuela 134 8 13N 72 15W
Friant, U.S.A. 124 36 59N 119 43W
Frías, Argentina 140 28 40 S 65 5W
Fribourg, Switz. 31 46 49N 7 9 E
Fribourg □, Switz. 31 46 40N 7 0 E
Fridafors, Sweden 11 56 25N 14 39 E
Friday Harbor, U.S.A. 124 48 32N 123 1W
Friedberg, Bayern, W. Germany 31 48 21N 10 59 E
Friedberg, Hessen, W. Germany 31 50 21N 8 46 E
Friedland, E. Germany 30 53 40N 13 33 E
Friedrichshafen, W. Germany 31 47 39N 9 29 E
Friedrichskoog, W. Germany 30 54 1N 8 52 E
Friedrichsort, W. Germany 30 54 24N 10 11 E
Friedrichstadt, W. Germany 30 54 23N 9 6 E
Friendly Is. = Tonga ■, Pac. Oc. 68 19 50 S 174 30W
Friesack, E. Germany 30 52 43N 12 35 E
Friesche Wad, Neths. 16 53 22N 5 44 E
Friesland □, Neths. 16 53 5N 5 50 E
Friesoythe, W. Germany 30 53 1N 7 51 E
Frillesås, Sweden 11 57 20N 12 12 E
Frinnaryd, Sweden 11 57 55N 14 50 E
Frio →, U.S.A. 121 28 30N 98 10W
Friona, U.S.A. 121 34 40N 102 42W
Frisian Is., Europe 30 53 30N 6 0 E
Fristad, Sweden 11 57 50N 13 0 E
Fritch, U.S.A. 121 35 40N 101 35W
Fritsla, Sweden 11 57 33N 12 47 E
Fritzlar, W. Germany 30 51 8N 9 19 E
Friuli-Venezia Giulia □, Italy 27 46 0N 13 0 E
Frobisher B., Canada 103 62 30N 66 0W
Frobisher Bay, Canada 103 63 44N 68 31W
Frobisher L., Canada 111 56 20N 108 15W
Frogmore, Australia 76 34 15 S 148 52 E
Frohavet, Norway 8 63 50N 9 35 E
Froid, U.S.A. 120 48 20N 104 29W
Froid-Chapelle, Belgium 17 50 9N 4 19 E
Frolovo, U.S.S.R. 39 49 45N 43 40 E
Fromberg, U.S.A. 122 42 25N 108 58W
Frome, U.K. 13 51 16N 2 17W
Frome, L., Australia 73 30 45 S 139 45 E
Frome Downs, Australia 73 31 13 S 139 45 E
Frómista, Spain 22 42 16N 4 25W
Front Range, U.S.A. 122 40 0N 105 40W
Front Royal, U.S.A. 114 38 55N 78 10W
Fronteira, Portugal 23 39 3N 7 39W
Fronteiras, Brazil 138 7 5 S 40 37W
Frontera, Canary Is. 25 27 47N 17 59W
Frontera, Mexico 127 18 30N 92 40W
Frontignan, France 20 43 27N 3 45 E
Frosinone, Italy 28 41 38N 13 20 E
Frosolone, Italy 29 41 34N 14 27 E
Frostburg, U.S.A. 114 39 43N 78 57W
Frostisen, Norway 8 68 14N 17 10 E
Frouard, France 19 48 47N 6 8 E
Frövi, Sweden 10 59 28N 15 24 E
Frøya, Norway 8 63 43N 8 40 E
Fruges, France 19 50 30N 2 8 E
Frumoasa, Romania 34 46 28N 25 48 E
Frunze, U.S.S.R. 40 42 54N 74 46 E
Frutal, Brazil 139 20 0 S 49 0W
Frutigen, Switz. 31 46 35N 7 38 E
Frýdek-Místek, Czech. 32 49 40N 18 20 E
Frýdlant, Czech. 32 50 56N 15 9 E
Fryvaldov = Jeseník, Czech. 32 50 0N 17 8 E
Fu Jiang →, China 58 30 0N 106 16 E
Fu Xian, Liaoning, China 61 39 38N 121 58 E
Fu Xian, Shaanxi, China 60 36 0N 109 20 E
Fu'an, China 59 27 11N 119 36 E
Fubian, China 58 31 17N 102 22 E
Fucécchio, Italy 26 43 44N 10 51 E
Fucheng, China 60 37 50N 116 10 E
Fuchou = Fuzhou, China 59 26 5N 119 16 E
Fuchū, Hiroshima, Japan 64 34 34N 133 14 E
Fūchū, Tōkyō, Japan 65 35 40N 139 29 E
Fuchuan, China 59 24 50N 111 5 E
Fuchun Jiang →, China 59 30 5N 120 5 E
Fúcino, Conca del, Italy 27 42 1N 13 31 E
Fuding, China 59 27 20N 120 12 E
Fuencaliente, Canary Is. 25 28 28N 17 50W
Fuencaliente, Spain 23 38 25N 4 18W
Fuencaliente, Pta., Canary Is. 25 28 27N 17 51W
Fuengirola, Spain 23 36 32N 4 41W
Fuente Alamo, Albacete, Spain 25 38 44N 1 24W
Fuente Álamo, Murcia, Spain 25 37 42N 1 6W
Fuente de Cantos, Spain 23 38 15N 6 18W
Fuente de San Esteban, La, Spain 22 40 49N 6 15W
Fuente del Maestre, Spain 23 38 31N 6 28W
Fuente el Fresno, Spain 23 39 14N 3 46W
Fuente Ovejuna, Spain 23 38 15N 5 25W
Fuentes de Andalucía, Spain 23 37 28N 5 20W
Fuentes de Ebro, Spain 24 41 31N 0 38W
Fuentes de León, Spain 23 38 5N 6 32W
Fuentes de Oñoro, Spain 22 40 33N 6 52W
Fuentesaúco, Spain 22 41 15N 5 30W
Fuerte →, Mexico 126 25 50N 109 25W
Fuerte Olimpo, Paraguay 140 21 0 S 57 51W
Fuerteventura, Canary Is. 25 28 30N 14 0W
Fufeng, China 60 34 22N 108 0 E
Fugløysund, Norway 8 70 15N 20 20 E
Fugong, China 58 27 5N 98 47 E
Fugou, China 60 34 3N 114 25 E
Fugu, China 60 39 2N 111 3 E
Fuhai, China 62 47 2N 87 25 E
Fuji, Japan 65 35 9N 138 39 E
Fuji-no-miya, Japan 65 35 10N 138 40 E
Fuji-San, Japan 65 35 22N 138 44 E
Fuji-yoshida, Japan 65 35 30N 138 46 E
Fujian □, China 59 26 0N 118 0 E
Fujieda, Japan 65 34 52N 138 16 E
Fujioka, Japan 65 36 15N 139 5 E
Fujisawa, Japan 65 35 22N 139 29 E
Fukaya, Japan 65 36 12N 139 12 E
Fukien = Fujian □, China 59 26 0N 118 0 E
Fukuchiyama, Japan 65 35 19N 135 9 E
Fukue-Shima, Japan 63 32 40N 128 45 E
Fukui, Japan 65 36 0N 136 10 E
Fukui □, Japan 65 36 0N 136 12 E
Fukuma, Japan 64 33 46N 130 28 E
Fukuoka, Japan 64 33 39N 130 21 E
Fukuoka □, Japan 64 33 30N 131 0 E

Gestro, Wabi →, *Ethiopia* **89** 4 12N 42 2 E
Gesves, *Belgium* **17** 50 24N 5 4 E
Getafe, *Spain* **22** 40 18N 3 44W
Gethsémani, *Canada* **105** 50 13N 60 40W
Gettysburg, *Pa., U.S.A.* **114** 39 47N 77 18W
Gettysburg, *S. Dak., U.S.A.* **120** 45 3N 99 56W
Getz Ice Shelf, *Antarctica* **143** 75 0 S 130 0W
Geul →, *Neths.* **17** 50 53N 5 43 E
Geurie, *Australia* **76** 32 22 S 148 50 E
Gévaudan, *France* **20** 44 40N 3 40 E
Gevgelija, *Yugoslavia* **35** 41 9N 22 30 E
Gévora →, *Spain* **23** 38 53N 6 57W
Gex, *France* **21** 46 21N 6 3 E
Geyser, *U.S.A.* **122** 47 17N 110 30W
Geyserville, *U.S.A.* **124** 38 42N 122 54W
Geysir, *Iceland* **8** 64 19N 20 18W
Ghâbat el Arab = Wang Kai, *Sudan* **89** 9 3N 29 23 E
Ghaghara →, *India* **49** 25 45N 84 40 E
Ghalla, Wadi el →, *Sudan* **89** 10 25N 27 32 E
Ghallamane, *Mauritania* **84** 23 15N 10 0W
Ghana ■, *W. Afr.* **91** 8 0N 1 0W
Ghansor, *India* **49** 22 39N 80 1 E
Ghanzi, *Botswana* **96** 21 50 S 21 34 E
Ghanzi □, *Botswana* **96** 21 50 S 21 45 E
Gharb el Istiwa'iya □, *Sudan* **89** 5 0N 30 0 E
Gharbîya, Es Sahrâ el, *Egypt* **88** 27 40N 26 30 E
Ghard Abû Muharik, *Egypt* **88** 26 50N 30 0 E
Ghardaïa, *Algeria* **85** 32 20N 3 37 E
Ghârib, G., *Egypt* **88** 28 6N 32 54 E
Ghârib, Râs, *Egypt* **88** 28 6N 33 18 E
Gharyān, *Libya* **86** 32 10N 13 0 E
Gharyān □, *Libya* **86** 30 35N 12 0 E
Ghat, *Libya* **86** 24 59N 10 11 E
Ghatal, *India* **49** 22 40N 87 46 E
Ghatampur, *India* **49** 26 8N 80 13 E
Ghatere, *Solomon Is.* **68** 7 55 S 159 0 E
Ghatprabha →, *India* **51** 16 15N 75 20 E
Ghayl, *Si. Arabia* **46** 21 40N 46 20 E
Ghazal, Bahr el →, *Chad* **87** 13 0N 15 47 E
Ghazâl, Bahr el →, *Sudan* **89** 9 31N 30 25 E
Ghazaouet, *Algeria* **85** 35 8N 1 50W
Ghaziabad, *India* **48** 28 42N 77 26 E
Ghazipur, *India* **49** 25 38N 83 35 E
Ghaznī, *Afghan.* **47** 33 30N 68 28 E
Ghaznī □, *Afghan.* **47** 32 10N 68 20 E
Ghedi, *Italy* **26** 45 24N 10 16 E
Ghèlinsor, *Somali Rep.* **98** 6 28N 46 39 E
Ghent = Gent, *Belgium* **17** 51 2N 3 42 E
Gheorghe Gheorghiu-Dej, *Romania* **34** 46 17N 26 47 E
Gheorgheni, *Romania* **34** 46 43N 25 41 E
Ghergani, *Romania* **34** 44 37N 25 37 E
Gherla, *Romania* **34** 47 0N 23 57 E
Ghilarza, *Italy* **28** 40 8N 8 50 E
Ghisonaccia, *France* **21** 42 1N 9 26 E
Ghisoni, *France* **21** 42 7N 9 12 E
Ghizao, *Afghan.* **48** 33 20N 65 44 E
Ghizar →, *Pakistan* **49** 36 15N 73 43 E
Ghod →, *India* **50** 18 30N 74 35 E
Ghogha, *India* **48** 21 40N 72 20 E
Ghot Ogrein, *Egypt* **88** 31 10N 25 20 E
Ghotaru, *India* **48** 27 20N 70 1 E
Ghotki, *Pakistan* **48** 28 5N 69 21 E
Ghowr □, *Afghan.* **47** 34 0N 64 20 E
Ghudāmis, *Libya* **86** 30 11N 9 29 E
Ghughri, *India* **49** 22 39N 80 41 E
Ghugus, *India* **50** 19 58N 79 12 E
Ghulam Mohammad Barrage, *Pakistan* **48** 25 30N 68 20 E
Ghūrīān, *Afghan.* **47** 34 17N 61 25 E
Gia Dinh, *Vietnam* **55** 10 49N 106 42 E
Gia Lai = Pleiku, *Vietnam* **54** 13 57N 108 0 E
Gia Nghia, *Vietnam* **55** 12 0N 107 42 E
Gia Ngoc, *Vietnam* **54** 14 50N 108 58 E
Gia Vuc, *Vietnam* **54** 14 42N 108 34 E
Giamama, *Somali Rep.* **98** 0 4N 42 44 E
Gian, *Phil.* **57** 5 45N 125 20 E
Giannutri, *Italy* **26** 42 16N 11 5 E
Giant Forest, *U.S.A.* **124** 36 36N 118 43W
Giant Mts. = Krkonoše, *Czech.* **32** 50 50N 15 35 E
Giant's Causeway, *U.K.* **15** 55 15N 6 30W
Giarabub = Al Jaghbūb, *Libya* **86** 29 42N 24 38 E
Giarre, *Italy* **29** 37 44N 15 10 E
Giaveno, *Italy* **26** 45 3N 7 20 E
Gibara, *Cuba* **128** 21 9N 76 11W
Gibb River, *Australia* **78** 16 26 S 126 26 E
Gibbo, Mt., *Australia* **75** 36 38 S 147 58 E
Gibbon, *U.S.A.* **120** 40 49N 98 45W
Gibe →, *Ethiopia* **89** 7 20N 37 36 E
Gibellina, *Italy* **28** 37 48N 13 0 E
Gibraléon, *Spain* **23** 37 23N 6 58W
Gibraltar, *Europe* **23** 36 7N 5 22W
Gibraltar, Str. of, *Medit. S.* **23** 35 55N 5 40W
Gibson City, *U.S.A.* **119** 40 28N 88 22W
Gibson Desert, *Australia* **78** 24 0 S 126 0 E
Gibsonburg, *U.S.A.* **119** 41 23N 83 19W
Gibsons, *Canada* **110** 49 24N 123 32W
Gibsonville, *U.S.A.* **124** 39 46N 120 54W
Giddalur, *India* **51** 15 20N 78 57 E
Giddings, *U.S.A.* **121** 30 11N 96 58W
Gidole, *Ethiopia* **89** 5 40N 37 25 E
Gien, *France* **19** 47 40N 2 36 E
Giessen, *W. Germany* **30** 50 34N 8 40 E
Gieten, *Neths.* **16** 53 0N 6 46 E
Gifatin, Geziret, *Egypt* **88** 27 10N 33 50 E
Giffard, *Canada* **107** 46 51N 71 12W
Gifford Creek, *Australia* **79** 24 3 S 116 16 E
Gifhorn, *W. Germany* **30** 52 29N 10 32 E
Gifu, *Japan* **65** 35 30N 136 45 E
Gifu □, *Japan* **65** 35 40N 137 0 E
Gigant, *U.S.S.R.* **39** 46 28N 41 20 E
Giganta, Sa. de la, *Mexico* **126** 25 30N 111 30W
Gigen, *Bulgaria* **34** 43 40N 24 28 E
Gigha, *U.K.* **14** 55 42N 5 45W
Giglei, *Somali Rep.* **98** 5 25N 45 20 E
Giglio, *Italy* **26** 42 20N 10 52 E
Gignac, *France* **20** 43 39N 3 32 E
Gigüela →, *Spain* **25** 39 8N 3 44W
Gijón, *Spain* **22** 43 32N 5 42W
Gil Gil, Cr. →, *Australia* **77** 30 19 S 148 42 E
Gil I., *Canada* **110** 53 12N 129 15W
Gila →, *U.S.A.* **123** 32 43N 114 33W
Gila Bend, *U.S.A.* **123** 33 0N 112 46W
Gila Bend Mts., *U.S.A.* **123** 33 15N 113 0W
Gīlān □, *Iran* **46** 37 0N 50 0 E
Gilbert →, *Australia* **72** 16 35 S 141 15 E
Gilbert Is., *Kiribati* **66** 1 0N 176 0 E
Gilbert Plains, *Canada* **111** 51 9N 100 28W
Gilbert River, *Australia* **72** 18 9 S 142 52 E
Gilberton, *Australia* **72** 19 16 S 143 35 E
Gilbués, *Brazil* **138** 9 50 S 45 21W
Gilf el Kebîr, Hadabat el, *Egypt* **88** 23 50N 25 50 E
Gilford I., *Canada* **110** 50 40N 126 30W
Gilgai, *Australia* **77** 29 50 S 151 9 E
Gilgandra, *Australia* **76** 31 43 S 148 39 E
Gilgil, *Kenya* **92** 0 30 S 36 20 E
Gilgit, *India* **49** 35 50N 74 15 E
Gilgit →, *Pakistan* **49** 35 44N 74 37 E
Giljeva Planina, *Yugoslavia* **33** 43 9N 20 0 E
Gillam, *Canada* **111** 56 20N 94 40W
Gilleleje, *Denmark* **11** 56 8N 12 19 E
Gillen, L., *Australia* **79** 26 11 S 124 38 E
Gilles, L., *Australia* **73** 32 50 S 136 45 E
Gillespie, *U.S.A.* **118** 39 7N 89 49W
Gillespies Pt., *N.Z.* **81** 43 24 S 169 49 E
Gillette, *U.S.A.* **120** 44 20N 105 30W
Gilliat, *Australia* **72** 20 40 S 141 28 E
Gillingham, *U.K.* **13** 51 23N 0 34 E
Gilly, *Belgium* **17** 50 25N 4 29 E
Gilman, *U.S.A.* **119** 40 46N 88 0W
Gilman City, *U.S.A.* **118** 40 8N 93 53W
Gilmer, *U.S.A.* **121** 32 44N 94 55W
Gilmore, *Australia* **76** 35 20 S 148 12 E
Gilmore, L., *Australia* **79** 32 29 S 121 37 E
Gilmour, *Canada* **109** 44 48N 77 37W
Gilo →, *Ethiopia* **89** 8 10N 33 15 E
Gilort →, *Romania* **34** 44 38N 23 32 E
Gilroy, *U.S.A.* **124** 37 1N 121 37W
Giluwe, Mt., *Papua N. G.* **69** 6 8 S 143 52 E
Gilze, *Neths.* **17** 51 32N 4 57 E
Gimbi, *Ethiopia* **89** 9 3N 35 42 E
Gimigliano, *Italy* **29** 38 58N 16 32 E
Gimli, *Canada* **111** 50 40N 97 0W
Gimo, *Sweden* **10** 60 11N 18 12 E
Gimone →, *France* **20** 44 0N 1 6 E
Gimont, *France* **20** 43 38N 0 52 E
Gimzo, *Israel* **44** 31 56N 34 56 E
Gin →, *Sri Lanka* **51** 6 5N 80 7 E
Gin Gin, *Australia* **73** 25 0 S 151 58 E
Ginâh, *Egypt* **88** 25 21N 30 30 E
Gindie, *Australia* **72** 23 44 S 148 8 E
Gineta, La, *Spain* **25** 39 8N 2 1W
Gingin, *Australia* **79** 31 22 S 115 54 E
Gîngiova, *Romania* **34** 43 54N 23 50 E
Ginir, *Ethiopia* **89** 7 6N 40 40 E
Ginosa, *Italy* **29** 40 35N 16 45 E
Ginzo de Limia, *Spain* **22** 42 3N 7 47W
Giohar, *Somali Rep.* **98** 2 48N 45 30 E
Gióia, G. di, *Italy* **29** 38 30N 15 50 E
Gióia del Colle, *Italy* **29** 40 49N 16 55 E
Gióia Táuro, *Italy* **29** 38 26N 15 53 E
Gioiosa Iónica, *Italy* **29** 38 20N 16 19 E
Gióna, Óros, *Greece* **35** 38 38N 22 14 E
Giovi, Passo dei, *Italy* **26** 44 33N 8 57 E
Giovinazzo, *Italy* **29** 41 10N 16 40 E
Gir Hills, *India* **48** 21 0N 71 0 E
Girab, *India* **48** 26 2N 70 38 E
Giraltovce, *Czech.* **32** 49 7N 21 32 E
Girard, *Ill., U.S.A.* **118** 39 27N 89 48W
Girard, *Kans., U.S.A.* **121** 37 30N 94 50W
Girard, *Ohio, U.S.A.* **116** 41 10N 80 42W
Girard, *Pa., U.S.A.* **116** 42 1N 80 21W
Girardot, *Colombia* **134** 4 18N 74 48W
Girardville, *Canada* **107** 49 0N 72 32W
Girdle Ness, *U.K.* **14** 57 9N 2 2W
Giresun, *Turkey* **46** 40 55N 38 30 E
Girga, *Egypt* **88** 26 17N 31 55 E
Girgarre, *Australia* **74** 36 18 S 145 2 E
Girgir, C., *Papua N. G.* **69** 3 50 S 144 35 E
Giridih, *India* **49** 24 10N 86 21 E
Girifalco, *Italy* **29** 38 49N 16 25 E
Girilambone, *Australia* **73** 31 16 S 146 57 E
Giro, *Nigeria* **91** 11 7N 4 42 E
Giromagny, *France* **19** 47 45N 6 50 E
Gironde □, *France* **20** 44 45N 0 30W
Gironde →, *France* **20** 45 32N 1 7W
Gironella, *Spain* **24** 42 2N 1 53 E
Giru, *Australia* **72** 19 30 S 147 5 E
Girvan, *U.K.* **14** 55 15N 4 50W
Gisborne, *Australia* **74** 37 29 S 144 36 E
Gisborne, *N.Z.* **80** 38 39 S 178 5 E
Gisenyi, *Rwanda* **92** 1 41 S 29 15 E
Gislaved, *Sweden* **11** 57 19N 13 32 E
Gisors, *France* **19** 49 15N 1 47 E
Gistel, *Belgium* **17** 51 9N 2 59 E
Gitega, *Burundi* **92** 3 26 S 29 56 E
Gits, *Belgium* **17** 51 0N 3 6 E
Giuba →, *Somali Rep.* **98** 1 30N 42 35 E
Giugliano in Campania, *Italy* **29** 40 55N 14 12 E
Giulianova, *Italy* **27** 42 45N 13 58 E
Giurgeni, *Romania* **34** 44 45N 27 48 E
Giurgiu, *Romania* **34** 43 52N 25 57 E
Giv'at Brenner, *Israel* **44** 31 52N 34 47 E
Giv'atayim, *Israel* **44** 32 4N 34 49 E
Give, *Denmark* **11** 55 51N 9 13 E
Givet, *France* **19** 50 8N 4 49 E
Givors, *France* **21** 45 35N 4 45 E
Givry, *Belgium* **17** 50 23N 4 2 E
Givry, *France* **19** 46 41N 4 46 E
Giyon, *Ethiopia* **89** 8 33N 38 1 E
Giza = El Gîza, *Egypt* **88** 30 0N 31 10 E
Gizhiga, *U.S.S.R.* **41** 62 3N 160 30 E
Gizhiginskaya, Guba, *U.S.S.R.* **41** 61 0N 158 0 E
Gizo, *Solomon Is.* **68** 8 7 S 156 50 E
Giżycko, *Poland* **32** 54 2N 21 48 E
Gizzeria, *Italy* **29** 38 57N 16 10 E
Gjegjan, *Albania* **35** 41 58N 20 3 E
Gjerstad, *Norway* **10** 58 54N 9 0 E
Gjirokastra, *Albania* **35** 40 7N 20 10 E
Gjoa Haven, *Canada* **102** 68 20N 96 8W
Gjøl, *Denmark* **11** 57 4N 9 42 E
Gjøvik, *Norway* **10** 60 47N 10 43 E
Glace Bay, *Canada* **105** 46 11N 59 58W
Glacier B., *U.S.A.* **110** 58 30N 136 10W
Glacier Nat. Park, *Canada* **110** 51 15N 117 30W
Glacier Park, *U.S.A.* **122** 48 30N 113 18W
Glacier Peak Mt., *U.S.A.* **122** 48 7N 121 7W
Gladewater, *U.S.A.* **121** 32 30N 94 58W
Gladstone, *Queens., Australia* **72** 23 52 S 151 16 E
Gladstone, *S. Austral., Australia* **73** 33 15 S 138 22 E
Gladstone, *W. Austral., Australia* **79** 25 57 S 114 17 E
Gladstone, *Canada* **111** 50 13N 98 57W
Gladstone, *Mich., U.S.A.* **114** 45 52N 87 1W
Gladstone, *Mo., U.S.A.* **118** 39 13N 94 35W
Gladwin, *U.S.A.* **114** 43 59N 84 29W
Gladys L., *Canada* **110** 59 50N 133 0W
Glafsfjorden, *Sweden* **10** 59 30N 12 37 E
Gláma, *Iceland* **8** 65 48N 23 0W
Glåma →, *Norway* **10** 59 12N 10 57 E
Glamis, *U.S.A.* **125** 33 0N 115 4W
Glamoč, *Yugoslavia* **27** 44 3N 16 51 E
Glan, *Sweden* **11** 58 37N 16 0 E
Glanerbrug, *Neths.* **16** 52 13N 6 58 E
Glarus, *Switz.* **31** 47 3N 9 4 E
Glasco, *Kans., U.S.A.* **120** 39 25N 97 50W
Glasco, *N.Y., U.S.A.* **117** 42 3N 73 57W
Glasgow, *U.K.* **14** 55 52N 4 14W
Glasgow, *Ky., U.S.A.* **114** 37 2N 85 55W
Glasgow, *Mo., U.S.A.* **118** 39 14N 92 51W
Glasgow, *Mont., U.S.A.* **122** 48 12N 106 35W
Glastonbury, *U.K.* **13** 51 9N 2 42W
Glastonbury, *U.S.A.* **117** 41 42N 72 27W
Glauchau, *E. Germany* **30** 50 50N 12 33 E
Glazov, *U.S.S.R.* **37** 58 9N 52 40 E
Gleiwitz = Gliwice, *Poland* **32** 50 22N 18 41 E
Glen, *U.S.A.* **117** 44 7N 71 10W
Glen Affric, *U.K.* **14** 57 15N 5 0W
Glen Afton, *N.Z.* **80** 37 37 S 175 4 E
Glen Alice, *Australia* **76** 33 2 S 150 14 E
Glen Almond, *Canada* **106** 45 42N 75 29W
Glen Canyon Dam, *U.S.A.* **123** 37 0N 111 25W
Glen Canyon Nat. Recreation Area, *U.S.A.* **123** 37 30N 111 0W
Glen Coe, *U.K.* **12** 56 40N 5 0W
Glen Cove, *U.S.A.* **117** 40 51N 73 37W
Glen Davis, *Australia* **76** 33 5 S 150 18 E
Glen Garry, *U.K.* **14** 57 3N 5 7W
Glen Innes, *Australia* **77** 29 44 S 151 44 E
Glen Lyon, *U.S.A.* **117** 41 10N 76 7W
Glen Massey, *N.Z.* **80** 37 38 S 175 2 E
Glen Mor, *U.K.* **14** 57 12N 4 37W
Glen Moriston, *U.K.* **14** 57 10N 4 58W
Glen Orchy, *U.K.* **14** 56 27N 4 52W
Glen Spean, *U.K.* **14** 56 53N 4 40W
Glen Ullin, *U.S.A.* **120** 46 48N 101 46W
Glen Valley, *Australia* **75** 36 54 S 147 28 E
Glénans, Is. de, *France* **18** 47 42N 4 0W
Glenavy, *N.Z.* **81** 44 54 S 171 7 E
Glenbawn, L., *Australia* **77** 32 5 S 151 0 E
Glenbrook, *Australia* **76** 33 45 S 150 37 E
Glenburgh, *Australia* **79** 25 26 S 116 6 E
Glenburn, *Australia* **74** 37 27 S 145 26 E
Glencoe, *Canada* **108** 42 45N 81 43W
Glencoe, *S. Africa* **97** 28 11 S 30 11 E
Glencoe, *U.S.A.* **120** 44 45N 94 10W
Glendale, *Ariz., U.S.A.* **123** 33 40N 112 8W
Glendale, *Calif., U.S.A.* **125** 34 7N 118 18W
Glendale, *Oreg., U.S.A.* **122** 42 44N 123 29W
Glendale, *Zambia* **93** 17 22 S 31 5 E
Glendive, *U.S.A.* **120** 47 7N 104 40W
Glendo, *U.S.A.* **120** 42 30N 105 0W
Glenelg, *Australia* **73** 34 58 S 138 31 E
Glenelg →, *Australia* **74** 38 4 S 140 59 E
Glenflorrie, *Australia* **78** 22 55 S 115 59 E
Glengarriff, *Ireland* **15** 51 45N 9 33W
Glengarry, *Australia* **75** 38 7 S 146 37 E
Glengyle, *Australia* **72** 24 48 S 139 37 E
Glenham, *N.Z.* **81** 46 26 S 168 52 E
Glenhope, *N.Z.* **81** 41 40 S 172 39 E
Glenisla, *Australia* **74** 37 14 S 142 12 E
Glenmaggie, *Australia* **75** 37 54 S 146 43 E
Glenmary, Mt., *N.Z.* **81** 44 0 S 169 55 E
Glenmora, *U.S.A.* **121** 31 1N 92 34W
Glenmorgan, *Australia* **77** 27 14 S 149 42 E
Glenn, *U.S.A.* **124** 39 31N 122 1W
Glenns Ferry, *U.S.A.* **122** 43 0N 115 15W
Glenorchy, *Tas., Australia* **72** 42 49 S 147 18 E
Glenorchy, *Vic., Australia* **74** 36 55 S 142 41 E
Glenore, *Australia* **72** 17 50 S 141 12 E
Glenormiston, *Australia* **72** 22 55 S 138 50 E
Glenreagh, *Australia* **77** 30 2 S 153 1 E
Glenrock, *U.S.A.* **122** 42 53N 105 55W
Glenrothes, *U.K.* **14** 56 12N 3 11W
Glenrowan, *Australia* **75** 36 29 S 146 13 E
Glens Falls, *U.S.A.* **117** 43 20N 73 40W
Glenthompson, *Australia* **74** 37 38 S 142 38 E
Glenties, *Ireland* **15** 54 48N 8 18W
Glenville, *U.S.A.* **114** 38 56N 80 50W
Glenwood, *Alta., Canada* **110** 49 21N 113 31W
Glenwood, *Nfld., Canada* **105** 49 0N 54 58W
Glenwood, *Ark., U.S.A.* **121** 34 20N 93 30W
Glenwood, *Hawaii, U.S.A.* **112** 19 29N 155 10W
Glenwood, *Iowa, U.S.A.* **120** 41 7N 95 41W
Glenwood, *Minn., U.S.A.* **120** 45 38N 95 21W
Glenwood, *Wash., U.S.A.* **124** 46 1N 121 17W
Glenwood Sprs., *U.S.A.* **122** 39 39N 107 21W
Glina, *Yugoslavia* **27** 45 20N 16 6 E
Glittertind, *Norway* **10** 61 40N 8 32 E
Gliwice, *Poland* **32** 50 22N 18 41 E
Globe, *U.S.A.* **123** 33 25N 110 53W
Glödnitz, *Austria* **33** 46 53N 14 7 E
Głogów, *Poland* **32** 51 37N 16 5 E
Gloria, La, *Colombia* **134** 8 37N 73 48W
Glorieuses, Is., *Ind. Oc.* **97** 11 30 S 47 20 E
Glossop, *U.K.* **12** 53 27N 1 56W
Gloucester, *Australia* **77** 32 0 S 151 59 E
Gloucester, *U.K.* **13** 51 52N 2 15W
Gloucester, *U.S.A.* **117** 42 38N 70 39W
Gloucester, C., *Papua N. G.* **69** 5 26 S 148 21 E
Gloucester I., *Australia* **72** 20 0 S 148 30 E
Gloucestershire □, *U.K.* **13** 51 44N 2 10W
Gloversville, *U.S.A.* **117** 43 5N 74 18W
Glovertown, *Canada* **105** 48 40N 54 3W
Główno, *Poland* **32** 51 59N 19 42 E
Głubczyce, *Poland* **32** 50 13N 17 52 E
Glubokiy, *U.S.S.R.* **39** 48 35N 40 25 E
Glubokoye, *U.S.S.R.* **36** 55 10N 27 45 E
Głuchołazy, *Poland* **32** 50 19N 17 24 E
Glücksburg, *W. Germany* **30** 54 48N 9 34 E
Glückstadt, *W. Germany* **30** 53 46N 9 28 E
Glukhov, *U.S.S.R.* **36** 51 40N 33 58 E
Glussk, *U.S.S.R.* **36** 52 53N 28 41 E
Glyngøre, *Denmark* **11** 56 46N 8 52 E
Gmünd, *Kärnten, Austria* **33** 46 54N 13 31 E
Gmünd, *Niederösterreich, Austria* **32** 48 45N 15 0 E
Gnali, *Gabon* **94** 2 34 S 11 18 E
Gnarp, *Sweden* **10** 62 3N 17 16 E
Gnarput, L., *Australia* **74** 38 4 S 143 24 E
Gnesta, *Sweden* **10** 59 3N 17 17 E
Gniew, *Poland* **32** 53 50N 18 50 E
Gniezno, *Poland* **32** 52 30N 17 35 E
Gnoien, *E. Germany* **30** 53 58N 12 41 E
Gnosjö, *Sweden* **11** 57 22N 13 43 E
Gnowangerup, *Australia* **79** 33 58 S 117 59 E
Go Cong, *Vietnam* **55** 10 22N 106 40 E
Gō-no-ura, *Japan* **64** 33 44N 129 40 E
Go Quao, *Vietnam* **55** 9 43N 105 17 E
Goa, *India* **51** 15 33N 73 59 E
Goa □, *India* **51** 15 33N 73 59 E
Goalen Hd., *Australia* **75** 36 33 S 150 4 E
Goalpara, *India* **52** 26 10N 90 40 E
Goalundo Ghat, *Bangla.* **49** 23 50N 89 47 E
Goaso, *Ghana* **90** 6 48N 2 30W
Goat Fell, *U.K.* **14** 55 37N 5 11W
Goba, *Ethiopia* **89** 7 1N 39 59 E

Goba, *Mozam.* **97** 26 15 S 32 13 E
Gobabis, *Namibia* **96** 22 30 S 19 0 E
Gobernador Gregores, *Argentina* **142** 48 46 S 70 15W
Gobi, *Asia* **60** 44 0N 111 0 E
Gobichettipalayam, *India* **51** 11 31N 77 21 E
Gobles, *U.S.A.* **119** 42 22N 85 53W
Gobō, *Japan* **65** 33 53N 135 10 E
Gobo, *Sudan* **89** 5 40N 31 10 E
Goch, *W. Germany* **30** 51 40N 6 9 E
Gochas, *Namibia* **96** 24 59 S 18 55 E
Godavari →, *India* **50** 16 25N 82 18 E
Godavari Point, *India* **50** 17 0N 82 20 E
Godbout, *Canada* **105** 49 20N 67 38W
Godda, *India* **49** 24 50N 87 13 E
Goddua, *Libya* **86** 26 26N 14 19 E
Godegård, *Sweden* **11** 58 43N 15 8 E
Goderich, *Canada* **108** 43 45N 81 41W
Goderville, *France* **18** 49 38N 0 22 E
Godfrey, *U.S.A.* **118** 38 57N 90 11W
Godfreys Creek, *Australia* **76** 34 8 S 148 43 E
Godhavn, *Greenland* **144** 69 15N 53 38W
Godhra, *India* **48** 22 49N 73 40 E
Godinlave, *Somali Rep.* **98** 5 54N 46 38 E
Gödöllö, *Hungary* **33** 47 38N 19 25 E
Godoy Cruz, *Argentina* **140** 32 56 S 68 52W
Gods →, *Canada* **111** 56 22N 92 51W
Gods L., *Canada* **111** 54 40N 94 15W
Godthåb, *Greenland* **144** 64 10N 51 35W
Godwin Austen = K2, Mt., *Pakistan* **49** 35 58N 76 32 E
Goeie Hoop, Kaap die = Good Hope, C. of, *S. Africa* **96** 34 24 S 18 30 E
Goéland, L. au, *Canada* **106** 49 50N 76 48W
Goeree, *Neths.* **16** 51 50N 4 0 E
Goes, *Neths.* **17** 51 30N 3 55 E
Gogama, *Canada* **104** 47 35N 81 43W
Gogango, *Australia* **72** 23 40 S 150 2 E
Gogebic, L., *U.S.A.* **120** 46 20N 89 34W
Gogra = Ghaghara →, *India* **49** 25 45N 84 40 E
Gogriâl, *Sudan* **89** 8 30N 28 8 E
Goiana, *Brazil* **138** 7 33 S 34 59W
Goianésia, *Brazil* **139** 15 18 S 49 7W
Goiânia, *Brazil* **139** 16 43 S 49 20W
Goiás, *Brazil* **139** 15 55 S 50 10W
Goiás □, *Brazil* **138** 12 10 S 48 0W
Goiatuba, *Brazil* **139** 18 1 S 49 23W
Goio-Ere, *Brazil* **141** 24 12 S 53 1W
Goirle, *Neths.* **17** 51 31N 5 4 E
Góis, *Portugal* **22** 40 10N 8 6W
Gojam □, *Ethiopia* **89** 10 55N 36 30 E
Gojeb, Wabi →, *Ethiopia* **89** 7 12N 36 40 E
Gojō, *Japan* **65** 34 21N 135 42 E
Gojra, *Pakistan* **48** 31 10N 72 40 E
Gokak, *India* **51** 16 11N 74 52 E
Gokarannath, *India* **49** 27 57N 80 39 E
Gokarn, *India* **51** 14 33N 74 17 E
Gökçeada, *Turkey* **35** 40 10N 25 50 E
Gokurt, *Pakistan* **48** 29 40N 67 26 E
Gola, *India* **49** 28 3N 80 32 E
Golaghat, *India* **52** 26 30N 94 0 E
Golakganj, *India* **49** 26 8N 89 52 E
Golan Heights = Hagolan, *Syria* **44** 33 0N 35 45 E
Golaya Pristen, *U.S.S.R.* **38** 46 29N 32 32 E
Golchikha, *U.S.S.R.* **144** 71 45N 83 30 E
Golconda, *U.S.A.* **122** 40 58N 117 32W
Gold Beach, *U.S.A.* **122** 42 25N 124 25W
Gold Coast, *Australia* **77** 28 0 S 153 25 E
Gold Coast, *W. Afr.* **91** 4 0N 1 40W
Gold Hill, *U.S.A.* **122** 42 28N 123 2W
Goldberg, *E. Germany* **30** 53 34N 12 6 E
Golden, *Canada* **110** 51 20N 116 59W
Golden, *Colo., U.S.A.* **120** 39 42N 105 15W
Golden, *Ill., U.S.A.* **118** 40 7N 91 1W
Golden Bay, *N.Z.* **81** 40 40 S 172 50 E
Golden Gate, *U.S.A.* **122** 37 54N 122 30W
Golden Hinde, *Canada* **110** 49 40N 125 44W
Golden Lake, *Canada* **106** 45 34N 77 21W
Golden Prairie, *Canada* **111** 50 13N 109 37W
Golden Rock, *India* **51** 10 45N 78 48 E
Golden Vale, *Ireland* **15** 52 33N 8 17W
Goldendale, *U.S.A.* **122** 45 53N 120 48W
Goldfield, *U.S.A.* **123** 37 45N 117 13W
Goldfields, *Canada* **111** 59 28N 108 29W
Goldsand L., *Canada* **111** 57 2N 101 8W
Goldsboro, *U.S.A.* **115** 35 24N 77 59W
Goldsmith, *U.S.A.* **121** 32 0N 102 40W
Goldsworthy, *Australia* **78** 20 21 S 119 30 E
Goldthwaite, *U.S.A.* **121** 31 25N 98 32W
Golegã, *Portugal* **23** 39 24N 8 29W
Golęniów, *Poland* **32** 53 35N 14 50 E
Goleta, *U.S.A.* **125** 34 27N 119 50W
Golfito, *Costa Rica* **128** 8 41N 83 5W
Golfo Aranci, *Italy* **28** 41 0N 9 35 E
Goliad, *U.S.A.* **121** 28 40N 97 22W
Golija, *Yugoslavia* **33** 43 22N 20 15 E
Gollan, *Australia* **77** 32 16 S 149 5 E
Golo →, *France* **21** 42 31N 9 32 E
Golol, *Somali Rep.* **98** 3 38N 43 49 E
Golovanevsk, *U.S.S.R.* **38** 48 25N 30 30 E
Golra, *Pakistan* **48** 33 37N 72 56 E
Golspie, *Australia* **76** 34 20 S 149 42 E
Golspie, *U.K.* **14** 57 58N 3 58W
Golungo Alto, *Angola* **95** 9 8 S 14 46 E
Golyama Kamchiya →, *Bulgaria* **34** 43 10N 27 55 E
Goma, *Rwanda* **92** 2 11 S 29 18 E
Goma, *Zaïre* **92** 1 37 S 29 10 E
Gomati →, *India* **49** 25 32N 83 11 E
Gombari, *Zaïre* **92** 2 45N 29 3 E
Gombe, *Nigeria* **91** 10 19N 11 2 E
Gombe →, *Tanzania* **92** 4 38 S 31 40 E
Gombi, *Nigeria* **91** 10 12N 12 30 E
Gomel, *U.S.S.R.* **36** 52 28N 31 0 E
Gomera, *Canary Is.* **25** 28 7N 17 14W
Gómez Palacio, *Mexico* **126** 25 40N 104 0W
Gommern, *E. Germany* **30** 52 5N 11 47 E
Gomogomo, *Indonesia* **57** 6 39 S 134 43 E
Gompa = Ganta, *Liberia* **90** 7 15N 8 59W
Gonābād, *Iran* **47** 34 15N 58 45 E
Gonaïves, *Haiti* **129** 19 20N 72 42W
Gonâve, G. de la, *Haiti* **129** 19 29N 72 42W
Gonâve, I. de la, *Haiti* **129** 18 45N 73 0W
Gonbab-e Kāvūs, *Iran* **47** 37 20N 55 25 E
Gonda, *India* **49** 27 9N 81 58 E
Gondal, *India* **48** 21 58N 70 52 E
Gonder, *Ethiopia* **89** 12 39N 37 30 E
Gonder □, *Ethiopia* **89** 12 55N 37 30 E
Gondia, *India* **50** 21 23N 80 10 E
Gondola, *Mozam.* **93** 19 10 S 33 37 E
Gondomar, *Portugal* **22** 41 10N 8 35W
Gondomar, *Spain* **22** 42 7N 8 45W
Gondrecourt-le-Château, *France* **19** 48 31N 5 30 E
Gong Xian, *China* **58** 28 23N 104 47 E
Gong'an, *China* **59** 30 7N 112 12 E
Gongcheng, *China* **59** 24 50N 110 49 E
Gongga Shan, *China* **58** 29 40N 101 55 E
Gongguan, *China* **58** 21 48N 109 36 E
Gonghe, *China* **62** 36 18N 100 32 E
Gongola □, *Nigeria* **91** 8 0N 12 0 E
Gongola →, *Nigeria* **91** 9 30N 12 4 E
Gongolgon, *Australia* **73** 30 21 S 146 54 E
Gongshan, *China* **58** 27 43N 98 29 E
Gongtan, *China* **58** 28 55N 108 20 E
Goniadz, *Poland* **32** 53 30N 22 44 E
Goniri, *Nigeria* **91** 11 30N 12 15 E
Gonjo, *China* **58** 30 52N 98 17 E
Gonnesa, *Italy* **28** 39 17N 8 27 E
Gónnos, *Greece* **35** 39 52N 22 29 E
Gonnosfanadiga, *Italy* **28** 39 30N 8 39 E
Gonzales, *Calif., U.S.A.* **124** 36 35N 121 30W
Gonzales, *Tex., U.S.A.* **121** 29 30N 97 30W
González Chaves, *Argentina* **140** 38 2 S 60 5W
Goobang Creek, *Australia* **76** 33 6 S 147 10 E
Good Hope, C. of, *S. Africa* **96** 34 24 S 18 30 E
Goodenough I., *Papua N. G.* **69** 9 20 S 150 15 E
Gooderham, *Canada* **109** 44 54N 78 21W
Goodeve, *Canada* **111** 51 4N 103 10W
Gooding, *U.S.A.* **122** 43 0N 114 44W
Goodland, *U.S.A.* **120** 39 22N 101 44W
Goodnight, *U.S.A.* **121** 35 4N 101 13W
Goodooga, *Australia* **73** 29 3 S 147 28 E
Goodsoil, *Canada* **111** 54 24N 109 13W
Goodsprings, *U.S.A.* **123** 35 51N 115 30W
Goole, *U.K.* **12** 53 42N 0 52W
Goolgowi, *Australia* **74** 33 58 S 145 41 E
Gooloogong, *Australia* **76** 33 36 S 148 26 E
Goomalling, *Australia* **79** 31 15 S 116 49 E
Goombalie, *Australia* **73** 29 59 S 145 26 E
Goombungee, *Australia* **77** 27 18 S 151 51 E
Goonda, *Mozam.* **93** 19 48 S 33 57 E
Goondiwindi, *Australia* **77** 28 30 S 150 21 E
Goongarrie, *Australia* **79** 30 3 S 121 9 E
Goonumbla, *Australia* **76** 32 59 S 148 11 E
Goonyella, *Australia* **72** 21 47 S 147 58 E
Goor, *Neths.* **16** 52 13N 6 33 E
Goorambat, *Australia* **74** 36 24 S 145 56 E
Gooray, *Australia* **77** 28 25 S 150 2 E
Goose →, *Canada* **105** 53 20N 60 35W
Goose L., *U.S.A.* **122** 42 0N 120 30W
Gooty, *India* **51** 15 7N 77 41 E
Gopalganj, *Bangla.* **52** 23 1N 89 50 E
Gopalganj, *India* **49** 26 28N 84 30 E
Göppingen, *W. Germany* **31** 48 42N 9 40 E
Gor, *Spain* **25** 37 23N 2 58W
Góra, *Poland* **32** 51 40N 16 31 E
Gorakhpur, *India* **49** 26 47N 83 23 E
Gorbatov, *U.S.S.R.* **37** 56 12N 43 2 E
Gorbea, Peña, *Spain* **24** 43 1N 2 50W
Gorda, *U.S.A.* **124** 35 53N 121 26W
Gorda, Pta., *Nic.* **128** 14 20N 83 10W
Gorda, Pta., *Canary Is.* **25** 28 45N 18 0W
Gordan B., *Australia* **78** 11 35 S 130 10 E
Gordon, *S. Austral., Australia* **73** 32 7 S 138 20 E
Gordon, *Vic., Australia* **74** 37 34 S 144 6 E
Gordon, *U.S.A.* **120** 42 49N 102 12W
Gordon →, *Australia* **72** 42 27 S 145 30 E
Gordon, I., *Chile* **142** 54 55 S 69 30W
Gordon Downs, *Australia* **78** 18 48 S 128 33 E
Gordon L., *Alta., Canada* **111** 56 30N 110 25W
Gordon L., *N.W.T., Canada* **110** 63 5N 113 11W
Gordon River, *Australia* **79** 34 10 S 117 15 E
Gordonia, *S. Africa* **96** 28 13 S 21 10 E
Gordonvale, *Australia* **72** 17 5 S 145 50 E
Gore, *Australia* **77** 28 17 S 151 30 E
Goré, *Chad* **87** 7 59N 16 31 E
Gore, *Ethiopia* **89** 8 12N 35 32 E
Gore, *N.Z.* **81** 46 5 S 168 58 E
Gore Bay, *Canada* **108** 45 57N 82 28W
Gorey, *Ireland* **15** 52 41N 6 18W
Gorgān, *Iran* **47** 36 55N 54 30 E
Gorgona, *Italy* **26** 43 27N 9 52 E
Gorgona, I., *Colombia* **136** 3 0N 78 10W
Gorgora, *Ethiopia* **89** 12 15N 37 17 E
Gorham, *U.S.A.* **117** 44 23N 71 10W
Gori, *U.S.S.R.* **39** 42 0N 44 7 E
Gorin, *U.S.A.* **118** 40 22N 92 1W
Gorinchem, *Neths.* **16** 51 50N 4 59 E
Gorinhatã, *Brazil* **139** 19 15 S 49 45W
Goritsy, *U.S.S.R.* **37** 57 4N 36 43 E
Gorízia, *Italy* **27** 45 56N 13 37 E
Gorki = Gorkiy, *U.S.S.R.* **37** 56 20N 44 0 E
Gorki, *U.S.S.R.* **36** 54 17N 30 59 E
Gorkiy, *U.S.S.R.* **37** 56 20N 44 0 E
Gorkovskoye Vdkhr., *U.S.S.R.* **37** 57 2N 43 4 E
Gørlev, *Denmark* **11** 55 30N 11 15 E
Gorlice, *Poland* **32** 49 35N 21 11 E
Görlitz, *E. Germany* **30** 51 10N 14 59 E
Gorlovka, *U.S.S.R.* **38** 48 19N 38 5 E
Gorman, *Calif., U.S.A.* **125** 34 47N 118 51W
Gorman, *Tex., U.S.A.* **121** 32 15N 98 43W
Gormandale, *Australia* **75** 38 18 S 146 44 E
Gorna Dzhumayo = Blagoevgrad, *Bulgaria* **35** 42 2N 23 5 E
Gorna Oryakhovitsa, *Bulgaria* **34** 43 7N 25 40 E
Gornja Radgona, *Yugoslavia* **27** 46 40N 16 2 E
Gornja Tuzla, *Yugoslavia* **33** 44 35N 18 46 E
Gornji Grad, *Yugoslavia* **27** 46 20N 14 52 E
Gornji Milanovac, *Yugoslavia* **33** 44 0N 20 29 E
Gornji Vakuf, *Yugoslavia* **33** 43 57N 17 34 E
Gorno-Altaysk, *U.S.S.R.* **40** 51 50N 86 5 E
Gorno Slinkino, *U.S.S.R.* **40** 60 5N 70 0 E
Gornyy, *U.S.S.R.* **37** 51 50N 48 30 E
Gorodenka, *U.S.S.R.* **38** 48 41N 25 29 E
Gorodets, *U.S.S.R.* **37** 56 38N 43 28 E
Gorodishche, *R.S.F.S.R., U.S.S.R.* **37** 53 13N 45 40 E
Gorodishche, *Ukraine S.S.R., U.S.S.R.* **38** 49 17N 31 27 E
Gorodnitsa, *U.S.S.R.* **36** 50 46N 27 19 E
Gorodnya, *U.S.S.R.* **36** 51 55N 31 33 E
Gorodok, *Byelorussian S.S.R., U.S.S.R.* **36** 55 30N 30 3 E
Gorodok, *Ukraine S.S.R., U.S.S.R.* **36** 49 46N 23 32 E
Goroka, *Papua N. G.* **69** 6 7 S 145 25 E
Goroke, *Australia* **74** 36 43 S 141 29 E
Gorokhov, *U.S.S.R.* **36** 50 30N 24 45 E
Gorokhovets, *U.S.S.R.* **37** 56 13N 42 39 E
Gorom Gorom, *Burkina Faso* **91** 14 26N 0 14W
Goromonzi, *Zambia* **93** 17 52 S 31 22 E
Gorongose →, *Mozam.* **97** 20 30 S 34 40 E
Gorongoza, *Mozam.* **93** 18 44 S 34 2 E
Gorongoza, Sa. da, *Mozam.* **93** 18 27 S 34 2 E
Gorontalo, *Indonesia* **57** 0 35N 123 5 E
Goronyo, *Nigeria* **91** 13 29N 5 39 E
Gorredijk, *Neths.* **16** 53 0N 6 3 E
Gorron, *France* **18** 48 25N 0 50W
Gorssel, *Neths.* **16** 52 12N 6 12 E
Gort, *Ireland* **15** 53 4N 8 50W
Gorumahisani, *India* **50** 22 20N 86 24 E
Gorzkowice, *Poland* **32** 51 13N 19 36 E
Gorzów Śląski, *Poland* **32** 51 3N 18 22 E
Gorzów Wielkopolski, *Poland* **32** 52 43N 15 15 E
Gose, *Japan* **65** 34 27N 135 44 E
Gosford, *Australia* **76** 33 23 S 151 18 E
Goshen, *S. Africa* **96** 25 50 S 25 0 E
Goshen, *Calif., U.S.A.* **124** 36 21N 119 25W
Goshen, *Ind., U.S.A.* **119** 41 36N 85 46W
Goshen, *N.Y., U.S.A.* **117** 41 23N 74 21W
Goslar, *W. Germany* **30** 51 55N 10 23 E
Gospič, *Yugoslavia* **27** 44 35N 15 23 E
Gosport, *U.K.* **13** 50 48N 1 8W
Gosport, *U.S.A.* **119** 39 21N 86 40W
Gosse →, *Australia* **72** 19 32 S 134 37 E
Gostivar, *Yugoslavia* **35** 41 48N 20 57 E
Gostyń, *Poland* **32** 51 50N 17 3 E
Gostynin, *Poland* **32** 52 26N 19 29 E
Göta älv →, *Sweden* **11** 57 42N 11 54 E
Göta kanal, *Sweden* **9** 58 50N 13 58 E
Göteborg, *Sweden* **11** 57 43N 11 59 E
Göteborgs och Bohus län □, *Sweden* **9** 58 30N 11 30 E
Gotemba, *Japan* **65** 35 18N 138 56 E
Götene, *Sweden* **11** 58 32N 13 30 E
Gotha, *E. Germany* **30** 50 56N 10 42 E
Gothenburg, *U.S.A.* **120** 40 58N 100 8W
Gotland, *Sweden* **11** 57 30N 18 33 E
Gotse Delchev, *Bulgaria* **35** 41 43N 23 46 E
Gotska Sandön, *Sweden* **9** 58 24N 19 15 E
Gōtsu, *Japan* **64** 35 0N 132 14 E
Göttingen, *W. Germany* **30** 51 31N 9 55 E
Gottwald, *U.S.S.R.* **38** 49 39N 36 27 E
Gottwaldov, *Czech.* **32** 49 14N 17 40 E
Goubangzi, *China* **61** 41 20N 121 52 E
Gouda, *Neths.* **16** 52 1N 4 42 E
Goudiry, *Senegal* **90** 14 15N 12 45W
Gough I., *Atl. Oc.* **4** 40 10 S 9 45W
Gouin, Rés., *Canada* **106** 48 35N 74 40W
Gouitafla, *Ivory C.* **90** 7 30N 5 53W
Goulburn, *Australia* **76** 34 44 S 149 44 E
Goulburn →, *Australia* **74** 36 6 S 144 55 E
Goulburn Is., *Australia* **72** 11 40 S 133 20 E
Goulia, *Ivory C.* **90** 10 1N 7 11W
Goulimine, *Morocco* **84** 28 56N 10 0W
Goulmina, *Morocco* **84** 31 41N 4 57W
Gounou-Gaya, *Chad* **87** 9 38N 15 31 E
Goúra, *Greece* **35** 37 56N 22 20 E
Gouraya, *Algeria* **85** 36 31N 1 56 E
Gourdon, *France* **20** 44 44N 1 23 E
Gouré, *Niger* **91** 14 0N 10 10 E
Gouri, *Chad* **87** 19 36N 19 36 E
Gourits →, *S. Africa* **96** 34 21 S 21 52 E
Gourma Rharous, *Mali* **91** 16 55N 1 50W
Gournay-en-Bray, *France* **19** 49 29N 1 44 E
Gourock Ra., *Australia* **76** 36 0 S 149 25 E
Goursi, *Burkina Faso* **90** 12 42N 2 37W
Gouvêa, *Brazil* **139** 18 27 S 43 44W
Gouverneur, *U.S.A.* **117** 44 18N 75 30W
Gouzon, *France* **20** 46 12N 2 14 E
Govan, *Canada* **111** 51 20N 105 0W
Governador Valadares, *Brazil* **139** 18 15 S 41 57W
Governor's Harbour, *Bahamas* **128** 25 10N 76 14W
Gowan Ra., *Australia* **72** 25 0 S 145 0 E
Gowanda, *U.S.A.* **116** 42 29N 78 58W
Gowd-e Zirreh, *Afghan.* **47** 29 45N 62 0 E
Gower, The, *U.K.* **13** 51 35N 4 10W
Gowna, L., *Ireland* **15** 53 52N 7 35W
Gowrie, *U.S.A.* **118** 42 17N 94 17W
Gowrie, Carse of, *U.K.* **14** 56 30N 3 10W
Goya, *Argentina* **140** 29 10 S 59 10W
Goyder Lagoon, *Australia* **73** 27 3 S 138 58 E
Goyllarisquisga, *Peru* **136** 10 31 S 76 24W
Goz Beîda, *Chad* **87** 12 10N 21 20 E
Goz Regeb, *Sudan* **89** 16 3N 35 33 E
Graaff-Reinet, *S. Africa* **96** 32 13 S 24 32 E
Grabill, *U.S.A.* **119** 41 13N 84 57W
Grabow, *E. Germany* **30** 53 17N 11 31 E
Gračac, *Yugoslavia* **27** 44 18N 15 57 E
Gračanica, *Yugoslavia* **33** 44 43N 18 18 E
Graçay, *France* **19** 47 10N 1 50 E
Grace, *U.S.A.* **122** 42 38N 111 46W
Grace, L. (North), *Australia* **79** 33 10 S 118 20 E
Grace, L. (South), *Australia* **79** 33 15 S 118 25 E
Gracefield, *Canada* **106** 46 6N 76 3W
Graceville, *U.S.A.* **120** 45 36N 96 23W
Gracias a Dios, C., *Honduras* **128** 15 0N 83 10W
Graciosa, I., *Canary Is.* **25** 29 15N 13 32W
Gradaús, *Brazil* **138** 7 43 S 51 11W
Gradaús, Serra dos, *Brazil* **138** 8 0 S 50 45W
Gradets, *Bulgaria* **34** 42 46N 26 30 E
Gradgery, *Australia* **76** 31 12 S 147 52 E
Grado, *Italy* **27** 45 40N 13 20 E
Grado, *Spain* **22** 43 23N 6 4W
Gradule, *Australia* **77** 28 32 S 149 15 E
Grady, *U.S.A.* **121** 34 52N 103 15W
Graeca, Lacul, *Romania* **34** 44 5N 26 10 E
Graénalon, L., *Iceland* **8** 64 10N 17 20W
Grafenau, *W. Germany* **31** 48 51N 13 24 E
Gräfenberg, *W. Germany* **31** 49 39N 11 15 E
Grafton, *Australia* **77** 29 38 S 152 58 E
Grafton, *Ill., U.S.A.* **118** 38 58N 90 26W
Grafton, *N. Dak., U.S.A.* **120** 48 30N 97 25W
Gragnano, *Italy* **29** 40 42N 14 30 E
Graham, *Canada* **104** 49 20N 90 30W
Graham, *N.C., U.S.A.* **115** 36 5N 79 22W
Graham, *Tex., U.S.A.* **121** 33 7N 98 38W
Graham →, *Canada* **110** 56 31N 122 17W
Graham Bell, Os., *U.S.S.R.* **40** 80 5N 70 0 E
Graham I., *Canada* **110** 53 40N 132 30W
Graham Land, *Antarctica* **143** 65 0 S 64 0W
Graham Mt., *U.S.A.* **123** 32 46N 109 58W
Grahamdale, *Canada* **111** 51 23N 98 30W
Grahamstown, *S. Africa* **96** 33 19 S 26 31 E
Graïba, *Tunisia* **86** 34 30N 10 13 E
Graide, *Belgium* **17** 49 58N 5 4 E
Graie, Alpi, *Europe* **26** 45 30N 7 10 E
Grain Coast, *W. Afr.* **90** 4 20N 10 0W
Grajaú, *Brazil* **138** 5 50 S 46 4W
Grajaú →, *Brazil* **138** 3 41 S 44 48W
Grajewo, *Poland* **32** 53 39N 22 30 E
Gramada, *Bulgaria* **34** 43 49N 22 39 E
Graman, *Australia* **77** 29 28 S 150 56 E
Gramat, *France* **20** 44 48N 1 43 E
Grammichele, *Italy* **29** 37 12N 14 37 E
Grampian □, *U.K.* **14** 57 0N 3 0W
Grampian Mts., *U.K.* **14** 56 50N 4 0W

Greenwater Lake Prov. Park

Grampians, The, Australia 74 37 0 S 142 20 E
Gran →, Surinam 135 4 1N 55 30W
Gran Altiplanicie Central, Argentina 142 49 0 S 69 30W
Gran Canaria, Canary Is. 25 27 55N 15 35W
Gran Chaco, S. Amer. 140 25 0 S 61 0W
Gran Paradiso, Italy 26 45 33N 7 17 E
Gran Sabana, La, Venezuela 135 5 30N 61 30W
Gran Sasso d'Italia, Italy 27 42 25N 13 30 E
Granada, Nic. 128 11 58N 86 0W
Granada, Spain 25 37 10N 3 35W
Granada, U.S.A. 121 38 5N 102 20W
Granada □, Spain 23 37 18N 3 0W
Granadilla de Abona, Canary Is. 25 28 7N 16 33W
Granard, Ireland 15 53 47N 7 30W
Granbury, U.S.A. 121 32 28N 97 48W
Granby, Canada 107 45 25N 72 45W
Grand →, Canada 108 42 51N 79 34W
Grand →, Mich., U.S.A. 119 43 4N 86 15W
Grand →, Mo., U.S.A. 118 39 23N 93 6W
Grand →, S. Dak., U.S.A. 120 45 40N 100 32W
Grand Bahama, Bahamas 128 26 40N 78 30W
Grand Bank, Canada 105 47 6N 55 48W
Grand Bassam, Ivory C. 90 5 10N 3 49W
Grand Bend, Canada 108 43 19N 81 45W
Grand Béréby, Ivory C. 90 4 38N 6 55W
Grand Blanc, U.S.A. 119 42 56N 83 38W
Grand-Bourg, Guadeloupe 129 15 53N 61 19W
Grand Calumet, Île du, Canada 106 45 44N 76 41W
Grand Canal = Yun Ho →, China 61 39 10N 117 10 E
Grand Canyon, U.S.A. 123 36 3N 112 9W
Grand Canyon National Park, U.S.A. 123 36 15N 112 20W
Grand Cayman, Cayman Is. 128 19 20N 81 20W
Grand Cess, Liberia 90 4 40N 8 12W
Grand-Combe, La, France 21 44 13N 4 2 E
Grand Coulee, U.S.A. 122 47 48N 119 1W
Grand Coulee Dam, U.S.A. 122 48 0N 118 50W
Grand Erg de Bilma, Niger 87 18 30N 14 0 E
Grand Erg Occidental, Algeria 85 30 20N 1 0 E
Grand Erg Oriental, Algeria 85 30 0N 6 30 E
Grand Falls, Canada 105 48 56N 55 40W
Grand Forks, Canada 110 49 0N 118 30W
Grand Forks, U.S.A. 120 48 0N 97 3W
Grand-Fougeray, France 18 47 44N 1 43W
Grand Haven, U.S.A. 119 43 3N 86 13W
Grand I., U.S.A. 104 46 30N 86 40W
Grand Island, U.S.A. 120 40 59N 98 25W
Grand Isle, U.S.A. 121 29 15N 89 58W
Grand Junction, Colo., U.S.A. 123 39 0N 108 30W
Grand Junction, Iowa, U.S.A. 118 42 2N 94 14W
Grand Lac Victoria, Canada 106 47 35N 77 35W
Grand Lahou, Ivory C. 90 5 10N 5 0W
Grand L., N.B., Canada 105 45 57N 66 7W
Grand L., Nfld., Canada 105 49 0N 57 30W
Grand L., Nfld., Canada 105 53 40N 60 30W
Grand L., La., U.S.A. 121 29 55N 92 45W
Grand L., Ohio, U.S.A. 119 40 32N 84 25W
Grand Lake, U.S.A. 122 40 20N 105 54W
Grand Ledge, U.S.A. 119 42 45N 84 45W
Grand-Leez, Belgium 17 50 35N 4 45 E
Grand-Lieu, L. de, France 18 47 6N 1 40W
Grand-Lucé, Le, France 18 47 52N 0 28 E
Grand Manan I., Canada 105 44 45N 66 52W
Grand Marais, Canada 120 47 45N 90 25W
Grand Marais, U.S.A. 104 46 39N 85 59W
Grand-Mère, Canada 107 46 36N 72 40W
Grand Piles, Canada 107 46 40N 72 40W
Grand Popo, Benin 91 6 15N 1 57 E
Grand Portage, U.S.A. 104 47 58N 89 41W
Grand-Pressigny, Le, France 18 46 55N 0 48 E
Grand Rapids, Canada 111 53 12N 99 19W
Grand Rapids, Mich., U.S.A. 119 42 57N 86 40W
Grand Rapids, Minn., U.S.A. 120 47 15N 93 29W
Grand River, U.S.A. 118 40 49N 93 58W
Grand St-Bernard, Col du, Switz. 31 45 50N 7 10 E
Grand Santi, Fr. Guiana 135 4 20N 54 24W
Grand Teton, U.S.A. 122 43 54N 111 50W
Grand Valley, U.S.A. 122 39 30N 108 2W
Grand View, Canada 111 51 10N 100 42W
Grandas de Salime, Spain 22 43 13N 6 53W
Grande →, Jujuy, Argentina 140 24 20 S 65 2W
Grande →, Mendoza, Argentina 140 36 52 S 69 45W
Grande →, Bolivia 137 15 51 S 64 39W
Grande →, Bahia, Brazil 138 11 30 S 44 30W
Grande →, Minas Gerais, Brazil 139 20 6 S 51 4W
Grande →, Spain 25 39 6N 0 48W
Grande →, U.S.A. 121 25 57N 97 9W
Grande →, Venezuela 135 8 36N 61 39W
Grande, B., Argentina 142 50 30 S 68 20W
Grande, I., Brazil 139 23 9 S 44 14W
Grande, La, U.S.A. 122 45 15N 118 0W
Grande, Serra, Goiás, Brazil 138 11 15 S 46 30W
Grande, Serra, Piauí, Brazil 138 8 0 S 45 0W
Grande Baie, Canada 107 48 19N 70 52W
Grande Baleine, R. de la →, Canada 104 55 16N 77 47W
Grande Cache, Canada 110 53 53N 119 8W
Grande de Santiago →, Mexico 126 21 20N 105 50W
Grande-Entrée, Canada 105 47 30N 61 40W
Grande-Motte, La, France 21 43 23N 4 5 E
Grande Prairie, Canada 110 55 10N 118 50W
Grande-Rivière, Canada 105 48 26N 64 30W
Grande Sauldre →, France 19 47 27N 2 5 E
Grande-Vallée, Canada 105 49 14N 65 8W
Grandes-Bergeronnes, Canada 107 48 16N 69 35W
Grandfalls, U.S.A. 121 31 21N 102 51W
Grandoe Mines, Canada 110 56 29N 129 54W
Grândola, Portugal 23 38 12N 8 35W
Grandpré, France 19 49 20N 4 50 E
Grandview, Mo., U.S.A. 118 38 53N 94 32W
Grandview, Wash., U.S.A. 122 46 13N 119 58W
Grandview Heights, U.S.A. 119 39 58N 83 2W
Grandvilliers, France 19 49 40N 1 57 E
Graneros, Chile 140 34 5 S 70 45W
Granet, L., Canada 106 47 47N 77 31W
Grange, La, Ga., U.S.A. 115 33 4N 85 0W
Grange, La, Ky., U.S.A. 114 38 20N 85 20W
Grange, La, Mo., U.S.A. 118 40 3N 91 35W
Grange, La, Tex., U.S.A. 121 29 54N 96 52W
Grange, La, U.S.A. 124 37 42N 120 27W
Grangemouth, U.K. 14 56 1N 3 43W
Granger, Wash., U.S.A. 122 46 25N 120 5W
Granger, Wyo., U.S.A. 122 41 35N 109 58W
Grängesberg, Sweden 10 60 6N 15 1 E
Grangeville, U.S.A. 122 45 57N 116 4W
Granite City, U.S.A. 118 38 45N 90 3W
Granite Falls, U.S.A. 120 44 45N 95 35W
Granite Mtn., U.S.A. 125 33 5N 116 28W
Granite Peak, Australia 79 25 40 S 121 20 E
Granite Pk., U.S.A. 122 45 8N 109 52W
Granity, N.Z. 81 41 39 S 171 51 E
Granja, Brazil 138 3 7 S 40 50W
Granja de Moreruela, Spain 22 41 48N 5 44W
Granja de Torrehermosa, Spain 23 38 19N 5 35W
Gränna, Sweden 11 58 1N 14 28 E
Granollers, Spain 24 41 39N 2 18 E
Gransee, E. Germany 30 53 0N 13 10 E
Grant, U.S.A. 120 40 53N 101 42W
Grant, I., Australia 78 11 10 S 132 52 E
Grant, Mt., U.S.A. 122 38 34N 118 48W
Grant, Pt., Australia 74 38 32 S 145 6 E
Grant City, U.S.A. 118 40 30N 94 25W
Grant Range Mts., U.S.A. 123 38 30N 115 30W
Grantham, Australia 77 27 35 S 152 12 E
Grantham, U.K. 12 52 55N 0 39W
Grantown-on-Spey, U.K. 14 57 19N 3 36W
Grants, U.S.A. 123 35 14N 107 51W
Grants Pass, U.S.A. 122 42 30N 123 22W
Grantsburg, U.S.A. 120 45 46N 92 44W
Grantsville, U.S.A. 122 40 35N 112 32W
Granville, France 18 48 50N 1 35W
Granville, N. Dak., U.S.A. 120 48 18N 100 48W
Granville, N.Y., U.S.A. 114 43 24N 73 16W
Granville, U.S.A. 118 41 17N 89 15W
Granville L., Canada 111 56 18N 100 30W
Granya, Australia 75 36 8 S 147 15 E
Grao de Gandía, Spain 25 39 0N 0 7W
Grapeland, U.S.A. 121 31 30N 95 31W
Gras, L. de, Canada 102 64 30N 110 30W
Graskop, S. Africa 97 24 56 S 30 49 E
Gräsö, Sweden 10 60 28N 18 35 E
Grass →, Canada 111 56 3N 96 33W
Grass Range, U.S.A. 122 47 0N 109 0W
Grass River Prov. Park, Canada 111 54 40N 100 50W
Grass Valley, Calif., U.S.A. 124 39 18N 121 0W
Grass Valley, Oreg., U.S.A. 122 45 22N 120 48W
Grassano, Italy 29 40 38N 16 17 E
Grasse, France 21 43 38N 6 56 E
Grasset, L., Canada 106 49 55N 78 10W
Grassmere, Australia 73 31 24 S 142 38 E
Gratis, U.S.A. 119 39 38N 84 32W
Gratz, U.S.A. 119 38 28N 84 57W
Graubünden □, Switz. 31 46 45N 9 30 E
Graulhet, France 20 43 45N 1 59 E
Graus, Spain 24 42 11N 0 20 E
Gravatá, Brazil 138 8 10 S 35 29W
Grave, Neths. 16 51 46N 5 44 E
Grave, Pte. de, France 20 45 34N 1 4W
's-Graveland, Neths. 16 52 15N 5 7 E
Gravelbourg, Canada 111 49 50N 106 35W
Gravelines, France 19 51 0N 2 10 E
's-Gravendeel, Neths. 16 51 47N 4 37 E
's-Gravenhage, Neths. 16 52 7N 4 17 E
Gravenhurst, Canada 106 44 52N 79 20W
's-Gravenpolder, Neths. 17 51 28N 3 54 E
's-Gravensande, Neths. 16 52 0N 4 9 E
Gravesend, Australia 77 29 35 S 150 20 E
Gravesend, U.K. 13 51 25N 0 22 E
Gravina di Púglia, Italy 29 40 48N 16 25 E
Gravois, Pointe-à-, Haiti 129 18 15N 73 56W
Gravone →, France 21 41 58N 8 45 E
Gray, France 19 47 22N 5 35 E
Grayling, U.S.A. 104 44 40N 84 42W
Grayling →, Canada 110 59 21N 125 0W
Grays Harbor, U.S.A. 122 46 55N 124 8W
Grays L., U.S.A. 122 43 8N 111 30W
Grays River, U.S.A. 124 46 21N 123 37W
Graysholm, Australia 77 28 22 S 151 22 E
Grayson, Canada 111 50 45N 102 40W
Grayville, U.S.A. 119 38 16N 88 0W
Graz, Austria 33 47 4N 15 27 E
Grazalema, Spain 23 36 46N 5 23W
Greasy L., Canada 110 62 55N 122 12W
Great Abaco I., Bahamas 128 26 25N 77 10W
Great Australia Basin, Australia 72 26 0 S 140 0 E
Great Australian Bight, Australia 79 33 30 S 130 0 E
Great Bahama Bank, Bahamas 128 23 15N 78 0W
Great Barrier I., N.Z. 80 36 11 S 175 25 E
Great Barrier Reef, Australia 72 18 0 S 146 50 E
Great Barrington, U.S.A. 117 42 11N 73 22W
Great Basin, U.S.A. 122 40 0N 116 30W
Great Bear →, Canada 102 65 0N 124 0W
Great Bear L., Canada 102 65 30N 120 0W
Great Bena, U.S.A. 117 41 57N 75 45W
Great Bend, U.S.A. 120 38 25N 98 55W
Great Blasket I., Ireland 15 52 5N 10 30W
Great Britain, Europe 6 54 0N 2 15W
Great Central, Canada 110 49 20N 125 10W
Great Dividing Ra., Australia 72 23 0 S 146 0 E
Great Duck I., Canada 108 45 40N 82 57W
Great Exuma I., Bahamas 128 23 30N 75 50W
Great Falls, Canada 111 50 27N 96 1W
Great Falls, U.S.A. 122 47 27N 111 12W
Great Fish → = Groot Vis →, S. Africa 96 33 28 S 27 5 E
Great Guana Cay, Bahamas 128 24 0N 76 20W
Great Harbour Deep, Canada 105 50 25N 56 32W
Great Inagua I., Bahamas 129 21 0N 73 20W
Great Indian Desert = Thar Desert, India 48 28 0N 72 0 E
Great I., Canada 111 58 53N 96 35W
Great Karoo, S. Africa 96 31 55 S 21 0 E
Great Lake, Australia 72 41 50 S 146 40 E
Great Orme's Head, U.K. 12 53 20N 3 52W
Great Ouse →, U.K. 12 52 47N 0 22 E
Great Palm I., Australia 72 18 45 S 146 40 E
Great Papuan Plateau, Papua N. G. 69 6 30 S 142 25 E
Great Plains, N. Amer. 100 47 0N 105 0W
Great Ruaha →, Tanzania 92 7 56 S 37 52 E
Great Saint Bernard P. = Grand St-Bernard, Col du, Switz. 31 45 50N 7 10 E
Great Salt Lake, U.S.A. 122 41 0N 112 30W
Great Salt Lake Desert, U.S.A. 122 40 20N 113 50W
Great Salt Plains Res., U.S.A. 121 36 40N 98 15W
Great Sandy Desert, Australia 78 21 0 S 124 0 E
Great Scarcies →, S. Leone 90 9 0N 13 0W
Great Sea Reef, Fiji 68 16 15 S 179 0 E
Great Slave L., Canada 110 61 23N 115 38W
Great Smoky Mts. Nat. Park, U.S.A. 115 35 39N 83 30W
Great Stour = Stour →, U.K. 13 51 15N 1 20 E
Great Victoria Desert, Australia 79 29 30 S 126 30 E
Great Wall, China 60 38 30N 109 30 E
Great Western, Australia 74 37 10 S 142 50 E
Great Whernside, U.K. 12 54 9N 1 59W
Great Yarmouth, U.K. 12 52 40N 1 45 E
Greater Antilles, W. Indies 129 17 40N 74 0W
Greater London □, U.K. 13 51 30N 0 5W
Greater Manchester □, U.K. 12 53 30N 2 15W
Greater Sunda Is., Indonesia 56 7 0 S 112 0 E
Grebbestad, Sweden 11 58 42N 11 15 E
Grebenka, U.S.S.R. 36 50 9N 32 22 E
Greco, Mte., Italy 28 41 48N 14 0 E
Gredgwin, Australia 74 35 59 S 143 38 E
Gredos, Sierra de, Spain 22 40 20N 5 0W
Greece, U.S.A. 116 43 13N 77 41W
Greece ■, Europe 35 40 0N 23 0 E
Greeley, Colo., U.S.A. 120 40 30N 104 40W
Greeley, Nebr., U.S.A. 120 41 36N 98 32W
Green →, Ky., U.S.A. 114 37 54N 87 30W
Green →, Utah, U.S.A. 123 38 11N 109 53W
Green B., U.S.A. 114 45 0N 87 30W
Green Bay, U.S.A. 114 44 30N 88 0W
Green C., Australia 75 37 13 S 150 1 E
Green City, U.S.A. 118 40 16N 92 57W
Green Cove Springs, U.S.A. 115 29 59N 81 40W
Green Hd., Australia 79 30 5 S 114 56 E
Green Is., Papua N. G. 69 4 35 S 154 10 E
Green Island, N.Z. 81 45 55 S 170 26 E
Green River, U.S.A. 123 38 59N 110 10W
Greenbank, U.S.A. 124 48 6N 122 34W
Greenbush, Mich., U.S.A. 116 44 35N 83 19W
Greenbush, Minn., U.S.A. 120 48 46N 96 10W
Greencastle, U.S.A. 119 39 40N 86 48W
Greene, Iowa, U.S.A. 118 42 54N 92 48W
Greene, N.Y., U.S.A. 117 42 20N 75 45W
Greenethorpe, Australia 76 34 0 S 148 26 E
Greenfield, Calif., U.S.A. 124 36 19N 121 15W
Greenfield, Calif., U.S.A. 125 35 15N 119 0W
Greenfield, Ill., U.S.A. 118 39 21N 90 12W
Greenfield, Ind., U.S.A. 119 39 47N 85 51W
Greenfield, Iowa, U.S.A. 118 41 18N 94 28W
Greenfield, Mass., U.S.A. 117 42 38N 72 38W
Greenfield, Miss., U.S.A. 121 37 28N 93 50W
Greenfield, Ohio, U.S.A. 119 39 21N 83 23W
Greenfield Park, Canada 117 45 29N 73 29W
Greenland ■, N. Amer. 144 66 0N 45 0W
Greenland Sea, Arctic 144 73 0N 10 0W
Greenock, U.K. 14 55 57N 4 46W
Greenore, Ireland 15 54 2N 6 8W
Greenore Pt., Ireland 15 52 15N 6 20W
Greenough →, Australia 79 28 51 S 114 38 E
Greenough Pt., Canada 108 44 58N 81 26W
Greenport, U.S.A. 117 41 5N 72 23W
Greens Creek, Australia 74 36 57 S 143 0 E
Greensboro, Ga., U.S.A. 115 33 34N 83 12W
Greensboro, N.C., U.S.A. 115 36 7N 79 46W
Greensburg, Ind., U.S.A. 119 39 20N 85 30W
Greensburg, Kans., U.S.A. 121 37 38N 99 20W
Greensburg, Pa., U.S.A. 116 40 18N 79 31W
Greentown, U.S.A. 119 40 29N 85 58W
Greenup, U.S.A. 119 39 15N 88 10W
Greenville, Liberia 90 5 1N 9 6W
Greenville, Ala., U.S.A. 115 31 50N 86 37W
Greenville, Calif., U.S.A. 124 40 8N 120 57W
Greenville, Ill., U.S.A. 118 38 53N 89 22W
Greenville, Ind., U.S.A. 119 38 22N 85 59W
Greenville, Maine, U.S.A. 105 45 30N 69 32W
Greenville, Mich., U.S.A. 119 43 12N 85 14W
Greenville, Miss., U.S.A. 121 33 25N 91 0W
Greenville, N.C., U.S.A. 115 35 37N 77 26W
Greenville, Ohio, U.S.A. 119 40 5N 84 38W
Greenville, Pa., U.S.A. 116 41 23N 80 22W
Greenville, S.C., U.S.A. 115 34 54N 82 24W
Greenville, Tenn., U.S.A. 115 36 13N 82 51W
Greenville, Tex., U.S.A. 121 33 5N 96 5W
Greenwater Lake Prov. Park, Canada 111 52 32N 103 30W

Hallandsås

Guerrara, *Oasis, Algeria* **85** 32 51N 4 22 E
Guerrara, *Saoura, Algeria* **85** 28 5N 0 8W
Guerrero □, *Mexico* **127** 17 30N 100 0W
Guerzim, *Algeria* **85** 29 39N 1 40W
Gueugnon, *France* **21** 46 36N 4 4 E
Gueydan, *U.S.A.* **121** 30 3N 92 30W
Guglionesi, *Italy* **29** 41 55N 14 54 E
Gui Jiang →, *China* **59** 23 30N 111 15 E
Gui Xian, *China* **58** 23 8N 109 35 E
Guia, *Canary Is.* **25** 28 8N 15 38W
Guia de Isora, *Canary Is.* **25** 28 12N 16 46W
Guia Lopes da Laguna, *Brazil* **141** 21 26 S 56 7W
Guichi, *China* **59** 30 39N 117 27 E
Guider, *Cameroon* **91** 9 56N 13 57 E
Guidimouni, *Niger* **91** 13 42N 9 31 E
Guiding, *China* **58** 26 34N 107 11 E
Guidong, *China* **59** 26 7N 113 57 E
Guiglo, *Ivory C.* **90** 6 45N 7 30W
Guigues, *Canada* **106** 47 28N 79 26W
Guijá, *Mozam.* **97** 24 27 S 33 0 E
Guijo de Coria, *Spain* **22** 40 6N 6 28W
Guildford, *Australia* **74** 37 9 S 144 11 E
Guildford, *U.K.* **13** 51 14N 0 34W
Guilford, *U.S.A.* **105** 45 12N 69 25W
Guilin, *China* **59** 25 18N 110 15 E
Guillaumes, *France* **21** 44 5N 6 52 E
Guillestre, *France* **21** 44 39N 6 40 E
Guilvinec, *France* **18** 47 48N 4 17W
Güimar, *Canary Is.* **25** 28 18N 16 24W
Guimarães, *Brazil* **138** 2 9 S 44 42W
Guimarães, *Portugal* **22** 41 28N 8 24W
Guimaras, *Phil.* **57** 10 35N 122 37 E
Guinda, *U.S.A.* **124** 38 50N 122 12W
Guinea ■, *W. Afr.* **90** 10 20N 11 30W
Guinea, Gulf of, *Atl. Oc.* **91** 3 0N 2 30 E
Guinea-Bissau ■, *Africa* **90** 12 0N 15 0W
Güines, *Cuba* **128** 22 50N 82 0W
Guingamp, *France* **18** 48 34N 3 10W
Guipavas, *France* **18** 48 26N 4 29W
Guiping, *China* **59** 23 21N 110 2 E
Guipúzcoa □, *Spain* **24** 43 12N 2 15W
Guir, O. →, *Algeria* **85** 31 29N 2 17W
Guiratinga, *Brazil* **137** 16 21 S 53 45W
Güiria, *Venezuela* **135** 10 32N 62 18W
Guiscard, *France* **19** 49 40N 3 1 E
Guise, *France* **19** 49 52N 3 35 E
Guitiriz, *Spain* **22** 43 11N 7 50W
Guiuan, *Phil.* **57** 11 5N 125 55 E
Guixi, *China* **59** 28 16N 117 15 E
Guiyang, *Guizhou, China* **58** 26 32N 106 40 E
Guiyang, *Hunan, China* **59** 25 46N 112 42 E
Guizhou □, *China* **58** 27 0N 107 0 E
Gujan-Mestras, *France* **20** 44 38N 1 4W
Gujarat □, *India* **48** 23 20N 71 0 E
Gujiang, *China* **59** 27 11N 114 47 E
Gujranwala, *Pakistan* **48** 32 10N 74 12 E
Gujrat, *Pakistan* **48** 32 40N 74 2 E
Gukovo, *U.S.S.R.* **39** 48 1N 39 58 E
Gular, *Australia* **76** 31 19 S 148 27 E
Gulargambone, *Australia* **76** 31 20 S 148 30 E
Gulbarga, *India* **50** 17 20N 76 50 E
Gulbene, *U.S.S.R.* **36** 57 8N 26 52 E
Guledagudda, *India* **51** 16 3N 75 48 E
Gulf, The, *Asia* **47** 27 0N 50 0 E
Gulfport, *U.S.A.* **121** 30 21N 89 3W
Gulgong, *Australia* **76** 32 20 S 149 49 E
Gulin, *China* **58** 28 1N 105 50 E
Gulistan, *Pakistan* **48** 30 30N 66 35 E
Gull Lake, *Canada* **111** 50 10N 108 29W
Gullegem, *Belgium* **17** 50 51N 3 13 E
Gullringen, *Sweden* **11** 57 48N 15 44 E
Gulma, *Nigeria* **91** 12 40N 4 23 E
Gulmarg, *India* **49** 34 3N 74 25 E
Gulpen, *Neths.* **17** 50 49N 5 53 E
Gulshad, *U.S.S.R.* **40** 46 45N 74 25 E
Gulsvik, *Norway* **10** 60 24N 9 38 E
Gulu, *Uganda* **92** 2 48N 32 17 E
Gulwe, *Tanzania* **92** 6 30 S 36 25 E
Gulyaypole, *U.S.S.R.* **38** 47 45N 36 21 E
Gum Lake, *Australia* **73** 32 42 S 143 9 E
Gumal →, *Pakistan* **48** 31 40N 71 50 E
Gumbaz, *Pakistan* **48** 30 2N 69 0 E
Gumel, *Nigeria* **91** 12 39N 9 22 E
Gumiel de Hizán, *Spain* **24** 41 46N 3 41W
Gumlu, *Australia* **72** 19 53 S 147 41 E
Gumma □, *Japan* **65** 36 30N 138 20 E
Gummersbach, *W. Germany* **30** 51 2N 7 32 E
Gummi, *Nigeria* **91** 12 4N 5 9 E
Gümüsane, *Turkey* **46** 40 30N 39 30 E
Gümüşhaciköy, *Turkey* **38** 40 50N 35 18 E
Gumzai, *Indonesia* **57** 5 28 S 134 42 E
Guna, *India* **48** 24 40N 77 19 E
Guna Mt., *Ethiopia* **89** 11 50N 37 40 E
Gunbower, *Australia* **74** 35 59 S 144 24 E
Gundagai, *Australia* **76** 35 3 S 148 6 E
Gundaroo, *Australia* **76** 35 2 S 149 16 E
Gundelfingen, *W. Germany* **31** 48 33N 10 22 E
Gundih, *Indonesia* **57** 7 10 S 110 56 E
Gundlakamma →, *India* **51** 15 30N 80 15 E
Gungal, *Australia* **76** 32 17 S 150 32 E
Gungu, *Zaïre* **95** 5 43 S 19 20 E
Gunisao →, *Canada* **111** 53 56N 97 53W
Gunisao L., *Canada* **111** 53 33N 96 15W
Gunnbjørn Fjeld, *Greenland* **144** 68 45N 31 0W
Gunnedah, *Australia* **77** 30 59 S 150 15 E
Gunning, *Australia* **76** 34 47 S 149 14 E
Gunningbar Cr. →, *Australia* **76** 31 14 S 147 6 E
Gunnison, *Colo., U.S.A.* **123** 38 32N 106 56W
Gunnison, *Utah, U.S.A.* **122** 39 11N 111 48W
Gunnison →, *U.S.A.* **123** 39 3N 108 30W
Guntakal, *India* **51** 15 11N 77 27 E
Guntersville, *U.S.A.* **115** 34 18N 86 16W
Guntong, *Malaysia* **55** 4 36N 101 3 E
Guntur, *India* **51** 16 23N 80 30 E
Gunungapi, *Indonesia* **57** 6 45 S 126 30 E
Gunungsitoli, *Indonesia* **56** 1 15N 97 30 E
Gunupur, *India* **50** 19 5N 83 50 E
Günz →, *W. Germany* **31** 48 27N 10 16 E
Gunza, *Angola* **95** 10 50 S 13 50 E
Günzburg, *W. Germany* **31** 48 27N 10 16 E
Gunzenhausen, *W. Germany* **31** 49 6N 10 45 E
Guo He →, *China* **61** 32 59N 117 10 E
Guoyang, *China* **60** 33 32N 116 12 E
Gupis, *Pakistan* **49** 36 15N 73 20 E
Gura Humorului, *Romania* **34** 47 35N 25 53 E
Gürchañ, *Iran* **46** 34 55N 49 25 E
Gurdaspur, *India* **48** 32 5N 75 31 E
Gurdon, *U.S.A.* **121** 33 55N 93 10W
Gurdzhaani, *U.S.S.R.* **39** 41 43N 45 52 E
Gurgaon, *India* **48** 28 27N 77 1 E
Gurguéia →, *Brazil* **138** 6 50 S 43 24W
Gurha, *India* **48** 25 12N 71 39 E
Guri Dam, *Venezuela* **135** 7 50N 62 52W
Gurk →, *Austria* **33** 46 35N 14 31 E
Gurkha, *Nepal* **49** 28 5N 84 40 E
Gurley, *Australia* **77** 29 45 S 149 48 E
Gurnee, *U.S.A.* **119** 42 22N 87 55W
Gurué, *Mozam.* **93** 15 25 S 36 58 E
Gurun, *Malaysia* **55** 5 49N 100 27 E
Gurupá, *Brazil* **138** 1 25 S 51 35W
Gurupá, I. Grande de, *Brazil* **135** 1 25 S 51 45W
Gurupi, *Brazil* **139** 11 43 S 49 4W
Gurupi →, *Brazil* **138** 1 13 S 46 6W
Gurupi, Serra do, *Brazil* **138** 5 0 S 47 30W
Guryev, *U.S.S.R.* **39** 47 5N 52 0 E
Gus-Khrustalnyy, *U.S.S.R.* **37** 55 42N 40 44 E
Gusau, *Nigeria* **91** 12 12N 6 40 E
Gusev, *U.S.S.R.* **36** 54 35N 22 10 E
Gushan, *China* **61** 39 50N 123 35 E
Gushi, *China* **59** 32 11N 115 41 E
Gushiago, *Ghana* **91** 9 55N 0 15W
Gusinje, *Yugoslavia* **33** 42 35N 19 50 E
Gúspini, *Italy* **28** 39 32N 8 38 E
Gusselby, *Sweden* **10** 59 38N 15 14 E
Gustanj, *Yugoslavia* **27** 46 36N 14 49 E
Gustine, *U.S.A.* **124** 37 14N 121 0W
Güstrow, *E. Germany* **30** 53 47N 12 12 E
Gusum, *Sweden* **11** 58 16N 16 30 E
Guta = Kalárovo, *Czech.* **33** 47 54N 18 0 E
Gütersloh, *W. Germany* **30** 51 54N 8 25 E
Gutha, *Australia* **79** 28 58 S 115 55 E
Guthalongra, *Australia* **72** 19 52 S 147 50 E
Guthega Dam, *Australia* **75** 36 20 S 148 27 E
Guthrie, *U.S.A.* **121** 35 55N 97 30W
Guthrie Center, *U.S.A.* **118** 41 41N 94 30W
Gutian, *China* **59** 26 32N 118 43 E
Gutiérrez, *Bolivia* **137** 19 25 S 63 34W
Guttenberg, *U.S.A.* **118** 42 46N 91 10W
Guyana ■, *S. Amer.* **136** 5 0N 59 0W
Guyang, *China* **60** 41 0N 110 5 E
Guyenne, *France* **20** 44 30N 0 40 E
Guymon, *U.S.A.* **121** 36 45N 101 30W
Guyra, *Australia* **77** 30 15 S 151 40 E
Guyuan, *Hebei, China* **60** 41 37N 115 40 E
Guyuan, *Ningxia Huizu, China* **60** 36 0N 106 20 E
Guzhang, *China* **58** 28 42N 109 58 E
Guzhen, *China* **61** 33 22N 117 18 E
Guzinozersk, *U.S.S.R.* **41** 51 20N 106 35 E
Guzmán, L. de, *Mexico* **126** 31 25N 107 25W
Gwa, *Burma* **52** 17 36N 94 34 E
Gwaai, *Zambia* **93** 19 15 S 27 45 E
Gwabegar, *Australia* **77** 30 31 S 149 0 E
Gwadabawa, *Nigeria* **91** 13 28N 5 15 E
Gwādar, *Pakistan* **47** 25 10N 62 18 E
Gwagwada, *Nigeria* **91** 10 15N 7 15 E
Gwalia, *Australia* **79** 28 54 S 121 20 E
Gwalior, *India* **48** 26 12N 78 10 E
Gwanda, *Zambia* **93** 20 55 S 29 0 E
Gwandu, *Nigeria* **91** 12 30N 4 41 E
Gwane, *Zaïre* **92** 4 45N 25 48 E
Gwaram, *Nigeria* **91** 10 15N 10 25 E
Gwarzo, *Nigeria* **91** 12 20N 8 55 E
Gweebarra B., *Ireland* **15** 54 52N 8 21W
Gweedore, *Ireland* **15** 55 4N 8 15W
Gwent □, *U.K.* **13** 51 45N 2 55W
Gweru, *Zambia* **93** 19 28 S 29 45 E
Gwi, *Nigeria* **91** 9 0N 7 10 E
Gwinn, *U.S.A.* **114** 46 15N 87 29W
Gwio Kura, *Nigeria* **91** 12 40N 11 2 E
Gwol, *Ghana* **90** 10 58N 1 59W
Gwoza, *Nigeria* **91** 11 5N 13 40 E
Gwydir →, *Australia* **77** 29 27 S 149 48 E
Gwynedd □, *U.K.* **12** 53 0N 4 0W
Gyaring Hu, *China* **62** 34 50N 97 40 E
Gydanskiy P-ov., *U.S.S.R.* **40** 70 0N 78 0 E
Gympie, *Australia* **73** 26 11 S 152 38 E
Gyobingauk, *Burma* **52** 18 13N 95 39 E
Gyoda, *Japan* **65** 36 10N 139 30 E
Gyoma, *Hungary* **33** 46 56N 20 50 E
Gyöngyös, *Hungary* **33** 47 48N 19 56 E
Györ, *Hungary* **33** 47 41N 17 40 E
Gypsum Pt., *Canada* **110** 61 53N 114 35W
Gypsumville, *Canada* **111** 51 45N 98 40W
Gyttorp, *Sweden* **10** 59 31N 14 58 E
Gyula, *Hungary* **33** 46 38N 21 17 E
Gzhatsk = Gagarin, *U.S.S.R.* **36** 55 38N 35 0 E

H

Ha 'Arava →, *Israel* **44** 30 50N 35 20 E
Ha Coi, *Vietnam* **54** 21 26N 107 46 E
Ha Dong, *Vietnam* **54** 20 58N 105 46 E
Ha Giang, *Vietnam* **54** 22 50N 104 59 E
Ha Tien, *Vietnam* **55** 10 23N 104 29 E
Ha Tinh, *Vietnam* **54** 18 20N 105 54 E
Ha Trung, *Vietnam* **54** 20 0N 105 50 E
Haacht, *Belgium* **17** 50 59N 4 37 E
Ha'afeva, *Tonga* **68** 19 57 S 174 43W
Haag, *W. Germany* **31** 48 11N 12 12 E
Haaksbergen, *Neths.* **16** 52 9N 6 45 E
Haaltert, *Belgium* **17** 50 55N 4 1 E
Haamstede, *Neths.* **17** 51 42N 3 45 E
Ha'ano, *Tonga* **68** 19 41 S 174 18W
Ha'apai Group, *Tonga* **68** 19 47 S 174 27W
Haapamäki, *Finland* **8** 62 18N 24 28 E
Haapsalu, *U.S.S.R.* **36** 58 56N 23 30 E
Haarlem, *Neths.* **16** 52 23N 4 39 E
Haast, *N.Z.* **81** 43 51 S 169 1 E
Haast →, *N.Z.* **81** 43 50 S 169 2 E
Haast P., *N.Z.* **81** 44 6 S 169 21 E
Haastrecht, *Neths.* **16** 52 0N 4 47 E
Hab Nadi Chauki, *Pakistan* **48** 25 0N 66 50 E
Habana, La, *Cuba* **128** 23 8N 82 22W
Habaswein, *Kenya* **92** 1 2N 39 30 E
Habay, *Canada* **110** 58 50N 118 44W
Habay-la-Neuve, *Belgium* **17** 49 44N 5 38 E
Habiganj, *Bangla.* **52** 24 24N 91 30 E
Hablingbo, *Sweden* **11** 57 12N 18 16 E
Habo, *Sweden* **11** 57 55N 14 6 E
Haccourt, *Belgium* **17** 50 44N 5 40 E
Hachenburg, *W. Germany* **30** 50 40N 7 49 E
Hachijō-Jima, *Japan* **65** 33 5N 139 45 E
Hachinohe, *Japan* **63** 40 30N 141 29 E
Hachiōji, *Japan* **65** 35 40N 139 20 E
Hachy, *Belgium* **17** 49 42N 5 41 E
Hackensack, *U.S.A.* **117** 40 53N 74 3W
Hadali, *Pakistan* **48** 32 16N 72 11 E
Hadarba, Ras, *Sudan* **88** 22 4N 36 51 E
Hadd, Ras al, *Oman* **47** 22 35N 59 50 E
Haddington, *U.K.* **14** 55 57N 2 48W
Haddon Rig, *Australia* **76** 31 27 S 147 52 E
Haded Plain, *Somali Rep.* **98** 9 46N 48 2 E
Hadejia, *Nigeria* **91** 12 30N 10 5 E
Hadejia →, *Nigeria* **91** 12 50N 10 51 E
Haden, *Australia* **77** 27 13 S 151 54 E
Ḥadera, *Israel* **44** 32 27N 34 55 E
Ḥadera, N. →, *Israel* **44** 32 28N 34 52 E
Haderslev, *Denmark* **11** 55 15N 9 30 E
Hadhramaut = Ḥadramawt, *S. Yemen* **45** 15 30N 49 30 E
Hadjeb El Aïoun, *Tunisia* **86** 35 21N 9 32 E
Ḥadramawt, *S. Yemen* **45** 15 30N 49 30 E
Hadrians Wall, *U.K.* **12** 55 0N 2 30W
Hadsten, *Denmark* **11** 56 19N 10 3 E
Hadsund, *Denmark* **11** 56 44N 10 8 E
Haeju, *N. Korea* **61** 38 3N 125 45 E
Haerhpin = Harbin, *China* **61** 45 48N 126 40 E
Hafar al Bāṭin, *Si. Arabia* **46** 28 25N 46 0 E
Hafizabad, *Pakistan* **48** 32 5N 73 40 E
Haflong, *India* **52** 25 10N 93 5 E
Hafnarfjörður, *Iceland* **8** 64 4N 21 57W
Haft-Gel, *Iran* **46** 31 30N 49 32 E
Hafun, Ras, *Somali Rep.* **45** 10 29N 51 30 E
Hagalil, *Israel* **44** 32 53N 35 18 E
Hagari →, *India* **51** 15 40N 77 0 E
Hagen, *W. Germany* **30** 51 21N 7 29 E
Hagenow, *E. Germany* **30** 53 25N 11 10 E
Hagerman, *U.S.A.* **121** 33 5N 104 22W
Hagerstown, *Ind., U.S.A.* **119** 39 55N 85 10W
Hagerstown, *Md., U.S.A.* **114** 39 39N 77 46W
Hagersville, *Canada* **108** 42 58N 80 3W
Hagetmau, *France* **20** 43 39N 0 37W
Hagfors, *Sweden* **10** 60 3N 13 45 E
Häggenås, *Sweden* **10** 63 24N 14 55 E
Hagi, *Iceland* **8** 65 28N 23 25W
Hagi, *Japan* **64** 34 30N 131 22 E
Hagolan, *Syria* **44** 33 0N 35 45 E
Hagondange-Briey, *France* **19** 49 16N 6 11 E
Hags Hd., *Ireland* **15** 52 57N 9 30W
Hague, C. de la, *France* **18** 49 44N 1 56W
Hague, The = 's-Gravenhage, *Neths.* **16** 52 7N 4 17 E
Haguenau, *France* **19** 48 49N 7 47 E
Hai □, *Tanzania* **92** 3 10 S 37 10 E
Hai Duong, *Vietnam* **54** 20 56N 106 19 E
Hai'an, *Guangdong, China* **59** 20 18N 110 11 E
Hai'an, *Jiangsu, China* **59** 32 37N 120 27 E
Haicheng, *Fujian, China* **59** 24 23N 117 48 E
Haicheng, *Liaoning, China* **61** 40 50N 122 45 E
Haidar Khel, *Afghan.* **48** 33 58N 68 38 E
Haifa = Ḥefa, *Israel* **44** 32 46N 35 0 E
Haifeng, *China* **59** 22 58N 115 10 E
Haig, *Australia* **79** 30 55 S 126 10 E
Haiger, *W. Germany* **30** 50 44N 8 12 E
Haikang, *China* **59** 20 52N 110 8 E
Haikou, *China* **54** 20 1N 110 16 E
Ḥā'il, *Si. Arabia* **46** 27 28N 41 45 E
Hailakandi, *India* **52** 24 42N 92 34 E
Hailar, *China* **62** 49 10N 119 38 E
Hailey, *U.S.A.* **122** 43 30N 114 15W
Haileybury, *Canada* **106** 47 30N 79 38W
Hailin, *China* **61** 44 37N 129 30 E
Hailing Dao, *China* **59** 21 35N 111 47 E
Hailong, *China* **61** 42 32N 125 40 E
Hailun, *China* **62** 47 28N 126 50 E
Hailuoto, *Finland* **8** 65 3N 24 45 E
Haimen, *Guangdong, China* **59** 23 15N 116 38 E
Haimen, *Jiangsu, China* **59** 31 52N 121 10 E
Haimen, *Zhejiang, China* **59** 28 40N 121 24 E
Hainan Dao, *China* **54** 19 0N 109 30 E
Hainaut □, *Belgium* **17** 50 30N 4 0 E
Haines, *U.S.A.* **122** 44 51N 117 59W
Haines City, *U.S.A.* **115** 28 6N 81 35W
Haines Junction, *Canada* **110** 60 45N 137 30W
Haining, *China* **59** 30 28N 120 40 E
Haiphong, *Vietnam* **54** 20 47N 106 41 E
Haiti ■, *W. Indies* **129** 19 0N 72 30W
Haiya Junction, *Sudan* **88** 18 20N 36 21 E
Haiyan, *China* **59** 30 28N 120 58 E
Haiyang, *China* **61** 36 47N 121 9 E
Haiyuan, *Guangxi Zhuangzu, China* **58** 22 8N 107 35 E
Haiyuan, *Ningxia Huizu, China* **60** 36 35N 105 52 E
Haizhou, *China* **61** 34 37N 119 7 E
Haizhou Wan, *China* **61** 34 50N 119 20 E
Haja, *Indonesia* **57** 3 19 S 129 37 E
Hajar Bangar, *Sudan* **87** 10 40N 22 45 E
Hajdúböszörmény, *Hungary* **33** 47 40N 21 30 E
Hajdúszoboszló, *Hungary* **33** 47 27N 21 22 E
Hajiganj, *Bangla.* **52** 23 15N 90 50 E
Hajipur, *India* **49** 25 45N 85 13 E
Hajr, *Oman* **47** 24 0N 56 34 E
Haka, *Burma* **52** 22 39N 93 37 E
Hakansson, Mts., *Zaïre* **93** 8 40 S 25 45 E
Håkantorp, *Sweden* **11** 58 18N 12 55 E
Hakataramea, *N.Z.* **81** 44 43 S 170 30 E
Hakken-Zan, *Japan* **65** 34 10N 135 54 E
Hakodate, *Japan* **63** 41 45N 140 44 E
Hakota, *Japan* **65** 36 5N 140 30 E
Haku-San, *Japan* **65** 36 9N 136 46 E
Hakun, *Burma* **52** 26 46N 95 42 E
Ḥalab, *Syria* **46** 36 10N 37 15 E
Ḥalabjah, *Iraq* **46** 35 10N 45 58 E
Ḥalaib, *Sudan* **88** 22 12N 36 30 E
Halanzy, *Belgium* **17** 49 33N 5 44 E
Halberstadt, *E. Germany* **30** 51 53N 11 2 E
Halcombe, *N.Z.* **80** 40 8 S 175 30 E
Halcon, Mt., *Phil.* **57** 13 0N 121 30 E
Halden, *Norway* **10** 59 9N 11 23 E
Haldensleben, *E. Germany* **30** 52 17N 11 30 E
Haldwani, *India* **49** 29 31N 79 30 E
Hale, *U.S.A.* **118** 39 36N 93 20W
Hale →, *Australia* **72** 24 56 S 135 53 E
Haleakala Crater, *U.S.A.* **112** 20 43N 156 12W
Halen, *Belgium* **17** 50 57N 5 6 E
Haleyville, *U.S.A.* **115** 34 15N 87 40W
Half Assini, *Ghana* **90** 5 1N 2 50W
Halfmoon Bay, *N.Z.* **81** 46 50 S 168 5 E
Halfway →, *Canada* **110** 56 12N 121 32W
Halfway Creek, *Australia* **77** 29 54 S 153 5 E
Ḥalḥul, *Jordan* **44** 31 35N 35 7 E
Haliburton, *Canada* **109** 45 3N 78 30W
Halifax, *Australia* **72** 18 32 S 146 22 E
Halifax, *Canada* **105** 44 38N 63 35W
Halifax, *U.K.* **12** 53 43N 1 51W
Halifax B., *Australia* **72** 18 50 S 147 0 E
Halifax I., *Namibia* **96** 26 38 S 15 4 E
Halīl →, *Iran* **47** 27 40N 58 30 E
Halin, *Somali Rep.* **98** 9 6N 48 37 E
Hall, *Australia* **76** 35 12 S 149 1 E
Hall, *Austria* **31** 47 17N 11 30 E
Hall Beach, *Canada* **103** 68 46N 81 12W
Hall Pt., *Australia* **78** 15 40 S 124 23 E
Hallabro, *Sweden* **11** 56 22N 15 5 E
Hallands län □, *Sweden* **11** 56 50N 12 50 E
Hallands Väderö, *Sweden* **11** 56 27N 12 34 E
Hallandsås, *Sweden* **11** 56 22N 13 0 E

Herbignac

Hassi Rhénami, Algeria 85 31 50N 5 58 E
Hassi Tartrat, Algeria 85 30 5N 6 28 E
Hassi Zerzour, Morocco 84 30 51N 3 56W
Hastière-Lavaux, Belgium 17 50 13N 4 49 E
Hastings, Australia 74 38 18 S 145 12 E
Hastings, Canada 109 44 18N 77 57W
Hastings, N.Z. 80 39 39 S 176 52 E
Hastings, U.K. 13 50 51N 0 36 E
Hastings, Mich., U.S.A. 119 42 40N 85 20W
Hastings, Minn., U.S.A. 120 44 41N 92 51W
Hastings, Nebr., U.S.A. 120 40 34N 98 22W
Hastings →, Australia 77 31 25 S 152 55 E
Hastings Ra., Australia 77 31 15 S 152 14 E
Hästveda, Sweden 11 56 17N 13 55 E
Hat Yai, Thailand 55 7 1N 100 27 E
Hatanbulag, Mongolia 60 43 8N 109 5 E
Hatano, Japan 65 35 22N 139 14 E
Hatch, U.S.A. 123 32 45N 107 8W
Hatches Creek, Australia 72 20 56 S 135 12 E
Hatchet L., Canada 111 58 36N 103 40W
Haţeg, Romania 34 45 36N 22 55 E
Haţeg, Mţii., Romania 34 45 25N 23 0 E
Hatert, Neths. 16 51 49N 5 50 E
Hatfield P.O., Australia 73 33 54 S 143 49 E
Hatgal, Mongolia 62 50 26N 100 9 E
Hathras, India 48 27 36N 78 6 E
Hato de Corozal, Colombia 134 6 11N 71 45W
Hato Mayor, Dom. Rep. 129 18 46N 69 15W
Hattah, Australia 74 34 48 S 142 17 E
Hattem, Neths. 16 52 28N 6 4 E
Hatteras, C., U.S.A. 115 35 10N 75 30W
Hattiesburg, U.S.A. 121 31 20N 89 20W
Hatvan, Hungary 33 47 40N 19 45 E
Hau Bon = Cheo Reo, Vietnam 54 13 25N 108 28 E
Hau Duc, Vietnam 54 15 20N 108 13 E
Haubstadt, U.S.A. 119 38 12N 87 34W
Haug, Norway 10 60 23N 10 26 E
Haugastøl, Norway 10 60 30N 7 50 E
Haugesund, Norway 9 59 23N 5 13 E
Hauhungaroa Ra., N.Z. 80 38 42 S 175 40 E
Haulerwijk, Neths. 16 53 4N 6 20 E
Haultain →, Canada 111 55 51N 106 46W
Haungpa, Burma 52 25 29N 96 7 E
Hauraki Gulf, N.Z. 80 36 35 S 175 5 E
Hauran, Syria 44 32 50N 36 15 E
Haut Atlas, Morocco 84 32 30N 5 0W
Haut-Rhin □, France 19 48 0N 7 15 E
Haut Zaïre □, Zaïre 92 2 20N 26 0 E
Hautah, Wahāt al, Si. Arabia 46 23 40N 47 0 E
Haute-Corse □, France 21 42 30N 9 30 E
Haute-Garonne □, France 20 43 30N 1 30 E
Haute-Loire □, France 20 45 5N 3 50 E
Haute-Marne □, France 19 48 10N 5 20 E
Haute-Saône □, France 19 47 45N 6 10 E
Haute-Savoie □, France 21 46 0N 6 20 E
Haute-Vienne □, France 20 45 50N 1 10 E
Hauterive, Canada 107 49 10N 68 16W
Hautes-Alpes □, France 21 44 42N 6 20 E
Hautes Fagnes, Belgium 17 50 34N 6 6 E
Hautes-Pyrénées □, France 20 43 0N 0 10 E
Hauteville-Lompnès, France 21 45 58N 5 36 E
Hautmont, France 19 50 15N 3 55 E
Hautrage, Belgium 17 50 29N 3 46 E
Hauts-de-Seine □, France 19 48 52N 2 15 E
Hauts Plateaux, Algeria 85 35 0N 1 0 E
Hauzenberg, W. Germany 31 48 39N 13 38 E
Havana = Habana, La, Cuba 128 23 8N 82 22W
Havana, U.S.A. 118 40 19N 90 3W
Havant, U.K. 13 50 51N 0 59W
Havasu, L., U.S.A. 125 34 18N 114 28W
Havdhem, Sweden 11 57 10N 18 20 E
Havel →, E. Germany 30 52 40N 12 1 E
Havelange, Belgium 17 50 23N 5 15 E
Havelian, Pakistan 48 34 2N 73 10 E
Havelock, N.B., Canada 105 46 2N 65 24W
Havelock, Ont., Canada 109 44 26N 77 53W
Havelock, N.Z. 81 41 17 S 173 48 E
Havelte, Neths. 16 52 46N 6 14 E
Haverfordwest, U.K. 13 51 48N 4 59W
Haverhill, U.S.A. 117 42 50N 71 2W
Haveri, India 51 14 53N 75 24 E
Havering, U.K. 13 51 33N 0 20 E
Haverstraw, U.S.A. 117 41 12N 73 58W
Håverud, Sweden 11 58 50N 12 28 E
Havilah, Australia 76 32 37 S 149 45 E
Havlíčkův Brod, Czech. 32 49 36N 15 33 E
Havneby, Denmark 11 55 5N 8 34 E
Havre, U.S.A. 122 48 34N 109 40W
Havre, Le, France 18 49 30N 0 5 E
Havre-Aubert, Canada 105 47 12N 61 56W
Havre-St.-Pierre, Canada 105 50 18N 63 33W
Havza, Turkey 46 41 0N 35 35 E
Haw →, U.S.A. 115 35 36N 79 3W
Hawaii □, U.S.A. 112 20 30N 157 0W
Hawaii I., Pac. Oc. 112 20 0N 155 0W
Hawaiian Is., Pac. Oc. 112 20 30N 156 0W
Hawaiian Ridge, Pac. Oc. 67 24 0N 165 0W
Hawarden, Canada 111 51 25N 106 36W
Hawarden, U.S.A. 120 43 2N 96 28W
Hawea Flat, N.Z. 81 44 40 S 169 19 E
Hawea Lake, N.Z. 81 44 28 S 169 19 E
Hawera, N.Z. 80 39 35 S 174 19 E
Hawesville, U.S.A. 119 37 54N 86 45W
Hawick, U.K. 14 55 25N 2 48W
Hawk Junction, Canada 104 48 5N 84 38W
Hawk Point, U.S.A. 118 38 58N 91 8W
Hawkdun Ra., N.Z. 81 44 53 S 170 5 E
Hawke, C., Australia 77 32 13 S 152 34 E
Hawke B., N.Z. 80 39 25 S 177 20 E
Hawke's Bay □, N.Z. 80 39 45 S 176 35 E
Hawkesbury, Canada 104 45 37N 74 37W
Hawkesbury I., Canada 110 53 37N 129 3W
Hawkesbury Pt., Australia 72 11 55 S 134 5 E
Hawkesdale, Australia 74 38 7 S 142 20 E
Hawkinsville, U.S.A. 115 32 17N 83 30W
Hawkwood, Australia 73 25 45 S 150 50 E
Hawley, U.S.A. 120 46 58N 96 20W
Hawrān, Syria 44 32 45N 36 15 E
Hawthorne, U.S.A. 122 38 31N 118 37W
Hawzen, Ethiopia 89 13 58N 39 28 E
Haxtun, U.S.A. 120 40 40N 102 39W
Hay, Australia 74 34 30 S 144 51 E
Hay →, Australia 72 24 50 S 138 0 E
Hay →, Canada 110 60 50N 116 26W
Hay, C., Australia 78 14 5 S 129 29 E
Hay I., Canada 108 44 53N 80 58W
Hay L., Canada 110 58 50N 118 50W
Hay Lakes, Canada 110 53 12N 113 2W
Hay-on-Wye, U.K. 13 52 4N 3 9W
Hay River, Canada 110 60 51N 115 44W
Hay Springs, U.S.A. 120 42 40N 102 38W
Hayange, France 19 49 20N 6 2 E
Hayato, Japan 64 31 40N 130 43 E
Hayden, Ariz., U.S.A. 123 33 2N 110 48W
Hayden, Colo., U.S.A. 122 40 30N 107 22W
Haydon, Australia 72 18 0 S 141 30 E
Haye-du-Puits, La, France 18 49 17N 1 33W
Hayes, U.S.A. 120 44 22N 101 1W
Hayes →, Canada 111 57 3N 92 12W
Haynesville, U.S.A. 121 33 0N 93 7W
Hays, Canada 110 50 6N 111 48W
Hays, U.S.A. 120 38 55N 99 25W
Haysdale, Australia 74 34 54 S 143 18 E
Haystack Mountain, Australia 77 28 37 S 152 30 E
Haysville, U.S.A. 119 38 28N 86 55W
Hayward, Calif., U.S.A. 124 37 40N 122 5W
Hayward, Wis., U.S.A. 120 46 2N 91 30W
Hayward's Heath, U.K. 13 51 0N 0 5W
Hazard, U.S.A. 114 37 18N 83 10W
Hazaribag, India 49 23 58N 85 26 E
Hazaribag Road, India 49 24 12N 85 57 E
Hazebrouck, France 19 50 42N 2 31 E
Hazelton, Canada 110 55 20N 127 42W
Hazelton, U.S.A. 120 46 30N 100 15W
Hazen, N. Dak., U.S.A. 120 47 18N 101 38W
Hazen, Nev., U.S.A. 122 39 37N 119 2W
Hazerswoude, Neths. 16 52 5N 4 36 E
Hazlehurst, Ga., U.S.A. 115 31 50N 82 35W
Hazlehurst, Miss., U.S.A. 121 31 52N 90 24W
Hazleton, Ind., U.S.A. 119 38 29N 87 34W
Hazleton, Pa., U.S.A. 117 40 58N 76 0W
Hazlett, L., Australia 78 21 30 S 128 48 E
Ḥazor, Israel 44 33 2N 35 32 E
He Xian, Anhui, China 59 31 45N 118 20 E
He Xian, Guangxi Zhuangzu, China 59 24 27N 111 30 E
Head of Bight, Australia 79 31 30 S 131 25 E
Headlands, Zambia 93 18 15 S 32 2 E
Healdsburg, U.S.A. 124 38 33N 122 51W
Healdton, U.S.A. 121 34 16N 97 31W
Healesville, Australia 74 37 35 S 145 30 E
Heanor, U.K. 12 53 1N 1 20W
Heard I., Ind. Oc. 53 53 0 S 74 0 E
Hearne, U.S.A. 121 30 54N 96 35W
Hearne B., Canada 111 60 10N 99 10W
Hearne L., Canada 110 62 20N 113 10W
Hearst, Canada 104 49 40N 83 41W
Heart →, U.S.A. 120 46 40N 100 51W
Heart's Content, Canada 105 47 54N 53 27W
Heath →, Bolivia 136 12 31 S 68 38W
Heath Mts., N.Z. 81 45 39 S 167 9 E
Heath Pt., Canada 105 49 8N 61 40W
Heath Steele, Canada 105 47 17N 66 5W
Heathcote, Australia 74 36 56 S 144 45 E
Heathmere, Australia 74 38 12 S 141 35 E
Heavener, U.S.A. 121 34 54N 94 36W
Hebbronville, U.S.A. 121 27 20N 98 40W
Hebei □, China 60 39 0N 116 0 E
Hebel, Australia 73 28 58 S 147 47 E
Heber, U.S.A. 125 32 44N 115 32W
Heber Springs, U.S.A. 121 35 29N 91 59W
Hebert, Canada 111 50 30N 107 10W
Hebgen, L., U.S.A. 122 44 50N 111 15W
Hebi, China 60 35 57N 114 7 E
Hebrides, U.K. 14 57 30N 7 0W
Hebrides, Inner Is., U.K. 14 57 20N 6 40W
Hebrides, Outer Is., U.K. 14 57 30N 7 40W
Hebron = Al Khalīl, Jordan 44 31 32N 35 6 E
Hebron, Canada 103 58 5N 62 30W
Hebron, N. Dak., U.S.A. 120 46 56N 102 2W
Hebron, Nebr., U.S.A. 120 40 15N 97 33W
Heby, Sweden 10 59 56N 16 53 E
Hecate Str., Canada 110 53 10N 130 30W
Hechi, China 58 24 40N 108 2 E
Hechingen, W. Germany 31 48 20N 8 58 E
Hechtel, Belgium 17 51 8N 5 22 E
Hechuan, China 58 30 2N 106 12 E
Hecla, U.S.A. 120 45 56N 98 8W
Hecla I., Canada 111 51 10N 96 43W
Heddal, Norway 10 59 36N 9 9 E
Hédé, France 18 48 18N 1 49W
Hede, Sweden 10 62 23N 13 30 E
Hedemora, Sweden 10 60 18N 15 58 E
Hedgehope, N.Z. 81 46 12 S 168 34 E
Hedley, U.S.A. 121 34 53N 100 39W
Hedmark fylke □, Norway 10 61 17N 11 40 E
Hedrick, U.S.A. 118 41 11N 92 19W
Hedrum, Norway 10 59 7N 10 5 E
Heeg, Neths. 16 52 58N 5 37 E
Heegermeer, Neths. 16 52 56N 5 32 E
Heemskerk, Neths. 16 52 31N 4 40 E
Heemstede, Neths. 16 52 22N 4 37 E
Heer, Neths. 17 50 50N 5 43 E
Heerde, Neths. 16 52 24N 6 2 E
's Heerenburg, Neths. 16 51 53N 6 16 E
Heerenveen, Neths. 16 52 57N 5 55 E
Heerhugowaard, Neths. 16 52 40N 4 51 E
Heerlen, Neths. 17 50 55N 6 0 E
Heers, Belgium 17 50 45N 5 18 E
Heesch, Neths. 16 51 44N 5 32 E
Heestert, Belgium 17 50 47N 3 25 E
Heeze, Neths. 17 51 23N 5 35 E
Ḥefa, Israel 44 32 46N 35 0 E
Hefei, China 59 31 52N 117 18 E
Hegang, China 62 47 20N 130 19 E
Hegyalja, Hungary 33 48 25N 21 25 E
Heichengzhen, China 60 36 24N 106 3 E
Heide, W. Germany 30 54 10N 9 7 E
Heidelberg, C. Prov., S. Africa 96 34 6 S 20 59 E
Heidelberg, Trans., S. Africa 97 26 30 S 28 23 E
Heidelberg, W. Germany 31 49 23N 8 41 E
Heidenheim, W. Germany 31 48 40N 10 10 E
Heigun-To, Japan 64 33 47N 132 14 E
Heijing, China 58 25 22N 101 44 E
Heilbron, S. Africa 97 27 16 S 27 59 E
Heilbronn, W. Germany 31 49 8N 9 13 E
Heiligenblut, Austria 33 47 2N 12 51 E
Heiligenhafen, W. Germany 30 54 21N 10 58 E
Heiligenstadt, E. Germany 30 51 22N 10 9 E
Heilongjiang □, China 61 48 0N 126 0 E
Heilunkiang = Heilongjiang □, China 61 48 0N 126 0 E
Heino, Neths. 16 52 26N 6 14 E
Heinola, Finland 9 61 13N 26 2 E
Heinsch, Belgium 17 49 42N 5 44 E
Heinsun, Burma 52 25 52N 95 35 E
Heirnkut, Burma 52 25 14N 94 44 E
Heishan, China 61 41 40N 122 5 E
Heishui, Liaoning, China 61 42 8N 119 30 E
Heishui, Sichuan, China 58 32 4N 103 2 E
Heist, Belgium 17 51 20N 3 15 E
Heist-op-den-Berg, Belgium 17 51 5N 4 44 E
Hejaz = Al Ḥijāz, Si. Arabia 46 26 0N 37 30 E
Hejian, China 60 38 25N 116 5 E
Hejiang, China 58 28 43N 105 46 E
Hejin, China 60 35 35N 110 42 E
Hekelgem, Belgium 17 50 55N 4 7 E
Hekimhan, Turkey 46 38 50N 38 0 E
Hekinan, Japan 65 34 52N 137 0 E
Hekla, Iceland 8 63 56N 19 35W
Hekou, Gansu, China 60 36 10N 103 28 E
Hekou, Guangdong, China 59 23 13N 112 45 E
Hekou, Yunnan, China 62 22 30N 103 59 E
Helagsfjället, Sweden 10 62 54N 12 25 E
Helan Shan, China 60 39 0N 105 55 E
Helchteren, Belgium 17 51 4N 5 22 E
Helden, Neths. 17 51 19N 6 0 E
Helechosa, Spain 23 39 22N 4 53W
Helena, Ark., U.S.A. 121 34 30N 90 35W
Helena, Mont., U.S.A. 122 46 40N 112 0W
Helendale, U.S.A. 125 34 44N 117 19W
Helensburgh, Australia 76 34 11 S 151 1 E
Helensburgh, U.K. 14 56 0N 4 44W
Helensville, N.Z. 80 36 41 S 174 29 E
Ḥelez, Israel 44 31 36N 34 39 E
Helgasjön, Sweden 11 57 0N 14 50 E
Helgeroa, Norway 10 59 0N 9 45 E
Helgoland, W. Germany 30 54 10N 7 51 E
Heligoland = Helgoland, W. Germany 30 54 10N 7 51 E
Heliopolis, Egypt 88 30 6N 31 17 E
Hellebæk, Denmark 11 56 4N 12 32 E
Hellendoorn, Neths. 16 52 24N 6 27 E
Hellevoetsluis, Neths. 16 51 50N 4 8 E
Hellín, Spain 25 38 31N 1 40W
Helmand □, Afghan. 47 31 20N 64 0 E
Helmand →, Afghan. 47 31 12N 61 34 E
Helmand, Hamun, Iran 47 31 15N 61 15 E
Helme →, E. Germany 30 51 40N 11 20 E
Helmond, Neths. 17 51 29N 5 41 E
Helmsdale, U.K. 14 58 7N 3 40W
Helmstedt, W. Germany 30 52 16N 11 0 E
Helnæs, Denmark 11 55 9N 10 0 E
Helong, China 61 42 40N 129 0 E
Helper, U.S.A. 122 39 44N 110 56W
Helsingborg, Sweden 11 56 3N 12 42 E
Helsinge, Denmark 11 56 2N 12 12 E
Helsingfors, Finland 9 60 15N 25 3 E
Helsingør, Denmark 11 56 2N 12 35 E
Helsinki, Finland 9 60 15N 25 3 E
Helston, U.K. 13 50 7N 5 17W
Helvellyn, U.K. 12 54 31N 3 1W
Helvoirt, Neths. 17 51 38N 5 14 E
Helwân, Egypt 88 29 50N 31 20 E
Hemavati →, India 51 12 30N 76 20 E
Hemet, U.S.A. 125 33 45N 116 59W
Hemingford, U.S.A. 120 42 21N 103 4W
Hemmingford, Canada 107 45 3N 73 35W
Hemphill, U.S.A. 121 31 21N 93 49W
Hempstead, U.S.A. 121 30 5N 96 5W
Hemse, Sweden 11 57 15N 18 22 E
Hemsö, Sweden 10 62 43N 18 5 E
Hen & Chickens Is., N.Z. 80 35 58 S 174 45 E
Henan □, China 60 34 0N 114 0 E
Henares →, Spain 24 40 24N 3 30W
Hendaye, France 20 43 23N 1 47W
Henderson, Argentina 140 36 18 S 61 43W
Henderson, Ky., U.S.A. 119 37 50N 87 38W
Henderson, N.C., U.S.A. 115 36 20N 78 25W
Henderson, Nev., U.S.A. 125 36 2N 115 0W
Henderson, Pa., U.S.A. 115 35 25N 88 40W
Henderson, Tex., U.S.A. 121 32 5N 94 49W
Hendersonville, U.S.A. 115 35 21N 82 28W
Hendon, Australia 77 28 5 S 151 50 E
Heng Xian, China 58 22 40N 109 17 E
Hengcheng, China 60 38 18N 106 28 E
Hengdaohezi, China 61 44 52N 129 0 E
Hengelo, Gelderland, Neths. 16 52 3N 6 19 E
Hengelo, Overijssel, Neths. 16 52 16N 6 48 E
Hengfeng, China 59 28 12N 115 48 E
Hengshan, Hunan, China 59 27 16N 112 45 E
Hengshan, Shaanxi, China 60 37 58N 109 5 E
Hengshui, China 60 37 41N 115 40 E
Hengyang, Hunan, China 59 26 52N 112 33 E
Hengyang, Hunan, China 59 26 59N 112 22 E
Hénin-Beaumont, France 19 50 25N 2 58 E
Henlopen, C., U.S.A. 114 38 48N 75 5W
Hennan, Sweden 10 62 3N 15 46 E
Hennebont, France 18 47 49N 3 19W
Hennenman, S. Africa 96 27 59 S 27 1 E
Hennepin, U.S.A. 118 41 15N 89 21W
Hennessey, U.S.A. 121 36 8N 97 53W
Hennigsdorf, E. Germany 30 52 38N 13 13 E
Henrichemont, France 19 47 20N 2 30 E
Henrietta, U.S.A. 121 33 50N 98 15W
Henrietta, Ostrov, U.S.S.R. 41 77 6N 156 30 E
Henrietta Maria C., Canada 104 55 9N 82 20W
Henry, U.S.A. 118 41 5N 89 20W
Henryetta, U.S.A. 121 35 30N 96 0W
Henryville, Canada 107 45 8N 73 11W
Hensall, Canada 108 43 26N 81 30W
Hentiyn Nuruu, Mongolia 62 48 30N 108 30 E
Henty, Australia 76 35 30 S 147 0 E
Henzada, Burma 52 17 38N 95 26 E
Hepburn Springs, Australia 74 37 19 S 144 9 E
Heping, China 59 24 29N 115 0 E
Heppner, U.S.A. 122 45 21N 119 34W
Hepu, China 58 21 40N 109 12 E
Hepworth, Canada 108 44 37N 81 9W
Heqing, China 58 26 37N 100 11 E
Hequ, China 60 39 20N 111 15 E
Héraðsflói, Iceland 8 65 42N 14 12W
Héraðsvötn →, Iceland 8 65 45N 19 25W
Herald Cays, Australia 72 16 58 S 149 9 E
Herāt, Afghan. 47 34 20N 62 7 E
Herāt □, Afghan. 47 35 0N 62 0 E
Hérault □, France 20 43 34N 3 15 E
Hérault →, France 20 43 17N 3 26 E
Herbault, France 18 47 36N 1 8 E
Herbert →, Australia 72 18 31 S 146 17 E
Herbert Downs, Australia 72 23 7 S 139 9 E
Herberton, Australia 72 17 20 S 145 25 E
Herbiers, Les, France 18 46 52N 1 1W
Herbignac, France 18 47 27N 2 18W

Herborn

Herborn, *W. Germany* **30** 50 40N 8 19 E
Herby, *Poland* **32** 50 45N 18 50 E
Hercegnovi, *Yugoslavia* **33** 42 30N 18 33 E
Hercegovina = Bosna i Hercegovina □, *Yugoslavia* **33** 44 0N 18 0 E
Herculaneum, *U.S.A.* **118** 38 16N 90 23W
Herðubreið, *Iceland* **8** 65 11N 16 21W
Hereford, *U.K.* **13** 52 4N 2 42W
Hereford, *U.S.A.* **121** 34 50N 102 28W
Hereford, Mt., *Canada* **107** 45 5N 71 36W
Hereford and Worcester □, *U.K.* **13** 52 10N 2 30W
Herefoss, *Norway* **11** 58 32N 8 23 E
Herekino, *N.Z.* **80** 35 18 S 173 11 E
Herent, *Belgium* **17** 50 54N 4 40 E
Herentals, *Belgium* **17** 51 12N 4 51 E
Herenthout, *Belgium* **17** 51 8N 4 45 E
Herfølge, *Denmark* **11** 55 26N 12 9 E
Herford, *W. Germany* **30** 52 7N 8 40 E
Héricourt, *France* **19** 47 32N 6 45 E
Herington, *U.S.A.* **120** 38 43N 97 0W
Herisau, *Switz.* **31** 47 22N 9 17 E
Hérisson, *France* **20** 46 32N 2 42 E
Herjehogna, *Norway* **9** 61 43N 12 7 E
Herk →, *Belgium* **17** 50 56N 5 12 E
Herkenbosch, *Neths.* **17** 51 9N 6 4 E
Herkimer, *U.S.A.* **117** 43 0N 74 59W
Herlong, *U.S.A.* **124** 40 8N 120 8W
Herm, *Chan. Is.* **18** 49 30N 2 28W
Hermagor-Pressegger See, *Austria* **33** 46 38N 13 23 E
Herman, *U.S.A.* **120** 45 51N 96 8W
Hermann, *U.S.A.* **120** 38 40N 91 25W
Hermannsburg, *W. Germany* **30** 52 49N 10 6 E
Hermannsburg Mission, *Australia* **78** 23 57 S 132 45 E
Hermanus, *S. Africa* **96** 34 27 S 19 12 E
Herment, *France* **20** 45 45N 2 24 E
Hermidale, *Australia* **73** 31 30 S 146 42 E
Hermiston, *U.S.A.* **122** 45 50N 119 16W
Hermitage, *N.Z.* **81** 43 44 S 170 5 E
Hermitage, *U.S.A.* **118** 37 56N 93 19W
Hermite, I., *Chile* **142** 55 50 S 68 0W
Hermon, Mt. = Ash Shaykh, J., *Lebanon* **46** 33 25N 35 50 E
Hermosillo, *Mexico* **126** 29 10N 111 0W
Hernád →, *Hungary* **33** 47 56N 21 8 E
Hernandarias, *Paraguay* **141** 25 20 S 54 40W
Hernandez, *U.S.A.* **124** 36 24N 120 46W
Hernando, *Argentina* **140** 32 28 S 63 40W
Hernando, *U.S.A.* **121** 34 50N 89 59W
Herne, *Belgium* **17** 50 44N 4 2 E
Herne, *W. Germany* **17** 51 33N 7 12 E
Herne Bay, *U.K.* **13** 51 22N 1 8 E
Herning, *Denmark* **11** 56 8N 8 58 E
Heroica = Caborca, *Mexico* **126** 30 40N 112 10W
Heroica Nogales = Nogales, *Mexico* **126** 31 20N 110 56W
Heron Bay, *Canada* **104** 48 40N 86 25W
Herradura, Pta. de la, *Canary Is.* **25** 28 26N 14 8W
Herreid, *U.S.A.* **120** 45 53N 100 5W
Herrera, *Spain* **23** 37 26N 4 55W
Herrera de Alcántar, *Spain* **23** 39 39N 7 25W
Herrera de Pisuerga, *Spain* **22** 42 35N 4 20W
Herrera del Duque, *Spain* **23** 39 10N 5 3W
Herrick, *Australia* **72** 41 5 S 147 55 E
Herrin, *U.S.A.* **118** 37 50N 89 0W
Herrljunga, *Sweden* **11** 58 5N 13 1 E
Hersbruck, *W. Germany* **31** 49 30N 11 25 E
Herseaux, *Belgium* **17** 50 43N 3 15 E
Herselt, *Belgium* **17** 51 3N 4 53 E
Herstal, *Belgium* **17** 50 40N 5 38 E
Hertford, *U.K.* **13** 51 47N 0 4W
Hertford □, *U.K.* **13** 51 51N 0 5W
's-Hertogenbosch, *Neths.* **17** 51 42N 5 17 E
Hertzogville, *S. Africa* **96** 28 9 S 25 30 E
Hervás, *Spain* **22** 40 16N 5 52W
Herve, *Belgium* **17** 50 38N 5 48 E
Hervey Bay, *Australia* **72** 25 3 S 153 5 E
Herwijnen, *Neths.* **16** 51 50N 5 7 E
Herzberg, *E. Germany* **30** 51 40N 13 13 E
Herzberg, *W. Germany* **30** 51 38N 10 20 E
Herzele, *Belgium* **17** 50 53N 3 53 E
Herzliyya, *Israel* **44** 32 10N 34 50 E
Hesdin, *France* **19** 50 21N 2 0 E
Hesel, *W. Germany* **30** 53 18N 7 36 E
Heshui, *China* **60** 36 0N 108 0 E
Heshun, *China* **60** 37 22N 113 32 E
Hesperange, *Lux.* **17** 49 35N 6 10 E
Hesperia, *U.S.A.* **125** 34 25N 117 18W
Hesse = Hessen □, *W. Germany* **30** 50 40N 9 20 E
Hessen □, *W. Germany* **30** 50 40N 9 20 E
Hetch Hetchy Aqueduct, *U.S.A.* **124** 37 36N 121 25W
Hettinger, *U.S.A.* **120** 46 0N 102 38W
Hettstedt, *E. Germany* **30** 51 39N 11 30 E
Heugem, *Neths.* **17** 50 49N 5 42 E
Heule, *Belgium* **17** 50 51N 3 15 E
Heusden, *Belgium* **17** 51 2N 5 17 E
Heusden, *Neths.* **16** 51 44N 5 8 E
Hève, C. de la, *France* **18** 49 30N 0 5 E
Heverlee, *Belgium* **17** 50 52N 4 42 E
Hevron →, *Asia* **44** 31 12N 34 42 E
Hewett, C., *Canada* **103** 70 16N 67 45W
Hexham, *Australia* **74** 38 0 S 142 41 E
Hexham, *U.K.* **12** 54 58N 2 7W
Hexi, *Yunnan, China* **58** 24 9N 102 38 E
Hexi, *Zhejiang, China* **59** 27 58N 119 38 E
Hexigten Qi, *China* **61** 43 18N 117 30 E
Hexrivier, *S. Africa* **96** 33 30 S 19 35 E
Heysham, *U.K.* **12** 54 5N 2 53W
Heythuysen, *Neths.* **17** 51 15N 5 55 E
Heyuan, *China* **59** 23 39N 114 40 E
Heywood, *Australia* **74** 38 8 S 141 37 E
Heze, *China* **60** 35 14N 115 20 E
Hezhang, *China* **58** 27 8N 104 41 E
Hi-no-Misaki, *Japan* **64** 35 26N 132 38 E
Hi Vista, *U.S.A.* **125** 34 45N 117 46W
Hialeach, *U.S.A.* **115** 25 49N 80 17W
Hiawatha, *Kans., U.S.A.* **120** 39 55N 95 33W
Hiawatha, *Utah, U.S.A.* **122** 39 29N 111 1W
Hibbing, *U.S.A.* **120** 47 30N 93 0W
Hibbs B., *Australia* **72** 42 35 S 145 15 E
Hibernia Reef, *Australia* **78** 12 0 S 123 23 E
Hibiki-Nada, *Japan* **64** 34 0N 130 0 E
Hickory, *U.S.A.* **115** 35 46N 81 17W
Hicks Bay, *N.Z.* **80** 37 34 S 178 21 E
Hicks Pt., *Australia* **75** 37 49 S 149 17 E
Hicksville, *N.Y., U.S.A.* **117** 40 46N 73 30W
Hicksville, *Ohio, U.S.A.* **119** 41 18N 84 46W
Hida, *Romania* **34** 47 10N 23 19 E
Hida-Gawa →, *Japan* **65** 35 26N 137 3 E
Hida-Sammyaku, *Japan* **65** 36 30N 137 40 E
Hida-Sanchi, *Japan* **65** 36 10N 137 0 E
Hidaka, *Japan* **64** 35 30N 134 44 E
Hidalgo, *Mexico* **127** 24 15N 99 26W
Hidalgo, *U.S.A.* **119** 39 9N 88 9W
Hidalgo □, *Mexico* **127** 20 30N 99 10W
Hidalgo, Presa M., *Mexico* **126** 26 30N 108 35W
Hidalgo, Pta. del, *Canary Is.* **25** 28 33N 16 19W
Hidalgo del Parral, *Mexico* **126** 26 58N 105 40W
Hiddensee, *E. Germany* **30** 54 30N 13 6 E
Hidrolândia, *Brazil* **139** 17 0 S 49 15W
Hieflau, *Austria* **33** 47 36N 14 46 E
Hiendelaencina, *Spain* **24** 41 5N 3 0W
Hienghène, *N. Cal.* **68** 20 41 S 164 56 E
Hierro, *Canary Is.* **25** 27 44N 18 0 E
Higashi-matsuyama, *Japan* **65** 36 2N 139 25 E
Higashiōsaka, *Japan* **65** 34 40N 135 37 E
Higasi-Suidō, *Japan* **64** 34 0N 129 30 E
Higbee, *U.S.A.* **118** 39 19N 92 31W
Higgins, *U.S.A.* **121** 36 9N 100 1W
Higgins Corner, *U.S.A.* **124** 39 2N 121 5W
Higginsville, *Australia* **79** 31 42 S 121 38 E
Higginsville, *U.S.A.* **118** 39 4N 93 43W
High Atlas = Haut Atlas, *Morocco* **84** 32 30N 5 0W
High I., *Canada* **105** 56 40N 61 10W
High Island, *U.S.A.* **121** 29 32N 94 22W
High Level, *Canada* **110** 58 31N 117 8W
High Point, *U.S.A.* **115** 35 57N 79 58W
High Prairie, *Canada* **110** 55 30N 116 30W
High River, *Canada* **110** 50 30N 113 50W
High Springs, *U.S.A.* **115** 29 50N 82 40W
High Wycombe, *U.K.* **13** 51 37N 0 45W
Highbury, *Australia* **72** 16 25 S 143 9 E
Highland, *Ill., U.S.A.* **118** 38 44N 89 41W
Highland, *Ind., U.S.A.* **119** 41 33N 87 28W
Highland, *Wis., U.S.A.* **118** 43 6N 90 21W
Highland □, *U.K.* **14** 57 30N 5 0W
Highland Park, *U.S.A.* **119** 42 10N 87 50W
Highmore, *U.S.A.* **120** 44 35N 99 26W
Highrock L., *Canada* **111** 57 5N 105 32W
Higüay, *Dom. Rep.* **129** 18 37N 68 42W
Hihya, *Egypt* **88** 30 40N 31 36 E
Hiiumaa, *U.S.S.R.* **36** 58 50N 22 45 E
Híjar, *Spain* **24** 41 10N 0 27W
Ḥijārah, Ṣaḥrā' al, *Iraq* **46** 30 25N 44 30 E
Ḥijāz □, *Si. Arabia* **45** 24 0N 40 0 E
Hiji, *Japan* **64** 33 22N 131 32 E
Hijken, *Neths.* **16** 52 54N 6 30 E
Hijo = Tagum, *Phil.* **57** 7 33N 125 53 E
Hikari, *Japan* **64** 33 58N 131 58 E
Hiketa, *Japan* **64** 34 13N 134 24 E
Hiko, *U.S.A.* **124** 37 30N 115 13W
Hikone, *Japan* **65** 35 15N 136 10 E
Hilawng, *Burma* **52** 21 23N 93 48 E
Hildburghhausen, *E. Germany* **31** 50 24N 10 43 E
Hildesheim, *W. Germany* **30** 52 9N 9 55 E
Hill →, *Australia* **79** 30 23 S 115 3 E
Hill City, *Idaho, U.S.A.* **122** 43 20N 115 2W
Hill City, *Kans., U.S.A.* **120** 39 25N 99 51W
Hill City, *Minn., U.S.A.* **120** 46 57N 93 35W
Hill City, *S. Dak., U.S.A.* **120** 43 58N 103 35W
Hill End, *Australia* **75** 38 1 S 146 9 E
Hill Island L., *Canada* **111** 60 30N 109 50W
Hillared, *Sweden* **11** 57 37N 13 10 E
Hillcrest Center, *U.S.A.* **125** 35 23N 118 57W
Hillegom, *Neths.* **16** 52 18N 4 35 E
Hillerød, *Denmark* **11** 55 56N 12 19 E
Hillerstorp, *Sweden* **11** 57 20N 13 52 E
Hilli, *Bangla.* **52** 25 17N 89 1 E
Hillingdon, *U.K.* **13** 51 33N 0 29W
Hillman, *U.S.A.* **114** 45 5N 83 52W
Hillmond, *Canada* **111** 53 26N 109 41W
Hillsboro, *Ill., U.S.A.* **118** 39 9N 89 29W
Hillsboro, *Iowa, U.S.A.* **118** 40 50N 91 42W
Hillsboro, *Kans., U.S.A.* **120** 38 22N 97 10W
Hillsboro, *Mo., U.S.A.* **118** 38 14N 90 34W
Hillsboro, *N. Dak., U.S.A.* **120** 47 23N 97 9W
Hillsboro, *N.H., U.S.A.* **117** 43 8N 71 56W
Hillsboro, *N. Mex., U.S.A.* **123** 33 0N 107 35W
Hillsboro, *Ohio, U.S.A.* **119** 39 12N 83 37W
Hillsboro, *Oreg., U.S.A.* **124** 45 31N 123 0W
Hillsboro, *Tex., U.S.A.* **121** 32 0N 97 10W
Hillsborough, *Grenada* **129** 12 28N 61 28W
Hillsdale, *Mich., U.S.A.* **119** 41 55N 84 40W
Hillsdale, *N.Y., U.S.A.* **117** 42 11N 73 30W
Hillside, *Australia* **78** 21 45 S 119 23 E
Hillsport, *Canada* **104** 49 27N 85 34W
Hillston, *Australia* **73** 33 30 S 145 31 E
Hilo, *U.S.A.* **112** 19 44N 155 5W
Hilton, *U.S.A.* **116** 43 16N 77 48W
Hilton Beach, *Canada* **108** 46 15N 83 53W
Hilvarenbeek, *Neths.* **17** 51 29N 5 8 E
Hilversum, *Neths.* **16** 52 14N 5 10 E
Himachal Pradesh □, *India* **48** 31 30N 77 0 E
Himalaya, Mts., *Asia* **49** 29 0N 84 0 E
Himara, *Albania* **35** 40 8N 19 43 E
Hime-Jima, *Japan* **64** 33 43N 131 40 E
Himeji, *Japan* **64** 34 50N 134 40 E
Himi, *Japan* **65** 36 50N 137 0 E
Himmerland, *Denmark* **11** 56 45N 9 30 E
Ḥimṣ, *Syria* **46** 34 40N 36 45 E
Hinche, *Haiti* **129** 19 9N 72 1W
Hinchinbrook I., *Australia* **72** 18 20 S 146 15 E
Hinckley, *U.K.* **13** 52 33N 1 21W
Hinckley, *U.S.A.* **122** 39 18N 112 41W
Hindås, *Sweden* **11** 57 42N 12 27 E
Hindaun, *India* **48** 26 44N 77 5 E
Hindmarsh L., *Australia* **74** 36 5 S 141 55 E
Hindol, *India* **50** 20 40N 85 10 E
Hinds, *N.Z.* **81** 43 59 S 171 36 E
Hindsholm, *Denmark* **11** 55 30N 10 40 E
Hindu Bagh, *Pakistan* **48** 30 56N 67 50 E
Hindu Kush, *Asia* **47** 36 0N 71 0 E
Hindupur, *India* **51** 13 49N 77 32 E
Hines Creek, *Canada* **110** 56 20N 118 40W
Hinganghat, *India* **50** 20 30N 78 52 E
Hingeon, *Belgium* **17** 50 32N 4 59 E
Hingham, *U.S.A.* **122** 48 34N 110 29W
Hingoli, *India* **50** 19 41N 77 15 E
Hinlopenstretet, *Svalbard* **144** 79 35N 18 40 E
Hinna = Imi, *Ethiopia* **89** 6 28N 42 10 E
Hinna, *Nigeria* **91** 10 25N 11 35 E
Hino, *Japan* **65** 35 0N 136 15 E
Hinojosa del Duque, *Spain* **23** 38 30N 5 9W
Hinokage, *Japan* **64** 32 39N 131 24 E
Hinsdale, *U.S.A.* **122** 48 26N 107 2W
Hinterrhein →, *Switz.* **31** 46 40N 9 25 E
Hinton, *Canada* **110** 53 26N 117 34W
Hinton, *U.S.A.* **114** 37 40N 80 51W
Hippolytushoef, *Neths.* **16** 52 54N 4 58 E
Hirado, *Japan* **64** 33 22N 129 33 E
Hirado-Shima, *Japan* **64** 33 20N 129 30 E
Hirakarta, *Japan* **65** 34 48N 135 40 E
Hirakud, *India* **50** 21 32N 83 51 E
Hirakud Dam, *India* **50** 21 32N 83 45 E
Hirata, *Japan* **64** 35 24N 132 49 E
Hiratsuka, *Japan* **65** 35 19N 139 21 E
Hirhafok, *Algeria* **85** 23 49N 5 45 E
Hîrlău, *Romania* **34** 47 23N 27 0 E
Hiromi, *Japan* **64** 33 13N 132 36 E
Hirosaki, *Japan* **63** 40 34N 140 28 E
Hiroshima, *Japan* **64** 34 24N 132 30 E
Hiroshima □, *Japan* **64** 34 50N 133 0 E
Hiroshima-Wan, *Japan* **64** 34 5N 132 20 E
Hirsholmene, *Denmark* **11** 57 30N 10 36 E
Hirson, *France* **19** 49 55N 4 4 E
Hîrşova, *Romania* **34** 44 40N 27 59 E
Hirtshals, *Denmark* **11** 57 36N 9 57 E
Hisar, *India* **48** 29 12N 75 45 E
Hispaniola, *W. Indies* **129** 19 0N 71 0W
Hita, *Japan* **64** 33 20N 130 58 E
Hitachi, *Japan* **65** 36 36N 140 39 E
Hitachiota, *Japan* **65** 36 30N 140 30 E
Hitchin, *U.K.* **13** 51 57N 0 16W
Hitoyoshi, *Japan* **64** 32 13N 130 45 E
Hitra, *Norway* **8** 63 30N 8 45 E
Hitzacker, *W. Germany* **30** 53 9N 11 1 E
Hiu, *Vanuatu* **68** 13 10 S 166 35 E
Hiuchi-Nada, *Japan* **64** 34 5N 133 20 E
Ḥiyyon, N. →, *Israel* **44** 30 25N 35 10 E
Hjalmar L., *Canada* **111** 61 33N 109 25W
Hjälmare kanal, *Sweden* **10** 59 20N 15 59 E
Hjälmaren, *Sweden* **10** 59 18N 15 40 E
Hjartdal, *Norway* **10** 59 37N 8 41 E
Hjerkinn, *Norway* **10** 62 13N 9 33 E
Hjørring, *Denmark* **11** 57 29N 9 59 E
Hjorted, *Sweden* **11** 57 37N 16 19 E
Hjortkvarn, *Sweden* **11** 58 54N 15 26 E
Hko-ut, *Burma* **52** 20 58N 98 2 E
Hkyenhpa, *Burma* **52** 27 43N 97 25 E
Hlaingbwe, *Burma* **52** 17 8N 97 50 E
Hlinsko, *Czech.* **32** 49 45N 15 54 E
Hluhluwe, *S. Africa* **97** 28 1 S 32 15 E
Hlwaze, *Burma* **52** 18 54N 96 37 E
Hńak, *Greenland* **144** 70 40N 52 10W
Ho, *Ghana* **91** 6 37N 0 27 E
Ho Chi Minh City = Phanh Bho Ho Chi Minh, *Vietnam* **55** 10 58N 106 40 E
Ho Thuong, *Vietnam* **54** 19 32N 105 48 E
Hoa Binh, *Vietnam* **54** 20 50N 105 20 E
Hoa Da, *Vietnam* **55** 11 16N 108 40 E
Hoa Hiep, *Vietnam* **55** 11 34N 105 51 E
Hoai Nhon, *Vietnam* **54** 14 28N 109 1 E
Hoare B., *Canada* **103** 65 17N 62 30W
Hobart, *Australia* **72** 42 50 S 147 21 E
Hobart, *Ind., U.S.A.* **119** 41 32N 87 15W
Hobart, *Okla., U.S.A.* **121** 35 0N 99 5W
Hobbs, *U.S.A.* **121** 32 40N 103 3W
Hobbs Coast, *Antarctica* **143** 74 50 S 131 0W
Hobo, *Colombia* **134** 2 35N 75 30W
Hoboken, *Belgium* **17** 51 11N 4 21 E
Hoboken, *U.S.A.* **117** 40 45N 74 4W
Hobro, *Denmark* **11** 56 39N 9 46 E
Hobscheid, *Lux.* **17** 49 42N 5 57 E
Hoburgen, *Sweden* **11** 56 55N 18 7 E
Hochschwab, *Austria* **33** 47 35N 15 0 E
Höchst, *W. Germany* **31** 50 6N 8 33 E
Höchstadt, *W. Germany* **31** 49 42N 10 48 E
Hockenheim, *W. Germany* **31** 49 18N 8 33 E
Hodaka-Dake, *Japan* **65** 36 17N 137 39 E
Hodgson, *Canada* **111** 51 13N 97 36W
Hódmezövásárhely, *Hungary* **33** 46 28N 20 22 E
Hodna, Chott el, *Algeria* **85** 35 30N 5 0 E
Hodna, Monts du, *Algeria* **85** 35 52N 4 42 E
Hodonín, *Czech.* **32** 48 50N 17 10 E
Hœdic, I. de, *France* **18** 47 20N 2 53W
Hoegaarden, *Belgium* **17** 50 47N 4 53 E
Hoek van Holland, *Neths.* **16** 52 0N 4 7 E
Hoeksche Waard, *Neths.* **16** 51 46N 4 25 E
Hoenderloo, *Neths.* **16** 52 7N 5 52 E
Hoensbroek, *Neths.* **17** 50 55N 5 55 E
Hoeselt, *Belgium* **17** 50 51N 5 29 E
Hoëveld, *S. Africa* **97** 26 30 S 30 0 E
Hoeven, *Neths.* **17** 51 35N 4 35 E
Hof, *Iceland* **8** 64 33N 14 40W
Hof, *W. Germany* **31** 50 18N 11 55 E
Höfðakaupstaður, *Iceland* **8** 65 50N 20 19W
Hofgeismar, *W. Germany* **30** 51 29N 9 23 E
Hofmeyr, *S. Africa* **96** 31 39 S 25 50 E
Hofors, *Sweden* **10** 60 31N 16 15 E
Hofsjökull, *Iceland* **8** 64 49N 18 48W
Hofsós, *Iceland* **8** 65 53N 19 26W
Hōfu, *Japan* **64** 34 3N 131 34 E
Hogan Group, *Australia* **72** 39 13 S 147 1 E
Hogansville, *U.S.A.* **115** 33 14N 84 50W
Hogeland, *U.S.A.* **122** 48 51N 108 40W
Hogenakai Falls, *India* **51** 12 6N 77 50 E
Högfors, *Sweden* **10** 59 58N 15 3 E
Hōgo-Kaikyō, *Japan* **64** 33 20N 131 58 E
Högsäter, *Sweden* **11** 58 38N 12 5 E
Högsby, *Sweden* **11** 57 10N 16 1 E
Högsjö, *Sweden* **10** 59 4N 15 44 E
Hogsty Reef, *Bahamas* **129** 21 41N 73 48W
Hoh →, *U.S.A.* **124** 47 45N 124 29W
Hoh Xil Shan, *China* **62** 35 0N 89 0 E
Hohe Rhön, *W. Germany* **31** 50 24N 9 58 E
Hohe Tauern, *Austria* **33** 47 11N 12 40 E
Hohe Venn, *Belgium* **17** 50 30N 6 5 E
Hohenau, *Austria* **32** 48 36N 16 55 E
Hohenems, *Austria* **31** 47 22N 9 42 E
Hohenstein-Ernstthal, *E. Germany* **30** 50 48N 12 43 E
Hohenwald, *U.S.A.* **115** 35 35N 87 30W
Hohenwestedt, *W. Germany* **30** 54 6N 9 30 E
Hohhot, *China* **60** 40 52N 111 40 E
Hohoe, *Ghana* **91** 7 8N 0 32 E
Hoi An, *Vietnam* **54** 15 30N 108 19 E
Hoi Xuan, *Vietnam* **54** 20 25N 105 9 E
Hoisington, *U.S.A.* **120** 38 33N 98 50W
Højer, *Denmark* **11** 54 58N 8 42 E
Hōjō, *Japan* **64** 33 58N 132 46 E
Hok, *Sweden* **11** 57 31N 14 16 E
Hökensås, *Sweden* **11** 58 0N 14 5 E
Hökerum, *Sweden* **11** 57 51N 13 16 E
Hokianga Harbour, *N.Z.* **80** 35 31 S 173 22 E
Hokitika, *N.Z.* **81** 42 42 S 171 0 E
Hokkaidō □, *Japan* **63** 43 30N 143 0 E
Hokksund, *Norway* **10** 59 44N 9 59 E
Hol-Hol, *Djibouti* **89** 11 20N 42 50 E
Holbæk, *Denmark* **11** 55 43N 11 43 E
Holbrook, *Australia* **76** 35 42 S 147 18 E
Holbrook, *U.S.A.* **123** 35 54N 110 10W
Holden, *Canada* **110** 53 13N 112 11W
Holden, *Mo., U.S.A.* **118** 38 43N 94 0W
Holden, *Utah, U.S.A.* **122** 39 0N 112 26W
Holdenville, *U.S.A.* **121** 35 5N 96 25W
Holderness, *U.K.* **12** 53 45N 0 5W
Holdfast, *Canada* **111** 50 58N 105 25W

Huambo

Holdich, Argentina 142 45 57 S 68 13W
Holdrege, U.S.A. 120 40 26N 99 22W
Hole-Narsipur, India 51 12 48N 76 16 E
Holgate, U.S.A. 119 41 15N 84 8W
Holguín, Cuba 128 20 50N 76 20W
Hollabrunn, Austria 32 48 34N 16 5 E
Hollams Bird I., Namibia 96 24 40 S 14 30 E
Holland, U.S.A. 119 42 47N 86 7W
Hollandia = Jayapura, Indonesia 57 2 28 S 140 38 E
Hollandsch Diep, Neths. 17 51 41N 4 30 E
Hollandsch IJssel →, Neths. 16 51 55N 4 34 E
Holleton, Australia 79 31 55 S 119 0 E
Hollfeld, W. Germany 31 49 56N 11 18 E
Hollick Kenyon Plateau, Antarctica 143 82 0 S 110 0W
Hollidaysburg, U.S.A. 116 40 26N 78 25W
Hollis, U.S.A. 121 34 45N 99 55W
Hollister, Calif., U.S.A. 124 36 51N 121 24W
Hollister, Idaho, U.S.A. 122 42 21N 114 40W
Hollum, Neths. 16 53 26N 5 38 E
Holly, Colo., U.S.A. 120 38 7N 102 7W
Holly, Mich., U.S.A. 119 42 48N 83 38W
Holly Hill, U.S.A. 115 29 15N 81 3W
Holly Springs, U.S.A. 121 34 45N 89 25W
Hollywood, Calif., U.S.A. 112 34 7N 118 25W
Hollywood, Fla., U.S.A. 115 26 0N 80 9W
Holm, Sweden 10 62 40N 16 40 E
Holman Island, Canada 102 70 42N 117 41W
Hólmavík, Iceland 8 65 42N 21 40W
Holmegil, Norway 10 59 10N 11 44 E
Holmes Reefs, Australia 72 16 27 S 148 0 E
Holmestrand, Norway 10 59 31N 10 14 E
Holmsbu, Norway 10 59 32N 10 27 E
Holmsjön, Sweden 10 62 26N 15 20 E
Holmsland Klit, Denmark 11 56 0N 8 5 E
Holmsund, Sweden 8 63 41N 20 20 E
Holon, Israel 44 32 2N 34 47 E
Holroyd →, Australia 72 14 10 S 141 36 E
Holstebro, Denmark 11 56 22N 8 37 E
Holsworthy, U.K. 13 50 48N 4 21W
Holt, Iceland 8 63 33N 19 48W
Holte, Denmark 11 55 50N 12 29 E
Holten, Neths. 16 52 17N 6 26 E
Holton, Canada 105 54 31N 57 12W
Holton, U.S.A. 120 39 28N 95 44W
Holtville, U.S.A. 125 32 50N 115 27W
Holwerd, Neths. 16 53 22N 5 54 E
Holy Cross, U.S.A. 102 62 10N 159 52W
Holy I., England, U.K. 12 55 42N 1 48W
Holy I., Wales, U.K. 12 53 17N 4 37W
Holyhead, U.K. 12 53 18N 4 38W
Holyoke, Colo., U.S.A. 120 40 39N 102 18W
Holyoke, Mass., U.S.A. 117 42 14N 72 37W
Holyrood, Canada 105 47 27N 53 8W
Holzkirchen, W. Germany 31 47 53N 11 42 E
Holzminden, W. Germany 30 51 49N 9 31 E
Homa Bay, Kenya 92 0 36 S 34 30 E
Homa Bay □, Kenya 92 0 50 S 34 30 E
Homalin, Burma 52 24 55N 95 0 E
Homberg, W. Germany 30 51 2N 9 20 E
Hombori, Mali 91 15 20N 1 38W
Homburg, W. Germany 31 49 19N 7 21 E
Home B., Canada 103 68 40N 67 10W
Home Hill, Australia 72 19 43 S 147 25 E
Home Reef, Tonga 68 18 59 S 174 47W
Homedale, U.S.A. 122 43 42N 116 59W
Homer, Alaska, U.S.A. 102 59 40N 151 35W
Homer, Ill., U.S.A. 119 40 4N 87 57W
Homer, La., U.S.A. 121 32 50N 93 4W
Homer, Mich., U.S.A. 119 42 9N 84 49W
Homestead, Australia 72 20 20 S 145 40 E
Homestead, Fla., U.S.A. 115 25 29N 80 27W
Homestead, Oreg., U.S.A. 122 45 5N 116 57W
Homewood, Calif., U.S.A. 124 39 4N 120 8W
Homewood, Ill., U.S.A. 119 41 34N 87 40W
Hominy, U.S.A. 121 36 26N 96 24W
Homnabad, India 50 17 45N 77 11 E
Homoine, Mozam. 97 23 55 S 35 8 E
Homoljske Planina, Yugoslavia 33 44 10N 21 45 E
Homorod, Romania 34 46 5N 25 15 E
Homs = Ḥimş, Syria 46 34 40N 36 45 E
Hon Chong, Vietnam 55 10 25N 104 30 E
Hon Me, Vietnam 54 19 23N 105 56 E
Hon Quan, Vietnam 55 11 40N 106 50 E
Honan = Henan □, China 60 34 0N 114 0 E
Honbetsu, Japan 63 43 7N 143 37 E
Honcut, U.S.A. 124 39 20N 121 32W
Honda, Colombia 134 5 12N 74 45W
Hondeklipbaai, S. Africa 96 30 19 S 17 17 E
Hondo, Japan 64 32 27N 130 12 E
Hondo, U.S.A. 121 29 22N 99 6W
Hondo →, Belize 127 18 25N 88 21W
Honduras ■, Cent. Amer. 128 14 40N 86 30W
Honduras, G. de, Caribbean 128 16 50N 87 0W
Hønefoss, Norway 9 60 10N 10 18 E
Honesdale, U.S.A. 117 41 34N 75 17W
Honey Harbour, Canada 108 44 52N 79 49W
Honey L., U.S.A. 124 40 13N 120 14W
Honfleur, France 18 49 25N 0 13 E
Hong →, Vietnam 54 20 17N 106 34 E
Hong Gai, Vietnam 54 20 57N 107 5 E
Hong He →, China 60 32 25N 115 35 E
Hong Kong ■, Asia 59 22 11N 114 14 E
Hong'an, China 59 31 20N 114 40 E
Honghai Wan, China 59 22 40N 115 0 E
Honghu, China 59 29 50N 113 30 E
Hongjiang, China 58 27 7N 109 59 E
Hongliu He →, China 60 38 0N 109 50 E
Hongor, Mongolia 60 45 45N 112 50 E
Hongsa, Laos 54 19 43N 101 20 E
Hongshui He →, China 58 23 48N 109 30 E
Hongtong, China 60 36 16N 111 40 E
Honguedo, Détroit d', Canada 105 49 15N 64 0W
Hongya, China 58 29 57N 103 22 E
Hongyuan, China 58 32 51N 102 40 E
Hongze Hu, China 61 33 15N 118 35 E
Honiara, Solomon Is. 68 9 27 S 159 57 E
Honiton, U.K. 13 50 48N 3 11W
Honjō, Akita, Japan 63 39 23N 140 3 E
Honjō, Gumma, Japan 65 36 14N 139 11 E
Honkawane, Japan 65 35 5N 138 5 E
Honkorâb, Ras, Egypt 88 24 35N 35 10 E
Honolulu, U.S.A. 112 21 19N 157 52W
Honshū, Japan 63 36 0N 138 0 E
Hontoria del Pinar, Spain 24 41 50N 3 10W
Hood, Pt., Australia 79 34 23 S 119 34 E
Hood Mt., U.S.A. 122 45 24N 121 41W
Hood Pt., Papua N. G. 69 10 4 S 147 45 E
Hood River, U.S.A. 122 45 45N 121 31W
Hoodsport, U.S.A. 124 47 24N 123 7W
Hooge, W. Germany 30 54 31N 8 36 E
Hoogerheide, Neths. 17 51 26N 4 20 E
Hoogeveen, Neths. 16 52 44N 6 30 E
Hoogeveensche Vaart, Neths. 16 52 42N 6 12 E
Hoogezand, Neths. 16 53 11N 6 45 E
Hooghly → = Hughli →, India 49 21 56N 88 4 E
Hooghly-Chinsura = Chunchura, India 49 22 53N 88 27 E
Hoogkerk, Neths. 16 53 13N 6 30 E
Hooglede, Belgium 17 50 59N 3 5 E
Hoogstraten, Belgium 17 51 24N 4 46 E
Hoogvliet, Neths. 16 51 52N 4 21 E
Hook Hd., Ireland 15 52 8N 6 57W
Hook I., Australia 72 20 4 S 149 0 E
Hook of Holland = Hoek van Holland, Neths. 16 52 0N 4 7 E
Hooker, U.S.A. 121 36 55N 101 10W
Hooker Creek, Australia 78 18 23 S 130 38 E
Hoopeston, U.S.A. 119 40 30N 87 40W
Hoopstad, S. Africa 96 27 50 S 25 55 E
Hoorn, Neths. 16 52 38N 5 4 E
Hoover Dam, U.S.A. 125 36 0N 114 45W
Hooversville, U.S.A. 116 40 8N 78 57W
Hop Bottom, U.S.A. 117 41 41N 75 47W
Hopà, Turkey 39 41 28N 41 30 E
Hope, Canada 110 49 25N 121 25W
Hope, Ariz., U.S.A. 125 33 43N 113 42W
Hope, Ark., U.S.A. 121 33 40N 93 36W
Hope, Ind., U.S.A. 119 39 18N 85 46W
Hope, N. Dak., U.S.A. 120 47 21N 97 42W
Hope, L., Australia 73 28 24 S 139 18 E
Hope I., Canada 108 44 55N 80 11W
Hope Pt., U.S.A. 102 68 20N 166 50W
Hope Town, Bahamas 128 26 35N 76 57W
Hopedale, Canada 105 55 28N 60 13W
Hopefield, S. Africa 96 33 3 S 18 22 E
Hopei = Hebei □, China 60 39 0N 116 0 E
Hopelchén, Mexico 127 19 46N 89 50W
Hopetoun, Vic., Australia 74 35 42 S 142 22 E
Hopetoun, W. Austral., Australia 79 33 57 S 120 7 E
Hopetown, S. Africa 96 29 34 S 24 3 E
Hopin, Burma 52 24 58N 96 30 E
Hopkins, Mich., U.S.A. 119 42 37N 85 46W
Hopkins, Mo., U.S.A. 118 40 31N 94 45W
Hopkins →, Australia 74 38 25 S 142 30 E
Hopkins, L., Australia 78 24 15 S 128 35 E
Hopkinsville, U.S.A. 115 36 52N 87 26W
Hopland, U.S.A. 124 39 0N 123 7W
Hoptrup, Denmark 11 55 11N 9 28 E
Hoquiam, U.S.A. 124 46 50N 123 55W
Hōrai, Japan 65 34 58N 137 32 E
Horcajo de Santiago, Spain 24 39 50N 3 1W
Hordaland fylke □, Norway 9 60 25N 6 15 E
Horden Hills, Australia 78 20 15 S 130 0 E
Hordio, Somali Rep. 98 10 33N 51 6 E
Horezu, Romania 34 45 6N 24 0 E
Horgen, Switz. 31 47 15N 8 35 E
Horinger, China 60 40 28N 111 48 E
Horlick Mts., Antarctica 143 84 0 S 102 0W
Hormoz, Iran 47 27 35N 55 0 E
Hormoz, Jaz. ye, Iran 47 27 8N 56 28 E
Hormozgān □, Iran 47 27 30N 56 0 E
Hormuz Str., The Gulf 47 26 30N 56 30 E
Horn, Ísafjarðarsýsla, Iceland 8 66 28N 22 28W
Horn, Suður-Múlasýsla, Iceland 8 65 10N 13 31W
Horn, Neths. 17 51 12N 5 57 E
Horn →, Canada 110 61 30N 118 1W
Horn, Cape = Hornos, C. de, Chile 142 55 50 S 67 30W
Horn Head, Ireland 15 55 13N 8 0W
Horn I., Australia 72 10 37 S 142 17 E
Horn I., U.S.A. 115 30 17N 88 40W
Horn Mts., Canada 110 62 15N 119 15W
Hornachuelos, Spain 23 37 50N 5 14W
Hornavan, Sweden 8 66 15N 17 30 E
Hornbæk, Denmark 11 56 5N 12 26 E
Hornbeck, U.S.A. 121 31 22N 93 20W
Hornbrook, U.S.A. 122 41 58N 122 37W
Hornburg, E. Germany 30 52 2N 10 36 E
Hornby, N.Z. 81 43 33 S 172 33 E
Horncastle, U.K. 12 53 13N 0 8W
Horndal, Sweden 10 60 18N 16 23 E
Hornell, U.S.A. 116 42 23N 77 41W
Hornell L., Canada 110 62 20N 119 25W
Hornepayne, Canada 104 49 14N 84 48W
Hornings Mills, Canada 108 44 9N 80 12W
Hornitos, U.S.A. 124 37 30N 120 14W
Hornos, C. de, Chile 142 55 50 S 67 30W
Hornoy, France 19 49 50N 1 54 E
Hornsby, Australia 76 33 42 S 151 2 E
Hornsea, U.K. 12 53 55N 0 10W
Hornslandet, Sweden 10 61 35N 17 37 E
Hornslet, Denmark 11 56 18N 10 19 E
Hornu, Belgium 17 50 26N 3 50 E
Hörnum, W. Germany 30 54 44N 8 18 E
Horqin Youyi Qianqi, China 61 46 5N 122 3 E
Horqueta, Paraguay 140 23 15 S 56 55W
Horqueta, La, Venezuela 135 7 55N 60 20W
Horra, La, Spain 22 41 44N 3 53W
Horred, Sweden 11 57 22N 12 28 E
Horse Cr. →, U.S.A. 120 41 57N 103 58W
Horse Is., Canada 105 50 15N 55 50W
Horsefly L., Canada 110 52 25N 121 0W
Horsens, Denmark 11 55 52N 9 51 E
Horsens Fjord, Denmark 11 55 50N 10 0 E
Horsham, Australia 74 36 44 S 142 13 E
Horsham, U.K. 13 51 4N 0 20W
Horst, Neths. 17 51 27N 6 3 E
Horten, Norway 10 59 25N 10 32 E
Hortobágy →, Hungary 33 47 30N 21 6 E
Horton, U.S.A. 120 39 42N 95 30W
Horton →, Canada 102 69 56N 126 52W
Hörvik, Sweden 11 56 2N 14 45 E
Horwood, L., Canada 104 48 5N 82 20W
Hosaina, Ethiopia 89 7 30N 37 47 E
Hosdurga, India 51 13 49N 76 17 E
Hose, Gunung-Gunung, Malaysia 56 2 5N 114 6 E
Hoshangabad, India 48 22 45N 77 45 E
Hoshiarpur, India 48 31 30N 75 58 E
Hosingen, Lux. 17 50 1N 6 6 E
Hoskins, Papua N. G. 69 5 29 S 150 27 E
Hoskinstown, Australia 76 35 25 S 149 28 E
Hosmer, U.S.A. 120 45 36N 99 29W
Hososhima, Japan 64 32 26N 131 40 E
Hospet, India 51 15 15N 76 20 E
Hospitalet de Llobregat, Spain 24 41 21N 2 6 E
Hoste, I., Chile 142 55 0 S 69 0W
Hostens, France 20 44 30N 0 40W
Hot, Thailand 54 18 8N 98 29 E
Hot Creek Ra., U.S.A. 122 39 0N 116 0W
Hot Springs, Ark., U.S.A. 121 34 30N 93 0W
Hot Springs, S. Dak., U.S.A. 120 43 25N 103 30W
Hotagen, Sweden 8 63 50N 14 30 E
Hotan, China 62 37 25N 79 55 E
Hotazel, S. Africa 96 27 17 S 22 58 E
Hotchkiss, U.S.A. 123 38 47N 107 47W
Hotham, C., Australia 78 12 2 S 131 18 E
Hotham Heights, Australia 75 36 58 S 147 11 E
Hoting, Sweden 8 64 8N 16 15 E
Hotte, Massif de la, Haiti 129 18 30N 73 45W
Hottentotsbaai, Namibia 96 26 8 S 14 59 E
Hotton, Belgium 17 50 16N 5 26 E
Houailou, N. Cal. 68 21 17 S 165 38 E
Houat, I. de, France 18 47 24N 2 58W
Houck, U.S.A. 123 35 15N 109 15W
Houdan, France 19 48 48N 1 35 E
Houdeng-Goegnies, Belgium 17 50 29N 4 10 E
Houei Sai, Laos 54 20 18N 100 26 E
Houffalize, Belgium 17 50 8N 5 48 E
Houghton, U.S.A. 120 47 9N 88 39W
Houghton L., U.S.A. 114 44 20N 84 40W
Houghton-le-Spring, U.K. 12 54 51N 1 28W
Houhora, N.Z. 80 34 49 S 173 9 E
Houille →, Belgium 17 50 8N 4 50 E
Houlton, U.S.A. 105 46 5N 67 50W
Houma, U.S.A. 121 29 35N 90 44W
Houndé, Burkina Faso 90 11 34N 3 31W
Hourtin, France 20 45 11N 1 4W
Hourtin-Carcans, Étang d', France 20 45 10N 1 6W
Houston, Canada 110 54 25N 126 39W
Houston, Mo., U.S.A. 121 37 20N 92 0W
Houston, Tex., U.S.A. 121 29 50N 95 20W
Houten, Neths. 16 52 2N 5 10 E
Houthalen, Belgium 17 51 2N 5 23 E
Houthem, Belgium 17 50 48N 2 57 E
Houthulst, Belgium 17 50 59N 3 20 E
Houtman Abrolhos, Australia 79 28 43 S 113 48 E
Houyet, Belgium 17 50 11N 5 1 E
Hov, Denmark 11 55 55N 10 15 E
Hova, Sweden 11 58 53N 14 14 E
Høvåg, Norway 11 58 10N 8 16 E
Hovd, Mongolia 62 48 2N 91 37 E
Hove, U.K. 13 50 50N 0 10W
Hovmantorp, Sweden 11 56 47N 15 7 E
Hövsgöl, Mongolia 60 43 37N 109 39 E
Hövsgöl Nuur, Mongolia 62 51 0N 100 30 E
Hovsta, Sweden 10 59 22N 15 15 E
Howakil, Ethiopia 89 15 10N 40 16 E
Howar, Wadi →, Sudan 89 17 30N 27 8 E
Howard, Australia 73 25 16 S 152 32 E
Howard, Kans., U.S.A. 121 37 30N 96 16W
Howard, Pa., U.S.A. 116 41 0N 77 40W
Howard, S. Dak., U.S.A. 120 44 2N 97 30W
Howard I., Australia 72 12 10 S 135 24 E
Howard L., Canada 111 62 15N 105 57W
Howatharra, Australia 79 28 29 S 114 33 E
Howe, U.S.A. 122 43 48N 113 0W
Howe, C., Australia 75 37 30 S 150 0 E
Howe I., Canada 109 44 16N 76 17W
Howell, U.S.A. 104 42 38N 83 56W
Howes Valley, Australia 76 32 51 S 150 51 E
Howick, Canada 117 45 11N 73 51W
Howick, N.Z. 80 36 54 S 174 56 E
Howick, S. Africa 97 29 28 S 30 14 E
Howick Group, Australia 72 14 20 S 145 30 E
Howitt, L., Australia 73 27 40 S 138 40 E
Howley, Canada 105 49 12N 57 2W
Howqua →, Australia 75 37 12 S 146 29 E
Howrah = Haora, India 49 22 37N 88 20 E
Howth Hd., Ireland 15 53 21N 6 0W
Höxter, W. Germany 30 51 45N 9 26 E
Hoy I., U.K. 14 58 50N 3 15W
Hoya, W. Germany 30 52 47N 9 10 E
Høyanger, Norway 9 61 13N 6 4 E
Hoyerswerda, E. Germany 30 51 26N 14 14 E
Hoyos, Spain 22 40 9N 6 45W
Hpawlum, Burma 52 27 12N 98 12 E
Hpettintha, Burma 52 24 14N 95 23 E
Hpizow, Burma 52 26 57N 98 24 E
Hradec Králové, Czech. 32 50 15N 15 50 E
Hranice, Czech. 32 49 34N 17 45 E
Hron →, Czech. 33 47 49N 18 45 E
Hrubieszów, Poland 32 50 49N 23 51 E
Hrvatska, Yugoslavia 27 45 20N 16 0 E
Hrvatska □, Yugoslavia 27 45 20N 18 0 E
Hsenwi, Burma 52 23 22N 97 55 E
Hsiamen = Xiamen, China 59 24 25N 118 4 E
Hsian = Xi'an, China 60 34 15N 109 0 E
Hsinhailien = Lianyungang, China 61 34 40N 119 11 E
Hsipaw, Burma 52 22 37N 97 18 E
Hsüchou = Xuzhou, China 61 34 18N 117 10 E
Htawgaw, Burma 52 25 57N 98 23 E
Hu Xian, China 60 34 8N 108 42 E
Hua Hin, Thailand 54 12 34N 99 58 E
Hua Xian, Henan, China 60 35 30N 114 30 E
Hua Xian, Shaanxi, China 60 34 30N 109 48 E
Hua'an, China 59 25 1N 117 32 E
Huacaya, Bolivia 137 20 45 S 63 43W
Huacheng, China 59 24 4N 115 37 E
Huachinera, Mexico 126 30 9N 108 55W
Huacho, Peru 136 11 10 S 77 35W
Huachón, Peru 136 10 35 S 76 0W
Huade, China 60 41 55N 113 59 E
Huadian, China 61 43 0N 126 40 E
Huai He →, China 59 33 0N 118 30 E
Huai Yot, Thailand 55 7 45N 99 37 E
Huai'an, Hebei, China 60 40 30N 114 20 E
Huai'an, Jiangsu, China 61 33 30N 119 10 E
Huaide, China 61 43 30N 124 40 E
Huaidezhen, China 61 43 48N 124 50 E
Huaihua, China 58 27 32N 109 57 E
Huaiji, China 59 23 55N 112 12 E
Huainan, China 59 32 38N 116 58 E
Huaining, China 59 30 24N 116 40 E
Huairen, China 60 39 48N 113 20 E
Huairou, China 60 40 20N 116 35 E
Huaiyang, China 60 33 40N 114 52 E
Huaiyuan, Anhui, China 61 32 55N 117 10 E
Huaiyuan, Guangxi Zhuangzu, China 58 24 31N 108 22 E
Huajianzi, China 61 41 23N 125 20 E
Huajuapan de Leon, Mexico 127 17 50N 97 48W
Hualapai Pk., U.S.A. 123 35 8N 113 58W
Hualian, Taiwan 59 23 59N 121 37 E
Huallaga →, Peru 136 5 0 S 75 30W
Huallanca, Peru 136 8 50 S 77 56W
Huamachuco, Peru 136 7 50 S 78 5W
Huambo, Angola 95 12 42 S 15 54 E
Huambo □, Angola 95 13 0 S 16 0 E

Huan Jiang

Huan Jiang →, China 60 34 28N 109 0 E
Huan Xian, China 60 36 33N 107 7 E
Huancabamba, Peru 136 5 10 S 79 15W
Huancane, Peru 136 15 10 S 69 44W
Huancapi, Peru 136 13 40 S 74 0W
Huancavelica, Peru 136 12 50 S 75 5W
Huancavelica □, Peru 136 13 0 S 75 0W
Huancayo, Peru 136 12 5 S 75 12W
Huanchaca, Bolivia 136 20 15 S 66 40W
Huanchaca, Serranía de, Bolivia 137 14 30 S 60 39W
Huang Hai = Yellow Sea, China 61 35 0N 123 0 E
Huang He →, China 61 37 55N 118 50 E
Huang Xian, China 61 37 38N 120 30 E
Huangchuan, China 59 32 15N 115 10 E
Huanggang, China 59 30 29N 114 52 E
Huangling, China 60 35 34N 109 15 E
Huangliu, China 62 18 20N 108 50 E
Huanglong, China 60 35 30N 109 59 E
Huanglongtan, China 59 32 40N 110 33 E
Huangmei, China 59 30 5N 115 56 E
Huangpi, China 59 30 50N 114 22 E
Huangping, China 58 26 52N 107 54 E
Huangshi, China 59 30 10N 115 3 E
Huangsongdian, China 61 43 45N 127 25 E
Huangyan, China 59 28 38N 121 19 E
Huangyangsi, China 59 26 33N 111 39 E
Huaning, China 58 24 17N 102 56 E
Huanjiang, China 58 24 50N 108 18 E
Huanta, Peru 136 12 55 S 74 20W
Huantai, China 61 36 58N 117 56 E
Huánuco, Peru 136 9 55 S 76 15W
Huánuco □, Peru 136 9 55 S 76 14W
Huanuni, Bolivia 136 18 16 S 66 51W
Huanzo, Cordillera de, Peru 136 14 35 S 73 20W
Huaping, China 58 26 46N 101 25 E
Huaral, Peru 136 11 32 S 77 13W
Huaraz, Peru 136 9 30 S 77 32W
Huari, Peru 136 9 14 S 77 14W
Huarmey, Peru 136 10 5 S 78 5W
Huarochiri, Peru 136 12 9 S 76 15W
Huarocondo, Peru 136 13 26 S 72 14W
Huarong, China 59 29 29N 112 30 E
Huascarán, Peru 136 9 8 S 77 36W
Huascarán, Nevado, Peru 136 9 7 S 77 37W
Huasco, Chile 140 28 30 S 71 15W
Huasco →, Chile 140 28 27 S 71 13W
Huasna, U.S.A. 125 35 6N 120 24W
Huatabampo, Mexico 126 26 50N 109 50W
Huauchinango, Mexico 127 20 11N 98 3W
Huautla de Jiménez, Mexico 127 18 8N 96 51W
Huaxi, China 58 26 25N 106 40 E
Huay Namota, Mexico 126 21 56N 104 30W
Huayin, China 60 34 35N 110 5 E
Huayllay, Peru 136 11 3 S 76 21W
Huayuan, China 58 28 37N 109 29 E
Huazhou, China 59 21 33N 110 33 E
Hubbard, Iowa, U.S.A. 118 42 18N 93 18W
Hubbard, Tex., U.S.A. 121 31 50N 96 50W
Hubbart Pt., Canada 111 59 21N 94 41W
Hubei □, China 59 31 0N 112 0 E
Hubli-Dharwad = Dharwad, India 51 15 22N 75 15 E
Hückelhoven-Ratheim, W. Germany 30 51 6N 6 13 E
Huddersfield, U.K. 12 53 38N 1 49W
Hudi, Sudan 88 17 43N 34 18 E
Hudiksvall, Sweden 10 61 43N 17 10 E
Hudson, Canada 111 50 6N 92 9W
Hudson, Mass., U.S.A. 117 42 23N 71 35W
Hudson, Mich., U.S.A. 119 41 50N 84 20W
Hudson, N.Y., U.S.A. 117 42 15N 73 46W
Hudson, Wis., U.S.A. 120 44 57N 92 45W
Hudson, Wyo., U.S.A. 122 42 54N 108 37W
Hudson →, U.S.A. 117 40 42N 74 2W
Hudson Bay, Sask., Canada 111 52 51N 102 23W
Hudson Bay, Canada 103 60 0N 86 0W
Hudson Falls, U.S.A. 117 43 18N 73 34W
Hudson Mts., Antarctica 143 74 32 S 99 20W
Hudson Str., Canada 103 62 0N 70 0W
Hudson's Hope, Canada 110 56 0N 121 54W
Hudsonville, U.S.A. 119 42 52N 85 52W
Hue, Vietnam 54 16 30N 107 35 E
Huebra →, Spain 22 41 2N 6 48W
Huechucuicui, Pta., Chile 142 41 48 S 74 2W
Huedin, Romania 34 46 52N 23 2 E
Huehuetenango, Guatemala 128 15 20N 91 28W
Huejúcar, Mexico 126 22 21N 103 13W
Huelgoat, France 18 48 22N 3 46W
Huelma, Spain 25 37 39N 3 28W
Huelva, Spain 23 37 18N 6 57W
Huelva □, Spain 23 37 40N 7 0W
Huelva →, Spain 23 37 27N 6 0W
Huentelauquén, Chile 140 31 38 S 71 33W
Huércal Overa, Spain 25 37 23N 1 57W
Huerta, Sa. de la, Argentina 140 31 10 S 67 30W
Huertas, C. de las, Spain 25 38 21N 0 24W
Huerva →, Spain 24 41 39N 0 52W
Huesca, Spain 24 42 8N 0 25W
Huesca □, Spain 24 42 20N 0 1 E
Huéscar, Spain 25 37 44N 2 35W
Huetamo, Mexico 126 18 36N 100 54W
Huete, Spain 24 40 10N 2 43W
Hugh →, Australia 72 25 1 S 134 1 E
Hughenden, Australia 72 20 52 S 144 10 E
Hughes, Australia 79 30 42 S 129 31 E
Hughes, U.S.A. 102 66 0N 154 20W
Hughli →, India 49 21 56N 88 4 E
Hugo, U.S.A. 120 39 12N 103 27W
Hugoton, U.S.A. 121 37 11N 101 22W
Hui Xian, Gansu, China 60 33 50N 106 4 E
Hui Xian, Henan, China 60 35 27N 113 12 E
Hui'an, China 59 25 1N 118 43 E
Hui'anbu, China 60 37 28N 106 38 E
Huiarau Ra., N.Z. 80 38 45 S 176 55 E
Huichang, China 59 25 32N 115 45 E
Huichapán, Mexico 127 20 24N 99 40W
Huidong, China 58 26 34N 102 35 E
Huifa He →, China 61 43 0N 127 50 E
Huíla, Angola 95 15 4 S 13 32 E
Huila □, Colombia 134 2 30N 75 45W
Huila, Nevado del, Colombia 134 3 0N 76 0W
Huilai, China 59 23 0N 116 18 E
Huili, China 58 26 35N 102 17 E
Huimin, China 61 37 27N 117 28 E
Huinan, China 61 42 40N 126 2 E
Huinca Renancó, Argentina 140 34 51 S 64 22W
Huining, China 60 35 38N 105 0 E
Huinong, China 60 39 5N 106 35 E
Huiroa, N.Z. 80 39 15 S 174 30 E
Huise, Belgium 17 50 54N 3 36 E
Huishui, China 58 26 7N 106 38 E
Huisne →, France 18 47 59N 0 11 E
Huissen, Neths. 16 51 57N 5 57 E
Huiting, China 60 34 5N 116 5 E
Huitong, China 58 26 51N 109 45 E
Huixtla, Mexico 127 15 9N 92 28W
Huize, China 58 26 24N 103 15 E
Huizen, Neths. 16 52 18N 5 14 E
Huizhou, China 59 23 0N 114 23 E
Hukou, China 59 29 45N 116 21 E
Hukuntsi, Botswana 96 23 58 S 21 45 E
Hula, Ethiopia 89 6 33N 38 30 E
Hulan, China 62 46 1N 126 37 E
Ḩulayfā', Si. Arabia 46 25 58N 40 45 E
Huld, Mongolia 60 45 5N 105 30 E
Hulda, Israel 44 31 50N 34 51 E
Hulin He →, China 61 45 0N 122 10 E
Hull, Canada 106 45 25N 75 44W
Hull, U.K. 12 53 45N 0 20W
Hull, U.S.A. 118 39 43N 91 13W
Hull →, U.K. 12 53 43N 0 25W
Hulst, Neths. 17 51 17N 4 2 E
Hultsfred, Sweden 11 57 30N 15 52 E
Hulun Nur, China 62 49 0N 117 30 E
Humahuaca, Argentina 140 23 10 S 65 25W
Humaitá, Brazil 137 7 35 S 63 1W
Humaitá, Paraguay 140 27 2 S 58 31W
Humansdorp, S. Africa 96 34 2 S 24 46 E
Humansville, U.S.A. 118 37 48N 93 35W
Humbe, Angola 95 16 40 S 14 55 E
Humber →, U.K. 12 53 40N 0 10W
Humberside □, U.K. 12 53 50N 0 30W
Humbert River, Australia 78 16 30 S 130 45 E
Humble, U.S.A. 121 29 59N 93 18W
Humboldt, Canada 111 52 15N 105 9W
Humboldt, Iowa, U.S.A. 118 42 42N 94 15W
Humboldt, Tenn., U.S.A. 121 35 50N 88 55W
Humboldt →, U.S.A. 122 40 2N 118 31W
Humboldt Gletscher, Greenland 144 79 30N 62 0W
Humboldt Mts., N.Z. 81 44 30 S 168 15 E
Humbolt, Massif du, N. Cal. 68 21 53 S 166 25 E
Hume, Calif., U.S.A. 124 36 48N 118 54W
Hume, Kans., U.S.A. 118 38 5N 94 35W
Hume, L., Australia 75 36 0 S 147 0 E
Humenné, Czech. 32 48 55N 21 50 E
Humeston, U.S.A. 118 40 51N 93 30W
Humpata, Angola 95 15 2 S 13 24 E
Humphreys, Mt., U.S.A. 124 37 17N 118 40W
Humphreys Pk., U.S.A. 123 35 24N 111 38W
Humpolec, Czech. 32 49 31N 15 20 E
Humptulips, U.S.A. 124 47 14N 123 57W
Humula, Australia 76 35 30 S 147 46 E
Hūn, Libya 86 29 2N 16 0 E
Hun Jiang →, China 61 40 50N 125 38 E
Húnaflói, Iceland 8 65 50N 20 50W
Hunan □, China 59 27 30N 112 0 E
Hunchun, China 61 42 52N 130 28 E
Hundested, Denmark 11 55 58N 11 52 E
Hundred Mile House, Canada 110 51 38N 121 18W
Hunedoara, Romania 34 45 40N 22 50 E
Hünfeld, W. Germany 30 50 40N 9 47 E
Hung Yen, Vietnam 54 20 39N 106 4 E
Hunga, Tonga 68 18 41 S 174 7W
Hunga Ha'api, Tonga 68 20 41 S 175 7W
Hungary ■, Europe 33 47 20N 19 20 E
Hungary, Plain of, Europe 6 47 0N 20 0 E
Hungerford, Australia 73 28 58 S 144 24 E
Hŭngnam, N. Korea 61 39 49N 127 45 E
Huni Valley, Ghana 90 5 33N 1 56W
Hunsberge, Namibia 96 27 45 S 17 12 E
Hunsrück, W. Germany 31 49 30N 7 0 E
Hunstanton, U.K. 12 52 57N 0 30 E
Hunsur, India 51 12 16N 76 16 E
Hunte →, W. Germany 30 52 30N 8 19 E
Hunter, Australia 74 36 26 S 144 30 E
Hunter, N.Z. 81 44 36 S 171 2 E
Hunter, N. Dak., U.S.A. 120 47 12N 97 17W
Hunter, N.Y., U.S.A. 117 42 13N 74 13W
Hunter →, Australia 76 32 52 S 151 46 E
Hunter →, N.Z. 81 44 21 S 169 27 E
Hunter, C., Solomon Is. 68 9 48 S 159 50 E
Hunter Hills, The, N.Z. 81 44 26 S 170 46 E
Hunter I., Australia 72 40 30 S 144 45 E
Hunter I., Canada 110 51 55N 128 0W
Hunter Mts., N.Z. 81 45 43 S 167 25 E
Hunter Ra., Australia 76 32 45 S 150 15 E
Hunters Road, Zambia 93 19 9 S 29 49 E
Hunterville, N.Z. 80 39 56 S 175 35 E
Huntingburg, U.S.A. 119 38 20N 86 58W
Huntingdon, Canada 107 45 6N 74 10W
Huntingdon, U.K. 13 52 20N 0 11W
Huntingdon, U.S.A. 116 40 28N 78 1W
Huntington, Ind., U.S.A. 119 40 52N 85 30W
Huntington, N.Y., U.S.A. 117 40 52N 73 25W
Huntington, Oreg., U.S.A. 122 44 22N 117 21W
Huntington, Utah, U.S.A. 122 39 24N 111 1W
Huntington, W. Va., U.S.A. 114 38 20N 82 30W
Huntington Beach, U.S.A. 125 33 40N 118 0W
Huntington Park, U.S.A. 123 33 58N 118 15W
Huntley, U.S.A. 119 42 10N 88 26W
Huntly, N.Z. 80 37 34 S 175 11 E
Huntly, U.K. 14 57 27N 2 48W
Huntsville, Canada 108 45 20N 79 14W
Huntsville, Ala., U.S.A. 115 34 45N 86 35W
Huntsville, Mo., U.S.A. 118 39 26N 92 33W
Huntsville, Tex., U.S.A. 121 30 45N 95 35W
Hunyani →, Zambia 93 15 57 S 30 39 E
Hunyuan, China 60 39 42N 113 42 E
Hunza →, India 49 35 54N 74 20 E
Huo Xian, China 60 36 36N 111 42 E
Huon, G., Papua N. G. 69 7 0 S 147 30 E
Huon Pen., Papua N. G. 69 6 20 S 147 30 E
Huong Hoa, Vietnam 54 16 37N 106 45 E
Huong Khe, Vietnam 54 18 13N 105 41 E
Huonville, Australia 72 43 0 S 147 5 E
Huoqiu, China 59 32 20N 116 12 E
Huoshan, Anhui, China 59 32 28N 118 30 E
Huoshan, Anhui, China 59 31 25N 116 20 E
Huoshao Dao, Taiwan 59 22 40N 121 30 E
Hupeh □ = Hubei □, China 59 31 0N 112 0 E
Hure Qi, China 61 42 45N 121 45 E
Hurezani, Romania 34 44 49N 23 40 E
Hurghada, Egypt 88 27 15N 33 50 E
Hurley, N. Mex., U.S.A. 123 32 45N 108 7W
Hurley, Wis., U.S.A. 120 46 26N 90 10W
Huron, Calif., U.S.A. 124 36 12N 120 6W
Huron, Ohio, U.S.A. 116 41 22N 82 34W
Huron, S. Dak., U.S.A. 120 44 22N 98 12W
Huron, L., N. Amer. 108 45 0N 83 0W
Hurricane, U.S.A. 123 37 10N 113 12W
Hurso, Ethiopia 89 9 35N 41 33 E
Hurum, Norway 10 61 9N 8 46 E
Hurunui →, N.Z. 81 42 54 S 173 18 E
Hurup, Denmark 11 56 46N 8 25 E
Húsavík, Iceland 8 66 3N 17 21W
Huşi, Romania 34 46 41N 28 7 E
Huskisson, Australia 76 35 2 S 150 41 E
Huskvarna, Sweden 11 57 47N 14 15 E
Hussar, Canada 110 51 3N 112 41W
Husum, Sweden 10 63 21N 19 12 E
Husum, W. Germany 30 54 27N 9 3 E
Hutchinson, Kans., U.S.A. 121 38 3N 97 59W
Hutchinson, Minn., U.S.A. 120 44 50N 94 22W
Hutsonville, U.S.A. 119 39 6N 87 40W
Hüttental, W. Germany 30 50 52N 8 1 E
Huttig, U.S.A. 121 33 5N 92 10W
Hutton, Mt., Australia 73 25 51 S 148 20 E
Huwun, Ethiopia 89 4 23N 40 6 E
Ḩuwwārah, Jordan 44 32 9N 35 15 E
Huy, Belgium 17 50 31N 5 15 E
Hvammur, Iceland 8 65 13N 21 49W
Hvar, Yugoslavia 27 43 11N 16 28 E
Hvarski Kanal, Yugoslavia 27 43 15N 16 35 E
Hvítá, Iceland 8 64 40N 21 5W
Hvítá →, Iceland 8 64 0N 20 58W
Hvítárvatn, Iceland 8 64 37N 19 50W
Hwang Ho = Huang He →, China 61 37 55N 118 50 E
Hwange, Zambia 93 18 18 S 26 30 E
Hwange Nat. Park, Zambia 96 19 0 S 26 30 E
Hwekum, Burma 52 26 7N 95 22 E
Hyannis, U.S.A. 120 42 0N 101 45W
Hyargas Nuur, Mongolia 62 49 0N 93 0 E
Hybo, Sweden 10 61 49N 16 15 E
Hyde, N.Z. 81 45 18 S 170 16 E
Hyde Park, Guyana 135 6 30N 58 16W
Hyden, Australia 79 32 24 S 118 53 E
Hyderabad, India 50 17 22N 78 29 E
Hyderabad, Pakistan 48 25 23N 68 24 E
Hyères, France 21 43 8N 6 9 E
Hyères, Is. d', France 21 43 0N 6 20 E
Hyesan, N. Korea 61 41 20N 128 10 E
Hyland →, Canada 110 59 52N 128 12W
Hyland, Mt., Australia 77 30 10 S 152 27 E
Hylltebruk, Sweden 11 56 59N 13 15 E
Hymia, India 49 33 40N 78 2 E
Hyndman Pk., U.S.A. 122 43 50N 114 10W
Hyōgo □, Japan 64 35 15N 135 0 E
Hyrum, U.S.A. 122 41 35N 111 56W
Hysham, U.S.A. 122 46 21N 107 11W
Hythe, U.K. 13 51 4N 1 5 E
Hyūga, Japan 64 32 25N 131 35 E
Hyvinge = Hyvinkää, Finland 9 60 38N 24 50 E
Hyvinkää, Finland 9 60 38N 24 50 E

I

I-n-Échaï, Mali 84 20 10N 2 5W
I-n-Gall, Niger 91 16 51N 7 1 E
Iabès, Erg, Algeria 85 27 30N 2 2W
Iaco →, Brazil 136 9 3 S 68 34W
Iaçu, Brazil 139 12 45 S 40 13W
Iakora, Madag. 97 23 6 S 46 40 E
Iaşi, Romania 34 47 10N 27 40 E
Iauaretê, Colombia 134 0 36N 69 12W
Iba, Phil. 57 15 22N 120 0 E
Ibadan, Nigeria 91 7 22N 3 58 E
Ibagué, Colombia 134 4 20N 75 20W
Ibaiti, Brazil 139 23 50 S 50 10W
Iballja, Albania 34 42 12N 20 0 E
Ibăneşti, Romania 34 46 45N 24 50 E
Ibar →, Yugoslavia 33 43 43N 20 45 E
Ibara, Japan 64 34 36N 133 28 E
Ibaraki, Japan 65 34 49N 135 34 E
Ibaraki □, Japan 65 36 10N 140 10 E
Ibarra, Ecuador 134 0 21N 78 7W
Ibba, Sudan 89 4 49N 29 2 E
Ibba, Bahr el →, Sudan 89 5 30N 28 55 E
Ibbenbüren, W. Germany 30 52 16N 7 41 E
Ibembo, Zaïre 92 2 35N 23 35 E
Ibera, L., Argentina 140 28 30 S 57 9W
Iberia, U.S.A. 118 38 5N 92 18W
Iberian Peninsula, Europe 6 40 0N 5 0W
Iberville, Canada 107 45 19N 73 17W
Iberville, Lac D', Canada 104 55 55N 73 15W
Ibi, Nigeria 91 8 15N 9 44 E
Ibiá, Brazil 139 19 30 S 46 30W
Ibicaraí, Brazil 139 14 51 S 39 36W
Ibicuí, Brazil 139 14 51 S 39 59W
Ibicuy, Argentina 140 33 55 S 59 10W
Ibioapaba, Sa. da, Brazil 138 4 0 S 41 30W
Ibipetuba, Brazil 138 11 0 S 44 32W
Ibitiara, Brazil 139 12 39 S 42 13W
Ibiza, Spain 25 38 54N 1 26 E
Íblei, Monti, Italy 29 37 15N 14 45 E
Ibo, Mozam. 93 12 22 S 40 40 E
Ibonma, Indonesia 57 3 29 S 133 31 E
Ibotirama, Brazil 139 12 13 S 43 12W
Ibshawâi, Egypt 88 29 21N 30 40 E
Ibu, Indonesia 57 1 35N 127 33 E
Ibuki-Sanchi, Japan 65 35 25N 136 18 E
Iburg, W. Germany 30 52 10N 8 3 E
Ibusuki, Japan 64 31 12N 130 40 E
Icá, Peru 136 14 0 S 75 48W
Ica □, Peru 136 14 20 S 75 30W
Iça →, Brazil 136 2 55 S 67 58W
Icabarú, Venezuela 135 4 20N 61 45W
Icabarú →, Venezuela 135 4 45N 62 15W
Içana, Brazil 134 0 21N 67 19W
Içana →, Brazil 134 0 26N 67 19W
Icatu, Brazil 138 2 46 S 44 4W
Iceland ■, Atl. Oc. 8 65 0N 19 0W
Icha, U.S.S.R. 41 55 30N 156 0 E
Ich'ang = Yichang, China 59 30 40N 111 20 E
Ichchapuram, India 50 19 10N 84 40 E
Ichihara, Japan 65 35 28N 140 5 E
Ichikawa, Japan 65 35 44N 139 55 E
Ichilo →, Bolivia 137 15 57 S 64 50W
Ichinomiya, Gifu, Japan 65 35 18N 136 48 E
Ichinomiya, Kumamoto, Japan 64 32 58N 131 5 E
Ichinoseki, Japan 63 38 55N 141 8 E
Ichnya, U.S.S.R. 36 50 52N 32 24 E
Icht, Morocco 84 29 6N 8 54W
Ichtegem, Belgium 17 51 5N 3 1 E
Icó, Brazil 138 6 24 S 38 51W
Icod, Canary Is. 25 28 22N 16 43W
Icoraci, Brazil 138 1 18 S 48 28W
Icy Str., U.S.A. 110 58 20N 135 30W
Ida Grove, U.S.A. 120 42 20N 95 25W
Ida Valley, Australia 79 28 42 S 120 29 E
Idabel, U.S.A. 121 33 53N 94 50W
Idaga Hamus, Ethiopia 89 14 13N 39 48 E
Idah, Nigeria 91 7 5N 6 40 E
Idaho □, U.S.A. 122 44 10N 114 0W
Idaho City, U.S.A. 122 43 50N 115 52W
Idaho Falls, U.S.A. 122 43 30N 112 1W
Idaho Springs, U.S.A. 122 39 49N 105 30W

Inyanga

Idanha-a-Nova, *Portugal* **22** 39 50N 7 15W
Idar-Oberstein, *W. Germany* .... **31** 49 43N 7 19 E
Idd el Ghanam, *Sudan* **87** 11 30N 24 19 E
Iddan, *Somali Rep.* ... **98** 6 10N 48 55 E
Idehan, *Libya* .... **86** 27 10N 11 30 E
Idehan Marzūq, *Libya* **86** 24 50N 13 51 E
Idelès, *Algeria* .... **85** 23 50N 5 53 E
Idfû, *Egypt* .... **88** 25 0N 32 49 E
Ídhi Óros, *Greece* .... **35** 35 15N 24 45 E
Ídhra, *Greece* .... **35** 37 20N 23 28 E
Idi, *Indonesia* .... **56** 5 2N 97 37 E
Idiofa, *Zaïre* .... **94** 4 55 S 19 42 E
Idkerberget, *Sweden* .. **10** 60 22N 15 15 E
Idku, Bahra el, *Egypt* . **88** 31 18N 30 18 E
Idlip, *Syria* .... **46** 35 55N 36 38 E
Idna, *Jordan* .... **44** 31 34N 34 58 E
Idria, *U.S.A.* **124** 36 25N 120 41W
Idrija, *Yugoslavia* .... **27** 46 0N 14 5 E
Idritsa, *U.S.S.R.* ..... **36** 56 25N 28 30 E
Idstein, *W. Germany* .. **31** 50 13N 8 17 E
Idutywa, *S. Africa* .... **97** 32 8 S 28 18 E
Ieper, *Belgium* .... **17** 50 51N 2 53 E
Ierápetra, *Greece* ..... **35** 35 0N 25 44 E
Ierissós, *Greece* ...... **35** 40 22N 23 52 E
Ierzu, *Italy* .... **28** 39 48N 9 32 E
Ieshima-Shotō, *Japan* . **64** 34 40N 134 32 E
Iesi, *Italy* .... **27** 43 32N 13 12 E
Ifach, Punta, *Spain* ... **25** 38 38N 0 5 E
Ifanadiana, *Madag.* ... **97** 21 19 S 47 39 E
Ife, *Nigeria* .... **91** 7 30N 4 31 E
Iférouâne, *Niger* ..... **91** 19 5N 8 24 E
Iffley, *Australia* ...... **72** 18 53 S 141 12 E
Ifni, *Morocco* **84** 29 29N 10 12W
Ifon, *Nigeria* .... **91** 6 58N 5 40 E
Iforas, Adrar des, *Mali* **91** 19 40N 1 40 E
Ifrane, *Morocco* **84** 33 33N 5 7W
Iga, *Japan* .... **65** 34 45N 136 10 E
Iganga, *Uganda* ...... **92** 0 37N 33 28 E
Igara Paraná →, *Colombia* .... **134** 2 9 S 71 47W
Igarapava, *Brazil* ..... **139** 20 3 S 47 47W
Igarapé Açu, *Brazil* .. **138** 1 4 S 47 33W
Igarapé-Mirim, *Brazil* . **138** 1 59 S 48 58W
Igarka, *U.S.S.R.* ..... **41** 67 30N 86 33 E
Igatimi, *Paraguay* .... **141** 24 5 S 55 40W
Igatpuri, *India* .... **50** 19 40N 73 35 E
Igbetti, *Nigeria* .... **91** 8 44N 4 8 E
Igbo-Ora, *Nigeria* ..... **91** 7 29N 3 15 E
Igboho, *Nigeria* ...... **91** 8 53N 3 50 E
Iggesund, *Sweden* .... **10** 61 39N 17 10 E
Ighil Izane, *Algeria* ... **85** 35 44N 0 31 E
Iglésias, *Italy* .... **28** 39 19N 8 27 E
Igli, *Algeria* **85** 30 25N 2 19W
Igloolik, *Canada* **103** 69 20N 81 49W
Igma, Gebel el, *Egypt* **88** 28 55N 34 0 E
Ignace, *Canada* **104** 49 30N 91 40W
Igoshevo, *U.S.S.R.* ... **37** 59 25N 42 35 E
Iguaçu →, *Brazil* .... **141** 25 36 S 54 36W
Iguaçu, Cat. del, *Brazil* **141** 25 41 S 54 26W
Iguaçu Falls = Iguaçu, Cat. del, *Brazil* .... **141** 25 41 S 54 26W
Iguala, *Mexico* **127** 18 20N 99 40W
Igualada, *Spain* ...... **24** 41 37N 1 37 E
Iguana Creek, *Australia* **75** 37 46 S 147 23 E
Iguape, *Brazil* .... **139** 24 43 S 47 33W
Iguassu = Iguaçu →, *Brazil* .... **141** 25 36 S 54 36W
Iguatu, *Brazil* .... **138** 6 20 S 39 18W
Iguéla, *Gabon* .... **94** 2 0 S 9 16 E
Igunga □, *Tanzania* .. **92** 4 20 S 33 45 E
Ihiala, *Nigeria* .... **91** 5 51N 6 55 E
Ihosy, *Madag.* .... **97** 22 24 S 46 8 E
Ihotry, L., *Madag.* ... **97** 21 56 S 43 41 E
Ii, *Finland* .... **8** 65 19N 25 22 E
Iida, *Japan* .... **65** 35 35N 137 50 E
Iijoki →, *Finland* .... **8** 65 20N 25 20 E
Iisalmi, *Finland* ...... **8** 63 32N 27 10 E
Iizuka, *Japan* .... **64** 33 38N 130 42 E
Ijâfene, *Mauritania* ... **84** 20 40N 8 0W
Ijebu-Igbo, *Nigeria* ... **91** 6 56N 4 1 E
Ijebu-Ode, *Nigeria* ... **91** 6 47N 3 58 E
IJmuiden, *Neths.* ..... **16** 52 28N 4 35 E
IJssel →, *Neths.* ..... **16** 52 35N 5 50 E
IJsselmeer, *Neths.* .... **16** 52 45N 5 20 E
IJsselmuiden, *Neths.* .. **16** 52 34N 5 57 E
IJsselstein, *Neths.* .... **16** 52 1N 5 2 E
Ijuí →, *Brazil* .... **141** 27 58 S 55 20W
Ijūin, *Japan* .... **64** 31 37N 130 24 E
IJzendijke, *Neths.* .... **17** 51 19N 3 37 E
IJzer →, *Belgium* .... **17** 51 9N 2 44 E
Ikale, *Nigeria* .... **91** 7 40N 5 37 E
Ikare, *Nigeria* .... **91** 7 32N 5 40 E
Ikaría, *Greece* .... **35** 37 35N 26 10 E
Ikast, *Denmark* ...... **11** 56 8N 9 10 E
Ikawa, *Japan* .... **65** 35 13N 138 15 E
Ikeda, *Japan* .... **64** 34 1N 133 48 E
Ikeja, *Nigeria* .... **91** 6 36N 3 23 E
Ikela, *Zaïre* .... **94** 1 6 S 23 6 E
Ikenge, *Zaïre* .... **94** 0 8 S 18 8 E
Ikerre-Ekiti, *Nigeria* .. **91** 7 25N 5 19 E
Ikhtiman, *Bulgaria* ... **34** 42 27N 23 48 E
Iki, *Japan* .... **64** 33 45N 129 42 E
Iki-Kaikyō, *Japan* .... **64** 33 40N 129 45 E
Ikimba L., *Tanzania* .. **92** 1 30 S 31 20 E
Ikire, *Nigeria* .... **91** 7 23N 4 15 E
Ikitsuki-Shima, *Japan* . **64** 33 23N 129 26 E
Ikom, *Nigeria* .... **91** 6 0N 8 42 E
Ikopa →, *Madag.* .... **97** 16 45 S 46 40 E
Ikot Ekpene, *Nigeria* . **91** 5 12N 7 40 E
'Ikrimah, *Libya* ...... **86** 32 2N 23 41 E
Ikungu, *Tanzania* .... **92** 1 33 S 33 42 E
Ikuno, *Japan* .... **64** 35 10N 134 48 E
Ikurun, *Nigeria* ...... **91** 7 54N 4 40 E
Ila, *Nigeria* .... **91** 8 0N 4 39 E
Ilagan, *Phil.* .... **57** 17 7N 121 53 E
Īlām, *Iran* .... **46** 33 0N 46 0 E
Ilam, *Nepal* .... **49** 26 58N 87 58 E
Ilanskiy, *U.S.S.R.* .... **41** 56 14N 96 3 E
Ilaro, *Nigeria* .... **91** 6 53N 3 3 E
Iława, *Poland* .... **32** 53 36N 19 34 E
Ilayangudi, *India* ..... **51** 9 34N 78 37 E
Ilbilbie, *Australia* ..... **72** 21 45 S 149 20 E
Île-à-la Crosse, *Canada* **111** 55 27N 107 53W
Île-à-la-Crosse, Lac, *Canada* **111** 55 40N 107 45W
Île-Bouchard, L', *France* .... **18** 47 7N 0 26 E
Île-de-France, *France* . **19** 49 0N 2 20 E
Ile-Rousse, L', *France* **21** 42 38N 8 57 E
Ilebo, *Zaïre* .... **95** 4 17 S 20 55 E
Ileje □, *Tanzania* .... **93** 9 30 S 33 25 E
Ilek, *U.S.S.R.* .... **40** 51 32N 53 21 E
Ilek →, *U.S.S.R.* .... **40** 51 30N 53 22 E
Ilero, *Nigeria* .... **91** 8 0N 3 20 E
Îles, L. des, *Canada* .. **106** 46 20N 75 18W
Ilesha, *Kwara, Nigeria* **91** 8 57N 3 28 E
Ilesha, *Oyo, Nigeria* .. **91** 7 37N 4 40 E
Ilford, *Australia* ...... **76** 33 0 S 149 52 E
Ilford, *Canada* **111** 56 4N 95 35W
Ilfracombe, *Australia* . **72** 23 30 S 144 30 E
Ilfracombe, *U.K.* **13** 51 13N 4 8W
Ilha Grande, *Brazil* ... **135** 0 27 S 65 2W
Ilha Grande, B. da, *Brazil* .... **139** 23 9 S 44 30W
Ílhavo, *Portugal* **22** 40 33N 8 43W
Ilhéus, *Brazil* .... **139** 14 49 S 39 2W
Ili →, *U.S.S.R.* ...... **40** 45 53N 77 10 E
Ilich, *U.S.S.R.* .... **40** 40 50N 68 27 E
Iliff, *U.S.A.* **120** 40 50N 103 3W
Iligan, *Phil.* .... **57** 8 12N 124 13 E
Ilíki, L., *Greece* ...... **35** 38 24N 23 15 E
Iliodhrómia, *Greece* .. **35** 39 12N 23 50 E
Ilion, *U.S.A.* **117** 43 0N 75 3W
Ilirska-Bistrica, *Yugoslavia* .... **27** 45 34N 14 14 E
Ilkal, *India* .... **51** 15 57N 76 8 E
Ilkeston, *U.K.* **12** 52 59N 1 19W
Illampu = Ancohuma, Nevada, *Bolivia* .... **136** 16 0 S 68 50W
Illana B., *Phil.* .... **57** 7 35N 123 45 E
Illapel, *Chile* .... **140** 32 0 S 71 10W
'Illār, *Jordan* .... **44** 32 23N 35 7 E
Ille-et-Vilaine □, *France* **18** 48 10N 1 30W
Ille-sur-Têt, *France* ... **20** 42 40N 2 38 E
Iller →, *W. Germany* . **31** 48 23N 9 58 E
Illescas, *Spain* **22** 40 8N 3 51W
Illiers-Combray, *France* **18** 48 18N 1 15 E
Illimani, *Bolivia* ...... **136** 16 30 S 67 50W
Illinois □, *U.S.A.* **113** 40 15N 89 30W
Illinois →, *U.S.A.* ... **113** 38 55N 90 28W
Illiopolis, *U.S.A.* **118** 39 51N 89 15W
Illium = Troy, *Turkey* **46** 39 57N 26 12 E
Illizi, *Algeria* .... **85** 26 31N 8 32 E
Illora, *Spain* **23** 37 17N 3 53W
Ilm →, *E. Germany* .. **30** 51 7N 11 45 E
Ilmen, Oz., *U.S.S.R.* . **36** 58 15N 31 10 E
Ilmenau, *E. Germany* . **30** 50 41N 10 55 E
Ilo, *Peru* .... **136** 17 40 S 71 20W
Ilobu, *Nigeria* .... **91** 7 45N 4 25 E
Iloilo, *Phil.* .... **57** 10 45N 122 33 E
Ilora, *Nigeria* .... **91** 7 45N 3 50 E
Ilorin, *Nigeria* .... **91** 8 30N 4 35 E
Iloulya, *U.S.S.R.* ..... **39** 49 15N 44 2 E
Ilovatka, *U.S.S.R.* .... **37** 50 30N 45 50 E
Ilovlya →, *U.S.S.R.* .. **39** 49 14N 43 54 E
Ilubabor □, *Ethiopia* . **89** 7 25N 35 0 E
Ilukste, *U.S.S.R.* ..... **36** 55 55N 26 20 E
Ilva Mică, *Romania* ... **34** 47 17N 24 40 E
Ilwaco, *U.S.A.* **124** 46 19N 124 3W
Ilwaki, *Indonesia* ..... **57** 7 55 S 126 30 E
Ilyichevsk, *U.S.S.R.* .. **38** 46 10N 30 35 E
Imabari, *Japan* .... **64** 34 4N 133 0 E
Imaichi, *Japan* .... **65** 36 43N 139 46 E
Imaloto →, *Madag.* .. **97** 23 27 S 45 13 E
Imandra, Oz., *U.S.S.R.* **40** 67 30N 33 0 E
Imari, *Japan* .... **64** 33 15N 129 52 E
Imasa, *Sudan* .... **88** 18 0N 36 12 E
Imbâbah, *Egypt* ...... **88** 30 5N 31 12 E
Imbabura □, *Ecuador* **134** 0 30N 78 45W
Imbaimadai, *Guyana* . **135** 5 44N 60 17W
Imbler, *U.S.A.* **122** 45 31N 118 0W
Imdahane, *Morocco* .. **84** 32 8N 7 0W
Imeni Poliny Osipenko, *U.S.S.R.* .... **41** 52 30N 136 29 E
Imeri, Serra, *Brazil* ... **134** 0 50N 65 25W
Imerimandroso, *Madag.* **97** 17 26 S 48 35 E
Imesan, *Mauritania* ... **84** 22 54N 15 30W
Imi, *Ethiopia* .... **89** 6 28N 42 10 E
Imishly, *U.S.S.R.* .... **39** 39 49N 48 4 E
Imitek, *Morocco* **84** 29 43N 8 10W
Imlay, *U.S.A.* **122** 40 45N 118 9W
Imlay City, *U.S.A.* ... **116** 43 0N 83 2W
Immenstadt, *W. Germany* .... **31** 47 34N 10 13 E
Immingham, *U.K.* **12** 53 37N 0 12W
Immokalee, *U.S.A.* ... **115** 26 25N 81 26W
Imo □, *Nigeria* ...... **91** 5 15N 7 20 E
Imola, *Italy* .... **27** 44 20N 11 42 E
Imotski, *Yugoslavia* ... **33** 43 27N 17 12 E
Imperatriz, *Amazonas, Brazil* .... **136** 5 18 S 67 11W
Imperatriz, *Maranhão, Brazil* .... **138** 5 30 S 47 29W
Impéria, *Italy* .... **26** 43 52N 8 0 E
Imperial, *Canada* **111** 51 21N 105 28W
Imperial, *Peru* .... **136** 13 4 S 76 21W
Imperial, *Calif., U.S.A.* **125** 32 52N 115 34W
Imperial, *Nebr., U.S.A.* **120** 40 38N 101 39W
Imperial Beach, *U.S.A.* **125** 32 35N 117 8W
Imperial Dam, *U.S.A.* **125** 32 50N 114 30W
Imperial Res., *U.S.A.* **125** 32 53N 114 28W
Imperial Valley, *U.S.A.* **125** 32 55N 115 30W
Imperieuse Reef, *Australia* .... **78** 17 36 S 118 50 E
Impfondo, *Congo* .... **94** 1 40N 18 0 E
Imphal, *India* .... **52** 24 48N 93 56 E
Imphy, *France* .... **20** 46 55N 3 16 E
İmroz = Gökçeada, *Turkey* .... **35** 40 10N 25 50 E
Imst, *Austria* .... **31** 47 15N 10 44 E
Imuruan B., *Phil.* .... **57** 10 40N 119 10 E
In Belbel, *Algeria* .... **85** 27 55N 1 12 E
In Delimane, *Mali* .... **91** 15 52N 1 31 E
In Rhar, *Algeria* ..... **85** 27 10N 1 59 E
In Salah, *Algeria* ..... **85** 27 10N 2 32 E
In Tallak, *Mali* .... **91** 16 19N 3 15 E
Ina, *Japan* .... **65** 35 50N 138 0 E
Ina-Bonchi, *Japan* .... **65** 35 45N 137 58 E
Inajá, *Brazil* .... **138** 8 54 S 37 49W
Inangahua Junc., *N.Z.* **81** 41 52 S 171 59 E
Inanwatan, *Indonesia* . **57** 2 10 S 132 14 E
Iñapari, *Peru* .... **136** 11 0 S 69 40W
Inarajan, *Guam* ...... **68** 13 16N 144 45 E
Inari, *Finland* .... **8** 68 54N 27 5 E
Inarijärvi, *Finland* .... **8** 69 0N 28 0 E
Inazawa, *Japan* ...... **65** 35 15N 136 47 E
Inca, *Spain* .... **24** 39 43N 2 54 E
Incaguasi, *Chile* ...... **140** 29 12 S 71 5W
İnce-Burnu, *Turkey* ... **38** 42 7N 34 56 E
Inchon, *S. Korea* ..... **61** 37 27N 126 40 E
Incio, *Spain* **22** 42 39N 7 21W
Incomáti →, *Mozam.* . **97** 25 46 S 32 43 E
Incudine, L', *France* .. **21** 41 50N 9 12 E
Inda Silase, *Ethiopia* .. **89** 14 10N 38 15 E
Indalsälven →, *Sweden* **10** 62 36N 17 30 E
Indaw, *Burma* .... **52** 24 15N 96 5 E
Indbir, *Ethiopia* ..... **89** 8 7N 37 52 E
Independence, *Calif., U.S.A.* **124** 36 51N 118 14W
Independence, *Iowa, U.S.A.* **118** 42 27N 91 52W
Independence, *Kans., U.S.A.* **121** 37 10N 95 43W
Independence, *Ky., U.S.A.* **119** 38 57N 84 33W
Independence, *Mo., U.S.A.* **118** 39 3N 94 25W
Independence, *Oreg., U.S.A.* **122** 44 53N 123 12W
Independence Fjord, *Greenland* **144** 82 10N 29 0W
Independence Mts., *U.S.A.* **122** 41 30N 116 2W
Independência, *Brazil* . **138** 5 23 S 40 19W
Independencia, La, *Mexico* **127** 16 31N 91 47W
Independenţa, *Romania* **34** 45 25N 27 42 E
Inderborskiy, *U.S.S.R.* **39** 48 30N 51 42 E
Index, *U.S.A.* **124** 47 50N 121 33W
India ■, *Asia* .... **5** 20 0N 78 0 E
Indian →, *U.S.A.* **115** 27 59N 80 34W
Indian-Antarctic Ridge, *Ind. Oc.* .... **66** 49 0 S 120 0 E
Indian Cabins, *Canada* **110** 59 52N 117 40W
Indian Harbour, *Canada* **105** 54 27N 57 13W
Indian Head, *Canada* . **111** 50 30N 103 41W
Indian Ocean .... **53** 5 0 S 75 0 E
Indian Springs, *U.S.A.* **125** 36 35N 115 40W
Indiana, *U.S.A.* **116** 40 38N 79 9W
Indiana □, *U.S.A.* **119** 40 0N 86 0W
Indianapolis, *U.S.A.* .. **119** 39 42N 86 10W
Indianola, *Iowa, U.S.A.* **118** 41 20N 93 32W
Indianola, *Miss., U.S.A.* **121** 33 27N 90 40W
Indiapora, *Brazil* ..... **139** 19 57 S 50 17W
Indiga, *U.S.S.R.* ..... **40** 67 50N 48 50 E
Indigirka →, *U.S.S.R.* **41** 70 48N 148 54 E
Ind-ija, *Yugoslavia* .... **33** 45 6N 20 7 E
Indio, *U.S.A.* **125** 33 46N 116 15W
Indispensable Strait, *Solomon Is.* .... **68** 9 0 S 160 30 E
Indonesia ■, *Asia* .... **56** 5 0 S 115 0 E
Indore, *India* .... **48** 22 42N 75 53 E
Indramayu, *Indonesia* . **57** 6 20 S 108 19 E
Indravati →, *India* ... **50** 19 20N 80 20 E
Indre □, *France* ...... **19** 46 50N 1 39 E
Indre →, *France* ..... **18** 47 16N 0 11 E
Indre-et-Loire □, *France* .... **18** 47 20N 0 40 E
Indungo, *Angola* ..... **95** 14 48 S 16 17 E
Indus →, *Pakistan* ... **48** 24 20N 67 47 E
Indus, Mouth of the, *Pakistan* .... **48** 24 0N 68 0 E
Industry, *U.S.A.* **118** 40 20N 90 36W
İnebolu, *Turkey* ..... **46** 41 55N 33 40 E
İnegöl, *Turkey* .... **46** 40 5N 29 31 E
Inés, Mt., *Argentina* .. **142** 48 30 S 69 40W
Ineu, *Romania* .... **34** 46 26N 21 51 E
Inezgane, *Morocco* ... **84** 30 25N 9 29W
Infantes, *Spain* **25** 38 43N 3 1W
Infiernillo, Presa del, *Mexico* **126** 18 9N 102 0W
Infiesto, *Spain* **22** 43 21N 5 21W
Inganda, *Zaïre* .... **94** 0 5 S 20 57 E
Ingapirca, *Ecuador* ... **134** 2 38 S 78 56W
Ingebyra, *Australia* ... **75** 36 39 S 148 31 E
Ingelgar, *Australia* .... **76** 31 21 S 147 50 E
Ingelmunster, *Belgium* **17** 50 56N 3 16 E
Ingende, *Zaïre* .... **94** 0 12 S 18 57 E
Ingeniero Jacobacci, *Argentina* .... **142** 41 20 S 69 36W
Ingenio, *Canary Is.* ... **25** 27 55N 15 26W
Ingenio Santa Ana, *Argentina* .... **140** 27 25 S 65 40W
Ingersoll, *Canada* **108** 43 4N 80 55W
Ingham, *Australia* .... **72** 18 43 S 146 10 E
Ingleborough, *U.K.* ... **12** 54 11N 2 23W
Inglewood, *Queens., Australia* .... **77** 28 25 S 151 2 E
Inglewood, *Vic., Australia* .... **74** 36 29 S 143 53 E
Inglewood, *N.Z.* ...... **80** 39 9 S 174 14 E
Inglewood, *U.S.A.* ... **125** 33 58N 118 21W
Ingólfshöfði, *Iceland* .. **8** 63 48N 16 39W
Ingolstadt, *W. Germany* **31** 48 45N 11 26 E
Ingomar, *U.S.A.* **122** 46 35N 107 21W
Ingonish, *Canada* **105** 46 42N 60 18W
Ingore, *Guinea-Biss.* .. **90** 12 24N 15 48W
Ingraj Bazar, *India* ... **49** 24 58N 88 10 E
Ingrid Christensen Coast, *Antarctica* ... **143** 69 30 S 76 0 E
Ingul →, *U.S.S.R.* ... **38** 46 50N 32 15 E
Ingulec, *U.S.S.R.* .... **38** 47 42N 33 14 E
Ingulets →, *U.S.S.R.* . **38** 46 41N 32 48 E
Inguri →, *U.S.S.R.* .. **39** 42 38N 41 35 E
Ingwavuma, *S. Africa* . **97** 27 9 S 31 59 E
Inhaca, I., *Mozam.* ... **97** 26 1 S 32 57 E
Inhafenga, *Mozam.* ... **97** 20 36 S 33 53 E
Inhambane, *Mozam.* .. **97** 23 54 S 35 30 E
Inhambane □, *Mozam.* **97** 22 30 S 34 20 E
Inhambupe, *Brazil* ... **139** 11 47 S 38 21W
Inhaminga, *Mozam.* .. **93** 18 26 S 35 0 E
Inharrime, *Mozam.* ... **97** 24 30 S 35 0 E
Inharrime →, *Mozam.* **97** 24 30 S 35 0 E
Inhuma, *Brazil* .... **138** 6 40 S 41 42W
Inhumas, *Brazil* ...... **139** 16 22 S 49 30W
Iniesta, *Spain* **25** 39 27N 1 45W
Ining = Yining, *China* **62** 43 58N 81 10 E
Inini □, *Fr. Guiana* ... **135** 4 0N 53 0W
Inírida →, *Colombia* . **134** 3 55N 67 52W
Inishbofin, *Ireland* **15** 53 35N 10 12W
Inishmore, *Ireland* **15** 53 8N 9 45W
Inishowen, *Ireland* **15** 55 14N 7 15W
Injune, *Australia* ..... **73** 25 53 S 148 32 E
Inklin, *Canada* **110** 58 56N 133 5W
Inklin →, *Canada* **110** 58 50N 133 10W
Inkom, *U.S.A.* **122** 42 51N 112 15W
Inle L., *Burma* .... **52** 20 30N 96 58 E
Inn →, *Austria* ...... **31** 48 35N 13 28 E
Innamincka, *Australia* . **73** 27 44 S 140 46 E
Inner Hebrides, *U.K.* . **14** 57 0N 6 30W
Inner Mongolia = Nei Monggol Zizhiqu □, *China* .... **60** 42 0N 112 0 E
Inner Sound, *U.K.* ... **14** 57 30N 5 55W
Innerkip, *Canada* **108** 43 13N 80 42W
Innerste →, *W. Germany* .... **30** 52 45N 9 40 E
Innetalling I., *Canada* . **104** 56 0N 79 0W
Innisfail, *Australia* .... **72** 17 33 S 146 5 E
Innisfail, *Canada* **110** 52 0N 113 57W
Innisplain, *Australia* .. **77** 28 11 S 152 54 E
In'no-shima, *Japan* ... **64** 34 19N 133 10 E
Innsbruck, *Austria* .... **31** 47 16N 11 23 E
Inny →, *Ireland* **15** 53 30N 7 50W
Ino, *Japan* .... **64** 33 33N 133 26 E
Inocência, *Brazil* ..... **139** 19 47 S 51 48W
Inongo, *Zaïre* .... **94** 1 55 S 18 30 E
Inoni, *Congo* .... **94** 3 4 S 15 39 E
Inoucdjouac, *Canada* . **103** 58 25N 78 15W
Inowrocław, *Poland* ... **32** 52 50N 18 12 E
Inquisivi, *Bolivia* ..... **136** 16 50 S 67 10W
Inscription, C., *Australia* .... **79** 25 29 S 112 59 E
Insein, *Burma* .... **52** 16 50N 96 5 E
Însurăţei, *Romania* ... **34** 44 50N 27 40 E
Intendente Alvear, *Argentina* .... **140** 35 12 S 63 32W
Interior, *U.S.A.* **120** 43 46N 101 59W
Interlaken, *Switz.* ..... **31** 46 41N 7 50 E
International Falls, *U.S.A.* **120** 48 36N 93 25W
Intiyaco, *Argentina* ... **140** 28 43 S 60 5W
Intutu, *Peru* .... **134** 3 32 S 74 48W
Inubō-Zaki, *Japan* .... **65** 35 42N 140 52 E
Inútil, B., *Chile* ...... **142** 53 30 S 70 15W
Inuvik, *Canada* **102** 68 16N 133 40W
Inuyama, *Japan* ...... **65** 35 23N 136 56 E
Inveralochy, *Australia* . **76** 34 57 S 149 40 E
Inveraray, *U.K.* **14** 56 13N 5 5W
Inverbervie, *U.K.* **14** 56 50N 2 17W
Invercargill, *N.Z.* .... **81** 46 24 S 168 24 E
Inverell, *Australia* .... **77** 29 45 S 151 8 E
Invergordon, *U.K.* **14** 57 41N 4 10W
Inverleigh, *Australia* .. **74** 38 6 S 144 3 E
Inverloch, *Australia* ... **74** 38 38 S 145 45 E
Invermere, *Canada* ... **110** 50 30N 116 2W
Inverness, *Canada* **105** 46 15N 61 19W
Inverness, *U.K.* **14** 57 29N 4 12W
Inverness, *U.S.A.* **115** 28 50N 82 20W
Inverurie, *U.K.* **14** 57 15N 2 21W
Inverway, *Australia* ... **78** 17 50 S 129 38 E
Investigator Group, *Australia* .... **73** 34 45 S 134 20 E
Investigator Str., *Australia* .... **73** 35 30 S 137 0 E
Inya, *U.S.S.R.* .... **40** 50 28N 86 37 E
Inyanga, *Zambia* ..... **93** 18 12 S 32 40 E

Inyangani

Inyangani, *Zambia* **93** 18 5 S 32 50 E
Inyantue, *Zambia* **93** 18 30 S 26 40 E
Inyo Mts., *U.S.A.* **123** 37 0N 118 0W
Inyokern, *U.S.A.* **125** 35 38N 117 48W
Inywa, *Burma* **52** 23 56N 96 17 E
Inza, *U.S.S.R.* **37** 53 55N 46 25 E
Inzhavino, *U.S.S.R.* **37** 52 22N 42 30 E
Ioánnina, *Greece* **35** 39 42N 20 47 E
Iola, *U.S.A.* **121** 38 0N 95 20W
Ioma, *Papua N. G.* **69** 8 19 S 147 52 E
Ion Corvin, *Romania* **34** 44 7N 27 50 E
Iona, *U.K.* **14** 56 20N 6 25W
Ione, *Calif., U.S.A.* **124** 38 20N 120 56W
Ione, *Wash., U.S.A.* **122** 48 44N 117 29W
Ionia, *U.S.A.* **119** 42 59N 85 7W
Ionian Is. = Iónioi Nísoi, *Greece* **35** 38 40N 20 0 E
Ionian Sea, *Europe* **6** 37 30N 17 30 E
Iónioi Nísoi, *Greece* **35** 38 40N 20 0 E
Iori →, *U.S.S.R.* **39** 41 3N 46 17 E
Íos, *Greece* **35** 36 41N 25 20 E
Iowa □, *U.S.A.* **120** 42 18N 93 30W
Iowa →, *U.S.A.* **118** 41 10N 91 1W
Iowa City, *U.S.A.* **118** 41 40N 91 35W
Iowa Falls, *U.S.A.* **118** 42 30N 93 15W
Ipala, *Tanzania* **92** 4 30 S 32 52 E
Ipameri, *Brazil* **139** 17 44 S 48 9W
Iparía, *Peru* **136** 9 17 S 74 29W
Ipáti, *Greece* **35** 38 52N 22 14 E
Ipatinga, *Brazil* **139** 19 32 S 42 30W
Ipatovo, *U.S.S.R.* **39** 45 45N 42 50 E
Ipel →, *Europe* **33** 48 10N 19 35 E
Ipiales, *Colombia* **134** 0 50N 77 37W
Ipiaú, *Brazil* **139** 14 8 S 39 44W
Ipin = Yibin, *China* **58** 28 45N 104 32 E
Ipirá, *Brazil* **139** 12 10 S 39 44W
Ipiranga, *Brazil* **134** 3 13 S 65 57W
Ipixuna, *Brazil* **136** 7 0 S 71 40W
Ipixuna →, *Amazonas, Brazil* **136** 7 11 S 71 51W
Ipixuna →, *Amazonas, Brazil* **137** 5 45 S 63 2W
Ipoh, *Malaysia* **55** 4 35N 101 5 E
Iporá, *Brazil* **139** 11 23 S 50 40W
Ippy, *C.A.R.* **94** 6 5N 21 7 E
Ipsárion Óros, *Greece* **35** 40 40N 24 40 E
Ipswich, *Australia* **77** 27 35 S 152 40 E
Ipswich, *U.K.* **13** 52 4N 1 9 E
Ipswich, *Mass., U.S.A.* **117** 42 40N 70 50W
Ipswich, *S. Dak., U.S.A.* **120** 45 28N 99 1W
Ipu, *Brazil* **138** 4 23 S 40 44W
Ipueiras, *Brazil* **138** 4 33 S 40 43W
Ipupiara, *Brazil* **139** 11 49 S 42 37W
Iput →, *U.S.S.R.* **36** 52 26N 31 2 E
Iquique, *Chile* **136** 20 19 S 70 5W
Iquitos, *Peru* **134** 3 45 S 73 10W
Iracoubo, *Fr. Guiana* **135** 5 30N 53 10W
Iráklia, *Greece* **35** 36 50N 25 28 E
Iráklion, *Greece* **35** 35 20N 25 12 E
Irako-Zaki, *Japan* **65** 34 35N 137 1 E
Irala, *Paraguay* **141** 25 55 S 54 35W
Iramba □, *Tanzania* **92** 4 30 S 34 30 E
Iran ■, *Asia* **47** 33 0N 53 0 E
Iran, Gunung-Gunung, *Malaysia* **56** 2 20N 114 50 E
Iranamadu Tank, *Sri Lanka* **51** 9 23N 80 29 E
Īrānshahr, *Iran* **47** 27 15N 60 40 E
Irapa, *Venezuela* **135** 10 34N 62 35W
Irapuato, *Mexico* **126** 20 40N 101 30W
Iraq ■, *Asia* **46** 33 0N 44 0 E
Irarrar, O. →, *Mali* **85** 20 0N 1 30 E
Irati, *Brazil* **141** 25 25 S 50 38W
Irbid, *Jordan* **44** 32 35N 35 48 E
Irebu, *Zaïre* **94** 0 40 S 17 46 E
Irecê, *Brazil* **138** 11 18 S 41 52W
Iregua →, *Spain* **24** 42 27N 2 24 E
Ireland ■, *Europe* **15** 53 0N 8 0W
Ireland's Eye, *Ireland* **15** 53 25N 6 4W
Irele, *Nigeria* **91** 7 40N 5 40 E
Ireng →, *Brazil* **135** 3 33N 59 51W
Iret, *U.S.S.R.* **41** 60 3N 154 20 E
Irgiz, Bolshaya →, *U.S.S.R.* **37** 52 10N 49 10 E
Irhârharene, *Algeria* **85** 27 37N 7 30 E
Irharrhar, O. →, *Algeria* **85** 28 3N 6 15 E
Irherm, *Morocco* **84** 30 7N 8 18W
Irhil Mgoun, *Morocco* **84** 31 30N 6 28W
Iri, *S. Korea* **61** 35 59N 127 0 E
Irian Jaya □, *Indonesia* **57** 4 0 S 137 0 E
Iriba, *Chad* **87** 15 7N 22 15 E
Irié, *Guinea* **90** 8 15N 9 10W
Iringa, *Tanzania* **92** 7 48 S 35 43 E
Iringa □, *Tanzania* **92** 7 48 S 35 43 E
Irinjalakuda, *India* **51** 10 21N 76 14 E
Iriona, *Honduras* **128** 15 57N 85 11W
Iriri →, *Brazil* **135** 3 52 S 52 37W
Iriri Novo →, *Brazil* **137** 8 46 S 53 22W
Irish Republic ■, *Europe* **15** 53 0N 8 0W
Irish Sea, *Europe* **12** 54 0N 5 0W
Irkineyeva, *U.S.S.R.* **41** 58 30N 96 49 E
Irkutsk, *U.S.S.R.* **41** 52 18N 104 20 E
Irma, *Canada* **111** 52 55N 111 14W
Irō-Zaki, *Japan* **65** 34 36N 138 51 E
Iroise, Mer d', *France* **18** 48 15N 4 45W
Iron Baron, *Australia* **73** 32 58 S 137 11 E
Iron Bridge, *Canada* **108** 46 17N 83 14W
Iron Gate = Portile de Fier, *Europe* **34** 44 42N 22 30 E
Iron Knob, *Australia* **73** 32 46 S 137 8 E
Iron Mountain, *U.S.A.* **114** 45 49N 88 4W
Iron River, *U.S.A.* **120** 46 6N 88 40W
Ironbridge, *U.K.* **13** 52 38N 2 29W
Irondequoit, *U.S.A.* **116** 43 13N 77 35W
Ironstone Kopje, *Botswana* **96** 25 17 S 24 5 E
Ironton, *Mo., U.S.A.* **121** 37 40N 90 40W
Ironton, *Ohio, U.S.A.* **114** 38 35N 82 40W
Ironwood, *U.S.A.* **120** 46 30N 90 10W
Iroquois, *Canada* **109** 44 51N 75 19W
Iroquois →, *U.S.A.* **119** 41 5N 87 49W
Iroquois Falls, *Canada* **106** 48 46N 80 41W
Irpen, *U.S.S.R.* **36** 50 30N 30 15 E
Irrara Cr. →, *Australia* **73** 29 35 S 145 31 E
Irrawaddy □, *Burma* **52** 17 0N 95 0 E
Irrawaddy →, *Burma* **52** 15 50N 95 6 E
Irsina, *Italy* **29** 40 45N 16 15 E
Irtysh →, *U.S.S.R.* **40** 61 4N 68 52 E
Irumu, *Zaïre* **92** 1 32N 29 53 E
Irún, *Spain* **24** 43 20N 1 52W
Irurzun, *Spain* **24** 42 55N 1 50W
Irvine, *Canada* **111** 49 57N 110 16W
Irvine, *U.K.* **14** 55 37N 4 40W
Irvine, *Calif., U.S.A.* **125** 33 41N 117 46W
Irvine, *U.S.A.* **119** 37 42N 83 58W
Irvinestown, *U.K.* **15** 54 28N 7 38W
Irvington, *U.S.A.* **119** 37 53N 86 17W
Irvona, *U.S.A.* **116** 40 46N 78 35W
Irwin →, *Australia* **79** 29 15 S 114 54 E
Irwin, Pt., *Australia* **79** 35 5 S 116 55 E
Irymple, *Australia* **74** 34 14 S 142 8 E
Is-sur-Tille, *France* **19** 47 30N 5 8 E
Isa, *Nigeria* **91** 13 14N 6 24 E
Isaac →, *Australia* **72** 22 55 S 149 20 E
Isabel, *U.S.A.* **120** 45 27N 101 22W
Isabela, I., *Mexico* **126** 21 51N 105 55W
Isabela, La, *Dom. Rep.* **129** 19 58N 71 2W
Isabella, *Phil.* **57** 6 40N 122 10 E
Isabella, Cord., *Nic.* **128** 13 30N 85 25W
Isabella Ra., *Australia* **78** 21 0 S 121 4 E
Ísafjarðardjúp, *Iceland* **8** 66 10N 23 0W
Ísafjörður, *Iceland* **8** 66 5N 23 9W
Isagarh, *India* **48** 24 48N 77 51 E
Isahaya, *Japan* **64** 32 52N 130 2 E
Isaka, *Tanzania* **92** 3 56 S 32 59 E
Isana → = Içana →, *Brazil* **134** 0 26N 67 19W
Isangi, *Zaïre* **94** 0 52N 24 10 E
Isar →, *W. Germany* **31** 48 49N 12 58 E
Isarco →, *Italy* **27** 46 57N 11 18 E
Ísari, *Greece* **35** 37 22N 22 0 E
Isbergues, *France* **19** 50 36N 2 28 E
Iscayachi, *Bolivia* **137** 21 31 S 65 3W
Íschia, *Italy* **28** 40 45N 13 51 E
Iscuandé, *Colombia* **134** 2 28N 77 59W
Isdell →, *Australia* **78** 16 27 S 124 51 E
Ise, *Japan* **65** 34 25N 136 45 E
Ise-Heiya, *Japan* **65** 34 40N 136 30 E
Ise-Wan, *Japan* **65** 34 43N 136 43 E
Isefjord, *Denmark* **11** 55 53N 11 50 E
Iseo, *Italy* **26** 45 40N 10 3 E
Iseo, L. d', *Italy* **26** 45 45N 10 3 E
Iseramagazi, *Tanzania* **92** 4 37 S 32 10 E
Isère □, *France* **21** 45 15N 5 40 E
Isère →, *France* **21** 44 59N 4 51 E
Iserlohn, *W. Germany* **30** 51 22N 7 40 E
Isérnia, *Italy* **29** 41 35N 14 12 E
Isesaki, *Japan* **65** 36 19N 139 12 E
Iseyin, *Nigeria* **91** 8 0N 3 36 E
Isherton, *Guyana* **135** 2 20N 59 25W
Ishikari-Wan, *Japan* **63** 43 25N 141 1 E
Ishikawa □, *Japan* **65** 36 30N 136 30 E
Ishim, *U.S.S.R.* **40** 56 10N 69 30 E
Ishim →, *U.S.S.R.* **40** 57 45N 71 10 E
Ishinomaki, *Japan* **63** 38 32N 141 20 E
Ishioka, *Japan* **65** 36 11N 140 16 E
Ishizuchi-Yama, *Japan* **64** 33 45N 133 6 E
Ishkuman, *Pakistan* **49** 36 30N 73 50 E
Ishpeming, *U.S.A.* **104** 46 30N 87 40W
Ishurdi, *Bangla.* **52** 24 9N 89 3 E
Isigny-sur-Mer, *France* **18** 49 19N 1 6W
Isil Kul, *U.S.S.R.* **40** 54 55N 71 16 E
Isiolo, *Kenya* **92** 0 24N 37 33 E
Isiolo □, *Kenya* **92** 2 30N 37 30 E
Isipingo Beach, *S. Africa* **97** 30 0 S 30 57 E
Isiro, *Zaïre* **92** 2 53N 27 40 E
Isisford, *Australia* **72** 24 15 S 144 21 E
İskenderun, *Turkey* **46** 36 32N 36 10 E
İskilip, *Turkey* **38** 40 50N 34 20 E
Iskŭr →, *Bulgaria* **34** 43 45N 24 25 E
Iskut →, *Canada* **110** 56 45N 131 49W
Isla →, *U.K.* **14** 56 32N 3 20W
Isla Cristina, *Spain* **23** 37 13N 7 17W
Isla Vista, *U.S.A.* **125** 34 27N 119 52W
Islamabad, *Pakistan* **48** 33 40N 73 10 E
Islamkot, *Pakistan* **48** 24 42N 70 13 E
Islampur, *India* **50** 17 2N 74 20 E
Island →, *Canada* **110** 60 25N 121 12W
Island Bend, *Australia* **75** 36 19 S 148 31 E
Island Falls, *Canada* **104** 49 35N 81 20W
Island Falls, *U.S.A.* **105** 46 0N 68 16W
Island L., *Canada* **111** 53 47N 94 25W
Island Lagoon, *Australia* **73** 31 30 S 136 40 E
Island Pt., *Australia* **79** 30 20 S 115 1 E
Island Pond, *U.S.A.* **117** 44 50N 71 50W
Islands, B. of, *Canada* **105** 49 11N 58 15W
Islands, B. of, *N.Z.* **80** 35 15 S 174 6 E
Islay, *U.K.* **14** 55 46N 6 10W
Isle →, *France* **20** 44 55N 0 15W
Isle-Adam, L', *France* **19** 49 6N 2 14 E
Isle aux Morts, *Canada* **105** 47 35N 59 0W
Isle-Jourdain, L', *Gers, France* **20** 43 36N 1 5 E
Isle-Jourdain, L', *Vienne, France* **20** 46 13N 0 31 E
Isle of Wight □, *U.K.* **13** 50 40N 1 20W
Isle Royale, *U.S.A.* **120** 48 0N 88 50W
Isle-sur-le-Doubs, L', *France* **19** 47 26N 6 34 E
Isle Verte, L', *Canada* **107** 48 1N 69 20W
Isleta, *U.S.A.* **123** 34 58N 106 46W
Isleton, *U.S.A.* **124** 38 10N 121 37W
Ismail, *U.S.S.R.* **38** 45 22N 28 46 E
Ismâ'ilîya, *Egypt* **88** 30 37N 32 18 E
Ismaning, *W. Germany* **31** 48 14N 11 41 E
Ismay, *U.S.A.* **120** 46 33N 104 44W
Isna, *Egypt* **88** 25 17N 32 30 E
Isogstalo, *India* **49** 34 15N 78 46 E
Isola del Gran Sasso d'Italia, *Italy* **27** 42 30N 13 40 E
Ísola del Liri, *Italy* **28** 41 39N 13 32 E
Ísola della Scala, *Italy* **26** 45 16N 11 0 E
Ísola di Capo Rizzuto, *Italy* **29** 38 56N 17 5 E
İsparta, *Turkey* **46** 37 47N 30 30 E
Isperikh, *Bulgaria* **34** 43 43N 26 50 E
Íspica, *Italy* **29** 36 47N 14 53 E
İspir, *Turkey* **39** 40 40N 40 50 E
Israel ■, *Asia* **44** 32 0N 34 50 E
Issano, *Guyana* **135** 5 49N 59 26W
Isseka, *Australia* **79** 28 30 S 114 35 E
Issia, *Ivory C.* **90** 6 33N 6 33W
Issoire, *France* **20** 45 32N 3 15 E
Issoudun, *Canada* **107** 46 35N 71 38W
Issoudun, *France* **19** 46 57N 2 0 E
Issyk-Kul, Ozero, *U.S.S.R.* **40** 42 25N 77 15 E
Ist, *Yugoslavia* **27** 44 17N 14 47 E
İstanbul, *Turkey* **46** 41 0N 29 0 E
Istmina, *Colombia* **134** 5 10N 76 39W
Istok, *Yugoslavia* **33** 42 45N 20 24 E
Istokpoga, L., *U.S.A.* **115** 27 22N 81 14W
Istra, *U.S.S.R.* **37** 55 55N 36 50 E
Istra, *Yugoslavia* **27** 45 10N 14 0 E
Istranca Dağları, *Turkey* **35** 41 48N 27 30 E
Istres, *France* **21** 43 31N 4 59 E
Istria = Istra, *Yugoslavia* **27** 45 10N 14 0 E
Itá, *Paraguay* **140** 25 29 S 57 21W
Itabaiana, *Paraíba, Brazil* **138** 7 18 S 35 19W
Itabaiana, *Sergipe, Brazil* **138** 10 41 S 37 37W
Itabaianinha, *Brazil* **138** 11 16 S 37 47W
Itaberaba, *Brazil* **139** 12 32 S 40 18W
Itaberaí, *Brazil* **139** 16 2 S 49 48W
Itabira, *Brazil* **139** 19 37 S 43 13W
Itabirito, *Brazil* **139** 20 15 S 43 48W
Itaboca, *Brazil* **135** 4 50 S 62 40W
Itabuna, *Brazil* **139** 14 48 S 39 16W
Itacajá, *Brazil* **138** 8 19 S 47 46W
Itacaunas →, *Brazil* **138** 5 21 S 49 8W
Itacoatiara, *Brazil* **135** 3 8 S 58 25W
Itacuaí →, *Brazil* **136** 4 20 S 70 12W
Itaguaçu, *Brazil* **139** 19 48 S 40 51W
Itaguari →, *Brazil* **139** 14 11 S 44 40W
Itaguatins, *Brazil* **138** 5 47 S 47 29W
Itaim →, *Brazil* **138** 7 2 S 42 2W
Itainópolis, *Brazil* **138** 7 24 S 41 31W
Itaipu Dam, *Brazil* **141** 25 30 S 54 30W
Itaituba, *Brazil* **135** 4 10 S 55 50W
Itajaí, *Brazil* **141** 27 50 S 48 39W
Itajubá, *Brazil* **139** 22 24 S 45 30W
Itajuípe, *Brazil* **139** 14 41 S 39 22W
Itaka, *Tanzania* **93** 8 50 S 32 49 E
Itako, *Japan* **65** 35 56N 140 33 E
Italy ■, *Europe* **7** 42 0N 13 0 E
Itamaraté, *Brazil* **138** 2 16 S 46 24W
Itambacuri, *Brazil* **139** 18 1 S 41 42W
Itambé, *Brazil* **139** 15 15 S 40 37W
Itampolo, *Madag.* **97** 24 41 S 43 57 E
Itanhauã →, *Brazil* **135** 4 45 S 63 48W
Itanhém, *Brazil* **139** 17 9 S 40 20W
Itano, *Japan* **64** 34 7N 134 28 E
Itapaci, *Brazil* **139** 14 57 S 49 34W
Itapagé, *Brazil* **138** 3 41 S 39 34W
Itaparica, I. de, *Brazil* **139** 12 54 S 38 42W
Itapebi, *Brazil* **139** 15 56 S 39 32W
Itapecuru-Mirim, *Brazil* **138** 3 24 S 44 20W
Itaperuna, *Brazil* **139** 21 10 S 41 54W
Itapetinga, *Brazil* **139** 15 15 S 40 15W
Itapetininga, *Brazil* **141** 23 36 S 48 7W
Itapeva, *Brazil* **141** 23 59 S 48 59W
Itapicuru →, *Bahia, Brazil* **138** 11 47 S 37 32W
Itapicuru →, *Maranhão, Brazil* **138** 2 52 S 44 12W
Itapinima, *Brazil* **137** 5 25 S 60 44W
Itapipoca, *Brazil* **138** 3 30 S 39 35W
Itapiranga, *Brazil* **135** 2 45 S 58 1W
Itapiúna, *Brazil* **138** 4 33 S 38 57W
Itaporanga, *Brazil* **138** 7 18 S 38 0W
Itapuá □, *Paraguay* **141** 26 40 S 55 40W
Itapuranga, *Brazil* **139** 15 40 S 49 59W
Itaquari, *Brazil* **139** 20 20 S 40 25W
Itaquatiara, *Brazil* **136** 2 58 S 58 30W
Itaquí, *Brazil* **140** 29 8 S 56 30W
Itararé, *Brazil* **141** 24 6 S 49 23W
Itarsi, *India* **48** 22 36N 77 51 E
Itarumã, *Brazil* **139** 18 42 S 51 25W
Itatí, *Argentina* **140** 27 16 S 58 15W
Itatira, *Brazil* **138** 4 30 S 39 37W
Itatuba, *Brazil* **137** 5 46 S 63 20W
Itatupa, *Brazil* **135** 0 37 S 51 12W
Itaueira, *Brazil* **138** 7 36 S 43 2W
Itaueira →, *Brazil* **138** 6 41 S 42 55W
Itaúna, *Brazil* **139** 20 4 S 44 34W
Itchen →, *U.K.* **13** 50 57N 1 20W
Ite, *Peru* **136** 17 55 S 70 57W
Ithaca = Itháki, *Greece* **35** 38 25N 20 40 E
Ithaca, *U.S.A.* **117** 42 25N 76 30W
Itháki, *Greece* **35** 38 25N 20 40 E
Itinga, *Brazil* **139** 16 36 S 41 47W
Itiquira, *Brazil* **137** 17 12 S 54 7W
Itiquira →, *Brazil* **137** 17 18 S 56 44W
Itiruçu, *Brazil* **139** 13 31 S 40 9W
Itiúba, *Brazil* **138** 10 43 S 39 51W
Ito, *Japan* **65** 34 58N 139 5 E
Itomamo, L., *Canada* **107** 49 11N 70 28W
Iton →, *France* **18** 49 9N 1 12 E
Itonamas →, *Bolivia* **136** 12 28 S 64 24W
Itsa, *Egypt* **88** 29 15N 30 47 E
Itsukaichi, *Japan* **64** 34 22N 132 22 E
Itsuki, *Japan* **64** 32 24N 130 50 E
Íttiri, *Italy* **28** 40 38N 8 32 E
Itu, *Brazil* **141** 23 17 S 47 15W
Itu, *Nigeria* **91** 5 10N 7 58 E
Ituaçu, *Brazil* **139** 13 50 S 41 18W
Ituango, *Colombia* **134** 7 4N 75 45W
Ituiutaba, *Brazil* **139** 19 0 S 49 25W
Itumbiara, *Brazil* **139** 18 20 S 49 10W
Ituna, *Canada* **111** 51 10N 103 24W
Itunge Port, *Tanzania* **93** 9 40 S 33 55 E
Ituni, *Guyana* **135** 5 28N 58 15W
Itupiranga, *Brazil* **138** 5 9 S 49 20W
Iturama, *Brazil* **139** 19 44 S 50 11W
Iturbe, *Argentina* **140** 23 0 S 65 25W
Ituri →, *Zaïre* **92** 1 40N 27 1 E
Iturup, Ostrov, *U.S.S.R.* **41** 45 0N 148 0 E
Ituverava, *Brazil* **139** 20 20 S 47 47W
Ituxi →, *Brazil* **137** 7 18 S 64 51W
Ituyuro →, *Argentina* **140** 22 40 S 63 50W
Itzehoe, *W. Germany* **30** 53 56N 9 31 E
Iuka, *U.S.A.* **119** 38 37N 88 47W
Ivaí →, *Brazil* **141** 23 18 S 53 42W
Ivalo, *Finland* **8** 68 38N 27 35 E
Ivalojoki →, *Finland* **8** 68 40N 27 40 E
Ivangorod, *U.S.S.R.* **36** 59 37N 28 40 E
Ivanhoe, *N.S.W., Australia* **73** 32 56 S 144 20 E
Ivanhoe, *N. Terr., Australia* **78** 15 41 S 128 41 E
Ivanhoe, *U.S.A.* **124** 36 25N 119 13W
Ivanhoe L., *Canada* **111** 60 25N 106 30W
Ivanić Grad, *Yugoslavia* **27** 45 41N 16 25 E
Ivanjica, *Yugoslavia* **33** 43 35N 20 12 E
Ivanjšcice, *Yugoslavia* **27** 46 12N 16 13 E
Ivankoyskoye Vdkhr., *U.S.S.R.* **37** 56 37N 36 32 E
Ivano-Frankovsk, *U.S.S.R.* **36** 48 40N 24 40 E
Ivanovo, *Byelorussian S.S.R., U.S.S.R.* **36** 52 7N 25 29 E
Ivanovo, *R.S.F.S.R., U.S.S.R.* **37** 57 5N 41 0 E
Ivato, *Madag.* **97** 20 37 S 47 10 E
Ivaylovgrad, *Bulgaria* **35** 41 32N 26 8 E
Ivindo →, *Gabon* **94** 0 9 S 12 9 E
Ivinheima →, *Brazil* **141** 23 14 S 53 42W
Iviza = Ibiza, *Spain* **25** 38 54N 1 26 E
Ivohibe, *Madag.* **97** 22 31 S 46 57 E
Ivolândia, *Brazil* **139** 16 34 S 50 51W
Ivory Coast ■, *Africa* **90** 7 30N 5 0W
Ivösjön, *Sweden* **11** 56 8N 14 25 E
Ivrea, *Italy* **26** 45 30N 7 52 E
Ivugivik, *Canada* **103** 62 24N 77 55W
Iwahig, *Phil.* **56** 8 36N 117 32 E
Iwai-Jima, *Japan* **64** 33 47N 131 58 E
Iwaki, *Japan* **63** 37 3N 140 55 E
Iwakuni, *Japan* **64** 34 15N 132 8 E
Iwami, *Japan* **64** 35 32N 134 15 E
Iwamizawa, *Japan* **63** 43 12N 141 46 E
Iwanai, *Japan* **63** 42 58N 140 30 E
Iwanuma, *Japan* **63** 38 7N 140 51 E
Iwase, *Japan* **65** 36 21N 140 6 E
Iwata, *Japan* **65** 34 42N 137 51 E
Iwate-San, *Japan* **63** 39 51N 141 0 E
Iwo, *Nigeria* **91** 7 39N 4 9 E
Iwungu, *Zaïre* **95** 5 16 S 19 17 E
Ixiamas, *Bolivia* **136** 13 50 S 68 5W
Ixopo, *S. Africa* **97** 30 11 S 30 5 E
Ixtepec, *Mexico* **127** 16 32N 95 10W
Ixtlán del Río, *Mexico* **126** 21 5N 104 21W
Iyo, *Japan* **64** 33 45N 132 45 E
Iyo-mishima, *Japan* **64** 33 58N 133 30 E
Iyo-Nada, *Japan* **64** 33 40N 132 20 E
Izabal, L. de, *Guatemala* **128** 15 30N 89 10W
Izamal, *Mexico* **127** 20 56N 89 1W
Izberbash, *U.S.S.R.* **39** 42 35N 47 52 E
Izegem, *Belgium* **17** 50 55N 3 12 E
Izhevsk = Ustinov, *U.S.S.R.* **40** 56 51N 53 14 E
İzmir, *Turkey* **46** 38 25N 27 8 E
İzmit, *Turkey* **46** 40 45N 29 50 E
Iznajar, *Spain* **23** 37 15N 4 19W
Iznalloz, *Spain* **25** 37 24N 3 30W
Izobil'nyy, *U.S.S.R.* **39** 45 25N 41 44 E
Izola, *Yugoslavia* **27** 45 32N 13 39 E
Izozog, Bañados de, *Bolivia* **137** 18 48 S 62 10W
Izra, *Syria* **44** 32 51N 36 15 E
Iztochni Rodopi, *Bulgaria* **35** 41 45N 25 30 E

Jersey

Izu-Hantō, *Japan* **65** 34 45N 139 0 E
Izuhara, *Japan* **64** 34 12N 129 17 E
Izumi, *Japan* **64** 32 5N 130 22 E
Izumi-sano, *Japan* **65** 34 23N 135 18 E
Izumiotsu, *Japan* **65** 34 30N 135 24 E
Izumo, *Japan* **64** 35 20N 132 46 E
Izyaslav, *U.S.S.R.* **36** 50 5N 26 50 E
Izyum, *U.S.S.R.* **38** 49 12N 37 19 E

J

J.F. Rodrigues, *Brazil* **138** 2 55 S 50 20W
Jaba, *Ethiopia* **89** 6 20N 35 7 E
Jaba', *Jordan* **44** 32 20N 35 13 E
Jabal el Awlîya, *Sudan* **89** 15 10N 32 31 E
Jabalón →, *Spain* **23** 38 53N 4 5W
Jabalpur, *India* **49** 23 9N 79 58 E
Jabālyah, *Egypt* **44** 31 32N 34 27 E
Jablah, *Syria* **46** 35 20N 36 0 E
Jablanac, *Yugoslavia* **27** 44 42N 14 56 E
Jablonec, *Czech.* **32** 50 43N 15 10 E
Jabłonowo, *Poland* **32** 53 23N 19 10 E
Jaboatão, *Brazil* **138** 8 7 S 35 1W
Jaboticabal, *Brazil* **141** 21 15 S 48 17W
Jaburu, *Brazil* **137** 5 30 S 64 0W
Jaca, *Spain* **24** 42 35N 0 33W
Jacaré →, *Brazil* **138** 10 3 S 42 13W
Jacareí, *Brazil* **141** 23 20 S 46 0W
Jacarèzinho, *Brazil* **141** 23 5 S 50 0W
Jaciara, *Brazil* **137** 15 59 S 54 57W
Jacinto, *Brazil* **139** 16 10 S 40 17W
Jaciparaná, *Brazil* **137** 9 15 S 64 23W
Jackadgery, *Australia* **77** 29 35 S 152 34 E
Jackman, *U.S.A.* **105** 45 35N 70 17W
Jacksboro, *U.S.A.* **121** 33 14N 98 15W
Jackson, *Australia* **73** 26 39 S 149 39 E
Jackson, *Ala., U.S.A.* **115** 31 32N 87 53W
Jackson, *Calif., U.S.A.* **124** 38 19N 120 47W
Jackson, *Ky., U.S.A.* **114** 37 35N 83 22W
Jackson, *Mich., U.S.A.* **119** 42 18N 84 25W
Jackson, *Minn., U.S.A.* **120** 43 35N 95 0W
Jackson, *Miss., U.S.A.* **121** 32 20N 90 10W
Jackson, *Mo., U.S.A.* **121** 37 25N 89 42W
Jackson, *Ohio, U.S.A.* **114** 39 0N 82 40W
Jackson, *Tenn., U.S.A.* **115** 35 40N 88 50W
Jackson, *Wyo., U.S.A.* **122** 43 30N 110 49W
Jackson, C., *N.Z.* **81** 40 59 S 174 20 E
Jackson, L., *U.S.A.* **122** 43 55N 110 40W
Jackson Bay, *N.Z.* **81** 43 58 S 168 42 E
Jackson Center, *U.S.A.* **119** 40 27N 84 4W
Jacksons, *N.Z.* **81** 42 46 S 171 32 E
Jacksonville, *Ala., U.S.A.* **115** 33 49N 85 45W
Jacksonville, *Calif., U.S.A.* **124** 37 52N 120 24W
Jacksonville, *Fla., U.S.A.* **115** 30 15N 81 38W
Jacksonville, *Ill., U.S.A.* **118** 39 42N 90 15W
Jacksonville, *N.C., U.S.A.* **115** 34 50N 77 29W
Jacksonville, *Oreg., U.S.A.* **122** 42 19N 122 56W
Jacksonville, *Tex., U.S.A.* **121** 31 58N 95 19W
Jacksonville Beach, *U.S.A.* **115** 30 19N 81 26W
Jacmel, *Haiti* **129** 18 14N 72 32W
Jacob Lake, *U.S.A.* **123** 36 45N 112 12W
Jacobabad, *Pakistan* **48** 28 20N 68 29 E
Jacobina, *Brazil* **138** 11 11 S 40 30W
Jacob's Well, *Jordan* **44** 32 13N 35 13 E
Jacques-Cartier →, *Canada* **107** 46 40N 71 45W
Jacques-Cartier, L., *Canada* **107** 47 35N 71 13W
Jacques-Cartier, Mt., *Canada* **105** 48 57N 66 0W
Jacqueville, *Ivory C.* **90** 5 12N 4 25W
Jacuí →, *Brazil* **141** 30 2 S 51 15W
Jacumba, *U.S.A.* **125** 32 37N 116 11W
Jacundá →, *Brazil* **138** 1 57 S 50 26W
Jade, *W. Germany* **30** 53 22N 8 14 E
Jadebusen, *W. Germany* **30** 53 30N 8 15 E
Jadoigne, *Belgium* **17** 50 43N 4 52 E
Jadotville = Likasi, *Zaïre* **93** 10 55 S 26 48 E
Jadraque, *Spain* **24** 40 55N 2 55W
Jādū, *Libya* **86** 32 0N 12 0 E
Jaén, *Peru* **136** 5 25 S 78 40W
Jaén, *Spain* **23** 37 44N 3 43W
Jaén □, *Spain* **23** 37 50N 3 30W
Jafène, *Africa* **84** 20 35N 5 30W
Jaffa = Tel Aviv-Yafo, *Israel* **44** 32 4N 34 48 E
Jaffa, C., *Australia* **73** 36 58 S 139 40 E
Jaffna, *Sri Lanka* **51** 9 45N 80 2 E
Jagadhri, *India* **48** 30 10N 77 20 E
Jagadishpur, *India* **49** 25 30N 84 21 E
Jagdalpur, *India* **50** 19 3N 82 0 E
Jagersfontein, *S. Africa* **96** 29 44 S 25 27 E
Jagst →, *W. Germany* **31** 49 14N 9 11 E
Jagtial, *India* **50** 18 50N 79 0 E
Jaguaquara, *Brazil* **139** 13 32 S 39 58W
Jaguariaíva, *Brazil* **141** 24 10 S 49 50W
Jaguaribe, *Brazil* **138** 5 53 S 38 37W
Jaguaribe →, *Brazil* **138** 4 25 S 37 45W
Jaguaruana, *Brazil* **138** 4 50 S 37 47W
Jagüey Grande, *Cuba* **128** 22 35N 81 7W
Jagungal, Mt., *Australia* **76** 36 8 S 148 22 E
Jahangirabad, *India* **48** 28 19N 78 4 E
Jahrom, *Iran* **47** 28 30N 53 31 E
Jaicós, *Brazil* **138** 7 21 S 41 8W
Jailolo, *Indonesia* **57** 1 5N 127 30 E
Jailolo, Selat, *Indonesia* **57** 0 5N 129 5 E
Jaintiapur, *Bangla.* **52** 25 8N 92 7 E
Jaipur, *India* **48** 27 0N 75 50 E
Jajce, *Yugoslavia* **33** 44 19N 17 17 E
Jajpur, *India* **50** 20 53N 86 22 E
Jakarta, *Indonesia* **57** 6 9 S 106 49 E
Jakobstad, *Finland* **8** 63 40N 22 43 E
Jakupica, *Yugoslavia* **35** 41 45N 21 22 E
Jal, *U.S.A.* **121** 32 8N 103 8W
Jalalabad, *Afghan.* **47** 34 30N 70 29 E
Jalalabad, *India* **49** 27 41N 79 42 E
Jalalpur Jattan, *Pakistan* **48** 32 38N 74 11 E
Jalama, *U.S.A.* **125** 34 29N 120 29W
Jalapa, *Guatemala* **128** 14 39N 89 59W
Jalapa Enríquez, *Mexico* **127** 19 32N 96 55W
Jalas, Jabal al, *Si. Arabia* **46** 27 30N 36 30 E
Jalaun, *India* **49** 26 8N 79 25 E
Jales, *Brazil* **139** 20 10 S 50 33W
Jaleswar, *Nepal* **49** 26 38N 85 48 E
Jalgaon, *Maharashtra, India* **50** 21 2N 76 31 E
Jalgaon, *Maharashtra, India* **50** 21 0N 75 42 E
Jalhay, *Belgium* **17** 50 33N 5 58 E
Jalingo, *Nigeria* **91** 8 55N 11 25 E
Jalisco □, *Mexico* **126** 20 0N 104 0W
Jalkot, *Pakistan* **49** 35 14N 73 24 E
Jallas →, *Spain* **22** 42 54N 9 8W
Jallumba, *Australia* **74** 36 55 S 141 57 E
Jalna, *India* **50** 19 48N 75 38 E
Jalón →, *Spain* **24** 41 47N 1 4W
Jalpa, *Mexico* **126** 21 38N 102 58W
Jalpaiguri, *India* **52** 26 32N 88 46 E
Jalq, *Iran* **47** 27 35N 62 46 E
Jaluit I., *Pac. Oc.* **66** 6 0N 169 30 E
Jamaari, *Nigeria* **91** 11 44N 9 53 E
Jamaica, *U.S.A.* **118** 41 51N 94 18W
Jamaica ■, *W. Indies* **128** 18 10N 77 30W
Jamalpur, *Bangla.* **52** 24 52N 89 56 E
Jamalpur, *India* **49** 25 18N 86 28 E
Jamalpurganj, *India* **49** 23 2N 88 1 E
Jamanxim →, *Brazil* **137** 4 43 S 56 18W
Jamari, *Brazil* **137** 8 45 S 63 27W
Jamari →, *Brazil* **137** 8 27 S 63 30W
Jambe, *Indonesia* **57** 1 15 S 132 10 E
Jambes, *Belgium* **17** 50 27N 4 52 E
Jambi, *Indonesia* **56** 1 38 S 103 30 E
Jambi □, *Indonesia* **56** 1 30 S 102 30 E
Jambusar, *India* **48** 22 3N 72 51 E
James →, *U.S.A.* **120** 42 52N 97 18W
James B., *Canada* **104** 51 30N 80 0W
James Ranges, *Australia* **78** 24 10 S 132 30 E
James Ross I., *Antarctica* **143** 63 58 S 57 50W
Jamesport, *U.S.A.* **118** 39 58N 93 48W
Jamestown, *Australia* **73** 33 10 S 138 32 E
Jamestown, *S. Africa* **96** 31 6 S 26 45 E
Jamestown, *Ind., U.S.A.* **119** 39 56N 86 38W
Jamestown, *Ky., U.S.A.* **114** 37 0N 85 5W
Jamestown, *Mo., U.S.A.* **118** 38 48N 92 30W
Jamestown, *N. Dak., U.S.A.* **120** 46 54N 98 42W
Jamestown, *N.Y., U.S.A.* **116** 42 5N 79 18W
Jamestown, *Ohio, U.S.A.* **119** 39 39N 83 44W
Jamestown, *Pa., U.S.A.* **116** 41 32N 80 27W
Jamestown, *Tenn., U.S.A.* **115** 36 25N 85 0W
Jamieson, *Australia* **75** 37 19 S 146 9 E
Jamiltepec, *Mexico* **127** 16 17N 97 49W
Jamkhandi, *India* **50** 16 30N 75 15 E
Jammā'īn, *Jordan* **44** 32 8N 35 12 E
Jammalamadugu, *India* **51** 14 51N 78 25 E
Jammerbugt, *Denmark* **11** 57 15N 9 20 E
Jammu, *India* **48** 32 43N 74 54 E
Jammu & Kashmir □, *India* **49** 34 25N 77 0 E
Jamnagar, *India* **48** 22 30N 70 6 E
Jamner, *India* **50** 20 45N 75 52 E
Jamoigne, *Belgium* **17** 49 41N 5 24 E
Jampur, *Pakistan* **48** 29 39N 70 40 E
Jamrud, *Pakistan* **48** 33 59N 71 24 E
Jamshedpur, *India* **49** 22 44N 86 12 E
Jamtara, *India* **49** 23 59N 86 49 E
Jämtlands län □, *Sweden* **10** 62 40N 13 50 E
Jamuna →, *Bangla.* **52** 23 51N 89 45 E
Jamurki, *Bangla.* **52** 24 9N 90 2 E
Jan Kempdorp, *S. Africa* **96** 27 55 S 24 51 E
Jan L., *Canada* **111** 54 56N 102 55W
Jan Mayen Is., *Arctic* **144** 71 0N 9 0W
Janaúba, *Brazil* **139** 15 48 S 43 19W
Janaucu, I., *Brazil* **138** 0 30N 50 10W
Jand, *Pakistan* **48** 33 30N 72 6 E
Janda, L. de la, *Spain* **23** 36 15N 5 45W
Jandaia, *Brazil* **139** 17 6 S 50 7W
Jandaq, *Iran* **47** 34 3N 54 22 E
Jandia, *Canary Is.* **25** 28 6N 14 21W
Jandia, Pta. de, *Canary Is.* **25** 28 3N 14 31W
Jandiatuba →, *Brazil* **134** 3 28 S 68 42W
Jandola, *Pakistan* **48** 32 20N 70 9 E
Jandowae, *Australia* **73** 26 45 S 151 7 E
Jandrain-Jandrenouilles, *Belgium* **17** 50 40N 4 58 E
Jándula →, *Spain* **23** 38 3N 4 6W
Jane Pk., *N.Z.* **81** 45 15 S 168 20 E
Janesville, *U.S.A.* **118** 42 39N 89 1W
Janga, *Ghana* **91** 10 5N 1 0W
Jango, *Brazil* **137** 20 27 S 55 29W
Jangoon, *India* **50** 17 44N 79 5 E
Janhtang Ga, *Burma* **52** 26 32N 96 38 E
Janīn, *Jordan* **44** 32 28N 35 18 E
Janjina, *Yugoslavia* **33** 42 58N 17 25 E
Janos, *Mexico* **126** 30 45N 108 10W
Jánosháza, *Hungary* **33** 47 8N 17 12 E
Janów Podlaski, *Poland* **32** 52 11N 23 11 E
Januária, *Brazil* **139** 15 25 S 44 25W
Janub Dârfûr □, *Sudan* **89** 11 0N 25 0 E
Janub Kordofân □, *Sudan* **89** 12 0N 30 0 E
Janville, *France* **19** 48 10N 1 50 E
Janzé, *France* **18** 47 55N 1 28W
Jaora, *India* **48** 23 40N 75 10 E
Japan ■, *Asia* **63** 36 0N 136 0 E
Japan, Sea of, *Asia* **63** 40 0N 135 0 E
Japan Trench, *Pac. Oc.* **66** 32 0N 142 0 E
Japen = Yapen, *Indonesia* **57** 1 50 S 136 0 E
Japurá →, *Brazil* **134** 3 8 S 64 46W
Jaque, *Panama* **134** 7 27N 78 8W
Jara, La, *U.S.A.* **123** 37 16N 106 0W
Jaraguá, *Brazil* **139** 15 45 S 49 20W
Jaraguari, *Brazil* **137** 20 9 S 54 35W
Jaraicejo, *Spain* **23** 39 40N 5 49W
Jaraiz, *Spain* **22** 40 4N 5 45W
Jarama →, *Spain* **24** 40 2N 3 39W
Jaramillo, *Argentina* **142** 47 10 S 67 7W
Jarandilla, *Spain* **22** 40 8N 5 39W
Jaranwala, *Pakistan* **48** 31 15N 73 26 E
Jarash, *Jordan* **44** 32 17N 35 54 E
Jarauçu →, *Brazil* **135** 1 48 S 52 22W
Jardas al 'Abīd, *Libya* **86** 32 18N 20 59 E
Jardim, *Brazil* **140** 21 28 S 56 2W
Jardín →, *Spain* **25** 38 50N 2 10W
Jardines de la Reina, Is., *Cuba* **128** 20 50N 78 50W
Jargalang, *China* **61** 43 5N 122 55 E
Jargalant = Hovd, *Mongolia* **62** 48 2N 91 37 E
Jargalant, *Mongolia* **62** 48 2N 91 37 E
Jargeau, *France* **19** 47 50N 2 1 E
Jari →, *Brazil* **135** 1 9 S 51 54W
Jarmen, *E. Germany* **30** 53 56N 13 20 E
Jarnac, *France* **20** 45 40N 0 11W
Jarny, *France* **19** 49 9N 5 53 E
Jarocin, *Poland* **32** 51 59N 17 29 E
Jarosław, *Poland* **32** 50 2N 22 42 E
Järpås, *Sweden* **11** 58 23N 12 57 E
Järpen, *Sweden* **10** 63 21N 13 26 E
Jarrahdale, *Australia* **79** 32 24 S 116 5 E
Jarres, Plaine des, *Laos* **54** 19 27N 103 10 E
Jarso, *Ethiopia* **89** 5 15N 37 30 E
Jartai, *China* **60** 39 45N 105 48 E
Jaru, *Brazil* **137** 10 26 S 62 27W
Jaru →, *Brazil* **137** 10 5 S 61 59W
Jarud Qi, *China* **61** 44 28N 120 50 E
Jarvis, *Canada* **108** 42 53N 80 6W
Jarvis I., *Pac. Oc.* **67** 0 15 S 159 55W
Jarwa, *India* **49** 27 38N 82 30 E
Jaša Tomić, *Yugoslavia* **33** 45 26N 20 50 E
Jasin, *Malaysia* **55** 2 20N 102 26 E
Jāsk, *Iran* **47** 25 38N 57 45 E
Jasło, *Poland* **32** 49 45N 21 30 E
Jason, Is., *Falk. Is.* **142** 51 0 S 61 0W
Jasonville, *U.S.A.* **119** 39 10N 87 13W
Jasper, *Alta., Canada* **110** 52 55N 118 5W
Jasper, *Ont., Canada* **109** 44 50N 75 56W
Jasper, *Ont., Canada* **117** 44 52N 75 57W
Jasper, *Ala., U.S.A.* **115** 33 48N 87 16W
Jasper, *Fla., U.S.A.* **115** 30 31N 82 58W
Jasper, *Ind., U.S.A.* **119** 38 24N 86 56W
Jasper, *Minn., U.S.A.* **120** 43 52N 96 22W
Jasper, *Tex., U.S.A.* **121** 30 59N 93 58W
Jasper Nat. Park, *Canada* **110** 52 50N 118 8W
Jassy = Iaşi, *Romania* **34** 47 10N 27 40 E
Jastrebarsko, *Yugoslavia* **27** 45 41N 15 39 E
Jastrzębie Zdrój, *Poland* **32** 49 57N 18 35 E
Jászárokszállás, *Hungary* **33** 47 39N 20 1 E
Jászberény, *Hungary* **33** 47 30N 19 55 E
Jászladány, *Hungary* **33** 47 23N 20 10 E
Jataí, *Brazil* **139** 17 58 S 51 48W
Jatapu →, *Brazil* **135** 2 13 S 58 17W
Jati, *Pakistan* **48** 24 20N 68 19 E
Jatibarang, *Indonesia* **57** 6 28 S 108 18 E
Jatinegara, *Indonesia* **57** 6 13 S 106 52 E
Játiva, *Spain* **25** 39 0N 0 32W
Jatobal, *Brazil* **138** 4 35 S 49 33W
Jatt, *Israel* **44** 32 24N 35 2 E
Jáu, *Angola* **95** 15 12 S 13 31 E
Jaú, *Brazil* **141** 22 10 S 48 30W
Jaú →, *Brazil* **135** 1 54 S 61 26W
Jauaperí →, *Brazil* **135** 1 26 S 61 35W
Jauche, *Belgium* **17** 50 41N 4 57 E
Jauja, *Peru* **136** 11 45 S 75 15W
Jaunjelgava, *U.S.S.R.* **36** 56 35N 25 0 E
Jaunpur, *India* **49** 25 46N 82 44 E
Jauru →, *Brazil* **137** 16 22 S 57 46W
Java = Jawa, *Indonesia* **57** 7 0 S 110 0 E
Java Sea, *Indonesia* **56** 4 35 S 107 15 E
Java Trench, *Ind. Oc.* **66** 10 0 S 110 0 E
Javadi Hills, *India* **51** 12 40N 78 40 E
Jávea, *Spain* **25** 38 48N 0 10 E
Javhlant = Ulyasutay, *Mongolia* **62** 47 56N 97 28 E
Javier, I., *Chile* **142** 47 5 S 74 25W
Javla, *India* **50** 17 18N 75 9 E
Javron, *France* **18** 48 25N 0 25W
Jawa, *Indonesia* **57** 7 0 S 110 0 E
Jawor, *Poland* **32** 51 4N 16 11 E
Jaworzno, *Poland* **32** 50 13N 19 11 E
Jay, *U.S.A.* **121** 36 25N 94 46W
Jaya, Puncak, *Indonesia* **57** 3 57 S 137 17 E
Jayanca, *Peru* **136** 6 24 S 79 50W
Jayanti, *India* **52** 26 45N 89 40 E
Jayapura, *Indonesia* **57** 2 28 S 140 38 E
Jayawijaya, Pegunungan, *Indonesia* **57** 5 0 S 139 0 E
Jayton, *U.S.A.* **121** 33 17N 100 35W
Jazminal, *Mexico* **126** 24 56N 101 25W
Jean, *U.S.A.* **125** 35 47N 115 20W
Jean Marie River, *Canada* **102** 61 32N 120 38W
Jean Rabel, *Haiti* **129** 19 50N 73 5W
Jeanerette, *U.S.A.* **121** 29 52N 91 38W
Jeanette, Ostrov, *U.S.S.R.* **41** 76 43N 158 0 E
Jeannette, *U.S.A.* **116** 40 20N 79 36W
Jebba, *Morocco* **84** 35 11N 4 43W
Jebba, *Nigeria* **91** 9 9N 4 48 E
Jebel, Bahr el →, *Sudan* **89** 9 30N 30 25 E
Jebel Qerri, *Sudan* **89** 16 16N 32 50 E
Jeberos, *Peru* **136** 5 15 S 76 10W
Jedburgh, *U.K.* **14** 55 28N 2 33W
Jedda = Jiddah, *Si. Arabia* **46** 21 29N 39 10 E
Jędrzejów, *Poland* **32** 50 35N 20 15 E
Jedway, *Canada* **110** 52 17N 131 14W
Jeetze →, *W. Germany* **30** 53 9N 11 6 E
Jefferson, *Iowa, U.S.A.* **118** 42 3N 94 25W
Jefferson, *Ohio, U.S.A.* **116** 41 40N 80 46W
Jefferson, *Tex., U.S.A.* **121** 32 45N 94 23W
Jefferson, *Wis., U.S.A.* **119** 43 0N 88 49W
Jefferson, Mt., *Nev., U.S.A.* **122** 38 51N 117 0W
Jefferson, Mt., *Oreg., U.S.A.* **122** 44 45N 121 50W
Jefferson City, *Mo., U.S.A.* **118** 38 34N 92 10W
Jefferson City, *Tenn., U.S.A.* **115** 36 8N 83 30W
Jeffersontown, *U.S.A.* **119** 38 17N 85 44W
Jeffersonville, *Ind., U.S.A.* **119** 38 20N 85 42W
Jeffersonville, *Ohio, U.S.A.* **119** 39 38N 83 34W
Jega, *Nigeria* **91** 12 15N 4 23 E
Jekabpils, *U.S.S.R.* **36** 56 29N 25 57 E
Jelenia Góra, *Poland* **32** 50 50N 15 45 E
Jelgava, *U.S.S.R.* **36** 56 41N 23 49 E
Jelli, *Sudan* **89** 5 25N 31 45 E
Jellicoe, *Canada* **104** 49 40N 87 30W
Jemaja, *Indonesia* **56** 3 5N 105 45 E
Jemaluang, *Malaysia* **55** 2 16N 103 52 E
Jemappes, *Belgium* **17** 50 27N 3 54 E
Jember, *Indonesia* **57** 8 11 S 113 41 E
Jembongan, *Malaysia* **56** 6 45N 117 20 E
Jemeppe, *Belgium* **17** 50 37N 5 30 E
Jemnice, *Czech.* **32** 49 1N 15 34 E
Jena, *E. Germany* **30** 50 56N 11 33 E
Jena, *U.S.A.* **121** 31 41N 92 7W
Jendouba, *Tunisia* **86** 36 29N 8 47 E
Jenkins, *U.S.A.* **114** 37 13N 82 41W
Jenner, *U.S.A.* **124** 38 27N 123 7W
Jennings, *La., U.S.A.* **121** 30 10N 92 45W
Jennings, *Mo., U.S.A.* **118** 38 43N 90 16W
Jennings →, *Canada* **110** 59 38N 132 5W
Jenny, *Sweden* **11** 57 47N 16 35 E
Jenolan Caves, *Australia* **76** 33 49 S 150 1 E
Jeparit, *Australia* **74** 36 8 S 142 1 E
Jequié, *Brazil* **139** 13 51 S 40 5W
Jequitaí →, *Brazil* **139** 17 4 S 44 50W
Jequitinhonha, *Brazil* **139** 16 30 S 41 0W
Jequitinhonha →, *Brazil* **139** 15 51 S 38 53W
Jerada, *Morocco* **85** 34 17N 2 10W
Jerangle, *Australia* **76** 35 52 S 149 23 E
Jerantut, *Malaysia* **55** 3 56N 102 22 E
Jérémie, *Haiti* **129** 18 40N 74 10W
Jeremoabo, *Brazil* **138** 10 4 S 38 21W
Jerez, Punta, *Mexico* **127** 22 58N 97 40W
Jerez de García Salinas, *Mexico* **126** 22 39N 103 0W
Jerez de la Frontera, *Spain* **23** 36 41N 6 7W
Jerez de los Caballeros, *Spain* **23** 38 20N 6 45W
Jericho = El Arīḥā, *Jordan* **44** 31 52N 35 27 E
Jericho, *Australia* **72** 23 38 S 146 6 E
Jerichow, *E. Germany* **30** 52 30N 12 2 E
Jerico Springs, *U.S.A.* **118** 37 37N 94 1W
Jerilderie, *Australia* **74** 35 20 S 145 41 E
Jermyn, *U.S.A.* **117** 41 31N 75 31W
Jerome, *U.S.A.* **123** 34 50N 112 0W
Jerrys Plains, *Australia* **76** 32 29 S 150 53 E
Jersey, *Chan. Is.* **18** 49 13N 2 7W

Kamenka Dneprovskaya

Jungfrau, Switz. 31 46 32N 7 58 E
Junggar Pendi, China 62 44 30N 86 0 E
Junglinster, Lux. 17 49 43N 6 15 E
Jungshahi, Pakistan 48 24 52N 67 44 E
Juniata →, U.S.A. 116 40 30N 77 40W
Junín, Argentina 140 34 33 S 60 57W
Junín, Peru 136 11 12 S 76 0W
Junín □, Peru 136 11 30 S 75 0W
Junín de los Andes, Argentina 142 39 45 S 71 0W
Jūniyah, Lebanon 46 33 59N 35 38 E
Junnar, India 50 19 12N 73 58 E
Junquera, La, Spain 24 42 25N 2 53 E
Junta, La, U.S.A. 121 38 0N 103 30W
Juntura, U.S.A. 122 43 44N 118 4W
Juparanã, L., Brazil 139 19 16 S 40 8W
Jupiter →, Canada 105 49 29N 63 37W
Juquiá, Brazil 139 24 19 S 47 38W
Jur, Nahr el →, Sudan 89 8 45N 29 15 E
Jura, Europe 19 46 35N 6 5 E
Jura, U.K. 14 56 0N 5 50W
Jura □, France 19 46 47N 5 45 E
Jura, Mts., Europe 21 46 40N 6 5 E
Jura, Sd. of, U.K. 14 55 57N 5 45W
Jura Suisse, Switz. 31 47 10N 7 0 E
Jurado, Colombia 134 7 7N 77 46W
Jurilovca, Romania 34 44 46N 28 52 E
Jurong, China 59 31 57N 119 9 E
Juruá →, Brazil 134 2 37 S 65 44W
Juruena, Brazil 137 13 0 S 58 10W
Juruena →, Brazil 137 7 20 S 58 3W
Juruti, Brazil 135 2 9 S 56 4W
Jussey, France 19 47 50N 5 55 E
Justo Daract, Argentina 140 33 52 S 65 12W
Jutaí, Brazil 136 5 11 S 68 54W
Jutaí →, Brazil 134 2 43 S 66 57W
Jüterbog, E. Germany 30 52 0N 13 6 E
Juticalpa, Honduras 128 14 40N 86 12W
Jutland = Jylland, Denmark 11 56 25N 9 30 E
Jutphaas, Neths. 16 52 2N 5 6 E
Juventud, I. de la, Cuba 128 21 40N 82 40W
Juvigny-sous-Andaine, France 18 48 32N 0 30W
Juvisy-sur-Orge, France 19 48 42N 2 22 E
Juwain, Afghan. 47 31 45N 61 30 E
Juye, China 60 35 22N 116 5 E
Juzennecourt, France 19 48 10N 4 58 E
Jylland, Denmark 11 56 25N 9 30 E
Jyväskylä, Finland 8 62 14N 25 50 E

K

K2, Mt., Pakistan 49 35 58N 76 32 E
Kaala-Gomén, N. Cal. 68 20 40 S 164 25 E
Kaap die Goeie Hoop, S. Africa 96 34 24 S 18 30 E
Kaap Plateau, S. Africa 96 28 30 S 24 0 E
Kaapkruis, Namibia 96 21 55 S 13 57 E
Kaapstad = Cape Town, S. Africa 96 33 55 S 18 22 E
Kaatsheuvel, Neths. 17 51 39N 5 2 E
Kabaena, Indonesia 57 5 15 S 122 0 E
Kabala, S. Leone 90 9 38N 11 37W
Kabale, Uganda 92 1 15 S 30 0 E
Kabalo, Zaïre 92 6 0 S 27 0 E
Kabambare, Zaïre 92 4 41 S 27 39 E
Kabango, Zaïre 93 8 35 S 28 30 E
Kabanjahe, Indonesia 56 3 6N 98 30 E
Kabara, Mali 90 16 40N 2 50W
Kabardinka, U.S.S.R. 38 44 40N 37 57 E
Kabardino-Balkar-A.S.S.R. □, U.S.S.R. 39 43 30N 43 30 E
Kabare, Indonesia 57 0 4 S 130 58 E
Kabarega Falls, Uganda 92 2 15N 31 30 E
Kabasalan, Phil. 57 7 47N 122 44 E
Kabba, Nigeria 91 7 50N 6 3 E
Kabe, Japan 64 34 31N 132 31 E
Kabi, Niger 87 13 30N 12 35 E
Kabin Buri, Thailand 54 13 57N 101 43 E
Kabinakagami L., Canada 104 48 54N 84 25W
Kabīr, Zab al →, Iraq 46 36 0N 43 0 E
Kabīr Kūh, Iran 46 33 0N 47 30 E
Kabkabīyah, Sudan 87 13 50N 24 0 E
Kablungu, C., Papua N. G. 69 6 20 S 150 1 E
Kabna, Sudan 88 19 6N 32 40 E
Kabo, C.A.R. 94 7 35N 18 38 E
Kabompo, Zambia 93 13 36 S 24 14 E
Kabondo, Zaïre 93 8 58 S 25 40 E
Kabongo, Zaïre 92 7 22 S 25 33 E
Kabou, Togo 91 9 28N 0 55 E
Kaboudia, Rass, Tunisia 86 35 13N 11 10 E
Kabra, Australia 72 23 25 S 150 25 E
Kabūd Gonbad, Iran 47 37 5N 59 45 E
Kābul, Afghan. 47 34 28N 69 11 E
Kābul □, Afghan. 47 34 30N 69 0 E
Kabul →, Pakistan 48 33 55N 72 14 E
Kabunga, Zaïre 92 1 38 S 28 3 E
Kaburuang, Indonesia 57 3 50N 126 30 E
Kabushiya, Sudan 89 16 54N 33 41 E
Kabwe, Zambia 93 14 30 S 28 29 E
Kabwum, Papua N. G. 69 6 11 S 147 15 E
Kačanik, Yugoslavia 33 42 13N 21 12 E
Kachanovo, U.S.S.R. 36 57 25N 27 38 E
Kachchh, Gulf of, India 48 22 50N 69 15 E
Kachchh, Rann of, India 48 24 0N 70 0 E
Kachebera, Zambia 93 13 50 S 32 50 E
Kachin □, Burma 52 26 0N 97 30 E
Kachira, L., Uganda 92 0 40 S 31 7 E
Kachiry, U.S.S.R. 40 53 10N 75 50 E
Kachisi, Ethiopia 89 9 40N 37 50 E
Kachot, Cambodia 55 11 30N 103 3 E
Kackar, Turkey 46 40 45N 41 10 E
Kadaingti, Burma 52 17 37N 97 32 E
Kadaiyanallur, India 51 9 3N 77 22 E
Kadan Kyun, Burma 56 12 30N 98 20 E
Kadanai →, Afghan. 48 31 22N 65 45 E
Kadarkút, Hungary 33 46 13N 17 39 E
Kade, Ghana 91 6 7N 0 56W
Kadi, India 48 23 18N 72 23 E
Kadina, Australia 73 34 0 S 137 43 E
Kadiri, India 51 14 12N 78 13 E
Kadirli, Turkey 46 37 23N 36 5 E
Kadiyevka = Stakhanov, U.S.S.R. 39 48 35N 38 40 E
Kadoka, U.S.A. 120 43 50N 101 31W
Kadom, U.S.S.R. 37 54 37N 42 30 E
Kadoma, Zambia 93 18 20 S 29 52 E
Kâdugli, Sudan 89 11 0N 29 45 E
Kaduna, Nigeria 91 10 30N 7 21 E
Kaduna □, Nigeria 91 11 0N 7 30 E
Kadungle, Australia 76 32 45 S 147 36 E
Kaédi, Mauritania 90 16 9N 13 28W
Kaelé, Cameroon 91 10 7N 14 27 E
Kaeng Khoï, Thailand 54 14 35N 101 0 E
Kaeo, N.Z. 80 35 6 S 173 49 E
Kaesŏng, N. Korea 61 37 58N 126 35 E
Kāf, Si. Arabia 46 31 25N 37 29 E
Kafakumba, Zaïre 95 9 38 S 23 46 E
Kafanchan, Nigeria 91 9 40N 8 20 E
Kafareti, Nigeria 91 10 25N 11 12 E
Kaffrine, Senegal 90 14 8N 15 36W
Kafia Kingi, Sudan 94 9 20N 24 25 E
Kafinda, Zambia 93 12 32 S 30 20 E
Kafirévs, Ákra, Greece 35 38 9N 24 38 E
Kafr 'Ayn, Jordan 44 32 3N 35 7 E
Kafr el Dauwâr, Egypt 88 31 8N 30 8 E
Kafr el Sheikh, Egypt 88 31 15N 30 50 E
Kafr Kammā, Israel 44 32 44N 35 26 E
Kafr Kannā, Israel 44 32 45N 35 20 E
Kafr Mālik, Jordan 44 32 0N 35 18 E
Kafr Mandā, Israel 44 32 49N 35 15 E
Kafr Quaddūm, Jordan 44 32 14N 35 7 E
Kafr Rā'ī, Jordan 44 32 23N 35 9 E
Kafr Şīr, Lebanon 44 33 19N 35 23 E
Kafr Yāsīf, Israel 44 32 58N 35 10 E
Kafue, Zambia 93 15 46 S 28 9 E
Kafue Flats, Zambia 93 15 40 S 27 25 E
Kafulwe, Zambia 93 9 0 S 29 1 E
Kaga, Afghan. 48 34 14N 70 10 E
Kaga, Japan 65 36 16N 136 15 E
Kaga Bandoro, C.A.R. 94 7 0N 19 10 E
Kagan, U.S.S.R. 40 39 43N 64 33 E
Kagawa □, Japan 64 34 15N 134 0 E
Kagawong L., Canada 108 45 54N 82 15W
Kagera □, Tanzania 92 2 0 S 31 30 E
Kagera →, Uganda 92 0 57 S 31 47 E
Kağizman, Turkey 46 40 5N 43 10 E
Kagoshima, Japan 64 31 35N 130 33 E
Kagoshima □, Japan 64 31 30N 130 30 E
Kagoshima-Wan, Japan 64 31 25N 130 40 E
Kagul, U.S.S.R. 38 45 50N 28 15 E
Kahama, Tanzania 92 4 8 S 32 30 E
Kahama □, Tanzania 92 3 50 S 32 0 E
Kahang, Malaysia 55 2 12N 103 32 E
Kahayan →, Indonesia 56 3 40 S 114 0 E
Kahe, Tanzania 92 3 30 S 37 25 E
Kahemba, Zaïre 95 7 18 S 18 55 E
Kaherekoau Mts., N.Z. 81 45 45 S 167 15 E
Kahil, Djebel bou, Algeria 85 34 26N 4 0 E
Kahniah →, Canada 110 58 15N 120 55W
Kahnūj, Iran 47 27 55N 57 40 E
Kahoka, U.S.A. 118 40 25N 91 42W
Kahoolawe, U.S.A. 112 20 33N 156 35W
Kahramanmaras, Turkey 46 37 37N 36 53 E
Kahurangi, Pt., N.Z. 81 40 50 S 172 10 E
Kahuta, Pakistan 48 33 35N 73 24 E
Kai, Kepulauan, Indonesia 57 5 55 S 132 45 E
Kai Besar, Indonesia 57 5 35 S 133 0 E
Kai-Ketil, Indonesia 57 5 45 S 132 40 E
Kai Xian, China 58 31 11N 108 21 E
Kaiama, Nigeria 91 9 36N 4 1 E
Kaiapit, Papua N. G. 69 6 18 S 146 18 E
Kaiapoi, N.Z. 81 42 24 S 172 40 E
Kaibara, Japan 65 35 8N 135 5 E
Kaieteur Falls, Guyana 135 5 1N 59 10W
Kaifeng, China 60 34 48N 114 21 E
Kaihua, China 59 29 12N 118 20 E
Kaiingveld, S. Africa 96 30 0 S 22 0 E
Kaikohe, N.Z. 80 35 25 S 173 49 E
Kaikoura, N.Z. 81 42 25 S 173 43 E
Kaikoura Pen., N.Z. 81 42 25 S 173 43 E
Kaikoura Ra., N.Z. 81 41 59 S 173 41 E
Kailahun, S. Leone 90 8 18N 10 39W
Kailashahar, Bangla. 52 24 19N 92 0 E
Kaili, China 58 26 33N 107 59 E
Kailu, China 61 43 38N 121 18 E
Kailua, U.S.A. 112 19 39N 156 0W
Kaimana, Indonesia 57 3 39 S 133 45 E
Kaimanawa Mts., N.Z. 80 39 15 S 175 56 E
Kaimata, N.Z. 81 42 34 S 171 28 E
Kaimganj, India 49 27 33N 79 24 E
Kaimon-Dake, Japan 64 31 11N 130 32 E
Kaimur Hill, India 49 24 30N 82 0 E
Kainan, Japan 64 34 9N 135 12 E
Kainantu, Papua N. G. 69 6 18 S 145 52 E
Kaingaroa Forest, N.Z. 80 38 24 S 176 30 E
Kainji Res., Nigeria 91 10 1N 4 40 E
Kaipara Harbour, N.Z. 80 36 25 S 174 14 E
Kaiping, China 59 22 23N 112 42 E
Kaipokok B., Canada 105 54 54N 59 47W
Kairana, India 48 29 24N 77 15 E
Kaironi, Indonesia 57 0 47 S 133 40 E
Kairouan, Tunisia 86 35 45N 10 5 E
Kairuku, Papua N. G. 69 8 51 S 146 35 E
Kaiserslautern, W. Germany 31 49 30N 7 43 E
Kaitaia, N.Z. 80 35 8 S 173 17 E
Kaitangata, N.Z. 81 46 17 S 169 51 E
Kaithal, India 48 29 48N 76 26 E
Kaitu →, Pakistan 48 33 10N 70 30 E
Kaiwi Channel, U.S.A. 112 21 13N 157 30W
Kaiyang, China 58 27 4N 106 59 E
Kaiyuan, Liaoning, China 61 42 28N 124 1 E
Kaiyuan, Yunnan, China 58 23 40N 103 12 E
Kajaani, Finland 8 64 17N 27 46 E
Kajabbi, Australia 72 20 0 S 140 1 E
Kajana = Kajaani, Finland 8 64 17N 27 46 E
Kajang, Malaysia 55 2 59N 101 48 E
Kajiado, Kenya 92 1 53 S 36 48 E
Kajiado □, Kenya 92 2 0 S 36 30 E
Kajiki, Japan 64 31 44N 130 40 E
Kajo Kaji, Sudan 89 3 58N 31 40 E
Kaka, Sudan 89 10 38N 32 10 E
Kakabeka Falls, Canada 104 48 24N 89 37W
Kakamas, S. Africa 96 28 45 S 20 33 E
Kakamega, Kenya 92 0 20N 34 46 E
Kakamega □, Kenya 92 0 20N 34 46 E
Kakamigahara, Japan 65 35 28N 136 48 E
Kakanj, Yugoslavia 33 44 9N 18 7 E
Kakanui Mts., N.Z. 81 45 10 S 170 30 E
Kake, Japan 64 34 36N 132 19 E
Kakegawa, Japan 65 34 45N 138 1 E
Kakhib, U.S.S.R. 39 42 28N 46 34 E
Kakhovka, U.S.S.R. 38 46 40N 33 15 E
Kakhovskoye Vdkhr., U.S.S.R. 38 47 5N 34 16 E
Kakinada, India 50 16 57N 82 11 E
Kakisa →, Canada 110 61 3N 118 10W
Kakisa L., Canada 110 60 56N 117 43W
Kakogawa, Japan 64 34 46N 134 51 E
Kakwa →, Canada 110 54 37N 118 28W
Kala, Nigeria 91 12 2N 14 40 E
Kala Oya →, Sri Lanka 51 8 20N 79 45 E
Kalaa-Kebira, Tunisia 86 35 59N 10 32 E
Kalabagh, Pakistan 48 33 0N 71 28 E
Kalabahi, Indonesia 57 8 13 S 124 31 E
Kalabáka, Greece 35 39 42N 21 39 E
Kalabo, Zambia 95 14 58 S 22 40 E
Kalach, U.S.S.R. 37 50 22N 41 0 E
Kalach na Donu, U.S.S.R. 39 48 43N 43 32 E
Kaladar, Canada 109 44 37N 77 5W
Kalahari, Africa 96 24 0 S 21 30 E
Kalahari Gemsbok Nat. Park, S. Africa 96 25 30 S 20 30 E
Kalakamati, Botswana 97 20 40 S 27 25 E
Kalakan, U.S.S.R. 41 55 15N 116 45 E
K'alak'unlun Shank'ou, Pakistan 49 35 33N 77 46 E
Kalam, Pakistan 49 35 34N 72 30 E
Kalama, U.S.A. 124 46 0N 122 55W
Kalama, Zaïre 92 2 52 S 28 35 E
Kalamariá, Greece 35 40 33N 22 55 E
Kalamata, Greece 35 37 3N 22 10 E
Kalamazoo, U.S.A. 119 42 20N 85 35W
Kalamazoo →, U.S.A. 119 42 40N 86 12W
Kalamb, India 50 18 3N 74 48 E
Kalambo Falls, Tanzania 93 8 37 S 31 35 E
Kálamos, Greece 35 38 37N 20 55 E
Kalan, Turkey 46 39 7N 39 32 E
Kalannie, Australia 79 30 22 S 117 5 E
Kalao, Indonesia 57 7 21 S 121 0 E
Kalaotoa, Indonesia 57 7 20 S 121 50 E
Kälarne, Sweden 10 62 59N 16 8 E
Kalárovo, Czech. 33 47 54N 18 0 E
Kalasin, Thailand 54 16 26N 103 30 E
Kalat, Pakistan 47 29 8N 66 31 E
Kálathos, Greece 35 36 9N 28 8 E
Kalaus →, U.S.S.R. 39 45 40N 44 7 E
Kalávrita, Greece 35 38 3N 22 8 E
Kalaw, Burma 52 20 38N 96 34 E
Kalbarri, Australia 79 27 40 S 114 10 E
Kalecik, Turkey 38 40 4N 33 26 E
Kalehe, Zaïre 92 2 6 S 28 50 E
Kalema, Tanzania 92 1 12 S 31 55 E
Kalemie, Zaïre 92 5 55 S 29 9 E
Kalemyo, Burma 52 23 11N 94 4 E
Kalety, Poland 32 50 35N 18 52 E
Kalewa, Burma 52 23 10N 94 15 E
Kálfafellsstaður, Iceland 8 64 11N 15 53W
Kalgan = Zhangjiakou, China 60 40 48N 114 55 E
Kalgoorlie-Boulder, Australia 79 30 40 S 121 22 E
Kaliakra, Nos, Bulgaria 34 43 21N 28 30 E
Kalianda, Indonesia 56 5 50 S 105 45 E
Kalibo, Phil. 57 11 43N 122 22 E
Kaliganj Town, Bangla. 49 22 25N 89 8 E
Kalima, Zaïre 92 2 33 S 26 32 E
Kalimantan, Indonesia 56 0 0 114 0 E
Kalimantan Barat □, Indonesia 56 0 0 110 30 E
Kalimantan Selatan □, Indonesia 56 2 30 S 115 30 E
Kalimantan Tengah □, Indonesia 56 2 0 S 113 30 E
Kalimantan Timur □, Indonesia 56 1 30N 116 30 E
Kálimnos, Greece 35 37 0N 27 0 E
Kalimpong, India 49 27 4N 88 35 E
Kalinadi →, India 51 14 50N 74 7 E
Kalinin, U.S.S.R. 37 56 55N 35 55 E
Kaliningrad, R.S.F.S.R., U.S.S.R. 36 54 42N 20 32 E
Kaliningrad, R.S.F.S.R., U.S.S.R. 37 55 58N 37 54 E
Kalinkovichi, U.S.S.R. 36 52 12N 29 20 E
Kalinovik, Yugoslavia 33 43 31N 18 29 E
Kalipetrovo, Bulgaria 34 44 5N 27 14 E
Kaliro, Uganda 92 0 56N 33 30 E
Kalispell, U.S.A. 122 48 10N 114 22W
Kalisz, Poland 32 51 45N 18 8 E
Kaliua, Tanzania 92 5 5 S 31 48 E
Kaliveli Tank, India 51 12 5N 79 50 E
Kalix →, Sweden 8 65 50N 23 11 E
Kalka, India 48 30 46N 76 57 E
Kalkaska, U.S.A. 104 44 44N 85 11W
Kalkfeld, Namibia 96 20 57 S 16 14 E
Kalkfontein, Botswana 96 22 4 S 20 57 E
Kalkrand, Namibia 96 24 1 S 17 35 E
Kallakkurichchi, India 51 11 44N 79 1 E
Kållandsö, Sweden 11 58 40N 13 5 E
Kallia, Jordan 44 31 46N 35 30 E
Kallidaikurichi, India 51 8 38N 77 31 E
Kallinge, Sweden 11 56 15N 15 18 E
Kallithéa, Greece 35 37 55N 23 41 E
Kallonís, Kólpos, Greece 35 39 10N 26 10 E
Kallsjön, Sweden 8 63 38N 13 0 E
Kalmalo, Nigeria 91 13 40N 5 20 E
Kalmar, Sweden 11 56 40N 16 20 E
Kalmar län □, Sweden 11 57 25N 16 0 E
Kalmar sund, Sweden 11 56 40N 16 25 E
Kalmthout, Belgium 17 51 23N 4 29 E
Kalmyk A.S.S.R. □, U.S.S.R. 39 46 5N 46 1 E
Kalmykovo, U.S.S.R. 39 49 0N 51 47 E
Kalna, India 49 23 13N 88 25 E
Kalo, Papua N. G. 69 10 1 S 147 48 E
Kalocsa, Hungary 33 46 32N 19 0 E
Kaloko, Zaïre 92 6 47 S 25 48 E
Kalol, Gujarat, India 48 22 37N 73 31 E
Kalol, Gujarat, India 48 23 15N 72 33 E
Kalolímnos, Greece 35 37 4N 27 8 E
Kalomo, Zambia 93 17 0 S 26 30 E
Kalona, U.S.A. 118 41 29N 91 43W
Kalpi, India 49 26 8N 79 47 E
Kalrayan Hills, India 51 11 45N 78 40 E
Kalsubai, India 50 19 35N 73 45 E
Kaltungo, Nigeria 91 9 48N 11 19 E
Kalu, Pakistan 48 25 5N 67 39 E
Kaluga, U.S.S.R. 37 54 35N 36 10 E
Kalulushi, Zambia 93 12 50 S 28 3 E
Kalundborg, Denmark 11 55 41N 11 5 E
Kalush, U.S.S.R. 36 49 3N 24 23 E
Kałuszyn, Poland 32 52 13N 21 52 E
Kalutara, Sri Lanka 51 6 35N 80 0 E
Kalyan, India 50 20 30N 74 3 E
Kalyazin, U.S.S.R. 37 57 15N 37 55 E
Kama, Burma 52 19 1N 95 4 E
Kama, Zaïre 92 3 30 S 27 5 E
Kama →, U.S.S.R. 40 55 45N 52 0 E
Kamachumu, Tanzania 92 1 37 S 31 37 E
Kamae, Japan 64 32 48N 131 56 E
Kamaing, Burma 52 25 26N 96 35 E
Kamaishi, Japan 63 39 20N 142 0 E
Kamakura, Japan 65 35 19N 139 33 E
Kamalia, Pakistan 48 30 44N 72 42 E
Kamamaung, Burma 52 17 21N 97 40 E
Kamandorskiye Ostrava, U.S.S.R. 41 55 0N 167 0 E
Kamapanda, Zambia 93 12 5 S 24 0 E
Kamaran, Yemen 45 15 21N 42 35 E
Kamativi, Zambia 93 18 15 S 27 27 E
Kamba, Nigeria 91 11 50N 3 45 E
Kambalda, Australia 79 31 10 S 121 37 E
Kambam, India 51 9 45N 77 16 E
Kambar, Pakistan 48 27 37N 68 1 E
Kambia, S. Leone 90 9 3N 12 53W
Kambolé, Zambia 93 8 47 S 30 48 E
Kambove, Zaïre 93 10 51 S 26 33 E
Kambuie, Zaïre 95 6 59 S 22 19 E
Kamchatka, P-ov., U.S.S.R. 41 57 0N 160 0 E
Kamen, U.S.S.R. 40 53 50N 81 30 E
Kamen Kashirskiy, U.S.S.R. 36 51 39N 24 56 E
Kamenets-Podolskiy, U.S.S.R. 38 48 45N 26 10 E
Kamenjak, Rt., Yugoslavia 27 44 47N 13 55 E
Kamenka, R.S.F.S.R., U.S.S.R. 37 53 10N 44 5 E
Kamenka, R.S.F.S.R., U.S.S.R. 37 50 47N 39 20 E
Kamenka, Ukraine S.S.R., U.S.S.R. 38 49 3N 32 6 E
Kamenka Bugskaya, U.S.S.R. 36 50 8N 24 16 E
Kamenka Dneprovskaya, U.S.S.R. 38 47 29N 34 14 E

Kamenolomini

Kamenolomini, U.S.S.R. 39 47 40N 40 14 E
Kamensk-Shakhtinskiy, U.S.S.R. 39 48 23N 40 20 E
Kamensk Uralskiy, U.S.S.R. 40 56 25N 62 2 E
Kamenskiy, R.S.F.S.R., U.S.S.R. 37 50 48N 45 25 E
Kamenskiy, R.S.F.S.R., U.S.S.R. 39 49 20N 41 15 E
Kamenskoye, U.S.S.R. 41 62 45N 165 30 E
Kamenyak, Bulgaria 34 43 24N 26 57 E
Kamenz, E. Germany 30 51 17N 14 7 E
Kameoka, Japan 65 35 0N 135 35 E
Kameyama, Japan 65 34 51N 136 27 E
Kami-Jima, Japan 64 32 27N 130 20 E
Kami-koshiki-Jima, Japan 64 31 50N 129 52 E
Kamiah, U.S.A. 122 46 12N 116 2W
Kamień Pomorski, Poland 32 53 57N 14 43 E
Kamieskroon, S. Africa 96 30 9 S 17 56 E
Kamiita, Japan 64 34 6N 134 22 E
Kamilukuak, L., Canada 111 62 22N 101 40W
Kamina, Zaïre 93 8 45 S 25 0 E
Kaminak L., Canada 111 62 10N 95 0W
Kamioka, Japan 65 36 25N 137 15 E
Kamituga, Zaïre 92 3 2 S 28 10 E
Kamloops, Canada 110 50 40N 120 20W
Kamnik, Yugoslavia 27 46 14N 14 37 E
Kamo, N.Z. 80 35 42 S 174 20 E
Kamo, U.S.S.R. 39 40 21N 45 7 E
Kamoa Mts., Guyana 135 1 30N 59 0W
Kamogawa, Japan 65 35 5N 140 5 E
Kamoke, Pakistan 48 32 4N 74 4 E
Kamouraska, Canada 107 47 34N 69 52W
Kamp →, Austria 33 48 23N 15 42 E
Kampala, Uganda 92 0 20N 32 30 E
Kampar, Malaysia 55 4 18N 101 9 E
Kampar →, Indonesia 56 0 30N 103 8 E
Kampen, Neths. 16 52 33N 5 53 E
Kamperland, Neths. 17 51 34N 3 43 E
Kamphaeng Phet, Thailand 54 16 28N 99 30 E
Kampolombo, L., Zambia 93 11 37 S 29 42 E
Kampong To, Thailand 55 6 3N 101 13 E
Kampot, Cambodia 55 10 36N 104 10 E
Kampsville, U.S.A. 118 39 18N 90 37W
Kamptee, India 50 21 9N 79 19 E
Kampti, Burkina Faso 90 10 7N 3 25W
Kampuchea = Cambodia ■, Asia 54 12 15N 105 0 E
Kampung →, Indonesia 57 5 44 S 138 24 E
Kampung Air Putih, Malaysia 55 4 15N 103 10 E
Kampung Jerangau, Malaysia 55 4 50N 103 10 E
Kampung Raja, Malaysia 55 5 45N 102 35 E
Kampungbaru = Tolitoli, Indonesia 57 1 5N 120 50 E
Kamrau, Teluk, Indonesia 57 3 30 S 133 36 E
Kamsack, Canada 111 51 34N 101 54W
Kamskoye Ustye, U.S.S.R. 37 55 10N 49 20 E
Kamuchawie L., Canada 111 56 18N 101 59W
Kamui-Misaki, Japan 63 43 20N 140 21 E
Kamyshin, U.S.S.R. 37 50 10N 45 24 E
Kamyzyak, U.S.S.R. 39 46 4N 48 10 E
Kan, Burma 52 22 25N 94 5 E
Kanaaupscow, Canada 104 54 2N 76 30W
Kanab, U.S.A. 123 37 3N 112 29W
Kanab Creek, U.S.A. 123 37 0N 112 40W
Kanagawa □, Japan 65 35 20N 139 20 E
Kanairiktok →, Canada 105 55 2N 60 18W
Kanakapura, India 51 12 33N 77 28 E
Kanália, Greece 35 39 30N 22 53 E
Kananga, Zaïre 95 5 55 S 22 18 E
Kanarraville, U.S.A. 123 37 34N 113 12W
Kanash, U.S.S.R. 37 55 30N 47 32 E
Kanaskat, U.S.A. 124 47 19N 121 54W
Kanata, Canada 109 45 20N 75 59W
Kanawha →, U.S.A. 114 38 50N 82 8W
Kanazawa, Japan 65 36 30N 136 38 E
Kanbalu, Burma 52 23 12N 95 31 E
Kanchanaburi, Thailand 54 14 2N 99 31 E
Kanchenjunga, Nepal 49 27 50N 88 10 E
Kanchipuram, India 51 12 52N 79 45 E
Kanda Kanda, Zaïre 95 6 52 S 23 48 E
Kandahar = Qandahār, Afghan. 47 31 32N 65 30 E
Kandalaksha, U.S.S.R. 40 67 9N 32 30 E
Kandangan, Indonesia 56 2 50 S 115 20 E
Kandavu, Fiji 68 19 0 S 178 15 E
Kandavu Passage, Fiji 68 18 45 S 178 0 E
Kandep, Papua N. G. 69 5 54 S 143 32 E
Kandhíla, Greece 35 37 46N 22 22 E
Kandhkot, Pakistan 48 28 16N 69 8 E
Kandhla, India 48 29 18N 77 19 E
Kandi, Benin 91 11 7N 2 55 E
Kandi, India 49 23 58N 88 5 E
Kandla, India 48 23 0N 70 10 E
Kandos, Australia 76 32 45 S 149 58 E
Kandrian, Papua N. G. 69 6 14 S 149 37 E
Kandy, Sri Lanka 51 7 18N 80 43 E
Kane, U.S.A. 116 41 39N 78 53W
Kane Basin, Canada 144 79 1N 73 0W
Kanevskaya, U.S.S.R. 39 46 3N 39 3 E
Kanfanar, Yugoslavia 27 45 7N 13 50 E
Kangaba, Mali 90 11 56N 8 25W
Kangar, Malaysia 55 6 27N 100 12 E
Kangaroo I., Australia 73 35 45 S 137 0 E
Kangaroo Mts., Australia 72 23 25 S 142 0 E
Kangaroo Valley, Australia 76 34 42 S 150 32 E
Kangavar, Iran 46 34 40N 48 0 E
Kangding, China 58 30 2N 101 57 E
Kangean, Kepulauan, Indonesia 56 6 55 S 115 23 E
Kangerdlugsuak, Greenland 144 68 10N 32 20W
Kanggye, N. Korea 61 41 0N 126 35 E
Kangnŭng, S. Korea 61 37 45N 128 54 E
Kango, Gabon 94 0 11N 10 5 E
Kangoya, Zaïre 95 9 55 S 22 48 E
Kangping, China 61 42 43N 123 18 E
Kangpokpi, India 52 25 8N 93 58 E
Kangyidaung, Burma 52 16 56N 94 54 E
Kanhangad, India 51 12 21N 74 58 E
Kanheri, India 50 19 13N 72 50 E
Kani, Ivory C. 90 8 29N 6 36W
Kaniama, Zaïre 92 7 30 S 24 12 E
Kaniapiskau →, Canada 105 56 40N 69 30W
Kaniapiskau L., Canada 105 54 10N 69 55W
Kanin, P-ov., U.S.S.R. 40 68 0N 45 0 E
Kanin Nos, Mys, U.S.S.R. 40 68 45N 43 20 E
Kaniva, Australia 74 36 22 S 141 18 E
Kanjiža, Yugoslavia 33 46 3N 20 4 E
Kanjut Sar, Pakistan 49 36 7N 75 25 E
Kankakee, U.S.A. 119 41 6N 87 50W
Kankakee →, U.S.A. 119 41 23N 88 16W
Kankan, Guinea 90 10 23N 9 15W
Kanker, India 50 20 10N 81 40 E
Kankunskiy, U.S.S.R. 41 57 37N 126 8 E
Kanmuri-Yama, Japan 64 34 30N 132 4 E
Kannabe, Japan 64 34 32N 133 23 E
Kannapolis, U.S.A. 115 35 32N 80 37W
Kannauj, India 49 27 3N 79 56 E
Kano, Nigeria 91 12 2N 8 30 E
Kano □, Nigeria 91 11 45N 9 0 E
Kan'onji, Japan 64 34 7N 133 39 E
Kanoroba, Ivory C. 90 9 7N 6 8W
Kanowha, U.S.A. 118 42 57N 93 47W
Kanowit, Malaysia 56 2 14N 112 20 E
Kanowna, Australia 79 30 32 S 121 31 E
Kanoya, Japan 64 31 25N 130 50 E
Kanpetlet, Burma 52 21 10N 93 59 E
Kanpur, India 49 26 28N 80 20 E
Kansas, U.S.A. 119 39 33N 87 56W
Kansas □, U.S.A. 120 38 40N 98 0W
Kansas →, U.S.A. 120 39 7N 94 36W
Kansas City, Kans., U.S.A. 118 39 0N 94 40W
Kansas City, Mo., U.S.A. 118 39 3N 94 30W
Kansenia, Zaïre 93 10 20 S 26 0 E
Kansk, U.S.S.R. 41 56 20N 95 37 E
Kansu = Gansu □, China 60 36 0N 104 0 E
Kantang, Thailand 55 7 25N 99 31 E
Kantché, Niger 91 13 31N 8 30 E
Kanté, Togo 91 9 57N 1 3 E
Kantemirovka, U.S.S.R. 39 49 43N 39 55 E
Kantharalak, Thailand 54 14 39N 104 39 E
Kantō □, Japan 65 36 15N 139 30 E
Kantō-Heiya, Japan 65 36 0N 139 30 E
Kantō-Sanchi, Japan 65 35 59N 138 50 E
Kantu-long, Burma 52 19 57N 97 36 E
Kanturk, Ireland 15 52 10N 8 55W
Kanuma, Japan 65 36 34N 139 42 E
Kanumbra, Australia 74 37 3 S 145 40 E
Kanus, Namibia 96 27 50 S 18 39 E
Kanye, Botswana 96 25 0 S 25 28 E
Kanzenze, Zaïre 93 10 30 S 25 12 E
Kanzi, Ras, Tanzania 92 7 1 S 39 33 E
Kao, Fiji 68 19 40 S 175 1W
Kaohsiung = Gaoxiong, Taiwan 59 22 38N 120 18 E
Kaokoveld, Namibia 96 19 15 S 14 30 E
Kaolack, Senegal 90 14 5N 16 8W
Kaoshan, China 61 44 38N 124 50 E
Kaouar, Niger 87 19 5N 12 52 E
Kapadvanj, India 48 23 5N 73 0 E
Kapagere, Papua N. G. 69 9 46 S 147 42 E
Kapanga, Zaïre 95 8 30 S 22 40 E
Kapchagai, U.S.S.R. 40 43 51N 77 14 E
Kapellen, Belgium 17 51 19N 4 25 E
Kapéllo, Ákra, Greece 35 36 9N 23 3 E
Kapema, Zaïre 93 10 45 S 28 22 E
Kapfenberg, Austria 33 47 26N 15 18 E
Kapia, Zaïre 95 4 17 S 19 46 E
Kapiri Mposhi, Zambia 93 13 59 S 28 43 E
Kāpīsā □, Afghan. 47 35 0N 69 20 E
Kapiskau →, Canada 104 52 47N 81 55W
Kapit, Malaysia 56 2 0N 112 55 E
Kapiti I., N.Z. 80 40 50 S 174 56 E
Kapka, Massif du, Chad 87 15 7N 21 45 E
Kaplice, Czech. 32 48 42N 14 30 E
Kapoe, Thailand 55 9 34N 98 32 E
Kapoeta, Sudan 89 4 50N 33 35 E
Kaponga, N.Z. 80 39 29 S 174 9 E
Kapos →, Hungary 33 46 44N 18 30 E
Kaposvár, Hungary 33 46 25N 17 47 E
Kapowsin, U.S.A. 124 46 59N 122 13W
Kappeln, W. Germany 30 54 37N 9 56 E
Kapps, Namibia 96 22 32 S 17 18 E
Kaprije, Yugoslavia 27 43 42N 15 43 E
Kaprijke, Belgium 17 51 13N 3 38 E
Kapsukas, U.S.S.R. 36 54 33N 23 19 E
Kapuas →, Indonesia 56 0 25 S 109 20 E
Kapuas Hulu, Pegunungan, Malaysia 56 1 30N 113 30 E
Kapulo, Zaïre 93 8 18 S 29 15 E
Kapunda, Australia 73 34 20 S 138 56 E
Kapurthala, India 48 31 23N 75 25 E
Kapuskasing, Canada 104 49 25N 82 30W
Kapuskasing →, Canada 104 49 49N 82 0W
Kapustin Yar, U.S.S.R. 39 48 37N 45 40 E
Kaputar, Mt., Australia 77 30 15 S 150 10 E
Kaputir, Kenya 92 2 5N 35 28 E
Kapuvár, Hungary 33 47 36N 17 1 E
Kara, U.S.S.R. 40 69 10N 65 0 E
Kara Bogaz Gol, Zaliv, U.S.S.R. 40 41 0N 53 30 E
Kara Kalpak A.S.S.R. □, U.S.S.R. 40 43 0N 60 0 E
Kara Kum = Karakum, Peski, U.S.S.R. 40 39 30N 60 0 E
Kara-Saki, Japan 64 34 41N 129 30 E
Kara Sea, U.S.S.R. 40 75 0N 70 0 E
Karabük, Turkey 38 41 12N 32 37 E
Karaburuni, Albania 35 40 25N 19 20 E
Karabutak, U.S.S.R. 40 49 59N 60 14 E
Karachala, U.S.S.R. 39 39 45N 48 53 E
Karachayevsk, U.S.S.R. 39 43 50N 42 0 E
Karachev, U.S.S.R. 36 53 10N 35 5 E
Karachi, Pakistan 48 24 53N 67 0 E
Karad, India 50 17 15N 74 10 E
Karadeniz Boğazı, Turkey 46 41 10N 29 10 E
Karaga, Ghana 91 9 58N 0 28W
Karaganda, U.S.S.R. 40 49 50N 73 10 E
Karagayly, U.S.S.R. 40 49 26N 76 0 E
Karaginskiy, Ostrov, U.S.S.R. 41 58 45N 164 0 E
Karagwe □, Tanzania 92 2 0 S 31 0 E
Karaikal, India 51 10 59N 79 50 E
Karaikkudi, India 51 10 0N 78 45 E
Karaitivu, I., Sri Lanka 51 9 45N 79 52 E
Karaj, Iran 47 35 48N 51 0 E
Karak, Malaysia 55 3 25N 102 2 E
Karakas, U.S.S.R. 40 48 20N 83 30 E
Karakitang, Indonesia 57 3 14N 125 28 E
Karakoram Pass, Pakistan 49 35 33N 77 50 E
Karakoram Ra., Pakistan 49 35 30N 77 0 E
Karakum, Peski, U.S.S.R. 40 39 30N 60 0 E
Karal, Chad 87 12 50N 14 46 E
Karalon, U.S.S.R. 41 57 5N 115 50 E
Karaman, Turkey 46 37 14N 33 13 E
Karamay, China 62 45 30N 84 58 E
Karambu, Indonesia 56 3 53 S 116 6 E
Karamea, N.Z. 81 41 14 S 172 6 E
Karamea →, N.Z. 81 41 13 S 172 26 E
Karamea Bight, N.Z. 81 41 22 S 171 40 E
Karamoja □, Uganda 92 3 0N 34 15 E
Karamsad, India 48 22 35N 72 50 E
Karanganyar, Indonesia 57 7 38 S 109 37 E
Karanja, India 50 20 29N 77 31 E
Karapiro, N.Z. 80 37 53 S 175 32 E
Karara, Australia 77 28 12 S 151 37 E
Karasburg, Namibia 96 28 0 S 18 44 E
Karasino, U.S.S.R. 40 66 50N 86 50 E
Karasjok, Norway 8 69 27N 25 30 E
Karasuk, U.S.S.R. 40 53 44N 78 2 E
Karasuyama, Japan 65 36 39N 140 9 E
Karatau, U.S.S.R. 40 43 10N 70 28 E
Karatau, Khrebet, U.S.S.R. 40 43 30N 69 30 E
Karativu, Sri Lanka 51 8 22N 79 47 E
Karatoya →, India 52 24 7N 89 36 E
Karauli, India 48 26 30N 77 4 E
Karawa, Zaïre 94 3 18N 20 17 E
Karawanken, Europe 33 46 30N 14 40 E
Karazhal, U.S.S.R. 40 48 2N 70 49 E
Karbalā, Iraq 46 32 36N 44 3 E
Kårböle, Sweden 10 61 59N 15 22 E
Karcag, Hungary 33 47 19N 20 57 E
Karcha →, Pakistan 49 34 45N 76 10 E
Karda, U.S.S.R. 41 55 0N 103 16 E
Kardhámila, Greece 35 38 35N 26 5 E
Kardhítsa, Greece 35 39 23N 21 54 E
Kärdla, U.S.S.R. 36 58 50N 22 40 E
Kareeberge, S. Africa 96 30 59 S 21 50 E
Kareima, Sudan 88 18 30N 31 49 E
Karelian A.S.S.R. □, U.S.S.R. 40 65 30N 32 30 E
Karema, Papua N. G. 69 9 12 S 147 18 E
Kargānrūd, Iran 46 37 55N 49 0 E
Kargasok, U.S.S.R. 40 59 3N 80 53 E
Kargat, U.S.S.R. 40 55 10N 80 15 E
Kargı, Turkey 38 41 11N 34 30 E
Kargil, India 49 34 32N 76 12 E
Karguéri, Niger 91 13 27N 10 30 E
Karia ba Mohammed, Morocco 84 34 22N 5 12W
Kariba, Zambia 93 16 28 S 28 50 E
Kariba Dam, Zambia 93 16 30 S 28 35 E
Kariba Gorge, Zambia 93 16 30 S 28 50 E
Kariba L., Zambia 93 16 40 S 28 25 E
Karibib, Namibia 96 22 0 S 15 56 E
Karimata, Kepulauan, Indonesia 56 1 25 S 109 0 E
Karimata, Selat, Indonesia 56 2 0 S 108 40 E
Karimnagar, India 50 18 26N 79 10 E
Karimunjawa, Kepulauan, Indonesia 56 5 50 S 110 30 E
Karin, Somali Rep. 98 10 50N 45 52 E
Kariya, Japan 65 34 58N 137 1 E
Karkal, India 51 13 15N 74 56 E
Karkar I., Papua N. G. 69 4 40 S 146 0 E
Karkaralinsk, U.S.S.R. 40 49 26N 75 30 E
Karkinitskiy Zaliv, U.S.S.R. 38 45 56N 33 0 E
Karkur, Israel 44 32 29N 34 57 E
Karkur Tohl, Egypt 88 22 5N 25 5 E
Karl Libknekht, U.S.S.R. 36 51 40N 35 35 E
Karl-Marx-Stadt, E. Germany 30 50 50N 12 55 E
Karl-Marx-Stadt □, E. Germany 30 50 45N 13 0 E
Karla, L. = Voiviïs Límni, Greece 35 39 30N 22 45 E
Karlobag, Yugoslavia 27 44 32N 15 5 E
Karlovac, Yugoslavia 27 45 31N 15 36 E
Karlovka, U.S.S.R. 38 49 29N 35 8 E
Karlovy Vary, Czech. 32 50 13N 12 51 E
Karlsborg, Sweden 11 58 33N 14 33 E
Karlshamn, Sweden 11 56 10N 14 51 E
Karlskoga, Sweden 10 59 22N 14 33 E
Karlskrona, Sweden 11 56 10N 15 35 E
Karlsruhe, W. Germany 31 49 3N 8 23 E
Karlstad, Sweden 10 59 23N 13 30 E
Karlstad, U.S.A. 120 48 38N 96 30W
Karlstadt, W. Germany 31 49 57N 9 46 E
Karnal, India 48 29 42N 77 2 E
Karnali →, Nepal 49 28 45N 81 16 E
Karnaphuli Res., Bangla. 52 22 40N 92 20 E
Karnataka □, India 51 13 15N 77 0 E
Karnes City, U.S.A. 121 28 53N 97 53W
Karnische Alpen, Europe 33 46 36N 13 0 E
Karo, Mali 90 12 16N 3 18W
Karoi, Zambia 93 16 48 S 29 45 E
Karonga, Malawi 93 9 57 S 33 55 E
Karoonda, Australia 73 35 1 S 139 59 E
Karora, Sudan 88 17 44N 38 15 E
Káros, Greece 35 36 54N 25 40 E
Karousádhes, Greece 35 39 47N 19 45 E
Kárpathos, Greece 35 35 37N 27 10 E
Karpáthos, Stenón, Greece 35 36 0N 27 30 E
Karrebæk, Denmark 11 55 12N 11 39 E
Kars, Turkey 46 40 40N 43 5 E
Karsakpay, U.S.S.R. 40 47 55N 66 40 E
Karsha, U.S.S.R. 39 49 45N 51 35 E
Karshi, U.S.S.R. 40 38 53N 65 48 E
Karsiyang, India 49 26 56N 88 18 E
Karst, Yugoslavia 27 45 35N 14 0 E
Karsun, U.S.S.R. 37 54 14N 46 57 E
Kartaly, U.S.S.R. 40 53 3N 60 40 E
Kartapur, India 48 31 27N 75 32 E
Karthaus, U.S.A. 116 41 8N 78 9W
Kartuzy, Poland 32 54 22N 18 10 E
Karuah, Australia 76 32 37 S 151 56 E
Karufa, Indonesia 57 3 50 S 133 20 E
Karumba, Australia 72 17 31 S 140 50 E
Karumo, Tanzania 92 2 25 S 32 50 E
Karumwa, Tanzania 92 3 12 S 32 38 E
Karungu, Kenya 92 0 50 S 34 10 E
Karup, Denmark 11 56 19N 9 10 E
Karur, India 51 10 59N 78 2 E
Karviná, Czech. 32 49 53N 18 25 E
Karwi, India 49 25 12N 80 57 E
Kasache, Malawi 93 13 25 S 34 20 E
Kasai, Japan 64 34 55N 134 52 E
Kasai →, Zaïre 95 3 30 S 16 10 E
Kasai Occidental □, Zaïre 95 6 0 S 22 0 E
Kasai Oriental □, Zaïre 92 5 0 S 24 30 E
Kasaji, Zaïre 93 10 25 S 23 27 E
Kasama, Japan 65 36 23N 140 16 E
Kasama, Zambia 93 10 16 S 31 9 E
Kasane, Namibia 96 17 34 S 24 50 E
Kasanga, Tanzania 93 8 30 S 31 10 E
Kasangulu, Zaïre 95 4 33 S 15 15 E
Kasaoka, Japan 64 34 30N 133 30 E
Kasaragod, India 51 12 30N 74 58 E
Kasat, Burma 52 15 56N 98 13 E
Kasba, Bangla. 52 23 45N 91 2 E
Kasba L., Canada 111 60 20N 102 10W
Kasba Tadla, Morocco 84 32 36N 6 17W
Kaseda, Japan 64 31 25N 130 19 E
Kasempa, Zambia 93 13 30 S 25 44 E
Kasenga, Zaïre 93 10 20 S 28 45 E
Kasese, Uganda 92 0 13N 30 3 E
Kasewa, Zambia 93 14 28 S 28 53 E
Kasganj, India 49 27 48N 78 42 E
Kashabowie, Canada 104 48 40N 90 26W
Kāshān, Iran 47 34 5N 51 30 E
Kashi, China 62 39 30N 76 2 E
Kashihara, Japan 65 34 27N 135 46 E
Kashima, Ibaraki, Japan 65 35 58N 140 38 E
Kashima, Saga, Japan 64 33 7N 130 6 E
Kashima-Nada, Japan 65 36 0N 140 45 E
Kashimbo, Zaïre 93 11 12 S 26 19 E
Kashin, U.S.S.R. 37 57 20N 37 36 E
Kashipur, Orissa, India 50 19 16N 83 3 E
Kashipur, Ut. P., India 49 29 15N 79 0 E
Kashira, U.S.S.R. 37 54 45N 38 10 E
Kashiwa, Japan 65 35 52N 139 59 E
Kashiwazaki, Japan 63 37 22N 138 33 E

Kingman, *Ind., U.S.A.* **119** 39 58N 87 18W
Kingman, *Kans., U.S.A.* **121** 37 41N 98 9W
Kings →, *U.S.A.* **124** 36 10N 119 50W
Kings Canyon National Park, *U.S.A.* **124** 37 0N 118 35W
King's Lynn, *U.K.* **12** 52 45N 0 25 E
Kings Mountain, *U.S.A.* **115** 35 13N 81 20W
King's Peak, *U.S.A.* **122** 40 46N 110 27W
Kingsbridge, *U.K.* **13** 50 17N 3 46W
Kingsburg, *U.S.A.* **124** 36 35N 119 36W
Kingsbury, *U.S.A.* **119** 41 31N 86 42W
Kingscliff-Fingal, *Australia* **77** 28 16 S 153 34 E
Kingscote, *Australia* **73** 35 40 S 137 38 E
Kingscourt, *Ireland* **15** 53 55N 6 48W
Kingsey Falls, *Canada* **107** 45 51N 72 4W
Kingsley, *U.S.A.* **120** 42 37N 95 58W
Kingsport, *U.S.A.* **115** 36 33N 82 36W
Kingston, *Canada* **109** 44 14N 76 30W
Kingston, *Jamaica* **128** 18 0N 76 50W
Kingston, *N.Z.* **81** 45 20 S 168 43 E
Kingston, *Mo., U.S.A.* **118** 39 38N 94 2W
Kingston, *N.Y., U.S.A.* **117** 41 55N 74 0W
Kingston, *Pa., U.S.A.* **117** 41 19N 75 58W
Kingston, *R.I., U.S.A.* **117** 41 29N 71 30W
Kingston Pk., *U.S.A.* **125** 35 45N 115 54W
Kingston South East, *Australia* **73** 36 51 S 139 55 E
Kingston-upon-Thames, *U.K.* **13** 51 23N 0 20W
Kingstown, *Australia* **77** 30 29 S 151 6 E
Kingstown, *St. Vincent* **129** 13 10N 61 10W
Kingstree, *U.S.A.* **115** 33 40N 79 48W
Kingsville, *Canada* **108** 42 2N 82 45W
Kingsville, *U.S.A.* **121** 27 30N 97 53W
Kingussie, *U.K.* **14** 57 5N 4 2W
Kinistino, *Canada* **111** 52 57N 105 2W
Kinkala, *Congo* **95** 4 18 S 14 49 E
Kinki □, *Japan* **65** 33 30N 136 0 E
Kinleith, *N.Z.* **80** 38 20 S 175 56 E
Kinmount, *Canada* **109** 44 48N 78 45W
Kinmundy, *U.S.A.* **119** 38 46N 88 51W
Kinna, *Sweden* **11** 57 32N 12 42 E
Kinnaird, *Canada* **110** 49 17N 117 39W
Kinnairds Hd., *U.K.* **14** 57 40N 2 0W
Kinnared, *Sweden* **11** 57 2N 13 7 E
Kinneret, *Israel* **44** 32 44N 35 34 E
Kino, *Mexico* **126** 28 45N 111 59W
Kinoje →, *Canada* **104** 52 8N 81 25W
Kinomoto, *Japan* **65** 35 30N 136 13 E
Kinoni, *Uganda* **92** 0 41 S 30 28 E
Kinrooi, *Belgium* **17** 51 9N 5 45 E
Kinross, *U.K.* **14** 56 13N 3 25W
Kinsale, *Ireland* **15** 51 42N 8 31W
Kinsale, Old Hd. of, *Ireland* **15** 51 37N 8 32W
Kinshasa, *Zaïre* **95** 4 20 S 15 15 E
Kinsley, *U.S.A.* **121** 37 57N 99 30W
Kinston, *U.S.A.* **115** 35 18N 77 35W
Kintampo, *Ghana* **91** 8 5N 1 41W
Kintap, *Indonesia* **56** 3 51 S 115 13 E
Kintore Ra., *Australia* **78** 23 15 S 128 47 E
Kintyre, *U.K.* **14** 55 30N 5 35W
Kintyre, Mull of, *U.K.* **14** 55 17N 5 55W
Kinu, *Burma* **52** 22 46N 95 37 E
Kinu-Gawa →, *Japan* **65** 35 36N 139 57 E
Kinushseo →, *Canada* **104** 55 15N 83 45W
Kinuso, *Canada* **110** 55 20N 115 25W
Kinyangiri, *Tanzania* **92** 4 25 S 34 37 E
Kinzig →, *W. Germany* **31** 48 37N 7 49 E
Kinzua, *U.S.A.* **116** 41 52N 78 58W
Kinzua Dam, *U.S.A.* **116** 41 53N 79 0W
Kiosk, *Canada* **109** 46 6N 78 53W
Kiowa, *Kans., U.S.A.* **121** 37 3N 98 30W
Kiowa, *Okla., U.S.A.* **121** 34 45N 95 50W
Kipahigan L., *Canada* **111** 55 20N 101 55W
Kipanga, *Tanzania* **92** 6 15 S 35 20 E
Kiparissía, *Greece* **35** 37 15N 21 40 E
Kiparissiakós Kólpos, *Greece* **35** 37 25N 21 25 E
Kipawa, *Canada* **106** 46 47N 78 59W
Kipawa, Parc de, *Canada* **106** 47 0N 78 50W
Kipawa L., *Canada* **106** 46 50N 79 0W
Kipembawe, *Tanzania* **92** 7 38 S 33 27 E
Kipengere Ra., *Tanzania* **93** 9 12 S 34 15 E
Kipili, *Tanzania* **92** 7 28 S 30 32 E
Kipini, *Kenya* **92** 2 30 S 40 32 E
Kipling, *Canada* **111** 50 6N 102 38W
Kippure, *Ireland* **15** 53 11N 6 23W
Kipushi, *Zaïre* **93** 11 48 S 27 12 E
Kira Kira, *Solomon Is.* **68** 10 27 S 161 56 E
Kirandul, *India* **50** 18 33N 81 10 E
Kiratpur, *India* **48** 29 32N 78 12 E
Kirchhain, *W. Germany* **30** 50 49N 8 54 E
Kirchheim, *W. Germany* **31** 48 38N 9 20 E
Kirchheim-Bolanden, *W. Germany* **31** 49 40N 8 0 E
Kirensk, *U.S.S.R.* **41** 57 50N 107 55 E
Kirgella Rocks, *Australia* **79** 30 5 S 122 50 E
Kirgiz S.S.R. □, *U.S.S.R.* **40** 42 0N 75 0 E
Kiri, *Zaïre* **94** 1 29 S 19 0 E
Kiri Buru, *India* **50** 22 0N 85 0 E
Kiribati ■, *Pac. Oc.* **66** 1 0N 176 0 E
Kırıkkale, *Turkey* **46** 39 51N 33 32 E
Kirikopuni, *N.Z.* **80** 35 50 S 174 1 E
Kirillov, *U.S.S.R.* **37** 59 51N 38 14 E
Kirin = Jilin, *China* **61** 43 44N 126 30 E
Kirin □ = Jilin □, *China* **61** 44 0N 124 0 E
Kirindi →, *Sri Lanka* **51** 6 15N 81 20 E
Kirishi, *U.S.S.R.* **36** 59 28N 31 59 E
Kirishima-Yama, *Japan* **64** 31 58N 130 55 E
Kiritimati, *Kiribati* **67** 1 58N 157 27W
Kirkcaldy, *U.K.* **14** 56 7N 3 10W
Kirkcudbright, *U.K.* **14** 54 50N 4 3W
Kirkee, *India* **50** 18 34N 73 56 E
Kirkenær, *Norway* **10** 60 27N 12 3 E
Kirkenes, *Norway* **8** 69 40N 30 5 E
Kirkfield, *Canada* **109** 44 34N 78 59W
Kirkintilloch, *U.K.* **14** 55 57N 4 10W
Kirkjubæjarklaustur, *Iceland* **8** 63 47N 18 4W
Kirkland, *Ariz., U.S.A.* **123** 34 29N 112 46W
Kirkland, *Ill., U.S.A.* **119** 42 5N 88 51W
Kirkland Lake, *Canada* **104** 48 9N 80 2W
Kırklareli, *Turkey* **46** 41 44N 27 15 E
Kirklin, *U.S.A.* **119** 40 12N 86 22W
Kirkliston Ra., *N.Z.* **81** 44 25 S 170 34 E
Kirksville, *U.S.A.* **118** 40 8N 92 35W
Kirkūk, *Iraq* **46** 35 30N 44 21 E
Kirkwall, *U.K.* **14** 58 59N 2 59W
Kirkwood, *S. Africa* **96** 33 22 S 25 15 E
Kirkwood, *U.S.A.* **118** 38 35N 90 24W
Kirlampudi, *India* **50** 17 12N 82 12 E
Kirn, *W. Germany* **31** 49 46N 7 29 E
Kirov, *R.S.F.S.R., U.S.S.R.* **36** 54 3N 34 20 E
Kirov, *R.S.F.S.R., U.S.S.R.* **37** 58 35N 49 40 E
Kirovabad, *U.S.S.R.* **39** 40 45N 46 20 E
Kirovakan, *U.S.S.R.* **39** 40 48N 44 30 E
Kirovo-Chepetsk, *U.S.S.R.* **37** 58 28N 50 0 E
Kirovograd, *U.S.S.R.* **38** 48 35N 32 20 E
Kirovsk, *R.S.F.S.R., U.S.S.R.* **40** 67 48N 33 50 E
Kirovsk, *Turkmen S.S.R., U.S.S.R.* **40** 37 42N 60 23 E
Kirovsk, *Ukraine S.S.R., U.S.S.R.* **39** 48 35N 38 30 E
Kirovski, *U.S.S.R.* **39** 45 51N 48 11 E
Kirovskiy, *U.S.S.R.* **41** 54 27N 155 42 E
Kirriemuir, *U.K.* **14** 56 41N 3 0W
Kirsanov, *U.S.S.R.* **37** 52 35N 42 40 E
Kırşehir, *Turkey* **46** 39 14N 34 5 E
Kirstonia, *S. Africa* **96** 25 30 S 23 45 E
Kirtachi, *Niger* **91** 12 52N 2 30 E
Kīrteh, *Afghan.* **47** 32 15N 63 0 E
Kirthar Range, *Pakistan* **48** 27 0N 67 0 E
Kiruna, *Sweden* **8** 67 52N 20 15 E
Kirundu, *Zaïre* **92** 0 50 S 25 35 E
Kirup, *Australia* **79** 33 40 S 115 50 E
Kirya, *U.S.S.R.* **37** 55 5N 46 45 E
Kiryū, *Japan* **65** 36 24N 139 20 E
Kisa, *Sweden* **11** 58 0N 15 39 E
Kisaga, *Tanzania* **92** 4 30 S 34 23 E
Kisalaya, *Nic.* **128** 14 40N 84 3W
Kisambo, *Zaïre* **95** 6 25 S 18 14 E
Kisanga, *Zaïre* **92** 2 30N 26 35 E
Kisangani, *Zaïre* **92** 0 35N 25 15 E
Kisantu, *Zaïre* **95** 5 7 S 15 5 E
Kisar, *Indonesia* **57** 8 5 S 127 10 E
Kisaran, *Indonesia* **56** 3 0N 99 37 E
Kisarawe, *Tanzania* **92** 6 53 S 39 0 E
Kisarawe □, *Tanzania* **92** 7 3 S 39 0 E
Kisarazu, *Japan* **65** 35 23N 139 55 E
Kisbér, *Hungary* **33** 47 30N 18 0 E
Kiselevsk, *U.S.S.R.* **40** 54 5N 86 39 E
Kishanganga →, *Pakistan* **49** 34 18N 73 28 E
Kishanganj, *India* **49** 26 3N 88 14 E
Kishangarh, *India* **48** 27 50N 70 30 E
Kishi, *Nigeria* **91** 9 1N 3 52 E
Kishinev, *U.S.S.R.* **38** 47 0N 28 50 E
Kishiwada, *Japan* **65** 34 28N 135 22 E
Kishon, *Israel* **44** 32 49N 35 2 E
Kishorganj, *Bangla.* **52** 24 26N 90 40 E
Kishtwar, *India* **49** 33 20N 75 48 E
Kishwaukee →, *U.S.A.* **118** 42 12N 89 8W
Kisii, *Kenya* **92** 0 40 S 34 45 E
Kisii □, *Kenya* **92** 0 40 S 34 45 E
Kisiju, *Tanzania* **92** 7 23 S 39 19 E
Kısır, Dağ, *Turkey* **39** 41 0N 43 5 E
Kisizi, *Uganda* **92** 1 0 S 29 58 E
Kiska I., *U.S.A.* **102** 52 0N 177 30 E
Kiskatinaw →, *Canada* **110** 56 8N 120 10W
Kiskittogisu L., *Canada* **111** 54 13N 98 20W
Kiskörös, *Hungary* **33** 46 37N 19 20 E
Kiskundorozsma, *Hungary* **33** 46 16N 20 5 E
Kiskunfélegyháza, *Hungary* **33** 46 42N 19 53 E
Kiskunhalas, *Hungary* **33** 46 28N 19 37 E
Kiskunmajsa, *Hungary* **33** 46 30N 19 48 E
Kislovodsk, *U.S.S.R.* **39** 43 50N 42 45 E
Kismayu = Chisimaio, *Somali Rep.* **98** 0 22 S 42 32 E
Kiso-Gawa →, *Japan* **65** 35 20N 136 45 E
Kiso-Sammyaku, *Japan* **65** 35 45N 137 45 E
Kisofukushima, *Japan* **65** 35 52N 137 43 E
Kisoro, *Uganda* **92** 1 17 S 29 48 E
Kispest, *Hungary* **33** 47 27N 19 9 E
Kissidougou, *Guinea* **90** 9 5N 10 0W
Kissimmee, *U.S.A.* **115** 28 18N 81 22W
Kissimmee →, *U.S.A.* **115** 27 20N 80 55W
Kississing L., *Canada* **111** 55 10N 101 20W
Kistanje, *Yugoslavia* **27** 43 58N 15 55 E
Kisújszállás, *Hungary* **33** 47 12N 20 50 E
Kisuki, *Japan* **64** 35 17N 132 54 E
Kisumu, *Kenya* **92** 0 3 S 34 45 E
Kisvárda, *Hungary* **33** 48 14N 22 4 E
Kiswani, *Tanzania* **92** 4 5 S 37 57 E
Kiswere, *Tanzania* **93** 9 27 S 39 30 E
Kit Carson, *U.S.A.* **120** 38 48N 102 45W
Kita, *Mali* **90** 13 5N 9 25W
Kita-Ura, *Japan* **65** 36 0N 140 34 E
Kitab, *U.S.S.R.* **40** 39 7N 66 52 E
Kitakami-Gawa →, *Japan* **63** 38 25N 141 19 E
Kitakyūshū, *Japan* **64** 33 50N 130 50 E
Kitale, *Kenya* **92** 1 0N 35 0 E
Kitami, *Japan* **63** 43 48N 143 54 E
Kitangiri, L., *Tanzania* **92** 4 5 S 34 20 E
Kitano-Kaikyō, *Japan* **64** 34 17N 134 58 E
Kitaya, *Tanzania* **93** 10 38 S 40 8 E
Kitchener, *Australia* **79** 30 55 S 124 8 E
Kitchener, *Canada* **108** 43 27N 80 29W
Kitega = Gitega, *Burundi* **92** 3 26 S 29 56 E
Kitengo, *Zaïre* **92** 7 26 S 24 8 E
Kiteto □, *Tanzania* **92** 5 0 S 37 0 E
Kitgum, *Uganda* **92** 3 17N 32 52 E
Kíthira, *Greece* **35** 36 9N 23 0 E
Kíthnos, *Greece* **35** 37 26N 24 27 E
Kitikmeot □, *Canada* **102** 70 0N 110 0W
Kitimat, *Canada* **110** 54 3N 128 38W
Kitinen →, *Finland* **8** 67 34N 26 40 E
Kitiyab, *Sudan* **89** 17 13N 33 35 E
Kítros, *Greece* **35** 40 22N 22 34 E
Kitsuki, *Japan* **64** 33 25N 131 37 E
Kittakittaooloo, L., *Australia* **73** 28 3 S 138 14 E
Kittanning, *U.S.A.* **116** 40 49N 79 30W
Kittatinny Mts., *U.S.A.* **117** 41 0N 75 0W
Kittery, *U.S.A.* **117** 43 7N 70 42W
Kitui, *Kenya* **92** 1 17 S 38 0 E
Kitui □, *Kenya* **92** 1 30 S 38 25 E
Kitwe, *Zambia* **93** 12 54 S 28 13 E
Kitzbühel, *Austria* **31** 47 27N 12 24 E
Kitzingen, *W. Germany* **31** 49 44N 10 9 E
Kivalo, *Finland* **8** 66 18N 26 0 E
Kivarli, *India* **48** 24 33N 72 46 E
Kivu □, *Zaïre* **92** 3 10 S 27 0 E
Kivu, L., *Zaïre* **92** 1 48 S 29 0 E
Kiwai I., *Papua N. G.* **69** 8 35 S 143 30 E
Kiyev, *U.S.S.R.* **36** 50 30N 30 28 E
Kiyevskoye Vdkhr., *U.S.S.R.* **36** 51 0N 30 0 E
Kiziguru, *Rwanda* **92** 1 46 S 30 23 E
Kızıl Irmak →, *Turkey* **38** 39 15N 36 0 E
Kizil Jilga, *India* **49** 35 26N 78 50 E
Kizil Yurt, *U.S.S.R.* **39** 43 13N 46 54 E
Kızılcahamam, *Turkey* **38** 40 30N 32 30 E
Kizimkazi, *Tanzania* **92** 6 28 S 39 30 E
Kizlyar, *U.S.S.R.* **39** 43 51N 46 40 E
Kizyl-Arvat, *U.S.S.R.* **40** 38 58N 56 15 E
Kjellerup, *Denmark* **11** 56 17N 9 25 E
Kladanj, *Yugoslavia* **33** 44 14N 18 42 E
Kladno, *Czech.* **32** 50 10N 14 7 E
Kladovo, *Yugoslavia* **33** 44 36N 22 33 E
Klaeng, *Thailand* **54** 12 47N 101 39 E
Klagenfurt, *Austria* **33** 46 38N 14 20 E
Klagshamn, *Sweden* **11** 55 32N 12 53 E
Klagstorp, *Sweden* **11** 55 22N 13 23 E
Klaipeda, *U.S.S.R.* **36** 55 43N 21 10 E
Klamath →, *U.S.A.* **122** 41 40N 124 4W
Klamath Falls, *U.S.A.* **122** 42 20N 121 50W
Klamath Mts., *U.S.A.* **122** 41 20N 123 0W
Klangklang, *Burma* **52** 22 41N 93 26 E
Klanjec, *Yugoslavia* **27** 46 3N 15 45 E
Klappan →, *Canada* **110** 58 0N 129 43W
Klarälven →, *Sweden* **9** 59 23N 13 32 E
Klaten, *Indonesia* **57** 7 43 S 110 36 E
Klatovy, *Czech.* **32** 49 23N 13 18 E
Klawak, *U.S.A.* **110** 55 35N 133 0W
Klawer, *S. Africa* **96** 31 44 S 18 36 E
Klazienaveen, *Neths.* **16** 52 44N 7 0 E
Kleczew, *Poland* **32** 52 22N 18 9 E
Kleena Kleene, *Canada* **110** 52 0N 124 59W
Klein, *U.S.A.* **122** 46 26N 108 31W
Klein-Karas, *Namibia* **96** 27 33 S 18 7 E
Kleine Gette →, *Belgium* **17** 50 51N 5 6 E
Kleine Nete →, *Belgium* **17** 51 12N 4 46 E
Klekovača, *Yugoslavia* **27** 44 25N 16 32 E
Klenovec, *Czech.* **32** 48 36N 19 54 E
Klenovec, *Yugoslavia* **35** 41 32N 20 49 E
Klerksdorp, *S. Africa* **96** 26 53 S 26 38 E
Kletnya, *U.S.S.R.* **36** 53 23N 33 12 E
Kletsk, *U.S.S.R.* **36** 53 5N 26 45 E
Kletskaïa Kletskiy, *U.S.S.R.* **40** 49 20N 43 0 E
Kletskiy, *U.S.S.R.* **39** 49 20N 43 0 E
Kleve, *W. Germany* **30** 51 46N 6 10 E
Klickitat, *U.S.A.* **122** 45 50N 121 10W
Klickitat →, *U.S.A.* **124** 45 42N 121 17W
Klimovichi, *U.S.S.R.* **36** 53 36N 32 0 E
Klin, *U.S.S.R.* **37** 56 20N 36 48 E
Klinaklini →, *Canada* **110** 51 21N 125 40W
Klintsey, *U.S.S.R.* **36** 52 50N 32 10 E
Klipdale, *S. Africa* **96** 34 19 S 19 57 E
Klipplaat, *S. Africa* **96** 33 1 S 24 22 E
Klitmøller, *Denmark* **11** 57 3N 8 30 E
Kljajićevo, *Yugoslavia* **33** 45 45N 19 17 E
Ključ, *Yugoslavia* **27** 44 32N 16 48 E
Kłobuck, *Poland* **32** 50 55N 18 55 E
Kłodzko, *Poland* **32** 50 28N 16 38 E
Kloetinge, *Neths.* **17** 51 30N 3 56 E
Klondike, *Canada* **102** 64 0N 139 26W
Kloosterzande, *Neths.* **17** 51 22N 4 1 E
Klosterneuburg, *Austria* **33** 48 18N 16 19 E
Klosters, *Switz.* **31** 46 52N 9 52 E
Klötze, *E. Germany* **30** 52 38N 11 9 E
Klouto, *Togo* **91** 6 57N 0 44 E
Kluane L., *Canada* **102** 61 15N 138 40W
Kluczbork, *Poland* **32** 50 58N 18 12 E
Klundert, *Neths.* **17** 51 40N 4 32 E
Klyuchevskaya, Guba, *U.S.S.R.* **41** 55 50N 160 30 E
Knaresborough, *U.K.* **12** 54 1N 1 29W
Knee L., *Man., Canada* **111** 55 3N 94 45W
Knee L., *Sask., Canada* **111** 55 51N 107 0W
Kneïss, Is., *Tunisia* **86** 34 22N 10 18 E
Knesselare, *Belgium* **17** 51 9N 3 26 E
Knezha, *Bulgaria* **34** 43 30N 24 5 E
Knić, *Yugoslavia* **33** 43 53N 20 45 E
Knight Inlet, *Canada* **110** 50 45N 125 40W
Knighton, *U.K.* **13** 52 21N 3 2W
Knights Ferry, *U.S.A.* **124** 37 50N 120 40W
Knight's Landing, *U.S.A.* **124** 38 50N 121 43W
Knightstown, *U.S.A.* **119** 39 49N 85 32W
Knin, *Yugoslavia* **27** 44 1N 16 17 E
Knittelfeld, *Austria* **33** 47 13N 14 51 E
Knjaževac, *Yugoslavia* **33** 43 35N 22 18 E
Knob, C., *Australia* **79** 34 32 S 119 16 E
Knockmealdown Mts., *Ireland* **15** 52 16N 8 0W
Knokke, *Belgium* **17** 51 20N 3 17 E
Knowlton, *Canada* **107** 45 13N 72 31W
Knowsley, *Australia* **74** 36 50 S 144 35 E
Knox, *U.S.A.* **119** 41 18N 86 36W
Knox, C., *Canada* **110** 54 11N 133 5W
Knox City, *U.S.A.* **121** 33 26N 99 49W
Knox Coast, *Antarctica* **143** 66 30 S 108 0 E
Knoxville, *Iowa, U.S.A.* **118** 41 20N 92 55W
Knoxville, *Tenn., U.S.A.* **115** 35 58N 83 57W
Knutshø, *Norway* **10** 62 18N 9 41 E
Knysna, *S. Africa* **96** 34 2 S 23 2 E
Knyszyn, *Poland* **32** 53 20N 22 56 E
Ko Kha, *Thailand* **54** 18 11N 99 24 E
Kō-Saki, *Japan* **64** 34 5N 129 13 E
Ko Tao, *Thailand* **55** 10 6N 99 48 E
Koartac, *Canada* **103** 60 55N 69 40W
Koba, *Aru, Indonesia* **57** 6 37 S 134 37 E
Koba, *Bangka, Indonesia* **56** 2 26 S 106 14 E
Kobarid, *Yugoslavia* **27** 46 15N 13 30 E
Kobayashi, *Japan* **64** 31 56N 130 59 E
Kobdo = Hovd, *Mongolia* **62** 48 2N 91 37 E
Kobdo = Jargalant, *Mongolia* **62** 48 2N 91 37 E
Kōbe, *Japan* **65** 34 45N 135 10 E
Kobelyaki, *U.S.S.R.* **38** 49 11N 34 9 E
København, *Denmark* **11** 55 41N 12 34 E
Koblenz, *W. Germany* **31** 50 21N 7 36 E
Kobo, *Ethiopia* **89** 12 2N 39 56 E
Kobo, *Zaïre* **95** 4 54 S 17 9 E
Kobrin, *U.S.S.R.* **36** 52 15N 24 22 E
Kobroor, Kepulauan, *Indonesia* **57** 6 10 S 134 30 E
Kobuchizawa, *Japan* **65** 35 52N 138 19 E
Kobuleti, *U.S.S.R.* **39** 41 55N 41 45 E
Kobyłka, *Poland* **32** 52 21N 21 10 E
Kobylkino, *U.S.S.R.* **37** 54 8N 43 56 E
Kobylnik, *U.S.S.R.* **36** 54 58N 26 39 E
Kočani, *Yugoslavia* **35** 41 55N 22 25 E
Koceljevo, *Yugoslavia* **33** 44 28N 19 50 E
Kočevje, *Yugoslavia* **27** 45 39N 14 50 E
Koch Bihar, *India* **52** 26 22N 89 29 E
Kochas, *India* **49** 25 15N 83 56 E
Kocher →, *W. Germany* **31** 49 14N 9 12 E
Kocheya, *U.S.S.R.* **41** 52 32N 120 42 E
Kōchi, *Japan* **64** 33 30N 133 35 E
Kōchi □, *Japan* **64** 33 40N 133 30 E
Kōchi-Heiya, *Japan* **64** 33 28N 133 30 E
Kochiu = Gejiu, *China* **58** 23 20N 103 10 E
Kodaira, *Japan* **65** 35 44N 139 29 E
Koddiyar Bay, *Sri Lanka* **51** 8 33N 81 15 E
Kodiak, *U.S.A.* **102** 57 30N 152 45W
Kodiak I., *U.S.A.* **102** 57 30N 152 45W
Kodinar, *India* **48** 20 46N 70 46 E
Kodori →, *U.S.S.R.* **39** 42 47N 41 10 E
Koekelare, *Belgium* **17** 51 5N 2 59 E
Koersel, *Belgium* **17** 51 3N 5 17 E
Koes, *Namibia* **96** 26 0 S 19 15 E
Koetong, *Australia* **75** 36 10 S 147 30 E
Koffiefontein, *S. Africa* **96** 29 30 S 25 0 E
Kofiau, *Indonesia* **57** 1 11 S 129 50 E
Koforidua, *Ghana* **91** 6 3N 0 17W
Kōfu, *Japan* **65** 35 40N 138 30 E
Koga, *Japan* **65** 36 11N 139 43 E
Kogaluk →, *Canada* **105** 56 12N 61 44W
Kogan, *Australia* **77** 27 2 S 150 40 E
Kogin Baba, *Nigeria* **91** 7 55N 11 35 E
Kogota, *Japan* **63** 38 33N 141 3 E
Koh-i-Bābā, *Afghan.* **47** 34 30N 67 0 E
Koh-i-Khurd, *Afghan.* **48** 33 30N 65 59 E
Kohat, *Pakistan* **48** 33 40N 71 29 E
Kohima, *India* **52** 25 35N 94 10 E
Kohkīlūyeh va Būyer Aḥmadi □, *Iran* **47** 31 30N 50 30 E
Kohler Ra., *Antarctica* **143** 77 0 S 110 0W
Kohtla Järve, *U.S.S.R.* **36** 59 20N 27 20 E
Kohukohu, *N.Z.* **80** 35 22 S 173 38 E
Kojima, *Japan* **64** 34 30N 133 50 E
Kōjo, *Japan* **64** 34 33N 133 55 E

Kojonup

Kojonup, *Australia* **79** 33 48 S 117 10 E
Koka, *Sudan* **88** 20 5N 30 35 E
Kokand, *U.S.S.R.* **40** 40 30N 70 57 E
Kokanee Glacier Prov. Park, *Canada* **110** 49 47N 117 10W
Kokas, *Indonesia* **57** 2 42 S 132 26 E
Kokchetav, *U.S.S.R.* **40** 53 20N 69 25 E
Kokemäenjoki, *Finland* **9** 61 32N 21 44 E
Kokerite, *Guyana* **135** 7 12N 59 35W
Kokhma, *U.S.S.R.* **37** 56 55N 41 18 E
Kokiri, *N.Z.* **81** 42 29 S 171 25 E
Kokkola, *Finland* **8** 63 50N 23 8 E
Koko, *Nigeria* **91** 11 28N 4 29 E
Kokoda, *Papua N. G.* **69** 8 54 S 147 47 E
Kokolopozo, *Ivory C.* **90** 5 8N 6 5W
Kokomo, *U.S.A.* **119** 40 30N 86 6W
Kokonau, *Indonesia* **57** 4 43 S 136 26 E
Kokopo, *Papua N. G.* **69** 4 22 S 152 19 E
Kokoro, *Niger* **91** 14 12N 0 55 E
Koksoak →, *Canada* **103** 58 30N 68 10W
Kokstad, *S. Africa* **97** 30 32 S 29 29 E
Kokubu, *Japan* **64** 31 44N 130 46 E
Kokuora, *U.S.S.R.* **41** 71 35N 144 50 E
Kola, *Indonesia* **57** 5 35 S 134 30 E
Kola, *U.S.S.R.* **40** 68 45N 33 8 E
Kola Pen. = Kolskiy Poluostrov, *U.S.S.R.* **40** 67 30N 38 0 E
Kolachel, *India* **51** 8 10N 77 15 E
Kolahoi, *India* **49** 34 12N 75 22 E
Kolahun, *Liberia* **90** 8 15N 10 4W
Kolaka, *Indonesia* **57** 4 3 S 121 46 E
Kolar, *India* **51** 13 12N 78 15 E
Kolar Gold Fields, *India* **51** 12 58N 78 16 E
Kolari, *Finland* **8** 67 20N 23 48 E
Kolby Kås, *Denmark* **11** 55 48N 10 32 E
Kolchugino, *U.S.S.R.* **37** 56 17N 39 22 E
Kolda, *Senegal* **90** 12 55N 14 57W
Kolding, *Denmark* **11** 55 30N 9 29 E
Kole, *Zaïre* **94** 3 16 S 22 42 E
Koléa, *Algeria* **85** 36 38N 2 46 E
Kolepom = Yos Sudarso, Pulau, *Indonesia* **57** 8 0 S 138 30 E
Kolguyev, Ostrov, *U.S.S.R.* **40** 69 20N 48 30 E
Kolham, *Neths.* **16** 53 11N 6 44 E
Kolhapur, *India* **50** 16 43N 74 15 E
Kolia, *Ivory C.* **90** 9 46N 6 28W
Kolín, *Czech.* **32** 50 2N 15 9 E
Kolind, *Denmark* **11** 56 21N 10 34 E
Kölleda, *E. Germany* **30** 51 11N 11 14 E
Kollegal, *India* **51** 12 9N 77 9 E
Kolleru L., *India* **50** 16 40N 81 10 E
Kollum, *Neths.* **16** 53 17N 6 10 E
Kolmanskop, *Namibia* **96** 26 45 S 15 14 E
Köln, *W. Germany* **30** 50 56N 6 58 E
Koło, *Poland* **32** 52 14N 18 40 E
Kołobrzeg, *Poland* **32** 54 10N 15 35 E
Kologriv, *U.S.S.R.* **37** 58 48N 44 25 E
Kolokani, *Mali* **90** 13 35N 7 45W
Kolombangara, *Solomon Is.* **68** 8 0 S 157 5 E
Kolomna, *U.S.S.R.* **37** 55 8N 38 45 E
Kolomyya, *U.S.S.R.* **38** 48 31N 25 2 E
Kolondiéba, *Mali* **90** 11 5N 6 54W
Kolonodale, *Indonesia* **57** 2 3 S 121 25 E
Koloona, *Australia* **77** 29 37 S 150 46 E
Kolosib, *India* **52** 24 15N 92 45 E
Kolpashevo, *U.S.S.R.* **40** 58 20N 83 5 E
Kolpino, *U.S.S.R.* **36** 59 44N 30 39 E
Kolpny, *U.S.S.R.* **37** 52 12N 37 10 E
Kolskiy Poluostrov, *U.S.S.R.* **40** 67 30N 38 0 E
Kolubara →, *Yugoslavia* **33** 44 35N 20 15 E
Koluszki, *Poland* **32** 51 45N 19 46 E
Kolwezi, *Zaïre* **93** 10 40 S 25 25 E
Kolyberovo, *U.S.S.R.* **37** 55 15N 38 40 E
Kolyma →, *U.S.S.R.* **41** 69 30N 161 0 E
Kolymskoye, Okhotsko, *U.S.S.R.* **41** 63 0N 157 0 E
Kôm Ombo, *Egypt* **88** 24 25N 32 52 E
Komagene, *Japan* **65** 35 44N 137 58 E
Komaki, *Japan* **65** 35 17N 136 55 E
Komárno, *Czech.* **33** 47 49N 18 5 E
Komárom, *Hungary* **33** 47 43N 18 7 E
Komarovo, *U.S.S.R.* **36** 58 38N 33 40 E
Komatipoort, *S. Africa* **97** 25 25 S 31 55 E
Komatsu, *Japan* **65** 36 25N 136 30 E
Komatsujima, *Japan* **64** 34 0N 134 35 E
Kombissiri, *Burkina Faso* **91** 12 4N 1 20W
Kombo, *Gabon* **94** 0 20 S 12 22 E
Kombori, *Burkina Faso* **90** 13 26N 3 56W
Komen, *Yugoslavia* **27** 45 49N 13 45 E
Komenda, *Ghana* **91** 5 4N 1 28W
Komi A.S.S.R. □, *U.S.S.R.* **40** 64 0N 55 0 E
Komiža, *Yugoslavia* **27** 43 3N 16 11 E
Komló, *Hungary* **33** 46 15N 18 16 E
Kommamur Canal, *India* **51** 16 0N 80 25 E
Kommunarsk, *U.S.S.R.* **39** 48 30N 38 45 E
Kommunizma, Pik, *U.S.S.R.* **47** 39 0N 72 2 E
Komodo, *Indonesia* **57** 8 37 S 119 20 E
Komoé, *Ivory C.* **90** 5 12N 3 44W
Komono, *Congo* **94** 3 10 S 13 20 E
Komoran, Pulau, *Indonesia* **57** 8 18 S 138 45 E
Komoro, *Japan* **65** 36 19N 138 26 E
Komotini, *Greece* **35** 41 9N 25 26 E
Kompasberg, *S. Africa* **96** 31 45 S 24 32 E
Kompong Bang, *Cambodia* **55** 12 24N 104 40 E
Kompong Cham, *Cambodia* **55** 12 0N 105 30 E
Kompong Chhnang, *Cambodia* **55** 12 20N 104 35 E
Kompong Chikreng, *Cambodia* **54** 13 5N 104 18 E
Kompong Kleang, *Cambodia* **54** 13 6N 104 8 E
Kompong Luong, *Cambodia* **55** 11 49N 104 48 E
Kompong Pranak, *Cambodia* **54** 13 35N 104 55 E
Kompong Som, *Cambodia* **55** 10 38N 103 30 E
Kompong Som, Chhung, *Cambodia* **55** 10 50N 103 32 E
Kompong Speu, *Cambodia* **55** 11 26N 104 32 E
Kompong Sralao, *Cambodia* **54** 14 5N 105 46 E
Kompong Thom, *Cambodia* **54** 12 35N 104 51 E
Kompong Trabeck, *Cambodia* **54** 13 6N 105 14 E
Kompong Trabeck, *Cambodia* **55** 11 9N 105 28 E
Kompong Trach, *Cambodia* **55** 11 25N 105 48 E
Kompong Tralach, *Cambodia* **55** 11 54N 104 47 E
Komrat, *U.S.S.R.* **38** 46 18N 28 40 E
Komsberg, *S. Africa* **96** 32 40 S 20 45 E
Komsomolets, Ostrov, *U.S.S.R.* **41** 80 30N 95 0 E
Komsomolsk, *R.S.F.S.R., U.S.S.R.* **37** 57 2N 40 20 E
Komsomolsk, *R.S.F.S.R., U.S.S.R.* **41** 50 30N 137 0 E
Komsomolskiy, *U.S.S.R.* **37** 53 30N 49 30 E
Konakovo, *U.S.S.R.* **37** 56 52N 36 45 E
Konarhá □, *Afghan.* **47** 35 30N 71 3 E
Konawa, *U.S.A.* **121** 34 59N 96 46W
Konch, *India* **49** 26 0N 79 10 E
Kondagaon, *India* **50** 19 35N 81 35 E
Kondakovo, *U.S.S.R.* **41** 69 36N 152 0 E
Konde, *Tanzania* **92** 4 57 S 39 45 E
Kondinin, *Australia* **79** 32 34 S 118 8 E
Kondo, *Zaïre* **95** 5 35 S 13 0 E
Kondoa, *Tanzania* **92** 4 55 S 35 50 E
Kondoa □, *Tanzania* **92** 5 0 S 36 0 E
Kondratyevo, *U.S.S.R.* **41** 57 22N 98 15 E
Konduga, *Nigeria* **91** 11 35N 13 26 E
Kondukur, *India* **51** 15 12N 79 57 E
Koné, *N. Cal.* **68** 21 4 S 164 52 E
Kong, *Ivory C.* **90** 8 54N 4 36W
Kong →, *Cambodia* **54** 13 32N 105 58 E
Kong, Koh, *Cambodia* **55** 11 20N 103 0 E
Kong Christian IX.s Land, *Greenland* **144** 68 0N 36 0W
Kong Christian X.s Land, *Greenland* **144** 74 0N 29 0W
Kong Franz Joseph Fd., *Greenland* **144** 73 20N 24 30W
Kong Frederik IX.s Land, *Greenland* **144** 67 0N 52 0W
Kong Frederik VI.s Kyst, *Greenland* **144** 63 0N 43 0W
Kong Frederik VIII.s Land, *Greenland* **144** 78 30N 26 0W
Kong Oscar Fjord, *Greenland* **144** 72 20N 24 0W
Konga, *Sweden* **11** 56 30N 15 6 E
Kongbo, *C.A.R.* **94** 4 44N 21 23 E
Kongeå, *Denmark* **11** 55 24N 9 39 E
Kongju, *S. Korea* **61** 36 30N 127 0 E
Konglu, *Burma* **52** 27 13N 97 57 E
Kongolo, *Kasai Or., Zaïre* **92** 5 26 S 24 49 E
Kongolo, *Shaba, Zaïre* **92** 5 22 S 27 0 E
Kongor, *Sudan* **89** 7 1N 31 27 E
Kongoussi, *Burkina Faso* **91** 13 19N 1 32W
Kongsberg, *Norway* **10** 59 39N 9 39 E
Kongsvinger, *Norway* **10** 60 12N 12 2 E
Kongwa, *Tanzania* **92** 6 11 S 36 26 E
Kongwak, *Australia* **74** 38 30 S 145 42 E
Koni, *Zaïre* **93** 10 40 S 27 11 E
Koni, Mts., *Zaïre* **93** 10 36 S 27 10 E
Königsberg = Kaliningrad, *U.S.S.R.* **36** 54 42N 20 32 E
Königshofen, *W. Germany* **31** 50 18N 10 29 E
Königslutter, *W. Germany* **30** 52 14N 10 50 E
Königswusterhausen, *E. Germany* **30** 52 19N 13 38 E
Konin, *Poland* **32** 52 12N 18 15 E
Kónitsa, *Greece* **35** 40 5N 20 48 E
Konjice, *Yugoslavia* **27** 46 20N 15 28 E
Konkiep, *Namibia* **96** 26 49 S 17 15 E
Konkouré →, *Guinea* **90** 9 50N 13 42W
Könnern, *E. Germany* **30** 51 40N 11 45 E
Konnur, *India* **51** 16 14N 74 49 E
Kono, *S. Leone* **90** 8 30N 11 5W
Konongo, *Ghana* **91** 6 40N 1 15W
Konos, *Papua N. G.* **69** 3 10 S 151 44 E
Konosha, *U.S.S.R.* **40** 61 0N 40 5 E
Kōnosu, *Japan* **65** 36 3N 139 31 E
Konotop, *U.S.S.R.* **36** 51 12N 33 7 E
Konqi He →, *China* **62** 40 45N 90 10 E
Końskie, *Poland* **32** 51 15N 20 23 E
Konstantinovka, *U.S.S.R.* **38** 48 32N 37 39 E
Konstantinovski, *U.S.S.R.* **39** 47 33N 41 10 E
Konstanz, *W. Germany* **31** 47 39N 9 10 E
Kontagora, *Nigeria* **91** 10 23N 5 27 E
Kontich, *Belgium* **17** 51 8N 4 26 E
Kontum, *Vietnam* **54** 14 24N 108 0 E
Kontum, Plateau du, *Vietnam* **54** 14 30N 108 0 E
Konya, *Turkey* **46** 37 52N 32 35 E
Konya Ovasi, *Turkey* **46** 38 30N 33 0 E
Konyin, *Burma* **52** 22 58N 94 42 E
Konz, *W. Germany* **31** 49 41N 6 36 E
Konza, *Kenya* **92** 1 45 S 37 7 E
Koo-wee-rup, *Australia* **74** 38 13 S 145 28 E
Kookynie, *Australia* **79** 29 17 S 121 22 E
Kooline, *Australia* **78** 22 57 S 116 20 E
Kooloonong, *Australia* **74** 34 48 S 143 10 E
Koolyanobbing, *Australia* **79** 30 48 S 119 36 E
Koondrook, *Australia* **74** 35 33 S 144 8 E
Koorawatha, *Australia* **76** 34 2 S 148 33 E
Koorda, *Australia* **79** 30 48 S 117 35 E
Kooskia, *U.S.A.* **122** 46 9N 115 59W
Kootenai →, *Canada* **122** 49 15N 117 39W
Kootenay L., *Canada* **110** 49 45N 116 50W
Kootenay Nat. Park, *Canada* **110** 51 0N 116 0W
Kootjieskolk, *S. Africa* **96** 31 15 S 20 21 E
Kopanovka, *U.S.S.R.* **39** 47 28N 46 50 E
Kopaonik Planina, *Yugoslavia* **33** 43 10N 21 50 E
Kopargaon, *India* **50** 19 51N 74 28 E
Kópavogur, *Iceland* **8** 64 6N 21 55W
Koper, *Yugoslavia* **27** 45 31N 13 44 E
Kopervik, *Norway* **9** 59 17N 5 17 E
Kopeysk, *U.S.S.R.* **40** 55 7N 61 37 E
Kopi, *Australia* **73** 33 24 S 135 40 E
Köping, *Sweden* **10** 59 31N 16 3 E
Kopiste, *Yugoslavia* **27** 42 48N 16 42 E
Köpmanholmen, *Sweden* **10** 63 10N 18 35 E
Koppal, *India* **51** 15 23N 76 5 E
Koppang, *Norway* **10** 61 34N 11 3 E
Kopparberg, *Sweden* **9** 59 52N 15 0 E
Kopparbergs län □, *Sweden* **10** 61 20N 14 15 E
Koppeh Dāgh, *Asia* **47** 38 0N 58 0 E
Kopperå, *Norway* **10** 63 24N 11 50 E
Koppies, *S. Africa* **97** 27 20 S 27 30 E
Koppom, *Sweden* **10** 59 43N 12 10 E
Koprivnica, *Yugoslavia* **27** 46 12N 16 45 E
Kopychintsy, *U.S.S.R.* **36** 49 7N 25 58 E
Kopys, *U.S.S.R.* **36** 54 20N 30 17 E
Korab, *Yugoslavia* **35** 41 44N 20 40 E
Koraput, *India* **50** 18 50N 82 40 E
Korba, *India* **49** 22 20N 82 45 E
Korbach, *W. Germany* **30** 51 17N 8 50 E
Korbu, G., *Malaysia* **55** 4 41N 101 18 E
Korça, *Albania* **35** 40 37N 20 50 E
Korce = Korça, *Albania* **35** 40 37N 20 50 E
Korčula, *Yugoslavia* **27** 42 57N 17 8 E
Korčulanski Kanal, *Yugoslavia* **27** 43 3N 16 40 E
Kordestan, *Asia* **46** 35 30N 42 0 E
Kordestān □, *Iran* **46** 36 0N 47 0 E
Korea, North ■, *Asia* **61** 40 0N 127 0 E
Korea, South ■, *Asia* **61** 36 0N 128 0 E
Korea Strait, *Asia* **61** 34 0N 129 30 E
Koregaon, *India* **50** 17 40N 74 10 E
Korenevo, *U.S.S.R.* **36** 51 27N 34 55 E
Korenovsk, *U.S.S.R.* **39** 45 30N 39 22 E
Korets, *U.S.S.R.* **36** 50 40N 27 5 E
Korgus, *Sudan* **88** 19 16N 33 29 E
Korhogo, *Ivory C.* **90** 9 29N 5 28W
Koribundu, *S. Leone* **90** 7 41N 11 46W
Korim, *Indonesia* **57** 0 58 S 136 10 E
Korinthiakós Kólpos, *Greece* **35** 38 16N 22 30 E
Kórinthos, *Greece* **35** 37 56N 22 55 E
Korioumé, *Mali* **90** 16 35N 3 0W
Kōriyama, *Japan* **63** 37 24N 140 23 E
Körmend, *Hungary* **33** 47 5N 16 35 E
Kornat, *Yugoslavia* **27** 43 50N 15 20 E
Korneshty, *U.S.S.R.* **38** 47 21N 28 1 E
Kornsjø, *Norway* **10** 58 57N 11 39 E
Kornstad, *Norway* **10** 62 59N 7 27 E
Koro, *Fiji* **68** 17 19 S 179 23 E
Koro, *Ivory C.* **90** 8 32N 7 30W
Koro, *Mali* **90** 14 1N 2 58W
Koro Sea, *Fiji* **68** 17 30 S 179 45W
Koro Toro, *Chad* **87** 16 5N 18 30 E
Koroba, *Papua N. G.* **69** 5 44 S 142 47 E
Korocha, *U.S.S.R.* **37** 50 55N 37 30 E
Korogoro Pt., *Australia* **77** 31 3 S 153 4 E
Korogwe, *Tanzania* **92** 5 5 S 38 25 E
Korogwe □, *Tanzania* **92** 5 0 S 38 20 E
Koroit, *Australia* **74** 38 18 S 142 24 E
Korong Vale, *Australia* **74** 36 22 S 143 45 E
Koronowo, *Poland* **32** 53 19N 17 55 E
Koror, *Pac. Oc.* **57** 7 20N 134 28 E
Körös →, *Hungary* **33** 46 43N 20 12 E
Korosten, *U.S.S.R.* **36** 50 57N 28 25 E
Korotoyak, *U.S.S.R.* **37** 51 1N 39 2 E
Korraraika, Helodranon' i, *Madag.* **97** 17 45 S 43 57 E
Korsakov, *U.S.S.R.* **41** 46 36N 142 42 E
Korshunovo, *U.S.S.R.* **41** 58 37N 110 10 E
Korsör, *Denmark* **9** 55 20N 11 9 E
Korsun Shevchenkovskiy, *U.S.S.R.* **38** 49 26N 31 16 E
Korsze, *Poland* **32** 54 11N 21 9 E
Kortemark, *Belgium* **17** 51 2N 3 3 E
Kortessem, *Belgium* **17** 50 52N 5 23 E
Korti, *Sudan* **88** 18 6N 31 33 E
Kortrijk, *Belgium* **17** 50 50N 3 17 E
Korumburra, *Australia* **74** 38 26 S 145 50 E
Korwai, *India* **48** 24 7N 78 5 E
Koryakskiy Khrebet, *U.S.S.R.* **41** 61 0N 171 0 E
Kos, *Greece* **35** 36 50N 27 15 E
Kosa, *Ethiopia* **89** 7 50N 36 50 E
Kosaya Gora, *U.S.S.R.* **37** 54 10N 37 30 E
Kościan, *Poland* **32** 52 5N 16 40 E
Kościerzyna, *Poland* **32** 54 8N 17 59 E
Kosciusko, *U.S.A.* **121** 33 3N 89 34W
Kosciusko, Mt., *Australia* **75** 36 27 S 148 16 E
Kosciusko I., *U.S.A.* **110** 56 0N 133 40W
Kösély →, *Hungary* **33** 47 25N 21 5 E
Kosgi, *India* **50** 16 58N 77 43 E
Kosha, *Sudan* **88** 20 50N 30 30 E
Koshigaya, *Japan* **65** 35 54N 139 48 E
K'oshih = Kashi, *China* **62** 39 30N 76 2 E
Koshiki-Rettō, *Japan* **64** 31 45N 129 49 E
Koshkonong, L., *U.S.A.* **119** 42 53N 88 58W
Kōshoku, *Japan* **65** 36 38N 138 6 E
Kosi, *India* **48** 27 48N 77 29 E
Kosi-meer, *S. Africa* **97** 27 0 S 32 50 E
Košice, *Czech.* **32** 48 42N 21 15 E
Kosjerić, *Yugoslavia* **33** 44 0N 19 55 E
Kosŏng, *N. Korea* **61** 38 40N 128 22 E
Kosovska-Mitrovica, *Yugoslavia* **33** 42 54N 20 52 E
Kostajnica, *Yugoslavia* **27** 45 17N 16 30 E
Kostanjevica, *Yugoslavia* **27** 45 51N 15 27 E
Kostelec, *Czech.* **32** 50 14N 16 35 E
Koster, *S. Africa* **96** 25 52 S 26 54 E
Kôstî, *Sudan* **89** 13 8N 32 43 E
Kostopol, *U.S.S.R.* **36** 50 51N 26 22 E
Kostroma, *U.S.S.R.* **37** 57 50N 40 58 E
Kostromskoye Vdkhr., *U.S.S.R.* **37** 57 52N 40 49 E
Kostyukovichi, *U.S.S.R.* **36** 53 20N 32 4 E
Koszalin, *Poland* **32** 54 11N 16 8 E
Köszeg, *Hungary* **33** 47 23N 16 33 E
Kot Addu, *Pakistan* **48** 30 30N 71 0 E
Kot Moman, *Pakistan* **48** 32 13N 73 0 E
Kota, *India* **48** 25 14N 75 49 E
Kota Baharu, *Malaysia* **55** 6 7N 102 14 E
Kota Belud, *Malaysia* **56** 6 21N 116 26 E
Kota Kinabalu, *Malaysia* **56** 6 0N 116 4 E
Kota Tinggi, *Malaysia* **55** 1 44N 103 53 E
Kotaagung, *Indonesia* **56** 5 38 S 104 29 E
Kotabaru, *Indonesia* **56** 3 20 S 116 20 E
Kotabumi, *Indonesia* **56** 4 49 S 104 54 E
Kotagede, *Indonesia* **57** 7 54 S 110 26 E
Kotamobagu, *Indonesia* **57** 0 57N 124 31 E
Kotaneelee →, *Canada* **110** 60 11N 123 42W
Kotawaringin, *Indonesia* **56** 2 28 S 111 27 E
Kotchandpur, *Bangla.* **52** 23 24N 89 1 E
Kotcho L., *Canada* **110** 59 7N 121 12W
Kotelnich, *U.S.S.R.* **37** 58 20N 48 10 E
Kotelnikovo, *U.S.S.R.* **39** 47 38N 43 8 E
Kotelnyy, Ostrov, *U.S.S.R.* **41** 75 10N 139 0 E
Kothagudam, *India* **50** 17 30N 80 40 E
Kothapet, *India* **50** 19 21N 79 28 E
Köthen, *E. Germany* **30** 51 44N 11 59 E
Kothi, *India* **49** 24 45N 80 40 E
Kotiro, *Pakistan* **48** 26 17N 67 13 E
Kotka, *Finland* **9** 60 28N 26 58 E
Kotlas, *U.S.S.R.* **40** 61 15N 47 0 E
Kotli, *Pakistan* **48** 33 30N 73 55 E
Kotmul, *Pakistan* **49** 35 32N 75 10 E
Kotohira, *Japan* **64** 34 11N 133 49 E
Kotonkoro, *Nigeria* **91** 11 3N 5 58 E
Kotor, *Yugoslavia* **33** 42 25N 18 47 E
Kotoriba, *Yugoslavia* **27** 46 23N 16 48 E
Kotovo, *U.S.S.R.* **37** 50 22N 44 45 E
Kotovsk, *U.S.S.R.* **38** 47 45N 29 35 E
Kotputli, *India* **48** 27 43N 76 12 E
Kotri, *Pakistan* **48** 25 22N 68 22 E
Kotri →, *India* **50** 19 15N 80 35 E
Kótronas, *Greece* **35** 36 38N 22 29 E
Kottayam, *India* **51** 9 35N 76 33 E
Kottur, *India* **51** 10 34N 76 56 E
Kotuy →, *U.S.S.R.* **41** 71 54N 102 6 E
Kotzebue, *U.S.A.* **102** 66 50N 162 40W
Kouango, *C.A.R.* **94** 5 0N 20 10 E
Koudekerke, *Neths.* **17** 51 29N 3 33 E
Koudougou, *Burkina Faso* **90** 12 10N 2 20W
Koufonísi, *Greece* **35** 34 56N 26 8 E
Kougaberge, *S. Africa* **96** 33 48 S 23 50 E
Kouibli, *Ivory C.* **90** 7 15N 7 14W
Kouilou →, *Congo* **95** 4 10 S 12 5 E
Kouki, *C.A.R.* **94** 7 22N 17 3 E
Koula Moutou, *Gabon* **94** 1 15 S 12 25 E
Koulen, *Cambodia* **54** 13 50N 104 40 E
Koulikoro, *Mali* **90** 12 40N 7 50W
Koumac, *N. Cal.* **68** 20 33 S 164 17 E
Koumala, *Australia* **72** 21 38 S 149 15 E
Koumankou, *Mali* **90** 11 58N 6 6W
Koumbia, *Burkina Faso* **90** 11 10N 3 50W
Koumbia, *Guinea* **90** 11 48N 13 29W

Kungala

Koumboum, *Guinea* **90** 10 25N 13 0W
Koumpenntoum, *Senegal* **90** 13 59N 14 34W
Koumra, *Chad* **87** 8 50N 17 35 E
Koundara, *Guinea* **90** 12 29N 13 18W
Koundé, *C.A.R.* **94** 6 7N 14 38 E
Kounradskiy, *U.S.S.R.* **40** 46 59N 75 0 E
Kountze, *U.S.A.* **121** 30 20N 94 22W
Koupéla, *Burkina Faso* **91** 12 11N 0 21W
Kourizo, Passe de, *Chad* **86** 22 28N 15 27 E
Kourou, *Fr. Guiana* **135** 5 9N 52 39W
Kouroussa, *Guinea* **90** 10 45N 9 45W
Koussané, *Mali* **90** 14 53N 11 14W
Kousseri, *Cameroon* **87** 12 0N 14 55 E
Koutiala, *Mali* **90** 12 25N 5 23W
Kouto, *Ivory C.* **90** 9 53N 6 25W
Kouts, *U.S.A.* **119** 41 18N 87 2W
Kouvé, *Togo* **91** 6 25N 1 25 E
Kovačica, *Yugoslavia* **33** 45 5N 20 38 E
Kovel, *U.S.S.R.* **36** 51 10N 24 20 E
Kovilpatti, *India* **51** 9 10N 77 50 E
Kovin, *Yugoslavia* **33** 44 44N 20 59 E
Kovrov, *U.S.S.R.* **37** 56 25N 41 25 E
Kovur, *Andhra Pradesh, India* **50** 17 3N 81 39 E
Kovur, *Andhra Pradesh, India* **51** 14 30N 80 1 E
Kowkash, *Canada* **104** 50 20N 87 12W
Kowloon, *H.K.* **59** 22 20N 114 15 E
Koyabuti, *Indonesia* **57** 2 36 S 140 37 E
Kōyama, *Japan* **64** 31 20N 130 56 E
Koyuk, *U.S.A.* **102** 64 55N 161 20W
Koyukuk →, *U.S.A.* **102** 64 56N 157 30W
Koyulhisar, *Turkey* **38** 40 20N 37 52 E
Kozan, *Turkey* **46** 37 35N 35 50 E
Kozáni, *Greece* **35** 40 19N 21 47 E
Kozara, *Yugoslavia* **27** 45 0N 17 0 E
Kozarac, *Yugoslavia* **27** 44 58N 16 48 E
Kozelsk, *U.S.S.R.* **36** 54 2N 35 48 E
Kozhikode = Calicut, *India* **51** 11 15N 75 43 E
Kozje, *Yugoslavia* **27** 46 5N 15 35 E
Kozlovets, *Bulgaria* **34** 43 30N 25 20 E
Koźmin, *Poland* **32** 51 48N 17 27 E
Kozmodemyansk, *U.S.S.R.* **37** 56 20N 46 36 E
Kōzu-Shima, *Japan* **65** 34 13N 139 10 E
Kpabia, *Ghana* **91** 9 10N 0 20W
Kpalimé, *Togo* **91** 6 57N 0 44 E
Kpandae, *Ghana* **91** 8 30N 0 2W
Kpessi, *Togo* **91** 8 4N 1 16 E
Kra, Isthmus of = Kra, Kho Khot, *Thailand* **55** 10 15N 99 30 E
Kra, Kho Khot, *Thailand* **55** 10 15N 99 30 E
Kra Buri, *Thailand* **55** 10 22N 98 46 E
Krabbendijke, *Neths.* **17** 51 26N 4 7 E
Krabi, *Thailand* **55** 8 4N 98 55 E
Kragan, *Indonesia* **57** 6 43 S 111 38 E
Kragerø, *Norway* **10** 58 52N 9 25 E
Kragujevac, *Yugoslavia* **33** 44 2N 20 56 E
Krakatau = Rakata, Pulau, *Indonesia* **56** 6 10 S 105 20 E
Krakor, *Cambodia* **54** 12 32N 104 12 E
Kraków, *Poland* **32** 50 4N 19 57 E
Kraksaan, *Indonesia* **57** 7 43 S 113 23 E
Kråkstad, *Norway* **10** 59 39N 10 55 E
Kralanh, *Cambodia* **54** 13 35N 103 25 E
Králiky, *Czech.* **32** 50 6N 16 45 E
Kraljevo, *Yugoslavia* **33** 43 44N 20 41 E
Kralovice, *Czech.* **32** 49 59N 13 29 E
Kralupy, *Czech.* **32** 50 13N 14 20 E
Kramatorsk, *U.S.S.R.* **38** 48 50N 37 30 E
Krambach, *Australia* **77** 32 4 S 152 16 E
Kramfors, *Sweden* **10** 62 55N 17 48 E
Kramis, C., *Algeria* **85** 36 26N 0 45 E
Krångede, *Sweden* **10** 63 9N 16 10 E
Kranj, *Yugoslavia* **27** 46 16N 14 22 E
Kranjska Gora, *Yugoslavia* **27** 46 29N 13 48 E
Krankskop, *S. Africa* **97** 28 0 S 30 47 E
Krapina, *Yugoslavia* **27** 46 10N 15 52 E
Krapina →, *Yugoslavia* **27** 45 50N 15 50 E
Krapivna, *U.S.S.R.* **37** 53 58N 37 10 E
Krapkowice, *Poland* **32** 50 29N 17 56 E
Kraskino, *U.S.S.R.* **41** 42 44N 130 48 E
Kraslice, *Czech.* **32** 50 19N 12 31 E
Krasnaya Gorbatka, *U.S.S.R.* **37** 55 52N 41 45 E
Krasnaya Polyana, *U.S.S.R.* **39** 43 40N 40 13 E
Kraśnik, *Poland* **32** 50 55N 22 5 E
Kraśnik Fabryczny, *Poland* **32** 50 58N 22 11 E
Krasnoarmeisk, *U.S.S.R.* **38** 48 18N 37 11 E
Krasnoarmeysk, *R.S.F.S.R., U.S.S.R.* **37** 51 0N 45 42 E
Krasnoarmeysk, *R.S.F.S.R., U.S.S.R.* **39** 48 30N 44 25 E
Krasnodar, *U.S.S.R.* **39** 45 5N 39 0 E
Krasnodon, *U.S.S.R.* **39** 48 17N 39 44 E
Krasnodonetskaya, *U.S.S.R.* **39** 48 5N 40 50 E
Krasnogorskiy, *U.S.S.R.* **37** 56 10N 48 28 E
Krasnograd, *U.S.S.R.* **38** 49 27N 35 27 E
Krasnogvardeyskoye, *U.S.S.R.* **39** 45 52N 41 33 E
Krasnogvardyesk, *U.S.S.R.* **38** 45 32N 34 16 E
Krasnokutsk, *U.S.S.R.* **36** 50 10N 34 50 E
Krasnoperekopsk, *U.S.S.R.* **38** 46 0N 33 54 E
Krasnoselkupsk, *U.S.S.R.* **40** 65 20N 82 10 E
Krasnoslobodsk, *R.S.F.S.R., U.S.S.R.* **37** 54 25N 43 45 E
Krasnoslobodsk, *R.S.F.S.R., U.S.S.R.* **39** 48 42N 44 33 E
Krasnoturinsk, *U.S.S.R.* **40** 59 46N 60 12 E
Krasnoufimsk, *U.S.S.R.* **40** 56 57N 57 46 E
Krasnouralsk, *U.S.S.R.* **40** 58 21N 60 3 E
Krasnovodsk, *U.S.S.R.* **40** 40 0N 52 52 E
Krasnoyarsk, *U.S.S.R.* **41** 56 8N 93 0 E
Krasnoye = Krasnyy, *U.S.S.R.* **36** 54 25N 31 30 E
Krasnoye, *Kalmyk A.S.S.R., U.S.S.R.* **39** 46 16N 45 0 E
Krasnoye, *R.S.F.S.R., U.S.S.R.* **37** 59 15N 47 40 E
Krasnozavodsk, *U.S.S.R.* **37** 56 27N 38 25 E
Krasny Liman, *U.S.S.R.* **38** 48 58N 37 50 E
Krasny Sulin, *U.S.S.R.* **39** 47 52N 40 8 E
Krasnystaw, *Poland* **32** 50 57N 23 5 E
Krasnyy, *U.S.S.R.* **36** 54 25N 31 30 E
Krasnyy Kholm, *U.S.S.R.* **37** 58 10N 37 10 E
Krasnyy Kut, *U.S.S.R.* **37** 50 50N 47 0 E
Krasnyy Luch, *U.S.S.R.* **39** 48 13N 39 0 E
Krasnyy Profintern, *U.S.S.R.* **37** 57 45N 40 27 E
Krasnyy Yar, *Kalmyk A.S.S.R., U.S.S.R.* **39** 46 43N 48 23 E
Krasnyy Yar, *R.S.F.S.R., U.S.S.R.* **37** 53 30N 50 22 E
Krasnyy Yar, *R.S.F.S.R., U.S.S.R.* **37** 50 42N 44 45 E
Krasnyye Baki, *U.S.S.R.* **37** 57 8N 45 10 E
Krasnyyoskolskoye Vdkhr., *U.S.S.R.* **38** 49 30N 37 30 E
Kraszna →, *Hungary* **33** 48 0N 22 20 E
Kratie, *Cambodia* **54** 12 32N 106 10 E
Kratke Ra., *Papua N. G.* **69** 6 45 S 146 0 E
Krau, *Indonesia* **57** 3 19 S 140 5 E
Kravanh, Chuor Phnum, *Cambodia* **55** 12 0N 103 32 E
Krawang, *Indonesia* **57** 6 19N 107 18 E
Krefeld, *W. Germany* **30** 51 20N 6 32 E
Krémaston, Límni, *Greece* **35** 38 52N 21 30 E
Kremenchug, *U.S.S.R.* **38** 49 5N 33 25 E
Kremenchugskoye Vdkhr., *U.S.S.R.* **38** 49 20N 32 30 E
Kremenets, *U.S.S.R.* **38** 50 8N 25 43 E
Kremennaya, *U.S.S.R.* **38** 49 1N 38 10 E
Kremges = Svetlovodsk, *U.S.S.R.* **36** 49 2N 33 13 E
Kremikovtsi, *Bulgaria* **34** 42 46N 23 28 E
Kremmen, *E. Germany* **30** 52 45N 13 1 E
Kremmling, *U.S.A.* **122** 40 10N 106 30W
Krems, *Austria* **33** 48 25N 15 36 E
Kremsmünster, *Austria* **33** 48 3N 14 8 E
Kretinga, *U.S.S.R.* **36** 55 53N 21 15 E
Krettamia, *Algeria* **84** 28 47N 3 27W
Krettsy, *U.S.S.R.* **36** 58 15N 32 30 E
Kreuzberg, *W. Germany* **31** 50 22N 9 58 E
Kribi, *Cameroon* **91** 2 57N 9 56 E
Krichem, *Bulgaria* **34** 42 8N 24 28 E
Krichev, *U.S.S.R.* **36** 53 45N 31 50 E
Krim, *Yugoslavia* **27** 45 53N 14 30 E
Krimpen, *Neths.* **16** 51 55N 4 34 E
Krishna →, *India* **50** 15 57N 80 59 E
Krishnagiri, *India* **51** 12 32N 78 16 E
Krishnanagar, *India* **49** 23 24N 88 33 E
Krishnaraja Sagara, *India* **51** 12 20N 76 30 E
Kristiansand, *Norway* **9** 58 9N 8 1 E
Kristianstad, *Sweden* **11** 56 2N 14 9 E
Kristianstads län □, *Sweden* **9** 56 15N 14 0 E
Kristiansund, *Norway* **10** 63 7N 7 45 E
Kristiinankaupunki, *Finland* **8** 62 16N 21 21 E
Kristinehamn, *Sweden* **10** 59 18N 14 13 E
Kristinestad, *Finland* **8** 62 16N 21 21 E
Kríti, *Greece* **35** 35 15N 25 0 E
Kriva →, *Yugoslavia* **34** 42 5N 21 47 E
Kriva Palanka, *Yugoslavia* **34** 42 11N 22 19 E
Krivaja →, *Yugoslavia* **33** 44 27N 18 9 E
Krivoy Rog, *U.S.S.R.* **38** 47 51N 33 20 E
Križevci, *Yugoslavia* **27** 46 3N 16 32 E
Krk, *Yugoslavia* **27** 45 8N 14 40 E
Krka →, *Yugoslavia* **27** 45 50N 15 30 E
Krkonoše, *Czech.* **32** 50 50N 15 35 E
Krnov, *Czech.* **32** 50 5N 17 40 E
Krobia, *Poland* **32** 51 47N 16 59 E
Krokeaí, *Greece* **35** 36 53N 22 32 E
Krokodil →, *Mozam.* **97** 25 14 S 32 18 E
Krokom, *Sweden* **10** 63 20N 14 30 E
Krolevets, *U.S.S.R.* **36** 51 35N 33 20 E
Kroměříz, *Czech.* **32** 49 18N 17 21 E
Krommenie, *Neths.* **16** 52 30N 4 46 E
Kromy, *U.S.S.R.* **36** 52 48N 35 48 E
Kronach, *W. Germany* **31** 50 14N 11 19 E
Kronobergs län □, *Sweden* **11** 56 45N 14 30 E
Kronprins Olav Kyst, *Antarctica* **143** 69 0 S 42 0 E
Kronprinsesse Märtha Kyst, *Antarctica* **143** 73 30 S 10 0 E
Kronshtadt, *U.S.S.R.* **36** 60 5N 29 45 E
Kroonstad, *S. Africa* **96** 27 43 S 27 19 E
Kröpelin, *E. Germany* **30** 54 4N 11 48 E
Kropotkin, *R.S.F.S.R., U.S.S.R.* **39** 45 28N 40 28 E
Kropotkin, *R.S.F.S.R., U.S.S.R.* **41** 59 0N 115 30 E
Kropp, *W. Germany* **30** 54 24N 9 32 E
Krościenko, *Poland* **32** 49 29N 20 25 E
Krosno, *Poland* **32** 49 42N 21 46 E
Krosno Odrzańskie, *Poland* **32** 52 3N 15 7 E
Krotoszyn, *Poland* **32** 51 42N 17 23 E
Krško, *Yugoslavia* **27** 45 57N 15 30 E
Kruger Nat. Park, *S. Africa* **97** 23 30 S 31 40 E
Krugersdorp, *S. Africa* **97** 26 5 S 27 46 E
Kruiningen, *Neths.* **17** 51 27N 4 2 E
Kruisfontein, *S. Africa* **96** 33 59 S 24 43 E
Kruishoutem, *Belgium* **17** 50 54N 3 32 E
Kruisland, *Neths.* **17** 51 34N 4 25 E
Kruja, *Albania* **35** 41 32N 19 46 E
Krulevshchina, *U.S.S.R.* **36** 55 5N 27 45 E
Kruma, *Albania* **34** 42 14N 20 28 E
Krumbach, *W. Germany* **31** 48 15N 10 22 E
Krung Thep = Bangkok, *Thailand* **54** 13 45N 100 35 E
Krupanj, *Yugoslavia* **33** 44 25N 19 22 E
Krupinica →, *Czech.* **33** 48 15N 18 52 E
Kruševac, *Yugoslavia* **33** 43 35N 21 28 E
Kruzof I., *U.S.A.* **110** 57 10N 135 40W
Krylbo, *Sweden* **10** 60 7N 16 15 E
Krymsk Abinsk, *U.S.S.R.* **38** 44 50N 38 0 E
Krymskiy Poluostrov, *U.S.S.R.* **38** 45 0N 34 0 E
Krynica Morska, *Poland* **32** 54 23N 19 28 E
Krynki, *Poland* **32** 53 17N 23 43 E
Krzywiń, *Poland* **32** 51 58N 16 50 E
Krzyz, *Poland* **32** 52 52N 16 0 E
Ksabi, *Morocco* **84** 32 51N 4 13W
Ksar Chellala, *Algeria* **85** 35 13N 2 19 E
Ksar el Boukhari, *Algeria* **85** 35 51N 2 52 E
Ksar el Kebir, *Morocco* **84** 35 0N 6 0W
Ksar es Souk = Ar Rachidiya, *Morocco* **84** 31 58N 4 20W
Ksar Rhilane, *Tunisia* **86** 33 0N 9 39 E
Ksour, Mts. des, *Algeria* **85** 32 45N 0 30W
Kstovo, *U.S.S.R.* **37** 56 12N 44 13 E
Kuala, *Indonesia* **56** 2 55N 105 47 E
Kuala Berang, *Malaysia* **55** 5 5N 103 1 E
Kuala Dungun, *Malaysia* **55** 4 45N 103 25 E
Kuala Kangsar, *Malaysia* **55** 4 46N 100 56 E
Kuala Kelawang, *Malaysia* **55** 2 56N 102 5 E
Kuala Kerai, *Malaysia* **55** 5 30N 102 12 E
Kuala Kubu Baharu, *Malaysia* **55** 3 34N 101 39 E
Kuala Lipis, *Malaysia* **55** 4 10N 102 3 E
Kuala Lumpur, *Malaysia* **55** 3 9N 101 41 E
Kuala Nerang, *Malaysia* **55** 6 16N 100 37 E
Kuala Pilah, *Malaysia* **55** 2 45N 102 15 E
Kuala Rompin, *Malaysia* **55** 2 49N 103 29 E
Kuala Selangor, *Malaysia* **55** 3 20N 101 15 E
Kuala Trengganu, *Malaysia* **55** 5 20N 103 8 E
Kualajelai, *Indonesia* **56** 2 58 S 110 46 E
Kualakapuas, *Indonesia* **56** 2 55 S 114 20 E
Kualakurun, *Indonesia* **56** 1 10 S 113 50 E
Kualapembuang, *Indonesia* **56** 3 14 S 112 38 E
Kualasimpang, *Indonesia* **56** 4 17N 98 3 E
Kuancheng, *China* **61** 40 37N 118 30 E
Kuandang, *Indonesia* **57** 0 56N 123 1 E
Kuandian, *China* **61** 40 45N 124 45 E
Kuangchou = Guangzhou, *China* **59** 23 5N 113 10 E
Kuantan, *Malaysia* **55** 3 49N 103 20 E
Kuba, *U.S.S.R.* **39** 41 21N 48 32 E
Kuban →, *U.S.S.R.* **39** 45 20N 37 30 E
Kubenskoye, Oz., *U.S.S.R.* **37** 59 40N 39 25 E
Kuberle, *U.S.S.R.* **39** 47 0N 42 20 E
Kubokawa, *Japan* **64** 33 12N 133 8 E
Kubor, Mt., *Papua N. G.* **69** 6 10 S 144 44 E
Kubrat, *Bulgaria* **34** 43 49N 26 31 E
Kučevo, *Yugoslavia* **33** 44 30N 21 40 E
Kucha Gompa, *India* **49** 34 25N 76 56 E
Kuchaman, *India* **48** 27 13N 74 47 E
Kuchinotsu, *Japan* **64** 32 36N 130 11 E
Kucing, *Malaysia* **56** 1 33N 110 25 E
Kuçove = Qytet Stalin, *Albania* **35** 40 47N 19 57 E
Kud →, *Pakistan* **48** 26 5N 66 20 E
Kudalier →, *India* **50** 18 35N 79 48 E
Kudamatsu, *Japan* **64** 34 0N 131 52 E
Kudat, *Malaysia* **56** 6 55N 116 55 E
Kudremukh, Mt., *India* **51** 13 15N 75 20 E
Kudus, *Indonesia* **57** 6 48 S 110 51 E
Kudymkar, *U.S.S.R.* **40** 59 1N 54 39 E
Kueiyang = Guiyang, *China* **58** 26 32N 106 40 E
Kufrinjah, *Jordan* **44** 32 20N 35 41 E
Kufstein, *Austria* **31** 47 35N 12 11 E
Kugong I., *Canada* **104** 56 18N 79 50W
Kūh-e 'Alījūq, *Iran* **47** 31 30N 51 41 E
Kūh-e Dīnār, *Iran* **47** 30 40N 51 0 E
Kūh-e-Hazārām, *Iran* **47** 29 35N 57 20 E
Kūh-e-Jebāl Bārez, *Iran* **47** 29 0N 58 0 E
Kūh-e Sorkh, *Iran* **47** 35 30N 58 45 E
Kūh-e Taftān, *Iran* **47** 28 40N 61 0 E
Kūhak, *Iran* **47** 27 12N 63 10 E
Kūhhā-ye-Bashākerd, *Iran* **47** 26 45N 59 0 E
Kūhhā-ye Sabalān, *Iran* **46** 38 15N 47 45 E
Kuhnsdorf, *Austria* **33** 46 37N 14 38 E
Kūhpāyeh, *Iran* **47** 32 44N 52 20 E
Kui Buri, *Thailand* **55** 12 3N 99 52 E
Kuinre, *Neths.* **16** 52 47N 5 51 E
Kuito, *Angola* **95** 12 22 S 16 55 E
Kuji, *Japan* **63** 40 11N 141 46 E
Kujū-San, *Japan* **64** 33 5N 131 15 E
Kujukuri-Heiya, *Japan* **65** 35 45N 140 30 E
Kukawa, *Nigeria* **91** 12 58N 13 27 E
Kukerin, *Australia* **79** 33 13 S 118 0 E
Kukmor, *U.S.S.R.* **37** 56 11N 50 54 E
Kukup, *Malaysia* **55** 1 20N 103 27 E
Kukvidze, *U.S.S.R.* **37** 50 40N 43 15 E
Kula, *Yugoslavia* **33** 45 37N 19 32 E
Kula Gulf, *Solomon Is.* **68** 8 5 S 157 18 E
Kulai, *Malaysia* **55** 1 44N 103 35 E
Kulal, Mt., *Kenya* **92** 2 42N 36 57 E
Kulaly, Os., *U.S.S.R.* **39** 45 0N 50 0 E
Kulasekarappattinam, *India* **51** 8 20N 78 0 E
Kuldiga, *U.S.S.R.* **36** 56 58N 21 59 E
Kuldja = Yining, *China* **62** 43 58N 81 10 E
Kuldu, *Sudan* **89** 12 50N 28 30 E
Kulebaki, *U.S.S.R.* **37** 55 22N 42 25 E
Kulen Vakuf, *Yugoslavia* **27** 44 35N 16 2 E
Kulgam, *India* **49** 33 36N 75 2 E
Kuli, *U.S.S.R.* **39** 42 2N 47 12 E
Kulim, *Malaysia* **55** 5 22N 100 34 E
Kulin, *Australia* **79** 32 40 S 118 2 E
Kulja, *Australia* **79** 30 28 S 117 18 E
Kulm, *U.S.A.* **120** 46 22N 98 58W
Kulmbach, *W. Germany* **31** 50 6N 11 27 E
Kulsary, *U.S.S.R.* **40** 46 59N 54 1 E
Kultay, *U.S.S.R.* **39** 45 5N 51 40 E
Kulti, *India* **49** 23 43N 86 50 E
Kulumbura, *Australia* **78** 13 55 S 126 35 E
Kulunda, *U.S.S.R.* **40** 52 35N 78 57 E
Kulungar, *Afghan.* **48** 34 0N 69 2 E
Kulwin, *Australia* **74** 35 0 S 142 42 E
Kulyab, *U.S.S.R.* **40** 37 55N 69 50 E
Kum Tekei, *U.S.S.R.* **40** 43 10N 79 30 E
Kuma, *Japan* **64** 33 39N 132 54 E
Kuma →, *U.S.S.R.* **39** 44 55N 47 0 E
Kumaganum, *Nigeria* **91** 13 8N 10 38 E
Kumagaya, *Japan* **65** 36 9N 139 22 E
Kumai, *Indonesia* **56** 2 44 S 111 43 E
Kumamba, Kepulauan, *Indonesia* **57** 1 36 S 138 45 E
Kumamoto, *Japan* **64** 32 45N 130 45 E
Kumamoto □, *Japan* **64** 32 55N 130 55 E
Kumano, *Japan* **65** 33 54N 136 5 E
Kumano-Nada, *Japan* **65** 33 47N 136 20 E
Kumanovo, *Yugoslavia* **34** 42 9N 21 42 E
Kumara, *N.Z.* **81** 42 37 S 171 12 E
Kumarkhali, *Bangla.* **52** 23 51N 89 15 E
Kumarl, *Australia* **79** 32 47 S 121 33 E
Kumasi, *Ghana* **90** 6 41N 1 38W
Kumba, *Cameroon* **91** 4 36N 9 24 E
Kumbakonam, *India* **51** 10 58N 79 25 E
Kumbarilla, *Australia* **77** 27 15 S 150 55 E
Kumbo, *Cameroon* **91** 6 15N 10 36 E
Kumbukkan Oya →, *Sri Lanka* **51** 6 35N 81 40 E
Kumdok, *India* **49** 33 32N 78 10 E
Kumeny, *U.S.S.R.* **37** 58 10N 49 47 E
Kumi, *Uganda* **92** 1 30N 33 58 E
Kumla, *Sweden* **10** 59 8N 15 10 E
Kummerower See, *E. Germany* **30** 53 47N 12 52 E
Kumo, *Nigeria* **91** 10 1N 11 12 E
Kumon Bum, *Burma* **52** 26 30N 97 15 E
Kumotori-Yama, *Japan* **65** 35 51N 138 57 E
Kumta, *India* **51** 14 29N 74 25 E
Kumtorkala, *U.S.S.R.* **39** 43 2N 46 50 E
Kumusi →, *Papua N. G.* **69** 8 16 S 148 13 E
Kumylzhenskaya, *U.S.S.R.* **39** 49 51N 42 38 E
Kunama, *Australia* **76** 35 35 S 148 4 E
Kunashir, Ostrov, *U.S.S.R.* **41** 44 0N 146 0 E
Kunda, *U.S.S.R.* **36** 59 30N 26 34 E
Kundiawa, *Papua N. G.* **69** 6 2 S 145 1 E
Kundip, *Australia* **79** 33 42 S 120 10 E
Kundla, *India* **48** 21 21N 71 25 E
Kungala, *Australia* **77** 29 58 S 153 7 E

Kungälv

Kungälv, *Sweden* **11** 57 53N 11 59 E
Kunghit I., *Canada* **110** 52 6N 131 3W
Kungrad, *U.S.S.R.* **40** 43 6N 58 54 E
Kungsbacka, *Sweden* **11** 57 30N 12 5 E
Kungu, *Zaïre* **94** 2 47N 19 12 E
Kungur, *U.S.S.R.* **40** 57 25N 56 57 E
Kungurri, *Australia* **72** 21 3 S 148 46 E
Kungyangon, *Burma* **52** 16 27N 96 20 E
Kunhar →, *Pakistan* **49** 34 20N 73 30 E
Kunhegyes, *Hungary* **33** 47 22N 20 36 E
Kunimi-Dake, *Japan* **64** 32 33N 131 1 E
Kuningan, *Indonesia* **57** 6 59 S 108 29 E
Kunisaki, *Japan* **64** 33 33N 131 45 E
Kunlong, *Burma* **52** 23 20N 98 50 E
Kunlun Shan, *Asia* **62** 36 0N 86 30 E
Kunming, *China* **58** 25 1N 102 41 E
Kunnamkulam, *India* **51** 10 38N 76 7 E
Kunrade, *Neths.* **17** 50 53N 5 57 E
Kunsan, *S. Korea* **61** 35 59N 126 45 E
Kunshan, *China* **59** 31 22N 120 58 E
Kununurra, *Australia* **78** 15 40 S 128 50 E
Kunwarara, *Australia* **72** 22 55 S 150 9 E
Kunya-Urgench, *U.S.S.R.* **40** 42 19N 59 10 E
Künzelsau, *W. Germany* **31** 49 17N 9 41 E
Kuopio, *Finland* **8** 62 53N 27 35 E
Kuopion lääni □, *Finland* **8** 63 25N 27 10 E
Kupa →, *Yugoslavia* **27** 45 28N 16 24 E
Kupang, *Indonesia* **57** 10 19 S 123 39 E
Kupiano, *Papua N. G.* **69** 10 4 S 148 14 E
Kupres, *Yugoslavia* **33** 44 1N 17 15 E
Kupyansk, *U.S.S.R.* **38** 49 52N 37 35 E
Kupyansk-Uzlovoi, *U.S.S.R.* **38** 49 45N 37 34 E
Kuqa, *China* **62** 41 35N 82 30 E
Kur →, *Bhutan* **52** 26 50N 91 0 E
Kura →, *U.S.S.R.* **39** 39 50N 49 20 E
Kurahashi-Jima, *Japan* **64** 34 8N 132 31 E
Kuranda, *Australia* **72** 16 48 S 145 35 E
Kurashiki, *Japan* **64** 34 40N 133 50 E
Kurayoshi, *Japan* **64** 35 26N 133 50 E
Kurduvadi, *India* **50** 18 8N 75 29 E
Kŭrdzhali, *Bulgaria* **35** 41 38N 25 21 E
Kure, *Japan* **64** 34 14N 132 32 E
Kuressaare = Kingisepp, *U.S.S.R.* **36** 58 15N 22 30 E
Kurgaldzhino, *U.S.S.R.* **40** 50 35N 70 20 E
Kurgan, *U.S.S.R.* **40** 55 26N 65 18 E
Kurganinsk, *U.S.S.R.* **39** 44 54N 40 34 E
Kurgannaya = Kurganinsk, *U.S.S.R.* **39** 44 54N 40 34 E
Kuria Maria Is. = Khūrīyā Mūrīyā, Jazā 'ir, *Oman* **45** 17 30N 55 58 E
Kurichchi, *India* **51** 11 36N 77 35 E
Kuridala, *Australia* **72** 21 16 S 140 29 E
Kurigram, *Bangla.* **52** 25 49N 89 39 E
Kurihashi, *Japan* **65** 36 8N 139 42 E
Kuril Is. = Kurilskiye Ostrova, *U.S.S.R.* **41** 45 0N 150 0 E
Kuril Trench, *Pac. Oc.* **66** 44 0N 153 0 E
Kurilsk, *U.S.S.R.* **41** 45 14N 147 53 E
Kurilskiye Ostrova, *U.S.S.R.* **41** 45 0N 150 0 E
Kuringen, *Belgium* **17** 50 56N 5 18 E
Kurino, *Japan* **64** 31 57N 130 43 E
Kurkur, *Egypt* **88** 23 50N 32 0 E
Kurkūrah, *Libya* **86** 31 30N 20 1 E
Kurla, *India* **50** 19 5N 72 52 E
Kurlovskiy, *U.S.S.R.* **37** 55 25N 40 40 E
Kurmuk, *Sudan* **89** 10 33N 34 21 E
Kurnool, *India* **51** 15 45N 78 0 E
Kurobe-Gawe →, *Japan* **65** 36 55N 137 25 E
Kurogi, *Japan* **64** 33 12N 130 40 E
Kurovskoye, *U.S.S.R.* **37** 55 35N 38 55 E
Kurow, *N.Z.* **81** 44 44 S 170 29 E
Kurrajong, *Australia* **76** 33 33 S 150 42 E
Kurram →, *Pakistan* **48** 32 36N 71 20 E
Kurri Kurri, *Australia* **76** 32 50 S 151 28 E
Kursavka, *U.S.S.R.* **39** 44 29N 42 32 E
Kuršenai, *U.S.S.R.* **36** 56 1N 23 3 E
Kursk, *U.S.S.R.* **37** 51 42N 36 11 E
Kuršumlija, *Yugoslavia* **33** 43 9N 21 19 E
Kuru, Bahr el →, *Sudan* **89** 8 10N 26 50 E
Kuruktag, *China* **62** 41 0N 89 0 E
Kuruman, *S. Africa* **96** 27 28 S 23 28 E
Kuruman →, *S. Africa* **96** 26 56 S 20 39 E
Kurumbul →, *Australia* **77** 28 38 S 150 35 E
Kurume, *Japan* **64** 33 15N 130 30 E
Kurunegala, *Sri Lanka* **51** 7 30N 80 23 E
Kurupukari, *Guyana* **135** 4 43N 58 37W
Kurya, *U.S.S.R.* **41** 61 15N 108 10 E
Kusatsu, *Gumma, Japan* **65** 36 37N 138 36 E
Kusatsu, *Shiga, Japan* **65** 34 58N 135 57 E
Kusawa L., *Canada* **110** 60 20N 136 13W
Kusel, *W. Germany* **31** 49 31N 7 25 E
Kushchevskaya, *U.S.S.R.* **39** 46 33N 39 35 E
Kushikino, *Japan* **64** 31 44N 130 16 E
Kushima, *Japan* **64** 31 29N 131 14 E
Kushimoto, *Japan* **65** 33 28N 135 47 E
Kushiro, *Japan* **63** 43 0N 144 25 E
Kushiro →, *Japan* **63** 42 59N 144 23 E
Kushka, *U.S.S.R.* **40** 35 20N 62 18 E
Kushol, *India* **49** 33 40N 76 36 E
Kushtia, *Bangla.* **52** 23 55N 89 5 E
Kushum →, *U.S.S.R.* **39** 49 0N 50 20 E
Kuskokwim →, *U.S.A.* **102** 60 17N 162 27W
Kuskokwim Bay, *U.S.A.* **102** 59 50N 162 56W
Kustanay, *U.S.S.R.* **40** 53 10N 63 35 E
Kusu, *Japan* **64** 33 16N 131 9 E
Kut, Ko, *Thailand* **55** 11 40N 102 35 E
Kütahya, *Turkey* **46** 39 30N 30 2 E
Kutaisi, *U.S.S.R.* **39** 42 19N 42 40 E
Kutaraja = Banda Aceh, *Indonesia* **56** 5 35N 95 20 E
Kutch, Gulf of = Kachchh, Gulf of, *India* **48** 22 50N 69 15 E
Kutch, Rann of = Kachchh, Rann of, *India* **48** 24 0N 70 0 E
Kutina, *Yugoslavia* **27** 45 29N 16 48 E
Kutiyana, *India* **48** 21 36N 70 2 E
Kutkai, *Burma* **52** 23 27N 97 56 E
Kutkashen, *U.S.S.R.* **39** 40 58N 47 47 E
Kutná Hora, *Czech.* **32** 49 57N 15 16 E
Kutno, *Poland* **32** 52 15N 19 23 E
Kuttabul, *Australia* **72** 21 5 S 148 48 E
Kutu, *Zaïre* **94** 2 40 S 18 11 E
Kutum, *Sudan* **89** 14 10N 24 40 E
Kuujjuaq, *Canada* **103** 58 6N 68 15W
Kuurne, *Belgium* **17** 50 51N 3 18 E
Kuvango, *Angola* **95** 14 28 S 16 20 E
Kuvshinovo, *U.S.S.R.* **36** 57 2N 34 11 E
Kuwait = Al Kuwayt, *Kuwait* **46** 29 30N 48 0 E
Kuwait ■, *Si. Arabia* **46** 29 30N 47 30 E
Kuwana, *Japan* **65** 35 0N 136 43 E
Kuybyshev, *R.S.F.S.R., U.S.S.R.* **37** 53 8N 50 6 E
Kuybyshev, *R.S.F.S.R., U.S.S.R.* **40** 55 27N 78 19 E
Kuybyshevo, *U.S.S.R.* **38** 47 25N 36 40 E
Kuybyshevskoye Vdkhr., *U.S.S.R.* **37** 55 2N 49 30 E
Kuye He →, *China* **60** 38 23N 110 46 E
Kūysanjaq, *Iraq* **46** 36 5N 44 38 E
Kuyumba, *U.S.S.R.* **41** 60 58N 96 59 E
Kuzey Anadolu Dağlari, *Turkey* **46** 41 30N 35 0 E
Kuzhitturai, *India* **51** 8 18N 77 11 E
Kuznetsk, *U.S.S.R.* **37** 53 12N 46 40 E
Kvænangen, *Norway* **8** 70 5N 21 15 E
Kvam, *Norway* **10** 61 40N 9 42 E
Kvareli, *U.S.S.R.* **39** 41 27N 45 47 E
Kvarner, *Yugoslavia* **27** 44 50N 14 10 E
Kvarnerič, *Yugoslavia* **27** 44 43N 14 37 E
Kvillsfors, *Sweden* **11** 57 24N 15 29 E
Kviteseid, *Norway* **10** 59 24N 8 29 E
Kwabhaca, *S. Africa* **97** 30 51 S 29 0 E
Kwadacha →, *Canada* **110** 57 28N 125 38W
Kwakhanai, *Botswana* **96** 21 39 S 21 16 E
Kwakoegron, *Surinam* **135** 5 12N 55 25W
Kwale, *Kenya* **92** 4 15 S 39 31 E
Kwale, *Nigeria* **91** 5 46N 6 26 E
Kwale □, *Kenya* **92** 4 15 S 39 10 E
KwaMashu, *S. Africa* **97** 29 45 S 30 58 E
Kwamouth, *Zaïre* **94** 3 9 S 16 12 E
Kwando →, *Africa* **95** 18 27 S 23 32 E
Kwangju, *S. Korea* **61** 35 9N 126 54 E
Kwango →, *Zaïre* **94** 3 14 S 17 22 E
Kwangsi-Chuang = Guangxi Zhuangzu Zizhiqu □, *China* **58** 24 0N 109 0 E
Kwangtung = Guangdong □, *China* **59** 23 0N 113 0 E
Kwara □, *Nigeria* **91** 8 0N 5 0 E
Kwataboahegan →, *Canada* **104** 51 9N 80 50W
Kwatisore, *Indonesia* **57** 3 18 S 134 50 E
Kweichow = Guizhou □, *China* **58** 27 0N 107 0 E
Kwekwe, *Zambia* **93** 18 58 S 29 48 E
Kwiguk, *U.S.A.* **102** 63 45N 164 35W
Kwikila, *Papua N. G.* **69** 9 49 S 147 38 E
Kwimba □, *Tanzania* **92** 3 0 S 33 0 E
Kwinana New Town, *Australia* **79** 32 15 S 115 47 E
Kwoka, *Indonesia* **57** 0 31 S 132 27 E
Kya-in-Seikkyi, *Burma* **52** 16 2N 98 8 E
Kyabé, *Chad* **87** 9 30N 19 0 E
Kyabra Cr. →, *Australia* **73** 25 36 S 142 55 E
Kyabram, *Australia* **74** 36 19 S 145 4 E
Kyaiklat, *Burma* **52** 16 25N 95 40 E
Kyaikmaraw, *Burma* **52** 16 23N 97 44 E
Kyaikthin, *Burma* **52** 23 32N 95 40 E
Kyaikto, *Burma* **54** 17 20N 97 3 E
Kyakhta, *U.S.S.R.* **41** 50 30N 106 25 E
Kyangin, *Burma* **52** 18 20N 95 20 E
Kyaukhnyat, *Burma* **52** 18 15N 97 31 E
Kyaukse, *Burma* **52** 21 36N 96 10 E
Kyauktaw, *Burma* **52** 20 51N 92 59 E
Kyawkku, *Burma* **52** 21 48N 96 56 E
Kyburz, *U.S.A.* **124** 38 47N 120 18W
Kyeamba, *Australia* **76** 35 26 S 147 40 E
Kyeintali, *Burma* **52** 18 0N 94 29 E
Kyenjojo, *Uganda* **92** 0 40N 30 37 E
Kyidaunggan, *Burma* **52** 19 53N 96 12 E
Kyle Dam, *Zambia* **93** 20 15 S 31 0 E
Kyle of Lochalsh, *U.K.* **14** 57 17N 5 43W
Kyll →, *W. Germany* **31** 49 48N 6 42 E
Kyllburg, *W. Germany* **31** 50 2N 6 35 E
Kyneton, *Australia* **74** 37 10 S 144 29 E
Kynuna, *Australia* **72** 21 37 S 141 55 E
Kyō-ga-Saki, *Japan* **65** 35 45N 135 15 E
Kyoga, L., *Uganda* **92** 1 35N 33 0 E
Kyogle, *Australia* **77** 28 40 S 153 0 E
Kyongju, *S. Korea* **61** 35 51N 129 14 E
Kyōto, *Japan* **65** 35 0N 135 45 E
Kyōto □, *Japan* **65** 35 15N 135 45 E
Kyren, *U.S.S.R.* **41** 51 45N 101 45 E
Kyrenia, *Cyprus* **46** 35 20N 33 20 E
Kyritz, *E. Germany* **30** 52 57N 12 25 E
Kystatyam, *U.S.S.R.* **41** 67 20N 123 10 E
Kytal Ktakh, *U.S.S.R.* **41** 65 30N 123 40 E
Kyu-hkok, *Burma* **52** 24 4N 98 4 E
Kyulyunken, *U.S.S.R.* **41** 64 10N 137 5 E
Kyunhla, *Burma* **52** 23 25N 95 15 E
Kyuquot, *Canada* **110** 50 3N 127 25W
Kyurdamir, *U.S.S.R.* **39** 40 25N 48 3 E
Kyūshū, *Japan* **64** 33 0N 131 0 E
Kyūshū □, *Japan* **64** 33 0N 131 0 E
Kyūshū-Sanchi, *Japan* **64** 32 35N 131 17 E
Kyustendil, *Bulgaria* **34** 42 16N 22 41 E
Kyusyur, *U.S.S.R.* **41** 70 39N 127 15 E
Kywong, *Australia* **75** 34 58 S 146 44 E
Kyzyl, *U.S.S.R.* **41** 51 50N 94 30 E
Kyzyl-Kiya, *U.S.S.R.* **40** 40 16N 72 8 E
Kyzylkum, Peski, *U.S.S.R.* **40** 42 30N 65 0 E
Kzyl-Orda, *U.S.S.R.* **40** 44 48N 65 28 E

L

Laaber →, *W. Germany* **31** 49 0N 12 3 E
Laage, *E. Germany* **30** 53 55N 12 21 E
Laanecoorie Res., *Australia* **74** 36 52 S 143 50 E
Laasphe, *W. Germany* **30** 50 56N 8 23 E
Laba →, *U.S.S.R.* **39** 45 11N 39 42 E
Laban, *Burma* **52** 25 52N 96 40 E
Labastide-Murat, *France* **20** 44 39N 1 33 E
Labastide-Rouairoux, *France* **20** 43 28N 2 39 E
Labbézenga, *Mali* **91** 15 2N 0 48 E
Labdah = Leptis Magna, *Libya* **86** 32 40N 14 12 E
Labe = Elbe →, *Europe* **30** 53 50N 9 0 E
Labé, *Guinea* **90** 11 24N 12 16W
Laberec →, *Czech.* **32** 48 37N 21 58 E
Laberge, L., *Canada* **110** 61 11N 135 12W
Labin, *Yugoslavia* **27** 45 5N 14 8 E
Labinsk, *U.S.S.R.* **39** 44 40N 40 48 E
Labis, *Malaysia* **55** 2 22N 103 2 E
Laboe, *W. Germany* **30** 54 25N 10 13 E
Laboka, *Gabon* **94** 0 19N 11 32 E
Labouheyre, *France* **20** 44 13N 0 55W
Laboulaye, *Argentina* **140** 34 10 S 63 30W
Labra, Peña, *Spain* **22** 43 3N 4 26W
Labrador, Coast of □, *Canada* **105** 53 20N 61 0W
Labrador City, *Canada* **105** 52 57N 66 55W
Lábrea, *Brazil* **137** 7 15 S 64 51W
Labrède, *France* **20** 44 41N 0 32W
Labrieville, *Canada* **107** 49 18N 69 34W
Labuan, Pulau, *Malaysia* **56** 5 21N 115 13 E
Labuha, *Indonesia* **57** 0 30 S 127 30 E
Labuhan, *Indonesia* **57** 6 22 S 105 50 E
Labuhanbajo, *Indonesia* **57** 8 28 S 120 1 E
Labuissière, *Belgium* **17** 50 19N 4 11 E
Labuk, Telok, *Malaysia* **56** 6 10N 117 50 E
Labutta, *Burma* **52** 16 9N 94 46 E
Labytnangi, *U.S.S.R.* **40** 66 39N 66 21 E
Lac Allard, *Canada* **105** 50 33N 63 24W
Lac-aux-Sables, *Canada* **107** 46 51N 72 24W
Lac Bouchette, *Canada* **107** 48 16N 72 11W
Lac Carré, *Canada* **107** 46 7N 74 29W
Lac-des-Écorces, *Canada* **106** 46 34N 75 22W
Lac du Flambeau, *U.S.A.* **120** 46 1N 89 51W
Lac Édouard, *Canada* **107** 47 40N 72 16W
Lac-Etchemin, *Canada* **107** 46 24N 70 30W
Lac La Biche, *Canada* **110** 54 45N 111 58W
Lac la Martre, *Canada* **102** 63 8N 117 16W
Lac-Mégantic, *Canada* **107** 45 35N 70 53W
Lac-Rémi, *Canada* **106** 46 1N 74 46W
Lac-Ste-Marie, *Canada* **106** 45 57N 75 57W
Lac Seul, Res., *Canada* **104** 50 25N 92 30W
Lac Thien, *Vietnam* **54** 12 25N 108 11 E
Lacanau, *France* **20** 44 58N 1 5W
Lacanau, Étang de, *France* **20** 44 58N 1 7W
Lacantúm →, *Mexico* **127** 16 36N 90 40W
Lacara →, *Spain* **23** 38 55N 6 25W
Lacaune, *France* **20** 43 43N 2 40 E
Lacaune, Mts. de, *France* **20** 43 43N 2 50 E
Laccadive Is. = Lakshadweep Is., *Ind. Oc.* **5** 10 0N 72 30 E
Lacepede B., *Australia* **73** 36 40 S 139 40 E
Lacepede Is., *Australia* **78** 16 55 S 122 0 E
Lacerdónia, *Mozam.* **93** 18 3 S 35 35 E
Lacey, *U.S.A.* **124** 47 7N 122 49W
Lachay, Pta., *Peru* **136** 11 17 S 77 44W
Lachen, *India* **52** 27 46N 88 36 E
Lachhmangarh, *India* **48** 27 50N 75 4 E
Lachi, *Pakistan* **48** 33 25N 71 20 E
Lachine, *Canada* **107** 45 30N 73 40W
Lachlan →, *Australia* **73** 34 22 S 143 55 E
Lachute, *Canada* **107** 45 39N 74 21W
Lackawanna, *U.S.A.* **116** 42 49N 78 50W
Lacolle, *Canada* **117** 45 5N 73 22W
Lacombe, *Canada* **110** 52 30N 113 44W
Lacon, *U.S.A.* **118** 41 2N 89 24W
Lacona, *Iowa, U.S.A.* **118** 41 11N 93 23W
Lacona, *N.Y., U.S.A.* **117** 43 37N 76 5W
Láconi, *Italy* **28** 39 54N 9 4 E
Laconia, *U.S.A.* **117** 43 32N 71 30W
Lacq, *France* **20** 43 25N 0 35W
Lacrosse, *U.S.A.* **122** 46 51N 117 58W
Ladakh Ra., *India* **49** 34 0N 78 0 E
Ladário, *Brazil* **137** 19 1 S 57 35W
Ladd, *U.S.A.* **118** 41 23N 89 13W
Laddonia, *U.S.A.* **118** 39 15N 91 39W
Ládhon →, *Greece* **35** 37 40N 21 50 E
Ladik, *Turkey* **38** 40 57N 35 58 E
Ladismith, *S. Africa* **96** 33 28 S 21 15 E
Lādīz, *Iran* **47** 28 55N 61 15 E
Ladnun, *India* **48** 27 38N 74 25 E
Ladoga, L. = Ladozhskoye Ozero, *U.S.S.R.* **40** 61 15N 30 30 E
Ladon, *France* **19** 48 0N 2 30 E
Ladozhskoye Ozero, *U.S.S.R.* **40** 61 15N 30 30 E
Ladrillero, G., *Chile* **142** 49 20 S 75 35W
Lady Grey, *S. Africa* **96** 30 43 S 27 13 E
Lady Julia Percy I., *Australia* **74** 38 25 S 142 0 E
Ladybrand, *S. Africa* **96** 29 9 S 27 29 E
Ladysmith, *Canada* **110** 49 0N 123 49W
Ladysmith, *S. Africa* **97** 28 32 S 29 46 E
Ladysmith, *U.S.A.* **120** 45 27N 91 4W
Lae, *Papua N. G.* **69** 6 40 S 147 2 E
Laem Ngop, *Thailand* **55** 12 10N 102 26 E
Laem Pho, *Thailand* **55** 6 55N 101 19 E
Læsø, *Denmark* **11** 57 15N 10 53 E
Læsø Rende, *Denmark* **11** 57 20N 10 45 E
Lafayette, *Colo., U.S.A.* **120** 40 0N 105 2W
Lafayette, *Ga., U.S.A.* **115** 34 44N 85 15W
Lafayette, *Ind., U.S.A.* **114** 40 22N 86 52W
Lafayette, *Ind., U.S.A.* **119** 40 25N 86 54W
Lafayette, *La., U.S.A.* **121** 30 18N 92 0W
Lafayette, *Tenn., U.S.A.* **115** 36 35N 86 0W
Laferte →, *Canada* **110** 61 53N 117 44W
Lafia, *Nigeria* **91** 8 30N 8 34 E
Lafiagi, *Nigeria* **91** 8 52N 5 20 E
Laflamme →, *Canada* **106** 49 17N 77 9W
Lafleche, *Canada* **111** 49 45N 106 40W
Lafon, *Sudan* **89** 5 5N 32 29 E
Laforce, *Canada* **106** 47 32N 78 44W
Laforsen, *Sweden* **10** 61 56N 15 3 E
Lagaip →, *Papua N. G.* **69** 5 4 S 142 52 E
Lagan →, *Sweden* **11** 56 56N 13 58 E
Lagan →, *U.K.* **15** 54 35N 5 55W
Lagarfljót →, *Iceland* **8** 65 40N 14 18W
Lagarto, *Brazil* **138** 10 54 S 37 41W
Lage, *Spain* **22** 43 13N 9 0W
Lage, *W. Germany* **30** 52 0N 8 47 E
Lage-Mierde, *Neths.* **17** 51 25N 5 9 E
Lågen →, *Norway* **9** 61 8N 10 25 E
Lägerdorf, *W. Germany* **30** 53 53N 9 35 E
Laggan, *Australia* **76** 34 23 S 149 31 E
Laghmān □, *Afghan.* **47** 34 20N 70 0 E
Laghouat, *Algeria* **85** 33 50N 2 59 E
Lagnieu, *France* **21** 45 55N 5 20 E
Lagny, *France* **19** 48 52N 2 44 E
Lago, *Italy* **29** 39 9N 16 8 E
Lago Posadas, *Argentina* **142** 47 30 S 71 40W
Lago Ranco, *Chile* **142** 40 19 S 72 30W
Lagôa, *Portugal* **23** 37 8N 8 27W
Lagoaça, *Portugal* **22** 41 11N 6 44W
Lagodekhi, *U.S.S.R.* **39** 41 50N 46 22 E
Lagónegro, *Italy* **29** 40 8N 15 45 E
Lagonoy Gulf, *Phil.* **57** 13 50N 123 50 E
Lagos, *Nigeria* **91** 6 25N 3 27 E
Lagos, *Portugal* **23** 37 5N 8 41W
Lagos de Moreno, *Mexico* **126** 21 21N 101 55W
Lagrange, *Australia* **78** 18 45 S 121 43 E
Lagrange, *U.S.A.* **119** 41 39N 85 25W
Lagrange B., *Australia* **78** 18 38 S 121 42 E
Laguardia, *Spain* **24** 42 33N 2 35W
Laguépie, *France* **20** 44 8N 1 57 E
Laguna, *Brazil* **141** 28 30 S 48 50W
Laguna, *U.S.A.* **123** 35 3N 107 28W
Laguna, La, *Canary Is.* **25** 28 28N 16 18W
Laguna Beach, *U.S.A.* **125** 33 31N 117 52W
Laguna de la Janda, *Spain* **23** 36 15N 5 45W
Laguna Limpia, *Argentina* **140** 26 32 S 59 45W
Laguna Madre, *U.S.A.* **127** 27 0N 97 20W
Lagunas, *Chile* **140** 21 0 S 69 45W
Lagunas, *Peru* **136** 5 10 S 75 35W
Lagunillas, *Bolivia* **137** 19 38 S 63 43W
Lahad Datu, *Malaysia* **57** 5 0N 118 20 E
Lahan Sai, *Thailand* **54** 14 25N 102 52 E
Lahanam, *Laos* **54** 16 16N 105 16 E
Laharpur, *India* **49** 27 43N 80 56 E
Lahat, *Indonesia* **56** 3 45 S 103 30 E
Lahe, *Burma* **52** 26 20N 95 26 E
Lahewa, *Indonesia* **56** 1 22N 97 12 E
Lahijan, *Iran* **46** 37 10N 50 6 E
Lahn →, *W. Germany* **31** 50 17N 7 38 E
Laholm, *Sweden* **11** 56 30N 13 2 E
Laholmsbukten, *Sweden* **11** 56 30N 12 45 E
Lahontan Res., *U.S.A.* **122** 39 28N 118 58W
Lahore, *Pakistan* **48** 31 32N 74 22 E
Lahpongsel, *Burma* **52** 27 7N 98 25 E
Lahr, *W. Germany* **31** 48 20N 7 52 E

Las Marismas

Lahti, *Finland* **9** 60 58N 25 40 E
Lahtis = Lahti, *Finland* **9** 60 58N 25 40 E
Laï, *Chad* **87** 9 25N 16 18 E
Lai Chau, *Vietnam* **54** 22 5N 103 3 E
Lai-hka, *Burma* **52** 21 16N 97 40 E
Laiagam, *Papua N. G.* **69** 5 33 S 143 30 E
Lai'an, *China* **59** 32 28N 118 30 E
Laibin, *China* **58** 23 42N 109 14 E
Laidley, *Australia* **77** 27 39 S 152 20 E
Laifeng, *China* **59** 29 27N 109 20 E
Laignes, *France* **19** 47 50N 4 20 E
Laikipia □, *Kenya* **92** 0 30N 36 30 E
Laingsburg, *S. Africa* **96** 33 9 S 20 52 E
Lairg, *U.K.* **14** 58 1N 4 24W
Laishui, *China* **60** 39 23N 115 45 E
Laiwu, *China* **61** 36 15N 117 40 E
Laixi, *China* **61** 36 50N 120 31 E
Laiyang, *China* **61** 36 59N 120 45 E
Laiyuan, *China* **60** 39 20N 114 40 E
Laizhou Wan, *China* **61** 37 30N 119 30 E
Laja →, *Mexico* **126** 20 55N 100 46W
Lajere, *Nigeria* **91** 12 10N 11 25 E
Lajes, *Rio Grande do N., Brazil* **138** 5 41 S 36 14W
Lajes, *Sta. Catarina, Brazil* **141** 27 48 S 50 20W
Lajinha, *Brazil* **139** 20 9 S 41 37W
Lajkovac, *Yugoslavia* **33** 44 27N 20 14 E
Lajosmizse, *Hungary* **33** 47 3N 19 32 E
Lak Sao, *Laos* **54** 18 11N 104 59 E
Lakaband, *Pakistan* **48** 31 2N 69 15 E
Lakar, *Indonesia* **57** 8 15 S 128 17 E
Lakatoro, *Vanuatu* **68** 16 0 S 167 0 E
Lake Alpine, *U.S.A.* **124** 38 29N 120 0W
Lake Andes, *U.S.A.* **120** 43 10N 98 32W
Lake Anse, *U.S.A.* **114** 46 42N 88 25W
Lake Arthur, *U.S.A.* **121** 30 8N 92 40W
Lake Boga, *Australia* **74** 35 26 S 143 38 E
Lake Bolac, *Australia* **74** 37 42 S 142 49 E
Lake Cargelligo, *Australia* **73** 33 15 S 146 22 E
Lake Charles, *U.S.A.* **121** 30 15N 93 10W
Lake Charm, *Australia* **74** 35 36 S 143 46 E
Lake City, *Colo., U.S.A.* **123** 38 3N 107 27W
Lake City, *Fla., U.S.A.* **115** 30 10N 82 40W
Lake City, *Iowa, U.S.A.* **118** 42 12N 94 42W
Lake City, *Mich., U.S.A.* **114** 44 20N 85 10W
Lake City, *Minn., U.S.A.* **120** 44 28N 92 21W
Lake City, *Pa., U.S.A.* **116** 42 2N 80 20W
Lake City, *S.C., U.S.A.* **115** 33 51N 79 44W
Lake Coleridge, *N.Z.* **81** 43 17 S 171 30 E
Lake Cowal, *Australia* **76** 33 41 S 147 21 E
Lake Cullulleraine, *Australia* **74** 34 15 S 141 37 E
Lake Forest, *U.S.A.* **119** 42 15N 87 50W
Lake Geneva, *U.S.A.* **119** 42 36N 88 26W
Lake George, *U.S.A.* **117** 43 25N 73 43W
Lake Grace, *Australia* **79** 33 7 S 118 28 E
Lake Harbour, *Canada* **103** 62 50N 69 50W
Lake Havasu City, *U.S.A.* **125** 34 25N 114 29W
Lake Hughes, *U.S.A.* **125** 34 41N 118 26W
Lake Isabella, *U.S.A.* **125** 35 38N 118 28W
Lake King, *Australia* **79** 33 5 S 119 45 E
Lake Lenore, *Canada* **111** 52 24N 104 59W
Lake Louise, *Canada* **110** 51 30N 116 10W
Lake Mead Nat. Rec. Area, *U.S.A.* **125** 36 0N 114 30W
Lake Michigan Beach, *U.S.A.* **119** 42 13N 86 25W
Lake Mills, *Iowa, U.S.A.* **120** 43 23N 93 33W
Lake Mills, *Wis., U.S.A.* **119** 43 5N 88 55W
Lake Murray, *Papua N. G.* **69** 6 48 S 141 29 E
Lake Nash, *Australia* **72** 20 57 S 138 0 E
Lake Odessa, *U.S.A.* **119** 42 47N 85 8W
Lake Orion, *U.S.A.* **119** 42 47N 83 14W
Lake Providence, *U.S.A.* **121** 32 49N 91 12W
Lake River, *Canada* **104** 54 30N 82 31W
Lake St. Peter, *Canada* **109** 45 18N 78 2W
Lake Superior Prov. Park, *Canada* **104** 47 45N 84 45W
Lake Tekapo, *N.Z.* **81** 44 0 S 170 30 E
Lake Varley, *Australia* **79** 32 48 S 119 30 E
Lake Villa, *U.S.A.* **119** 42 25N 88 5W
Lake Village, *U.S.A.* **121** 33 20N 91 19W
Lake Wales, *U.S.A.* **115** 27 55N 81 32W
Lake Worth, *U.S.A.* **115** 26 36N 80 3W
Lakefield, *Canada* **109** 44 25N 78 16W
Lakeland, *U.S.A.* **115** 28 0N 82 0W
Lakemba, *Fiji* **68** 18 13 S 178 47W
Lakeport, *U.S.A.* **124** 39 1N 122 56W
Lakes Entrance, *Australia* **75** 37 50 S 148 0 E
Lakeside, *Ariz., U.S.A.* **123** 34 12N 109 59W
Lakeside, *Calif., U.S.A.* **125** 32 52N 116 55W
Lakeside, *Nebr., U.S.A.* **120** 42 5N 102 24W
Lakeview, *U.S.A.* **122** 42 15N 120 22W
Lakewood, *Colo., U.S.A.* **120** 39 44N 105 3W
Lakewood, *N.J., U.S.A.* **117** 40 5N 74 13W
Lakewood, *Ohio, U.S.A.* **116** 41 28N 81 50W
Lakewood Center, *U.S.A.* **124** 47 11N 122 32W
Lakhaniá, *Greece* **35** 35 58N 27 54 E
Lakhipur, *Assam, India* **52** 24 48N 93 0 E
Lakhipur, *Assam, India* **52** 26 2N 90 18 E
Lakhonpheng, *Laos* **54** 15 54N 105 34 E
Lakhpat, *India* **48** 23 48N 68 47 E
Laki, *Iceland* **8** 64 4N 18 14W
Lakin, *U.S.A.* **121** 37 58N 101 18W
Lakitusaki →, *Canada* **104** 54 21N 82 25W
Lakonikós Kólpos, *Greece* **35** 36 40N 22 40 E
Lakota, *Ivory C.* **90** 5 50N 5 30W
Lakota, *U.S.A.* **120** 48 0N 98 22W
Laksefjorden, *Norway* **8** 70 45N 26 50 E
Lakselv, *Norway* **8** 70 2N 24 56 E
Lakshadweep Is., *Ind. Oc.* **5** 10 0N 72 30 E
Laksham, *Bangla.* **52** 23 14N 91 8 E
Lakshmeshwar, *India* **51** 15 9N 75 28 E
Lakshmikantapur, *India* **49** 22 5N 88 20 E
Lakshmipur, *Bangla.* **52** 22 58N 90 50 E
Lakuramau, *Papua N. G.* **69** 2 54 S 151 15 E
Lal Lal, *Australia* **74** 37 38 S 144 1 E
Lala Musa, *Pakistan* **48** 32 40N 73 57 E
Lalago, *Tanzania* **92** 3 28 S 33 58 E
Lalapanzi, *Zambia* **93** 19 20 S 30 15 E
Lalbert, *Australia* **74** 35 38 S 143 20 E
Lalbert Creek, *Australia* **74** 35 23 S 143 4 E
Lalganj, *India* **49** 25 52N 85 13 E
Lalibela, *Ethiopia* **89** 12 2N 39 2 E
Lalin, *China* **61** 45 12N 127 0 E
Lalín, *Spain* **22** 42 40N 8 5W
Lalin He →, *China* **61** 45 32N 125 40 E
Lalinde, *France* **20** 44 50N 0 44 E
Lalitpur, *India* **49** 24 42N 78 28 E
Lam, *Vietnam* **54** 21 21N 106 31 E
Lam Pao Res., *Thailand* **54** 16 50N 103 15 E
Lama Kara, *Togo* **91** 9 30N 1 15 E
Lamaipum, *Burma* **52** 25 40N 97 57 E
Lamap, *Vanuatu* **68** 16 26 S 167 43 E
Lamar, *Colo., U.S.A.* **120** 38 9N 102 35W
Lamar, *Mo., U.S.A.* **121** 37 30N 94 20W
Lamarque, *Argentina* **142** 39 24 S 65 40W
Lamas, *Peru* **136** 6 28 S 76 31W
Lamastre, *France* **21** 44 59N 4 35 E
Lamballe, *France* **18** 48 29N 2 31W
Lambaréné, *Gabon* **94** 0 41 S 10 12 E
Lambasa, *Fiji* **68** 16 30 S 179 10 E
Lambay I., *Ireland* **15** 53 30N 6 0W
Lambayeque □, *Peru* **136** 6 45 S 80 0W
Lambert, *U.S.A.* **120** 47 44N 104 39W
Lambert, C., *Papua N. G.* **69** 4 11 S 151 31 E
Lambert Glacier, *Antarctica* **143** 71 0 S 70 0 E
Lamberts Bay, *S. Africa* **96** 32 5 S 18 17 E
Lambesc, *France* **21** 43 39N 5 16 E
Lambeth, *Canada* **108** 42 54N 81 18W
Lámbia, *Greece* **35** 37 52N 21 53 E
Lambon, *Papua N. G.* **69** 4 45 S 152 48 E
Lambro →, *Italy* **26** 45 8N 9 32 E
Lambton, *Canada* **107** 45 50N 71 5W
Lame, *Nigeria* **91** 10 30N 9 20 E
Lame Deer, *U.S.A.* **122** 45 45N 106 40W
Lamego, *Portugal* **22** 41 5N 7 52W
Lamèque, *Canada* **105** 47 45N 64 38W
Lameroo, *Australia* **73** 35 19 S 140 33 E
Lamesa, *U.S.A.* **121** 32 45N 101 57W
Lamía, *Greece* **35** 38 55N 22 26 E
Lammermuir Hills, *U.K.* **14** 55 50N 2 40W
Lamon Bay, *Phil.* **57** 14 30N 122 20 E
Lamoni, *U.S.A.* **118** 40 37N 93 56W
Lamont, *Canada* **110** 53 46N 112 50W
Lamont, *Calif., U.S.A.* **125** 35 15N 118 55W
Lamont, *Iowa, U.S.A.* **118** 42 35N 91 40W
Lampa, *Peru* **136** 15 22 S 70 22W
Lampang, *Thailand* **54** 18 16N 99 32 E
Lampasas, *U.S.A.* **121** 31 5N 98 10W
Lampaul, *France* **18** 48 28N 5 7W
Lampazos de Naranjo, *Mexico* **126** 27 2N 100 32W
Lampeter, *U.K.* **13** 52 6N 4 6W
Lampione, *Medit. S.* **86** 35 33N 12 20 E
Lampman, *Canada* **111** 49 25N 102 50W
Lamprey, *Canada* **111** 58 33N 94 8W
Lampung □, *Indonesia* **56** 5 30 S 104 30 E
Lamu, *Burma* **52** 19 14N 94 10 E
Lamu, *Kenya* **92** 2 16 S 40 55 E
Lamu □, *Kenya* **92** 2 0 S 40 45 E
Lamud, *Peru* **136** 6 10 S 77 57W
Lamy, *U.S.A.* **123** 35 30N 105 58W
Lan Xian, *China* **60** 38 15N 111 35 E
Lan Yu, *Taiwan* **59** 22 5N 121 35 E
Lanai I., *U.S.A.* **112** 20 50N 156 55W
Lanak La, *India* **49** 34 27N 79 32 E
Lanaken, *Belgium* **17** 50 53N 5 39 E
Lanak'o Shank'ou = Lanak La, *India* **49** 34 27N 79 32 E
Lanao, L., *Phil.* **57** 7 52N 124 15 E
Lanark, *Canada* **106** 45 1N 76 22W
Lanark, *U.K.* **14** 55 40N 3 48W
Lancang, *China* **58** 22 36N 99 58 E
Lancang Jiang →, *China* **58** 21 40N 101 10 E
Lancashire □, *U.K.* **12** 53 40N 2 30W
Lancaster, *Canada* **106** 45 10N 74 30W
Lancaster, *U.K.* **12** 54 3N 2 48W
Lancaster, *Calif., U.S.A.* **125** 34 47N 118 8W
Lancaster, *Ky., U.S.A.* **114** 37 40N 84 40W
Lancaster, *Mo., U.S.A.* **118** 40 31N 92 32W
Lancaster, *N.H., U.S.A.* **117** 44 27N 71 33W
Lancaster, *N.Y., U.S.A.* **116** 42 53N 78 43W
Lancaster, *Pa., U.S.A.* **117** 40 4N 76 19W
Lancaster, *S.C., U.S.A.* **115** 34 45N 80 47W
Lancaster, *Wis., U.S.A.* **118** 42 48N 90 43W
Lancaster Sd., *Canada* **103** 74 13N 84 0W
Lancefield, *Australia* **74** 37 18 S 144 45 E
Lancer, *Canada* **111** 50 48N 108 53W
Lanchow = Lanzhou, *China* **60** 36 1N 103 52 E
Lanciano, *Italy* **27** 42 15N 14 22 E
Lanco, *Chile* **142** 39 24 S 72 46W
Lancones, *Peru* **136** 4 30 S 80 30W
Lancun, *China* **61** 36 25N 120 10 E
Łancut, *Poland* **32** 50 10N 22 13 E
Landau, *Bayern, W. Germany* **31** 48 41N 12 41 E
Landau, *Rhld-Pfz., W. Germany* **31** 49 12N 8 7 E
Landeck, *Austria* **31** 47 9N 10 34 E
Landen, *Belgium* **17** 50 45N 5 3 E
Lander, *U.S.A.* **122** 42 50N 108 49W
Lander →, *Australia* **78** 22 0 S 132 0 E
Landerneau, *France* **18** 48 28N 4 17W
Landeryd, *Sweden* **11** 57 7N 13 15 E
Landes, *France* **20** 44 0N 1 0W
Landes □, *France* **20** 43 57N 0 48W
Landete, *Spain* **24** 39 56N 1 25W
Landi Kotal, *Pakistan* **48** 34 7N 71 6 E
Landivisiau, *France* **18** 48 31N 4 6W
Landor, *Australia* **79** 25 10 S 116 54 E
Landquart, *Switz.* **31** 46 58N 9 32 E
Landrecies, *France* **19** 50 7N 3 40 E
Landrienne, *Canada* **106** 48 30N 77 50W
Land's End, *U.K.* **13** 50 4N 5 43W
Landsberg, *W. Germany* **31** 48 3N 10 52 E
Landsborough Cr. →, *Australia* **72** 22 28 S 144 35 E
Landsbro, *Sweden* **11** 57 24N 14 56 E
Landshut, *W. Germany* **31** 48 31N 12 10 E
Landskrona, *Sweden* **11** 55 53N 12 50 E
Landstuhl, *W. Germany* **31** 49 25N 7 34 E
Landvetter, *Sweden* **11** 57 41N 12 17 E
Laneffe, *Belgium* **17** 50 17N 4 30 E
Lanesboro, *U.S.A.* **117** 41 57N 75 34W
Lanett, *U.S.A.* **115** 33 0N 85 15W
Lang Bay, *Canada* **110** 49 45N 124 21W
Lang Lang, *Australia* **74** 38 15 S 145 34 E
Lang Qua, *Vietnam* **54** 22 16N 104 27 E
Lang Shan, *China* **60** 41 0N 106 30 E
Lang Son, *Vietnam* **54** 21 52N 106 42 E
Lang Suan, *Thailand* **55** 9 57N 99 4 E
La'nga Co, *China* **49** 30 45N 81 15 E
Lángadhás, *Greece* **35** 40 46N 23 2 E
Langádhia, *Greece* **35** 37 43N 22 1 E
Långan →, *Sweden* **10** 63 19N 14 44 E
Langara I., *Canada* **110** 54 14N 133 1W
Langatabbetje, *Surinam* **135** 4 59N 54 28W
Langdai, *China* **58** 26 6N 105 21 E
Langdon, *U.S.A.* **120** 48 47N 98 24W
Langdorp, *Belgium* **17** 50 59N 4 52 E
Langeac, *France* **20** 45 7N 3 29 E
Langeais, *France* **18** 47 20N 0 24 E
Langeb Baraka →, *Sudan* **88** 17 28N 36 50 E
Langeberg, *S. Africa* **96** 33 55 S 21 0 E
Langeberge, *S. Africa* **96** 28 15 S 22 33 E
Langeland, *Denmark* **11** 54 56N 10 48 E
Langemark, *Belgium* **17** 50 55N 2 55 E
Langen, *W. Germany* **31** 49 59N 8 40 E
Langenburg, *Canada* **111** 50 51N 101 43W
Langeness, *W. Germany* **30** 54 34N 8 35 E
Langeoog, *W. Germany* **30** 53 44N 7 33 E
Langeskov, *Denmark* **11** 55 22N 10 35 E
Langesund, *Norway* **10** 59 0N 9 45 E
Länghem, *Sweden* **11** 57 36N 13 14 E
Langhirano, *Italy* **26** 44 39N 10 16 E
Langholm, *U.K.* **14** 55 9N 2 59W
Langjökull, *Iceland* **8** 64 39N 20 12W
Langkawi, P., *Malaysia* **55** 6 25N 99 45 E
Langklip, *S. Africa* **96** 28 12 S 20 20 E
Langkon, *Malaysia* **56** 6 30N 116 40 E
Langlade, *St- P. & M.* **105** 46 50N 56 20W
Langlois, *U.S.A.* **122** 42 54N 124 26W
Langnau, *Switz.* **31** 46 56N 7 47 E
Langogne, *France* **20** 44 43N 3 50 E
Langon, *France* **20** 44 33N 0 16W
Langøya, *Norway* **8** 68 45N 14 50 E
Langres, *France* **19** 47 52N 5 20 E
Langres, Plateau de, *France* **19** 47 45N 5 3 E
Langsa, *Indonesia* **56** 4 30N 97 57 E
Långsele, *Sweden* **10** 63 12N 17 4 E
Långshyttan, *Sweden* **10** 60 27N 16 2 E
Langtao, *Burma* **52** 27 15N 97 34 E
Langting, *India* **52** 25 31N 93 7 E
Langtry, *U.S.A.* **121** 29 50N 101 33W
Langu, *Thailand* **55** 6 53N 99 47 E
Languedoc, *France* **20** 43 58N 4 0 E
Langxi, *China* **59** 31 10N 119 12 E
Langxiangzhen, *China* **60** 39 43N 116 8 E
Langzhong, *China* **58** 31 38N 105 58 E
Lanigan, *Canada* **111** 51 51N 105 2W
Lankao, *China* **60** 34 48N 114 50 E
Lannemezan, *France* **20** 43 8N 0 23 E
Lannilis, *France* **18** 48 35N 4 32W
Lannion, *France* **18** 48 46N 3 29W
Lanoraie, *Canada* **107** 45 58N 73 13W
Lanouaille, *France* **20** 45 24N 1 9 E
Lanping, *China* **58** 26 28N 99 15 E
Lansdale, *U.S.A.* **117** 40 14N 75 18W
Lansdowne, *Australia* **77** 31 48 S 152 30 E
Lansdowne, *Canada* **109** 44 24N 76 1W
Lansdowne House, *Canada* **104** 52 14N 87 53W
Lansford, *U.S.A.* **117** 40 48N 75 55W
Lanshan, *China* **59** 25 24N 112 10 E
Lansing, *U.S.A.* **119** 42 47N 84 40W
Lanslebourg-Mont-Cenis, *France* **21** 45 17N 6 52 E
Lanta Yai, Ko, *Thailand* **55** 7 35N 99 3 E
Lantian, *China* **60** 34 11N 109 20 E
Lanus, *Argentina* **140** 34 44 S 58 27W
Lanusei, *Italy* **28** 39 53N 9 31 E
Lanxi, *China* **59** 29 13N 119 28 E
Lanzarote, *Canary Is.* **25** 29 0N 13 40W
Lanzhou, *China* **60** 36 1N 103 52 E
Lanzo Torinese, *Italy* **26** 45 16N 7 29 E
Lao →, *Italy* **29** 39 45N 15 45 E
Lao Bao, *Laos* **54** 16 35N 106 30 E
Lao Cai, *Vietnam* **54** 22 30N 103 57 E
Laoag, *Phil.* **57** 18 7N 120 34 E
Laoang, *Phil.* **57** 12 32N 125 8 E
Laoha He →, *China* **61** 43 25N 120 35 E
Laois □, *Ireland* **15** 53 0N 7 20W
Laon, *France* **19** 49 33N 3 35 E
Laona, *U.S.A.* **114** 45 32N 88 41W
Laos ■, *Asia* **54** 17 45N 105 0 E
Lapa, *Brazil* **141** 25 46 S 49 44W
Lapalisse, *France* **20** 46 15N 3 38 E
Laparan, *Phil.* **57** 6 0N 120 0 E
Lapeer, *U.S.A.* **104** 43 3N 83 20W
Lapi □, *Finland* **8** 67 0N 27 0 E
Lapland = Lappland, *Europe* **8** 68 7N 24 0 E
Laporte, *U.S.A.* **117** 41 27N 76 30W
Lapovo, *Yugoslavia* **33** 44 10N 21 2 E
Lappland, *Europe* **8** 68 7N 24 0 E
Laprida, *Argentina* **140** 37 34 S 60 45W
Laptev Sea, *U.S.S.R.* **41** 76 0N 125 0 E
Lăpuşul →, *Romania* **34** 47 25N 23 40 E
Lār, *Iran* **47** 27 40N 54 14 E
Lara, *Australia* **74** 38 2 S 144 26 E
Lara □, *Venezuela* **134** 10 10N 69 50W
Larabanga, *Ghana* **90** 9 16N 1 56W
Laracha, *Spain* **22** 43 15N 8 35W
Larache, *Morocco* **84** 35 10N 6 5W
Laragne-Montéglin, *France* **21** 44 18N 5 49 E
Laramie, *U.S.A.* **120** 41 20N 105 38W
Laramie Mts., *U.S.A.* **120** 42 0N 105 30W
Laranjeiras, *Brazil* **138** 10 48 S 37 10W
Laranjeiras do Sul, *Brazil* **141** 25 23 S 52 23W
Larantuka, *Indonesia* **57** 8 21 S 122 55 E
Larap, *Phil.* **57** 14 18N 122 39 E
Larat, *Indonesia* **57** 7 0 S 132 0 E
Laravale, *Australia* **77** 28 6 S 152 57 E
Larde, *Mozam.* **93** 16 28 S 39 43 E
Larder Lake, *Canada* **106** 48 5N 79 40W
Lárdhos, Ákra, *Greece* **35** 36 4N 28 10 E
Laredo, *Spain* **24** 43 26N 3 28W
Laredo, *U.S.A.* **121** 27 34N 99 29W
Laredo Sd., *Canada* **110** 52 30N 128 53W
Laren, *Neths.* **16** 52 16N 5 14 E
Largentière, *France* **21** 44 34N 4 18 E
Largs, *U.K.* **14** 55 48N 4 51W
Lari, *Italy* **26** 43 34N 10 35 E
Lariang, *Indonesia* **57** 1 26 S 119 17 E
Larimore, *U.S.A.* **120** 47 55N 97 35W
Larino, *Italy* **29** 41 48N 14 54 E
Lárisa, *Greece* **35** 39 49N 22 28 E
Larkana, *Pakistan* **48** 27 32N 68 18 E
Larnaca, *Cyprus* **46** 35 0N 33 35 E
Larne, *U.K.* **15** 54 52N 5 50W
Larned, *U.S.A.* **120** 38 15N 99 10W
Larochette, *Belgium* **17** 49 47N 6 13 E
Laroquebrou, *France* **20** 44 58N 2 12 E
Larrimah, *Australia* **78** 15 35 S 133 12 E
Larsen Ice Shelf, *Antarctica* **143** 67 0 S 62 0W
Larvik, *Norway* **10** 59 4N 10 0 E
Laryak, *U.S.S.R.* **40** 61 15N 80 0 E
Larzac, Causse du, *France* **20** 43 50N 3 17 E
Las Animas, *U.S.A.* **121** 38 8N 103 18W
Las Anod, *Somali Rep.* **98** 8 26N 47 19 E
Las Blancos, *Spain* **25** 37 38N 0 49W
Las Brenãs, *Argentina* **140** 27 5 S 61 7W
Las Cabezas de San Juan, *Spain* **23** 37 0N 5 58W
Las Chimeneas, *Mexico* **125** 32 8N 116 5W
Las Coloradas, *Argentina* **142** 39 34 S 70 36W
Las Cruces, *U.S.A.* **123** 32 18N 106 50W
Las Flores, *Argentina* **140** 36 10 S 59 7W
Las Heras, *Argentina* **140** 32 51 S 68 49W
Las Horquetas, *Argentina* **142** 48 14 S 71 11W
Las Khoreh, *Somali Rep.* **98** 11 10N 48 20 E
Las Lajas, *Argentina* **142** 38 30 S 70 25W
Las Lomas, *Peru* **136** 4 40 S 80 10W
Las Lomitas, *Argentina* **140** 24 43 S 60 35W
Las Marismas, *Spain* **23** 37 5N 6 20W

Lindesberg

Leping, China 59 28 47N 117 7 E
Lepontine, Alpi, Italy 31 46 22N 8 27 E
Leptis Magna, Libya 86 32 40N 14 12 E
Lequeitio, Spain 24 43 20N 2 32W
Lercara Friddi, Italy 28 37 42N 13 36 E
Lerdo, Mexico 126 25 32N 103 32W
Léré, C.A.R. 94 6 46N 17 25 E
Léré, Chad 87 9 39N 14 13 E
Lere, Nigeria 91 9 43N 9 18 E
Leribe, Lesotho 97 28 51 S 28 3 E
Lérici, Italy 26 44 4N 9 58 E
Lérida, Spain 24 41 37N 0 39 E
Lérida □, Spain 24 42 6N 1 0 E
Lérins, Is. de, France 21 43 31N 7 3 E
Lerma, Spain 22 42 0N 3 47W
Léros, Greece 35 37 10N 26 50 E
Lérouville, France 19 48 44N 5 30 E
Lerwick, U.K. 14 60 10N 1 10W
Léry, Canada 107 45 21N 73 48W
Lesbos, I. = Lésvos, Greece 35 39 10N 26 20 E
Leshan, China 58 29 33N 103 41 E
Lésina, L. di, Italy 27 41 53N 15 25 E
Lesja, Norway 10 62 7N 8 51 E
Lesjaverk, Norway 10 62 12N 8 34 E
Leskov I., Antarctica 143 56 0 S 28 0W
Leskovac, Yugoslavia 33 43 0N 21 58 E
Leslie, Ark., U.S.A. 121 35 50N 92 35W
Leslie, Mich., U.S.A. 119 42 27N 84 26W
Lesneven, France 18 48 35N 4 20W
Lešnica, Yugoslavia 33 44 39N 19 20 E
Lesnoye, U.S.S.R. 36 58 15N 35 18 E
Lesotho ■, Africa 97 29 40 S 28 0 E
Lesozavodsk, U.S.S.R. 41 45 30N 133 29 E
Lesparre-Médoc, France 20 45 18N 0 57W
Lessay, France 18 49 14N 1 30W
Lesse →, Belgium 17 50 15N 4 54 E
Lesser Antilles, W. Indies 129 15 0N 61 0W
Lesser Slave L., Canada 110 55 30N 115 25W
Lesser Sunda Is., Indonesia 57 7 0 S 120 0 E
Lessines, Belgium 17 50 42N 3 50 E
Lester, U.S.A. 124 47 12N 121 29W
Lestock, Canada 111 51 19N 103 59W
Lesuer I., Australia 78 13 50 S 127 17 E
Lésvos, Greece 35 39 10N 26 20 E
Leszno, Poland 32 51 50N 16 30 E
Letchworth, U.K. 13 51 58N 0 13W
Letea, Ostrov, Romania 34 45 18N 29 20 E
Lethbridge, Australia 74 37 58 S 144 6 E
Lethbridge, Canada 110 49 45N 112 45W
Lethem, Guyana 135 3 20N 59 50W
Leti, Kepulauan, Indonesia 57 8 10 S 128 0 E
Letiahau →, Botswana 96 21 16 S 24 0 E
Leticia, Colombia 134 4 9 S 70 0W
Leting, China 61 39 23N 118 55 E
Letjiesbos, S. Africa 96 32 34 S 22 16 E
Letlhakeng, Botswana 96 24 0 S 24 59 E
Letpadan, Burma 52 17 45N 95 45 E
Letpan, Burma 52 19 28N 94 10 E
Letterkenny, Ireland 15 54 57N 7 42W
Leu, Romania 34 44 10N 24 0 E
Léua, Angola 95 11 34 S 20 32 E
Leucadia, U.S.A. 125 33 4N 117 18W
Leucate, France 20 42 56N 3 3 E
Leucate, Étang de, France 20 42 50N 3 0 E
Leuk, Switz. 31 46 19N 7 37 E
Leupegem, Belgium 17 50 50N 3 36 E
Leuser, G., Indonesia 56 3 46N 97 12 E
Leutkirch, W. Germany 31 47 49N 10 1 E
Leuven, Belgium 17 50 52N 4 42 E
Leuze, Hainaut, Belgium 17 50 36N 3 37 E
Leuze, Namur, Belgium 17 50 33N 4 54 E
Lev Tolstoy, U.S.S.R. 37 53 13N 39 29 E
Levack, Canada 108 46 38N 81 23W
Levádhia, Greece 35 38 27N 22 54 E
Levan, U.S.A. 122 39 37N 111 52W
Levanger, Norway 8 63 45N 11 19 E
Levant, I. du, France 21 43 3N 6 28 E
Lévanto, Italy 26 44 10N 9 37 E
Levanzo, Italy 28 38 0N 12 19 E
Levelland, U.S.A. 121 33 38N 102 23W
Leven, U.K. 14 56 12N 3 0W
Leven, L., U.K. 14 56 12N 3 22W
Leven, Toraka, Madag. 97 12 30 S 47 45 E
Levens, France 21 43 50N 7 12 E
Leveque C., Australia 78 16 20 S 123 0 E
Leverano, Italy 29 40 16N 18 0 E
Leverkusen, W. Germany 30 51 2N 6 59 E
Leverville, Zaïre 95 4 50 S 18 44 E
Levet, France 19 46 56N 2 22 E
Levice, Czech. 33 48 13N 18 35 E
Levico, Italy 27 46 0N 11 18 E
Levie, France 21 41 40N 9 7 E
Levier, France 19 46 58N 6 8 E
Levin, N.Z. 80 40 37 S 175 18 E
Lévis, Canada 107 46 48N 71 9W
Levis, L., Canada 110 62 37N 117 58W
Levítha, Greece 35 37 0N 26 28 E
Levittown, N.Y., U.S.A. 117 40 41N 73 31W
Levittown, Pa., U.S.A. 117 40 10N 74 51W
Lévka, Greece 35 35 18N 24 3 E
Levkás, Greece 35 38 40N 20 43 E
Levkôsia = Nicosia, Cyprus 46 35 10N 33 25 E
Levoča, Czech. 32 49 2N 20 35 E
Levroux, France 19 46 59N 1 38 E
Levski, Bulgaria 34 43 21N 25 10 E
Levskigrad, Bulgaria 34 42 38N 24 47 E
Levuka, Fiji 68 17 34 S 179 0 E
Lewe, Burma 52 19 38N 96 7 E
Lewellen, U.S.A. 120 41 22N 102 5W
Lewes, U.K. 13 50 53N 0 2 E
Lewes, U.S.A. 114 38 45N 75 8W
Lewis, U.K. 14 58 10N 6 40W
Lewis →, U.S.A. 124 45 51N 122 48W
Lewis, Butt of, U.K. 14 58 30N 6 12W
Lewis Ra., Australia 78 20 3 S 128 50 E
Lewis Ra., U.S.A. 122 48 0N 113 15W
Lewisburg, Ohio, U.S.A. 119 39 51N 84 33W
Lewisburg, Pa., U.S.A. 116 40 57N 76 57W
Lewisburg, Tenn., U.S.A. 115 35 29N 86 46W
Lewisport, U.S.A. 119 37 56N 86 54W
Lewisporte, Canada 105 49 15N 55 3W
Lewiston, U.S.A. 122 46 25N 117 0W
Lewistown, Ill., U.S.A. 118 40 24N 90 9W
Lewistown, Mont., U.S.A. 122 47 0N 109 25W
Lewistown, Pa., U.S.A. 116 40 37N 77 33W
Lexington, Ill., U.S.A. 118 40 37N 88 47W
Lexington, Ky., U.S.A. 119 38 6N 84 30W
Lexington, Miss., U.S.A. 121 33 8N 90 2W
Lexington, Mo., U.S.A. 118 39 7N 93 55W
Lexington, N.C., U.S.A. 115 35 50N 80 13W
Lexington, Nebr., U.S.A. 120 40 48N 99 45W
Lexington, Ohio, U.S.A. 116 40 39N 82 35W
Lexington, Oreg., U.S.A. 122 45 29N 119 46W
Lexington, Tenn., U.S.A. 115 35 38N 88 25W
Lexington Park, U.S.A. 114 38 16N 76 27W
Lexton, Australia 74 37 16 S 143 31 E
Leyburn, Australia 77 28 1 S 151 35 E
Leye, China 58 24 48N 106 29 E
Leyre →, France 20 44 39N 1 1W
Leyte, Phil. 57 11 0N 125 0 E
Lezay, France 20 46 15N 0 1 E
Lezha, Albania 35 41 47N 19 42 E
Lezhi, China 58 30 19N 104 58 E
Lézignan-Corbières, France 20 43 13N 2 43 E
Lezoux, France 20 45 49N 3 21 E
Lgov, U.S.S.R. 36 51 42N 35 16 E
Lhasa, China 62 29 25N 90 58 E
Lhazê, China 62 29 5N 87 38 E
Lhokkruet, Indonesia 56 4 55N 95 24 E
Lhokseumawe, Indonesia 56 5 10N 97 10 E
Lhuntsi Dzong, India 52 27 39N 91 10 E
Li, Thailand 54 17 48N 98 57 E
Li Shui →, China 59 29 24N 112 1 E
Li Xian, Gansu, China 60 34 10N 105 5 E
Li Xian, Hebei, China 60 38 30N 115 35 E
Li Xian, Hunan, China 59 29 36N 111 42 E
Li Xian, Sichuan, China 58 31 23N 103 13 E
Lia-Moya, C.A.R. 94 6 54N 16 17 E
Liádhoi, Greece 35 36 50N 26 11 E
Liamena, Australia 77 31 58 S 149 22 E
Lian Xian, China 59 24 51N 112 22 E
Liancheng, China 59 25 42N 116 40 E
Lianga, Phil. 57 8 38N 126 6 E
Liangcheng, Nei Mongol Zizhiqu, China 60 40 28N 112 25 E
Liangcheng, Shandong, China 61 35 32N 119 37 E
Liangdang, China 60 33 56N 106 18 E
Lianghekou, China 58 29 11N 108 44 E
Liangping, China 58 30 38N 107 47 E
Lianhua, China 59 27 3N 113 54 E
Lianjiang, Fujian, China 59 26 12N 119 27 E
Lianjiang, Guangdong, China 59 21 40N 110 20 E
Lianping, China 59 24 26N 114 30 E
Lianshan, China 59 24 38N 112 8 E
Lianshanguan, China 61 40 53N 123 43 E
Lianshui, China 61 33 42N 119 20 E
Lianyuan, China 59 27 40N 111 38 E
Lianyungang, China 61 34 40N 119 11 E
Liao He →, China 61 41 0N 121 50 E
Liaocheng, China 60 36 28N 115 58 E
Liaodong Bandao, China 61 40 0N 122 30 E
Liaodong Wan, China 61 40 20N 121 10 E
Liaoning □, China 61 42 0N 122 0 E
Liaoyang, China 61 41 15N 122 58 E
Liaoyuan, China 61 42 58N 125 2 E
Liaozhong, China 61 41 23N 122 50 E
Liapádhes, Greece 35 39 42N 19 40 E
Liard →, Canada 110 61 51N 121 18W
Liari, Pakistan 48 25 37N 66 30 E
Líbano, Colombia 134 4 55N 75 4W
Libau = Liepaja, U.S.S.R. 36 56 30N 21 0 E
Libby, U.S.A. 122 48 20N 115 33W
Libenge, Zaïre 94 3 40N 18 55 E
Liberal, Kans., U.S.A. 121 37 4N 101 0W
Liberal, Mo., U.S.A. 121 37 35N 94 30W
Liberdade, Brazil 136 10 5 S 70 20W
Liberdade →, Brazil 137 9 40 S 52 17W
Liberec, Czech. 32 50 47N 15 7 E
Liberia, Costa Rica 128 10 40N 85 30W
Liberia ■, W. Afr. 90 6 30N 9 30W
Libertad, Venezuela 134 8 20N 69 37W
Libertad, La, Guatemala 128 16 47N 90 7W
Libertad, La, Mexico 126 29 55N 112 41W
Libertad, La □, Peru 136 8 0 S 78 30W
Liberty, Ind., U.S.A. 119 39 38N 84 56W
Liberty, Mo., U.S.A. 118 39 15N 94 24W
Liberty, Tex., U.S.A. 121 30 5N 94 50W
Liberty Center, U.S.A. 119 41 27N 84 1W
Libertyville, U.S.A. 119 42 18N 87 57W
Libibi, Angola 95 14 42 S 17 44 E
Libin, Belgium 17 49 59N 5 15 E
Libo, China 58 25 22N 107 53 E
Libobo, Tanjung, Indonesia 57 0 54 S 128 28 E
Libode, S. Africa 97 31 33 S 29 2 E
Libonda, Zambia 95 14 28 S 23 12 E
Libourne, France 20 44 55N 0 14W
Libramont, Belgium 17 49 55N 5 23 E
Libreville, Gabon 94 0 25N 9 26 E
Libya ■, N. Afr. 86 27 0N 17 0 E
Libyan Desert, Africa 82 25 0N 25 0 E
Libyan Plateau = Ed-Déffa, Egypt 88 30 40N 26 30 E
Licantén, Chile 140 35 55 S 72 0W
Licata, Italy 28 37 6N 13 55 E
Licheng, China 60 36 28N 113 20 E
Lichfield, U.K. 12 52 40N 1 50W
Lichinga, Mozam. 93 13 13 S 35 11 E
Lichtaart, Belgium 17 51 13N 4 55 E
Lichtenburg, S. Africa 96 26 8 S 26 8 E
Lichtenfels, W. Germany 31 50 7N 11 4 E
Lichtenvoorde, Neths. 16 51 59N 6 34 E
Lichtervelde, Belgium 17 51 2N 3 9 E
Lichuan, Hubei, China 58 30 18N 108 57 E
Lichuan, Jiangxi, China 59 27 18N 116 55 E
Licking, South Fork →, U.S.A. 119 38 40N 84 19W
Licola, Australia 75 37 39 S 146 39 E
Licosa, Punta, Italy 29 40 15N 14 53 E
Lida, U.S.A. 123 37 30N 117 30W
Lida, U.S.S.R. 36 53 53N 25 15 E
Lidhult, Sweden 11 56 50N 13 27 E
Lidingö, Sweden 10 59 22N 18 8 E
Lidköping, Sweden 11 58 31N 13 14 E
Lido, Italy 27 45 25N 12 23 E
Lido, Niger 91 12 54N 3 44 E
Lido di Roma = Óstia, Lido di, Italy 28 41 43N 12 17 E
Lidzbark Warminski, Poland 32 54 7N 20 34 E
Liebenwalde, E. Germany 30 52 51N 13 23 E
Lieberose, E. Germany 30 51 59N 14 18 E
Liechtenstein ■, Europe 31 47 8N 9 35 E
Liederkerke, Belgium 17 50 52N 4 5 E
Liège, Belgium 17 50 38N 5 35 E
Liège □, Belgium 17 50 32N 5 35 E
Liegnitz = Legnica, Poland 32 51 12N 16 10 E
Liempde, Neths. 17 51 35N 5 23 E
Lienart, Zaïre 92 3 3N 25 31 E
Lienyünchiangshih = Lianyungang, China 61 34 40N 119 11 E
Lienz, Austria 33 46 50N 12 46 E
Liepaja, U.S.S.R. 36 56 30N 21 0 E
Lier, Belgium 17 51 7N 4 34 E
Lierneux, Belgium 17 50 17N 5 47 E
Lieshout, Neths. 17 51 31N 5 36 E
Liévin, France 19 50 24N 2 47 E
Lièvre →, Canada 106 45 31N 75 26W
Liezen, Austria 33 47 34N 14 15 E
Liffey →, Ireland 15 53 21N 6 20W
Lifford, Ireland 15 54 50N 7 30W
Liffré, France 18 48 12N 1 30W
Lifjell, Norway 10 59 27N 8 45 E
Lifuka, Tonga 68 19 48 S 174 21W
Lightning Ridge, Australia 73 29 22 S 148 0 E
Lignano, Italy 27 45 42N 13 8 E
Ligny-en-Barrois, France 19 48 36N 5 20 E
Ligny-le-Châtel, France 19 47 54N 3 45 E
Ligoúrion, Greece 35 37 37N 23 2 E
Ligua, La, Chile 140 32 30 S 71 16W
Ligueil, France 18 47 2N 0 49 E
Liguria □, Italy 26 44 30N 9 0 E
Ligurian Sea, Italy 26 43 20N 9 0 E
Lihir Group, Papua N. G. 69 3 0 S 152 35 E
Lihou Reefs and Cays, Australia 72 17 25 S 151 40 E
Lihue, U.S.A. 112 21 59N 159 24W
Lijiang, China 58 26 55N 100 20 E
Likasi, Zaïre 93 10 55 S 26 48 E
Likati, Zaïre 94 3 20N 24 0 E
Likhoslavl, U.S.S.R. 36 57 12N 35 30 E
Likhovski, U.S.S.R. 39 48 10N 40 10 E
Likokou, Gabon 94 0 12 S 12 48 E
Likoma I., Malawi 93 12 3 S 34 45 E
Likumburu, Tanzania 93 9 43 S 35 8 E
Liling, China 59 27 42N 113 29 E
Lille, Belgium 17 51 15N 4 50 E
Lille, France 19 50 38N 3 3 E
Lille Bælt, Denmark 11 55 20N 9 45 E
Lillebonne, France 18 49 30N 0 32 E
Lillehammer, Norway 10 61 8N 10 30 E
Lillers, France 19 50 35N 2 28 E
Lillesand, Norway 11 58 15N 8 23 E
Lilleshall, U.K. 13 52 45N 2 22W
Lillestrøm, Norway 10 59 58N 11 5 E
Lillian Point, Mt., Australia 79 27 40 S 126 6 E
Lillimur, Australia 74 36 23 S 141 11 E
Lillo, Spain 24 39 45N 3 20W
Lillooet →, Canada 110 49 15N 121 57W
Lilongwe, Malawi 93 14 0 S 33 48 E
Liloy, Phil. 57 8 4N 122 39 E
Lilydale, Australia 74 37 46 S 145 20 E
Lim →, Yugoslavia 33 43 0N 19 40 E
Lima, Indonesia 57 3 37 S 128 4 E
Lima, Peru 136 12 0 S 77 0W
Lima, Sweden 10 60 55N 13 20 E
Lima, Mont., U.S.A. 122 44 41N 112 38W
Lima, Ohio, U.S.A. 119 40 42N 84 5W
Lima □, Peru 136 12 3 S 77 3W
Lima →, Portugal 22 41 41N 8 50W
Limages, Canada 106 45 20N 75 16W
Liman, U.S.S.R. 39 45 45N 47 12 E
Limassol, Cyprus 46 34 42N 33 1 E
Limavady, U.K. 15 55 3N 6 58W
Limavady □, U.K. 15 55 0N 6 55W
Limay →, Argentina 142 39 0 S 68 0W
Limay Mahuida, Argentina 140 37 10 S 66 45W
Limbang, Brunei 56 4 42N 115 6 E
Limbara, Monti, Italy 28 40 50N 9 10 E
Limbdi, India 48 22 34N 71 51 E
Limbe, Cameroon 91 4 1N 9 10 E
Limbourg, Belgium 17 50 37N 5 56 E
Limbri, Australia 77 31 3 S 151 5 E
Limbueta, Angola 95 12 30 S 18 42 E
Limbunya, Australia 78 17 14 S 129 50 E
Limburg, W. Germany 31 50 22N 8 4 E
Limburg □, Belgium 17 51 2N 5 25 E
Limburg □, Neths. 17 51 20N 5 55 E
Limedsforsen, Sweden 10 60 52N 13 25 E
Limeira, Brazil 141 22 35 S 47 28W
Limerick, Ireland 15 52 40N 8 38W
Limerick □, Ireland 15 52 30N 8 50W
Limestone, U.S.A. 116 42 2N 78 39W
Limestone →, Canada 111 56 31N 94 7W
Limevale, Australia 77 28 44 S 151 12 E
Limfjorden, Denmark 11 56 55N 9 0 E
Limia → = Lima →, Portugal 22 41 41N 8 50W
Limmared, Sweden 11 57 34N 13 20 E
Limmen, Neths. 16 52 34N 4 42 E
Limmen Bight, Australia 72 14 40 S 135 35 E
Limmen Bight →, Australia 72 15 7 S 135 44 E
Límni, Greece 35 38 43N 23 18 E
Límnos, Greece 35 39 50N 25 5 E
Limoeiro, Brazil 138 7 52 S 35 27W
Limoeiro do Norte, Brazil 138 5 5 S 38 0W
Limoges, Canada 109 45 20N 75 15W
Limoges, France 20 45 50N 1 15 E
Limón, Costa Rica 128 10 0N 83 2W
Limon, U.S.A. 120 39 18N 103 38W
Limone Piemonte, Italy 26 44 12N 7 32 E
Limousin, France 20 45 30N 1 30 E
Limousin, Plateaux du, France 20 45 45N 1 15 E
Limoux, France 20 43 4N 2 12 E
Limpopo →, Africa 97 25 5 S 33 30 E
Limuru, Kenya 92 1 2 S 36 35 E
Lin Xian, China 60 37 57N 110 58 E
Lin'an, China 59 30 15N 119 42 E
Linares, Chile 140 35 50 S 71 40W
Linares, Colombia 134 1 23N 77 31W
Linares, Mexico 127 24 50N 99 40W
Linares, Spain 25 38 10N 3 40W
Linares □, Chile 140 36 0 S 71 0W
Línas Mte., Italy 28 39 25N 8 38 E
Lincang, China 58 23 58N 100 1 E
Lincheng, China 60 37 25N 114 30 E
Linchuan, China 59 27 57N 116 15 E
Lincoln, Argentina 140 34 55 S 61 30W
Lincoln, Canada 108 43 10N 79 29W
Lincoln, N.Z. 81 43 38 S 172 30 E
Lincoln, U.K. 12 53 14N 0 32W
Lincoln, Calif., U.S.A. 124 38 54N 121 17W
Lincoln, Ill., U.S.A. 118 40 10N 89 20W
Lincoln, Kans., U.S.A. 120 39 6N 98 9W
Lincoln, Maine, U.S.A. 105 45 27N 68 29W
Lincoln, N.H., U.S.A. 117 44 3N 71 40W
Lincoln, N. Mex., U.S.A. 123 33 30N 105 26W
Lincoln, Nebr., U.S.A. 120 40 50N 96 42W
Lincoln □, U.K. 12 53 14N 0 32W
Lincoln Park, U.S.A. 119 42 15N 83 11W
Lincoln Sea, Arctic 144 84 0N 55 0W
Lincoln Wolds, U.K. 12 53 20N 0 5W
Lincolnton, U.S.A. 115 35 30N 81 15W
Lind, U.S.A. 122 47 0N 118 33W
Linda, U.S.A. 124 39 6N 121 34W
Lindås, Sweden 11 56 38N 15 35 E
Lindau, W. Germany 31 47 33N 9 41 E
Linde →, Neths. 16 52 50N 5 57 E
Linden, Guyana 136 6 0N 58 10W
Linden, Calif., U.S.A. 124 38 1N 121 5W
Linden, Ind., U.S.A. 119 40 11N 86 54W
Linden, Mich., U.S.A. 119 42 49N 83 47W
Linden, Tex., U.S.A. 121 33 0N 94 20W
Lindenheuvel, Neths. 17 50 59N 5 48 E
Lindenhurst, U.S.A. 117 40 41N 73 23W
Lindenow, Australia 75 37 48 S 147 28 E
Linderöd, Sweden 11 55 56N 13 47 E
Linderödsåsen, Sweden 11 55 53N 13 53 E
Lindesberg, Sweden 10 59 36N 15 15 E

Luangwa

Loji, *Indonesia* **57** 1 38 S 127 28 E
Loka, *Sudan* **89** 4 13N 31 0 E
Lokandu, *Zaïre* **92** 2 30 S 25 45 E
Løken, *Norway* **10** 59 48N 11 29 E
Lokeren, *Belgium* **17** 51 6N 3 59 E
Lokhvitsa, *U.S.S.R.* **36** 50 25N 33 18 E
Lokichokio, *Kenya* **92** 4 19N 34 13 E
Lokitaung, *Kenya* **92** 4 12N 35 48 E
Lokka, *Finland* **8** 67 55N 27 35 E
Løkken, *Denmark* **11** 57 22N 9 41 E
Løkken Verk, *Norway* **10** 63 7N 9 43 E
Loknya, *U.S.S.R.* **36** 56 49N 30 4 E
Lokoja, *Nigeria* **91** 7 47N 6 45 E
Lokolama, *Zaïre* **94** 2 35 S 19 50 E
Lokuru, *Solomon Is.* **68** 8 20 S 157 0 E
Lol →, *Sudan* **89** 9 13N 26 30 E
Lola, *Guinea* **90** 7 52N 8 29W
Lola, Mt., *U.S.A.* **124** 39 26N 120 22W
Lolibai, Gebel, *Sudan* **89** 3 50N 33 0 E
Lolimi, *Sudan* **89** 4 35N 34 0 E
Loliondo, *Tanzania* **92** 2 2 S 35 39 E
Lolland, *Denmark* **11** 54 45N 11 30 E
Lollar, *W. Germany* **30** 50 39N 8 43 E
Lolo, *U.S.A.* **122** 46 50N 114 8W
Lolodorf, *Cameroon* **91** 3 16N 10 49 E
Lolowai, *Vanuatu* **68** 15 18 S 168 0 E
Lom, *Bulgaria* **34** 43 48N 23 12 E
Lom →, *Bulgaria* **34** 43 45N 23 15 E
Lom Kao, *Thailand* **54** 16 53N 101 14 E
Lom Sak, *Thailand* **54** 16 47N 101 15 E
Loma, *U.S.A.* **122** 47 59N 110 29W
Loma Linda, *U.S.A.* **125** 34 3N 117 16W
Lomaloma, *Fiji* **68** 17 17 S 178 59W
Lomami →, *Zaïre* **92** 0 46N 24 16 E
Lomas de Zamóra, *Argentina* **140** 34 45 S 58 25W
Lombadina, *Australia* **78** 16 31 S 122 54 E
Lombard, *U.S.A.* **119** 41 53N 88 1W
Lombardia □, *Italy* **26** 45 35N 9 45 E
Lombardy = Lombardia □, *Italy* **26** 45 35N 9 45 E
Lombe, *Angola* **95** 9 27 S 16 13 E
Lombez, *France* **20** 43 29N 0 55 E
Lomblen, *Indonesia* **57** 8 30 S 123 32 E
Lombok, *Indonesia* **56** 8 45 S 116 30 E
Lomé, *Togo* **91** 6 9N 1 20 E
Lomela, *Zaïre* **94** 2 19 S 23 15 E
Lomela →, *Zaïre* **94** 0 15 S 20 40 E
Lomello, *Italy* **26** 45 5N 8 46 E
Lometa, *U.S.A.* **121** 31 15N 98 25W
Lomié, *Cameroon* **94** 3 13N 13 38 E
Lomma, *Sweden* **11** 55 43N 13 6 E
Lomme →, *Belgium* **17** 50 8N 5 10 E
Lommel, *Belgium* **17** 51 14N 5 19 E
Lomond, *Canada* **110** 50 24N 112 36W
Lomond, L., *U.K.* **14** 56 8N 4 38W
Lomonosov, *U.S.S.R.* **36** 59 57N 29 53 E
Lomphat, *Cambodia* **54** 13 30N 106 59 E
Lompobatang, *Indonesia* **57** 5 24 S 119 56 E
Lompoc, *U.S.A.* **125** 34 41N 120 32W
Lomsegga, *Norway* **10** 61 49N 8 21 E
Lomza, *Poland* **32** 53 10N 22 2 E
Lonavale, *India* **50** 18 46N 73 29 E
Loncoche, *Chile* **142** 39 20 S 72 50W
Loncopuè, *Argentina* **142** 38 4 S 70 37W
Londa, *India* **51** 15 30N 74 30 E
Londe-les-Maures, La, *France* **21** 43 8N 6 14 E
Londerzeel, *Belgium* **17** 51 0N 4 19 E
Londiani, *Kenya* **92** 0 10 S 35 33 E
Londinières, *France* **18** 49 50N 1 25 E
London, *Canada* **108** 42 59N 81 15W
London, *U.K.* **13** 51 30N 0 5W
London, *Ky., U.S.A.* **114** 37 11N 84 5W
London, *Ohio, U.S.A.* **119** 39 54N 83 28W
London, Greater □, *U.K.* **13** 51 30N 0 5W
London Mills, *U.S.A.* **118** 40 43N 90 11W
Londonderry, *U.K.* **15** 55 0N 7 20W
Londonderry □, *U.K.* **15** 55 0N 7 20W
Londonderry, C., *Australia* **78** 13 45 S 126 55 E
Londonderry, I., *Chile* **142** 55 0 S 71 0W
Londrina, *Brazil* **141** 23 18 S 51 10W
Londuimbale, *Angola* **95** 12 15 S 15 19 E
Lone Pine, *U.S.A.* **124** 36 35N 118 2W
Lonely I., *Canada* **108** 45 34N 81 28W
Long Beach, *Calif., U.S.A.* **125** 33 46N 118 12W
Long Beach, *N.Y., U.S.A.* **117** 40 35N 73 40W
Long Beach, *Wash., U.S.A.* **124** 46 20N 124 1W
Long Branch, *U.S.A.* **117** 40 19N 74 0W
Long Creek, *U.S.A.* **122** 44 43N 119 6W
Long Eaton, *U.K.* **12** 52 54N 1 16W
Long I., *Australia* **72** 22 8 S 149 53 E
Long I., *Bahamas* **129** 23 20N 75 10W
Long I., *Papua N. G.* **69** 5 20 S 147 5 E
Long I., *U.S.A.* **117** 40 50N 73 20W
Long I. Sd., *U.S.A.* **117** 41 10N 73 0W
Long L., *Canada* **104** 49 30N 86 50W
Long Lake, *U.S.A.* **117** 43 57N 74 25W
Long Pine, *U.S.A.* **120** 42 33N 99 41W
Long Pt., *Nfld., Canada* **105** 48 47N 58 46W
Long Pt., *Ont., Canada* **108** 42 35N 80 2W
Long Pt., *N.Z.* **81** 46 34 S 169 36 E
Long Point B., *Canada* **108** 42 40N 80 10W
Long Range Mts., *Canada* **105** 49 30N 57 30W
Long Str. = Longa, Proliv, *U.S.S.R.* **144** 70 0N 175 0 E
Long Thanh, *Vietnam* **55** 10 47N 106 57 E
Long Xian, *China* **60** 34 55N 106 55 E
Long Xuyen, *Vietnam* **55** 10 19N 105 28 E
Longa, *Angola* **95** 14 42 S 18 32 E
Longá, *Greece* **35** 36 53N 21 55 E
Longa, Proliv, *U.S.S.R.* **144** 70 0N 175 0 E
Long'an, *China* **58** 23 10N 107 40 E
Longarone, *Italy* **27** 46 15N 12 18 E
Longburn, *N.Z.* **80** 40 23 S 175 35 E
Longchang, *China* **58** 29 18N 105 15 E
Longchi, *China* **58** 29 25N 103 24 E
Longchuan, *Guangdong, China* **59** 24 5N 115 17 E
Longchuan, *Yunnan, China* **58** 24 23N 97 58 E
Longde, *China* **60** 35 30N 106 20 E
Longeau, *France* **19** 47 47N 5 20 E
Longford, *Australia* **72** 41 32 S 147 3 E
Longford, *Ireland* **15** 53 43N 7 50W
Longford □, *Ireland* **15** 53 42N 7 45W
Longguan, *China* **60** 40 45N 115 30 E
Longhua, *China* **61** 41 18N 117 45 E
Longhui, *China* **59** 27 7N 111 2 E
Longido, *Tanzania* **92** 2 43 S 36 42 E
Longiram, *Indonesia* **56** 0 5 S 115 45 E
Longkou, *Jiangxi, China* **59** 26 8N 115 10 E
Longkou, *Shandong, China* **61** 37 40N 120 18 E
Longlac, *Canada* **104** 49 45N 86 25W
Longli, *China* **58** 26 25N 106 58 E
Longlier, *Belgium* **17** 49 52N 5 27 E
Longlin, *China* **58** 24 47N 105 20 E
Longling, *China* **58** 24 37N 98 39 E
Longmen, *China* **59** 23 40N 114 18 E
Longming, *China* **58** 22 59N 107 7 E
Longmont, *U.S.A.* **120** 40 10N 105 4W
Longnan, *China* **59** 24 55N 114 47 E
Longnawan, *Indonesia* **56** 1 51N 114 55 E
Longobucco, *Italy* **29** 39 27N 16 37 E
Longquan, *China* **59** 28 7N 119 10 E
Longreach, *Australia* **72** 23 28 S 144 14 E
Longshan, *China* **58** 29 29N 109 25 E
Longsheng, *China* **58** 25 48N 110 0 E
Longton, *Australia* **72** 20 58 S 145 55 E
Longtown, *U.K.* **13** 51 58N 2 59W
Longué-Jumelles, *France* **18** 47 22N 0 8W
Longueau, *France* **19** 49 52N 2 21 E
Longueuil, *Qué., Canada* **107** 45 32N 73 30W
Longueuil, *Canada* **117** 45 32N 73 28W
Longuyon, *France* **19** 49 27N 5 35 E
Longview, *Canada* **110** 50 32N 114 10W
Longview, *Tex., U.S.A.* **121** 32 30N 94 45W
Longview, *Wash., U.S.A.* **124** 46 9N 122 58W
Longvilly, *Belgium* **17** 50 2N 5 50 E
Longwarry, *Australia* **74** 38 8 S 145 48 E
Longwood, *Australia* **74** 36 48 S 145 26 E
Longwy, *France* **19** 49 30N 5 46 E
Longxi, *China* **60** 34 53N 104 40 E
Longyou, *China* **59** 29 1N 119 8 E
Longzhou, *China* **58** 22 22N 106 50 E
Lonigo, *Italy* **27** 45 23N 11 22 E
Löningen, *W. Germany* **30** 52 43N 7 44 E
Lonja →, *Yugoslavia* **27** 45 30N 16 40 E
Lonkin, *Burma* **52** 25 39N 96 22 E
Lonoke, *U.S.A.* **121** 34 48N 91 57W
Lonquimay, *Chile* **142** 38 26 S 71 14W
Lons-le-Saunier, *France* **19** 46 40N 5 31 E
Lønstrup, *Denmark* **11** 57 29N 9 47 E
Loogootee, *U.S.A.* **119** 38 41N 86 55W
Lookout, C., *Canada* **104** 55 18N 83 56W
Lookout, C., *U.S.A.* **115** 34 30N 76 30W
Loolmalasin, *Tanzania* **92** 3 0 S 35 53 E
Loon →, *Alta., Canada* **110** 57 8N 115 3W
Loon →, *Man., Canada* **111** 55 53N 101 59W
Loon Lake, *Canada* **111** 54 2N 109 10W
Loon-op-Zand, *Neths.* **17** 51 38N 5 5 E
Loongana, *Australia* **79** 30 52 S 127 5 E
Loop Hd., *Ireland* **15** 52 34N 9 55W
Loosduinen, *Neths.* **16** 52 3N 4 14 E
Lop Buri, *Thailand* **54** 14 48N 100 37 E
Lop Nor = Lop Nur, *China* **62** 40 20N 90 10 E
Lop Nur, *China* **62** 40 20N 90 10 E
Lopare, *Yugoslavia* **33** 44 39N 18 46 E
Lopatin, *U.S.S.R.* **39** 43 50N 47 35 E
Lopatina, G., *U.S.S.R.* **41** 50 47N 143 10 E
Lopaye, *Sudan* **89** 6 37N 33 40 E
Lopera, *Spain* **23** 37 56N 4 14W
Lopevi, *Vanuatu* **68** 16 30 S 168 21 E
Lopez, C., *Gabon* **94** 0 47 S 8 40 E
Lopez I., *Gabon* **94** 0 50 S 8 47 E
Loppersum, *Neths.* **16** 53 20N 6 44 E
Lopphavet, *Norway* **8** 70 27N 21 15 E
Lora →, *Afghan.* **47** 32 0N 67 15 E
Lora, Hamun-i-, *Pakistan* **47** 29 38N 64 58 E
Lora, La, *Spain* **22** 42 45N 4 0W
Lora Cr. →, *Australia* **73** 28 10 S 135 22 E
Lora del Río, *Spain* **23** 37 39N 5 33W
Lorain, *U.S.A.* **116** 41 28N 82 55W
Loraine, *U.S.A.* **118** 40 9N 91 13W
Loralai, *Pakistan* **48** 30 20N 68 41 E
Lorca, *Spain* **25** 37 41N 1 42W
Lord Howe I., *Pac. Oc.* **66** 31 33 S 159 6 E
Lord Howe Ridge, *Pac. Oc.* **66** 30 0 S 162 30 E
Lordsburg, *U.S.A.* **123** 32 22N 108 45W
Lorengau, *Papua N. G.* **69** 2 1 S 147 15 E
Loreto, *Bolivia* **137** 15 13 S 64 40W
Loreto, *Brazil* **138** 7 5 S 45 10W
Loreto, *Italy* **27** 43 26N 13 36 E
Loreto, *Mexico* **126** 26 1N 111 21W
Loreto □, *Peru* **134** 5 0 S 75 0W
Loreto Aprutina, *Italy* **27** 42 24N 13 59 E
Loretteville, *Canada* **107** 46 51N 71 21W
Lorgues, *France* **21** 43 28N 6 22 E
Lorica, *Colombia* **134** 9 14N 75 49W
Lorient, *France* **18** 47 45N 3 23W
Lorimor, *U.S.A.* **118** 41 7N 94 3W
Loristān □, *Iran* **46** 33 20N 47 0 E
Lorn, *U.K.* **14** 56 26N 5 10W
Lorn, Firth of, *U.K.* **14** 56 20N 5 40W
Lorne, *N.S.W., Australia* **77** 31 36 S 152 39 E
Lorne, *Vic., Australia* **74** 38 33 S 143 59 E
Lörrach, *W. Germany* **31** 47 36N 7 38 E
Lorraine, *France* **19** 48 30N 6 0 E
Lorrainville, *Canada* **106** 47 21N 79 23W
Los, Îles de, *Guinea* **90** 9 30N 13 50W
Los Alamos, *Calif., U.S.A.* **125** 34 44N 120 17W
Los Alamos, *N. Mex., U.S.A.* **123** 35 57N 106 17W
Los Altos, *U.S.A.* **124** 37 23N 122 7W
Los Andes, *Chile* **140** 32 50 S 70 40W
Los Angeles, *Chile* **140** 37 28 S 72 23W
Los Angeles, *U.S.A.* **125** 34 0N 118 10W
Los Angeles Aqueduct, *U.S.A.* **125** 35 25N 118 0W
Los Antiguos, *Argentina* **142** 46 35 S 71 40W
Los Banos, *U.S.A.* **124** 37 8N 120 56W
Los Barrios, *Spain* **23** 36 11N 5 30W
Los Blancos, *Argentina* **140** 23 40 S 62 30W
Los Cristianos, *Canary Is.* **25** 28 3N 16 42W
Los Gatos, *U.S.A.* **124** 37 14N 121 59W
Los Hermanos, *Venezuela* **129** 11 45N 64 25W
Los Islotes, *Canary Is.* **25** 29 4N 13 44W
Los Lagos, *Chile* **142** 39 51 S 72 50W
Los Llanos de Aridane, *Canary Is.* **25** 28 38N 17 54W
Los Lomas, *Peru* **136** 4 40 S 80 10W
Los Lunas, *U.S.A.* **123** 34 48N 106 47W
Los Menucos, *Argentina* **142** 40 50 S 68 10W
Los Mochis, *Mexico* **126** 25 45N 109 5W
Los Monegros, *Spain* **24** 41 29N 0 13W
Los Monos, *Argentina* **142** 46 1 S 69 36W
Los Olivos, *U.S.A.* **125** 34 40N 120 7W
Los Palacios, *Cuba* **128** 22 35N 83 15W
Los Palacios y Villafranca, *Spain* **23** 37 10N 5 55W
Los Reyes, *Mexico* **126** 19 34N 102 30W
Los Ríos □, *Ecuador* **134** 1 30 S 79 25W
Los Roques, *Venezuela* **134** 11 50N 66 45W
Los Santos de Maimona, *Spain* **23** 38 27N 6 22W
Los Teques, *Venezuela* **134** 10 21N 67 2W
Los Testigos, *Venezuela* **135** 11 23N 63 6W
Los Vilos, *Chile* **140** 32 10 S 71 30W
Los Yébenes, *Spain* **23** 39 36N 3 55W
Losada →, *Colombia* **134** 2 12N 73 55W
Loshkalakh, *U.S.S.R.* **41** 62 45N 147 20 E
Lošinj, *Yugoslavia* **27** 44 30N 14 30 E
Losser, *Neths.* **16** 52 16N 7 1 E
Lossiemouth, *U.K.* **14** 57 43N 3 17W
Losuia, *Papua N. G.* **69** 8 30 S 151 4 E
Lot □, *France* **20** 44 39N 1 40 E
Lot →, *France* **20** 44 18N 0 20 E
Lot-et-Garonne □, *France* **20** 44 22N 0 30 E
Lota, *Chile* **140** 37 5 S 73 10W
Løten, *Norway* **10** 60 51N 11 21 E
Lothair, *S. Africa* **97** 26 22 S 30 27 E
Lothian □, *U.K.* **14** 55 50N 3 0W
Lothiers, *France* **19** 46 42N 1 33 E
Lotofaga, *W. Samoa* **68** 14 1 S 171 30W
Lotschbergtunnel, *Switz.* **31** 46 26N 7 43 E
Lottefors, *Sweden* **10** 61 25N 16 24 E
Loubomo, *Congo* **94** 4 9 S 12 47 E
Loudéac, *France* **18** 48 11N 2 47W
Loudi, *China* **59** 27 42N 111 59 E
Loudima, *Congo* **94** 4 6 S 13 5 E
Loudon, *U.S.A.* **115** 35 35N 84 22W
Loudonville, *U.S.A.* **116** 40 40N 82 15W
Loudun, *France* **18** 47 0N 0 5 E
Loué, *France* **18** 47 59N 0 9W
Loue →, *France* **19** 47 1N 5 28 E
Louga, *Senegal* **90** 15 45N 16 5W
Loughborough, *U.K.* **12** 52 46N 1 11W
Loughrea, *Ireland* **15** 53 11N 8 33W
Loughros More B., *Ireland* **15** 54 48N 8 30W
Louhans, *France* **21** 46 38N 5 12 E
Louis Trichardt, *S. Africa* **97** 23 1 S 29 43 E
Louis XIV, Pte., *Canada* **104** 54 37N 79 45W
Louisa, *U.S.A.* **114** 38 5N 82 40W
Louisbourg, *Canada* **105** 45 55N 60 0W
Louisburg, *U.S.A.* **118** 38 37N 94 41W
Louise I., *Canada* **110** 52 55N 131 50W
Louiseville, *Canada* **107** 46 20N 72 56W
Louisiade Arch., *Papua N. G.* **69** 11 10 S 153 0 E
Louisiana, *U.S.A.* **118** 39 25N 91 0W
Louisiana □, *U.S.A.* **121** 30 50N 92 0W
Louisville, *Ky., U.S.A.* **119** 38 15N 85 45W
Louisville, *Miss., U.S.A.* **121** 33 7N 89 3W
Loukouo, *Congo* **94** 3 38 S 14 39 E
Loulay, *France* **20** 46 3N 0 30W
Loulé, *Portugal* **23** 37 9N 8 0W
Louny, *Czech.* **32** 50 20N 13 48 E
Loup City, *U.S.A.* **120** 41 19N 98 57W
Loupe, La, *France* **18** 48 29N 1 1 E
Lourdes, *France* **20** 43 6N 0 3W
Lourdes-du-Blanc-Sablon, *Canada* **105** 51 24N 57 12W
Lourenço, *Brazil* **135** 2 30N 51 40W
Lourenço-Marques = Maputo, *Mozam.* **97** 25 58 S 32 32 E
Loures, *Portugal* **23** 38 50N 9 9W
Lourinhã, *Portugal* **23** 39 14N 9 17W
Louroux-Béconnais, Le, *France* **18** 47 30N 0 55W
Lousã, *Portugal* **22** 40 7N 8 14W
Louth, *Australia* **73** 30 30 S 145 8 E
Louth, *Ireland* **15** 53 47N 6 33W
Louth, *U.K.* **12** 53 23N 0 0 E
Louth □, *Ireland* **15** 53 55N 6 30W
Louvain = Leuven, *Belgium* **17** 50 52N 4 42 E
Louveigné, *Belgium* **17** 50 32N 5 42 E
Louvière, La, *Belgium* **17** 50 27N 4 10 E
Louviers, *France* **18** 49 12N 1 10 E
Louwsburg, *S. Africa* **97** 27 37 S 31 7 E
Lovat →, *U.S.S.R.* **36** 58 14N 30 28 E
Love, *Canada* **111** 53 29N 104 10W
Lovech, *Bulgaria* **34** 43 8N 24 42 E
Loveland, *Colo., U.S.A.* **120** 40 27N 105 4W
Loveland, *Ohio, U.S.A.* **119** 39 16N 84 16W
Lovell, *U.S.A.* **122** 44 51N 108 20W
Lovelock, *U.S.A.* **122** 40 17N 118 25W
Lóvere, *Italy* **26** 45 50N 10 4 E
Loves Park, *U.S.A.* **118** 42 19N 89 3W
Loviisa = Lovisa, *Finland* **9** 60 28N 26 12 E
Lovilia, *U.S.A.* **118** 41 8N 92 55W
Loving, *U.S.A.* **121** 32 17N 104 4W
Lovington, *Ill., U.S.A.* **119** 39 43N 88 38W
Lovington, *N. Mex., U.S.A.* **121** 33 0N 103 20W
Lovios, *Spain* **22** 41 55N 8 4W
Lovisa, *Finland* **9** 60 28N 26 12 E
Lovran, *Yugoslavia* **27** 45 18N 14 15 E
Lövstabukten, *Sweden* **10** 60 35N 17 45 E
Low, *Canada* **106** 45 50N 76 0W
Low Pt., *Australia* **79** 32 25 S 127 25 E
Lowa, *Zaïre* **92** 1 25 S 25 47 E
Lowa →, *Zaïre* **92** 1 24 S 25 51 E
Lowden, *U.S.A.* **118** 41 52N 90 56W
Lowell, *Ind., U.S.A.* **119** 41 18N 87 25W
Lowell, *Mass., U.S.A.* **117** 42 38N 71 19W
Lower Arrow L., *Canada* **110** 49 40N 118 5W
Lower California = Baja California, *Mexico* **126** 31 10N 115 12W
Lower Hutt, *N.Z.* **80** 41 10 S 174 55 E
Lower L., *U.S.A.* **122** 41 17N 120 3W
Lower Lake, *U.S.A.* **124** 38 56N 122 36W
Lower Post, *Canada* **110** 59 58N 128 30W
Lower Red L., *U.S.A.* **120** 48 0N 94 50W
Lower Saxony = Niedersachsen □, *W. Germany* **30** 52 45N 9 0 E
Lower Tunguska = Tunguska, Nizhnyaya →, *U.S.S.R.* **41** 65 48N 88 4 E
Lowestoft, *U.K.* **13** 52 29N 1 44 E
Lowicz, *Poland* **32** 52 6N 19 55 E
Lowry City, *U.S.A.* **118** 38 8N 93 44W
Lowville, *U.S.A.* **117** 43 48N 75 30W
Lowyar □, *Afghan.* **47** 34 0N 69 0 E
Loxton, *Australia* **73** 34 28 S 140 31 E
Loxton, *S. Africa* **96** 31 30 S 22 22 E
Loyalton, *U.S.A.* **124** 39 41N 120 14W
Loyalty Is. = Loyauté, Is., *N. Cal.* **68** 21 0 S 167 30 E
Loyang = Luoyang, *China* **60** 34 40N 112 26 E
Loyauté, Is., *N. Cal.* **68** 21 0 S 167 30 E
Loyev, *U.S.S.R.* **36** 51 56N 30 46 E
Loyoro, *Uganda* **92** 3 22N 34 14 E
Lož, *Yugoslavia* **27** 45 43N 14 30 E
Lozère □, *France* **20** 44 35N 3 30 E
Loznica, *Yugoslavia* **33** 44 32N 19 14 E
Lozovaya, *U.S.S.R.* **38** 49 0N 36 20 E
Luachimo, *Angola* **95** 7 23 S 20 48 E
Luacono, *Angola* **95** 11 15 S 21 37 E
Lualaba →, *Zaïre* **92** 0 26N 25 20 E
Luampa, *Zambia* **93** 15 4 S 24 20 E
Lu'an, *China* **59** 31 45N 116 29 E
Luan Chau, *Vietnam* **54** 21 38N 103 24 E
Luan He →, *China* **61** 39 20N 119 5 E
Luan Xian, *China* **61** 39 40N 118 40 E
Luancheng, *Guangxi Zhuangzu, China* **58** 22 48N 108 55 E
Luancheng, *Hebei, China* **60** 37 53N 114 40 E
Luanda, *Angola* **95** 8 50 S 13 15 E
Luanda □, *Angola* **95** 9 0 S 13 10 E
Luang Prabang, *Laos* **54** 19 52N 102 10 E
Luang Thale, *Thailand* **55** 7 30N 100 15 E
Luangwa, *Zambia* **93** 15 35 S 30 16 E

Luangwa

Luangwa →, *Zambia* . **93** 14 25 S 30 25 E
Luangwa Valley, *Zambia* . . . . **93** 13 30 S 31 30 E
Luanne, *China* . . . . . . **61** 40 55N 117 40 E
Luanping, *China* . . . . . **61** 40 53N 117 23 E
Luanshya, *Zambia* . . . . **93** 13 3 S 28 28 E
Luapula □, *Zambia* . . **93** 11 0 S 29 0 E
Luapula →, *Africa* . . . **93** 9 26 S 28 33 E
Luarca, *Spain* **22** 43 32N 6 32W
Luashi, *Zaïre* . . . . **93** 10 50 S 23 36 E
Luau, *Angola* . . . . **95** 10 40 S 22 10 E
Lubalo, *Angola* . . . . . . **95** 9 10 S 19 15 E
Lubań, *Poland* . . . . **32** 51 5N 15 15 E
Lubana, Ozero, *U.S.S.R.* . . . . **36** 56 45N 27 0 E
Lubang Is., *Phil.* . . . . . **57** 13 50N 120 12 E
Lubango, *Angola* . . . . . **95** 14 55 S 13 30 E
Lubartów, *Poland* . . . . **32** 51 28N 22 42 E
Lubawa, *Poland* . . . . . . **32** 53 30N 19 48 E
Lubbeek, *Belgium* . . . . **17** 50 54N 4 50 E
Lübben, *E. Germany* . . **30** 51 56N 13 54 E
Lübbenau, *E. Germany* **30** 51 49N 13 59 E
Lubbock, *U.S.A.* **121** 33 40N 101 53W
Lubeck, *Australia* . . . . **74** 36 45 S 142 34 E
Lübeck, *W. Germany* . **30** 53 52N 10 41 E
Lübecker Bucht, *W. Germany* . . . . **30** 54 3N 11 0 E
Lubefu, *Zaïre* . . . . **92** 4 47 S 24 27 E
Lubefu →, *Zaïre* . . . . . **92** 4 10 S 23 0 E
Lubero = Luofu, *Zaïre* **92** 0 10 S 29 15 E
Lubicon L., *Canada* . . **110** 56 23N 115 56W
Lublin, *Poland* . . . . **32** 51 12N 22 38 E
Lubliniec, *Poland* . . . . **32** 50 43N 18 45 E
Lubny, *U.S.S.R.* . . . . . **36** 50 3N 32 58 E
Lubon, *Poland* . . . . **32** 52 21N 16 51 E
Lubongola, *Zaïre* . . . . . **92** 2 35 S 27 50 E
Lubsko, *Poland* . . . . . . **32** 51 45N 14 57 E
Lübtheen, *E. Germany* **30** 53 18N 11 4 E
Lubuagan, *Phil.* . . . . . . **57** 17 21N 121 10 E
Lubudi →, *Zaïre* . . . . . **93** 9 0 S 25 35 E
Lubuk Antu, *Malaysia* **56** 1 3N 111 50 E
Lubuklinggau, *Indonesia* . . . . **56** 3 15 S 102 55 E
Lubuksikaping, *Indonesia* . . . . **56** 0 10N 100 15 E
Lubumbashi, *Zaïre* . . . **93** 11 40 S 27 28 E
Lubunda, *Zaïre* . . . . . . **92** 5 12 S 26 41 E
Lubungu, *Zambia* . . . . **93** 14 35 S 26 24 E
Lubutu, *Zaïre* . . . . **92** 0 45 S 26 30 E
Luc, Le, *France* . . . . . . **21** 43 23N 6 21 E
Luc An Chau, *Vietnam* **54** 22 6N 104 43 E
Luc-en-Diois, *France* . **21** 44 36N 5 28 E
Lucala, *Angola* . . . . **95** 9 7 S 15 58 E
Lucan, *Canada* **108** 43 11N 81 24W
Lucca, *Italy* . . . . **26** 43 50N 10 30 E
Luce Bay, *U.K.* **14** 54 45N 4 48W
Lucea, *Jamaica* **128** 18 25N 78 10W
Lucedale, *U.S.A.* **115** 30 55N 88 34W
Lucena, *Phil.* . . . . **57** 13 56N 121 37 E
Lucena, *Spain* **23** 37 27N 4 31W
Lucena del Cid, *Spain* **24** 40 9N 0 17W
Lučenec, *Czech.* . . . . . **33** 48 18N 19 42 E
Lucera, *Italy* . . . . **29** 41 30N 15 20 E
Lucerne = Luzern, *Switz.* . . . . **31** 47 3N 8 18 E
Lucerne, *U.S.A.* **124** 39 6N 122 48W
Lucerne Valley, *U.S.A.* **125** 34 27N 116 57W
Lucero, *Mexico* **126** 30 49N 106 30W
Luceville, *Canada* **107** 48 32N 68 22W
Luchena →, *Spain* . . . **25** 37 44N 1 50W
Lucheng, *China* . . . . . . **60** 36 20N 113 11 E
Lucheringo →, *Mozam.* . . . . **93** 11 43 S 36 17 E
Lüchow, *W. Germany* . **30** 52 58N 11 8 E
Luchuan, *China* . . . . . . **59** 22 21N 110 12 E
Lucie →, *Surinam* . . . **135** 3 35N 57 38W
Lucira, *Angola* . . . . **95** 14 0 S 12 35 E
Luckau, *E. Germany* . **30** 51 50N 13 43 E
Luckenwalde, *E. Germany* . . . . **30** 52 5N 13 11 E
Luckey, *U.S.A.* **119** 41 27N 83 29W
Lucknow, *Australia* . . . **76** 33 21 S 149 11 E
Lucknow, *Canada* **108** 43 57N 81 31W
Lucknow, *India* . . . . . . **49** 26 50N 81 0 E
Luçon, *France* **20** 46 28N 1 10W
Lucusse, *Angola* . . . . . **95** 12 32 S 20 48 E
Lüda = Dalian, *China* **61** 38 50N 121 40 E
Luda Kamchiya →, *Bulgaria* . . . . **34** 43 3N 27 29 E
Ludbreg, *Yugoslavia* . . **27** 46 15N 16 38 E
Lüdenscheid, *W. Germany* . . . . **30** 51 13N 7 37 E
Lüderitz, *Namibia* . . . . **96** 26 41 S 15 8 E
Ludewe □, *Tanzania* . **93** 10 0 S 34 50 E
Ludhiana, *India* . . . . . . **48** 30 57N 75 56 E
Ludian, *China* . . . . **58** 27 10N 103 33 E
Luding Qiao, *China* . . **58** 29 53N 102 12 E
Lüdinghausen, *W. Germany* . . . . **30** 51 46N 7 28 E
Ludington, *U.S.A.* . . . **114** 43 58N 86 27W
Ludlow, *U.K.* **13** 52 23N 2 42W
Ludlow, *Calif., U.S.A.* **125** 34 43N 116 10W
Ludlow, *Vt., U.S.A.* . . **117** 43 25N 72 40W
Ludus, *Romania* . . . . . **34** 46 29N 24 5 E
Ludvika, *Sweden* . . . . . **10** 60 8N 15 14 E
Ludwigsburg, *W. Germany* . . . . **31** 48 53N 9 11 E
Ludwigshafen, *W. Germany* . . . . **31** 49 27N 8 27 E
Ludwigslust, *E. Germany* . . . . **30** 53 19N 11 28 E
Ludza, *U.S.S.R.* . . . . . **36** 56 32N 27 43 E
Lue, *Australia* . . . . **76** 32 38 S 149 50 E
Luebo, *Zaïre* . . . . **95** 5 21 S 21 23 E
Lueki, *Zaïre* . . . . **92** 3 20 S 25 48 E
Luena, *Angola* . . . . **95** 12 13 S 19 51 E
Luena, *Zaïre* . . . . **93** 9 28 S 25 43 E
Luena, *Zambia* . . . . . . **93** 10 40 S 30 25 E
Luepa, *Venezuela* **135** 5 43N 61 31W
Lüeyang, *China* . . . . . . **60** 33 22N 106 10 E
Lufeng, *Guangdong, China* . . . . **59** 22 57N 115 38 E
Lufeng, *Yunnan, China* **58** 25 0N 102 5 E
Lufico, *Angola* . . . . **95** 6 24 S 13 23 E
Lufira →, *Zaïre* . . . . . **93** 9 30 S 27 0 E
Lufkin, *U.S.A.* **121** 31 25N 94 40W
Lufupa, *Zaïre* . . . . **93** 10 37 S 24 56 E
Luga, *U.S.S.R.* . . . . . . **36** 58 40N 29 55 E
Luga →, *U.S.S.R.* . . . **36** 59 40N 28 18 E
Lugang, *Taiwan* . . . . . . **59** 24 4N 120 23 E
Lugano, *Switz.* . . . . **31** 46 0N 8 57 E
Lugano, L. di, *Switz.* . **31** 46 0N 9 0 E
Lugansk = Voroshilovgrad, *U.S.S.R.* . . . . **39** 48 38N 39 15 E
Lugard's Falls, *Kenya* . **92** 3 6 S 38 41 E
Lugela, *Mozam.* . . . . . **93** 16 25 S 36 43 E
Lugenda →, *Mozam.* . **93** 11 25 S 38 33 E
Lugh Ganana, *Somali Rep.* . . . . **98** 3 48N 42 34 E
Lugnaquilla, *Ireland* . . **15** 52 58N 6 28W
Lugnvik, *Sweden* . . . . **10** 62 56N 17 55 E
Lugo, *Italy* . . . . **27** 44 25N 11 53 E
Lugo, *Spain* **22** 43 2N 7 35W
Lugo □, *Spain* **22** 43 0N 7 30W
Lugoj, *Romania* . . . . . . **34** 45 42N 21 57 E
Lugones, *Spain* **22** 43 26N 5 50W
Lugovoye, *U.S.S.R.* . . **40** 42 55N 72 43 E
Luhe, *China* . . . . **59** 32 19N 118 50 E
Luhe →, *W. Germany* **30** 53 18N 10 11 E
Luhuo, *China* . . . . **58** 31 21N 100 48 E
Luiana, *Angola* . . . . . . **95** 17 25 S 22 59 E
Luino, *Italy* . . . . **26** 46 0N 8 42 E
Luís Correia, *Brazil* . . **138** 3 0 S 41 35W
Luís Gonçalves, *Brazil* **138** 5 37 S 50 25W
Luitpold Coast, *Antarctica* . . . . **143** 78 30 S 32 0W
Luiza, *Zaïre* . . . . **95** 7 40 S 22 30 E
Luizi, *Zaïre* . . . . **92** 6 0 S 27 25 E
Luján, *Argentina* . . . . . **140** 34 45 S 59 5W
Lujiang, *China* . . . . **59** 31 20N 117 15 E
Lukala, *Zaïre* . . . . **95** 5 31 S 14 32 E
Lukanga Swamp, *Zambia* . . . . **93** 14 30 S 27 40 E
Lukenie →, *Zaïre* . . . . **94** 3 0 S 18 50 E
Lukhisaral, *India* . . . . . **49** 25 11N 86 5 E
Lŭki, *Bulgaria* . . . . **35** 41 50N 24 43 E
Lukk, *Libya* . . . . **86** 32 1N 24 46 E
Lukolela, *Equateur, Zaïre* . . . . **94** 1 10 S 17 12 E
Lukolela, *Kasai Or., Zaïre* . . . . **92** 5 23 S 24 32 E
Lukosi, *Zambia* . . . . . . **93** 18 30 S 26 30 E
Lukovit, *Bulgaria* . . . . **34** 43 13N 24 11 E
Łuków, *Poland* . . . . **32** 51 55N 22 23 E
Lukoyanov, *U.S.S.R.* . . **37** 55 2N 44 29 E
Lule älv →, *Sweden* . . **8** 65 35N 22 10 E
Luleå, *Sweden* . . . . **8** 65 35N 22 10 E
Lüleburgaz, *Turkey* . . . **46** 41 23N 27 22 E
Luliang, *China* . . . . **58** 25 0N 103 40 E
Luling, *U.S.A.* **121** 29 45N 97 40W
Lulong, *China* . . . . **61** 39 53N 118 51 E
Lulonga →, *Zaïre* . . . . **94** 1 0N 18 10 E
Lulua →, *Zaïre* . . . . . . **95** 4 30 S 20 30 E
Luluabourg = Kananga, *Zaïre* . . . . **95** 5 55 S 22 18 E
Lumai, *Angola* . . . . **95** 13 13 S 21 25 E
Lumajang, *Indonesia* . **57** 8 8 S 113 13 E
Lumbala Kaquengue, *Angola* . . . . **95** 12 39 S 22 34 E
Lumbala N'guimbo, *Angola* . . . . **95** 14 18 S 21 18 E
Lumberton, *Miss., U.S.A.* **121** 31 4N 89 28W
Lumberton, *N.C., U.S.A.* **115** 34 37N 78 59W
Lumberton, *N. Mex., U.S.A.* **123** 36 58N 106 57W
Lumbres, *France* . . . . . **19** 50 40N 2 5 E
Lumbwa, *Kenya* . . . . . . **92** 0 12 S 35 28 E
Lumding, *India* . . . . . . **52** 25 46N 93 10 E
Lumi, *Papua N. G.* . . . **69** 3 30 S 142 2 E
Lummen, *Belgium* . . . . **17** 50 59N 5 12 E
Lumsden, *N.Z.* . . . . **81** 45 44 S 168 27 E
Lumut, *Malaysia* . . . . . **55** 4 13N 100 37 E
Lumut, Tg., *Indonesia* **56** 3 50 S 105 58 E
Lunan, *China* . . . . **58** 24 40N 103 18 E
Lunavada, *India* . . . . . . **48** 23 8N 73 37 E
Lunca, *Romania* . . . . . . **34** 47 22N 25 1 E
Lund, *Sweden* . . . . **11** 55 44N 13 12 E
Lund, *U.S.A.* **122** 38 53N 115 0W
Lunda Norte □, *Angola* **95** 8 0 S 20 0 E
Lunda Sul □, *Angola* . **95** 10 0 S 20 0 E
Lundazi, *Zambia* . . . . . **93** 12 20 S 33 7 E
Lunde, *Norway* . . . . . . **10** 59 17N 9 5 E
Lunderskov, *Denmark* **11** 55 29N 9 19 E
Lundi →, *Zambia* . . . . **93** 21 43 S 32 34 E
Lundu, *Malaysia* . . . . . **56** 1 40N 109 50 E
Lundy, *U.K.* **13** 51 10N 4 41W
Lune →, *U.K.* **12** 54 0N 2 51W
Lüneburg, *W. Germany* **30** 53 15N 10 23 E
Lüneburg Heath = Lüneburger Heide, *W. Germany* . . . . **30** 53 0N 10 0 E
Lüneburger Heide, *W. Germany* . . . . **30** 53 0N 10 0 E
Lunel, *France* . . . . **21** 43 39N 4 9 E
Lünen, *W. Germany* . . **30** 51 36N 7 31 E
Lunenburg, *Canada* . . **105** 44 22N 64 18W
Lunéville, *France* . . . . . **19** 48 36N 6 30 E
Lunga →, *Zambia* . . . **93** 14 34 S 26 25 E
Lungi Airport, *S. Leone* **90** 8 40N 13 17W
Lunglei, *India* . . . . **52** 22 55N 92 45 E
Lungngo, *Burma* . . . . . **52** 21 57N 93 36 E
Luni, *India* . . . . **48** 26 0N 73 6 E
Luni →, *India* . . . . **48** 24 41N 71 14 E
Luninets, *U.S.S.R.* . . . **36** 52 15N 26 50 E
Luning, *U.S.A.* **122** 38 30N 118 10W
Lunino, *U.S.S.R.* . . . . . **37** 53 35N 45 6 E
Lunner, *Norway* . . . . . . **10** 60 19N 10 35 E
Lunsemfwa →, *Zambia* **93** 14 54 S 30 12 E
Lunsemfwa Falls, *Zambia* . . . . **93** 14 30 S 29 6 E
Lunteren, *Neths.* . . . . . **16** 52 5N 5 38 E
Luo He →, *China* . . . . **60** 34 35N 110 20 E
Luocheng, *China* . . . . . **58** 24 48N 108 53 E
Luochuan, *China* . . . . . **60** 35 45N 109 26 E
Luoci, *China* . . . . **58** 25 19N 102 18 E
Luodian, *China* . . . . . . **58** 25 24N 106 43 E
Luoding, *China* . . . . . . **59** 22 45N 111 40 E
Luodong, *Taiwan* . . . . **59** 24 41N 121 46 E
Luofu, *Zaïre* . . . . **92** 0 10 S 29 15 E
Luohe, *China* . . . . **60** 33 32N 114 2 E
Luojiang, *China* . . . . . . **58** 31 18N 104 33 E
Luonan, *China* . . . . **60** 34 5N 110 10 E
Luoning, *China* . . . . . . **60** 34 35N 111 40 E
Luoshan, *China* . . . . . . **59** 32 13N 114 30 E
Luotian, *China* . . . . **59** 30 46N 115 22 E
Luoyang, *China* . . . . . . **60** 34 40N 112 26 E
Luoyuan, *China* . . . . . . **59** 26 28N 119 30 E
Luozi, *Zaïre* . . . . **95** 4 54 S 14 0 E
Luozigou, *China* . . . . . **61** 43 42N 130 18 E
Lupeni, *Romania* . . . . . **34** 45 21N 23 13 E
Lupilichi, *Mozam.* . . . . **93** 11 47 S 35 13 E
Lupire, *Angola* . . . . **95** 14 36 S 19 29 E
Lupoing, *China* . . . . . . **58** 24 53N 104 21 E
Luquan, *China* . . . . **58** 25 35N 102 25 E
Luque, *Paraguay* . . . . . **140** 25 19 S 57 25W
Luque, *Spain* **23** 37 35N 4 16W
Luray, *U.S.A.* **114** 38 39N 78 26W
Lure, *France* . . . . **19** 47 40N 6 30 E
Luremo, *Angola* . . . . . . **95** 8 30 S 17 50 E
Lurgan, *U.K.* **15** 54 28N 6 20W
Luribay, *Bolivia* . . . . . **136** 17 6 S 67 39W
Lurin, *Peru* . . . . **136** 12 17 S 76 52W
Lusaka, *Zambia* . . . . . . **93** 15 28 S 28 16 E
Lusambo, *Zaïre* . . . . . . **92** 4 58 S 23 28 E
Lusangaye, *Zaïre* . . . . . **92** 4 54 S 26 0 E
Luseland, *Canada* **111** 52 5N 109 24W
Lushan, *Henan, China* **60** 33 45N 112 55 E
Lushan, *Sichuan, China* **58** 30 12N 102 52 E
Lushih, *China* . . . . **60** 34 3N 111 3 E
Lushnja, *Albania* . . . . . **35** 40 55N 19 41 E
Lushoto, *Tanzania* . . . **92** 4 47 S 38 20 E
Lushoto □, *Tanzania* . **92** 4 45 S 38 20 E
Lushui, *China* . . . . **58** 25 58N 98 44 E
Lüshun, *China* . . . . **61** 38 45N 121 15 E
Lusignan, *France* . . . . . **20** 46 26N 0 8 E
Lusigny-sur-Barse, *France* . . . . **19** 48 16N 4 15 E
Lusk, *U.S.A.* **120** 42 47N 104 27W
Lussac-les-Châteaux, *France* . . . . **20** 46 24N 0 43 E
Lussanvira, *Brazil* . . . . **139** 20 42 S 51 7W
Luta = Dalian, *China* . **61** 38 50N 121 40 E
Lutembo, *Angola* . . . . . **95** 13 26 S 21 16 E
Luti, *Solomon Is.* . . . . **68** 7 14 S 157 0 E
Luton, *U.K.* **13** 51 53N 0 24W
Lutong, *Malaysia* . . . . **56** 4 28N 114 0 E
Lutsk, *U.S.S.R.* . . . . . . **36** 50 50N 25 15 E
Lutuai, *Angola* . . . . **95** 12 41 S 20 7 E
Lützow Holmbukta, *Antarctica* . . . . **143** 69 10 S 37 30 E
Lutzputs, *S. Africa* . . . **96** 28 3 S 20 40 E
Luverne, *U.S.A.* **120** 43 35N 96 12W
Luvo, *Angola* . . . . **95** 5 51 S 14 5 E
Luvua, *Zaïre* . . . . **93** 8 48 S 25 17 E
Luvua →, *Zaïre* . . . . . . **92** 6 50 S 27 30 E
Luwegu →, *Tanzania* . **93** 8 31 S 37 23 E
Luwuk, *Indonesia* . . . . **57** 0 56 S 122 47 E
Luxembourg, *Lux.* . . . . **17** 49 37N 6 9 E
Luxembourg □, *Belgium* . . . . **17** 49 58N 5 30 E
Luxembourg ■, *Europe* **17** 50 0N 6 0 E
Luxeuil-les-Bains, *France* . . . . **19** 47 49N 6 24 E
Luxi, *Hunan, China* . . **59** 28 20N 110 7 E
Luxi, *Yunnan, China* . **58** 24 40N 103 55 E
Luxi, *Yunnan, China* . **58** 24 27N 98 36 E
Luxor = El Uqsur, *Egypt* . . . . **88** 25 41N 32 38 E
Luy →, *France* **20** 43 39N 1 9W
Luy-de-Béarn →, *France* **20** 43 39N 0 48W
Luy-de-France →, *France* **20** 43 39N 0 48W
Luyi, *China* . . . . **60** 33 50N 115 35 E
Luyksgestel, *Neths.* . . . **17** 51 17N 5 20 E
Luz-St.-Sauveur, *France* **20** 42 53N 0 0 E
Luzern, *Switz.* . . . . **31** 47 3N 8 18 E
Luzern □, *Switz.* . . . . . **31** 47 2N 7 55 E
Luzhai, *China* . . . . **58** 24 29N 109 42 E
Luzhou, *China* . . . . **58** 28 52N 105 20 E
Luziânia, *Brazil* . . . . . . **139** 16 20 S 48 0W
Luzilândia, *Brazil* . . . . **138** 3 28 S 42 22W
Luzon, *Phil.* . . . . **57** 16 0N 121 0 E
Luzy, *France* . . . . **19** 46 47N 3 58 E
Luzzi, *Italy* . . . . **29** 39 28N 16 17 E
Lvov, *U.S.S.R.* . . . . . . **36** 49 50N 24 0 E
Lyakhovichi, *U.S.S.R.* **36** 53 2N 26 32 E
Lyakhovskiye, Ostrova, *U.S.S.R.* . . . . **41** 73 40N 141 0 E
Lyaki, *U.S.S.R.* . . . . . . **39** 40 34N 47 22 E
Lyal I., *Canada* **108** 44 57N 81 24W
Lyall Mt., *N.Z.* . . . . . . **81** 45 16 S 167 32 E
Lyallpur = Faisalabad, *Pakistan* . . . . **48** 31 30N 73 5 E
Lychen, *E. Germany* . . **30** 53 13N 13 20 E
Lyckeby, *Sweden* . . . . . **11** 56 12N 15 37 E
Lycksele, *Sweden* . . . . . **8** 64 38N 18 40 E
Lydda = Lod, *Israel* . . **44** 31 57N 34 54 E
Lydenburg, *S. Africa* . . **97** 25 10 S 30 29 E
Lyell, *N.Z.* . . . . **81** 41 48 S 172 4 E
Lyell I., *Canada* **110** 52 40N 131 35W
Lyell Range, *N.Z.* . . . . **81** 41 38 S 172 20 E
Lygnern, *Sweden* . . . . . **11** 57 30N 12 15 E
Lyman, *U.S.A.* **122** 41 24N 110 15W
Lyme Regis, *U.K.* **13** 50 44N 2 57W
Lymington, *U.K.* **13** 50 46N 1 32W
Lynchburg, *Ohio, U.S.A.* **119** 39 15N 83 48W
Lynchburg, *Va., U.S.A.* **114** 37 23N 79 10W
Lynd →, *Australia* . . . **72** 16 28 S 143 18 E
Lynd Ra., *Australia* . . . **73** 25 30 S 149 20 E
Lynden, *Canada* **116** 43 14N 80 9W
Lynden, *U.S.A.* **124** 48 56N 122 32W
Lyndhurst, *N.S.W., Australia* . . . . **76** 33 41 S 149 2 E
Lyndhurst, *S. Austral., Australia* . . . . **73** 30 15 S 138 18 E
Lyndon →, *Australia* . **79** 23 29 S 114 6 E
Lyndonville, *N.Y., U.S.A.* **116** 43 19N 78 25W
Lyndonville, *Vt., U.S.A.* **117** 44 32N 72 1W
Lyngdal, *Norway* . . . . . **10** 59 54N 9 32 E
Lynher Reef, *Australia* **78** 15 27 S 121 55 E
Lynn, *Ind., U.S.A.* **119** 40 3N 84 56W
Lynn, *Mass., U.S.A.* . . **117** 42 28N 70 57W
Lynn Canal, *U.S.A.* . . **110** 58 50N 135 20W
Lynn Lake, *Canada* . . . **111** 56 51N 101 3W
Lynnwood, *U.S.A.* **124** 47 49N 122 19W
Lynton, *U.K.* **13** 51 14N 3 50W
Lyntupy, *U.S.S.R.* . . . . **36** 55 4N 26 23 E
Lynx L., *Canada* **111** 62 25N 106 15W
Lyø, *Denmark* . . . . **11** 55 3N 10 9 E
Lyon, *France* . . . . **21** 45 46N 4 50 E
Lyonnais, *France* . . . . . **21** 45 45N 4 15 E
Lyons = Lyon, *France* **21** 45 46N 4 50 E
Lyons, *Australia* . . . . . . **74** 38 2 S 141 28 E
Lyons, *Colo., U.S.A.* . . **120** 40 17N 105 15W
Lyons, *Ga., U.S.A.* . . . **115** 32 10N 82 15W
Lyons, *Kans., U.S.A.* . . **120** 38 24N 98 13W
Lyons, *N.Y., U.S.A.* . . . **116** 43 3N 77 0W
Lyrestad, *Sweden* . . . . . **11** 58 48N 14 4 E
Lys → = Leie →, *Belgium* . . . . **19** 51 2N 3 45 E
Lysekil, *Sweden* . . . . . . **11** 58 17N 11 26 E
Lyskovo, *U.S.S.R.* . . . . **37** 56 0N 45 3 E
Lyster, *Canada* **107** 46 22N 71 37W
Lysvik, *Sweden* . . . . . . **10** 60 1N 13 9 E
Lytle, *U.S.A.* **121** 29 14N 98 46W
Lyttelton, *N.Z.* . . . . . . **81** 43 35 S 172 44 E
Lytton, *Canada* **110** 50 13N 121 31W
Lyuban, *U.S.S.R.* . . . . . **36** 59 16N 31 18 E
Lyubcha, *U.S.S.R.* . . . . **36** 53 46N 26 1 E
Lyubertsy, *U.S.S.R.* . . . **37** 55 39N 37 50 E
Lyubim, *U.S.S.R.* . . . . . **37** 58 20N 40 39 E
Lyuboml, *U.S.S.R.* . . . . **36** 51 11N 24 4 E
Lyubotin, *U.S.S.R.* . . . . **38** 50 0N 36 0 E
Lyubytino, *U.S.S.R.* . . . **36** 58 50N 33 16 E
Lyudinovo, *U.S.S.R.* . . **36** 53 52N 34 28 E

M

Ma →, *Vietnam* . . . . . **54** 19 47N 105 56 E
Mā'ad, *Jordan* . . . . **44** 32 37N 35 36 E
Ma'alah, *Si. Arabia* . . . **46** 26 31N 47 20 E
Maamba, *Zambia* . . . . . **96** 17 17 S 26 28 E
Ma'ān, *Jordan* . . . . **46** 30 12N 35 44 E
Ma'anshan, *China* . . . . **59** 31 44N 118 29 E
Maarheeze, *Neths.* . . . . **17** 51 19N 5 36 E
Maarianhamina, *Finland* . . . . **9** 60 5N 19 55 E
Maarn, *Neths.* . . . . **16** 52 3N 5 22 E
Ma'arrat un Nu'man, *Syria* . . . . **46** 35 38N 36 40 E
Maarssen, *Neths.* . . . . . **16** 52 9N 5 2 E
Maartensdijk, *Neths.* . . **16** 52 9N 5 10 E
Maas →, *Neths.* . . . . . **16** 51 45N 4 32 E
Maasbracht, *Belgium* . **17** 51 9N 5 54 E
Maasbree, *Neths.* . . . . . **17** 51 22N 6 3 E
Maasdam, *Neths.* . . . . . **16** 51 48N 4 34 E
Maasdijk, *Neths.* . . . . . **16** 51 58N 4 13 E
Maaseik, *Belgium* . . . . **17** 51 6N 5 45 E
Maasland, *Neths.* . . . . . **16** 51 57N 4 16 E
Maasniel, *Neths.* . . . . . **17** 51 12N 6 1 E
Maassluis, *Neths.* . . . . . **16** 51 56N 4 16 E
Maastricht, *Neths.* . . . . **17** 50 50N 5 40 E
Maave, *Mozam.* . . . . . . **97** 21 4 S 34 47 E
Mabaruma, *Guyana* . . **135** 8 10N 59 50W
Mabein, *Burma* . . . . . . **52** 23 29N 96 37 E
Mabel L., *Canada* **110** 50 35N 118 43W
Mabenge, *Zaïre* . . . . . . **92** 4 15N 24 12 E
Maberly, *Canada* **109** 44 50N 76 32W
Mabian, *China* . . . . **58** 28 47N 103 37 E
Mablethorpe, *U.K.* . . . . **12** 53 21N 0 14 E
Maboma, *Zaïre* . . . . . . **92** 2 30N 28 10 E

Maguse L.

Maboukou, Congo 94 3 39 S 12 31 E
Mabrouk, Mali 91 19 29N 1 15W
Mabton, U.S.A. 122 46 15N 120 12W
Mabungo, Somali Rep. 98 0 49N 42 35 E
Mac Bac, Vietnam 55 9 46N 106 7 E
Macachín, Argentina 140 37 10 S 63 43W
Macaé, Brazil 139 22 20 S 41 43W
Macaíba, Brazil 138 5 51 S 35 21W
Macajuba, Brazil 139 12 9 S 40 22W
McAlester, U.S.A. 121 34 57N 95 46W
McAllen, U.S.A. 121 26 12N 98 15W
Macallister →, Australia 75 38 2 S 146 59 E
Macamic, Canada 106 48 45N 79 0W
Macao = Macau ■, China 62 22 16N 113 35 E
Macão, Portugal 23 39 35N 7 59W
Macapá, Brazil 138 0 5N 51 4W
Macará, Ecuador 134 4 23 S 79 57W
Macarani, Brazil 139 15 33 S 40 24W
Macarena, Serranía de la, Colombia 134 2 45N 73 55W
Macarthur, Australia 74 38 5 S 142 0 E
McArthur →, Australia 72 15 54 S 136 40 E
McArthur River, Australia 72 16 27 S 136 7 E
Macas, Ecuador 134 2 19 S 78 7W
Macate, Peru 136 8 48 S 78 7W
Macau, Brazil 138 5 0 S 36 40W
Macau ■, China 62 22 16N 113 35 E
Macaúbas, Brazil 139 13 2 S 42 42W
Macaya →, Colombia 134 0 59N 72 20W
McBride, Canada 110 53 20N 120 19W
McCall, U.S.A. 122 44 55N 116 6W
McCamey, U.S.A. 121 31 8N 102 15W
McCammon, U.S.A. 122 42 41N 112 11W
McCauley I., Canada 110 53 40N 130 15W
McCleary, U.S.A. 124 47 3N 123 16W
Macclesfield, U.K. 12 53 16N 2 9W
McClintock, Canada 111 57 50N 94 10W
McClintock Ra., Australia 78 18 44 S 127 38 E
McCloud, U.S.A. 122 41 14N 122 5W
McClure, U.S.A. 116 40 42N 77 20W
McClure, L., U.S.A. 124 37 35N 120 16W
McClure Str., Canada 144 75 0N 119 0W
McClusky, U.S.A. 120 47 30N 100 31W
McComb, U.S.A. 121 31 13N 90 30W
McConaughy, L., U.S.A. 120 41 20N 101 40W
McCook, U.S.A. 120 40 15N 100 35W
McCullough Mt., U.S.A. 125 35 35N 115 13W
McCusker →, Canada 111 55 32N 108 39W
McDame, Canada 110 59 44N 128 59W
McDermitt, U.S.A. 122 42 0N 117 45W
Macdonald →, N.S.W., Australia 76 33 22 S 151 0 E
MacDonald →, Queens., Australia 77 30 45 S 150 45 E
Macdonald, Mt., Vanuatu 68 17 36 S 168 23 E
McDonald Is., Ind. Oc. 53 53 0 S 73 0 E
Macdonald L., Australia 78 23 30 S 129 0 E
Macdonnell Ranges, Australia 78 23 40 S 133 0 E
McDouall Peak, Australia 73 29 51 S 134 55 E
Macdougall L., Canada 102 66 0N 98 27W
MacDowell L., Canada 104 52 15N 92 45W
Macduff, U.K. 14 57 40N 2 30W
Maceda, Spain 22 42 16N 7 39W
Macedon, Australia 74 37 24 S 144 35 E
Macedonia = Makedonija □, Yugoslavia 35 41 53N 21 40 E
Maceió, Brazil 138 9 40 S 35 41W
Maceira, Portugal 23 39 41N 8 55W
Macenta, Guinea 90 8 35N 9 32W
Macerata, Italy 27 43 19N 13 28 E
McFarland, U.S.A. 125 35 41N 119 14W
McFarlane →, Canada 111 59 12N 107 58W
Macfarlane, L., Australia 73 32 0 S 136 40 E
McGehee, U.S.A. 121 33 40N 91 25W
McGill, U.S.A. 122 39 27N 114 50W
Macgillycuddy's Reeks, Ireland 15 52 2N 9 45W
MacGregor, Canada 111 49 57N 98 48W
McGregor, U.S.A. 118 43 0N 91 15W
McGregor →, Canada 110 55 10N 122 0W
McGregor Ra., Australia 73 27 0 S 142 45 E
Mach, Pakistan 47 29 50N 67 20 E
Machacalis, Brazil 139 17 5 S 40 45W
Machado = Jiparaná →, Brazil 137 8 3 S 62 52W
Machagai, Argentina 140 26 56 S 60 2W
Machakos, Kenya 92 1 30 S 37 15 E
Machakos □, Kenya 92 1 30 S 37 15 E
Machala, Ecuador 134 3 20 S 79 57W
Machanga, Mozam. 97 20 59 S 35 0 E
Machattie, L., Australia 72 24 50 S 139 48 E
Machava, Mozam. 97 25 54 S 32 28 E
Machece, Mozam. 93 19 15 S 35 32 E
Machecoul, France 18 47 0N 1 49W
Machelen, Belgium 17 50 55N 4 26 E
Macheng, China 59 31 12N 115 2 E
McHenry, U.S.A. 119 42 21N 88 16W
Machevna, U.S.S.R. 41 61 20N 172 20 E
Machezo, Spain 23 39 21N 4 20W
Machias, U.S.A. 105 44 40N 67 28W
Machichaco, C., Spain 24 43 28N 2 47W
Machichi →, Canada 111 57 3N 92 6W
Machida, Japan 65 35 28N 139 23 E
Machilipatnam, India 51 16 12N 81 8 E
Machine, La, France 19 46 54N 3 27 E
Machiques, Venezuela 134 10 4N 72 34W
Machupicchu, Peru 136 13 8 S 72 30W
Machynlleth, U.K. 13 52 36N 3 51W
McIlwraith Ra., Australia 72 13 50 S 143 20 E
Măcin, Romania 34 45 16N 28 8 E
Macina, Mali 90 14 50N 5 0W
McIntosh, U.S.A. 120 45 57N 101 20W
McIntosh L., Canada 111 55 45N 105 0W
Macintyre →, Australia 77 28 37 S 150 47 E
Macizo Galaico, Spain 22 42 30N 7 30W
Mackay, Australia 72 21 8 S 149 11 E
Mackay, U.S.A. 122 43 58N 113 37W
MacKay →, Canada 110 57 10N 111 38W
Mackay, L., Australia 78 22 30 S 129 0 E
McKay Ra., Australia 78 23 0 S 122 30 E
McKeesport, U.S.A. 116 40 21N 79 50W
McKellar, Canada 108 45 30N 79 55W
McKenna, U.S.A. 124 46 56N 122 33W
Mackenzie, Canada 110 55 20N 123 5W
Mackenzie, Guyana 135 6 0N 58 17W
McKenzie, U.S.A. 115 36 10N 88 31W
Mackenzie →, Australia 72 23 38 S 149 46 E
Mackenzie →, Canada 102 69 10N 134 20W
McKenzie →, U.S.A. 122 44 2N 123 6W
Mackenzie City = Linden, Guyana 136 6 0N 58 10W
Mackenzie Highway, Canada 110 58 0N 117 15W
Mackenzie Mts., Canada 102 64 0N 130 0W
Mackenzie Plains, N.Z. 81 44 10 S 170 25 E
McKerrow L., N.Z. 81 44 25 S 168 5 E
Mackinaw, U.S.A. 118 40 32N 89 21W
Mackinaw →, U.S.A. 118 40 33N 89 44W
Mackinaw City, U.S.A. 104 45 47N 84 44W
McKinlay, Australia 72 21 16 S 141 18 E
McKinlay →, Australia 72 20 50 S 141 28 E
McKinley, Mt., U.S.A. 102 63 2N 151 0W
McKinley Sea, Arctic 144 84 0N 10 0W
McKinney, U.S.A. 121 33 10N 96 40W
Mackinnon Road, Kenya 92 3 40 S 39 1 E
Mackintosh Ra., Australia 79 27 39 S 125 32 E
Macksville, Australia 77 30 40 S 152 56 E
McLaughlin, U.S.A. 120 45 50N 100 50W
Maclean, Australia 77 29 26 S 153 16 E
McLean, Ill., U.S.A. 118 40 19N 89 10W
McLean, Tex., U.S.A. 121 35 15N 100 35W
McLeansboro, U.S.A. 119 38 5N 88 30W
Maclear, S. Africa 97 31 2 S 28 23 E
Macleay →, Australia 77 30 56 S 153 0 E
McLennan, Canada 110 55 42N 116 50W
MacLeod, B., Canada 111 62 53N 110 0W
McLeod L., Australia 79 24 9 S 113 47 E
MacLeod Lake, Canada 110 54 58N 123 0W
M'Clintock Chan., Canada 102 72 0N 102 0W
McLoughlin, Mt., U.S.A. 122 42 10N 122 19W
McLure, Canada 110 51 2N 120 13W
McMahon's Reef, Australia 76 34 39 S 148 26 E
McMechen, U.S.A. 116 39 57N 80 44W
McMillan L., U.S.A. 121 32 40N 104 20W
McMinnville, Oreg., U.S.A. 122 45 16N 123 11W
McMinnville, Tenn., U.S.A. 115 35 43N 85 45W
McMorran, Canada 111 51 19N 108 42W
McMurdo Sd., Antarctica 143 77 0 S 170 0 E
McMurray = Fort McMurray, Canada 110 56 44N 111 7W
McMurray, U.S.A. 124 48 19N 122 19W
McNary, U.S.A. 123 34 4N 109 53W
MacNutt, Canada 111 51 5N 101 36W
Macocolo, Angola 95 6 47 S 16 8 E
Macodoene, Mozam. 97 23 32 S 35 5 E
Macomb, U.S.A. 118 40 25N 90 40W
Macomer, Italy 28 40 16N 8 48 E
Mâcon, France 21 46 19N 4 50 E
Macon, Ga., U.S.A. 115 32 50N 83 37W
Macon, Ill., U.S.A. 118 39 43N 89 0W
Macon, Miss., U.S.A. 115 33 7N 88 31W
Macon, Mo., U.S.A. 118 39 40N 92 26W
Macondo, Angola 95 12 37 S 23 46 E
Macossa, Mozam. 93 17 55 S 33 56 E
Macoun L., Canada 111 56 32N 103 40W
Macoupin Cr. →, U.S.A. 118 39 11N 90 38W
Macovane, Mozam. 97 21 30 S 35 0 E
McPherson, U.S.A. 120 38 25N 97 40W
McPherson Pk., U.S.A. 125 34 53N 119 53W
Macpherson Ra., Australia 77 28 15 S 153 15 E
Macquarie, L., Australia 76 33 4 S 151 36 E
Macquarie, Mt., Australia 76 33 37 S 149 10 E
Macquarie Harbour, Australia 72 42 15 S 145 23 E
Macquarie Is., Pac. Oc. 66 54 36 S 158 55 E
MacRobertson Land, Antarctica 143 71 0 S 64 0 E
Macroom, Ireland 15 51 54N 8 57W
Macroy, Australia 78 20 53 S 118 2 E
MacTier, Ont., Canada 108 45 8N 79 47W
MacTier, Canada 116 45 9N 79 46W
Macubela, Mozam. 93 16 53 S 37 49 E
Macugnaga, Italy 26 45 57N 7 58 E
Macuiza, Mozam. 93 18 7 S 34 29 E
Macujer, Colombia 134 0 24N 73 10W
Macusani, Peru 136 14 4 S 70 29W
Macuse, Mozam. 93 17 45 S 37 10 E
Macuspana, Mexico 127 17 46N 92 36W
Macusse, Angola 95 17 48 S 20 23 E
McVille, U.S.A. 120 47 46N 98 11W
Madadeni, S. Africa 97 27 43 S 30 3 E
Madadi, Chad 87 18 28N 20 45 E
Madagali, Nigeria 91 10 56N 13 33 E
Madagascar ■, Africa 97 20 0 S 47 0 E
Madā'in Sālih, Si. Arabia 46 26 46N 37 57 E
Madama, Niger 87 22 0N 13 40 E
Madame I., Canada 105 45 30N 60 58W
Madanapalle, India 51 13 33N 78 28 E
Madang, Papua N. G. 69 5 12 S 145 49 E
Madaoua, Niger 91 14 5N 6 27 E
Madara, Nigeria 91 11 45N 10 35 E
Madaripur, Bangla. 52 23 19N 90 15 E
Madauk, Burma 52 17 56N 96 52 E
Madawaska, Canada 106 45 30N 78 0W
Madawaska →, Canada 109 45 27N 76 21W
Madaya, Burma 52 22 12N 96 10 E
Madbar, Sudan 89 6 17N 30 45 E
Maddalena, La, Italy 28 41 13N 9 25 E
Maddaloni, Italy 29 41 4N 14 23 E
Made, Neths. 17 51 41N 4 49 E
Madeira, Atl. Oc. 84 32 50N 17 0W
Madeira, U.S.A. 119 39 11N 84 22W
Madeira →, Brazil 135 3 22 S 58 45W
Madeleine, Is. de la, Canada 105 47 30N 61 40W
Madera, U.S.A. 124 36 58N 120 1W
Madgaon, India 51 15 12N 73 58 E
Madha, India 50 18 0N 75 30 E
Madhubani, India 49 26 21N 86 7 E
Madhumati →, Bangla. 52 22 53N 89 52 E
Madhya Pradesh □, India 48 21 50N 81 0 E
Madian, China 59 33 0N 116 6 E
Madidi →, Bolivia 136 12 32 S 66 52W
Madikeri, India 51 12 30N 75 45 E
Madill, U.S.A. 121 34 5N 96 49W
Madimba, Angola 95 6 36 S 14 23 E
Madimba, Zaïre 95 5 0 S 15 0 E
Madīnat ash Sha'b, S. Yemen 45 12 50N 45 0 E
Madingou, Congo 94 4 10 S 13 33 E
Madirovalo, Madag. 97 16 26 S 46 32 E
Madison, Calif., U.S.A. 124 38 41N 121 59W
Madison, Fla., U.S.A. 115 30 29N 83 39W
Madison, Ind., U.S.A. 119 38 42N 85 20W
Madison, Mo., U.S.A. 118 39 28N 92 13W
Madison, Nebr., U.S.A. 120 41 53N 97 25W
Madison, Ohio, U.S.A. 116 41 45N 81 4W
Madison, S. Dak., U.S.A. 120 44 0N 97 8W
Madison, Wis., U.S.A. 118 43 5N 89 25W
Madison →, U.S.A. 122 45 56N 111 30W
Madisonville, Ky., U.S.A. 114 37 20N 87 30W
Madisonville, Tex., U.S.A. 121 30 57N 95 55W
Madista, Botswana 96 21 15 S 25 6 E
Madiun, Indonesia 57 7 38 S 111 32 E
Madley, U.K. 13 52 3N 2 51W
Madoc, Canada 109 44 30N 77 28W
Madol, Sudan 89 9 3N 27 45 E
Madon →, France 19 48 36N 6 6 E
Madona, U.S.S.R. 36 56 53N 26 5 E
Madonie, Le, Italy 28 37 50N 13 50 E
Madras = Tamil Nadu □, India 51 11 0N 77 0 E
Madras, India 51 13 8N 80 19 E
Madras, U.S.A. 122 44 40N 121 10W
Madre, L., Mexico 127 25 0N 97 30W
Madre, L., U.S.A. 121 26 0N 97 40W
Madre, Sierra, Mexico 127 16 0N 93 0W
Madre, Sierra, Phil. 57 17 0N 122 0 E
Madre de Dios □, Peru 136 12 0 S 70 15W
Madre de Dios →, Bolivia 136 10 59 S 66 8W
Madre de Dios, I., Chile 142 50 20 S 75 10W
Madre del Sur, Sierra, Mexico 127 17 30N 100 0W
Madre Occidental, Sierra, Mexico 126 27 0N 107 0W
Madre Oriental, Sierra, Mexico 126 25 0N 100 0W
Madri, India 48 24 16N 73 32 E
Madrid, Spain 22 40 25N 3 45W
Madrid, U.S.A. 118 41 53N 93 49W
Madrid □, Spain 22 40 30N 3 45W
Madridejos, Spain 23 39 28N 3 33W
Madrigal de las Altas Torres, Spain 22 41 5N 5 0W
Madrona, Sierra, Spain 23 38 27N 4 16W
Madroñera, Spain 23 39 26N 5 42W
Madu, Sudan 89 14 37N 26 4 E
Madura, Selat, Indonesia 57 7 30 S 113 20 E
Madura Motel, Australia 79 31 55 S 127 0 E
Madurai, India 51 9 55N 78 10 E
Madurantakam, India 51 12 30N 79 50 E
Madzhalis, U.S.S.R. 39 42 9N 47 47 E
Mae Chan, Thailand 54 20 9N 99 52 E
Mae Hong Son, Thailand 54 19 16N 98 1 E
Mae Khlong →, Thailand 54 13 24N 100 0 E
Mae Phrik, Thailand 54 17 27N 99 7 E
Mae Ramat, Thailand 54 16 58N 98 31 E
Mae Rim, Thailand 54 18 54N 98 57 E
Mae Sot, Thailand 54 16 43N 98 34 E
Mae Suai, Thailand 54 19 39N 99 33 E
Mae Tha, Thailand 54 18 28N 99 8 E
Maebaru, Japan 64 33 33N 130 12 E
Maebashi, Japan 65 36 24N 139 4 E
Maella, Spain 24 41 8N 0 7 E
Măeruş, Romania 34 45 53N 25 31 E
Maesteg, U.K. 13 51 36N 3 40W
Maestra, Sierra, Cuba 128 20 15N 77 0W
Maestrazgo, Mts. del, Spain 24 40 30N 0 25W
Maevatanana, Madag. 97 16 56 S 46 49 E
Maewo, Vanuatu 68 15 10 S 168 10 E
Ma'fan, Libya 86 25 56N 14 29 E
Mafeking, Canada 111 52 40N 101 10W
Maféré, Ivory C. 90 5 30N 3 2W
Mafeteng, Lesotho 96 29 51 S 27 15 E
Maffe, Belgium 17 50 21N 5 19 E
Maffra, Australia 75 37 53 S 146 58 E
Mafia I., Tanzania 92 7 45 S 39 50 E
Mafikeng, S. Africa 96 25 50 S 25 38 E
Mafra, Brazil 141 26 10 S 50 0W
Mafra, Portugal 23 38 55N 9 20W
Mafungabusi Plateau, Zambia 93 18 30 S 29 8 E
Magadan, U.S.S.R. 41 59 38N 150 50 E
Magadi, Kenya 92 1 54 S 36 19 E
Magadi, L., Kenya 92 1 54 S 36 19 E
Magaliesburg, S. Africa 97 26 0 S 27 32 E
Magallanes □, Chile 142 52 0 S 72 0W
Magallanes, Estrecho de, Chile 142 52 30 S 75 0W
Magangué, Colombia 134 9 14N 74 45W
Magaria, Niger 91 13 4N 9 5 E
Magburaka, S. Leone 90 8 47N 12 0W
Magdalena, Argentina 140 35 5 S 57 30W
Magdalena, Bolivia 137 13 13 S 63 57W
Magdalena, Malaysia 56 4 25N 117 55 E
Magdalena, Mexico 126 30 50N 112 0W
Magdalena, U.S.A. 123 34 10N 107 20W
Magdalena □, Colombia 134 10 0N 74 0W
Magdalena →, Colombia 134 11 6N 74 51W
Magdalena →, Mexico 126 30 40N 112 25W
Magdalena, B., Mexico 126 24 30N 112 10W
Magdalena, I., Chile 142 44 40 S 73 0W
Magdalena, Llano de la, Mexico 126 25 0N 111 30W
Magdeburg, E. Germany 30 52 8N 11 36 E
Magdeburg □, E. Germany 30 52 20N 11 30 E
Magdelaine Cays, Australia 72 16 33 S 150 18 E
Magdi'el, Israel 44 32 10N 34 54 E
Magdub, Sudan 89 13 42N 25 5 E
Magee, U.S.A. 121 31 53N 89 45W
Magee, I., U.K. 15 54 48N 5 44W
Magelang, Indonesia 57 7 29 S 110 13 E
Magellan's Str. = Magallanes, Estrecho de, Chile 142 52 30 S 75 0W
Magenta, Italy 26 45 28N 8 53 E
Magenta, L., Australia 79 33 30 S 119 2 E
Maggia →, Switz. 31 46 18N 8 36 E
Maggiorasca, Mte., Italy 26 44 33N 9 29 E
Maggiore, L., Italy 26 46 0N 8 35 E
Maghama, Mauritania 90 15 32N 12 57W
Maghār, Israel 44 32 54N 35 24 E
Magherafelt, U.K. 15 54 44N 6 37W
Maghnia, Algeria 85 34 50N 1 43W
Magione, Italy 27 43 10N 12 12 E
Magliano in Toscana, Italy 27 42 36N 11 18 E
Máglie, Italy 29 40 8N 18 17 E
Magnac-Laval, France 20 46 13N 1 11 E
Magnetawan, Canada 108 45 40N 79 39W
Magnetic Pole (North), Canada 144 77 5N 102 6W
Magnetic Pole (South), Antarctica 143 65 2 S 139 4 E
Magnitogorsk, U.S.S.R. 40 53 27N 59 4 E
Magnolia, Ark., U.S.A. 121 33 18N 93 12W
Magnolia, Miss., U.S.A. 121 31 8N 90 28W
Magnor, Norway 10 59 56N 12 15 E
Magnus, Mt., Australia 77 28 30 S 151 50 E
Magny-en-Vexin, France 19 49 9N 1 47 E
Magog, Canada 107 45 18N 72 9W
Magoro, Uganda 92 1 45N 34 12 E
Magosa = Famagusta, Cyprus 46 35 8N 33 55 E
Magoye, Zambia 93 16 1 S 27 30 E
Magpie L., Canada 105 51 0N 64 41W
Magrath, Canada 110 49 25N 112 50W
Magro →, Spain 25 39 11N 0 25W
Magrur, Wadi →, Sudan 89 16 5N 26 30 E
Magu □, Tanzania 92 2 31 S 33 28 E
Maguan, China 58 23 0N 104 21 E
Maguarinho, C., Brazil 138 0 15 S 48 30W
Maguse L., Canada 111 61 40N 95 10W

Marathon

Manapire →, Venezuela 134 7 42N 66 7W
Manapouri, N.Z. 81 45 34 S 167 39 E
Manapouri, L., N.Z. 81 45 32 S 167 32 E
Manar →, India 50 18 50N 77 20 E
Manas, China 62 44 17N 85 56 E
Manas, Somali Rep. 98 2 57N 43 28 E
Manasir, Si. Arabia 47 24 30N 51 10 E
Manaslu, Mt., Nepal 49 28 33N 84 33 E
Manasquan, U.S.A. 117 40 7N 74 3W
Manassa, U.S.A. 123 37 12N 105 58W
Manaung, Burma 52 18 45N 93 40 E
Manaus, Brazil 135 3 0 S 60 0W
Manawan L., Canada 111 55 24N 103 14W
Manawatu →, N.Z. 80 40 28 S 175 12 E
Manay, Phil. 57 7 17N 126 33 E
Mancelona, U.S.A. 104 44 54N 85 5W
Mancha, La, Spain 25 39 10N 2 54W
Mancha Real, Spain 23 37 48N 3 39W
Manche □, France 18 49 10N 1 20W
Manchester, U.K. 12 53 30N 2 15W
Manchester, Calif., U.S.A. 124 38 58N 123 41W
Manchester, Conn., U.S.A. 117 41 47N 72 30W
Manchester, Ga., U.S.A. 115 32 53N 84 32W
Manchester, Iowa, U.S.A. 118 42 28N 91 27W
Manchester, Ky., U.S.A. 114 37 9N 83 45W
Manchester, Mich., U.S.A. 119 42 9N 84 2W
Manchester, N.H., U.S.A. 117 42 58N 71 29W
Manchester, N.Y., U.S.A. 116 42 56N 77 16W
Manchester, Vt., U.S.A. 117 43 10N 73 5W
Manchester L., Canada 111 61 28N 107 29W
Manchuria = Dongbei, China 61 42 0N 125 0 E
Manciano, Italy 27 42 35N 11 30 E
Mancifa, Ethiopia 89 6 53N 41 50 E
Mancora, Pta., Peru 136 4 9 S 81 1W
Mand →, Iran 47 28 20N 52 30 E
Manda, Chunya, Tanzania 92 6 51 S 32 29 E
Manda, Ludewe, Tanzania 93 10 30 S 34 40 E
Mandabé, Madag. 97 21 0 S 44 55 E
Mandaguari, Brazil 141 23 32 S 51 42W
Mandah, Mongolia 60 44 27N 108 2 E
Mandal, Norway 9 58 2N 7 25 E
Mandalay, Burma 52 22 0N 96 4 E
Mandale = Mandalay, Burma 52 22 0N 96 4 E
Mandalgovi, Mongolia 60 45 45N 106 10 E
Mandalī, Iraq 46 33 43N 45 28 E
Mandan, U.S.A. 120 46 50N 101 0W
Mandapeta, India 50 16 47N 81 56 E
Mandar, Teluk, Indonesia 57 3 35 S 119 15 E
Mandas, Italy 28 39 40N 9 8 E
Mandasor = Mandsaur, India 48 24 3N 75 8 E
Mandaue, Phil. 57 10 20N 123 56 E
Mandelieu-la-Napoule, France 21 43 34N 6 57 E
Mandera, Kenya 92 3 55N 41 53 E
Mandera □, Kenya 92 3 30N 41 0 E
Manderfeld, Belgium 17 50 20N 6 20 E
Mandi, India 48 31 39N 76 58 E
Mandimba, Mozam. 93 14 20 S 35 40 E
Mandioli, Indonesia 57 0 40 S 127 20 E
Mandioré, L., S. Amer. 137 18 8 S 57 33W
Mandji I. = Lopez I., Gabon 94 0 50 S 8 47 E
Mandla, India 49 22 39N 80 30 E
Mandø, Denmark 11 55 18N 8 33 E
Mandoto, Madag. 97 19 34 S 46 17 E
Mandoúdhion, Greece 35 38 48N 23 29 E
Mandra, Pakistan 48 33 23N 73 12 E
Mandrare →, Madag. 97 25 10 S 46 30 E
Mandritsara, Madag. 97 15 50 S 48 49 E
Mandsaur, India 48 24 3N 75 8 E
Mandurah, Australia 79 32 36 S 115 48 E
Mandúria, Italy 29 40 25N 17 38 E
Mandvi, India 48 22 51N 69 22 E
Mandya, India 51 12 30N 77 0 E
Mandzai, Pakistan 48 30 55N 67 6 E
Mané, Burkina Faso 91 12 59N 1 21W
Manengouba, Mts., Cameroon 91 5 0N 9 50 E
Maner →, India 50 18 30N 79 40 E
Maneroo, Australia 72 23 22 S 143 53 E
Maneroo Cr. →, Australia 72 23 21 S 143 53 E
Manfalût, Egypt 88 27 20N 30 52 E
Manfred, Australia 73 33 19 S 143 45 E
Manfredónia, Italy 29 41 40N 15 55 E
Manfredónia, G. di, Italy 29 41 30N 16 10 E
Manga, Brazil 139 14 46 S 43 56W
Manga, Burkina Faso 91 11 40N 1 4W
Manga, Niger 91 15 0N 14 0 E
Mangabeiras, Chapada das, Brazil 138 10 0 S 46 30W
Mangalagiri, India 51 16 26N 80 36 E
Mangaldai, India 52 26 26N 92 2 E
Mangalia, Romania 34 43 50N 28 35 E
Mangalore, Australia 74 36 56 S 145 10 E
Mangalore, India 51 12 55N 74 47 E
Manganeses, Spain 22 41 45N 5 43W
Mangaon, India 50 18 15N 73 20 E
Mange, Zaïre 94 0 54N 20 30 E
Manggar, Indonesia 56 2 50 S 108 10 E
Manggawitu, Indonesia 57 4 8 S 133 32 E
Mangin Range, Burma 52 24 15N 95 45 E
Mangkalihat, Tanjung, Indonesia 57 1 2N 118 59 E
Mangla Dam, Pakistan 49 33 9N 73 44 E
Manglares, C., Colombia 134 1 36N 79 2W
Manglaur, India 48 29 44N 77 49 E
Mangnai, China 62 37 52N 91 43 E
Mango, Fiji 68 17 27 S 179 9W
Mango, Togo 91 10 20N 0 30 E
Mangoche, Malawi 93 14 25 S 35 16 E
Mangoky →, Madag. 97 21 29 S 43 41 E
Mangole, Indonesia 57 1 50 S 125 55 E
Mangombe, Zaïre 92 1 20 S 26 48 E
Mangonui, N.Z. 80 35 1 S 173 32 E
Mangoplah, Australia 76 35 23 S 147 17 E
Mangualde, Portugal 22 40 38N 7 48W
Mangueigne, Chad 87 10 30N 21 15 E
Mangueira, L. da, Brazil 141 33 0 S 52 50W
Manguéni, Hamada, Niger 86 22 35N 12 40 E
Mangum, U.S.A. 121 34 50N 99 30W
Mangyshlak Poluostrov, U.S.S.R. 39 44 30N 52 30 E
Mangyshlakskiy Zaliv, U.S.S.R. 39 44 40N 50 50 E
Manhattan, U.S.A. 120 39 10N 96 40W
Manhatten, U.S.A. 119 41 26N 87 59W
Manhiça, Mozam. 97 25 23 S 32 49 E
Manhuaçu, Brazil 139 20 15 S 42 2W
Manhumirim, Brazil 139 20 22 S 41 57W
Maní, Colombia 134 4 49N 72 17W
Mania →, Madag. 97 19 42 S 45 22 E
Maniago, Italy 27 46 11N 12 40 E
Manica, Mozam. 97 18 58 S 32 59 E
Manica e Sofala □, Mozam. 97 19 10 S 33 45 E
Manicaland □, Zambia 93 19 0 S 32 30 E
Manicoré, Brazil 137 5 48 S 61 16W
Manicoré →, Brazil 137 5 51 S 61 19W
Manicouagan →, Canada 107 49 30N 68 30W
Manīfah, Si. Arabia 46 27 44N 49 0 E
Manifold, Australia 72 22 41 S 150 40 E
Manifold, C., Australia 72 22 41 S 150 50 E
Maniganggo, China 58 31 56N 99 10 E
Manigotagan, Canada 111 51 6N 96 18W
Manihiki, Cook Is. 67 10 24 S 161 1W
Manika, Plateau de la, Zaïre 93 10 0 S 25 5 E
Manikganj, Bangla. 52 23 52N 90 0 E
Manila, Phil. 57 14 40N 121 3 E
Manila, U.S.A. 122 41 0N 109 44W
Manila Bay, Phil. 57 14 0N 120 0 E
Manildra, Australia 76 33 11 S 148 41 E
Manilla, Australia 77 30 45 S 150 43 E
Manimpé, Mali 90 14 11N 5 28W
Manipur □, India 52 25 0N 94 0 E
Manipur →, Burma 52 23 45N 94 20 E
Manisa, Turkey 46 38 38N 27 30 E
Manistee, U.S.A. 114 44 15N 86 20W
Manistee →, U.S.A. 114 44 15N 86 21W
Manistique, U.S.A. 114 45 59N 86 18W
Manito, U.S.A. 118 40 25N 89 47W
Manito L., Canada 111 52 43N 109 43W
Manitoba □, Canada 111 55 30N 97 0W
Manitoba, L., Canada 111 51 0N 98 45W
Manitou, Canada 111 49 15N 98 32W
Manitou Beach, U.S.A. 119 41 58N 84 19W
Manitou I., U.S.A. 104 47 22N 87 30W
Manitou Is., U.S.A. 114 45 8N 86 0W
Manitou L., Ont., Canada 108 45 51N 82 0W
Manitou L., Qué., Canada 105 50 55N 65 17W
Manitou Springs, U.S.A. 120 38 52N 104 55W
Manitoulin I., Canada 108 45 40N 82 30W
Manitowaning, Canada 108 45 46N 81 49W
Manitowoc, U.S.A. 114 44 8N 87 40W
Manitsauá-Missu →, Brazil 137 10 58 S 53 20W
Maniwaki, Canada 106 46 23N 75 58W
Manizales, Colombia 134 5 5N 75 32W
Manja, Madag. 97 21 26 S 44 20 E
Manjacaze, Mozam. 97 24 45 S 34 0 E
Manjakandriana, Madag. 97 18 55 S 47 47 E
Manjeri, India 51 11 7N 76 11 E
Manjhand, Pakistan 48 25 50N 68 10 E
Manjil, Iran 46 36 46N 49 30 E
Manjimup, Australia 79 34 15 S 116 6 E
Manjra →, India 50 18 49N 77 52 E
Mankato, Kans., U.S.A. 120 39 49N 98 11W
Mankato, Minn., U.S.A. 120 44 8N 93 59W
Mankayane, Swaziland 97 26 40 S 31 4 E
Mankono, Ivory C. 90 8 1N 6 10W
Mankota, Canada 111 49 25N 107 5W
Manlay, Mongolia 60 44 9N 107 0 E
Manlleu, Spain 24 42 2N 2 17 E
Manly, Australia 76 33 48 S 151 17 E
Manmad, India 50 20 18N 74 28 E
Mann Ranges, Mts., Australia 79 26 6 S 130 5 E
Manna, Indonesia 56 4 25 S 102 55 E
Mannahill, Australia 73 32 25 S 140 0 E
Mannar, Sri Lanka 51 9 1N 79 54 E
Mannar, G. of, Asia 51 8 30N 79 0 E
Mannar I., Sri Lanka 51 9 5N 79 45 E
Mannargudi, India 51 10 45N 79 51 E
Mannheim, W. Germany 31 49 28N 8 29 E
Manning, Canada 110 56 53N 117 39W
Manning, Oreg., U.S.A. 124 45 45N 123 13W
Manning, S.C., U.S.A. 115 33 40N 80 9W
Manning →, Australia 77 31 52 S 152 43 E
Manning Prov. Park, Canada 110 49 5N 120 45W
Manning Str., Solomon Is. 68 7 30 S 158 0 E
Mannington, U.S.A. 114 39 35N 80 25W
Mannu →, Italy 28 39 15N 9 32 E
Mannu, C., Italy 28 40 2N 8 24 E
Mannum, Australia 73 34 50 S 139 20 E
Mannus, Australia 76 35 45 S 147 55 E
Mano, S. Leone 90 8 3N 12 2W
Manoa, Bolivia 137 9 40 S 65 27W
Manokwari, Indonesia 57 0 54 S 134 0 E
Manombo, Madag. 97 22 57 S 43 28 E
Manono, Zaïre 92 7 15 S 27 25 E
Manosque, France 21 43 49N 5 47 E
Manotick, Canada 109 45 13N 75 41W
Manouane, L., Qué., Canada 105 50 45N 70 45W
Manouane, L., Qué., Canada 107 47 33N 74 6W
Manouro, Pt., Vanuatu 68 17 41 S 168 36 E
Manresa, Spain 24 41 48N 1 50 E
Mans, Le, France 18 48 0N 0 10 E
Mansa, Gujarat, India 48 23 27N 72 45 E
Mansa, Punjab, India 48 30 0N 75 27 E
Mansa, Zambia 93 11 13 S 28 55 E
Manseau, Canada 107 46 22N 72 0W
Mansehra, Pakistan 48 34 20N 73 15 E
Mansel I., Canada 103 62 0N 80 0W
Mansfield, Australia 75 37 4 S 146 6 E
Mansfield, U.K. 12 53 8N 1 12W
Mansfield, La., U.S.A. 121 32 2N 93 40W
Mansfield, Mass., U.S.A. 117 42 2N 71 12W
Mansfield, Ohio, U.S.A. 116 40 45N 82 30W
Mansfield, Pa., U.S.A. 116 41 48N 77 4W
Mansfield, Wash., U.S.A. 122 47 51N 119 44W
Mansi, Burma 52 24 48N 95 52 E
Mansidão, Brazil 138 10 43 S 44 2W
Mansilla de las Mulas, Spain 22 42 30N 5 25W
Mansle, France 20 45 52N 0 12 E
Manso →, Brazil 139 13 50 S 47 0W
Mansoa, Guinea-Biss. 90 12 0N 15 20W
Manson, U.S.A. 118 42 32N 94 32W
Manson Creek, Canada 110 55 37N 124 32W
Mansoura, Algeria 85 36 1N 4 31 E
Manta, Ecuador 134 1 0 S 80 40W
Manta, B. de, Ecuador 134 0 54 S 80 44W
Mantalingajan, Mt., Phil. 56 8 55N 117 45 E
Mantare, Tanzania 92 2 42 S 33 13 E
Manteca, U.S.A. 124 37 50N 121 12W
Mantecal, Venezuela 134 7 34N 69 17W
Mantena, Brazil 139 18 47 S 40 59W
Manteno, U.S.A. 119 41 15N 87 50W
Manteo, U.S.A. 115 35 55N 75 41W
Mantes-la-Jolie, France 19 49 0N 1 41 E
Manthani, India 50 18 40N 79 35 E
Manthelan, France 18 47 9N 0 47 E
Manti, U.S.A. 122 39 23N 111 32W
Mantiqueira, Serra da, Brazil 141 22 0 S 44 0W
Manton, U.S.A. 104 44 23N 85 25W
Mantorp, Sweden 11 58 21N 15 20 E
Mántova, Italy 26 45 20N 10 42 E
Mänttä, Finland 8 62 0N 24 40 E
Mantua = Mántova, Italy 26 45 20N 10 42 E
Manturovo, U.S.S.R. 37 58 30N 44 30 E
Manu, Peru 136 12 10 S 70 51W
Manu →, Peru 136 12 16 S 70 55W
Manua Is., Amer. Samoa 68 14 13 S 169 35W
Manuae, Cook Is. 67 19 30 S 159 0W
Manuel Alves →, Brazil 139 11 19 S 48 28W
Manuel Alves Grande →, Brazil 138 7 27 S 47 35W
Manuel Urbano, Brazil 136 8 53 S 69 18W
Manui, Indonesia 57 3 35 S 123 5 E
Manukau, N.Z. 80 37 1 S 174 55 E
Manukau Harbour, N.Z. 80 37 3 S 174 45 E
Manunui, N.Z. 80 38 54 S 175 21 E
Manuripi →, Bolivia 136 11 6 S 67 36W
Manus I., Papua N. G. 69 2 0 S 147 0 E
Manvi, India 51 15 57N 76 59 E
Manville, U.S.A. 120 42 48N 104 36W
Manwath, India 50 19 19N 76 32 E
Many, U.S.A. 121 31 36N 93 28W
Manyara, L., Tanzania 92 3 40 S 35 50 E
Manych →, U.S.S.R. 39 47 15N 40 0 E
Manych-Gudilo, Oz., U.S.S.R. 39 46 24N 42 38 E
Manyonga →, Tanzania 92 4 10 S 34 15 E
Manyoni, Tanzania 92 5 45 S 34 55 E
Manyoni □, Tanzania 92 6 30 S 34 30 E
Manzai, Pakistan 48 32 12N 70 15 E
Manzala, Bahra el, Egypt 88 31 10N 31 56 E
Manzanares, Spain 25 39 0N 3 22W
Manzaneda, Cabeza de, Spain 22 42 12N 7 15W
Manzanillo, Cuba 128 20 20N 77 31W
Manzanillo, Mexico 126 19 0N 104 20W
Manzanillo, Pta., Panama 128 9 30N 79 40W
Manzano Mts., U.S.A. 123 34 30N 106 45W
Manzhouli, China 62 49 35N 117 25 E
Manzini, Swaziland 97 26 30 S 31 25 E
Mao, Chad 87 14 4N 15 19 E
Maoke, Pegunungan, Indonesia 57 3 40 S 137 30 E
Maolin, China 61 43 58N 123 30 E
Maoming, China 59 21 50N 110 54 E
Maowen, China 58 31 41N 103 49 E
Maoxing, China 61 45 28N 124 40 E
Mapam Yumco, China 49 30 45N 81 28 E
Mapastepec, Mexico 127 15 26N 92 54W
Mapia, Kepulauan, Indonesia 57 0 50N 134 20 E
Mapimí, Mexico 126 25 50N 103 50W
Mapimí, Bolsón de, Mexico 126 27 30N 104 15W
Maping, China 59 31 34N 113 32 E
Mapinga, Tanzania 92 6 40 S 39 12 E
Mapinhane, Mozam. 97 22 20 S 35 0 E
Mapire, Venezuela 135 7 45N 64 42W
Maple →, U.S.A. 119 42 58N 84 56W
Maple Creek, Canada 111 49 55N 109 29W
Maple Valley, U.S.A. 124 47 25N 122 3W
Mapleton, U.S.A. 122 44 4N 123 58W
Maprik, Papua N. G. 69 3 44 S 143 3 E
Mapuca, India 51 15 36N 73 46 E
Mapuera →, Brazil 135 1 5 S 57 2W
Maputo, Mozam. 97 25 58 S 32 32 E
Maputo, B. de, Mozam. 97 25 50 S 32 45 E
Maqiaohe, China 61 44 40N 130 30 E
Maqnā, Si. Arabia 46 28 25N 34 50 E
Maqteïr, Mauritania 84 21 50N 11 40W
Maquela do Zombo, Angola 95 6 0 S 15 15 E
Maquinchao, Argentina 142 41 15 S 68 50W
Maquoketa, U.S.A. 118 42 4N 90 40W
Mar, Serra do, Brazil 141 25 30 S 49 0W
Mar Chiquita, L., Argentina 140 30 40 S 62 50W
Mar del Plata, Argentina 140 38 0 S 57 30W
Mar Menor, L., Spain 25 37 40N 0 45W
Mara, Guyana 135 6 0N 57 36W
Mara, India 52 28 11N 94 14 E
Mara, Tanzania 92 1 30 S 34 32 E
Mara □, Tanzania 92 1 45 S 34 20 E
Maraã, Brazil 134 1 52 S 65 25W
Marabá, Brazil 138 5 20 S 49 5W
Maracá, I. de, Brazil 138 2 10N 50 30W
Maracaibo, Venezuela 134 10 40N 71 37W
Maracaibo, L. de, Venezuela 134 9 40N 71 30W
Maracaju, Brazil 141 21 38 S 55 9W
Maracajú, Serra de, Brazil 137 23 57 S 55 1W
Maracanã, Brazil 138 0 46 S 47 27W
Maracás, Brazil 139 13 26 S 40 18W
Maracay, Venezuela 134 10 15N 67 28W
Marādah, Libya 86 29 15N 19 15 E
Maradi, Niger 91 13 29N 7 20 E
Maradun, Nigeria 91 12 35N 6 18 E
Marāgheh, Iran 46 37 30N 46 12 E
Maragogipe, Brazil 139 12 46 S 38 55W
Marāh, Si. Arabia 46 25 0N 45 35 E
Marajó, B. de, Brazil 138 1 0 S 48 30W
Marajó, I. de, Brazil 138 1 0 S 49 30W
Maralal, Kenya 92 1 0N 36 38 E
Maralinga, Australia 79 30 13 S 131 32 E
Marama, Australia 73 35 10 S 140 10 E
Maramasike, Solomon Is. 68 9 30 S 161 25 E
Marampa, S. Leone 90 8 45N 12 28W
Maran, Malaysia 55 3 35N 102 45 E
Marana, U.S.A. 123 32 30N 111 9W
Maranboy, Australia 78 14 40 S 132 39 E
Maranchón, Spain 24 41 6N 2 15W
Marand, Iran 46 38 30N 45 45 E
Marang, Malaysia 55 5 12N 103 13 E
Maranguape, Brazil 138 3 55 S 38 50W
Maranhão = São Luís, Brazil 138 2 39 S 44 15W
Maranhão □, Brazil 138 5 0 S 46 0W
Marano, L. di, Italy 27 45 42N 13 13 E
Maranoa →, Australia 73 27 50 S 148 37 E
Marañón →, Peru 136 4 30 S 73 35W
Marão, Mozam. 97 24 18 S 34 2 E
Marapi →, Brazil 135 0 37N 55 58W
Marari, Brazil 136 5 43 S 67 47W
Mărăşeşti, Romania 34 45 52N 27 14 E
Maratea, Italy 29 39 59N 15 43 E
Marateca, Portugal 23 38 34N 8 40W
Marathókambos, Greece 35 37 43N 26 42 E
Marathon, Australia 72 20 51 S 143 32 E
Marathon, Canada 104 48 44N 86 23W
Marathón, Greece 35 38 11N 23 58 E
Marathon, Iowa, U.S.A. 118 42 52N 94 59W
Marathon, N.Y., U.S.A. 117 42 25N 76 3W
Marathon, Tex., U.S.A. 121 30 15N 103 15W

Maratua

Maratua, *Indonesia* ... **57** 2 10N 118 35 E
Maraú, *Brazil* .... **139** 14 6 S 39 0W
Maravae, *Solomon Is.* **68** 7 54 S 156 44 E
Maravatío, *Mexico* ... **126** 19 51N 100 25W
Marbella, *Spain* **23** 36 30N 4 57W
Marble Bar, *Australia* . **78** 21 9 S 119 44 E
Marble Falls, *U.S.A.* . **121** 30 30N 98 15W
Marblehead, *U.S.A.* .. **117** 42 29N 70 51W
Marbleton, *Canada* ... **107** 45 37N 71 35W
Marburg, *W. Germany* **30** 50 49N 8 36 E
Marby, *Sweden* ...... **10** 63 7N 14 18 E
Marcal →, *Hungary* .. **33** 47 41N 17 32 E
Marcapata, *Peru* ..... **136** 13 31 S 70 52W
Marcaria, *Italy* .... **26** 45 7N 10 34 E
Marceline, *U.S.A.* **118** 39 43N 92 57W
March, *U.K.* .... **13** 52 33N 0 5 E
Marchal, *Zaïre* .... **95** 5 16 S 14 58 E
Marchand = Rommani, *Morocco* **84** 33 31N 6 40W
Marche, *France* ...... **20** 46 5N 1 20 E
Marche □, *Italy* ...... **27** 43 22N 13 10 E
Marche-en-Famenne, *Belgium* .... **17** 50 14N 5 19 E
Marchena, *Spain* **23** 37 18N 5 23W
Marches = Marche □, *Italy* .... **27** 43 22N 13 10 E
Marciana Marina, *Italy* **26** 42 44N 10 12 E
Marcianise, *Italy* ..... **29** 41 3N 14 16 E
Marcigny, *France* ..... **21** 46 17N 4 2 E
Marcillat-en-Combraille, *France* . **20** 46 12N 2 38 E
Marcinelle, *Belgium* .. **17** 50 24N 4 26 E
Marck, *France* .... **19** 50 57N 1 57 E
Marckolsheim, *France* **19** 48 10N 7 30 E
Marcona, *Peru* .... **136** 15 10 S 75 0W
Marcos Juárez, *Argentina* .... **140** 32 42 S 62 5W
Marcus, *Pac. Oc.* ..... **66** 24 0N 153 45 E
Marcus Necker Ridge, *Pac. Oc.* .... **66** 20 0N 175 0 E
Marcy Mt., *U.S.A.* ... **117** 44 7N 73 55W
Mardan, *Pakistan* ..... **48** 34 20N 72 0 E
Mardie, *Australia* ..... **78** 21 12 S 115 59 E
Mardin, *Turkey* .... **46** 37 20N 40 43 E
Maré, I., *N. Cal.* ..... **68** 21 30 S 168 0 E
Marechal Deodoro, *Brazil* .... **138** 9 43 S 35 54W
Maree L., *U.K.* **14** 57 40N 5 30W
Mareeba, *Australia* ... **72** 16 59 S 145 28 E
Marek = Stanke Dimitrov, *Bulgaria* . **34** 42 17N 23 9 E
Marek, *Indonesia* ..... **57** 4 41 S 120 24 E
Maremma, *Italy* ...... **26** 42 45N 11 15 E
Maréna, *Mali* **90** 14 0N 7 20W
Marenberg, *Yugoslavia* **27** 46 38N 15 13 E
Marengo, *U.S.A.* **118** 41 42N 92 5W
Marennes, *France* **20** 45 49N 1 7W
Marenyi, *Kenya* ...... **92** 4 22 S 39 8 E
Marerano, *Madag.* ... **97** 21 23 S 44 52 E
Marèttimo, *Italy* ...... **28** 37 58N 12 5 E
Mareuil-sur-Lay, *France* **20** 46 32N 1 14W
Marfa, *U.S.A.* **121** 30 15N 104 0W
Marganets, *U.S.S.R.* .. **38** 47 40N 34 40 E
Margaret Bay, *Canada* **110** 51 20N 127 35W
Margaret L., *Canada* . **110** 58 56N 115 25W
Margarita, I. de, *Venezuela* **135** 11 0N 64 0W
Margarítion, *Greece* .. **35** 39 22N 20 26 E
Margate, *S. Africa* .... **97** 30 50 S 30 20 E
Margate, *U.K.* .... **13** 51 23N 1 24 E
Margelan, *U.S.S.R.* ... **40** 40 27N 71 42 E
Margeride, Mts. de la, *France* .... **20** 44 43N 3 38 E
Margherita, *India* .... **52** 27 16N 95 40 E
Margherita di Savola, *Italy* .... **29** 41 25N 16 5 E
Marguerite, *Canada* .. **110** 52 30N 122 25W
Marhoum, *Algeria* **85** 34 27N 0 11W
Mari A.S.S.R. □, *U.S.S.R.* .... **37** 56 30N 48 0 E
María Elena, *Chile* ... **140** 22 18 S 69 40W
María Grande, *Argentina* .... **140** 31 45 S 59 55W
Maria I., *N. Terr.*, *Australia* .... **72** 14 52 S 135 45 E
Maria I., *Tas.*, *Australia* .... **72** 42 35 S 148 0 E
Maria van Diemen, C., *N.Z.* .... **80** 34 29 S 172 40 E
Mariager, *Denmark* ... **11** 56 40N 10 0 E
Mariager Fjord, *Denmark* .... **11** 56 42N 10 19 E
Mariakani, *Kenya* .... **92** 3 50 S 39 27 E
Marian L., *Canada* ... **110** 63 0N 116 15W
Mariana Trench, *Pac. Oc.* .... **66** 13 0N 145 0 E
Marianao, *Cuba* **128** 23 8N 82 24W
Mariani, *India* .... **52** 26 39N 94 19 E
Marianna, *Ark.*, *U.S.A.* **121** 34 48N 90 48W
Marianna, *Fla.*, *U.S.A.* **115** 30 45N 85 15W
Mariannelund, *Sweden* **11** 57 37N 15 35 E
Mariánské Lázně, *Czech.* .... **32** 49 48N 12 41 E
Marias →, *U.S.A.* ... **122** 47 56N 110 30W
Mariato, Punta, *Panama* **128** 7 12N 80 52W
Mariazell, *Austria* .... **33** 47 47N 15 19 E
Ma'rib, *Yemen* .... **45** 15 25N 45 21 E
Maribo, *Denmark* .... **11** 54 48N 11 30 E
Maribor, *Yugoslavia* .. **27** 46 36N 15 40 E
Marico →, *Africa* .... **96** 23 35 S 26 57 E
Maricopa, *Ariz.*, *U.S.A.* **123** 33 5N 112 2W
Maricopa, *Calif.*, *U.S.A.* **125** 35 7N 119 27W
Marîdî, *Sudan* .... **89** 4 55N 29 25 E
Maridi, Wadi →, *Sudan* .... **89** 6 15N 29 21 E
Marié →, *Brazil* ..... **134** 0 27 S 66 26W
Marie-Galante, *Guadeloupe* **129** 15 56N 61 16W
Mariecourt, *Canada* .. **103** 61 30N 72 0W
Mariefred, *Sweden* ... **10** 59 15N 17 12 E
Mariehamn, *Finland* .. **9** 60 5N 19 55 E
Marienberg, *E. Germany* .... **30** 50 40N 13 10 E
Marienberg, *Neths.* ... **16** 52 30N 6 35 E
Marienbourg, *Belgium* **17** 50 6N 4 31 E
Mariental, *Namibia* ... **96** 24 36 S 18 0 E
Marienville, *U.S.A.* ... **116** 41 27N 79 8W
Mariestad, *Sweden* ... **11** 58 43N 13 50 E
Marietta, *Ga.*, *U.S.A.* **115** 34 0N 84 30W
Marietta, *Ohio*, *U.S.A.* **114** 39 27N 81 27W
Marieville, *Canada* ... **117** 45 26N 73 10W
Marignane, *France* ... **21** 43 25N 5 13 E
Mariinsk, *U.S.S.R.* ... **40** 56 10N 87 20 E
Mariinskiy Posad, *U.S.S.R.* .... **37** 56 10N 47 45 E
Marília, *Brazil* .... **141** 22 13 S 50 0W
Marillana, *Australia* .. **78** 22 37 S 119 16 E
Marimba, *Angola* .... **95** 8 28 S 17 8 E
Marín, *Spain* **22** 42 23N 8 42W
Marina, *U.S.A.* **124** 36 41N 121 48W
Mariña, La, *Spain* **22** 43 30N 7 40W
Marina di Cirò, *Italy* .. **29** 39 22N 17 8 E
Marina Plains, *Australia* **72** 14 37 S 143 57 E
Marinduque, *Phil.* .... **57** 13 25N 122 0 E
Marine City, *U.S.A.* .. **114** 42 45N 82 29W
Marinel, Le, *Zaïre* .... **93** 10 25 S 25 17 E
Marineo, *Italy* .... **28** 37 57N 13 23 E
Marinette, *U.S.A.* **114** 45 4N 87 40W
Maringá, *Brazil* ...... **141** 23 26 S 52 2W
Marinha Grande, *Portugal* **23** 39 45N 8 56W
Marion, *Ala.*, *U.S.A.* . **115** 32 33N 87 20W
Marion, *Ill.*, *U.S.A.* .. **118** 37 45N 88 55W
Marion, *Ind.*, *U.S.A.* . **119** 40 35N 85 40W
Marion, *Iowa*, *U.S.A.* **118** 42 2N 91 36W
Marion, *Kans.*, *U.S.A.* **120** 38 25N 97 2W
Marion, *Mich.*, *U.S.A.* **114** 44 7N 85 8W
Marion, *N.C.*, *U.S.A.* **115** 35 42N 82 0W
Marion, *Ohio*, *U.S.A.* **119** 40 38N 83 8W
Marion, *S.C.*, *U.S.A.* . **115** 34 11N 79 22W
Marion, *Va.*, *U.S.A.* .. **115** 36 51N 81 29W
Marion, L., *U.S.A.* ... **115** 33 30N 80 15W
Marion I., *Ind. Oc.* ... **53** 47 0 S 38 0 E
Maripa, *Venezuela* **135** 7 26N 65 9W
Maripasoula, *Fr. Guiana* **135** 3 40N 54 4W
Mariposa, *U.S.A.* **124** 37 31N 119 59W
Mariscal Estigarribia, *Paraguay* .... **140** 22 3 S 60 40W
Maritime Alps = Maritimes, Alpes, *Europe* .... **21** 44 10N 7 10 E
Maritimes, Alpes, *Europe* .... **21** 44 10N 7 10 E
Marīvān, *Iran* .... **46** 35 30N 46 25 E
Mariyampole = Kapsukas, *U.S.S.R.* **36** 54 33N 23 19 E
Markam, *China* ...... **58** 29 42N 98 38 E
Markapur, *India* ..... **51** 15 44N 79 19 E
Markaryd, *Sweden* ... **11** 56 28N 13 35 E
Markazī □, *Iran* ...... **47** 35 0N 49 30 E
Markdale, *Canada* **108** 44 19N 80 39W
Marke, *Belgium* ...... **17** 50 48N 3 14 E
Marked Tree, *U.S.A.* . **121** 35 35N 90 24W
Markelsdorfer Huk, *W. Germany* .... **30** 54 33N 11 0 E
Marken, *Neths.* ...... **16** 52 26N 5 12 E
Markermeer, *Neths.* .. **16** 52 33N 5 15 E
Market Drayton, *U.K.* **12** 52 55N 2 30W
Market Harborough, *U.K.* **13** 52 29N 0 55W
Markham, *Canada* **108** 43 52N 79 16W
Markham →, *Papua N. G.* .... **69** 6 41 S 147 2 E
Markham L., *Canada* . **111** 62 30N 102 35W
Markham Mt., *Antarctica* .... **143** 83 0 S 164 0 E
Marki, *Poland* .... **32** 52 20N 21 2 E
Markleeville, *U.S.A.* .. **124** 38 44N 119 47W
Markoupoulon, *Greece* **35** 37 53N 23 57 E
Markovo, *U.S.S.R.* ... **41** 64 40N 169 40 E
Markoye, *Burkina Faso* **91** 14 39N 0 2 E
Marks, *U.S.S.R.* ..... **37** 51 45N 46 50 E
Markstay, *Canada* **108** 46 29N 80 32W
Marksville, *U.S.A.* ... **121** 31 10N 92 2W
Markt Schwaben, *W. Germany* .... **31** 48 14N 11 49 E
Marktredwitz, *E. Germany* .... **31** 50 1N 12 2 E
Marla, *Australia* ..... **73** 27 19 S 133 33 E
Marlbank, *Canada* **109** 44 26N 77 6W
Marlboro, *U.S.A.* **117** 42 19N 71 33W
Marlborough, *Australia* **72** 22 46 S 149 52 E
Marlborough □, *N.Z.* . **81** 41 45 S 173 33 E
Marlborough Downs, *U.K.* **13** 51 25N 1 55W
Marle, *France* .... **19** 49 43N 3 47 E
Marlee, *Australia* ..... **77** 31 47 S 152 20 E
Marlin, *U.S.A.* **121** 31 25N 96 50W
Marlo, *Australia* ...... **75** 37 46 S 148 31 E
Marlow, *E. Germany* . **30** 54 8N 12 34 E
Marlow, *U.S.A.* **121** 34 40N 97 58W
Marmagao, *India* ..... **51** 15 25N 73 56 E
Marmande, *France* ... **20** 44 30N 0 10 E
Marmara, *Turkey* .... **38** 40 35N 27 38 E
Marmara, Sea of = Marmara Denizi, *Turkey* .... **46** 40 45N 28 15 E
Marmara Denizi, *Turkey* .... **46** 40 45N 28 15 E
Marmaris, *Turkey* .... **46** 36 50N 28 14 E
Marmarth, *U.S.A.* **120** 46 21N 103 52W
Marmelos →, *Brazil* . **137** 6 6 S 61 46W
Marmion L., *Canada* . **104** 48 55N 91 20W
Marmion Mt., *Australia* **79** 29 16 S 119 50 E
Marmolada, Mte., *Italy* **27** 46 25N 11 55 E
Marmolejo, *Spain* **23** 38 3N 4 13W
Marmora, *Canada* **109** 44 28N 77 41W
Marnay, *France* ...... **19** 47 16N 5 48 E
Marne, *W. Germany* .. **30** 53 57N 9 1 E
Marne □, *France* .... **19** 48 50N 4 10 E
Marne →, *France* .... **19** 48 48N 2 24 E
Marnueli, *U.S.S.R.* ... **39** 41 30N 44 48 E
Maro, *Chad* .... **87** 8 30N 19 0 E
Maroa, *Venezuela* **134** 2 43N 67 33W
Maroala, *Madag.* ..... **97** 15 23 S 47 59 E
Maroantsetra, *Madag.* . **97** 15 26 S 49 44 E
Maromandia, *Madag.* . **97** 14 13 S 48 5 E
Marondera, *Zambia* .. **93** 18 5 S 31 42 E
Marong, *Australia* .... **74** 36 44 S 144 8 E
Maroni →, *Fr. Guiana* **135** 5 30N 54 0W
Maronne →, *France* .. **20** 45 5N 1 56 E
Maroochydore, *Australia* .... **73** 26 29 S 153 5 E
Maroona, *Australia* ... **74** 37 27 S 142 54 E
Maros →, *Hungary* .. **33** 46 15N 20 13 E
Marosakoa, *Madag.* .. **97** 15 26 S 46 38 E
Marostica, *Italy* ...... **27** 45 44N 11 40 E
Maroua, *Cameroon* ... **91** 10 40N 14 20 E
Marovoay, *Madag.* ... **97** 16 6S 46 39 E
Marowijne □, *Surinam* **135** 4 0N 55 0W
Marowijne →, *Surinam* **135** 5 45N 53 58W
Marquard, *S. Africa* .. **96** 28 40 S 27 28 E
Marqueira, *Portugal* .. **23** 38 41N 9 9W
Marquesas Is., *Pac. Oc.* **67** 9 30 S 140 0W
Marquette, *U.S.A.* ... **104** 46 30N 87 21W
Marquette, L., *Canada* **107** 48 54N 73 54W
Marquise, *France* ..... **19** 50 50N 1 40 E
Marra, Gebel, *Sudan* . **89** 7 20N 27 35 E
Marracuene, *Mozam.* . **97** 25 45 S 32 35 E
Marradi, *Italy* .... **27** 44 5N 11 37 E
Marrakech, *Morocco* . **84** 31 9N 8 0W
Marrar, *Australia* ..... **76** 34 50 S 147 23 E
Marrawah, *Australia* .. **72** 40 55 S 144 42 E
Marrecas, Serra das, *Brazil* .... **138** 9 0 S 41 0W
Marree, *Australia* .... **73** 29 39 S 138 1 E
Marrilla, *Australia* .... **78** 22 31 S 114 25 E
Marrimane, *Mozam.* .. **97** 22 58 S 33 34 E
Marromeu, *Mozam.* .. **97** 18 15 S 36 25 E
Marroquí, Punta, *Spain* **23** 36 0N 5 37W
Marrowie Creek, *Australia* .... **73** 33 23 S 145 40 E
Marrubane, *Mozam.* .. **93** 18 0 S 37 0 E
Marrum, *Neths.* ...... **16** 53 19N 5 48 E
Marrupa, *Mozam.* .... **93** 13 8 S 37 30 E
Mars, Le, *U.S.A.* **120** 43 0N 96 0W
Marsa Brega, *Libya* .. **86** 30 24N 19 37 E
Marsá Matrûh, *Egypt* . **88** 31 19N 27 9 E
Marsá Susah, *Libya* .. **86** 32 52N 21 59 E
Marsabit, *Kenya* ..... **92** 2 18N 38 0 E
Marsabit □, *Kenya* ... **92** 2 45N 37 45 E
Marsala, *Italy* .... **28** 37 48N 12 25 E
Marsciano, *Italy* ...... **27** 42 54N 12 20 E
Marsden, *Australia* ... **76** 33 47 S 147 32 E
Marsdiep, *Neths.* ..... **16** 52 58N 4 46 E
Marseillan, *France* .... **20** 43 23N 3 31 E
Marseille, *France* .... **21** 43 18N 5 23 E
Marseilles = Marseille, *France* .... **21** 43 18N 5 23 E
Marseilles, *U.S.A.* **119** 41 20N 88 43W
Marsh I., *U.S.A.* **121** 29 35N 91 50W
Marsh L., *U.S.A.* **120** 45 5N 96 0W
Marshall, *Liberia* **90** 6 8N 10 22W
Marshall, *Ark.*, *U.S.A.* **121** 35 58N 92 40W
Marshall, *Ill.*, *U.S.A.* . **119** 39 23N 87 42W
Marshall, *Mich.*, *U.S.A.* **119** 42 17N 84 59W
Marshall, *Minn.*, *U.S.A.* **120** 44 25N 95 45W
Marshall, *Mo.*, *U.S.A.* **118** 39 8N 93 15W
Marshall, *Tex.*, *U.S.A.* **121** 32 29N 94 20W
Marshall →, *Australia* **72** 22 59 S 136 59 E
Marshall Is., *Pac. Oc.* **66** 9 0N 171 0 E
Marshalltown, *U.S.A.* . **118** 42 5N 92 56W
Marshfield, *Mo.*, *U.S.A.* **121** 37 20N 92 58W
Marshfield, *Wis.*, *U.S.A.* **120** 44 42N 90 10W
Mársico Nuovo, *Italy* . **29** 40 26N 15 43 E
Märsta, *Sweden* ...... **10** 59 37N 17 52 E
Marstal, *Denmark* .... **11** 54 51N 10 30 E
Marstrand, *Sweden* ... **11** 57 53N 11 35 E
Mart, *U.S.A.* **121** 31 34N 96 51W
Marta →, *Italy* ...... **27** 42 14N 11 42 E
Martaban, *Burma* .... **52** 16 30N 97 35 E
Martaban, G. of, *Burma* .... **52** 16 5N 96 30 E
Martano, *Italy* .... **29** 40 14N 18 18 E
Martapura, *Kalimantan*, *Indonesia* .... **56** 3 22 S 114 47 E
Martapura, *Sumatera*, *Indonesia* .... **56** 4 19 S 104 22 E
Marte, *Nigeria* .... **91** 12 23N 13 46 E
Martel, *France* .... **20** 44 57N 1 37 E
Martelange, *Belgium* .. **17** 49 49N 5 43 E
Marten River, *Canada* **108** 46 44N 79 49W
Martensdale, *U.S.A.* .. **118** 41 23N 93 45W
Martés, Sierra, *Spain* . **25** 39 20N 1 0W
Martha's Vineyard, *U.S.A.* **117** 41 25N 70 35W
Martigné-Ferchaud, *France* **18** 47 50N 1 20W
Martigny, *Switz.* ..... **31** 46 6N 7 3 E
Martigues, *France* .... **21** 43 24N 5 4 E
Martil, *Morocco* **84** 35 36N 5 15W
Martin, *Czech.* .... **32** 49 6N 18 48 E
Martin, *S. Dak.*, *U.S.A.* **120** 43 11N 101 45W
Martin, *Tenn.*, *U.S.A.* **121** 36 23N 88 51W
Martín →, *Spain* **24** 41 18N 0 19W
Martin, L., *U.S.A.* ... **115** 32 45N 85 50W
Martina Franca, *Italy* . **29** 40 42N 17 20 E
Martinborough, *N.Z.* . **80** 41 14 S 175 29 E
Martindale, *Australia* . **76** 32 27 S 150 40 E
Martinez, *U.S.A.* **124** 38 1N 122 8W
Martinho Campos, *Brazil* .... **139** 19 20 S 45 13W
Martinique, *W. Indies* . **129** 14 40N 61 0W
Martinique Passage, *W. Indies* **129** 15 15N 61 0W
Martínon, *Greece* ..... **35** 38 35N 23 15 E
Martinópolis, *Brazil* .. **141** 22 11 S 51 12W
Martins Ferry, *U.S.A.* **116** 40 5N 80 46W
Martinsburg, *Pa.*, *U.S.A.* **116** 40 18N 78 21W
Martinsburg, *W. Va.*, *U.S.A.* **114** 39 30N 77 57W
Martinsville, *Ill.*, *U.S.A.* **119** 39 20N 87 53W
Martinsville, *Ind.*, *U.S.A.* **119** 39 29N 86 23W
Martinsville, *Va.*, *U.S.A.* **115** 36 41N 79 52W
Marton, *N.Z.* .... **80** 40 4 S 175 23 E
Martorell, *Spain* ...... **24** 41 28N 1 56 E
Martos, *Spain* **23** 37 44N 3 58W
Martūbah, *Libya* ..... **86** 32 35N 22 46 E
Martuni, *U.S.S.R.* .... **39** 40 9N 45 10 E
Maru, *Nigeria* .... **91** 12 22N 6 22 E
Marudi, *Malaysia* ..... **56** 4 11N 114 19 E
Ma'ruf, *Afghan.* ...... **47** 31 30N 67 6 E
Marugame, *Japan* .... **64** 34 15N 133 40 E
Marúggio, *Italy* ...... **29** 40 20N 17 33 E
Marui, *Papua N. G.* .. **69** 4 4 S 143 2 E
Maruim, *Brazil* ...... **138** 10 45 S 37 5W
Marulan, *Australia* ... **76** 34 43 S 150 3 E
Marulan South, *Australia* .... **76** 34 47 S 150 3 E
Marum, *Neths.* .... **16** 53 9N 6 16 E
Marum, Mt., *Vanuatu* **68** 16 15 S 168 7 E
Marunga, *Angola* ..... **95** 17 28 S 20 2 E
Marungu, Mts., *Zaïre* . **92** 7 30 S 30 0 E
Maruoka, *Japan* ...... **65** 36 9N 136 16 E
Marvejols, *France* .... **20** 44 33N 3 19 E
Marwar, *India* .... **48** 25 43N 73 45 E
Mary, *U.S.S.R.* ...... **40** 37 40N 61 50 E
Mary Frances L., *Canada* **111** 63 19N 106 13W
Mary Kathleen, *Australia* .... **72** 20 44 S 139 48 E
Maryborough = Port Laoise, *Ireland* **15** 53 2N 7 20W
Maryborough, *Queens.*, *Australia* .... **73** 25 31 S 152 37 E
Maryborough, *Vic.*, *Australia* .... **74** 37 0 S 143 44 E
Maryfield, *Canada* **111** 49 50N 101 35W
Maryland □, *U.S.A.* .. **114** 39 10N 76 40W
Maryland Jct., *Zambia* **93** 17 45 S 30 31 E
Maryport, *U.K.* **12** 54 43N 3 30W
Mary's Harbour, *Canada* **105** 52 18N 55 51W
Marystown, *Canada* .. **105** 47 10N 55 10W
Marysvale, *U.S.A.* **123** 38 25N 112 17W
Marysville, *Australia* .. **74** 37 33 S 145 45 E
Marysville, *Canada* ... **110** 49 35N 116 0W
Marysville, *Calif.*, *U.S.A.* **124** 39 14N 121 40W
Marysville, *Kans.*, *U.S.A.* **120** 39 50N 96 49W
Marysville, *Mich.*, *U.S.A.* **116** 42 55N 82 29W
Marysville, *Ohio*, *U.S.A.* **119** 40 15N 83 20W
Marysville, *Wash.*, *U.S.A.* **124** 48 3N 122 11W
Maryvale, *Australia* .. **77** 28 4 S 152 12 E
Maryville, *Mo.*, *U.S.A.* **118** 40 21N 94 52W
Maryville, *Tenn.*, *U.S.A.* **115** 35 50N 84 0W
Marzo, Punta, *Colombia* **134** 6 50N 77 42W
Marzūq, *Libya* .... **86** 25 53N 13 57 E
Masada = Mesada, *Israel* .... **44** 31 20N 35 19 E
Masahunga, *Tanzania* . **92** 2 6 S 33 18 E
Masai, *Malaysia* ...... **55** 1 29N 103 55 E
Masai Steppe, *Tanzania* **92** 4 30 S 36 30 E
Masaka, *Uganda* ..... **92** 0 21 S 31 45 E
Masalembo, Kepulauan, *Indonesia* **56** 5 35 S 114 30 E
Masalima, Kepulauan, *Indonesia* .... **56** 5 4 S 117 5 E
Masamba, *Indonesia* .. **57** 2 30 S 120 15 E
Masan, *S. Korea* ..... **61** 35 11N 128 32 E
Masanasa, *Spain* **25** 39 25N 0 25W
Masandam, Ras, *Oman* **47** 26 30N 56 30 E
Masasi, *Tanzania* ..... **93** 10 45 S 38 52 E

Monte Cristi

Moberly, *U.S.A.* **118** 39 25N 92 25W
Moberly →, *Canada* **110** 56 12N 120 55W
Mobile, *U.S.A.* **115** 30 41N 88 3W
Mobile B., *U.S.A.* **115** 30 30N 88 0W
Mobridge, *U.S.A.* **120** 45 31N 100 28W
Mobutu Sese Seko, L., *Africa* **92** 1 30N 31 0 E
Moc Chau, *Vietnam* **54** 20 50N 104 38 E
Moc Hoa, *Vietnam* **55** 10 46N 105 56 E
Mocaba, Sa. de, *Angola* **95** 7 12 S 15 0 E
Mocabe Kasari, *Zaïre* **93** 9 58 S 26 12 E
Mocajuba, *Brazil* **138** 2 35 S 49 30W
Moçambique, *Mozam.* **93** 15 3 S 40 42 E
Moçâmedes = Namibe, *Angola* **95** 15 7 S 12 11 E
Mocapra →, *Venezuela* **134** 7 56N 66 46W
Mocha, I., *Chile* **142** 38 22 S 73 56W
Mochudi, *Botswana* **96** 24 27 S 26 7 E
Mocimboa da Praia, *Mozam.* **93** 11 25 S 40 20 E
Möckeln, *Sweden* **11** 56 40N 14 15 E
Moclips, *U.S.A.* **124** 47 14N 124 10W
Mocoa, *Colombia* **134** 1 7N 76 35W
Mococa, *Brazil* **141** 21 28 S 47 0W
Mocorito, *Mexico* **126** 25 30N 107 53W
Moctezuma, *Mexico* **126** 29 50N 109 0W
Moctezuma →, *Mexico* **127** 21 59N 98 34W
Mocuba, *Mozam.* **93** 16 54 S 36 57 E
Mocúzari, Presa, *Mexico* **126** 27 10N 109 10W
Moda, *Burma* **52** 24 22N 96 29 E
Modane, *France* **21** 45 12N 6 40 E
Modasa, *India* **48** 23 30N 73 21 E
Modave, *Belgium* **17** 50 27N 5 18 E
Modder →, *S. Africa* **96** 29 2 S 24 37 E
Modderrivier, *S. Africa* **96** 29 2 S 24 38 E
Módena, *Italy* **26** 44 39N 10 55 E
Modena, *U.S.A.* **123** 37 55N 113 56W
Modesto, *U.S.A.* **124** 37 43N 121 0W
Módica, *Italy* **29** 36 52N 14 45 E
Modigliana, *Italy* **27** 44 9N 11 48 E
Modjamboli, *Zaïre* **94** 2 28N 22 6 E
Modo, *Sudan* **89** 5 31N 30 33 E
Modra, *Czech.* **33** 48 19N 17 20 E
Moe, *Australia* **75** 38 12 S 146 19 E
Moebase, *Mozam.* **93** 17 3 S 38 41 E
Moëlan-sur-Mer, *France* **18** 47 49N 3 38W
Moengo, *Surinam* **135** 5 45N 54 20W
Moergestel, *Neths.* **17** 51 33N 5 11 E
Moers, *W. Germany* **17** 51 27N 6 38 E
Moffat, *U.K.* **14** 55 20N 3 27W
Moga, *India* **48** 30 48N 75 8 E
Mogadishu = Muqdisho, *Somali Rep.* **98** 2 2N 45 25 E
Mogador = Essaouira, *Morocco* **84** 31 32N 9 42W
Mogadouro, *Portugal* **22** 41 22N 6 47W
Mogalakwena →, *S. Africa* **97** 22 38 S 28 40 E
Mogami →, *Japan* **63** 38 45N 140 0 E
Mogán, *Canary Is.* **25** 27 53N 15 43W
Mogaung, *Burma* **52** 25 20N 97 0 E
Møgeltønder, *Denmark* **11** 54 57N 8 48 E
Mogente, *Spain* **25** 38 52N 0 45W
Mogho, *Ethiopia* **89** 4 54N 40 16 E
Mogi das Cruzes, *Brazil* **141** 23 31 S 46 11W
Mogi-Guaçu →, *Brazil* **141** 20 53 S 48 10W
Mogi-Mirim, *Brazil* **141** 22 29 S 47 0W
Mogielnica, *Poland* **32** 51 42N 20 41 E
Mogilev, *U.S.S.R.* **36** 53 55N 30 18 E
Mogilev-Podolskiy, *U.S.S.R.* **38** 48 20N 27 40 E
Mogilno, *Poland* **32** 52 39N 17 55 E
Mogincual, *Mozam.* **93** 15 35 S 40 25 E
Mogliano Véneto, *Italy* **27** 45 33N 12 15 E
Mogo, *Australia* **76** 35 48 S 150 10 E
Mogocha, *U.S.S.R.* **41** 53 40N 119 50 E
Mogoi, *Indonesia* **57** 1 55 S 133 10 E
Mogok, *Burma* **52** 23 0N 96 40 E
Mogriguy, *Australia* **76** 32 3 S 148 40 E
Moguer, *Spain* **23** 37 15N 6 52W
Mogumber, *Australia* **79** 31 2 S 116 3 E
Mohács, *Hungary* **33** 45 58N 18 41 E
Mohaka →, *N.Z.* **80** 39 7 S 177 12 E
Mohales Hoek, *Lesotho* **96** 30 7 S 27 26 E
Mohall, *U.S.A.* **120** 48 46N 101 30W
Moḩammadābād, *Iran* **47** 37 52N 59 5 E
Mohammadia, *Algeria* **85** 35 33N 0 3 E
Mohammedia, *Morocco* **84** 33 44N 7 21W
Mohave, L., *U.S.A.* **125** 35 25N 114 36W
Mohawk →, *U.S.A.* **117** 42 47N 73 42W
Moheda, *Sweden* **11** 57 1N 14 35 E
Möhne →, *W. Germany* **30** 51 29N 7 57 E
Mohnyin, *Burma* **52** 24 47N 96 22 E
Moholm, *Sweden* **11** 58 37N 14 5 E
Mohoro, *Tanzania* **92** 8 6 S 39 8 E
Moia, *Sudan* **89** 5 3N 28 2 E
Moidart, L., *U.K.* **14** 56 47N 5 40W
Moille, La, *U.S.A.* **118** 41 32N 89 17W
Moinabad, *India* **50** 17 44N 77 16 E
Moindou, *N. Cal.* **68** 21 42 S 165 41 E
Moine, La →, *U.S.A.* **118** 39 58N 90 32W
Moineşti, *Romania* **34** 46 28N 26 31 E
Mointy, *U.S.S.R.* **40** 47 10N 73 18 E
Moira →, *Canada* **109** 44 21N 77 24W
Moirans, *France* **21** 45 20N 5 33 E
Moirans-en-Montagne, *France* **21** 46 26N 5 43 E
Moisakula, *U.S.S.R.* **36** 58 3N 25 12 E
Moisie, *Canada* **105** 50 12N 66 1W
Moisie →, *Canada* **105** 50 14N 66 5W
Moissac, *France* **20** 44 7N 1 5 E
Moïssala, *Chad* **87** 8 21N 17 46 E
Moita, *Portugal* **23** 38 38N 8 58W
Mojácar, *Spain* **25** 37 6N 1 55W
Mojados, *Spain* **22** 41 26N 4 40W
Mojave, *U.S.A.* **125** 35 8N 118 8W
Mojave Desert, *U.S.A.* **125** 35 0N 116 30W
Mojiang, *China* **58** 23 37N 101 35 E
Mojo, *Bolivia* **140** 21 48 S 65 33W
Mojo, *Ethiopia* **89** 8 35N 39 5 E
Mojokerto, *Indonesia* **57** 7 28 S 112 26 E
Mojos, Llanos de, *Bolivia* **137** 15 0 S 65 0W
Moju →, *Brazil* **138** 1 40 S 48 25W
Mokai, *N.Z.* **80** 38 32 S 175 56 E
Mokambo, *Zaïre* **93** 12 25 S 28 20 E
Mokameh, *India* **49** 25 24N 85 55 E
Mokane, *U.S.A.* **118** 38 41N 91 53W
Mokau →, *N.Z.* **80** 38 35 S 174 35 E
Mokelumne →, *U.S.A.* **124** 38 23N 121 25W
Mokelumne Hill, *U.S.A.* **124** 38 18N 120 43W
Mokhós, *Greece* **35** 35 16N 25 27 E
Mokhotlong, *Lesotho* **97** 29 22 S 29 2 E
Mokihinui →, *N.Z.* **81** 41 33 S 171 58 E
Moknine, *Tunisia* **86** 35 35N 10 58 E
Mokoan, L., *Australia* **74** 36 27 S 146 5 E
Mokpalin, *Burma* **52** 17 26N 96 53 E
Mokra Gora, *Yugoslavia* **33** 42 50N 20 30 E
Mokronog, *Yugoslavia* **27** 45 57N 15 9 E
Moksha →, *U.S.S.R.* **37** 54 45N 41 53 E
Mokshan, *U.S.S.R.* **37** 53 25N 44 35 E
Mol, *Belgium* **17** 51 11N 5 5 E
Mola, C. de la, *Spain* **24** 39 40N 4 20 E
Mola di Bari, *Italy* **29** 41 3N 17 5 E
Moláoi, *Greece* **35** 36 49N 22 56 E
Molat, *Yugoslavia* **27** 44 15N 14 50 E
Molchanovo, *U.S.S.R.* **40** 57 40N 83 50 E
Mold, *U.K.* **12** 53 10N 3 10W
Moldavia = Moldova, *Romania* **34** 46 30N 27 0 E
Moldavian S.S.R. □, *U.S.S.R.* **38** 47 0N 28 0 E
Molde, *Norway* **8** 62 45N 7 9 E
Moldova, *Romania* **34** 46 30N 27 0 E
Moldova Nouă, *Romania* **34** 44 45N 21 41 E
Moldoveanu, *Romania* **34** 45 36N 24 45 E
Mole →, *Australia* **77** 29 0 S 151 32 E
Molepolole, *Botswana* **96** 24 28 S 25 28 E
Molesworth, *N.Z.* **81** 42 5 S 173 16 E
Molfetta, *Italy* **29** 41 12N 16 35 E
Molina de Aragón, *Spain* **24** 40 46N 1 52W
Moline, *U.S.A.* **118** 41 30N 90 30W
Molinella, *Italy* **27** 44 38N 11 40 E
Molinos, *Argentina* **140** 25 28 S 66 15W
Moliro, *Zaïre* **92** 8 12 S 30 30 E
Molise □, *Italy* **27** 41 45N 14 30 E
Moliterno, *Italy* **29** 40 14N 15 50 E
Mollahat, *Bangla.* **49** 22 56N 89 48 E
Mölle, *Sweden* **11** 56 17N 12 31 E
Molledo, *Spain* **22** 43 8N 4 6W
Mollendo, *Peru* **136** 17 0 S 72 0W
Mollerin, L., *Australia* **79** 30 30 S 117 35 E
Mollerusa, *Spain* **24** 41 37N 0 54 E
Mollina, *Spain* **23** 37 8N 4 38W
Mölln, *W. Germany* **30** 53 37N 10 41 E
Mölltorp, *Sweden* **11** 58 30N 14 26 E
Mollymook, *Australia* **76** 35 21 S 150 29 E
Mölndal, *Sweden* **11** 57 40N 12 3 E
Molo, *Burma* **52** 23 22N 96 53 E
Molochansk, *U.S.S.R.* **38** 47 15N 35 35 E
Molochnaya →, *U.S.S.R.* **38** 47 0N 35 30 E
Molodechno, *U.S.S.R.* **36** 54 20N 26 50 E
Molokai, *U.S.A.* **112** 21 8N 157 0W
Moloma →, *U.S.S.R.* **37** 58 20N 48 15 E
Molong, *Australia* **76** 33 5 S 148 54 E
Molopo →, *Africa* **96** 27 30 S 20 13 E
Mólos, *Greece* **35** 38 47N 22 37 E
Molotov = Perm, *U.S.S.R.* **40** 58 0N 57 10 E
Moloundou, *Cameroon* **94** 2 8N 15 15 E
Molsheim, *France* **19** 48 33N 7 29 E
Molson L., *Canada* **111** 54 22N 96 40W
Molteno, *S. Africa* **96** 31 22 S 26 22 E
Molu, *Indonesia* **57** 6 45 S 131 40 E
Molucca Sea, *Indonesia* **57** 4 0 S 124 0 E
Moluccas = Maluku, *Indonesia* **57** 1 0 S 127 0 E
Moma, *Mozam.* **93** 16 47 S 39 4 E
Moma, *Zaïre* **92** 1 35 S 23 52 E
Mombaça, *Brazil* **138** 5 43 S 39 45W
Mombasa, *Kenya* **92** 4 2 S 39 43 E
Mombetsu, *Japan* **63** 42 27N 142 4 E
Mombil, *Burma* **52** 27 46N 98 6 E
Mombuey, *Spain* **22** 42 3N 6 20W
Momchilgrad, *Bulgaria* **35** 41 33N 25 23 E
Momence, *U.S.A.* **119** 41 10N 87 40W
Momi, *Zaïre* **92** 1 42 S 27 0 E
Momignies, *Belgium* **17** 50 2N 4 10 E
Mompós, *Colombia* **134** 9 14N 74 26W
Møn, *Denmark* **11** 54 57N 12 15 E
Mona, Canal de la, *W. Indies* **129** 18 30N 67 45W
Mona, I., *Puerto Rico* **129** 18 5N 67 54W
Mona, Pta., *Costa Rica* **128** 9 37N 82 36W
Mona, Punta, *Spain* **23** 36 43N 3 45W
Mona Quimbundo, *Angola* **95** 9 55 S 19 58 E
Monach Is., *U.K.* **14** 57 32N 7 40W
Monaco ■, *Europe* **21** 43 46N 7 23 E
Monadhliath Mts., *U.K.* **14** 57 10N 4 4W
Monagas □, *Venezuela* **135** 9 20N 63 0W
Monaghan, *Ireland* **15** 54 15N 6 58W
Monaghan □, *Ireland* **15** 54 10N 7 0W
Monahans, *U.S.A.* **121** 31 35N 102 50W
Monapo, *Mozam.* **93** 14 56 S 40 19 E
Monarch Mt., *Canada* **110** 51 55N 125 57W
Monastier-sur-Gazeille, Le, *France* **20** 44 57N 3 59 E
Monastir = Bitola, *Yugoslavia* **35** 41 5N 21 10 E
Monastir, *Tunisia* **86** 35 50N 10 49 E
Monastyriska, *U.S.S.R.* **36** 49 8N 25 14 E
Monbetsu, *Japan* **63** 44 21N 143 22 E
Moncada, *Spain* **24** 39 30N 0 24W
Moncalieri, *Italy* **26** 45 0N 7 40 E
Moncalvo, *Italy* **26** 45 3N 8 15 E
Moncão, *Portugal* **22** 42 4N 8 27W
Moncarapacho, *Portugal* **23** 37 5N 7 46W
Moncayo, Sierra del, *Spain* **24** 41 48N 1 50W
Mönchengladbach, *W. Germany* **30** 51 12N 6 23 E
Monchique, *Portugal* **23** 37 19N 8 38W
Monclova, *Mexico* **126** 26 50N 101 30W
Moncontour, *France* **18** 48 22N 2 38W
Moncouche, L., *Canada* **107** 48 45N 70 42W
Moncoutant, *France* **20** 46 43N 0 35W
Moncton, *Canada* **105** 46 7N 64 51W
Mondego →, *Portugal* **22** 40 9N 8 52W
Mondego, C., *Portugal* **22** 40 11N 8 54W
Mondeodo, *Indonesia* **57** 3 34 S 122 9 E
Mondo, *Chad* **87** 13 47N 15 32 E
Mondolfo, *Italy* **27** 43 45N 13 8 E
Mondonac, L., *Canada* **107** 47 24N 73 58W
Mondoñedo, *Spain* **22** 43 25N 7 23W
Mondovì, *Italy* **26** 44 23N 7 49 E
Mondovi, *U.S.A.* **120** 44 37N 91 40W
Mondragon, *France* **21** 44 13N 4 44 E
Mondragone, *Italy* **28** 41 8N 13 52 E
Mondrain I., *Australia* **79** 34 9 S 122 14 E
Monduli □, *Tanzania* **92** 3 0 S 36 0 E
Monemvasía, *Greece* **35** 36 41N 23 3 E
Monessen, *U.S.A.* **116** 40 9N 79 50W
Monesterio, *Spain* **23** 38 6N 6 15W
Monestier-de-Clermont, *France* **21** 44 55N 5 38 E
Monêtier-les-Bains, Le, *France* **21** 44 58N 6 30 E
Monett, *U.S.A.* **121** 36 55N 93 56W
Monfalcone, *Italy* **27** 45 49N 13 32 E
Monflanquin, *France* **20** 44 32N 0 47 E
Monforte, *Portugal* **23** 39 6N 7 25W
Monforte de Lemos, *Spain* **22** 42 31N 7 33W
Mong Hta, *Burma* **52** 19 50N 98 35 E
Mong Ket, *Burma* **52** 23 8N 98 22 E
Mong Kung, *Burma* **52** 21 35N 97 35 E
Mong Kyawt, *Burma* **52** 19 56N 98 45 E
Mong Nai, *Burma* **52** 20 32N 97 46 E
Mong Ping, *Burma* **52** 21 22N 99 2 E
Mong Pu, *Burma* **52** 20 55N 98 44 E
Mong Ton, *Burma* **52** 20 17N 98 45 E
Mong Tung, *Burma* **52** 22 2N 97 41 E
Mong Yai, *Burma* **52** 22 21N 98 3 E
Monga, *Zaïre* **94** 4 12N 22 49 E
Mongalla, *Sudan* **89** 5 8N 31 42 E
Mongers, L., *Australia* **79** 29 25 S 117 5 E
Monghyr = Munger, *India* **49** 25 23N 86 30 E
Mongla, *Bangla.* **52** 22 8N 89 35 E
Mongngaw, *Burma* **52** 22 47N 96 59 E
Mongo, *Chad* **87** 12 14N 18 43 E
Mongó, *Eq. Guin.* **94** 1 52N 10 10 E
Mongolia ■, *Asia* **62** 47 0N 103 0 E
Mongomo, *Eq. Guin.* **94** 1 38N 11 19 E
Mongonu, *Nigeria* **91** 12 40N 13 32 E
Mongororo, *Chad* **87** 12 3N 22 26 E
Mongu, *Zambia* **95** 15 16 S 23 12 E
Môngua, *Angola* **95** 16 43 S 15 20 E
Monistrol-d'Allier, *France* **20** 44 58N 3 38 E
Monistrol-sur-Loire, *France* **21** 45 17N 4 11 E
Monkey Bay, *Malawi* **93** 14 7 S 35 1 E
Monkey River, *Belize* **127** 16 22N 88 29W
Monkira, *Australia* **72** 24 46 S 140 30 E
Monkoto, *Zaïre* **94** 1 38 S 20 35 E
Monkton, *Canada* **108** 43 35N 81 5W
Monmouth, *U.K.* **13** 51 48N 2 43W
Monmouth, *U.S.A.* **118** 40 50N 90 40W
Mono, *Solomon Is.* **68** 7 20 S 155 35 E
Mono, L., *U.S.A.* **124** 38 0N 119 9W
Monolith, *U.S.A.* **125** 35 7N 118 22W
Monon, *U.S.A.* **119** 40 52N 86 53W
Monona, *Iowa, U.S.A.* **118** 43 3N 91 24W
Monona, *Wis., U.S.A.* **118** 43 4N 89 20W
Monongahela, *U.S.A.* **116** 40 12N 79 56W
Monópoli, *Italy* **29** 40 57N 17 18 E
Monor, *Hungary* **33** 47 21N 19 27 E
Monóvar, *Spain* **25** 38 28N 0 53W
Monowai, *N.Z.* **81** 45 53 S 167 31 E
Monowai, L., *N.Z.* **81** 45 53 S 167 25 E
Monqoumba, *C.A.R.* **94** 3 33N 18 40 E
Monreal del Campo, *Spain* **24** 40 47N 1 20W
Monreale, *Italy* **28** 38 6N 13 16 E
Monroe, *Ga., U.S.A.* **115** 33 47N 83 43W
Monroe, *Iowa, U.S.A.* **118** 41 31N 93 6W
Monroe, *La., U.S.A.* **121** 32 32N 92 4W
Monroe, *Mich., U.S.A.* **119** 41 55N 83 26W
Monroe, *N.C., U.S.A.* **115** 35 2N 80 37W
Monroe, *N.Y., U.S.A.* **117** 41 19N 74 11W
Monroe, *Ohio, U.S.A.* **119** 39 27N 84 22W
Monroe, *Utah, U.S.A.* **123** 38 45N 112 5W
Monroe, *Wash., U.S.A.* **124** 47 51N 121 58W
Monroe, *Wis., U.S.A.* **118** 42 38N 89 40W
Monroe, Res., *U.S.A.* **119** 39 1N 86 31W
Monroe City, *U.S.A.* **118** 39 40N 91 40W
Monroeville, *Ala., U.S.A.* **115** 31 33N 87 15W
Monroeville, *Ind., U.S.A.* **119** 40 59N 84 52W
Monroeville, *Pa., U.S.A.* **116** 40 26N 79 45W
Monrovia, *Liberia* **90** 6 18N 10 47W
Monrovia, *U.S.A.* **123** 34 7N 118 1W
Mons, *Belgium* **17** 50 27N 3 58 E
Monsaraz, *Portugal* **23** 38 28N 7 22W
Monse, *Indonesia* **57** 4 0 S 123 10 E
Monsefú, *Peru* **136** 6 52 S 79 52W
Monségur, *France* **20** 44 38N 0 4 E
Monsélice, *Italy* **27** 45 16N 11 46 E
Monster, *Neths.* **16** 52 1N 4 10 E
Mont-Carmel, *Canada* **107** 47 26N 69 52W
Mont-de-Marsan, *France* **20** 43 54N 0 31W
Mont Dore, *N. Cal.* **68** 22 16 S 166 34 E
Mont-Dore, Le, *France* **20** 45 35N 2 49 E
Mont-Joli, *Canada* **107** 48 37N 68 10W
Mont-Laurier, *Canada* **106** 46 35N 75 30W
Mont-St.-Michel, Le, *France* **18** 48 40N 1 30W
Mont-sous-Vaudrey, *France* **19** 46 58N 5 36 E
Mont-sur-Marchienne, *Belgium* **17** 50 23N 4 24 E
Mont-Tremblant, *Canada* **106** 46 13N 74 36W
Mont Tremblant Prov. Park, *Canada* **107** 46 30N 74 30W
Montabaur, *W. Germany* **30** 50 26N 7 49 E
Montagnac, *France* **20** 43 29N 3 28 E
Montagnana, *Italy* **27** 45 13N 11 29 E
Montagu, *S. Africa* **96** 33 45 S 20 8 E
Montagu I., *Antarctica* **143** 58 25 S 26 20W
Montague, *Canada* **105** 46 10N 62 39W
Montague, *U.S.A.* **122** 41 47N 122 30W
Montague, I., *Mexico* **126** 31 40N 114 56W
Montague I., *Australia* **75** 36 16 S 150 13 E
Montague I., *U.S.A.* **102** 60 0N 147 0W
Montague Ra., *Australia* **79** 27 15 S 119 30 E
Montague Sd., *Australia* **78** 14 28 S 125 20 E
Montaigu, *France* **18** 46 59N 1 18W
Montalbán, *Spain* **24** 40 50N 0 45W
Montalbano di Elicona, *Italy* **29** 38 1N 15 0 E
Montalbano Iónico, *Italy* **29** 40 17N 16 33 E
Montalbo, *Spain* **24** 39 53N 2 42W
Montalcino, *Italy* **27** 43 4N 11 30 E
Montalegre, *Portugal* **22** 41 49N 7 47W
Montalto di Castro, *Italy* **27** 42 20N 11 36 E
Montalto Uffugo, *Italy* **29** 39 25N 16 9 E
Montalvo, *U.S.A.* **125** 34 15N 119 12W
Montamarta, *Spain* **22** 41 39N 5 49W
Montaña, *Peru* **136** 6 0 S 73 0W
Montana □, *U.S.A.* **112** 47 0N 110 0W
Montaña Clara, I., *Canary Is.* **25** 29 17N 13 33W
Montánchez, *Spain* **23** 39 15N 6 8W
Montañita, *Colombia* **134** 1 22N 75 28W
Montargis, *France* **19** 47 59N 2 43 E
Montauban, *France* **20** 44 0N 1 21 E
Montauk, *U.S.A.* **117** 41 3N 71 57W
Montauk Pt., *U.S.A.* **117** 41 4N 71 52W
Montbard, *France* **19** 47 38N 4 20 E
Montbéliard, *France* **19** 47 31N 6 48 E
Montblanch, *Spain* **24** 41 23N 1 4 E
Montbrison, *France* **21** 45 36N 4 3 E
Montcalm, Pic de, *France* **20** 42 40N 1 25 E
Montceau-les-Mines, *France* **19** 46 40N 4 23 E
Montcerf, *Canada* **106** 46 32N 76 3W
Montchanin, *France* **21** 46 47N 4 30 E
Montclair, *U.S.A.* **117** 40 53N 74 13W
Montcornet, *France* **19** 49 40N 4 1 E
Montcuq, *France* **20** 44 21N 1 13 E
Montdidier, *France* **19** 49 38N 2 35 E
Monte, La, *U.S.A.* **118** 38 47N 93 27W
Monte Albán, *Mexico* **127** 17 2N 96 45W
Monte Alegre, *Brazil* **135** 2 0 S 54 0W
Monte Alegre de Goiás, *Brazil* **139** 13 14 S 47 10W
Monte Alegre de Minas, *Brazil* **139** 18 52 S 48 52W
Monte Azul, *Brazil* **139** 15 9 S 42 53W
Monte Bello Is., *Australia* **78** 20 30 S 115 45 E
Monte-Carlo, *Monaco* **21** 43 46N 7 23 E
Monte Carmelo, *Brazil* **139** 18 43 S 47 29W
Monte Caseros, *Argentina* **140** 30 10 S 57 50W
Monte Comán, *Argentina* **140** 34 40 S 67 53W
Monte Cristi, *Dom. Rep.* **129** 19 52N 71 39W

Monte Dinero

Monte Dinero, Argentina 142 52 18 S 68 33W
Monte Lindo →, Paraguay 140 23 56 S 57 12W
Monte Quemado, Argentina 140 25 53 S 62 41W
Monte Redondo, Portugal 22 39 53N 8 50W
Monte Rio, U.S.A. 124 38 28N 123 0W
Monte San Giovanni, Italy 28 41 39N 13 33 E
Monte San Savino, Italy 27 43 20N 11 42 E
Monte Sant' Ángelo, Italy 29 41 42N 15 59 E
Monte Santu, C. di, Italy 28 40 5N 9 42 E
Monte Vista, U.S.A. 123 37 40N 106 8W
Monteagudo, Argentina 141 27 14 S 54 8W
Monteagudo, Bolivia 137 19 49 S 63 59W
Montealegre, Spain 25 38 48N 1 17W
Montebello, Canada 106 45 40N 74 55W
Montebelluna, Italy 27 45 47N 12 3 E
Montebourg, France 18 49 30N 1 20W
Montecastrilli, Italy 27 42 40N 12 30 E
Montecatini Terme, Italy 26 43 55N 10 48 E
Montecito, U.S.A. 125 34 26N 119 40W
Montecristi, Ecuador 134 1 0 S 80 40W
Montecristo, Italy 26 42 20N 10 20 E
Montefalco, Italy 27 42 53N 12 38 E
Montefiascone, Italy 27 42 31N 12 2 E
Montefrío, Spain 23 37 20N 4 0W
Montegnée, Belgium 17 50 38N 5 31 E
Montego Bay, Jamaica 128 18 30N 78 0W
Montegranaro, Italy 27 43 13N 13 38 E
Monteiro, Brazil 138 7 48 S 37 2W
Montejicar, Spain 25 37 33N 3 30W
Montejinnie, Australia 78 16 40 S 131 38 E
Montelíbano, Colombia 134 8 5N 75 29W
Montélimar, France 21 44 33N 4 45 E
Montella, Italy 29 40 50N 15 0 E
Montellano, Spain 23 36 59N 5 36W
Montello, U.S.A. 120 43 49N 89 21W
Montelupo Fiorentino, Italy 26 43 44N 11 2 E
Montemor-o-Novo, Portugal 23 38 40N 8 12W
Montemor-o-Velho, Portugal 22 40 11N 8 40W
Montemorelos, Mexico 127 25 11N 99 42W
Montendre, France 20 45 16N 0 26W
Montenegro = Crna Gora □, Yugoslavia 33 42 40N 19 20 E
Montenegro, Brazil 141 29 39 S 51 29W
Montenero di Bisaccia, Italy 27 42 0N 14 47 E
Montepuez, Mozam. 93 13 8 S 38 59 E
Montepuez →, Mozam. 93 12 32 S 40 27 E
Montepulciano, Italy 27 43 5N 11 46 E
Montereale, Italy 27 42 31N 13 13 E
Montereau-Fault-Yonne, France 19 48 22N 2 57 E
Monterey, Calif., U.S.A. 124 36 35N 121 57W
Monterey, Ind., U.S.A. 119 41 11N 86 30W
Monterey B., U.S.A. 124 36 50N 121 55W
Montería, Colombia 134 8 46N 75 53W
Montero, Bolivia 137 17 20 S 63 15W
Monteros, Argentina 140 27 11 S 65 30W
Monterotondo, Italy 27 42 3N 12 36 E
Monterrey, Mexico 126 25 40N 100 30W
Montes Altos, Brazil 138 5 50 S 47 4W
Montes Claros, Brazil 139 16 30 S 43 50W
Montesano, U.S.A. 124 46 58N 123 39W
Montesárchio, Italy 29 41 5N 14 37 E
Montescaglioso, Italy 29 40 34N 16 40 E
Montesilvano, Italy 27 42 30N 14 8 E
Montevarchi, Italy 27 43 30N 11 32 E
Montevideo, Uruguay 141 34 50 S 56 11W
Montevideo, U.S.A. 120 44 55N 95 40W
Montezuma, Ind., U.S.A. 119 39 47N 87 22W
Montezuma, Iowa, U.S.A. 118 41 32N 92 35W
Montfaucon, France 19 49 16N 5 8 E
Montfaucon-en-Velay, France 21 45 11N 4 20 E
Montfort, France 18 48 9N 1 58W
Montfort, Neths. 17 51 7N 5 58 E
Montfort-l'Amaury, France 19 48 47N 1 49 E
Montgenèvre, France 21 44 56N 6 43 E
Montgomery = Sahiwal, Pakistan 48 30 45N 73 8 E
Montgomery, U.K. 13 52 34N 3 9W
Montgomery, Ala., U.S.A. 115 32 20N 86 20W
Montgomery, Ill., U.S.A. 119 41 44N 88 21W
Montgomery, W. Va., U.S.A. 114 38 9N 81 21W
Montgomery City, U.S.A. 118 38 59N 91 30W
Montguyon, France 20 45 12N 0 12W
Monthey, Switz. 31 46 15N 6 56 E
Monticelli d'Ongina, Italy 26 45 3N 9 56 E
Monticello, Ark., U.S.A. 121 33 40N 91 48W
Monticello, Fla., U.S.A. 115 30 35N 83 50W
Monticello, Ill., U.S.A. 119 40 1N 88 34W
Monticello, Ind., U.S.A. 119 40 40N 86 45W
Monticello, Iowa, U.S.A. 118 42 18N 91 12W
Monticello, Ky., U.S.A. 115 36 52N 84 50W
Monticello, Minn., U.S.A. 120 45 17N 93 52W
Monticello, Miss., U.S.A. 121 31 35N 90 8W
Monticello, Mo., U.S.A. 118 40 7N 91 43W
Monticello, N.Y., U.S.A. 117 41 37N 74 42W
Monticello, Utah, U.S.A. 123 37 55N 109 27W
Montichiari, Italy 26 45 28N 10 29 E
Montier-en-Der, France 19 48 30N 4 45 E
Montignac, France 20 45 4N 1 10 E
Montignies-sur-Sambre, Belgium 17 50 24N 4 29 E
Montigny, France 19 49 7N 6 10 E
Montigny-sur-Aube, France 19 47 57N 4 45 E
Montijo, Spain 23 38 52N 6 39W
Montijo, Presa de, Spain 23 38 55N 6 26W
Montilla, Spain 23 37 36N 4 40W
Montlhéry, France 19 48 39N 2 15 E
Montluçon, France 20 46 22N 2 36 E
Montmagny, Canada 107 46 58N 70 34W
Montmarault, France 20 46 19N 2 57 E
Montmartre, Canada 111 50 14N 103 27W
Montmédy, France 19 49 30N 5 20 E
Montmélian, France 21 45 30N 6 4 E
Montmirail, France 19 48 51N 3 30 E
Montmoreau-St.-Cybard, France 20 45 23N 0 8 E
Montmorency, Canada 105 46 53N 71 11W
Montmorillon, France 20 46 26N 0 50 E
Montmort, France 19 48 55N 3 49 E
Monto, Australia 72 24 52 S 151 6 E
Montoir-sur-le-Loir, France 18 47 45N 0 52 E
Montório al Vomano, Italy 27 42 35N 13 38 E
Montoro, Spain 23 38 1N 4 27W
Montour Falls, U.S.A. 116 42 20N 76 51W
Montpelier, Idaho, U.S.A. 122 42 15N 111 20W
Montpelier, Ind., U.S.A. 119 40 33N 85 17W
Montpelier, Ohio, U.S.A. 119 41 34N 84 40W
Montpelier, Vt., U.S.A. 117 44 15N 72 38W
Montpellier, France 20 43 37N 3 52 E
Montpezat-de-Quercy, France 20 44 15N 1 30 E
Montpon-Ménestérol, France 20 45 0N 0 11 E
Montréal, Canada 107 45 31N 73 34W
Montréal, France 20 43 13N 2 8 E
Montreal L., Canada 111 54 20N 105 45W
Montreal Lake, Canada 111 54 3N 105 46W
Montredon-Labessonnié, France 20 43 45N 2 18 E
Montréjeau, France 20 43 6N 0 35 E
Montrésor, France 18 47 10N 1 10 E
Montreuil, France 19 50 27N 1 45 E
Montreuil, L., Canada 106 50 12N 77 40W
Montreuil-Bellay, France 18 47 8N 0 9W
Montreux, Switz. 31 46 26N 6 55 E
Montrevault, France 18 47 17N 1 2W
Montrevel-en-Bresse, France 21 46 21N 5 8 E
Montrichard, France 18 47 20N 1 10 E
Montrose, U.K. 14 56 43N 2 28W
Montrose, Colo., U.S.A. 123 38 30N 107 52W
Montrose, Pa., U.S.A. 117 41 50N 75 55W
Montrose, L., U.S.A. 118 38 18N 93 50W
Monts, Pte. des, Canada 105 49 20N 67 12W
Monts-sur-Guesnes, France 18 46 55N 0 13 E
Montsalvy, France 20 44 41N 2 30 E
Montsant, Sierra de, Spain 24 41 17N 1 0 E
Montsauche, France 19 47 13N 4 2 E
Montsech, Sierra del, Spain 24 42 0N 0 45 E
Montseny, Spain 24 41 55N 2 25W
Montserrat, Spain 24 41 36N 1 49 E
Montserrat, W. Indies 129 16 40N 62 10W
Montuenga, Spain 22 41 3N 4 38W
Montuiri, Spain 24 39 34N 2 59 E
Monveda, Zaïre 94 2 52N 21 30 E
Monyo, Burma 52 17 59N 95 30 E
Monywa, Burma 52 22 7N 95 11 E
Monza, Italy 26 45 35N 9 15 E
Monze, Zambia 93 16 17 S 27 29 E
Monze, C., Pakistan 48 24 47N 66 37 E
Monzón, Spain 24 41 52N 0 10 E
Mooi River, S. Africa 97 29 13 S 29 50 E
Mook, Neths. 16 51 46N 5 54 E
Mo'oka, Japan 65 36 26N 140 1 E
Moolawatana, Australia 73 29 55 S 139 45 E
Mooliabeenee, Australia 79 31 20 S 116 2 E
Mooloogool, Australia 79 26 2 S 119 5 E
Moomin, Cr. →, Australia 77 29 44 S 149 20 E
Moonah →, Australia 72 22 3 S 138 33 E
Moonan Flat, Australia 77 31 55 S 151 14 E
Moonbeam, Canada 104 49 20N 82 10W
Moondarra, Australia 75 38 2 S 146 30 E
Moonie, Australia 77 27 46 S 150 20 E
Moonie →, Australia 77 29 19 S 148 43 E
Moonta, Australia 73 34 6 S 137 32 E
Moora, Australia 79 30 37 S 115 58 E
Mooraberree, Australia 72 25 13 S 140 54 E
Mooralla, Australia 74 37 25 S 142 10 E
Moorarie, Australia 79 25 56 S 117 35 E
Moorcroft, U.S.A. 120 44 17N 104 58W
Moore, Australia 77 30 57 S 150 52 E
Moore →, Australia 79 31 22 S 115 30 E
Moore, L., Australia 79 29 50 S 117 35 E
Moore Reefs, Australia 72 16 0 S 149 5 E
Moorefield, U.S.A. 114 39 5N 78 59W
Moores Res., U.S.A. 117 44 45N 71 50W
Mooresville, Ind., U.S.A. 119 39 37N 86 22W
Mooresville, N.C., U.S.A. 115 35 36N 80 45W
Moorfoot Hills, U.K. 14 55 44N 3 8W
Moorhead, U.S.A. 120 46 51N 96 44W
Moorland, Australia 77 31 46 S 152 38 E
Mooroopna, Australia 74 36 25 S 145 22 E
Moorpark, U.S.A. 125 34 17N 118 53W
Moorreesburg, S. Africa 96 33 6 S 18 38 E
Moorslede, Belgium 17 50 54N 3 4 E
Moosburg, W. Germany 31 48 28N 11 57 E
Moose →, Canada 104 51 20N 80 25W
Moose Creek, Canada 109 45 15N 74 58W
Moose Factory, Canada 104 51 16N 80 32W
Moose I., Canada 111 51 42N 97 10W
Moose Jaw, Canada 111 50 24N 105 30W
Moose Jaw →, Canada 111 50 34N 105 18W
Moose Lake, Canada 111 53 43N 100 20W
Moose Lake, U.S.A. 120 46 27N 92 48W
Moose Mountain Cr. →, Canada 111 49 13N 102 12W
Moose Mountain Prov. Park, Canada 111 49 48N 102 25W
Moose River, Canada 104 50 48N 81 17W
Moosehead L., U.S.A. 105 45 34N 69 40W
Moosomin, Canada 111 50 9N 101 40W
Moosonee, Canada 104 51 17N 80 39W
Moosup, U.S.A. 117 41 44N 71 52W
Mopeia Velha, Mozam. 93 17 30 S 35 40 E
Mopipi, Botswana 96 21 6 S 24 55 E
Mopoi, C.A.R. 92 5 6N 26 54 E
Mopti, Mali 90 14 30N 4 0W
Moqatta, Sudan 89 14 38N 35 50 E
Moquegua, Peru 136 17 15 S 70 46W
Moquegua □, Peru 136 16 50 S 70 55W
Mór, Hungary 33 47 25N 18 12 E
Móra, Portugal 23 38 55N 8 10W
Mora, Sweden 10 61 2N 14 38 E
Mora, Minn., U.S.A. 120 45 52N 93 19W
Mora, N. Mex., U.S.A. 123 35 58N 105 21W
Mora de Ebro, Spain 24 41 6N 0 38 E
Mora de Rubielos, Spain 24 40 15N 0 45W
Mora la Nueva, Spain 24 41 7N 0 39 E
Morača →, Yugoslavia 33 42 20N 19 9 E
Morada Nova, Brazil 138 5 7 S 38 23W
Morada Nova de Minas, Brazil 139 18 37 S 45 22W
Moradabad, India 49 28 50N 78 50 E
Morafenobe, Madag. 97 17 50 S 44 53 E
Morąg, Poland 32 53 55N 19 56 E
Moral de Calatrava, Spain 25 38 51N 3 33W
Moraleja, Spain 22 40 6N 6 43W
Morales, Colombia 134 2 45N 76 38W
Moramanga, Madag. 97 18 56 S 48 12 E
Moran, Kans., U.S.A. 121 37 53N 94 35W
Moran, Wyo., U.S.A. 122 43 53N 110 37W
Moranbah, Australia 72 22 1 S 148 6 E
Morangarell, Australia 76 34 8 S 147 42 E
Morano Cálabro, Italy 29 39 51N 16 8 E
Morant Cays, Jamaica 128 17 22N 76 0W
Morant Pt., Jamaica 128 17 55N 76 12W
Morar L., U.K. 14 56 57N 5 40W
Moratalla, Spain 25 38 14N 1 49W
Moratuwa, Sri Lanka 51 6 45N 79 55 E
Morava →, Czech. 32 48 10N 16 59 E
Moravia, U.S.A. 118 40 50N 92 50W
Moravian Hts. = Ceskomoravská Vrchovina, Czech. 32 49 30N 15 40 E
Moravica →, Yugoslavia 33 43 52N 20 8 E
Moravice →, Czech. 32 49 50N 17 43 E
Moravița, Romania 33 45 17N 21 14 E
Moravská Třebová, Czech. 32 49 45N 16 40 E
Morawa, Australia 79 29 13 S 116 0 E
Morawhanna, Guyana 135 8 30N 59 40W
Moray Firth, U.K. 14 57 50N 3 30W
Morbach, W. Germany 31 49 48N 7 7 E
Morbegno, Italy 26 46 8N 9 34 E
Morbi, India 48 22 50N 70 42 E
Morbihan □, France 18 47 55N 2 50W
Morcenx, France 20 44 0N 0 55W
Mordelles, France 18 48 5N 1 52W
Morden, Canada 111 49 15N 98 10W
Mordialloc, Australia 74 38 1 S 145 6 E
Mordovian A.S.S.R. □, U.S.S.R. 37 54 20N 44 30 E
Mordovo, U.S.S.R. 37 52 6N 40 50 E
Møre og Romsdal fylke □, Norway 10 62 30N 8 0 E
Morea, Australia 74 36 45 S 141 18 E
Morea, Greece 6 37 45N 22 10 E
Moreau →, U.S.A. 120 45 15N 100 43W
Morecambe, U.K. 12 54 5N 2 52W
Morecambe B., U.K. 12 54 7N 3 0W
Moree, Australia 77 29 28 S 149 54 E
Morehead, Papua N. G. 69 8 41 S 141 41 E
Morehead, U.S.A. 119 38 12N 83 22W
Morehead City, U.S.A. 115 34 46N 76 44W
Morelia, Mexico 126 19 40N 101 11W
Morella, Australia 72 23 0 S 143 52 E
Morella, Spain 24 40 35N 0 5W
Morelos, Mexico 126 26 42N 107 40W
Morelos □, Mexico 127 18 40N 99 10W
Morena, Sierra, Spain 23 38 20N 4 0W
Morenci, Ariz., U.S.A. 123 33 7N 109 20W
Morenci, Mich., U.S.A. 119 41 43N 84 13W
Moreni, Romania 34 44 59N 25 36 E
Morero, Bolivia 137 11 9 S 66 15W
Moreru →, Brazil 137 10 10 S 59 15W
Moresby I., Canada 110 52 30N 131 40W
Morestel, France 21 45 40N 5 28 E
Moret-sur-Loing, France 19 48 22N 2 58 E
Moreton, Australia 72 12 22 S 142 30 E
Moreton I., Australia 77 27 10 S 153 25 E
Moreuil, France 19 49 46N 2 30 E
Morez, France 21 46 31N 6 2 E
Morgan, Australia 73 34 0 S 139 35 E
Morgan, U.S.A. 122 41 3N 111 44W
Morgan City, U.S.A. 121 29 40N 91 15W
Morgan Hill, U.S.A. 124 37 8N 121 39W
Morganfield, U.S.A. 114 37 40N 87 55W
Morganton, U.S.A. 115 35 46N 81 48W
Morgantown, Ind., U.S.A. 119 39 22N 86 16W
Morgantown, W. Va., U.S.A. 114 39 39N 79 58W
Morgat, France 18 48 15N 4 32W
Morgenzon, S. Africa 97 26 45 S 29 36 E
Morges, Switz. 31 46 31N 6 29 E
Morhange, France 19 48 55N 6 38 E
Mori, Italy 26 45 51N 10 59 E
Morialmée, Belgium 17 50 17N 4 35 E
Morice L., Canada 110 53 50N 127 40W
Morichal, Colombia 134 2 10N 70 34W
Morichal Largo →, Venezuela 135 9 27N 62 25W
Moriguchi, Japan 65 34 44N 135 34 E
Moriki, Nigeria 91 12 52N 6 30 E
Morin-Heights, Canada 107 45 54N 74 15W
Morinville, Canada 110 53 49N 113 41W
Morioka, Japan 63 39 45N 141 8 E
Moris, Mexico 126 28 8N 108 32W
Morisset, Australia 76 33 6 S 151 30 E
Morlaàs, France 20 43 21N 0 18W
Morlaix, France 18 48 36N 3 52W
Morlanwelz, Belgium 17 50 28N 4 15 E
Mormanno, Italy 29 39 53N 15 59 E
Mormant, France 19 48 37N 2 52 E
Mornington, Vic., Australia 74 38 15 S 145 5 E
Mornington, W. Austral., Australia 78 17 31 S 126 6 E
Mornington, I., Chile 142 49 50 S 75 30W
Mornington I., Australia 72 16 30 S 139 30 E
Mórnos →, Greece 35 38 30N 22 0 E
Moro, Sudan 89 10 50N 30 9 E
Moro G., Phil. 57 6 30N 123 0 E
Morobe, Papua N. G. 69 7 49 S 147 38 E
Morocco, U.S.A. 119 40 57N 87 27W
Morocco ■, N. Afr. 84 32 0N 5 50W
Morococha, Peru 136 11 40 S 76 5W
Moroga, Solomon Is. 68 10 30 S 161 40 E
Morogoro, Tanzania 92 6 50 S 37 40 E
Morogoro □, Tanzania 92 8 0 S 37 0 E
Moroleón, Mexico 126 20 8N 101 32W
Morombe, Madag. 97 21 45 S 43 22 E
Moron, Argentina 140 34 39 S 58 37W
Morón, Cuba 128 22 8N 78 39W
Mörön →, Mongolia 62 47 14N 110 37 E
Morón de Almazán, Spain 24 41 29N 2 27W
Morón de la Frontera, Spain 23 37 6N 5 28W
Morona →, Peru 134 4 40 S 77 10W
Morona-Santiago □, Ecuador 134 2 30 S 78 0W
Morondava, Madag. 97 20 17 S 44 17 E
Morondo, Ivory C. 90 8 57N 6 47W
Morongo Valley, U.S.A. 125 34 3N 116 37W
Moronou, Ivory C. 90 6 16N 4 59W
Morotai, Indonesia 57 2 10N 128 30 E
Moroto, Uganda 92 2 28N 34 42 E
Moroto Summit, Kenya 92 2 30N 34 43 E
Morozovsk, U.S.S.R. 39 48 25N 41 50 E
Morpeth, Australia 76 32 44 S 151 39 E
Morpeth, U.K. 12 55 11N 1 41W
Morphou, Cyprus 46 35 12N 32 59 E
Morrelganj, Bangla. 52 22 28N 89 51 E
Morrilton, U.S.A. 121 35 10N 92 45W
Morrinhos, Ceará, Brazil 138 3 14 S 40 7W
Morrinhos, Minas Gerais, Brazil 139 17 45 S 49 10W
Morrinsville, N.Z. 80 37 40 S 175 32 E
Morris, Canada 111 49 25N 97 22W
Morris, Ill., U.S.A. 119 41 20N 88 20W
Morris, Minn., U.S.A. 120 45 33N 95 56W
Morris, Mt., Australia 79 26 9 S 131 4 E
Morrisburg, Canada 109 44 55N 75 7W

Nanutarra

Nanutarra, *Australia* .. **78** 22 32 S 115 30 E
Nanxiong, *China* ..... **59** 25 6N 114 15 E
Nanyang, *China* ...... **60** 33 11N 112 30 E
Nanyi Hu, *China* ..... **59** 31 5N 119 0 E
Nan'yō, *Japan* .... **64** 34 3N 131 49 E
Nanyuan, *China* ...... **60** 39 44N 116 22 E
Nanyuki, *Kenya* ...... **92** 0 2N 37 4 E
Nanzhang, *China* ..... **59** 31 45N 111 50 E
Náo, C. de la, *Spain* .. **25** 38 44N 0 14 E
Naococane L., *Canada* **105** 52 50N 70 45W
Naoetsu, *Japan* ...... **63** 37 12N 138 10 E
Naogaon, *Bangla.* .... **52** 24 52N 88 52 E
Náousa, *Greece* ...... **35** 40 42N 22 9 E
Naozhou Dao, *China* . **59** 20 55N 110 20 E
Napa, *U.S.A.* **124** 38 18N 122 17W
Napa →, *U.S.A.* **124** 38 10N 122 19W
Napanee, *Canada* **109** 44 15N 77 0W
Napanoch, *U.S.A.* **117** 41 44N 74 22W
Nape, *Laos* .... **54** 18 18N 105 6 E
Nape Pass = Keo Neua, Deo, *Vietnam* **54** 18 23N 105 10 E
Naperville, *U.S.A.* ... **119** 41 46N 88 9W
Napier, *N.Z.* .... **80** 39 30 S 176 56 E
Napier Broome B., *Australia* .... **78** 14 2 S 126 37 E
Napier Downs, *Australia* .... **78** 17 11 S 124 36 E
Napier Pen., *Australia* **72** 12 4 S 135 43 E
Napierville, *Canada* .. **107** 45 11N 73 25W
Napierville □, *Canada* **107** 45 10N 73 30W
Naples = Nápoli, *Italy* **29** 40 50N 14 17 E
Naples, *U.S.A.* **115** 26 10N 81 45W
Napo, *China* .... **58** 23 22N 105 50 E
Napo □, *Ecuador* .... **134** 0 30 S 77 0W
Napo →, *Peru* .... **134** 3 20 S 72 40W
Napoleon, *N. Dak., U.S.A.* **120** 46 32N 99 49W
Napoleon, *Ohio, U.S.A.* **119** 41 24N 84 7W
Nápoli, *Italy* .... **29** 40 50N 14 17 E
Nápoli, G. di, *Italy* ... **29** 40 40N 14 10 E
Napopo, *Zaïre* .... **92** 4 15N 28 0 E
Nappa Merrie, *Australia* .... **73** 27 36 S 141 7 E
Nappanee, *U.S.A.* **119** 41 27N 86 0W
Naqâda, *Egypt* .... **88** 25 53N 32 42 E
Nara, *Japan* .... **65** 34 40N 135 49 E
Nara, *Mali* **90** 15 10N 7 20W
Nara □, *Japan* .... **65** 34 30N 136 0 E
Nara, Canal, *Pakistan* . **48** 24 30N 69 20 E
Nara Visa, *U.S.A.* **121** 35 39N 103 10W
Naracoorte, *Australia* . **73** 36 58 S 140 45 E
Naradhan, *Australia* .. **75** 33 34 S 146 17 E
Narasapur, *India* ..... **51** 16 26N 81 40 E
Narasaropet, *India* ... **51** 16 14N 80 4 E
Narathiwat, *Thailand* . **55** 6 30N 101 48 E
Narayanganj, *Bangla.* . **52** 23 40N 90 33 E
Narayanpet, *India* .... **50** 16 45N 77 30 E
Narbonne, *France* .... **20** 43 11N 3 0 E
Narcea →, *Spain* **22** 43 33N 6 44W
Nardò, *Italy* .... **29** 40 10N 18 0 E
Narembeen, *Australia* . **79** 32 7 S 118 24 E
Nares Stræde, *Arctic* . **100** 80 0N 70 0W
Naretha, *Australia* .... **79** 31 0 S 124 45 E
Narew →, *Poland* .... **32** 52 26N 20 41 E
Nari →, *Pakistan* .... **48** 29 40N 68 0 E
Narindra, Helodranon' i, *Madag.* .... **97** 14 55 S 47 30 E
Narino □, *Colombia* .. **134** 1 30N 78 0W
Narita, *Japan* .... **65** 35 47N 140 19 E
Narmada →, *India* ... **48** 21 38N 72 36 E
Narnaul, *India* .... **48** 28 5N 76 11 E
Narni, *Italy* .... **27** 42 30N 12 30 E
Naro, *Ghana* **90** 10 22N 2 27W
Naro, *Italy* .... **28** 37 18N 13 48 E
Naro Fominsk, *U.S.S.R.* .... **37** 55 23N 36 43 E
Narodnaya, *U.S.S.R.* . **6** 65 5N 60 0 E
Narok, *Kenya* .... **92** 1 55 S 35 52 E
Narok □, *Kenya* ..... **92** 1 20 S 36 30 E
Narón, *Spain* **22** 43 32N 8 9W
Narooma, *Australia* ... **75** 36 14 S 150 4 E
Narowal, *Pakistan* .... **48** 32 6N 74 52 E
Narrabri, *Australia* ... **77** 30 19 S 149 46 E
Narrabri West, *Australia* .... **77** 30 21 S 149 46 E
Narran →, *Australia* . **73** 28 37 S 148 12 E
Narrandera, *Australia* . **75** 34 42 S 146 31 E
Narraway →, *Canada* **110** 55 44N 119 55W
Narrogin, *Australia* ... **79** 32 58 S 117 14 E
Narromine, *Australia* . **76** 32 12 S 148 12 E
Narsampet, *India* ..... **50** 17 57N 79 58 E
Narsimhapur, *India* ... **49** 22 54N 79 14 E
Nartkala, *U.S.S.R.* ... **39** 43 33N 43 51 E
Naruto, *Kantō, Japan* . **64** 34 11N 134 37 E
Narutō, *Shikoku, Japan* **65** 35 36N 140 25 E
Naruto-Kaikyō, *Japan* **64** 34 14N 134 39 E
Narva, *U.S.S.R.* ...... **36** 59 23N 28 12 E
Narva →, *U.S.S.R.* .. **36** 59 27N 28 2 E
Narvik, *Norway* ...... **8** 68 28N 17 26 E
Narvskoye Vdkhr., *U.S.S.R.* .... **36** 59 18N 28 14 E
Narwana, *India* ...... **48** 29 39N 76 6 E
Naryan-Mar, *U.S.S.R.* **40** 68 0N 53 0 E
Naryilco, *Australia* ... **73** 28 37 S 141 53 E
Narym, *U.S.S.R.* ..... **40** 59 0N 81 30 E
Narymskoye, *U.S.S.R.* **40** 49 10N 84 15 E
Naryn, *U.S.S.R.* ..... **40** 41 26N 75 58 E
Nasa, *Norway* .... **8** 66 29N 15 23 E
Nasarawa, *Nigeria* .... **91** 8 32N 7 41 E
Năsăud, *Romania* .... **34** 47 19N 24 29 E
Nasawa, *Vanuatu* .... **68** 15 0 S 168 0 E
Naseby, *N.Z.* .... **81** 45 1 S 170 10 E
Naselle, *U.S.A.* **124** 46 22N 123 49W
Naser, Buheirat en, *Egypt* .... **88** 23 0N 32 30 E
Nashua, *Iowa, U.S.A.* **118** 42 55N 92 34W
Nashua, *Mont., U.S.A.* **122** 48 10N 106 25W
Nashua, *N.H., U.S.A.* **117** 42 50N 71 25W
Nashville, *Ark., U.S.A.* **121** 33 56N 93 50W
Nashville, *Ga., U.S.A.* **115** 31 3N 83 15W
Nashville, *Ill., U.S.A.* . **118** 38 21N 89 23W
Nashville, *Ind., U.S.A.* **119** 39 12N 86 14W
Nashville, *Mich., U.S.A.* **119** 42 36N 85 5W
Nashville, *Tenn., U.S.A.* **115** 36 12N 86 46W
Našice, *Yugoslavia* ... **33** 45 32N 18 4 E
Nasielsk, *Poland* ..... **32** 52 35N 20 50 E
Nasik, *India* .... **50** 19 58N 73 50 E
Nasirabad, *India* ..... **48** 26 15N 74 45 E
Naskaupi →, *Canada* . **105** 53 47N 60 51W
Naso, *Italy* .... **29** 38 8N 14 46 E
Nass →, *Canada* **110** 55 0N 129 40W
Nassau, *Bahamas* **128** 25 0N 77 20W
Nassau, *U.S.A.* **117** 42 30N 73 34W
Nassau, B., *Chile* .... **142** 55 20 S 68 0W
Nasser, L. = Naser, Buheirat en, *Egypt* . **88** 23 0N 32 30 E
Nasser City = Kôm Ombo, *Egypt* ...... **88** 24 25N 32 52 E
Nassian, *Ivory C.* **90** 8 28N 3 28W
Nässjö, *Sweden* ...... **11** 57 39N 14 42 E
Näsum, *Sweden* ...... **11** 56 10N 14 29 E
Näsviken, *Sweden* .... **10** 61 46N 16 52 E
Nata, *Botswana* ...... **96** 20 12 S 26 12 E
Natagaima, *Colombia* . **134** 3 37N 75 6W
Natal, *Brazil* .... **138** 5 47 S 35 13W
Natal, *Canada* **110** 49 43N 114 51W
Natal, *Indonesia* ...... **56** 0 35N 99 7 E
Natal □, *S. Africa* .... **97** 28 30 S 30 30 E
Natalinci, *Yugoslavia* . **33** 44 15N 20 49 E
Naṭanz, *Iran* .... **47** 33 30N 51 55 E
Natashquan, *Canada* .. **105** 50 14N 61 46W
Natashquan →, *Canada* **105** 50 7N 61 50W
Natchez, *U.S.A.* **121** 31 35N 91 25W
Natchitoches, *U.S.A.* . **121** 31 47N 93 4W
Natewa B., *Fiji* ...... **68** 16 35 S 179 40 E
Nathalia, *Australia* ... **74** 36 1 S 145 13 E
Nathdwara, *India* ..... **48** 24 55N 73 50 E
Natimuk, *Australia* ... **74** 36 42 S 142 0 E
Nation →, *Canada* ... **110** 55 30N 123 32W
National City, *U.S.A.* . **125** 32 39N 117 7W
Natitingou, *Benin* .... **91** 10 20N 1 26 E
Natividad, I., *Mexico* . **126** 27 50N 115 10W
Natogyi, *Burma* ...... **52** 21 25N 95 39 E
Natoma, *U.S.A.* **120** 39 14N 99 0W
Natron, L., *Tanzania* . **92** 2 20 S 36 0 E
Natrona Heights, *U.S.A.* **116** 40 39N 79 43W
Natrûn, W. el →, *Egypt* .... **88** 30 25N 30 13 E
Nattai River, *Australia* **76** 34 3 S 150 26 E
Natuna Besar, Kepulauan, *Indonesia* **55** 4 0N 108 15 E
Natuna Selatan, Kepulauan, *Indonesia* **55** 2 45N 109 0 E
Natural Bridge, *U.S.A.* **117** 44 5N 75 30W
Naturaliste C., *Australia* .... **72** 40 50 S 148 15 E
Natya, *Australia* ..... **74** 34 57 S 143 13 E
Nau Qala, *Afghan.* ... **48** 34 5N 68 5 E
Naubinway, *U.S.A.* ... **104** 46 7N 85 27W
Naucelle, *France* ..... **20** 44 13N 2 20 E
Nauders, *Austria* ..... **31** 46 54N 10 30 E
Nauen, *E. Germany* .. **30** 52 36N 12 52 E
Naugatuck, *U.S.A.* ... **117** 41 28N 73 4W
Naughton, *Canada* ... **108** 46 24N 81 12W
Naujoji Vilnia, *U.S.S.R.* .... **36** 54 48N 25 27 E
Naumburg, *E. Germany* **30** 51 10N 11 48 E
Nauru ■, *Pac. Oc.* ... **66** 1 0 S 166 0 E
Nausori, *Fiji* .... **68** 18 2 S 178 32 E
Nauta, *Peru* .... **134** 4 31 S 73 35W
Nautla, *Mexico* **127** 20 20N 96 50W
Nauvoo, *U.S.A.* **118** 40 33N 91 23W
Nava, *Mexico* **126** 28 25N 100 46W
Nava del Rey, *Spain* .. **22** 41 22N 5 6W
Navacerrada, Puerto de, *Spain* **22** 40 47N 4 0W
Navadwip, *India* ..... **49** 23 34N 88 20 E
Navahermosa, *Spain* .. **23** 39 41N 4 28W
Navajo Res., *U.S.A.* .. **123** 36 55N 107 30W
Navalcarnero, *Spain* .. **22** 40 17N 4 5W
Navalmoral de la Mata, *Spain* **22** 39 52N 5 33W
Navalvillar de Pela, *Spain* **23** 39 9N 5 24W
Navan = An Uaimh, *Ireland* **15** 53 39N 6 40W
Navarino, I., *Chile* ... **142** 55 0 S 67 40W
Navarra □, *Spain* **24** 42 40N 1 40W
Navarre, *Australia* .... **74** 36 53 S 143 11 E
Navarre, *U.S.A.* **116** 40 43N 81 31W
Navarrenx, *France* **20** 43 20N 0 45W
Navarro, *U.S.A.* **124** 39 10N 123 32W
Navas del Marqués, Las, *Spain* **22** 40 36N 4 20W
Navasota, *U.S.A.* **121** 30 20N 96 5W
Navassa, *W. Indies* ... **129** 18 30N 75 0W
Nave, *Italy* .... **26** 45 35N 10 17 E
Naver →, *U.K.* **14** 58 34N 4 15W
Navia, *Spain* **22** 43 35N 6 42W
Navia →, *Spain* **22** 43 15N 6 50W
Navia de Suarna, *Spain* **22** 42 58N 6 59W
Navidad, *Chile* .... **140** 33 57 S 71 50W
Naviti, *Fiji* .... **68** 17 7 S 177 15 E
Navlya, *U.S.S.R.* ..... **36** 52 53N 34 30 E
Navoi, *U.S.S.R.* ...... **40** 40 9N 65 22 E
Navojoa, *Mexico* **126** 27 0N 109 30W
Navolato, *Mexico* **126** 24 47N 107 42W
Návpaktos, *Greece* ... **35** 38 23N 21 50 E
Návplion, *Greece* ..... **35** 37 33N 22 50 E
Navrongo, *Ghana* **91** 10 51N 1 3W
Navsari, *India* .... **50** 20 57N 72 59 E
Navua, *Fiji* .... **68** 18 6 S 178 10 E
Nawa Kot, *Pakistan* .. **48** 28 21N 71 24 E
Nawabganj, *Bangla.* .. **52** 24 35N 88 14 E
Nawabganj, *Ut. P., India* .... **49** 26 56N 81 14 E
Nawabganj, *Ut. P., India* .... **49** 28 32N 79 40 E
Nawabshah, *Pakistan* . **48** 26 15N 68 25 E
Nawada, *India* .... **49** 24 50N 85 33 E
Nawakot, *Nepal* ...... **49** 27 55N 85 10 E
Nawalgarh, *India* ..... **48** 27 50N 75 15 E
Nawanshahr, *India* ... **49** 32 33N 74 48 E
Nawapara, *India* ..... **50** 20 46N 82 33 E
Nawāsīf, Harrat, *Si. Arabia* .... **46** 21 20N 42 10 E
Nawi, *Sudan* .... **88** 18 32N 30 50 E
Nawng Hpa, *Burma* .. **52** 22 30N 98 30 E
Náxos, *Greece* .... **35** 37 8N 25 25 E
Nay, *France* **20** 43 10N 0 18W
Nāy Band, *Iran* ...... **47** 27 20N 52 40 E
Naya →, *Colombia* .. **134** 3 13N 77 22W
Nayakhan, *U.S.S.R.* .. **41** 61 56N 159 0 E
Nayarit □, *Mexico* **126** 22 0N 105 0W
Nayé, *Senegal* **90** 14 28N 12 12W
Nayong, *China* ...... **58** 26 50N 105 20 E
Nazaré, *Bahia, Brazil* . **139** 13 2 S 39 0W
Nazaré, *Goiás, Brazil* . **138** 6 23 S 47 40W
Nazaré, *Pará, Brazil* .. **137** 6 25 S 52 29W
Nazaré, *Portugal* **23** 39 36N 9 4W
Nazareth = Nazerat, *Israel* .... **44** 32 42N 35 17 E
Nazas, *Mexico* **126** 25 10N 104 6W
Nazas →, *Mexico* **126** 25 35N 103 25W
Naze, The, *U.K.* ..... **13** 51 53N 1 19 E
Nazerat, *Israel* .... **44** 32 42N 35 17 E
Nazir Hat, *Bangla.* ... **52** 22 35N 91 49 E
Nazko, *Canada* **110** 53 1N 123 37W
Nazko →, *Canada* ... **110** 53 7N 123 34W
Nazret, *Ethiopia* ..... **89** 8 32N 39 22 E
Nchanga, *Zambia* .... **93** 12 30 S 27 49 E
Ncheu, *Malawi* ...... **93** 14 50 S 34 47 E
Ndala, *Tanzania* ..... **92** 4 45 S 33 15 E
Ndalatando, *Angola* .. **95** 9 12 S 14 48 E
Ndali, *Benin* .... **91** 9 50N 2 46 E
Ndareda, *Tanzania* ... **92** 4 12 S 35 30 E
Ndélé, *C.A.R.* .... **61** 8 25N 20 36 E
Ndendé, *Gabon* ...... **94** 2 22 S 11 23 E
Ndjamena, *Chad* ..... **87** 12 10N 14 59 E
Ndjolé, *Gabon* .... **94** 0 10 S 10 45 E
Ndola, *Zambia* ...... **93** 13 0 S 28 34 E
Ndoto Mts., *Kenya* ... **92** 2 0N 37 0 E
Ndoua, C., *N. Cal.* ... **68** 22 24 S 166 56 E
Nduguti, *Tanzania* .... **92** 4 18 S 34 41 E
Nduindui, *Vanuatu* ... **68** 15 24 S 167 46 E
Nea →, *Norway* ..... **10** 63 15N 11 0 E
Néa Flippiás, *Greece* .. **35** 39 12N 20 53 E
Neagari, *Japan* ...... **65** 36 26N 136 25 E
Neagh, Lough, *U.K.* .. **15** 54 35N 6 25W
Neah Bay, *U.S.A.* **124** 48 25N 124 40W
Neale L., *Australia* ... **78** 24 15 S 130 0 E
Neápolis, *Kozan, Greece* .... **35** 40 20N 21 24 E
Neápolis, *Lakonia, Greece* .... **35** 36 27N 23 8 E
Near Is., *U.S.A.* ..... **102** 53 0N 172 0 E
Neath, *U.K.* **13** 51 39N 3 49W
Neba, I., *N. Cal.* ..... **68** 20 9 S 163 56 E
Nebbou, *Burkina Faso* **91** 11 9N 1 51W
Nebine Cr. →, *Australia* .... **73** 29 27 S 146 56 E
Nebit Dag, *U.S.S.R.* .. **40** 39 30N 54 22 E
Nebolchy, *U.S.S.R.* .. **36** 59 8N 33 18 E
Nebraska □, *U.S.A.* .. **120** 41 30N 100 0W
Nebraska City, *U.S.A.* **120** 40 40N 95 52W
Nébrodi, Monti, *Italy* . **28** 37 55N 14 50 E
Necedah, *U.S.A.* **120** 44 2N 90 7W
Nechako →, *Canada* . **110** 53 30N 122 44W
Neches →, *U.S.A.* ... **121** 29 55N 93 52W
Neckar →, *W. Germany* .... **31** 49 31N 8 26 E
Necochea, *Argentina* .. **140** 38 30 S 58 50W
Nedelišće, *Yugoslavia* . **27** 46 23N 16 22 E
Neder Rijn →, *Neths.* **16** 51 57N 6 2 E
Nederbrakel, *Belgium* . **17** 50 48N 3 46 E
Nederweert, *Neths.* ... **17** 51 17N 5 45 E
Nédha →, *Greece* .... **35** 37 25N 21 45 E
Nedroma, *Algeria* **85** 35 1N 1 45W
Neede, *Neths.* .... **16** 52 8N 6 37 E
Needles, *U.S.A.* **125** 34 50N 114 35W
Needles, Pt., *N.Z.* .... **80** 36 3 S 175 25 E
Needles, The, *U.K.* ... **13** 50 39N 1 35W
Ñeembucú □, *Paraguay* **140** 27 0 S 58 0W
Neemuch = Nimach, *India* .... **48** 24 30N 74 56 E
Neenah, *U.S.A.* **114** 44 10N 88 30W
Neepawa, *Canada* **111** 50 15N 99 30W
Neer, *Neths.* .... **17** 51 16N 5 59 E
Neerim, *Australia* .... **74** 37 59 S 145 57 E
Neerim South, *Australia* **74** 38 1 S 145 58 E
Neerpelt, *Belgium* .... **17** 51 13N 5 26 E
Neeworra, *Australia* .. **77** 29 2 S 149 3 E
Nefta, *Tunisia* .... **86** 33 53N 7 50 E
Neftah Sidi Boubekeur, *Algeria* .... **85** 35 1N 0 4 E
Neftegorsk, *U.S.S.R.* . **39** 44 25N 39 45 E
Negapatam = Nagappattinam, *India* **51** 10 46N 79 51 E
Negaunee, *U.S.A.* **104** 46 30N 87 36W
Negba, *Israel* .... **44** 31 40N 34 41 E
Negele, *Ethiopia* ..... **89** 5 20N 39 36 E
Negev Desert = Hanegev, *Israel* .... **44** 30 50N 35 0 E
Negombo, *Sri Lanka* . **51** 7 12N 79 50 E
Negotin, *Yugoslavia* .. **33** 44 16N 22 37 E
Negra, La, *Chile* ..... **140** 23 46 S 70 18W
Negra, Peña, *Spain* ... **22** 42 11N 6 30W
Negra, Pta., *Mauritania* **84** 22 54N 16 18W
Negra, Pta., *Peru* .... **136** 6 6 S 81 10W
Negra Pt., *Phil.* ...... **57** 18 40N 120 50 E
Negrais C., *Burma* ... **52** 16 0N 94 12 E
Negreira, *Spain* **22** 42 54N 8 45W
Négrine, *Algeria* ..... **85** 34 30N 7 30 E
Negro →, *Argentina* .. **142** 41 2 S 62 47W
Negro →, *Bolivia* .... **137** 14 11 S 63 7W
Negro →, *Brazil* ..... **135** 3 0 S 60 0W
Negro →, *Uruguay* ... **141** 33 24 S 58 22W
Negros, *Phil.* .... **57** 9 30N 122 40 E
Nehalem →, *U.S.A.* . **124** 45 40N 123 56W
Nehbandān, *Iran* ..... **47** 31 35N 60 5 E
Neheim-Hüsten, *W. Germany* .... **30** 51 27N 7 58 E
Nehoiaşu, *Romania* ... **34** 45 24N 26 20 E
Nei Monggol Zizhiqu □, *China* .. **60** 42 0N 112 0 E
Neiafu, *Tonga* .... **68** 18 39 S 173 59W
Neidpath, *Canada* **111** 50 12N 107 20W
Neihart, *U.S.A.* **122** 47 0N 110 44W
Neijiang, *China* ...... **58** 29 35N 104 55 E
Neilrex, *Australia* .... **77** 31 44 S 149 20 E
Neilton, *U.S.A.* **122** 47 24N 123 52W
Neiqiu, *China* .... **60** 37 15N 114 30 E
Neira de Jusá, *Spain* .. **22** 42 53N 7 14W
Neisse →, *Europe* ... **30** 52 4N 14 46 E
Neiva, *Colombia* **134** 2 56N 75 18W
Neixiang, *China* ..... **60** 33 10N 111 52 E
Nejanilini L., *Canada* . **111** 59 33N 97 48W
Nejo, *Ethiopia* .... **89** 9 30N 35 28 E
Nekemte, *Ethiopia* ... **89** 9 4N 36 30 E
Nêkheb, *Egypt* .... **88** 25 10N 32 48 E
Neksø, *Denmark* ..... **11** 55 4N 15 8 E
Nelas, *Portugal* **22** 40 32N 7 52W
Nelia, *Australia* ...... **72** 20 39 S 142 12 E
Nelidovo, *U.S.S.R.* ... **36** 56 13N 32 49 E
Neligh, *U.S.A.* **120** 42 11N 98 2W
Nelkan, *U.S.S.R.* .... **41** 57 40N 136 4 E
Nelligen, *Australia* ... **76** 35 39 S 150 8 E
Nellikuppam, *India* ... **51** 11 46N 79 43 E
Nellore, *India* .... **51** 14 27N 79 59 E
Nelma, *U.S.S.R.* ..... **41** 47 39N 139 0 E
Nelson, *Australia* .... **74** 38 3 S 141 2 E
Nelson, *Canada* **110** 49 30N 117 20W
Nelson, *N.Z.* .... **81** 41 18 S 173 16 E
Nelson, *U.K.* **12** 53 50N 2 14W
Nelson, *U.S.A.* **123** 35 35N 113 16W
Nelson □, *N.Z.* ...... **81** 42 11 S 172 15 E
Nelson →, *Canada* .. **111** 54 33N 98 2W
Nelson, C., *Australia* . **74** 38 26 S 141 32 E
Nelson, C., *Papua N. G.* .... **69** 9 0 S 149 20 E
Nelson, Estrecho, *Chile* **142** 51 30 S 75 0W
Nelson Bay, *Australia* . **76** 32 43 S 152 9 E
Nelson Forks, *Canada* **110** 59 30N 124 0W
Nelson House, *Canada* **111** 55 47N 98 51W
Nelson L., *Canada* ... **111** 55 48N 100 7W
Nelspoort, *S. Africa* .. **96** 32 7 S 23 0 E
Nelspruit, *S. Africa* ... **97** 25 29 S 30 59 E
Nelungaloo, *Australia* . **76** 33 7 S 148 0 E
Néma, *Mauritania* **90** 16 40N 7 15W
Neman →, *U.S.S.R.* . **36** 55 25N 21 10 E
Nemeiben L., *Canada* **111** 55 20N 105 20W
Nemingha, *Australia* .. **77** 31 6 S 151 0 E
Nemira, *Romania* .... **34** 46 17N 26 19 E
Némiscachingue, L., *Canada* **106** 47 25N 74 30W
Nemours, *France* .... **19** 48 16N 2 40 E
Nemunas = Neman →, *U.S.S.R.* .... **36** 55 25N 21 10 E
Nemuro, *Japan* ...... **63** 43 20N 145 35 E
Nemuro-Kaikyō, *Japan* **63** 43 30N 145 30 E
Nemuy, *U.S.S.R.* .... **41** 55 40N 136 9 E
Nen Jiang →, *China* . **61** 45 28N 124 30 E
Nenagh, *Ireland* **15** 52 52N 8 11W
Nenana, *U.S.A.* **102** 64 30N 149 20W
Nenasi, *Malaysia* ..... **55** 3 9N 103 23 E
Nendiarene, Pte., *N. Cal.* .... **68** 20 14 S 164 19 E
Nene →, *U.K.* ...... **12** 52 38N 0 13 E
Nenjiang, *China* ..... **62** 49 10N 125 10 E
Neno, *Malawi* .... **93** 15 25 S 34 40 E
Nenusa, Kepulauan, *Indonesia* .... **57** 4 45N 127 1 E
Neodesha, *U.S.A.* **121** 37 30N 95 37W
Neoga, *U.S.A.* **119** 39 19N 88 27W
Neópolis, *Brazil* ..... **138** 10 18 S 36 35W
Neosho, *U.S.A.* **121** 36 56N 94 28W
Neosho →, *U.S.A.* .. **121** 35 59N 95 10W
Nepal ■, *Asia* ...... **49** 28 0N 84 30 E
Nepalganj, *Nepal* .... **49** 28 5N 81 40 E
Nephi, *U.S.A.* **122** 39 43N 111 52W
Nephin, *Ireland* **15** 54 1N 9 21W
Neptune City, *U.S.A.* . **117** 40 13N 74 4W
Néra →, *Romania* ... **34** 44 48N 21 25 E
Nérac, *France* .... **20** 44 8N 0 21 E
Nerang, *Australia* .... **77** 27 58 S 153 20 E
Nerastro, Sarīr, *Libya* **86** 24 20N 20 37 E

Nganglong Kangri

Nganglong Kangri, China 49 33 0N 81 0 E
Nganjuk, Indonesia 57 7 32 S 111 55 E
Ngao, Thailand 54 18 46N 99 59 E
Ngaoundéré, Cameroon 94 7 15N 13 35 E
Ngapara, N.Z. 81 44 57 S 170 46 E
Ngara, Tanzania 92 2 29 S 30 40 E
Ngara □, Tanzania 92 2 29 S 30 40 E
Ngaruawahia, N.Z. 80 37 42 S 175 11 E
Ngatapa, N.Z. 80 38 32 S 177 45 E
Ngathainggyaung, Burma 52 17 24N 95 5 E
Ngauruhoe, Mt., N.Z. 80 39 13 S 175 45 E
Ngawi, Indonesia 57 7 24 S 111 26 E
Nggamea, Fiji 68 16 46 S 179 46W
Nggela, Solomon Is. 68 9 5 S 160 15 E
Nghia Lo, Vietnam 54 21 33N 104 28 E
Ngidinga, Zaïre 95 5 37 S 15 17 E
Ngo, Congo 94 2 29 S 15 45 E
N'Gola, Angola 95 14 10 S 14 30 E
Ngoma, Malawi 93 13 8 S 33 45 E
Ngomahura, Zambia 93 20 26 S 30 43 E
Ngomba, Tanzania 93 8 20 S 32 53 E
Ngop, Sudan 89 6 17N 30 9 E
Ngoring Hu, China 62 34 55N 97 5 E
Ngorkou, Mali 90 15 40N 3 41W
Ngorongoro, Tanzania 92 3 11 S 35 32 E
Ngouri, Chad 87 13 38N 15 22 E
Ngourti, Niger 87 15 19N 13 12 E
Ngozi, Burundi 92 2 54 S 29 50 E
Ngudu, Tanzania 92 2 58 S 33 25 E
Nguigmi, Niger 87 14 20N 13 20 E
Ngukurr, Australia 72 14 44 S 134 44 E
Ngunga, Tanzania 92 3 37 S 33 37 E
Nguru, Nigeria 91 12 56N 10 29 E
Nguru Mts., Tanzania 92 6 0 S 37 30 E
Nguyen Binh, Vietnam 54 22 39N 105 56 E
Nha Trang, Vietnam 55 12 16N 109 10 E
Nhacoongo, Mozam. 97 24 18 S 35 14 E
Nhambiquara, Brazil 137 12 50 S 59 49W
Nhamundá, Brazil 135 2 14 S 56 43W
Nhamundá →, Brazil 135 2 12 S 56 41W
Nhangutazi, L., Mozam. 97 24 0 S 34 30 E
Nhecolândia, Brazil 137 19 17 S 56 58W
Nhill, Australia 74 36 18 S 141 40 E
Nho Quan, Vietnam 54 20 18N 105 45 E
Nhulunbuy, Australia 72 12 10 S 137 20 E
Nhundo, Angola 95 14 25 S 21 23 E
Nia-nia, Zaïre 92 1 30N 27 40 E
Niafounké, Mali 90 16 0N 4 5W
Niagara, U.S.A. 114 45 45N 88 0W
Niagara Falls, Canada 108 43 7N 79 5W
Niagara Falls, U.S.A. 116 43 5N 79 0W
Niagara-on-the-Lake, Canada 108 43 15N 79 4W
Niah, Malaysia 56 3 58N 113 46 E
Niamey, Niger 91 13 27N 2 6 E
Nianforando, Guinea 90 9 37N 10 36W
Nianfors, Sweden 10 61 36N 16 46 E
Niangala, Australia 77 31 18 S 151 25 E
Niangara, Zaïre 92 3 42N 27 50 E
Niangua →, U.S.A. 118 38 0N 92 48W
Nias, Indonesia 56 1 0N 97 30 E
Niassa □, Mozam. 93 13 30 S 36 0 E
Nibbiano, Italy 26 44 54N 9 20 E
Nibe, Denmark 11 56 59N 9 38 E
Nicaragua ■, Cent. Amer. 128 11 40N 85 30W
Nicaragua, L. de, Nic. 128 12 0N 85 30W
Nicastro, Italy 29 39 0N 16 18 E
Nice, France 21 43 42N 7 14 E
Niceville, U.S.A. 115 30 30N 86 30W
Nichinan, Japan 64 31 38N 131 23 E
Nicholás, Canal, W. Indies 128 23 30N 80 5W
Nicholasville, U.S.A. 119 37 54N 84 31W
Nichols, U.S.A. 117 42 1N 76 22W
Nicholson, Australia 78 18 2 S 128 54 E
Nicholson, U.S.A. 117 41 37N 75 47W
Nicholson →, Australia 72 17 31 S 139 36 E
Nicholson Ra., Australia 79 27 15 S 116 45 E
Nickerie □, Surinam 135 4 0N 57 0W
Nickerie →, Surinam 135 5 58N 57 0W
Nicobar Is., Ind. Oc. 53 9 0N 93 0 E
Nicoclí, Colombia 134 8 26N 76 48W
Nicola, Canada 110 50 12N 120 40W
Nicolet, Canada 107 46 17N 72 35W
Nicolls Town, Bahamas 128 25 8N 78 0W
Nicosia, Cyprus 46 35 10N 33 25 E
Nicosia, Italy 29 37 45N 14 22 E
Nicótera, Italy 29 38 33N 15 57 E
Nicoya, Costa Rica 128 10 9N 85 27W
Nicoya, G. de, Costa Rica 128 10 0N 85 0W
Nicoya, Pen. de, Costa Rica 128 9 45N 85 40W
Nidd →, U.K. 12 54 1N 1 32W
Nidda, W. Germany 30 50 24N 9 2 E
Nidda →, W. Germany 31 50 6N 8 34 E
Nidzica, Poland 32 53 25N 20 28 E
Niebüll, W. Germany 30 54 47N 8 49 E
Nied →, W. Germany 19 49 23N 6 40 E
Niederaula, W. Germany 30 50 48N 9 37 E
Niederbronn-les-Bains, France 19 48 57N 7 39 E
Niedere Tauern, Austria 33 47 20N 14 0 E
Niedermarsberg, W. Germany 30 51 28N 8 52 E
Niedersachsen □, W. Germany 30 52 45N 9 0 E
Niefang, Eq. Guin. 94 1 50N 10 14 E
Niekerkshoop, S. Africa 96 29 19 S 22 51 E
Niel, Belgium 17 51 7N 4 20 E
Niellé, Ivory C. 90 10 5N 5 38W
Niem, C.A.R. 94 6 12N 15 14 E
Niemba, Zaïre 92 5 58 S 28 24 E
Nienburg, W. Germany 30 52 38N 9 15 E
Niers →, W. Germany 30 51 35N 6 13 E
Niesky, E. Germany 30 51 18N 14 48 E
Nieu Bethesda, S. Africa 96 31 51 S 24 34 E
Nieuw-Amsterdam, Neths. 16 52 43N 6 52 E
Nieuw Amsterdam, Surinam 135 5 53N 55 5W
Nieuw Beijerland, Neths. 16 51 49N 4 20 E
Nieuw-Dordrecht, Neths. 16 52 45N 6 59 E
Nieuw Loosdrecht, Neths. 16 52 12N 5 8 E
Nieuw Nickerie, Surinam 135 6 0N 56 59W
Nieuw-Schoonebeek, Neths. 16 52 39N 7 0 E
Nieuw-Vennep, Neths. 16 52 16N 4 38 E
Nieuw-Vossemeer, Neths. 17 51 34N 4 12 E
Nieuwe-Niedorp, Neths. 16 52 44N 4 54 E
Nieuwe-Pekela, Neths. 16 53 5N 6 58 E
Nieuwe-Schans, Neths. 16 53 11N 7 12 E
Nieuwendijk, Neths. 16 51 46N 4 55 E
Nieuwerkerken, Belgium 17 50 52N 5 12 E
Nieuwkoop, Neths. 16 52 9N 4 48 E
Nieuwleusen, Neths. 16 52 34N 6 17 E
Nieuwnamen, Neths. 17 51 18N 4 9 E
Nieuwolda, Neths. 16 53 15N 6 58 E
Nieuwoudtville, S. Africa 96 31 23 S 19 7 E
Nieuwpoort, Belgium 17 51 8N 2 45 E
Nieuwveen, Neths. 16 52 12N 4 46 E
Nieves, Spain 22 42 7N 8 26W
Nieves, Pico de las, Canary Is. 25 27 57N 15 35W
Nièvre □, France 19 47 10N 3 40 E
Nigata, Japan 64 34 13N 132 39 E
Niğde, Turkey 46 38 0N 34 40 E
Nigel, S. Africa 97 26 27 S 28 25 E
Niger □, Nigeria 91 10 0N 5 0 E
Niger ■, W. Afr. 91 17 30N 10 0 E
Niger →, W. Afr. 91 5 33N 6 33 E
Nigeria ■, W. Afr. 91 8 30N 8 0 E
Nightcaps, N.Z. 81 45 57 S 168 2 E
Nigríta, Greece 35 40 56N 23 29 E
Nihtaur, India 49 29 20N 78 23 E
Nii-Jima, Japan 65 34 20N 139 15 E
Niigata, Japan 63 37 58N 139 0 E
Niihama, Japan 64 33 55N 133 16 E
Niihau, U.S.A. 112 21 55N 160 10W
Niimi, Japan 64 34 59N 133 28 E
Níjar, Spain 25 36 53N 2 15W
Nijkerk, Neths. 16 52 13N 5 30 E
Nijlen, Belgium 17 51 10N 4 40 E
Nijmegen, Neths. 16 51 50N 5 52 E
Nijverdal, Neths. 16 52 22N 6 28 E
Nike, Nigeria 91 6 26N 7 29 E
Nikel, U.S.S.R. 8 69 24N 30 12 E
Nikiniki, Indonesia 57 9 49 S 124 30 E
Nikki, Benin 91 9 58N 3 12 E
Nikkō, Japan 65 36 45N 139 35 E
Nikolayev, U.S.S.R. 38 46 58N 32 0 E
Nikolayevsk, U.S.S.R. 37 50 0N 45 35 E
Nikolayevsk-na-Amur, U.S.S.R. 41 53 8N 140 44 E
Nikolsk, U.S.S.R. 37 59 30N 45 28 E
Nikolskoye, U.S.S.R. 41 55 12N 166 0 E
Nikopol, Bulgaria 34 43 43N 24 54 E
Nikopol, U.S.S.R. 38 47 35N 34 25 E
Niksar, Turkey 38 40 31N 37 2 E
Nīkshahr, Iran 47 26 15N 60 10 E
Nikšić, Yugoslavia 33 42 50N 18 57 E
Nîl, Nahr en →, Africa 88 30 10N 31 6 E
Nîl el Abyad →, Sudan 89 15 38N 32 31 E
Nîl el Azraq →, Sudan 89 15 38N 32 31 E
Niland, U.S.A. 125 33 16N 115 30W
Nile = Nîl, Nahr en →, Africa 88 30 10N 31 6 E
Nile □, Uganda 92 2 0N 31 30 E
Nile Delta, Egypt 88 31 40N 31 0 E
Niles, U.S.A. 116 41 8N 80 40W
Nilgiri Hills, India 51 11 30N 76 30 E
Nilo Peçanha, Brazil 139 13 37 S 39 6W
Nimach, India 48 24 30N 74 56 E
Nimbahera, India 48 24 37N 74 45 E
Nimbin, Australia 77 28 36 S 153 13 E
Nîmes, France 21 43 50N 4 23 E
Nimfaíon, Ákra-, Greece 35 40 5N 24 20 E
Nimmitabel, Australia 75 36 29 S 149 15 E
Nimneryskiy, U.S.S.R. 41 57 50N 125 10 E
Nīmrūz □, Afghan. 47 30 0N 62 0 E
Nimule, Sudan 89 3 32N 32 3 E
Nin, Yugoslavia 27 44 16N 15 12 E
Nīnawá, Iraq 46 36 25N 43 10 E
Ninda, Angola 95 14 47 S 21 24 E
Nindigully, Australia 73 28 21 S 148 50 E
Ninemile, U.S.A. 110 56 0N 130 7W
Ninety Mile Beach, The, Australia 75 38 15 S 147 24 E
Nineveh = Nīnawá, Iraq 46 36 25N 43 10 E
Ning Xian, China 60 35 30N 107 58 E
Ningaloo, Australia 78 22 41 S 113 41 E
Ning'an, China 61 44 22N 129 20 E
Ningbo, China 59 29 51N 121 28 E
Ningcheng, China 61 41 32N 119 53 E
Ningde, China 59 26 38N 119 23 E
Ningdu, China 59 26 25N 115 59 E
Ninggang, China 59 26 42N 113 55 E
Ningguo, China 59 30 35N 119 0 E
Ninghai, China 59 29 15N 121 27 E
Ninghua, China 59 26 14N 116 45 E
Ningjin, China 60 37 35N 114 57 E
Ningjing Shan, China 58 30 0N 98 20 E
Ninglang, China 58 27 20N 100 55 E
Ningling, China 60 34 25N 115 22 E
Ningming, China 58 22 8N 107 4 E
Ningnan, China 58 27 5N 102 36 E
Ningpo = Ningbo, China 59 29 51N 121 28 E
Ningqiang, China 60 32 47N 106 15 E
Ningshan, China 60 33 21N 108 21 E
Ningsia Hui A.R. = Ningxia Huizu Zizhiqu □, China 60 38 0N 106 0 E
Ningwu, China 60 39 0N 112 18 E
Ningxia Huizu Zizhiqu □, China 60 38 0N 106 0 E
Ningxiang, China 59 28 15N 112 30 E
Ningyang, China 60 35 47N 116 45 E
Ningyuan, China 59 25 37N 111 57 E
Ninh Binh, Vietnam 54 20 15N 105 55 E
Ninh Giang, Vietnam 54 20 44N 106 24 E
Ninh Hoa, Vietnam 54 12 30N 109 7 E
Ninh Ma, Vietnam 54 12 48N 109 21 E
Ninove, Belgium 17 50 51N 4 2 E
Nioaque, Brazil 141 21 5 S 55 50W
Niobrara, U.S.A. 120 42 48N 97 59W
Niobrara →, U.S.A. 120 42 45N 98 0W
Nioki, Zaïre 94 2 47 S 17 40 E
Niono, Mali 90 14 15N 6 0W
Nioro du Rip, Senegal 90 13 40N 15 50W
Nioro du Sahel, Mali 90 15 15N 9 30W
Niort, France 20 46 19N 0 29W
Nipa, Papua N. G. 69 6 9 S 143 29 E
Nipani, India 51 16 20N 74 25 E
Nipawin, Canada 111 53 20N 104 0W
Nipawin Prov. Park, Canada 111 54 0N 104 37W
Nipigon, Canada 104 49 0N 88 17W
Nipigon, L., Canada 104 49 50N 88 30W
Nipin →, Canada 111 55 46N 108 35W
Nipishish L., Canada 105 54 12N 60 45W
Nipissing L., Canada 108 46 20N 80 0W
Nipomo, U.S.A. 125 35 4N 120 29W
Nipton, U.S.A. 125 35 28N 115 16W
Niquelândia, Brazil 139 14 33 S 48 23W
Nira →, India 50 17 58N 75 8 E
Nirasaki, Japan 65 35 42N 138 27 E
Nirmal, India 50 19 3N 78 20 E
Nirmali, India 49 26 20N 86 35 E
Niš, Yugoslavia 33 43 19N 21 58 E
Nisa, Portugal 23 39 30N 7 41W
Nişāb, S. Yemen 45 14 25N 46 29 E
Nišava →, Yugoslavia 33 43 20N 21 46 E
Niscemi, Italy 29 37 8N 14 21 E
Nishi-Sonogi-Hantō, Japan 64 32 55N 129 45 E
Nishinomiya, Japan 65 34 45N 135 20 E
Nishio, Japan 65 34 52N 137 3 E
Nishiwaki, Japan 64 34 59N 134 58 E
Nísíros, Greece 35 36 35N 27 12 E
Niskibi →, Canada 104 56 29N 88 9W
Nispen, Neths. 17 51 29N 4 28 E
Nisqually →, U.S.A. 124 47 6N 122 42W
Nissafors, Sweden 11 57 25N 13 37 E
Nissan →, Sweden 11 56 40N 12 51 E
Nissedal, Norway 10 59 10N 8 30 E
Nisser, Norway 10 59 7N 8 28 E
Nissum Fjord, Denmark 11 56 20N 8 11 E
Nistelrode, Neths. 17 51 42N 5 34 E
Nisutlin →, Canada 110 60 14N 132 34W
Niţā', Si. Arabia 46 27 15N 48 35 E
Nitchequon, Canada 105 53 10N 70 58W
Niterói, Brazil 139 22 52 S 43 0W
Nith →, Canada 108 43 12N 80 23W
Nith →, U.K. 14 55 20N 3 5W
Nitra, Czech. 33 48 19N 18 4 E
Nittedal, Norway 10 60 1N 10 57 E
Nittendau, W. Germany 31 49 12N 12 16 E
Niue I., Cook Is. 67 19 2 S 169 54W
Niulan Jiang →, China 58 27 30N 103 5 E
Niut, Indonesia 56 0 55N 110 6 E
Niutou Shan, China 59 29 5N 121 59 E
Niuzhuang, China 61 40 58N 122 28 E
Nivelles, Belgium 17 50 35N 4 20 E
Nivernais, France 19 47 0N 3 20 E
Nixon, U.S.A. 121 29 17N 97 45W
Nizam Sagar, India 50 18 10N 77 58 E
Nizamabad, India 50 18 45N 78 7 E
Nizamghat, India 52 28 20N 95 45 E
Nizhne Kolymsk, U.S.S.R. 41 68 34N 160 55 E
Nizhneangarsk, U.S.S.R. 41 55 47N 109 30 E
Nizhnegorskiy, U.S.S.R. 38 45 27N 34 38 E
Nizhneudinsk, U.S.S.R. 41 54 54N 99 3 E
Nizhnevartovsk, U.S.S.R. 40 60 56N 76 38 E
Nizhneyansk, U.S.S.R. 41 71 26N 136 4 E
Nizhniy Lomov, U.S.S.R. 37 53 34N 43 38 E
Nizhniy Novgorod = Gorkiy, U.S.S.R. 37 56 20N 44 0 E
Nizhniy Tagil, U.S.S.R. 40 57 55N 59 57 E
Nizhnyaya Tunguska →, U.S.S.R. 41 64 20N 93 0 E
Nizip, Turkey 46 37 5N 37 50 E
Nizké Tatry, Czech. 32 48 55N 20 0 E
Nizza Monferrato, Italy 26 44 46N 8 22 E
Njakwa, Malawi 93 11 1 S 33 56 E
Njanji, Zambia 93 14 25 S 31 46 E
Njinjo, Tanzania 93 8 48 S 38 54 E
Njombe, Tanzania 93 9 20 S 34 50 E
Njombe □, Tanzania 93 9 20 S 34 49 E
Njombe →, Tanzania 92 6 56 S 35 6 E
Nkambe, Cameroon 91 6 35N 10 40 E
Nkana, Zambia 93 12 50 S 28 8 E
Nkawkaw, Ghana 91 6 36N 0 49W
Nkayi, Zambia 93 19 41 S 29 20 E
Nkhota Kota, Malawi 93 12 56 S 34 15 E
Nkolabona, Gabon 94 1 14N 11 43 E
Nkone, Zaïre 94 1 2 S 22 20 E
Nkongsamba, Cameroon 91 4 55N 9 55 E
Nkunga, Zaïre 95 4 41 S 18 34 E
Nkurenkuru, Namibia 96 17 42 S 18 32 E
Nkwanta, Ghana 90 6 10N 2 10W
Noakhali = Maijdi, Bangla. 52 22 48N 91 10 E
Noatak, U.S.A. 102 67 32N 162 59W
Nobel, Canada 108 45 25N 80 6W
Nobeoka, Japan 64 32 36N 131 41 E
Nōbi-Heiya, Japan 65 35 15N 136 45 E
Noble, U.S.A. 119 38 42N 88 14W
Noblejas, Spain 24 39 58N 3 26W
Noblesville, U.S.A. 119 40 1N 85 59W
Noce →, Italy 26 46 9N 11 4 E
Nocera Inferiore, Italy 29 40 45N 14 37 E
Nocera Terinese, Italy 29 39 2N 16 9 E
Nocera Umbra, Italy 27 43 8N 12 47 E
Noci, Italy 29 40 47N 17 7 E
Nockatunga, Australia 73 27 42 S 142 42 E
Nocona, U.S.A. 121 33 48N 97 45W
Noda, Japan 65 35 56N 139 52 E
Noel, U.S.A. 121 36 36N 94 29W
Noelville, Canada 108 46 8N 80 26W
Nogal Valley, Somali Rep. 98 8 35N 48 35 E
Nogales, Mexico 126 31 20N 110 56W
Nogales, U.S.A. 123 31 33N 110 56W
Nōgata, Japan 64 33 48N 130 44 E
Nogent-en-Bassigny, France 19 48 1N 5 20 E
Nogent-le-Rotrou, France 18 48 20N 0 50 E
Nogent-sur-Seine, France 19 48 30N 3 30 E
Noggerup, Australia 79 33 32 S 116 5 E
Noginsk, Moskva, U.S.S.R. 37 55 50N 38 25 E
Noginsk, Sib., U.S.S.R. 41 64 30N 90 50 E
Nogoa →, Australia 72 23 40 S 147 55 E
Nogoyá, Argentina 140 32 24 S 59 48W
Nogueira de Ramuin, Spain 22 42 21N 7 43W
Noguera Pallaresa →, Spain 24 42 15N 1 0 E
Noguera Ribagorzana →, Spain 24 41 40N 0 43 E
Nohar, India 48 29 11N 74 49 E
Noire →, Canada 106 45 54N 76 57W
Noire, Mt., France 18 48 11N 3 40W
Noirétable, France 20 45 48N 3 46 E
Noirmoutier, I. de, France 18 46 58N 2 10W
Noirmoutier-en-l'Ile, France 18 47 0N 2 14W
Nojane, Botswana 96 23 15 S 20 14 E
Nojima-Zaki, Japan 65 34 54N 139 53 E
Nok Kundi, Pakistan 47 28 50N 62 45 E
Nokaneng, Botswana 96 19 40 S 22 17 E
Nokhtuysk, U.S.S.R. 41 60 0N 117 45 E
Nokomis, Canada 111 51 35N 105 0W
Nokomis, U.S.A. 118 39 18N 89 18W
Nokomis L., Canada 111 57 0N 103 0W
Nokou, Chad 87 14 35N 14 47 E
Nol, Sweden 11 57 56N 12 5 E
Nola, C.A.R. 94 3 35N 16 4 E
Nola, Italy 29 40 54N 14 29 E
Nolay, France 19 46 58N 4 35 E
Noli, C. di, Italy 26 44 12N 8 26 E
Nolinsk, U.S.S.R. 37 57 28N 49 57 E
Noma Omuramba →, Namibia 96 18 52 S 20 53 E
Noma-Saki, Japan 64 31 25N 130 7 E
Nomad, Papua N. G. 69 6 19 S 142 13 E
Noman L., Canada 111 62 15N 108 55W
Nombre de Dios, Panama 128 9 34N 79 28W
Nome, U.S.A. 102 64 30N 165 24W
Nominingue, Canada 106 46 24N 75 2W
Nominingue, L., Canada 106 46 26N 74 59W
Nomo-Zaki, Japan 64 32 35N 129 44 E
Nomuka, Tonga 68 20 17 S 174 48W
Nomuka Group, Tonga 68 20 20 S 174 48W
Nonacho L., Canada 111 61 42N 109 40W
Nonancourt, France 18 48 47N 1 11 E
Nonant-le-Pin, France 18 48 42N 0 12 E
Nonda, Australia 72 20 40 S 142 28 E

Nová Baňa

Nong Chang, *Thailand* **54** 15 23N 99 51 E
Nong Het, *Laos* **54** 19 29N 103 59 E
Nong Khai, *Thailand* **54** 17 50N 102 46 E
Nong'an, *China* **61** 44 25N 125 5 E
Nongoma, *S. Africa* **97** 27 58 S 31 35 E
Nonoava, *Mexico* **126** 27 28N 106 44W
Nonthaburi, *Thailand* **54** 13 51N 100 34 E
Nontron, *France* **20** 45 31N 0 40 E
Nonza, *France* **21** 42 47N 9 21 E
Noojee, *Australia* **74** 37 57 S 146 1 E
Noonamah, *Australia* **78** 12 40 S 131 4 E
Noonan, *U.S.A.* **120** 48 51N 102 59W
Noondoo, *Australia* **73** 28 35 S 148 30 E
Noonkanbah, *Australia* **78** 18 30 S 124 50 E
Noorat, *Australia* **74** 38 12 S 142 55 E
Noord-Bergum, *Neths.* **16** 53 14N 6 1 E
Noord Brabant □, *Neths.* **17** 51 40N 5 0 E
Noord Holland □, *Neths.* **16** 52 30N 4 45 E
Noordbeveland, *Neths.* **17** 51 35N 3 50 E
Noordeloos, *Neths.* **16** 51 55N 4 56 E
Noordhollandsch Kanaal, *Neths.* **16** 52 55N 4 48 E
Noordhorn, *Neths.* **16** 53 16N 6 24 E
Noordoostpolder, *Neths.* **16** 52 45N 5 45 E
Noordwijk aan Zee, *Neths.* **16** 52 14N 4 26 E
Noordwijk-Binnen, *Neths.* **16** 52 14N 4 27 E
Noordwijkerhout, *Neths.* **16** 52 16N 4 30 E
Noordzee Kanaal, *Neths.* **16** 52 28N 4 35 E
Noorinbee, *Australia* **75** 37 32 S 149 10 E
Noorwolde, *Neths.* **16** 52 54N 6 8 E
Nootka, *Canada* **110** 49 38N 126 38W
Nootka I., *Canada* **110** 49 32N 126 42W
Nóqui, *Angola* **95** 5 55 S 13 30 E
Nora, *Ethiopia* **89** 16 6N 40 4 E
Nora, *Sweden* **10** 59 32N 15 2 E
Nora Springs, *U.S.A.* **118** 43 9N 93 0W
Noradjuha, *Australia* **74** 36 50 S 141 58 E
Norah Hd., *Australia* **76** 33 18 S 151 32 E
Noranda, *Canada* **106** 48 20N 79 0W
Norberg, *Sweden* **10** 60 4N 15 56 E
Norborne, *U.S.A.* **118** 39 18N 93 40W
Nórcia, *Italy* **27** 42 50N 13 5 E
Norco, *U.S.A.* **125** 33 56N 117 33W
Nord □, *France* **19** 50 15N 3 30 E
Nord-Ostsee Kanal, *W. Germany* **30** 54 15N 9 40 E
Nord-Süd Kanal, *W. Germany* **30** 53 0N 10 32 E
Nord-Trøndelag fylke □, *Norway* **8** 64 20N 12 0 E
Nordagutu, *Norway* **10** 59 25N 9 20 E
Nordaustlandet, *Svalbard* **144** 79 14N 23 0 E
Nordborg, *Denmark* **11** 55 5N 9 50 E
Nordby, *Århus, Denmark* **11** 55 58N 10 32 E
Nordby, *Ribe, Denmark* **11** 55 27N 8 24 E
Norddeich, *W. Germany* **30** 53 37N 7 10 E
Nordegg, *Canada* **110** 52 29N 116 5W
Norden, *W. Germany* **30** 53 35N 7 12 E
Nordenham, *W. Germany* **30** 53 29N 8 28 E
Norderhov, *Norway* **10** 60 7N 10 17 E
Norderney, *W. Germany* **30** 53 42N 7 15 E
Nordfriesische Inseln, *W. Germany* **30** 54 40N 8 20 E
Nordhausen, *E. Germany* **30** 51 29N 10 47 E
Nordhorn, *W. Germany* **30** 52 27N 7 4 E
Nordjyllands Amtskommune □, *Denmark* **11** 57 0N 10 0 E
Nordkapp, *Norway* **8** 71 10N 25 44 E
Nordkapp, *Svalbard* **144** 80 31N 20 0 E
Nordkinn, *Norway* **6** 71 8N 27 40 E
Nordland fylke □, *Norway* **8** 65 40N 13 0 E
Nördlingen, *W. Germany* **31** 48 50N 10 30 E
Nordrhein-Westfalen □, *W. Germany* **30** 51 45N 7 30 E
Nordstrand, *W. Germany* **30** 54 27N 8 50 E
Nordvik, *U.S.S.R.* **41** 74 2N 111 32 E
Nore, *Norway* **10** 60 10N 9 0 E
Nore →, *Ireland* **15** 52 40N 7 20W
Norefjell, *Norway* **10** 60 16N 9 29 E
Norembega, *Canada* **106** 48 59N 80 43W
Noresund, *Norway* **10** 60 11N 9 37 E
Norfolk, *Nebr., U.S.A.* **120** 42 3N 97 25W
Norfolk, *Va., U.S.A.* **114** 36 40N 76 15W
Norfolk □, *U.K.* **12** 52 39N 1 0 E
Norfolk Broads, *U.K.* **12** 52 30N 1 15 E
Norfolk I., *Pac. Oc.* **66** 28 58 S 168 3 E
Norfork Res., *U.S.A.* **121** 36 13N 92 15W
Norg, *Neths.* **16** 53 4N 6 28 E
Norilsk, *U.S.S.R.* **41** 69 20N 88 6 E
Norley, *Australia* **73** 27 45 S 143 48 E
Norma, Mt., *Australia* **72** 20 55 S 140 42 E
Normal, *U.S.A.* **118** 40 30N 89 0W
Norman, *U.S.A.* **121** 35 12N 97 30W
Norman →, *Australia* **72** 17 28 S 140 49 E
Norman Wells, *Canada* **102** 65 17N 126 51W
Normanby, *N.Z.* **80** 39 32 S 174 18 E
Normanby →, *Australia* **72** 14 23 S 144 10 E
Normanby I., *Papua N. G.* **69** 10 55 S 151 5 E
Normandie, *France* **18** 48 45N 0 10 E
Normandie, Collines de, *France* **18** 48 45N 0 45W
Normandin, *Canada* **107** 48 49N 72 31W
Normandy = Normandie, *France* **18** 48 45N 0 10 E
Normanhurst, Mt., *Australia* **79** 25 4 S 122 30 E
Normanton, *Australia* **72** 17 40 S 141 10 E
Normétal, *Canada* **106** 49 0N 79 22W
Norquay, *Canada* **111** 51 53N 102 5W
Norquinco, *Argentina* **142** 41 51 S 70 55W
Norrahammar, *Sweden* **11** 57 43N 14 7 E
Norrbotten □, *Sweden* **8** 66 30N 22 30 E
Norrby, *Sweden* **8** 64 55N 18 15 E
Nørre Åby, *Denmark* **11** 55 27N 9 52 E
Nørre Nebel, *Denmark* **11** 55 47N 8 17 E
Nørresundby, *Denmark* **11** 57 5N 9 52 E
Norris, *U.S.A.* **122** 45 40N 111 40W
Norris City, *U.S.A.* **119** 37 59N 88 20W
Norristown, *U.S.A.* **117** 40 9N 75 21W
Norrköping, *Sweden* **11** 58 37N 16 11 E
Norrland □, *Sweden* **8** 66 50N 18 0 E
Norrtälje, *Sweden* **10** 59 46N 18 42 E
Norseman, *Australia* **79** 32 8 S 121 43 E
Norsholm, *Sweden* **11** 58 31N 15 59 E
Norsk, *U.S.S.R.* **41** 52 30N 130 0 E
Norsup, *Vanuatu* **68** 16 3 S 167 24 E
Norte, Pta., *Argentina* **142** 42 5 S 63 46W
Norte, Pta. del, *Canary Is.* **25** 27 51N 17 57W
Norte de Santander □, *Colombia* **134** 8 0N 73 0W
Nortelândia, *Brazil* **137** 14 25 S 56 48W
North Adams, *U.S.A.* **117** 42 42N 73 6W
North America **100** 40 0N 100 0W
North Atlantic Ocean, *Atl. Oc.* **130** 30 0N 50 0W
North Baltimore, *U.S.A.* **119** 41 11N 83 41W
North Battleford, *Canada* **111** 52 50N 108 17W
North Bay, *Canada* **108** 46 20N 79 30W
North Belcher Is., *Canada* **104** 56 50N 79 50W
North Bend, *Canada* **110** 49 50N 121 27W
North Bend, *Oreg., U.S.A.* **122** 43 28N 124 14W
North Bend, *Pa., U.S.A.* **116** 41 20N 77 42W
North Bend, *Wash., U.S.A.* **124** 47 30N 121 47W
North Berwick, *U.K.* **14** 56 4N 2 44W
North Berwick, *U.S.A.* **117** 43 18N 70 43W
North Buganda □, *Uganda* **92** 1 0N 32 0 E
North Canadian →, *U.S.A.* **121** 35 17N 95 31W
North C., *Canada* **105** 47 2N 60 20W
North C., *N.Z.* **80** 34 23 S 173 4 E
North C., *Papua N. G.* **69** 2 32 S 150 50 E
North Caribou L., *Canada* **104** 52 50N 90 40W
North Carolina □, *U.S.A.* **115** 35 30N 80 0W
North Channel, *Canada* **108** 46 0N 83 0W
North Channel, *U.K.* **14** 55 0N 5 30W
North Chicago, *U.S.A.* **119** 42 19N 87 50W
North College Hill, *U.S.A.* **119** 39 13N 84 33W
North Dakota □, *U.S.A.* **120** 47 30N 100 0W
North Dandalup, *Australia* **79** 32 30 S 115 57 E
North Down □, *U.K.* **15** 54 40N 5 45W
North Downs, *U.K.* **13** 51 17N 0 30 E
North East, *U.S.A.* **116** 42 17N 79 50W
North East Frontier Agency = Arunachal Pradesh □, *India* **52** 28 0N 95 0 E
North East Providence Chan., *W. Indies* **128** 26 0N 76 0W
North Eastern □, *Kenya* **92** 1 30N 40 0 E
North English, *U.S.A.* **118** 41 31N 92 5W
North Esk →, *U.K.* **14** 56 44N 2 25W
North European Plain, *Europe* **6** 55 0N 20 0 E
North Fabius →, *U.S.A.* **118** 39 54N 91 28W
North Foreland, *U.K.* **13** 51 22N 1 28 E
North Fork, *U.S.A.* **124** 37 14N 119 21W
North Fork, American →, *U.S.A.* **124** 38 45N 121 8W
North Fork, Feather →, *U.S.A.* **124** 39 17N 121 38W
North Fork, Salt →, *U.S.A.* **118** 39 26N 91 53W
North Frisian Is. = Nordfriesische Inseln, *W. Germany* **30** 54 40N 8 20 E
North Gower, *Canada* **109** 45 8N 75 43W
North Hatley, *Canada* **107** 45 17N 71 58W
North Henik L., *Canada* **111** 61 45N 97 40W
North Highlands, *U.S.A.* **124** 38 40N 121 25W
North Horr, *Kenya* **92** 3 20N 37 8 E
North I., *Kenya* **92** 4 5N 36 5 E
North I., *N.Z.* **81** 38 0 S 175 0 E
North Judson, *U.S.A.* **119** 41 13N 86 46W
North Kingsville, *U.S.A.* **116** 41 53N 80 42W
North Knife →, *Canada* **111** 58 53N 94 45W
North Koel →, *India* **49** 24 45N 83 50 E
North Korea ■, *Asia* **61** 40 0N 127 0 E
North Lakhimpur, *India* **52** 27 14N 94 7 E
North Las Vegas, *U.S.A.* **125** 36 15N 115 6W
North Liberty, *U.S.A.* **119** 41 32N 86 26W
North Loup →, *U.S.A.* **120** 41 17N 98 23W
North Manchester, *U.S.A.* **119** 41 0N 85 46W
North Minch, *U.K.* **14** 58 5N 5 55W
North Nahanni →, *Canada* **110** 62 15N 123 20W
North Olmsted, *U.S.A.* **116** 41 25N 81 56W
North Ossetian A.S.S.R. □, *U.S.S.R.* **39** 43 30N 44 30 E
North Palisade, *U.S.A.* **124** 37 6N 118 32W
North Platte, *U.S.A.* **120** 41 10N 100 50W
North Platte →, *U.S.A.* **120** 41 15N 100 45W
North Pt., *Canada* **105** 47 5N 64 0W
North Pt., *Vanuatu* **68** 14 56 S 168 6 E
North Pole, *Arctic* **144** 90 0N 0 0 E
North Portal, *Canada* **111** 49 0N 102 33W
North Powder, *U.S.A.* **122** 45 2N 117 59W
North Ronaldsay, *U.K.* **14** 59 20N 2 30W
North Saskatchewan →, *Canada* **111** 53 15N 105 5W
North Sea, *Europe* **6** 56 0N 4 0 E
North Solitary I., *Australia* **77** 29 56 S 153 24 E
North Sporades = Voríai Sporádhes, *Greece* **35** 39 15N 23 30 E
North Sydney, *Canada* **105** 46 12N 60 15W
North Thompson →, *Canada* **110** 50 40N 120 20W
North Tonawanda, *U.S.A.* **116** 43 5N 78 50W
North Troy, *U.S.A.* **117** 44 59N 72 24W
North Truchas Pk., *U.S.A.* **123** 36 0N 105 30W
North Twin I., *Canada* **104** 53 20N 80 0W
North Tyne →, *U.K.* **12** 54 59N 2 7W
North Uist, *U.K.* **14** 57 40N 7 15W
North Vancouver, *Canada* **110** 49 25N 123 3W
North Vernon, *U.S.A.* **119** 39 0N 85 35W
North Wabasca L., *Canada* **110** 56 0N 113 55W
North Walsham, *U.K.* **12** 52 49N 1 22 E
North Webster, *U.S.A.* **119** 41 25N 85 48W
North West C., *Australia* **78** 21 45 S 114 9 E
North West Christmas I. Ridge, *Pac. Oc.* **67** 6 30N 165 0W
North West Frontier □, *Pakistan* **48** 34 0N 71 0 E
North West Highlands, *U.K.* **14** 57 35N 5 2W
North West Providence Channel, *W. Indies* **128** 26 0N 78 0W
North West River, *Canada* **105** 53 30N 60 10W
North West Solitary I., *Australia* **77** 30 1 S 153 16 E
North West Territories □, *Canada* **102** 67 0N 110 0W
North Western □, *Zambia* **93** 13 30 S 25 30 E
North York Moors, *U.K.* **12** 54 25N 0 50W
North Yorkshire □, *U.K.* **12** 54 15N 1 25W
Northallerton, *U.K.* **12** 54 20N 1 26W
Northam, *S. Africa* **96** 24 56 S 27 18 E
Northampton, *Australia* **79** 28 27 S 114 33 E
Northampton, *U.K.* **13** 52 14N 0 54W
Northampton, *Mass., U.S.A.* **117** 42 22N 72 31W
Northampton, *Pa., U.S.A.* **117** 40 38N 75 24W
Northampton □, *U.K.* **13** 52 16N 0 55W
Northampton Downs, *Australia* **72** 24 35 S 145 48 E
Northbridge, *U.S.A.* **117** 42 12N 71 40W
Northcliffe, *Australia* **79** 34 39 S 116 7 E
Northeim, *W. Germany* **30** 51 42N 10 0 E
Northern □, *Malawi* **93** 11 0 S 34 0 E
Northern □, *Uganda* **92** 3 5N 32 30 E
Northern □, *Zambia* **93** 10 30 S 31 0 E
Northern Circars, *India* **50** 17 30N 82 30 E
Northern Indian L., *Canada* **111** 57 20N 97 20W
Northern Ireland □, *U.K.* **15** 54 45N 7 0W
Northern Light, L., *Canada* **104** 48 15N 90 39W
Northern Marianas, *Pac. Oc.* **66** 17 0N 145 0 E
Northern Province □, *S. Leone* **90** 9 15N 11 30W
Northern Territory □, *Australia* **78** 16 0 S 133 0 E
Northfield, *U.S.A.* **120** 44 30N 93 10W
Northland □, *N.Z.* **80** 35 30 S 173 30 E
Northome, *U.S.A.* **120** 47 53N 94 15W
Northport, *Ala., U.S.A.* **115** 33 15N 87 35W
Northport, *Mich., U.S.A.* **114** 45 8N 85 39W
Northport, *Wash., U.S.A.* **122** 48 55N 117 48W
Northumberland □, *U.K.* **12** 55 12N 2 0W
Northumberland, C., *Australia* **73** 38 5 S 140 40 E
Northumberland Is., *Australia* **72** 21 30 S 149 50 E
Northumberland Str., *Canada* **105** 46 20N 64 0W
Northwich, *U.K.* **12** 53 16N 2 30W
Northwood, *Iowa, U.S.A.* **120** 43 27N 93 0W
Northwood, *N. Dak., U.S.A.* **120** 47 44N 97 30W
Norton, *U.S.A.* **120** 39 50N 99 53W
Norton, *Zambia* **93** 17 52 S 30 40 E
Norton Sd., *U.S.A.* **102** 64 0N 164 0W
Norton Shores, *U.S.A.* **119** 43 8N 86 15W
Nortorf, *W. Germany* **30** 54 14N 9 47 E
Norwalk, *Calif., U.S.A.* **125** 33 54N 118 5W
Norwalk, *Conn., U.S.A.* **117** 41 9N 73 25W
Norwalk, *Ohio, U.S.A.* **116** 41 13N 82 38W
Norway, *U.S.A.* **114** 45 46N 87 57W
Norway ■, *Europe* **9** 63 0N 11 0 E
Norway House, *Canada* **111** 53 59N 97 50W
Norwegian Dependency □, *Antarctica* **143** 66 0 S 15 0 E
Norwegian Sea, *Atl. Oc.* **144** 66 0N 1 0 E
Norwich, *Canada* **108** 42 59N 80 36W
Norwich, *U.K.* **12** 52 38N 1 17 E
Norwich, *Conn., U.S.A.* **117** 41 33N 72 5W
Norwich, *N.Y., U.S.A.* **117** 42 32N 75 30W
Norwood, *Canada* **109** 44 23N 77 59W
Norwood, *U.S.A.* **119** 39 10N 84 27W
Noshiro, *Japan* **63** 40 12N 140 0 E
Nosok, *U.S.S.R.* **40** 70 10N 82 20 E
Nosovka, *U.S.S.R.* **36** 50 50N 31 37 E
Noşratābād, *Iran* **47** 29 55N 60 0 E
Noss Hd., *U.K.* **14** 58 29N 3 4W
Nossa Senhora da Glória, *Brazil* **138** 10 14 S 37 25W
Nossa Senhora das Dores, *Brazil* **138** 10 29 S 37 13W
Nossa Senhora do Livramento, *Brazil* **137** 15 48 S 56 22W
Nossebro, *Sweden* **11** 58 12N 12 43 E
Nossob →, *S. Africa* **96** 26 55 S 20 45 E
Nosy Boraha, *Madag.* **97** 16 50 S 49 55 E
Nosy Varika, *Madag.* **97** 20 35 S 48 32 E
Noteć →, *Poland* **32** 52 44N 15 26 E
Notigi Dam, *Canada* **111** 56 40N 99 10W
Notikewin →, *Canada* **110** 57 2N 117 38W
Notios Evvoïkos Kólpos, *Greece* **35** 38 20N 24 0 E
Noto, *Italy* **29** 36 52N 15 4 E
Noto, G. di, *Italy* **29** 36 50N 15 10 E
Notodden, *Norway* **10** 59 35N 9 17 E
Notre-Dame, *Canada* **105** 46 18N 64 46W
Notre Dame B., *Canada* **105** 49 45N 55 30W
Notre Dame de Koartac = Koartac, *Canada* **103** 60 55N 69 40W
Notre-Dame-de-la-Doré, *Canada* **107** 48 43N 72 39W
Notre-Dame-des-Bois, *Canada* **107** 45 24N 71 4W
Notre Dame d'Ivugivic = Ivugivik, *Canada* **103** 62 24N 77 55W
Notre-Dame-du-Bon-Conseil, *Canada* **107** 46 0N 72 21W
Notre Dame du Lac, *Ont., Canada* **108** 46 18N 80 11W
Notre-Dame-du-Lac, *Qué., Canada* **107** 47 36N 68 48W
Notre-Dame-du-Laus, *Canada* **106** 46 5N 75 37W
Notre-Dame-du-Nord, *Canada* **106** 47 36N 79 30W
Notre-Dame-du-Portage, *Canada* **107** 47 46N 69 37W
Notsé, *Togo* **91** 7 0N 1 17 E
Nottawasaga B., *Canada* **108** 44 35N 80 15W
Nottaway →, *Canada* **104** 51 22N 78 55W
Nøtterøy, *Norway* **10** 59 14N 10 24 E
Nottingham, *U.K.* **12** 52 57N 1 10W
Nottingham □, *U.K.* **12** 53 10N 1 0W
Nottoway →, *U.S.A.* **114** 36 33N 76 55W
Notwane →, *Botswana* **96** 23 35 S 26 58 E
Nouâdhibou, *Mauritania* **84** 20 54N 17 0W
Nouâdhibou, Ras, *Mauritania* **84** 20 50N 17 0W
Nouakchott, *Mauritania* **90** 18 9N 15 58W
Nouméa, *N. Cal.* **68** 22 17 S 166 30 E
Noupoort, *S. Africa* **96** 31 10 S 24 57 E
Nouveau Comptoir, *Canada* **104** 53 0N 78 49W
Nouvelle Calédonie = New Caledonia, *Pac. Oc.* **68** 21 0 S 165 0 E
Nouzonville, *France* **19** 49 48N 4 44 E
Nová Baňa, *Czech.* **33** 48 28N 18 39 E

Nová Bystřice

Nová Bystřice, *Czech.* **32** 49 2N 15 8 E
Nova Casa Nova, *Brazil* **138** 9 25 S 41 5W
Nova Cruz, *Brazil* **138** 6 28 S 35 25W
Nova Era, *Brazil* **139** 19 45 S 43 3W
Nova Esperança, *Brazil* **141** 23 8 S 52 24W
Nova Friburgo, *Brazil* **139** 22 16 S 42 30W
Nova Gaia, *Angola* **95** 10 10 S 17 35 E
Nova Gradiška, *Yugoslavia* **33** 45 17N 17 28 E
Nova Granada, *Brazil* **139** 20 30 S 49 20W
Nova Iguaçu, *Brazil* **139** 22 45 S 43 28W
Nova Iorque, *Brazil* **138** 7 0 S 44 5W
Nova Lamego, *Guinea-Biss.* **90** 12 19N 14 11W
Nova Lima, *Brazil* **141** 19 59 S 43 51W
Nova Lisboa = Huambo, *Angola* **95** 12 42 S 15 54 E
Nova Lusitânia, *Mozam.* **93** 19 50 S 34 34 E
Nova Mambone, *Mozam.* **97** 21 0 S 35 3 E
Nova Mesto, *Yugoslavia* **27** 45 47N 15 12 E
Nova Ponte, *Brazil* **139** 19 8 S 47 41W
Nova Scotia □, *Canada* **105** 45 10N 63 0W
Nova Sofala, *Mozam.* **97** 20 7 S 34 42 E
Nova Venécia, *Brazil* **139** 18 45 S 40 24W
Nova Vida, *Brazil* **137** 10 11 S 62 47W
Nova Zagora, *Bulgaria* **34** 42 32N 25 59 E
Noval Iorque, *Brazil* **138** 6 48 S 44 0W
Novaleksandrovskaya, *U.S.S.R.* **39** 45 29N 41 17 E
Novannenskiy, *U.S.S.R.* **37** 50 32N 42 39 E
Novar, *Canada* **108** 45 27N 79 15W
Novara, *Italy* **26** 45 27N 8 36 E
Novata, *U.S.A.* **124** 38 6N 122 35W
Novaya Kakhovka, *U.S.S.R.* **38** 46 42N 33 27 E
Novaya Lyalya, *U.S.S.R.* **40** 59 10N 60 35 E
Novaya Sibir, Ostrov, *U.S.S.R.* **41** 75 10N 150 0 E
Novaya Zemlya, *U.S.S.R.* **40** 75 0N 56 0 E
Novelda, *Spain* **25** 38 24N 0 45W
Novellara, *Italy* **26** 44 50N 10 43 E
Novelty, *U.S.A.* **118** 40 1N 92 12W
Noventa Vicentina, *Italy* **27** 45 18N 11 30 E
Novgorod, *U.S.S.R.* **36** 58 30N 31 25 E
Novgorod-Severskiy, *U.S.S.R.* **36** 52 2N 33 10 E
Novi Bečej, *Yugoslavia* **33** 45 36N 20 10 E
Novi Grad, *Yugoslavia* **27** 45 19N 13 33 E
Novi Krichim, *Bulgaria* **34** 42 8N 24 31 E
Novi Lígure, *Italy* **26** 44 45N 8 47 E
Novi Pazar, *Bulgaria* **34** 43 25N 27 15 E
Novi Pazar, *Yugoslavia* **33** 43 12N 20 28 E
Novi Sad, *Yugoslavia* **33** 45 18N 19 52 E
Novi Vinodolski, *Yugoslavia* **27** 45 10N 14 48 E
Novigrad, *Yugoslavia* **27** 44 10N 15 32 E
Noville, *Belgium* **17** 50 4N 5 46 E
Novinger, *U.S.A.* **118** 40 14N 92 43W
Novo Acôrdo, *Brazil* **138** 10 10 S 46 48W
Novo Aripuanã, *Brazil* **135** 5 8 S 60 22W
Nôvo Cruzeiro, *Brazil* **139** 17 29 S 41 53W
Nôvo Hamburgo, *Brazil* **141** 29 37 S 51 7W
Novo Horizonte, *Brazil* **139** 21 25 S 49 10W
Novo Remanso, *Brazil* **138** 9 41 S 42 4W
Novo-Zavidovskiy, *U.S.S.R.* **37** 56 32N 36 29 E
Novoakrainka, *U.S.S.R.* **38** 48 25N 31 30 E
Novoaltaysk, *U.S.S.R.* **40** 53 30N 84 0 E
Novoazovsk, *U.S.S.R.* **38** 47 15N 38 4 E
Novobelitsa, *U.S.S.R.* **36** 52 27N 31 2 E
Novobogatinskoye, *U.S.S.R.* **39** 47 20N 51 11 E
Novocherkassk, *U.S.S.R.* **39** 47 27N 40 5 E
Novodevichye, *U.S.S.R.* **37** 53 37N 48 50 E
Novograd-Volynskiy, *U.S.S.R.* **36** 50 34N 27 35 E
Novogrudok, *U.S.S.R.* **36** 53 40N 25 50 E
Novokayakent, *U.S.S.R.* **39** 42 30N 47 52 E
Novokazalinsk, *U.S.S.R.* **40** 45 48N 62 6 E
Novokhopersk, *U.S.S.R.* **37** 51 5N 41 39 E
Novokuybyshevsk, *U.S.S.R.* **37** 53 7N 49 58 E
Novokuznetsk, *U.S.S.R.* **40** 53 45N 87 10 E
Novomirgorod, *U.S.S.R.* **38** 48 45N 31 33 E
Novomoskovsk, *R.S.F.S.R., U.S.S.R.* **37** 54 5N 38 15 E
Novomoskovsk, *Ukraine S.S.R., U.S.S.R.* **38** 48 33N 35 17 E
Novopolotsk, *U.S.S.R.* **36** 55 32N 28 37 E
Novorossiysk, *U.S.S.R.* **38** 44 43N 37 46 E
Novorybnoye, *U.S.S.R.* **41** 72 50N 105 50 E
Novorzhev, *U.S.S.R.* **36** 57 3N 29 25 E
Novoselitsa, *U.S.S.R.* **38** 48 14N 26 15 E
Novoshakhtinsk, *U.S.S.R.* **39** 47 46N 39 58 E
Novosibirsk, *U.S.S.R.* **40** 55 0N 83 5 E
Novosibirskiye Ostrava, *U.S.S.R.* **41** 75 0N 142 0 E
Novosil, *U.S.S.R.* **37** 52 59N 37 2 E
Novosokolniki, *U.S.S.R.* **36** 56 33N 30 5 E
Novotroitsk, *U.S.S.R.* **40** 51 10N 58 15 E
Novotulskiy, *U.S.S.R.* **37** 54 10N 37 43 E
Novouzensk, *U.S.S.R.* **37** 50 32N 48 17 E
Novovolynsk, *U.S.S.R.* **36** 50 45N 24 4 E
Novovyatsk, *U.S.S.R.* **37** 58 24N 49 45 E
Novozybkov, *U.S.S.R.* **36** 52 30N 32 0 E
Novska, *Yugoslavia* **33** 45 19N 17 0 E
Novvy Port, *U.S.S.R.* **40** 67 40N 72 30 E
Novy Bug, *U.S.S.R.* **38** 47 34N 32 29 E
Nový Bydzov, *Czech.* **32** 50 14N 15 29 E
Novy Dwór Mazowiecki, *Poland* **32** 52 26N 20 44 E
Novyy Afon, *U.S.S.R.* **39** 43 7N 40 50 E
Novyy Oskol, *U.S.S.R.* **37** 50 44N 37 55 E
Now Shahr, *Iran* **47** 36 40N 51 30 E
Nowa Deba, *Poland* **32** 50 26N 21 41 E
Nowa Nowa, *Australia* **75** 37 44 S 148 3 E
Nowa Ruda, *Poland* **32** 50 35N 16 30 E
Nowa Sól, *Poland* **32** 51 48N 15 44 E
Nowe, *Poland* **32** 53 41N 18 44 E
Nowe Warpno, *Poland* **33** 53 42N 14 18 E
Nowendoc, *Australia* **77** 31 32 S 151 44 E
Nowgong, *India* **52** 26 20N 92 50 E
Nowingi, *Australia* **74** 34 33 S 142 15 E
Nowogard, *Poland* **32** 53 41N 15 10 E
Nowogród, *Poland* **32** 53 14N 21 53 E
Nowra, *Australia* **76** 34 53 S 150 35 E
Nowy Korczyn, *Poland* **32** 50 19N 20 48 E
Nowy Sącz, *Poland* **32** 49 40N 20 41 E
Noxen, *U.S.A.* **117** 41 25N 76 4W
Noxon, *U.S.A.* **122** 48 0N 115 43W
Noya, *Spain* **22** 42 48N 8 53W
Noyant, *France* **18** 47 30N 0 6 E
Noyers, *France* **19** 47 40N 4 0 E
Noyes I., *U.S.A.* **110** 55 30N 133 40W
Noyon, *France* **19** 49 34N 3 0 E
Noyon, *Mongolia* **60** 43 2N 102 4 E
Nozay, *France* **18** 47 34N 1 38W
Nsa, O. en →, *Algeria* **85** 32 28N 5 24 E
Nsa, Plateau de, *Congo* **94** 2 26 S 15 20 E
Nsah, *Congo* **94** 2 22 S 15 19 E
Nsanje, *Malawi* **93** 16 55 S 35 12 E
Nsawam, *Ghana* **91** 5 50N 0 24W
Nsomba, *Zambia* **93** 10 45 S 29 51 E
Nsopzup, *Burma* **52** 25 51N 97 30 E
Nsukka, *Nigeria* **91** 6 51N 7 29 E
Ntoum, *Gabon* **94** 0 22N 9 47 E
Nu Jiang →, *China* **58** 29 58N 97 25 E
Nu Shan, *China* **58** 26 0N 99 20 E
Nuba Mts. = Nubah, Jibalan, *Sudan* **89** 12 0N 31 0 E
Nubah, Jibalan, *Sudan* **89** 12 0N 31 0 E
Nubian Desert = Nûbîya, Es Sahrâ En, *Sudan* **88** 21 30N 33 30 E
Nûbîya, Es Sahrâ En, *Sudan* **88** 21 30N 33 30 E
Ñuble □, *Chile* **140** 37 0 S 72 0W
Nuboai, *Indonesia* **57** 2 10 S 136 30 E
Nubra →, *India* **49** 34 35N 77 35 E
Nueces →, *U.S.A.* **121** 27 50N 97 30W
Nueima →, *Jordan* **44** 31 54N 35 25 E
Nueltin L., *Canada* **111** 60 30N 99 30W
Nuenen, *Neths.* **17** 51 29N 5 33 E
Nueva, I., *Chile* **142** 55 13 S 66 30W
Nueva Antioquia, *Colombia* **134** 6 5N 69 26W
Nueva Esparta □, *Venezuela* **135** 11 0N 64 0W
Nueva Gerona, *Cuba* **128** 21 53N 82 49W
Nueva Imperial, *Chile* **142** 38 45 S 72 58W
Nueva Palmira, *Uruguay* **140** 33 52 S 58 20W
Nueva Rosita, *Mexico* **126** 28 0N 101 11W
Nueva San Salvador, *El Salv.* **128** 13 40N 89 18W
Nuéve de Julio, *Argentina* **140** 35 30 S 61 0W
Nuevitas, *Cuba* **128** 21 30N 77 20W
Nuevo, G., *Argentina* **142** 43 0 S 64 30W
Nuevo Guerrero, *Mexico* **127** 26 34N 99 15W
Nuevo Laredo, *Mexico* **127** 27 30N 99 30W
Nuevo León □, *Mexico* **126** 25 0N 100 0W
Nuevo Mundo, Cerro, *Bolivia* **136** 21 55 S 66 53W
Nuevo Rocafuerte, *Ecuador* **134** 0 55 S 75 27W
Nugget Pt., *N.Z.* **81** 46 27 S 169 50 E
Nugrus, Gebel, *Egypt* **88** 24 47N 34 35 E
Nuhaka, *N.Z.* **80** 39 3 S 177 45 E
Nuits-St.-Georges, *France* **19** 47 10N 4 56 E
Nukey Bluff, Mt., *Australia* **73** 32 26 S 135 29 E
Nukheila, *Sudan* **88** 19 1N 26 21 E
Nukiki, *Solomon Is.* **68** 6 45 S 156 29 E
Nuku'alofa, *Tonga* **68** 21 10 S 174 0W
Nukus, *U.S.S.R.* **40** 42 20N 59 7 E
Nuland, *Neths.* **16** 51 44N 5 26 E
Nulato, *U.S.A.* **102** 64 40N 158 10W
Nules, *Spain* **24** 39 51N 0 9W
Nullagine →, *Australia* **78** 21 20 S 120 20 E
Nullarbor, *Australia* **79** 31 28 S 130 55 E
Nullarbor Plain, *Australia* **79** 31 10 S 129 0 E
Nullawarre, *Australia* **74** 38 30 S 142 45 E
Nullawil, *Australia* **74** 35 49 S 143 10 E
Numalla, L., *Australia* **73** 28 43 S 144 20 E
Numan, *Nigeria* **91** 9 29N 12 3 E
Numansdorp, *Neths.* **16** 51 43N 4 26 E
Numata, *Japan* **65** 36 45N 139 4 E
Numatinna →, *Sudan* **89** 7 38N 27 20 E
Numazu, *Japan* **65** 35 7N 138 51 E
Numbulwar, *Australia* **72** 14 15 S 135 45 E
Numfoor, *Indonesia* **57** 1 0 S 134 50 E
Numurkah, *Australia* **74** 36 5 S 145 26 E
Nunaksaluk I., *Canada* **105** 55 49N 60 20W
Nundle, *Australia* **77** 31 29 S 151 9 E
Nuneaton, *U.K.* **13** 52 32N 1 29W
Nungatta, *Australia* **75** 37 11 S 149 20 E
Nungo, *Mozam.* **93** 13 23 S 37 43 E
Nungwe, *Tanzania* **92** 2 48 S 32 2 E
Nunivak, *U.S.A.* **102** 60 0N 166 0W
Nunkun, *India* **49** 33 57N 76 2 E
Nunspeet, *Neths.* **16** 52 21N 5 45 E
Nuoro, *Italy* **28** 40 20N 9 20 E
Nuqayy, Jabal, *Libya* **86** 23 11N 19 30 E
Nuquí, *Colombia* **134** 5 42N 77 17W
Nure →, *Italy* **26** 45 3N 9 49 E
Nuremburg = Nürnberg, *W. Germany* **31** 49 26N 11 5 E
Nuri, *Mexico* **126** 28 2N 109 22W
Nurina, *Australia* **79** 30 56 S 126 33 E
Nuriootpa, *Australia* **73** 34 27 S 139 0 E
Nurlat, *U.S.S.R.* **37** 54 29N 50 45 E
Nürnberg, *W. Germany* **31** 49 26N 11 5 E
Nurran, L. = Terewah, L., *Australia* **73** 29 52 S 147 35 E
Nurrari Lakes, *Australia* **79** 29 1 S 130 5 E
Nurri, *Italy* **28** 39 43N 9 13 E
Nusa Barung, *Indonesia* **57** 8 10 S 113 30 E
Nusa Kambangan, *Indonesia* **57** 7 40 S 108 10 E
Nusa Tenggara Barat □, *Indonesia* **56** 8 50 S 117 30 E
Nusa Tenggara Timur □, *Indonesia* **57** 9 30 S 122 0 E
Nushki, *Pakistan* **48** 29 35N 66 0 E
Nutak, *Canada* **103** 57 28N 61 59W
Nuth, *Neths.* **17** 50 55N 5 53 E
Nutwood Downs, *Australia* **72** 15 49 S 134 10 E
Nuwakot, *Nepal* **49** 28 10N 83 55 E
Nuwara Eliya, *Sri Lanka* **51** 6 58N 80 48 E
Nuweiba', *Egypt* **88** 28 59N 34 39 E
Nuweveldberge, *S. Africa* **96** 32 10 S 21 45 E
Nuyts, C., *Australia* **79** 32 2 S 132 21 E
Nuyts Arch., *Australia* **73** 32 35 S 133 20 E
Nuzvid, *India* **50** 16 47N 80 53 E
Nxau-Nxau, *Botswana* **96** 18 57 S 21 4 E
Nyaake, *Liberia* **90** 4 52N 7 37W
Nyack, *U.S.A.* **117** 41 5N 73 57W
Nyadal, *Sweden* **10** 62 48N 17 59 E
Nyah, *Australia* **74** 35 12 S 143 25 E
Nyah West, *Australia* **74** 35 16 S 143 21 E
Nyahanga, *Tanzania* **92** 2 20 S 33 37 E
Nyahua, *Tanzania* **92** 5 25 S 33 23 E
Nyahururu, *Kenya* **92** 0 2N 36 27 E
Nyainqentanglha Shan, *China* **62** 30 0N 90 0 E
Nyakanazi, *Tanzania* **92** 3 2 S 31 10 E
Nyakrom, *Ghana* **91** 5 40N 0 50W
Nyâlâ, *Sudan* **89** 12 2N 24 58 E
Nyamandhlovu, *Zambia* **93** 19 55 S 28 16 E
Nyambiti, *Tanzania* **92** 2 48 S 33 27 E
Nyamwaga, *Tanzania* **92** 1 27 S 34 33 E
Nyandekwa, *Tanzania* **92** 3 57 S 32 32 E
Nyanding →, *Sudan* **89** 8 40N 32 41 E
Nyanga →, *Gabon* **94** 2 58 S 10 15 E
Nyangana, *Namibia* **96** 18 0 S 20 40 E
Nyanguge, *Tanzania* **92** 2 30 S 33 12 E
Nyankpala, *Ghana* **91** 9 21N 0 58W
Nyanza, *Burundi* **92** 4 21 S 29 36 E
Nyanza, *Rwanda* **92** 2 20 S 29 42 E
Nyanza □, *Kenya* **92** 0 10 S 34 15 E
Nyarling →, *Canada* **110** 60 41N 113 23W
Nyarrin, *Australia* **74** 35 22 S 142 43 E
Nyasa, L. = Malawi, L., *Africa* **93** 12 30 S 34 30 E
Nyaunglebin, *Burma* **52** 17 52N 96 42 E
Nyazura, *Zambia* **93** 18 40 S 32 16 E
Nyazwidzi →, *Zambia* **93** 20 0 S 31 17 E
Nyborg, *Denmark* **11** 55 18N 10 47 E
Nybro, *Sweden* **11** 56 44N 15 55 E
Nyda, *U.S.S.R.* **40** 66 40N 72 58 E
Nyeri, *Kenya* **92** 0 23 S 36 56 E
Nyerol, *Sudan* **89** 8 41N 32 1 E
Nyhem, *Sweden* **10** 62 54N 15 37 E
Nyiel, *Sudan* **89** 6 9N 31 13 E
Nyinahin, *Ghana* **90** 6 43N 2 3W
Nyirbátor, *Hungary* **33** 47 49N 22 9 E
Nyíregyháza, *Hungary* **33** 47 58N 21 47 E
Nykarleby, *Finland* **8** 63 22N 22 31 E
Nykøbing, *Sjælland, Denmark* **11** 55 55N 11 40 E
Nykøbing, *Storstrøm, Denmark* **11** 54 56N 11 52 E
Nykøbing, *Viborg, Denmark* **11** 56 48N 8 51 E
Nyköping, *Sweden* **11** 58 45N 17 0 E
Nykroppa, *Sweden* **10** 59 37N 14 18 E
Nykvarn, *Sweden* **10** 59 11N 17 25 E
Nyland, *Sweden* **10** 63 1N 17 45 E
Nylstroom, *S. Africa* **97** 24 42 S 28 22 E
Nymagee, *Australia* **73** 32 7 S 146 20 E
Nymboida →, *Australia* **77** 29 22 S 152 32 E
Nymburk, *Czech.* **32** 50 10N 15 1 E
Nynäshamn, *Sweden* **10** 58 54N 17 57 E
Nyngan, *Australia* **76** 31 30 S 147 8 E
Nyon, *Switz.* **31** 46 23N 6 14 E
Nyong →, *Cameroon* **91** 3 17N 9 54 E
Nyons, *France* **21** 44 22N 5 10 E
Nyora, *Australia* **74** 38 20 S 145 41 E
Nyord, *Denmark* **11** 55 4N 12 13 E
Nyou, *Burkina Faso* **91** 12 42N 2 1W
Nysa, *Poland* **32** 50 30N 17 22 E
Nysa →, *Europe* **32** 52 4N 14 46 E
Nyssa, *U.S.A.* **122** 43 56N 117 2W
Nysted, *Denmark* **11** 54 40N 11 44 E
Nyūgawa, *Japan* **64** 33 56N 133 5 E
Nyunzu, *Zaïre* **92** 5 57 S 27 58 E
Nyurba, *U.S.S.R.* **41** 63 17N 118 28 E
Nzega, *Tanzania* **92** 4 10 S 33 12 E
Nzega □, *Tanzania* **92** 4 10 S 33 10 E
N'Zérékoré, *Guinea* **90** 7 49N 8 48W
Nzeto, *Angola* **95** 7 10 S 12 52 E
Nzilo, Chutes de, *Zaïre* **93** 10 18 S 25 27 E
Nzubuka, *Tanzania* **92** 4 45 S 32 50 E

O

Ō-Shima, *Fukuoka, Japan* **64** 33 54N 130 25 E
Ō-Shima, *Nagasaki, Japan* **64** 34 29N 129 33 E
Ō-Shima, *Shizuoka, Japan* **65** 34 44N 139 24 E
Oacoma, *U.S.A.* **120** 43 50N 99 26W
Oahe Dam, *U.S.A.* **120** 44 28N 100 25W
Oahe L., *U.S.A.* **120** 45 30N 100 25W
Oahu, *U.S.A.* **112** 21 30N 158 0W
Oak Creek, *Colo., U.S.A.* **122** 40 15N 106 59W
Oak Creek, *Wis., U.S.A.* **119** 42 52N 87 55W
Oak Harb., *U.S.A.* **124** 48 20N 122 38W
Oak Hill, *U.S.A.* **114** 38 0N 81 7W
Oak Lawn, *U.S.A.* **119** 41 43N 87 44W
Oak Park, *Ill., U.S.A.* **119** 41 53N 87 47W
Oak Park, *U.S.A.* **114** 41 55N 87 45W
Oak Ridge, *U.S.A.* **115** 36 1N 84 12W
Oak View, *U.S.A.* **125** 34 24N 119 18W
Oakbank, *Australia* **73** 33 4 S 140 33 E
Oakdale, *Calif., U.S.A.* **124** 37 45N 120 55W
Oakdale, *La., U.S.A.* **121** 30 50N 92 38W
Oakengates, *U.K.* **12** 52 42N 2 29W
Oakes, *U.S.A.* **120** 46 14N 98 4W
Oakesdale, *U.S.A.* **122** 47 11N 117 15W
Oakey, *Australia* **77** 27 25 S 151 43 E
Oakford, *U.S.A.* **118** 40 6N 89 58W
Oakham, *U.K.* **12** 52 40N 0 43W
Oakhurst, *U.S.A.* **124** 37 19N 119 40W
Oakland, *Calif., U.S.A.* **124** 37 50N 122 18W
Oakland, *Ill., U.S.A.* **119** 39 39N 88 2W
Oakland, *Oreg., U.S.A.* **122** 43 23N 123 18W
Oakland City, *U.S.A.* **119** 38 20N 87 20W
Oakleigh, *Australia* **74** 37 54 S 145 6 E
Oakley, *Idaho, U.S.A.* **122** 42 14N 113 55W
Oakley, *Kans., U.S.A.* **120** 39 8N 100 51W
Oakley Creek, *Australia* **77** 31 37 S 149 46 E
Oakover →, *Australia* **78** 21 0 S 120 40 E
Oakridge, *U.S.A.* **122** 43 47N 122 31W
Oaktown, *U.S.A.* **119** 38 52N 87 27W
Oakville, *Canada* **108** 43 27N 79 41W
Oakville, *U.S.A.* **124** 46 50N 123 14W
Oakwood, *Australia* **77** 29 38 S 151 4 E
Oakwood, *U.S.A.* **119** 41 6N 84 23W
Oamaru, *N.Z.* **81** 45 5 S 170 59 E
Ōamishirasato, *Japan* **65** 35 31N 140 18 E
Oarai, *Japan* **65** 36 21N 140 34 E
Oasis, *Calif., U.S.A.* **125** 33 28N 116 6W
Oasis, *Nev., U.S.A.* **124** 37 29N 117 55W
Oates Coast, *Antarctica* **143** 69 0 S 160 0 E
Oatman, *U.S.A.* **125** 35 1N 114 19W
Oaxaca, *Mexico* **127** 17 2N 96 40W
Oaxaca □, *Mexico* **127** 17 0N 97 0W
Ob →, *U.S.S.R.* **40** 66 45N 69 30 E
Oba, *Canada* **104** 49 4N 84 7W
Obala, *Cameroon* **91** 4 9N 11 32 E
Obalski, L., *Canada* **106** 48 43N 77 58W
Obama, *Fukui, Japan* **65** 35 30N 135 45 E
Obama, *Nagasaki, Japan* **64** 32 43N 130 13 E
Obamsca, L., *Canada* **106** 50 24N 78 16W
Oban, *U.K.* **14** 56 25N 5 30W
Obbia, *Somali Rep.* **98** 5 25N 48 30 E
Obdam, *Neths.* **16** 52 41N 4 55 E
Obed, *Canada* **110** 53 30N 117 10W
Obedjwan, *Canada* **106** 48 40N 74 56W
Obera, *Argentina* **141** 27 21 S 55 2W
Oberammergau, *W. Germany* **31** 47 35N 11 3 E
Oberdrauburg, *Austria* **33** 46 44N 12 58 E
Oberengadin, *Switz.* **31** 46 35N 9 55 E
Oberhausen, *W. Germany* **30** 51 28N 6 50 E
Oberkirch, *W. Germany* **31** 48 31N 8 5 E
Oberland, *Switz.* **31** 46 30N 7 30 E
Oberlin, *Kans., U.S.A.* **120** 39 52N 100 31W
Oberlin, *La., U.S.A.* **121** 30 42N 92 42W
Oberlin, *Ohio, U.S.A.* **116** 41 15N 82 10W
Obernai, *France* **19** 48 28N 7 30 E
Oberndorf, *W. Germany* **31** 48 17N 8 35 E
Oberon, *Australia* **76** 33 45 S 149 52 E

Oberpfälzer Wald, *W. Germany* **31** 49 30N 12 25 E
Oberstdorf, *W. Germany* **31** 47 25N 10 16 E
Oberting, *Gabon* **94** 0 22 S 9 46 E
Obi, Kepulauan, *Indonesia* **57** 1 23 S 127 45 E
Obiaruku, *Nigeria* **91** 5 51N 6 9 E
Óbidos, *Brazil* **135** 1 50 S 55 30W
Óbidos, *Portugal* **23** 39 19N 9 10W
Obihiro, *Japan* **63** 42 56N 143 12 E
Obilatu, *Indonesia* **57** 1 25 S 127 20 E
Obilnoye, *U.S.S.R.* **39** 47 32N 44 30 E
Obing, *W. Germany* **31** 48 0N 12 25 E
Öbisfelde, *E. Germany* **30** 52 27N 10 57 E
Objat, *France* **20** 45 16N 1 24 E
Oblong, *U.S.A.* **119** 39 0N 87 55W
Obluchye, *U.S.S.R.* **41** 49 1N 131 4 E
Obninsk, *U.S.S.R.* **37** 55 8N 36 37 E
Obo, *C.A.R.* **92** 5 20N 26 32 E
Obo, *Ethiopia* **89** 3 46N 38 52 E
Oboa, Mt., *Uganda* **92** 1 45N 34 45 E
Obock, *Djibouti* **89** 12 0N 43 20 E
Oborniki, *Poland* **32** 52 39N 16 50 E
Obouya, *Congo* **94** 0 56 S 15 43 E
Oboyan, *U.S.S.R.* **37** 51 13N 36 37 E
Obozerskaya, *U.S.S.R.* **40** 63 20N 40 15 E
Obrovac, *Yugoslavia* **27** 44 11N 15 41 E
Observatory Inlet, *Canada* **110** 55 10N 129 54W
Obshchi Syrt, *U.S.S.R.* **6** 52 0N 53 0 E
Obskaya Guba, *U.S.S.R.* **40** 69 0N 73 0 E
Obuasi, *Ghana* **91** 6 17N 1 40W
Obubra, *Nigeria* **91** 6 8N 8 20 E
Obzor, *Bulgaria* **34** 42 50N 27 52 E
Ocala, *U.S.A.* **115** 29 11N 82 5W
Ocamo →, *Venezuela* **135** 2 48N 65 14W
Ocampo, *Mexico* **126** 28 9N 108 24W
Ocaña, *Colombia* **134** 8 15N 73 20W
Ocaña, *Spain* **24** 39 55N 3 30W
Ocanomowoc, *U.S.A.* **120** 43 7N 88 30W
Ocate, *U.S.A.* **121** 36 12N 104 59W
Occidental, Cordillera, *Colombia* **134** 5 0N 76 0W
Occidental, Cordillera, *Peru* **136** 14 0 S 74 0W
Ocean, I. = Banaba, *Kiribati* **66** 0 45 S 169 50 E
Ocean City, *N.J., U.S.A.* **114** 39 18N 74 34W
Ocean City, *Wash., U.S.A.* **124** 47 4N 124 10W
Ocean Grove, *Australia* **74** 38 16 S 144 32 E
Ocean Park, *U.S.A.* **124** 46 30N 124 2W
Oceano, *U.S.A.* **125** 35 6N 120 37W
Oceanport, *U.S.A.* **117** 40 20N 74 3W
Oceanside, *U.S.A.* **125** 33 13N 117 26W
Ochagavia, *Spain* **24** 42 55N 1 5W
Ochamchire, *U.S.S.R.* **39** 42 46N 41 32 E
Ochamps, *Belgium* **17** 49 56N 5 16 E
Ochiai, *Japan* **64** 35 1N 133 45 E
Ochil Hills, *U.K.* **14** 56 14N 3 40W
Ochre River, *Canada* **111** 51 4N 99 47W
Ochsenfurt, *W. Germany* **31** 49 38N 10 3 E
Ochsenhausen, *W. Germany* **31** 48 4N 9 57 E
Ocilla, *U.S.A.* **115** 31 35N 83 12W
Ockelbo, *Sweden* **10** 60 54N 16 45 E
Ocmulgee →, *U.S.A.* **115** 31 58N 82 32W
Ocna Sibiului, *Romania* **34** 45 52N 24 2 E
Ocoña, *Peru* **136** 16 26 S 73 8W
Ocoña →, *Peru* **136** 16 28 S 73 8W
Oconee →, *U.S.A.* **115** 31 58N 82 32W
Oconomowoc, *U.S.A.* **119** 43 6N 88 30W
Oconto, *U.S.A.* **114** 44 52N 87 53W
Oconto Falls, *U.S.A.* **114** 44 52N 88 10W
Ocosingo, *Mexico* **127** 17 10N 92 15W
Ocotal, *Nic.* **128** 13 41N 86 31W
Ocotlán, *Mexico* **126** 20 21N 102 42W
Ocquier, *Belgium* **17** 50 24N 5 24 E
Ocreza →, *Portugal* **23** 39 32N 7 50W
Octave, *U.S.A.* **123** 34 10N 112 43W
Octeville, *France* **18** 49 38N 1 40W
Ocumare del Tuy, *Venezuela* **134** 10 7N 66 46W
Ocuri, *Bolivia* **137** 18 45 S 65 50W
Oda, *Ghana* **91** 5 50N 0 51W
Oda, *Ehime, Japan* **64** 33 36N 132 53 E
Ōda, *Shimane, Japan* **64** 35 11N 132 30 E
Oda, Jebel, *Sudan* **88** 20 21N 36 39 E
Ódáðahraun, *Iceland* **8** 65 5N 17 0W
Ödåkra, *Sweden* **11** 56 7N 12 45 E
Odate, *Japan* **63** 40 16N 140 34 E
Odawara, *Japan* **65** 35 20N 139 6 E
Odda, *Norway* **9** 60 3N 6 35 E
Odder, *Denmark* **11** 55 58N 10 10 E
Oddur, *Somali Rep.* **98** 4 11N 43 52 E
Ödeborg, *Sweden* **11** 58 32N 11 58 E
Odei →, *Canada* **111** 56 6N 96 54W
Odell, *U.S.A.* **119** 41 0N 88 31W
Odemira, *Portugal* **23** 37 35N 8 40W
Ödemiş, *Turkey* **46** 38 15N 28 0 E
Odendaalsrus, *S. Africa* **96** 27 48 S 26 45 E
Odense, *Denmark* **11** 55 22N 10 23 E
Odenwald, *W. Germany* **31** 49 40N 9 0 E
Oder →, *W. Germany* **30** 53 33N 14 38 E
Oderzo, *Italy* **27** 45 47N 12 29 E
Odessa, *Canada* **109** 44 17N 76 43W
Odessa, *Mo., U.S.A.* **118** 39 0N 93 57W
Odessa, *Tex., U.S.A.* **121** 31 51N 102 23W
Odessa, *Wash., U.S.A.* **122** 47 19N 118 35W
Odessa, *U.S.S.R.* **38** 46 30N 30 45 E
Odiakwe, *Botswana* **96** 20 12 S 25 17 E
Odiel →, *Spain* **23** 37 10N 6 55W
Odienné, *Ivory C.* **90** 9 30N 7 34W
Odintsovo, *U.S.S.R.* **37** 55 39N 37 15 E
Odobeşti, *Romania* **34** 45 43N 27 4 E
O'Donnell, *U.S.A.* **121** 33 0N 101 48W
Odoorn, *Neths.* **16** 52 51N 6 51 E
Odorheiu Secuiesc, *Romania* **34** 46 21N 25 21 E
Odoyevo, *U.S.S.R.* **37** 53 56N 36 42 E
Odra →, *Poland* **32** 53 33N 14 38 E
Odra →, *Spain* **22** 42 14N 4 17W
Odweina, *Somali Rep.* **98** 9 25N 45 4 E
Odžaci, *Yugoslavia* **33** 45 30N 19 17 E
Odzi, *Zambia* **97** 19 0 S 32 20 E
Oedelem, *Belgium* **17** 51 10N 3 21 E
Oegstgeest, *Neths.* **16** 52 11N 4 29 E
Oeiras, *Brazil* **138** 7 0 S 42 8W
Oeiras, *Portugal* **23** 38 41N 9 18W
Oelrichs, *U.S.A.* **120** 43 11N 103 14W
Oelsnitz, *E. Germany* **30** 50 24N 12 11 E
Oelwein, *U.S.A.* **120** 42 41N 91 55W
Oenpelli, *Australia* **78** 12 20 S 133 4 E
O'Fallon, *U.S.A.* **118** 38 50N 90 43W
Ofanto →, *Italy* **29** 41 22N 16 13 E
Offa, *Nigeria* **91** 8 13N 4 42 E
Offaly □, *Ireland* **15** 53 15N 7 30W
Offenbach, *W. Germany* **31** 50 6N 8 46 E
Offenburg, *W. Germany* **31** 48 29N 7 56 E
Offerdal, *Sweden* **10** 63 28N 14 0 E
Officer, *Australia* **74** 38 3 S 145 22 E
Offida, *Italy* **27** 42 56N 13 40 E
Offranville, *France* **18** 49 52N 1 1 E
Ofidhousa, *Greece* **35** 36 33N 26 8 E
Ofotfjorden, *Norway* **8** 68 27N 16 40 E
Ofu, *Amer. Samoa* **68** 14 11 S 169 41W
Oga-Hantō, *Japan* **63** 39 58N 139 47 E
Ogaden, *Ethiopia* **98** 7 30N 45 30 E
Ogahalla, *Canada* **104** 50 6N 85 51W
Ōgaki, *Japan* **65** 35 21N 136 37 E
Ogallala, *U.S.A.* **120** 41 12N 101 40W
Ogascanane, L., *Canada* **106** 47 5N 78 25W
Ogbomosho, *Nigeria* **91** 8 1N 4 11 E
Ogden, *Iowa, U.S.A.* **118** 42 3N 94 0W
Ogden, *Utah, U.S.A.* **122** 41 13N 112 1W
Ogdensburg, *U.S.A.* **117** 44 40N 75 27W
Ogeechee →, *U.S.A.* **115** 31 51N 81 6W
Ogilby, *U.S.A.* **125** 32 49N 114 50W
Oglesby, *U.S.A.* **118** 41 21N 89 3W
Oglio →, *Italy* **26** 45 2N 10 39 E
Ogmore, *Australia* **72** 22 37 S 149 35 E
Ognon →, *France* **19** 47 16N 5 28 E
Ogoja, *Nigeria* **91** 6 38N 8 39 E
Ogoki →, *Canada* **104** 51 38N 85 57W
Ogoki L., *Canada* **104** 50 50N 87 10W
Ogoki Res., *Canada* **104** 50 45N 88 15W
Ogooué →, *Gabon* **94** 1 0 S 9 0 E
Ōgori, *Japan* **64** 34 6N 131 24 E
Ogosta →, *Bulgaria* **34** 43 48N 23 55 E
Ogowe = Ogooué →, *Gabon* **94** 1 0 S 9 0 E
Ogr = Sharafa, *Sudan* **89** 11 59N 27 7 E
Ogrein, *Sudan* **88** 17 55N 34 50 E
Ogulin, *Yugoslavia* **27** 45 16N 15 16 E
Ogun □, *Nigeria* **91** 7 0N 3 0 E
Oguni, *Japan* **64** 33 11N 131 8 E
Oguta, *Nigeria* **91** 5 44N 6 44 E
Ogwashi-Uku, *Nigeria* **91** 6 15N 6 30 E
Ogwe, *Nigeria* **91** 5 0N 7 14 E
Ohai, *N.Z.* **81** 44 55 S 168 0 E
Ohakune, *N.Z.* **80** 39 24 S 175 24 E
Ohanet, *Algeria* **85** 28 44N 8 46 E
Ōhara, *Japan* **65** 35 15N 140 23 E
Ohau, L., *N.Z.* **81** 44 15 S 169 53 E
Ohaupo, *N.Z.* **80** 37 56 S 175 20 E
Ohey, *Belgium* **17** 50 26N 5 8 E
Ohio □, *U.S.A.* **114** 40 20N 84 10W
Ohio →, *U.S.A.* **114** 38 0N 86 0W
Ohio City, *U.S.A.* **119** 40 46N 84 37W
Ohiwa Harbour, *N.Z.* **80** 37 59 S 177 10 E
Ohre →, *Czech.* **32** 50 30N 14 10 E
Ohre →, *E. Germany* **30** 52 18N 11 47 E
Ohrid, *Yugoslavia* **35** 41 8N 20 52 E
Ohridsko, Jezero, *Yugoslavia* **35** 41 8N 20 52 E
Ohrigstad, *S. Africa* **97** 24 39 S 30 36 E
Öhringen, *W. Germany* **31** 49 11N 9 31 E
Oiapoque →, *Brazil* **135** 4 8N 51 40W
Oikou, *China* **61** 38 35N 117 42 E
Oil City, *U.S.A.* **116** 41 26N 79 40W
Oil Springs, *Canada* **108** 42 47N 82 7W
Oildale, *U.S.A.* **125** 35 25N 119 1W
Oirschot, *Neths.* **17** 51 30N 5 18 E
Oise □, *France* **19** 49 28N 2 30 E
Oise →, *France* **19** 49 0N 2 4 E
Oisterwijk, *Neths.* **17** 51 35N 5 12 E
Ōita, *Japan* **64** 33 14N 131 36 E
Ōita □, *Japan* **64** 33 15N 131 30 E
Oiticica, *Brazil* **138** 5 3 S 41 5W
Ojai, *U.S.A.* **125** 34 28N 119 16W
Ojinaga, *Mexico* **126** 29 34N 104 25W
Ojos del Salado, Cerro, *Argentina* **140** 27 0 S 68 40W
Oka →, *U.S.S.R.* **37** 56 20N 43 59 E
Okaba, *Indonesia* **57** 8 6 S 139 42 E
Okahandja, *Namibia* **96** 22 0 S 16 59 E
Okahukura, *N.Z.* **66** 38 48 S 175 14 E
Okaihau, *N.Z.* **80** 35 19 S 173 47 E
Okanagan L., *Canada* **110** 50 0N 119 30W
Okandja, *Gabon* **94** 0 35 S 13 45 E
Okanogan, *U.S.A.* **122** 48 6N 119 43W
Okanogan →, *U.S.A.* **122** 48 6N 119 43W
Okapa, *Papua N. G.* **69** 6 38 S 145 39 E
Okaputa, *Namibia* **96** 20 5 S 17 0 E
Okara, *Pakistan* **48** 30 50N 73 31 E
Okarito, *N.Z.* **81** 43 15 S 170 9 E
Okato, *N.Z.* **80** 39 12 S 173 53 E
Okaukuejo, *Namibia* **96** 19 10 S 16 0 E
Okavango Swamps, *Botswana* **96** 18 45 S 22 45 E
Okawa, *Japan* **64** 33 9N 130 21 E
Okawville, *U.S.A.* **118** 38 26N 89 33W
Okaya, *Japan* **65** 36 0N 138 10 E
Okayama, *Japan* **64** 34 40N 133 54 E
Okayama □, *Japan* **64** 35 0N 133 50 E
Okazaki, *Japan* **65** 34 57N 137 10 E
Oke-Iho, *Nigeria* **91** 8 1N 3 18 E
Okeechobee, *U.S.A.* **115** 27 16N 80 46W
Okeechobee, L., *U.S.A.* **115** 27 0N 80 50W
Okefenokee Swamp, *U.S.A.* **115** 30 50N 82 15W
Okehampton, *U.K.* **13** 50 44N 4 1W
Okene, *Nigeria* **91** 7 32N 6 11 E
Oker →, *W. Germany* **30** 52 30N 10 22 E
Okha, *U.S.S.R.* **41** 53 40N 143 0 E
Ókhi Óros, *Greece* **35** 38 5N 24 25 E
Okhotsk, *U.S.S.R.* **41** 59 20N 143 10 E
Okhotsk, Sea of, *Asia* **41** 55 0N 145 0 E
Okhotskiy Perevoz, *U.S.S.R.* **41** 61 52N 135 35 E
Okhotsko Kolymskoye, *U.S.S.R.* **41** 63 0N 157 0 E
Oki-no-Shima, *Japan* **64** 32 44N 132 33 E
Oki-Shotō, *Japan* **64** 36 5N 133 15 E
Okiep, *S. Africa* **96** 29 39 S 17 53 E
Okigwi, *Nigeria* **91** 5 52N 7 20 E
Okija, *Nigeria* **91** 5 54N 6 55 E
Okitipupa, *Nigeria* **91** 6 31N 4 50 E
Oklahoma □, *U.S.A.* **121** 35 20N 97 30W
Oklahoma City, *U.S.A.* **121** 35 25N 97 30W
Okmulgee, *U.S.A.* **121** 35 38N 96 0W
Oknitsa, *U.S.S.R.* **38** 48 25N 27 30 E
Okolo, *Uganda* **92** 2 37N 31 8 E
Okolona, *Ky., U.S.A.* **119** 38 8N 85 41W
Okolona, *Miss., U.S.A.* **121** 34 0N 88 45W
Okrika, *Nigeria* **91** 4 40N 7 10 E
Oktabrsk, *U.S.S.R.* **40** 49 28N 57 25 E
Oktyabrsk, *U.S.S.R.* **37** 53 11N 48 40 E
Oktyabrskiy, *U.S.S.R.* **36** 52 38N 28 53 E
Oktyabrskoy Revolyutsii, Os., *U.S.S.R.* **41** 79 30N 97 0 E
Oktyabrskoye = Zhovtnevoye, *U.S.S.R.* **38** 46 54N 32 3 E
Oktyabrskoye, *U.S.S.R.* **40** 62 28N 66 3 E
Ōkuchi, *Japan* **64** 32 4N 130 37 E
Okulovka, *U.S.S.R.* **36** 58 25N 33 19 E
Okuru, *N.Z.* **81** 43 55 S 168 55 E
Okushiri-Tō, *Japan* **63** 42 15N 139 30 E
Okuta, *Nigeria* **91** 9 14N 3 12 E
Okwa →, *Botswana* **96** 22 30 S 23 0 E
Ola, *U.S.A.* **121** 35 2N 93 10W
Ólafsfjörður, *Iceland* **8** 66 4N 18 39W
Ólafsvík, *Iceland* **8** 64 53N 23 43W
Olancha, *U.S.A.* **125** 36 15N 118 1W
Olancha Pk., *U.S.A.* **125** 36 15N 118 7W
Olanchito, *Honduras* **128** 15 30N 86 30W
Öland, *Sweden* **11** 56 45N 16 38 E
Olargues, *France* **20** 43 34N 2 53 E
Olary, *Australia* **73** 32 18 S 140 19 E
Olascoaga, *Argentina* **140** 35 15 S 60 39W
Olathe, *U.S.A.* **120** 38 50N 94 50W
Olavarría, *Argentina* **140** 36 55 S 60 20W
Oława, *Poland* **32** 50 57N 17 20 E
Ólbia, *Italy* **28** 40 55N 9 30 E
Ólbia, G. di, *Italy* **28** 40 55N 9 35 E
Old Bahama Chan. = Bahama, Canal Viejo de, *W. Indies* **128** 22 10N 77 30W
Old Baldy Pk. = San Antonio, Mt., *U.S.A.* **125** 34 17N 117 38W
Old Castile = Castilla La Vieja, *Spain* **22** 41 55N 4 0W
Old Castle, *Ireland* **15** 53 46N 7 10W
Old Cork, *Australia* **72** 22 57 S 141 52 E
Old Crow, *Canada* **102** 67 30N 139 55W
Old Dale, *U.S.A.* **125** 34 8N 115 47W
Old Dongola, *Sudan* **88** 18 11N 30 44 E
Old Forge, *N.Y., U.S.A.* **117** 43 43N 74 58W
Old Forge, *Pa., U.S.A.* **117** 41 20N 75 46W
Old Fort →, *Canada* **111** 58 36N 110 24W
Old Junee, *Australia* **76** 34 49 S 147 31 E
Old Shinyanga, *Tanzania* **92** 3 33 S 33 27 E
Old Speck, Mt., *U.S.A.* **117** 44 35N 70 57W
Old Town, *U.S.A.* **105** 45 0N 68 41W
Old Wives L., *Canada* **111** 50 5N 106 0W
Oldbury, *U.K.* **13** 51 38N 2 30W
Oldeani, *Tanzania* **92** 3 22 S 35 35 E
Oldenburg, *Niedersachsen, W. Germany* **30** 53 10N 8 10 E
Oldenburg, *Schleswig-Holstein, W. Germany* **30** 54 16N 10 53 E
Oldenzaal, *Neths.* **16** 52 19N 6 53 E
Oldham, *U.K.* **12** 53 33N 2 8W
Oldman →, *Canada* **110** 49 57N 111 42W
Olds, *Canada* **110** 51 50N 114 10W
Olean, *U.S.A.* **116** 42 8N 78 25W
Oléggio, *Italy* **26** 45 36N 8 38 E
Oleiros, *Portugal* **22** 39 56N 7 56W
Olekma →, *U.S.S.R.* **41** 60 22N 120 42 E
Olekminsk, *U.S.S.R.* **41** 60 25N 120 30 E
Olema, *U.S.A.* **124** 38 3N 122 47W
Olen, *Belgium* **17** 51 9N 4 52 E
Olenek, *U.S.S.R.* **41** 68 28N 112 18 E
Olenek →, *U.S.S.R.* **41** 73 0N 120 10 E
Olenino, *U.S.S.R.* **36** 56 15N 33 30 E
Oléron, I. d', *France* **20** 45 55N 1 15W
Oleśnica, *Poland* **32** 51 13N 17 22 E
Olesno, *Poland* **32** 50 51N 18 26 E
Olevsk, *U.S.S.R.* **36** 51 12N 27 39 E
Olga, *U.S.S.R.* **41** 43 50N 135 14 E
Olga, L., *Canada* **106** 49 47N 77 15W
Olga, Mt., *Australia* **79** 25 20 S 130 50 E
Olgastretet, *Svalbard* **144** 78 35N 25 0 E
Ølgod, *Denmark* **11** 55 49N 8 36 E
Olhão, *Portugal* **23** 37 3N 7 48W
Olib, *Yugoslavia* **27** 44 23N 14 44 E
Oliena, *Italy* **28** 40 18N 9 22 E
Oliete, *Spain* **24** 41 1N 0 41W
Olifants →, *Africa* **97** 23 57 S 31 58 E
Olifantshoek, *S. Africa* **96** 27 57 S 22 42 E
Ólimbos, *Greece* **35** 35 44N 27 11 E
Ólimbos, Óros, *Greece* **35** 40 6N 22 23 E
Olímpia, *Brazil* **141** 20 44 S 48 54W
Olimpo □, *Paraguay* **140** 20 30 S 58 45W
Olin, *U.S.A.* **118** 42 0N 91 9W
Olinda, *Australia* **76** 32 50 S 150 10 E
Olinda, *Brazil* **138** 8 1 S 34 51W
Olindiná, *Brazil* **138** 11 22 S 38 21W
Olite, *Spain* **24** 42 29N 1 40W
Oliva, *Argentina* **140** 32 0 S 63 38W
Oliva, *Spain* **25** 38 58N 0 9W
Oliva, La, *Canary Is.* **25** 28 36N 13 57W
Oliva, Punta del, *Spain* **22** 43 37N 5 28W
Oliva de la Frontera, *Spain* **23** 38 17N 6 54W
Olivares, *Spain* **24** 39 46N 2 20W
Olive Hill, *U.S.A.* **119** 38 18N 83 13W
Olivehurst, *U.S.A.* **124** 39 6N 121 34W
Oliveira, *Brazil* **139** 20 39 S 44 50W
Oliveira de Azemeis, *Portugal* **22** 40 49N 8 29W
Oliveira dos Brejinhos, *Brazil* **139** 12 19 S 42 54W
Olivenza, *Spain* **23** 38 41N 7 9W
Oliver, *Canada* **110** 49 13N 119 37W
Oliver L., *Canada* **111** 56 56N 103 22W
Olivine Ra., *N.Z.* **81** 44 15 S 168 30 E
Olkhovka, *U.S.S.R.* **39** 49 48N 44 32 E
Olkusz, *Poland* **32** 50 18N 19 33 E
Ollagüe, *Chile* **140** 21 15 S 68 10W
Olloy, *Belgium* **17** 50 5N 4 36 E
Olmedo, *Spain* **22** 41 20N 4 43W
Olmos, *Peru* **136** 5 59 S 79 46W
Olney, *Ill., U.S.A.* **119** 38 40N 88 0W
Olney, *Tex., U.S.A.* **121** 33 25N 98 45W
Olofström, *Sweden* **11** 56 17N 14 32 E
Oloma, *Cameroon* **91** 3 29N 11 19 E
Olomane →, *Canada* **105** 50 14N 60 37W
Olombo, *Congo* **94** 1 18 S 15 53 E
Olomouc, *Czech.* **32** 49 38N 17 12 E
Olongapo, *Phil.* **57** 14 50N 120 18 E
Oloron, Gave d' →, *France* **20** 43 33N 1 5W
Oloron-Ste.-Marie, *France* **20** 43 11N 0 38W
Olot, *Spain* **24** 42 11N 2 30 E
Olovo, *Yugoslavia* **33** 44 8N 18 35 E
Olovyannaya, *U.S.S.R.* **41** 50 58N 115 35 E
Oloy →, *U.S.S.R.* **41** 66 29N 159 29 E
Olpe, *W. Germany* **30** 51 2N 7 50 E
Olshanka, *U.S.S.R.* **38** 48 16N 30 58 E
Olshany, *U.S.S.R.* **38** 50 3N 35 53 E
Olst, *Neths.* **16** 52 20N 6 7 E
Olsztyn, *Poland* **32** 53 48N 20 29 E
Olt →, *Romania* **34** 43 43N 24 51 E
Olten, *Switz.* **31** 47 21N 7 53 E
Olteniţa, *Romania* **34** 44 7N 26 42 E
Olton, *U.S.A.* **121** 34 16N 102 7W
Oltu, *Turkey* **46** 40 35N 41 58 E
Olvega, *Spain* **24** 41 47N 2 0W
Olvera, *Spain* **23** 36 55N 5 18W
Olympia, *Greece* **35** 37 39N 21 39 E
Olympia, *U.S.A.* **124** 47 0N 122 58W
Olympic Mts., *U.S.A.* **124** 47 50N 123 45W
Olympic Nat. Park, *U.S.A.* **124** 47 48N 123 30W
Olympus, Mt. = Ólimbos, Óros, *Greece* **35** 40 6N 22 23 E
Olympus, Mt., *U.S.A.* **124** 47 52N 123 40W
Olyphant, *U.S.A.* **117** 41 27N 75 36W
Om →, *U.S.S.R.* **40** 54 59N 73 22 E
Om Hajer, *Ethiopia* **89** 14 20N 36 41 E
Om Koi, *Thailand* **54** 17 48N 98 22 E
Ōmachi, *Japan* **65** 36 30N 137 50 E
Omae-Zaki, *Japan* **65** 34 36N 138 14 E
Omagh, *U.K.* **15** 54 36N 7 20W
Omagh □, *U.K.* **15** 54 35N 7 15W
Omaha, *U.S.A.* **120** 41 15N 96 0W
Omak, *U.S.A.* **122** 48 24N 119 31W
Oman ■, *Asia* **45** 23 0N 58 0 E
Oman, G. of, *Asia* **47** 24 30N 58 30 E
Omar Combon, *Somali Rep.* **98** 3 10N 45 47 E
Omaruru, *Namibia* **96** 21 26 S 16 0 E
Omaruru →, *Namibia* **96** 22 7 S 14 15 E
Omate, *Peru* **136** 16 45 S 71 0W

Öyeren

Ortles, Italy 26 46 31N 10 33 E
Ortón →, Bolivia 136 10 50 S 67 0W
Ortona, Italy 27 42 21N 14 24 E
Orūmīyeh, Iran 46 37 40N 45 0 E
Orūmīyeh, Daryācheh-ye, Iran 46 37 50N 45 30 E
Orune, Italy 28 40 25N 9 20 E
Oruro, Bolivia 136 18 0 S 67 9W
Oruro □, Bolivia 136 18 40 S 67 30W
Orust, Sweden 11 58 10N 11 40 E
Oruzgān □, Afghan. 47 33 30N 66 0 E
Orvault, France 18 47 17N 1 38W
Orvieto, Italy 27 42 43N 12 8 E
Orwell, U.S.A. 116 41 32N 80 52W
Orwell →, U.K. 13 52 2N 1 12 E
Oryakhovo, Bulgaria 34 43 40N 23 57 E
Orzinuovi, Italy 26 45 24N 9 55 E
Orzysz, Poland 32 53 50N 21 58 E
Osa, Pen. de, Costa Rica 128 8 0N 84 0W
Osage, Iowa, U.S.A. 120 43 15N 92 50W
Osage, Wyo., U.S.A. 120 43 59N 104 25W
Osage →, U.S.A. 118 38 35N 91 57W
Osage City, U.S.A. 120 38 43N 95 51W
Ōsaka, Japan 65 34 40N 135 30 E
Ōsaka □, Japan 65 34 30N 135 30 E
Ōsaka-Wan, Japan 65 34 30N 135 18 E
Osawatomie, U.S.A. 120 38 30N 94 55W
Osborne, U.S.A. 120 39 30N 98 45W
Osby, Sweden 11 56 23N 13 59 E
Osceola, Ark., U.S.A. 121 35 40N 90 0W
Osceola, Iowa, U.S.A. 118 41 0N 93 20W
Osceola, Mo., U.S.A. 118 38 3N 93 42W
Oschatz, E. Germany 30 51 17N 13 8 E
Oschersleben, E. Germany 30 52 2N 11 13 E
Óschiri, Italy 28 40 43N 9 7 E
Oscoda, U.S.A. 116 44 26N 83 20W
Ösel = Saaremaa, U.S.S.R. 36 58 30N 22 30 E
Osëry, U.S.S.R. 37 54 52N 38 28 E
Osgood, U.S.A. 119 39 8N 85 18W
Osgoode, Canada 109 45 8N 75 36W
Osh, U.S.S.R. 40 40 37N 72 49 E
Oshawa, Canada 109 43 50N 78 50W
Oshima, Japan 64 33 55N 132 14 E
Oshkosh, Nebr., U.S.A. 120 41 27N 102 20W
Oshkosh, Wis., U.S.A. 120 44 3N 88 35W
Oshmyany, U.S.S.R. 36 54 26N 25 52 E
Oshogbo, Nigeria 91 7 48N 4 37 E
Oshwe, Zaïre 94 3 25 S 19 28 E
Osijek, Yugoslavia 33 45 34N 18 41 E
Ósilo, Italy 28 40 45N 8 41 E
Osimo, Italy 27 43 28N 13 30 E
Osintorf, U.S.S.R. 36 54 40N 30 39 E
Osipenko = Berdyansk, U.S.S.R. 38 46 45N 36 50 E
Osipovichi, U.S.S.R. 36 53 19N 28 33 E
Osizweni, S. Africa 97 27 49 S 30 7 E
Oskaloosa, U.S.A. 118 41 18N 92 40W
Oskarshamn, Sweden 11 57 15N 16 27 E
Oskélanéo, Canada 106 48 5N 75 15W
Oskol →, U.S.S.R. 37 49 6N 37 25 E
Oslo, Norway 10 59 55N 10 45 E
Oslob, Phil. 57 9 31N 123 26 E
Oslofjorden, Norway 10 59 20N 10 35 E
Osmanabad, India 50 18 5N 76 10 E
Osmancık, Turkey 38 40 45N 34 47 E
Osmaniye, Turkey 46 37 5N 36 10 E
Ösmo, Sweden 10 58 58N 17 55 E
Osnabrück, W. Germany 30 52 16N 8 2 E
Osor, Italy 26 44 42N 14 24 E
Osorio, Brazil 141 29 53 S 50 17W
Osorno, Chile 142 40 25 S 73 0W
Osorno, Spain 22 42 24N 4 22W
Osorno □, Chile 142 40 34 S 73 9W
Osorno, Vol., Chile 142 41 0 S 72 30W
Osoyoos, Canada 110 49 0N 119 30W
Ospika →, Canada 110 56 20N 124 0W
Osprey Reef, Australia 72 13 52 S 146 36 E
Oss, Neths. 16 51 46N 5 32 E
Ossa, Mt., Australia 72 41 52 S 146 3 E
Óssa, Oros, Greece 35 39 47N 22 42 E
Ossa de Montiel, Spain 25 38 58N 2 45W
Ossabaw I., U.S.A. 115 31 45N 81 8W
Osse →, France 20 44 7N 0 17 E
Ossendrecht, Neths. 17 51 24N 4 20 E
Ossining, U.S.A. 117 41 9N 73 50W
Ossipee, U.S.A. 117 43 41N 71 9W
Ossokmanuan L., Canada 105 53 25N 65 0W
Ossora, U.S.S.R. 41 59 20N 163 13 E
Ostaboningue, L., Canada 106 47 9N 78 53W
Ostashkov, U.S.S.R. 36 57 4N 33 2 E
Oste →, W. Germany 30 53 30N 9 12 E
Ostend = Oostende, Belgium 17 51 15N 2 54 E
Oster, U.S.S.R. 36 50 57N 30 53 E
Osterburg, E. Germany 30 52 47N 11 44 E
Osterburken, W. Germany 31 49 26N 9 25 E
Österbybruk, Sweden 10 60 13N 17 55 E
Österbymo, Sweden 11 57 49N 15 15 E
Österdalälven →, Sweden 9 61 30N 13 45 E
Östergötlands län □, Sweden 11 58 35N 15 45 E
Osterholz-Scharmbeck, W. Germany 30 53 14N 8 48 E
Østerild, Denmark 11 57 2N 8 51 E
Österkorsberga, Sweden 11 57 18N 15 6 E
Östersund, Sweden 10 63 10N 14 38 E
Østfold fylke □, Norway 10 59 25N 11 25 E
Ostfriesische Inseln, W. Germany 30 53 45N 7 15 E
Ostfriesland, W. Germany 30 53 20N 7 30 E
Óstia, Lido di, Italy 28 41 43N 12 17 E
Ostiglía, Italy 27 45 4N 11 9 E
Ostra, Italy 27 43 40N 13 5 E
Ostrava, Czech. 32 49 51N 18 18 E
Ostróda, Poland 32 53 42N 19 58 E
Ostrog, U.S.S.R. 36 50 20N 26 30 E
Ostrogozhsk, U.S.S.R. 37 50 55N 39 7 E
Ostrogróg Sźamotuly, Poland 32 52 37N 16 33 E
Ostrołęka, Poland 32 53 4N 21 32 E
Ostrov, Bulgaria 34 43 40N 24 9 E
Ostrov, Romania 34 44 6N 27 24 E
Ostrov, U.S.S.R. 36 57 25N 28 20 E
Ostrów Mazowiecka, Poland 32 52 50N 21 51 E
Ostrów Wielkopolski, Poland 32 51 36N 17 44 E
Ostrowiec-Świętokrzyski, Poland 32 50 55N 21 22 E
Ostrzeszów, Poland 32 51 25N 17 52 E
Ostseebad-Külungsborn, E. Germany 30 54 10N 11 40 E
Ostuni, Italy 29 40 44N 17 34 E
Osum →, Bulgaria 34 43 40N 24 50 E
Osumi →, Albania 35 40 40N 20 10 E
Ōsumi-Hantō, Japan 64 31 20N 130 55 E
Ōsumi-Kaikyō, Japan 63 30 55N 131 0 E
Osuna, Spain 23 37 14N 5 8W
Oswego, U.S.A. 117 43 29N 76 30W
Oswestry, U.K. 12 52 52N 3 3W
Oświecim, Poland 32 50 2N 19 11 E
Ōta, Japan 65 36 18N 139 22 E
Ota-Gawa →, Japan 64 34 21N 132 18 E
Otago □, N.Z. 81 44 44 S 169 10 E
Otago Harb., N.Z. 81 45 47 S 170 42 E
Otago Pen., N.Z. 81 45 48 S 170 39 E
Otahuhu, N.Z. 80 36 56 S 174 51 E
Ōtake, Japan 64 34 12N 132 13 E
Ōtaki, Japan 65 35 17N 140 15 E
Otaki, N.Z. 80 40 45 S 175 10 E
Otane, N.Z. 80 39 54 S 176 39 E
Otaru, Japan 63 43 10N 141 0 E
Otaru-Wan = Ishikari-Wan, Japan 63 43 25N 141 1 E
Otautau, N.Z. 81 46 9 S 168 1 E
Otava →, Czech. 32 49 26N 14 12 E
Otavalo, Ecuador 134 0 13N 78 20W
Otavi, Namibia 96 19 40 S 17 24 E
Otchinjau, Angola 95 16 30 S 13 56 E
Otelec, Romania 34 45 36N 20 50 E
Otero de Rey, Spain 22 43 6N 7 36W
Othello, U.S.A. 122 46 53N 119 8W
Othonoí, Greece 35 39 52N 19 22 E
Óthris, Óros, Greece 35 39 4N 22 42 E
Otira, N.Z. 81 42 49 S 171 35 E
Otira Gorge, N.Z. 81 42 53 S 171 33 E
Otis, U.S.A. 120 40 12N 102 58W
Otjiwarongo, Namibia 96 20 30 S 16 33 E
Oto Tolu Group, Tonga 68 20 21 S 174 32W
Otočac, Yugoslavia 27 44 53N 15 12 E
Otoineppu, Japan 63 44 44N 142 16 E
Otorohanga, N.Z. 80 38 12 S 175 14 E
Otoskwin →, Canada 104 52 13N 88 6W
Otosquen, Canada 111 53 17N 102 1W
Ōtoyo, Japan 64 33 43N 133 45 E
Otranto, Italy 29 40 9N 18 28 E
Otranto, C. d', Italy 29 40 7N 18 30 E
Otranto, Str. of, Italy 29 40 15N 18 40 E
Otse, S. Africa 96 25 2 S 25 45 E
Otsego, U.S.A. 119 42 27N 85 42W
Ōtsu, Japan 65 35 0N 135 50 E
Ōtsuki, Japan 65 35 36N 138 57 E
Otta, Norway 10 61 46N 9 32 E
Ottapalam, India 51 10 46N 76 23 E
Ottawa, Canada 109 45 27N 75 42W
Ottawa, Ill., U.S.A. 119 41 20N 88 55W
Ottawa, Kans., U.S.A. 120 38 40N 95 6W
Ottawa, Ohio, U.S.A. 119 41 1N 84 3W
Ottawa → = Outaouais →, Canada 107 45 27N 74 8W
Ottawa Is., Canada 103 59 35N 80 10W
Ottélé, Cameroon 91 3 38N 11 19 E
Ottenby, Sweden 11 56 15N 16 24 E
Otter L., Canada 111 55 35N 104 39W
Otter Rapids, Ont., Canada 104 50 11N 81 39W
Otter Rapids, Sask., Canada 111 55 38N 104 44W
Otterbein, U.S.A. 119 40 29N 87 6W
Otterberg, W. Germany 31 49 30N 7 46 E
Otterndorf, W. Germany 30 53 47N 8 52 E
Otterup, Denmark 11 55 30N 10 22 E
Otterville, Canada 108 42 55N 80 36W
Otterville, U.S.A. 118 38 42N 93 0W
Otteys Cr. →, Australia 77 28 45 S 150 33 E
Ottignies, Belgium 17 50 40N 4 33 E
Otto Beit Bridge, Zambia 93 15 59 S 28 56 E
Ottosdal, S. Africa 96 26 46 S 25 59 E
Ottoshoop, S. Africa 96 25 45 S 25 58 E
Ottoville, U.S.A. 119 40 57N 84 22W
Ottsjö, Sweden 10 63 13N 13 2 E
Ottumwa, U.S.A. 118 41 0N 92 25W
Otu, Nigeria 91 8 14N 3 22 E
Otukpa, Nigeria 91 7 9N 7 41 E
Oturkpo, Nigeria 91 7 16N 8 8 E
Otway, B., Chile 142 53 30 S 74 0W
Otway, C., Australia 74 38 52 S 143 30 E
Otwock, Poland 32 52 5N 21 20 E
Ötz, Austria 31 47 13N 10 53 E
Ötz →, Austria 31 47 14N 10 50 E
Ötztaler Alpen, Austria 31 46 45N 11 0 E
Ou →, Laos 54 20 4N 102 13 E
Ou Neua, Laos 54 22 18N 101 48 E
Ouachita →, U.S.A. 121 31 38N 91 49W
Ouachita, L., U.S.A. 121 34 40N 93 25W
Ouachita Mts., U.S.A. 121 34 50N 94 30W
Ouaco, N. Cal. 68 20 50 S 164 29 E
Ouadâne, Mauritania 84 20 50N 11 40W
Ouadda, C.A.R. 94 8 15N 22 20 E
Ouagadougou, Burkina Faso 91 12 25N 1 30W
Ouagam, Chad 87 14 22N 14 42 E
Ouahigouya, Burkina Faso 90 13 31N 2 25W
Ouahila, Algeria 84 27 50N 5 0W
Ouahran = Oran, Algeria 85 35 45N 0 39W
Oualâta, Mauritania 90 17 20N 6 55W
Ouallene, Algeria 85 24 41N 1 11 E
Ouanda Djallé, C.A.R. 94 8 55N 22 53 E
Ouandago, C.A.R. 94 7 13N 18 50 E
Ouango, C.A.R. 94 4 19N 22 30 E
Ouarâne, Mauritania 84 21 0N 10 30W
Ouareau, L., Rés., Canada 107 46 17N 74 9W
Ouargla, Algeria 85 31 59N 5 16 E
Ouarkziz, Djebel, Algeria 84 28 50N 8 0W
Ouarzazate, Morocco 84 30 55N 6 50W
Ouasiemsca →, Canada 107 49 0N 72 30W
Ouatagouna, Mali 91 15 11N 0 43 E
Ouatere, C.A.R. 94 5 30N 19 8 E
Oubangi →, Zaïre 94 0 30 S 17 50 E
Oubarakai, O. →, Algeria 85 27 20N 9 0 E
Oubatche, N. Cal. 68 20 26 S 164 39 E
Ouche →, France 19 47 6N 5 16 E
Oud-Beijerland, Neths. 16 51 50N 4 25 E
Oud-Gastel, Neths. 17 51 35N 4 28 E
Oud Turnhout, Belgium 17 51 19N 5 0 E
Ouddorp, Neths. 16 51 50N 3 57 E
Oude-Pekela, Neths. 16 53 6N 7 0 E
Oude Rijn →, Neths. 16 52 12N 4 24 E
Oudega, Neths. 16 53 8N 6 0 E
Oudenaarde, Belgium 17 50 50N 3 37 E
Oudenbosch, Neths. 17 51 35N 4 32 E
Oudenburg, Belgium 17 51 11N 3 1 E
Ouderkerk, Utrecht, Neths. 16 52 18N 4 55 E
Ouderkerk, Zuid-Holland, Neths. 16 51 56N 4 38 E
Oudeschild, Neths. 16 53 2N 4 50 E
Oudewater, Neths. 16 52 2N 4 52 E
Oudkarspel, Neths. 16 52 43N 4 49 E
Oudon, France 18 47 22N 1 19W
Oudtshoorn, S. Africa 96 33 35 S 22 14 E
Oued Zem, Morocco 84 32 52N 6 34W
Ouégoa, N. Cal. 68 20 20 S 164 26 E
Ouellé, Ivory C. 90 7 26N 4 1W
Ouen, I., N. Cal. 68 22 26 S 166 49 E
Ouenza, Algeria 85 35 57N 8 4 E
Ouessa, Burkina Faso 90 11 4N 2 47W
Ouessant, I. d', France 18 48 28N 5 6W
Ouesso, Congo 94 1 37N 16 5 E
Ouest, Pte., Canada 105 49 52N 64 40W
Ouezzane, Morocco 84 34 51N 5 35W
Ouffet, Belgium 17 50 26N 5 28 E
Ouidah, Benin 91 6 25N 2 0 E
Ouistreham, France 18 49 17N 0 18W
Oujda, Morocco 85 34 41N 1 55W
Oujeft, Mauritania 84 20 2N 13 0W
Ould Yenjé, Mauritania 90 15 38N 12 16W
Ouled Djellal, Algeria 85 34 28N 5 2 E
Ouled Naïl, Mts. des, Algeria 85 34 30N 3 30 E
Oulmès, Morocco 84 33 17N 6 0W
Oulu, Finland 8 65 1N 25 29 E
Oulu □, Finland 8 65 10N 27 20 E
Oulujärvi, Finland 8 64 25N 27 15 E
Oulujoki →, Finland 8 65 1N 25 30 E
Oulx, Italy 26 45 2N 6 49 E
Oum Chalouba, Chad 87 15 48N 20 46 E
Oum-el-Bouaghi, Algeria 85 35 55N 7 6 E
Oum el Ksi, Algeria 84 29 4N 6 59W
Oum-er-Rbia, O. →, Morocco 84 33 19N 8 21W
Oumè, Ivory C. 90 6 21N 5 27W
Ounane, Dj., Algeria 85 25 4N 7 19 E
Ounguati, Namibia 96 22 0 S 15 46 E
Ounianga-Kébir, Chad 87 19 4N 20 29 E
Ounianga Sérir, Chad 87 18 54N 20 51 E
Our →, Lux. 17 49 55N 6 5 E
Ouray, U.S.A. 123 38 3N 107 40W
Ourcq →, France 19 49 1N 3 1 E
Oureg, Oued el →, Algeria 85 32 34N 2 10 E
Ourém, Brazil 138 1 33 S 47 6W
Ouricuri, Brazil 138 7 53 S 40 5W
Ourinhos, Brazil 141 23 0 S 49 54W
Ourique, Portugal 23 37 38N 8 16W
Ouro Fino, Brazil 141 22 16 S 46 25W
Ouro Prêto, Brazil 141 20 20 S 43 30W
Ouro Sogui, Senegal 90 15 36N 13 19W
Oursi, Burkina Faso 91 14 41N 0 27W
Ourthe →, Belgium 17 50 29N 5 35 E
Ouse, Australia 72 42 38 S 146 42 E
Ouse →, E. Sussex, U.K. 13 50 43N 0 3 E
Ouse →, N. Yorks., U.K. 12 54 3N 0 7 E
Oust, France 20 42 52N 1 13 E
Oust →, France 18 47 35N 2 6W
Outaouais →, Canada 107 45 27N 74 8W
Outardes, Canada 107 50 20N 69 10W
Outardes →, Canada 107 49 24N 69 30W
Outat Oulad el Haj, Morocco 85 33 22N 3 42W
Outer Hebrides, U.K. 14 57 30N 7 40W
Outer I., Canada 105 51 10N 58 35W
Outes, Spain 22 42 52N 8 55W
Outjo, Namibia 96 20 5 S 16 7 E
Outlook, Canada 111 51 30N 107 0W
Outlook, U.S.A. 120 48 53N 104 46W
Outreau, France 19 50 40N 1 36 E
Ouvèze →, France 21 43 59N 4 51 E
Ouyen, Australia 74 35 1 S 142 22 E
Ouzouer-le-Marché, France 19 47 54N 1 32 E
Ovada, Italy 26 44 39N 8 40 E
Ovalle, Chile 140 30 33 S 71 18W
Ovar, Portugal 22 40 51N 8 40W
Ovejas, Colombia 134 9 32N 75 14W
Ovens, Australia 75 36 35 S 146 46 E
Ovens →, Australia 75 36 2 S 146 12 E
Overdinkel, Neths. 16 52 14N 7 2 E
Overflakkee, Neths. 16 51 44N 4 10 E
Overijse, Belgium 17 50 47N 4 32 E
Overijssel □, Neths. 16 52 25N 6 35 E
Overijsselsch Kanaal →, Neths. 16 52 31N 6 6 E
Overland, U.S.A. 118 38 41N 90 23W
Overpelt, Belgium 17 51 12N 5 20 E
Overton, U.S.A. 125 36 32N 114 31W
Övertorneå, Sweden 8 66 23N 23 38 E
Overum, Sweden 11 58 0N 16 20 E
Ovid, Colo., U.S.A. 120 41 0N 102 17W
Ovid, Mich., U.S.A. 119 43 1N 84 22W
Ovidiopol, U.S.S.R. 38 46 15N 30 30 E
Oviedo, Spain 22 43 25N 5 50W
Oviedo □, Spain 22 43 20N 6 0W
Oviken, Sweden 10 63 0N 14 23 E
Oviksfjällen, Sweden 10 63 0N 13 49 E
Övör Hangay □, Mongolia 60 45 0N 102 30 E
Ovoro, Nigeria 91 5 26N 7 16 E
Ovruch, U.S.S.R. 36 51 25N 28 45 E
Owaka, N.Z. 81 46 27 S 169 40 E
Owando, Congo 94 0 29 S 15 55 E
Owase, Japan 65 34 7N 136 12 E
Owatonna, U.S.A. 120 44 3N 93 10W
Owbeh, Afghan. 47 34 28N 63 10 E
Owego, U.S.A. 117 42 6N 76 17W
Owen Falls, Uganda 92 0 30N 33 5 E
Owen Mt., N.Z. 81 41 35 S 172 33 E
Owen Sound, Canada 108 44 35N 80 55W
Owen Stanley Range, Papua N. G. 69 8 30 S 147 0 E
Owendo, Gabon 94 0 17N 9 30 E
Owens →, U.S.A. 124 36 32N 117 59W
Owens L., U.S.A. 125 36 20N 118 0W
Owensboro, U.S.A. 119 37 40N 87 5W
Owensville, Ind., U.S.A. 119 38 16N 87 41W
Owensville, Mo., U.S.A. 118 38 20N 91 30W
Owenton, U.S.A. 119 38 32N 84 50W
Owerri, Nigeria 91 5 29N 7 0 E
Owhango, N.Z. 80 39 0 S 175 23 E
Owingsville, U.S.A. 119 38 9N 83 46W
Owl →, Canada 111 57 51N 92 44W
Owo, Nigeria 91 7 10N 5 39 E
Owosso, U.S.A. 104 43 0N 84 10W
Owyhee, U.S.A. 122 42 0N 116 3W
Owyhee →, U.S.A. 122 43 46N 117 2W
Owyhee, L., U.S.A. 122 43 40N 117 16W
Ox Mts., Ireland 15 54 6N 9 0W
Oxapampa, Peru 136 10 33 S 75 26W
Oxberg, Sweden 10 61 7N 14 11 E
Oxelösund, Sweden 11 58 43N 17 15 E
Oxford, N.Z. 81 43 18 S 172 11 E
Oxford, U.K. 13 51 45N 1 15W
Oxford, Iowa, U.S.A. 118 41 43N 91 47W
Oxford, Mich., U.S.A. 119 42 49N 83 16W
Oxford, Miss., U.S.A. 121 34 22N 89 30W
Oxford, N.C., U.S.A. 115 36 19N 78 36W
Oxford, Ohio, U.S.A. 119 39 30N 84 40W
Oxford □, U.K. 13 51 45N 1 15W
Oxford L., Canada 111 54 51N 95 37W
Oxley, N.S.W., Australia 74 34 11 S 144 6 E
Oxley, Vic., Australia 75 36 35 S 146 22 E
Oxnard, U.S.A. 125 34 10N 119 14W
Oxus → = Amudarya →, U.S.S.R. 40 43 40N 59 0 E
Oya, Malaysia 56 2 55N 111 55 E
Oyabe, Japan 65 36 47N 136 56 E
Oyama, Japan 65 36 18N 139 48 E
Oyana, Japan 64 32 32N 130 30 E
Oyapock →, Fr. Guiana 135 4 8N 51 40W
Oyem, Gabon 94 1 34N 11 31 E
Oyen, Canada 111 51 22N 110 28W
Öyeren, Norway 10 59 50N 11 15 E

Oykel

Oykel →, *U.K.* **14** 57 55N 4 26W
Oymyakon, *U.S.S.R.* **41** 63 25N 142 44 E
Oyo, *Nigeria* **91** 7 46N 3 56 E
Oyo □, *Nigeria* **91** 8 0N 3 30 E
Oyón, *Peru* **136** 10 37 S 76 47W
Oyonnax, *France* **21** 46 16N 5 40 E
Oyster Bay, *U.S.A.* **117** 40 52N 73 32W
Ozamis, *Phil.* **57** 8 15N 123 50 E
Ozark, *Ala., U.S.A.* **115** 31 29N 85 39W
Ozark, *Ark., U.S.A.* **121** 35 30N 93 50W
Ozark, *Mo., U.S.A.* **121** 37 0N 93 15W
Ozark Plateau, *U.S.A.* **121** 37 20N 91 40W
Ozarks, L. of the, *U.S.A.* **118** 38 10N 92 40W
Ózd, *Hungary* **33** 48 14N 20 15 E
Ozette, L., *U.S.A.* **124** 48 6N 124 38W
Ozieri, *Italy* **28** 40 35N 9 0 E
Ozona, *U.S.A.* **121** 30 43N 101 11W
Ozorków, *Poland* **32** 51 57N 19 16 E
Ozu, *Ehime, Japan* **64** 33 30N 132 33 E
Ozu, *Kumamoto, Japan* **64** 32 52N 130 52 E
Ozuluama, *Mexico* **127** 21 40N 97 50W

P

P.K. le Roux Dam, *S. Africa* **96** 30 4 S 24 40 E
Pa, *Burkina Faso* **90** 11 33N 3 19W
Pa-an, *Burma* **52** 16 51N 97 40 E
Pa Mong Dam, *Thailand* **54** 18 0N 102 22 E
Paagoumène, *N. Cal.* **68** 20 29 S 164 11 E
Paal, *Belgium* **17** 51 2N 5 10 E
Paama, *Vanuatu* **68** 16 28 S 168 14 E
Paar →, *W. Germany* **31** 48 13N 10 59 E
Paarl, *S. Africa* **96** 33 45 S 18 56 E
Paatsi →, *U.S.S.R.* **8** 68 55N 29 0 E
Paauilo, *U.S.A.* **112** 20 3N 155 22W
Pab Hills, *Pakistan* **48** 26 30N 66 45 E
Pabianice, *Poland* **32** 51 40N 19 20 E
Pabna, *Bangla.* **52** 24 1N 89 18 E
Pabo, *Uganda* **92** 3 1N 32 10 E
Pacaás Novos, Serra dos, *Brazil* **137** 10 45 S 64 15W
Pacaipampa, *Peru* **136** 5 35 S 79 39W
Pacaja →, *Brazil* **138** 1 56 S 50 50W
Pacajus, *Brazil* **138** 4 10 S 38 31W
Pacaraima, Sierra, *Venezuela* **135** 4 0N 62 30W
Pacarán, *Peru* **136** 12 50 S 76 3W
Pacaraos, *Peru* **136** 11 12 S 76 42W
Pacasmayo, *Peru* **136** 7 20 S 79 35W
Pacaudière, La, *France* **20** 46 11N 3 52 E
Paceco, *Italy* **28** 37 59N 12 32 E
Pachacamac, *Peru* **136** 12 14 S 77 53W
Pachhar, *India* **48** 24 40N 77 42 E
Pachino, *Italy* **29** 36 43N 15 4 E
Pachitea →, *Peru* **136** 8 46 S 74 33W
Pachiza, *Peru* **136** 7 16 S 76 46W
Pacho, *Colombia* **134** 5 8N 74 10W
Pachora, *India* **50** 20 38N 75 29 E
Pachuca, *Mexico* **127** 20 10N 98 40W
Pacific, *Canada* **110** 54 48N 128 28W
Pacific, *U.S.A.* **118** 38 29N 90 45W
Pacific-Antarctic Basin, *Pac. Oc.* **67** 46 0 S 95 0W
Pacific-Antarctic Ridge, *Pac. Oc.* **67** 43 0 S 115 0W
Pacific Grove, *U.S.A.* **124** 36 38N 121 58W
Pacific Ocean, *Pac. Oc.* **66** 10 0N 140 0W
Pacifica, *U.S.A.* **124** 37 36N 122 30W
Pacitan, *Indonesia* **57** 8 12 S 111 7 E
Packenham, *Canada* **109** 45 22N 76 25W
Packwood, *U.S.A.* **124** 46 36N 121 40W
Pacuí →, *Brazil* **139** 16 46 S 45 1W
Padaido, Kepulauan, *Indonesia* **57** 1 5 S 138 0 E
Padang, *Indonesia* **56** 1 0 S 100 20 E
Padangpanjang, *Indonesia* **56** 0 40 S 100 20 E
Padangsidempuan, *Indonesia* **56** 1 30N 99 15 E
Padatchuang, *Burma* **52** 19 46N 94 48 E
Padauari →, *Brazil* **135** 0 15 S 64 5W
Padborg, *Denmark* **11** 54 49N 9 21 E
Padcaya, *Bolivia* **137** 21 52 S 64 48W
Paddockwood, *Canada* **111** 53 30N 105 30W
Paderborn, *W. Germany* **30** 51 42N 8 44 E
Padilla, *Bolivia* **137** 19 19 S 64 20W
Padloping Island, *Canada* **103** 67 0N 62 50W
Padma →, *Bangla.* **52** 23 22N 90 32 E
Padmanabhapuram, *India* **51** 8 16N 77 17 E
Pádova, *Italy* **27** 45 24N 11 52 E
Padra, *India* **48** 22 15N 73 7 E
Padrauna, *India* **49** 26 54N 83 59 E
Padre I., *U.S.A.* **121** 27 0N 97 20W
Padro, Mte., *France* **21** 42 28N 8 59 E
Padrón, *Spain* **22** 42 41N 8 39W
Padstow, *U.K.* **12** 50 33N 4 57W
Padua = Pádova, *Italy* **27** 45 24N 11 52 E
Paducah, *Ky., U.S.A.* **114** 37 0N 88 40W
Paducah, *Tex., U.S.A.* **121** 34 3N 100 16W
Padul, *Spain* **23** 37 1N 3 38W
Padula, *Italy* **29** 40 20N 15 40 E
Padwa, *India* **50** 18 27N 82 47 E
Paekakariki, *N.Z.* **80** 40 59 S 174 58 E
Paengaroa, *N.Z.* **80** 37 49 S 176 29 E
Paeroa, *N.Z.* **80** 37 23 S 175 41 E
Paesana, *Italy* **26** 44 40N 7 18 E
Pafúri, *Mozam.* **97** 22 28 S 31 17 E
Pag, *Yugoslavia* **27** 44 30N 14 50 E
Paga, *Ghana* **91** 11 1N 1 8W
Pagadian, *Phil.* **57** 7 55N 123 30 E
Pagai Selatan, P., *Indonesia* **56** 3 0 S 100 15 E
Pagai Utara, *Indonesia* **56** 2 35 S 100 0 E
Pagalu = Annobón, *Atl. Oc.* **83** 1 25 S 5 36 E
Pagastikós Kólpos, *Greece* **35** 39 15N 23 0 E
Pagatan, *Indonesia* **56** 3 33 S 115 59 E
Page, *Ariz., U.S.A.* **123** 36 57N 111 27W
Page, *N. Dak., U.S.A.* **120** 47 11N 97 37W
Paglieta, *Italy* **27** 42 10N 14 30 E
Pagny-sur-Moselle, *France* **19** 48 59N 6 0 E
Pago Pago, *Amer. Samoa* **68** 14 16 S 170 43W
Pagosa Springs, *U.S.A.* **123** 37 16N 107 4W
Pagwa River, *Canada* **104** 50 2N 85 14W
Pahala, *U.S.A.* **112** 19 12N 155 25W
Pahang →, *Malaysia* **55** 3 30N 103 9 E
Pahiatua, *N.Z.* **80** 40 27 S 175 50 E
Pahokee, *U.S.A.* **115** 26 50N 80 40W
Pahrump, *U.S.A.* **125** 36 15N 116 0W
Pahute Mesa, *U.S.A.* **124** 37 25N 116 50W
Pai, *Thailand* **54** 19 19N 98 27 E
Paia, *U.S.A.* **112** 20 54N 156 22W
Paicines, *U.S.A.* **124** 36 44N 121 17W
Paide, *U.S.S.R.* **36** 58 57N 25 31 E
Paignton, *U.K.* **13** 50 26N 3 33W
Paiján, *Peru* **136** 7 42 S 79 20W
Päijänne, L., *Finland* **9** 61 30N 25 30 E
Paimbœuf, *France* **18** 47 17N 2 0W
Paimpol, *France* **18** 48 48N 3 4W
Painan, *Indonesia* **56** 1 21 S 100 34 E
Painesville, *U.S.A.* **116** 41 42N 81 18W
Paint Hills = Nouveau Comptoir, *Canada* **104** 53 0N 78 49W
Paint L., *Canada* **111** 55 28N 97 57W
Paint Rock, *U.S.A.* **121** 31 30N 99 56W
Painted Desert, *U.S.A.* **123** 36 0N 111 30W
Paintsville, *U.S.A.* **114** 37 50N 82 50W
Pais Vasco □, *Spain* **24** 43 0N 2 30W
Paisley, *Canada* **108** 44 18N 81 16W
Paisley, *U.K.* **14** 55 51N 4 27W
Paisley, *U.S.A.* **122** 42 43N 120 40W
Païta, *N. Cal.* **68** 22 8 S 166 22 E
Paita, *Peru* **136** 5 11 S 81 9W
Paiva →, *Portugal* **22** 41 4N 8 16W
Paizhou, *China* **59** 30 12N 113 55 E
Pajares, *Spain* **22** 43 1N 5 46W
Pajares, Puerto de, *Spain* **22** 43 0N 5 46W
Pak Lay, *Laos* **54** 18 15N 101 27 E
Pak Phanang, *Thailand* **55** 8 21N 100 12 E
Pak Sane, *Laos* **54** 18 22N 103 39 E
Pak Song, *Laos* **54** 15 11N 106 14 E
Pak Suong, *Laos* **54** 19 58N 102 15 E
Pakala, *India* **51** 13 29N 79 8 E
Pakaraima Mts., *Guyana* **135** 6 0N 60 0W
Pakenham, *Australia* **74** 38 6 S 145 30 E
Pakenham, *Canada* **106** 45 18N 76 18W
Pakistan ■, *Asia* **47** 30 0N 70 0 E
Pakistan, East = Bangladesh ■, *Asia* **52** 24 0N 90 0 E
Pakkading, *Laos* **54** 18 19N 103 59 E
Pakokku, *Burma* **52** 21 20N 95 0 E
Pakpattan, *Pakistan* **48** 30 25N 73 27 E
Pakrac, *Yugoslavia* **33** 45 27N 17 12 E
Paks, *Hungary* **33** 46 38N 18 55 E
Pakse, *Laos* **54** 15 5N 105 52 E
Paktīā □, *Afghan.* **47** 33 0N 69 15 E
Pakwach, *Uganda* **92** 2 28N 31 27 E
Pala, *Chad* **87** 9 25N 15 5 E
Pala, *U.S.A.* **125** 33 22N 117 5W
Pala, *Zaïre* **92** 6 45 S 29 30 E
Palabek, *Uganda* **92** 3 22N 32 33 E
Palacios, *U.S.A.* **121** 28 44N 96 12W
Palafrugell, *Spain* **24** 41 55N 3 10 E
Palagiano, *Italy* **29** 40 35N 17 0 E
Palagonía, *Italy* **29** 37 20N 14 43 E
Palagruža, *Yugoslavia* **27** 42 24N 16 15 E
Palaiokhóra, *Greece* **35** 35 16N 23 39 E
Palais, Le, *France* **18** 47 20N 3 10W
Palakol, *India* **51** 16 31N 81 46 E
Palam, *India* **50** 19 0N 77 0 E
Palamás, *Greece* **35** 39 26N 22 4 E
Palamós, *Spain* **24** 41 50N 3 10 E
Palampur, *India* **48** 32 10N 76 30 E
Palana, *Australia* **72** 39 45 S 147 55 E
Palana, *U.S.S.R.* **41** 59 10N 159 59 E
Palanan, *Phil.* **57** 17 8N 122 29 E
Palanan Pt., *Phil.* **57** 17 17N 122 30 E
Palandri, *Pakistan* **49** 33 42N 73 40 E
Palangkaraya, *Indonesia* **56** 2 16 S 113 56 E
Palani, *India* **51** 10 30N 77 30 E
Palani Hills, *India* **51** 10 14N 77 33 E
Palanpur, *India* **48** 24 10N 72 25 E
Palapye, *Botswana* **96** 22 30 S 27 7 E
Palar →, *India* **51** 12 27N 80 13 E
Palas, *Pakistan* **49** 35 4N 73 14 E
Palatine, *U.S.A.* **119** 42 7N 88 3W
Palatka, *U.S.A.* **115** 29 40N 81 40W
Palatka, *U.S.S.R.* **41** 60 6N 150 54 E
Palawan, *Phil.* **56** 9 30N 118 30 E
Palayankottai, *India* **51** 8 45N 77 45 E
Palazzo, Pte., *France* **21** 42 28N 8 30 E
Palazzo San Gervásio, *Italy* **29** 40 53N 15 58 E
Palazzolo Acreide, *Italy* **29** 37 4N 14 54 E
Palca, *Chile* **136** 19 7 S 69 9W
Paldiski, *U.S.S.R.* **36** 59 23N 24 9 E
Palel, *India* **52** 24 27N 94 2 E
Paleleh, *Indonesia* **57** 1 10N 121 50 E
Palembang, *Indonesia* **56** 3 0 S 104 50 E
Palen Creek, *Australia* **77** 28 17 S 152 48 E
Palena →, *Chile* **142** 43 50 S 73 50W
Palena, L., *Chile* **142** 43 55 S 71 40W
Palencia, *Spain* **22** 42 1N 4 34W
Palencia □, *Spain* **22** 42 31N 4 33W
Palermo, *Colombia* **134** 2 54N 75 26W
Palermo, *Italy* **28** 38 8N 13 20 E
Palermo, *U.S.A.* **122** 39 30N 121 37W
Palestine, *Asia* **44** 32 0N 35 0 E
Palestine, *U.S.A.* **121** 31 42N 95 35W
Palestrina, *Italy* **28** 41 50N 12 52 E
Paletwa, *Burma* **52** 21 10N 92 50 E
Palghat, *India* **51** 10 46N 76 42 E
Palgrave, Mt., *Australia* **78** 23 22 S 115 58 E
Pali, *India* **48** 25 50N 73 20 E
Palinuro, C., *Italy* **29** 40 1N 15 14 E
Palisade, *U.S.A.* **120** 40 21N 101 10W
Paliseul, *Belgium* **17** 49 54N 5 8 E
Palitana, *India* **48** 21 32N 71 49 E
Palizada, *Mexico* **127** 18 18N 92 8W
Palizzi, *Italy* **29** 37 58N 15 59 E
Palk Bay, *Asia* **51** 9 30N 79 15 E
Palk Strait, *Asia* **51** 10 0N 79 45 E
Palkonda, *India* **50** 18 36N 83 48 E
Palkonda Ra., *India* **51** 13 50N 79 20 E
Palla Road = Dinokwe, *Botswana* **96** 23 29 S 26 37 E
Pallamallawa, *Australia* **77** 29 29 S 150 10 E
Pallanza = Verbánia, *Italy* **26** 45 56N 8 43 E
Pallasovka, *U.S.S.R.* **37** 50 4N 47 0 E
Palleru →, *India* **50** 16 45N 80 2 E
Pallinup, *Australia* **79** 34 0 S 117 55 E
Pallisa, *Uganda* **92** 1 12N 33 43 E
Palliser, C., *N.Z.* **80** 41 37 S 175 14 E
Palliser Bay, *N.Z.* **80** 41 26 S 175 5 E
Pallu, *India* **48** 28 59N 74 14 E
Palm Beach, *U.S.A.* **115** 26 46N 80 0W
Palm Desert, *U.S.A.* **125** 33 43N 116 22W
Palm Is., *Australia* **72** 18 40 S 146 35 E
Palm Springs, *U.S.A.* **125** 33 51N 116 35W
Palma, *Mozam.* **93** 10 46 S 40 29 E
Palma →, *Brazil* **139** 12 33 S 47 52W
Palma, B. de, *Spain* **25** 39 30N 2 39 E
Palma, La, *Canary Is.* **25** 28 40N 17 50W
Palma, La, *Panama* **128** 8 15N 78 0W
Palma, La, *Spain* **23** 37 21N 6 38W
Palma de Mallorca, *Spain* **24** 39 35N 2 39 E
Palma del Río, *Spain* **23** 37 43N 5 17W
Palma di Montechiaro, *Italy* **28** 37 12N 13 46 E
Palma Soriano, *Cuba* **128** 20 15N 76 0W
Palmahim, *Israel* **44** 31 56N 34 44 E
Palmanova, *Italy* **27** 45 54N 13 18 E
Palmares, *Brazil* **138** 8 41 S 35 28W
Palmarito, *Venezuela* **134** 7 37N 70 10W
Palmarola, *Italy* **28** 40 57N 12 50 E
Palmarolle, *Canada* **106** 48 40N 79 12W
Palmas, *Brazil* **141** 26 29 S 52 0W
Palmas, C., *Liberia* **90** 4 27N 7 46W
Pálmas, G. di, *Italy* **28** 39 0N 8 30 E
Palmas de Monte Alto, *Brazil* **139** 14 16 S 43 10W
Palmdale, *U.S.A.* **125** 34 36N 118 7W
Palmeira, *Brazil* **139** 25 25 S 50 0W
Palmeira dos Índios, *Brazil* **138** 9 25 S 36 37W
Palmeirais, *Brazil* **138** 6 0 S 43 0W
Palmeiras →, *Brazil* **139** 12 22 S 47 8W
Palmeirinhas, Pta. das, *Angola* **95** 9 2 S 12 57 E
Palmela, *Portugal* **23** 38 32N 8 57W
Palmelo, *Brazil* **139** 17 20 S 48 27W
Palmer, *U.S.A.* **102** 61 35N 149 10W
Palmer →, *Australia* **72** 15 34 S 142 26 E
Palmer Arch., *Antarctica* **143** 64 15 S 65 0W
Palmer Lake, *U.S.A.* **120** 39 10N 104 52W
Palmer Land, *Antarctica* **143** 73 0 S 60 0W
Palmerston, *Canada* **108** 43 50N 80 51W
Palmerston North, *N.Z.* **81** 40 21 S 175 39 E
Palmerton, *U.S.A.* **117** 40 47N 75 36W
Palmetto, *U.S.A.* **115** 27 33N 82 33W
Palmi, *Italy* **29** 38 21N 15 51 E
Palmira, *Argentina* **140** 32 59 S 68 34W
Palmira, *Colombia* **134** 3 32N 76 16W
Palmyra = Tudmur, *Syria* **46** 34 36N 38 15 E
Palmyra, *Ill., U.S.A.* **118** 39 26N 90 0W
Palmyra, *Mo., U.S.A.* **118** 39 45N 91 30W
Palmyra, *N.Y., U.S.A.* **116** 43 5N 77 18W
Palmyra, *Wis., U.S.A.* **119** 42 52N 88 36W
Palmyra Is., *Pac. Oc.* **67** 5 52N 162 5W
Palo Alto, *U.S.A.* **124** 37 25N 122 8W
Palo del Colle, *Italy* **29** 41 4N 16 43 E
Palo Verde, *U.S.A.* **125** 33 26N 114 45W
Paloma, La, *Chile* **140** 30 35 S 71 0W
Palombara Sabina, *Italy* **27** 42 4N 12 45 E
Palopo, *Indonesia* **57** 3 0 S 120 16 E
Palos, C. de, *Spain* **25** 37 38N 0 40W
Palos Verdes, *U.S.A.* **125** 33 48N 118 23W
Palos Verdes, Pt., *U.S.A.* **125** 33 43N 118 26W
Palouse, *U.S.A.* **122** 46 59N 117 5W
Palpa, *Peru* **136** 14 30 S 75 15W
Palparara, *Australia* **72** 24 47 S 141 28 E
Pålsboda, *Sweden* **11** 59 3N 15 22 E
Palu, *Indonesia* **57** 1 0 S 119 52 E
Palu, *Turkey* **46** 38 45N 40 0 E
Paluan, *Phil.* **57** 13 26N 120 29 E
Palwal, *India* **48** 28 8N 77 19 E
Pama, *Burkina Faso* **91** 11 19N 0 44 E
Pamanukan, *Indonesia* **57** 6 16 S 107 49 E
Pamban I., *India* **51** 9 15N 79 20 E
Pambula, *Australia* **75** 36 55 S 149 53 E
Pamekasan, *Indonesia* **57** 7 10 S 113 28 E
Pamiers, *France* **20** 43 7N 1 39 E
Pamirs, *U.S.S.R.* **40** 37 40N 73 0 E
Pamlico →, *U.S.A.* **115** 35 25N 76 30W
Pamlico Sd., *U.S.A.* **115** 35 20N 76 0W
Pampa, *U.S.A.* **121** 35 35N 100 58W
Pampa, La □, *Argentina* **140** 36 50 S 66 0W
Pampa de Agma, *Argentina* **142** 43 45 S 69 40W
Pampa de las Salinas, *Argentina* **140** 32 1 S 66 58W
Pampa Grande, *Bolivia* **137** 18 5 S 64 6W
Pampa Hermosa, *Peru* **136** 7 7 S 75 4W
Pampanua, *Indonesia* **57** 4 16 S 120 8 E
Pamparato, *Italy* **26** 44 16N 7 54 E
Pampas, *Argentina* **140** 35 0 S 63 0W
Pampas, *Peru* **136** 12 20 S 74 50W
Pampas →, *Peru* **136** 13 24 S 73 12W
Pamplona, *Colombia* **134** 7 23N 72 39W
Pamplona, *Spain* **24** 42 48N 1 38W
Pampoenpoort, *S. Africa* **96** 31 3 S 22 40 E
Pan Xian, *China* **58** 25 46N 104 38 E
Pana, *U.S.A.* **118** 39 25N 89 10W
Panaca, *U.S.A.* **123** 37 51N 114 23W
Panache, L., *Canada* **108** 46 15N 81 20W
Panagyurishte, *Bulgaria* **34** 42 30N 24 15 E
Panaitan, *Indonesia* **57** 6 36 S 105 12 E
Panaji, *India* **51** 15 25N 73 50 E
Panamá, *Panama* **128** 9 0N 79 25W
Panama ■, *Cent. Amer.* **128** 8 48N 79 55W
Panamá, G. de, *Panama* **128** 8 4N 79 20W
Panama Canal, *Panama* **128** 9 10N 79 37W
Panama City, *U.S.A.* **115** 30 10N 85 41W
Panamint Range, *U.S.A.* **125** 36 20N 117 20W
Panamint Ra., *U.S.A.* **123** 36 30N 117 20W
Panamint Springs, *U.S.A.* **125** 36 20N 117 28W
Panão, *Peru* **136** 9 55 S 75 55W
Panare, *Thailand* **55** 6 51N 101 30 E
Panarea, *Italy* **29** 38 38N 15 3 E
Panaro →, *Italy* **26** 44 55N 11 25 E
Panarukan, *Indonesia* **57** 7 42 S 113 56 E
Panay, *Phil.* **57** 11 10N 122 30 E
Panay, G., *Phil.* **57** 11 0N 122 30 E
Pancake Ra., *U.S.A.* **123** 38 30N 116 0W
Pančevo, *Yugoslavia* **33** 44 52N 20 41 E
Pancorbo, Paso, *Spain* **24** 42 32N 3 5W
Pandan, *Phil.* **57** 11 45N 122 10 E
Pandegelang, *Indonesia* **57** 6 25 S 106 0 E
Pandharpur, *India* **50** 17 41N 75 20 E
Pandhurna, *India* **50** 21 36N 78 35 E
Pandilla, *Spain* **24** 41 32N 3 43W
Pando, *Uruguay* **141** 34 44 S 56 0W
Pando □, *Bolivia* **136** 11 20 S 67 40W
Pando, L. = Hope, L., *Australia* **73** 28 24 S 139 18 E
Pandu, *Zaïre* **94** 4 59N 19 16 E
Panevezys, *U.S.S.R.* **36** 55 42N 24 25 E
Panfilov, *U.S.S.R.* **40** 44 10N 80 0 E
Panfilovo, *U.S.S.R.* **37** 50 25N 42 46 E
Panga, *Zaïre* **92** 1 52N 26 18 E
Pangala, *Congo* **94** 4 1 S 13 52 E
Pangalanes, Canal des, *Madag.* **97** 22 48 S 47 50 E
Pangani, *Tanzania* **92** 5 25 S 38 58 E
Pangani □, *Tanzania* **92** 5 25 S 39 0 E
Pangani →, *Tanzania* **92** 5 26 S 38 58 E
Pange Creek, *Australia* **76** 31 45 S 147 8 E
Pangfou = Bengbu, *China* **61** 32 58N 117 20 E
Pangil, *Zaïre* **92** 3 10 S 26 35 E
Pangkah, Tanjung, *Indonesia* **57** 6 51 S 112 33 E
Pangkai, *Burma* **52** 22 40N 98 40 E
Pangkajene, *Indonesia* **57** 4 46 S 119 34 E
Pangkalanbrandan, *Indonesia* **56** 4 1N 98 20 E
Pangkalanbuun, *Indonesia* **56** 2 41 S 111 37 E
Pangkalansusu, *Indonesia* **56** 4 2N 98 13 E
Pangkalpinang, *Indonesia* **56** 2 0 S 106 0 E
Pangkoh, *Indonesia* **56** 3 5 S 114 8 E
Pangnirtung, *Canada* **103** 66 8N 65 54W
Pangrango, *Indonesia* **57** 6 46 S 107 1 E
Pangsau Pass, *Burma* **52** 27 15N 96 10 E
Pangtara, *Burma* **52** 20 57N 96 40 E
Panguipulli, *Chile* **142** 39 38 S 72 20W
Panguitch, *U.S.A.* **123** 37 52N 112 30W
Pangutaran Group, *Phil.* **57** 6 18N 120 34 E
Panhandle, *U.S.A.* **121** 35 23N 101 23W
Pani Mines, *India* **48** 22 29N 73 50 E
Pania-Mutombo, *Zaïre* **92** 5 11 S 23 51 E
Panié, Mt., *N. Cal.* **68** 20 36 S 164 46 E
Panipat, *India* **48** 29 25N 77 2 E

Pavlograd

Panitya, Australia .... 74 35 15 S 141 0 E
Panjal Range, India .. 48 32 30N 76 50 E
Panjgur, Pakistan .... 47 27 0N 64 5 E
Panjim = Panaji, India 51 15 25N 73 50 E
Panjinad Barrage,
Pakistan .... 47 29 22N 71 15 E
Panjwai, Afghan. ..... 48 31 26N 65 27 E
Pankshin, Nigeria .... 91 9 16N 9 25 E
Panmure, Australia ... 74 38 20 S 142 43 E
Panna, India .... 49 24 40N 80 15 E
Panna Hills, India .... 49 24 40N 81 15 E
Panora, U.S.A. 118 41 41N 94 22W
Panorama, Brazil ..... 141 21 21 S 51 51W
Panruti, India .... 51 11 46N 79 35 E
Panshan, China ...... 61 41 3N 122 2 E
Panshi, China .... 61 42 58N 126 5 E
Pantar, Indonesia ..... 57 8 28 S 124 10 E
Pantelleria, Italy ..... 28 36 52N 12 0 E
Pantha, Burma .... 52 23 55N 94 35 E
Pantin Sakan, Burma . 52 18 38N 97 33 E
Pantón, Spain 22 42 31N 7 37W
Panton Hill, Australia . 74 37 39 S 145 14 E
Pánuco, Mexico 127 22 0N 98 15W
Panyam, Nigeria ..... 91 9 27N 9 8 E
Panyu, China .... 59 22 51N 113 20 E
Pao →, Anzoátegui,
Venezuela 135 8 6N 64 17W
Pao →, Apure,
Venezuela 134 8 33N 68 1W
Páola, Italy .... 29 39 21N 16 2 E
Paola, U.S.A. 120 38 36N 94 50W
Paoli, U.S.A. 119 38 33N 86 28W
Paonia, U.S.A. 123 38 56N 107 37W
Paoting = Baoding,
China .... 60 38 50N 115 28 E
Paot'ou = Baotou,
China .... 60 40 32N 110 2 E
Paoua, C.A.R. .... 94 7 9N 16 20 E
Pápa, Hungary .... 33 47 22N 17 30 E
Papagayo →, Mexico . 127 16 36N 99 43W
Papagayo, G. de,
Costa Rica 128 10 30N 85 50W
Papagni →, India .... 51 15 35N 77 45 E
Papakura, N.Z. ...... 80 37 4 S 174 59 E
Papantla, Mexico 127 20 30N 97 30W
Papar, Malaysia ...... 56 5 45N 116 0 E
Papara, Tahiti .... 68 17 45 S 149 21W
Paparoa, N.Z. .... 81 36 6 S 174 16 E
Paparoa Range, N.Z. . 81 42 5 S 171 35 E
Pápas, Ákra, Greece .. 35 38 13N 21 20 E
Papatoetoe, N.Z. ..... 80 36 59 S 174 51 E
Papeete, Tahiti .... 68 17 32 S 149 34W
Papenburg,
W. Germany .... 30 53 7N 7 25 E
Papenoo, Tahiti ...... 68 17 30 S 149 25W
Papetoai, Tahiti ...... 68 17 29 S 149 52W
Papien Chiang =
Da →, Vietnam .... 54 21 15N 105 20 E
Papigochic →, Mexico 126 29 9N 109 40W
Papineau-Labelle, Parc
Prov., Canada 106 46 10N 75 15W
Papineauville, Canada 106 45 37N 75 1W
Paposo, Chile .... 140 25 0 S 70 30W
Papua, Gulf of,
Papua N. G. .... 69 9 0 S 144 50 E
Papua New Guinea ■,
Oceania .... 69 8 0 S 145 0 E
Papuča, Yugoslavia ... 27 44 22N 15 30 E
Papudo, Chile .... 140 32 29 S 71 27W
Papuk, Yugoslavia .... 33 45 30N 17 30 E
Papun, Burma .... 52 18 0N 97 30 E
Pará = Belém, Brazil . 138 1 20 S 48 30W
Pará □, Brazil .... 137 3 20 S 52 0W
Pará □, Surinam 135 5 20N 55 5W
Parábita, Italy .... 29 40 3N 18 8 E
Paraburdoo, Australia . 78 23 14 S 117 32 E
Paracas, Pen., Peru ... 136 13 53 S 76 20W
Paracatu, Brazil ...... 139 17 10 S 46 50W
Paracatu →, Brazil ... 139 16 30 S 45 4W
Parachilna, Australia .. 73 31 10 S 138 21 E
Parachinar, Pakistan .. 48 33 55N 70 5 E
Paraćin, Yugoslavia ... 33 43 54N 21 27 E
Paracuru, Brazil ...... 138 3 24 S 39 4W
Parada, Punta, Peru .. 136 15 22 S 75 11W
Paradas, Spain 23 37 18N 5 29W
Paradela, Spain 22 42 44N 7 37W
Paradip, India .... 50 20 15N 86 35 E
Paradis, Canada 106 48 15N 76 35W
Paradise, Calif., U.S.A. 124 39 46N 121 37W
Paradise, Mont.,
U.S.A. 122 47 27N 114 17W
Paradise, Nev., U.S.A. 125 36 4N 115 7W
Paradise →, Canada . 105 53 27N 57 19W
Paradise Valley, U.S.A. 122 41 30N 117 28W
Parado, Indonesia .... 57 8 42 S 118 30 E
Paragould, U.S.A. 121 36 5N 90 30W
Paraguá →, Bolivia .. 137 13 34 S 61 53W
Paragua →, Venezuela 135 6 55N 62 55W
Paragua, La, Venezuela 135 6 50N 63 20W
Paraguaçu →, Brazil . 139 12 45 S 38 54W
Paraguaçu Paulista,
Brazil .... 141 22 22 S 50 35W
Paraguaipoa, Venezuela 134 11 21N 71 57W
Paraguaná, Pen. de,
Venezuela 134 12 0N 70 0W
Paraguarí, Paraguay .. 140 25 36 S 57 0W
Paraguarí □, Paraguay 140 26 0 S 57 10W
Paraguay ■, S. Amer. 140 23 0 S 57 0W
Paraguay →, Paraguay 140 27 18 S 58 38W
Paraíba = João Pessoa,
Brazil .... 138 7 10 S 34 52W
Paraíba □, Brazil .... 138 7 0 S 36 0W
Paraíba do Sul →,
Brazil .... 139 21 37 S 41 3W
Parainen, Finland .... 9 60 18N 22 18 E
Paraiso, Mexico 127 18 24N 93 14W
Parakhino Paddubye,
U.S.S.R. .... 36 58 26N 33 10 E
Parakou, Benin ...... 91 9 25N 2 40 E
Paramakkudi, India ... 51 9 31N 78 39 E
Paramaribo, Surinam . 135 5 50N 55 10W
Parambu, Brazil ...... 138 6 13 S 40 43W
Paramillo, Nudo del,
Colombia 134 7 4N 75 55W
Paramirim, Brazil .... 139 13 26 S 42 15W
Paramirim →, Brazil . 139 11 34 S 43 18W
Paramithiá, Greece ... 35 39 30N 20 35 E
Paramushir, Ostrov,
U.S.S.R. .... 41 50 24N 156 0 E
Paran →, Israel ...... 44 30 20N 35 10 E
Paraná, Argentina .... 140 31 45 S 60 30W
Paranã, Brazil .... 139 12 30 S 47 48W
Paraná □, Brazil ..... 141 24 30 S 51 0W
Paraná →, Argentina . 140 33 43 S 59 15W
Paranaguá, Brazil .... 141 25 30 S 48 30W
Paranaíba →, Brazil . 139 20 6 S 51 4W
Paranapanema →,
Brazil .... 141 22 40 S 53 9W
Paranapiacaba, Serra
do, Brazil .... 141 24 31 S 48 35W
Paranavaí, Brazil ..... 141 23 4 S 52 56W
Parang, Jolo, Phil. ... 57 5 55N 120 54 E
Parang, Mindanao,
Phil. .... 57 7 23N 124 16 E
Parangaba, Brazil .... 138 3 45 S 38 33W
Parangippettai, India . 51 11 30N 79 38 E
Paraparauma, N.Z. ... 80 40 57 S 175 3 E
Parapóla, Greece ..... 35 36 55N 23 27 E
Paraspóri, Ákra, Greece 35 35 55N 27 15 E
Paratinga, Brazil ..... 139 12 40 S 43 10W
Paratoo, Australia .... 73 32 42 S 139 40 E
Parattah, Australia ... 72 42 22 S 147 23 E
Paraúna, Brazil ...... 139 16 55 S 50 26W
Paray-le-Monial, France 21 46 27N 4 7 E
Parbati →, India ..... 48 25 50N 76 30 E
Parbatipur, Bangla. ... 52 25 39N 88 55 E
Parbhani, India ...... 50 19 8N 76 52 E
Parchim, E. Germany . 30 53 25N 11 50 E
Parczew, Poland ..... 32 51 40N 22 52 E
Pardes Hanna, Israel .. 44 32 28N 34 57 E
Pardilla, Spain 22 41 33N 3 43W
Pardo →, Bahia, Brazil 139 15 40 S 39 0W
Pardo →,
Mato Grosso, Brazil 141 21 46 S 52 9W
Pardo →,
Minas Gerais, Brazil 139 15 48 S 44 48W
Pardo →, São Paulo,
Brazil .... 139 20 10 S 48 38W
Pardubice, Czech. .... 32 50 3N 15 45 E
Pare, Indonesia ...... 57 7 43 S 112 12 E
Pare □, Tanzania .... 92 4 10 S 38 0 E
Pare Mts., Tanzania .. 92 4 0 S 37 45 E
Parecis, Serra dos,
Brazil .... 137 13 0 S 60 0W
Paredes de Nava, Spain 22 42 9N 4 42W
Parelhas, Brazil ...... 138 6 41 S 36 39W
Paren, U.S.S.R. ...... 41 62 30N 163 15 E
Parengarenga Harbour,
N.Z. .... 80 34 31 S 173 0 E
Parent, Canada 106 47 55N 74 35W
Parent, L., Canada ... 106 48 31N 77 1W
Parentis-en-Born,
France 20 44 21N 1 4W
Parepare, Indonesia .. 57 4 0 S 119 40 E
Parfino, U.S.S.R. .... 36 57 59N 31 34 E
Parham, Canada 109 44 39N 76 43W
Paria, G. de, Venezuela 134 10 20N 62 0W
Paria, Pen. de,
Venezuela 135 10 50N 62 30W
Pariaguán, Venezuela . 135 8 51N 64 34W
Pariaman, Indonesia .. 56 0 47 S 100 11 E
Paricatuba, Brazil .... 135 4 26 S 61 53W
Paricutín, Cerro,
Mexico 126 19 28N 102 15W
Parigi, Java, Indonesia 57 7 42 S 108 29 E
Parigi, Sulawesi,
Indonesia .... 57 0 50 S 120 5 E
Parika, Guyana 135 6 50N 58 20W
Parima, Serra, Brazil . 135 2 30N 64 0W
Parinari, Peru .... 136 4 35 S 74 25W
Parîng, Romania ..... 34 45 20N 23 37 E
Parintins, Brazil ..... 135 2 40 S 56 50W
Paris, Canada 108 43 12N 80 25W
Paris, France .... 19 48 50N 2 20 E
Paris, Idaho, U.S.A. .. 122 42 13N 111 30W
Paris, Ill., U.S.A. 119 39 36N 87 42W
Paris, Ky., U.S.A. 119 38 12N 84 12W
Paris, Mo., U.S.A. 118 39 29N 92 0W
Paris, Tenn., U.S.A. .. 115 36 20N 88 20W
Paris, Tex., U.S.A. ... 121 33 40N 95 30W
Paris, Ville de □,
France .... 19 48 50N 2 20 E
Parish, U.S.A. 117 43 24N 76 9W
Pariti, Indonesia ..... 57 10 15 S 123 45 E
Park, U.S.A. 124 48 45N 122 18W
Park City, U.S.A. 122 40 42N 111 35W
Park Falls, U.S.A. 120 45 58N 90 27W
Park Forest, U.S.A. .. 119 41 29N 87 40W
Park Range, U.S.A. .. 122 40 0N 106 30W
Park Rapids, U.S.A. .. 120 46 56N 95 0W
Park Ridge, U.S.A. ... 119 42 2N 87 51W
Park River, U.S.A. ... 120 48 25N 97 43W
Park Rynie, S. Africa . 97 30 25 S 30 45 E
Parker, Ariz., U.S.A. . 125 34 8N 114 16W
Parker, S. Dak.,
U.S.A. 120 43 25N 97 7W
Parker Dam, U.S.A. .. 125 34 13N 114 5W
Parkersburg, Iowa,
U.S.A. 118 42 35N 92 47W
Parkersburg, W. Va.,
U.S.A. 114 39 18N 81 31W
Parkerview, Canada .. 111 51 21N 103 18W
Parkes, Australia ..... 76 33 9 S 148 11 E
Parkfield, U.S.A. 124 35 54N 120 26W
Parkhill, Canada 108 43 15N 81 38W
Parkland, U.S.A. 124 47 9N 122 26W
Parkside, Canada 111 53 10N 106 33W
Parkston, U.S.A. 120 43 25N 98 0W
Parksville, Canada 110 49 20N 124 21W
Parkville, Australia ... 77 31 58 S 150 53 E
Parlakimidi, India .... 50 18 45N 84 5 E
Parli, India .... 50 18 50N 76 35 E
Parma, Italy .... 26 44 50N 10 20 E
Parma, Idaho, U.S.A. 122 43 49N 116 59W
Parma, Ohio, U.S.A. . 116 41 25N 81 42W
Parma →, Italy ...... 26 44 56N 10 26 E
Parnaguá, Brazil ..... 138 10 10 S 44 38W
Parnaíba, Piauí, Brazil 138 2 54 S 41 47W
Parnaíba, São Paulo,
Brazil .... 137 19 34 S 51 14W
Parnaíba →, Brazil .. 138 3 0 S 41 50W
Parnamirim, Brazil ... 138 8 5 S 39 34W
Parnarama, Brazil .... 138 5 31 S 43 6W
Parnassós, Greece .... 35 38 35N 22 30 E
Parnassus, N.Z. ..... 81 42 42 S 173 23 E
Párnis, Greece .... 35 38 14N 23 45 E
Párnon Óros, Greece . 35 37 15N 22 45 E
Pärnu, U.S.S.R. ...... 36 58 28N 24 33 E
Parola, India .... 50 20 47N 75 7 E
Paroo →, Australia .. 73 31 28 S 143 32 E
Páros, Greece .... 35 37 5N 25 12 E
Parowan, U.S.A. 123 37 54N 112 56W
Parpaillon, France .... 21 44 30N 6 40 E
Parral, Chile .... 140 36 10 S 71 52W
Parramatta, Australia . 76 33 48 S 151 1 E
Parras, Mexico 126 25 30N 102 20W
Parrett →, U.K. 13 51 7N 2 58W
Parris I., U.S.A. 115 32 20N 80 30W
Parrsboro, Canada ... 105 45 30N 64 25W
Parry Is., Canada 144 77 0N 110 0W
Parry Sound, Canada . 108 45 20N 80 0W
Parsberg, W. Germany 31 49 10N 11 43 E
Parshall, U.S.A. 120 47 56N 102 11W
Parsnip →, Canada .. 110 55 10N 123 2W
Parsons, U.S.A. 121 37 20N 95 17W
Parsons Ra., Australia 72 13 30 S 135 15 E
Partabpur, India ..... 50 20 0N 80 42 E
Partanna, Italy .... 28 37 43N 12 51 E
Parthenay, France 18 46 38N 0 16W
Partinico, Italy .... 28 38 3N 13 6 E
Partur, India .... 50 19 40N 76 14 E
Paru →, Brazil ...... 135 1 33 S 52 38W
Parú →, Venezuela .. 134 4 20N 66 27W
Paru de Oeste →,
Brazil 135 1 30N 56 0W
Parucito →, Venezuela 134 5 18N 65 59W
Parur, India .... 51 10 13N 76 14 E
Paruro, Peru .... 136 13 45 S 71 50W
Parvān □, Afghan. ... 47 35 0N 69 0 E
Parvatipuram, India .. 50 18 50N 83 25 E
Parys, S. Africa ...... 96 26 52 S 27 29 E
Pas-de-Calais □, France 19 50 30N 2 10 E
Pasadena, Calif.,
U.S.A. 125 34 5N 118 9W
Pasadena, Tex., U.S.A. 121 29 45N 95 14W
Pasaje, Ecuador ...... 134 3 23 S 79 50W
Pasaje →, Argentina . 140 25 39 S 63 56W
Pascagoula, U.S.A. ... 121 30 21N 88 30W
Pascagoula →, U.S.A. 121 30 21N 88 35W
Paşcani, Romania .... 34 47 14N 26 45 E
Pasco, U.S.A. 122 46 10N 119 0W
Pasco □, Peru .... 136 10 40 S 75 0W
Pasco, Cerro de, Peru 136 10 45 S 76 10W
Pasewalk, E. Germany 30 53 30N 14 0 E
Pasfield L., Canada ... 111 58 24N 105 20W
Pasha →, U.S.S.R. ... 36 60 29N 32 55 E
Pashiwari, Pakistan ... 49 34 40N 75 10 E
Pashmakli = Smolyan,
Bulgaria .... 35 41 36N 24 38 E
Pasighat, India .... 52 28 4N 95 21 E
Pasing, W. Germany .. 31 48 9N 11 27 E
Pasirian, Indonesia ... 57 8 13 S 113 8 E
Pasley, C., Australia .. 79 33 52 S 123 35 E
Pašman, Yugoslavia .. 27 43 58N 15 20 E
Pasni, Pakistan ...... 47 25 15N 63 27 E
Paso Cantinela, Mexico 125 32 33N 115 47W
Paso de Indios,
Argentina .... 142 43 55 S 69 0W
Paso de los Libres,
Argentina .... 140 29 44 S 57 10W
Paso de los Toros,
Uruguay .... 140 32 45 S 56 30W
Paso Flores, Argentina 142 40 35 S 70 38W
Paso Robles, U.S.A. .. 123 35 40N 120 45W
Pasorapa, Bolivia .... 137 18 16 S 64 37W
Paspébiac, Canada ... 105 48 3N 65 17W
Pasrur, Pakistan ...... 48 32 16N 74 43 E
Passage West, Ireland . 15 51 52N 8 20W
Passaic, U.S.A. 117 40 50N 74 8W
Passau, W. Germany .. 31 48 34N 13 27 E
Passendale, Belgium .. 17 50 54N 3 2 E
Passero, C., Italy ..... 29 36 42N 15 8 E
Passo Fundo, Brazil .. 141 28 10 S 52 20W
Passos, Brazil .... 139 20 45 S 46 37W
Passow, E. Germany .. 30 53 13N 14 10 E
Passy, France .... 21 45 55N 6 41 E
Pastaza □, Ecuador .. 134 2 0 S 77 0W
Pastaza →, Peru ..... 134 4 50 S 76 52W
Pastęk, Poland .... 32 54 3N 19 41 E
Pasto, Colombia 134 1 13N 77 17W
Pastos Bons, Brazil ... 138 6 36 S 44 5W
Pastrana, Spain 24 40 27N 2 53W
Pasuruan, Indonesia .. 57 7 40 S 112 44 E
Patagonia, Argentina .. 142 45 0 S 69 0W
Patagonia, U.S.A. 123 31 35N 110 45W
Patan, Gujarat, India . 50 17 22N 73 57 E
Patan, Maharashtra,
India .... 48 23 54N 72 14 E
Patani, Indonesia ..... 57 0 20N 128 50 E
Pataudi, India .... 48 28 18N 76 48 E
Patay, France .... 19 48 2N 1 40 E
Patchewollock,
Australia .... 74 35 22 S 142 12 E
Patchogue, U.S.A. ... 117 40 46N 73 1W
Patea, N.Z. .... 80 39 45 S 174 30 E
Pategi, Nigeria ...... 91 8 50N 5 45 E
Patensie, S. Africa .... 96 33 46 S 24 49 E
Paternò, Italy .... 29 37 34N 14 53 E
Pateros, U.S.A. 122 48 4N 119 58W
Paterson, Australia ... 76 32 35 S 151 36 E
Paterson, U.S.A. 117 40 55N 74 10W
Paterson, C., Australia 74 38 41 S 145 37 E
Paterson Inlet, N.Z. .. 81 46 56 S 168 12 E
Paterson Ra., Australia 78 21 45 S 122 10 E
Paterswolde, Neths. ... 16 53 9N 6 34 E
Pathankot, India ..... 48 32 18N 75 45 E
Patharghata, Bangla. . 52 22 2N 89 58 E
Pathfinder Res., U.S.A. 122 42 30N 107 0W
Pathiu, Thailand ..... 55 10 42N 99 19 E
Pathum Thani,
Thailand .... 54 14 1N 100 32 E
Pati, Indonesia .... 57 6 45 S 111 1 E
Pati Pt., Guam .... 68 13 40N 144 50 E
Patía, Colombia 134 2 4N 77 4W
Patía →, Colombia ... 134 2 13N 78 40W
Patiala, India .... 48 30 23N 76 26 E
Patine Kouka, Senegal 90 12 45N 13 45W
Pativilca, Peru .... 136 10 42 S 77 48W
Patkai Bum, India .... 52 27 0N 95 30 E
Pátmos, Greece ...... 35 37 21N 26 36 E
Patna, India .... 49 25 35N 85 12 E
Patonga, Uganda ..... 92 2 45N 33 15 E
Patos, Brazil .... 138 6 55 S 37 16W
Patos, L. dos, Brazil .. 141 31 20 S 51 0W
Patos de Minas, Brazil 139 18 35 S 46 32W
Patquía, Argentina .... 140 30 2 S 66 55W
Pátrai, Greece .... 35 38 14N 21 47 E
Pátraikós, Kólpos,
Greece .... 35 38 17N 21 30 E
Patricio Lynch, I., Chile 142 48 35 S 75 30W
Patrie, La, Canada ... 107 45 24N 71 15W
Patrocínio, Brazil .... 139 18 57 S 47 0W
Patta, Kenya .... 92 2 10 S 41 0 E
Pattada, Italy .... 28 40 35N 9 7 E
Pattanapuram, India .. 51 9 6N 76 50 E
Pattani, Thailand ..... 55 6 48N 101 15 E
Patten, U.S.A. 105 45 59N 68 28W
Patterson, Calif.,
U.S.A. 124 37 30N 121 9W
Patterson, La., U.S.A. 121 29 44N 91 20W
Patterson, Mt., U.S.A. 124 38 29N 119 20W
Patteson, Passage,
Vanuatu .... 68 15 26 S 168 12 E
Patti, India .... 48 31 17N 74 54 E
Patti, Italy .... 29 38 8N 14 57 E
Pattoki, Pakistan ..... 48 31 5N 73 52 E
Patton, U.S.A. 116 40 38N 78 40W
Pattonsburg, U.S.A. .. 118 40 3N 94 8W
Pattukkattai, India ... 51 10 25N 79 20 E
Patu, Brazil .... 138 6 6 S 37 38W
Patuakhali, Bangla. ... 52 22 20N 90 25 E
Patuca →, Honduras . 128 15 50N 84 18W
Patuca, Punta,
Honduras 128 15 49N 84 14W
Pâturages, Belgium ... 17 50 25N 3 52 E
Pátzcuaro, Mexico 126 19 30N 101 40W
Pau, France 20 43 19N 0 25W
Pau, Gave de →,
France 20 43 33N 1 12W
Pau d' Arco, Brazil ... 138 7 30 S 49 22W
Pau dos Ferros, Brazil 138 6 7 S 38 10W
Paucartambo, Peru ... 136 13 19 S 71 35W
Pauillac, France 20 45 11N 0 46W
Pauini, Brazil .... 136 7 40 S 66 58W
Pauini →, Brazil ..... 135 1 42 S 62 50W
Pauk, Burma .... 52 21 27N 94 30 E
Paul I., Canada 105 56 30N 61 20W
Paul Isnard, Fr. Guiana 135 4 47N 54 1W
Paul-Sauvé, L., Canada 106 50 15N 78 20W
Paulding, U.S.A. 119 41 8N 84 35W
Paulhan, France ...... 20 43 33N 3 28 E
Paulis = Isiro, Zaïre .. 92 2 53N 27 40 E
Paulista, Brazil .... 138 7 57 S 34 53W
Paulistana, Brazil .... 138 8 9 S 41 9W
Paullina, U.S.A. 120 42 55N 95 40W
Paulo Afonso, Brazil . 138 9 21 S 38 15W
Paulo de Faria, Brazil 139 20 2 S 49 24W
Paulpietersburg,
S. Africa .... 97 27 23 S 30 50 E
Pauls Valley, U.S.A. .. 121 34 40N 97 17W
Pauma Valley, U.S.A. 125 33 16N 116 58W
Paungde, Burma ..... 52 18 29N 95 30 E
Pauni, India .... 50 20 48N 79 40 E
Pausa, Peru .... 136 15 16 S 73 22W
Pauto →, Colombia .. 134 5 9N 70 55W
Pavelets, U.S.S.R. .... 37 53 49N 39 14 E
Pavia, Italy .... 26 45 10N 9 10 E
Pavlikeni, Bulgaria ... 34 43 14N 25 20 E
Pavlodar, U.S.S.R. ... 40 52 33N 77 0 E
Pavlograd, U.S.S.R. .. 38 48 30N 35 52 E

Pavlovo

Pavlovo, *Gorkiy, U.S.S.R.* .... **37** 55 58N 43 5 E
Pavlovo, *Yakut A.S.S.R., U.S.S.R.* .... **41** 63 5N 115 25 E
Pavlovsk, *U.S.S.R.* ... **37** 50 26N 40 5 E
Pavlovskaya, *U.S.S.R.* **39** 46 17N 39 47 E
Pavlovskiy-Posad, *U.S.S.R.* .... **37** 55 47N 38 42 E
Pavullo nel Frignano, *Italy* .... **26** 44 20N 10 50 E
Pavuvu, *Solomon Is.* .. **68** 9 4 S 159 8 E
Paw Paw, *U.S.A.* **119** 42 13N 85 53W
Pawahku, *Burma* ..... **52** 26 11N 98 40 E
Pawhuska, *U.S.A.* **121** 36 40N 96 25W
Pawling, *U.S.A.* **117** 41 35N 73 37W
Pawnee, *Ill., U.S.A.* .. **118** 39 35N 89 35W
Pawnee, *Okla., U.S.A.* **121** 36 24N 96 50W
Pawnee City, *U.S.A.* . **120** 40 8N 96 10W
Pawpaw, *U.S.A.* **118** 41 41N 88 59W
Pawtucket, *U.S.A.* ... **117** 41 51N 71 22W
Paxoí, *Greece* .... **35** 39 14N 20 12 E
Paxton, *Ill., U.S.A.* ... **119** 40 25N 88 7W
Paxton, *Nebr., U.S.A.* **120** 41 12N 101 27W
Payakumbuh, *Indonesia* **56** 0 20 S 100 35 E
Payerne, *Switz.* ...... **31** 46 49N 6 56 E
Payette, *U.S.A.* **122** 44 0N 117 0W
Paymogo, *Spain* **23** 37 44N 7 21W
Payne, *U.S.A.* **119** 41 5N 84 44W
Payne Bay = Bellin, *Canada* **103** 60 0N 70 0W
Payne L., *Canada* **103** 59 30N 74 30W
Paynes Find, *Australia* **79** 29 15 S 117 42 E
Paynesville, *Australia* . **75** 37 55 S 147 43 E
Paynesville, *Liberia* ... **90** 6 20N 10 45W
Paynesville, *U.S.A.* ... **120** 45 21N 94 44W
Paysandú, *Uruguay* ... **140** 32 19 S 58 8W
Payson, *Ariz., U.S.A.* **123** 34 17N 111 15W
Payson, *Utah, U.S.A.* . **122** 40 8N 111 41W
Paz →, *Guatemala* ... **128** 13 44N 90 10W
Paz, B. de la, *Mexico* . **126** 24 15N 110 25W
Paz, La, *Entre Ríos, Argentina* .... **140** 30 50 S 59 45W
Paz, La, *San Luis, Argentina* .... **140** 33 30 S 67 20W
Paz, La, *Bolivia* ...... **136** 16 20 S 68 10W
Paz, La, *Honduras* ... **128** 14 20N 87 47W
Paz, La, *Mexico* **126** 24 10N 110 20W
Paz, La □, *Bolivia* ... **136** 15 30 S 68 0W
Paz Centro, La, *Nic.* .. **128** 12 20N 86 41W
Pazar, *Turkey* .... **46** 41 10N 40 50 E
Pazardzhik, *Bulgaria* .. **34** 42 12N 24 20 E
Pazin, *Yugoslavia* .... **27** 45 14N 13 56 E
Pazña, *Bolivia* .... **136** 18 36 S 66 55W
Pčinja →, *Yugoslavia* . **35** 41 50N 21 45 E
Pe Ell, *U.S.A.* **124** 46 30N 123 18W
Peabody, *U.S.A.* **117** 42 31N 70 56W
Peace →, *Canada* **110** 59 0N 111 25W
Peace Point, *Canada* .. **110** 59 7N 112 27W
Peace River, *Canada* . **110** 56 15N 117 18W
Peach Springs, *U.S.A.* **123** 35 36N 113 30W
Peak, The, *U.K.* **12** 53 24N 1 53W
Peak Downs, *Australia* **72** 22 14 S 148 0 E
Peak Downs Mine, *Australia* .... **72** 22 17 S 148 11 E
Peak Hill, *N.S.W., Australia* .... **76** 32 47 S 148 11 E
Peak Hill, *W. Austral., Australia* .... **79** 25 35 S 118 43 E
Peak Range, *Australia* **72** 22 50 S 148 20 E
Peake, *Australia* ...... **73** 35 25 S 140 0 E
Peake Cr. →, *Australia* **73** 28 2 S 136 7 E
Peale Mt., *U.S.A.* **123** 38 25N 109 12W
Pearblossom, *U.S.A.* . **125** 34 30N 117 55W
Pearl, *U.S.A.* **118** 39 28N 90 38W
Pearl →, *U.S.A.* **121** 30 23N 89 45W
Pearl Banks, *Sri Lanka* **51** 8 45N 79 45 E
Pearl City, *Hawaii, U.S.A.* **112** 21 24N 158 0W
Pearl City, *Ill., U.S.A.* **118** 42 16N 89 50W
Pearsall, *U.S.A.* **121** 28 55N 99 8W
Pearse I., *Canada* **110** 54 52N 130 14W
Peary Land, *Greenland* **144** 82 40N 33 0W
Pease →, *U.S.A.* **121** 34 12N 99 7W
Pebane, *Mozam.* ..... **93** 17 10 S 38 8 E
Pebas, *Peru* .... **134** 3 10 S 71 46W
Pebble, I., *Falk. Is.* ... **142** 51 20 S 59 40W
Pebble Beach, *U.S.A.* **124** 36 34N 121 57W
Peč, *Yugoslavia* ...... **33** 42 40N 20 17 E
Peçanha, *Brazil* ...... **139** 18 33 S 42 34W
Pecatonica, *U.S.A.* ... **118** 42 19N 89 22W
Pecatonica →, *U.S.A.* **118** 42 26N 89 17W
Péccioli, *Italy* .... **26** 43 32N 10 43 E
Pechea, *Romania* ..... **34** 45 36N 27 49 E
Pechenezhin, *U.S.S.R.* **38** 48 30N 24 48 E
Pechenga, *U.S.S.R.* ... **40** 69 30N 31 25 E
Pechiguera, Pta., *Canary Is.* **25** 28 51N 13 53W
Pechnezhskoye Vdkhr., *U.S.S.R.* .... **37** 50 0N 37 10 E
Pechora →, *U.S.S.R.* . **40** 68 13N 54 15 E
Pechorskaya Guba, *U.S.S.R.* .... **40** 68 40N 54 0 E
Pechory, *U.S.S.R.* .... **36** 57 48N 27 40 E
Pecica, *Romania* ..... **34** 46 10N 21 3 E
Pečka, *Yugoslavia* .... **33** 44 18N 19 33 E
Pécora, C., *Italy* ..... **28** 39 28N 8 23 E
Pecos, *U.S.A.* **121** 31 25N 103 35W
Pecos →, *U.S.A.* **121** 29 42N 102 30W
Pécs, *Hungary* .... **33** 46 5N 18 15 E
Peddapalli, *India* ..... **50** 18 40N 79 24 E
Peddapuram, *India* ... **50** 17 6N 82 8 E
Pedder, L., *Australia* . **72** 42 55 S 146 10 E
Peddie, *S. Africa* ..... **97** 33 14 S 27 7 E
Pédernales, *Dom. Rep.* **129** 18 2N 71 44W
Pedirka, *Australia* .... **73** 26 40 S 135 14 E
Pedra Azul, *Brazil* ... **139** 16 2 S 41 17W
Pedra Grande, Recifes de, *Brazil* .... **139** 17 45 S 38 58W
Pedras Negras, *Brazil* . **137** 12 51 S 62 54W
Pedreiras, *Brazil* ..... **138** 4 32 S 44 40W
Pedrera, La, *Colombia* **134** 1 18 S 69 43W
Pedro Afonso, *Brazil* . **138** 9 0 S 48 10W
Pedro Cays, *Jamaica* .. **128** 17 5N 77 48W
Pedro Chico, *Colombia* **134** 1 4N 70 25W
Pedro de Valdivia, *Chile* .... **140** 22 55 S 69 38W
Pedro Juan Caballero, *Paraguay* .... **141** 22 30 S 55 40W
Pedro Muñoz, *Spain* .. **25** 39 25N 2 56W
Pedrógão Grande, *Portugal* **22** 39 55N 8 9W
Peduyim, *Israel* ...... **44** 31 20N 34 37 E
Peebinga, *Australia* ... **73** 34 52 S 140 57 E
Peebles, *U.K.* **14** 55 40N 3 12W
Peebles, *U.S.A.* **119** 38 57N 83 23W
Peechelba, *Australia* .. **75** 36 12 S 146 15 E
Peekskill, *U.S.A.* **117** 41 18N 73 57W
Peel, *Australia* .... **76** 33 20 S 149 38 E
Peel, *I. of Man* **12** 54 14N 4 40W
Peel →, *Australia* .... **77** 30 50 S 150 29 E
Peel →, *Canada* **102** 67 0N 135 0W
Peelwood, *Australia* .. **76** 34 7 S 149 27 E
Peene →, *E. Germany* **30** 54 9N 13 46 E
Peera Peera Poolanna L., *Australia* .... **73** 26 30 S 138 0 E
Peers, *Canada* **110** 53 40N 116 0W
Pegasus Bay, *N.Z.* ... **81** 43 20 S 173 10 E
Pegnitz, *W. Germany* . **31** 49 45N 11 33 E
Pegnitz →, *W. Germany* .... **31** 49 29N 10 59 E
Pego, *Spain* **25** 38 51N 0 8W
Pegu, *Burma* .... **52** 17 20N 96 29 E
Pegu Yoma, *Burma* .. **52** 19 0N 96 0 E
Pehuajó, *Argentina* ... **140** 35 45 S 62 0W
Pei Xian, *China* ...... **60** 34 44N 116 55 E
Peine, *Chile* .... **140** 23 45 S 68 8W
Peine, *W. Germany* ... **30** 52 19N 10 12 E
Peip'ing = Beijing, *China* .... **60** 39 55N 116 20 E
Peiss, *W. Germany* ... **31** 47 58N 11 47 E
Peissenberg, *W. Germany* .... **31** 47 48N 11 4 E
Peitz, *E. Germany* .... **30** 51 50N 14 23 E
Peixe, *Brazil* .... **139** 12 0 S 48 40W
Peixe →, *Brazil* ..... **139** 21 31 S 51 58W
Peixoto de Azeredo →, *Brazil* .... **137** 10 6 S 55 31W
Peize, *Neths.* .... **16** 53 9N 6 30 E
Pek →, *Yugoslavia* ... **33** 44 45N 21 29 E
Pekalongan, *Indonesia* **57** 6 53 S 109 40 E
Pekan, *Malaysia* ...... **55** 3 30N 103 25 E
Pekanbaru, *Indonesia* . **56** 0 30N 101 15 E
Pekin, *U.S.A.* **118** 40 35N 89 40W
Peking = Beijing, *China* .... **60** 39 55N 116 20 E
Pelabuhan Kelang, *Malaysia* .... **55** 3 0N 101 23 E
Pelabuhan Ratu, Teluk, *Indonesia* .... **57** 7 5 S 106 30 E
Pelabuhanratu, *Indonesia* .... **57** 7 0 S 106 32 E
Pélagos, *Greece* ...... **35** 39 17N 24 4 E
Pelaihari, *Indonesia* ... **56** 3 55 S 114 45 E
Pelat, Mt., *France* .... **21** 44 16N 6 42 E
Peleaga, *Romania* .... **34** 45 22N 22 55 E
Pelechuco, *Bolivia* .... **136** 14 48 S 69 4W
Pelée, Mt., *Martinique* **129** 14 48N 61 0W
Pelee, Pt., *Canada* ... **108** 41 54N 82 31W
Pelee I., *Canada* **108** 41 47N 82 40W
Pelejo, *Peru* .... **136** 6 10 S 75 49W
Pelekech, *Kenya* ..... **92** 3 52N 35 8 E
Peleng, *Indonesia* .... **57** 1 20 S 123 30 E
Pelham, *U.S.A.* **115** 31 5N 84 6W
Pelhřimov, *Czech.* .... **32** 49 24N 15 12 E
Pelican L., *Canada* ... **111** 52 28N 100 20W
Pelican Narrows, *Canada* **111** 55 10N 102 56W
Pelican Rapids, *Canada* **111** 52 45N 100 42W
Pelkosenniemi, *Finland* **8** 67 6N 27 28 E
Pella, *S. Africa* ...... **96** 29 1 S 19 6 E
Pella, *U.S.A.* **118** 41 30N 93 0W
Péllaro, *Italy* .... **29** 38 1N 15 40 E
Pelletier Sta., *Canada* . **107** 47 33N 69 26W
Pellworm, *W. Germany* **30** 54 30N 8 40 E
Pelly →, *Canada* **102** 62 47N 137 19W
Pelly Bay, *Canada* **103** 68 38N 89 50W
Pelly L., *Canada* **102** 66 0N 102 0W
Peloponnese = Pelopónnisos □, *Greece* .... **35** 37 10N 22 0 E
Pelopónnisos □, *Greece* **35** 37 10N 22 0 E
Peloritani, Monti, *Italy* **29** 38 2N 15 25 E
Peloro, C., *Italy* ...... **29** 38 15N 15 40 E
Pelorus Sound, *N.Z.* .. **81** 40 59 S 173 59 E
Pelotas, *Brazil* .... **141** 31 42 S 52 23W
Pelvoux, Massif de, *France* .... **21** 44 52N 6 20 E
Pemalang, *Indonesia* .. **57** 6 53 S 109 23 E
Pematangsiantar, *Indonesia* .... **56** 2 57N 99 5 E
Pemba, *Mozam.* ...... **93** 12 58 S 40 30 E
Pemba, *Zambia* ...... **93** 16 30 S 27 28 E
Pemba Channel, *Tanzania* .... **92** 5 0 S 39 37 E
Pemba I., *Tanzania* ... **92** 5 0 S 39 45 E
Pemberton, *Australia* . **79** 34 30 S 116 0 E
Pemberton, *Canada* .. **110** 50 25N 122 50W
Pembina, *U.S.A.* **111** 48 58N 97 15W
Pembina →, *U.S.A.* ... **111** 49 0N 98 12W•
Pembine, *U.S.A.* **114** 45 38N 87 59W
Pembino, *U.S.A.* **120** 48 58N 97 15W
Pembroke, *Canada* ... **109** 45 50N 77 7W
Pembroke, *U.K.* **13** 51 41N 4 57W
Pembroke, *U.S.A.* **115** 32 5N 81 32W
Pen-y-Ghent, *U.K.* ... **12** 54 10N 2 15W
Peña, Sierra de la, *Spain* **24** 42 32N 0 45W
Peña de Francia, Sierra de, *Spain* **22** 40 32N 6 10W
Penafiel, *Portugal* **22** 41 12N 8 17W
Peñafiel, *Spain* **22** 41 35N 4 7W
Peñaflor, *Spain* **23** 37 43N 5 21W
Peñalara, Pico, *Spain* . **22** 40 51N 3 57W
Penalva, *Brazil* .... **138** 3 18 S 45 10W
Penamacôr, *Portugal* .. **22** 40 10N 7 10W
Penang = Pinang, *Malaysia* .... **55** 5 25N 100 15 E
Penápolis, *Brazil* .... **141** 21 30 S 50 0W
Peñaranda de Bracamonte, *Spain* . **22** 40 53N 5 13W
Peñarroya-Pueblonuevo, *Spain* **23** 38 19N 5 16W
Peñas, C. de, *Spain* ... **22** 43 42N 5 52W
Penas, G. de, *Chile* ... **142** 47 0 S 75 0W
Peñas, Pta., *Venezuela* **135** 11 17N 62 0W
Peñas de San Pedro, *Spain* **25** 38 44N 2 0W
Peñas del Chache, *Canary Is.* **25** 29 6N 13 33W
Peñausende, *Spain* ... **22** 41 17N 5 52W
Pench'i = Benxi, *China* **61** 41 20N 123 48 E
Pend Oreille →, *U.S.A.* **122** 49 4N 117 37W
Pend Oreille, L., *U.S.A.* **122** 48 0N 116 30W
Pendembu, *S. Leone* .. **90** 9 7N 12 14W
Pendências, *Brazil* .... **138** 5 15 S 36 43W
Pender B., *Australia* .. **78** 16 45 S 122 42 E
Pendleton, *Calif., U.S.A.* **125** 33 16N 117 23W
Pendleton, *Ind., U.S.A.* **119** 40 0N 85 45W
Pendleton, *Oreg., U.S.A.* **122** 45 35N 118 50W
Penedo, *Brazil* .... **138** 10 15 S 36 36W
Penetanguishene, *Canada* **108** 44 50N 79 55W
Peng Xian, *China* .... **58** 31 4N 103 32 E
Pengalengan, *Indonesia* **57** 7 9 S 107 30 E
Penge, *Kasai Or., Zaïre* **92** 5 30 S 24 33 E
Penge, *Kivu, Zaïre* ... **92** 4 27 S 28 25 E
Penglai, *China* .... **61** 37 48N 120 42 E
Pengshui, *China* ...... **58** 29 17N 108 12 E
Penguin, *Australia* .... **72** 41 8 S 146 6 E
Pengxi, *China* .... **58** 30 44N 105 45 E
Pengze, *China* .... **59** 29 52N 116 32 E
Penhalonga, *Zambia* .. **93** 18 52 S 32 40 E
Peniche, *Portugal* **23** 39 19N 9 22W
Penicuik, *U.K.* **14** 55 50N 3 14W
Penida, *Indonesia* .... **56** 8 45 S 115 30 E
Peninsular Malaysia □, *Malaysia* .... **55** 4 0N 102 0 E
Peñíscola, *Spain* ...... **24** 40 22N 0 24 E
Penitente, Serra dos, *Brazil* .... **138** 8 45 S 46 20W
Penmarch, *France* **18** 47 49N 4 21W
Penmarch, Pte. de, *France* **18** 47 48N 4 22W
Penn Hills, *U.S.A.* ... **116** 40 28N 79 52W
Penn Yan, *U.S.A.* **116** 42 39N 77 7W
Pennabilli, *Italy* ...... **27** 43 50N 12 17 E
Pennant, *Canada* **111** 50 32N 108 14W
Penne, *Italy* .... **27** 42 28N 13 56 E
Penner →, *India* ..... **51** 14 35N 80 10 E
Pennine, Alpi, *Alps* .. **26** 46 4N 7 30 E
Pennines, *U.K.* **12** 54 50N 2 20W
Pennington, *U.S.A.* ... **124** 39 15N 121 47W
Pennino, Mte., *Italy* .. **27** 43 6N 12 54 E
Pennsylvania □, *U.S.A.* **114** 40 50N 78 0W
Pennville, *U.S.A.* **119** 40 30N 85 9W
Penny, *Canada* **110** 53 51N 121 20W
Peno, *U.S.S.R.* ...... **36** 57 2N 32 49 E
Penola, *Australia* ..... **73** 37 25 S 140 21 E
Penonomé, *Panama* ... **128** 8 31N 80 21W
Penot, Mt., *Vanuatu* .. **68** 16 20 S 167 31 E
Penrhyn Is., *Cook Is.* . **67** 9 0 S 158 30W
Penrith, *Australia* .... **76** 33 43 S 150 38 E
Penrith, *U.K.* **12** 54 40N 2 45W
Pensacola, *U.S.A.* **115** 30 30N 87 10W
Pensacola Mts., *Antarctica* .... **143** 84 0 S 40 0W
Pense, *Canada* **111** 50 25N 104 59W
Penshurst, *Australia* .. **74** 37 49 S 142 20 E
Pentecost = Pentecôte, *Vanuatu* .... **68** 15 42 S 168 10 E
Pentecoste, *Brazil* .... **138** 3 48 S 39 17W
Pentecôte, *Vanuatu* ... **68** 15 42 S 168 10 E
Penticton, *Canada* **110** 49 30N 119 38W
Pentland, *Australia* ... **72** 20 32 S 145 25 E
Pentland Firth, *U.K.* .. **14** 58 43N 3 10W
Pentland Hills, *U.K.* .. **14** 55 48N 3 25W
Penukonda, *India* .... **51** 14 5N 77 38 E
Penylan L., *Canada* .. **111** 61 50N 106 20W
Penza, *U.S.S.R.* ...... **37** 53 15N 45 5 E
Penzance, *U.K.* **13** 50 7N 5 32W
Penzberg, *W. Germany* **31** 47 46N 11 23 E
Penzhino, *U.S.S.R.* ... **41** 63 30N 167 55 E
Penzhinskaya Guba, *U.S.S.R.* .... **41** 61 30N 163 0 E
Penzlin, *E. Germany* . **30** 53 32N 13 6 E
Peoria, *Ariz., U.S.A.* . **123** 33 40N 112 15W
Peoria, *Ill., U.S.A.* ... **118** 40 40N 89 40W
Peoria Heights, *U.S.A.* **118** 40 45N 89 35W
Peotone, *U.S.A.* **119** 41 20N 87 48W
Pepingen, *Belgium* ... **17** 50 46N 4 10 E
Pepinster, *Belgium* ... **17** 50 34N 5 47 E
Pera Hd., *Australia* ... **72** 12 55 S 141 37 E
Perabumilih, *Indonesia* **56** 3 27 S 104 15 E
Perakhóra, *Greece* .... **35** 38 2N 22 56 E
Perales de Alfambra, *Spain* **24** 40 38N 1 0W
Perales del Puerto, *Spain* **22** 40 10N 6 40W
Peralta, *Spain* **24** 42 21N 1 49W
Pérama, *Greece* ...... **35** 35 20N 24 40 E
Percé, *Canada* **105** 48 31N 64 13W
Perche, *France* .... **18** 48 31N 1 1 E
Perche, Collines du, *France* .... **18** 48 30N 0 40 E
Percival Lakes, *Australia* .... **78** 21 25 S 125 0 E
Percy, *France* **18** 48 55N 1 11W
Percy, *U.S.A.* **118** 38 5N 89 41W
Percy Is., *Australia* ... **72** 21 39 S 150 16 E
Perdido →, *Argentina* **142** 42 55 S 67 0W
Perdido, Mte., *Spain* . **20** 42 40N 0 5 E
Perdu, Mt. = Perdido, Mte., *Spain* .... **20** 42 40N 0 5 E
Pereira, *Colombia* **134** 4 49N 75 43W
Pereira Barreto, *Brazil* **139** 20 38 S 51 7W
Perekerten, *Australia* . **74** 34 55 S 143 40 E
Perekop, *U.S.S.R.* .... **38** 46 10N 33 42 E
Perené →, *Peru* ..... **136** 11 9 S 74 14W
Perenjori, *Australia* ... **79** 29 26 S 116 16 E
Pereslavl-Zalesskiy, *U.S.S.R.* .... **37** 56 45N 38 50 E
Pereyaslav Khmelnitskiy, *U.S.S.R.* .... **36** 50 3N 31 28 E
Pérez, I., *Mexico* **127** 22 24N 89 42W
Pergamino, *Argentina* . **140** 33 52 S 60 30W
Pérgine Valsugano, *Italy* .... **27** 46 4N 11 15 E
Pérgola, *Italy* .... **27** 43 35N 12 50 E
Perham, *U.S.A.* **120** 46 36N 95 36W
Perhentian, Kepulauan, *Malaysia* .... **55** 5 54N 102 42 E
Periam, *Romania* ..... **34** 46 2N 20 59 E
Péribonca →, *Canada* **107** 48 45N 72 5W
Péribonca, L., *Canada* **107** 50 1N 71 10W
Péribonka, *Canada* **107** 48 46N 72 3W
Perico, *Argentina* .... **140** 24 20 S 65 5W
Pericos, *Mexico* **126** 25 3N 107 42W
Périers, *France* **18** 49 11N 1 25W
Périgord, *France* ..... **20** 45 0N 0 40 E
Périgueux, *France* .... **20** 45 10N 0 42 E
Perijá, Sierra de, *Colombia* **134** 9 30N 73 3W
Peristéra, *Greece* ..... **35** 39 15N 23 58 E
Perito Moreno, *Argentina* .... **142** 46 36 S 70 56W
Peritoró, *Brazil* ...... **138** 4 20 S 44 18W
Periyakulam, *India* ... **51** 10 5N 77 30 E
Periyar →, *India* ..... **51** 10 15N 76 10 E
Periyar, L., *India* ..... **51** 9 25N 77 10 E
Perković, *Yugoslavia* .. **27** 43 41N 16 10 E
Perlas, Arch. de las, *Panama* **128** 8 41N 79 7W
Perlas, Punta de, *Nic.* . **128** 12 30N 83 30W
Perleberg, *E. Germany* **30** 53 5N 11 50 E
Perlevka, *U.S.S.R.* ... **37** 51 48N 38 57 E
Perm, *U.S.S.R.* ...... **40** 58 0N 57 10 E
Pernambuco = Recife, *Brazil* .... **138** 8 0 S 35 0W
Pernambuco □, *Brazil* **138** 8 0 S 37 0W
Pernatty Lagoon, *Australia* .... **73** 31 30 S 137 12 E
Pernik, *Bulgaria* ...... **34** 42 35N 23 2 E
Peron, C., *Australia* .. **79** 25 30 S 113 30 E
Peron Is., *Australia* ... **78** 13 9 S 130 4 E
Peron Pen., *Australia* . **79** 26 0 S 113 10 E
Péronne, *France* ...... **19** 49 55N 2 57 E
Péronnes, *Belgium* ... **17** 50 27N 4 9 E
Perosa Argentina, *Italy* **26** 44 57N 7 11 E
Perouse Str., La, *Asia* **66** 45 40N 142 0 E
Perow, *Canada* **110** 54 35N 126 10W
Perpendicular Pt., *Australia* .... **77** 31 37 S 152 52 E
Perpignan, *France* .... **20** 42 42N 2 53 E
Perris, *U.S.A.* **125** 33 47N 117 14W
Perros-Guirec, *France* . **18** 48 49N 3 28W
Perry, *Fla., U.S.A.* ... **115** 30 9N 83 40W
Perry, *Ga., U.S.A.* ... **115** 32 25N 83 41W
Perry, *Iowa, U.S.A.* .. **118** 41 48N 94 5W
Perry, *Maine, U.S.A.* . **115** 44 59N 67 20W
Perry, *Mich., U.S.A.* . **119** 42 50N 84 13W
Perry, *Mo., U.S.A.* ... **118** 39 26N 91 40W
Perry, *Okla., U.S.A.* . **121** 36 20N 97 20W
Perrysburg, *U.S.A.* ... **119** 41 34N 83 38W
Perryton, *U.S.A.* **121** 36 28N 100 48W
Perryville, *U.S.A.* **118** 37 42N 89 50W
Persberg, *Sweden* .... **10** 59 47N 14 15 E
Persepolis, *Iran* ...... **47** 29 55N 52 50 E
Perseverancia, *Bolivia* **137** 14 44 S 62 48W
Persia = Iran ■, *Asia* . **47** 33 0N 53 0 E
Persian Gulf = Gulf, The, *Asia* .... **47** 27 0N 50 0 E
Perstorp, *Sweden* ..... **11** 56 10N 13 25 E
Perth, *Australia* ...... **79** 31 57 S 115 52 E
Perth, *Canada* **109** 44 55N 76 15W
Perth, *U.K.* **14** 56 24N 3 27W
Perth Amboy, *U.S.A.* . **117** 40 31N 74 16W

Pingguo

Perthus, Le, France 20 42 30N 2 53 E
Perthville, Australia 76 33 30 S 149 31 E
Pertuis, France 21 43 42N 5 30 E
Peru, Ill., U.S.A. 118 41 18N 89 12W
Peru, Ind., U.S.A. 119 40 42N 86 0W
Peru ■, S. Amer. 134 8 0 S 75 0W
Peru-Chile Trench, Pac. Oc. 67 20 0 S 72 0W
Perúgia, Italy 27 43 6N 12 24 E
Perušić, Yugoslavia 27 44 40N 15 22 E
Péruwelz, Belgium 17 50 31N 3 36 E
Pervomaysk, R.S.F.S.R., U.S.S.R. 37 54 56N 43 58 E
Pervomaysk, Ukraine S.S.R., U.S.S.R. 38 48 10N 30 46 E
Pervouralsk, U.S.S.R. 40 56 55N 60 0 E
Perwez, Belgium 17 50 38N 4 48 E
Pésaro, Italy 27 43 55N 12 53 E
Pesca, La, Mexico 127 23 46N 97 47W
Pescara, Italy 27 42 28N 14 13 E
Pescara →, Italy 27 42 28N 14 13 E
Peschanokopskoye, U.S.S.R. 39 46 14N 41 4 E
Péscia, Italy 26 43 54N 10 40 E
Pescina, Italy 27 42 0N 13 39 E
Peshawar, Pakistan 48 34 2N 71 37 E
Peshtigo, U.S.A. 114 45 4N 87 46W
Peski, U.S.S.R. 37 51 14N 42 29 E
Peskovka, U.S.S.R. 37 59 23N 52 20 E
Pêso da Régua, Portugal 22 41 10N 7 47W
Pesqueira, Brazil 138 8 20 S 36 42W
Pessac, France 20 44 48N 0 37W
Pessoux, Belgium 17 50 17N 5 11 E
Pestovo, U.S.S.R. 36 58 33N 35 42 E
Pestravka, U.S.S.R. 37 52 28N 49 57 E
Petah Tiqwa, Israel 44 32 6N 34 53 E
Petaling Jaya, Malaysia 55 3 4N 101 42 E
Petaluma, U.S.A. 124 38 13N 122 39W
Petange, Lux. 17 49 33N 5 55 E
Petatlán, Mexico 126 17 31N 101 16W
Petauke, Zambia 93 14 14 S 31 20 E
Petawawa, Canada 109 45 54N 77 17W
Petegem, Belgium 17 50 59N 3 32 E
Petén Itzá, L., Guatemala 128 16 58N 89 50W
Peter 1st, I., Antarctica 143 69 0 S 91 0W
Peter Pond L., Canada 111 55 55N 108 44W
Peterbell, Canada 104 48 36N 83 21W
Peterborough, Australia 73 32 58 S 138 51 E
Peterborough, Canada 109 44 20N 78 20W
Peterborough, U.K. 13 52 35N 0 14W
Peterborough, U.S.A. 117 42 55N 71 59W
Peterhead, U.K. 14 57 30N 1 49W
Petermann Bjerg, Greenland 100 73 7N 28 25W
Peter's Mine, Guyana 135 6 14N 59 20W
Petersburg, Alaska, U.S.A. 102 56 50N 133 0W
Petersburg, Ill., U.S.A. 118 40 1N 89 51W
Petersburg, Ind., U.S.A. 119 38 30N 87 15W
Petersburg, Va., U.S.A. 114 37 17N 77 26W
Petersburg, W. Va., U.S.A. 114 38 59N 79 10W
Petford, Australia 72 17 20 S 144 58 E
Petília Policastro, Italy 29 39 7N 16 48 E
Petit Bois I., U.S.A. 115 30 16N 88 25W
Petit-Cap, Canada 105 49 3N 64 30W
Petit Goâve, Haiti 129 18 27N 72 51W
Petit Lac Manicouagan, Canada 105 51 25N 67 40W
Petit Saint Bernard, Col du, Italy 26 45 40N 6 52 E
Petitcodiac, Canada 105 45 57N 65 11W
Petite Baleine →, Canada 104 56 0N 76 45W
Petite-Rivière, Canada 107 47 20N 70 33W
Petite Saguenay, Canada 107 48 15N 70 4W
Petitsikapau, L., Canada 105 54 37N 66 25W
Petlad, India 48 22 30N 72 45 E
Peto, Mexico 127 20 10N 88 53W
Petone, N.Z. 80 41 13 S 174 53 E
Petoskey, U.S.A. 104 45 22N 84 57W
Petra, Jordan 44 30 20N 35 22 E
Petra, Spain 24 39 37N 3 6 E
Petra, Ostrova, U.S.S.R. 144 76 15N 118 30 E
Petralia, Italy 29 37 49N 14 4 E
Petrel, Spain 25 38 30N 0 46W
Petreto-Bicchisano, France 21 41 47N 8 58 E
Petrich, Bulgaria 35 41 24N 23 13 E
Petrijanec, Yugoslavia 27 46 23N 16 17 E
Petrikov, U.S.S.R. 36 52 11N 28 29 E
Petrinja, Yugoslavia 27 45 28N 16 18 E
Petrolândia, Brazil 138 9 5 S 38 20W
Petrolia, Canada 108 42 54N 82 9W
Petrolina, Brazil 138 9 24 S 40 30W
Petropavlovsk, U.S.S.R. 40 54 53N 69 13 E
Petropavlovsk-Kamchatskiy, U.S.S.R. 41 53 3N 158 43 E
Petropavlovskiy = Akhtubinsk, U.S.S.R. 39 48 13N 46 7 E
Petrópolis, Brazil 139 22 33 S 43 9W
Petroşeni, Romania 34 45 28N 23 20 E
Petroskey, U.S.A. 114 45 22N 84 57W
Petrova Gora, Yugoslavia 27 45 15N 15 45 E
Petrovac, Yugoslavia 33 42 13N 18 57 E
Petrovsk, U.S.S.R. 37 52 22N 45 19 E
Petrovsk-Zabaykalskiy, U.S.S.R. 41 51 20N 108 55 E
Petrovskoye = Svetlograd, U.S.S.R. 39 45 25N 42 58 E
Petrozavodsk, U.S.S.R. 40 61 41N 34 20 E
Petrus Steyn, S. Africa 97 27 38 S 28 8 E
Petrusburg, S. Africa 96 29 4 S 25 26 E
Pettitts, Australia 76 34 56 S 148 10 E
Petukhovka, U.S.S.R. 36 53 42N 30 54 E
Peumo, Chile 140 34 21 S 71 12W
Peureulak, Indonesia 56 4 48N 97 45 E
Pevek, U.S.S.R. 41 69 41N 171 19 E
Peveragno, Italy 26 44 20N 7 37 E
Peyrehorade, France 20 43 34N 1 7W
Peyruis, France 21 44 1N 5 56 E
Pézenas, France 20 43 28N 3 24 E
Pfaffenhofen, W. Germany 31 48 31N 11 31 E
Pfarrkirchen, W. Germany 31 48 25N 12 57 E
Pfeffenhausen, W. Germany 31 48 40N 11 58 E
Pforzheim, W. Germany 31 48 53N 8 43 E
Pfullendorf, W. Germany 31 47 55N 9 15 E
Pfungstadt, W. Germany 31 49 47N 8 36 E
Phala, Botswana 96 23 45 S 26 50 E
Phalera = Phulera, India 48 26 52N 75 16 E
Phalodi, India 48 27 12N 72 24 E
Phalsbourg, France 19 48 46N 7 15 E
Phan, Thailand 54 19 28N 99 43 E
Phan Rang, Vietnam 55 11 34N 109 0 E
Phan Ri = Hoa Da, Vietnam 55 11 16N 108 40 E
Phan Thiet, Vietnam 55 11 1N 108 9 E
Phanat Nikhom, Thailand 54 13 27N 101 11 E
Phangan, Ko, Thailand 55 9 45N 100 0 E
Phangnga, Thailand 55 8 28N 98 30 E
Phanh Bho Ho Chi Minh, Vietnam 55 10 58N 106 40 E
Phanom Sarakham, Thailand 54 13 45N 101 21 E
Pharenda, India 49 27 5N 83 17 E
Phatthalung, Thailand 55 7 39N 100 6 E
Phayao, Thailand 54 19 11N 99 55 E
Phelps, N.Y., U.S.A. 116 42 57N 77 5W
Phelps, Wis., U.S.A. 120 46 2N 89 2W
Phelps L., Canada 111 59 15N 103 15W
Phenix City, U.S.A. 115 32 30N 85 0W
Phet Buri, Thailand 54 13 1N 99 55 E
Phetchabun, Thailand 54 16 25N 101 8 E
Phetchabun, Thiu Khao, Thailand 54 16 0N 101 20 E
Phi Phi, Ko, Thailand 55 7 45N 98 46 E
Phiafay, Laos 54 14 48N 106 0 E
Phibun Mangsahan, Thailand 54 15 14N 105 14 E
Phichai, Thailand 54 17 22N 100 10 E
Phichit, Thailand 54 16 26N 100 22 E
Philadelphia, Miss., U.S.A. 121 32 47N 89 5W
Philadelphia, N.Y., U.S.A. 117 44 9N 75 40W
Philadelphia, Pa., U.S.A. 117 40 0N 75 10W
Philip, U.S.A. 120 44 4N 101 42W
Philippeville, Belgium 17 50 12N 4 33 E
Philippi L., Australia 72 24 20 S 138 55 E
Philippines ■, Asia 57 12 0N 123 0 E
Philippolis, S. Africa 96 30 15 S 25 16 E
Philippopolis = Plovdiv, Bulgaria 34 42 8N 24 44 E
Philipsburg, Canada 107 45 2N 73 5W
Philipsburg, Mont., U.S.A. 122 46 20N 113 21W
Philipsburg, Pa., U.S.A. 116 40 53N 78 10W
Philipstown, S. Africa 96 30 28 S 24 30 E
Phillip, I., Australia 74 38 30 S 145 12 E
Phillips, Tex., U.S.A. 121 35 48N 101 17W
Phillips, Wis., U.S.A. 120 45 41N 90 22W
Phillipsburg, Kans., U.S.A. 120 39 48N 99 20W
Phillipsburg, Pa., U.S.A. 117 40 43N 75 12W
Phillott, Australia 73 27 53 S 145 50 E
Philmont, U.S.A. 117 42 14N 73 37W
Philomath, U.S.A. 122 44 28N 123 21W
Phimai, Thailand 54 15 13N 102 30 E
Phitsanulok, Thailand 54 16 50N 100 12 E
Phnom Dangrek, Thailand 54 14 20N 104 0 E
Phnom Penh, Cambodia 55 11 33N 104 55 E
Phoenix, Ariz., U.S.A. 123 33 30N 112 10W
Phoenix, N.Y., U.S.A. 117 43 13N 76 18W
Phoenix Is., Kiribati 66 3 30 S 172 0W
Phoenixville, U.S.A. 117 40 12N 75 29W
Phon, Thailand 54 15 49N 102 36 E
Phon Tiou, Laos 54 17 53N 104 37 E
Phong →, Thailand 54 16 23N 102 56 E
Phong Saly, Laos 54 21 42N 102 9 E
Phong Tho, Vietnam 54 22 32N 103 21 E
Phonhong, Laos 54 18 30N 102 25 E
Phonum, Thailand 55 8 49N 98 48 E
Photharam, Thailand 54 13 41N 99 51 E
Phra Chedi Sam Ong, Thailand 54 15 16N 98 23 E
Phra Nakhon Si Ayutthaya, Thailand 54 14 25N 100 30 E
Phra Thong, Ko, Thailand 55 9 5N 98 17 E
Phrae, Thailand 54 18 7N 100 9 E
Phrom Phiram, Thailand 54 17 2N 100 12 E
Phu Dien, Vietnam 54 18 58N 105 31 E
Phu Loi, Laos 54 20 14N 103 14 E
Phu Ly, Vietnam 54 20 35N 105 50 E
Phu Tho, Vietnam 54 21 24N 105 13 E
Phuc Yen, Vietnam 54 21 16N 105 45 E
Phuket, Thailand 55 7 52N 98 22 E
Phuket, Ko, Thailand 55 8 0N 98 22 E
Phulbari, India 52 25 55N 90 2 E
Phulera, India 48 26 52N 75 16 E
Phun Phin, Thailand 55 9 7N 99 12 E
Piacá, Brazil 138 7 42 S 47 18W
Piacenza, Italy 26 45 2N 9 42 E
Piaçubaçu, Brazil 138 10 24 S 36 25W
Piádena, Italy 26 45 8N 10 22 E
Pialba, Australia 73 25 20 S 152 45 E
Pian Cr. →, Australia 73 30 2 S 148 12 E
Piana, France 21 42 15N 8 34 E
Pianella, Italy 27 42 24N 14 5 E
Piangil, Australia 74 35 5 S 143 20 E
Pianoro, Italy 27 44 20N 11 20 E
Pianosa, Puglia, Italy 27 42 12N 15 44 E
Pianosa, Toscana, Italy 26 42 36N 10 4 E
Piapot, Canada 111 49 59N 109 8W
Piare →, Italy 27 45 32N 12 44 E
Pias, Portugal 23 38 1N 7 29W
Piaseczno, Poland 32 52 5N 21 2 E
Piatã, Brazil 139 13 9 S 41 48W
Piatra, Romania 34 43 51N 25 9 E
Piatra Neamţ, Romania 34 46 56N 26 21 E
Piauí □, Brazil 138 7 0 S 43 0W
Piaui →, Brazil 138 6 38 S 42 42W
Piave →, Italy 27 45 32N 12 44 E
Piazza Ármerina, Italy 29 37 21N 14 20 E
Pibor →, Sudan 89 7 35N 33 0 E
Pibor Post, Sudan 89 6 47N 33 3 E
Pica, Chile 136 20 35 S 69 25W
Picardie, France 19 49 50N 3 0 E
Picardie, Plaine de, France 19 50 0N 2 0 E
Picardy = Picardie, France 19 49 50N 3 0 E
Picayune, U.S.A. 121 30 31N 89 40W
Picerno, Italy 29 40 40N 15 37 E
Pichilemu, Chile 140 34 22 S 72 0W
Pichincha, □, Ecuador 134 0 10 S 78 40W
Pickerel L., Canada 104 48 40N 91 25W
Pickle Lake, Canada 104 51 30N 90 12W
Pico Truncado, Argentina 142 46 40 S 68 0W
Picola, Australia 74 36 0 S 145 3 E
Picos, Brazil 138 7 5 S 41 28W
Picos Ancares, Sierra de, Spain 22 42 51N 6 52W
Picota, Peru 136 6 54 S 76 24W
Picquigny, France 19 49 56N 2 10 E
Picton, Australia 76 34 12 S 150 34 E
Picton, Canada 109 44 1N 77 9W
Picton, N.Z. 81 41 18 S 174 3 E
Picton, I., Chile 142 55 2 S 66 57W
Pictou, Canada 105 45 41N 62 42W
Picture Butte, Canada 110 49 55N 112 45W
Picuí, Brazil 138 6 31 S 36 21W
Picún Leufú, Argentina 142 39 30 S 69 5W
Pidurutalagala, Sri Lanka 51 7 10N 80 50 E
Piedad, La, Mexico 126 20 20N 102 1W
Piedecuesta, Colombia 134 6 59N 73 3W
Piedicavallo, Italy 26 45 41N 7 57 E
Piedmont = Piemonte □, Italy 26 45 0N 7 30 E
Piedmont, U.S.A. 115 33 55N 85 39W
Piedmont Plateau, U.S.A. 115 34 0N 81 30W
Piedmonte d'Alife, Italy 29 41 22N 14 22 E
Piedra →, Spain 24 41 18N 1 47W
Piedra del Anguila, Argentina 142 40 2 S 70 4W
Piedra Lais, Venezuela 134 3 10N 65 50W
Piedrabuena, Spain 23 39 0N 4 10W
Piedrahita, Spain 22 40 28N 5 23W
Piedras, R. de las →, Peru 136 12 30 S 69 15W
Piedras Negras, Mexico 126 28 35N 100 35W
Piemonte □, Italy 26 45 0N 7 30 E
Pier Millan, Australia 74 35 14 S 142 40 E
Pierce, U.S.A. 122 46 29N 115 53W
Piercefield, U.S.A. 117 44 13N 74 35W
Pierre, U.S.A. 120 44 23N 100 20W
Pierre Benite, Barrage, France 21 45 42N 4 49 E
Pierre-de-Bresse, France 21 46 54N 5 13 E
Pierrefeu-du-Var, France 21 43 13N 6 9 E
Pierrefonds, France 19 49 20N 3 0 E
Pierrefontaine-les-Varans, France 19 47 14N 6 32 E
Pierrefort, France 20 44 55N 2 50 E
Pierrelatte, France 21 44 23N 4 43 E
Pierreville, Canada 107 46 4N 72 49W
Piešťany, Czech. 32 48 38N 17 55 E
Piesting →, Austria 33 48 6N 16 40 E
Piet Retief, S. Africa 97 27 1 S 30 50 E
Pietarsaari = Jakobstad, Finland 8 63 40N 22 43 E
Pietermaritzburg, S. Africa 97 29 35 S 30 25 E
Pietersburg, S. Africa 97 23 54 S 29 25 E
Pietraperzia, Italy 29 37 26N 14 8 E
Pietrasanta, Italy 26 43 57N 10 12 E
Pietrosu, Romania 34 47 12N 25 8 E
Pietrosul, Romania 34 47 35N 24 43 E
Pieve di Cadore, Italy 27 46 25N 12 22 E
Pieve di Teco, Italy 26 44 3N 7 54 E
Pievepélago, Italy 26 44 12N 10 35 E
Pigádhia, Greece 35 35 30N 27 12 E
Pigeon, U.S.A. 114 43 50N 83 17W
Pigeon I., India 51 14 2N 74 20 E
Pigeon L., Canada 109 44 27N 78 30W
Piggott, U.S.A. 121 36 20N 90 10W
Pigna, Italy 26 43 57N 7 40 E
Pigüe, Argentina 140 37 36 S 62 25W
Pihani, India 49 27 36N 80 15 E
Pijnacker, Neths. 16 52 1N 4 26 E
Pikalevo, U.S.S.R. 36 59 37N 34 0 E
Pikedale, Australia 77 28 39 S 151 38 E
Pikes Peak, U.S.A. 120 38 50N 105 10W
Piketberg, S. Africa 96 32 55 S 18 40 E
Pikeville, U.S.A. 114 37 30N 82 30W
Pikou, China 61 39 18N 122 22 E
Pikwitonei, Canada 111 55 35N 97 9W
Piła, Poland 32 53 10N 16 48 E
Pila, Spain 25 38 16N 1 11W
Pilani, India 48 28 22N 75 33 E
Pilar, Brazil 138 9 36 S 35 56W
Pilar, Paraguay 140 26 50 S 58 20W
Pilas Group, Phil. 57 6 45N 121 35 E
Pilaya →, Bolivia 137 20 55 S 64 4W
Pilbara, Australia 78 21 15 S 118 16 E
Pilcomayo →, Paraguay 140 25 21 S 57 42W
Pilibhit, India 49 28 40N 79 50 E
Pilica →, Poland 32 51 52N 21 17 E
Pilkhawa, India 48 28 43N 77 42 E
Pillar Valley, Australia 77 29 46 S 153 7 E
Pillaro, Ecuador 134 1 10 S 78 32W
Pílos, Greece 35 36 55N 21 42 E
Pilot Grove, U.S.A. 118 38 53N 92 55W
Pilot Mound, Canada 111 49 15N 98 54W
Pilot Point, U.S.A. 121 33 26N 97 0W
Pilot Rock, U.S.A. 122 45 30N 118 50W
Pilsen = Plzeň, Czech. 32 49 45N 13 22 E
Pilštanj, Yugoslavia 27 46 8N 15 39 E
Pima, U.S.A. 123 32 54N 109 50W
Pimba, Australia 73 31 18 S 136 46 E
Pimenta Bueno, Brazil 137 11 35 S 61 10W
Pimentel, Peru 136 6 45 S 79 55W
Pimpinio, Australia 74 36 34 S 142 7 E
Pin-Blanc, L., Canada 106 46 45N 78 8W
Pina, Spain 24 41 29N 0 33W
Pinang, Malaysia 55 5 25N 100 15 E
Pinar del Río, Cuba 128 22 26N 83 40W
Pinchang, China 58 31 36N 107 3 E
Pincher Creek, Canada 110 49 30N 113 57W
Pinchi L., Canada 110 54 38N 124 30W
Pinckneyville, U.S.A. 118 38 5N 89 20W
Pîncota, Romania 34 46 20N 21 45 E
Pind Dadan Khan, Pakistan 48 32 36N 73 7 E
Pindar, Australia 79 28 30 S 115 47 E
Pindaré →, Brazil 138 3 17 S 44 47W
Pindaré Mirim, Brazil 138 3 37 S 45 21W
Pindi Gheb, Pakistan 48 33 14N 72 21 E
Pindiga, Nigeria 91 9 58N 10 53 E
Pindobal, Brazil 138 3 16 S 48 25W
Pindos Óros, Greece 35 40 0N 21 0 E
Pindus Mts. = Pindos Óros, Greece 35 40 0N 21 0 E
Pine, U.S.A. 123 34 27N 111 30W
Pine →, Canada 111 58 50N 105 38W
Pine, C., Canada 105 46 37N 53 32W
Pine, La, U.S.A. 122 43 40N 121 30W
Pine Bluff, U.S.A. 121 34 10N 92 0W
Pine City, U.S.A. 120 45 46N 93 0W
Pine Falls, Canada 111 50 34N 96 11W
Pine Flat Res., U.S.A. 124 36 50N 119 20W
Pine Pass, Canada 110 55 25N 122 42W
Pine Point, Canada 110 60 50N 114 28W
Pine Ridge, Australia 76 31 10 S 147 30 E
Pine Ridge, U.S.A. 120 43 0N 102 35W
Pine River, Canada 111 51 45N 100 30W
Pine River, U.S.A. 120 46 43N 94 24W
Pine Valley, U.S.A. 125 32 50N 116 32W
Pinecrest, U.S.A. 124 38 12N 120 1W
Pinedale, U.S.A. 124 36 50N 119 48W
Pinega →, U.S.S.R. 40 64 8N 46 54 E
Pinehill, Australia 72 23 38 S 146 57 E
Pinerolo, Italy 26 44 47N 7 21 E
Pineto, Italy 27 42 36N 14 4 E
Pinetop, U.S.A. 123 34 10N 109 57W
Pinetown, S. Africa 97 29 48 S 30 54 E
Pinetree, U.S.A. 122 43 42N 105 52W
Pineville, Ky., U.S.A. 115 36 42N 83 42W
Pineville, La., U.S.A. 121 31 22N 92 30W
Piney, France 19 48 22N 4 21 E
Piney Range, Australia 76 33 50 S 147 58 E
Ping →, Thailand 54 15 42N 100 9 E
Pingaring, Australia 79 32 40 S 118 32 E
Pingba, China 58 26 23N 106 12 E
Pingchuan, China 58 27 35N 101 55 E
Pingding, China 60 37 47N 113 38 E
Pingdingshan, China 60 33 43N 113 27 E
Pingdong, Taiwan 59 22 39N 120 30 E
Pingdu, China 61 36 42N 119 59 E
Pingelly, Australia 79 32 32 S 117 5 E
Pingguo, China 58 23 19N 107 36 E

Porter L.

Poland ■, Europe 32 52 0N 20 0 E
Polanów, Poland 32 54 7N 16 41 E
Polar Sub-Glacial Basin, Antarctica 143 85 0 S 110 0 E
Polcura, Chile 140 37 17 S 71 43W
Polden Hills, U.K. 13 51 7N 2 50W
Polessk, U.S.S.R. 36 54 50N 21 8 E
Polesye, U.S.S.R. 36 52 0N 28 10 E
Polewali, Indonesia 57 3 21 S 119 23 E
Polgar, Hungary 33 47 54N 21 6 E
Poli, Cameroon 94 8 34N 13 15 E
Políaigos, Greece 35 36 45N 24 38 E
Policastro, G. di, Italy 29 39 55N 15 35 E
Police, Poland 32 53 33N 14 33 E
Polignano a Mare, Italy 29 41 0N 17 12 E
Poligny, France 19 46 50N 5 42 E
Políkhnitas, Greece 35 39 4N 26 10 E
Polillo Is., Phil. 57 14 56N 122 0 E
Polístena, Italy 29 38 25N 16 4 E
Políyiros, Greece 35 40 23N 23 25 E
Polk, U.S.A. 116 41 22N 79 57W
Polla, Italy 29 40 31N 15 27 E
Pollachi, India 51 10 35N 77 0 E
Pollensa, Spain 24 39 54N 3 1 E
Pollensa, B. de, Spain 24 39 53N 3 8 E
Póllica, Italy 29 40 13N 15 3 E
Pollino, Mte., Italy 29 39 54N 16 13 E
Pollock, U.S.A. 120 45 58N 100 18W
Polna, U.S.S.R. 36 58 31N 28 0 E
Polnovat, U.S.S.R. 40 63 50N 65 54 E
Polo, Ill., U.S.A. 118 41 59N 89 38W
Polo, Mo., U.S.A. 118 39 33N 94 3W
Pologi, U.S.S.R. 38 47 29N 36 15 E
Polonnoye, U.S.S.R. 36 50 6N 27 30 E
Polotsk, U.S.S.R. 36 55 30N 28 50 E
Polson, U.S.A. 122 47 45N 114 12W
Poltava, U.S.S.R. 38 49 35N 34 35 E
Poltimore, Canada 106 45 47N 75 43W
Polunochnoye, U.S.S.R. 40 60 52N 60 25 E
Polur, India 51 12 32N 79 11 E
Polynesia, Pac. Oc. 67 10 0 S 162 0W
Pomarance, Italy 26 43 18N 10 51 E
Pomarico, Italy 29 40 31N 16 33 E
Pomaro, Mexico 126 18 20N 103 18W
Pombal, Brazil 138 6 45 S 37 50W
Pombal, Portugal 22 39 55N 8 40W
Pómbia, Greece 35 35 0N 24 51 E
Pomeroy, Ohio, U.S.A. 114 39 0N 82 0W
Pomeroy, Wash., U.S.A. 122 46 30N 117 33W
Pomio, Papua N. G. 69 5 32 S 151 33 E
Pomme de Terre, Res., U.S.A. 118 37 54N 93 19W
Pomona, U.S.A. 125 34 2N 117 49W
Pomorie, Bulgaria 34 42 32N 27 41 E
Pomoshnaya, U.S.S.R. 38 48 13N 31 36 E
Pompano Beach, U.S.A. 115 26 12N 80 6W
Pompei, Italy 29 40 45N 14 30 E
Pompey, France 19 48 46N 6 6 E
Pompeys Pillar, U.S.A. 122 46 0N 108 0W
Ponape = Pohnpei, Pac. Oc. 66 6 55N 158 10 E
Ponask, L., Canada 104 54 0N 92 41W
Ponass L., Canada 111 52 16N 103 58W
Ponca, U.S.A. 120 42 38N 96 41W
Ponca City, U.S.A. 121 36 40N 97 5W
Ponce, Puerto Rico 129 18 1N 66 37W
Ponchatoula, U.S.A. 121 30 27N 90 25W
Poncheville, L., Canada 106 50 10N 76 55W
Poncin, France 21 46 6N 5 25 E
Pond, U.S.A. 125 35 43N 119 20W
Pond Inlet, Canada 103 72 40N 77 0W
Pondicherry, India 51 11 59N 79 50 E
Pondrôme, Belgium 17 50 6N 5 0 E
Ponds, I. of, Canada 105 53 27N 55 52W
Ponérihouen, N. Cal. 68 21 5 S 165 24 E
Ponferrada, Spain 22 42 32N 6 35W
Pongo, Wadi →, Sudan 89 8 42N 27 40 E
Poniatowa, Poland 32 51 11N 22 3 E
Ponikva, Yugoslavia 27 46 16N 15 26 E
Ponnaiyar →, India 51 11 50N 79 45 E
Ponnani, India 51 10 45N 75 59 E
Ponneri, India 51 13 20N 80 15 E
Ponnuru, India 51 16 5N 80 34 E
Ponoi →, U.S.S.R. 40 66 59N 41 17 E
Ponoka, Canada 110 52 42N 113 40W
Ponorogo, Indonesia 57 7 52 S 111 27 E
Pons, France 20 45 35N 0 34W
Pons, Spain 24 41 55N 1 12 E
Ponsul →, Portugal 23 39 40N 7 31W
Pont-à-Celles, Belgium 17 50 30N 4 22 E
Pont-à-Mousson, France 19 48 54N 6 1 E
Pont-Audemer, France 18 49 21N 0 30 E
Pont-Aven, France 18 47 51N 3 47W
Pont Canavese, Italy 26 45 24N 7 33 E
Pont-de-Roide, France 19 47 23N 6 45 E
Pont-de-Salars, France 20 44 18N 2 44 E
Pont-de-Vaux, France 19 46 26N 4 56 E
Pont-de-Veyle, France 21 46 17N 4 53 E
Pont-l'Abbé, France 18 47 52N 4 15W
Pont-l'Évêque, France 18 49 18N 0 11 E
Pont-Rouge, Canada 107 46 45N 71 42W
Pont-St.-Esprit, France 21 44 16N 4 40 E
Pont-sur-Yonne, France 19 48 18N 3 10 E
Ponta de Pedras, Brazil 138 1 23 S 48 52W
Ponta Grossa, Brazil 141 25 7 S 50 10W
Ponta Pora, Brazil 141 22 20 S 55 35W
Pontacq, France 20 43 11N 0 8W
Pontailler-sur-Saône, France 19 47 13N 5 25 E
Pontal →, Brazil 138 9 8 S 40 12W
Pontalina, Brazil 139 17 31 S 49 27W
Pontarlier, France 19 46 54N 6 20 E
Pontassieve, Italy 27 43 47N 11 25 E
Pontaubault, France 18 48 40N 1 20W
Pontaumur, France 20 45 52N 2 40 E
Pontcharra, France 21 45 26N 6 1 E
Pontchartrain, L., U.S.A. 121 30 12N 90 0W
Pontchâteau, France 18 47 25N 2 5W
Ponte Alta, Serra do, Brazil 139 19 42 S 47 40W
Ponte Alta do Norte, Brazil 138 10 45 S 47 34W
Ponte Branca, Brazil 137 16 27 S 52 40W
Ponte da Barca, Portugal 22 41 48N 8 25W
Ponte de Sor, Portugal 23 39 17N 7 57W
Ponte dell 'Olio, Italy 26 44 52N 9 39 E
Ponte di Legno, Italy 26 46 15N 10 30 E
Ponte do Lima, Portugal 22 41 46N 8 35W
Ponte do Pungué, Mozam. 93 19 30 S 34 33 E
Ponte-Leccia, France 21 42 28N 9 13 E
Ponte Macassar, Indonesia 57 9 30 S 123 58 E
Ponte nell' Alpi, Italy 27 46 10N 12 18 E
Ponte Nova, Brazil 139 20 25 S 42 54W
Ponte San Martino, Italy 26 45 36N 7 47 E
Ponte San Pietro, Italy 26 45 42N 9 35 E
Pontebba, Italy 27 46 30N 13 17 E
Pontecorvo, Italy 28 41 28N 13 40 E
Pontedera, Italy 26 43 40N 10 37 E
Pontefract, U.K. 12 53 42N 1 19W
Ponteix, Canada 111 49 46N 107 29W
Pontelandolfo, Italy 29 41 17N 14 41 E
Pontevedra, Spain 22 42 26N 8 40W
Pontevedra □, Spain 22 42 25N 8 39W
Pontevedra, R. de →, Spain 22 42 22N 8 45W
Pontevico, Italy 26 45 16N 10 6 E
Pontiac, Ill., U.S.A. 119 40 50N 88 40W
Pontiac, Mich., U.S.A. 104 42 40N 83 20W
Pontiac, Parc, Canada 106 46 30N 76 30W
Pontian Kecil, Malaysia 55 1 29N 103 23 E
Pontianak, Indonesia 56 0 3 S 109 15 E
Pontine Is. = Ponziane, Isole, Italy 28 40 55N 13 0 E
Pontine Mts. = Kuzey Anadolu Dağlari, Turkey 46 41 30N 35 0 E
Pontínia, Italy 28 41 25N 13 2 E
Pontivy, France 18 48 5N 2 58W
Pontoise, France 19 49 3N 2 5 E
Ponton →, Canada 110 58 27N 116 11W
Pontorson, France 18 48 34N 1 30W
Pontrémoli, Italy 26 44 22N 9 52 E
Pontrieux, France 18 48 42N 3 10W
Ponts-de-Cé, Les, France 18 47 25N 0 30W
Pontypool, Canada 109 44 6N 78 38W
Pontypool, U.K. 13 51 42N 3 1W
Pontypridd, U.K. 13 51 36N 3 21W
Ponza, Italy 28 40 55N 12 57 E
Ponziane, Isole, Italy 28 40 55N 13 0 E
Poochera, Australia 73 32 43 S 134 51 E
Poole, U.K. 13 50 42N 1 58W
Pooley I., Canada 110 52 45N 128 15W
Poona = Pune, India 50 18 29N 73 57 E
Poonamallee, India 51 13 3N 80 10 E
Pooncarie, Australia 73 33 22 S 142 31 E
Poopelloe, L., Australia 73 31 40 S 144 0 E
Poopó, Bolivia 136 18 23 S 66 59W
Poopó, L. de, Bolivia 136 18 30 S 67 35W
Poor Knights Is., N.Z. 80 35 29 S 174 43 E
Poowong, Australia 74 38 21 S 145 46 E
Popanyinning, Australia 79 32 40 S 117 2 E
Popayán, Colombia 134 2 27N 76 36W
Poperinge, Belgium 17 50 51N 2 42 E
Popigay, U.S.S.R. 41 72 1N 110 39 E
Popilta, L., Australia 73 33 10 S 141 42 E
Popio, L., Australia 73 33 10 S 141 52 E
Poplar, U.S.A. 120 48 3N 105 9W
Poplar →, Man., Canada 111 53 0N 97 19W
Poplar →, N.W.T., Canada 110 61 22N 121 52W
Poplar Bluff, U.S.A. 121 36 45N 90 22W
Poplarville, U.S.A. 121 30 55N 89 30W
Popocatepetl, Mexico 127 19 10N 98 40W
Popokabaka, Zaïre 95 5 41 S 16 40 E
Pópoli, Italy 27 42 12N 13 50 E
Popondetta, Papua N. G. 69 8 48 S 148 17 E
Popovača, Yugoslavia 27 45 30N 16 41 E
Popovo, Bulgaria 34 43 21N 26 18 E
Poppel, Belgium 17 51 27N 5 2 E
Poprád, Czech. 32 49 3N 20 18 E
Poprád →, Czech. 32 49 38N 20 42 E
Poradaha, Bangla. 52 23 51N 89 1 E
Porali →, Pakistan 48 25 35N 66 26 E
Porangaba, Brazil 136 8 48 S 70 36W
Porangahau, N.Z. 80 40 17 S 176 37 E
Porangatu, Brazil 139 13 26 S 49 10W
Porbandar, India 48 21 44N 69 43 E
Porce →, Colombia 134 7 28N 74 53W
Porcher I., Canada 110 53 50N 130 30W
Porco, Bolivia 137 19 50 S 65 59W
Porcos →, Brazil 139 12 42 S 45 7W
Porcuna, Spain 23 37 52N 4 11W
Porcupine, Canada 106 48 30N 81 11W
Porcupine →, Canada 111 59 11N 104 46W
Porcupine →, U.S.A. 102 66 35N 145 15W
Pordenone, Italy 27 45 58N 12 40 E
Poreč, Yugoslavia 27 45 14N 13 36 E
Porecatu, Brazil 139 22 43 S 51 24W
Porepunkah, Australia 75 36 42 S 146 55 E
Poretskoye, U.S.S.R. 37 55 9N 46 21 E
Pori, Finland 9 61 29N 21 48 E
Porjus, Sweden 8 66 57N 19 50 E
Porkhov, U.S.S.R. 36 57 45N 29 38 E
Porkkala, Finland 9 59 59N 24 26 E
Porlamar, Venezuela 135 10 57N 63 51W
Porlezza, Italy 26 46 2N 9 8 E
Porma →, Spain 22 42 49N 5 28W
Pornic, France 18 47 7N 2 5W
Poronaysk, U.S.S.R. 41 49 13N 143 0 E
Póros, Greece 35 37 30N 23 30 E
Poroshiri-Dake, Japan 63 42 41N 142 52 E
Poroto Mts., Tanzania 93 9 0 S 33 30 E
Porpoise B., Antarctica 143 66 0 S 127 0 E
Porquerolles, I. de, France 21 43 0N 6 13 E
Porrentruy, Switz. 31 47 25N 7 6 E
Porreras, Spain 24 39 31N 3 2 E
Porretta, Passo di, Italy 26 44 2N 10 56 E
Porsangen, Norway 8 70 40N 25 40 E
Porsgrunn, Norway 10 59 10N 9 40 E
Port Adelaide, Australia 73 34 46 S 138 30 E
Port Alberni, Canada 110 49 14N 124 50W
Port Albert, Australia 75 38 42 S 146 42 E
Port Alfred, Canada 107 48 18N 70 53W
Port Alfred, S. Africa 96 33 36 S 26 55 E
Port Alice, Canada 110 50 20N 127 25W
Port Allegany, U.S.A. 116 41 49N 78 17W
Port Allen, U.S.A. 121 30 30N 91 15W
Port Alma, Australia 72 23 38 S 150 53 E
Port Angeles, U.S.A. 124 48 7N 123 30W
Port Antonio, Jamaica 128 18 10N 76 30W
Port Aransas, U.S.A. 121 27 49N 97 4W
Port Arthur = Lüshun, China 61 38 45N 121 15 E
Port Arthur, Australia 72 43 7 S 147 50 E
Port Arthur, U.S.A. 121 30 0N 94 0W
Port au Port B., Canada 105 48 40N 58 50W
Port-au-Prince, Haiti 129 18 40N 72 20W
Port Augusta, Australia 73 32 30 S 137 50 E
Port Augusta West, Australia 73 32 29 S 137 29 E
Port Austin, U.S.A. 116 44 3N 82 59W
Port Bell, Uganda 92 0 18N 32 35 E
Port Bergé Vaovao, Madag. 97 15 33 S 47 40 E
Port Blandford, Canada 105 48 20N 54 10W
Port Bou, Spain 24 42 25N 3 9 E
Port Bouët, Ivory C. 90 5 16N 3 57W
Port Bradshaw, Australia 72 12 30 S 137 20 E
Port Broughton, Australia 73 33 37 S 137 56 E
Port Burwell, Canada 108 42 40N 80 48W
Port Campbell, Australia 74 38 37 S 143 1 E
Port Canning, India 49 22 23N 88 40 E
Port Carling, Canada 108 45 7N 79 35W
Port-Cartier, Canada 105 50 2N 66 50W
Port Chalmers, N.Z. 81 45 49 S 170 30 E
Port Chester, U.S.A. 117 41 0N 73 41W
Port Clements, Canada 110 53 40N 132 10W
Port Clinton, U.S.A. 119 41 30N 82 58W
Port Colborne, Canada 108 42 50N 79 10W
Port Coquitlam, Canada 110 49 15N 122 45W
Port Credit, Canada 108 43 33N 79 35W
Port Curtis, Australia 72 23 57 S 151 20 E
Port Dalhousie, Canada 116 43 13N 79 16W
Port Darwin, Australia 78 12 24 S 130 45 E
Port Darwin, Falk. Is. 142 51 50 S 59 0W
Port Davey, Australia 72 43 16 S 145 55 E
Port-de-Bouc, France 21 43 24N 4 59 E
Port-de-Paix, Haiti 129 19 50N 72 50W
Port Dickson, Malaysia 55 2 30N 101 49 E
Port Douglas, Australia 72 16 30 S 145 30 E
Port Dover, Canada 108 42 47N 80 12W
Port Edward, Canada 110 54 12N 130 10W
Port Elgin, Canada 108 44 25N 81 25W
Port Elizabeth, S. Africa 96 33 58 S 25 40 E
Port Ellen, U.K. 14 55 38N 6 10W
Port-en-Bessin, France 18 49 21N 0 45W
Port Erin, I. of Man 12 54 5N 4 45W
Port Essington, Australia 78 11 15 S 132 10 E
Port Etienne = Nouâdhibou, Mauritania 84 20 54N 17 0W
Port Fairy, Australia 74 38 22 S 142 12 E
Port Fitzroy, N.Z. 80 36 8 S 175 20 E
Port Fouâd = Bûr Fuad, Egypt 88 31 15N 32 20 E
Port Gamble, U.S.A. 124 47 51N 122 35W
Port-Gentil, Gabon 94 0 40 S 8 50 E
Port Gibson, U.S.A. 121 31 57N 91 0W
Port Glasgow, U.K. 14 55 57N 4 40W
Port Harcourt, Nigeria 91 4 40N 7 10 E
Port Hardy, Canada 110 50 41N 127 30W
Port Harrison = Inoucdjouac, Canada 103 58 25N 78 15W
Port Hawkesbury, Canada 105 45 36N 61 22W
Port Hedland, Australia 78 20 25 S 118 35 E
Port Henry, U.S.A. 117 44 0N 73 30W
Port Hood, Canada 105 46 0N 61 32W
Port Hope, Canada 109 43 56N 78 20W
Port Hueneme, U.S.A. 125 34 7N 119 12W
Port Huron, U.S.A. 104 43 0N 82 28W
Port Isabel, U.S.A. 121 26 4N 97 9W
Port Jackson, Australia 76 33 50 S 151 18 E
Port Jefferson, U.S.A. 117 40 58N 73 5W
Port Jervis, U.S.A. 117 41 22N 74 42W
Port-Joinville, France 18 46 45N 2 23W
Port Katon, U.S.S.R. 39 46 52N 38 46 E
Port Kembla, Australia 76 34 52 S 150 49 E
Port-la-Nouvelle, France 20 43 1N 3 3 E
Port Laoise, Ireland 15 53 2N 7 20W
Port Lavaca, U.S.A. 121 28 38N 96 38W
Port-Leucate, France 20 42 53N 3 3 E
Port Lincoln, Australia 73 34 42 S 135 52 E
Port Loko, S. Leone 90 8 48N 12 46W
Port Loring, Canada 108 45 55N 80 0W
Port Louis, France 18 47 42N 3 22W
Port Louis, Mauritius 53 20 10 S 57 30 E
Port Lyautey = Kenitra, Morocco 84 34 15N 6 40W
Port Macdonnell, Australia 73 38 0 S 140 48 E
Port Macquarie, Australia 77 31 25 S 152 25 E
Port Maria, Jamaica 128 18 25N 77 5W
Port Mellon, Canada 110 49 32N 123 31W
Port-Menier, Canada 105 49 51N 64 15W
Port Morant, Jamaica 128 17 54N 76 19W
Port Moresby, Papua N. G. 69 9 24 S 147 8 E
Port Mourant, Guyana 135 6 15N 57 20W
Port Mouton, Canada 105 43 58N 64 50W
Port Musgrave, Australia 72 11 55 S 141 50 E
Port-Navalo, France 18 47 34N 2 54W
Port Nelson, Canada 111 57 3N 92 36W
Port Nicholson, N.Z. 80 41 20 S 174 52 E
Port Nolloth, S. Africa 96 29 17 S 16 52 E
Port Nouveau-Québec, Canada 103 58 30N 65 59W
Port O'Connor, U.S.A. 121 28 26N 96 24W
Port of Spain, Trin. & Tob. 129 10 40N 61 31W
Port Orchard, U.S.A. 124 47 31N 122 38W
Port Orford, U.S.A. 122 42 45N 124 28W
Port Pegasus, N.Z. 81 47 12 S 167 41 E
Port Perry, Canada 109 44 6N 78 56W
Port Phillip B., Australia 74 38 10 S 144 50 E
Port Pirie, Australia 73 33 10 S 138 1 E
Port Radium = Echo Bay, Canada 102 66 5N 117 55W
Port Renfrew, Canada 110 48 30N 124 20W
Port Roper, Australia 72 14 45 S 135 25 E
Port Rowan, Canada 108 42 40N 80 30W
Port Safaga = Bûr Safâga, Egypt 88 26 43N 33 57 E
Port Said = Bûr Sa'îd, Egypt 88 31 16N 32 18 E
Port St. Joe, U.S.A. 115 29 49N 85 20W
Port St. Johns, S. Africa 97 31 38 S 29 33 E
Port-St.-Louis-du-Rhône, France 21 43 23N 4 49 E
Port Sanilac, U.S.A. 116 43 26N 82 33W
Port Saunders, Canada 105 50 40N 57 18W
Port Severn, Canada 108 44 48N 79 43W
Port Shepstone, S. Africa 97 30 44 S 30 28 E
Port Simpson, Canada 110 54 30N 130 20W
Port Stanley, Canada 108 42 40N 81 10W
Port Stephens, Australia 76 32 38 S 152 12 E
Port Sudan = Bûr Sûdân, Sudan 88 19 32N 37 9 E
Port-sur-Saône, France 19 47 42N 6 2 E
Port Talbot, U.K. 13 51 35N 3 48W
Port Taufiq = Bûr Taufiq, Egypt 88 29 54N 32 32 E
Port Townsend, U.S.A. 124 48 7N 122 50W
Port-Vendres, France 20 42 32N 3 8 E
Port Wakefield, Australia 73 34 12 S 138 10 E
Port Washington, U.S.A. 114 43 25N 87 52W
Port Weld, Malaysia 55 4 50N 100 38 E
Port Welshpool, Australia 75 38 42 S 146 28 E
Portachuelo, Bolivia 137 17 10 S 63 20W
Portadown, U.K. 15 54 27N 6 26W
Portage, Mich., U.S.A. 118 42 12N 85 35W
Portage, U.S.A. 120 43 31N 89 25W
Portage →, U.S.A. 119 41 32N 82 58W
Portage La Prairie, Canada 111 49 58N 98 18W
Portageville, U.S.A. 121 36 25N 89 40W
Portalegre, Portugal 23 39 19N 7 25W
Portalegre □, Portugal 23 39 20N 7 40W
Portales, U.S.A. 121 34 12N 103 25W
Portarlington, Australia 74 38 7 S 144 40 E
Portarlington, Ireland 15 53 10N 7 10W
Porte, La, U.S.A. 119 41 36N 86 43W
Porte City, La, U.S.A. 118 42 19N 92 12W
Porteirinha, Brazil 139 15 44 S 43 2W
Portel, Brazil 138 1 57 S 50 49W
Portel, Portugal 23 38 19N 7 41W
Porter, U.S.A. 119 41 36N 87 4W
Porter L., N.W.T., Canada 111 61 41N 108 5W
Porter L., Sask., Canada 111 56 20N 107 20W

Pyaye

Prinsesse Astrid Kyst, *Antarctica* **143** 70 45 S 12 30 E
Prinsesse Ragnhild Kyst, *Antarctica* **143** 70 15 S 27 30 E
Prinzapolca, *Nic.* **128** 13 20N 83 35W
Prior, C., *Spain* **22** 43 34N 8 17W
Pripet = Pripyat →, *U.S.S.R.* **36** 51 20N 30 9 E
Pripet Marshes = Polesye, *U.S.S.R.* **36** 52 0N 28 10 E
Pripyat →, *U.S.S.R.* **36** 51 20N 30 9 E
Pripyat Marshes = Polesye, *U.S.S.R.* **36** 52 0N 28 10 E
Prislop, Pasul, *Romania* **34** 47 37N 25 15 E
Pristen, *U.S.S.R.* **37** 51 15N 36 44 E
Priština, *Yugoslavia* **33** 42 40N 21 13 E
Pritzwalk, *E. Germany* **30** 53 10N 12 11 E
Privas, *France* **21** 44 45N 4 37 E
Priverno, *Italy* **28** 41 29N 13 10 E
Privolzhsk, *U.S.S.R.* **37** 57 23N 41 16 E
Privolzhskaya Vozvyshennost, *U.S.S.R.* **37** 51 0N 46 0 E
Privolzhskiy, *U.S.S.R.* **37** 51 25N 46 3 E
Privolzhye, *U.S.S.R.* **37** 52 52N 48 33 E
Priyutnoye, *U.S.S.R.* **39** 46 12N 43 40 E
Prizren, *Yugoslavia* **33** 42 13N 20 45 E
Prizzi, *Italy* **28** 37 44N 13 24 E
Prnjavor, *Yugoslavia* **33** 44 52N 17 43 E
Probolinggo, *Indonesia* **57** 7 46 S 113 13 E
Procida, *Italy* **28** 40 46N 14 0 E
Proddatur, *India* **51** 14 45N 78 30 E
Proença-a-Nova, *Portugal* **23** 39 45N 7 54W
Prof. Van Blommestein Meer, *Surinam* **135** 4 45N 55 5W
Profondeville, *Belgium* **17** 50 23N 4 52 E
Progreso, *Mexico* **127** 21 20N 89 40W
Prokhladnyy, *U.S.S.R.* **39** 43 50N 44 2 E
Prokletije, *Albania* **34** 42 30N 19 45 E
Prokopyevsk, *U.S.S.R.* **40** 54 0N 86 45 E
Prokuplje, *Yugoslavia* **33** 43 16N 21 36 E
Proletarskaya, *U.S.S.R.* **39** 46 42N 41 50 E
Prome = Pyè, *Burma* **52** 18 49N 95 13 E
Prophet →, *Canada* **110** 58 48N 122 40W
Prophetstown, *U.S.A.* **118** 41 40N 89 56W
Propriá, *Brazil* **138** 10 13 S 36 51W
Propriano, *France* **21** 41 41N 8 52 E
Proserpine, *Australia* **72** 20 21 S 148 36 E
Prosser, *U.S.A.* **122** 46 11N 119 52W
Prostějov, *Czech.* **32** 49 30N 17 9 E
Proston, *Australia* **73** 26 8 S 151 32 E
Protection, *U.S.A.* **121** 37 16N 99 30W
Próti, *Greece* **35** 37 5N 21 32 E
Provadiya, *Bulgaria* **34** 43 12N 27 30 E
Proven, *Belgium* **17** 50 54N 2 40 E
Provence, *France* **21** 43 40N 5 46 E
Providence, *Ky., U.S.A.* **114** 37 25N 87 46W
Providence, *R.I., U.S.A.* **117** 41 50N 71 28W
Providence Bay, *Canada* **108** 45 41N 82 15W
Providence C., *N.Z.* **81** 45 59 S 166 29 E
Providence Mts., *U.S.A.* **123** 35 0N 115 30W
Providencia, *Ecuador* **134** 0 28 S 76 28W
Providencia, I. de, *Colombia* **128** 13 25N 81 26W
Provideniya, *U.S.S.R.* **41** 64 23N 173 18W
Provins, *France* **19** 48 33N 3 15 E
Provo, *U.S.A.* **122** 40 16N 111 37W
Provost, *Canada* **111** 52 25N 110 20W
Prozor, *Yugoslavia* **33** 43 50N 17 34 E
Prudentópolis, *Brazil* **139** 25 12 S 50 57W
Prud'homme, *Canada* **111** 52 20N 105 54W
Prudnik, *Poland* **32** 50 20N 17 38 E
Prüm, *W. Germany* **31** 50 14N 6 22 E
Pruszcz Gd., *Poland* **32** 54 17N 18 40 E
Pruszków, *Poland* **32** 52 9N 20 49 E
Prut →, *Romania* **34** 45 28N 28 10 E
Pruzhany, *U.S.S.R.* **36** 52 33N 24 28 E
Prvič, *Yugoslavia* **27** 44 55N 14 47 E
Prydz B., *Antarctica* **143** 69 0 S 74 0 E
Pryor, *U.S.A.* **121** 36 17N 95 20W
Przasnysz, *Poland* **32** 53 2N 20 45 E
Przedbórz, *Poland* **32** 51 6N 19 53 E
Przemysl, *Poland* **32** 49 50N 22 45 E
Przeworsk, *Poland* **32** 50 6N 22 32 E
Przewóz, *Poland* **32** 51 28N 14 57 E
Przhevalsk, *U.S.S.R.* **40** 42 30N 78 20 E
Przysuchla, *Poland* **32** 51 22N 20 38 E
Psakhná, *Greece* **35** 38 34N 23 35 E
Psará, *Greece* **35** 38 37N 25 38 E
Psel →, *U.S.S.R.* **38** 49 5N 33 20 E
Pserimos, *Greece* **35** 36 56N 27 12 E
Pskov, *U.S.S.R.* **36** 57 50N 28 25 E
Psunj, *Yugoslavia* **33** 45 25N 17 19 E
Pszczyna, *Poland* **32** 49 59N 18 58 E
Pteleón, *Greece* **35** 39 3N 22 57 E
Ptich →, *U.S.S.R.* **36** 52 9N 28 52 E
Ptolemaís, *Greece* **35** 40 30N 21 43 E
Ptuj, *Yugoslavia* **27** 46 28N 15 50 E
Ptujska Gora, *Yugoslavia* **27** 46 23N 15 47 E
Pu Xian, *China* **60** 36 24N 111 6 E
Pua, *Thailand* **54** 19 11N 100 55 E
Puán, *Argentina* **140** 37 30 S 62 45W
Pu'an, *China* **58** 25 46N 104 57 E
Pu'apu'a, *W. Samoa* **68** 13 34 S 172 9W
Pubei, *China* **58** 22 16N 109 31 E
Pucacuro →, *Peru* **134** 3 20 S 74 58W
Pucallpa, *Peru* **136** 8 25 S 74 30W
Pucará, *Bolivia* **137** 18 43 S 64 11W
Pucará, *Peru* **136** 15 5 S 70 24W
Pucarani, *Bolivia* **136** 16 23 S 68 30W
Pucheng, *China* **59** 27 59N 118 31 E
Pučišće, *Yugoslavia* **27** 43 22N 16 43 E
Pucka, Zatoka, *Poland* **32** 54 30N 18 40 E
Puckapunyal, *Australia* **74** 37 0 S 145 3 E
Puding, *China* **58** 26 18N 105 44 E
Pudukkottai, *India* **51** 10 28N 78 47 E
Puebla, *Mexico* **127** 19 0N 98 10W
Puebla □, *Mexico* **127** 18 30N 98 0W
Puebla, La, *Spain* **24** 39 46N 3 1 E
Puebla de Alcocer, *Spain* **23** 38 59N 5 14W
Puebla de Cazalla, La, *Spain* **23** 37 10N 5 20W
Puebla de Don Fadrique, *Spain* **25** 37 58N 2 25W
Puebla de Don Rodrigo, *Spain* **23** 39 5N 4 37W
Puebla de Guzmán, *Spain* **23** 37 37N 7 15W
Puebla de los Infantes, La, *Spain* **23** 37 47N 5 24W
Puebla de Montalbán, La, *Spain* **22** 39 52N 4 22W
Puebla de Sanabria, *Spain* **22** 42 4N 6 38W
Puebla de Trives, *Spain* **22** 42 20N 7 10W
Puebla del Caramiñal, *Spain* **22** 42 37N 8 56W
Pueblo, *U.S.A.* **120** 38 20N 104 40W
Pueblo Hundido, *Chile* **140** 26 20 S 70 5W
Pueblo Nuevo, *Venezuela* **134** 8 26N 71 26W
Puelches, *Argentina* **140** 38 5 S 65 51W
Puelén, *Argentina* **140** 37 32 S 67 38W
Puente Alto, *Chile* **140** 33 32 S 70 35W
Puente del Arzobispo, *Spain* **22** 39 48N 5 10W
Puente-Genil, *Spain* **23** 37 22N 4 47W
Puente la Reina, *Spain* **24** 42 40N 1 49W
Puenteareas, *Spain* **22** 42 10N 8 28W
Puentedeume, *Spain* **22** 43 24N 8 10W
Puentes de Garcia Rodriguez, *Spain* **22** 43 27N 7 50W
Pu'er, *China* **58** 23 0N 101 15 E
Puerco →, *U.S.A.* **123** 34 22N 107 50W
Puerta, La, *Spain* **25** 38 22N 2 45W
Puerto, *Canary Is.* **25** 28 5N 17 20W
Puerto Acosta, *Bolivia* **136** 15 32 S 69 15W
Puerto Aisén, *Chile* **142** 45 27 S 73 0W
Puerto Ángel, *Mexico* **127** 15 40N 96 29W
Puerto Arista, *Mexico* **127** 15 56N 93 48W
Puerto Armuelles, *Panama* **128** 8 20N 82 51W
Puerto Ayacucho, *Venezuela* **134** 5 40N 67 35W
Puerto Barrios, *Guatemala* **128** 15 40N 88 32W
Puerto Bermejo, *Argentina* **140** 26 55 S 58 34W
Puerto Bermúdez, *Peru* **136** 10 20 S 75 0W
Puerto Bolívar, *Ecuador* **134** 3 19 S 79 55W
Puerto Cabello, *Venezuela* **134** 10 28N 68 1W
Puerto Cabezas, *Nic.* **128** 14 0N 83 30W
Puerto Cabo Gracias á Dios, *Nic.* **128** 15 0N 83 10W
Puerto Capaz = Jebba, *Morocco* **84** 35 11N 4 43W
Puerto Carreño, *Colombia* **134** 6 12N 67 22W
Puerto Castilla, *Honduras* **128** 16 0N 86 0W
Puerto Chicama, *Peru* **136** 7 45 S 79 20W
Puerto Coig, *Argentina* **142** 50 54 S 69 15W
Puerto Cortes, *Costa Rica* **128** 8 55N 84 0W
Puerto Cortés, *Honduras* **128** 15 51N 88 0W
Puerto Cumarebo, *Venezuela* **134** 11 29N 69 30W
Puerto de Gran Tarajal, *Canary Is.* **25** 28 13N 14 1W
Puerto de la Cruz, *Canary Is.* **25** 28 24N 16 32W
Puerto de Pozo Negro, *Canary Is.* **25** 28 19N 13 55W
Puerto de Santa María, *Spain* **23** 36 36N 6 13W
Puerto del Rosario, *Canary Is.* **25** 28 30N 13 52W
Puerto Deseado, *Argentina* **142** 47 55 S 66 0W
Puerto Guaraní, *Paraguay* **137** 21 18 S 57 55W
Puerto Heath, *Bolivia* **136** 12 34 S 68 39W
Puerto Huitoto, *Colombia* **134** 0 18N 74 3W
Puerto Inca, *Peru* **136** 9 22 S 74 54W
Puerto Juárez, *Mexico* **127** 21 11N 86 49W
Puerto La Cruz, *Venezuela* **135** 10 13N 64 38W
Puerto Leguízamo, *Colombia* **134** 0 12 S 74 46W
Puerto Limón, *Colombia* **134** 3 23N 73 30W
Puerto Lobos, *Argentina* **142** 42 0 S 65 3W
Puerto López, *Colombia* **134** 4 5N 72 58W
Puerto Lumbreras, *Spain* **25** 37 34N 1 48W
Puerto Madryn, *Argentina* **142** 42 48 S 65 4W
Puerto Maldonado, *Peru* **136** 12 30 S 69 10W
Puerto Manotí, *Cuba* **128** 21 22N 76 50W
Puerto Mazarrón, *Spain* **25** 37 34N 1 15W
Puerto Mercedes, *Colombia* **134** 1 11N 72 53W
Puerto Miraña, *Colombia* **134** 1 20 S 70 19W
Puerto Montt, *Chile* **142** 41 28 S 73 0W
Puerto Morelos, *Mexico* **127** 20 49N 86 52W
Puerto Nariño, *Colombia* **134** 4 56N 67 48W
Puerto Natales, *Chile* **142** 51 45 S 72 15W
Puerto Nuevo, *Colombia* **134** 5 53N 69 56W
Puerto Nutrias, *Venezuela* **134** 8 5N 69 18W
Puerto Ordaz, *Venezuela* **135** 8 16N 62 44W
Puerto Padre, *Cuba* **128** 21 13N 76 35W
Puerto Páez, *Venezuela* **134** 6 13N 67 28W
Puerto Peñasco, *Mexico* **126** 31 20N 113 33W
Puerto Pinasco, *Paraguay* **140** 22 36 S 57 50W
Puerto Pirámides, *Argentina* **142** 42 35 S 64 20W
Puerto Plata, *Dom. Rep.* **129** 19 48N 70 45W
Puerto Portillo, *Peru* **136** 9 45 S 72 42W
Puerto Princesa, *Phil.* **57** 9 46N 118 45 E
Puerto Quellón, *Chile* **142** 43 7 S 73 37W
Puerto Quepos, *Costa Rica* **128** 9 29N 84 6W
Puerto Real, *Spain* **23** 36 33N 6 12W
Puerto Rico, *Bolivia* **136** 11 5 S 67 38W
Puerto Rico ■, *W. Indies* **129** 18 15N 66 45W
Puerto Saavedra, *Chile* **142** 38 47 S 73 24W
Puerto Sastre, *Paraguay* **140** 22 2 S 57 55W
Puerto Siles, *Bolivia* **137** 12 48 S 65 5W
Puerto Suárez, *Bolivia* **137** 18 58 S 57 52W
Puerto Tejada, *Colombia* **134** 3 14N 76 24W
Puerto Umbría, *Colombia* **134** 0 52N 76 33W
Puerto Vallarta, *Mexico* **126** 20 36N 105 15W
Puerto Varas, *Chile* **142** 41 19 S 72 59W
Puerto Villazón, *Bolivia* **137** 13 32 S 61 57W
Puerto Wilches, *Colombia* **134** 7 21N 73 54W
Puertollano, *Spain* **23** 38 43N 4 7W
Puertomarin, *Spain* **22** 42 48N 7 36W
Puesto Cunambo, *Peru* **134** 2 10 S 76 0W
Pueyrredón, L., *Argentina* **142** 47 20 S 72 0W
Pugachev, *U.S.S.R.* **37** 52 0N 48 49 E
Puge, *China* **58** 27 20N 102 31 E
Puge, *Tanzania* **92** 4 45 S 33 11 E
Puget Sd., *U.S.A.* **122** 47 15N 122 30W
Puget-Théniers, *France* **21** 43 58N 6 53 E
Púglia □, *Italy* **29** 41 0N 16 30 E
Pugu, *Tanzania* **92** 6 55 S 39 4 E
Puha, *N.Z.* **80** 38 30 S 177 50 E
Pui, *Romania* **34** 45 30N 23 4 E
Puica, *Peru* **136** 15 0 S 72 33W
Puig Mayor, Mte., *Spain* **24** 39 48N 2 47 E
Puigcerdá, *Spain* **24** 42 24N 1 50 E
Puigmal, *Spain* **24** 42 23N 2 7 E
Puisaye, Collines de la, *France* **19** 47 37N 3 20 E
Puiseaux, *France* **19** 48 11N 2 30 E
Pujilí, *Ecuador* **134** 0 57 S 78 41W
Puka, *Albania* **34** 42 2N 19 53 E
Pukaki L., *N.Z.* **81** 44 4 S 170 1 E
Pukapuka, *Cook Is.* **67** 10 53 S 165 49W
Pukatawagan, *Canada* **111** 55 45N 101 20W
Pukearuhe, *N.Z.* **80** 38 55 S 174 31 E
Pukekohe, *N.Z.* **80** 37 12 S 174 55 E
Puketeraki Ra., *N.Z.* **81** 42 58 S 172 13 E
Pukeuri, *N.Z.* **81** 45 4 S 171 2 E
Pukou, *China* **59** 32 7N 118 38 E
Pula, *Italy* **28** 39 0N 9 0 E
Pula, *Yugoslavia* **27** 44 54N 13 57 E
Pulacayo, *Bolivia* **136** 20 25 S 66 41W
Pulaski, *N.Y., U.S.A.* **117** 43 32N 76 9W
Pulaski, *Tenn., U.S.A.* **115** 35 10N 87 0W
Pulaski, *Va., U.S.A.* **114** 37 4N 80 49W
Pulawy, *Poland* **32** 51 23N 21 59 E
Pulga, *U.S.A.* **124** 39 48N 121 29W
Pulgaon, *India* **50** 20 44N 78 21 E
Pulicat, L., *India* **51** 13 40N 80 15 E
Puliyangudi, *India* **51** 9 11N 77 24 E
Pullabooka, *Australia* **76** 33 44 S 147 46 E
Pullman, *U.S.A.* **122** 46 49N 117 10W
Pulog, Mt., *Phil.* **57** 16 40N 120 50 E
Púlpito do Sul, *Angola* **95** 15 46 S 12 0 E
Pultusk, *Poland* **32** 52 43N 21 6 E
Pumlumon Fawr, *U.K.* **13** 52 29N 3 47W
Puna, *Bolivia* **137** 19 45 S 65 28W
Puná, I., *Ecuador* **134** 2 55 S 80 5W
Punakha, *Bhutan* **52** 27 42N 89 52 E
Punalur, *India* **51** 9 0N 76 56 E
Punasar, *India* **48** 27 6N 73 6 E
Punata, *Bolivia* **137** 17 32 S 65 50W
Punavia, *Tahiti* **68** 17 38 S 149 36W
Punch, *India* **49** 33 48N 74 4 E
Pune, *India* **50** 18 29N 73 57 E
Pungue, Ponte de, *Mozam.* **93** 19 0 S 34 0 E
Puning, *China* **59** 23 20N 116 12 E
Punjab □, *India* **48** 31 0N 76 0 E
Punjab □, *Pakistan* **48** 30 0N 72 0 E
Puno, *Peru* **136** 15 55 S 70 3W
Punta Alta, *Argentina* **142** 38 53 S 62 4W
Punta Arenas, *Chile* **142** 53 10 S 71 0W
Punta Cardón, *Venezuela* **134** 11 38N 70 14W
Punta Coles, *Peru* **136** 17 43 S 71 23W
Punta de Bombón, *Peru* **136** 17 10 S 71 48W
Punta de Díaz, *Chile* **140** 28 0 S 70 45W
Punta de Piedras, *Venezuela* **134** 10 54N 64 6W
Punta Delgado, *Argentina* **142** 42 43 S 63 38W
Punta Gorda, *Belize* **127** 16 10N 88 45W
Punta Gorda, *U.S.A.* **115** 26 55N 82 0W
Punta Prieta, *Mexico* **126** 28 58N 114 17W
Puntabie, *Australia* **73** 32 12 S 134 13 E
Puntarenas, *Costa Rica* **128** 10 0N 84 50W
Punto Fijo, *Venezuela* **134** 11 50N 70 13W
Punxsutawney, *U.S.A.* **116** 40 56N 79 0W
Puqi, *China* **59** 29 40N 113 50 E
Puquio, *Peru* **136** 14 45 S 74 10W
Pur →, *U.S.S.R.* **40** 67 31N 77 55 E
Purace, Vol., *Colombia* **134** 2 21N 76 23W
Purari →, *Papua N. G.* **69** 7 49 S 145 0 E
Purbeck, Isle of, *U.K.* **13** 50 40N 2 5W
Purcell, *U.S.A.* **121** 35 0N 97 25W
Purchena Tetica, *Spain* **25** 37 21N 2 21W
Puri, *India* **50** 19 50N 85 58 E
Purificación, *Colombia* **134** 3 51N 74 55W
Purísima, La, *Mexico* **126** 26 10N 112 4W
Purlewaugh, *Australia* **77** 31 20 S 149 30 E
Purmerend, *Neths.* **16** 52 30N 4 58 E
Purna →, *India* **50** 19 6N 77 2 E
Purnia, *India* **49** 25 45N 87 31 E
Purnim, *Australia* **74** 38 16 S 142 36 E
Purukcahu, *Indonesia* **56** 0 35 S 114 35 E
Puruliya, *India* **49** 23 17N 86 24 E
Purus →, *Brazil* **135** 3 42 S 61 28W
Pŭrvomay, *Bulgaria* **34** 42 8N 25 17 E
Purwakarta, *Indonesia* **57** 6 35 S 107 29 E
Purwodadi, *Jawa, Indonesia* **57** 7 7 S 110 55 E
Purwodadi, *Jawa, Indonesia* **57** 7 51 S 110 0 E
Purwokerto, *Indonesia* **57** 7 25 S 109 14 E
Purworejo, *Indonesia* **57** 7 43 S 110 2 E
Pus →, *India* **50** 19 55N 77 55 E
Pusad, *India* **50** 19 56N 77 36 E
Pusan, *S. Korea* **61** 35 5N 129 0 E
Push, La, *U.S.A.* **124** 47 55N 124 38W
Pushchino, *U.S.S.R.* **41** 54 10N 158 0 E
Pushkin, *U.S.S.R.* **36** 59 45N 30 25 E
Pushkino, *R.S.F.S.R., U.S.S.R.* **37** 51 16N 47 0 E
Pushkino, *R.S.F.S.R., U.S.S.R.* **37** 56 2N 37 49 E
Püspökladány, *Hungary* **33** 47 19N 21 6 E
Pustoshka, *U.S.S.R.* **36** 56 20N 29 30 E
Putahow L., *Canada* **111** 59 54N 100 40W
Putao, *Burma* **52** 27 28N 97 30 E
Putaruru, *N.Z.* **80** 38 2 S 175 50 E
Putbus, *E. Germany* **30** 54 19N 13 29 E
Putian, *China* **59** 25 23N 119 0 E
Putignano, *Italy* **29** 40 50N 17 5 E
Putina, *Peru* **136** 14 55 S 69 55W
Puting, Tanjung, *Indonesia* **56** 3 31 S 111 46 E
Putlitz, *E. Germany* **30** 53 15N 12 3 E
Putna →, *Romania* **34** 45 42N 27 26 E
Putnam, *U.S.A.* **117** 41 55N 71 55W
Putorana, Gory, *U.S.S.R.* **41** 69 0N 95 0 E
Putorino, *N.Z.* **80** 39 4 S 177 0 E
Putre, *Chile* **136** 18 12 S 69 35W
Puttalam Lagoon, *Sri Lanka* **51** 8 15N 79 45 E
Putte, *Neths.* **17** 51 22N 4 24 E
Putten, *Neths.* **16** 52 16N 5 36 E
Puttgarden, *E. Germany* **30** 54 28N 11 15 E
Puttur, *India* **51** 12 46N 75 12 E
Putty, *Australia* **76** 32 57 S 150 42 E
Putumayo →, *S. Amer.* **134** 3 7 S 67 58W
Putuo, *China* **59** 29 56N 122 20 E
Putussibau, *Indonesia* **56** 0 50N 112 56 E
Puurs, *Belgium* **17** 51 5N 4 17 E
Puy, Le, *France* **20** 45 3N 3 52 E
Puy-de-Dôme, *France* **20** 45 46N 2 57 E
Puy-de-Dôme □, *France* **20** 45 40N 3 5 E
Puy-Guillaume, *France* **20** 45 57N 3 29 E
Puy-l'Évêque, *France* **20** 44 31N 1 9 E
Puyallup, *U.S.A.* **124** 47 10N 122 22W
Puyang, *China* **60** 35 40N 115 1 E
Puyehue, *Chile* **142** 40 40 S 72 37W
Puylaurens, *France* **20** 43 35N 2 0 E
Puyo, *Ecuador* **134** 1 28 S 77 59W
Pwani □, *Tanzania* **92** 7 0 S 39 0 E
Pweto, *Zaïre* **93** 8 25 S 28 51 E
Pwinbyu, *Burma* **52** 20 23N 94 40 E
Pwllheli, *U.K.* **12** 52 54N 4 26W
Pyalong, *Australia* **74** 37 7 S 144 51 E
Pyana →, *U.S.S.R.* **37** 55 30N 46 0 E
Pyapon, *Burma* **52** 16 20N 95 40 E
Pyasina →, *U.S.S.R.* **41** 73 30N 87 0 E
Pyatigorsk, *U.S.S.R.* **39** 44 2N 43 6 E
Pyatikhatki, *U.S.S.R.* **38** 48 28N 33 38 E
Pyaye, *Burma* **52** 19 12N 95 10 E

Pyè, Burma 52 18 49N 95 13 E
Pyinbauk, Burma 52 19 10N 95 12 E
Pyinmana, Burma 52 19 45N 96 12 E
Pyŏngyang, N. Korea 61 39 0N 125 30 E
Pyote, U.S.A. 121 31 34N 103 5W
Pyramid Hill, Australia 74 36 2S 144 6 E
Pyramid L., U.S.A. 122 40 0N 119 30W
Pyramid Pk., U.S.A. 125 36 25N 116 37W
Pyramids, Egypt 88 29 58N 31 9 E
Pyrénées, Europe 20 42 45N 0 18 E
Pyrénées-Atlantiques □, France 20 43 10N 0 50W
Pyrénées-Orientales □, France 20 42 35N 2 26 E
Pyrzyce, Poland 32 53 10N 14 55 E
Pyshchug, U.S.S.R. 37 58 57N 45 47 E
Pytalovo, U.S.S.R. 36 57 5N 27 55 E
Pyttegga, Norway 10 62 13N 7 42 E
Pyu, Burma 52 18 30N 96 28 E

Q

Qabalān, Jordan 44 32 8N 35 17 E
Qabātiyah, Jordan 44 32 25N 35 16 E
Qachasnek, S. Africa 97 30 6S 28 42 E
Qādib, S. Yemen 45 12 37N 53 57 E
Qā'emshahr, Iran 47 36 30N 52 55 E
Qagan Nur, China 60 43 30N 114 55 E
Qahar Youyi Zhongqi, China 60 41 12N 112 40 E
Qahremānshahr = Bākhtarān, Iran 46 34 23N 47 0 E
Qaidam Pendi, China 62 37 0N 95 0 E
Qala-i-Jadid, Afghan. 48 31 1N 66 25 E
Qala Yangi, Afghan. 48 34 20N 66 30 E
Qalāt, Afghan. 47 32 15N 66 58 E
Qal'at al Akhḍar, Si. Arabia 46 28 0N 37 10 E
Qal'eh-ye Now, Afghan. 47 35 0N 63 5 E
Qalqīlya, Israel 44 32 12N 34 58 E
Qalyûb, Egypt 88 30 12N 31 11 E
Qam, Jordan 44 32 36N 35 43 E
Qamar, Ghubbat al, S. Yemen 45 16 20N 52 30 E
Qamdo, China 58 31 15N 97 6 E
Qamruddin Karez, Pakistan 48 31 45N 68 20 E
Qāna, Lebanon 44 33 12N 35 17 E
Qandahār, Afghan. 47 31 32N 65 30 E
Qâra, Egypt 88 29 38N 26 30 E
Qara Qash →, India 49 35 0N 78 30 E
Qarachuk, Syria 46 37 0N 42 2 E
Qārah, Si. Arabia 46 29 55N 40 3 E
Qardud, Sudan 89 10 20N 29 56 E
Qarqan, China 62 38 5N 85 20 E
Qarqan He →, China 62 39 30N 88 30 E
Qarrasa, Sudan 89 14 38N 32 5 E
Qāsim, Syria 44 32 59N 36 2 E
Qaṣr Bū Hadi, Libya 86 31 1N 16 45 E
Qaṣr-e Qand, Iran 47 26 15N 60 45 E
Qasr Farâfra, Egypt 88 27 0N 28 1 E
Qatar ■, Asia 47 25 30N 51 15 E
Qattâra, Egypt 88 30 12N 27 3 E
Qattâra, Munkhafed el, Egypt 88 29 30N 27 30 E
Qattâra Depression = Qattâra, Munkhafed el, Egypt 88 29 30N 27 30 E
Qāyen, Iran 47 33 40N 59 10 E
Qazvin, Iran 46 36 15N 50 0 E
Qena, Egypt 88 26 10N 32 43 E
Qena, Wadi →, Egypt 88 26 12N 32 44 E
Qeshm, Iran 47 26 55N 56 10 E
Qezi'ot, Israel 44 30 52N 34 26 E
Qi Xian, China 60 34 40N 114 48 E
Qian Gorlos, China 61 45 5N 124 42 E
Qian Xian, China 60 34 31N 108 15 E
Qiancheng, China 58 27 12N 109 50 E
Qianjiang, Guangxi Zhuangzu, China 58 23 38N 108 58 E
Qianjiang, Hubei, China 59 30 24N 112 55 E
Qianjiang, Sichuan, China 58 29 33N 108 47 E
Qianshan, China 59 30 37N 116 35 E
Qianwei, China 58 29 13N 103 56 E
Qianxi, China 58 27 3N 106 3 E
Qianyang, Hunan, China 59 27 18N 110 10 E
Qianyang, Shaanxi, China 60 34 40N 107 8 E
Qianyang, Zhejiang, China 59 30 11N 119 25 E
Qiaojia, China 58 26 56N 102 58 E
Qichun, China 59 30 18N 115 25 E
Qidong, Hunan, China 59 26 49N 112 7 E
Qidong, Jiangsu, China 59 31 48N 121 38 E
Qijiang, China 58 28 57N 106 35 E
Qila Safed, Pakistan 47 29 0N 61 30 E
Qila Saifullāh, Pakistan 48 30 45N 68 17 E
Qilian Shan, China 62 38 30N 96 0 E
Qimen, China 59 29 50N 117 42 E
Qin He →, China 60 35 1N 113 22 E
Qin Jiang →, China 59 26 15N 115 55 E
Qin Ling = Qinling Shandi, China 60 33 50N 108 10 E
Qin'an, China 60 34 48N 105 40 E
Qing Xian, China 60 38 35N 116 45 E
Qingcheng, China 61 37 15N 117 40 E
Qingdao, China 61 36 5N 120 20 E
Qingfeng, China 60 35 52N 115 8 E
Qinghai □, China 62 36 0N 98 0 E
Qinghai Hu, China 62 36 40N 100 10 E
Qinghecheng, China 61 41 15N 124 30 E
Qinghemen, China 61 41 48N 121 25 E
Qingjian, China 60 37 8N 110 8 E
Qingjiang, Jiangsu, China 61 33 30N 119 2 E
Qingjiang, Jiangxi, China 59 28 4N 115 29 E
Qingliu, China 59 26 11N 116 48 E
Qinglong, China 58 25 49N 105 12 E
Qingping, China 58 26 39N 107 47 E
Qingpu, China 59 31 10N 121 6 E
Qingshui, China 60 34 48N 106 8 E
Qingshuihe, China 60 39 55N 111 35 E
Qingtian, China 59 28 12N 120 15 E
Qingtongxia Shuiku, China 60 37 50N 105 58 E
Qingxi, China 58 27 8N 108 43 E
Qingxu, China 60 37 34N 112 22 E
Qingyang, Anhui, China 59 30 38N 117 50 E
Qingyang, Gansu, China 60 36 2N 107 55 E
Qingyi Jiang →, China 58 29 32N 103 44 E
Qingyuan, Guangdong, China 59 23 40N 112 59 E
Qingyuan, Liaoning, China 61 42 10N 124 55 E
Qingyuan, Zhejiang, China 59 27 36N 119 3 E
Qingyun, China 61 37 45N 117 20 E
Qingzhen, China 58 26 31N 106 25 E
Qinhuangdao, China 61 39 56N 119 30 E
Qinling Shandi, China 60 33 50N 108 10 E
Qinshui, China 60 35 40N 112 8 E
Qinyang, China 60 35 7N 112 57 E
Qinyuan, China 60 36 29N 112 20 E
Qinzhou, China 58 21 58N 108 38 E
Qionghai, China 54 19 15N 110 26 E
Qionglai, China 58 30 25N 103 31 E
Qionglai Shan, China 58 31 0N 102 30 E
Qiongshan, China 54 19 51N 110 26 E
Qiongzhou Haixia, China 54 20 10N 110 15 E
Qiqihar, China 62 47 26N 124 0 E
Qiryat 'Anavim, Israel 44 31 49N 35 7 E
Qiryat Ata, Israel 44 32 47N 35 6 E
Qiryat Bialik, Israel 44 32 50N 35 5 E
Qiryat Gat, Israel 44 31 32N 34 46 E
Qiryat Ḥayyim, Israel 44 32 49N 35 4 E
Qiryat Mal'akhi, Israel 44 31 44N 34 44 E
Qiryat Shemona, Israel 44 33 13N 35 35 E
Qiryat Yam, Israel 44 32 51N 35 4 E
Qishan, China 60 34 25N 107 38 E
Qishan, Taiwan 59 22 52N 120 25 E
Qishon →, Israel 44 32 49N 35 2 E
Qitai, China 62 44 2N 89 35 E
Qiubei, China 58 24 2N 104 12 E
Qixia, China 61 37 17N 120 52 E
Qiyang, China 59 26 35N 111 50 E
Qom, Iran 47 34 40N 51 0 E
Qomsheh, Iran 47 32 0N 51 55 E
Qondūz, Afghan. 47 36 50N 68 50 E
Qondūz □, Afghan. 47 36 50N 68 50 E
Qu Jiang →, China 58 30 1N 106 24 E
Qu Xian, Sichuan, China 58 30 48N 106 58 E
Qu Xian, Zhejiang, China 59 28 57N 118 54 E
Quaama, Australia 75 36 27S 149 55 E
Quackenbrück, W. Germany 30 52 40N 7 59 E
Quairading, Australia 79 32 0S 117 21 E
Quakertown, U.S.A. 117 40 27N 75 20W
Qualeup, Australia 79 33 48S 116 48 E
Quambatook, Australia 75 35 49S 143 34 E
Quambone, Australia 76 30 57S 147 53 E
Quan Long, Vietnam 55 9 7N 105 8 E
Quanah, U.S.A. 121 34 20N 99 45W
Quandialla, Australia 76 34 1S 147 47 E
Quang Ngai, Vietnam 54 15 13N 108 58 E
Quang Yen, Vietnam 54 20 56N 106 52 E
Quannan, China 59 24 45N 114 33 E
Quantock Hills, U.K. 13 51 8N 3 10W
Quantong, Australia 74 36 43S 142 3 E
Quanzhou, Fujian, China 59 24 55N 118 34 E
Quanzhou, Guangxi Zhuangzu, China 59 25 57N 111 5 E
Quaraí, Brazil 140 30 15S 56 20W
Quarré-les-Tombes, France 19 47 21N 4 0 E
Quartu Sant' Elena, Italy 28 39 15N 9 10 E
Quartzsite, U.S.A. 125 33 44N 114 16W
Quatsino, Canada 110 50 30N 127 40W
Quatsino Sd., Canada 110 50 25N 127 58W
Qubab = Mishmar Ayyalon, Israel 44 31 52N 34 57 E
Qūchān, Iran 47 37 10N 58 27 E
Queanbeyan, Australia 76 35 17S 149 14 E
Québec, Canada 107 46 52N 71 13W
Québec □, Canada 105 50 0N 70 0W
Quedlinburg, E. Germany 30 51 47N 11 9 E
Queen Alexandra Ra., Antarctica 143 85 0S 170 0 E
Queen Charlotte, Canada 110 53 15N 132 2W
Queen Charlotte Bay, Falk. Is. 142 51 50S 60 40W
Queen Charlotte Is., Canada 110 53 20N 132 10W
Queen Charlotte Sd., N.Z. 81 41 10S 174 15 E
Queen Charlotte Str., Canada 110 51 0N 128 0W
Queen City, U.S.A. 118 40 25N 92 34W
Queen Elizabeth Is., Canada 4 76 0N 95 0W
Queen Elizabeth Nat. Park, Uganda 92 0 0 30 0 E
Queen Mary Land, Antarctica 143 70 0S 95 0 E
Queen Maud G., Canada 102 68 15N 102 30W
Queen Maud Mts., Antarctica 143 86 0S 160 0W
Queens Chan., Australia 78 15 0S 129 30 E
Queenscliff, Australia 74 38 16S 144 39 E
Queensland □, Australia 72 22 0S 142 0 E
Queenstown, Australia 72 42 4S 145 35 E
Queenstown, N.Z. 81 45 1S 168 40 E
Queenstown, S. Africa 96 31 52S 26 52 E
Queets, U.S.A. 124 47 32N 124 20W
Queguay Grande →, Uruguay 140 32 9S 58 9W
Queimadas, Brazil 138 11 0S 39 38W
Queiros, C., Vanuatu 68 14 55S 167 1 E
Quela, Angola 95 9 10S 16 56 E
Quelimane, Mozam. 93 17 53S 36 58 E
Quelpart = Cheju Do, S. Korea 61 33 29N 126 34 E
Quemado, N. Mex., U.S.A. 123 34 17N 108 28W
Quemado, Tex., U.S.A. 121 28 58N 100 35W
Quemú-Quemú, Argentina 140 36 3S 63 36W
Quequén, Argentina 140 38 30S 58 30W
Querco, Peru 136 13 50S 74 52W
Querétaro, Mexico 126 20 40N 100 23W
Querétaro □, Mexico 126 20 30N 100 0W
Querfurt, E. Germany 30 51 22N 11 33 E
Quesada, Spain 25 37 51N 3 4W
Queshan, China 60 32 55N 114 2 E
Quesnel, Canada 110 53 0N 122 30W
Quesnel →, Canada 110 52 58N 122 29W
Quesnel L., Canada 110 52 30N 121 20W
Quesnoy, Le, France 19 50 15N 3 38 E
Questa, U.S.A. 123 36 45N 105 35W
Questembert, France 18 47 40N 2 28W
Quetena, Bolivia 136 22 10S 67 25W
Quetico Prov. Park, Canada 104 48 30N 91 45W
Quetrequile, Argentina 142 41 33S 69 22W
Quetta, Pakistan 47 30 15N 66 55 E
Quevedo, Ecuador 134 1 2S 79 29W
Quévillon, L., Canada 106 49 4N 76 57W
Quezaltenango, Guatemala 128 14 50N 91 30W
Quezon City, Phil. 57 14 38N 121 0 E
Qui Nhon, Vietnam 54 13 40N 109 13 E
Quiaca, La, Argentina 140 22 5S 65 35W
Quibala, Angola 95 10 46S 14 59 E
Quibaxe, Angola 95 8 24S 14 27 E
Quibdo, Colombia 134 5 42N 76 40W
Quiberon, France 18 47 29N 3 9W
Quíbor, Venezuela 134 9 56N 69 37W
Quick, Canada 110 54 36N 126 54W
Quickborn, W. Germany 30 53 42N 9 52 E
Quiet L., Canada 110 61 5N 133 5W
Quiévrain, Belgium 17 50 24N 3 41 E
Quiindy, Paraguay 140 25 58S 57 14W
Quila, Mexico 126 24 23N 107 13W
Quilán, C., Chile 142 43 15S 74 30W
Quilcene, U.S.A. 124 47 49N 122 53W
Quilengues, Angola 95 14 12S 14 12 E
Quilimarí, Chile 140 32 5S 71 30W
Quilino, Argentina 140 30 14S 64 29W
Quillabamba, Peru 136 12 50S 72 50W
Quillacollo, Bolivia 136 17 26S 66 17W
Quillagua, Chile 140 21 40S 69 40W
Quillaicillo, Chile 140 31 17S 71 40W
Quillan, France 20 42 53N 2 10 E
Quillebeuf-sur-Seine, France 18 49 28N 0 30 E
Quillota, Chile 140 32 54S 71 16W
Quilmes, Argentina 140 34 43S 58 15W
Quilon, India 51 8 50N 76 38 E
Quilpie, Australia 73 26 35S 144 11 E
Quilpué, Chile 140 33 5S 71 33W
Quilua, Mozam. 93 16 17S 39 54 E
Quimbele, Angola 95 6 17S 16 41 E
Quimbonge, Angola 95 8 36S 18 30 E
Quime, Bolivia 136 17 2S 67 15W
Quimilí, Argentina 140 27 40S 62 30W
Quimper, France 18 48 0N 4 9W
Quimperlé, France 18 47 53N 3 33W
Quinault →, U.S.A. 124 47 23N 124 18W
Quincemil, Peru 136 13 15S 70 40W
Quincy, Calif., U.S.A. 124 39 56N 120 56W
Quincy, Fla., U.S.A. 115 30 34N 84 34W
Quincy, Ill., U.S.A. 120 39 55N 91 20W
Quincy, Mass., U.S.A. 117 42 14N 71 0W
Quincy, Wash., U.S.A. 122 47 22N 119 56W
Quines, Argentina 140 32 13S 65 48W
Quinga, Mozam. 93 15 49S 40 15 E
Quingey, France 19 47 7N 5 52 E
Quintana de la Serena, Spain 23 38 45N 5 40W
Quintana Roo □, Mexico 127 19 0N 88 0W
Quintanar de la Orden, Spain 24 39 36N 3 5W
Quintanar de la Sierra, Spain 24 41 57N 2 55W
Quintanar del Rey, Spain 25 39 21N 1 56W
Quintero, Chile 140 32 45S 71 30W
Quintin, France 18 48 26N 2 56W
Quinto, Spain 24 41 25N 0 32W
Quinyambie, Australia 73 30 15S 141 0 E
Quinze, L. des, Canada 106 47 35N 79 5W
Quípar →, Spain 25 38 15N 1 40W
Quipungo, Angola 95 14 37S 14 40 E
Quirihue, Chile 140 36 15S 72 35W
Quirimbo, Angola 95 10 36S 14 12 E
Quirindi, Australia 77 31 28S 150 40 E
Quiriquire, Venezuela 134 9 59N 63 13W
Quiroga, Spain 22 42 28N 7 18W
Quiruvilca, Peru 136 8 1S 78 19W
Quissac, France 21 43 55N 4 0 E
Quissanga, Mozam. 93 12 24S 40 28 E
Quitapa, Angola 95 10 20S 18 19 E
Quitilipi, Argentina 140 26 50S 60 13W
Quitman, Ga., U.S.A. 115 30 49N 83 35W
Quitman, Miss., U.S.A. 115 32 2N 88 42W
Quitman, Tex., U.S.A. 121 32 48N 95 25W
Quito, Ecuador 134 0 15S 78 35W
Quixadá, Brazil 138 4 55S 39 0W
Quixaxe, Mozam. 93 15 17S 40 4 E
Quixeramobim, Brazil 138 5 12S 39 17W
Quixinge, Angola 95 9 52S 14 23 E
Quizenga, Angola 95 9 21S 15 28 E
Qujing, China 58 25 32N 103 41 E
Qul'ân, Jazâ'ir, Egypt 88 24 22N 35 31 E
Qumbu, S. Africa 97 31 10S 28 48 E
Qumrān, Jordan 44 31 43N 35 27 E
Quneitra, Syria 44 33 7N 35 48 E
Quoin I., Australia 78 14 54S 129 32 E
Quoin Pt., S. Africa 96 34 46S 19 37 E
Quondong, Australia 73 33 6S 140 18 E
Quorn, Australia 73 32 25S 138 0 E
Qurein, Sudan 89 13 30N 34 50 E
Qûs, Egypt 88 25 55N 32 50 E
Quseir, Egypt 88 26 7N 34 16 E
Qusrah, Jordan 44 32 5N 35 20 E
Quthing, Lesotho 97 30 25S 27 36 E
Quwo, China 60 35 38N 111 25 E
Quyang, China 60 38 35N 114 40 E
Quynh Nhai, Vietnam 54 21 49N 103 33 E
Quyon, Canada 106 45 31N 76 14W
Quzi, China 60 36 20N 107 20 E
Qytet Stalin, Albania 35 40 47N 19 57 E

R

Ra, Ko, Thailand 55 9 13N 98 16 E
Råå, Sweden 11 56 0N 12 45 E
Raahe, Finland 8 64 40N 24 28 E
Raalte, Neths. 16 52 23N 6 16 E
Raamsdonksveer, Neths. 17 51 43N 4 52 E
Ra'ananna, Israel 44 32 12N 34 52 E
Raasay, U.K. 14 57 25N 6 4W
Raasay, Sd. of, U.K. 14 57 30N 6 8W
Rab, Yugoslavia 27 44 45N 14 45 E
Raba, Indonesia 57 8 36S 118 55 E
Rába →, Hungary 33 47 38N 17 38 E
Rabaçal →, Portugal 22 41 30N 7 12W
Rabah, Nigeria 91 13 5N 5 30 E
Rabai, Kenya 92 3 50S 39 31 E
Rabaraba, Papua N. G. 69 9 58S 149 49 E
Rabastens, France 20 43 50N 1 43 E
Rabastens-de-Bigorre, France 20 43 23N 0 9 E
Rabat, Morocco 84 34 2N 6 48W
Rabaul, Papua N. G. 69 4 24S 152 18 E
Rabbit →, Canada 110 59 41N 127 12W
Rabbit Lake, Canada 111 53 8N 107 46W
Rabbitskin →, Canada 110 61 47N 120 42W
Rābigh, Si. Arabia 46 22 50N 39 5 E
Rabka, Poland 32 49 37N 19 59 E
Rácale, Italy 29 39 57N 18 6 E
Racalmuto, Italy 28 37 25N 13 41 E
Racconigi, Italy 26 44 47N 7 41 E
Raccoon →, U.S.A. 118 41 35N 93 37W
Raccoon Cr. →, U.S.A. 119 39 47N 87 23W
Race, C., Canada 105 46 40N 53 5W
Rach Gia, Vietnam 55 10 5N 105 5 E
Raciąż, Poland 32 52 46N 20 10 E
Racibórz, Poland 32 50 7N 18 18 E
Racine, U.S.A. 119 42 41N 87 51W
Rackerby, U.S.A. 124 39 26N 121 22W
Radama, Nosy, Madag. 97 14 0S 47 47 E
Radama, Saikanosy, Madag. 97 14 16S 47 53 E
Rădăuţi, Romania 34 47 50N 25 59 E
Radbuza →, Czech. 32 49 35N 13 5 E
Radcliff, U.S.A. 119 37 51N 85 57W
Radeburg, E. Germany 30 51 6N 13 55 E
Radeče, Yugoslavia 27 46 5N 15 14 E
Radekhov, U.S.S.R. 36 50 25N 24 32 E
Radford, U.S.A. 114 37 8N 80 32W
Radhanpur, India 48 23 50N 71 38 E

Red Deer

Radhwa, Jabal, *Si. Arabia* **46** 24 34N 38 18 E
Radiska →, *Yugoslavia* **35** 41 38N 20 37 E
Radisson, *Canada* **111** 52 30N 107 20W
Radium Hot Springs, *Canada* **110** 50 35N 116 2W
Radna, *Romania* **34** 46 7N 21 41 E
Radnor Forest, *U.K.* **13** 52 17N 3 10W
Radolfzell, *W. Germany* **31** 47 44N 8 58 E
Radom, *Poland* **32** 51 23N 21 12 E
Radomir, *Bulgaria* **34** 42 37N 23 4 E
Radomsko, *Poland* **32** 51 5N 19 28 E
Radomyshl, *U.S.S.R.* **36** 50 30N 29 12 E
Radoviš, *Yugoslavia* **35** 41 38N 22 28 E
Radovljica, *Yugoslavia* **27** 46 22N 14 12 E
Radstock, *U.K.* **13** 51 17N 2 25W
Radstock, C., *Australia* **73** 33 12 S 134 20 E
Răducăneni, *Romania* **34** 46 58N 27 54 E
Radviliškis, *U.S.S.R.* **36** 55 49N 23 33 E
Radville, *Canada* **111** 49 30N 104 15W
Rae, *Canada* **110** 62 50N 116 3W
Rae Bareli, *India* **49** 26 18N 81 20 E
Rae Isthmus, *Canada* **103** 66 40N 87 30W
Raeren, *Belgium* **17** 50 41N 6 7 E
Raeside, L., *Australia* **79** 29 20 S 122 0 E
Raetihi, *N.Z.* **80** 39 25 S 175 17 E
Rafaela, *Argentina* **140** 31 10 S 61 30W
Rafah, *Egypt* **88** 31 18N 34 14 E
Rafai, *C.A.R.* **92** 4 59N 23 58 E
Raffadali, *Italy* **28** 37 23N 13 29 E
Rafḥā, *Si. Arabia* **46** 29 35N 43 35 E
Rafsanjān, *Iran* **47** 30 30N 56 5 E
Raft Pt., *Australia* **78** 16 4 S 124 26 E
Ragag, *Sudan* **89** 10 59N 24 40 E
Ragged Mt., *Australia* **79** 33 27 S 123 25 E
Raglan, *Australia* **72** 23 42 S 150 49 E
Raglan, *N.Z.* **80** 37 55 S 174 55 E
Ragunda, *Sweden* **10** 63 6N 16 23 E
Ragusa, *Italy* **29** 36 56N 14 42 E
Raha, *Indonesia* **57** 4 55 S 123 0 E
Rahad, Nahr ed →, *Sudan* **89** 14 28N 33 31 E
Rahad al Bardī, *Sudan* **87** 11 20N 23 40 E
Rahaeng = Tak, *Thailand* **54** 16 52N 99 8 E
Rahden, *W. Germany* **30** 52 26N 8 36 E
Raheita, *Ethiopia* **89** 12 46N 43 4 E
Rahimyar Khan, *Pakistan* **48** 28 30N 70 25 E
Rahotu, *N.Z.* **80** 39 20 S 173 49 E
Raichur, *India* **51** 16 10N 77 20 E
Raiganj, *India* **49** 25 37N 88 10 E
Raigarh, *India* **50** 21 56N 83 25 E
Raighar, *India* **50** 19 51N 82 6 E
Raijua, *Indonesia* **57** 10 37 S 121 36 E
Railton, *Australia* **72** 41 25 S 146 28 E
Rainbow, *Australia* **74** 35 55 S 142 0 E
Rainbow Lake, *Canada* **110** 58 30N 119 23W
Rainier, *U.S.A.* **124** 46 4N 122 58W
Rainier, Mt., *U.S.A.* **124** 46 50N 121 50W
Rainy L., *Canada* **111** 48 42N 93 10W
Rainy River, *Canada* **111** 48 43N 94 29W
Raipur, *India* **50** 21 17N 81 45 E
Ra'is, *Si. Arabia* **46** 23 33N 38 43 E
Raj Nandgaon, *India* **50** 21 5N 81 5 E
Raja, Ujung, *Indonesia* **56** 3 40N 96 25 E
Raja Ampat, Kepulauan, *Indonesia* **57** 0 30 S 130 0 E
Rajahmundry, *India* **50** 17 1N 81 48 E
Rajajooseppi, *Finland* **8** 68 28N 28 29 E
Rajang →, *Malaysia* **56** 2 30N 112 0 E
Rajapalaiyam, *India* **51** 9 25N 77 35 E
Rajasthan □, *India* **48** 26 45N 73 30 E
Rajasthan Canal, *India* **48** 28 0N 72 0 E
Rajauri, *India* **49** 33 25N 74 21 E
Rajbari, *Bangla.* **52** 23 47N 89 41 E
Rajgarh, *Mad. P., India* **48** 24 2N 76 45 E
Rajgarh, *Raj., India* **48** 28 40N 75 25 E
Rajhenburg, *Yugoslavia* **27** 46 1N 15 29 E
Rajkot, *India* **48** 22 15N 70 56 E
Rajmahal Hills, *India* **49** 24 30N 87 30 E
Rajpipla, *India* **50** 21 50N 73 30 E
Rajpura, *India* **48** 30 25N 76 32 E
Rajshahi, *Bangla.* **52** 24 22N 88 39 E
Rajshahi □, *Bangla.* **49** 25 0N 89 0 E
Rakaia, *N.Z.* **81** 43 45 S 172 1 E
Rakaia →, *N.Z.* **81** 43 36 S 172 15 E
Rakan, Ra's, *Qatar* **47** 26 10N 51 20 E
Rakaposhi, *Pakistan* **49** 36 10N 74 25 E
Rakata, Pulau, *Indonesia* **56** 6 10 S 105 20 E
Rakhni, *Pakistan* **48** 30 4N 69 56 E
Rakkestad, *Norway* **10** 59 25N 11 21 E
Rakops, *Botswana* **96** 21 1 S 24 28 E
Rákospalota, *Hungary* **33** 47 30N 19 5 E
Rakov, *U.S.S.R.* **36** 53 58N 26 59 E
Rakovica, *Yugoslavia* **27** 44 59N 15 38 E
Rakovník, *Czech.* **32** 50 6N 13 42 E
Rakovski, *Bulgaria* **34** 42 21N 24 57 E
Rakvere, *U.S.S.R.* **36** 59 30N 26 25 E
Raleigh, *Australia* **77** 30 27 S 153 2 E
Raleigh, *U.S.A.* **115** 35 47N 78 39W
Raleigh B., *U.S.A.* **115** 34 50N 76 15W
Ralja, *Yugoslavia* **33** 44 33N 20 34 E
Ralls, *U.S.A.* **121** 33 40N 101 20W
Ram →, *Canada* **110** 62 1N 123 41W
Rām Allāh, *Jordan* **44** 31 55N 35 10 E
Ram Hd., *Australia* **75** 37 47 S 149 30 E
Rama, *Israel* **44** 32 56N 35 21 E
Rama, *Nic.* **128** 12 9N 84 15W
Ramacca, *Italy* **29** 37 24N 14 40 E
Ramachandrapuram, *India* **50** 16 50N 82 4 E
Ramales de la Victoria, *Spain* **24** 43 15N 3 28W
Ramalho, Serra do, *Brazil* **139** 13 45 S 44 0W
Raman, *Thailand* **55** 6 29N 101 18 E
Ramanathapuram, *India* **51** 9 25N 78 55 E
Ramanetaka, B. de, *Madag.* **97** 14 13 S 47 52 E
Ramas C., *India* **51** 15 5N 73 55 E
Ramat Gan, *Israel* **44** 32 4N 34 48 E
Ramat HaSharon, *Israel* **44** 32 7N 34 50 E
Ramatlhabama, *S. Africa* **96** 25 37 S 25 33 E
Ramban, *India* **49** 33 14N 75 12 E
Rambervillers, *France* **19** 48 20N 6 38 E
Rambi, *Fiji* **68** 16 30 S 179 59W
Rambipuji, *Indonesia* **57** 8 12 S 113 37 E
Rambla, La, *Spain* **23** 37 37N 4 45W
Rambouillet, *France* **19** 48 39N 1 50 E
Ramdurg, *India* **51** 15 58N 75 22 E
Ramea, *Canada* **105** 47 31N 57 23W
Ramechhap, *Nepal* **49** 27 25N 86 10 E
Ramelau, *Indonesia* **57** 8 55 S 126 22 E
Ramenskoye, *U.S.S.R.* **37** 55 32N 38 15 E
Ramgarh, *Bihar, India* **49** 23 40N 85 35 E
Ramgarh, *Raj., India* **48** 27 16N 75 14 E
Ramgarh, *Raj., India* **48** 27 30N 70 36 E
Rāmhormoz, *Iran* **46** 31 15N 49 35 E
Ramla, *Israel* **44** 31 55N 34 52 E
Ramlat Zalṭan, *Libya* **86** 28 30N 19 30 E
Ramlu, *Ethiopia* **89** 13 32N 41 40 E
Ramme, *Denmark* **11** 56 30N 8 11 E
Rammūn, *Jordan* **44** 31 55N 35 17 E
Ramnad = Ramanathapuram, *India* **51** 9 25N 78 55 E
Ramnagar, *India* **49** 32 47N 75 18 E
Ramnäs, *Sweden* **10** 59 46N 16 12 E
Ramon, *U.S.S.R.* **37** 51 55N 39 21 E
Ramon, Har, *Israel* **44** 30 30N 34 38 E
Ramona, *U.S.A.* **125** 33 1N 116 56W
Ramore, *Canada* **106** 48 30N 80 25W
Ramotswa, *Botswana* **96** 24 50 S 25 52 E
Rampart, *U.S.A.* **102** 65 0N 150 15W
Rampur, *H.P., India* **48** 31 26N 77 43 E
Rampur, *Mad. P., India* **48** 23 25N 73 53 E
Rampur, *Orissa, India* **50** 21 48N 83 58 E
Rampur, *Ut. P., India* **49** 28 50N 79 5 E
Rampur Hat, *India* **49** 24 10N 87 50 E
Rampura, *India* **48** 24 30N 75 27 E
Ramsel, *Belgium* **17** 51 2N 4 50 E
Ramsey, *Canada* **104** 47 25N 82 20W
Ramsey, *U.K.* **12** 54 20N 4 21W
Ramsey, *U.S.A.* **118** 39 8N 89 7W
Ramsgate, *U.K.* **13** 51 20N 1 25 E
Ramshai, *India* **52** 26 44N 88 51 E
Ramsjö, *Sweden* **10** 62 11N 15 37 E
Ramtek, *India* **50** 21 20N 79 15 E
Ramu →, *Papua N. G.* **69** 4 0 S 144 41 E
Ramvik, *Sweden* **10** 62 49N 17 51 E
Ranaghat, *India* **49** 23 15N 88 35 E
Ranahu, *Pakistan* **48** 25 55N 69 45 E
Ranau, *Malaysia* **56** 6 2N 116 40 E
Rancagua, *Chile* **140** 34 10 S 70 50W
Rance, *Belgium* **17** 50 9N 4 16 E
Rance →, *France* **18** 48 34N 1 59W
Rance, Barrage de la, *France* **18** 48 30N 2 3W
Rancharia, *Brazil* **139** 22 15 S 50 55W
Rancheria →, *Canada* **110** 60 13N 129 7W
Ranchester, *U.S.A.* **122** 44 57N 107 12W
Ranchi, *India* **49** 23 19N 85 27 E
Ranco, L., *Chile* **142** 40 15 S 72 25W
Randan, *France* **20** 46 2N 3 21 E
Randazzo, *Italy* **29** 37 53N 14 56 E
Randers, *Denmark* **11** 56 29N 10 1 E
Randers Fjord, *Denmark* **11** 56 37N 10 20 E
Randfontein, *S. Africa* **97** 26 8 S 27 45 E
Randle, *U.S.A.* **124** 46 32N 121 57W
Randolph, *Mass., U.S.A.* **117** 42 10N 71 3W
Randolph, *N.Y., U.S.A.* **116** 42 10N 78 59W
Randolph, *Utah, U.S.A.* **122** 41 43N 111 10W
Randolph, *Vt., U.S.A.* **117** 43 55N 72 39W
Randsfjord, *Norway* **10** 60 15N 10 25 E
Råne älv →, *Sweden* **8** 65 50N 22 20 E
Ranfurly, *N.Z.* **81** 45 7 S 170 6 E
Rangae, *Thailand* **55** 6 19N 101 44 E
Rangamati, *Bangla.* **52** 22 38N 92 12 E
Rangaunu, *N.Z.* **80** 39 26 S 175 28 E
Rangaunu B., *N.Z.* **80** 34 51 S 173 15 E
Rångedala, *Sweden* **11** 57 47N 13 9 E
Rangeley, *U.S.A.* **117** 44 58N 70 33W
Rangely, *U.S.A.* **122** 40 3N 108 53W
Ranger, *U.S.A.* **121** 32 30N 98 42W
Rangia, *India* **52** 26 28N 91 38 E
Rangiora, *N.Z.* **81** 43 19 S 172 36 E
Rangitaiki →, *N.Z.* **80** 37 54 S 176 49 E
Rangitata →, *N.Z.* **81** 43 45 S 171 15 E
Rangitikei →, *N.Z.* **80** 40 17 S 175 15 E
Rangitoto Range, *N.Z.* **80** 38 25 S 175 35 E
Rangkasbitung, *Indonesia* **57** 6 21 S 106 15 E
Rangoon, *Burma* **52** 16 45N 96 20 E
Rangpur, *Bangla.* **52** 25 42N 89 22 E
Rangsit, *Thailand* **54** 13 59N 100 37 E
Ranibennur, *India* **51** 14 35N 75 30 E
Raniganj, *India* **49** 23 40N 87 5 E
Ranippettai, *India* **51** 12 56N 79 23 E
Ranken →, *Australia* **72** 20 31 S 137 36 E
Rankin, *Ill., U.S.A.* **119** 40 28N 87 54W
Rankin, *Tex., U.S.A.* **121** 31 16N 101 56W
Rankin Inlet, *Canada* **102** 62 30N 93 0W
Rankins Springs, *Australia* **75** 33 49 S 146 14 E
Rannoch, L., *U.K.* **14** 56 41N 4 20W
Rannoch Moor, *U.K.* **14** 56 38N 4 48W
Ranobe, Helodranon' i, *Madag.* **97** 23 3 S 43 33 E
Ranohira, *Madag.* **97** 22 29 S 45 24 E
Ranomafana, *Toamasina, Madag.* **97** 18 57 S 48 50 E
Ranomafana, *Toliara, Madag.* **97** 24 34 S 47 0 E
Ranon, *Vanuatu* **68** 16 10 S 168 7 E
Ranong, *Thailand* **55** 9 56N 98 40 E
Ransiki, *Indonesia* **57** 1 30 S 134 10 E
Ransom, *U.S.A.* **119** 41 9N 88 39W
Rantau, *Indonesia* **56** 2 56 S 115 9 E
Rantauprapat, *Indonesia* **56** 2 15N 99 50 E
Rantekombola, *Indonesia* **57** 3 15 S 119 57 E
Rantīs, *Jordan* **44** 32 4N 35 3 E
Rantoul, *U.S.A.* **119** 40 18N 88 10W
Ranum, *Denmark* **11** 56 54N 9 14 E
Raon l'Étape, *France* **19** 48 24N 6 50 E
Raoui, Erg er, *Algeria* **85** 29 0N 2 0W
Raoyang, *China* **60** 38 15N 115 45 E
Rapa Iti, *Pac. Oc.* **67** 27 35 S 144 20W
Rapallo, *Italy* **26** 44 21N 9 12 E
Rāpch, *Iran* **47** 25 40N 59 15 E
Rapid →, *Canada* **110** 59 15N 129 5W
Rapid City, *U.S.A.* **120** 44 0N 103 0W
Rapid River, *U.S.A.* **114** 45 55N 87 0W
Rapide-Blanc, *Canada* **107** 47 48N 73 2W
Rapide-Sept, *Canada* **106** 47 46N 78 19W
Rapides des Joachims, *Canada* **106** 46 13N 77 43W
Rapla, *U.S.S.R.* **36** 59 1N 24 52 E
Rappville, *Australia* **77** 29 6 S 152 57 E
Rarotonga, *Cook Is.* **67** 21 30 S 160 0W
Ra's al Khaymah, *U.A.E.* **47** 25 50N 56 5 E
Ra's al-Unuf, *Libya* **86** 30 25N 18 15 E
Ras Bânâs, *Egypt* **88** 23 57N 35 59 E
Ras Dashen, *Ethiopia* **89** 13 8N 38 26 E
Ras el Ma, *Algeria* **85** 34 26N 0 50W
Ras Mallap, *Egypt* **88** 29 18N 32 50 E
Râs Timirist, *Mauritania* **90** 19 21N 16 30W
Rasa, Punta, *Argentina* **142** 40 50 S 62 15W
Rasca, Pta. de la, *Canary Is.* **25** 27 59N 16 41W
Raseiniai, *U.S.S.R.* **36** 55 25N 23 5 E
Rashad, *Sudan* **89** 11 55N 31 0 E
Rashîd, *Egypt* **88** 31 21N 30 22 E
Rashîd, Masabb, *Egypt* **88** 31 22N 30 17 E
Rasht, *Iran* **46** 37 20N 49 40 E
Rasi Salai, *Thailand* **54** 15 20N 104 9 E
Rasipuram, *India* **51** 11 30N 78 15 E
Raška, *Yugoslavia* **33** 43 19N 20 39 E
Rason, L., *Australia* **79** 28 45 S 124 25 E
Raşova, *Romania* **34** 44 15N 27 55 E
Rasra, *India* **49** 25 50N 83 50 E
Rass el Oued, *Algeria* **85** 35 57N 5 2 E
Rasskazovo, *U.S.S.R.* **37** 52 35N 41 50 E
Rastatt, *W. Germany* **31** 48 50N 8 12 E
Rat Buri, *Thailand* **54** 13 30N 99 54 E
Rat Is., *U.S.A.* **102** 51 50N 178 15 E
Rat River, *Canada* **110** 61 7N 112 36W
Ratangarh, *India* **48** 28 5N 74 35 E
Rath, *India* **49** 25 36N 79 37 E
Rath Luirc, *Ireland* **15** 52 21N 8 40W
Rathbun Res., *U.S.A.* **118** 40 49N 92 53W
Rathdowney, *Australia* **77** 28 13 S 152 52 E
Rathdrum, *Ireland* **15** 52 57N 6 13W
Rathedaung, *Burma* **52** 20 29N 92 45 E
Rathenow, *E. Germany* **30** 52 38N 12 23 E
Rathkeale, *Ireland* **15** 52 32N 8 57W
Rathlin I., *U.K.* **15** 55 18N 6 14W
Rathlin O'Birne I., *Ireland* **15** 54 40N 8 50W
Ratibor = Racibórz, *Poland* **32** 50 7N 18 18 E
Ratlam, *India* **48** 23 20N 75 0 E
Ratnagiri, *India* **50** 16 57N 73 18 E
Ratnapura, *Sri Lanka* **51** 6 40N 80 20 E
Raton, *U.S.A.* **121** 37 0N 104 30W
Rats, R. aux →, *Canada* **107** 48 53N 72 14W
Rattaphum, *Thailand* **55** 7 8N 100 16 E
Rattray Hd., *U.K.* **14** 57 38N 1 50W
Rättvik, *Sweden* **10** 60 52N 15 7 E
Ratz, Mt., *Canada* **110** 57 23N 132 12W
Ratzeburg, *W. Germany* **30** 53 41N 10 46 E
Raub, *Malaysia* **55** 3 47N 101 52 E
Rauch, *Argentina* **140** 36 45 S 59 5W
Raufarhöfn, *Iceland* **8** 66 27N 15 57W
Raufoss, *Norway* **10** 60 44N 10 37 E
Raukumara Ra., *N.Z.* **80** 38 5 S 177 55 E
Raul Soares, *Brazil* **139** 20 5 S 42 22W
Rauland, *Norway* **10** 59 43N 8 0 E
Rauma, *Finland* **9** 61 10N 21 30 E
Rauma →, *Norway* **10** 62 34N 7 43 E
Raurkela, *India* **49** 22 14N 84 50 E
Rava Russkaya, *U.S.S.R.* **36** 50 15N 23 42 E
Ravanusa, *Italy* **28** 37 16N 13 58 E
Rāvar, *Iran* **47** 31 20N 56 51 E
Ravels, *Belgium* **17** 51 22N 5 0 E
Ravena, *U.S.A.* **117** 42 28N 73 49W
Ravenna, *Italy* **27** 44 28N 12 15 E
Ravenna, *Ky., U.S.A.* **119** 37 42N 83 55W
Ravenna, *Nebr., U.S.A.* **120** 41 3N 98 58W
Ravenna, *Ohio, U.S.A.* **116** 41 11N 81 15W
Ravensburg, *W. Germany* **31** 47 48N 9 38 E
Ravenshoe, *Australia* **72** 17 37 S 145 29 E
Ravenstein, *Neths.* **16** 51 47N 5 39 E
Ravensthorpe, *Australia* **79** 33 35 S 120 2 E
Ravenswood, *Queens., Australia* **72** 20 6 S 146 54 E
Ravenswood, *Vic., Australia* **74** 36 53 S 144 15 E
Ravenswood, *U.S.A.* **114** 38 58N 81 47W
Ravensworth, *Australia* **76** 32 26 S 151 4 E
Ravenwood, *U.S.A.* **118** 40 23N 94 41W
Ravi →, *Pakistan* **48** 30 35N 71 49 E
Ravna Gora, *Yugoslavia* **27** 45 24N 14 50 E
Rawa Mazowiecka, *Poland* **32** 51 46N 20 12 E
Rawalpindi, *Pakistan* **48** 33 38N 73 8 E
Rawāndūz, *Iraq* **46** 36 40N 44 30 E
Rawang, *Malaysia* **55** 3 20N 101 35 E
Rawdon, *Canada* **107** 46 3N 73 40W
Rawene, *N.Z.* **80** 35 25 S 173 32 E
Rawicz, *Poland* **32** 51 36N 16 52 E
Rawlinna, *Australia* **79** 30 58 S 125 28 E
Rawlins, *U.S.A.* **122** 41 50N 107 20W
Rawlinson Range, *Australia* **79** 24 40 S 128 30 E
Rawson, *Argentina* **142** 43 15 S 65 0W
Ray, *U.S.A.* **120** 48 21N 103 6W
Ray, C., *Canada* **105** 47 33N 59 15W
Rayachoti, *India* **51** 14 4N 78 50 E
Rayadurg, *India* **51** 14 40N 76 50 E
Rayagada, *India* **50** 19 15N 83 20 E
Raychikhinsk, *U.S.S.R.* **41** 49 46N 129 25 E
Raymond, *Canada* **110** 49 30N 112 35W
Raymond, *Calif., U.S.A.* **124** 37 13N 119 54W
Raymond, *Ill., U.S.A.* **118** 39 19N 89 34W
Raymond, *Wash., U.S.A.* **124** 46 45N 123 48W
Raymond Terrace, *Australia* **76** 32 45 S 151 44 E
Raymondville, *U.S.A.* **121** 26 30N 97 50W
Raymore, *Canada* **111** 51 25N 104 31W
Rayne, *U.S.A.* **121** 30 16N 92 16W
Rayón, *Mexico* **126** 29 43N 110 35W
Rayong, *Thailand* **54** 12 40N 101 20 E
Raytown, *U.S.A.* **118** 39 1N 94 28W
Rayville, *U.S.A.* **121** 32 30N 91 45W
Raywood, *Australia* **74** 36 30 S 144 15 E
Raz, Pte. du, *France* **18** 48 2N 4 47W
Ražana, *Yugoslavia* **33** 44 6N 19 55 E
Ražanj, *Yugoslavia* **33** 43 40N 21 31 E
Razdel'naya, *U.S.S.R.* **38** 46 50N 30 2 E
Razdolnoye, *U.S.S.R.* **38** 45 46N 33 29 E
Razelm, Lacul, *Romania* **34** 44 50N 29 0 E
Razgrad, *Bulgaria* **34** 43 33N 26 34 E
Razmak, *Pakistan* **48** 32 45N 69 50 E
Razole, *India* **51** 16 36N 81 48 E
Ré, I. de, *France* **20** 46 12N 1 30W
Reading, *U.K.* **13** 51 27N 0 57W
Reading, *Mich., U.S.A.* **119** 41 50N 84 45W
Reading, *Ohio, U.S.A.* **119** 39 13N 84 26W
Reading, *Pa., U.S.A.* **117** 40 20N 75 53W
Real, Cordillera, *Bolivia* **136** 17 0 S 67 10W
Realicó, *Argentina* **140** 35 0 S 64 15W
Réalmont, *France* **20** 43 48N 2 10 E
Reata, *Mexico* **126** 26 8N 101 5W
Rebais, *France* **19** 48 50N 3 10 E
Rebecca L., *Australia* **79** 30 0 S 122 15 E
Rebi, *Indonesia* **57** 6 23 S 134 7 E
Rebiana, *Libya* **86** 24 12N 22 10 E
Rebun-Tō, *Japan* **63** 45 23N 141 2 E
Recanati, *Italy* **27** 43 24N 13 32 E
Recaş, *Romania* **34** 45 46N 21 30 E
Recherche, Arch. of the, *Australia* **79** 34 15 S 122 50 E
Rechitsa, *U.S.S.R.* **36** 52 13N 30 15 E
Recht, *Belgium* **17** 50 20N 6 3 E
Recife, *Brazil* **138** 8 0 S 35 0W
Recklinghausen, *W. Germany* **17** 51 36N 7 10 E
Reconquista, *Argentina* **140** 29 10 S 59 45W
Recreio, *Brazil* **137** 8 0 S 58 25W
Recreo, *Argentina* **140** 29 25 S 65 10W
Recuay, *Peru* **136** 9 43 S 77 28W
Red → = Hong →, *Vietnam* **54** 20 17N 106 34 E
Red →, *N. Amer.* **120** 50 24N 96 48W
Red →, *U.S.A.* **121** 31 0N 91 40W
Red Bank, *U.S.A.* **117** 40 21N 74 4W
Red Bay, *Canada* **105** 51 44N 56 25W
Red Bluff, *U.S.A.* **122** 40 11N 122 11W
Red Bluff L., *U.S.A.* **121** 31 59N 103 58W
Red Bud, *U.S.A.* **118** 38 13N 90 0W
Red Cliffs, *Australia* **74** 34 19 S 142 11 E
Red Cloud, *U.S.A.* **120** 40 8N 98 33W
Red Deer, *Canada* **110** 52 20N 113 50W
Red Deer →, *Alta., Canada* **111** 50 58N 110 0W
Red Deer →, *Man., Canada* **111** 52 53N 101 1W

Red Deer L.

Red Deer L., *Canada* . **111** 52 55N 101 20W
Red Indian L., *Canada* **105** 48 35N 57 0W
Red Lake, *Canada* ... **111** 51 3N 93 49W
Red Lake Falls, *U.S.A.* **120** 47 54N 96 15W
Red Lodge, *U.S.A.* ... **122** 45 10N 109 10W
Red Mountain, *U.S.A.* **125** 35 22N 117 38W
Red Oak, *U.S.A.* **120** 41 0N 95 10W
Red Range, *Australia* . **77** 29 46 S 151 57 E
Red Rock, *Australia* .. **77** 29 59 S 153 14 E
Red Rock, *Canada* ... **104** 48 55N 88 15W
Red Rock, L., *U.S.A.* **118** 41 30N 93 15W
Red Rock's Pt., *Australia* .... **79** 32 13 S 127 32 E
Red Sea, *Asia* .... **45** 25 0N 36 0 E
Red Slate Mt., *U.S.A.* **124** 37 31N 118 52W
Red Sucker L., *Canada* **111** 54 9N 93 40W
Red Tower Pass = Turnu Rosu Pasul, *Romania* .... **34** 45 33N 24 17 E
Red Wing, *U.S.A.* **120** 44 32N 92 35W
Rédange, *Lux.* .... **17** 49 46N 5 52 E
Redbank, *Australia* ... **74** 36 56 S 143 21 E
Redbridge, *U.K.* ..... **13** 51 35N 0 7 E
Redcar, *U.K.* **12** 54 37N 1 4W
Redcliff, *Canada* **111** 50 10N 110 50W
Redcliffe, *Australia* ... **77** 27 12 S 153 0 E
Redcliffe, Mt., *Australia* .... **79** 28 30 S 121 30 E
Reddersburg, *S. Africa* **96** 29 41 S 26 10 E
Redding, *U.S.A.* **122** 40 30N 122 25W
Redditch, *U.K.* **13** 52 18N 1 57W
Redenção, *Brazil* .... **138** 4 13 S 38 43W
Redesdale, *Australia* .. **74** 37 2 S 144 31 E
Redfield, *U.S.A.* **120** 45 0N 98 30W
Redkey, *U.S.A.* **119** 40 21N 85 9W
Redknife →, *Canada* . **110** 61 14N 119 22W
Redlands, *U.S.A.* **125** 34 0N 117 11W
Redmond, *Australia* .. **79** 34 55 S 117 40 E
Redmond, *Oreg., U.S.A.* **122** 44 19N 121 11W
Redmond, *Wash., U.S.A.* **124** 47 40N 122 7W
Redon, *France* **18** 47 40N 2 6W
Redonda, *Antigua* **129** 16 58N 62 19W
Redondela, *Spain* **22** 42 15N 8 38W
Redondo, *Portugal* ... **23** 38 39N 7 37W
Redondo Beach, *U.S.A.* **124** 33 50N 118 23W
Redrock Pt., *Canada* . **110** 62 11N 115 2W
Redruth, *U.K.* **13** 50 14N 5 14W
Redvers, *Canada* **111** 49 35N 101 40W
Redwater, *Canada* **110** 53 55N 113 6W
Redwood, *U.S.A.* **117** 44 18N 75 48W
Redwood City, *U.S.A.* **124** 37 30N 122 15W
Redwood Falls, *U.S.A.* **120** 44 30N 95 2W
Ree, L., *Ireland* **15** 53 35N 8 0W
Reed, L., *Canada* **111** 54 38N 100 30W
Reed City, *U.S.A.* **114** 43 52N 85 30W
Reeder, *U.S.A.* **120** 46 7N 102 52W
Reedley, *U.S.A.* **124** 36 36N 119 27W
Reedsburg, *U.S.A.* **120** 43 34N 90 5W
Reedsport, *U.S.A.* ... **122** 43 45N 124 4W
Reefton, *Australia* ... **76** 34 15 S 147 27 E
Reefton, *N.Z.* .... **81** 42 6 S 171 51 E
Reeve, L., *Australia* .. **75** 38 0 S 147 35 E
Reftele, *Sweden* ...... **11** 57 11N 13 35 E
Refugio, *U.S.A.* **121** 28 18N 97 17W
Rega →, *Poland* ..... **32** 54 10N 15 18 E
Regalbuto, *Italy* ...... **29** 37 40N 14 38 E
Regavim, *Israel* ...... **44** 32 32N 35 2 E
Regen, *W. Germany* .. **31** 48 58N 13 9 E
Regen →, *W. Germany* **31** 49 2N 12 6 E
Regeneração, *Brazil* .. **138** 6 15 S 42 41W
Regensburg, *W. Germany* .... **31** 49 1N 12 7 E
Réggio di Calábria, *Italy* .... **29** 38 7N 15 38 E
Réggio nell' Emilia, *Italy* .... **26** 44 42N 10 38 E
Regina, *Canada* **111** 50 27N 104 35W
Régina, *Fr. Guiana* ... **135** 4 19N 52 8W
Registro, *Brazil* ...... **141** 24 29 S 47 49W
Reguengos de Monsaraz, *Portugal* . **23** 38 25N 7 32W
Rehar →, *India* ...... **49** 23 55N 82 40 E
Rehoboth, *Namibia* ... **96** 23 15 S 17 4 E
Rehovot, *Israel* ...... **44** 31 54N 34 48 E
Rei-Bouba, *Cameroon* **94** 8 40N 14 15 E
Reichenbach, *E. Germany* .... **30** 50 36N 12 19 E
Reid, *Australia* .... **79** 30 49 S 128 26 E
Reid River, *Australia* . **72** 19 40 S 146 48 E
Reids Flat, *Australia* .. **76** 34 7 S 149 0 E
Reidsville, *U.S.A.* **115** 36 21N 79 40W
Reigate, *U.K.* **13** 51 14N 0 11W
Reillo, *Spain* **24** 39 54N 1 53W
Reims, *France* .... **19** 49 15N 4 1 E
Reina, *Israel* .... **44** 32 43N 35 18 E
Reina Adelaida, Arch., *Chile* .... **142** 52 20 S 74 0W
Reinbeck, *U.S.A.* **118** 42 18N 92 40W
Reindeer →, *Canada* . **111** 55 36N 103 11W
Reindeer I., *Canada* .. **111** 52 30N 98 0W
Reindeer L., *Canada* . **111** 57 15N 102 15W
Reine, La, *Canada* ... **106** 48 50N 79 30W
Reinga, C., *N.Z.* ..... **80** 34 25 S 172 43 E
Reinosa, *Spain* **22** 43 2N 4 15W
Reinosa, Paso, *Spain* . **22** 42 56N 4 10W
Reitdiep, *Neths.* ...... **16** 53 20N 6 20 E
Reitz, *S. Africa* ...... **97** 27 48 S 28 29 E
Reivilo, *S. Africa* ..... **96** 27 36 S 24 8 E
Rejmyre, *Sweden* ..... **11** 58 50N 15 55 E
Reka →, *Yugoslavia* . **27** 45 40N 14 0 E
Rekinniki, *U.S.S.R.* .. **41** 60 51N 163 40 E
Reliance, *Canada* **111** 63 0N 109 20W
Remad, Oued →, *Algeria* **85** 33 28N 1 20W
Rémalard, *France* .... **18** 48 26N 0 47 E
Remarkable, Mt., *Australia* .... **73** 32 48 S 138 10 E
Rembang, *Indonesia* .. **57** 6 42 S 111 21 E
Remchi, *Algeria* **85** 35 2N 1 26W
Remedios, *Colombia* . **134** 7 2N 74 41W
Remedios, *Panama* ... **128** 8 15N 81 50W
Remeshk, *Iran* .... **47** 26 55N 58 50 E
Remich, *Lux.* .... **17** 49 32N 6 22 E
Rémigny, *Canada* **106** 47 46N 79 12W
Remington, *U.S.A.* ... **119** 40 45N 87 8W
Rémire, *Fr. Guiana* .. **135** 4 53N 52 17W
Remiremont, *France* .. **19** 48 0N 6 36 E
Remo, *Ethiopia* ...... **89** 6 48N 41 20 E
Remontnoye, *U.S.S.R.* **39** 46 34N 43 37 E
Remoulins, *France* ... **21** 43 55N 4 35 E
Remscheid, *W. Germany* .... **30** 51 11N 7 12 E
Ren Xian, *China* ..... **60** 37 8N 114 40 E
Renascença, *Brazil* ... **134** 3 50 S 66 21W
Rend L., *U.S.A.* **118** 38 2N 88 58W
Rende, *Italy* .... **29** 39 19N 16 11 E
Rendeux, *Belgium* .... **17** 50 14N 5 30 E
Rendína, *Greece* ..... **35** 39 4N 21 58 E
Rendova, *Solomon Is.* **68** 8 33 S 157 17 E
Rendsburg, *W. Germany* .... **30** 54 18N 9 41 E
Rene, *U.S.S.R.* **41** 66 2N 179 25W
Renfrew, *Canada* **109** 45 30N 76 40W
Renfrew, *U.K.* **14** 55 52N 4 24W
Rengat, *Indonesia* .... **56** 0 30 S 102 45 E
Rengo, *Chile* .... **140** 34 24 S 70 50W
Renhua, *China* .... **59** 25 5N 113 40 E
Renhuai, *China* ...... **58** 27 48N 106 24 E
Reni, *U.S.S.R.* .... **38** 45 28N 28 15 E
Renigunta, *India* ..... **51** 13 38N 79 30 E
Renk, *Sudan* .... **89** 11 50N 32 50 E
Renkum, *Neths.* ...... **16** 51 58N 5 43 E
Renmark, *Australia* ... **73** 34 11 S 140 43 E
Rennell, *Solomon Is.* . **68** 11 40 S 160 10 E
Rennell Sd., *Canada* .. **110** 53 23N 132 35W
Renner Springs T.O., *Australia* .... **72** 18 20 S 133 47 E
Rennes, *France* **18** 48 7N 1 41W
Rennes, Bassin de, *France* **18** 48 0N 1 30W
Reno, *U.S.A.* **124** 39 30N 119 50W
Reno →, *Italy* .... **27** 44 37N 12 17 E
Renovo, *U.S.A.* **116** 41 20N 77 47W
Renqiu, *China* .... **60** 38 43N 116 5 E
Rensselaer, *Ind., U.S.A.* **119** 40 57N 87 10W
Rensselaer, *N.Y., U.S.A.* **117** 42 38N 73 41W
Rentería, *Spain* **24** 43 19N 1 54W
Renton, *U.S.A.* **124** 47 30N 122 9W
Renwick, *N.Z.* .... **81** 41 30 S 173 51 E
Réo, *Burkina Faso* ... **90** 12 28N 2 35W
Réole, La, *France* **20** 44 35N 0 1W
Reotipur, *India* ...... **49** 25 33N 83 45 E
Repalle, *India* .... **51** 16 2N 80 45 E
Repentigny, *Canada* .. **107** 45 44N 73 28W
Republic, *Mich., U.S.A.* **104** 46 25N 87 59W
Republic, *Wash., U.S.A.* **122** 48 38N 118 42W
Republican →, *U.S.A.* **120** 39 3N 96 48W
Republican City, *U.S.A.* **120** 40 9N 99 20W
Republiek, *Surinam* .. **135** 5 30N 55 13W
Repulse B., *Antarctica* **143** 64 30 S 99 30 E
Repulse Bay, *Canada* . **103** 66 30N 86 30W
Requena, *Peru* .... **136** 5 5 S 73 52W
Requena, *Spain* **25** 39 30N 1 4W
Resele, *Sweden* ...... **10** 63 20N 17 5 E
Reserve, *Canada* **111** 52 28N 102 39W
Reserve, *U.S.A.* **123** 33 50N 108 54W
Resht = Rasht, *Iran* .. **46** 37 20N 49 40 E
Resistencia, *Argentina* **140** 27 30 S 59 0W
Reşiţa, *Romania* ..... **34** 45 18N 21 53 E
Resolution I., *Canada* **103** 61 30N 65 0W
Resolution I., *N.Z.* ... **81** 45 40 S 166 40 E
Resplandes, *Brazil* ... **138** 6 17 S 45 13W
Resplendor, *Brazil* ... **139** 19 20 S 41 15W
Ressano Garcia, *Mozam.* .... **97** 25 25 S 32 0 E
Restinga, La, *Canary Is.* **25** 27 38N 17 59W
Reston, *Canada* **111** 49 33N 101 6W
Retalhuleu, *Guatemala* **128** 14 33N 91 46W
Reteag, *Romania* ..... **34** 47 10N 24 0 E
Retenue, L. de, *Zaïre* . **93** 11 0 S 27 0 E
Rethel, *France* .... **19** 49 30N 4 20 E
Rethem, *W. Germany* . **30** 52 47N 9 25 E
Réthímnon, *Greece* ... **35** 35 18N 24 30 E
Retiche, Alpi, *Switz.* . **31** 46 30N 10 0 E
Retie, *Belgium* ...... **17** 51 16N 5 5 E
Retiers, *France* **18** 47 55N 1 23W
Retortillo, *Spain* **22** 40 48N 6 21W
Reuland, *Belgium* .... **17** 50 12N 6 8 E
Réunion, *Ind. Oc.* .... **53** 21 0 S 56 0 E
Reus, *Spain* .... **24** 41 10N 1 5 E
Reusel, *Neths.* .... **17** 51 21N 5 9 E
Reuss →, *Switz.* ..... **31** 47 16N 8 24 E
Reuterstadt Stavenhagen, *E. Germany* .... **30** 53 41N 12 54 E
Reutlingen, *W. Germany* .... **31** 48 28N 9 13 E
Reutte, *Austria* ...... **31** 47 29N 10 42 E
Reuver, *Neths.* .... **17** 51 17N 6 5 E
Reval = Tallinn, *U.S.S.R.* .... **36** 59 22N 24 48 E
Revel, *France* .... **20** 43 28N 2 0 E
Revelganj, *India* ..... **49** 25 50N 84 40 E
Revelstoke, *Canada* .. **110** 51 0N 118 10W
Reventazón, *Peru* .... **136** 6 10 S 80 58W
Revigny-sur-Ornain, *France* .... **19** 48 49N 4 59 E
Revilla Gigedo, Is., *Pac. Oc.* **67** 18 40N 112 0W
Revillagigedo I., *U.S.A.* **110** 55 50N 131 20W
Revin, *France* .... **19** 49 55N 4 39 E
Revuè →, *Mozam.* ... **93** 19 50 S 34 0 E
Rewa, *India* .... **49** 24 33N 81 25 E
Rewa →, *Guyana* **135** 3 19N 58 42W
Rewari, *India* .... **48** 28 15N 76 40 E
Rexburg, *U.S.A.* **122** 43 55N 111 50W
Rey, Rio del →, *Nigeria* .... **91** 4 30N 8 48 E
Rey Malabo, *Eq. Guin.* **91** 3 45N 8 50 E
Reyes, *Bolivia* .... **136** 14 19 S 67 23W
Reyes, Pt., *U.S.A.* ... **124** 37 59N 123 2W
Reykjahlið, *Iceland* ... **8** 65 40N 16 55W
Reykjanes, *Iceland* ... **8** 63 48N 22 40W
Reykjavík, *Iceland* ... **8** 64 10N 21 57W
Reynolds, *Canada* **111** 49 40N 95 55W
Reynolds, *U.S.A.* **118** 41 20N 90 40W
Reynolds Ra., *Australia* **78** 22 30 S 133 0 E
Reynoldsville, *U.S.A.* . **116** 41 5N 78 58W
Reynosa, *Mexico* **127** 26 5N 98 18W
Rezekne, *U.S.S.R.* ... **36** 56 30N 27 17 E
Rharis, O. →, *Algeria* **85** 26 0N 5 4 E
Rhayader, *U.K.* **13** 52 19N 3 30W
Rheden, *Neths.* ...... **16** 52 0N 6 3 E
Rhein, *Canada* **111** 51 25N 102 15W
Rhein →, *Europe* .... **30** 51 52N 6 2 E
Rhein-Main-Donau-Kanal →, *W. Germany* .... **31** 49 1N 11 27 E
Rheinbach, *W. Germany* .... **30** 50 38N 6 54 E
Rheine, *W. Germany* . **30** 52 17N 7 25 E
Rheinland-Pfalz □, *W. Germany* .... **31** 50 0N 7 0 E
Rheinsberg, *E. Germany* .... **30** 53 6N 12 52 E
Rhenen, *Neths.* ...... **16** 51 58N 5 33 E
Rheola, *Australia* ..... **74** 36 39 S 143 42 E
Rheriss, Oued →, *Morocco* **84** 30 50N 4 34W
Rheydt, *W. Germany* . **30** 51 10N 6 24 E
Rhin = Rhein →, *Europe* .... **30** 51 52N 6 2 E
Rhinau, *France* ...... **19** 48 19N 7 43 E
Rhine = Rhein →, *Europe* .... **30** 51 52N 6 2 E
Rhineland-Palatinate □ = Rheinland-Pfalz □, *W. Germany* .... **31** 50 0N 7 0 E
Rhinelander, *U.S.A.* .. **120** 45 38N 89 29W
Rhino Camp, *Uganda* . **92** 3 0N 31 22 E
Rhir, Cap, *Morocco* .. **84** 30 38N 9 54W
Rhisnes, *Belgium* ..... **17** 50 31N 4 48 E
Rho, *Italy* .... **26** 45 31N 9 2 E
Rhode Island □, *U.S.A.* **117** 41 38N 71 37W
Rhodes = Ródhos, *Greece* .... **35** 36 15N 28 10 E
Rhodes' Tomb, *Zambia* **93** 20 30 S 28 30 E
Rhodesia = Zimbabwe ■, *Africa* **93** 19 0 S 30 0 E
Rhodope Mts. = Rhodopi Planina, *Bulgaria* .... **35** 41 40N 24 20 E
Rhodopi Planina, *Bulgaria* .... **35** 41 40N 24 20 E
Rhondda, *U.K.* **13** 51 39N 3 30W
Rhône □, *France* ..... **21** 45 54N 4 35 E
Rhône →, *France* .... **21** 43 28N 4 42 E
Rhum, *U.K.* **14** 57 0N 6 20W
Rhyl, *U.K.* **12** 53 19N 3 29W
Rhymney, *U.K.* **13** 51 32N 3 7W
Ri-Aba, *Eq. Guin.* .... **91** 3 28N 8 40 E
Riachão, *Brazil* ...... **138** 7 20 S 46 37W
Riacho de Santana, *Brazil* .... **139** 13 37 S 42 57W
Rialma, *Brazil* .... **139** 15 18 S 49 34W
Riang, *India* .... **52** 27 31N 92 56 E
Riaño, *Spain* **22** 42 59N 5 0W
Rians, *France* .... **21** 43 37N 5 44 E
Riansares →, *Spain* .. **24** 39 32N 3 18W
Riasi, *India* .... **49** 33 10N 74 50 E
Riau □, *Indonesia* .... **56** 0 0 102 35 E
Riau, Kepulauan, *Indonesia* .... **56** 0 30N 104 20 E
Riaza, *Spain* **24** 41 18N 3 30W
Riaza →, *Spain* **24** 41 42N 3 55W
Riba de Saelices, *Spain* **24** 40 55N 2 17W
Ribadavia, *Spain* **22** 42 17N 8 8W
Ribadeo, *Spain* **22** 43 35N 7 5W
Ribadesella, *Spain* ... **22** 43 30N 5 7W
Ribamar, *Brazil* ...... **138** 2 33 S 44 3W
Ribas, *Spain* .... **24** 42 19N 2 15 E
Ribas do Rio Pardo, *Brazil* .... **137** 20 27 S 53 46W
Ribble →, *U.K.* **12** 54 13N 2 20W
Ribe, *Denmark* ...... **11** 55 19N 8 44 E
Ribeauvillé, *France* ... **19** 48 10N 7 20 E
Ribécourt, *France* .... **19** 49 30N 2 55 E
Ribeira, *Spain* **22** 42 36N 8 58W
Ribeira do Pombal, *Brazil* .... **138** 10 50 S 38 32W
Ribeirão Prêto, *Brazil* **141** 21 10 S 47 50W
Ribeiro Gonçalves, *Brazil* .... **138** 7 32 S 45 14W
Ribemont, *France* .... **19** 49 47N 3 27 E
Ribera, *Italy* .... **28** 37 30N 13 13 E
Ribérac, *France* ...... **20** 45 15N 0 20 E
Riberalta, *Bolivia* .... **137** 11 0 S 66 0W
Ribnica, *Yugoslavia* .. **27** 45 45N 14 45 E
Ribnitz-Damgarten, *E. Germany* .... **30** 54 14N 12 24 E
Riccarton, *N.Z.* ...... **81** 43 32 S 172 37 E
Riccia, *Italy* .... **29** 41 30N 14 50 E
Riccione, *Italy* .... **27** 44 0N 12 39 E
Rice, *U.S.A.* **125** 34 5N 114 51W
Rice L., *Canada* **109** 44 12N 78 10W
Rice Lake, *U.S.A.* **120** 45 30N 91 42W
Riceys, Les, *France* ... **19** 47 59N 4 22 E
Rich, *Morocco* **84** 32 16N 4 30W
Rich, C., *Canada* **108** 44 43N 80 38W
Rich Hill, *U.S.A.* **121** 38 5N 94 22W
Richards Bay, *S. Africa* **97** 28 48 S 32 6 E
Richards L., *Canada* .. **111** 59 10N 107 10W
Richardson →, *Australia* .... **74** 36 40 S 142 47 E
Richardson →, *Canada* **111** 58 25N 111 14W
Richardson Mts., *N.Z.* **81** 44 49 S 168 34 E
Richardson Springs, *U.S.A.* **124** 39 51N 121 46W
Richardton, *U.S.A.* ... **120** 46 56N 102 22W
Riche, C., *Australia* .. **79** 34 36 S 118 47 E
Richelieu, *France* ..... **18** 47 0N 0 20 E
Richey, *U.S.A.* **120** 47 42N 105 5W
Richfield, *Idaho, U.S.A.* **122** 43 2N 114 5W
Richfield, *Utah, U.S.A.* **123** 38 50N 112 0W
Richford, *U.S.A.* **117** 45 0N 72 40W
Richibucto, *Canada* ... **105** 46 42N 64 54W
Richland, *Ga., U.S.A.* **115** 32 7N 84 40W
Richland, *Iowa, U.S.A.* **118** 41 13N 92 0W
Richland, *Mo., U.S.A.* **118** 37 51N 92 26W
Richland, *Oreg., U.S.A.* **122** 44 49N 117 9W
Richland, *Wash., U.S.A.* **122** 46 15N 119 15W
Richland Center, *U.S.A.* **120** 43 21N 90 22W
Richlands, *U.S.A.* **114** 37 7N 81 49W
Richmond, *N.S.W., Australia* .... **76** 33 35 S 150 42 E
Richmond, *Queens., Australia* .... **72** 20 43 S 143 8 E
Richmond, *Ont., Canada* **109** 45 11N 75 50W
Richmond, *Qué., Canada* **107** 45 40N 72 9W
Richmond, *N.Z.* ..... **81** 41 20 S 173 12 E
Richmond, *S. Africa* .. **97** 29 51 S 30 18 E
Richmond, *N. Yorks., U.K.* **12** 54 24N 1 43W
Richmond, *Surrey, U.K.* **13** 51 28N 0 18W
Richmond, *Calif., U.S.A.* **124** 37 58N 122 21W
Richmond, *Ind., U.S.A.* **119** 39 50N 84 50W
Richmond, *Ky., U.S.A.* **119** 37 40N 84 20W
Richmond, *Mich., U.S.A.* **116** 42 47N 82 45W
Richmond, *Mo., U.S.A.* **120** 39 15N 93 58W
Richmond, *Tex., U.S.A.* **121** 29 32N 95 42W
Richmond, *Utah, U.S.A.* **122** 41 55N 111 48W
Richmond, *Va., U.S.A.* **114** 37 33N 77 27W
Richmond →, *Australia* **77** 28 52 S 153 35 E
Richmond, Mt., *N.Z.* . **81** 41 32 S 173 22 E
Richmond Hill, *Canada* **108** 43 52N 79 27W
Richmond Ra., *Australia* .... **77** 29 0 S 152 45 E
Richmond Ra., *N.Z.* . **81** 41 32 S 173 22 E
Richton, *U.S.A.* **115** 31 23N 88 58W
Richwood, *Ohio, U.S.A.* **119** 40 26N 83 18W
Richwood, *W. Va., U.S.A.* **114** 38 17N 80 32W
Ricla, *Spain* **24** 41 31N 1 24W
Ricupe, *Angola* ...... **95** 14 37 S 21 25 E
Riddarhyttan, *Sweden* . **10** 59 49N 15 33 E
Riddell, *Australia* .... **74** 37 28 S 144 42 E
Ridderkerk, *Neths.* ... **16** 51 52N 4 35 E
Ridge Farm, *U.S.A.* .. **119** 39 54N 87 39W
Ridgecrest, *U.S.A.* ... **125** 35 37N 117 40W
Ridgedale, *Canada* ... **111** 53 0N 104 10W
Ridgefield, *U.S.A.* ... **124** 45 49N 122 45W
Ridgeland, *U.S.A.* **115** 32 30N 80 58W
Ridgelands, *Australia* . **72** 23 16 S 150 17 E
Ridgetown, *Canada* ... **108** 42 26N 81 52W
Ridgeville, *U.S.A.* **119** 40 18N 85 2W
Ridgewood, *U.S.A.* ... **117** 40 59N 74 7W
Ridgway, *Ill., U.S.A.* . **119** 37 48N 88 16W
Ridgway, *Pa., U.S.A.* . **116** 41 25N 78 43W
Riding Mt. Nat. Park, *Canada* **111** 50 50N 100 0W
Ridley Mt., *Australia* . **79** 33 12 S 122 7 E
Ried, *Austria* .... **33** 48 14N 13 30 E
Riedlingen, *W. Germany* .... **31** 48 9N 9 28 E
Riel, *Neths.* .... **17** 51 31N 5 1 E
Rienza →, *Italy* ..... **27** 46 49N 11 47 E
Riesa, *E. Germany* ... **30** 51 19N 13 19 E

St.-André-de-Cubzac

St.-André-de-Cubzac, *France* **20** 44 59N 0 26W
St.-André-de-l'Eure, *France* . . . . **18** 48 54N 1 16 E
St-André-Est, *Canada* **107** 45 34N 74 20W
St.-André-les-Alpes, *France* . . . . **21** 43 58N 6 30 E
St. Andrew's, *Canada* . **105** 47 45N 59 15W
St. Andrews, *N.Z.* . . . . **81** 44 33 S 171 10 E
St. Andrews, *U.K.* . . . **14** 56 20N 2 48W
St-Anicet, *Canada* **117** 45 8N 74 22W
St. Ann B., *Canada* . . **105** 46 22N 60 25W
St. Anne, *U.K.* **18** 49 43N 2 11W
St. Anne, *U.S.A.* **119** 41 1N 87 43W
St. Ann's Bay, *Jamaica* **128** 18 26N 77 15W
St-Anselme, *Canada* . . **107** 46 37N 70 58W
St. Anthony, *Canada* . **105** 51 22N 55 35W
St. Anthony, *U.S.A.* . . **122** 44 0N 111 40W
St-Antonin, *Canada* . . **107** 47 46N 69 29W
St.-Antonin-Noble-Val, *France* . . . . **20** 44 10N 1 45 E
St-Apolline, *Canada* . . **107** 46 48N 70 12W
St. Arnaud, *Australia* . **74** 36 40 S 143 16 E
St. Arnaud Ra., *N.Z.* . **81** 42 1 S 172 53 E
St. Arthur, *Canada* . . . **105** 47 33N 67 46W
St. Asaph, *U.K.* **12** 53 15N 3 27W
St.-Astier, *France* . . . . **20** 45 8N 0 31 E
St-Aubert, *Canada* . . . **107** 47 11N 70 13W
St.-Aubin-du-Cormier, *France* **18** 48 15N 1 26W
St-Augustin-Saguenay, *Canada* **105** 51 13N 58 38W
St. Augustine, *U.S.A.* **115** 29 52N 81 20W
St. Austell, *U.K.* **13** 50 20N 4 48W
St.-Avold, *France* . . . . **19** 49 6N 6 43 E
St-Barthélémy, *Canada* **107** 46 11N 73 8W
St.-Barthélemy, I., *W. Indies* **129** 17 50N 62 50W
St-Basile-Sud, *Canada* **107** 46 45N 71 49W
St. Bathans, *N.Z.* . . . . **81** 44 53 S 169 50 E
St. Bathan's Mt., *N.Z.* **81** 44 45 S 169 45 E
St. Bee's Hd., *U.K.* . . **12** 54 30N 3 38W
St.-Benoît-du-Sault, *France* . . . . **20** 46 26N 1 24 E
St. Bernard, Col du Grand, *Europe* . . . . . **31** 45 53N 7 11 E
St.-Bernard, Col du Petit, *France* . . . . **21** 45 41N 6 51 E
St. Boniface, *Canada* . **111** 49 53N 97 5W
St.-Bonnet, *France* . . . **21** 44 40N 6 5 E
St.-Brévin-les-Pins, *France* **18** 47 14N 2 10W
St.-Brice-en-Coglès, *France* **18** 48 25N 1 22W
St. Bride's, *Canada* . . . **105** 46 56N 54 10W
St. Brides B., *U.K.* . . . **13** 51 48N 5 15W
St.-Brieuc, *France* **18** 48 30N 2 46W
St-Bruno, *Canada* **107** 48 28N 71 39W
St.-Calais, *France* . . . . **18** 47 55N 0 45 E
St-Casimir, *Canada* . . . **107** 46 40N 72 8W
St.-Cast-le-Guildo, *France* **18** 48 37N 2 18W
St. Catharines, *Canada* **108** 43 10N 79 15W
St. Catherines I., *U.S.A.* **115** 31 35N 81 10W
St. Catherine's Pt., *U.K.* **13** 50 34N 1 18W
St.-Céré, *France* . . . . . . **20** 44 51N 1 54 E
St.-Cergue, *Switz.* . . . . **31** 46 27N 6 10 E
St.-Cernin, *France* . . . . **20** 45 5N 2 25 E
St-Césaire, *Canada* . . . **107** 45 25N 73 0W
St.-Chamond, *France* . **21** 45 28N 4 31 E
St. Charles, *Ill., U.S.A.* **119** 41 55N 88 21W
St. Charles, *Mo., U.S.A.* **118** 38 46N 90 30W
St.-Chély-d'Apcher, *France* . . . . **20** 44 48N 3 17 E
St.-Chinian, *France* . . . **20** 43 25N 2 56 E
St. Christopher, *W. Indies* **129** 17 20N 62 40W
St. Christopher-Nevis ■, *W. Indies* . **129** 17 20N 62 40W
St-Chrysostôme, *Canada* **107** 45 6N 73 46W
St.-Ciers-sur-Gironde, *France* **20** 45 17N 0 37W
St. Clair, *Mich., U.S.A.* **116** 42 47N 82 27W
St. Clair, *Mo., U.S.A.* **118** 38 21N 90 59W
St. Clair, *Pa., U.S.A.* . **117** 40 42N 76 12W
St. Clair, L., *Canada* . **108** 42 30N 82 45W
St. Clair Shores, *U.S.A.* **119** 42 30N 82 53W
St. Clairsville, *U.S.A.* . **116** 40 5N 80 53W
St.-Claud, *France* . . . . . **20** 45 54N 0 28 E
St. Claude, *Canada* . . . **111** 49 40N 98 20W
St.-Claude, *France* . . . . **21** 46 22N 5 52 E
St-Clet, *Canada* **107** 45 21N 74 13W
St. Cloud, *Fla., U.S.A.* **115** 28 15N 81 15W
St. Cloud, *Minn., U.S.A.* **120** 45 30N 94 11W
St-Coeur de Marie, *Canada* **107** 48 39N 71 43W
St-Côme, *Canada* **107** 46 16N 73 47W
St. Cricq, C., *Australia* **79** 25 17 S 113 6 E
St. Croix, *Virgin Is.* . . **129** 17 45N 64 45W
St. Croix →, *U.S.A.* . **120** 44 45N 92 50W
St. Croix Falls, *U.S.A.* **120** 45 18N 92 22W
St.-Cyr-sur-Mer, *France* **21** 43 11N 5 43 E
St-Cyrille-de-L'Islet, *Canada* **107** 47 2N 70 17W
St. David, *U.S.A.* **118** 40 30N 90 3W
St. David's, *Canada* . . **105** 48 12N 58 52W
St. David's, *U.K.* **13** 51 54N 5 16W
St. David's Head, *U.K.* **13** 51 55N 5 16W
St.-Denis, *France* . . . . . **19** 48 56N 2 22 E
St.-Denis, *Réunion* . . . **53** 20 52 S 55 27 E
St.-Denis-d'Orques, *France* **18** 48 2N 0 17W
St.-Dié, *France* . . . . **19** 48 17N 6 56 E
St.-Dizier, *France* . . . . . **19** 48 38N 4 56 E
St-Donat-de-Montcalm, *Canada* **107** 46 19N 74 13W
St.-Égrève, *France* . . . . **21** 45 14N 5 41 E
St. Elias, Mt., *U.S.A.* . **102** 60 14N 140 50W
St. Elias Mts., *Canada* **110** 60 33N 139 28W
St.-Élie, *Fr. Guiana* . . **135** 4 49N 53 17W
St. Elmo, *U.S.A.* **119** 39 2N 88 51W
St-Éloi, *Canada* **107** 48 2N 69 14W
St-Élouthère, *Canada* . **107** 47 30N 69 15W
St.-Eloy-les-Mines, *France* . . . . **20** 46 10N 2 51 E
St.-Émilion, *France* . . . **20** 44 53N 0 9W
St-Éphrem-de-Tring, *Canada* **107** 46 2N 70 59W
St.-Étienne, *France* . . . **21** 45 27N 4 22 E
St.-Étienne-de-Tinée, *France* . . . . **21** 44 16N 6 56 E
St. Eugène, *Canada* . . **106** 45 30N 74 28W
St-Eusèbe, *Canada* . . . **107** 47 33N 68 55W
St-Eustache, *Canada* . . **107** 45 33N 73 54W
St. Eustatius, *W. Indies* **129** 17 20N 63 0W
St-Fabien, *Canada* **107** 48 18N 68 52W
St-Félicien, *Canada* . . . **107** 48 40N 72 25W
St-Félix-de-Valois, *Canada* **107** 46 10N 73 26W
St.-Florent, *France* . . . **21** 42 41N 9 18 E
St.-Florent-sur-Cher, *France* . . . . **19** 46 59N 2 15 E
St.-Florentin, *France* . . **19** 48 0N 3 45 E
St.-Flour, *France* . . . . . **20** 45 2N 3 6 E
St.-Fons, *France* . . . . . . **21** 45 42N 4 52 E
St. Francis, *U.S.A.* . . . **120** 39 48N 101 47W
St. Francis →, *U.S.A.* **121** 34 38N 90 36W
St. Francis, C., *S. Africa* . . . . **96** 34 14 S 24 49 E
St. Francisville, *Ill., U.S.A.* **119** 38 36N 87 39W
St. Francisville, *La., U.S.A.* **121** 30 48N 91 22W
St-François, *Canada* . . **107** 46 48N 70 49W
St-François →, *Canada* **107** 46 7N 72 55W
St-François, L., *Qué., Canada* **107** 45 10N 74 22W
St-François, L., *Qué., Canada* **117** 45 10N 74 22W
St-François-du-Lac, *Canada* **107** 46 5N 72 50W
St-Fulgence, *Canada* . . **107** 48 27N 70 54W
St.-Fulgent, *France* . . . **18** 46 50N 1 10W
St-Gabriel-de-Brandon, *Canada* **107** 46 17N 73 24W
St-Gabriel-de-Rimouski, *Canada* . . **107** 48 25N 68 10W
St.-Gaudens, *France* . . **20** 43 6N 0 44 E
St-Gédéon, *Canada* . . . **107** 48 30N 71 46W
St-Gédéon-de-Beauce, *Canada* **107** 45 45N 70 40W
St.-Gengoux-le-National, *France* . . . **21** 46 37N 4 40 E
St.-Geniez-d'Olt, *France* . . . . **20** 44 27N 2 58 E
St. George, *Australia* . **73** 28 1 S 148 30 E
St. George, *N.B., Canada* **105** 45 11N 66 50W
St. George, *Ont., Canada* **108** 43 15N 80 15W
St. George, *S.C., U.S.A.* **115** 33 13N 80 37W
St. George, *Utah, U.S.A.* **123** 37 10N 113 35W
St. George, C., *Canada* **105** 48 30N 59 16W
St. George, C., *Papua N. G.* . . . . **69** 4 49 S 152 53 E
St. George, C., *U.S.A.* **115** 29 36N 85 2W
St. George Ra., *Australia* . . . . **78** 18 40 S 125 0 E
St-Georges, *Belgium* . . **17** 50 37N 5 20 E
St. George's, *Canada* . **105** 48 26N 58 31W
St-Georges, *Canada* . . **107** 46 8N 70 40W
St.-Georges, *Fr. Guiana* **135** 4 0N 52 0W
St. George's, *Grenada* **129** 12 5N 61 43W
St. George's B., *Canada* **105** 48 24N 58 53W
St. George's Channel, *Papua N. G.* . . . . **69** 4 10 S 152 20 E
St. George's Channel, *U.K.* **15** 52 0N 6 0W
St-Georges-de-Cacouna, *Canada* **107** 47 55N 69 30W
St.-Georges-de-Didonne, *France* . . . **20** 45 36N 1 0W
St. Georges Head, *Australia* . . . . **76** 35 12 S 150 42 E
St-Georges-Ouest, *Canada* **107** 46 7N 70 40W
St.-Gérard, *Belgium* . . **17** 50 21N 4 44 E
St-Gérard, *Canada* . . . **107** 45 46N 71 25W
St.-Germain-de-Calberte, *France* . . . **20** 44 13N 3 48 E
St-Germain-de-Grantham, *Canada* . **107** 45 50N 72 34W
St.-Germain-des-Fossés, *France* . . . . **20** 46 12N 3 26 E
St.-Germain-du-Plain, *France* . . . . **19** 46 42N 4 58 E
St.-Germain-en-Laye, *France* . . . . **19** 48 54N 2 6 E
St.-Germain-Laval, *France* . . . . **21** 45 50N 4 1 E
St.-Germain-Lembron, *France* . . . . **20** 45 27N 3 14 E
St.-Gervais-d'Auvergne, *France* . . . . **20** 46 4N 2 50 E
St.-Gervais-les-Bains, *France* . . . . **21** 45 53N 6 42 E
St.-Gildas, Pte. de, *France* **18** 47 8N 2 14W
St.-Gilles, *France* . . . . . **21** 43 40N 4 26 E
St.-Gilles-Croix-de-Vie, *France* **20** 46 41N 1 55W
St.-Girons, *France* . . . . **20** 42 59N 1 8 E
St. Goar, *W. Germany* **31** 50 12N 7 43 E
St. Gotthard P. = San Gottardo, Paso del, *Switz.* . . . . **31** 46 33N 8 33 E
St.-Gualtier, *France* . . **18** 46 39N 1 26 E
St.-Guénolé, *France* . . **18** 47 49N 4 23W
St-Guillaume-d'Upton, *Canada* **107** 45 53N 72 46W
St. Helena, *Atl. Oc.* . . **4** 15 55 S 5 44W
St. Helena, *U.S.A.* . . . **122** 38 29N 122 30W
St Helena, Mt., *U.S.A.* **124** 38 40N 122 36W
St. Helena B., *S. Africa* **96** 32 40 S 18 10 E
St. Helens, *Australia* . . **72** 41 20 S 148 15 E
St. Helens, *U.K.* **12** 53 28N 2 44W
St. Helens, *U.S.A.* . . . **124** 45 55N 122 50W
St. Helens, Mt., *U.S.A.* **124** 46 12N 122 11W
St. Helier, *U.K.* **18** 49 11N 2 6W
St.-Hilaire-du-Harcouët, *France* . . . **18** 48 35N 1 5W
St-Hilarion, *Canada* . . **107** 47 34N 70 24W
St.-Hippolyte, *France* . **19** 47 19N 6 50 E
St.-Hippolyte-du-Fort, *France* . . . . **20** 43 58N 3 52 E
St-Honoré, *Canada* . . . **107** 48 32N 71 5W
St.-Honoré-les-Bains, *France* . . . . **19** 46 54N 3 50 E
St.-Hubert, *Belgium* . . **17** 50 2N 5 23 E
St-Hubert-de-Témiscouata, *Canada* **107** 47 49N 69 9W
St-Hyacinthe, *Canada* . **107** 45 40N 72 58W
St. Ignace, *U.S.A.* **104** 45 53N 84 43W
St. Ignace I., *Canada* . **104** 48 45N 88 0W
St. Ignatius, *U.S.A.* . . **122** 47 19N 114 8W
St-Imier, *Switz.* . . . . . . **31** 47 9N 6 58 E
St-Isidore, *Canada* **107** 45 20N 73 42W
St. Ives, *Cambs., U.K.* **13** 52 20N 0 5W
St. Ives, *Cornwall, U.K.* **13** 50 13N 5 29W
St-Jacques, *Canada* . . . **107** 45 57N 73 34W
St.-James, *France* **18** 48 31N 1 20W
St. James, *Minn., U.S.A.* **120** 43 57N 94 40W
St. James, *Mo., U.S.A.* **118** 38 0N 91 37W
St-Jean, *Canada* **107** 45 20N 73 20W
St-Jean →, *Canada* . . **105** 50 17N 64 20W
St-Jean, L., *Canada* . . **107** 48 40N 72 0W
St. Jean Baptiste, *Canada* **111** 49 15N 97 20W
St.-Jean-d'Angély, *France* **20** 45 57N 0 31W
St.-Jean-de-Bournay, *France* . . . . **21** 45 30N 5 9 E
St-Jean-de-Dieu, *Canada* **107** 48 0N 69 3W
St.-Jean-de-Luz, *France* **20** 43 23N 1 39W
St.-Jean-de-Maurienne, *France* . . . . **21** 45 16N 6 21 E
St.-Jean-de-Monts, *France* **18** 46 47N 2 4W
St.-Jean-du-Gard, *France* . . . . **20** 44 7N 3 52 E
St.-Jean-en-Royans, *France* . . . . **21** 45 1N 5 18 E
St-Jean-Port-Joli, *Canada* **107** 47 15N 70 13W
St-Jérôme, *Qué., Canada* **107** 48 26N 71 53W
St-Jérôme, *Qué., Canada* **107** 45 47N 74 0W
St-Joachim, *Canada* . . **107** 47 4N 70 50W
St. Joe, *U.S.A.* **119** 41 19N 84 54W
St. John, *Canada* **105** 45 20N 66 8W
St. John, *Kans., U.S.A.* **121** 37 59N 98 45W
St. John, *N. Dak., U.S.A.* **120** 48 58N 99 40W
St. John →, *N. Amer.* **105** 45 15N 66 4W
St. John, C., *Canada* . **105** 50 0N 55 32W
St. John's, *Antigua* . . . **129** 17 6N 61 51W
St. John's, *Canada* . . . **105** 47 35N 52 40W
St. Johns, *Ariz., U.S.A.* **123** 34 31N 109 26W
St. Johns, *Mich., U.S.A.* **119** 43 0N 84 31W
St. John's →, *U.S.A.* . **115** 30 20N 81 30W
St. Johnsbury, *U.S.A.* . **117** 44 25N 72 1W
St. Johnsville, *U.S.A.* . **117** 43 0N 74 43W
St.-Joseph, *N. Cal.* . . . . **68** 20 27 S 166 36 E
St. Joseph, *Ill., U.S.A.* **119** 40 7N 88 2W
St. Joseph, *La., U.S.A.* **121** 31 55N 91 15W
St. Joseph, *Mich., U.S.A.* **119** 42 5N 86 30W
St. Joseph, *Mo., U.S.A.* **118** 39 46N 94 50W
St. Joseph →, *U.S.A.* **119** 42 7N 86 30W
St. Joseph, I., *Canada* **108** 46 12N 83 58W
St. Joseph, L., *Canada* **104** 51 10N 90 35W
St-Joseph-de-Beauce, *Canada* **107** 46 18N 70 53W
St-Joseph-de-la-Rivière-Bleue, *Canada* **107** 47 26N 69 3W
St-Joseph-de-Sorel, *Canada* **107** 46 2N 73 7W
St-Jovite, *Canada* **106** 46 8N 74 38W
St-Jude, *Canada* **107** 45 46N 72 59W
St.-Juéry, *France* . . . . . **20** 43 57N 2 12 E
St.-Julien-Chapteuil, *France* . . . . **21** 45 2N 4 4 E
St.-Julien-du-Sault, *France* . . . . **19** 48 1N 3 17 E
St.-Julien-en-Genevois, *France* . . . . **21** 46 9N 6 5 E
St.-Junien, *France* . . . . **20** 45 53N 0 55 E
St.-Just-en-Chaussée, *France* . . . . **19** 49 30N 2 25 E
St.-Just-en-Chevalet, *France* . . . . **20** 45 55N 3 50 E
St.-Justin, *France* **20** 43 59N 0 14W
St-Justine, *Canada* **107** 46 24N 70 21W
St. Kilda, *N.Z.* . . . . **81** 45 53 S 170 31 E
St. Kitts = St. Christopher, *W. Indies* **129** 17 20N 62 40W
St. Laurent, *Canada* . . . **111** 50 25N 97 58W
St.-Laurent, *Fr. Guiana* **135** 5 29N 54 3W
St.-Laurent-du-Pont, *France* . . . . **21** 45 23N 5 45 E
St.-Laurent-en-Grandvaux, *France* . **21** 46 35N 5 58 E
St. Lawrence, *Australia* **72** 22 16 S 149 31 E
St. Lawrence, *Canada* **105** 46 54N 55 23W
St. Lawrence →, *Canada* **105** 49 30N 66 0W
St. Lawrence, Gulf of, *Canada* **105** 48 25N 62 0W
St. Lawrence I., *U.S.A.* **102** 63 0N 170 0W
St.-Léger, *Belgium* . . . **17** 49 37N 5 39 E
St. Leonard, *Canada* . . **105** 47 12N 67 58W
St.-Léonard-de-Noblat, *France* . . . . **20** 45 49N 1 29 E
St-Léonard-de-Portneuf, *Canada* . . **107** 46 53N 71 55W
St. Lewis →, *Canada* . **105** 52 26N 56 11W
St.-Lô, *France* **18** 49 7N 1 5W
St-Louis, *Senegal* **90** 16 8N 16 27W
St. Louis, *Mich., U.S.A.* **114** 43 27N 84 38W
St. Louis, *Mo., U.S.A.* **118** 38 40N 90 12W
St. Louis →, *U.S.A.* . **120** 47 15N 92 45W
St.-Loup-sur-Semouse, *France* . . . . **19** 47 53N 6 16 E
St-Luc, *Canada* **107** 45 22N 73 18W
St. Lucia ■, *W. Indies* **129** 14 0N 60 50W
St. Lucia, L., *S. Africa* **97** 28 5 S 32 30 E
St. Lucia Channel, *W. Indies* **129** 14 15N 61 0W
St-Ludger, *Canada* . . . **107** 45 45N 70 42W
St. Lunaire-Griquet, *Canada* **105** 51 31N 55 28W
St. Maarten, *W. Indies* **129** 18 0N 63 5W
St-Magloire, *Canada* . . **107** 46 35N 70 17W
St.-Maixent-l'École, *France* **20** 46 24N 0 12W
St.-Malo, *France* **18** 48 39N 2 1W
St.-Malo, G. de, *France* **18** 48 50N 2 30W
St.-Mandrier-sur-Mer, *France* . . . . **21** 43 4N 5 57 E
St-Marc, *Haiti* **129** 19 10N 72 41W
St.-Marcellin, *France* . **21** 45 9N 5 20 E
St.-Marcouf, Is., *France* **18** 49 30N 1 10W
St. Margaret I., *Australia* . . . . **75** 38 38 S 146 50 E
St. Maries, *U.S.A.* . . . **122** 47 17N 116 34W
St-Martin, I., *W. Indies* **129** 18 0N 63 0W
St.-Martin-de-Ré, *France* **20** 46 12N 1 21W
St. Martin L., *Canada* **111** 51 40N 98 30W
St.-Martin-Vésubie, *France* . . . . **21** 44 4N 7 15 E
St. Martins, *Canada* . . **105** 45 22N 65 34W
St. Martinsville, *U.S.A.* **121** 30 10N 91 50W
St.-Martory, *France* . . . **20** 43 9N 0 56 E
St. Mary, Mt., *Papua N. G.* . . . . **69** 8 8 S 147 2 E
St. Mary Is., *India* . . . . **51** 13 20N 74 35 E
St. Mary Pk., *Australia* **73** 31 32 S 138 34 E
St. Marys, *N.S.W., Australia* . . . . **76** 33 44 S 150 49 E
St. Marys, *Tas., Australia* . . . . **72** 41 35 S 148 11 E
St. Marys, *Canada* **108** 43 20N 81 10W
St. Mary's, *U.K.* **13** 49 55N 6 17W
St. Marys, *Mo., U.S.A.* **118** 37 53N 89 57W
St. Marys, *Pa., U.S.A.* **116** 41 27N 78 33W
St. Mary's, C., *Canada* **105** 46 50N 54 12W
St. Mary's B., *Canada* **105** 46 50N 53 50W
St. Marys Bay, *Canada* **105** 44 25N 66 10W
St.-Mathieu, Pte. de, *France* **18** 48 20N 4 45W
St. Matthews, *U.S.A.* . **119** 38 15N 85 39W
St. Matthews, I. = Zadetkyi Kyun, *Burma* . . . . **55** 10 0N 98 25 E
St. Matthias Grp., *Papua N. G.* . . . . **69** 1 30 S 150 0 E
St.-Maur-des-Fossés, *France* . . . . **19** 48 48N 2 30 E
St-Maurice →, *Canada* **107** 46 21N 72 31W
St-Maurice, Parc Prov. du, *Canada* **107** 47 5N 73 15W
St.-Médard-de-Guizières, *France* . . . **20** 45 1N 0 4W
St.-Méen-le-Grand, *France* **18** 48 11N 2 12W

Santa Cruz

Santa Cruz →, *Argentina* .... **142** 50 10 S 68 20W
Santa Cruz, I., *Solomon Is.* .... **66** 10 30 S 166 0 E
Santa Cruz Cabrália, *Brazil* .... **139** 16 17 S 39 2W
Santa Cruz de la Palma, *Canary Is.* **25** 28 41N 17 46W
Santa Cruz de Mudela, *Spain* **25** 38 39N 3 28W
Santa Cruz de Tenerife, *Canary Is.* **25** 28 28N 16 15W
Santa Cruz del Norte, *Cuba* **128** 23 9N 81 55W
Santa Cruz del Retamar, *Spain* **22** 40 8N 4 14W
Santa Cruz del Sur, *Cuba* **128** 20 44N 78 0W
Santa Cruz do Rio Pardo, *Brazil* ...... **141** 22 54 S 49 37W
Santa Cruz do Sul, *Brazil* .... **141** 29 42 S 52 25W
Santa Cruz I., *U.S.A.* . **125** 34 0N 119 45W
Santa Domingo, Cay, *Bahamas* **128** 21 25N 75 15W
Santa Elena, *Argentina* **140** 30 58 S 59 47W
Santa Elena, *Ecuador* . **134** 2 16 S 80 52W
Santa Elena, C., *Costa Rica* **128** 10 54N 85 56W
Sant' Eufémia, G. di, *Italy* .... **29** 38 50N 16 10 E
Santa Eugenia, Pta., *Mexico* **126** 27 50N 115 5W
Santa Eulalia, *Spain* .. **25** 38 59N 1 32 E
Santa Fe, *Argentina* .. **140** 31 35 S 60 41W
Santa Fe, *Spain* **23** 37 11N 3 43W
Santa Fe, *U.S.A.* **123** 35 40N 106 0W
Santa Fé □, *Argentina* **140** 31 50 S 60 55W
Santa Filomena, *Brazil* **138** 9 6 S 45 50W
Santa Helena, *Brazil* .. **138** 2 14 S 45 18W
Santa Helena de Goiás, *Brazil* .... **139** 17 53 S 50 35W
Santa Inês, *Brazil* .... **139** 13 17 S 39 48W
Santa Inés, *Spain* **23** 38 32N 5 37W
Santa Inés, I., *Chile* .. **142** 54 0 S 73 0W
Santa Isabel = Rey Malabo, *Eq. Guin.* . **91** 3 45N 8 50 E
Santa Isabel, *Argentina* **140** 36 10 S 66 54W
Santa Isabel, *Brazil* ... **139** 11 45 S 51 30W
Santa Isabel, *Solomon Is.* .... **68** 8 0 S 159 0 E
Santa Isabel, Pico, *Eq. Guin.* .... **91** 3 36N 8 49 E
Santa Isabel do Araguaia, *Brazil* ... **138** 6 7 S 48 19W
Santa Isabel do Morro, *Brazil* .... **139** 11 34 S 50 40W
Santa Lucía, *Corrientes, Argentina* .... **140** 28 58 S 59 5W
Santa Lucía, *San Juan, Argentina* .... **140** 31 30 S 68 30W
Santa Lucía, *Spain* ... **25** 37 35N 0 58W
Santa Lucía, *Uruguay* . **140** 34 27 S 56 24W
Santa Lucia Range, *U.S.A.* **124** 36 0N 121 20W
Santa Magdalena, I., *Mexico* **126** 24 40N 112 15W
Santa Margarita, *Argentina* .... **140** 38 28 S 61 35W
Santa Margarita, *Mexico* **126** 24 30N 111 50W
Santa Margarita, *U.S.A.* **124** 35 23N 120 37W
Santa Margarita →, *U.S.A.* **125** 33 13N 117 23W
Santa Margherita, *Italy* **26** 44 20N 9 11 E
Santa María, *Argentina* **140** 26 40 S 66 0W
Santa Maria, *Brazil* ... **141** 29 40 S 53 48W
Santa María, *Spain* ... **24** 39 38N 2 47 E
Santa Maria, *U.S.A.* .. **125** 34 58N 120 29W
Santa Maria, *Zambia* . **93** 11 5 S 29 58 E
Santa María →, *Mexico* **126** 31 0N 107 14W
Santa María, B. de, *Mexico* **126** 25 10N 108 40W
Santa Maria, C. de, *Portugal* **23** 36 58N 7 53W
Santa Maria Capua Vetere, *Italy* .... **29** 41 3N 14 15 E
Santa Maria da Vitória, *Brazil* .... **139** 13 24 S 44 12W
Santa María de Ipire, *Venezuela* **135** 8 49N 65 19W
Santa Maria di Leuca, C., *Italy* .... **29** 39 48N 18 20 E
Santa Maria do Suaçuí, *Brazil* .... **139** 18 12 S 42 25W
Santa Maria dos Marmelos, *Brazil* ... **137** 6 7 S 61 51W
Santa María la Real de Nieva, *Spain* **22** 41 4N 4 24W
Santa Marta, *Colombia* **134** 11 15N 74 13W
Santa Marta, *Spain* ... **23** 38 37N 6 39W
Santa Marta, Ría de, *Spain* **22** 43 44N 7 45W
Santa Marta, Sierra Nevada de, *Colombia* **134** 10 55N 73 50W
Santa Marta Grande, C., *Brazil* .... **141** 28 43 S 48 50W
Santa Maura = Levkás, *Greece* .... **35** 38 40N 20 43 E
Santa Monica, *U.S.A.* **125** 34 0N 118 30W
Santa Olalla, *Huelva, Spain* **23** 37 54N 6 14W
Santa Olalla, *Toledo, Spain* **22** 40 2N 4 25W
Santa Ona, *Solomon Is.* **68** 10 0 S 162 0 E
Sant' Onofrio, *Italy* ... **29** 38 42N 16 10 E
Santa Pola, *Spain* **25** 38 13N 0 35W
Santa Quitéria, *Brazil* . **138** 4 20 S 40 10W
Santa Rita, *U.S.A.* ... **123** 32 50N 108 0W
Santa Rita, *Guarico, Venezuela* **134** 8 8N 66 16W
Santa Rita, *Zulia, Venezuela* **134** 10 32N 71 32W
Santa Rita do Araquaia, *Brazil* ... **137** 17 20 S 53 12W
Santa Rosa, *La Pampa, Argentina* .... **140** 36 40 S 64 17W
Santa Rosa, *San Luis, Argentina* .... **140** 32 21 S 65 10W
Santa Rosa, *Bolivia* ... **136** 10 36 S 67 20W
Santa Rosa, *Brazil* ... **141** 27 52 S 54 29W
Santa Rosa, *Colombia* **134** 3 32N 69 48W
Santa Rosa, *Ecuador* . **134** 3 27 S 79 58W
Santa Rosa, *Peru* ..... **136** 14 30 S 70 50W
Santa Rosa, *Calif., U.S.A.* **124** 38 26N 122 43W
Santa Rosa, *N. Mex., U.S.A.* **121** 34 58N 104 40W
Santa Rosa, *Venezuela* **134** 1 29N 66 55W
Santa Rosa de Cabal, *Colombia* **134** 4 52N 75 38W
Santa Rosa de Copán, *Honduras* **128** 14 47N 88 46W
Santa Rosa de Osos, *Colombia* **134** 6 39N 75 28W
Santa Rosa de Río Primero, *Argentina* . **140** 31 8 S 63 20W
Santa Rosa de Viterbo, *Colombia* **134** 5 53N 72 59W
Santa Rosa del Palmar, *Bolivia* .... **137** 16 54 S 62 24W
Santa Rosa I., *Calif., U.S.A.* **125** 34 0N 120 6W
Santa Rosa I., *Fla., U.S.A.* **115** 30 23N 87 0W
Santa Rosa Ra., *U.S.A.* **122** 41 45N 117 30W
Santa Rosalía, *Mexico* **126** 27 20N 112 20W
Santa Sofia, *Italy* ..... **27** 43 57N 11 55 E
Santa Sylvina, *Argentina* .... **140** 27 50 S 61 10W
Santa Tecla = Nueva San Salvador, *El Salv.* **128** 13 40N 89 18W
Santa Teresa, *Argentina* **140** 33 25 S 60 47W
Santa Teresa, *Brazil* .. **139** 19 55 S 40 36W
Santa Teresa, *Mexico* . **127** 25 17N 97 51W
Santa Teresa, *Venezuela* **135** 4 43N 61 4W
Santa Teresa di Riva, *Italy* .... **29** 37 58N 15 21 E
Santa Teresa Gallura, *Italy* .... **28** 41 14N 9 12 E
Santa Vitória, *Brazil* .. **139** 18 50 S 50 8W
Santa Vitória do Palmar, *Brazil* ..... **141** 33 32 S 53 25W
Santa Ynez, *U.S.A.* ... **125** 34 37N 120 5W
Santa Ynez →, *U.S.A.* **125** 34 37N 120 41W
Santa Ysabel, *U.S.A.* . **125** 33 7N 116 40W
Santadi, *Italy* .... **28** 39 5N 8 42 E
Santahar, *Bangla.* .... **52** 24 48N 88 59 E
Santai, *China* .... **58** 31 5N 104 58 E
Santaluz, *Brazil* ...... **138** 11 15 S 39 22W
Santana, *Brazil* ...... **139** 13 2 S 44 5W
Santana, Coxilha de, *Brazil* .... **141** 30 50 S 55 35W
Santana do Ipanema, *Brazil* .... **138** 9 22 S 37 14W
Santana do Livramento, *Brazil* .... **141** 30 55 S 55 30W
Santanayi, *Spain* ..... **25** 39 20N 3 5 E
Santander, *Colombia* . **134** 3 1N 76 28W
Santander, *Spain* **22** 43 27N 3 51W
Santander □, *Spain* ... **22** 43 25N 4 0W
Santander Jiménez, *Mexico* **127** 24 11N 98 29W
Santaquin, *U.S.A.* **122** 40 0N 111 51W
Santarém, *Brazil* ..... **135** 2 25 S 54 42W
Santarém, *Portugal* ... **23** 39 12N 8 42W
Santarém □, *Portugal* . **23** 39 10N 8 40W
Santaren Channel, *W. Indies* **128** 24 0N 79 30W
Santee, *U.S.A.* **125** 32 50N 116 58W
Santéramo in Colle, *Italy* .... **29** 40 48N 16 45 E
Santerno →, *Italy* .... **27** 44 10N 11 38 E
Santhia, *Italy* .... **26** 45 20N 8 10 E
Santiago, *Bolivia* ..... **137** 18 19 S 59 34W
Santiago, *Brazil* ...... **141** 29 11 S 54 52W
Santiago, *Chile* ...... **140** 33 24 S 70 40W
Santiago, *Panama* **128** 8 0N 81 0W
Santiago, *Peru* .... **136** 14 11 S 75 43W
Santiago □, *Chile* .... **140** 33 30 S 70 50W
Santiago →, *Peru* .... **134** 4 27 S 77 38W
Santiago, C., *Chile* ... **142** 50 46 S 75 27W
Santiago, Punta de, *Eq. Guin.* .... **91** 3 12N 8 40 E
Santiago, Serranía de, *Bolivia* .... **137** 18 25 S 59 25W
Santiago de Chuco, *Peru* .... **136** 8 9 S 78 11W
Santiago de Compostela, *Spain* . **22** 42 52N 8 37W
Santiago de Cuba, *Cuba* **128** 20 0N 75 49W
Santiago de los Cabelleros, *Dom. Rep.* **129** 19 30N 70 40W
Santiago del Estero, *Argentina* .... **140** 27 50 S 64 15W
Santiago del Estero □, *Argentina* .... **140** 27 40 S 63 15W
Santiago del Teide, *Canary Is.* **25** 28 17N 16 48W
Santiago do Cacém, *Portugal* **23** 38 1N 8 42W
Santiago Ixcuintla, *Mexico* **126** 21 50N 105 11W
Santiago Papasquiaro, *Mexico* **126** 25 0N 105 20W
Santiaguillo, L. de, *Mexico* **126** 24 50N 104 50W
Santillana del Mar, *Spain* **22** 43 24N 4 6W
Santisteban del Puerto, *Spain* **25** 38 17N 3 15W
Santo, *Vanuatu* ...... **68** 15 27 S 167 10 E
Santo →, *Peru* ...... **136** 8 56 S 78 37W
Santo Amaro, *Brazil* .. **139** 12 30 S 38 43W
Santo Anastácio, *Brazil* **141** 21 58 S 51 39W
Santo André, *Brazil* .. **141** 23 39 S 46 29W
Santo Ângelo, *Brazil* . **141** 28 15 S 54 15W
Santo Antonio, *Brazil* **137** 15 50 S 56 0W
Santo Antônio de Jesus, *Brazil* .... **139** 12 58 S 39 16W
Santo Antônio do Içá, *Brazil* .... **134** 3 5 S 67 57W
Santo Antônio do Leverger, *Brazil* .... **137** 15 52 S 56 5W
Santo Corazón, *Bolivia* **137** 18 0 S 58 45W
Santo Domingo, *Dom. Rep.* **129** 18 30N 69 59W
Santo Domingo, *Baja Calif. N., Mexico* **126** 30 43N 116 2W
Santo Domingo, *Baja Calif. S., Mexico* **126** 25 32N 112 2W
Santo Domingo, *Nic.* . **128** 12 14N 84 59W
Santo Domingo de la Calzada, *Spain* **24** 42 26N 2 57W
Santo Domingo de los Colorados, *Ecuador* **134** 0 15 S 79 9W
Santo Stéfano di Camastro, *Italy* .... **29** 38 1N 14 22 E
Santo Stino di Livenza, *Italy* .... **27** 45 45N 12 40 E
Santo Tirso, *Portugal* . **22** 41 21N 8 28W
Santo Tomás, *Mexico* . **126** 31 33N 116 24W
Santo Tomás, *Peru* ... **136** 14 26 S 72 8W
Santo Tomé, *Argentina* **141** 28 40 S 56 5W
Santo Tomé de Guayana = Ciudad Guayana, *Venezuela* **135** 8 0N 62 30W
Santoña, *Spain* **22** 43 29N 3 27W
Santos, *Brazil* .... **141** 24 0 S 46 20W
Santos, Sierra de los, *Spain* **23** 38 7N 5 12W
Santos Dumont, *Brazil* **141** 22 55 S 43 10W
Santpoort, *Neths.* ..... **16** 52 26N 4 39 E
Sānūr, *Jordan* .... **44** 32 22N 35 15 E
Sanvignes-les-Mines, *France* .... **19** 46 40N 4 18 E
San'yō, *Japan* .... **64** 34 2N 131 5 E
Sanyuan, *China* ...... **60** 34 35N 108 58 E
Sanyuki-Sammyaku, *Japan* .... **64** 34 5N 133 0 E
Sanza Pombo, *Angola* **95** 7 18 S 15 56 E
São Anastácio, *Brazil* . **141** 22 0 S 51 40W
São Bartolomeu de Messines, *Portugal* . **23** 37 15N 8 17W
São Benedito, *Brazil* .. **138** 4 3 S 40 53W
São Bento, *Brazil* .... **138** 2 42 S 44 50W
São Bento do Norte, *Brazil* .... **138** 5 4 S 36 2W
São Bernado de Campo, *Brazil* ..... **139** 23 45 S 46 34W
São Borja, *Brazil* ..... **141** 28 39 S 56 0W
São Bras d'Alportel, *Portugal* **23** 37 8N 7 37W
São Caitano, *Brazil* ... **138** 8 21 S 36 6W
São Carlos, *Brazil* .... **141** 22 0 S 47 50W
São Cristóvão, *Brazil* . **138** 11 1 S 37 15W
São Domingos, *Brazil* . **139** 13 25 S 46 19W
São Domingos do Maranhão, *Brazil* .. **138** 5 42 S 44 22W
São Félix, *Brazil* ..... **139** 11 36 S 50 39W
São Francisco, *Brazil* . **139** 16 0 S 44 50W
São Francisco →, *Brazil* .... **138** 10 30 S 36 24W
São Francisco do Maranhão, *Brazil* .. **138** 6 15 S 42 52W
São Francisco do Sul, *Brazil* .... **141** 26 15 S 48 36W
São Gabriel, *Brazil* ... **141** 30 20 S 54 20W
São Gabriel da Palha, *Brazil* .... **139** 18 47 S 40 39W
São Gonçalo, *Brazil* .. **139** 22 48 S 43 5W
São Gotardo, *Brazil* .. **139** 19 19 S 46 3W
Sao Hill, *Tanzania* ... **93** 8 20 S 35 12 E
São João da Boa Vista, *Brazil* .... **141** 22 0 S 46 52W
São João da Pesqueira, *Portugal* **22** 41 8N 7 24W
São João da Ponte, *Brazil* .... **139** 15 56 S 44 1W
São João del Rei, *Brazil* .... **139** 21 8 S 44 15W
São João do Araguaia, *Brazil* .... **138** 5 23 S 48 46W
São João do Paraíso, *Brazil* .... **139** 15 19 S 42 1W
São João do Piauí, *Brazil* .... **138** 8 21 S 42 15W
São João dos Patos, *Brazil* .... **138** 6 30 S 43 42W
São Joaquim da Barra, *Brazil* .... **139** 20 35 S 47 53W
São José, B. de, *Brazil* **138** 2 38 S 44 4W
São José da Laje, *Brazil* .... **138** 9 1 S 36 3W
São José de Mipibu, *Brazil* .... **138** 6 5 S 35 15W
São José do Peixe, *Brazil* .... **138** 7 24 S 42 34W
São José do Rio Prêto, *Brazil* .... **141** 20 50 S 49 20W
São José dos Campos, *Brazil* .... **141** 23 7 S 45 52W
São Leopoldo, *Brazil* . **141** 29 50 S 51 10W
São Lourenço, *Brazil* . **139** 22 7 S 45 3W
São Lourenço →, *Brazil* .... **137** 17 53 S 57 27W
São Lourenço, Pantanal do, *Brazil* .... **137** 17 30 S 56 20W
São Luís, *Brazil* ...... **138** 2 39 S 44 15W
São Luís do Curu, *Brazil* .... **138** 3 40 S 39 14W
São Luís Gonzaga, *Brazil* .... **141** 28 25 S 55 0W
São Marcos →, *Brazil* **139** 18 15 S 47 37W
São Marcos, B. de, *Brazil* .... **138** 2 0 S 44 0W
São Martinho, *Portugal* **22** 40 18N 8 8W
São Mateus, *Brazil* ... **139** 18 44 S 39 50W
São Mateus →, *Brazil* **139** 18 35 S 39 44W
São Miguel do Araguaia, *Brazil* ... **139** 13 19 S 50 13W
São Miguel dos Campos, *Brazil* .... **138** 9 47 S 36 5W
São Nicolau →, *Brazil* **138** 5 45 S 42 2W
São Paulo, *Brazil* ..... **141** 23 32 S 46 37W
São Paulo □, *Brazil* .. **141** 22 0 S 49 0W
Sao Paulo, I., *Atl. Oc.* **4** 0 50N 31 40W
São Paulo de Olivença, *Brazil* .... **134** 3 27 S 68 48W
São Pedro do Sul, *Portugal* **22** 40 46N 8 4W
São Rafael, *Brazil* .... **138** 5 47 S 36 55W
São Raimundo das Mangabeiras, *Brazil* **138** 7 1 S 45 29W
São Raimundo Nonato, *Brazil* .... **138** 9 1 S 42 42W
São Romão, *Brazil* ... **139** 16 22 S 45 4W
São Roque, C. de, *Brazil* .... **138** 5 30 S 35 16W
São Sebastião, I. de, *Brazil* .... **141** 23 50 S 45 18W
São Sebastião do Paraíso, *Brazil* ..... **141** 20 54 S 46 59W
São Simão, *Brazil* .... **139** 18 56 S 50 30W
São Teotónio, *Portugal* **23** 37 30N 8 42W
São Tomé, *Atl. Oc.* ... **87** 0 10N 6 39 E
São Tomé, *Brazil* .... **138** 5 58 S 36 4W
São Tomé, C. de, *Brazil* .... **139** 22 0 S 40 59W
São Tomé & Principe ■, *Africa* .. **95** 0 12N 6 39 E
São Vicente, *Brazil* ... **141** 23 57 S 46 23W
São Vicente, C. de, *Portugal* **23** 37 0N 9 0W
Saona, I., *Dom. Rep.* . **129** 18 10N 68 40W
Saône →, *France* .... **21** 45 44N 4 50 E
Saône-et-Loire □, *France* .... **19** 46 30N 4 50 E
Saonek, *Indonesia* .... **57** 0 22 S 130 55 E
Saoura, O. →, *Algeria* **85** 29 0N 0 55W
Sapão →, *Brazil* ..... **138** 11 1 S 45 32W
Saparua, *Indonesia* ... **57** 3 33 S 128 40 E
Sapé, *Brazil* .... **138** 7 6 S 35 13W
Sapele, *Nigeria* .... **91** 5 50N 5 40 E
Sapelo I., *U.S.A.* **115** 31 28N 81 15W
Sapiéntza, *Greece* .... **35** 36 45N 21 43 E
Sapone, *Burkina Faso* **91** 12 3N 1 35W
Saposoa, *Peru* .... **136** 6 55 S 76 45W
Sapozhok, *U.S.S.R.* .. **37** 53 59N 40 41 E
Sappemeer, *Neths.* .... **16** 53 10N 6 48 E
Sappho, *U.S.A.* **124** 48 4N 124 16W
Sapporo, *Japan* ...... **63** 43 0N 141 21 E
Sapri, *Italy* .... **29** 40 5N 15 37 E
Sapudi, *Indonesia* .... **57** 7 6 S 114 20 E
Sapulpa, *U.S.A.* **121** 36 0N 96 0W
Saqqez, *Iran* .... **46** 36 15N 46 20 E
Sar-e Pol, *Afghan.* .... **47** 36 10N 66 0 E
Sar Planina, *Yugoslavia* **34** 42 10N 21 0 E
Sara, *Burkina Faso* ... **90** 11 40N 3 53W
Sara Buri, *Thailand* ... **54** 14 30N 100 55 E
Sarāb, *Iran* .... **46** 38 0N 47 30 E
Saragossa = Zaragoza, *Spain* **24** 41 39N 0 53W
Saraguro, *Ecuador* ... **134** 3 35 S 79 16W
Saraipali, *India* .... **50** 21 20N 82 59 E
Sarajevo, *Yugoslavia* .. **33** 43 52N 18 26 E
Saramacca □, *Surinam* **135** 5 0N 56 0W
Saramacca →, *Surinam* **135** 5 50N 55 55W
Saramati, *Burma* ..... **52** 25 44N 95 2 E
Saran, G., *Indonesia* .. **56** 0 30 S 111 25 E
Saranac, *U.S.A.* **119** 42 56N 85 13W
Saranac Lake, *U.S.A.* . **117** 44 20N 74 10W

Scordia

Saranda, Tanzania 92 5 45 S 34 59 E
Sarandí del Yi, Uruguay 141 33 18 S 55 38W
Sarandí Grande, Uruguay 140 33 44 S 56 20W
Sarangani B., Phil. 57 6 0N 125 13 E
Sarangani Is., Phil. 57 5 25N 125 25 E
Sarangarh, India 50 21 30N 83 5 E
Saransk, U.S.S.R. 37 54 10N 45 10 E
Sarapul, U.S.S.R. 40 56 28N 53 48 E
Sarar Plain, Somali Rep. 98 9 25N 46 17 E
Sarasota, U.S.A. 115 27 20N 82 30W
Saratoga, Calif., U.S.A. 124 37 16N 122 2W
Saratoga, Wyo., U.S.A. 122 41 30N 106 48W
Saratoga Springs, U.S.A. 117 43 5N 73 47W
Saratov, U.S.S.R. 37 51 30N 46 2 E
Saravane, Laos 54 15 43N 106 25 E
Sarawak □, Malaysia 56 2 0N 113 0 E
Saraya, Senegal 90 12 50N 11 45W
Sarbāz, Iran 47 26 38N 61 19 E
Sarbīsheh, Iran 47 32 30N 59 40 E
Sarca →, Italy 26 45 52N 10 52 E
Sardalas, Libya 86 25 50N 10 34 E
Sardarshahr, India 48 28 30N 74 29 E
Sardegna, Italy 28 39 57N 9 0 E
Sardhana, India 48 29 9N 77 39 E
Sardina, Pta., Canary Is. 25 28 9N 15 44W
Sardinata, Colombia 134 8 5N 72 48W
Sardinia = Sardegna, Italy 28 39 57N 9 0 E
Sardinia, U.S.A. 119 39 0N 83 49W
Saréyamou, Mali 90 16 7N 3 10W
Sargasso Sea, Atl. Oc. 130 27 0N 72 0W
Sargent, U.S.A. 120 41 42N 99 24W
Sargodha, Pakistan 48 32 10N 72 40 E
Sarh, Chad 87 9 5N 18 23 E
Sarhro, Djebel, Morocco 84 31 6N 5 0W
Sārī, Iran 47 36 30N 53 4 E
Sária, Greece 35 35 54N 27 17 E
Saricumbe, Angola 95 12 12 S 19 46 E
Sarida →, Jordan 44 32 4N 34 45 E
Sarikamiş, Turkey 46 40 22N 42 35 E
Sarikei, Malaysia 56 2 8N 111 30 E
Sarina, Australia 72 21 22 S 149 13 E
Sariñena, Spain 24 41 47N 0 10W
Sarīr Tibasti, Libya 86 22 50N 18 30 E
Sarita, U.S.A. 121 27 14N 97 49W
Sariyer, Turkey 35 41 10N 29 3 E
Sark, Chan. Is. 18 49 25N 2 20W
Sarkad, Hungary 33 46 47N 21 23 E
Sarlat-la-Canéda, France 20 44 54N 1 13 E
Sarles, U.S.A. 120 48 58N 99 0W
Sărmaşu, Romania 34 46 45N 24 13 E
Sarmi, Indonesia 57 1 49 S 138 44 E
Sarmiento, Argentina 142 45 35 S 69 5W
Särna, Sweden 10 61 41N 13 8 E
Sarnano, Italy 27 43 2N 13 17 E
Sarnen, Switz. 31 46 53N 8 13 E
Sarnia, Canada 108 42 58N 82 23W
Sarno, Italy 29 40 48N 14 35 E
Sarny, U.S.S.R. 36 51 17N 26 40 E
Särö, Sweden 11 57 31N 11 57 E
Sarolangun, Indonesia 56 2 19 S 102 42 E
Saronikós Kólpos, Greece 35 37 45N 23 45 E
Saronno, Italy 26 45 38N 9 2 E
Sárospatak, Hungary 33 48 18N 21 33 E
Sarova, U.S.S.R. 37 54 55N 43 19 E
Sarpsborg, Norway 10 59 16N 11 12 E
Sarracín, Spain 24 42 15N 3 45W
Sarralbe, France 19 49 0N 7 1 E
Sarre = Saar →, Europe 19 49 41N 6 32 E
Sarre, La, Canada 106 48 45N 79 15W
Sarre-Union, France 19 48 57N 7 4 E
Sarrebourg, France 19 48 43N 7 3 E
Sarreguemines, France 19 49 5N 7 4 E
Sarriá, Spain 22 42 49N 7 29W
Sarrión, Spain 24 40 9N 0 49W
Sarro, Mali 90 13 40N 5 15W
Sarstedt, W. Germany 30 52 13N 9 50 E
Sartène, France 21 41 38N 8 58 E
Sarthe □, France 18 47 58N 0 10 E
Sarthe →, France 18 47 33N 0 31W
Sartilly, France 18 48 45N 1 28W
Sartynya, U.S.S.R. 40 63 22N 63 11 E
Sárvár, Hungary 33 47 15N 16 56 E
Sarvestān, Iran 47 29 20N 53 10 E
Särvfjället, Sweden 10 62 42N 13 30 E
Sárviz →, Hungary 33 46 24N 18 41 E
Sary-Tash, U.S.S.R. 40 39 44N 73 15 E
Sarych, Mys., U.S.S.R. 38 44 25N 33 45 E
Saryshagan, U.S.S.R. 40 46 12N 73 38 E
Sarzana, Italy 26 44 5N 9 59 E
Sarzeau, France 18 47 31N 2 48W
Sas van Gent, Neths. 17 51 14N 3 48 E
Sasa, Israel 44 33 2N 35 23 E
Sasabeneh, Ethiopia 98 7 59N 44 43 E
Sasamungga, Solomon Is. 68 7 0 S 156 50 E
Sasaram, India 49 24 57N 84 5 E
Sasayama, Japan 65 35 4N 135 13 E
Sasebo, Japan 64 33 10N 129 43 E
Saseginaga, L., Canada 106 47 6N 78 35W
Saser, India 49 34 50N 77 50 E
Saskatchewan □, Canada 111 54 40N 106 0W
Saskatchewan →, Canada 111 53 37N 100 40W
Saskatoon, Canada 111 52 10N 106 38W
Saskylakh, U.S.S.R. 41 71 55N 114 1 E
Sasnovka, U.S.S.R. 37 56 20N 51 4 E
Sasolburg, S. Africa 97 26 46 S 27 49 E
Sasovo, U.S.S.R. 37 54 25N 41 55 E
Sassandra, Ivory C. 90 5 0N 6 8W
Sassandra →, Ivory C. 90 4 58N 6 5W
Sássari, Italy 28 40 44N 8 33 E
Sassenheim, Neths. 16 52 14N 4 31 E
Sassnitz, E. Germany 30 54 29N 13 39 E
Sasso Marconi, Italy 27 44 22N 11 12 E
Sassocorvaro, Italy 27 43 47N 12 30 E
Sassoferrato, Italy 27 43 26N 12 51 E
Sassuolo, Italy 26 44 31N 10 47 E
Sástago, Spain 24 41 19N 0 21W
Sastown, Liberia 90 4 45N 8 27W
Sasumua Dam, Kenya 92 0 45 S 36 40 E
Sata-Misaki, Japan 64 30 59N 130 40 E
Satadougou, Mali 90 12 25N 11 25W
Satanta, U.S.A. 121 37 30N 101 0W
Satara, India 50 17 44N 73 58 E
Sataua, W. Samoa 68 13 28 S 172 40W
Satilla →, U.S.A. 115 30 59N 81 28W
Satipo, Peru 136 11 15 S 74 25W
Satkania, Bangla. 52 22 4N 92 3 E
Satkhira, Bangla. 52 22 43N 89 8 E
Satmala Hills, India 50 20 15N 74 40 E
Satna, India 49 24 35N 80 50 E
Šator, Yugoslavia 27 44 11N 16 37 E
Sátoraljaújhely, Hungary 33 48 25N 21 41 E
Satpura Ra., India 48 21 25N 76 10 E
Satrup, W. Germany 30 54 39N 9 38 E
Satsuma-Hantō, Japan 64 31 25N 130 25 E
Sattahip, Thailand 54 12 41N 100 54 E
Sattenapalle, India 51 16 25N 80 6 E
Satu Mare, Romania 34 47 46N 22 55 E
Satui, Indonesia 56 3 50 S 115 27 E
Satun, Thailand 55 6 43N 100 2 E
Satupe'itea, W. Samoa 68 13 45 S 172 18W
Saturnina →, Brazil 137 12 15 S 58 10W
Sauce, Argentina 140 30 5 S 58 46W
Sauceda, Mexico 126 25 55N 101 18W
Saucillo, Mexico 126 28 1N 105 17W
Sauda, Norway 9 59 40N 6 20 E
Saúde, Brazil 138 10 56 S 40 24W
Sauðarkrókur, Iceland 8 65 45N 19 40W
Saudi Arabia ■, Asia 46 26 0N 44 0 E
Sauer →, W. Germany 17 49 44N 6 31 E
Saugatuck, U.S.A. 119 42 40N 86 12W
Saugeen →, Canada 108 44 30N 81 22W
Saugerties, U.S.A. 117 42 4N 73 58W
Saugues, France 20 44 58N 3 32 E
Sauherad, Norway 10 59 25N 9 15 E
Saujon, France 20 45 41N 0 55W
Sauk Centre, U.S.A. 120 45 42N 94 56W
Sauk City, U.S.A. 118 43 17N 89 43W
Sauk Rapids, U.S.A. 120 45 35N 94 10W
Saül, Fr. Guiana 135 3 37N 53 12W
Saulgau, W. Germany 31 48 4N 9 32 E
Saulieu, France 19 47 17N 4 14 E
Sault, France 21 44 6N 5 24 E
Sault-au-Moulton, Canada 107 48 33N 69 15W
Sault aux Cochons →, Canada 107 48 44N 69 4W
Sault Ste. Marie, Canada 108 46 30N 84 20W
Sault Ste. Marie, U.S.A. 104 46 27N 84 22W
Saumlaki, Indonesia 57 7 55 S 131 20 E
Saumur, France 18 47 15N 0 5W
Saunders C., N.Z. 81 45 53 S 170 45 E
Saunders I., Antarctica 143 57 48 S 26 28W
Saunders Point, Mt., Australia 79 27 52 S 125 38 E
Saunemin, U.S.A. 119 40 54N 88 24W
Saurbær, Borgarfjarðarsýsla, Iceland 8 64 24N 21 35W
Saurbær, Eyjafjarðarsýsla, Iceland 8 65 27N 18 13W
Sauri, Nigeria 91 11 42N 6 44 E
Saurimo, Angola 95 9 40 S 20 12 E
Sausalito, U.S.A. 124 37 51N 122 29W
Sautatá, Colombia 134 7 50N 77 4W
Sauvage, L., Canada 106 50 6N 74 30W
Sauveterre-de-Béarn, France 20 43 24N 0 57W
Sauzé-Vaussais, France 20 46 8N 0 8 E
Savá, Honduras 128 15 32N 86 15W
Sava →, Yugoslavia 33 44 50N 20 26 E
Savage, U.S.A. 120 47 27N 104 20W
Savage I. = Niue I., Cook Is. 67 19 2 S 169 54W
Savai'i, W. Samoa 68 13 28 S 172 24W
Savalou, Benin 91 7 57N 1 58 E
Savane, Mozam. 93 19 37 S 35 8 E
Savanna, U.S.A. 118 42 5N 90 10W
Savanna la Mar, Jamaica 128 18 10N 78 10W
Savannah, Ga., U.S.A. 115 32 4N 81 4W
Savannah, Mo., U.S.A. 118 39 55N 94 46W
Savannah, Tenn., U.S.A. 115 35 12N 88 18W
Savannah →, U.S.A. 115 32 2N 80 53W
Savannakhet, Laos 54 16 30N 104 49 E
Savant L., Canada 104 50 16N 90 44W
Savant Lake, Canada 104 50 14N 90 40W
Savantvadi, India 51 15 55N 73 54 E
Savanur, India 51 14 59N 75 21 E
Savda, India 50 21 9N 75 56 E
Savé, Benin 91 8 2N 2 29 E
Save →, France 20 43 47N 1 17 E
Save →, Mozam. 97 21 16 S 34 0 E
Sāveh, Iran 46 35 2N 50 20 E
Savelugu, Ghana 91 9 38N 0 54W
Savenay, France 18 47 20N 1 55W
Saverdun, France 20 43 14N 1 34 E
Saverne, France 19 48 43N 7 20 E
Savigliano, Italy 26 44 39N 7 40 E
Savigny-sur-Braye, France 18 47 53N 0 49 E
Saviñao, Spain 22 42 35N 7 38W
Savio →, Italy 27 44 19N 12 20 E
Savo, Solomon Is. 68 9 8 S 159 48 E
Savoie □, France 21 45 26N 6 25 E
Savona, Italy 26 44 19N 8 29 E
Sävsjö, Sweden 11 57 20N 14 40 E
Sävsjøström, Sweden 11 57 1N 15 25 E
Savusavu, Fiji 68 16 34 S 179 15 E
Savusavu B., Fiji 68 16 45 S 179 15 E
Sawahlunto, Indonesia 56 0 40 S 100 52 E
Sawai, Indonesia 57 3 0 S 129 5 E
Sawai Madhopur, India 48 26 0N 76 25 E
Sawang Daen Din, Thailand 54 17 28N 103 28 E
Sawankhalok, Thailand 54 17 19N 99 50 E
Sawara, Japan 65 35 55N 140 30 E
Sawatch Mts., U.S.A. 123 38 30N 106 30W
Sawdā, Jabal as, Libya 86 28 51N 15 12 E
Sawel, Mt., U.K. 15 54 48N 7 5W
Sawfajjin, W. →, Libya 86 31 46N 14 30 E
Sawi, Thailand 55 10 14N 99 5 E
Sawmills, Zambia 93 19 30 S 28 2 E
Sawtell, Australia 77 30 19 S 153 6 E
Sawu, Indonesia 57 10 35 S 121 50 E
Sawu Sea, Indonesia 57 9 30 S 121 50 E
Sawyerville, Canada 107 45 20N 71 34W
Saxby →, Australia 72 18 25 S 140 53 E
Saxony, Lower = Niedersachsen □, W. Germany 30 52 45N 9 0 E
Saxton, U.S.A. 116 40 12N 78 18W
Say, Niger 91 13 8N 2 22 E
Saya, Nigeria 91 9 30N 3 18 E
Sayabec, Canada 105 48 35N 67 41W
Sayaboury, Laos 54 19 15N 101 45 E
Sayán, Peru 136 11 8 S 77 12W
Sayan, Vostochnyy, U.S.S.R. 41 54 0N 96 0 E
Sayan, Zapadnyy, U.S.S.R. 41 52 30N 94 0 E
Sayasan, U.S.S.R. 39 42 56N 46 15 E
Saydā, Lebanon 46 33 35N 35 25 E
Sayghān, Afghan. 47 35 10N 67 55 E
Sayhan-Ovoo, Mongolia 60 45 27N 103 54 E
Sayhandulaan, Mongolia 60 44 40N 109 1 E
Sayḥut, S. Yemen 45 15 12N 51 10 E
Saylorville Res., U.S.A. 118 41 43N 93 41W
Saynshand, Mongolia 60 44 55N 110 11 E
Sayō, Japan 64 34 59N 134 22 E
Sayre, Okla., U.S.A. 121 35 20N 99 40W
Sayre, Pa., U.S.A. 117 42 0N 76 30W
Sayula, Mexico 126 19 50N 103 40W
Sazin, Pakistan 49 35 35N 73 30 E
Sazlika →, Bulgaria 35 41 59N 25 50 E
Sbeïtla, Tunisia 86 35 12N 9 7 E
Scaër, France 18 48 2N 3 42W
Scafell Pikes, U.K. 12 54 26N 3 14W
Scalea, Italy 29 39 49N 15 47 E
Scalpay, U.K. 14 57 51N 6 40W
Scandia, Canada 110 50 20N 112 0W
Scandiano, Italy 26 44 36N 10 40 E
Scandinavia, Europe 8 64 0N 12 0 E
Scansano, Italy 27 42 40N 11 20 E
Scapa Flow, U.K. 14 58 52N 3 6W
Scappoose, U.S.A. 124 45 45N 122 53W
Scarborough, Trin. & Tob. 129 11 11N 60 42W
Scarborough, U.K. 12 54 17N 0 24W
Scargill, N.Z. 81 42 56 S 172 58 E
Scarsdale, Australia 74 37 41 S 143 39 E
Scebeli, Wabi →, Somali Rep. 89 2 0N 44 0 E
Šćedro, Yugoslavia 27 43 6N 16 43 E
Scenic, U.S.A. 120 43 49N 102 32W
Schaal See, W. Germany 30 53 40N 10 57 E
Schaesberg, Neths. 17 50 54N 6 0 E
Schaffen, Belgium 17 51 0N 5 5 E
Schaffhausen □, Switz. 31 47 42N 8 36 E
Schagen, Neths. 16 52 49N 4 48 E
Schaijk, Neths. 16 51 44N 5 38 E
Schalkhaar, Neths. 16 52 17N 6 12 E
Schalkwijk, Neths. 16 52 0N 5 11 E
Schanck, C., Australia 74 38 30 S 144 55 E
Schärding, Austria 32 48 27N 13 27 E
Scharhörn, W. Germany 30 53 58N 8 24 E
Scharnitz, Austria 31 47 23N 11 15 E
Scheessel, W. Germany 30 53 10N 9 33 E
Schefferville, Canada 105 54 48N 66 50W
Schelde →, Belgium 17 51 15N 4 16 E
Schell City, U.S.A. 118 38 1N 94 7W
Schell Creek Ra., U.S.A. 122 39 15N 114 30W
Schenectady, U.S.A. 117 42 50N 73 58W
Scherfede, W. Germany 30 51 32N 9 2 E
Scherpenheuvel, Belgium 17 50 58N 4 58 E
Scherpenisse, Neths. 17 51 33N 4 6 E
Scherpenzeel, Neths. 16 52 5N 5 30 E
Schesslitz, W. Germany 31 49 59N 11 2 E
Scheveningen, Neths. 16 52 6N 4 16 E
Schiedam, Neths. 16 51 55N 4 25 E
Schiermonnikoog, Neths. 16 53 30N 6 15 E
Schifferstadt, W. Germany 31 49 22N 8 23 E
Schifflange, Lux. 17 49 30N 6 1 E
Schijndel, Neths. 17 51 37N 5 27 E
Schiltigheim, France 19 48 35N 7 45 E
Schio, Italy 27 45 42N 11 21 E
Schipbeek, Neths. 16 52 14N 6 10 E
Schipluiden, Neths. 16 51 59N 4 19 E
Schirmeck, France 19 48 29N 7 12 E
Schlei →, W. Germany 30 54 45N 9 52 E
Schleiden, W. Germany 30 50 32N 6 26 E
Schleiz, E. Germany 30 50 35N 11 49 E
Schleswig, W. Germany 30 54 32N 9 34 E
Schleswig-Holstein □, W. Germany 30 54 10N 9 40 E
Schlüchtern, W. Germany 31 50 20N 9 32 E
Schmalkalden, E. Germany 30 50 43N 10 28 E
Schmölln, E. Germany 30 50 54N 12 22 E
Schmölln, E. Germany 30 53 15N 14 6 E
Schneeberg, Austria 33 47 47N 15 48 E
Schneeberg, E. Germany 30 50 35N 12 39 E
Schneider, U.S.A. 119 41 13N 87 28W
Schoenberg, Belgium 17 50 17N 6 16 E
Schofield, U.S.A. 120 44 54N 89 39W
Scholls, U.S.A. 124 45 24N 122 56W
Schönberg, E. Germany 30 53 50N 10 55 E
Schönberg, W. Germany 30 54 23N 10 20 E
Schönebeck, E. Germany 30 52 2N 11 42 E
Schongau, W. Germany 31 47 49N 10 54 E
Schöningen, W. Germany 30 52 8N 10 57 E
Schoolcraft, U.S.A. 119 42 7N 85 38W
Schoondijke, Neths. 17 51 21N 3 33 E
Schoonebeek, Neths. 16 52 39N 6 52 E
Schoonhoven, Neths. 16 51 57N 4 51 E
Schoorl, Neths. 16 52 42N 4 42 E
Schortens, W. Germany 30 53 37N 7 51 E
Schoten, Belgium 17 51 16N 4 30 E
Schouten I., Australia 72 42 20 S 148 20 E
Schouwen, Neths. 17 51 43N 3 45 E
Schramberg, W. Germany 31 48 12N 8 24 E
Schrankogl, Austria 31 47 3N 11 7 E
Schreiber, Canada 104 48 45N 87 20W
Schrobenhausen, W. Germany 31 48 33N 11 16 E
Schruns, Austria 31 47 5N 9 56 E
Schuler, Canada 111 50 20N 110 6W
Schumacher, Canada 104 48 30N 81 16W
Schurz, U.S.A. 122 38 57N 118 48W
Schuyler, U.S.A. 120 41 30N 97 3W
Schuylkill Haven, U.S.A. 117 40 37N 76 11W
Schwabach, W. Germany 31 49 19N 11 3 E
Schwäbisch Gmünd, W. Germany 31 48 49N 9 48 E
Schwäbisch Hall, W. Germany 31 49 7N 9 45 E
Schwäbische Alb, W. Germany 31 48 30N 9 30 E
Schwabmünchen, W. Germany 31 48 11N 10 45 E
Schwandorf, W. Germany 31 49 20N 12 7 E
Schwaner, Pegunungan, Indonesia 56 1 0 S 112 30 E
Schwarmstedt, W. Germany 30 52 41N 9 37 E
Schwärze, E. Germany 30 52 50N 13 49 E
Schwarzenberg, E. Germany 30 50 31N 12 49 E
Schwarzwald, W. Germany 31 48 0N 8 0 E
Schwaz, Austria 31 47 20N 11 44 E
Schwedt, E. Germany 30 53 4N 14 18 E
Schweinfurt, W. Germany 31 50 3N 10 12 E
Schweizer-Reneke, S. Africa 96 27 11 S 25 18 E
Schwerin, E. Germany 30 53 37N 11 22 E
Schwerin □, E. Germany 30 53 35N 11 20 E
Schweriner See, E. Germany 30 53 45N 11 26 E
Schwetzingen, W. Germany 31 49 22N 8 35 E
Schwyz, Switz. 31 47 2N 8 39 E
Schwyz □, Switz. 31 47 2N 8 39 E
Sciacca, Italy 28 37 30N 13 3 E
Sciao, Somali Rep. 98 3 26N 45 21 E
Scicli, Italy 29 36 48N 14 41 E
Scie, La, Canada 105 49 57N 55 36W
Scilla, Italy 29 38 18N 15 44 E
Scilly, Isles of, U.K. 13 49 55N 6 15W
Ścinawa, Poland 32 51 25N 16 26 E
Scioto →, U.S.A. 114 38 44N 83 0W
Scobey, U.S.A. 120 48 47N 105 30W
Scone, Australia 77 32 5 S 150 52 E
Scone, U.K. 14 56 25N 3 26W
Scordia, Italy 29 37 19N 14 50 E

Shibogama L.

Shibogama L., *Canada* 104 53 35N 88 15W
Shibukawa, *Japan* 65 36 29N 139 0 E
Shibushi, *Japan* 64 31 25N 131 8 E
Shibushi-Wan, *Japan* 64 31 24N 131 8 E
Shicheng, *China* 59 26 22N 116 20 E
Shidao, *China* 61 36 50N 122 25 E
Shidian, *China* 58 24 40N 99 5 E
Shido, *Japan* 64 34 19N 134 10 E
Shiel, L., *U.K.* 14 56 48N 5 32W
Shield, C., *Australia* 72 13 20S 136 20 E
Shiga □, *Japan* 65 35 20N 136 0 E
Shigaib, *Sudan* 87 15 5N 23 35 E
Shigaraki, *Japan* 65 34 57N 136 2 E
Shigu, *China* 58 26 51N 99 56 E
Shiguaigou, *China* 60 40 52N 110 15 E
Shihchiachuangi = Shijiazhuang, *China* 60 38 2N 114 28 E
Shiiba, *Japan* 64 32 29N 131 4 E
Shijiazhuang, *China* 60 38 2N 114 28 E
Shijiu Hu, *China* 59 31 25N 118 50 E
Shikarpur, *India* 48 28 17N 78 7 E
Shikarpur, *Pakistan* 48 27 57N 68 39 E
Shikine-Jima, *Japan* 65 34 19N 139 13 E
Shikoku, *Japan* 64 33 30N 133 30 E
Shikoku □, *Japan* 64 33 30N 133 30 E
Shikoku-Sanchi, *Japan* 64 33 30N 133 30 E
Shilabo, *Ethiopia* 45 6 22N 44 32 E
Shiliguri, *India* 52 26 45N 88 25 E
Shilka, *U.S.S.R.* 41 52 0N 115 55 E
Shilka →, *U.S.S.R.* 41 53 20N 121 26 E
Shillelagh, *Ireland* 15 52 46N 6 32W
Shillong, *India* 52 25 35N 91 53 E
Shilo, *Jordan* 44 32 4N 35 18 E
Shilong, *China* 59 23 5N 113 52 E
Shilou, *China* 60 37 0N 110 48 E
Shilovo, *U.S.S.R.* 37 54 25N 40 57 E
Shima-Hantō, *Japan* 65 34 22N 136 45 E
Shimabara, *Japan* 64 32 48N 130 20 E
Shimada, *Japan* 65 34 49N 138 10 E
Shimane □, *Japan* 64 35 0N 132 30 E
Shimane-Hantō, *Japan* 64 35 30N 133 0 E
Shimanovsk, *U.S.S.R.* 41 52 15N 127 30 E
Shimen, *China* 59 29 35N 111 20 E
Shimenjie, *China* 59 29 29N 116 48 E
Shimian, *China* 58 29 17N 102 23 E
Shimizu, *Japan* 65 35 0N 138 30 E
Shimo-Jima, *Japan* 64 32 15N 130 7 E
Shimo-Koshiki-Jima, *Japan* 64 31 40N 129 43 E
Shimoda, *Japan* 65 34 40N 138 57 E
Shimodate, *Japan* 65 36 20N 139 55 E
Shimoga, *India* 51 13 57N 75 32 E
Shimoni, *Kenya* 92 4 38S 39 20 E
Shimonita, *Japan* 65 36 13N 138 47 E
Shimonoseki, *Japan* 64 33 58N 131 0 E
Shimotsuma, *Japan* 65 36 11N 139 58 E
Shimpuru Rapids, *Angola* 95 17 45S 19 55 E
Shimsha →, *India* 51 13 15N 77 10 E
Shimsk, *U.S.S.R.* 36 58 15N 30 50 E
Shin, L., *U.K.* 14 58 7N 4 30W
Shin-Tone →, *Japan* 65 35 44N 140 51 E
Shinan, *China* 58 22 44N 109 53 E
Shinano →, *Japan* 63 36 50N 138 30 E
Shīndand, *Afghan.* 47 33 12N 62 8 E
Shingbwiyang, *Burma* 52 26 41N 96 13 E
Shingleton, *U.S.A.* 104 46 25N 86 33W
Shingū, *Japan* 65 33 40N 135 55 E
Shinji, *Japan* 64 35 24N 132 54 E
Shinji Ko, *Japan* 64 35 26N 132 57 E
Shinjō, *Japan* 63 38 46N 140 18 E
Shinkafe, *Nigeria* 91 13 8N 6 29 E
Shinminato, *Japan* 65 36 47N 137 4 E
Shinonoi, *Japan* 65 36 35N 138 9 E
Shinshiro, *Japan* 65 34 54N 137 30 E
Shinyanga, *Tanzania* 92 3 45S 33 27 E
Shinyanga □, *Tanzania* 92 3 50S 34 0 E
Shio-no-Misaki, *Japan* 65 33 25N 135 45 E
Shiogama, *Japan* 63 38 19N 141 1 E
Shiojiri, *Japan* 65 36 6N 137 58 E
Ship I., *U.S.A.* 121 30 16N 88 55W
Shipehenski Prokhod, *Bulgaria* 34 42 45N 25 15 E
Shiping, *China* 58 23 45N 102 23 E
Shippegan, *Canada* 105 47 45N 64 45W
Shippensburg, *U.S.A.* 116 40 4N 77 32W
Shiprock, *U.S.A.* 123 36 51N 108 45W
Shiqian, *China* 58 27 32N 108 13 E
Shiqma, N. →, *Israel* 44 31 37N 34 30 E
Shiquan, *China* 60 33 5N 108 15 E
Shīr Kūh, *Iran* 47 31 39N 54 3 E
Shiragami-Misaki, *Japan* 63 41 24N 140 12 E
Shirahama, *Japan* 65 33 41N 135 20 E
Shirakawa, *Japan* 65 36 17N 136 56 E
Shirane-San, *Gumma, Japan* 65 36 48N 139 22 E
Shirane-San, *Yamanashi, Japan* 65 35 42N 138 9 E
Shiraoi, *Japan* 63 42 33N 141 21 E
Shīrāz, *Iran* 47 29 42N 52 30 E
Shirbin, *Egypt* 88 31 11N 31 32 E
Shire →, *Africa* 93 17 42S 35 19 E
Shirinab →, *Pakistan* 48 30 15N 66 28 E
Shiringushi, *U.S.S.R.* 37 53 51N 42 46 E
Shiriya-Zaki, *Japan* 63 41 25N 141 30 E
Shirley, *U.S.A.* 119 39 53N 85 35W
Shirol, *India* 50 16 47N 74 41 E
Shirpur, *India* 50 21 21N 74 57 E
Shīrvān, *Iran* 47 37 30N 57 50 E
Shirwa, L. = Chilwa, L., *Malawi* 93 15 15S 35 40 E
Shishou, *China* 59 29 38N 112 22 E
Shitai, *China* 59 30 12N 117 25 E
Shively, *U.S.A.* 119 38 12N 85 49W
Shivpuri, *India* 48 25 26N 77 42 E
Shivta, *Israel* 44 30 53N 34 40 E
Shixian, *China* 61 43 5N 129 50 E
Shixing, *China* 59 24 46N 114 5 E
Shiyan, *China* 59 32 35N 110 45 E
Shiyata, *Egypt* 88 29 25N 25 7 E
Shizhu, *China* 58 29 58N 108 7 E
Shizong, *China* 58 24 50N 104 0 E
Shizuishan, *China* 60 39 15N 106 50 E
Shizuoka, *Japan* 65 35 0N 138 24 E
Shizuoka □, *Japan* 65 35 15N 138 40 E
Shklov, *U.S.S.R.* 36 54 16N 30 15 E
Shkoder = Shkodra, *Albania* 34 42 6N 19 20 E
Shkodra, *Albania* 34 42 6N 19 20 E
Shkumbini →, *Albania* 35 41 5N 19 50 E
Shmidt, O., *U.S.S.R.* 41 81 0N 91 0 E
Shō-Gawa →, *Japan* 65 36 47N 137 4 E
Shoal Cr. →, *U.S.A.* 118 39 39N 93 35W
Shoal Lake, *Canada* 111 50 30N 100 35W
Shoalhaven →, *Australia* 76 34 54S 150 42 E
Shoals, *U.S.A.* 119 38 40N 86 47W
Shōbara, *Japan* 64 34 51N 133 1 E
Shōdo-Shima, *Japan* 64 34 30N 134 15 E
Shoeburyness, *U.K.* 13 51 31N 0 49 E
Sholapur = Solapur, *India* 50 17 43N 75 56 E
Shologontsy, *U.S.S.R.* 41 66 13N 114 0 E
Shomera, *Israel* 44 33 4N 35 17 E
Shōmrōn, *Jordan* 44 32 15N 35 13 E
Shoranur, *India* 51 10 46N 76 19 E
Shorapur, *India* 51 16 31N 76 48 E
Shortland I., *Solomon Is.* 69 7 0S 155 45 E
Shoshone, *Calif., U.S.A.* 125 35 58N 116 16W
Shoshone, *Idaho, U.S.A.* 122 43 0N 114 27W
Shoshone L., *U.S.A.* 122 44 30N 110 40W
Shoshone Mts., *U.S.A.* 122 39 30N 117 30W
Shoshong, *Botswana* 96 22 56S 26 31 E
Shoshoni, *U.S.A.* 122 43 13N 108 5W
Shostka, *U.S.S.R.* 36 51 57N 33 32 E
Shou Xian, *China* 59 32 37N 116 42 E
Shouchang, *China* 59 29 18N 119 12 E
Shouguang, *China* 61 37 52N 118 45 E
Shouning, *China* 59 27 27N 119 31 E
Shouyang, *China* 60 37 54N 113 8 E
Show Low, *U.S.A.* 123 34 16N 110 0W
Shpola, *U.S.S.R.* 38 49 1N 31 30 E
Shreveport, *U.S.A.* 121 32 30N 93 50W
Shrewsbury, *U.K.* 12 52 42N 2 45W
Shrirampur, *India* 49 22 44N 88 21 E
Shrirangapattana, *India* 51 12 26N 76 43 E
Shropshire □, *U.K.* 13 52 36N 2 45W
Shuangbai, *China* 58 24 42N 101 38 E
Shuangcheng, *China* 61 45 20N 126 15 E
Shuangfeng, *China* 59 27 29N 112 11 E
Shuanggou, *China* 61 34 2N 117 30 E
Shuangjiang, *China* 58 23 26N 99 58 E
Shuangliao, *China* 61 43 29N 123 30 E
Shuangshanzi, *China* 61 40 20N 119 8 E
Shuangyang, *China* 61 43 28N 125 40 E
Shuangyashan, *China* 62 46 28N 131 5 E
Shu'ayb, Wadi →, *Jordan* 44 31 54N 35 38 E
Shucheng, *China* 59 31 28N 116 57 E
Shuguri Falls, *Tanzania* 93 8 33S 37 22 E
Shuicheng, *China* 58 26 38N 104 48 E
Shuiji, *China* 59 27 13N 118 20 E
Shuiye, *China* 60 36 7N 114 8 E
Shujalpur, *India* 48 23 18N 76 46 E
Shukpa Kunzang, *India* 49 34 22N 78 22 E
Shulan, *China* 61 44 28N 127 0 E
Shule, *China* 62 39 25N 76 3 E
Shullsburg, *U.S.A.* 118 42 35N 90 15W
Shumagin Is., *U.S.A.* 102 55 0N 159 0W
Shumerlya, *U.S.S.R.* 37 55 30N 46 25 E
Shumikha, *U.S.S.R.* 40 55 10N 63 15 E
Shunchang, *China* 59 26 54N 117 48 E
Shunde, *China* 59 22 42N 113 14 E
Shungay, *U.S.S.R.* 39 48 30N 46 45 E
Shungnak, *U.S.A.* 102 66 55N 157 10W
Shuo Xian, *China* 60 39 20N 112 33 E
Shūr →, *Iran* 47 28 30N 55 0 E
Shurkhua, *Burma* 52 22 15N 93 38 E
Shurma, *U.S.S.R.* 37 56 58N 50 21 E
Shurugwi, *Zambia* 93 19 40S 30 0 E
Shūsf, *Iran* 47 31 50N 60 5 E
Shūshtar, *Iran* 46 32 0N 48 50 E
Shuswap L., *Canada* 110 50 55N 119 3W
Shuwaykah, *Jordan* 44 32 20N 35 1 E
Shuya, *U.S.S.R.* 37 56 50N 41 28 E
Shuyang, *China* 61 34 10N 118 42 E
Shuzenji, *Japan* 65 34 58N 138 56 E
Shwebo, *Burma* 52 22 30N 95 45 E
Shwegu, *Burma* 52 24 15N 96 26 E
Shwegun, *Burma* 52 17 9N 97 39 E
Shwenyaung, *Burma* 52 20 46N 96 57 E
Shyok, *India* 49 34 15N 78 12 E
Shyok →, *Pakistan* 49 35 13N 75 53 E
Si Chon, *Thailand* 55 9 0N 99 54 E
Si Kiang = Xi Jiang →, *China* 59 22 5N 113 20 E
Si Prachan, *Thailand* 54 14 37N 100 9 E
Si Racha, *Thailand* 54 13 10N 100 48 E
Si Xian, *China* 61 33 30N 117 50 E
Siah, *Si. Arabia* 46 22 0N 47 0 E
Siahan Range, *Pakistan* 47 27 30N 64 40 E
Siaksrindrapura, *Indonesia* 56 0 51N 102 0 E
Sialkot, *Pakistan* 48 32 32N 74 30 E
Sialsuk, *India* 52 23 24N 92 45 E
Siam = Thailand ■, *Asia* 54 16 0N 102 0 E
Sian = Xi'an, *China* 60 34 15N 109 0 E
Siantan, P., *Indonesia* 55 3 10N 106 15 E
Siàpo →, *Venezuela* 134 2 7N 66 28W
Sīāreh, *Iran* 47 28 5N 60 14 E
Siargao, *Phil.* 57 9 52N 126 3 E
Siari, *Pakistan* 49 34 55N 76 40 E
Siasi, *Phil.* 57 5 34N 120 50 E
Siassi, *Papua N. G.* 69 5 40S 147 51 E
Siátista, *Greece* 35 40 15N 21 33 E
Siau, *Indonesia* 57 2 50N 125 25 E
Siauliai, *U.S.S.R.* 36 55 56N 23 15 E
Siaya □, *Kenya* 92 0 0 34 20 E
Siazan, *U.S.S.R.* 39 41 3N 49 10 E
Sibâi, Gebel el, *Egypt* 88 25 45N 34 10 E
Sibang, *Gabon* 94 0 25N 9 31 E
Sibari, *Italy* 29 39 47N 16 27 E
Sibasa, *S. Africa* 97 22 53S 30 33 E
Sibayi, L., *S. Africa* 97 27 20S 32 45 E
Šibenik, *Yugoslavia* 27 43 48N 15 54 E
Siberia, *U.S.S.R.* 144 60 0N 100 0 E
Siberut, *Indonesia* 56 1 30S 99 0 E
Sibi, *Pakistan* 48 29 30N 67 54 E
Sibil, *Indonesia* 57 4 59S 140 35 E
Sibiti, *Congo* 94 3 38S 13 19 E
Sibiu, *Romania* 34 45 45N 24 9 E
Sibley, *Ill., U.S.A.* 119 40 35N 88 23W
Sibley, *Iowa, U.S.A.* 120 43 21N 95 43W
Sibley, *La., U.S.A.* 121 32 34N 93 16W
Sibolga, *Indonesia* 56 1 42N 98 45 E
Sibret, *Belgium* 17 49 58N 5 38 E
Sibsagar, *India* 52 27 0N 94 36 E
Sibu, *Malaysia* 56 2 18N 111 49 E
Sibuco, *Phil.* 57 7 20N 122 10 E
Sibuguey B., *Phil.* 57 7 50N 122 45 E
Sibutu, *Phil.* 57 4 45N 119 30 E
Sibutu Passage, *E. Indies* 57 4 50N 120 0 E
Sibuyan, *Phil.* 57 12 25N 122 40 E
Sibuyan Sea, *Phil.* 57 12 30N 122 20 E
Sicamous, *Canada* 110 50 49N 119 0W
Sichuan □, *China* 58 31 0N 104 0 E
Sicilia, *Italy* 29 37 30N 14 30 E
Sicilia □, *Italy* 29 37 30N 14 30 E
Sicilia, Canale di, *Italy* 28 37 25N 12 30 E
Sicilian Channel = Sicilia, Canale di, *Italy* 28 37 25N 12 30 E
Sicily = Sicilia, *Italy* 29 37 30N 14 30 E
Sicuani, *Peru* 136 14 21S 71 10W
Siculiana, *Italy* 28 37 20N 13 23 E
Sidamo □, *Ethiopia* 89 5 0N 37 50 E
Sidaouet, *Niger* 91 18 34N 8 3 E
Siddeburen, *Neths.* 16 53 15N 6 52 E
Siddhapur, *India* 48 23 56N 72 25 E
Siddipet, *India* 50 18 0N 78 51 E
Sidell, *U.S.A.* 119 39 55N 87 49W
Sidéradougou, *Burkina Faso* 90 10 42N 4 12W
Siderno Marina, *Italy* 29 38 16N 16 17 E
Sidheros, Ákra, *Greece* 35 35 19N 26 19 E
Sidhirókastron, *Greece* 35 41 13N 23 24 E
Sîdi Abd el Rahmân, *Egypt* 88 30 55N 29 44 E
Sîdi Barrâni, *Egypt* 88 31 38N 25 58 E
Sidi-bel-Abbès, *Algeria* 85 35 13N 0 39W
Sidi Bennour, *Morocco* 84 32 40N 8 25W
Sidi Haneish, *Egypt* 88 31 10N 27 35 E
Sidi Kacem, *Morocco* 84 34 11N 5 49W
Sidi Omar, *Egypt* 88 31 24N 24 57 E
Sidi Slimane, *Morocco* 84 34 16N 5 56W
Sidi Smaïl, *Morocco* 84 32 50N 8 31W
Sidi 'Uzayz, *Libya* 86 31 41N 24 55 E
Sidlaw Hills, *U.K.* 14 56 32N 3 10W
Sidley, Mt., *Antarctica* 143 77 2S 126 2W
Sidmouth, *U.K.* 13 50 40N 3 13W
Sidmouth, C., *Australia* 72 13 25S 143 36 E
Sidney, *Canada* 110 48 39N 123 24W
Sidney, *Mont., U.S.A.* 120 47 42N 104 7W
Sidney, *N.Y., U.S.A.* 117 42 18N 75 20W
Sidney, *Nebr., U.S.A.* 120 41 12N 103 0W
Sidney, *Ohio, U.S.A.* 119 40 18N 84 6W
Sidoarjo, *Indonesia* 57 7 27S 112 43 E
Sidoktaya, *Burma* 52 20 27N 94 15 E
Sidon = Saydā, *Lebanon* 46 33 35N 35 25 E
Sidra, G. of = Surt, Khalīj, *Libya* 86 31 40N 18 30 E
Siedlce, *Poland* 32 52 10N 22 20 E
Sieg →, *W. Germany* 30 50 46N 7 7 E
Siegburg, *W. Germany* 30 50 48N 7 12 E
Siegen, *W. Germany* 30 50 52N 8 2 E
Siem Pang, *Cambodia* 54 14 7N 106 23 E
Siem Reap, *Cambodia* 54 13 20N 103 52 E
Siena, *Italy* 27 43 20N 11 20 E
Sieradź, *Poland* 32 51 37N 18 41 E
Sierck-les-Bains, *France* 19 49 26N 6 20 E
Sierpc, *Poland* 32 52 55N 19 43 E
Sierpe, Bocas de la, *Venezuela* 134 10 0N 61 30W
Sierra Blanca, *U.S.A.* 123 31 11N 105 17W
Sierra Blanca Pk., *U.S.A.* 123 33 20N 105 54W
Sierra City, *U.S.A.* 124 39 34N 120 42W
Sierra Colorada, *Argentina* 142 40 35S 67 50W
Sierra de Yeguas, *Spain* 23 37 7N 4 52W
Sierra Gorda, *Chile* 140 22 50S 69 15W
Sierra Grande, *Argentina* 142 41 36S 65 22W
Sierra Leone ■, *W. Afr.* 90 9 0N 12 0W
Sierra Mojada, *Mexico* 126 27 19N 103 42W
Sierraville, *U.S.A.* 124 39 36N 120 22W
Sierre, *Switz.* 31 46 17N 7 31 E
Sif Fatima, *Algeria* 85 31 6N 8 41 E
Sífnos, *Greece* 35 37 0N 24 45 E
Sifton, *Canada* 111 51 21N 100 8W
Sifton Pass, *Canada* 110 57 52N 126 15W
Sig, *Algeria* 85 35 32N 0 12W
Sigdal, *Norway* 10 60 4N 9 38 E
Sigean, *France* 20 43 2N 2 58 E
Sighetu-Marmatiei, *Romania* 34 47 57N 23 52 E
Sighişoara, *Romania* 34 46 12N 24 50 E
Sigli, *Indonesia* 56 5 25N 96 0 E
Siglufjörður, *Iceland* 8 66 12N 18 55W
Sigmaringen, *W. Germany* 31 48 5N 9 13 E
Signakhi, *U.S.S.R.* 39 41 40N 45 57 E
Signal, *U.S.A.* 125 34 30N 113 38W
Signal Pk., *U.S.A.* 125 33 25N 114 4W
Signy I., *Antarctica* 143 60 45S 45 56W
Signy-l'Abbaye, *France* 19 49 40N 4 25 E
Sigourney, *U.S.A.* 118 41 20N 92 12W
Sigsig, *Ecuador* 134 3 0S 78 50W
Sigtuna, *Sweden* 10 59 36N 17 44 E
Sigüenza, *Spain* 24 41 3N 2 40W
Siguiri, *Guinea* 90 11 31N 9 10W
Sigulda, *U.S.S.R.* 36 57 10N 24 55 E
Sigurd, *U.S.A.* 123 38 49N 112 0W
Sihanoukville = Kompong Som, *Cambodia* 55 10 38N 103 30 E
Sihaus, *Peru* 136 8 40S 77 40W
Sihui, *China* 59 23 20N 112 40 E
Si'ir, *Jordan* 44 31 35N 35 9 E
Siirt, *Turkey* 46 37 57N 41 55 E
Sijarira Ra., *Zambia* 93 17 36S 27 45 E
Sikao, *Thailand* 55 7 34N 99 21 E
Sikar, *India* 48 27 33N 75 10 E
Sikasso, *Mali* 90 11 18N 5 35W
Sikeston, *U.S.A.* 121 36 52N 89 35W
Sikhote Alin, Khrebet, *U.S.S.R.* 41 46 0N 136 0 E
Sikiá., *Greece* 35 40 2N 23 56 E
Síkinos, *Greece* 35 36 40N 25 8 E
Sikkani Chief →, *Canada* 110 57 47N 122 15W
Sikkim □, *India* 52 27 50N 88 30 E
Sil →, *Spain* 22 42 27N 7 43W
Sila, La, *Italy* 29 39 15N 16 35 E
Silacayoapan, *Mexico* 127 17 30N 98 9W
Silandro, *Italy* 26 46 38N 10 48 E
Sīlat az Zahr, *Jordan* 44 32 19N 35 11 E
Silba, *Yugoslavia* 27 44 24N 14 41 E
Silchar, *India* 52 24 49N 92 48 E
Silcox, *Canada* 111 57 12N 94 10W
Silenrieux, *Belgium* 17 50 14N 4 27 E
Siler City, *U.S.A.* 115 35 44N 79 30W
Sileru →, *India* 50 17 49N 81 24 E
Silesia = Śląsk, *Poland* 32 51 0N 16 30 E
Silet, *Algeria* 85 22 44N 4 37 E
Silgarhi Doti, *Nepal* 49 29 15N 81 0 E
Silghat, *India* 52 26 35N 93 0 E
Silifke, *Turkey* 46 36 22N 33 58 E
Siling Co, *China* 62 31 50N 89 20 E
Silíqua, *Italy* 28 39 20N 8 49 E
Silistra, *Bulgaria* 34 44 6N 27 19 E
Siljan, *Sweden* 10 60 55N 14 45 E
Silkeborg, *Denmark* 11 56 10N 9 32 E
Sillajhuay, Cordillera, *Chile* 136 19 46S 68 40W
Sillé-le-Guillaume, *France* 18 48 10N 0 8W
Sillustani, *Peru* 136 15 50S 70 7W
Siloam Springs, *U.S.A.* 121 36 15N 94 31W
Silsbee, *U.S.A.* 121 30 20N 94 8W
Silute, *U.S.S.R.* 36 55 21N 21 33 E
Silva Porto = Kuito, *Angola* 95 12 22S 16 55 E
Silver City, *N. Mex., U.S.A.* 123 32 50N 108 18W
Silver City, *Nev., U.S.A.* 122 39 15N 119 48W
Silver Cr. →, *U.S.A.* 122 43 16N 119 13W
Silver Creek, *U.S.A.* 116 42 33N 79 9W
Silver Grove, *U.S.A.* 119 39 2N 84 24W
Silver L., *U.S.A.* 124 38 39N 120 6W
Silver Lake, *Calif., U.S.A.* 125 35 21N 116 7W
Silver Lake, *Ind., U.S.A.* 119 41 4N 85 53W
Silver Lake, *Oreg., U.S.A.* 122 43 9N 121 4W
Silver Lake, *Wis., U.S.A.* 119 42 33N 88 13W
Silver Streams, *S. Africa* 96 28 20S 23 33 E
Silver Water, *Canada* 108 45 52N 82 52W
Silverspur, *Australia* 77 28 52S 151 17 E
Silverton, *Colo., U.S.A.* 123 37 51N 107 45W
Silverton, *Tex., U.S.A.* 121 34 30N 101 16W
Silves, *Portugal* 23 37 11N 8 26W
Silvi, *Italy* 27 42 32N 14 5 E
Silvia, *Colombia* 134 2 37N 76 21W
Silvies →, *U.S.A.* 122 43 22N 118 48W
Silvolde, *Neths.* 16 51 55N 6 23 E
Silvretta Gruppe, *Switz.* 31 46 50N 10 6 E
Silwa Bahari, *Egypt* 88 24 45N 32 55 E

Smartt Syndicate Dam

Smartt Syndicate Dam, S. Africa 96 30 45 S 23 10 E
Smartville, U.S.A. 124 39 13N 121 18W
Smeaton, Canada 111 53 30N 104 49W
Smederevo, Yugoslavia 33 44 40N 20 57 E
Smederevska Palanka, Yugoslavia 33 44 22N 20 58 E
Smela, U.S.S.R. 38 49 15N 31 58 E
Smethport, U.S.A. 116 41 50N 78 28W
Smidovich, U.S.S.R. 41 48 36N 133 49 E
Smilde, Neths. 16 52 58N 6 28 E
Smiley, Canada 111 51 38N 109 29W
Smith, Canada 110 55 10N 114 0W
Smith →, Canada 110 59 34N 126 30W
Smith Arm, Canada 102 66 15N 123 0W
Smith Center, U.S.A. 120 39 50N 98 50W
Smith Sund, Greenland 144 78 30N 74 0W
Smithburne →, Australia 72 17 3 S 140 57 E
Smithers, Canada 110 54 45N 127 10W
Smithfield, S. Africa 97 30 9 S 26 30 E
Smithfield, N.C., U.S.A. 115 35 31N 78 16W
Smithfield, Utah, U.S.A. 122 41 50N 111 50W
Smiths Falls, Canada 109 44 55N 76 0W
Smithton, Australia 72 40 53 S 145 6 E
Smithtown, Australia 77 30 58 S 152 48 E
Smithville, Canada 108 43 6N 79 33W
Smithville, Mo., U.S.A. 118 39 23N 94 35W
Smithville, Tex., U.S.A. 121 30 2N 97 12W
Smoky →, Canada 110 56 10N 117 21W
Smoky Bay, Australia 73 32 22 S 134 13 E
Smoky Cape, Australia 77 30 55 S 153 5 E
Smoky Falls, Canada 104 50 4N 82 10W
Smoky Hill →, U.S.A. 120 39 3N 96 48W
Smoky Lake, Canada 110 54 10N 112 30W
Smøla, Norway 10 63 23N 8 3 E
Smolensk, U.S.S.R. 36 54 45N 32 0 E
Smolikas, Óros, Greece 35 40 9N 20 58 E
Smolník, Czech. 32 48 43N 20 44 E
Smolyan, Bulgaria 35 41 36N 24 38 E
Smooth Rock Falls, Canada 104 49 17N 81 37W
Smoothstone L., Canada 111 54 40N 106 50W
Smorgon, U.S.S.R. 36 54 20N 26 24 E
Smyadovo, Bulgaria 34 43 2N 27 1 E
Smyrna = İzmir, Turkey 46 38 25N 27 8 E
Snaefell, U.K. 12 54 18N 4 26W
Snæfellsjökull, Iceland 8 64 49N 23 46W
Snake →, U.S.A. 122 46 12N 119 2W
Snake I., Australia 75 38 47 S 146 33 E
Snake L., Canada 111 55 32N 106 35W
Snake Ra., U.S.A. 122 39 0N 114 30W
Snake River Plain, U.S.A. 122 43 13N 113 0W
Snake Valley, Australia 74 37 37 S 143 35 E
Snapper Point, Australia 77 35 34 S 150 23 E
Snarum, Norway 10 60 1N 9 54 E
Snedsted, Denmark 11 56 55N 8 32 E
Sneek, Neths. 16 53 2N 5 40 E
Sneeker-meer, Neths. 16 53 2N 5 45 E
Sneeuberge, S. Africa 96 31 46 S 24 20 E
Snejbjerg, Denmark 11 56 8N 8 54 E
Snelling, U.S.A. 124 37 31N 120 26W
Snezhnoye, U.S.S.R. 39 48 0N 38 58 E
Snežnik, Yugoslavia 27 45 36N 14 35 E
Snigirevka, U.S.S.R. 38 47 2N 32 49 E
Snizort, L., U.K. 14 57 33N 6 28W
Snøhetta, Norway 10 62 19N 9 16 E
Snohomish, U.S.A. 124 47 53N 122 6W
Snoul, Cambodia 55 12 4N 106 26 E
Snow Hill, U.S.A. 114 38 10N 75 21W
Snow Lake, Canada 111 54 52N 100 3W
Snow Mt., U.S.A. 124 39 22N 122 44W
Snowbird L., Canada 111 60 45N 103 0W
Snowdon, U.K. 12 53 4N 4 8W
Snowdrift, Canada 111 62 24N 110 44W
Snowdrift →, Canada 111 62 24N 110 44W
Snowflake, U.S.A. 123 34 30N 110 4W
Snowshoe Pk., U.S.A. 122 48 13N 115 41W
Snowtown, Australia 73 33 46 S 138 14 E
Snowville, U.S.A. 122 41 59N 112 47W
Snowy →, Australia 75 37 46 S 148 30 E
Snowy Mts., Australia 75 36 30 S 148 20 E
Snug Corner, Bahamas 129 22 33N 73 52W
Snyatyn, U.S.S.R. 38 48 30N 25 50 E
Snyder, Okla., U.S.A. 121 34 40N 99 0W
Snyder, Tex., U.S.A. 121 32 45N 100 57W
Soacha, Colombia 134 4 35N 74 13W
Soahanina, Madag. 97 18 42 S 44 13 E
Soalala, Madag. 97 16 6 S 45 20 E
Soan →, Pakistan 48 33 1N 71 44 E
Soanierana-Ivongo, Madag. 97 16 55 S 49 35 E
Soap Lake, U.S.A. 122 47 23N 119 31W
Sobat, Nahr →, Sudan 89 9 22N 31 33 E
Sobhapur, India 48 22 47N 78 17 E
Sobinka, U.S.S.R. 37 56 0N 40 0 E
Sobo-Yama, Japan 64 32 51N 131 22 E
Sobótka, Poland 32 50 54N 16 44 E
Sobrado, Spain 22 43 2N 8 2W
Sobral, Brazil 138 3 50 S 40 20W
Sobreira Formosa, Portugal 23 39 46N 7 51W
Soc Giang, Vietnam 54 22 54N 106 1 E
Soc Trang, Vietnam 55 9 37N 105 50 E
Soča →, Europe 27 46 20N 13 40 E
Sochaczew, Poland 32 52 15N 20 13 E
Soch'e = Shache, China 62 38 20N 77 10 E
Sochi, U.S.S.R. 39 43 35N 39 40 E
Société, Is. de la, Pac. Oc. 67 17 0 S 151 0W
Society Is. = Société, Is. de la, Pac. Oc. 67 17 0 S 151 0W
Socompa, Portezuelo de, Chile 140 24 27 S 68 18W
Socorro, Colombia 134 6 29N 73 16W
Socorro, U.S.A. 123 34 4N 106 54W
Socorro, I., Mexico 126 18 45N 110 58W
Socotra, Ind. Oc. 45 12 30N 54 0 E
Socúellmos, Spain 25 39 16N 2 47W
Soda L., U.S.A. 123 35 7N 116 2W
Soda Plains, India 49 35 30N 79 0 E
Soda Springs, U.S.A. 122 42 40N 111 40W
Söderfors, Sweden 10 60 23N 17 25 E
Söderhamn, Sweden 10 61 18N 17 10 E
Söderköping, Sweden 10 58 31N 16 20 E
Södermanlands län □, Sweden 10 59 10N 16 30 E
Södertälje, Sweden 10 59 12N 17 39 E
Sodiri, Sudan 89 14 27N 29 0 E
Sodo, Ethiopia 89 7 0N 37 41 E
Södra Vi, Sweden 11 57 45N 15 45 E
Sodražica, Yugoslavia 27 45 45N 14 39 E
Sodus, U.S.A. 116 43 13N 77 5W
Soekmekaar, S. Africa 97 23 30 S 29 55 E
Soest, Neths. 16 52 9N 5 19 E
Soest, W. Germany 30 51 34N 8 7 E
Soestdijk, Neths. 16 52 11N 5 17 E
Sofádhes, Greece 35 39 20N 22 4 E
Sofala, Australia 76 33 4 S 149 43 E
Sofara, Mali 90 13 59N 4 9W
Sofia = Sofiya, Bulgaria 34 42 45N 23 20 E
Sofia →, Madag. 97 15 27 S 47 23 E
Sofievka, U.S.S.R. 38 48 6N 33 55 E
Sofiiski, U.S.S.R. 41 52 15N 133 59 E
Sofikón, Greece 35 37 47N 23 3 E
Sofiya, Bulgaria 34 42 45N 23 20 E
Sogakofe, Ghana 91 6 2N 0 39 E
Sogamoso, Colombia 134 5 43N 72 56W
Sögel, W. Germany 30 52 50N 7 32 E
Sogeri, Papua N. G. 69 9 26 S 147 35 E
Sogn og Fjordane fylke □, Norway 9 61 40N 6 0 E
Sogndalsfjøra, Norway 9 61 14N 7 5 E
Sognefjorden, Norway 9 61 10N 5 50 E
Sohâg, Egypt 88 26 33N 31 43 E
Sohano, Papua N. G. 69 5 22 S 154 37 E
Soignies, Belgium 17 50 35N 4 5 E
Soira, Mt., Ethiopia 89 14 45N 39 30 E
Soissons, France 19 49 25N 3 19 E
Sōja, Japan 64 34 40N 133 45 E
Sojat, India 48 25 55N 73 45 E
Sok →, U.S.S.R. 37 53 24N 50 8 E
Sokal, U.S.S.R. 36 50 31N 24 15 E
Söke, Turkey 46 37 48N 27 28 E
Sokelo, Zaïre 93 9 55 S 24 36 E
Sokki, Oued In →, Algeria 85 29 30N 3 42 E
Sokna, Norway 10 60 16N 9 50 E
Soknedal, Norway 10 62 57N 10 13 E
Soko Banja, Yugoslavia 33 43 40N 21 51 E
Sokodé, Togo 91 9 0N 1 11 E
Sokol, U.S.S.R. 37 59 30N 40 5 E
Sokółka, Poland 32 53 25N 23 30 E
Sokolo, Mali 90 14 53N 6 8W
Sokołów Małpolski, Poland 32 50 12N 22 7 E
Sokołów Podlaski, Poland 32 52 25N 22 15 E
Sokoto, Nigeria 91 13 2N 5 16 E
Sokoto □, Nigeria 91 12 30N 5 0 E
Sokoto →, Nigeria 91 11 20N 4 10 E
Sol Iletsk, U.S.S.R. 40 51 10N 55 0 E
Solai, Kenya 92 0 2N 36 12 E
Solana, La, Spain 25 38 59N 3 14W
Solano, Phil. 57 16 31N 121 15 E
Solapur, India 50 17 43N 75 56 E
Solares, Spain 22 43 23N 3 43W
Solberga, Sweden 11 57 45N 14 43 E
Solec Kujawski, Poland 32 53 5N 18 14 E
Soledad, Colombia 134 10 55N 74 46W
Soledad, U.S.A. 124 36 27N 121 16W
Soledad, Venezuela 135 8 10N 63 34W
Solent, The, U.K. 13 50 45N 1 25W
Solenzara, France 21 41 53N 9 23 E
Solesmes, France 19 50 10N 3 30 E
Solfonn, Norway 9 60 2N 6 57 E
Soligalich, U.S.S.R. 37 59 5N 42 10 E
Soligorsk, U.S.S.R. 36 52 51N 27 27 E
Solikamsk, U.S.S.R. 40 59 38N 56 50 E
Solila, Madag. 97 21 25 S 46 37 E
Solimões → = Amazonas →, S. Amer. 135 0 5 S 50 0W
Solingen, W. Germany 17 51 10N 7 4 E
Sollebrunn, Sweden 11 58 8N 12 32 E
Sollefteå, Sweden 10 63 12N 17 20 E
Sollentuna, Sweden 10 59 26N 17 56 E
Sóller, Spain 24 39 46N 2 43 E
Solling, W. Germany 30 51 44N 9 36 E
Solna, Sweden 10 59 22N 18 1 E
Solnechnogorsk, U.S.S.R. 37 56 10N 36 57 E
Sologne, France 19 47 40N 1 45 E
Solok, Indonesia 56 0 45 S 100 40 E
Sololá, Guatemala 128 14 49N 91 10 E
Solomon, N. Fork →, U.S.A. 120 39 29N 98 26W
Solomon, S. Fork →, U.S.A. 120 39 25N 99 12W
Solomon Is. ■, Pac. Oc. 68 6 0 S 155 0 E
Solomon Sea, Papua N. G. 69 7 0 S 150 0 E
Solomon's Pools = Birak Sulaymān, Jordan 44 31 42N 35 7 E
Solon, China 62 46 32N 121 10 E
Solon Springs, U.S.A. 120 46 19N 91 47W
Solonópole, Brazil 138 5 44 S 39 1W
Solor, Indonesia 57 8 27 S 123 0 E
Solotcha, U.S.S.R. 37 54 48N 39 53 E
Solothurn, Switz. 31 47 13N 7 32 E
Solothurn □, Switz. 31 47 18N 7 40 E
Solsona, Spain 24 42 0N 1 31 E
Solta, Yugoslavia 27 43 24N 16 15 E
Solṭānābād, Iran 47 36 29N 58 5 E
Soltau, W. Germany 30 52 59N 9 50 E
Soltsy, U.S.S.R. 36 58 10N 30 30 E
Solunska Glava, Yugoslavia 35 41 44N 21 31 E
Solvang, U.S.A. 125 34 36N 120 8W
Solvay, U.S.A. 117 43 5N 76 17W
Sölvesborg, Sweden 11 56 5N 14 35 E
Solway Firth, U.K. 12 54 45N 3 38W
Solwezi, Zambia 93 12 11 S 26 21 E
Somali Rep. ■, Africa 98 7 0N 47 0 E
Sombe Dzong, Bhutan 52 27 13N 89 8 E
Sombernon, France 19 47 20N 4 40 E
Sombor, Yugoslavia 33 45 46N 19 9 E
Sombra, Canada 108 42 43N 82 29W
Sombrerete, Mexico 126 23 40N 103 40W
Sombrero, Anguilla 129 18 37N 63 30W
Someren, Neths. 17 51 23N 5 42 E
Somers, U.S.A. 122 48 4N 114 18W
Somerset, Canada 111 49 25N 98 39W
Somerset, Colo., U.S.A. 123 38 55N 107 30W
Somerset, Ky., U.S.A. 114 37 5N 84 40W
Somerset, Mass., U.S.A. 117 41 45N 71 10W
Somerset, Pa., U.S.A. 116 40 1N 79 4W
Somerset □, U.K. 13 51 9N 3 0W
Somerset East, S. Africa 96 32 42 S 25 35 E
Somerset I., Canada 102 73 30N 93 0W
Somerset West, S. Africa 96 34 8 S 18 50 E
Somerton, Australia 77 30 55 S 150 38 E
Somerton, U.S.A. 123 32 35N 114 47W
Somerville, Australia 74 38 14 S 145 11 E
Somerville, U.S.A. 117 40 34N 74 36W
Someş →, Romania 34 47 49N 22 43 E
Someşul Mare →, Romania 34 47 18N 24 30 E
Somma Lombardo, Italy 26 45 41N 8 42 E
Somma Vesuviana, Italy 29 40 52N 14 23 E
Sommariva, Australia 73 26 24 S 146 36 E
Sommatino, Italy 28 37 20N 14 0 E
Somme □, France 19 50 0N 2 20 E
Somme →, France 19 50 11N 1 38 E
Somme, B. de la, France 18 50 14N 1 33 E
Sommelsdijk, Neths. 16 51 46N 4 9 E
Sommen, Jönköping, Sweden 11 58 12N 15 0 E
Sommen, Östergötland, Sweden 11 58 0N 15 15 E
Sommepy-Tahure, France 19 49 15N 4 31 E
Sömmerda, E. Germany 30 51 10N 11 8 E
Sommesous, France 19 48 44N 4 12 E
Sommières, France 21 43 47N 4 6 E
Somosomo Str., Fiji 68 16 0 S 180 0 E
Somoto, Nic. 128 13 28N 86 37W
Sompolno, Poland 32 52 26N 18 30 E
Somport, Paso, Spain 24 42 48N 0 31W
Somport, Puerto de, Spain 24 42 48N 0 31W
Somuncurá, Meseta de, Argentina 142 41 30 S 67 0W
Son, Neths. 17 51 31N 5 30 E
Son, Norway 10 59 32N 10 42 E
Son, Spain 22 42 43N 8 58W
Son Ha, Vietnam 54 15 3N 108 34 E
Son Hoa, Vietnam 54 13 2N 108 58 E
Son La, Vietnam 54 21 20N 103 50 E
Son Tay, Vietnam 54 21 8N 105 30 E
Soná, Panama 128 8 0N 81 20W
Sonamarg, India 49 34 18N 75 21 E
Sonamukhi, India 49 23 18N 87 27 E
Sonamura, India 52 23 29N 91 15 E
Soncino, Italy 26 45 24N 9 52 E
Sondag →, S. Africa 96 33 44 S 25 51 E
Sóndalo, Italy 26 46 20N 10 20 E
Sondar, India 49 33 28N 75 56 E
Sønder Omme, Denmark 11 55 50N 8 54 E
Sønder Ternby, Denmark 11 57 31N 9 58 E
Sønderborg, Denmark 11 54 55N 9 49 E
Sønderjyllands Amtskommune □, Denmark 11 55 10N 9 10 E
Sondershausen, E. Germany 30 51 22N 10 50 E
Sóndrio, Italy 26 46 10N 9 53 E
Sone, Mozam. 93 17 23 S 34 55 E
Sonepur, India 50 20 55N 83 50 E
Song, Thailand 54 18 28N 100 11 E
Song Cau, Vietnam 54 13 27N 109 18 E
Song Xian, China 60 34 12N 112 8 E
Songea, Tanzania 93 10 40 S 35 40 E
Songea □, Tanzania 93 10 30 S 36 0 E
Songeons, France 19 49 32N 1 50 E
Songhua Hu, China 61 43 35N 126 50 E
Songhua Jiang →, China 61 47 45N 132 30 E
Songjiang, China 59 31 1N 121 12 E
Songkan, China 58 28 35N 106 52 E
Songkhla, Thailand 55 7 13N 100 37 E
Songming, China 58 25 12N 103 2 E
Songo, Angola 95 7 22 S 14 51 E
Songololo, Zaïre 95 5 42 S 14 2 E
Songpan, China 58 32 40N 103 30 E
Songtao, China 58 28 11N 109 10 E
Songwe, Zaïre 92 3 20 S 26 16 E
Songwe →, Africa 93 9 44 S 33 58 E
Songxi, China 59 27 31N 118 44 E
Songzi, China 59 30 12N 111 45 E
Sonid Youqi, China 60 42 45N 112 48 E
Sonipat, India 48 29 0N 77 5 E
Sonkovo, U.S.S.R. 37 57 50N 37 5 E
Sonmiani, Pakistan 48 25 25N 66 40 E
Sonnino, Italy 28 41 25N 13 13 E
Sono →, Goiás, Brazil 138 9 58 S 48 11W
Sono →, Minas Gerais, Brazil 139 17 2 S 45 32W
Sonobe, Japan 65 35 6N 135 28 E
Sonora, Calif., U.S.A. 124 37 59N 120 27W
Sonora, Tex., U.S.A. 121 30 33N 100 37W
Sonora □, Mexico 126 29 0N 111 0W
Sonora →, Mexico 126 28 50N 111 33W
Sonora Desert, U.S.A. 125 33 40N 114 15W
Sonoyta, Mexico 126 31 51N 112 50W
Sonsonate, El Salv. 128 13 43N 89 44W
Sonthofen, W. Germany 31 47 31N 10 16 E
Soochow = Suzhou, China 59 31 19N 120 38 E
Sop Hao, Laos 54 20 33N 104 27 E
Sop Prap, Thailand 54 17 53N 99 20 E
Sopachuy, Bolivia 137 19 29 S 64 31W
Sopi, Indonesia 57 2 34N 128 28 E
Sopo, Nahr →, Sudan 89 8 40N 26 30 E
Sopot, Poland 32 54 27N 18 31 E
Sopotnica, Yugoslavia 35 41 23N 21 13 E
Sopron, Hungary 33 47 45N 16 32 E
Sop's Arm, Canada 105 49 46N 56 56W
Sopur, India 49 34 18N 74 27 E
Sør-Rondane, Antarctica 143 72 0 S 25 0 E
Sør-Trøndelag fylke □, Norway 10 63 0N 10 0 E
Sora, Italy 28 41 45N 13 36 E
Sorada, India 50 19 45N 84 26 E
Sorah, Pakistan 48 27 13N 68 56 E
Söråker, Sweden 10 62 30N 17 32 E
Sorano, Italy 27 42 40N 11 42 E
Sorata, Bolivia 136 15 50 S 68 40W
Sorbas, Spain 25 37 6N 2 7W
Sorel, Canada 107 46 0N 73 10W
Sorento, Australia 74 38 22 S 144 47 E
Sorento, U.S.A. 118 39 0N 89 34W
Soreq, N. →, Israel 44 31 57N 34 43 E
Soresina, Italy 26 45 17N 9 51 E
Sorgono, Italy 28 40 1N 9 6 E
Sorgues, France 21 44 1N 4 53 E
Soria, Spain 24 41 43N 2 32W
Soria □, Spain 24 41 46N 2 28W
Soriano, Uruguay 140 33 24 S 58 19W
Soriano nel Cimino, Italy 27 42 25N 12 14 E
Sorkh, Kuh-e, Iran 47 35 40N 58 30 E
Sorø, Denmark 11 55 26N 11 32 E
Soro, Guinea 90 10 9N 9 48W
Sorocaba, Brazil 141 23 31 S 47 27W
Soroki, U.S.S.R. 38 48 8N 28 12 E
Soron, India 49 27 55N 78 45 E
Sorong, Indonesia 57 0 55 S 131 15 E
Soroti, Uganda 92 1 43N 33 35 E
Sørøya, Norway 8 70 40N 22 30 E
Sørøysundet, Norway 8 70 25N 23 0 E
Sorraia →, Portugal 23 38 55N 8 53W
Sorrento, Italy 29 40 38N 14 23 E
Sorsele, Sweden 8 65 31N 17 30 E
Sorso, Italy 28 40 50N 8 34 E
Sorsogon, Phil. 57 13 0N 124 0 E
Sortino, Italy 29 37 9N 15 1 E
Sorvizhi, U.S.S.R. 37 57 52N 48 32 E
Sos, Spain 24 42 30N 1 13W
Soscumica, L., Canada 106 50 15N 77 27W
Sosna →, U.S.S.R. 37 52 42N 38 55 E
Sosnovka, R.S.F.S.R., U.S.S.R. 37 53 13N 41 24 E
Sosnovka, R.S.F.S.R., U.S.S.R. 41 54 9N 109 35 E
Sosnowiec, Poland 32 50 20N 19 10 E
Sospel, France 21 43 52N 7 27 E
Šoštanj, Yugoslavia 27 46 23N 15 4 E
Soto la Marina →, Mexico 127 23 40N 97 40W
Soto y Amío, Spain 22 42 46N 5 53W
Sotteville-lès-Rouen, France 18 49 24N 1 5 E
Sotuta, Mexico 127 20 29N 89 43W
Souanké, Congo 94 2 10N 14 3 E
Soucy, Canada 106 48 10N 75 30W
Soufflay, Congo 94 2 1N 14 54 E
Sougne-Remouchamps, Belgium 17 50 29N 5 42 E
Souillac, France 20 44 53N 1 29 E
Souk-Ahras, Algeria 85 36 23N 7 57 E

Stagnone

Souk el Arba du Rharb, *Morocco* **84** 34 43N 5 59W
Soukhouma, *Laos* **54** 14 38N 105 48 E
Sŏul, *S. Korea* **61** 37 31N 126 58 E
Soulac-sur-Mer, *France* **20** 45 30N 1 7W
Soultz-sous-Forêts, *France* **19** 48 57N 7 52 E
Soumagne, *Belgium* **17** 50 37N 5 44 E
Sound, The, *Denmark* **9** 56 7N 12 30 E
Soúnion, Ákra, *Greece* **35** 37 37N 24 1 E
Sour el Ghozlane, *Algeria* **85** 36 10N 3 45 E
Sources, Mt. aux, *Lesotho* **97** 28 45 S 28 50 E
Sourdeval, *France* **18** 48 43N 0 55W
Soure, *Brazil* **138** 0 35 S 48 30W
Soure, *Portugal* **22** 40 4N 8 38W
Souris, *Man., Canada* **111** 49 40N 100 20W
Souris, *P.E.I., Canada* **105** 46 21N 62 15W
Souris →, *Canada* **120** 49 40N 99 34W
Sousa, *Brazil* **138** 6 45 S 38 10W
Sousel, *Brazil* **138** 2 38 S 52 29W
Sousel, *Portugal* **23** 38 57N 7 40W
Souss, O. →, *Morocco* **84** 30 27N 9 31W
Sousse, *Tunisia* **86** 35 50N 10 38 E
Soustons, *France* **20** 43 45N 1 19W
Souterraine, La, *France* **20** 46 15N 1 30 E
South Africa, Rep. of ■, *Africa* **96** 32 0 S 23 0 E
South America **132** 10 0 S 60 0W
South Atlantic Ocean **131** 20 0 S 10 0W
South Aulatsivik I., *Canada* **105** 56 45N 61 30W
South Australia □, *Australia* **73** 32 0 S 139 0 E
South Baldy, Mt., *U.S.A.* **123** 34 6N 107 27W
South Baymouth, *Canada* **108** 45 33N 82 1W
South Beloit, *U.S.A.* **118** 42 29N 89 2W
South Bend, *Ind., U.S.A.* **119** 41 38N 86 20W
South Bend, *Wash., U.S.A.* **124** 46 44N 123 52W
South Boston, *U.S.A.* **115** 36 42N 78 58W
South Branch, *Canada* **105** 47 55N 59 2W
South Brook, *Canada* **105** 49 26N 56 5W
South Buganda □, *Uganda* **92** 0 15 S 31 30 E
South Carolina □, *U.S.A.* **115** 33 45N 81 0W
South Charleston, *U.S.A.* **114** 38 20N 81 40W
South China Sea, *Asia* **66** 10 0N 113 0 E
South Dakota □, *U.S.A.* **120** 45 0N 100 0W
South Downs, *U.K.* **13** 50 53N 0 10W
South East C., *Australia* **72** 43 40 S 146 50 E
South-East Indian Rise, *Ind. Oc.* **66** 43 0 S 80 0 E
South East Is., *Australia* **79** 34 17 S 123 30 E
South Esk →, *U.K.* **14** 56 44N 3 3W
South Foreland, *U.K.* **13** 51 7N 1 23 E
South Fork →, *U.S.A.* **122** 47 54N 113 15W
South Fork, American →, *U.S.A.* **124** 38 45N 121 5W
South Fork, Feather →, *U.S.A.* **124** 39 17N 121 36W
South Georgia, *Antarctica* **143** 54 30 S 37 0W
South Glamorgan □, *U.K.* **13** 51 30N 3 20W
South Grand →, *U.S.A.* **118** 38 17N 93 55W
South Haven, *U.S.A.* **119** 42 22N 86 20W
South Henik, L., *Canada* **111** 61 30N 97 30W
South Honshu Ridge, *Pac. Oc.* **66** 23 0N 143 0 E
South Horr, *Kenya* **92** 2 12N 36 56 E
South I., *Kenya* **92** 2 35N 36 35 E
South I., *N.Z.* **81** 44 0 S 170 0 E
South Invercargill, *N.Z.* **81** 46 26 S 168 23 E
South Knife →, *Canada* **111** 58 55N 94 37W
South Korea ■, *Asia* **61** 36 0N 128 0 E
South Lake Tahoe, *U.S.A.* **124** 38 57N 120 2W
South Loup →, *U.S.A.* **120** 41 4N 98 40W
South Lyon, *U.S.A.* **119** 42 28N 83 39W
South Magnetic Pole, *Antarctica* **143** 65 2 S 139 4 E
South Milwaukee, *U.S.A.* **119** 42 50N 87 52W
South Molton, *U.K.* **13** 51 1N 3 50W
South Nahanni →, *Canada* **110** 61 3N 123 21W
South Nation →, *Canada* **109** 45 34N 75 6W
South Negril Pt., *Jamaica* **128** 18 14N 78 30W
South Orkney Is., *Antarctica* **143** 63 0 S 45 0W
South Pass, *U.S.A.* **122** 42 20N 108 58W
South Pekin, *U.S.A.* **118** 40 30N 89 39W
South Pines, *U.S.A.* **115** 35 10N 79 25W
South Pittsburg, *U.S.A.* **115** 35 1N 85 42W
South Platte →, *U.S.A.* **120** 41 7N 100 42W
South Pole, *Antarctica* **143** 90 0 S 0 0 E
South Porcupine, *Canada* **104** 48 30N 81 12W
South River, *Canada* **108** 45 52N 79 23W
South River, *U.S.A.* **117** 40 27N 74 23W
South Ronaldsay, *U.K.* **14** 58 46N 2 58W
South Sandwich Is., *Antarctica* **143** 57 0 S 27 0W
South Saskatchewan →, *Canada* **111** 53 15N 105 5W
South Seal →, *Canada* **111** 58 48N 98 8W
South Shetland Is., *Antarctica* **143** 62 0 S 59 0W
South Shields, *U.K.* **12** 54 59N 1 26W
South Sioux City, *U.S.A.* **120** 42 30N 96 24W
South Solitary I., *Australia* **77** 30 12 S 153 16 E
South Taranaki Bight, *N.Z.* **80** 39 40 S 174 5 E
South Thompson →, *Canada* **110** 50 40N 120 20W
South Twin I., *Canada* **104** 53 7N 79 52W
South Tyne →, *U.K.* **12** 54 46N 2 25W
South Uist, *U.K.* **14** 57 20N 7 15W
South Wayne, *U.S.A.* **118** 42 34N 89 53W
South West Africa = Namibia ■, *Africa* **96** 22 0 S 18 9 E
South West C., *Australia* **72** 43 34 S 146 3 E
South West Rocks, *Australia* **77** 30 52 S 153 3 E
South Whitley, *U.S.A.* **119** 41 5N 85 38W
South Yemen ■, *Asia* **45** 15 0N 48 0 E
South Yorkshire □, *U.K.* **12** 53 30N 1 20W
Southampton, *Canada* **108** 44 30N 81 25W
Southampton, *U.K.* **13** 50 54N 1 23W
Southampton, *U.S.A.* **117** 40 54N 72 22W
Southampton I., *Canada* **103** 64 30N 84 0W
Southbridge, *N.Z.* **81** 43 48 S 172 16 E
Southbridge, *U.S.A.* **117** 42 4N 72 2W
Southeast Pacific Basin, *Pac. Oc.* **67** 16 30 S 92 0W
Southend, *Canada* **111** 56 19N 103 22W
Southend-on-Sea, *U.K.* **13** 51 32N 0 42 E
Southern □, *Malawi* **93** 15 0 S 35 0 E
Southern □, *S. Leone* **90** 8 0N 12 30W
Southern □, *Zambia* **93** 16 20 S 26 20 E
Southern Alps, *N.Z.* **81** 43 41 S 170 11 E
Southern Cross, *Australia* **79** 31 12 S 119 15 E
Southern Hills, *Australia* **79** 32 15 S 122 40 E
Southern Indian L., *Canada* **111** 57 10N 98 30W
Southern Ocean, *Antarctica* **143** 62 0 S 60 0 E
Southern Uplands, *U.K.* **14** 55 30N 3 3W
Southfield, *U.S.A.* **119** 42 29N 83 17W
Southington, *U.S.A.* **117** 41 37N 72 53W
Southland □, *N.Z.* **81** 45 51 S 168 13 E
Southold, *U.S.A.* **117** 41 4N 72 26W
Southport, *Australia* **77** 27 58 S 153 25 E
Southport, *U.K.* **12** 53 38N 3 1W
Southport, *U.S.A.* **115** 33 55N 78 0W
Southwestern Pacific Basin, *Pac. Oc.* **66** 42 0 S 170 0W
Southwold, *U.K.* **13** 52 19N 1 41 E
Soutpansberg, *S. Africa* **97** 23 0 S 29 30 E
Souvigny, *France* **20** 46 33N 3 10 E
Sovetsk, *Lithuania, U.S.S.R.* **36** 55 6N 21 50 E
Sovetsk, *R.S.F.S.R., U.S.S.R.* **37** 57 38N 48 53 E
Sovetskaya Gavan, *U.S.S.R.* **41** 48 50N 140 0 E
Sovicille, *Italy* **27** 43 16N 11 12 E
Soviet Union = Union of Soviet Socialist Republics ■, *Eurasia* **41** 60 0N 100 0 E
Sovra, *Yugoslavia* **33** 42 44N 17 34 E
Soweto, *S. Africa* **97** 26 14 S 27 54 E
Sōya-Kaikyō = Perouse Str., La, *Asia* **66** 45 40N 142 0 E
Sōya-Misaki, *Japan* **63** 45 30N 142 0 E
Soyo, *Angola* **95** 6 13 S 12 20 E
Sozh →, *U.S.S.R.* **36** 51 57N 30 48 E
Sozopol, *Bulgaria* **34** 42 23N 27 42 E
Spa, *Belgium* **17** 50 29N 5 53 E
Spain ■, *Europe* **7** 40 0N 5 0W
Spakenburg, *Neths.* **16** 52 15N 5 22 E
Spalding, *Australia* **73** 33 30 S 138 37 E
Spalding, *U.K.* **12** 52 47N 0 9W
Spalding, *U.S.A.* **120** 41 45N 98 27W
Spangler, *U.S.A.* **116** 40 39N 78 48W
Spaniard's Bay, *Canada* **105** 47 38N 53 20W
Spanish, *Canada* **108** 46 12N 82 20W
Spanish →, *Canada* **108** 46 11N 82 19W
Spanish Fork, *U.S.A.* **122** 40 10N 111 37W
Spanish Town, *Jamaica* **128** 18 0N 76 57W
Sparks, *U.S.A.* **124** 39 30N 119 45W
Sparta = Spárti, *Greece* **35** 37 5N 22 25 E
Sparta, *Ga., U.S.A.* **115** 33 18N 82 59W
Sparta, *Ill., U.S.A.* **118** 38 7N 89 42W
Sparta, *Mich., U.S.A.* **119** 43 10N 85 42W
Sparta, *Wis., U.S.A.* **120** 43 55N 90 47W
Spartanburg, *U.S.A.* **115** 35 0N 82 0W
Spartansburg, *U.S.A.* **116** 41 48N 79 43W
Spartel, C., *Morocco* **84** 35 47N 5 56W
Spárti, *Greece* **35** 37 5N 22 25 E
Spartivento, C., *Calabria, Italy* **29** 37 56N 16 4 E
Spartivento, C., *Sard., Italy* **28** 38 52N 8 50 E
Spas-Demensk, *U.S.S.R.* **36** 54 20N 34 0 E
Spas-Klepiki, *U.S.S.R.* **37** 55 10N 40 10 E
Spassk-Dalniy, *U.S.S.R.* **41** 44 40N 132 48 E
Spassk-Ryazanskiy, *U.S.S.R.* **37** 54 24N 40 25 E
Spátha, Akra, *Greece* **35** 35 42N 23 43 E
Spatsizi →, *Canada* **110** 57 42N 128 7W
Spearfish, *U.S.A.* **120** 44 32N 103 52W
Spearman, *U.S.A.* **121** 36 15N 101 10W
Speed, *Australia* **74** 35 21 S 142 27 E
Speedway, *U.S.A.* **119** 39 47N 86 15W
Speers, *Canada* **111** 52 43N 107 34W
Speightstown, *Barbados* **129** 13 15N 59 39W
Speke Gulf, *Tanzania* **92** 2 20 S 32 50 E
Spekholzerheide, *Neths.* **17** 50 51N 6 2 E
Spence Bay, *Canada* **102** 69 32N 93 32W
Spencer, *Idaho, U.S.A.* **122** 44 18N 112 8W
Spencer, *Ind., U.S.A.* **119** 39 17N 86 46W
Spencer, *Iowa, U.S.A.* **120** 43 5N 95 19W
Spencer, *N.Y., U.S.A.* **117** 42 14N 76 30W
Spencer, *Nebr., U.S.A.* **120** 42 52N 98 43W
Spencer, *W. Va., U.S.A.* **114** 38 47N 81 24W
Spencer, C., *Australia* **73** 35 20 S 136 53 E
Spencer B., *Namibia* **96** 25 30 S 14 47 E
Spencer G., *Australia* **73** 34 0 S 137 20 E
Spencerville, *Canada* **109** 44 51N 75 33W
Spencerville, *U.S.A.* **119** 40 43N 84 21W
Spences Bridge, *Canada* **110** 50 25N 121 20W
Spenser Mts., *N.Z.* **81** 42 15 S 172 45 E
Sperkhiós →, *Greece* **35** 38 57N 22 3 E
Sperrin Mts., *U.K.* **15** 54 50N 7 0W
Spessart, *W. Germany* **31** 50 10N 9 20 E
Spétsai, *Greece* **35** 37 15N 23 10 E
Spey →, *U.K.* **14** 57 26N 3 25W
Speyer, *W. Germany* **31** 49 19N 8 26 E
Speyer →, *W. Germany* **31** 49 19N 8 27 E
Spézia, La, *Italy* **26** 44 8N 9 50 E
Spezzano Albanese, *Italy* **29** 39 41N 16 19 E
Spickard, *U.S.A.* **118** 40 14N 93 36W
Spiekeroog, *W. Germany* **30** 53 45N 7 42 E
Spielfeld, *Austria* **27** 46 43N 15 38 E
Spiez, *Switz.* **31** 46 40N 7 40 E
Spijk, *Neths.* **16** 53 24N 6 50 E
Spijkenisse, *Neths.* **16** 51 51N 4 20 E
Spilimbergo, *Italy* **27** 46 7N 12 53 E
Spin Baldak = Qala-i-Jadid, *Afghan.* **48** 31 1N 66 25 E
Spinazzola, *Italy* **29** 40 58N 16 5 E
Spirit Lake, *Idaho, U.S.A.* **122** 47 56N 116 56W
Spirit Lake, *Wash., U.S.A.* **124** 46 15N 122 9W
Spirit River, *Canada* **110** 55 45N 118 50W
Spiritwood, *Canada* **111** 53 24N 107 33W
Spišská Nová Ves, *Czech.* **32** 48 58N 20 34 E
Spithead, *U.K.* **13** 50 43N 1 5W
Spittal, *Austria* **33** 46 48N 13 31 E
Spitzbergen = Svalbard, *Arctic* **144** 78 0N 17 0 E
Split, *Yugoslavia* **27** 43 31N 16 26 E
Split L., *Canada* **111** 56 8N 96 15W
Splitski Kanal, *Yugoslavia* **27** 43 31N 16 20 E
Splügenpass, *Switz.* **31** 46 30N 9 20 E
Spoffard, *U.S.A.* **121** 29 10N 100 27W
Spokane, *U.S.A.* **122** 47 45N 117 25W
Spoleto, *Italy* **27** 42 46N 12 47 E
Spoon →, *U.S.A.* **118** 40 19N 90 4W
Spooner, *U.S.A.* **120** 45 49N 91 51W
Sporyy Navolok, Mys, *U.S.S.R.* **40** 75 50N 68 40 E
Spragge, *Canada* **108** 46 15N 82 40W
Sprague, *U.S.A.* **122** 47 18N 117 59W
Sprague River, *U.S.A.* **122** 42 28N 121 31W
Spratly, I., *S. China Sea* **56** 8 20N 112 0 E
Spray, *U.S.A.* **122** 44 50N 119 46W
Spree →, *E. Germany* **30** 52 32N 13 13 E
Spremberg, *E. Germany* **30** 51 33N 14 21 E
Sprimont, *Belgium* **17** 50 30N 5 40 E
Spring City, *U.S.A.* **122** 39 31N 111 28W
Spring Garden, *U.S.A.* **124** 39 52N 120 47W
Spring Green, *U.S.A.* **118** 43 11N 90 4W
Spring Hill, *Australia* **76** 33 23 S 149 9 E
Spring Mts., *U.S.A.* **123** 36 20N 115 43W
Spring Ridge, *Australia* **77** 32 15 S 149 21 E
Spring Valley, *Calif., U.S.A.* **125** 32 45N 117 0W
Spring Valley, *Ill., U.S.A.* **118** 41 20N 89 14W
Spring Valley, *Minn., U.S.A.* **120** 43 40N 92 23W
Springbok, *S. Africa* **96** 29 42 S 17 54 E
Springdale, *Canada* **105** 49 30N 56 6W
Springdale, *Ark., U.S.A.* **121** 36 10N 94 5W
Springdale, *Wash., U.S.A.* **122** 48 1N 117 50W
Springe, *W. Germany* **30** 52 12N 9 35 E
Springer, *U.S.A.* **121** 36 22N 104 36W
Springerville, *U.S.A.* **123** 34 10N 109 16W
Springfield, *Canada* **108** 42 50N 80 56W
Springfield, *N.Z.* **81** 43 19 S 171 56 E
Springfield, *Colo., U.S.A.* **121** 37 26N 102 40W
Springfield, *Ill., U.S.A.* **118** 39 48N 89 40W
Springfield, *Ky., U.S.A.* **119** 37 41N 85 13W
Springfield, *Mass., U.S.A.* **117** 42 8N 72 37W
Springfield, *Mo., U.S.A.* **121** 37 15N 93 20W
Springfield, *Ohio, U.S.A.* **119** 39 58N 83 48W
Springfield, *Oreg., U.S.A.* **122** 44 2N 123 0W
Springfield, *Tenn., U.S.A.* **115** 36 35N 86 55W
Springfield, *Vt., U.S.A.* **117** 43 20N 72 30W
Springfield, L., *U.S.A.* **118** 39 46N 89 36W
Springfontein, *S. Africa* **96** 30 15 S 25 40 E
Springhill, *Canada* **105** 45 40N 64 4W
Springhouse, *Canada* **110** 51 56N 122 7W
Springhurst, *Australia* **75** 36 10 S 146 31 E
Springs, *S. Africa* **97** 26 13 S 28 25 E
Springsure, *Australia* **72** 24 8 S 148 6 E
Springvale, *Queens., Australia* **72** 23 33 S 140 42 E
Springvale, *W. Austral., Australia* **78** 17 48 S 127 41 E
Springvale, *U.S.A.* **117** 43 28N 70 48W
Springville, *Calif., U.S.A.* **124** 36 8N 118 49W
Springville, *N.Y., U.S.A.* **116** 42 31N 78 41W
Springville, *Utah, U.S.A.* **122** 40 14N 111 35W
Springwater, *Canada* **111** 51 58N 108 23W
Springwood, *Australia* **76** 33 41 S 150 33 E
Spruce-Creek, *U.S.A.* **116** 40 36N 78 9W
Sprucedale, *Canada* **108** 45 29N 79 28W
Spur, *U.S.A.* **121** 33 28N 100 50W
Spurgeon, *U.S.A.* **119** 38 14N 87 15W
Spurn Hd., *U.K.* **12** 53 34N 0 8 E
Spuž, *Yugoslavia* **33** 42 32N 19 10 E
Spuzzum, *Canada* **110** 49 37N 121 23W
Squam L., *U.S.A.* **117** 43 45N 71 32W
Squamish, *Canada* **110** 49 45N 123 10W
Square Islands, *Canada* **105** 52 47N 55 47W
Squatec, *Canada* **107** 47 53N 68 43W
Squillace, G. di, *Italy* **29** 38 43N 16 35 E
Squinzano, *Italy* **29** 40 27N 18 1 E
Squires, Mt., *Australia* **79** 26 14 S 127 28 E
Sragen, *Indonesia* **57** 7 26 S 111 2 E
Srbac, *Yugoslavia* **33** 45 7N 17 30 E
Srbija □, *Yugoslavia* **33** 43 30N 21 0 E
Srbobran, *Yugoslavia* **33** 45 32N 19 48 E
Sre Khtum, *Cambodia* **55** 12 10N 106 52 E
Sre Umbell, *Cambodia* **55** 11 8N 103 46 E
Srebrnica, *Yugoslavia* **33** 44 10N 19 18 E
Sredinnyy Khrebet, *U.S.S.R.* **41** 57 0N 160 0 E
Sredinnyy Ra. = Sredinnyy Khrebet, *U.S.S.R.* **41** 57 0N 160 0 E
Središče, *Yugoslavia* **27** 46 24N 16 17 E
Sredna Gora, *Bulgaria* **34** 42 40N 24 20 E
Sredne Tambovskoye, *U.S.S.R.* **41** 50 55N 137 45 E
Srednekolymsk, *U.S.S.R.* **41** 67 27N 153 40 E
Srednevilyuysk, *U.S.S.R.* **41** 63 50N 123 5 E
Śrem, *Poland* **32** 52 6N 17 2 E
Sremska Mitrovica, *Yugoslavia* **33** 44 59N 19 33 E
Srepok →, *Cambodia* **54** 13 33N 106 16 E
Sretensk, *U.S.S.R.* **41** 52 10N 117 40 E
Sri Kalahasti, *India* **51** 13 45N 79 44 E
Sri Lanka ■, *Asia* **51** 7 30N 80 50 E
Sriharikota, I., *India* **51** 13 40N 80 20 E
Srikakulam, *India* **50** 18 14N 83 58 E
Srinagar, *India* **49** 34 5N 74 50 E
Sripur, *Bangla.* **52** 24 14N 90 30 E
Srirangam, *India* **51** 10 54N 78 42 E
Srivardhan, *India* **50** 18 4N 73 3 E
Srivilliputtur, *India* **51** 9 31N 77 40 E
Środa Wielkopolski, *Poland* **32** 52 15N 17 19 E
Srpska Itabej, *Yugoslavia* **33** 45 35N 20 44 E
Staaten →, *Australia* **72** 16 24 S 141 17 E
Staberhuk, *E. Germany* **30** 54 23N 11 18 E
Stabroek, *Belgium* **17** 51 20N 4 22 E
Stad Delden, *Neths.* **16** 52 16N 6 43 E
Stade, *W. Germany* **30** 53 35N 9 31 E
Staden, *Belgium* **17** 50 59N 3 1 E
Staðarhólskirkja, *Iceland* **8** 65 23N 21 58W
Städjan, *Sweden* **10** 61 56N 12 52 E
Stadlandet, *Norway* **8** 62 10N 5 10 E
Stadskanaal, *Neths.* **16** 53 4N 6 55 E
Stadthagen, *W. Germany* **30** 52 20N 9 14 E
Stadtlohn, *W. Germany* **30** 52 0N 6 52 E
Stadtroda, *E. Germany* **30** 50 51N 11 44 E
Stafafell, *Iceland* **8** 64 25N 14 52W
Staffa, *U.K.* **14** 56 26N 6 21W
Stafford, *U.K.* **12** 52 49N 2 9W
Stafford, *U.S.A.* **121** 38 0N 98 35W
Stafford □, *U.K.* **12** 52 53N 2 10W
Stafford Springs, *U.S.A.* **117** 41 58N 72 20W
Stagnone, *Italy* **28** 37 50N 12 28 E

Suwannee

Strzyżów, Poland **32** 49 52N 21 47 E
Stuart, Fla., U.S.A. **115** 27 11N 80 12W
Stuart, Iowa, U.S.A. **118** 41 30N 94 19W
Stuart, Nebr., U.S.A. **120** 42 39N 99 8W
Stuart →, Canada **110** 54 0N 123 35W
Stuart L., Canada **110** 54 30N 124 30W
Stuart Mts., N.Z. **81** 45 2 S 167 39 E
Stuart Range, Australia **73** 29 10 S 134 56 E
Stuart Town, Australia **76** 32 44 S 149 4 E
Stubbekøbing, Denmark **11** 54 53N 12 9 E
Studholme Junc., N.Z. **81** 44 42 S 171 9 E
Stugun, Sweden **10** 63 10N 15 40 E
Stühlingen, W. Germany **31** 47 44N 8 26 E
Stull, L., Canada **104** 54 24N 92 34W
Stung Treng, Cambodia **54** 13 31N 105 58 E
Stupart →, Canada **111** 56 0N 93 25W
Stupino, U.S.S.R. **37** 54 57N 38 2 E
Sturgeon →, Canada **108** 46 35N 80 11W
Sturgeon B., Canada **111** 52 0N 97 50W
Sturgeon Bay, U.S.A. **114** 44 52N 87 20W
Sturgeon Falls, Canada **108** 46 25N 79 57W
Sturgeon L., Alta., Canada **110** 55 6N 117 32W
Sturgeon L., Ont., Canada **104** 50 0N 90 45W
Sturgeon L., Ont., Canada **109** 44 28N 78 43W
Sturgis, Mich., U.S.A. **119** 41 50N 85 25W
Sturgis, S. Dak., U.S.A. **120** 44 25N 103 30W
Sturkö, Sweden **11** 56 5N 15 42 E
Sturt Cr. →, Australia **78** 19 8 S 127 50 E
Sturt Creek, Australia **78** 19 12 S 128 8 E
Stutterheim, S. Africa **96** 32 33 S 27 28 E
Stuttgart, U.S.A. **121** 34 30N 91 33W
Stuttgart, W. Germany **31** 48 46N 9 10 E
Stuyvesant, U.S.A. **117** 42 23N 73 45W
Stykkishólmur, Iceland **8** 65 2N 22 40W
Styr →, U.S.S.R. **36** 52 7N 26 35 E
Styria = Steiermark □, Austria **33** 47 26N 15 0 E
Su-no-Saki, Japan **65** 34 58N 139 45 E
Su Xian, China **60** 33 41N 116 59 E
Suakin, Sudan **88** 19 8N 37 20 E
Suapure →, Venezuela **134** 6 48N 67 1W
Suaqui, Mexico **126** 29 12N 109 41W
Suatá →, Venezuela **135** 7 52N 65 22W
Subang, Indonesia **57** 6 34 S 107 45 E
Subansiri →, India **52** 26 48N 93 50 E
Subi, Indonesia **55** 2 58N 108 50 E
Subiaco, Italy **27** 41 56N 13 5 E
Subotica, Yugoslavia **33** 46 6N 19 49 E
Success, Canada **111** 50 28N 108 6W
Suceava, Romania **34** 47 38N 26 16 E
Suceava →, Romania **34** 47 38N 26 16 E
Sucha-Beskidzka, Poland **32** 49 44N 19 35 E
Suchan, Poland **32** 53 18N 15 18 E
Suchitoto, El Salv. **128** 13 56N 89 0W
Suchou = Suzhou, China **59** 31 19N 120 38 E
Süchow = Xuzhou, China **61** 34 18N 117 10 E
Suchowola, Poland **32** 53 33N 23 3 E
Sucio →, Colombia **134** 7 27N 77 7W
Suck →, Ireland **15** 53 17N 8 18W
Suckling, Mt., Papua N. G. **69** 9 49 S 148 53 E
Sucre, Bolivia **137** 19 0 S 65 15W
Sucre, Colombia **134** 8 49N 74 44W
Sucre □, Colombia **134** 8 50N 75 40W
Sucre □, Venezuela **135** 10 25N 63 30W
Sucuaro, Colombia **134** 4 34N 68 50W
Sućuraj, Yugoslavia **27** 43 10N 17 8 E
Sucuriju, Brazil **138** 1 39N 49 57W
Sucuriú →, Brazil **137** 20 47 S 51 38W
Sud, Pte., Canada **105** 49 3N 62 14W
Sud-Ouest, Pte. du, Canada **105** 49 23N 63 36W
Suda →, U.S.S.R. **37** 59 0N 37 40 E
Sudair, Si. Arabia **46** 26 0N 45 0 E
Sudak, U.S.S.R. **38** 44 51N 34 57 E
Sudan, U.S.A. **121** 34 4N 102 32W
Sudan ■, Africa **89** 15 0N 30 0 E
Suday, U.S.S.R. **37** 59 0N 43 0 E
Sudbury, Canada **108** 46 30N 81 0W
Sudbury, U.K. **13** 52 2N 0 44 E
Sûdd, Sudan **89** 8 20N 30 0 E
Suddie, Guyana **135** 7 8N 58 29W
Süderbrarup, W. Germany **30** 54 38N 9 47 E
Süderlügum, W. Germany **30** 54 50N 8 55 E
Süderoog-Sand, W. Germany **30** 54 27N 8 30 E
Sudetan Mts. = Sudety, Europe **32** 50 20N 16 45 E
Sudety, Europe **32** 50 20N 16 45 E
Sudi, Tanzania **93** 10 11 S 39 57 E
Sudirman, Pegunungan, Indonesia **57** 4 30 S 137 0 E
Sudogda, U.S.S.R. **37** 55 55N 40 50 E
Sudr, Egypt **88** 29 40N 32 42 E
Sudzha, U.S.S.R. **36** 51 14N 35 17 E
Sueca, Spain **25** 39 12N 0 21W
Suedala, Sweden **11** 55 30N 13 15 E
Sueur, Le, U.S.A. **120** 44 25N 93 52W
Suez = El Suweis, Egypt **88** 29 58N 32 31 E
Suez, G. of = Suweis, Khalîg el, Egypt **88** 28 40N 33 0 E
Suez Canal = Suweis, Qanâl es, Egypt **88** 31 0N 32 20 E
Sūf, Jordan **44** 32 19N 35 49 E
Suffield, Canada **111** 50 12N 111 10W
Suffolk, U.S.A. **114** 36 47N 76 33W
Suffolk □, U.K. **13** 52 16N 1 0 E
Suga no-Sen, Japan **64** 35 25N 134 25 E
Sugar →, Ill., U.S.A. **118** 42 25N 89 15W
Sugar →, Ind., U.S.A. **119** 39 50N 87 23W
Sugar City, U.S.A. **120** 38 18N 103 38W
Sugar Cr. →, U.S.A. **118** 40 12N 89 41W
Sugluk = Saglouc, Canada **103** 62 14N 75 38W
Sugny, Belgium **17** 49 49N 4 54 E
Suhaia, L., Romania **34** 43 45N 25 15 E
Suhār, Oman **47** 24 20N 56 40 E
Suhbaatar, Mongolia **62** 50 17N 106 10 E
Sühbaatar □, Mongolia **60** 45 30N 114 0 E
Suhl, E. Germany **30** 50 35N 10 40 E
Suhl □, E. Germany **30** 50 37N 10 43 E
Sui Xian, Henan, China **59** 31 42N 113 24 E
Sui Xian, Henan, China **60** 34 25N 115 2 E
Suiá Missu →, Brazil **137** 11 13 S 53 15W
Suichang, China **59** 28 29N 119 15 E
Suichuan, China **59** 26 20N 114 32 E
Suide, China **60** 37 30N 110 12 E
Suifenhe, China **61** 44 25N 131 10 E
Suihua, China **62** 46 32N 126 55 E
Suijiang, China **58** 28 40N 103 59 E
Suining, Hunan, China **59** 26 35N 110 10 E
Suining, Jiangsu, China **61** 33 56N 117 58 E
Suining, Sichuan, China **58** 30 26N 105 35 E
Suiping, China **60** 33 10N 113 59 E
Suippes, France **19** 49 8N 4 30 E
Suir →, Ireland **15** 52 15N 7 10W
Suita, Japan **65** 34 45N 135 32 E
Suixi, China **59** 21 19N 110 18 E
Suiyang, Guizhou, China **58** 27 58N 107 18 E
Suiyang, Heilongjiang, China **61** 44 30N 130 56 E
Suizhong, China **61** 40 21N 120 20 E
Sujangarh, India **48** 27 42N 74 31 E
Sukabumi, Indonesia **57** 6 56 S 106 50 E
Sukadana, Kalimantan, Indonesia **56** 1 10 S 110 0 E
Sukadana, Sumatera, Indonesia **56** 5 5 S 105 33 E
Sukaraja, Indonesia **56** 2 28 S 110 25 E
Sukarnapura = Jayapura, Indonesia **57** 2 28 S 140 38 E
Sukhinichi, U.S.S.R. **36** 54 8N 35 10 E
Sukhona →, U.S.S.R. **40** 60 30N 45 0 E
Sukhothai, Thailand **54** 17 1N 99 49 E
Sukhumi, U.S.S.R. **39** 43 0N 41 0 E
Sukkur, Pakistan **48** 27 42N 68 54 E
Sukkur Barrage, Pakistan **48** 27 40N 68 50 E
Sukma, India **50** 18 24N 81 45 E
Sukumo, Japan **64** 32 56N 132 44 E
Sukunka →, Canada **110** 55 45N 121 15W
Sul, Canal do, Brazil **138** 0 10 S 48 30W
Sula →, U.S.S.R. **36** 49 40N 32 41 E
Sula, Kepulauan, Indonesia **57** 1 45 S 125 0 E
Sulaco →, Honduras **128** 15 2N 87 44W
Sulaiman Range, Pakistan **48** 30 30N 69 50 E
Sulak →, U.S.S.R. **39** 43 20N 47 34 E
Sulam Tsor, Israel **44** 33 4N 35 6 E
Sulawesi □, Indonesia **57** 2 0 S 120 0 E
Sulechów, Poland **32** 52 5N 15 40 E
Sulejów, Poland **32** 51 26N 19 53 E
Sulima, S. Leone **90** 6 58N 11 32W
Sulina, Romania **34** 45 10N 29 40 E
Sulingen, W. Germany **30** 52 41N 8 47 E
Sulitälma, Sweden **8** 67 17N 17 28 E
Sulitjelma, Norway **8** 67 9N 16 3 E
Sullana, Peru **136** 4 52 S 80 39W
Sullivan, Canada **106** 48 7N 77 50W
Sullivan, Ill., U.S.A. **119** 39 40N 88 40W
Sullivan, Ind., U.S.A. **119** 39 5N 87 26W
Sullivan, Mo., U.S.A. **118** 38 10N 91 10W
Sullivan Bay, Canada **110** 50 55N 126 50W
Sully, U.S.A. **118** 41 34N 92 50W
Sully-sur-Loire, France **19** 47 45N 2 20 E
Sulmona, Italy **27** 42 3N 13 55 E
Sulphur, La., U.S.A. **121** 30 13N 93 22W
Sulphur, Okla., U.S.A. **121** 34 35N 97 0W
Sulphur Pt., Canada **110** 60 56N 114 48W
Sulphur Springs, U.S.A. **121** 33 5N 95 36W
Sulphur Springs Draw →, U.S.A. **121** 32 12N 101 36W
Sulsul, Ethiopia **98** 5 5N 44 50 E
Sultan, Canada **104** 47 36N 82 47W
Sultan, U.S.A. **124** 47 51N 121 49W
Sultanpur, India **49** 26 18N 82 4 E
Sulu Arch., Phil. **57** 6 0N 121 0 E
Sulu Sea, E. Indies **57** 8 0N 120 0 E
Sululta, Ethiopia **89** 9 10N 38 43 E
Suluq, Libya **86** 31 44N 20 14 E
Sulzbach, W. Germany **31** 49 18N 7 4 E
Sulzbach-Rosenberg, W. Germany **31** 49 30N 11 46 E
Sulzberger Ice Shelf, Antarctica **143** 78 0 S 150 0 E
Sumalata, Indonesia **57** 1 0N 122 31 E
Sumampa, Argentina **140** 29 25 S 63 29W
Sumatera □, Indonesia **56** 0 40N 100 20 E
Sumatra = Sumatera □, Indonesia **56** 0 40N 100 20 E
Sumatra, U.S.A. **122** 46 38N 107 31W
Sumba, Indonesia **57** 9 45 S 119 35 E
Sumba, Selat, Indonesia **57** 9 0 S 118 40 E
Sumbawa, Indonesia **56** 8 26 S 117 30 E
Sumbawa Besar, Indonesia **56** 8 30 S 117 26 E
Sumbawanga □, Tanzania **92** 8 0 S 31 30 E
Sumbe, Angola **95** 11 10 S 13 48 E
Sumburgh Hd., U.K. **14** 59 52N 1 17W
Sumdo, India **49** 35 6N 78 41 E
Sumé, Brazil **138** 7 39 S 36 55W
Sumedang, Indonesia **57** 6 52 S 107 55 E
Šumen, Bulgaria **34** 43 18N 26 55 E
Sumenep, Indonesia **57** 7 1 S 113 52 E
Sumgait, U.S.S.R. **39** 40 34N 49 38 E
Sumisu-Jima, Japan **65** 31 27N 140 3 E
Summer L., U.S.A. **122** 42 50N 120 50W
Summerland, Canada **110** 49 32N 119 41W
Summerside, Canada **105** 46 24N 63 47W
Summerville, Ga., U.S.A. **115** 34 30N 85 20W
Summerville, S.C., U.S.A. **115** 33 2N 80 11W
Summit Lake, Canada **110** 54 20N 122 40W
Summit Pk., U.S.A. **123** 37 20N 106 48W
Sumner, N.Z. **81** 43 35 S 172 48 E
Sumner, Ill., U.S.A. **119** 38 42N 87 53W
Sumner, Iowa, U.S.A. **118** 42 49N 92 7W
Sumner, Wash., U.S.A. **124** 47 12N 122 14W
Sumner L., N.Z. **81** 42 42 S 172 15 E
Sumoto, Japan **64** 34 21N 134 54 E
Sumprabum, Burma **52** 26 33N 97 36 E
Sumter, U.S.A. **115** 33 55N 80 22W
Sumy, U.S.S.R. **36** 50 57N 34 50 E
Sun City, Ariz., U.S.A. **123** 33 41N 112 16W
Sun City, Calif., U.S.A. **125** 33 41N 117 11W
Sun Prairie, U.S.A. **118** 43 11N 89 13W
Sunart, L., U.K. **14** 56 42N 5 43W
Sunburst, U.S.A. **122** 48 56N 111 59W
Sunbury, Australia **74** 37 35 S 144 44 E
Sunbury, U.S.A. **117** 40 50N 76 46W
Sunchales, Argentina **140** 30 58 S 61 35W
Suncho Corral, Argentina **140** 27 55 S 63 27W
Sunchon, S. Korea **61** 34 52N 127 31 E
Suncook, U.S.A. **117** 43 8N 71 27W
Sunda, Selat, Indonesia **56** 6 20 S 105 30 E
Sunda Is., Indonesia **66** 5 0 S 105 0 E
Sundance, U.S.A. **120** 44 27N 104 27W
Sundarbans, The, Asia **52** 22 0N 89 0 E
Sundargarh, India **50** 22 4N 84 5 E
Sunday I., Australia **75** 38 43 S 146 38 E
Sundays = Sondag →, S. Africa **96** 33 44 S 25 51 E
Sundbyberg, Sweden **10** 59 22N 17 58 E
Sunderland, Canada **109** 44 16N 79 4W
Sunderland, U.K. **12** 54 54N 1 22W
Sundre, Canada **110** 51 49N 114 38W
Sundridge, Canada **108** 45 45N 79 25W
Sunds, Denmark **11** 56 13N 9 1 E
Sundsjö, Sweden **10** 62 59N 15 9 E
Sundsvall, Sweden **10** 62 23N 17 17 E
Sung Hei, Vietnam **55** 10 20N 106 2 E
Sungai Kolok, Thailand **55** 6 2N 101 58 E
Sungai Lembing, Malaysia **55** 3 55N 103 3 E
Sungai Patani, Malaysia **55** 5 37N 100 30 E
Sungaigerong, Indonesia **56** 2 59 S 104 52 E
Sungailiat, Indonesia **56** 1 51 S 106 8 E
Sungaipakning, Indonesia **56** 1 19N 102 0 E
Sungaipenuh, Indonesia **56** 2 1 S 101 20 E
Sungaitiram, Indonesia **56** 0 45 S 117 8 E
Sungari = Songhua Jiang →, China **61** 47 45N 132 30 E
Sungguminasa, Indonesia **57** 5 17 S 119 30 E
Sunghua Chiang = Songhua Jiang →, China **61** 47 45N 132 30 E
Sungikai, Sudan **89** 12 20N 29 51 E
Sungurlu, Turkey **38** 40 12N 34 21 E
Sunja, Yugoslavia **27** 45 21N 16 35 E
Sunne, Sweden **10** 59 52N 13 5 E
Sunnyside, Utah, U.S.A. **122** 39 34N 110 24W
Sunnyside, Wash., U.S.A. **122** 46 24N 120 2W
Sunnyvale, U.S.A. **124** 37 23N 122 2W
Sunray, U.S.A. **121** 36 1N 101 47W
Sunshine, Australia **74** 37 48 S 144 52 E
Suntar, U.S.S.R. **41** 62 15N 117 30 E
Sunyani, Ghana **90** 7 21N 2 22W
Suō-Nada, Japan **64** 33 50N 131 30 E
Supai, U.S.A. **123** 36 14N 112 44W
Supamo →, Venezuela **135** 6 48N 61 50W
Supaul, India **49** 26 10N 86 40 E
Supe, Peru **136** 11 0 S 77 30W
Superior, Ariz., U.S.A. **123** 33 19N 111 9W
Superior, Mont., U.S.A. **122** 47 15N 114 57W
Superior, Nebr., U.S.A. **120** 40 3N 98 2W
Superior, Wis., U.S.A. **120** 46 45N 92 5W
Superior, L., N. Amer. **113** 47 40N 87 0W
Supetar, Yugoslavia **27** 43 25N 16 32 E
Suphan Buri, Thailand **54** 14 14N 100 10 E
Suphan Dağı, Turkey **46** 38 54N 42 48 E
Supriori, Kepulauan, Indonesia **57** 1 0 S 136 0 E
Suq al Jum'ah, Libya **86** 32 58N 13 12 E
Suqian, China **61** 33 54N 118 8 E
Sūr, Lebanon **44** 33 19N 35 16 E
Sūr, Oman **47** 22 34N 59 32 E
Sur, Pt., U.S.A. **124** 36 18N 121 54W
Sura →, U.S.S.R. **37** 56 6N 46 0 E
Surab, Pakistan **48** 28 25N 66 15 E
Surabaja = Surabaya, Indonesia **57** 7 17 S 112 45 E
Surabaya, Indonesia **57** 7 17 S 112 45 E
Surahammar, Sweden **10** 59 43N 16 13 E
Suraia, Romania **34** 45 40N 27 25 E
Surakarta, Indonesia **57** 7 35 S 110 48 E
Surakhany, U.S.S.R. **39** 40 25N 50 1 E
Surandai, India **51** 8 58N 77 26 E
Surat, Australia **77** 27 10 S 149 6 E
Surat, India **50** 21 12N 72 55 E
Surat Thani, Thailand **55** 9 6N 99 20 E
Suratgarh, India **48** 29 18N 73 55 E
Surazh, Byelorussian S.S.R., U.S.S.R. **36** 55 25N 30 44 E
Surazh, R.S.F.S.R., U.S.S.R. **36** 53 5N 32 27 E
Surduc Pasul, Romania **34** 45 21N 23 23 E
Surdulica, Yugoslavia **33** 42 41N 22 11 E
Sûre = Sauer →, W. Germany **17** 49 44N 6 31 E
Surendranagar, India **48** 22 45N 71 40 E
Surf, U.S.A. **125** 34 41N 120 36W
Surfers Paradise, Australia **77** 28 0 S 153 25 E
Surgères, France **20** 46 7N 0 47W
Surgut, U.S.S.R. **40** 61 14N 73 20 E
Surhuisterveen, Neths. **16** 53 11N 6 10 E
Suriapet, India **50** 17 10N 79 40 E
Şūrīf, Jordan **44** 31 40N 35 4 E
Surigao, Phil. **57** 9 47N 125 29 E
Surin, Thailand **54** 14 50N 103 34 E
Surin Nua, Ko, Thailand **55** 9 30N 97 55 E
Surinam ■, S. Amer. **135** 4 0N 56 0W
Suriname □, Surinam **135** 5 30N 55 0W
Suriname →, Surinam **135** 5 50N 55 15W
Surmene, Turkey **39** 41 0N 40 1 E
Surovikino, U.S.S.R. **39** 48 32N 42 55 E
Surprise, L., Canada **106** 49 20N 74 55W
Surprise L., Canada **110** 59 40N 133 15W
Surrey □, U.K. **13** 51 16N 0 30W
Sursee, Switz. **31** 47 11N 8 6 E
Sursk, U.S.S.R. **37** 53 3N 45 40 E
Surt, Libya **86** 31 11N 16 39 E
Surt, Al Hammadah al, Libya **86** 30 0N 17 50 E
Surt, Khalīj, Libya **86** 31 40N 18 30 E
Surtsey, Iceland **8** 63 20N 20 30W
Surubim, Brazil **138** 7 50 S 35 45W
Surud Ad, Somali Rep. **98** 10 42N 47 9 E
Suruga-Wan, Japan **65** 34 45N 138 30 E
Surumu →, Brazil **135** 3 22N 60 19W
Susa, Italy **26** 45 8N 7 3 E
Suså →, Denmark **11** 55 20N 11 42 E
Sušac, Yugoslavia **27** 42 46N 16 30 E
Susak, Yugoslavia **27** 44 30N 14 18 E
Susaki, Japan **64** 33 22N 133 17 E
Sūsangerd, Iran **46** 31 35N 48 6 E
Susanino, U.S.S.R. **41** 52 50N 140 14 E
Susanville, U.S.A. **122** 40 28N 120 40W
Susong, China **59** 30 10N 116 5 E
Susquehanna →, U.S.A. **117** 39 33N 76 5W
Susquehanna Depot, U.S.A. **117** 41 55N 75 36W
Susques, Argentina **140** 23 35 S 66 25W
Sussex, Canada **105** 45 45N 65 37W
Sussex, U.S.A. **117** 41 12N 74 38W
Sussex, E. □, U.K. **13** 51 0N 0 20 E
Sussex, W. □, U.K. **13** 51 0N 0 30W
Susteren, Neths. **17** 51 4N 5 51 E
Sustut →, Canada **110** 56 20N 127 30W
Susubona, Solomon Is. **68** 8 19 S 159 27 E
Susuman, U.S.S.R. **41** 62 47N 148 10 E
Susunu, Indonesia **57** 3 20 S 133 25 E
Sutherland, Australia **76** 34 2 S 151 4 E
Sutherland, S. Africa **96** 32 24 S 20 40 E
Sutherland, U.S.A. **120** 41 12N 101 11W
Sutherland Falls, N.Z. **81** 44 48 S 167 46 E
Sutherlin, U.S.A. **122** 43 28N 123 16W
Sutivan, Yugoslavia **27** 43 23N 16 30 E
Sutlej →, Pakistan **48** 29 23N 71 3 E
Sutter, U.S.A. **124** 39 10N 121 45W
Sutter Creek, U.S.A. **124** 38 24N 120 48W
Sutton, Australia **76** 35 10 S 149 15 E
Sutton, Ont., Canada **108** 44 18N 79 22W
Sutton, Qué., Canada **107** 45 6N 72 37W
Sutton, N.Z. **81** 45 34 S 170 8 E
Sutton, U.S.A. **120** 40 40N 97 50W
Sutton →, Canada **104** 55 15N 83 45W
Sutton-in-Ashfield, U.K. **12** 53 7N 1 20W
Suttor →, Australia **72** 21 36 S 147 2 E
Su'u, Solomon Is. **68** 9 11 S 160 56 E
Suva, Fiji **68** 18 6 S 178 30 E
Suva Reka, Yugoslavia **33** 42 21N 20 50 E
Suvo Rudište, Yugoslavia **33** 43 17N 20 49 E
Suvorov, U.S.S.R. **37** 54 7N 36 30 E
Suvorov Is. = Suwarrow Is., Cook Is. **67** 15 0 S 163 0W
Suwa, Japan **65** 36 2N 138 8 E
Suwa-Ko, Japan **65** 36 3N 138 5 E
Suwałki, Poland **32** 54 8N 22 59 E
Suwannaphum, Thailand **54** 15 33N 103 47 E
Suwannee →, U.S.A. **115** 29 18N 83 9W

T

Tarrington

Talamanca, Cordillera de, Cent. Amer. 128 9 20N 83 20W
Talara, Peru 136 4 38 S 81 18W
Talas, U.S.S.R. 40 42 30N 72 13 E
Talasea, Papua N. G. 69 5 20 S 150 2 E
Talata Mafara, Nigeria 91 12 38N 6 4 E
Talaud, Kepulauan, Indonesia 57 4 30N 127 10 E
Talavera de la Reina, Spain 22 39 55N 4 46W
Talawana, Australia 78 22 51 S 121 9 E
Talawgyi, Burma 52 25 4N 97 19 E
Talayan, Phil. 57 6 52N 124 24 E
Talbert, Sillon de, France 18 48 53N 3 5W
Talbingo Dam, Australia 76 35 40 S 148 20 E
Talbor, Australia 74 37 10 S 143 44 E
Talbot, C., Australia 78 13 48 S 126 43 E
Talbragar →, Australia 76 32 12 S 148 37 E
Talca, Chile 140 35 28 S 71 40W
Talca □, Chile 140 35 20 S 71 46W
Talcahuano, Chile 140 36 40 S 73 10W
Talcher, India 50 21 0N 85 18 E
Talcho, Niger 91 14 44N 3 28 E
Taldy Kurgan, U.S.S.R. 40 45 10N 78 45 E
Ṭalesh, Kūhhā-ye, Iran 46 39 0N 48 30 E
Talfīt, Jordan 44 32 5N 35 17 E
Talguharai, Sudan 88 18 19N 35 56 E
Tali Post, Sudan 89 5 55N 30 44 E
Taliabu, Indonesia 57 1 45 S 125 0 E
Talibon, Phil. 57 10 9N 124 20 E
Talibong, Ko, Thailand 55 7 15N 99 23 E
Talihina, U.S.A. 121 34 45N 95 1W
Talikota, India 51 16 29N 76 17 E
Taliwang, Indonesia 56 8 50 S 116 55 E
Talkeetna, U.S.A. 102 62 20N 150 9W
Tall, Jordan 44 33 0N 35 6 E
Tall 'Afar, Iraq 46 36 22N 42 27 E
Tall 'Asūr, Jordan 44 31 59N 35 17 E
Talla, Egypt 88 28 5N 30 43 E
Talladega, U.S.A. 115 33 28N 86 2W
Tallahassee, U.S.A. 115 30 25N 84 15W
Tallangatta, Australia 75 36 15 S 147 19 E
Tallarook, Australia 74 37 5 S 145 6 E
Tallawang, Australia 77 32 12 S 149 28 E
Tällberg, Sweden 10 60 51N 15 2 E
Tallering Pk., Australia 79 28 6 S 115 37 E
Tallinn, U.S.S.R. 36 59 22N 24 48 E
Tallulah, U.S.A. 121 32 25N 91 12W
Ṭallūzā, Jordan 44 32 17N 35 18 E
Talmalmo, Australia 76 35 55 S 147 29 E
Talmest, Morocco 84 31 48N 9 21W
Talmont, France 20 46 27N 1 37W
Talnoye, U.S.S.R. 38 48 50N 30 44 E
Taloda, India 50 21 34N 74 11 E
Talodi, Sudan 89 10 35N 30 22 E
Talovaya, U.S.S.R. 37 51 6N 40 45 E
Talpa de Allende, Mexico 126 20 23N 104 51W
Talsi, U.S.S.R. 36 57 10N 22 30 E
Talsinnt, Morocco 85 32 33N 3 27W
Taltal, Chile 140 25 23 S 70 33W
Taltson →, Canada 110 61 24N 112 46W
Talwood, Australia 77 28 29 S 149 29 E
Talyawalka Cr. →, Australia 73 32 28 S 142 22 E
Tam Chau, Vietnam 55 10 48N 105 12 E
Tam Ky, Vietnam 54 15 34N 108 29 E
Tam Quan, Vietnam 54 14 35N 109 3 E
Tama, U.S.A. 118 41 56N 92 37W
Tamala, Australia 79 26 42 S 113 47 E
Tamalameque, Colombia 134 8 52N 73 49W
Tamale, Ghana 91 9 22N 0 50W
Taman, U.S.S.R. 38 45 14N 36 41 E
Tamana, Japan 64 32 58N 130 32 E
Tamanar, Morocco 84 31 1N 9 46W
Tamano, Japan 64 34 29N 133 59 E
Tamanrasset, Algeria 85 22 50N 5 30 E
Tamanrasset, O. →, Algeria 85 22 0N 2 0 E
Tamanthi, Burma 52 25 19N 95 17 E
Tamaqua, U.S.A. 117 40 46N 75 58W
Tamar →, U.K. 13 50 33N 4 15W
Támara, Colombia 134 5 50N 72 10W
Tamarang, Australia 77 31 27 S 150 5 E
Tamarite de Litera, Spain 24 41 52N 0 25 E
Tamaroa, U.S.A. 118 38 8N 89 14W
Tamashima, Japan 64 34 32N 133 40 E
Tamaské, Niger 91 14 49N 5 43 E
Tamaulipas □, Mexico 127 24 0N 99 0W
Tamaulipas, Sierra de, Mexico 127 23 30N 98 20W
Tamazula, Mexico 126 24 55N 106 58W
Tamazunchale, Mexico 127 21 16N 98 47W
Tamba-Dabatou, Guinea 90 11 50N 10 40W
Tambacounda, Senegal 90 13 45N 13 40W
Tambar Springs, Australia 77 31 20 S 149 51 E
Tambelan, Kepulauan, Indonesia 56 1 0N 107 30 E
Tambellup, Australia 79 34 4 S 117 37 E
Tambo, Australia 72 24 54 S 146 14 E
Tambo, Peru 136 12 57 S 74 1W
Tambo →, Australia 75 37 50 S 147 50 E
Tambo →, Peru 136 10 42 S 73 47W
Tambo de Mora, Peru 136 13 30 S 76 8W
Tambobamba, Peru 136 13 54 S 72 8W
Tambohorano, Madag. 97 17 30 S 43 58 E
Tambopata →, Peru 136 13 21 S 69 36W
Tambora, Indonesia 56 8 12 S 118 5 E
Tamboritha, Mt., Australia 75 37 31 S 146 40 E
Tambov, U.S.S.R. 37 52 45N 41 28 E
Tambre →, Spain 22 42 49N 8 53W
Tambuku, Indonesia 57 7 8 S 113 40 E
Tamburâ, Sudan 89 5 40N 27 25 E
Tâmchekket, Mauritania 90 17 25N 10 40W
Tame, Colombia 134 6 28N 71 44W
Tamega →, Portugal 22 41 5N 8 21W
Tamelelt, Morocco 84 31 50N 7 32W
Tamenglong, India 52 25 0N 93 35 E
Tamerza, Tunisia 86 34 23N 7 58 E
Tamiahua, L. de, Mexico 127 21 30N 97 30W
Tamil Nadu □, India 51 11 0N 77 0 E
Tamines, Belgium 17 50 26N 4 36 E
Tamis →, Yugoslavia 34 44 51N 20 39 E
Tamluk, India 49 22 18N 87 58 E
Tammerfors = Tampere, Finland 9 61 30N 23 50 E
Tammisaari, Finland 9 60 0N 23 26 E
Ṭammūn, Jordan 44 32 18N 35 23 E
Tämnaren, Sweden 10 60 10N 17 25 E
Tamo Abu, Pegunungan, Malaysia 56 3 10N 115 0 E
Tampa, U.S.A. 115 27 57N 82 38W
Tampa B., U.S.A. 115 27 40N 82 40W
Tampere, Finland 9 61 30N 23 50 E
Tampico, Mexico 127 22 20N 97 50W
Tampico, U.S.A. 118 41 38N 89 47W
Tampin, Malaysia 55 2 28N 102 13 E
Tamri, Morocco 84 30 49N 9 50W
Tamrida = Qādib, S. Yemen 45 12 37N 53 57 E
Tamsalu, U.S.S.R. 36 59 11N 26 8 E
Tamuja →, Spain 23 39 38N 6 29W
Tamworth, Australia 77 31 7 S 150 58 E
Tamworth, Canada 109 44 29N 77 0W
Tamworth, U.K. 13 52 38N 1 41W
Tan An, Vietnam 55 10 32N 106 25 E
Tan-tan, Morocco 84 28 29N 11 1W
Tana, Norway 8 70 26N 28 14 E
Tana →, Kenya 92 2 32 S 40 31 E
Tana →, Norway 8 70 30N 28 23 E
Tana, L., Ethiopia 89 13 5N 37 30 E
Tana River, Kenya 92 2 0 S 39 30 E
Tanabe, Japan 65 33 44N 135 22 E
Tanabi, Brazil 139 20 37 S 49 37W
Tanafjorden, Norway 8 70 45N 28 25 E
Tanaga, Pta., Canary Is. 25 27 42N 18 10W
Tanagro →, Italy 29 40 35N 15 25 E
Tanahbala, Indonesia 56 0 30 S 98 30 E
Tanahgrogot, Indonesia 56 1 55 S 116 15 E
Tanahjampea, Indonesia 57 7 10 S 120 35 E
Tanahmasa, Indonesia 56 0 12 S 98 39 E
Tanahmerah, Indonesia 57 6 5 S 140 16 E
Tanami, Australia 78 19 59 S 129 43 E
Tanami Desert, Australia 78 18 50 S 132 0 E
Tanana, U.S.A. 102 65 10N 152 15W
Tanana →, U.S.A. 102 65 9N 151 55W
Tananarive = Antananarivo, Madag. 97 18 55 S 47 31 E
Tanannt, Morocco 84 31 54N 6 56W
Tánaro →, Italy 26 45 1N 8 47 E
Tanaunella, Italy 28 40 42N 9 45 E
Tanba-Sanchi, Japan 65 35 7N 135 48 E
Tancarville, France 18 49 29N 0 28 E
Tancheng, China 61 34 25N 118 20 E
Tanchŏn, N. Korea 61 40 27N 128 54 E
Tanda, Ut. P., India 49 26 33N 82 35 E
Tanda, Ut. P., India 49 28 57N 78 56 E
Tanda, Ivory C. 90 7 48N 3 10W
Tandag, Phil. 57 9 4N 126 9 E
Tandaia, Tanzania 93 9 25 S 34 15 E
Tăndărei, Romania 34 44 39N 27 40 E
Tandaué, Angola 95 16 58 S 18 5 E
Tandil, Argentina 140 37 15 S 59 6W
Tandil, Sa. del, Argentina 140 37 30 S 59 0W
Tandlianwala, Pakistan 48 31 3N 73 9 E
Tando Adam, Pakistan 48 25 45N 68 40 E
Tandou L., Australia 73 32 40 S 142 5 E
Tandsbyn, Sweden 10 63 0N 14 45 E
Tandur, India 50 19 11N 79 30 E
Tane-ga-Shima, Japan 63 30 30N 131 0 E
Taneatua, N.Z. 80 38 4 S 177 1 E
Tanen Tong Dan, Burma 54 16 30N 98 30 E
Tanezrouft, Algeria 85 23 9N 0 11 E
Tang, Koh, Cambodia 55 10 16N 103 7 E
Tang Krasang, Cambodia 54 12 34N 105 3 E
Tanga, Tanzania 92 5 5 S 39 2 E
Tanga □, Tanzania 92 5 20 S 38 0 E
Tanga Is., Papua N. G. 69 3 20 S 153 15 E
Tangail, Bangla. 52 24 15N 89 55 E
Tanganyika, L., Africa 92 6 40 S 30 0 E
Tanger, Morocco 84 35 50N 5 49W
Tangerang, Indonesia 57 6 11 S 106 37 E
Tangerhütte, E. Germany 30 52 26N 11 50 E
Tangermünde, E. Germany 30 52 32N 11 57 E
Tanggu, China 61 39 2N 117 40 E
Tanggula Shan, China 62 32 40N 92 10 E
Tanghe, China 60 32 47N 112 50 E
Tangier = Tanger, Morocco 84 35 50N 5 49W
Tangorin P.O., Australia 72 21 47 S 144 12 E
Tangshan, China 61 39 38N 118 10 E
Tangtou, China 61 35 28N 118 30 E
Tanguiéta, Benin 91 10 35N 1 21 E
Tangxi, China 59 29 3N 119 25 E
Tangyan He →, China 58 28 54N 108 19 E
Tanimbar, Kepulauan, Indonesia 57 7 30 S 131 30 E
Taninges, France 21 46 7N 6 36 E
Taniyama, Japan 64 31 31N 130 31 E
Tanjay, Phil. 57 9 30N 123 5 E
Tanjong Malim, Malaysia 55 3 42N 101 31 E
Tanjore = Thanjavur, India 51 10 48N 79 12 E
Tanjung, Indonesia 56 2 10 S 115 25 E
Tanjungbalai, Indonesia 56 2 55N 99 44 E
Tanjungbatu, Indonesia 56 2 23N 118 3 E
Tanjungkarang Telukbetung, Indonesia 56 5 20 S 105 10 E
Tanjungpandan, Indonesia 56 2 43 S 107 38 E
Tanjungpinang, Indonesia 56 1 5N 104 30 E
Tanjungpriok, Indonesia 57 6 8 S 106 55 E
Tanjungredeb, Indonesia 56 2 9N 117 29 E
Tanjungselor, Indonesia 56 2 55N 117 25 E
Tank, Pakistan 48 32 14N 70 25 E
Tanna, Vanuatu 68 19 30 S 169 20 E
Tänndalen, Sweden 10 62 33N 12 18 E
Tannis Bugt, Denmark 11 57 40N 10 15 E
Tannu-Ola, U.S.S.R. 41 51 0N 94 0 E
Tano →, Ghana 90 5 7N 2 56W
Tanout, Niger 91 14 50N 8 55 E
Tanquinho, Brazil 139 11 58 S 39 6W
Tanta, Egypt 88 30 45N 30 57 E
Tantangara Res., Australia 76 35 45 S 148 38 E
Tantoyuca, Mexico 127 21 21N 98 10W
Tantung = Dandong, China 61 40 10N 124 20 E
Tantūra = Dor, Israel 44 32 37N 34 55 E
Tanuku, India 50 16 45N 81 44 E
Tanumshede, Sweden 11 58 42N 11 20 E
Tanunda, Australia 73 34 30 S 139 0 E
Tanur, India 51 11 1N 75 52 E
Tanus, France 20 44 8N 2 19 E
Tanzania ■, Africa 92 6 0 S 34 0 E
Tanzawa-Sanchi, Japan 65 35 27N 139 0 E
Tanzilla →, Canada 110 58 8N 130 43W
Tao Ko, Thailand 55 10 5N 99 52 E
Tao'an, China 61 45 22N 122 40 E
Tao'er He →, China 61 45 45N 124 5 E
Taohua Dao, China 59 29 50N 122 20 E
Taolanaro, Madag. 97 25 2 S 47 0 E
Taole, China 60 38 48N 106 40 E
Taormina, Italy 29 37 52N 15 16 E
Taos, U.S.A. 123 36 28N 105 35W
Taoudenni, Mali 84 22 40N 3 55W
Taoudrart, Adrar, Algeria 85 24 25N 2 24 E
Taounate, Morocco 84 34 25N 4 41W
Taourirt, Algeria 85 26 37N 0 20 E
Taourirt, Morocco 85 34 25N 2 53W
Taouz, Morocco 84 30 53N 4 0W
Taoyuan, China 59 28 55N 111 16 E
Taoyuan, Taiwan 59 25 0N 121 13 E
Tapa, U.S.S.R. 36 59 15N 25 50 E
Tapa Shan = Daba Shan, China 58 32 0N 109 0 E
Tapachula, Mexico 127 14 54N 92 17W
Tapah, Malaysia 55 4 12N 101 15 E
Tapajós →, Brazil 135 2 24 S 54 41W
Tapaktuan, Indonesia 56 3 15N 97 10 E
Tapanahoni →, Surinam 135 4 20N 54 25W
Tapanui, N.Z. 81 45 56 S 169 18 E
Tapauá, Brazil 137 5 40 S 64 20W
Tapauá →, Brazil 137 5 40 S 64 21W
Tapeta, Liberia 90 6 29N 8 52W
Taphan Hin, Thailand 54 16 13N 100 26 E
Tapi →, India 50 21 8N 72 41 E
Tapia, Spain 22 43 34N 6 56W
Tapini, Papua N. G. 69 8 19 S 147 0 E
Tápiószele, Hungary 33 47 25N 19 55 E
Tapiraí, Brazil 139 19 52 S 46 1W
Tapirapé →, Brazil 138 10 41 S 50 38W
Tapirapecó, Serra, Venezuela 135 1 10N 65 0W
Tapirapuã, Brazil 137 14 51 S 57 45W
Tapoeripa, Surinam 135 5 22N 56 34W
Tapolca, Hungary 33 46 53N 17 29 E
Tappahannock, U.S.A. 114 37 56N 76 50W
Tapuaenuku, Mt., N.Z. 81 42 0 S 173 39 E
Tapul Group, Phil. 57 5 35N 120 50 E
Tapun, India 52 27 35N 96 22 E
Tapurucuará, Brazil 135 0 24 S 65 2W
Taquara, Brazil 141 29 36 S 50 46W
Taquari →, Brazil 137 19 15 S 57 17W
Taquaritinga, Brazil 139 21 24 S 48 30W
Tara, Australia 77 27 17 S 150 31 E
Tara, Canada 108 44 28N 81 9W
Tara, Japan 64 33 2N 130 11 E
Tara, U.S.S.R. 40 56 55N 74 24 E
Tara, Zambia 93 16 58 S 26 45 E
Tara →, U.S.S.R. 40 56 42N 74 36 E
Tara-Dake, Japan 64 32 58N 130 6 E
Tarabagatay, Khrebet, U.S.S.R. 40 48 0N 83 0 E
Tarabuco, Bolivia 137 19 10 S 64 57W
Tarābulus, Lebanon 46 34 31N 35 50 E
Tarābulus, Libya 86 32 49N 13 7 E
Taradale, N.Z. 80 39 33 S 176 53 E
Tarago, Australia 76 35 6 S 149 39 E
Tarahouahout, Algeria 85 22 41N 5 59 E
Tarajalejo, Canary Is. 25 28 12N 14 7W
Tarakan, Indonesia 56 3 20N 117 35 E
Tarakit, Mt., Kenya 92 2 2N 35 10 E
Taralga, Australia 76 34 26 S 149 52 E
Taramakau →, N.Z. 81 42 34 S 171 8 E
Tarana, Australia 76 33 31 S 149 52 E
Taranagar, India 48 28 43N 74 50 E
Taranaki □, N.Z. 80 39 5 S 174 51 E
Tarancón, Spain 24 40 1N 3 1W
Taranga, India 48 23 56N 72 43 E
Taranga Hill, India 48 24 0N 72 40 E
Táranto, Italy 29 40 30N 17 11 E
Táranto, G. di, Italy 29 40 0N 17 15 E
Tarapacá, Colombia 134 2 56 S 69 46W
Tarapacá □, Chile 140 20 45 S 69 30W
Tarapoto, Peru 136 6 30 S 76 20W
Taraquá, Brazil 134 0 6N 68 28W
Tarare, France 21 45 54N 4 26 E
Tararua Range, N.Z. 80 40 45 S 175 25 E
Tarasag, Vanuatu 68 14 13 S 167 35 E
Tarascon, France 21 43 48N 4 39 E
Tarascon-sur-Ariège, France 20 42 50N 1 36 E
Tarashcha, U.S.S.R. 38 49 30N 30 31 E
Tarata, Peru 136 17 27 S 70 2W
Tarauacá, Brazil 136 8 6 S 70 48W
Tarauacá →, Brazil 136 6 42 S 69 48W
Taravo →, France 21 41 42N 8 49 E
Tarawera, N.Z. 80 39 2 S 176 36 E
Tarawera L., N.Z. 80 38 13 S 176 27 E
Tarawera Mt., N.Z. 80 38 14 S 176 32 E
Tarazona, Spain 24 41 55N 1 43W
Tarazona de la Mancha, Spain 25 39 16N 1 55W
Tarbat Ness, U.K. 14 57 52N 3 48W
Tarbela Dam, Pakistan 48 34 8N 72 52 E
Tarbert, Strathclyde, U.K. 14 55 55N 5 25W
Tarbert, W. Isles, U.K. 14 57 54N 6 49W
Tarbes, France 20 43 15N 0 3 E
Tarboro, U.S.A. 115 35 55N 77 30W
Tarbrax, Australia 72 21 7 S 142 26 E
Tarbū, Libya 86 26 0N 15 5 E
Tarcento, Italy 27 46 12N 13 12 E
Tarcoola, Australia 73 30 44 S 134 36 E
Tarcoon, Australia 73 30 15 S 146 43 E
Tarcutta, Australia 76 35 16 S 147 44 E
Tardets-Sorholus, France 20 43 8N 0 52W
Tardoire →, France 20 45 52N 0 14 E
Taree, Australia 77 31 50 S 152 30 E
Tarentaise, France 21 45 30N 6 35 E
Tarf, Ras, Morocco 84 35 40N 5 11W
Tarfa, Wadi el →, Egypt 88 28 25N 30 50 E
Tarfaya, Morocco 84 27 55N 12 55W
Targon, France 20 44 44N 0 16W
Targuist, Morocco 84 34 59N 4 14W
Tarhbalt, Morocco 84 30 39N 5 20W
Tarhit, Algeria 85 30 58N 2 0W
Tarhūnah, Libya 86 32 27N 13 36 E
Tari, Papua N. G. 69 5 54 S 142 59 E
Táriba, Venezuela 134 7 49N 72 13W
Tarifa, Spain 23 36 1N 5 36W
Tarija, Bolivia 140 21 30 S 64 40W
Tarija □, Bolivia 140 21 30 S 63 30W
Tariku →, Indonesia 57 2 55 S 138 26 E
Tarim →, China 62 39 30N 88 30 E
Tarim Basin = Tarim Pendi, China 62 40 0N 84 0 E
Tarim Pendi, China 62 40 0N 84 0 E
Tarime □, Tanzania 92 1 15 S 34 0 E
Taritatu →, Indonesia 57 2 54 S 138 27 E
Tarka →, S. Africa 96 32 10 S 26 0 E
Tarkastad, S. Africa 96 32 0 S 26 16 E
Tarkhankut, Mys, U.S.S.R. 38 45 25N 32 30 E
Tarko Sale, U.S.S.R. 40 64 55N 77 50 E
Tarkwa, Ghana 90 5 20N 2 0W
Tarlac, Phil. 57 15 29N 120 35 E
Tarlton Downs, Australia 72 22 40 S 136 45 E
Tarm, Denmark 11 55 56N 8 31 E
Tarma, Peru 136 11 25 S 75 45W
Tarn □, France 20 43 49N 2 8 E
Tarn →, France 20 44 5N 1 6 E
Tarn-et-Garonne □, France 20 44 8N 1 20 E
Tarna →, Hungary 33 47 31N 19 59 E
Tarnagulla, Australia 74 36 45 S 143 49 E
Tårnby, Denmark 11 55 37N 12 36 E
Tarnobrzeg, Poland 32 50 35N 21 41 E
Tarnów, Poland 32 50 3N 21 0 E
Táro →, Italy 26 45 0N 10 15 E
Taroom, Australia 73 25 36 S 149 48 E
Taroudannt, Morocco 84 30 30N 8 52W
Tarp, W. Germany 30 54 40N 9 25 E
Tarpon Springs, U.S.A. 115 28 8N 82 42W
Tarquinia, Italy 27 42 15N 11 45 E
Tarqūmiyah, Jordan 44 31 35N 35 1 E
Tarragona, Spain 24 41 5N 1 17 E
Tarragona □, Spain 24 41 0N 1 0 E
Tarrasa, Spain 24 41 34N 2 1 E
Tárrega, Spain 24 41 39N 1 9 E
Tarrington, Australia 74 37 46 S 142 7 E

Tarrytown

Tarrytown, *U.S.A.* 117 41 5N 73 52W
Tarshiha = Me'ona, *Israel* 44 33 1N 35 15 E
Tarso Emissi, *Chad* 87 21 27N 18 36 E
Tarso Ourari, *Chad* 87 21 27N 17 27 E
Tarsus, *Turkey* 46 36 58N 34 55 E
Tartagal, *Argentina* 140 22 30 S 63 50W
Tartas, *France* 20 43 50N 0 49W
Tartu, *U.S.S.R.* 36 58 20N 26 44 E
Tarţūs, *Syria* 46 34 55N 35 55 E
Tarumirim, *Brazil* 139 19 16 S 41 59W
Tarumizu, *Japan* 64 31 29N 130 42 E
Tarussa, *U.S.S.R.* 37 54 44N 37 10 E
Tarutao, Ko, *Thailand* 55 6 33N 99 40 E
Tarutung, *Indonesia* 56 2 0N 98 54 E
Tarvisio, *Italy* 27 46 31N 13 35 E
Tarz Ulli, *Libya* 86 25 32N 10 8 E
Tasahku, *Burma* 52 27 33N 97 52 E
Tasāwah, *Libya* 86 26 0N 13 30 E
Taschereau, *Canada* 106 48 40N 78 40W
Taseko →, *Canada* 110 52 8N 123 45W
Tasgaon, *India* 50 17 2N 74 39 E
Tash-Kumyr, *U.S.S.R.* 40 41 40N 72 10 E
Tashauz, *U.S.S.R.* 40 41 49N 59 58 E
Tashi Chho Dzong = Thimphu, *Bhutan* 52 27 31N 89 45 E
Tashkent, *U.S.S.R.* 40 41 20N 69 10 E
Tashtagol, *U.S.S.R.* 40 52 47N 87 53 E
Tasikmalaya, *Indonesia* 57 7 18 S 108 12 E
Tåsjön, *Sweden* 8 64 15N 16 0 E
Taskan, *U.S.S.R.* 41 62 59N 150 20 E
Taskopru, *Turkey* 38 41 30N 34 15 E
Tasman →, *N.Z.* 81 43 48 S 170 8 E
Tasman, Mt., *N.Z.* 81 43 34 S 170 12 E
Tasman B., *N.Z.* 81 40 59 S 173 25 E
Tasman Mts., *N.Z.* 81 41 3 S 172 25 E
Tasman Pen., *Australia* 72 43 10 S 148 0 E
Tasman Sea, *Pac. Oc.* 66 36 0 S 160 0 E
Tasmania □, *Australia* 72 42 0 S 146 30 E
Tăşnad, *Romania* 34 47 30N 22 33 E
Tassil Tin-Rerhoh, *Algeria* 85 20 5N 3 55 E
Tassili n-Ajjer, *Algeria* 85 25 47N 8 1 E
Tassili-Oua-n-Ahaggar, *Algeria* 85 20 41N 5 30 E
Tasu Sd., *Canada* 110 52 47N 132 2W
Tata, *Morocco* 84 29 46N 7 56W
Tatabánya, *Hungary* 33 47 32N 18 25 E
Tatahouine, *Tunisia* 86 32 57N 10 29 E
Tatar A.S.S.R. □, *U.S.S.R.* 40 55 30N 51 30 E
Tatarbunary, *U.S.S.R.* 38 45 50N 29 39 E
Tatarsk, *U.S.S.R.* 40 55 14N 76 0 E
Tatebayashi, *Japan* 65 36 15N 139 32 E
Tateshina-Yama, *Japan* 65 36 8N 138 11 E
Tateyama, *Japan* 65 35 0N 139 50 E
Tatham, *Australia* 77 28 56 S 153 9 E
Tathlina L., *Canada* 110 60 33N 117 39W
Tathra, *Australia* 75 36 44 S 149 59 E
Tatinnai L., *Canada* 111 60 55N 97 40W
Tatnam, C., *Canada* 111 57 16N 91 0W
Tatong, *Australia* 75 36 43 S 146 9 E
Tatra = Tatry, *Czech.* 32 49 20N 20 0 E
Tatry, *Czech.* 32 49 20N 20 0 E
Tatsuno, *Japan* 64 34 52N 134 33 E
Tatta, *Pakistan* 48 24 42N 67 55 E
Tatuí, *Brazil* 141 23 25 S 47 53W
Tatum, *U.S.A.* 121 33 16N 103 16W
Tat'ung = Datong, *China* 60 40 6N 113 18 E
Tatura, *Australia* 74 36 29 S 145 16 E
Tatvan, *Turkey* 46 38 31N 42 15 E
Tau, *Amer. Samoa* 68 14 15 S 169 30W
Tauá, *Brazil* 138 6 1 S 40 26W
Taubaté, *Brazil* 141 23 0 S 45 36W
Tauberbischofsheim, *W. Germany* 31 49 37N 9 40 E
Taucha, *E. Germany* 30 51 22N 12 31 E
Taufikia, *Sudan* 89 9 24N 31 37 E
Taumarunui, *N.Z.* 80 38 53 S 175 15 E
Taumaturgo, *Brazil* 136 8 54 S 72 51W
Taung, *S. Africa* 96 27 33 S 24 47 E
Taungdwingyi, *Burma* 52 20 1N 95 40 E
Taunggyi, *Burma* 52 20 50N 97 0 E
Taungtha, *Burma* 52 21 12N 95 25 E
Taungup, *Burma* 52 18 51N 94 14 E
Taungup Pass, *Burma* 52 18 40N 94 45 E
Taunsa Barrage, *Pakistan* 48 30 42N 70 50 E
Taunton, *U.K.* 13 51 1N 3 7W
Taunton, *U.S.A.* 117 41 54N 71 6W
Taunus, *W. Germany* 31 50 15N 8 20 E
Taupo, *N.Z.* 80 38 41 S 176 7 E
Taupo, L., *N.Z.* 80 38 46 S 175 55 E
Taurage, *U.S.S.R.* 36 55 14N 22 16 E
Tauranga, *N.Z.* 80 37 42 S 176 11 E
Tauranga Harb., *N.Z.* 80 37 30 S 176 5 E
Tauri →, *Papua N. G.* 69 8 8 S 146 8 E
Taurianova, *Italy* 29 38 22N 16 1 E
Taurus Mts. = Toros Dağlari, *Turkey* 46 37 0N 35 0 E
Tauste, *Spain* 24 41 58N 1 18W
Tautira, *Tahiti* 68 17 44 S 149 9W
Tauz, *U.S.S.R.* 39 41 0N 45 40 E
Tavaar, *Somali Rep.* 98 3 6N 46 1 E
Tavda, *U.S.S.R.* 40 58 7N 65 8 E
Tavda →, *U.S.S.R.* 40 59 20N 63 28 E
Taverny, *France* 19 49 2N 2 13 E
Taveta, *Tanzania* 92 3 23 S 37 37 E
Taveuni, *Fiji* 68 16 51 S 179 58W
Tavignano →, *France* 21 42 7N 9 33 E
Tavira, *Portugal* 23 37 8N 7 40W
Tavistock, *Canada* 108 43 19N 80 50W
Tavistock, *U.K.* 13 50 33N 4 9W
Tavolara, *Italy* 28 40 55N 9 40 E
Távora →, *Portugal* 22 41 8N 7 35W
Tavoy, *Burma* 54 14 2N 98 12 E
Tavua, *Fiji* 68 17 37 S 177 5 E
Taw →, *U.K.* 13 51 4N 4 11W
Tawas City, *U.S.A.* 104 44 16N 83 31W
Tawau, *Malaysia* 56 4 20N 117 55 E
Tawitawi, *Phil.* 57 5 10N 120 0 E
Tawngche, *Burma* 52 26 34N 95 38 E
Tawonga, *Australia* 75 36 41 S 147 8 E
Tāwurgha', *Libya* 86 32 1N 15 2 E
Taxila, *Pakistan* 48 33 42N 72 52 E
Tay →, *U.K.* 14 56 37N 3 38W
Tay, Firth of, *U.K.* 14 56 25N 3 8W
Tay, L., *Australia* 79 32 55 S 120 48 E
Tay, L., *U.K.* 14 56 30N 4 10W
Tay Ninh, *Vietnam* 55 11 20N 106 5 E
Tayabamba, *Peru* 136 8 15 S 77 16W
Taylakovy, *U.S.S.R.* 40 59 13N 74 0 E
Taylor, *Canada* 110 56 13N 120 40W
Taylor, *Mich., U.S.A.* 119 42 14N 83 16W
Taylor, *Nebr., U.S.A.* 120 41 46N 99 23W
Taylor, *Pa., U.S.A.* 117 41 23N 75 43W
Taylor, *Tex., U.S.A.* 121 30 30N 97 30W
Taylor, Mt., *N.Z.* 81 43 30 S 171 20 E
Taylor Mt., *U.S.A.* 123 35 16N 107 36W
Taylors Arm, *Australia* 77 30 45 S 152 45 E
Taylorsville, *U.S.A.* 119 38 2N 85 21W
Taylorville, *U.S.A.* 118 39 32N 89 20W
Taymā, *Si. Arabia* 46 27 35N 38 45 E
Taymyr, Poluostrov, *U.S.S.R.* 41 75 0N 100 0 E
Tayport, *U.K.* 14 56 27N 2 52W
Ţayr Zibnā, *Lebanon* 44 33 14N 35 23 E
Tayshet, *U.S.S.R.* 41 55 58N 98 1 E
Tayside □, *U.K.* 14 56 25N 3 30W
Taytay, *Phil.* 57 10 45N 119 30 E
Taz →, *U.S.S.R.* 40 67 32N 78 40 E
Taza, *Morocco* 84 34 16N 4 6W
Taze, *Burma* 52 22 57N 95 24 E
Tazenakht, *Morocco* 84 30 35N 7 12W
Tazerbo, *Libya* 86 25 45N 21 0 E
Tazin L., *Canada* 111 59 44N 108 42W
Tazoult, *Algeria* 85 35 29N 6 11 E
Tazovskiy, *U.S.S.R.* 40 67 30N 78 44 E
Tbilisi, *U.S.S.R.* 39 41 43N 44 50 E
Tchad = Chad ■, *Africa* 87 15 0N 17 15 E
Tchad, L., *Chad* 87 13 30N 14 30 E
Tchaourou, *Benin* 91 8 58N 2 40 E
Tch'eng-tou = Chengdu, *China* 58 30 38N 104 2 E
Tchentlo L., *Canada* 110 55 15N 125 0W
Tchibanga, *Gabon* 94 2 45 S 11 0 E
Tchien, *Liberia* 90 5 59N 8 15W
Tchikala-Tcholohanga, *Angola* 95 12 38 S 16 3 E
Tchin Tabaraden, *Niger* 91 15 58N 5 56 E
Tchingou, Massif de, *N. Cal.* 68 20 54 S 165 0 E
Tcholliré, *Cameroon* 94 8 24N 14 10 E
Tch'ong-k'ing = Chongqing, *China* 58 29 35N 106 25 E
Tczew, *Poland* 32 54 8N 18 50 E
Te Anau, L., *N.Z.* 81 45 15 S 167 45 E
Te Araroa, *N.Z.* 80 37 39 S 178 25 E
Te Aroha, *N.Z.* 80 37 32 S 175 44 E
Te Awamutu, *N.Z.* 80 38 1 S 175 20 E
Te Kaha, *N.Z.* 80 37 44 S 177 52 E
Te Karaka, *N.Z.* 80 38 26 S 177 53 E
Te Kauwhata, *N.Z.* 80 37 25 S 175 9 E
Te Kopuru, *N.Z.* 80 36 2 S 173 56 E
Te Kuiti, *N.Z.* 80 38 20 S 175 11 E
Te Puke, *N.Z.* 80 37 46 S 176 22 E
Te Waewae B., *N.Z.* 81 46 13 S 167 33 E
Tea →, *Brazil* 134 0 30 S 65 9W
Tea Gardens, *Australia* 76 32 38 S 152 10 E
Tea Tree, *Australia* 72 22 5 S 133 22 E
Teague, *U.S.A.* 121 31 40N 96 20W
Teano, *Italy* 29 41 15N 14 1 E
Teapa, *Mexico* 127 18 35N 92 56W
Teba, *Spain* 23 36 59N 4 55W
Tebakang, *Malaysia* 56 1 6N 110 30 E
Teberda, *U.S.S.R.* 39 43 30N 41 46 E
Tébessa, *Algeria* 85 35 22N 8 8 E
Tebicuary →, *Paraguay* 140 26 36 S 58 16W
Tebingtinggi, *Indonesia* 56 3 20N 99 9 E
Tébourba, *Tunisia* 86 36 49N 9 51 E
Téboursouk, *Tunisia* 86 36 29N 9 10 E
Tebulos, *U.S.S.R.* 39 42 36N 45 17 E
Tecate, *Mexico* 126 32 34N 116 38W
Tech →, *France* 20 42 36N 3 3 E
Techiman, *Ghana* 90 7 35N 1 58W
Tecka, *Argentina* 142 43 29 S 70 48W
Tecomán, *Mexico* 126 18 55N 103 53W
Tecopa, *U.S.A.* 125 35 51N 116 14W
Tecoripa, *Mexico* 126 28 37N 109 57W
Tecuala, *Mexico* 126 22 23N 105 27W
Tecuci, *Romania* 34 45 51N 27 27 E
Tecumseh, *Canada* 108 42 19N 82 54W
Tecumseh, *U.S.A.* 119 42 1N 83 59W
Ted, *Somali Rep.* 98 4 24N 43 55 E
Teddywaddy, *Australia* 74 36 12 S 143 21 E
Tedzhen, *U.S.S.R.* 40 37 23N 60 31 E
Tee Lake, *Canada* 106 46 40N 79 0W
Tees →, *U.K.* 12 54 36N 1 25W
Teesdale, *Australia* 74 38 2 S 144 2 E
Teesside, *U.K.* 12 54 37N 1 13W
Teeswater, *Canada* 108 43 59N 81 17W
Tefé, *Brazil* 135 3 25 S 64 50W
Tefé →, *Brazil* 135 3 35 S 64 47W
Tegal, *Indonesia* 57 6 52 S 109 8 E
Tegelen, *Neths.* 17 51 20N 6 9 E
Tegernsee, *W. Germany* 31 47 43N 11 46 E
Teggiano, *Italy* 29 40 24N 15 32 E
Teghra, *India* 49 25 30N 85 34 E
Tegid, L. = Bala, L., *U.K.* 12 52 53N 3 38W
Tegina, *Nigeria* 91 10 5N 6 11 E
Tegua, *Vanuatu* 68 13 15 S 166 37 E
Tegucigalpa, *Honduras* 128 14 5N 87 14W
Tehachapi, *U.S.A.* 125 35 11N 118 29W
Tehachapi Mts., *U.S.A.* 125 35 0N 118 40W
Tehamiyam, *Sudan* 88 18 20N 36 32 E
Tehilla, *Sudan* 88 17 42N 36 6 E
Téhini, *Ivory C.* 90 9 39N 3 40W
Tehrān, *Iran* 47 35 44N 51 30 E
Tehuacán, *Mexico* 127 18 30N 97 30W
Tehuantepec, *Mexico* 127 16 21N 95 13W
Tehuantepec, G. de, *Mexico* 127 15 50N 95 0W
Tehuantepec, Istmo de, *Mexico* 127 17 0N 94 30W
Teide, *Canary Is.* 25 28 15N 16 38W
Teifi →, *U.K.* 13 52 4N 4 14W
Teign →, *U.K.* 13 50 41N 3 42W
Teignmouth, *U.K.* 13 50 33N 3 30W
Teil, Le, *France* 21 44 33N 4 40 E
Teilleul, Le, *France* 18 48 32N 0 53W
Teixeira, *Brazil* 138 7 13 S 37 15W
Teixeira Pinto, *Guinea-Biss.* 90 12 3N 16 0W
Tejo →, *Europe* 23 38 40N 9 24W
Tejon Pass, *U.S.A.* 125 34 49N 118 53W
Tekamah, *U.S.A.* 120 41 48N 96 22W
Tekapo, L., *N.Z.* 81 43 53 S 170 33 E
Tekax, *Mexico* 127 20 11N 89 18W
Tekeli, *U.S.S.R.* 40 44 50N 79 0 E
Tekeze →, *Ethiopia* 89 14 20N 35 50 E
Tekija, *Yugoslavia* 33 44 42N 22 26 E
Tekirdağ, *Turkey* 46 40 58N 27 30 E
Tekkali, *India* 50 18 37N 84 15 E
Tekoa, *U.S.A.* 122 47 19N 117 4W
Tekouiât, O. →, *Algeria* 85 22 25N 2 35 E
Tel Adashim, *Israel* 44 32 30N 35 17 E
Tel Aviv-Yafo, *Israel* 44 32 4N 34 48 E
Tel Lakhish, *Israel* 44 31 34N 34 51 E
Tel Megiddo, *Israel* 44 32 35N 35 11 E
Tel Mond, *Israel* 44 32 15N 34 56 E
Tela, *Honduras* 128 15 40N 87 28W
Télagh, *Algeria* 85 34 51N 0 32W
Telanaipura = Jambi, *Indonesia* 56 1 38 S 103 30 E
Telavi, *U.S.S.R.* 39 42 0N 45 30 E
Telde, *Canary Is.* 25 27 59N 15 25W
Telefomin, *Papua N. G.* 69 5 10 S 141 31 E
Telegraph Cr. →, *Canada* 110 58 0N 131 10W
Telegraph Point, *Australia* 77 31 20 S 152 49 E
Telekhany, *U.S.S.R.* 36 52 30N 25 46 E
Telemark fylke □, *Norway* 10 59 25N 8 30 E
Telén, *Argentina* 140 36 15 S 65 31W
Teleño, *Spain* 22 42 23N 6 22W
Teleorman →, *Romania* 34 44 15N 25 20 E
Teles Pires →, *Brazil* 137 7 21 S 58 3W
Telescope Peak, *U.S.A.* 125 36 6N 117 7W
Teletaye, *Mali* 91 16 31N 1 30 E
Telford, *U.K.* 12 52 42N 2 31W
Telfs, *Austria* 31 47 19N 11 4 E
Telgte, *W. Germany* 30 51 59N 7 46 E
Télimélé, *Guinea* 90 10 54N 13 2W
Telkwa, *Canada* 110 54 41N 127 5W
Tell City, *U.S.A.* 119 38 0N 86 44W
Tellicherry, *India* 51 11 45N 75 30 E
Tellin, *Belgium* 17 50 5N 5 13 E
Telluride, *U.S.A.* 123 37 58N 107 48W
Teloloapán, *Mexico* 127 18 21N 99 51W
Telpos Iz, *U.S.S.R.* 6 63 35N 57 30 E
Telsen, *Argentina* 142 42 30 S 66 50W
Telšiai, *U.S.S.R.* 36 55 59N 22 14 E
Teltow, *E. Germany* 30 52 24N 13 15 E
Teluk Anson, *Malaysia* 55 4 3N 101 0 E
Teluk Betung = Tanjungkarang Telukbetung, *Indonesia* 56 5 20 S 105 10 E
Teluk Intan = Teluk Anson, *Malaysia* 55 4 3N 101 0 E
Telukbutun, *Indonesia* 55 4 13N 108 12 E
Telukdalem, *Indonesia* 56 0 33N 97 50 E
Tema, *Ghana* 91 5 41N 0 0 E
Temanggung, *Indonesia* 57 7 18 S 110 10 E
Temapache, *Mexico* 127 21 4N 97 38W
Temax, *Mexico* 127 21 10N 88 50W
Temba, *S. Africa* 97 25 20 S 28 17 E
Tembe, *Zaïre* 92 0 16 S 28 14 E
Temblador, *Venezuela* 135 8 59N 62 44W
Tembleque, *Spain* 24 39 41N 3 30W
Temblor Ra., *U.S.A.* 125 35 30N 120 0W
Teme →, *U.K.* 13 52 23N 2 15W
Temecula, *U.S.A.* 125 33 26N 117 6W
Temerloh, *Malaysia* 55 3 27N 102 25 E
Temir, *U.S.S.R.* 40 49 21N 57 3 E
Temirtau, *Kazakh S.S.R., U.S.S.R.* 40 50 5N 72 56 E
Temirtau, *R.S.F.S.R., U.S.S.R.* 40 53 10N 87 30 E
Témiscaming, *Canada* 106 46 44N 79 5W
Témiscamingue, L., *Canada* 106 47 10N 79 25W
Temma, *Australia* 72 41 12 S 144 48 E
Temnikov, *U.S.S.R.* 37 54 40N 43 11 E
Temo →, *Italy* 28 40 20N 8 30 E
Temora, *Australia* 76 34 30 S 147 30 E
Temosachic, *Mexico* 126 28 58N 107 50W
Tempe, *U.S.A.* 123 33 26N 111 59W
Tempe Downs, *Australia* 78 24 22 S 132 24 E
Tempio Pausania, *Italy* 28 40 53N 9 6 E
Tempiute, *U.S.A.* 124 37 39N 115 38W
Temple, *U.S.A.* 121 31 5N 97 22W
Temple B., *Australia* 72 12 15 S 143 3 E
Templemore, *Ireland* 15 52 48N 7 50W
Templeton, *U.S.A.* 124 35 33N 120 42W
Templeton →, *Australia* 72 21 0 S 138 40 E
Templeuve, *Belgium* 17 50 39N 3 17 E
Templin, *E. Germany* 30 53 8N 13 31 E
Tempoal, *Mexico* 127 21 31N 98 23W
Temryuk, *U.S.S.R.* 38 45 15N 37 24 E
Temse, *Belgium* 17 51 7N 4 13 E
Temska →, *Yugoslavia* 33 43 17N 22 33 E
Temuco, *Chile* 142 38 45 S 72 40W
Temuka, *N.Z.* 81 44 14 S 171 17 E
Ten Boer, *Neths.* 16 53 16N 6 42 E
Tena, *Ecuador* 134 0 59 S 77 49W
Tenabo, *Mexico* 127 20 2N 90 12W
Tenaha, *U.S.A.* 121 31 57N 94 25W
Tenali, *India* 51 16 15N 80 35 E
Tenancingo, *Mexico* 127 19 0N 99 33W
Tenango, *Mexico* 127 19 7N 99 33W
Tenasserim, *Burma* 55 12 6N 99 3 E
Tenasserim □, *Burma* 54 14 0N 98 30 E
Tenay, *France* 21 45 55N 5 31 E
Tenby, *U.K.* 13 51 40N 4 42W
Tenda, Col di, *France* 21 44 7N 7 36 E
Tendaho, *Ethiopia* 89 11 48N 40 54 E
Tende, *France* 21 44 5N 7 35 E
Tendelti, *Sudan* 89 13 1N 31 55 E
Tendjedi, Adrar, *Algeria* 85 23 41N 7 32 E
Tendrara, *Morocco* 85 33 3N 1 58W
Teneida, *Egypt* 88 25 30N 29 19 E
Tenente Marques →, *Brazil* 137 11 10 S 59 56W
Ténéré, *Niger* 91 19 0N 10 30 E
Ténéré, Erg du, *Niger* 87 17 35N 10 55 E
Tenerife, *Canary Is.* 25 28 15N 16 35W
Tenerife, Pico, *Canary Is.* 25 27 43N 18 1W
Ténès, *Algeria* 85 36 31N 1 14 E
Teng Xian, *Guangxi Zhuangzu, China* 59 23 21N 110 56 E
Teng Xian, *Shandong, China* 61 35 5N 117 10 E
Tengah □, *Indonesia* 57 2 0 S 122 0 E
Tengah Kepulauan, *Indonesia* 56 7 5 S 118 15 E
Tengchong, *China* 58 25 0N 98 28 E
Tengchowfu = Penglai, *China* 61 37 48N 120 42 E
Tenggara □, *Indonesia* 57 3 0 S 122 0 E
Tenggarong, *Indonesia* 56 0 24 S 116 58 E
Tenggol, P., *Malaysia* 55 4 48N 103 41 E
Tengiz, Ozero, *U.S.S.R.* 40 50 30N 69 0 E
Tenino, *U.S.A.* 124 46 51N 122 51W
Tenkasi, *India* 51 8 55N 77 20 E
Tenke, *Shaba, Zaïre* 93 11 22 S 26 40 E
Tenke, *Shaba, Zaïre* 93 10 32 S 26 7 E
Tenkodogo, *Burkina Faso* 91 11 54N 0 19W
Tenna →, *Italy* 27 43 12N 13 47 E
Tennant Creek, *Australia* 72 19 30 S 134 15 E
Tennessee □, *U.S.A.* 113 36 0N 86 30W
Tennessee →, *U.S.A.* 114 37 4N 88 34W
Tenneville, *Belgium* 17 50 6N 5 32 E
Tennille, *U.S.A.* 115 32 58N 82 50W
Tennsift, Oued →, *Morocco* 84 32 3N 9 28W
Tennyson, *U.S.A.* 119 38 5N 87 7W
Teno, Pta. de, *Canary Is.* 25 28 21N 16 55W
Tenom, *Malaysia* 56 5 4N 115 57 E
Tenosique, *Mexico* 127 17 30N 91 24W
Tenri, *Japan* 65 34 39N 135 49 E
Tenryū, *Japan* 65 34 52N 137 49 E
Tenryū-Gawa →, *Japan* 65 35 39N 137 48 E
Tent L., *Canada* 111 62 25N 107 54W
Tenterfield, *Australia* 77 29 0 S 152 0 E
Teófilo Otoni, *Brazil* 139 17 50 S 41 30W
Teotihuacán, *Mexico* 127 19 44N 98 50W
Tepa, *Indonesia* 57 7 52 S 129 31 E
Tepalcatepec →, *Mexico* 126 18 35N 101 59W
Tepehuanes, *Mexico* 126 25 21N 105 44W
Tepequem, Serra, *Brazil* 135 3 45N 61 45W
Tepetongo, *Mexico* 126 22 28N 103 9W
Tepic, *Mexico* 126 21 30N 104 54W
Tepoca, C., *Mexico* 126 30 20N 112 25W
Tequila, *Mexico* 126 20 54N 103 47W
Ter →, *Spain* 24 42 0N 3 12 E
Ter Apel, *Neths.* 16 52 53N 7 5 E
Téra, *Niger* 91 14 0N 0 45 E
Tera →, *Spain* 22 41 54N 5 44W
Teraina, I., *Kiribati* 67 4 43N 160 25W
Téramo, *Italy* 27 42 40N 13 40 E

Ti-n-Medjerdam, O.

Terang, *Australia* **74** 38 15 S 142 55 E
Terawhiti, C., *N.Z.* **80** 41 16 S 174 38 E
Terazit, Massif de, *Niger* **87** 20 2N 8 30 E
Terborg, *Neths.* **16** 51 56N 6 22 E
Tercero →, *Argentina* **140** 32 58 S 61 47W
Terdal, *India* **50** 16 33N 75 3 E
Terebovlya, *U.S.S.R.* **36** 49 18N 25 44 E
Terek →, *U.S.S.R.* **39** 44 0N 47 30 E
Terenos, *Brazil* **137** 20 26 S 54 50W
Tereshka →, *U.S.S.R.* **37** 51 48N 46 26 E
Teresina, *Brazil* **138** 5 9 S 42 45W
Teresinha, *Brazil* **135** 0 58N 52 2W
Terewah, L., *Australia* **73** 29 52 S 147 35 E
Terges →, *Portugal* **23** 37 49N 7 41W
Tergnier, *France* **19** 49 40N 3 17 E
Terhazza, *Mali* **84** 23 38N 5 22W
Terheijden, *Neths.* **17** 51 38N 4 45 E
Teridgerie, *Australia* **76** 30 53 S 148 50 E
Teridgerie Cr. →, *Australia* **73** 30 25 S 148 50 E
Terlizzi, *Italy* **29** 41 8N 16 32 E
Terme, *Turkey* **38** 41 11N 37 0 E
Termeil, *Australia* **76** 35 30 S 150 22 E
Termez, *U.S.S.R.* **40** 37 15N 67 15 E
Términi Imerese, *Italy* **28** 37 58N 13 42 E
Términos, L. de, *Mexico* **127** 18 35N 91 30W
Térmoli, *Italy* **27** 42 0N 15 0 E
Ternate, *Indonesia* **57** 0 45N 127 25 E
Terneuzen, *Neths.* **17** 51 20N 3 50 E
Terney, *U.S.S.R.* **41** 45 3N 136 37 E
Terni, *Italy* **27** 42 34N 12 38 E
Ternitz, *Austria* **33** 47 43N 16 2 E
Ternopol, *U.S.S.R.* **36** 49 30N 25 40 E
Terowie, *Australia* **76** 32 27 S 147 52 E
Terra Bella, *U.S.A.* **125** 35 58N 119 3W
Terra Nova B., *Antarctica* **143** 74 50 S 164 40 E
Terrace, *Canada* **110** 54 30N 128 35W
Terrace Bay, *Canada* **104** 48 47N 87 5W
Terracina, *Italy* **28** 41 17N 13 12 E
Terralba, *Italy* **28** 39 42N 8 38 E
Terranova = Ólbia, *Italy* **28** 40 55N 9 30 E
Terranuova Bracciolini, *Italy* **27** 43 31N 11 35 E
Terrasini Favarotta, *Italy* **28** 38 10N 13 4 E
Terrasson-la-Villedieu, *France* **20** 45 8N 1 18 E
Terre Haute, *U.S.A.* **119** 39 28N 87 24W
Terrebonne, *Canada* **107** 45 42N 73 38W
Terrebonne B., *U.S.A.* **121** 29 15N 90 28W
Terrecht, *Mali* **85** 20 10N 0 10W
Terrell, *U.S.A.* **121** 32 44N 96 19W
Terrenceville, *Canada* **105** 47 40N 54 44W
Terrick Terrick, *Australia* **72** 24 44 S 145 5 E
Territoire de Belfort □, *France* **19** 47 40N 6 55 E
Terry, *U.S.A.* **120** 46 47N 105 20W
Terry Hie Hie, *Australia* **77** 29 47 S 150 10 E
Terschelling, *Neths.* **16** 53 25N 5 20 E
Terter →, *U.S.S.R.* **39** 40 35N 47 22 E
Teruel, *Spain* **24** 40 22N 1 8W
Teruel □, *Spain* **24** 40 48N 1 0W
Tervel, *Bulgaria* **34** 43 45N 27 28 E
Tervola, *Finland* **8** 66 6N 24 49 E
Teryaweyna L., *Australia* **73** 32 18 S 143 22 E
Tešanj, *Yugoslavia* **33** 44 38N 17 59 E
Teseney, *Ethiopia* **89** 15 5N 36 42 E
Tesha →, *U.S.S.R.* **37** 55 38N 42 9 E
Teshio, *Japan* **63** 44 53N 141 44 E
Teshio-Gawa →, *Japan* **63** 44 53N 141 45 E
Tesiyn Gol →, *Mongolia* **62** 50 40N 93 20 E
Teslin, *Canada* **102** 60 10N 132 43W
Teslin →, *Canada* **110** 61 34N 134 35W
Teslin L., *Canada* **110** 60 15N 132 57W
Tesouro, *Brazil* **137** 16 4 S 53 34W
Tessalit, *Mali* **91** 20 12N 1 0 E
Tessaoua, *Niger* **91** 13 47N 7 56 E
Tessenderlo, *Belgium* **17** 51 4N 5 5 E
Tessin, *E. Germany* **30** 54 2N 12 28 E
Tessit, *Mali* **91** 15 13N 0 18 E
Test →, *U.K.* **13** 51 7N 1 30W
Testa del Gargano, *Italy* **29** 41 50N 16 10 E
Teste, La, *France* **20** 44 37N 1 8W
Têt →, *France* **20** 42 44N 3 2 E
Tetachuck L., *Canada* **110** 53 18N 125 55W
Tetas, Pta., *Chile* **140** 23 31 S 70 38W
Tete, *Mozam.* **93** 16 13 S 33 33 E
Tete □, *Mozam.* **93** 15 15 S 32 40 E
Tetepari, I., *Solomon Is.* **68** 8 45 S 157 35 E
Teterev →, *U.S.S.R.* **36** 51 1N 30 5 E
Teteringen, *Neths.* **17** 51 37N 4 49 E
Teterow, *E. Germany* **30** 53 45N 12 34 E
Teteven, *Bulgaria* **34** 42 58N 24 17 E
Tethul →, *Canada* **110** 60 35N 112 12W
Tetiyev, *U.S.S.R.* **38** 49 22N 29 38 E
Teton →, *U.S.A.* **122** 47 58N 111 0W
Tétouan, *Morocco* **84** 35 35N 5 21W
Tetovo, *Yugoslavia* **34** 42 1N 21 2 E
Tetuán = Tétouan, *Morocco* **84** 35 35N 5 21W
Tetyushi, *U.S.S.R.* **37** 54 55N 48 49 E
Teuco →, *Argentina* **140** 25 35 S 60 11W
Teulada, *Italy* **28** 38 59N 8 47 E
Teulon, *Canada* **111** 50 23N 97 16W
Teun, *Indonesia* **57** 6 59 S 129 8 E
Teutoburger Wald, *W. Germany* **30** 52 5N 8 20 E
Tevere →, *Italy* **27** 41 44N 12 14 E
Teverya, *Israel* **44** 32 47N 35 32 E
Teviot →, *U.K.* **14** 55 21N 2 51W
Tewantin, *Australia* **73** 26 27 S 153 3 E
Tewkesbury, *U.K.* **13** 51 59N 2 8W
Texada I., *Canada* **110** 49 40N 124 25W
Texarkana, *Ark., U.S.A.* **121** 33 25N 94 0W
Texarkana, *Tex., U.S.A.* **121** 33 25N 94 3W
Texas, *Australia* **77** 28 49 S 151 9 E
Texas □, *U.S.A.* **121** 31 40N 98 30W
Texas City, *U.S.A.* **121** 29 20N 94 55W
Texel, *Neths.* **16** 53 5N 4 50 E
Texhoma, *U.S.A.* **121** 36 32N 101 47W
Texline, *U.S.A.* **121** 36 26N 103 0W
Texoma L., *U.S.A.* **121** 34 0N 96 38W
Teykovo, *U.S.S.R.* **37** 56 55N 40 30 E
Teyvareh, *Afghan.* **47** 33 30N 64 24 E
Teza →, *U.S.S.R.* **37** 56 32N 41 53 E
Tezin, *Afghan.* **48** 34 24N 69 30 E
Teziutlán, *Mexico* **127** 19 50N 97 22W
Tezpur, *India* **52** 26 40N 92 45 E
Tezzeron L., *Canada* **110** 54 43N 124 30W
Tha-anne →, *Canada* **111** 60 31N 94 37W
Tha Deua, *Laos* **54** 17 57N 102 53 E
Tha Deua, *Laos* **54** 19 26N 101 50 E
Tha Pla, *Thailand* **54** 17 48N 100 32 E
Tha Rua, *Thailand* **54** 14 34N 100 44 E
Tha Sala, *Thailand* **55** 8 40N 99 56 E
Tha Song Yang, *Thailand* **54** 17 34N 97 55 E
Thaba Nchu, *S. Africa* **96** 29 17 S 26 52 E
Thaba Putsoa, *Lesotho* **97** 29 45 S 28 0 E
Thabana Ntlenyana, *Lesotho* **97** 29 30 S 29 16 E
Thabazimbi, *S. Africa* **97** 24 40 S 27 21 E
Thabeikkyin, *Burma* **52** 22 53N 95 59 E
Thai Binh, *Vietnam* **54** 20 35N 106 1 E
Thai Hoa, *Vietnam* **54** 19 20N 105 20 E
Thai Muang, *Thailand* **55** 8 24N 98 16 E
Thai Nguyen, *Vietnam* **54** 21 35N 105 55 E
Thailand ■, *Asia* **54** 16 0N 102 0 E
Thailand, G. of, *Asia* **55** 11 30N 101 0 E
Thakhek, *Laos* **54** 17 25N 104 45 E
Thakurgaon, *Bangla.* **52** 26 2N 88 34 E
Thal, *Pakistan* **48** 33 28N 70 33 E
Thal Desert, *Pakistan* **48** 31 10N 71 30 E
Thala, *Tunisia* **86** 35 35N 8 40 E
Thalabarivat, *Cambodia* **54** 13 33N 105 57 E
Thallon, *Australia* **73** 28 39 S 148 49 E
Thalwil, *Switz.* **31** 47 17N 8 35 E
Thame →, *U.K.* **13** 51 35N 1 8W
Thames, *N.Z.* **80** 37 7 S 175 34 E
Thames →, *Canada* **108** 42 20N 82 25W
Thames →, *U.K.* **13** 51 30N 0 35 E
Thames →, *U.S.A.* **117** 41 18N 72 9W
Thames, Firth of, *N.Z.* **80** 37 0 S 175 25 E
Thamesford, *Canada* **108** 43 4N 81 0W
Thamesville, *Canada* **108** 42 33N 81 59W
Thāmit, W. →, *Libya* **86** 30 51N 16 14 E
Than Uyen, *Vietnam* **54** 22 0N 103 54 E
Thanbyuzayat, *Burma* **52** 15 58N 97 44 E
Thane, *India* **50** 19 12N 72 59 E
Thanesar, *India* **48** 30 1N 76 52 E
Thanet, I. of, *U.K.* **13** 51 21N 1 20 E
Thangoo, *Australia* **78** 18 10 S 122 22 E
Thangool, *Australia* **72** 24 38 S 150 42 E
Thanh Hoa, *Vietnam* **54** 19 48N 105 46 E
Thanh Hung, *Vietnam* **55** 9 55N 105 43 E
Thanh Pho Ho Chi Minh = Phanh Bho Ho Chi Minh, *Vietnam* **55** 10 58N 106 40 E
Thanh Thuy, *Vietnam* **54** 22 55N 104 51 E
Thanjavur, *India* **51** 10 48N 79 12 E
Thann, *France* **19** 47 48N 7 5 E
Thaon-les-Vosges, *France* **19** 48 15N 6 24 E
Thap Sakae, *Thailand* **55** 11 30N 99 37 E
Thap Than, *Thailand* **54** 15 27N 99 54 E
Thar Desert, *India* **48** 28 0N 72 0 E
Tharad, *India* **48** 24 30N 71 44 E
Thargomindah, *Australia* **73** 27 58 S 143 46 E
Tharrawaddy, *Burma* **52** 17 38N 95 48 E
Tharrawaw, *Burma* **52** 17 41N 95 28 E
Tharwa, *Australia* **76** 35 31 S 149 4 E
Thásos, *Greece* **35** 40 40N 24 40 E
That Khe, *Vietnam* **54** 22 16N 106 28 E
Thatcher, *Ariz., U.S.A.* **123** 32 54N 109 46W
Thatcher, *Colo., U.S.A.* **121** 37 38N 104 6W
Thaton, *Burma* **52** 16 55N 97 22 E
Thau, Bassin de, *France* **20** 43 23N 3 36 E
Thaungdut, *Burma* **52** 24 30N 94 40 E
Thayer, *U.S.A.* **121** 36 34N 91 34W
Thayetmyo, *Burma* **52** 19 20N 95 10 E
The Alberga →, *Australia* **73** 27 6 S 135 33 E
The Bight, *Bahamas* **129** 24 19N 75 24W
The Blue Mt., *Australia* **77** 30 50 S 151 41 E
The Dalles, *U.S.A.* **122** 45 40N 121 11W
The English Company's Is., *Australia* **72** 11 50 S 136 32 E
The Entrance, *Australia* **76** 33 21 S 151 30 E
The Frome →, *Australia* **73** 29 8 S 137 54 E
The Grenadines, Is., *W. Indies* **129** 12 40N 61 20W
The Hague = 's-Gravenhage, *Neths.* **16** 52 7N 4 17 E
The Hamilton →, *Australia* **73** 26 40 S 135 19 E
The Lynd, *Australia* **72** 19 12 S 144 20 E
The Macumba →, *Australia* **73** 27 52 S 137 12 E
The Neales →, *Australia* **73** 28 8 S 136 47 E
The Oaks, *Australia* **76** 34 3 S 150 34 E
The Officer →, *Australia* **79** 27 46 S 132 30 E
The Pas, *Canada* **111** 53 45N 101 15W
The Range, *Zambia* **93** 19 2 S 31 2 E
The Rock, *Australia* **76** 35 15 S 147 2 E
The Salt Lake, *Australia* **73** 30 6 S 142 8 E
The Stevenson →, *Australia* **73** 27 6 S 135 33 E
The Warburton →, *Australia* **73** 28 4 S 137 28 E
Thebes = Thívai, *Greece* **35** 38 19N 23 19 E
Thebes, *Egypt* **88** 25 40N 32 35 E
Thedford, *Canada* **108** 43 9N 81 51W
Thedford, *U.S.A.* **120** 41 59N 100 31W
Theebine, *Australia* **73** 25 57 S 152 34 E
Theil, Le, *France* **18** 48 16N 0 42 E
Thekulthili L., *Canada* **111** 61 3N 110 0W
Thelon →, *Canada* **111** 62 35N 104 3W
Thénezay, *France* **18** 46 44N 0 2W
Thenia, *Algeria* **85** 36 44N 3 33 E
Thenon, *France* **20** 45 9N 1 4 E
Theodore, *Australia* **72** 24 55 S 150 3 E
Thepha, *Thailand* **55** 6 52N 100 58 E
Thérain →, *France* **19** 49 15N 2 27 E
Theresa, *U.S.A.* **117** 44 13N 75 50W
Thermaïkos Kólpos, *Greece* **35** 40 15N 22 45 E
Thermopolis, *U.S.A.* **122** 43 35N 108 10W
Thermopylae P., *Greece* **35** 38 48N 22 35 E
Thessalía □, *Greece* **35** 39 30N 22 0 E
Thessalon, *Canada* **108** 46 20N 83 30W
Thessaloníki, *Greece* **35** 40 38N 22 58 E
Thessaloniki, Gulf of = Thermaïkos Kólpos, *Greece* **35** 40 15N 22 45 E
Thessaly = Thessalía □, *Greece* **35** 39 30N 22 0 E
Thetford, *U.K.* **13** 52 25N 0 44 E
Thetford Mines, *Canada* **107** 46 8N 71 18W
Theun →, *Laos* **54** 18 19N 104 0 E
Theunissen, *S. Africa* **96** 28 26 S 26 43 E
Theux, *Belgium* **17** 50 32N 5 49 E
Thevenard, *Australia* **73** 32 9 S 133 38 E
Thiámis →, *Greece* **35** 39 15N 20 6 E
Thiberville, *France* **18** 49 8N 0 27 E
Thibodaux, *U.S.A.* **121** 29 48N 90 49W
Thicket Portage, *Canada* **111** 55 19N 97 42W
Thief River Falls, *U.S.A.* **120** 48 15N 96 48W
Thiel Mts., *Antarctica* **143** 85 15 S 91 0W
Thiene, *Italy* **27** 45 42N 11 29 E
Thiérache, *France* **19** 49 51N 3 45 E
Thiers, *France* **20** 45 52N 3 33 E
Thies, *Senegal* **90** 14 50N 16 51W
Thiet, *Sudan* **89** 7 37N 28 49 E
Thika, *Kenya* **92** 1 1 S 37 5 E
Thille-Boubacar, *Senegal* **90** 16 31N 15 5W
Thillot, Le, *France* **19** 47 53N 6 46 E
Thimphu, *Bhutan* **52** 27 31N 89 45 E
þingvallavatn, *Iceland* **8** 64 11N 21 9W
Thio, *N. Cal.* **68** 21 37 S 166 14 E
Thionville, *France* **19** 49 20N 6 10 E
Thíra, *Greece* **35** 36 23N 25 27 E
Thirasía, *Greece* **35** 36 26N 25 21 E
Thirlmere, *Australia* **76** 34 11 S 150 35 E
Thirsk, *U.K.* **12** 54 15N 1 20W
Thiruvarur, *India* **51** 10 46N 79 38 E
Thisted, *Denmark* **9** 56 58N 8 40 E
Thistle I., *Australia* **73** 35 0 S 136 8 E
Thitgy, *Burma* **52** 18 15N 96 13 E
Thithia, *Fiji* **68** 17 45 S 179 18W
Thitpokpin, *Burma* **52** 19 24N 95 58 E
Thívai, *Greece* **35** 38 19N 23 19 E
Thiviers, *France* **20** 45 25N 0 54 E
Thizy, *France* **21** 46 2N 4 18 E
þjórsá →, *Iceland* **8** 63 47N 20 48W
Thlewiaza →, *Man., Canada* **111** 59 43N 100 5W
Thlewiaza →, *N.W.T., Canada* **111** 60 29N 94 40W
Thmar Puok, *Cambodia* **54** 13 57N 103 4 E
Tho Vinh, *Vietnam* **54** 19 16N 105 42 E
Thoa →, *Canada* **111** 60 31N 109 47W
Thoen, *Thailand* **54** 17 43N 99 12 E
Thoeng, *Thailand* **54** 19 41N 100 12 E
Thoissey, *France* **21** 46 12N 4 48 E
Tholdi, *Pakistan* **49** 35 5N 76 6 E
Tholen, *Neths.* **17** 51 32N 4 13 E
Thomas, *Okla., U.S.A.* **121** 35 48N 98 48W
Thomas, *W. Va., U.S.A.* **114** 39 10N 79 30W
Thomas, L., *Australia* **73** 26 4 S 137 58 E
Thomas Hill Res., *U.S.A.* **118** 39 34N 92 39W
Thomaston, *U.S.A.* **115** 32 54N 84 20W
Thomasville, *Ala., U.S.A.* **115** 31 55N 87 42W
Thomasville, *Ga., U.S.A.* **115** 30 50N 84 0W
Thomasville, *N.C., U.S.A.* **115** 35 55N 80 4W
Thommen, *Belgium* **17** 50 14N 6 5 E
Thompson, *Canada* **111** 55 45N 97 52W
Thompson, *U.S.A.* **123** 39 0N 109 50W
Thompson →, *Canada* **110** 50 15N 121 24W
Thompson →, *U.S.A.* **120** 39 46N 93 37W
Thompson Falls, *U.S.A.* **122** 47 37N 115 20W
Thompson Landing, *Canada* **111** 62 56N 110 40W
Thompson Pk., *U.S.A.* **122** 41 0N 123 3W
Thomson, *U.S.A.* **118** 41 58N 90 6W
Thomson →, *Queens., Australia* **72** 25 11 S 142 53 E
Thomson →, *Vic., Australia* **75** 36 52 S 141 4 E
Thomson's Falls = Nyahururu, *Kenya* **92** 0 2N 36 27 E
Thon Buri, *Thailand* **55** 13 43N 100 29 E
Thônes, *France* **21** 45 54N 6 18 E
Thongwa, *Burma* **52** 16 45N 96 33 E
Thonon-les-Bains, *France* **21** 46 22N 6 29 E
Thonze, *Burma* **52** 17 38N 95 47 E
Thorez, *U.S.S.R.* **39** 48 4N 38 34 E
þórisvatn, *Iceland* **8** 64 20N 18 55W
þorlákshöfn, *Iceland* **8** 63 51N 21 22W
Thornaby on Tees, *U.K.* **12** 54 36N 1 19W
Thornbury, *Canada* **108** 44 34N 80 26W
Thornbury, *N.Z.* **81** 46 17 S 168 9 E
Thornton, *U.S.A.* **118** 42 57N 93 23W
Thornton-Beresfield, *Australia* **76** 32 50 S 151 40 E
Thorntown, *U.S.A.* **119** 40 8N 86 36W
Thorold, *Canada* **108** 43 7N 79 12W
Thorpedale, *Australia* **75** 38 19 S 146 13 E
þórshöfn, *Iceland* **8** 66 12N 15 20W
Thouarcé, *France* **18** 47 17N 0 30W
Thouars, *France* **18** 46 58N 0 15W
Thouin, C., *Australia* **78** 20 20 S 118 10 E
Thousand Oaks, *U.S.A.* **125** 34 10N 118 50W
Thrakikón Pélagos, *Greece* **35** 40 30N 25 0 E
Thredbo Village, *Australia* **75** 36 31 S 148 20 E
Three Forks, *U.S.A.* **122** 45 55N 111 32W
Three Hills, *Canada* **110** 51 43N 113 15W
Three Hummock I., *Australia* **72** 40 25 S 144 55 E
Three Lakes, *U.S.A.* **120** 45 48N 89 10W
Three Oaks, *U.S.A.* **119** 41 48N 86 36W
Three Points, C., *Ghana* **90** 4 42N 2 6W
Three Rivers, *Australia* **79** 25 10 S 119 5 E
Three Rivers, *Calif., U.S.A.* **124** 36 26N 118 54W
Three Rivers, *Mich., U.S.A.* **119** 41 57N 85 38W
Three Rivers, *Tex., U.S.A.* **121** 28 30N 98 10W
Three Sisters, Mt., *U.S.A.* **122** 44 10N 121 46W
Three Sisters Is., *Solomon Is.* **68** 10 10 S 161 57 E
Throssell, L., *Australia* **79** 27 33 S 124 10 E
Throssell Ra., *Australia* **78** 22 3 S 121 43 E
Thuan Hoa, *Vietnam* **55** 8 58N 105 30 E
Thubun Lakes, *Canada* **111** 61 30N 112 0W
Thuddungra, *Australia* **76** 34 8 S 148 8 E
Thueyts, *France* **21** 44 41N 4 9 E
Thuillies, *Belgium* **17** 50 18N 4 20 E
Thuin, *Belgium* **17** 50 20N 4 17 E
Thuir, *France* **20** 42 38N 2 45 E
Thule, *Antarctica* **143** 59 27 S 27 19W
Thule, *Greenland* **144** 77 40N 69 0W
Thun, *Switz.* **31** 46 45N 7 38 E
Thundelarra, *Australia* **79** 28 53 S 117 7 E
Thunder B., *U.S.A.* **116** 45 0N 83 20W
Thunder Bay, *Canada* **104** 48 20N 89 15W
Thunersee, *Switz.* **31** 46 43N 7 39 E
Thung Song, *Thailand* **55** 8 10N 99 40 E
Thunkar, *Bhutan* **52** 27 55N 91 0 E
Thuong Tra, *Vietnam* **54** 16 2N 107 42 E
Thur →, *Switz.* **31** 47 32N 9 10 E
Thurgau □, *Switz.* **31** 47 34N 9 10 E
Thüringer Wald, *E. Germany* **30** 50 35N 11 0 E
Thurles, *Ireland* **15** 52 40N 7 53W
Thurloo Downs, *Australia* **73** 29 15 S 143 30 E
Thurn P., *Austria* **31** 47 20N 12 25 E
Thursday I., *Australia* **72** 10 30 S 142 3 E
Thurso, *Canada* **106** 45 36N 75 15W
Thurso, *U.K.* **14** 58 34N 3 31W
Thurston I., *Antarctica* **143** 72 0 S 100 0W
Thury-Harcourt, *France* **18** 48 59N 0 30W
Thutade L., *Canada* **110** 57 0N 126 55W
Thuy, Le, *Vietnam* **54** 17 14N 106 49 E
Thyborøn, *Denmark* **11** 56 42N 8 12 E
Thylungra, *Australia* **73** 26 4 S 143 28 E
Thyolo, *Malawi* **93** 16 7 S 35 5 E
Thysville = Mbanza Ngungu, *Zaïre* **95** 5 12 S 14 53 E
Ti-n-Barraouene, O. →, *Africa* **91** 18 40N 4 5 E
Ti-n-Medjerdam, O. →, *Algeria* **85** 25 45N 1 30 E

Townsend

Togtoh, *China* **60** 40 15N 111 10 E
Toi, *Japan* **65** 34 54N 138 47 E
Toinya, *Sudan* **89** 6 17N 29 46 E
Tojo, *Indonesia* **57** 1 20 S 121 15 E
Tōjō, *Japan* **64** 34 53N 133 16 E
Toka, *Guyana* **135** 3 58N 59 17W
Tokaanu, *N.Z.* **80** 38 58 S 175 46 E
Tokachi-Gawa →, *Japan* **63** 42 44N 143 42 E
Tokai, *Japan* **65** 35 2N 136 55 E
Tokaj, *Hungary* **33** 48 8N 21 27 E
Tokala, *Indonesia* **57** 1 30 S 121 40 E
Tokanui, *N.Z.* **81** 46 34 S 168 56 E
Tokar, *Sudan* **88** 18 27N 37 56 E
Tokara Kaikyō, *Japan* **63** 30 0N 130 0 E
Tokarahi, *N.Z.* **81** 44 56 S 170 39 E
Tokat, *Turkey* **46** 40 22N 36 35 E
Tokeland, *U.S.A.* **124** 46 42N 123 59W
Tokelau Is., *Pac. Oc.* **66** 9 0 S 171 45W
Toki, *Japan* **65** 35 18N 137 8 E
Tokmak, *U.S.S.R.* **40** 42 49N 75 15 E
Toko Ra., *Australia* **72** 23 5 S 138 20 E
Tokomaru Bay, *N.Z.* **80** 38 8 S 178 22 E
Tokoname, *Japan* **65** 34 53N 136 51 E
Tokoroa, *N.Z.* **80** 38 13 S 175 50 E
Tokorozawa, *Japan* **65** 35 47N 139 28 E
Toku, *Tonga* **68** 18 10 S 174 11W
Tokuji, *Japan* **64** 34 11N 131 42 E
Tokushima, *Japan* **64** 34 4N 134 34 E
Tokushima □, *Japan* **64** 34 15N 134 0 E
Tokuyama, *Japan* **64** 34 3N 131 50 E
Tōkyō, *Japan* **65** 35 45N 139 45 E
Tōkyō □, *Japan* **65** 35 40N 139 30 E
Tōkyō-Wan, *Japan* **65** 35 25N 139 47 E
Tolbukhin, *Bulgaria* **34** 43 37N 27 49 E
Toledo, *Spain* **22** 39 50N 4 2W
Toledo, *Ill., U.S.A.* **119** 39 16N 88 15W
Toledo, *Iowa, U.S.A.* **118** 42 0N 92 35W
Toledo, *Ohio, U.S.A.* **119** 41 37N 83 33W
Toledo, *Oreg., U.S.A.* **122** 44 40N 123 59W
Toledo, *Wash., U.S.A.* **122** 46 29N 122 51W
Toledo, Montes de, *Spain* **23** 39 33N 4 20W
Tolentino, *Italy* **27** 43 12N 13 17 E
Tolga, *Algeria* **85** 34 40N 5 22 E
Tolga, *Norway* **10** 62 26N 11 1 E
Toliara, *Madag.* **97** 23 21 S 43 40 E
Toliara □, *Madag.* **97** 21 0 S 45 0 E
Tolima □, *Colombia* **134** 3 45N 75 15W
Tolima, Vol., *Colombia* **134** 4 40N 75 19W
Tolitoli, *Indonesia* **57** 1 5N 120 50 E
Tolkamer, *Neths.* **16** 51 52N 6 6 E
Tollarp, *Sweden* **11** 55 55N 13 58 E
Tolleson, *U.S.A.* **123** 33 29N 112 10W
Tollhouse, *U.S.A.* **124** 37 1N 119 24W
Tolmachevo, *U.S.S.R.* **36** 58 56N 29 51 E
Tolmezzo, *Italy* **27** 46 23N 13 0 E
Tolmin, *Yugoslavia* **27** 46 11N 13 45 E
Tolo, *Zaïre* **94** 2 55 S 18 34 E
Tolo, Teluk, *Indonesia* **57** 2 20 S 122 10 E
Tolochin, *U.S.S.R.* **36** 54 25N 29 42 E
Tolono, *U.S.A.* **119** 39 59N 88 16W
Tolosa, *Spain* **24** 43 8N 2 5W
Tolox, *Spain* **23** 36 41N 4 54W
Toltén, *Chile* **142** 39 13 S 74 14W
Toluca, *Mexico* **127** 19 20N 99 40W
Tom Burke, *S. Africa* **97** 23 5 S 28 0 E
Tom Price, *Australia* **78** 22 40 S 117 48 E
Tomah, *U.S.A.* **120** 43 59N 90 30W
Tomahawk, *U.S.A.* **120** 45 28N 89 40W
Tomakomai, *Japan* **63** 42 38N 141 36 E
Tomales, *U.S.A.* **124** 38 15N 122 53W
Tomales B., *U.S.A.* **124** 38 15N 123 58W
Tomanlivi, *Fiji* **68** 17 37 S 178 1 E
Tomar, *Portugal* **23** 39 36N 8 25W
Tomás Barrón, *Bolivia* **136** 17 35 S 67 31W
Tomaszów Mazowiecki, *Poland* **32** 51 30N 19 57 E
Tomatlán, *Mexico* **126** 19 56N 105 15W
Tombador, Serra do, *Brazil* **137** 12 0 S 58 0W
Tombé, *Sudan* **89** 5 53N 31 40 E
Tombigbee →, *U.S.A.* **115** 31 4N 87 58W
Tombôco, *Angola* **95** 6 48 S 13 18 E
Tombong, *Australia* **75** 36 54 S 148 56 E
Tombouctou, *Mali* **90** 16 50N 3 0W
Tombstone, *U.S.A.* **123** 31 40N 110 4W
Tombua, *Angola* **95** 15 55 S 11 55 E
Tomé, *Chile* **140** 36 36 S 72 57W
Tomé-Açu, *Brazil* **138** 2 25 S 48 9W
Tomelilla, *Sweden* **11** 55 33N 13 58 E
Tomelloso, *Spain* **25** 39 10N 3 2W
Tomiko L., *Canada* **108** 46 32N 79 49W
Tomingley, *Australia* **76** 32 6 S 148 16 E
Tomini, *Indonesia* **57** 0 30N 120 30 E
Tomini, Teluk, *Indonesia* **57** 0 10 S 122 0 E
Tominian, *Mali* **90** 13 17N 4 35W
Tomiño, *Spain* **22** 41 59N 8 46W
Tomioka, *Japan* **65** 37 20N 141 0 E
Tomkinson Ranges, *Australia* **79** 26 11 S 129 5 E
Tommot, *U.S.S.R.* **41** 59 4N 126 20 E
Tomnavoulin, *U.K.* **14** 57 19N 3 18W
Tomnop Ta Suos, *Cambodia* **55** 11 20N 104 15 E
Tomo, *Colombia* **134** 2 38N 67 32W
Tomo, *Japan* **64** 34 23N 133 23 E
Tomo →, *Colombia* **134** 5 20N 67 48W
Tomobe, *Japan* **65** 36 20N 140 20 E
Toms Place, *U.S.A.* **124** 37 34N 118 41W
Toms River, *U.S.A.* **117** 39 59N 74 12W
Tomsk, *U.S.S.R.* **40** 56 30N 85 5 E
Tomtabacken, *Sweden* **11** 57 30N 14 30 E
Tonalá, *Mexico* **127** 16 8N 93 41W
Tonale, Passo del, *Italy* **26** 46 15N 10 34 E
Tonalea, *U.S.A.* **123** 36 17N 110 58W
Tonami, *Japan* **65** 36 40N 136 58 E
Tonantins, *Brazil* **134** 2 45 S 67 45W
Tonasket, *U.S.A.* **122** 48 45N 119 30W
Tonate, *Fr. Guiana* **135** 5 0N 52 28W
Tonawanda, *U.S.A.* **116** 43 0N 78 54W
Tonbridge, *U.K.* **13** 51 12N 0 18 E
Tondano, *Indonesia* **57** 1 35N 124 54 E
Tondela, *Portugal* **22** 40 31N 8 5W
Tønder, *Denmark* **11** 54 58N 8 50 E
Tondi, *India* **51** 9 45N 79 4 E
Tondi Kiwindi, *Niger* **91** 14 28N 2 2 E
Tondibi, *Mali* **91** 16 39N 0 14W
Tonekābon, *Iran* **47** 36 45N 51 12 E
Tong Xian, *China* **60** 39 55N 116 35 E
Tonga ■, *Pac. Oc.* **68** 19 50 S 174 30W
Tonga Trench, *Pac. Oc.* **66** 18 0 S 175 0W
Tongaat, *S. Africa* **97** 29 33 S 31 9 E
Tongala, *Australia* **74** 36 14 S 144 56 E
Tong'an, *China* **59** 24 37N 118 8 E
Tongareva, *Cook Is.* **67** 9 0 S 158 0W
Tongatapu, *Tonga* **68** 21 10 S 174 0W
Tongatapu Group, *Tonga* **68** 21 0 S 175 0W
Tongbai, *China* **59** 32 20N 113 23 E
Tongcheng, *Anhui, China* **59** 31 4N 116 56 E
Tongcheng, *Hubei, China* **59** 29 15N 113 50 E
Tongchuan, *China* **60** 35 6N 109 3 E
Tongdao, *China* **58** 26 10N 109 42 E
Tongeren, *Belgium* **17** 50 47N 5 28 E
Tonggu, *China* **59** 28 31N 114 20 E
Tongguan, *China* **60** 34 40N 110 25 E
Tonghai, *China* **58** 24 10N 102 53 E
Tonghua, *China* **61** 41 42N 125 58 E
Tongjiang, *Heilongjiang, China* **62** 47 40N 132 27 E
Tongjiang, *Sichuan, China* **58** 31 58N 107 11 E
Tongking, G. of = Tonkin, G. of, *Asia* **54** 20 0N 108 0 E
Tongliang, *China* **58** 29 50N 106 3 E
Tongliao, *China* **61** 43 38N 122 18 E
Tongling, *China* **59** 30 55N 117 48 E
Tonglu, *China* **59** 29 45N 119 37 E
Tongnan, *China* **58** 30 9N 105 50 E
Tongoa, *Vanuatu* **68** 16 54 S 168 34 E
Tongobory, *Madag.* **97** 23 32 S 44 20 E
Tongoy, *Chile* **140** 30 16 S 71 31W
Tongren, *China* **58** 27 43N 109 11 E
Tongres = Tongeren, *Belgium* **17** 50 47N 5 28 E
Tongsa Dzong, *Bhutan* **52** 27 31N 90 31 E
Tongue, *U.K.* **14** 58 29N 4 25W
Tongue →, *U.S.A.* **120** 46 24N 105 52W
Tongwei, *China* **60** 35 0N 105 5 E
Tongxin, *China* **60** 36 59N 105 58 E
Tongyu, *China* **61** 44 45N 123 4 E
Tongzi, *China* **58** 28 9N 106 49 E
Tonica, *U.S.A.* **118** 41 13N 89 4W
Tonj, *Sudan* **89** 7 20N 28 44 E
Tonk, *India* **48** 26 6N 75 54 E
Tonkawa, *U.S.A.* **121** 36 44N 97 22W
Tonkin = Bac Phan, *Vietnam* **54** 22 0N 105 0 E
Tonkin, G. of, *Asia* **54** 20 0N 108 0 E
Tonlé Sap, *Cambodia* **54** 13 0N 104 0 E
Tonnay-Charente, *France* **20** 45 56N 0 55W
Tonneins, *France* **20** 44 23N 0 19 E
Tonnerre, *France* **19** 47 51N 3 59 E
Tönning, *W. Germany* **30** 54 18N 8 57 E
Tonopah, *U.S.A.* **123** 38 4N 117 12W
Tonoshō, *Japan* **64** 34 29N 134 11 E
Tonosí, *Panama* **128** 7 20N 80 20W
Tønsberg, *Norway* **10** 59 19N 10 25 E
Tonumea, *Tonga* **68** 20 30 S 174 30W
Tonzang, *Burma* **52** 23 36N 93 42 E
Tonzi, *Burma* **52** 24 39N 94 57 E
Toobeah, *Australia* **77** 28 25 S 149 54 E
Tooele, *U.S.A.* **122** 40 30N 112 20W
Toogong, *Australia* **76** 33 19 S 148 38 E
Toolleen, *Australia* **74** 36 45 S 144 42 E
Toolondo, *Australia* **74** 36 58 S 141 58 E
Tooloom, *Australia* **77** 28 36 S 152 27 E
Tooma, *Australia* **76** 35 57 S 148 3 E
Toompine, *Australia* **73** 27 15 S 144 19 E
Toongi, *Australia* **76** 32 28 S 148 30 E
Toonpan, *Australia* **72** 19 28 S 146 48 E
Toonumbar, *Australia* **77** 28 34 S 152 46 E
Toora, *Australia* **75** 38 39 S 146 23 E
Toora-Khem, *U.S.S.R.* **41** 52 28N 96 17 E
Tooradin, *Australia* **74** 38 13 S 145 23 E
Tooraweenah, *Australia* **76** 31 26 S 148 52 E
Toowoomba, *Australia* **77** 27 32 S 151 56 E
Topalu, *Romania* **34** 44 31N 28 3 E
Topaz, *U.S.A.* **124** 38 41N 119 30W
Topeka, *U.S.A.* **120** 39 3N 95 40W
Topki, *U.S.S.R.* **40** 55 20N 85 35 E
Topl'a →, *Czech.* **32** 48 45N 21 45 E
Topley, *Canada* **110** 54 49N 126 18W
Toplica →, *Yugoslavia* **33** 43 15N 21 49 E
Toplița, *Romania* **34** 46 55N 25 20 E
Topocalma, Pta., *Chile* **140** 34 10 S 72 2W
Topock, *U.S.A.* **125** 34 46N 114 29W
Topola, *Yugoslavia* **33** 44 17N 20 41 E
Topoľčany, *Czech.* **32** 48 35N 18 12 E
Topoli, *U.S.S.R.* **39** 47 59N 51 38 E
Topolnitsa →, *Bulgaria* **34** 42 11N 24 18 E
Topolobampo, *Mexico* **126** 25 40N 109 4W
Topolovgrad, *Bulgaria* **34** 42 5N 26 20 E
Toppenish, *U.S.A.* **122** 46 27N 120 16W
Topusko, *Yugoslavia* **27** 45 18N 15 59 E
Toquepala, *Peru* **136** 17 24 S 70 25W
Torá, *Spain* **24** 41 49N 1 25 E
Tora Kit, *Sudan* **89** 11 2N 32 36 E
Toraka Vestale, *Madag.* **97** 16 20 S 43 58 E
Torata, *Peru* **136** 17 23 S 70 1W
Torbat-e Heydārīyeh, *Iran* **47** 35 15N 59 12 E
Torbat-e Jām, *Iran* **47** 35 16N 60 35 E
Torbay, *Canada* **105** 47 40N 52 42W
Torbay, *U.K.* **13** 50 26N 3 31W
Torbreck, Mt., *Australia* **74** 37 23 S 145 58 E
Tørdal, *Norway* **10** 59 10N 8 45 E
Tordesillas, *Spain* **22** 41 30N 5 0W
Tordoya, *Spain* **22** 43 6N 8 36W
Töreboda, *Sweden* **11** 58 41N 14 7 E
Torey, *U.S.S.R.* **41** 50 33N 104 50 E
Torfajökull, *Iceland* **8** 63 54N 19 0W
Torgau, *E. Germany* **30** 51 32N 13 0 E
Torgelow, *E. Germany* **30** 53 40N 13 59 E
Torhout, *Belgium* **17** 51 5N 3 7 E
Tori, *Ethiopia* **89** 7 53N 33 35 E
Torigni-sur-Vire, *France* **18** 49 3N 0 58W
Torija, *Spain* **24** 40 44N 3 2W
Torin, *Mexico* **126** 27 33N 110 15W
Toriñana, C., *Spain* **22** 43 3N 9 17W
Torino, *Italy* **26** 45 4N 7 40 E
Torit, *Sudan* **89** 4 27N 32 31 E
Torkovichi, *U.S.S.R.* **36** 58 51N 30 21 E
Tormes →, *Spain* **22** 41 18N 6 29W
Tornado Mt., *Canada* **110** 49 55N 114 40W
Torne älv →, *Sweden* **8** 65 50N 24 12 E
Torneå = Tornio, *Finland* **8** 65 50N 24 12 E
Torneträsk, *Sweden* **8** 68 24N 19 15 E
Tornio, *Finland* **8** 65 50N 24 12 E
Tornionjoki →, *Finland* **8** 65 50N 24 12 E
Tornquist, *Argentina* **140** 38 8 S 62 15W
Toro, *Spain* **22** 41 35N 5 24W
Torö, *Sweden* **11** 58 48N 17 50 E
Toro, Cerro del, *Chile* **140** 29 10 S 69 50W
Toro Pk., *U.S.A.* **125** 33 34N 116 24W
Törökszentmiklós, *Hungary* **33** 47 11N 20 27 E
Toroníos Kólpos, *Greece* **35** 40 5N 23 30 E
Toronto, *Australia* **76** 33 0 S 151 30 E
Toronto, *Canada* **108** 43 39N 79 20W
Toronto, *U.S.A.* **116** 40 27N 80 36W
Toropets, *U.S.S.R.* **36** 56 30N 31 40 E
Tororo, *Uganda* **92** 0 45N 34 12 E
Toros Dağlari, *Turkey* **46** 37 0N 35 0 E
Torotoro, *Bolivia* **137** 18 7 S 65 46W
Torowie, *Australia* **73** 33 8 S 138 55 E
Torpshammar, *Sweden* **10** 62 29N 16 20 E
Torquay, *Australia* **74** 38 20 S 144 19 E
Torquay, *Canada* **111** 49 9N 103 30W
Torquay, *U.K.* **13** 50 27N 3 31W
Torquemada, *Spain* **22** 42 2N 4 19W
Torralba de Calatrava, *Spain* **23** 39 1N 3 44W
Torrance, *U.S.A.* **125** 33 50N 118 19W
Torrão, *Portugal* **23** 38 16N 8 11W
Torre Annunziata, *Italy* **29** 40 45N 14 26 E
Tôrre de Moncorvo, *Portugal* **22** 41 12N 7 8W
Torre del Greco, *Italy* **29** 40 47N 14 22 E
Torre del Mar, *Spain* **23** 36 44N 4 6W
Torre-Pacheco, *Spain* **25** 37 44N 0 57W
Torre Pellice, *Italy* **26** 44 49N 7 13 E
Torreblanca, *Spain* **24** 40 14N 0 12 E
Torrecampo, *Spain* **23** 38 29N 4 41W
Torrecilla en Cameros, *Spain* **24** 42 15N 2 38W
Torredembarra, *Spain* **24** 41 9N 1 24 E
Torredonjimeno, *Spain* **23** 37 46N 3 57W
Torrejoncillo, *Spain* **22** 39 54N 6 28W
Torrelaguna, *Spain* **24** 40 50N 3 38W
Torrelavega, *Spain* **22** 43 20N 4 5W
Torremaggiore, *Italy* **29** 41 42N 15 17 E
Torremolinos, *Spain* **23** 36 38N 4 30W
Torrens, L., *Australia* **73** 31 0 S 137 50 E
Torrens Cr. →, *Australia* **72** 22 23 S 145 9 E
Torrens Creek, *Australia* **72** 20 48 S 145 3 E
Torrente, *Spain* **25** 39 27N 0 28W
Torrenueva, *Spain* **25** 38 38N 3 22W
Torreón, *Mexico* **126** 25 33N 103 25W
Torreperogil, *Spain* **25** 38 2N 3 17W
Torres, *Mexico* **126** 28 46N 110 47W
Torres, Is., *Vanuatu* **68** 13 15 S 166 37 E
Torres Novas, *Portugal* **23** 39 27N 8 33W
Torres Strait, *Australia* **69** 9 50 S 142 20 E
Torres Vedras, *Portugal* **23** 39 5N 9 15W
Torrevieja, *Spain* **25** 37 59N 0 42W
Torrey, *U.S.A.* **123** 38 18N 111 25W
Torridge →, *U.K.* **13** 50 51N 4 10W
Torridon, L., *U.K.* **14** 57 35N 5 50W
Torrijos, *Spain* **22** 39 59N 4 18W
Torrington, *Australia* **77** 29 19 S 151 44 E
Torrington, *Conn., U.S.A.* **117** 41 50N 73 9W
Torrington, *Wyo., U.S.A.* **120** 42 5N 104 8W
Torroella de Montgrí, *Spain* **24** 42 2N 3 8 E
Torrox, *Spain* **23** 36 46N 3 57W
Torsås, *Sweden* **11** 56 24N 16 0 E
Torsby, *Sweden* **10** 60 7N 13 0 E
Torsö, *Sweden* **11** 58 48N 13 45 E
Tortola, *Virgin Is.* **129** 18 19N 65 0W
Tórtoles de Esgueva, *Spain* **22** 41 49N 4 2W
Tortona, *Italy* **26** 44 53N 8 54 E
Tortoreto, *Italy* **27** 42 50N 13 55 E
Tortorici, *Italy* **29** 38 2N 14 48 E
Tortosa, *Spain* **24** 40 49N 0 31 E
Tortosa, C., *Spain* **24** 40 41N 0 52 E
Tortosendo, *Portugal* **22** 40 15N 7 31W
Tortue, I. de la, *Haiti* **129** 20 5N 72 57W
Tortuga, La, *Venezuela* **129** 11 0N 65 22W
Torūd, *Iran* **47** 35 25N 55 5 E
Toruń, *Poland* **32** 53 0N 18 39 E
Torup, *Denmark* **11** 57 5N 9 5 E
Torup, *Sweden* **11** 56 57N 13 5 E
Tory I., *Ireland* **15** 55 17N 8 12W
Torysa →, *Czech.* **32** 48 39N 21 21 E
Torzhok, *U.S.S.R.* **36** 57 5N 34 55 E
Tosa, *Japan* **64** 33 24N 133 23 E
Tosa-Shimizu, *Japan* **64** 32 52N 132 58 E
Tosa-Wan, *Japan* **64** 33 15N 133 30 E
Tosa-yamada, *Japan* **64** 33 36N 133 38 E
Toscana, *Italy* **26** 43 30N 11 5 E
Toscano, Arcipelago, *Italy* **26** 42 30N 10 30 E
Tosno, *U.S.S.R.* **36** 59 38N 30 46 E
Tossa, *Spain* **24** 41 43N 2 56 E
Tostado, *Argentina* **140** 29 15 S 61 50W
Tostaree, *Australia* **75** 37 44 S 148 10 E
Tostedt, *W. Germany* **30** 53 17N 9 42 E
Tostón, Pta. de, *Canary Is.* **25** 28 42N 14 2W
Tosu, *Japan* **64** 33 22N 130 31 E
Tosya, *Turkey* **46** 41 1N 34 2 E
Totana, *Spain* **25** 37 45N 1 30W
Toten, *Norway* **10** 60 37N 10 53 E
Toteng, *Botswana* **96** 20 22 S 22 58 E
Tôtes, *France* **18** 49 41N 1 3 E
Tótkomlós, *Hungary* **33** 46 24N 20 45 E
Totma, *U.S.S.R.* **37** 60 0N 42 40 E
Totnes, *U.K.* **13** 50 26N 3 41W
Totness, *Surinam* **135** 5 53N 56 19W
Totonicapán, *Guatemala* **128** 14 58N 91 12W
Totora, *Bolivia* **137** 17 42 S 65 9W
Totoya, I., *Fiji* **68** 18 57 S 179 50W
Totten Glacier, *Antarctica* **143** 66 45 S 116 10 E
Tottenham, *Australia* **76** 32 14 S 147 21 E
Tottenham, *Canada* **108** 44 1N 79 49W
Tottori, *Japan* **64** 35 30N 134 15 E
Tottori □, *Japan* **64** 35 30N 134 12 E
Touat, *Algeria* **85** 27 27N 0 30 E
Touba, *Ivory C.* **90** 8 22N 7 40W
Toubkal, Djebel, *Morocco* **84** 31 0N 8 0W
Toucy, *France* **19** 47 44N 3 15 E
Tougan, *Burkina Faso* **90** 13 11N 2 58W
Touggourt, *Algeria* **85** 33 6N 6 4 E
Tougué, *Guinea* **90** 11 25N 11 50W
Touho, *N. Cal.* **68** 20 47 S 165 14 E
Toukley, *Australia* **76** 33 14 S 151 31 E
Toukmatine, *Algeria* **85** 24 49N 7 11 E
Toul, *France* **19** 48 40N 5 53 E
Toulepleu, *Ivory C.* **90** 6 32N 8 24W
Toulon, *France* **21** 43 10N 5 55 E
Toulon, *U.S.A.* **118** 41 6N 89 52W
Toulouse, *France* **20** 43 37N 1 27 E
Toummo, *Niger* **86** 22 45N 14 8 E
Toummo Dhoba, *Niger* **86** 22 30N 14 31 E
Toumodi, *Ivory C.* **90** 6 32N 5 4W
Tounassine, Hamada, *Algeria* **84** 28 48N 5 0W
Toungoo, *Burma* **52** 19 0N 96 30 E
Touques →, *France* **18** 49 22N 0 8 E
Touquet-Paris-Plage, Le, *France* **19** 50 30N 1 36 E
Tour-du-Pin, La, *France* **21** 45 33N 5 27 E
Touraine, *France* **18** 47 20N 0 30 E
Tourane = Da Nang, *Vietnam* **54** 16 4N 108 13 E
Tourcoing, *France* **19** 50 42N 3 10 E
Tourine, *Mauritania* **84** 22 23N 11 50W
Tournai, *Belgium* **17** 50 35N 3 25 E
Tournan-en-Brie, *France* **19** 48 44N 2 46 E
Tournay, *France* **20** 43 13N 0 13 E
Tournon, *France* **21** 45 4N 4 50 E
Tournon-St.-Martin, *France* **18** 46 45N 0 58 E
Tournus, *France* **21** 46 35N 4 54 E
Touros, *Brazil* **138** 5 12 S 35 28W
Tours, *France* **18** 47 22N 0 40 E
Touside, Pic, *Chad* **87** 21 1N 16 29 E
Touwsrivier, *S. Africa* **96** 33 20 S 20 2 E
Tovar, *Venezuela* **134** 8 20N 71 46W
Tovarkovskiy, *U.S.S.R.* **37** 53 40N 38 14 E
Tovdal, *Norway* **11** 58 47N 8 10 E
Tovdalselva →, *Norway* **11** 58 15N 8 5 E
Towamba, *Australia* **75** 37 6 S 149 43 E
Towanda, *Ill., U.S.A.* **119** 40 36N 88 53W
Towanda, *N.Y., U.S.A.* **117** 41 46N 76 30W
Tower, *U.S.A.* **120** 47 49N 92 17W
Towerhill Cr. →, *Australia* **72** 22 28 S 144 35 E
Towner, *U.S.A.* **120** 48 25N 100 26W
Townsend, *U.S.A.* **122** 46 25N 111 32W

Townsend Mt.

Townsend Mt., *Australia* .... **75** 36 25 S 148 16 E
Townshend I., *Australia* **72** 22 10 S 150 31 E
Townsville, *Australia* . **72** 19 15 S 146 45 E
Towong, *Australia* .... **75** 36 8 S 147 59 E
Towson, *U.S.A.* **114** 39 26N 76 34W
Toyah, *U.S.A.* **121** 31 20N 103 48W
Toyahvale, *U.S.A.* ... **121** 30 58N 103 45W
Toyama, *Japan* ...... **65** 36 40N 137 15 E
Toyama □, *Japan* .... **65** 36 45N 137 30 E
Toyama-Wan, *Japan* .. **63** 37 0N 137 30 E
Tōyō, *Japan* .... **64** 33 26N 134 16 E
Toyohashi, *Japan* .... **65** 34 45N 137 25 E
Toyokawa, *Japan* .... **65** 34 48N 137 27 E
Toyonaka, *Japan* .... **65** 34 50N 135 28 E
Toyooka, *Japan* ...... **64** 35 35N 134 48 E
Toyota, *Japan* .... **65** 35 3N 137 7 E
Toyoura, *Japan* ...... **64** 34 6N 130 57 E
Tozeur, *Tunisia* ...... **86** 33 56N 8 8 E
Tra On, *Vietnam* ..... **55** 9 58N 105 55 E
Trabancos →, *Spain* .. **22** 41 36N 5 15W
Traben Trarbach, *W. Germany* .... **31** 49 57N 7 7 E
Trabzon, *Turkey* ..... **46** 41 0N 39 45 E
Tracadie, *Canada* **105** 47 30N 64 55W
Tracy, *Canada* **107** 46 1N 73 9W
Tracy, *Calif., U.S.A.* . **124** 37 46N 121 27W
Tracy, *Minn., U.S.A.* . **120** 44 12N 95 38W
Tradate, *Italy* .... **26** 45 43N 8 54 E
Traer, *U.S.A.* **118** 42 12N 92 28W
Trafalgar, *Australia* ... **75** 38 14 S 146 12 E
Trafalgar, C., *Spain* .. **23** 36 10N 6 2W
Trāghān, *Libya* ...... **86** 26 0N 14 30 E
Tragowel, *Australia* ... **74** 35 50 S 144 0 E
Traiguén, *Chile* ...... **142** 38 15 S 72 41W
Trail, *Canada* **110** 49 5N 117 40W
Trainor L., *Canada* ... **110** 60 24N 120 17W
Traíra →, *Brazil* ..... **134** 1 4 S 69 26W
Tralee, *Ireland* **15** 52 16N 9 42W
Tralee B., *Ireland* **15** 52 17N 9 55W
Tramore, *Ireland* **15** 52 10N 7 10W
Tran Ninh, Cao Nguyen, *Laos* ...... **54** 19 30N 103 10 E
Tranås, *Sweden* ...... **11** 58 3N 14 59 E
Trancas, *Argentina* ... **140** 26 11 S 65 20W
Tranche-sur-Mer, La, *France* **18** 46 20N 1 27W
Trancoso, *Portugal* ... **22** 40 49N 7 21W
Tranebjerg, *Denmark* . **11** 55 51N 10 36 E
Tranemo, *Sweden* .... **11** 57 30N 13 20 E
Trang, *Thailand* ...... **55** 7 33N 99 38 E
Trangahy, *Madag.* .... **97** 19 7 S 44 31 E
Trangan, *Indonesia* ... **57** 6 40 S 134 20 E
Trangie, *Australia* .... **76** 32 4 S 148 0 E
Trångsviken, *Sweden* . **10** 63 19N 14 0 E
Trani, *Italy* .... **29** 41 17N 16 24 E
Tranoroa, *Madag.* .... **97** 24 42 S 45 4 E
Tranquebar, *India* .... **51** 11 1N 79 54 E
Tranqueras, *Uruguay* . **141** 31 13 S 55 45W
Trans Nzoia □, *Kenya* **92** 1 0N 35 0 E
Transantarctic Mts., *Antarctica* .... **143** 85 0 S 170 0W
Transcaucasia = Zakavkazye, *U.S.S.R.* .... **39** 42 0N 44 0 E
Transcona, *Canada* ... **111** 49 55N 97 0W
Transilvania, *Romania* **34** 46 19N 25 0 E
Transkei □, *S. Africa* . **97** 32 15 S 28 15 E
Transtrand, *Sweden* ... **10** 61 6N 13 20 E
Transvaal □, *S. Africa* **96** 25 0 S 29 0 E
Transylvania = Transilvania, *Romania* .... **34** 46 19N 25 0 E
Transylvanian Alps, *Romania* .... **6** 45 30N 25 0 E
Trápani, *Italy* .... **28** 38 1N 12 30 E
Trapper Peak, *U.S.A.* **122** 45 56N 114 29W
Traralgon, *Australia* .. **75** 38 12 S 146 34 E
Traryd, *Sweden* ...... **11** 56 35N 13 45 E
Trarza □, *Mauritania* . **90** 17 30N 15 0W
Trás-os-Montes, *Angola* **95** 10 17 S 19 5 E
Trasacco, *Italy* .... **27** 41 58N 13 30 E
Trăscău, Munţii, *Romania* .... **34** 46 14N 23 14 E
Trasimeno, L., *Italy* .. **27** 43 10N 12 5 E
Trat, *Thailand* .... **55** 12 14N 102 33 E
Traun, *Austria* .... **33** 48 14N 14 15 E
Traunstein, *W. Germany* .... **31** 47 52N 12 40 E
Tråvad, *Sweden* ...... **11** 58 15N 13 5 E
Traveller's L., *Australia* **73** 33 20 S 142 0 E
Travemünde, *W. Germany* .... **30** 53 58N 10 52 E
Travers, Mt., *N.Z.* ... **81** 42 1 S 172 45 E
Traverse City, *U.S.A.* . **114** 44 45N 85 39W
Travnik, *Yugoslavia* .. **33** 44 17N 17 39 E
Trawalla, *Australia* ... **74** 37 25 S 143 28 E
Trayning, *Australia* ... **79** 31 7 S 117 16 E
Trazo, *Spain* **22** 43 0N 8 30W
Trbovlje, *Yugoslavia* .. **27** 46 12N 15 5 E
Treasury Is., *Solomon Is.* .... **68** 7 22 S 155 37 E
Trébbia →, *Italy* ..... **26** 45 4N 9 41 E
Trebel →, *E. Germany* **30** 53 55N 13 1 E
Trebinje, *Yugoslavia* .. **33** 42 44N 18 22 E
Trebisacce, *Italy* ...... **29** 39 52N 16 32 E
Trebišnica →, *Yugoslavia* .... **33** 42 47N 18 8 E
Trebišov, *Czech.* ..... **32** 48 38N 21 41 E
Trebižat →, *Yugoslavia* **33** 43 15N 17 30 E
Trebnje, *Yugoslavia* .. **27** 45 54N 15 1 E
Třeboň, *Czech.* ...... **32** 48 59N 14 48 E
Trebujena, *Spain* **23** 36 52N 6 11W
Trecate, *Italy* .... **26** 45 26N 8 42 E
Tredegar, *U.K.* **13** 51 47N 3 16W
Tregaron, *U.K.* **13** 52 14N 3 56W
Trégastel-Plage, *France* **18** 48 49N 3 31W
Tregnago, *Italy* .... **27** 45 31N 11 10 E
Tregrosse Is., *Australia* **72** 17 41 S 150 43 E
Tréguier, *France* **18** 48 47N 3 16W
Trégunc, *France* **18** 47 51N 3 51W
Treherne, *Canada* **111** 49 38N 98 42W
Tréia, *Italy* .... **27** 43 20N 13 20 E
Treignac, *France* ..... **20** 45 32N 1 48 E
Treinta y Tres, *Uruguay* **141** 33 16 S 54 17W
Treis, *W. Germany* ... **31** 50 9N 7 19 E
Trekveld, *S. Africa* ... **96** 30 35 S 19 45 E
Trelde Næs, *Denmark* **11** 55 38N 9 53 E
Trelew, *Argentina* .... **142** 43 10 S 65 20W
Trélissac, *France* ..... **20** 45 11N 0 47 E
Trelleborg, *Sweden* ... **11** 55 20N 13 10 E
Trélon, *France* .... **19** 50 5N 4 6 E
Tremblade, La, *France* **20** 45 46N 1 8W
Tremblant, Mt., *Canada* **106** 46 16N 74 35W
Tremiti, *Italy* .... **27** 42 8N 15 30 E
Tremonton, *U.S.A.* ... **122** 41 45N 112 10W
Tremp, *Spain* .... **24** 42 10N 0 52 E
Trenche →, *Canada* .. **107** 47 46N 72 53W
Trenčín, *Czech.* ...... **32** 48 52N 18 4 E
Trenggalek, *Indonesia* **57** 8 3 S 111 43 E
Trenque Lauquen, *Argentina* .... **140** 36 5 S 62 45W
Trent →, *Canada* **109** 44 6N 77 34W
Trent →, *U.K.* **12** 53 33N 0 44W
Trente et un Milles, L. des, *Canada* **106** 46 12N 75 49W
Trentham, *Australia* .. **74** 37 23 S 144 21 E
Trentino-Alto Adige □, *Italy* .... **26** 46 30N 11 0 E
Trento, *Italy* .... **26** 46 5N 11 8 E
Trenton, *Canada* **109** 44 10N 77 34W
Trenton, *Mich., U.S.A.* **119** 42 8N 83 11W
Trenton, *Mo., U.S.A.* **118** 40 5N 93 37W
Trenton, *N.J., U.S.A.* **117** 40 15N 74 41W
Trenton, *Nebr., U.S.A.* **120** 40 14N 101 4W
Trenton, *Tenn., U.S.A.* **121** 35 58N 88 57W
Trepassey, *Canada* ... **105** 46 43N 53 25W
Tréport, Le, *France* .. **18** 50 3N 1 20 E
Trepuzzi, *Italy* .... **29** 40 26N 18 4 E
Tres Arroyos, *Argentina* .... **140** 38 26 S 60 20W
Três Corações, *Brazil* . **141** 21 44 S 45 15W
Três Lagoas, *Brazil* ... **139** 20 50 S 51 43W
Tres Lagos →, *Argentina* .... **142** 49 35 S 71 25W
Tres Marías, *Mexico* .. **126** 21 25N 106 28W
Três Marias, Reprêsa, *Brazil* .... **139** 18 12 S 45 15W
Tres Montes, C., *Chile* **142** 46 50 S 75 30W
Tres Pinos, *U.S.A.* ... **124** 36 48N 121 19W
Três Pontas, *Brazil* ... **139** 21 23 S 45 29W
Tres Puentes, *Chile* ... **140** 27 50 S 70 15W
Tres Puntas, C., *Argentina* .... **142** 47 0 S 66 0W
Três Rios, *Brazil* ..... **139** 22 6 S 43 15W
Tres Valles, *Mexico* .. **127** 18 15N 96 8W
Treska →, *Yugoslavia* **35** 42 0N 21 20 E
Trespaderne, *Spain* ... **24** 42 47N 3 24W
Trets, *France* .... **21** 43 27N 5 41 E
Treuchtlingen, *W. Germany* .... **31** 48 58N 10 55 E
Treuenbrietzen, *E. Germany* .... **30** 52 6N 12 51 E
Treungen, *Norway* ... **9** 59 1N 8 31 E
Trêve, L. la, *Canada* . **106** 49 56N 75 30W
Treviglio, *Italy* .... **26** 45 31N 9 35 E
Trevinca, Peña, *Spain* . **22** 42 15N 6 46W
Treviso, *Italy* .... **27** 45 40N 12 15 E
Trévoux, *France* ..... **21** 45 57N 4 47 E
Treysa, *W. Germany* .. **30** 50 55N 9 12 E
Trgovište, *Yugoslavia* . **33** 42 20N 22 10 E
Triabunna, *Australia* .. **72** 42 30 S 147 55 E
Trial B., *Australia* .... **77** 30 48 S 153 2 E
Triang, *Malaysia* ..... **55** 3 15N 102 26 E
Triaucourt-en-Argonne, *France* .... **19** 48 59N 5 2 E
Tribsees, *E. Germany* . **30** 54 4N 12 46 E
Tribulation, C., *Australia* .... **72** 16 5 S 145 29 E
Tribune, *U.S.A.* **120** 38 30N 101 45W
Tricárico, *Italy* .... **29** 40 37N 16 9 E
Tricase, *Italy* .... **29** 39 56N 18 20 E
Trichinopoly = Tiruchchirappalli, *India* .... **51** 10 45N 78 45 E
Trichur, *India* .... **51** 10 30N 76 18 E
Trida, *Australia* ...... **73** 33 1 S 145 1 E
Trier, *W. Germany* ... **31** 49 45N 6 37 E
Trieste, *Italy* .... **27** 45 39N 13 45 E
Trieste, G. di, *Italy* ... **27** 45 37N 13 40 E
Trieux →, *France* **18** 48 43N 3 9W
Triggiano, *Italy* ...... **29** 41 4N 16 58 E
Triglav, *Yugoslavia* ... **27** 46 21N 13 50 E
Trigno →, *Italy* ...... **27** 42 4N 14 48 E
Trigueros, *Spain* **23** 37 24N 6 50W
Trikhonis, Límni, *Greece* .... **35** 38 34N 21 30 E
Tríkkala, *Greece* ..... **35** 39 34N 21 47 E
Trikora, Puncak, *Indonesia* .... **57** 4 15 S 138 45 E
Trilj, *Yugoslavia* ..... **27** 43 38N 16 42 E
Trillo, *Spain* **24** 40 42N 2 35W
Trim, *Ireland* **15** 53 34N 6 48W
Trincomalee, *Sri Lanka* **51** 8 38N 81 15 E
Trindade, *Brazil* ..... **139** 16 40 S 49 30W
Trindade, I., *Atl. Oc.* . **4** 20 20 S 29 50W
Tring-Jonction, *Canada* **107** 46 16N 70 59W
Trinidad, *Bolivia* ..... **137** 14 46 S 64 50W
Trinidad, *Colombia* ... **134** 5 25N 71 40W
Trinidad, *Cuba* **128** 21 48N 80 0W
Trinidad, *Uruguay* .... **140** 33 30 S 56 50W
Trinidad, *U.S.A.* **121** 37 15N 104 30W
Trinidad, *W. Indies* ... **129** 10 30N 61 15W
Trinidad →, *Mexico* .. **127** 17 49N 95 9W
Trinidad, G., *Chile* ... **142** 49 55 S 75 25W
Trinidad, I., *Argentina* **142** 39 10 S 62 0W
Trinidad & Tobago ■, *W. Indies* **129** 10 30N 61 20W
Trinitápoli, *Italy* ..... **29** 41 22N 16 5 E
Trinity, *Canada* **105** 48 59N 53 55W
Trinity, *U.S.A.* **121** 30 59N 95 25W
Trinity →, *Calif., U.S.A.* **122** 41 11N 123 42W
Trinity →, *Tex., U.S.A.* **121** 30 30N 95 0W
Trinity B., *Canada* ... **105** 48 20N 53 10W
Trinity Mts., *U.S.A.* .. **122** 40 20N 118 50W
Trinkitat, *Sudan* ...... **88** 18 45N 37 51 E
Trino, *Italy* .... **26** 45 10N 8 18 E
Trion, *U.S.A.* **115** 34 35N 85 18W
Trionto, C., *Italy* ..... **29** 39 38N 16 47 E
Triora, *Italy* .... **26** 44 0N 7 46 E
Tripoli = Tarābulus, *Lebanon* .... **46** 34 31N 35 50 E
Tripoli = Tarābulus, *Libya* .... **86** 32 49N 13 7 E
Tripoli, *U.S.A.* **118** 42 49N 92 16W
Tripp, *U.S.A.* **120** 43 16N 97 58W
Tripura □, *India* ..... **52** 24 0N 92 0 E
Trischen, *W. Germany* **30** 54 3N 8 32 E
Tristan da Cunha, *Atl. Oc.* .... **4** 37 6 S 12 20W
Trivandrum, *India* .... **51** 8 41N 77 0 E
Trivento, *Italy* .... **29** 41 48N 14 31 E
Trnava, *Czech.* .... **33** 48 23N 17 35 E
Trobriand Is., *Papua N. G.* .... **69** 8 30 S 151 0 E
Trochu, *Canada* **110** 51 50N 113 13W
Trodely I., *Canada* ... **104** 52 15N 79 26W
Trogir, *Yugoslavia* .... **27** 43 32N 16 15 E
Troglav, *Yugoslavia* .. **27** 43 56N 16 36 E
Trøgstad, *Norway* .... **10** 59 37N 11 16 E
Tróia, *Italy* .... **29** 41 22N 15 19 E
Troilus, L., *Canada* ... **104** 50 50N 74 35W
Troina, *Italy* .... **29** 37 47N 14 34 E
Trois Fourches, Cap des, *Morocco* **85** 35 26N 2 58W
Trois-Pistoles, *Canada* **107** 48 5N 69 10W
Trois-Rivières, *Canada* **107** 46 25N 72 34W
Troisvierges, *Belgium* . **17** 50 8N 6 0 E
Troitsk, *U.S.S.R.* ..... **40** 54 10N 61 35 E
Troitsko Pechorsk, *U.S.S.R.* .... **40** 62 40N 56 10 E
Trölladyngja, *Iceland* . **8** 64 54N 17 16W
Trollhättan, *Sweden* .. **11** 58 17N 12 20 E
Trollheimen, *Norway* .. **10** 62 46N 9 1 E
Trombetas →, *Brazil* . **135** 1 55 S 55 35W
Tromelin I., *Ind. Oc.* . **53** 15 52 S 54 25 E
Troms fylke □, *Norway* **8** 68 56N 19 0 E
Tromsø, *Norway* ..... **8** 69 40N 18 56 E
Trona, *U.S.A.* **125** 35 46N 117 23W
Tronador, *Argentina* .. **142** 41 10 S 71 50W
Trondheim, *Norway* .. **10** 63 36N 10 25 E
Trondheimsfjorden, *Norway* .... **8** 63 35N 10 30 E
Trönninge, *Sweden* ... **11** 56 37N 12 51 E
Trönö, *Sweden* .... **10** 61 22N 16 54 E
Tronto →, *Italy* ...... **27** 42 54N 13 55 E
Troon, *U.K.* **14** 55 33N 4 40W
Tropea, *Italy* .... **29** 38 40N 15 53 E
Tropic, *U.S.A.* **123** 37 36N 112 4W
Tropoja, *Albania* ..... **34** 42 23N 20 10 E
Trossachs, The, *U.K.* . **14** 56 14N 4 24W
Trostan, *U.K.* **15** 55 4N 6 10W
Trostberg, *W. Germany* **31** 48 2N 12 33 E
Trostyanets, *U.S.S.R.* . **36** 50 33N 34 59 E
Trotternish, *U.K.* **14** 57 32N 6 15W
Troup, *U.S.A.* **121** 32 10N 95 3W
Trout →, *Canada* **110** 61 19N 119 51W
Trout Creek, *Canada* . **108** 45 59N 79 22W
Trout L., *N.W.T., Canada* **110** 60 40N 121 14W
Trout L., *Ont., Canada* **111** 51 20N 93 15W
Trout Lake, *Mich., U.S.A.* **104** 46 10N 85 2W
Trout Lake, *Wash., U.S.A.* **124** 46 0N 121 32W
Trout River, *Canada* .. **105** 49 29N 58 8W
Trouville-sur-Mer, *France* .... **18** 49 21N 0 5 E
Trowbridge, *U.K.* **13** 51 18N 2 12W
Troy, *Turkey* .... **46** 39 57N 26 12 E
Troy, *Ala., U.S.A.* ... **115** 31 50N 85 58W
Troy, *Idaho, U.S.A.* .. **122** 46 44N 116 46W
Troy, *Ill., U.S.A.* **118** 38 44N 89 54W
Troy, *Ind., U.S.A.* ... **119** 38 0N 86 48W
Troy, *Kans., U.S.A.* .. **120** 39 47N 95 2W
Troy, *Mich., U.S.A.* .. **119** 42 37N 83 9W
Troy, *Mo., U.S.A.* ... **118** 38 56N 90 59W
Troy, *Mont., U.S.A.* .. **122** 48 30N 115 58W
Troy, *N.Y., U.S.A.* ... **117** 42 45N 73 39W
Troy, *Ohio, U.S.A.* ... **119** 40 0N 84 10W
Troyan, *Bulgaria* ..... **34** 42 57N 24 43 E
Troyes, *France* .... **19** 48 19N 4 3 E
Trpanj, *Yugoslavia* ... **33** 43 1N 17 15 E
Trstena, *Czech.* ...... **32** 49 21N 19 37 E
Trstenik, *Yugoslavia* .. **33** 43 36N 21 0 E
Trubchevsk, *U.S.S.R.* . **36** 52 33N 33 47 E
Trucial States = United Arab Emirates ■, *Asia* .... **47** 23 50N 54 0 E
Truckee, *U.S.A.* **124** 39 20N 120 11W
Truite, L. à la, *Canada* **106** 47 20N 78 20W
Trujillo, *Colombia* **134** 4 10N 76 19W
Trujillo, *Honduras* ... **128** 16 0N 86 0W
Trujillo, *Peru* .... **136** 8 6 S 79 0W
Trujillo, *Spain* **23** 39 28N 5 55W
Trujillo, *U.S.A.* **121** 35 34N 104 44W
Trujillo, *Venezuela* ... **134** 9 22N 70 38W
Trujillo □, *Venezuela* . **134** 9 25N 70 30W
Truk, *Pac. Oc.* .... **66** 7 25N 151 46 E
Trumann, *U.S.A.* **121** 35 42N 90 32W
Trumbull, Mt., *U.S.A.* **123** 36 25N 113 8W
Trun, *France* .... **18** 48 50N 0 2 E
Trundle, *Australia* .... **76** 32 53 S 147 35 E
Trung-Phan, *Vietnam* . **54** 16 0N 108 0 E
Truro, *Canada* **105** 45 21N 63 14W
Truro, *U.K.* **13** 50 17N 5 2W
Truslove, *Australia* ... **79** 33 20 S 121 45 E
Trustrup, *Denmark* ... **11** 56 20N 10 46 E
Truth or Consequences, *U.S.A.* **123** 33 9N 107 16W
Trutnov, *Czech.* ...... **32** 50 37N 15 54 E
Truyère →, *France* ... **20** 44 38N 2 34 E
Tryavna, *Bulgaria* .... **34** 42 54N 25 25 E
Tryon, *U.S.A.* **115** 35 15N 82 16W
Tryonville, *U.S.A.* **116** 41 42N 79 48W
Trzcianka, *Poland* .... **32** 53 3N 16 25 E
Trzebiatów, *Poland* ... **32** 54 3N 15 18 E
Trzebiez, *Poland* ..... **32** 53 38N 14 31 E
Trzebinia-Siersza, *Poland* .... **32** 50 11N 19 18 E
Trzebnica, *Poland* .... **32** 51 20N 17 1 E
Tržič, *Yugoslavia* ..... **27** 46 22N 14 18 E
Tsageri, *U.S.S.R.* .... **39** 42 39N 42 46 E
Tsaratanana, *Madag.* . **97** 16 47 S 47 39 E
Tsaratanana, Mt. de, *Madag.* .... **97** 14 0 S 49 0 E
Tsarevo = Michurin, *Bulgaria* .... **34** 42 9N 27 51 E
Tsarichanka, *U.S.S.R.* **38** 48 55N 34 30 E
Tsau, *Botswana* ...... **96** 20 8 S 22 22 E
Tsebrikovo, *U.S.S.R.* . **38** 47 9N 30 10 E
Tselinograd, *U.S.S.R.* . **40** 51 10N 71 30 E
Tsetserleg, *Mongolia* .. **62** 47 36N 101 32 E
Tshabong, *Botswana* .. **96** 26 2 S 22 29 E
Tshane, *Botswana* .... **96** 24 5 S 21 54 E
Tshela, *Zaïre* .... **95** 4 57 S 13 4 E
Tshesebe, *Botswana* .. **97** 21 51 S 27 32 E
Tshibeke, *Zaïre* ...... **92** 2 40 S 28 35 E
Tshibinda, *Zaïre* ..... **92** 2 23 S 28 43 E
Tshikapa, *Zaïre* ...... **95** 6 28 S 20 48 E
Tshilenge, *Zaïre* ..... **92** 6 17 S 23 48 E
Tshinsenda, *Zaïre* .... **93** 12 20 S 28 0 E
Tshofa, *Zaïre* .... **92** 5 13 S 25 16 E
Tshwane, *Botswana* ... **96** 22 24 S 22 1 E
Tsigara, *Botswana* .... **96** 20 22 S 25 54 E
Tsihombe, *Madag.* ... **97** 25 18 S 45 29 E
Tsimlyansk, *U.S.S.R.* . **39** 47 40N 42 6 E
Tsimlyanskoye Vdkhr., *U.S.S.R.* .... **39** 48 0N 43 0 E
Tsinan = Jinan, *China* **60** 36 38N 117 1 E
Tsineng, *S. Africa* .... **96** 27 5 S 23 5 E
Tsinghai = Qinghai □, *China* .... **62** 36 0N 98 0 E
Tsingtao = Qingdao, *China* .... **61** 36 5N 120 20 E
Tsinjomitondraka, *Madag.* .... **97** 15 40 S 47 8 E
Tsiroanomandidy, *Madag.* .... **97** 18 46 S 46 2 E
Tsivilsk, *U.S.S.R.* .... **37** 55 50N 47 25 E
Tsivory, *Madag.* ..... **97** 24 4 S 46 5 E
Tskhinvali, *U.S.S.R.* .. **39** 42 14N 44 1 E
Tsna →, *U.S.S.R.* ... **37** 54 55N 41 58 E
Tso Moriri, L., *India* . **49** 32 50N 78 20 E
Tsodilo Hill, *Botswana* **96** 18 49 S 21 43 E
Tsogttsetsiy, *Mongolia* **60** 43 43N 105 35 E
Tsolo, *S. Africa* ..... **97** 31 18 S 28 37 E
Tsomo, *S. Africa* ..... **97** 32 0 S 27 42 E
Tsu, *Japan* .... **65** 34 45N 136 25 E
Tsu L., *Canada* **110** 60 40N 111 52W
Tsuchiura, *Japan* ..... **65** 36 5N 140 15 E
Tsugaru-Kaikyō, *Japan* **63** 41 35N 141 0 E
Tsukumi, *Japan* ...... **64** 33 4N 131 52 E
Tsukushi-Sanchi, *Japan* **64** 33 25N 130 30 E
Tsumeb, *Namibia* ..... **96** 19 9 S 17 44 E
Tsumis, *Namibia* ..... **96** 23 39 S 17 29 E
Tsuna, *Japan* .... **64** 34 28N 134 56 E
Tsuno-Shima, *Japan* .. **64** 34 21N 130 52 E
Tsuru, *Japan* .... **65** 35 31N 138 57 E
Tsuruga, *Japan* ...... **65** 35 45N 136 2 E
Tsuruga-Wan, *Japan* .. **65** 35 50N 136 3 E
Tsurugi, *Japan* ...... **65** 36 29N 136 37 E
Tsurugi-San, *Japan* ... **64** 33 51N 134 6 E
Tsurumi-Saki, *Japan* .. **64** 32 56N 132 5 E
Tsuruoka, *Japan* ..... **63** 38 44N 139 50 E
Tsurusaki, *Japan* ..... **64** 33 14N 131 41 E
Tsushima, *Gifu, Japan* **65** 35 10N 136 43 E
Tsushima, *Nagasaki, Japan* .... **64** 34 20N 129 20 E
Tsvetkovo, *U.S.S.R.* .. **38** 49 8N 31 33 E
Tu →, *Burma* .... **52** 21 50N 96 15 E
Tua →, *Portugal* **22** 41 13N 7 26W
Tuai, *N.Z.* .... **80** 38 47 S 177 10 E
Tuakau, *N.Z.* .... **80** 37 16 S 174 59 E
Tual, *Indonesia* ...... **57** 5 38 S 132 44 E
Tuam, *Ireland* **15** 53 30N 8 50W
Tuamarina, *N.Z.* ..... **81** 41 25 S 173 59 E
Tuamotu Arch., *Pac. Oc.* .... **67** 17 0 S 144 0W

Varangerfjorden

Uslar, W. Germany 30 51 39N 9 39 E
Usman, U.S.S.R. 37 52 5N 39 48 E
Usoke, Tanzania 92 5 8S 32 24 E
Usolye Sibirskoye, U.S.S.R. 41 52 48N 103 40 E
Usoro, Nigeria 91 5 33N 6 11 E
Uspallata, P. de, Argentina 140 32 37S 69 22W
Uspenskiy, U.S.S.R. 40 48 41N 72 43 E
Usquert, Neths. 16 53 24N 6 36 E
Ussel, France 20 45 32N 2 18 E
Ussuriysk, U.S.S.R. 41 43 48N 131 59 E
Ust-Aldan = Batamay, U.S.S.R. 41 63 30N 129 15 E
Ust Amginskoye = Khandyga, U.S.S.R. 41 62 42N 135 35 E
Ust-Bolsheretsk, U.S.S.R. 41 52 50N 156 15 E
Ust Buzulukskaya, U.S.S.R. 37 50 8N 42 11 E
Ust chaun, U.S.S.R. 41 68 47N 170 30 E
Ust-Donetskiy, U.S.S.R. 39 47 35N 40 55 E
Ust'-Ilga, U.S.S.R. 41 55 5N 104 55 E
Ust Ilimpeya = Yukti, U.S.S.R. 41 63 26N 105 42 E
Ust-Ilimsk, U.S.S.R. 41 58 3N 102 39 E
Ust Ishim, U.S.S.R. 40 57 45N 71 10 E
Ust-Kamchatsk, U.S.S.R. 41 56 10N 162 28 E
Ust-Kamenogorsk, U.S.S.R. 40 50 0N 82 36 E
Ust-Karenga, U.S.S.R. 41 54 25N 116 30 E
Ust Khayryuzova, U.S.S.R. 41 57 15N 156 45 E
Ust-Kut, U.S.S.R. 41 56 50N 105 42 E
Ust Kuyga, U.S.S.R. 41 70 1N 135 43 E
Ust-Labinsk, U.S.S.R. 39 45 15N 39 41 E
Ust Luga, U.S.S.R. 36 59 35N 28 20 E
Ust Maya, U.S.S.R. 41 60 30N 134 28 E
Ust-Mil, U.S.S.R. 41 59 40N 133 11 E
Ust-Nera, U.S.S.R. 41 64 35N 143 15 E
Ust-Nyukzha, U.S.S.R. 41 56 34N 121 37 E
Ust Olenek, U.S.S.R. 41 73 0N 119 48 E
Ust-Omchug, U.S.S.R. 41 61 9N 149 38 E
Ust Port, U.S.S.R. 40 69 40N 84 26 E
Ust Tsilma, U.S.S.R. 40 65 25N 52 0 E
Ust-Tungir, U.S.S.R. 41 55 25N 120 36 E
Ust Urt = Ustyurt, Plato, U.S.S.R. 40 44 0N 55 0 E
Ust Vorkuta, U.S.S.R. 40 67 24N 64 0 E
Ustaoset, Norway 10 60 30N 8 2 E
Ustaritz, France 20 43 24N 1 27W
Uste, U.S.S.R. 37 59 35N 39 40 E
Ústí nad Labem, Czech. 32 50 41N 14 3 E
Ústí nad Orlicí, Czech. 32 49 58N 16 24 E
Ustica, Italy 28 38 42N 13 10 E
Ustinov, U.S.S.R. 40 56 51N 53 14 E
Ustka, Poland 32 54 35N 16 55 E
Ustrzyki Dolne, Poland 32 49 27N 22 40 E
Ustye, U.S.S.R. 41 57 46N 94 37 E
Ustyurt, Plato, U.S.S.R. 40 44 0N 55 0 E
Ustyuzhna, U.S.S.R. 37 58 50N 36 32 E
Usu, China 62 44 27N 84 40 E
Usuki, Japan 64 33 8N 131 49 E
Usulután, El Salv. 128 13 25N 88 28W
Usumacinta →, Mexico 127 17 0N 91 0W
Usumbura = Bujumbura, Burundi 92 3 16S 29 18 E
Usure, Tanzania 92 4 40S 34 22 E
Uta, Indonesia 57 4 33S 136 0 E
'Uta Vava'u, Tonga 68 18 36S 174 0W
Utah □, U.S.A. 122 39 30N 111 30W
Utah, L., U.S.A. 122 40 10N 111 58W
Ute Cr. →, U.S.A. 121 35 21N 103 45W
Utena, U.S.S.R. 36 55 27N 25 40 E
Ütersen, W. Germany 30 53 40N 9 40 E
Utete, Tanzania 92 8 0S 38 45 E
Uthai Thani, Thailand 54 15 22N 100 3 E
Uthal, Pakistan 48 25 44N 66 40 E
Utiariti, Brazil 137 13 0S 58 10W
Utica, N.Y., U.S.A. 117 43 5N 75 18W
Utica, Ohio, U.S.A. 116 40 13N 82 26W
Utiel, Spain 24 39 37N 1 11W
Utik L., Canada 111 55 15N 96 0W
Utikuma L., Canada 110 55 50N 115 30W
Utinga, Brazil 139 12 6S 41 5W
Uto, Japan 64 32 41N 130 40 E
Utrecht, Neths. 16 52 5N 5 8 E
Utrecht, S. Africa 97 27 38S 30 20 E
Utrecht □, Neths. 16 52 6N 5 7 E
Utrera, Spain 23 37 12N 5 48W
Utsjoki, Finland 8 69 51N 26 59 E
Utsunomiya, Japan 65 36 30N 139 50 E
Uttar Pradesh □, India 49 27 0N 80 0 E
Uttaradit, Thailand 54 17 36N 100 5 E
Uttoxeter, U.K. 12 52 53N 1 50W
Ütze, W. Germany 30 52 28N 10 11 E
Uudenmaan lääni □, Finland 9 60 25N 25 0 E
Uusikaarlepyy, Finland 8 63 32N 22 31 E
Uusikaupunki, Finland 9 60 47N 21 25 E
Uva, U.S.S.R. 37 56 59N 52 13 E
Uvá →, Colombia 134 3 41N 70 3W
Uvalde, U.S.A. 121 29 15N 99 48W
Uvarovo, U.S.S.R. 37 51 59N 42 14 E
Uvat, U.S.S.R. 40 59 5N 68 50 E
Uvéa, I., Vanuatu 68 20 30S 166 35 E
Uvinza, Tanzania 92 5 5S 30 24 E
Uvira, Zaïre 92 3 22S 29 3 E
Uvs Nuur, Mongolia 62 50 20N 92 30 E
Uwa, Japan 64 33 22N 132 31 E
Uwajima, Japan 64 33 10N 132 35 E
Uweinat, Jebel, Sudan 88 21 54N 24 58 E
Uxbridge, Canada 108 44 6N 79 7W
Uxin Qi, China 60 38 50N 109 5 E
Uxmal, Mexico 127 20 22N 89 46W
Uyandi, U.S.S.R. 41 69 19N 141 0 E
Uyo, Nigeria 91 5 1N 7 53 E
Uyu →, Burma 52 24 51N 94 57 E
Uyuni, Bolivia 136 20 28S 66 47W
Uzbek S.S.R. □, U.S.S.R. 40 41 30N 65 0 E
Uzen, Bol. →, U.S.S.R. 37 50 0N 49 30 E
Uzen, Mal. →, U.S.S.R. 37 50 0N 48 30 E
Uzerche, France 20 45 25N 1 34 E
Uzès, France 21 44 1N 4 26 E
Uzh →, U.S.S.R. 36 51 15N 30 12 E
Uzhgorod, U.S.S.R. 36 48 36N 22 18 E
Uzlovaya, U.S.S.R. 37 54 0N 38 5 E
Uzunköprü, Turkey 35 41 16N 26 43 E

V

Vaal →, S. Africa 96 29 4S 23 38 E
Vaal Dam, S. Africa 97 27 0S 28 14 E
Vaals, Neths. 17 50 46N 6 1 E
Vaalwater, S. Africa 97 24 15S 28 8 E
Vaasa, Finland 8 63 6N 21 38 E
Vaasan lääni □, Finland 8 63 2N 22 50 E
Vaassen, Neths. 16 52 17N 5 58 E
Vabre, France 20 43 42N 2 24 E
Vác, Hungary 33 47 49N 19 10 E
Vacaria, Brazil 141 28 31S 50 52W
Vacaville, U.S.A. 124 38 21N 122 0W
Vaccarès, Étang de, France 21 43 32N 4 34 E
Vach →, U.S.S.R. 40 60 45N 76 45 E
Vache, I.-à-, Haiti 129 18 2N 73 35W
Väddö, Sweden 10 59 55N 18 50 E
Vadnagar, India 48 23 47N 72 40 E
Vado Lígure, Italy 26 44 16N 8 26 E
Vadodara, India 48 22 20N 73 10 E
Vadsø, Norway 8 70 3N 29 50 E
Vadstena, Sweden 11 58 28N 14 54 E
Vaduz, Liech. 31 47 8N 9 31 E
Værøy, Norway 8 67 40N 12 40 E
Vagnhärad, Sweden 10 58 57N 17 33 E
Vagos, Portugal 22 40 33N 8 42W
Váh →, Czech. 33 47 55N 18 0 E
Vahsel B., Antarctica 143 75 0S 35 0W
Vaigach, U.S.S.R. 40 70 10N 59 0 E
Vaigai →, India 51 9 15N 79 10 E
Vaiges, France 18 48 2N 0 30W
Vaihingen, W. Germany 31 48 55N 8 58 E
Vaijapur, India 50 19 58N 74 45 E
Vaikam, India 51 9 45N 76 25 E
Vailly-sur-Aisne, France 19 49 24N 3 31 E
Vaippar →, India 51 9 0N 78 25 E
Vaison-la-Romaine, France 21 44 14N 5 4 E
Vaitogi, Amer. Samoa 68 14 21S 170 44W
Vajpur, India 50 21 24N 73 17 E
Val-Alain, Canada 107 46 24N 71 45W
Val-Barrette, Canada 106 46 30N 75 21W
Val Caron, Canada 108 46 37N 81 1W
Val-d'Ajol, Le, France 19 47 55N 6 30 E
Val-de-Marne □, France 19 48 45N 2 28 E
Val-des-Bois, Canada 106 45 54N 75 35W
Val-d'Oise □, France 19 49 5N 2 10 E
Val d'Or, Canada 106 48 7N 77 47W
Val Marie, Canada 111 49 15N 107 45W
Valadares, Portugal 22 41 5N 8 38W
Valahia, Romania 34 44 35N 25 0 E
Valais □, Switz. 31 46 12N 7 45 E
Valandovo, Yugoslavia 35 41 19N 22 34 E
Valcheta, Argentina 142 40 40S 66 8W
Valcourt, Canada 107 45 29N 72 18W
Valdagno, Italy 27 45 38N 11 18 E
Valday, U.S.S.R. 36 57 58N 33 9 E
Valdayskaya Vozvyshennost, U.S.S.R. 36 57 0N 33 30 E
Valdeazogues →, Spain 23 38 45N 4 55W
Valdemarsvik, Sweden 11 58 14N 16 40 E
Valdepeñas, Ciudad Real, Spain 23 38 43N 3 25W
Valdepeñas, Jaén, Spain 23 37 33N 3 47W
Valderaduey →, Spain 22 41 31N 5 42W
Valderrobres, Spain 24 40 53N 0 9 E
Valdés, Pen., Argentina 142 42 30S 63 45W
Valdez, Ecuador 134 1 15N 79 0W
Valdez, U.S.A. 102 61 14N 146 17W
Valdivia, Chile 142 39 50S 73 14W
Valdivia, Colombia 134 7 11N 75 27W
Valdivia □, Chile 142 40 0S 73 0W
Valdobbiádene, Italy 27 45 53N 12 0 E
Valdosta, U.S.A. 115 30 50N 83 20W
Valdoviño, Spain 22 43 36N 8 8W
Valdres, Norway 10 60 55N 9 28 E
Vale, U.S.A. 122 44 0N 117 15W
Vale, U.S.S.R. 39 41 30N 42 58 E
Valea lui Mihai, Romania 34 47 32N 22 11 E
Valença, Brazil 139 13 20S 39 5W
Valença, Portugal 22 42 1N 8 34W
Valença do Piauí, Brazil 138 6 20S 41 45W
Valençay, France 19 47 9N 1 34 E
Valence, Drôme, France 21 44 57N 4 54 E
Valence, Tarn-et-Garonne, France 20 44 6N 0 53 E
Valencia, Spain 25 39 27N 0 23W
Valencia, Venezuela 134 10 11N 68 0W
Valencia □, Spain 25 39 20N 0 40W
Valencia, Albufera de, Spain 25 39 20N 0 27W
Valencia, G. de, Spain 25 39 30N 0 20 E
Valencia de Alcántara, Spain 23 39 25N 7 14W
Valencia de Don Juan, Spain 22 42 17N 5 31W
Valencia del Ventoso, Spain 23 38 15N 6 29W
Valenciennes, France 19 50 20N 3 34 E
Valensole, France 21 43 50N 5 59 E
Valentia Harbour, Ireland 15 51 56N 10 17W
Valentia I., Ireland 15 51 54N 10 22W
Valentim, Sa. do, Brazil 138 6 0S 43 30W
Valentine, Nebr., U.S.A. 120 42 50N 100 35W
Valentine, Tex., U.S.A. 121 30 36N 104 28W
Valenza, Italy 26 45 2N 8 39 E
Valera, Venezuela 134 9 19N 70 37W
Valga, U.S.S.R. 36 57 44N 26 0 E
Valguarnera Caropepe, Italy 29 37 30N 14 22 E
Valier, U.S.A. 122 48 25N 112 9W
Valinco, G. de, France 21 41 40N 8 52 E
Valjevo, Yugoslavia 33 44 18N 19 53 E
Valkeakoski, Finland 9 61 16N 24 2 E
Valkenburg, Neths. 17 50 52N 5 50 E
Valkenswaard, Neths. 17 51 21N 5 29 E
Vall de Uxó, Spain 24 39 49N 0 15W
Valla, Sweden 10 59 2N 16 20 E
Valladolid, Mexico 127 20 40N 88 11W
Valladolid, Spain 22 41 38N 4 43W
Valladolid □, Spain 22 41 38N 4 43W
Vallata, Italy 29 41 3N 15 16 E
Valldemosa, Spain 24 39 43N 2 37 E
Valle d'Aosta □, Italy 26 45 45N 7 22 E
Valle de Arán, Spain 24 42 50N 0 55 E
Valle de Cabuérniga, Spain 22 43 14N 4 18W
Valle de la Pascua, Venezuela 134 9 13N 66 0W
Valle de las Palmas, Mexico 125 32 20N 116 43W
Valle de Santiago, Mexico 126 20 25N 101 15W
Valle de Suchil, Mexico 126 23 38N 103 55W
Valle de Zaragoza, Mexico 126 27 28N 105 49W
Valle del Cauca □, Colombia 134 3 45N 76 30W
Valle Fértil, Sierra del, Argentina 140 30 20S 68 0W
Valle Hermoso, Mexico 127 25 35N 97 40W
Vallecas, Spain 22 40 23N 3 41W
Valledupar, Colombia 134 10 29N 73 15W
Vallée-Jonction, Canada 107 46 22N 70 55W
Vallehermoso, Canary Is. 25 28 10N 17 15W
Vallejo, U.S.A. 124 38 12N 122 15W
Vallenar, Chile 140 28 30S 70 50W
Valleraugue, France 20 44 6N 3 39 E
Vallet, France 18 47 10N 1 15W
Valletta, Malta 86 35 54N 14 30 E
Valley Center, U.S.A. 125 33 13N 117 2W
Valley City, U.S.A. 120 46 57N 98 0W
Valley Falls, U.S.A. 122 42 33N 120 16W
Valley Park, U.S.A. 118 38 33N 90 29W
Valley Springs, U.S.A. 124 38 11N 120 50W
Valley Station, U.S.A. 118 38 10N 85 50W
Valley Wells, U.S.A. 125 35 27N 115 46W
Valleyview, Canada 110 55 5N 117 17W
Valli di Comácchio, Italy 27 44 40N 12 15 E
Vallimanca, Arroyo, Argentina 140 35 40S 59 10W
Vallo della Lucánia, Italy 29 40 14N 15 16 E
Vallon-Pont-d'Arc, France 21 44 24N 4 24 E
Vallorbe, Switz. 31 46 42N 6 20 E
Valls, Spain 24 41 18N 1 15 E
Vallsta, Sweden 10 61 31N 16 22 E
Valmaseda, Spain 24 43 11N 3 12W
Valmeyer, U.S.A. 118 38 18N 90 19W
Valmiera, U.S.S.R. 36 57 37N 25 29 E
Valmont, France 18 49 45N 0 30 E
Valmontone, Italy 28 41 48N 12 55 E
Valmy, France 19 49 5N 4 45 E
Valnera, Mte., Spain 24 43 9N 3 40W
Valognes, France 18 49 30N 1 28W
Valona = Vlóra, Albania 35 40 32N 19 28 E
Valongo, Portugal 22 41 8N 8 30W
Valpaços, Portugal 22 41 36N 7 17W
Valparaíso, Chile 140 33 2S 71 40W
Valparaíso, Mexico 126 22 50N 103 32W
Valparaiso, U.S.A. 119 41 27N 87 2W
Valparaíso □, Chile 140 33 2S 71 40W
Valpovo, Yugoslavia 33 45 39N 18 25 E
Valréas, France 21 44 24N 5 0 E
Vals, Switz. 31 46 39N 9 11 E
Vals →, S. Africa 96 27 23S 26 30 E
Vals, Tanjung, Indonesia 57 8 26S 137 25 E
Vals-les-Bains, France 21 44 42N 4 24 E
Valsad, India 50 20 40N 72 58 E
Valskog, Sweden 10 59 27N 15 57 E
Válta, Greece 35 40 3N 23 25 E
Valtellina, Italy 26 46 9N 9 55 E
Valuyki, U.S.S.R. 37 50 10N 38 5 E
Valverde, Canary Is. 25 27 48N 17 55W
Valverde del Camino, Spain 23 37 35N 6 47W
Valverde del Fresno, Spain 22 40 15N 6 51W
Vama, Romania 34 47 34N 25 42 E
Vámos, Greece 35 35 24N 24 13 E
Vamsadhara →, India 50 18 21N 84 8 E
Van, Turkey 46 38 30N 43 20 E
Van, L. = Van Gölü, Turkey 46 38 30N 43 0 E
Van Alstyne, U.S.A. 121 33 25N 96 36W
Van Bruyssel, Canada 107 47 56N 72 9W
Van Buren, Canada 105 47 10N 67 55W
Van Buren, Ark., U.S.A. 121 35 28N 94 18W
Van Buren, Maine, U.S.A. 115 47 10N 68 1W
Van Buren, Mo., U.S.A. 121 37 0N 91 0W
Van Canh, Vietnam 54 13 37N 109 0 E
Van Diemen, C., N. Terr., Australia 78 11 9S 130 24 E
Van Diemen, C., Queens., Australia 72 16 30S 139 46 E
Van Diemen G., Australia 78 11 45S 132 0 E
Van Gölü, Turkey 46 38 30N 43 0 E
Van Horn, U.S.A. 121 31 3N 104 55W
Van Horne, U.S.A. 118 42 1N 92 4W
Van Ninh, Vietnam 54 12 42N 109 14 E
Van Reenen P., S. Africa 97 28 22S 29 27 E
Van Rees, Pegunungan, Indonesia 57 2 35S 138 15 E
Van Tassell, U.S.A. 120 42 40N 104 3W
Van Tivu, India 51 8 51N 78 15 E
Van Wert, U.S.A. 119 40 52N 84 31W
Van Yen, Vietnam 54 21 4N 104 42 E
Vanavara, U.S.S.R. 41 60 22N 102 16 E
Vanceburg, U.S.A. 119 38 36N 83 19W
Vancouver, Canada 110 49 15N 123 10W
Vancouver, U.S.A. 124 45 44N 122 41W
Vancouver, C., Australia 79 35 2S 118 11 E
Vancouver I., Canada 110 49 50N 126 0W
Vandalia, Ill., U.S.A. 118 38 57N 89 4W
Vandalia, Mo., U.S.A. 118 39 18N 91 30W
Vandalia, Ohio, U.S.A. 119 39 54N 84 12W
Vandavasi, India 51 12 30N 79 30 E
Vandeloos Bay, Sri Lanka 51 8 0N 81 45 E
Vandenburg, U.S.A. 125 34 35N 120 33W
Vanderbijlpark, S. Africa 97 26 42S 27 54 E
Vandergrift, U.S.A. 116 40 36N 79 33W
Vanderhoof, Canada 110 54 0N 124 0W
Vanderlin I., Australia 72 15 44S 137 2 E
Vandry, Canada 107 47 50N 73 34W
Vandyke, Australia 72 24 10S 147 51 E
Vänern, Sweden 11 58 47N 13 30 E
Vänersborg, Sweden 11 58 26N 12 19 E
Vang Vieng, Laos 54 18 58N 102 32 E
Vanga, Kenya 92 4 35S 39 12 E
Vangaindrano, Madag. 97 23 21S 47 36 E
Vanguard, Canada 111 49 55N 107 20W
Vangunu, Solomon Is. 68 8 40S 158 5 E
Vanier, Canada 109 45 27N 75 40W
Vanimo, Papua N. G. 69 2 42S 141 21 E
Vanivilasa Sagara, India 51 13 45N 76 30 E
Vaniyambadi, India 51 12 46N 78 44 E
Vankarem, U.S.S.R. 41 67 51N 175 50 E
Vankleek Hill, Canada 109 45 32N 74 40W
Vanna, Norway 8 70 6N 19 50 E
Vännäs, Sweden 8 63 58N 19 48 E
Vannes, France 18 47 40N 2 47W
Vanoise, Massif de la, France 21 45 25N 6 40 E
Vanrhynsdorp, S. Africa 96 31 36S 18 44 E
Vanrook, Australia 72 16 57S 141 57 E
Vans, Les, France 21 44 25N 4 7 E
Vansbro, Sweden 10 60 32N 14 15 E
Vansittart B., Australia 78 14 3S 126 17 E
Vanthli, India 48 21 28N 70 25 E
Vanua Levu, Fiji 68 16 33S 179 15 E
Vanua Mbalavu, Fiji 68 17 40S 178 57W
Vanuatu ■, Pac. Oc. 68 15 0S 168 0 E
Vanwyksvlei, S. Africa 96 30 18S 21 49 E
Vanzylsrus, S. Africa 96 26 52S 22 4 E
Vapnyarka, U.S.S.R. 38 48 32N 28 45 E
Var □, France 21 43 27N 6 18 E
Var →, France 21 43 39N 7 12 E
Vara, Sweden 11 58 16N 12 55 E
Varada →, India 51 15 0N 75 40 E
Varades, France 18 47 25N 1 1W
Varaita →, Italy 26 44 49N 7 36 E
Varallo, Italy 26 45 50N 8 13 E
Varanasi, India 49 25 22N 83 0 E
Varangerfjorden, Norway 8 70 3N 29 25 E

Varaždin

Varaždin, Yugoslavia 27 46 20N 16 20 E
Varazze, Italy 26 44 21N 8 36 E
Varberg, Sweden 11 57 6N 12 20 E
Vardak □, Afghan. 47 34 0N 68 0 E
Vardar → = Axiós →, Greece 35 40 57N 22 35 E
Varde, Denmark 11 55 38N 8 29 E
Varde Å, Denmark 11 55 35N 8 19 E
Varel, W. Germany 30 53 23N 8 9 E
Varella, Mui, Vietnam 54 12 54N 109 26 E
Varena, U.S.S.R. 36 54 12N 24 30 E
Varennes-sur-Allier, France 20 46 19N 3 24 E
Vareš, Yugoslavia 33 44 12N 18 23 E
Varese, Italy 26 45 49N 8 50 E
Varese Lígure, Italy 26 44 22N 9 33 E
Vårgårda, Sweden 11 58 2N 12 49 E
Vargem Bonita, Brazil 139 20 20 S 46 22W
Vargem Grande, Brazil 138 3 33 S 43 56W
Varginha, Brazil 141 21 33 S 45 25W
Vargön, Sweden 11 58 22N 12 20 E
Variadero, U.S.A. 121 35 43N 104 17W
Varillas, Chile 140 24 0 S 70 10W
Väring, Sweden 11 58 30N 14 0 E
Värmeln, Sweden 10 59 35N 12 54 E
Värmlands län □, Sweden 10 60 0N 13 20 E
Varna, Bulgaria 34 43 13N 27 56 E
Varna, U.S.A. 118 41 2N 89 14W
Varna →, India 50 16 48N 74 32 E
Värnamo, Sweden 11 57 10N 14 3 E
Värö, Sweden 11 57 16N 12 11 E
Vars, Canada 106 45 21N 75 21W
Varsseveld, Neths. 16 51 56N 6 29 E
Varvarin, Yugoslavia 33 43 43N 21 20 E
Varzaneh, Iran 47 32 25N 52 40 E
Várzea Alegre, Brazil 138 6 47 S 39 17W
Várzea da Palma, Brazil 139 17 36 S 44 44W
Várzea Grande, Brazil 137 15 39 S 56 8W
Varzi, Italy 26 44 50N 9 12 E
Varzo, Italy 26 46 12N 8 15 E
Varzy, France 19 47 22N 3 20 E
Vasa, Finland 8 63 6N 21 38 E
Vasa Barris →, Brazil 138 11 10 S 37 10W
Vascão →, Portugal 23 37 31N 7 31W
Vaşcău, Romania 34 46 28N 22 30 E
Vascongadas □, Spain 24 42 50N 2 45W
Väse, Sweden 10 59 23N 13 52 E
Vasht = Khāsh, Iran 47 28 15N 61 15 E
Vasilevichi, U.S.S.R. 36 52 15N 29 50 E
Vasilikón, Greece 35 38 25N 23 40 E
Vasilkov, U.S.S.R. 36 50 7N 30 15 E
Vaslui, Romania 34 46 38N 27 42 E
Väsman, Sweden 10 60 9N 15 5 E
Vassar, Canada 111 49 10N 95 55W
Vassar, U.S.A. 114 43 23N 83 33W
Västerås, Sweden 10 59 37N 16 38 E
Västerbottens län □, Sweden 8 64 58N 18 0 E
Västernorrlands län □, Sweden 10 63 30N 17 30 E
Västervik, Sweden 11 57 43N 16 43 E
Västmanlands län □, Sweden 10 59 45N 16 20 E
Vasto, Italy 27 42 8N 14 40 E
Vasvár, Hungary 33 47 3N 16 47 E
Vatan, France 19 47 4N 1 50 E
Vaté = Efate, I., Vanuatu 68 17 40 S 168 25 E
Vathí, Greece 35 37 46N 27 1 E
Váthia, Greece 35 36 29N 22 29 E
Vatican City ■, Italy 27 41 54N 12 27 E
Vaticano, C., Italy 28 38 40N 15 48 E
Vatnajökull, Iceland 8 64 30N 16 48W
Vatnås, Norway 10 59 58N 9 37 E
Vatneyri, Iceland 8 65 35N 24 0W
Vatoloha, Mt., Madag. 97 17 52 S 47 48 E
Vatomandry, Madag. 97 19 20 S 48 59 E
Vatra-Dornei, Romania 34 47 22N 25 22 E
Vättern, Sweden 11 58 25N 14 30 E
Vatulele, Fiji 68 18 33 S 177 37 E
Vaucluse □, France 21 43 50N 5 20 E
Vaucouleurs, France 19 48 37N 5 40 E
Vaud □, Switz. 31 46 35N 6 30 E
Vaughn, Mont., U.S.A. 122 47 37N 111 36W
Vaughn, N. Mex., U.S.A. 123 34 37N 105 12W
Vaupe □, Colombia 134 1 0N 71 0W
Vaupés → = Uaupés →, Brazil 134 0 2N 67 16W
Vauvert, France 21 43 42N 4 17 E
Vauxhall, Canada 110 50 5N 112 9W
Vavoua, Ivory C. 90 7 23N 6 29W
Vaxholm, Sweden 10 59 25N 18 20 E
Växjö, Sweden 11 56 52N 14 50 E
Vaygach, Ostrov, U.S.S.R. 40 70 0N 60 0 E
Veadeiros, Brazil 139 14 7 S 47 31W
Vechta, W. Germany 30 52 47N 8 18 E
Vechte →, Neths. 30 52 34N 6 6 E
Vecilla, La, Spain 22 42 51N 5 27W
Vecsés, Hungary 33 47 26N 19 19 E
Vedaranniyam, India 51 10 25N 79 50 E
Veddige, Sweden 11 57 17N 12 20 E
Vedea →, Romania 34 43 53N 25 59 E
Vedia, Argentina 140 34 30 S 61 31W
Vedra, I. del, Spain 25 38 52N 1 12 E
Vedrin, Belgium 17 50 30N 4 52 E
Veendam, Neths. 16 53 5N 6 52 E
Veenendaal, Neths. 16 52 2N 5 34 E
Veerle, Belgium 17 51 4N 4 59 E
Vefsna →, Norway 8 65 48N 13 10 E
Vega, Norway 8 65 40N 11 55 E
Vega, U.S.A. 121 35 18N 102 26W
Vega, La, Dom. Rep. 129 19 20N 70 30W
Vega, La, Peru 136 10 41 S 77 44W
Vegadeo, Spain 22 43 27N 7 4W
Vegafjorden, Norway 8 65 37N 12 0 E
Vegesack, W. Germany 30 53 10N 8 38 E
Veghel, Neths. 17 51 37N 5 32 E
Vegorritis, Límni, Greece 35 40 45N 21 45 E
Vegreville, Canada 110 53 30N 112 5W
Vegusdal, Norway 11 58 32N 8 10 E
Veii, Italy 27 42 0N 12 24 E
Vejen, Denmark 11 55 30N 9 9 E
Vejer de la Frontera, Spain 23 36 15N 5 59W
Vejle, Denmark 11 55 43N 9 30 E
Vejle Fjord, Denmark 11 55 40N 9 50 E
Vela, La, Venezuela 134 11 27N 69 34W
Vela Luka, Yugoslavia 27 42 59N 16 44 E
Velanai I., Sri Lanka 51 9 45N 79 45 E
Velas, C., Costa Rica 128 10 21N 85 52W
Velasco, Sierra de, Argentina 140 29 20 S 67 10W
Velay, Mts. du, France 20 45 0N 3 40 E
Velddrif, S. Africa 96 32 42 S 18 11 E
Veldegem, Belgium 17 51 7N 3 10 E
Velden, Neths. 17 51 25N 6 10 E
Veldhoven, Neths. 17 51 24N 5 25 E
Velebit Planina, Yugoslavia 27 44 50N 15 20 E
Velebitski Kanal, Yugoslavia 27 44 45N 14 55 E
Veleka →, Bulgaria 34 42 4N 27 58 E
Velenje, Yugoslavia 27 46 23N 15 8 E
Velestínon, Greece 35 39 23N 22 43 E
Veleta, La, Spain 23 37 1N 3 22W
Vélez, Colombia 134 6 1N 73 41W
Vélez Blanco, Spain 25 37 41N 2 5W
Vélez Málaga, Spain 23 36 48N 4 5W
Vélez Rubio, Spain 25 37 41N 2 5W
Velhas →, Brazil 139 17 13 S 44 49W
Velika, Yugoslavia 33 45 27N 17 40 E
Velika Gorica, Yugoslavia 27 45 44N 16 5 E
Velika Kapela, Yugoslavia 27 45 10N 15 5 E
Velika Kladuša, Yugoslavia 27 45 11N 15 48 E
Velika Morava →, Yugoslavia 33 44 43N 21 3 E
Velikaya →, U.S.S.R. 36 57 48N 28 20 E
Velikaya Lepetikha, U.S.S.R. 38 47 2N 33 58 E
Velike Lašče, Yugoslavia 27 45 49N 14 45 E
Velikiye Luki, U.S.S.R. 36 56 25N 30 32 E
Velikonda Range, India 51 14 45N 79 10 E
Velikoye, Oz., U.S.S.R. 37 55 15N 40 10 E
Velingrad, Bulgaria 35 42 4N 23 58 E
Velino, Mte., Italy 27 42 10N 13 20 E
Velizh, U.S.S.R. 36 55 36N 31 11 E
Velke Meziřici, Czech. 32 49 21N 16 1 E
Vella G., Solomon Is. 68 8 0 S 156 50 E
Vella Lavella, Solomon Is. 68 7 45 S 156 40 E
Vellar →, India 51 11 30N 79 36 E
Velletri, Italy 28 41 43N 12 43 E
Vellinge, Sweden 11 55 29N 13 0 E
Vellore, India 51 12 57N 79 10 E
Velp, Neths. 16 52 0N 5 59 E
Velsen-Noord, Neths. 16 52 27N 4 40 E
Velten, E. Germany 30 52 40N 13 11 E
Veluwe Meer, Neths. 16 52 24N 5 44 E
Velva, U.S.A. 120 48 6N 100 56W
Vembanad L., India 51 9 36N 76 15 E
Veme, Norway 10 60 14N 10 7 E
Ven, Sweden 11 55 55N 12 45 E
Vena, Sweden 11 57 31N 16 0 E
Venaco, France 21 42 14N 9 11 E
Venado Tuerto, Argentina 140 33 50 S 62 0W
Venafro, Italy 29 41 28N 14 3 E
Venarey-les-Laumes, France 19 47 32N 4 26 E
Venaria, Italy 26 45 6N 7 39 E
Venčane, Yugoslavia 33 44 24N 20 28 E
Vence, France 21 43 43N 7 6 E
Venda □, S. Africa 97 22 40 S 30 35 E
Vendas Novas, Portugal 23 38 39N 8 27W
Vendée □, France 18 46 50N 1 35W
Vendée →, France 18 46 20N 1 10W
Vendéen, Bocage, France 20 46 40N 1 20W
Vendeuvre-sur-Barse, France 19 48 14N 4 28 E
Vendôme, France 18 47 47N 1 3 E
Vendrell, Spain 24 41 10N 1 30 E
Vendsyssel, Denmark 11 57 22N 10 0 E
Vénéta, L., Italy 27 45 23N 12 25 E
Véneto □, Italy 27 45 40N 12 0 E
Venev, U.S.S.R. 37 54 22N 38 17 E
Venézia, Italy 27 45 27N 12 20 E
Venézia, G. di, Italy 27 45 20N 13 0 E
Venezuela ■, S. Amer. 134 8 0N 66 0W
Venezuela, G. de, Venezuela 134 11 30N 71 0W
Vengurla, India 51 15 53N 73 45 E
Vengurla Rocks, India 51 15 55N 73 22 E
Venice = Venézia, Italy 27 45 27N 12 20 E
Venkatagiri, India 51 14 0N 79 35 E
Venkatapuram, India 50 18 20N 80 30 E
Venlo, Neths. 17 51 22N 6 11 E
Venosta, Canada 106 45 52N 76 1W
Venraij, Neths. 17 51 31N 6 0 E
Vent, Îs. du, Pac. Oc. 68 17 30 S 149 30W
Venta, La, Mexico 127 18 8N 94 3W
Venta de Cardeña, Spain 23 38 16N 4 20W
Venta de San Rafael, Spain 22 40 42N 4 12W
Ventana, Punta de la, Mexico 126 24 4N 109 48W
Ventana, Sa. de la, Argentina 140 38 0 S 62 30W
Ventersburg, S. Africa 96 28 7 S 27 9 E
Venterstad, S. Africa 96 30 47 S 25 48 E
Ventimíglia, Italy 26 43 50N 7 39 E
Ventnor, U.K. 13 50 35N 1 12W
Ventotene, Italy 28 40 48N 13 25 E
Ventoux, Mt., France 21 44 10N 5 17 E
Ventspils, U.S.S.R. 36 57 25N 21 32 E
Ventuarí →, Venezuela 134 3 58N 67 2W
Ventucopa, U.S.A. 125 34 50N 119 29W
Ventura, U.S.A. 125 34 16N 119 18W
Ventura, La, Mexico 126 24 38N 100 54W
Venturosa, La, Colombia 134 6 8N 68 48W
Venus B., Australia 74 38 40 S 145 42 E
Vera, Argentina 140 29 30 S 60 20W
Vera, Spain 25 37 15N 1 51W
Veracruz, Mexico 127 19 10N 96 10W
Veracruz □, Mexico 127 19 0N 96 15W
Veraval, India 48 20 53N 70 27 E
Verbánia, Italy 26 45 56N 8 43 E
Verbicaro, Italy 29 39 46N 15 54 E
Vercelli, Italy 26 45 19N 8 25 E
Verchères, Canada 107 45 47N 73 21W
Verchovchevo, U.S.S.R. 38 48 32N 34 10 E
Verdalsøra, Norway 8 63 48N 11 30 E
Verde →, Argentina 142 41 56 S 65 5W
Verde →, Goiás, Brazil 139 19 11 S 50 44W
Verde →, Goiás, Brazil 139 18 1 S 50 14W
Verde →, Mato Grosso, Brazil 137 21 25 S 52 20W
Verde →, Mato Grosso, Brazil 137 11 54 S 55 48W
Verde →, Chihuahua, Mexico 126 26 29N 107 58W
Verde →, Oaxaca, Mexico 127 15 59N 97 50W
Verde →, Veracruz, Mexico 126 21 10N 102 50W
Verde →, Paraguay 140 23 9 S 57 37W
Verde, Cay, Bahamas 128 23 0N 75 5W
Verde Grande →, Brazil 139 16 13 S 43 49W
Verde Pequeno →, Brazil 139 14 48 S 43 31W
Verden, W. Germany 30 52 58N 9 18 E
Verdi, U.S.A. 124 39 31N 119 59W
Verdigre, U.S.A. 120 42 38N 98 0W
Verdon →, France 21 43 43N 5 46 E
Verdon-sur-Mer, Le, France 20 45 33N 1 4W
Verdun, France 19 49 9N 5 24 E
Verdun-sur-le-Doubs, France 19 46 54N 5 2 E
Vereeniging, S. Africa 97 26 38 S 27 57 E
Vérendrye, Parc Prov. de la, Canada 106 47 20N 76 40W
Verga, C., Guinea 90 10 30N 14 10W
Vergato, Italy 26 44 18N 11 8 E
Vergemont, Australia 72 23 33 S 143 1 E
Vergemont Cr. →, Australia 72 24 16 S 143 16 E
Vergennes, U.S.A. 117 44 9N 73 15W
Vergt, France 20 45 2N 0 43 E
Verín, Spain 22 41 57N 7 27W
Veriña, Spain 22 43 32N 5 43W
Verkhnedvinsk, U.S.S.R. 36 55 45N 27 58 E
Verkhnevilyuysk, U.S.S.R. 41 63 27N 120 18 E
Verkhneye Kalinino, U.S.S.R. 41 59 54N 108 8 E
Verkhniy Baskunchak, U.S.S.R. 39 48 14N 46 44 E
Verkhovye, U.S.S.R. 37 52 55N 37 15 E
Verkhoyansk, U.S.S.R. 41 67 35N 133 25 E
Verkhoyansk Ra. = Verkhoyanskiy Khrebet, U.S.S.R. 41 66 0N 129 0 E
Verkhoyanskiy Khrebet, U.S.S.R. 41 66 0N 129 0 E
Verlo, Canada 111 50 19N 108 35W
Verma, Norway 10 62 21N 8 3 E
Vermenton, France 19 47 40N 3 42 E
Vermilion, Canada 111 53 20N 110 50W
Vermilion →, Alta., Canada 111 53 22N 110 51W
Vermilion →, Qué., Canada 107 47 38N 72 56W
Vermilion →, Ill., U.S.A. 118 41 19N 89 5W
Vermilion →, Ind., U.S.A. 119 39 57N 87 27W
Vermilion, B., U.S.A. 121 29 45N 91 55W
Vermilion Bay, Canada 111 49 51N 93 34W
Vermilion Chutes, Canada 110 58 22N 114 51W
Vermilion L., U.S.A. 120 47 53N 92 25W
Vermillion, U.S.A. 120 42 50N 96 56W
Vermont, U.S.A. 118 40 18N 90 26W
Vermont □, U.S.A. 117 43 40N 72 50W
Vernal, U.S.A. 122 40 28N 109 35W
Vernalis, U.S.A. 124 37 36N 121 17W
Verner, Canada 108 46 25N 80 8W
Verneuil-sur-Avre, France 18 48 45N 0 55 E
Verneukpan, S. Africa 96 30 0 S 21 0 E
Vernon, Canada 110 50 20N 119 15W
Vernon, France 18 49 5N 1 30 E
Vernon, Ill., U.S.A. 118 38 48N 89 5W
Vernon, Ind., U.S.A. 119 38 59N 85 36W
Vernon, Tex., U.S.A. 121 34 10N 99 20W
Vernonia, U.S.A. 124 45 52N 123 11W
Vero Beach, U.S.A. 115 27 39N 80 23W
Véroia, Greece 35 40 34N 22 12 E
Verolanuova, Italy 26 45 20N 10 5 E
Véroli, Italy 28 41 43N 13 24 E
Verona, Canada 109 44 29N 76 42W
Verona, Italy 26 45 27N 11 0 E
Verona, U.S.A. 118 42 59N 89 32W
Veropol, U.S.S.R. 41 65 15N 168 40 E
Versailles, France 19 48 48N 2 8 E
Versailles, Ill., U.S.A. 118 39 53N 90 39W
Versailles, Ind., U.S.A. 119 39 4N 85 15W
Versailles, Ky., U.S.A. 119 38 3N 84 44W
Versailles, Mo., U.S.A. 118 38 26N 92 51W
Versailles, Ohio, U.S.A. 119 40 13N 84 29W
Versalles, Bolivia 137 12 44 S 63 18W
Vert, C., Senegal 90 14 45N 17 30W
Verte, I., Canada 107 48 2N 69 26W
Vertou, France 18 47 10N 1 28W
Vertus, France 19 48 54N 4 0 E
Verulam, S. Africa 97 29 38 S 31 2 E
Verviers, Belgium 17 50 37N 5 52 E
Vervins, France 19 49 50N 3 53 E
Verzej, Yugoslavia 27 46 34N 16 13 E
Vescavoto, France 21 42 30N 9 27 E
Vesdre →, Belgium 17 50 36N 6 0 E
Veselí nad Lužnicí, Czech. 32 49 12N 14 43 E
Veselovskoye Vdkhr., U.S.S.R. 39 47 0N 41 0 E
Veshenskaya, U.S.S.R. 39 49 35N 41 44 E
Vesle →, France 19 49 23N 3 28 E
Vesoul, France 19 47 40N 6 11 E
Vessigebro, Sweden 11 56 58N 12 40 E
Vest-Agder fylke □, Norway 9 58 30N 7 15 E
Vesta, Costa Rica 128 9 43N 83 3W
Vesterålen, Norway 8 68 45N 15 0 E
Vestersche Veld, Neths. 16 52 52N 6 9 E
Vestfjorden, Norway 8 67 55N 14 0 E
Vestfold fylke □, Norway 9 59 15N 10 0 E
Vestmannaeyjar, Iceland 8 63 27N 20 15W
Vestmarka, Norway 10 59 56N 11 59 E
Vestone, Italy 26 45 43N 10 25 E
Vestsjællands Amtskommune □, Denmark 11 55 30N 11 20 E
Vestspitsbergen, Svalbard 144 78 40N 17 0 E
Vestvågøy, Norway 8 68 18N 13 50 E
Vesuvio, Italy 29 40 50N 14 22 E
Vesuvius, Mt. = Vesuvio, Italy 29 40 50N 14 22 E
Vesyegonsk, U.S.S.R. 37 58 40N 37 16 E
Veszprém, Hungary 33 47 8N 17 57 E
Vésztő, Hungary 33 46 55N 21 16 E
Vetapalem, India 51 15 47N 80 18 E
Vetlanda, Sweden 11 57 24N 15 3 E
Vetluga, U.S.S.R. 37 57 53N 45 45 E
Vetlugu →, U.S.S.R. 40 56 18N 46 24 E
Vetluzhskiy, U.S.S.R. 37 57 17N 45 12 E
Vetovo, Bulgaria 34 43 42N 26 16 E
Vetralia, Italy 27 42 20N 12 2 E
Vettore, Monte, Italy 27 42 49N 13 16 E
Veurne, Belgium 17 51 5N 2 40 E
Vevay, U.S.A. 119 38 45N 85 4W
Vevey, Switz. 31 46 28N 6 51 E
Veynes, France 21 44 32N 5 49 E
Veys, Iran 46 31 30N 49 0 E
Vézelise, France 19 48 30N 6 5 E
Vézère →, France 20 44 53N 0 53 E
Vi Thanh, Vietnam 55 9 42N 105 26 E
Viacha, Bolivia 136 16 39 S 68 18W
Viadana, Italy 26 44 55N 10 30 E
Viamão, Brazil 141 30 5 S 51 0W
Viana, Brazil 138 3 13 S 45 0W
Viana, Spain 24 42 31N 2 22W
Viana del Bollo, Spain 22 42 11N 7 6W
Viana do Alentejo, Portugal 23 38 17N 7 59W
Viana do Castelo, Portugal 22 41 42N 8 50W
Vianden, Belgium 17 49 56N 6 12 E
Vianen, Neths. 16 51 59N 5 5 E
Vianna do Castelo □, Portugal 22 41 50N 8 30W
Vianópolis, Brazil 139 16 40 S 48 35W
Viar →, Spain 23 37 36N 5 50W
Viaréggio, Italy 26 43 52N 10 13 E
Viaur →, France 20 44 8N 1 58 E
Vibank, Canada 111 50 20N 103 56W
Vibo Valéntia, Italy 29 38 40N 16 5 E
Viborg, Denmark 11 56 27N 9 23 E
Vibraye, France 18 48 3N 0 44 E
Vic-en-Bigorre, France 20 43 24N 0 3 E
Vic-Fézensac, France 20 43 47N 0 19 E

W

Wasior

Wasior, *Indonesia* **57** 2 43 S 134 30 E
Waskaiowaka, L., *Canada* **111** 56 33N 96 23W
Waskesiu Lake, *Canada* **111** 53 55N 106 5W
Wasmes, *Belgium* **17** 50 25N 3 50 E
Waspik, *Neths.* **17** 51 41N 4 57 E
Wassenaar, *Neths.* **16** 52 8N 4 24 E
Wasserburg, *W. Germany* **31** 48 4N 12 15 E
Wasserkuppe, *W. Germany* **30** 50 30N 9 56 E
Wassy, *France* **19** 48 30N 4 58 E
Waswanipi, *Canada* **106** 49 40N 76 29W
Waswanipi →, *Canada* **106** 49 40N 76 25W
Waswanipi, L., *Canada* **106** 49 35N 76 40W
Watangpone, *Indonesia* **57** 4 29 S 120 25 E
Watchem, *Australia* **74** 36 9 S 142 52 E
Water Park Pt., *Australia* **72** 22 56 S 150 47 E
Water Valley, *U.S.A.* **121** 34 9N 89 38W
Waterberge, *S. Africa* **97** 24 10 S 28 0 E
Waterbury, *Conn., U.S.A.* **117** 41 32N 73 0W
Waterbury, *Vt., U.S.A.* **117** 44 22N 72 44W
Waterbury L., *Canada* **111** 58 10N 104 22W
Waterdown, *Canada* **108** 43 20N 79 53W
Waterford, *Australia* **77** 27 42 S 153 9 E
Waterford, *Canada* **108** 42 56N 80 17W
Waterford, *Ireland* **15** 52 16N 7 8W
Waterford, *Calif., U.S.A.* **124** 37 38N 120 46W
Waterford, *Wis., U.S.A.* **119** 42 46N 88 13W
Waterford □, *Ireland* **15** 52 10N 7 40W
Waterford Harb., *Ireland* **15** 52 10N 6 58W
Waterhen L., *Man., Canada* **111** 52 10N 99 40W
Waterhen L., *Sask., Canada* **111** 54 28N 108 25W
Wateringen, *Neths.* **16** 52 2N 4 16 E
Waterloo, *Belgium* **17** 50 43N 4 25 E
Waterloo, *Ont., Canada* **108** 43 30N 80 32W
Waterloo, *Qué., Canada* **117** 45 22N 72 32W
Waterloo, *S. Leone* **90** 8 26N 13 8W
Waterloo, *Ill., U.S.A.* **118** 38 22N 90 6W
Waterloo, *Ind., U.S.A.* **119** 41 24N 85 2W
Waterloo, *Iowa, U.S.A.* **118** 42 27N 92 20W
Waterloo, *N.Y., U.S.A.* **116** 42 54N 76 53W
Waterloo, *Wis., U.S.A.* **118** 43 11N 88 59W
Waterman, *U.S.A.* **119** 41 46N 88 47W
Watermeal-Boitsford, *Belgium* **17** 50 48N 4 25 E
Watersmeet, *U.S.A.* **120** 46 15N 89 12W
Waterton Glacier Int. Peace Park, *U.S.A.* **122** 48 35N 113 40W
Watertown, *Conn., U.S.A.* **117** 41 36N 73 7W
Watertown, *N.Y., U.S.A.* **117** 43 58N 75 57W
Watertown, *S. Dak., U.S.A.* **120** 44 57N 97 5W
Watertown, *Wis., U.S.A.* **119** 43 15N 88 45W
Waterval-Boven, *S. Africa* **97** 25 40 S 30 18 E
Waterville, *Canada* **117** 45 16N 71 54W
Waterville, *Maine, U.S.A.* **105** 44 35N 69 40W
Waterville, *N.Y., U.S.A.* **117** 42 56N 75 23W
Waterville, *Pa., U.S.A.* **116** 41 19N 77 21W
Waterville, *Wash., U.S.A.* **122** 47 38N 120 1W
Watervliet, *Belgium* **17** 51 17N 3 38 E
Watervliet, *Mich., U.S.A.* **119** 42 11N 86 18W
Watervliet, *N.Y., U.S.A.* **117** 42 46N 73 43W
Wates, *Indonesia* **57** 7 51 S 110 10 E
Watford, *Canada* **108** 42 57N 81 53W
Watford, *U.K.* **13** 51 38N 0 23W
Watford City, *U.S.A.* **120** 47 50N 103 23W
Wathaman →, *Canada* **111** 57 16N 102 59W
Watheroo, *Australia* **79** 30 15 S 116 0 E
Wating, *China* **60** 35 40N 106 38 E
Watkins Glen, *U.S.A.* **116** 42 25N 76 55W
Watling I. = San Salvador, *Bahamas* **129** 24 0N 74 40W
Watonga, *U.S.A.* **121** 35 51N 98 24W
Watou, *Belgium* **17** 50 51N 2 38 E
Watrous, *Canada* **111** 51 40N 105 25W
Watrous, *U.S.A.* **121** 35 50N 104 55W
Watsa, *Zaïre* **92** 3 4N 29 30 E
Watseka, *U.S.A.* **119** 40 45N 87 45W
Watson, *Australia* **79** 30 29 S 131 31 E
Watson, *Canada* **111** 52 10N 104 30W
Watson Lake, *Canada* **102** 60 6N 128 49W
Watsonville, *U.S.A.* **124** 36 55N 121 49W
Wattiwarriganna Cr. →, *Australia* **73** 28 57 S 136 10 E
Wattle Flat, *Australia* **76** 33 8 S 149 43 E
Wattwil, *Switz.* **31** 47 18N 9 6 E
Watuata = Batuata, *Indonesia* **57** 6 12 S 122 42 E
Watubela, Kepulauan, *Indonesia* **57** 4 28 S 131 35 E
Wau, *Papua N. G.* **69** 7 21 S 146 47 E
Waubach, *Neths.* **17** 50 55N 6 3 E
Waubamik, *Canada* **108** 45 27N 80 1W
Waubaushene, *Canada* **108** 44 45N 79 42W
Waubay, *U.S.A.* **120** 45 22N 97 17W
Waubra, *Australia* **74** 37 21 S 143 39 E
Wauchope, *Australia* **77** 31 28 S 152 45 E
Wauchula, *U.S.A.* **115** 27 35N 81 50W
Waugh, *Canada* **111** 49 40N 95 11W
Waukegan, *U.S.A.* **119** 42 22N 87 54W
Waukesha, *U.S.A.* **119** 43 0N 88 15W
Waukon, *U.S.A.* **120** 43 14N 91 33W
Wauneta, *U.S.A.* **120** 40 27N 101 25W
Waupaca, *U.S.A.* **120** 44 22N 89 8W
Waupun, *U.S.A.* **120** 43 38N 88 44W
Waurika, *U.S.A.* **121** 34 12N 98 0W
Wausau, *U.S.A.* **120** 44 57N 89 40W
Wauseon, *U.S.A.* **119** 41 33N 84 8W
Wautoma, *U.S.A.* **120** 44 3N 89 20W
Wauwatosa, *U.S.A.* **119** 43 6N 87 59W
Wave Hill, *Australia* **78** 17 32 S 131 0 E
Waveland, *U.S.A.* **119** 39 53N 87 3W
Waveney →, *U.K.* **13** 52 24N 1 20 E
Waverley, *N.Z.* **80** 39 46 S 174 37 E
Waverly, *Ill., U.S.A.* **118** 39 36N 89 57W
Waverly, *Iowa, U.S.A.* **118** 42 40N 92 30W
Waverly, *Mo., U.S.A.* **118** 39 13N 93 31W
Waverly, *N.Y., U.S.A.* **117** 42 0N 76 33W
Wavre, *Belgium* **17** 50 43N 4 38 E
Wavreille, *Belgium* **17** 50 7N 5 15 E
Wâw, *Sudan* **89** 7 45N 28 1 E
Wāw al Kabīr, *Libya* **86** 25 20N 16 43 E
Wāw an Nāmūs, *Libya* **86** 24 55N 17 46 E
Wawa, *Canada* **104** 47 59N 84 47W
Wawa, *Nigeria* **91** 9 54N 4 27 E
Wawa, *Sudan* **88** 20 30N 30 22 E
Wawagosic →, *Canada* **106** 49 58N 79 6W
Wawanesa, *Canada* **111** 49 36N 99 40W
Wawasee, L., *U.S.A.* **119** 41 24N 85 42W
Wawoi →, *Papua N. G.* **69** 7 48 S 143 16 E
Wawona, *U.S.A.* **124** 37 32N 119 39W
Waxahachie, *U.S.A.* **121** 32 22N 96 53W
Waxweiler, *W. Germany* **31** 50 6N 6 22 E
Way, L., *Australia* **79** 26 45 S 120 16 E
Wayabula Rau, *Indonesia* **57** 2 29N 128 17 E
Wayagamac, L., *Canada* **107** 47 21N 72 39W
Wayatinah, *Australia* **72** 42 19 S 146 27 E
Waycross, *U.S.A.* **115** 31 12N 82 25W
Wayi, *Sudan* **89** 5 8N 30 10 E
Wayland, *U.S.A.* **119** 42 40N 85 39W
Wayne, *Nebr., U.S.A.* **120** 42 16N 97 0W
Wayne, *W. Va., U.S.A.* **114** 38 15N 82 27W
Wayne City, *U.S.A.* **119** 38 21N 88 35W
Waynesboro, *Ga., U.S.A.* **115** 33 6N 82 1W
Waynesboro, *Miss., U.S.A.* **115** 31 40N 88 39W
Waynesboro, *Pa., U.S.A.* **114** 39 46N 77 32W
Waynesboro, *Va., U.S.A.* **114** 38 4N 78 57W
Waynesburg, *U.S.A.* **114** 39 54N 80 12W
Waynesville, *Kans., U.S.A.* **118** 37 50N 92 12W
Waynesville, *N.C., U.S.A.* **115** 35 31N 83 0W
Waynesville, *Ohio, U.S.A.* **119** 39 32N 84 5W
Waynoka, *U.S.A.* **121** 36 38N 98 53W
Wāzin, *Libya* **86** 31 58N 10 40 E
Wazirabad, *Pakistan* **48** 32 30N 74 8 E
We, *Indonesia* **56** 5 51N 95 18 E
Weald, The, *U.K.* **13** 51 7N 0 9 E
Wear →, *U.K.* **12** 54 55N 1 22W
Weatherford, *Okla., U.S.A.* **121** 35 30N 98 45W
Weatherford, *Tex., U.S.A.* **121** 32 45N 97 48W
Weaubleau, *U.S.A.* **118** 37 54N 93 32W
Weaverville, *U.S.A.* **122** 40 44N 122 56W
Webb City, *U.S.A.* **121** 37 9N 94 30W
Webbwood, *Canada* **108** 46 16N 81 52W
Weber, *N.Z.* **80** 40 24 S 176 20 E
Webo = Nyaake, *Liberia* **90** 4 52N 7 37W
Webster, *Mass., U.S.A.* **117** 42 4N 71 54W
Webster, *N.Y., U.S.A.* **116** 43 11N 77 27W
Webster, *S. Dak., U.S.A.* **120** 45 24N 97 33W
Webster, *Wis., U.S.A.* **120** 45 53N 92 25W
Webster City, *U.S.A.* **118** 42 30N 93 50W
Webster Green, *U.S.A.* **120** 38 38N 90 20W
Webster Springs, *U.S.A.* **114** 38 30N 80 25W
Weda, *Indonesia* **57** 0 21N 127 50 E
Weda, Teluk, *Indonesia* **57** 0 30N 127 50 E
Weddell I., *Falk. Is.* **142** 51 50 S 61 0W
Weddell Sea, *Antarctica* **143** 72 30 S 40 0W
Wedderburn, *Australia* **74** 36 26 S 143 33 E
Wedgeport, *Canada* **105** 43 44N 65 59W
Wedza, *Zambia* **93** 18 40 S 31 33 E
Wee Jasper, *Australia* **76** 35 8 S 148 40 E
Wee Waa, *Australia* **77** 30 11 S 149 26 E
Weed, *U.S.A.* **122** 41 29N 122 22W
Weed Heights, *U.S.A.* **124** 38 59N 119 13W
Weedon-Centre, *Canada* **107** 45 42N 71 27W
Weedsport, *U.S.A.* **117** 43 3N 76 35W
Weedville, *U.S.A.* **116** 41 17N 78 28W
Weemelah, *Australia* **77** 29 2 S 149 15 E
Weenen, *S. Africa* **97** 28 48 S 30 7 E
Weener, *W. Germany* **30** 53 10N 7 23 E
Weert, *Neths.* **17** 51 15N 5 43 E
Weesp, *Neths.* **16** 52 18N 5 2 E
Weetaliba, *Australia* **77** 31 35 S 149 39 E
Wegliniec, *Poland* **32** 51 18N 15 10 E
Węgorzewo, *Poland* **32** 54 13N 21 43 E
Węgrów, *Poland* **32** 52 24N 22 0 E
Wehl, *Neths.* **16** 51 58N 6 13 E
Wei He →, *Hebei, China* **60** 36 10N 115 45 E
Wei He →, *Shaanxi, China* **60** 34 38N 110 15 E
Weichang, *China* **61** 41 58N 117 49 E
Weichuan, *China* **60** 34 20N 113 59 E
Weida, *E. Germany* **30** 50 47N 12 3 E
Weiden, *W. Germany* **31** 49 40N 12 10 E
Weifang, *China* **61** 36 44N 119 7 E
Weihai, *China* **61** 37 30N 122 6 E
Weilburg, *W. Germany* **30** 50 28N 8 17 E
Weilheim, *W. Germany* **31** 47 50N 11 9 E
Weimar, *E. Germany* **30** 51 0N 11 20 E
Weinan, *China* **60** 34 31N 109 29 E
Weingarten, *W. Germany* **31** 47 49N 9 39 E
Weinheim, *W. Germany* **31** 49 33N 8 40 E
Weining, *China* **58** 26 50N 104 17 E
Weipa, *Australia* **72** 12 40 S 141 50 E
Weir →, *Australia* **77** 28 20 S 149 50 E
Weir →, *Canada* **111** 56 54N 93 21W
Weir River, *Canada* **111** 56 49N 94 6W
Weirton, *U.S.A.* **116** 40 23N 80 35W
Weiser, *U.S.A.* **122** 44 10N 117 0W
Weishan, *Shandong, China* **61** 34 47N 117 5 E
Weishan, *Yunnan, China* **58** 25 12N 100 20 E
Weissenburg, *W. Germany* **31** 49 2N 10 58 E
Weissenfels, *E. Germany* **30** 51 11N 12 0 E
Weisswasser, *E. Germany* **30** 51 30N 14 36 E
Weiswampach, *Belgium* **17** 50 8N 6 5 E
Weixi, *China* **58** 27 10N 99 10 E
Weixin, *China* **58** 27 48N 105 3 E
Weiyuan, *China* **60** 35 7N 104 10 E
Weiz, *Austria* **33** 47 13N 15 39 E
Weizhou Dao, *China* **58** 21 0N 109 5 E
Wejherowo, *Poland* **32** 54 35N 18 12 E
Wekusko L., *Canada* **111** 54 40N 99 50W
Welbourn Hill, *Australia* **73** 27 21 S 134 6 E
Welch, *U.S.A.* **114** 37 29N 81 36W
Weldya, *Ethiopia* **89** 11 50N 39 34 E
Welega □, *Ethiopia* **89** 9 25N 34 20 E
Welkenraedt, *Belgium* **17** 50 39N 5 58 E
Welkite, *Ethiopia* **89** 8 15N 37 42 E
Welkom, *S. Africa* **96** 28 0 S 26 46 E
Welland, *Canada* **108** 43 0N 79 15W
Welland →, *U.K.* **12** 52 43N 0 10W
Wellen, *Belgium* **17** 50 50N 5 21 E
Wellesley Is., *Australia* **72** 16 42 S 139 30 E
Wellin, *Belgium* **17** 50 5N 5 6 E
Wellingborough, *U.K.* **13** 52 18N 0 41W
Wellington, *Australia* **76** 32 35 S 148 59 E
Wellington, *Canada* **109** 43 57N 77 20W
Wellington, *N.Z.* **80** 41 19 S 174 46 E
Wellington, *S. Africa* **96** 33 38 S 19 1 E
Wellington, *Salop, U.K.* **12** 52 42N 2 31W
Wellington, *Somerset, U.K.* **13** 50 58N 3 13W
Wellington, *Colo., U.S.A.* **120** 40 43N 105 0W
Wellington, *Kans., U.S.A.* **121** 37 15N 97 25W
Wellington, *Mo., U.S.A.* **118** 39 8N 93 59W
Wellington, *Nev., U.S.A.* **124** 38 47N 119 28W
Wellington, *Ohio, U.S.A.* **116** 41 9N 82 12W
Wellington, *Tex., U.S.A.* **121** 34 55N 100 13W
Wellington □, *N.Z.* **81** 40 8 S 175 36 E
Wellington, C., *Australia* **75** 39 4 S 146 29 E
Wellington, I., *Chile* **142** 49 30 S 75 0W
Wellington, L., *Australia* **75** 38 6 S 147 20 E
Wells, *Norfolk, U.K.* **12** 52 57N 0 51 E
Wells, *Somerset, U.K.* **13** 51 12N 2 39W
Wells, *Maine, U.S.A.* **117** 43 18N 70 35W
Wells, *Minn., U.S.A.* **120** 43 44N 93 45W
Wells, *Nev., U.S.A.* **122** 41 8N 115 0W
Wells Gray Prov. Park, *Canada* **110** 52 30N 120 15W
Wells L., *Australia* **79** 26 44 S 123 15 E
Wells River, *U.S.A.* **117** 44 9N 72 4W
Wellsboro, *U.S.A.* **116** 41 45N 77 20W
Wellsburg, *U.S.A.* **116** 40 15N 80 36W
Wellsford, *N.Z.* **80** 36 16 S 174 32 E
Wellsville, *Mo., U.S.A.* **118** 39 4N 91 30W
Wellsville, *N.Y., U.S.A.* **116** 42 9N 77 53W
Wellsville, *Ohio, U.S.A.* **116** 40 36N 80 40W
Wellsville, *Utah, U.S.A.* **122** 41 35N 111 59W
Wellton, *U.S.A.* **123** 32 39N 114 6W
Welmel, Wabi →, *Ethiopia* **89** 5 38N 40 47 E
Welo, *Somali Rep.* **98** 9 25N 48 55 E
Welo □, *Ethiopia* **89** 11 50N 39 48 E
Wels, *Austria* **33** 48 9N 14 1 E
Welshpool, *Australia* **75** 38 42 S 146 26 E
Welshpool, *U.K.* **13** 52 40N 3 9W
Wem, *U.K.* **12** 52 52N 2 45W
Wembere →, *Tanzania* **92** 4 10 S 34 15 E
Wemmel, *Belgium* **17** 50 55N 4 18 E
Wen Xian, *Gansu, China* **60** 32 43N 104 36 E
Wen Xian, *Henan, China* **60** 34 55N 113 5 E
Wenatchee, *U.S.A.* **122** 47 30N 120 17W
Wenchang, *China* **54** 19 38N 110 42 E
Wencheng, *China* **59** 27 46N 120 4 E
Wenchi, *Ghana* **90** 7 46N 2 8W
Wenchow = Wenzhou, *China* **59** 28 0N 120 38 E
Wenchuan, *China* **58** 31 22N 103 35 E
Wendell, *U.S.A.* **122** 42 50N 114 42W
Wendeng, *China* **61** 37 15N 122 5 E
Wendesi, *Indonesia* **57** 2 30 S 134 17 E
Wendo, *Ethiopia* **89** 6 40N 38 27 E
Wendon, *U.S.A.* **125** 33 49N 113 33W
Wendover, *U.S.A.* **122** 40 49N 114 1W
Wenduine, *Belgium* **17** 51 18N 3 5 E
Weng'an, *China* **58** 27 5N 107 25 E
Wengcheng, *China* **59** 24 22N 113 50 E
Wengyuan, *China* **59** 24 20N 114 9 E
Wenjiang, *China* **58** 30 44N 103 55 E
Wenling, *China* **59** 28 21N 121 20 E
Wenlock →, *Australia* **72** 12 2 S 141 55 E
Wenona, *U.S.A.* **118** 41 3N 89 3W
Wenshan, *China* **58** 23 20N 104 18 E
Wenshang, *China* **60** 35 45N 116 30 E
Wenshui, *Guizhou, China* **58** 28 27N 106 28 E
Wenshui, *Shanxi, China* **60** 37 26N 112 1 E
Wensu, *China* **62** 41 15N 80 10 E
Wentworth, *Australia* **74** 34 2 S 141 54 E
Wentzville, *U.S.A.* **118** 38 49N 90 51W
Wenut, *Indonesia* **57** 3 11 S 133 19 E
Wenxi, *China* **60** 35 20N 111 10 E
Wenzhou, *China* **59** 28 0N 120 38 E
Weott, *U.S.A.* **122** 40 19N 123 56W
Wepener, *S. Africa* **96** 29 42 S 27 3 E
Werbomont, *Belgium* **17** 50 23N 5 41 E
Werda, *Botswana* **96** 25 24 S 23 15 E
Werdau, *E. Germany* **30** 50 45N 12 20 E
Werder, *E. Germany* **30** 52 23N 12 56 E
Werder, *Ethiopia* **98** 6 58N 45 1 E
Werdohl, *W. Germany* **30** 51 15N 7 47 E
Weri, *Indonesia* **57** 3 10 S 132 38 E
Werkendam, *Neths.* **16** 51 50N 4 53 E
Werne, *W. Germany* **30** 51 38N 7 38 E
Werneck, *W. Germany* **31** 49 59N 10 6 E
Wernigerode, *E. Germany* **30** 51 49N 10 45 E
Werombi, *Australia* **76** 33 58 S 150 34 E
Werra →, *W. Germany* **30** 51 26N 9 39 E
Werribee, *Australia* **74** 37 54 S 144 40 E
Werribee →, *Australia* **74** 37 51 S 144 37 E
Werrimull, *Australia* **74** 34 25 S 141 38 E
Werris Creek, *Australia* **77** 31 18 S 150 38 E
Wersar, *Indonesia* **57** 1 30 S 131 55 E
Wertach →, *W. Germany* **31** 48 24N 10 53 E
Wertheim, *W. Germany* **31** 49 44N 9 32 E
Wertingen, *W. Germany* **31** 48 33N 10 41 E
Wervershoof, *Neths.* **16** 52 44N 5 10 E
Wervik, *Belgium* **17** 50 47N 3 3 E
Wesel, *W. Germany* **30** 51 39N 6 34 E
Weser →, *W. Germany* **30** 53 33N 8 30 E
Wesiri, *Indonesia* **57** 7 30 S 126 30 E
Weslemkoon L., *Canada* **109** 45 2N 77 25W
Wesley Vale, *U.S.A.* **123** 35 3N 106 2W
Wesleyville, *Canada* **105** 49 8N 53 36W
Wesleyville, *U.S.A.* **116** 42 9N 80 1W
Wessel, C., *Australia* **72** 10 59 S 136 46 E
Wessel Is., *Australia* **72** 11 10 S 136 45 E
Wesselburen, *W. Germany* **30** 54 11N 8 53 E
Wessem, *Neths.* **17** 51 11N 5 49 E
Wessington, *U.S.A.* **120** 44 30N 98 40W
Wessington Springs, *U.S.A.* **120** 44 10N 98 35W
West, *U.S.A.* **121** 31 50N 97 5W
West Allis, *U.S.A.* **119** 43 1N 87 0W
West B., *U.S.A.* **121** 29 5N 89 27W
West Baines →, *Australia* **78** 15 38 S 129 59 E
West Bend, *U.S.A.* **114** 43 25N 88 10W
West Bengal □, *India* **49** 23 0N 88 0 E
West Branch, *U.S.A.* **104** 44 16N 84 13W
West Bromwich, *U.K.* **13** 52 32N 2 1W
West Cape Howe, *Australia* **79** 35 8 S 117 36 E
West Carrollton, *U.S.A.* **119** 39 40N 84 17W
West Chazy, *U.S.A.* **117** 44 49N 73 28W
West Chester, *U.S.A.* **114** 39 58N 75 36W
West Chicago, *U.S.A.* **119** 41 53N 88 12W
West Columbia, *U.S.A.* **121** 29 10N 95 38W
West Covina, *U.S.A.* **125** 34 4N 117 54W
West Des Moines, *U.S.A.* **118** 41 30N 93 45W
West End, *Bahamas* **128** 26 41N 78 58W
West Falkland, *Falk. Is.* **142** 51 40 S 60 0W
West Frankfort, *U.S.A.* **118** 37 56N 89 0W
West Germany ■, *Europe* **30** 52 0N 9 0 E
West Glamorgan □, *U.K.* **13** 51 40N 3 55W
West Hartford, *U.S.A.* **117** 41 45N 72 45W

Willandra Billabong Creek

Willandra Billabong Creek →, Australia 73 33 22 S 145 52 E
Willapa, B., U.S.A. 122 46 44N 124 0W
Willapa Hills, U.S.A. 124 46 35N 123 25W
Willard, N. Mex., U.S.A. 123 34 35N 106 1W
Willard, Utah, U.S.A. 122 41 28N 112 1W
Willaura, Australia 74 37 31 S 142 45 E
Willcox, U.S.A. 123 32 13N 109 53W
Willebroek, Belgium 17 51 4N 4 22 E
Willemstad, Neth. Ant. 129 12 5N 69 0W
Willeroo, Australia 78 15 14 S 131 37 E
William →, Canada 111 59 8N 109 19W
William, Mt., Australia 74 37 17 S 142 35 E
William Creek, Australia 73 28 58 S 136 22 E
Williambury, Australia 79 23 45 S 115 12 E
Williams, Australia 79 33 2 S 116 52 E
Williams, Ariz., U.S.A. 123 35 16N 112 11W
Williams, Calif., U.S.A. 124 39 9N 122 9W
Williams Lake, Canada 110 52 10N 122 10W
Williamsburg, Ky., U.S.A. 115 36 45N 84 10W
Williamsburg, Pa., U.S.A. 116 40 27N 78 14W
Williamsburg, Va., U.S.A. 114 37 17N 76 44W
Williamsfield, U.S.A. 118 40 55N 90 1W
Williamson, N.Y., U.S.A. 116 43 14N 77 15W
Williamson, W. Va., U.S.A. 114 37 46N 82 17W
Williamsport, Ind., U.S.A. 119 40 17N 87 17W
Williamsport, Pa., U.S.A. 116 41 18N 77 1W
Williamston, Mich., U.S.A. 119 42 41N 84 17W
Williamston, S.C., U.S.A. 115 35 50N 77 5W
Williamstown, Australia 74 37 51 S 144 52 E
Williamstown, Ky., U.S.A. 119 38 38N 84 34W
Williamstown, Mass., U.S.A. 117 42 41N 73 12W
Williamstown, N.Y., U.S.A. 117 43 25N 75 54W
Williamsville, Ill., U.S.A. 118 39 57N 89 33W
Williamsville, Mo., U.S.A. 121 37 0N 90 33W
Williamtown, Australia 76 32 48 S 151 50 E
Willimantic, U.S.A. 117 41 45N 72 12W
Willis Group, Australia 72 16 18 S 150 0 E
Willisburg, U.S.A. 119 37 49N 85 8W
Williston, S. Africa 96 31 20 S 20 53 E
Williston, Fla., U.S.A. 115 29 25N 82 28W
Williston, N. Dak., U.S.A. 120 48 10N 103 35W
Williston L., Canada 110 56 0N 124 0W
Willits, U.S.A. 122 39 28N 123 17W
Willmar, U.S.A. 120 45 5N 95 0W
Willoughby, U.S.A. 116 41 38N 81 26W
Willow Bunch, Canada 111 49 20N 105 35W
Willow L., Canada 110 62 10N 119 8W
Willow Lake, U.S.A. 120 44 40N 97 40W
Willow Springs, U.S.A. 121 37 0N 92 0W
Willow Tree, Australia 77 31 40 S 150 45 E
Willow Wall, The, China 61 42 10N 122 0 E
Willowlake →, Canada 110 62 42N 123 8W
Willowmore, S. Africa 96 33 15 S 23 30 E
Willows, Australia 72 23 39 S 147 25 E
Willows, U.S.A. 124 39 30N 122 10W
Willowvale = Gatyana, S. Africa 97 32 16 S 28 31 E
Wills, L., Australia 78 21 25 S 128 51 E
Wills Cr. →, Australia 72 22 43 S 140 2 E
Wills Point, U.S.A. 121 32 42N 95 57W
Willunga, Australia 73 35 15 S 138 30 E
Wilmette, U.S.A. 114 42 6N 87 44W
Wilmington, Australia 73 32 39 S 138 7 E
Wilmington, Del., U.S.A. 114 39 45N 75 32W
Wilmington, Ill., U.S.A. 119 41 19N 88 10W
Wilmington, N.C., U.S.A. 115 34 14N 77 54W
Wilmington, Ohio, U.S.A. 119 39 27N 83 50W
Wilpena Cr. →, Australia 73 31 25 S 139 29 E
Wilrijk, Belgium 17 51 9N 4 22 E
Wilsall, U.S.A. 122 45 59N 110 40W
Wilson, U.S.A. 115 35 44N 77 54W
Wilson →, Queens., Australia 73 27 38 S 141 24 E
Wilson →, W. Austral., Australia 78 16 48 S 128 16 E
Wilson Bluff, Australia 79 31 41 S 129 0 E
Wilson Str., Solomon Is. 68 8 0 S 156 39 E
Wilsons Promontory, Australia 75 38 55 S 146 25 E
Wilster, W. Germany 30 53 55N 9 23 E
Wilton, U.K. 13 51 5N 1 52W
Wilton, U.S.A. 120 47 12N 100 47W
Wilton →, Australia 72 14 45 S 134 33 E
Wiltshire □, U.K. 13 51 20N 2 0W
Wiltz, Lux. 17 49 57N 5 55 E
Wiluna, Australia 79 26 36 S 120 14 E
Wimereux, France 19 50 45N 1 37 E
Wimmera, Australia 74 36 30 S 142 0 E
Wimmera →, Australia 74 36 8 S 141 56 E
Winam G., Kenya 92 0 20 S 34 15 E
Winamac, U.S.A. 119 41 3N 86 36W
Winburg, S. Africa 96 28 30 S 27 2 E
Winchelsea, Australia 74 38 10 S 144 1 E
Winchendon, U.S.A. 117 42 40N 72 3W
Winchester, Canada 109 45 6N 75 21W
Winchester, N.Z. 81 44 11 S 171 17 E
Winchester, U.K. 13 51 4N 1 19W
Winchester, Conn., U.S.A. 117 41 53N 73 9W
Winchester, Idaho, U.S.A. 122 46 11N 116 32W
Winchester, Ill., U.S.A. 118 39 38N 90 27W
Winchester, Ind., U.S.A. 119 40 10N 84 56W
Winchester, Ky., U.S.A. 119 38 0N 84 8W
Winchester, N.H., U.S.A. 117 42 47N 72 22W
Winchester, Nev., U.S.A. 125 36 6N 115 10W
Winchester, Ohio, U.S.A. 119 38 57N 83 40W
Winchester, Tenn., U.S.A. 115 35 11N 86 8W
Winchester, Va., U.S.A. 114 39 14N 78 8W
Wind →, U.S.A. 122 43 8N 108 12W
Wind Pt., U.S.A. 119 42 47N 87 46W
Wind River Range, U.S.A. 122 43 0N 109 30W
Windber, U.S.A. 116 40 14N 78 50W
Windermere, L., U.K. 12 54 20N 2 57W
Windeyer, Australia 76 32 46 S 149 32 E
Windfall, Canada 110 54 12N 116 13W
Windfall, U.S.A. 119 40 22N 85 57W
Windflower L., Canada 110 62 52N 118 30W
Windhoek, Namibia 96 22 35 S 17 4 E
Windigo →, Canada 107 47 46N 73 19W
Windom, U.S.A. 120 43 48N 95 3W
Windorah, Australia 72 25 24 S 142 36 E
Window Rock, U.S.A. 123 35 47N 109 4W
Windrush →, U.K. 13 51 48N 1 35W
Windsor, Australia 76 33 37 S 150 50 E
Windsor, N.S., Canada 105 44 59N 64 5W
Windsor, Nfld., Canada 105 48 57N 55 40W
Windsor, Ont., Canada 108 42 18N 83 0W
Windsor, Qué., Canada 107 45 34N 72 0W
Windsor, N.Z. 81 44 59 S 170 49 E
Windsor, U.K. 13 51 28N 0 36W
Windsor, Colo., U.S.A. 120 40 33N 104 45W
Windsor, Conn., U.S.A. 117 41 50N 72 40W
Windsor, Ill., U.S.A. 119 39 26N 88 36W
Windsor, Mo., U.S.A. 118 38 32N 93 31W
Windsor, N.Y., U.S.A. 117 42 5N 75 37W
Windsor, Vt., U.S.A. 117 43 30N 72 25W
Windsorton, S. Africa 96 28 16 S 24 44 E
Windward Is., Pac. Oc. 67 18 0 S 149 0W
Windward Is., W. Indies 129 13 0N 63 0W
Windward Passage = Vientos, Paso de los, Caribbean 129 20 0N 74 0W
Windy L., Canada 111 60 20N 100 2W
Winefred L., Canada 111 55 30N 110 30W
Winejok, Sudan 89 9 1N 27 30 E
Winfield, Ill., U.S.A. 118 41 5N 91 30W
Winfield, Kans., U.S.A. 121 37 15N 97 0W
Winfield, Mo., U.S.A. 118 39 0N 90 44W
Wingate Mts., Australia 78 14 25 S 130 40 E
Wingello, Australia 76 34 42 S 150 10 E
Wingen, Australia 77 31 54 S 150 54 E
Wingene, Belgium 17 51 3N 3 17 E
Wingham, Australia 77 31 48 S 152 22 E
Wingham, Canada 108 43 55N 81 20W
Winifred, U.S.A. 122 47 30N 109 28W
Winisk, Canada 104 55 20N 85 15W
Winisk →, Canada 104 55 17N 85 5W
Winisk L., Canada 104 52 55N 87 22W
Wink, U.S.A. 121 31 49N 103 9W
Winkler, Canada 111 49 10N 97 56W
Winlock, U.S.A. 124 46 29N 122 56W
Winneba, Ghana 91 5 25N 0 36W
Winnebago, Ill., U.S.A. 118 42 15N 89 18W
Winnebago, Minn., U.S.A. 120 43 43N 94 8W
Winnebago L., U.S.A. 114 44 0N 88 20W
Winnecke Cr. →, Australia 78 18 35 S 131 34 E
Winnemucca, U.S.A. 122 41 0N 117 45W
Winnemucca, L., U.S.A. 122 40 25N 119 21W
Winner, U.S.A. 120 43 23N 99 52W
Winnett, U.S.A. 122 47 2N 108 21W
Winnfield, U.S.A. 121 31 57N 92 38W
Winnibigoshish L., U.S.A. 120 47 25N 94 12W
Winning, Australia 78 23 9 S 114 30 E
Winnipeg, Canada 111 49 54N 97 9W
Winnipeg →, Canada 111 50 38N 96 19W
Winnipeg, L., Canada 111 52 0N 97 0W
Winnipeg Beach, Canada 111 50 30N 96 58W
Winnipegosis, Canada 111 51 39N 99 55W
Winnipegosis L., Canada 111 52 30N 100 0W
Winnipesaukee, L., U.S.A. 117 43 38N 71 21W
Winnsboro, La., U.S.A. 121 32 10N 91 41W
Winnsboro, S.C., U.S.A. 115 34 23N 81 5W
Winnsboro, Tex., U.S.A. 121 32 56N 95 15W
Winokapau, L., Canada 105 53 15N 62 50W
Winona, Miss., U.S.A. 121 33 30N 89 42W
Winona, Wis., U.S.A. 120 44 2N 91 39W
Winooski, U.S.A. 117 44 31N 73 11W
Winschoten, Neths. 16 53 9N 7 3 E
Winsen, W. Germany 30 53 21N 10 11 E
Winslow, Ariz., U.S.A. 123 35 2N 110 41W
Winslow, Ind., U.S.A. 119 38 23N 87 13W
Winslow, Wash., U.S.A. 124 47 37N 122 31W
Winsted, U.S.A. 117 41 55N 73 5W
Winston-Salem, U.S.A. 115 36 7N 80 15W
Winsum, Neths. 16 53 20N 6 32 E
Winter Garden, U.S.A. 115 28 33N 81 35W
Winter Haven, U.S.A. 115 28 0N 81 42W
Winter Park, U.S.A. 115 28 34N 81 19W
Winterberg, W. Germany 30 51 12N 8 30 E
Winterhaven, U.S.A. 125 32 47N 114 39W
Winters, Calif., U.S.A. 124 38 32N 121 58W
Winters, Tex., U.S.A. 121 31 58N 99 58W
Winterset, U.S.A. 118 41 18N 94 0W
Wintersville, U.S.A. 116 40 22N 80 38W
Winterswijk, Neths. 16 51 58N 6 43 E
Winterthur, Switz. 31 47 30N 8 44 E
Winthrop, Minn., U.S.A. 120 44 31N 94 25W
Winthrop, Wash., U.S.A. 122 48 27N 120 6W
Winton, Queens., Australia 72 22 24 S 143 3 E
Winton, Vic., Australia 74 36 32 S 146 7 E
Winton, N.Z. 81 46 8 S 168 20 E
Winton, U.S.A. 115 36 25N 76 58W
Winton Swamp, Australia 74 36 27 S 146 5 E
Wintzenheim, France 19 48 4N 7 17 E
Wipper →, E. Germany 30 51 17N 11 10 E
Wirral, U.K. 12 53 25N 3 0W
Wirrinya, Australia 76 33 39 S 147 48 E
Wirrulla, Australia 73 32 24 S 134 31 E
Wisbech, U.K. 12 52 39N 0 10 E
Wisconsin □, U.S.A. 120 44 30N 90 0W
Wisconsin →, U.S.A. 120 43 0N 91 15W
Wisconsin Dells, U.S.A. 120 43 38N 89 45W
Wisconsin Rapids, U.S.A. 120 44 25N 89 50W
Wisdom, U.S.A. 122 45 37N 113 27W
Wisemans Ferry, Australia 76 33 22 S 150 59 E
Wishaw, U.K. 14 55 46N 3 55W
Wishek, U.S.A. 120 46 20N 99 35W
Wisła, Poland 32 49 38N 18 53 E
Wisła →, Poland 32 54 22N 18 55 E
Wisłok →, Poland 32 50 13N 22 32 E
Wisłoka →, Poland 32 50 27N 21 23 E
Wismar, E. Germany 30 53 53N 11 23 E
Wismar, Guyana 135 5 59N 58 18W
Wisner, U.S.A. 120 42 0N 96 46W
Wissant, France 19 50 52N 1 40 E
Wissembourg, France 19 49 2N 7 57 E
Wissenkerke, Neths. 17 51 35N 3 45 E
Witbank, S. Africa 97 25 51 S 29 14 E
Witdraai, S. Africa 96 26 58 S 20 48 E
Witham →, U.K. 12 53 3N 0 8W
Withernsea, U.K. 12 53 43N 0 2 E
Witmarsum, Neths. 16 53 6N 5 28 E
Witney, U.K. 13 51 47N 1 29W
Witnossob →, Namibia 96 26 55 S 20 37 E
Wittdün, W. Germany 30 54 38N 8 23 E
Witten, W. Germany 17 51 26N 7 19 E
Wittenberg, E. Germany 30 51 51N 12 39 E
Wittenberge, E. Germany 30 53 0N 11 44 E
Wittenburg, E. Germany 30 53 30N 11 4 E
Wittenoom, Australia 78 22 15 S 118 20 E
Wittingen, W. Germany 30 52 43N 10 43 E
Wittlich, W. Germany 31 50 0N 6 54 E
Wittmund, W. Germany 30 53 39N 7 45 E
Wittow, E. Germany 30 54 37N 13 21 E
Wittstock, E. Germany 30 53 10N 12 30 E
Witzenhausen, Germany 30 51 60N 9 46 E
Wlingi, Indonesia 57 8 5 S 112 25 E
Włocławek, Poland 32 52 40N 19 3 E
Włodawa, Poland 32 51 33N 23 31 E
Włoszczowa, Poland 32 50 50N 19 55 E
Woburn, U.S.A. 117 42 31N 71 7W
Wodian, China 60 32 50N 112 35 E
Wodonga, Australia 75 36 5 S 146 50 E
Woerden, Neths. 16 52 5N 4 54 E
Woerth, France 19 48 57N 7 45 E
Woëvre, France 19 49 15N 5 45 E
Wognum, Neths. 16 52 40N 5 1 E
Woinbogoin, China 58 32 51N 98 39 E
Wokam, Indonesia 57 5 45 S 134 28 E
Wokha, India 52 26 6N 94 16 E
Wolbrom, Poland 32 50 24N 19 45 E
Wolcottville, U.S.A. 119 41 32N 85 22W
Woldegk, E. Germany 30 53 27N 13 35 E
Wolf →, Canada 110 60 17N 132 33W
Wolf Creek, U.S.A. 122 47 1N 112 2W
Wolf L., Canada 110 60 24N 131 40W
Wolf Point, U.S.A. 120 48 6N 105 40W
Wolfe I., Canada 109 44 7N 76 20W
Wolfenbüttel, W. Germany 30 52 10N 10 33 E
Wolfheze, Neths. 16 52 0N 5 48 E
Wolfsberg, Austria 33 46 50N 14 52 E
Wolfsburg, W. Germany 30 52 27N 10 49 E
Wolgast, E. Germany 30 54 3N 13 46 E
Wolhusen, Switz. 31 47 4N 8 4 E
Wolin, Poland 32 53 50N 14 37 E
Wollar, Australia 76 32 20 S 149 56 E
Wollaston, Is., Chile 142 55 40 S 67 30W
Wollaston L., Canada 111 58 7N 103 10W
Wollaston Pen., Canada 102 69 30N 115 0W
Wollogorang, Australia 72 17 13 S 137 57 E
Wollombi, Australia 76 32 56 S 151 8 E
Wollomombi, Australia 77 30 30 S 152 4 E
Wollondilly →, Australia 76 34 12 S 150 18 E
Wollongong, Australia 76 34 25 S 150 54 E
Wolmaransstad, S. Africa 96 27 12 S 25 59 E
Wolmirstedt, E. Germany 30 52 15N 11 35 E
Wolseley, Australia 73 36 23 S 140 54 E
Wolseley, Canada 111 50 25N 103 15W
Wolseley, S. Africa 96 33 26 S 19 7 E
Wolstenholme, C., Canada 100 62 35N 77 30W
Wolstenholme Fjord, Canada 144 76 0N 70 0W
Wolsztyn, Poland 32 52 8N 16 5 E
Wolumla, Australia 75 36 51 S 149 50 E
Wolvega, Neths. 16 52 52N 6 0 E
Wolverhampton, U.K. 13 52 35N 2 6W
Wombat, Australia 76 34 24 S 148 16 E
Wombeyan Caves, Australia 76 34 17 S 149 59 E
Wommels, Neths. 16 53 6N 5 36 E
Wonarah, Australia 72 19 55 S 136 20 E
Wonboyn, Australia 75 37 15 S 149 55 E
Wonck, Belgium 17 50 46N 5 38 E
Wondai, Australia 73 26 20 S 151 49 E
Wondalga, Australia 76 35 24 S 148 8 E
Wondelgem, Belgium 17 51 5N 3 44 E
Wonder Gorge, Zambia 93 14 40 S 29 0 E
Wongalarroo L., Australia 73 31 32 S 144 0 E
Wongan Hills, Australia 79 30 51 S 116 37 E
Wongarbon, Australia 76 32 20 S 148 45 E
Wongawol, Australia 79 26 5 S 121 55 E
Wongungarra →, Australia 75 37 12 S 147 3 E
Wŏnju, S. Korea 61 37 22N 127 58 E
Wonnangatta →, Australia 75 37 32 S 147 15 E
Wonosari, Indonesia 57 7 58 S 110 36 E
Wŏnsan, N. Korea 61 39 11N 127 27 E
Wonthaggi, Australia 74 38 37 S 145 37 E
Wonwron, Australia 75 38 27 S 146 45 E
Woocalla, Australia 73 31 42 S 137 12 E
Wood Buffalo Nat. Park, Canada 110 59 0N 113 41W
Wood Is., Australia 78 16 24 S 123 19 E
Wood L., Canada 111 55 17N 103 17W
Wood Lake, U.S.A. 120 42 38N 100 14W
Wood River, U.S.A. 118 38 52N 90 5W
Woodah I., Australia 72 13 27 S 136 10 E
Woodanilling, Australia 79 33 31 S 117 24 E
Woodbridge, Canada 108 43 47N 79 36W
Woodburn, Australia 77 29 6 S 153 23 E
Woodenbong, Australia 77 28 24 S 152 39 E
Woodend, Australia 74 37 20 S 144 33 E
Woodfords, U.S.A. 124 38 47N 119 50W
Woodgreen, Australia 72 22 26 S 134 12 E
Woodlake, U.S.A. 124 36 25N 119 6W
Woodland, U.S.A. 124 38 40N 121 50W
Woodlands, Australia 79 24 46 S 118 8 E
Woodlark I., Papua N. G. 69 9 10 S 152 50 E
Woodpecker, Canada 110 53 30N 122 40W
Woodridge, Canada 111 49 20N 96 9W
Woodroffe, Mt., Australia 79 26 20 S 131 45 E
Woodruff, Ariz., U.S.A. 123 34 51N 110 1W
Woodruff, Utah, U.S.A. 122 41 30N 111 4W
Woods, L., Australia 72 17 50 S 133 30 E
Woods, L., Canada 105 54 30N 65 13W
Woods, L. of the, Canada 111 49 15N 94 45W
Woods Point, Australia 75 37 32 S 146 16 E
Woods Reef, Australia 77 30 22 S 150 45 E
Woodside, Australia 73 38 31 S 146 52 E
Woodstock, N.S.W., Australia 76 33 45 S 148 53 E
Woodstock, Queens., Australia 72 19 35 S 146 50 E
Woodstock, W. Austral., Australia 78 21 41 S 118 57 E
Woodstock, N.B., Canada 105 46 11N 67 37W
Woodstock, Ont., Canada 108 43 10N 80 45W
Woodstock, U.K. 13 51 51N 1 20W
Woodstock, Ill., U.S.A. 119 42 17N 88 30W
Woodstock, Vt., U.S.A. 117 43 37N 72 31W
Woodsville, U.S.A. 117 44 10N 72 0W
Woodville, N.Z. 80 40 20 S 175 53 E
Woodville, Ohio, U.S.A. 119 41 27N 83 22W
Woodville, Tex., U.S.A. 121 30 45N 94 25W

X

Y